W9-AQS-199

THE OXFORD COMPANION TO BRITISH HISTORY

Til min kone og veninde Minna med kaerlighed og taknemmelighed

EDITED BY JOHN CANNON

Oxford New York
OXFORD UNIVERSITY PRESS
1997

Oxford University Press, Great Clarendon Street, Oxford OX2 6DP

Oxford New York
Athens Auckland Bangkok Bogota Bombay Buenos Aires
Calcutta Cape Town Dar es Salaam Delhi Florence Hong Kong Istanbul
Karachi Kuala Lumpur Madras Madrid Melbourne Mexico City
Nairobi Paris Singapore Taipei Tokyo Toronto Warsaw

and associated companies in
Berlin Ibadan

Oxford is a trade mark of Oxford University Press

© Oxford University Press 1997
First published 1997

All rights reserved. No part of this publication may be reproduced, stored in a retrieval system, or transmitted, in any form or by any means, without the prior permission in writing of Oxford University Press. Within the UK, exceptions are allowed in respect of any fair dealing for the purpose of research or private study, or criticism or review, as permitted under the Copyright, Designs and Patents Act, 1988, or in the case of reprographic reproduction in accordance with the terms of the licences issued by the Copyright Licensing Agency. Enquiries concerning reproduction outside these terms and in other countries should be sent to the Rights Department, Oxford University Press, at the address above

British Library Cataloguing in Publication Data
Data available

Library of Congress Cataloging in Publication Data
Data available

ISBN 0-19-866176-2

Typeset by Interactive Sciences Ltd, Gloucester

Printed in Great Britain
on acid-free paper by
Butler & Tanner Ltd
Frome, Somerset

CONTENTS

PREFACE

No two historians would agree on what should be included in a *Companion to British History*, nor perhaps is it desirable that they should. Much 'history' was partisan and contentious when taking place: Saxons killed Danes, Jacobites despised Hanoverians, methodists mistrusted Anglicans, chartists hated whigs; Gladstone was admired as a man of stern moral purpose and denounced as a fraud and humbug. We should not drain away controversy in order to try for some agreed verdict. It may be of some consolation to readers provoked by an omission or questionable inclusion that certain entries have been included, excised, and reinstated. I do not know of any infallible or purely objective test for inclusion and have often wished that I did.

Some features certainly call for explanation. We have devoted considerable space to 'local history', with a general article on the subject and shorter entries on all the English and Welsh counties, the Scottish provinces, ancient kingdoms, modern regions, and on most important towns, together with entries on a number of castles, cathedrals, and country houses. This reflects not only the interest felt by many people in their immediate surroundings, but also that the distinction commonly made between national and local history is, in practice, difficult to sustain. The one-hour skirmish at Newburn, five miles west of Newcastle, on 28 August 1640, when the Scottish army crossed the Tyne with little trouble, helped to bring about the execution of Charles I and the abolition of the monarchy. National events must take place somewhere, and not necessarily in London, while local events can cast long shadows. The industrial revolution—if the phrase is still permissible—was in practice an agglomeration of forges and furnaces, mills and mines, shipyards and turnpikes, all over the British Isles.

This raises a further difficulty. The term 'national' begs the question 'which nation and whose nation?'—not in the sense beloved by Marxist historians (for whom nation was a tedious distraction from the class struggle)—but because though there was a British state, there was never a British nation, unless the term is used to describe the seventh-century Welsh. Packed into these small islands are four nations, and within each nation are further divisions and differences. Welsh and English, Irish and Scots differ, but so do north and south Wales, Portnaguran and Motherwell, Belfast and Dingle, Wolverhampton and Wisbech. The book attempts, within severe limits, to do justice to each nation, with articles on the kingdoms of England, Ireland, and Scotland and on the principality of Wales. What is difficult, in a book of this nature, is to register the changing relationships between the component nations, though the entry on nationalism suggests some lines of enquiry. Other relationships are discussed in the entries on foreign policy, the Commonwealth of Nations, and the European Economic Community.

There is no way of avoiding the question 'what is history?' In the course of preparing this volume, I was told by many kind friends that I did not know what history was about. I fear they may be right. But, in my less submissive moments, I think a broad and eclectic 'seamless web' approach may be defended. It allows the readers to decide—even if they decide merely that a particular entry should have been omitted. We have, for example, included an article on the development of sport and brief references to individual sports. They will not be enough to please enthusiasts. But they make the point that most sports, as we know them, developed in the later nineteenth century and were in response to mass urbanization. They had an important political and national role. Indeed, post-Marxists, if conceding that religion is no longer the opiate of the masses, might wonder whether sport has taken its place, judging from the attention paid to it by radio, television, and newspapers. Irish nationalists were well aware in the nineteenth century of the relevance of sport to their own aspirations and begged their fellow countrymen to shun English games like soccer and tennis in favour of traditional Gaelic pastimes like hurling. In 1990 Norman Tebbit pointed out, in a pithy phrase, the connection between cricket and national identity, though he had little thanks for his pains.

Sport is but one example of the balance to be struck between traditional political and military history, and social, cultural, scientific, and economic history. Few readers would doubt that Handel's *Messiah*, Marks and Spencer, and the Grand National are as much part of the fabric of English life as the political parties, newspapers, and constitutional arrangements. Should one exclude the Proms (even if they represent only a part of a part of English life) in favour of longer articles on the Bedchamber crisis of 1839, the Field of the Cloth of Gold, or the battle of Blore Heath? Are inventors, industrialists, and entrepreneurs, like Dunlop, Watt, Brunel, Royce, and Harland, intrinsically of less consequence than foreign secretaries, however transient? We have, I hope rightly, included substantial entries on the great industries—mining, gas, shipbuilding, motor manufacture, cotton, aeronautics—which have given employment to millions of people. We have tried to explore aspects of private and domestic life with articles on childbirth, housing, health, food and drink, retailing, holidays, and funerals, which attempt to chart some of those 'noiseless revolutions' which Macaulay, essentially a political historian, thought more significant than 'important events'. It is for the reader to decide whether the balance is right.

The 'seamless web' approach involves even more difficult and controversial decisions. Though sport is included, sportsmen are not (save for W. G. Grace and Sir Stanley Matthews), since their fame, like that of performing artists, is usually by its nature fleeting. In relation to architects, painters, and men of letters, the problem is even more acute. Most people appreciate the importance of images and would acknowledge that we see the Tudor monarchy largely through the eyes of Holbein. Should we exclude him as not British and only a painter? Does the work of Vanbrugh at Blenheim or Castle Howard, or that of Sir George Gilbert Scott at St Pancras have no bearing on British history? Has any minister left a greater impression on the national mind (if there is such a thing) than Capability Brown? Do the lives of Robert Burns and Dylan Thomas not resonate today in the identity of Scotland and Wales? We have included short entries on many authors, partly because not all readers will have the *Oxford Companion to English Literature* at their elbows, but more because to exclude them would leave a gaping hole in historical comprehension. Many authors, of course, played an important political role and would be included in even the most traditional survey—Milton, Dryden, Addison, Sheridan, Shelley, Byron, O'Casey. But even those less directly interested in politics—Shakespeare, Johnson, Jane Austen, Scott, Dickens, Wilde—illuminate the life and concerns of their own times. We cannot hope to do justice to them as writers, but we can suggest how they contribute to our understanding of and feel for the past—Trollope for the cathedral close, Wells for the draper's counter, Bennett the provincial printing office, Kipling the hill-station, Wodehouse the jolly weekend.

It is hardly possible to produce a work of this complexity without errors surviving. I would be glad to be told of them, preferably with compassion. Though we have tried to provide clear and authoritative entries, taking account of the most recent scholarship, contributors have also been encouraged to express their own opinions rather than offer bland and lifeless summaries. It would be a strange reader who agreed with all their judgements and some may not agree with any. Some opinions are bound to seem intrusive, unfair, or irritating. But if certain entries appear irreverent, we rely upon the irreverence of the reader who is, after all, at perfect liberty to dissent from dissent.

John Cannon
University of Newcastle upon Tyne
May 1997

CONTRIBUTORS

GA Professor Geoffrey Alderman, Pro-Vice-Chancellor, Middlesex University

DDA Dr David Denis Aldridge, formerly Lecturer in History, University of Newcastle upon Tyne

SAA Dr Stephen Alford, Honorary Lecturer in Modern History, University of St Andrews

DJA Mr Douglas J. Allen, Senior Lecturer in Media Studies, Motherwell College

SDB Dr Stephen Badsey, Senior Lecturer, Department of War Studies, Royal Military Academy Sandhurst

RNB Professor Richard N. Bailey, Pro-Vice-Chancellor, University of Newcastle upon Tyne

CJB Professor C. J. Bartlett, formerly Professor of International History, University of Dundee

DB Professor David Richard Bates, Head of Department of Medieval History, Head of School of History & Archaeology, Director of Centre for Medieval & Renaissance Studies, University of Glasgow

JVB Professor John Beckett, Professor of English Regional History, University of Nottingham

HB Professor Hugh Berrington, Emeritus Professor, University of Newcastle upon Tyne

CB Dr Clyde Binfield, Reader in History, University of Sheffield

JPB Dr Jeremy Boulton, Senior Lecturer in History, Department of History, University of Newcastle upon Tyne

KB Professor Keith Branigan, Professor of Prehistory & Archaeology, University of Sheffield

RB Professor Roy C. Bridges, Professor of History, University of Aberdeen

DEB Dr Dauvit Broun, Lecturer in Scottish History, University of Glasgow

NJB Mr Nicholas J. Bryars, Head of History at the Cambridge High School, Abu Dhabi, UAE

RAB Professor R. Angus Buchanan, Hon. Director, Centre for the History of Technology, University of Bath

JB Professor John Butt, Emeritus Professor, University of Strathclyde

KJB Professor Kenneth Button, Distinguished Research Professor, Institute of Public Policy, George Mason University, Fairfax, Va., USA

EC Professor Euan Cameron, Professor in Reformation History, University of Newcastle upon Tyne

JCa Professor James Campbell, Professor of Medical History, Oxford University, Fellow of Worcester College

JAC Professor J. A. Cannon, Emeritus Professor of Modern History, University of Newcastle upon Tyne

SMC Ms Sue Minna Cannon, formerly at the University of Newcastle upon Tyne

HC Professor Harold Carter, Emeritus Professor, University of Wales

SC Mr Stuart Carter, Ph.D. student, University of Newcastle upon Tyne

MEC Professor Muriel Evelyn Chamberlain, Professor of History, University of Wales, Swansea

JFC Dr Judith Champ, Pastoral Adviser, Roman Catholic Diocese of Portsmouth (formerly at Department of Theology & Religious Studies, King's College, London)

JCh Professor J. A. Chartres, Professor, Leeds University Business School

TOC Dr Thomas Owen Clancy, Lecturer, Department of Celtic, University of Glasgow

ASEC Dr Alan Simon Esmonde Cleary, Senior Lecturer, University of Birmingham

CMC Dr Colin M. Coates, Lecturer, Centre of Canadian Studies, University of Edinburgh

JC Mrs June Cochrane, formerly at the University of Newcastle upon Tyne

BIC Dr Bruce Coleman, Senior Lecturer, Department of History & Archaeology, University of Exeter

JRC Professor John Collis, Department of Archaeology & Prehistory, University of Sheffield

ECr Dr Eric Cross, Senior Lecturer in Music (also Head of Department & Dean of Arts), University of Newcastle upon Tyne

AC Dr Anne Curry, Senior Lecturer in History, University of Reading

JWD Professor John W. Derry, Professor of Modern British History, University of Newcastle upon Tyne

ID Dr Ian Donnachie, Staff Tutor & Senior Lecturer in History, the Open University in Scotland

JAD Professor J. A. Downie, Professor of English & Pro-Warden (Academic) Goldsmiths College, London

SD Dr Sean Duffy, Lecturer, Department of Medieval History, Trinity College, Dublin

SMD Ms Sandra M. Dunkin, Research Student, University of Newcastle upon Tyne

Contributors

DJD Dr David Dutton, Senior Lecturer in History, University of Liverpool

TEF Mr T. E. Faulkner, Senior Lecturer in the History of Design, University of Northumbria

DF Professor David French, Professor of History, University College London

IJG Professor Ian Gentles, Professor of History, Glendon College, York University (Toronto)

JG Professor John Gillingham, Professor of History, LSE

BJG Dr Brian Golding, Senior Lecturer, Department of History, University of Southampton

PG Professor Peter Gordon, Emeritus Professor of Education, University of London Institute of Education

TSG Dr Tim S. Gray, Head of Department of Politics, University of Newcastle upon Tyne

RAG Professor Ralph Alan Griffiths, Professor of Medieval History, University of Wales, Swansea

JRG Revd Dr John R. Guy, Editor, *The Journal of Welsh Religious History*

AAH Dr Andrew Hanham, Senior Research Officer, History of Parliament Trust

ASH Dr A. S. Hargreaves, University of Newcastle upon Tyne

JFCH Professor John F. C. Harrison, Emeritus Professor of History, University of Sussex

RH Dr Robert Holland, Reader in History at the Institute of Commonwealth Studies, University of London

MAH Dr Michael Hopkinson, Lecturer in History, University of Stirling

KI Professor Kenneth Ingham, Emeritus Professor of History, University of Bristol

AJ Dr Alvin Jackson, Reader in Modern History, Queen's University of Belfast

AJe Dr Andrew Jennings, Lecturer in Scandinavian History, University of Edinburgh

CJ Dr Clyve Jones, Assistant Librarian, Institute of Historical Research, University of London

JRJ Professor J. R. Jones, Emeritus Professor, University of East Anglia

IJEK Dr Ian John Ernest Keil, formerly Senior Lecturer in Economic & Social History, Loughborough University

DK Professor David Knight, Professor of History and Philosophy of Science, University of Durham

CNL Mr Christopher N. Lanigan, Postgraduate Ridley Fellow, Department of Politics, University of Newcastle upon Tyne

CHL Professor Clive H. Lee, Professor of Historical Economics, University of Aberdeen

BPL Professor Bruce Philip Lenman, Professor of Modern History, University of St Andrews

AIL Mr Andrew Iain Lewer, Graduate Student, Downing College, Cambridge

SL Dr S. D. Lloyd, Senior Lecturer, Department of History, University of Newcastle upon Tyne

RL Mr Roger Lockyer, Emeritus Reader in History in the University of London

HL Professor Henry Loyn, Emeritus Professor, Queen Mary and Westfield College, University of London

CML Miss Charlotte M. Lythe, Senior Lecturer, Economic Studies, University of Dundee

NMcC Professor Norman McCord, Emeritus Professor of Social History, University of Newcastle upon Tyne

AM Mrs Audrey MacDonald, formerly at the University of Newcastle upon Tyne

NATM Dr Norman Macdougall, Senior Lecturer, Department of Scottish History, University of St Andrews

GAM Dr Gordon Macmullan, Lecturer, Department of English, King's College, London

WMM Revd Dr William M. Marshall, Former Head of History, Millfield, Somerset

GM Professor Ged Martin, Director, Centre of Canadian Studies, University of Edinburgh

RAM Dr Roger A. Mason, Reader in Scottish History, University of St Andrews

LHM Mr Lewis Mates, graduate student, Department of History, University of Newcastle upon Tyne

HCGM Professor H. C. G. Matthew, Professor of Modern History, University of Oxford

RJM Professor R. J. Morris, Personal Chair in Economic & Social History, University of Edinburgh

MM Mrs Maureen Mulholland, Lecturer in Law, Faculty of Law, University of Manchester

DMP Professor David M. Palliser, Professor of Medieval History, School of History, University of Leeds

RACP Dr R. A. C. Parker, Fellow, Queen's College, Oxford

NTP Dr Nicholas Phillipson, Reader in History, University of Edinburgh

JLP Dr John Pimlott, Head, Department of War Studies, Royal Military Academy Sandhurst

AJP Professor Anthony James Pollard, Director, Centre for Local Historical Research, University of Teesside

BJP Professor Bernard Porter, Professor of Modern History & Head of Department of History, University of Newcastle upon Tyne

JRP Professor John R. Presley, Professor of Economics, Department of Economics, Loughborough University

MCP Professor Michael Prestwich, Pro-Vice-Chancellor & Professor of History, University of Durham

MDP Professor Martin Pugh, Professor of Modern British History, University of Newcastle upon Tyne

AER Miss A. E. Redgate, Lecturer, Department of History, University of Newcastle upon Tyne

GBR Dr Glynis B. Ridley, Lecturer in English Literature, University of Huddersfield

PER Miss Pamela E. Ritchie, Research Student, University of St Andrews

LR Mrs Lynda Rollason, Part-time Tutor with Department of Adult Education, University of Durham

ER Dr Edward Royle, Reader in History, University of York

AS Professor Andrew Sanders, Professor of English, University of Durham

JNRS Mr John Saunders, Senior Lecturer in English, University of Newcastle upon Tyne

ES Dr Eleanor Scott, Lecturer in History & Archaeology, King Alfred's College, Winchester. Associate Lecturer in Classical Studies, Open University

JAS Dr J. A. Sharpe, Senior Lecturer, Department of History, University of York

GDS Dr Gary Sheffield, Senior Lecturer, Department of War Studies, Royal Military Academy Sandhurst

RCS Professor Richard C. Simmons, Professor of American History, University of Birmingham

AS Dr Alan Sked, Senior Lecturer in International History, LSE

EAS Dr E. A. Smith, formerly Reader in Modern History, University of Reading

RAS Mr Richard A. Smith, Research Student at the University of Newcastle upon Tyne

RLS Professor R. L. Storey, Emeritus Professor of Medieval History, University of Nottingham

KJS Dr Keith J. Stringer, Reader in Medieval British History at the University of Lancaster

RJT Mr Roland Tanner, Research Assistant, Department of Scottish History, University of Glasgow

JBT Professor J. B. Trapp, Director Emeritus & Honorary Fellow, Warburg Institute, University of London

JKW Professor John K. Walton, Professor of Modern Social History, University of Lancaster

DAW Dr David Anthony Washbrook, Reader in Modern South Asian History, Oxford University, Fellow of St Antony's College

MJW Professor Martyn Webb [Emeritus Professor], Honorary Research Fellow, University of Western Australia

BW Mr Bruce Webster, Honorary Senior Research Fellow, the University of Kent at Canterbury

DCW Dr D. C. Whaley, Senior Lecturer, Department of English Literary and Linguistic Studies, University of Newcastle upon Tyne

DW Mr David Wilkinson, Research Officer, The History of Parliament Trust

MW Ms Margaret Wilkinson, Senior Lecturer in Economics, University of Bradford

PW Dr Peter Willis, formerly Reader in the History of Architecture, University of Newcastle upon Tyne

AHW Professor Austin Woolrych, Emeritus Professor of History, University of Lancaster

BAEY Dr Barbara Yorke, Reader, Department of History & Archaeology, King Alfred's College, Winchester

ACKNOWLEDGEMENTS

So many people have helped with the production of this volume that it is impossible to acknowledge them all individually, but I hope they will accept my thanks here and will approve of the book. I must however mention the staff of the Robinson Library in the University of Newcastle upon Tyne, particularly for their patience and kindness during the long stages of proofreading and checking. I would like especially to acknowledge the administrative skills of Sandra Dunkin, the organiser of victory—if victory it be—and the assistance of Dr Anne Hargreaves, whose help in the later stages was unstinted and who finished, as often happens, by supervising her supervisor. I would also like to express my gratitude to my collaborators at Oxford University Press, and in particular to Pam Coote, Alysoun Owen, Wendy Tuckey, and Alison Jones, who succeeded in turning a sometimes laborious task into a positive pleasure and whose contribution to this work has been so important.

NOTE TO THE READER

Entries are arranged in letter-by-letter alphabetical order up to the first punctuation in the headword. For example, the entry on **Quebec, capture of** precedes **Quebec Act**. We have tried in all cases to use the most appropriate headword, particularly the name by which people were best known. It would be unhelpful to have entered **Disraeli** under 'Beaconsfield', a name by which he was known for only the last five years of his life, and it would be unreasonable to expect all readers to remember that Lord **Melbourne** was William Lamb. Where there have been second or third creations of a title, all the holders of that title are arranged together in straightforward alphabetical order for simplicity of reference. Holders of titles created in the Scottish peerage are distinguished by [S] after the headword, for example **Melville, George Melville, 1st earl of [S]**, and similarly [I] denotes titles created in the Irish peerage.

An asterisk within the text indicates a cross-reference to another relevant headword. An item is normally marked with an asterisk only at its first appearance in any entry, and if the reference is merely incidental it has not been marked. We have not asterisked sovereigns after 1066 for England, or after Malcolm II (d. 1034) for Scotland, since they all have entries. 'See also' at the end of an entry indicates that there is another substantial entry with a bearing on the subject. Further reading lists have been confined to longer entries and are limited to key works, partly to save space, and partly because they tend to date rather quickly.

The subject index at the back of the book is intended to reinforce the system of cross-reference and make it easier for readers to identify entries of kindred interest. General entries are listed first, followed by specific examples. The words 'see also' in the index refer the reader to headwords within the index, not within the *Companion* text itself. The accompanying genealogies are not exhaustive lists of all the members of a dynasty, but are designed to illuminate specific family relationships, for example the important reconciliation of Norman and Saxon interests by the marriage of Henry I to a Saxon princess.

abbeys and priories. Both are titles of status applied to monasteries. An abbey is presided over by an abbot in the case of a male religious community (monks) or an abbess in the case of a female (nuns). A priory has no resident abbot or abbess. It may be the dependency of an abbey or a daughter house. Before the Reformation several English cathedrals (e.g. *Canterbury, *Durham, and *Winchester) had been served by monastic communities, and these too were designated as priories. Such communities were under the presidency of a prior.

'Abbey' and 'priory' are titles most properly applied to religious communities during the fullest development of monasticism in the Middle Ages. They were the home of the men and women who could, in the apostle Paul's words, continue 'instant in prayer; distributing to the necessity of the saints; given to hospitality'. A life dedicated to prayer and the worship of God, to hospitality and to almsgiving, as well as to work and study, lived as far as possible detached from the distractions and temptations of society, was the objective of these communities.

Benedict, who founded a monastery at Monte Cassino in Italy in 529, compiled for his community a rule of life which was later to be the inspiration for much of monasticism in medieval Europe. Followers of Benedict's rule accompanied *Augustine's mission to England in 597. During the Middle Ages, many of the greater monasteries housed Benedictine communities, including all but one (*Carlisle) of the cathedral priories. Even today, 450 years after Henry VIII (1509–47) dissolved the monasteries, there are substantial remains of Benedictine churches, such as Glastonbury and Whitby. Several of the Benedictine abbeys, e.g. *Gloucester and—briefly—Westminster, became the cathedrals of new dioceses. Others (*Sherborne, *Tewkesbury, Romsey, Shrewsbury, and *Selby among them) became parish churches. Although now shorn of many of their conventual buildings, enough remains to remind us of the prestige and vigour of these communities in their heyday. However, not all abbeys and priories belonged to the Benedictine order. At the time of their dissolution in the late 1530s, ten other orders were represented in England and Wales, including the Bonshommes. Peculiar to Britain, these were priests who followed the rule of St Augustine and who possessed only two monasteries (Ashridge, Herts., and Edington, Wilts.) in England. Next to the *Benedictines, it was perhaps the *Cistercians who made the most enduring impact, both spiritually and architecturally. Dissatisfied with the observance of the Benedictine rule at the monastery of Molesme in Burgundy, the abbot Robert with several monks left in 1098 and settled in Cîteaux to follow a stricter way of life. His work was consolidated by Bernard of Clairvaux in the 12th cent. At the dissolution the order possessed some 80 houses in England and Wales. Often built in remote places, the ruins of their churches (e.g. *Fountains and *Rievaulx in Yorkshire, *Tintern in Gwent) are among the finest in the British Isles. JRG

Abbey theatre. First permanent home of the Irish National Theatre, founded by Lady *Gregory, Edward Martyn, and W. B. *Yeats to foster native drama. Yeats's verse play *On Baile's Strand* was the opening production in 1904 but more dramatic scenes came four years later with riots at the first night of J. M. *Synge's *The Playboy of the Western World*. Controversy also surrounded the staging of plays by *Shaw and *O'Casey, though the latter's *The Shadow of a Gunman* marked a decisive shift from Celtic twilight to Dublin tenement. The original building, on the corner of Abbey Street, was destroyed by fire in 1951. JNRS

Abbot, George (1562–1633). Bishop of Lichfield (1609), London (1610), and archbishop of Canterbury (1611–33). Born in Guildford, Abbot was educated there and at Balliol College, Oxford. As a fellow of Balliol (1583) and master of University College (1597) he established a reputation as a preacher. His sermons are eloquent and reveal his Calvinist theology. In 1604 he was among those appointed to prepare a new translation of the Bible. His defence of hereditary monarchy and work in Scotland promoting episcopacy (1608) coupled with the support of the earl of Dunbar won him the favour of James I and the primacy. From 1621 his ministry was overshadowed by his accidental killing of one of his gamekeepers, and under Charles I his influence over the king's religious policy was eclipsed by that of William *Laud. He was pious and kindly, but a poor administrator. JRG

abdication crisis, 1936. A constitutional *scandale* stemming from the determination of King Edward VIII, who succeeded his father George V on 20 January 1936, to marry Mrs Wallis *Simpson, an American lady who had divorced her first husband and was about to divorce her second. At first Edward hoped that he might enter into morganatic marriage: Wallis would become his wife but not queen.

*Baldwin, prime minister, issued an ultimatum: the king must choose between the throne and Mrs Simpson. Edward chose the latter, and abdicated on 11 December. British public opinion was genuinely outraged at the prospect of the king marrying a twice-divorced American commoner, and there is much truth in the assertion that many Conservatives had been irritated by Edward's public indignation at unemployment and slum housing. None the less, had the king stood firm, it is difficult to see what the government could have done, short of denying him an income. GA

Aberconwy, peace of, 1277. This treaty, which brought to a conclusion the war between Llywelyn ap Gruffydd and Edward I marked the beginning of the end of Llywelyn's considerable ambitions. His rule was confined to 'Lesser' Gwynedd, west of the Conwy, and five years later he was killed near Builth in a new rising. JAC

Aberdeen, an ancient royal burgh (1178) and centre for education with two universities by 1600, became a significant port and developed a range of industries after 1750. A diversified industrial economy including linen, cotton and woollens, shipbuilding and engineering, distilling, paper, white fish, and granite reduced the strains of economic change. In 1911 nearly half of total employment was in services, a sector which has grown rapidly in the 20th cent. In 1970 oil was first tapped in the North Sea, and in 1975 the Forties field came on stream; Aberdeen became the capital of the British offshore oil industry. JB

Aberdeen, battle of, 1644. After his victory at *Tippermuir on 1 September 1644, *Montrose advanced upon Aberdeen with less than 2,000 men against a superior covenanting force under Lord Balfour. After heavy fighting on the 13th, Montrose's troops entered the city. Incensed by the murder of a drummer-boy while negotiations were in progress, Montrose gave Aberdeen over to sack and pillage. JAC

Aberdeen, cathedrals. St Machar's cathedral, built on the site of a church founded by one of St *Columba's disciples (*c.*580) and a subsequent Norman cathedral burnt by Edward III (1336), was battlemented against possible English attack from the sea and Highlanders from the mountains; its 15th-cent. ashlar facing was the first large-scale use of dressed granite in the area. Alternately under presbyterian and episcopal rule 1560–1690, then wholly presbyterian, the glory of its surviving interior is the nave's oak ceiling bearing 48 heraldic shields (1520). The central tower, weakened in the Cromwellian period by removal of some of the buttresses to construct a barracks, fell after a storm (1688). The episcopal cathedral, erected 1816–17 as St Andrew's chapel, is regarded by American episcopalians as the mother church, since their first bishop (Samuel Seabury) was consecrated in Aberdeen in 1784 after reluctance by the Anglican authorities to perform the rite. ASH

Aberdeen, George Hamilton-Gordon, 4th earl of (1784–1860). Aberdeen represents a classic case of a politician whose reputation has been permanently sullied by an unfortunate premiership. As prime minister during the *Crimean War he paid a high price for underestimating public anxiety about the conduct of the war. Yet he had a long career of public service behind him. Educated at Harrow and Cambridge he first made his mark as a diplomat. In the closing stages of the war against Napoleon he was closely involved with the maintenance of the Grand Alliance against France and with the negotiation of the peace of Paris in 1814. In 1828 he became foreign secretary in *Wellington's administration and he was briefly secretary for war and the colonies in 1834–5. In 1841 he was once again foreign secretary under *Peel. Through patience and sound judgement he achieved some improvement in Anglo-French relations, despite British suspicions of French policy in Spain and the South Seas, and happily settled the long-standing border dispute between Canada and the USA. He ended the war with China by the treaty of *Nanking in 1842, which opened up five Chinese ports to British trade and leased Hong Kong to Britain. In domestic affairs Aberdeen loyally supported Peel, resigning with him after the repeal of the Corn Laws in 1846. Aberdeen did not lack political courage. He opposed *Palmerston over the 'Don *Pacifico' incident in 1850, believing that Palmerston was unnecessarily bellicose, and did not shrink from criticizing *Russell over the Ecclesiastical Titles Bill in 1851.

When Russell's government fell in 1852 Aberdeen headed a ministry which held out every prospect of stability. He was widely respected as a man of sober judgement and sound temperament, and with Palmerston, *Gladstone, Russell, *Graham, and *Herbert in the administration, the government lacked neither talent nor experience. But Aberdeen was unlucky in that he was drawn into war with Russia. Despite its notoriety the Crimean War was not without justification. British suspicions of Russia were well founded and of long standing, but although the political nation was convinced of the wisdom of containing Russian designs, public opinion was soon appalled by the incompetence exposed by the war and demanded scapegoats. Critics forgot that they had often called for economies in defence spending and any recognition of improvements which had been effected in the army was overlaid by an obsession with those defects which had been revealed with brutal clarity. It was sad that a government which was drawn towards cautious domestic reform should fall victim to war hysteria, but Aberdeen could not resolve conflicting reactions among his colleagues to the pressures of war. He had little choice but to resign when *Roebuck's motion calling for an inquiry into the condition of the army was carried in the Commons by 305 votes to 148 on 29 January 1855. A further complication was that Aberdeen could not call on party loyalty to see him through. His government was a coalition of Whigs, Peelites, radicals, and independents and the issues raised by the war accentuated differences between them. Aberdeen also faced clashes of personality within the government, Russell being the most difficult of several touchy colleagues. Aberdeen was a politician of integrity, intelligence, and goodwill, and a man of culture and discernment, but thrust into a position of leadership at a uniquely trying time, he was tested beyond endurance. JWD

Aberfan disaster. On 21 October 1966 an avalanche of waste and sludge from a coal tip buried the primary school of this south Wales village, causing the loss of 144 lives, mostly young children. The subsequent inquiry blamed the tragedy on the lack of any National Coal Board tipping policy. SC

Abernethy, submission of, 1072. After the *Norman Conquest, the boundary between England and Scotland remained in doubt and Malcolm Canmore, king of Scotland, gave refuge to *Edgar the Atheling, whose sister he married. The north, having been harried by William the Conqueror in 1069–70, was once more harried by Malcolm. In 1072 William led an expedition to Scotland and at Abernethy, near Perth, forced Malcolm to submit, do homage, expel Edgar, and give hostages. JAC

Abyssinian War, 1935–41. Conflict between Abyssinia and Italy. Mussolini used a border incident on 5 December 1934 at Walwal, on the Eritrean and Somali frontier, as a pretext for pursuing his aim of imperial expansion in north Africa. The Italians invaded Abyssinia on 3 October 1935 without declaring war and captured the capital Addis Ababa on 5 May 1936. The League of Nations branded Italy the aggressor and imposed limited sanctions but to no avail. In 1941 the British evicted the Italians with the aid of Abyssinian nationalists. RAS

Aclea, battle of, 851. This was a major victory for King Æthelwulf of Wessex over Danish raiders. From 835 the Danes had launched a series of heavy plundering attacks on the south of England, and in 850, for the first time, wintered on Thanet in Kent. Men from 350 ships stormed Canterbury and London, driving the Mercian king Beorhtwulf and his army to flight, before facing the West Saxon king and his son Æthelbald south of the Thames. The Wessex men made 'the greatest slaughter of a heathen host' heard of to that day. AM

Acre, defence of, 1799. Bonaparte, in Egypt, advanced into Syria to menace the Turks, then in alliance with Britain. Sir Sidney *Smith flung troops and guns into the fort of Acre, which resisted the French for two months. Bonaparte attempted to represent the rebuff as a great victory, explaining that there was no point in occupying a pile of rubble. But three months later he abandoned his troops and sailed back to France. JAC

Acre, siege of, 1189–91. The siege and capture of Acre during the Third Crusade was a great event. Acre was the largest port and chief town of the kingdom of Jerusalem and the siege commenced in 1189. Richard I joined the besiegers in June 1191, bringing heavy siege-engines. Despite efforts by Saladin to relieve the city, it surrendered on terms in July. But the crusaders' advance south on Jerusalem stalled and in October 1192 Richard left Acre on his ill-fated journey home. JAC

Acton, Sir John, 1st Baron Acton (1834–1902). Historian and liberal Roman catholic. From an old Shropshire family on his father's side, Acton had a German mother and was brought up as a Roman catholic mainly on the continent, and especially in Germany. He first came to public attention writing articles for liberal catholic periodicals, many of them reprinted in *The History of Freedom* and *Lectures and Essays in Modern History*. He reported the 1870–1 Vatican Council from a liberal catholic perspective, opposing papal infallibility. Acton was an MP 1858–65 (for Carlow) and was created a peer by *Gladstone in 1869. He was a lord-in-waiting at court, 1892–5. To this point, Acton had a great reputation as a cosmopolitan historical polymath, whose great work on the history of liberty awaited publication. In 1895 he became regius professor at Cambridge, and delivered a famous inaugural lecture (11 June 1895). He edited, but did not contribute to, the *Cambridge Modern History*, which set the pattern for a century for the Cambridge approach to multi-authored textbooks. Acton never finished any of his own grand projects (his note-boxes in Cambridge University Library reflect a mind almost mad with compilation) but his published output was far larger than is often allowed. Central to Acton's interest in history was the role of freedom and the capacity of the individual, if correctly imbued with moral and political righteousness, to promote freedom and progress in church and state. Gladstone, for Acton, most nearly epitomized this capacity. Though not an easy author to read, Acton was a sharp epigrammist; his most famous epigram—'Power tends to corrupt and absolute power corrupts absolutely'—was written in a letter to Mandell Creighton on 3 April 1887. HCGM

Acton Burnell, statute of, 1283. Edward I's chancellor, Robert *Burnell, owned the castle of Acton Burnell in Shropshire. A Parliament there in 1283 provided for the easier recovery of debts by merchants by authorizing the mayors of London, York, and Bristol to take action. The intention was to encourage foreign merchants to trade in England by affording fair treatment. Defaulting debtors could be kept in prison on bread and water at their own expense. The statute was amended two years later by the statute of *Merchants. JAC

Acts of Parliament. See PARLIAMENT.

Adam, Robert (1728–92). Scottish architect who, with his brothers John (1721–92) and James (1730–94), trained in the office of their father William Adam (1689–1748), the leading architect of his day in Scotland. After a spell at Edinburgh University, and a grand tour, Robert Adam started his architectural practice in London in 1758 and soon developed a light and decorative style inspired by his travels in Greece and Italy. His interiors combine domes, columned screens, and apses with classically derived surface patterns in delicate colours. The unity of the 'Adam style' can be seen in Kedleston (1760–1), Syon (1760–9), Osterley (1761–80), or Kenwood (1767–9), with their elegant plasterwork, furnishings, and fabrics. Robert Adam's finest civic work was in Edinburgh, notably Charlotte Square (1791–1807), the *Register House (1774–92), and the first stage of the university (1789–93). To this later period belong such buildings as Seton (1790–1) and Culzean (1777–92), both in the castle style, which reflect Robert Adam's interest in the Picturesque. In 1773 there appeared the first engraved volume of the *Works in Architecture of Robert and James Adam*. PW

Addington, Henry, 1st Viscount Sidmouth (1757–1844). Prime minister. During a long political career Addington suffered from the denigration of foes and the condescension of friends, yet like other underrated politicians he had remarkable powers of survival. The son of a country doctor, he was educated at Winchester and Oxford. Entering the Commons in 1784 he made little impact until *Pitt pushed him as speaker in 1789. He proved himself to be capable and fair-minded, and because of his opposition to *catholic emancipation he was George III's choice to succeed Pitt as prime minister in 1801. Addington appealed to the backbench country gentlemen, whose prejudices he shared and whom he intuitively understood. Despite its defects the peace of *Amiens was initially popular and Addington's policies of fiscal economy were generally approved. His management of public finance was competent, but the breakdown of the peace settlement exposed his limitations and in 1804 he was replaced by Pitt. Raised to the peerage in 1805 he served at various times and with mixed fortunes in Pitt's second ministry, in the Ministry of All the *Talents, and in *Perceval's administration. When *Liverpool formed his ministry in 1812 Sidmouth became home secretary, holding the office until 1821, when he remained in the government as minister without portfolio. At the Home Office Sidmouth was responsible for the surveillance of radical activity. His views were conservative and consistent. He opposed catholic emancipation and parliamentary reform. He believed in the traditional constitution and was convinced that concessions made to popular pressure would be dangerous and unsettling. Yet during several industrial disputes in the troubled post-Waterloo years he sympathized with the strikers, believing that employers should keep faith with their men. If his advice had been followed in 1819 there would have been no *'Peterloo massacre': he had cautioned the magistrates at Manchester against seeking any confrontation with large crowds. Nevertheless, whatever his misgivings about their conduct, he thought it necessary to support the magistrates in the face of criticism. Though he had to rely on informers and spies for information about radical activists, he had a healthy scepticism about many of the alarmist stories passed on to the Home Office. He was dubious about the likely benefits of government intervention in matters of trade and had no wish to extend the powers of central government. After he left office in 1824 he remained a staunch opponent of catholic relief and parliamentary reform, voting against both measures in 1829 and 1832. Throughout his career he voiced the unspoken convictions of many country gentlemen with a tenacity they admired, and while at times he annoyed colleagues by vacillation, Sidmouth's proudest boast was that he had never deliberately hurt anyone. JWD

Addison, Joseph (1672–1719). English writer and politician. Educated at Charterhouse, Queen's College, and Magdalen College, Oxford, where he became a fellow, Addison found favour with the Whigs on account of *The Campaign* (1705), a poem celebrating *Marlborough's victory at *Blenheim. Appointed under-secretary of state in 1706, he was elected MP for Lostwithiel in 1708, accompanying the lord-lieutenant, Lord Wharton, to Ireland in 1709. Addison's close friendship with Richard *Steele and Jonathan *Swift led to his involvement in the **Tatler* (1709–10), but he is best known for his contributions to the **Spectator*, which included most of the 'Sir Roger de Coverley' papers and important essays on *Milton and *Locke. Addison was a crucial figure in the development of a 'polite and commercial' Whig ideology, and the morality propounded in the *Spectator* is the basis of his description as 'The First Victorian'. Addison's other works included the seminal travel book *Remarks on Several Parts of Italy* (1705), a tragedy, *Cato* (1713), which was favourably compared to Shakespeare by his contemporaries, and the stridently anti-Jacobite periodical the *Freeholder* (1715–16). Returning to office on the accession of George I in 1714, Addison became secretary of state, marrying the countess of Warwick in 1716. JAD

'Addled Parliament' (5 April–7 June 1614). The second Parliament of James I was bedevilled by rumours that certain members had undertaken to manage the crown's business, to ensure a positive outcome. Suspicion that their freedom of debate was thereby being undermined added to members' fears that James, by levying *impositions, would be rich enough to rule without Parliament. James took his stand on the 1606 legal judgment in favour of impositions, but the Commons insisted that the judges had acted 'above their commission'. Deadlock ensued, and James therefore dissolved Parliament before any bills were passed. RL

Adela of Louvain (*c.*1100–51), queen of Henry I. Henry's second wife, Adela married him after the death of his only legitimate son in the **White Ship* disaster. The marriage's chief—and unfulfilled—purpose was to provide Henry with a male heir. When it had manifestly failed to do so, Henry persuaded his chief subjects to agree to the succession of his daughter, the Empress *Matilda, in January 1127. After Henry's death, Adela married William d'Aubigny, earl of Arundel, for whom she produced an heir. DB

Adelaide (1792–1849), queen of William IV. Adelaide of Saxe-Meiningen was suggested by Queen *Charlotte as a suitable wife for her son William Henry, then duke of Clarence, hoping that he would end his relationship with Mrs Jordan, actress and mother of his ten children. Marrying in July 1818, Adelaide's reserved personality complemented William's exuberant nature and, despite their differences, the marriage proved happy. The death of two infant daughters clouded Adelaide's life. But following William's accession in 1830, she performed her royal duties with dedication. Initial unpopularity sparked by a belief that she meddled in politics gave way to respect for her charitable works. Her health deteriorated after William's death in 1837 and she died twelve years later. SMC

Aden. A port in the Middle East, commanding the entrance to the Red Sea. In 1839 Aden was ceded to the British by the Turkish sultan and administered from British India. It became a free port in 1850 and was developed as a coaling station on the steamship route from Suez to Bombay. In April 1937 it became a British crown colony and in 1963 part of the South Arabian Federation of Arab Emirates. After the civil war (1965–7) the British withdrew from Aden and it became the capital of the People's Republic of South Yemen. RAS

Admiralty. The relationship of a highly skilled professional service with civilian control is bound to be difficult. With the navy, problems were multiplied by the very high cost of building and maintaining a fleet, which caused acute tensions when the era of the *dreadnoughts coincided in the 1900s with demands for democratic welfare provision; together with the fact that until recently communications were so difficult that great discretion had to be allowed to the man on the spot. In 1798, before the critical battle of the *Nile, the cabinet did not know where *Nelson's fleet was in the Mediterranean, and Nelson did not know where Napoleon was.

Until a permanent royal navy came into being, organization did not need to be elaborate. Medieval and early modern fleets have neatly been called 'less an institution than an event'. A commander was appointed for the campaign, after which most of the vessels, being converted merchantmen, returned to their home ports. The first admirals were appointed in the late 13th cent., and in the 14th the custom grew up of naming one to command north of the Thames, one for the south and west. But Henry VIII made a considerable effort to strengthen naval power. In 1540 Lord *Bedford was named lord admiral and in 1545 a Council for Marine Causes was established—the genesis of the Navy Board, the four commissioners having specified duties and fixed salaries. *Buckingham, Charles I's favourite, was made lord high admiral and after his murder in 1628 the office was put into commission, largely to save money. This arrangement, with a 1st lord of the Admiralty, became permanent after 1708. Only between 1827 and 1828 was the office of lord high admiral revived, for the duke of Clarence (the future William IV), and the experiment was not an unmitigated success. The growing importance of the navy in the 17th cent. was underlined by the fact that the lord high admiralship was taken at the highest level—by James, duke of York, 1660–73, Charles II himself 1673–84, and Anne's husband, Prince *George of Denmark, 1702–8. In 1673–9 the 1st lord was Prince *Rupert, cousin to the king: it is understandable that when, in 1877, the post went to W. H. *Smith, eyebrows were raised.

The Navy Board took responsibility for administration and implementation, the Admiralty Board for appointments and strategy. Though a recipe for friction, this dual system survived for two centuries and presided over some of the navy's most glorious victories, the balance of power between the boards fluctuating as personalities changed. The fleet to which Charles I had devoted considerable care deserted him at the Civil War. The Commonwealth regime abolished both boards, but found it necessary to replace them with commissioners of the Admiralty and naval commissioners, under whom the navy, particularly with *Blake's leadership, acquitted itself well. Charles II in 1660 restored the old order and was fortunate enough to find in Samuel *Pepys a remarkably capable civil servant, first as clerk of the acts and then as secretary to the Board of Admiralty. The same efficiency was scarcely maintained in the 18th cent. and the great victories were won more by tactics, morale, and personnel than by administration. Since the 1st lord was always a politician, often with no experience of the sea, professional naval advice came from a 1st sea lord, under a variety of names.

The dual system came to an end in 1832, again partly as a measure of economy, when Sir James *Graham brought the Navy Board into the Admiralty structure and redefined channels of responsibility.

In the 20th cent. the degree of autonomy built up by the Admiralty was weakened by a number of factors—spiralling cost, an acceleration of technological change, and, not least, after 1945, by the remarkable shrinking of the navy itself. Winston *Churchill as 1st lord and *Fisher as 1st sea lord both convulsed and improved the navy before 1914, but they may also be seen as agents undermining the Admiralty's inherited position. In 1931, for the first time since 1709, the 1st lord was briefly not a member of the cabinet, and in 1964, after a great run-down of the navy in the wake of the Second World War, the post of 1st lord was discontinued. In a unified Ministry of *Defence the spokesman for the navy was the chief of naval staff and 1st sea lord. Ironically, the grandiose Admiralty Arch was completed in 1911, when the first challenge to British naval supremacy was becoming apparent: a mean-spirited administration in the 1990s proposed to sell it. DDA; JAC

Admiralty, Court of. The High Court of Admiralty, whose first record dates from 1361, dealt with matters relating to crime on the high seas and cases involving maritime questions and foreign merchants. It applied principles of civil law and hence was popular with the cosmopolitan mercantile community. Its heyday was the Tudor period, when it was used to settle disputes relating to maritime contracts and matters of shipwreck and salvage. The court excited the hostility of Parliament and of the common lawyers, especially *Coke, and declined in the 17th cent., losing most of its commercial jurisdiction to the common law courts. Admiralty remained a separate court until merged with the matrimonial and probate courts into the Probate, Divorce, and Admiralty division of the High Court in 1873. MM

Admonition to the Parliament, 1572. A puritan manifesto, composed by John Field and others, arguing against the authority of bishops and urging a presbyterian church government. It was not presented to Parliament but was published in June 1572 after a puritan bill had been abandoned, when the House was informed that the queen 'utterly misliketh it'. An *Answer to the Admonition* was offered by John *Whitgift, future archbishop of Canterbury. JAC

Adomnán, St (*c.*628–704). Irish scholar, diplomat, and ninth abbot of Iona. Born into the royal Uí Néill dynasty and educated at Durrow, probably where he taught the future King Aldfrith of Northumbria, he moved in the 670s to

Iona, where he wrote his *Holy Places*, based on a conversation with a Frankish bishop, Arculf. He visited Aldfrith twice (incorporating at least one journey to Abbot Ceolfrith of Monkwearmouth-Jarrow), in 686, as emissary of the king of Brega, and in 688, when he accepted the Roman Easter. Failure to convert his monks perhaps influenced his writing (688–92) a life of his kinsman *Columba, the monastery's founder, and his return to Ireland in 692. A second visit there saw negotiation with Irish, Scottish, and Pictish kings, and promulgation of his *Law of the Innocents*, protecting non-combatants from violence, at the 697 Synod of Birr (Co. Offaly). Adomnán's cult flourished in Ireland and Scotland. AER

Adrian IV (*c.*1100–59). Name taken by Nicholas Breakspear, still the only Englishman to be elected pope. After studying at Paris, he became abbot of St Rufus in Avignon and then a cardinal in 1149. As papal legate to Scandinavia in 1152–3, he reorganized the churches there. Elected pope in 1154, he soon found himself at odds with the Emperor Frederick I (Barbarossa). In 1155–6 he granted lordship over Ireland to Henry II. According to a papal bull (known from its opening word as **Laudabiliter*), Adrian made the grant so that Henry could reform 'a rough and ignorant people'—and scholars still debate whether or not the bull is a forgery. JG

Adrian, Edgar Douglas, 1st Baron Adrian (1889–1977). Scientist. Born in London, Adrian went to Westminster School and Trinity College, Cambridge, where he read science. Specializing in physiology, he became a fellow of his college in 1913 and then, obtaining a medical degree in record time, spent the First World War treating nervous disorders and cases of shell-shock. Adrian returned to Cambridge in 1919 and published extensively on the nervous system. He shared the Nobel prize in 1932, held the chair of physiology from 1937 to 1951, and was master of Trinity from 1951 to 1965. Among his many distinctions was the presidency of the Royal Society 1950–5. He was given the OM in 1942 and a barony in 1955. JAC

Adullamites was the name derisively given to Robert *Lowe and nearly 40 Liberal MPs who opposed Lord *Russell's programme of parliamentary reform in 1866. They were dubbed by John *Bright on 13 March in allusion to the cave of Adullam (1 Sam. 22), to which David fled and was joined by everyone who was discontented. Their opposition brought about the fall of the government but a further measure of reform was then introduced by the Conservative government of *Derby and *Disraeli. JAC

advowsons are the right of appointing a parson in the Church of England to a parish or other church benefice. They can be held by the bishop of the diocese or by a patron (individual or corporate) who has the right to 'present' someone to the living, i.e. nominate a person to the bishop or ecclesiastical superior. The system survived from pre-Reformation power struggles between church and state until the right became protected in English civil law. Two Church of England reports in the 1960s recommended reform of the system and the Benefice Measure of 1978 provided for involvement of the parish in appointments but not for abolition of this form of patronage. JFC

Adwalton Moor, battle of, 1643. *Newcastle and the *Fairfaxes were manœuvring in the spring of 1643 for control of Yorkshire. In the battle on Adwalton Moor, 30 June, 5 miles east of Bradford, the royalists outnumbered their opponents and after heavy fighting achieved an important victory. Bradford and Leeds fell immediately and Newcastle settled down to the siege of Hull. JAC

Æd (d. 878), 'king of the Picts' (876–8), anachronistically regarded as 4th king of Scotland. Son of *Kenneth I, he succeeded his brother *Constantine I. This was the worst period of Scandinavian devastation, and defeat and occupation in 875–6 must have left the kingdom shattered, affording an opportunity for those who wished to challenge the dominance of Æd's family, which had monopolized the kingship for more than three decades. Two rivals on record are the obscure *Giric and Æd's nephew *Eochaid, son of Rhun of Strathclyde. Either of these may have been Æd's final opponent in battle at Strathallan (7 miles north of Stirling), which left Æd fatally wounded. A debatable source says that he was buried on Iona. DEB

Ædan mac Gabhrain (d. *c.*608), king of Dalriada. He was crowned on Iona in 574 by St *Columba, his spiritual adviser, and was politically significant. Ædan established a powerful kingdom, first gaining authority over the Irish Dalriada at the convention of Druim Cett in 575. Successful campaigns included expeditions to the Orkneys and the Isle of Man. But in 603 he led a great army against the powerful Northumbrian king *Æthelfryth at *Degsastan, thought to be in Liddesdale. Soundly defeated and his army destroyed, he fled, which may be why, in Welsh tradition, he is known as 'Ædan the traitor of the North'. AM

Ælfheah (954–1012), archbishop of Canterbury, was a monk at Deerhurst and at Bath before being appointed bishop of Winchester in 984. In 994 he is said to have visited Olaf of Norway, then on a raid at Southampton, converted him, and obtained a promise to leave England alone. In 1006 he succeeded Ælfric as archbishop of Canterbury. A Danish host burned Canterbury in 1011 and took the archbishop prisoner: 'Then was he a captive, he who had been | The head of England, and of Christendom' (*Anglo-Saxon Chronicle*). Ælfheah refused to be ransomed and on 19 April 1012 at Greenwich was battered to death. He was buried in St Paul's and then in his own cathedral at Canterbury. He is recognized as a saint, usually as St Alphege. JAC

Ælle (d. *c.*514), founder of the South Saxon kingdom, is said to have landed near Selsey Bill in 477, traditionally with three sons and three ships, driving the Britons back into Andredesweald, a great wood across south-eastern Britain. His next recorded battle, in 485, took place near an unknown stream, Mearcredes burna, and in 491, Ælle and his son Cissa successfully stormed the fort of Anderida, near Pevensey, wiping out the Britons. Named by *Bede as first of the *bretwaldas, a powerful overlord, he was probably leader of a general Anglo-Saxon push against Britons in the south, but his disappearance from records after Anderida seems to coincide with a revival of the Britons, who, led by *Ambrosius Aurelianus, were victorious in battle at *Mount Badon. The site is uncertain and the date debatable (516 in the Annals Cambriae), but Bede placed the event *c.*493. AM

Ælle (d. 867), king of Northumbria (*c.*863–7 or, possibly, his reign was confined to 867). He was the last independent English king of Northumbria. Though probably not of royal birth, he sought to usurp power from his predecessor Osberht at a dire time. Danish armies were in sight of taking York, and in November 866 they did. Ælle and Osberht united in an effort to regain the city on 21 March 867. They penetrated the walls, but both were then killed. JCa

aeronautical industry. Following the rapid development of powered flight at the beginning of the 20th cent., aircraft manufacture, in common with many other strategic industries, was given a great stimulus during the *First World War. The military potential of fixed-wing aircraft for observation and combat was proved for the first time on any scale. Non-rigid airships were used on coastal patrol and anti-submarine work and later large rigid airships, the R33 and R34, were built, based on German designs. In July 1919 the R34 was the first aircraft to cross the Atlantic from Britain to America.

Regular civil aviation developed after the war, with the first daily service from London to Paris commencing in 1919. Several British companies joined to form Imperial Airways in 1924 and the network for both mail and passenger transport was gradually extended beyond Europe to outposts of the empire in Africa and Asia. In 1931 the company adopted the Handley Page aircraft, which could carry 40 passengers at 100 m.p.h. From 1934 the Empire Flying Boat, nicknamed the 'Queen of the Skies', carrying its passengers in considerable comfort, could cruise for 800 miles at 165 m.p.h. The British Overseas Airways Corporation (BOAC) was established 1939.

The *Second World War changed the face of aviation and again brought major advances in aircraft design and propulsion, particularly turbo-prop and jet engines, leading to the development of much larger and faster civilian aircraft. Post-war expansion to meet military and civil aviation requirements brought further significant innovations, but at considerable cost. One prestige project typified the 'white-heat of technology' era of the 1960s, when Britain, in co-operation with France, operated at the limits of known technology in the race to produce a supersonic passenger transport aircraft. Concorde was developed, in spite of escalating cost and the uncertainty of its financial viability, swallowing hundreds of millions of pounds, in an exercise described by one expert as 'an unmitigated disaster without historical parallel'.

Despite an impressive performance in aero-engines and in other sectors of aerospace during the 1960s and 1970s, the commercial viability of some projects was questionable and deprived routine manufacturing of talented engineers and scientists. While remaining the third largest in the world after the USA and France, the British aerospace industry suffered badly during the periodic crises experienced by civil aviation and from reductions in defence orders. During the 1980s, collaborative development of civil and military aircraft, particularly with European partners, increased to save on costs of new production programmes. ID

Æthelbald (d. 757), king of Mercia (716–57). In his time any member of an extended royal family had an accepted chance to capture the throne. This is the background to the young Æthelbald's being driven into exile in the reign of his second cousin Ceolred, and to his succeeding Ceolred as king. *Bede tells us something weighty about Æthelbald's success as king. Writing in 731 he says that all the kingdoms of the English, south of the Humber, are under the authority of Æthelbald. A charter of 736 describes Æthelbald in language which supports this claim, one terming him king of all the kingdoms of the South English and even king of Britain. His relations with the church were forceful. He seems to have established a firm exploitation of monasteries and he misconducted himself with nuns. He died at the hands of his own military household. Our fragments of knowledge suggest the creative authority of a mighty ruler. JCa

Æthelbert (d. 616), king of Kent (560–616) has a special importance as the king who welcomed the Christian missionaries led by St *Augustine to England in 597. He exercised overlordship over all the English peoples south of the Humber, and as a direct result of his support the Christian mission was firmly established in the south-east, with bishoprics set up at his principal centre, *Canterbury (where Augustine became the first archbishop), *Rochester, and *London. Sources suggest that he began his reign as early as 560 or 565, but it is likely that these dates refer to his possible date of birth and that his reign commenced in the late 570s or early 580s. At that stage Kent had firm contacts with the continent and sometime before 589 Æthelbert married Bertha, daughter of Charibert, a Frankish king of Paris. She was a Christian, and brought a Christian priest, the bishop Liudhard, with her. They practised their faith in a church on the site of St Martin's, east of the city wall: a fragment of the pre-Augustinian structure survives. Æthelbert allowed Augustine to preach, allotting him the church at St Martin's and a site in the city which became the cathedral church, and later a site for the monks outside the wall on which was built St Augustine's abbey, a burial place for kings and archbishops. The king was quickly converted, probably in 597, and many of his people with him. The new faith drew him into yet closer contact with Francia and ultimately with Rome, and provided him with literate servants. As a result the first extant Anglo-Saxon laws were drawn up, after the example of the Romans, making provision among other things for the incorporation of the Christian church into the social fabric of the kingdom. Æthelbert continued to exercise effective authority in the south-east but Kentish pre-eminence weakened after his death in 616, a perilous time both for his kingdom and for the Christian mission. HL

Æthelburg (b. *c.*605) was the Christian daughter of Æthelbert of Kent. Her marriage to the Northumbrian king

Edwin (625) brought about his baptism and the initial conversion of his kingdom by Bishop *Paulinus, who had accompanied her north. Edwin's defeat and death in 633 forced queen and bishop to flee back to Kent. AM

Æthelfleda, lady of the Mercians (d. 918), was the last independent ruler of Mercia. The daughter of Alfred of Wessex and his Mercian wife Ealhswith, she was married to Æthelred of Mercia, probably in the second half of the 880s. Even before his death in 911, Æthelfleda is recorded as exercising regalian power in the province in the 'Mercian Register', a fragment of a Mercian chronicle incorporated into some versions of the **Anglo-Saxon Chronicle*. In particular she is noted for providing a ring of burhs (fortified centres) around western Mercia and for conducting successful military campaigns against the Welsh, the Hiberno-Norse Vikings who were establishing settlements in Lancashire and Cheshire, and the Danes of York and the east midlands. Her campaigns against the Danes were in co-operation with her brother King Edward the Elder of Wessex and, although Æthelfleda has often been cited as evidence for the relative independence of women in Anglo-Saxon England, her position must be viewed in the context of the ambitions of her father and brother to annex western Mercia. These were realized after Æthelfleda's death in 918, when Edward deposed her daughter Ælfwynn and took over control of the province. BAEY

Æthelfryth (d. *c*.616), king of Northumbria (*c*.593–*c*.616), was said by *Bede to be the cruellest enemy of the Britons, slaughtering, enslaving, and opening the way for further Anglo-Saxon settlement. It was probably Æthelfryth who defeated the British at Catterick (north Yorks.), lamented in the Welsh poem, *Gododdin*. His defeat of King *Ædan at *Degsastan in 603 effectively subdued the Irish in Scotland. His victory over the men of Powys at *Chester *c*.616 was significant, separating Britons in Wales from their northern compatriots. But Æthelfryth's demise was at the hands of Anglo-Saxons. Threatened by Æthelfryth if he did not murder or hand over Edwin, claimant to the Northumbrian kingdom of *Deira, who had taken refuge at his East Anglian court, *Rædwald attacked, killing Æthelfryth in battle near the *river Idle (Lincs.) *c*.616. AM

Æthelheard, king of the West Saxons (726–40). Little is known of this king who succeeded to the throne of Wessex when *Ine, described in some sources as his kinsman, abdicated to go on pilgrimage to Rome. His succession was challenged by Atheling Oswald, who claimed descent from King *Ceawlin. Æthelheard suffered from the expansion of Mercian power; Æthelbald of Mercia is recorded as taking control of Somerton in 733 and seems to have been able to grant land in northern Somerset and Wiltshire. Æthelheard was probably married to Frithugyth whose departure to Rome with Bishop Forthhere is recorded for 737. BAEY

Æthelnoth (d. 1038). Archbishop of Canterbury from 1020. Often referred to as 'the Good', and thought to have influenced *Cnut, who was generous to Canterbury and granted him extensive powers of jurisdiction. Æthelnoth restored the church at Canterbury, damaged during Danish raids, and in 1023 had the remains of his martyred predecessor, *Ælfheah, translated there with great ceremony. An arm of St Augustine of Hippo, bought by him at Pavia, was given to the abbey church at Coventry. An improbable account claims that, after Cnut's death, pledged to consecrate none but his son Harthacnut, he refused to crown *Harold Harefoot. AM

Æthelred (d. *c*.716), king of Mercia (675–704). All we know of Æthelred, son of *Penda, comes from episodic indications of a career whose apparent paradoxes signal a world no less pious than brutal. Its realities can be glimpsed, not recaptured. In 676 he ravaged Kent, and not least its churches. In 679 he won an important victory over the Northumbrians at the battle on the *Trent. In 697 his nobles murdered his royal Northumbrian wife Osthryth. In 704 he abdicated to become a monk. JCa

Æthelred (d. 796), king of Northumbria (774–8/9, 790–6). Knowledge of Northumbrian history at this time is 'nasty, brutish, and short'. Æthelred was displaced after five years' rule by a member of another line, Ælfwald. Regaining power upon Ælfwald's murder in 790, Æthelred butchered Ælfwald's sons and sought to secure himself by marrying the daughter of *Offa of Mercia, and faced the shock of the Viking sack of *Lindisfarne in 793. In 796 he was murdered. With better sources we could better interpret these miseries. JCa

Æthelred I (d. 871), king of Wessex (865–71). The third son of *Æthelwulf to succeed to the kingship of the West Saxons, Æthelred had to endure the first major onslaught of the Danes in their systematic attempt to conquer England. From bases set up in *East Anglia in 866 they first turned their attention to *Northumbria and *Mercia, delaying moves against *Wessex until the autumn of 870. After a series of skirmishes and battles with varying fortunes, Æthelred died on campaign in April 871, to be succeeded by his younger brother *Alfred. HL

Æthelred, lord of the Mercians (d. 911). Of unknown origins, by 883 Æthelred was in control of that western part of Mercia which had been left under Anglo-Saxon control when Vikings conquered the rest of the province. Æthelred found it expedient to accept the overlordship of *Alfred of Wessex and married his eldest daughter *Æthelfleda, perhaps soon after Alfred had ceded control of London to him in 886. The two provinces co-ordinated activities against the Vikings, but Æthelred seems to have become increasingly plagued by ill-health so that well before his death in 911 Æthelfleda had become the effective leader of the Mercians. BAEY

Æthelred II (d. 1016), king of England (978–1016). Æthelred *Unræd*, the 'Unready', or more accurately the 'ill-advised', lost his kingship 1013–14, when the Danish king, *Sweyn Forkbeard, forced him into exile in Normandy, the home of his second wife *Emma, whom Æthelred had married in 1002. The Anglo-Saxon Chronicler who composed a full account late in Æthelred's reign was heavily biased against the king, painting a grim picture of impotence, vacillation, and treachery. Modern approaches have been kinder, noting solid evidence for effective government in the legal and financial spheres and pointing to the cultural and religious elements of strength in a period which produced in Ælfric the most polished master of Old English prose and in *Wulfstan, bishop of Worcester and archbishop of York, one of the most competent statesmen and framers of secular and ecclesiastical law. No one denies the periods of political incompetence notably later in the reign, after 1006, when Æthelred relied too much on the advice of the treacherous ealdorman Eadric Streona. It was indeed the king's deep misfortune that, no military leader himself, he had to face renewed Viking onslaught which reached a peak after the defeat and death of the ealdorman Byrhtnoth at the battle of *Maldon in 991. This was followed by attempts to buy off the Danes by the payment of immense sums as *Danegeld, a course of action suggested by Archbishop Sigeric. £10,000 was paid to them in 993, and further immense sums were levied sporadically throughout the reign, a wry tribute to the efficiency of Æthelred's tax collectors. Sporadic violent reaction also occurred as when on the morrow of *St Brice's day, 13 November 1002, Æthelred ordered 'all the Danish men in England' to be slain. In the later stages of the reign things got completely out of hand, in spite of the bravery of individual leaders such as Ulfketel, ealdorman of East Anglia, and *Edmund Ironside, Æthelred's son and successor. *Ælfheah, archbishop of Canterbury, was martyred by the Danes in 1012, and Sweyn's success the following year may be attributed in part to English war-weariness and disenchantment with their natural leaders. After Sweyn's death, Æthelred was recalled on promise to rule justly and institute reforms but died on 23 April 1016 in London which was itself under immediate threat from *Cnut's invading and ultimately victorious army. HL

Æthelthryth (Ætheldreda, Audrey), **St** (*c.*630–79). Daughter of King Anna of East Anglia, and virgin wife of Tondbert, of the south Gyrwe, and secondly of Ecgfrith of Northumbria, who eventually released her to monastic life at Coldingham, north of Berwick. Æthelthryth founded a double monastery at Ely on the East Anglian–Mercian frontier, perhaps the first south-eastern house for women. The promotion of her cult (in 695), by *Wilfrid (who had received land for St Andrew's, Hexham, from her) and by her sister and successor Sexburh, showed Gallic influence and, after *Æthelwold refounded Ely (*c.*970), gave title to church and to lands, to her community, and respectability as rulers of East Anglia to her royal West Saxon devotees. Her usefulness was as great as her sanctity. Bede wrote a hymn on virginity in her honour. Her cult survived the Norman Conquest. AER

Æthelwold, St (*c.*908–84). Winchester-born leader of the 10th-cent. reformation, and major influence on King *Edgar. Probably a noble, Æthelwold served King *Æthelstan, was ordained priest by Bishop Ælfheah of Winchester, became a monk under *Dunstan at Glastonbury, and was made, by King Edred, abbot of Abingdon (*c.*955) and, by Edgar, bishop of Winchester (963). He replaced the clerks of the Old and New Minsters with monks (964), and developed Winchester as a centre of art and learning. One of its products was Ælfric, later his biographer. Æthelwold's *Benedictional* (collection of blessings), which combined two liturgical traditions, proved very influential. Besides Abingdon, Æthelwold revived the monasteries of Peterborough, Ely, and Thorney, thereby reintroducing monasticism to the Danelaw. He was behind the *Regularis concordia*, a version of the rule of St Benedict, which he himself translated into English, with additions regulating communal prayer, prescribed by the council of Winchester (*c.*970) for all English religious houses.

Perhaps the most forceful and austere of the reformers, Æthelwold was a wealthy patron of building, and ruthlessly efficient in acquiring estates. Historical tradition and cults of earlier saints were promoted to buttress his houses' claims, as was the cult of the Virgin. An inspiration was continental practice, especially that at Fleury-sur-Loire. Another was the golden age of monasticism as portrayed by Bede, which may explain Æthelwold's unusual policy that cathedral chapters should be monastic. Heavily involved in politics, he worked closely with Edgar and Queen Ælfthryth. Æthelwold elevated royal authority, for example implying parallels between king and Christ. The popularity of his cult, promoted by his pupil *Wulfstan (of Winchester) possibly at his own request, was limited, though his biography was widely circulated until the 15th cent. AER

Æthelwulf (d. 858), king of Wessex (839–58). The son of *Egbert (802–39) and father of four kings, the youngest of whom was *Alfred the Great (871–99), Æthelwulf is a far from negligible figure in Anglo-Saxon history. He was a competent military leader, acting as a subking in the south-east in his father's lifetime (829–39), and conducting substantial campaigns against the Danes at *Aclea in Kent in 851 and against the Welsh of Powys (in support of his Mercian allies) in 853. Much of his personal interest seemed, however, to lie in ecclesiastical directions. He made generous provision for the financing of churches (his Decimations), apparently in the form of grants of a tenth of royal lands into the hands of thegns empowered to transfer proceeds to religious foundations. In 855 he yielded his authority to his eldest son Æthelbald, and went on pilgrimage to Rome, possibly accompanied by his young son Alfred, who would have been about 6. Æthelwulf was away from his kingdom for a twelvemonth, and on his return with a Frankish princess as a bride (a young girl, Judith, held to be only 12 years old) he was forced to agree to a division of the kingdom with his own authority confined effectively to the south-east until his death in 858. Æthelbald then succeeded to the whole kingdom, and also, in spite of the fact that she was his stepmother, married Judith. HL

Aetius, Flavius (d. 454). Roman general. Gildas's work *On the Ruin of Britain* contains the passage known as The Groans of the Britons: 'To Agitius thrice consul, the groans of the Britons. . . . the barbarians push us back to the sea, the sea pushes us back to the barbarians. Between these two types of death we are either slaughtered or drowned.' The Agitius of the text is usually identified as Flavius Aetius, consul for the third time in 446 and last effective Roman commander in Gaul. Other possibilities are Aegidius, appointed by the Emperor Majorian (457–61) as commander in Gaul and subsequently ruling independently till his death in 464 but never thrice consul; or another Flavius Aetius of similar date who was consul but whose career lay mainly in the eastern part of the empire. There is no evidence that any of these intervened in Britain. ASEC

Afghan wars. From 1807, when the armies of Tsar Alexander I reached its northern borders, Afghanistan came to represent an uneasy neutral zone between the Russian and the British Indian empires around which 'the Great Game' was played. The British attempted to bring the kingdom under 'informal influence' but, when this broke down, launched three military interventions—in 1838–42, 1878–81, and 1919–21. None was successful. The first Afghan War against Dost Mohammed saw a British expeditionary force reach and capture the capital, Kabul. However, surrounding tribes rose up and forced a desperate retreat through mountainous country. Only one member of the original army of 16,000 lived to cross the Khyber pass back into India. The second war was precipitated by Lord *Lytton's forward policies, which subsequently were repudiated by *Gladstone's incoming 1880 government. The third war arose when Habibullah Khan demanded recognition by the British of the absolute independence of his kingdom. At first this was refused but British arms, once more, found the Afghan terrain and peoples intractable. Afghanistan's sovereignty at international law was formally recognized on 21 November 1921. DAW

Africa, partition of. Africa is the nearest continent to western Europe, yet its colonization lagged far behind more distant parts of the world. That was partly because of the health risks it presented to Europeans, and partly because for years there seemed little to take them there. The main exception was trade, in slaves and other goods, which could be carried on perfectly well through African and Arab middlemen at the coasts. A number of maritime nations had posts in Africa from the 16th cent. onwards, including the Portuguese, Spaniards, and—a little later—the Dutch and British in the west and south. As late as the 1860s, however, their presence in tropical Africa was marginal. Britain seemed content with this. In 1865 a parliamentary select committee recommended withdrawing from three of her four west coast settlements altogether. It was shortly after that, however, that interest in Africa hotted up again.

The reasons for this were the use of quinine as a prophylaxis against malaria; missionary activities; a new demand for Africa's natural products; booming trade to the East, which passed round Africa on two sides after the Suez canal was opened in 1869; and native rebellions, which tended to suck British troops and government inland. (The relative importance of each of these factors is controversial.) Other European countries also became involved, especially France in the north and west. In 1882 Britain took control of Egypt after a rebellion there against the local khedive and his growing dependence on European financiers threatened her own interests, particularly in Suez. That sparked off the main stage of the 'scramble for Africa', in which several European nations vied for control over different regions.

To prevent that leading to conflict, the German chancellor Bismarck called a conference in Berlin in 1884, which parcelled west and central Africa out amongst the claimants. That was done with relatively little fuss, mainly because none of the latter felt desperately strongly about it. The only new colony to feel the effects of this immediately was the Congo 'Free State', chiefly because of its bloody exploitation by its new owner, the Belgian King Leopold II.

In the 1890s the action shifted to the east and south. Here the lion's share went to Britain, including the *Sudan, most of east-central Africa, and the *Rhodesias. This time the competition was somewhat keener, threatening conflicts with France over *Fashoda in 1898, and Germany on the eve of the second *Boer War. The risk, however, was felt to be worth it, both because of the reputed riches of the area and because these countries were seen as indirectly vital to the protection of Britain's trade routes to the East. By 1900 the process was more or less completed, leaving virtually the whole of Africa—barring only Ethiopia and Liberia—in European hands. BJP

Africa Company. See ROYAL AFRICA COMPANY.

Agadir crisis, 1911. A Franco-German colonial crisis triggered by a German gunboat in a Moroccan port (July 1911) led ministers to resolve an inter-service dispute over the role of the army in a hypothetical war with Germany by agreeing 'in principle' that it should be sent to the continent. CJB

Agincourt, battle of, 1415. Henry V landed in France on 13 August 1415 with an army of *c.*2,500 men-at-arms and 7,500 archers, laying siege to *Harfleur. He may have intended a more extensive campaign, but as the town held out until 23 September, and his army was much depleted by dysentery, he decided to return forthwith to England via Calais. The march north was lengthier than expected as he was forced far inland in search of a crossing of the Somme. The French army, perhaps over 20,000 strong, attempted to block his approach to Calais. Henry had little choice but to give battle on 25 October though he now had only about 900 men-at-arms and 5,000 archers. He drew up his well-disciplined troops, all on foot, within 300 yards of the enemy, across a narrow front bordered by trees, with archers on the flanks. The French cavalry charged into this funnel, hampered by volleys of arrows and by the wet ground; the rear lines piled into the front. Many were killed or captured, amongst them the duke of Orléans. Against chivalric practice, Henry had some prisoners killed when he thought the French were regrouping and after an attack on his baggage, but this did not diminish the renown gained from this unexpected victory. AC

Agreement of the People, 1647. A set of counter-proposals from the more radical members of the army, largely in the lower ranks, who were concerned at the concessions which the army council had offered the king in the *Heads of the Proposals. The Agreement, formulated in October 1647, became the basis for the discussions at the army debates in *Putney. It wished the reformed electoral system to be related to the number of inhabitants rather than property or taxation and urged a substantial widening of the parliamentary franchise. *Cromwell and *Ireton retorted that the security of property would be undermined. When the Agreement was submitted to Parliament, it was rejected.

JAC

Agricola, Gnaeus Iulius. Governor of Britain 77–83. Thanks to the fortunate circumstances first of Agricola's daughter having married the historian *Tacitus and second that Tacitus' biography of his father-in-law survived, we are better informed about Agricola than any other provincial governor in the Roman empire. Agricola came of a senatorial family in southern Gaul. He progressed through the usual career of a senator, but was exceptional in spending all three of his periods of provincial service in Britain, culminating in an unusually long governorship. He first served in Britain as a military tribune (legion unknown) at the time of the *Boudiccan revolt (60/1). He returned as legate (commander) of *legio XX Valeria Victrix* 69–73, during which time his legion took part in the advance north of the Humber–Mersey line. He served as a consul in the year 77 and probably arrived in Britain as governor late in that year. Tacitus' account of Agricola's governorship is dominated by narratives of the seven seasons of campaigning, advancing Roman power far into Scotland and culminating in the defeat of the Caledonian tribes under *Calgacus at the battle of Mons Graupius (83/4). The route of advance east of the Highland massif can be traced through the sites of 'marching camps', temporary campaign fortifications. In the intervals from fighting he is shown governing wisely and promoting Roman ways amongst the Britons. But our view of Agricola has been over-influenced by Tacitus' laudatory biography, portraying him as an exceptional general and a just governor. His undoubted feats of arms have been over-emphasized to the detriment of his predecessors, and there is little in the archaeological record to suggest his governorship saw significant development in the civil sphere.

ASEC

agricultural revolution. This was traditionally regarded as a movement which took place simultaneously with the *industrial revolution, and involved the invention and introduction of new crop rotations in which roots and artificial crops were cultivated, and which involved also improvements in livestock breeding, and the reorganization of the land as a result of parliamentary enclosure. Taken together, these changes were held to have raised the output and productivity of land in such a way that the population was fed (with some help from imports) without resort to massive labour inputs which would have slowed down the industrial revolution by restricting the flow of labour from the countryside to the town. Consequently agricultural productivity and labour productivity must both have risen; indeed, the twin achievements of 18th- and 19th-cent. agriculture are seen as the ability to match population growth with rising agricultural production, and structural economic change with major gains in labour productivity.

Without much doubt the end results deduced by this argument are correct. Food supply did more or less keep pace with population and urbanization, although there was some slack in demand *c.*1750 and a shortfall by 1815 of about 5 per cent, which was largely met by importing grain from Ireland. By 1850 an estimated 6.5 million extra mouths were being fed from home production compared with 1750. However, questions have been raised about the nature, and particularly the timing, of the agricultural revolution. Originally it was believed to have taken place alongside, and to have been a necessary concomitant to, the industrial revolution. Recent research has raised questions about this linkage. Although there is general agreement that English agriculture underwent a fundamental technological transformation between the mid-16th and the mid-19th cents. which had a decisive impact on 'productivity' in terms of grain yields per acre, the timing and mechanics of this transformation remain in question.

Modern understanding of the agricultural revolution sees it loosely as a three-stage, overlapping, process. The first phase, completed by *c.*1750–70, saw two developments: first, the introduction of new crops, particularly root crops such as turnips and swedes, and legumes such as clover, trefoil, and lucerne, which could be grown in the fields between grain crops; and second, a considerable rise in the productivity of labour. As a result of these changes less land needed to be left fallow in order to restore its fertility, additional animal feedstuffs were grown allowing farmers to keep more cattle, and greater quantities (and quality) of manure became available which, when spread on the fields, gradually raised the yield. Farmers acted empirically because the scientific principles behind this process of fixing the nitrogen in the soil were not understood until well into the 19th cent., but from early beginnings in Norfolk the new crops were gradually adopted across the country, as and when soils permitted. At the same time, rising labour productivity ensured that the new farming was not a drain on industrial production.

During the second phase of the agricultural revolution, lasting from around 1750 to 1830, demand increased rapidly. In this period the slack in the agricultural economy which had been partly taken up by grain exports disappeared and by the early 19th cent. an import balance existed despite a considerable growth in output. Few new crops were introduced in this period, but the reorganization of the land through enclosure (first by agreement and then by parliamentary means), and the gradual growth of larger farms, with their savings on capital inputs and their supposed higher quality of husbandry, brought a slow rise in productivity, and a growing trend towards regional specialization. Norfolk farmers had pioneered the cultivation of clover in England, but it was only after 1740 that the principal benefits of the new crop were felt and yields began to rise rapidly. The pressure on agricultural resources during the French *Revolutionary and Napoleonic wars (1793–1815) led to additional land being brought (temporarily) into cultivation but also to higher prices as farm produce occasionally failed to keep pace with demand, and higher rents.

The third phase, beginning in about 1830, and sometimes called the second agricultural revolution, saw for the first time farmers using substantial inputs purchased off their farms, in the form of new fertilizers for their land and artificial feedstuffs for their animals. Together with the introduction of improved methods of drainage, of particular importance for the heavier claylands, the results were seen in the era of high farming—a phrase used of more or less any progressive practices—between the 1840s and 1870s, which soon gave way to a severe and prolonged agricultural depression.

Perhaps the most remarkable feature of the agricultural revolution was the absence of real technological advances. Although steam-powered machines were introduced for various processes in the agricultural cycle, the availability of labour, especially in the corn-growing areas of southern and eastern England, seems artificially to have slowed down the shift from labour to machinery, and it was not until the flight from the land during the late 19th-cent. depression that farmers began actively to introduce machinery.

In Scotland the agricultural revolution took a rather different form. Although, as in England, there has been a tendency to view it as a long-term change, it is now thought that, at least in the Lowlands, this underplays the transformation which occurred in the second half of the 18th cent. A rapid move towards single tenancies and production for the market was partly stimulated by the pace of population growth, and particularly of urbanization (notably Glasgow and Edinburgh) in the second half of the 18th cent., although Scottish industrialization prior to 1815 was partly at least a rural phenomenon, often via planned new settlements.

The result, in the second half of the 18th cent., was seen in the adoption of new technologies and crops, a shift to long leases with improving clauses written in, and higher productivity. Many of the existing farmers successfully adapted to the new demands upon them, so that there was no Lowland equivalent of the Highland clearances, although the traditional cottar class did suffer in these years. The absence of protest on their part seems to have reflected the alternative labour opportunities in the towns and new settlements, and indeed in the countryside where demand remained high and little technology was introduced. In the long run the new agriculture enabled more food to be produced at lower cost and labour productivity rose as a part of this process. Overall the result was a radical departure from the patterns of the past in the last quarter of the 18th cent., not simply measured in terms of physical enclosure, but also in the more effective use of land involving liming, sown grasses, and the organization of labour. It was a structural change, and not simply a perpetuation and intensification of existing trends, since it produced a dramatic increase in crop yields, allowing Scottish cultivators to catch up on English levels of output in the space of a few decades, and resulted in a visible alteration of the rural social system in an equally short time. JVB

Beckett, J. V., *The Agricultural Revolution* (Oxford, 1990); Kerridge, E., *The Agricultural Revolution* (1967); Mingay, G. E., *The Agricultural Revolution: Changes in Agriculture 1650–1880* (1977).

agriculture is the process of cultivating the land to grow crops. It reflects a level of civilization beyond that of early man, who lived by hunting wild animals and by eating natural produce of the earth such as berries.

The system of agriculture which spread across much of northern Europe in the late Saxon period including much of the British Isles, was that of common field, alternatively known as open field, farming. In this system land around the village was gradually colonized from the waste (assarted), and cultivated for crops. As each parcel of land was brought under the plough, it was divided between the various serfs or villeins in such a way as to ensure a reasonable mix of soil qualities, and the result was that each farmer acquired a selection of 'strips' scattered around the village. The system was adopted across much of the country but not everywhere. In parts of northern England, and in Kent, for example, other systems prevailed.

The common field system was best suited to a small population of predominantly rural people providing for their own needs, which could be supplemented by trading weekly in the local market. It ran into trouble as population increased through the 16th cent., and piecemeal attempts were made to enclose the land. Initially these were resisted by the government on the grounds that enclosure produced engrossing and might eventually lead to a monopoly of landholdings, and also because it was believed to bring unemployment. By the second half of the 17th cent., and the early years of the 18th cent., however, the situation was changing. As grain prices fell, or remained static, after about 1650, farmers tried to raise their output. On the claylands this was achieved by diversifying into the more lucrative dairying and rearing business. This put pressure on the resources of grass, and considerable enclosing activity took place with the intention of shifting out of mixed farming (with its traditional balance of animals and crops) into pasture farming, with an emphasis on the rearing and fattening of animals. In addition this regional specialization pointed towards more sophisticated marketing mechanisms and lower transport costs. It also enjoyed legal protection through the courts, and probably well over 20 per cent of the land area was enclosed by private means prior to 1750.

Enclosure meant, in effect, the abandoning of the old open field system with its emphasis on communal rights and obligations. Each farmer, far from having strips in each field, now had his own holding usually with an accompanying farmstead within the fields, and the village community began to take on a new shape.

From about 1760 the most common means of enclosing land was by parliamentary legislation—a reversal of the days in the 16th cent. when government opposed enclosure—and between 1750 and 1830 about 21 per cent of the land area of Britain was enclosed by this means. As a result, large tracts of the countryside were reorganized. The great expanses of the open fields were replaced by hedges, fences, and, in upland areas, dry stone walling. Closely associated with this change was a move towards larger and more compact farms. However, the speed of change, and the impact of enclosure on the productivity of farms, has been questioned. Enclosure raised rents, often between 50 and 100 per cent, and many landowners undoubtedly promoted enclosure because they anticipated a windfall in higher rental income, but these alterations were not a necessary reflection of either greater efficiency or greater productivity. These may have come in time as farmers were left to experiment and to adopt improved rotations and methods as they saw fit once they were no longer expected to conform to the rules of the manor court. Commoners, squatters, and others who had lived on the land but without a specific landholding were expropriated at enclosure, and few seem to have been able to make a living thereafter.

By the 19th cent. the typical pattern of farming was one in which individual farmers worked a designated holding, altering the balance of animals and crops according no longer to the rules of a manorial court—most courts lapsed at enclosure, and they were abolished in 1926 except in the Nottinghamshire village of Laxton where open field farming still continues—but to the covenants in their leases. Even so, many farms remained small, family concerns, rather than the larger holdings favoured by agricultural experts.

Agriculture enjoyed a period of considerable prosperity in the middle decades of the 19th cent. From the 1830s farmers began to use increasing quantities of artificial fertilizers and animal feedstuffs, pushing up productivity to new levels. In the wake of *Corn Law repeal in 1846, drainage loans enabled many landowners to improve the quality of their clay lands, and the 1850s and 1860s are often known as the golden age of farming.

In the course of the 1870s a series of bad harvests, coupled with a rapid increase in the flow of food imports (grain and meat) from the Americas, led to depression. From 1879 until the Second World War, with only occasional respites, the agricultural sector of the economy was under considerable strain. Landowners, faced with falling rents and falling land values, sold out, particularly after 1918. Farmers, faced with competing in a market which was loaded against them by the policy of free trade, turned to smaller holdings employing less labour. One result, the so-called 'flight from the land', saw a rapid outflow of population from the predominantly arable counties, and the first serious shift into agricultural machinery by those farmers who remained.

Agriculture benefited briefly in the 20th cent. from plough-up campaigns and intensive cropping during the two world wars. Since 1945, and particularly since Britain entered the *European Economic Community in 1971, the position has changed again. On average, farms are now much larger than they were in the 19th cent., and much more specialized. Output has risen spectacularly, and considerable areas of land have been removed from cultivation altogether under the European Community's 'set aside' scheme, to try to prevent the recurrence of food mountains. Small farms have now very largely disappeared, and the countryside has been transformed once again into large 'open' fields with the grubbing-up of the old enclosure hedges which had surrounded much smaller fields than those of today. JVB

Beckett, J. V., *The Agricultural Revolution* (Oxford, 1990); Finberg, H. P. R., *et al.* (eds.), *The Agrarian History of England and Wales* (Cambridge, 1967–).

Aidan, St (d. 651). First abbot of *Lindisfarne, site of his see (634–51). Sent from *Iona, replacing a severer colleague, to work closely with King *Oswald in restoring Christianity in Northumbria, Aidan's legacy was profound: Lindisfarne, and his royal pupil *Hilda were stars in the later 7th-cent. firmament. Aidan's rejection of worldly behaviour and elevated associations partly explains the eclipse of his cult by *Cuthbert's and his relative obscurity. We depend on *Bede, in whose portrait, combining contemplation, industry in evangelization (royal estates providing his bases for preaching tours), study, sternness, asceticism, moderation, humility, and discretion, he embodies the episcopal ideals of Pope Gregory I and is a model for Bede's slothful contemporaries. His only defect was failure to accept the Roman Easter. Here Bede may have been defending Lindisfarne against *Wilfrid's negative assessment of its traditions as expounded, apparently, at the Synod of *Whitby. Some of Aidan's relics were taken from Lindisfarne to Ireland by Colman, and his cult was revived at *Glastonbury in the 10th cent. AER

aids, feudal. See FEUDAL AIDS.

Ailred of Rievaulx (1110–67), known as the 'St Bernard of the North', was the leading figure in the *Cistercian order in England in the mid-12th cent. The son of a priest of Hexham (Northd.), he seemed set for a secular career, entering the service of David I of Scotland, *c.*1130. But in 1134 he entered the abbey of *Rievaulx (north Yorks.), where he remained for nine years as novice and monk before being chosen as first abbot of Revesby (Lincs.), daughter house of Rievaulx. Just four years later he was recalled to be abbot of Rievaulx itself. Largely because of Ailred's inspiration and guidance, his gentleness and humanism, Rievaulx emerged as the chief centre of Cistercian influence in England. The monastery itself prospered and expanded, its numbers increasing to 150 choir monks and 500 lay brothers and servants, and four more daughter houses were established in England and Scotland. Ailred himself became a figure of national importance, beyond Cistercian circles, through his many friends, contacts, and writings. These include his treatise on friendship, the *Speculum caritatis*, and his Sermons on Isaiah, probably his finest work. Of delicate health, he was constantly ill and in pain in the last ten years of his life. He died in his beloved Rievaulx on 12 January 1167, and was buried in the chapter house. He was never formally canonized, but it is no surprise that there was a local cult, approved by the Cistercians. SL

air travel. Commercial carriage of passengers by aircraft or airship began only at the end of the First World War in 1919, based on war surplus, with the direct involvement of manufacturers—Handley Page in the UK, Junkers in Germany—in airline development. For much of the next 40 years, air travel offered an outstanding parable of British international economic failure, with route development lagging behind the market leaders, the imperial preoccupation in international travel, and modest aircraft design leading to the operation of a multiplicity of uncompetitive types. Paris and near-European routes were established in the early 1920s, and supported by subsidy from 1921. The Hambling Committee's recommendations led to the amalgamation into Imperial Airways in 1924, as the UK's 'chosen instrument', embodying an explicit British aircraft and engine policy. Imperial developed the routes to Singapore and the Cape to the neglect of Europe, and even there lagged behind the Dutch KLM (running services to Singapore by 1933).

Early routes combined air, rail, and sea: in 1932, Imperial's service to the Cape involved 33 stages and six changes of vehicle. Only with the flying boat did the routes to Alexandria (1937), Singapore and Sydney (1938), and the USA (1939) become fully 'airways'. The railways helped develop domestic routes, which proved largely uneconomic even with mail subsidy (1934), and were grouped into the UK's second 'chosen instrument', British Airways (1935). Continuing poor performance led the Conservative government to nationalize and integrate both under Lord *Reith into the new British Overseas Airways Corporation in 1940.

The war established air travel, accelerated aircraft technology, and created rapid growth by national carriers into the early 1950s, in which BOAC was a major participant. Continuing 'buy British' policy produced the first jet in the Comet (1952) and the first non-stop transatlantic aircraft, the Britannia (1957), but only one international commercial success, the Vickers Viscount (1953) which served British European Airways. The jet age truncated the competitive life of both the latter with the introduction of the Sud-Aviation Caravelle (1956) on European routes, and the Boeing 707 for the Atlantic crossing (1958), ironically after BOAC had established the first scheduled jet service with the Comet 4.

Despite control by nationalistic and arcane regulations under the International Air Traffic Association (1945), real costs fell as larger and more efficient aircraft were introduced, especially with the Boeing 747. Aircraft displaced from premium routes were applied to the package holiday trade, in which Britain led development through the 1950s and 1960s, and liberalization favoured renewed growth by independent carriers from 1965: passengers carried by UK charters increased fourteen times in the decade from 1963. The consequent introduction of reduced fares to scheduled flights with the ABC (1973) and APEX (1975) schemes further expanded the market, in which British Airways, recreated by merging BOAC and BEA in 1974, faced real competition. Rationalization and subsequent privatization (1986) made BA an international leader and aggressive competitor, notably in respect of Freddie Laker's 'Skytrain' in the late 1970s, and Richard Branson's Virgin in the later 1980s. Air travel continued to grow as real fares fell. JCh

Aix-la-Chapelle, treaty of, 1748. Between March and November 1748 all the belligerents in the War of the *Austrian Succession met here to negotiate a settlement. The British and French put together an agreement that they persuaded their respective (and less powerful) allies to sign. There had been no clear victor in the war and the peace merely acknowledged the status quo. Prussia had made a separate peace with Austria in 1745, but her conquest of Austrian Silesia was recognized at Aix-la-Chapelle. Don Philip of Spain was granted the dukedom of Parma, and Anglo-Spanish trade disputes were adjudicated. The British handed back Louisbourg in America to France and the French withdrew from the Austrian Netherlands. The outbreak of the *Seven Years War, after less than a decade, illustrates the fragility of the peace settlement. AIL

Akeman Street. This Roman road linked *Cirencester and *Verulamium, running across the south midlands via Alchester (Oxon.). It was probably laid out in the 50s AD. The modern name derives from the Anglo-Saxon words meaning 'oak-man'. No Roman name is known. ASEC

***Alabama* case.** The *Alabama* was the largest (990 tons) of several potential commerce raiders built in Britain for the Confederate South in the American Civil War. They all broke early steam power records for Atlantic crossings. Like them, the *Alabama* collected her armament outside Britain, and in two years of high seas raiding made 62 seizures of merchantmen. She was finally sunk in international waters off Cherbourg in June 1864 by the Union warship *Kearsage*. Arbitration in Switzerland in 1871 awarded higher damages against Britain, whose moral case was weak, than the sums claimed by the US government. Convention XIII of the 1909 London naval conference accepted that neutral powers were physically restricted in their dealings with belligerent warships; rights of passage for such ships were conceded. DDA

Alanbrooke, Alan Brooke, 1st Viscount (1883–1963). Soldier. Chief of the imperial general staff for much of the Second World War, Brooke was the son of an Irish baronet from Fermanagh and a member of the protestant ascendancy. After the Royal Military Academy at Woolwich from 1902 he spent the Great War on the western front as an artillery officer. During the inter-war period he had spells at staff college and at Imperial Defence College and at the outbreak of the Second World War was a lieutenant-general in charge of anti-aircraft defence. After commanding in France, he was appointed commander-in-chief home forces in 1940 after Dunkirk and the following year took over as chief of the imperial general staff. He was capable of standing up to and working with *Churchill, whose boldness and imagination he complemented with sober planning, worked well with *Cunningham (navy) and *Portal (RAF), and appointed winning generals in *Alexander, *Montgomery, and *Slim. Brooke was given a barony in 1945 and a viscountcy in 1946. JAC

Alba, kingdom of. The name 'Alba' was Irish and originally applied to Britain ('Albion'). It was then adopted by the kingdom created by *Kenneth MacAlpin of *Dalriada when he took over the kingdom of the Picts in the 840s. This was far from being the whole of Scotland, since Lothian south of the Forth was still held by the Northumbrians and much of the north, west, and the islands were under Norse influence. By the 11th cent. it was more commonly known as Scotia or Scotland. The dukedom of Albany, which merged with the Scottish crown, took its title from Alba, and it remains the Gaelic name for Scotland today. See also FORTRIU; SCOTS, KINGDOM OF. JAC

Alban, St. Protomartyr of Britain, known from early medieval hagiographies. These portray him as a Roman officer who sheltered a priest during one of the persecutions and was martyred at *Verulamium. No date is given but dates in the early and the late 3rd cent. have been put forward. The description of the trial and passion of Alban reflects the actual topography of Verulamium and the medieval St Albans abbey may perpetuate the site of his death or burial; the shrine was in existence to be visited by Bishop *Germanus of Auxerre in 429. ASEC

Albany, Alexander Stewart, 1st duke of [S] (*c*.1454–85). Second son of James II of Scotland, created earl of March [S] (1455), lord of Annandale, and duke of Albany (1458). As admiral of Scotland and march warden in the 1470s, Albany was an obvious focus for Scottish opposition to his brother James III's English alliance (October 1474). Indicted for treason in October 1479, Albany fled to France, where he married and fathered the son who, as John, duke of *Albany, would act as governor (1515–24) for James V.

The remainder of his life consisted of a series of spectacular but unsuccessful come-backs—with English aid as 'Alexander IV' (July 1482), as lieutenant-general for James III (October 1482), with Douglas support in Annandale (battle of Lochmaben, 1484), and a remarkable gaolbreak from Edinburgh castle in the spring of 1485. Later the same year Albany was killed by a lance splinter at a tournament in Paris. NATM

Albany, John Stewart, 2nd duke of [S] (1484–1536). When James IV of Scotland was killed at *Flodden in 1513, his son was 17 months old. Albany, a grandson of James II, was heir presumptive. His father had laid claim to the Scottish throne but was defeated and fled to France. Albany was summoned to become regent to his young cousin and held office from 1515 until 1524. Bred in France, Albany strove to restore the *Franco-Scottish alliance and by the treaty of *Rouen (1517) negotiated marriage for James V to a French princess. From 1517 to 1521 Albany was in France, weakening his Scottish position. In 1521 he effected a reconciliation with *Margaret, the king's mother and sister to Henry VIII, and there were rumours of a possible marriage. In 1522 Henry VIII went to war, protesting that the king's life was in jeopardy, but Albany's grand preparations came to nothing. He resumed the contest in 1523 but again the campaign against northern England misfired, and he returned to France for good in 1524. The enduring legacy of his regency was a French marriage for James, though it did not take place until 1537. JAC

Albany, Murdac Stewart, 2nd duke of [S] (*c*.1362–1425). Son and heir of Robert, 1st duke of Albany (d. 1420), Murdac served as royal justiciar north of Forth. Captured by the English at *Homildon Hill (1402), he spent more than thirteen years in captivity. Between 1413 and 1415 Murdac and his cousin James I were fellow-captives in the Tower of London and at Windsor.

Murdac returned to Scotland in 1416 and succeeded his father as governor in 1420. Less effective than Duke Robert, possibly because of his inability to control his surviving sons, yet a major political figure as heir presumptive to the throne, Murdac neither initiated nor firmly opposed James I's release in 1424. He officiated at James's coronation at Scone (21 May 1424), but was arrested in Parliament the following March, and beheaded with other members of his family at Stirling on 25 May 1425, victim of the political ambitions of James I. NATM

Albany, Robert Stewart, 1st duke of [S] (1339–1420). Third son of Robert II by his first wife Elizabeth Mure, and uncrowned ruler of Scotland for 32 years (1388–1420). While still a young man, Robert acquired the earldoms of Menteith [S] (1361) and Fife [S] (1371); he became royal chamberlain in 1382; and in December 1388 was made guardian for his infirm elder brother John, earl of Carrick [S] (later Robert III, 1390–1406). In 1398 Robert was created duke of Albany, a title which reflected his ambitions for his family in the north, especially in Buchan and Ross.

Albany's guardianship—and from 1406 governorship for the captive, uncrowned James I—was characterized by intermittent hostility towards England, consistent support (until 1418) of the antipope Benedict XIII, a growing commitment to the French alliance, and a ruthless elimination of political opponents, probably in pursuit of his family's claim to the throne. This final ambition remained unfulfilled. NATM

Albert, prince consort (1819–61). Albert was the second son of Ernest, duke of Saxe-Coburg, and Louise, daughter of Duke Augustus of Saxe-Coburg-Altenburg. His parents were divorced in 1826. He was a shy and delicate child and always lacked stamina but was exceptionally diligent and serious-minded. His tutor, Christoph Florschutz, was the dominant influence on his early years and gave him a love of learning, particularly in languages, history, the natural sciences, and music, which lasted throughout his life. He became a gifted composer and organist and made the Victorian court something of a centre of musical life.

The possibility of a match with his cousin Queen Victoria, who was the same age, was fostered by their uncle Leopold, king of the Belgians, and by Baron Stockmar, one of her advisers, but they did not meet until 1836 when they were both 17 years old. Victoria then found him 'extremely handsome', but at that stage neither thought of a lifetime's companionship. Albert enrolled at Bonn University and eagerly applied himself to study in natural science, political economy, and philosophy as well as developing his musical talent. When they met again at Windsor three years later Victoria fell instantly in love and Albert, unsure of himself at first, soon responded. Five days after their meeting she proposed to him and they were married on 10 February 1840.

If Albert was unexpectedly swept off his feet by Victoria's ardour, he was less enthusiastic about her country, nor did her subjects take to him. He was not thought important enough to marry the queen of England, and the facts that he was German, Victoria's first cousin, lacked wealth and position, and was hardly known in England all counted against him. He was variously (and wrongly) supposed to be a 'Coburg adventurer on the make', a political radical, a papist by inclination, and (even worse because accurately) an intellectual. Parliament reduced the allowance that was proposed for him from £50,000 to £30,000 p.a., and refused to grant him precedence next to the queen. Precedence was nevertheless conferred on him by letters patent, but he received no title and was not officially designated prince consort until 1857.

Victoria adored her husband and insisted that he should be by her side on state and ceremonial occasions which often made her nervous, but she was reluctant to admit him to a share in her political duties, so that in spite of their private happiness he was frustrated by his lack of influence and of opportunity to practise his slowly acquired theoretical knowledge of his new country's constitution and its social problems. He did however guide his wife towards political neutrality, weaning her from her previous Whig partisanship and reconciling her after 1841 to *Peel, for whom he felt a strong affinity and intellectual sympathy. After 1842 he acted as Victoria's informal counsellor, private secretary, and sole confidant. He also strongly influenced her taste in music and art, with a strong bias towards early Renaissance style, as evidenced in his reconstruction of *Osborne as their private family home. He took an interest in the workings of the royal household and set about modernizing and pruning household offices. In many ways he was a natural bureaucrat—he was efficient, painstaking, and absorbed by detail. He was happy to become, on Peel's suggestion, chairman of the Fine Arts Royal Commission and he threw himself energetically into his favourite project to make South Kensington a centre for the arts and for education. In 1847 he was elected chancellor of Cambridge University and he devoted a substantial share of his time thereafter to the reform and modernization of the university, with a particular concern for the development of scientific education and the raising of intellectual and pedagogic standards. His attempt to promote the causes of social improvement, science and technology, and the public patronage of the arts and sciences was summed up in the organization of the *Great Exhibition of 1851, which he did a great deal to bring about. Nor was he inactive in other public fields. He attempted to guide British foreign policy in peaceful directions and tried to insist that *Palmerston should submit his policies and dispatches to the queen. Palmerston's refusal led to his dismissal from the Foreign Office in 1851. Nevertheless, Albert was unable to avert the outbreak of the *Crimean War in 1854 and Palmerston's return as prime minister in 1855. Almost his last act on his death-bed in 1861 was to tone down an aggressive dispatch to Washington on the **Trent* affair which probably averted war with the USA.

Perhaps Albert's most lasting contribution to his adopted country was the example he set, with Victoria, of a respectable and devout private life. They produced nine children, to whom Albert was a loving and devoted though heavy-handed father. His relations with his eldest son, the future King Edward VII, suffered from 'Bertie's' resistance to the ambitious and sometimes oppressive system of education which his father devised and supervised, aided by Victoria, who wished her son to become a second Albert, despite their temperamental difference. The relentless pressure placed on the prince of Wales resulted in his alienation from his parents and increased the anxieties from which Albert increasingly suffered. His habits of overwork and his consequently weakened physical constitution resulted in an inability, and perhaps a lack of will, to resist the attacks of ill-health which set in during the last year of his life and he died of typhoid fever on 14 December 1861 at the age of 42.

Albert has been described as 'perhaps the most astute and ambitious politician of his age', but his political successes were few. It was his fate to be a highly sensitive and intelligent man who failed to understand the mentality of his adopted countrymen or to realize how alien to them were his passions for intellect, hard work, and the patronage of the arts and sciences. His marriage was not always easy, for Victoria was a strong and determined personality, but it was founded upon a genuine and profound love which by its example exerted a deep influence on the character of Victorian England. EAS

Albert Memorial. When Prince *Albert died in 1861 a competition was held for a national monument to him, which Sir G. G. *Scott, inevitably, won. It took ten years to build, from 1863 to 1872. It stands in Hyde Park, just across Kensington Gore from the Albert Hall. The latter is cheap and rather boring, designed by an army engineer. The memorial makes up for that—tall, Gothic, spiky, colourful, and crammed with decorations and sculptures meant to celebrate the glorious achievements of the high Victorian age. Underneath, however, there is an iron skeleton, which is corroding. There may be a certain symbolism in that. BJP

Albion is a poetical personification for Britain. It was first used in classical literature in the 6th cent. BC and referred either to the Celtic name or to the white cliffs of Dover. *Camden mentions that it had been related to Albion, son of Neptune. The phrase 'perfidious Albion' has been attributed to the marquis de Ximenes (1726–1817), though Bossuet in the 17th cent. had mentioned 'L'Angleterre perfide'. It was soon superseded by *Britannia. JAC

Albuera, battle of, 1811. On 16 May 1811 an Anglo-Spanish-Portuguese force of 35,000 men under Marshal Beresford blocked Marshal Soult's French army of 24,000 moving to lift the siege of Badajoz in Spain. Both sides lost heavily—two British brigades took 60 and 80 per cent casualties respectively. However the allied army succeeded in repulsing the French in a confused battle which featured the epic action of the 'astonishing infantry' of the Fusilier Brigade. Albuera, along with *Fuentes de Onoro fought two weeks earlier, stabilized the situation along the Spanish–Portuguese frontier, but as Wellington said, 'another such battle would ruin us'. GDS

alchemy, an art of ancient but uncertain origins, can be interpreted as an enquiry into man's relationship with the cosmos and the will of the Creator, manifested as either a devotional philosophy transforming sinful man into perfect being ('esoteric'), or attempted transmutation of base metals into gold or silver ('exoteric'), or an inextricable mixture of both. The catalyst required was the elixir of life, tincture, or philosophers' stone, the preparation of which long obsessed men of all ranks, despite its futility.

Probably arising in Hellenistic Alexandria, alchemy (*alkimia*) was transmitted to Europe through Islamic culture, via 12th-cent. translations into Latin by men like Robert of Chester, Adelard of Bath, and the encyclopedist Bartholomaeus Anglicus. Whilst earlier Taoist alchemists had aimed principally for longevity, if not immortality, medieval western alchemists' objectives were gold-making or creating superior medicines, drawing on Aristotelian theory of the four 'elements' (air, fire, earth, water), old ideas that the planets were connected to certain metals, animistic beliefs, and current technical knowledge. The medieval idea of unity of matter justified the approach that if lead and gold were both dense and soft, then merely changing greyness to yellowness should convert the common metal into the precious one. Obsession with chemical colour changes (series of black, white, iridescent, yellow, purple, red) was matched by symbolic and enigmatic language, as the basic procedures of calcination, sublimation, fusion, crystallization, and distillation absorbed much time and expense.

Since the gold-makers' skills rendered them vulnerable to avaricious magnates, caution and circumspection were advisable, but public credulity encouraged conjuring and dishonesty; *Chaucer's bitterness in 'The Canon's Yeoman's Tale' suggests that he himself had been taken in. Practical alchemy, nevertheless, had much to offer medicine, giving rise to metallic rather than herbal remedies, much favoured by Paracelsus, and eventually to iatrochemistry.

Despite interest from John Dee, Kenelm Digby, the 'Wizard' 9th earl of *Northumberland, Walter *Ralegh, and even Charles II, alchemy received its death-warrant in the mid-17th cent. when Robert *Boyle demolished the theory of the four 'elements'. Although it had led to the discovery of alcohol and the mineral acids, historians of chemistry view alchemy in general as fraudulent. Yet growing dissatisfaction with the mechanistic objectives of modern science has renewed interest in the alchemists' wider goals and debate about man and Creator. ASH

Alcock, John (1430–1500). Ecclesiastical statesman. Born in Beverley, Alcock attended the University of Cambridge and rose rapidly in the church. From 1472 to 1476 he was bishop of Rochester, transferring to Worcester in 1476, and to Ely in 1486. He was in high favour with Edward IV, holding office as master of the rolls, lord chancellor (joint), president of the Council of Wales, and as tutor to Edward, prince of Wales. Henry VII brought him back into service, employing him to baptize Prince *Arthur, and appointing him again as lord chancellor and as comptroller of the royal works. Alcock was a benefactor of Peterhouse, Cambridge, and the founder of Jesus College. He is buried in the Alcock chapel in Ely cathedral. JAC

Alcuin (*c.*735–804) was a Northumbrian, probably noble, deacon, adviser to Charlemagne, and architect of the Carolingian Renaissance. He was born between 735 and 745, and succeeded his teacher Ælbert as master of the school at York in 767. He travelled on the continent, with Ælbert, and for Archbishop Eanbald, and after meeting Charlemagne at Parma in 781 was invited to his court. Traditionally described as head of the palace school, he was more a personal tutor to Charlemagne, who gave him several monasteries, including that of St Martin's at Tours, where he died.

Alcuin became involved in political life and influenced Charlemagne's thinking. Authorship of some of Charlemagne's texts is still credited to Alcuin, though not as many as was once the case. He wrote against the heresy of adoptionism (a political as well as a religious concern), he probably composed the letter to Pope Leo III wherein pope's and king's functions are defined, and he may have been partly responsible for Charlemagne's taking the Roman imperial title in the west (in 800). His writings include one of the earliest, medieval, political essays. An ideal of warrior kingship is presented in Alcuin's poem on *The Bishops, Kings and Saints of York*, the first major extant Latin verse history in the medieval West, finished possibly as late as 792/3. This is a work of patriotism, centred on a unified Northumbria and the church at York; pro-Roman in outlook (omitting the controversies in the career of *Wilfrid), it offers *Edwin as supreme kingly example and Ælbert as ideal prelate, and advocates concord between political and spiritual rulers. It complements the exhortatory letters Alcuin sent to kings and his view of bishops.

Alcuin's correspondence also reveals that both he and Charlemagne were involved in English, particularly Mercian and Northumbrian, politics. Alcuin returned twice to England, once with papal legates (786) and in 790, for three years when he hoped to guide the conduct of King *Æthelred of Northumbria.

Alcuin's writings include textbooks, saints' lives (including his kinsman *Willibrord's in prose and verse), compilations of commentaries, missals, and other texts requested by correspondents, and Charlemagne's epitaph for Pope Hadrian I. His epitaph for himself became a literary model. His revisions of the lectionary (lessons to be read at mass) and of the (Latin) Vulgate text of the Bible became standard. He helped to introduce singing the Creed at mass and to disseminate the performance of penance on the continent. He encouraged the cults of the archangel Michael and the Virgin and of St Martin. His reception of visitors at Tours, and his acquisition of books from England, spread English influence. His pupils were many, often distinguished and influential.

Alcuin's thinking was influenced by Pope Gregory I and by *Bede. His originality is to be found in his York poem, his intense interest in number symbolism, and his application of logic to theology.

He offers historians evidence (in his letters, more than 300 of which survive, mostly written between 794 and 804) for low standards in the late 8th-cent. English church and amongst the Northumbrian élite, and (in his York poem) for 8th-cent. Northumbrian history, the development of the York school, and York's wealth and commercial activity.

Alcuin's driving forces were friendship and teaching. Though devoted to Charlemagne, he protested against the treatment of the Saxons in conversion, and disagreed with him about the law of *sanctuary. He believed it better to write books to serve the soul, than to dig vines for the body. AER

Aldhelm (*c.*639–709) was one of the most learned men of his time. Thought to be related to West Saxon kings and educated at Malmesbury under the Irish scholar Maildubh, he also studied briefly at the Canterbury school flourishing under Archbishop *Theodore and Abbot Hadrian after 669. A distinguished scholar, teacher, ecclesiastically energetic, appointed abbot of Malmesbury *c.*675, and first bishop of *Sherborne *c.*705, Aldhelm founded monasteries, built churches, and a surviving letter shows him writing to Geraint, king of *Dumnonia, urging conformity with the Roman observance of Easter. He comments on being weighed down 'with the burdens of pastoral care' and 'great tumultuous uproars in secular affairs'. Yet it is said he would sing, minstrel-like, to attract passers-by in order to preach to them.

His sophisticated style of writing and use of obscure vocabulary and difficult Latin was greatly admired and imitated. Widely studied in England, his works were transmitted by missionaries to continental centres of learning, then reimported for the late 9th- and 10th-cent. revival of English learning. Extant works include ecclesiastical poems, rhythmical verse, and a number of letters. His *Letter to Acircius*, a metrical treatise incorporating a hundred 'riddles' or 'mysteries', was addressed to the Northumbrian king Aldfrith, probably his godson. His largest work, *De virginitate*, dedicated to the nuns at Barking (Essex), is a twofold treatise in prose and verse, which became a stylistic model for subsequent Anglo-Latin works. None of the vernacular poems he is said to have written has survived. AM

Alexander I (*c.*1077–1124), king of Scots (1107–24). The second of the three sons of *Malcolm Canmore and Queen (later St) *Margaret to become king, he succeeded his elder brother Edgar. He ruled north of the Forth–Clyde line while his younger brother David (later David I) governed Strathclyde and much of Lothian in his name, a power-sharing arrangement which indicates that these southern territories were still not fully incorporated into 'Scotland'. He maintained friendly relations with England by marrying Sybil, one of Henry I's illegitimate daughters, and by campaigning with Henry in Wales in 1114. Committed to reforming religious practices in accordance with European norms, he invited Augustinian canons to Scone, a key royal centre, and some Englishmen were appointed to bishoprics—though great care was taken to preserve the independence of the Scottish church from Canterbury and York. But his achievements as a modernizer were limited and much overshadowed by those of David I. KJS

Alexander II (1198–1249), king of Scots (1214–49). Son and successor of William the Lion, his ability as a ruler was 'above average'. He swiftly asserted himself against King John by allying with the barons of *Magna Carta, who formally recognized Scottish claims to Northumberland, Cumberland, and Westmorland. In 1216 the Yorkshire rebels paid homage to him, and he marched as far south as Dover to meet Prince Louis of France who, as claimant to the English throne, acknowledged his right to the border counties (but not to Yorkshire). Following John's death and the royalist victory at *Lincoln, the ground was cut from beneath the Scots, and in December 1217 Alexander made peace with Henry III and relinquished his war gains. These events introduced a new realism into Anglo-Scottish relations, and both kingdoms adopted more conciliatory policies. Unlike John, Henry III accepted Scotland's right to exist as a separate sovereign state, and Alexander recognized the futility of continuing to pursue the traditional Scottish goal of southern expansion. His marriage to Henry III's sister *Joan reinforced the new understanding between the crowns, and by the treaty of *York (1237) he renounced all claims to the border shires. Scottish resources were now concentrated on the vigorous assertion of authority in the north and west of Scotland, which were thereby brought more firmly under royal oversight and control. Alexander campaigned in Argyll in the early 1220s; Ross and Caithness had finally been pacified by the early 1230s; and Galloway was at last brought to heel in 1234–5. He died of a fever on the island of Kerrera in Oban Bay while leading a major expedition against the Western Isles. KJS

Alexander III (1241–86), king of Scots (1249–86). Only son of Alexander II and his second wife, Marie de Coucy. The view that his reign from 1249 was a 'golden age' for Scotland was first fully articulated by 14th- and 15th-cent. Scottish chroniclers, who boosted his reputation in order to stress Scottish national identity and the political independence of the kingdom. Nevertheless, there is much to be said for their retrospective assessments. The reign began badly with the factional squabbles of Alexander's minority (1249–60), notably between the Comyns and the Durwards. Thereafter, however, Alexander dealt with the great lords firmly but sensitively, and crown–magnate relations were stable. Continuing earlier processes of consolidation and expansion, he and his war captains campaigned extensively in the west, and brought matters to a successful conclusion in 1266, when sovereignty over Man and the Western Isles was relinquished by Norway. Their annexation to Scotland, one of the greatest triumphs of Scottish state-building, was facilitated by amicable relations with England. Alexander had married Henry III's daughter *Margaret in 1251, and although Henry intervened in the minority power struggles, he repeatedly reassured the Scots of his respect for their liberties, thus implicitly recognizing Scotland's status as an independent realm. It was a cruel set of circumstances which jeopardized this 'golden age'—the deaths of Alexander's three children between 1281 and 1284, and his own untimely death at the age of 44, when he was thrown from his horse while travelling during a storm to visit his second wife, Yolande de Dreux. Even so, by 1286 Scotland had emerged as a unified and sturdily autonomous state, able to meet and ultimately to overcome the challenges posed by both dynastic misfortune and the Anglo-Scottish warfare ignited by Edward I's imperialist ambitions in 1296. KJS

Alexander, Harold Rupert Leofric George, 1st Earl Alexander (1891–1969). From an Anglo-Irish aristocratic family, Alexander fought throughout the First World War, imperturbably and courageously, commanding a brigade at the age of 27. In 1919 he led a Baltic-German unit against the Red Army. In 1939–40 he served in France, and, until 1942, in Britain. Then he took charge of the British retreat from Burma. In August 1942, he became commander-in-chief, Middle East, but left *Montgomery a free hand with the 8th Army.

Polite, elegant, and tactful, Alexander's 'easy smiling grace won all hearts' (*Churchill). In ground command of Anglo-American forces in Tunisia he 'won the adulation of his American subordinates' (Bradley) while successfully directing the capture of Tunis and 250,000 enemy troops. Soon, however, the Anglo-American campaign in Sicily exposed Alexander's inability to impose his orders on self-willed subordinates when Montgomery seized priority for his army over Patton's. In May 1944, when the break-out from the Anzio beachhead followed the allied breakthrough further south, the American general Mark Clark, out of vanity, went north to seize Rome rather than carrying out his orders to block the retreat of part of the German 10th Army. Perhaps Alexander's diffidence in enforcing his thoughts was because they came from his staff; 'Alex' himself had only 'the average brain of an average English gentleman' (*Mountbatten). His style and amenability entranced civilian politicians, notably Churchill and *Macmillan. On 12 December 1944 he became allied C.-in-C., Mediterranean, and field marshal, backdated to 4 June to restore his seniority over Montgomery. In 1946–52 he was the last non-Canadian governor-general of Canada, was given an earldom as Alexander of Tunis, and became minister of defence in Churchill's government until 1954. RACP

Alexander, Sir William, 1st earl of Stirling [S] (*c.*1576–1640). Alexander was born at Menstrie in Clackmannanshire. He established an early reputation as poet and dramatist, served at the court of Prince *Henry, and was knighted. In 1614 James VI and I made him master of requests [S], a post he held until his death. He was given *Nova Scotia to colonize in 1621, with baronetcies to provide support, but made little progress, and was eventually reduced to poverty. From 1626 until his death he served as secretary of state [S], was granted a viscountcy in 1630, and raised to the earldom of Stirling [S] in 1633. But his record was not distinguished. 'Unactable plays and unreadable poems' is a verdict on his literary output. His sojourn at Charles I's court at Westminster left him out of touch with Scottish opinion and he did little to arrest the drift towards collision in Scotland, which ultimately brought his master, Charles I, to trial and execution. JAC

Alexandra (1844–1925), queen of Edward VII. Born in Copenhagen, eldest daughter of the future Christian IX of Denmark, Alexandra retained warm Danish sympathies all her life. Her marriage to Edward, then prince of Wales, took place in 1863: she was hailed by *Tennyson, poet laureate, as 'sea-king's daughter from over the sea'. The couple, popular with the public, took much of the attention shunned by the widowed Victoria, and became society figures. Alexandra, with her stately beauty, fitted the part admirably, acting as a foil for Edward's ebullience. The marriage was affectionate, though Edward was far from faithful. Alexandra's tolerance is revealed by her insistence, when it became clear that the king was dying, that Mrs Keppel, his mistress, be sent for. Family life was the focus of her existence, partly because of her initial difficulty with English, and then her growing deafness. She did not engage in politics but devoted much of her time to nursing and hospitals: Alexandra Day was instituted in 1913 to sell paper roses for hospital funds. Privately she was a keen photographer and collected Fabergé eggs, adding to the great royal collection. Following Edward's death in 1910 she led a quiet, private life, mainly at Sandringham, surrounding herself with her family. She is buried at Windsor. SMC

Alexandria, battle of, 1801. Napoleon's expedition to Egypt was cut off in August 1798 by *Nelson's victory of the *Nile, and a year later Napoleon abandoned his men and returned to France. In March 1801 a British force of 14,000 men was landed under Sir Ralph Abercromby and fought its way towards Alexandria. On the 21st, after heavy fighting in which Abercromby was killed, the French capitulated. Egypt was restored to Turkish rule. Abercromby's widow was given a barony in his honour. JAC

Alford, battle of, 1645. Alford was one of *Montrose's brilliant victories. Pursued by William Baillie's troops, Montrose took his men up the glens and over the hills until Baillie retired on Inverness. On 2 July he found Montrose at Alford, 20 miles to the west of Aberdeen. Each side had between 2,000 and 3,000 men. Baillie's forces could not withstand the ferocity of Montrose's charge and were badly beaten. JAC

Alfred (849–99), king of Wessex (871–99). A popular image of Alfred is of national superman; destined by his father's (*Æthelwulf) will to be king, despite having three surviving older brothers (Æthelbald, Æthelbert, and *Æthelred I); saviour of the English from the Vikings; architect of a united England; founder of the navy, reformer of the army, town-planner, exponent of time and resource management; patron of the church; promoter of universal education and father of English prose; saintly, and easy to know, since we have more evidence for him than for any earlier king. Extreme revisionists emphasize his skill as propagandist, downgrading his achievements.

Perception of Alfred's personality, policies, and methods depends largely, and sometimes entirely, upon his seemingly intimate hagiographical biography by *Asser. But there was probably a different side to Alfred's character. And if the denial of the text's authenticity, powerfully reasserted in 1995, should carry the day, then significant elements of the traditional reconstruction of Alfred's career will disappear.

Asser says Alfred was born in 849 in Wantage and married a Mercian lady in 868. The quality of his own writings suggests that he had a sound education in Latin. He assisted Æthelred against the 'great army' which invaded in 865, and his accession in 871 was most likely not a certainty. The 870s saw continuing war against the Danes, who were numerous, skilled, treacherous, well led, wanting conquest and settlement, not unattractive as allies or lords to rivals. They also damaged Christian faith and institutions. In 878, surprised by King *Guthrum at *Chippenham, Alfred fled to Athelney (Somerset), but defeated the Danes in a desperate last-stand battle at *Edington. The results were the treaty of *Wedmore, Guthrum's baptism and retirement to be king of East Anglia. The army of Hæsten invaded in 892, and proved more difficult, but left in 896.

The West Saxon dynasty was the only one to survive the Viking threat and to this achievement Alfred added authority over all the English outside Danish control. Mercia (under Burgred) had been an ally, and was handled tactfully. Alfred married his daughter *Æthelfleda to Ealdorman *Æthelred, probably of Mercian royal stock, allowed him to operate as subking, and the Mercian *witan to survive, and ceded London after its recapture from the Danes (886). After this, all the English not subject to the Danes submitted to Alfred, and he represented them all in a treaty with Guthrum. Asser asserts that the Welsh too submitted.

Alfred's success depended on his own abilities and on the excellence of his administration. Earlier dynastic stability will have contributed to royal control over local government, though Alfred's rota system for *thegns' attendance at court and the system of division of his revenues are recorded by Asser alone. His new 60-oared design for 'long ships' was not immediately successful, his division of the *fyrd into two (home and away) was perhaps to safeguard agriculture, or to allow military expense to be shared. His most ambitious and effective reform was the development between the wars of *burhs* (33 of them recorded in the slightly later Burghal Hidage). Various sites—old Roman towns, new towns, old or new forts—chosen so that nowhere in Wessex was further than 20 miles from one, were fortified and their defence and maintenance imposed on the people. Some 27,000 men were required in all. The *burhs* caused the 890s wars to be fought largely outside Wessex.

Some *burhs*, including *Winchester, were given a common town-plan, suggesting that they were intended to be permanently inhabited commercial centres. Alfred's government was expensive. It is probable that he bought peace with heavy *Danegelds, for example in 896. Wealth was necessary to ensure aristocratic support, for building, against Vikings, and also against dynastic rivals. Alfred's nephews Æthelhelm and Æthelwold challenged his disposition of Æthelred's property before the witan and could be expected to challenge his son *Edward for the kingship. Asser asserts that Alfred spent lavishly on art, architecture, alms, and gifts to the church. His coinage shows he was not short of silver, and his will that he was hugely wealthy in 899.

Alfred's relationship with the church seems superficially harmonious. Ninth-cent. West Saxon kings seem not to have pressured the church economically: the **Anglo-Saxon Chronicle* records Alfred sending alms to Rome, and receiving gifts from Pope Marinus, and Asser recounts his foundation of monasteries at Athelney and Shaftesbury (for women). Churchmen took part in war, and the archbishop of Canterbury was influential and probably predisposed towards the creation of one, unified kingdom. Ecclesiastical support may have facilitated Alfred's success. Yet evidence from Abingdon suggests Alfred was resented there as a despoiler, other evidence that he appropriated monastic properties right across Wessex, and it is as a threat to the church that he appears in a papal letter in 878.

The support Alfred needed was not automatic, so he attempted to teach his subjects about their duties, his authority, and their collective destiny. The authorship and dates of texts produced in his reign have been much discussed, and depend in part on the degree of credence given to Asser's account of Alfred's intellectual development. Acceptance suggests that most of the work was done in the 890s, denial that it was mostly complete by 892. Alfred's law code referred to the laws of *Æthelbert of Kent and of *Offa of Mercia, and included *Ine's, perhaps to appeal to Kentish and Mercian sentiment and to indicate historical continuity. A law on treason and an oath of allegiance to the king (more fully documented in later codes) were introduced. The code's purpose was to promote the king as lawgiver on Roman and biblical models, rather than to serve as a handbook, and Alfred's preface offers a history of law beginning with the Ten Commandments, suggesting that his people were a new people of God. The *Chronicle* was perhaps composed in 896–7 under Alfred's direction, its content and structure suggesting that it was commissioned to tie Alfred into West Saxon history and Wessex into world history, to emphasize Alfred's fitness to rule, to represent the West Saxon kings as struggling for Christianity against paganism, to set Alfred's cause and people in a context of contemporary world powers and events, and to celebrate his achievement (strong, peaceful rule in Wessex, destined to rule all England) as an inevitable result of history. The translations of Orosius' *History against the Pagans* and Bede's *Ecclesiastical History*, both likewise offering 9th-cent. Wessex a historical context, were also, probably, composed at Alfred's request.

Alfred proposed, in his prose preface to his translation of Pope Gregory I's *Pastoral Rule* (a treatise about the role of bishops but also applied to the kingly office), a programme of translation of books 'most necessary for all men to know'. He complained that clerical knowledge of Latin and educational standards generally had greatly declined. But his own and his team's activities betray this to be an exaggeration. Alfred himself refers to Asser, Plegmund, Wærferth, Grimbald, and John. For their attendance on and education of Alfred, some of their work, the plans for mass education, and for reading tests for ealdormen and reeves (administrators and judges), we depend on Asser. Alfred's *Pastoral Rule* was sent to his bishops, to educate them and to urge them to teach. He wanted all free men to be literate in English, and Latin teaching to be available to those intended for holy orders. Alfred also translated, more freely, two contemplative works, Boethius' *Consolation of Philosophy* and Augustine's *Soliloquies*, and a number of psalms.

Alfred's guiding principle in selecting texts and his intended audience are subjects of debate. One factor was belief that to defeat their enemies the people needed God's help, and to deserve it they needed help in understanding his message. Contemplation was recommended by Gregory to prevent pride, the greatest danger of office. The translations emphasized what the authors thought, or implied, about power, authority, and social cohesion: the power of the king is awesome, the subject's duty to be his tool; wisdom, acquired through reading and study, will lead to office, power, success, and riches as well as happiness in the next world. These messages are deeply political.

The West Saxon take-over of England, 10th-cent. economic development, the *burhs* as sites of mints and centres of administration, can all be traced back to Alfred. Though vernacular literature failed to take off, the education of bishops may have contributed to the 10th-cent. reform movement since its leaders were bishops. Alfred's legal innovations may have laid a foundation for the English common law of Henry II's time.

That Alfred was open to Carolingian influence is detectable in the oath of allegiance, his bridge-building, his educational programme, and his concept of kingship. Asser exaggerated his contemplative quality into something approaching neurosis. The reality was a ruthless, shrewd ruler with a keen historical sense, a sensitivity to public opinion, and a genuine sense of duty. He had learned his lesson from Pope Gregory, with whose character and situation he had much in common, and whom he may have made in part his model. The only early medieval monarch to combine significant personal activity in both rule and scholarship, he was doing what he wanted of his underlings and what Gregory enjoined. The man at the top must set a good example. AER

Frantzen, A. J., *King Alfred* (Boston, 1986); Keynes, S., and Lapidge, M. (trans.), *Alfred the Great: Asser's Life of King Alfred and Other Contemporary Sources* (Harmondsworth, 1983); Smyth, A. P., *King Alfred the Great* (Oxford, 1995).

Alfred the Atheling (*c.*1008–*c.*1037) was a younger son of *Æthelred by *Emma, daughter of the count of Normandy. Her second marriage, to *Cnut, dispossessed the sons by her first marriage and they were brought up in Normandy. In 1035, on the death of Cnut, Alfred made an ill-judged visit to England. He was captured by Earl *Godwine, blinded, and died in Ely. His elder brother *Edward succeeded to the throne in 1042. Alfred's murder was quoted by Norman supporters in 1066 in justification for the deposition of *Harold, son of Godwine. JAC

Algeciras. A great-power conference (January–April 1906), which resolved the first Moroccan crisis of 1905–6, during which Germany had vainly tried to weaken or destroy the Anglo-French *Entente. The British gave solid backing to France. The crisis is often seen as the first direct step to August 1914. CJB

Algiers, bombardment of, 1816. On 27 August 1816, Lord Exmouth, in command of nineteen British warships and assisted by a Dutch squadron under Admiral van Capellan, bombarded Algiers for eight hours, destroying much of the town. The Dey then agreed to abolish Christian slavery in his dominions, which he had earlier refused to do. RAS

Allectus. Imperial usurper based in Britain, AD 293–6. In 293 the western Roman empire was administered by Maximian and his junior *Constantius Chlorus, and the usurper *Carausius was operating in Britain and northern Gaul. In 293 Constantius took Boulogne, and Carausius was assassinated by his finance minister Allectus. Allectus himself then became a usurper. Recent archaeological excavations in London, south of St Paul's cathedral, indicate the presence of a palace which dendrochronological studies suggest dates to 293–4; Allectus may well have built it. In 296 Constantius invaded Britain and Allectus was slain in a battle near Silchester. ES

allegiance, oaths of. The vicissitudes of oaths of allegiance reflect not merely dynastic fortunes but the changing priorities of different generations. The first oath of which we know, to *Edmund in the 10th cent., offered 'fealty as a man ought to be faithful to his lord'. It was presumably to guard against a vassal putting his lord before the king that William I imposed the oath at *Salisbury in 1086 on his tenants-in-chief, and homage between vassal and lord normally included the phrase 'save the duty owed to the king'. Matters became more complex when religious and party issues were added in the 16th and 17th cents. Elizabeth's oath of allegiance in 1559 required the specific repudiation of any jurisdiction by any foreign prince, person, prelate, or potentate. After the *Gunpowder plot, James I demanded an oath repudiating papal authority and promising to divulge 'all treasons and traiterous conspiracies which I shall know or hear of'. As soon as Charles I had been executed in 1649, Parliament asked for an oath approving the measure and accepting the abolition of the monarchy, and all the changes of regime up to the Restoration were accompanied by debates on an appropriate oath. Charles II made his office-holders swear that it was not lawful 'upon any pretence whatsoever' to take up arms against the king. During the excitement of the *Popish plot, Parliament added oaths against transubstantiation, which James II promptly ruled aside in his *Declaration of Indulgence of 1687. The next *bouleversement*, which brought in William and Mary, declared that Charles II's oath against taking up arms was no longer necessary, but the repudiation of non-resistance forced 400 *non-jurors to resign their benefices. Dynastic and religious considerations continued to complicate allegiance until the 19th cent. Jacobites could not take the oath to George I and his successors, and catholics, Jews, and atheists remained excluded from Parliament until the oath was amended in 1829, 1858, and 1888. The existing oath of allegiance, based upon the Promissory Oaths Act of 1868, is nearly as simple as that of Edmund. JAC

Allen, William (1532–94). Founding principal of Douai College (1568–85) and cardinal (1587). A Lancashireman, educated at Oriel College, Oxford, he became principal of St Mary's Hall (1556–60), then joined catholic exiles at Louvain

(1561). Briefly in England (1562–5), he was ordained at Mechlin, visited Rome, and founded the college at Douai (1568) to give English catholics university education and train missionary priests for reconverting England. He also instigated the Douai translation of the Bible (1582). Visiting Rome again (1575, 1579), he advised the pope about founding the English college there and inspired the Jesuit mission to England (1580). He retired to Rome (1585) in poor health, became cardinal-priest, and died there. Despite his political ineptitude in corresponding with Mary, queen of Scots, supporting the Armada, and misjudging the strength of English catholic patriotism, he was a fine teacher, ardent for the reconversion of England. His college kept the core of English catholicism alive against government attempts to extinguish it. WMM

Allenby, Edmund, 1st Viscount Allenby (1861–1936). Soldier and administrator. After extensive service in Africa before 1914, Allenby fought in France as a divisional, corps, and army commander before being posted to Palestine in June 1917. In the Middle East he proved himself a master of mobile warfare. In October 1917 his troops defeated the Turks at Gaza and by Christmas he had occupied Jerusalem. Further rapid progress was halted when his army was milked of reinforcements to be sent to France. But when he resumed his offensive in September 1918, operating in co-operation with the Arab forces organized by Colonel T. E. *Lawrence (of Arabia), he destroyed the Turkish armies in Palestine and Syria at the battle of Megiddo. Between 1919 and 1925 he served as high commissioner in Egypt. His notoriously bad temper earned him the nickname of 'the bull'. He received his peerage in 1919. DF

Alliance Party. Formed in April 1970 against the backdrop of accelerating communal violence to bridge the gap between the unionists and nationalists of Northern Ireland. The party was represented at the Sunningdale conference (December 1973) and in the power-sharing executive (January–May 1974): it has remained loyal to the broad principles embodied in the Sunningdale agreement (power-sharing between unionists and nationalists within a Union framework). Its share of the vote peaked in 1977, when its candidates secured 14.4 per cent in the district council elections: recent electoral performance has been weaker, settling usually at 7–8 per cent. The party has never been able to expand its base beyond middle-class liberals and the small, anti-sectarian section of the working class who once voted for the *Northern Ireland Labour Party. However, as with other centrist parties, Alliance commands a respect and wields an influence beyond its formal electoral support. AJ

Alma, battle of, 1854. On 20 September, a week after disembarking in the *Crimea, British, French, and Turkish troops under *Raglan and St Arnaud launched an attack on Menshikov's forces blocking their advance on Sebastopol at the Alma river. After heavy fighting at bayonet point, the Russians were forced to retreat. Though Lord *Aberdeen told Queen Victoria that 'we may fairly hope that the fall of Sebastopol cannot long be delayed', the fortress held out for another year. JAC

almanacks were booklets, of varying length, containing astronomical and astrological information, details of weights and measures, a calendar, and other matters of practical use. They frequently included predictions of political events or natural disasters, proverbs, and other moral sayings, while some of the longer ones were designed to be of use to specific trades or callings. The almanack was therefore useful, and, from about 1650, might also be entertaining, as the astrological aspects became taken less seriously and almanack writers began to satirize the genre. What is clear is that almanacks were sold in vast numbers: some 400,000 a year in England in the 1660s, which suggests that one in every three families might own one. Many were published annually, and some almanack writers, especially in the 17th cent., enjoyed a steady living. The almanack gradually became more utilitarian, and as such remained in use well into the 19th cent. JAS

Almanza, battle of, 1707. On 25 April an allied force under the command of Lord Galway and the marquis de Ruvigny, comprising about 15,000 English, Dutch, and Portuguese troops, attacked a Franco-Spanish army under Marshal Berwick that was twice its size near Valencia. Despite initial allied success, a Portuguese defeat on the right flank exposed the English and Dutch, over 3,000 of whom were forced to surrender. The battle marked the effective end of Archduke Charles of Austria's attempts to gain Spain, confirming the Bourbon succession under Philip V in all but Catalonia. JLP

Almenara, battle of, 1710. On the river Noguera in Aragon, on 27 July, an allied army of 24,000 troops, commanded by the Austrian Count Stahremberg, and including an English contingent under *Stanhope, attacked a Spanish army of roughly equal size, commanded by General Villadarias with Philip V in attendance. Caught by surprise, the Spanish were defeated, chiefly by Stanhope's men, and the bulk of the army survived only because of the onset of night. Casualties were relatively light—about 400 allied and 1,300 Spanish. The battle marked a resurgence of allied fortunes in Aragon. JLP

almshouses, also known as bede-houses, are buildings, usually purpose-designed, to provide accommodation for aged or frail people. They were established at a time when there was no alternative welfare provision. Usually they were paid for by a benefactor, whose intentions were set out in a deed stipulating who might be given help.

The origin of almshouses lay in medieval monasteries, which built houses from which alms and hospitality were dispensed. The religious links remained: often almshouses were intended to contain small communities who had to attend regular services to pray for the souls of the benefactor and such other persons as might be specified. The houses frequently included a chapel and generally the priest who took the services supervised the residents. The range of care for the bedesmen or bedeswomen varied. Generous benefactors established funds to pay for fuel, clothing (sometimes a uniform), and even some food and drink. Some almshouses had the character of a 20th-cent. hospice and cared for the terminally ill. Nursing was sometimes a duty for those who were well enough to care for their less fortunate fellow-residents.

Benefactors usually specified that residents should come from a particular locality and be persons who had led respectable lives. Many permitted the admission of husbands and wives.

By the early 14th cent. the endowment of almshouses had become a favoured form of charitable bequest. Medieval examples still surviving include the Hospital of St Cross at Winchester (Hants). After the Reformation, almshouses continued to be established in many towns and villages, and are often architecturally agreeable or even distinguished. Benefactors often specified that only members of the Church of England were eligible. But when Thomas Cook of travel agency fame founded an almshouse in his native town of Melbourne (Derbys.), he did not insist on membership of any religious denomination, though he was himself a committed Baptist; he did, however, restrict admission to people living in the town. *Trollope's novels *The Warden* (1855) and *Barchester Towers* (1857) turned on the wardenship of Hiram's Hospital at Barchester. IJEK

Alnwick, battle of, 1093. During the reign of Malcolm III of Scotland there were repeated clashes over the border with England. After William Rufus had taken possession of Cumberland and Westmorland, negotiations broke down. Malcolm invaded Northumberland and besieged Alnwick castle. A relief force on 13 November 1093 killed both Malcolm and his eldest son Edward. JAC

Alnwick, battle of, 1174. In pursuit of his claims to the northern shires, William I 'the Lion', king of Scotland, invaded England in 1173 and 1174. In 1174, having failed to take Carlisle, Wark, and Prudhoe castles, William in frustration decided to ravage the coastal plain of Northumberland. On the morning of 13 July, while most of his men were scattered across the countryside, William and the few knights he had with him were caught completely by surprise just outside Alnwick castle by a force loyal to Henry II led by Ranulf *Glanvill. A sharp fight followed before William was led away in captivity to Henry II who imposed severe terms. The battle effectively ended the Great Rebellion (1173–4) in England. SL

Alnwick castle is a major medieval fortress in Northumberland and a principal residence of the Percy family since the early 14th cent. It stands above the river Aln amongst parkland created by Capability *Brown around 1765. In its present form the castle is mostly mid-19th cent., the creation of Algernon, 4th duke of Northumberland, who employed Salvin to restore and improve the exterior and a team of Italian artists under Canina and Montiroli to decorate the interior. Probably founded soon after the Conquest, the castle was constructed in stone in the mid-12th cent., a shell keep clasped by two large baileys. There are extensive 14th-cent. additions; notably the main gatehouse and barbican, one of the most complete in the country. Alnwick is strategically placed straddling the eastern route into England and was frequently involved in Anglo-Scottish affairs. A cross in the park commemorates the death of Malcolm, king of Scots, at the siege of *Alnwick in 1093. LR

Alresford, battle of. See CHERITON.

Althorp, John Charles Spencer, Viscount, 3rd Earl Spencer (1782–1845). By temperament Althorp preferred the pleasures of private life to the tribulations of politics. He was not an eloquent speaker but won the confidence of the Commons by his honesty and ability to convince back-benchers that he was one of themselves. In both the *Grey and *Melbourne administrations he was important as chancellor of the Exchequer. He welcomed the 1832 Reform Bill, was involved in drafting it, and prominent in securing its passage through Parliament, but in 1834 he could not support an Irish Coercion Bill and this contributed to Grey's decision to resign as premier. Melbourne believed Althorp's presence in the Commons was essential for the survival of his ministry and it was a great blow when Althorp succeeded his father as Earl Spencer in November 1834. The result was Melbourne's resignation. Althorp was happy to leave politics. He refused to be either lord-lieutenant of Ireland or governor-general of Canada and immersed himself in farming and country sports. Yet he had been both popular and effective as leader of the House of Commons. His career confirms that in politics character often counts for more than intellect. JWD

Amboyna massacre, 1623. The island of Amboyna in the Moluccas became the focus of Anglo-Dutch rivalry in the spice trade. In 1623, the English settlement was wiped out by the Dutch, who were the dominant power in the region, and the English East India Company turned its attention towards the Indian subcontinent. The massacre soured relations between Dutch and English for many years. DAW

Ambrosius Aurelianus, 'the last of the Romans', was a British leader who emerged during the twilight years of Roman Britain to resist the onslaught of invading Saxons. Ever since the Saxons (under *Hengist and Horsa?) had established themselves in Kent in AD 455, other areas of southern Britain had fallen under Saxon rule. The Britons fought back, and their greatest successes occurred in the late 5th cent. under Ambrosius Aurelianus. This resistance culminated in the battle of *Mount Badon at which the Saxons were defeated; the Britons won a generation of peace. ES

America. The thirteen colonies later formed the United States of America. Contemporaries did not distinguish them from Britain's Caribbean or other mainland settlements. All except Georgia, founded in 1732, resulted from 17th-cent. crown grants, mainly to companies or proprietors. Most were eventually taken under crown control, so that by 1750 they had similar institutional and political systems. The original Indian inhabitants were gradually dispossessed and marginalized by armed, aggressive settlers.

In the south, Virginia (1607) became a royal province in 1624. Its neighbour, Maryland (see BALTIMORE), was taken under royal control, but reverted to proprietary rule in 1715. Tobacco, a major export crop, shaped the development of both colonies. The demand for labour was met by indentured servants from the British Isles, young persons who worked for a term of years in return for a free passage and the promise of future benefits. After about 1680 African slaves gradually displaced them. In South Carolina (1663) rice became the great export crop; here slavery was more concentrated and harsher. South Carolina and North Carolina, which had pockets of slavery and of free subsistence farmers, became royal colonies. In Georgia, founded by humanitarians as a refuge for poor persons and oppressed protestants, attempts to ban slavery and strong drink failed; it developed as a plantation-based society.

In the north, no staples dominated. Families rather than indentured servants went to Massachusetts (see MASSACHUSETTS BAY COMPANY), and to Connecticut, which received a royal charter in 1662. In both, the religious convictions of the early settlers and a congregational church system helped shape social and political institutions. Hostilities between congregationalists, baptists, and quakers played a major role in the development of religious toleration in Rhode Island, settled from 1636. New Hampshire, first settled by New England congregationalists and by more latitudinarian Anglican colonists, was chartered in 1679. These northern colonies had economies based on farming and maritime undertakings, including shipbuilding (and timber exports from New Hampshire).

The middle colonies, founded after 1660, became the great receptacles of continuing white migration, of both independent families and servants. New York was granted to James, duke of York (later James II) in 1664. From it he granted New Jersey, in which there was a substantial Presbyterian Scottish interest, to a number of proprietors. Both territories later came under direct royal control. Pennsylvania's (see PENN, WILLIAM) early life was dominated by members of the Society of Friends. The Penns held it until the American Revolution. Its southern neighbour, Delaware, was formed from Pennsylvania's three lower counties. New York City and, especially, Philadelphia became substantial urban centres; their hinterlands and the region generally were characterized by successful farming, with a surplus of foodstuffs finding markets elsewhere.

In the 17th cent. the colonies were seen in Britain as receptacles for a surplus population. Traditional arguments that migration would relieve unemployment and reduce poverty as well as create markets for British goods and provide valuable sources of precious metals and raw materials persisted. By the end of the century, the need for a large labour force at home was stressed. Although immigration continued from mainland Britain, its major sources became northern Ireland and protestant Germany. This led to increasing religious diversity as Ulster presbyterians ('Scotch-Irish') and a variety of German baptists, Lutherans, and Moravians arrived. Even so, natural increase more than migration fed population growth. This was formidable, a distinguishing feature in the development of the colonies, underpinning a burgeoning self-confidence and a conviction that because of the availability of land a modest independence was attainable by the majority of white males in the New World, as it was not in the Old.

	1660	1720	1740	1780
New England				
White	30,594	166,937	281,163	650,832
Black	562	3,956	8,541	14,377
Middle colonies				
White	4,846	92,259	204,093	680,493
Black	630	10,825	16,452	42,365
Southern colonies				
White	34,718	138,110	270,283	779,754
Black	1,728	54,098	125,031	509,928
Totals				
Whites	70,158	397,306	755,539	2,111,079
Blacks	2,920	68,879	150,024	566,670
All	73,078	466,185	905,563	2,677,749

Westwards expansion and the settlement of the interior valleys filled the 'back country' from western Pennsylvania to South Carolina and settlers also moved into western New York and the Ohio region. Land speculation became a fact of colonial life. Land companies with American and British participants sought political favours from the colonial authorities and from the British government, while population pressures in the older settled regions caused social tensions. Intercolonial and back-country versus seaboard rivalries lasted to and beyond the American Revolution. From the 1750s the British government began to increase its attempts to create an imperial policy embracing western settlement and Indian relations.

British opinion was that the colonies were primarily of value to the development of a profitable maritime commercial empire. An appreciation of the trading interdependence of the Atlantic colonies, for which southern Europe also became an important market, and of their direct trade with Great Britain, including their great potential as markets for English manufactured goods, grew in the century after 1650. Regulatory measures included various acts of trade (*'Navigation Acts') from 1651 onwards in the face of Dutch competition. Foreign-built and/or -crewed ships were excluded from colonial trade and most exports and imports were to be carried via English and (after 1707) Scottish ports. From 1673 a Customs Service was created in the colonies. In 1696 the foundation of the Board of *Trade provided a focus for colonial administration and attempts were made to tighten British control, especially during times of war.

These were not continued with any force under Sir Robert *Walpole and the duke of *Newcastle, a period characterized as one of 'salutary neglect'. Only renewed struggles with Spain and France, particularly from the late 1740s, and the rise of a group of imperially minded politicians and colonial governors, created demands for stronger executive control and greater colonial obedience. By this time colonial political identities were almost fully formed. The original crown charters had conferred large powers of self-government on the colonies, notably in allowing them representative assemblies with substantial legislative powers, chosen by wide electorates. These assemblies assumed fiscal authority and control of local government, a process shaped by the concurrent emergence of élite groups of successful families.

Such developments were accompanied by the growth of a political culture, with roots in English opposition to Stuart absolutism, drawing on 17th-cent. puritanism and vulgarized Lockianism, later mingled with the opposition rhetoric of country against court, and against Walpole's system, and a belief in New World purity and British corruption. The Great Awakening of the 1740s also revitalized protestant dissent and further distanced many Americans from the claims of an Anglican political and church establishment to authority. But denominational and other interest group rivalries, like those over land, caused internal conflicts. Yet a degree of cultural cohesion and awareness of shared political, commercial, and economic interests was stimulated by the productions of the colonial printing presses, particularly by newspapers. Virginians and New Englanders recounted their short histories as the successful creation of quasi-independent New World societies.

Warfare between France and England in North America in 1754, arising from rivalries in the Ohio valley, therefore necessitated co-operation between a mother country and colonies whose differences were masked by shared ambitions for commercial and territorial victory over a catholic power believed to be seeking universal monarchy. British plans for colonial union in 1754 failed in the colonial assemblies. The course of the *Seven Years War revealed the jealous self-interest of the colonial assemblies towards each other and towards London, despite royal governors' and English ministers' orders. Overwhelming advantages in terms of wealth and population enjoyed, for example, by New York and New England over French Canada, together with the deployment of British regular troops, failed to bring victory until 1759–60.

Success brought rejoicing for a God-ordained triumph of protestantism and liberty, even prophecies of a forthcoming millennium. The reality was a huge increase in the British national debt, provoking anxieties about bankruptcy and fears that colonial expansion, no longer checked by the French and their Indian allies, would precipate expensive new conflicts with the frontier tribes, concerns fed by the Cherokee War (1759–61) and by a major middle-colony Indian war in 1763. These and British official memories of colonial military non-cooperation and illegal trade during the Seven Years War suggested that colonial dependence on crown and Parliament might need to be ensured by new British measures. The mood in America also altered as wartime spending was succeeded by deflation and depression and as credit crises in the mother country were increasingly felt. When British ministers introduced new measures to raise larger revenues from America, colonial political awareness was stimulated and diffused and intercolonial co-operation increased. Resistance and then revolution followed.

The loss of the thirteen colonies occurred, however, as British–American trade was again increasing and as British politicians were becoming more involved in schemes to profit from the opening up of western lands. Tobacco imports were changing Glasgow's commerce, Chesapeake wheat was beginning to feed Britain's own growing population, and enormous quantities of American products were being shipped to the sugar islands. British manufactured goods were also pouring into America, leading some historians to claim that the colonies were experiencing a 'consumer revolution'. Benjamin Franklin believed that the future prosperity of Britain depended on America and that the centre of the British empire might one day be found there. Isaac *Barré told the House of Commons in March 1774 that 'You have not a loom nor an anvil but what is stamped with America.' Even George III mused on the interdependence of commerce and power, prophesying the West Indies following the Americans 'not [into] Independence but must for its own interest be dependent on North America: then Ireland would soon follow the same plan . . . then this Island would be reduced to itself, and soon would be a poor Island indeed, for reduced in her Trade Merchants would retire with their Wealth to climates more to their Advantage, and Shoals of Manufacturers would leave this country for the New Empire.'

Such views illustrate the impact of successful colonial growth on some contemporaries and hinted at the need for an imaginative readjustment of the view that the colonies were still the dependent children of the mother country. But the political nation upheld the sovereignty of crown and Parliament over America. This must not be sacrificed to colonial or trading interests. Schemes on both sides of the Atlantic, either for granting the colonial assemblies a form of equality with the British Parliament or for managing the thirteen colonies by admitting their representatives to the British Parliament, as Scotland had been managed since the Act of Union, found no vital support. In 1776 the thirteen colonies, bolstered by the experience of more than a century of successful growth and a large degree of self-government, declared themselves 'free and independent states absolved from all allegiance to, or dependence upon, the crown and parliament of Great Britain'. RCS

Greene, J. P., and Pole, J. R. (eds.), *Colonial British America: Essays in the New History of the Early Modern Era* (Baltimore, 1984); Simmons, R. C., *The American Colonies from Settlement to Independence* (New York, 1976).

American War. See WAR OF 1812.

American War of Independence, 1775–83. The roots of American independence go as deep as the original settlements—colonists of a dissenting disposition with little cause for affection for their mother country, the development of a more egalitarian society without bishops or noblemen, colonial assemblies gaining political experience and anxious to extend their privileges, and a population increasing in size, prosperity, and confidence. In 1715 the colonists numbered fewer than half a million, of whom 70,000 were negro slaves. By 1770 there were more than 2 million. The ties with England were already weakening as many of the new settlers—Germans, Swiss, or Ulster-Irish—had no English connections. (See AMERICA.)

The crisis was triggered off by the *Seven Years War, during which the British drove the French out of Canada. It had often been remarked that only the threat of falling prey to Spain or France kept the colonists in check. That check was removed at exactly the moment that the British became alarmed at the rising cost of the plantations: they were anxious to reduce clashes with the Indians and determined that the Americans should bear more of the imperial burden. The first objective produced a prohibition on expansion across the Allegheny mountains, the second produced *Grenville's *Stamp Act of 1764, which led to a storm of protest. Though the Stamp Act was repealed in 1766, the *Declaratory Act which reaffirmed British sovereignty deprived the gesture of much of its appeal. The imposition of the *Townshend duties provoked violence and the situation escalated. The *Boston massacre of 1770 was followed by the seizure of the Gaspée in 1772 and the *Boston Tea Party in 1773. By 1774 the Americans had summoned a congress to concert resistance and most Britons were convinced that the lawlessness of the colonists could not be tolerated.

Once fighting began at *Lexington in 1775, Britain faced a difficult military task. To occupy and garrison so vast a country was out of the question. But many Americans, especially in the south, remained loyal to the crown and British armed intervention could give them the upper hand against the patriots. The first phase finished when *Burgoyne's grandiose plan to drive down the Hudson river from Canada and cut off *New England ended in capitulation at *Saratoga in October 1777. Though the disaster could have been retrieved, it brought France and Spain into the conflict and placed in jeopardy Britain's command of the seas. Nevertheless the issue remained in doubt and *Washington experienced great difficulty in holding his troops together. In 1780 *Cornwallis led a major expedition to the southern colonies. He was cut off and his surrender at *Yorktown in October 1781 brought the conflict to an end. American independence was recognized by the treaty of *Versailles in 1783.

The short-term consequences were less dramatic than many expected. Though Britain's eclipse as a world power was confidently predicted, her economic recovery was swift, and the colonial development of Australia, New Zealand, India, and parts of Africa went some way to compensating for the loss of the first British empire. But in the long run there was a great shift of power across the Atlantic and the population of the USA passed that of the mother country soon after the American Civil War, in the 1860s. In the long perspective of world events, the colonization and the loss of America, together with the spread of the English language and English parliamentary institutions, seems the single most important development in British history.

JAC

Amherst, Jeffrey Amherst, 1st Baron (1717–97). Amherst, a career soldier, was the son of a lawyer from Kent and advanced under the patronage of the Dorset family. He entered the army at an early age and was lieutenant-colonel by 28. After serving with distinction in the War of the *Austrian Succession at *Dettingen and *Fontenoy, he was made commander-in-chief in America in 1758, and acquired a great reputation by the conquest of Canada. In 1761 he was created KB. At the outbreak of hostilities with the American colonies, Amherst was brought into the cabinet, raised to the peerage in 1776, and made formally C.-in-C. 1778–82. He seems to have acted more as a chief of staff than a strategist. He was dismissed at the fall of North's ministry, but brought back as C.-in-C. from 1793 to 1795. Systematic and methodical rather than dashing, he had a reputation for honesty and directness. George III, however, remarked sardonically in 1772 that Amherst's services, undoubtedly great, 'would not be lessened if he left the appreciating them to others'. JAC

Amiens, mise of, 1264. After the struggle between Henry III and the baronial party had gone on for several years, it was agreed to put the validity of the provisions of *Oxford (1258) to Louis IX of France for arbitration. The point at issue was mainly whether the king should have an unrestricted right to appoint and dismiss his advisers. Each side sent representatives to the meeting at Amiens in January 1263, where Louis decided emphatically in favour of his fellow king, declaring the Provisions null and void. The result was not to settle the dispute but to force de *Montfort and his supporters into open rebellion. JAC

Amiens, treaty of, 1802. The treaty provided the only break in the long war between Britain and revolutionary and Napoleonic France from 1793 to 1814. By 1801 the conflict was near to stalemate. Britain had been unable to co-ordinate effective coalitions and her raids on the continent had proved unsuccessful: France had lost control of the seas and was unable to deliver a knock-out blow. The resignation of *Pitt in 1801 made it easier for his successor *Addington to seek peace. Britain retained Ceylon and Trinidad but restored the Cape of Good Hope to the Dutch. Malta was to be given back to the Knights of St John and guaranteed. The French were to withdraw from Naples and central Italy and Egypt was to return to Turkish rule. Each side dragged its feet on fulfilling the terms and the peace, little more than an armed truce, lasted only until May 1803, when Britain declared war. Napoleon then began planning an invasion of England. JAC

Amritsar massacre, 1919. On 13 April 1919 at Jallianwalla Bagh in Amritsar, General R. E. H. Dyer ordered his soldiers to fire on a protesting though unarmed crowd, killing 400 people. The shootings were for defiance of a martial law ban on assembly imposed under the Rowlatt Act, passed against sedition at the end of the First World War. The Act and the massacre became symbols of British oppression to the Indian freedom struggle, then developing a mass political following. Mahatma *Gandhi led nation-wide demonstrations, which brought him to leadership of the Indian national movement. DAW

anabaptists or re-baptizers held that baptism should be postponed until people were capable of understanding the promises made and obligations accepted. But the hatred and persecution they encountered stemmed from the widespread belief that they intended to overthrow the whole social order. There were different groups within the movement but those anabaptists who held power in Münster 1533–5 were radical, advocating common property and practising polygamy. This served to smear the whole movement and 'anabaptist' became a term of abuse. Henry VIII thought them 'a detestable sect' and burned a number:

James I in the preface to *Basilikon Doron* denounced them as 'a vile sect' and burned more. Their doctrinal influence was on the Brownists, *baptists, Hutterites and Mennonites. JAC

anarchism. Though mistrust of the state and a desire for cheap and limited government is a commonplace in the British political tradition, formal anarchism has received little support. Anarchist elements have been traced in the Commonwealth period, though they were more probably collective agrarianists, and the theory developed only after the French Revolution in the 1790s. *Paine declared that government was, at best, a necessary evil: 'a great part of what is called government is mere imposition.' *Spence and *Godwin went further. Spence's vision of the future was of parish communities, with minimal powers reserved for the state, while Godwin insisted that government was a 'brute engine', which had caused all the vices of mankind. Neither had many disciples, though *Shelley followed his father-in-law Godwin in calling government 'a mighty calamity'. The *Cato Street conspiracy to murder the cabinet in 1820, the work of some of Spence's supporters, gave anarchism a lurid image. The First International split in 1871 between the supporters of Marx, who wanted a proletarian state, and those of Bakunin who argued, with some prescience, that it might itself become an engine of despotism. The small British groups made little impact. Sheffield anarchists in 1891 produced a short-lived paper and a group of Walsall anarchists were convicted at Stafford assizes in 1892 of conspiring to manufacture bombs. An even more sensational episode was the siege of 100 Sidney Street, Stepney, in 1911, with two foreign anarchists holed up, while the home secretary, Winston *Churchill, helped to supervise a shoot-out. Peter the Painter (otherwise Peter Piaktoff) escaped the flames and disappeared from history. There was some interest in anarchist theory among left-wing circles involved in the Spanish Civil War in the 1930s. But fear of anarchy, an important ingredient of the conservative tradition, was always in Britain more influential than anarchism itself. JAC

anchorites, who had their origin in the early church, were solitary holy men or women (anchoresses) living an ascetic life of contemplation and confined to a strictly enclosed cell that was often attached to, or inside, a church. Though initially subject to no rules, by the 12th cent. they were required to be licensed and controlled by the diocesan bishop. In England they were particularly numerous during the 11th and 12th cents. and were supported by many patrons, while treatises, including the *Ancrene Wisse*, were written for their spiritual guidance. BJG

Ancrum Moor, battle of, 1545. The death of James V after the disaster at *Solway Moss in 1542 encouraged Henry VIII to propose a marriage between his only son Edward and the infant queen of Scotland, Mary. When the negotiations faltered, Henry resolved on a strong-arm policy, the famous *'rough wooing'. In 1544 Hertford (*Somerset) led a punitive raid which sacked Edinburgh. The following year another expedition, led by Sir Ralph Evers and Sir Brian Latoun, gutted Melrose. But the regent, *Arran, and the earl of *Angus gathered a Scottish army just outside the town and on 17 February inflicted a heavy defeat on the invaders, killing both the leaders. JAC

Anderson, Elizabeth Garrett (1836–1917). First Englishwoman to qualify in medicine. Elizabeth Garrett was born in Aldeburgh (Suffolk), where she is buried. Inspired by the beginning of the organized women's movement, and aware that the liberal professions were closed to them, her tenacious efforts led to her becoming a licentiate of the Society of Apothecaries (1865) and the first female MD in France (1870). Concentrating on treating women and children, she founded a dispensary and then the first hospital wholly staffed by women, eventually becoming dean of the London School of Medicine for Women. Marriage to Skelton Anderson proved a help rather than a hindrance in her career. Always concerned with education and social improvement, Anderson's greatest service to the women's cause was her normality. A sense of duty, courage, and unaffected manner combined to disarm a hostile profession, and served as a role model for others. ASH

Andrew, St (d. *c.* AD 60). Fisherman of Galilee, among the first of Jesus' disciples, and first missionary, bringing his brother Simon (Peter) to Christ. Little is known of his life after the Crucifixion, though it is generally thought he was crucified at Patras in Achaia. Among various legends is the claim that his relics were carried to Scotland by the 4th-cent. abbot St Rule, divinely led to present-day *St Andrews. There he built his church, an evangelistic centre for the area. Patron saint of Scotland, the saltire cross associated with his death represents Scotland on the Union Jack. St Andrew's day is 30 November. AM

Andrewes, Lancelot (1555–1626). Bishop of Chichester (1605), Ely (1609), and Winchester (1619–26). Educated at Pembroke Hall, Cambridge, Andrewes was a scholar of great erudition, conversant with fifteen languages. One of those appointed to prepare a new translation of the Bible (1604), he was largely responsible for the Pentateuch and historical books of the Old Testament.

Both in his lifetime and subsequently his fame has largely rested on his ability as a preacher and devotional writer. His sermons were influential in formulating a distinctive Anglican theology. They owe much to the Greek fathers, particularly Chrysostom, but are none the less firmly founded in western catholic thought. In style they are complex, abounding in puns and containing untranslated quotations from Latin, Greek, and Hebrew, thus making great demands upon his hearers. His *Preces privatae* are carefully arranged, revealing Andrewes's rare but precious gift for the expression in writing of devotion and prayer. JRG

Aneurin (late 6th cent.). Bard. Almost everything known about Aneurin has to be conjectured from the epic poem he composed, *Y Gododdin*, recounting a disastrous raid on the Anglo-Saxons of *Bernicia and *Deira by the Britons of *Gododdin in Lothian (*c.*600). But the text has been added to. *Nennius, *Historia Brittonum* (*c.*796), named him along with *Taliesin as one of the five Welsh bards during the struggle against the Northumbrians. Aneurin speaks as an eye-witness of the battle and of the dead heroes as his kinsmen, from which it has been inferred that he belonged to the Gododdin: others have suggested that he was a visiting bard, possibly from *Elmet. A case has been made that he could have been a brother of St Deiniol, patron saint of Bangor. JAC

Angevin empire. The term is commonly used to describe the collection of lands held, or claimed, by Henry II and his immediate successors before Henry III renounced his claims in the treaty of *Paris (1259). Henry II first brought the constituent parts of the empire together by combining under his rulership three distinct inheritances. These were, first, the former Anglo-Norman realm, comprising the duchy of Normandy and the kingdom of England, brought into being in 1066, split apart during Stephen's reign, and reunited under Henry in 1154 on his accession. He had become duke of Normandy in 1150, when his father *Geoffrey of Anjou, who had conquered the duchy in 1144, abdicated in his favour. Henry also claimed suzerainty over the duchy of Brittany, a claim inherited from his Norman ducal predecessors, and over Wales and Scotland, claims inherited from previous kings of England. Together, this was Henry's inheritance from his mother, the Empress *Matilda, daughter of Henry I. From his father Henry inherited the county of Anjou (hence *Angevin* empire), and the counties of Maine and Touraine, the three lordships together conventionally described as Greater Anjou. Thirdly, there was *Aquitaine, the inheritance of the heiress *Eleanor of Aquitaine, which came to Henry as prince consort following their marriage in 1152. The core of the duchy consisted of Poitou and Gascony, with a host of other lordships over which the dukes of Aquitaine claimed suzerainty. As if this was not enough, Ireland also came into the Angevin orbit following Henry's invasion of 1171–2. Henry, accordingly, was lord of a vast block of territory stretching from the Pyrenees to Scotland, making him the most powerful ruler in western Europe at the time.

There has been much discussion of the origins of the empire. Was it fundamentally the product of Henry's opportunism in the early 1150s, or the result of a good deal of genealogical chance and fortuitous development, or had any of Henry's dynastic predecessors planned the long-term union of the three inheritances? The latter seems distinctly unlikely. First, no one could have predicted that, through genealogical chance, Eleanor of Aquitaine would become heiress to the duchy in 1137, and that, since she and her first husband, Louis VII of France, had only daughters, the duchy would revert to her on the annulment of the marriage in 1152. This meant that Eleanor brought the duchy with her on marrying Henry in the same year. It is clear that she only accepted Henry's overtures because marriage to him made sense since, by then, he had possession of Anjou, which marched with her beloved Poitou to the north, was duke of Normandy, and was poised to take England. Second, there is no indication that either of Henry's parents envisaged the union of the Anglo-Norman realm and Anjou. Geoffrey, in particular, gave little help to Matilda in her fight for England against Stephen and, although he took over Normandy in 1144, he did so in his son's name, associating Henry in the government of the duchy from 1146. He kept the administrations of Normandy and Anjou separate, and abdicated in Normandy (but not Anjou) in Henry's favour in 1150. These are scarcely the actions of an empire-builder. Moreover, most historians now agree that Geoffrey intended permanent partition: Anjou to go to his younger son, Geoffrey the Younger, and the Anglo-Norman realm to Henry, a disposition reflected in the still contentious report of the death-bed will that he supposedly made in 1151. Third, although Henry was born of the marriage in 1128 between Geoffrey and Matilda, that does not necessarily mean that either of the negotiating parties, Henry II's grandparents, Henry I or Fulk of Anjou, envisaged a territorial union. There were, of course, successional implications, since Matilda, by then, was heiress to the Anglo-Norman realm, and Geoffrey was Fulk's heir, but it is inconceivable that anyone could have considered the union of the two inheritances as inevitable. Who could know what the future would hold? Who could have predicted in 1128 that Matilda and Geoffrey would produce three sons?

In short, the evidence suggests strongly that it was Henry II himself who created the Angevin empire. His acquisitiveness and ambition led him to exploit the possibilities and, brushing aside his younger brother, to bring together the three different inheritances between 1150 and 1156, when Geoffrey the Younger rebelled but was forced to submit. The implications of this are of profound importance in considering the reasons for the failure of the Angevin empire to survive. If the empire was essentially the product of unforeseen developments and Henry's opportunism, and if, accordingly, its roots were shallow and artificial, then its decline and collapse in 1204, within fifteen years of its creator's own demise in 1189, is more explicable.

Naturally, there is more to it than that. Those who maintain that the empire's collapse was inevitable stress the fact that neither Henry II, Richard I, nor John sought to centralize. Rather, each lordship remained apart in its institutions, laws, and customs, with a bare minimum of 'imperial legislation', no common currency, and no single political centre. Moreover, even England and Normandy, the most intimately linked provinces, because of the consequences of the Norman Conquest, were going their separate ways by the end of the 12th cent. In particular, cross-channel landholding patterns were breaking up, with ever more distinct baronages residing either side of the Channel. No attempt was made to create one sovereign, independent entity. On the contrary, changing circumstances forced the Angevin lords to accept ever greater implications in their feudal relationship to the Capetian kings of France, so far as their French fiefs were concerned, culminating in the terms of the treaty of *Le Goulet (1200). Only in England were they juridically equal to their French overlords. Again, there was no intention that the different dominions should pass as one inheritance. As early as 1169, at Montmirail, Henry II made plain his wish that each of his sons should receive a part, each part descending to that son's own heirs as a distinct unit. In addition, the sheer extent of the Angevin lands made effective government difficult, a problem exacerbated by the extraordinary rivalries and tensions within the ruling family itself.

Powerful though these arguments are, the fact remains that until 1202–3 the Angevin empire remained essentially intact. Structural weaknesses and deep historical trends at work there may have been, but do these alone explain the proximate timing of the collapse? Allowance must also be made for the growth of an external force that could make these internal 'weaknesses' count for something in the real world, and the comparative abilities of John and Philip II, the Capetian king at the time. Here, there can be no doubt that Philip was much more of a match than his father Louis VII had been, partly because of his own abilities, but also because he commanded far greater resources, the result of Capetian territorial expansion combined with a much more intensive exploitation of royal rights in the 1190s. Philip also had a far more compact principality to defend than the sprawling land mass of the Angevin empire in France, which took up in expenditure much of the revenue generated. In addition, perhaps crucially, John played into Philip's hands. Between 1200 and 1204 he somehow managed to fritter away the advantages he had enjoyed, in particular by his gross mismanagement of the natural defenders of the Angevin empire in France, the social élite such as the Lusignans, lords of La Marche, the Norman baronage, and William des Roches, the leader of the great lords of Anjou, Maine, and Touraine.

The combination of these factors meant that by the end of 1204 only the *Channel Islands and a much reduced Gascony remained in John's hands. Neither he nor his son, Henry III, accepted the losses, but despite their considerable efforts they were unable to retrieve the situation. In 1259 Henry bowed to what now can be seen as almost the inevitable and renounced his claims to Henry II's French inheritance. In return, Louis IX acknowledged him as rightful duke of Gascony. An era had come to an end. SL

Gillingham, J. B., *The Angevin Empire* (1984); Holt, J. C., 'The End of the Anglo-Norman Realm', *Proceedings of the British Academy*, 59 (1975), 3–45; Le Patourel, J., *Feudal Empires: Norman and Plantagenet*, ed. M. Jones (1984).

Angles. See ANGLO-SAXONS.

Anglesey. Island county of north-west Wales, separated from the mainland by the Menai Straits. In 1974 it became the district of Ynys Môn in the county of Gwynedd, but was reconstituted as a county in 1996. Its location, together with the protective barrier of the Snowdonian mountains, made it a traditional centre of resistance to invaders, Roman and Norman. But after conquest by Edward I it was created a county of the principality of Wales in 1284, a status confirmed at the Act of Union of 1536.

Anglesey is a low plateau with hills rising no more than 500 feet. It was known as 'Môn mam Cymru' (Môn, mother of Wales) because of its productive cereal-growing, but present farming is primarily dairy. Economic development is also related to the major road/rail crossings of the island to the port of Holyhead, the major British link to Ireland. Two bridges cross the Menai Straits; *Telford's Menai suspension bridge (1819–20) and *Stephenson's Britannia tubular bridge (1846–50), originally rail but now both rail and road. Copper was mined on Anglesey but recent economic activity is related to a nuclear power station at Wylfa Head and an aluminium smelter. Tourism is also a significant employer, mainly along the coastline.

The population of the county was 69,149 in 1991. The island has been one of the cores of Welsh speech: 91.7 per cent spoke Welsh in 1901, a figure fallen to 62.0 per cent in 1991. HC

Anglesey, Henry William Paget, 1st marquis of (1768–1854). Soldier and administrator. In 1793 Anglesey raised the Staffordshire Volunteers (later the 80th Foot) and the following year served in Flanders under the duke of York. In 1808 he commanded the cavalry with distinction during the *Corunna campaign. At *Waterloo he showed undaunted bravery whilst directing the cavalry and horse artillery. He led the heavy brigade in the terrible charge which overwhelmed the comte d'Erlon's division. He lost a leg in the battle and was created marquis for his services. In 1828 Anglesey became lord-lieutenant of Ireland. He favoured catholic emancipation, an opinion which led to his recall in 1829 by Prime Minister *Wellington. Anglesey was reappointed by *Grey and faced opposition from *O'Connell. In 1846 he was made a field marshal and master-general of ordnance. Anglesey is buried in the family vault at Lichfield cathedral. RAS

Anglicanism. See CHURCH OF ENGLAND.

angling is the art of catching fish with rod, line, and hook, with live or artificial bait, and can be pursued at many different levels and in different ways. The name derives from the Old English *angle*, a hook. The success of Izaak Walton's *The Compleat Angler* (1653) testifies to the popularity of the pastime in the 17th cent. Competitive events were organized by local clubs, often based upon pubs, and commanded a very large following, particularly as the expanding railway network improved access to rivers, lakes, and canals. A National Federation of Anglers was formed in 1903. JAC

Anglo-catholicism. Developing rapidly from original *tractarianism in the late 19th cent., it reached its peak in the 1920s and 1930s. Charles *Gore, with Halifax as lay leader for 50 years, transformed old tractarianism from a marginal phenomenon into the central force in the church; he achieved what *Newman could not. Whereas tractarianism had stressed Anglican continuity from ancient times, extreme Anglo-catholicism became eventually a copy of ultramontane Roman catholicism, but at its best it was socialist in ethos, pastorally vigorous in socially deprived areas, such as east London and Portsea, with *Lang and Garbett as incumbents, where the rest of the church was apathetic. After establishing more frequent communion, they added the trappings of candles, vestments, incense, reservation of the sacrament, and confession, but extremists went further with every Roman practice, including weekly non-communicating high mass and benediction, which appalled old tractarians. Bishop King of *Lincoln was tried for excess (1890). *Davidson, favouring comprehension, nevertheless prohibited benediction and devotions to the sacrament, but in vain. In the 1920s, with *evangelicalism weakened, Anglo-catholicism was the moving force. The failure of Prayer Book revision (1928) encouraged extremists to use the Roman rite, just when a continental contrary wind, the liturgical movement, was blowing and young intellectuals such as *Ramsey, Dix, and Farrer were developing a liberal catholicism. The 1960s devastated old Anglo-catholicism, while the evangelicals at Keele, by responding, weathered the radical storm. Moreover, the second Vatican Council (1962–5) by 'protestantizing' catholic liturgy and throwing out petty liturgical paraphernalia and birettas left the old-style Anglo-catholics an isolated group, for whom the ordination of women (1990s) became a major stumbling-block. WMM

Anglo-Dutch wars. Three wars, 1652–4, 1665–7, 1672–4, provide a unique element of continuity between the Commonwealth and the restored monarchy. All were intended to redress the commercial imbalance between England and the Dutch Republic, transferring trade and wealth to the former. In the first war security was also an objective. The Dutch rejected a union which the Commonwealth demanded (1651), and sent a fleet into English waters to prevent Dutch ships being searched. An accidental clash precipitated war, but the *Rump soon identified commercial supremacy as its objective. The lighter-armed Dutch navy suffered heavy defeats, one in 1652, three in 1653, and their trade was paralysed. After *Cromwell dissolved the Rump in April 1653 the majority in *Barebone's Parliament wished to continue to total victory, but when his followers voted to dissolve Parliament Cromwell conceded lenient terms (April 1654). He did this because, by a separate agreement, the leading province of Holland excluded the house of Orange from all offices. As William II (d. 1650) had been the chief European champion of the exiled Stuarts and the Dutch were the only state with a navy that could cover an invasion (as 1688 was to show) this made the Commonwealth secure against external enemies.

James, duke of York (later James II), brought about the second war, assuming that victory was assured and that increased wealth could strengthen the crown. He defeated a rebuilt and stronger Dutch fleet off *Lowestoft (June 1665) but failed to exploit the success. Each side won an expensive victory in 1666 but this campaign exhausted English finances. No fleet could be sent out in 1667. Shore defences failed to prevent the Dutch destroying English ships in the river *Medway. The third war aimed to annihilate the Dutch Republic. The French overran its eastern provinces, but the English fleet could only fight drawn battles, one in 1672, three in 1673. An army was unable to land on the Dutch coast. This war, launched by the pro-catholic *cabal, with France as an ally, became unpopular. Opposition, stimulated by William of Orange's propaganda, made Parliament refuse further money, forcing Charles to make peace. JRJ

Anglo-Irish agreement, 1985, signed at Hillsborough, Co. Down, on 15 November 1985, by Margaret *Thatcher and the taoiseach (prime minister) of Ireland, Dr Garret FitzGerald. The agreement was intended to promote reconciliation within Northern Ireland, a greater understanding between the unionist and nationalist traditions in Ireland, and co-operation between the British and Irish governments. It established an intergovernmental conference and an attendant secretariat, the latter based at Maryfield, Co. Down. Although the document recognized the constitutional rights of the majority, Ulster Unionists saw it as establishing a form of joint authority, and mounted a ferocious campaign of opposition in 1985–6. AJ

Anglo-Irish ascendancy (protestant ascendancy). Problematic labels generally applied to the dominant Church of Ireland landed interest: 'protestant ascendancy' appears to have been first coined in 1782. However, the origins of this interest lay with the land confiscations of the 17th cent. The Ulster plantation (1608–9) brought a substantial transfer of property from the Gaelic lords to English investors and settlers; the Cromwellian confiscations (1652–3) brought the expropriation of the great majority of catholic landowners throughout the rest of Ireland. The Restoration land settlement brought a minor catholic recovery, but this was short-lived. The victory of the Williamite cause in the war of 1689–91 paved the way for further confiscations, and—more importantly—for a series of measures designed to bolster the new protestant landed interest. These 'penal laws' targeted the residual catholic gentry, and ensured a virtual protestant monopoly over freehold proprietorship until the end of the 18th cent.

The 18th cent. was, therefore, the golden age of the ascendancy. Rural economic growth after *c.*1740 helped to finance the widespread construction or remodelling of the 'big houses' (mansions), and the building of lavish town houses, most spectacularly in Dublin. The height of ascendancy political power came after 1782–3, with the grant of legislative independence to the gentry-dominated Irish Parliament. But increasingly powerful and vocal catholic and dissenter interests effectively challenged this dominance in the 1790s, and the apparent helplessness of the ascendancy during the 1798 rising made it vulnerable to English intervention. The Act of *Union (1800) abolished the Dublin Parliament, and represented a severe blow to the political authority and prestige of the Irish landed interest. Further political set-backs came with *catholic emancipation (1829) and with the rise of an ambitious and radical peasant nationalism. The land legislation of the British government at the end of the 19th cent. weakened the rights of Irish proprietors, and encouraged a transfer of land to the former tenant farmers. Land purchase legislation, especially the *Land Act of 1903, facilitated this transfer, and brought a swift if relatively cushioned end to the economic predominance of the Anglo-Irish ascendancy. AJ

Anglo-Irish treaty, 1921. A truce on 11 July ended the war between the *Irish Republican Army and the British army which had been raging since 1919. Eamon *de Valera, president of Dáil Éireann, the constituent assembly of Ireland, met with *Lloyd George to discuss a settlement. Deadlock ensued with Lloyd George wanting dominion Home Rule for Ireland and de Valera insisting on an independent Irish Republic. Negotiations began in earnest in October with

Arthur *Griffith and Michael *Collins representing Ireland. After much debate a treaty was signed on 6 December whereby Ireland became a free state, with the six counties of Ulster remaining as part of the UK, but with full dominion status. It followed an ultimatum from the British that the Irish agree to their terms or face the renewal of war. The Dáil eventually accepted the treaty on 7 January 1922 by 64 votes to 57 and it came into effect on 6 December.

RAS

Anglo-Japanese treaty, 1902. Concluded on 30 January to improve British security against France and Russia in the Far East, each party agreed to fight only if the other became involved in war with at least two other powers. The treaty promised to localize any war, and facilitated Japan's decision to attack Russia in 1904. It was renewed in 1905, each party agreeing to assist the other in a war with only one opponent. From 1911 the British also tried to use the alliance as a restraining influence on Japan. American objections brought about its demise in 1921–2. CJB

Anglo-Russian entente, 1907. The convention was concluded on 31 August 1907 to try to resolve the long-running Anglo-Russian rivalries in Persia, Tibet, and Afghanistan. The Foreign Office also looked to the entente to improve the balance of power in Europe and the Near East against Germany. Only Russian weaknesses after defeat by Japan and revolution at home made agreement possible at that time. As Russia recovered from the war so rivalries began to revive in Persia, and some competition continued in Asia even after Britain and Russia found themselves fighting on the same side against Germany from 1914. CJB

Anglo-Saxon art and architecture now only survives fragmentarily and even what remains is not necessarily representative of what once existed. Our view of architecture, for example, is distorted by the near-total loss of all wooden buildings and by the Norman destruction of all pre-Conquest cathedrals. Similarly art in wood and fabric is now rare and whilst 5th- and 6th-cent. metalwork has been well preserved by burial in pagan graves, Christian material remained above ground and thus vulnerable to the destructive forces of changing taste, Viking and Norman looting, or the zealous cleansing of the Reformation.

Wood was the medium of almost all secular architecture and our information consequently has to rely on the excavated post-holes and foundation-trenches of structures which have otherwise totally vanished. Essentially two types of building are represented in the archaeological record. One was the so-called 'sunken-featured building' with a half-subterranean floor or cellar. These seem largely to have functioned as workshops alongside a second type of structure, the rectangular 'hall'. These halls vary in their size and their constructional techniques, but at the royal level represented by palaces at *Yeavering (Northd.) and Cheddar (Som.) they were obviously impressive structures reaching up to 100 feet in length.

Wood was also the natural medium for churches built in the Irish tradition brought to Northumbria by St *Aidan and his followers in the 7th cent., and it continued to be an important medium throughout the period. Only Greenstead (Essex), however, now remains as an example of this once-widespread form. The alternative tradition of masonry architecture survives much more extensively. It was this tradition which was reintroduced to lowland Britain by the Augustinian mission to Kent in the late 6th cent. and enthusiastically exploited by Northumbrians such as *Wilfrid and *Benedict Biscop later in the following century. For such early ecclesiastics it is clear that the use of stone represented a statement of their identity with the rest of the Christian world and it is the same identification which is reflected in the fact that their early churches, such as Reculver (Kent) or Hexham (Northd.), show links in their plans, technology, and ornament to buildings in Gaul and Italy.

The great cultural renaissance of the late 8th and early 9th cents. under the Carolingian monarchy brought with it an attempt to emulate the scale and forms of classical antiquity; churches at *Brixworth (Northants), Wareham (Dorset), and Cirencester (Glos.) seem to represent English responses to these continental movements, particularly in the form of their crypts. Despite the disruptions of *Viking activity ambitious churches incorporating Carolingian features were still being erected or modified in the later 9th cent. *Deerhurst (Glos.) and *Repton (Derbys.) provide two well-dated examples and early in the following century the new minster at *Winchester, with its great aisled nave and projecting transepts, clearly echoes continental types. More typical, however, of a persistent characteristic of English architectural taste is a work which is broadly contemporary with the new minster, the church of St Oswald at Gloucester whose earliest phases lie between *c.*880 and 918. It has a crypt and western apse of Carolingian type but its basic unaisled form is highly conservative and could be paralleled as far back as King *Cenwalh's 7th-cent. church at Winchester. The excavated sequence of the old minster at Winchester, indeed, shows that same conservatism persisting through into the period of the *Benedictine reform movement: the building was extensively altered at both its east and west ends in 980 and 993–4 to give a total length exceeding 240 feet, but at its core, preserved like a relic, remained the building erected by Cenwalh in *c.*648.

Anglo-Saxon art mirrors the characteristics of ecclesiastical architecture; it responds creatively to foreign models but remains highly conservative in its tastes. In the pagan period, where our information now depends largely on surviving metalwork, it is essentially a non-representational art whose effects rely upon contrasts of line and colour and on the ambiguities of stylized animal motifs. This Germanic art found its most striking expression in the gold and garnet jewellery of *Sutton Hoo. The Christian conversion brought with it both new media for Anglo-Saxon artists, such as books and stone carving, and an alien Late Antique aesthetic from the Mediterranean world. 7th- and 8th-cent. artists developed a fascinating range of responses to these imported concepts and their native inherited traditions. The range is well exemplified by two contemporary works of *c.*700, the Codex Amiatinus and the *Lindisfarne Gospels. The Codex, written and illuminated at *Jarrow, meticulously reproduced the art of its Italian model, whilst the

Lindisfarne Gospels reinterpreted similar models in a more linear style and combined them with zoomorphic forms which reach back to Sutton Hoo. Analogous combinations of eclectic borrowing and conservative traditionalism characterize later English art of the 9th cent. and beyond.

The Viking invasions and settlements of the later 9th cent. divided the artistic culture of the country in two. In the north we see Scandinavian animal ornament and mythology grafted onto native Anglo-Saxon monuments like the crosses and grave-slabs of York minster, Leeds, and Gosforth (Cumbria). In the south, building upon the cultural realignments encouraged by King *Alfred and his immediate successors, there was an artistic revival in the later years of the 10th cent. associated with the Benedictine reform movement which cautiously fused Carolingian and Ottonian motifs with long-established insular forms. By the end of the Anglo-Saxon period, in work like the Romsey Rood, Romanesque art was already emerging. RNB

Backhouse, J., *et al.*, *The Golden Age of Anglo-Saxon Art* (1984); Fernie, E., *The Architecture of the Anglo-Saxons* (1983); Webster, L., *et al.*, *The Making of England* (1991); Wilson, D. M., *Anglo-Saxon Art* (1984).

Anglo-Saxon Chronicle. Records of historical events, normally in Latin, were kept from the early days of Christian Anglo-Saxon England, notably in the form of genealogies, Easter tables, and monastic writings. For example, *Bede, the greatest scholar of the age, was deeply interested in chronology. It was King *Alfred, however, in the early 890s who was directly responsible for putting into shape the *Anglo-Saxon Chronicle* as we have it, providing a record of events on an annalar basis in the vernacular Old English language. The *Chronicle* was kept up to date, clearly with encouragement from the royal court, at great ecclesiastical centres where literate clerks could be found. Surviving manuscripts associated with Canterbury, Worcester, York, and Abingdon provide very full accounts for some periods (the reign of Alfred and the reign of *Æthelred conspicuously, and then the reign of *Edward the Confessor and the Norman kings), but give only distressingly jejune entries at others. At Peterborough the *Chronicle*, initially copied from a Canterbury manuscript *c.*1121, continued to be kept as late as 1155, giving a full and lurid account of Stephen's reign in a language which was visibly changing from Old English into Early Middle English. HL

Anglo-Saxons is the name collectively applied to the descendants of the Germanic people who settled in Britain between the late 4th and early 7th cents. and retrospectively to their ancestors. Their backgrounds varied. Some came as mercenaries, others as invaders. They included, besides Angles and Saxons, Jutes and other groups. Some had experience of Frankish Gaul and hence some acquaintance with Roman institutions and culture. The eventual use of the name 'English' and 'England' for people and territory probably owes something to the influence of *Bede, whose *History of the English People* dealt with the whole. He followed Pope Gregory I, who knew the people as Angles.

Much about the invasion and settlement period is obscure, but for most of its history Anglo-Saxon England is one of the best-documented early medieval European societies. Besides Bede's *History*, historical sources include a number of saints' lives, and the **Anglo-Saxon Chronicle*. Many letters survive, those of the Anglo-Saxon missionary to the continent, *Boniface, of particular importance in our knowledge of the 8th cent. church. Poetry, in the vernacular (Old English) and in Latin, religious and secular, composed for several purposes, can convey historical fact, religious ideal, ethics, and values. Some poets are anonymous, others, like *Aldhelm and Cynewulf, can be studied. A great body of evidence relates to royal ideology, government, and administration: vernacular law codes (beginning with that of *Æthelbert of Kent), charters, writs, and wills. Historians also benefit from the study of the language of vernacular texts, from that of place-names, of art (including sculpture), and of architecture. Art was often didactic, and choice of particular styles might indicate values and allegiances, as, perhaps in the cases of the Codex Amiatinus, and *Wilfrid's churches. Archaeology, of burials, settlements, towns, kings' halls (for example *Yeavering, Cheddar), monasteries, and churches, is critically important. Yet there are still uncertainties. Gaps in the evidence, problems of its interpretation and of reconciling different types, generate lively debate. Some may never be solved: it is salutary to realize how important subjects depend on chance survivals or discoveries—the ship-burial at *Sutton Hoo (mound 1) and the poem **Beowulf* for example. Many themes intertwine: these two sources must be considered, along with problems concerning land tenure, and coinage, in the study of kings as portrayed by Bede.

From obscure beginnings the Anglo-Saxons formed a number of kingdoms. The 7th-cent. trend was a shift in the balance of power from south and east (*Kent and *East Anglia) to north and west (*Northumbria, *Mercia, *Wessex), and the take-over of smaller kingdoms by larger ones, the so-called *Heptarchy. The 8th cent. was a period of Mercian dominance and Northumbrian independence, the 9th of the rise of Wessex, and of the threat of the Vikings. They established their own kingdoms (of East Anglia and Northumbria): their invasions and settlements had both positive and negative effects. In the 10th cent. Wessex united England.

To the forging of one people and one state *Alfred, *Athelstan, and *Edgar made significant contributions. Encouragement of its desirability was to be found in the pages of Bede and in the needs of the church and the principles of its organization. Its cause was furthered by the leaders of the 10th-cent. reform movement. But the England of 1066 was not inevitable. Quite different borders could have been established. In the late 7th cent., for example, one kingdom south of the Humber and another north, including southern Scotland, was a possibility; in the 10th a kingdom pushing into Wales rather than the Scandinavian-held north. The 11th cent., marred by the unsuccessful *Æthelred II (the Unready), the conquest by the Danish *Cnut, *Edward the Confessor, and the *Norman Conquest, is not properly representative of the history, culture, and achievements of the Anglo-Saxons.

Society and culture had of course changed over time.

Anglo-Saxon paganism is not fully known. The great period of conversion was the 7th cent., an age of saints, especially in Northumbria (the missionary *Aidan, the home-grown Wilfrid, *Cuthbert, and others) and monastic foundations (including *Lindisfarne, *Whitby, *Ripon, *Hexham, *Monkwearmouth-Jarrow) which were to be very rich. A stratified society, in which, for example *ceorls and gesiths (royal companions) had different *wergelds, its political life was dominated by the aristocracy, and it was subject to certain tensions. That between the bonds of lordship and of kinship was in-built. Historical development brought a growth in royal power and authority in a society wherein freedom and the participation in government of free men had a long history. On some issues—marriage and war, for example—the new religion might conflict with traditional values and necessities. Some features of Anglo-Saxon society seem alien, even incomprehensible, to some modern eyes at first sight: the practice of blood-feud, the institution of the retinue (war-band), both of which could contribute to a high level of violence and instability in élite society, the combination of genuine piety with ferocity in warfare, and its condoning by clerics. Yet others seem modern: the status of women has been seen as comparatively high, some queens and royal ladies, particularly *Æthelfleda, lady of the Mercians, and abbesses, notably *Hilda and Ælfflæd of Whitby, played an important part in political and religious life. Many aspects of government have, from Alfred onwards, a recognizably modern flavour.

The Anglo-Saxon arrival had ended Britain's involvement with Roman culture and institutions, but this was recreated in the late 6th cent. Christianity, purveyed to the Anglo-Saxons almost entirely by non-British teachers, from the Irish, from Frankish Gaul, and from Rome (beginning with the mission of *Augustine), brought England into the Mediterranean, Christian, Roman world, to which in the 8th cent. the English themselves contributed. Missionaries worked amongst the Anglo-Saxons' still pagan continental kin. *Boniface was also prominent in Frankish church reform and functioned as representative of the pope to the Franks. Anglo-Saxon veneration of the papacy was strong and contributed to the growth of papal authority in the West. *Alcuin of York was adviser to Charlemagne and a leading figure in the Carolingian Renaissance. After the disintegration of the Carolingian empire, Athelstan, who involved himself with foreign dynasties and politics, was perhaps the most powerful monarch in the West.

But England owed much to Europe. The books collected on the continent by *Benedict Biscop, and the school of Canterbury, established by Archbishop *Theodore, himself from Tarsus, brought her Christian culture and scholarship. From an early period Frankish support and influence were factors in English dynastic politics, most clearly visible in Charlemagne's support for some of *Offa of Mercia's enemies, and in his involvement in Northumbrian affairs, but continuing in the 9th cent. Carolingian ideas concerning church reform and kingship, Carolingian administrative and governmental institutions and practices, Carolingian coinage, and Carolingian art all had an impact in the 8th cent. Alfred learned much from Carolingian example. The 10th-cent. reformers worked under the influence of continental ones, particularly the houses of St Peter's, Ghent, and of Fleury-sur-Loire. Government in the 10th and 11th cents. has much about it that seems Carolingian. Involvement with Normandy came in the late 10th cent. Trade, especially in slaves in the early period and wool in the later, brought great wealth, probably the main attraction for Cnut and William the Conqueror.

The Anglo-Saxon achievement was cultural, religious, economic, and political. Art, architecture, vernacular and Anglo-Latin writing, and scholarship are all remarkable. There were tensions between tradition and Christianity, but there were also compromises and accommodations, a fusion of cultures, in which old values were expressed in new contexts and vice versa. Not, originally, an urban people, Scandinavian activity and the development of Alfred's *burhs* lay behind their 10th- and 11th-cent. towns. Coinage was firmly under royal control, changed, after the great coin reform of Edgar, at regular intervals. Prosperity sustained the frequent collection of large *Danegelds. Government had in fact been well organized and ambitious quite early, as the Tribal Hidage and Offa's Dike testify. By the 11th cent., with its hundreds, shires, ealdormen and reeves, law courts, and tax-collecting, Anglo-Saxon England was, by European standards, remarkably sophisticated and advanced. There was no capital, but *Winchester was almost a capital city. The country was united, though it was not uniform in every particular, and there are hints of a lingering separatism in Northumbria. The compilation of William I's *Domesday Book, which offers much information about late Anglo-Saxon England, would not have been possible without Anglo-Saxon administrative genius. This genius, largely West Saxon, is visible elsewhere, in the rational distribution of mints in the 10th cent., and in the shire system, almost unchanged until 1974.

In administration and, ultimately, in language, the Anglo-Saxon legacy was long-lasting. Anglo-Saxon legal developments may have contributed to the English common law of the 12th cent. and may explain some of the differences between England and the other territories ruled by (the Angevin) Henry II, even after his legal reforms.

Anglo-Saxon history was of interest to some 12th-cent. scholars, for example Henry of Huntingdon and *William of Malmesbury. In the 16th cent. it was studied for possibilities of precedent and justification for rejecting papal authority, in the 17th for advancing the claims of Parliament and people against despots, as descendants of witans and free assemblies. It was popular again in the Victorian period, as an important element in constitutional history and a theatre for national heroes and empire-builders.

There are many gaps and puzzles to stimulate and delight the modern enquirer, like the condition of the upper peasantry, minsters, and the origins of the parish system; the major overlordship attained by some kings, now popularly referred to as *bretwaldas, and its role in the unification of England; continuity from the Romano-British past and into the Norman period, including the vexed matter of *'feudalism' and its origins; and, of course, why the Normans won.

AER

Campbell, J. (ed.), *The Anglo-Saxons* (Oxford, 1982); Hill, D., *An Atlas of Anglo-Saxon England* (Oxford, 1981); Whitelock, D. (ed.), *English Historical Documents c.500–1042* (2nd edn. London, 1979).

Anglo-Scottish border. See MARCHES OF SCOTLAND.

Anglo-Scottish wars. See SCOTTISH WARS OF INDEPENDENCE.

Angus, Archibald Douglas, 5th earl of [S] (*c.*1449–1513). Son and heir of George, 4th earl of Angus [S] (d. 1463), father of the poet Gavin *Douglas, and the great political maverick of late 15th and early 16th-cent. Scotland. Angus was involved in the seizure of James III at Lauder bridge (July 1482)—hence the much later nickname 'Bell-the-Cat'—his English treasons spanned more than a decade, and he rebelled against James III in 1488. Yet Angus was a friend of James IV, providing the king with his first mistress, Marion Boyd, the earl's niece, in 1492; he subsequently shared another mistress, Janet Kennedy, with the king; and he was chancellor from 1492 to 1497. Losing royal trust, Angus was warded (imprisoned) in Dumbarton and on Bute from 1501 to 1509. He opposed war with England in 1513, and missed *Flodden (though two of his sons perished there), dying at Whithorn late in 1513. NATM

Angus, Archibald Douglas, 6th earl of [S] (*c.*1490–1557). Douglas's father was killed at *Flodden and he inherited the earldom from his grandfather in 1513. Later that year he married *Margaret, queen dowager of Scotland. The daughter of the marriage became countess of *Lennox and was mother of Lord *Darnley, briefly king of Scotland. Angus was a member of the Council of Regency for James V 1517–21 and 1523–6 and chancellor in 1527. On bad terms with the young king and divorced by his wife, he was in exile in England from 1528 to 1542. He returned to Scotland in 1542 after the death of James, abandoned the English connection, and fought with some distinction at *Ancrum and *Pinkie. His great-nephew, the 8th earl, was active in the *Ruthven raid of 1582. JAC

Angus (Oengus) **MacFergus** (*c.*690–761), king of the Picts. Under Angus Pictish power was at its height. Succeeding in 729 after a fierce internal struggle, Angus established himself as over-king and waged war on all his neighbours. The king of Atholl was defeated *c.*734 and his son drowned (a formal ritual killing): the king himself was drowned *c.*739. In 736 Angus attacked *Dalriada and captured Dunedd. Next he is reported at war with the Northumbrians, his immediate neighbours to the south of the Forth. But when he turned his attention to the Britons of *Strathclyde he was not so successful. With the aid of Eadberht of Northumbria, he captured their stronghold of Dumbarton in 756, but his army was wiped out ten days later. Though the details are suspect, Angus was clearly a formidable ruler, and the continuator of *Bede's chronology bade farewell to him in 761 without regret: 'a tyrant murderer who from the beginning to the end of his reign persisted in bloody crime.' JAC

Anjou. District around the city of Angers in France ruled by counts from the 10th cent. onwards. The counts of Anjou won control of neighbouring regions (Maine and Touraine) and played a crucial role in the politics of northern France. This led, in 1127, to Henry I marrying his daughter *Matilda to the young count, Geoffrey 'le Bel'—otherwise known as *Geoffrey Plantagenet, allegedly because of his habit of wearing a sprig of broom (*planta genista*) in his cap. After Henry I's death, Geoffrey of Anjou conquered Normandy and bequeathed it, together with Anjou, Maine, and Touraine, to his elder son Henry in 1151. In 1154 Henry of Anjou became King Henry II of England and for the next fifty years Anjou remained the homeland of three successive kings of England: Henry II, Richard I, and John. Since Henry had married *Eleanor, duchess of Aquitaine, in 1152, this meant that a count of Anjou had become ruler of huge dominions stretching from the Scottish border to the Pyrenees: the *Angevin empire. Henry II, Eleanor, and Richard were all buried in Fontevraud (in Anjou), but in 1203–5 John's incompetence allowed Philip Augustus of France to wrest Anjou as well as Normandy from the family's grasp. In 1259, by the treaty of *Paris, Henry III reluctantly acknowledged that Anjou belonged to the king of France. Later, at the highpoint of their success in the *Hundred Years War, the English briefly won control of Maine. JG

Annates, Acts in Restraint of, 1532, 1534. These formed part of the campaign by Henry VIII's government, designed either to cajole the papacy into granting an annulment of the king's first marriage, or to give statutory authority for the English church to act independently of Rome. 'Annates' were taxes levied by the papacy on recently appointed, mostly senior, clergy. The Act in Conditional Restraint of Annates (23 Hen. VIII c. 20), passed in spring 1532, required that these payments be suspended; any papal retaliation was to be ignored. This legislation passed both Houses of Parliament with much opposition. Henry VIII at once suspended the Act: Archbishop Thomas *Cranmer was consecrated with papal approval in 1533. In the November–December 1534 session, after the pope had excommunicated Henry, the Act in Absolute Restraint of Annates (25 Hen. VIII c. 20) abolished annates entirely and ordered that bishops be elected by deans and chapters acting on royal nomination. Both statutes were repealed by 1 & 2 P. & M. c. 8 in 1554–5. EC

Anne (1665–1714), queen of England, Scotland (Great Britain from 1707), and Ireland (1702–14). The conventional picture of Queen Anne as a weak-willed and ineffectual monarch has been subjected to substantial revision. Reexamination of her political role has revealed a much less insipid personality, a woman of considerable assertiveness who, despite chronic ill-health, was a shrewd political operator and above all was determined to rule. Her adherence to her own principles and prejudices often thwarted her ministers' more self-interested ends; and though she sometimes found herself having to give way to larger political pressures, it was seldom without prolonged struggle.

Her early experiences played an important part in forming her for the role she later assumed. She was the younger daughter of James, duke of York and his first wife Anne *Hyde. The doctrines of the Church of England in which she was educated provided an important political and emotional prop for the rest of her life. In 1683, aged 18, she was married to Prince *George of Denmark, a distant cousin, and their relationship quickly blossomed into one of lasting devotion. She made no secret of her growing antipathy towards her father on account of his catholicism, and after his accession as king in 1685 her small household and social circle stood out as a rallying point for protestant courtiers. Anne deserted her father at the revolution in 1688 and joined William of Orange and his wife, her elder sister Mary. Before long, however, relations with them became strained with bitterness and jealousy, especially after Anne succeeded where they had failed and produced a healthy son, the duke of Gloucester, in 1689. Anne's hatred of the king deepened as William persistently excluded Prince George from any share in government. Once more, therefore, she was forced during most of the 1690s to operate in a delicate adversarial situation in which she had her position to defend. But the experience sharpened her skills of political infighting and prepared her for the day-to-day dealings she would have with her ministers. Her particular intimates were the *Marlboroughs and Lord *Godolphin. In Sarah Marlborough, especially, she found the feminine comfort and support she needed as she endured one failed pregnancy after another. These gradually took their physical toll. By 1700, when her seventeenth and last pregnancy ended in miscarriage, she was, at 35, practically an invalid and prone to serious rheumatism. That same year her one surviving child, William of Gloucester, succumbed to illness and died.

Anne became queen on William III's death in March 1702. She had patiently waited for what she had said would be her 'sunshine day'. In the early years of her reign, while her health allowed, she gave fresh impetus to court life and ceremonial in a conscious effort to elevate her regal image. Marlborough's martial triumphs on the continent were duly embodied in this process, and wherever she travelled she was received with acclamation. She stoutly opposed politically inspired suggestions that her Hanoverian heir be invited to reside in England in the firm belief that a rival court would diminish her own authority and *gloire*. Away from royal panoply, Anne industriously fulfilled the position she occupied at the centre of government. She presided once or twice weekly at cabinet meetings, conferred with individual ministers, regularly attended debates in the Lords, and gave active encouragement to major national ventures, such as the war with France, the union with Scotland (1707), and after 1710 the drive for peace.

Until 1710 her administrations were headed by the 'duumvirs', her old friends Godolphin, at the treasury, and Marlborough, in command of the army and directing the campaigns in the *Spanish Succession war. Neither of them were party men in the conventional sense, but acted primarily as 'political managers' holding together ministries containing both Whigs and Tories. Like her predecessor, she was anxious to preserve her independence of manœuvre and to avoid becoming the captive of 'party'. Indeed, much of her discernible political activity took the form of long and stressful feuds with senior politicians to avoid appointing party nominees whom she considered anathema. In 1702 the high Tory grandees, mindful of Anne's affinity with Toryism, expected the lion's share of governmental appointments, but she resisted their demands for a purge of Whigs. After 1705 Godolphin's efforts to persuade her to placate the powerful and well-organized *Junto Whig faction, whom she knew would dominate her entirely, placed a growing strain on their association, but she reluctantly yielded to a series of Whig appointments. Sarah Marlborough's less tactful bullying on behalf of the Junto was a major source of irritation to the queen, but though the duchess frequently behaved abominably, Anne could ill afford to dismiss her, fearing that she would use her influence with Marlborough and Godolphin to induce them to resign.

The queen's third 'manager', Robert *Harley, gradually gained her confidence and friendship with his notion of a 'moderate' ministry of both parties, a venture in which he was assisted by his cousin Abigail Masham, who had replaced Sarah as Anne's closest friend and confidante. However, in 1708 Harley's attempt to implement this plan with the queen's co-operation backfired when the 'duumvirs' forced Anne to dismiss him from his post of secretary of state. The Whig election victory later that year increased Junto demands for places in the administration, but it was only during the queen's desolation following the death of Prince George in October that Godolphin was able to override her wishes and impose more Junto appointees.

By 1710 Anne was willing to sacrifice Godolphin for Harley (later Lord Oxford), though the Tories' huge electoral success in the summer ruled out her favoured objective of 'moderation' and forced her to accept an exclusively Tory government under Harley's lead. Long accustomed to Godolphin's tact, Anne disliked Oxford's high-handedness and equivocation, and by August 1713 had begun to turn against him. As her health became more precarious in 1714, Lord *Bolingbroke seemed increasingly likely to succeed Oxford, by now ill and demoralized, although the queen remained non-committal. Two days after dismissing Oxford on 27 July, Anne fell mortally ill, but her acceptance of the politically neutral duke of *Shrewsbury as next lord treasurer on the 30th was crucial in ensuring that after her death on 1 August the transition to the Hanoverian dynasty occurred without the political turmoil which many had feared. AAH

Bucholz, R. O., *The Augustan Court* (Stanford, Calif., 1993); Gregg, E., *Queen Anne* (1980).

Anne of Bohemia (1366–94), queen of Richard II. Born in Prague, the eldest daughter of Emperor Charles IV, Anne was the first wife of Richard II, king of England, chosen for her nobility and gentleness and later known as 'Good Queen Anne'. The marriage took place on 14 January 1382 at St Stephen's chapel, Westminster, followed by her coronation on the 22nd. Plain and unassuming, Anne was devoted to Richard, helping him through severe depression. An educated woman, she used her influence, notably for the citizens of London (1392). On her death of the plague in 1394 at Richmond palace, Surrey, she was greatly mourned by Richard, who commissioned a magnificent tomb for her in Westminster abbey. She died childless. SMC

Anne Boleyn (*c*.1507–36), 2nd queen of Henry VIII. The entanglement of personal motives with great political issues, which makes history both difficult and fascinating, is rarely more apparent than in Anne Boleyn's three years as queen to Henry VIII. She has been accused of bringing about the Reformation single-handedly. Sir Thomas Boleyn, descended from London merchants, was a courtier and became gentleman of the bedchamber to Henry VIII. Anne spent several years at the court of France. Returning in 1522 she was given a post in the household of *Catherine of Aragon. The king's interest at this time was in her sister Mary, who became his mistress. Anne was dark-haired, with large eyes, composed and cultivated, with a mole on her neck and a malformed finger. By 1527 Henry was initiating annulment proceedings against Catherine, but not until 1532, it seems, did he and Anne become lovers—suggesting some steadiness of purpose on her part. Meanwhile her father had been given the Garter in 1523, created Viscount Rochford in 1525, and advanced to be earl of Wiltshire in 1529: her brother George was created Baron Rochford *c*.1530. Anne herself was made marchioness of Pembroke in September 1532. Henry's suit to the papacy had stalled. But early in January 1533 Anne knew she was pregnant and was married privately to Henry on the 24th. The birth of a princess, Elizabeth, on 7 September 1533 was a disappointment, but more ominous was a miscarriage in September 1534. The king was already beginning to look elsewhere: perhaps the excitement of the protracted chase had made the joys of possession rather brief. Publicly, Anne's position was strong—the Princess Mary had been declared illegitimate, and Anne's marriage was protected by a new Treason Law. But in January 1536 Catherine of Aragon died—ironically a mishap for Anne, since it opened up the possibility of another marriage free from any dubiety. Anne was once more pregnant but at the end of the month, alarmed by news of Henry's heavy fall at a joust, she gave premature birth to a dead son. Henry was now paying marked attention to *Jane Seymour, one of Anne's ladies-in-waiting. At the end of April 1536, Anne was accused of adultery with several men and incest with her brother George. On 2 May she was taken to the Tower, and just over a fortnight later, after a trial presided over by her uncle *Norfolk, she was executed. The charges against her were preposterous and she denied them with dignity, but she had never been popular and they served their turn. Her daughter Elizabeth was deprived of her rank, but succeeded to the throne 22 years later.
JAC

Anne of Cleves (1515–57), 4th queen of Henry VIII. The daughter of John, 3rd duke of Cleves, Anne was suggested by Thomas *Cromwell as a wife for Henry VIII to strengthen the protestant alliance. On first meeting, in December 1539, Henry was dismayed to find her 'well and seemly . . . but nothing so fair as reported', alluding to *Holbein's flattering portrait. He was persuaded to go through with the marriage in January 1540. Anne spoke little English and was not well educated, not sharing Henry's passion either for dance or music. Her jovial nature was not enough and Henry found her plain and homely. After Cromwell's fall and the swing in favour of catholicism, Henry sought swiftly to extricate himself, citing grounds of non-consummation, her earlier betrothal to a son of the duke of Lorraine, and, most tellingly, that he had never inwardly consented. The annulment was declared in July 1540, according Anne a handsome settlement and residences, on condition that she remain in England and accept the status of royal sister. Not surprisingly, Anne felt that she had fared rather well. Henry quickly remarried, making *Catherine Howard his fifth wife. After Catherine's execution, there were rumours that Anne was to be recalled, and even that she was pregnant, but nothing came of it. She lived at Chelsea until her death in July 1557 and was buried with considerable ceremony at Westminster abbey. SMC

Anne of Denmark (1574–1619), queen of James VI and I. Anne was daughter of Frederick II of Denmark and Norway. The marriage to James VI on 23 November 1589 was followed by her coronation in May 1590. She was later suspected of favouring catholicism since she refused the sacrament at her coronation in England in July 1603. Her eldest son *Henry Frederick, later prince of Wales, died in 1612, leaving his brother Charles (b. 1600) heir to the throne. Anne was interested in the arts, patronizing both Ben *Jonson and Inigo *Jones. An amiable woman, who enjoyed masques and dancing, her husband James, with a taste for theological disputation, found her frivolous. She suffered from gout and dropsy for many years, though her death in 1619 was sudden. She died intestate, leaving heavy debts, an indication of earlier extravagance. SMC

Anne Neville (1456–85), queen of Richard III. Anne was an important pawn in the ferocious political game of the later 15th cent. She was the second daughter of Richard Neville, earl of *Warwick ('the Kingmaker'). Her elder sister Isabella married George, duke of *Clarence, one of Edward IV's brothers. In 1470 Anne was married to the young *Edward, prince of Wales, heir to Henry VI. But her father was killed at *Barnet in 1470 and her new husband at *Tewkesbury, three weeks later. With the *Yorkists temporarily on top, Anne was transferred to the other side and in 1472 became wife of Richard, duke of Gloucester, another of Edward IV's brothers, taking with her much of Warwick's former property. On Edward IV's death in 1483, Richard usurped the throne and Anne was crowned on 6 July. Her only son *Edward, aged 8, was created prince of Wales in September 1483 but died in April 1484, leaving the royal couple childless. Richard became increasingly bitter and relations may have become strained. When Anne herself died in March 1485, speculation was rife and Richard was said to be casting around for a second wife. Her life as queen had lasted less than two years and her husband's as king did not last much longer. SMC

Anselm, St (1033–1109). Archbishop of Canterbury (1093–1109). Anselm was born at Aosta in northern Italy. We are especially well informed about his life because of the biographies written by Eadmer and the archbishop's own voluminous correspondence. Inspired by a monastic vocation, he travelled to northern France in the late 1050s, where he became a monk at Le Bec and a pupil of *Lanfranc.

Thereafter he rose to be both prior and abbot of the monastery. A great philosopher whose works include the *Monologion*, the *Proslogion*, and *Cur Deus homo*, his promotion to Canterbury in March 1093 occurred after William II had kept the archbishopric vacant for four years after Lanfranc's death in order to exploit its revenues. Anselm subsequently quarrelled bitterly with both William II and Henry I. His disputes with both kings ultimately focused on his belief that obedience was owed first and foremost to the papacy; those with Rufus also concerned Anselm's desire to protect the rights of Canterbury and his wish to reform clerical and lay morals. The arguments were given a much sharper edge by the way in which the late 11th-cent. papacy, during the period known as the Gregorian reform, was seeking to assert its moral and spiritual authority at the expense of long-established customs. By 1097 the breach between Rufus and Anselm was irreparable and the archbishop went into voluntary exile. He was recalled in 1100 by Henry I, who was anxious to give an appearance of legitimacy to his rule, and Anselm was for a time able to hold ecclesiastical councils and rule the church as he wished. In time fresh quarrels developed about the practice of lay investiture of bishops, still practised in England, although prohibited by the papacy since the 1070s, and in 1103 Anselm again went into exile. A settlement was not finally reached until 1106–7. The causes of these protracted quarrels remain difficult to interpret. In particular, the question of whether Anselm was a principled but other-worldly monk out of his depth in the rough-and-tumble of politics or an astute politician who calculatingly sought to increase the church's authority is currently the subject of a highly charged debate. Equally, while there is probably agreement that the kings should be seen as the protectors of the long-established rights of the monarchy over the church in the face of new and dangerous innovations, some commentators regard the blasphemous and apparently cynical William Rufus as an oppressor whom no principled churchman could ultimately tolerate, while others think that he was mostly bluff and bluster. It is impossible to see Anselm as in any serious sense a revolutionary figure; his often-expressed wish to co-operate with kings and his determination to protect the property rights of his archbishopric—even against the papacy—clearly show this. But he possessed a sharper sense of the nature of authority and obedience than his Anglo-Norman contemporaries, a consequence undoubtedly of an outstanding philosophical mind, which made it very difficult for him to accept compromises which the less acute and scrupulous found possible. He is in some respects representative of a changing intellectual and political climate, in which notions of authority were being redefined. His consistently expressed preference for the quiet world of the contemplative monk should not be allowed to conceal a robust personality who saw it as his God-given duty to engage with the world. DB

Anson, George, 1st Baron Anson (1697–1762). A circumnavigator of the world, Anson shared some attributes with plundering Elizabethan 'sea-dogs' but his work also pointed Britain towards a modern commercial imperialism in the Pacific region. Entering the navy in 1712, Anson rose to command a Pacific expedition in 1739. He captured a Spanish treasure ship and sailed on westwards to reach home in 1744 a rich man. Further active service and politics qualified him for a peerage and spells as 1st lord of the Admiralty from 1751 to 1762. His careful reforms helped to ensure the naval triumphs of the *Seven Years War. RB

anticlericalism, hostility towards the church, occurs in every age, despite the existence of individual sanctity and devotion. One driving force behind the Cathar movement was abhorrence of ecclesiastical corruption and wealth. Later in England *Wyclif criticized bishops as 'dumb fools in the realm of hell' and 'devil's proctors for dispersing the flock of Christ'. *Chaucer drew attention to clerical avarice and worldliness. In 1376 the Commons, in presenting a petition 'against the Pope and the cardinals', said that clergy and chivalry had given place to simony and greed; the pope in Avignon did not feed his flock but sheared it. The statutes of *Provisors (1351) and *Praemunire (1353) reflected not just the king's desire to protect his own authority, but also popular hostility towards clerical influence. This was also one of the driving forces of the 16th-cent. Reformation. Though ironically in England the years 1480 to 1530 were a great age of church building and piety, anticlericalism, strongly fuelled by *lollardy and Lutheranism, was intense in the 1520s, for the church owned one-fifth of the wealth of England and its revenue was three times that of the crown. Besides 'the pomp and splendour' of worldly prelates, such as *Wolsey, and criticism of ecclesiastical courts, pluralities, and tithes, articulated by increasingly well-educated lay contemporaries, many felt that this wealth could be better managed for educational and social needs. Even after the Reformation extreme sectarians despised Anglican clergy as 'magicians, sorcerers, enchanters . . .'. The clergy's time-serving attitude in 1689 lost them further respect, for 95 per cent retained their benefices by readily transferring their allegiance from James II to William III. The removal of press censorship (1695) let loose a torrent of abuse which in *Atterbury's words encouraged 'a settled contempt of religion and the priesthood'. Clerical internecine strife and electoral machination under Anne caused another tidal wave of Whig anticlerical legislation in the 1730s. Later in 18th- and 19th-cent. England anticlericalism rumbled on, though never with the political or religious intensity of catholic Europe; Anglican prelates were seen to add 'plural livings almost as monopoly players acquire first houses, then hotels, in desirable sites'. A strong anticlerical strain in *chartism designated the clergy as 'the Church of a Selfish Aristocracy' (1841). More dedicated clerical attitudes engendered by both *evangelical and *tractarian movements did much to dissipate this age-old antipathy. WMM

Anti-Corn Law League. Agitation against the *Corn Laws, which imposed duties on imported foodstuffs to protect British producers, increased after the Corn Law of 1815, and peaked in 1838–46. The creation of a Manchester Anti-Corn Law Association in 1838 led in 1839 to the establishment there of a national league. In 1839–40, it functioned solely as a propaganda organ, publishing attacks on the

Corn Laws and sending out agents to preach free trade. This achieved nothing; the movement was short of money and had little prestige. Its leader, Richard *Cobden, advocated direct political involvement, and the league contested a by-election at Walsall early in 1841. Its candidate was beaten, but his intervention forced the withdrawal of a moderate Whig opponent of free trade, gave the seat to a Conservative, and showed that the league did have some muscle. In the general election of 1841, a few free traders were returned, including Cobden himself, who proved a competent parliamentary spokesman. The league's organization became increasingly sophisticated, and in 1843 *The Times* described it as 'a great fact' and claimed that 'a new power has arisen in the State'. Centred in Manchester, despite a nominal move to London early in 1843, the league, under the chairmanship of an able organizer, George Wilson, became a model for later political agitations. It fought elections, and sought to multiply supporters on the electoral registers and expel opponents, by exploiting the registration provisions of the 1832 Reform Act. Propaganda continually increased in scope and variety. Considerable sums of money were raised, much of it from industrial interests who resented the dominance of the landed aristocracy and believed that protection of agriculture was an impediment to other commerce. In 1843 Cobden was joined in Parliament by John *Bright, and their rhetorical partnership proved effective in and out of Parliament. Prevailing economic doctrines advocated the removal of impediments to trade, while the league mobilized moral and even religious arguments against the Corn Laws, which allegedly increased the price of 'the poor man's bread'. The irruption of the league into electoral politics quickened Whig conversion to free trade. The Conservative leader *Peel won the 1841 election, but his commitment to the Corn Laws weakened. Peel's budgets of 1842 and 1845, together with other measures such as the Canada Corn Act of 1843, cut tariffs and increased the isolation of the Corn Laws. No disaster followed this sequence of reforms, but instead a substantial recovery from the depression years of 1838–42. In 1845 and again in 1846, the potato crop, on which many Irish had become dependent, suffered a catastrophic failure, threatening widespread starvation. Peel decided that all obstructions to the import of food must go, including the Corn Laws. This split the governing Conservative Party, but with the aid of opposition forces, including Whigs and the league, Peel was able to repeal the Corn Laws in 1846. The league would never have been able to secure repeal by its own power, and its role in the final crisis was exaggerated at the time and later. NMcC

Antigua is one of the Leeward Islands in the eastern Caribbean. With Barbuda it forms an independent state within the Commonwealth. It was visited and named by Columbus but colonized in the 17th cent. by English settlers. The island relies upon agricultural exports and tourism. JAC

Anti-Jacobin. A weekly journal which ran from November 1797 until July 1798 under the editorship of William Gifford. Its prospectus declared its prejudices in favour of the established institutions of church and state, and its satire was directed against British radicals—*Paine, *Godwin, Holcroft, Thelwall—and their Whig allies, with side-swipes at the Noble Savage, sensibility, and Gothick. The contributors included *Canning, George Ellis, John Hookham Frere, and the cartoonist James *Gillray. On its demise it was succeeded by a monthly periodical review of the same name. Among its more savage and memorable items is the denunciation of the Whig as 'the friend of every country but his own', and Canning's celebrated 'The Friend of Humanity and the Knife-Grinder', in which the latter's supine contentment provokes the Friend to 'kick the Knife-Grinder, overturn his wheel, and exit in a transport of republican enthusiasm and universal philanthropy'. JAC

antinomianism ('against the law') held that the moral law was not a rule of life for believers, the opposition of matter and spirit implying the indifference of bodily functions. It was an occupational hazard of *Lutheranism and *Calvinism alike, lurking in the doctrine of justification by faith alone and the righteousness implied by such faith. Propounded during the Reformation by the Lutheran John Agricola, it was taken up by some *anabaptists, and championed in England by Tobias Crisp (1600–43), flourishing in the 1650s. Its most egregious 18th-cent. representative was William Huntington, Sinner Saved (1745–1813), and its most telling refutation was Fletcher of Madeley's *Checks to Antinomianism* (1771). CB

Antiquaries, Society of. Founded in 1707 by a group of like-minded men meeting weekly at the Bear tavern in the Strand (London), it has had continuous existence since 1717. Gaining a royal charter (1751), then launching *Archaeologia* (1779), it moved to its present home, Burlington House, in 1875. ASH

anti-slavery. Slavery was regarded in later 18th-cent. Britain as essential to the exploitation of the West Indian colonies where, it was believed, only negroes were capable of working on the sugar plantations. As those colonies were thought to be the keystone of imperial prosperity there was strong opposition to any interference with the institution, particularly from centres like Bristol and Liverpool whose economies depended on the plantations or on the Atlantic slave trade which supplied them.

The moral objections to slavery arose mainly from the *evangelical movement of the second half of the century, reflecting concern for the spiritual and physical welfare of all mankind. A national committee of nine quakers and three Anglicans was set up in London in 1787, headed by Granville *Sharp with Thomas *Clarkson as secretary. It was decided to aim first at the suppression of the slave trade, whose cruelty was the subject of widespread propaganda. In 1788 William *Wilberforce, the son of a Hull merchant, joined the cause after his evangelical conversion, and supplied parliamentary leadership. He persuaded his friend William *Pitt to give it unofficial backing and commitees were set up in provincial towns, the most active being in Manchester. Over a hundred petitions were submitted in support of Wilberforce's parliamentary motion to end the trade in 1789. However, the economic arguments in favour of the trade prevailed, and after another unsuccessful attempt in 1791, the abolitionist cause suffered from the reaction against the French Revolution. The agitation was revived by Clarkson's speaking tours in 1804, by which time the economic importance of the West Indies had lessened, and in 1807 Lord *Grenville, an early convert, gave his government's backing to an abolition bill, forcing it through the Lords.

The campaign to abolish slavery itself throughout the British empire began in earnest in 1823, when the Anti-Slavery Society was formed in London by evangelicals, quakers, and methodists. The leaders included James Cropper, a quaker merchant from Liverpool, Joseph Sturge, a Birmingham corn merchant, and in Parliament Henry *Brougham, T. F. *Buxton, T. B. *Macaulay, and Wilberforce. A campaign during the 1830 general election encouraged *Grey's government to put through a bill abolishing slavery in the British empire in 1833, substituting apprenticeship for seven years. This vestige of slavery was abolished from 1 August 1838. The movements against slavery and the slave trade marked an important stage in the development of middle-class pressure groups both in London and in the industrial provinces. EAS

Antonine Wall. The second and more northerly of the two walls constructed across northern Britain by the Romans in the 2nd cent. On the death of *Hadrian in AD 138 his successor Antoninus Pius demonstrated his military capabilities by reoccupying Scotland up to the Forth–Clyde line. Following the example of his predecessor he had a linear barrier constructed, running from the Forth, west of modern Edinburgh, to the Clyde, west of modern Glasgow. Only half the length (37 miles) of Hadrian's Wall, the Antonine Wall was constructed of turf on a stone base. It apparently differed from the earlier wall in having forts of varying sizes at intervals, supposedly the better to deal with local conditions. It also seemingly lacked the milecastles and turrets of Hadrian's Wall. Recent excavations have shown that in fact the Antonine Wall was laid out as a version of Hadrian's Wall and construction was well advanced before the changes which distinguish it were implemented. The wall was briefly abandoned, then reoccupied in the mid-150s, and abandoned for good after Antoninus' death in 161. ASEC

Antrim was until 1973 one of the six counties of Northern Ireland, with close links with Scotland, 13 miles distant from Torr Head: there is a major ferry route from Larne to Stranraer and Cairnryan. The county is bounded on the west by the Bann, and to the south by Lough Neagh and the Lagan. The Giant's Causeway is off the north coast and Belfast Lough indents the south-east coastline. The Glens of Antrim are in the north-east corner. Carrickfergus castle was built by John de *Courcy in the 1170s and Antrim, Lisburne, Larne, Ballymena, and Coleraine developed as market towns before the spectacular growth of Belfast in the 18th and early 19th cents. Farming was diversified by the linen industry and in the 20th cent. by synthetic fibre production. The county has the smallest Roman catholic population in Northern Ireland and its three parliamentary seats were held in 1992 with large majorities by the Ulster Unionist Party (two) and the Democratic Unionist Party (one, Ian Paisley). JAC

Anzacs. The Australian and New Zealand Army Corps was raised at the beginning of the First World War. Australia, with a population of 5 million, raised 322,000 volunteers, of whom 60,000 lost their lives—one of the highest casualty rates. New Zealand, with 1.1 million people, raised 124,000 troops, of whom 17,000 died. They took a major part in the 1915 landings at *Gallipoli, a plan imaginative in concept, disastrous in execution. The Anzac establishment of a bridgehead on 25 April was met by savage resistance from the Turks, stiffened by their German allies. Anzac cove was evacuated in December 1915 and most of the survivors moved to the Western Front. 25 April is commemorated as Anzac day. JAC

Apology of the Commons, 1604. Less an apology than a vigorous assertion of parliamentary rights. It arose out of a dispute over the electoral return for Buckinghamshire, the Commons insisting that they were the sole judge of their own elections. Though the matter was compromised, they resolved to address the king. The apology was couched in respectful terms—James I was 'a king of such understanding and wisdom as is rare to find in any prince in the world'—but the House maintained that its privileges were of right, not of grace. 'The prerogatives of princes may easily and do daily grow,' James was advised. In these exchanges may be seen the shape of things to come. JAC

Appeals, Act in Restraint of (1533). The Act (24 Hen. VIII c. 12), largely the work of Thomas *Cromwell, was a crucial step in Henry VIII's assertion of royal supremacy against the papacy. He had already moved against the clergy with accusations of *praemunire and in 1532 forbade the payment of *annates or first fruits to Rome. The Act, passed in the first week of April, forbade appeals to Rome and had two objectives—to allow *Cranmer to give a ruling on Henry's marriage to *Catherine of Aragon which could not be appealed, and to intimidate the pope generally. The preamble declared majestically that 'this realm of England is an empire . . . governed by one supreme head and king . . . furnished with plenary, whole and entire power . . . without restraint or provocation to any foreign princes or potentates of the world'. A week later *Anne Boleyn appeared as queen and six weeks later Cranmer declared that Henry's marriage to Catherine had been invalid. JAC

appeasement is generally used to describe the policy towards Nazi Germany pursued by Prime Minister Neville *Chamberlain between 1937 and 1939, and has purely negative connotations. In fact, appeasement had a more respectable history and passed through several phases. British unhappiness with the vindictive reparations required to be paid by Germany after the First World War led to a policy of economic appeasement. Originally fixed, in 1921, at £6,600 million, the reparations total was reduced by almost three-quarters under the Young Plan of 1929. During the early years of Nazi rule in Germany (1933–6) a policy of economic appeasement also operated in relation to trade; in April 1933 an Anglo-German Trade Pact was concluded by

Ramsay *MacDonald's National Government, in the belief that although the Nazis were not likeable, one ought to do business with them.

Anglo-French acquiescence in Hitler's remilitarization of the Rhineland (March 1936), in violation of the treaties of *Versailles and *Locarno, marked a new phase of appeasement. In political circles in Britain, the Versailles settlement was widely blamed for the rise of the Nazis, and of Nazi sympathies amongst many ethnic Germans who, after 1918, found themselves excluded from Germany proper. In March 1938 Hitler ordered the anschluss, the union with Austria forbidden at Versailles, and almost at once indicated his determination also to meet the demands (real or imaginary) of Germans living in the Sudetenland, in Czechoslovakia, for union with Germany. Chamberlain could count on British public opinion for support of a policy aimed at giving the Nazis what they wanted. At Munich, on 29 September 1938, the Sudetenland was transferred to Germany, whilst more Czech territory was ceded to Poland and Hungary. Chamberlain, who visited Hitler twice during this crisis, was a national hero. Only after the German occupation of Prague (March 1939) was appeasement abandoned.

In its final phase, appeasement was an emergency measure. But it gave Britain a valuable year in which to rearm. GA

appellants. Richard II's political opponents of 1387–8 are known as the appellants, for it was by means of the legal process of appeal that they proceeded in Parliament against the king's ministers and friends. The king had been humiliated in Parliament in 1386, when his chancellor Michael de la *Pole, earl of Suffolk, was impeached. Richard's attempts to restore royal authority in the next year led to a short civil war, in which his favourite Robert de Vere, earl of *Oxford, was defeated at *Radcot Bridge. In the *'Merciless Parliament' of February 1388, Richard's five chief opponents, the earls of *Gloucester, Arundel, Warwick, Derby, and *Nottingham, appealed Suffolk, de Vere, the archbishop of York, Robert *Tresilian (the chief justice), and Nicholas Brembre of London, accusing them of treason. The appeal was a long-established process in common law, but had not been employed in this way previously in Parliament. Legal argument was dismissed, and judicial combat rejected; the process permitted no right of reply. Tresilian and Brembre were promptly executed; the archbishop of York was translated to St Andrews, while Suffolk and de Vere both died in exile. In 1397 Richard II revenged himself on the appellants, engineering an appeal against Gloucester, Warwick, and Arundel. MCP

Apprentice Boys. The Apprentice Boys are an Ulster loyalist organization whose title celebrates the thirteen apprentices who shut the city gates of Derry before the Jacobite siege (April–July 1689). The commemoration of the siege by the Williamites of Derry began possibly in 1692, though it only became an annual event after *c.*1790: the first Apprentice Boys Club appears to have been formed in 1714. With the shifting sectarian balance in the city in the 19th cent. the Apprentice Boys took on a more defensively protestant character. Like the *Orange order, the movement appears to have been in abeyance in the second quarter of the 19th cent., but to have enjoyed a growth after *c.*1850. The Apprentice Boys remain in existence, with a membership of around 10,000. AJ

apprenticeship refers to the period of service as a learner of a trade or handicraft. The apprentice, usually a boy at the beginning of his working life, is bound by a legal agreement to serve an employer for a fixed number of years in which the employer is reciprocally bound to instruct him. The system developed during the Middle Ages when guilds of craftsmen in particular trades such as silversmiths and shoemakers, established control of their trades by regulating the number of recruits and their training. Contracts, or indentures, were enforced strictly and governed the premium to be paid for learning, the length of the training (usually seven years), and, in some cases, where apprentices lived. The statute of *Artificers of 1563 gave magistrates power to compel compliance with apprenticeships. At the end of their apprenticeships trainees became journeymen, fully skilled tradesmen. If they could afford to set up in business they became masters in their own right. Apprenticeships were criticized as a system by which employers were enabled to pay low wages to a person whose skills might have been acquired in a relatively short time. Over time the power of many trade guilds declined and there were changes in the apprenticeship contracts. Amongst the more important was a reduction in the length of time to be served.

Apprenticeship in a wide variety of traditional skilled work continued in the second half of the 20th cent. However, challenges to such 'training on the job' combined with expanding provision of formal technical education led to a decline in traditional apprenticeship and the growth of full- and part-time education as a means of entry into skilled work. IJEK

Aquitaine. Rich wine-producing region in the south-west of France. Originally a province in Roman Gaul, after the 9th cent. Aquitaine became a more or less independent duchy in the kingdom of France. In 1154 when *Eleanor of Aquitaine's husband became King Henry II, the duchy became one of the king of England's dominions and remained so, though within fluctuating borders, until 1453. Until Edward III claimed the French throne for himself, the kings of England (as dukes of Aquitaine) owed homage to the kings of France. In 1202 King Philip Augustus pronounced the confiscation of all John's fiefs in France. While Eleanor of Aquitaine lived this had little effect in her duchy, but when she died in 1204 most of the lords and towns of inland Poitou (northern Aquitaine) transferred their allegiance to Philip. In 1224 Louis VIII conquered La Rochelle and the remainder of Plantagenet Poitou. This left a duchy of Aquitaine comprising little more than *Gascony and from then on the two names were used interchangeably. Continuing Anglo-French disputes over the status of Aquitaine contributed to the outbreak of the *Hundred Years War in the 1330s. By the treaty of *Brétigny (1360) Edward III obtained Poitou and in consequence the Black Prince was briefly prince of a greater Aquitaine, but when war was renewed in

1369 these gains were soon lost. From then on the history of 'English' Aquitaine was essentially the history of Gascony. JG

Arbroath, declaration of. The name usually given to the letter of the Scottish barons to Pope John XXII, dated at Arbroath on 6 April 1320, which proclaimed the ancient independence of Scotland and denounced English efforts at conquest. It was part of Robert I of Scotland's response to his threatened excommunication for failing to observe papal demands for a truce. On receipt of the letter, the pope suspended the proceedings which he had taken against the Scots, and called on Edward II to make peace. The letter attracted little attention till the late 17th cent. when it was published during efforts to maintain the integrity of Scotland; since then it has often been described as a Scottish 'Declaration of Independence'. BW

Arbroath abbey. The *Tironensian (reformed Benedictine) abbey of Aberbrothoc was founded in 1178 by King William the Lion (buried there, 1214); munificently endowed by him, it became one of the wealthiest and most privileged religious houses, with 'mitred' abbots. The declaration of *Arbroath was signed there in 1320. After 1502 the abbots were replaced by 'commendators' (loyal servants of the crown); with the Reformation, the abbey estates passed to the Hamilton family, while the ruinous buildings became quarry material for much of the modern burgh. ASH

Arch, Joseph (1826–1919). Trade unionist and politician. Arch was the son of a Warwickshire farm labourer and began work on the farm at the age of 9 scaring birds. He gained experience in public speaking as a primitive methodist lay preacher and in 1872 launched a National Agricultural Labourers' Union. It had considerable success and wages on farms improved, though numbers dwindled in the face of strong counter-attacks by landlords and farmers. Arch entered Parliament as a Liberal in 1885 but was defeated the following year: he served again from 1892 until 1900—the first farm labourer in the House of Commons. He published an autobiography in 1898. JAC

archaeology as a discipline attempts to reconstruct the origin, prehistory, and history of the human race using material remains such as artefacts, settlements, earthworks, burials, and skeletal remains. It also uses evidence for human impact on the natural environment such as pollen, soil erosion, and animal and plant remains. Though it had its origins in history and art history in the last century, it has developed its own theoretical and methodological base, drawing on anthropology and geography for models and analogues, on biology for environmental reconstruction, geology for excavation techniques, and the natural sciences for analytical and dating methods. It thus encompasses in a unique way the arts, social sciences, and natural sciences.

Its relationship with history started as merely a means of illustrating or verifying information derived from written sources. However, increasingly archaeology has been able to fill in gaps, for areas and periods where written sources are rare or lacking, for aspects of society not covered in the texts, or even providing alternative or contradictory hypotheses to those based on historical evidence. However, like written sources, there are inbuilt biases, due to the processes of deposition and survival of archaeological data, the selection of field methods and excavation techniques, and the skills of observation and academic viewpoint of the excavator ('archaeologists only find what they are looking for').

In the 19th cent. archaeology rapidly established itself as the only means of studying pre-literate societies, and the great civilizations such as those of Egypt and Mesopotamia where written archives could be recovered. For societies where historical sources already existed, archaeology was marginal, and concerned primarily with antiquarianism or art history, the discovery of objects primarily for their intrinsic artistic quality, such as the sculpture and painted pottery of classical Greece, or the uncovering of plans of temples, churches, and castles, generally with little concern for the stratigraphical context or associations.

With the shift in interest to social and economic questions, such as the nature of early farms, villages, and settlement patterns, archaeology came into its own, not only to illustrate the physical nature of, for instance, buildings described in the written documents, but also to answer questions on which the written sources are silent. In the period between the wars the lead was taken by southern Scandinavia. In northern Germany there were excavations such as those of the Viking trading port of Hedeby, or of the raised villages or terps of the Frisian coast. In Denmark the leading archaeologist was Gudmund Hatt who concentrated on settlements of the Germanic and Viking Iron Ages, reflecting the interests of the politically important Danish farming communities in their origins and environmental setting.

In Britain it was not until the 1950s that social and economic paradigms made their mark on archaeology, with excavations such as those by Brian Hope-Taylor of the Northumbrian palace complex at *Yeavering, or Maurice Beresford and John Hurst who initiated the study of the origin and demise of the deserted medieval village of Wharram Percy in North Yorkshire. In both cases the excavators consciously introduced the Scandinavian techniques of 'open area excavation', the stripping of large surfaces which are then systematically cleaned and recorded layer by layer. While respecting the stratigraphical sequence, this technique allows a better understanding of the ephemeral stone and timber buildings which are the norm in peasant societies. In the 1960s it was gradually adopted by prehistorians and finally Roman archaeologists, as their interests shifted from narrow culture-historical and historical interpretations to more socio-economic problems.

The new methods especially had a major impact on urban archaeology, as the town became envisaged more as an organic whole. Massive open area excavations of complex stratified sites in cities such as *Winchester and *York in the 1960s produced huge quantities of data and finds, forcing an increased specialization of archaeology in the 1970s. In many cases permanent teams, or 'units', were established to monitor urban renewal and excavate threatened sites, though only now has computerization allowed adequate recording techniques to be developed. This work has revolutionized our knowledge of urban development, and new scientific techniques such as dendrochronological dating are providing detail of a precision which can rival that of the written sources. JRC

archbishops are, literally, chief bishops. By the 5th cent. AD the title was applied to the occupants of sees of major ecclesiastical importance, particularly those of metropolitan bishops. This designation originated in the bishop of the principal city of a district or division of a country, the *metropolis*, being the usual president of any assembly of bishops of that area. Ecclesiastically, such a district or division formed a province.

In western catholic Christianity many provinces reflected the divisions of the Roman empire. Thus Milan, residence of the emperors during the 4th cent., became the metropolitan see for much of northern Italy, and Arles, capital of Gaul and residence of the Roman governor, attained metropolitical status in 417. There is little evidence to suggest that, prior to the withdrawal of the Roman legions, the church in Britain was organized along provincial or metropolitical lines. Not until the arrival of *Augustine (597) was *Canterbury established as an archbishopric, and *York did not become a separate province until the 8th cent.

In the Middle Ages the archbishops of Canterbury possessed wide powers. They could hold visitations of all the dioceses in the province and exercise spiritual oversight of any vacant see. They also confirmed and consecrated (but did not nominate) bishops-elect of dioceses in their province, and, by delegation to their archdeacons, enthroned them in their cathedrals.

However, attempts by Canterbury to assert its precedence over York were fiercely resisted, particularly in the 11th and 12th cents. The argument was not resolved until the 14th cent.—in Canterbury's favour. The attempt to establish a third archbishopric, at *Lichfield, in the late 8th cent., was short-lived.

The independence of the Scottish bishops from the province of York was recognized by Pope Celestine III in 1192, though the primatial see (*St Andrews) was not raised to archiepiscopal status until 1472. *Glasgow became an archbishopric in 1492. The title of archbishop ceased to be used for these two sees of the episcopal church in Scotland after the revolution of 1688. Since 1704 the chief bishop of the Anglican church, designated the Primus, is elected from among the Scottish diocesans.

In Ireland *Armagh, *Cashel, *Dublin, and *Tuam all achieved archiepiscopal status during the 12th cent., the primatial see being at Armagh. The number of Anglican archbishoprics was reduced to two (Armagh and Dublin) by the Ecclesiastical Commission in the 1830s. JRG

archdeacons. Literally chiefs of the deacons. The office traces its origins to the New Testament church, where the ministry of Stephen and others is described in the Acts of the Apostles as their *diaconia*. The term *archidiaconus* emerged in the 4th cent., when Caecilianus was referred to as archdeacon of Carthage. He was the chief administrative assistant of the bishop in the diocese. As dioceses were established and grew in size, their bishops delegated administrative authority in a specified area to an archdeacon, thus giving him a territorial title, e.g. archdeacon of Cleveland, a practice discernible in England by the late 12th cent. The archdeacon became in effect an intermediary between the bishop and the parochial clergy. From the mid-12th cent. archdeacons held regular visitations, and following the third Lateran Council they became responsible for ensuring that church buildings and other church property in their jurisdiction were kept in repair. JRG

archery developed as a sport from the use of the bow and arrow in hunting and warfare. The English and Welsh long bow dominated the battlefield from the 11th to the 15th cent., and governments frequently forbade other sports, particularly football, in order to encourage archery practice. When guns developed and the bow became redundant as a weapon, the sport was maintained. The Company of Archers, founded in Edinburgh in 1676, eventually became a royal bodyguard. The Royal Toxophilite Society was established in 1781. The Grand National Archery Society, set up in 1861, developed into the national body and an international organization, the Fédération International de Tir à l'Arc (FITA) was established in 1931. Archery was introduced into the Olympics in 1900, dropped in the 1920s, but brought back in 1972. JAC

Arches, Court of. This was one of the ecclesiastical courts. Before and after the Reformation, appeal from the consistory court of the diocese lay to the court of one of the two archbishops, York or Canterbury. The Court of Arches was the court of the Archbishop of Canterbury. It sat in the church of St Mary-le-Bow in London, acquiring its name from that venue since that church is built over arches. The court still hears appeals relating to clergy discipline in the Church of England as well as disputes over the ordering of churches and the rules relating to burials in church grounds. MM

architecture. British architecture has a strongly national character, often nurturing indigenous traditions while at the same time developing distinctive, and occasionally imitative, versions of European or international styles. Scottish architecture tended to develop independently (to some extent even after the union of the crowns in 1603), until the Act of *Union of 1707. Here castles, towers, and fortified manor houses, often with turrets and 'crow-stepped' gables, predominated during the Middle Ages; the 16th and 17th cents. saw the beginnings of the *Renaissance, with a distinct French influence.

In England, after the Norman Conquest, Saxon architecture, often of wooden construction, was replaced by 'Norman'; this was, in effect, a version of the European Romanesque style, with fine ashlar masonry, heavy columns, and round arches. The Normans built castles and cathedrals which were not only centres of power in their own right, but symbolized the cultural and political superiority of the new regime.

The Gothic style flourished from *c.*1200 to the early 16th

cent., with many uniquely British developments such as the late 'Perpendicular' phase. Further potential development along Gothic lines was curtailed by Henry VIII's *dissolution of the monasteries in 1536. Henry's break with Rome over his divorce from Catherine of Aragon inhibited possible Italian Renaissance influence, then permeating Europe, as a result of which Tudor architecture often exhibits a curious mixture of Gothic, and half-digested Renaissance forms borrowed from German or Flemish pattern books. However, the Elizabethan and Jacobean periods saw the development of the first great aristocratic country houses (the so-called 'prodigy houses' such as *Longleat, Wiltshire (from 1553), Burghley, near Stamford (1575–85), Wollaton, Nottinghamshire (1580–8), and *Hatfield, Hertfordshire (from 1611)). The era also witnessed the emergence of the first designers to whom the word 'architect' was applied: John Shute (fl. 1550–70) was the first native architect to go to Italy and published in 1563 *The First and Chief Groundes of Architecture*, while Robert Smythson (*c.*1536–1614) had a substantial hand in the design of both Longleat and Wollaton.

Meanwhile, a more European culture was developing around the Stuart court; Rubens and *Van Dyck were given patronage as was Inigo *Jones (1573–1652), who made at least two lengthy visits to Italy. Jones's surviving works, much inspired by Andrea Palladio (1508–80), include the Queen's House, *Greenwich (1616–35) and the *Banqueting House, Whitehall (1619–22). Jones brought Britain once again into the mainstream of European architecture but was essentially a court architect and the Civil War prevented any widespread dissemination of his ideas. The Restoration saw the reintroduction of classicism, but in a different form. The architects of the 'English baroque' (*c.*1660–*c.*1720) turned for inspiration to the Italian baroque and to contemporary French architecture, although adapting this to English, and in ecclesiastical terms, specifically Protestant, taste. They include: Sir Christopher *Wren (1632–1723)—many churches in the city of London following the Great Fire of 1666 and, above all, *St Paul's cathedral (begun 1666); Nicholas *Hawksmoor (1661–1736)—the churches of St Mary Woolnoth (1716–27) and St George, Bloomsbury (1720–30), both in London, and Easton Neston House, Northamptonshire (completed 1702); and Sir John *Vanbrugh (1664–1726)—*Castle Howard, Yorkshire (1699–1726), *Blenheim, Oxfordshire (1704–20), and Seaton Delaval, Northumberland (*c.*1718–29).

Following the Act of Union and the establishment of the Hanoverian dynasty, a desire to create a specifically British, rather than English, national identity saw the rise of the Palladian style (*c.*1720–*c.*1760). Numerous country houses (invariably surrounded by landscaped parks) and villas were built in this style: harmonious, symmetrical, and perfectly proportioned, so much so that practical considerations were often sacrificed for the correct adherence to classical rules.

The country house during the first half of the 18th cent. became virtually an emblem of cultural and political authority (e.g. *Holkham Hall, Norfolk, mainly by William *Kent, from 1734). One of the initiators of Palladianism was Richard Boyle, 3rd earl of *Burlington (1694–1753), whose villa, Chiswick House, near London (*c.*1723–9) was inspired by the Villa Rotunda, near Vicenza, by Palladio himself. Palladian architects include Colen Campbell (1676–1729), William *Kent (1685–1748), the latter closely associated with Burlington and also a painter, designer, and landscape gardener, and James Paine (1717–89). Palladian principles were also successfully adopted in the planning of cities and towns, as at Bath, and in the development of London's Georgian streets and squares.

By the third quarter of the century there was some reaction against this established taste; Robert *Adam (1728–92) was able to create a fashionable style based on the introduction of neo-classical elements culled principally from the antique. Indeed, increasing interest in antiquity led to the 'Greek Revival' and to the further development of the *Gothic Revival, the origins of which lie earlier in the century. Sir John *Soane (1753–1837) developed an extremely personal neo-classical style, as in his now largely demolished works at the Bank of England from 1788, and played a part in architectural education and in furthering the status of the profession. His rival John *Nash (1752–1835) was a versatile exponent of Picturesque architecture and was responsible for George IV's metropolitan 'improvements' in the area of what is now Regent's Park, London (1821–30).

The 19th cent. saw a continuing emphasis on stylistic revivals, particularly the Gothic Revival; Victorian architecture tends to be large in scale and highly decorative, reflecting the era's wealth and prosperity. Major Victorian architects include: Sir Charles *Barry (1795–1860), A. W. N. *Pugin (1812–52)—collaborators in the neo-Gothic rebuilding of the Houses of *Parliament after 1835—Sir G. G. *Scott (1811–78), Norman Shaw (1831–1912), and G. E. Street (1824–81). Late in the century, the Arts and Crafts movement, influenced by the ideas of William *Morris (1834–96), rejected the dependence upon historical styles in design. An extremely talented exponent of Arts and Crafts ideas in his early work, and of classicism in his later, was Sir Edwin *Lutyens (1869–1944).

Twentieth-cent. British architecture has tended to be conservative, apart from the work of comparatively isolated figures such as the Glaswegian Charles Rennie *Mackintosh (1868–1928), at least until the Second World War; after this European modernism, with its simplified, functional forms, became universally accepted, partly due to the need for urban reconstruction. Major works of British modernism include the Royal Festival Hall, London (completed 1951 to the designs of Leslie Martin and Robert Matthew) and Coventry cathedral by Sir Basil *Spence (completed 1961); also the New Towns of the 1950s and 1960s and many inner city housing estates (some of which are now regarded less sympathetically than at the time of their construction). A version of modernism, emphasizing the use of exposed concrete, became known as 'brutalism'; Sir Denys Lasdun's National theatre, South Bank, London, and the nearby Hayward Gallery/Queen Elizabeth Hall complex are examples of this (both designed in the 1960s). More recently, 'high-tech.' architecture, which celebrates the most up-to-date use of technology, has become important, as with Sir Richard Rogers's Lloyd's of London Building and Sir Norman Foster's Stansted Airport, Essex (both completed during the 1980s).

Throughout the British Isles there was a strong tradition of vernacular architecture until at least the 19th cent., when more standardized forms of design took over as a result of improved communications, the growth of the architectural profession (the Institute, later the Royal Institute, of British Architects founded 1834), and, with this, the influence of books and magazines. This makes use of local materials and techniques and therefore differs according to the region in which it is found. It tends to be relatively plain and functional, although it may incorporate features from 'high' or 'polite' styles. TEF

Colvin, H. M., *A Biographical Dictionary of British Architects, 1600–1840* (3rd edn. 1995); Summerson, J., *Architecture in Britain 1530–1830* (9th edn. 1993); Watkin, D., *English Architecture* (1979).

archives. See RECORD OFFICES.

Arcot, siege of, 1751. Robert *Clive, a young captain in the army of the *East India Company, while attempting to relieve Mahomet Ali in Trichinopoly, was besieged in Arcot by a vastly superior French and Indian force. He defended it for fifty days until help came. It was Clive's first major victory and a check to French progress in the Carnatic. JAC

Areopagitica, an impassioned plea by John *Milton (1644) for liberation of the press to a Parliament occupied with perceived offences by writers and printers, was written in response to the Licensing Ordinance of 1643 that no book should be printed unless previously approved by an authorized officer. Although aware that liberty was double-edged, Milton abhorred such control before rather than after publication, associating it with censorship in catholic countries and regarding it as discouragement to learning. He was ignored. The licensing system eventually lapsed in 1694, but moral and practical problems relating to censorship remain. ASH

Argyll, Archibald Campbell, 5th earl of [S] (1532–73). A committed protestant whose political allegiances frequently changed and, at times, seemed inconsistent with his religious convictions. Signing the first 'Common Band' of the protestant nobles as Lord Lorne (1557), Argyll succeeded his father in 1558. However, he did not formally join the lords of the *Congregation until May 1559. During the personal reign of Mary, queen of Scots, Argyll was a favoured privy counsellor until charged with treason on 5 December 1565, for his part in *Moray's rebellion against *Darnley. Having been reconciled with Mary in the spring of 1566, Argyll was later appointed lieutenant of her forces, losing at *Langside in 1568. Abandoning the Marian cause to support James VI, he was made a privy counsellor by *Mar in September 1571. On 17 January 1573, Argyll was appointed chancellor by *Morton, an office he held until his death nine months later. PER

Argyll, Archibald Campbell, 1st marquis of [S] (*c*.1607–61). Campbell's father, the 7th earl, became a catholic, fought in the Spanish army in the Netherlands, and was declared a traitor in 1619. Campbell, as a protestant, took over the enormous estates at the age of 12, and succeeded to the earldom in 1638. His subsequent conduct was erratic, even granted the confused situation. A violent *covenanter in 1639–40, he made terms with Charles I in 1641 and was advanced to the marquisate. He then rejoined the covenanting party but was routed by *Montrose at *Inverlochy and *Kilsyth in 1645. Next he joined in welcoming Cromwell but in 1651 took part in Charles II's coronation at Scone, having been promised a dukedom and the Garter. He made his peace with the Cromwellian regime and served in the Parliament of 1659 as MP for Aberdeenshire. In 1660, at the Restoration, he set off to London to welcome back Charles II, but was arrested, and executed at Edinburgh. A small, red-headed, squinting man, Clarendon described him as of 'extraordinary cunning', though in the end his contorted tergiversations overwhelmed him. But he explained ruefully that he had lived in a 'distracted time'. JAC

Argyll, Archibald Campbell, 9th earl of [S] (1629–85). Campbell's father, the 1st marquis, had played an equivocal part in the civil wars and in 1661 was executed for treason. Campbell, who had fought on the royal side at *Dunbar and *Worcester, was restored to the earldom in 1663. His presbyterian sympathies placed him in jeopardy during James, duke of York's government of Scotland, and in 1681 he was accused of treason and lodged in Edinburgh castle. He escaped in disguise and joined *Monmouth in Holland. Involved in the *Rye House plot, he led an expedition to raise the west of Scotland in May 1685 to coincide with Monmouth's rising in the south-west of England. There was little support, divided counsels, and he was captured. Executed at Edinburgh, where his father had suffered before him, Argyll died with composure and bravery. JAC

Argyll, Archibald Campbell, 10th earl of (d. 1703). Scottish politician. Following the attainder and execution in 1685 of his father, the 9th earl, Argyll's chief objective was to assume his patrimony as head of the Campbell clan. Failing to obtain recognition from James II, he joined William of Orange in 1688 and accompanied him to England. Accordingly, he was admitted as earl of Argyll to the convention of Scottish estates in April 1689 which declared in favour of William and Mary, and in June his father's attainder and forfeiture of Campbell lands was rescinded. The political restoration of the house of Argyll, with its assertive leadership over the presbyterian Campbells, did much to quell lingering Jacobite unrest among other clans. By the mid-1690s he and the marquis of *Queensberry effectively led the court interest in Scotland, though their alliance was frequently under stress. He was created a duke in 1701. AAH

Argyll, Archibald Campbell, 3rd duke of [S] (1682–1761). Campbell succeeded his brother John in 1743, having been created earl of Islay [S] in 1706. He was a keen supporter of the Union and fought on the government side at *Sheriffmuir in 1715. He held the privy seal [S] 1721–33 and the great seal [S] from 1733 until his death. From 1707 to 1713 and again from 1715 until his death he was a representative peer of Scotland. For many years he was the Whig government's adviser on Scottish affairs and, though his brother broke with Walpole in 1737, Islay remained in control of Scottish patronage. While his brother was high-spirited, imperious, and a celebrated orator, Islay was a man of business; Horace Walpole called him 'dark and shrewd' but a most useful man. JAC

Argyll, Colin Campbell, Lord Lorne, 1st earl of [S] (d. December 1492/January 1493). Colin Campbell was the grandson of Sir Duncan Campbell of Lochawe, 1st Lord Campbell [S] (1445), who died in 1453. Colin's elevation to earl (1458) was followed by a steady acquisition of lands and offices—justiciar south of Forth by 1462, master of the royal household a few years later, and Lord Lorne by 1470.

Argyll's life was one of contrasts, combining the attributes of a shrewd and hard-working royal councillor and the ambitions of an immensely powerful Highland clan chief. He supported the English alliance of 1474, yet opposed James III at Lauder (July 1482). In 1483 Argyll became chancellor, but was suddenly sacked by James III in February 1488. Joining the formidable magnate coalition against the king, Argyll recovered the chancellorship on James's death at *Sauchie Burn, and held it throughout the troubled early years of the next reign. NATM

Argyll, Colin Campbell, 6th earl of [S] (*c.*1542–84). Campbell succeeded his half-brother in the earldom in 1573. After a quarrel with Regent *Morton over certain crown jewels, brought to Argyll by his second wife, the widow of Regent *Moray, he seized the young king James at Stirling in 1578 and forced him to dismiss Morton. Argyll was appointed lord chancellor [S] and held the post until his death. A reconciliation with Morton did not last and Argyll voted for his execution in 1581. JAC

Argyll, John Campbell, 2nd duke of (1678–1743). Soldier and politician. While still in his twenties, Argyll, as head of the powerful Campbell faction, emerged pre-eminent among the Scottish magnates, and as lord high commissioner (1705) played a key role in opening negotiations for the Anglo-Scottish union. He afterwards commanded with distinction in the War of the *Spanish Succession, though he conceived a lasting hatred of the duke of *Marlborough, much to Tory delight. But his association with *Harley's Tory administration turned sour during an embittered spell as commander-in-chief in Spain (1711–12). In 1712 he became commander of the army in Scotland, and in 1715 suppressed the Jacobite uprising, though with reluctance. He lost office during the Whig divisions of 1716–19 but was reinstated, and by 1725 his following was in control of Scottish affairs. His relations with *Walpole deteriorated after the *Porteous episode (1736–7), and in 1742 his Scottish contingent in the Commons contributed appreciably to the minister's downfall. AAH

aristocracy. A vague term, derived from the Greek *aristokratia*, meaning the rule of the best. In ancient Roman society it was represented by the patricians. It is broader than *peerage or even nobility. In common parlance, it was usually taken to mean the upper classes or 'betters' and was confined largely to landowners. Since, unlike peerage, there was no legal definition, it was a matter of opinion who constituted the aristocracy, whether the concept included the *gentry, and, if so, how far down that group it went.

In origin, nobility applied largely to kings and their immediate families. As kingdoms grew larger, the surviving members of previous royal families were often incorporated into the aristocracy, together with particularly trusted advisers and supporters. A characteristic of aristocracy was therefore a tendency for it to grow larger. The early 7th-cent. laws of *Æthelbert of Kent already distinguished eorls from ceorls for the payment of *wergeld. Elaborate justification was scarcely needed. It was assumed that an eorl was a man of honour, whose word could be trusted on oath. Noble blood guaranteed bravery in youth and sage counsel in age.

Hereditary membership of the aristocracy was established at an early period, save for upheavals like the *Norman Conquest, which brought in a new governing élite, and in most parts of the country the practice of primogeniture ensured the survival of estates intact. Only in Kent and in Wales did the custom of *gavelkind produce the partible inheritance which reduced many noble families to penury on the continent.

In *Alfred's day, governors of counties or regions were called *ealdormen, though the reassertion of Danish influence in the early 11th cent. meant that the word gave way to *eorl*, which remained for three centuries the only recognized title. After the Norman Conquest the high aristocracy consisted of the 1,400 tenants-in-chief, to whom had been allocated all the land not expressly reserved for the crown or the church, and who held it directly from the king. But some of the subtenants also accumulated substantial property and formed part of the governing élite. The *knightly class soon ceased to be purely professional soldiers and became landed proprietors in their own right, acting as seigneurs or lords of the manor. The local jurisdiction which they exercised under the crown gave them great power at a time when government at Westminster was very distant.

The *'barons' who confronted John in 1215 were not peers in the formal sense and titles were so rare that in the reign of Henry I there were only eight earldoms in existence. Two developments in the 13th and 14th cents. transformed the situation. The summoning of parliaments, with a separate upper chamber, made it necessary to establish which lords were entitled to attend and began the process of separating lords of Parliament from the rest of the aristocracy. Secondly, a diversification of titles led to a considerable increase in peerage numbers. To the old title of earl was added dukedoms (1337) which were at first reserved for the royal family, marquisates (1385), baronies (1387), and viscountcies (1440). By the end of Henry VI's reign the peerage had grown to about 60. In the Tudor period, commentators like Sir Thomas *Smith began to distinguish a greater nobility from a lesser nobility, or gentry. But the size of the greater nobility remained small, making it inevitable that it should rely upon the gentry for help in governing the country.

Two further developments in the Tudor period strengthened the position of the aristocracy. At the *dissolution of the monasteries most of the estates found their way, sooner or later, into the hands of the nobility and gentry. The Russells were one of many families whose fortunes were established at this time, picking up many monastic estates, including Covent Garden and Woburn abbey. The removal of abbots from the upper house of Parliament after the Reformation left that chamber dominated by secular lords. The growing prestige of Parliament as an institution gave the aristocracy a powerful base from which to challenge the monarchy and defend itself against the commonalty.

The 17th cent. was full of vicissitudes. The lavish creation of titles by the early Stuarts, including the introduction of *baronetcies, threatened to dilute the aristocracy and weaken its powers of resistance. The long struggle with the crown, which was attempting to find non-parliamentary sources of revenue, seemed at one stage to have brought down aristocracy and monarchy alike: in 1649, with the king executed and the House of Lords declared useless and dangerous, it looked as though the split in the upper classes had handed power to the forces of radical dissent. For many aristocratic families, the 1650s were particularly hard, their houses and property plundered, their church disestablished and derided, their income subject to swingeing taxes levied by the parliamentary victors. Worst of all was the short rule of the *major-generals, several of them men of humble origins.

After the Restoration, the aristocracy recovered much of its wealth and influence. But the underlying rivalry with the crown re-emerged in the 1680s. This time the outcome was decisive, with gentry and nobility united against James II, and supported by most of the nation.

The 150 years following the *Glorious Revolution of 1688 was the golden age of aristocrats, victorious on both flanks. They were no longer menaced by radicals or republicans, nor by a quasi-absolutist monarchy. Decades of Hanoverian prosperity saw the manor-houses rebuilt and enlarged, the old muddy villages and duck ponds removed to a respectful distance, the parks enclosed and embellished. The greater aristocracy built up their estates, often in several counties, and protected them from the follies of spendthrift heirs by the *entail or strict settlement. Their monopoly of office, national and local, was almost complete: cabinets were composed almost exclusively of noblemen, while the gentry, as justices of the peace, looked after the shires. Parliament itself was firmly under the control of the landed interest, though the trading towns sent their own merchants and businessmen to protect their concerns.

In an increasingly utilitarian age, rather less was heard of noble blood and more of service to the nation. Though the aristocracy retained a particular interest in the armed forces, and especially the cavalry, the invention of guns and the introduction of standing armies had deprived them of their former rationale as a military class. In *Pitt's words, the iron barons were replaced by silken barons. Nevertheless, their claims were still formidable—that they were superior in education, experienced in making decisions, enjoyed the leisure necessary to consider public affairs, and, above all, that their great possessions gave them a unique concern for the well-being of the country, since they had so much to lose. They also claimed a distinctive political role, as a balancing or stabilizing force, which prevented the country from sliding into royal despotism or democratic licence.

Ideological challenge to noble ascendancy came with the American and French Revolutions, in which titles were abolished and aristocrats denounced. But the identification of egalitarianism with national enemies may have given the British aristocracy a further lease of life. More insidious dangers were developments not overtly political—the growing complexity of public business, which put the amateur at a disadvantage; the growth of new industrial towns, where the symbols of aristocracy were less obvious; the improvements in schooling, which meant that education was no longer the preserve of the wealthy; the eventual decline of agriculture until the great landed interest looked less a national concern than a farming lobby; perhaps, most of all, the gradual effects of new forms of taxation which steadily encroached upon aristocratic fortunes. Significantly, the introduction of a tax upon incomes, which Charles *Fox rightly saw must do vast damage to aristocracy, came in the darkest moment of the war against revolutionary France in 1799. Nevertheless, judicious concessions, like the *Great Reform Act of 1832 and the repeal of the *Corn Laws in 1846, enabled the landed classes to preserve much of their influence throughout the 19th cent. But signs of decay were increasingly apparent and the extravagance of the Edwardian period had all the hallmarks of an Indian summer. The Great War of 1914 proved a cataclysm, but it was a crumbling building that was knocked down.

Gentry and aristocracy survive into the late 20th cent. in their own world, but it is shrunken and private. They retain many houses and much social prestige, but the houses are often open to the public, with tea served in the stables; others, like Lambton castle, have been turned into fun-fairs, taken over as schools, or developed as conference centres. Aristocrats are still much sought after as patrons, presidents, chancellors, and board members, but the days when a cabinet of nine could contain eight peers of the realm, the ninth being merely the son of a peeress in her own right, have vanished into the past. JAC

Beckett, J. V., *The Aristocracy in England, 1660–1914* (Oxford, 1986); Bush, M. L., *The English Aristocracy: A Comparative Synthesis* (Manchester, 1984); Cannadine, D., *The Decline and Fall of the British Aristocracy* (New Haven, 1990); Cannon, J. A., *Aristocratic Century: The Peerage of Eighteenth-Century England* (Cambridge, 1984).

Arkinholm, battle of, 1455. In the spring of 1455 James II of Scotland moved to rid himself of the powerful 'Black Douglases'—James, earl of *Douglas, and his three brothers, Ormond, Moray, and Balvenie—ravaging their estates. Douglas fled to England but the three brothers gave battle at Arkinholm on the Esk near Langholm on 1 May. They were utterly defeated. Moray was killed in the battle, Ormond captured and executed, and Balvenie fled. The power of the Black Douglases was broken and a Parliament in Edinburgh in June declared them and their adherents traitors. JAC

Arklow, battle of, 1798. Despite the repulse at *New Ross on 5 June 1798 the Wexford rebels remained dangerous. They had captured Gorey, and threatened Arklow, opening a line of advance north to Dublin. But the government was given time to reinforce the small garrison at Arklow and when the rebels attacked on 9 June, in great numbers, they were driven back, largely by artillery. The rebellion lost impetus and Wexford was recaptured on 21 June. JAC

Ark Royal. The name given to a series of warships in the Royal Navy. The first *Ark Royal*, originally called *Ark Raleigh*, was purchased by the crown in 1588. It was used as the flagship of Lord *Howard of Effingham against the *Armada. In the 20th cent. the name has been given mainly to aircraft carriers. RAS

Arkwright, Sir Richard (1732–92). Born in Preston, one of thirteen children, Arkwright was apprenticed to a barber, and established a business in Bolton. Travelling around northern textile districts to buy hair for wig-making, Arkwright met craftsmen attempting to improve cotton production and lured John *Kay away from his employer in the 1760s; together they produced the water frame, a roller-spinning machine which Arkwright patented (1769). This, powered by water or a horse capstan, was the basis of Arkwright's fortune. His first horse-driven factory was established at Nottingham (1769) to supply Midland hosiers in partnership with Samuel Need and Jedediah Strutt of Derby. In 1771 he moved to Cromford (Derbys.) and was dominant in the early cotton industry. Lancashire cottonmasters successfully attacked his patent (1781 and 1785), but Arkwright deserves the title of 'father of the factory system' because of his organization of production. Knighted (1786), he became high sheriff of Derbyshire in 1787. JB

Arlington, Henry Bennet, 1st earl of (1618–85). Having fought for the crown in the Civil War, the future foreign minister of Charles II represented him at Madrid during Cromwell's alliance with France against Spain. Bennet believed in Anglo-Spanish friendship even if this conflicted with the Portuguese alliance strengthened through Charles II's marriage in 1662: like all future members of the *'cabal' Arlington was the inveterate foe of that marriage's promoter, *Clarendon. Financially dependent on office, he was weak in ameliorating Anglo-Dutch relations, though in 1666 he married a Dutch wife. Distrustful of France, as secretary of state Bennet was similarly flaccid in falling in with Charles II's French policies. Neither conscience (he professed himself a catholic on his death-bed) nor better judgement prevented his contriving Charles's first secret treaty of *Dover with Louis XIV in May 1670. He was granted a barony in 1665 and promoted to an earldom in 1672. Disgraced as secretary in 1673, Arlington became an Admiralty commissioner, and assisted in withdrawing the garrison at Tangier. Latterly he played the 'Maecenas' at his seat at Euston (Norfolk). DDA

Armada, Spanish. The invasion fleet sent against England by Philip II of Spain in July 1588 comprised some 138 vessels (including warships, ancillary craft, and requisitioned transports), perhaps 7,000 seamen, and 17,000 soldiers, and siege equipment for use in England. The number of soldiers would be doubled once the forces of the duke of Parma in Flanders were embarked in the Armada at Calais for passage to England. The English naval forces comprised 34 royal warships and some 170 privately owned ships, preponderantly drawn from East Anglia and Kent. Variable in quality though these ships were they did have a national identity, whereas the Armada included ships from Portugal, Naples/Sicily, Venice, Ragusa, and north Germany. Quite apart from the unmanageable scale of the Armada's preparation and the Spanish government's financial weakness, the quality of English guns and their handling on board ship were of an order with which the Spaniards could not compete. Yet the English, in their turn, could not compete with Spanish soldiery if it came to hand-to-hand fighting at sea, or in a land campaign. Hence the English fleet, under Lord *Howard of Effingham's overall command out of Plymouth, and including Lord Henry Seymour's patrols in the Dover Straits, looked to its more manœuvrable ships and more effective fire-power to avoid being grappled by the enemy.

Philip II's purposes behind the Armada were to end English attacks on Spain's commerce with her American dominions, to assert his sovereignty in Flanders, which Elizabeth had been impugning since 1585, and, above all, to bring heretic England back into the fold of Rome. He had himself a claim to Elizabeth's crown which, if success was granted to the enterprise, Philip would use in the best interests of Spain and the true faith. On the English side the issues were the defence of a protestant realm that included catholic Ireland, vigilance against the threat posed by Spanish power in Flanders, and the protection of Elizabeth's person and the 'Englishness' of her queenship.

Under the command of the duke of Medina-Sidonia, not a professional commander but uniquely experienced in fleet logistics, the Armada took three weeks to make Corunna from Lisbon. From the Lizard Point in Cornwall on 29 July its disciplined crescent formation was only twice broken by English forces (two of its ships were lost) before it reached Calais on 6 August. Here Parma had failed to prepare his troops, and had critically underrated Dutch naval forces, which sealed off his sea exits. The Armada's congestion made it vulnerable to Howard's fireship attack on the night of 7 August, and on the following day there was heavy Spanish loss of life in a sustained battle off Gravelines. The shoaling coast and southerlies of increasing strength prevented Medina-Sidonia from standing in again for Calais, and deteriorating weather drove a dispersed Armada up the North Sea, pursued by Howard whose ordnance, and the health of his crews, were now spent. Driven round Scotland and Ireland, in unseasonably severe weather, two-thirds of the Armada were brilliantly navigated back home, but upwards of 30 ships were lost in the Hebrides and western Ireland. Some 11,000 Spaniards may have died. Although the elements had principally saved England, the campaign brought her high international repute, while Spain proved she could place a huge naval force in northern latitudes. The campaign's outcome saw neither state radically altering its policies. DDA

Armagh was the smallest of the six counties of Northern Ireland. It borders the Irish Republic to the south, Co. Down to the east, Tyrone and Lough Neagh to the north and north-west. The chief town is Armagh which has been an archbishopric since the 12th cent.: there is also a Roman catholic archbishopric. Portadown and Lurgan in the north are of local importance. The northern parts of the county grow fruit and there is farming and light industry. The catholic population is strong in the south and in 1921 Armagh council protested against the creation of Northern Ireland and was dissolved. Armagh forms a parliamentary constituency with Newry and in 1992 returned a Social Democratic and Labour Party member with a comfortable majority. JAC

Armagh (Ard Machae), **archiepiscopal diocese of.** Its strong associations with St *Patrick make Armagh inevitably the seat of both the Catholic and Anglican primates of all Ireland. Traditionally founded by St Patrick in 444, the original church community, contrary to Celtic tradition, was headed by bishops, but from the 8th cent., in Celtic style, the 'heir of Patrick' was always an abbot with bishops subordinate. With the advent of 10th/11th-cent. Roman reform Abbot Cellach was consecrated bishop (1106). By the Council of Raithbressail (1111) Armagh became the metropolitan see of Leth Cuinn (northern half of Ireland) with twelve dioceses. Later, by the Council of Kells-Mellifont (1152) when Ireland was divided further into four provinces, the province of *Tuam for western Ireland was carved out of Armagh, while Armagh, with its eleven dioceses, still retained overall primacy. In the late 20th-cent. troubles both primates of Armagh have worked for reconciliation. Armagh has two cathedrals, both dedicated to St Patrick. The Anglican one on the site of a 5th-cent. church is 19th cent. with a 10th-cent. crypt. The catholic cathedral is neo-Gothic (1840–73). A notable Anglican archbishop was James *Ussher (1625–56). WMM

Arminianism. Under Elizabeth I, though against her will, the Church of England eschewed ritual and adopted the grim Calvinist belief that God, when creating human beings, had predestined them to either salvation or damnation. The 1590s saw a reaction set in, similar to that which was taking place in Holland under the impetus of Jacob Arminius, and English anti-predestinarians came to be called Arminians, even though they were an autonomous movement. The Arminians were given only limited advancement by James I, but with the accession of the high-church Charles I in 1625 they came to dominate the episcopal bench, especially after the appointment of *Laud as archbishop in 1633. Not all Arminians were ritualists, but their critics lumped them together as crypto-catholics and Charles's identification with them was one of the principal causes of the lack of trust between him and his subjects which led to the collapse of royal rule. RL

armour. There are relatively few surviving pieces of medieval date, so the study of armour is largely dependent on the evidence of monumental effigies, manuscript illuminations, and documentary sources such as accounts and inventories. Three periods of development have been identified. The first period, *c.*11th–13th cents., saw the predominance of mail. A knee-length mail hauberk, sometimes hooded, was worn over a padded garment (aketon). By the mid- to late 12th cent., a surcoat of linen was commonly worn over the hauberk. Helmets were at first conical with a descending plate to protect the nose, but developed into rounder, cylindrical forms with visors (the great helm). In the third period, from the late 14th to early 16th cents., full plate armour was worn, covering the trunk as well as the legs and arms. A padded coat (or arming doublet) would be worn under a solid breast- and backplate. Helmets came in many shapes, often protecting the whole head by means of a visor. It is a myth that this plate armour was heavy and that it limited a man's mobility. It was very well articulated, and often lighter than the mail hauberk. Even in this third period mail might still be worn to protect the groin and armpits. The second period links the first and the third but overlapped with both. It saw the development of the coat of plates, a cloth-covered body armour which was essentially a fabric garment reinforced internally with metal plates (subsequently called the brigandine). This might be worn with mail, and also with solid, and later articulated, plate protection on the arms, hands, legs, and feet. The great helm persisted but was giving way to the head-hugging bascinet, which sometimes had a visor. Changes in armour appeared gradually, and armies would have sported many different styles. Our picture of armour is too often derived from the top of the range—the most expensive, up-to-date apparel of the aristocratic and knightly classes. The rank and file continued to rely well into the later Middle Ages on mail shirts, reinforced cloth armours (brigandine and jak) and simpler headgear (sallets, kettle hats, etc.). Moreover, tournament armour can be misleading. Because of the desire to protect life in what was, after all, a sport, it tended to be heavier and more defensive than armour for war: visors, for instance, were *de rigueur*, whereas there is strong evidence that faces might be left uncovered in battle. The most expensive and most fashionable armours in the later Middle Ages came from northern Italy and southern Germany, each with a distinctive style. These armours were exported in large quantities. In 1512 for instance Henry VIII purchased 2,000 light armours (i.e. protecting the body and arms only) from Florence and a further 5,000 the following year from Milan. Generally speaking, however, the rank and file had to make do with locally produced, and probably often recycled, armour. Armours developed in tandem with weapons. Swords of the first period were long and weighty, designed to deliver a heavy blow capable of cutting through mail. As both the coat of plates and the fully articulated armour left certain body areas vulnerable, a thinner, lighter, sharply pointed sword was more appropriate, used in thrusting as well as cutting fashion. The move to plate left the shield largely redundant. Heraldic devices shifted from the surcoat to the material covering the plates, although armour of the third period was often decorated by etching and painting. Breastplates and helmets continued well into the age of artillery and survive today in ceremonial armours. AC

Arms, Assize of. Henry II made an Assize of Arms in 1181. It bound all freemen of England to swear on oath that they would possess and bear arms in the service of king and realm. The assize stipulated precisely the military equipment that each man should have according to his rank and wealth. Every knight, for example, was to have a hauberk, helmet, shield, and lance, whilst lesser men with rent or chattels valued at 10 marks were to possess a short coat of mail, an iron headpiece, and a lance. At first, the assize was applied by itinerant justices, who were to proclaim the assize in the shires, take the oaths required, enroll the names of all those liable, and arrange for local juries to make assessments of individuals' wealth. In the 13th cent., however, this became the responsibility of each sheriff and two knights of the shire. The assize, frequently renewed, effectively revived the old Anglo-Saxon *fyrd duty. SL

Arms, College of. See COLLEGE OF ARMS.

Armstrong, William Armstrong, 1st Baron (1810–1900). Armstrong was the son of a Newcastle merchant. Although trained as a solicitor, he was interested in technical experiments from boyhood. Financial backing from fellow-members of Newcastle's business community facilitated in 1847 his establishment of the Elswick engine works near Newcastle to manufacture hydraulic machinery. During the *Crimean War he became involved in gun-making and this led in 1859 to the Elswick Ordnance Company. Between 1859 and 1863 this company supplied 3,000 guns to the British forces. During the later 19th cent. it became one of the world's leading engineering, shipbuilding, and armaments firms, taking over the rival Whitworth company in 1897. In 1900 the company employed 25,028 workers and had a weekly wage bill of nearly £37,000. Armstrong acquired a Northumberland estate at Cragside in 1863 and commissioned the architect Norman Shaw to build a mansion for him there. He received a knighthood in 1859, and a peerage in 1887. NMcC

army. The exact origins of the British army are lost to history, although its red parade uniforms have been fancifully traced back to the colour of the tunics of King *Arthur's bodyguard. A vestige of late Roman military customs and practice can be seen in the law codes and military organization of the earliest British kingdoms. Long before the Norman Conquest, military obligation seems to have divided into two basic forms which have remained constant until modern times. One was an obligation for common service by all adult males, established in English law as the *militia by the Assize of *Arms of 1181. The other was a small permanent standing army, usually represented in the medieval period by the warriors of the royal household. To these were added an obligation upon individuals to serve the crown on a temporary basis, and a tradition of employing and paying mercenary troops, who might on occasion be the same people. Although women have always played a major part in warfare, they have been almost entirely excluded from combat roles until very recently.

By early modern times, English armies consisted almost entirely of troops paid in some fashion. However, any form of standing army was considered a potential instrument of royal despotism, and was also beyond the financial resources of the monarchy to maintain. The *Yeomen of the Guard, founded by Henry VII in 1485 as a small royal bodyguard, is the earliest unit of the British army that has survived to the present day. Other modern units trace their descent from mercenary forces in the service of various kingdoms during the same period. The granting of money by Parliament to finance armies on a temporary basis became one of the most important issues between crown and Parliament. It reached a crisis in 1639–41 when Parliament refused Charles I money to repel a Scots invasion, and would not trust him with control of an army to suppress the Irish rebellion.

The direct ancestor of the modern British army is usually considered to be the parliamentary *New Model Army of 1645. However, its part in enforcing Cromwell's rule in England and in subjugating Scotland and Ireland helped to establish a prejudice against soldiers which lasted well into modern times. The first properly constituted standing army, of tiny proportions, was created in 1661 by Charles II from royalist and parliamentary units of the Civil War, and entitled 'His Majesty's Guards and Garrisons'. For the next century the army grew at an irregular rate, partly from the need to find garrisons for overseas possessions, and partly for European wars. The existence and function of the army (unlike that of the Royal Navy) was based on royal prerogative rather than statute, an issue which came to a head in the reign of James II and played a part in his overthrow. Thereafter the 1689 *Declaration of Rights established that a standing army was illegal without Parliament's approval, granted every year in the *Mutiny Act until 1953, when this was replaced by a five-yearly Armed Forces Act. The issue of direct royal control over the army largely died away during the reign of Queen Anne and the Hanoverians. George II became the last British monarch to lead his army personally into battle at *Dettingen in 1743.

Particularly after the Act of *Union with Scotland of 1707, and the subsequent defeat of *Jacobite uprisings a large army at home was not required. Instead, the British needed a minimum force to keep order (particularly before the establishment of police forces in the 19th cent.), garrisons for their overseas possessions, and small forces to contribute to coalitions for European wars. The British army developed in a manner regarded by European standards as both eccentric and old-fashioned, with a central core of units providing the basis for a much larger army that could be expanded and disbanded according to need. The existence of this permanent standing army was first acknowledged by a royal warrant of 1751 setting out the official precedence of units.

Whereas in some countries the army became the focus of political and social reform, in Britain it was always seen as the last bastion of reaction. Particularly after the French Revolution, the army was deliberately kept apart from British society (through the building of barracks), and practices regarded as obsolete in continental warfare, such as officers purchasing their commissions, regiments having considerable autonomy from central authority, and the flogging of soldiers, persisted well into the 19th cent. Parliamentary fears of militarism meant rigid control of the army's budget, a deliberately divided command system, and a toleration of inefficiency in order to keep the army politically weak. Officers were drawn largely from the lesser gentry, with an admixture of the aristocracy, and recruits from the poorest classes. By the middle of the 19th cent. the army had become so socially and politically separated from the bulk of the British population that the Victorian historian Sir John Seeley (1834–95) described in his *The Expansion of England* (1883) how the empire had been acquired 'in a fit of absence of mind'.

It was equally easy to forget that by the end of the 19th cent. Britain was a major continental land power with a large permanent army, because neither the continent nor most of the army was European. Particularly after the loss of the American colonies in the *American War of Independence (1775–83), the largest single focus for the British army was India, following the crown's absorption of the East India Company army as the Indian army in 1858. Garrisoning British India (the frontiers of which stretched from modern Iran to Thailand) with both British and Indian troops became the major army role of the late 19th cent. A series of reforms following the *Crimean War (1853–6), associated in particular with the abolition of purchase by Edward *Cardwell in 1871 and with the creation of the 'county regiments' structure ten years later, produced a largely infantry army to serve overseas. Experiences such as the inability of the British to intervene effectively in the Franco-Prussian War (1870–1) and the revelation of serious military deficiencies in the Second *Boer War (1899–1902) produced more reforms to prepare the army for warfare in Europe, most particularly associated with Richard *Haldane. Like many other late Victorian or Edwardian reforms, these actions have continued to determine much of the structure and ethos of the late 20th-cent. army, despite the removal of their original justification.

The British tradition of a small long-service army for use overseas, virtually unique in European historical development, meant that at the start of the *First World War (1914–18) Britain was the only belligerent country without conscription, introduced with reluctance in January 1916. The creation of a mass citizen army for the war, at first entirely by voluntary methods, was of great social as well as political significance for Britain, marking the first real contact between the army and British society since the Civil War. Ultimately the British army was the most successful of the war, inflicting a crushing defeat upon Germany, previously regarded as the dominant European land power. Although all belligerents suffered terribly from the effects of mass mechanized warfare, British losses were not markedly worse than those of any other major power. However, with no shared military tradition to draw upon, the social and cultural impact of the war upon Britain was devastating, and has persisted to the end of the 20th cent. At the war's end, the mass conscript army structure was abandoned, and the army returned to its role as a long-service garrison for the empire by 1922, with considerable enthusiasm on all sides.

The experience of the First World War enabled Britain to cope rather better with the *Second World War (1939–45). For the first time in British history peacetime conscription was introduced in 1939, shortly before the outbreak of war. However, the demands of a genuinely global war for naval and air forces, and the growing erosion of distinctions between naval and land warfare, or even between civilian and military occupations, all contrived to keep the British army in the field considerably smaller than in the First World War. Although Britain (the only country save Germany to fight, with its empire, from the start in 1939 to the end) once more emerged victorious, it faced in 1945 a changed military situation. In particular the traditional roles of the British army of garrisoning the empire and fighting in Europe were ceasing to be relevant. After 1945 Britain maintained, again for the first time in its history, peacetime conscription (known as National Service) until 1963, after which, largely for cultural and social reasons, the army reverted once more to an all-volunteer force. Its two major roles were from 1949 membership of *NATO (the North Atlantic Treaty Organization) as part of the collective defence of western Europe against the Soviet Union until 1991, and covering the 'Retreat from Empire', a succession of wars as Britain dismantled its empire, beginning with the independence and partition of India in 1947. The most significant war for the army in this period was in Northern Ireland (1969–94), Britain's longest war since medieval times.

The army in the last decades of the 20th cent. was faced with the same issues that had confronted it since the 18th. It was once more largely separate from its own society, subject to rigid budgetary control, generally ill-equipped to cope either with changes in the nature of warfare or of Britain's role in the world, socially reactionary, and badly in need of reform. However, it has also remained the most effective military instrument obtainable for the minimum financial, political, and social cost which successive governments have been prepared to pay. SDB

Ascoli, D., *A Companion to the British Army, 1660–1983* (1983); Carver, M., *The Seven Ages of the British Army* (1984); French, D., *The British Way in Warfare, 1688–2000* (1990); Pimlott, J., *The Guinness History of the British Army* (1993); Strachan, H., *European Armies and the Conduct of War* (1983).

Arnhem, battle of, 1944. British and Polish parachute troops attempted to secure bridges at Arnhem over the Rhine in September 1944, while US forces seized crossings further south over rivers and canals at Eindhoven and Nijmegen. *Montgomery expected to exploit operation Market-garden by outflanking German defences and surrounding the Ruhr even before using Antwerp for supplies. The Americans succeeded; the British drop met overwhelming counter-attack from SS Panzer divisions resting nearby, organized by Model's Army Group HQ, which actually saw the parachutists descend. Montgomery's decision to attack in spite of warnings from ULTRA intelligence was a gamble in an attempt to finish the European war in 1944. RACP

Arnold, Matthew (1822–88). Poet and critic. Son of Thomas *Arnold, headmaster of Rugby school, Matthew was educated also at Winchester and Oxford, before election to an Oriel fellowship (1845). From 1851 to 1883 he was an inspector of schools, sent to study systems in Europe, and became a leading propagandist for improved secondary education in England. Emerging as a mature poet by 1853, with a recognizably Celtic temperament (from his mother), he was professor of poetry at Oxford 1857–67, but subsequently turned to literary then social criticism. He broadened the accepted form of the critical essay, and in *Culture and Anarchy* (1869) famously classified English society into 'Barbarians, Philistines and Populace' as it lagged behind continental ideas; refusal to comply with Victorian complacency about England's perceived world-wide supremacy was unforgivable to many. Arnold's religious liberalism found voice in subsequent works which sought to free Christianity from doctrinal lumber, despite his own admiration for *Newman. ASH

Arnold, Thomas (1795–1842). Headmaster of Rugby School. Arnold was educated at Winchester and Corpus Christi College, Oxford, obtaining a first in classics. In 1818 he was ordained deacon and became vicar of Laleham, Middlesex. Appointed to the mastership of Rugby, a prosperous public school, in 1828, he built a chapel at the school, then an unusual feature. Dr Arnold brought with him what has been termed 'muscular Christianity', a good picture of which can be found in Tom Hughes's *Tom Brown's Schooldays* (1857). Arnold's weekly sermons were aimed at improving the character of the pupils and imbuing them with a sense of duty to the community. At the same time, games were seen as a means of stimulating team spirit. Arnold stamped his imprint on public school education of his day. PG

Arran, Thomas Boyd, earl of [S] (d. *c.*1474). As son of Robert, Lord Boyd, Thomas benefited greatly from the coup of July 1466, when James III (1460–88) was seized at Linlithgow. By his father's influence he was made earl of Arran, given extensive lands, and was married to Mary, elder sister of the king (1467). This was resented by James III and many nobles, who felt Mary should have been married abroad. Arran was one of the ambassadors who concluded the treaty of Copenhagen, by which *Margaret of Denmark married James III, and Orkney and Shetland were pawned to the Scottish crown (1468). However, while on the embassy, the Boyds were removed from power. Arran fled to Bruges with Mary, and was forfeited (1469). An attempt to return to Scotland in 1471 was abandoned when James III detained his wife, following her earlier return. He subsequently resided in England until his death. RJT

Arran, James Hamilton, 2nd earl of [S] (*c.*1517–75). Arran was a great-grandson of James II of Scotland and succeeded to the earldom in 1529. On the death of James V in 1542 he was heir presumptive to the Scottish throne, Mary being a tiny infant. From 1543 he was regent on her behalf. At first pro-English and anxious for a marriage between Mary and Edward VI, when this fell through and war followed, he abjured protestantism and moved towards the French interest. When Mary was sent to be brought up in France, Arran was created duke of Chatelherault. In 1554 he gave up the regency to *Mary of Guise, though he retained hopes of a marriage between Queen Mary and his own son. He opposed the *Darnley marriage and was obliged to leave the kingdom between 1565 and 1569. On his return, he supported the queen's party. Even allowing for the vicissitudes of Scottish politics, his course seems vacillating and uncertain. JAC

Arran, James Hamilton, 3rd earl of [S] (*c.*1538–1609). Arran's father was regent of Scotland and heir presumptive from 1542 until James VI was born in 1566. Arran himself was one of the many contenders for the hand of Elizabeth, and, failing that, of Mary, queen of Scots. He was abroad from 1550 to 1559 and on his return to Scotland became a leader of the protestant party. But in 1562 he was declared insane and in 1581 was persuaded to resign his earldom in favour of his relative James Stewart. The resignation was cancelled in 1586 on grounds of incapacity, but Arran played no further part in public life. JAC

Arran, James Stewart, 4th earl of [S] (*c.*1550–95). James Stewart was a second son of Lord Ochiltree [S]. After service with the Dutch he returned to Scotland in 1579 and was soon in favour with James VI, who appointed him a gentleman of the bedchamber in 1580. He took an active part in the prosecution of *Morton for complicity in the murder of *Darnley, James's father. His relative the 3rd earl of Arran, who was insane, was placed in his charge and in 1581 consented to renounce the earldom in Stewart's favour. In 1583 he was temporarily ousted by the protestant lords in the *Ruthven raid, but recovered his position in 1584 and had *Gowrie executed. He became chancellor [S] and for a time wielded great power. But he was overthrown in the coup of November 1585, attainted, and exiled. Though he returned, he never recaptured his former influence and in 1595 was murdered by Sir James Douglas in revenge for his part in Morton's downfall. JAC

Arras, Congress of, 1435. Marked an attempt by the papacy and the Council of Basle to bring about peace between England and France. It was presided over by two cardinals and attended by embassies representing Henry VI (who claimed to be king of France by the terms of the treaty of *Troyes), Charles VII of France, and Philip, duke of Burgundy, still technically in alliance with the English but already moving towards a *rapprochement* with Charles. It came to naught because the English refused to abandon Henry VI's rights to the French throne. They withdrew their delegation on 6 September, leaving the way clear for a Franco-Burgundian alliance, the treaty of Arras, finalized on 21 September. AC

array, commissions of. This was a means of raising local troops between the *fyrd and the feudal levy and the militia of modern times. The commissions instructed individuals, usually gentry or noblemen, to raise troops in their area and were first issued by Edward I. They were a heavy burden, particularly if the cost fell upon the township or locality and Parliament succeeded in obtaining a number of concessions. Edward III promised in 1327 not to employ the men outside their county, save in case of invasion; in 1344 that the crown would pay wages if they were asked to serve outside the kingdom; in 1350 that they would only be issued with the consent of Parliament. A statute of Henry IV in 1402 repeated the limitations, declaring that they 'shall be firmly holden and kept in all points'. After mid-16th cent. it was more convenient to ask the *lords-lieutenant to raise levies and commissions fell into disuse. Charles I in desperation, on the eve of civil war, revived them, issuing the first in May 1642 to some Lancashire gentry. *Clarendon thought it had been a mistake to resort to antique procedures, 'a thing they had not before heard of', and they were at once declared unlawful by Parliament. JAC

***Arrow* War,** 1856–60. The *casus belli* of the war occurred when the ship *Arrow* was boarded at Canton, in October 1856, by the Chinese, who arrested the crew on suspicion of piracy. Although the crew and owner were Chinese, the ship was registered in Hong Kong and flew the Union Jack. The incident was used by western powers as an opportunity to extract concessions from China. On 29 December 1857 an Anglo-French force occupied Canton and then proceeded to *Tientsin where a treaty was signed in June 1858. China agreed to open ports and receive legations at Peking. However, in 1859 British and French ministers were refused permission to enter Peking. A second Anglo-French force landed at Pei-Tang on 1 August 1860 and took Peking in October. On 18 October the treaty of Peking ended hostilities, the Chinese agreed to honour the Tientsin treaty and ceded Kowloon, the mainland opposite Hong Kong, to Britain. See also CHINA WARS. RAS

Arsuf, battle of, 1191. On 22 August 1191 Richard I led the armies of the Third Crusade out of Acre southwards towards Jaffa, whence they would strike inland to Jerusalem. Nothing better demonstrates Richard's tactical sense and generalship than the march and the battle that followed. The army marched close to the sea-shore, its right flank protected by Richard's fleet, which accompanied it and kept it supplied. Saladin's forces harassed the crusaders, but could not break their close formation and Saladin realized that he would have to risk open battle if he were to halt the advance. On 7 September, on the plain to the north of Arsuf (some 12 miles from Jaffa), the two armies met. The day was won when the massed crusader cavalry charged and forced Saladin to withdraw. The march to Jaffa was resumed. SL

art galleries. In medieval England, as elsewhere in Europe, the church was the most important patron of art, and the first paintings and statues seen by the public were in churches and monasteries, many of whose collections were dispersed or destroyed at the Reformation. Private collections in palaces and noble houses began in the 16th cent., but only a few could see them. Charles I was a great English patron, particularly of painting, but after 1649 the royal collection was dispersed in a period of puritan disdain for art.

Art collecting was at its peak in the 18th cent., a gentleman's pride demanding that this evidence of his family, wealth, and good taste should be on show. Noblemen on the grand tour often sent back large numbers of paintings and sculptures, of varying quality. Some collections in country houses were open to visitors on specific days, though admission fees and difficulty of access filtered out the lower orders.

The first London institution to open its art collection to the public was the Foundling hospital in the 1740s, partly sponsored by William *Hogarth. After 1768 the Royal Academy exhibitions were popular, though again the poor were excluded by admission charges. Not until the 19th cent. did public art galleries develop, although governments remained slow to grant funds. The lead was taken by private patrons. In 1814 Dulwich Gallery became the first major public gallery after Sir Peter Bourgeois left his collection to Dulwich College. The Fitzwilliam Museum at Cambridge, endowed by the 7th viscount, opened in 1848, the Bowes Museum at Barnard Castle in 1892, and the Burrell Collection at Glasgow in 1983. Government funds were voted for the National Gallery in 1824. The National Portrait Gallery (1856) and the National Galleries of Scotland (1859) and Ireland (1864) were largely privately funded.

Legislation in 1845 and 1850 encouraged local authorities to provide public museums and art galleries, and the great provision of municipal galleries was largely a Victorian achievement, often assisted by private donors. Birmingham opened its art gallery in 1867 (Rossetti, Brown); Dundee 1873; Liverpool's Walker Gallery 1877; Nottingham 1878; York 1879 (Etty); Manchester 1882 (Hunt and Millais); Leicester 1885; Aberdeen 1885 (Dyce); Leeds 1888; Norwich 1894 (Crome and Cotman); Glasgow 1902; Newcastle's Laing Gallery 1904; Bristol 1905; Cardiff 1912. Two notable galleries, the Tate and the Wallace Collection in London, were launched by private donations in the 1890s, Kenwood House and the Courtauld Institute in the 1920s and 1930s.

Concern that many great works of art were leaving the country, especially to the USA, prompted the foundation of the National Art Collections Fund in 1903 to assist British galleries to make purchases. From 1946 the Arts Council of Great Britain has paid subsidies to the arts, including galleries. Other funding comes from the National Heritage Memorial Fund and, in recent years, the National Lottery. JC

Arthur. King Arthur and his circle are creations of medieval writers drawing on history, folklore, mythology, and imagination. Though British in his historical dimension, as a figure of legend and romance Arthur belongs to European culture and has been transplanted to that of America. Arthurian material has been continually reshaped and developed, reflecting aspects of contemporary life, morality, and aspirations. The literature is vast, embracing literary scholarship, historical and archaeological investigations of British responses to the Anglo-Saxon invasions, fiction, and enthusiastic attempts to identify sites and persons.

The 'real' Arthur is a hero referred to in the British poem the **Gododdin* (*c.*600), in the 9th-cent. *Nennius' *Historia Brittonum* (as victorious 'leader of battles', including *Mount Badon, against Anglo-Saxons), and in two entries in the 10th-cent. *Annales Cambriae*. The original warlord, who defies identification, was developed by the 9th- and 10th-cent. Welsh into a great Welsh victor. British tradition from areas conquered by the Anglo-Saxons had migrated to unconquered Wales, and the 9th and 10th cents. saw both Welsh cultural revival and a prospect of Welsh success against the English. An inspirational national figure was needed. His manufacture both used and influenced early Welsh poetry. Arthur grew into a ruler and hero, possibly absorbing other heroes.

Welsh tradition in turn contributed to oral traditions in Cornwall, and in Brittany, where it came to be believed that he still lived. It was probably Breton bards who were responsible for the Round Table motif and who spread the material in French and Norman lands.

But Arthur and his world were definitively formed in the 1130s by *Geoffrey of Monmouth in his fictional *History of the Kings of Britain*. In this, Arthur is the ideal king, conqueror of much of Europe, attacking even Rome. Finally defeated and mortally wounded, he is borne to Avalon. Geoffrey's purposes perhaps included justifying the desire of the current rulers of England to be independent of France, and consoling the Welsh for English domination by giving them a glorious history.

Arthur's court proved a magnet for heroes and their deeds, and in much Arthurian material Arthur's own profile is low, his function that of a reference point. The legend of Tristan and Isolde, one of the most popular, was tacked on to Arthur's. Other tales, however, developed out of it. The Grail element, combining Celtic traditions of magical testing-vessels and blessed food-producing horns with Christian sentiment, first crystallized in French. Chrétien of Troyes in the 1170s and 1180s also introduced courtly love, made the Round Table a centre of chivalry, and identified Arthur's capital as Camelot. The first treatment in (Middle) English was Layamon's *Brut* (late 12th cent.), which introduced the element of faerie. The greatest English production was the late 14th-cent. *Sir Gawain and the Green Knight*.

The cult of chivalry was a European phenomenon. Arthurian romances portrayed its ideals, and some of its organization and trappings. Arthurian characters and deeds were emulated in tournaments, sometimes in Arthurian dress, and in ceremonial, as in Edward III's foundation of the Order of the *Garter. The material had a religious element, yet the ethos was not ecclesiastical; the lesson was that the path of the Christian knight could lead to salvation, and one of its implicit ideas was that of crusade. Arthurian matters could be politically useful. Honour paid by Edward I to what were apparently bones of Arthur and Guinevere, at Glastonbury in 1278, was flattering to the Welsh, while emphasizing that hope for a Messianic delivery from him was pointless.

In the early modern period the popularity of Arthurian material declined. Changes in war, government, and economy made the chivalrous, aristocratic, knight obsolete and the Renaissance made classical literature more popular. It survived in the English-speaking world because of Sir Thomas *Malory. His work, completed about 1469, retailed the story as a tragedy. It was printed in 1485 by *Caxton, who saw it as a moral, didactic work, as the *Morte Darthur*.

Henry VII exploited Welsh interest, for example naming his elder son *Arthur, and making him prince of Wales in 1489, but Arthur's significance under the Tudors was chiefly in pageantry and in literature. He featured in some pageant decorations, but he was not alone, and there was little attempt to connect him with Tudor monarchs. There was some drama and poetry, and Arthur was taken up by Edmund *Spenser in his *Faerie Queene*. *Shakespeare, however, gave him no attention.

Arthur's historicity had not been accepted by everyone. William of Newburgh, *Gerald of Wales, and Ranulf Higden were openly critical of Geoffrey of Monmouth's history, but Geoffrey carried the day until the late 16th cent. The Italian Polydore Vergil had sparked controversy in his *Anglica historia*, written at Henry VII's request and published in 1534. John *Leland defended Arthur against him in 1544. Scottish perception was subtly different. Hector *Boece's *History of the Scots* (1526) incorporated some reworkings, mostly to Arthur's detriment, as if Arthur were an Englishman and offensive to Scottish pride. The development of historical scholarship was fuelled in part by perceptions that Anglo-Saxon history might yield support for protestantism and the break with Rome, and that the ancient British might have been rather like the indigenous people of the recently discovered New World.

Arthurian romance was next popular in the 19th cent., though *Dryden wrote a play which was set to music by *Purcell. Sir Walter *Scott and William *Wordsworth wrote some Arthurian material, but the boom began with *Tennyson's poems, from 1832, based on Malory. Tennyson's characters often symbolize particular qualities, and his works are moralizing. Other Arthurian writers include Algernon Swinburne, William *Morris, Matthew *Arnold, and (satirically) the American Mark Twain.

Emphases similar to those in literature have been apparent in the visual arts. Most Arthurian art has been in the Gothic style, with a consistent range of images. The medieval period generated manuscript illumination, sculptured decoration of churches, tiles, misericords, caskets, embroidery, *objets d'art*, and frescos, in England and on the continent. Tristan and Isolde was the most popular legend, particularly with women in convents. The Round Table now in Winchester castle was built probably for Edward I, and painted for Henry VIII. Above a Tudor rose is Arthur, originally with Henry's face, and royal symbols. Early modern art preferred secular, contemporary themes, and neglected the elements with Roman catholic implications, the Grail quests.

Nineteenth-cent. didacticism found numerous expressions, including the decoration (1851–64) of the Queen's Robing Room in the new palace of Westminster with Arthurian scenes, in fresco, to illustrate moral qualities. Arthurian scenes were also used for the Oxford Union murals in 1857, undertaken by a group of *Pre-Raphaelite artists, who produced many Arthurian works. In general Arthur seldom appears; he is eclipsed as a hero by Galahad and Lancelot, and the most influential of Tennyson's poems were *The Lady of Shalott* and *Elaine*.

In the 20th cent. Arthurian settings and circles have proved an enduring theme for novelists and poets of very different kinds. British musical treatments include works by Boughton, Bax, *Parry, and *Elgar. There have been a number of films.

Many attempts have been made to identify Arthurian sites. Through the ages Camelot has been located at Cadbury (where an Iron Age hill-fort was a centre of British power in the late 5th cent.), Caerleon, Colchester, Winchester, Tintagel, and, recently and controversially, near Stirling. The origin of Arthur's association with Cornwall is not clear. According to Welsh tradition, Kelliwic, possibly Killibury castle, was his base. Dozmary Pool and Loe Pool are associated with the Lady of the Lake. Castle Dore and Tintagel (with their late 5th- and early 6th-cent. secular aristocratic dwellings) are 'identified' as settings for Tristan and Isolde. Glastonbury (where the Tor was occupied in the Dark Ages) was associated in the mid-12th cent. with an abduction of Guinevere, and became identified with Avalon. In 1190 or 1191 the monks 'discovered', fraudulently, the burial of Arthur and Guinevere, and in the mid-13th cent. they added Joseph of Arimathea, with whom the Holy Grail was associated, to their history. The enduring resonance of Arthurian romance was underlined in the hopeful application to John F. Kennedy's presidency of the USA of the name of Camelot. AER

Barber, R., *King Arthur: Hero and Legend* (Woodbridge, 1986); Morris, R., *The Character of King Arthur in Medieval Literature* (Cambridge, 1982); Whitaker, M., *The Legends of King Arthur in Art* (Woodbridge, 1990).

Arthur, Prince (1187–*c.*1203). A young Plantagenet prince murdered by his uncle King John. As the posthumous only son of Geoffrey and Constance of Brittany, Arthur was duke of Brittany from the moment of his birth. Greater prospects opened up in 1190 when his uncle, Richard I, nominated him as heir presumptive to the throne, but by 1199, when Richard died, John had taken over as the acknowledged successor. Some of the barons of *Anjou revived Arthur's claim but were soon outmanœuvred. His moment came in 1202 when King Philip Augustus, at war against John, decided to recognize Arthur as rightful ruler of Normandy and Anjou. Unfortunately for Arthur he was captured by John at Mirebeau in August 1202, imprisoned at Rouen, and never seen again. Ever since the image of the murdered young prince has done much damage to John's reputation. JG

Arthur, prince of Wales (1486–1502), was the eldest son of Henry VII and *Elizabeth of York and the elder brother of Henry VIII. At the age of 15 he was married to *Catherine of Aragon and set up court at Ludlow. Five months later he was dead of consumption and buried in Worcester cathedral. It is doubtful whether the marriage was ever consummated and Catherine married Henry VIII in 1509. JAC

Articles of Grievances, 1689. The *Glorious Revolution gave both the English and Scottish *Conventions the opportunity to reassert parliamentary powers. The English *Declaration of Rights in February 1689 was followed by a Scottish *Claim of Right and Articles of Grievances in April 1689. The Articles protested against the *Committee of Articles which, by arranging the business of Parliament, had usurped much of its power. William's commissioner *Hamilton was reluctant to give way, fearing to lose control, but his successor *Melville conceded the point in 1690 and the committee was abolished. JAC

Artificers, statute of, 1563. A regulation of labour, which sought to banish idleness, advance husbandry, and yield 'a convenient proportion' of wages. Growing concern at the number of masterless men, increasing vagabondage, and escalating crime underlay the outline of terms and conditions of service between masters and servants, in an effort to reduce notorious discord. All unmarried persons below 30 who had received craft training could not refuse to serve if requested, those between 12 and 60 compellable to serve in husbandry were defined, and unmarried women between 12 and 40 could also be made to serve. Wage rates were to be set yearly at the Court of Chancery, after receipt of local recommendations, and then proclaimed in every county. To control undue mobility, anyone failing to carry letters testimonial was punishable for vagrancy. Regulations for apprenticeship concerned eligibility, age, duration, and grievance; refusal to be bound was punishable. ASH

Arundel, Henry Fitz Alan, 12th earl of (1512–80). Arundel steered a dextrous course through the rapids of mid-Tudor politics. He was in high favour with Henry VIII, who was his godfather, served with distinction against the French, and was awarded the Garter. He succeeded his father in 1544. During the reign of Edward VI Arundel was at odds with the duke of *Northumberland and spent a year in the Tower. In 1553 he ostensibly supported Lady Jane *Grey, doing homage to her, but took out an insurance by reporting everything to Mary. At the crisis he arrested Northumberland at Cambridge. Under Mary he was Lord Steward and, as a fellow-catholic, once more in favour. In Elizabeth's reign, he was mentioned as a possible husband. But he was implicated in the *Ridolfi plot in 1571, spent more years in captivity, and in the later 1570s lived in quiet retirement. JAC

Arundel, Philip Howard, 13th earl of (1557–95). Philip Howard's father was the 4th duke of *Norfolk, executed in 1572: his mother, daughter of Henry, earl of *Arundel, died soon after his birth. The dukedom was under attainder from 1572 but in 1580 Howard succeeded his grandfather as earl of Arundel. He was accused of complicity in the *Throckmorton plot. In 1584, much under the influence of his wife, he converted to catholicism, and the following year was arrested while attempting to leave the country. He was attainted and imprisoned in the Tower. In 1588 he was tried for treason as having prayed for the success of the *Armada, was condemned to death and died after seven more years in prison. His son Thomas was restored to the titles by James I in 1604 and created earl of Norfolk by Charles I in 1644. JAC

Arundel, Thomas Howard, 14th earl of (1585–1646). Howard's father was a catholic convert and spent the last eleven years of his life in the Tower, where he died in 1595. Howard was restored to the title by James I in 1604, received the Garter in 1611, and converted back to protestantism in 1615. In 1621 he was made earl marshal for life. In 1639 he was put in charge of the army to restore order among the Scots, but since the campaign ended without fighting, his military qualities were not tested. He was lord steward 1640–1 and presided over the trial of *Strafford. He escorted Princess Mary to Holland in 1642, was created earl of Norfolk in 1644, and died at Padua in 1646. *Clarendon disliked him, finding him pompous and self-interested. He was also disparaging about Howard's pretensions to learning—'willing to be thought a scholar'—but Howard was an assiduous collector of works of art and a patron of men of scholarship. JAC

Arundel, Thomas (1352–1414). Archbishop of Canterbury. The third son of Richard FitzAlan, 8th earl of Arundel, Thomas was an Oxford undergraduate when he became bishop of Ely in 1374. When the baronial critics of Richard II took control of his government in 1386, Arundel was appointed chancellor and promoted to the archbishopric of York in 1388. He was replaced as chancellor after Richard's resumption of authority in 1389, but again held the office from 1391 until he was translated to Canterbury in 1396. Next year, Richard destroyed the leadership of the former opposition. Arundel's brother, the 9th earl, was beheaded, and Arundel exiled and deprived of his archbishopric by fictitious translation to St Andrews. He regained Canterbury in 1399 by supporting Henry IV's usurpation, most prominently as principal spokesman in the quasi-parliamentary assembly which seemingly legalized Richard's deposition. In the new reign, Arundel had considerable influence in the king's council, and was again chancellor from 1407 to 1410, when his resignation marked the rise of a faction headed by Prince Henry (later Henry V). On its fall, Henry IV reappointed Arundel as chancellor, in 1412. The accession of Henry V in 1413 ended Arundel's role as a power behind the throne. Despite his obvious personal interest in the revolution of 1399, he was also a vigorous defender of the English church from heresy and anticlerical threats. RLS

Arundel castle in Sussex was started by Roger, earl of Shrewsbury, soon after the *Norman Conquest. It was later in the possession of the Aubigny family until 1243, passed by marriage to the Fitz Alans until 1580, and subsequently to the Howards, dukes of Norfolk. Pevsner is scathing about the 19th-cent. restoration of the castle—'silly, appalling, a piece of open-air fancy dress'. JAC

Ascham, Roger (1515/16–68). Protestant classical scholar and educator, born in Yorkshire. He went up about 1530 to St John's College, Cambridge, which was already famous for piety and learning, and was there influenced by Sir John *Cheke, whom he supported on Greek pronunciation. Ascham himself taught Latin, Greek, and logic, being also university public orator, and, though seemingly always subject to health and money difficulties, sought wider responsibilities. His *Toxophilus, the School of Shooting* (1545), a finely observed and beautifully written account of the merits of archery, 'English matter, in the English tongue, for English men', secured him patronage. After tutoring both Princess Elizabeth and the future Edward VI, Ascham went on embassy to Germany in 1550, and briefly visited Venice, where he found 'all service to God lacking'. A sympathizer with Lady Jane *Grey, he suffered little under Mary, for whom he acted as Latin secretary; and was in favour with Elizabeth. Ascham's best-known work, *The Schoolmaster, or Plain and Perfect Way of Teaching Children the Latin Tongue* (1570), advocated an education based ultimately on Quintilian, applied so as to persuade rather than force English young people to live, speak, and write well. This patriotic purpose is reinforced with dispraise of the current Italianized English fashion. Like *The Schoolmaster*, Ascham's Report on Germany was published posthumously. JBT

Ashanti (Asante) **wars.** The Ashanti empire, located in the hinterland of the Gold Coast of west Africa, reached its peak in the late 18th cent. An attempt by the Ashanti to establish their dominion over the territory adjacent to British trading posts in 1807 threatened British legitimate trade, but because of Britain's vacillation over its role in the region did not lead to armed conflict until 1824 when the Ashanti were victorious. The judicious intervention of George Maclean, chief administrator of the British Gold Coast settlements, induced the Ashanti to waive their claims over the coastal peoples, but the British government's ambivalence emboldened the Ashanti to seize the coastal territory again in 1863. After another reversal of policy, Britain sent a military force under Sir Garnet *Wolseley to challenge Ashanti claims in 1873. Wolseley marched north and destroyed the Ashanti capital, Kumasi. In 1874 the land south of Ashanti was declared to be a British crown colony. The rapid expansion of French and German colonization in the region induced Britain to demand Ashanti submission in 1896. When the Ashanti resisted, another British expedition (1900–1) finally destroyed the empire, which became a British crown colony in 1902. KI

Ashburton treaty, 1842. After the *War of 1812, relations between Britain and the USA remained difficult, with a number of problems including border disputes in Maine. In 1841 when *Peel took office, the situation was bad enough to call for naval deployments in case of war. Peel dispatched Lord Ashburton, who had an American wife, as a special envoy. By the treaty, signed in April 1842, Britain dropped the right of maritime search, the Maine border was adjusted, and the rest of the boundary with Canada agreed as the 49th parallel. The Oregon question remained at issue but one of the last acts of Peel's government in 1846 was to reach a settlement on that as well. JAC

Ashdown, battle of, 871. In 870 a large Danish army established camp at Reading and began raiding the surrounding countryside. *Æthelred, king of Wessex, and his brother *Alfred gave battle at Ashdown on the Berkshire downs about 8 January 871: this was Alfred's home territory since he was born at Wantage. The struggle raged round a stunted thorn-bush and, according to the *Anglo-Saxon Chronicle*, 'fighting went on till nightfall'. The Danes were driven back—the first major check to their advance—but a follow-up against their camp failed. Æthelred died within weeks and, his sons being too young to lead in battle, Alfred became king. JAC

Ashingdon, battle of, 1016. This was the final battle in the struggle between *Edmund Ironside and *Cnut and took place south of the river Crouch in Essex. The defection of Eadric, ealdorman of Mercia, who led the Magonsaete from Herefordshire and Shropshire from the field, contributed to a crushing Danish victory, with 'all the flower of the English nation' cut down. The two leaders met subsequently at Deerhurst in Gloucestershire to divide the kingdom but Edmund's death weeks afterwards gave the whole realm into Cnut's hands. JAC

asiento (Spanish: contract) was the concession made by Spain to Britain at *Utrecht in 1713 of the right to supply negro slaves to the Spanish empire. It had previously been held by the Portuguese and the French. Intended to last for thirty years, the trade was never as profitable as the British hoped and disputes about its implementation were among the causes of the War of *Jenkins's Ear in 1739. At *Aix-la-Chapelle in 1748 the British argued for an addition of the four years lost by warfare, but in 1750 relinquished the concession for £100,000 compensation. JAC

Aske, Robert (d. 1537). A Lincolnshire attorney, Aske led the *Pilgrimage of Grace in 1536–7, a widespread rising against the *dissolution of the monasteries and in favour of the old religion. An outbreak in Lincolnshire was followed by Aske's Yorkshire rising, strong enough to persuade Henry VIII to offer pardons and agree in November 1536 to grant Aske an audience. But after renewed activity in January 1537, Aske was seized, sent to the Tower of London, and in July executed in York. A moderate who had persistently tried to restrain his followers and urged them to trust Henry's honour and good faith, Aske paid with his life for such naïvety. JAC

Askew, Anne (1521–46). Protestant martyr. A Lincolnshire gentlewoman devoted to biblical study, Anne Askew regularly entered into textual debates with the clergy and was ultimately dismissed by her husband for offending them. Examined in London for heretical views on the sacrament in 1545, she was arraigned again the following year and sentenced to burn. She was racked in the Tower, her prosecutors vainly seeking evidence against suspected reformists at court, including *Catherine Parr. Weakened by torture, she was carried by chair to the stake and supported there by a chain, refusing a final offer of pardon for recantation. AM

Asquith, Herbert Henry, 1st earl of Oxford and Asquith (1852–1928). Prime minister. Between 1908 and 1914 Asquith enjoyed an outstanding record, pushing through a series of major constitutional and social reforms. However, he had less success as a wartime premier from 1914 to 1916, and his reputation declined during the undignified period of infighting within the Liberal Party from 1918 to 1926.

Asquith's early life was spent in Morley and Huddersfield where his relatives were minor employers in the woollen trade. He soon left these modest origins behind him and advanced by means of a scholarship to Balliol College (1896), to the bar, and to a safe seat in Parliament—East Fife—which he held from 1885 to 1918. His first wife Helen, by whom he had five children, died in 1891, and when he remarried in 1894 it was to a very different character, Margot Tennant, the daughter of a wealthy Scots chemicals magnate, Sir Charles Tennant. Margot was a terrible snob who insisted on calling her husband Henry not Herbert, and described him as 'incorrigibly middle-class'. Her chief motive in marrying him seems to have been ambition; she correctly saw him as prime ministerial material. Yet despite Margot's undoubted loyalty to Asquith and his party, the marriage was, for him, a very mixed blessing. Margot's extravagance severely stretched his barrister's income; her involvement with high society accelerated his own pronounced taste for the pleasures of metropolitan life; and her tactlessness and perpetual interference in politics compounded his hostility towards the enfranchisement of women.

Though his attendance at Westminster was restricted by the need to maintain his legal income, Asquith's abilities were quickly recognized. His systematic working habits, skill in mastering a brief, and capacity for retaining huge quantities of information made him a formidable parliamentarian. 'Bring out the sledgehammer,' *Campbell-Bannerman used to cry when he wished to strengthen his front bench with Asquith's debating talents. In 1892 *Gladstone gave him the vital experience as home secretary which placed him in line for the premiership.

Subsequently, however, Asquith's career entered the doldrums for a time. In 1898 he declined the chance to lead the Liberals in the Commons, largely for financial reasons, though this problem was eased in 1901 when Sir Charles Tennant settled an annual income of £5,000 on Margot. Worse, Asquith became associated with the *Liberal Imperialist cause during the South African War which detached him from the mainstream of the party. He even joined a cabal designed to force Campbell-Bannerman to go to the House of Lords when the Liberals next took office. However, between 1903 and 1905 he worked his passage back into favour by championing the *free trade cause against the protectionism propagated by Joseph *Chamberlain. When offered the Exchequer in December 1905 he quickly accepted.

Asquith proved to be one of the most important, innovative chancellors of modern times. He made it compulsory to provide an annual return of income to the Inland Revenue; he drew up the scheme for non-contributory old-age pensions; and he prepared the ground for the 'People's Budget' of 1909 by forcing the Treasury to abandon its opposition to a supertax on incomes above £5,000. This record puts Asquith in the school of New Liberalism, but he was too good a politician not to respect the traditional Liberal causes. He was, for example, a first-rate temperance speaker, notwithstanding his pronounced fondness for alcohol.

When Campbell-Bannerman retired in 1908 Asquith seemed to be the natural successor as prime minister. He presided over a highly talented cabinet, and was never afraid to promote able and ambitious men like *Lloyd George and Winston *Churchill. His working partnership with Lloyd George, whom he made chancellor, proved to be an immense source of strength to the party and the government until it broke down during the Great War. As premier Asquith played a key role in supporting Lloyd George's 1909 budget against criticism in the cabinet. As a result of the ensuing controversy he led the Liberals through two general elections in 1910 and ultimately resolved the problem that had hampered them since Gladstone's days; the 1911 *Parliament Act curtailed the powers of the House of Lords and excluded it altogether from financial legislation.

The outbreak of war brought further proof of Asquith's skills. Against expectations he succeeded in taking his cabinet to war with only two resignations and thus kept the Liberal Party together; it was widely accepted that his leadership helped to maintain national unity over British participation in the war. However, his cold, legalistic temperament was not well suited to the emotional atmosphere of wartime. He began to suffer from a failure to cultivate the press and from a feeling that he lacked the determination to win the war. Asquithian cabinets—during which the prime minister often wrote long letters to Venetia Stanley, a young woman with whom he had become infatuated—were protracted and inconclusive affairs. But he was essentially unlucky that neither the generals nor the admirals proved capable of scoring a military victory. His decision to form a coalition government with the Conservative and Labour parties in May 1915 was the beginning of the end for Asquith, though it seemed a clever move at the time. Increasingly the Liberals began to blame him for right-wing policies like conscription. When presented with an ultimatum by Bonar *Law and Lloyd George in December 1916, he misjudged his strength by resigning. The result was a new coalition under Lloyd George and a split in the Liberal party. This led to the disastrous 'coupon' election in 1918 in which Asquith lost his seat and the Liberals were displaced by Labour on the opposition front bench. Though he achieved a come-back by winning a by-election at Paisley in 1920, he was by then a largely negative force, intent upon keeping the party out of the hands of Lloyd George. He finally surrendered the leadership in 1926. MDP

Jenkins, R., *Asquith* (1964); Koss, S., *Asquith* (1976); Spender, J. A., and Asquith, C., *Asquith* (2 vols., 1932).

Asser (d. 909). Bishop of Sherborne. Author of the *Life of King Alfred*, Asser was a Welshman who was a monk and priest at St David's in Dyfed until recruited by Alfred of Wessex in 885 to become one of a group of scholars at his court who assisted the king with his own studies and translations. His famous biography of Alfred was written by 893 and makes use of the recently completed **Anglo-Saxon Chronicle*. Asser added to the work his own observations and discussions with the king and others at the court. It is a major source for the reign, but it must be remembered that the portrait of Alfred has been carefully modelled to fit 9th-cent. perceptions of a good Christian king. Asser lovingly records the many gifts he received from Alfred, and he may have been created a suffragan bishop based in Exeter before succeeding Wulfsige *c.*900 as bishop of Sherborne. BAEY

assizes. The word has a number of different meanings in legal history. It was used to describe (*a*) a session (or sitting) of an official body, especially the king's council (e.g. the Assize of *Clarendon 1166); (*b*) the edicts or enactments made at such sessions; (*c*) the forms of action or procedures instituted by such edicts and available as writs to would-be litigants in the royal court (e.g. the Grand Assize and the petty assizes of novel disseisin, mort d'ancestor, and darrein presentment, all introduced by Henry II); (*d*) the system of travelling courts which became part of English life from the reign of Henry II until 1971. From the time of Henry I, the king's justice was locally administered by justices appointed by the king, sometimes administered by itinerant 'justices in Eyre'. From Henry II's reign the General *Eyre became a familiar institution until its decline in the 14th cent. The country was divided by Henry II into six judicial circuits for the purpose of bringing royal justice to all regions.

The Assizes of Clarendon and *Northampton (1166 and 1176) provided that those suspected of serious crime should be presented on oath by twelve men of each hundred to the king's justices, members of the *Great Council and later the judges of the common law courts—who therefore travelled round the country receiving these presentments and, after the abolition of the ordeals in 1215, presiding at trials by jury for serious crime. At first in the General Eyre and later under the commissions of *oyer and terminer and *gaol delivery, they would hear criminal cases.

When the petty or possessory assizes were instituted by Henry II, the writs which set them in motion called on the sheriff to summon a group of neighbours (the 'inquest' or jury) to give an answer under oath, before the royal justices, to a specific question relating to disseisin. The justices were therefore said to 'take the assizes'; indeed, the barons demanded in *Magna Carta that the justices should travel round regularly for this purpose.

So the 'justices of assize' travelled round to hear cases of serious crime and at the same time to take the assizes, i.e. receive the verdicts of the inquest jury in the possessory assizes. Increasingly with the growth of royal justice into the common law, and especially after the reign of Edward I, they also in effect heard civil cases under the nisi prius system.

In the 13th cent. the term 'assize' came to be the general term applied to the visits of the judges on circuit. After 1340 the justices of assize were required to be justices of the Court of *Common Pleas or *King's Bench or serjeants at law.

The assizes continued until 1971 on the circuits ordained by Henry II, the assize towns, which were centres of importance in the Middle Ages, being visited periodically and with considerable ceremony by assize judges, who would hear serious criminal and important civil cases. Although the Courts Act 1971 abolished the assizes, senior judges still go 'on circuit' to hear cases in important modern centres of population. MM

associations were a stage in the development of lobbies to express opinion and influence policy. They began innocuously as demonstrations of loyalty at times of crisis. *Burghley and *Walsingham sponsored an association to protect Queen Elizabeth in 1584 against the machinations of Mary, queen of Scots' supporters. Another association to support and, if necessary, avenge William III followed the discovery of Fenwick's conspiracy in 1696: the signatories wore orange ribbons with gold letters declaring 'National Association for King William'. The archbishop of York launched an association in 1745 to repulse the young pretender and safeguard the Hanoverians. But associations could be turned to other purposes. The *Yorkshire Association in 1780 called for economical reform and Lord George *Gordon's Protestant Association deplored concessions to the catholics. The speaker of the House of Commons reflected conservative attitudes when he expressed his 'total disapproval of the committees and associations: they were in his opinion extremely improper.' In the 1790s, under the shadow of the French Revolution, Lord Henderland denounced the *Friends of the People—an association for parliamentary reform: 'what occasion for such associations, with such names?' *Shelburne in 1795 referred to associations as a discovery as momentous in politics as any in science, and J. F. *Stephen, in his sardonic way, observed in 1850 that 'for the diffusion of any blessing of which mankind can partake, there is a committee'. JAC

Astley, Sir Jacob (1579–1652). A professional soldier who fought for the king all through the Civil War and was given a barony in 1644. He was present at the beginning and end of the conflict. At Edgehill on 23 October 1642 he led his troops into battle with a soldier's prayer: 'O Lord, thou knowest how busy I must be this day. If I forget thee, do not thou forget me.' At the end, in the market-place of Stow-on-the-Wold, on 21 March 1646, he surrendered the king's last sizeable force. Sitting on a drum, he told his captors, 'you may now go to play, boys, unless you fall out among yourselves.' JAC

Astor, Nancy W. (1879–1964). Politician, and daughter of an American railway developer in Virginia. Nancy Astor had an unhappy first marriage, which ended in divorce in 1903. The following year she travelled to England, marrying Waldorf Astor three years later; when Waldorf, Conservative MP for Plymouth, Sutton, succeeded to the peerage in 1919, Nancy was returned in his stead at the subsequent by-election, becoming only the second woman to be elected to Parliament and the first to take her seat (Constance Gore-Booth having declined, along with the other Sinn Fein MPs, to sit in 1918). As a parliamentarian (1919–45) Nancy was outspoken—perhaps too much so—in favour of those causes she held dear: opposition to divorce (despite her own experience); raising to 18 the age at which it was legal to purchase alcohol; lowering to 21 the voting age for women; above all, appeasement of Nazi Germany. The Astor home, Cliveden, became a by-word for appeasement, but in fact Nancy was anti-Nazi, refused to meet Hitler, and had her name included on a Nazi blacklist. GA

astrology. The idea that the motion of the stars and the planets might affect human life dates from ancient times, although astrology as a rigorous, 'scientific' system originated with the Greek mathematician Ptolemy in the 2nd cent. AD. In the Middle Ages, astrology, by then rendered compatible with Christianity, was thought to fall into two broad subcategories: natural astrology, the everyday influence of the planets in normal activities, such as the practice of medicine; and judicial astrology, which aimed at predicting events and giving advice.

The influence of astrological thinking was considerable, and many educated Britons between the 15th and late 17th cents. accepted its principles. It was especially important in medicine, where the casting of a horoscope was thought an important aid in diagnosing disease and in prescribing remedies. It also had ramifications in physiology, botany, and metallurgy. More dangerously, astrology acquired political overtones, and more than one astrologer found himself in trouble for predicting the death of the monarch or other significant events.

The golden age of astrology in Britain was the 17th cent., with several astrologers gaining considerable reputation, status, and income. The two most important figures were William Lilly (1602–81) and John Gadbury (1627–1704). Lilly, who also operated as a medical practitioner and almanack writer, acquired a wide fame and a good income, some impression of the seriousness with which astrology was taken being conveyed by the fact that his predictive talents were enlisted by Parliament during the civil wars. Gadbury, conversely, rejected his early parliamentarian sympathies, became an ardent royalist, and flourished after the Restoration of 1660.

The early 18th cent., however, marked the point at which educated opinion, under the influence of new scientific thinking, was beginning to reject astrology. Yet it continued to enjoy a wide currency outside the educated élite, while even at that social level the issue was one of the recategorization of astrological terms rather than total rejection. More research is needed, but even preliminary investigations have uncovered groups of provincial astrologers who found a ready clientele among the middling sorts in their localities, and, as modern tabloid newspapers and women's magazines demonstrate, this ancient science, while having moved downmarket, is not entirely dead. JAS

asylum was the right Britons proudly afforded generations of foreign refugees fleeing from religious or political tyrannies in their own countries to Britain's relatively more tolerant shores. Early beneficiaries were the French Huguenots who came there after Louis XIV's outlawing of protestantism in 1685. Like most best British liberties it rested on the absence of any laws to exclude them, rather than one to protect them specifically. (Theoretically the monarch could have exercised his or her royal prerogative against them, but after the 18th cent. that was not feasible.) During the French wars this was modified, by an Alien Act passed in 1793; but still thousands of royalists sought shelter in Britain, and the Act was repealed in 1826. A similar Act in 1848–50 was never implemented.

Throughout Victoria's reign, therefore, refugees poured in, mostly left-wingers. They included Mazzini, Marx, Victor Hugo, Herzen, Kropotkin, and Louis Napoleon (from the other side). Some of them brought valuable skills, as the Huguenots had done: the Rossettis, for example, were refugees originally, and another Italian exile, Panizzi, became principal librarian of the British Museum; but they also caused problems with governments abroad. In 1858 a great row blew up with France after the ex-refugee Orsini's attempt on the life of Napoleon III with a bomb. That led to *Palmerston's fall when he tried to appease the tyrant emperor. No 19th-cent. government tried that again.

When Britain's free-entry policy was eventually dropped, it was for social rather than political reasons. None the less the 1905 Alien Act, directed against Jews, did specifically exempt refugees. The first real inroad into this traditional British freedom, as with many others, came during the *First World War. Refugees still entered Britain after that, but on sufferance, rather than as a right. In the 1980s and 1990s, when the increase in persecution in the world made asylum more necessary than ever, Britain was noticeably meaner than many other countries in granting it. What had once been a distinctive British tradition was now at an end.

BJP

asylums for the insane had medieval origins in Britain, with London's Bethlem Hospital (*Bedlam) the most famous. Its shortened name passed into the language in association with foolishness, loss of control, and the abdication of reason and humanity, as befitted a prevailing frame of mind in which madness was equated with descent into brutishness and kept in check with chains and whips. The patients in Bedlam were a spectacle for curious visitors in the 17th and 18th cents. During the latter century a private madhouse system developed, as medical entrepreneurs made claims for cure as well as management and security. At the turn of the 18th and 19th cents. reformers such as Pinel in France began to claim that asylums could be turned into therapeutic environments, in which insanity could be cured by seclusion from external stresses and a system of moral management could lead patients back into recognizing the need for acceptable, self-disciplined behaviour. This line was taken by the Tuke family at their York Retreat, an asylum for quakers which became a model for later developments. An Act in 1808 empowered counties to set up asylums for pauper lunatics with a view to possible cure as well as custody. Such asylums gradually spread, and the emergence of the 'non-restraint' system under practitioners like John Conolly provided an additional legitimacy, as locks and chains were struck off and a humane regime based on an appeal to reason supposedly took over. In 1845 legislation required the general establishment of pauper asylums, and commissioners in lunacy were established to inspect, remedy abuses, prescribe best practice, and deal with alleged cases of wrongful confinement, when patients were certified and confined at the behest of relatives who would benefit financially from their incarceration. Charles Reade's mid-Victorian novel *Hard Cash* dealt forcefully with this issue; but the promise of cure made asylums seem more legitimate and less frightening even as the pauper asylums became less able to live up to the reformers' promises. As they filled up with incurable patients and were unable to attract or train staff with appropriate attitudes, patient–staff ratios increased, pauper asylums reverted to custodial control rather than cure, and doctors' pretensions to understanding and treating insanity failed to develop beyond asylum management. Huge 'museums of madness' proliferated in the late 19th cent., and silted up with long-term inmates. The abuses of the system came to seem to outweigh its humanitarian and therapeutic pretensions, and physical as well as moral restraints were reintroduced. The emergent psychiatric profession had used 'moral treatment' to enhance its credibility, but failed to deliver cures in significant numbers. The sheer scale of Victorian investment in the system, and the administrative power of the psychiatrists, kept it in being until the last quarter of the 20th cent., when a fashion for decarceration and the liberation of inmates led to replacement with so-called care in the community, whose limitations were quickly made apparent in the absence of appropriate funding. With all its defects, the asylum was more than (as one critic suggested) 'a convenient place to get rid of inconvenient people': it was a refuge for those who could not cope, and the failure of alternative systems showed that it had its virtues as well as its drawbacks for patients, as well as for those who sought to shape and sanitize the social order through the promotion of custodial care.

JKW

atheism is a philosophical term derived from the Greek ἄθεος, meaning the absence of a god, but is usually translated as disbelief in or denial of the existence of God. Dogmatic denials of God have been rare outside popular unbelief. More usual is the argument from the insufficiency of evidence for the existence of a God, which might more properly be termed scepticism or agnosticism. Speculative atheism goes further in denying the possibility of evidence to demonstrate the existence of God.

Atheistic views were held among the Greek Atomists of the 5th cent. BC, but within Christendom such views have been marginal. In the 16th cent., when the word atheism came into use in English, it was a term of abuse, and English philosophers long preferred the theory of Isaac *Newton (1642–1727) that the origin of motion is external to matter rather than the materialist theory that motion is a property of matter. Natural theology in 18th-cent. England meant not scientific materialism (atheism) but the existence of at least a remote external first cause of the universe (*deism). In this respect, English thought differed from that of continental Europe where Spinoza (1632–77) argued that God and the material world were the same thing. Materialistic ideas, however, could be derived from the philosophy of John *Locke by writers such as Anthony Collins (1676–1729)—the first author to use the term 'free thinker'.

Collins was spurned in England but read on the continent, where atheism became a commonplace of the French Enlightenment, especially in the writings of Baron d'Holbach (1723–89), whose *Système de la nature* (*System of Nature*) was influential in popular atheistic thought for the next hundred years. Atheism remained a dangerous creed to profess. Aikenhead, a youth, was hanged at Edinburgh in 1697; Whiston lost his chair at Cambridge in 1710 because his religious views were unsound; and *Shelley, the poet, was expelled from Oxford as an undergraduate in 1811 for distributing a tract on 'The Necessity of Atheism'. In Britain the best-known atheist, Thomas *Paine (1737–1809), was in fact a deist whose *Age of Reason* was written to counter the progress of French atheism. As loyalist propaganda in the 1790s was directed against those radical ideas in religion and politics associated with the French Revolution, atheism became identified with lower-class subversion, though only a few radicals, such as William *Godwin (1756–1836) and Jeremy *Bentham (1748–1832), were actually atheists.

In the 19th cent., materialistic atheism was taken up in the radical anticlerical publications of Richard *Carlile (1790–1843), Charles Southwell (1814–60), George Jacob *Holyoake (1817–1906), and Charles *Bradlaugh (1833–91). Holyoake was an atheist in the sense that he saw no evidence for the existence of God, and to avoid the opprobrium associated with atheism he adopted the word *secularism instead; but Bradlaugh was a speculative atheist, influenced by Spinoza, who argued that in a world in which matter is all there can be no evidence for any God beyond nature. Though one could argue that this philosophy, known as monism, is actually pantheism rather than atheism, the two were equated in popular thought. Not until 1886 was Bradlaugh, an avowed atheist, allowed to take his seat in Parliament.

With the development of scientific ideas in the 19th cent., theories of the universe and of biological evolution which dispensed with explanations requiring the existence of God gained influential support, though many intellectuals preferred Thomas *Huxley's word 'agnosticism' to describe their views rather than outright atheism. Even in the later 20th cent., when large numbers of people live a materialistic life-style of practical atheism, the word atheism still lacks social respectability and public figures prefer to avoid its use. ER

Athelstan (d. 939), King of England (924–39). One of the greatest of Anglo-Saxon kings, Athelstan, son of *Edward the Elder, succeeded in uniting all of England under his rule. Early in his reign he consolidated his position south of the Humber. Brought up in the household of his father and of his aunt, *Æthelfleda, effective ruler of the Mercians, he was well received by the Mercian as well as by the West Saxon nobility. At a meeting held at Hereford he brought the Welsh to submission, and their princes, notably *Hywel Dda, the ablest among them, regularly attended his courts. His military successes were great. From 927 he established direct control of York. He led expeditions against the Scots, culminating in a battle at *Brunanburh in 937 when he and his brother and successor, *Edmund, led a joint force of West Saxons and Mercians to victory against a composite force of Scandinavians, Irish, and Scots, aiming to overthrow his domination in the north. No fewer than five kings and seven earls from Ireland and the son of the Scottish king were killed in the battle. Athelstan established a firm internal peace, issuing important codes of law, calculated to apply to all his subjects, and also confirming local peace agreements. His central courts developed into virtual national assemblies, attended by magnates drawn from all England, as well as Welsh princes. On the international scale he extended the range of the monarchy, arranging marriages for his sisters with Hugh, duke of the Franks, and with the future Otto the Great of Germany. He protected in exile Louis IV (d'Outremer), king of France (936–54), and brought up at his court a future king of Norway in the person of Haakon Haraldsson, known as Athelstan's foster-child. His charters, written in a very elaborate Latin style, betray an advanced secretariat for the age, and accord the king formal titles that indicate effort to express his special dignity. His coinage was placed under strong royal control, and after 927 his style on coins was normally given as *rex totius Britanniae*, king of all Britain. Not all his work proved immediately enduring. After his death, the English hold on the north weakened and Scandinavian princes returned to York. Athelstan's reign, nevertheless, marks a vital stage in the move towards the unification of England under the West Saxon dynasty. HL

Athenry, battle of, 1316. The battle, east of Galway, on 10 August 1316, was a heavy defeat for the O'Connors, who were in alliance with Edward *Bruce. They were opposed by an Anglo-Irish force led by Richard de Bermingham and William de Burgh. Their chief Felim O'Connor was slain, and their power broken. But Edward Bruce continued his struggle to create an Irish kingdom for himself. JAC

athletics covers a large and increasing number of events, including sprints, marathons, discus, pole-vaulting, shot-putting, high and long jump, pentathlon, and triple jump. Running races, especially for wagers, have always been common but the first organized meeting in Britain seems to have been held at the Royal Military Academy, Woolwich, in 1849. The supervising body in Britain is the Amateur Athletic Association and world-wide the International Amateur Athletics Federation (IAAF), whose Olympics Organizing Committee is responsible for the Olympic Games. The IAAF has been much exercised in recent years by the problem of drug use, which can dramatically improve performances, and a number of competitors have been disqualified. In Scotland there is a strong tradition of professional athletics. The Powderhall Sprint was first run in Edinburgh in 1870 and professional meetings continue to be held, usually in the Meadowbank stadium. JAC

Atholl, James Murray, 2nd duke of [S] (*c.*1690–1764). Though not chief of a major clan, Atholl was one of the greatest men in the Highlands because of his vast estates and because of his possession of the extensive regality of Atholl, two-thirds of the county of Perthshire, in which he exercised powers just short of full sovereignty.

His elder brother William, marquis of Tullibardine, was attainted after the '15. His father had not countenanced the rising, so it proved possible to obtain an Act of Parliament in 1715 transferring the succession to James. He succeeded in 1724. His rights were confirmed by an Act in 1733, when he also succeeded Islay (*Argyll) as lord privy seal. In 1738, through Stanley ancestry, he inherited the sovereignty of the *Isle of Man.

In 1745 James fled safely south, leaving Tullibardine, the Jacobite duke, to take control of the Perthshire complex. By joining *Cumberland's army on its march north, Duke James secured his return. Among the beneficiaries was John, son of Lord George *Murray, who despite his father's attainder was allowed to succeed as 3rd duke, after selling to the crown the lordship of Man. BPL

Atholl, John Murray, 1st marquis of [S] (1631–1703). Murray's grandfather was earl of Tullibardine but resigned the title in 1626 on promise of the earldom of Atholl, given to his son in 1629. Murray succeeded in 1642 at the age of 11 and in 1653 joined Lord *Middleton in the Highland rising on behalf of Charles II. At the Restoration he was in favour. From 1663 to 1676 he served as justice-general [S] and in 1670 succeeded a cousin as earl of Tullibardine. From 1672 to 1689 he was keeper of the privy seal and in 1676 was raised to the rank of marquis. In 1679 he fought with *Monmouth against the covenanters at *Bothwell Bridge, and took an active part against *Argyll's invasion of 1685, earning a reputation for brutality. In 1687 James II gave him the Thistle. His vacillation at the *Glorious Revolution earned him widespread mistrust and, in the end, he took refuge in visiting Bath to take the waters, while *Dundee was raising the clans for James II. He played little part subsequently but his son, a staunch Williamite, was secretary of state [S] 1696–8. Macaulay declared that 'his abilities were mean, his temper false, pusillanimous and cruel'. JAC

Atholl, John Murray, 1st duke of [S] (1660–1724). Murray was a strong supporter of the *Glorious Revolution, was created earl of Tullibardine in 1696, and succeeded his father as marquis of Atholl in May 1703. A month later he was raised to the dukedom and was given the Thistle in 1704. From 1696 to 1698 he served as secretary of state [S], resigning on losing ground to the *Queensberry interest, and lord privy seal from 1703. But in 1705 he resigned and offered vigorous opposition to the *Union, arguing that Scottish opinion had not been properly consulted and that Scotland would be underrepresented at Westminster. Henceforth he acted with the Tories. His first son was killed at *Malplaquet; his second son took part in the '15 and the '45; his third son succeeded him; his fourth son was out in the '15, and his fifth son, Lord George *Murray, was a pillar of the Jacobite cause in both the '15 and the '45. JAC

Atholl, John Stewart, 4th earl of [S] (*c*.1528–79). Atholl succeeded his father as a boy. He was a strong Roman catholic and supported the cause of Mary, queen of Scots. He opposed the religious reforms of 1560 and was appointed to the council in 1561 on Mary's return from France. At *Corrichie in 1562 he helped to put down a rising by his father-in-law, Lord *Huntly. He gave support to the *Darnley marriage but opposed *Bothwell and was against Mary in the confrontation at *Carberry Hill. He was in the Council of Regency until *Moray's return in 1567. In 1578 Atholl joined forces with *Argyll to challenge the regent *Morton and was appointed chancellor [S]. A reconciliation restored Morton to the council but in April 1579, immediately after banqueting with Morton at Stirling, Atholl fell ill and died. Rumours of poison circulated at once but Morton denied it at his own execution in 1581. JAC

Atholl, Walter Stewart, earl of [S] (*c*.1360–1437). Second son of Robert II's second marriage, to Euphemia Ross, and the only one of Robert's sons not to acquire an earldom in his father's lifetime. Lord of Brechin until 1402, Walter Stewart acquired the earldom of Caithness [S] in that year, and that of Atholl [S] and the lordship of Methven in 1404. His main territorial ambitions centred on the earldom of Strathearn [S], which he received in life-rent from his nephew James I in 1427.

Atholl was already an old man when his sons David and Alan predeceased him. Fears that James I was seeking to undermine his position in Perthshire led Atholl and his grandson Robert to organize a successful assassination plot. The king was murdered at the Perth Blackfriars (20 February 1437), but Atholl failed to win the ensuing struggle to control the young James II, and was beheaded for regicide on 26 March 1437. NATM

Atholl, John of Strathbogie, earl of (d. 1306). Scottish earl who played a leading if inconsistent role in the Wars of Independence. He was captured at the battle of *Dunbar (1296) and imprisoned in the Tower of London. Reconciled with Edward I, he became warden of northern Scotland in 1304. He subsequently reverted to the Scottish allegiance, attended the coronation of Robert Bruce, his brother-in-law, in 1306, and was retaken by the English three months later, shortly after the Scottish defeat at *Methven. Hanged in London from an exceptionally high gallows, then decapitated and burned, he was the first earl to be executed in England since 1076. His fate shows Edward I's cruelty and vindictiveness, but it was also a logical development of the English view that the Scots, far from fighting a just war, were rebels and traitors against their lawful sovereign lord. KJS

Atlantic, battle of the, 1939–45. A decisive Second World War battle, the struggle diverged from pre-war expectations. Before the war British naval experts thought 'Asdic' countered submarines and, like the highest German authorities, considered surface warships the best means of interrupting transport to Britain of food, munitions, and troops. Hitler allotted priority to submarines only after the fall of France, which gave German submarines greater range from Bay of Biscay harbours. In the first half of 1941 the Germans began to win, using 'wolf-packs' of submarines to overwhelm convoys. Ships sunk exceeded new building. In June, however, the British began to decode orders, generated by German 'Enigma' machines, giving U-boat assembly areas in the Atlantic. In July 1941, shipping losses from submarine attack fell to less than one-third of those in June in spite of more U-boats. Early in 1942, the Germans recovered; they began to read allied convoy orders and again made their own orders indecipherable. Losses to allied ships exceeded combined British and American building. In 1943, however, at twelve times the volume of 1941, US construction far exceeded losses. Greater numbers and better weapons now gave victory to the British, Canadians, and Americans. 'Very long-range' aircraft and small escort aircraft carriers improved allied reconnaissance and attack, as did airborne and shipborne short-wave radar, together with high-frequency direction finding, which enabled warships to locate U-boats as soon as they made radio signals. Depth charges, to destroy submerged U-boats, were improved. The allies won the battle of the Atlantic for good in summer 1943. Victory, first over German surface vessels—most dramatically the defeat of the pocket-battleship *Graf Spee* in 1939 and of the *Bismarck* in 1941—and then over German submarines enabled British survival and the build-up of American forces in Britain for the liberation of France in 1944 and the defeat of the Germans in 1945. RACP

Atlantic charter. This was drawn up at the first of the *Churchill–Roosevelt wartime meetings (9–12 August 1941) during one of the darkest periods of the war. Above all a political gesture and propaganda exercise, the charter had less effect on American isolationists than hoped. The two powers renounced territorial aggrandizement; condemned territorial changes contrary to the wishes of the people concerned; pledged that peoples should be free to choose their own form of government, and to live in freedom from want and fear. The two leaders were not in entire agreement. Churchill insisted on qualifying American proposals to guarantee equal access to the world's riches to 'all States, great or small' by calling for 'due respect for . . . existing obligations' within the empire. Roosevelt for his part diluted Churchill's plea for an 'effective' post-war international organization by agreeing to no more than the ultimate 'establishment of a wider and permanent system of general security'. A British bid for Soviet endorsement elicited only a vague statement of approval. CJB

atom bomb. See NUCLEAR ENERGY.

Atrebates. A British tribe and *civitas*. The tribe seems to have either origins or close relationships in Gaul (France) where a tribe of the same name is recorded by *Caesar. Indeed, the king of the Gallic Atrebates, *Commius, fled to Britain and appears to have established a dynasty ruling over the British tribe. From about 15 BC, the Atrebates seem to have re-established friendly relations with Rome, and it was an appeal for help from the last Atrebatic king, Verica, which provided *Claudius with the pretext for the invasion of Britain in AD 43. The tribal capital was Calleva, which after the granting of *civitas* status in the later 1st cent. was known as Calleva Atrebatum. The tribal territory administered from here lay south of the Thames in Berkshire and the adjacent parts of Wiltshire, Hampshire, and Surrey. The name Atrebates means 'settlers' or 'inhabitants'. KB

Attacotti. A British tribe or people. Little is known of the Attacotti, whose name means 'oldest inhabitants', perhaps a reference to their ancient origins. They seem to have inhabited a corner of north-western Britain, most probably the Outer Hebrides, although Ireland and north-west Scotland have also been suggested as their homeland. They are mentioned only in late Roman sources such as Ammianus Marcellinus and St Jerome, amongst whom they had a reputation for savagery. St Jerome, in particular, accused them of cannibalism. According to Ammianus they took part in raids on the province of Britain in AD 365, and two years later joined with other enemies of Rome in the *barbarica conspiratio* which overwhelmed the frontier defences of Britain. Nevertheless by the end of the 4th cent. Attacotti are recorded serving with the Roman army, one unit even being attached to the imperial bodyguard, the *auxilia palatina*. KB

attainder, Acts of. These were unpleasant political weapons whereby the accused was denied a proper trial and the normal laws of evidence could be set aside. In form they were bills of Parliament, passed by both Houses and receiving the royal assent: life, property, and titles were all forfeit. Parliamentary indictment was used against the *Despensers, favourites of Edward II, and during the Wars of the *Roses, Lancastrians and Yorkists in turn used attainders against their opponents. Thomas *Cromwell was attainted in 1540 without being heard in his own defence. The attainder of *Strafford, after his impeachment had broken down, was a crucial episode in the power struggle before the Civil War and Charles I's assent was both imprudent and shabby. In 1689 the Jacobite Parliament at Dublin used attainder wholesale against the supporters of William III. One of the last attainders in England was against Sir John Fenwick for plotting to assassinate William III, but there was uneasiness at the method of proceeding. *Ormond and *Bolingbroke were deprived by Acts of attainder in 1715 after they had fled rather than face impeachments. Accusations which did not demand death, such as the bill against Francis *Atterbury, bishop of Rochester, in 1722, were known as bills of pains and penalties. JAC

Atterbury, Francis (1663–1732). Anglican priest and high-church Tory. A King's Scholar at Westminster school, Atterbury was then educated in the fiercely royalist and high Anglican Christ Church, Oxford, where he became a don. When James II tried to catholicize Oxford University, the leading seminary of the Church of England, Atterbury was prominent in opposition. By 1710 Atterbury was the leading Tory spokesman for the high-church vision of a revitalized Anglican church–state and a strong defender of the rights of *convocation. By the time he became bishop of Rochester and dean of Westminster in 1713, he was of the radical Tory school epitomized by Henry St John (*Bolingbroke). The destruction of the Tory Party after 1715 appalled him. No Jacobite before 1716, he was driven to Jacobite intrigue by one-party tyranny and Whig Erastianism. Detected and exiled by a bill of pains and penalties forced through by *Walpole in 1723, he was a minister of the exiled court until 1728, but long before his death had become totally disillusioned by its incompetence and incorrigible proselytizing. BPL

Attlee, Clement, 1st Earl Attlee (1883–1967). Prime minister. The son of a solicitor, Attlee grew up in a comfortably middle-class environment. He was educated at Haileybury and University College, Oxford, where he read history. Called to the bar in 1905, he forsook the law for a career in social work after viewing poverty at first hand in London's East End. Meanwhile Attlee became committed to socialism, joining the *Fabians in 1907 and the *Independent Labour Party in 1908. He volunteered for military service in the *First World War, fighting with distinction in Gallipoli, Mesopotamia, and France. In later years he retained the title of 'Major', clearly setting himself apart from the strong antimilitarist strain within the Labour movement.

With the war over Attlee became mayor of Stepney and was elected to Parliament as member for Limehouse in 1922. He immediately became parliamentary private secretary to Ramsay *MacDonald and was appointed under-secretary at the War Office in the short-lived Labour government of 1924. Attlee broadened his experience when serving under Sir John *Simon on the Statutory Commission on India after 1927. There he revealed those qualities of moderation, diligence, and attention to detail which were to characterize his political life. He became chancellor of the duchy of Lancaster in November 1930, but was soon promoted to be postmaster-general. When this second Labour government collapsed in the summer of 1931, Attlee refused to follow MacDonald when the latter re-emerged as prime minister of an all-party *National Government.

Ironically, Labour's catastrophic performance in the general election of that year worked to Attlee's advantage. So depleted was the party's front bench that Attlee faced no opposition when the pacifist George *Lansbury was forced out of the leadership in 1935. Even so, it was widely expected that Attlee would be only a stop-gap leader pending the return of some of the party's senior figures to the House of Commons. After the general election of 1935, however, he successfully retained his position in a contest with Herbert *Morrison and Arthur Greenwood. Few imagined that he would hold on to the leadership—without serious challenge—for the next 20 years.

For many Labour activists Attlee's greatest virtue lay in the fact that he was unlikely to follow MacDonald in abusing the office of party leader. Yet it was always easy to underestimate his qualities. He was no orator. Even his private conversation was clipped and uninformative. But Attlee emerged as a consummate politician and expert party manager, capable of controlling difficult and wilful colleagues. During the 1930s he played his part in curbing the excesses of Labour's left and re-establishing Labour as a viable party of government. Attlee was ill at the outbreak of war in September 1939, but in May 1940, following the debate on the ill-fated Norwegian campaign, he made it clear that Labour would not serve in a government headed by Neville *Chamberlain.

Under Winston *Churchill Attlee served successively as lord privy seal, dominions secretary, and lord president. From 1942 he was also designated deputy prime minister and was the most powerful figure on the home front. This certainly gave him more opportunity than Churchill enjoyed—or perhaps desired—to think about the challenges of the post-war world. With the resumption of party politics in the general election of 1945 Attlee was the beneficiary of the mood of popular radicalism which had swept through the electorate during the war years. He emerged as the head of the first majority Labour government in British history.

As prime minister 1945–51 Attlee helped shape the development of British politics, in both the domestic and foreign arenas, for the next quarter-century. The administration presided over a substantial extension of the public ownership of British industry, the development of the welfare state including the creation of the National Health Service, and the establishment of Britain's position within the western alliance. Attlee headed a talented, if not always harmonious, group of senior ministers, which included Ernest *Bevin, Hugh Dalton, and Herbert *Morrison. The overall coherence of the government was testimony to his qualities. Despite considerable difficulties, Labour sustained its public support and never lost a by-election throughout the Parliament.

Though Labour was again victorious in the general election of 1950, its massive majority of 1945 was all but wiped out. Party unity came under severe strain, while the outbreak of the *Korean War imposed new difficulties. The government struggled on but its creative energy was largely exhausted. Conservative tactics in the House of Commons made the business of government difficult and Attlee went to the country again in October 1951. Labour was narrowly defeated and the moment was perhaps opportune for Attlee to resign the leadership. Mounting problems within the party, the emergence of a clear left–right split, and the absence of an obvious successor convinced him that he should carry on. But as leader of the opposition Attlee engaged in little more than an exercise in damage limitation, failing to define a new role for the Labour movement. After a further electoral defeat in 1955, Attlee resigned and went to the House of Lords with an earldom.

A modest man by nature, Attlee came to enjoy great respect from the majority of those who worked under him and the electorate at large. Though the ideas of central planning, state intervention, and welfarism, which dominated his government, have been less in vogue over the last two decades, his historical reputation remains high. Attlee's standing as one of the most successful of peacetime prime ministers this century seems beyond challenge. DJD

Burridge, T., *Clement Attlee* (1985); Harris, K., *Attlee* (1985).

attorney-general. The chief law officer of the crown who acts as the crown's representative in legal proceedings. The origins of the office are disputed but have been attributed to the medieval king's attorney and the king's serjeant. The title attorney-general of England was first used in 1461. The attorney-general acted as assistant to the House of Lords but had ceased to attend by 1700. After some dispute, it was confirmed in 1670 that the attorney-general could be a member of the House of Commons and this has been the case since then. During the 17th cent. the attorney-general was often accused of undue subservience to the monarch and of being over-zealous and overbearing in prosecuting in state trials, as in the notorious prosecution of Sir Walter *Ralegh by *Coke in 1603. The modern attorney-general is a hybrid member of the government in that he is the government's legal adviser and representative, but also has historic functions relating to the administration of the law, e.g. the issue of a *nolle prosequi* to prevent the continuance of a prosecution, the giving of consent to certain prosecutions and the bringing of 'relator actions' on behalf of the public in certain cases, e.g. public nuisance. In these cases he is required to be non-political. MM

Attwood, Thomas (1783–1856). Banker, currency reformer, and founder of the *Birmingham Political Union, Attwood argued that the economic ills of the nation were caused by hard money, and that the cure lay in an abundant supply of paper currency instead of gold. Although now remembered chiefly for his support of parliamentary reform, he always saw this as secondary to the need for a change in monetary policy. Attwood regarded himself as the representative of the Birmingham 'industrious' classes, meaning businessmen, masters, and skilled workers in the small-scale industries of the midlands. This was the basis on which he built the middle–working-class alliance in the BPU in 1830–2, which he attempted (less successfully) to incorporate in 1837 in the early *chartist movement. He was returned for Birmingham in the reformed Parliament of 1832 and wrote continuously on monetary reform from 1816 to 1847. JFCH

Aubrey, John (1626–97). A Wiltshire country gentleman of antiquarian interests, reduced to penury by litigation and imprudence. The only work he published himself was *Miscellanies* (1696), dealing with astrology and the occult, but his copious notes on antiquity and topography were used by others. In 1680 he sent to Anthony à Wood at Oxford his *Minutes of Lives*, sketches mainly of contemporaries. They were not published until 1813 and a full, though bowdlerized, edition waited until 1898. They became a classic of quizzical humour. The best known is his description of Thomas *Hobbes, also from north Wiltshire and, though forty years older, educated by the same schoolmaster. To Aubrey, we owe Hobbes at 40 taking up Euclid's theorems and declaring, '"By God, this is impossible" . . . This made him in love with Geometry.' But the other lives contain vivid glimpses of 17th-cent. characters. Dr Kettell, president of Aubrey's college, Trinity, Oxford, who 'dragged with one foot a little, by which he gave warning (like a rattlesnake) of his coming'; *Prynne, with his 'long, quil cap, which came 2 or 3, at least, inches over his eyes, which served him as an umbrella'; Dr Corbet, bishop of Oxford, at confirmation—'there was a man with a great venerable beard; sayd the Bishop, *You, behind the Beard.*' Aubrey quarrelled with Wood, whose unkind description has something of Aubrey's own vivacity: 'a shiftless person, roving and magotieheaded, and sometimes little better than crazed.' JAC

Auchinleck, Claude (1884–1981). British general and field marshal. Originally an officer in the Indian army, Auchinleck succeeded Wavell as commander-in-chief, Middle East, in July 1941. On 17 November the 8th Army, under Alan Cunningham, attacked westward into Cyrenaica. Rommel counter-attacked on 22 November and Cunningham decided to retreat, but Auchinleck took direct command and replaced Cunningham by Neil Ritchie on 26 November. The 'Crusader' offensive continued, clearing Cyrenaica by 6 January. Rommel counter-attacked again on 21 January and drove the 8th Army back to the Gazala line by 4 February. Churchill felt Auchinleck to be dilatory in offensive action and Rommel struck first in May 1942. The 8th Army was defeated by concentrations of German armour, outflanking ill-coordinated resistance. By mid-June the 8th Army's retreat, with the rapid fall of Tobruk, became near rout. On 25 June Auchinleck took over direct command, organized a defence at El Alamein, and finally stopped Rommel. However, in August, Churchill flew to Cairo, and substituted *Alexander and *Montgomery respectively as C.-in-C. and army commander. Montgomery blackened Auchinleck's reputation by suggesting that he planned further retreat if Rommel resumed serious attacks. Auchinleck ended his career as C.-in-C. of the Indian army. He refused a peerage, distressed by the partition of India. RACP

Auchinleck manuscript. This manuscript, presented to the Advocates' Library by Alexander Boswell of Auchinleck (1744), now in the National Library of Scotland, is one of the most important surviving manuscripts of pre-Chaucerian poetry (assigned 1330–40). Its wide-ranging miscellany of religious and secular material, dominated by metrical romances, is almost entirely in English. ASH

Auckland, George Eden, 1st earl (1784–1849). Auckland was a Whig who served as president of the Board of Trade under *Grey and as 1st lord of the Admiralty under *Melbourne. In 1835, he was appointed governor-general of India. The most important developments of his period in office concerned external relations. He pursued commercial expansion from India into Afghanistan and central Asia. He was responsible for undertaking the first *Afghan War, which initially was prosecuted with success and gained him an earldom. However, incautious policies towards 'the tribes' soon stirred revolt. In the winter of 1841–2, British forces were obliged to retreat and were shot down or frozen to death in the snow. Of 16,000 men who set out from Kabul only one, Dr Brydon, survived beyond the Khyber pass to proclaim himself, famously, 'the army of the Indus'. Lord Auckland was recalled in disgrace in February 1842. DAW

Auckland, William Eden, 1st Baron (1744–1814). Politician and diplomat. A younger son of the well-known Durham family, Eden trained as a lawyer after leaving Oxford. He entered Parliament in 1774 for Woodstock and quickly established himself as a useful man, with a particular interest in economic matters and in penal reform. He was employed by Lord *North in the abortive negotiations in 1778 with the American rebels, served as chief secretary in Ireland from 1780 until 1782, and stayed with North during the coalition. But soon afterwards, he accepted an invitation from *Pitt to negotiate a commercial treaty with France and was pilloried in the *Rolliad* as a chief rat. He was subsequently employed as ambassador to Spain and then Holland, raised to the Irish peerage in 1789 and to the British in 1793. From 1798 until 1804 he served as joint postmaster-general, and during the Ministry of All the Talents was president of the Board of Trade. Eden was a capable man of business and an agreeable companion but acquired a reputation for self-seeking. JAC

Auden, W. H. (1907–73). Poet, essayist, and dramatist, whose name is often given to the literary generation of the 1930s when, it has been said, 'the red flag was intertwined with the old school tie'. After Oxford, time in Berlin offered release and a new perspective on his own society, Marx, Freud, and *Eliot all influencing *Poems* (1930). Yet he was as ready to write 'in praise of limestone', the Icelandic sagas, or simple human love. Intellectually restless, a brilliant chronicler of the times, in 'Spain' (1937) he wrote one of the definitive poems of a 'low, dishonest decade'. On the eve of war he emigrated. American Auden omits the line from 'Spain' about 'the conscious acceptance of guilt in the necessary murder' and the long 'New Year Letter' (1941) shows a new engagement with Christianity. Increasingly the benign man of letters, he wrote the libretto for Stravinsky's *The Rake's Progress* (1951), returning to Oxford four years later as professor of poetry. JNRS

Audley, Thomas, 1st Baron Audley of Walden (1488–1544). Audley was a lawyer from Essex, who became town clerk of Colchester in 1514 and was elected to Parliament for the borough in 1523. He was a member of *Wolsey's household but avoided going down with his master. He succeeded *More as speaker, an influential role in the Reformation Parliament. On More's resignation as chancellor in 1532, Audley was appointed keeper of the great seal and in 1533 lord chancellor. In this capacity he presided over the trials of More, *Fisher, and the accomplices of *Anne Boleyn. In 1538 he was given a barony and he acquired the estates of the abbey of Walden at the *dissolution of the monasteries. In 1540 he received the Garter and saw through the attainder against Thomas *Cromwell. His property passed, via a daughter, to a grandson, created Lord Howard de Walden, then earl of *Suffolk, who built Audley End. Audley's reputation was as a complete time-server and his motto was said to have been 'Had I done nothing I had not been seen; if I had done much, I had not been suffered.' JAC

Audley End (Essex) lies on the river Cam, near Saffron Walden. It was originally Walden abbey and passed at the *dissolution of the monasteries to Lord *Audley. It then descended to Lord *Suffolk, who rebuilt from 1603 onwards. Only half of the original house survives, the rest having been pulled down in 1749. Robert *Adam worked on the interior and built the bridge, and the gardens were landscaped by Capability *Brown. JAC

Aughrim, battle of, 1691. The battle of the *Boyne in July 1690 did not end the conflict in Ireland. The Jacobites held Limerick and Galway and much territory west of the Shannon. The task of subduing them was left to William's Dutch commander, Ginkel, who took Athlone on 30 June 1691 and crossed the Shannon. The Jacobites, under the command of Saint-Ruth, a French nobleman, dug in near Aughrim, defended by bogs, streams, and stone walls. On 12 July Ginkel, with just over 20,000 men, launched his attack against the same number. Heavy fighting continued all day but after Saint-Ruth had been killed the Jacobites broke, losing guns and ammunition. Galway surrendered later in July, Limerick in October. JAC

Augustine, St (d. *c*.604). Prior in the pope's own monastery, Augustine was chosen by Gregory the Great to lead an evangelistic mission to the Anglo-Saxons. On the journey, his companions sent Augustine back to Rome to express their growing apprehension. Gregory returned him with messages of encouragement, and his authority confirmed as their abbot. In 597 they landed on Thanet in Kent, where *Æthelbert was the most powerful king south of the Humber, and his Frankish wife *Bertha was a Christian. Fearing witchcraft, the superstitious Æthelbert received the monks outdoors. Impressed by their sincerity, he supplied them with food, a house in Canterbury, shared use of an old Roman church with Bertha, and permission to preach. *Bede records that the simplicity of their lives and their comforting heavenly message led some to conversion, and Æthelbert himself was ultimately baptized. Augustine returned to Arles, in Gaul, for episcopal consecration, after which he is said to have converted thousands. He established his see in *Canterbury, where he built his church, and outside the walls founded the monastery of SS Peter and Paul (St Augustine's).

Augustine turned to Gregory for instructions on organization, management, and discipline. Gregory advised tolerance of irregularities committed in ignorance, recognized the difficulty of eradicating old customs immediately, and suggested adapting existing festivals and temples for Christian worship. He supplied more personnel, books, relics, and furnishings for the churches, sent an archbishop's pallium for Augustine, and a plan for the organization of all England.

Augustine is perhaps overshadowed by Gregory, perceived apostle of the English, who conceived and directed the mission. Yet Gregory's letters reveal a diligent servant who faced enormous difficulties in securing a new church based on orthodox Roman lines. Although he failed to win the co-operation of British clergy in his few available years, Augustine established Christianity, and introduced to an illiterate Germanic society the influence of Mediterranean civilization, through Latin learning and classical architecture. With him, Æthelbert produced the first written law code, providing for matters secular and ecclesiastical. With Æthelbert's crucial support, he consecrated two bishops, establishing sees at *Rochester in Kent and in East Saxon *London. To secure continuity, he consecrated his successor, *Laurentius, before he died. Although the church suffered early set-backs, it was rooted in Kent where Augustine, first archbishop of Canterbury, established his see and provided training for those who would continue his work. AM

Augustinian canons (or 'Regular' or 'Black' canons) had their origin in the mid-11th-cent. ecclesiastical reform movement. Earlier communities of clerics (or 'canons') staffing cathedrals and large churches and organized (sometimes loosely) in a quasi-monastic rule had long existed, and following the Carolingian reform many observed the mid-8th-cent. rule of Chrodegang of Metz. This had largely fallen into disuse by the 11th cent. and reformed canons, particularly in southern France, Italy, and Germany, increasingly adopted a rule based on that drawn up for communities founded by St Augustine of Hippo (354–430). This was usually expanded by local communities, and in the 12th cent. some versions were as ascetic in character as that of the *Cistercians. Many, though not all, Augustinian priories were sited in towns, particularly in continental Europe, where their canons fulfilled a wide range of roles, serving in parish churches and cathedrals, running hospitals (such as St Bartholomew's, London), and functioning as teachers. They were perhaps the most ubiquitous of all monasteries in the medieval world, appealing to a wide cross-section of lay patrons. In England, where the first truly Augustinian priory was founded at Colchester *c.*1100, they tended to be more contemplative, often emerging from communities of hermits, being sited in remote places, and were barely distinguishable from the reformed *Benedictines, such as the Cistercians. The majority of English foundations were made in the first half of the 12th cent.: many were small, but some, like Leicester or Cirencester, retained their prosperity and prestige till the *dissolution. BJG

Augustinian (or Austin) **friars** were founded by Pope Alexander IV in 1256 from a number of small hermit communities in Italy. They were given the rule of St Augustine of Hippo (see AUGUSTINIAN CANONS) which the *Dominicans, whose constitution they largely followed, also observed. Though they were a mendicant order they continued some eremetical observances and their first foundations were located away from towns. Soon, however, they established themselves in urban areas and in England, where their first community was founded in 1248–9 at Clare, by the *dissolution they were found in nearly 40 places, usually substantial towns or ports, such as Grimsby, Hull, and King's Lynn, as well as Oxford and Cambridge. The Cambridge house was a centre of the early Reformation in England, and Luther was an Augustinian friar at Erfurt. BJG

Auld Alliance. See FRANCO-SCOTTISH ALLIANCE.

Auldearn, battle of, 1645. *Montrose was unable to follow up his great victory at *Inverlochy in February 1645 when many of his followers returned home. The campaign resumed the pattern of march and counter-march. This time a covenanting army under Sir John Hurry tried to surprise Montrose on 9 May at Auldearn, east of Nairn. The issue was decided by a spirited cavalry counter-attack by the Gordons and Hurry fled to Inverness. JAC

Aulus Plautius was the general commanding the Roman invasion of Britain in AD 43. Consul in 29, he had probably governed the military province of Pannonia on the middle Danube; experience together with political and family influence made him a suitable choice for *Claudius' British expedition. After a delay caused by the troops' fear of Britain as the island beyond Ocean, the invasion was successfully mounted with four legions and an equivalent number (*c.*20,000) of auxiliary troops. The major settlement at Camulodunum (*Colchester) surrendered in the presence of the emperor. By the time Plautius left Britain in 47, the greater part of the island south-east of the Humber–Severn line was under Roman control. On his return to Rome he was accorded an *ovatio* (a lesser form of triumph), the last recorded instance of this ceremony. ASEC

Auray, battle of, 1364. Sir John *Chandos, who had fought at *Crécy and *Poitiers, was engaged in 1364 in supporting the claims of John de Montfort to the duchy of Brittany against those of Charles de Blois. On 27 September, while besieging Auray, he was attacked by Bertrand du Guesclin. The French were defeated, Blois killed, and du Guesclin captured. JAC

Austen, Jane (1775–1817). Country parson's daughter who became one of England's best-loved novelists. As she says in *Emma* (1816), 'one half of the world cannot understand the pleasures of the other', and for some, minute attention to nuances of bygone manners makes her simple romances vapidly parochial. For others, her awareness of the realities of money and class and their bearing on human happiness will always be compelling. Though she rejected suggestions to try her hand at historical subjects, confident that '3 or 4 families in a Country Village is the very thing to work on', it is misleading to think of her as a miniaturist. The Napoleonic wars occupy her only in letters from her sailor brothers, and she is less consciously concerned with the condition of England than novelists later in the century, but her penetration and seriousness reflect an admiration for Dr *Johnson. He could not have matched the sprightly ironic comedy of *Pride and Prejudice* (1813) but would have appreciated the more sombre moral dilemmas of *Mansfield Park* (1814). Three years later, still unmarried, she was dead, leaving her sister Cassandra to supervise the publication of *Northanger Abbey* and *Persuasion* (1818). JNRS

Austin, Herbert (1866–1941). Motor car manufacturer. Austin served his engineering apprenticeship at Langlands Foundry, Melbourne. He became manager of the Wolseley Sheep Shearing Company and in 1893 returned to England to work for the company in Birmingham. He was one of the first British engineers to envisage the possibilities of the petrol-driven car and built his first three-wheeled Wolseley car in 1895. In 1905 he went into business for himself as the Austin Motor Company Ltd. at a 2.5-acre site at Longbridge, Birmingham. By the following year he produced 120 cars with a work-force of 270. Invention, design, and technical skill were Austin's strengths. The Austin Seven (Baby Austin), launched in 1922, brought motoring within the means of the masses. Along with the Austin Twenty (1919) and the Twelve (1921), these models enabled the company to survive the difficult post-war period and expand. By 1939 the company employed 20,000 people and produced 76,482 cars on a 200-acre site. RAS

Australia, Commonwealth of. A federation of six states, *New South Wales (founded 1788), Western Australia (1829), Tasmania (formerly Van Diemen's Land, 1825), South Australia (1834), Victoria (1851), and Queensland (1859) and the self-governing Northern Territory (1863), together with Australian Capital Territory (1911), Norfolk (1856), Heard and McDonald (1947), Cocos (1955), Christmas (1958), and Coral Sea (1969) Islands, and the Australian Antarctic Territory (1933).

Australia is the smallest, most arid, and least populated of the world's continents. Its mainland, together with Tasmania, is nearly 3 million square miles—i.e. 35 times the size of Great Britain—and had a population of 18 million in 1991. Australia took its name from the mythical Southern Continent first postulated by classical geographers, *Terra Australis Incognita*. First sighted by Portuguese and Spanish navigators during the late 15th cent., it became known through 17th- and 18th-cent. Dutch, British, and later French voyages.

Australia's Aboriginal people entered the country more than 40,000 years ago across a land-bridge created during a low sea-level period. They greatly modified the Australian environment by the extensive use of fire and hunting to extinction of its mega-fauna, and developed a distinctive way of life centred around hunting and gathering, in which women and children played a key role. Aborigines gave animate and inanimate things quasi-religious properties and their cultures revolved round a seasonal cycle of life, whose origins were explained by a creation known (in translation) as the Dream Time. Completely isolated from the rest of the world, Aborigines developed a strong attachment to and intimate knowledge of the land (which they regarded as Mother). Although they appeared to have no socio-political system, they developed a complex web of social, lineal, and trade relations, which could extend over large areas. Estimates put their population at the time of the coming of the British at 500,000.

The modern era began with the arrival on 26 January 1788 of the 1st Fleet of eleven vessels under the command of Captain Arthur Phillip RN, who took formal possession of land already named New South Wales and claimed on Britain's behalf in 1770 by Captain James *Cook. Extending westward as far as longitude east 135 degrees (extended to 129 degrees E. in 1834), New South Wales, with Sydney its capital, excluded New Holland, known to the Dutch East India Company from about 1610, but thought of little value. The British began to occupy New Holland in 1827, and with the formal possession and change of name to Western Australia and the founding of the Swan River Colony under Captain Stirling RN in 1829, Britain laid claim to the whole of the continent. New South Wales, the first colony, was subsequently divided into five separate colonies.

Britain's decision in 1786 to occupy New South Wales was partly to compensate for the loss of the American colonies to which unwanted convicts (some 50,000 before the *Declaration of Independence in 1776) had been sent; and partly to protect Britain's control of the sea route to Asia via the Southern Ocean.

On arrival at *Botany Bay on 18 January 1788, Captain Phillip, finding it less fertile than he had anticipated, sailed a few miles into Port Jackson (now Sydney Harbour), where, on 26 January, he commenced landing 736 convicts (including 188 women) along with a military guard of 210 officers and men. He was followed by the commercially organized 2nd and 3rd Fleets, which embarked a further 3,100 convicts, of whom nearly 300 died from maltreatment during the voyage. The transportation of convicts to New South Wales ceased in 1840, to Van Diemen's Land in 1853 (shortly afterwards renamed Tasmania), and to Norfolk Island in 1855. Between 1850 and 1868, 10,000 convicts were shipped as a subsidy to poverty-stricken Western Australia, making a grand total of 160,000 convicts transported before 1868. Convictism's real legacy is Australia's distinctively authoritarian executive-style government. The Aborigines offered no effective resistance to the British who, presuming them to be 'savages', applied the principle of *vacuum domicilium* (or *terra nullius*) which accorded the Aborigines a natural but not a civil right to the land.

The early days of New South Wales were under near famine conditions and the colony was not self-sufficient in wheat until 1797. Free settlers were loathe to emigrate to such a distant land because it lacked a staple product and was tainted by convictism. However, the crossing of the Blue Mountains behind Sydney in 1813 revealed a belt of millions of acres of rich savannah grasslands. Here, flocks of fine wool-bearing merino sheep (first imported from the Cape Colony in 1797) spread out and by 1880 it supported over 60 million sheep. The export of wool provided the staple upon which to found a viable economy, helped end convict transportation, and created a new class of politically powerful and capitalist large-landholding squatters (graziers).

Exploration by sea from Sydney had already established that Tasmania was an island (George Bass, 1796) and a later circumnavigation (Matthew Flinders, 1803) established the true extent of the Australian continent. Inland exploration was initially directed toward the discovery of a supposed inland sea and new grasslands (Charles Sturt, 1830 and 1845; Hamilton Hume and William Hovell, 1824; and Thomas Mitchell, 1836). Later explorations culminated in a series of trans-Australian expeditions, the most famous of which were E. J. Eyre (1851), L. Leichhardt (1844–5), Augustus Gregory (1855–6), John McDouall Stuart (1860–2), R. O'H. Burke and W. J. Wills (1861), and John Forrest (1874).

The discovery of gold in 1851 caused a dramatic leap in immigration and the combined population of New South Wales and Victoria rose from 267,000 in 1850 to 886,000 in 1860; 538,000 were located in the newly proclaimed colony of Victoria. Melbourne, its capital, rapidly became Australia's financial and industrial centre. A miners' revolt at Eureka Stockade near Ballarat in 1854 eventually forced the introduction of democratic reforms far in advance of those in England. These included the adoption of secret ballot (1856), adult male franchise (1857), paid parliamentarians (1870), and eventually votes for women (1908). The electoral power of the surplus population created by the gold rushes led to the breakup of the squatters' vast landholdings into family-operated cereal, hay, and dairy farms 1869–91.

After the repeal of the British *Corn Laws in 1846, South Australians began to develop 'dry-land' wheat farming technologies in the 1850s. These were later adopted by new-land farmers in Victoria and New South Wales. Land clearing boomed, using rollers (Mullenizing, invented 1868), the stump plough (1876), harvesters (strippers, 1835), and with the introduction of refrigerated shipping (1882) came the export of dairy products and fresh meat to Britain.

The gold rushes and the rise of agriculture encouraged commerce, finance, trade, and industry in Sydney and Melbourne, the latter growing to more than half a million by 1900. The spread of wage labour in mines, factories, ports, and shearing sheds saw the rise of trade unionism during the 1870s. The defeat of the great strikes of 1888–95 led to the setting-up of union-backed Labour parties. The first, but short-lived, minority Labour governments took office in Queensland in 1899, and federally in 1904.

The 1880s was an era of reckless bank lending, and even more reckless borrowing by the land boomers. The inevitable bank crash of 1893 caused great distress and unemployment and also brought to an end 'marvellous Melbourne'. The discovery of gold in Western Australia (Coolgardie, 1892, and Kalgoorlie, 1893) partly alleviated the recession.

The latter part of the 19th cent. was also a highly formative period for Australian culture: the founding of universities (Sydney, 1850; Melbourne, 1853; Adelaide, 1874; Tasmania, 1890); the writing of Australian novels and poetry, among them works by Henry Lawson (1867–1922); the beginnings of Australian science and technology (Australasian Association for the Advancement of Science, Sydney, 1888); the development of Australian-rules football (first game 1858) and of Australian prowess in sport (the 'Ashes', 1882).

Following a series of meetings during the 1890s, six colonies agreed by referendum to become a federation. This was inaugurated on 1 January 1901 as the Commonwealth of Australia under a written constitution, based on that of the USA. One of the Commonwealth government's first acts was to introduce the so-called 'White Australia policy' to protect the Australian working man's standard of living. The outbreak of the First World War in 1914 severely tested the new federation. An Australian Imperial Force (AIF) comprising 330,000 troops was sent overseas to fight alongside the allies, of whom 60,000 died or were killed in action. The period between the First and Second World Wars was at first prosperous with assisted British immigration until development was stopped by the Great Depression of the 1930s. At times, unemployment exceeded 25 per cent of the work-force. Australia's support for British empire preference helped maintain her exports to Britain. High gold prices, a devalued Australian currency, and the introduction of tariffs, subsidies, and marketing boards to protect local industry and primary producers may have staved off an even worse calamity, but Australia's dependence upon overseas capital and markets remained unchanged.

With the fall of Singapore in 1942, the withdrawal of the British to India, and the Japanese invasion of Papua New Guinea, the Second World War came to the shores of Australia with the bombing of Darwin. Wartime Labour Prime Minister John Curtin turned to America for military help. Australian forces played an important part in the Pacific War and were the first to defeat the Japanese on land in the battle for New Guinea (Kokoda).

After 1945, the wartime industrialization of Australia was continued behind tariff walls. The nationalization and welfare state ambitions of the governing Australian Labour Party were brought to a halt with the Australian High Court's rejection of the ALP's Bank Nationalization Act (1948) as unconstitutional, and the electoral success of Robert Menzies and his conservative coalition government in 1949. The coalition governed in times of increasing prosperity until defeated by the ALP in 1972 under the leadership of Gough Whitlam in a revolt against the conservatism and alleged uniformity of the Menzies era. The Menzies era (he served as prime minister until 1966) was one of the *embourgeoisement* of urban Australia involving the spread of the suburban family owner-occupied house (the 'quarter acre block') and car ownership.

Post-war mass European immigration, assisted by the Labour government, was made possible by an assured British market, a high Australian tariff wall, a 1960s boom in mining, especially for bauxite and iron ore, and the discovery of new reserves of petroleum, natural gas, and coal. 500,000 European immigrants, one-third from the British Isles, came to Australia 1945–9. Immigration peaked at 170,000 in 1952. The balance shifted toward Asian migration after the end of the war in Vietnam in 1972, whence Australia had accepted more than 100,000 refugees. Australia's population, which had passed the million mark by 1860 and the 5 million mark by 1920, was by 1970 more than 12.5 million.

Under the Whitlam Labour government (1972–5) tariffs were reduced and some economic reforms introduced. But the government ended in turmoil, was dismissed by the governor-general, Sir John Kerr, in 1975 and replaced after a general election by a coalition (Liberal and Country Party) under the leadership of Malcolm Fraser (1975–83). The Whitlam government's initiatives in Aboriginal affairs (already made full citizens by referendum in 1966), heritage, environment, family law, and health care were continued by the new government.

Despite massive majorities, the Fraser government was thought indecisive and, because of Kerr's action, regarded by some as lacking legitimacy. Labour was returned to power in 1983 under the leadership of former labour union leader, Robert Hawke. Replaced by his rival and federal treasurer Paul Keating in 1992, Hawke's government sought accord with the labour unions, introduced a programme of financial and industrial deregulation, improved health and welfare, superintended the 200th anniversary of the British settlement of Australia, and failed in its attempt to change the constitution.

The rise of a new nationalism, epitomized by Whitlam's recognition of China and North Vietnam, and his tour of Asian countries, the Fraser government's multi-cultural initiatives, and Hawke's celebration of the winning of the America's Cup in 1983, sought to include the new Asia-Pacific and multi-cultural horizon. Keating took the new nationalism further by forging closer links with Asia and pushing his republican ideas. He was returned to office in 1993 when coalition leader John Hewson failed to convince the people of the need to introduce a goods and services tax. Keating, with his self-proclaimed republican 'big picture vision' for Australia, his polemical style, and what was believed to be his arrogance, was roundly defeated in the 1996 election by a John Howard-led coalition. The 1996 election represented the third occasion (the others in 1949 and 1975) on which a reformist Labour government, often using ideas taken from the conservatives (deregulation and market economics being most recent), had been rejected by an electorate saturated with change.

Australia looks west to Europe, east to the USA, and north to her burgeoning Asian neighbours. Although now officially multi-cultural, Australia has still not resolved her relation with her own indigenous people, the Aborigines. The granting of native title by federal law in 1993 will in the long run markedly change the position of Aborigines, but unlike Australia's European and Asian immigrants, a high proportion of the nearly 300,000 Aboriginal people are still both culturally and geographically 'fringe dwellers'.

With the rise of the new industrializing countries of east Asia, Australia's relative industrial and economic strength has dramatically declined. Australia has yet to face the fact, for example, that personal incomes in Singapore are on a par with those of an Australian worker. Furthermore, since Australia no longer has preferential access to European markets, it is now in direct competition with other primary raw material producers. Though retaining all the political, organizational and governmental structures inherited from Britain, Australia is no longer the Anglo-Celtic culture that she was before 1945. MJW

Blainey, G., *The Rush that Never Ended: A History of Australian Mining* (Melbourne, 1963); Blainey, G., *The Tyranny of Distance: How Distance Shaped Australia's History* (Melbourne, 1966); Elder, B. (ed.), *Great Events in Australia's History* (Frenchs Forest, 1988); Molony, J., *The Penguin History of Australia* (Ringwood, 1987).

Austria, relations with. At the end of the First World War, the Austro-Hungarian empire, which had fought alongside Germany, was dismembered by the treaty of *Saint-Germain-en-Laye. Austria was reduced to a state of just over six millions, one-third of whom lived in Vienna—'a pathetic relic' in Harold Nicolson's words. Many Austrians concluded that only union with Germany—Anschluss—could make a viable state, but this was specifically forbidden by the treaty of *Versailles. The new state suffered severe economic and financial difficulties. A plan in 1931 for a customs union with Germany was vetoed by France and the subsequent collapse of the Creditanstalt bank helped to precipitate the world economic crisis. In 1934 the Austrian Chancellor Dollfuss, who had suppressed the Social Democrat opposition and taken emergency powers, was murdered by Austrian Nazis. Austria was briefly protected by Mussolini's Italy, but Mussolini's stock fell after the inglorious invasion of Abyssinia and he was obliged to come to terms with Hitler, who had made the Anschluss his top priority. In March 1938 when Dollfuss's successor, Schuschnigg, announced a plebiscite on union with Germany, Hitler sent in troops. Anthony *Eden, British foreign secretary, resigned over Chamberlain's insistence on trying to conciliate Mussolini and the British ambassador in Berlin, Sir Neville Henderson, could scarcely be persuaded to make even a token protest: 'I was always convinced that Austria was bound to become part of Germany in some form sooner or later. Austria is now eliminated and without bloodshed,' he wrote. A plebiscite, conducted under Hitler's auspices, produced a 99 per cent vote for union.

During the Second World War the British government considered the possibility of Austria as part of a post-war confederation to remedy its economic isolation but was frustrated by the Soviet Union. After the war, Austria was reconstituted with its 1937 boundaries and occupied by the four allies for ten years. A peace treaty was postponed until 1955, when Austria was declared a neutral power and joined the United Nations. Its political stability, in contrast to the pre-war position, was remarkable, but the search for economic breadth continued. In 1959 it joined EFTA which, as an economic bloc, did not infringe Austrian neutrality, and in 1973, when Britain joined the EEC, Austria negotiated associated status. In 1995 Austria joined the EEC. JAC

Austrian Succession, War of the. Most of western Europe was plunged into war through Frederick the Great's invasion of Austrian Silesia in December 1740 (though Britain was already fighting the War of *Jenkins's Ear with Spain). There followed eight years of continental and colonial warfare that killed half a million people. The European fighting took place in three theatres, the Low Countries, Italy, and central Europe. Spain and France were closely allied, with periodic links to Prussia. Britain, Piedmont-Sardinia, the United Provinces, and Austria were ranged against them. British, Austrian, and Dutch troops, often under the duke of *Cumberland's command, fought against the French in the Low Countries. George II himself fought at *Dettingen (1743), but before the peace of *Aix-la-Chapelle in 1748, the French army had thrust deep into Dutch territory. In Italy, Britain provided financial and naval support for the Austrians and Piedmont-Sardinians against a Franco-Spanish army seeking to carve a kingdom for Don Philip of Spain. In central Europe, British money helped Maria Theresa in her fight for the territorial survival of Austria against the powerful onslaughts of France and Prussia. At sea Britain was triumphant, the French navy having been destroyed by late 1747, largely due to the skill of *Anson and *Hawke. This placed the French economy under great strain by barring access to her colonies. In India the French had moderate success, but in America the British predominated, capturing the fort of Louisbourg in June 1745.

At home, the war helped to end the career of *Walpole and assisted the rise of *Carteret. The suggestion that Britain was supporting others for little gain was used by the *Pelham brothers to oust Carteret in 1744, but the policy of subsidizing allies continued. Apart from the Jacobite rising of 1745–6, the conflict seemed remote to the British people and was not a 'popular war' in the manner of the *Seven Years War. Its inconclusiveness demonstrated its futility. AIL

Authorized Version. See BIBLE.

Avon was a new county, formed under the Local Government Act of 1972. It was based upon Bristol, Bath, and

Weston-super-Mare, but incorporated a slice of Gloucestershire, including Sodbury, Thornbury, and Marshfield, and a part of north Somerset, including Clevedon, Chew Magna, Radstock, Midsomer Norton, and Steep Holme. The name was taken from the river Avon, which runs through Bath and Bristol. There was considerable opposition to the proposal, particularly from Somerset. The county town was Bristol. Avon was abolished in 1996. JAC

Avranches, compromise of. On 21 May 1172, at Avranches cathedral (Normandy), Henry II was publicly absolved by papal legates from complicity in the murder of Archbishop Thomas *Becket on condition that he provide 200 knights to serve in the Holy Land for one year, take the cross himself and fight either in the Holy Land or against the Moors in Spain, restore all properties seized from the church of Canterbury, allow appeals from the English church to Rome, and abolish all evil customs prejudicial to the church which he had introduced. The agreement paved the way for the re-establishment of sound relations between church and state in England after the Becket affair. SL

Aylesbury case. This was a protracted legal wrangle which led to a dispute between the two Houses of Parliament. Matthew Ashby, a Whig elector at Aylesbury in 1700, was prevented by the mayor from voting. He took his case to the House of Lords, which supported him: the House of Commons then insisted that it was the sole judge of election matters. The rivalry between the two houses was exacerbated by party feeling, the Whigs being strong in the House of Lords. The matter was unresolved when Parliament was prorogued. JAC

Babbage, Charles (1792–1871) Babbage made the first (clockwork) computers. He studied mathematics at Peterhouse, Cambridge, and in 1828 was elected to the Lucasian chair of mathematics, which *Newton had earlier held. Meanwhile Babbage had been one of a group including John *Herschel and William *Whewell who had brought the Cambridge syllabus up to date. He hoped to eliminate errors in mathematical tables by calculating and printing them mechanically, and in 1834 oversaw the construction of his difference engine. Before it was finished, he saw how much more powerful it would be as an analytical engine, but the government cut off finance: the principles were later realized electronically. He was an irascible man, writing on *The Decline of Science in England* (1830), and in 1837 a *Bridgewater Treatise* in which the world was a great computer programmed by God. DK

Babington plot, 1586. Anthony Babington (1561–86), a Derbyshire gentleman and a catholic page in Mary Stuart's service in England, was contacted by John Ballard, a catholic priest. The plan involved twelve men, six of whom were detailed to kill Elizabeth; the others, with Spanish and papal help, were to secure the freedom of Mary. Babington's failure was engineered by Sir Francis *Walsingham, who recruited a catholic, Gilbert Gifford, as an agent. Trusted by Babington and his fellow-conspirators, Gifford's job was to pass messages, hidden in a beer barrel, from Mary to the French ambassador: in fact the whole network was set up by Walsingham, who read the notes in transit. Babington was executed in September 1586. The plot sealed the fate of Mary by convincing Elizabeth that she was incorrigible. SA

Bacon, Francis, 1st Baron Verulam, 1st Viscount St Albans (1561–1626). Lawyer, philosopher, and essayist. The son of a prominent lawyer, Bacon went to Trinity College, Cambridge, and then to the Inns of Court. In constant need of money, in 1584 he became an MP. In the course of his public career, he prosecuted the earl of *Essex, his former patron: he became much disliked. On the accession of James I Bacon achieved rapid promotion, prosecuting *Ralegh, raised to the peerage, and ending up as lord chancellor. But in 1621 he was convicted of taking bribes, and though soon pardoned and released, he had to give up public life.

His witty and pithy *Essays* were first published in 1597, and are splendid examples of English prose; and in 1605 he brought out his *Advancement of Learning*. In this first exercise in writing about science, he was highly critical of the humanistic education he had received at Cambridge, and saw classical texts as flotsam carried down on the river of time. He believed that the Bible and the Book of Nature were, rightly understood, compatible; and that scientific knowledge properly applied would bring us back to the state of Adam and Eve in the garden of Eden. In 1620 he published his *Novum organum*, presenting his philosophy of science in the form of aphorisms, many of them striking and memorable. In retirement, he collected and published information of a rather miscellaneous kind, in what was to be the *Great Instauration*: his title-pages indicate that he saw himself as an intellectual Columbus, revealing the new world of science to his contemporaries, and bringing back ships freighted with useful knowledge. He died a martyr to science, from a chill caught trying to preserve a chicken by stuffing it with snow. After his death, the fragmentary *New Atlantis* was published in 1627: with its vision of an island governed by an Academy of Sciences, founded 'for the knowledge of causes, and secret motions of things; and the enlarging the bounds of human empire, to the effecting of all things possible'. This is the most accessible and exciting of his writings on science.

Bacon is an important figure in the *scientific revolution; Robert *Boyle and other founders of the *Royal Society saw themselves as his disciples. His was a cautious experimental method, the mind being cleared of preconceptions or 'idols' and proceeding by induction and generalization to the discovery of causes or 'forms'. He was sceptical about mathematics, as Aristotle had been; and was similarly doubtful about the motion of the earth, and the atomic theory. He was scornful about his contemporary William *Gilbert, who had done careful studies of magnetism. Galileo praised Copernicus for defying common sense; Bacon's science was organized common sense; and his vision of utility was gripping.

Britain's industrial revolution did indeed depend upon this kind of thinking, but the systematic application of science was a feature only of the 19th cent., for example with Humphry *Davy. Britons in the 1790s saw Baconian science as safe; the French *philosophes* had been led into dangerous speculation, and had brought atheism and revolution upon their country. Baconian induction lay behind the public health measures of the 19th cent., and John Stuart *Mill sought to formalize his methods in his *System of Logic* of 1843. All efforts to show that inductive inference can bring certainty seem, however, to have failed; and in the 20th cent., while Baconian induction has often been taught to schoolchildren as 'the scientific method', it has been out of favour amongst philosophers of science. Nevertheless, we can appreciate his vision of the scientist not as a spider, which spins webs; nor as an ant, which rushes around seizing upon everything; but as a bee, which collects nectar and turns it laboriously into honey. DK

Bacon, Sir Nicholas (1510–79). Statesman. Nicholas Bacon, a great work-horse of Elizabeth's government, owed his rise in part to college friendship. He came from Suffolk and was at Corpus Christi College, Cambridge, with Matthew *Parker, afterwards archbishop of Canterbury. Later, he formed a friendship with William Cecil (*Burghley), whose wife's sister he married in 1553. He read law at Gray's Inn and was employed on the *dissolution of the monasteries: though his suggestion of an academy for statesmen was not followed up, he managed to acquire a number of estates for himself. He served as MP for Westmorland (1542) and for Dartmouth (1545). From 1540 to 1547 he was solicitor to the Court of Augmentations and from 1547 to 1561 attorney to the Court of *Wards. Though a protestant, sympathetic towards puritanism, he survived Mary's reign without disaster. Bacon's boat came in, with that of his two friends, at Elizabeth's accession. Cecil was reappointed secretary of state in November 1558, Bacon became keeper of the great seal in December 1558, and Parker archbishop of Canterbury in 1559. Bacon was capable of offering independent advice and increasingly hostile towards Mary, queen of Scots. He received Elizabeth frequently at his house at Gorhambury, completed in 1568. Fat and cheerful, he was also efficient and honest. Elizabeth's reluctance to grant peerages presumably deprived Bacon of that honour, though he was knighted in 1558. His son Francis *Bacon, lawyer and scholar, was created Baron Verulam in 1618 and Viscount St Albans in 1621. JAC

Bacon, Roger (*c.*1214–92). Philosopher. A Franciscan friar, much of Bacon's life is obscure, but he was born in Somerset and probably studied at Oxford before teaching in Paris. From *c.*1250–7 he was again in Oxford but his Franciscan superiors returned him to Paris, where he was under a cloud and in confinement. In 1265 Pope Clement IV asked him to prepare a treatise on the knowledge of the day. This high patronage did not last, for Clement died in 1268, and Bacon was soon in trouble again. His *Opus majus*, dating from the 1260s, attacked authority and sophistry and has been hailed as a foundation work in modern science. Bacon laid stress on useful knowledge, on ascertaining facts, and on the need for experimentation. He proved that air is necessary for combustion, and his prophecies included flight and submarine travel. His work in alchemy gained him a popular reputation as a magician, exploited by Robert Greene in *Friar Bacon and Friar Bungay* (*c.*1590). This showed Bacon at Brasenose College making a brazen head which would prophesy, 'read a lecture in philosophy', and build a brazen wall to keep England safe. JAC

Baden-Powell, Robert (1857–1941). Founder of the *Boy Scouts. Baden-Powell joined the army in 1876 and specialized in reconnaissance and scouting. In 1897 he was appointed to command the 5th Dragoon Guards stationed in India. He used the opportunity to develop scouting training methods based on powers of observation, deduction, and initiative. He explained his methods in *Aids to Scouting* (1899). During the Boer War he took part in the defence of *Mafeking. His improvisation and organization helped the British to hold out for 217 days against overwhelming forces. Mafeking was relieved on 17 May 1900 to wild rejoicing in London and Baden-Powell returned to England a popular hero. He was made inspector-general of the cavalry in 1903 and from 1908 held a post with the Territorials. He retired from the army in 1910 to devote his energies to the Boy Scout movement he had founded several years earlier. He was awarded the OM in 1937. RAS

badminton took its name from the Gloucestershire seat of the dukes of Beaufort, where it is believed to have evolved in the 1870s from the older game of shuttlecock. It was much played in the Indian army and rules were drawn up in Poona. A Badminton Association was founded in 1893, an Irish Union in 1899, a Scottish in 1911, and a Welsh in 1928. An International Federation was formed in 1934. The convenience of a vigorous and sociable under-cover game led to its rapid spread, particularly in Scandinavia and the Far East. JAC

Baffin, William (d. 1622). Explorer. Baffin, believed to be a Londoner, made a number of voyages in the 1610s looking for the North-West Passage. His measurements and observations were remarkably accurate. He was killed in India in a skirmish with the Portuguese. In 1821 the large island he had discovered to the north of Hudson Bay was named after him. JAC

Bagehot, Walter (1826–77). Journalist. From a banking family in Langport (Som.), his father a unitarian, Bagehot attended University College, London, and began to study law. But he moved into banking, wrote copiously, particularly for the *National Review*, and from 1860 edited his father-in-law James Wilson's paper *The Economist*. Though capable of brilliant writing and subtle insights, much of Bagehot's work is marred by a habitual superciliousness towards the 'stupid' masses and his inability to resist a *bon mot*. His best-known work, *The English Constitution*, which came out in the 1860s, was enormously successful and seriously misleading. Written at the time of Victoria's seclusion after Albert's death, it is understandable that Bagehot should have underestimated both the weakness of the monarchy and its non-party character: 'the queen must sign her own death warrant if the two Houses unanimously send it up to her' is more piquant than profound. The distinction between the efficient and the dignified parts of the constitution, so much admired, was hardly novel, and the suggestion that the only rights the monarch had were to 'be consulted, encourage and warn' is too pat. But since the book became recommended reading for George V and George VI when princes, it helped to establish the position it claimed to describe. G. M. Young thought Bagehot 'the wisest man of his generation', but a less respectful commentator called him merely 'a television man before his time'. JAC

Baginbun, battle of, 1170. In 1169 Richard de Clare, earl of *Pembroke, known as Strongbow, decided to seek territory in Ireland. A small advance party commanded by Raymond le Gros dug in on the coast at Baginbun Head, between Hook Head and Wexford, and was attacked by a vastly superior force of Norsemen and Irish. The invaders were successful. Strongbow then joined them, took Waterford and Dublin, and declared himself king of Leinster. The first English foothold in Ireland had been obtained. JAC

Bahamas. These islands lie off the coast of Florida and form an independent state within the Commonwealth. The larger islands include Grand Bahama and Andros: the capital, Nassau, is situated on New Providence Island. Their strategic position covering the entrance to the Gulf of Mexico gave them more than local importance. The economy depends greatly on tourism and on the large mercantile fleet flying the Bahamian flag. The queen is head of state and appoints the governor-general. Originally sighted by Columbus, they were first claimed by Spain and then, in the 17th cent., colonized by English settlers, some of them from Bermuda. For decades they remained bases for pirates. Some of the islands changed hands during the *American War of Independence but were restored to Britain in 1783. The duke of Windsor was governor during the Second World War. JAC

Baillie, Robert (1599–1662). Cleric. Baillie was born in Glasgow and educated at the university there. Appointed to a living at Kilwinning in Ayrshire, he took part in the Glasgow Assembly, protested against *Arminian innovations, and served with the army of the *covenant. In 1642 he was appointed professor of divinity at Glasgow and rapidly became one of the leading presbyterian spokesmen. He represented the Scottish kirk at the *Westminster Assembly and was dismayed at the Erastianism and tolerance of many of the English. *Cromwell he thought lax and that his power should be broken: the independents, shockingly, 'expressed themselves for toleration not only to themselves, but to other sects'. But, with the cunning of the righteous, Baillie wrote of the independents: 'we purpose not to meddle in haste, till it please God to advance our army, which we expect will much assist our arguments.' Later, Baillie became a leader of the *resolutionists. In 1660 he declined a bishopric but was appointed principal of Glasgow University. His *Letters and Journals* have been much used. JAC

Baird, John Logie (1888–1946). Television inventor. Baird came from Helensburgh (Dumbartonshire) and studied electrical engineering at Glasgow University. In poor health, he moved to Hastings in 1922, where he experimented with a crude home-made transmitting apparatus. By 1925 he was able to demonstrate shadowy television in Selfridge's store and followed with a public demonstration to members of the Royal Institution. His machine is preserved in the Science Museum at south Kensington. In 1927 he formed his own company. An experimental BBC television service was started in 1929 and regular broadcasts from Alexandra palace in 1936. Baird was greatly disappointed that, after trials, the service used a rival high-definition transmitting system, developed by Marconi-EMI. In 1937 the Cup Final and in 1938 the Boat Race were shown on television, but when the service closed down at the start of the Second World War, there were still only 20,000 sets in use. JAC

Bakewell, Robert (1725–95). Bakewell was considered by Lord Ernle to be one of the pioneers of the agricultural revolution as a result of his animal breeding activities at Dishley, near Loughborough, particularly the 'New Leicester' breed of sheep. The principle of selective breeding was known before Bakewell began his experiments in 1745, and his work was not unique. However, he gained considerable contemporary prominence because he was solely a specialist breeder. He is thought to have borrowed the pedigree concept from racehorse trainers. He selected more rigorously than other landlords and was more sophisticated in the choice of animals he selected from. Earlier breeders had lacked his foresight and patience, and had not enjoyed the resources to breed exclusively from the finest animals. Bakewell also played an important role in cattle breeding, and by applying the same principles that had given him success with the New Leicesters he developed the New Longhorn. JVB

Balaclava, battle of, 1854. On 25 October 1854 the Russian commander in the Crimea, Menshikov, attempted to lift the siege of Sebastopol by attacking with 25,000 troops towards the British base at Balaclava. The 'thin red line' of 93rd Highlanders repulsed a charge by Russian cavalry. This was followed by a successful attack on the main body of the Russian horse by the numerically inferior British heavy [cavalry] brigade and by the notorious *Charge of the Light Brigade. The battle was a victory for the allies, commanded by Lord *Raglan and General Canrobert, although the Russians retained the Causeway Heights. GDS

balance of power meant different things at different times and operated centuries before it was ever defined. Article I of the first treaty of *Paris of May 1814 spoke of establishing 'a system of real and permanent Balance of Power' in Europe. Writing of the period before 1914 the British foreign secretary, Sir Edward *Grey, said, 'I imagine it to mean that when one Power or group of Powers is the strongest "bloc" in Europe, our policy has been, or should be, that of creating, or siding with, some other combination of Powers, in order to make a counterpoise to the strongest Power or Group and so to preserve equilibrium in Europe.' Grey had in mind the balance between the Triple Alliance of Germany, Austria, and Italy and the Dual Alliance of France and Russia. In 1864 another foreign secretary, Lord *Palmerston, had provided a definition which was still closer to that of 1814 than to that of 1914. He said, 'It means that it is to the interest of the community of nations that no one nation should acquire such a preponderance as to endanger the security of the rest; and it is for the advantage of all that the smaller Powers should be respected in their independence and not swallowed up by their more powerful neighbours. That is the doctrine of the balance of power and it is a doctrine worthy of being acted upon.' The doctrine was always strongly attacked by radicals. Richard *Cobden called it a 'figment', which he could never understand. John *Bright rejoiced that it was dead, intemperately proclaiming that it had burdened the nation with debts, killed hundreds of thousands of Englishmen, and 'desolated' millions of families. Cobden and Bright objected to it, in part, because it was associated with the preservation of the Vienna settlement, arrived at at the end of the Napoleonic wars. The aim had been to ensure stability. So long as the territorial balance then created between the five great powers was preserved, no one power would be strong enough to disturb the peace. If any tried, the other four would automatically form a coalition against it. It has convincingly been argued that Bismarck destroyed the open self-balancing Vienna system by his obsessional creation of tight alliances to protect the newly unified Germany. MEC

Baldwin (d. 1190). Archbishop of Canterbury. Native of Exeter, after a spell as archdeacon of Totnes, where he became a celebrated canonist, Baldwin entered the Cistercian monastery at Ford, Devonshire (*c.*1170), becoming abbot and then bishop of Worcester (1180). He was Henry II's own choice as archbishop in 1184, after an election disputed by the Benedictine monks of Canterbury whose hostility he soon provoked in a struggle famous throughout Europe. He took the cross (1188), preaching the crusade in Wales with 'the energy and style of Bernard of Clairvaux'. Henry sent him unsuccessfully to patch up a peace with Philip Augustus, as a prelude to the crusade. After attending Henry on his death-bed and crowning Richard I, he set out for the East. Heading the English advance guard, he arrived at the siege of *Acre (October 1190), deputized for Patriarch Heraclius, but died soon after. WMM

Baldwin, Stanley (1867–1947). Prime Minister. Educated at Harrow and Cambridge, Baldwin entered the family ironmaster's business but on his father's death in 1908 was elected to succeed him as Conservative MP for Bewdley (Worcs.), thus entering Parliament at a comparatively late age, though with much industrial experience. Baldwin served in the Lloyd George coalition governments from 1917 to 1922, but became increasingly alarmed at the amorality and adventurism associated with the later years of Lloyd George's premiership. Baldwin made the key speech at the Carlton Club meeting of Conservative backbenchers in 1922 that brought down Lloyd George, after which he served as chancellor of the Exchequer in the short-lived Conservative administration of the dying Andrew Bonar *Law, succeeding to the premiership in May 1923. Baldwin's industrial experience told him that free trade had had its day, and, acting more from impulse than from guile, he determined on its abolition. But he had already told a Conservative conference that he was not 'a clever man' and knew 'nothing of political tactics'. The truth of this was demonstrated by his decision to call a general election almost at once on the issue of protection. The Conservatives lost their overall majority, thus permitting the formation of the first Labour government.

But while Baldwin lacked Lloyd George's political cunning, he preserved in public life values of probity, charity, and conciliation which struck chords with British public opinion. He was known to be a man of simple country pleasures who had, during the Great War, donated one-fifth of his private fortune to reduce the size of the war loan. In a political atmosphere heavy with the rhetoric of class antagonism, Baldwin's conciliatory spirit and appeal to moderation seemed far preferable to a Labour Party tinged with extremism and a Liberal Party in a state of civil war. Following the general election of 1924, which saw the Liberal Party reduced to 40 seats, the Conservatives emerged with a majority of over 200 in the Commons. Baldwin was once more prime minister.

The composition of the cabinet was not, however, conducive to the pursuit of the policy of national unity which Baldwin had preached. In order to make peace with the Conservative free traders, Baldwin gave the Exchequer to Winston *Churchill, and in order to appease the Tory evangelical moralists he appointed as home secretary William Joynson-Hicks, a man who held deep anti-Jewish prejudices. His one inspired appointment was to put Neville *Chamberlain in charge of the Ministry of Health. Churchill's return to the gold standard (1925) had a very predictable effect on employment, and the cabinet took an equally predictable line on the *General Strike the following year. Baldwin brushed aside George V's advice to pursue a military solution (packing the king off to Sandringham), and appealed instead to the quietist instincts of the British public and to the moderate elements within the Labour movement. This policy paid handsome dividends, since the Trades Union Congress abandoned the miners and called off the industrial action. However, in 1927, and against his own better judgement, the cabinet pushed through the vindictive Trade Disputes Act, by which the principle of 'contracting out' of the political levy collected by trade unions was replaced by 'contracting in'. It was hoped that this provision would reduce Labour Party membership and income, which it did, but the Act did Baldwin's government little credit, and may have played a part in the Conservative defeat at the polls in 1929.

Between 1929 and 1931 Baldwin fought a bitter duel with the empire free traders, led by the press barons Lords *Beaverbrook and *Rothermere. The experience of 1924 lay heavily upon him. The age of free trade was clearly drawing to a close, but Baldwin understood better than most the sensitivities this issue aroused within his party, and he grew ever more indignant at the challenge which the protectionists were mounting to his leadership. On 17 March 1931 he made a dramatic appeal to the Conservative public to choose between him and 'the engines of propaganda for the constantly changing policies, desires, personal wishes, personal likes and personal dislikes of two men . . . What the proprietorship of these papers is aiming at is power, but power without responsibility—the prerogative of the harlot throughout the ages.'

Baldwin survived, and his leadership of the Conservative

Party was never again seriously challenged. In 1931 he agreed to serve under Ramsay *MacDonald as lord president of the council, succeeding MacDonald as prime minister in 1935. Baldwin was not slow in perceiving the vital necessity of a programme of rearmament in the face of international aggression. But he overestimated the strength of pacifism within British society, wrongly fearing the effect of a policy of rearmament on his own popularity, and (through higher taxation) on economic recovery. The result was a strategy as hypocritical as it was cynical, and does not redound to Baldwin's credit. In November 1935 he called a general election, during the course of which he protested his support for the *League of Nations. The election resulted in a resounding Conservative victory, but Baldwin's advocacy of the League was in fact a sham. Baldwin knew that the League's sanctions against Italy (which had invaded Abyssinia) would not be effective if they excluded oil; it was precisely for this reason that he supported them. When his foreign secretary, Sir Samuel *Hoare, signed an agreement with Pierre Laval, the French prime minister, proposing the cession of Abyssinian territory to Italy, Baldwin forced him to resign, though in the view of many he ought to have resigned himself.

Baldwin's handling of the abdication crisis, the following year, cannot be faulted. In advising Edward VIII against a morganatic marriage to Mrs *Simpson he acted with the utmost constitutional propriety, and with the backing of the Labour leader Clement *Attlee, and of the dominion prime ministers, all of whom he had been careful to consult. The smoothness of George VI's succession was due primarily to Baldwin's calm assuredness. He stayed in office long enough to attend the new king's coronation; two weeks later, aged almost 70, he resigned, accepting the customary earldom.

Stanley Baldwin, pipe in hand, was an avuncular figure, the epitome of British middle-class moderation against a turbulent and menacing European backcloth. He also symbolized the inter-war Conservative Party's suspicion of intellectuals and preference for second-class minds. Baldwin cannot be called a great thinker, or a great statesman: he is dwarfed by Lloyd George who preceded him and Winston Churchill who came afterwards, and in his own premiership was outclassed by his chancellor, Neville Chamberlain. Yet he could act decisively (witness the speedy passage of the 1936 Public Order Act, to curb the pseudo-military provocations of the *British Union of Fascists) and he was more honourable than most politicians of his generation. Perhaps for this reason he and Clement Attlee had a high regard for each other. There is much truth in the view that Baldwin helped 'tame' the Labour Party, and that the triumph of constitutionalism within its ranks, and its increasing respectability within British society (leading, ultimately, to Labour's 1945 election victory), owed something to Baldwin's patronage. GA

Baldwin, A. W., *My Father* (1955); Jenkins, R., *Baldwin* (1987); Middlemass, R. K., and Barnes, A. J. L., *Baldwin* (1969); Young, G. M., *Stanley Baldwin* (1952).

Balfour, Arthur James, 1st earl of (1848–1930). Prime Minister. Essentially a mid-Victorian, Arthur Balfour seems miscast as a 20th-cent. prime minister. He was the last representative of the traditional landed class to rise to the top and achieved it largely through the patronage of the 3rd marquis of *Salisbury. Naturally fitted for life in a rural vicarage or an Oxford college, Balfour did in fact produce an original work, *A Defence of Philosophic Doubt* (1879), which his critics thought summed up his approach to politics admirably.

Balfour grew up on the family estate at Whittingehame in the Scottish borders; his father had been a Tory MP and his mother was a sister of Robert Cecil, the future Lord Salisbury. Though a member of the Souls (a cross-party group of gifted young politicians), the young Balfour remained a solitary, intellectual figure, especially after the death in 1875 of his intended wife, May Lyttelton. He never married. Having no particular purpose in life, he decided to enter politics, and from 1874 to 1885 represented Hertford, the Cecil family's pocket borough. A poor speaker, Balfour underlined his rather detached position by involvement with Lord Randolph *Churchill's *'Fourth Party'.

However, around 1885–6 Balfour's career took off. He left the security of Hertford and, despite his distaste for mixing with the electorate, contested a new, popular constituency, East Manchester, which he held until 1906. Acting as, in effect, his uncle's secretary, he entered upon a lengthy apprenticeship for the prime ministership. He served briefly as president of the Local Government Board (1885) and as secretary of state for Scotland (1886), but really made his reputation as chief secretary for Ireland (1887–91). In that role Balfour adopted a twofold strategy. First he ruthlessly suppressed rural violence, earning thereby the epithet 'Bloody Balfour'. Second, he attempted to conciliate nationalist opinion by policies of social interventionism, including the sale of land to tenant farmers on easy terms, and investment in light railways and seed potatoes.

By promoting his nephew as leader of the House in 1891–2 and 1895–1902, Salisbury placed him in line for succession as prime minister in the latter year. Unhappily, Salisbury also bequeathed to Balfour the accumulated problems of his own prolonged reign. In particular, the financial cost of the South African War led Joseph *Chamberlain to take up the cause of tariff reform. Though Balfour cleverly manœuvred Chamberlain into resigning from the cabinet, this only led him to launch a campaign from 1903 onwards which largely captured the party for protectionism. Balfour struggled to maintain party unity by offering a compromise acceptable to Tory free traders and protectionists. This meant adopting 'retaliation', in effect to use the threat of tariffs to force other states to reduce their barriers against British goods. However, Balfour's clever dialectics merely convinced colleagues that he did not care very much about the issue, and earned him the contempt of both sides. Free traders felt he had failed to support them in their constituencies, while the protectionists blamed his ambiguous approach for losing the 1906 election. None the less, although immersed in this controversy, Balfour's government did take several important initiatives including the passage of the 1902 *Education Act, the Anglo-French *Entente of 1904, and the establishment of the Committee of Imperial Defence and the Royal Commission on the Poor Laws.

After 1906 the parliamentary party became predominantly protectionist in sympathy and Balfour exercised little effective leadership. In 1909 he made no attempt to stop the Tory majority in the Lords from rejecting *Lloyd George's budget. This proved to be a serious error. It resulted in Balfour having to lead his party through two unsuccessful elections in 1910, and as a result 1911 saw the development of a 'Balfour Must Go' campaign. He resigned—the first in a long line of modern Tory leaders to fall victim to their own backbenchers.

Yet a remarkably long career as a respected elder statesman still awaited Balfour. From the outbreak of war in 1914 he became an unofficial adviser to the Liberal government, and not surprisingly, *Asquith appointed him 1st lord of the Admiralty in the coalition of May 1915. Subsequently he served Lloyd George as foreign secretary (1916–19) in which capacity he produced the famous *Balfour declaration committing the government to the establishment of a national homeland in Palestine for the Jews. His last role was as lord president of the council under Lloyd George (1919–22) and under *Baldwin (1925–9). MDP

Balfour declaration. Partly with a view to securing the support of world Jewry for the allied war effort, *Lloyd George's government authorized Foreign Secretary A. J. *Balfour to send a letter (2 November 1917) to Lord Rothschild (lay leader of Anglo-Jewry) pledging the support of the British government for the establishment, in Palestine, of a 'National Home' for the Jewish people, but safeguarding the rights of Palestine's non-Jewish inhabitants. The terms of this declaration were incorporated into the *mandate for Palestine granted to Britain by the League of Nations, on the basis of which considerable Jewish settlement there was permitted between the two world wars. Growing Arab resentment and violence led to the abrogation of the declaration by Neville *Chamberlain's government in 1939. GA

Ball, John (d. 1381). Contemporary chroniclers saw John Ball as the evil genius behind the *Peasants' Revolt of 1381. Very little is known about this man, who in a letter ascribed to him described himself as formerly a priest of St Mary's, York, and then of Colchester. A member of the ecclesiastical underworld, he had been formally prohibited from preaching in 1366. Early in 1381 his attacks on the established church order led to his excommunication and imprisonment at Maidstone in Kent, from where the rebels released him. He was soon linked by chroniclers with *lollardy, but his preaching during the revolt, with its egalitarian message, was in a well-established tradition. After the rising, Ball was sentenced to be hanged, drawn, and quartered. MCP

ballads. Defining a ballad is difficult, since it is an adaptable and flexible art-form which has changed with the times. Intended for singing, the metre and language is usually simple and direct, the colours bold, the humour broad, with a chorus to encourage the company to join in. The earliest ballads were often heroic narratives—'Sir Patrick Spens', 'The Battle of Otterburn', 'Flodden Field'. They were meant for minstrels to sing in baronial halls. But with the advent of printing, ballads could be sold as broadsheets and could appeal to a wider audience. They soon acquired a satirical and disrespectful tone which made the authorities uneasy. The ballads of *Robin Hood were particularly popular, and Bishop *Latimer complained that he had once found an empty church because the congregation was off on Robin Hood's Day—'a traitor and a thief'. The first collection of ballads seems to have been *A Handful of Pleasant Delights* (1566). Samuel *Pepys was a great collector of ballads and left 1,400 to his Cambridge college, Magdalene. The great revival of interest in old ballads came with the publication of Thomas *Percy's *Reliques of Ancient English Poetry* in 1765, which helped to kindle the enthusiasm for the medieval past that characterized the Romantic movement. But by this time ballads were of great variety—love-sick swains, horrible murders, betrayals, pirates, and domestic infighting. Charles *Burney deplored the vulgarization of ballads when he remarked in 1802 that a ballad was 'a mean and trifling song such as is generally sung in the streets'. But the ballad had still some way to fall—to Mrs Dyer baby farmer, the dying cowboy, Frankie and Johnnie, and irreverent wartime ditties about the sergeant-major. Their value as a guide to changing taste was put by John *Selden in his *Table Talk* in the 17th cent.: 'more solid things do not show the complexion of the times so well as ballads and libels.' JAC

ballet is a dramatic entertainment by dancers, usually in costume with scenery and accompanied by music. Originating as elaborations of social dances in the lavish court spectacles of Renaissance Italy, it developed in France following the marriage of Catherine de Medici to Henri II in 1533. The *ballet de cour* mixed poetry, vocal and instrumental music, dancing, costumes, and scenery—the same recipe as that of the English *masque, a similar celebratory entertainment including both professional dancers and members of the court.

The establishment of the Académie Royale de Danse in 1661 was rapidly followed by Lully and Molière's numerous *comédie-ballets*, and the strong influence of French dance and Lully's music is clearly apparent in late 17th-cent. English stage works such as *Purcell's *Dido and Aeneas*. Dance continued to be incorporated into opera. When Marie Sallé came to Covent Garden in 1734, creating a stir in the ballet *Pygmalion* with her loose muslin dress and free hair rather than panniered skirts and wig, *Handel included dance music for her troupe in his operas. Also popular in London at this time was pantomime, often performed between the acts of plays or operas. The dancing-master John Weaver claimed credit for the first pantomime with *The Tavern Bilkers*: probably the 'Comical Entertainment in a Tavern between Scaramouch, Harlequin and Punchanello' advertised at Drury Lane theatre in 1703. The theatre director John Rich was a famous Harlequin in many productions, although Weaver's *The Loves of Mars and Venus* (1717) ignored grotesque *commedia* characters and offered what he termed 'scenical dancing' and mime.

Sallé's expressive dancing, together with the English pantomime and the acting style of David *Garrick, influenced

Jean-Georges Noverre, the greatest proponent of the new *ballet d'action* whose central dramatic narrative was conveyed entirely by dance, mime, and music without spoken or sung text. Among Noverre's pupils was Charles-Louis Didelot, who worked in London at the turn of the 19th cent. Carlotta Grisi, the first Giselle (Paris, 1841), married choreographer Jules Perrot, formerly partner of the great Romantic ballerina Marie Taglioni. The couple worked at Her Majesty's Theatre, London, in the 1840s, and Perrot's *Pas de quatre* (1845) brought together four of the world's leading ballerinas: Taglioni, Grisi, Cerrito, and Grahn.

As with Noverre, the concept of a unified art-work was also central to Sergei Diaghilev's Ballets Russes, whose company had annual London seasons from 1911 to 1914. Diaghilev commissioned many of the leading artists of his time: choreographers Fokine, Massine, and Balanchine; designers Bakst, Picasso, and Cocteau; and numerous composers including Stravinsky, Debussy, Satie, and Ravel. Diaghilev helped establish classical ballet as a serious art-form and trained many of the key figures in British ballet: Marie Rambert, who in 1926 formed the company that became known as the Ballet Rambert (from 1987 the Rambert Dance Company); Ninette de Valois, who established the Vic-Wells Ballet at Sadler's Wells (known as the Royal Ballet from 1956); and Alicia Markova, whose mantle as the leading British ballerina was passed on to Margot Fonteyn. Renowned for her effortless technique, grace, and dramatic involvement, Fonteyn's later career included an acclaimed partnership with Rudolf Nureyev.

Among leading British choreographers this century are Frederick Ashton, John Cranko, Kenneth MacMillan, and Antony Tudor, while important composers writing specific ballet scores include *Vaughan Williams, Bliss, and *Britten. Britten also exploited dance in his operas *Gloriana* (1953) and *Death in Venice* (1974). There are now numerous touring dance companies in Britain, some of which specialize in modern dance. ECr

Balliol, Edward (*c*.1280–1365). Son of John *Balliol, king of Scots, and himself titular king of Scots (1332–56). He had good prospects in youth, being betrothed in 1295 to the niece of the French king, and recognized as heir to the Scottish throne as late as 1301. But the Wars of Independence marginalized the Balliols, and after his father's death in 1313 Edward lived in obscurity in Picardy.

Edward III's coup in England (1330), and his distaste for the settlement with Robert I which *Isabella and *Mortimer had accepted in 1328, opened up new possibilities. There were others who had lost Scottish estates in the wars, and in 1331, Balliol returned to England and put himself at the head of a group of 'disinherited', who hoped to take advantage of the youth of David II. Landing at Kinghorn they were at first dramatically successful: after a victory at *Dupplin Moor outside Perth (11 August 1332), Balliol was made king at Scone. By the end of the year, however, he had been forced to flee ignominiously to England. This provoked Edward III to intervene in person, defeating the Scots at *Halidon Hill outside Berwick (19 July 1333), and reimposing Balliol as king. In 1334 Balliol had to pay the price, performing liege homage to Edward for his kingdom, and ceding much of southern Scotland to Edward III's direct rule.

There followed five years of devastating guerrilla warfare before Balliol's attempt was proven to have failed. Though he himself took part in several expeditions, he was evidently only the agent of Edward III, and for much of the time remained in England. However he did not abandon his claims, and after David II's capture at *Neville's Cross (17 October 1346) even made moves to reassert his position; but to no avail. In 1356, disgusted with his prospects and burdened by age, he resigned his title to Edward III in return for a pension.

He has been slightingly treated by many Scottish historians, but he had little opportunity to reveal his abilities and there is no contemporary comment on his character.

BW

Balliol, John (*c*.1250–1313), king of Scots (1292–6). The son of John Balliol of Barnard Castle, he was descended through his mother from David earl of *Huntingdon, the brother of William the Lion, king of Scots (1165–1214). The Balliol family held lands in France, in northern England, and in Galloway. These last gave John a stake in Scotland and a number of strong supporters when the crown became vacant on the death of *Margaret, the 'Maid of Norway', in 1290. In addition, he was linked with the very powerful Comyn family through the marriage of his sister to John *Comyn of Badenoch.

The verdict of Edward I's Parliament at Norham went to Balliol as being descended from the eldest of the three daughters of William the Lion's brother; and he was duly enthroned as king of Scots on 30 November 1292. There is every reason to think that this judgment was acceptable to the majority of Scots.

Edward I, however, had insisted that all the claimants acknowledged his right to be lord superior of Scotland, a claim for which there was little unambiguous evidence. Balliol therefore had to perform homage and fealty to Edward before his enthronement. This enabled Edward to assert what he believed to be his rights over Scotland and Edward's claims were to plague John's entire reign. He faced nine appeals to Edward from disgruntled litigants, in the course of which he had in 1293 to appear in Edward's Parliament and was humiliatingly adjudged to be in default. Far more serious was Edward's demand in 1294 for military service in his French wars by John himself and all the most prominent nobles of Scotland. Edward was for the moment distracted by a very serious Welsh revolt, and the Scots were able to get away with excuses. But it was clear that Edward would not let this go on indefinitely, and the Scottish nobles, distrusting King John's determination to resist, set up in July 1295 a council of twelve which took power out of John's hands. The council allied formally with Philip IV of France in October 1295; and prepared to resist Edward by force. From this point, John had lost control. In 1296 Edward I took Berwick. Scottish resistance was destroyed by Earl *Warenne at *Dunbar, and John was forced to resign his kingdom into Edward's hands at Montrose in July. Balliol was brought a prisoner to London; and the rest of his career had little impact. Though the Scottish opponents of Edward continued till 1304 to act in his name, and though in 1302 Edward I clearly recognized that his restoration was still a possibility, Balliol himself in 1298 declared formally that he never wanted to have anything to do with Scotland again, because of the malice and treachery of the Scots. In 1299 he was transferred to papal custody and in 1301 was released to his ancestral lands in Picardy, where he died in 1313. Balliol was clearly not able to resist Edward I; yet his only Parliament enacted sensible measures to administer the western Highlands, which suggests that in other circumstances he could have been an effective king. BW

Ballymore Hill, battle of, 1798. Father Murphy, leading the Wexford rebels, ambushed a small detachment of British troops on 4 June near Enniscorthy, killing their commander, Colonel Lambert Walpole, and taking several guns. Though no more than a skirmish, it gave great encouragement to the rebels. JAC

Balmoral (Aberdeenshire). The Scottish holiday home of the royal family. The present house was built in 1853–6 for Queen Victoria by the architect William Smith of Aberdeen (1817–91) as a replacement for an earlier house in Jacobethan style erected in 1834–9 by his father, John Smith (1781–1852). After leasing Balmoral for four years, the queen bought the estate in 1852. 'This dear paradise', as she called it, is a white granite mansion in Scots baronial style, and embodies modifications suggested by Prince *Albert. The design of *Osborne, the Queen's stuccoed Italianate villa on the Isle of Wight overlooking the Solent, had also benefited from the prince's involvement from 1845 to 1851, in this instance as a collaborator with Thomas *Cubitt (1788–1855)—the builder and property developer described by Robert Kerr as 'perhaps as near an approach to an architect as any man not an architect could be'. Queen Victoria spent part of every spring and autumn at Balmoral, her love of Scotland finding public expression in her books *Leaves from the Journal of Our Life in the Highlands* published in 1869, with a second part, *More Leaves*, appearing in 1883. PW

Baltimore, George Calvert, 1st Lord (*c*.1580–1632). Royal servant, MP, and secretary of state from 1619 to 1625, Calvert relinquished office when he openly declared his conversion to catholicism. He shared with his catholic father-in-law, Lord Arundell of Wardour, a wish for an American lordship, beginning a settlement at Ferryland, in his short-lived Province of Avalon, in Newfoundland. Calvert, who visited the Chesapeake, obtained from Charles I in 1632 proprietary rights to land carved out of Virginia north of the Potomac. The Maryland (named after Charles I's catholic wife) charter gave the Baltimore family palatinate powers of government and has been characterized as representing Charles's 'idealized picture of a restored monarchical authority in England'. Calvert died in 1632; his sons, Cecilius, the second baron, and Leonard, the first governor, introduced religious toleration in order to encourage Roman catholic settlement but protestants later became numerous and dominant. RCS

Bamburgh castle in Northumberland is sited on an outcrop of basalt rock, overlooking the North Sea. A citadel of the Anglo-Saxon kings of *Bernicia, it was close to their palace at *Yeavering and the royal monastery of *Lindisfarne. Later the site became a centre of power of the earls of Northumbria. Between the 10th and 12th cents. control of the north of England was disputed between the kings of England and of Scotland, the earls being a powerful independent force. In 1095 William Rufus took it by force from the then earl, Robert Mowbray, as part of his bid to control the north. After that the castle remained in royal hands until the 16th cent., except when held by Henry, earl of Northumberland, son of King David of Scots, during the reign of Stephen, when Scottish influence in Northumberland was in the ascendant. It is likely that the keep was begun by David and Henry, and completed by Henry II of England, after he recovered the castle in 1157; and that the castle had achieved its full extent, of three wards each with its own gate, by 1250. It was allowed to fall into decay after being severely damaged in the siege of 1464, when held by the Lancastrians against Edward IV. *Warwick the Kingmaker pounded it with heavy guns, despite the king's wish that it be taken 'whole, unbroken with ordinance'. Its present condition is due to modern restorations, especially by Lord *Armstrong. LR

Bamford, Samuel (1788–1872). Lancashire radical and poet. Brought up a Wesleyan in Middleton near Manchester, he worked as a warehouse boy, farm labourer, on coal ships plying between Tyneside and London, and as a bookseller before setting up as a hand-loom weaver. Under the influence of William *Cobbett he became a radical, founding the Middleton Hampden Club in 1816 and being arrested for treason for advocating parliamentary reform in 1817. Acquitted of this charge, he was present at the *'Peterloo' massacre of 16 August 1819 as leader of the Middleton contingent and was sentenced to a year in Lincoln gaol for treason. This ended his radical career. He returned to hand-loom weaving and when this failed turned unsuccessfully to writing and public readings of his poetry. His autobiography was written in 1841–3 to justify his turbulent past and warn *chartists against the use of violence. ER

Banbury, battle of. See EDGECOTE.

Bancroft, Richard (1544–1610). Archbishop of Canterbury. Born in Lancashire and educated at Christ's College, Cambridge, Bancroft was successively canon of Westminster (1587), chaplain to Archbishop *Whitgift (1592), bishop of London (1597), and archbishop (1604). From 1597 he was virtually acting primate during Whitgift's illness and attended Elizabeth at her death. A powerful advocate of episcopacy, whether preaching as canon of Westminster or making overtures to secular catholic clergy rather than Jesuits, his profound animosity towards presbyterianism was evident at the *Hampton Court conference (1604). As archbishop, he was tough with potential schismatics, helped restore episcopacy to Scotland, and secured the passage through convocation of the canons of 1604, the Latin corpus of Anglican canon law, virtually unmodified until *Fisher. A man of scholarly interests, Bancroft zealously supported work on the 1611 translation of the Bible and sought to improve intellectual standards of the clergy. WMM

Banda, Hastings Kamuzo (b. *c.*1902). Malawian nationalist statesman. Banda trained as a doctor in the USA and in Scotland and practised medicine in England (1945–53) and in Ghana (1953–8). He protested ineffectively against the creation of the Central African Federation in 1953, but returned home to lead the campaign against federation as president of the Nyasaland African Congress in 1958. In 1959 the colonial government declared a state of emergency and Banda was imprisoned. He was released a year later and became successively minister of natural resources and local government in 1961 and prime minister in 1963. In the latter year, the Federation was dissolved, Banda retaining his office when Nyasaland became independent and was renamed *Malawi in 1964. Malawi became a republic in 1966 with Banda as president, an office he assumed for life in 1971. He remained consistently pro-western in his foreign policy but governed autocratically at home. KI

Bangladesh proclaimed itself an independent and sovereign state on 25 March 1971 although it was not until 15 December that *Pakistan conceded this status. Previously, the country had been known as East Pakistan, united with West Pakistan in the state created at the time of India's partition in 1947. Prior to this, the region consisted of the most eastern districts of the British Indian presidency of *Bengal. These were marked by a Muslim-majority population in contrast to the Hindu majority of West Bengal. Religious tensions, reinforced by class cleavages, began to rise towards the end of the 19th cent. and reached fever-pitch in the 1940s. The proposal for the 1947 partition won the support of the majority of both Muslims and Hindus in the Bengal Legislative Assembly. However, East Bengal's place in the new Pakistan was never comfortable. Power was narrowly concentrated in the landed-military élites of the West. The East felt itself to be an exploited and alien colony. In the 1960s, a movement developed around the Awami League demanding, at the very least, provincial autonomy. It was repressed but reasserted itself strongly in 1970 when President Yahya was obliged by US pressure to hold Pakistan's first general elections. The Awami League won 160 of the 162 East Pakistan constituencies. West Pakistan's military and political leaders struck back, arresting the president of the Awami League and unleashing tanks on Dakha. A *Mukti Bahini* guerrilla movement responded. Brutalizing violence drove 10 million refugees into neighbouring India, whose army then intervened. On 15 December 1971, West Pakistan forces surrendered and the 'liberation' of Bangladesh was confirmed. DAW

Bangor, diocese of. The foundation of the church at Bangor is ascribed to Deiniol in the 6th cent., his sphere of influence as a bishop extending throughout the principality of *Gwynedd in north-west Wales. Work on the cathedral began in the 12th cent. under Bishop David (1120–39). It was extended during the episcopates of Anian I (1267–1307) and Anian II (1309–28). The nave and aisles were rebuilt late in the 14th cent., and the tower by Bishop Skevington in the 16th. Much alteration and restoration was undertaken in the 19th cent. under the direction of Gilbert *Scott.

The diocese has an area of over 1,500 square miles and includes the island of Anglesey, the holy island of Bardsey, burial place of many of the Welsh saints, and the mountainous countryside of Snowdonia. Worship in many of the churches is conducted in the Welsh language. William *Morgan, translator of the Bible into Welsh (1588), was born in the diocese. His work was revised later by John Davies, rector of Mallwyd, the chaplain of the bishop of Bangor. More recently the notable priest and poet R. S. Thomas was rector of Aberdaron on the Lleyn peninsula, drawing much of his inspiration from the area. JRG

Bangorian controversy. Loosed by Benjamin *Hoadly, a low-church Whig cleric, appointed to the bishopric of Bangor in 1715. The following year he launched an attack on the *non-jurors, arguing that their deposition had been lawful. In 1717 he followed with a sermon 'My kingdom is not of this world', in which he adopted a most extreme position—that Christ had not vested authority in any secular persons, that private judgement was sacrosanct, and that sincerity of belief was the ultimate test. Hoadly appeared to his opponents to open the floodgates to religious anarchy and William *Law and others commenced vigorous pamphlet warfare. The revival of religious controversy was extremely unwelcome to Whig ministers and when the matter was raised in the lower house of *convocation, that body was hastily prorogued, not to meet again until 1852. JAC

Bank Charter Act, 1844. The culmination of government efforts to create an effective legal framework to achieve a stable currency, the Act defined the roles of the Bank of England. One department had the exclusive duty of issuing notes having a minimum value of £5 as legal tender in England and Wales. It was to ensure that notes had an equivalent backing of bullion in its vaults, combined with a fiduciary issue defined by the Treasury. The other department undertook banking business, acting as the regulatory body for the banking system with powers which included fixing the minimum cost (interest) of borrowing money. IJEK

Bank Holiday Act, 1871. Introduced by Sir John Lubbock, this Act compelled the clearing banks to close on certain days, thus making them public holidays. In England and Wales Easter Monday, Whit Monday, the first Monday in August, and Boxing Day became public holidays. In Scotland New Year's Day, the first Monday in May and August, and Christmas Day were declared holidays. RAS

banking. A system of trading in money which involved safeguarding deposits and making funds available for borrowers, banking developed in the Middle Ages in response to the growing need for credit in commerce. The lending functions of banks were undertaken in England by money-lenders. Until their expulsion by Edward I in 1291, the most important money-lenders were Jews, since they were not bound by canon law which forbade usury. They were replaced by Italian merchants who had papal dispensations to lend money at interest. In the 13th cent. credit was essential to finance commerce and major projects. The most important was the wool trade but other examples included large buildings such as Edward's castles in north Wales. When Italians had their activities in England curtailed in the early 14th cent., they were replaced by English merchants and goldsmiths, whose rates of interest were sufficiently low to avoid the usury laws. These sources of banking activity were the mainstay of commerce until the later 17th cent.

Monarchs had borrowed from merchants and landowners for centuries. By the late 17th cent., constitutional changes, particularly the growth of parliamentary power over government expenditures, required a more regulated framework. The *Bank of England, founded in 1694, gave the government and other users of credit access to English funds. Similar developments occurred in Scotland and Ireland. These banks remained without serious competition until the later 18th cent., when expanding commercial and manufacturing activities gave scope to merchants, brewers, and landowners to establish banks based on their own cash reserves. These commercial banks took deposits, made loans, usually for limited periods, and issued promissory notes whose value was backed by bullion in the vaults combined with a fiduciary issue which depended on the likely scale of withdrawals. Errors of judgement sometimes occurred and 'runs on the bank' took place when depositors feared for the security of their money and demanded its return.

Fluctuations in the value of money because of the return to a gold-based currency after the end of the Napoleonic wars (1815) precipitated a series of crises. To stabilize the currency the government eventually introduced the 1844 *Bank Charter Act, which gave the Bank of England two functions, that of supervising the note issue as part of the currency and that of monitoring the activities of the banking system. Regulatory powers were put in place in 1845 to control banking in Scotland and Ireland.

From their earliest days, banks required loyal staff who did not accept bribes, steal money, or give information about accounts to unauthorized persons. Literate and numerate staff received high salaries, retirement pensions, and various privileges including holidays and social facilities. Infringement of the rules was punished by loss of job and all privileges. Their work required systematic record keeping which grew in volume and complexity during the 19th cent. when cheques replaced banknotes for many business transactions. In 1773 banks established the London Clearing House to process cheques rapidly.

In the 19th cent., overseas trade and the expanding British empire reinforced the place of London as a centre of merchant banking. The probity, knowledge, and skills of these specialist bankers attracted business from foreign firms and governments seeking loans in Britain. Some British firms employed merchant banks to arrange their supply of capital finance. This usually involved share or bond issues which were traded on the stock markets. Such arrangements made possible the rapid development of railways, heavy engineering, mines, and large commercial developments. Many of these merchant banks survive, including Rothschilds, Lazard Brothers, Baring, Kleinwort Benson, and Schroders. Internal commerce and trade were funded mainly by a larger number of separate local banks which, after the middle of the 19th cent., became consolidated into a much smaller number of banks covering much of England. Numbers continued to diminish so that by 1980 banking was dominated by four companies: Barclays, Lloyds, Midland, and National Westminster.

London's dominance as the banking centre, not only of Britain but of the financial world, was not challenged until the 20th cent. with the growth of competing international economies such as the USA and Japan. None the less, London remains a major centre of merchant banking.

Within Britain, banking has been characterized, largely because of technological innovation, by an increasingly sophisticated provision of traditional banking services and an expansion of services associated with consumer credit. The business of safeguarding and lending money is often arranged through machine-readable cards and continuous access by telephone. Since the Financial Services Act of 1986, banks face more competition with many banking services being provided by building societies, trustee savings banks, and the Post Office. IJEK

Banks, Sir Joseph (1743–1820). Explorer, and for over forty years president of the *Royal Society. Educated at Harrow, Eton, and Christ Church, Oxford, Banks developed an extra-curricular interest in botany. Graduating in 1763, instead of going on a grand tour, he sailed to Newfoundland and Labrador on HMS *Niger*. Inheriting great wealth in land in 1764, he resolved to join Captain *Cook's voyage to observe Venus from Tahiti and then to search for the unknown southern continent (1768–71). Accompanied by a staff including artists and the botanist Carl Solander, he observed ethnography and botany in Tahiti, New Zealand, and New South Wales. Returning a hero, he was in 1778 elected president of the Royal Society, holding the office to his death. Having learned his science as one of a large and expensive team involving the armed forces, not unlike modern 'big science', he spent his working life administering it. Seeing unity as strength, putting down what he saw as rival institutions, but promoting the *Royal Institution, *Kew Gardens, and the colonization of Australia, he became the formidable autocrat of science in Regency Britain. DK

Banks of England, Ireland, and Scotland. Founded in 1694, the Bank of England was a private company, the first to offer services in England. By the 19th cent. it had become the central bank and the currency manager for the state, although these powers were not formally enshrined until the Bank Charter Act of 1844. In 1946 it was taken into public ownership.

The Bank of Ireland was created by legislative charter of the Irish Parliament in 1783. Although it dominated banking in Ireland during its first half-century, its position was never that of a central bank. It continues to function as a commercial bank whose head office is in Dublin.

The Scottish Parliament in 1695 licensed a partnership to establish the Bank of Scotland with the intention of providing coherence for the finances in Scotland. However, the bank ran into difficulties which encouraged others to set up competing banks. After the Act of *Union in 1707 the Scottish financial system was linked to that of England although the Bank of Scotland together with other Scottish banks retains the right to issue its own banknotes. IJEK

banneret and banret. By origin, a knight who brought his men into the field under his own banner and who ranked next to a baron. By extension, a title granted for deeds of valour in the field in the presence of the king, who shaped the pennon by cutting off its points. Edward III made John de Copeland a knight banneret for capturing the king of Scotland at *Neville's Cross in 1346 and Sir Richard Croft was created by Henry VII after the battle of *Stoke in 1487. Though knights banneret took precedence over the new order of baronets established by James I, they died out, partly because, after the civil wars, few kings took the field in person. JAC

Bannockburn, battle of, 1314. Early in 1314 Edward II assembled a large army to restore his crumbling authority in Scotland and to relieve Stirling castle, besieged by supporters of Robert I Bruce. The English had a marked superiority in numbers and thought it unlikely that the Scots would offer a pitched battle. But Bruce massed his spearmen, dug pits to protect them from the cavalry, and in a preliminary encounter on 23 June, the English knights suffered badly. On the following day, the Scots gained the upper hand in heavy fighting and the English fell back in confusion. Edward was forced to flee and narrowly escaped capture. The Scottish victory was decisive and reaffirmed the independence of the country. JAC

Banqueting House (Whitehall). The Banqueting House is one of the finest rooms in the country. Built by Inigo *Jones for James I, between 1619 and 1622, it was one of the few buildings to survive the fire at Whitehall palace in 1698. It was intended to be part of a great new complex which was never completed. The severe and classical features, based on Palladio's designs, were a new form of architecture. The ceiling was finished in 1634 by Rubens and is largely devoted to themes illustrating the wisdom and virtue of James I: its baroque exuberance is in strange contrast with the restraint of the hall. It was from this building that Charles I stepped through a window to the scaffold in 1649. Cromwell declined the crown there in 1657 and William and Mary accepted it there in 1689. In the 18th cent. it was used as a royal chapel. The Banqueting House is open to the public and still used on grand occasions. JAC

baptists formed one of the main protestant dissenting groups, holding that baptism should be undertaken by adults who could understand the ceremony and its significance, and that it should involve total immersion in water. These views may have been inherited from the 16th-cent. *anabaptists, but baptists managed to shed the odium which had attached to the earlier group. The first baptist community was established in London in 1612 and the movement spread rapidly, in Britain and in the American colonies. The writings of John *Bunyan in the Restoration period gained for baptists widespread respect. They did little more than maintain their numbers in early Hanoverian England but in the early 19th cent. expanded greatly and by 1851 had more than 2,700 congregations in England and Wales. Of these the large majority were Particular Baptists, who had retained a *Calvinist outlook, as against the General Baptists who had moved towards *unitarianism. Baptist churches and educational institutions are extremely strong in the United States. JAC

Barbados. An island in the eastern Caribbean some 200 miles north-east of Trinidad. Extending 21 miles by 14, it is a little larger than the Isle of Wight. It was uninhabited in 1627 when settled by the English, who began growing sugar cane in the 1630s. In 1665 it survived an attack by the Dutch. The capital is Bridgetown and tourism is augmented by light industry. The population in 1996 was 259,000 and since 1966 it has been an independent state within the Commonwealth. JAC

Barbour, John (d. 1395). Medieval Scottish poet, author of *The Bruce*. Barbour was probably born in south-west Scotland (*c.*1325), and became archdeacon of Aberdeen diocese (1357). In this position he played a significant role in political and ecclesiastical affairs, attending general council to discuss David II's ransom (1357), and travelling abroad to Oxford and France.

From the accession of Robert II (1371) he was closely associated with the royal court, acting as a clerk of audit and auditor of Exchequer regularly until 1385. He also received considerable financial patronage from the king, some undoubtedly for his compositions. *The Bruce* (written 1375–7) is the earliest substantial poem in Scots to survive. It deals with the reign of Robert I (1306–29), and is based on oral and written testaments, often of contemporaries. He is also known to have written *The Brut* and *The Stewartis Original*, which do not survive. RJT

Barebone's Parliament. When Cromwell expelled the *Rump on 20 April 1653, he had no plans for an alternative government and no authority to call elections to a new Parliament. After deliberation, he and his council of officers decided to vest the supreme authority in a nominated assembly, initially for sixteen months. Together they chose 144 members to represent all the English counties, and also Ireland, Scotland, and Wales. The assembly met on 4 July and soon voted to call itself a Parliament; it gets its familiar sobriquet from Praise-God Barebone, leather-seller, lay preacher, and MP for London. Barebone was not a typical member, however, for at least four-fifths of the House were gentlemen, and moderate men clearly outnumbered religious and political radicals. But the latter strove disruptively for extreme changes in religion and the law, until the moderate majority, to Cromwell's relief, staged a walk-out on 12 December and resigned their authority back into his hands. AHW

Barham, Charles Middleton, 1st Lord (1726–1813). Middleton was a cousin of Henry *Dundas, the future intimate of Pitt the Younger, treasurer of the navy and secretary at war. Hence Middleton had access to the centre of government almost from the time he became comptroller of the navy in 1778, when still in the rank of captain, and was the better able to outface critics. His active naval career had been more profitable than distinguished, but he found his métier in the comptrollership, held until 1790 in weekly communication with Pitt and in combination with his parliamentary seat at Rochester. Appointed to the Admiralty Board in 1794 Middleton was to resign in 1795; but 10 years later his enduring reputation brought him to the 1st lordship in succession to Dundas, when Middleton was created Lord Barham. His outstanding administrative record was crowned by a provident foresight which ensured the ship-strength available to *Nelson at *Trafalgar. DDA

Baring, Evelyn, 1st earl of Cromer (1841–1917). Proconsul. Baring's father was an MP and younger brother of the great banker Lord Ashburton, his mother the daughter of an admiral, and the family seat at Cromer Hall (Norfolk). Baring spent the years 1858–72 in the Royal Artillery and then went to India as private secretary to his cousin, Lord *Northbrook, the viceroy. In 1877 he began his life's work when he was sent as commissioner to Egypt to attempt the enormous task of placing its finances and administration on a firm footing. For thirty years he was the effective power in the land, comptroller-general from 1879 to 1880, consul-general 1883–1907. Restoration of Egyptian solvency meant withdrawal from the Sudan and Baring acquiesced, with misgivings, in the choice of *Gordon to carry out the task, watching helplessly when Gordon was trapped and overwhelmed at Khartoum. Not until the 1890s was *Kitchener able to restore Egyptian control over the Sudan. Baring, meanwhile, accumulated honours—a barony in 1892, viscountcy in 1899, and earldom in 1901. Edward VII gave him the Order of Merit in 1906. He retired from ill-health in 1907 and published a two-volume work on *Modern Egypt* the following year. JAC

Barnardo, Thomas John (1845–1905). Philanthropist. During the protestant religious revival in Dublin in 1862, Barnardo gave up his job to devote his time to evangelizing work. In 1866 he entered the London Hospital as a missionary medical student and visited slums where he was saddened by the number of homeless and neglected children. Barnardo abandoned his plans to go to China as a missionary in order to help them. On 15 July 1867 he founded the East End Juvenile Mission for the care of sick and destitute children. Under the patronage of Lord *Shaftesbury he opened a boy's home at 18 Stepney Causeway, later followed by a series of similar houses known as 'Dr Barnardo's Homes'. In 1876 he started the Girls' Village Home in Barkingside (Essex). In 1882 he began sending children to Canada for training and resettlement. His work expanded both at home and in Canada and before his death he had rescued 59,384 children and assisted as many as 500,000. RAS

Barnes, Robert (1495–1540). Protestant martyr. Barnes, born in Norfolk, became prior of an Augustinian friary in Cambridge. He adopted Lutheranism and in 1526 was brought before *Wolsey to answer charges of heresy. Barnes recanted and subsequently spent several years in Germany, where he stayed with Luther. He was recalled to England by Thomas *Cromwell, to whom his support of the royal supremacy against the papacy might be of use. Barnes was employed on several diplomatic missions in Germany and Scandinavia and was involved in negotiating Henry VIII's marriage with *Anne of Cleves. The breakdown of that marriage weakened his position and that of his patron. Cromwell was beheaded on 28 July 1540 and two days later Barnes, attainted for heresy, was burned at Smithfield. JAC

Barnet, battle of, 1471. *Warwick, Edward IV's great ally at *Towton, turned against him in 1470 and drove him out of the kingdom. Returning in March 1471, Edward landed near Hull and moved south. Warwick, in possession of London, marched out to confront him. They met at Barnet, 14 miles north, on 14 April. Warwick had some 15,000 troops, Edward rather fewer. The action began early in the morning with mist still thick on the ground. Warwick's men won initial success, but confusion and mistaken identity led to cries of treason and a fatal collapse of morale. Warwick himself, fighting on foot, was cut down trying to reach his horse. Three weeks later, Edward secured his position beyond doubt with his crushing victory over Queen *Margaret at *Tewkesbury. JAC

baronets are hereditary knights and at first their elder sons could be knighted on their 21st birthday. The order was instituted by James I in 1611 as a means of raising money for the army in Ulster. Irish baronetcies followed in 1619 and Scottish in 1625. The latter were originally of *Nova Scotia since the intention was to support that colony. Baronets remained commoners and were therefore eligible for membership of the House of Commons. Pledges to limit the number granted were soon broken. JAC

barons. The name was first used loosely to mean any great landowners or lords and then acquired a precise meaning as the lowest of the five ranks in the peerage. The word came into use after the Conquest to describe the more important tenants-in-chief. Their special privileges released them from the authority of the *sheriff: they led their own men whereas lesser lords brought their men to the sheriff's levy. In time a class of greater barons emerged who were summoned specifically to the host or the king's council. The emergence of Parliament in the 13th cent. meant that barons were summoned by writ to the House of Lords and then sought to make the privilege hereditary. From 1387 onwards, barons could be created by letters patent, which in time replaced summons by writ as the normal method of creation. But from 1385, the establishment of superior titles of duke, marquis, and viscount pushed barons into the lowest rank of the nobility. The hereditary principle was first breached in 1876 when law lords were given life baronies and in 1958 life peers were admitted to the House of Lords, holding baronies. JAC

baroque is a term widely applied by art historians over the past 200 years to the whole spectrum of European art in the 17th and early 18th cents. Possibly used by Iberian jewellers to categorize imperfectly formed pearls, or originating in the Italian *baroco*, dismissal of a dubious theory with an extravagant conclusion, baroque meant a style in architecture, painting, music, and furniture which flouted classical standards.

In 17th-cent. Britain baroque was never whole-heartedly embraced or ever permitted to overwhelm classical models. Here a protestant ethos was decisive because, quintessentially, the baroque was represented by the grandeur of Counter-Reformation Rome as projected by Bernini, Borromini, and their demanding Barberini patron Pope Urban VIII (reigned 1623–44); the fulsome interior decoration of the Pitti palace in Florence by Pietro da Cortona (1641–6) would never have been wanted, or even afforded, for an English great house.

No painter who has been labelled 'baroque' has surpassed Rubens, the supreme colourist. While it should be remembered that he was ever a master of line, and had a practical knowledge of contemporary architecture, it is striking how, in England, Rubens's greatest surviving decorative scheme, the ceiling of the Whitehall *Banqueting House (late 1630s) is 'reined in' by the building's austerely basilica-like character. This situation is reversed in Nicholas Stone's porch for St Mary's church, Oxford (1633), where barley-sugar ('solomonic') columns, redolent of Bernini, support a traditional fan-vaulted roof. In drawing, *Lely's 31 depictions in black and white chalk of a Garter procession, made in the 1660s, are regarded as among the most accomplished of baroque drawings. Their swagger is exactly suited to their theme. In baroque woodwork, Grinling *Gibbons's choir stalls in St Paul's cathedral are unsurpassed in England. While the English and Dutch shared in an ebullient use of brick, in stone (emanating from the fertile minds of *Vanbrugh, *Hawksmoor, Talman, and Archer) there was a profoundly native adaptation of baroque. With these men there arrived a startlingly exaggerated interpretation of such classical features as entablatures, finials, pedestals, and pilasters, above all at *Blenheim, *Castle Howard, Seaton Delaval, *Chatsworth (all built between 1685 and 1725), but also in Hawksmoor's London churches.

The Vanbrugh-esque had no counterpart in music because Britain shared sufficiently in the common currency of continental music. The ever-developing organ catered splendidly for the observational requirements of reformed churches, and it was symptomatic of the era that musicians such as Tomkins, Lawes, Locke, and *Purcell benefited from royal rather than ecclesiastical patronage: the two latter furnished music for great occasions of state which would have sounded no less appropriate in catholic milieux. There seems, indeed, to be a paradox in the architectural disciplines of neo-Palladianism suppressing the fantasies of a Vanbrugh just when *Handel, a mighty dramatic as well as musical genius, was beguiling audiences with elaborately staged operas manifestly indebted to Italian practice.

DDA

barrier treaties. After their experience in 1672, when they were almost overrun by the French, the Dutch sought guarantees against renewed aggression. Their proposal was to garrison certain fortresses in the southern Netherlands, under Spanish sovereignty until *Utrecht, under Austrian subsequently. Britain supported these demands while being anxious at the commercial advantage the Dutch might obtain. In 1715, as part of the Utrecht settlement, the Dutch were given the right to fortify seven towns, including Tournai and Namur, and to share one other with the Austrians. The Austrians were to provide the cost out of local revenues. The fortresses were a persistent cause of irritation between the Dutch and the Austrians and served little military purpose, being easily overrun in 1745. JAC

Barrosa, battle of, 1811. Since 1810 Cadiz had been besieged by the French under General Victor. In January 1811 an Anglo-Spanish force attempted to lift the blockade by landing 50 miles to the south at Tafira and marching north to attack the French from the rear at Chiclana. On 5 March Victor, hiding in Chiclana Forest, attacked the allied flank and captured Barrosa ridge, the key strategic point on the field. General Graham (*Lynedoch), commanding the British troops, in a bold but bloody counter-attack managed to repulse the French. The Spanish army, under General La Peña, did not intervene and allowed the French to escape when the English were too tired to pursue. RAS

Barrow, Henry (*c.*1550–93). An early puritan separatist, Barrow was born in Norfolk, educated at Clare Hall, Cambridge, and became a member of Gray's Inn. While living a dissolute life, he had a conversion experience (*c.*1580) and dedicated himself to theology, especially *Brownist ideas. Arrested in 1586, he was examined personally by *Whitgift and *Burghley. From prison he smuggled his illicit writings to the Netherlands. Eventually he and John Greenwood were tried for writing 'with malicious intent' and hanged. Separatism multiplied rapidly, but the separatist churches of London and Amsterdam deriving from Barrow were regarded as the 'ancient' churches of the separation. Some historians have ascribed the Martin *Marprelate tracts to him; he has also been regarded as a founder of the independents. WMM

Barrow, Isaac (1630–77). Scholar. Barrow was born in London and sent to Trinity College, Cambridge, where he became a fellow. His royalist sympathies led him to spend 1655–9 abroad but at the Restoration he rose rapidly. In 1660 he was elected to the chair of Greek at Cambridge and in 1663 became the first professor of mathematics at Cambridge, resigning in 1669 to make room for Newton. In 1673 he was elected master of Trinity, where he began building the great Wren library. Barrow's reputation was largely as a mathematician and as a preacher: his sermons, though extremely long, were regarded as models of lucidity. His attack upon the doctrine of papal supremacy, published posthumously, was also highly regarded. JAC

Barrow, Sir John (1764–1848). Promoter of exploration. As a member of Lord *Macartney's staff, Barrow was on the famous embassy to China in 1793 and then with him at the *Cape of Good Hope after the British take-over; he wrote accounts of both ventures. Barrow had made some useful travels in the little-known South African interior and drew maps. He became 2nd secretary at the Admiralty in 1806 and remained there using the position to promote British exploration, official and semi-official, most notably of west

Africa and of the north polar region. Barrow was a founder member and key figure in the foundation of the Royal Geographical Society in 1830 and set it on its path as the premier promoter of 19th-cent. exploration. RB

Barry, Sir Charles (1795–1860). Versatile Victorian architect who espoused a diverse range of styles. After travel in 1817–20 through France, Italy, Greece, Turkey, Egypt, and Syria, he returned to London and built several churches in a Gothic idiom, including St Peter's, Brighton (1824–8). Turning to the Greek revival, he designed first the Royal Institution of Fine Arts (1824–35) and then the Athenaeum (1837–9), both in Manchester. By this time he was using Italian *palazzi* as models for the Travellers' (1830–2) and Reform Clubs (1838–41) in Pall Mall. Barry never lost his genius for flexibility, and elsewhere used Tudor Gothic (as at Canford Manor), Jacobethan (as at Highclere castle), and even Scottish baronial (as at Dunrobin). His *magnum opus*, the Houses of *Parliament, won in competition in 1836, was in the required 'Gothic or Elizabethan' style, but its construction took its toll on Barry's health and hastened his death in 1860. PW

Barry, James (1741–1806). A history painter, Barry was brought from Ireland to London by Edmund *Burke, who also paid for him to visit Italy, where he was influenced by the Renaissance great masters. He was elected ARA in 1772, RA in 1773, and appointed professor of painting in 1782, but his truculence alienated other Royal Academy members who petitioned the king to have him expelled in 1799. Between 1777 and 1783/4 he worked for almost no payment on six large pictures on the theme of the Progress of Human Culture, in the Society of Arts, London. *Johnson said of this, 'There is a grasp of much there which you find nowhere else.' Grand-manner history painting was little appreciated by British patrons, yet Barry persisted, enduring poverty and squalor, to become the only British painter to follow consistently the precepts set by *Reynolds for this style. JC

Bartholomew (d. 1184). Bishop of Exeter. Eminent Norman theologian and expert canon lawyer, Bartholomew was appointed archdeacon in 1155. His election to the see in 1161, urged by *Theobald of Canterbury, was supported by Thomas *Becket. After Theobald's death, he was chosen by Henry II to help secure Becket's election to Canterbury, then in 1164 took part in an embassy seeking papal intervention in the crisis between king and archbishop. During the Becket controversy, he seemed to steer a middle course. Bartholomew's presence at the controversial crowning of *Henry the Young King (1170) is uncertain, but Becket asked that he should not be papally censured with others involved. Considered by Pope Alexander III to be a great luminary of the English church, in his later years Bartholomew often acted as judge-delegate for the papal court. AM

Barton, Elizabeth (*c.*1506–34). Prophetess. Known as the Maid of Kent, Elizabeth Barton, a domestic servant, developed religious mania, with trances and visions. She was taken up by local catholic priests and used to discredit Lutheran ideas. But when she took up the cause of *Catherine of Aragon and declared that Henry VIII would die if he divorced her, the Maid moved into deep waters. For a time she was protected by *Warham, *More, and *Fisher, but when *Cranmer succeeded Warham as archbishop he interrogated Barton and obtained a confession that her revelations were feigned. With several of her associates she was executed at Tyburn in April 1534. JAC

Basilikon doron (1598), a manual on the practice of kingship, was written by James I and VI for his eldest son, Prince *Henry. Though less polemical in tone than *The Trew Law of Free Monarchies*, composed about the same time, it made apparent James's exalted view of kingly power. James wrote the *Basilikon doron* for his own enjoyment and initially distributed it only among his family and close friends. Mass publication, in England, came in March 1603, on the eve of James's accession to the English throne, when the *Basilikon* quickly became a best seller and fuelled fears of the new king's absolutist tendencies. RL

bastard feudalism. The term bastard feudalism, seemingly invented in 1885, has come to be adopted as a convenient label to distinguish a social structure different from its predecessor in the post-Conquest period. The essence of the original feudal system introduced by William I was that tenants of manors or other substantial units of land had obligations to their lords, of which fealty, suit of court, and military service were the most common. With bastard feudalism the bond between a man and his lord was not tenurial but financial, not hereditary but personal; it was often made by a written contract, an indenture, by which a retainer undertook, in return for a pension, to attend and ride with his lord whenever required, suitably armed and equipped.

The proliferation—if not the origin—of this pattern of relationships coincided with the *Hundred Years War. Edward III and his successors raised their invading armies by indentures with lords and other captains who undertook to provide certain numbers of mounted men and archers. They in turn recruited parts of their contingents by similar contracts. All were to be paid wages of war: these were not feudal armies. The core of a lord's company would be the men already retained to follow him 'in peace and war'. It was therefore in the king's interest that lords had organized companies available for military service, not only for campaigns abroad but for emergencies like foreign invasion or domestic rebellion.

The political hazards of this dependency could be reduced by good kingship. Public order was assisted if lords kept their retainers in order, as by arbitrating in their quarrels. It was otherwise when lords competed for regional dominance, as did the dukes of Norfolk and Suffolk, and the Nevilles and Percies, in a period of weak monarchy. 'Livery and maintenance' could weaken the administration of justice. In 1384 the parliamentary Commons complained that wrongdoers expected to escape retribution through the patronage of the lords whose liveries of cloth or badges they wore. Sheriffs and justices of the peace retained by a lord would not be impartial: juries could be packed or intimidated.

For many landed gentry, the best safeguard available was to have the 'good lordship' of a noble protector by becoming his retainer, probably without a pension. Social aspirations may have helped to swell retinues, because tradesmen and rustic tenants able to wear a lord's livery could describe themselves as 'yeomen'; while those of more dignified standing were known as 'gentlemen'. Both these personal descriptions became widely used in the 15th cent., particularly in indictments of riotous assemblies. Eventually bastard feudalism was curbed, though not abolished, by Henry VII's conciliar jurisdiction and his statute of 1504, which prohibited retaining without royal licence. RLS

Bastwick, John (1593–1654). Bastwick was an indefatigable opponent of *Laud and the bishops. Born in Essex, he went to Emmanuel College, Cambridge, and then practised as a physician. In the 1630s he published several pamphlets urging presbyterianism and denouncing the church which was 'as full of ceremonies as a dog is of fleas'. In 1637, with *Prynne and Burton, he was sentenced to the pillory, to a fine, life imprisonment, and to have his ears cropped. *Clarendon subsequently described him as 'a half-witted, cracked-brained fellow', but admitted that it was unwise to treat gentlemen 'as the poorest and most mechanic malefactors used to be', since it was much resented by professional men and 'treasured up wrath for the time to come'. Bastwick was exiled to the Scillies but brought back in triumph by the *Long Parliament in 1640. He subsequently served in the parliamentary army and continued to wage pamphlet warfare until his death. JAC

Basutoland. See LESOTHO.

Bath (Roman). The Roman settlement of Aquae Sulis developed where a number of thermal springs erupt from the floor of the Avon valley. Chief of these is the King's Bath Spring which delivers nearly 250,000 gallons of water a day and was the focus of Roman activity. Also within the Roman site were the far smaller Hetlin (Hot Bath) and Cross Bath Springs. Late Iron Age coins recovered from the spring and the presence of a presiding Celtic goddess, Sulis (assimilated to Minerva), suggest pre-Roman veneration. The religious and thermal precinct at Bath is the earliest and grandest Roman civil building complex in Britain. Constructed probably from the 60s, it comprised a precinct containing a tetrastyle classical temple, on axis with which was an altar. Laid out on a series of cross-axes were the reservoir capturing the King's Bath Spring and the baths complex, which consisted of a large, covered, lead-lined bath (the Great Bath) with subsidiary baths to east and west. The date, size, plan, classical style of the temple, and detail of the architectural stonework and sculpture mark the complex out as exceptional in the western part of the empire. Round about 200, major refurbishment of the buildings included modifications to the temple, the replacing of the timber roofs of the baths with a tile barrel-vault, and the enclosing of the reservoir within a barrel-vaulted containing building. Excavation of the main spring has yielded over 12,000 Roman coins and 130 lead tablets inscribed in Latin with curses (*defixiones*) as well as intaglios and other offerings to the deity, where the steaming spring issues from the underworld. In the later 4th cent. maintenance of the complex started to lapse, with silt accumulating. After the end of Roman rule and technology, the waters backed up and eventually the complex fell into ruin, though the town is mentioned in the *Anglo-Saxon Chronicle* for 577. Protected in the 3rd cent. by a defensive/precinct wall enclosing 25 acres, the springs and their temples and baths lay west of the Avon. To the east, in the Walcot area, seems to have been the main focus of a town presumably serving both the sacred complex and the local country-dwellers. ASEC

(post-Roman) After the collapse of Roman power, Bath did not slide into total insignificance. *Edgar was crowned there in 973 and in 1090 the diocese was transferred from Wells to Bath. The *Gesta Stephani* of 1138 referred to visitors from all over England making their way to the baths. *Leland, in the 1530s, commented that Bath was much frequented by people 'diseased with lepre, pokkes, scabbes and great aches'. Queen Elizabeth paid a brief visit in 1591 but found the smell disagreeable. Anne of Denmark went there in 1615 but in 1631 Dr Edward Jorden warned that the water was too dirty to drink. A regulation by the corporation in 1648 does not inspire confidence: 'no person shall presume to cast or throw any dog, bitch or other live beast into any of the said baths.' *Pepys visited in 1668, enjoyed the music, but thought it could not be clean to have so many bodies in the same water. *Mary of Modena was said to have conceived her son James in September 1687 while visiting.

The transformation of Bath into the fashionable spa of Georgian England was primarily the work of two men—Richard 'Beau' *Nash and John Wood. Nash was master of ceremonies from 1705 to 1761 and imposed order and decency upon what was potentially an unruly and difficult clientele, insisting that rank be put aside—the 'happy secret of uniting the vulgar and the great'. To the baths were added concerts, receptions, balls, fireworks, the theatre, milliners, booksellers, coffee-houses, card parties, and pleasure walks in Spring Gardens (1735) and Sydney Gardens (1795). Wood began the massive reconstruction of Bath from medieval huddle to Georgian spaciousness, under the patronage of Ralph Allen, whose estate at Prior Park above the city provided the stone. Queen Square (1729–36) was followed by the Mineral Water hospital (1737–42), North and South Parades (1740–8) and Gay Street (1750s). John Wood, junior, added the Circus (1754–8) to his father's design, Royal Crescent (1767–75), and the Assembly Rooms (1769–71). The glory of Bath lasted until the early 19th cent., by which time success had bred disaster and Nash's vulgarians had taken over. Catherine Morland in Jane Austen's *Northanger Abbey* (1818) found that in the Pump Room on Sundays there was 'not a genteel face to be seen'. JAC

Bath, Order of the. Bathing as a symbol of purification was an element in the creation of spotless knights and the practice grew up of dubbing numbers of knights on grand occasions like coronations. By the time of Henry V they were known as knights of the Bath, though no order existed. In 1725 John Anstis, Garter King of Arms, suggested the 'revival' of the order. *Walpole and George I agreed, partly to add lustre to the new regime, partly to fend off aspirants. The red ribbon became coveted. The Order was extended in 1815 and 1847. It has a military and civilian division, with three categories in each—the Knights Grand Cross (GCB), Knights Commander (KCB), and Companions (CB). Women members are dames. The dean of Westminster is usually its dean and the chapel of the order is Henry VII's chapel in Westminster abbey. JAC

Bath abbey is a fine example of late Perpendicular building. Begun in 1499 by Bishop Oliver King, it replaced a larger Norman foundation. The architects, the Vertue brothers, were also responsible for Henry VII's chapel at Westminster: each has magnificent fan vaulting. The bishop is said to have been encouraged by a dream showing the ladder to heaven, and the scene is reproduced on the west front. The abbey was a Benedictine foundation and fell into neglect after the *dissolution of the monasteries, but, being in the middle of the town, was taken over in 1573 as the parish church. JAC

Bath and Wells, diocese of. The present see, created in 909, is roughly conterminous with the old county of Somerset. Though Wells itself was founded in *c.*704 as a religious centre by *Ine, king of Wessex, and his nephew *Aldhelm, first bishop of *Sherborne, it was not until 909 that *Edward the Elder split the bishopric of Sherborne into four, Wells being the new see for Somerset, and Athelm, a monk from Glastonbury nearby, the first bishop. In 973 *Dunstan crowned *Edgar as king of all England at *Bath abbey. The first Norman bishop, John de Villula (1088–1122), became abbot of Bath, to which in accordance with the Council of London (1075) he transferred his see (1090). This led to friction between the monks of Bath and the canons of Wells over episcopal elections. In 1176 Pope Alexander III resolved the dispute by declaring the cities to be joint-sees and ordering the chapters to hold elections together. Complications intensified when Savaric, bishop of Bath and Wells (1192–1205), became abbot of Glastonbury and styled himself 'bishop of Glastonbury'. In 1245 Pope Innocent IV finally resolved the matter in favour of joint elections and the retention of the title 'Bath and Wells'. Later bishops were often important nationally. Robert *Burnell (1275–92), chancellor of England, Edward I's friend and adviser, Thomas Beckington (1443–65), Latin secretary to Henry VI, and Thomas *Wolsey (1518–23) held the see *in commendam*. Though at the Reformation the bishopric lost over half its estates it nevertheless had further notable bishops, including William *Laud (1626–8), later Charles I's archbishop, and Thomas *Ken (1685–91), the saintly non-juror. Despite the bishopric's relative lack of importance, its bishops still retain the shadow of former glory, the privilege, along with bishops of Durham, of supporting the sovereign during the coronation. The magnificent 13th-cent. cathedral stands within a complex of buildings, including the moated bishop's palace, started by Burnell, and the 14th-cent. Vicars' Close. WMM

Bathurst, Henry, 2nd Earl Bathurst (1714–94). Bathurst's career spanned politics and the law. He was an MP from 1735 to 1751 and became a king's counsel in 1746 and a judge of the common pleas in 1754. As a politician Bathurst opposed the Walpole ministry and was later active in the interest of *Frederick, prince of Wales. After the latter's death Bathurst supported government and his elevation to the bench was at the recommendation of Lord *Hardwicke. The untimely death of Lord Chancellor Yorke in 1770 resulted in Bathurst serving as a commissioner for the great seal until he was unexpectedly promoted to the chancellorship in January 1771. He was consequently raised to the peerage as Baron Apsley and, in 1775, succeeded as Earl Bathurst. As chancellor he was competent and even-handed, but not especially noteworthy. A loyal Northite, he surrendered the chancellorship to Thurlow in 1778, but served as lord president from 1779 until the fall of the ministry in 1782. DW

Bathurst, Henry, 3rd Earl Bathurst (1762–1834). Bathurst's grandfather was one of the twelve Tory peers created in 1712 to carry the treaty of *Utrecht and in 1772, aged 88, had been promoted earl; his father was lord chancellor 1771–8 and lord president of the council 1779–82. As Lord Apsley, Bathurst entered Parliament on the family interest at Cirencester as soon as he was of age and was appointed a lord of the Admiralty by *Pitt, a personal friend. He held the post until 1789 when he became a lord of the Treasury, and from 1793 to 1802 was a commissioner of the Board of Control. He had a long career in the Tory ministries of the early 19th cent.—president of the Board of Trade 1807–12, secretary for war 1812–27, and lord president of the council 1828–30. He was given the Garter in 1817. He held a number of valuable sinecures and according to *Greville, once his secretary, made moderate talents go a long way. JAC

'Bats, Parliament of', 1426. Competition between Humphrey, duke of *Gloucester, and Henry *Beaufort, bishop of Winchester, to dominate government in the minority of Henry VI assumed dangerous proportions with a riot on London bridge, 30 October 1425. A Parliament was called to Leicester for 18 February 1426, then adjourned to Northampton. Members and their attendants had orders not to come armed, but many carried clubs or 'bats'. The quarrel was submitted to arbitration. Peace was made, for the time being. Beaufort resigned as chancellor and went abroad. RLS

Battle abbey. Founded by William I in fulfilment of a vow made before the battle of *Hastings, it was commenced on lower ground to the west nearer water and shelter, but the Marmoutier monks were angrily ordered to rebuild with the high altar over the spot where Harold II fell; it was consecrated to St Martin (1094). The Benedictine house had a remarkable range of privileges as well as generous endowments, and grew in wealth and fame despite intermittent havoc from plague. It was surrendered in 1538 and the church destroyed, but the great gatehouse and other abbey buildings still stand. ASH

Baugé, battle of, 1421. On 22 March 1421 Thomas, duke of *Clarence, while campaigning in Anjou, was killed in a rash sortie. Lord Tankerville was also killed, and *Somerset, Fitzwalter, and Huntingdon captured. No more than a nasty reverse, Baugé heralded the French recovery after *Agincourt. Henry V left for France to restore the situation and died on the campaign in 1422. JAC

Baxter, Richard (1615–91). Puritan divine. A Shropshireman, Baxter was educated locally. Sickened by a brief spell at the royal court, he returned home to study for ordination, after which he became master of Bridgnorth Grammar School (1638). Contact with nonconformists, however, sowed doubts about Anglicanism and episcopacy. After a spell as vicar of Kidderminster (1642) and parliamentary army chaplain, he became disillusioned by both sides in the Civil War. In 1660 he welcomed Charles II back, but his inflexibility at the *Savoy conference helped its breakdown. After refusing the see of Hereford, he preached in London until ejected after the Act of *Uniformity (1662). The outstanding personality among the dissenters of 1662, he was imprisoned on several occasions for preaching without licence. Having helped overthrow James II, he welcomed William and Mary. A prolific writer and man of conscience, he occupied a unique place in contemporary religious life. WMM

Bayeux Tapestry. An extraordinary work: simultaneously, it is a major work of art, unique for its time, a stunning piece of political propaganda in support of the Norman claim to the English throne in 1066, and, archaeologically speaking, a record of immense importance for the study of a host of subjects ranging from contemporary ship construction and navigation, military tactics, and equipment, to the more homely—clothes and fashions, furniture and fittings. In considerable detail, it portrays 626 people, 202 horses, 55 dogs, 505 animals of various sorts, 37 fortresses and/or buildings, 41 boats and ships, and innumerable weapons, clothes, and agricultural implements.

Strictly speaking, the tapestry is an embroidery, some 230 feet long and around 20 inches high. It is worked in eight coloured wools on a plain linen ground, its masses of colour, in couched and laid work, defined by stem or outline stitch. It was produced in six separate pieces, the consistent quality indicating very close monitoring by the overall designer. It consists of one single horizontal line of action set within two borders (above and below), and takes the form of a sequence of vignettes, which together provide an episodic account of events.

Politically, the tapestry records some of the events of 1064/5–6 which culminated in the death of Harold II at the battle of *Hastings. But it is certainly not objective. The tapestry seeks to impart a political message which splices with its overarching moral—the inevitable fate that awaits any man who breaks a solemn oath sworn on the relics of Bayeux cathedral. Since Harold is shown swearing such an oath to Duke William of Normandy in full public view, the tapestry's essential story is that of Harold's downfall after he committed perjury by taking the English throne on Edward the Confessor's death. William in this context is but the rod of divine vengeance.

Internal evidence indicates that the tapestry was produced for Bishop *Odo of Bayeux, William's half-brother. It is now generally accepted that it was made in England, famous for its embroidery work, probably in Kent, of which Odo was earl (1067–82). If the attribution to Odo is correct, then it must have been made between 1066 and 1097, when Odo died; and if it is English, then a date in the 1070s or early 1080s is most likely as Odo rebelled in 1082, was imprisoned for five years, and lost Kent. SL

Beachy Head, battle of, 1690. Command of the Channel was of critical importance in 1690, when William III and James II struggled for control of Ireland and the French threatened to invade England as a diversion. In June, de Tourville put to sea with a French fleet of 78 vessels. *Torrington, commanding the joint Anglo-Dutch fleet, was apprehensive and cautious: 'the odds are great,' he wrote, and his main objective was not to hazard his fleet. On 29 June the brunt of the action fell upon the Dutch, who lost six ships. Torrington withdrew to the safety of the Thames estuary, leaving the French to dominate the Channel. Torrington was sent to the Tower, court-martialled, but acquitted. JAC

beagling is the hunting of hares on foot with the aid of beagle hounds, specially bred for the purpose. It was practised in the classical world and held its popularity in England until gradually replaced in the 18th cent. by fox-hunting. The mounted version, practised by harriers, was common in the 19th cent. but has since declined. Many of the remaining packs of beagles are owned by military establishments or by public schools. JAC

Beale, Dorothea (1831–1906). Headmistress. Born into a pious family, Dorothea Beale's religious convictions led her into teaching and a lifetime's commitment to the cause of education for women. She entered Queen's College, London, in 1848 where her ability was recognized by the offer of the post of mathematics tutor, followed by the headship of the college's preparatory school. But it is as principal of Cheltenham Ladies' College that she is best remembered. In 1858 the college was in danger of closure. Beale improved the calibre of the teaching staff and broadened the syllabus, with dramatic results. 'A benevolent despot' in the words of *DNB*, she enforced a rule of silence, hoping to eliminate what she considered the female vice of gossiping. She was instrumental in establishing St Hilda's Hall, Oxford, as a teachers' training institution. She died from cancer in 1906 leaving £55,000 to the college. SMC

bear-baiting. Reputedly introduced from Italy in the 12th cent., the spectator sport of setting dogs onto a bear chained to a stake occurred usually in an arena known as a bear garden, such as that at Bankside, south of the Thames, attended by Henry VIII and Elizabeth. Many Tudor nobles kept bear 'sleuths' (packs), generally well looked after, but they were not a purely aristocratic indulgence: town councils had official bears, and baits were held at markets and fairs. In Paris Garden, another regular venue in Southwark, a grandstand collapsed in 1583, killing or injuring many of the spectators. Despite Macaulay's remark that the puritans hated bear-baiting for the pleasure afforded the spectators rather than concern for the bear, there were stirrings of disapproval, but the sport remained popular and declined only slowly, not legally banned until 1835. Street-names such as Bear Lane, near Blackfriars Bridge, attest to its place in social life. ASH

Beatles. The Beatles, a 1960s Liverpool pop group, were the decade's most commercially successful rock-pop musicians and a social phenomenon ('Beatlemania') in crystallizing youth culture. The later musical experimentalism of John Lennon (murdered, 1980) and Paul McCartney, the songwriters of the 'Fab Four', subverted, revolutionized, and continues to influence popular culture for younger generations. ASH

Beaton, David (*c.*1494–1546). Cardinal. Beaton was the nephew of Archbishop Beaton or Bethune of Glasgow and St Andrews, whom he succeeded as archbishop in 1539. He already held a French bishopric, was a cardinal, and had been much employed in James V's French matrimonial negotiations. After James's death in 1542 *Mary of Guise relied upon him greatly and he was chancellor [S] 1543–6. He strongly resisted the proposed marriage between the infant Mary, queen of Scots, and Prince Edward of England (later Edward VI). His life-style was magnificent and his behaviour profligate. In March 1546 Beaton was instrumental in the burning of George *Wishart, a reformer. Two months later, friends of Wishart burst into the castle of St Andrews and murdered the archbishop. His nephew, James Beaton, was the last catholic archbishop of Glasgow, serving from 1552 until 1560, when he retired to France. JAC

Beatty, Sir David, later 1st Earl Beatty (1871–1936). Admiral. In 1914 Beatty was one of the youngest admirals in the Royal Navy, and, as commander of the battle-cruiser squadron of the Grand Fleet, held one of the navy's most prestigious appointments. He led the battle-cruisers at the *Dogger Bank and *Jutland, where he lost three of his ships. Beatty was a demonstrative, flamboyant, and aggressive commander, much admired by those who served under him. In December 1916 he succeeded *Jellicoe as commander of the Grand Fleet. But despite his own criticisms of Jellicoe's lack of aggression at Jutland, for the rest of the war he pursued the same Fabian strategy designed to keep the German surface fleet bottled up in harbour. At the end of the war he was appointed 1st sea lord, a post he held until 1927. During this period he was responsible for the post-war reorganization of the navy and acted as a member of the British delegation which helped to draft the Washington naval treaty, an agreement which prevented the outbreak of a naval arms race between Britain and the USA. DF

Beauchamp, Guy de, 10th earl of Warwick (*c.*1270–1315). Warwick's father was prominent in Edward I's reign in campaigns against the Welsh and Scots. Warwick succeeded to the earldom in 1298 and fought at *Falkirk with distinction. But at Edward II's accession, he quarrelled violently with the favourite *Gaveston and in 1310 was one of the *Ordainers trying to control the king, and working closely with *Thomas of Lancaster. In 1312 he handed over Gaveston to be executed after he had been held in Warwick castle. He refused to serve in the *Bannockburn campaign and died the following year: in the circumstances suggestions of poison were inevitable. JAC

Beauchamp, Richard, 13th earl of Warwick (1382–1439). Warwick's early years were spent fighting Welsh rebels with Prince Henry (later Henry V) and winning an international reputation as a paragon of chivalry. His pilgrimage to Jerusalem in 1408–10 was punctuated with 'feats of arms' in France, Italy, and Prussia. He served Henry in major embassies and the conquest of Normandy. Although a regular member of Henry VI's council, and in charge of the young king's education from 1428 to 1436, he still periodically campaigned in France. He was appointed lieutenant-general there in 1437 and died in Rouen. With his great landed wealth, well-served administration, and enjoyment of royal favour, Warwick dominated the west midlands. He is commemorated by a gilded bronze effigy in his chapel in St Mary's, Warwick, and an illustrated panegyric by the Warwickshire antiquary John Rous (d. 1491). RLS

Beaufort, Edmund, duke of Somerset. See SOMERSET, EDMUND BEAUFORT, DUKE OF.

Beaufort, Henry (*c.*1375–1447), cardinal bishop of Winchester. The second son of *John of Gaunt and Catherine Swynford, Beaufort rose rapidly in the church, becoming bishop of Lincoln in his early twenties, translating to Winchester in 1404. As half-brother of Henry IV, he was rarely far from the heart of Lancastrian government, being chancellor of England under three kings in 1403–5, 1413–17, and 1424–6. A capable administrator and tireless diplomat, his skills and wealth were indispensable to the regime for over forty years. Yet his relationship with the royal family was ambivalent. He quarrelled both with Henry V, over his acceptance of a cardinal's red hat, and with Humphrey of *Gloucester for pre-eminence in England during the minority of Henry VI. His immense wealth secured him in power, guaranteed by extensive loans made to the crown from 1417. He shamelessly used his position to the advantage of his family, but there can be no doubting his commitment to the dynasty. In his later years he endeavoured, without success, to achieve a peace settlement with France. Being created cardinal legate in 1427, he was content to be the papal representative in England. Proud, ambitious, and avaricious, delegating his spiritual responsibility in his diocese to subordinates, he stands as the exemplar of a worldly political prelate in late medieval England, outshining even Thomas *Wolsey. He was buried in Winchester cathedral. AJP

Beaufort, Joan. See JOAN BEAUFORT.

Beaufort, Lady Margaret (1443–1509). The mother of Henry VII, Margaret Beaufort was one of the most remarkable women of the 15th cent. She was married to Edmund Tudor, earl of Richmond, as a child and conceived Henry when she was only 12. Tudor died when she was six months pregnant; she outlived two further husbands, but had no more children. She was separated from her son in 1461, when he was 4, and apart from a one-week reunion in 1470, did not see him again until he was king. Nevertheless, she devoted herself to his cause. By 1482 she was near to completing terms for his return from exile in Brittany. However, Edward IV's death and the accession of Richard III intervened. Tudor now became the pretender to the throne and Margaret threw herself into the conspiracy which triumphed on the field of Bosworth. As mother of the king, for 24 years Margaret wielded immense political influence. She was the only person to whom he deferred. She outlived Henry, her last service being to help manipulate the succession of her grandson Henry VIII, dying two weeks after his coronation. A small, birdlike woman, in later years troubled by failing eyesight and arthritis, she was renowned for her piety, sponsoring the publication of devotional literature. She was the founder of two colleges at Cambridge, Christ's and St John's. Her portrait hangs in both colleges, whose great gates are adorned with her heraldic imagery. At Oxford, she founded the first chair of divinity, and the first women's college, Lady Margaret Hall (1879), was named after her. AJP

Beaufort, Thomas, duke of Exeter. See EXETER, THOMAS BEAUFORT, DUKE OF.

Beaumaris castle, on the south coast of Anglesey, was started for Edward I after the Welsh revolt of September 1294, although it may have been planned as early as 1283/4. Edward's castle-building was directed at maintaining control of Wales by isolating the area of Snowdonia, the focus of Welsh resistance, and separating it from Anglesey, the main grain-growing region. Beaumaris formed part of a strategic ring of fortresses designed to make Edward's conquest permanent. The castle was built over the site of Llanfaes, a Welsh royal manor and principal port of the island. The houses of the town were dismantled and re-erected in the new English borough of Beaumaris, close by, the inhabitants being transported to Newborough or re-established in the English town. Work, under the direction of Master James of St George, was pushed forward rapidly, and the project demonstrates the resources Edward was able to deploy. By the end of the first building season, in November 1295, over £6,700 had been expended. This included over £2,000 on materials, together with the wages of the 450 masons, 375 quarriers, and 1,800 other workmen employed, plus payment of the garrison. Master James reported to the Exchequer that nowhere were the walls less than 20 feet high; that the majority of the towers had been begun and that gates had been hung and could be locked at night. Although Master James urged that more money be sent to continue the works, activity tailed off and by 1300 all work on the castle had ceased, as Edward diverted resources into the Scottish wars. Work was resumed between 1306 and 1330 but the castle was not completed. The castle's defences were not threatened until 1646, when it was garrisoned for Charles I in the Civil War. LR

Beaverbrook, Lord (1879–1964). Newspaper proprietor. Born to a Scots-Canadian family in Ontario, William Aitken worked as a company negotiator, and used his business acumen to become a millionaire. In 1910 he journeyed to England, where his fellow Scots-Canadian, Andrew Bonar *Law, found him a seat as a Conservative MP. Beaverbrook's penchant for making friends with men and women of influence served him well. He cultivated the acquaintance of *Lloyd George, played a murky part in Lloyd George's overthrow of *Asquith, and was rewarded with a peerage (1916) and membership of the Privy Council (1918).

Beaverbrook had, meanwhile, bought the *Daily Express*. He discovered he had a natural flair for journalism and this, combined with his business sense, helped boost the paper's popularity: by 1936 it had achieved a world-record circulation of 2.25 million copies per day. In 1923 he acquired control of the *Evening Standard*. Beaverbrook used his newspapers as vehicles for his own idiosyncratic views: empire free trade, support of Edward VIII during the *abdication crisis, and for Neville *Chamberlain over Munich. In 1940 Churchill made him minister of aircraft production. The choice was inspired. Beaverbrook's ruthless methods helped ensure the victory of the Royal Air Force in the Battle of Britain. GA

Bechuanaland. See BOTSWANA.

Becket, Thomas (*c.*1120–70). Archbishop of Canterbury who was murdered in his own cathedral and so became a saint. Son of a Norman merchant settled in London, Becket worked as an accounts clerk to a banker (a cousin of his) before entering the service of Archbishop *Theobald of Canterbury in 1145. He became Theobald's confidential agent and was rewarded with the rich archdeaconry of Canterbury. Soon after being crowned by Theobald, Henry II appointed Thomas chancellor. In this office he displayed a wide range of talents, administrative, diplomatic, and military. He also enjoyed an ostentatiously lavish life-style. His zeal in the king's interests, even when they appeared to conflict with the church's, gave Theobald cause for concern and, not surprisingly, led Henry to believe that Thomas was his loyal friend. When Theobald died, Henry decided that Thomas should succeed him. This ran counter to the strong Canterbury tradition that the archbishop ought to be a monk. Reluctantly the cathedral monks agreed to elect the king's good servant. On 2 June 1162 Becket was ordained priest, and the next day consecrated archbishop.

At once Becket began to oppose the king, even on fairly routine matters which raised issues of principle only for someone who was determined to find them. He began to campaign for the canonization of *Anselm, a monk-archbishop who had defied kings. Many more or less imaginative attempts have been made to explain the volte-face but, in the absence of good evidence for Becket's state of mind in 1162–3, they remain highly speculative. The earliest lives of Becket, in Latin by *John of Salisbury, Edward Grim, and William fitzStephen, in French by Guernes of Pont-Sainte-Maxence, do little to unravel the mystery; written in the shadow of his murder and canonization, they present the martyred saint.

Whatever Becket's motives, Henry felt betrayed. Twelfth-cent. church–state relations bristled with problems which could be, and since the ending of the *Investiture contest normally were, shelved by men of goodwill, but which could provide a field day for men who were determined to quarrel. King and archbishop were soon quarrelling over a wide range of issues, among them the question of 'criminous clerks', i.e. *benefit of clergy. In January 1164 Thomas reluctantly but publicly accepted the constitutions of *Clarendon, and then infuriated the king and confused his fellow-bishops by trying to wriggle out of his commitment. At the Council of Northampton (October 1164) Henry brought charges against Becket arising out of his conduct while chancellor. Becket, seeing that the king was determined to break him, fled in disguise to France, where he remained in exile until 1170, studying canon law, leading an ascetic life, and claiming to be defending the rights not only of the church of Canterbury but of the church as a whole. Both Louis VII of France and Pope Alexander III urged a reconciliation, but neither Henry nor Thomas could trust the other. After years of protracted and fruitless negotiations, the coronation of *Henry the Young King in June 1170 by the archbishop of York brought matters to a swift conclusion. In Becket's eyes crowning the king was a Canterbury privilege. He agreed terms with Henry. This enabled him to return to England with the intention of punishing those who had infringed that privilege. In November he excommunicated the archbishop of York and two other bishops. They complained to the king, then in Normandy. Henry's angry words prompted four knights to cross the Channel and kill Becket on 29 December 1170, a murder that shocked Christendom. Little more than two years later, in February 1173, he was canonized by Alexander III.

During his lifetime few churchmen thought that Becket's truculence did much to help the cause of Canterbury, of the English church, or of the church in general. Probably no one thought his conduct was that of a saint, even if he had taken to wearing coarse and lice-ridden undergarments. But his murder changed everything. It put Henry in the wrong. It forced him to do penance and to make concessions, though none of lasting significance. The church of Canterbury clearly gained. *The *Canterbury Tales* bear eloquent witness to the fact that for centuries Becket's tomb in the cathedral was the greatest pilgrimage shrine in England. In 1538 Henry VIII declared Becket a traitor, but though he destroyed the shrine, he could not eliminate the cult. JG

Beckett, Samuel (1900–89). Irish novelist and playwright, whose *Waiting for Godot* (1952) was to the 1950s what *The Waste Land* was to the 1920s. A play in which 'nothing happens, twice', it was followed by others paring away character and action in a *reductio ad absurdum* raised to the level of metaphysical inquiry. *Not I* (1972) lasts only fifteen minutes and all we see is a shadowy auditor and a woman's mouth from which words stream, expressing, in Beckett's words, 'that there is nothing to express . . . together with the obligation to express'. From 1937 settled in Paris and writing in French, his affinities were with Sartre and Heidegger, though an earlier Cartesian dualism often shaped his work. As a story-teller and novelist he was indebted to James *Joyce, and his trilogy, completed in 1953 with *The Unnameable*, though not for the faint-hearted, is redeemed by touches of the master's sly humour. JNRS

Beckford, William (1709–70). Beckford was a new man in the aristocratic world of Hanoverian politics and a link between traditional Toryism and *Wilkite radicalism. His great wealth came from Jamaican estates and he was frequently reminded, when tribune of the people, that he was a slave-owner. Sent to England to be educated at Westminster and Oxford, he remained and was elected MP for Shaftesbury in 1747. In 1754 he transferred to London, where he had built up an electoral interest, strengthening his position by bringing two brothers into Parliament. From 1756 onwards he was a supporter of *Pitt. Early in the reign of George III he launched a series of attacks upon aristocratic oligarchy and called for a measure of parliamentary reform. He was lord mayor of London in 1762/3 and again in 1769/70 when he presented a Wilkite petition to the king, accompanying it with a well-publicized rebuke, which was subsequently inscribed on his statue in the Guildhall. He died unexpectedly a month later, leaving several illegitimate children, and a 10-year old son, who became the author of *Vathek* and the recluse of Fonthill. JAC

Bedchamber crisis, 1839. After the resignation of Lord *Melbourne in 1839 Robert *Peel was summoned to form a ministry. Peel mentioned casually to the queen the changes he thought should be made to the royal household. He wanted the queen to dismiss those ladies of the bedchamber whose husbands were Whigs. Subsequently Peel received a letter from the queen stating that the removal of the ladies of her bedchamber would be repugnant to her feelings. Peel objected in particular to Lord Morpeth's sister and Lady Normanby and refused to give way. The queen appealed to Melbourne and, in their desire to support her, the Whig statesmen reluctantly returned to their posts. With the fall of the Whig administration in 1841 the question rose again. This time the prince consort arranged for the ladies in question to resign voluntarily and this compromise settled the difficulty. RAS

Bede, St (672/3–735). First English historian, author of the *Ecclesiastical History of the English People* (*c.*731). Deacon, priest, and monk, Bede is generally associated with *Jarrow, but probably lived mostly in the monastery of *Monkwearmouth, which he entered in 679/80. Bede owed his scholarship, and much of his outlook, to their founder, *Benedict Biscop. He travelled a little to Lindisfarne and York.

History was not his prime concern. He wrote biblical commentaries, hagiography, hymns and homilies, textbooks of instruction in Latin, and scientific texts, and, to Egbert (bishop of York), a letter criticizing episcopal and monastic standards in Northumbria.

Bede was particularly interested in miracles and in the calculation of dates and time. Some of his scientific scholarship was advanced and his historical influence profound. His commentaries were soon in heavy demand on the continent. He was the first systematically to use the *anno domini* dating system and his idealized portrait of the 7th-cent. church inspired King *Alfred and Bishop *Æthelwold, who attempted its re-creation. Modern scholars, attempting reconstruction and deconstruction, depend heavily upon him.

In historical writing Bede was influenced by the 4th-cent. Eusebius of Caesarea, but the greatest non-biblical influence upon him was probably Pope Gregory I. His purposes were varied. The prime one was to facilitate the salvation of his people. The *Ecclesiastical History*'s parade of exemplars, like *Aidan, *Cuthbert, and *Oswald, to remedy contemporary defects entailed, inconveniently for modern scholars, much selection. The English are given a Roman historical context and destiny. To Bede's imposition of order on a more complex past, his so-called list of *bretwaldas can be related. He may have felt that a 'national' history would encourage 'national' unity. He may have been offering a Christian alternative to traditional secular sagas.

Bede was in touch with highly placed people (including King *Ceolwulf, Acca, bishop of Hexham, and Egbert), his contacts brought information, and he was interested in the wider world. Yet lack of experience outside his monastery may have made him so idealistic as to be considered isolated, not sharing other clerics' interests. But the quarrels generated by *Wilfrid may have inspired his presentation of an alternative version of 7th-cent. ecclesiastical history to that offered in Wilfrid's biography. Whether considered as the 'opposition' view or a 'compromise' to reconcile two parties, it suggests sensitivity to, and perhaps involvement in, politics.

Well written and researched, Bede's works are subtle and complex. Some attempt was made to promote his cult, but Viking raids caused Monkwearmouth and Jarrow to be abandoned *c.*800. Remains claimed to be Bede's were discovered in the mid-11th cent., and moved to Durham cathedral, where they remain. Bede was recognized as a doctor of the church by Pope Leo XIII in 1899. AER

Bedford, John of Lancaster, duke of (1389–1435). The third son of King Henry IV, John was created duke of Bedford by his brother Henry V in 1414. Throughout his life he identified himself with his brother's policies, especially in pursuing English claims to the French throne. He was lieutenant of the kingdom during Henry's absences in France. He also proved himself an able soldier, commanding the ships which defeated the French fleet at the mouth of the Seine before relieving *Harfleur in August 1416. After Henry's death in August 1422 he was appointed regent of France. In alliance with John, duke of Brittany, and Philip, duke of Burgundy, whose sister Anne he married in June 1423, Bedford prosecuted the war in France, at first with considerable success. But his position in France was made difficult by both lack of funds and the uneasy state of England induced partly by the actions of his brother Humphrey, duke of *Gloucester, who was acting as lord protector to the infant Henry VI. After the failure of the siege of *Orléans in 1429 Bedford resigned the regency in favour of Philip of Burgundy but retained the government of Normandy, where he continued to pursue English policy, securing the coronation of the young Henry VI in Paris in December 1431. The death of Duchess Anne and Bedford's marriage to Jacqueline, daughter of the comte de Saint-Pol, in 1433 destroyed friendly relations between England and Burgundy and seriously undermined the English position in France. Bedford died at Rouen in September 1435, his policies in ruins, after the failure of peace negotiations at the Congress of *Arras, which had seen Duke Philip finally desert the English cause and make his peace with France. There is a contemporary portrait of the duke in the manuscript known as the Bedford Hours (BL Add. MS 18850) where he is shown kneeling before St George. His rule in France was deliberately mild; he lowered taxation, reformed the debased coinage, and sought to impose a fair administration. Bedford, though pursuing the English cause, was universally respected. Some years after his death King Louis XI of France, on being counselled to deface his tomb, is said to have replied, 'let his body rest in quiet; which when he was living, would have disquieted the proudest of us all; and as for the tomb, which, I assure you, is not so worthy as his acts deserve, I account it an honour to have him remain in my dominions.' LR

Bedford, Francis Russell, 4th earl of (1593–1641). Bedford hoped to resolve the political crisis of early 1641, since he was acceptable to Charles I as well as the parliamentary leaders. In concert with his client John *Pym, a key figure in the Commons, he planned to accept office in the king's government, take control of the Treasury, and restore the royal finances with the aid of a substantial parliamentary grant. In return, Charles would abandon both *Strafford and the *Arminians and return to traditional rule in church and state. Bedford was prepared to save Strafford's life, which Charles made a condition, but could not carry his parliamentary associates with him. At this critical moment, he was struck down by smallpox and died on 9 May. RL

Bedford, John Russell, 1st earl of (*c.*1485–1555). The founder of the fortunes of the house of Russell was born in Dorset of gentry stock and became a gentleman of the bedchamber to Henry VII and Henry VIII. In the 1520s he was much employed in diplomatic and military matters. From 1529 to 1536 he was MP for Buckinghamshire and in 1537 became comptroller of the household. In 1539 he was created baron and given the Garter. From 1540 to 1543 he served as lord high admiral and from 1542 to his death as lord privy seal. His gains from the *dissolution of the monasteries were gigantic, and included Tavistock in Devon, Woburn in Bedfordshire, and Covent Garden in London. In 1549 he helped to suppress the western rising and was advanced to the earldom of Bedford. Though he endorsed the proclamation of Lady Jane *Grey in 1553, he succeeded in retaining the favour of Mary. The *DNB* remarks demurely that he was 'by no means in favour of the restoration of the abbey lands to their original uses'. In his *Letter to a Noble Lord*, *Burke declared that 'the grants to the House of Russell were so enormous . . . as to stagger credibility'. Russell he dismissed as 'the prompt and greedy instrument of a *levelling* tyrant'. JAC

Bedford, John Russell, 4th duke of (1710–71). Succeeding to one of the wealthiest dukedoms in Britain in 1732,

Bedford developed a political following which made him a valuable catch for any ministry. He served as 1st lord of the Admiralty (1744–8) and as southern secretary (1748–51), resigning after lengthy bickering with *Newcastle. Bedford returned to office in 1757 and was lord-lieutenant of Ireland until 1761. In September 1762 he went to Paris as ambassador responsible for the peace negotiations and signed the resultant treaty in February 1763. After a brief estrangement from administration, he joined the *Grenville ministry as lord president in September 1763. Thereafter his followers often acted with those of Grenville, fully supporting a hardline attitude towards the American colonies. Following protracted negotiations in 1767 the Bedfordites entered the *Grafton ministry; the duke himself, though approving the junction, was in poor health and chose not to accept office. Bedford's life was conterminous with the era of 'personal parties' and the office-hungry Bedfordites were criticized, even by contemporaries, as a faction motivated principally by material self-interest. DW

Bedford level was by far the most ambitious drainage scheme attempted in the Fens. A group of 'adventurers', under Francis, 4th earl of *Bedford, was granted authority in 1630 to proceed and Vermuyden, the Dutch engineer, put in charge. The main objective was to shorten the course of the river Ouse in order to increase its outfall: the most important cut was the old Bedford river from Earith to Salter's Lock, 21 miles long, and bypassing Ely. There was strong opposition from local people, acute financial and technological difficulties, and an interruption caused by the civil wars. The work was officially declared complete in 1652, though much of the reclaimed land was of dubious value and maintenance proved expensive, because of silting and peat shrinkage. See also CAMBRIDGESHIRE. JAC

Bedfordshire is a small, low-lying, and predominantly agricultural county, drained largely by the river Ouse, which meanders across it from west to east, and its tributaries, the Ivel, Ouzel, Flit, and Hiz. The southern boundary runs along the chalk ridge of the Chilterns. In pre-Roman times it formed part of the kingdom of the Catuvellauni. The Roman road Watling Street crossed the south-west corner. In 571 a victory of the English over the Britons seems to have secured the northern parts of the area for the kingdom of the *Middle Angles, and later for *Mercia. In the 9th cent., Alfred, king of *Wessex, divided the region with Guthrum, the Danish leader, who took the lands east and north of a line from the Lea to Bedford and up the Ouse to Stony Stratford. Forty years later, it was recovered by *Edward the Elder, king of Wessex, who fortified the town of Bedford in 919. It proved strong enough to beat off a Danish raid in 921 but succumbed once more to the Danes in the early 11th cent. By that time Bedfordshire was taking shape as a county and was mentioned in the *Anglo-Saxon Chronicle* for 1011. Bedford itself commanded an important river crossing over the Ouse, became a local route centre, and was the point from which the river was navigable by barges. In *Domesday Book it was, like the other county towns nearby, given separate treatment, but the report was unusually brief.

County and borough received parliamentary representation in the 13th cent. There were several long-established county interests. The Greys held Wrest Park from the 13th cent. onwards; the St Johns Bletso and Melchbourne Park from the 15th cent.; the Osborns Chicksands Priory from the 16th; and the owners of estates at Luton Hoo, Southill, and Ampthill also had influence. But the emerging and dominating interest was that of the Russells, whose acquisitions at the *dissolution of the monasteries included Covent Garden and Woburn abbey, and who became earls of Bedford in 1550 and dukes in 1694.

Despite its nearness to London, Bedfordshire remained something of a backwater. Celia Fiennes in the 1690s and *Defoe in the 1720s found Bedford a pleasant town, with a sprinkling of gentry, and Defoe admired the quantities of wheat the county produced. The cottage industry of straw-plaiting brought a modest prosperity, but in 1793 John Byng described Bedford as a 'vile, unimproved place'. The 19th cent. saw dramatic changes. By 1851 Luton had overtaken Bedford as the largest town. A boost to the local economy was the coming of the railways: the line from Bedford to St Pancras opened in 1868. Brick-making developed as an alternative to the declining hat trade and Luton turned to engineering. The Vauxhall car company established its headquarters in the town in 1907. In the extreme south of the county, on Dunstable downs, lies Whipsnade Zoo, opened in 1931. By 1961 Bedford's population had risen to 63,000, Luton's to 131,000.

The most famous native of the county was John *Bunyan, author of the **Pilgrim's Progress*. He was born at Elstow, just south of Bedford, and his cottage survives in the village. He spent twelve years in Bedford gaol after the Restoration for his nonconformist views but in 1874 a statue was erected in the town in his honour.

In 1994 the Banham commission proposed to abolish the county, save for ceremonial purposes, setting up three unitary authorities, Bedford borough, Luton borough, and Central Bedfordshire. JAC

Bedlam, more properly **Bethlem hospital,** was originally attached to the priory of St Mary Bethlehem outside Bishopsgate, founded in 1247 by Simon FitzMary, sheriff of London, and used for the 'distracted' from 1377. After the priory's dissolution (1546), it was granted to the city, and from 1557 jointly managed with *Bridewell. The only public madhouse and a popular resort for sightseers from the early 17th cent., it became infamous for the callous cruelty meted out to the insane—'bedlam' is still used figuratively for any place of uproar. The hospital was relocated from Moorfields to Lambeth (1815), and is now at Beckenham (Kent), linked with the Maudsley Hospital. ASH

Beecham, Sir Thomas (1879–1961). Self-taught English conductor. Financed by the family business (for which his spell in advertising produced 'Hark! the herald angels sing! | Beecham's Pills are just the thing'), Beecham founded many leading orchestras, including the Beecham Symphony Orchestra (1909), London Philharmonic Orchestra (1932), and Royal Philharmonic Orchestra (1946), with whom he made many fine recordings. He also created the Beecham

Opera Company (1915), performing in London and the provinces, and was artistic director at Covent Garden (1932–9), where he conducted several *Ring* cycles. His vast repertoire included many small-scale 'lollipops', although he was an early champion of the operas of Richard Strauss and, most notably, the music of *Delius. His elegant, meticulously phrased performances of Haydn and Mozart became legendary, as did his caustic, witty *bons mots*. Although he maintained that he simply chose the best players and let them do the rest, his genius as a conductor is indisputable. ECr

Beechey, Sir William (1753–1839). Portrait painter. Beechey was born in Burford (Oxon.), entered the Royal Academy Schools in 1772, and from his first exhibition four years later, enjoyed a modest success. He moved to Norwich in 1781 before returning to London, where for many years he was a fashionable painter. In 1793 he was elected ARA and in the same year appointed portrait painter to Queen Charlotte and instructor to the princesses. A careful painter, he paid meticulous attention to making his paintings durable. Ironically, the painting considered his best and certainly his most ambitious work, for which he was knighted and elected RA in 1798, *King George III Reviewing the 10th Hussars and the 3rd Dragoons*, was destroyed by fire at Windsor castle in 1992. JC

Beeton, Mrs (1836–65). Isabella Mary Beeton, née Mayson, was born in 1836 in London. Although her father died when she was 4, she received a rounded education, attending finishing school in Heidelburg and becoming an accomplished pianist. However, it is for her cookery and household management books that she is remembered. In 1856 she married Samuel Orchard Beeton, a publisher. Mrs Beeton became a regular contributor to his monthly household publication, writing both a cookery column and a fashion feature. Despite her own poor health, she gave sound advice on diet and domestic science. Her practical style coupled with attractive illustrations ensured popular and enduring success for her book, *Household Management*, published originally in instalments between 1859 and 1860. Mrs Beeton died following the birth of her fourth son. SMC

Beggar's Opera, The. John Gay's ballad opera began its record-breaking run at the theatre in Lincoln's Inn Fields on 29 January 1728. A satire on Italian opera set in Newgate prison and making use of folk-tunes and popular songs, the ubiquitous references to statesmen, politicians, and 'great men' were interpreted as reflections on the conduct of Sir Robert *Walpole, the prime minister, who, through the characters of Macheath and Peachum, was likened both to a highwayman and to the thief-taker and racketeer Jonathan *Wild. Although the sequel, *Polly*, was suppressed, Bertolt Brecht subsequently extended the range of Gay's satire in *Die Dreigroschenoper* (*The Threepenny Opera*) to indict the capitalist system *tout court*. JAD

Behn, Aphra (1640–89). Dramatist and novelist, Aphra Behn was born on 10 July 1640 at Wye, Kent. Her early childhood, spent in the West Indies, later provided inspiration for her novel *Oroonoko*, a forerunner to Rousseau's 'natural man'. Her marriage to a wealthy merchant in 1663 gave her entrance to the court of Charles II. In 1666, Charles chose Behn, then widowed, to carry out spying missions in Holland. She returned to England to concentrate on writing, her reputation as an intelligent and intrepid woman much enhanced. Acclaimed as the first professional female writer, Behn's output was prolific. Although much of her work was published anonymously to overcome male prejudice, fellow Restoration writers, including *Dryden, held her in esteem. Behn's continual efforts to promote herself and her works eventually affected her health. She died on 16 April 1689 and was buried in Westminster abbey. A sour epitaph read, 'Here lies a proof that wit can never be defence enough against mortality.' SMC

Bek, Anthony (*c.*1240–1311). Bishop of Durham. Bek came from Lincolnshire, went to Oxford University, and in 1270 entered the household of Prince Edward. He accompanied Edward on crusade and returned with him when he succeeded as Edward I in 1274. A year later he was made constable of the Tower. Henceforth he was one of the king's closest advisers, accompanying him on campaigns in Wales and Scotland, fighting at *Falkirk, and given the lordship of the Isle of Man. In 1283 he was elected bishop of Durham, where he possessed palatine powers. Extremely wealthy, Bek lived in great pomp and was given the title patriarch of Jerusalem by Pope Clement V. A protracted dispute with the priory of Durham caused him to lose favour with Edward I, but Edward II, from 1307 onwards, supported him, and he was able to bring his feud with the priory to a successful conclusion. JAC

Belfast is the second largest city in Ireland, and the economic and political capital of Northern Ireland. Although the Normans established a fort at Belfast in the 12th cent., a substantial town only developed at the beginning of the 17th cent.: Belfast benefited from the Ulster plantation, and from the patronage of the lord deputy, Sir Arthur *Chichester, and was incorporated by royal charter in 1613. The economic collapse of Chichester's descendants, the earls of Donegall, after the mid-18th cent. liberated the town from a constrictive leasing policy, and—in combination with the success of the local cotton industry—induced a period of rapid growth. But the most remarkable years of expansion were from *c.*1860 to the First World War, which coincided with the marked development of the shipbuilding and engineering industries, and the consolidation of linen manufacturing: the population of Belfast grew from 87,000 in 1851 to 349,000 by 1901. Belfast was incorporated as a city in 1888, and its chief magistrate raised to the dignity of lord mayor in 1892. With the Government of *Ireland Act (1920), and the partition of the island, Belfast became the administrative capital of the newly created Northern Ireland.

The swift expansion of Belfast partly determined its politics. Rapid, uneven growth was accompanied by an alteration of the sectarian demography: the proportion of catholic citizens grew from virtually nothing at the beginning of the 18th cent. to one-third by the late 19th and 20th cents. A shifting denominational balance in company with rapid growth brought fluid sectarian frontiers within the city, and political instability: intercommunal violence, notably in 1857, 1864, 1886, and 1921–2, became almost endemic. The industrial growth of the city—unique in an Irish context—brought closer links with the British economy and with the empire: this, in combination with a protestant domination of capital, helped to determine the predominantly unionist character of the city's politics. AJ

Belgae. A British *civitas*. The Romans applied the name Belgae to a whole group of tribes in north-west Gaul, but the appearance of a *civitas* of this name in Britain is something of a mystery. According to Ptolemy its territory included not only *Winchester but *Bath and a nearby, but as yet unidentified, settlement called Ischalis. It seems likely that Ptolemy has made an error here (he made others) since the resulting shape of the territory of the Belgae would bear little resemblance to pre-Roman tribal geography and would be something of an administrative nightmare. If the *civitas* was actually focused around Winchester there is still a problem, since this area seems to have been part of the old kingdom of the *Atrebates. The *civitas* of the Belgae was therefore most probably an artificial creation of the Roman administration, like the neighbouring *civitas* of the *Regni, and was created at about the same time in *c.* AD 80 following the death of King *Cogidubnus. Its administrative capital at Winchester was known as Venta Belgarum. The town walls enclosed about 140 acres, and though there were extra-mural suburbs, its population was probably no more than 3,000–4,000. KB

Belgium, relations with. The British played a major part in the creation of the state of Belgium 1830–9, the government soon deciding after the initial success of the Belgian revolt against the Dutch that an independent state was compatible with national interest, provided it was not subject to French influence and its neutrality was internationally recognized. Fears of French ambitions in Belgium intermittently surfaced until 1870, and help to explain British distrust of Napoleon III. From 1905 the German threat did much to give British military planning a primarily continental emphasis, and it was German defiance of Belgian neutrality in August 1914 which moved public opinion so decisively in favour of war. Germany again infringed Belgian neutrality in 1940, but the Franco-British advance to assist the victim only facilitated the success of the German outflanking drive through the Ardennes. The massive evacuation from Dunkirk followed. CJB

Belize in central America, south of Mexico, is a little larger than Wales. It was originally part of the Maya empire. English colonists were repeatedly driven out by the Spaniards. In 1862 it was formed into a colony as British Honduras and was renamed Belize in 1973. Though it became independent in 1981, British troops remained as protection against Guatemalan claims. Belize is a constitutional monarchy, with the queen as head of state, within the Commonwealth. Its main exports are sugar, bananas, and mahogany. JAC

Bell, Alexander Graham (1847–1922). Inventor of the telephone. Bell followed his father, who was a distinguished authority on the physiology of the voice, in teaching his system of 'visible speech' to the deaf. In 1870 he emigrated with his parents to Canada and in 1873 was appointed professor of vocal physiology at Boston University. It was during his research that Bell conceived the idea of the electrical transmission of speech. The American physicist Joseph Henry encouraged him to perform practical experiments and in June 1875 the first rough telephone was constructed. In March 1876 the first complete intelligible sentence was transmitted. Bell took out a patent which was fiercely contested but eventually upheld by the US Supreme Court. In 1877 Bell went to Europe to promote the new telephone. He won a 50,000-franc prize for his invention which he used to establish the Volta laboratory at Washington for research into deafness. RAS

Bell, Andrew (1753–1852). Founder of the Madras system of education. Bell was educated at St Andrews University, Scotland, after which he settled in Virginia, becoming a tutor. He returned to England, gaining a doctorate of divinity at St Andrews, and sailed for India in 1787. Two years later, Bell became superintendent of the Madras Male Orphan Asylum, founded by the East India Company. The teachers were few and inefficient, so Bell experimented with a system of mutual instruction whereby clever young boys were placed in charge of other boys. This system was described in a pamphlet written by Bell in 1797 shortly after he returned to England and was adopted in a number of schools. There was open rivalry with Joseph *Lancaster, who claimed to have originated the system. The Church of England in 1811 formed the *National Schools Society for Promoting the Education of the Poor with Bell as its first superintendent. PG

Bell, George (1883–1958). Bishop of Chichester (1929–58) and leading ecumenist. Born in Hampshire and educated at Christ Church, Oxford, Bell was successively chaplain to Archbishop *Davidson (1914), dean of Canterbury (1924), and bishop of Chichester. From 1919 he strove tirelessly for Christian unity and, as chairman of Life and Work (1932), was a leading international protagonist, responsible for founding the World Council of Churches. Present in Berlin at Hitler's accession (1933) and later personally confronting Hess and Ribbentrop, he foretold the evils of Nazism. A confidant of Bonhoeffer, the German dissident pastor—whom he met secretly in wartime Stockholm—and of the anti-Nazi confessing church, he tried in vain to obtain British support for wartime German resistance; he persistently opposed demands for German unconditional surrender and condemned obliteration bombing. With vast ecclesiastical experience, he seemed the obvious choice for Canterbury (1944), but his outspokenness possibly cost the nation and the church the benefit of his primacy. A profoundly pastoral diocesan bishop, he was a lover of English literature. He reintroduced religious drama—the first since the Reformation—to cathedral life, commissioning for Canterbury Masefield's *Coming of Christ* (1928) with music by *Holst, and *Eliot's *Murder in the Cathedral* (1935). WMM

Bell, Gertrude (1868–1926). Traveller, archaeologist, and diplomatist in the Middle East. Bell took a first in modern history at Oxford at the age of 18 and then made herself expert in Persian before turning to Arabic in 1899 when she first visited the Middle East. Four major caravan journeys through the Syrian and Arabian region and some archaeological digs between 1905 and 1913 led to an RGS medal and several books, the best known being *The Desert and the Sown*. With her large knowledge of the Turkish empire she was recruited as a British political officer in the Great War. Although not always able to reconcile Foreign Office and government of India policies and herself sometimes erratic in her general support of the Arab cause, she became an important figure, especially in the mandated territory of *Iraq, which emerged after the war. One result of her influence with King Feisal and British officials was the opportunity to build on her earlier scholarly interests by setting up the museum in Baghdad. RB

Bell, Henry (1767–1830). Bell was apprenticed as a millwright, but spent part of his career as the proprietor of a hotel in Helensburgh, where he conceived the idea of a steamboat to bring his clients more easily from Glasgow. Another Scotsman, William Symington, had already demonstrated the effectiveness of a steam-engine in a canal boat in 1789, and Robert Fulton was experimenting with small steam-powered vessels in France and America around the same time. Bell, however, deserves the credit for converting the idea into an economically viable proposition, commissioning the first commercially successful steam vessel, *Comet*, which was launched on the river Clyde in 1812. *Comet*, a 30-ton boat equipped with a 3-horse-power steam-engine, plied regularly between Glasgow and Greenock until it was wrecked in 1820. RAB

Benbow, John (1653–1702). Admiral. Of the 'tarpaulin' rather than 'gentleman' breed of naval commander, Benbow was born in Shrewsbury. Entering the navy he showed diligence in navigation which a later, and enforced, spell in the merchant service only enhanced. In the Mediterranean he entered the circle of those favoured by Arthur *Herbert and, after the revolution, such valuable patronage brought him dockyard posts and naval commands. Benbow was master of the fleet at *Beachy Head in 1690, and prominent at Barfleur in 1692, when he also bombarded St Malo. Promoted admiral in 1696 Benbow then commanded a squadron before Dunkirk, and in the western Channel. His chief claim to fame was his West Indies command 1701–2, of great consequence at the start of the *Spanish Succession War. In May 1702, in action against a French force under Du Casse, Benbow was mortally wounded, at the same time being deserted by his captains, two of whom were shot after trial. He died at Port Royal (Jamaica), but lived on in a celebrated sea-song as 'Brave Benbow'. DDA

Benburb, battle of, 1646. After the Irish rebellion of 1641, the situation was extremely confused. The Irish catholic confederacy fought against royalists, parliamentarians, and with a Scottish army sent over under Monro to protect the Ulstermen. In 1643 a truce or 'cessation' enabled *Ormond to begin sending troops back to England to fight on behalf of the king. After Charles surrendered to the Scots in May 1646 hostilities in Ireland continued. In June, Monro's troops were badly beaten at Benburb on the Blackwater by Owen Roe *O'Neill and the confederates, a victory celebrated at Rome with a Te Deum. Parliament's response was to send first Michael Jones, then Oliver *Cromwell, to restore English rule. JAC

Benedict Biscop (628–*c*.690) at 25 left his position at *Oswui's Northumbrian court to undertake the first of several pilgrimages to Rome. Twenty years later, after becoming a monk at Lerins (near Cannes), accompanying Archbishop *Theodore from Rome to Canterbury, and spending two years supervising the monastery there, he returned to Northumbria, founding the twin monasteries of *Monkwearmouth (674) and *Jarrow (681/2). He imported stonemasons and glaziers from Gaul, on his frequent travels he collected books, relics, pictures, and other 'spiritual treasures', and not least brought John the arch-cantor from Rome to teach Roman monastic office. Concerned to establish not only a centre of learning, but also a stable, obedient order, his rule, with Benedictine overtones, combined the best of seventeen monasteries observed on his travels. Enriched by his own experiences of Mediterranean culture and monasticism, the foundations became centres of intellectual achievement, notably producing the saint and historian *Bede. AM

Benedictines. The monastic order of St Benedict of Nursia (*c*.480–*c*.550) had its origins at Monte Cassino, south of Rome, where *c*.540 Benedict drew up a rule, drawing heavily on antecedent Rules, such as those of St Augustine of Hippo and Caesarius of Arles. This concise codification, detailing the practice of communal spiritual and contemplative life, remained one of several monastic rules in western Europe but gradually, partly through the unifying influence of the Carolingian empire, became dominant, until challenged by the rule of St Augustine in the 11th cent. Apart from its structured articulation of the monastic life, one of its chief strengths was its adaptability, and many interpretations were introduced, often in an effort to enforce greater asceticism and discipline, of which amongst the most influential were those of Benedict of Aniane (*c*.750–821) in the Carolingian empire, Cluny, founded in Burgundy in 909, and Cîteaux, also in Burgundy (1098).

The first Benedictine abbeys in England were probably those founded by *Wilfrid of York at Ripon and Hexham at the end of the 7th cent. Thereafter the order spread rapidly in England, and soon supplanted communities of Celtic and other observance, though these survived for many years in Celtic Britain. Important abbeys were established in the north, e.g. at *Jarrow-Monkwearmouth; in the south-east, especially at *Canterbury, where the existing monasteries of Christ Church and St Augustine's were reformed on Benedictine lines; in the south-west, e.g. at *Glastonbury and *Malmesbury. With the rise of the kingdom of *Mercia further notable foundations were made in the midlands, especially in the Severn valley, while others emerged in the fenlands, such as Peterborough. The Viking raids of the 9th cent. severely affected most Benedictine houses, some of which were totally destroyed; others were refounded, and some new ones founded in the mid-10th cent. under the influence of *Æthelwold, bishop of Winchester, Archbishop *Dunstan of Canterbury, and *Wulfstan, bishop of Worcester, all themselves monks. Though the extent of this monastic reform has been questioned there remains little doubt that there was a considerable revitalization of the monastic movement. Following the Norman Conquest some abbeys lost land, but most soon recovered under new, Norman abbots, and attracted widespread patronage, as did St Albans and Westminster, and new abbeys were founded, such as Chester, St Mary's York, Durham, and Selby. There was also an increase in the number of Benedictine nunneries, though the most prestigious were Anglo-Saxon foundations like Shaftesbury or Wilton. Though later challenged by the emerging universities the following two centuries perhaps marked the high point of Benedictine cultural, artistic, and scholarly influence, at centres such as Winchester, Bury St Edmunds, and St Albans.

The Benedictines were also challenged by the rising appeal to lay society of new orders, like the *Cistercians and the *Augustinians, and the *friars who presented a new spirituality, and attempts were made at internal reform and centralization of an order that now numbered several hundred houses. By the 16th cent. the number of Benedictine monks had declined significantly and, though many remained wealthy institutions till their *dissolution, their dynamic had largely been lost. BJG

benefit of clergy was fought for by Archbishop Thomas *Becket and conceded by Henry II in 1176 in the aftermath of Becket's murder. It exempted clergy from trial or sentence in a secular court on charges arising from a range of felonies and offences. This exemption extended from tonsured clerics to include nuns, and later it was allowed to all who could prove themselves literate by reading a verse of Scripture when charged with certain violations of the law. The reasoning was that literacy was the accepted test of clerical status. It was abolished by Parliament in 1827. JRG

benevolences. These so-called free gifts, offered out of the goodwill or *benevolentia* of the subjects, were outlawed by statute in 1484, but monarchs continued to solicit them at times of financial crisis or when parliamentary grants were not available. They eventually fell into disuse because of their low yield. *Forced loans were more effective. RL

Bengal, acquisition of. On 12 August 1765 the Mughal emperor Shah Alam proclaimed the English *East India Company his *diwan* (administrator) for the revenues of the provinces of Bengal, Bihar, and Orissa. This confirmed the company's transformation from a trading to a political power in India and made Bengal the 'bridgehead' of its new empire. The transformation had begun in south India in 1746 when the company and its French rival had backed different candidates for the nawabi of Arcot. It continued in Bengal between 1757 and 1764 when, first, Robert *Clive had defeated the army of Siraj-ud-Daula, the nawab of Bengal, at Panipat; and then Sir Hector Munro had overcome the forces of the Mughal emperor at Buxar. The process was brought to completion in 1773 by Warren *Hastings, who removed the last residual powers of the nawab of Bengal and took not only revenue but all aspects of the administration of the region into company hands. DAW

Bennett, Arnold (1867–1931). Like George *Eliot, Bennett was a fine novelist of provincial middle-class society—in his case that of the Potteries, a landscape of canals and kilns and trams and chimneys and dust. *The Old Wives' Tale* (1908) tells the story of two sisters, daughters of a draper in Bursley (Burslem). *Clayhanger* (1910) recalls the introduction of steam-printing into the Potteries and begins with two lads watching a horse-drawn canal barge bringing china clay up from Cornwall. *Riceyman Steps* (1923) moves the scene to Clerkenwell and the date to the 1920s, but stays with the same kind of people running a second-hand bookshop and a grocer's with pretensions to be a confectionery. Bennett, born in Hanley, started by following his father's career as a solicitor but went to London in 1888 where he made a living editing and writing reviews and short stories. From 1902 until 1912 he lived in Paris. Bennett's shabby, hard-working characters have something in common with those of Gissing, whom he tried to help, and with those of H. G. *Wells, with whom he maintained a lengthy friendship and literary correspondence. JAC

Bennington, battle of, 1777. On his march south from Canada to split the rebellious American colonies, *Burgoyne found himself at Fort Edward short of supplies. He dispatched a raiding force under a German officer, Baum, with 800 scratch troops to Bennington. There they were confronted on 16 August by a force twice their size under John Stark. Baum was killed and his expedition wiped out. The loss of men made Burgoyne's position still more hazardous. JAC

Benson, battle of, *c.*777. This was an important victory in Oxfordshire in the fluctuating struggle between *Mercia and *Wessex. *Offa of Mercia defeated *Cynewulf of Wessex and took possession of territories south of the Thames. JAC

Benson, Edward (1829–96). Archbishop of Canterbury. Born in Birmingham and educated at Trinity College, Cambridge, he taught at *Rugby and was successively first master of Wellington College (1859–72), first bishop of Truro (1877), and archbishop (1883). Close to Frederick Temple, he wrote supporting him over *Essays and Reviews* (1860). At Truro he successfully campaigned for a cathedral and planned the first service of Nine Lessons and Carols. Less at home in politics than *Tait, as a friend of *Gladstone he firmly supported church establishment. A lover of pageantry, with a high sense of the dignity of Canterbury, he dealt with the ritualist case against the saintly Bishop Edward King of Lincoln in a revived archiepiscopal court, thus reclaiming for Canterbury oversight of common worship. Benson acquitted King on all but two counts—'the most courageous thing that has come from Lambeth for the last 200 years'. WMM

Bentham, Jeremy (1748–1832). English utilitarian and philosophical radical. Educated at Oxford University, Bentham qualified as a barrister before he was 20, though he never practised law. He was highly critical of English law for its obscurantism, and devoted his life to systematizing it on the basis of utility. In his first substantial publication *A *Fragment on Government* (1776), Bentham launched a broadside against *Blackstone's defence of England's constitution. He dismissed the concept of inalienable natural rights as contemptuously as he dismissed precedent; the only rights that existed were legal rights, and they could never be unqualified. His most important contribution to moral philosophy was contained in his *Introduction to the Principles of Morals and Legislation* (1789), where he elaborated his theory of utility in terms of the greatest happiness of the greatest number, and thereby established utilitarianism as a systematic theory of moral and political decision-making. In his 'felicific calculus', he demonstrated how alternative courses of action could be evaluated by estimating the total quantity of pleasure they would generate; the action that promised the most pleasure was rationally the one to be chosen. Bentham became famous with Dumont's exposition of his views in *Traités de législation civile et pénale* (1802) and was honoured in various countries, including France, Russia, and the USA. His most lasting achievement, however, was to inspire the radical forces in England calling for reform. His intellectual leadership of the philosophical radicals was a critical factor in achieving many of the legal, social, industrial, economic, and political reforms that took place in England during the 19th cent. Towards the end of his life Bentham had become a legendary figure in the reform movement. He had established its literary organ in the *Westminster Review*, and he was instrumental in creating University College, London, to disseminate rational ideas to future leaders of society. TSG

Bentinck, Lord George (1802–48). Bentinck personified integrity in politics and sport. A son of the duke of Portland, Bentinck was private secretary to *Canning, his uncle by marriage, and an MP from 1828. With other Canningites he abandoned *Wellington in the late 1820s, though supporting *catholic emancipation, and backed *Grey's ministry and, with reservations, the Reform Bill. With the *Derby Dilly, he moved back towards the Tories. Declining office from *Peel in 1841, as he had from Grey, Bentinck remained silent in the House and devoted his time to sport, above all the turf, where as owner, breeder, rider, and enemy of sharp practice he became a leading figure. In 1845–6 he emerged as an enraged opponent of Peel's policy of *Corn Law repeal, which he saw as betrayal: 'What I cannot bear is being sold!' His personal and social standing helped to give him the leadership of the protectionist revolt in the Commons and, though failing to prevent repeal, he succeeded in bringing down Peel's government. Bentinck, who had sold his stud and immersed himself in economic statistics, continued to champion protectionism but, liberal in religious matters, he alienated his party by voting for the admission of *Jews to Parliament in late 1847 and resigned the leadership. Returning briefly, he died suddenly of a heart attack. *Disraeli's *Lord George Bentinck* (1852) was a notable work of political piety and self-promotion. BIC

Bentinck, Lord William (1774–1839). Soldier and administrator. Bentinck joined Marshal Suwarrof's army in Italy and served with the Austrian forces during the campaigns of 1799 and 1801. In 1803 he became governor of Madras but was recalled after being held responsible for the sepoy mutiny at Velore in July 1806. He subsequently saw action in the Mediterranean, commanding the British forces in Sicily (1811) and conducting a successful expedition against Genoa (1814). From 1827 to 1835 Bentinck acted as governor-general of Bengal. He instituted financial reforms to eradicate debts created by the recent Burmese War, reorganized the legal system, abolishing such practices as suttee (widow-burning), improved communications, introduced education programmes, and opened up official posts to natives. In 1833 he became the first governor-general of India after the East India Company Charter Act. RAS

Bentley, Richard (1662–1742). Scholar and polemicist. After attending Wakefield Grammar School and St John's College, Cambridge, Bentley came under the patronage of Stillingfleet, later bishop of Worcester, and was appointed royal librarian in 1694. His reputation as an outstanding classicist was established by the controversy over the *Letters of Phalaris*, which Bentley showed to be forgeries. In 1700, he was elected master of Trinity, Cambridge, where he remained until his death. His relations with the fellows were acrimonious and there were repeated attempts to deprive him of his mastership, all of which Bentley managed to defeat. Of his later publications, his edition of *Horace* (1711) was most admired. Despite their political differences, *Johnson wrote handsomely of him that 'the many attacks on him were owing to envy, and to a desire of being known, by being in competition with such a man'. JAC

Beowulf. Anglo-Saxon poem. This anonymous epic of 3,182 lines is preserved in BL Cotton Vitellius A. XV, written *c.*1000. Provenance, date, and genesis are uncertain: Northumbria or Mercia in the 8th cent. have long been favoured, although some recent scholarship proposes Viking Age alternatives.

The principal setting is southern Scandinavia *c.*500, but there is also reference, direct or indirect, to *Hengist, King *Offa, and other figures from English history. The stately and complex narrative is composed in the alliterative metre common to most early Germanic poetry, and is enhanced by rich description, decorous speeches, and moral reflection. It surveys Danish dynastic legend before depicting three great monster fights which conform to international story-types. In the first two, the young Geat hero Beowulf frees King Hrothgar and the Danes from the predations of the evil fen-dwellers Grendel and his mother; in the last, Beowulf, now an aged king, loses his life while slaying a treasure-guarding dragon. Interlacing the main plot are quasi-historical feuds and wars which emphasize the rhythms of joy and sorrow, youth and age, life and death which permeate the poem. *Beowulf* is deeply concerned with the ideals and tensions of the heroic life, especially strength, wisdom, loyalty, and the quest for glory. Whether it is also a 'mirror for princes', Scandinavian propaganda, a Christian critique of heroism, or a Christian allegory of salvation is more contentious. DCW

Berengaria (*c.*1164/5–*c.*1230), queen of Richard I. The daughter of Sancho VI of Navarre, Berengaria was married to Richard in an alliance intended to protect his southern frontiers while he was occupied on the Third Crusade. On her journey to the Holy Land, Berengaria was shipwrecked off Cyprus and threatened by the ruler, Isaac Comnenus. Richard captured the island, thus ensuring a strategic supply base for campaigns in Palestine, and married Berengaria, who was also crowned queen, in Limassol in May 1191. Thereafter, she saw her husband only rarely and England never. There were no children. After Richard's death in 1199, Berengaria lived on her dower lands at Le Mans, France, where she was famed for her almsgiving. Denied by King John, she only received her marriage settlement under Henry III. Just before her death, she founded a Cistercian monastery at L'Épau, where she is buried. JC

Beresford, John (1738–1805). Irish politician. Beresford was a pillar of the *Anglo-Irish ascendancy and strongly opposed to concessions to the catholics. The second son of the earl of Tyrone, he was elected to the Irish Parliament in 1760 for Waterford, which he represented until his death, first at Dublin and from 1801 at Westminster. He held office as a commissioner of revenue and from 1780 as first commissioner and was the centre of a powerful family interest. His position was threatened in 1795 by *Fitzwilliam, the new lord-lieutenant, who described Beresford as 'virtually king of Ireland' and dismissed him. 'An old rotten, stinking jobber' was Fitzwilliam's private opinion to *Burke. Beresford fought back and Fitzwilliam told *Pitt he must choose between them. Pitt did so and Fitzwilliam was recalled. A duel between him and Beresford was averted by the dramatic intervention of a magistrate. Beresford resumed office and gave strong support to the Act of *Union. His brother became archbishop of Tuam in 1794. JAC

Berkeley, George (1685–1753). Philosopher and bishop. One of the most renowned philosophers of his day, Berkeley was born in Kilkenny of English descent. He became a fellow of Trinity College, Dublin, but spent 1713–20 in London or on continental travel, becoming well acquainted with *Pope, *Swift, and Arbuthnot. In 1720 his essay 'Towards Preventing the Ruin of Great Britain', provoked by the South Sea crisis, attacked luxury and the new commercialism. In 1724 he was appointed dean of Derry but his main interest was in raising support for a college in Bermuda to preach the gospel and he was in America 1728–32. From 1734 he was bishop of Cloyne and spent almost all his later years in the diocese, apart from a last few months in Oxford. His idealist philosophy, attacking the materialism of *Locke and *Newton, is to be found largely in *Treatise Concerning the Principles of Human Knowledge* (1710) and *Three Dialogues* (1713). JAC

Berkeley castle (Glos.) is unusual in being still a family residence, having been in the hands of one family, the Berkeleys, since the Norman Conquest. The shell keep was built soon after 1067, the curtain walls in the late 12th cent., and the great hall in the mid-14th cent. Edward II was brought here in 1327 and, it seems, brutally murdered. JAC

Berkshire is an area south of the upper Thames, which separated the county from Oxfordshire and Buckinghamshire, flowing from Lechlade, via Oxford, Abingdon, Wallingford, Reading, Henley, Marlow, Maidenhead, to Windsor. The southern parts are drained by the Kennet, which flows through Hungerford and Newbury to join the Thames at Reading. Through the centre of the county run the chalk hills, from Uffington, via Wantage, to Streatley—the line of the *Icknield Way and the Berkshire Ridgeway. There were therefore two east–west corridors—one north of the downs, one south.

In Roman times, the area was the territory of the *Atrebates. From the early days of the Saxon occupation, it was disputed between *Mercia and *Wessex. Mercia gained the upper hand in the mid-7th cent. and the region was still held by *Offa of Mercia in the 770s. It was recaptured by King *Egbert for Wessex in the early 9th cent. and became an important part of the kingdom: Wantage was a royal estate and *Alfred the Great was born there. It was probably one of the earliest shires to be organized and placed under an *ealdorman: it was first mentioned by the *Anglo-Saxon Chronicle* under 860, when Æthelwulf, earldorman of Berkshire, fought against the Danes with the men of Hampshire. The name has caused difficulty. In the *Chronicle* it appears as Berrocscire, and *Asser, Alfred's biographer, explained it as a wood, where box was abundant: this seems rather slight for a place-name. It was first in the diocese of *Dorchester, just across the river in Oxfordshire, then in *Winchester, and from 909 in *Ramsbury in Wiltshire, whence it was finally transferred to the new diocese of *Salisbury. This suggests that it was border country, lacking a powerful capital. A large monastery was established at Abingdon in 675 and, well before the Conquest, the crossing-points at Wallingford, Reading, and Windsor had grown into small towns. In 1066 William crossed the Thames at Wallingford on his triumphant march from Hastings. He took over many of the estates of the previous royal family and began building the castle at *Windsor, soon established as a major royal residence. Its position astride some of the main routes to London gave Berkshire strategic importance. In the civil war between King Stephen and *Matilda in the 12th cent., Wallingford castle was held for the latter and withstood repeated sieges. In John's reign, it was again held for the king against his barons, and in Henry III's reign was taken by Simon de *Montfort before the battle of *Lewes. During the 17th-cent. civil wars, the county was on the border between royalist and parliamentarian: Wallingford was held throughout the war for the king, Windsor for his opponents. The two battles of *Newbury in 1643 and 1644 were fierce but inconclusive: Donnington castle held out for the king until the last month of the war.

Berkshire remained a quiet rural area, the downs feeding the sheep, and Newbury and Abingdon gaining reputations for cloth. The wealth of John Winchcombe, 'Jack of Newbury', in the early Tudor period was legendary and his exploits were commemorated in ballads and chapbooks.

Reading's place on the river gave it steady prosperity: in the 1720s, Defoe found it 'large and wealthy, the inhabitants rich and driving a very great trade'. But the extensive areas of downland and the barren, sandy heathland in the east kept the population down. The Kennet and Avon canal in the south, opened in 1810, gave a modest boost to trade, but the Wiltshire and Berkshire, a narrow canal completed in 1809, had desultory traffic from the beginning. The market towns of the shire remained small, until the great expansion of Reading itself—9,000 in 1801, 60,000 by 1901, 134,000 by 1991: Huntley and Palmer's biscuit partnership dates from 1841. Didcot grew considerably in the 20th cent. as a rail junction, but Wantage, Wallingford, and Faringdon, bypassed by the main lines, stayed small: Wallingford had a population of 2,800 in 1851 and 2,700 in 1901; Faringdon declined from 3,400 to 2,900; Wantage increased slowly from 3,000 to 3,700. Berkshire remained essentially a shire to be passed through, from east to west. Brunel's Great Western railway cut a large swathe through the north of the county in the 1830s by way of the valley of the White Horse, and the Taunton to Reading line, through Hungerford and Newbury, opened in 1847. The M4 motorway, completed in 1971, bisected the county from Bray in the east to Membury in the west. Many of the industries retained farming connections—brewing or horse-racing, with stables at Lambourn and East Ilsley, and important courses at Ascot and Newbury. Twentieth-cent. industries included atomic research at Harwell and Aldermaston. By the local government reorganization of 1972, the county gained Slough and Eton from Buckinghamshire, but lost Abingdon, Faringdon, Wantage, and Wallingford to Oxfordshire—Mercia's belated triumph. At the same time, the growth of Bracknell, one of the earliest post-war new towns, meant that the balance of the county population had tipped dramatically towards the east, succumbing to the pull of London.

The Banham commission on local government in 1994 recommended that the county be abolished, save for ceremonial purposes, and replaced by five unitary authorities, Reading, Wokingham, Slough, Newbury, and Bracknell Forest with Windsor and Maidenhead. JAC

Berlin, Congress of, 1878. A summit conference which met in the German capital, under the presidency of Bismarck, in June 1878. All the European great powers and Turkey were represented. Lord *Salisbury and Lord Beaconsfield (Benjamin *Disraeli) represented Britain. It had been summoned because European opinion was uneasy at the gains Russia had made by the treaty of San Stefano at the end of the recent Russo-Turkish War. Many questions were settled by secret agreements before the congress assembled. San Stefano had provided for a 'Big Bulgaria', an autonomous principality including half the Balkan peninsula, which seemed likely to be under Russian influence. This was divided and part returned to Turkish jurisdiction. Austria was to 'occupy and administer' Bosnia and Herzegovina, although they remained under Turkish suzerainty. Britain was to lease Cyprus from Turkey. This gave her a forward base in the eastern Mediterranean to cover the Suez canal, opened in 1869. In return, Britain promised to maintain Turkish interests in Asia Minor. The independence of Serbia, Montenegro, and Romania was recognized but Romania had to cede southern Bessarabia to Russia. Disraeli returned to London boasting that he had secured 'peace with honour' but Salisbury later concluded that they had 'backed the wrong horse' in trying to prop up the Turkish empire. Panslavism was temporarily checked but the emerging Balkan nations remained dissatisfied. MEC

Bermuda is a group of islands in the western Atlantic, some 600 miles from the east coast of the United States. It has the status of a dependent territory with internal self-government. It was named after the Spanish explorer Juan Bermudez, though it remained in British hands from 1612 onwards. The economy relies heavily upon tourism. JAC

Bernicia, kingdom of. This kingdom may have had its origins in Anglo-Saxon settlements around the rivers Tyne and Wear, but it expanded rapidly in the late 6th and 7th cents. to control all the land between the Tees and the Forth, largely through absorption of British kingdoms, including *Rheged and that of the *Gododdin. The first recorded king was *Ida (*c.*547–59). His grandson *Æthelfryth (592–616) and great-grandsons *Oswald (634–42) and *Oswui (642–70) were responsible for the aggressive military expansion which enabled Oswald and Oswui to establish a wide-ranging overlordship over other Anglo-Saxon and Celtic kingdoms. The supremacy of the Bernician dynasty in northern England was only seriously challenged by *Edwin of Deira (617–33) who ruled in both Bernicia and Deira, but by the end of the reign of *Ecgfrith (670–85) the Deiran dynasty had been obliterated in the male line and Deira integrated with Bernicia to form the province of *Northumbria. The disastrous defeat of Ecgfrith by the Picts at *Nechtansmere put an end to further overlordship or conquest of the northern Celtic peoples.

In spite of some evangelization in the province by Bishop *Paulinus of York, the main period of conversion for Bernicia was in the reign of Oswald, through a mission of Irish monks from *Iona who were established at *Lindisfarne. In Oswui's reign problems became apparent because of variations in customs, including methods of calculating Easter followed by the Ionan church, and that of Deira which had been established by missionaries from Rome. At a synod at *Whitby in 664 Oswui decided that Deira's 'Roman' customs would prevail.

When much of Deira was overrun by Scandinavians after 867, Bernicia (or a substantial part of it) re-emerged in effect as a separate province in which the main powers were a dynasty known as 'ealdormen of Bamburgh' and the community of St *Cuthbert from Lindisfarne, which eventually settled in Durham. BAEY

Bertha, daughter of the Frankish king Charibert, married King *Æthelbert of Kent sometime before 597, on condition that she could continue to practise her Christian faith. With her personal bishop, Liudhard of Senlis, she used the old Roman church of St Martin, Canterbury. She did not convert her pagan husband. Pope Gregory the Great, writing to her in 601, rebuked her for this, but it seems likely that the relationship with the greater Merovingian rulers influenced Æthelbert's acceptance of *Augustine's Christian mission in 597. Praising her recent part in the English conversion, Gregory compared her to Helena, mother of Constantine the Great. Described by him as educated, Bertha would be able to read and possibly write Latin, and may be perceived as a figurehead of change in Anglo-Saxon society, heralding the advent of Christianity and literacy. Dates are unknown, but she died before 616. AM

Berwick, James FitzJames, 1st duke of (1670–1734). Berwick spent almost all his life abroad in foreign military service. He was a natural son of James, duke of York, by Arabella Churchill, sister of the future duke of *Marlborough. Born and educated in France, Berwick volunteered to join the emperor's forces besieging the Turkish redoubt of Buda in 1686. His father's succession as James II suggested a great career in Britain. He was created duke in 1687, made governor of Portsmouth (a post of responsibility in troubled times), and awarded the Garter. But James's flight in 1688 condemned Berwick to a life of distinguished exile. He fought for his father in Ireland and then settled down in France, being naturalized in 1702 and created a marshal of France in 1706. Sent to Spain to restore the flagging fortunes of Philip V, he won a great victory at *Almanza in 1707. He was given French and Spanish dukedoms, which still survive in the family. In 1734, at the age of 64, still fighting for his adopted country in the War of the Polish Succession, he was killed outside Philipburg by a stray cannon-ball. His reputation was as a brave soldier and a sensible adviser. Montesquieu wrote of him that 'he was brought up to support a sinking cause'. JAC

Berwick, treaty of, 1357. David II, king of Scotland, was captured at *Neville's Cross in 1346. Eleven years later, by the treaty of Berwick, he was ransomed for 100,000 marks, with hostages given for security. JAC

Berwick, treaty of, 1560. The years 1558–60 were critical in Anglo-Scottish relations. The death of Mary Tudor in 1558 placed a protestant on the English throne. Mary, queen of Scots, became queen of France in 1559, with her mother *Mary of Guise as regent for her in Scotland. Her catholicizing policy was opposed by the lords of the *Congregation, a group of noblemen, supported by the zeal of John *Knox. The regent held the port of Leith, vital for communication with France. By the treaty of Berwick of February 1560, Elizabeth I undertook to support the rebellious lords. In June 1560 Mary of Guise died and later in the year Mary, queen of Scots, was widowed. Though one must be careful before hailing the treaty as the turning-point towards a protestant Scotland and union with England, there is little doubt that it turned the scales in the struggle between the old and new religions. JAC

Berwick-on-Tweed. Northumbrian coastal town at the mouth of the river Tweed. Berwick was a disputed Anglo-Scottish border town and changed hands thirteen times before finally being recognized as English in 1482. The Elizabethan fortifications, built in 1558, followed the latest Italian system, designed to give fire cover to every part of the wall, and are the only surviving walls of their kind. The castle was an important border fortress but declined after the 1707 Union. It was eventually demolished to make way for a railway station, the platform of which runs over the great hall where Edward I made his famous decision to support John *Balliol for the Scottish crown in 1291. The barracks, built in 1719 following complaints by townsfolk against billeting and probably designed by *Vanbrugh, were among the first to be built in Britain. Berwick has three very different bridges. The 17th-cent. Old Bridge is an elegant structure which took a quarter of a century to build. The Royal Border Bridge, an impressive railway viaduct, was designed by Robert *Stephenson and built 1847–50. It has 28 arches and stands 126 feet above the water. The Royal Tweed Bridge, of concrete construction, was built in 1928 to carry the main road north. RAS

Besant, Annie (1847–1933). Secularist, socialist, and theosophist. Born in London of Irish descent, Annie Wood married the Revd Frank Besant in 1867, but the marriage broke up in 1873 over her religious doubts. She moved to London where in 1874 she made her first public speech, on 'The Political Status of Women', and joined Charles *Bradlaugh's National Secular Society. Largely at her insistence, in 1877 they republished *The Fruits of Philosophy*, an old birth-control pamphlet by Charles Knowlton. The subsequent trial, which was inconclusive, gave unprecedented publicity to birth-control arguments. She now worked closely with Bradlaugh to promote *secularism, but after 1884 was drawn into socialist politics and in 1887 helped plan the *'Bloody Sunday' demonstration in Trafalgar Square. The following year she organized the Bryant & May's match-girls' strike and was elected to the London School Board. In 1889 her views shifted to theosophy of which she became the leader, and in 1894 she moved to India, where she devoted the rest of her life to Indian nationalism. ER

Bessemer, Sir Henry (1813–94). Bessemer distinguished himself as a professional inventor responsible for many ingenious ideas. By far his most successful invention was the process which bears his name for making steel—previously an expensive material in short supply—available in bulk. Invented in 1856, the process involved blowing air through molten cast iron so that it combined with excess carbon in the melt to produce mild steel in substantial quantities. This caused a brief but spectacular display while the reaction took place. Steel from 'Bessemer converters' came to be used extensively in railway lines, ship plate, and forgings for large guns. Despite the occurrence of technical problems in its early development, the process was widely adopted in iron- and steelworks in Britain and elsewhere during the following decades. The invention secured public recognition and many honours for Bessemer, including a knighthood in 1879. RAB

Betjeman, Sir John (1906–84). Poet laureate and essayist, whose eccentricity and accessibility have encouraged an undervaluation of his literary gifts. His *Collected Poems* (1958) sold over a million copies and as broadcaster he became a national institution, championing Victoriana and the disappearing 'Metro-land' of his youth. Unhappy at Marlborough, he blossomed at Oxford, where he moved in literary circles and went on to write for the *Architectural Review.* His first book, *Mount Sion* (1931), testifies to an enduring fascination with the Anglican church, and hymn forms are often reflected in his traditional metrics. Cornwall and the home counties repeatedly engage his 'topographical predilection', and he documents the doings of middle-class suburbia with a mixture of nostalgia and irony. He has something of Thomas *Hardy's sadness and simplicity, but a greater capacity for enjoyment—of remembered tennis parties, for example, with Miss J. Hunter Dunn, 'furnish'd and burnish'd by Aldershot sun'. JNRS

Bevan, Aneurin (1897–1960). Perhaps the greatest and certainly one of the most controversial of Labour Party politicians, Bevan was born in Tredegar, a miner's son in a dissenting family. His creation of the National Health Service in 1948 remains Labour's most enduring legacy to the people of the United Kingdom. During the war years he was virtually a one-man opposition to *Churchill and had no ministerial experience when *Attlee appointed him minister of health in 1945. He resigned when his cabinet colleagues in 1951 imposed charges on dental and ophthalmic treatment in order to pay inflated defence estimates during the Korean War, a resignation they must have anticipated. He was not an easy colleague to work with. He twice lost the party whip (1939 and 1955) and in the 1950s he opposed party leadership on defence and foreign affairs. He and his wife Jenny Lee, also an MP, were regarded by many party workers as the socialist soul of Labour. His followers became known as Bevanites and were accused of forming a party within a party around the *Tribune* newspaper. But they also found Bevan difficult, especially after he denounced unilateral nuclear disarmament at the 1957 party conference, declaring that no Labour foreign secretary should be sent 'naked into the conference chamber'. Thereafter he was reconciled with *Gaitskell.

A brilliant orator, who mastered a residual stammer, he was capable of taking on Churchill and *Lloyd George. His jeer in 1948 (much interpreted) that the Tories were 'lower than vermin' gave his adversaries a propaganda feast. He was the most loved and hated politician of his time. AS

Beveridge, William H. (1879–1963). Social reformer. Educated at Oxford, Beveridge joined Toynbee Hall, in London's East End, where he met Sidney and Beatrice *Webb. Impressed by social-insurance arrangements in Prussia, he used his position as a leader-writer for the *Morning Post* to press the case for comprehensive welfare provision in Britain. In 1908 he joined the Board of Trade and played a major part in drafting the Labour Exchanges Act of 1909 and the National Insurance Act of 1911.

In 1919 Beveridge became director of the London School of Economics (LSE), which the Webbs had founded. While firmly establishing LSE's reputation in the social sciences, his inclination to autocracy caused inevitable clashes; in 1937 he resigned, to become master of University College, Oxford. At the outbreak of war in 1939 Beveridge hoped to be put in charge of wartime manpower administration. But his unhappy relationship with the trade unions in the First World War (he had helped to draft legislation restricting wartime collective bargaining) ruled this out. Instead he was asked to chair an inquiry into post-war social services. His two reports on social insurance (1942) and full employment (1944) formed the basis of the Labour government's welfare legislation in the later 1940s. He was given a peerage in 1946. GA

Beverley. Yorkshire town, in the marshlands of the Hull valley. John, bishop of York, founded or restored a monastery there, where he was buried (721); he was later canonized as St John of Beverley (1037). The monastery was succeeded by a collegiate church or minster, which became a major pilgrimage centre thanks to John's shrine. A town developed north of the church, and its rights of sanctuary included the whole town. The archbishops of York were lords of the town, and in the 1120s *Thurstan granted its burgesses the same liberties as York. The minster, rebuilt *c.*1220–1400, surpasses in both size and beauty some English cathedrals. The town flourished not only as an ecclesiastical centre, but through textiles, and by 1377 was one of the twelve largest English towns. Its trade and industry decayed in the 15th and 16th cents., and the suppression of the college (1548) further impoverished the town. In the 17th and 18th cents. prosperity returned as Beverley became effectively the administrative and social capital of east Yorkshire. In the 19th cent. it became a byword for electoral corruption, and was disfranchised in 1870 after a scandalous election, in which the novelist *Trollope unsuccessfully contested the seat. DMP

Bevin, Ernest (1881–1951). Trade unionist and Labour politician. The illegitimate son of a village midwife, Bevin left school at 11 but rose to become one of Britain's most respected foreign secretaries. After a succession of manual jobs and considering becoming a Baptist minister, Bevin became a full-time official of the Dockers' Union in 1911. By 1914 he was one of the union's three national organizers. By 1920 he had become assistant general secretary. Bevin gained national attention in the immediate post-war years through his evidence to the Shaw Inquiry in 1920 on dock labour and his efforts to use trade union power to end British intervention in the Russian civil war. He was convinced of the need to consolidate union organization and masterminded the amalgamation of eighteen unions into the Transport and General Workers' Union, of which he became the first general secretary in 1922. The failure of the *General Strike of 1926 underlined his belief that unions should negotiate from strength.

The collapse of the Labour government of 1929–31 compelled Bevin further into the political arena and he played a major role during the 1930s in committing Labour to realistic policies on the economy and rearmament. A devastating speech at the 1935 party conference helped remove the pacifist George *Lansbury from the leadership. By 1937 Bevin was chairman of the TUC and one of the most influential figures in the Labour movement.

When Labour joined *Churchill's wartime coalition in May 1940, the prime minister made the surprise but inspired appointment of Bevin to the ministry of Labour. At the age of 59 he entered Parliament. Though he did not always fit easily into the Commons, his contribution to the war effort was invaluable. Probably no other figure could have secured the same level of co-operation from the work-force.

With the election of a majority Labour government in 1945 Bevin went, not as he had expected to the Treasury, but to the Foreign Office. Here he laid the foundation stones of British foreign policy for the next 40 years. To the disappointment of Labour's left wing but the approval of the Conservative opposition, Bevin took a consistently strong line towards the Soviet Union in the developing Cold War. Indeed he saw it as Britain's task to contain Soviet expansion until the USA was persuaded to commit its resources fully to the same end. Under Bevin's powerful influence the government went ahead with the construction of a British atomic bomb, seized the opportunities offered under the Marshall Plan, and played a leading role in the creation of *NATO in 1949. Only over the question of Palestine was his stewardship a failure. Many considered he would make a better prime minister than Attlee, but he refused to be drawn into any intrigues.

Bevin had been in poor health since the 1930s. After the 1950 general election he was no longer capable of fulfilling his duties and in the end had to be eased reluctantly out of office by Attlee. He died within a month. Bevin was a man of great intelligence, despite his lack of formal education. He won the unqualified respect of his ministry and left an enduring mark on British diplomacy. DJD

Bewcastle cross (Cumbria). This carving is a major example of Anglo-Saxon sculpture. Stylistically it is closely linked to the nearby Ruthwell cross and can be similarly dated to the first half of the 8th cent. Panels of vine-scroll, interlace, and key-pattern cover three sides of the now-headless monument, whilst on the west face there are depictions of John the Baptist and Christ in Majesty. These are set over a lengthy runic inscription whose damaged text shows that the cross was commemorative; the falconer depicted at the bottom of this face may be a portrait of the deceased. RNB

Bewick, Thomas (1755–1828). English animal artist and engraver, born near Newcastle upon Tyne, where he spent most of his life and established a school of engraving. He was apprenticed at 14 to Ralph Beilby, an engraver and jeweller with whom he was later in partnership for 20 years. A bird-watcher and countryman, Bewick's finest work is in natural history illustrations particularly to a number of his books, including *A General History of Quadrupeds* (1790) and *A History of British Birds* (1797, 1804). He is equally admired for his tailpieces, which are exquisite miniature scenes of shrewdly observed incidents of rustic life and manners in Georgian England. Regarded as the father of modern wood engraving, Bewick halted the decline of engraving into a primarily reproductive technique and brought to it new expressive possibilities. His *Memoirs* were published in part in 1862 and in full in 1975. JC

Bible. The Bible is a library of different literary types rather than a single book (Greek *biblia*—books (plural)). The larger part, the Old Testament (OT), is a collection of Jewish sacred writings, originally in Hebrew and consisting of teaching (or Law—*Torah*), history, prophecy, and poetry, all expressing the Jewish experience of God—a literature of faith rather than of scientific or historical observation. The 'canon' of the Hebrew OT was not endorsed by Jewish authority until *c.* AD 100 by which time the Septuagint, its Greek translation (Alexandria, 3rd cent. BC) combined with other Greek writings (the Apocrypha), was prevalent amongst Hellenistic Jews. Though the western church accepted 'old Latin' versions of the Septuagint, Jerome made a new Latin translation from the original Hebrew (390–410). Known as the Vulgate, this, with the Apocrypha, was authorized by the Council of Trent (1545–63) and the first Vatican Council (1870). Protestant churches never gave the Apocrypha similar authorization. The New Testament (NT), originally in Greek, also includes diverse literary forms from early Christian experience—letters of Paul and other apostles, historical narrative (Acts), apocalyptic writing (Revelation), and four gospels which are not history but arrangements of remembered acts and sayings of Jesus, retold with the eyes of faith specifically to promote faith. The New Testament 'canon' gradually emerged and was not fixed until *c.*382.

The first English translations were patchy and spasmodic—paraphrases attributed to *Cædmon (*c.*680), *Bede's translation of part of John's Gospel (673–735), 9th–10th-cent. glosses, free translations of Genesis 1–12, Psalms 1–50, the gospels (10th cent.), and Middle English metrical versions. The first full versions were 14th-cent. NT translations from the Vulgate, made under *lollard influence. Illicit MS translations continued to appear, until a powerful impetus was provided by printing of the Vulgate (1456), the Hebrew text (1488), and Erasmus' Greek NT (1516), which inspired *Tyndale to make the first English NT translation from the original Greek in Worms (1526) and of the Pentateuch from the original Hebrew (1529–30). *Coverdale, whose first complete English Bible (1535) was partly based on Tyndale, superintended publication of the Great Bible (1539–40), which Thomas *Cromwell ordered to be placed in churches. A new version (1557), issued in Geneva—the first with verse-divisions—formed the basis of the so-called Geneva Bible, dedicated to Elizabeth (1560) and widely read at all levels in her reign. *Parker, however, authorized yet another, this time more Latinate, revision of the Great Bible, the Bishops' Bible (1568)—also with verse-divisions, but 'incompetent, both in its scholarship and verbosity'. Meanwhile exiled English catholics in Rheims translated their own NT from the Vulgate (1582), followed by the OT at Douai (1609–10). At the *Hampton Court conference (1604) James I commissioned a panel of 54 to produce the King James (or so-called Authorized) Version of 1611, a comprehensive revision of previous translations, using the Latinate Bishops' Bible as the basis. In fact, the translators wisely relied heavily on the Geneva version and therefore Tyndale (without attribution), though with some unfortunate Latinized-English amendments. Its superb quality enabled it to supplant all previous versions, and for 250 years it was the only one used. It supplied the epistles and gospels for the 1662 Prayer Book, though Coverdale was retained for the psalms. The next two centuries saw little new, except for slight revisions in John *Wesley's *Explanatory Notes on the New Testament* (1755) and in the catholic Rheims–Douai version (1749–50). Though new scholarship led to a conservative Revised Version (1881–5), translations proliferated in the 20th cent.: James Moffatt (1922, 1924), Ronald Knox (1945, 1949), followed by the Revised Standard Version (1952)—embodying modern scholarship and meaning, but retaining the Tyndale–King James style—the New English Bible (1961, 1970), Jerusalem Bible (catholic) (1966), and others. The influence of the Bible, especially of the 1611 version and thus Tyndale, on English culture and language has been incalculable, not only in literature, but in daily aphorisms and forms of thought. This version spread to America and round the growing British empire. It has been admired for 'its simplicity, its dignity, its power, its happy turns of expression . . . the music of its cadences, and the felicities of its rhythm'. For Victor Hugo England had 'two books, the Bible and Shakespeare; England made Shakespeare, but the Bible made England.' The emphasis placed on Bible reading was a great incentive to book publication. Though protestant fundamentalists regard it as literally inspired, most Christians, catholic, evangelical, or liberal, for whom Christianity is a religion of a person not a book, use it as a basic source. Politically too it has been rummaged for causes both revolutionary and reactionary. It can be all things to all men. As William *Blake put it 'Both read the bible day and night, but thou read'st black where I read white.' For *Macaulay, 'if everything else in our language should perish, [the Bible] would alone suffice to show the whole extent of its beauty and power'. WMM

Bible Christians were a methodist connexion founded in 1815 in north Devon by William O'Bryan (1778–1868), a Wesleyan farmer of Anglican and quaker descent, an attractive but refractory personality. Despite a stress on lay representation, it maintained a strong view of the ministry, which included women. Closest in temper to *primitive methodism, its political attitudes aligned it with *dissent. Its emphases on mission and education were reflected in Samuel Pollard (1864–1915) of south-west China, and Shebbear College (founded 1841) under Thomas Ruddle (1839–1909), 'the North Devon Arnold'. The Bible Christians joined with the New Connexion and United Free Churches in 1907 to form the United Methodist Church which, in turn, entered the methodist church in 1932. CB

Bible Society. The evangelical revival's largest pan-denominational organization was formed in 1804 to promote the international distribution of the Scriptures. Based in London, with a committee of fifteen Anglicans, fifteen dissenters, and six foreigners, its fundamental principle was that only bibles authorized by public authority should be circulated, without note or comment. By 1825 it had issued 4,252,000 bibles in 140 languages and its auxiliaries flourished nation-wide. Buffeted by crises over the inclusion of the Apocrypha (1823–6) and trinitarianism as a basis of membership (1831), it maintained its interdenominational appeal and by the 1970s issued 1,000,000 bibles annually, in over 1,000 languages. CB

Biddle, John (1615–62). Religious controversialist. Biddle, a bright lad from Wotton under Edge (Glos.), was sent to Magdalen College, Oxford, and became a schoolmaster at Gloucester. But he developed and published doubts of the divinity of the Holy Ghost and was repeatedly imprisoned during the Commonwealth, spending 1655–8 in confinement on the Scilly Islands. The Restoration did not assist him and in 1662 he was once more arrested, dying in prison. JAC

Biedcanford, battle of, *c.*571. Though Biedcanford was clearly an important battle, it is difficult to identify. The *Anglo-Saxon Chronicle* seems precise, attributing a victory over the Britons to Cutha, brother of *Ceawlin of Wessex, who went on to take the towns of Lygeabyrig, Aeglesbyrig, Benesingtun, and Egonsham. These have with some confidence been identified as Limbury (now part of north Luton), Aylesbury, Benson, and Eynsham. But the detail is much disputed. Stenton denied that the name referred to Bedford. Historians have puzzled whether Britons could have been holding the vale of Aylesbury as late as 571. Hence Oman suggested that the struggle must have been between fellow-Saxons, while Myres argued that the event had been misplaced by at least 100 years and must refer to a 5th-cent. Saxon breakthrough. JAC

Big Ben, the name given to the clock in the eastern tower of the Houses of Parliament, Westminster, was originally applied only to its 13-ton bell, supposedly named after Sir Benjamin Hall, commissioner of works (1859). Famous for its accuracy, its chimes have become familiar nation-wide through radio and television. ASH

Bignor. Roman villa. Situated on the edge of the Weald to the north of Chichester, the villa at Bignor was uncovered by the antiquary Samuel Lysons (also responsible for the uncovering of *Woodchester) between 1812 and 1820. Starting from modest beginnings at the turn of the 1st and 2nd cents., the villa had developed by the middle of the 4th cent. into one of the largest and most palatial in Britain. It is particularly noteworthy for the number and quality of its mosaics. ASEC

Bigod, Roger, 4th earl of Norfolk (*c.*1212–70). Bigod's grandfather had been one of the barons who enforced *Magna Carta on John. He succeeded his father in 1225 at the age of 12 or so, having been brought up at the Scottish court of Alexander II, whose sister he married. In 1246 he succeeded as hereditary earl marshal. He fought in campaigns in Wales and France on behalf of Henry III, but in 1258 became a leader of the baronial opposition to restrain the king. In the ensuing conflict he seems to have steered a careful course, siding with de *Montfort when he was in power, but making his peace with the king after *Evesham. JAC

Bigod, Roger, 5th earl of Norfolk (1245–1306). Bigod was one of the most powerful barons in Edward I's reign. He succeeded his father Hugh Bigod, justiciar, in 1266 and his uncle as earl and hereditary marshal of England in 1270. His life was spent in the service of Edward I and he saw much campaigning in Wales and Scotland: he was present at the defeat of *Wallace at *Falkirk in 1298. But relations with the king, who made heavy demands on his subjects, were by no means easy. In 1297 Bigod refused to lead a campaign in Gascony. 'You will either go or hang', Edward is reported to have said, to be met with the retort, 'I will neither go nor hang.' Edward was forced to give way and confirm charters, but the dispute simmered on and surfaced once more on the Scottish campaign of 1298. Bigod's political position was weakened by heavy debt and in his last years he was obliged to come to terms with Edward. JAC

billeting. The right of the crown to demand accommodation for its troops was always part of the royal prerogative, and derived from the subject's duty to help the king against his enemies. Though it was never popular, since remuneration was often inadequate and slow, it did not become a major constitutional issue until the 17th cent., when Parliament was watchful for encroachments upon the liberties of the subject and the Stuart kings were very short of money. The *petition of right (1628) complained that 'great companies of soldiers and mariners have been dispersed into divers counties and the inhabitants against their will have been compelled to receive them into their houses . . . to the great grievance and vexation of the people'. Though Charles accepted the petition, the grievance continued, and in 1640 he told Yorkshire petitioners sharply that the right of billeting was a 'necessary power'. After the *Glorious Revolution, the law was modified: ordinary citizens were not required to find billets, but innkeepers were obliged to accept troops and a scale of charges laid down. Not until a programme of barrack-building was carried through in the 19th cent. was the issue finally put to rest. JAC

billiards and snooker. Billiards is a game of some antiquity which evolved as a popular pursuit in the 19th cent. A version was played in the 16th and 17th cents. with a hoop and a king-pin as a skittle. A modern billiards room was opened in Covent Garden and then in many London clubs, with a slate base, three balls, and rubber cushions. A Billiards Association was founded in 1885, a Control Club in 1908, and the two amalgamated in 1919 into the Billiards Association and Control Council. Snooker developed from it in the Indian army and is believed to have taken its name from the slang term for a new cadet. Billiards has never achieved wide popularity but snooker acquired a considerable TV following and its simpler variant, pool, is played in many pubs, since the tables are smaller. JAC

Bill of Rights. Passed by Parliament in December 1689 this gave statutory force to the *Declaration of Rights presented to William and Mary on 13 February 1689, and agreed by them after they had jointly accepted the crown of Great Britain. The bill closely followed the declaration in its recital of ancient rights, and the recent abuses of the royal prerogative by the catholic James II, deemed to have abdicated and hence vacated the throne. The question of any contractual character the crown might possess was skirted. The succession was now stated to lie in the heirs of the bodies of the protestant Mary, and then her younger sister Anne. None could succeed who were of the catholic faith, or had married catholics. Prerogative power to dispense with law in specific instances was rendered subject to statutory sanction; and Parliament claimed the right to override a royal pardon. This received statutory recognition in 1701 through the *Act of Settlement. DDA

Birgham, treaty of, 1290. Anglo-Scottish treaty, initially drawn up at Birgham (Berwickshire) on 18 July and ratified at Northampton on 28 August 1290. It provided for the marriage of *Margaret 'the Maid of Norway', granddaughter and successor of Alexander III, to Edward of Caernarfon (later Edward II), son and heir of Edward I, on condition that Scotland should remain an independent sovereign kingdom ruled by Margaret. It became redundant on Margaret's death in September 1290; but had the marriage taken place and children issued from it, it is possible that a lasting Anglo-Scottish union, similar to the union of the crowns of 1603, would have been achieved. KJS

Birkbeck, George (1776–1841). Son of a Yorkshire banker, Birkbeck qualified in medicine at Edinburgh and at 23 was appointed to succeed Thomas Garnett as second holder of the chair of natural philosophy (science) at the new Andersonian Institution in Glasgow. The course of free lectures he introduced on science for working men was highly successful, 500 attending with 'striking regularity, good order, with the most ardent attention'. In 1823 these led to the foundation of the Glasgow Mechanics' Institute, with Birkbeck as patron. Birkbeck had moved to London in 1804 to obtain greater security and better remuneration and practised medicine with success. In 1824 he helped to found the London Mechanics' Institute, renamed the Birkbeck Institution in 1866, and Birkbeck College in 1907. With his friend *Brougham he was one of the founders of the University of London and served on its council. JAC

***Birkenhead*, HMS,** 1852. On 25 February 1852 at night the paddle-steamer *Birkenhead* taking 480 soldiers and 13 women and children for the Kaffir War struck a rock and sank off Cape Town. The troops were ordered to stand fast on deck to avoid swamping the women's boat and almost all perished in shark-infested waters. Hailed by the Victorians as a matchless example of courage, it has also been condemned as a needless sacrifice. JAC

Birkett, William Norman (1883–1962). Lawyer. Birkett was the son of an Ulverston draper. He was educated at Barrow Grammar School and served in his father's shop in Ulverston before going to Cambridge to read theology. He was called to the bar in 1913, took silk in 1924, and was appointed a judge of the Queen's Bench Division in 1941, having briefly sat in Parliament as a Liberal. In 1946 he was one of two British judges who sat on the International War Crimes Tribunal at Nuremberg. He was appointed to the Court of Appeal in 1950 and in 1957 he became a life peer. A great English advocate, in the tradition of Marshall *Hall and Edward *Carson, he was outstanding as counsel in many cases, criminal and civil. He was also an accomplished broadcaster and after-dinner speaker. MM

Birmingham. The rise of Birmingham from local to national importance was largely an 18th-cent. development, when improvements in turnpike roads and canals enabled it to turn to advantage its central situation. The name indicates the ham or settlement of the people of Beorma, presumably a Saxon leader, and at the time of Domesday Book (1086) it was no more than a tiny hamlet, with five villeins and four smallholders. It grew during the Middle Ages, acquiring a market, but was overshadowed politically by Warwick and Coventry. Birmingham's reputation for cutlery began early, for in the 1530s *Leland found it 'a good market town', with one long street by the brook: 'there be many smiths in the town that use to make knives and all manner of cutting tools,' exploiting the local coal and iron. *Camden, 40 years later, was more enthusiastic—it was 'swarming with inhabitants and echoing with the noise of anvils': the upper part of the town had 'an abundance of handsome buildings'. During the civil wars, Birmingham declared for the Parliament, which must have found its guns, pikes, and swords of great value: *Clarendon, on the king's side, accused it of 'hearty, wilful, disloyalty'. Being near the front line of each side, it was repeatedly harassed but suffered no permanent damage. By 1700 it had well over 10,000 inhabitants. It still had no parliamentary representation and no corporation, which cynics thought a great advantage, since it allowed the people to shun politics and concentrate on business. But by 1830 the *Birmingham Political Union had taken the lead in pressing for reform and the town acquired two MPs in 1832 and a council in 1838. Under the mayoralty of Joseph *Chamberlain in the 1870s Birmingham became celebrated for municipal enterprise, and Mason's College, founded in 1870, received a charter as a university in 1900. Birmingham's economy diversified, with Cadbury's established at Bournville in 1879, General Electric in 1896, the Dunlop Rubber Company at Castle Bromwich in the 1890s, and the Austin Motor Company in 1905. The development of the railway system in the 19th cent. and the motorway network in the 20th helped Birmingham to continue to exploit its geographical position, and during the Edwardian period it overtook Liverpool and Manchester as the second city in England and Wales. JAC

Birmingham, diocese of. Largely conterminous with north Warwickshire and including the city of Birmingham, the see was created mainly out of the diocese of Worcester in 1905, after a campaign which had been launched in 1888 by Bishop Philpott of Worcester. Other great industrial cities such as Bristol (1542), Manchester (1848), Liverpool (1880), and Newcastle (1882) already had their own sees. Charles *Gore, who had been bishop of Worcester from 1902, transferred to the new see and held it until 1911, when he moved to Oxford. Bishop Barnes, a local man, who held the see from 1924 until 1953, was a mathematician, whose attacks on the doctrine of the real presence and impatience with miracles caused him to be accused of heresy. Bishop Wilson, his successor (1953–69), had been bishop of Singapore at the time of the Japanese occupation and had ministered the gospel in captivity. The cathedral is the former parish church of St Philip, built in baroque style by Thomas Archer (1711–19) with 19th-cent. windows by *Burne-Jones and William *Morris. JAC

Birmingham Political Union. Formed in 1830 by Thomas *Attwood to press for parliamentary reform as a remedy for economic distress and inspired by the successful campaign for *catholic emancipation. Led by local businessmen and manufacturers, the BPU aimed to unite middle- and working-class reformers in a programme of peaceful and orderly change based on currency reform and household suffrage. It rapidly became a preponderant factor in Birmingham political life; and as the Reform Bill crisis deepened, the BPU organized a series of huge reform demonstrations, becoming the pattern for similar political unions elsewhere. After the passing of the 1832 Reform Bill, the BPU fell apart and was virtually dissolved in 1834. A revival came in 1837, but the BPU was soon swallowed up by *chartism, which possessed a more powerful working-class dynamic. JFCH

Birmingham riots, 1791. A foretaste of the great conservative revulsion against the French Revolution, directed against its sympathizers. Joseph *Priestley, a unitarian scientist, had foolishly written of placing gunpowder beneath superstition and error, and was henceforth known as 'Gunpowder Priestley'. On 14 July 1791, after a dinner to celebrate the storming of the Bastille, his house, library, and scientific apparatus were destroyed by the mob, while the authorities were suspiciously inactive. Several dissenting meeting-houses were also burned before dragoons from Nottingham arrived to restore order. Four rioters were executed. JAC

birth control techniques appear to have been widely available long before the 19th cent. Herbal mixtures were advocated to reduce the sex drive or induce abortion. Such mixtures usually worked by causing violent vomiting or diarrhoea, although recent research has indicated that some ingredients, such as the herb savin, might well have produced uterine contractions. Contemporaries also seem to have been aware of the withdrawal technique since at least the early 18th cent., when the practice of coitus interruptus was linked by quack literature to an awesome list of debilitating medical complaints, including deafness, blindness, and loss of memory. Male contraceptives, known since at least the 16th cent., were advertised by the early 18th cent., when such 'armour', made of animal gut, was used, largely by upper-class men, to avoid contracting venereal infections from prostitutes. The 1820s and 1830s saw the first open discussion of birth control techniques, and the dissemination of (sometimes inaccurate) contraceptive knowledge amongst the working classes. More public debate followed the creation of the so-called Malthusian League (1877–1927) which distributed some 3 million pamphlets advocating birth control during its existence.

Before the third quarter of the 19th cent., however, there is little statistical evidence that English couples were practising much family limitation. The only important qualification is that marital fertility was on the low side (i.e. significantly lower than its potential biological maximum) due apparently to the contraceptive effect of relatively long periods of breast-feeding. Birth control before 1870 was restricted to higher social classes and some groups of industrial workers, such as those in the textile industry.

All this changed after 1870 when, within a few generations, Britain, in common with most other European countries, underwent the so-called fertility transition. Between 1880 and 1930 the fertility of women of child-bearing age declined by over 60 per cent and the average size of British families fell by almost two-thirds. This declining birth rate was due largely to the adoption of birth control within marriage. It is also clear that the contraceptive techniques used in the early stages of this decline were largely traditional methods such as abstinence, coitus interruptus, and 'safe periods' rather than mechanical aids such as condoms, caps, or sponges. It remains unclear why couples, particularly working-class couples, chose to limit the size of their families from the late 19th cent. Since traditional birth control methods were used, fertility decline was not 'caused' by any increase in the supply of mechanical contraceptives. It is unlikely, too, that improving survival chances of infants promoted a desire to reduce completed family size, since the fertility decline appears to have antedated the fall in infant mortality. In the end, the adoption of birth control within marriage may have been due to a new determination of women to limit the size of their families, prompted by the impact of feminist arguments, growing medical information regarding the dangers of repeated childbirth, and the impact of universal compulsory schooling in 1880, which reduced the contribution children might make to the household economy. JPB

bishops. The office and work of a bishop has evolved from that of the apostles in the New Testament church. That church recognized two differing forms of ministry, that which was local and settled (pastors and teachers) and the itinerant ministry of apostles, prophets, and evangelists. The scope of the apostolic ministry is clearly revealed in the work of Paul as founder of churches, arbiter in matters of doctrine, faith, and discipline, and in his appointment of elders to supervise individual Christian communities. The word *episcopus* (bishop), literally 'overseer', well defines this apostolic ministry. The letters of Ignatius of Antioch (*c.* AD 100) show that by that date the work of the bishop as chief pastor, preacher, and liturgical president was becoming established, and by the time of Irenaeus of Lyons (*c.* AD 170) the office of bishop was widely recognized and accepted.

The jurisdiction of a bishop, within which he exercises his ministry, is a diocese, a word taken from a territorial administrative unit of the Roman empire. There were certainly Christians in the British Isles by the beginning of the 3rd cent. AD (they were mentioned by Tertullian *c.*208) and several bishops in the country by 314, when three of them attended the Council of Arles. The churches in Wales, Ireland, and Scotland remained episcopal during the period Christianity was forced underground in England after the withdrawal of the Romans.

The gradual re-establishment of the Christian church in England and revival of episcopal government followed the mission of *Augustine (597), but early Anglo-Saxon dioceses could be vast in extent and often conterminous with the kingdom in which their see was placed. After the Norman conquest, the sees of a number of bishops were transferred to larger towns (e.g. *Sherborne to *Salisbury, *Selsey to *Chichester), thus creating the diocesan map which endured until the Reformation. The reformed Church of England retained bishops and Henry VIII established five new dioceses (*Bristol, *Chester, *Gloucester, *Oxford, and, briefly, Westminster). With the development of major conurbations in the 19th cent. further dioceses were founded (*Ripon 1836, *Manchester 1848, *St Albans and *Truro 1877, *Liverpool 1880, *Newcastle 1882, *Southwell 1884, and *Wakefield 1888), a process which continued into the 20th (*Birmingham and *Southwark 1905, *Chelmsford, *Bury St Edmunds, and *Sheffield 1914, *Bradford 1920, *Blackburn 1926, *Derby, *Guildford, *Leicester, and *Portsmouth 1927). JRG

Bishops' wars, 1639–40. Charles I assumed, with good reason, that religious diversity was a source of weakness in a state. In 1637, therefore, he ordered the Scottish presbyterian church to use a new prayer book on the English model. This provoked a protest movement which culminated in the drawing up of a national *covenant to defend 'the true religion'. Charles raised an army to enforce his will but his troops were an undisciplined rabble and rather than risk fighting he accepted the pacification of Berwick in June 1639. This brought to an end the first of the so-called Bishops' wars, but in 1640 Charles again took up arms. The outcome was worse. The Scots promptly invaded England, brushed aside Charles's army at *Newburn, outside Newcastle, on 28 August, and occupied the north-east of the country. They were now secretly collaborating with the king's opponents and refused to contemplate withdrawing unless and until he summoned Parliament. Charles's policy had collapsed. RL

Black, Joseph (1728–99). Chemist who showed that gases enter into chemical reactions. Black studied medicine at Glasgow University with William Cullen, and then migrated to Edinburgh where in 1754 he submitted his MD dissertation on *magnesia alba*, a remedy for stomach aches. This he extended into a paper in 1756. He followed a cycle of reactions, in which 'fixed air' (carbon dioxide) is driven off from the stone on heating, leaving a powder akin to quicklime. With water it is slaked; and then slowly absorbs or fixes air or gas again to turn back into the starting substance. In 1756 he succeeded Cullen as professor of chemistry (within the medical school) at Glasgow, and in 1766 in Edinburgh. He also noted how much heat was needed to turn ice into cold water, or boiling water into steam: the phenomenon of *latent heat*. He was an early convert to Lavoisier's new chemistry. DK

Black and Tans was the nickname, derived from a Limerick hound pack, or the colour of the uniform, for an auxiliary police force recruited in Britain 1920–1 from ex-servicemen to reinforce the hard-pressed Royal *Irish Constabulary (RIC). The ill-disciplined force was associated with drunken brutality and reprisals against the Irish community following *Irish Republican Army (IRA) atrocities. It is frequently confused with auxiliaries formed from army officers, established several months later. The Black and Tans soon became synonymous with talk of British oppression, and in the Irish Republic the conflict 1919–21 is often called 'The Tan War'. MAH

Blackburn, diocese of. The see, created in 1927 mostly out of the *Manchester diocese, comprises much of Lancashire except for Liverpool and Manchester, a mixture of countryside and cotton-mill towns. The cathedral is the former parish church of St Mary's, built in 1818, early Gothic Revival in style, extended in the 1930s, 1950s, and 1960s. WMM

Black Death. An epidemic of catastrophic proportions, the Black Death first struck England in the summer of 1348, and spread rapidly from the south coast, reaching virtually all parts of the country within twelve months. This first outbreak probably killed between a third and a half of the population, as is shown by figures showing death rates for the clergy, and for peasant landholders. The plague struck again in 1361, and further outbreaks followed as the disease became endemic. It is usually considered to have been bubonic plague, spread by fleas and rats, but its rapidity and morbidity were much greater than any previous outbreak, perhaps because it took a highly infectious pneumonic form. The Black Death had major economic effects, although these did not become fully apparent until the 1370s. The area under arable cultivation was sharply reduced, as demand for cereals fell, and some lands were turned over to pasture. Labour became more expensive, and attempts to revive peasant labour services were unsuccessful. The plague also caused social dislocation, notably with a rapid turnover of peasant holdings. The aristocracy suffered less than the population at large, and the workings of government were little affected. MCP

'Black Dinner', 1440. Later title given to the beheading, following a banquet in Edinburgh castle on 24 November 1440, of William 6th earl of Douglas [S] and his brother David, on the orders of Chancellor Crichton. Neither Douglas was forfeited, and their removal was probably planned by their uncle James 'the Gross', who became 7th earl of Douglas. NATM

Blackheath, battle of, 1497. A formidable rising of Cornishmen in the summer of 1497 protested against taxation to support Henry VII's campaign against James IV of Scotland, arguing that this was a purely northern responsibility. Under the leadership of Thomas Flammock and James, Lord Audley, the rebels marched through Wells, Salisbury, and Winchester towards London, where they caused great panic. But Lord Daubeney and the earl of Oxford led the army prepared for Scotland against the insurgents at Blackheath and dispersed them. Flammock and Audley were executed. JAC

Black Hole of Calcutta. By legend, on 20 June 1756 Nawab Siraj-ud-Daula, Robert *Clive's great enemy, packed 146 Englishmen captured at Calcutta into a small guardroom. The next day only 21 were left alive. There is today much dispute about Siraj-ud-Daula's culpability and the actual number of victims, which may only have been 43. DAW

Black Parliament, 1320. A parliament held at Scone on 4 August 1320 to try conspirators who had intended to kill Robert I and place Sir William Soulis, the son of a competitor in the *Great Cause, on the throne. Soulis was sentenced to life imprisonment, while five others were acquitted. Some were not so fortunate. Sir Roger Mowbray, dead before the trial, was none the less sentenced to be drawn, hanged, and beheaded, although Robert I's clemency prevented the mutilation. Four others were drawn behind horses, hanged, and beheaded. These punishments were unusual by Scottish standards, and shocked Scots more than the initial treason. RJT

'Black Prince'. See EDWARD THE BLACK PRINCE.

Blackstone, Sir William (1723–80). Blackstone is acknowledged as one of the greatest writers on the common law. He was both a practising barrister and an academic—an unusual combination at the time—and in 1758 was appointed as the first Vinerian professor of law in the University of Oxford. It was not yet possible in the 18th cent. to study the common law in the universities of Oxford and Cambridge and his lectures in Oxford, designed to enlighten undergraduates, were a masterly survey of the subject. His *Commentaries* have been one of the most authoritative and revered sources of English law and have frequently been acknowledged as such in the courts (e.g. his description of the prerogative). Like a number of distinguished lawyers, he was not quite at home in the House of Commons, where he sat from 1761 until 1770, when he was appointed to the bench of Common Pleas. MM

Blackwater, battle of. See YELLOW FORD.

Blackwood, William (1776–1834). Born in Edinburgh, Blackwood established himself in the book trade and then went into publishing. In 1817 he launched a magazine to counter the Whig tendencies of the **Edinburgh Review*, founded in 1802, but less ponderous than the Tory **Quarterly Review* (1809). After a faltering start, *Blackwood's* established itself, with Lockhart, John Galt, John Wilson, and James *Hogg among its authors. During its first year, *Blackwood's* published a series of severe attacks on 'the Cockney school of poetry'. Lockhart dismissed *Keats's *Endymion* as 'calm, settled, imperturbable drivelling idiocy', and the comments on *Hazlitt were so virulent that he was able to get damages from Blackwood. The magazine was continued by his son John Blackwood, and survived until 1980. JAC

Bladensburg, battle of, 1814. The defeat of Napoleon in 1814 allowed Britain to take the offensive in the *War of 1812

against the USA. A force of 4,000 men, under General Robert Ross, some of them peninsular veterans, was landed at Chesapeake Bay. A militia force at Bladensburg on 24 August was brushed aside and the British entered Washington, burning the White House in retaliation for the American sack of Toronto in 1813. JAC

Blair, Anthony ('Tony') (b. 1953). Prime minister. Educated at Fettes College, Edinburgh and St John's College, Oxford, Tony Blair followed his elder brother William to Lincoln's Inn and qualified as a lawyer. He entered Parliament in 1983 as Labour MP for Sedgfield, Durham, and soon made his mark as an articulate and forceful speaker and an adroit TV performer. He was elected to the shadow cabinet in 1988 and was spokesman on Home Affairs when John *Smith died in 1994. Blair won the leadership contest with ease, defeating John Prescott and Margaret Beckett. He pursued Neil *Kinnock's policy of working to shed Labour's 'loony left' image: 'New Labour''s reward was a massive majority at the general election of May 1997. JAC

Blake, Robert (1599–1657). Admiral. Educated at Oxford, where he was said to have expressed republican views, Blake volunteered for the parliamentary army in 1642, and distinguished himself at the sieges of Lyme and Taunton. In February 1649 he was one of three colonels appointed admiral and general at sea by the Commonwealth. His first assignment was to neutralize the royalist navy under Prince Rupert besieging Kinsale. Having done this, he chased Rupert to Lisbon. By mauling Rupert's forces, blockading Lisbon, and seizing the annual fleet returning from Brazil, Blake forced Portugal and Spain to recognize the authority of the Commonwealth. He well merited the thanks which Parliament bestowed upon him for he had completed a revolution in naval warfare. Fleets permanently in the service of the state had now been substituted for ships impressed or hired from merchants for the occasion. This achievement he shared with the *Council of State and Sir Henry *Vane of the Admiralty Committee, but it was Blake who won the loyalty and maintained the efficiency of the new navy. However, while an inspiring commander, he could boast no innovating skill in naval tactics. Defeated by the Dutch commander Tromp at *Dungeness (30 November 1652), he avenged his humiliation at *Portland and Beachy Head (18–20 February 1653). In 1654 he was given command of the Mediterranean fleet, where he campaigned against Turkey and Spain. His victory over the Spanish West Indies fleet in April 1657 was the occasion of a public thanksgiving in London. Blake suffered from chronic illness, especially after being wounded in 1653, and died at sea while returning to England after the Spanish campaign in August 1657. IJG

Blake, William (1757–1827). Artist, engraver, philosopher, visionary, and poet, Blake regarded art, imagination, and religion as one and aimed to create, through poetry and painting, a 'visual symbolism' to express his 'spiritual vision' and 'mystical philosophy'. After drawing school and apprenticeship to an engraver, Blake briefly attended the Royal Academy where he was at odds with Joshua *Reynolds. Returning to engraving, he became engrossed in what he called 'illuminated painting', an attempt to produce books in the style of medieval illuminated manuscripts. His first major work was *Songs of Innocence* in 1789, and *Songs of Experience* was published in 1794. Blake longed for fame and an enthusiastic audience, to build a New Jerusalem, but refused to compromise to make his work more accessible. He spent many years in poverty, saved only by the patronage of artist John Linnell and others. He spent his later years drawing rather than writing, surrounded by admirers, who included Samuel *Palmer. Individual, nonconformist, experimental, Blake's work still challenges and mystifies, yet it includes two of the best-known poems in the English language, 'Tyger, tyger' and 'Jerusalem'. JC

Blanketeers, March of the, 1817. This was another episode in the troubled post-war period. After the *Spa Fields riots of November 1816, the government suspended habeas corpus and banned meetings of more than 50 people unless authorized by a magistrate. A large gathering of some 5,000 weavers met in St Peter's Fields (Manchester), on 10 March 1817, intending to march to London to petition the prince regent for redress. They carried blankets and rugs with them. After the Riot Act had been read, most were dispersed by the cavalry, but 300 reached the bridge at Stockport, where almost all were turned back. A handful reached Leek. The episode is described by Samuel *Bamford in *Passages in the Life of a Radical*. JAC

blasphemy is open to wide definition, but within the Christian tradition is normally defined as a profane utterance or an impious speech against God or established religion. Blasphemy occasionally troubled the medieval church, but became more common after the Reformation, when a plurality of views coexisted with an increased official concern over religious orthodoxy. Perhaps the most celebrated victim of the blasphemy laws was James Nayler, who in 1656 parodied Christ's entry into Jerusalem by riding a donkey into Bristol. He was whipped in both London and Bristol, stood on the pillory, bored through the tongue, branded on the forehead, and kept in *Bridewell at Parliament's pleasure. As late as 1832 a bookseller named Eaton was imprisoned and pilloried for attacking the Bible. The 19th cent., however, saw a modification of the law on blasphemy. The key case was *Ramsay* v. *Foote* (1883), which established that it was not blasphemous to attack the fundamentals of religion if 'the decencies of controversy' were observed. This remains the legal position. JAS

Blatchford, Robert Peel Granville (1851–1943). English socialist and nationalist. Author and journalist, Blatchford wrote for the British newspaper the *Sunday Chronicle* 1885–91, before co-founding the *Clarion* in 1891, a popular socialist weekly, which he edited for 20 years. He had become a socialist as a result of his revulsion at the conditions of the slums of Manchester, but his socialism was uneasily combined with a fierce nationalism arising out of his seven years' service in the army. He became involved in the labour movement, and used the *Clarion* as a vehicle for his socialist views conveyed in a low-brow style of writing, pitched to working-class and lower middle-class readers.

Blatchford's socialism was the homely message of William *Morris, not the revolutionary doctrine of Karl *Marx, and it was so successfully transmitted that it spawned a host of organizations—such as the Clarion Scouts, the Clarion Field Clubs, and the National Clarion Cycling Club—established to promote socialist fellowship. Blatchford became leader of an influential group within the labour movement—the Clarionettes, siding with the *Social Democratic Federation against the *Independent Labour Party. His most important book *Merrie England* (1894), which sold over 2 million copies, has been described as the best recruiting document ever produced by socialists in Britain. However, Blatchford's nationalistic beliefs gradually pulled him away from the labour movement. His support for the *Boer War alienated fellow-socialists, and his advocacy of *conscription, when war broke out in 1914, finally severed his connections with the labour movement. TSG

Blenheim, battle of, 1704. In early 1704 the French and Bavarians in the War of the Spanish Succession were threatening the imperial capital of Vienna. The duke of *Marlborough marched from the Low Countries to the Danube to link up with his allies and force battle on the enemy. On 19 May 1704 Marlborough's multi-national army set off from Bedburg. He kept his objective secret, to deceive both the enemy and also his Dutch allies, who might have objected to such a risky strategy. The ploy worked and the Anglo-Dutch army united with the armies of the margrave of Baden and Eugene of Savoy. On 13 August 1704 Marlborough attacked the 60,000-strong Franco-Bavarian forces under Marshal Tallard at the village of Blindheim (or Blenheim) in Bavaria. Marlborough and Eugene attacked on the flanks of the enemy position, forcing Tallard to weaken his centre. A major French counter-attack was beaten off with the aid of Eugene's cavalry. The battle was decided by a major blow against Tallard's centre, which gave way as Eugene pushed forward on the right flank. The Franco-Bavarian force lost 38,000 men while the victors lost 12,000. The threat to Vienna was lifted and Bavaria fell to the allies. GDS

Blenheim palace (Oxon.). Home of the dukes of Marlborough and birthplace of Sir Winston *Churchill. Situated in Woodstock, close to Oxford, Blenheim palace was given to John Churchill, 1st duke of *Marlborough, in gratitude for his victory in 1704 over the French at the battle of *Blenheim during the War of the Spanish Succession. The architect was Sir John *Vanbrugh, soldier and dramatist, whose genius (in Swift's words) 'without single thought or lecture, [had] hugely turn'd to architecture'. In 1699 Vanbrugh had prepared drawings for *Castle Howard for the earl of *Carlisle, and here and at Blenheim he was assisted by Nicholas *Hawksmoor. Blenheim is the more dramatic and confident of the two designs, in part due to its striking situation high on a hill; Henry Wise (1653–1738) was largely responsible for the formal gardens near the palace, and a plan of 1709 signed by *Bridgeman shows the main avenue stretching across Vanbrugh's bridge into the park beyond. From about 1764 this area was planted and flooded by Capability *Brown. The palace itself consists of a pedimented centre block, with flanking courts on each side; the forms are imaginative, powerful, and highly modelled, with that abstraction of classical elements typical of the two architects. Inside the heroic scale is sustained in the great hall, saloon, library, and other rooms, with their paintings, furniture, bronzes, and tapestries: Grinling *Gibbons, Laguerre, *Rysbrack, and Sir James Thornhill are among the artists and craftsmen represented. During the early 20th cent. the 9th duke of Marlborough engaged the Frenchman Achille Duchêne to restore the north forecourt, replant the elm avenue leading to it, and create formal gardens on the east and two water terraces (completed 1930) on the west. Sir Winston Churchill is buried in the churchyard at Bladon, on the south-east edge of Blenheim Park. PW

Bligh, William (1754–1817). Sailor. Born in Plymouth, Bligh joined the navy at 16 and sailed with *Cook on his last voyage. In 1787 he was given command of an expedition to the Pacific to procure bread-fruits, taking HMS *Bethia* renamed *Bounty*. Fletcher Christian, his mate and the leader of the mutiny, was a friend and Bligh's own choice. Bligh was an excellent navigator, not a brutal commander by the standards of his day, but irritable and prone to bad language. After the mutiny on 28 April 1789, he and eighteen men were placed in an open boat. They reached Timor after 41 days and well over 3,500 miles, with the loss of only one man, killed by natives. On his return to Britain, Bligh was court-martialled and exonerated. He resumed his career, served as governor of New South Wales, and died a vice-admiral. JAC

Blitz. British colloquialism for air attacks on UK towns, particularly at night in 1940–1, especially on London, derived from *Blitzkrieg*, lightning war, said to be the preferred German method. Night air attacks meant, however, German acceptance of slow attrition. Towns important for war, like Belfast, Manchester, Sheffield, Glasgow, Hull, Plymouth, Coventry, suffered but the main 'Blitz' descended on London, which was bombed every night but one for over two months. Human casualties were less than feared; damage to buildings greater. The indirect effect of homelessness on war production was greater than the destruction of factories. Death, injury, and homelessness lowered morale; survivors drew strength from self-esteem and comradeship. This was especially true in London where size enabled effective concentration of help for victims. In 1940–1, before the attack on the USSR diverted the German air force, about 42,000 were killed in the UK and more than 50,000 seriously wounded. RACP

Bloemfontein, convention of, 1854. The British government was puzzled by the Great Trek of 1836–7 when thousands of Boer farmers moved out of the Cape and left British jurisdiction. In 1845 it annexed *Natal and in 1848 Sir Harry Smith followed up by annexing the *Orange River Territory, pursuing the Boers. But it was difficult to establish effective control and in 1852 the British signed the *Sand river convention acknowledging the independence of the Boers in the Transvaal in the hope that they would not assist the Boers in the Orange River Territory. But the Orange River Territory remained unstable and, in a startling switch of policy in 1854, by the Bloemfontein convention, power was handed back to the Boers in the form of a provisional government. This arrangement did not prove satisfactory and two Boer wars later resulted. JAC

Blois, treaty of, 1572. Elizabeth I, excommunicated by the pope in 1570, was in a very vulnerable position and in 1571 the *Ridolfi plot against her life was exposed. To protect herself, she sought reconciliation with the French, who had supported Mary, queen of Scots, but were in rivalry with Spain. *Walsingham conducted negotiations and on 21 April 1572 Charles IX of France agreed at Blois to a treaty of mutual defence. The main result was that the French ceased to support Mary's followers in Scotland, preparing the way for a protestant settlement there. JAC

Bloody Assizes was the name given to the mass trials of *Monmouth's rebels in 1685, presided over by *Jeffreys and four other judges. Nearly all the 1,300 prisoners were undoubtedly guilty of treason, for which the sentence was death by hanging, disembowelling, and quartering. The revulsion against the treatment of the rebels, and the legend which subsequently developed, were provoked by the conduct of the trials. The judges indicated that pleas of not guilty would invariably mean death sentences by ordering execution on the day of conviction. These examples produced pleas of guilty which enabled courts to sentence 500 in two days at Taunton, 540 at Wells in one. Most of those convicted were kept in suspense for weeks before being executed or ordered for transportation. The executions of some 250 were dispersed in towns over the area of the rebellion, and to increase the impact further pickled heads and quartered bodies were publicly displayed throughout the western region. James II's queen and courtiers took profits from the sale of those transported to the West Indies. The emotion generated by the repression is still very much alive locally. JRJ

'Bloody Sunday', 1887, 1920. The encounter on 13 November 1887 in Trafalgar Square between radicals and Irish and police, supported by troops, attempting to enforce a ban, left two demonstrators killed, though no shots were fired. A small incident by most standards, it shocked Victorian England. 'Bloody Sunday' in Dublin on 21 November 1920 saw a different scale of savagery. Fourteen British officers were murdered in their homes or hotels by the *Irish Republican Army, and in the afternoon *Black and Tan troops opened fire on a Gaelic football crowd at Croke Park, killing twelve. JAC

Bloomsbury Group. A circle of artists, writers, and critics meeting in private houses in Bloomsbury, London, who in their revolt against the artistic, social, and sexual restrictions of Victorian society were an important influence on cultural and intellectual life in the early decades of the 20th cent. Most had studied at Cambridge, and were influenced by the philosopher G. E. Moore, whose *Principia ethica* (1903) emphasized the importance of personal relationships and aesthetic experience. Among leading members were Clive and Vanessa Bell, E. M. *Forster, Roger Fry, J. Maynard *Keynes, and Virginia *Woolf. JC

Blore Heath, battle of, 1459. *Warwick's father, the earl of *Salisbury, supported the duke of *York in 1459 when he rebelled against Henry VI. He marched from Yorkshire to join York, who was in Wales, near Ludlow. Royalist forces mustered under Lord Audley at Market Drayton to prevent the junction and attacked Salisbury's men on Blore Heath, 3 miles east of the town, on 23 September. Audley was defeated and slain, and Salisbury joined York. The following year he fought on York's side in the defeat at *Wakefield and was beheaded after the battle. JAC

Blyton, Enid Mary (1897–1968). Children's author. Born in East Dulwich (London), Blyton trained as a kindergarten teacher. Her first books, collections of poems in *Child Whispers* and stories in *The Enid Blyton Book of Fairies*, were published in 1922 and 1924. She edited a number of publications such as *Sunny Stories* and the *Enid Blyton Magazine*. Her wide range of books included a popular series of school stories beginning with *The Naughtiest Girl in the School* (1940) and the well-known 'Famous Five' and 'Secret Seven' adventures. Noddy and his Toyland friends became television personalities reproduced in numerous commercial products. A prolific writer, widely translated, her work has been severely criticized for its limited style, moral attitudes, and for perceived racist, sexist, and snobbish elements in the middle-class, privileged world of her stories, which nevertheless have been popular with children. AM

Boat Race. The Oxford and Cambridge universities' challenge race for eights was first rowed at Henley in 1829, with Oxford winning. It moved to London in 1836 and became an annual event in 1839. The race is over $4\frac{1}{4}$ miles from Putney to Mortlake. JAC

Bodiam castle, 15 miles north of Hastings (Sussex), has often been cited as a typical late medieval castle in which the defensive provision was secondary to domestic comfort. Its present appearance, a picturesque ruin surrounded by a wide moat full of water lilies, masks its serious military purpose. Built in 1385, at a time of threatened French invasion, to fortify the river Rother, which was at that time navigable by sea-going ships as far as Bodiam, the castle has wide water defences to keep attackers at a distance and to control access, and was one of the earliest castles to incorporate gunports. The main approach to Bodiam, via a causeway protected by a 90-degree turn, three drawbridges, a tower and barbican, in addition to a heavily defended gatehouse, is a prime example of the principle of multiple defence. As evidence of its importance, the castle was not slighted in the 17th cent. but maintained as part of the south coast defences against attack. LR

Bodley, Sir Thomas (1545–1613). Bodley, a benefactor to the University of Oxford, was born in Exeter. His family were protestants and took refuge in Germany and Switzerland during Mary's reign. Bodley was educated at Magdalen College, Oxford, and elected a fellow of Merton. About 1583 he became gentleman usher to the queen, probably through the patronage of *Walsingham or *Leicester. In 1584 he was returned to Parliament for Portsmouth and in 1586 for St Germans. Bodley was then employed on a number of diplomatic missions to Denmark, France, and Holland, returning to England in 1596. He was considered as a possible secretary of state but devoted the rest of his life to restoring the Duke Humphrey Library at Oxford. It was reopened in 1602, and named after Bodley in 1604, when he was knighted. James I visited the new library in 1605. Bodley is buried in Merton chapel, where there is a monument.

JAC

Boece (Boethius), **Hector** (*c.*1465–1536). Scottish historian. A contemporary of Scottish historian John Major, with whom he attended the University of Paris (*c.*1485), he became a professor at Montaigu College (*c.*1492–8). In 1498, Boece made the acquaintance of William Elphinstone, bishop of Aberdeen, who enlisted his aid for the establishment of a university (later King's College) where Boece became principal. His first publication was his lives of the bishops of Mortlach and Aberdeen, printed in Paris in 1522. His only other published work, the *History of Scotland*, was printed in 1527. It ranged from the earliest times to the reign of James III: a second edition, continued by Ferrerius, was published in Paris in 1574. This is the earliest history of Scotland with the exception of the summary work of Major. In 1530–3 it was translated into Scottish prose from the Latin by John Bellenden, archdean of Moray, at the request of James V. Prone to the legendary, it lacks credibility as a historical narrative.

SMD

Boer wars. The first Boer War (1880–1) was hardly more than a skirmish, won by the Boers (Dutch-origin South African farmers) after a famous victory over a British force at *Majuba on the northern frontier of *Natal. That gave the Boer republics of the *Transvaal and *Orange Free State the independence they craved from the British empire, in most things except foreign policy. Britain accepted this while they were poor and backward. That soon changed, however, when the vast Witwatersrand goldfield was discovered in the Transvaal in 1886, offering untold riches to whichever power controlled it. In 1899 Britain went to war again against the Boers, and got it back. It would be too simplistic, however, to assume that this was out of mere cupidity.

Britain had other reasons for noticing the Boers' new wealth. One worry was that if it made them too powerful, they could threaten her supremacy in the rest of South Africa, possibly in league with Germany. The aftermath of the *Jameson Raid fuelled that fear. The kaiser sent a telegram congratulating the Boer president for repelling the raid. Britain regarded that as unwonted interference in the one aspect of the Transvaal's affairs she had not surrendered control over. The republic was behaving cockily in other ways too. A lot was made of its slightly less liberal 'native policy' by comparison with Britain's, which had been one of the reasons for setting up the independent Boer states in the first place. There were also complaints of mistreatment of immigrant diggers ('uitlanders') in the goldfields, though these were mostly invented or exaggerated. Britain negotiated to ease these grievances, but possibly not genuinely. Her main agent in South Africa, *Milner, seems to have wanted war. British troops were poured in. In the end, on 10 October 1899, it was the Boers who issued the ultimatum, but under provocation. Most foreign opinion saw Britain as the aggressor, an evil Goliath against the David who was pluckily standing up to his bullying.

David did surprisingly well initially. The first months of the war went disastrously against Britain, with the Boers advancing deep into Natal and holding several British garrisons under siege. Only in May 1900 did the tide begin to turn, mainly through the sheer force of the numbers Britain could deploy. By October the Transvaal had been largely reconquered, Kruger, its president, had fled, and both republics were annexed to the British flag. Back in London the government used the opportunity to call a snap 'khaki' election, which it won. But the war was not over yet. The Boers continued a 'guerrilla' kind of warfare, which was only crushed in the end by a policy of methodical land-razing, farm-burning, and herding non-combatant Boers—mainly women—into unhealthy 'concentration camps'. In June 1901 *Campbell-Bannerman, the Liberal leader, publicly attacked all this as 'methods of barbarism', which shocked patriots, but seemed to touch a wider chord.

When the last Boers eventually surrendered, in May 1902, most Britons were heartily sick of the war. They had won, but at a price. 5,774 Britons had been killed (more than on the other side), and 22,829 injured. The Boers had been beaten, but not bowed. In the treaty of *Vereeniging (31 May) they stuck out in defence of their racial policies, and got their new masters to back down on that. Resentment continued to simmer, contributing to more Boer rebellions later, and South Africa's withdrawal from the *Commonwealth in 1961. In Britain, the army's poor showing proved salutary, leading to a cessation of aggressive *imperialism for a while, and a great national self-examination, especially of her 'decadence'. The war also boosted anti-imperialism. Overall, therefore, the Boer War was probably not a good one to have won.

BJP

Bohun, Humphry de, 3rd earl of Hereford (*c.*1249–98). Bohun succeeded his grandfather as earl of Hereford in 1275. As constable of England and one of the great marcher lords he was employed against Llywelyn and the Welsh. But he was one of the lords who became increasingly irritated by Edward I's incessant demands for military service and heavy taxation. In 1297 he and Roger *Bigod, earl of Norfolk (constable and marshal respectively), refused to serve in Gascony unless the king was also present. Though deprived of his office, he had to be reinstated, obtaining confirmation of *Magna Carta and the Forest Charter against arbitrary taxation. He took part in Edward's successful Scottish campaign in 1298 with some reluctance and continued friction with the king over the rights of the baronage meant that the victory at *Falkirk was not followed up. He died at the end of that year.

JAC

Bohun, Humphry de, 4th earl of Hereford (*c.*1276–1322). Bohun succeeded his father as earl of Hereford and constable of England in 1298 when there was still considerable tension between Edward I and his leading barons. But in 1302 he married a daughter of Edward I, widow of

John, earl of Holland. In the reign of Edward II, Bohun was a leading *Ordainer and took part in the murder of *Gaveston. He was taken prisoner by the Scots after the defeat at *Bannockburn, but exchanged. His opposition to the *Despensers in 1321 led him to take up arms with *Thomas of Lancaster, and he was killed at their disaster at *Boroughbridge. JAC

Bolingbroke, Henry St John, 1st Viscount (1678–1751). St John was Tory MP for the family seat of Wootton Bassett (1701–8) and Berkshire (1710–12), secretary at war (1704–8), secretary of state for the northern department (1710–13) and for the southern department (1713–14). He was in charge of the negotiations for the peace of Utrecht (1713) ending the War of the Spanish Succession. In 1712 he had been, to his disappointment, created Viscount Bolingbroke, hoping to become an earl. This 'snub' contributed to the growing rift between him and Prime Minister Robert *Harley, which effectively paralysed the Tory ministry. Dismissed office by George I he was impeached and attainted. He fled to France into the service of the pretender as his secretary of state, from which post he was also dismissed in 1716. He was pardoned and returned to England in 1723, and was restored to his estates in 1725, though barred from the House of Lords. Moving into opposition to *Walpole, he provided much of the intellectual backbone to the 'patriot' and Tory parties with his philosophical and political writings, particularly in the *Craftsman*. He retired to France in 1735, and wrote essays on history, including his most famous work *Patriot King* (1738). CJ

Bombay. An island off the west coast of India originally in Portuguese possession. It was given to Charles II in 1661 as part of the dowry of *Catherine of Braganza. In 1673, the English *East India Company moved its west-coast station there from Surat. Initially, the town grew quickly, reaching a population of 60,000 by 1677. But it stagnated through the 18th cent. under the shadow of the Maratha empire on the mainland. Following the defeat of the Maratha Peshwa in 1818, Bombay city became the capital of a large presidency embracing Maharashtra, Gujarat, and Sindh. Its port thrived on trade to China and the Far East and was served by a cosmopolitan commercial community. From the 1860s, it began to develop as an industrial centre. By 1901 its population had reached 850,000, making it the third largest city in the British empire after London and *Calcutta. DAW

Bondfield, Margaret G. (1873–1953). Trade union leader and first woman cabinet minister. Bondfield left school at 13 and became a shop assistant. She immersed herself in socialist politics, eventually joining the Fabian Society. Her first-hand knowledge of the plight of shop-workers assisted her promotion within the National Union of Shop Assistants, of which she became assistant secretary (1898), but she also identified with a number of feminist causes, including women's suffrage and campaigns for maternity and child welfare schemes. Elected to Parliament in 1923, she served in the Labour government of 1924 as parliamentary secretary to the ministry of labour, and in the second Labour government (1929–31) as minister of labour. Her deep nonconformist outlook and her devotion to teetotalism were in part responsible for an increasingly conservative outlook on problems of unemployment and family welfare. She identified herself with the fiscal conservatism of Philip *Snowden, and in August 1931 supported the cabinet's decision to cut unemployment benefit. At the general election, she lost her seat. GA

Boniface, St (*c*.675–754). St Boniface was possibly the greatest of early Anglo-Saxon missionaries. Named Wynfrith, trained in monasteries at Exeter and Nursling (Hants), he left England in 718, working first with *Willibrord in Frisia before beginning his own work in Hesse and Thuringia as regional bishop. Appointed archbishop in 731 and ultimately papal legate, supported by Frankish rulers, he became a leading ecclesiastical figure in Europe. In 754 he returned to evangelize in Frisia, where he and his followers were killed by heathen robbers. In establishing an organized church under the authority of the pope, setting up sees in Bavaria, and effecting the reform of the Frankish church, he contributed to the extension of papal authority in Europe. His success depended on fellow Anglo-Saxons joining him, as bishops in new sees, monks, nuns, and teachers in new foundations, which, like his great abbey of Fulda on the borders of Hesse and Thuringia, became centres of English learning. Surviving correspondence shows Boniface engaged in formal consultation with the pope and leading Anglo-Saxon churchmen, in personal exchanges, particularly with nuns and abbesses who sent him books and vestments, and actively concerned about religious and moral affairs in England. AM

Bonner, Edmund (*c*.1500–69). Bishop of London. Born in Cheshire and educated at Broadgates Hall, Oxford, Bonner in turn loyally served *Wolsey as his chaplain until his death and then, strongly anti-papalist, Henry VIII and Thomas *Cromwell by courageously pleading Henry's divorce (1532) and his appeal to the pope against excommunication (1534). Successively bishop of Hereford (1538) and London (1539), he was deprived and imprisoned under Edward VI for objecting to the new *Book of Common Prayer (1549). He was restored by Mary (1553) to his London see, which was now enthusiastically puritan. Coerced by the court, he had to implement repression under the re-enacted medieval statutes. His contemporary description, 'bloody Bonner', was ill deserved, for the council accused him of leniency. To accompany repression with positive re-education, he published *Profitable and Necessarye Doctrine* (1555–6). Deprived again by Elizabeth, he died in Marshalsea prison. WMM

Book of Common Order. Published (1564) as the Church of Scotland's regulations for public worship. Its predecessor, brought from Geneva by John *Knox (1559), possibly originated among English refugees in Frankfurt. Because a metrical psalter was added (1564), it was known as the 'Psalm-book'. A Gaelic version was published (1567). Often revised since 1867, the Book's 1940 version, incorporating insights of the modern liturgical movement, was perhaps the most progressive liturgy until the second Vatican Council (1961–5). Newer versions have appeared (1979 and 1994) affirming the centrality of the eucharist as the principal Sunday service. WMM

Book of Common Prayer. By a proclamation of 23 September 1548, Edward VI set up a commission of twelve bishops and clergy to oversee the preparation of 'one uniform order [of service] throughout the kingdom'. This 'Windsor Commission' (so-called from its meeting-place) seems to have refined and emended a draft prayer book prepared by Archbishop Thomas *Cranmer, for the bench of bishops approved its work only a month later. The Act of *Uniformity (March 1549) ordered the exclusive use of the new Book of Common Prayer from Whitsunday (9 June) that year. The Prayer Book contained morning and evening offices, and forms for the administration of the sacraments (e.g. baptism and the eucharist) as well as the psalter. It was a response to the desire of Cranmer and other reformers for a single, convenient provision for the public worship of the church in the vernacular. It drew heavily upon the work of the continental reformers as well as upon existing Latin service books.

After 1549, reformed ideas, particularly from Germany and Switzerland, rapidly gained ground among English scholars, and these were reflected in the Second Prayer Book, issued in 1552. This book was probably little used, as the accession of Mary I saw a temporary return to the older Latin services.

In 1559 a modified 1552 Prayer Book came into use under Elizabeth I, and this in its turn formed the basis of the 1662 book, which remained the norm of Anglican worship until the 20th cent. Attempts to revise the Prayer Book in 1928 were frustrated by Parliament, but since 1980 there has been an authorized *Alternative Service Book* in England. JRG

Book of Homilies. Published soon after the accession of Edward VI, though written five years before, the *Book of Homilies* contained twelve sermons composed by some of the leading reformers of the English church, including *Cranmer and *Latimer. The homilies were to be read to the people by the clergy in place of a sermon. By supporting justification by faith, ignoring teaching on the eucharist, and attacking some popular religious customs, they revealed the reforming sympathies of their composers. Contributions of more conservative scholars such as Bishop *Bonner were confined to less contentious subjects, e.g. love and charity. JRG

book of sports. Sunday, the one non-working day in the week, was traditionally a time for recreation, but *puritan clergy and local officials, equating it with the sabbath, kept it 'holy' by banning customary pastimes. This threatened to alienate public sentiment from the established church and to endanger social stability by dividing communities. In 1618, therefore, James I issued a declaration asserting the right of all persons to engage in 'lawful recreation' on Sundays after divine service. Charles I reissued this 'book of sports' in 1633, thereby further widening the gap between royal government and the 'godly'. RL

Books of Discipline, 1560, 1578. Both works expounded an ideal never fully realized. The *First Book of Discipline* (1560) was largely the work of the uncompromising Calvinist John *Knox, a blueprint for the government of the reformed church in Scotland. It was heavily dependent upon the *Ordinances* of Calvin's church in Geneva, with which Knox was personally acquainted. The book's implementation was, however, opposed by many of the Scottish nobility. Knox died in 1572 and three years later Andrew *Melville, principal of Glasgow University, began drawing up a *Second Book of Discipline*, intended to purge the Scottish church of the last vestiges of episcopal government. JRG

Boot, Jesse (1850–1931). Boot was born in Nottingham, where his father, a Wesleyan lay preacher, ran a herbal medicines shop. Jesse followed in his father's footsteps. Their sales to co-religionists benefited from John *Wesley's advocacy of herbal medicines. During the later 19th cent., Boot saw the advantages of meeting demands for mainstream medicine and employed a legally licensed pharmacist to dispense drugs in every shop. Retailing activities grew by offering a wide range of general items as well as Boot's own pharmaceuticals. The business became nation-wide by establishing branches and by purchasing chains of other retailers, for example Day's in the London area. In 1920 Jesse Boot sold the business to the American company Rexall. However, in 1933 the latter's financial difficulties enabled the Boot family to regain control. Currently the firm is an international corporation based in Nottingham. IJEK

Booth, Charles (1840–1916). Booth, a wealthy Liverpool shipowner and social investigator, refused to accept the findings of the *Social Democratic Federation that about 25 per cent of the working population were living in poverty. He found that official statistics were substantially defective and began his own investigation using statistical techniques to come to accurate conclusions. Booth published seventeen volumes on the life and labour of London's poor between 1889 and 1903. His main finding was that the SDF estimate was too low: 30.7 per cent were living in poverty. Only 0.9 per cent were responsible for their own poverty: the main causes were inadequate wages and precarious employment. He drew a poverty line at £1.05 per week for a 'moderate family' and felt that the state should help the honest poor and, in particular, provide old-age pensions. Booth greatly influenced the practice of later social investigators and the Liberal government (1906–14). JB

Booth, William (1829–1912). Revivalist and founder of the *Salvation Army. Of lower middle-class background, Booth joined the methodists in Nottingham and in 1844 was converted. After experience in several different methodist connexions (including a ministry in 1858 in the methodist new connexion) he rejected them all as too staid and middle class to reach the mass of people needing salvation. Strongly supported by his wife Catherine, also an active methodist, he set up a mission in London's East End in 1865, from which developed the Salvation Army. For some time Booth waged his holy war solely on the spiritual front; but experience showed that poverty was a great impediment to salvation, and in his book *In Darkest England* (1890) he outlined plans for social reform. Booth was extremely authoritarian and the military structure of the Salvation Army reflected his temperament. No theologian, he was at times anti-intellectual: 'do not argue, but pray,' he advised his officers. JFCH

Booth's rising, 1659, was one of many attempts by royalists to overthrow the commonwealth regime. *Penruddock's rising in Wiltshire in 1655 had failed completely but in 1659 Sir George Booth succeeded in rousing a substantial number of supporters in Cheshire to exploit the uncertainty following the death of Oliver *Cromwell. Anticipated risings elsewhere failed to get off the ground and John *Lambert crushed the rebels without difficulty at Winnington bridge on 19 August. Booth was imprisoned in the Tower but released in 1660 and formed part of the deputation sent to Breda to beg Charles II to return. He was created a peer in Charles's coronation honours. JAC

Borders. From 1973, an administrative region of Scotland, comprising the counties of Berwick, Peebles, Roxburgh, and Selkirk and a small part of Midlothian; these counties together, historically, formed much of the frontier zone facing England. From 1973 to 1996 it shared local government functions with its districts of Berwickshire, Ettrick and Lauderdale, Roxburgh and Tweeddale, but in 1996 it became an all-purpose local authority. A hilly area, its economy has continued to be dominated by sheep-farming and textile-manufacturing and services, with a growing presence of tourism attracted by its legends (perpetuated in the border ballads), its castles and abbeys, its peaceful countryside, and its small towns. CML

Borneo, North. North Borneo is ethnologically part of the southern Philippines. Although the Spanish touched the region in the 16th cent., it was not until Alexander Dalrymple's expedition of 1759 that it was connected to the outside world. The *East India Company opened and closed several settlements and, in 1846, Labuan was occupied as a crown colony. In 1877 the British North Borneo Company began to move inland and, effectively, to establish a government. The Japanese invasion of 1941–2 ended this informal arrangement and eventually led to crown colony status in 1946. Representative government and membership of the Malaysian Federation followed in 1963. DAW

Boroughbridge, battle of, 1322. *Thomas of Lancaster and the earl of Hereford, in rebellion against Edward II and the *Despensers, retreated into Yorkshire to join the Scots. At Boroughbridge, on 16 March 1322, they found the crossing of the Ure blocked by a strong force of infantry and archers commanded by Sir Andrew Harcla, sheriff of Cumberland. Hereford was killed and Lancaster, who surrendered, was executed for treason. Harcla, created earl of Carlisle, enjoyed his new honours for only a year, hanged by Edward in 1323 for treasonable contacts with the Scots. JAC

borough English was the custom that lands should descend to the youngest son or daughter, or, in default of issue, to the youngest brother of the deceased. Also known as ultimogeniture, it was therefore the opposite of primogeniture, the more widespread convention. The name originated from a case in Nottingham in 1327 when the English borough, or part of the town, held to ultimogeniture, the French (Norman) part to primogeniture. In fact it was not particularly common in boroughs. It was found more especially in the south-east and not at all in the north. The origin and intention of the custom has been much discussed but scarcely illuminated. Even *Maitland is less persuasive than usual, suggesting that the youngest is the 'hearth-child' and that the custom may be a trace of an ancient religion centred on the hearth. It survived in some places until 1925. JAC

boroughs. The word 'borough' ('burgh' in Scotland) has caused endless confusion in British history through its changing meanings and through its relationship to other terms for urban settlements. The Old English (Anglo-Saxon) terms *burg*, *burh*, and *byrig* were used originally for fortified places, including villages and royal halls. By 1086, however, *Domesday Book was using the word, in its Latin form *burgus*, to mean 'town', whether fortified or not, and was referring to its inhabitants as *burgenses* (burgesses), or at least to those who paid their share of borough dues. In the 12th cent. burgage tenure came to be seen as the normal characteristic of an English borough: each burgess held a burgage, usually a house with little other land, for a money rent. In the 13th cent. the larger towns developed rules to define who were 'free burgesses' (or, in cathedral towns, citizens), and to ensure that burgesses, the only townspeople with political rights, were defined as those who were sons (or sometimes widows or daughters) of burgesses, who had served an apprenticeship, or had paid a fee. These rules were enforced in many towns until the 17th and 18th cents., ensuring that a restricted proportion of the urban population (mostly male) were the only ones who could run businesses and elect municipal officials and councillors.

Between the 13th and 17th cents., as many towns grew in importance and acquired privileges from the crown or from their lords, 'borough' developed multiple meanings. From the late 13th cent. royal officials tended to confine the word 'borough' to the more privileged urban places, and to distinguish certain boroughs as having separate juries for the administration of justice; they have been called 'juridical boroughs'. Others, not always the same, have been termed 'taxation boroughs' because they paid royal taxes at different rates from other towns and rural settlements, especially after 1334. Finally, sheriffs in the 13th and 14th cents. had to choose which places in their counties were suited to be represented in parliaments: these are often called 'parliamentary boroughs', though the concept is a later one. By the 16th and 17th cents. 'borough' was being used chiefly in two senses: as a legally corporate town, usually with privileges granted by royal charters, and as a town which sent members ('burgesses') to Parliament. Most important towns were both by the 17th cent., but a few places without chartered privileges were parliamentary boroughs (e.g. Gatton), while some important and growing towns were not represented in Parliament, and either had no borough privileges, or had lost them after having enjoyed them in the Middle Ages (e.g. Birmingham and Manchester).

The problem had become one of fossilized and self-perpetuating rights: the crown could create new boroughs in both senses, but rarely chose to disfranchise those old boroughs which had ceased to be important. Furthermore, corporate boroughs often changed their regulations to ensure self-perpetuating and unelected bodies of aldermen and councillors, while the crown was concerned to ensure that they also returned conformist members of Parliament. After the Restoration commissioners appointed under the *Corporation Act remodelled many urban corporations, and many more were remodelled by new charters imposed by the government in 1681–8. These charters were cancelled after the revolution of 1688, which reintroduced the old system in all its variety, and it remained intact throughout the 18th cent. while the anomalies between boroughs and other towns became more glaring.

Modern boroughs begin with the 1830s. The 1832 *Reform Act revised the parliamentary franchise, both in terms of which boroughs were represented and of who was entitled to vote. In 1835 the *Municipal Corporations Act dissolved the corporations of nearly 200 boroughs, and replaced them by councils elected by ratepayers. New places were incorporated as boroughs, such as Birmingham and Manchester in 1838. Successive Acts since the 1830s have continued to revise the numbers and areas of boroughs in both senses, and in 1888–9 many larger boroughs or burghs were excluded from the new county councils and made all-purpose authorities (county boroughs in England and Wales, counties of cities in Scotland). Since the 1974–5 reorganizations of British local government, the title 'borough' has also been applied to some districts which are more rural than urban (e.g. east Yorkshire and north Bedfordshire). The semantic confusions of the word clearly continue.

DMP

Boscawen, Edward (1711–61). Boscawen was a younger son of Viscount Falmouth. He went to sea at 14 and was given his first command in 1741. Wounded in the action off *Cape Finisterre in 1747, he was promoted admiral—the youngest in the navy—and sent in charge of an expedition to India. From 1742 until his death he was MP for Truro, and from 1751 a lord of the Admiralty. In 1758 he commanded the naval force sent to take Louisbourg, and the following year was dispatched to the Mediterranean to prevent a French squadron at Toulon joining a Channel invasion fleet. In August he pursued the squadron of seven ships under de la Clue into *Lagos Bay in Portugal and destroyed it. Boscawen was a determined and pugnacious sailor and, though a stern disciplinarian, was noted for the attention he paid to the health of his men.

JAC

Boston, on the river Witham in Lincolnshire, was once one of the greatest English ports. It became a town only after 1066, but rapidly flourished by exporting wool. In the 13th cent. it paid more tax than any port except London, and was home to one of England's international fairs. It declined in the 15th cent., but was still enough of a port to send emigrants to America in 1630, giving its name to the state capital of Massachusetts. It is still dominated by the medieval church of St Botolph ('Boston stump') with its 272-foot tower, 'the most prodigious of English parochial steeples' (Pevsner).

DMP

Boston 'massacre', 1770. The 'massacre' resulted from the clash, probably engineered by radical elements, between British troops, who fired without orders, and an urban crowd, on 5 March 1770 in Boston (Mass.). Three persons were killed and two later died from wounds. Its propaganda value was quickly utilized, notably by Paul Revere, the engraver; radical patriots, who controlled the Boston town meeting, used traditional arguments against redcoats and 'standing armies' to force the withdrawal of troops to an island fort. In an ensuing trial, the soldiers and their officer were acquitted of manslaughter. The incident alarmed moderate colonial opponents of British measures as well as the British government.

RCS

Boston Tea Party, 1773. This marked a distinct stage on the road from resistance to insurrection in North America. The unpopular tea duty was continued after the repeal of the other *Townshend duties. In 1773 the East India Company was allowed to export dutied tea directly to America. The patriotic leadership in Boston failed to gain undertakings that tea would not be landed. A group of men disguised as 'Mohawks or Indians' 'emptied every chest of tea' on board three ships into Boston harbour on 16 December 1773. This unchecked attack on British property provoked the *'Intolerable Acts' of 1774.

RCS

Boswell, James (1740–95). Writer. Educated at Edinburgh High School and Edinburgh University, the son of Lord Auchinleck, Boswell owes his significance to the writer and poet Samuel *Johnson. Their friendship enabled him to write *Life of Johnson* (1791) as well as *Journal of a Tour to the Hebrides* (1785). Boswell's non-Johnsonian literary achievement was his *Account of Corsica* (1768). The *Life* is a milestone in English literature. It provides witty yet profound insights into one of Britain's finest writers and a strong flavour of 18th-cent. society. The power of Johnson's personality shines through every page. However, Boswell and Johnson met for the first time only in 1763 with the latter already in his fifties, and though they had a strong friendship, they were not as inseparable as the *Life* may suggest. Boswell was a vain man who found it difficult to control his emotions, being prone to depression, drink, and whoring. He was a fame hunter, obsequious to his targets (notably Corsican General Paoli, the reckless politician John *Wilkes, and Johnson), but occasionally rude and haughty to those he considered 'lesser men'. He lacked sufficient dedication to be a successful lawyer and his hopes of entering Parliament were never realized. Without Johnson, Boswell's life would have been one of high but unfulfilled aspirations.

AIL

Bosworth, battle of, 1485. Richard III's usurpation of the throne of his nephew Edward V was challenged by Henry Tudor, the future Henry VII, whose own remote claim came through his descent from *John of Gaunt. Henry landed at Milford Haven and advanced by way of Shrewsbury and Lichfield. Richard concentrated his forces at Leicester where he could watch events. The armies met on open ground on 22 August near Market Bosworth, 11 miles west of Leicester. Richard chose a strong position on Ambien hill, but his considerable superiority in numbers was offset by the defection of Lord *Stanley and his brother and the inactivity of the earl of *Northumberland, who commanded the royalist rearguard. Richard was cut down fighting on foot and his body slung on horseback for burial at Grey Friars, in Leicester. JAC

Botany Bay, discovered on 29 April 1770 by Captain *Cook, who first named it Stingray Bay, later Botanists' (Harbour and Bay), and finally Botany Bay in his journal, probably to honour the botanists aboard HMS *Endeavour* led by Sir Joseph *Banks as well as to mark its floral novelties. Banks later (1786) advocated Botany Bay as an ideal place for a penal colony on account of its supposed fertility. The first fleet under Captain Arthur Phillip landed there on 20 January 1788 and, finding Banks's account much exaggerated, moved on to Port Jackson, landing there at Sydney Cove. Nevertheless, the name Botany Bay became synonymous with Australia, first as a convict settlement, and later as a generic name for fine-quality Australian yarn. Today much of the shores of Botany Bay are taken up with Sydney's southern suburban residential development. Botany Bay is also the site of Sydney's (Kingsford-Smith) international airport. MJW

Bothwell, James Hepburn, 4th earl of (*c*.1535–78). Bothwell's grandfather perished at Flodden. The family influence was in Liddisdale and the south of Scotland. He succeeded as earl in 1556. Though a protestant, he was at first a supporter of *Mary of Guise and strongly anti-English. He had no part in the murder of *Rizzio, and as relations between Mary, queen of Scots, and *Darnley deteriorated, he became close to the queen. In 1567 events moved to a melodramatic climax. In February, Bothwell was the chief instigator of the murder of Darnley, blown up at Kirk o' Field. On 7 May he was divorced, on 12 May created duke of Orkney, and on 15 May married to Mary at Holyrood palace. The marriage lasted no more than a month. Outraged at his elevation, his enemies confronted him. Mary and Bothwell fled to Borthwick castle, from which Bothwell escaped, but after the encounter at *Carberry Hill on 15 June, they parted for ever—Mary to captivity in Lochleven castle, Bothwell to Orkney and Shetland. Thence he fled to Norway, under Danish rule. The king of Denmark resisted appeals to extradite or execute him but as a useful pawn, he was kept in prison, first in Malmö, then in Dragsholm on Zealand, where he died insane. His embalmed body is preserved in a crypt in the church at Faarvejle nearby. Bothwell's rough wooing may have appealed to Mary, neither of whose previous husbands were powerful men—she would 'go with him to the world's end in a white petticoat', she was reported to have said. Bothwell's behaviour does not suggest high intelligence—kidnapping or offers of single combat were his mainstay—and his brief spell at the top suggests Mary's folly rather than his ability. JAC

Bothwell, Francis Stewart, 1st earl of [S] (*c*.1563–*c*.1612). Stewart was the nephew of the 4th earl, who was the third husband of Mary, queen of Scots, and a grandson of James V. His uncle having died in Denmark in 1578, Stewart was created earl of Bothwell in 1581 and in 1583 appointed lord high admiral. Though a strong supporter of the reformed religion, his behaviour was as turbulent as that of his uncle. In 1588 his men killed Sir William Stewart in an affray in Edinburgh. For a time he remained a favourite with James VI and was appointed joint governor of the realm when the king went to Denmark to fetch his bride. But the following year he was accused of consulting witches about the king's death and stripped of his offices. In retaliation, Bothwell raided Holyrood palace in December 1591 to seize the king, but failed. He tried again in July 1593 at Falkland and once more failed. Meanwhile the king's efforts to capture Bothwell had also failed. Next Bothwell forced himself into the king's presence to beseech pardon and in April 1594 there was another confrontation at Leith, which decided nothing. But having lost the support of the kirk, Bothwell fled to France in 1595 and spent the rest of his life abroad in poverty. The association with his uncle's murder of James's father *Darnley and the connection with witchcraft go far to explain James's terror, but Bothwell's actions appear to be purely factious and random. JAC

Bothwell Bridge, battle of, 1679. After the murder in May 1679 of Archbishop James *Sharp of St Andrews, a zealous episcopalian, the *covenanters rose in the south-west. They defeated John Graham of Claverhouse (Viscount *Dundee) at *Drumclog on 1 June and occupied Glasgow, but were routed by James, duke of *Monmouth, at Bothwell Bridge on the Clyde on 22 June. JAC

Botswana. Former British protectorate of Bechuanaland. British influence in the region was established by representatives of the *London Missionary Society and traders operating northward from Cape Colony in the early 19th cent. Its importance in British eyes was as the road to the interior of Africa from the Cape, but it was not until pressure from the Boers of the South African Republic (*Transvaal) to the east and the establishment of a German colony to the west threatened that road that the British government declared a protectorate in 1885. South African claims to the territory were resisted and it became independent in 1966. KI

Boudicca. British queen of the *Iceni tribe. Boudicca made her mark on history by leading the British rebellion against the Romans in AD 60/1, which came close to driving them out of Britain. Her husband Prasutagus had become a client king of the Romans at the time of the invasion, and the arrangement had survived the succession of Nero in AD 54. However, when Prasutagus died in AD 60 the Romans decided to incorporate his kingdom into the province of Britain. The take-over seems to have been badly handled and, according to the Roman historian Tacitus, ended up with Boudicca being flogged and her two young daughters raped. The rebellion which she instigated was joined by the Iceni's neighbours, the *Trinovantes, and by other disaffected British tribesmen. They captured and destroyed the new Roman colony at *Colchester, repeated their success at the flourishing port of *London, and then settled old scores by destroying *Verulamium, the capital of their traditional foes the *Catuvellauni. The Roman governor *Suetonius Paullinus eventually managed to assemble a large enough force somewhere in the midlands on the line of *Watling Street to take on the rebels in a pitched battle. The British were defeated and the rebellion collapsed. Boudicca died shortly afterwards, by her own hand according to Tacitus. Of Boudicca herself we know little, although Dio Cassius describes her as tall and severe, with long fair hair, a penetrating gaze and a rasping voice. She seems to have been no figurehead but a formidable leader. KB

Boulton, Matthew (1728–1809). Birmingham entrepreneur and engineer. Boulton developed his father's button and stamping business from 1759, applying a dowry to establish his new Soho Works (1760–2). Like his associate *Wedgwood, he integrated manufacturing with mercantile functions and a coherent marketing approach to his products. Already chronically short of water power by 1771, he acquired a two-thirds share of *Watt's 1769 patent (1773), and entered partnership (1775), managing the business and the defence of patent rights. Their new engine (1776) particularly suited Cornwall, where coal was expensive, and 40 per cent of their reciprocating horsepower had been installed by 1800. Their distinctive rotative engine was complete by 1787, and 4,000 horsepower was in use by 1800, over half in Lancashire, Staffordshire, London, and Yorkshire. They joined the Albion Flour Mill project (1784), and centralized production in their new Soho Foundry (1796). As the partnership ended, Boulton applied steam to minting at Soho (*c.*1800) and the Tower (1805), and exported mints to Russia, Denmark, and Brazil (1800–11). JCh

boundary commission. Redistribution of parliamentary constituencies had always been accompanied by accusations that they were made for party advantage, but movements of population, particularly in the 20th cent. from city centres to suburbs, meant that readjustment of boundaries was a constant need. The problem was tackled by the Redistribution of Seats Act of 1949 which set up four permanent boundary commissions, for England, Scotland, Wales, and Northern Ireland, to review and report regularly. The chairmanship was to be taken by the Speaker. Schedule 2 of the Act defined the rules the commissions were to follow and laid down that each constituency should have one MP. JAC

***Bounty*, HMS.** A 215-ton armed vessel, originally the *Bethia* but renamed after extensive alterations and refitting at Deptford (1787) for a specific mission to transport breadfruit trees from Tahiti in the South Seas to the West Indies. She was small, overcrowded, and undermanned, so fragile discipline contributed to mutiny by some of the crew under the leadership of master's mate Fletcher Christian, near Tonga (28 April 1789); Captain William *Bligh and eighteen loyal crewmen were set adrift in the long boat. The mutineers sailed eastwards, to settle eventually on Pitcairn Island (1790), where the *Bounty* was stripped and then burned. ASH

Bourchier, Thomas (*c.*1410–86). Archbishop of Canterbury. A great-grandson of Edward III, Bourchier became chancellor of the university and bishop of Worcester while studying at Oxford. Because of his 'great blood', he was chosen as archbishop in 1454 by the baronial council ruling during Henry VI's insanity. He welcomed the Yorkist descent on London in 1460, and was one of the nobles who agreed to Edward IV's assumption of the crown. He probably applied himself to his pastoral duties, for he held no political office (apart from a short term as chancellor in 1455–6) and seemed ready to accept *force majeure*, crowning both Richard III and Henry VII. From 1473, Bourchier was the first archbishop of Canterbury to hold the title of cardinal. RLS

Bourges, treaty of, 1412. This agreement between *Henry IV, king of England, and a group of French lords headed by the duke of Orléans arose out of the French civil war. In return for Henry's aid against the Burgundians, Orléans was prepared to accept English claims to sovereignty over the duchy of Aquitaine. Henry duly dispatched an army of 4,000 under his second son, Thomas, duke of *Clarence, in July 1412, but as the Orléanists had meanwhile come to a temporary peace with Burgundy, the terms of the treaty were never fulfilled. AC

Bouvines, battle of, 1214. On 27 July 1214 was fought one of the most decisive battles in European history. Near Bouvines (Flanders), the army of Philip II 'Augustus', king of France (1179–1223), crushed the forces of the coalition ranged against him: an expeditionary corps from England, dispatched by King John under the command of William Longspee I, earl of Salisbury; the detachments of Rhineland princes beholden to John through English silver; and Otto of Brunswick, John's nephew and Holy Roman emperor, eager to destroy Philip since he supported Otto's rival for the imperial throne, Frederick II of Hohenstaufen. Philip's victory laid open the way to Hohenstaufen dominance in Germany and Italy, confirmed the Capetian gains made at John's expense in Normandy, Anjou, and elsewhere in the years 1202–4, and set John upon the road to Runnymede and *Magna Carta. SL

Bower, Walter (d. 1449). Author of the *Scotichronicon*, and abbot of Inchcolm (1417–49). He was born in Haddington in east Lothian (1385), entering St Andrews cathedral priory as a youth, and probably graduated from St Andrews University shortly after its foundation (1410). As abbot of Inchcolm he promoted the revival in interest in Scottish saints at his abbey, dedicated to *Columba. He was intimately involved in government in the reigns of James I and II, administering collection of taxes raised for James I's ransom in 1424, and attending parliaments and general councils as late as 1445.

He is best remembered for the *Scotichronicon*, a Latin chronicle of Scotland composed in the 1440s, based on Fordun's 14th-cent. chronicle, but altering and continuing it to the death of James I. Bower's intimate knowledge of the contemporary government and church makes the *Scotichronicon* an invaluable source for late medieval Scotland. RJT

bowls is one of the oldest and most popular of all sports and like many others blossomed in late Victorian Britain: London, which had only one municipal green in 1895, had 76 by 1907. The modern game developed when biased bowls were brought into use, permitting considerable tactical play. Hereford has a bowling green within the city walls which is said to date from the 15th cent. and to be the oldest in existence: James IV of Scotland had a green at Holyrood palace in the early 16th cent. Standard rules were drawn up in 1848–9 by W. W. Mitchell, a Glasgow solicitor, and were widely accepted. The Scottish Bowling Association was formed in 1892, the English in 1903, and the International Board in 1905. Crown green bowls, played on a convex green, was popular in the midlands and north. By 1914 there were said to be 600,000 crown green players in the north of England, competing for considerable money prizes. The English Bowling Association, strong in London and the south, remained resolutely amateur. Indoor bowls has made much progress in recent years, partly through the advent of television. JAC

Bow Street runners were constables attached to the Bow Street Police Office. Professional thief-takers had been established there by the magistrate Sir John Fielding in the mid-18th cent., but were too few to cope with escalating crime. Seven police offices were established in London in 1792 on the Bow Street pattern, though for defined districts; the unlimited jurisdiction of Bow Street enabled its six 'runners' to range widely and gain prestige for their vigilance and detective skills. Valuable public servants but poorly paid, hence increasingly corrupt, they were superseded by the Metropolitan Police Act (1829). ASH

Boxer Rising, 1900. The spread of European influence led to strong anti-foreign feelings in northern China. Encouraged by Dowager Empress Tzu Hsi, young Chinese formed an organization called the Society of Harmonious Fists or 'Boxers'. They attacked converts to Christianity, missionaries, and workers on foreign-controlled railways. British Admiral Seymour led reinforcements to safeguard foreign nationals but was fired upon from the forts at Taku. On 20 June a Boxer uprising occurred in Peking where the German minister, Baron von Ketteler, was killed and other foreign legations besieged. A six-nation force landed at Tientsin on 14 July and marched 80 miles north-west to relieve Peking on 14 August. RAS

boxing developed from uncontrolled encounters, in which wrestling, kicking, gouging, biting, hair-pulling, and kicking opponents when down were practised. Early prize fights went on until one of the combatants could not continue: Mendoza fought Henry Lee over 53 rounds in 1806. James Figg in the 1720s was hailed as the champion of All England and his protégé Jack Broughton tried in the 1740s to introduce some elementary rules, such as rounds. By 1838 London Prize Ring rules were in use, with a roped-off ring. The Queensberry rules from 1867 onwards took some time to establish themselves: they included padded gloves, 3-minute rounds, and a 10-second knock-out. Weight divisions were gradually introduced where previously heavyweights had dominated. The Amateur Boxing Association was set up in 1880 and boxing was brought into the Olympic Games in 1904. In professional boxing, the British Board of Control has supervised since 1919, though international authorities have proliferated. The introduction of radio and then television has vastly increased the purses which boxers can command. JAC

Boycott, Charles Cunningham (1837–97). Boycott came from Norfolk and after a career in the army retired as a captain. He was engaged in 1873 as land agent by Lord Erne for his Mayo estates. In September 1880 at Ennis, *Parnell announced a new policy of ostracizing an opponent of the *Irish Land League 'by putting him into a sort of moral Coventry . . . as if he were a leper of old'. Boycott was an early victim and the following month his crops had to be harvested by Orange volunteers, protected by hundreds of police and military at great cost. John *Dillon used the phrase 'boycotting' on 17 November in a speech at Cashel and it was reported in *The Times*. The verb made its way into French, German, and Russian, as well as English. JAC

Boyd, Robert, Lord [S] (d. *c.*1482). Created Lord Boyd (1452), he took a minor role in government until orchestrating his family's seizure of the young James III at Linlithgow (July 1466). He was subsequently politically ruthless, excluding his brother Alexander from power, and appointing himself governor of the persons of the king and his brothers (October 1466). He pursued a policy of self-aggrandizement, elevating his son to the earldom of *Arran, and marrying him to Mary, the king's sister, a deeply unpopular action (1467). He successfully arranged the treaty of Copenhagen (1468), by which the king married *Margaret of Denmark, and the Scottish crown eventually gained possession of Orkney and Shetland. However, the Boyd faction's hold on power remained tenuous, and they were ousted while Boyd was in England (1469). Forfeited by Parliament (1469), Boyd fled to Bruges and later England (1471), following a failed attempt to return to Scotland. RJT

Boyle, Robert (1627–91). Famous for his work on air pressure, Boyle was the youngest son of the 1st earl of Cork. After Eton, he went on a grand tour in 1639–44, and during the 1650s belonged to the 'invisible college', so called because they never all met together at once, associated with John *Wilkins at Wadham College, Oxford. Crucial in the *scientific revolution in England, this was a nucleus for the *Royal Society, in which, though very important, Boyle would never take office. With Robert *Hooke in Oxford he made and experimented with an air pump, and hit upon the law of gas pressure, discovering a new variable. A godly man who brought prestige to natural philosophy, he was a great advocate for a version of the atomic, or *corpuscular*, theory of matter: having been impressed by the Strasbourg clock, he sought mechanical explanations of all phenomena. DK

Boyne, battle of the, 1690. James II's attempt in the summer of 1689 to reassert his rule over all Ireland faltered on the resistance of *Derry and Enniskillen. The Williamite victory at *Newtown Butler in July 1689 was the start of the counter-attack. Derry was relieved the following day and *Schomberg landed on 13 August. In June 1690 William III arrived to take personal command and began his advance south. The Jacobites decided to give battle on the line of the Boyne, 30 miles north of Dublin. When they met on 1 July, James's army was some 25,000 strong, William's a little more. William hoped to outflank his opponents by crossing the river to the west towards Rosnaree, but the attack bogged down. In the end, the day was decided largely by a frontal assault across the Boyne, with the advantage of numbers beginning to tell. The Jacobites managed an orderly retreat and William's forces were in no condition to pursue. Though casualties were not heavy, the outcome was decisive. Schomberg was killed in action; William was in Dublin for a Te Deum on 6 July; James, explaining rather unnecessarily to his supporters 'I do now resolve to shift for myself', was safe on board a boat at Duncannon within two days. JAC

Boys' Brigade. Founded by William Alexander Smith in Glasgow in 1883. Smith started the brigade as a means of controlling the boys who attended his Scottish free church Sunday school. He sought to use military drill and discipline for the religious and moral improvement of the boys. The first meeting was held on 4 October 1883 in the Mission Hall, North Woodside Road, Glasgow. The crest of the brigade was an anchor and its motto 'Sure and Steadfast'. The uniform consisted of a 'pill-box' cap, belt, and haversack. During the 1890s the organization spread across Scotland and then into England. It remained primarily a religious organization despite the efforts of the War Office to incorporate the brigade into a national cadet force administered by the Territorials. The appeal of the brigade has been reduced in the modern era by alternative leisure interests for youth. RAS

Boy Scouts. Youth movement founded by *Baden-Powell in 1908. Baden-Powell was inspired to establish the Boy Scouts by the interest shown in his army training manual, *Aids to Scouting*, by younger boys and by the example of the *Boys' Brigade. He held a trial camp on Brownsea Island in Poole Harbour from 29 July to 9 August 1907. It mixed boys from different social backgrounds and split them into small units of five, each with its own leader, to promote independence and self-reliance. The camp was a success and the following year Baden-Powell established the Boy Scouts, with the financial aid of Sir C. Arthur Pearson, and wrote *Scouting for Boys*. Groups sprang up all over the country and within two years there were 100,000 members. His aim was 'to counteract if possible the deterioration moral and physical which shortened our rising generation, and to train the boys to be more efficient and characterful citizens'. Scouting was accused of simply being military training under a different name but Baden-Powell placed emphasis on personal development, with the motto 'Be Prepared'. Unlike the Boys' Brigade, he did not believe in drilling boys as it destroyed individuality and dulled enthusiasm. Scouting had an imperial influence, as Baden-Powell explained: 'Scoutcraft includes the qualities of our frontier colonists, such as resourcefulness, endurance, pluck, trustworthiness etc.'

Other branches were added to the organization; the Wolf Cubs in 1914, the Rover Scouts in 1919, and the Beavers in 1982. In 1920, at London Olympia, a Jamboree was held consisting of Scout troops from around the world. It was here that Baden-Powell was named Chief Scout of the World. Today the movement has spread to 150 countries and has around 16 million members. RAS

Bracton, Sir Henry (*c.*1210–68). Bracton, 'the flower and crown of English Jurisprudence' (Maitland) and one of the greatest writers on the common law, was born in Devon and became the dean of Exeter cathedral, where he is buried. He served during the reign of Henry III as a justice in Eyre and a justice of King's Bench, but his fame rests on his great work *De legibus et consuetudinibus Angliae* ('On the Laws and Customs of England'). This remarkable work is one of the most important books in English legal history. It was much influenced by notions of canon law and Roman law, which at this time was being 'received' in many European countries. But Bracton's authorship of *De legibus* is now doubted and it has been suggested that most of the book was written by others, and merely revised by Bracton himself. MM

Braddock Down, battle of, 1643. Parliament and the king were still contending for local supremacy in the south-west in the early days of 1643. At Braddock Down, near Liskeard, on 19 January 1643, Sir Ralph *Hopton defeated a parliamentary force, taking 1,250 men and all their guns. JAC

Bradford. In medieval times, *York and *Hull were the chief Yorkshire towns. Though Bradford received a charter as early as 1251, it remained a cloth town of local importance: a fulling mill is recorded for 1311. *Leland, visiting in the 1530s, thought it a 'praty quik market toune' (busy), 'standing much by clothing', the same size as *Leeds, but only half the size of Wakefield. During the 17th cent. it lost ground. Celia Fiennes in the 1690s did not mention it and *Defoe in the 1720s ignored it, though he devoted a long description to Leeds. Its revival was due to the development of the worsted trade and the growth of the canal network. Bradford canal, completed in 1774, and the link to the Leeds and Liverpool canal (1777), gave access to the east and west coasts. By the early decades of the 19th cent., Bradford had begun its prodigious growth. In 1832 it was given two MPs, elected its first borough council in 1847, and by 1851 was the seventh largest town in the country, with a population of well over 100,000. From 1846 onwards it was also joined to the rapidly growing railway system, via Leeds. Two remarkable Bradford entrepreneurs were S. C. Lister and Titus *Salt. Lister, son of Bradford's first MP, was an inventor and mill-owner, gave Lister Park to the borough, and finished as Baron Masham. Salt developed in the 1850s the extraordinary community of Saltaire, round the great mill—an influential example of early town-planning. In the 20th cent. Bradford was less well served. It suffered comparatively little from the attentions of the Luftwaffe but severely at the hands of post-war town planners. Many evocations of Edwardian Bradford, when wool was still king, are to be found in the works of J. B. Priestley, particularly *Bright Day*, a threnody for 'Bruddersford' trams. JAC

Bradford, diocese of. The see was created in 1919 out of sections of the *Wakefield and *Ripon dioceses, to accommodate the increasing population in this heartland of the woollen industry. It comprises parts of western Yorkshire and a small area of Lancashire. Among notable bishops were A. W. F. Blunt (1931–55), whose address to his diocesan conference on 1 December 1936 began the chain reaction culminating in Edward VIII's abdication. Roy Williamson (1984–91) was noted for his interfaith work and community relations. The cathedral is the former 15th-cent. parish church with 18th-cent. fittings and notable modern extensions (1953–65). WMM

Bradford on Avon, Anglo-Saxon chapel of St Laurence. This small but ambitious Wiltshire building has a lofty nave from which low arches lead into a square-ended chancel, a north chapel, and a now-destroyed southern chamber. Its masonry is of very high-quality ashlar which is elaborately decorated externally with pilaster strips, string courses, and blind arcading. These features, together with the manuscript analogues for the carved angels above the chancel arch, suggest a Late Saxon construction date; the recorded grant of the minster to Shaftesbury nuns in 1001 would provide an appropriate context. RNB

Bradlaugh, Charles (1833–91). Radical, atheist, and republican lecturer and journalist. Born in London, he rose from solicitor's clerk and part-time *Secularist lecturer to become one of the most formidable public speakers and unofficial legal advocates in Victorian Britain. He owned and largely edited the *National Reformer* from 1862, formed the National Secular Society in 1866, and launched the National Republican League in 1873. New heights of notoriety were achieved with the republication and prosecution of the 'Knowlton Pamphlet' with Annie *Besant in 1877. In 1880 he was elected to Parliament for Northampton, but as an avowed atheist was not allowed to take the oath of allegiance. His attempt to secure entry to the Commons, not successful until 1886, made him the leader of democratic opinion in Britain. In Parliament, he took a special interest in Indian affairs and gained some credit for his resolute opposition to socialism. ER

Bradshaw, John (1602–59). President of the High Court of Justice which tried and condemned Charles I to death. An undistinguished lawyer, Bradshaw may have been selected because he had assisted John *Lilburne in his judicial appeal in 1645, and because none of the leading judges would act. At the trial he found himself out of his depth. Discomfited by the king's challenge to the court's legality, Bradshaw twice ordered him removed. At the end of the trial, after sentencing Charles as a 'tyrant, traitor and murderer', he denied the king's request to be heard. Elected president of the *Council of State, Bradshaw nevertheless challenged *Cromwell's right to dismiss the *Rump Parliament in 1653. A committed republican, he continued to be a thorn in Cromwell's side, being elected to the protector's parliaments of 1654 and 1656, but prevented from taking his seat. When the Rump was recalled in 1659, Bradshaw resumed his presidency of the Council of State, but died a few months before the Restoration. He was posthumously attainted of treason, and along with those of other deceased regicides, his corpse was exhumed and hanged, and his skull impaled in Westminster Hall. IJG

Bradwardine, Thomas (1290–1349). Archbishop of Canterbury. Probably born in Sussex and educated at Merton College, Oxford, and often regarded as the most eminent English mathematician of the age, he earned the title of 'Doctor Profundus' by writing *De causa Dei contra Pelagium*, stressing Augustinian views of grace and election. As university proctor during a dispute between the university and the archdeacon of Oxford (1325), he achieved the university's royal exemption from episcopal jurisdiction despite an appeal to the pope in Avignon. Later, accompanying Edward III as royal confessor to Flanders and France, he was at Crécy and the siege of Calais and helped negotiate the subsequent treaty. He became archdeacon of Norwich (1347) and, as Edward's choice, archbishop (1349). After being consecrated, at the king's request, by the pope in Avignon, he returned to London only to die of the plague almost immediately. WMM

Bramham Moor, battle of, 1408. Henry Percy, earl of *Northumberland, who had been lucky to escape disaster in 1403 when the revolt of his son Hotspur was crushed at *Shrewsbury, raised rebellion against Henry IV again in 1408. He marched south to Thirsk but, in the middle of a bitter winter, found little support. He was defeated and killed at Bramham Moor, near Wetherby, on 20 February 1408 by Sir Thomas Rokeby, sheriff of Yorkshire. JAC

Brandywine, battle of, 1777. *Burgoyne set out from Canada on his march south against the American rebels in June 1777. The following month, *Howe took a large force from New York by sea, landed in Maryland, and moved north. *Washington moved south to protect Philadelphia and took up position on the Brandywine Creek. On 11 September Howe outflanked him, pushed him back, and went on to occupy Philadelphia, driving out the Congress. But British elation was short-lived when news came through in October that Burgoyne had surrendered at *Saratoga. JAC

Braose, William de (d. 1211). King John's treatment of William is the most notorious example of his capricious approach towards his subjects. William, a major Welsh marcher lord, and lord of Limerick (Ireland), supported John's disputed claim to the throne in 1199 and served the king well in the early years of the reign. But his capture of John's nephew and dynastic rival *Arthur of Brittany, at Mirebeau (Poitou) in 1201, proved his downfall, for he was one of the few who knew that Arthur had been murdered. There is no evidence that William sought to use this knowledge against John, but John became increasingly concerned about his loyalty. From 1205, he determined to destroy him after Matilda, William's wife, blabbed something about Arthur's fate when John, typically, demanded their sons as hostages. John ruthlessly hounded the family. Matilda and her sons disappeared, and William died in exile in France in 1211. SL

brass bands are wind bands comprising brass instruments, sometimes with percussion, as opposed to military bands which mix brass and woodwind. The standard British scoring is: 1 soprano cornet in E flat, 8 or 9 cornets in B flat playing in four parts (3 or 4 solo, 2 second, 2 third, and 1 ripieno), 1 flugelhorn in B flat (often doubling the ripieno cornet), 3 tenor horns in E flat (solo, first, and second), 2 baritones in B flat (first and second), 2 euphoniums in B flat (one part), 2 tenor trombones (first and second), 1 bass trombone, 2 basses in E flat (bass tubas playing one part), and two basses in B flat (one part), with optional percussion.

The rise of the brass band in England coincided with the development of valved brass instruments, particularly the cornet, allowing a wider chromatic range. These powerful new instruments were ideal for open-air performance. Many cavalry regiments had mounted brass bands, while amateur civilian bands rapidly became popular. Throughout their history brass bands have been particularly associated with the north of England, often being attached to collieries or factories. The Stalybridge Old Band (1818) may have been the earliest band; others were soon formed in Wales (1832) and Scotland by the 1860s. Some of today's leading bands, including Black Dyke Mills Band and Besses o'th'Barn Band, have a history stretching back to the mid-19th cent. Estimates suggest over 20,000 British bands in existence around 1900; many were associated with religious organizations, and for more than a century brass bands have been very successfully promoted by the Salvation Army.

Increasingly high standards of performance were fostered by the many brass band competitions, such as those at Belle Vue (Manchester), and the National Brass Band Festival held at Crystal Palace, London, until 1936. The strict rules of the National Brass Band Club lay down the standard scoring required and ensure the amateur status of all but the conductor. Contests are rigorously judged and include a compulsory test piece. Although much of the band repertoire comprises arrangements of variable quality, original works have been written by many leading composers, including *Elgar, *Holst, and Rubbra, and, more recently, Henze, McCabe, Horowitz, and Edward Gregson. ECr

Breadalbane, John Campbell, 1st earl of [S] (1635–1717). Campbell took part in *Middleton's rising in 1653, which was defeated by *Monck. He obtained his peerage in a curious way, becoming creditor to the earl of Caithness, on whose death he was given estates and title, and married the widow. When in 1681 the Privy Council decided in favour of Caithness's male heir, Campbell was compensated with a new title as earl of Breadalbane. In 1689, though sympathetic to James II, he made his peace with William after *Killiecrankie and from 1692 to 1696 was a lord of the Treasury [S]. He was much involved in the negotiations which led to the proclamation of August 1691 and the subsequent *Glencoe massacre, though a later inquiry cleared him. He did not take part in the discussions on the *Union, though he served as a representative peer 1713–15. In 1715 he sent some of his men to join *Mar's rising, but escaped punishment, perhaps because he was 80 years of age. He was described as cheerful and agreeable, but Macky wrote that he was 'wise as a serpent, and as slippery as an eel'. JAC

'Bread or blood' riots, 1816. The years after *Waterloo saw high prices, unemployment, and a trade recession, causing widespread distress. The agricultural labourers of the fenland were a depressed group, badly paid and housed. They complained of tithes, enclosures, threshing-machines, and the hiring of Irish labour, and arson, tree-cutting, sheep-stealing, and cattle-maiming were not infrequent. The worst disturbance was at Littleport in May 1816 when a large crowd was dispersed by the yeomanry, with two killed and nearly 100 arrests. Tried by special commission at Ely on 17 June, 24 were sentenced to death. In the event, five were hanged and nine transported. The protesters were said to have carried placards threatening 'Bread or blood'. JAC

Brecon cathedral. See SWANSEA.

Breconshire. Border county of south Wales taking its name from the Welsh kingdom of *Brycheiniog which can be identified from the 8th cent. Its Norman successor was the lordship of Brecon, one of the lordships of the *march. At the Act of *Union with England in 1536 the lordships of Brecon and of Builth to the north, together with the smaller lordships of Blaenllynfi and Hay, were merged to form the county which was sometimes called Brecknockshire. In 1974 it became a district of the new county of Powys and remained part of that county after the revision of 1996.

Breconshire is dominated by highland, including the Brecon Beacons (Pen-y-Fan 2,906 feet), one of the country's national parks, the Black Mountains, and Fforest Fawr. Only some 6 per cent of the county is below 500 feet, the lower land being formed by the valleys of the rivers Wye and Usk.

Breconshire is predominantly agricultural with the Old Red Sandstone rocks giving the soil a distinctive red character in the south. Livestock farming includes cattle and sheep on the lower land, but extensive sheep runs on the higher ground. The southernmost fringe overlaps with the South Wales Coalfield where, although mining has ceased, some light industry has replaced it.

The county retains its distinctive border character, highly Anglicized in the east, less so in the west. Welsh speakers constitute only 5.7 per cent in the vale of Grwney on the English border but 40.7 per cent in Llywel on the western fringe. The percentage for the county was 23.0 in 1991. The total population is 41,488. HC

Breda, declaration of, 1660. In April 1660, while he was still in exile in Holland, Charles II issued the Breda declaration. It was a skilful political document, rightly described as 'Hyde's masterpiece', conciliatory but vague. It promised a general amnesty, save for some regicides, payment of arrears to *Monck's troops, and an assurance that 'tender consciences' in religion would be respected. Most contentious issues were left to a free Parliament. But after the king's return in May 1660 and the breakdown of the *Savoy conference, persecution of dissenters was resumed. JAC

Breda, treaty of, 1667. Signed on 31 July, the treaty brought to an end the second *Anglo-Dutch War. The most important clause in the long run left England in possession of New Netherlands, including New Amsterdam, renamed New York. The *Navigation Act of 1651 was modified to allow the Dutch to bring to England exports from the southern Netherlands and from Germany. The vexed questions of search, contraband, and saluting were compromised. JAC

Breedon church, dramatically set on a Leicestershire hill, stands on the site of an Anglo-Saxon monastery and houses an extensive collection of 8th- and 9th-cent. stone sculpture. The most important are fragmentary sections of two lengthy friezes. The narrower frieze is now some 24 feet long and carries scroll-work whose details can be paralleled in Carolingian manuscripts and Italian sculpture of *c.*800; this was set internally. The contemporary broader frieze was placed externally and is some 45 feet long. It employs a wide range of plant, animal, bird, and human motifs which draw on both Carolingian and Byzantine sources. RNB

Brémule, battle of, 1119. Fought on 20 August between Henry I and Louis VI of France. Louis invaded Normandy in support of William Clito's claim to the duchy and was keen to bring Henry to battle. His enthusiasm led him to launch poorly controlled cavalry attacks against the English and Norman household troops, most of whom were fighting on foot. Henry himself received some blows on his helmet, but the French were beaten off and fled in disorder. The contemporary Norman historian Orderic Vitalis noted that the quality of their armour and the chivalrous preference for capturing (and presumably ransoming) the enemy meant that of the 900 knights engaged in 'the battle of the two kings' only three were killed. JG

Brentford, Patrick Ruthven, 1st earl of (*c.*1573–1651). Ruthven was a professional soldier who spent most of his life in the Swedish service, rising to lieutenant-general. In 1638, well over the age of 60, and with war clouds gathering, he returned to Scotland, was created Lord Ruthven [S], and appointed governor of Edinburgh castle, which he was forced to surrender to the *covenanters in 1640. He was advanced to the earldom of Forth [S], fought at *Edgehill, and won a smart encounter a little later at Brentford, taking it as his title in 1644 when he was given an English earldom. After the wars, he was in exile with Charles II but returned to Scotland with him and died at Dundee. Ruthven was a brave, battered, and resourceful soldier of vast experience, but *Clarendon complained that his understanding had been impaired by 'immoderate drinking'. JAC

Brétigny, treaty of, 1360. After the Black Prince's great victory at *Poitiers in 1356, Edward III resumed campaigning in 1359. But though inflicting great damage he was unable to land a knock-out blow and negotiations commenced in May 1360 at Brétigny, near Chartres. King John's ransom was to be cut and, in exchange for abandoning his claim to the throne of France, Edward was to have Guînes and Aquitaine in full sovereignty. These sweeping gains could not be substantiated and, after John's death, Charles V of France continued to claim suzerainty. See also CALAIS, TREATY OF. JAC

bretwalda. It would be a venial sin, but sinful all the same, to regard the term 'bretwalda' as having caused more trouble than it is worth. It first appears in the **Anglo-Saxon Chronicle*'s annal for 829. The A version says *Egbert of Wessex was the eighth king who was bretwalda (ruler of Britain). The other versions use 'brytenwalda' (wide ruler). There is dispute as to which term is 'right'. It is not helped by a questioned charter of *Athelstan (934) which in its English version uses 'brytenwalda', but in its Latin uses 'King and ruler of this whole island of Britain' as the equivalent. More significant is the relationship of the term to *Bede's statement that there were seven rulers who had *imperium* over much or all of our island: the earliest *Ælle of Sussex (late 5th cent.), the latest *Oswui of Northumbria (d. 670). The 9th-cent. annalist plainly had this passage in mind. Historians have long employed the term 'bretwalda' in relation to Bede's crucial statement. Thus, independently of the question 'which is the "right" form?', the use of 'bretwalda', 'bretwaldaship' as terms of historical art is the focus of dispute on the organization of power in early England.

If, as is likely, 'bretwalda' is an early term, it is of a poetically glorifying kind, not relating to any position which could or can be specifically defined. By a related argument Bede's observation on *imperium*, and who held it, derives from some topos of grouping rulers in sevens (to be found later in *'Nennius's' idea of seven Roman emperors who ruled in Britain). Two questions arise. First, whence did Bede get his information, or 'information'? Why, for example, dig up the exceedingly obscure Ælle? Second, granted the almost infinite obscurity of early political arrangements, may not Bede (who could have known more about these matters than we do) be transmitting traditions which derive from something which lay between the poetically rhetorical and the institutionally defined? Historians' discussion of what they call 'bretwaldaship' also involves discussion of elements in early 'overlordship', such as the right to tribute and to participation in land grants. JCa

brewing is as ancient as distilling, and had a long evolution prior to its expansion during the 18th and 19th cents. to become a large-scale industry pioneering mass production. Its basic raw materials are barley, hops, and water, and the process involves the infusion of malted barley and water, followed by fermentation of the liquid or wort drawn from the mixture. In the medieval period ale-brewing prevailed and it was not until the early 15th cent. that hops were added to the wort for flavouring and as a preservative. The resulting beverage was known as 'beere' or 'biere' to distinguish it from ale, which was rarely hopped. Many householders from the gentry downwards, and most retailers, brewed their own beer.

From the beginning of the 18th cent. rising population accelerated a long-term trend towards larger breweries. Among the more important firms established at the time were Whitbread, Guinness, and Younger. From the outset these and other family firms dominated an industry which expanded rapidly along parallel paths. Every town of consequence had its brewery, while in the cities like London, Edinburgh, and Dublin much larger units began to evolve. The spectacular growth of Burton upon Trent was in part due to the excellence of the local water, but it also benefited from the town's central position once a national canal network had been established. The size of a brewery generally reflected the size of its immediate market, since beer is a bulky commodity and transport costs were high. Partly to counter this, brewing had its own peculiar marketing arrangements, with a high proportion of output sold through tied houses under the ownership of the brewing companies themselves. Concentration also made the industry an increasingly easy target for the excise, though the strength of beer and the duties payable have varied considerably since the 18th cent.

The expansion of the industry during the latter half of the 19th cent. outstripped its earlier growth. Brewing benefited from rapid advances in science and technology, especially from a deeper understanding of the chemistry involved, and from developments like refrigeration and bottling. The Institute of Brewing was set up in 1886 to disseminate this research. By this time the brewing industry encompassed hundreds of firms of various sizes across Britain, retailing beer through thousands of outlets. The industry was pervasive in other respects. Through its raw material needs it retained close links with agriculture and the countryside; it continued to be conspicuously taxed; and the sale of beer was increasingly enmeshed in complex licensing laws. In all these areas, especially when the *temperance movement was active, the industry was forced into the forefront of national politics.

The years from the First World War to the late 1950s were characterized by rationalization and amalgamation, an almost continuous decline in production, and increased taxation. Notable product changes, begun in the Victorian era, saw a shift from dark, heavy beers to lighter, brighter beers and ales. Lager, pioneered by Tennent in Glasgow and Jeffrey in Edinburgh, along with bottled beers, increased greatly in popularity. Experimental canning was tried in the 1930s. After some painful readjustment in the 1950s and early 1960s, the industry was dominated by six conglomerates, mainly producing keg and lager beers. However, about 80 regional and local brewers managed to maintain their independence, and partly encouraged by the Campaign for Real Ale, successfully maintained the production of traditional cask beers. ID

Brian Boru (d. 1014), usually regarded as the greatest of Ireland's *high kings, belonged to what had been a minor *Munster dynasty, Dál Cais (based in the lower Shannon basin), which rose to prominence in the mid-10th cent., ending the supremacy of the Eóganacht dynastic federation. Brian's father, Cennétig mac Lorcáin, began the family's rise to power and died in 951 as king of north Munster (Thomond). Brian succeeded his brother Mathgamain in 976 and rose swiftly, dominating the Viking towns of Limerick and Waterford, and quickly establishing himself as king of all Munster. At this point he emerged as a challenger to the reigning high king, the midlands ruler Mael Sechnaill mac Domnaill of the southern Uí Néill, who in 997 acknowledged Brian as king over the southern half of Ireland and who finally submitted to Brian as high king in 1002. Brian set about asserting his dominance throughout the island, adopting the title 'Emperor of the Irish' in 1005. A revolt by the Leinstermen and the Hiberno-Norse of Dublin led to Brian's great victory over them in the battle of *Clontarf in 1014, at which, however, he himself was slain. His descendants, who remained powerful in Thomond for centuries, bear the surname O'Brien. SD

Bridewell. The London Bridewell, set up in 1555, was the first 'House of Correction' and the term was often used henceforth to describe such institutions. The 16th cent. saw a massive increase in the numbers of poor and indigent, and houses of correction, with stern regimes of hard work, were used for the punishment and reformation of petty offenders or groups who were regarded as anti-social or idle, such as players of unlawful games, fortune-tellers, minstrels, tinkers and pedlars, hedge-breakers, vagabonds, and gypsies. In 1610 houses of correction were set up generally throughout England. The distinction between them and prisons was abolished in 1865. MM

bridge developed in the 19th cent. from whist and is believed to have originated in the Near East. The word itself is doubtful, but may derive from the Russian *biritch* meaning no trumps. The essential difference from whist is the bidding process to establish the trump suit and the forecast. Contract bridge replaced auction bridge in the 1930s. A world championship was founded in the 1950s. The large number of local bridge clubs are affiliated to the English Bridge Union, which issues points, enabling players to qualify as club masters, district masters, and the like. JAC

Bridgeman, Charles (d. 1738). Royal Gardener to George II 1728–38, Bridgeman played a major role in the evolution of the English landscape garden. Stylistically his work lay between the geometric layouts of the late 1600s and early 1700s and the freer designs of William *Kent and Lancelot 'Capability' *Brown. Bridgeman fused formal elements (parterres, avenues, geometric ponds and lakes) with the transitional (mounts, lawns, irregular *cabinets*), and the progressive (ha-has, winding walks, irregular lawns and woods, and statuary and garden buildings used to exploit key vantage-points). For the crown he was active at *Hampton Court, *Kensington, *Richmond, *St James's Park, and *Windsor, whilst his private commissions included Claremont, Eastbury, and Wimpole. Outstanding among his independent clients was Viscount Cobham of Stowe in Buckinghamshire, whose celebrated landscape was recorded in the perspective views of Jacques Rigaud and Bernard Baron published by Sarah Bridgeman, the gardener's widow, in 1739. Bridgeman was a collaborator with *Vanbrugh, *Gibbs, *Kent, and Flitcroft, and friend of the painters Mercier, Thornhill, and Wootton, and of *Pope, Prior and other *literati*. As Horace *Walpole noted in his *Observations on Modern Gardening*, first published in 1780, Bridgeman had 'many detached thoughts, that strongly indicate the dawn of modern taste'. PW

bridges. Britain's pre-1100 wooden bridges do not survive, except as place-names, but extensive activity continued throughout the Middle Ages, and few new bridge sites were added before 1750 to those identifiable in 1500. Bridge-building was one of the three communal obligations, an object for pious work, and for seigneurial enterprise. There had been a Roman *London bridge, but its continuous history dates from that constructed of wood in 993, and rebuilt of stone from 1176. Some early bridging works were extensive: Aldreth Causeway (*c.*1100) was one of two constructed across the fenland to the Isle of Ely. Many towns levied *pontage* tolls to erect and maintain bridges, and there were also religious links: Queen *Matilda endowed Barking abbey to maintain Bow bridge, *c.*1150, and chapels were recurrent features of medieval bridges, as at Wakefield and Derby. Bridging points formed the core of medieval new towns, such as Chelmsford (*c.*1200) and Leeds (1207). Bridges replaced many fords and ferries in the later Middle Ages, and indicated widespread growth of vehicular traffic. Medieval stone bridge construction was robust and coped with much traffic growth, and widening and strengthening engineering works did not become generalized until after 1750.

Responsibility for bridges lay with parishes or landowners, but uncertainty led to the statute of Bridges (1531) providing for fall-back maintenance by the county, and by 1602 48 bridges had become the responsibility of the West Riding. Heavily used bridges also required special procedures: private Acts were employed increasingly in the 18th cent. to create commissions to finance major bridges and new crossings by tolls, beginning with Westminster (1736) initiated with a dedicated lottery. General county responsibility did not come until 1888. Private Acts were thus used for many of the eight bridges added to London before 1820 (including Kew in 1759), and three of these—Vauxhall, Waterloo, and Southwark (1816, 1817, 1819)—effectively created the new suburbs of Brixton, Kennington, and Camberwell. Trunk turnpike development built major bridges, notably on *Telford's Holyhead road at Conwy and the Menai Straits (1815–19).

Significant development functions came also with the great aqueducts at Barton on the Bridgwater canal (1761), which obviated the need for locks, and Telford's cast-iron construction at Pontcysyllte (1805) carrying the Ellesmere canal over the Dee at 127 feet. *Ironbridge, Coalport (1779), and Sunderland (1796) pioneered the application and diffusion of cast iron to bridge construction, and laid the basis for the railways, although *Brunel and *Cubitt still used timber extensively in the 1840s. Railways employed brick and cast and wrought iron to bridge Britain's great estuaries and rivers between the 1840s and the 1870s: the Dee, the Severn, the Tamar, the Solway Firth, the Menai Straits, and the Tay. Even before the failure of materials and design on the last (1879), steel had established itself as the critical construction material, and demonstrated its strength in the Forth bridge (completed 1890).

Twentieth-cent. bridge-building has been correspondingly dominated by steel and concrete for roads. The great railway crossings were replicated from the 1960s by road bridges, all bar the Tay on the suspension principle, and new crossings of the Thames and Humber were added. Lightweight box-girder construction speeded the building of over-bridges from the 1960s, despite initial collapses, and *motorway and trunk road building provided an immense stimulus to their use: the first stretch of the M1, opened in 1959, had 183 bridges in its 75 miles, and was constructed in 586 days. JCh

Bridgwater, Francis Egerton, 3rd duke of (1736–1803). Bridgwater succeeded his brother as duke in 1748 at the age of 11. His education was neglected and he grew up slovenly and uncouth. After the collapse of his proposed marriage to the widowed duchess of Hamilton (one of the Gunning sisters) in 1758, he devoted almost all his time to exploiting the coal resources on his Lancashire estates. To this end he employed *Brindley in 1761 to construct a 6-mile canal from Worsley to Salford, with a famous aqueduct at Barton over the river Irwell and followed it with the Manchester to Liverpool canal, of 28 miles, along which he ran a passenger service taking nine hours. Though his enterprises imposed vast financial burdens on him, in the end they paid off and made him one of the richest men in the kingdom. He died unmarried and was buried at Little Gaddesden (Herts.), near his Ashridge estate, where his memorial inscription read: 'he sent barges across fields the farmers formerly tilled.' JAC

Brigantes. A British tribal federation and *civitas*. The name means 'upland people' or 'hill-dwellers', which is appropriate to the Pennine heartland of the tribe. Their territory, however, included coastal plains as well, for Ptolemy confirms that they held most of northern England from coast to coast. Not surprisingly, such a vast area was not the fiefdom of a single tribe but rather of a loose confederation. Some of the federal tribes are known to us by name—the Setanti, the Lopocares, the Gabrantovices, the Tectoverdi, and the *Carvetii. Each tribe no doubt had its own capital but there may also have been a central place for the whole federation, possibly at Almondsbury near Huddersfield or at Stanwick near Scotch Corner. Certainly by the time the Romans reached their southern borders, the Brigantes were led by a single ruler, Queen *Cartimandua, with whom the Romans established treaty relations. Internal schism and instability led to Roman invasion and occupation in the later 1st cent. Eventually a *civitas* was established, perhaps during *Hadrian's visit to the province, with its capital at Aldborough (*Isurium*), but much of Brigantian territory probably remained under direct military government throughout the Roman occupation. KB

Briggitines. Established *c.*1346 as a double order of men and women by St Bridget of Sweden (*c.*1303–73). They followed the *Augustinian rule and constitutions drawn up by Bridget, including the 'Rule of the Saviour'. There was only one English house, Twickenham, founded and richly endowed by Henry V in 1415 and transferred to Syon in 1431. This had a considerable reputation for contemplative devotion until its *dissolution in 1539, after which it was briefly refounded by Queen Mary in 1557, before its nuns fled in 1559 to Flanders, whence, after many vicissitudes and travels, their successors returned to England in 1809. BJG

Bright, John (1811–89). Radical politician and son of a Rochdale textile manufacturer, his first public speech (on temperance, 1830) and first political campaign (against church rates in Rochdale, 1834) mark the strong quaker influence on him. A leading public speaker for the *Anti-Corn Law League (1839–46), Bright was elected MP for Durham (1843), Manchester (1847–57), and thereafter Birmingham. He supported *free trade, opposed legislation limiting the hours of adult workers in textile factories, and, in the 1850s, called for peace, retrenchment, and reform, gaining unpopularity for his opposition to the *Crimean War. He also took up the cause of India, opposing the renewal of the East India Company's Charter in 1853 and advocating devolved government in India under Westminster control, but when offered the secretaryship of state for India by *Gladstone in 1868 he declined it because of its military responsibilities. He favoured extending the franchise to adult male householders in 1866, but was never a true democrat. He entered Liberal cabinets as president of the Board of Trade (1868–70) and chancellor of the duchy of Lancaster (1873–4, 1880–2), resigning on the latter occasion in protest at the naval bombardment of Alexandria. He was a long-standing advocate of church and land reform in Ireland, but attacked Gladstone's *Home Rule proposals in 1886. Said to be the most belligerent of pacifists, Bright was one of the greatest orators of the 19th cent. ER

Brighton. This was originally Brithelmston, a Sussex fishing village where, according to tradition, Charles II spent a night during his escape to France. Brighton developed rapidly from the mid-18th cent., when Dr Richard Russell recommended its health-giving air. It was patronized by Fanny *Burney, Samuel *Johnson (1770), and from 1784 by George, prince of Wales, five years before George III favoured Weymouth as a resort. Brighton's original classical Royal Pavilion, built by Henry Holland (1784), was redeveloped by *Nash in oriental style with an Indian exterior and Chinese interior (1817). Queen Victoria sold the building to the town. Charles *Dickens was a frequent visitor. The population in the 1990s was over 150,000. WMM

Brigit, St (*c.*450–*c.*525). Patron saint of Ireland, with *Columba and *Patrick. Born in Faughart (Co. Louth), she took the veil in her youth, having evaded marriage by disfiguring her face. Her monastery of Cill-Dara (Kildare), founded *c.*470, developed as a centre of learning and spirituality. Her school of art was renowned for illuminated manuscripts, notably the Book of Kildare, which disappeared three centuries ago. A remarkable woman, head of a group of nunneries, influential in church affairs, her great compassion was accompanied by practical measures to relieve the needy. Numerous miracles are attributed to her. Often identified with the Virgin Mary and known as 'the Mary of the Gael' in Ireland, her popularity spread abroad through Irish missionary monks. AM

Brihuega, battle of, 1710. Under pressure from a revitalized Franco-Spanish army of 12,000 troops under the command of the duc de Vendôme, an English force of 4,000 men commanded by Lord *Stanhope was forced to retreat from Madrid into Catalonia. Caught at Brihuega on 9 December, Stanhope's troops stood firm until their powder ran out, after which they organized a bayonet charge against the superior enemy surrounding them. Reduced to less than 500 men, Stanhope had no choice but to surrender. The victory cost the French and Spanish about 1,500 casualties. JLP

Brindley, James (1716–72). Brindley, an engineer, was born in Derbyshire and set up as millwright at Leek in Staffordshire. In 1759 he was put in charge of the duke of *Bridgwater's canal between his coal pits at Worsley and Manchester. Brindley subsequently supervised the building of a number of canals, including the Liverpool to Manchester, opened in 1767; the Trent and Mersey, 140 miles long and involving a 2,880-yard tunnel at Harecastle; and the Staffordshire and Worcester. 'The great Mr. Brindley', wrote an observer in 1767, 'is as plain a looking man as one of the boors of the Peak, or one of his own carters, but when he speaks, all ears listen.' Hard-working and inventive, Brindley was largely self-taught and barely literate: 'midlin louk' was his laconic account of an early attempt to improve a steam-engine. JAC

Bristol. A city at the junction of the rivers Avon and Frome, just inland from the Severn estuary. It is not recorded before *c.*1020, but by 1066 was a flourishing port, shipping slaves to Ireland. The Normans built there one of the key strategic castles of England, and Earl *Robert of Gloucester (1107–47) made it his power base in supporting his half-sister *Matilda in the civil wars from 1138. The original centre lay between the two rivers, just inside Gloucestershire, but the Redcliffe area south of the Avon (and in Somerset) quickly became an important suburb. By 1216 Bristol was influential enough to have an elected mayor, and by *c.*1240 enterprising enough to divert the river Frome to make a better harbour. Trade until the 15th cent. was chiefly with Ireland, Gascony, and the Iberian peninsula, with Bordeaux wines the main imports. By 1377 Bristol ranked in the poll tax as the largest provincial town after York; its importance was recognized in 1373 when the king took it out of Gloucestershire and Somerset and made it a county corporate; later its status was further enhanced when it became a cathedral city (1542) and when its traders were incorporated as the Society of Merchant Venturers (1552). Bristol suffered severely in the Civil War of 1642–6, but enjoyed a golden age in the late 17th and 18th cents. as the largest and wealthiest English town after London. Its wealth by then came chiefly from transatlantic trade (especially in slaves) and its associated new industries (sugar and tobacco). By 1800, however, it was overtaken in importance by Liverpool, Manchester, and Birmingham, and in 1831 it was the scene of serious riots during the passage of the first Reform Bill. More positively, in the 1830s and 1840s I. K. *Brunel helped to make Bristol an important terminus for railways and for Atlantic steamships, and from 1868 new docks at Avonmouth helped the city recover prosperity. In the 20th cent. it has developed into a large and thriving conurbation. DMP

Bristol, diocese of. The see, founded in 1542 by Henry VIII, is now roughly conterminous with the city of Bristol, but at first included all Dorset, taken from the *Salisbury diocese. It incurred Archbishop *Laud's displeasure in the 17th cent. for its puritan ethos and lax discipline. As one of the poorest dioceses, from which bishops wanted rapid preferment, Bristol proved a useful tool for 18th-cent. managers of political patronage. Its poverty, and the need to create the Ripon and Manchester dioceses without increasing the total bench of bishops, led to its brief union with the *Gloucester diocese in 1836. Dorset returned to Salisbury, though Bristol retained a number of north Wiltshire parishes. Rising population made this merger clearly undesirable, and the bishopric had its independence restored by an Act of 1884. The first 32 women priests of the Church of England were ordained here in 1994. The cathedral is the former St Augustine's abbey, dissolved at the Reformation and rededicated to the Holy Trinity. The 13th-cent. choir remains, and there is a fine Norman chapter house. WMM

Bristol, St Mary, Redcliffe. 'The most famous, absolute and goodliest parish church in England', declared Queen Elizabeth I. The church, of cathedralesque proportions, stone-vaulted throughout, is a monument to the piety of the inhabitants of Redcliffe, a wealthy suburb of Bristol. Its foundation goes back certainly to 1158 and possibly earlier, but the building that stands today is Gothic. The transepts and nave, completed by *c.*1376, are attributed to William Canynges the Elder, merchant, six times mayor and MP for the city. The east end was rebuilt by William Canynges the Younger, his grandson, also mayor and MP, who, after his wife's death, took holy orders and became dean of the college at Westbury-on-Trym. In the south transept are two effigies of William, one as a merchant with his wife, the other as a priest. At some time between *c.*1200 and *c.*1320 the church became the focus of a popular cult of the Virgin, which centred round an image housed in the north porch. This explains the curious double form of the porch. The inner porch of *c.*1200 housed the image: the outer porch of *c.*1320 was built around it to serve as a vestibule to the cult area and to the church as a whole. The spire was part of the original design but completed only in 1872. The young poet Chatterton worshipped in the church and is buried outside. LR

Bristol riots, 1831. The rejection of *Grey's second Reform Bill by the House of Lords was greeted by widespread demonstrations and rioting. Bristol had a reputation for disorder and the riots there were as much against an oligarchical corporation as against the Lords' action. The flash-point was a visit on 29 October by the recorder, Sir Charles Wetherell, an outspoken opponent of the bill, to open the assizes. Troops had been drafted in but were badly handled and obliged to withdraw. The Mansion House, Customs House, Bishop's palace, and half of Queen Square were then attacked and looted. After two days, more troops cleared the streets, with twelve killed and 100 arrested. Thirty-one persons were condemned to death and five eventually executed. The commander of the dragoons was court-martialled, and shot himself. Though the disorders added greatly to political tension, it is not clear that they affected the final outcome. JAC

Britain, Battle of, 1940. On 18 June 1940 *Churchill declared 'the Battle of France is over; I expect that the Battle of Britain is about to begin'. On 2 July Hitler reluctantly ordered planning for the invasion of England, preferring a peaceful acceptance by the British of German dominance in continental Europe. The Churchill government, supported by most public opinion, chose to fight on and challenge Hitler who knew, Churchill declared, 'that he will have to break us in this island or lose the war'. The German army had ample resources to conquer the UK. Could they be landed, and, if landed, supplied when the Royal Navy had overwhelming superiority? The German navy thought they could not, even if the Luftwaffe could beat the RAF and then attack British warships. Certainly, the invasion was impossible without German air supremacy. The battle was a German attempt to destroy RAF Fighter Command and so win air superiority over the Channel and south-east England.

The single-seat aircraft in the decisive encounters were evenly matched. The Messerschmitt 109E was as fast as the British Spitfire and faster than the Hurricane; the British types were more manœuvrable. The British fought over their own air space with a chain of radar stations, supplemented by observers who reported approaching aircraft to sector headquarters, from which fighter squadrons were directed at the enemy by radio. The German bombers began by attacking shipping from mid-July to mid-August. The plan was to force the RAF to attack German fighter escorts. On 13 August, 'Eagle Day', the Germans began the main battle, attacking airfields and aircraft factories. The British came closest to defeat in late August and early September. The Germans made repeated attacks on airfields in the south-east and put out of action many sector control posts. British losses in aircraft and pilots began to exceed replacements. The Germans exaggerated their success and thought the RAF beaten: throughout the Second World War air crews constantly believed they had destroyed more hostile aircraft than post-war evidence confirmed. On 7 and 9 September heavy attacks hit London; the Germans lost 84 aircraft. Evidently the RAF was not defeated and Hitler postponed the decision to invade. On 15 September a renewed attack on London gave the RAF another success: 60 German aircraft and only 26 British were lost. On 17 September Hitler again postponed the invasion and on 12 October it was abandoned.

The Battle of Britain helped, especially since British successes were overstated, to reinforce British support for Churchill's decision to continue the war. The battle encouraged Roosevelt's decision to assist Britain to fight on. In 1941 it forced Hitler to attack the USSR without first solving the problem of the British and American threat. The Battle of Britain was a highly visible contest between small numbers in summer skies. The British lost less than 800 aircraft, the Germans nearly 1,400. It was a fierce, limited struggle. Less than 3,000 British air crew took part, of whom 507 were killed and about the same number seriously wounded. Churchill was correct: 'Never in the field of human conflict was so much owed by so many to so few.' RACP

Britannia, the Roman name for the British Isles revived by *Camden (1586), has become the poetic name for Britain. Personified as a seated female figure, adapting a 2nd-cent. Roman design, she appeared emblematically (modelled by Frances Stewart, later duchess of Richmond) on Charles II's 1667 peace of *Breda medal and copper coinage (1672); the 'union' shield resting alongside bore the crosses of St George and St Andrew. The spear was replaced by a trident (1797) after naval triumphs to represent her ruling the waves. She became helmeted (1825), before appearing on the silver groat (1836), and continues on today's 50p piece. ASH

British Academy. In response to a resolve for a world-wide Association of Scientific and Literary Academies (Wiesbaden, 1899), the British Academy was established in 1901 to promote 'Historical, Philosophical and Philological Studies'. It soon received a royal charter, but many years passed before it affected the humanities' world as the *Royal Society did science. Despite endowments for periodical lectures, published in annual *Proceedings*, it contented itself with achieved eminence rather than new ideas and rising scholars; no government support came until 1924, nor permanent quarters (Burlington Gardens) until 1927, and Beatrice *Webb, the first elected woman fellow (1932), found it 'a funny little body of elderly and aged men'. By the mid-1940s it was moribund, choked by age, complacent, and out of touch, but under Sir Charles Webster (president, 1950–4) and Mortimer Wheeler (secretary), efficiency and scope slowly broadened: by 1970 it had active research committees, funds to support and encourage younger scholars, an improved government grant, new premises in Burlington House, foreign exchanges, and domestic partnerships. More recent reorganization (language and literature; history and archaeology; philosophy, law, and social sciences) has been accompanied by schemes for the support of advanced scholarship in the humanities and social sciences. ASH

British and Foreign School Society. The society stemmed from the work of Joseph *Lancaster, a pioneer of English elementary education, who established a school and a training institution at Borough Road, Southwark, in 1798. With the promise of £100 p.a. from George III, Lancaster formed 'The Society for Promoting the Royal British or Lancasterian System for the Education of the Poor' in 1808, later changed to the British and Foreign School Society. The main object was to enable poor children to read the Bible. The schools were not confined to any one denomination, in the words of the Royal Charter 'all sects and parties sinking their differences in the provision of the best educational means, and using them in the common school on equal terms'. Nevertheless, the Anglicans soon established their own *National Schools Society. The training institution at Borough Road was moved to Isleworth (Middx.) in 1890, retaining the name of Borough Road Training College. Almost 4,000 British schools were established by the Society. Many became board schools after 1870 and either closed or transferred to local education authorities after the 1902 Education Act. PG

British Association for the Advancement of Science. This peripatetic body, founded in 1831, with an open membership, has been very important in promoting public awareness of science. The *Royal Society was London-based and like a gentleman's club; the *Royal Institution, where Humphry *Davy and then Michael *Faraday lectured, fashionable and expensive. In Germany, with then no single capital city, meetings were organized each year in a different city: and this became the model for Great Britain and Ireland. Provincial pride and fear of scientific decline were important factors; the first meeting was in York, then came Oxford and Cambridge (where the word *scientist* was coined), and then commercial and industrial cities: by 1914 there had also been meetings in Montreal, Cape Town, and Melbourne. Cities competed to attract meetings, often opening museums or mechanics' institutes; famous debates took place there; and women were, rather grudgingly, admitted. The proceedings were widely reported, and subsequently published; research grants were awarded; and office-holding became an important part of a scientist's career. DK

British Broadcasting Corporation (BBC). Britain's key media organization, which oversaw the introduction of *radio (1922) and *television (1936), and set standards of broadcasting admired throughout the world. Founded in 1922 as the British Broadcasting Company, funded by a licence fee under government auspices, it became a corporation with a royal charter five years later. From the start it was a monopoly organization designed to regulate the British airwaves, to avoid what was seen as the 'chaos' of free enterprise broadcasting in the USA. Whether this strictly regulated 'public service' approach to broadcasting—symbolized by the BBC's nickname 'Auntie'—has proved conservative and paternalistic or a safeguard against shoddy commercialism is a continuing subject of debate.

The tone for the BBC was set by its founder, John *Reith, managing director of the company 1922–6, and director-general of the corporation 1927–38. His Scottish presbyterian values ensured that the BBC fulfilled its remit to inform, educate, and entertain, and observe due impartiality in politics, news, and current affairs. The BBC's reputation for news coverage was made in 1926, when the *General Strike halted other forms of news production; and received international recognition during the Second World War, when the overseas broadcasting service (established 1932) and foreign-language section (1938) came into their own.

To ensure its impartiality, the early BBC was banned from dealing with controversial issues, and even when the ban was removed by the government in 1928, the BBC trod so carefully that many felt it did a totally inadequate job of dealing with the domestic and international crises of the 1930s. Only certain maverick producers in the devolved regional services, such as Olive Shapley in the north-west, dared to feature the experiences of the unemployed on air.

The BBC introduced more varied fare to supplement its Home Service during the war, with a forces programme of light music (to become the Light Programme in 1945) and a Third Programme of high art and classical music. This pattern remained until the 1960s saw it reshaped into Radios 1, 2, 3, and 4 (with the addition of Radio 5 in the 1990s) and the start of BBC Local Radio in 1967. In television, BBC broadcasting became popular with its post-war relaunch, with innovations such as schools educational TV from 1952, and a second channel, BBC2, from 1962.

Though technically independent of government control, with its own—government-appointed—board of governors, the BBC has been subject to varying degrees of political pressure at times of crisis such as Suez, the Falklands War, the Ulster crisis, and has reacted with varying degrees of independence or compliance.

In general the BBC has tried to steer a middle course, reflecting the spirit of the times—thus being noted for its liberal and progressive approach in the 1960s under Director-General Hugh Greene; while from the 1980s, it has had to adapt to the free market values of Thatcherite Conservatism under Michael Checkland and John Birt. At the end of the century, in the era of cable, satellite, and interactive media, the BBC's privileged status as a publicly funded body is increasingly being questioned. DJA

British empire. At its apogee, around 1920, the British empire was the greatest—the biggest, at any rate—ever known. It was reputed to cover a quarter of the world's land area, and a fifth of its population. Most of that, however, was of recent provenance. Like all mighty oaks, this one had a tiny origin. When exactly that was is hard to say. A medieval English proto-empire can be dimly made out, in 12th–13th-cent. Ireland and Gascony. Most historians date the beginnings of the empire proper, however, from Tudor times. It grew out of the great seafaring voyages of that age. Britain was a little behind the Spanish and Portuguese, so initially her empire did not compare with theirs. They took the plums. Britain had to make do with North America and the Caribbean, which were not so obviously valuable. The first British colony was Virginia, which was settled in 1585, but not for long. A ship returning four years later found that the colonists had disappeared. In 1607 the colony was re-established, and this time survived. Other places were also colonized, especially some Caribbean islands, and more of the North American coast. Trading posts were established in India. These became the two main focuses of British imperial dominion for the next two centuries.

It was mainly a commercial empire, run by chartered monopoly *companies, and defended by the Royal *Navy. Britain made sure its benefits accrued to her exclusively, by a series of *Navigation Acts passed in the mid-17th cent. to prevent the colonies dealing with anyone else. That was to cause trouble later on. Meanwhile, however, the empire expanded steadily, partly through the extension of British trade, and partly as a result of wars with other colonial powers. The *Seven Years War, for example, saw Britain take control of much of India (1756–7). That marked the peak of what later came to be called the 'first' British empire, which came to an end with the rebellion of the thirteen American colonies, originally against Britain's trading restrictions, in 1776.

The loss of America (except Canada) threatened to mark the beginning of the end of the British empire as a whole. That was because the idea of *exclusive* trading colonies was coming under attack on other fronts. Adam *Smith, for example, taught that they undermined the 'wealth of nations', rather than promoting it. In the early 19th cent. most liberals believed that empires were things of the past. For years historians followed them in assuming that the early and mid-19th cent. was one of the British empire's low points. In fact, however, it continued to expand. Even while America was being lost, Captain *Cook was sniffing out new imperial possibilities in the antipodes. The first colony there, *New South Wales, was established in 1788. *Sierra Leone in west Africa was established as a home for freed slaves at around the same time. Other gains—*Trinidad, *Malta, *Gibraltar, the *Cape of Good Hope—were made as a result of the French Revolutionary wars. Later came *Tasmania, *Singapore, *Burma, Western Australia, *New Zealand, *Aden, *Hong Kong, *Natal . . . a full list would be tedious, but would also illustrate the continuity of Britain's imperial history at this time. Most of this expansion was due to the requirements of Britain's ever-expanding trade. By the 1880s, when the conventional view used to be that the empire picked up again, the bulk of it was already in place.

The difference about the 1880s was that Britons thereafter became infused with a conscious mood of *imperial*ism*. They sought empire deliberately, instead of merely accepting its growth in what the imperialist J. R. Seeley called 'a fit of absence of mind'. That may have had some effect on this phase of its expansion, though it has to be said that much of it took place under non-imperialists, like *Gladstone. It was he who took control of *Egypt in 1882, for example, though strictly—perhaps to save his anti-imperialist face—this was never called a colony. That sparked off the Scramble for *Africa, which added much of the eastern and southern part of the continent to Britain's collection. The culmination of this phase was the second *Boer War (1899–1902), after which things calmed down a little. The only substantial additions to the British empire after this were the *'mandated' territories—ex-German and Ottoman possessions, including much of the Middle East—which were allocated to it in the wake of the *First World War. They too were not meant to be 'colonies', though most people at the time regarded them as such.

This was the empire's zenith. It was huge. In 1901 an imperial census reckoned its total population was 398,401,404, but even that may have been an underestimate, as it apparently never occurred to the heads of households in some colonies that the British wanted them to count their women too. It had a presence in every habitable continent, giving rise to the boast that 'the sun never set' on it: though one subversive joke suggested that this was only because 'God doesn't trust the Brits in the dark'. Most Britons felt it was beneficial: 'the greatest secular agency for good that the world has seen', according to Lord *Rosebery, though there were other opinions, voiced by J. A. *Hobson. The wonder was that so small a country as Britain, at the very edge of Europe, was able to exercise so wide a sway. How was it done?

The simple answer to that is: 'with difficulty'. Britain's empire would have been far too much for her, if she really had tried to dominate it. She succeeded in holding it mainly by being flexible, and persuading others to take much of the strain. In the 'white' dominions these were the European settlers, who were given effective self-government from early on in the 19th cent., in exchange for which they agreed to look after their 'natives' themselves. That often meant exploiting, enslaving, and even extirpating them, while the Colonial Office in London looked on helplessly. Elsewhere local governors utilized divisions amongst natives cleverly, or adopted a policy of preserving native social and power structures, so as to keep disruption to a minimum. Every colony had its class of collaborators. This, however, diluted Britain's real control. Collaborators needed to be appeased. Later they proved less willing, especially as Britain's prosperity and strength came to look more vulnerable. That, in the end, was what brought the empire down, in the aftermath of the *Second World War, when the process of *decolonization began.

The empire left legacies on both sides. For the ex-colonies it brought stability for a while, though sometimes only by bottling up natural conflicts that were bound to erupt later. It helped the spread of capitalism, Christianity, parliamentary institutions, English as a lingua franca, and (most beneficially) cricket. Afterwards it conferred automatic membership of a new club, the *Commonwealth of Nations, of which most ex-colonies availed themselves. So far as Britain is concerned, the balance sheet is controversial. She may not have profited as much as she thought from the empire. It can be argued that it held her back industrially; for example, by boosting the *public schools, whose paternalist ethos was necessary to furnish its governors, but disastrous for the entrepreneurial spirit. Its collapse was felt as a loss, however, economically and emotionally. Many of the country's problems in the second half of the 20th cent. were undoubtedly aggravated by her difficulty in coming to terms with its disappearance. On the other hand it provided the later British film industry, while it lasted, with some splendid locations and plots. BJP

Lloyd, T., *The British Empire, 1558–1983* (Oxford, 1984); Porter, B., *The Lion's Share: A Short History of British Imperialism 1850–1983* (1985).

British Empire, Order of the. This was the first democratic or meritocratic order and, significantly, was established in June 1917 in the darkest days of the First World War. Though far less aristocratic than previous orders, it was nevertheless divided into five sections—the Knights Grand Cross, the Knights Commander, Commanders, Officers, and Members. Associated with the order was the British Empire Medal. Of equal significance was that a large number of women were, for the first time, admitted to honours. The prelate of the Order is the bishop of London, the dean is the dean of St Paul's, and the chapel of the order is in the crypt of St Paul's. *Punch* complained that decorations were given in handfuls and that to remain undecorated was a distinction in its own right. JAC

British Guiana. See GUYANA.

British Honduras. See BELIZE.

British Museum and Library. Founded in 1753 to house three historic collections (Cotton, Harley, Sloane) of books, manuscripts, and curiosities acquired by the nation, the museum was funded by public lottery and established in Montagu House, Bloomsbury, 'for publick use to all Posterity'. Created in the era of the *Encyclopédistes*, it amassed appropriately, acquiring *inter alia* the Royal library (1757), the Rosetta Stone, George III's library (1823), and the *Elgin marbles, to become a centre for both scholarship and tourism through its extensive coverage of world cultures. The British Library was established by statute (1973) as the national centre for reference, and is a copyright deposit library. The museum has outgrown its original home since opening in 1759, but removal of the library to the new, much-criticized building at St Pancras will enable the great court to be opened up to improve facilities while retaining the round reading room. ASH

British Somaliland. Former British protectorate near the mouth of the Red Sea. In 1884, during the 19th-cent. partition of Africa by European powers, Britain declared a protectorate over the part of Somali territory lying strategically opposite its important naval base in *Aden. The country's natural resources were poor and development was hampered by a rebellion against British administration in the north from 1899 to 1920. In the Second World War British troops occupied the neighbouring Somali territory, previously controlled by Italy, and in 1960 the two former dependencies were united to create the independent state of Somalia. KI

British Union of Fascists. The BUF was founded in 1932 between Sir Oswald *Mosley's New Party and various small British fascist groups. The BUF was partly funded by Mussolini and given valuable publicity in the papers of Lord Rothermere (*Harmsworth). The fascist salute was adopted and Black House established in Chelsea as an organizational and social centre. The Blackshirts, a paramilitary organization, were formed in self-defence against attacks from militant Jewish youths and communists.

However, the crisis in British society, which Mosley expected to capitalize on, failed to materialize in the 1930s. The factors which fed fascism on the continent—chronic unemployment, the threat of communism, and national grievances—were not as extreme in Britain. The BUF failed to create a nation-wide, mass movement. It suffered a set-back after the Olympia meeting in June 1934 when unnecessarily strong action was taken by the Blackshirts to silence hecklers. Its link with political violence and its increasingly anti-Semitic stance alienated moderate opinion, including Rothermere.

When on 4 October 1936 1,900 fascist marchers were turned back by 100,000 opponents at the 'Battle of Cable Street' in the East End of London, the government feared for public order and decided to take action. The Public Order Act (1936) prohibited political uniforms and gave the police powers to ban marches.

Many BUF members were interned in 1940 but in reality the movement had always been marginal and was never a threat to the stability of government. RAS

Britons. The peoples living in Britain during the Roman occupation. The name, which the people of Britain seem to have given themselves, first appears in the account of the voyages of the Greek explorer Pytheas of Marseilles in the late 4th cent. BC. The Greek form of the name is Prettani (or Pritani) and this form was used by later Greek writers such as Polybius (2nd cent. BC), Diodorus, and Strabo (1st cent. BC). Strabo, however, writing after Caesar's expeditions, also used the form Brettani, and Latin authors such as Catullus and Caesar wrote of the Brittani from the first, and from the name of the people came the name of the Roman province, Britannia. The meaning of the name is uncertain, but is thought to be something like 'the tattooed people'. Tattooing, however, barely figured amongst the descriptions of the Britons provided by ancient authors. Only Herodian (3rd cent. AD) wrote of tattoos of patterns and animals on the naked bodies of the Britons, and he referred specifically only to the people of the most northern regions. Caesar claimed far more widespread use of the blue dye woad, but this was used over the whole body and not for painting or tattooing patterns.

In general, Roman authors presented a rather dismal picture of the Britons, as barbarians who wore skins or went naked, practised a form of polygamy, and lived a simple and frugal life. Strabo, who claimed he had seen British youths in Rome, described them as relatively tall, but bow-legged and graceless. But Caesar recognized that not all Britons were the same, identifying those around the south-east coast as more civilized and of different stock from the people of the interior. Tacitus, whose father-in-law *Agricola had campaigned widely in Britain in the mid-1st cent. AD, also observed that the Britons varied widely in physical type, and specifically compared the red-haired, heavily built *Caledonii to the swarthy, curly-haired *Silures of south Wales.

It is clear, from the writings of Strabo and Caesar, that, even before the invasion, the Britons in the south-east corner of the island were becoming socially and politically sophisticated and acquiring a taste for things Roman. They were using gold and bronze coins, and were exporting raw materials (gold, silver, and iron) along with grain and hides. Archaeology reveals that, in exchange, they received manufactured goods such as bronze- and silverware and fine pottery, together with amphorae full of wine. These products are found mainly at a limited number of major tribal centres like Camulodunum (*Colchester) and *Verulamium (St Albans) and in a small number of adjacent burials. They were acquired mainly by tribal élites from whom came the chieftains, and increasingly the kings, who wielded power in Britain at the time of the Roman invasion.

To some extent, therefore, political and social developments in the last century before the Claudian invasion of AD 43 paved the way for the sort of political system and settlement that conquest by Rome brought with it. Nucleated settlements which acted as centres of administration for large tribal territories were known to both the invaders and the natives—the Romans called them towns, and the Britons *oppida*. Equally, both Romans and Britons were by now used to a society in which ultimate power was in the hands of a single individual, supported by, and who in return patronized, an élite class.

The Romans were pragmatic enough to develop a system of provincial administration which perpetuated, at least initially, the existing tribal framework. Thus in Britain they created, between AD 70 and AD 120, about fifteen self-governing tribal authorities (*civitates*), each with elected magistrates and council and each based on a major town. The first such grants of local self-government were in the areas which had shown the most political sophistication before the invasion—Kent, Essex, Hertfordshire, and Buckinghamshire, where the *civitates* of the *Cantiaci, the *Trinovantes, and the *Catuvellauni were established. Other *civitates* were added later, and there is little doubt that the first magistrates and councillors in these authorities were drawn from the old tribal élites. Nor should we be surprised that they reacted in the same way as other native élites have reacted throughout history, by attempting to emulate the life-style of their conquerors. By AD 80, according to Tacitus, the Britons were widely adopting Roman fashion in housing, clothing, language, and diet, and this is borne out by the archaeological evidence. Houses with mosaics, plastered walls and ceilings, under-floor heating, and their own bath-suites were built in town and country alike. Roman shoes and sandals were made and worn, and although there is little evidence to support Tacitus' claim that the toga was to be seen everywhere in Britain, fragments of imported silk and tombstones showing natives in Roman-style clothes testify to the fashionable aspirations of some Britons. The same tombstones, inscribed in Latin, together with private messages varying from a simple word or two scratched on a pot to a full letter written on a waxed tablet reveal the spread of Latin. Along with wine, a variety of amphorae demonstrate that olive oil, fish-sauce, and other exotic foodstuffs were imported by the shipload from the Mediterranean. These developments spawned others, as the demand for both manufactured and imported products created a growing class of craftsmen and middle-men. Accumulating wealth, and other routes to social advancement such as the army, provided opportunities for social mobility which extended the franchise and the opportunity for public service and positions of power and influence to families previously excluded from them. 'And so the Britons were slowly introduced to the luxuries that make vice agreeable', wrote Tacitus.

Just how widespread, socially, the adoption of a Romanized life-style was is hotly debated. It is reasonable to claim that all those living in towns were to some extent exposed to a way of life unknown before the Roman occupation, and certainly the families who built and lived in 'villas' in the country were displaying their adoption of a Romanized life-style. But there were probably less than a hundred towns in Roman Britain, mostly very small, and with a total population which is unlikely to have much exceeded 200,000 people. The villas, even if we assume 3,000 of them (three times the number of probable examples presently known), would add little to this total, since the greatest part of a villa estate's population would be the agricultural labour force and servants. If we compare this to recent estimates of the total population of Roman Britain, at around 2–3 million, we can see that the more obviously Romanized element of the population was very much in the minority.

What is more difficult to assess is the extent to which the lives of the agrarian population were significantly changed by the Roman occupation. Even in rural settlements which show few signs of Romanized architecture, imported pottery and glass, coins, Roman-style jewellery, and occasional Latin graffiti are found. There were some changes in agricultural practice too, with new agricultural implements and crops, new methods of land management, and an increasing emphasis on cash-crops and farming for profit. But these changes, not surprisingly, are best attested in those areas where villas were most prolific—roughly in the area south and east of the *Fosse Way. Outside this area, the clearest signs of Romanization are often found in the civilian settlements that grew up to serve the soldiers in the garrison forts of the north and west. By providing for the needs of the troops, by intermarriage, and by social intercourse, the native Britons of these areas were introduced to a Roman way of life different perhaps from that of the towns in the south-east but equally quite different from anything they had known before the conquest.

It would be easy to make much of this and claim that the life of the British was totally transformed by the Roman conquest and occupation. But this would be to go too far. For a minority, changes in life-style, and even in attitudes, were dramatic, but for the vast majority of the population, the general impression is that much of life went on as before. KB

Alcock, L., *Economy, Society and Warfare among the Britons and Saxons* (Cardiff, 1987); Cunliffe, B. W., *Iron Age Communities in Britain* (3rd edn. New York, 1991); Laing, L. R., *Celtic Britain and Ireland, AD 200–800: The Myth of the Dark Ages* (New York, 1990).

Britten, Benjamin (1913–76). The most distinguished English composer of his generation, Britten showed original talent from an early age. Educated at the *Royal College of Music (London), he was impatient with the parochialism of much English musical life, though his roots were firmly in East Anglia, where he had his home for 30 years. In 1945 Britten's opera *Peter Grimes* was premièred in London. Its impact was remarkable: Britten had written an opera which quickly established itself in the international repertoire and which combined a distinctively modern style with the ability to appeal to the general musical public. Thereafter Britten's prolific output demonstrated his fluency in writing for the human voice and his capacity to match musical subtlety with psychological insight. A brilliant pianist, Britten's commitment to musical performance was reflected in the foundation of the Aldeburgh Festival in 1948. He was created a life peer in 1976. JWD

Brixworth church in Northamptonshire is the most impressive church to survive from Anglo-Saxon England. Built from reused brick and tile pillaged from Roman Leicester, its earliest parts probably date to the 8th cent. At the core is a spacious nave flanked by a series of side-chapels, now known only from excavations, which were entered through great archways. To the east was a square choir and apsed sanctuary surrounded by an external ring-crypt. To the west, chambers flanked a two-storey porch. In the late Anglo-Saxon period the nave walls were raised and a stair turret added to the porch. RNB

'broad-bottom administration' was the facetious name given to the coalition formed in December 1744, at the expense of *Carteret and *Pulteney. Henry *Pelham, his brother *Newcastle and Lord *Hardwicke were joined by *Chesterfield, George Lyttelton, Gower, *Bedford, Hinde Cotton, and *Dodington. The Pelhams promised to bring in William *Pitt as soon as George II's dislike could be overcome. Hardwicke told the king that there was not one man left in the Commons 'capable of leading or conducting an opposition'. The coalition represented a significant development in the rehabilitation of the *Tories and the reunification of the *Whigs. The opportunities given by the nickname to cartoonists were not overlooked. JAC

broad church is a term applied from the late 1840s to Anglicans who were neither *evangelicals nor *tractarians, and became common currency after W. J. Conybeare's *Edinburgh Review* article on 'Church Parties' (1853). It embraced prominent churchmen who, influenced by Thomas *Arnold and *Coleridge, worked to restate catholic doctrines and reposition the national church, unafraid of contemporary scholarship. With F. D. *Maurice (1805–72) as their representative divine, F. W. Robertson of Brighton (1816–53) their preacher, *Jowett of Balliol (1817–93) their academic, and Dean Stanley of Westminster (1815–81) their ecclesiastic, they were influential, even dominant, in their church by 1900 and attractive to many nonconformists, especially *congregationalists. CB

Brontë family. In 1820, the Irish-born Patrick Brontë brought his Cornish wife and their six young children to Haworth parsonage on the bleak Yorkshire moors, near Bradford. After the deaths of Mrs Brontë and the two eldest girls (possibly hastened by time at a clergy daughters' school), the children were cared for by an aunt but thrown very much on their own resources, creating imaginary worlds and writing. After erratic schooling, then short teaching or governess posts, Charlotte, Emily, and Anne returned to Haworth to care for their father; anxiety over their irresponsible debt-laden brother Branwell, for whom there had been great hopes, deepened as he became addicted to alcohol and opium, and all struggled against ill-health. Charlotte's discovery of some of Emily's poems led to publication of *Poems by Currer, Ellis, and Acton Bell* (pseudonyms corresponding to their initials), which, if selling poorly, nevertheless encouraged them towards novels. Charlotte (*Jane Eyre*, 1847; *Shirley*, 1849; *Villette*, 1853, based on her time in Brussels) became a literary celebrity, but Emily's *Wuthering Heights* (1848) was too innovative and passionate for many tastes; Anne (*Agnes Grey*, 1847; *Tenant of Wildfell Hall*, 1848) might have been overpowered by her more brilliant sisters, but continues to be quietly appreciated. Although Branwell's debts were discharged, he died in 1848, to be followed shortly by Emily, then Anne the following summer. Charlotte eventually married her father's curate (1854), but died soon after, similarly from tuberculosis. ASH

Brooke, Sir Basil, 1st Lord Brookeborough (1880–1974). Prime minister of Northern Ireland 1943–63 and indelibly associated with the comment 'a Protestant Parliament and a Protestant State'. Descended from Ulster plantation landowners, Brooke came late to politics after a military career. He was behind the establishment of the Ulster Special Constabulary, minister of agriculture 1933–40, and the most active of Sir James *Craig's administration. Minister of commerce 1940–3, his criticism of the ineffective response to wartime emergency led to his assuming premiership. He was an intransigent opponent of any concessions to catholic minority and conservative in economic affairs while premier. During the tumultuous years following his retirement, he was an outdated and all-too-easily ridiculed man. MAH

Brooke, Sir James (1803–68). Brooke, 'the White Raja of Sarawak', was born at Benares, educated in England, and recruited to the Madras army in 1819. Wounded in the first *Burmese War (1824–6), he resigned his commission in 1830. Inheriting a fortune five years later, he became an explorer in south-east Asia. In 1841, while recuperating at Singapore, he heard that his friend, the raja of Sarawak, was facing a major rebellion but that no official relief expedition was planned. He rushed to the raja's aid and helped to crush the rebellion. As a reward, and after the death of the raja, he was offered the rajadom by its overlord, the sultan of *Brunei. He accepted and established a dynasty. He cleared the region of pirates and established the Borneo Company to promote development. He was recognized by the USA as the ruler of an independent state in 1850; and by the British in 1864. DAW

Brooks's, one of the most famous of London clubs, began life in Pall Mall in 1764 as Almack's, its proprietor William McCall wisely reversing his name to avoid anti-Scottish prejudice. In 1778 it moved to new premises in St James's Street built by Henry Holland and changed its name to Brooks's. It was noted for high gambling and Whig politics. In its possession are fine busts of *Fox and *Pitt by *Nollekens. JAC

Brougham, Henry Peter, 1st Baron Brougham and Vaux (1778–1868). A member of a minor gentry family in Westmorland, educated at Edinburgh University, Brougham was one of the most eminent lawyers and intellectuals of his time, renowned for the breadth of his interests. He helped to found the **Edinburgh Review* and his contributions made it the leading political journal of the day. He qualified for the English bar in 1802 and entered the House of Commons in 1810 in pursuit of fame and political distinction. He was a brilliant if too frequent speaker, supporting the liberal wing of the Whig Party and espousing the causes of anti-slavery, popular education, and legal reform. He played a leading part in forming the Society for the Diffusion of Useful Knowledge in 1825 and in founding the University of London in 1828, both established on utilitarian and secular principles.

Brougham was mistrusted by his party leaders who considered his support of Queen *Caroline, whose adviser he became in 1819–20, to be motivated by desire for personal advancement. His support of popular causes, particularly anti-slavery, gained him election as MP for Yorkshire in 1830, though he had no property in the county, and when the Whigs came to power he expected high office. He reluctantly accepted the post of lord chancellor with a peerage because it meant giving up the House of Commons and a lucrative income at the bar. He carried through a series of important legal reforms but continued disagreements with his colleagues, especially over the credit for the Reform Act, led *Melbourne not to reappoint him in 1834. He never returned to office and became markedly eccentric in later life. EAS

Brown, George (1914–85). Brown was one of the Labour Party's most colourful characters, becoming deputy leader (1960–70) and foreign secretary (1966–8). He entered Parliament in 1945 and occupied several minor government positions under *Attlee. Defeated by Harold *Wilson for the leadership of the party in 1963, he was both first secretary of state and secretary of state for economic affairs in Wilson's first government (1964–6). He lost his seat at the general election of 1970 and was made Lord George-Brown the same year. Notorious for his drinking and his social gaffes, he acquired a certain personal popularity. But in office he proved an outstanding failure, helping to discredit the concept of detailed economic management. His eventual resignation in 1968 confirmed his political irrelevance. AS

Brown, Lancelot (1715/16–83). English landscape designer, generally known as 'Capability' because of his references to the 'capabilities' of the places about which he was consulted. Born in Northumberland, he worked first for Sir William Loraine at Kirkharle Hall but by 1741 had moved south to Stowe. Charles *Bridgeman had died in 1738, and Brown took a prominent part in the evolution of the Stowe landscape for which *Gibbs and *Kent were providing buildings. Soon Brown established his own distinctive landscape style with its clumps, belts, bridges, irregular lakes, and encircling woodland and lawns. Major commissions (sometimes involving the design of buildings) began to come his way, among them Croome Court (from 1750), *Longleat, Burton Constable, *Chatsworth (from 1761), and *Blenheim (from about 1764). In 1764 Brown was appointed master gardener at Hampton Court, a post which carried with it an official residence within the palace grounds, Wilderness House. In 1771 he went into partnership with the younger Henry Holland (1745–1806), later his son-in-law, and together they undertook architectural commissions such as Claremont (1771–4), Cadland (1775–8), and Nuneham (1781–2). On his death in 1783 Brown was buried at Fenstanton in Huntingdonshire, where he had bought the manor in 1767. Horace *Walpole wrote of him: 'such was the effect of his genius, that when he was the happiest man, he will be least remembered. So closely did he copy nature that his work will be mistaken for it.' PW

Browne, Robert (*c.*1550–1633). An early puritan separatist preacher and pamphleteer, Browne was born in Rutland of a wealthy family. After graduating from Corpus Christi College, Cambridge (1572), where he was under *Cartwright's influence, he had a spell in London as a schoolmaster and open-air preacher (1572–8) and then in Cambridgeshire. Hostile to any form of church government, he and Robert Harrison established independent congregations, later known as Brownists, in East Anglia. Arrested for heresy (1581), but protected by his kinsman *Burghley, he emigrated to Middelburg (the Netherlands), where he continued publishing heretical literature. At odds with other puritan exiles, he returned to England (1583), was imprisoned, but, after submitting to the church, became master of Stamford Grammar School (1586–91). Accepting episcopal ordination (1591), he was rector of Achurch (Northants) until his death. A turbulent, unstable character, he is still regarded by many as a founder of *congregationalism. WMM

Browne, Sir Thomas (1605–82). Physician and author. London-born, educated at Oxford, Montpellier, and Padua, Browne received a Leiden MD (1633) before returning to practise near Halifax. He settled in Norwich (1637), was admitted MD Oxon., and in 1643 published the authorized version of his most famous work *Religio medici*, printed without apparent permission the preceding year. Its reflections on the mysteries of God, creation, and man were an immediate success throughout Europe, though papal authorities placed it in the 'Index expurgatorius'. *Pseudodoxia epidemica* (1646) attempted to dispel some popular superstitions, while *Urn Burial* and *The Garden of Cyrus* (1658) reflected antiquarian interests. Despite all-embracing curiosity and encyclopedic knowledge, Browne remained credulous, as illustrated by his involvement in the conviction of two women as witches (1664). He corresponded with *Evelyn, *Dugdale, and *Aubrey, and, ever a royalist, received a knighthood on Charles II's state visit to Norwich in 1671. ASH

Browning, Robert (1812–89). Born in Camberwell, son of a clerk in the Bank of England, Browning read widely as a boy in his father's library, greatly admiring *Keats, *Shelley, and *Byron. He spent only two terms at the University of London, but travelled in Russia and Italy. Much of his early work was historically based. *Paracelsus* (1835) was a verse drama about the 16th-cent. physician. *Strafford* (1837), which *Macready persuaded him to write, was a lifeless poetic drama; *King Victor and King Charles* was on the unpromising subject of a dynastic dispute in 18th-cent. Piedmont and was never performed; *A Blot on the 'Scutcheon* (1843) ran for three nights and convinced Browning to abandon the theatre. *Dramatic Lyrics* (1842) included 'My Last Duchess', 'Soliloquy in a Spanish Cloister', and 'The Pied Piper': *Dramatic Romances and Lyrics* (1845) added 'Home Thoughts from Abroad', 'The Lost Leader', and 'How they Brought the Good News from Ghent to Aix'. In 1846 Browning married Elizabeth Barrett, already an established poet, and they lived mainly in Italy until her death in 1861. His greatest success, *The Ring and the Book* (1868–9), took a melodramatic murder story from late 17th-cent. Italy and presented it from different viewpoints. Some of Browning's poems seem inconsequential and others suggest unpleasant feelings not far below the surface. He was overpraised towards the end of his life and is in some danger of being underrated today. JAC

Bruce, Edward (d. 1318). Brother of Robert I king of Scots, earl of Carrick from 1313, titular king of Ireland (1315–18). Edward Bruce was an outstanding if savage soldier, but, it seems, an arrogant and over-ambitious man, with too little political sense. As soon as Robert I took the throne in 1306, Edward became one of his foremost commanders. In 1308 he ravaged Galloway, confining English authority in the area to a few castles, which were gradually reduced until 1313; further campaigns followed, culminating in the siege of Stirling castle which began in 1313. It is likely that a wearisome siege was not quite Edward's idea of war; and he made an agreement with the English commander Philip Mowbray that the castle would surrender if not relieved within a year. This meant that Edward II would have to attempt to relieve it, which displeased Robert I, since his policy was always to avoid a pitched battle and rely on guerrilla tactics. However, battle could not be avoided. At *Bannockburn (24 June 1314), Edward was in command of the leading brigade. In August 1314, he was among the leaders of a raid into north-east England, which caused widespread damage. In the Parliament of 1315, he was rewarded by being made heir presumptive to the Scottish throne, in the (unlikely) event that Robert I would die without a direct male heir.

It seems that Edward was not satisfied, and felt that, while his brother was king, he could not achieve what he deserved in Scotland. With Robert's full backing, he embarked on an expedition to Ireland, which has been the subject of much controversy. He seems to have landed in Ulster at the end of May 1315, with the support of Ulster nobles, who had close links with Scotland; but then forced them, reluctantly according to one account, to acknowledge him as king of Ireland, which implied an intention to conquer the whole island. He proceeded to the south, ravaging as usual as he went; but did not find the support he expected. By October 1316, he wrote to the Welsh suggesting that he should join them in an attempt to expel the English from Wales, and that he should become prince of Wales as well as king of Ireland! There was so little reality in all this that in 1317, his brother had to come briefly to his aid in Ireland, but with little success. Edward's position as king was impossible to sustain; and in October 1318 he was killed in battle at Faughart, near Dundalk, and his army destroyed.

He was described by a chronicler as 'a little headstrong and impetuous (*aliquantulum preceps et impetuosus*)'. The judgement seems just. BW

Bruce, James (1730–94). British explorer. Bruce established his claim to fame by revealing to the western world that the Blue Nile had its source in Lake Tana, in Abyssinia (Ethiopia). As British consul in Algiers from 1763 he became interested in the antiquities of north Africa and travelled extensively around the Mediterranean. From Cairo in 1768 he set out to discover the source of the Nile, travelling upstream as far as Aswan. From there he struck eastward to the Red Sea and then inland again to Gondar. Although the country was troubled by political disturbances, he continued his journey to Lake Tana which he reached in November 1770. After a perilous homeward journey he reached England in 1774, only to encounter serious doubts about the validity of his discoveries. His claims were vindicated by later travellers. KI

Bruce, Marjorie (d. 1316). Eldest daughter of King Robert I, and joint founder of the royal house of Stewart (Stuart). Born before 1297, she was the only child of her father's first wife Isabel, daughter of Donald, earl of Mar. Her short life was blighted by personal misfortune. She was captured and handed over to Edward I in 1306, spent the next eight years as a prisoner of the English, and shortly after her return to Scotland was killed by a fall from her horse. But in 1315 she had been married to Walter Stewart, and her son Robert Stewart became king of Scots as Robert II in 1371, when her stepbrother David II died childless. KJS

Bruce, Robert (1210–95). Known as the 'Competitor'. Leading member of the 13th-cent. Scottish nobility and grandfather of the future King Robert I. His extensive lands stretched from Middlesex to Aberdeenshire, the most important concentrations lying in Essex, Co. Durham, and south-west Scotland, where he held the great lordship of Annandale, granted to the Bruces (who came originally from Brix in Normandy) by David I. His long career vividly illustrates the comparatively easy-going nature of Anglo-Scottish relations before the Wars of Independence, when a significant number of landowners held prominence on both sides of the border. His transnational interests are reflected in his marriage to Isabel de Clare, daughter of the earl of Gloucester. He also served as sheriff of Cumberland and supported Henry III against Simon de *Montfort at the battle of *Lewes. A truly cosmopolitan figure, he went on crusade to the Holy Land (1271–2), and on his return journey granted lands, probably in Annandale, to Clairvaux abbey in Burgundy. Descended through his mother from David I, he was one of the chief claimants or 'competitors' for the vacant Scottish throne in 1291–2, and was bitterly disappointed when Edward I declared in favour of John *Balliol, though Balliol's case was in fact legally stronger. He did not contest the decision, but the family never abandoned its claims to the kingdom, which were finally realized in 1306. He died at Lochmaben castle in Annandale, and was buried in Guisborough priory (Yorks.), founded by the Bruces in the early 12th cent. KJS

Bruce, Robert (d. 1304). Eldest son of Robert *Bruce (d. 1295) and father of Robert I. His marriage to Marjorie, widow of Adam of Kilconquhar, brought him the earldom of Carrick in about 1272—a promotion which involved the Bruces in territorial rivalry with their neighbour John *Balliol, lord of Galloway—and he succeeded to his family's Anglo-Scottish patrimony some 20 years later. Bruce–Balliol rivalry intensified when Robert's father and John Balliol were the main challengers for the Scottish throne in 1291–2. When Balliol was enthroned, Robert refused to recognize him, thereby keeping his family's claims to the Scottish crown alive. He provided his son, the future king, with a power base by assigning Carrick to him, and on the outbreak of the *Scottish Wars of Independence, his anti-Balliol stance led him to support Edward I. After the English victory at *Dunbar (27 April 1296), he asked for the Scottish throne—a request to which Edward famously responded: 'Have we nothing else to do but win kingdoms for you?' Despite this rebuff, Robert remained in the English allegiance until his death, when he was buried in Holm Cultram abbey (Cumberland). KJS

Bruce, Robert I of Scotland. See ROBERT I.

Brudenell, James Thomas. See CARDIGAN, 7TH EARL OF.

Bruges, treaty of, 1375. After years of warfare, Charles V of France and Edward III agreed a truce, under papal auspices, and established a conference at Bruges to negotiate a permanent settlement. But after Edward's death in June 1377, fighting was resumed. JAC

Brummell, George (1778–1840), known as 'Beau' Brummell. English dandy. Son of Lord North's private secretary, with a reputation for fastidiousness and ready repartee apparent even at Eton, he utilized a generous inheritance to settle in Mayfair and devote himself to becoming an arbiter of fashion, promoting personal cleanliness and refinement in dress through moderation, in contrast to the Macaronis' slovenliness. Supremely self-centred, cold, and arrogant, he was an intimate friend of George, prince of Wales until royal favour was withdrawn in 1811, after which he lost commercial credit but increased gaming. Accumulating debt eventually forced retirement to Calais (1816), where he received assistance from friends and was briefly consul at Caen (post abolished in 1832). A subsequent slide into poverty was accompanied by two paralytic strokes, until extreme degradation and imbecility led to admission to an asylum at Caen, where he died. ASH

Brunanburh, battle of, 937. Brunanburh was the crowning military achievement of Athelstan's reign, which saw *Wessex advances into Devon, south Wales, and the north. In 937 a formidable coalition attempted to hold him at bay. Constantine II of Scotland was joined by Owain of Strathclyde and Olaf Guthfrithsson from Dublin (whose father had been driven out of Northumbria by Athelstan). The site of the battle remains uncertain, though if the Dublin fleet did use the Humber, Brough or Aldborough are possibilities. In savage fighting, Athelstan and his brother Edmund prevailed: five young kings, including a son of Constantine, are said to have been killed. The *Anglo-Saxon Chronicle* thought the victory the greatest ever won by the Saxons and broke into sombre verse:

Likewise the English king and the prince,
Brothers triumphant in war, together
Returned to their home, the land of Wessex.
To enjoy the carnage, they left behind
The horn-beaked raven with dusky plumage,
And the hungry hawk of battle, the dun-coated
Eagle, who with white-tipped tail shared
The feast with the wolf, grey beast of the forest. JAC

Brunei rose as a powerful Islamic sultanate in the 15th cent. When Magellan visited it in 1521, it held sway over most of lowland Borneo and the surrounding archipelago. However, after it was destroyed by a Spanish fleet, it passed into obscurity. In 1888, surrounded by the Brookes' Sarawak and the domains of the British North Borneo Company, it was taken under a British protectorate. From 1906 to 1959, it was administered by the British resident. Rich oil reserves were discovered. The sultan was restored to his government and, in 1963, declined to join the *Malaysian Federation. DAW

Brunel, Isambard Kingdom (1806–59). Engineer. Son of the distinguished émigré Sir Marc, Brunel was scientifically educated in Paris (unusual when the engineering profession was entered through practical pupillage) and consistently applied first principles to problems, making him more admired by subsequent engineers than contemporary shareholders. Sickness incurred at his father's Thames Tunnel (1826–8) led Brunel to convalesce at Bristol, where he gained appointments as engineer of the Clifton bridge (1829–31), the floating harbour (1830–1), and the Great Western Railway (from 1833). Brunel's engineering of the GWR demonstrated his vision and his failings: the commitment to the broad (7-inch) gauge and his own design for bolstering track promised quality and speed, but delivered inflexibility; his vision of the Atlantic crossing from Bristol encapsulated by his first two major ships, *Great Western* (1837) and **Great Britain* (1843), displayed the temptation to exceed the bounds of commercial technology proven in the outstandingly advanced **Great Eastern* (1858); his remarkable bridges of brick, timber, and iron; and locomotive failings from which Gooch rescued the line. A driven man, his genius produced the monitor to attack Sebastopol and the prefabricated hospital for Kronstadt, railways in Italy and India, hectored assistants and neglected pupils, and chronic overwork that contributed to early death as his two greatest achievements, the Albert bridge at Saltash and the *Great Eastern*, neared commissioning. JCh

Brussels, treaty of. Signed on 17 March 1948 between the United Kingdom, France, Belgium, the Netherlands, and Luxembourg, it set up the Brussels Treaty Organization, also known as *Western European Union. This purported to be a security pact based on shared cultural heritage of its members and against any revival of German expansionism. There was also an important, veiled motivation. The treaty was intended to demonstrate that west European states were willing to co-operate with each other and therefore make a US commitment to a role in the security of western Europe more acceptable to Congress. The Brussels treaty was therefore a vital step on the road to the formation of *NATO. CNL

'Brutus'. The extraordinary legend that Britain had been 'founded' by Brutus, great-grandson of Aeneas of Troy, haunted men's imagination for centuries. *Geoffrey of Monmouth, in the 12th cent., related how Brutus, after many adventures, visited England (landing at Totnes), subdued the race of giants who inhabited it, gave his name to it, and founded London as New Troy.

The implausibility of a myth is no great obstacle to its popularity and 'Brutus' ran and ran. Tudor historians deeply resented the suggestion of Polydore Vergil (a foreigner) that the story was not very likely as a slur upon the nation. The myth had important political consequences. First it put heart into the Welsh after centuries of defeat. They could comfort themselves with a heroic past which must foretell a glorious future: William of Newburgh, writing some 40 years after Geoffrey, remarked sourly that the story had only been told to please the Welsh. Secondly, Geoffrey's account of King *Arthur, a direct descendant of Brutus, told how he had conquered Ireland, Iceland, Orkney, Sweden, Norway, Denmark, Normandy, and had challenged Rome itself. Tudor imperialists seized upon it. John Dee and others improved upon Arthur's conquests by adding America, visited by *Madog in the 12th cent., and called for a great new British empire. Until deep into the 20th cent. the imperialist vision inspired and helped to bind together the nations of the British Isles. JAC

Brut y tywysogyon ('Chronicle of the Princes') is the most valuable narrative source for the history of medieval Wales. Translated from a lost Latin original, three independent versions in Welsh survive from the 14th cent. as continuations of *Geoffrey of Monmouth's *Historia regum Britanniae*. These versions are in Peniarth 20, Red Book of Hergest, and Cotton, Cleopatra B V, with a continuation in Black Book of Basingwerk; all three have fine modern editions by Thomas Jones. They begin with Cadwaladr Fendigaid whose death (682) was regarded as a key event in the history of Britons and Saxons. They end with the equally crucial death of Llywelyn ap Gruffydd (1282); Peniarth 20 continues to 1332, drawing on other lost annals, and Black Book of Basingwerk has a continuation to 1461 of little value. The Latin original used church and monastic annals from the 8th cent. and, for 900–1100, others kept at St Davids and possibly Llanbadarn Fawr. It was perhaps composed at the Cistercian abbey of Strata Florida (Cardiganshire). Sometimes cryptic, often bloody, the extant versions are also eloquent and rhetorical with moving laments of great kings. Their compilation reflects the strong sense of identity of the Welsh faced with foreign conquest. RAG

Bryce, James (1838–1922). Political analyst and Liberal politician. Bryce was from Belfast and educated there and in Glasgow and Oxford universities. In 1863 he won the Arnold history prize with *The Holy Roman Empire*, the first of many works on the character and morphology of states. After a spell as an education commissioner, in 1870 he became professor of Roman law at Oxford, and began the revival of that subject. Bryce was one of a group of Oxford liberal intellectuals who provided the party with a cogent programme of reform, much of it education oriented. He was a keen mountaineer and travelled widely. In 1877 he published *Transcaucasia and Ararat*, reflecting his interest in the Eastern Question, a subject which preoccupied him for the rest of his life; he became an especial champion of the rights of the Armenians, including their right to nationhood after the disintegration of the Turkish empire in 1918. In 1880 Bryce became a Liberal MP. He was in *Gladstone's last cabinet of 1892–4, becoming president of the Board of Trade 1894–5. He chaired a royal commission on education in 1895. A home-ruler despite his Ulster protestant background, he was an uneasy Irish secretary 1906–7, when he went to Washington as ambassador (until 1913), a very successful appointment. Bryce's greatest (and still influential) book was *The American Commonwealth* (1888), a practical as well as theoretical analysis, based on interviews and travels. Bryce became Viscount Bryce in 1914. That year he chaired the Bryce commission on war atrocities and was a member of the small group which promoted a *League of Nations. In 1921 he published *Modern Democracies*, an encomium for a fast-disappearing liberalism. HCGM

Brycheiniog was a medieval Welsh kingdom whose dynasty is traditionally said to have begun with Brychan, the son of a 5th-cent. Irish chieftain and the daughter of the king of Garthmadrun in the Vale of Usk. His line ended *c*.940, when Brycheiniog fell under *Deheubarth's influence. It was conquered by Bernard of Neufmarché (1093), whose new marcher lordship was known as Brecon (a corruption of Brychan). Brecknock is the English version of Brycheiniog. The lordship was the basis (with Builth lordship) of the new county of Brecon in 1536; it lasted until 1974 when it was incorporated in Co. Powys. Brycheiniog is used as the Welsh version of Breconshire. RAG

Buchan, Alexander Comyn, earl of [S] (d. before 14 March 1290). Earl from 1244, and one of the six guardians of the realm from 1286 till his death. In youth, he was involved in many of the turbulent acts of his family, including the ravaging of the lands of the Bissets in 1242, and the violent seizure of the young Alexander III in 1257. During the minority of Alexander III he and his relatives repeatedly clashed with the supporters of Alan Durward in their efforts to control the council, but a compromise was reached in 1258; and thereafter Alexander appears more as a loyal and effective agent of the king. In 1264 he led the punishment of those in the Isles and Caithness who had supported the king of Norway in his campaign of 1263; and became constable of Scotland by 1275. He died just before the crisis of 1290. From being a disturber of order in his youth, he had become a respected elder statesman. BW

Buchan, John Comyn, earl of [S] (d. 1308). Buchan's career shows the difficulties faced by prominent Scots who wished to maintain the integrity of their country. Like the rest of his family he was a supporter of John *Balliol, and hostile to the claims of Edward I. Yet he had at times to compromise, submitting to Edward in 1296 and being sent by him to suppress the rising of Andrew Murray in 1297. Instead, he joined the rising himself, fought at *Falkirk against Edward, and was a leading figure on the Scottish side till what seemed to be Edward's final victory in 1304, after which he was prepared to co-operate in Edward's reorganization of Scottish government. We cannot say what he would have done in 1306 but for Bruce's murder of his cousin John *Comyn of Badenoch, which forced him finally onto the English side. He was routed by Bruce at *Inverurie in 1308, and his earldom was ravaged. He fled to England where he died soon after. BW

Buchan, William Comyn, earl of [S] (d. 1233). Comyn was justiciar [S]. By his first wife he was grandfather of the Red Comyn, and great-grandfather of the Red *Comyn who was a competitor for the Scottish throne in 1291. His son Walter became earl of Menteith [S] and was one of the leaders of the powerful Comyn interest in the early years of Alexander III. His second marriage was to Margaret, countess of Buchan, in whose right he was recognized as earl. His son Alexander, by his second wife, was also justiciar 1251–5 and 1257–89. In 1200 Comyn was one of the noblemen sent by William the Lion to make friendly overtures to King John and in 1221 he was a witness to the marriage contract between Alexander II and John's daughter *Joan. He was buried in the Cistercian abbey of Deer (Aberdeenshire), which he had founded. JAC

Buchan, Alexander Stewart, 1st earl of [S] (d. *c*.1406). Lord of Badenoch. The fourth son of Robert II, he was made a justiciar in northern Scotland (1372), in which post he earned his nickname of 'Wolf of Badenoch'. He became earl of Buchan in 1382 as a result of his marriage to Euphemia, countess of Ross. He was associated with bands of caterans, and was sacked from his justiciarship in 1388. Buchan had been extorting large sums from the bishop of Moray since 1370, in return for protection. In 1389 Moray excommunicated him, and from 1390 took protection from the sheriff of Inverness. In 1390, on Robert II's death, Buchan and his caterans burned Forres, and then Elgin burgh and cathedral, in reprisals for Moray's actions. His royal connections saved him from harsh criticism, but his and his bastard son's northern power proved problematic for the crown well into the 15th cent. RJT

Buchan, John Stewart, 3rd earl of [S] (d. 1424). A younger son of Robert, duke of Albany, governor of Scotland, who made him earl of Buchan (1406). Albany appointed Buchan chamberlain (1407), in which post he oversaw widespread embezzling of royal funds. In 1419 Buchan travelled to France with 6,000 Scots to fight for the Dauphin Charles (later Charles VII) against the English. They played an important role and won a small victory at *Baugé in Anjou (1421). Made constable of France, and leader of the French forces, Buchan came close to fighting

James I, involved on the English side, at Beaugency (1421). Buchan was killed, with most of his army, at *Verneuil (1424). This outcome was as welcome to James I as to the English, as it enabled him to turn against Buchan's family, the Albany Stewarts, and their estates, without fear of reprisal. RJT

Buchanan, George (1506–82). The most distinguished Scottish humanist of his era, Buchanan was born near Killearn in Stirlingshire and educated primarily at Paris, where he quickly gained a reputation as a neo-Latin poet and dramatist of rare distinction. Deeply influenced by Erasmus, his strongly anticlerical views led to frequent brushes with authority culminating in imprisonment by the Portuguese Inquisition. The date of his conversion to protestantism is unknown, but on his return to Scotland in 1561 he was associated both with the court of the catholic Mary Stuart and with the new protestant kirk. Following the queen's deposition in 1567, he emerged as the most influential of Mary's detractors, justifying resistance to tyranny in his elegant dialogue *De jure regni apud Scotos* (1579) and his monumental *Rerum Scoticarum historia* (1582). Both were dedicated to Mary's son James VI, whose education at Buchanan's hands profoundly influenced the king's own belief in his *divine right to rule. RAM

Buckingham, John Sheffield, 1st duke of (1647–1721). Buckingham succeeded as 3rd earl of Mulgrave at the age of 10, served in the army and navy, and was gentleman of the bedchamber to Charles II. He was in favour with James II, who appointed him lord chamberlain. He stayed with James until the end, but accepted William and Mary and was created marquis of Normanby in 1694. Anne, whom he had courted in 1682, made him lord privy seal and promoted him in 1703 to the dukedom made available by the death of the second Villiers duke. Until 1714 he was an influential high Tory, serving on the commission to negotiate union with Scotland, as lord steward 1710–11 and lord president of the council 1711–14. After 1714 his political career was over. He was a poet of some repute, though *Johnson was disparaging. His house at the end of the Mall, built in 1703, was sold to George III in 1761 and became the nucleus of Buckingham palace. JAC

Buckingham, Edward Stafford, 3rd duke of (1478–1521). Stafford's great-great-grandfather was killed at *Shrewsbury in 1403 fighting for Henry IV; his great-grandfather, the 1st duke, died fighting for the Lancastrians at *Northampton in 1460. His father, a prominent supporter of Richard III, was seized and executed at Salisbury in 1483, when Stafford was 6. He was restored to his title by Henry VII and given the Garter when he was 21. In 1509, at the coronation of Henry VIII, he claimed the right to act as lord high chamberlain. He had royal blood, through Thomas, duke of *Gloucester, younger son of Edward III, and his mother, Catherine Woodville, sister to Edward IV's queen. Under a suspicious king, this was a dangerous heritage. In addition, his connection by marriages with the Percies, de la Poles, and Howards made him one of the greatest magnates of the day. His life-style was lavish and his behaviour grand. In 1520, an anonymous letter to *Wolsey accused the duke of treasonable words. He was summoned from Thornbury, placed in the Tower, and executed on 17 May 1521. JAC

Buckingham, Henry Stafford, 2nd duke of (1455–83). Buckingham came from a staunchly Lancastrian family. His father was killed at the first battle of *St Albans, just before he was born: his grandfather (from whom he inherited the title), was killed at *Northampton when he was 6. He could expect little favour from the Yorkist establishment. Edward IV's death opened the door. Allying himself with Richard of Gloucester, the two dukes swept to power in the summer of 1483. With Gloucester crowned as Richard III, Buckingham, lavishly rewarded, looked well set. Yet within four months he joined dissident southern gentry in rebellion. Betrayed to the king, he was summarily executed at Salisbury on 2 November. Buckingham's volte-face remains an enigma. He may have been converted to Henry Tudor's cause; he might have judged that he was again joining the winning side; or he might even have had his own fantasies about the crown. His behaviour suggests that Edward IV had correctly judged him to be dangerously untrustworthy. AJP

Buckingham, George Villiers, 1st duke of (1592–1628). Buckingham attracted James I's attention by his good looks, and by 1616 had replaced Robert *Carr as the reigning favourite. Unlike Carr, however, he displayed considerable administrative ability, carrying through a major programme of naval reform after James appointed him lord admiral. The king's repeated affirmations of his dependence upon Buckingham meant that he was blamed for unpopular policies such as the 'Spanish match' (for Prince Charles) of which he was merely the executant. Only in 1623, during his enforced stay in Spain, did he emancipate himself from James's tutelage, and not until Charles became king in 1625 did he have a free hand in making policy. He planned to build up an anti-Spanish alliance, of which France was to be the linchpin, but religion, as always, complicated the situation, for the French protestants of La Rochelle were under attack from their own king and appealed to Charles to save them. Military operations would require massive funding from Parliament, but Buckingham's involvement in dubious practices such as the sale of titles and offices had brought him an unsavoury reputation, and his catholic connections—his mother was a catholic convert and his wife had abandoned catholicism only in order to marry him—further undermined parliamentary trust. Despite all obstacles he sent out expeditions against Cadiz in 1625 and in support of La Rochelle in 1627, but both ended in humiliating defeat. The Commons attempted to impeach him in 1626, and two years later denounced him as the cause of all England's evils. This inspired an army officer, John Felton, to assassinate him at Portsmouth in August 1628. Buckingham was in fact a patriot, dedicated to the king's service and his country's safety, and although his death was welcomed as a deliverance, subsequent events were to show that he was a symptom rather than the cause of malfunctioning in the English polity. RL

Buckingham, George Villiers, 2nd duke of (1628–87). Heir to his renowned father the 1st duke (assassinated August 1628), he was brought up with the royal children and, despite frequent provocations, Charles II always felt a fraternal bond with Buckingham. He fought in the Civil War, but his youth recovered his estates for him in 1647. Personally involved in the Scottish invasion on Charles II's behalf in 1651, Buckingham was able to return to England from exile in 1657, when he married a daughter of Sir Thomas *Fairfax. Naturally enjoying preferment at the Restoration, lack of managerial capacity combined with pathological irresponsibility rendered Buckingham the least weighty of 'the *cabal's' members. His public support for the dissenting community, and the personal standing he acquired with Louis XIV, together bear out contemporary estimates of Buckingham's capricious shallowness. Pope's account, in the *Epistle to Bathurst*, of Buckingham's wretched end is a ludicrous exaggeration. DDA

Buckingham palace (London). The official London residence of Her Majesty the Queen. Buckingham House (as it then was) was built in 1702–5 for John Sheffield, 1st duke of *Buckingham, by the architect William Winde (d. 1722). Its style is classical, essentially that of a country house set in an English park. Buckingham House was bought in 1762 by George III, who had it altered and enlarged by Sir William *Chambers in 1762–9. In 1825 George IV approached his friend John *Nash for designs, and in 1825–30 Nash incorporated Buckingham House in Buckingham palace. On Nash's dismissal in 1830 he was replaced by Edward Blore (1787–1879), who had assisted with Abbotsford for Sir Walter *Scott. Blore completed Nash's work at Buckingham palace, adding an attic on the garden front (1832–7), then converting the south-east conservatory into a chapel (1842–3), and in 1847–50 building the east wing facing the Mall; in 1913 this was refaced by Sir Aston Webb, who also laid out the *rond point* with radiating avenues in front of the palace. Its interiors are sumptuous, and some of the rooms were opened to the public in 1993 to help pay for the rebuilding of parts of *Windsor castle after the fire in 1992. Apart from the rich décor, the visitor may see examples of works of art from the royal collections, supplemented by the changing exhibitions in the nearby Queen's Gallery, converted in 1962 from the palace chapel. PW

Buckinghamshire has little geographical unity and seems to be an entirely artificial creation. The chalk hills of the Chilterns run across the middle of the county from south-west to north-east. The area to the south drains into the Thames, which forms the southern boundary. North of the Chilterns stretches the vale of Aylesbury, rich clay farming land, and north of that again the valley of the Ouse, looking towards Northampton, Bedford, and the midlands. Communications between north and south have always been poor, and Olney in the north, where William Cowper lived, was in a different world from Stoke Poges in the south, where *Gray wrote 'Elegy in a Country Churchyard'.

The diffuseness of the shire was increased by the fact that the county town was not Aylesbury, near the middle, but the smaller town of Buckingham in the extreme north-west corner. For centuries there was rivalry between the two and in the 1740s the assizes were moved to Aylesbury and then back again. Tradition looked upon Buckingham as deeply conservative and Aylesbury as radical. But Aylesbury in the Hanoverian period was venal rather than progressive. Most of the numerous Buckinghamshire parliamentary boroughs were under the secure control of the neighbouring gentry families—the Drakes at Amersham, or the Wallers and Pettys at Wycombe. The powerful county families included the Verneys of Claydon and, when their money ran out, the Grenvilles of Stowe, who had complete command over Buckingham itself.

Pre-Roman Buckinghamshire was in *Catuvellauni territory, and *Cunobelinus, grandson of *Cassivellaunus, is believed to be commemorated in Great and Little Kimble, near *Chequers. The Roman road *Watling Street ran across the north-east of the county through Stony Stratford, intersecting with the older *Icknield Way just east of the county near Dunstable. In the 6th cent. the area was disputed between the Britons and the English, the latter reported by the *Anglo-Saxon Chronicle* to have captured Aylesbury in 571. The region became part of the kingdom of *Mercia. As a county Buckinghamshire probably developed after *Edward the Elder, king of Wessex, launched his great advance against the Danes and fortified Buckingham as a frontier outpost in 918. It was first mentioned as a county in 1010 when most of it was overrun by a second Danish advance. In *Domesday Book, Buckingham was the only town to be separately assessed and appears to have been substantial. It did not maintain its pre-eminence and was overtaken by Aylesbury, Wycombe, Marlow, Chesham, and other towns. *Leland, in early Tudor times, found Aylesbury a 'fair town' with a celebrated market and the county gaol. Wycombe had parliamentary representation from early on, Buckingham and Aylesbury from the 16th cent., and Wendover, Amersham, and Marlow as late as the 17th cent.

Industrial development also came late to Buckinghamshire. Lace-making gave the county considerable prosperity in the 17th and 18th cents. but declined sharply in the 19th. Slough did not even merit a separate entry in the 1801 census but was included in the parish of Upton. The 19th cent. gave the county a network of railways, which stimulated the growth of Wolverton, Slough, and Wycombe. Proximity to London led to great changes in the 20th cent., the balance of population moving south. Between 1931 and 1951 the rate of growth was third in the whole country, largely due to Wycombe and Slough, which, by 1961, had grown to 50,000 and 80,000, while Buckingham remained at just over 4,000. The development of Milton Keynes in the north-east as a new town promises to restore the balance. By the Local Government Act of 1972 Buckinghamshire lost Slough and Eton in the extreme south to Berkshire. The Banham commission on local government reported in 1994 in favour of abolishing the county, save for ceremonial purposes, and substituting four unitary authorities, Milton Keynes, Aylesbury Vale, Wycombe, and South Buckinghamshire. JAC

budget. The practice of devising an annual programme for financial legislation has been attributed to William Lowndes, an official in the Treasury throughout the half-century after 1675. The term dates from the 1730s and is derived from the wallet or 'bougette' in which the chancellor of the Exchequer carried his proposals. Early in the 18th cent. the principle was established that funding and expenditure proposals should be the preserve of the House of Commons, and that financial initiatives within the Commons should be the preserve of the Treasury ministers. In the 19th cent. the practice developed by which the annual budget comprised an assessment of Exchequer income and expenditures for the past financial year, together with estimates of expected spending needs in the forthcoming year and the fiscal steps required to provide for them. Since the Second World War, when economic management has become a more important part of the political process, the budget has become a means of indicating government economic strategies to other economic agencies, a statement of the state of the economy, and a means of political and media manipulation. As the range of economic instruments at the disposal of the state has increased, together with the need to respond far more frequently to changing events, the budget has lost some of its importance. CHL

'Bulge, battle of the', 1944. In September 1944 Hitler decided to counter Anglo-American success in France and Belgium by secretly preparing powerful forces, including twelve Panzer divisions, to break through in the Ardennes, cross the Meuse, and retake Antwerp. Allied supplies would be blocked and allied troops north of Antwerp isolated. Selecting a period of bad weather to palliate allied air superiority, the Germans attacked on 16 December 1944. They used their remaining trucks to support rapid advance into a salient; now, however, the British and Americans had superior mobility and contained the initial surprise success gained by the Germans. Moreover, the American defenders held road junctions, notably at Bastogne where 101 Airborne, hurriedly moved there, withstood a six-day siege. At the time, the surprise German attack caused dismay at an unexpected reassertion of enemy strength and, later, doubts about the efficiency of allied intelligence. *Montgomery reinforced his unpopularity by seeming publicly to criticize American generals. RACP

Buller, Sir Redvers Henry (1839–1906). Soldier. Buller was a man of outstanding personal bravery, but his indecisiveness in high command cast a shadow over his later career. He took part in the *Zulu War (1878–9), winning the Victoria Cross, and in the *Gordon relief expedition in the Sudan (1884–5). He then climbed the army ladder steadily until refusing the post of commander-in-chief in India, before reluctantly agreeing to command in South Africa in 1899 at the beginning of the second Anglo-Boer War. He then made the unwise decision to divide his force into three columns, he himself commanding one. This resulted in a series of piecemeal defeats and his replacement in overall command by Lord *Roberts. Buller's subsequent leadership of his own column demonstrated the same qualities of hesitation, and his later public attempt to refute his critics was not well received. KI

Bunker Hill, battle of, 1775. After the encounter at *Lexington in April 1775, General Gage found himself trapped in Boston by the American rebels. The town was dominated by Dorchester heights to the south and the Charlestown peninsula to the north. On 16 June the Americans dug in on Bunker Hill, near Charlestown, and the following day Gage sent 2,000 troops to dislodge them. This they accomplished but at the cost of more than 1,000 killed and wounded. The British paid tribute to the courage and tenacity which the rebels had shown. JAC

Bunyan, John (1628–88). Puritan author. Son of a brazier near Bedford, but mustered in a parliamentary levy and stationed at Newport Pagnell 1644–6, Bunyan resumed his father's trade, then suffered a severe religious crisis initiated by his wife's piety. Subsequently joining a nonconformist group in Bedford under John Gifford, he began to preach (1657). The Restoration revived hostilities against conventicles, so his refusal to give any undertaking not to continue preaching led to imprisonment for most of the next twelve years, until the *Declaration of Indulgence (1672); the county gaol being less brutal than portrayed by legend, the enforced leisure produced a stream of theological and devotional works. After further brief confinement (1677), he became pastor of the Bedford separatist church, was nicknamed 'Bishop Bunyan' for his zeal in pastoral work and preaching, and continued to write. The vitality of **Pilgrim's Progress*, written in gaol, made him a household name. ASH

Burbage, Richard (*c.*1567–1619). Actor. Son of an actor/manager, Burbage gained from his lifelong experience of permanent (then a novelty) rather than travelling theatre to become an outstanding actor, esteemed by playwrights and audiences. Talented, versatile, and a leading player in the Chamberlain's Men by 1594, his relationship with *Shakespeare soon extended beyond that of fellow-players, or script-writer and player, as they shared the enterprise of constructing and running the *Globe theatre in Southwark, where he mainly performed. Burbage's versatility, suggesting a flexible rather than sonorous voice, and ability to get into the skin of a part (as in Richard III) was exploited by *Jonson and Shakespeare, and led to demand for his services for new productions. Excelling in tragedy (Hamlet, Lear, Othello) despite small stature and some stoutness, he also acted in plays by Kyd, Webster, Beaumont and Fletcher, and was additionally a competent oil-painter. ASH

Burdett, Sir Francis (1770–1844). A wealthy, patrician landowner, Burdett was an outstanding example of gentry or Tory-radical leadership of popular radical movements. For 30 years (1807–37) he was MP for the radical borough of Westminster, championing the cause of parliamentary reform and speaking out against corruption and patronage. When he was imprisoned in 1810 for a breach of parliamentary privilege, troops had to be called to disperse the crowds, in a manner reminiscent of *Wilkes. Burdett provided leadership for the radical reformers during the lean years of the Napoleonic wars; but when the parliamentary reform movement grew after 1816, with strong working-class roots in the industrial districts, his popularity waned. His ideas, like those of his early mentor *Horne Tooke, were derived from the past, and he justified reform by appeals to antiquity and custom, and the historic 'rights of Englishmen'. JFCH

Burford, battle of, *c.*752. *Æthelbald of Mercia was defeated by *Cuthred of Wessex, enabling Wessex temporarily to extend its territories north of the Thames. Henry of Huntingdon gives a very detailed account, some of which may be authentic. On the evidence of place-names, Stenton denied that Beorhford could be Burford in Oxfordshire. Wessex's gains were wiped out by *Offa's victory at *Benson *c.*777. JAC

burgages were forms of tenure. In the royal burghs of Scotland, they were properties held from the crown for rent and with the obligation of performing *watch and ward. In England, they were properties in certain boroughs held freehold: in parliamentary boroughs they could carry the right to vote, which gave them a value far in excess of their economic worth. Before the *Great Reform Act of 1832 there were 29 burgage boroughs. Since it was not difficult for patrons to buy up a majority of burgage properties, many burgage boroughs, particularly in Wiltshire and Yorkshire, were soon closed up and saw few elections: Thirsk was not contested between 1673 and 1832. The burgage boroughs had many idiosyncrasies. At Droitwich the properties were dried-up salt-pans; at Downton some of them were at the bottom of a stream into which the property had long since fallen; Old Sarum had only seven voters. In the 18th cent. patrons controlled the voters by issuing snatch-papers—title deeds to the property to be produced at the hustings to prove freehold, but at once taken away for safe keeping. In 1832 thirteen burgage boroughs lost both their seats and another nine lost one seat. JAC

Burgh, Hubert de (*c.*1175–1243). A younger son from a family of Norfolk gentry, he rose to govern Plantagenet England and marry a sister of a king of Scotland. Hubert entered John's service in the 1190s. His reputation was made by his obstinate defence of the castle of Chinon in Anjou against Philip Augustus in 1205. Appointed seneschal of Poitou in 1212 he held that province against French attack. Recalled to England he was appointed *justiciar at the height of the *Magna Carta crisis and remained in that office, with overall responsibility for the administration of England, until 1232. He played a decisive part in the war of 1215–17, first successfully resisting Prince Louis of France's long siege of Dover castle (1216–17), and then commanding the victorious English fleet at the August 1217 battle of *Sandwich (or Dover) which finally ended Louis's hopes of becoming king of England. From 1219 onwards Hubert was the most influential figure in Henry III's minority government, successfully presenting himself as a moderate and patriotic Englishman opposed to the arbitrary excesses of foreigners such as Fawkes de Breauté and Peter des *Roches. In 1221 he married, as his third wife, Margaret, sister of Alexander II of Scotland, and four years later was created earl of Kent. In 1232 his lifelong rival for royal favour, Peter des Roches, finally persuaded Henry to dismiss and imprison him. He made a dramatic escape from prison in 1233 and was reconciled to the king next year, but never recovered his former influence. JG

Burghley, William Cecil, 1st Lord (1520–98). Cecil, created Lord Burghley in February 1571, was the son of Lincolnshire gentleman Richard Cecil. After education at Grantham and Stamford grammar schools, he matriculated at St John's College, Cambridge, in 1535. He became part of the important humanist circle of Roger *Ascham, Thomas *Smith, John *Cheke, and Walter Haddon. Cecil married Cheke's daughter Mary in 1541, which may explain why he left Cambridge for London in the same year. Cecil entered Gray's Inn in May 1541. Mary died a year after the birth of their first son Thomas, but Cecil remarried in December 1545. His new wife was Mildred, daughter of the prominent protestant humanist Sir Anthony Cooke; Mildred, like Cecil, was a Greek scholar of some reputation.

His political career gathered pace after the early 1540s. According to Cecil's own chronology of his life, he sat in Parliament in 1543. He was knighted in 1551, and became a member of the Privy Council (and the principal secretary) from 1550 until 1553. He was central to the duke of *Northumberland's reconstitution of the council. Cecil did not go abroad during the reign of Mary, but offered his diplomatic services in 1554 and 1555; still, he seems to have been a member of a group of crown critics in the Parliament of 1555 and spent the last three years of the reign privately in Wimbledon.

Cecil's public life began again in November 1558, when he started working on the day of Mary Tudor's death to secure a comfortable accession for Elizabeth. Until he was appointed lord treasurer in 1572, Cecil was principal secretary and the queen's private secretary. He was a key link between Elizabeth and her Privy Council: this meant hard administrative work—collecting and analysing information from diplomats, preparing council agendas, and drafting papers for Elizabeth—but it also put him in a position to press his own concerns in council and present them to the queen. Cecil was at the centre of the campaign in 1559–60 to support the protestant lords of the *Congregation in Scotland. Like his Privy Council colleagues, Cecil wanted Elizabeth to marry and have heirs to settle the English succession; this was the central political issue of the decade because it involved Mary Stuart, her French connections, Scotland, and the competing ideologies of protestantism and catholicism.

Cecil was prepared to experiment with radical solutions to England's political problems. In 1563 he devised a plan for the 'interregnum' government of the Privy Council in the event of Elizabeth's death. He collaborated with Sir Francis *Walsingham in 1584 to involve Englishmen in a 'bond of association' to take action in the event of Elizabeth's assassination by catholic foreigners; in fact, Cecil had privately worked out the project in 1569. Although the second part of his Elizabethan career—between 1585 and his death in

1598—is generally viewed as more 'conservative', Cecil was still active as a parliamentary patron, co-ordinator of the Privy Council, master of the court of wards (which he had held since 1561), and lord treasurer; on top of this, he held the more 'local' offices of lord-lieutenant and justice of the peace in the eastern counties. He became, in a very real sense, the elder statesman of the Elizabethan regime.

Cecil's reputation is a mixed one. Some of his earliest biographers and contemporaries—John Clapham, his 'anonymous' biographer, George Whetstone, and Hugh Broughton—emphasized Cecil's anxiety over England's Roman catholic enemies, his political success, and his patronage of learning. *Macaulay argued that Cecil was purely an administrator, and this assessment stuck. Because Cecil did not flee abroad during the reign of Mary, historians have often assumed that he was not a strong protestant. In fact, he was part of a solid reformed culture at Cambridge; he knew and patronized radicals like Bishop John *Hooper and an English printer of Calvin in the 1540s and 1560s, John Day. Cecil had a keen sense of providence and a strongly apocalyptic view of the struggle between the protestant and catholic European kingdoms.

Cecil understood Britain and knew its geography intimately; he wrote his own historical account of the imperial nature of the English crown in 1584 or 1585. He also patronized historians and scholars like William *Camden. Socially, Cecil was determined to acquire the trappings of court, council, and noble status. He owned and built three houses—Cecil House in London; Burghley House in Northamptonshire; and Theobalds in Hertfordshire—and developed estates in Lincolnshire, Rutland, and Northamptonshire. Cecil suffered regularly with gout from 1566. He was interested in works on cosmography and genealogy and, as a political man with a classical education, owned a substantial library of Greek, Latin, and Italian books.

SA

burghs, a variant spelling of boroughs, is the Scottish term for privileged towns. David I is traditionally credited with the first foundations of royal burghs; after 1450, burghs founded by subjects (burghs of barony and burghs of regality) became more numerous. Scottish burghs differed in many respects from English boroughs: they were more uniform in their laws and customs; they had a more unified voice in national politics until 1707; and indeed the royal burghs (generally the most important towns) had their own *Convention from the 16th cent. Furthermore, four burghs acquired universities between 1411 and 1583, so that until the 19th cent. Scotland had more university towns than England. Since 1707 the differences between English boroughs and Scottish burghs have diminished, but not altogether disappeared.

DMP

Burgoyne, John (1723–92). Soldier and playwright. Of an impecunious Bedfordshire gentry family, Burgoyne was reputed to be the natural son of Lord Bingley. His career began with a runaway marriage to Lady Charlotte Stanley, daughter of the earl of Derby. The following year Burgoyne joined the army, retired in the 1750s, but rejoined at the start of the Seven Years War, serving with distinction in Portugal. In 1761 he was brought into Parliament for Midhurst, transferring in 1768 to Preston, a noisy open borough where the Stanleys had influence. He was fined £1,000 for violent conduct and was lucky to keep his seat. He spoke often in the House, shone in society, wrote verse and plays, and acquired the nickname 'Gentleman Johnny'. His big chance came with the war against America. The ambitious expedition from Canada down the Hudson valley was his own plan and he was appointed to the command. After a bright start, he was forced to surrender at *Saratoga in October 1777. He returned to England to clear his name, declared that he was a scapegoat, and became a vocal member of the opposition. When the Rockinghams took office in 1782 he was made commander-in-chief Ireland, resigning in 1784. He remained an active member of the Commons and in 1786 scored a stage success with *The Heiress*. Horace *Walpole called him 'General Swagger' and wrote that 'he had a half-understanding, which was worse than none'.

JAC

Burke, Edmund (1729–97). Whig politician and conservative political philosopher. Burke was born in Ireland to a catholic mother and protestant father. Brought up as a protestant, he was sent to a quaker school and then to Trinity College, Dublin. He studied law in London, but quickly turned his attention to writing. However, Burke's first love was politics and he became a member of Parliament in 1766. He remained an MP for virtually the rest of his life, and became a towering figure in the House of Commons, captivating his audience with spellbinding oratory. Burke had an unrivalled gift for portraying the wider significance of the issues of the day in terms of general principles, and as a result many of his speeches contain disquisitions on political philosophy. Indeed this was the way in which Burke understood the activity of political philosophy—as reflection on the principles which lay behind current political practice. He rejected the radical and utopian thinking of 18th-cent. writers such as Rousseau, who allowed their imaginations to run away with them, regarding them as little less than sacrilegious; for him the political traditions of a mature society were embodiments of the divine will. Moreover, for Burke, politics is the art of the possible; all social arrangements fall short of the ideal, but we should not reject them for that reason, since they may well be the best that are practicable in the circumstances.

Burke has often been accused of inconsistency. His stance on the plight of catholics in Ireland—he deplored their savage treatment by the protestant ascendancy—and of Indians in Bengal—he denounced the barbarisms perpetrated by the East India Company—is contrasted with his rejection of the idea of natural rights advanced by the French revolutionaries, and his defence of customary patterns of government. Similarly, Burke's sympathy for the American colonists chafing at the imposition of taxes by the British government appears to contradict his insistence on the sovereign authority of Parliament. However, if we bear in mind the above organizing ideas of his political philosophy, we can see that there is an underlying coherence in his writing. In his defence of the Irish catholics, the Bengali Indians, and the American colonists, Burke was not arguing that they had natural rights to determine their own destiny, or that the system of imperial authority exercised over them was fundamentally illegitimate. Far from it; what Burke was asserting was that there had been abuse of legitimate (i.e. traditional) authority, and that such abuse must be corrected to prevent a backlash which could lead to the overthrow of that authority. Similarly, we can see consistency in Burke's apparently contradictory endorsement of the 1688/9 Whig revolution in England, yet denunciation of the 1789 revolution in France. In both cases he sought to defend traditional modes of political authority. The Whig revolution in England was a revolution averted, in that it preserved the established Anglican state from an unconstitutional conversion by James II into a Roman catholic polity. By contrast the French Revolution was a real revolution, perpetrated illegitimately against the wholesome foundations of a 'noble and venerable castle', the traditional and settled French state.

Burke's enduring reputation as a political thinker rests on the claim that he is the founder of conservative ideology. His **Reflections on the Revolution in France* (1790) is generally regarded as the epitome of conservatism, defending traditional political cultures. However, he recognized that some change was inevitable—indeed he held that a state without the means of change was without the means of its own conservation. He also strongly affirmed the modern principle of popular government. Although he was no democrat, Burke held that the primary organ of the British constitution was the House of Commons, and that Parliament owed its authority to the approval of the people.

As a practising politician and statesman, Burke also left his mark. His impassioned defence of the formation of political parties as a means of resisting the unconstitutional influence of the crown—he argued that when bad men combine, good men must unite—was an important step in the process of legitimizing party politics in Britain. This is not to say that Burke's endorsement of party loyalty was unconditional. On the contrary, he was himself responsible for splitting the Whig party over the issue of the French Revolution, by refusing to follow *Fox's approval of the revolution, and he has been accused by historians of thereby depriving the Whigs of office for the next 40 years. Moreover, although he only held minor office (that of paymaster-general) for two short spells under Lord *Rockingham, Burke exerted considerable influence on the government. His vehement condemnation of the revolution in France helped to stiffen anti-French policy in Britain. Similarly the sympathetic tone he adopted toward the American colonists contributed towards the *rapprochement* which was eventually reached by the British government. Finally Burke's obsessive pursuit of the impeachment of Warren *Hastings in the House of Lords for his iniquitous rule as governor-general of Bengal, though it failed to secure Hastings's conviction, succeeded in creating an irresistible momentum for the subsequent reform of the East India Company.

Perhaps Burke's epitaph should be that he was an extremist in pursuit of moderation. TSG

Burke and Hare. Edinburgh's reputation for medical excellence was jeopardized in the 1820s by growing public vigilance against grave-robbing for dissection purposes. Rather than turn resurrectionists, Burke and Hare smothered a sick lodger and sold his body, before murdering a further fifteen vagrants and street folk in 1827–8 for similar gain; encouraged by the easy money forthcoming, they were helped by the anatomist Dr Knox's lack of suspicion at the freshness of the corpses. After the discovery of a body in Burke's bedstraw, Hare turned king's evidence, Knox remained silent, and Burke was hanged and publicly dissected. Their activities hastened the Anatomy Act (1832). ASH

Burlington, Richard Boyle, 3rd earl of Burlington and 4th earl of Cork (1684–1753). Patron and architect. Following visits to Italy in 1714–19, Burlington determined to restore *Palladian architecture to the prominence it held in England during the time of Inigo *Jones. Burlington's protégé was William *Kent, and together they promoted Palladianism for the next thirty years. Burlington arranged for the publication of Kent's *The Designs of Inigo Jones* (1727) and after 1730 published Palladio's engraved drawings of Roman baths as *Fabbriche antiche disegnate da Andrea Palladio*. Notable among Burlington's own buildings are the dormitory at Westminster School, London (1722–30, rebuilt 1947), and the Assembly Rooms, York (1731–2, refronted 1828), which is a model of Palladio's Egyptian Hall, based on Vitruvius. Examples of Burlington's collaboration with Kent include *Holkham Hall, Norfolk (about 1734) and Chiswick House, Middlesex (from 1717), a Palladian villa whose garden layout and buildings reflect ideas expressed in Robert Castell's *The Villas of the Ancients, Illustrated* (1729) which was dedicated to Burlington. PW

Burma was ruled by the Alaungpaya dynasty from 1752 to 1885. Initially, the dynasty was expansionary, conquering (although failing to hold) Thailand and pressing west towards Arakan and Assam. However, it was severely checked and ultimately defeated by a counter-expansionary drive coming from the British in India. The British conquest of Burma was piecemeal, beginning in 1826 and not reaching completion until 1885. It partly came about as a reaction to deep Burmese hostility and the failures of 'informal empire'. But it also reflected growing economic ambitions. In colonial Burma, valuable resources of oil, tin, and rubber were more fully exploited and commercial rice cultivation was developed. Originally ruled as a province of British India, the country was given its own administration in 1937. Between 1942 and 1945, Burma was overrun by the Japanese—many of the British, famously, 'walking out' to India. After the war, hopes continued in the Colonial Office for a restoration of British dominance. However, an Anti-Fascist People's Freedom League had arisen under the leadership of Aung San to organize large-scale popular resistance to the Japanese. Now it was turned against the British. On 4 January 1948, the Independent Republic of Burma came into existence. DAW

Burma campaigns (1941–5). These involved three issues. One commanded American support, the attempt to reopen the land route to nationalist-held China to strengthen resistance to, and prepare for an attack on, Japan. In 1944 the Japanese, by extending their conquests in China, made this strategy futile. The second involved guarding British-controlled India; the third the reconquest of lost British territories, particularly Malaya, rich in rubber and tin. In 1944 General *Slim defeated a Japanese offensive and in 1945 *Mountbatten's South-East Asia Command organized the reconquest of Burma followed by operation Zipper, landings in Malaya, shortly after the Japanese surrender.

RACP

Burmese wars. The British in India fought three wars against the Alaungpaya dynasty (1752–1885), kings of Burma. The first, between 1824 and 1826, was a reaction to Burmese expansion which had reached Assam and was considered to threaten *Calcutta. Following a victory notable for its heavy casualties, the East India Company annexed Assam, Arakan, and Tenasserim and established a resident at the royal court. The second war in 1852 was provoked by a revolt against interference in Burmese affairs by the resident and led to the annexation of Pegu. The third war, in 1885–6, was a response to the throne's attempts to promote anti-British sentiments and to establish friendly relations with the French in Indo-China. In its wake, the dynasty was displaced, upper Burma was annexed, and the whole of the country was ruled directly as a province of British India.

DAW

Burnell, Robert (d. 1292). Clerical statesman. One of Edward I's chief advisers, Burnell was born at Acton Burnell in Shropshire, took holy orders, and came under the patronage of Edward when prince, accompanying him on many journeys. He acted as a guardian of the realm when Henry III died in 1272 while Edward was on crusade. On the king's return in 1274 he nominated Burnell chancellor, a post he held for the rest of his life. The following year he was made bishop of Bath and Wells. He took a prominent part in Welsh and Scottish affairs and in legal reform. By the end of his life he was said to have acquired more than 80 manors in nineteen counties. He was reputed to have fathered a number of children and, despite the king's powerful support, was passed over for promotion either to Winchester or to Canterbury. JAC

Burnet, Gilbert (1643–1715). Whig bishop and historian. Born in Edinburgh and educated at Aberdeen University, Burnet became professor of divinity at Glasgow at the age of 26. When he moved in the 1670s to London, he was for a time in favour with Charles II, whom he rebuked for 'sinful pleasures', but increasingly was involved with the opposition Whigs, and attended Lord *Russell on the scaffold in 1683. He then moved to Holland, was in high favour with William of Orange, accompanied him on the expedition of 1688, and wrote the declaration on landing. His reward was the bishopric of Salisbury, which he held for the rest of his life. He was governor of Prince William of Gloucester, who died in 1700. Burnet's best-known historical work is the *History of my Own Time*, published posthumously and dealing with the Restoration to the treaty of Utrecht. *Macaulay made great use of it and offered a strong defence of Burnet's character and writings. A more scholarly work was the *History of the Reformation*, which used archival sources (1679) and for which Burnet received the thanks of Parliament. A large, powerful, and confident man, Burnet was a vigorous preacher and a diligent bishop. He was in the thick of controversy all his life, a thorn in the side of the Tories, and lived to see the Hanoverian succession established.

JAC

Burney, Charles (1726–1814). Musical historian, composer, and organist, Burney was educated in his birthplace Shrewsbury and in Chester. In 1744 he went to London as apprentice to Thomas Arne, the composer of 'Rule Britannia', through whom he met *Handel. In 1746 Burney was introduced to Fulke Greville, who bought out his apprenticeship, enabling him to continue his studies and develop his career as an organist and composer. He obtained an Oxford doctorate in 1769. Burney travelled widely in Europe, researching his *History of Music*, published between 1776 and 1789. The entertaining account of his travels (1773) established his literary reputation and helped ensure the success of the *History* in the face of competition from a similar work by Sir John Hawkins. His biography, written by his daughter Fanny, incorporating some of his memoirs, was published in 1832. JC

Burney, Frances (Fanny) (1752–1840). Novelist and dramatist. Frances was one of the daughters of music historian Charles *Burney, in whose circle she met Samuel *Johnson and Edmund *Burke. A quiet observer of mankind, her first novel, *Evelina*, was published anonymously in 1778 and well received. The second, *Cecilia*, published in 1782, brought her society introductions, which led to a minor appointment at the court of Queen *Charlotte in 1786. Five years later, to the surprise of her friends and family, she married General d'Arblay, an impoverished French refugee. Between 1802 and 1812 they lived in France, and at the time of Waterloo she was in Brussels.

Fanny Burney edited her father's memoirs, which were published in 1832. Her own *Early Diary* (1768–78), first published in 1889, includes sketches of Johnson, *Garrick, and Mrs Thrale, and her later diaries, published 1842–6, give interesting insights into the court of George III, which she found dreary. JC

Burns, John E. (1858–1943). Trade union organizer and exponent of 'Lib-Labism'. Burns was born in south London. Despite little formal education he became an engineer, and involved himself in the Amalgamated Society of Engineers and more generally in working-class politics in London's dockland. An accomplished orator, he was one of the organizers of the great London dock strike of 1889, which marked a watershed in the development of trade unionism among unskilled manual workers. In 1884 Burns had joined the *Social Democratic Federation, and acquired a reputation as a socialist militant. But by the 1890s he had broken both with Marxism and with trade unionism, supporting instead the furtherance of working-class interests within the Liberal Party. Elected as an independent Labour MP for Battersea in 1892, in 1905 he accepted office as president of the

Local Government Board in the newly formed Liberal administration. Burns resigned from the government in 1914, apparently in protest against the declaration of war with Germany. He retired from Parliament in 1918. GA

Burns, Robert (1759–96). Poet, son of an Ayrshire tenant farmer. Well educated by an enlightened parish schoolmaster, Burns grew up with an appetite for literature which constantly jostled with his love of the vernacular culture of his region and country. His first creative period coincided with his father's death in 1784, his own unsuccessful attempts at farming, and a passionate affair with Jean Armour. It culminated in the publication of the so-called Kilmarnock edition of his *Poems Chiefly in the Scottish Dialect* (1786). This carefully crafted selection of poems, which was designed to show that Scots could be used as a vehicle of polite literature, was a literary sensation and marks the beginning of a Burns cult that has survived and prospered until the present day. It earned Burns the quite unwarranted reputation for being an untaught natural genius and quickly established him as Scotland's national bard, the man whose loyalties to the refined polite conventions of the English neo-classical literary tradition and to the simplicities of vernacular verse seemed to typify the cultural dilemmas of educated and ambitious post-Union Scots. Being lionized in Edinburgh proved an unnerving and complicated experience for Burns, who was on the point of emigrating to Jamaica when marriage, the offer of a farm, and an appointment in the excise in 1789 made him decide to stay in Scotland. The second creative period of his career was marked by his contributions to James Johnson's *The Scots Musical Museum* (1789–1803). These took the form of more than 100 brilliantly and delicately reworked vernacular songs and lyrics which some modern critics think are the ultimate vindication of his claim that he had transformed the literary potential of Scots and, indeed, of vernacular literature generally. He died in poverty in Dumfries in 1796 at the age of 37. NTP

Burton, Sir Richard (1821–90). Traveller, Arabist, and great Victorian outsider, Burton joined the Indian army in 1842. In India he learned numerous languages and much obscure lore, not least about Islam. Hence he was credible when he travelled to Mecca disguised as an Arab in 1853. Now famous, he led an expedition to Harar in north-east Africa before being chosen by the Royal Geographical Society to lead their great east African expedition of 1856. Burton discovered Lake Tanganyika in 1858. He was led by increasingly acrimonious arguments with his companion *Speke to insist for a time that Tanganyika was the source of the Nile. Burton was in fact happier as a traveller than as a strictly scientific explorer and his best monuments are more than 50 books with their masses of cultural information. He had tended to see Africans through the eyes of Arab traders, disliked the missionary approach to Africa, and favoured the racist outlook of the Anthropological Society. Later travels, sometimes as a British consul, took him to the Gold Coast, Mount Cameroon, Dahomey, Brazil, and the American West. He published translations of the *Arabian Nights* and the *Kama Sutra*. This and other exploits shocked many Victorians, including his wife, who destroyed most of his papers. RB

Bury St Edmunds and Ipswich, diocese of. The see, roughly conterminous with Suffolk, was created in 1914 out of the *Norwich diocese. Suffolk then had its own see for the first time since the *Dunwich bishopric collapsed under the weight of the Danish invasions, though Hoxne and Bury St Edmunds are reported to have been sees in the 11th cent. St Edmund's abbey, founded by *Cnut in memory of the East Anglian king martyred by the Danes (868), was from the first richly endowed and, with its 170 manors, ranked amongst the foremost in England. The cathedral at Bury St Edmunds is the former 15th-cent. Perpendicular parish church adjoining the tower of the ruined former Norman abbey. Transepts and central tower have been added to the cathedral in the 20th cent.; further extensions were completed in 1990. The bishop's residence is at Ipswich. Suffolk is well known for its many magnificent parish churches. WMM

Busaco, battle of, 1810. After making peace with Austria by the treaty of Schönbrunn, Napoleon resolved to drive the English out of Spain and Portugal. Masséna was dispatched with a large force while *Wellington prepared his defensive line at *Torres Vedras. On 27 September 1810 Masséna, with considerable numerical superiority, launched an attack at Busaco, 125 miles north-east of Lisbon, but failed to make progress and took heavy losses. Wellington retired to Torres Vedras, from which he counter-attacked the following year. JAC

buses are road vehicles carrying passengers by short stages on fixed routes, picking up and setting down by request. The word is an abbreviation of 'omnibus'. They were introduced by Shillibeer to London from Paris in July 1829, carrying 20 passengers drawn by three horses, soon reduced for economy to two-horse traction, with twelve inside and three outside seats. During the 1830s and 1840s buses spread to Manchester, Glasgow, Birmingham, and other major centres. Successive reductions in their taxation 1842–70 raised capacity and reduced fares: the introduction of 'knifeboard' seats on the roof in the 1840s increased capacity to 22; and the double-deck, 'garden seat' horse-bus, which carried 26, proved the limit of its development. Expensive to run, buses were restricted to the middle-class market, and were uneconomic by comparison with trams, which relegated them to a support role in many towns. By contrast, in London where trams were excluded from the city, the bus predominated, and passenger journeys grew fivefold to 300 million, 1860–96.

The motor bus, introduced to Edinburgh in 1898, spread rapidly with more reliable and efficient designs from 1908, transformed the market, raising capacity and reducing fares, and democratized usage. In London passenger journeys reached over 750 million in 1914, near parity with the total for trams and trolleybuses, and had overtaken them by the early 1920s. With the two-horse bus team producing up to 8 tons of manure per annum, motorization was also critical to the cleansing of city streets, and the horse bus disappeared from London in 1914, and everywhere else during the 1920s. By the late 1930s, there were 50,000 buses on the road, performing around two-thirds of road passenger journeys, and as many passenger miles as the railways.

Organizationally, growth outside London was chaotic before 1930: much bus business was highly competitive, with easy entry, variable standards, and the majority of firms operating pirate or irregular services; in some towns, by contrast, municipal or private operators enjoyed near monopoly. The London General Omnibus Company, a French foundation of 1855, experienced strong competition as motor vehicles were introduced, but re-established monopoly in the London Electric Railways grouping of 1912. Competition returned, from the *Chocolate Express* and around 200 others 1922–4, when it was restrained by Labour's co-ordinating regulation in the aftermath of a bus strike, and unification came with the London Passenger Transport Board in 1933. Elsewhere, the Road Traffic Act of 1930 introduced control and fostered concentration, and by 1939 the majority of services were provided by around 100 municipal operators, and the Tilling/British Electric Traction and Scottish Motor Traction private groups, both with substantial railway involvement. Britain was largely mapped out into regional monopolies or cartels such as Crosville, Ribble, and Southdown, akin to the situation in London, with strong backward linkages to manufacturers like Leyland and AEC.

Bus services were not nationalized directly by the Transport Act of 1947, but the British Transport Commission acquired railway bus interests under it (1948), and Tilling (1948) and Scottish Motor Traction (1949) by purchase. Many independent and municipal undertakings remained, along with the large group of British Electric Traction. Further acquisitions by BTC were debarred by legislation in 1953, when the Thesiger Committee also endorsed existing regulation by licence. Usage began to fall from 1952 in London, and from 1955 outside, as car ownership rose. The Transport Act of 1968 brought full public ownership of an industry half its 1952 peak, declining further to one-third by 1988. Local government reform in 1986 led to the breakup of this regime, and combined with doctrinaire deregulation to open the industry once more, producing in such cities as Glasgow a rainbow traffic jam of buses. By the mid-1990s the industry was less competitive, and was coming to be dominated by new private regional monopolies, as companies such as Stagecoach grew rapidly by acquisition.

JCh

Buss, Frances Mary (1827–94). A pioneer of higher education for women, Frances Buss started teaching at 14. She entered Queen's College, London, in 1849 and went on to found the North London Collegiate School for Girls the following year. Starting with 35 pupils, a year later it had 135 and a long waiting list. Buss was a fervent supporter of women's suffrage and campaigned to have university examinations opened to girls, giving much help to Emily *Davies in founding Girton College, Cambridge. Convinced of girls' intellectual equality with boys, she saw education as a means of providing women with careers and financial independence. In 1871 she added the Camden Lower School to the Collegiate. She was closely involved in establishing St Hilda's Hall, Oxford, as well as lobbying the Schools Commission to regard education for women as part of its remit. A contemporary jingle, attacking Buss and her fellow-campaigner Dorothea Beale, hints at sternness of purpose:

Miss Buss and Miss Beale
Cupid's darts do not feel.
How different from us
Miss Beale and Miss Buss.

PG; SMC

Bute, John Crichton-Stuart, 3rd marquis of (1847–1900). Philanthropist and scholar. Bute inherited the title and large estates at the age of 6 months. After education at Harrow and Christ Church, Oxford, he converted to the catholic church. Much of his time was devoted to the development of Cardiff docks and to the family estates in Glamorgan. He was twice mayor of Cardiff and president of the University College. In Scotland, he was a benefactor of Glasgow and St Andrews universities, and took a keen interest in Scottish history, on which he published. From 1892 to 1898 he was rector of St Andrews. A retiring disposition prevented him taking a prominent political role, but he is a good example of a late Victorian nobleman dedicated to university and municipal matters. The *Daily Chronicle* wrote, on his death, that 'there is probably no similar estate in the country where an immense commercial empire has been fostered on one man's property'.

JAC

Bute, John Stuart, 3rd earl of [S] (1713–92). Prime minister. Bute served as tutor to the prince of Wales from 1755, thereby acquiring a level of influence which gave rise to political controversy after the latter's succession as George III in 1760. Initially holding only a court appointment, Bute rose to become secretary of state in 1761 and then 1st lord of the Treasury in May 1762 until his resignation the following April. Disheartened by the difficulties in implementing the theoretical reign of virtue which had so impressed his royal pupil, Bute gave up the struggle. If he therefore appears a political coward, some mitigating circumstances can be found in the campaign of vilification conducted against him. This offensive was grounded in blatant anti-Scottish prejudice and included the scurrilous accusation of sexual involvement with the king's mother. Political antagonism towards Bute continued after his resignation; and exaggerated fears about his influence (as a 'minister behind the curtain') destabilized the administrations of both *Grenville and *Rockingham. The Bute myth provided some understandable consolation for politicians who found themselves excluded from power, but, in the case of the Rockinghamites, it also supplied the starting-point for a broader ideology of opposition to secret influence. The precise date at which Bute ceased to hold any sway over the king cannot be absolutely determined; that his influence was waning towards extinction from as early as 1765 is plausible, not least because the king outgrew his earlier dependence. Bute was by no means an incompetent statesman and his diplomacy leading to the peace of *Paris of 1763 is now recognized on its merits. Beyond the sphere of politics, he was not only a patron of education, literature, and the fine arts, but also a keen student of science, with a particular interest in botany. DW

butler. The Norman office of chief butler did not develop into one of the great offices of state. The main duty was to supervise the coronation banquets, which were abandoned after the fiasco of 1821. In England the office was hereditary in the earls of Arundel and their successors the dukes of Norfolk. The chief butler of Ireland gave the name to the Butler family, earls and dukes of Ormond. JAC

Butler, Joseph (1692–1752). Bishop. Butler attended a dissenting academy in Gloucestershire before conforming to the Church of England and graduating from Oriel College, Oxford. He advanced in his profession under the patronage of Bishop Talbot (of Salisbury and Durham) and Lord Chancellor Talbot, and also gained the favour of Queen Caroline, who commended him to George II on her deathbed. He was appointed bishop of Bristol in 1738, dean of St Paul's in 1740, and bishop of Durham in 1750. His major publications were *Fifteen Sermons* (1726) and *The Analogy of Religion* (1736). His contribution to the deistic controversy stressed the role of conscience in opposition to Hobbesian self-interest. Though Butler's reasoning was greatly admired, for example by *Gladstone, who spent the last years of his life editing his works, he assumed too readily that conscience always speaks clearly and that it says the same thing in all societies, and his argument that conscience and self-interest necessarily coincide seems facile: 'conscience and self-love, if we understand our true happiness, always lead us the same way.' JAC

Butler, Josephine (1828–1906). Campaigner for women. Born in Northumberland, daughter of John Grey, a political agent for the Whigs, she married George Butler, an academic and later dean of Winchester, in 1852. She first took up philanthropic work amongst poor women in Oxford and continued it after moving to Liverpool in 1864. She became president of the North of England Council for the Higher Education of Women (1869–70) and secretary (1869–85) of the Ladies' National Association for the Repeal of the Contagious Diseases Acts, passed in 1866–9 to regulate prostitution in garrison towns and ports. She campaigned against this abuse of women's rights and its double standard of morality until repeal in 1883–6. In 1874 she took up the cause of girls exported for prostitution, and later supported W. T. Stead's National Vigilance Association. She withdrew from public life after the death of her husband in 1890. ER

Butler, Richard Austen (1902–82). Born in India and educated at Cambridge, 'Rab' Butler entered Parliament in 1929 as MP for Saffron Walden. As president of the Board of Education he was responsible for the Education Act (1944) which introduced a tripartite secondary system and the '11-plus' examination. During his time as chairman of the Conservative research department, Butler helped to reconcile the Tories to the welfare state, reviving their fortunes in the post-war era. He served in all three of the great offices of state, as chancellor (1951–5), home secretary (1957–62), and foreign secretary (1963–5). He was twice passed over for leadership of the party in favour of *Macmillan in 1957 and Douglas-*Home in 1963. Butler retired from politics in 1965, became a life peer, and accepted the mastership of Trinity College, Cambridge. RAS

Butler, Samuel (1612–80). Poet and satirist. Few records of Butler's life survive, but after education at Worcester he served as clerk or secretary to a succession of noble families, gaining easy access to libraries. His commonplace books, however, say much about his ideas and opinions: in many respects a Baconian, with a practical and realistic outlook though temperamentally gloomy unless elevated by claret, he was deeply conscious of the self-deception, hypocrisy, and folly of mankind. His scepticism found outlet in satire, where even the newly founded *Royal Society was mocked. Publication of the burlesque **Hudibras* (1662) brought a brief period of fame before he relapsed into comparative obscurity again. Although the legend of his poverty and neglect was probably exaggerated, it was not until 1677 that a royal pension was forthcoming, and he died poor and disappointed. ASH

Butler, Samuel (1835–1902). Butler's grandfather was a bishop and his father a canon of Lincoln and he would have followed them into the church had he not developed religious doubts after graduating with a first from St John's College, Cambridge. He then spent five years sheep-farming in New Zealand, partly to escape from his father. Butler had many talents, was a very competent painter and photographer, and wrote music. As a man of letters, he turned to many forms, including scientific exposition, poetry, theological disputation, Greek translation, art, and travel. His first success was a satirical novel *Erewhon* ('Nowhere'), published in 1872, and depicting a country in which illness was a crime and the use of machinery forbidden. His posthumous novel *The Way of all Flesh* (1903) was written over many years and is partly autobiographical. It contained thinly disguised and brutal portraits of his father and grandfather—'could any decrepitude be so awful as childhood in a happy, united god-fearing family?'. That Butler was 'in an odd way dependent on the disapproval of his father' is a perceptive comment. JAC

Butt, Dame Clara (1872–1936). English contralto, who studied with Daniel Rootham and at the Royal College of Music with J. H. Blower. Her first major success was as Orpheus in Gluck's opera at the Royal College in 1892, a role she recreated in 1920 at Covent Garden under *Beecham, the year in which she was made DBE for wartime services to charity. Her career, however, centred on the concert platform, where her tall, imposing figure was matched by a powerful voice with a strident lower register. She was particularly associated with the music of Elgar, singing the première of his *Sea Pictures* (Norwich, 1899), conducted by the composer, in a dress reminiscent of a mermaid. ECr

Butt, Isaac (1813–79). Founder of the *Home Rule movement. At the outset of his political and legal career, Butt was a vigorous defender of an Orange Toryism. Increasingly, however, his unionism and his commitment to property right were tinctured with a strong national feeling: this was encouraged by the haphazard nature of government action during the years of the Great Famine. Defending the *Young Irelanders in May 1848, he urged that the detrimental economic consequences of the British connection might be offset through a subordinate parliament in Dublin. Although he sat for Youghal in the House of Commons (1852–65), he languished for a time on the margins of national politics. His defence of the *Fenian conspirators in 1868 restored his patriotic reputation. His federalist sympathies and broad political appeal were most clearly evident in his Home Government Association (1870): he was returned to Parliament in 1871 as a Home Ruler, representing Limerick. Butt helped to create a national organization for his cause through the Home Rule League (1873), but by the time of his death in 1879 he had been superseded by angrier and more militant lieutenants. AJ

Butterfield, William (1814–1900). Architect. Undoubtedly the most original of Victorian Gothic Revival architects, though not to the taste of those who like their buildings restrained. He was greatly influenced by *Pugin, and his early churches—he mainly built churches—were at least as stylistically correct as the latter's. He then discovered north Italian Gothic, however, which seems to have liberated his spirit. His first characteristic masterpiece is All Saints, Margaret Street, in his native London (1859); his most famous—or notorious—is Keble College, Oxford (1873–6), to which a common reaction is 'Who knitted it?'; and his biggest single building is that part of Melbourne Anglican cathedral (1877–84) which was built before its commissioners lost their nerve and contracted a duller architect to finish it. (It is worth the trip to Australia on its own.) All are distinguished by their polychromaticism, and by their Anglo-catholic atmosphere; although in fact Butterfield hated ritual, and never worked for the Roman church on principle. Photographs of him make him appear dour, and he lived a monkish kind of life. BJP

Butterworth, George (1885–1916). English composer and one of countless examples of the pity and waste of war. Educated at Eton and Trinity College, Oxford, Butterworth was a leading member of a group of musicians, including Cecil Sharp and Ralph *Vaughan Williams, interested in English *folk-song. His compositions were few and small scale, but Butterworth developed a distinctive voice, with a full and at times lush orchestration in his idylls *A Shropshire Lad* (1912) and *The Banks of Green Willow* (1913). In his setting for *Housman's poem 'The lads in their hundreds to Ludlow come in for the fair', Butterworth paid moving tribute to 'the lads who will die in their glory and never be old'. At the outbreak of war in 1914 he joined up, was awarded the MC, and died in action on the Somme on 5 August 1916. Vaughan Williams dedicated to his memory the Second ('London') Symphony. JAC

Buxton, Thomas Fowell (1786–1845). Anti-slavery campaigner and quaker philanthropist, Buxton married Hannah Gurney (sister of Elizabeth *Fry). In 1808 he joined the quaker brewers Truman, Hanbury & Co. (his mother was a Hanbury), which brought him into contact with the London poor of Spitalfields. Elected MP for Weymouth (1818–37) he advocated prison reform and ending the death penalty for forgery. He was a founder of the *Anti-Slavery Society in 1823, taking over from *Wilberforce as its parliamentary spokesman the following year. He carried resolutions in the Commons against slavery in 1824 and 1831, leading to the successful bill for gradual abolition in 1833. In 1836 he moved an inquiry into the apprenticeship system which was being introduced in place of slavery. Following his electoral defeat in 1837, he devoted himself to the ill-fated Niger expedition designed to end slavery in Africa. He was made a baronet in 1840. ER

Bye plot, 1603. James VI and I, plagued by plots in Scotland, was confronted by fresh ones as soon as he arrived in his new kingdom. The Bye plot was a hare-brained scheme, hatched by William Watson, a catholic priest, to seize the king at Greenwich and force him to grant a general toleration. It fizzled out, but the subsequent investigations led to the *Main plot, which brought down Lord Cobham, *Cecil's brother-in-law, and *Ralegh. JAC

Byland, battle of, 1322. The victory of his supporters at *Boroughbridge in March 1322 encouraged Edward II to undertake another campaign against the Scots in the summer. After besieging Berwick without success, he retired, pursued by Robert I Bruce. While the king was at Rievaulx abbey, Bruce's men attacked over the hills from Northallerton. They dispersed the royal rearguard at Old Byland, just west of Rievaulx on 14 October, but Edward escaped to York, losing most of his personal possessions. The battle was no more than a skirmish, but a king of England in flight in his own country was mortifying. JAC

Byng, George, 1st Viscount Torrington (1664–1733). Byng entered the navy at 14 from a family in straitened circumstances. In 1688, while serving as a lieutenant in *Dartmouth's fleet, he acted as intermediary with William of Orange and was rewarded with his own command. By 1703 he was rear admiral and was brought into Parliament in 1705 for Plymouth. From 1709 he was a lord of the Admiralty and commanded squadrons frustrating Jacobite invasions in 1708 and 1715. In 1718 he became admiral of the fleet and the same year won a crushing victory over a Spanish force at *Cape Passaro, though he was assisted by the ineptness of Spanish tactics. He was given his viscountcy in 1721 and served as 1st lord of the Admiralty from 1727 until his death. His fourth son was the ill-fated Admiral *Byng. JAC

Byng, John (1704–57). Byng's naval career got off to a flying start. He was a younger son of Viscount Torrington (George *Byng), the hero of the naval victory over the Spaniards at *Cape Passaro and 1st lord of the Admiralty 1727–33. He entered the navy at 14, was present at Cape Passaro, and reached rear admiral in 1745. Six years later he was brought into Parliament as a government supporter for Rochester. On the outbreak of war in 1756 he was dispatched to the Mediterranean with a squadron to protect *Minorca, under threat from the French. He found an enemy force landed on the island and a French fleet cruising outside. Byng's ships engaged the enemy but came off worse and Byng retired to Gibraltar, leaving Minorca to its fate. When it surrendered, the outcry was thunderous. Byng was recalled at once, court-martialled, and sentenced to death for not doing his utmost to engage, though with a recommendation to mercy. The recommendation was ignored and he was shot on the quarter-deck of the *Monarque* in Portsmouth harbour. Byng died with courage and composure and the memorial at Southill insisted that he had been the victim of political persecution. Voltaire's *Candide*, published in 1759, contained the famous observation that the English liked to shoot an admiral from time to time, *pour encourager les autres*. JAC

Byrd, William (*c.*1543–1632). Britain's leading composer during the Elizabethan and Jacobean periods, Byrd's large, varied output included English anthems and consort songs, Latin motets and masses, and keyboard and instrumental consort music. A pupil of Thomas *Tallis, he was appointed organist and choirmaster at Lincoln cathedral in 1563. In 1570 he became a gentleman of the Chapel Royal, where he was joint organist with Tallis, with whom he was granted a royal monopoly of music printing. Byrd published three collections setting English texts (1588, 1589, and 1611), yet he wrote few true madrigals, preferring the contrapuntal consort song for solo voice and viols (such as the elegy 'Ye sacred muses', written on Tallis's death in 1585).

Byrd's finest music was inspired by Latin texts. He was regularly listed as a recusant, virtually retiring from the Chapel Royal (where Elizabeth allowed Latin in the services) to live in Essex close to leading members of the catholic nobility. His two books of *Gradualia* (1605, 1607) supply music for the proper of the mass, complementing three masterly settings of the ordinary, whose finely balanced counterpoint matches the best of Palestrina and Lassus. Many of Byrd's Latin motets set penitential texts, treating Jerusalem as a metaphor for catholic England with powerfully expressive music. Joyful exuberance, however, pervades works like the madrigalian 'Laudibus in sanctis', as it does his virtuoso keyboard variations. ECr

Byron, George Gordon, 6th Baron Byron (1788–1824). Succeeded to the barony and Newstead abbey in 1798. After Harrow and Cambridge he embarked on the grand tour and a life of dissipation which provided material for his verses, in 1812 waking to find himself famous with the publication of the first two cantos of *Childe Harold*. In politics associated with the *Holland House set, his maiden speech was on the Nottinghamshire frame-breakers' bill, but he left England in 1816 after separating from his wife, heiress Annabella Milbanke. On the continent he befriended *Shelley, was present at the inception of *Frankenstein*, and published a stream of verse romances refining the features of the 'Byronic hero', a gloomy self-projection of their author, which shocked and fascinated Regency England. Affecting an aristocratic disdain for writers who were 'all inky thumbs', he was a more serious artist than he admitted. Saluted in Italy as 'il poeta della rivoluzione', in 1824 his love of liberty took him to fight in the Greek War for Independence. He died of fever at Missolonghi, his masterpiece *Don Juan* unfinished. Though the obituaries regretted such 'elaborate lampoons', the 20th cent. has generally preferred his more satirical vein. JNRS

Byron, John, 1st Baron Byron (1599–1652). A royalist commander in the Civil War, Byron was one of seven brothers who fought for the king. He was in action as a cavalry commander at *Edgehill, *Roundway Down, the first battle of *Newbury, and at *Marston Moor. Defeated at *Nantwich in January 1644, Byron managed to hold Chester for the king until February 1646. He then retired to Caernarfon castle, which he surrendered in June 1646. The rest of his life was spent in exile. JAC

cabal. Word meaning secret clique or conspiracy, given to Charles II's administration of 1671–3 which covered the time of the third *Anglo-Dutch War, the alliance with Louis XIV, and the suspension of the religious penal laws. The cabal was not a cabinet or unified ministry. The ministers, whose initials formed the word cabal, each had different principles and objectives. Lord *Clifford, who climbed from being a poor Devonshire squire to become lord treasurer, became a catholic and advocated war to seize Dutch commercial wealth and to make the crown more absolute. *Arlington, a courtier and careerist, always tried to implement what he interpreted as Charles's wishes. *Buckingham wanted to become chief minister: he affected popularity and favoured religious toleration. Lord Ashley, advanced to be earl of *Shaftesbury, also advocated toleration. The cynical *Lauderdale governed Scotland for Charles. The cabal disintegrated under parliamentary pressure in 1673: Clifford died, Buckingham and Shaftesbury went into opposition. JRJ

cabinet. The executive committee of the government, appointed by and answerable to the *prime minister. It evolved in the later 17th cent. out of the *Privy Council, which had become too large and too miscellaneous to be efficient. During Anne's reign, the inner group of ministers called themselves the cabinet when the queen was present, the lords of the committee when she was not. In 1710/11 there were 62 cabinet meetings and 106 committee meetings, the attendance at cabinet averaging eleven and at the committee five or six. Two developments of crucial importance were the withdrawal of the monarch from attendance during George I's reign, allowing the first minister to take the chair and impose his views on his colleagues, and the slow growth of the principle of cabinet solidarity.

In the 18th cent., the cabinet was overwhelmingly aristocratic. George *Grenville in the 1760s had a cabinet of nine, in which he was the only commoner—yet he was the nephew of a viscount and younger brother of an earl. Not until the later 19th cent. did commoners predominate: in 1892 *Gladstone's cabinet had five peers and twelve commoners. Like most committees, the cabinet has tended to grow, with periodic attempts to prune it, particularly in wartime. The Fox–North coalition in 1783 had seven cabinet members; *Liverpool in 1812 had thirteen; *Peel in 1841 had fourteen; *Salisbury in 1895 had nineteen; *MacDonald in 1924 had 20, and John *Major in July 1995 had 23. JAC

In *Bagehot's words, the cabinet links the legislative part of the state to the executive. Its members are normally drawn from the majority party in the House of Commons, together with some peers: at the same time, they head the executive departments and effectively constitute the leadership of the party. The government as a whole consists of about 100 ministers, ministers of state, junior ministers, and whips: as a body, it never meets. The decisions of the cabinet are the decisions of the government. Its internal disagreements are governed by the hallowed doctrine of collective responsibility, which declares that decisions taken by the cabinet are binding on all its members, and indeed on all members of the government. A minister who disagrees with his cabinet colleagues may express those differences within the cabinet room, but unless he resigns, he may not voice them outside. To the world beyond, the cabinet presents a united front, however harsh the disputes may have been.

The 20th cent. saw the transformation of the 19th-cent. cabinet under the twin impact of war and welfare. The First World War led to the introduction of the cabinet secretariat, one of whose tasks was to minute the decisions of the cabinet. What is remarkable is that the cabinet had for so long been run on the basis of human memory. The exigencies of war meant that the cabinet could no longer work in such a casual way, but the growing functions of the state in economic and social matters would, in any case, have required the development.

The extension of the state's functions imposed a further burden on an institution better suited to the minimal state of the 19th cent. Committees had long been a feature of the cabinet but they were *ad hoc* and temporary. The modern system of permanent standing committees of the cabinet dates effectively from the Second World War. Small committees of ministers, chaired by either the prime minister or a senior member of the government and including ministers not in the cabinet, deal with matters too important, too sensitive, or too broad to be determined within a single department. Over the years the system developed, so that by 1995 there were nineteen cabinet committees or subcommittees. These included the committee on economic and domestic policy, chaired by the prime minister; another on the environment, presided over by the deputy prime minister; and a committee on public expenditure whose chairman was the chancellor of the Exchequer.

These committees have, in effect, become subcabinets. Membership is small and largely consists of those ministers whose departments are most closely concerned. Their brief is to resolve as many issues as possible without going to the full cabinet, and if they cannot reach a decision to refer the question to that body. The powers of cabinet committees are therefore extensive and the principle of collective responsibility applies as forcefully there as to the cabinet itself.

The permanent committees are not the only way in which decisions are taken outside the full cabinet. Quite apart from decisions ministers reach in their departments, decisions may be taken by officially constituted *ad hoc* committees or by the prime minister after consultation with another minister or after discussion with informal groups of ministers. Many decisions going beyond departmental boundaries, or involving questions of general government policy, are taken outside the traditional full cabinet.

The crucial problem of 20th-cent. cabinet government has been to adapt an institution which developed in the 19th cent. Though the cabinet has grown in size in absolute terms, a smaller proportion of ministers are appointed to it. Cabinet committees were one response: another solution has been to create super-ministries, e.g. the Department of the Environment, headed by a secretary of state who sits in the cabinet, containing a number of subordinate ministers who, in earlier years, would have been heads of their department and would have had a seat in the cabinet.

The growth of cabinet committees has meant that the cabinet itself no longer has the central importance it once had. 'Cabinet meetings', said Nigel Lawson, former chancellor of the Exchequer, 'are ninety per cent of the time a dignified [rather than an] efficient part of cabinet government.'

Recent discussion has emphasized the increasing power of the prime minister and the declining status of the cabinet. The argument has perhaps been overdone, but there is little doubt that during the 20th cent. the office of prime minister has expanded in power, partly at the expense of the cabinet. However, the cabinet remains the ultimate court of appeal within the government. Moreover, it remains, along with Parliament and in certain fields the judiciary, one of the organs which confers legitimacy possessed neither by cabinet committees nor by the prime minister himself. HB

Cabot, John (d. 1498) and **Sebastian** (1474–1557). Much obscurity surrounds the lives of the Cabots, father and son, and their precise roles in the discovery of the Americas. But they discovered and defined the north-east American coast as part of a continent and Sebastian set the British on the long and fruitless search for polar passages to the Orient. Genoese born, but working for Venice and Spain, John came to Bristol in 1493 and was inspired by Columbus to try to cross the Atlantic. After one failure, he reached Cape Breton and Newfoundland in the *Matthew* in 1497, thinking initially that he had reached Cathay. He died on an attempted repeat voyage. Sebastian may have been with him in 1497 but certainly attempted the North-West Passage to the Orient in 1508. Possibly he reached the entrance to Hudson's Bay before navigating to a disputed extent southwards along the North American coast. With a decline in English interest, Sebastian sailed with a Spanish expedition to the river Plate in 1526–30 and was influential as a cartographer and trainer of pilots. In 1547, he returned to English service, advised on maritime matters, and helped to found the Company of *Merchant Venturers which, in searching for a North-East Passage, opened up trade with Russia. RB

Cade, Jack (d. 1450). Leader of Kentish rebellion. Cade's identity remains a mystery. Military experience is suggested by his capacity to organize, lead, and attempt to discipline the thousands of men from Kent and adjoining counties who began to rise late in May 1450. He adopted the name of John Mortimer, apparently for propaganda purposes: there is no proof that he had any connection with that family or its head, Richard of *York. Cade harnessed a seemingly spontaneous movement of protest against the incompetence and corruption of Henry VI's government which, divided and demoralized, could not prevent the rebels entering London on 3 July. Here Cade's control of his followers crumbled, the citizens united to expel them, and the rebels were persuaded to accept pardons and disperse. Although himself pardoned (as 'Mortimer'), Cade remained belligerent and was fatally wounded when resisting arrest on 12 July. RLS

Cadoc, St. A leading 6th-cent. Welsh scholar. Trained by an Irish monk in Wales, he sought further instruction in Ireland, allegedly under Mochuta, abbot of Lismore, returning to study rhetoric at Llanspyddyd. His principal foundation at Llancarfan became a centre of religious and literary learning. Cadoc is known for his use of didactic aphorisms (e.g. 'conscience is the eye of God in the soul of man'), possibly reflected in a 17th-cent. collection of early Welsh sayings entitled 'The Wisdom of Cadoc'. An 11th-cent. biographer claims travels and foundations in Scotland, Cornwall, and Brittany. Cadoc's reported martyrdom in Italy is doubted. AM

Cadwaladr (d. 664), Welsh king. Son of *Cadwallon who devastated Northumbria before being killed by King *Oswald in 633, Cadwaladr himself suffered a serious defeat by the West Saxons at Pinhoe near Exeter in 658. His death in the widespread plague of 664–5 seems to mark the end of British hopes of recovery from the Saxon invasion. Though his deeds are not recorded, he is a significant figure in later prophetic poems, becoming, like King *Arthur, a semi-mythical hero, one who would rise again and lead his people to victory. The 12th-cent. *Geoffrey of Monmouth's *Historia regum Brittaniae*, which ends with Cadwaladr's death, and his 'Life of Merlin' also popularized such prophecies. Said to be peaceful and pious, Cadwaladr is the dedicatee of a number of churches in Wales, the church of Llangadwaldr in Anglesey claiming him as patron saint and founder. AM

Cadwaladr (d. 1172), prince of Gwynedd. Son of *Gruffydd ap Cynan and younger brother of *Owain Gwynedd, Cadwaladr played a prominent but tortuous role in 12th-cent. Wales. In 1137 he seized the northern part of Ceredigion but was prevented by the resistance of Cardigan castle from overrunning the south. Next he plunged into the English civil war on the side of the Empress *Matilda, possibly because of a marriage connection to Ralph, earl of Chester, and was present at *Lincoln in 1141 when Stephen was captured. He was then involved in serious family quarrels in Wales—first with his brother Owain in 1143 and then with two nephews who attacked his territory of Ceredigion. A fresh quarrel with Owain in 1152 drove him into exile in England until Henry II insisted on his restoration in 1157. Cadwaladr took part in the attempt to subdue *Rhys ap Gruffydd of Deheubarth, who had thrown off allegiance to Henry II (1159), but joined Owain and the other Welsh princes in resisting Henry's second campaign in Wales, which ended in English withdrawal. Cadwaladr was clearly of consequence but his hold on power was precarious.

JAC

Cadwallon (d. 634), king of Gwynedd. With his ally *Penda of Mercia, Cadwallon was responsible for the death of *Edwin of Northumbria at the battle of *Heathfield in 633 and for those of his successors Osric of Deira and Eanfrith of Bernicia the following year. In 634 he was himself defeated and slain by Eanfrith's brother *Oswald at the battle of *Heavenfield, near Hexham. Not surprisingly Cadwallon gets a consistently bad press in *Bede's *Ecclesiastical History*, especially for his brutal ravaging within Northumbria. In Welsh poetry he is celebrated as a 'lion of hosts over the Saxons' and his hostility to Northumbria is explained as a reaction to previous attacks on north Wales by the deceitful Edwin.

BAEY

Cadwgan (Cadogan) (d. 1111), Welsh prince. Cadwgan was one of the sons of Bleddyn ap Cynfyn who ruled Gwynedd and Powys from 1063 to 1075. He began in the 1080s by waging war against *Rhys ap Tewdwr of Deheubarth, who was killed in 1093 by the Normans. The following year Cadwgan led a great counter-attack against the Norman advance in Wales, in league with *Gruffydd ap Cynan, king of Gwynedd. A number of castles were seized, much of the Hereford–Gloucester border overrun, and Rufus himself led two expeditions to restore control. In 1102 Cadwgan joined with *Robert of Bellême, earl of Shrewsbury, in revolt against Henry I but was defeated. The last years of his life were taken up with the activities of his son Owain, who in 1109 abducted Nest, wife of Gerald of Windsor. This led Henry to depose Cadwgan and he was murdered by his nephew's followers while trying to re-establish himself in Powys.

JAC

Cædmon (d. 680). An elderly uneducated herdsman at the monastery of Whitby who, in a dream, miraculously received the gift of composing vernacular religious poetry. When he awoke, he remembered his song in praise of God the creator and added more verses. Learning of his new-found ability, the abbess *Hilda took him into the monastic community to receive instruction. He learned about Old Testament history, the Gospels and apostolic teachings, the Last Judgement, heaven, hell, and the judgements of God. According to *Bede, what he learned he turned into vernacular poems and songs. Only a few lines survive, recorded by Bede in his *Ecclesiastical History*. In an age when few could read or write, much less understand ecclesiastical Latin, Cædmon must have made a valuable contribution to the propagation of the Scriptures and Christian doctrine.

AM

Cædwalla (*c.*659–89), king of Wessex (685–7). A member of the royal kin of Wessex, Cædwalla is first met as an exile in the wild lands (*deserti*) of the Chilterns and the Weald. He made himself king of Wessex and extended his power widely. In particular he conquered the Isle of Wight, exterminating its royal dynasty. In this conquest he was associated with the great bishop *Wilfrid. Not long after, he abdicated and went to Rome. There he was baptized, died, and was buried in St Peter's with a noble Latin epitaph. Anyone who claims to understand the inwardness of 7th-cent. England should think again about Cædwalla.

JCa

Caen, treaty of, 1091. On his death-bed in 1087 William the Conqueror gave England to his second son William Rufus, and the duchy of *Normandy to his first son, *Robert. But each retained estates and supporters in the other's territories and relations broke down. In 1091 Rufus led an expedition to Normandy, forcing Robert to a treaty at Caen or Rouen. Rufus kept his Normandy possessions, but agreed to help Robert recover lost estates in Cotentin and Maine. Each named the other as successor should there be no children. They joined forces to dispossess their younger brother Henry (later Henry I) in Cotentin but by 1094 were at war with each other again.

JAC

Caerleon in Gwent was the legionary base of the *legio* (Roman legion) *II Augusta*. It became its permanent headquarters in the mid/late 70s AD, probably under the governor *Frontinus, subsequent to its postings at Exeter and Gloucester. Excavations at Caerleon have revealed impressive structures such as the military bath-house. Epigraphic and literary evidence connected with Caerleon has provided invaluable insights into the workings of both legion and province. An inscription from Goldcliff, a few miles from the fortress, implies that *II Augusta* was involved in the reclamation of waterlogged land. An inscription on a statue-base from nearby *Caerwent records that it was set up 'by decree of the council of the *civitas Silurum*' to Tiberius Claudius Paulinus, a legate of *II Augusta* at Caerleon, who went on to become governor. Two Christian martyrs, Aaron and Julius, died at Caerleon during the 3rd-cent. persecutions.

ES

Caernarfon castle (Gwynedd) was begun in June 1283 during the second Welsh War. In its form Caernarfon is different from any of the other Edwardian castles and, it can be argued, its distinctive features are deliberately symbolic of Edward I's political attitudes and his ambitions in Wales. First, Edward always maintained that his conquest was merely the reassertion of established right. Caernarfon castle incorporates the ancient motte of the castle of Hugh, earl of Chester, built at the end of the 11th cent. during the first Norman penetration into Wales, and thus resumes a lordship symbolized by the earlier fortification. Secondly, national monarchies of the time viewed their own power in imperial terms. Thus lawyers of Philip IV in France insisted that 'the king of France is emperor in his kingdom' and it is certain that Edward shared this interest. Caernarfon's Christian Roman associations were consciously fostered. The site of Caernarfon is Roman Segontium. In 1283, during building work, a body, thought to be that of *Magnus Maximus (383–8), alleged father of the Emperor *Constantine, was discovered and, on Edward's orders, reburied in the new church in the town. The castle, alone among the Welsh castles, was built with polygonal towers and banded masonry, imitating the land walls at Constantinople, believed at that time to be the work of Constantine himself. The king's tower in the castle, seat of government in the principality, was decorated with imperial eagles. Finally, Edward chose the castle to be the birthplace of his son, the future Edward II, but also Edward of Caernarfon and the first English prince of Wales. LR

Caernarfonshire. County of north Wales. It was part of the tribal territory of the Celtic Venedotae, later the Welsh kingdom of *Gwynedd. 'Arfon' is the land over against Môn (*Anglesey) and the county's name is derived from the Roman fortress Castrum (or Caer) of Segontium—Caer yn Arfon. With the destruction of Gwynedd by Edward I, Arfon, together with the Llŷn peninsula, Eifionydd to the south, and Arllechwedd, the land west of the Conwy river, were joined together by the statute of *Rhuddlan in 1284 as Caernarfonshire, a county of the principality of Wales. At the Act of *Union with England in 1536 the county remained, but in 1974 became part of the county of Gwynedd and was divided into three districts, Arfon, Dwyfor (Llŷn), and Aberconwy. In 1996 Môn was detached and Caernarfonshire, Eifionydd, and Aberconwy remain as the new county of Gwynedd.

The county was dominated by the Snowdon massif (Eryri) with the highest peaks in Wales (yr Wyddfa, 3,560 feet), a glaciated terrain of steep mountain slopes, deeply eroded valleys, and lakes. It is one of Wales's national parks. It is predominantly agricultural with sheep-farming as the main enterprise but extensive slate-quarrying and mining in the 18th and 19th cents. have scarred the landscape. There is still some slate production, but tourism, particularly hill-walking and rock-climbing, is a significant element in the economy. Hydroelectric schemes exploit the steep slopes and fast-flowing rivers.

Regarded as the primary mountain fastness of Wales, it has retained Welsh speech. In 1901, 89.6 per cent spoke Welsh with 47.7 being monoglot Welsh. By 1991 the percentage speaking Welsh had fallen to 61.5. In 1991 the total population was 133,338. HC

Caerphilly castle, in mid-Glamorgan, a baronial castle begun in 1271 by Gilbert de Clare, earl of *Gloucester, is 'one of the most remarkable defensive complexes ever completed by an individual [private] patron in the Middle Ages'. This huge castle is an early example of the principle of concentric fortification and heavily defended gatehouse. It is notable for its extensive water defences, a major engineering feat, involving the construction of a fortified dam to hold the waters in place. This aspect of the castle's defence seems to have been influenced by Gilbert's participation in the siege of *Kenilworth in 1266, in which the mere had played an important part in the successful defence of the castle. Caerphilly's scale was possible because Gilbert de Clare was very wealthy. Also as lord of Glamorgan he was subject to the law of the march, which meant that he could build a castle without licence from the king. Further he felt threatened by the possibility of Welsh rebellion and unsure of the king's friendship, as after Simon de *Montfort's rebellion he had promoted the cause of the disinherited, supporters of Simon. The result of particular circumstances, it played no significant part in subsequent Welsh history and on *Leland's visit 1535–45 was in a ruinous condition. LR

Caerwent. Roman town in Gwent and tribal capital of the *Silures (Venta Silurum). Roman occupation in south Wales pivoted around the legionary fortress at Caerleon until the Hadrianic stimulation of AD 121–2. Hadrian clearly considered the area ready for local self-government and formal constitution, and the Roman town of Caerwent was developed. Much of the town has been excavated and a partial plan is known, featuring forum, temple, baths, amphitheatre, and housing. The administration of the tribe and its capital by the town council is specifically attested in an inscription, carved on a pedestal for a statue. ES

Caesar, Julius. Roman politician and general. Born in 100 BC of a leading patrician family, Caesar rose to be consul in 59 BC. His provincial command included the Roman province of southern Gaul. In a series of brilliant campaigns from 58 to 54 BC he conquered Gaul as far as the Rhine, earning himself glory, money, and a battle-trained army. Late in the campaigning season of 55 BC he invaded Britain with a small force, but retreated when his fleet was wrecked by storms. The following year he returned with a larger army and defeated the tribes of south-eastern Britain under *Cassivellaunus, concluding a treaty. For these abortive incursions into a semi-mythical island the Senate voted a longer thanksgiving than for the conquest of Gaul; the expeditions were more for propaganda at home than as a preliminary to conquest. ASEC

Cairns, Hugh, 1st Earl Cairns (1819–85). The leading Conservative lawyer of the *Disraeli era. Of Ulster protestant stock and educated at Belfast Academy and Trinity College, Dublin, Cairns became a successful barrister in London and was Conservative MP for Belfast 1852–66. Solicitor-general and attorney-general to *Derby, he became lord chancellor under Disraeli, who valued his judgement, in 1868 and 1874–80. A vigorous defender of Conservative and protestant interests, he was party leader in the Lords 1868–70 (some would have preferred him to *Salisbury even in 1881) and led the peers' opposition to Irish church disestablishment until forced to compromise. An active legal reformer, he worked closely with *Selborne, his Liberal equivalent. Cairns's evangelical protestantism and firmness over Ireland gave him a wider party appeal than his legal distinction alone would have done. Austere and dour in personality, determined and logical in argument, Cairns, though often troubled by ill-health, was active in evangelical and philanthropic causes and a long-serving Sunday school teacher. BIC

Caistor by Norwich, Venta Icenorum, was the chief town of the *civitas* of the *Iceni, which covered present Norfolk and much of Suffolk. The site lies on the river Tas south of modern Norwich in the parish of Caistor St Edmund. There is no known Iron Age antecedent to the Roman site, indeed most significant late Iron Age sites lie in western Norfolk. The town was probably laid out late in the 1st cent. with a street-grid covering some 50 acres. A simple forum and basilica complex and an unpretentious public baths date around the middle of the 2nd cent. Also known are two Romano-Celtic temples, a large house, and evidence for pottery manufacture and glass-working. In the 3rd cent. walls enclosing 33 acres were built. By comparison with other towns of like status, Caistor by Norwich seems a late underdeveloper. This has been attributed to the after-effects of the *Boudiccan revolt, but it seems unlikely they could have cast a baleful shadow so far on. Its position away from the main centres of the Iceni may be part of the explanation. ASEC

Calais, possession of. Calais was in English hands from its capture by Edward III in 1347 to its loss in 1558. It was essentially a 'little bit of England overseas', being represented in the English Parliament from 1536. Soon after its capture, some of the French were expelled and English settlement was deliberately encouraged. Thenceforward, the town's officials, garrison, and merchants were almost exclusively drawn from the homeland. Its strategic significance was as both an outer defence for England and a base for campaigns into France, but it proved a constant drain on English resources. It was heavily defended, often housing 1,000 troops alongside a civilian population of *c.*5,000. It also played a key role as the staple through which all exported wool had to be directed. As a result, its company of merchants became increasingly powerful in the government and financing of the town. AC

Calais, treaty of, 1360. By this treaty, based on terms agreed at *Brétigny in May, Edward III gained Aquitaine, Poitou, Ponthieu, Guînes, and Calais in full sovereignty, giving up in return his claim to the French throne and to Normandy, Anjou, and Maine, and agreeing to ransom the French king, John II, for 3 million *écus*. The renunciations—by Edward of his French claim and by John II of sovereignty—were never formally made. Thus although the treaty marked a triumph for Edward III, John II's son, Charles V, was able to reopen the war in 1369 on the grounds that its terms had never been fulfilled. AC

Calcutta was founded on 24 August 1690 by Job Charnock of the English *East India Company at the village of Kalikata on the banks of the Hooghly river in *Bengal. It grew quickly as Bengal displaced *Madras as the company's leading commercial region. Following Robert *Clive's victory at the battle of *Plassey in 1757, a new Fort William was built and came to constitute the centre from which the company's political expansion in India took place. The town attracted a large British community and in 1834 became recognized as the official capital of British India. From the 1870s, a jute industry also developed to complement Calcutta's already advanced commercial and administrative functions. In 1901 the city had a population of 1 million and was the second largest in the British empire after London. However, in 1912 the capital was removed to *New Delhi and Calcutta began what has been a long decline. DAW

Caledonii. The people of the Scottish Highlands. For a people on the very fringes of the known world, the Caledonians make an appearance in the works of a surprising number of Roman writers including Lucan, Martial, Ptolemy, Dio Cassius, and several lesser authors. Xiphilinus tells us that they were actually a confederation of tribes rather than a single entity, and given the size and broken nature of their territory this is to be expected. Confederation is confirmed by Tacitus, who records that *Calgacus, who addressed the Caledonians before the battle of Mons Graupius, was 'one of many leaders'. If Dio Cassius is to be believed Calgacus would have been chosen for leadership for his boldness. Dio praised the ability of the Caledonians to endure cold, hunger, and hardship, and recorded that they lived on flocks, game, and fruit. Tacitus, whose father-in-law *Agricola fought the Caledonians, described them as red-haired and large-limbed, but little else is known of them except that they maintained their independence of the Romans throughout the occupation. They fought against Agricola in the late 1st cent., against *Septimius Severus in the early 3rd, and are recorded as one of Rome's most persistent enemies in the Verona List of AD 312–14. KB

calendar reform, 1751. To remedy the imperfections introduced by Julius Caesar, most of Europe adopted after 1582 the reform proposed by Pope Gregory XIII. Reluctant to follow popish examples, some protestant countries stayed with the old calendar, which became increasingly out of line. The Act 24 Geo. II c. 23 remedied this by eliminating eleven days in September 1752. At the same time, England fell into line with Scotland by starting the year on 1 January instead of 25 March. The protests were less concerned with 'give us back our eleven days' than with the genuine difficulties when contracts or birthdays fell between 2 and 14 September 1752, which disappeared. The 'new style' introduced a new anomaly, still with us, whereby the seventh month, September, became the ninth month. JAC

Calgacus is the name given by *Tacitus to the leader of the Caledonian confederacy at the climactic battle against the Romans under *Agricola at Mons Graupius in 83/4. Calgacus appears only to give a speech inveighing against the evils of Rome and exhorting his followers to resist as last of the free Britons. It contains the famous epigram 'ubi solitudinem faciunt pacem appellant', 'they create a desert and call it peace'. However, such set-piece speeches are a convention of Graeco-Roman histories; and as such we are hearing the words and thoughts of Tacitus, not Calgacus. ASEC

Callaghan, James (b. 1912). Prime minister. Callaghan has the unique record of having held all the highest offices of state: chancellor of the Exchequer (1964–7), home secretary

(1967–70), foreign secretary (1974–6), and finally prime minister (1976–9). His background was unassuming and he grew up in relative poverty after the early death of his father. He left school at 16 to obtain a secure job as a tax officer in the civil service. He joined the union and rose steadily, becoming assistant general secretary of the Inland Revenue Staff Federation in 1936. In the late 1930s he met Harold Laski, the Labour intellectual, who encouraged him to read widely and turned his mind to politics.

In 1945 Callaghan was elected to Parliament as Labour MP for Cardiff South. He quickly established his reputation as an effective debater and in the 1950s became recognized as a Gaitskellite. In 1960 he was defeated in the deputy leadership election by George *Brown. After Gaitskell's untimely death in 1963 Callaghan stood for leader but came third behind Harold *Wilson and Brown.

When Labour assumed power in 1964 Callaghan became chancellor of the Exchequer. However, his authority was challenged by the creation of a new Department of Economic Affairs under Brown. Callaghan's term was dogged by speculation against sterling which prompted a series of financial crises resulting in the devaluation of the pound on 17 November 1967. He was unhappy in the post, aware of his own limitations when it came to economic management.

Callaghan moved to the Home Office, where he attempted to deal with the problem of immigration from Commonwealth countries and was responsible for sending British troops into Northern Ireland in August 1969. As the only senior minister with trade union connections, Callaghan thwarted measures put forward by Barbara Castle and Wilson, in 1969, to reform trade union law.

Callaghan's term as foreign secretary coincided with the controversy surrounding Britain's entry into the EEC. The issue had split the Labour Party, Callaghan having criticized the idea of entry without fully opposing it. He set out to renegotiate the terms of entry agreed by the Heath government. Between June 1974 and March 1975 he visited foreign capitals using his union skills as a negotiator to settle details concerning the EEC budget, Common Agricultural Policy, and arrangements for Commonwealth countries. But the changes were largely cosmetic.

In 1976 Wilson announced his resignation and Callaghan beat Michael *Foot to assume the party leadership and prime ministership. The election was won mainly due to the desire of the party centre-right to stop Foot rather than on Callaghan's own merits. The outlook for Callaghan's term was gloomy from the outset, a fact he recognized. Inflation was rampant and he was aware that the country was not earning the standard of living it enjoyed, the deficit being covered by borrowing. In September 1976, the government was forced to apply to the International Monetary Fund for stand-by credit of £2.3 billion. The government had no effective majority and in 1977 Callaghan had to strike a deal with the Liberals to survive, the price being devolution bills for Scotland and Wales.

During the 'winter of discontent' (1978–9) the country was crippled by strikes as protests against wage restraint, despite the 'social contract' which Labour claimed to have with the unions. In March 1979 the devolution referenda failed. The Labour government lost a vote of no confidence by one vote and the subsequent general election. In October 1980 Callaghan resigned as leader and in 1987 became a life peer. An experienced and capable politician with a conciliatory and pleasant manner, he lacked the vision and decisiveness necessary for leadership. RAS

Calvert, George. See BALTIMORE, 1ST LORD OF.

Calvinism, the creed of Jean Calvin (1509–64), was largely as formulated in his *Institutes*, published 1536. Calvin was greatly influenced by St Augustine in inferring predestination from divine foreknowledge, and he therefore presumed that the elect, chosen for salvation, were known to God from before the creation. Free will was an illusion: 'we call predestination God's eternal decree, by which he determined with himself what he willed to become of each man . . . eternal life is fore-ordained for some, eternal damnation for others . . . it is very wicked merely to investigate the causes of God's will . . . when one asks why God has so done, we must reply, because he has willed it.' [*Institutes*, III. xxi. 5; xxiii. 2.] Church organization followed from that basic premiss, that the chosen of God—the elect—were entitled to no inferior place in worship, but should share government with the ministers. While Luther subordinated church to state, Calvin insisted on the supremacy of the church, with a *presbyterian form of government. Doctrinally, Calvin shared with Luther belief in the absolute authority of the bible and in justification by faith alone.

Taken into Scotland from Calvin's Geneva in 1559 by John *Knox, Calvinism became the national creed and was recognized as the established church in 1690. In England it struggled first to influence Anglicanism, then to overthrow it, and was in command from the Civil War to the Restoration. After 1660 it was at first the most powerful of the dissenting sects but lost ground rapidly to the *baptists and *congregationalists and in the early 18th cent. was infiltrated by *socinianism and *unitarianism. Its theology continued to influence groups within the protestant dissenting churches, particularly the Countess of *Huntingdon's Connexion and the Welsh Calvinistic Methodists. But the appeal of so austere and harsh a creed faded in an age of enlightenment and humanitarianism, and at the religious census of 1851 the Presbyterian churches had no more than 160 places of worship, while the Huntingdon Connexion had 109, the Welsh Calvinist Methodists 828, the congregationalists more than 3,000, and the *methodists more than 10,000. JAC

Cambridge, George, 2nd duke of (1819–1904). Cambridge, first cousin to Queen Victoria, was born in Hanover where his father was viceroy. He followed his father into the army, fought in the Crimea, reaching field marshal by 1862. In the 1830s he was considered by some a possible husband for Victoria but in the end married an actress. As commander-in-chief of the army for nearly forty years between 1856 and 1895, Cambridge was known for his resistance to reform, particularly those initiated by *Cardwell. The equestrian statue in Whitehall was erected in 1907. JAC

Cambridge, Great St Mary's. Commonly called the university church, this is a fine very late perpendicular parish church on a splendid site between King's Parade and the Market Square. Rebuilding of the original church was begun in the late 15th cent. but was protracted. The west tower, started in 1491, was only half-finished in 1550, completed in 1608, but the proposed spire was never added. Until the Senate House was built in 1730, St Mary's was used for the award of degrees. JAC

Cambridge, Richard of Conisborough, 1st earl of (1385–1415). Richard was the younger son of Edmund, duke of *York, and a grandson of Edward III. With no lands, he depended on Exchequer annuities which were irregularly paid until after his clandestine marriage to Anne Mortimer, sister of Edmund *Mortimer, earl of March, in 1408. No landed endowment accompanied his creation as earl by Henry V: it was really a courtesy title, recognizing Richard as heir to his childless brother Duke Edward. Apparently unhinged by resentment, Richard devised hare-brained seditious schemes in conversation with the Northumberland knight Thomas Gray of Heton and persuaded himself that Edmund Mortimer shared his motives for rebellion. It remains a mystery how Henry, Lord Scrope of Masham, became entangled in this half-baked conspiracy. Convicted for plotting the deaths of Henry V and his brothers, Cambridge, Scrope, and Gray were beheaded at Southampton. RLS

Cambridgeshire is a quiet, thinly populated, agricultural county, pleasantly hilly in the chalk south, flat in the north where it joins the Fens. The river Cam bisects the southern part of the county, flowing north to join the Ouse near Ely. It fell into three sections—the area around Cambridge, with a considerable number of small villages; that part of the Isle of Ely which centred on Ely itself; and a northern part of the isle, around March and Wisbech, which looked more towards Peterborough or up to the Wash, and retained a certain autonomy from Ely. It was a county of small landowners, puritan and nonconformist in sympathy, and politically independent. By the Local Government Act of 1972, Cambridgeshire took over Huntingdonshire and the soke of Peterborough, adding more than 50 per cent to its area.

Cambridge was a Roman settlement, the centre of a network of roads, joining to cross the Cam. Its importance was enhanced by the fact that it became the southern point of a complex pattern of inland navigation, centred on the Ouse, and supported by Roman cuts, as at Reach Lode and Swaffham Lode. It was early colonized by the Angles and a second settlement grew up south of the bridge. In the 7th cent. it was much disputed between the East Angles and the Mercians, and seems to have been devastated, since *Bede referred to it, late in the century, as 'a small, deserted fortress'.

A development in 673 was the foundation by St *Æthelthryth of a monastery at Ely, on a small hill rising from the fens. It rapidly prospered and survived sacking by the Danes in 870. Work on the Norman cathedral began in 1083 and it was given cathedral status in 1109. Ely's unique position was responsible for the bishop being granted quasi-*palatine status. It retained separate judicial and administrative systems and, though the Isle of Ely was made a division of Cambridgeshire in 1836, it was given its own county council in 1888, March becoming the county town. It was once more merged with Cambridgeshire in 1958.

Cambridge town went down before the first Danish onslaught in 870, was liberated by *Edward the Elder in the early 10th cent., but fell to the Danes once more in 1011. After the Norman Conquest, William I built the castle in 1068 and the town received a charter in 1201. Stourbridge fair on Midsummer common was one of the largest in Europe. The growth of the university in the 13th cent. produced prolonged antagonism between town and gown, and is responsible for that strange mixture of seat of learning and East Anglian market town which characterizes Cambridge today.

The northern parts of the county remained for centuries almost completely cut off by fen and water and developed their own unique way of life. Their inaccessibility made them a natural shelter for refugees, of whom *Hereward, leader of resistance to the Normans, was the most famous. Proposals for draining the fens were put forward repeatedly. *Camden wrote laconically in 1586 that the speeches in Parliament on the subject were 'a specious pretence of doing good to the publick'. In the 17th cent. a start was made, and the earl of *Bedford, through the work of Vermuyden, the Dutch engineer, succeeded in reclaiming vast areas. The results were not always successful, however, since the land dried out, shrank, and was often well below the level of the dikes. For decades to come, great stretches remained lake or quagmire in wet weather.

The fen part of the county, with its vast horizons and lonely windswept fields, has always been an acquired taste. Camden wrote of the 'Fen-men, a sort of people (much like the place) of brutish, uncivilized tempers, envious of all others . . . and usually walking aloft on a sort of stilts'. *Pepys paid a visit in 1663 to his poor relations living near Wisbech, was plagued by gnats, and did not much enjoy his journey 'over most sad fens, all the way observing the sad life the people of this place do live . . . sometimes rowing from one spot to another, and then wading'. Admiration for Ely cathedral was usually tempered by disgust at the town itself. Celia Fiennes nearly fell off her horse in 1698 and found Ely 'the dirtiest place I ever saw . . . a perfect quagmire, the whole city . . . I had frogs and slow-worms and snails in my room.' More than a hundred years later, things were little better, *Cobbett finding Ely in 1830 'a miserable little town'. Wisbech was a flourishing port and displayed some elegant buildings, but Pevsner wrote laconically in 1954 that the Fens 'grow much potato, sugar-beet and other root crops, and wheat, but they have never grown much architecture'. JAC

Cambridge University dates back to 1209, when, after a serious clash with the townspeople, some of the clerks at Oxford migrated to Cambridge. The first college, on a very modest scale, was Peterhouse, established in 1284 by Hugh de Balsham, bishop of Ely. Although it modelled itself mainly on the Oxford pattern, with the teachers forming the *studium generale* or corporation, Cambridge did not escape ecclesiastical control from Ely until the 15th cent. Royal patronage led to expansion: Henry VI founded King's College in 1441 and Henry VIII established Trinity College in 1546.

After the Reformation, the poor students largely disappeared, to be replaced by the sons of aristocratic and wealthy families. Many of the leading figures of the Renaissance of learning were associated with Cambridge, including Erasmus, long resident at Queen's College, *Ascham, and *Fisher. An Elizabethan statute of 1570 had the effect of making the wealthy constituent colleges more independent of the university. As puritanism flourished in East Anglia, and many of the students were local, Cambridge supported the parliamentary cause in the Civil War, while Oxford was the headquarters of the royalists: these political sympathies died hard and in the 18th cent. Whiggish Cambridge gave a much more enthusiastic welcome to the Hanoverians than did Oxford. Academically, Cambridge was characterized by the growth of science, or natural philosophy as it was called, with *Newton at Trinity its best-known exponent.

By the middle of the 19th cent. reform was long overdue. Cambridge supported the notion of a royal commission which investigated the two universities from 1850. Two Acts, in 1856 and 1877, did much to break the oligarchical nature of the government of the university. In 1871 Anglican religious exclusiveness was ended. Cambridge's scientific reputation was further enhanced with the opening of the Cavendish Laboratory in 1873, which became famous for its work in experimental physics. Two women's colleges were established at this time, Girton in 1869, Newnham in 1871.

The majority of the heads of colleges are called master. For the first six centuries of its existence, Cambridge, like Oxford, was a seminary, and until 1871 fellows were required to be celibates in holy orders. There are now over 30 colleges. The older foundations date from the Middle Ages, like Corpus Christi College (1352), Pembroke (1357), and Trinity Hall (1390). Several are Tudor, such as Christ's (1505), Trinity, and Emmanuel (1584). Downing was founded in 1800 after a protracted and troublesome legal action over the original bequest by Sir George Downing in 1717. Selwyn and St Edmunds came in the late 19th cent. (1882, 1896). During the 1960s, no fewer than six new colleges came into existence, Churchill (1960), Darwin (1964), Lucy Cavendish (1965), Clare Hall (1966), Fitzwilliam (1966), and Wolfson (1969). Robinson College opened in 1977. PG

Cambuskenneth abbey (Stirling) was one of several *Augustinian priories founded by David I of Scotland in the 1140s. It was situated close to Stirling castle and belonged to the Arrouaisian congregation. Though like many Scottish communities it suffered from English raids and entered a period of decline in the 14th cent., during which time the Scots Parliament sometimes met here, it later recovered; the abbot was granted episcopal status in 1406, James III was buried here in 1488 and a lavish rebuilding occurred early in the 16th cent. Later it fell under the control of lay commendators and after the Reformation became a temporal lordship of the Erskine family which had held the commendation since the 1560s, when it had an income of over £3,000. Little now remains but a 14th-cent. detached bell-tower. BJG

Camden, battle of, 1780. In December 1779 *Clinton took an expedition from New York to South Carolina in the hope of drawing on loyalist support. In May 1780 Charleston was captured with 6,000 rebel prisoners. Clinton then handed over to *Cornwallis. A counter-thrust by De Kalb and Gates from North Carolina was met at Camden on 16 August. Though Cornwallis was heavily outnumbered, the Americans were routed and De Kalb killed. JAC

Camden, Charles Pratt, 1st Earl (1714–94). Camden joined Middle Temple and was called to the bar in 1738. At first he found it difficult to obtain a brief but eventually found work and established his reputation. In 1757 he became attorney-general under *Pitt and Whig MP for Downton. In 1761 he was promoted to chief justice of Common Pleas. His most famous case came in 1763 involving *Wilkes and the libellous **North Briton*. Camden ruled that *general warrants were illegal and gained great popularity. He strongly opposed the taxation of the American colonies, declaring the *Stamp Act unconstitutional. He became lord chancellor in Chatham's second administration and although he opposed the ministry's American policy, retained the great seal until 1770. He remained in opposition until the death of Chatham, but became president of the council in the *Rockingham administration and retained the post until his death. RAS

Camden, John Jeffreys Pratt, 2nd Earl and 1st Marquis (1759–1840). Statesman. Son of the famous lawyer, Pratt came into Parliament in 1780 and succeeded to the earldom in 1794. After a number of minor offices, he followed *Fitzwilliam in 1795 as lord-lieutenant of Ireland, holding the post until 1798. The situation in Ireland was extremely tense: Lecky's opinion was that Camden was well intentioned but bewildered, and his lord-lieutenancy ended in the Irish rebellion. In 1799 he was given the Garter. He served in a number of Tory governments, as secretary for war 1804–5 and as lord president of the council 1805–6 and 1807–12. On his retirement he was promoted marquis. From 1780 to 1834 he held the lucrative sinecure of teller of the Exchequer. Canning's private opinion was that, by the end, Camden had become 'useless lumber' in cabinet. JAC

Camden, William (1551–1623). Camden was one of the finest of schoolmaster-historians. Born in London, he was educated at St Paul's and then at Oxford. From 1575 until 1597 he taught at Westminster School, where he became headmaster. From 1597 his position as Clarenceux king-of-arms gave him more time to devote to his passion for history. He produced two major works—*Britannia* (1586), a survey, county by county, of the antiquities of Britain as a successor to *Leland, and *Annals of Queen Elizabeth* (1615), which established the view of her reign as a *via media*. Camden's work was an example of the new civic history, intended as a handbook for statesmen: he eschewed invented rhetorical speeches, made use of state papers obtained through his patron Lord *Burghley, and wrote beautifully, with piquant and jocular personal touches. Worcestershire perry he dismissed as 'cold and flatulent'; the ruggedness of Northumberland 'seems to have hardened the very carcases of its inhabitants'; Britain is certainly 'the masterpiece of Nature, performed when she was in her best and gayest humour; which she placed as a little world in itself, by the side of the greater, for the diversion of mankind'. He endowed the Camden chair of history in his University of Oxford.

JAC

Cameron, Donald (1695–1748). Jacobite. Cameron of Lochiel's grandfather had taken part in *Glencairn's royalist rising in 1652 and fought for the Stuarts at *Killiecrankie in 1689: his father was out in the '15 and attainted. When Prince Charles Edward landed at Moidart in 1745, Cameron was the first chief to whom he applied. He advised caution, but agreed to lead his clan to Glenfinnan, where it provided the bulk of Charles's small force. Lochiel took part in the march to Derby and was badly wounded at *Culloden. Though he reached France with the prince in September 1746, he died after a few months in the French service. His brother Archibald, a physician, was out in the '45 with him and was hanged in 1753 when captured on a visit to Scotland.

JAC

Cameron, Richard (1648–80). Covenanting leader. Born in Falkland in Fife where he was a schoolteacher, Cameron became a presbyterian field preacher in the south-west of Scotland. In 1678–80 he was in Holland, missing the covenanting defeat at *Bothwell Bridge in June 1679. On his return he joined in issuing the Sanquhar declaration, which denounced Charles II and his brother James and declared them deposed. Tracked down by royal troops, Cameron and his brother were killed at Aird's Moss, near Auchinleck in Ayrshire. His followers, the reformed presbyterians, refused to accept the 1689 church settlement in Scotland. See CAMERONIANS.

JAC

Cameronians. Known as the 'Society people' until 1690, these covenanters of south-west Scotland followed the extensive field preaching of Richard *Cameron (1648–80) and Donald Cargill (*c.*1627–1681). After Cameron was killed in battle and Cargill hanged for publicly defying Charles II with excommunication, the various dissident societies combined to speak against the *Test Act and to forbid listening to presbyterians who had responded to the *Declaration of Indulgence (1672). After 1690 they raised the prestigious Cameronian regiment against James. Unlike other leading ministers, Cameronians refused to join the restored presbyterian Church of Scotland which they saw as Erastian, and finally became the free church (1876).

WMM

Cameroon is an independent republic on the west coast of Africa with a population of 12 million. It attracted Portuguese, Dutch, and British interest but from 1884 until 1916 was under German rule. After the First World War, France administered east Cameroon under a League of Nations *mandate and Britain south Cameroon. They became independent in 1960 and a plebiscite supported their union. The capital is Yaoundé and the chief exports are cocoa, coffee, bananas, and cotton.

JAC

Campaign for Nuclear Disarmament (CND). The largest and most politically orthodox organization associated with the two waves of mass agitation against the British nuclear deterrent and US nuclear bases in Britain during the late 1950s and again in the early 1980s. It was formed in 1958 by establishment intellectuals such as Bertrand *Russell and J. B. Priestley and urged unilateral British nuclear disarmament. It soon became involved in demonstrations and protests organized by the smaller anarchist-orientated Direct Action Committee. The Easter 1958 march to the Aldermaston nuclear base in Berkshire attracted up to 10,000 supporters and 1959 and 1960 saw the numbers approaching 100,000. The success of a unilateralist motion at the 1960 Labour Party Conference was a high point, but *Gaitskell managed to reverse the decision in 1961 and the signing of the 1963 Test Ban treaty caused CND to lose momentum.

It re-emerged as a mass movement in the 1980s as a result of the expansion of nuclear weapons systems and a new iciness in American–Soviet relations. It again proved to be a broad church, with strong trade union, youth, Labour, Liberal, Christian, and Green subgroups, though some radical protesters, such as the Greenham Common women's Peace Camp, were not part of CND. By 1982 it had about 100,000 members and drew an estimated 400,000 people to its Hyde Park rally. One consequence of the Labour Party's move to the left was the Gang of Four's decision to defect and set up the *Social Democratic Party. Further multilateral agreements to control nuclear weapons were both welcome to CND and blunted its cutting edge. Though it did not succeed in its main objective, CND was a remarkable organizational feat and showed more stamina than most political lobbies, even if its main achievement was to damage the Labour Party.

CNL

Campbell, Sir Colin, 1st Baron Clyde (1792–1863). Campbell was born in Glasgow and entered the army in 1807. He fought in many of the most celebrated campaigns of his era: the Peninsular War (1808–14); the Demerara insurrection (1823); the Opium War (1839–42); the second *Sikh War (1848–9); and the *Crimean War (1854), where he commanded a brigade at both *Alma and *Balaclava. However, he lacked connections and it took him thirty years to rise from captain to colonel; and another ten to become a general. On the outbreak of the mutiny in 1857, he was appointed commander-in-chief of the Indian army and was principally responsible for putting down the rebellion and relieving the sieges of *Lucknow and *Cawnpore. He was knighted in 1849 and made a peer in 1858. He was nicknamed 'Old Khabadar' (Old Careful) in the Indian army for his cautious tactics, most notably at the relief of Lucknow.

DAW

Campbell-Bannerman, Sir Henry (1836–1908). Prime minister. A genial and popular politician, Campbell-Bannerman none the less acquired a reputation, which still clings to him, as uninspired and unlikely to reach the top in politics. In fact he proved to be much more shrewd and determined than his apparently more talented rivals in both parties. He managed to hold the Liberal Party together during a difficult, post-Gladstonian period, and led it to its greatest electoral victory in 1906.

A typical Lowland Scot, 'C-B' was educated in Glasgow and at Cambridge, became a partner in the family firm, and married Charlotte Bruce in 1860; the marriage proved to be a long and happy one. As MP for the Stirling Burghs from 1868 C-B showed himself a radical Gladstonian, supporting Scottish disestablishment and *Irish Home Rule. Indeed, throughout his career he derived strength from his capacity to foster the confidence of radical Liberals for his loyal advocacy of progressive causes including women's suffrage, Labour representation, and Scottish devolution; on hearing of the dissolution of the Russian Duma by the tsar he uttered one of his two memorable remarks: 'La duma est morte; vive la duma.'

However, as a young member C-B spoke infrequently and made little impact as a junior minister in *Gladstone's 1868 and 1880 governments. In 1884–5 he served briefly as chief secretary for Ireland and reached the cabinet as secretary of state for war prior to the Home Rule crisis in 1886. He retained this post in Gladstone's last administration in 1892 and under *Rosebery in 1894–5, though by that time he harboured ambitions to become Speaker. Instead he was destined to fill the vacuum left by Gladstone's retirement. Rosebery quit in 1896, and Sir William *Harcourt resigned as leader in 1898. When both John *Morley and H. H. *Asquith declined the poisoned chalice, C-B became leader almost by default.

He was promptly faced with the task of guiding the divided Liberal Party through a period dominated by the *Boer War when his leadership was challenged by Rosebery and undermined by the *Liberal Imperialists who supported the government's South African policy. The use of concentration camps by *Kitchener to quell the Boers provoked C-B's other memorable words: 'When is a war not a war? When it is carried on by methods of barbarism in South Africa.' His prospects were rapidly transformed during 1902–4 as the *Balfour government wrestled with the consequences of the war and split over tariff reform. As prime minister 1905–8 he successfully bridged the gap between New Liberal policies and Gladstonian traditions. Adopting the role of a firm chairman, he gave free rein to his exceptionally able ministers; Ernest *Bevin once described Clement *Attlee as Labour's Campbell-Bannerman. Though some legislation was lost in the House of Lords, important reforms were enacted in connection with trade unions and school meals; old-age pensions were devised by Asquith and the British army reorganized by *Haldane. By the time of his retirement through ill-health in 1908, C-B had pointed the Liberals towards their next great goal—the reduction of the powers of the Lords. MDP

Campbell family. Originating in Argyll, the Campbells first came to prominence under Robert I (1306–29), already aiding the crown against other Highland families. From 1457, led by the Campbell earls of Argyll, they expanded their power in the south-western Highlands and Islands with royal approval, filling the vacuum left by the forfeiture of the MacDonald lord of the Isles (1493). The family successfully balanced its role in the Highlands with Lowland political aspirations, and branches spread to Breadalbane, Ayrshire, Nairnshire, Fife, and Angus. In the 16th cent. they became indispensable royal proxies in the Highlands for a crown unable to govern directly. Such power eventually produced problems—by the 17th cent. some saw the Campbell clan as little better than those they supplanted. As leaders of the *covenanters, and strong supporters of the Scottish kirk, they came into conflict with Charles I and James VII. In the 18th cent. the Campbells were once more crown agents, associated with the *Glencoe massacre (1692), the Act of *Union (1707), opposition to the Jacobites (1745–6), and the *Highland clearances. Often criticized, the family's consistent ability over seven centuries made it one of the most successful Scottish dynasties. RJT

Campden Wonder. Perhaps the most baffling of all historical mysteries. In August 1660 William Harrison, an elderly rent-collector in the small market town of Chipping Campden, disappeared. When a bloodstained hat was found, it was presumed that he had been murdered. A local youth, John Perry, confessed that he had helped his brother and mother to kill Harrison, and all three were duly hanged. Two years later Harrison reappeared and resumed a placid life. His explanation was that he had been kidnapped, sold as a slave to a Turkish physician near Smyrna, and released as a favour. Why the youth confessed is a matter for abnormal psychology and, though false confessions to murders are not uncommon, confessions to false murders are rather rare. The absurdity of Harrison's story—70-year-old rent-collectors are not normally much sought after for the white slave traffic—suggests that it might be true, since it would not have been difficult to invent a more plausible explanation. One obvious answer, that the whole tale was made up by Sir Thomas Overbury, the local gentleman who first published it in 1676, is contradicted by the fact that Anthony à Wood at Oxford on 6 August 1662 had heard and noted that 'Mr. Harrison, supposed to be murdered two years ago, came out of Turkey to his home in the country.' JAC

Camperdown, battle of, 1797. Camperdown is a coastal village in Holland about 10 miles north-west of Alkmaar. Some 10 to 18 miles offshore the Dutch fleet was defeated by a British fleet under the command of Admiral *Duncan on 11 October 1797. By then the Dutch, as the Batavian Republic, were effectively under the rule of revolutionary France, and their navy had been designated to assist in an invasion of Ireland. In strength there was little to choose between the opponents, and there was a bravery on both sides which recalled the great 17th-cent. encounters. Both Dutch flagships and nine other ships were taken during a $2\frac{1}{2}$-hour action, more than half their force. Duncan's ships sustained heavy damage but none was lost, and the victory was the more notable because Duncan's watch on the Dutch had been earlier hampered by the *Nore mutiny. DDA

Campion, Edmund (1540–81). Jesuit martyr. Son of a London bookseller, Campion was enabled to study at Oxford, where, with brilliant prospects as scholar and orator, he was ordained deacon (1568) despite catholic inclinations. Conscience prevailing, he was received at Douai (1573), then sent from Rome by the Jesuits to Bohemia to serve his novitiate, before being reordained in Prague. Part of the Jesuits' 1580 mission to English catholics and carefully non-political, unlike his companion Robert *Parsons, Campion's 'sweetness of disposition' and eloquent preaching were so successful that the authorities were alerted, especially after *Decem rationes*, denouncing Anglicanism, appeared at St Mary's, Oxford. Captured at Lyford (Berks.) through a servant's treachery, and taken to the Tower, his refusal to recant led to torture on the rack, but he remained steadfast. Trumped-up charges of conspiracy to overthrow the queen, and an unjustly conducted prosecution, brought conviction of treason and hanging at Tyburn. ASH

Canada. A self-governing dominion since 1867, much of what is today called Canada was earlier colonized by the British and the French. British interest in the area initially focused not on the land but on the sea. Ships leaving the west country probably located the Grand Banks fisheries even before John *Cabot's explorations of 1497. Despite official discouragement of settlement, *Newfoundland became *de facto* the first overseas British colony, a status it relinquished later than other parts of what would become Canada.

In 17th- and 18th-cent. usage, the name Canada referred primarily to the St Lawrence lowlands. Here the British involvement is usually dated from *Wolfe's victory on the Plains of Abraham (1759), but this was not the first British attempt to capture the French colony. In 1629 the Kirke brothers seized the small fort at Quebec. The colony was returned to the French three years later. Subsequent large-scale but unsuccessful attacks took place in 1690 and 1711.

From 1670, through the royally chartered *Hudson's Bay Company, England claimed sovereignty over Rupert's Land, an area including much of the central plains and northern Canada. The control the Hudson's Bay Company exercised was largely at the sufferance of the native peoples of the area, but the expanding fur trade eventually led the company to set up posts in the far north and on the west coast, establishing British claims to this contested region.

In the long-running 18th-cent. conflict with France, the British definitively acquired Acadia, renamed *Nova Scotia, in 1713. For some forty years, the British laid few claims to the area. Unable to secure a pledge of allegiance from the Acadian population, British authorities dispossessed and deported them. Nova Scotia was then available for Anglo-American settlement.

With the fall of Quebec in 1759, and the 1763 treaty of *Paris, British control over the northern half of North America was unrivalled by any other European power. The attempt to integrate the French, catholic population of the St Lawrence valley into the British empire formed a large part of the political agenda for the next century. A series of constitutions was enacted to address the evolving relationship. The *Quebec Act (1774) guaranteed religious freedoms and legal customs, providing greater privileges to the Canadians than catholics enjoyed in Britain. In doing so, it heightened tensions between Britain and its colonies to the south.

When conflict between Britain and its other North American colonies broke out, Nova Scotia, though populated in large part by recent arrivals from Massachusetts, obeyed the military garrison at Halifax. Quebec maintained its allegiance, not necessarily out of love for the British rulers, but for fear of the more radical protestants of the rebel colonies. In the aftermath of the American Revolution, loyalist refugees streamed north to the colonies that had refused to join the rebels.

The arrival of the Anglo-American refugees created new exigencies. Nova Scotia was divided into two colonies, *New Brunswick and peninsular Nova Scotia. *Prince Edward Island had already acquired a separate administration from Nova Scotia in 1769, and *Cape Breton Island enjoyed a separate status as a refuge for loyalists for forty years. In 1791, Quebec was divided essentially along the Ottawa river to create Upper and Lower Canada. Henceforth, Upper Canada contained primarily an English-speaking population.

As they had been for the French, the North American colonies were often more of strategic than economic importance to the British. With the fisheries secured, the colonies served two other main purposes. They provided other primary resources, such as wheat, timber, and minerals. Also, they offered a place for British emigrants. Until the 1810s, relatively few made the rough transatlantic voyage to settle in the British North American colonies. But after 1815, Highland Scots and northern Irish flocked to Canada. In the 1830s and 1840s, tens of thousands arrived at the various ports of call. These huge influxes of population exacerbated tensions between colonial politicians and the mother country and were important factors in the rebellions of 1837–8 in Lower Canada. In turn, these rebellions suggested to the British government that the attempt to integrate the French-Canadian population into the empire had not been successful.

A third constitution, the Union Act, tried to address the problems. It united the two Canadas, in the hope of swamping the French-speaking population, and gradually assimilating it. However, brilliant French-Canadian politicians made alliances with reformist English-speaking colleagues to defeat the attempts. The fourth constitution, the British North America Act of 1867, essentially rejected the assimilationist policy, by separating again Upper and Lower Canada, and joining them with Nova Scotia and New Brunswick, much to the dismay of many people in the latter two colonies. The four provinces received important degrees of autonomy, within a federal system. This constitution, the longest lasting of all the attempts, has proved the most malleable, and despite increasing tensions since the 1960s, the most successful. But Quebec separatism, as demonstrated by the referendum of 1995, remains strong.

With the BNA Act, the name Canada extended to take in the provinces involved. Other provinces and territories were either annexed or joined the federation subsequently: the Northwest Territories through purchase from the Hudson's Bay Company in 1870; Manitoba (1870); British Columbia (1871); Prince Edward Island (1873); the Arctic Islands (1880), Yukon (1898); Alberta and Saskatchewan (1905); Newfoundland (1949). Canada was a self-governing dominion, the 'eldest daughter' of the empire. Constitutionally equal in status to Britain according to the statute of *Westminster (1931), until 1949 the final court of appeal remained the Judicial Committee of the Privy Council in London, and until 1982 any amendments to the constitution had to be requested of the Westminster Parliament.

Due to further waves of migration, Canada retained and extended its British character. Between 1902 and 1912 alone, over 1.5 million British emigrants left for Canada. A similarly large proportion of immigrants arrived following the Second World War. In part because of these continuing migrations, cultural and emotional links to Britain in English-speaking Canada remained strong until relatively recently and Canada contributed greatly to the allied war effort in both world wars. However, following the Second World War, Canadian politicians and diplomats have attempted to carve out a separate space in world affairs. For instance, Lester B. Pearson won the Nobel peace prize for negotiating an end to the *Suez crisis in 1956 despite British consternation at Canada's role in the matter.

Economically, Canada has at times relied heavily on British markets and investment. Though in slow decline for a long period, since the Second World War trade between Canada and Britain has levelled out at a lower, but not inconsequential, level. As the economic clout of the USA has expanded in the 20th cent., so has its influence over Canada. The passage of the Free Trade Agreement in 1989 (and later the North American Free Trade Agreement) recognized and indeed enhanced Canada's continental orientation. CMC

Conrad, M., *et al.*, *History of the Canadian Peoples* (2 vols., Toronto, 1993); Francis, R. D., *et al.*, *Origins: Canadian History to Confederation* (Toronto, 1992); —— *et al.*, *Destinies: Canadian History since Confederation* (Toronto, 1992).

canal system. Though the Roman Fossdyke at Lincoln was restored in the 1120s, Britain was late to develop its canal network, being well endowed with improvable rivers and ready access to coastal shipping. Four main phases of river navigation preceded the first canals—1634–8, 1662–5, 1697–1700, and 1719–21—and provided the experience essential to their creation, demonstrating the benefits of enhanced inland water carriage. *Exeter had been linked to Topsham by a new cut in 1564–6, perhaps the first English canal, certainly the first recorded use of the pound lock, the critical technology for inland navigation. By the 1630s, it had been applied on the Lea, the Thames, and Warwickshire Avon.

The first modern development was the Newry canal (opened 1745), which linked Lough Neagh and the Tyrone coalfield with seaborne access to the Dublin market. The first English canal, the Sankey Brook navigation, linked St Helens coal to the river Mersey and *Liverpool (1757). Its engineer, Henry Berry, had assisted on the Newry canal. While the Sankey was an extensive parallel cut, the duke of *Bridgwater's canal (1761) was the first to take a route independent of any river and holds traditional place as the beginning of the 'Canal Age'. When completed in 1767, it linked the duke's pits north-west of Manchester to Runcorn in the south-west, a broad 30-mile contour route without locks but with one lengthy aqueduct and a major embankment.

Trunk route development followed from the promotion boom of 1766–72, when most schemes involved James *Brindley or his circle, drawing upon the expertise proven on the Bridgwater. The key links were those of the Grand Trunk canal (1777), which connected the Trent and Mersey, and through the Birmingham canal (1772) connected the midland manufacturing regions with the ports of *Hull and Liverpool; the Staffordshire and Worcestershire (1772), tying both to the river Severn; the Thames and Severn (1789), the Coventry (1790), and Oxford (1790) canals which completed links from the north-west to London. *Birmingham, in 1700 the most important manufacturing centre more than 15 miles from water transport, had become the hub of the English canal system. The route from Liverpool to London, around 600 miles by sea, had been cut by 1790 to around 360 by canal, and fell to 290 in 1805 when the Grand Junction canal bypassed the Thames navigation. Lateral trunk routes linked Bristol and London through the Kennet and Avon Canal (1810), and Leeds and Liverpool (1815); the first trans-Pennine crossing was the Rochdale canal (1804); in Scotland, the Forth and Clyde canal (1790) linked Edinburgh and Glasgow, and the Caledonian canal through the Great Glen (1822) cut out the hazardous journey by way of the Pentland Firth. Wales developed a limited canal system for the transport of iron and coal in the valleys from the 1790s. No significant trunk routes were initiated after the Grand Union in 1810, and building was effectively over by 1830, with approximately 4,000 miles completed.

Medium-length hauls of coal and minerals proved the staple traffic of the canal system, and canals cut the cost of carriage by up to two-thirds, releasing the growing urban and industrial economy from critical fuel shortages. For such traffic, the half of the Leeds and Liverpool open by 1777 was rather more significant than the completion of the trunk route as a whole in 1815. From the 1790s the directness of the Grand Junction route was combined with the intensive use of horsepower to provide for the carriage of shop goods and parcels by 'flyboats', thus breaking down regional barriers and allowing for the reduction of inventory costs. Canal carriage was conducted by large specialist firms such as Pickfords, the canal companies themselves sometimes before 1845 in legal disguise, and by smaller companies: unlike railways, no practical monopoly of transport was gained by the canal proprietors.

The canals had creative effects: new towns were established, notably Stourport, Runcorn, Ellesmere Port, and Goole. Birmingham exemplified the impact of canals in making pathways through established towns, and the Leeds and Liverpool coast-to-coast development. They created employment: around 37,000 men and 2,500 women were recorded as canal employees in 1851, less than 1 per cent of the work-force, but a distinct and culturally separate community, containing specialist occupations, such as the 'leggers' who conveyed boats through some tunnels. Canal building engaged many of the greatest engineers of the era—Brindley, *Smeaton, *Rennie, and *Telford for example—and created in the 1790s the financial precursors of the railway in attracting purely investment capital. Many were very profitable, returning dividends in 1825 in excess of 40 per cent, but profit performance was highly polarized, because costs were commonly underestimated, and the average of about 6 per cent left half the 80 companies making no real return.

The system was completed as such only in the 1820s, and immediately proved inflexible in the face of growing traffic. Mixed gauge development reduced real integration, with the bulk of the system being Brindley model narrow (7-foot) canals; inflexible locks, tunnels, pumping capacity, and inclined planes all represented bottle-necks to further expansion. Water shortages limited carriage, and stemmed from the problems of maintaining summit reservoirs in the face of traffic growth, especially where wasteful staircases of locks had been employed, or where routes were insolubly porous. By the mid-1840s, carriers such as Pickfords were rapidly abandoning canals in favour of the railway. Many canals did remain important bulk carriers and the Leeds and Liverpool's trunk carriage peaked after 1870.

Canal usage continued to fall in the First World War, and declined further in the inter-war years, reviving little between 1939 and 1945, and carrying only 5 per cent of all goods conveyed at the peak of the war effort in 1944. Nationalization in 1948 left trends unchanged: although the volume of goods carried on all inland waterways grew until 1953, 36 per cent of the remaining 2,100 miles were seen as redundant in 1955, with a mere 16 per cent, largely rivers, identified for development. By the 1968 Transport Act, around 1,000 miles were identified as 'cruising waterways' and leisure usage has predominated in subsequent decades, with some restoration by preservation groups, notably of the Kennet and Avon and Rochdale canals. JCh

Bagwell, P. S., *The Transport Revolution from 1770* (1974); Dyos, H. J., and Aldcroft, D. H., *British Transport: An Economic Survey from the Seventeenth Century to the Twentieth* (Leicester, 1969); Rolt, L. T. C., *Navigable Waterways* (1969); Turnbull, G. L., *Traffic and Transport: An Economic History of Pickfords* (1979).

Canning, Charles John, 1st Earl (1812–63). Canning served as an under-secretary to Robert *Peel and as postmaster-general to Lord *Aberdeen before being appointed governor-general of India in 1856. His years in office were dominated by the *Indian mutiny of 1857. At first, he stood firm against the entreaties of several of his lieutenants to appease the rebels and declare an amnesty. He recalled an army from China and insisted on military reconquest. Afterwards he resisted demands for widespread vengeance and bloodshed, earning the nickname 'Clemency Canning'. His post-mutiny policies centred on reorganizing the army and promoting the loyalty of Indians to Britain. He founded the first Indian universities, passed tenancy legislation, guaranteed the continuity of princely states, and banned interference in Indian religion and custom. Following the abolition of the *East India Company in 1858, he became the first viceroy of India. Ill-health led him to resign from office in 1862. DAW

Canning, George (1770–1827). Prime minister. The most brilliant of the disciples of the younger *Pitt, Canning was distrusted for much of his career as an ambitious intriguer. He also suffered from the prejudices of those who could not forget that his father had died in penury and that his mother had been an actress. Rescued by a wealthy uncle, Canning was educated at Eton and Oxford. Entering the Commons in 1794 he shone as an eloquent orator and the writer of witty polemical verses. He denounced the French Revolution and supported the war against France. In opposition he was devastating when criticizing the *Addington and *Grenville administrations. When *Portland became prime minister in 1807 Canning was made foreign secretary. His conduct of affairs was bold and energetic. He prevented the Danish fleet from falling into French hands and supported the Spaniards and Portuguese in their struggle against Napoleon. But the failure of the *Walcheren expedition heightened distrust of Canning and he sought to make *Castlereagh the scapegoat for failure. The outcome was the famous duel which consigned both men to the back benches. Only in 1818 did Canning return to office as president of the Board of Control and in 1822 he was about to sail for India as governor-general when Castlereagh's suicide led to his appointment as foreign secretary. His success was as dazzling as it was controversial. Always opposed to the *Congress system, he disengaged from Europe with enthusiasm. By recognizing the independence of the Spanish American colonies, he opened up Latin America for British commerce. He astutely supported the Greeks in their fight for independence while preventing Russia from overwhelming Turkey. But some Tories thought Canning's policy dangerously opportunistic and when he was asked to form a government in 1827 *Wellington and *Peel refused to serve under him. Canning's ministry was a coalition of liberal Tories and conservative Whigs. He had long supported *catholic emancipation and his sensitivity to the public mood might have led him to change his mind on parliamentary reform. But his unexpected death in August 1827 after only three months in office meant that his premiership did not fulfil its promise. He is remembered as a great foreign secretary and an outstanding orator. JWD

canon law was the law of the universal church and from the 4th cent. became a complete legal system, taking much inspiration from the civil (Roman) law. All European countries accepted the authority of canon law and the conflict between church and state in many countries, and in England notably between Henry II and Thomas *Becket, arose from disputes over the boundaries between canon law and domestic law of the kingdom in such matters as *advowsons (the right to present to a clergy living), criminous clerks, or other jurisdictional disputes.

In 1066 William I had established a dual system of secular and ecclesiastical courts. In the latter canon law was administered, and they were acknowledged as having authority in all matters spiritual. The jurisdiction of these courts was wide. They dealt with offences against religion and morals, for which clergy and laity alike could be brought before the court and penance imposed, and with matters relating to marriage, legitimacy, and other aspects of the family, and succession to personal property.

Until the Reformation and the reign of Henry VIII the ultimate authority in matters spiritual lay with the papal curia, to which appeal ultimately lay, and this authority was accepted by all, though there were many examples of tensions and rivalries between the canon law and the common law courts, e.g. the common law courts would not allow the church courts to deal with questions of title to freehold land, nor to impose fines nor grant damages. The statutes of *Praemunire were specifically passed to forbid Englishmen to appeal to Rome in cases which were exclusively the concern of the common law.

After Henry VIII's break with Rome, appeal was no longer allowed to the papal curia and was abolished by statute in 1533. After the Reformation, therefore, the English ecclesiastical courts, although much influenced still by canon law, were no longer applying the canon law of the universal church, and a special English ecclesiastical law developed in the tribunals of the Church of England. This tendency was enhanced by the fact that doctors of civil law were increasingly appointed in place of churchmen as judges in the church courts. Ecclesiastical law became part of and subordinate to the common law, though until the 19th cent. the church courts retained jurisdiction over succession in cases of personal property and over questions of family law. MM

Canterbury (Roman). Succeeding an important late Iron Age settlement, the *civitas*-capital of Durovernum was laid out on either side of the Great Stour in the later 1st cent., with a rather irregular street-grid. Canterbury had an above-average range of public buildings. The site of a forum/basilica complex is known; adjacent to it was a large temple precinct with associated masonry theatre, and a public baths with portico. All date from the late 1st and early 2nd cents. In the late 3rd cent. walls enclosing 130 acres were constructed. Excavations have shown artisan buildings and larger private houses alongside the public buildings. By the later 4th cent. the town was in decay. The relationship of Roman to Anglo-Saxon Canterbury is vexed; there was activity within the walls for much of the 5th cent., and some of the earliest Anglo-Saxon churches might have late Roman origins. ASEC

(post-Roman) Canterbury re-emerged as the capital of a pagan English kingdom of *Kent, to which St *Augustine was sent by Pope Gregory the Great in 597. Gregory intended the new English church to have archbishops at London and York, but a series of historical accidents led to Augustine and his successors remaining at Canterbury instead of moving to London. Canterbury became one of the larger English walled towns, with a self-governing corporation, but it was dominated until the 1530s by its two great abbeys of Christ Church (the cathedral) and St Augustine's. The many distinguished archbishops included Thomas *Becket, whose murder in the cathedral in 1170 led to his canonization; when the cathedral was rebuilt after a fire in 1174, it was designed to focus on his tomb, which became one of the great pilgrimage shrines of the West. The city suffered economically from the dissolutions at the Reformation, but revived modestly through silk-weaving introduced by Walloon refugees, and later as a social centre for gentry and clergy. In the Second World War the historic core was heavily bombed, but enough is left for the city to remain a major tourist centre. Pride of place goes to the cathedral and close, with a rich legacy of surviving and well-documented buildings. DMP

Canterbury, metropolitan diocese of. The diocese, comprising east Kent, was founded in 601 at the instigation of Pope Gregory the Great, four years after *Augustine's arrival in Kent in 597. The boundaries of the diocese itself have changed little, though from 1375 to 1558 Calais fell within it. The number of sees in the Canterbury province, however, has varied from 12 in 735 to 29 today (30 including the modern diocese of Europe). Disestablishment removed the Welsh bishoprics in 1920. Despite Gregory's intention that London should be the metropolitan see after Augustine's death, respect for the latter and the fragility of Christianity in Essex reinforced Canterbury's primatial position. Its early vigour, responsible for *Paulinus' successful mission to Northumbria in 625, soon declined so much that there was a vacancy in mid-century. In the late 8th-cent. the short-lived metropolitan status of *Lichfield almost eclipsed Canterbury. Pope Leo's decision to restore the primacy to Canterbury was confirmed by a synod at Clofesho in 803. Since Gregory's blueprint for two provinces of Canterbury and York, each with twelve sees, left their relationship unclear, York claimed independence from Canterbury. The dispute reached a peak in 1070 when *Lanfranc demanded obedience from Thomas of York, but following a visit to Rome and a council at Winchester in 1072, Canterbury's precedence, albeit possibly proved with forged evidence, was confirmed temporarily. It arose again in 1118 and continued until Innocent VI (1352–62) resolved the question. York was to have metropolitan authority over the north as 'primate of England', Canterbury to have national precedence as 'primate of all England'. Though still retaining his diocesan seat at Canterbury, the archbishop's official residence as primate since *c.*1185 has been at *Lambeth palace, suitably close to Westminster and Whitehall. In imperial days all colonial sees looked to Canterbury for oversight. Today, though all Anglican provinces are autonomous, Canterbury is accorded unofficial primacy of honour in the Anglican communion, from Japan to Jerusalem, from the USA and Uganda to Polynesia. Thus the archbishop presides over the Lambeth conference each decade and, as universal leader, has represented world-wide Anglicanism in visits to the pope and at the historic visit of Pope John Paul II to Canterbury in 1982. Increasingly the archbishop has found himself spokesman in the House of Lords not only for Christian communities, but for British adherents of non-Christian faiths. The present cathedral, originally monastic, begun by William of Sens in 1174, is a fine blend of French and English styles. WMM

Canterbury, quitclaim of, 1189. Anglo-Scottish treaty. Immediately after Henry II's death, William the Lion petitioned Richard I for full release from the oppressive terms imposed on Scotland by the treaty of *Falaise. Richard, needing to raise finance for the Third Crusade, accepted William's offer of 10,000 marks (about £6,500), and at Canterbury on 5 December 1189 released him from all allegiance and subjection for the kingdom of Scotland, which remained an independent realm until Edward I's successful revival of English claims of overlordship in 1291–2. KJS

Canterbury Tales. Late 14th-cent. unfinished masterpiece by Chaucer. The General Prologue presents portraits, whose colour and vigour transcend stereotype, of diverse pilgrims congregated at the Tabard inn (Southwark), including a battle-worn Knight, sweetly pretentious Prioress, and emaciated scholar-Clerk. They lighten the journey to Thomas *Becket's shrine at Canterbury by exchanging twenty-four tales (all but four complete, all but two in rhyming verse), which range from high romance set in ancient Greece (Knight) to low comedy in contemporary England (Miller, Reeve), and from animal fable whimsically laced with erudition (Nun's Priest) to a concluding prose homily (Parson). DCW

Cantiaci. A British tribal grouping and *civitas*. The Cantiaci seem to be an artificial creation of the Roman government, for there is no record of either a tribe or federation of this name before the Roman conquest. *Caesar records the existence of at least four small tribes in Cantium (Kent), but although he gives the names of their kings he does not know the names of the tribes. Nevertheless it was probably these and other small tribes who were brought together in the later 1st cent. AD to form the *civitas* of the Cantiaci. Its territory will have included all of Kent, and the eastern parts of Surrey and Sussex, but Ptolemy's attribution of London to the Cantiaci is clearly in error. The capital of the new *civitas* was established at *Canterbury, where there had been an important native settlement before the invasion, and was given the name of Durovernum Cantiacorum. KB

Cape Breton Island has formed part of *Nova Scotia since 1820. Named Île Royale by the French, who built *Louisbourg, it was ceded to Britain in 1763. There are French- and Gaelic-speaking communities, coal-mining, and an ailing steel industry. A causeway was built to the mainland in 1955. GM

Cape Finisterre, battles of, 1747. The two encounters, in May and October 1747, were very similar in character, since they arose from the Royal Navy's attempt to cut off French communication with its American possessions. In the first, *Anson annihilated a smaller squadron protecting a convoy. In the second, *Hawke sank six out of nine warships, though most of the merchantmen managed to escape. JAC

Cape of Good Hope. Cape Town was captured by the British from the Dutch in 1795 and formally ceded in 1814. Strained relations between British immigrants and the Dutch settlers (Boers) over slavery and religion led to the Boers' Great Trek in 1835 to re-establish their own territories. The Cape became a crown colony in 1853. The discovery of diamonds (1867) and gold (1886) on Boer land renewed the struggle for political control in southern Africa, leading finally to the *Boer War (1899–1902). In 1910 the Cape became a province of the Union of South Africa along with the Boer republics of Natal, Transvaal, and the Orange Free State. RAS

Cape Passaro, battle of, 1718. Cape Passaro is the extreme southerly cape of Sicily. On 31 July 1718 a British fleet under Sir George *Byng defeated a Spanish fleet of twice its numerical strength, destroying or capturing 17 Spanish warships. The Spanish fleet was newly built and hardly fit for action, but it was supporting an invasion of Sicily by Philip V to wrest the island from the Emperor Charles VI. Britain was not yet at war with Spain but, in part owing to the 'personal union' with Hanover, was already committed to supporting Charles's ambitions in southern Italy. DDA

Cape St Vincent, battle of, 1797. On 14 February 1797, four months after the start of hostilities with Spain and after the British fleet had been forced to evacuate the Mediterranean for the first time in a century, 15 ships under Sir John *Jervis met the Spanish grand fleet of 27 more heavily gunned ships 25 miles off the south-western cape of Portugal. The Spanish line was disordered and, in a westerly wind, Jervis steered through a wide gap from the north. *Nelson in *Captain* broke out of the line to prevent the westerly Spaniards rounding the British rear to re-unite with their easterly ships. *Captain*, only later 'nobly supported' by *Excellent* and *Culloden*, was fought to a standstill; Nelson then vaulted with boarding parties first into the *San Nicolas* and then into *San Josef*: his 'patent bridge'. In all, four Spaniards were taken, Nelson's irregularity in leaving the line matching Jervis's expressed resolve upon 'a considerable degree of enterprise'. Jervis was sent to the Lords as Earl St Vincent. DDA

capitalism. Since Marx's great work this term has acquired pejorative overtones indicating criticism rather than approval or even neutral exposition. Capitalism is the name given to the market economy system, which had its roots in earliest history in exchange between communities, but which did not come to full fruition until the restrictive practices of the medieval and mercantilist eras had been gradually eroded. The upsurge in international and intercontinental trade, especially from the 18th cent. onwards, together with the beginnings of modern economic growth in western Europe and North America, was rooted in the operation of competitive markets. During the past two centuries world economic growth has been achieved very largely through the free market system and mainstream economic theory has provided a theoretical justification for it. But it has also been subject to sustained criticism, both in the relatively mild form that its inherent limitations required that its operation should be modified by government intervention and, at the extreme, that its inherent flaws and corruption would ensure its eventual collapse.

The positive case for free market capitalism is based on the liberty of the individual to pursue his or her objectives subject only to the constraint of law. The state should be involved principally, and some would say exclusively, in providing a legal framework within which property rights and contracts are upheld as a basic protection against crime. Given such a constitutional framework, the most efficient economic system allows markets to operate freely, as individuals buy or sell commodities and services including their own labour. The competitive environment, idealized in perfect competition, represents the most efficient structure. In such a market, all parties are fully informed and are price takers, since no group or individual has sufficient power to control either prices or supplies. Such a structure implies that all participants benefit, so that the interaction of individuals within the market is mutually advantageous. Competition weeds out costly or inefficient producers and ensures that consumers pay the lowest possible price.

It is, of course, generally recognized that this is not an entirely accurate description of either the modern economy or its precursors. The theoretical tradition supporting the free-market system has passed from classical economics to the neo-classical school, which is the current mainstream, and on the more radical right to monetarism, new classical, and Austrian economics. All offer a similar explanation for the divergence between the idealized system outlined above and the reality of human experience. This depends heavily on the concepts of market imperfection and market failure, which suggest that a range of obstacles inhibit the free working of markets. Monopoly power constitutes such an obstacle. Companies with such an advantage can restrict sales or charge high prices, creating an inefficiency in the market system at the expense of consumers. The legislation passed in the late 19th cent. in the USA was spurred by the fear of the monopoly power accumulated in the hands of conglomerates like Standard Oil and broke up the trusts into smaller and competitive units. After 1979 the British government sought to break the monopoly of state industries in telephones, gas, and electricity by returning them to the private sector and exposing them to competition. Another type of perceived imperfection has been the interference of government policy. Monetarist theorists like Friedman have explained inflation as the result of weak control of the monetary system by the state. Even the Thatcher administration failed to live up to the strictures of Professor Friedman's policy prescription.

According to this perspective, the market system is efficient and totally satisfactory provided various imperfections can be eliminated. But one area of difficulty lies in the provision of public goods by the state because market failure means they are not adequately supplied by private producers. Examples include transport networks, law and order, welfare benefits, defence, health, and education. The difficulty lies in the fact that payment is indirect, through taxation, rather than in the direct way in which individuals buy themselves a coat or a book. An important market imperfection, as perceived by those on the right, lies in the oversupply of public goods by the vested interests of bureaucrats and politicians, while concealing the true cost to the taxpayer by financing provision through fiscal deficits.

More familiar criticisms have come from those whose vision of capitalism is not of an ideal state marred temporarily by imperfections. The Keynesian tradition, following the work of John Maynard *Keynes, makes the basic assumption that the market system needs to be supplemented and managed by the state because it will seldom produce outcomes optimal for society as a whole. Adherents to this tradition believe, for example, that state intervention can reduce unemployment and generate economic growth, both of which claims would be denied by scholars like Friedman. A far more radical view of capitalism is taken by the Marxian tradition. Marx argued that capitalism was based not on complementarity of interest but upon conflict between the classes. Further, he argued, capitalism contained the seeds of its own destruction through that conflict. As capitalists cut wages to sustain profits in the face of ever more severe competition, they must reduce the capacity of workers to buy their products, leading to a crisis of underconsumption. The acquisition of colonies was one means of postponing eventual collapse by securing new and additional markets. An important 20th-cent. variant of the radical critique has been dependency theory. This asserts that the industrialization of the western economies was funded by the expropriation of resources from the Third World, through cheap labour and imperialist control, a further potent manifestation of the inherent corruption within capitalist development. Others have explained the continued failure of the capitalist world to collapse, as predicted by Marx, as a result of artificial demand created by governments in the form of military expenditure. This brings together the external exploitation of colonialism with internal exploitation based on class. CHL

Backhouse, R., *A History of Modern Economic Analysis* (Oxford, 1985); Howard, M. C., and King, J. E., *A History of Marxian Economics* (2 vols., 1989, 1992); Mair, D., and Miller, A. G. (eds.), *A Modern Guide to Economic Thought* (Aldershot, 1991).

capital punishment was formerly of central importance in all European criminal justice systems. Although the history of capital punishment in Scotland has been little studied, it is clear that hanging was the standard method of executing on both sides of the border. Under English law, decapitation, hanging, drawing, and quartering, or (in the case of women) burning at the stake were reserved for traitors, while some independent jurisdictions, notably Halifax, where a primitive guillotine was in use, had their own methods. But generally, capital punishment meant hanging.

Evidence from burial sites suggests that capital punishment was known in Anglo-Saxon England. Calculating levels of capital punishment for this and the medieval period is impossible, although it seems they were low. This changed drastically in the Tudor period. Certainly by Elizabeth's reign large numbers of convicted criminals were executed, a trend which continued after 1603. To take an extreme example, an estimated 150 were hanged annually in the London area in the mid-Jacobean period. Put differently, between a quarter and a fifth of those standing trial for felony in Elizabethan or Jacobean England were executed. Overwhelmingly, they suffered for property offences: of 337 death sentences passed by the main criminal court in Cheshire 1580–1619, 294 (or 87 per cent) were for property offences (mainly theft and burglary), 35 for homicide, and 8 for other offences.

The Elizabethan and Stuart periods also saw an elaboration of rituals at executions, a trend which probably began with treason cases, and a marked contribution from the clergy. The speech made by the convicted person assumed a central importance, taking a stereotyped form in which convicted persons confessed their crimes, admitted earlier sins, sought forgiveness from monarch, God, and the spectators, and thus publicly reintegrated themselves into society before dying.

The 18th cent. provides better documentation on ceremonies and crowd reactions at executions. It also experienced a lower level of executions than the early 17th, with large numbers of convicted persons being reprieved, notably before being transported to the American colonies. A system of selectivity was in operation. The capacity to execute widely was retained but usually those executed were persistent offenders, persons with no influential patrons, perpetrators of unusually atrocious crimes, or offenders convicted at a time when the authorities wanted to make examples.

The early 19th cent. experienced a rapid transition in thinking on punishment. Transportation to Australia or incarceration in one of the new penitentiary prisons became the standard punishment for serious, non-homicidal offenders. By the mid-19th cent. capital punishment was restricted to murderers and, after 1868, was carried out inside prisons rather than in public, while the adoption of the drop (a trapdoor device) made death quicker and less agonizing. By that date the abolition of the death penalty was already being mooted. Debate on this issue surfaced intermittently in the 20th cent., leading to its abolition for all practical purposes in 1965. JAS

Caracalla. Roman emperor. The eldest son of the Emperor *Septimius Severus, his real name was Marcus Aurelius Antoninus, Caracalla being a nickname from his habit of wearing the military cloak. He came to Britain with his father in 208 to take part in the campaign into Scotland, to get him away from the flesh-pots, according to one source. After his father's death at York in 211 he negotiated terms with the tribes of central and southern Scotland and withdrew the troops to the *Hadrian's Wall area before returning to Rome to substantiate his claim to the throne by murdering his brother. He was assassinated in 218. ASEC

Caratacus, British king and opponent of the Roman invasion. Caratacus was one of several sons of the great British king *Cunobelinus and on his father's death around AD 40 he and his brother Togodumnus appear to have divided the *Catuvellaunian kingdom between them. Their forces jointly opposed the Roman invasion in AD 43 but Togodumnus died shortly after the battle at the Thames and Caratacus, escaping capture, seems to have fled west. He re-emerged five years later leading the *Silures of south-east Wales in their initially successful attempts to repel the Roman conquest of their territory. When the Romans planted legionary fortresses at Kingsholm (*Gloucester) and *Wroxeter, he withdrew into central Wales and began to organize the *Ordovices to oppose the Roman advance. In a pitched battle on well-chosen ground, perhaps near Caersws, his forces fought well but lost. He himself escaped and fled to *Brigantia, but he was betrayed and handed over to the Romans by Queen *Cartimandua. Taken in chains to Rome, he made a bold and defiant speech before *Claudius (imaginatively recorded by Tacitus) which won him and his family a pardon. He spent the rest of his life in exile in Rome. KB

Carausius. Roman imperial usurper, AD 286–93. In 286 Carausius revolted against official Roman command in advance of disciplinary action by the western *Augustus* (emperor) Maximian. Appointed to command patrols of the English Channel, which was plagued by barbarians, Carausius had exploited the booty profits too successfully for Maximian's liking, and Maximian sentenced him to death. Carausius declared himself emperor and controlled Britain and north-western Gaul 286–93. In 293 Constantius Chlorus (Maximian's *Caesar* or deputy) made military gains against Carausius in Gaul and captured the great fleet base at Boulogne. Carausius was assassinated by his finance minister *Allectus. ES

Carberry Hill, encounter at, 1567. Mary, queen of Scots' marriage to *Bothwell in May 1567 provoked widespread protest. They took refuge in Borthwick castle to the south of Edinburgh but were forced to flee. On 15 June at Carberry Hill, east of the city, they were confronted by a superior force. While negotiations continued, Mary's troops began to desert. Bothwell fled north and finished up in lifelong captivity in Denmark. Mary was imprisoned in Lochleven castle and, on 24 July, abdicated in favour of her infant son James. JAC

Carbisdale, battle of, 1650. Early in 1650 *Montrose sailed from Bergen to Orkney with a small force. He moved to the mainland without gathering much support and on 27 April was surprised at Carbisdale, on the Kyle of Sutherland, west of Dornoch. His supporters were routed, Montrose captured and hanged in Edinburgh the following month. JAC

Cardiff. The capital of Wales located at the mouth of the river Taff. Cardiff was the site of a Roman fort constructed in AD 76, controlling the crossing of the Taff. But little is clear as to its post-Roman history. During the Dark Ages the Celtic St *Teilo founded his church at Llandaff to the north and there is some slight place-name evidence of Viking presence. But it is with the coming of the Normans that the site was revitalized. Robert *Fitzhamon set up his castle within the Roman fort. A settlement was established about the castle which became the military and administrative centre of the lordship of Glamorgan, and was protected by stone walls by the beginning of the 14th cent. A charter was granted sometime after 1147. Although large by Welsh standards, later evidence suggests a town of no great significance. Its population, estimated by the Hearth Tax of 1660–70, was some 1,600, and at the first census of 1801, with a population of 1,870, it ranked only 21st amongst Welsh towns.

With the beginning of the iron industry on the northern edge of the coalfield, Cardiff began its rapid growth as the main port, linked to the interior by the Glamorgan canal (1798) and then the Taff Vale railway (1840–1). But from the middle of the century, coal export rose to dominance, reaching 13.5 million tons by 1913. Cardiff was the world's premium coal port and its population rose in parallel with coal. In 1881, when its population was 82,761, it became, and has remained ever since, the largest Welsh town. By 1901 the population was 164,333.

The rise of Cardiff is intimately associated with the successive marquises of Bute, who owned great swathes of urban estate, initially by marriage, subsequently by purchase. The series of docks, constructed by the estate (Bute West, 1839; Bute East, 1856; Roath Basin, 1808; Roath Dock, 1887; Alexander Dock, 1907), was unique in Britain, since the development was provided by a single private estate. But financial pressures meant that provision was slow and exclusively for coal export. Cardiff never developed a general trade or a port-based industry.

Even so, its size, twice that of the next largest town, made it dominant in Wales. It became a county borough in 1889, was designated a city in 1905, and slowly acquired a new role as the Welsh metropolis. As the gradual run down of coal-mining led to the decline of the docks, Cardiff emerged as an administrative and financial centre and high-technology industries began to accumulate. Cardiff was transformed into a thriving regional city and, after its designation in 1955 as the capital of Wales, a significant administrative centre.

These changes were accompanied by a physical transformation. In 1897 Cathays Park, an area of some 58 acres, was purchased from the Bute estate and laid out as a civic centre. With local, regional, and national buildings, it is one of the most distinctive of administrative areas in Britain. The gift of Cardiff castle and its surrounding lands by the marquis of Bute in 1947 provided an extensive parkland in the heart of the city.

Internal reorganization has given four large shopping malls within the centre, the St David's centre having a major concert hall, whilst Millennium funds are contributing to a national stadium. But perhaps the most significant development is that of Cardiff Bay, where the old docklands are being transformed in a characteristic 'inner harbour' development, which will see a barrage to provide a permanent waterfront and such buildings as a new combined theatre, opera, and museum centre. The population of Cardiff in 1991 was 279,055 and of south Glamorgan 392,780 (of whom 6.4 per cent spoke Welsh). HC

Cardigan, James Brudenell, 7th earl of (1797–1868). Born at Hambledon Manor (Bucks.), as Lord Brudenell he was commissioned in the 8th Hussars in 1824, purchased command of the 15th Hussars in 1832, and was removed for misconduct in 1834. Nothing daunted, in 1836 he purchased command of the 11th Hussars, and in 1837 succeeded to the family title. In 1841 he was tried by the House of Lords for fighting a duel, and acquitted on a technicality. He survived repeated scandals over both his military and private life, marrying twice, first in 1826 the divorcée Elizabeth Johnstone (née Tollemache), from whom he separated in 1846, then in 1858 Adeline de Horsey immediately following his first wife's death. Cardigan's fame and notoriety rest with his command of the light cavalry brigade in the *Crimean War, particularly the *'Charge of the Light Brigade' at Balaclava in 1854. He was inspector-general of cavalry 1855–60, and gave his name to the woollen 'Cardigan' jacket popularized by the war. SDB

Cardiganshire. A west-coast county of Wales bordering the Irish Sea. In 1974 it became the district of Ceredigion in the county of *Dyfed, but in 1996 was reconstituted as a county, retaining the name Ceredigion. That name, from which Cardigan is derived, is supposedly after Ceredig, founder of a post-Roman Celtic chiefdom (*gwlad*) and the son of *Cunedda, a leader of the *Votadini, who moved or were moved from Strathclyde in the 5th cent. Its territorial extent was confirmed under Norman occupation and, after its conquest by Edward I in 1277, it was created one of the shires of the principality by the statute of *Rhuddlan in 1284. At the Act of *Union with England in 1536 it was retained as a county virtually within its ancient limits and has remained as such to the present, apart from the period 1974–96.

Cardiganshire is the land between the sea and the Plynlimon (Pumlumon) range and between the Teifi and Dyfi rivers. It consists of an interior high plateau (1,700–2,000 feet) falling in a series of lower plateaux, seamed by deeply incised rivers, to the coast. Economically there are three dominant activities, livestock farming, tourism, and education. Two of the institutes of the University of Wales are located in the county at Aberystwyth and Lampeter.

The population, which was 63,940 in 1991, has been growing after 100 years of rural depopulation. Its western location has meant that it has been a bastion of the Welsh language. But although it was spoken by 93 per cent in 1901, with 50.4 monoglot, the proportion had declined to 59.1 per cent in 1991.

Cardiganshire constitutes a parliamentary constituency and, in line with Welsh radicalism, its political representation was predominantly Liberal, but more recently *Plaid Cymru has taken the seat. HC

cards, playing. Of ancient and uncertain origin, but known in Europe by the 1370s, playing cards were probably introduced into England by soldiers returning from the French wars. The early suit signs of coins, clubs, swords, and cups soon gave way to cœurs (hearts, possibly representing the church), carreaux (arrowheads or diamonds, symbolic of vassals/archers), trèfles (clover or clubs, for husbandmen), and piques (lance-points or spades, for knights), which French pattern has since become international; fortune-telling preferred the larger tarot packs, but games of chance generally utilized those with just court and numerical cards. Whilst reflecting changing tastes and outstanding events, colours and characteristics have remained remarkably constant, though now more formalized and sophisticated. An established part of upper-class Christmas festivities by 1484, but castigated by puritans as inventions of the devil, playing cards were so popular by 1628 that the London card-makers formed a company and received a royal charter. Repeated petitions against foreign imports eventually resulted in imposition of duties and establishment of an office for sealing all those of English manufacture and regulating prices; since 1712, the duty mark has decorated the ace of spades, thereby providing date approximation. Political designs have included the *Rump Parliament, *Popish plot, Marlborough's victories, reign of Queen Anne (with her *touching for the evil), *South Sea bubble, and caricatures of 1880s figures. Social designs have reflected costume, especially on court cards, and included London cries, lyrics and music for *The *Beggar's Opera*, and educational themes. ASH

Cardwell, Edward (1813–85). Son of a Liverpool merchant, educated at Winchester and Balliol College, Oxford, Cardwell became a Conservative MP in 1841. Close to the leader *Peel, he followed the Peelite free traders after the party split of 1846. Elected for Liverpool in 1847, he was defeated in 1852 for supporting repeal of the Navigation Acts. In ministerial posts under *Aberdeen and *Palmerston, including colonial secretary, he stood out as an administrative reformer and economizer. *Gladstone's secretary at war from 1868, he ended flogging in the army and undertook major reforms, prompted partly by a sense of Britain's military weakness. Infantry regiments were given territorial designations and linked to reserves, short service was introduced, and the commander-in-chief's office was brought under clearer ministerial authority. The abolition of purchase of commissions was controversial; when the 1871 Army Regulation Bill was blocked by the Lords, the change was implemented by royal warrant. Cardwell became a viscount on the Liberal defeat in 1874. Strains of prolonged office may have contributed to later insanity. Historians have become sceptical about the military significance of his army reforms. BIC

Carey, George (b. 1935). Archbishop of Canterbury. Born and educated in Essex, after national service in the RAF, Carey graduated from the London College of Divinity and King's College, London. He was successively curate in Islington, theological college lecturer, vicar of St Nicholas's, Durham (1975), principal of Trinity College, Bristol (1982), bishop of Bath and Wells (1987), and archbishop (1991). A man of considerable scholarship and missionary flair, his primacy's most notable and controversial achievements have been the ordination of women to the priesthood (1994) and synod's acceptance of the Porvoo declaration establishing intercommunion with continental Lutheran churches (1995). Controversies over homosexuality and church finance remain. Originally an evangelical, he nurtures tolerance within Anglicanism and progress towards unity with Rome and eastern orthodoxy. He continues his predecessors' world-wide quasi-patriarchal role. WMM

Carey, Henry. See HUNSDON, 1ST BARON.

Carham, battle of, 1018. *Malcolm II of Scotland with his ally Owain of Strathclyde took advantage of *Cnut's efforts to establish himself as ruler of England to invade Northumbria and reverse a defeat at Durham in 1006. He inflicted a severe defeat on the Northumbrians at Carham, south-west of Coldstream. Simeon of Durham wrote that 'all the people who dwelt between Tees and Tweed were well-nigh exterminated'. It meant a significant shift in the balance of power in the north, confirming Scotland's hold on Lothian, and helping to establish the Tweed as the border. JAC

Carisbrooke castle. A small royal castle near Newport on the Isle of Wight. Occupied by parliamentary forces during the civil wars, the castle and its garrison of twelve soldiers was governed by Colonel Robert Hammond from 1647. Perhaps influenced by a report of Hammond's disenchantment with the parliamentary cause, Charles I fled from Hampton Court to Carisbrooke on 14 November 1647. At the end of December Charles negotiated a secret treaty with the Scots, after which point the garrison was strengthened, and Parliament ordered that the king should be detained in custody. Charles twice attempted but failed to escape from the castle, though he was let out on parole during the *Newport treaty of September 1648. Prior to their seizure of power, the army leaders dismissed Hammond. They then transferred Charles from Carisbrooke to Windsor in preparation for his trial and execution. IJG

Carlile, Richard (1790–1843). Free thinker and republican publisher. Born in Ashburton (Devon), Carlile moved to London as a journeyman tinplateman in 1813 but in 1816 began selling radical newspapers. He took up the ideas of Thomas *Paine which he published in the 'blasphemous and seditious press', and was imprisoned for blasphemous libel in 1817 and 1819–25. Between 1819 and 1826 he edited the weekly *Republican*, where he expressed views which changed from *deism to *atheism. He advocated *birth control but his Malthusian economics divided him from other popular radical leaders. In 1830 he rented the Blackfriars Rotunda theatre in south London for lectures by the charismatic deist the Revd Robert Taylor, but was imprisoned for seditious libel (1831–3). In the 1830s he preached allegorical Christianity, left his wife for a 'moral marriage' with the feminist Elizabeth Sharples, and lost much of his influence in the radical movement. ER

Carlisle, Charles Howard, 1st earl of (1628–85). Howard's nimble political footwork enabled him to make the awkward transition from ardent Cromwellian to ardent royalist. He was too young when the Civil War started to need a political stance but later gave strong support to *Cromwell, serving as captain of his bodyguard and fighting with distinction at *Worcester. His father-in-law, Lord Howard of Escrick, was a member of Cromwell's Council of State and his mother's cousin, Lord Eure, was in Cromwell's 'other house' of peers. Howard was made a viscount by Cromwell in 1657 and also served in the 'other house'. But he kept his options open. After Cromwell's death he supported his son as protector but was accused of complicity in *Booth's royalist rising in Cheshire in 1659. In 1660, returned to the *Convention, he changed sides and helped to bring back Charles II. He also moved to Anglicanism, having been catholic, presbyterian, and independent in turn. The new regime forgave old sins. Howard was lord-lieutenant for Cumberland and Westmorland 1660–85, and for Co. Durham 1672–85. In the coronation honours, he was created earl of Carlisle. He served on various diplomatic missions and from 1677 to 1681 was governor of Jamaica. A broadsheet described him, not unfairly, as 'of very complying principles' and *Burnet wrote charitably that he was 'apt to go forth and backward in public affairs'. JAC

Carlisle, Charles Howard, 3rd earl of (1669–1738). Though twice 1st lord of the Treasury, Carlisle's political career was episodic and inconsequential, and his lasting achievement was the building of *Castle Howard. He entered Parliament as a Whig in 1689 on the family interest at Morpeth, succeeded to the earldom in 1692, and was appointed lord-lieutenant of Cumberland and Westmorland in 1694. William III showed him favour, making him a gentleman of the bedchamber in 1700 and 1st lord of the Treasury in December 1701. But on Anne's succession in 1702, he was dismissed. He was reappointed 1st lord in May 1715 by George I, giving way to Walpole in October. Henceforth he held only minor court office. Increasing gout and his love for Castle Howard made him reluctant to leave Yorkshire: Walpole wrote in 1730 of 'the retired country life which you seem to make your choice'. He was buried in the vast mausoleum at Castle Howard designed by *Hawksmoor. JAC

Carlisle, diocese of. The see, created in 1133, was conterminous with Cumbria until the 19th cent. The region where *Ninian brought Celtic Christianity in the 4th cent. and which Kentigern secured in 573 came under the bishops of *Lindisfarne until the Danish invasions obliterated all trace of the see. The diocese was restored with its seat at Carlisle in 1133, following Rufus's annexation of Cumbria (1092). Initially the see had a complex history, for, though ecclesiastically always under the metropolitan jurisdiction of York, it fell politically under the Scottish kings for 21 years (1136–57). In 1856 the see was enlarged to take in northern parts of the Chester diocese. The cathedral, originally founded as an Augustinian priory in 1102, is noted for its fine 14th-cent. curvilinear east window. It suffered severely at the hands of the Scots during the Civil War. WMM

Carlisle, statute of, 1307. The activities in 1306 of William Testa, an over-zealous collector of *Peter's Pence on behalf of Pope Clement V, led to an urgent petition at Edward I's last Parliament at Carlisle. This statute responded by prohibiting payment of Peter's Pence other than was customary and forbidding foreign prelates from raising revenue in England from houses of their order. It constituted a precedent for subsequent anti-papal measures and particularly Henry VIII's legislation in 1533 abolishing payment totally. JAC

Carlton Club. Founded in 1832 after the Tories' sharp electoral defeat over the Great Reform Act as a means of rallying the party, of ensuring that supporters registered their right to vote, and of co-ordinating press campaigns. It met first at Carlton House Terrace, then at the Carlton Hotel, and finally at its own premises in Pall Mall, designed by Smirke. Smirke's building was bombed during the Second World War and the club moved to St James's Street. Members are still expected to hold conservative principles. At a meeting in the club on 19 October 1922 the Tories took their decision to withdraw from the *Lloyd George coalition. JAC

Carlyle, Thomas (1795–1881). Historian and man of letters. Born in Ecclefechan, the son of a strict presbyterian stonemason, and educated for the kirk at Edinburgh University, Carlyle showed a particular aptitude for mathematics, and earned a living as a tutor, schoolmaster, and journalist, developing a deep interest in contemporary German literature; his *Life of Schiller* appeared in 1823, his translation of *Wilhelm Meister* in 1824. His marriage to Jane Welsh Carlyle marked the beginning of a long, celebrated, and difficult marriage. By the late 1820s he had become a noted reviewer and commentator on contemporary politics, society, and morals, his collection *Sartor resartus* appearing in 1833–4. He abandoned Edinburgh for London in 1834 and began a career as a historian and political moralist. His essays on *Chartism* (1839) and *Past and Present* (1843) dramatized the moral demands subjects make on their rulers with remarkable power. His *French Revolution* (1837), his edition of Cromwell's speeches (1845), and his enormous study of Frederick the Great (1858–65) are brilliant imaginative accounts of the moral power of political leadership. By the end of his life Carlyle had become a fashionably unfashionable prophet who refused an honour from Disraeli and preferred burial at Ecclefechan to Westminster abbey. NTP

Carmarthenshire. County of south-west Wales. It was part of the early Welsh kingdom of *Dyfed and later its core—the vale of Towy (Ystrad Tywi)—became the heart of the later kingdom of *Deheubarth, one of the centres of resistance to Norman occupation. At the Norman conquest, a royal lordship was created about the royal borough of Carmarthen, an indication of its strategic significance. The shire was created at the statute of *Rhuddlan, by the addition of Ystrad Tywi to the lordship of Carmarthen. At the Act of *Union with England, other royal lordships and sublordships, including Llandovery (Llanymddyfri), St Clears, Kidwelly (Cydweli), and Newcastle Emlyn, were added to the county. In 1974 Carmarthen became a district in the county of Dyfed, but the old Ystrad Tywi was made into a separate district of Dinefwr and another district was based on Llanelli. In 1996 Carmarthenshire was restored as a county within its traditional bounds. The county is centred on the Tywi valley and the river's source areas in the Black Mountain to the east and the Carmarthen Vans to the north. To the east and west there are separate drainage systems, the Taff (Tâf) to the east and the Gwendraeth, Loughor/Amman to the west, where the county overlaps on to the anthracite section of the South Wales Coalfield.

The rich valley lowlands constitute the major dairying areas of south Wales. To the east, coal-mining in the 19th and 20th cents. gave rise to extensive village settlement. Llanelli was the main port and steel and tinplate were widely distributed, until rationalized after the Second World War. There is now one integrated plant at Trostre, but other smaller metal-using and engineering industries survive.

Carmarthenshire is a county of rich Welsh tradition. The name, an Anglicization of the Welsh Caerfyrddin, is derived from the Welsh name of Merlin. Welsh is spoken by 58.0 per cent in the district of Carmarthen, although it rises to 66.5 per cent in Dinefwr and falls to 46.5 in Llanelli. The population of the new county was 166,854 in 1991, with almost half in Llanelli. HC

Carmelites were originally established as a monastic order in Palestine in the mid-12th cent., claiming descent via early hermits on Mount Carmel from Elijah and the Old Testament prophets. They were given a rule of great asceticism in 1209. Following the decline of the crusading states they returned to Europe in the mid-13th cent. Several communities were established in England *c.*1242. Shortly afterwards the Carmelites were reorganized as mendicant *friars (the 'white friars'), perhaps under the influence of the English 'general' of the order, St Simon Stock. They remained especially popular in England, where there were nearly 40 friaries at the *dissolution. In England, as elsewhere, the order was notable for its scholars and theologians, while the 16th-cent. Spanish poet and mystic St John of the Cross was a Carmelite. BJG

Carnarvon, Henry Molyneux Herbert, 4th earl of (1831–90). Inheriting the earldom between Eton and Christ Church, Oxford, Carnarvon became a leading advocate of colonial federation, both amongst colonies and between them and the mother country. Colonial secretary under *Derby and *Disraeli, he federated the Canadian provinces into a self-governing dominion by the British North America Act (1867) but his similar attempt in southern Africa, including the Boer *Transvaal, came to grief. Carnarvon, distrustful of democracy, had been one of the cabinet to resign over the Conservatives' Reform Bill in 1867. In 1878, insistent on British neutrality and, as a high churchman sympathetic to Orthodox Christians, he resigned over Disraeli's policy on the Eastern Question. Lord-lieutenant of Ireland under *Salisbury in 1885, he pursued a policy of conciliation and held secret talks with the nationalist leader *Parnell, who later claimed *Home Rule had been discussed. Carnarvon resigned (again) as his policy crumbled, though he opposed Gladstone's *Irish Home Rule initiative. BIC

Carnatic wars. The Carnatic region covers the Eastern Ghats and Coromandel plain in south India and witnessed the initial struggle of the British and French for power in the subcontinent. Rivalry between Chanda Sahib and Mohammed Ali to be nawab of Arcot became entangled with rivalry between the English and French *East India Companies for trading supremacy. The French backed Chanda Sahib and the English Mohammed Ali. The hostilities, which brought the European War of Austrian Succession and Seven Years War to Asia, lasted with brief respites from 1746 until 1760 and saw the emergence of Robert *Clive. In 1760, the English won a decisive victory at the battle of *Wandewash. However, peace did not come to the region for another forty years. English hegemony was challenged by Hyder Ali and Tipu Sultan of Mysore, who received occasional support from France, and south India was not fully secured by the British until Arthur Wellesley's (*Wellington) victory over Tipu in 1799. DAW

Carnegie, Andrew (1835–1919). Philanthropist. Carnegie was born in Dunfermline but brought up in the USA. He made a vast entrepreneurial fortune, mainly in railroads and the iron industry, retiring in 1901 to supervise the 'wide distribution' of his great wealth. He had already begun in 1882 with the gift of a library to Dunfermline and he followed it with endowments to hundreds of libraries in Britain, the USA, and Canada. He also gave generously to the Scottish universities and served as rector at St Andrews, Edinburgh, and Aberdeen. He contributed to the palace of peace at The Hague and was hard hit by the outbreak of the First World War. His autobiography appeared in 1920. JAC

Caroline of Brandenburg-Anspach (1683–1737), queen of George II. Daughter of John Frederick, margrave of Brandenburg-Anspach, Caroline was brought up at the courts of Dresden and Berlin after her father had died when she was 4. In 1705 she married George Augustus, electoral prince of Hanover and, from 1727, king of Great Britain. Her life in England from 1714 was far from tranquil. Her husband was testy and choleric. Relations between him, as prince of Wales, and his father George I were bad, and in turn George and Caroline quarrelled bitterly with their son *Frederick, prince of Wales: 'there he goes, that wretch, that villain' was one of Caroline's many unflattering references to her first-born. She did not particularly resent her husband's attentions to other women which, at least, kept him occupied. An incomparable account of their domestic life is given in Lord *Hervey's published memoirs of the court. Her influence over the king, which was considerable, was exercised in favour of Sir Robert *Walpole, and she acted as regent in 1729, 1732, 1735, and 1736–7 in her husband's absences in Hanover. A woman of intelligence and learning, she was a benefactress of the Queen's College, Oxford. She died in great pain on 20 November 1737 from an undisclosed rupture, her husband characteristically fussing over her death-bed, and was buried in Westminster abbey. SMC

Caroline of Brunswick (1768–1821), queen of George IV. Caroline's marriage to her cousin George, prince of Wales, in March 1795 was a spectacular disaster. According to her own testimony, intimacy was confined to the first night, and certainly the couple separated after the birth of their daughter Princess *Charlotte in January 1796. Thereafter, Caroline spent much time on the continent with a strange entourage, which led to much gossip. A 'delicate investigation' into her conduct in 1806 cleared her of adultery but declared that she had been indiscreet. In 1815 Lady Bessborough, at a ball, found her 'a short, very fat, elderly woman, with an extremely red face', wearing a white frock cut 'disgustingly low'. When George became king in 1820, Caroline rejected an offer of £50,000 p.a. to stay abroad and returned to England to claim her place as queen. Her cause was taken up by George's not inconsiderable number of enemies and she won a good deal of popular support. A government-sponsored bill to annul the marriage had to be withdrawn. *Denman, one of her counsel, in a theatrical flourish, begged the Lords to remember that Christ himself had forgiven the woman taken in adultery, laying himself open to a celebrated riposte:

Most gracious Queen, we thee implore
To go away and sin no more;
Or, if the effort be too great,
To go away at any rate.

When Caroline appeared at Westminster abbey in July 1821 at George's coronation, demanding to be let in, she overplayed her hand. She died a fortnight afterwards. SMC

carols. The word 'carol' probably derives ultimately from the Greek *choros* via the Italian *carola* meaning a circle-dance. In England from medieval times 'carol' has signified a joyful religious seasonal song, usually sung in the vernacular. In his *English Folk Song*, Cecil Sharp says that it 'stands midway between the hymn and the ballad'. Although overwhelmingly associated with the Christmas season, it can reflect any religious theme.

Although today the distinction between carols, hymns, and popular Christmas songs has tended to become blurred, the true carol has certain characteristics. It usually gives indirect praise to God, through picturesque references to people, objects, or events which are tangential to the theme. The traditional west country carol 'A Merry Christmas', with its call for 'figgy-pudding' is a good example of this—the joy and fellowship engendered by the yearly commemoration of the incarnation being underlined.

Another characteristic of the true carol is that it is less based upon poetic narrative, than upon imagery and symbolism. In 'The Holly and the Ivy', another traditional carol, the white blossom and red berry stand for Mary and the sacrifice of Christ.

Some of the most delightful carols date from the 18th and early 19th cents., when bands of village musicians playing stringed and wind instruments formed the usual accompaniment to church choirs. The surviving part-books from country churches (e.g. Puddletown in Dorset) and the recorded performance of the music by singers and instrumentalists such as the Mellstock Band reveal, in such works as 'Arise and Hail the Joyful Day' and 'Hail Happy Morn', the vitality of this musical tradition, before it was swamped by congregational hymn-singing to organ accompaniment. In recent years the radio and television broadcasting of the service of Nine Lessons and Carols from *King's College, Cambridge, has done much to heighten awareness of the rich English Christian heritage of both traditional and modern carols. JRG

Carr, Robert, 1st Viscount Rochester, 1st earl of Somerset (*c.*1587–1645). Carr, a royal favourite, began his career as page to James VI of Scotland, whom he accompanied to London in 1603 when James ascended the English throne. By 1607 he was established as the king's favourite, but he only acquired political significance after the death of James's chief minister Robert *Cecil in 1612, acting as the king's secretary and building up a considerable clientage. His main alliance was with Henry *Howard, the pro-Spanish and pro-catholic earl of Northampton, and this was reinforced when he fell in love with Northampton's relative Frances Howard. She was the wife of the earl of *Essex—son of Elizabeth I's favourite—but James, ever indulgent, set up a tribunal which annulled the marriage, and in 1613 Frances married Carr, now earl of Somerset. Meanwhile Carr's former friend and adviser Sir Thomas Overbury, who had opposed the match on political and personal grounds, was removed from the scene when James sent him to the Tower of London, where he died, apparently of natural causes. Only in 1615 did James become aware that in fact Overbury had been poisoned by Frances. Carr and his wife were tried for murder, and although Carr protested his innocence, they were both found guilty. They were saved from execution by James, who issued a pardon, and after a few years' comfortable imprisonment they retired into private life, taking with them the very fine collection of works of art which Carr had acquired. His place as favourite was filled by *Buckingham. RL

Carrington, Peter, 6th Baron Carrington (b. 1919). Carrington is one of the few hereditary peers to hold high office through the modern Conservative Party. After junior ministerial appointments, Carrington served as high commissioner in Australia 1956–9. He rose to prominence as opposition leader in the Lords after 1964 and became defence secretary in 1970. One of *Heath's closest advisers, he was also party chairman (1972–4) and energy secretary (1974), advising Heath to call an election during the miners' strike of that year. Surprisingly, his career flourished under Margaret *Thatcher, who found him one of the more congenial Tory grandees. But his appointment as foreign secretary ended in 1982 when he resigned, having failed to foresee the Argentinian invasion of the Falkland Islands. Public reincarnation came as secretary-general of NATO (1984–8) and subsequently as an unsuccessful mediator for the European Community in war-torn Yugoslavia. Endowed with geniality and good humour, Mrs Thatcher described Carrington as a 'jolly Whig'. DJD

Carroll, Lewis, pseudonym of Charles Lutwidge Dodgson (1832–98). Author and mathematician. Brought up in a country parsonage, excelling in mathematical and classical studies at Oxford, Dodgson was appointed lecturer in mathematics at Christ Church (1855–81), and ordained deacon (1861) according to the terms of his fellowship endowment; feeling unsuited to parish work, he remained unpriested, hence unmarried. Shyness and a stammer were forgotten in the company of children, whom he amused with stories, puzzles, and riddles; some of these, invented for Dean Liddell's daughters, were recast and immortalized in *Alice's Adventures in Wonderland* (1865) and its sequel *Through the Looking-Glass* (1871), which continue to delight children of all ages. The pseudonym derived from retranslation of the Latin form of his first names (Carolus Ludovicus) reversed. Dodgson, ingenious and extremely methodical, also published mathematical works, verse, and pamphlets on university affairs, all combining logic and humour, and was a fine photographer. ASH

Carson, Sir Edward (1854–1935). Carson is still seen as the arch-opponent of *Irish Home Rule but was a more complex figure than traditionally depicted. Of middle-class southern protestant background, he became a successful lawyer and Unionist politician. In 1893 he moved his political and legal career to London, becoming solicitor-general for both Ireland and Britain and a major figure within the Tory Party. Carson was elected leader of the Unionist Party in 1910, and associated with Ulster resistance to the third Home Rule Bill, as a means of resisting devolution throughout Ireland. Less intransigent in private negotiations on the Ulster crisis than he appeared, he reluctantly accepted the need for partition by 1914. He became a member of the war cabinet and played a significant role in the removal of *Asquith from office in 1916. Attorney-general 1915–16, and 1st lord of the Admiralty 1917–18, his administrative ability was heavily criticized. Carson took a less central part in Irish Unionist politics after 1918 and resigned the leadership of Ulster Unionists in 1921 before Northern Ireland was established. His denunciation of the Anglo-Irish treaty was more heartfelt than his welcome of the Northern Irish government. In a characteristically melancholy manner, Carson regarded his career as a failure, whereas Northern Unionists have seen him as iconic. MAH

Carstares, William (1649–1715). Ecclesiastical statesman. Carstares was born near Glasgow, the son of a presbyterian minister who took part in the 1666 covenanting rising. After attending Edinburgh University, he lived in Holland, where he was ordained. On his return to Scotland, he was imprisoned by *Lauderdale 1674–9. When released, he resumed exile on the continent, in touch with *Shaftesbury and William of Orange. He was again arrested after the *Rye House plot in 1683 and sent to Scotland, where he was tortured before again being set free. He was then appointed chaplain by William and accompanied him on the 1688 expedition, conducting the thanksgiving service on their safe arrival at Torbay. Carstares became an influential adviser in religious matters and helped to persuade William to opt for a presbyterian settlement in Scotland. His political influence ceased with William's death in 1701 but from 1703 he was rector of the University of Edinburgh. JAC

Carteret, John, 2nd Baron Carteret, 1st Earl Granville (1690–1763). Carteret achieved prominence through Baltic diplomacy, 1719–20, and emerged untainted by the *South Sea bubble crisis to become secretary of state for the southern department in 1721. *Walpole and *Townshend's jealousy led to his demotion to the lord-lieutenancy of Ireland in 1724 and dismissal in 1730, whereupon he became a leader of the Whig opposition. Upon Walpole's fall in 1742, Carteret was appointed secretary of state for the northern department. He quickly became George II's favourite minister and developed complex diplomatic schemes to assist Austria, Britain's ally in the War of the Austrian Succession. In the Commons there was outrage at the lack of apparent benefit and cost of Carteret's policies, led by *Pitt but abetted by the *Pelham brothers; in November 1744 Granville (as he had become) was forced to resign. After some years of semi-retirement, Granville was persuaded by *Newcastle in 1751 to become lord president. He acted as an adviser to the king, Pitt, and Newcastle throughout the *Seven Years War. Though often ill or inebriated, his opinions were much respected by the cabinet. An accomplished classicist, linguist, and wit, Granville's career was restricted by his laziness and an insufficient regard for the power of the Commons. AIL

Carthusians. Part of an 11th-cent. revival of Egyptian solitary 'desert life', they were founded as a group of hermits near Grenoble, later La Grande Chartreuse (1084), by Bruno (d. 1101), formerly canon and teacher at Rheims. Their rule was written by Guigo (prior 1110–36), who also founded six other charterhouses in France, all strictly centralized on Chartreuse. A wise combination of the communal and solitary elements of monasticism, Carthusians lived in separate cells with more private than common prayer. As penance for *Becket's murder, Henry II established the first English house at Witham, Somerset (1178), whose saintly third prior became Bishop *Hugh of Lincoln. Six more houses followed (1342–1414), including London (1371) and the largest, Henry V's foundation at Sheen. Never relaxing their austerity, nor ambitious to proliferate, they were noted for their holiness—many distinguished men took vows—and for their powerful mystical tradition, nourished by writings such as *The Cloud of Unknowing*. Carthusian observance uniquely has never changed: *Nunquam reformata quia nunquam deformata*, 'Never reformed, because never deformed'. The quiet holiness of the early 16th-cent. London Charterhouse, a 'desert in the city', contrasting with the 'noisy, restless, ambitious and sordid whirl of the city streets' drew many notables for spiritual direction and even resident retreat. Its last prior, John Houghton, 'a character of rarest strength and beauty', and his monks were all heroically martyred at the *dissolution. WMM

Cartimandua, British queen of the *Brigantes. Cartimandua is said to have come from a long and distinguished ancestry, and was queen in her own right. She made her first appearance in history when in AD 51 she handed over to the Romans *Caratacus, the leader of the Welsh resistance. Her treaty relationship with the Romans probably began at this time, providing them with a friendly native state on the northern frontiers of the new province. However both personal and political differences with her consort Venutius led to considerable instability in her kingdom, which was in any case a confederation of tribes spread over most of northern England. Venutius' ambitions were initially thwarted by repeated Roman intervention in support of Cartimandua, but during the civil wars of AD 69 he took his opportunity to seize the kingdom. The queen was rescued by Roman cavalry, but never regained her throne. KB

Cartwright, Edmund (1743–1828). Inventor. A younger brother of John Cartwright, the parliamentary reformer, who also had a taste for inventing, Edmund Cartwright was an Anglican clergyman and from 1779 held the living of Goadby Marwood (Leics.). In 1785 he patented a loom driven by water, which he developed later in a factory near Doncaster. In 1789 he invented a wool-combing machine, which saved labour and caused great agitation among the workers. Cartwright was obliged to abandon his own factory, but his inventions were widely adopted, and in 1809 he was awarded a grant of £10,000 by Parliament. JAC

Cartwright, Major John (1740–1824). The 'Father of Reform' was a Lincolnshire squire who devoted the best years of his long life to radical agitation and propaganda. From support of the American colonists, Cartwright moved to a critique of the political system. His most famous book, *Take your Choice* (1776), argued the case for manhood suffrage, secret ballot, annual elections, equal electoral districts, and payment of MPs, by reference to Anglo-Saxon precedent, thus foreshadowing the claims of advanced political reformers until chartist times and beyond. In 1780 he founded the *Society for Constitutional Information. He welcomed the first stages of the French Revolution, but did not support Painite radicalism or the London *Corresponding Society. For some years after 1805 he was involved in the politics of the radical borough of Westminster, and from 1812 in the *Hampden Club movement. JFCH

Cartwright, Thomas (1535–1603). A leading early presbyterian, Cartwright was born in Hertfordshire and graduated from St John's College, Cambridge. Expelled on Mary's accession, he returned as fellow of Trinity (1562), but disputes over surplices and church government led him to depart for Ireland (1565–7). After his return as Lady Margaret professor of divinity (1569) his advocacy of presbyterian church government brought him into frequent conflict with *Whitgift, master of Trinity. Deprived of his professorship (1570) and his Trinity fellowship (1571), he emigrated to Geneva. After a brief spell in England (1572), he became (1573) minister to exiled English congregations in Antwerp and Middelburg. Back in England (1585), he continued to preach despite two spells of imprisonment, after which he retired to Guernsey (1592). Intellectually the leading puritan of his day, he refused to associate with the *Brownists and *Barrowists. WMM

Carvetii. A British tribe and *civitas*. The Carvetii are one of the many smaller tribes that made up the *Brigantian confederation of northern England. Their name means 'the Deer Men', and their principal deity seems to have been a war-god called Belatucadrus. They occupied the extreme north-west corner of Brigantian territory comprising Cumberland and part of Westmorland. Roman authors make no mention of the Carvetii, but the existence of the *Civitas Carvetiorum* is recorded on two inscriptions—a milestone and a tombstone from Brougham and Old Penrith respectively. The former is important because, dated to AD 258–68, it confirms that the *civitas* was in existence by the middle of the 3rd cent. at the latest. It was possibly created as part of a reorganization of the northern frontier in the early 3rd cent. A capital was established at Carlisle, known to the Romans as Luguvalium. KB

Casablanca conference. On 14–24 January 1943 *Churchill and Roosevelt met in Morocco to determine allied strategy. Stalin refused to attend as he was overseeing operations around Stalingrad. The prospect of opening a second front in northern France was discussed but the British considered it premature and instead the invasion of Sicily was planned. It was agreed to increase the bombing of Germany and to give priority to defeating the U-boats in the North Atlantic. It was decided to accept only the unconditional surrender of the axis powers, which ruled out any prospect of a negotiated peace. RAS

Casement, Sir Roger (1864–1916). Humanitarian and Irish hero. As British consul in the Congo Free State and then on the Amazon, Casement uncovered European atrocities against natives which stimulated powerful and mainly effective protest campaigns in Britain, and earned him a knighthood in 1911. He then returned to his Irish roots, and collaborated with Britain's German enemies during the *First World War, for which he was hanged in 1916 after landing from a German submarine near Tralee to help the *Easter Rising. In order to mute the predicted Irish-American protest, the British *secret services surreptitiously circulated private diaries revealing his homosexual proclivities, to their lasting shame. BJP

Cashel, archiepiscopal diocese of. The Irish archbishopric of Cashel (Caisel Muman—stone fort of Munster) was established by the Council of Raithbressail (1111), initially with oversight of the twelve dioceses of Leth Moga (southern half of Ireland), but when the Council of Kells-Mellifont (1152) further restructured Ireland into four provinces, Cashel's authority was reduced to the south-west by the creation of the *Dublin province for the south-east. *Patrick is said to have baptized King Aengus here (450) at the famous Rock, fortified in the 4th cent. The Council of Cashel in 1171 reformed Irish canon law. In the 13th–14th cents. its archbishops were still Irish, though the diocesan bishops were equally divided between Irish and Anglo-Norman. Cashel is still a catholic archiepiscopal see, but in 1838 the Anglican see was united with Dublin. Cashel, though still a diocese (also including Waterford and Lismore since 1833), ceased to be an Anglican archbishopric. The 13th-cent. cathedral, now roofless, was restored in 1686, but abandoned in 1749. Cormac's chapel (1127–32), enclosed by the choir and south transept, is reputed to be the most interesting Romanesque church in Ireland. St John Baptist's cathedral is neo-classical (1750–83). WMM

Cashel, Council of, 1171. After Henry II's invasion of Ireland and the submission of the princes (1171), he summoned a council of prelates to Cashel under Christian, bishop of Lismore, and the papal legate in the archbishop of Armagh's absence through old age. By reforming Irish canon law, revising the baptismal rite, introducing tithes, and thus removing Irish irregularities, they brought the church into line with the English church and with Rome. Letters they sent to Pope Alexander III were enthusiastically answered, recognizing Henry's new title as lord of Ireland, despite the horror of *Becket's murder the year before. WMM

Casket Letters. The contents of a small silver casket, uncovered in 1567, allegedly incriminating Mary Stuart and her lover *Bothwell in the murder of her second husband Lord *Darnley. The papers consist of eight letters from Mary to Bothwell, a sequence of 'sonnets' (totalling 158 lines), and two contracts for the marriage of Mary to Bothwell. The authenticity of the material cannot now be certainly established as the originals vanished in 1584. However, surviving copies suggest that, while not outright forgeries, the material was clumsily doctored by Mary's opponents at the York–Westminster conference in 1568–9. RAM

Cassivellaunus. British chief or king. Cassivellaunus is known only from the war diaries of Julius *Caesar and Dio Cassius' later derivative account of Caesar's invasions of 55 and 54 BC. Nevertheless, he may well have been a key figure in the political development of south-eastern Britain before the Roman conquest. Caesar recounts that before his invasions, Cassivellaunus had been in a continual state of warfare with neighbouring tribes. His territory is described as beginning some 75 miles from the sea, and on the far side (that is, on the north bank) of the Thames. This places him in the Chilterns and suggests that he may have been the first local chieftain to found a kingdom here which was later to dominate most of south-east England under the tribal name of the *Catuvellauni. His abilities as a war leader are confirmed by his selection by the British, even those he had recently been fighting, to lead the opposition to Caesar. His subsequent handling of his forces and his use of guerrilla tactics, which prevented Caesar from achieving the total victory he was seeking, suggest a shrewd military mind. The location of his stronghold is uncertain but Wheathamstead near Welwyn is possible. KB

Castillon, battle of, 1453. On 17 July 1453, the English lost Gascony, which they had held for 300 years. An Anglo-Gascon attack on a fortified artillery park a mile or two on the right bank of the Dordogne upstream from Castillon was probably launched without knowledge of the strength of its defence. For a short while, despite the hail of shot and ball, the rampart was gained. But the assault was repulsed and the English overrun, *Shrewsbury, their legendary 65-year-old commander, being killed in the rout. Thus, in a suicidal frontal attack on artillery, not unlike the *Charge of the Light Brigade, the *Hundred Years War came to an end. Only *Calais was left to the English. AJP

'Castlebar races', 1798. A small French expedition under Humbert landed at Killala in August 1798 to assist the Irish rebels. On 27 August at Castlebar they engaged militia, stiffened by regulars under General Lake, and routed them. Casualties on the loyalist side would have been heavier had not the militia shown an instinct for self-preservation—hence the mocking name 'Castlebar races'. But Humbert's force was a forlorn hope and surrendered at Ballinamuck a fortnight later. JAC

Castle Howard, near Malton (Yorks.), is one of the grandest houses privately built, comparable with *Chatsworth, which may have influenced its design. It was commissioned by the 3rd earl of *Carlisle, who began in 1699 to transform what had been the sprawling hamlet and ruined castle of Henderskelfe. The main house was designed by *Vanbrugh, with the west wing finished in the 1750s to the design of Sir Thomas Robinson of Rokeby, brother-in-law to the 4th earl. The three great features are a superb south front, the imposing dome and entrance hall, and an extensive park, dominated by Vanbrugh's Temple of the Four Winds and *Hawksmoor's sombre mausoleum. JAC

Castlereagh, Robert Stewart, Viscount, 2nd marquess of Londonderry (1769–1822). Castlereagh's career is remarkable in that he outgrew his background in Ulster politics and became an advocate of the union between Britain and Ireland, a capable war secretary, and finally a distinguished foreign secretary, whose comprehension of the craft of diplomacy had a depth and subtlety exceeding that of most of his contemporaries. Robert Stewart entered the Irish House of Commons at a by-election for Co. Down in 1790. He had the support of the reformist interest but while he never lost his belief in the necessity for reform in Ireland, he soon felt drawn to the policies of the younger *Pitt. His kinsman Lord *Camden encouraged him to look beyond merely Irish perspectives and he was elected to the Westminster Parliament in 1794. Castlereagh sympathized with reform in France but was unhappy about the decline of the French Revolution into violence. He was anxious about the impact of Jacobin ideas in Ireland through the secret society the *United Irishmen, and believed Ireland's destiny to be inextricably bound up with that of Britain. He supported the war against France, became prominent in the suppression of the *Irish rebellion of 1798, though always advocating clemency and reconciliation, and bore the main burden in carrying the Irish Act of *Union in Dublin. Like Pitt he saw the Union as preliminary to a comprehensive programme of reform. He supported *catholic emancipation, argued that the tithe should be abolished, and suggested that catholic clergy should be paid by the British crown. Castlereagh resigned with Pitt when George III thwarted the prospect for catholic emancipation. He was, however, prepared to serve in *Addington's administration from 1802 and in Pitt's second ministry in 1804. On the death of Pitt he left office but became war secretary in the *Portland ministry. He was an outstanding war minister. He saw the struggle against Napoleon in global terms, appreciated the need for European allies, improved recruitment to the militia and to the army, and organized an expeditionary force for continental intervention if possible. He was also eager to convey to the public the broader principles on which the war was being waged, though he lacked *Canning's ability to capture the enthusiasm of the public. The *Peninsular War was supported by Castlereagh from the start and he took the initiative in bringing Wellesley (*Wellington) forward and in restoring him to command after the death of *Moore. The failure of the *Walcheren expedition meant that Castlereagh left the war department as the scapegoat. He had strenuously urged an attack on French bases in the Scheldt, in order to disrupt French invasion plans and support the Austrians by a diversionary tactic. Although he had prepared the expedition with meticulous care, the campaign was bungled. The decision to withdraw was a bitter one, the more so because Canning was eager to ensure that Castlereagh carried the chief responsibility for failure. On learning that he was to be moved from the War Office, Castlereagh believed himself to be the victim of intrigue. The result was the collapse of the Portland ministry and the duel with Canning, which shocked contemporaries and relegated both men to the back benches for several years.

Castlereagh's great opportunity came when he was appointed foreign secretary and leader of the House of Commons on the formation of *Liverpool's ministry in 1812. He built up the final coalition against Napoleon and his personal diplomacy strengthened allied determination. Although not a brilliant orator, Castlereagh was a successful leader in the Commons, winning the trust of MPs by his patience, courtesy, and understanding. At Vienna he did much to frame the peace settlement. He was committed to regular meetings of the powers in congress not, as many have imagined, in order to perpetuate the status quo, but to enable peace to be preserved by considered adjustment to inevitable change. He did not believe in collective intervention in the domestic affairs of sovereign states. Castlereagh became alienated from Metternich and by 1820 had dissociated Britain from the *Holy Alliance, which he had condemned on its inception as 'a piece of sublime mysticism and nonsense'. Although his distrust of Russian expansion in the Near East drew Castlereagh closer to Metternich over the Greek revolt, he seriously contemplated the recognition of the independence of the Spanish American colonies. In 1822, worn out by overwork and saddened by the failure of the congress system to work as he had hoped, he suffered a nervous breakdown and committed suicide. For many years the tragedy of his death and sustained misrepresentation obscured his greatness as foreign secretary. He saw himself as applying the principles of Pitt, believing that peace could be preserved by carrying into peacetime the co-operation and concern for mutual interests which had been necessary in war. He combined the defence of British interests with the preservation of equilibrium in Europe, but disliked attempts to build policy on speculative and abstract theories. JWD

castles. Many man-made structures are called 'castles'; they are very diverse in character and date, ranging from the Iron Age fortification of *Maiden castle (Dorset), to *Dover castle, to Eastnor castle (Herefordshire) built as a stately home for the 1st Earl Somers in 1812. Of these only Dover is truly a castle, but the others tell us something about the way castles generally are regarded. Castles are fortifications, some of considerable size and complexity. But unlike Maiden castle, which housed and protected a whole people, they were built by a medieval lord for his own protection. Eastnor was built at a time when medievalism was fashionable, and castles were seen as the suitable residences of the aristocracy, symbols of their hereditary status and right to rule. True castles were also residences; the greatest were palaces of considerable size and luxuriousness. They were also status symbols and centres of government. The donjon or keep of a castle seems to have become a symbol of lordship, which may explain why Ralph, Lord Cromwell, built a tower keep as the centre of his castle at Tattershall in 1434, when towers as parts of the fortification had been superseded. Royal castles, especially those planted by William the Conqueror in the shire towns of England after the Conquest, became centres of royal government. They were county gaols, places where royal courts sat, and where documents, treasure, and weapons were securely held. Baronial castles were the caputs or heads of estates, where local government and business of the estate was transacted. Finally, all castles were privately owned. Whether the castle was built by the king to control or to protect the kingdom or by one of his barons to subdue his estate, it remained the property of the builder. Royal castles were not built for national defence, did not and still do not belong to the state. The king might require the owner of a castle to maintain it in readiness against an enemy of the kingdom, but the castle remained private property. If a castle was thought relevant to the defence of the realm it could be appropriated for the period of the emergency by the king, but was always returned to its owner. The castle of Norham on the Tweed was the centre of the bishop of Durham's estates in Norhamshire. It was built originally at the king's request and later taken several times into the king's hands during the protracted wars against the Scots.

Castles developed first in France, in Anjou, in the 10th cent. The first castles in England were built in Edward the Confessor's reign by his nephew Ralph and his Norman followers, and were strongly resented by the English, as foreign imports. Lordly residences in late Saxon England appear to have been enclosed with a palisade and a ditch, as excavations at Sulgrave (Northants) and Goltho (Lincs.) have shown, but the defences were slight. Castles were an introduction into England and a direct consequence of the Norman invasion of 1066.

Orderic Vitalis, a Norman historian writing in the 12th cent. about the Norman Conquest, said that the English fought bravely but lost to William because they lacked castles. William's victory was based on his successful use of castles. He secured his first landing in England with a wooden castle, which he brought with him in ready-made sections from Normandy. On entering London, after the battle of Hastings, one of William's first acts was to order the creation of a castle to control the city: the *Tower of London. His various campaigns to secure the country or to suppress rebellion are notable for castle-building at centres up and down the line of his march.

William used castles to secure his new kingdom; the nobles to whom he granted estates did the same in taking control of their new lands. The extent and rapidity of the military revolution which the Conquest introduced can be gauged from two accounts of rebellions recorded in the *Anglo-Saxon Chronicle*, either side of 1066. The first, in 1050–1, describes how the Godwine family rose against Edward the Confessor, took to their ships, and raided along the south coast. The second was that led by Bishop *Odo of Bayeux against William II in 1088 where each rebel provisioned a castle and sat inside the walls.

The castles built immediately after the Conquest, whether by the king or his followers, were generally rapidly constructed of earth and timber, using locally impressed Saxon labour. In form, they were either a fortified enclosure surrounded by a ditch (known as a ringwork) or a motte and bailey, that is an earth mound topped with a fortification and surrounded by a ditch connected to a further lower fortified enclosure. These castles vary considerably in size. This suggests that their owners had differing resources and also that their roles were different. Large castles like *Windsor, *Dover, or *Richmond seem to have been conceived from the first as residences as well as fortresses. The White Tower built by William I to subdue London incorporated two large suites of rooms plus a grand chapel and extensive storage space within the defensive keep. Excavations of the motte at Abinger (Surrey) have shown that the top of the motte had a raised fighting platform or perhaps a look-out tower surrounded by a palisade. All the accommodation, if there was any, must have been in the bailey and suggests that the smaller castles were principally fortresses.

This distinction is important, for it helps to explain the development of castles after the Conquest. During the Conquest all Norman barons, great or small, seem to have built castles; however, the wooden fortresses of the first generation were not very durable and their owners were soon forced to decide whether they should be replaced in stone. Further, the castle's importance in warfare meant that its design was constantly being refined so that to maintain its military efficiency meant a constant outlay. Many smaller landowners seem to have ceased to be castle owners, preferring instead a fortified manor house, which provided security and domestic comfort within their means. Castles became the prerogative of the wealthy baronage and the crown. Thus the castles which are notable monuments today are those which were rebuilt and updated in the 12th cent. and later, with both defensive systems and residential arrangements brought to considerable sophistication. Amongst the most developed examples in Britain are the castles built for Edward I in north Wales, for example, *Conwy, *Caernarfon, and *Harlech. These played a crucial role in the subjugation of the principality, and also provided palatial accommodation for the king and his officers.

Such castles were extremely expensive to build, and castles constructed in the later Middle Ages, such as *Bodiam, were consequently smaller, although they retained considerable sophistication. Despite the introduction of gunpowder in that period, castles retained their importance. Late examples, such as *Raglan (Monmouthshire), were designed to include cannon as part of their defences. Castles were again important in the English Civil War, when large numbers were refortified and held for the king. Several, including *Corfe, suffered major sieges. In recognition of the part that castles had played in the war, the majority of surviving buildings were deliberately slighted by the victorious parliamentarians. LR

Brown, R. A., *English Castles* (2nd edn. 1976); McNeill, T., *Castles* (1992); Pounds, N. J. G., *The Medieval Castle in England and Wales: A Social and Political History* (Cambridge, 1990); Thompson, M. W., *The Decline of the Castle* (Cambridge, 1987).

Cat and Mouse Act, 1913. Exasperated by the tactics of militant suffragettes in going on hunger strike, *Asquith's government passed the Prisoners' Temporary Discharge for Ill-Health Act, known commonly as the Cat and Mouse Act (3 Geo. V c. 4). Prisoners could be released and subsequently rearrested. McKenna, the home secretary, argued that the suffragettes, by arson and destruction, had 'declared war on society' and that the measure would reduce the disgusting practice of forcible feeding. Keir *Hardie opposed the bill as futile and unfair and Lord Robert Cecil suggested deportation instead. JAC

Cateau-Cambrésis, treaty of, 1559. Mary Tudor's marriage to Philip of Spain dragged her into a disastrous war against France in 1557 in the course of which *Calais was lost. When Elizabeth succeeded in November 1558, her position was precarious and she was anxious for peace. The treaty was signed on 3 April 1559. The French ceased to support the claims of Mary, queen of Scots (then married to the dauphin) to the English throne, and the English, by implication, gave up hopes of regaining Calais, since the French were to retain it for eight years and then restore it on conditions certain to be broken. JAC

cathedrals are the chief churches of a diocese, where the archbishop or bishop has his throne (*cathedra*). The fabric and worship of the church itself is the responsibility of the dean. The oldest dioceses of the Church of England are Canterbury (597), London (604), Rochester (604), York (625), Norwich (631), Lincoln (Lindsey) (634), Durham (Lindisfarne) (635), Lichfield (656), Hereford (676), and Worcester (680). The newest are Birmingham (1905), Southwark (1905), Chelmsford (1914), Bury St Edmunds (1914), Coventry (1918), Bradford (1920), Derby (1927), Guildford (1927), Leicester (1927), and Portsmouth (1927). There are also more than eighty suffragan bishoprics.

Little pre-Norman work remains, though *Wilfrid's 7th-cent. crypts at Ripon and Hexham survive. Among the more remarkable features of the other cathedrals are the Norman nave at Durham (late 12th cent.), the chapter house at Bristol (late 12th cent.), the west front at Wells (13th cent.), the carvings at Southwell (late 13th cent.), the spires at Lichfield (early 14th cent.), the cloisters at Gloucester (late 14th cent.), the towers of Lincoln (14th and 15th cent.), and the great dome of St Paul's (late 17th cent.). Modern Anglican cathedrals are at Truro (1880+), Liverpool (1904+), Guildford (1936+), and Coventry (1956–62), this last to the design of Sir Basil *Spence. *Westminster Roman catholic cathedral, with its enormous campanile, was built between 1895 and 1903. Two remarkable 20th-cent. catholic cathedrals are at Liverpool, designed by Sir Frederick Gibberd (1962–7), and at Clifton, Bristol (1970–3). [There are separate entries for all the sees of the Church of England, the Church of Ireland, the Church in Wales, and the episcopal Church of Scotland.] JAC

Catherine of Aragon (1485–1536), 1st queen of Henry VIII. Catherine was a tragic victim of brutal dynastic politics. The daughter of Ferdinand and Isabella of Spain, she was sent to England in October 1501 to marry Prince *Arthur, eldest son of Henry VII and one year her junior. The young couple were sent to Ludlow, where Arthur died five months after the marriage. Catherine stayed in England and in 1503 it was arranged that she should marry Arthur's younger brother Henry. Henry VII was in no haste to expedite the matter and for some years Catherine was in an unpleasant position. But on Henry VIII's accession in 1509 he hastened to fulfil the agreement. The marriage was at first affectionate, though not until 1516 was a living child, Princess Mary, born. By 1526, for a mixture of public and private reasons, Henry was clearly thinking of divorce, it having belatedly occurred to him that he had married his brother's wife. From this time forward, the fate of her marriage was out of Catherine's hands, though she continued to protest and refused to enter a nunnery. In July 1531 Henry left her and never saw her again. In 1533 his marriage to *Anne Boleyn took place and *Cranmer declared Catherine's marriage invalid. Her later years were spent at Buckden and Kimbolton, comforted by her faith, deprived of her title as queen, forbidden to see her daughter, and in constant fear of poison. She died in January 1536 and was buried in Peterborough abbey. To the end she maintained that her marriage to Arthur had never been consummated and that her marriage to Henry was consequently valid. JAC

Catherine of Braganza (1638–1705), queen of Charles II. Daughter of John, king of Portugal, Catherine's marriage to Charles II on 21 May 1662 was regarded by English merchants as 'the most beneficial that ever our nation was engaged in'. Her dowry included Bombay, and Tangier, which was subsequently evacuated. Dark-haired, petite, and amiable, Catherine was badly educated, with little command of languages. She had, however, some charm. Pepys thought her 'mighty pretty' when he saw her hand in hand with the king in 1663 and the following year remarked on her pretty broken English. Tension inevitably arose between her and Charles's mistress Lady Castlemaine. Catherine miscarried several times and had no live children. This, and the growth of anti-catholic feeling, fuelled suggestions of a divorce, but Charles stood by her. After Charles's death in February 1685, she moved to Somerset House and established a convent, before returning to Portugal after the Glorious Revolution, in March 1692. SMC

Catherine Howard (1520–42), 5th queen of Henry VIII. Catherine, the daughter of Lord Edmund Howard and niece of the duke of *Norfolk, was 19 when Henry became interested in her. The annulment of his marriage to *Anne of Cleves on 9 July 1540 was followed a fortnight later by his marriage to Catherine. She was tiny, pretty, and vivacious, her sparkle compensating for a lack of education. Henry showered her with gifts but by the end of 1541 he had heard rumours of her adultery, before and after marriage. The illness of his only son Edward, and no sign that she was pregnant, heralded her downfall. Pre-marital affairs with Francis Dereham and her cousin Thomas Culpeper were the basis for a charge of treason, that she had contaminated the royal blood. Members of the Norfolk household were imprisoned, Catherine placed under house arrest at Syon House, and then beheaded on 13 February 1542. She died with notable composure and is reported to have said, 'I die a queen, but would rather have died a wife of Culpeper.' Henry remained in good spirits and began thinking of a sixth marriage or of recalling Anne of Cleves. SMC

Catherine Parr (1512–48), 6th queen of Henry VIII. Daughter of Sir Thomas Parr of Kendal, Catherine was well educated with protestant sympathies. She was 32 and had been twice married when she attracted Henry's attention. She is said to have had strong reservations about marrying him—'better mistress than wife'—but the marriage was performed at Hampton Court on 12 July 1543. Her maturity served her well and the marriage was the most adult Henry had experienced. She provided something of a home for the royal family, intervened on behalf of both Mary and Elizabeth, and interested herself in their education. During 1544, while Henry led the invasion of France, Catherine acted as regent and took her duties seriously, adding her initials, KP, to documents. On Henry's death in 1547 she was disappointed not to be made regent for the young Edward VI. She went on to marry the ambitious Thomas *Seymour, a former admirer, and promoted Baron Seymour of Sudeley. She died on 7 September 1548 shortly after the birth of a daughter. SMC

Catherine of Valois (1401–37), queen of Henry V. Youngest daughter of Charles VI of France, Catherine was sent at an early age to a convent. Her marriage to Henry on 2 June 1420, after bitter warfare between France and England, was an affair of state. At the same time, the treaty of *Troyes was signed, whereby Henry was to become Charles's heir. A son, the later Henry VI, was born in December 1421 at Windsor. Catherine accompanied Henry to Harfleur, where war against the dauphin, Charles, continued, and returned a widow in May 1422 when Henry died of dysentry. Though an affair with Owain *Tudor resulted in an Act forbidding her to remarry without royal permission, she was already secretly married. The grandson of this marriage took the throne as Henry VII. Catherine died in February 1437, was buried in the Lady Chapel, Westminster abbey, and later placed alongside Henry V. On his 30th birthday in February 1669, Pepys was shown her corpse, 'and did kiss her mouth'. SMC

Catholic Apostolic Church. This millennialist denomination, notable for its liturgy and aristocratic tone, derived from meetings held from 1826 at Albury Park, the Surrey home of the London banker and Tory politician, Henry Drummond (1786–1860). Their intention was to explore the implications of biblical prophecy. Among those attending was Edward *Irving, minister of Regent Square Scottish Church, London, then at the peak of his wayward genius, but increasingly suspect for his views on the human nature of Christ and further isolated when speaking in tongues broke out among his people in 1831. Excluded from Regent Square in 1832, and from the *Church of Scotland in 1833, Irving established a congregation in Newman Street. This became the first Holy Catholic Apostolic Church, but Irving was not its leader for, though its adherents were popularly known as 'Irvingites', he was not held to possess apostolic gifts. Liberally supported by Drummond, the new body developed a hierarchy of apostles, prophets, evangelists, and pastors, with deacons to superintend material needs. Its remarkable liturgy drew on Church of Scotland, Anglican, Roman Catholic, and Eastern Orthodox elements, aptly reflected in the architecture of its main London church, Christ the King, Gordon Square (1854), which remains, though unfinished, one of Britain's finest expressions of the gothic revival. Since only apostles could ordain, the Church, which claimed 6,000 members in 30 congregations in 1851, lost its impetus after the last apostle's death in 1901. CB

Catholic Association, 1823–9. Daniel *O'Connell's Catholic Association, founded in Ireland in 1823, was one of the most successful pressure groups of the 19th cent. Its object was to persuade or force the British government to grant *catholic emancipation, allowing catholics to sit in Parliament. It organized petitions, held monster meetings, collected the 'catholic rent' of a penny a month, and was accused of drilling and intimidation. Attempts to suppress the association in 1825 failed, since it merely reconstituted itself. When O'Connell (unable as a catholic to take the oath) was returned to Parliament at the Co. Clare by-election in July 1828, *Wellington gave way rather than risk civil war. As a sop to the die-hards, the grant of catholic emancipation was preceded by an Act suppressing the association, but it had already voluntarily dissolved itself, its work done. JAC

catholic emancipation was achieved by an Act of Parliament of 1829, enabling Roman catholics in Britain to participate fully in public and political life by abolishing the *Test and *Corporation Acts. It resulted from Daniel *O'Connell's campaign to liberate the Irish majority from the political and economic domination of the *Anglo-Irish ascendancy. O'Connell's electoral success in the Co. Clare by-election convinced *Wellington that, short of a standing army, there was no means of controlling Ireland, other than to accede to the demands of the majority. English catholics played little part in the campaign. Its effect in resolving the Irish question was only partial, but the impact on British constitutional and religious history was immense. By splitting the Tory Party, with the ultra Tories regarding the actions of Wellington and *Peel in bringing in the measure as a gross betrayal, it prepared the way for the Whig victory of 1830 and for the decade of reform which followed.

The Act itself (10 Geo. IV c. 7), entitled *An Act for the Relief of His Majesty's Roman Catholic Subjects*, was carried against the strong opposition of the king and passed on 13 April 1829. It made provision for catholics to serve as members of lay corporations and (except catholic clergy) to sit in Parliament. Most crown offices were opened to catholics, save those of lord chancellor, keeper of the great seal, lord-lieutenant of Ireland and high commissioner of the Church of Scotland. No catholic prelate was to assume a title used by the Church of England, clergy were not to wear clerical dress outside church, and an unenforced ban was placed on religious orders.

The Act shattered the assumption that Britain was *de jure* and *de facto* a protestant nation, though the Act of *Settlement (1701) forbidding the monarch from being a catholic, or marrying a catholic, remained in force. But Parliament, henceforth open to both protestant and catholic dissenters, was no longer the political forum of the established church. Attempts by such a heterodox body to legislate for the Church of England were greeted with dismay by certain clerics. The unity of church and state, enshrined in the revolution settlement of 1689, had been shattered, with consequences few churchmen liked to consider. JFC

catholicism. The word derives from the universality of faith in the Christian church, but since the 16th cent. has referred to the portion of Christianity undivided from allegiance to papal authority and the beliefs and practices of the ancient church. In Britain, allegiance to the papacy and to those theological and doctrinal formulations rejected by reformers in the 16th cent. came to characterize a distinct brand of Christianity, as opposed to the *protestantism of the Church of England, which emerged from the Elizabethan settlement, and later dissenting groups. Since the 19th cent. parts of the Church of England have argued a case for adopting the term to include themselves, the Roman catholic church, and the orthodox churches as representing the undivided church of ancient times.

Commonly the word is used to delineate the distinctive post-Reformation communities in Britain which rejected the reform of the 16th cent. and the assertion of royal supremacy over the church in England. These catholic or papist communities survived and developed by resistance to legal proscription by *penal laws, eventually lifted in the late 18th and early 19th cents. That process can be understood in a series of phases, beginning with the period of survival as *recusant communities during the 17th cent. Up to 1688 and the fall of James II, catholics launched a missionary campaign to retain a foothold and maintain catholic life and worship in the teeth of hostile legislation. The sacramental nature of catholicism meant that the congregations, where they could exist, were dependent on priests who had to be trained in missionary seminaries in Europe. The first of these was founded by Cardinal William *Allen at Douai in Flanders and in Rome in the 1570s. The priests, subjected to the law of treason, went in fear of their lives and depended on the protection of lay families, mostly gentry, who risked safety and property to sustain catholic life. Lay and clerical catholics were executed up to the 1680s. The extent to which the penal laws were imposed varied according to the circumstances of the day and to local conditions, and in some areas catholicism flourished unmolested. Parts of Lancashire, the north-east, and the midlands became relatively safe territory, where recusant catholicism predominated. In Ireland, catholics formed the great majority outside Ulster, and in Scotland were strong in the Highlands and Islands.

In these areas it became possible, in the second phase from 1688 to the mid-18th cent., for catholic life to establish its existence, despite the fact that this was the lowest ebb in legal terms. The revolution of 1688 led to another and final wave of penal legislation and to renewed protestant antagonism towards catholicism. But the mood of the early 18th cent. turned against religious persecution and few of the laws were enforced. Almost the only lasting benefit to the catholics from the reign of James II was the appointment of vicars apostolic to govern the catholics in England and

Wales (and in Scotland later). This removed the organizational uncertainty from the community and eradicated some of the quarrelsomeness which had characterized an essentially insecure and haphazard operation. By the mid-18th cent., catholic practice was largely tolerated and life for the small congregations, served by travelling missionaries or gentry chaplains, fell into a pattern of quiet independence.

The final defeat of the *Jacobite cause in 1745 removed the political animus against catholicism, though not until 1829 was the prohibition on catholic MPs lifted. In the 1740s catholics were a negligible fraction of the population of England and Wales—perhaps 1 or 2 per cent—but from that time they entered a new phase of confidence and modest growth. Between about 1745 and the first Catholic Relief Act of 1778, catholics, along with their contemporaries, began to taste the first fruits of economic development. The drift to the towns began and though rural catholicism declined in some areas, urban catholicism in London, the midlands, and parts of the north began to emerge. New congregations, built around the independent self-determination of artisans and skilled craftsmen, grew up. They were able to persuade missioners to create settled missions, where there was a sufficiently stable population. Chapels and schools, though still technically illegal, began to appear. In these growing towns catholics were left to pursue their trades unmolested and were the basis of the emerging *nouveaux riches*, who were to take English catholicism into its 19th-cent. revival.

Between the Relief Acts of the late 18th cent. and about 1840, these emerging industrial catholics began to take greater responsibility for religious activities. At the same time this often brought them into conflict with the clergy. Tensions over the control and funding of the missionary enterprise had dogged English catholicism since the 16th cent. Clergy and laity had to be interdependent, but by the early 19th cent. both groups were asserting their rights and dignities. Numbers were increasing rapidly, from around 80,000 at the end of the 18th cent. to nearer 700,000 in the 1851 religious census. This growth was partly endogenous and partly due to massive migration of impoverished Irish catholics. Clerical training had been forced back onto British soil by the French Revolution and clerical numbers, organization, and ecclesiastical authority were increasing. Urban laity wanted at times to behave like the old gentry and were reluctant to relinquish the control over church life which money gave them.

The battle was ultimately resolved largely in favour of the clergy, whose role in an increasingly centralized and authoritarian contemporary catholicism was reinforced by enhanced papal discipline. The restoration of the catholic hierarchy to England and Wales in 1850, as well as resolving issues of control and organization, gave English catholicism a sense of belonging fully to the universal church under papal authority. The task after 1850 was to restore and rebuild English catholicism in the image of European catholicism and to create the churches, schools, society, devotions, and loyalty which built the powerful, close-knit catholic culture characteristic until the middle of the 20th cent. JFC

Bossy, J., *The English Catholic Community, 1570–1850* (1975); Butler, D., *Methodists and Papists: John Wesley and the Catholic Church in the 18th Century* (1994); Norman, E., *The English Catholic Church in the 19th Century* (1984); Quinn, D., *Patronage and Piety: The Politics of English Roman Catholicism 1850–1900* (1993).

Catholic University of Ireland. Though from 1793 catholics could take degrees at *Trinity College, Dublin, few chose to do so, and in 1844 *Peel proposed the establishment of undenominational colleges at Cork, Belfast, and Galway. The Irish catholic community split in response but the majority condemned them as godless, and the Synod of *Thurles in 1850 warned catholics not to attend. Archbishop *Cullen then presided over a committee to set up a catholic university. *Newman was installed as rector and the lectures he gave in Dublin formed the basis of his *Idea of a University*. The Catholic University opened in 1854 with twenty students but could make little progress without government assistance. It gained some help from the Royal University, set up in 1880 as an examining and funding body, which financed some fellowships. Augustine Birrell, chief secretary in the Liberal administration of 1906, introduced the major reconstruction of 1908, which established the National University, with component colleges at Dublin, Cork, and Galway. Though formally undenominational, it was under catholic control. *Queen's College, Belfast, was given university status at the same time. JAC

Cato Street conspiracy. A plot to murder Lord *Liverpool's cabinet at dinner at Lord *Harrowby's house in February 1820 was led by Arthur Thistlewood, a former army officer and a follower of the agrarian communist Thomas *Spence. It was the culmination of a series of conspiracies to overthrow the government and achieve democratic reform in the period after 1816. The plotters were betrayed by a government spy and arrested as they assembled in a stable in Cato Street. Thistlewood and four fellow-conspirators were executed on May Day, 1820. EAS

Catterick, battle of, 6th cent. *Aneurin's poem **Gododdin* relates how the North Britons from Edinburgh were defeated at Catterick by the men of *Bernicia and *Deira. He attributed their downfall to an immoderate consumption of mead. The battle was probably in the late 6th cent. It has been suggested that there may be confusion with *Æthelfryth of Bernicia's great victory at *Degsastan in 603. The battle was an important step in the development of Northumbria as a strong Saxon power. JAC

Catuvellauni. A British tribe and *civitas*. The Catuvellauni first appear in Roman records in Dio Cassius' account of the Claudian invasion of AD 43, where they led the opposition to the Roman forces. From the information Dio provides, we can trace the tribal kingdom back at least three generations to a king called Tasciovanus by the coins issued by him and his successor *Cunobelinus. In fact, it seems likely that the chief called *Cassivellaunus who had opposed Caesar in 54 BC had already begun to carve out the Catuvellaunian kingdom. The tribal name means 'good in battle', which seems particularly appropriate. By the time of the Claudian invasion, they had not only swallowed up smaller local tribes like the Ancalites, Bibroci, and Cassi but had captured large tracts of territory from the *Trinovantes and *Atrebates, and were pressing both the *Cantiaci and the *Iceni. The *civitas* which the Romans created in the mid-70s reflects this expansion, with its boundaries including Buckinghamshire, Hertfordshire, and Bedfordshire, much of Northamptonshire and parts of Oxfordshire and Cambridgeshire as well. The *civitas* capital was at *Verulamium (next to modern St Albans), which had been the original capital of Tasciovanus' kingdom. KB

Cavalier Parliament, 1661–79. This Parliament succeeded the *Convention, which had summoned Charles II back from exile. Though its members were overwhelmingly loyal to the monarchy—well over 100 had fought in the civil wars—they were by no means willing to yield Parliament's rights. The Anglican majority was noticeably less willing to forgive and forget than the king. It began by ordering that the *covenant be burned by the public hangman, supported a fierce penal code against dissenters, and forced Charles II in 1673 to withdraw his *Declaration of Indulgence. The unusual length of the Parliament gave opportunities for development of party organization, particularly under *Danby in the 1670s, even if party as such was still widely condemned and the names of 'court' and 'country' preferred. When Danby lost control in 1678, Charles dissolved the Parliament, but the three which succeeded were Whig-dominated, took up the issue of excluding James, duke of York (later James II), from the succession, and gave even more trouble. JAC

cavaliers. Nickname for the royalists who fought for Charles I during the civil wars. Like 'roundhead', 'cavalier' originated as a term of abuse. Stemming from the Spanish word *caballero*, it was meant to connote catholicism, foreignness, and immorality. The word was current by the summer of 1642, and referred to the disorganized and untrustworthy men who had backed the king in the *Bishops' wars (1639–40) and the army plots of 1641. Dissolute and turbulent individuals such as George, Lord *Goring, and ruthless and brutal soldiers of fortune such as Prince *Rupert, lent some plausibility to this caricature of the king's supporters. Parliamentary propagandists accordingly disseminated an image of the typical cavalier as a rakish individual consumed by the pursuit of illicit pleasure and personal gain, a man devoid of moral principles.

Rather than reject the nickname, the royalists redefined it for their own purposes. They saw themselves as well-born and -bred men who out of loyalty and conscience had chosen to defend their king. They stood for the old English tradition of gentility and valour at arms. Politically they asserted that Charles I, as supreme governor of the church, was God's anointed deputy. To defy him therefore was rebellion against God. Recent research has determined that, rather than being footloose young bachelors, most royalist officers were respectable married gentlemen. What bound them together was the principle of unconditional loyalty to the person of the king, whether or not they agreed with his particular words or actions. Combining contempt for the lower classes with a loathing for rebellion, many of them made enormous material sacrifices for their cause, in addition to hazarding their lives. Apart from a dislike for the Irish, they harboured little antagonism towards Roman catholics, many of whom supported the king as the lesser of two evils. The statement of Sir Beville Grenville prior to the outbreak of the Civil War sums up the simplicity and the curious pessimism of the royalist creed: 'The [king's] cause must make all those that die in it little inferior to martyrs. And for mine own part I desire to acquire an honest name or an honourable grave.' IJG

Cavell, Edith (1865–1915). The daughter of Frederick Cavell, vicar of Swardeston (Norfolk), Edith Cavell was a governess in Brussels before training as a nurse. In 1907 she returned to Brussels to become matron of the hospital of St Gilles and remained there at the outbreak of war in 1914. She set up escape routes for hundreds of Belgian and allied fugitives and was arrested by the Germans in August 1915. Under repeated interrogations and in solitary confinement, she made full confessions. Court-martialled on 7 October, she was shot on 12 October, dying with dignity and courage. The reaction world-wide to her death was enormous and elevated her to the status of martyr. Her body was later exhumed and reinterred in Norwich cathedral, 5 miles from her childhood home. A memorial was erected to her in St Martin's Place, off Trafalgar Square, London. SMC

Cavendish, Lord Frederick (1836–82). The second son of the 7th duke of Devonshire, Cavendish entered Parliament as a Liberal for the northern division of the West Riding of Yorkshire in 1865. His wife was the niece of Mrs Gladstone and Cavendish became Gladstone's private secretary. He held office as a junior lord of the Treasury in Gladstone's first administration and in 1882, when W. E. *Forster resigned, was sent to Ireland as chief secretary to replace him. Arriving in Dublin on 6 May he walked in Phoenix Park with T. H. Burke, the under-secretary, and was attacked and stabbed to death by a gang known as the *Invincibles. One of their number, James Carey, subsequently turned queen's evidence but was tracked down by his fellow-conspirators while on a vessel bound for South Africa under a false name and shot. Cavendish's murder caused a sensation and a new *Coercion Act was brought in. He was buried at *Chatsworth at the top end of Edensor churchyard at a funeral attended by 300 MPs, brought from London by special train, with the duke of Devonshire and Mr Gladstone leading 30,000 mourners. There is an impressive effigy in the church at Edensor and a copy at Cartmel priory. His widow appealed for conciliation, telling Gladstone, 'Uncle William, you did right to send him to Ireland.' JAC

Cavendish, Henry (1731–1810). Cavendish worked on the boundary of physics and chemistry. A nephew of the 3rd duke of Devonshire, and a wealthy man, he studied in Cambridge and in Paris, before living as a recluse in London, though he became an important figure in scientific life. He worked in the new field of pneumatic chemistry, isolating 'inflammable air' (hydrogen) and proving that water was not an element but a compound. Fascinated also by electricity, he made a model of the electric fish (torpedo), and many observations which he never published. He proved by means of a delicate torsion balance that, as *Newton had said, all particles of matter attract each other (whereas Aristotle had supposed that they were attracted to the centre of the universe), and calculated the mass of the earth. The Cavendish Laboratory in Cambridge was founded in his memory. DK

Cavendish, Thomas (1560–92). An enterprising and accomplished seaman but essentially a pirate, Cavendish helped explore North Carolina in 1585, before becoming the second English sailor to circumnavigate the world in 1586–8 in the ship *Desire*. After a very difficult passage through the Straits of Magellan, he sailed to California, captured a Spanish treasure ship, and returned home via the Moluccas and the Cape of Good Hope. Having lost most of his fortune at court, he tried to repeat his Pacific voyage in 1591 with John *Davis but failed to get through the Straits and died at sea in the South Atlantic. RB

Cavendish, William. See DEVONSHIRE, 4TH DUKE OF.

Cawnpore (Kanpur) was the scene of a bitter struggle during the *Indian mutiny and became a symbol of the violence of that conflict. Its British garrison, besieged for nineteen days, was obliged to surrender to Nana Sahib who, on hearing of the approach of Sir Henry *Havelock's relieving army, ordered all prisoners to be killed. Havelock retook the town and his forces wreaked a fearful revenge. However, the garrison he left behind proved unable to hold on and Tatya Tope, Nana Sahib's general, effected a reoccupation. It was not until December 1857 that Sir Colin *Campbell's army achieved the final reconquest. DAW

Caxton, William (*c.*1420–*c.*1492). A prominent merchant from Kent, Caxton established the first successful press in an England slow to adopt metallographic printing with movable type. Caxton learned printing in Cologne and the Low Countries, producing the first printed book in English—his own translation of *Le Receuil des histoires de Troye*—in Bruges *c.*1473–4. His press at Westminster, established in 1476, printed nearly 100 volumes, including works by *Chaucer, *Gower, *Lydgate, and *Malory, and translated writings on chivalry, morality, and religion. Formats varied, but volumes were typically in folio, on paper rather than vellum, in gatherings of four, with text in single columns. Illustrations were monochrome woodcuts. Although Caxton's printed books have been judged 'neither textually accurate nor aesthetically appealing', his impact on English culture is unquestionable. Apart from circulating numerous vernacular texts and taking the technological leap which provided the main means of disseminating information and ideas for the next four centuries, Caxton influenced English prose style and orthography, tending to standardize particular spellings at a time when linguistic upheavals such as the great vowel shift were still under way. DCW

Ceawlin (d. *c.*593), king of the West Saxons (560–91). Ceawlin, who began to reign in 560, fought against the Britons to extend Saxon power. At the battle of *Dyrham in 577 he is reported to have defeated three kings and to have taken Gloucester, Cirencester, and Bath, thus effectively separating Britons in the south-west from those north of the Bristol channel. In 584 he may have suffered a set-back at *Fethanleag, possibly near Bicester (Oxon.) for despite taking towns and booty, he is said to have returned home in anger. Ceawlin's final days are not easy to establish. Dissent may have produced another king or subking, Ceol, in 591, and in 592, after a defeat at Wodnesbeorh (near Alton Priors in the vale of Pewsey), he was expelled. He 'perished' the following year. Though the end of his reign was disastrous, he played an important role in Saxon expansion and *Bede lists him as the second great overlord, or *bretwalda. AM

Cecil, Sir Robert (1563–1612), Jacobean statesman, was the younger son, but political heir, of Elizabeth I's chief minister William Cecil (*Burghley). Small in stature, humpbacked, and physically frail, he devoted himself to the service of the monarchy which he venerated. Following in his father's footsteps, he entered Parliament in 1584 and quickly established his reputation. Knighted in 1591 and appointed privy counsellor, he was already acting secretary of state, though not formally appointed until 1596. In the last decade of Elizabeth's reign the Cecils' hold on power was challenged by a faction grouped around Elizabeth's young favourite, the ambitious earl of *Essex. Fortunately for the Cecils, Essex overreached himself and was executed. This left Cecil without rival as the queen's chief minister after the death of his father in 1598. Only the prospect of James VI's accession threatened him, for James had been a supporter of Essex, but Cecil neutralized this threat by opening secret communications with the Scottish king. His gamble paid off and he remained in office after James became king of England in 1603. James relied on Cecil, his 'little beagle', for the day-to-day business of government while he was away on frequent hunting expeditions. Cecil sometimes accompanied him, but apart from a love of hawking did not share the king's passion for the chase, and pressure of work meant he could rarely escape from his desk. While always treating James with deference, Cecil urged him to curtail his extravagance and also to restrain his partiality for Scots advisers and companions. Cecil was a staunch protestant but, like the king, took a relatively tolerant attitude towards catholics. His love of ceremony and of visual splendour—reflected in his pioneer collection of works of art—made him in some respects a precursor of the *Arminians. Like his royal master, Cecil loved peace, and in 1604 brought the long war with Spain to a close. Because James elevated him to the peerage shortly after his accession, Cecil had to leave the Commons, which made the management of the king's business in Parliament more difficult. In 1608, when he was earl of Salisbury, James appointed him lord treasurer, thereby saddling him with direct responsibility for restoring the royal revenue, eroded by inflation. Cecil's major attempt to refinance the crown, the *Great Contract, came close to success in 1610, but its eventual collapse diminished his reputation and influence, though he remained the king's principal adviser. However, although not yet 50, his health was in decline, and in 1612 he died. He had inherited the princely mansion called Theobalds which his father constructed, but its situation in good hunting country just north of London made James covet it. Cecil, ever the perfect courtier, therefore exchanged Theobalds for the ruinous palace at *Hatfield, some miles away, where he built the palatial house in which his descendants still live. RL

celibacy, clerical. Clerical celibacy, common since early Christian times, has scant scriptural authority. The Council of Elvira (*c.*305) forbade all western clergy to marry, a decision later confirmed by popes and western councils. The 11th-cent. Hildebrandine reforms, implemented in England sensitively by *Lanfranc, sought to eliminate renewed clerical concubinage. Lateran decrees (1123, 1139) reinforced this situation which remains the official catholic line, whereas the eastern church decreed (691) that, though bishops must be celibate, priests and deacons could continue already-established marriages. Clerical marriage was a major issue at the Reformation. Compulsory Anglican celibacy was abolished (1549), though *Cranmer was already secretly married. Elizabeth initially disapproved of married clergy, even of *Parker. After the second Vatican Council (1962–5) allowed a married diaconate, Paul VI in *Sacerdotalis caelibatus* resisted strong pressure to end celibacy (1967). Recent catholic reordination of married former Anglican bishops and priests (1995) has complicated the issue. WMM

céli Dé, 'clients of God' (often Anglicized as 'culdees'), was the name adopted by reforming ascetics in Ireland in the late 8th and early 9th cents. Based primarily in southern Irish monasteries such as Tallaght and Lismore, they sought to renew the monastic life-style of devotion, prayer, and asceticism. They were also keenly interested in wider structural reform, such as the provision of proper pastoral care.

Diarmait, abbot of *Iona 814–*c.*831, was influential on the reformers, who looked to early founders like *Columba as models of monastic behaviour. It may be Diarmait who helped to introduce the *céli Dé* to Scotland, where they were singularly successful. By *c.*940 there was a *céli Dé* community in St Andrews, where the Scottish king, *Constantine son of *Æd, retired into religion as their head. Through charters and church documents of the 11th cent. and later, we know of communities also in Abernethy, Brechin, Dunblane, Iona, probably Dunkeld, and many other monasteries. This frequency is unparalleled in Ireland.

The *céli Dé* lived in communities apart from the larger monastic or cathedral setting, in essence a monastery within a monastery. Although the membership of the community would appear to have been partly hereditary (members becoming celibate only later in life, upon entering strict observance), in places such as Kells in Ireland, the *céli Dé* were the observant monastics in an otherwise largely commercial and administrative religious power-centre. In Scotland, they continued to staff monasteries which did not change to continental rules, although many eventually became *Augustinian canons. Some conflict is observable between newly introduced orders and the now entrenched and conservative *céli Dé*, especially in St Andrews. Though tenacious, both communities and terminology gradually became obsolete in the course of the later Middle Ages. TOC

Celtic church. This term, which describes the Christian church as it developed in Wales, Ireland, and Scotland in the early Middle Ages, is useful to the extent that it recognizes that church practice in all three countries had many features in common (similar intellectual training, similar ideas on, for instance, pilgrimage and penance, similar styles of church building and art), but should not disguise the fact that there were very real differences between them in matters of organization. In particular, the concept of the territorial episcopal diocese was based on the administrative divisions of the Roman empire, with which Ireland had no formal link, and consequently, although it had its fair share of bishops, the diocesan system had difficulty in taking root there. Although *Christianity was present in Roman Britain by the early 3rd cent. AD, conversion was a slow and complex affair, and by the time of the Roman withdrawal much of Wales and Scotland was still heathen, and the earliest exact date for the presence of Christians in Ireland is a reference in 431 to Palladius, bishop to 'the Irish who believe in Christ'. While the earliest missionaries may have come from Gaul, Ireland was evangelized largely from Britain, its most famous British missionary being St *Patrick, whose activity probably dates to the early and mid-5th cent. The diffusion of the cult of Patrick, and the growth in the status of *Armagh, the ecclesiastical centre most closely associated with him, parallels that of St *David in south Wales, while the arrival of the Irish saint Colum Cille (*Columba) in *Iona, in the territory of *Dalriada in Scotland, in 563, marked the start of a lengthy period of Irish missionary activity in Britain and the continent. Those monasteries said to have been founded by Colum Cille were held together and administered in the form of a monastic *paruchia*, and while territorial dioceses were being established in Wales and Scotland, in Ireland ecclesiastical power was held largely by the abbatial, and frequently hereditary, heads of monastic centres, until the great 12th-cent. reform movement saw the establishment of an organized diocesan system along the lines of that operating throughout the Western church. SD

Celts. From the 5th cent. BC, Greek ethnographers such as Hecataeus of Miletus and Herodotus described the Celts as one of the major ethnic groups of central and western Europe, locating them inland from Marseilles, or around the headwaters of the Danube. Later Latin and Greek authors equated them with the Galli and Galatae who invaded northern Italy, Greece, and Asia Minor in the 4th and 3rd cents. BC, though Posidonius, writing around 100 BC, contrasted the Celts of Gaul with the less civilized Galatae of central Europe. Caesar, in the opening passage of the *De bello Gallico*, states that only the Gauls of central and southern Gaul called themselves Celts, with Belgae living in the north of Gaul and Aquitani in the south-west; these contrasted with surrounding ethnic groups such as the Germani and Britanni.

Interest was revived in the Celts during the Renaissance, as the earliest named inhabitants of temperate Europe. In 1582 George Buchanan claimed that the former inhabitants of Britain were Celts or Gauls on the basis of similarity in ancient place-names in Gaul and Britain. This linguistic similarity was developed by authors such as Pezron and Llywd in the 17th cent. to define a group of related languages spoken in ancient Gaul, and still surviving in parts of Brittany and Britain, and which they termed 'Celtic'. The term 'Celt' was thus extended to refer to speakers of these languages, or those whose recent ancestors had spoken it—Bretons, Celts, Cornish, Welsh, Irish, Manx, and Scottish.

To identify the ancient Celts, 18th- and 19th-cent. scholars turned to archaeology, describing certain objects and burial rites as 'Celtic'. In 1871 de Mortillet noted the similarity between burials in Champagne and northern Italy, suggesting this was the evidence for the historically documented Gallic invasion of northern Italy in the 4th cent. BC. Kemble and Franks, as early as 1863, had referred to objects from Britain decorated in a distinctive curvilinear art style as 'Celtic'. This art style was also found on the objects fished out at La Tène on Lake Neuchâtel in Switzerland, a site used by Hildebrand in 1874 to define the later Iron Age in central Europe; the cemetery of Hallstatt in Austria represented the earlier phase. Hildebrand considered both periods to be 'Celtic'.

By the late 19th cent. archaeologists had defined a La Tène 'culture', with distinctive artefact types (brooches, swords, etc.), art style, and burial rites, and following the theoretical assumptions of Kossinna and Childe that archaeological cultures could be equated with ancient peoples, the La Tène culture became that of the Celtic peoples, and La Tène art became 'Celtic' art. It was also assumed that there was a close correlation between ethnicity, language, art, and material culture, and by using classical and Irish sources that an ancient 'Celtic' society and 'Celtic' religion could also be defined, and the former distribution of the Celts mapped, using a combination of historical, archaeological, and linguistic (especially place-name) evidence. On this model, the modern existence of Celtic languages along the Atlantic seaboard implies a 'survival' of Celtic ways, supported further by the La Tène art style and early Christian art in Ireland, and also in descriptions of Irish society. Thus the Irish and the classical sources are often combined to produce a 'timeless' and 'placeless' description of Celtic society and religion.

Scholars such as Powell (1958) and Filip (1962) used archaeology to seek the origin and spread of the La Tène culture, and so of the Celts, and document their expansion. On the evidence of the continuity of burial rites from the preceding Hallstatt period, and of a concentration of richly decorated early La Tène art objects, the centre of origin was identified as northern France–western Germany, more specifically in Champagne, and the hill-ranges of the Hunsrück and Eifel on either side of the river Mosel. From these areas it was claimed the Celts expanded in the 4th and 3rd cents. BC by migrating into southern and western France, Britain, and central Europe, and, as documented by the historical sources, into Italy, Greece, Bulgaria, and Asia Minor. Subsequent revisions of this theory have extended the core area to include southern Germany and Bohemia, and back in time to the late Hallstatt period, to include the rich burials and 'princely residences' such as Asperg, the Heuneburg, and Mont Lassois.

This model has come under increasing criticism. It fails to account for Celtic-speaking groups in Iberia where La Tène objects are rare or unknown; the supposed invasion of Britain in the 4th–3rd cents. BC corresponds with the period in the first millennium BC when insular–continental contacts were at their lowest ebb; and continuity from the early to the late Iron Age is seen as the norm in virtually all areas where the archaeological record is sufficiently complete (e.g. Britain). The supposed 'expansion' of the Celts is largely a product of the misinterpretation of the archaeological record. Most art objects, ornaments, and weapons are deposited either in graves or in ritual contexts; neither of these are characteristic of the 6th–3rd cents. BC in much of Britain, and, more pertinently, in the areas of Gaul described by Caesar as 'Celtic'. It is therefore not surprising that early La Tène objects are rare or absent from these areas. Attempts to tie in the expansion of the Celts with early archaeological cultures (e.g. the late Bronze Age Urnfield culture) are equally unsatisfactory, and many archaeologists reject the simplistic correlation between language and material culture assumed by traditional approaches.

This new, and still disputed, view of the Celts is forcing us to adopt new models for the diffusion and adoption of language, material culture, and art styles, independent of one another. The naming of the language group as 'Celtic' is seen as an arbitrary choice by 17th-cent. scholars—it could have equally been Britannic, Belgic, or Gallic—as the Celts were only one of a number of ethnic groups using these languages. If we accept that there were never any Celts in antiquity in Britain, it follows that terms such as the 'Celtic' church (for the Scottish church of Bede), Celtic art (for early Christian Irish art), or indeed the description of the Welsh, Irish, and Scots as 'Celts' are without any historical foundations, and any direct connection between the ancient and modern Celts must be rejected. JRC

Collis, J., *The European Iron Age* (1984); James, S., *Exploring the World of the Celts* (1993); Kruta, V., Frey, O. H., Raftery, B., and Szabo, M. (eds.), *The Celts* (1991); Raftery, B. (ed.), *Celtic Art* (Paris, 1991).

censorship. The evolution of censorship has been a series of largely ineffective attempts by the authorities to suppress opinions of which they disapproved. Though they won many temporary victories, over time they were defeated by the growing liberalization of opinion, the difficulty of enforcing controls, and the proliferation of new vehicles of expression—pamphlets, plays, newspapers, film, radio, television, and computers. Before the invention of printing, arrangements for licensing were scarcely needed, though many authors, like Roger *Bacon and John *Wyclif, were subsequently taken to task for expressing heretical opinions. In 1529 Henry VIII issued a proclamation deploring the 'pestiferous, cursed and seditious errors' of Martin Luther, prohibiting the sale of books against the catholic religion, and mentioning by name several of *Tyndale's works. By 1538 it was declared that all books of Scripture needed a licence from the *Privy Council before publication. In 1557 the Stationers' Company was given the exclusive right of printing.

Elizabeth repeated the licensing arrangements in 1559 and in 1586 printing was restricted to London and the two universities. These regulations did not prevent the production of broadsheets and pamphlets, particularly of a puritan bent. Licensing regulations were continued under Charles I, Cromwell, and at the Restoration. The decision in 1695 not to renew the *Licensing Act freed authors from pre-publication inspection, but they were still liable to prosecution afterwards. In 1719 John Matthews, a Jacobite writer, was hanged for challenging the Hanoverian succession. Newspapers could be attacked by *general warrants, which authorized the arrest of all concerned with the production or distribution of offending literature. Not until the *Wilkes case in the 1760s were general warrants declared illegal.

Meanwhile, government had also moved against stage plays. As early as the 1570s the master of the revels had been given the task of licensing plays, but regulation was fitful. *Walpole, provoked by satirical performances by *Gay and *Fielding, sponsored a statute in 1737 giving the lord *chamberlain power to license theatres and plays. The later 18th cent. saw some relaxation. Another consequence of the Wilkes affair was that, in 1771, Parliament abandoned its efforts to prevent the publication of its debates in the newspapers. During the prosecution of William Woodfall in 1770, the jury insisted on its right to decide whether the passage complained of was libel (and not merely to declare the fact of publication), and this important extension of the right to comment was given statutory authority in Fox's *Libel Act of 1792.

The 20th-cent. position is extremely complex and changes rapidly, partly because of the number of outlets now available. The lord chamberlain's power to license stage plays was removed in 1968. The Victorian Act of 1857 against obscene publications, under which James *Joyce's *Ulysses* had been seized in 1923, was modified by an Act of 1959, which allowed a defence if artistic or literary merit could be proved. The first and most celebrated test of the new legislation was in 1960, when *Lady Chatterley's Lover* was cleared for publication after a parade of distinguished witnesses had testified to its deep moral integrity. Films are categorized under a British Board of Film Censors' code, set up by the industry itself. The home secretary has powers to intervene in BBC radio and television programmes, and the Independent Broadcasting Authority monitors commercial radio and television. To strike an appropriate balance on censorship is far from easy. *Milton's *Areopagitica* (1644) was a noble statement of the right 'to know, to utter, and to argue freely', but it does not seem likely that he had in mind the tabloid press or video nasties. JAC

Census Act, 1800. In 18th-cent. Britain there was much uncertainty about the size of the population and whether it was diminishing in relation to that of France. Sweden, Norway, Denmark, Iceland, and Austria, followed by Holland and Spain, instituted censuses in the course of the century. In 1753 Thomas Potter moved in Parliament for an annual census. His opponents retorted that it would give valuable information to enemies, complained of the affront to British liberty, and forecast widespread resistance. The bill was lost in the Lords. Arthur *Young proposed a census in a pamphlet of 1771 and an inconclusive debate about the trend rumbled on. The 1800 bill, which carried the day, was introduced by Charles Abbot, a future Speaker, at the suggestion of John Rickman. There was no opposition and the first census of Great Britain was carried out on 10 March 1801. The population of England and Wales was returned as 9.168 million and Scotland as 1.599 million, revealing an upwards trend. Contemporaries were struck by the size of London which, at 1 million, was as big as all the other towns together. Though simple and unsophisticated by later standards, the census was a milestone in the provision of statistical data and has subsequently been held at ten-year intervals. JAC

Central. An administrative region of Scotland, created in 1973 from Clackmannanshire, western parts of Perthshire, most of Stirlingshire, and the Bo'ness area of West Lothian. It was divided into three districts—Clackmannan, Falkirk, and Stirling. In April 1996 Central region was abolished, and all local government functions taken over by the previous districts. Parts of the area are mountainous, but most inhabitants live in a string of mainly industrial towns either in the Forth valley or along the line of the Forth–Clyde canal, which itself follows the natural east–west route used by the Romans for the *Antonine Wall. CML

Cenwalh (d. 672), king of Wessex (642–5, 648–72). Cenwalh was driven out by his powerful Mercian neighbours in 645 for repudiating his wife, sister of the Mercian king. He sought refuge at the court of East Anglia, where he was baptized. Returning in 648, he established a kinsman in Berkshire, probably as a bulwark against Mercian aggression. His main successes were against the Britons to the west, gaining victories at Bradford on Avon (652), Peonnan (658), and Posbury (possibly Pontesbury near Shrewsbury) in 661. Against the Mercians he was less successful and in 661 lost parts of Hampshire and the Isle of Wight to Mercia, which granted them to *Sussex. Cenwalh's creation of a second episcopal see at *Winchester, *c.*660, may have been prompted by the vulnerability of the one at *Dorchester-on-Thames, though *Bede claims that he had tired of his Frankish bishop, Agilbert, whose speech he could not understand. After Cenwalh's death, Bede says that Wessex was divided among under-kings for ten years, while the *Anglo-Saxon Chronicle* reports that his queen reigned for a year. AM

Cenwulf (d. 821), king of Mercia (796–821). Cenwulf became king after the brief reign of Ecgfrith, son of the great *Offa, doubtless by a coup, for he was only remotely related to his predecessor. He took over Offa's extensive authority in southern England. In 798 he repressed a revolt in Kent, brutally. His authority there was diminished by a long and bitter dispute with Archbishop *Wulfred of Canterbury, appointed in 805. He fought successful wars in Wales in 816 and 818. Founder, or a major benefactor, of Winchcombe abbey, he was buried there. JCa

Ceolnoth, archbishop of Canterbury (833–70), had the difficult task of establishing working relations with the West

Saxon kings who had won political control of Kent after many years of Mercian domination. In this he seems to have been largely successful, obtaining grants of land from King *Egbert and his son *Æthelwulf and confirmation of the cathedral's control of Kentish minsters which had been disputed in the archiepiscopate of his predecessor *Wulfred. His period in office saw an intensification of Viking raids and an attack on Canterbury in 850 or 851. By the time of his death in 870 there seems to have been a severe decline in standards of literacy and writing in the Canterbury scriptorium though the reasons for this may be complex and not simply the result of Viking harassment. BAEY

Ceolwulf (d. 764), king of Northumbria (729–31, 731–7). Such Anglo-Saxons of his day who can claim immortality, however humbly, owe this to *Bede. So with Ceolwulf. Bede, in dedicating his *Ecclesiastical History* to 'the most glorious King Ceolwulf', says that he had sent an earlier version to him 'to read and judge'. In the same year (731) Ceolwulf was, an annalist says, 'seized, tonsured [i.e. forced to become a monk] and restored to rule'. Six years later he was deposed for good. He lived long as a monk at *Lindisfarne and was (later) credited with the introduction of alcohol there. JCa

ceorl is one of the terms used in the early (7th- and 9th-cent.) English laws for the lowest class of freeman. Thus in Wessex his blood-price was 200 shillings: that of other free classes was 600 and 1,200. In Kent his relative status was higher. Even the West Saxon ceorl appears as the head of a free peasant household, owing military service, capable of owning slaves, and with significant legal status. At the same time such men could be in a condition of economic dependence. In the later period the term is one of several used for free peasants, though it occurs in the laws only as meaning 'husband'. An early 11th-cent. tract on status envisages the possibility of such a man's prospering to attain the rights of a thegn. Nevertheless in the 11th cent. the status of free peasants often fell. It is indicative that by 1300 the word was acquiring its modern sense of disparagement. JCa

ceramics. Historically ceramics production was widely dispersed, its main branches being brick and tile, pottery and porcelain manufacture. Brick-making was highly localized, wherever suitable clay deposits coincided with a lack of cheap building stone, or where coal, the main fuel used in firing the kilns, was itself cheap. The most primitive form of production was in clamps or piles, covered with earth or turves, and fired with small coal. By the late 18th cent. this was abandoned in favour of fixed kilns, which gradually became larger and more efficient. Continuous methods of firing were introduced during the second half of the 19th cent. Another important product, which played its part in the modernization of agriculture during the 18th and 19th cents., was the field drain. Decorative tile manufacture reached its peak during the Victorian and Edwardian eras.

Also widely manufactured, pottery was an important item of everyday use and of both short- and long-distance trade from prehistoric times, and hence can be an invaluable aid in the dating of archaeological and historic sites. Suitable clay is found in many parts of Britain, but the differences in quality arise from the variability of the raw material. According to material, methods of production, and finish, pottery can be classified in three categories—earthenware, stoneware, and porcelain. The high-domed furnace was introduced from the continent before 1600, but this was replaced in the 18th cent. by a bottle-shaped kiln, of the kind once common in the Potteries of Staffordshire, and still to be seen at the Gladstone Pottery Museum in Stoke-on-Trent or at the Ironbridge Gorge Museum, Telford.

Stoneware was probably the most common variety of pottery still in use in the 18th cent. It was made from a mixture of clay and 20 per cent ground flint, with a salt glaze, and was a typical product of the Staffordshire industry. Porcelain was imitated as a substitute for expensive East India Company imports from China, first pioneered by the Dutch in Delft. After 1740 imitation of Delft-ware was widespread, notably at Lambeth, Bristol, Liverpool, and Glasgow. Around the same time, fine porcelain began to be produced, among other locations, in Chelsea, Derby, and Worcester. Following Meissen and Sèvres products, British potters began to use china clay or kaolin, when in 1768 William Cookworthy, a Plymouth chemist, proved the potential of the kaolin reserves of Cornwall. Due to the availability of local skilled labour and cheap coal, this new industry concentrated on Staffordshire, where one of the best potters was Josiah *Wedgwood, whose Etruria works and products became world famous.

During the late 18th and early 19th cents. ceramics became one of the leading mass-production industries, though alongside cheap earthenware, high-quality porcelain was produced by potters like Spode, Minton, and Coalport. These and other famous names in the history of ceramics survive in the modern industry, which has become geographically more concentrated, but still manufactures a diverse range of products. The Arts and Crafts movement of the later 19th and early 20th cents. saw a revival of traditional pottery techniques, emphasizing artistic skill and design as a counter to mass production. ID

Cerdic, House of. By the late 9th cent., when the **Anglo-Saxon Chronicle* was compiled, Cerdic was regarded as the common ancestor of *Alfred and all previous kings of the West Saxons; however, the reality behind these claims is hard to ascertain. The arrival of Cerdic and his son Cynric is recorded in the *Chronicle* annal for 495, but the entries concerning them are riddled with so many inconsistencies that they cannot be taken as viable historical accounts. Not the least of the problems is that Cerdic is not in origin a Germanic name but Brittonic and may not have been borrowed into Old English until the period *c.*550–650. The last king who could claim to be a direct descendant in the male line from Cerdic was Edward the Confessor, but Henry I by marrying a great-niece of Edward ensured that subsequent rulers could continue to retain him as an ancestor.

BAEY

Ceylon. See SRI LANKA.

Chad (Ceadda), **St** (d. 673). One of four Northumbrian brothers who were 'famous priests', Chad studied in Ireland

and was a disciple of *Aidan. In 664 he succeeded his brother Cedd as abbot of Lastingham and was nominated to the see of Northumbria (his seat to be at York), by King *Oswui, retaliating to his son Alchfrith's nomination of *Wilfrid. Informed by Archbishop *Theodore that his consecration (*c.*665), by Wine and two British bishops, was irregular, he resigned the see. He became (fifth) bishop of the Mercians, the Middle Angles, and the people of Lindsey in 670, his seat at *Lichfield. As bishop he emulated Aidan, but his scope may have been limited by the earlier work of an active British church. Chad founded a monastery, possibly at Barrow-on-Humber, on land from *Wulfhere of Mercia. One of his monks, Trumbert, taught *Bede. The 8th-cent. Gospels of St Chad were probably associated with his shrine. AER

Chadwick, Edwin (1800–90). Reformer. John Stuart *Mill called Chadwick 'one of the organising and contriving minds of the age', and the great moment in his life came in 1829 when he met the aged Jeremy *Bentham and became his literary secretary. Henceforward, Chadwick was utilitarianism in action. He was born in Manchester, his family moved to London when he was 10, and he became a lawyer. In 1832 he was appointed to the Poor Law Commission and the following year to the commission on children in factories. His influence on both reports was very great and he was appointed secretary to the Poor Law Commission in 1834, a post which brought him savage criticism. Another of his abiding interests was sanitary reform and from 1848 to 1854 he served as a commissioner on the new Board of Health. He was then rather pointedly pensioned off and his public career closed, though he continued to campaign, particularly for competitive examinations in the civil service. Chadwick's character made him not only an exemplar but a caricature of utilitarian reform. He was hard-working, rigorous, and determined, but also tactless, unhumorous, impatient, dogmatic, and over-confident. Significantly, he was made to wait for his knighthood until he was 89. JAC

Chalgrove Field, battle of, 1643. Prince *Rupert disrupted *Essex's advance on Oxford in the summer of 1643 with a series of brilliant sorties. On 17 June he set out with nearly 2,000 men, mainly cavalry, and surprised several parliamentary garrisons, especially that at Chinnor. On the way back the following day, he turned on his pursuers at Chalgrove, between Watlington and Oxford, and inflicted a severe defeat. Fatally wounded in the battle was John *Hampden, of ship money fame. Shot in the shoulder, he could not reach his home at Great Hampden across the Chilterns but died in an inn at Thame. JAC

chamber. The chamber (*camera*) started life as the royal bedchamber, with treasure kept under the bed, and became the financial headquarters of the early Norman monarchy. The main treasure was at first kept in Winchester, as it had been in Anglo-Saxon times. As business grew rapidly in complexity, the office of *treasurer emerged. Much of the chamber's importance was lost in the reign of Henry III to the *wardrobe, though it regained influence under Edward II and Edward III. By the Tudor period, the *Exchequer had taken over most of the chamber's public responsibilities. JAC

Chamberlain, Sir Austen (1863–1937). The only 20th-cent. leader of the Conservative Party who failed to rise to the premiership, Chamberlain none the less enjoyed a ministerial career of considerable length and distinction. His rise owed much to the patronage of his father Joseph, but he ultimately emerged in his own right as a politician of standing. Chancellor of the Exchequer under Balfour (1903–5), he strongly supported tariff reform. During the First World War he accepted responsibility for the failure of the Mesopotamian campaign, resigning as secretary of state for India in 1917. But he was soon recalled to high office, returned to the Exchequer, and remained a leading supporter of *Lloyd George's coalition until its fall in October 1922. He succeeded Bonar *Law as Conservative leader in 1921 (having withdrawn from the leadership contest ten years earlier in the latter's favour), but lost his chance of the premiership through loyalty to Lloyd George.

As foreign secretary under *Baldwin (1924–9) he is best remembered for the *Locarno treaties of 1925, which, despite later misgivings, were hailed at the time as a great step towards European harmony, winning Chamberlain both the Garter and the Nobel peace prize. After a brief spell at the Admiralty, Chamberlain retired to the back benches in 1931, becoming one of very few British politicians who warned of the dangers posed by Hitler's Germany. Stiff and formal in appearance and manner, Chamberlain was often a difficult colleague. But he won respect for his loyalty and sense of principle. DJD

Chamberlain, Joseph (1836–1914). Radical and imperialist. Like many of the most interesting politicians, Chamberlain defies categorization. He made his fortune as a screw manufacturer, which enabled him to retire at the age of 38. He dedicated the rest of his life to politics, first on the Birmingham city council, where he rose to be mayor in 1873–5, and then as a Birmingham MP. He was an advanced social reformer for his time, clearing slums, building houses for the poor, setting up free public libraries and art galleries, and taking the gas, water, and sewage systems of Birmingham into municipal ownership. He also had sharp views on the aristocracy, which he regarded as useless ('they toil not, neither do they spin'), and he talked of making them pay a 'ransom' for their continued enjoyment of their privileges. That offended, as one might expect, Queen Victoria.

He rose to cabinet rank in 1880. But he was not altogether comfortable even on the radical wing of the *Liberal Party, because of his patriotic views on national issues. These were sorely tested by *Gladstone's limp policies, as he saw them, on South Africa and Egypt, and caused him to break formally with the Liberal party over the *Irish Home Rule issue in 1886. That was curious in some ways, because he was not an out-and-out unionist, and did not seem all that far away from Gladstone's views on Ireland when the crisis came. That led some of his contemporaries to suspect that he was really making a play for the leadership. If that was in his mind, however, he was soon disabused. The new

*Liberal Unionist group he attached himself to never made it up with the rump of the Liberal Party, and eventually allied with the *Conservatives. It was this camp that provided Chamberlain with his next major platform, as colonial secretary in *Salisbury's government of 1895.

As colonial secretary Chamberlain proved as radical as he had on the domestic scene, and in many of the same ways: advocating the development by central government, for example, of what he called Britain's 'imperial estates'. He also believed in their extension, particularly in southern Africa, where he was instrumental in trying to bring the Afrikaner republics to heel, first clandestinely (the *Jameson Raid) and then by helping to provoke the second *Boer War. That made him the leading imperialist of his time. But he was an unusual one. He sought to extend the empire, but also worried about its *over*-extension. With this in mind in 1898 he tried to fix a protective alliance with Germany behind Salisbury's back. He also wished to consolidate the colonies, in order to maximize their potential strength. In 1903 he came out publicly in favour of *imperial preference as a means of achieving this, resigning from the cabinet in order to press it at the next election (1906). The result was to split the Conservative Party (the second great party he had had this effect on), and give the Liberals a landslide victory.

He may have been right. In July 1906, however, he suffered a disabling stroke. Without his energy behind it the tariff reform campaign wilted. He died just before the Great War came to bear out his deepest fears. BJP

chamberlain, lord great. Originally in charge of the royal chamber and known as the master chamberlain, the office-holder had some financial responsibilities since part of the king's treasure was kept there. Later he lost most of his duties to the *treasurer and other officers, but retained responsibility for the palace of Westminster, the opening of Parliament, and the introduction of new peers. He also attended the coronation and handed water to the monarch before and after the banquet. From 1133 the office was hereditary in the de Vere family, though with interruptions and vicissitudes, until it passed in 1626 to their cousins the Berties, as Lords Willoughby de Eresby.

The office of lord chamberlain is quite distinct. He has direct charge of the royal household and in 1737 was given the power of licensing plays. This was strengthened by an Act of 1843 and not abolished until 1967. The vice-chamberlain is a deputy to the lord chamberlain. JAC

Chamberlain, (Arthur) Neville (1869–1940). Prime minister. Chamberlain was born in Birmingham, a son of Joseph *Chamberlain by his second wife. Educated at Rugby and Mason College, Birmingham, he seemed destined for a business career, but his election to the city council in 1911 provided an opportunity for him to display his considerable talents as a municipal reformer; in 1915 he became lord mayor of Birmingham and in 1916 he was instrumental in establishing in Birmingham the nation's first—and only—municipal savings bank. His record of conscientious and effective service in local government led to appointments first as a member of the control board established to oversee the liquor trade during the First World War, and then as director-general of national service (1916).

In 1918, at the late age of 49, he determined to enter politics, and was elected as a Conservative MP for Birmingham. Chamberlain had conceived a healthy dislike of *Lloyd George, but supported the coalition government (1918–22) as being in the national interest. In 1922 his half-brother Austen tried unsuccessfully to persuade the Conservative Party to continue in membership of the coalition; Neville agreed with *Baldwin and Bonar *Law that it had outlived its usefulness, and that Lloyd George's political judgement could no longer be trusted. In 1922, clearly marked out for high office, Chamberlain joined Bonar Law's government as postmaster-general, becoming minister of health in 1923, chancellor of the Exchequer 1923–4, and returning to the health portfolio in Baldwin's second government (1924–9).

Chamberlain's years at the Ministry of Health establish his claim to be one of the greatest social reformers in Britain in the 20th cent. It was at his urging that the cabinet agreed to finance a widows', orphans', and old-age pensions bill in 1925. He piloted through the Commons the Rating and Valuation Act of 1925, which gave relief from local rates to agriculture and industry, and he initiated the great Local Government Act of 1929, which abolished the Poor Law Guardians, transferring their powers, and the institutions they administered (including hospitals), to the counties and county boroughs. Meanwhile, he was able to bring about a partnership between private builders and local authorities to build almost 1 million houses for the working classes.

At the general election of 1929 Baldwin's government was voted out of office. Chamberlain agreed to Baldwin's suggestion that he undertake a reorganization of Conservative central office, establishing a research department, but he used this period (1929–31) and this position to work strenuously for the abandonment of free trade, which he correctly viewed as a millstone around the neck of British industry. During Baldwin's absence abroad Chamberlain represented the Conservative Party in the negotiations which led to the formation of the *National Government. He held office in that administration as chancellor of the Exchequer, until succeeding Baldwin as prime minister in 1937.

Neville Chamberlain's years at the Treasury, coinciding with the depression of the 1930s, were years of challenge: he stood the test. In 1932 he persuaded the cabinet to agree to the abandonment of free trade: a general duty of 10 per cent was placed on almost all imports, but goods originating from within the British empire were exempted. As Chancellor, Chamberlain professed a desire to balance the books: in fact, perhaps more by accident than design, his budgets were frankly inflationary. The first, in 1932, was meant to be orthodox, but was wrongly calculated, and led to an excess of expenditure over revenue of some £32 million; this sum was simply added to the national debt. In 1933 the sinking-fund was suspended: repayment of the national debt was met through borrowing. The war loan was converted from 5 per cent to 3.5 per cent, and bank rate reduced. In 1934 he was able to restore earlier cuts in unemployment pay, and in 1935 to lower income tax. It is true that this policy of financial good housekeeping was blown off course by the need to rearm in the face of the Nazi menace. It is equally true that his budgets assisted economic recovery, and put the nation's finances into a position whereby they were able to meet the early demands of war in 1939. In 1937 he had no hesitation in taxing business profits (the 'National Defence Contribution'), a move which delighted the socialists and caused a short-lived panic on the Stock Exchange.

In May 1937 Baldwin resigned the premiership; Chamberlain's succession was automatic. Almost exactly three years later he resigned in a welter of criticism, triggered by Britain's withdrawal from Norway but largely informed by public disenchantment with his pre-war foreign policy.

Chamberlain's policy towards Nazi Germany is commonly associated with *'appeasement'. It is as well to remember, therefore, that 'appeasement' of the Nazis was a popular policy in Britain in the 1930s. There was widespread agreement that Germany had been treated badly at Versailles in 1919, that if the principle of national self-determination had any meaning then the Austrian Germans could not be prohibited from joining Germany proper, and that the plight of ethnic Germans incorporated within other states created after the First World War needed attention. Neville Chamberlain believed in the *League of Nations, and would have joined France in bolstering the League in its efforts to counter the Italian invasion of Abyssinia. When that did not happen he became disenchanted with French diplomacy, and also unnerved by it. He saw it as his mission to prevent war with Germany and, if that could not be achieved, to postpone hostilities as long as possible in order to give the maximum time for rearmament.

But he had been unable to prevent or curtail Italian intervention in the Spanish Civil War, and Hitler's so-called 'invasion' of Austria caught him off guard. His policy during the Czech crisis (September 1938) was much affected, and undermined, by the unwillingness of the French to fulfil their treaty obligations towards the Czechs. Of course the 3 million Sudeten Germans living in Czechoslovakia were manipulated by the Nazis. None the less, Chamberlain's dramatic airline flight to Berchtesgaden (15 September), to meet Hitler, was tremendously popular at home, and his second visit, to sign the Munich agreement, though certainly paving the way for the Nazi take-over of the Czech state, was at the time widely hailed as a triumph.

In 1939, in relation to the British guarantee of Poland's borders, Chamberlain saw that appeasement was at an end. His honourable intentions were quickly erased from the public mind once Britain and Germany were at war. Chamberlain was then seen as a gullible English gentleman who had been totally outmanœuvred by a ruthless Führer. He had no stomach for war, and was not a war leader. In May 1940 he resigned to make way for Winston *Churchill, and died shortly afterwards. GA

Dilks, D., *Neville Chamberlain* (Cambridge, 1984); Feiling, K. G., *The Life of Neville Chamberlain* (1946); Macleod, I., *Neville Chamberlain* (1961); Neville, P., *Neville Chamberlain: A Study in Failure?* (1992).

Chambers, Ephraim (*c.*1680–1740). Encyclopedist, man of letters, and free thinker. Born in Kendal and apprenticed to a well-known map- and globe-maker, the publication of John Harris's *Lexicon technicum* (1704) gave him the idea of constructing an encyclopedia that would be a guide to universal knowledge and would be held together by an elaborate system of cross-referencing and a series of supplements on specialized topics. First published in 1728, subsequently republished in 1738, 1741, 1746, dedicated to the king, Chambers's title indicates the range of his work. *Cyclopaedia: or an universal dictionary of arts and sciences; containing an explanation of the terms and an account of the things signified thereby, in the several arts, both liberal and mechanical: and the several sciences human and divine . . . The whole intended as a course of ancient and modern learning. Extracted from the best authors, dictionaries, memoirs, translations, . . . in several languages.* The French translation of 1743–5 was an important influence on d'Alembert's and Diderot's *Encyclopédie.* NTP

Chambers, William (1800–83). Publisher and author born and educated in Peebles and apprenticed to an Edinburgh bookseller. Chambers set up his own bookselling business in 1819 and went into printing, entering the lucrative business of writing and publishing cheap, popular, improving periodicals. With his brother Robert, he made his reputation with *Chambers' Edinburgh Journal*, a $1\frac{1}{2}$ penny weekly begun in 1832. Crammed with entertaining and wholesome stories about Scottish history and biography, often written in vernacular Scots, it soon reached an English market. Chambers published a steady flow of periodicals and encyclopedias for the next four decades, made his fortune, and was an active and influential lord provost of Edinburgh in the 1880s. His interest in civic improvement and conservation left a permanent and wholly beneficent mark on the city's architectural development. He accepted a baronetcy from Gladstone but died before it could be awarded. NTP

Chambers, Sir William (1723–96). Architect. Born in Sweden, the son of Scottish parents, Chambers was educated in England, and travelled to the Far East, France, and Italy. On his return, he became architecture tutor to the prince of Wales, later George III, who advanced his career, and for whom he designed a coronation coach still used by the royal family. In 1757 he published *Designs of Chinese Buildings*, and his *Treatise of Civil Architecture* (1759) was long regarded as a standard work. As treasurer of the Royal Academy, his influence led to the development of the architectural profession. The pagoda and orangery at Kew are fine examples of his work, which led to a general interest in Britain in eastern architecture. He was extremely fastidious and correct, even dull, and his designs for Somerset House in London (1775) were criticized for lacking drama. From 1770 he was permitted to use his Swedish knighthood. JC

champion of England. The duty of the champion was to present himself in full armour on horseback at the *coronation banquet in Westminster Hall, to throw down the gauntlet, and challenge anyone who denied the king's title. The office was attached to the manor of Scrivelsby (Lincs.), which belonged in the 12th cent. to the Marmion family, who claimed to have been hereditary champions to the dukes of Normandy. Philip Marmion is said to have acted at the coronation of Edward I in 1274. The manor then passed to the Dymoke family and John Dymoke certainly acted as champion for Richard II. The Dymokes performed at subsequent ceremonies, the last being the coronation of George IV in 1821. William IV decided that the banquet was expensive and unseemly and it has not been held since. There is no record of any challenge being accepted, though it was rumoured that the Jacobites in 1761 might challenge George III. They did not. JAC

Chanak crisis, September–October 1922. Turkish nationalists under Mustapha Kemal were unhappy about the loss of territory to Greece under the Sèvres treaty of 1920. They expelled the Greeks from Smyrna by force in August 1922 and threatened to cross the Dardanelles. Britain feared for the security of the Straits. *Lloyd George reinforced British positions in Chanak, the neutral region on the Asiatic shore of the Dardanelles, thus blocking the Turks. Conflict was averted by an agreement settled on 11 October at Mudania. Eastern Thrace and Adrianople were returned to Turkey in return for recognition of the neutral zones of the Dardanelles. RAS

Chancellor, Richard (d. 1556). An explorer who opened up the first English contacts with Russia, Chancellor gained early experience of navigation and seamanship on voyages to the eastern Mediterranean. With the project to open a North-East Passage, he was chosen by *Willoughby to be pilot-major of the first expedition in 1553 and sailed the *Edward Bonaventure* into the White Sea. He then travelled overland to Moscow and made a preliminary trade agreement with Ivan IV which inspired backers in England to set up the Muscovy Company (*Russia Company). Chancellor made a second visit to Moscow in 1555 but was killed when his ship was wrecked off northern Scotland in 1556. However the contacts with Russia and further overland exploration continued. RB

chancellor of the Exchequer. This office is held by the head of the *Treasury. The critical changes were embodied in resolutions passed by the House of Commons in 1706 and 1713 that it would only consider proposals for public expenditure which came from the crown, endowing the executive with the sole authority to instigate financial initiatives. Together these decisions placed the Treasury under control of Parliament with its minister as a politician rather than an administrator. The subsequent growth of public expenditure and taxation, and the enhanced economic responsibilities assumed by government in the 20th cent., greatly increased the importance of the office. CHL

Chancery, Court of. The Chancery (*cancellaria*) began life as the royal secretariat during the Norman period. Its task was to draw up royal charters and writs under the authority of the great seal, which was in the possession of the chancellor. The chancellor, in medieval times, was often a bishop and was a leading member of the royal council.

By the 14th cent. common law had become the ordinary law of the land administered through courts independent of the crown, staffed by professional lawyers. Yet the king retained the power to administer justice outside the regular system if an aggrieved party could not obtain justice from common law. Petitions were presented to the king in council setting out the details of the case and asking for relief. Such petitions would be presented to the royal council for consideration. However, by the end of the 14th cent. petitions began to be addressed to the chancellor direct and by the end of the 15th cent. he was sitting alone hearing petitions and issuing decrees in his own name.

The rules of common law were bound by tradition and statute. The chancellor was not bound by such rigid procedures and intervened to correct the harshness of the common law on the grounds of 'conscience'. Procedure was simple and informal. The Chancery could sit anywhere, at any time, and once the chancellor felt he had enough information he would arrive at a decision. It was quick and inexpensive justice which especially benefited the poor and the weak. As Lord Ellesmere explained in 1615, 'men's actions are so diverse and infinite that it is impossible to make a general law which may aptly meet with every particular . . . The office of the chancellor is to correct men's consciences for frauds, breaches of trust, wrongs and oppressions of what nature soever they may be, and to soften and mollify the extremity of the law.' Business increased steadily and by the 16th cent. the court was overwhelmed with petitions.

The chancellor's form of justice acquired the name of 'equity'. Equity was not a new concept but the difference was that equity became distinct from common law. At first equity was not seen as a rival to common law, but resentment arose over the growth of Chancery business. In 1616, clashes over jurisdiction occurred between *Coke, chief justice of King's Bench, and Chancellor Ellesmere.

After the Reformation, chancellors tended to have a background in law and lost the intuition and common sense of their ecclesiastical predecessors. Equity became bound by precedent and Chancery litigation was expensive and slow, often taking thirty years by the 19th cent. Chancery clerks depended on fees, not a salary, so it was in their interest to prolong proceedings. The backlog of cases grew acute under Chancellor *Eldon (1801–27), who was too thorough to be efficient. Reform was piecemeal, a vice-chancellor appointed in 1813 and two more in 1842, the clerks were eliminated by 1852, procedure simplified, and a court of appeal established, but they were temporary measures. The 1873 Judicature Acts reduced the Court of Chancery to a division of the new High Court of Justice and judges were empowered to administer both law and equity.

In Ireland a chancellor presided over a separate court of equity which mirrored the development of the English equity system. In Scotland a chancellor existed from the 12th cent. and largely performed the same functions as his English counterpart. However, the chancellor became the chief administrator of law and not of a separate equitable system. Since the Union of 1707 there has been one lord chancellor for Great Britain. RAS

Chandos, Sir John (d. 1370). Chandos rose to prominence by military service, being present at the opening campaign of the *Hundred Years War in 1339, at *Crécy, and at the sea battle off Winchelsea in 1350. He became one of *Edward the Black Prince's most trusted friends, serving on the *chevauchée* of 1355 and at *Poitiers. Following the failure of the campaign of 1359, he was involved in negotiations leading to the treaties of *Brétigny and *Calais, but peace with France did not end his military activity. In 1364, leading the army of John IV, duke of Brittany, at the battle of *Auray, he defeated and killed the rival claimant, Charles de Blois, and captured Bertrand du Guesclin. Three years later, he commanded the right flank at the Black Prince's victory at *Najerà. When war reopened in 1369, he was seneschal of Poitou. Wounded in an engagement at Lussac on 31 December 1369, he died, unmarried, the following day. AC

Channel Islands. All that remains to the monarchy of its once extensive possessions in France, retained when John lost the rest of the duchy of *Normandy in 1204. They consist of the four larger islands of Jersey, Guernsey, Alderney, and Sark, with a number of smaller islands. A determined attempt by the French in 1781 to capture Jersey was beaten off by the heroic defence of Major Pierson. The population of Jersey in 1991 was 84,000, Guernsey 59,000, Alderney 2,300, and Sark 570. Alderney is no more than 10 miles from the French coast. Jersey, the largest of the islands, is some 10 miles from east to west and 5 from north to south; its capital, St Helier, is on the south coast. The official languages are English and French, with some Norman-French patois still in use. The queen appoints a lieutenant-governor as her representative in the two bailiwicks of Jersey and Guernsey. The islands have their own assemblies, legal systems, and currency. Their economy depends greatly upon tourism, but they also export fruit, flowers, and vegetables, and the low rate of income tax makes them a tax haven. During the Second World War, the islands were occupied by German troops and liberated on 9 May 1945. JAC

Channel Tunnel. The earliest detailed proposal for a tunnel dates from the peace of *Amiens in 1802, suggesting two tunnels with horse-drawn vehicles and stabling facilities. Mercifully it was not built. The invention of railways made the project more practical. The London, Chatham, and Dover Company made some exploratory digs and an English Channel Company was formed in 1872. A rival enterprise, sponsored by the South Eastern Company, began operations at Shakespeare Cliff in 1881. But in 1883 both schemes were abandoned, partly for strategic reasons. After the development of an *entente with France in the 1900s, the argument could be put into reverse. In 1966, the prime ministers of France and Britain pledged themselves to have the tunnel built. Financial difficulties caused the project to languish but a further agreement was signed in 1986. By this time opinion had hardened against a bridge and in favour of a rail tunnel only. Work began in December 1987, the main difficulties being financial rather than technological. The link from each side was established in December 1990 and the tunnelling completed by June 1991. The official opening by President Mitterrand and Queen Elizabeth II was in May 1994. After a series of embarrassing and entertaining mishaps, the first travellers passed through in November 1994. There are two rail tunnels, conveying cars and freight, and a smaller service tunnel. From Waterloo station to Paris is a three-hour run for passengers but the permanent terminal is intended for St Pancras. The tunnel is 31 miles long, second only to the Seikan tunnel in Japan. JAC

Chantrey, Sir Francis (1781–1841). English sculptor, born in Yorkshire. Although apprenticed to a woodcarver, Chantrey studied intermittently at the Royal Academy Schools, at first intending to be a portrait painter. About 1804, he decided to concentrate on sculpture and his bust of the radical politician John Horne Tooke (1811) made his reputation. He became, after *Nollekens, the most successful sculptor of portrait busts in England. His simple and natural sculptures of children, especially *The Sleeping Children* in Lichfield cathedral, were enormously popular, though now may be considered mawkishly sentimental. In 1817 Chantrey became a Royal Academician and he was knighted in 1837. He bequeathed £105,000 to the Royal Academy, the interest to be used to buy 'works of Fine Art of the highest merit executed within the shores of Great Britain'. The purchases, which have often caused controversy, are housed in the Tate Gallery (London). JC

chantries. Founded either by individuals, guilds, or corporations, chantries were endowments for offering masses usually near a person's tomb or effigy, for the soul's repose in purgatory. Wealthy men invested heavily; for example, Cardinal *Beaufort requested 10,000 masses for his soul. Humble villagers grouped together for an annual obit (memorial mass). Starting in the late 13th cent., with the greatest growth in the 14th, the number fluctuated, but by the Reformation there was a total of about 3,000 chantries. Most cathedrals had up to two dozen (in 1366 St Paul's had 74) and large churches had several. Many 'chantry priests' were employed specifically for this function and, as they had no pastoral duties, founders often provided for the mass-priest to teach in school. Ostensibly to rid the Church of superstitious practice, but incidentally increasing government revenue, chantries were dissolved in 1547. The small chantry chapels, such as Bishop Bubwith's (Wells), Cardinal Beaufort's (Winchester), and Humphrey, duke of *Gloucester's (St Albans), are 'a series unique in the history of European art'. WMM

Chaplin, Charles (1889–1977). Film actor and director. London-born of music-hall performers, with a wretched childhood as the family lost everything, Chaplin learned vaudeville techniques with the Fred Karno Company before being signed by the Keystone Company (Hollywood) in 1913. After an unpropitious start, he gained fame in silent films through portrayal of a baggy-trousered, moustachioed tramp, softening the original character with sentiment and pathos (*The Kid*, *The Gold Rush*, *City Lights*), so charming audiences. His rapid rise was due partly to the emergence of the star system but he contributed creatively if egotistically to cinema art: directing was merely an extension of his power as actor. He made few films after the introduction of sound, but received a special Academy Award in 1972 and was knighted (1975). Chaplin's personal life was frequently stormy, and he left America in 1952 because of political hostility and moral disapproval, to settle permanently in Switzerland. ASH

chapters and chapter houses. The chapter house of a monastery, cathedral, or collegiate foundation was second only to the church in importance, and was usually built in close proximity to it. Here the community assembled daily in pre-Reformation times for prayer, for the reading of a chapter in the rule (hence the name), and for the transaction of business. The importance of the chapter house in the life of the community was often reflected in its architectural splendour. Covered with a stone vault, well lit, and entered by an elaborate doorway, there are outstanding examples in England and Wales, including the ruins at *Rievaulx in Yorkshire and Margam in Glamorgan. At many cathedrals, too, there are fine chapter houses, notably at Wells (Som.), Southwell minster (Notts.), and Bristol cathedral.

Cathedrals which were not monastic foundations, and collegiate churches, were served by secular clergy, the canons or prebendaries, who constituted the capitular body or chapter. Each member of the chapter had his stall in the choir and seat in the chapter house, and initially each had a predetermined period of residence, when he was expected to assist with the conduct of the church's worship. As time passed these duties became increasingly the responsibility of a smaller group of residentiary canons, usually the precentor (responsible for the music and the ordering of the services), the chancellor (responsible for education), and the treasurer (responsible for the cathedral's fabric, and the vestments and vessels used in worship).

The reforms of the Ecclesiastical Commission in the 19th cent. deprived the prebendaries of their estates, income, and most of their obligations, and, except for the residentiary canons who, with the dean or provost of the cathedral, continue to be responsible for its management and worship, the title of canon or prebendary is now honorary. JRG

Charge of the Light Brigade, 1854. During the battle of *Balaclava (25 October 1854) Lord *Raglan ordered Lord *Lucan, his cavalry commander, to advance his forces to stop the Russians removing captured cannon from the Causeway Heights. Confusion among the British commanders led to Lucan mistakenly sending the Light Brigade to attack strong Russian positions at a different location, North valley. About one-third of the 673-strong brigade, commanded by Lord *Cardigan, became casualties. Thanks partly to *Tennyson's poem, the action has become a symbol of military stupidity and blindly obedient courage. GDS

charity schools. Although the practice of establishing charity schools for the poor by private donors had begun in Elizabethan times, a great increase in numbers occurred towards the end of the 17th cent. The Blue Coat School (Westminster), founded in 1688, educated, clothed, and apprenticed 50 boys. The main object was religious and moral, as well as enabling the poor to earn a livelihood. The *Society for Promoting Christian Knowledge (SPCK), at its first meeting in 1699, considered how best to establish 'Catechetical Schools' in every parish in London. Children between the ages of 7 and 12 were admitted and wore distinctive uniforms. Teaching was from 7.00 to 11.00 in the morning and 1.00 to 5.00 in the afternoon. Queen Anne took a personal interest and during her reign the schools made rapid advances. However, by 1760 the charity school movement was faltering. This was due to a number of factors, particularly the narrow curriculum offered, incompetent teachers, and the loss of royal patronage, because of suspicions that the schools were breeding-grounds for Jacobite sympathizers. PG

Charlemont, James Caulfeild, 1st earl of [I] (1728–99). Charlemont was a typical member of the *Anglo-Irish ascendancy, anxious to assert Irish rights against England but even more anxious not to encourage catholic demands. He was the son of an Irish viscount and succeeded to the title and the Ulster estates at the age of 6. He was created earl in 1763, having acted firmly in putting down disturbances in Armagh. Charlemont had literary and antiquarian tastes and, with *Burke, *Goldsmith, and *Johnson, belonged to the Club. Despite nervousness, which prevented him speaking in the Irish House of Lords, he became increasingly interested in politics, and played an important part as organizer, particularly through his contacts with Henry Flood and *Grattan. His aim, as he expressed it, was to serve Ireland in Ireland and to enhance her constitutional position. In 1768 he gave vigorous support to the *Octennial Bill, which limited the life of the Irish Parliament and strengthened its position, and in 1775 he brought Grattan into the Irish House of Commons as member for the family borough of Charlemont. His period of greatest influence was 1780–4 when he commanded the Irish *Volunteers and he rejoiced in the concessions obtained in 1782. After that, his role was to restrain. He disliked the growing radicalism of the Volunteers and helped to avoid a confrontation in 1783 between the Dublin Convention and the Irish Parliament. He continued as an active member of the Whig opposition in Ireland, helping to frustrate Pitt's commercial propositions in 1785, forming Whig clubs, and opposing the Act of *Union, which passed soon after his death. JAC

Charles I (1600–49), king of England, Scotland, and Ireland (1625–49). Charles was the second son of James VI and Anne of Denmark. Born in Scotland, he moved to England in 1604 after his father ascended the English throne. He developed into a somewhat reserved, scholarly boy, who hero-worshipped his charismatic elder brother Prince *Henry. Only after Henry was struck down by typhoid in 1612 did Charles, as heir apparent, move centre stage. In 1621 he was a regular attender at the House of Lords as Parliament considered whether England should intervene on the protestant side in the Thirty Years War. Public opinion favoured this, but James, as a leading protestant ruler, hoped to heal religious divisions by concluding a marriage between Charles and the Infanta Maria, sister of 'the most catholic king' of Spain.

Charles, now 22 and eager to be married, persuaded his father to let him make an incognito romantic journey to Spain. He set off in February 1623, accompanied by the royal favourite, *Buckingham, who had become a surrogate brother to him. Two weeks of hard riding through France brought them to Madrid, where Charles, after the Spaniards had recovered from the shock of his arrival, received a royal welcome. However, custom forbade him unchaperoned access to the infanta, and when he demonstrated his love by leaping over a garden wall to greet her, she ran away. Frustration, and the growing realization that the infanta was merely a pawn in a power game to keep James from intervening in the war, opened the eyes of Charles and Buckingham to the fact that the expansion of Spanish power threatened England. When they returned home in September, without the infanta, they began constructing an anti-Spanish coalition. The adhesion of France was essential, since protestant states by themselves could never match Spanish power, and Buckingham therefore arranged a marriage between Charles and Louis XIII's sister *Henrietta Maria.

James remained committed to peace, but was persuaded to call Parliament in 1624. Charles and Buckingham co-operated closely with its leading members in preparing the ground for war, but they only became free to act in March 1625, when the death of James brought Charles to the throne. The new king promptly summoned Parliament, assuming that it would complete what its predecessor had begun, but suspicion of Buckingham, who was associated with corruption and the Hispanophile attitude of James, led the Commons to make only a token grant of money. Charles could not comprehend this suspicion, and took attacks on the favourite personally. When the 1626 Parliament impeached Buckingham, following the failure of an expedition to attack Cadiz, Charles dissolved it. He then levied a *forced loan to pay for another expedition, this time in support of the French protestants. When this also ended in defeat a further clash with Parliament seemed inevitable. But Charles's acceptance of the *petition of right in 1628 defused the situation, and Buckingham, the bone of contention, was removed by an assassin's hand in August of that year.

When Parliament reassembled in 1629 Charles expected harmony, but now the religious issue came to the fore. Charles was a high churchman and promoted *Arminians, but members of Parliament were predominantly low church and equated Arminianism with 'popery', which they abhorred. The Commons drew up a resolution against Arminianism, and when Charles tried to prevent its discussion by dissolving Parliament, *Eliot and his associates held the Speaker down in his chair so that debate could continue. Charles responded to this outrage by imprisoning the offending members and dispensing with Parliament altogether. His personal rule was far from an *'Eleven Years Tyranny', but Charles's continued patronage of the Arminians—in particular Archbishop *Laud—outraged public opinion. So also did his resort to non-parliamentary taxation. Nevertheless, the personal rule was not threatened until the self-imposed débâcle of the *Bishops' wars, which left Charles with no choice but to summon Parliament. So weak was his position by late 1640 that he had to accept Acts severely curtailing his power. He also had to permit the impeachment and subsequent execution of Laud and his chief minister, *Strafford. However, by deciding to abandon the Arminians he attracted support from traditional Anglicans, and conservative opinion began rallying round him when Parliament broke with convention by trying to deprive him of control over the army.

Charles had skilfully transformed himself into the guardian of the constitution, but in January 1642 he unwisely yielded to pressure from his wife and others who advocated tough measures. After impeaching his principal opponents of treason, he went down to the House of Commons, accompanied by an armed guard, entered the chamber, and demanded their arrest. But, as Charles quickly noted, 'the birds are flown'. His attempted coup had failed and he decided to leave the unruly capital and appeal for support to the country. In August 1642 he raised the royal standard at Nottingham in the midlands, and shortly afterwards established his headquarters at Oxford. During the civil war that ensued, Charles showed qualities of endurance and decisiveness that had hitherto lain dormant. And although he left strategy in the hands of his nephew Prince *Rupert, he proved a successful commander in the field. But royalist resources were sufficient only for a short war, and Parliament had the longer purse. After his defeat at *Naseby in June 1645 Charles had no hope of winning, and in May 1646 gave himself up to his enemies. Yet even in defeat he was still a key figure, for everyone assumed that no blueprint for a post-war constitution could be implemented without his participation. The parliamentary army, which had emerged as a radical political force in its own right, was so concerned that in June 1647 it sent a troop of musketeers to remove the king from parliamentary guardianship and bring him closer to London. He was held captive in his own palace of Hampton Court until November, when fear for his personal safety drove him to escape and seek refuge in *Carisbrooke castle on the Isle of Wight.

The political situation was now chaotic, with Parliament, the army, and the Scots all putting proposals to Charles. Confronted by this evidence of disunity among his enemies, Charles took the understandable but risky course of playing them off against each other. All over the country sentiment was flowing, if not in favour of the king, then against those who had overthrown him, and the spring of 1648 saw a series of violent outbreaks called the second civil war. These convinced the army, which ruthlessly suppressed them, that Charles was not to be trusted and that a permanent peace settlement depended on removing him. In December 1648 they 'purged' Parliament of its conservative members, leaving the remaining 'rump' free to set up a high court to try the king. Charles refused to plead, insisting that he was accountable only to God, but although his dignity and fortitude impressed all those present, the outcome was a foregone conclusion. Charles was sentenced to death and beheaded, in front of the Banqueting House in Whitehall, on 30 January 1649.

Charles had many good qualities. He loved the arts, and assembled a collection of paintings among the best in Europe. He loved his wife and children, but above all he loved

God. Religion was central to his life, and was intimately involved with his commitment to order and ceremony. But his exalted view of the kingly office, his autocratic tendencies, and his lack of the common touch opened a chasm between him and his subjects which swallowed up the monarchy he tenaciously struggled to preserve. RL

Carlton, G., *Charles the First: The Personal Monarch* (1983); Gregg, P., *King Charles I* (1981); Wedgwood, C. V., *The Trial of Charles I* (1964).

Charles II (1630–85), king of England, Ireland, and Scotland (acceded 1649, restored 1660–85). Charles received his practical education in 1648–51 when he learnt how to adapt to rapidly changing circumstances, win and discard allies, make use of others, and trust absolutely no one. He also fathered his first bastards. He commissioned *Montrose to raise the Scottish Highlands, but withdrew his support to conclude an agreement with the more powerful *covenanting party, who defeated and then hanged Montrose (April 1650). Invited to Scotland by *Argyll, whom Charles executed in 1661, he took the covenant and publicly condemned the religions and policies of his father and mother. At first Argyll's puppet, Charles freed himself by devious manœuvring, but when *Cromwell's army advanced he took the gamble of invading England, where few rallied to him. After a disastrous defeat at *Worcester (September 1651) he made a romantic escape to France. Subsequent royalist plots to restore Charles failed. Foreign assistance proved ineffective: France preferred Cromwell as an ally, leaving Charles to an unhelpful combination with Spain, the weaker power. Divisions among the republican factions brought about his 1660 *Restoration, which was unconditional. It was old cavaliers who in 1661–2 imposed conditions by restoring strict Anglican religious uniformity and making Charles abandon his *Declaration of Indulgence (1662). In his first years Charles was advised by his principal minister, *Clarendon, to rule within the laws whereas younger ministers urged him to free the crown from constitutional restrictions. After the failure of the *Anglo-Dutch War of 1665–7 he abandoned Clarendon and initiated a new line of policy.

Charles, his brother James, and the *cabal ministers concluded treaties with France because it was the strongest European power. Victory in a new Dutch war would be assured. French subsidies and increased revenues from expanded trade (as occurred in 1681–8) would reduce, and might eventually eliminate, dependence on Parliament. War would enable the army to be expanded. Charles, James, and *Clifford also thought that they could become catholics and institute religious toleration: in the secret treaty of *Dover (1670) Louis XIV promised military aid if a rebellion resulted. In the event, unlike the other two, Charles delayed his conversion until his death-bed in 1685. For the first time no parliamentary session occurred in 1672, and had the Dutch War succeeded Charles would have been able to dictate from a position of strength. But stalemate at sea enabled Parliament to make Charles withdraw his Declaration of Indulgence and assent to the *Test Act barring catholics from office, forcing James and Clifford to resign. In 1673–4 Dutch propaganda fed MPs' suspicions of Charles's absolutist intentions: they refused to vote money, compelling Charles to desert France and make peace.

Charles also retreated in domestic politics, allowing his new lord treasurer *Danby to return to upholding the interests of the church, enforcing the penal laws against catholics and dissenters. Danby was needed to restore royal solvency and manage Parliament, but Charles never liked or trusted him (nor Danby, Charles). The king persisted in trying to maintain a personal connection with Louis XIV and barter English neutrality for subsidies. Danby was alarmed at the increase in French power and wished to balance it by championing William of Orange, furthering this policy by negotiating the marriage of William to James's daughter and heir Mary. Charles allowed the marriage in order to put up the price that Louis would pay for English neutrality, but Louis found it cheaper to bribe the opposition and give them secret papers incriminating Danby. This forced Charles to dismiss Danby and dissolve Parliament. At the same time 'revelations' broke of a *Popish plot to murder Charles. James's catholicism, absolutist and French sympathies, and the deciphering of correspondence by an employee, Coleman, made him seem the obvious beneficiary. By sending James into exile Charles raised doubts whether he would steadfastly resist the Whig bill to exclude James from the succession, since he had not protected ministers when they came under attack.

However Charles saw *exclusion of the rightful heir as changing the monarchy from a hereditary, divinely appointed institution into an elective, limited office that could soon give way to a new commonwealth. He stopped the first Exclusion Bill by dissolving Parliament (July 1679). When Charles fell ill and James returned from exile to defend his right, Charles sent him to rule Scotland, where he could prevent covenanting militants intervening in England (as they had done in 1639–45) to help the Whigs. In 1680 Charles blocked exclusion by encouraging the Lords to reject a second bill, and in March 1681 he dissolved the third Whig Parliament which he had ordered to meet at *Oxford, to separate the Whigs from their London supporters. No further meetings of Parliament were allowed, Charles being financially secure with a new secret treaty with France giving him subsidies in return for non-intervention in Europe.

The term 'Stuart revenge' does not accurately describe Charles's last years after 1681, apart from renewed prosecutions of dissenters. Charles strengthened the crown by obtaining the surrender or forfeiture of the charters of corporations. He purged Whigs from offices. When evidence surfaced of two separate Whig plots, one by popular activists to murder Charles and James, the other by aristocrats to stage a coup, he relentlessly prosecuted those involved. He used the law against opponents, but he cannot be said to have tried to undermine it or set up royal absolutism. His main interest at the end was politically trivial, to build a new palace near Winchester.

Charles had two great constructive achievements to his credit. He successfully resisted intense cavalier pressure in the early 1660s to go back on the Act of Indemnity that was intended to heal the divisions caused by the civil wars. This enabled him later to defend and conserve the rights of the crown without the nation being plunged into the catastrophe of another civil war. Secondly his personal tolerance, ineffective in trying to suspend religious persecution, found full play in his protection of intellectual freedom, although he did little more in the field of science than observe the experiments of the *Royal Society.

Charles's irregular private life resembled that of his French grandfather Henri IV. It seldom affected politics: the only politically active and influential mistress, the duchess of *Portsmouth, worked in the French interest, having been sent by Louis for that purpose. The barren Portuguese queen, *Catherine, counted for nothing. JRJ

Hutton, R., *Charles the Second: King of England, Scotland and Ireland* (1989); Jones, J. R., *Charles II, Royal Politician* (1987); Miller, J., *Charles II* (1991).

Charles, prince of Wales (b. 1948). Born during the reign of George VI, Prince Charles was 3 when his mother succeeded to the throne as Queen Elizabeth II. He was sent to Cheam School, Gordonstoun, Geelong Grammar School in Australia, Trinity College, Cambridge (where he took a degree in history), and University College, Aberystwyth, where he studied Welsh. Created prince of Wales in 1958, he was invested in *Caernarfon castle in 1969. He then entered the armed forces and pursued a vigorous training programme—flying a supersonic jet, qualifying as a helicopter pilot, catapulting from the deck of *Ark Royal* in a Buccaneer, training in minesweepers and submarines, and commanding a mine-hunter. His private pleasures included not only painting, music, and acting, but surfing, sailing, skiing, fishing, shooting, riding, and playing polo to international standard. His reward for these strenuous activities was to be increasingly portrayed in newspapers as a 'crank', 'a young twerp', and a 'wimp', who admitted talking to flowers and showed an interest in alternative medicine. Protest groups soon latched on to the fact that demonstrations, preferably violent, on a princely visit gained them publicity, and he was threatened with boycotts, hunger-strikes, air-fresheners, and bombs. His public utterances on matters like the environment, modern architecture, and the preservation of natural resources, on which he feels strongly, were greeted with indignation by interested groups. He is anxious to modernize the monarchy but not all of his suggestions have been well received. In 1994 he remarked that he would like to be defender of all faiths, and not merely that of the Church of England—which, as some newspaper correspondents tartly observed, sounded as if it did not matter what one believed provided one believed something. In 1981 the prince married Lady *Diana Spencer in St Paul's cathedral: the Clay Cross council in Derbyshire announced it would call a Republican Day (subsequently cancelled), and a Yorkshire councillor resolved to go on hunger-strike in protest at the cost of the ceremony. Two sons, Prince William and Prince Henry, were born in 1982 and 1984, but disharmony in the marriage was increasingly the subject of comment, and the royal couple separated in 1992 and divorced in 1996. Speculation at once began whether the prince would remarry. When, as a 14-year-old schoolboy at Gordonstoun the prince ordered a glass of cherry brandy at a Stornoway hotel, the ensuing sensation must have afforded him a glimpse that life might not be tranquil. JAC

Charles, Thomas (1755–1814). Welsh revivalist. Born in Carmarthenshire and educated at Jesus College, Oxford, Charles took holy orders in 1778. His sympathies were with the Calvinistic methodists and from a chapel in Bala he began building up an evangelical circle. In 1803 he established a press at Bala which produced catechisms and religious magazines in Welsh and he prepared for the British and Foreign Bible Society an edition of the Bible in Welsh. Charles fought off accusations of Jacobinism and democratical tendencies in *The Welsh Methodists Vindicated* (1802). In 1811 the ordaining of lay preachers led to a breach with the church which Charles, with reluctance, accepted. JAC

Charleston, battle of, 1780. In 1779 the British decided to concentrate on the southern states in America in order to encourage the loyalists. *Clinton took a strong expedition from New York to Georgia and moved north to besiege Charleston, the largest town in the south. After a close investment and heavy fighting, the defenders surrendered on 12 May 1780. Clinton took 6,000 prisoners and many guns. But the political response was disappointing. JAC

Charlotte Augusta, Princess (1796–1817). The daughter of George, prince of Wales, and Caroline of Brunswick, Charlotte bore the brunt of the hatred between her parents, who separated shortly after her birth. Much of her childhood was spent with little access to the outside world, though, largely through the efforts of her aunt, the duchess of Württemberg, she received a rounded education. In December 1813 she was betrothed to William, prince of Orange, but broke off the engagement, not wishing to move to Holland. Her stubbornness even managed momentarily to unite her warring parents, her father dismissing her entire household and her mother refusing to receive her. At length she was given lodgings at Windsor, but visitors were forbidden and letters had to be smuggled in. When, in 1816, Leopold of Saxe-Coburg proposed, Charlotte readily accepted and the marriage took place on 2 May at Carlton House (London). Charlotte died giving birth to a stillborn child on 5 November 1817. SMC

Charlotte of Mecklenburg-Strelitz (1744–1818), queen of George III. Though Charlotte was chosen unseen from lists of German princesses in 1761, her marriage to George III proved a great success. She was considered by many to be rather dull and distinctly plain, but George was devoted to her and their routine domestic life set a pattern for the future. She had little interest in political matters and was rarely accused of trying to influence her husband. Her fifteen children took up a great deal of her time and energy, but she was interested in music and literature. She cared for her husband during his long slide into insanity, though terrified by his occasional outbursts of violence. She predeceased him and was buried in November 1818 in St George's Chapel, Windsor. SMC

charters are grants of privilege. They are of fundamental importance to students of medieval legal, constitutional, and municipal history. They can also be used to establish where the king or lord was at a certain time, and they give some indication of his chief ministers from the frequency names appear as witnesses. But they need to be used with great caution since spurious charters are by no means uncommon, interpolations were frequently made, and contemporary phrases can be difficult to render precisely. Indeed, a number of learned controversies have turned on the exact meaning of charter terms. The oldest charters appear to be grants made to the Church in Kent during the reign of *Æthelbert in the 600s and were modelled on private Roman documents. Grants of land to individuals became common and the phrase 'bookland' indicated an estate held by charter. Next came charters to towns or cities, giving them the right to hold markets or fairs, to collect tolls, or to elect their own officials. William the Conqueror issued a charter to London, Norwich received one from Stephen, York from Richard I, Bristol from Henry III. Charters as regular instruments of royal policy seem to have been introduced into Scotland from 1095 during the reign of Edgar, who had close connections with the Anglo-Norman court of William Rufus. The 'coronation charters' of Henry I, Stephen, and Henry II were rather different in character and more like political manifestos, since they promised good government in accordance with the traditional laws of the realm. Though the promises were not always kept, the charters implied some limitation on royal authority and paved the way for *Magna Carta in 1215, itself constantly confirmed. Later came charters to guilds and to trading companies. The *Merchant Venturers, having obtained concessions from continental rulers, had their privileges confirmed by Edward III; the Royal College of Physicians of London was incorporated by Henry VIII in 1518; the *East India Company was granted its charter by Elizabeth in 1600. The sanctity of charters was regarded as the very bedrock of property. Consequently the campaigns by Charles II and James II after 1681 to call in the charters of parliamentary boroughs and remodel them roused fierce opposition. When the Fox–North coalition in 1783 introduced a bill to reform the East India Company, the opposition had much success with the argument that this was a gross and daring violation of the constitution. In the 19th and 20th cents. charters have been granted, under the supervision of the Privy Council, to universities and educational bodies.

JAC

chartism (1837–54) was the first attempt to build an independent political party representing the interests of the labouring and unprivileged sections of the nation. For many of its followers chartism was basically 'a knife and fork question'. Yet its programme was a series of political demands. The link between economic ills and political representation was constantly elaborated in chartist pamphlets and oratory.

The chartists were so named because they formulated their demands in a six-point charter: universal (manhood) suffrage, annual parliaments, vote by (secret) ballot, abolition of property qualifications for MPs, payment of MPs, and equal electoral districts. The object was to make the charter the law of the land by legal, constitutional means if possible, or by force if necessary—or by a mixture of both: 'peaceably if we can, forcibly if we must.' Great efforts were made to collect support for a petition to the House of Commons on behalf of the charter, but on each occasion the House rejected its demands. Alternative methods were therefore advocated. There were plans for making the central body of chartist delegates, the national convention, a people's parliament which would bypass Westminster; a general strike ('national holiday') was attempted in August 1839; and local riots, and perhaps an abortive insurrection (the *Newport rising) in November 1839, showed that 'physical force' might not be ruled out.

In its origins chartism was an umbrella movement which drew together many strands of radical grievance. In London and the provinces Working Men's Associations were formed in 1837, building on the remains of earlier radical reform organizations. In Birmingham, the movement at first was closely allied with middle-class radicals and currency reformers. In Leeds, *Owenite socialists combined with middle-class radicals and physical-force militants to launch the Leeds Working Men's Association. In other towns of the West Riding and the industrial North local movements and grievances (including the 1834 New Poor Law) provided a basis for chartism, which was thus not so much a national movement as a series of local and regional movements, loosely federated. This posed a problem of concerted action which was never solved. Attempts to build a national organization repeatedly fell apart; and the most effective link between chartists was the widely read chartist newspaper the *Northern Star*.

The geography of chartism reflected the national economic and social structure. Wherever there was a substantial number of skilled artisans, especially shoemakers, printers, tailors, and cabinet-makers, a chartist organization on the lines of the Working Men's Associations was to be expected, with an emphasis on self-help, independence, and propaganda for universal suffrage. Such was the movement in London or Birmingham. But in areas where there were substantial numbers of distressed hand-loom weavers or framework-knitters (as in Lancashire, the West Riding, and the midlands) chartism assumed a fiercer visage and adopted a more strident tone, expressed in mass demonstrations and torchlight meetings on the moors.

Just as the local variations of chartism were related to the structure of the economy, so the chronology of the movement reflected the cycle of booms and slumps between 1836 and 1851. The first climax of chartism came in the winter of 1839 during a severe trade depression. In 1842 a second peak of chartist activity was reached, arising out of mass unemployment in the northern towns. The last great flare-up of chartism came in 1848, following a winter of economic recession and inspired by revolutions on the continent. In periods of relative prosperity (1843–7 and after 1848) chartism lost its mass support. It then became a movement promoting education, temperance, municipal reforms, and settlement on the land—while never losing faith that universal suffrage would some day, somehow, be won. After 1848, as a curious epilogue, a group of chartists tried to steer the movement towards socialism and the international working-class movement of *Marx and *Engels.

The chartists failed to achieve their six points which, with the exception of annual parliaments, were realized later. JFCH

Chatham naval base. Henry VIII developed Deptford and Woolwich as naval bases and dockyards but in 1550 it was decided to develop Gillingham Water or Chatham, on the Medway, 20 miles nearer to the North Sea. During the Dutch wars of the 17th cent., Chatham became the major naval base. In 1667, in a surprise raid, De Ruyter burst through the boom at Sheerness, wreaked havoc on the ships at harbour, and towed away the *Royal Charles*. The dockyard closed in the 1980s. JAC

Chatsworth House (Derbys.). Country seat of the Cavendishes, dukes of Devonshire. The Elizabethan house, begun by Sir William Cavendish in 1552 and completed by his widow Bess of Hardwick (Lady *Shrewsbury) was replaced by the present building which has south and east fronts by William Talman (1687–96) and a north front by Thomas Archer (1704–7). Later architects at Chatsworth include James Paine, John Carr, and Sir Jeffry Wyatville, whose alterations and additions between 1820 and 1841 encompassed the library, the north wing and tower, and estate buildings. Chatsworth has painted ceilings by Verrio, Thornhill, and Laguerre, furniture by William *Kent, sculpture by Cibber and Canova, and paintings by Rembrandt, Frans Hals, *Van Dyck, Tintoretto, and *Lely. Of more recent date, there are sculptures by Angela Conner and paintings by *Landseer, *Sargent, and Lucien Freud. Among the contents of the library are major collections of drawings by Palladio and Rubens. The formal parterres at Chatsworth were designed by George London and Henry Wise, whilst the cascade by Grillet, a pupil of Le Nôtre, has a classical temple at its top by Thomas Archer (1702). From 1761 Capability *Brown made major changes in the grounds, incorporating new planting and a bridge by Paine (1760–4), and alterations to the course of the river Derwent. During the 19th cent. the 6th duke of Devonshire and his gardener Sir Joseph Paxton devised a system of cascades, fountains, and pools, culminating in the Emperor Fountain of 1843. They planted rare trees and specimen shrubs, and introduced rocks, buildings, and statuary to punctuate the landscape. The site of the conservatory (1836–40) by Paxton and Decimus Burton—which anticipated Paxton's design for the *Crystal Palace—is now covered by a maze. PW

Chaucer, Geoffrey (*c.*1343–1400). Chaucer's enduring fame reflects the range and quality of his poetry and prose, but also the accessibility of his midlands-based London English compared with that of works such as the north-western *Pearl* and *Sir Gawain and the Green Knight*. His impact on the English language and its poetics through the absorption of French words, ideas, and forms is considerable, as is his influence on writers from Hoccleve, *Lydgate, and the 'Scottish Chaucerians' onwards.

Born into a family of prosperous vintners, Chaucer served as page then esquire to various aristocratic households, including that of Richard II (1377–99). His wife Philippa Roet, with whom he probably had two sons, Lewis and Thomas, was also in royal service. Chaucer's specific assignments included fighting in the *Hundred Years War *c.*1359, undertaking trade and diplomatic missions to Italy and France, and acting as customs controller at the port of London and clerk of works at Westminster and elsewhere.

Chaucer's life experience doubtless contributed to his 'most wonderful, comprehensive nature' (Dryden), while his situation on the periphery of aristocratic circles perhaps underlies his self-presentation as 'an elvyssh man', a bystander at life's games of power and love. How closely the professional and artistic lives interlocked is unclear. A courtly audience seems implied, for instance, by *The Book of the Duchess*, probably a consolation for *John of Gaunt at the death of his duchess Blanche *c.*1369, while the ballade 'Lack of Steadfastness' offers advice to the king; yet no records exist of commissions or payments for poetry. Fellow poets and intellectuals such as 'moral *Gower' and 'philosophical Strode', saluted at the close of *Troilus and Criseyde*, must have been a valued part of Chaucer's readership.

Like other gifted contemporaries, Chaucer made an art of breathing new life into established conventions, and despite an increasing independence from sources, many of his late, masterly **Canterbury Tales* are modified translations of existing works. His sources and models include the allegorical love-vision *Le Roman de la Rose*, and works by Machaut, Froissart, Dante, Petrarch, Boccaccio, Ovid, Virgil, and Boethius.

Apart from the brilliant five-part tragedy *Troilus and Criseyde*, the poems are mainly small to medium scale, while in the broken ending of *The House of Fame* we perhaps see Chaucer losing his direction in an ambitious experimental project. Solemnity rarely goes unpunctured, yet Chaucer is also 'the noble philosophical poet of love' (Usk), preoccupied with questions about love, true nobility, and the Boethian opposition between false (worldly) felicity and true (spiritual) felicity. Notable, especially compared with the stiff rhetoric and unambiguous didacticism of much medieval literature, is Chaucer's ability not only to impersonate other voices (from the coy hen falcon in *The Parliament of Fowls* to the blustering Host in the *Canterbury Tales*), but also to articulate different world-views with apparent impartiality. This permits a fascinating range of interpretation for many individual poems (reflected in the abundant secondary literature), and occasions ongoing debates about the advancedness or otherwise of Chaucer's views on such issues as love, marriage, war, and the church. The only direct mention of 14th-cent. events is the jocular reference in the *Nun's Priest's Tale* to Jakke Straw, a leader of the 1381 *Peasants' Revolt, but the contemporary problems of religious charlatanry and the misuse of money and power are treated in the *Canterbury Tales* with pervasive irony. DCW

Chaumont, treaty of, 1814. Even after Napoleon's defeat at Leipzig in 1813 he remained dangerous, and Castlereagh, Britain's foreign secretary, was concerned lest he succeed in breaking the fifth coalition and signing a separate peace with one of the eastern powers. In March 1814 Castlereagh negotiated the treaty whereby Britain, Russia, Prussia, and Austria agreed to put 150,000 men each in the field until victory was achieved, and to guarantee Europe against French aggression for twenty years. The treaty was subsequently renewed. JAC

Chedworth. A large Romano-British villa in the Cotswolds 7 miles north-east of *Cirencester. Originating as simple, free-standing buildings in the early part of the 2nd cent., in the early 4th cent. it developed into an extensive complex. The excavated (and displayed) area comprised, at the south-western, uphill end, a court divided from the rest of the villa by a wall with gatehouse. On three sides this court was enclosed by buildings, including two sets of baths and many rooms floored with mosaic. Nearby lay a *nymphaeum* enclosing a spring. The north-western range was prolonged into a row of rooms. The outer court remains unexcavated. Nearby was a probable temple. This and other features of the design have led to the suggestion that rather than a villa, Chedworth may have been part of a sacred complex. ASEC

Cheke, Sir John (1514–57). Cambridge-born protestant Greek scholar, educator, and man of affairs, Cheke was fellow of St John's College from 1529. As regius professor 1540–51, he was supported by his friends Sir Thomas *Smith and Roger *Ascham in introducing the new 'Erasmian' pronunciation of Greek, against the vice-chancellor's ban. Under Henry VIII, Cheke was tutor to Prince Edward who, as Edward VI, gave him land, a knighthood, and the provostship of King's College, Cambridge; he was also member of Parliament, clerk to the council, and secretary of state. A supporter of Lady Jane *Grey, he was imprisoned for treason under Mary 1553–4 but allowed to migrate to Basle, whence he travelled in Italy and taught at Strasbourg before being enticed to Brussels by Mary's agents in 1556 and again imprisoned in London. Securing release by renouncing his religion, he died soon after. Cheke's edition of two sermons by St John Chrysostom, with his Latin translation, was the first text to be printed in England in Greek type (1543). His strongly nationalist feelings in favour of the English language are evident in his gospel translations and his preface to Hoby's translation of Castiglione's *Courtier* (1561). JBT

Chelmsford, diocese of. The present see, created in 1914, is conterminous with Essex. In 604 *Augustine consecrated *Mellitus bishop of London to convert the East Saxons, but success was short-lived. In *c.*650 *Oswui, king of Northumbria, sent Cedd as Celtic bishop of the East Saxons with two centres, at Tilbury and Ythancaestir near Bradwell. The Essex see was independent of London until 675, when Bishop Eorcenwald moved there. After that Essex remained within the London diocese until the 19th cent., though Simon *Sudbury, bishop of London (1362–75), resided in Essex, where he was better known. In 1845 Essex was removed from the overpopulated London diocese and united with *Rochester, only to be transferred again to the new see of *St Albans in 1877. With the creation of the see of Chelmsford in 1914, Essex again had a bishop of its own. The cathedral is the former 15th-cent. parish church with 19th-cent. additions. WMM

Chelsea hospital (London) was founded by Charles II for veteran soldiers. The pensioners wear an 18th-cent. uniform and celebrate the founder on Oak Apple Day (29 May). The buildings were by Christopher *Wren and the foundation stone was laid on 17 February 1682. The duke of *Wellington lay in state at the hospital in 1852, when several people died in the crush to pay respects. The Chelsea Flower Show is held annually in the gardens. JAC

Cheltenham Gold Cup. The most important steeplechase in England at level weights. The National Hunt Meeting at Cheltenham is held in mid-March and the Gold Cup is the main event, run over 3 miles, 2 furlongs, and 76 yards. First run in 1924, the most notable winner has been Golden Miller, winning five times in succession 1932–7. RAS

chemical industry. Chemicals have formed part of the industrial activity of Britain for centuries although the extraction of usable materials or their manufacture only came to be systematically related to scientific principles from the end of the 18th cent. Chemical processes were used in brewing and distillation of alcoholic drinks, in preparing medicines, making concrete, glass, and pottery, making soap, and in cleaning, bleaching, and dyeing textiles. By the later 15th cent. the manufacture of gunpowder had stimulated investigations of the properties of substances for use in warfare or in economic activities.

The period called the *industrial revolution in Britain saw the systematic exploitation of raw materials for use in the expanding economy. For example, town gas was made during the process of coking coal and it was used from 1808 at Soho in Birmingham to light the factory of Boulton and Watt. Within 20 years a number of gaslight companies were supplying many large towns. The by-products of coke and other chemicals, which began as waste, became of increasing importance as knowledge of their potential in other industries grew. Another example was the development of the lead chamber process which increased supplies of sulphuric acid, a necessity for many of the new industries.

Many heavy industries, such as iron, produced as by-products inorganic chemicals which, with further processing, found markets. Amongst these were agricultural fertilizers such as basic slag and essential components of products such as washing powders. Output of raw materials such as common salt became of increasing importance and firms led by Lever Brothers formed the Salt Union which lasted for some years, dominating its supply in the late 19th cent. Research and development in these fields of chemical manufacture were undertaken by Brunner and Mond. Their United Alkali Company merged with the explosives company Nobel Industries and the British Dyestuffs Corporation in 1926 to form Imperial Chemical Industries.

Applications of research in organic chemistry during the 19th cent. enabled the development of firms making solvents, synthetic dyes, and new materials. The most important of these were developments from combinations of cellulose which made possible a wide range of new products including parkesine (the first commercial plastic), photographic film, and viscose rayon.

During the 20th cent. the demands for new chemicals continued in order to reduce imports and to cut costs. Thus rayon was invented and marketed as artificial silk. Courtaulds sold this cheaper fibre which was used for clothing and furnishing fabrics. Similarly Lever Brothers and the Dutch company of Jurgens combined in 1929 to form Unilever, whose core businesses had depended on making soap, margarine, and cattle feed, but which then produced pharmaceuticals and food chemicals. Developments in long-chain polymer chemistry during the middle decades of the 20th cent. gave rise to many products: polythene, nylon, and terylene. The raw materials for these products derived from coal or crude oil. Major international oil companies became closely involved in chemical manufacturing and often undertook research to tailor-make some product for special uses such as materials for aircraft tyres.

The most modern chemical industries are those concerned with biochemistry, microbiology, and particularly pharmaceutical research. Associated with household names such as Boots, Fisons, Glaxo, and ICI and Zenaca, they all demand heavy research and development investment.

IJEK

Chepstow castle on the banks of the river Wye was one of the southernmost of the line of castles dominating the border with Wales. It was started immediately after the Norman Conquest by William *Fitzosbern, earl of Hereford, and added to by Walter de Clare and Richard de Clare, earl of *Pembroke ('Strongbow'), extending along the length of the river cliff. Later the castle passed to the Beauforts, who also owned *Raglan, nearby. During the first civil war, Chepstow was held for the king and surrendered after a brief siege in 1645: it was again besieged in the second civil war in 1648. After the Restoration, it was used as a prison: Henry Marten, the regicide, was confined there and gave his name to Marten's Tower. JAC

Chequers, in the Chilterns near Wendover (Bucks.), was given in 1917 by Lord Lee of Fareham as a country residence for the prime minister. It was first used by *Lloyd George in 1921. Lee, a Conservative MP first elected in 1900, was an admirer of Lloyd George, served as director-general of food production in 1917, and moved to agriculture in 1919 and to the Admiralty in 1921. He was given a barony in 1918 and left office when the coalition broke up in 1922. The house has a Tudor core, with Victorian additions and substantial remodelling by Lee 1909–12. Among its more remarkable features is a fine collection of paintings including Constables, Reynolds, Van Loos, and Raeburns. JAC

Cheriton, battle of, 1644. After *Roundway Down, *Hopton and *Waller continued their private struggle in Wessex, manœuvring for possession of Winchester. On 29 March they met at Cheriton, Waller with 10,000 men, Hopton with 6,000. The royalist cavalry suffered heavily when caught in deep rutted lanes and Hopton was obliged to retreat, first to Alresford, then to Winchester. The battle is sometimes known as Alresford.

JAC

Cheshire, a lowland county in north-western England, resembles a hammock slung between the south-west Pennines (east) and Flint–Denbighshire uplands (west); the southerly morainic barrier is crossed by the midland gap, now followed by road, rail, and canal. These barriers halted the early flood of Anglo-Saxon invaders to fertile meadowlands and ancient woodlands. The Romans had established a legionary fortress at Deva (*Chester), as a base for advances into Wales and west Brigantia, but place-names reflect subsequent traces of early Celtic church influence and Scandinavian invasions (Irish-Norse into Wirral, Danes into east). Initially part of *Mercia and 'shired' (=sheared) in the 10th cent., the county boundaries conformed to roughly their present extent by the 12th cent. *Palatinate from 1237 when the earldom passed to the crown, though sparsely inhabited, Cheshire was not rich in castles despite its border position; large country houses, characteristically half-timbered, were its greater glory. Of crucial importance during the Civil War because of its strategic position, the county saw much fighting. The royalist defeat at *Nantwich in 1644, followed by the surrender of Chester after siege in February 1646, effectively ended Charles I's hopes of help from Ireland.

Long known for its salt and famous for its cheese since the Middle Ages, Cheshire remained only moderately important agriculturally until specialization encouraged expansion of its dairying. The south and centre of the county have remained agricultural. Equal balance between rural and urban populations was affected by the revolutionary changes of the industrial period, with the extension of manufacturing industries and improving transport. Under the influence of the expanding cotton industry, Stockport (important for the manufacture of textile machinery) and other towns in north-east Cheshire grew rapidly; Birkenhead then developed around Cammell Laird's shipyard. As population quadrupled during the 19th cent., canals took coal and agricultural products to the labour forces, and salt all over England; railway networks radiating from Crewe and Chester were augmented by that growing around Manchester and a tunnel under the river Mersey, linking Birkenhead with Liverpool (1886). The emergence of the chemical industries, concentrated on Northwich (salt), Runcorn, and Port Sunlight (soap), lessened the dependence on textiles. Population has continued to increase, since much of northern Cheshire has become an overspill or dormitory area for nearby Lancashire urban centres. The county, once called 'the seedplot of Gentility', nevertheless remains the rich man's social playground, determined to maintain its distinctions. ASH

chess. The origins of chess have been much discussed but remain obscure, since it developed over time. It seems to have begun in India or China about the 6th cent. AD and to have been adopted in Persia, where it was known as *shatranj*. It spread to the west through the Arabs and the Vikings, and a Viking ivory chess set, discovered in the Hebrides in 1831, has been dated to the 12th cent. One of the earliest books to be issued by *Caxton (*c.*1481) was *Game* *and Playe of the Chesse*, a translation from a French translation of a Latin work. The medieval game was slow and was speeded up in the 16th cent. by giving the queen and bishop greater powers. Since then a reasonably standard game has developed, though with local variations. The game is controlled, with some difficulty, by the World Chess Federation, founded in 1924, which formulates rules, awards grandmasterships and masterships, and organizes the world championship. JAC

Chester (Roman), known to the Romans as Deva, was founded in the 70s as a legionary fortress, originally for *legio II Adiutrix*. From the 80s it became the long-term base of *legio XX Valeria Victrix*. Originally constructed in timber, it was rebuilt in stone *c*.100 and was larger than normal at 60 acres. Parts of the northern and eastern defences continued in use down to the English Civil War. Excavation within the fortress is restricted by later buildings, but it seems to have contained the usual complement of buildings, and an unexplained and elaborate complex known as the 'Elliptical Building'. Outside the south-eastern angle of the defences lay an amphitheatre, and traces of riverside works have been found to the west in the area of the Roodee. In the later Roman period the intensity of occupation declined, though was probably still military. ASEC

(post-Roman). After the Norman invasion of 1066, William quickly marched north to subdue the rebellious native population, particularly the Welsh; the castle was commenced and a hereditary earldom created, but this title reverted to the crown in 1237. Although Chester prospered as an administrative centre, the port was no longer viable by 1600 because of silting.

Granted a royal charter in 1506, Chester was severely affected by the Civil War since city and county supported opposing factions. Besieged 1644–6, the city was Charles's last important outlet to the sea and the nearest port for Ireland; he is said to have watched his army's defeat at *Rowton Heath in September 1645 from the medieval walls before escaping into Wales, leaving the city to starve. By mid-18th cent., it had recovered into quiet country-town prosperity, remaining untroubled by later industrial unrest. The continuous, rambling first-floor arcades of the medieval rows are unique, but many of the black-and-white half-timbered restorations are Victorian. ASH

Chester, battle of, *c*.616. *Æthelfryth of Northumbria defeated the Britons of Powys, killing their leader, Selyf. According to *Bede, the battle was preceded by a massacre of monks from Bangor-is-y-Coed (near Wrexham), who were praying for a British victory. Bede regarded this as just retribution for their refusal to accept *Augustine's invitation to adopt the Roman rites. The Saxon victory was part of a westwards expansion which ultimately drove a wedge between the Britons of Strathclyde and those of Wales, and represented an important step in the growth of Northumbrian power. JAC

Chester cathedral. The Benedictine abbey of St Werburgh was founded in 1092 on the site of an Anglo-Saxon foundation, in the diocese of Lichfield. It produced the earliest of the Chester mystery plays, and the *Polychronicon* of Ranulph Higden (d. 1364) was its main contribution to medieval learning. After the dissolution of the monasteries, the abbey was reconstituted as the cathedral of Christ and St Mary in 1541, in the newly formed diocese of Chester. Its revenues were sequestered when the city fell to parliamentary forces in 1646, and poverty was a recurrent theme for three centuries. Reorganization under the Ecclesiastical Commissioners Act (1840) proved beneficial, and relationships between the cathedral and the community steadily improved. The abbey buildings are among the best-preserved monastic remains in Britain. Parts of the Norman church survive, but most of it has been replaced by work of every century; built of the local, rather friable, red sandstone, it projects modest nobility rather than grandeur. The carved choir-stalls (*c*.1390) are particularly fine, though five misericords were destroyed by Dean Howson for being 'very improper', during the massive reconstruction carried out by Sir George Gilbert *Scott in 1868–76. ASH

Chesterfield, battle of, 1266. Despite Simon de *Montfort's death at *Evesham in 1265, the earl of Derby and other barons continued their resistance to Henry III. On 15 May 1266 they were defeated at Chesterfield and Derby was captured. Some of the survivors then took refuge in the fens of Ely, where they were suppressed by Henry's son Edward in 1267. JAC

Chesterfield, Philip Dormer Stanhope, 4th earl of (1694–1773). Politician and diplomat. Chesterfield owed his entrée into politics in 1714 to his kinsman James *Stanhope. He was elected an MP in 1715 and joined the household of the prince of Wales, the future George II. Inheriting his father's earldom in 1726, he served as ambassador to The Hague, 1728–32, but soon after his return joined the opposition to *Walpole. After Walpole's fall he made his peace in 1745 with the 'old corps' Whigs, led by the *Pelhams, and accepted office as lord-lieutenant of Ireland. He became one of the inner circle of ministers responsible for national policy, and in 1746 was appointed secretary of state (northern department), but his peace aims were frequently upstaged by the bellicosity of his senior colleague *Newcastle, and in 1748 he resigned. Chesterfield's *Letters to his son*, famously described by *Johnson as exhibiting 'the morals of a whore and the manners of a dancing master', were published by his widow the year after his death. AAH

Chester-le-Street, diocese of. Created in 883, when the monks of *Lindisfarne, evicted in 875, settled here on the south bank of the Tyne with *Cuthbert's relics. The cult of the saint made it the centre of wealth and power in the north-east until the see was moved to *Durham in 995. WMM

Chesterton, Gilbert Keith (1874–1936). Chesterton and his friend Hilaire Belloc (1870–1953), with whom he collaborated, were the best-known catholic writers of Edwardian England—*Shaw dubbed them 'Chesterbelloc'—though Chesterton did not join the catholic church until 1922. Busy journalists, they engaged in public controversy, particularly with Shaw, *Kipling, and *Wells. Chesterton's best works are probably *The Napoleon of Notting Hill* (1904), *The Club of Queer Trades* (1905) ('Major Brown, Major Brown, where does the jackal dwell?'), and *The Man who was Thursday* (1908), though his most popular books were the Father Brown detective stories from 1911. Chesterton's 'cheese and good ale' stance grows tedious at times, and the deep nostalgia which he shared with Belloc is perhaps best captured in the latter's poem 'Ha'nacker Mill'. JAC

Chevy Chase, battle of. See OTTERBURN.

Chichele, Henry (*c.*1362–1443). Archbishop of Canterbury. The son and brother of prominent London merchants, Chichele was an original fellow of New College, Oxford. As a doctor of civil law, he practised in church courts and diocesan administration. From 1406 he was in royal service as an ambassador, earning the bishopric of St Davids, a place in the council, and in 1414 promotion to Canterbury from Henry V. He never held a political office but was an assiduous member of royal councils for most of his life. He founded a collegiate church at his birthplace, Higham Ferrers (Northants), in 1422, and in 1438 the college of All Souls, Oxford, for 40 fellows praying for the souls of Henry V and other English casualties in the French war, while studying arts and law, but not theology. RLS

Chichester (Roman). The *civitas*-capital of the *Reg(i)ni; its Roman name was Noviomagus. Lying within the area of the possible late Iron Age *oppidum* defined by the Chichester entrenchments, after a brief military occupation the Roman town developed early. This can be ascribed to the influence of the pro-Roman king *Cogidubnus, mentioned on two exceptionally early Roman inscriptions from the town, one referring to a temple of Neptune and Minerva (location unknown). Otherwise, the development of the town seems to have been unexceptional. The main baths were in the north-western quadrant, the amphitheatre outside the south-eastern, walls were constructed in the 3rd/4th cents. Remains of a number of later Roman houses, some with mosaics, have been located. The town seems to have been in decline in the later 4th cent. ASEC

Chichester, Arthur, 1st Baron [I] (1563–1625). Lord deputy of Ireland. Chichester came from a Devon family, his mother being a Courtenay of Powderham. After serving against the Armada and taking part in the expedition against Cadiz in 1596, he went to Ireland and was appointed governor of Carrickfergus. In 1604 he was made lord deputy in succession to *Mountjoy and held the post for a remarkable eleven years, retiring in 1615. In 1613 he was made an Irish baron. There were two prominent features of his administration—to weaken the loyalty of the native Irish to their chiefs, which resulted in the *Flight of the Earls in 1607, and to encourage Scottish and English immigration to Ulster, where he acquired large estates. The moderation which has been perceived in his policy towards the catholics may have been more fatigue than principle, for he shared the current English contempt for the native Irish and believed their conversion to be essential, and his cautious approach to settlement was prudential rather than fundamental. JAC

Chichester, diocese of. The diocese was created by the transfer of the see from *Selsey under the terms of the Council of London (1075), and is roughly conterminous with Sussex. Among its bishops were Hilary (1147–69), who was at variance with Becket as Henry II's chancellor over Battle abbey (1157), and later refused total obedience to Becket as archbishop in his quarrel with the king. Later bishops include Ralph Neville (1224–44), chancellor of England, Richard de Wyche (1244–53), noted for his learning and sanctity and canonized in 1262, Reginald *Pecock (1450–9), theological writer and controversialist, deprived of his see, and Lancelot *Andrewes (1605–9), as a scholar and preacher one of the principal influences on Anglican theological development. Bishop George *Bell (1929–58) was a strong opponent of saturation bombing in the Second World War, a stance which is said to have cost him preferment to Canterbury in 1944. The cathedral, built between *c.*1091 and 1305, is Norman in origin, but was largely rebuilt between 1191 and 1210 in a style reminiscent of Canterbury. WMM

Chichester-Clark, James, Lord Moyola (b. 1923). Prime minister of Northern Ireland. Chichester-Clark, like his predecessor Terence *O'Neill, was from a landed background. He was Unionist chief whip in the Stormont Parliament (1963–6), leader of the House of Commons (1966–7), and minister of agriculture (1967–9). He deftly united support among both the allies and opponents of the prime minister, O'Neill, when he resigned from the cabinet in April 1969 in opposition to the new local government franchise: he succeeded O'Neill on 1 May. In August 1969 British troops were introduced into Northern Ireland, a development which weakened the authority of the Stormont government. The emergence of the more militant Provisional IRA in early 1971 forced Chichester-Clark to demand a new security initiative from London; and when this was not forthcoming, he resigned (20 March), taking a life peerage. An affable but unimaginative figure, Chichester-Clark was disorientated by high-handed British government action and by the rapid escalation of violence. Terence O'Neill observed that for the 22 months of his premiership Chichester-Clark bore a permanent expression of worry. AJ

Child, Sir Josiah, baronet (*c.*1630–99). Child made his money victualling the navy and lived at Portsmouth before developing a great estate at Wanstead in Essex. He sat in Parliament for Petersfield in 1658, Downton 1673, and Ludlow 1685. His baronetcy was awarded in 1678. From 1677 he was a director of the *East India Company, governor 1681–3 and 1686–8, and deputy governor 1684–6 and 1688–90. His brother John was governor of Bombay. Child's *Discourse on Trade* in 1668 praised the Dutch and argued for a low rate of interest to stimulate trade and manufactures. He disagreed with the commonly held view that high wages made England uncompetitive, maintaining that they were, in themselves, signs of prosperity. His prodigious wealth attracted much envy. *Evelyn described him as 'sordidly avaricious' and dismissed Wanstead, with its lakes and walnut trees, as 'a cursed and barren spot, as commonly these overgrown and suddenly moneyed men for the most part seat themselves'. Child's daughter married into the nobility, and his son Richard was made an Irish earl in 1731 as Tylney of Castlemaine. JAC

childbirth. Before the early 18th cent., childbirth was a social rather than medical event, prominently controlled by women and ritualistic. In late pregnancy, the expectant mother issued invitations to close female friends and relatives, known as 'gossips' (from 'god-siblings'), who were summoned by the husband on commencement of labour. The birth itself was supervised by the midwife (or 'grace-wife'), for which she was paid with a gift or 'grace'. The bedroom became a lying-in chamber, enclosed physically and symbolically (keyholes blocked, daylight excluded, use of candles), where the gossips prepared a special warmed drink, sweetened and spiced, known as the caudle. The actual birth depended on the midwife's method for swift, safe delivery, but once the 'navel-string' was tied and cut, the infant was swaddled, then shown to the mother. Although she had been brought to bed and completed her 'crying out', she was still 'in the straw' (alluding to early bed-fillings) and would remain so for a full month. Initially confined to bed in the darkened room, 'upsitting' was an important social occasion, when female visitors might drink the caudle; she then continued room- though not bed-bound, before moving around the house, though not outdoors. The rite of churching (originally purification, later just thanksgiving), unenforced but very popular, symbolically marked the end of lying-in. Men were excluded from the delivery, unless a surgeon was summoned to remove a dead foetus, using hooks, in the minority of difficult births. Since they were only called in as a last resort, medical knowledge of the birth mechanism and placental role was scant.

The Chamberlen family, Huguenot immigrants, were not the only male midwives in 17th-cent. London but were the most notable, though as their claimed special expertise remained a family secret for four generations (*ante* 1620–*c*.1730), their impact was limited. Their skills in delivering a living child by the head were instrumental rather than manual—forceps, vectis (=lever), fillet (=pliable noose)—but the disclosure of forceps was only coincidental with the rise of man-midwifery, not its cause. Replacing gossips with male pupils, William Smellie initiated large-scale teaching of midwifery in 1740s London and greatly enlarged experience of both normal labour and difficult births. Lying-in funds for poor mothers preceded establishment of lying-in hospitals and lying-in charities. Obstetric knowledge exploded, London supplanted Paris through its published treatises, and, by the end of the century, obstetrics had become firmly established within orthodox medical practice. But medical reform in the first half of the 19th cent. was accompanied by hardening of occupational boundaries and professional rivalry, and obstetrics became side-lined. Midwives, unregistered and generally untrained, still undertook the majority of deliveries in villages and large manufacturing towns, but lying-in hospitals were so bedevilled by epidemics of puerperal fever that poor women were more safely delivered in slums by these untrained women, despite Dickens's portrayal of Sairey Gamp as the epitome of disreputability.

By the end of the 19th cent. maternal mortality rates were causing public concern, but the introduction of antisepsis only impacted on the lying-in hospitals, and levels continued high until 1935. Maternal mortality was sensitive to standards of care, but although midwives could be monitored after the Midwives Act (1902), the newly created College of Obstetricians and Gynaecologists (1929) was more concerned with its own status than with general maternal care. Use of forceps and anaesthesia for normal deliveries had grown steadily from the 1870s, but surgical intervention may have sustained mortality rates until the introduction of sulphonamides (1936), then penicillin, which slashed deaths from puerperal fever. The 1936 Midwives Act, Second World War, and introduction of the National Health Service (1948) led to improvements in maternity services, and hospitals were increasingly used for normal as well as high-risk deliveries. By the 1980s, almost all births were hospitalized. Maternal and perinatal deaths are now rare, but the intense medicalization of childbirth is under challenge: women's expectations have changed, and dispute between doctors, midwives and mothers has spread to within the medical profession itself. ASH

Childers, Robert Erskine (1870–1922). Childers was a prim civil servant with a taste for high adventure. He was born in London and educated at Haileybury and Trinity College, Cambridge. His father, a distinguished oriental scholar, died when he was 6, and Childers was brought up by his mother, whose family came from Glendalough in the Wicklow Mountains. From 1895 to 1910 Childers was a clerk in the House of Commons. At the outbreak of the Boer War he volunteered and wrote two books on his experiences. In 1903 he achieved a sensational success with a brilliant novel, *The Riddle of the Sands*, about two yachtsmen who stumbled on German preparations, in the shelter of the Frisian Islands, for a barge-invasion of England: it touched public anxiety and sold copiously. From 1910 Childers became more involved in the Irish nationalist cause and in 1914 ran a quantity of arms to Howth in his yacht *Asgard*. During the Great War he worked as an intelligence officer and took part in the air raid on Zeppelin bases at Cuxhaven in November 1914—his old stamping-ground. He was secretary to the Irish delegation in 1921 but joined *de Valera in 1922 in opposition to the treaty and was shot by the new government of the Irish Free State. He died with composure, shaking hands with the firing squad. His son Erskine was president of Eire from 1973 to 1975. JAC

children. The proportion of children in British society has varied over time with little accurate documentation until censuses began in 1801. At that time, the proportion of children under 15 years was estimated to have been one-third of the total, increasing to almost 40 per cent by the mid-19th cent. By 1991 the proportion of children had decreased to about a quarter of the total population. These changes in relative proportions do not necessarily reflect differences in absolute numbers but are influenced by variations in life expectancy as well as birth rates. The numbers of children born in any family depended upon factors such as age at marriage, and the nutrition and health of parents, particularly the mother. Although many children were born, infant mortality rates were high until the major improvements in health care in the last quarter of the 19th cent. During the 18th and 19th cents. it was not uncommon for parents with a favourite or family Christian name to give it to several of their children in an attempt to guarantee its presence in the next generation. Official statistics indicate that the number of children per family varied little between social classes until the 1870s, when more reliable contraception was taken up by the better-off. The use of contraception to limit family size appears to have been associated with changing attitudes to women as well as the cost of the education of children in the rapidly expanding economy of Britain in the 19th cent. Access to contraception spread to all levels of society during the 20th cent., particularly after the introduction of the female contraceptive pill in the 1960s, which accelerated the decline in the birth rate and increased the proportion of childless couples. The numbers of children born have fallen below the rate needed to replace the population. Paradoxically, as the birth rate declined there was also a great deal of medical effort to understand and counter infertility.

Attitudes to children have varied over time, with gender, social status, and values about childhood shaping adult views and thus the children's experiences. The concept of childhood drawn from the old Roman catholic doctrine of original sin required that children be saved from the devil by a sound inculcation of Christian values beginning with the sacrament of baptism. Even very small children were expected to understand as though adult. The image of a child was not of innocence but of an imp, a little devil, likely to commit sin unless corrected. This concept continued after the Reformation when it was assumed that the young were likely to be corrupted by worldly ways and that a moral way of life could be attained only by strict, even forcible, guidance. It was accepted that all children at every level of society needed religious education whether formally in church or informally at home. Formal education and training for adult life assumed differing destinies for boys and for girls and for differing levels in society. The care of children was normally the task of parents and the immediate family, but, amongst the wealthy, care was the responsibility of special servants, such as nursemaids or 'nannies'. In the later Middle Ages, the sons of the aristocracy were sent as pages into another noble household at about the age of 12 years. Later, children of the upper classes were educated at home by a resident tutor or governess and it was more likely that the middle classes sent their sons away from home to boarding schools. The education of children in modern times has been characterized by its increasing formality and length.

A dramatic challenge to accepted ideas about children and childhood emerged in the 18th cent., expressed at its most controversial in the book *Émile* by J. J. Rousseau. The English edition appeared in 1763, a year after its first publication in French. Rousseau argued that children were born innocent and would continue so unless corrupted by adults. Although this remained a minority view for many years, it helped to modify some of the severity towards children. In addition, this new view of children stimulated the development of special toys and pastimes to help them learn. A major innovation, led by the publisher John Newberry in the later 18th cent., was literature specifically designed for child readers. This period also saw the establishment of Sunday schools for children's religious education.

The enjoyment of leisure in the ways suggested in the debates about childhood was completely outside the experience of the great majority of children. In rural areas, children of the less well-off had always performed household and other tasks. This pattern was continued in urban and industrial areas with children as young as 3 years being employed in textiles, mines, and other occupations. Charles *Kingsley's account of the London chimney sweeps in *The Water Babies*, and many of *Dickens's novels, drew attention in fiction to the reality of life for many children. During the 19th cent. there was increasing involvement of the state to protect children by controlling working practices and, eventually, to finance and regulate full-time education which removed children from full-time employment. State intervention continued in the 20th cent., raising the age at which children might leave compulsory full-time education and giving access to a range of non-compulsory educational opportunities including those at university level. Parallel developments occurred in the punishment of juvenile offenders by the state. In 1846 young offenders were separated from adults and sent to industrial schools, the precursors of borstal institutions, for treatment and rehabilitation. In 1908 the Children's Act established special courts to deal with child offenders, a system which continued for the rest of the 20th cent.

Children are both the newest members of society and its future. The history of British attitudes to children has demonstrated their importance in maintaining property and family position. At the highest levels of society, children were used to enhance the political and social strength of their families. At other levels they were educated and trained to contribute to the family's status and resources. Children at all levels were recognized as a cost during their time of dependency but as having the potential to repay their family line as adults. IJEK

Aries, P., *Centuries of Childhood* (1962); Walvin, J., *A Child's World: A Social History of English Childhood* (1982).

Chillingworth, William (1602–44). Theological controversialist. Born in Oxford, he was educated at Trinity College, where he became fellow. The Jesuits persuaded him, though *Laud's godson, to join the Roman church, but a brief spell of study in Douai (1630–1) caused him to leave catholic certainties for *Falkland's liberal group at Great Tew. Here he wrote his main work *The Religion of Protestants, a Safe Way of Salvation* (1637), supporting the right of free enquiry and denying any church monopoly of the truth. Taking Anglican orders (1638), he became chancellor of Salisbury (1638), but in the Civil War, while serving as a royalist army chaplain, he was captured at Arundel. Already in poor health, he died at Chichester. Ahead of his time, his rationalism and toleration, suspected by Romanists and puritans alike, were to be valued in later years. WMM

Chiltern hundreds. Members of Parliament cannot resign directly and must therefore, if they wish to retire before a general election, apply for an office of profit under the crown, which disqualifies them. By convention this is the stewardship of the Chiltern hundreds. The stewardships of the manor of Northstead, of East Hendred, and of Kempholme have also been used. JAC

Chimney Sweeps Act, 1875. The plight of small boys sent up to clean chimneys had been raised as early as the 1760s by Jonas *Hanway, who characteristically composed several pamphlets. Legislation to ensure decent treatment was largely ineffective, though an Act of 1788 specified that they should attend church on Sundays. Lord *Shaftesbury took up the matter towards the end of his life, drawing attention to two recent cases—the death of a 7-year-old boy in Co. Durham and a 14-year-old in Cambridgeshire. The 1875 Act (38 & 39 Vic. c. 70)—laid down that chimney sweeps should be registered by the police and certificates withheld if they disregarded safety. JAC

China, relations with. Direct British trading contacts with China began in 1637, and were soon followed by a considerable artistic and cultural interest in the world's longest-established civilization. Difficulties in finding suitable exports to China, coupled with the problem of dealing with an empire which acknowledged no equals in the world, led to the first *China (Opium) War in 1839–42. A British victory was rewarded with many privileges in five 'treaty' ports (a number later much increased), and by the acquisition of *Hong Kong. Further differences precipitated the second China War when the Chinese were finally forced (1860) to conform to western ideas of diplomatic practice. The British thereafter had no wish to see China weakened further since they already enjoyed the lion's share of trade and investment. Competition for trade and concessions increased in the 1890s, and Britain participated in an international force to raise the siege of the legations in Peking by the *Boxers (1900). In the 1920s and 1930s Chinese nationalism was strong enough to persuade the Foreign Office to start the renegotiation of the unequal treaties. On the other hand, from 1931 Britain was unable to assist China against growing Japanese pressure, while victory in 1945 temporarily made the USA the leading outside power in Chinese affairs. Britain, unlike the USA, recognized the new communist regime which came to power in China in 1949, and tried to moderate American policy towards Peking during and after the *Korean War (1950–3). China insisted on the return of Hong Kong when the lease expired in 1997, and firmly opposed British efforts in 1993–4 to extend democracy in the colony. CJB

China wars, 1839–42 and 1856–60. Otherwise known as the 'Opium wars', these were as much about clashes of imperial interests as the specific issue of opium, which was grown in British India and was one of the few commodities that China was prepared to trade. In 1839 the imperial Chinese government attempted to block the trade, seizing all opium held in the main trading port of Canton. The resulting war was an unequal conflict, with the Chinese having no answer to British fire-power, particularly from two East India Company gunboats with 32-pounder guns. The treaty of *Nanking gave Britain *Hong Kong and access to five other 'treaty ports' including Canton and Shanghai. China then collapsed into a brutal civil war known as the Tai Ping rebellion (1850–64), caught between a decadent government and religious fanaticism, in which about 20 million people died. Other powers took advantage of this, and in 1857 British and French forces occupied Canton. Although repulsed at the Taku Forts in June 1859, the Anglo-French force captured them next year, and founded the naval base at Port Arthur (modern Luda). After the convention of Peking had ceded Kowloon to Britain, in a notorious incident the Imperial Summer Palace at Peking was destroyed in reprisal for Chinese barbarities. Redvers *Buller, a famous participant in the war, refused to wear his campaign medal, believing the war to be immoral. See also ARROW WAR. SDB

Chippendale, Thomas (1718–79). Cabinet-maker and designer, the son of a Yorkshire joiner, he set up business in London about the 1750s. Employing varied styles and adapting to changing fashions, Chippendale designed an extensive range of furniture, carpets, wallpapers, and brassware, from the elaborate yet delicate for the homes of gentry, to the simple and unpretentious for their servants' quarters. In 1754 he published *The Gentleman and Cabinet-Maker's Director* which influenced style in Europe and America. Both Catherine the Great and Louis XVI had copies of the book. Chippendale's designs are in many distinguished houses, including Badminton, Harewood, and Alnwick castle. Probably his best work was after 1770, when he worked with Robert *Adam, a notoriously fastidious architect. Not highly regarded by his contemporaries and successors—*Sheraton said his designs were 'wholly antiquated and laid aside'—Chippendale's name has come to typify 18th-cent. mahogany furniture. JC

Chippenham, battle of, 878. *Alfred's Wessex forces were encamped at Chippenham in north Wiltshire on 6 January 878 when they were routed by a surprise attack from a Danish army at Gloucester, led by *Guthrum. Alfred was forced into hiding in the marshes of Somerset. JAC

Chippenham, treaty of. See WEDMORE.

chivalry. The French precursor of this term, *chevalerie*, indicates that this code of behaviour, to which the noble and gentle classes subscribed throughout the Middle Ages and beyond, derived initially from the special status and function of the mounted warrior. Developments in warfare *c.*800–1100 elevated this type of soldier in both a military and social context. The training was long, the costs of equipment high; the need for considered behaviour in the field and the praise attached to worthy actions spilled over into life in general. Thus was generated a moral, religious, and social code, which over the centuries became more closely defined and controlled through the conduct of *tournaments, laws of war, orders of chivalry, and *heraldry. The church, too, was keen to encourage the proper conduct of the warrior élite, and the crusades helped to shape 'the distinctive Christian strand in chivalry', even if its origins must still be sought in a secular context. Much of the early evidence derives from literary sources, such as the *chansons de geste*. Historians of chivalry always face the problem of deciding whether art and literature reflected realities of life or were intended to shape them. This is particularly relevant in the English context where Edward III's plans for a chivalric order, finally bearing fruit in the *Garter (*c.*1348), were much influenced by contemporary perceptions of the *Arthurian romance tradition. Although chivalry was to some degree institutionalized in the later Middle Ages through the military orders and through the writing of treatises, it remained a nebulous yet all-embracing concept. It was extremely important in creating a social bond between the crown, nobility, and gentry, and in generating the code of behaviour expected of a gentleman, demanding personal honour, generosity, loyalty, and courage. Thus it survived well beyond the era of the mounted knight. AC

choirs. A term used for groups of singers performing together, usually in parts with more than one singer per part. English usage often makes a distinction between 'choir', a small group of trained, often professional, and frequently ecclesiastical singers, and a larger, generally amateur and secular 'chorus'. Choruses in opera-houses, however, are traditionally professional.

The earliest recorded uses of choral singing are for Christian worship, in particular the unison singing of plainchant. Medieval monastic choirs often numbered over 50, while cathedrals, collegiate churches, and household chapels supported similar-sized choirs of men and boys. Convents, naturally, employed women's voices. Contrast was provided by alternating choral chant with passages sung by soloists. These sections were later set polyphonically and by the 15th cent. were assigned to a small choir, generally in four or five parts. By the mid-16th cent. London's Chapel Royal numbered around 32 men and 12 boys. The post-Reformation choir was usually split into two antiphonal groups: cantoris on the precentor's side and decani opposite on the dean's side.

During the Commonwealth (1649–60) choirs were disbanded, although at the Restoration Charles II conscripted the best choirboys throughout the country (including *Purcell) for his new Chapel Royal. Short choruses were an important element in the masque and Restoration stage works, and it was on this tradition that *Handel built his new genre, the English oratorio. Here the chorus (usually sung by around 24 singers including the soloists) often played an important dramatic role, as in the many double choruses of *Israel in Egypt* (1739). The 1784 Handel celebrations at Westminster abbey, with nearly 300 singers and almost as many instrumentalists, began a tradition of gargantuan performances that continued in the Handel festivals, using thousands of performers, inaugurated at London's Crystal Palace in 1857.

The 19th cent. saw the growth of countless amateur choral societies throughout Britain, now including female voices (except for male-voice choirs cultivated especially in Wales). Revivals of favourites by Handel (especially **Messiah*), Haydn, and, later, Bach were balanced by new commissions such as Mendelssohn's *Elijah* for the Birmingham Festival (1846). Evangelical movements formed choirs to sing hymns and gospel songs, and John Curwen's educational tonic sol-fa method opened up whole repertoires to singers unable to read conventional notation.

Some choirs, like the various Bach choirs around the country, concentrate on the music of a particular composer. During the last few decades, consorts of solo voices have specialized in early repertories such as madrigals, while small expert groups like the Monteverdi and Taverner choirs have adopted 'authentic' forces in an attempt to recreate earlier performing styles. ECr

cholera, an acute diarrhoeal disease transmitted by faecal contamination of water supplies and food, and long endemic in India, escaped from Bengal in 1817 to initiate the first of several world-wide pandemics. Asiatic cholera eventually appeared in England in October 1831 in the north-east port of Sunderland, supposedly imported from Hamburg; its presence was initially denied by those with mercantile interests, but it soon arose in Newcastle, Edinburgh, and London, before reaching France and then hurdling the Atlantic. Spreading capriciously, it caused some 31,000 estimated deaths in England and Scotland, and a further 20,000 in Ireland. A second outbreak commencing in London in 1848 was even more serious, despite a stream of regulations and recommendations, and affected all sections of the population rather than the 'destitute and reckless class' as before, with some 65,000 deaths in England, Wales, and Scotland and 30,000 in Ireland. The last two major outbreaks of 1853–4 and 1866 were milder. Mid-century attitudes of practical concern held by an enlightened minority (such as John Snow, who famously removed the handle of the Broad Street pump in 1854) spurred some sanitary reform, but there is disagreement amongst modern commentators about the impact of cholera on political, administrative, or social history. Despite its shock value, it was surpassed by tuberculosis and the fevers as a cause of death and debility, but local government reorganization facilitated progress in public health, and few cases occurred in Britain after 1893. ASH

Christadelphians. A Christian sect founded by John Thomas (New York, *c.*1848), but with adherents in Britain. Originally called Thomasites, the name Christadelphian ('Brother of Christ') was adopted during the American Civil War to justify objection to military service. Rejecting ministers and churches, and with no overall organization, the core belief is millennialist, with Christ expected to return and rule from Jerusalem; the Bible is regarded as infallible, the doctrine of the trinity is rejected, baptism is seen as valid only by immersion, and the unconverted will not be raised from the dead. ASH

Christianity, derived from Judaism to become the dominant religion of western Europe and the driving force behind its civilization, has underpinned much of Britain's cultural and artistic heritage for fourteen centuries; as the country's established religion, it has helped fashion attitudes, way of life, and public order. There is little evidence of widespread Christianity before the 4th cent., though it was probably introduced earlier by eastern traders along with Mithraism and Isis-worship, popular with the army and fortress-towns: archaeological evidence of a cryptogram has been found at Cirencester (2nd–3rd cents.), chi-rho signs elsewhere, and the first British martyr was *Alban. Urban Christianity was sufficiently vibrant to send three bishops (London, York, Colchester) to the Council of Arles (314); the little church at Silchester (*c.*360), wall-paintings at Lullingstone (Kent), and a Christian mosaic at Hinton St Mary (Dorset) further testify to its vigour. *Paganism, despite a brief revival 360–80, was in decline as the century ended, when historical figures such as *Ninian and *Patrick began to emerge and Christianity was becoming the religion not merely of towns and upper classes but of rural estates. On the arrival of Anglo-Saxon invaders with their gods Woden and Thor, British Christianity was virtually extinguished except for the western Celtic fringes relatively untouched by Romanization or Scandinavian conquest. *Monasticism (withdrawal from the world) had reached the Celts at a formative stage in their Christianity, and monks rather than bishops led the church. Patrick (*c.*390–461) evangelized Ireland, Ninian (*c.*360–*c.*432) the Picts of Galloway, and Kentigern (d. 612) Strathclyde; Illtud (d. *c.*540) and *David (*c.*530–*c.*589) worked in Wales, but had little wish to convert the pagan settlers, though they sent missions to the continent; *Columba settled in *Iona (*c.*563), whence *Aidan brought Christianity to *Lindisfarne (635). The great legacies of the Celtic church are illuminated manuscripts such as the Books of *Kells and Durrow, and the *Lindisfarne Gospels. When Roman missionaries under *Augustine arrived in Kent (597), divergences between the two strands arising from differences in administrative organization and details such as the date of Easter and style of monkish tonsure led to clashes unresolved until the Synod of *Whitby (664), when Roman customs prevailed. Conversion had sometimes been slow and patchy, though helped when a ruler embraced the new faith (*Æthelbert of Kent, *Edwin of Northumbria), but a brief golden age followed statesman-archbishop *Theodore's reorganization of scattered dioceses, which produced scholars such as *Bede, missionaries like *Boniface of Crediton, and growth in the church's status and prestige. Monasteries were not only centres of religion and education but functioned as law-courts, while large investments were made in buildings representing the church (stone replacing wood, built in 'the Roman style'); secular Anglo-Saxon and Christian cultural traditions began to fuse in both poetry and visual arts (metalwork, manuscripts, carvings). Attacks from *Viking raiders during the 9th cent., seen by churchmen as apocalyptic, destroyed religious houses and shifted power and wealth into secular hands, but did not totally destroy the church.

For two centuries after about 1050, when most of western Europe was formally Christian, sustained attempts were made to apply gospel principles and canon law to society generally, through Gregorian reform, clergy discipline, and then modification of lay life. The Norman Conquest, which joined England politically and ecclesiastically with Europe's main states, away from Scandinavia, led to a revival of religious life. *Edward the Confessor had already rebuilt the abbey church at *Westminster, but ecclesiastical administration was reorganized, cathedrals commenced (created 'to the glory of God'), and the cathedral school at Oxford grew into a university. Monasticism again flourished, but with changed structure: diverging from the original *Benedictines were *Cluniacs, *Cistercians, and *Augustinians, while *Hospitallers and *Templars were founded for service of Holy Land pilgrims; friars in the west, unlike monks, lived in rather than withdrawn from the world, the *Franciscans among the destitute, the *Dominicans as teachers, preachers, and scholars. Monasteries were not only repositories of learning but, through the concept of loving one's neighbour, cared for the sick (though the soul remained pre-eminent over the body). A redemptive religion centred on Christ's mediation with God, one of Christianity's attractions in a time of poverty, illness, and the ever-present consideration of early death was its promise of an afterlife with justice or consolation; chantries, schools, and hospitals were frequently founded on earth to buy grace in heaven. Since the prospect of punishment was more dramatic than that of bland paradise—art and literature reveal vividly imaginative interpretations of hell—the threat of eternal damnation was used to enforce a prescription of ethics and attitudes suitable for differing social ranks. High days and holy days punctuated the seasons' calendar, marriage laws for the laity contributed to a form of social welfare, while a knight's fidelity to his lord and protection of the needy was echoed in the adoption of a new position of prayer (kneeling with hands together) resembling feudal homage. At the same time, depictions of Christ in majesty yielded to images of his crucifixion, to encourage devotion. By the 15th cent. explorers, merchants, and colonizers had started to spread Christianity beyond Europe, a process that continued throughout the ensuing centuries. Empire-building not only involved colonization and growth of trade, but active and purposeful extension of religion; the cross followed the flag, sometimes vice versa. Nevertheless, with late 20th-cent. decolonization, Christianity, far from dying in these newly independent territories, has become even more vigorous, especially in Africa.

The principal sacraments (or 'mysteries') recognized by all Christians, except *quakers, are the eucharist and baptism. The eucharist or mass is the central act of most public worship as the re-presentation (*sic*) of Christ's last supper, death, and resurrection, symbolically feeding the faithful. Baptism is an initiation rite in which the use of water is an outward sign of death to the old self, washing, and fresh life; originally for converted adults, it is now usually administered to infants. Other sacraments, not universally acknowledged as such, are confirmation, marriage, ordination, confession, and anointing of the sick. Hymn-singing, preaching, reading of Scripture, and prayer form significant parts of worship. The Bible is an important primary written source for most Christians, taken literally by some, but regarded as no more than a history book, with all associated imperfections, by others. The greatest challenges to Christianity have been the doctrinal upheavals that led to the *Reformation (and the English church's rupture from Rome) and *secularism. The Census Report on Religious Worship (1851–3) caused alarm by its revelation that nearly 40 per cent of the population were unwilling or unable to attend a place of worship. While Christianity remains Britain's established religion at the end of the 20th cent., the challenge from secularism has increased, compounded by the increasing ethnic mix from immigrants with their own religions, and a growing interest in cults from the imminence of the millennium and a feeling that spirituality is lacking in a materialistic world. Desires for improvement in moral values repeatedly call for a return to 'Christian' ethics.

WMM; ASH

Christian socialism. See SOCIALISM, CHRISTIAN.

Christmas. Literally Christ-Mass, the liturgical commemoration of the birth of Christ. There is evidence of its observance on 25 December at Rome by the early 4th cent., and this date has remained the focus of the commemoration in the western, catholic, tradition ever since. There is no evidence to support the theory, which was seemingly first advanced by St Hippolytus (*c.* AD 170–*c.*236), that this was the actual birth-date of Christ. The choice was rather dictated by already well-established pagan celebrations on that day. In antiquity it was the winter solstice, celebrated as the birthday of both Sol Invictus and Mithras. In the Julian calendar, the solstice had fallen on 6 January, but because of its inaccuracy the date 'moved' back to 25 December. The other principal feast of the Incarnation, the Epiphany, which has the pre-eminence among orthodox Christians, is still celebrated on the old solstice, 6 January. Many of the features of modern Christmas, such as Christmas trees, cards, and boxes, are Victorian rather than earlier. JRG

Church Army. Founded in 1882 by the Revd Wilson Carlile, a 35-year-old Church of England curate in Kensington, its organization was consciously modelled on that of the *Salvation Army, even to the use of the military title of 'captain' for its officers. Like Booth's Salvation Army, Carlile's Church Army was dedicated to evangelism and social and moral welfare work among the poor and disadvantaged. A predominantly lay organization, including men and women, in recent years some members have been accepted for ordination. Carlile remained closely involved with the Church Army for sixty years, until his death in 1942. JRG

church commissioners. See ECCLESIASTICAL COMMISSIONERS.

churches. See ABBEYS; CATHEDRALS; PARISH CHURCHES.

Churchill, Lord Randolph (1849–95). An MP from 1874, Churchill was secretary to his father, the 7th duke of Marlborough, then lord-lieutenant of Ireland. After the Conservative defeat of 1880 he led a small ginger group known as the *Fourth Party undermining the party leadership of *Northcote. Contemptuous of the passivity and 'respectability' of the 'Old Gang', Churchill exploited the discontents of the neglected provincial associations in the National Union and claimed to speak for a 'Tory Democracy' derived from *Disraeli: 'Trust the people.' Audacious in language and style, compulsively self-publicizing, Churchill was a young man in a hurry, perhaps knowing that syphilis would shorten his career. His deal with *Salisbury in 1884, abandoning the National Union in return for admittance into the collective leadership, ended Northcote's chances of the premiership. Secretary for India in Salisbury's 1885 government, Churchill had Burma annexed. Though he flirted with Parnell's nationalists and pursued conciliation in Ireland, once *Gladstone had proposed *Home Rule Churchill hoisted unionist colours: 'Ulster will fight and Ulster will be right.' Chancellor of the Exchequer and leader of the Commons in 1886, he soon became impatient with cabinet colleagues and, seeking tactical alliance with *Chamberlain's wing of the Liberal Unionists, he began to challenge Salisbury's leadership. When Churchill, frustrated over cutting the services estimates, offered a tactical resignation, Salisbury called his bluff and accepted. Though he said he had 'forgotten *Goschen' (who took the Exchequer), rather he had underestimated the desire of those who mattered to rid themselves of a disruptive presence. Harassed by health and financial worries, Churchill never recovered politically. His marriage to New York heiress Jennie Jerome appeared, at least in public, to be a glamorous success. The biography published in 1908 by his son Winston, then a Liberal, celebrated Randolph as the frustrated hero of a democratic and radical Toryism: later historians have seen consistency in little but driving ambition. BIC

Churchill, Sir Winston Leonard Spencer (1874–1965). Britain's greatest prime minister, saviour of his country, inspiring orator, and winner of the Nobel prize for literature; Churchill was born at Blenheim palace in 1874, the elder son of Lord Randolph *Churchill and grandson of the 7th duke of Marlborough. His mother was the American heiress Jennie Jerome. Educated at Harrow and Sandhurst, he served with the 4th Hussars in Cuba, Malakand, Tirah, and Sudan (1895–8) and rode in the lancers' charge at *Omdurman. Between 1899 and 1900 he was a war correspondent in South Africa, where he was captured by the Boers but escaped. He enjoyed wars and was the first prime minister since the duke of *Wellington to have fought in battle. He saw active service in the trenches for a few months in 1916 and during the Second World War, when London was being bombed, confessed that he 'loved the bangs'. After 1945 his martial spirit was held against him and ill-founded accusations of war-mongering were made.

In 1900 he entered the House of Commons as a Conservative but crossed the floor within four years to join the Liberals on the issue of free trade. Returned as a Liberal at the next election, he gained his first ministerial experience under *Campbell-Bannerman as under-secretary for the colonies. *Asquith brought him into the cabinet at the age of 33 as president of the Board of Trade (1908) and moved him to the Home Office before he had reached the age of 35 (1910). By now Churchill had married Clementine Hozier (1908)—to whom he proposed four times before he won acceptance. She was to provide him with a stable emotional base for the rest of his life. Meanwhile, along with *Lloyd

George, he played a major part in laying the foundations of the *welfare state by establishing labour exchanges and social insurance. His tenure of the Home Office, on the other hand, is remembered for the myth that he sent troops to Wales to crush the striking miners of Tonypandy (1910) and for his appearance at the siege of Sidney Street (1911).

In 1911 he became 1st lord of the Admiralty and a historical figure of significance for the first time. Completing the work of the recently retired Admiral *Fisher, he replaced dreadnoughts with super-dreadnoughts, established a naval air service, and began the conversion of the fleet from coal to oil. In the words of historian M. D. R. Foot, 'the outbreak of war in 1914 found much the world's strongest fleet fully mobilised at its war stations, and able to exercise an international impact, which, over four and a quarter years proved decisive. It was as much Fisher's achievement as Churchill's, but neither could have achieved as much as he did without the other.'

Having the fleet ready was one of Churchill's contributions to the British war effort between 1914 and 1918. Another was the part he played in the development of the tank. However, he was remembered most of all for conceiving the 1915 Dardanelles campaign, designed to shorten the war by removing Turkey and allowing the western allies to link up with Russia. Approved by the war cabinet and given the half-hearted support of Fisher (who had been recalled in 1914 but who in Churchill's own words 'went mad' the following year), the attack on Gallipoli failed due to naval delays and the lack of troops to effect a surprise landing. In its wake, Asquith was forced to form a coalition with the Conservatives, who loathed Churchill as a renegade, and had him transferred from the Admiralty to become chancellor of the duchy of Lancaster. Lacking any influence over the course of the war, Churchill resigned the position and took command of a battalion of the Royal Scots Fusiliers in France. A few months later he was recalled by Lloyd George to become minister of munitions, although his influence on events remained minimal. Between 1918 and 1920 he was secretary of state for war and air, in which capacity he was responsible for running down the planned post-war Royal Air Force from 154 squadrons to 24, with only two for home defence. He was also responsible for ensuring that demobilization proceeded peacefully, a task which he fulfilled successfully. His attempts, on the other hand, to persuade his colleagues to overthrow the Bolsheviks in Russia were unsuccessful. Intervention did take place—to prevent allied stores falling into German hands—but Churchill had to organize the withdrawal of British troops. His true instincts, however, became well known and played their part in building up his image as an arch-enemy of the organized working class. The Tonypandy myth, plus his role during the 1926 *General Strike, helped consolidate this reputation.

In 1921 he became colonial secretary and made a treaty with the *Irish Free State. He also negotiated a peace settlement with the Arabs, advised by T. E. *Lawrence. Although he opposed Lloyd George's policy towards the Turks, he gave his prime minister vociferous support over the *Chanak crisis of 1922. When the coalition fell a few months later, he was defeated in the 1922 election and began work on his history of the First World War, the first volume of which was published in 1923 (it was completed in 1931). A friend quipped: 'Winston has written an enormous book about himself and called it *The World Crisis*.'

Returning to the Commons in October 1924, he was offered the chancellorship of the Exchequer by *Baldwin and rejoined the Conservative Party. In 1925 he put Great Britain back on the gold standard, unfortunately at the pre-war parity of £1 = $1, which was of little help to British exporters. Three years later he introduced the 'ten-year rule', whereby the service estimates would be prepared on the assumption that no war was likely for the next ten years. Meanwhile, he was only prevented from running down the navy as he had already run down the RAF by the threatened resignation of the entire Board of Admiralty. Even so, much of the grand fleet he had controlled before 1914 was broken up. In the General Strike of 1926, he took overall command of the government newspaper the *British Gazette*. This reinforced the hostility of organized labour towards him, but in fact he was not as bellicose against the miners as people assumed. Churchill's star, however, was set to wane. With the fall of Baldwin's government in 1929, he was out of office for the next ten years.

Churchill himself turned the 1930s into his wilderness years by choosing to wander in the political desert. His attacks on constitutional progress in India, inspired by a romantic vision of the India of his youth, and his defence of Edward VIII found little response among a British public used to the idea of independent dominions and determined not to have an American divorcee as queen at any price. Nor was Churchill able to capture the public imagination as the ideological foe of fascism. He admired Mussolini and sympathized with Franco during the Spanish Civil War. Finally, on the great economic questions of the day—unemployment, protection, recovery—he had little to say, unlike Lloyd George, who in the words of A. J. P. Taylor 'produced a rich stock of creative ideas'.

In the 1930s, however, Churchill did take up the cause of resistance to Nazi Germany. There were many obstacles to this and British governments were all too well aware of them: pacifist sentiment after the First World War; belief in the *League of Nations; sympathy for Germany's desire to rewrite the treaty of Versailles; not least, fear of the bomber. The Treasury in particular opposed rearmament, also with good cause: America's refusal to provide loans; war debts from the First World War; fear of inflation and the crowding-out of civilian investment; difficulties with management and labour if the economy had to be directed; a possible taxpayers' revolt; the lack of sufficient gold and foreign currency reserves to import both food and raw materials in wartime. After a year of war, Britain, it predicted, would be bankrupt. The chiefs of staff, for their part, advised that it would be impossible to fight a war on three fronts simultaneously against Germany, Italy, and Japan around the globe. Britain would simply lose. The Foreign Office, finally, asked just who our allies were going to be. America was neutral, the dominions unpredictable, and even if the Soviets could be brought in, an alliance with them might push Franco into the arms of the axis and close off the Mediterranean.

The appeasers, therefore, had a good case. Churchill, on the other hand, was a sort of appeaser too. He did not believe that war was inevitable and knew that Hitler wanted Britain as an ally. However, he believed that a grand alliance against the dictator would make him moderate his plans, at which stage his grievances could be considered. If not, perhaps he could be overthrown before it came to war. But if Germany would not see reason, then war it would be. He envisaged that war, however, as one in which Britain would make her contribution with sea and air power. He thought a continental army a mistake.

When war came, Churchill returned to the Admiralty, although he acted as if he were already prime minister. Almost immediately he became involved in a madcap scheme to send an expeditionary force to Norway, ostensibly to help save Finland from the Russians, but in practice to cut off Swedish iron ore from the Germans. The lack of air cover, however, plus shambolic planning meant that the whole campaign was a disaster. Ironically, *Chamberlain was blamed and Churchill became prime minister at the head of a national government.

As war leader, Churchill was a mixture of ruthlessness and impetuosity. Concerned to do everything possible to win the war, in practice he had few means of doing so. Still, he did what he could, which meant the bombing offensive, plus the Mediterranean campaign. Determined to have action, he prodded and sacked his generals and made many mistakes—sinking the French fleet at Oran, invading Greece, defending Crete, neglecting the Far East. Yet his position as prime minister was secure, since he had become in the summer of 1940 the spirit of British resistance incarnate, defying the Nazis with speeches of supreme eloquence that reflected the emotional mood of the nation precisely. His real hope of victory depended on the entry of the USA, and when that happened, Churchill persuaded the Americans both to make Europe the primary theatre of the war and to participate in the north African campaign. When Hitler attacked Stalin, he immediately offered aid to the Soviets, his only war aim being the destruction of Nazi Germany. Towards the end of the war, in October 1944, aware of US plans to send their troops home once the war was over, he signed the Percentages agreement with Stalin, dividing the Balkans into spheres of influence and saving Greece from communism.

As war leader, Churchill had little time for the home front. Nor was he much interested in post-war planning. When the *Beveridge Report was published in 1942, he doubted whether a bankrupt Britain would be able to afford the welfare state which it envisaged. In any case, he had left domestic affairs to *Attlee and his Labour colleagues, which proved a mistake. For it was to them that the electorate turned in July 1945 once victory had been secured over Germany. Churchill was still adored and respected, but the voters guessed correctly that he was not the man for post-war reconstruction. As leader of the Conservative Party and of the opposition, on the other hand, he was more politically secure than he had ever been before in peacetime. His voice continued to be heard in international affairs and, just as he had warned against the rising threat from Hitler, he now warned against the 'iron curtain' which was descending over Europe. He also spoke out in favour of a united Europe, although he never meant that Britain should be part of it.

In 1951 he returned as prime minister. He was now 77 years old, had suffered two strokes, and would suffer two more. Yet his government was highly successful. *Eden shone as foreign secretary, *Macmillan built a record number of council houses, and nothing was done to undermine the welfare state, inherited from Labour. Churchill attempted to arrange a summit conference with the Soviets after the death of Stalin in 1953, but Eisenhower would hear none of it. He in turn rejected Eisenhower's request the following year to involve the British in Vietnam to save the French. In April 1955 he agreed to retire as prime minister, completing a career without equal among democratic politicians. He died, still an MP, in 1965, was given a state funeral, and was buried in Bladon churchyard. No attempts to revise or belittle his reputation have yet proved successful. AS

Foot, M. R. D., 'Sir Winston Churchill', in Thal, H. van (ed.), *The Prime Ministers: From Lord John Russell to Edward Heath* (1975); Gilbert, M., *Churchill: A Life* (New York, 1991); Sked, A., and Cook, C., *Post-War Britain: A Political History, 1945–1992* (Harmondsworth, 1993).

Church in Wales. The Church in Wales as an autonomous province within the Anglican Communion came into being in 1920, when, on 31 March, the Act of 1914 disestablishing the Church of England in the principality came into force. The four ancient Welsh dioceses of Bangor, St Asaph, St Davids, and Llandaff, although remaining in full communion with the Church of England and the other Anglican churches, became a self-governing church, with the bishop of St Asaph, Alfred George Edwards, as the first archbishop of Wales. The 1914 Act, among other provisions, deprived the Welsh bishops of their seats in the House of Lords, and abolished private patronage. All endowments given to the church before 1662 were taken from it. Since 1920 there has been no established church in Wales; legally, all denominations have equal status. The Anglican church in Wales elects its own bishops, and manages its own affairs through an elected governing body of clergy and laity, and a representative body in which its property, including church buildings, is vested. The Disestablishment Act had been vehemently opposed by many—but not all—Anglicans in Wales, but was supported by the majority of free churchmen. JRG

Church Missionary Society. Founded in 1799 for missions in Africa and the East, the society became the Church of England's first effective body for such work despite far earlier establishment of the *Society for Promoting Christian Knowledge and the *Society for the Propagation of the Gospel. Consistently evangelical in its theology, it pioneered extensively throughout the world and continues to sponsor Bible translations. ASH

Church of England. Though, as an Erastian institution, the Church of England dates only from the 16th cent.,

*Christianity in these islands originated with merchants, administrators, and soldiers in 2nd- and 3rd-cent. Roman Britain. *Alban was martyred in the 3rd century and three British bishops were present at the Council of Arles (314), but the 5th-cent. Anglo-Saxon invasions virtually obliterated all trace of Christian presence, leaving a remnant in Wales whence Ireland and southern Scotland were converted. The present English church dates from the reintroduction of this Celtic Christianity into Northumbria by *Aidan (635) and Roman Christianity into Kent by *Augustine (597). After the union of these two streams at the Synod of *Whitby (664), *Theodore of Tarsus, archbishop of Canterbury, restructured the church to form the basis of the medieval ecclesiastical system. Though medieval kings exercised considerable authority over the church, it was the break with Rome (1534) which, by abrogating papal authority, fully established royal supremacy, from which date the established Church *of* England (*Ecclesia Anglicana*), as now understood, can be said to exist. The Act of *Supremacy (1534) declared Henry VIII to be 'the only supreme head of the Church' in place of the pope, which Elizabeth's Act (1559) moderated to the less offensive 'Supreme Governor'.

Apart from this the church remained legally and administratively much the same. The church courts and their penalties, diocesan administrative systems, the authority of bishops and archdeacons all continued. The non-monastic cathedrals—those of the old foundation—survived as before with the same legal standing and statutes. Only those which since Anglo-Saxon times had been monastic were perforce given revised constitutions. Ecclesiastical law remained as before. *Gibson's *Codex juris Ecclesiae Anglicani* (1713) still cited medieval ecclesiastical legislation. Though now under royal control the *convocations of Canterbury and York survived. Even crown appointments to bishoprics and cathedral deaneries showed little change, for royal nomination by *congé d'élire* and letters dimissory had been the norm until the late Middle Ages; even then 'the royal will was the final factor'. The church since Henry VIII was thoroughly Erastian, its officials little more than agents of the crown. Indeed post-Restoration clergy were also agents of royalist propaganda, parsons thundering from their pulpits the doctrines of *divine right, *non-resistance, and passive obedience. Every church building had to display the royal coat of arms on the chancel arch in place of the rood. All licensed Anglican clergy and ordinands still today take the loyal oath and licensed clergy have the right to administer marriage recognized by civil law without a civil registrar's presence. Though the last prelate holding senior political office was John *Robinson, bishop of London (1713–23), 18th-cent. episcopal appointments were a powerful means of government patronage, for the 26 bishops in the House of Lords, though sometimes breaking free, normally supported the government. More recently Archbishops *Tait and *Davidson in particular had substantial political influence, the latter, for instance, in the passage of the Parliament Act (1911). Though today there are 43 diocesan bishops, only 26 sit in the Lords where they try to represent the multi-cultural spiritual and ethical dimension of national life.

Though Henry VIII made virtually no theological or liturgical break with the past, there was under Edward VI a considerable influx of continental reform and liturgical innovation from Bucer, Zwingli, and Calvin. After a brief reversion to papal catholicism under Mary, the church moved towards a comprehensive settlement under Elizabeth. Enshrined in the Acts of *Supremacy and *Uniformity, the *Book of Common Prayer and the *Thirty-Nine Articles, this attempted to reconcile the diverse shades of English opinion. Provided citizens fulfilled the royal injunction to weekly church attendance, there was to be no test as to conscience, 'no windows into men's souls'. Episcopacy and royal supremacy marked the boundaries—presbyterianism and adherence to Rome were unacceptable. Most accepted, but minorities existed, some still adhering to Rome, others, though not yet schismatic, to presbyterianism or more extreme protestant views. Elizabeth and her first archbishop, Matthew *Parker, used strict liturgical uniformity to mask theological differences between catholic and Calvinistic wings within the church. After the heyday of the sects in the *Interregnum (1649–60), compromise became impossible. Moderate presbyterians' offer of limited episcopacy fell on deaf Anglican ears; instead, the Restoration settlement refused to recognize those already ordained non-episcopally, and demanded tests. A thousand incumbents were ejected—and thus became *nonconformists. From that time the church ceased to be the church of the whole nation.

Nevertheless a distinctive Anglican theology had already sprung up. The writings of John *Jewel (*Apologia Ecclesiae Anglicanae*, 1562) and Richard *Hooker (*Of the Laws of Ecclesiastical Polity*, 1593–7) demonstrated that *Ecclesia Anglicana*, in attempting a return to the early church before its infection with medieval accretions, was both 'catholic and reformed', appealing to the Scriptures, the early fathers, and reason. Seventeenth-cent. Caroline divines including Lancelot *Andrewes, John Cosin, George *Herbert, Jeremy *Taylor, and Nicholas Ferrar, through their personal sanctity, scholarship, and poetry, built on this foundation. The Prayer Book and the King James Bible became part of English culture.

After 1689 church life remained turbulent but settled down from 1714. Eighteenth-cent. ecclesiastics' reputation for idleness and rationalist indifference is undeserved. Modern research reveals that bishops and clergy were far more committed to their charges than hitherto supposed. Nor were they mere political hacks. Nevertheless liturgically the church was deadening. Medieval ecclesiastical corruption did not prevent the mysterious action of the medieval mass from touching the hearts of the humblest of men. Eighteenth-cent. Prayer Book liturgy and weighty preaching was another matter—too cerebral and unsuited to a mainly illiterate, uneducated people, about whose absence from, or misbehaviour in, church we often read in church court records. The preaching of the *Wesley brothers thus fell on ready ears, but it was to the church's shame that these two devoted Anglican priests, both high churchmen, and their followers were rejected. Enthusiasm was dangerous, leading to fanaticism.

Though there is evidence of both evangelical and Caroline high-church strands in the 18th cent., the full *evangelical revival spilled over into the 19th cent. and, with the *tractarian movement, invigorated church life. Evangelicalism following in the Wesley tradition produced many of note, clergy like Fletcher, Newton, and *Simeon and leading laymen such as *Wilberforce and *Shaftesbury. Tractarianism, led by *Keble, *Newman, and *Pusey, initially traced Anglicanism's traditions back to Augustine, but developed later into a powerful movement to restore fully the church's catholic wing. By 1900, in the shape of *Anglo-catholicism, it became increasingly ritualistic and caught the imagination and the hearts of the newly developed urban working class.

As the British empire spread throughout the world by commerce and the sword in the 18th and 19th cents., the church followed—or in some cases with its missionaries led the way. Two overseas dioceses in 1800 increased to 72 in 1882, and to 450 dioceses (in 28 provinces) in the 1990s. The *Ecclesia Anglicana* from having been merely the church of the English people became a world-wide communion of many nations and tongues. The archbishop of Canterbury, as St Augustine's successor, was not just 'Primate of all England' but came to hold a universal primacy of honour, 'a presidency of maturity and affection', though without authority. To provide cohesion and consensus, initially over the *Colenso affair, the first Lambeth conference with 67 bishops met in 1867, to be followed at *Tait's inspiration by the second in 1878. Tait and his successors kept increasingly frequent contact with the overseas churches. The archbishop still presides at the Lambeth conference each decade, and continuity is provided since 1968 by the Anglican Consultative Council and primates' meetings. *Davidson was the first archbishop to visit the Church abroad—in Canada and the USA (1904). It is now part of the archbishop's quasi-patriarchal role to visit provinces world-wide. Commonly held Anglican principles are enshrined in the so-called Lambeth Quadrilateral (1888)—the Scriptures, the creeds, the historic episcopate and threefold ministry, and the sacraments.

Twentieth-cent. liturgical scholarship has deeply affected all Christian denominations; Anglicanism is no exception. Recent liturgical modifications have meant that, with each Anglican province making its own modifications, the 1662 Prayer Book is no longer the global cohesive symbol. After England's attempt to produce a revised prayer book (1928) was foiled by Parliament, the Synod 50 years later introduced an *Alternative Service Book 1980*, providing services in modern English, embodying the fruit of liturgical study. Though worship is now closer to that of the early church and to modern practice in other denominations, the new forms have lost linguistic beauty, regarded by some as essential for true worship.

Because all religious orders were disbanded at the Reformation, there were no monasteries, convents or friaries until the restoration of the catholic hierarchy in the 19th cent., except for Nicholas Ferrar's short-lived 17th-cent. Little Gidding community, but the *Oxford movement spawned several Anglican religious orders in the monastic tradition, such as the Cowley Fathers (SSJE), Mirfield, and Kelham, while the Society of St Francis, founded in the 1920s, follows the Franciscan tradition, working in the Third World and in British inner cities.

Twentieth-cent. developments include women's ordination to the diaconate and the priesthood (in England 1987 and 1994), making the Anglican church the first episcopal church to take this step. Ecumenism, so much a part of 20th-cent. church life, has extended to dialogue with non-Christian faiths, which are now prominent in the English scene.

Though its regular practising members are fewer than the catholics, the *Ecclesia Anglicana* with its unique liturgical, musical, and architectural heritage is still the church of the nation. Through its parish system all citizens have a church building and the ministry of a parish priest. All citizens in a real sense belong, whatever their threshold of belief, and whether or not they are practising members. As a 'spiritual NHS', it remains a vital part of national life. Today with regular church-going at 7 per cent (Church of England 2.4 per cent, in all UK 2.9 per cent), but with 70 per cent believing in God, the ubiquitous church building in village or city, together with mosque, synagogue, and temple, is sacramental, a vital outward and visible sign of the spiritual dimension of man's existence. Quite by chance in its creation as a 'catholic and reformed' national church, the Church of England happens to be pivotal between Roman catholic and eastern orthodox churches on the one hand and protestant reformed churches on the other. Its diversity under a cloak of uniformity, though apparently a weakness, is also its greatest strength, recognizing as it does disparate, but equally valid, paths to God, hints of which appear as early as New Testament times. Today (1995) UK Anglicanism has a mere 1,718,000 practising members, whereas the UK catholic church can claim 1,952,000. WMM

Church of Ireland. Building on 4th-cent. traces, *Patrick evangelized Ireland (*c.*432) and developed a distinctively Celtic Christianity, but with the partial Anglo-Norman conquest of Ireland the church once again joined mainstream western Christendom. Though Henry VIII established the Church *of* Ireland after his Irish break with Rome (1536), the Reformation was weaker and less popular than in England. Despite parliamentary suppression of the monasteries (1537), they continued in Gaelic areas, friars pursued their ministry, and Jesuits arrived (*c.*1545). Elizabeth's Irish Parliament (1560), after hastily, but reluctantly, passing Irish Acts of Supremacy and Uniformity, was as hastily dissolved. The Reformation largely failed. Gaelic, which most Irishmen spoke, was forbidden in worship and the established church was inextricably associated with the colonizing offices of state. Only the 'new' colonizers were protestant; the Gaelic Irish and old Anglo-Irish remained catholic. After 1580 missionary priests poured in, but Anglo-Scottish colonization of Ulster (*c.*1610) made it the bastion of protestantism, *Ussher's 104 Irish Articles (1615) were Calvinistic in ethos and *Cromwell further antagonized Irish opinion by confiscating catholic land and allowing protestants economic predominance. Despite the spirituality of some, such as Jeremy *Taylor, the established church was increasingly associated with colonization, unpopular, and lacking vibrant spirituality. William III's promise of toleration (1691) was a dead letter until 1791. After the Anglican archbishoprics were reduced to two and bishoprics by eight (1833), the church, always predominantly evangelical, was disestablished (1869). The Book of Common Prayer was revised in 1870 and again in 1926 with an *Alternative Prayer Book* issued in 1984. Today with two archbishoprics and twelve dioceses, it has a total membership (1990) of 437,000 (340,000 in the North and 97,000 in the Republic). WMM

Church of Scotland. The church claims continuity from *Ninian and *Columba. Although the Scottish Reformation's first impact was *Lutheran, the return of John *Knox from Geneva in 1559 led to the Church's reconstruction on conciliar, that is to say *presbyterian, lines, a process not completed until 1690. In between kirk and crown battled as to whether Scotland's ecclesiastical system should be presbyterian or *episcopalian. Presbyterianism was advanced by the first *General Assembly (1560), the first presbytery (Edinburgh 1581), agreed by the monarch (1586) and ratified by Parliament (1642). Its popular status was affirmed by the National Covenant (1638), the *Solemn League and Covenant (1643), and the *Westminster Assembly (1643–52). Episcopalianism was advanced by the Stuart monarchs' steady preference, the imposition of the Prayer Book (1637), and the restoration of episcopacy (1660). The conflict was intensified by the assassination of Archbishop *Sharp of St Andrews (1679), and resolved by the revolution of 1688: all ministers must subscribe to the Westminster confession as the standard of their faith. In the 18th cent. the now dominant church was weakened by secession; and the growth of two parties, one favouring the rights of patronage in ministerial settlements, the other favouring congregational rights, led to the *Disruption of 1843, and the formation of the *Free Church. Thereafter a pattern of reunion developed, although each one also resulted in a remnant. The secession and relief churches formed the United Presbyterian Church in 1847; the United Presbyterian and Free Churches became the United Free Church in 1900. At the same time patronage was abolished (1874), there was a significant liturgical revival, and the Church of Scotland Act (1921), which explicitly declared the church's spiritual freedom, paved the way for union with the United Free Church (1929), in the context of an establishment purged of what had fuelled earlier secessions. The General Assembly was now equally composed of ministers and elders, and women were admitted to both eldership (1966) and ministry (1968). If the church's membership accounted for under a quarter of the adult population by the 1990s, its cultural impact on the nation remained profound. CB

churchwardens are representatives of the parish meeting or the vestry, generally assisted by sidesmen. From the 12th to the middle of the 16th cents. churchwardens were primarily responsible for providing and maintaining all that was necessary for public worship in their parish church or chapel. A subsidiary duty was that of presentment to the ecclesiastical courts of moral misdemeanours of the laity and clergy of the parish. From the mid-16th to the 19th cents. churchwardens were also civil officials with duties as various as providing arms for soldiers, poor relief, and vermin control. Until 1571 churchwardens were elected by the whole parish, and after that time it was usual for the parish to elect one warden and the minister the other. Their accounts, which were presented annually to the parish meeting, are a major source of information about parish life. LR

cinema was the most influential mass medium in the first half of the 20th cent. In world terms, British cinema has never been regarded highly, constantly overshadowed by Hollywood, and with only the occasional international breakthrough, such as producer Alexander Korda in the 1930s, Ealing films in the 1950s, and the James Bond films in the 1960s.

Only in non-fiction has British cinema been a world-leader, with John Grierson pioneering the documentary film with *Drifters* (1929) and his subsequent work with the Empire Marketing Board and GPO Film Unit. Though hailed as a major contributor to the art of cinema, Grierson's reputation has been dented by recent criticisms of the documentary movement's paternalistic, middle-class ideology—with the honourable exception of Humphrey Jennings, whose portraits of Britons at peace and war (*Spare Time, Listen to Britain*) have been elevated to classic status.

Recent research has unearthed a more authentic British people's cinema in the workers' film movement, a network of proletarian film groups documenting the struggles of the inter-war years under the influence of Soviet revolutionary cinema. Most recent work on British cinema history has moved away from attempting to champion British films in world terms, or from elevating directors to a pantheon of 'auteurs'. Only a few directors, such as Alfred Hitchcock, Anthony Asquith, David Lean, Carol Reed, Michael Powell, and American Joseph Losey could lay claim to a 'personal artistic vision' within British cinema.

Instead research has concentrated on Britain's previously unexplored mainstream commercial fiction cinema, looking at popular genre films such as horror, war, and comedy (the *Carry On* and *Doctor* series); at the industry, studios, and financial organizations which produced and distributed them; at institutions such as the British Board of Film Censors which influenced them; at the stars who acted in them; and at the mass audiences who enjoyed them—a complete map of the social, cultural, political, and ideological contours of British cinema as a whole.

Studies of the most popular stars of the 1930s, Gracie *Fields and George *Formby, reveal their films as sites of ideological struggle for the consent of the working class, with a vision of imaginary national unity 'magically' resolving the problems of the depression. The role of cinema in constructing a united nation is even more explicitly revealed in the films of the Second World War, under the more obvious propaganda influence of the Ministry of Information.

Cinema of the late 1940s and early 1950s reveals, most famously, Ealing films projecting Britain and the British character in the new era of austerity and Labour-Conservative welfare consensus; less obviously, Gainsborough's 'women's pictures' (*The Wicked Lady*) show deep-rooted male fears of women's wartime liberation.

Similar psychoanalytic critical methods applied to Hammer horror films of the 1950s reveal social fears and repressed sexuality translated into fictional vampire narratives. James Bond films of the 1960s incorporate themes of male sexual doubts, Cold War conflict, and Britain's declining imperial power in the creation of a mythical spy superhero. A more obvious reflection of changing British social attitudes to sex, race, class, rebellion, and youth is evident from the 'New Wave' films of the late 1950s and early 1960s (*A Taste of Honey*), and the 'Swinging London' films of the mid-1960s (*Alfie*). The dramatic decline in cinema attendance during the 1960s, following the spread of television, was halted in the 1990s and some recovery effected. Nevertheless, the cities of Britain are littered with old cinemas, now serving as supermarkets, warehouses, or bingo halls. See FILM INDUSTRY. DJA

Cinque Ports. A maritime confederation in Kent and Sussex, and the nearest England ever came to having an urban federation of the continental kind. Their privileges from the crown, in return for naval service, go back at least to the 12th cent., and they remained a formidable maritime power until Tudor times. The original 'Five Ports'—Hastings, New Romney, Hythe, Dover, and Sandwich—were later joined by Rye and Winchelsea, and other lesser ports were included as 'limbs' or members. Most of their special jurisdiction was abolished in 1855, but the office of lord warden remains a distinguished honour in the gift of the sovereign. DMP

Cintra, convention of, 1808. Concluded on 30 August after a British victory over the French at *Vimeiro early in the Peninsular War. Though it was in Britain's interest to conclude a treaty, the terms negotiated by Sir Hew Dalrymple, commander of the British forces, were ridiculous. All French troops, equipment, and loot were to be transported back to France in British ships and no guarantee was exacted to prevent them returning to Spain. The news of the treaty caused uproar in London and led to an official inquiry, which relieved Dalrymple of his command. RAS

Cirencester. *Civitas*-capital of the *Dobunni, Corinium grew to be one of the most considerable towns of Roman Britain. Probably replacing the late Iron Age *oppidum* at Bagendon 3 miles to the north, the town developed on the site of two successive forts on *Fosse Way. The large, early 2nd-cent. forum/basilica complex lay at the centre of the town beside a large enclosure, possibly religious. On the western side of the town was an earth and timber amphitheatre and a possible theatre lay at the northern end of the town. In the later 2nd cent. defences were constructed enclosing 240 acres, appreciably more than the built-up area of the street-grid. Originally these consisted of stone gates linked by earthwork, in the 3rd/4th cents. the latter fronted by a stone wall. A 4th-cent. inscription mentioning a *Rector* (governor) of Britannia Prima, one of the four late Roman provinces of Britain, may suggest that Cirencester was a provincial capital. The town had a number of large houses of the 2nd to 4th cents. Many contained fine mosaics such as the 2nd-cent. examples from under modern Dyer Street. In the 4th cent. Cirencester may have been the base for a 'school' or *officina* of mosaicists serving the Cotswold region. Though there is no evidence for occupation after *c.*400, Cirencester is one of the three former Roman towns mentioned in the *Anglo-Saxon Chronicle* entry for 577. ASEC

Cistercians (or 'white' monks) were a monastic order established in 1098 by Robert of Molesme at Cîteaux (Burgundy) in reaction to the perceived laxity of contemporary *Benedictine monasticism. Their constitutions, whose dating has been controversial, aimed at a literal observance of the Benedictine rule, and included the rejection of many types of revenue, including the possession of churches and manorial dues. Their estates were organized in self-contained 'granges' staffed by lay brothers ('conversi') who, while not monks, followed a rule and wore a distinctive habit. Early Cistercians owed much to contemporary eremitical practice and their administration, codified as the 'Carta caritatis' ('Charter of Love') during the abbacy of the Englishman Stephen Harding, by 1119, provided a clear command and disciplinary structure, articulated through annual visitations of daughter- by mother-communities. After initial difficulties the Cistercians enjoyed phenomenal success, particularly during the life of St Bernard, who entered Cîteaux in 1112 and was abbot of its daughter house of Clairvaux from 1115 till his death in 1153. By then *c.*300 abbeys had been founded across Europe (and in the crusading states), and though attempts were made in 1152 to limit new foundations there were *c.*530 houses by 1200. Thereafter the tide slackened and, though the Cistercians continued to influence other monastic groups, benefactions declined.

In England and Wales the first abbey was founded at Waverley (Surrey) in 1128, followed shortly afterwards by *Tintern and *Rievaulx. By 1152 there were about 40, as well as communities in Scotland (such as *Melrose) and Ireland. Moreover, there were several nunneries following Cistercian customs, as well as thirteen abbeys of the order of Savigny which were taken over by Cîteaux in 1147. In the later Middle Ages Cistercian influence declined, though there were a few new, urban foundations (e.g. at Oxford and London). Their economy underwent drastic changes following the *Black Death. BJG

Ciudad Rodrigo, battle of, 1812. The fortress of Ciudad Rodrigo was a strategic stronghold near the Portuguese–Spanish border held by a French garrison of roughly 2,500 men. In early 1812, *Wellington with 35,000 men marched through snow and laid siege to it. By 14 January the artillery and engineers had breached the walls in two places. On the morning of 19 January a fierce assault was launched and after heavy fighting the fortress was taken by storm. The British lost some 900 men killed and wounded including Generals Craufurd and Mackinnon. However, Wellington captured 153 heavy guns and gained a vital frontier gateway into Spain. RAS

civil law. The term has two meanings:

1. It is used as synonymous with Roman law, or with the Roman law tradition, which was accepted in most of the countries of Europe as the basis of their laws. The classical Roman law was the universal law and legal system of the Roman empire. With the fall of the Roman empire, the Roman or civil law which survived was heavily influenced by custom. Thus Roman law came to have two aspects—the pure classical Roman law and the bastardized Roman customary law which applied in the many barbarian and post-barbarian societies of western Europe. The codes of Roman law which most influenced western Europe were the code of Theodosius, and Justinian's *Corpus juris civilis*. These codes were much studied in the universities of Europe—especially in Italy where the first European law school was established in the 12th cent., at Bologna, the home of Irnerius, Azo, and Vacarius, who travelled from Bologna to Oxford and who influenced *Bracton. In the 13th cent. Accursius and Bartolus and his followers, as a reaction to the sophistication of the glossators, emphasized the practicalities of custom and conflict of laws. A further revival of Roman law took place in the 16th cent. in the University of Bourges under Cujas (1522–90) as part of the Renaissance and the revival of pure classical learning.

English law was undoubtedly influenced by civil law, though it never 'received' or adopted Roman law. There was little evidence of survival of Roman law from the Roman occupation of Britain, but the Norman Conquest brought England close to continental traditions, especially through the influence of *canon law. Further, *Lanfranc, William's first archbishop of Canterbury, had taught in the law school at Pavia before founding the school at Bec and coming to England. *Anselm and *Theobald, two more archbishops, were also from Bec and strongly versed in civil law and canon law.

The author of *Glanvill clearly had a sound grounding in Roman law, though the book makes it clear that English law is by no means the same. Bracton is commonly acknowledged to be heavily influenced by Roman law, though it has been disputed whether he was deeply imbued with Roman law ideas or merely using Roman principles to construct a synthesis of the emerging English common law. The great movement known as the Reception, under which many countries in Europe adopted the Roman civil law, passed England by, and although civilian ideas and procedures affected English law through the conciliar courts, including the courts of *Chancery and *Admiralty, and although later lawyers looked to Bracton and Britton for guidance and inspiration, civil law was never a serious threat to the common law in England. However, both through the canon law and through the interest of common law judges in civil law from time to time, Romanist ideas have been an undoubted if minor influence on the substantive law of England and Wales.

2. The other meaning of civil law is as distinct from criminal—i.e. the law relating to the adjustment and adjudication of the legal conflicts and disputes between individuals, as distinct from those matters where the state takes responsibility for dealing with conduct which is against the interests of society and which is therefore pursued and punished by that society. The common law was mainly civil law since the work of the courts of common law was primarily the development of the writ system to enable individuals to litigate in the king's courts. MM

civil list. The civil list is the grant made by Parliament for the monarch's personal support and for that of the household, and has frequently proved controversial. It was started in the reign of William and Mary and fixed at £700,000 p.a., out of which the monarchs had to pay pensions and salaries. *Walpole's desire to retain office in 1727 led to George II receiving an extremely generous settlement, since his income rose as trade increased. George III, young and inexperienced in 1760, agreed to a fixed sum of £800,000 p.a.—a 'most disastrous step', according to his biographer, since the growth of the royal family soon eroded the value of the grant and made repeated and embarrassing applications to Parliament necessary. The influence of the crown diminished accordingly. Although in later reigns pensions were dealt with separately, the civil list continued to provoke criticism. Victoria, a secluded widow for many years after Albert's death in 1861, spent very little and was repaid with a pamphlet entitled *What does she do with it?* It was presumed that vast savings were being transferred to the private purse. Edward VII and George V were given a basic £470,000 p.a. but post-war inflation in the 1960s brought the issue to the surface again in the reign of Elizabeth II. A select committee in 1971 recommended that any savings should return to the public purse and that there should be regular reviews of the civil list award. In the 1980s and 1990s there were persistent complaints that too many members of the royal family were supported at the taxpayers' expense. JAC

civil service. Despite repeated campaigns to reduce numbers, the civil service remains one of the great growth areas of modern British history. In the 17th cent. the civil service—i.e. persons directly employed by the government—was tiny. The royal household, it is true, numbered some 2,000 persons, but that included 210 Yeomen of the Guard, 55 gentlemen pensioners, together with cooks and porters, who were not civil servants in the modern sense. The two secretaries of state had a staff of about fifteen—four clerks of the signet, a French and a Latin secretary, a German translator, and between four and eight junior clerks. There was no career structure, posts were filled by patronage, and remuneration was by fees rather than salary. When the two secretaries of state were divided into foreign and home in 1782, the Home Office began with two under-secretaries, a chief clerk, ten other clerks, and some domestic staff. The Rockinghams began, and Pitt continued, a campaign of economical reform, and sinecures were snipped away, but the persistent warfare from 1793 led to further increases in numbers, particularly in the revenue and in naval administration.

The growth of the civil service in the 19th cent. was steady and moderate and hardly kept pace with the rise in population. In 1815 there were 25,000 civil servants; 39,000 by 1851; 54,000 by 1871; and 79,000 by 1891. Some reforms were introduced piecemeal by departments. In the Treasury, North had launched the concept of promotion by merit (1776), Shelburne had inaugurated fixed salaries (1782), and in 1805 an assistant secretary was appointed, the forerunner of the permanent secretary. A comprehensive review waited for the Northcote–Trevelyan Report of 1854, which recommended a division of labour between graduate policy-makers and humble administrators; entry by competitive examination; transfer between departments; and promotion by merit based on assessment. The proposals were implemented piecemeal, though a Civil Service Commission, to supervise recruitment, was set up at once in 1855.

The vast expansion of the civil service in the 20th cent. is not easy to calculate, since definitions are troublesome and one commentator has referred to the 'statistical conjuring tricks'—e.g. recategorizing thousands of civil servants—to give the impression that numbers are falling. The biggest growth has been in welfare and education services, beginning in the first decade of the century. By 1939 the numbers had risen to 387,000 and by 1979 to 730,000. These developments were accompanied by further reports. *Haldane in 1918 was concerned that senior civil servants had little time to think, though the proposals were modest. Plowden in 1961 complained that the Treasury had no adequate system for forecasting or controlling expenditure—a rather worrying observation—and the Fulton Committee in 1968 deplored the survival of the cult of the amateur gentleman, the generalist, and called for the expert or specialist: 'the cult is obsolete at all levels.' One consequence was the establishment of a Civil Service College in 1970 to conduct research and training.

Among other criticisms, it has often been suggested that the senior civil servants really run things and can frustrate the plans of all but the most determined of ministers. Generalization in so wide and imprecise an area is hard, but an equally cogent view is that the upper civil service has been too subservient to party whims and ideologies—what is sometimes known as the 'grovel factor'. Neutrality of the civil service is a concept readily conceded, but practice is more difficult, and the line between warning and frustrating not easy to establish.

Though the public image of the civil servant may remain a pin-striped bowler-hatted Whitehall mandarin, most civil servants work outside London and half of them are women. Of the non-industrial civil service, the large employers are the Ministry of Defence, the Department of Social Security, the Board of Inland Revenue, the Department of Education and Employment, the Department of the Environment, the Home Office, and Customs and Excise. JAC

civil wars, 1642–51. Armed conflict between king and Parliament, which also involved invasions of Ireland and Scotland by parliamentary armies. The early Stuart monarchy was hobbled in two critical respects. Without a standing army or paid bureaucracy, it lacked the power to coerce its subjects. Without adequate income from legal sources (including parliamentary taxation) it lacked financial power. James I and Charles I attempted to augment their income by raising customs duties, levying forced loans, exploiting feudal fiscal privileges, and inventing a new form of non-parliamentary taxation—*ship money. Although Parliament was, if anything, growing weaker during the decades prior to 1640, unparliamentary taxation, arbitrary arrest, and other Stuart high-handedness caused resentment and alienation among large segments of the nobility, gentry, lawyers, and merchants who comprised the political nation. A significant minority of these classes had imbibed puritan and common law doctrines that stiffened their defiance towards the absolutist pretensions of the king.

In 1629 Charles I dismissed Parliament, resolving never to call another. He might have succeeded but for the problem of the multiple kingdoms. During the 1630s he decided to bring Scottish religious practice into conformity with English by abolishing the presbyterian directory of worship and substituting an Anglican order of service. The Scots revolted, and Charles's two attempts to subdue them—the *Bishops' wars of 1639 and 1640—were abject failures. Tax revenues dried up and his soldiers deserted in droves. At the insistence of the nobility he summoned Parliament. Once convened, the Commons refused him the taxes he desperately needed, voting assistance to the Scots instead. They then set about dismantling the apparatus of prerogative government, abolishing ship money, the courts of *Star Chamber, *High Commission, *Wards, and others; passing a Triennial Act, depriving church courts of their punitive powers, and attainting Charles's chief minister *Strafford. Charles ratified all these changes, but with such ill grace that many doubted whether he would keep his word. Trust became a critical issue upon the outbreak of rebellion in Ireland in the autumn of 1641. As lord-lieutenant of Ireland, Strafford had ruled with a heavy hand. His absence, added to Charles's failure to guarantee the catholic inhabitants security of tenure on their estates, and fear of the resurgent strength of puritanism in the English Parliament, combined to ignite an uprising in Ulster which rapidly spread. Exaggerated reports of atrocities perpetrated against the protestant settlers in Ireland inflamed English opinion. It was universally accepted that an army should be mustered to crush the rebellion, but there was no agreement about entrusting the king with the command of that army. Charles's attempt to arrest five of the parliamentary ringleaders whom he suspected of plotting to impeach the queen, together with the rumour that he had actually authorized the Ulster catholics to rise in rebellion, contributed to the deepening distrust of him. Parliament's demand for control of the sword, and Charles's refusal, was the immediate cause of the outbreak of armed conflict in the autumn of 1642.

Mistrust of the king was compounded by fear that he could not be counted on to defend England against the military and political threat of international catholicism. Far from being a protestant champion, Charles was regarded by many as a crypto-papist. Thus legal and constitutional arguments about taxation, the rights of Parliament, and the extent of royal power were inflamed by religious panic. Religion more than any other single factor brought thousands of men to rally to the standard of either king or Parliament, to risk their lives, and to 'sheathe their swords in [their countrymen's] bowels'.

If the civil wars were in one sense Europe's last wars of religion, they were also in their early phase a baronial conflict. The armies on both sides were led by aristocrats, and in the king's view it was the nobility, particularly *Essex, 'the chief rebel', who had instigated the Civil War.

Despite its control of the midlands, the east, and the south-east including London, as well as its capture of the navy, there was nothing inevitable about Parliament's victory. Charles almost overthrew his foes at *Edgehill (October 1642), while in 1643 there were a number of royalist victories and a drawn battle between the king's and Essex's armies at *Newbury (September 1643). For all the efforts of John *Pym to hold together the parliamentary coalition and to finance the war with new excise and assessment taxes, parliamentary fortunes reached their nadir in that year. Popular demand for an end to the war became increasingly insistent.

What finally turned the tide against Charles I was again the reality of multiple kingdoms. In return for a promise to uphold the presbyterian form of church government and impose it in England, the Scots came to Parliament's aid with an army of 20,000. This bargain was sealed in the *Solemn League and Covenant of 1643, and the Scots army entered England early in 1644. The joint armies dealt a crushing blow to the king's forces under Prince *Rupert and the earl of Newcastle at *Marston Moor, near York (July 1644). However, this victory was almost frittered away by Essex when he allowed his army to become trapped by Charles at *Lostwithiel in Cornwall (September 1644). Now completely disenchanted with the aristocratic leadership of Parliament's armies, the win-the-war faction under Sir Henry *Vane and Oliver *Cromwell grasped the nettle, by purging the armies of their noble and parliamentary leadership, and creating the *New Model Army out of the remains of the armies of Essex, *Manchester, and *Waller. Led by Sir Thomas *Fairfax, and knit together by constant pay and religious indoctrination, this new army quickly put the royalist forces to flight at *Naseby (June 1645), *Langport (July 1645), and Bristol (September 1645). By May 1646 most royalists had surrendered and Charles had handed himself over to the Scots.

Refusing to accept the verdict of the battlefield, Charles dragged out peace negotiations with Parliament. Meanwhile, Denzil *Holles and Sir Philip Stapleton, the political heirs of Essex, who had died in September 1646, moved to disband the New Model with only a fraction of its arrears of pay. The consequence was an army revolt, the seizure of the king at Holdenby, and the invasion of London. Charles attempted to exploit the rift between army and Parliament and redoubled his efforts to persuade the Scots to assist him. At the same time Fairfax, Cromwell, and *Ireton struggled to control the *Levellers who were striving to seize political control of the army in order to implement their programme of democracy, religious and economic liberty, and decentralization.

Early in 1648 royalist risings erupted in Kent, Essex, Wales, and the navy in anticipation of a Scottish intervention on behalf of the king. But the Scots were late, and the New Model Army had no difficulty crushing the revolts one by one. When the duke of *Hamilton crossed the border in July with a small army, he attracted little support, so that Cromwell had no trouble destroying his forces between *Preston and Uttoxeter (August 1648). Everywhere triumphant in battle, the army found to its chagrin that Parliament was still intent on negotiating peace with the king. To prevent such an outcome it occupied London, purged the House of Commons of those who favoured negotiation, and engineered the trial and execution of the king. Once the *Rump Parliament had abolished monarchy and the House of Lords, it launched invasions of Ireland (1649) and Scotland (1650). In spite of Cromwellian ruthlessness at *Drogheda and Wexford, Ireland took three years to subjugate. The Scots were devastated at *Dunbar, east of Edinburgh (September 1650), but continued to resist, to the point of invading England a year later under Charles II. His forces scattered at *Worcester (September 1651), the hapless king fled to the continent where he sojourned until disunity within the army and a generalized fear of quakers and other radicals paved the way for a bloodless restoration of monarchy. Although the king, lords, and Church of England were brought back in 1660, prerogative government was not. The constitutional changes of 1641 were preserved, while the legacy of the civil wars in radical thought, religious liberty, and parliamentary domination of the state was to re-emerge in the *'Glorious' Revolution of 1688–9.

IJG

Gentles, I., *The New Model Army in England, Ireland and Scotland, 1645–1653* (Oxford, 1992); Kenyon, J., *The Civil Wars of England* (1988); Morrill, J., *The Nature of the English Revolution* (Harlow, 1993); Russell, C., *The Causes of the English Civil War* (Oxford, 1990).

Claim of Right, 1689. The Scottish equivalent of the English Bill of Rights, declaring that James VII had been deposed and that no Roman catholic could succeed to the throne of Scotland. But it also declared prelacy to be a great grievance and prepared the way for a presbyterian church settlement. On these terms the crown of Scotland was offered to William and Mary. JAC

clans. The Gaelic word *clann* means primarily children, but was also used synonymously with *cinel tuath* or *fine* to describe a family group of four generations from a common male ancestor. Clans are referred to in the reign of David I (1124–53) in the *Book of Deer*, where there are references to the toiseachs of the Clans Morgan and Canan. A toiseach was a royal official, so in these cases the post must have become hereditary. Mackintoshes are *Clann an Toiseach*, literally 'the toiseach's children'. In the Celtic church ecclesiastical positions could become hereditary, which is why Clan Macnab are in Gaelic *Clan an Abba* 'the children of the abbot'.

Clans Canan and Morgan did not survive. Nor did the two clans Chattan and Kay, who settled a dispute by sending 30 men each to fight at Perth before Robert III in 1397. Continual flux, constant rise and fall seems to have been typical of Scottish clans. Nevertheless, one can argue that the classic clans of the Highlands, and the much smaller border clans, were usually formed from a merging of feudal jurisdictions with kinship ties (real or imagined). Scottish feudalism, unlike Irish feudalism, became assimilated early into the Gaelic tradition. Most Highland clans were in origin Gaelic communities onto which feudal structures were grafted. Some of these communities in the west had originally been Norse. Especially in the province of *Moray, there were also feudal groups which adopted clanship. Such were the Frasers, Chisholms, Grants, and Rosses, as also the Inneses, Gordons, Stewarts, Sinclairs, and the Clan Menzies.

From feudalism a clan chief gained the concept of absolute ownership of land, and the system of succession by primogeniture. Female heirs, or wardship by a superior of a male minor, could threaten the tribal identity which was the other side of the clan coin. Control of the marriage of a female heiress by the cadet branches of the chiefly house, and the office of tutor or guardian within the clan, were partial answers. Kinship was largely bogus for the bulk of a clan, who only began to use surnames very late. Cadets of the chief, holding estates in tack or lease on generous terms, in exchange for military service, were the core of a clan and their multiplication its usual mode of expansion.

After the forfeiture of the lordship of the *Isles in 1493 broke the Clan Donald into smaller MacDonald clans, three great imperialist clans dominated Highland history, due to the support of the crown, whose agents they were. These were the Gordons in the north-east, the Mackenzies in the northern Highlands and Hebrides, and Clan Campbell in the west. Scots-speaking border clans like the Scotts, Nixons, and Maxwells became obsolete after the regal union of 1603 removed their defence function. Highland clans became deeply distrusted after a century of bloody intervention in Lowland politics between 1644 and 1746. After the last *Jacobite rebellion legislation effectively destroyed them as military, jurisdictional, and cultural units. Market economics and clearances completed the job in the 19th cent. BPL

Clapham sect. An influential evangelical network whose activity in the early 19th cent. found a base in Clapham, where ten of them are commemorated in the parish church. Often attributed to Sydney *Smith, the name was popularized and perhaps coined by Sir James Stephen in the **Edinburgh Review* (1844). The banker Henry Thornton (1760–1815) and his family provided the Clapham core but the 'sect's' dominant figure, their kinsman William *Wilberforce, also lived there (1797–1808), as did Zachary Macaulay (1768–1838) from 1803 to 1819, Lord Teignmouth (1751–1834) from 1802 to 1818, and John Venn (1759–1813), Clapham's rector from 1797. The original group, ranging from Granville *Sharp, the oldest, to Thomas *Clarkson, the last survivor, provided some 60 years of public service. Their commercial, legal, and administrative experience took them naturally into Parliament where their humanitarian concerns introduced an unusual but ineradicable note at a time when such reforms were regarded as business for individual members rather than government. Their greatest victories were the abolition of the *slave trade (1807) and of slavery itself in the British empire (1833), but their influence was decisive in promoting Christian missions in India and west Africa and in supporting such bodies as the Tract (1799) and *Bible (1804) societies at home. Mostly Anglican and significantly Tory, their links with Whigs and dissenters confirm their importance as midwives of *humanitarian reform. CB

Clapperton, Hugh (1788–1827). Scottish explorer of west Africa, Clapperton revealed the Fulani empire and tried to solve the problem of the Niger's course and termination. After an adventurous early career in the Royal Navy, Clapperton was retired on half-pay when in 1822 W. Oudney invited him and Denham to join an official expedition from Tripoli across the Sahara to the middle Niger region. Clapperton alone visited Kano and Sokoto in the newly created Fulani empire of Uthman dan Fodio and his son Mohamed Bello in 1824. On his return to Britain, the colonial secretary asked him immediately to go back to Sokoto to make treaties. With *Lander, he penetrated from the Guinea coast in the south, but Bello's disputes with neighbouring Bornu hampered Clapperton, who died of dysentery in April 1827 without solving the Niger problem. But three years later Lander showed that the Niger terminated in the Gulf of Guinea. RB

Clare, Gilbert de (d. 1230). See GLOUCESTER, 4TH EARL OF.

Clare, Gilbert de (1243–95). See GLOUCESTER, 6TH EARL OF.

Clare, Gilbert de (d. 1314). See GLOUCESTER, 7TH EARL OF.

Clare, Richard de (d. 1176). See PEMBROKE, EARL OF.

Clare, Richard de (d. 1262). See GLOUCESTER, 5TH EARL OF.

Clarence, Albert Victor Christian Edward, duke of (1864–92). Clarence was the first son of Edward, prince of Wales, and grandson of Queen Victoria. From the beginning, his health caused anxiety and he seems to have been congenitally handicapped: at the age of 5 he was described as 'languid and listless'. At 13 he went to Dartmouth Naval College and was then sent on a long world cruise with his brother George. He spent some time at Trinity College, Cambridge, though one tutor described his faculties as 'abnormally dormant' and another remarked that 'he hardly knows the meaning of the words *to read*'. The university obliged with an honorary degree. He was next placed in the army where the commander-in-chief reported that even elementary drill movements were beyond him. Known in the family as 'Eddie', he remained indolent and wayward and what vigour he did possess was devoted to sexual encounters of various kinds. 'His education and future', wrote his father in 1890, 'has been a matter of considerable anxiety to us and the difficulty of rousing him is very great.' Desperate remedies were suggested—even longer cruises or matrimony. In 1891 Princess *Mary of Teck, his cousin, accepted him, but he died of pneumonia at Sandringham on 14 January 1892, a month before the wedding. In due course his younger brother married his fiancée and succeeded as George V. The more lurid stories connected him with the Ripper murders. JAC

Clarence, George, Ist duke of (1446–78). Reputed to have been drowned in a butt of malmsey, Clarence was the younger brother of Edward IV. As an impressionable youth he was enticed by a promise of the crown to support *Warwick the Kingmaker (whose daughter Isabel he married) against his brother. In the event Henry VI was restored and in 1471 Clarence abandoned Warwick to help Edward IV recover the throne. In the early 1470s he was high in Edward's favour, lavishly rewarded with half of the Warwick inheritance. But his truculence (he quarrelled with Richard of Gloucester over the division of the spoils), incompetence, and insubordination exasperated the king. Arrested in 1477, and condemned for treason in a show trial before his peers, he was executed secretly in the Tower, by means never officially revealed. AJP

Clarence, Thomas, Ist duke of (1388–1421). The second son of Henry IV, Thomas was lieutenant of Ireland from 1401 to 1413, and was there, with guardians, until 1403, and again, more actively, in 1408–9. He also served in the Welsh war and at sea. He became more prominent when his father recovered control of government from Prince Henry (later Henry V): he was created duke and given command of the abortive expedition to support the Orléanist faction in France. Under Henry V, he took part in the Agincourt campaign and in the conquest of Normandy, sometimes in charge of successful detached operations. Clarence was lieutenant for the king's absence in England. Raiding Maine, he advanced with his cavalry ahead of the main army to attack a reported Franco-Scottish force at *Baugé, where he was killed. He had no legitimate heir. RLS

Clarendon, Assize of. An assize (set of instructions for the king's judges) issued on Henry II's orders from his palace at Clarendon in 1166. It required grand juries to name ('present') accused or suspected criminals in their area so that the sheriff could then have them arrested and brought for trial before royal judges in the county courts. Gaols were to be built in every county where they did not already exist. The assize is generally regarded as an important step in the development of common law machinery for the public prosecution of crime and of the integration of county courts into a national court system. JG

Clarendon, constitutions of. A written statement of Henry II's view of his customary rights over the English church. It was issued at a council held at the palace of Clarendon in January 1164 in an attempt to clarify and settle the issues at stake in the king's quarrel with *Becket. He required the bishops to promise to obey these customs in good faith, but since some of the constitutions, including one perceived as undermining *benefit of clergy, seemed to threaten the liberty of the church and in consequence were soon condemned by Pope Alexander III, the only outcome was to escalate the dispute. JG

Clarendon, Edward Hyde, 1st earl of (1609–74). Constitutionalism and the rule of law provided the guiding principles of Clarendon's life. In the first session of the *Long Parliament, 1640–1, he led the attack on Charles I's prerogative courts, but in the second he perceived John *Pym's radical policies as an equal threat to constitutional liberties and religious order. He co-authored Charles's declarations, joining him at York in May 1642. In 1643 as privy counsellor and chancellor of the Exchequer he persuaded Charles to convoke a parliament of royalist peers and MPs at Oxford to offset the absolutist advice of courtiers and soldiers. Similarly as adviser to the exiled Charles II he counselled him not to owe his restoration to Scottish, French, or Spanish intervention purchased by the abandonment of the Church of England.

In 1660 he became earl and lord chancellor. He did not think it proper to act as a prime minister, but his pregnant daughter *Anne's marriage to James, duke of York, provoked charges that he dominated the royal family. Nor would he engage in systematic parliamentary management. He opposed all governmental innovations and the second *Anglo-Dutch War, and lost control over junior ministers who combined against him when the war ended in failure. Charles cynically abandoned him, encouraging his impeachment. Clarendon fled to France, where he completed his monumental *History of the Rebellion*. JRJ

Clarendon, Henry Hyde, 2nd earl of (1638–1709). Clarendon was the son of the lord chancellor and historian, and brother of Anne Hyde, mother of Queen Mary and Queen Anne. He was returned to Parliament in 1661 and succeeded to the earldom in 1674. From 1662 he was in the service of Queen *Catherine, Charles II's Portuguese wife, as private secretary, lord chamberlain, and treasurer. On the accession of his brother-in-law James II in 1685, Clarendon and his younger brother *Rochester were given high office. From 1685 to 1687 Clarendon held the privy seal and was lord-lieutenant of Ireland. But his time in Dublin was difficult. As a protestant he was increasingly anxious at James's headlong catholicizing policy and as lord-lieutenant he was overshadowed by *Tyrconnel, a zealous catholic and commander-in-chief. In January 1687 both brothers were dismissed. At the revolution, his son Lord Cornbury was one of the first to join William, and Clarendon followed a fortnight later. Nevertheless he refused to take the oaths of allegiance to the new monarchs and had two spells in the Tower in 1690 and 1691 under suspicion of Jacobitism. The remainder of his life was spent in retirement. JAC

Clarendon, George Villiers, 4th earl of (1800–70). Whig politician. Clarendon served under such diverse leaders as *Aberdeen, *Palmerston, *Russell, and *Gladstone (1853–8, 1865–6, and 1868–70). The Tory leader, *Derby, twice offered him a place in government. A good linguist, he was an acknowledged expert on foreign affairs. Bismarck, with a touch of heavy Prussian humour, suggested in 1870 that had Clarendon lived longer he might have averted the Franco-Prussian War. Clarendon had learned the skills of diplomacy and politics as minister in Madrid during the Carlist wars and later as lord-lieutenant in Ireland (1847–52). As foreign secretary in 1853 he had the misfortune during the run-up to the *Crimean War to be in a divided cabinet. Clarendon's biggest opportunity to distinguish himself occurred during the Congress of *Paris in 1856 when he resisted the more extreme demands of Palmerston in London.

He also publicized ideas on friendly mediation before states resorted to war. If he perhaps missed an opportunity to discourage the Hohenzollern candidature which precipitated the Franco-Prussian War, he was far from inactive in the search for a peaceful settlement. CJB

Clarendon code. The title given, inaccurately, to the statutes passed after the Restoration re-establishing the Church of England under government by bishops and compelling the nation to conform. They embodied the principles, interests, and vindictiveness of the cavalier majority in Parliament rather than the judgement of Lord *Clarendon, Charles II's chief minister. The *Uniformity Act (1662) required clergy to have episcopal ordination and use only the Book of Common Prayer. Some 1,000 were ejected for refusing. The *Conventicle Act (1664) penalized all religious meetings outside the church. The *Five Mile Act (1665) banned dissenting ministers from corporate towns. In 1672 Charles tried to suspend these statutes by issuing a *Declaration of Indulgence. JRJ

Clarkson, Thomas (1760–1846). Anti-slavery campaigner. Born in Wisbech (Cambs.), son of a schoolmaster, Clarkson was educated at St Paul's School and St John's College, Cambridge, where he became concerned about slavery. In 1787 he helped found a committee for the suppression of the slave trade and lectured on behalf of the parliamentary campaign for abolition until his health collapsed in 1794. He resumed lecturing in 1805 until the ending of the trade in the British empire in 1807. In 1818 he took the case for international abolition to the Congress of Aix-la-Chapelle. With William *Wilberforce he was a vice-president of the *Anti-Slavery Society (founded 1823), and after the act was carried in 1833 for the gradual abolition of slavery in the British empire, he retained his concern for wider abolition and appeared on the platform at the 1840 international Anti-Slavery Convention in London. ER

class is about power. The history of social class is about the way in which men and women gained and used power over others, in matters of government and the state, in ideas, culture, and education, but above all in the relationships of production and consumption. The concept of social class has been and is used by historians in their struggle to understand the experience, social relationships, and social conflicts of past and present. The story of social class is part of the distinctive narrative of British history.

By the 1960s, historians had established the major outlines of this story. Sometime in the late 18th–early 19th cent., the way in which the British people began to think about their own society and the way in which the major conflicts and relationships of that society developed began to change. Eighteenth-cent. society was a hierarchy of ranks and orders held together by relationships of deference and patronage, although the sense of a bi-polar division of rich and poor, rulers and ruled, aristocracy and people might inform debates on poverty, consumption, and the nature of the constitution. The new relationships and consciousness of social class were associated with economic change, with the dominance of capitalist property relationships, with the intensity of competition in commerce, and, above all, with the reorganization of work through the division of labour and new machine-based, often steam-driven, technologies. Early conflicts were associated with trade unionism and the new technologies. The 1830s and 1840s were decades of intense conflict associated with constitutional change. There were key periods of industrial conflict in the 1880s and the quarter-century before 1926.

Social class was used to explain a wide variety of other changes and relationships. The demographic transition to low birth rates and low death rates was linked to middle-class experience in the second half of the 19th cent. and then filtered down to skilled and then unskilled working-class people. The voting patterns and political behaviour of the 20th cent. and the rise of the modern Labour and Tory Parties were related to middle- and working-class interests. Class was related to privilege in housing and education, to habits of dress, food consumption, and speech.

Behind this vast literature lay a varied selection of assumptions. British writing was dominated by a three-class model which was loosely related to the three factors of production identified by *Ricardo in 1817. The aristocracy were rent takers, the middle class were profit takers, and the working class wage earners. A rigid and deterministic Marxist presentation in which social development was dominated by an increasingly divisive conflict between capital and labour was rare, but the notion of a potential conflict derived from relationships to the means of production and the stabilization of this conflict in the 1850s and 1860s was central to the story. Explicit references to the ideas of Max Weber are even rarer, but his assumptions provide valuable guidance. Class was related to market position and hence involved privileges of education as well as property. Class was related to status which involved recognition by others in social status or 'social honour'.

This story has been questioned in a variety of ways. Eighteenth-cent. historians have identified a 'middling sort' not least in patterns of consumption. The re-examination of the political events of the 1830s and 1840s, especially the language of those contests, suggests little evidence of self-aware conflict groups based upon economic relationships. The closer study of work revealed a fundamental lack of homogeneity of experience within the major social classes. Divisions within classes, of gender, party, religion, region, ethnicity, were seen as providing identities and patterns of experience more dominant than class.

Social class has lost its privileged position in the narrative of British social history, but it remains a crucial means of explaining the conflicts and inequalities that arose and arise from the relationships of production and consumption, not least because, in the last 200 years, the language of class has been used in covert and overt ways by the people of Britain.

See also SOCIAL HISTORY. RJM

Classicianus. Procurator (chief financial administrator) of Britain AD 60–1. His origins and early career are unknown. His name suggests Gallic antecedents, like those of his wife, who was from Trier. He became procurator of Britain in the aftermath of the *Boudiccan revolt and was instrumental in having the victorious governor *Suetonius Paullinus recalled before the latter's military policies could do further fiscal damage. Much of what we know of Classicianus derives from the tombstone erected by his wife, parts of which were reused in late Roman towers added to the walls of London; clearly he died in office. ASEC

Classis Britannica was the name of the Roman fleet which policed the Channel. It does not appear in the evidence before the early 2nd cent., though fleets were used in the Claudian invasion and by *Agricola. Commanded by a procurator, its main base was at Boulogne, with an important installation at Dover. Bricks and tiles stamped *CL BR* (and variants) are widely distributed in present-day Kent and East Sussex, many associated with Wealden iron-working sites, which seem to have been under direct military exploitation. We have no direct evidence for the *Classis Britannica* after the early 3rd cent. ASEC

Claudius. Roman emperor AD 41–54. Because of his physical infirmities, Claudius had been denied the normal career of a Roman aristocrat. After the assassination of Caligula, the middle-aged Claudius was unexpectedly proclaimed emperor by the army. To reward the army and prove his martial prowess, Claudius decided to resume the work of his ancestor Julius *Caesar with an invasion of Britain in 43. Though the invasion force was commanded by *Aulus Plautius, the emperor himself came to Britain for the formal entry into Camulodunum (*Colchester). Having spent sixteen days in the new province, Claudius returned to Rome, where he celebrated a triumph. Claudius awarded the title *Britannicus* to his son, and the invasion was the most famous event of his reign. A large temple dedicated to him was constructed in Colchester. ASEC

Cleland, William (*c.*1661–89). Cleland joined the covenanting rising of 1679 and fought at *Drumclog and *Bothwell Bridge. In 1685 he took part in *Argyll's rising and at the revolution of 1688 gave allegiance to William III. On 21 August 1689 a small force led by Cleland was cut off by Jacobites at *Dunkeld, but drove off their assailants. Cleland was killed during the battle. JAC

clerk register (Scotland). First seen in 1286 (as clerk of the rolls), the office entailed custodianship of the records of crown charters, the Exchequer, and Parliament. The clerk register initially wrote the records himself, but by the mid-16th cent. he was a director of record-keeping. From 1532 the clerk register was an advocate, present at Parliament, Privy Council, and session as both a record keeper and judge. From 1689 the office was a well-paid political appointment, but after the *Union (1707), and the end of a separate Parliament and Privy Council, the job gradually declined into a sinecure. RJT

Cleveland was one of the new non-metropolitan counties created by the English local government reforms of 1972. It straddled the ancient border of the river Tees between Yorkshire and Co. Durham, which had become increasingly obsolete due to the industrialization of the Tees estuary. Middlesbrough and Stockton had been united in Teesside county borough (1968–74), and the town of Hartlepool, and the Yorkshire districts immediately adjacent to Middlesbrough, were added to form Cleveland county. Many people in these areas failed to identify with it and in 1996, following the recommendations of the Banham Commission, the county was abolished. CNL

Clifford, Thomas Clifford, 1st Baron (1630–73). Clifford was a Devon gentleman of modest means determined to make a mark after the Restoration. Elected in 1660 for the local borough of Totnes, he spoke frequently and in December 1660 was appointed a gentleman of the privy chamber. At that stage he belonged to Lord *Arlington's group. Bitterly opposed to the Dutch, he urged the second war in 1664 and volunteered for several naval actions. In 1666 he became comptroller of the household, held the post of treasurer 1668–72, and 1672–3 was lord high treasurer with a peerage. But as a member of the inner cabinet or *cabal, his judgement seems less good than his spirit. He advocated and signed the secret treaty of *Dover with Louis XIV, which involved Charles II in great embarrassment; suggested the stop on the Exchequer, a short-term expedient of doubtful wisdom; and pushed hard for a third Dutch War. But when the *Test Act, against which he argued, passed in 1673, he resigned all offices as an avowed catholic. He took his leave of John Evelyn, a close friend, with considerable solemnity, and a few weeks later was dead, it was rumoured by hanging himself. JAC

Clinton, Sir Henry (1730–95). Clinton was a grandson of the 6th earl of Lincoln, son of an admiral, and related to the dukes of Newcastle. He joined the army in 1745, fought in Canada during the War of Austrian Succession, and in Germany during the Seven Years War. By 1772 he was a major-general, acquired credit at *Bunker Hill, and was appointed second in command in America under *Howe. In 1778, after *Burgoyne's surrender at *Saratoga, he became commander-in-chief. In 1780 he scored a major victory at *Charleston, when 6,000 rebels surrendered with 300 guns, but outright victory eluded him and, like most generals, he called for reinforcements. He was allowed to resign in 1782 after the surrender of *Cornwallis at *Yorktown and was subsequently involved in acrimonious controversy. He has been severely criticized as peevish, neurotic, rising only to mediocrity, but it was not an easy war to win. JAC

Clitherow, St Margaret (1556–86). Catholic martyr. Daughter of a sheriff of York and a butcher's wife, she became a catholic (1574). She was tried at York for harbouring Jesuits and priests and hearing mass in her house. To save her children from giving evidence she refused to plead, was condemned and pressed to death. Her sons studied at Rheims and Rome for the priesthood and her daughter became a nun at Louvain. A fine example of recusant courage and the brutality of the age, she was canonized in 1970. WMM

Clive, Robert (1725–74). Soldier-statesman who helped to secure British control over India. Born in Shropshire, he was sent to Madras to join the *East India Company in 1743. Eight years later, when war broke out between Britain and France in India, he volunteered for military service and, against all the odds, seized and held the city of Arcot. In 1756 he moved to Bengal, where a dispute between the British and the French-supported Siraj-ud-Daula had led to the loss of Calcutta, where surviving Europeans had been incarcerated in the notorious *'Black Hole'. Clive organized a small force of European and Indian soldiers to retake the city in January 1757, but it soon became apparent that Siraj was still a major threat. Clive marched inland with no more than 3,200 troops to face Siraj's army of 50,000 at *Plassey on the Bhagirathi river. The battle was fought in a rainstorm on 23 June 1757; for the loss of only 23 men, Clive routed the enemy.

By now the undisputed master of Bengal, Clive returned to England in 1760, where he was raised to the Irish peerage as Baron Clive of Plassey (1762). He returned to India in 1765 as governor of Bengal, where he introduced a series of reforms to company administration. Corruption remained, however, and in 1772 he was forced to defend himself before Parliament. Although exonerated, the trial affected his health and, on 22 November 1774, he committed suicide. JLP

Clodius Albinus. Governor of Roman Britain 192–7 and claimant to the imperial throne. Probably from Hadrumetum (now Sousse) in north Africa, Albinus' career before his appointment to Britain is lost, nor do we know anything of his activities as governor. He came to prominence after the assassination of Commodus on 31 December 192, when he put himself forward as a successor. His chief rival was *Septimius Severus supported by the garrison of Pannonia Superior and the Senate. At first relations were outwardly cordial and Severus accorded Albinus the title of Caesar (junior partner). But in 195 Albinus crossed to Gaul, where the large army of Britain proclaimed him Augustus. After initial successes in 196 including the capture of Lugdunum (Lyons), he was defeated and killed by Severus outside that city on 19 February 197. ASEC

Clogher (Clochar mac nDaimine), **diocese of.** The Irish see of Clogher in the province of *Armagh was established by the Council of Raithbressail (1111). At Kells-Mellifont (1152) its territory was increased, though for a spell (1135–92) the see was transferred to Louth until the Anglo-Normans settled there. There were usually Irish, not Anglo-Norman, bishops until the 16th cent. Since the Reformation there have been both catholic and Anglican bishops of Clogher, though the Anglican diocese was vacant (1571–1604), and for a spell (1850–86) united with the Armagh diocese. There are cathedrals at Clogher and Enniskillen. WMM

Clontarf, battle of, 1014. *Brian Boru claimed the high kingship of Ireland, though resisted by Leinster and by the Norse kingdom of Dublin. After an inconclusive campaign in 1013, the Norse were reinforced from Orkney and the Isle of Man. On 23 April 1014 just outside Dublin, battle was joined. Brian Boru was too old to fight and his troops, largely from Munster, were led by his son Murchad. The Norsemen were led by Sihtric, king of Dublin. Though the Norse were defeated, Brian Boru, inadequately guarded, was killed and the victory was not followed up. JAC

cloth industry. See WOOLLEN INDUSTRY.

club-men. Not all Englishmen were keen to fight in the Civil War and by 1644 the depredations and extortions of each army had become unbearable. Groups of country folk, particularly in the royalist south and west, began to band together against troops from either side. Armed mainly with clubs, scythes, and spades, they were still formidable, and local commanders tried to enlist their help and turn their animosities against the other side. The Wiltshire club-men were hostile to Parliament, while their neighbours in Somerset were hostile to the king. *Cromwell had to deal with 2,000 of them on Hambledon Hill near Shaftesbury: his cavalry dispersed them with some loss of life, but he wrote to *Fairfax for permission to send the 'poor silly creatures' home. *Rupert tried to instill better discipline in the border counties in 1645, and it was in part to reduce looting and appease the club-men that Parliament strove to pay the *New Model Army regularly. JAC

clubs. The decades after the Restoration saw a proliferation of clubs and societies in London and the main provincial cities, many of them meeting in taverns or coffee-houses. They were prompted by greater prosperity, growth in the size of towns, and a marked increase in the membership of the professions. Contemporaries attached much importance to clubs as instruments of civility: one writer in 1739 remarked that though many clubs were run by 'the meanest and rudest of the citizens', they maintained 'the best order and decorum'. Though the most famous club, to which *Johnson, *Burke, and *Gibbon belonged, was literary, the majority were dining clubs, or political or gambling clubs. The Cocoa Tree Chocolate House, in Anne's reign, was a haunt of Tories and Jacobites; Read's Coffee House in Fleet Street was the home of Whigs. Sixty years later, Almack's and *Brooks's were famous gambling clubs. The 19th-cent. gentlemen's clubs were likely to have their own premises, not too far from the House of Commons, and to be run, not by a proprietor, but by a committee of members. The Athenaeum (1824), founded by J. W. *Croker, was literary; the *Carlton (1832) was established to restore the fortunes of the Tory Party after its shattering election defeat; the *Reform Club (1836) was a Whig and radical riposte to the Carlton's success. The heyday of the gentlemen's club was late Victorian and Edwardian England, with clubs offering overnight accommodation and libraries as well as good dining facilities. Trollope's old lawyer Abel Wharton, in *The Prime Minister*, 'twice a week, on Wednesdays and Saturdays, dined at that old law club, the Eldon, and played whist after dinner till twelve o'clock'. At the other end of the social scale were highly successful working men's clubs, where the drink was beer and the entertainment a local comedian, sing-song, or dominoes. JAC

Cluniacs were *Benedictine monks from the monastery of Cluny (Burgundy) founded by William, duke of Aquitaine, in 909. Cluny was a centre of reformed observance, laying great stress on the rule, the liturgy, and freedom from lay (and, indeed, episcopal) control. Under the leadership of its early abbots, especially Odo (927–42), Odilo (994–1048), and Hugh (1049–1109), Cluny enjoyed considerable prosperity, and exercised a wide influence on monastic reform elsewhere in Europe, while an increasing number of monasteries were taken under Cluniac control, or adopted Cluniac observances. The order was extremely centralized, Cluny's abbot possessed autocratic powers within the order, and other Cluniac foundations or 'priories' were subordinate to Cluny, where their monks made profession. The Cluniacs were closely involved with the papal reform movement of the late 11th cent. and Pope Urban II (1088–99) was himself a Cluniac. Under Hugh's abbacy, Cluny reached the height of its prestige as a spiritual and cultural centre, famous for its music and rebuilt abbey church, which, when consecrated in 1131–2, was perhaps the grandest in western Europe.

The first English Cluniac priory was founded by William de Warenne in 1077 near his castle at Lewes. His, the largest community, was joined by some 30 more, most being founded in the late 11th and 12th cents. Though initially subject to Cluny's authority and hence regarded as 'alien priories' and liable to sequestration during the Anglo-French wars, most purchased national identity as 'denizens'. BJG

Clwyd. A Welsh county created under the Local Government Act of 1972 and extant from 1974 to 1996. It was made up of the former counties of *Denbighshire and *Flintshire minus a north–south strip along the Conwy valley, allocated to *Gwynedd, but with the Edeyrnion rural district in the south-west, transferred from *Merioneth. The counties which emerged in 1972 from a long period of consultation were the result of attempts to balance historical tradition, minimum population to support services (usually taken as 250,000), and reasonable distances for internal administration. Clwyd was a compromise on all three bases. It had little in the way of common historical identity, although there was some common industrial inheritance, since it included the whole of the North Wales Coalfield. An earlier proposal had suggested amalgamation with Gwynedd. Another notion was amalgamation in *Powys. But while such schemes gave appropriate populations, they would have given unwieldy counties with severe communication problems. Clwyd, therefore, with a name of no historic significance, but derived from the river, was a compromise which gave an element of administrative identity to north-east Wales.

The county was divided into six districts: Colwyn; Rhuddlan; Delyn; Alyn and Deeside; Glyndŵr; and Wrexham Maelor. Its population was 390,200 in 1981 and 402,927 (1981 base) in 1991. In 1996 it was divided into three new unitary authorities, Denbighshire (91,000), Flintshire (144,000), and Wrexham (123,000), whilst Colwyn on the western border of Clwyd was joined with Aberconwy in Aberconwy and Colwyn (109,000). HC

Cnut (d. 1035), king of England (1016–35). Cnut, the younger son of the Danish king *Sweyn Forkbeard, came to prominence campaigning in England by the side of his father, 1013–14. Sweyn forced King *Æthelred into exile and received the submission of all England but died in February 1014. His son could then do no more than take his army back to Denmark after an act of savage brutality when he mutilated his hostages before putting them ashore at Sandwich. He returned in September 1015 and after hard battles with Æthelred's son *Edmund Ironside (d. Nov. 1016) conquered England. For close on 20 years this Danish prince, quickly recognized as legitimate successor to the Christian kingship of England, gave the kingdom a period of substantial peace and prosperity. At a great assembly at Oxford in 1018 he promised to adhere to the laws of King *Edgar, a promise reiterated in a letter sent to all the shire courts in 1019/20 in which he stated his intention to be a gracious lord and to support the rights of the church and just secular law. In 1019 he succeeded his elder brother as king of Denmark, and he also, after one major set-back at the hands of Olaf Haraldson (St Olaf) and the Swedes in 1026, gained mastery of Norway in 1028. Incongruously, Cnut attempted to govern Norway through the virtual regency of his English wife, Ælfgifu of Northampton, and their young son Sweyn (d. 1036), an experiment which ended in miserable failure in 1035, the year of Cnut's own death. Whether Cnut could have repaired the damage had he lived is a moot point: but the Norwegian fiasco is a reminder of the fragile nature of Cnut's so-called Scandinavian empire. England and to a lesser extent Denmark constituted the solid base of his political power. In England itself continuity is the main theme. There were occasional outbursts of ferocity, notably in the opening years of the reign, including the murder of the treacherous ealdorman Eadric Streona in 1017. Cnut made, primarily for political reasons, a Christian marriage to Æthelred's widow *Emma of Normandy, although continuing to consort with and recognize Ælfgifu of Northampton, and relied heavily on many of Æthelred's principal advisers, notably *Wulfstan, archbishop of York and bishop of Worcester (1002–23). Wulfstan was chiefly responsible for the framing of Cnut's law codes, the first of which dealt with ecclesiastical matters and the second, longer and more elaborate, with secular affairs. These codes proved the chief vehicles for the transmission of knowledge of Anglo-Saxon law deep into the Norman period. Local government continued to operate in shires, hundreds, and wapentakes, essential for the judicial and financial health of the local communities and of the monarchy. Cnut exploited to the full the wealth of a basically prosperous England. There were some major exactions recorded in the *Anglo-Saxon Chronicle*, £10,500 from London alone in 1018 to help pay off the victorious Danish fleet and £72,000 from the whole of England: but it was the regular exaction of geld from the country that provided the king with the means to set up stable government and to preserve internal peace. The advanced and sophisticated coinage that Cnut had inherited from his predecessors continued to be struck to a high and consistent standard, and urban communities, where mints were located, benefited from the range as well as from the strength of Cnut's regime. His piety was much more than skin deep and on an impressive visit to Rome in 1027 to attend the coronation of the Emperor Conrad—in itself a symptom of his prestige and confidence—Cnut took the opportunity to negotiate favourable terms for English traders and pilgrims *en route*. Prompted in part by his needs for reliable subordinates who would exercise more than traditional authority when the king was abroad, he deliberately built up the regional powers of some great men to whom was accorded the title of eorl, a step that has been interpreted, probably falsely, as potentially harmful to the integrity of the late Old English monarchy. In Cnut's day they, especially *Godwine, earl of Wessex, were kept firmly under royal discipline, serving a useful purpose as regional commanders. The reputation of Cnut suffered in one respect from sheer biological accident. He died relatively young (one later authority says at the age of 37, which is plausible) in 1035. His two sons *Harold Harefoot (by Ælfgifu) and *Harthacnut (by Emma) contended for the succession to England and to Denmark, and both died in their early twenties, Harold in 1040, Harthacnut in 1042. His other two children by Ælfgifu, Sweyn, much entangled in Norwegian politics, and Gunnhild, married to the future emperor Henry III, also died young in 1036 and 1038 respectively. The return of the ancient dynasty to England in the person of *Edward the Confessor (1042–66) left Cnut with no great apologist among English historical writers. The *Anglo-Saxon Chronicle* has comparatively little to say about him, and indeed his wife Emma, who lived on until 1052, has a better personal historical press. There can be no doubt, however, that Cnut's contribution to the institutional and economic life of England was considerable, and that medieval Scandinavian historians and chroniclers were well justified in referring to him as 'Cnut the Great'. HL

Coalbrookdale in Shropshire was the site of the great development of the iron industry by the Darby family, using local raw materials and the river Severn for transport. The valley also produced steam-engines in the early 18th cent. and at the end of the century the Coalport china factory was established. The museum complex based on *Ironbridge is one of the finest in the country. JAC

coal industry. This has the longest continuously recorded history of any British industry, beginning with monastic and manorial documents of the 13th cent. Pits were small, shallow, or outcrops, capital investment was minuscule, drainage was an insignificant problem, readily solved by adits or buckets, and markets were generally local. However, by the 14th cent. a water-borne export trade from the Forth and Tyne had developed. Expansion occurred in the 16th and 17th cents. as a consequence of the growth of markets. By 1690 coal output was approaching 3 million tons, with Northumberland and Durham accounting for 45 per cent of production.

Growth in output resulted from greater investment by landowners with coal on their estates. Supply was partly affected by the Reformation and secularization of ecclesiastical land. New owners exploited coal reserves more actively and sought markets within and beyond their localities. Where land was leased for mining, leases were often longer, encouraging investment and entrepreneurship. Mining methods improved considerably, and coal-mining was a major stimulus of invention, especially in the use of water-wheels to drive drainage pumps. Ultimately, between 1698 and 1705 the problem of drainage led to steam pumps devised by Thomas *Savery and Thomas *Newcomen. Demand from London accounted for the dominance of the seasale mines of the Great Northern Coalfield; domestic consumers were very important, but the industries of London—smiths, glass-makers, owners of sugarhouses, brick and tile kilns, breweries and distilleries—should not be ignored. A range of industries from lime-burning to dyeing encouraged landsale and seasale, the former operating close to the pit-head, thereby offsetting transport costs. Coal-mining was often combined with the promotion of other industries by landowners attempting to add value to their coal reserves.

Demand for coal escalated in the 18th cent. as the iron and metal industries altered their methods of production. Smelting by coke, achieved by Abraham *Darby I in 1709, spread rapidly after 1760. In the late 18th cent. the Cranage brothers, Peter Onions, and Henry *Cort applied coke to the puddling process in producing bar iron. New industries, notably gas, chemicals, the railways, and steam-power installations, also widened demand. Domestic consumers increased in number as urbanization proceeded. By 1800 output exceeded 11 million tons and in 1854 approached 65 million tons. It has been estimated that annual gross capital formation increased nearly sixfold between these years from over £480,000 to over £2.5 million. Technical and commercial constraints on growth were removed in this period. The steam-engine solved the problem of mine drainage; ventilation was improved in deeper pits by the sinking of air shafts; George *Stephenson's and Humphry *Davy's safety lamps began the improvement in underground lighting and mining safety, although gases remained a hazard; a labour-intensive industry which used ponies underground, as well as women and children in coal haulage, mining gained from the wire rope, the cage, and the rotary steam-engine, all features of substantial collieries by 1855. Cheaper transport was achieved by river improvement, canals, and railways. One per cent of national income in 1800, the coal industry accounted for about 6 per cent by 1900. Coal represented 5 per cent of the total value of exports up to the 1870s and by the early 20th cent. about 10 per cent. The industry was Britain's major male employer by 1914, when output reached 287.4 million tons, the highest figure ever reached.

After the war (1914–18) coal went into structural decline, encountering massive labour problems and declining productivity during a period of contraction, interrupted only by the Second World War (1939–45) and its immediate aftermath. Nationalized in 1947, the industry was extensively modernized at great public cost. Demand fell as alternative fuels gained ground. High-costing pits closed after 1959, and declining productivity was reversed. The number of collieries fell from 901 in 1951 to 438 in 1967, a process hastened in the 1970s and 1980s; one consequence was a substantial fall in the mining labour force. Despite a growing emphasis on open-cast working and new mechanized mines, such as the Selby complex, in an abortive attempt to compete with foreign imports, the industry continued its decline in the 1990s, returning to private ownership in 1994–5. JB

Cobbett, William (1763–1835). Radical journalist whose **Political Register* (1802–35) was the most influential radical paper of its time. Week after week Cobbett thundered against the political system ('Old Corruption') and championed the cause of labouring people, particularly the agricultural workers. His radicalism, blended with traditionalism, was individualistic, untheoretical, and non-revolutionary. He was, wrote *Hazlitt, 'a kind of 4th estate in the politics of the country'. Born and raised on a Surrey farm, Cobbett enlisted in 1784, served in Nova Scotia, and was promoted serjeant-major. On returning to England in 1791 he tried unsuccessfully to expose financial corruption in the regiment, and as a consequence had to flee to France and then to America. In Philadelphia (1792–9) Cobbett patriotically defended Great Britain, and when he returned to England in 1800 was welcomed as a Tory supporter. However, he soon became disenchanted with what he called 'The System' and from 1806 demanded parliamentary reform. Sentenced in 1810 to two years in Newgate gaol for seditious libel, Cobbett was henceforth regarded as a dangerous radical; and when habeas corpus was suspended in 1817 he deemed it prudent to flee to America. On his return home in 1819 he resumed farming and also wrote some of his finest pieces, published as *Rural Rides*. He was MP for Oldham in the reformed Parliament of 1833. JFCH

Cobden, Richard (1804–65). A British radical politician, Cobden was devoted to free trade and international peace, and hostile to aristocratic rule. After the successful campaign for the incorporation of Manchester, he joined the *Anti-Corn Law League. Dissatisfied with propaganda campaigns, early in 1841 he persuaded the league to fight a by-election. Although this was lost, by forcing a moderate Whig to withdraw the League had shown that it could affect election results. Cobden became MP for Southport in 1841 and proved a competent speaker both in and out of Parliament. His speaking style was simple and straightforward. In the aftermath of the Conservative victory in 1841, Cobden contemplated militant action, but eventually decided on exploiting all legitimate opportunities, both electorally and in the propaganda war. He was largely responsible for the League's increasing prominence. In 1846 he received from *Peel an exaggerated tribute as the man primarily responsible for repeal of the Corn Laws. Thereafter, Cobden remained a prominent reformer, but opposition to the *Crimean War and *Palmerston's popular foreign policy reduced his influence. In 1859–60 he negotiated an important commercial treaty with France. He died too early to take a place in the leadership of the emerging *Liberal Party.

NMcC

Cochrane, Thomas, 10th earl of Dundonald [S] (1775–1860). Cochrane had a long and colourful life. The family was impoverished and he had to make his own way in the world. In 1793 he joined the navy, in which his uncle was serving. During 1800–1 he commanded the *Speedy*, preying upon Spanish shipping, and captured a frigate three times the size of his own ship. Next he took up politics, was returned to Parliament in 1806 for Honiton, and then Westminster as partner to Sir Francis *Burdett. They formed a radical pair, urging parliamentary reform. In 1809 he was given charge of a fireship attack on a French squadron in Aix roads, quarrelled with Gambier, his superior officer, had him court-martialled, and lost. In 1814 Cochrane was involved in a Stock Exchange fraud, sentenced to a year in prison, stripped of his honours, and expelled from Parliament. His radical Westminster constituents returned him again, but he failed to become a second Wilkes. In 1818, abandoning Parliament, he left for South America, where Spain's colonies were in rebellion, and performed deeds of heroism on behalf of Chile, Peru, and Brazil. After that he commanded for the Greeks against the Turks without notable success. Returning to England, he succeeded as earl in 1831 and was given a free pardon in 1832. He was employed once more 1848–51 as commander-in-chief West Indies and promoted admiral. Cochrane was a vigorous and brave leader of men, but a bad subordinate and was never entrusted with supreme command. An uncomfortable national hero, he was buried in Westminster abbey. JAC

Cockburn, Henry (1779–1854). Scottish advocate, judge, and diarist, whose *Memorials of his Time* (1856) remains one of the most vivid and attractive accounts of Scottish politics and Edinburgh society and culture in what Cockburn called 'the last purely Scotch age'. A well-connected Whig who spent his whole life in Edinburgh, a successful and talented criminal advocate, Cockburn was a founder member of the **Edinburgh Review*. He became solicitor-general for Scotland in 1830, drafted the Scottish Reform Act, and was promoted to the Scottish bench in 1834. Cockburn's generous and unaffected prose did not make him a particularly trenchant Edinburgh reviewer or Whig pamphleteer. It did make him a diarist of near genius. His *Memorials* are his greatest work. His *Journals* which cover 1832–54 are less successful. His strongly topographical *Circuit Journeys*, written while he was a circuit judge, is a neglected masterpiece. In his later years he became a notable and ardent conservationist.

NTP

cock-fighting. A ferocious blood-sport, probably introduced by the Romans, in which intensively trained gamecocks with metal or bone spurs slipped over their natural ones were set to fight, usually to the death, on a stage in a circular pit. Mains (matches) were variously structured, with rules, the rowdy spectacles generally accompanied by heavy betting. A medieval Shrovetide schoolboy sport, and survivor of bans which claimed it interfered with archery practice, it flourished across all social classes and was a favourite pastime of royalty and the upper classes; numerous place-names involving the word 'cock' attest to the ease with which an arena could be set up. Forbidden briefly by the Commonwealth, its resurgence in Restoration England was typified by Charles II's own enthusiasm. The best cocks were valuable, and paintings frequently commissioned. County competition first showed itself in this sport, usually as three-day events and often associated with race meetings; Ireland quickly followed the English example. Opposition grew in the early 19th cent., but not all towns acquiesced readily; although banned in 1835 and 1849, it persisted in coal-mining areas, and may still occur secretly. ASH

Codrington, Sir Edward (1770–1851). Codrington was of the Gloucestershire family of baronets and entered the navy in 1783. He served with distinction at the *Glorious First of June in 1794 and was given his first command later that year. At *Trafalgar he captained the *Orion*. At the end of the war he was knighted and was promoted vice-admiral in 1825. In 1827 he was given a difficult command in the eastern Mediterranean, where the Greeks were in rebellion against the Turks. His squadron, with Russian and French contingents, was intended to enforce an armistice but on 20 October an accidental clash with a Turkish fleet led to the Turks' annihilation in *Navarino Bay, on the south-west of the Morea. The British government, while praising Codrington, explained the battle as an 'untoward event'. The sequel became acrimonious and Codrington's orders appear vague. He was promoted admiral of the blue in 1837 and commanded the Channel fleet from 1839 to 1842. JAC

coercion bills, under various names, were a sombre obbligato to Anglo-Irish relations throughout much of the 19th cent. Sometimes produced by threat of revolution or actual insurrection, or by widespread agrarian disorder, they also balanced measures of concession to improve their chance of getting through the Westminster Parliament. *Habeas corpus was not introduced in Ireland until 1781, most lords-lieutenant arguing that the country was not sufficiently settled, and it was suspended at frequent intervals thereafter. *Peel as chief secretary responded to agrarian violence in 1814 with an Insurrection Act, which suspended trials by jury in troubled areas and allowed a curfew and the recruitment of special constables. *Grey's ministry in 1833 replied to the disorders of the 'tithe war' and the murders by the 'whitefeet' with a coercion act which allowed the lord-lieutenant to ban public meetings and to proclaim martial law in disaffected areas: 'we coerce as do Metternich and the pope', *Palmerston wrote, 'but then we redress grievances, as they do not'. *Gladstone's first land reform in 1871 was accompanied by a Peace Preservation Act, which extended the powers of the lord-lieutenant to order search and arrest and made disturbed areas pay for the extra policing. His second land reform in 1881, at the height of the *Irish Land League agitation, was accompanied by another coercion act widening powers of arrest and detention, and strengthened after the murder of Lord Frederick *Cavendish. *Balfour, chief secretary 1887–91, declared coercion and concession his twin policy—'relentless as Cromwell in enforcing obedience . . . radical in redressing grievances'. His *Congested districts relief scheme was matched by a new Crime Act. The protracted opposition to coercive measures by *Parnell and his colleagues led to parliamentary devices like the closure to prevent business being brought to a standstill. JAC

coffee-houses. Coffee, tea, and chocolate became available through the *East India Company (founded 1600) and the first coffee-houses, as alternatives to taverns or ale-houses, appeared in Oxford (1650) and London (1652). They developed as centres for the exchange and distribution of domestic and foreign news, intelligence, and gossip in the days of unorganized delivery of letters and news-sheets. Concentrated in London mainly around the Royal Exchange, they rapidly became part of the daily life of the city, the business day often beginning and ending there. Frequented by stockbrokers, trading and livery companies, insurance schemes (spurred by the fire of 1666) were initiated, 'bubble' schemes hatched, and ships' passages announced there. *Pepys went to many, where the conversation ranged from Harrington's views on property to the reproductive mechanism of insects. The government of Charles II was soon alarmed at small groups of men meeting in private rooms and made a half-hearted attempt to ban them in 1675. Initially they worked in conjunction with the Post Office for the delivery of letters, but by 1700 the well-organized arrangements of the coffee-men (especially with the ship masters) were costing the Post Office much revenue: subsequent acts to curb the practice were ineffective, since postal administration remained unsavoury and inefficient. The coffee-men vied with each other to provide the broadest variety of intelligence, setting up individual arrangements with news publishers.

The class and type of customer varied according to locality, trade, and fashion. They soon became political headquarters, the Cocoa-Tree a famous Tory haunt, Ozinda's for Jacobites, and the Smyrna and St James's coffee-houses for Whigs. They were also used for educational purposes, lodge meetings, assignations, planning robberies, and occasionally for selling slaves, and attracted quacks, prostitutes, and press-gangs. With a growing population, rebuilding, improving communications, and more efficient public services, they were beginning to outlive their usefulness by 1830. As the original antagonism of the vintners had been replaced by acquisitiveness, the remaining coffee-houses reverted easily to taverns or wine-houses, or developed into clubs. ASH

Coggan, Donald (b. 1909). Archbishop of Canterbury. Coggan was born in London of a west country family and ultimately Welsh stock. He had a distinguished academic career at Cambridge and at Manchester University, where he taught Semitic languages and literature prior to ordination in 1934. After a brief curacy he returned to academic life, first in Canada, and then, after 1944, in London, where he transformed the moribund theological college of St John's Hall, Highbury, into the thriving London College of Divinity. A first-class scholar and administrator, steeped in the evangelical tradition, Coggan's merits were recognized in 1956 with appointment as bishop of Bradford, and in 1961 as archbishop of York. His translation at the age of 65 to Canterbury came as a surprise to many, but perceptions of him as a stop-gap or caretaker primate quickly faded. Before retirement in 1980 he proved an enthusiastic ecumenist and a prophetic leader, whilst giving the Church of England a period of stability. JRG

Cogidubnus, British king of the *Regni (Regnenses). The ancestry of Cogidubnus is obscure. It is possible that he was a prince of the *Atrebates, for his kingdom during the early years of the Roman occupation included the southern part of the old Atrebatic kingdom. Tacitus records that he was a loyal friend of Rome, and this is confirmed by his forenames—Tiberius Claudius—which reflect Claudius' grant of Roman citizenship to the king. He appears to have been installed in a newly created kingdom by the Romans at the time of the invasion, and to have provided them with a safe base at *Fishbourne on Chichester harbour for their campaign in south-west England. The palace which was built over the site of the Roman camp is likely to have been erected by Cogidubnus, although he may not have lived to see it completed in the late 70s. KB

coins and currency may be viewed from different angles—as symbols of monarchical or national authority; as art-forms reflecting the culture of a period and the influences at work; or as an economic weapon, control of which was essential for financial stability. For centuries coins were hammered out by hand and the quality of individual coins and the output of different mints varied considerably. Debased or worn coinage was bad for trade: in 1695 William Stout, a Lancaster shopkeeper, complained that 'the old silver coin of this nation continued to be more and more diminished, which made great distraction in trade'. If the intrinsic value of coins was more than their formal exchange value, they were hoarded or melted down; if markedly less, there was reluctance to accept them.

The king's coinage was one of the most visible manifestations of royal authority. The number of mints was carefully controlled and permission to subjects to strike coins granted sparingly: it was an indication of the weakness of government during Stephen's reign that so many magnates began to mint coins. Counterfeiting or clipping the coinage was regarded as a heinous crime. In 1350 Edward III declared counterfeiting to be high treason and Henry V extended treason to clipping or defacing. As late as 1742 gilding shillings to pass as guineas was made treason. Nor were these idle threats. Phoebe Harris was burned before 20,000 people in 1786 and Christian Murphy in 1789. It was an act of clemency in 1790 when Parliament substituted hanging and not until 1832 was the death sentence abolished.

At the time of Caesar's invasion in 55 BC coins were circulating in southern England. They were largely imitations of Gaulish coins, themselves imitations of Greek staters. Tasciovanus, king of the *Catuvellauni, minted gold, silver, and copper coins (*c.*20 BC), and his son *Cunobelinus had coins circulating in the Colchester area: the *Iceni and the *Coritani also had their own currency. After AD 43 the Romans substituted their own imperial coinage but by *c.* AD 430 the import and use of coins seems to have ended.

The peoples who penetrated the Roman empire—Vandals, Visigoths, Lombards, Franks, Angles, and Saxons—soon began to issue their own currency. At first the coins imitated Roman specimens, often without understanding the originals, but later kings substituted their own names and images. In England, gold thrymsas and silver sceats appeared around AD 600, minted mainly at Canterbury and London. The earliest coins to be struck by an identifiable king came from the short-lived *Peada of Mercia (656). King *Ecgfrith of Northumbria had his name on coins soon after (670–85), and Northumbrian coins showed some artistic originality, with a recurrent griffin or dragon. In the 750s, Pepin assumed the kingship of the Franks and introduced a completely new silver coinage, using the Latin term 'denarius'. When this was borrowed by the English, they used the name penny but retained the symbol *d.*: twelve denarii made one solidus, and twenty solidi one pound or libra, giving the term £*s.d.*, which survived until decimalization in 1971. Within a few years *Offa of Mercia was issuing his own silver pennies, which were the main form of currency for the next 600 years. Offa's coinage was produced largely at Canterbury, by named moneyers, was more plentiful than before, and of higher artistic merit. Two subsequent advances were *Athelstan's claim on his coins to be 'Rex Totius Britanniae' from 927, his insistence on one coinage, and the extension of his mints to Exeter, Shrewsbury, Chester, and York. *Edgar carried out a great reform of the coinage (*c.*973), with a system for calling in worn coins for reissue and a large increase in the number of mints.

There was little alteration in the design of the silver penny in the two centuries following the Norman Conquest. Richard and John not only kept the basic design but retained the name of their predecessor Henry II on their coins. A continuing problem was that of change. With only one denomination, pennies were cut to provide halves and quarters. The **Anglo-Saxon Chronicle* reported in 1124 that a man who took a pound of pennies (240) to market might find only twelve accepted. Henry I resolved on drastic action the following year, summoned nearly 100 moneyers to Winchester, and mutilated many of them for shoddy work. The coinage was at its worst during the civil war of Stephen's reign, when rival coins circulated, many of them crude. Henry III in 1257 introduced a new gold coin worth 20 silver pennies, but it was undervalued and therefore melted down: after three years he was obliged to abandon it.

The later Middle Ages saw a great increase in trade, accompanied by larger quantities of coin in circulation, and a marked improvement in sophistication. Edward I carried out a grand recoinage in 1279–80, minting new coins, silver halfpennies and farthings, to remove the need to cut, and a fourpence groat, which was not at first successful. Quality was improved, a mint master appointed, and the London mint moved to the Tower. The innovation of Edward III's reign was the introduction in 1344 of gold coins—a florin (6 shillings), half-florin, and quarter-florin. They were augmented by nobles (80 silver pennies), half- and quarter-nobles. Representations became more interesting. The half-florin had a rather benign leopard (which gave the coin its popular name): the noble had an elaborate scene of Edward III, sword drawn, in a two-castled ship, perhaps commemorating his naval victory at *Sluys in 1340. The noble was replaced during the reign of Edward IV by a coin of the same value, a noble-angel, which had a representation of the archangel Michael. It was accompanied by a ryal (from French *royaux*), valued at 10 shillings and with a large Yorkist rose—hence its popular name, rose-noble.

Tudor coinage was marked by three features—fluctuations in the value of the currency; the introduction of a great number of new coins; and the appearance of lifelike representations of the monarchs. Despite the political upheavals of the previous decades, Henry VII inherited a stable currency and bequeathed a strong position to his successor. But Henry VIII's systematic debasement of the currency from 1526 onwards drove up prices. Elizabeth brought the situation under control with some difficulty, admitting that her recoinage of 1560 was 'bitter medicine'. The new coins included a magnificent golden sovereign by Henry VII in 1489 and a half-sovereign; a gold Crown of the Rose at 5 shillings by Henry VIII and a half-crown which settled down later as a silver coin and ran until the 20th cent.; and a George noble in 1526 on which the patron saint made his first appearance. Edward VI introduced a treble sovereign, sixpence, and threepence; Mary a half-groat; and Elizabeth a rather strange silver $1\frac{1}{2}$*d.* and $\frac{3}{4}$*d.* to facilitate change. Henry VII's silver shilling carried a good likeness of the king in profile, known as the testoon (from French *tête*). Henceforth the national coinage carried some remarkable portraits—Henry VIII aged on a Bristol groat (1544–7); Edward VI's silver shilling (1550–3); Philip and Mary's sixpence (1554–8); an imperious Elizabeth gold pound (1561–82); a stylish Charles I shilling (1638–9), and a saturnine Charles II crown (1663).

James I celebrated the union of his two kingdoms in 1604 with a gold crown called 'unite' or 'unit', bearing the title 'King of Great Britain' and the legend 'I will make them one people.' But a more important development of his reign was the introduction of copper coinage. Lord Harington in 1613 was given a patent to produce copper farthings, known colloquially as Haringtons, with an intermediate status between coins and tokens.

Charles I had a keen interest in art and before 1642 his coinage was of a high standard. The Civil War produced some desperate expedients, particularly 'siege-money', made out of any metal to hand and cut into strange shapes. The Commonwealth issued its own coinage, with inscriptions in English: one legend 'God with us' prompted cavaliers to the obvious retort that 'the Commonwealth was on one side and God on the other'. Good likenesses of Cromwell were produced but never issued.

As soon as he returned from his travels in 1660, Charles II tackled the question of the currency. The following year he ordered all coins to be mechanically produced and called in the Commonwealth issues. An innovation was the use of Guinea gold from Africa, which settled at 21 shillings and was called a guinea. The need for small change remained a problem and thousands of tradesmen's tokens circulated. To meet this, Charles introduced copper halfpennies and farthings in 1672: on the new coins, Britannia made her appearance for the first time. But one further step, in 1684, to bring in tin coins proved disastrous, since the metal oxidized rapidly.

Charles was also king of Scotland and of Ireland. The Scottish coinage dated from David I's reign in the early 12th cent. But the number of coins struck was small, there were mints only at Edinburgh, Berwick, and Roxburgh, and what circulation there was came from England. The Scottish coinage had much in common with the English, partly through direct imitation, partly because each copied continental, and especially French, designs. But Scottish coins had their own peculiarities. Their international standing was undermined in the 15th and 16th cents. by persistent debasement. In 1423 the English government forbade the circulation of Scottish coins and at the union of the crowns in 1603 the Scottish pound was fixed at only one-twelfth that of the English. The falling value of the Scottish currency derived in part from the practice of mixing silver with alloy to produce the base metal billon. One result was that Scotland had less trouble about small change than England. James I introduced a billon penny and halfpenny: James III followed with a billon plack (from French *plaque*) valued at first at threepence and later at sixpence, a half-plack, and a copper farthing (1466); in James V's reign the bawbee ($1\frac{1}{2}$*d.*) and half-bawbee were issued, and in Mary's the hardhead was issued to help 'the common people' buy bread, drink, flesh, and fish. The billon coinage was discontinued after 1603, but twopence pieces in copper called hardheads, bodles, or turners continued to be issued until the Act of Union.

The earliest known Irish coins were minted by Sihtric Olafsson in the Viking kingdom of Dublin after 990 and were copies of English silver pennies. The circulation was probably very limited. No regular coinage was issued until after the Norman Conquest when John introduced coins stamped with a harp. There were no gold coins and, as in Scotland, silver was heavily alloyed. By the reign of Edward IV there were mints at Dublin, Waterford, Wexford, Cork, Drogheda, Limerick, and Trim, though the English government would not permit a national currency. In the Tudor period the Irish coinage suffered great debasement, as did the Scots and English, fuelling inflation and damaging trade. In 1689 James II issued a bronze currency known as 'gun-money' which, after his defeat at the Boyne, was bought in at metal value—less than 3 per cent of its face value. The fury caused by *Wood's halfpence in 1723 had less to do with the coins, which were of respectable quality and good design, than the state of Anglo-Irish relations.

In Wales, no coins were struck until after the Norman invasion. Coin hoards have been found in Wales dating to the 9th, 10th, and 11th cents., but the coins were foreign, mainly English, Viking, or Arabic. *Hywel Dda's silver penny (*c.*940) was minted at Chester, copied an English coin, and may have been a presentation piece. Subsequent Welsh rulers do not seem to have produced their own coins and what circulated were English, though there were mints at Cardiff and Rhuddlan.

One persistent problem was the weight of coins and the hazard of transporting large quantities. Individual merchants and financiers had long issued personal bills of exchange, from which developed the cheque and the banknote—at first for special named customers, then for general use. The earliest extant cheque, dated 1659, is preserved in the Institute of Banking Library and is for £400. On 29 February 1668 *Pepys recorded sending his father a goldsmith's note for £600. Paper credit expanded rapidly and by the end of the 17th cent. it was calculated that England and Wales had £11.6 million circulating as coins, but tallies, banknotes, and bills worth £15 million. The Bank of England began issuing large-denomination printed notes in 1725 with, in effect, the credit of the government behind them. Nevertheless, many people preferred their local banks. Banknotes are still issued on the authority of the Bank of England and contain the comforting message from the chief cashier 'I promise to pay the bearer on demand the sum of . . . pounds'. Scotland retains its own banknotes which also circulate in the north of England.

At the time of the great recoinage of 1696 bimetallism was still the basis of the British currency, silver and gold providing the mainstay. Later in the 18th cent. declining production of silver made it excessively expensive and the currency went over to gold almost completely. When in turn gold became in short supply during the Revolutionary wars, the government declared banknotes to be legal tender. There was continuing difficulty about small change. Some of George III's copper coins ('cartwheels') were too heavy to be practicable since they were intended to contain their own value in copper. The result was that the country was again flooded with token coins, many of them accepted only in small areas.

Reorganization of the currency after the Napoleonic wars became a major political question and it was decided to go to one standard—gold. Silver tokens were prohibited in 1813 and copper tokens in 1818. The gold standard was retained, with increasing difficulty, until the economic crisis of 1931.

Four developments in the 20th cent. may be noted. Substantial inflation, particularly after the Second World War, caused several coins to be abandoned as their purchasing power dwindled: the farthing, beloved of haberdashers, was withdrawn in 1960, and the halfpenny, which survived decimalization in 1971, succumbed in 1984. Secondly, in 1971 the whole coinage was decimalized in preparation for Britain's entry into the EEC. Decimalization had been advocated as early as 1849 when the florin had been introduced as one-tenth of a pound. Thirdly, there was fierce debate in the 1990s whether Britain should join a European currency and, if so, what inscriptions the coins should bear. Fourthly, the spread of credit cards and electronic banking meant that coinage played a smaller part in financial transactions than in the past, heralding the day when money would be carried only for sundry purchases like sweets and newspapers. JAC

Brooke, G. C., *English Coins* (1932); Davies, G., *A History of Money: From Ancient Times to the Present Day* (Cardiff, 1994); Feavearyear, A., *The Pound Sterling: A History of English Money* (2nd edn. Oxford, 1963); Oman, C., *The Coinage of England* (Oxford, 1931); Sutherland, C. H. V., *English Coinage 600–1900* (1973).

Coke, Sir Edward (1552–1634). Lawyer, judge, and parliamentary figure unrivalled in his day. Coke was called to the bar in 1578 and quickly gained a considerable reputation. In 1592 he became recorder of London and later that year solicitor-general. In 1593 the queen appointed him Speaker of the House of Commons and then attorney-general. Coke conducted a number of famous prosecutions for the crown, with unfeeling harshness, including the trials of *Essex (1601), Sir Walter *Ralegh (1603), and the Gunpowder plot conspirators (1605). In 1606 he became chief justice of Common Pleas. Although no advocate of a monarch subject to Parliament, Coke held that the royal prerogative was defined by law and could not be arbitrarily extended, a fact which brought him frequently into conflict with the crown. In 1613 he was transferred to the King's Bench, a post with more prestige but less influence. Then in 1616 Coke was removed from office altogether on the charge that in his decisions he had introduced several things in derogation of the royal prerogative. In 1621 Coke re-entered Parliament where he opposed monopolies and denounced interference with the liberties of Parliament. His last major political act was his role in drafting the *Petition of Right in 1628. RAS

Coke, Thomas William, 1st earl of Leicester (1754–1842). 'Coke of Norfolk' was an assertively Whig MP for Norfolk for over 50 years; there were two short intervals, when political excitement overwhelmed his local influence as a large landowner. He is remembered as an agricultural improver. Especially on the sandy soils of north-western Norfolk, new crop rotations raised production: turnips (winter food for sheep) preceded grain, followed by sown grass (summer food for sheep) leading again to grain; sheep fertilized for wheat and barley. Publicity for Coke's work and his agricultural shows ('sheep shearings'), where tenants mingled with prominent radicals and Whigs, has caused neglect of the agricultural improvements of his great-uncle Thomas Coke (1697–1759), Viscount Lovell (1728) and earl of Leicester (1744), who followed earlier aristocratic fashions, collected humanistic manuscripts and Roman and Italian art, and patronized architecture, building *Holkham Hall. He profited from Walpolean Whig connections in government; Coke of Norfolk's popularity among his tenantry enabled him, by contrast, vigorously to oppose governmental influence. RACP

Colchester. First 'capital' of Roman Britain. Camulodunum was the site of the most important late Iron Age *oppidum* of southern Britain, seat of *Cunobelinus (Cymbeline). After its surrender in AD 43 a legionary fortress was planted, succeeded in 49 by a *colonia* of retired legionaries living in the former barracks. A temple to the deified Claudius was under construction when the entire town was burned to the ground in the first fury of the revolt of *Boudicca. Town and temple were reconstructed, the latter being one of the few in Britain in the fully Roman style. It was the seat of the imperial cult and *concilium provinciae* (provincial council) for all Britain, and associated with a theatre. Walls to demonstrate the status of the *colonia* were constructed early in the 2nd cent. The town developed as a prosperous regional seat, its houses sheltering a fine collection of late 2nd-cent. mosaics. In the 4th cent. the density of occupation declined, though a rare example of a Roman-period church has been found outside the south walls. Medieval legend claimed for the town Helena, mother of the Emperor *Constantine I, as a daughter of Old King Coel. ASEC

Cold War. The antagonism between the USA and USSR lasting from the late 1940s until the late 1980s, 'cold' because it was waged through diplomatic and ideological means rather than force. Britain was allied to the USA. Britain's role in the emergence of the Cold War is controversial. One view is that war-ravaged Britain was marginal to the development of frosty American–Soviet relations, and that her encouragement of a permanent US military presence in Europe was largely related to fears of German revival. Cultural differences and the repressive nature of the Soviet regime would, in any case, have made lasting co-operation between the USSR, Britain, and the USA impossible. But others attach blame to Britain. Rather than seeking a 'third force Europe' or acting as a bridge between the USA and USSR, *Attlee's foreign secretary Ernest *Bevin (aided by *Churchill whose 1946 'iron curtain' speech had a great impact in America) pursued a policy of fanning the flames of anti-Soviet paranoia in Washington in order to obtain US financial aid and military presence in Europe, this giving Britain the resources to attempt to sustain her empire. The Cold War came to an end with the collapse of Soviet power, largely as a result of its intervention in Afghanistan, and its progress towards democracy. CNL

Coldstream Guards. The regiment is one of the oldest in the British army having been raised by *Cromwell for General *Monck in 1650. Their name derives from their march south in 1660 from Coldstream, on the Scottish border, to London where Monck helped to restore the monarchy. RAS

Colenso, John (1814–83). Bishop of *Natal. A Cornishman, Colenso was educated at St John's College, Cambridge, where he became mathematics fellow (1842–6). Originally an evangelical, he became, partly under F. D. *Maurice's influence, a naïve radical. As first bishop of Natal (from 1853), his over-simplistic *Commentary on the Epistle to the Romans* (1861) and *Pentateuch* (1862–70) dismayed Liberals and played into Conservative hands. Bishop Gray of Cape Town, his metropolitan, deposed him (1863). When the Privy Council annulled his deposition (1865), Colenso was warmly welcomed back. Gray nevertheless publicly excommunicated him (1866) and appointed a successor. Colenso continued his successful Zulu ministry, creating a schism that lasted until 1911. He publicly supported the Zulus before and after their resounding victory over British troops at *Isandhlwana (1879). He wrote a Zulu grammar, an English–Zulu dictionary, and a Zulu translation of the New Testament. His support of Cetewayo and the Zulus was worthier than his unwise sortie into theology. WMM

Coleridge, Samuel Taylor (1772–1834). Poet and polymath whose collaboration with *Wordsworth laid the foundations for English Romanticism. Their *Lyrical Ballads* (1798) opened with his 'Rime of the Ancient Mariner' and, although relations became strained, Coleridge's initial contribution cannot be gainsaid. Dogged by ill-health and self-doubt, his poetic career was brief and littered with unfulfilled projects: the incomplete 'Christabel'; 'Kubla Khan' famously interrupted by 'a person from Porlock'. As literary critic, if not the originator of the philosophical method he aspired to in *Biographia literaria* (1817), he gives a subtler account of language and morality than his predecessors. The charge of plagiarism from Schlegel, Schelling, and the German Idealists cannot be dismissed by his airy confidence that 'Truth is a divine ventriloquist', but there is a continuity in his thought from before his visit to Germany in 1798, when Immanuel Kant was still 'utterly unintelligible'. Though no friend to *Pitt's ministry, his 'baby trumpet of sedition' was already muted, and the political journalism of the *Watchman* (1796) and the *Friend* (1809) depended on 'placing the questions of the day in a moral point of view'. His last substantial work, *On the Constitution of Church and State* (1830), finds him staunchly defending them as 'two poles of the same magnet'. JNRS

Colet, John (1467–1519). Colet, a cleric and educator, was born in London as the eldest child of Sir Henry Colet, mercer and twice mayor of the city, and his wife Christian Knyvet. After schooling in London, he probably attended Cambridge University before travelling to Paris and Orléans, and to Italy. He was in Rome in 1493, and perhaps in Florence: certainly he read intensively the Florentine Platonists Marsilio Ficino and Pico della Mirandola. About 1496 Colet began to teach in Oxford, gaining a reputation for his exposition of the meaning and application to life of the Pauline Epistles as well as studying the Neoplatonist Pseudo-Dionysius and the Genesis account of creation. Colet's piety and eloquence impressed Erasmus from their first meeting in 1499; he was later Erasmus' patron and helper. As dean of St Paul's from 1505 to his death of the sweating sickness in 1519, Colet refounded and endowed St Paul's School (1509), making the Mercers its trustees. Erasmus advised him on its curriculum and in his *On the Basis of Study* (1511) characterized its Christian-humanist orientation; he also wrote for it pious, grammatical, and rhetorical handbooks. Colet's austerity and high-mindedness led him into conflict with his cathedral clergy. A forthright disputant, and powerful preacher to court and convocation, he was also from 1516—before Thomas *More—a member of the king's council. His works remained in manuscript almost completely until they were edited in the 19th cent. JBT

College of Arms. Established in 1484 by Richard III to bring order into the approval of heraldic designs. Garter king-of-arms has precedence though his concerns are mainly with his order. Clarenceux king-of-arms looks after the area south of the Trent, Norroys king-of-arms the area north and Ulster. There are also six heralds and four pursuivants, under the overall control of the earl marshal. Scottish heraldry is the responsibility of the Lyon Office under Lord Lyon king-of-arms, assisted by three heralds and three pursuivants. The office of Lord Lyon descends from that of Sennachie, bard to the ancient Celtic kings of Scotland. JAC

Collingwood, Cuthbert, 1st Baron (1750–1810). The Newcastle upon Tyne-born Collingwood had no influence behind him, unlike *Nelson, when he joined the navy in 1761; and again, unlike Nelson, with whom he was on terms of close friendship, Collingwood only obtained a captaincy when he was 30. The friends were strongly contrasted in temperament and physique, and Collingwood's reserve, which in fact concealed strong sensitivities, was very different from Nelson's transparent quality. A common devotion to the service excluded rancour when Collingwood succeeded Nelson in no less than three of their earliest commands in the Caribbean; and a shared experience cemented an association which continued through correspondence during their years ashore 1786–93. In dauntless courage Collingwood was unquestionably Nelson's equal, but a natural stoicism assisted Collingwood to more balanced judgements. Present at the *'Glorious First of June' battle 1794, and, pre-eminently, at *Cape St Vincent in February 1797, Collingwood ruefully accepted not being within Nelson's command which resulted in victory at the *Nile; and admiral rank only came in February 1799. At *Trafalgar Collingwood commanded the lee division in *Royal Sovereign*, devastatingly opening the action at midday, the most resplendent hour of his life, and taking command of the fleet on Nelson's death at 4.30 p.m. Raised to the peerage, the overworked Collingwood died at sea in March 1810, but was buried close to Nelson in St Paul's. DDA

Collins, Michael (1890–1922). Collins is the best-known 20th-cent. Irish revolutionary leader, a template for guerrillas, and has been very romanticized. From a west Cork farming background, he moved to London at 15, and was active among exiled nationalists. He played a background role in Dublin during the *Easter Rising. After internment, through an agency of *Irish Republican Brotherhood, Collins became the key figure in the reorganized Irish Volunteers/*Irish Republican Army. As director of IRA intelligence, he infiltrated all agencies of British rule in Ireland. Against his will, he was a negotiator at the Anglo-Irish conference of October–December 1921, revealing his pragmatism by signing the *Anglo-Irish treaty. As chairman of provisional government January–June 1922, Collins uneasily presided over the establishment of the new state while striving to appease anti-treaty former colleagues. British insistence on the treaty terms led to his ordering the Dublin Four Courts attack in June 1922, beginning the civil war. While visiting pro-treaty troops as commander-in-chief and searching for a basis for peace, he was killed in a west Cork ambush on 22 August 1922. Rumour and speculation have since run riot on the circumstances of his death. Lately debate has centred on what Collins might have contributed to Ireland had he lived. Undoubtedly the pro-treaty side lost its most charismatic figure and the Northern Ireland government its most fervent opponent. MAH

Colonial Office. The changes in the status and structure of the Colonial Office mirror fairly closely the vicissitudes of the British empire. For most of the 17th cent., while the American colonies were being established, there was no coordinating body at Westminster. The Privy Council exercised what supervision there was through a series of committees or councils, but distance and the chartered status of most of the colonies made control fitful. Not until 1696 was a Board of Trade and Plantations established under a president, working through the Privy Council. By 1768 the state of the American colonies was causing concern and a third secretaryship was created for the colonies, usually known as the American secretary. By 1782, with the rebellious colonies almost gone, both the third secretaryship and the Board of Trade were abolished, though the latter was revived in 1786. Colonial affairs went to the home secretary. In 1794, as part of the government reshuffle when the *Portland Whigs joined *Pitt, a third secretaryship was re-established under Henry *Dundas, with responsibility for war and the colonies. Indian affairs meanwhile fell to the Board of Control, set up in 1784. These rather makeshift arrangements sufficed until 1854, by which time the second British empire was growing, and a fourth secretary of state with special responsibility for the colonies was created. This was a powerful cabinet post, especially when held by men of the calibre of *Granville (1868–70, 1886) or Joseph *Chamberlain (1895–1903). A further reorganization took place in 1925 when a new Dominions Office was created with its own secretary of state. The extraordinarily rapid decolonization in the 1960s left the Colonial Office with few territories to administer. The secretaryship was abolished in 1966 and the Colonial Office merged with the Commonwealth Relations Office. They were both integrated into the Foreign Office in October 1968. JAC

Colquhoun, Patrick (1745–1820). Born in Dundee, his career was almost entirely in business, although he became lord provost of Glasgow (1782–3) and city magistrate in London (1792–1818). He is best known for his *Wealth, Power and Resources of the British Empire* (1814). In this he provided estimates of national income; this was an influence upon socialist writers since Colquhoun claimed that unproductive labour, estimated as 20 per cent of the labour force, received over 30 per cent of the output. As a social reformer he was concerned with poor relief and with policing in London. He believed that poverty could be removed by better standards of education. His pamphlet *New and Appropriate System of Education for the Labouring People* (1806) was extremely influential at that time. JRP

Columba, St (d. 597). Founder, in 565, of the monastery of *Iona, which contributed to conversion in Northumbria, Mercia, and Pictland. Born between 519 and 522 into the Cenél Conaill of Donegal branch of the northern royal Uí Néill, Columba had founded Derry in the 550s and possibly Durrow and Kells before his condemnation at the Synod of Teltown (Co. Meath), for involvement in the battle of Cúl Drebene (561), prompted him to be pilgrim-exile in the southern part of *Dalriada, where King Conall gave him Iona (574). Columba's major concern was the pastoral needs of Dalriada, but his visits to King Bridei facilitated 7th-cent. foundations in east Pictland. Revered in his foundations and their offshoots, including *Lindisfarne, he was belittled by *Wilfrid in debate at *Whitby (664). This perhaps prompted Abbot Cumméne the White to compose a (lost) biography, used by *Adomnán. Columba may have instigated the royal conference of Drumceat (Druim Cett) (575) which considered constitutional relations of the people of Irish Dalriada, with their king in Scotland, and with the Uí Néill high king. His political eminence may explain why he was regarded as one whose prayers gained victory for favoured kings, including *Oswald. His crozier and a psalter associated with him were, later, taken into battle. His relics were translated *c.*849, to *Dunkeld (Perthshire) in Pictland, and to Kells. AER

Columbanus, St (*c.*543–615). Born in Leinster (Ireland), Columbanus entered religious life as a young man. Fired with missionary zeal, he left the monastery at Bangor *c.*590 with twelve companions. His request to settle in the wastelands of Burgundy granted, he established monastic centres at Annegray, Luxeuil, and Fontaines. He greatly influenced the spread of monasticism in Gaul, attracting many followers. But adhering to Celtic traditions such as the dating of Easter, he provoked Frankish bishops whose authority he would not recognize, and whilst accepting the primacy of the papal see, he refused to conform with Roman practices. Driven out of Burgundy in 610 by Queen Brunhilde for criticizing her grandson's immorality, Columbanus worked briefly near Bregenz before settling in Lombardy, founding his great monastic centre at Bobbio, where he died. His rule reveals an extremely severe discipline and detailed penal code. AM

Combination Acts, 1799–1800. These Acts were directed against trade unions (combinations of workmen) when the government feared unrest and even revolution. Combinations were in fact already illegal under both common law and statute; the Acts were intended to simplify and speed up prosecution by summary trial. The Acts failed to crush the unions, consisting mainly of skilled artisans, but did force them to operate circumspectly or secretly. Repeal of the Acts came in 1824–5 after a campaign master-minded by *Place and presented by Joseph *Hume, and was followed by an immediate upsurge in trade union activity. JFCH

comics form the branch of the press and periodicals industry generally seen as providing children's entertainment. In their early days though, in the 18th and 19th cents., comics were very much an adult affair, often at the cutting edge of political reform struggles. Early examples include the satirical caricatures of *Hogarth, *Gillray, *Rowlandson, and *Cruikshank, often gathered together in 'strips' (with Rowlandson's Dr Syntax becoming one of the first cartoon heroes), or published in monthly magazines, such as the *Comick Magazine* (1796).

Influenced by European publications, broadsheet or tabloid 'picture sheets' appeared through the 19th cent., such as the *Glasgow Looking Glass* (1825); with the most famous satirical magazine **Punch* starting in 1841, and its later rival *Judy* (1867) launching the most popular Victorian cartoon character Ally Sloper.

The standard 'comic' format was pioneered by James Henderson's *Funny Folks* (1874), an eight-page black-and-white tabloid weekly mixing text and pictures and selling for 1 penny. This format was exploited by Alfred *Harmsworth, whose turn of the century Amalgamated Press revolution included the launch of the most successful of all comics, the half penny *Comic Cuts* (1890), with the perennially popular Weary Willie and Tired Tim. As part of the 'half penny boom', more comics offered sections for children, leading to a pre-First World War 'golden age' with comics like the *Rainbow*, and popular characters like Tiger Tim and the Bruin Boys. 'Twopenny coloureds' tended to be favoured by middle-class parents, while 'Penny Blacks' were the choice of the working-class reader. A famous entrant to the comic market in the 1930s was Dundee's D. C. Thomson, with the *Beano* and the *Dandy* gaining lasting popularity, while Amalgamated Press's *Film Fun* (1920), and *Mickey Mouse Weekly* (1930) showed the early influence of the cinema.

The comics industry was revolutionized from the 1930s and 1940s with the popularity of American 'comic books', especially Action Comics' superheroes such as Batman. A post-war 'moral panic' over some of the more lurid horror imports led to a temporary ban on US products, and a resurgence of the wholesome British tradition in *Eagle* (1950) and *Lion* (1952). The main phenomenon of the 1980s was the return of the 'adult' comic, with the success of the broad comedy of *Viz*, and the politically and ideologically complex world of *2000 A.D.* and *Judge Dredd*, reminding the public that comics were not just for kids. DJA

'commercial revolution'. This preceded major industrialization by two centuries and encompassed great upsurges in overseas trade with many consequences, not least the expansion of Britain's fleet. Essentially an English phenomenon, later the Scots were also heavily engaged. Trade experienced three long periods of growth, separated by virtual stagnation. Between 1475 and 1550 existing markets for English broadcloths and other woollens grew rapidly, because the importing regions became more prosperous and had greater purchasing power. In the second period, 1630–89, two general circumstances aided expansion. South European markets, previously the domain of Spanish and Italian industry, were won by the English and the Dutch in competition with one another. The second general circumstance was the rise of virtually new trades because cheaper English re-exports of sugar, tobacco, and calicoes created fresh markets. The third period, 1730–60, was linked to the growth of American and West Indian populations, production, and purchasing power, but also continued the advance of re-exports.

In the first period English woollen cloth exports were the bulwark of overseas trade, the wool trade declining sharply in the decade after 1510. In a period of inflation the quantity of cloth exported more than doubled by 1550; London gained at the expense of provincial ports, as trade with Antwerp grew and was controlled by the Company of *Merchant Venturers. Interruptions to the Antwerp trade caused by wars gradually brought this phase of growth to a halt, although English merchants trading with Hamburg accessed central European markets via the Elbe. Another change after 1580, the revival of some provincial ports, also resulted from the collapse of the Antwerp entrepôt trade.

The second expansion in the 17th cent. can be largely attributed to the growth of exports to southern Europe. Demand suddenly increased in Spain and was then supplemented from Portugal and Italy. The northern trade declined in relative importance, and by 1700 accounted for only half of English cloth exports compared with nine-tenths in the early 17th cent. Light cloths or 'New Draperies' were attractive to these markets and increasingly beat

Dutch competition, as English labour costs provided a cardinal advantage to these manufactures. Trade with Iberia also reached the Spanish and Portuguese colonies and thus the market was enlarged. The English cloth industry responded rapidly to changes in fashion and produced a greater variety of light cloths and textile mixtures. A substantial trade in salted and dried cod from the Grand Banks of Newfoundland was an additional source of exports to catholic Europe.

Several new imports in the period 1500–1750 provided exceptional profit margins and an incentive to exploration and mercantile enterprise. In the 16th cent. the chief imports were luxuries, especially French wine, but in the following century Spain and Portugal became important suppliers. Apart from wine, most imports were manufactures, bought in the Netherlands but produced in many parts of Europe. The gradual growth of British industry reduced the dependence on foreign manufactures in the 17th cent. One exception was European linens until the Scots and the Irish, protected by the *Navigation Laws and a rising tariff wall, learned to copy and outdo continental producers during the 18th cent. Trade with the Baltic, mainly conducted in the 16th and early 17th cents. via the Netherlands, became more direct, first because of the activities of the *Eastland Company (1579) and secondly because its profitability encouraged interlopers. In years of bad harvests Baltic corn was a standby, but after 1650 new raw materials were much more important. Amounts of timber, potash, tar, pitch, flax, and hemp increased as the navy and merchant marine grew, and Swedish iron also became important after 1650. From the Mediterranean came not only more wine but also wool, oil, raisins, figs and oranges, Italian silks, and Levant goods, including raw silk, mohair, cotton, and dyestuffs.

Trade with countries beyond Europe, insignificant before the Civil War, grew rapidly by 1700 when America and Asia accounted for a third of England's imports, and re-exports for nearly a third of all exports. The discoveries that Virginia could grow tobacco plants imported from Trinidad and that Brazilian sugar cane would flourish in the West Indies were fundamental to the later development of the Atlantic economy and of the triangular trade with Africa. The *East India Company (1600) began trading principally in pepper and then in cotton cloth; both tapped markets in Britain and Europe. Trade in slaves, sugar, coffee, tobacco, pepper, and oriental cottons underpinned the third great era of expansion in the 18th cent. before industrialization had proceeded far, America and the West Indies being much the most buoyant trading partners. Liverpool, Bristol, and Glasgow benefited most from these developments.

The Atlantic trade was controlled by merchant partnerships. If journeys were long or large capitals were required, the company form of organization was preferable. Once trade was established—even when companies claimed trading monopolies—the return to trading by partnerships was general. The *Russia Company (1555), the *Levant Company (1581), and the *Royal Africa Company (1672) all succumbed to this pattern; only the *Hudson's Bay Company (1670) retained control over its territory. The East India Company also survived and was much the most important in terms of trade and capital employed, but there were abortive attempts to displace it after 1698. In the 18th cent. it was markedly on the defensive, a highly profitable anachronism.

The 'commercial revolution' was important for its effects upon the British economy and the British state. It was buttressed by protective mercantilism, especially by the navigation laws; its result was the accumulation of capital from foreign trade and ultimately lower rates of interest than might have prevailed without this expansion. Foreign produce brought profits to distributors involved in inland trade. Merchant investment in land was probably more important than capital flows to industry, but the growth of London was exceptional in Europe. Pressure for domestic improvement was a major consequence of Britain's growing affluence, as her industries became increasingly attached to the international economy. JB

Committee of Articles (Lords of the Articles). A steering committee of the Scottish Parliament, dating back to the 15th cent. It prepared business and drafted legislation, each estate having equal representation. The royal government had strong influence over the committee and Parliament was given little opportunity for debate or dissent. In 1640 the committee was abolished, restored in 1660, and finally dismantled in 1690 after the *Glorious Revolution. JAC

Commius was a Gallic noble who allied himself with Julius *Caesar and was rewarded with the kingship of the Gallic *Atrebates. In 55 BC he was sent by Caesar to win over British tribes prior to the invasion, but was taken prisoner. Released at the end of the 55 BC invasion, he participated in the 54 BC invasion and was intermediary when *Cassivellaunus sued for terms. In 52 BC he sided with the revolt of Vercingetorix in Gaul, and on his defeat fled to Britain founding a new dynasty of the Atrebates in the Berkshire/north Hampshire area. ASEC

common law. The origins of the common law lay in the justice of the king, exercised through his *curia regis, rather than the customary law exercised in the old communal courts of shire and hundred, or the feudal law exercised by the lord in relation to his own vassals, free and unfree. In the reign of Henry I the justice of the king in his curia was sometimes invoked in favour of a subject, though justice was usually to be sought in the communal or feudal courts.

As overlord of all subjects, the king had a residual right to give justice to all, and as feudal lord of the tenants-in-chief he had the right and the duty to sit in his curia regis to hear their disputes, or to deal with matters relating to their feudal duties. Until the reign of Henry II, royal justice was available to subjects who were not tenants-in-chief only in exceptional cases, since the proper court for matters relating to land or tenure was the court of one's lord and other matters were the province of the court of shire or hundred. However, in the reign of Henry II, access to the king's justice was extended by the enactment of a principle that 'no man need answer for his freehold land without the king's writ being obtained'. As a result, the writ of right patent would issue to the lord ordering him to hear the case between his free tenants; where there was a dispute between tenants in chief, the alternative 'praecipe' form of the writ of right would be issued, ordering the defendant to return the disputed land or to appear before the king's justices to explain his refusal. Further, through the development of the Grand *Assize and the petty assizes, disputants over land would have their case tried by an inquest of neighbours who gave a verdict on oath before the royal justices. As these royal writs and particularly the petty assizes became popular with litigants, so they increasingly sought the justice of the king's courts rather than the local or feudal courts, which slowly declined. This decline was caused by a number of factors, legal, social, and economic, but the influence of royal justice and the effectiveness of its procedures (e.g. petty assizes, trial by jury) led inexorably to the decline of rival systems of justice and the triumph of the king's justice or, as it came to be known, the common law.

The king's justice was dispensed by the itinerant justices of the curia regis and gradually the principles and procedures of the king's law grew from their practice, drawing on the customs of different areas of the country. When the courts of Common Pleas, King's Bench, and Exchequer developed as separate entities, the law they applied was the common law. By the time of Edward I there was in existence a 'common law'—the law administered in the king's courts throughout the land and therefore 'common' to the whole kingdom.

The term 'common law' came to be used of the English legal system and, generally, to describe a system where the law is built up through the decisions of the courts. Hence it is used to describe the legal systems of former colonies such as the majority of the USA and the member countries of the Commonwealth, which share the common law tradition. The term is also used to describe those rules and principles of law which are based upon the decisions of the courts as distinct from the rules and remedies which were applied in the Court of Chancery. Finally the term is used to describe rules of law which have been established by the courts as against laws which are formally enacted by Parliament (statute law). MM

Common Market. See EUROPEAN ECONOMIC COMMUNITY.

Common Pleas, Court of. One of the three courts of common law. The Court of Common Pleas was an offshoot of the *curia regis, the court which followed the king on his travels around the country. The insistence of *Magna Carta led to a court being established in one place, clause 17 stating that 'Common Pleas shall not follow the king but be heard in some fixed place'. The court was based at Westminster Hall and decided controversies concerning civil cases between the king's subjects, cases involving claims to land, trespass, and debt. It kept its own records known as the *de Banco* rolls and in 1272 was given its own chief justice. In the Middle Ages it was the busiest of the common law courts and the most lucrative for the judges and early members of the legal profession who practised there. Over the centuries this position declined as other courts encroached on its jurisdiction and poached its cases. In the Judicature Act of 1873 the Court of Common Pleas along with the courts of Queen's Bench and Exchequer all became divisions of the High Court of Justice. Ultimately, they were all merged into the Queen's Bench Division in 1880. RAS

Commons, House of. From modest beginnings, the House of Commons has progressed until it shares effective sovereignty with the prime minister. Commoners were summoned to Parliament at first less for their advice than for their consent to taxation. Knights of the shire were first called to Parliament in 1254 and in Simon de *Montfort's Parliament of 1265 they were joined by representatives from certain boroughs and cities. They were not necessarily summoned to every parliament at first, and might be dismissed before the Parliament ended, or held back for separate discussions. Early usage was extremely fluid, with committees and groups joining for plenary sessions. From the early 14th cent. the Commons began to meet as a separate house, usually in the chapter house of the abbey of Westminster. The knights stayed with the citizens rather than joining the baronage, with whom they had much in common, adding great weight to the Commons house. The lesser clergy, who had been represented in some of the early parliaments, dropped out after 1340 and used *convocation, making it easier for the Commons to cohere as a body.

The Commons soon began to act as a channel for receiving petitions and took the lead in legislating to remove grievances. Their chief weapon was control of taxation and as early as 1395 the formula was in use that the grant was made 'by the Commons with the advice and assent of the Lords'. The principle of elective representation stood them in good stead in relation to both the crown and the Lords. At an early stage members took refuge in the reply that they must consult their constituents. The crown could and did intervene in elections and could create new parliamentary boroughs but its influence over the Lords was even more direct by the creation of peers. During the 18th and 19th cents. the House of Commons, through the prime minister, seized this prerogative and used it to bring the Lords to heel.

The use of Parliament by the Tudors to regulate the succession to the throne and to reform the church enhanced the standing of that body. Two further developments helped to confirm the Commons' identity. In 1547 they were granted St Stephen's chapel as their meeting place and stayed there until the great fire of 1834. At the same time, the House began a formal record of its own proceedings, the *Journals of the House of Commons*.

The result of the great struggles of the 17th cent. was to increase the power of the Commons at the expense of the Lords. Indeed, when the Commons in 1649 galloped out of control, Lords and monarchy were abolished as 'dangerous and useless'. Though the pendulum swung back after 1660, the strengthened position of Parliament after 1688 helped the Commons, particularly by limiting the power of the crown to govern without Parliament or to retain a complaisant Parliament. This helped to neutralize the advantage that lords had, that they could lobby the monarch through the court and their privilege of direct audience.

In addition the Commons reasserted its sole right to decide matters of taxation. Though the House of Lords retained considerable influence, the balance was further affected by the extensions of the franchise from 1832 onwards, which increased the Commons' claim to speak for the nation, and by a slow loss of faith in the hereditary principle. JAC

The starting-point of any discussion of the modern House of Commons is two related features—the near dominance of the executive and the ever-present power of the political parties. Romantic parliamentarianism looks back to a golden age in the mid-19th cent. that probably never was—the age of the private member.

Among the functions of the House of Commons, that of legislation would be given pride of place. But legislation bears the stamp of the executive, especially of the bureaucracy, rather than that of the Commons. Most important bills are introduced by the government of the day, which reflects both the privileges accorded in fact, if not always in name, to the government in the procedures of the House, and the quasi-monopoly of knowledge enjoyed by the executive. Popular criticism of the modern role of the House of Commons focuses on the alleged rigour of party control over the backbenchers, exercised through the whips, and tends to overlook the advantage the executive would have, even if the House were composed of 659 genuinely independent members.

Note first the long-standing rule that increases in taxation and expenditure can be imposed only on the proposal of the crown. Any private member who sponsors a bill that would increase public expenditure must either obtain the backing of the government or impose the new duties on local councils. More recent procedural changes allocate most of the time of the House to the government, an arrangement which rests ultimately on the government's control of its majority. Private members are allotted ten days a year for the discussion of their bills and the privilege of being awarded a day is decided by ballot. If a member's bill is controversial, there will be an attempt to 'talk it out'. If, at the end of the allotted time, the member seeks to move the closure, he faces two hurdles. The Speaker may think that the measure has not been adequately debated and may refuse to accept the motion: if a motion is accepted, it may not be passed by the numbers required—a majority, with at least 100 members voting in that majority. Lacking the organization of the whips' office, the backbencher may simply not be able to ensure the attendance of 100 supporters; and if it passes this test but faces obstruction in standing committee, he will not, as the government can, be able to propose and carry a guillotine motion to limit the time spent debating his bill.

A second element of the strength of the executive in and over the House of Commons lies in its near monopoly of knowledge. Ministers are backed by an experienced and informed department: the backbencher has only his personal resources. Moreover, the way in which the House of Commons deals with legislation deprives it of the information it might have to counter the accumulated wisdom of the department. The principle of the bill is debated by the whole House, normally at second or third reading, but the detail of the bill is discussed in standing committee. These standing committees are neither permanent in composition nor specialist in subject-matter. Members may indeed have knowledge derived in their personal capacity but they do not through their work on bills develop a corpus of information to match that available to ministers. In the 1960s, the House made fitful attempts to form specialized select committees to inquire into particular areas of government activity, and these arrangements were extended, systematized, and made permanent in 1979. Service on these select committees certainly makes for more informed backbenchers. But the select committees do not themselves examine legislation: this remains the province of the transient and unspecialized standing committees.

The third feature is party loyalty and party organization. Virtually every member (bar the Speaker) is elected as the candidate of a party, and members most of the time vote in the House with their party. The cohesion of parties in the division lobbies of the House dates from the 1890s and reached its peak in the 1950s. Since 1966 there has been a perceptible decline in party cohesion, but conformity rather than rebellion remains the most prominent feature of backbench life.

Many explanations have been offered for the strength of party cohesion in the British Parliament. The whips have the task of mobilizing their party's backbenchers: popular mythology ascribes to them powers beyond their reach. The whips cannot in themselves deny reselection to a dissident member, though withdrawal of the whip, itself rare, can rouse difficulties with the member's constituency association. In both parties the hope of office, and in the Conservative Party the thirst for honours, may prompt the potential rebel back into line, bearing out the truth of Napoleon's observation that 'men are governed by baubles'. Members, most of the time, follow the party line, in voting if not in debate. But such behaviour usually poses no strain on a member's conscience. Most of the time the House is debating humdrum questions on which many members are uninformed. When the division-bell rings, members stream into the House, many having heard not a word of the debate, and ask the whips, 'Which is our lobby?' Sanctions, threats, and rewards become important on the great dramatic issues. But most of the time the House is not witnessing drama, but an ill-attended tedious ritual of claim and counter-claim.

Nevertheless, ministers do sometimes give way to disquiet voiced on the floor of the House; more often, they yield to the importunities of their backbenchers expressed through party committees or behind-the-scenes deputations. When the government has a narrow majority, the discontents of small groups of backbenchers will be listened to even more attentively.

The government then is the dominant force in the legislation passed by the House. But in exercising these and other powers it is accountable to the House. Traditionally this accountability has been exercised most obviously through question time, an hour set aside four days a week. The value of question time, however, is greatly exaggerated. The ordinary process of debate is another way in which members can highlight blunders, abuse of power, or mismanagement. But members may well be inhibited from embarrassing a minister of their own party by the delight it affords their opponents. The sanction against ministerial, or indeed departmental, incompetence is supposed to be that ministers who fail to convince the House of their competence and integrity will be obliged to resign, but the doctrine of individual ministerial responsibility is more myth than reality.

Today, the select committees, with all their limitations, are becoming the chief means by which ministers are made accountable to the House. Even though they do not debate legislation, they enable the House to scrutinize the work of the departments, and the publicity given to their reports is a salutary check upon ministerial evasion and bureaucratic complacency. HB

Commonwealth. The Commonwealth took its origins from a vote by the *Rump Parliament on 4 January 1649, four weeks after *Pride's Purge, 'That the people are, under God, the original of all just power', and that they, the Commons, possessed supreme authority as the people's representatives. Two days later they set up the High Court of Justice which tried and sentenced Charles I. The abolition of the monarchy and the House of Lords followed, and another brief Act on 19 May formally declared England to be a Commonwealth. From February, executive authority was vested in a *Council of State, accountable to the Rump, elected annually by it, and drawn mainly from its own members. The army's general council of officers adopted and presented a written constitution called an *Agreement of the People (the second such), after modifying parts of it; it provided for biennial single-chamber parliaments, elected on a broad franchise by radically reformed constituencies. But the *Levellers, who were part-authors of the agreement and resented the officers' tampering with it, wrecked any chances of its acceptance by denouncing the Commonwealth as a new tyranny and raising a serious mutiny in the army. In face of this and other threats, including Scotland's proclamation of King Charles II, the Rump shelved the agreement and forgot its promises of early elections. Enlarged by many newly readmitted members who had held aloof from the act of regicide, it settled into a more prolonged and conservative regime than the army had ever envisaged. It fought shy of reforms that might add to the Commonwealth's already disturbing unpopularity and restricted religious toleration with a Blasphemy Act, though it repealed the laws which compelled attendance at parish worship.

The Commonwealth expanded to include Scotland and Ireland after the army's conquest of those countries. Its foreign policy became expansive too, and the *Navigation Act of 1651, which challenged Dutch domination of the carrying trade, was one factor that led it into war with the United Provinces in 1652. This dismayed *Cromwell, whose ideal was a united protestant interest in Europe. The Rump's materialist outlook and evident aversion to 'a godly reformation' brought it under increasing pressure from the army during 1652 to make way for a successor. Eventually it did introduce a bill for a new parliament to meet in November 1653, but its contents (which do not survive) left the army unsatisfied, and Cromwell in a rage expelled the Rump on 20 April. The brief experiment of a nominated assembly (*'Barebone's Parliament', July–December 1653) ended in its own abdication, and on 16 December the Commonwealth gave way to the Cromwellian *Protectorate.

It was briefly restored in May 1659, after a coup by the army against Richard *Cromwell, but renewed quarrels between the officers and the Rumpers soon exposed the political bankruptcy of both. Republicanism had struck few roots in England, and General *Monck was enthusiastically acclaimed when he opened the way to the Restoration by readmitting the members 'secluded' in Pride's Purge on 21 February 1660. AHW

Commonwealth of Nations. The husk of the old *British empire, an accidental by-product of history. The only thing its member states apart from Britain have in common is that they were once her colonies. Not all her ex-colonies are members: the future USA for example liberated themselves before the idea was thought of; some colonies, like *Burma and *British Somaliland, declined to join from the beginning; and the *Irish Free State, *South Africa, and *Pakistan were once members but later (in 1949, 1961, and 1972 respectively) left. Nevertheless the present Commonwealth comprises Britain and most of her old empire: around 50 states at the last count, scattered over all the inhabited continents, with a total area of 11 million square miles and a population estimated (in 1994) at 1.4 billion.

The term 'commonwealth', in this context, dates from the turn of the century, and grew out of the realization that already several of Britain's older-established colonies were self-governing in all essential respects. To call them 'colonies', or collectively an 'empire', appeared to undervalue their real independence, and the new word was felt by some to express better the form the empire would take: a union or federation of equal nation states, united for the common good of the whole. An important catalyst for this transformation was the *First World War. This had the dual effect of reminding the *dominions of their continued subjugation to Britain in some ways—when George V committed the whole empire to the war it was without formal consultation with them—while at the same time emphasizing their importance and sense of individual national identity. By the time the next world war came around, each dominion was allowed to decide for itself whether it would join in. (Canada, Australia, and New Zealand were generous with their contributions; South Africa, many of whose whites felt more affinity with the Nazis, less so.) This development was not to everyone's liking, however. Enthusiasts for the 'commonwealth ideal' had generally seen it as a means by which the dominions might take an equal share in the formulation of policies that would then be common to them all. Instead it took an entirely different turn, and came to mean that they would have equal rights to separate policies of their own.

This privilege was established in the early 1920s, after disputes within the Commonwealth over the Washington naval conference of 1921–2 and the *Chanak affair in 1922. In 1923 Canada became the first dominion to conclude a treaty with a foreign power (the Halibut Fish treaty) without reference to Britain; and the pattern for the future—of independent partnership—was set. It was formalized by an important pronouncement of the 1926 imperial conference, defining dominion status; and by the 1931 statute of *Westminster, which confirmed the dominions' legislative autonomy. For the moment this only applied to colonies of European settlement (the full list at that time was Canada, Newfoundland, Australia, New Zealand, Eire, and South Africa), and not to the 'non-white' colonies. That changed in 1947, when the newly independent nation of India was admitted to the Commonwealth. That established the character of the 'multiracial' Commonwealth as it exists today.

As *decolonization progressed, the other ex-colonies followed. Most old imperialists regarded this process with pride. Some of them indeed saw the new Commonwealth as the culmination of the empire, the goal to which its evolution had been directed for a hundred years or more. In a way it was, for there had always been a strong tradition of what was called 'trusteeship' in British imperial thought. It was also widely hoped that the Commonwealth might prove to be a powerful political and economic force in the world, all the more powerful for being free, and so revive Britain's flagging 'great power' status and role. Labour ministers were prone to this as well as Conservatives. For this reason the Commonwealth has been criticized for seducing Britain away from her continental neighbours, during the years when western Europe was evolving an alternative supranational structure of its own.

The idea that the Commonwealth could be a kind of empire-substitute, however, was shattered very soon. The newest members regarded their hard-won national independence jealously, and were unwilling to co-operate together merely to give Britain a further lease of international life. There were sharp clashes between members, arising from past memories that were hard to eradicate, conflicting economic interests, and differences of principle, especially over the issue of apartheid, which forced South Africa to leave in 1961. This was only to be expected. Widely dispersed as they were, and differentiated in almost every possible way, it would have been remarkable if the member states had easily and naturally cohered. So the Commonwealth became much less than the united 'third force' in the world that the imperial optimists had envisaged; something quite different, though still worthy of respect.

As it stands now, it is totally unlike any other international organization of states that has existed before. It has a secretariat, and a secretary-general (set up in 1965), but little else in common. It has no power, no united policy, no common principles, and no shared institutions. There used to be a common citizenship, with Britain allowing unrestricted entry to all Commonwealth citizens, but her Immigration Act of 1962 put an end to that. Most member states are parliamentary democracies, but not all. Most have retained English legal forms, but not all. Most play cricket, but not all. The single constitutional feature common to all member states is that they acknowledge the British monarch as symbolic head of the Commonwealth, but fewer than half recognize her or him as the head of their own states. It was once thought of as an economic unit, a potential free (or preferential) trade area, but that was never convincing, and collapsed when Britain joined the *European Economic Community in 1973. Another blow was the raising of British college fees for overseas students in 1979. The interchange of bright young people had been a valuable way of fostering Commonwealth solidarity. That was no longer felt to be a priority, however, in the narrowly utilitarian climate which prevailed at that time.

Nevertheless the Commonwealth still serves a purpose, as a forum for informal discussion and co-operation between nations of widely disparate cultures and material conditions. That function is served by a host of specialist Commonwealth institutions (the Commonwealth Institute in London, the Commonwealth Parliamentary Association, the Association of Commonwealth Universities, the Commonwealth of Learning, and so on); and by biennial conferences of Commonwealth heads of government. The ideal it represents still flickers, albeit fitfully. Only time will tell whether the Commonwealth is a mere footnote to history, or the beginning of a new chapter. BJP

Mansergh, P. N. S., *The Commonwealth Experience* (1969); Miller, J. D. B., *The Commonwealth in the World* (1965).

Common Wealth Party. Formed in 1942, Common Wealth was a merger of a movement Forward March, formed by the Liberal MP Sir Richard Acland, and the 1941 Committee of the playwright J. B. Priestley. An idealistic, socialist party, its membership was heavily middle class. Its two main themes were common ownership and vital democracy. The major parties had an electoral truce during the war. This gave a great fillip to Common Wealth, which won Conservative seats at Skipton and Eddisbury: it also supported an independent candidate who won easily in West Derbyshire. The party's application to Labour to affiliate was rejected, but it won another sweeping victory in April 1945 at Chelmsford, a safe Conservative seat.

Once the electoral truce was over, Common Wealth suffered the fate of most new parties in Britain. At the general election it held only Chelmsford, where Labour did not run a candidate. After the election, Acland called upon the party to dissolve and for its members to enrol with Labour as individuals. The leaders and many of the rank and file did so. The success of Common Wealth, though fragile, foreshadowed the Labour victory of 1945. HB

Communist Party of Great Britain. During the First World War the *Social Democratic Federation changed its name to the British Socialist Party, remaining affiliated to the *Labour Party. The success of the Bolshevik Revolution produced a realignment of the left and the Communist Party was founded in 1920. Its purely tactical request to the Labour Party for affiliation was rejected, but it gained two MPs in 1922, one of them under Labour colours. Such strength as the new party had was largely in south Wales and industrialized Scotland. The *Daily Worker* was started in 1930 but absorbed much of the energy of the party in trying to keep it going. Modest success came in 1935 when Harry

Pollitt polled 38 per cent of the vote in East Rhondda and Willie Gallacher won the West Fife seat. The party pursued a grimly Stalinist line and the outbreak of the Second World War produced vigorous intellectual gymnastics. The anti-fascist conflict to be won at all costs in September 1939 became an 'unjust and imperialist' war a month later when Stalin, now in alliance with Hitler, made it clear that his British comrades had made a false diagnosis. The German attack on the Soviet Union in 1941 produced another reappraisal and the Communist Party had some success, by association, in 1942. But no great breakthrough followed, and though the party returned two MPs in 1945, 12 of its 21 candidates lost their deposits. Worse was to follow when the development of the Cold War and the growing evidence of Stalin's tyranny forced it onto the defensive. At the general election of 1950, it put up 100 candidates, lost both its seats, and forfeited 97 deposits. The collapse of the Soviet Union in 1989 forced another reappraisal. One group resolved to change its name to the Democratic Left: their opponents retained the old name and put up four candidates at the general election of 1992, who polled an average of 150 votes. JAC

commutation was the change from meeting feudal obligations in labour or in kind to cash payments. It had obvious advantages for the lord, since serf labour was often grudging and unenthusiastic and hired labour did not need the same army of organizers: the serf or tenant knew more precisely what his obligations were and could plan his time. Boon work at harvest time was slowest to be commuted since there was bound to be a temporary shortage of labour then. The rate at which commutation took place varied from manor to manor and from region to region, according to local supply and demand of labour, nor was there a regular and steady progress towards a moneyed economy. But a process which began in the 12th cent. accelerated in the 14th, and was almost completed by the 16th cent. JAC

companies, trading. Trading companies monopolized overseas trade, made great fortunes, and played a part in the history of imperialism. The state supported their power and the companies made the state rich. The most important early English example was the Merchants of the *Staple which ran the wool trade from the 12th to 14th cents. It was followed, at the end of the 15th cent., by the *Merchant Venturers of London, monopolists of the expanding cloth industry's overseas trade. An Act of Parliament (1497) and a charter from Henry VII (1505) recognized the company's monopoly authority.

In the last quarter of the 16th cent. English overseas trade boomed and piracy was rampant. Company ships armed to fight pirates also defeated trading rivals and monopolized foreign trade. The French, Spanish, Russian, Barbary, Levant, and Eastland (Baltic) companies all date from this time. However the development of an effective navy at the end of the 17th cent. put an end to the need for monopoly trading in Europe; only those companies that went across the world still needed to protect themselves.

In the later 18th cent. trading companies became involved in imperialism: in Bengal, the *East India Company (royal charter, 1600) administered taxes and justice and the *Africa Company aided the growth of imperialism in Nigeria, east Africa, and Rhodesia. MW

compositions of delinquency was the term used by Parliament in the Civil War to describe the confiscation of property to be imposed on royalists wishing to compound or come to terms. They balanced between the need to raise revenue and the political desire to attract deserters from the royalist cause. An ordinance in March 1643 sequestered all property but in August one-fifth of the income was to be returned for the upkeep of wife and children. In January 1644 royalists were allowed to compound on the basis of two years' purchase of their estate, though they had first to take the covenant and swear never again to take up arms against Parliament. By the autumn of 1644 one royalist reported that 3,000 had compounded and 'daily more go'. JAC

comprehension. The Elizabethan religious settlement attempted to comprehend all from catholic to Calvinist under cover of liturgical uniformity, royal supremacy, episcopacy, and the Thirty-Nine Articles. Excepting recusants, this was largely successful until after the *Interregnum, the sectarians' heyday. By failing to achieve comprehension through modified episcopacy, the *Savoy conference of 1661 ended in schism—the exclusion of 936 non-episcopalians from their livings. Further attempts to include sectaries within the church through comprehension bills (1668, 1678, 1689) failed, for most bishops, including *Sheldon and *Sancroft, stood by the *Clarendon code. It was, for Tories, unthinkable to have a national church with sectaries outside. Despite the loss of 18th-cent. methodists, later archbishops have prevented further schism by retaining within tighter boundaries evangelicals, liberals, Anglo-catholics, and, more recently, opponents of women's ordination. Plurality of belief within defined limits of creeds, episcopacy, Scripture, and sacraments is a hallmark of Anglicanism. WMM

Compton, Henry (1632–1713). Bishop of London. Royalist son of the earl of Northampton, Compton had a spell in the new Horse Guards (from 1661), before graduating from Queen's College, Oxford (1666). Following ordination he was successively canon of Christ Church (1669–74), and bishop of Oxford (1674–5) and of London (1675–1713), where he was also responsible for the education of Princesses Mary and Anne, James's protestant daughters. Dedicated to national stability, he viewed sectarian turbulence and Romanism as equally dangerous. James II suspended him (1685). He was one of seven inviting William to England (1688) and in the crisis he appeared at Oxford in full military attire. Restored to his see, he briefly acted as primate, crowning William and Mary (April 1689), during *Sancroft's suspension, though soon afterwards the Canterbury chapter appointed *Tillotson to act instead. Essentially moderate, he was neither a dedicated Whig like *Tenison and *Burnet, nor a fervent Jacobite, like his friend *Atterbury. WMM

compurgation or law-wager was an Anglo-Saxon defence against an accusation by bringing a number of persons to testify to one's innocence as character witnesses. The laws of King *Ine laid down rules for the status of the compurgators and the number needed to answer to particular charges. The compurgators were not strictly witnesses nor jurymen, and the number varied, though was commonly twelve. The practice gradually fell into disuse after the Norman Conquest, though it survived for centuries in matters of debt. Clearly it contributed an element to the jury system which replaced it. JAC

computing and information technology. Computing science developed as an aid to mathematics. John *Napier, the discoverer of logarithms, described in 1617 a calculating machine made of ivory rods ('Napier's bones') which, he explained, would have helped the laborious calculations that 'ought to have been accomplished by many computers'. Pascal in France developed an arithmetical machine in the 1640s, which Leibniz improved upon, and Sir Samuel Morland, once *Pepys's tutor at Magdalene College, Cambridge, invented not only a speaking trumpet, writing-machine, and water-pump, but a calculating device: 'very pretty, but not very useful' was Pepys's laconic verdict. Charles *Babbage is rightly regarded as the immediate pioneer of computers, but the limitations of his work should not be ignored. His 'difference engine' was never completed (in *The Decline of Science* (1830) he blamed this on inadequate government funding—a cry that has been heard since) and his machine was purely mechanical, whereas modern computers depended upon electronic developments. But his later 'analytical engine', which Babbage admitted was no more than a 'shadowy vision', would have been not merely a calculator, using punched cards, but would have included a storage facility and a print-out. The Scheutze father and son in Sweden produced a commercially viable tabulating machine in the 1850s, one of which was used by the British registrar-general. In America, Hollerith, working on census returns, developed a machine using electric current and capable of analysing returns at speed. His Tabulating Machine Company (1896) was the forerunner of International Business Machines (IBM), which dominated the computer market for many years.

By the end of the 19th cent. the use of computers for purely statistical purposes was well established. Their introduction to a wider public came essentially after the Second World War. At Bletchley Park, a high-powered British team succeeded in cracking the German Enigma code, with the assistance of Colossus, specially designed to analyse German messages at speed and identify correlations. Early mainframe computers were enormous monsters. IBM's Automatic Sequence Controlled Calculator (ASCC, 1944) was 51 feet long and weighed 5 tons. Not until the invention of the microchip (integrated circuit), which evolved in the late 1950s out of work on semiconductors and transistors, did the possibility of personal computers arrive, changing access to computing out of all recognition and liberating users from the domination of experts. Digital Equipment Corporation introduced its PDP-8 microcomputer in 1963 and was followed by a host of competitors. Even so, the first acquaintance of ordinary people with the new technology was likely to have been with pocket calculators ('ready reckoners'), which led to a debate on whether they should be used in schools and universities and what effect they would have on mental arithmetic. But by the 1980s computers, long established in offices, turned up in stores, municipal administration, and libraries, and increasingly in spare bedrooms and basements. Babbage had been convinced that his work demonstrated the argument from design and that the world operated as a great calculating-machine, programmed by God. But, as with many discoveries, the excessive claims of pioneers and salesmen have become more sober. Computer manuals discuss chaos theory, expensive Ariane rockets blow up on launch (1996), and it is worth remembering that Babbage lost a great deal of money trying to invent an infallible scheme for winning on horses. JAC

Comyn, John (d. 1303), known as the 'Red Comyn'. A guardian (regent) of Scotland during the effective interregnum between Alexander III's death (1286) and John Balliol's accession (1292). Sometimes wrongly called the 'Black Comyn' by historians, he was in fact known to contemporaries as the 'Red Comyn', a title usually taken by the head of his family, the most influential baronial dynasty in 13th-cent. Scotland. He held the great Highland lordships of Badenoch and Lochaber, and estates in many other parts of Scotland. He helped to negotiate the treaty of *Birgham and subsequently supported Balliol, his brother-in-law, as king of Scots. He submitted to Edward I in 1296, but had joined William *Wallace by December 1297. KJS

Comyn, John (d. 1306), known as the 'Red Comyn'. Son and heir of John *Comyn, he was a leading Scottish patriot, despite appearances to the contrary—not least his murder by Robert Bruce, the future king. A devoted supporter of his uncle King John Balliol, he remained steadfastly loyal after Balliol's enforced abdication, and served from 1298 as a guardian or regent of Scotland in Balliol's name. Though he had established himself as the most powerful political figure in Scotland, he was unable to halt Edward I's massive campaign against the Scots in 1304, when he and other Scottish leaders had to submit. John's murder by Bruce and his companions in the Franciscan church, Dumfries, has been variously interpreted. Most likely, it was provoked by his refusal to desert Balliol and support Bruce's bid for the throne. KJS

Confederation of British Industry (CBI). The CBI emerged in 1965 from a group of older employers' organizations, the Federation of British Industries, the British Employers' Confederation, and the National Association of British Manufacturers, and like its predecessors aimed to influence economic decisions taken by governments. A subscription organization with a permanent staff, its origins in 1916 were relatively modest, but by 1939 the Federation of Business had a membership of about 2,900 firms and 180 trade associations, successfully lobbying the chancellor of the Exchequer. Governments in the 1960s and 1970s saw it as a partner with the *Trades Union Congress in attempting to impose prices and incomes policies. In the period since

1980 its quarterly forecasts for the British economy and its sectoral surveys have been an important element in testing the effects of fiscal and monetary policy. It is the most powerful lobbying group on behalf of employers. JB

Congested Districts Board (Ireland). The board was set up in 1891 by *Balfour when chief secretary for Ireland as the positive side of his policy of firmness and reform—to kill *Home Rule by kindness, it was suggested. The objective was to alleviate the dire poverty of the west of Ireland by providing funds for land purchase, building bridges and light railways, improving drainage, and sponsoring industries. Its resources were strengthened by George Wyndham in 1903. Before it was replaced in 1923, the board achieved much, but it did not kill Home Rule. JAC

Congregation, Lords of, 1557. A group of Scottish nobles who, in a 'Common Band' dated 3 December, pledged their lives to maintain, set forward, and establish the reformed religion in Scotland. Signed by the earls of Argyll, Glencairn, and *Morton, Lord Lorne, and Erskine of Dun, this 'Common Band', or covenant, was a protestant response to the increasing domination of Scotland by France during the regency of *Mary of Guise, and the maintenance of catholicism as the established religion. More significantly, this protestant manifesto signalled the emergence of the Lords of the Congregation as an organized political force in Scotland. PER

congregationalists were one of the main protestant dissenting sects. Since they believed strongly in the autonomy of each congregation, they were also known as independents or separatists. Their ideas, based on the priesthood of all believers, were developed by Robert *Browne and Henry *Barrow, and were *Calvinist in tone. The first congregations were established in the late 16th cent. and increased rapidly during the Civil War period, particularly in the parliamentary army and under the protection of *Cromwell, himself an independent. They made little progress in the 18th cent., but another great expansion took place in the early 19th cent. and at the time of the religious census of 1851 they were said to have 3,244 churches in England and Wales—more than the *baptists though less than a third of the *methodists. They were vigorous supporters of the *London Missionary Society (1796) and the *British and Foreign School Society (1807). The Congregational Union, formed in 1831, was necessarily a loose federation: in 1966 it was reorganized as the Congregational Church and in 1972 joined with the Presbyterian Church of England to form the United Reformed Church. JAC

Congress system. Formally set up by article VI of the *Quadruple Alliance, signed with the second treaty of *Paris (20 November 1815). It had been foreshadowed in the treaty of *Chaumont of March 1815, when the principal allies in the last coalition against Napoleon—Austria, Great Britain, Prussia, and Russia—resolved to remain united after the war to safeguard the peace settlements. Congresses met four times, at Aix-la-Chapelle (1818), Troppau (1820), Laibach (1821), and Verona (1822). The Aix-la-Chapelle meeting was harmonious. The allied army of occupation in France was to be withdrawn and France admitted to the union. Britain and France did not send representatives to the Troppau meeting, which had been called by the tsar to consider revolutionary outbreaks in Spain and Italy. The three eastern powers signed the Troppau declaration, asserting their right to intervene against revolutions. The British foreign secretary, Lord *Castlereagh, strongly resisted this interpretation in his State Paper of May 1820. The Troppau meeting was adjourned to Laibach but little was settled. The last congress, at Verona, discussed mainly Spain. Britain had to acquiesce in French intervention there. The congress system broke down because of the divergent aims of its members, the eastern powers wishing to use it to 'police' Europe, Britain insisting that it was intended only to secure the peace settlement and should not intervene in the domestic affairs of other countries. But it foreshadowed the peacekeeping efforts of the *League of Nations and the *United Nations in the 20th cent. MEC

Congreve, William (1670–1729). English poet and playwright. Educated at Kilkenny School and Trinity College, Dublin, at the same time as Jonathan *Swift, Congreve quickly gave up law for literature. After *Incognita* (1691)—a prose fiction more notable for its preface than its plot—Congreve found his *métier* in witty comedy, establishing his reputation with *The Old Batchelour* (1693), *The Double Dealer* (1693), and *Love for Love* (1695). Distinctive for their less ambiguous morality, epitomized by the love-match between Millamant and Mirabell which resolves *The Way of the World* (1700), Congreve's plays marked a significant development from earlier Restoration comedies. Disappointed by the reception of this last play, however, Congreve gave up writing for the stage, and the rest of his slim output was mostly poetic. Comfortably off as the holder of various government positions, but in poor health, Congreve was friendly with most of the literati of his day, regardless of party. JAD

Connacht (Connaught), taking its name from the mythical Irish figure, Conn of the Hundred Battles, was, by the 8th cent., dominated by the Uí Briúin dynasty, their ruling segment at the time of the Anglo-Norman invasion being the powerful O'Connor line, whose ecclesiastical capital at *Tuam was established as an archdiocese in 1152. Their hegemony was threatened by Anglo-Norman colonization in the 13th cent., led by the de Burgh family, but when the last member of the direct line of the de Burghs was killed in 1333, power in Connacht was shared between their cadet lines (generally known as Burkes) and several lines of the O'Connors and other Irish dynasties. The establishment of the presidency of Connacht in 1570 and the shiring of the province thereafter led to piecemeal plantation, while in the aftermath of the rebellion of *1641 surviving catholic landholders throughout Ireland were transported there, a process summed up in the aphorism ascribed to *Cromwell 'To hell or Connacht!' It played a significant part in the *1798 rebellion, witnessing the landing of the French General Humbert at Killala and a briefly successful campaign, and Connacht was also the scene of much activity in the Land

Wars of the late 19th cent., most memorably in the incident involving the land-agent Captain *Boycott which added the latter word to the English language. SD

Connolly, James (1868–1916). Author and union leader, Connolly was the most important Irish socialist in an intellectual and organizational sense. Though unsuccessful in an attempt to reconcile socialism and nationalism, he remains a great influence in Ireland and Scotland. Born in Edinburgh, Connolly joined the British army. Self-educated, he became a socialist organizer in Belfast and Dublin, founding the Irish Socialist Republican Party 1896 and 'the Workers' Republic' 1898. From 1902 to 1910 he was in the USA, where he set up the Irish Socialist Federation and published the *Harp*. Returning to Ireland in 1910, he organized the Irish Transport and General Workers' Union with James *Larkin and led the strike following a lock-out in 1913. Badly wounded in the *Easter Rising, he was executed strapped to a chair. Irish republican socialism has never recovered from his loss and has struggled to explain his blood-sacrifice. He published *Erin's Hope* (1897), *Labour in Irish History* and *Labour, Nationality and Religion* (1910), and *The Reconquest of Ireland* (1915). MAH

Conrad, Joseph (1857–1924). Writer. Conrad was born in the Ukraine, son of a revolutionary who was sent into internal exile. His mother died when he was 7, his father when he was 12. He went to sea, first visiting England in 1878 and becoming a British citizen in 1886. Though he never spoke English fluently, he wrote in it, publishing *Almayer's Folly* in 1895. It was followed rapidly by *An Outcast of the Islands* (1896), *The Nigger of the 'Narcissus'* (1897), *Lord Jim* (1900), and *Nostromo* (1904). Conrad published prolifically, making money on *Chance* (1914). He gained great recognition and declined a knighthood in his last year. Conrad drew on his own experiences at sea to write adventures with an important moral dimension. In *Lord Jim*, based upon a real episode, Jim, chief mate of the *Patna*, 'eaten up with rust', abandons ship unnecessarily, is disgraced, and redeems himself by sacrificing his life. 'Heart of Darkness' (1902), a long short story, based on Conrad's time in the Congo, is, among other things, a sharp critique of imperialism. JAC

conscription. In 1914 Britain was the only great power which relied upon volunteers to man its army. This tradition was continued until January 1916, by when nearly 2.5 million men had volunteered to join *Kitchener's New Armies. But by the summer of 1915 the flow of volunteers was failing to keep pace with the anticipated rate of casualties. Between June 1915 and May 1916 the *Asquith coalition government was convulsed by the conscription debate. Anti-conscriptionists argued that if more men were taken for the army, industry would have too little labour and Britain would be bankrupted before the army won the war. Pro-conscriptionists retorted that without conscription there would be no military victory. Asquith compromised. In January 1916 legislation was passed conscripting single men, followed in May by a second Act conscripting married men. By the end of the war nearly 2.3 million men had been conscripted, and without their efforts the British army would have collapsed long before the armistice. In 1939, conscription was introduced at once. DF

Conservative Party. The less reformist and progressive of the (normally) two main parties in British politics. It has a longer history than any other political party, perhaps anywhere, with an institutional continuity under that name from the early 1830s, though it drew upon older traditions including a church and king *Toryism. (In common currency 'Tory' has often been interchangeable with 'Conservative'.) The matrix of 19th-cent. Conservatism lay in the younger *Pitt's government and its support from the 1780s, a cause given wider appeal and sharper focus by its resistance to the *Jacobinism of revolutionary France. Constitutional and societal conservatism united the old *court party (largely placemen under Treasury patronage) and most of the country gentlemen in the Commons. A long near-monopoly of government ended only in 1830 when issues like *catholic emancipation and parliamentary reform broke up old solidarities. The loss of office and Treasury patronage (itself in decline) forced the organization of an independent party from a position of opposition. The Reform Bill struggle of 1831–2, though a defeat, was a crucible of party development and the newly named Conservative Party set itself to limit further damage to established institutions. The *Carlton Club, founded in 1832 and moved to Pall Mall in 1835, symbolized this development. *Wellington and *Peel were the recognized leaders, though the latter's *'Tamworth manifesto' of December 1834, a statement of political strategy, was not a party document.

The party operated within the framework of the parliamentary constitution and its organization helped to fill the gap left by the decline of the crown's influence in the 'making' of a House of Commons. It was politically adversarial, in competition for parliamentary power and government office with the rival Whig Party, which, with its radical allies, developed into the *Liberal Party. Victorian politics centred on this party competition. The disintegration of the Liberals in the early 20th cent. meant the Conservatives' main challenge came from the trade union-based Labour Party mobilizing the working-class vote. That change also involved a shift in the dominant issues. The Victorian Conservative Party was identified with the defence of the constitution and the causes and interests associated with it: the monarchy and House of Lords, the established churches, the Union with Ireland, landownership, property rights and inheritance, a limited franchise. Always associated, particularly at the parliamentary level, with wealth and privilege, it also reflected vertical divisions in society: church against chapel, land and agriculture against industry, the countryside against the larger towns. From around the Great War these traditional causes were largely superseded by socio-economic issues, a change assisted by the Irish settlement, the Bolshevik revolution, and economic depression. The main threats identified by the party were now trade unionism, egalitarianism, redistributive welfare, socialism, and Bolshevism. The Conservatives became more a party of business (companies and entrepreneurs took over its main financing) and more clearly the party of middle-class interests, including the suburban middle classes of the cities. Its leaders now came to be drawn from the business and professional classes rather than the landed and titled. The party was based more on horizontal than on vertical divisions in society. The 1951 general election's overwhelmingly Conservative middle-class vote represented a peak of class-based voting. At the same time nearly a third of the enfranchised working classes has usually supported the Conservatives for reasons of patriotic identity, resentment of immigrant groups, hostility to catholics or dissenters, or just a sense of economic interest.

The party's history has a pronounced periodization. After the long dominance of constitutional loyalism down to 1830, the Conservatives spent most of the period 1830–86 in opposition. Only two general elections, 1841 and 1874, were won. Franchise extensions and advancing urbanization and industrialization handicapped the party and its 1846 split over the *Corn Laws left long-term damage. It then benefited from the comparable Liberal split over *Irish Home Rule in 1886 and was maintained in office by the *Liberal Unionists for most of the next twenty years. (The two parties merged as the Conservative and Unionist Party in 1912.) Though hit by the Parliament Act removing the absolute veto of the Conservative-dominated House of Lords in 1911 and by the progress of Home Rule, the Conservatives gained from the Great War, which brought them back into government and divided the Liberals again. Faced with three-party politics and the first Labour governments in the 1920s, the Conservatives, who gained most of the disintegrating Liberal vote, established themselves as the dominant party, despite the impact of economic depression, and controlled the *National Government coalition from 1931. The Second World War undermined this position: it brought Labour into government and to the management of the 'home front', while the 1945 general election, lost decisively by the Conservatives, was the only one fought with the Soviet Union as ally rather than enemy. The 1945–51 Labour government established a 'post-war consensus' around a mixed economy, the welfare state, and a commitment to full employment. Conservative governments from 1951 to 1964 were founded on acceptance of this legacy as well as upon rising living standards and Cold War diplomacy. What was left of the colonial empire was liquidated, a process now seen even by most Conservatives as a legitimate application of democratic self-government. The party had come to terms with full democracy (except in its own internal structures where hierarchy and the notion of 'leadership' continued to appeal). With the breakdown of this domestic consensus by the 1970s under pressure of rising inflation, labour disputes, increasing unemployment, and declining economic competitiveness, the party turned (perhaps returned) sharply towards the free-market economics represented by the *Thatcher government of 1979–90. This tenure of office and four successive general election victories were, however, assisted by divisions within the Labour Party and the opposition generally. Though the 20th cent. stands more than the 19th as 'the Conservative century', Conservative dominance of government has owed much to the fragmentation of the political left and its consequences within the electoral system.

The Conservative Party has never had a clear ideological identity. Social paternalism, *laissez-faire*, state corporatism, religiosity and materialism, free trade and protectionism have all had their influence, though major division and damage have only rarely arisen from the tensions. Loyalties to the constitution and its symbols, social order, and patriotism have substituted for ideological coherence. Conservative political practice has generally been adaptive and pragmatic, geared to the needs of electoral success and office-holding. The long history of the party adds also to the blurring of ideological identity. The political right has never needed to recreate itself in Britain as in many continental countries. The Conservative Party's continuity reflects that of the state and nation which have not suffered conquest, major defeat, or social revolution. It also reflects the nature of economic and social development in Britain. The extent of social well-being among a large middle class and even sections of the working classes has facilitated the Conservative practice of defending great property through an alliance with small property. BIC

Blake, R., *The Conservative Party from Peel to Churchill* (1970); Coleman, B., *Conservatism and the Conservative Party in Nineteenth-Century Britain* (1988); Seldon, A., and Ball, S. (eds.), *Conservative Century: The Conservative Party since 1900* (Oxford, 1994).

consistory courts. After the Norman Conquest, separate ecclesiastical courts were set up to deal with pleas 'which belonged to the government of souls'. The consistory court was the court of a bishop for his diocese and was the normal forum for deciding serious cases of defamation and matters relating to wills of personal property. Where the consistory court found the defendant guilty of defamation it could impose penance. The church courts were not allowed to impose fines and where they required the defendant to pay back money as restitution they incurred the hostility of the common law courts and were subject to prohibition. The consistory court was normally presided over by the chancellor, a layman, and appeal lay from its decision to the court of the archbishop. MM

constable. One of the great medieval offices of state, derived from *comes stabuli*, count of the stables. The first lord high constable was a supporter of the Empress *Matilda, who made him earl of Hereford. It then passed to the Bohuns, on to *Thomas of Woodstock, and to his descendant Edward, duke of *Buckingham, executed by Henry VIII in 1521. It had acquired responsibility for the mobilization of the army, for the enforcement of martial law, and for adjudication on matters of chivalry. After Buckingham's death, the office was granted temporarily to noblemen so that they could act at coronations: the duke of *Wellington was lord high constable at three successive coronations in 1821, 1831, and 1838. Scottish constables commanded the army and from the time of Robert I the office became hereditary in the Hay family, earls of Erroll, who take precedence of all other Scottish subjects. JAC

Constable, Archibald (1774–1827). Publisher. Son of the earl of Kellie's land steward and apprenticed to Peter Hill, an Edinburgh bookseller, Constable soon established himself independently. Drawing on London and Scottish contacts, he ventured into publishing with theological and political pamphlets, before becoming proprietor of the *Scots Magazine* (1801) and then publisher of the prestigious **Edinburgh Review* (1802), which brought him into prominence. His liberality with authors confounded rivals. In 1805–8 and 1814–26 he published most of Sir Walter *Scott's works, and owned **Encyclopaedia Britannica* for a decade, introducing extended 'dissertations' as supplements. Dreams of a revolution in bookselling by offering easily affordable fiction to the 'millions' were ambushed by huge debts and bankruptcy (1826) from heady speculativeness; the firm's collapse (together with Ballantyne's) so rocked the publishing industry that ambition and innovation were stifled for years. Constable's efforts to recover lacked heart, and he soon succumbed to ill-health. ASH

Constable, John (1776–1837). Landscape painter, born at East Bergholt (Sussex), the son of a miller. At first intended for the church, then to follow his father, eventually Constable was allowed to go to London to study at the Royal Academy Schools. Encouraged by Benjamin *West, Constable concentrated on studying nature and rarely painted outside the genre of landscape: 'my art is to be found under every hedge.' Initially, he worked in the manner of *Gainsborough, but slowly developed his own style of conveying nature and humble subjects so as to appear spontaneous and without what he called 'fal-de-lal or fiddle-de-dee'. This gained him little recognition at home but a growing reputation in France where his *Hay Wain* (1821) influenced the modern school of landscape painters. In 1819 he became ARA, but a further ten years elapsed before he was elected a full academician. Today he is recognized with Turner as the major English landscape painter of the 19th cent. JC

Constans. Roman emperor. One of the three sons of *Constantine the Great amongst whom the empire was divided after Constantine's death in 337, Constans was awarded the central part of the empire including Italy. In 340 he invaded the possessions of his brother Constantine II in the West, defeating and killing him. Constans had to visit Britain in winter 342–3; the reasons for this risky crossing are unknown. Constans was in his turn overthrown in 350 by a cabal of Gallic nobles, who replaced him with an army commander in Britain, *Magnentius, who had Constans hunted down and killed. ASEC

Constantín, son of Fergus (d. 820), king of Picts (from 790) and of Scottish *Dalriada (from 811). Constantín was the first king to rule by right over both Picts and Scottish Gaels. After defeating a rival in 789, he reigned first as king of the Picts, only in 811 taking the kingship of Dalriada, which his father had held 778–81. His power base was the central Pictish territory of *Fortriu, and his dominance there is reflected in the recently discovered inscription on the Dupplin Cross (5 miles south-west of Perth), which bears his name set amidst the iconography of Christian kingship. The religious dimension of his reign is further demonstrated by his foundation of the monastery of *Dunkeld (*c.*818), by the presence of his name in the Durham *Liber vitae* (entered after that of Charlemagne), and by his commemoration as a saint in Irish martyrologies and a Scottish litany. He stands at the head of a short-lived Pictish dynasty, his brother, son, and nephew reigning in turn. TOC

Constantine (*c.*274–337), first Christian Roman emperor (306–37), known as 'the Great'. Born at Naissus (now Nis), Constantine was the son of *Constantius I by Helena. In 305 Constantius succeeded as *Augustus* (senior emperor) of the West. Constantine fled from the court of Galerius, eastern *Augustus*, in time to be at his father's death-bed at York in 306. He was illegally proclaimed *Augustus* by the army there. In 312 he invaded Italy and defeated Maxentius near Rome, apparently after a Christian vision. By 324 Constantine was sole *Augustus*. He was an energetic general and recast the Roman army. He also continued the administrative and fiscal reforms of Diocletian. Constantine promoted Christianity financially, legally, and theologically, being baptized on his death-bed in 337. He probably revisited Britain in 312 and 314, taking the title *Britannicus* in 315, and an edict of 319 is addressed to the *Vicarius* of the Britains, Pacatianus. ASEC

Constantine III (d. 411). Usurper, proclaimed emperor by Roman troops in Britain. At the beginning of the 5th cent. AD Roman Britain was not heavily defended, *Stilicho having withdrawn troops in 401–2 to help defend Italy against German invaders. This attack on Italy and the overrunning of Gaul by Germanic tribes left Britain as an isolated and relatively untroubled area from which came three successive attempts to usurp power. In AD 406 Marcus seized power in Britain, but after a few months was replaced by the equally short-lived Gratian. The new usurper, Constantine III, was more effective, managing to take substantial territories in Gaul and Spain, and enjoying some moderate successes against the Germans. Eventually he was defeated by the forces of the rightful western emperor Honorius: in 411 he was besieged at Arles, captured, and executed. ES

Constantine I (d. 876), 'king of the Picts' (862–76), anachronistically regarded as third king of Scotland. Son of *Kenneth I, he succeeded his uncle Donald I. Only for the second time in Pictish history had a family retained the kingship without a break beyond one generation. Constantine's ancestry in the male line was Gaelic, like most Pictish kings in the 9th cent. His career was chiefly consumed in a desperate struggle for survival against Scandinavian incursions. In 866 the Norwegian king of Dublin devastated Pictland (probably concentrating on Perthshire), and in 870–1 returned and took away many, including Picts, as slaves. In 875 Halfdan the Danish king of York inflicted a crushing defeat on Constantine at *Dollar (9 miles east of Stirling), driving him back to the Highlands. Constantine was killed the following year by the Danes at 'Inverdufata' (unidentified). A debatable source says that he was buried on Iona. The only record of Constantine as an aggressor beyond his kingdom was as sponsor of the assassination of Arthgal, king of *Strathclyde, in 872. DEB

Constantine II (d. 952), king of 'Scotland' (900–940/5). He retired to become abbot of the *céli Dé* ('Clients of God') at St Andrews. His father was *Æd (d. 878). Constantine II laid the foundations of the kingdom of Scotland. His victory over the Danes in the kingdom's heartland in Strathearn in 904 represented a turning-point in its struggle for survival against Scandinavian aggression, and after another victory at (probably) Corbridge (18 miles west of Newcastle) in 918 he initiated a policy of *rapprochement* with the Danes cemented with the marriage of his daughter to the Danish king Guthfrith. This was designed to support Danish York in its struggle for survival against kings of Wessex. The kings of Wessex began to threaten Scotland itself when *Athelstan invaded as far as Dunnottar (14 miles south of Aberdeen) in 934, and in 937 an invasion of England mounted by Constantine and the Danes from Dublin led by Guthfrith's son *Olaf ended in disaster at the battle of *Brunanburh, in which Constantine lost a son. Despite consorting with heathens, Constantine evidently had a genuine concern for the church, setting new standards of religious life and clerical freedom in an agreement proclaimed at Scone with Cellach, chief bishop of the Scots, in 905/6. Constantine probably established St Andrews as the seat of the chief bishop of his kingdom. DEB

Constantine III (d. 997), king of 'Scotland' (from 995). He reigned for only a year and a half following the assassination of *Kenneth II. He was a son of King *Cuilén, and the last of the descendants of King *Æd (d. 878) to hold the kingship. He was killed by *Kenneth III, a member of the rival branch of the royal dynasty, at 'Rathinveramon' (literally the 'fort on the mouth of the river Almond') which is unidentified, but probably near Scone, north of Perth. According to a late and debatable source he was buried on Iona. He is known from late medieval histories as Constantine the Bald. DEB

Constantius I (Constantius Chlorus), *Caesar* (deputy emperor) and then *Augustus* (emperor) of the western Roman empire (AD 292–306). In 293 Constantius was instrumental in wresting power back from the usurper *Carausius. Constantius' successes included taking Boulogne, home of the Channel fleet. Carausius was assassinated by *Allectus who in turn usurped imperial power. Constantius' forces attacked Allectus in Britain; Allectus was killed and Constantius made a triumphal entry into London. In AD 305–6 Constantius, then co-emperor with Maximian, conducted a military campaign in northern Britain. His son *Constantine joined him, and was declared emperor when Constantius died at York. ES

constitution. A constitution is a body of rules, formal or informal, which regulates the government of a state, or, indeed, a private association. It is concerned essentially not with 'What is to be done?' but 'How?' The procedures to be followed when taking decisions form the constitution. The distribution of power between the various organs of government, the limits of governmental authority, the methods of appointing or electing those who govern—these things are the staple of a constitution.

The existence of a constitution implies that there are some restraints upon those who govern. If decisions, for instance, depend upon the whim of an absolute monarch, or the fancy of a dictator, it is hard to speak of a constitution. Constitutions are about procedures, and arbitrary power, by its very arbitrariness, is not hedged around by prescribed procedures. Most states, and many private associations, have written constitutions—a code of written rules binding those who govern, which has been adopted at a specific time, together with any amendments which have been made in accordance with the procedures laid down in the constitution. Thus the US constitution is the document accepted in 1787, together with the 27 amendments which have been passed subsequently. Such a document, or collection of documents, is called the written, or, more aptly, the formal constitution.

A contrast is sometimes drawn between written and unwritten constitutions. Britain, it is said, has an unwritten constitution. But the distinction is overdrawn. Britain is indeed unusual in that there is no single document, or set of related documents, which can be called the formal constitution. The formal constitution in Britain is scattered through hundreds of Acts of Parliament and judicial rulings. There are, of course, many statutes that form part of the formal constitution in Britain: the *Bill of Rights of 1689 which limited royal power; the Act of *Settlement of 1701 which regulated the succession to the throne; the Representation of the People Acts from 1832 to the present day, which progressively widened the right to vote and regulated the conditions under which the right could be exercised. These statutes have not, however, been brought together in one legal document; the formal constitution of Britain, like truth, has to be collected and put together limb by limb.

But the description of Britain as having an unwritten constitution usually focuses on another attribute—the importance of conventions. Some of Britain's most important constitutional rules are constitutional *conventions*—rules which are generally observed but have no legal force. There is a convention that except for certain narrowly defined situations, the monarch acts on the advice of her ministers: there is no direct legal compulsion on the monarch to act on ministerial advice, but she invariably does. By convention, a government clearly defeated on a vote of confidence in the House of Commons either resigns or holds a general election. The most powerful organ in the constitution, the cabinet, is barely known to the law. Its composition, its time of meeting, its powers, are all regulated by convention and usage, not by law.

Conventions are rules which have evolved over decades of constitutional practice. They have grown up and are obeyed because people find them useful. It is as though opposing players in a game had reached informal understandings about what was to be considered 'foul play' without bothering to write them down in the rule book. Conventions play a most important part in British political life, but it is quite wrong to regard them as a unique feature of British politics. Conventions develop in both states and private clubs. They figure conspicuously in the constitutional practice of the USA, which has the oldest surviving written constitution in the world. The growth of conventions, for example, has changed the choice of the American president from the indirect election favoured and provided for by the framers of the constitution to direct election by the people.

The constitution, especially the formal part, is often regarded as having a superior status to the ordinary law; indeed, it is often seen as a fundamental law, a framework from which particular acts of legislation or executive decisions draw their legitimacy. It is held that it must be set apart from ordinary law and venerated as such, and be protected by change from chance majorities or the whims of a faction dominant for the time being. Many constitutions therefore specify that the constitution can be changed only by a special procedure. The constitution may lay down that an amendment must be passed by a special majority in the legislature, or must be approved by both houses of the legislature, or by the people in a referendum. Such measures emphasize the special status of the constitution and affirm that constitutional change can come about only through the deliberate and considered will of the people or their representatives. Such constitutions are called *rigid*; constitutions which can be changed in the same way as any ordinary mundane law are called *flexible*. Britain has a highly flexible constitution: that of the USA is highly rigid.

It is easy to assume that a constitutional state, one where the governors are themselves bound by rules, must also be democratic, but the assumption is false. A constitutional state is wholly compatible with a restricted franchise or oligarchic government. It is not the source of power which makes a state constitutional or otherwise, but the degree to which the various organs of the state check and control the use of arbitrary power. It is arbitrariness, not, say, traditional kingship, which is the opposite of constitutionalism.

Lastly, while it is true that a constitution may help to shape the political habits of a people, the converse is more likely to hold good. The world is littered with the parchment of dead constitutions—legal frameworks so remote from the experience of the peoples they sought to guide, so hostile to the most powerful interests in the land, that they collapsed at the first breath of challenge. HB

constitutional history once held a dominant and still holds a respectable position in historical output. The triumph of a reformed British Parliament in the 19th cent., and the desire to recommend parliamentary government to other nations as a guarantee of liberal stability, encouraged interest in its origins, in the evolution of the constitution, and in the Stuart period as its testing time. Two remarkable historians helped to establish the subject. In the preface to *Select Charters and Other Illustrations of English Constitutional History* (1866), William Stubbs wrote that he aimed to examine 'a distinct growth from a well-defined germ to full maturity'. He followed it with *The Constitutional History of England in its Origin and Development* (1873–8). S. R. Gardiner's contribution was *Constitutional Documents of the Puritan Revolution* (1889), and a sober and detailed *History of England from James I* (1863–), which reached sixteen volumes and 1656 before death intervened in 1902. One by-product of their initiative was the cult of documents. Volume after volume followed, and though the process was rather dull, the teaching sometimes mechanical, and the documents often divorced from their wider contexts, it was defended as systematic consultation of the evidence. The 20th cent. was less in awe of Parliament and a counter-attack developed. R. G. Usher, an American historian, launched a sharp attack on Gardiner's historical method in 1915. After the First World War, Herbert Butterfield and L. B. Namier, though differing on much else, agreed that the previous approach had been Whiggish and teleological. Interest in constitutional history waned as Britain's world position declined, in much the same way as imperial history dropped out of favour, and it suffered from competition from new forms of history, administrative, social, and economic. Though much work on constitutional history continued to be done, the emphasis was more on everyday working than on constitutional theory. The History of Parliament, which recommenced publication in 1964, eschewed documentary commentary or political narrative in favour of biographies of MPs and sketches of their constituencies. JAC

construction industry. The largest structures of the medieval and early modern periods were monasteries, churches, cathedrals, castles, and town walls. *York, with its 13th-cent. motte and bailey castle, known as Clifford's Tower, the massive minster (the largest Gothic church in England, 13th–15th cent.), and complete city walls, provides a classic composite. The city boundaries at the height of the pre-Reformation period contained 40 churches, 9 chapels, 4 monasteries, 4 friaries, 16 hospitals, and 9 guildhalls for the various trades.

Most of these were built of stone, while dwellings and other functional buildings like farmsteads or mills, depending on local materials, were of timber, clay, or brick. Roofing materials were thatch, turf, timber, tiles, slates, and lead. While there were many local styles, construction, especially in stone, was everywhere dependent on the mason's skill, hence the traditional importance and high status of the trade.

The most important 16th- and 17th-cent. buildings were town and country houses for the nobility and gentry, and public buildings, such as churches and town halls. In 1514 Cardinal *Wolsey began to build the largest house in England, *Hampton Court, further extended by Henry VIII. More typical, though still on a grand scale, was *Hardwick Hall (Derbys.), begun in 1591 by Elizabeth, countess of *Shrewsbury. Considering its size it was constructed incredibly quickly, being finished and occupied by 1597. Nearer the close of this period, and following the Great Fire of 1666, *St Paul's cathedral, designed by *Wren, was begun in 1673.

During the 18th cent. rising population and sustained economic prosperity generated greatly increased activity in construction. The urban building boom of the Georgian era is best appreciated in the splendid architecture of *Edinburgh, *Bath, *Stamford, and *Dublin, but can be seen in many other towns and villages. In the countryside the modernization of agriculture led to the construction of new farm houses and buildings, walls, roads, and ditches. Quarrying, both for stone and slate, and brick and tile manufacture, expanded rapidly to meet demand.

The *industrial revolution of the later 18th and early 19th cents. required major construction projects and a more functional architecture. The new factory buildings, such as the cotton-spinning mills still to be seen at Cromford, Styal, and New Lanark, were often large scale, and increased in size and complexity as industry expanded in centres like *Manchester and *Glasgow. The transport revolution, which accompanied industrialization, also engendered major canal, railway, bridge, and harbour building projects. The *Iron Bridge over the Severn at *Coalbrookdale (1777–9) was the first to use that great sinew of the industrial age in its construction. It was also put to good effect by Victorian engineers in the *Crystal Palace (1851) and the great train sheds at major railway stations like Waverley (Edinburgh), Temple Meads (Bristol), and St Pancras (London). Subsequently, in the late 19th and early 20th cents., steel and concrete were extensively used in construction, the largest engineering structures, apart from buildings, being bridges, motorways, tunnels, and gas and oil rigs.

The construction industry has always been an important barometer of the economy, seen, for example, in the building boom which coincided with the era of late 19th-cent. prosperity, more modestly in parts of Britain during the recovery of the 1930s, and during the years of reconstruction following the *Second World War. ID

Conventicles Act, 1664. This Act (16 Car. II c. 4) was one of the fiercest provisions of the *Clarendon code, which aimed at restoring Anglican supremacy after the Restoration. It forbade attendance at any meeting of more than five persons for religious purposes other than Church of England ceremonies, and was accompanied by a battery of fines, imprisonment, and transportation. It was strongly imposed at first but later ignored. In 1668 it was allowed to expire, replaced by a less severe act in 1670 (22 Car. II c. 1), and replaced by the *Toleration Act of 1689. JAC

Convention of Estates, 1689. The flight of James VII in 1688 made it impossible to summon a legal Scottish Parliament. It was therefore decided to fall back upon a Convention of Estates, which had often been summoned in emergencies, and which met on 14 March 1689 in Edinburgh. By the *Claim of Right it declared that James VII had been deposed and the *Articles of Grievances took the opportunity to protest against the organization of business by the *Lords of the Articles. In June the Convention declared itself a parliament. JAC

Convention of royal burghs. Meetings of the royal burghs in Scotland went back to the 14th cent. and in 1487 a statute authorized annual sessions. The conventions were in addition to the representation of the burghs in the Scottish Parliament and, after 1707, the British Parliament. The same commissioners often served in both bodies and the taxation distribution agreed by the burghs was usually confirmed by the Scottish Parliament. The conventions also had considerable political influence. They continued after the Act of *Union but in 1975, following the local government reorganization, the body was changed into a convention of local authorities. JAC

Convention Parliaments. The constitutional crisis of the 17th cent. produced two occasions when there were legal impediments to the summoning of a lawful parliament. The first was at the Restoration. On 25 April 1660, a month after the *Long Parliament had dissolved itself, a convention assembled and declared that the government should be in king, lords, and commons. Its first act was to declare itself a genuine parliament, 'notwithstanding any defect or default whatsoever'. It remained in existence until December 1660, establishing the terms of the Restoration, save for the church settlement, which was left to its successor. A similar procedure was adopted in 1689 after James II's flight meant that the calling of a lawful parliament was impossible. The Assembly which gathered at Westminster on 22 January was a parliament in all but name, and its first act, using the exact words of the 1660 measure, was to declare itself a parliament. By the *Declaration of Rights, later turned into the *Bill of Rights, it laid down the main features of the revolutionary settlement, accepted by William and Mary. In Scotland a *Convention of Estates was summoned in 1689 for the same purpose. JAC

conversion of England. See CHRISTIANITY.

convocations of Canterbury and York. These provincial assemblies, originally of bishops, date from Archbishop *Theodore (668–90), though York's, smaller and historically less significant, only developed separately *c.*733. Representatives (proctors) of cathedrals, monasteries, and parochial clergy attended later (13th cent.). Initially sitting together, bishops and lower clergy split into upper and lower houses (15th cent.). The archbishop presided over the whole convocation; the lower house, when sitting separately, was chaired by its elected prolocutor, its channel of communication to the bishops. Though kings watched warily, convocations normally legislated by canons, until compelled by Henry VIII to limit their powers drastically (Acts of *Submission 1532/1534). Despite Edward I's abortive attempts to prevent them, the clergy taxed themselves through convocations until 1664, after which the crown had less need to summon them. Acrimonious altercations between the Whiggish upper and Tory lower house of the Canterbury convocation (1689 and 1700–17)—reflecting contemporary political and ecclesiastical divisions—led the crown to suspend both convocations. They met only formally until the *evangelical and *tractarian revivals inspired them to resume discussion (1852 and 1861). Still exclusively clerical assemblies, the two convocations have existed alongside elected lay houses since 1885. The two sat jointly from 1904, a situation legalized as the Church Assembly (1920) which in turn gave way to the General Synod (1970). Though its 'last smile' lives on in the Synod's houses of bishops and clergy, convocation's loose federalism—and thus diocesan 'near-autonomy'—has given way to synodical centralism. WMM

Conway, treaty of. See ABERCONWY.

Conwy castle (Gwynedd), 13 miles north-east of Bangor, was begun in the spring of 1283 and was substantially complete by the autumn of 1287. The castle is similar to Caernarfon and like it was planned from the first with an adjoining walled town. The work involved the uprooting of the abbey of Aberconwy, the principal Cistercian abbey in Wales, to a new site at Maenan, 8 miles further up the river. The unfinished abbey church was taken over and completed as the parish church of the new town, which it still is. It was here that Richard II received Henry Percy, earl of *Northumberland, as Henry Bolingbroke's ambassador, and accepted assurances of safe conduct which proved to be false. During the Civil War the castle was repaired, supplied, and garrisoned, at his own expense, for the king by John *Williams, archbishop of York, a Conwy-born man. Parliamentary forces besieged the castle, which was eventually surrendered by Williams to prevent his native town from being destroyed. For the next five years it was kept on a war footing by Parliament before being slighted in 1655. LR

Cook, James (1728–79). Usually referred to as Captain Cook, he was arguably the greatest ever maritime explorer. Though not a great innovative scientist, he had 'the genius of the matter of fact' and a 'controlled imagination'. He established much of the basic geography of Australasia and the Pacific region, disposed of the myth of the southern continent, and, perhaps largely by accident, learned how to keep his men free of scurvy. Not by accident, he used Harrison's chronometer and lunar distances to calculate longitudes accurately. A brilliant hydrographical surveyor and navigator, he was also a great seaman and leader, behaving sensibly and honourably equally towards scientists like *Banks accompanying his expeditions, towards his crews, or the non-Europeans he encountered.

Cook was born in Yorkshire and apprenticed to a Whitby shipowner when he developed his 'passionately professional' approach to managing ships and their crews as well as learning navigation. In 1755 he entered the Royal Navy. Soon, his charts helped General *Wolfe up the St Lawrence and he also surveyed Newfoundland's coasts. Recognized as an expert navigator, he was chosen leader of the expedition in the *Endeavour* which took scientists to Tahiti to observe the transit of Venus between earth and sun in 1769. He also sought the reputed southern continent, circumnavigated the New Zealand islands, and explored the whole eastern coast of Australia. The results of this 1768–71 voyage added more reliable information about the Pacific than ever before. In the *Resolution* in 1772–5, Cook finally disproved the southern continent by sailing round Antarctica but also discovered Tonga and the New Hebrides. A third major expedition in 1776–9 was to the North Pacific to find the end of the North-West Passage. Of course he did not, though he sailed through the Bering Strait, but he did discover the Hawaiian Islands, where on a second visit he lost his life in a fracas with some natives over a stolen boat. RB

Cooper, Samuel (1609–72). English miniaturist who enjoyed a European reputation. He was active before, during, and after the English Civil War and Commonwealth and his patrons included *Cromwell and Charles II, *Milton and *Monck. Cooper regarded the miniature as a painting, not a piece of the jeweller's art; with his use of light and shade, combined with superb draughtsmanship, he broke away from his predecessors, especially *Hilliard. The diarist John *Evelyn described Cooper as 'the prince of limners' and *Pepys commissioned a miniature of his wife. The Royal Collection has several excellent examples of Cooper's work. There are also examples in London at the Victoria and Albert Museum and the National Portrait Gallery, in Cambridge, and at the Hague. JC

Co-operative movement. The Co-operative movement is often identified solely with retailing, and its foundation ascribed to the '*Rochdale Pioneers' who set up the first store to pay dividends to members on the basis of how much they had purchased from the society. It actually originated in the ideas of Robert *Owen, the visionary factory owner and social thinker of *New Lanark. During the 1820s and 1830s many groups of people started on the road to creating an alternative society based on mutual assistance rather than competitive individualism, the 'New Moral World' whose superiority, once established through the working of communities in which labour was the unit of currency, would drive out the irrationality of capitalism. The first step on the road to community-building was to set up a shop, whose surpluses could then be applied to manufacturing and ultimately farming; but most of the early co-operative societies fell at this first hurdle. The Rochdale Pioneers system rendered Co-operation attractive to those who sought to save as they spent, and brought the movement into line with prevailing social values. After the Pioneers began in 1844 the movement spread rapidly, supplying unadulterated foodstuffs at accessible prices and making a distinctive virtue of refusing credit. Co-operation was especially popular in the textile towns of Lancashire and west Yorkshire in the mid-Victorian years, later gaining a strong following in Scotland and colonizing the midlands and south. Membership had reached saturation point in some industrial towns by the turn of the century, and middle-class recruitment began in earnest in the inter-war years. Societies were locally based, but the Co-operative Wholesale Society co-ordinated purchasing and then manufacturing for the whole movement from 1863. Although most members came to view the dividend as the most important aspect, the Co-op never lost its idealism completely, providing classes and libraries, supporting strikes, and (through its Women's Guild) offering political confidence and empowerment to working-class women. The societies were democratically run and in 1918 a Co-operative Party was set up, which ran in harness with the Labour Party. The Co-op also diversified its retail services, went into banking and home loans, and built houses for its members. It sustained its strength into the mid-20th cent., despite campaigns against it by private traders, and came to hold a dominant position in retailing, which it gradually lost in the changing climate of the 1950s onwards.

Societies amalgamated, local identities were lost, the dividend itself was abandoned, and the Co-op seemed to many to have lost its way. Attempts are still being made to adapt it to modern circumstances without losing its distinctive identity, but the struggle is an uphill one. JKW

Coote, Sir Eyre (1726–83). Coote was born at Limerick and joined the army during the Jacobite uprising of 1745. His most distinguished service came in India where he fought under Robert *Clive at the battle of *Plassey in 1757. On 22 January 1760 he commanded at *Wandewash when the French threat to southern India was extirpated. He then went on to capture Pondicherry, the French capital in India, in 1761. Posted to *Calcutta, he rapidly quarrelled with members of the Bengal Council and left for England in 1762. In 1769 he returned as commander-in-chief of the Bengal army but soon resigned again for the same reason. In 1779, he came back once more as C.-in-C. under Warren *Hastings and led the army in the second Mysore War. But he was defeated by Hyder Ali, the Mysore sultan, at Porto Nuovo in 1781. Coote died at Madras in 1783. DAW

Copenhagen, battle of, 1801. This encounter with the Danish fleet was fought on 2 April in the narrow 3-mile-long King's Channel, of varying depth, which bounded the eastern defences of the Danish capital. These consisted of the formidable Trekronor fort, flanked to the north by 5 moored warships and to the south by a redoubtable line of 7 unmasted warships and 10 floating batteries, all moored, heavily gunned and manned. The British under Sir Hyde Parker with *Nelson as his second had 15 ships supported by a variety of assault craft and 600 soldiers. Following a daring navigation aided by a southerly wind the British attacked in line and broke the Danish defence, Danes and British each sustaining over 1,000 men killed. Nelson 'turned his blind eye' to Parker's premature signal to withdraw. The victory was as much a blow at Russia, leading the offensive 'Northern League', Nelson showing all his chivalry in subsequent armistice negotiations with the Danes. DDA

copyhold. Rack rents, or leasehold rents, in which the tenant pays an economic rent to the landlord, only became common across the country in the later 19th cent. Until then large parts of England, particularly in the north and west, but also in Norfolk, the home of the agricultural revolution, had a variety of arrangements offering more (or less) security to the tenant. These included copyhold, customaryhold, lifeleasehold, three-life, and 99-year leases, which gave the tenant virtual rights of ownership in return for a small annual rent, and occasional 'fines', payable usually on the death of the owner before the property could be transferred to his family. Copyhold literally meant 'by copy of the court roll', in other words by an agreement entered into the court rolls of the manor, and therefore approved by both landlord and tenant. These forms of tenure relieved the landlord of the responsibility of looking after the land, but were generally held not to have improved the quality of farming. By the 19th cent. the traditional rents were so out of line with real values that landlords sought to convert them to rack rents. However, copyhold was only abolished in 1926. JVB

copyright is the ownership of and right of control over the means of reproducing works of literature, art, drama, film, sound, and computer technology. Until the 18th cent. authors had little protection against pirate publication of their works. An important step forward, and the basis of modern legislation, was a statute of 1709 'to encourage learned men' (8 Anne c. 19) by granting the author sole right of publication for fourteen years, with the possibility of a further extension of another fourteen years. Publishers were required to submit nine copies of each work to be lodged in the royal library, the libraries of Oxford and Cambridge Universities, Sion College, London, the four Scottish universities, and the Faculty of Advocates in Edinburgh. The length of copyright was extended in 1814, 1842, and 1911 and comparable legislation brought in to protect plays, music, and engravings. Copyright now lasts 70 years after the death of an author. Under the terms of the Public Lending Rights scheme, introduced in 1983, authors can receive royalties on the use of their books in libraries in Britain and in Germany. JC

Coram, Thomas (1668–1751). Coram, a successful sea-captain, was an active philanthropist in the Walpole period, supporting the foundation of the colony of Georgia in America as a haven for debtors. Concerned at the plight of tiny children abandoned in the streets of London, he was the driving force behind the establishment of the Foundling hospital in 1739. *Hogarth, who painted a fine portrait of Coram, gave his support and *Handel conducted performances of *Messiah* to raise funds. In later life, Coram himself ran into financial difficulties and was assisted by a public subscription. He was buried in the chapel of his hospital and a statue raised outside. Though the hospital was demolished in 1928, the entrance lodges still stand in front of Coram's Fields, largely given over to children's playgrounds. JAC

Corbeil, treaty of, 1326. On 26 April 1326 Robert I Bruce and Charles IV of France agreed to a treaty of mutual aid against the English. This was an early step in the formation of the *Auld Alliance between Scotland and France. JAC

Corbridge. Coriostopitum was a major Roman military base and important town in the valley of the Tyne. The first base, dating to the campaigns of *Agricola (*c.*80), lay at Red House. Subsequently the base was moved three-quarters of a mile east to where the east–west road (the Stanegate) met the north–south road (Dere Street), just north of the Tyne bridge. A succession of forts was constructed through the late 1st and first half of the 2nd cents., one yielding two sets of Roman hoop armour, *lorica segmentata*. From the mid-2nd cent., the fort was abandoned and the military presence became a supply and works depot contained in two compounds at the centre of what was now largely a defended civil town. Inscriptions attest the continuing military importance of Corbridge whenever the Romans campaigned northwards. From *c.*200 dated an unfinished, large, square courtyard building in fine masonry at the centre of the town. Possibly a civil forum or a storehouse, similar continental buildings were markets for cross-border trade. The town consisted of buildings suggesting commercial activity tied to the military and the local populace, with little trace of high-status occupants. ASEC

Corfe castle (Dorset) stands on an isolated hill along the spine of the Isle of Purbeck, between Wareham and Swanage, guarding the routeways into Purbeck. Corfe was perhaps the site of an Anglo-Saxon royal residence and the place at which King *Edward, later known as 'the Martyr', was murdered by his stepmother Ælfthryth in 978. The castle was one of the first ordered to be built by William I after the battle of *Hastings and remained in royal hands until it was sold by Elizabeth I in 1572. Corfe, in the royal forest and warren of Purbeck, was a favourite residence of both King John and Henry III who spent large sums of money on the defences and on extensive domestic accommodation, the remains of which are known as the 'Gloriette'. During the Civil War the castle was held for the king, although most of Dorset was controlled by Parliament, and successfully withstood a siege in 1643, the defence being directed by Lady Bankes, wife of the owner. A second siege in 1646 ended when the attackers were secretly admitted to the castle. In recognition of her bravery Lady Bankes was allowed to retain the keys and seals of the castle, although the defences were systematically slighted. LR

Coritani. A British tribe and *civitas*. There has been much debate about the name of this tribe, and some believe it was called the Corieltauvi. There is no good reason, however, to discard the spelling provided by the geographer Ptolemy, who recorded them as the Coritani. The tribe occupied the territory between the rivers Welland and Humber, fringed on the west by the southern Pennines. To judge from their pre-invasion coinage, which often bears two names, it is possible that the leadership of the tribe was split between two kings or chiefs. If so, one might suggest that they ruled from the two major Iron Age centres known in the tribal territory at Old Sleaford and Leicester. The impression of the tribe at the time of the Roman conquest is that it was not yet united into a single powerful kingdom. This may explain the rapid Roman advance through their territory in the early years of the invasion, culminating in the foundation of a legionary fortress at *Lincoln *c.* AD 60. The pacified tribe were awarded local self-government as a *civitas* a decade or two later, and *Leicester, known as Ratae Coritanorum, was its administrative centre. KB

Cork (Corcach már Muman), **diocese of.** The Irish see of Cork was established in the province of *Cashel at the Council of Raithbressail (1111). St Finbar had founded a monastery in the 7th cent. Originally a Norse settlement, later colonized by the Anglo-Normans, it usually had English bishops from the 13th/14th cents. By the 1190s its cathedral had a secular chapter on the continental pattern. As part of a policy of Anglicization to establish sees in royal cities and so subordinate the Irish to English rule, Cork was eventually merged with Irish Cloyne (1411). This catholic diocese remained together until 1747, when Cork became separate again. Similarly the Anglican diocese of Cork has at times been held with Cloyne and Ross. There are cathedrals at all three sites. WMM

Corn Laws. First passed in 1815, these were always a controversial measure of agricultural protection. Britain's fast-growing population was making the country a food importer rather than exporter as before. The French wars had forced up domestic prices and encouraged agricultural investment, so there was fear of a post-war collapse of prices. Despite protests in some cities, Parliament passed a Corn Law that prohibited the importation of wheat until the domestic price reached 80 shillings a quarter. (Other cereals had similar provisions.) The 1820s still suffered agricultural depression despite a high ceiling for corn prices in years of poor harvests. In 1828 a sliding scale was introduced, which meant that duties would reduce as prices rose and vice versa. *Peel modified this in 1842 to a lower level of duties. Despite this trend to easier importation, the Corn Laws soon came under fierce attack from the *Anti-Corn Law League centred in the Lancashire cotton industry, which blamed recurrent industrial depressions on agricultural protection. It was also attacked as a system and symbol of aristocratic privilege. Under pressure the Whig government proposed to move to a fixed duty in 1841 but lost the election to the largely protectionist Conservatives. Peel, alarmed by the industrial crisis of 1842 and fearing the conjunction of high food prices with league agitation and mass unemployment, concluded that political stability required a sacrifice of the Corn Laws. Using the Irish potato famine of 1845 as an excuse, he proposed total repeal. This betrayal of party commitments and the landed interest produced a revolt of Conservative backbenchers and the farmers, led by the Central Agricultural Protection Society. Though Peel carried repeal of the Corn Laws in 1846 with full effect from 1849, he split his party into a free-trading minority and a protectionist majority. (Only in 1852 did the latter abandon the idea of protection.) Other free-trade measures followed and Corn Law repeal came to be seen as symbolizing the triumph of liberal and free-trading ideas. The main effect of repeal was delayed until the 1870s when cheap transatlantic grain flooded in and produced both sharp falls in food prices and acute agricultural depression. The United Kingdom was unusual among advanced countries in abandoning agricultural protection. BIC

Cornovii. British tribe and *civitas*. The Cornovii are a surprisingly obscure tribe, given that they lay well within the boundaries of the Roman province and their *civitas*-capital was one of the largest towns in Britain. They share their tribal name—which means 'the people of the horn'—with a Scottish tribe, but there is no reason to think they shared a common ancestry. Before the Roman invasion they issued no coinage and we know the names of none of their kings or chieftains. Equally there is no distinctive 'Cornovian' material culture by which to recognize them. Thus, the territory which we believe they occupied is effectively demarcated by the areas occupied by surrounding tribes rather than by any internal evidence from the Cornovii themselves. This suggests the *civitas* encompassed the modern counties of Shropshire, Staffordshire, and Cheshire. More or less at the heart of this territory lay the *civitas*-capital of Viriconium (*Wroxeter), which may have replaced, and borrowed the name of, the nearby Iron Age hill-fort on the Wrekin. It was from Wroxeter that an inscription was recovered which confirmed the existence of the *Civitas Cornoviorum*, previously known only from the writings of the Alexandrian geographer Ptolemy. KB

Cornwall. The oldest of English duchies (from 1337, though first a Norman earldom *c.*1140) has dimensions other than its peninsularity: the bulk of the course of the south-flowing Tamar forms the county boundary with Devon (some 45 miles), and but for the hills in which it rises could be canalized with the Marsland stream to render Cornwall an island. As the distant part of 'civitas *Dumnonia' the Romans may not have colonized Cornwall (any more than later Germanic invaders), but they monopolized its tin production as they did more precious metals elsewhere; and there is some evidence for a road system, including a link between Padstow and *Exeter (Isca). For Cornish people England is entered by crossing the Tamar, and in the Civil War, redoubtably though Cornish levies defended the crown within the county, they could not be brought to do so further east. Cornwall has a place in western prehistory at least as far back as the 3rd millennium BC, and in the 5th–6th cents. AD a church coloured by Irish and eastern Mediterranean practice; in later centuries it had a role not only in trade but in pilgrimage routes to southern Europe. Penzance is equidistant between Loch Foyle in Ulster and the Gironde; more intimately, perhaps, between Waterford and Quimper in Brittany. In the 5th cent. AD Brittany received an immigration from Dumnonia (Britons), and the disused Cornish language may still be studied in Breton schools. The Isles of *Scilly, 'a drowned landscape' integral to Cornwall's prehistory, lie on the same longitude as Ardnamurchan Point in Argyll and Cadiz; and, by extension, Cornwall has had its share in the evolution of the Atlantic world. The Falmouth mail service developed a proud record on its American run 1688–1850, and in the 19th cent. Cornish miners worked, and died, in the mines of South America and South Africa; in 1901 Marconi, in Newfoundland, received the first transatlantic radio transmission from Poldhu near the Lizard. Back home, it had taken all Brunel's genius to bridge the Tamar at Saltash 1857–9, and so bring the railway, and a holiday industry, to Cornwall.

Cornwall's geology is predominantly granite and slate, the latter used for walls as well as roofs, but china clay, around St Austell, is its one extractive industry today. In antiquity tin from Cornwall's streams, increasingly deep-mined by the later 16th cent., was the region's life-blood. As ingots the metal was exported far and wide, but the earliest traders appear to have used the two north coast havens, St Ives-Hayle and the Camel estuary, rather than those on the south coast towards which most of the tin-bearing streams flowed: while the western shores of Falmouth's estuary have rendered up hoards of Roman coins (in payment?), no place in Britain is so overwhelmingly rich in the remains of 5th–6th-cent. Mediterranean pottery (import containers?) as is Tintagel, on present evidence the prime entrepôt for this epoch. Few, if any, British sites have more romance and mystery than this inhospitable headland: its history prior to the cliff-hanging castle built there by Earl *Richard of Cornwall in the 1230s is at best elusive, and associations with 'King *Arthur' are solely attributable to the chronicler *Geoffrey of Monmouth, writing a century earlier. Not a vestige of corroborative evidence has surfaced since his time. More prosaically, at the time of *Domesday Book (1086), in which neither Tintagel nor tin receive mention, Cornwall was evidently underpopulated on the scale of one man per 160 acres. In 1346, however, Fowey was able to send over 40 ships to aid Edward III at Calais; in Armada year (1588) the port had only one ship in Queen Elizabeth's service, though Cornwall had become one of the most populous of southern counties. Its present-day population is some 480,000, much the most concentrated urban area being Redruth–Camborne. Truro (18,000) only became a centre in the early 19th cent., its cathedral, built 1890–1910, marking Cornwall as a diocese independent of Exeter for the first time in a millennium.

Domesday Book may confirm that Anglo-Saxon Cornwall was underdeveloped, but the special status of the tin-miners may have been established before the Conquest. When, in 1201, King John granted them their first charter confirming exceptional legal autonomies, in the Court of the *Stannaries, agriculture in Cornwall, which had once been exiguous, needed to give way to the territorial requirements of the tin-streamers; with the dukedom's establishment in 1336 their rights came under royal wardenship, though the court itself was only formally wound up in the mid-19th cent. By the 16th cent. the leading county families, Rashleighs, Eliots, Godolphins, formed closely knit groupings to which the Tudor monarchs were ready to respond by granting enfranchisement to some fifteen additional boroughs, including Bossiney and Penryn, famed respectively for their slate and granite quarries. The measure of their political evanescence, however, may be gauged by the *Great Reform Act of 1832 which disfranchised almost all of them, a quarter of the total number (56) which were then abolished in England and Wales. But great houses, Lanhydrock, Cotehele, Trerice, still attest to no mean aristocratic pride. By the end of the 18th cent. Cornishmen of a different stamp emerged: John Opie, the precocious portraitist and art theoretician, Richard Trevithick, wrestler and inventor of high-pressure steam traction, Humphry *Davy, perfecter of the miner's safety lamp. In the 19th cent. Robert Hunt became professor of London's School of Mines, a fellow of the Royal Society, and a stalwart supporter of the Royal Institution of Cornwall (1818) and the Polytechnic Society of Falmouth (1833). Such bodies sustained self-awareness in a county which, 150 years before, had been favoured with the first large-scale map of any English county. Today, though the pilchard no longer thrives along their coasts and their deep mines are derelict, the Cornish retain their cultural richness. Britain and the wider world would be poorer without their artists and potters, their cream, and Mr Lemon Hart's rum. DDA

Cornwall, duchy of. From the Norman Conquest onwards, Cornwall has had close links with the crown. William the Conqueror gave large estates there to his half-brother Robert; Reynold, an illegitimate son of Henry I, was created earl of Cornwall in 1141; John's second son *Richard was earl of Cornwall, but his line became extinct by 1300. In 1337 Edward III created his son, *Edward the Black Prince, duke of Cornwall—the first English dukedom. Henceforward the duchy belonged to the prince of Wales, reverting to the crown when there was no prince—for example, during much of the Tudor period. It was administered from Lostwithiel. It is a private estate, provides the prince of Wales with most of his income, and has property outside Cornwall. The lord warden of the stannaries, appointed by the duke, presides over the Council of the Duchy, and the duke appoints the sheriff of Cornwall. The great influence of the duchy may explain why there have been few great aristocratic families in Cornwall. The duke had considerable electoral influence before 1832, when Cornwall was full of parliamentary boroughs, which was the basis for the opposition interest built up by *Frederick, prince of Wales, against Sir Robert Walpole. The duchy owns 130,000 acres in some 23 counties, together with a number of shops, offices, and houses. The annual income from the duchy was estimated in 1996 as £4.5 million, but since 1993 the prince of Wales has paid standard income tax. JAC

Cornwallis, Charles, 1st Marquis Cornwallis (1738–1805). Soldier and administrator. Cornwallis served during the American War of Independence and from 1780 commanded the British forces in South Carolina. Though an able general, he was cut off at *Yorktown by American forces and the French fleet. He was forced to surrender on 19 October 1781 thus ending the war. In 1786–93 Cornwallis acted as governor-general and commander of the army in Bengal. He introduced the permanent settlement, concerning landownership, and judicial and revenue reforms. He also gained victory over Tipu Sahib of Mysore at the battle of Arikera (13 May 1791) and concluded settlements with other native powers. In 1798 Cornwallis left for Ireland as lord-lieutenant and succeeded in subduing the *Irish Rebellion. He presided over the Act of *Union (1800) but resigned a year later after the government's refusal to grant catholic emancipation. Cornwallis died on 5 October 1805 at Ghazipur shortly after resuming his former post in India. RAS

coronations. Though the monarch succeeds automatically on the death of his predecessor, the coronation is a public avowal of his new position. Indeed, earlier tradition held that he was not really king until he had been crowned. Consequently, coronations followed accessions very swiftly, particularly if there were rival candidates, allowing little time for elaborate preparations. Harold II was crowned on the very day of Edward the Confessor's burial and Henry I only three days after his brother William Rufus' death in 1100. The ceremony was, essentially, religious—a dedication to God's service. But the political opportunities were soon apparent. Monarchs wished for a widespread demonstration of their acceptance, especially by the most eminent in the land, with the chance to remind their subjects of the need for obedience: subjects found in the ceremony a chance to remind monarchs of their own rights. Hence, the evolution of the ceremony registers the ebb and flow of political power. It is also a remarkable example of the way in which new features can be grafted onto old stems.

The English ceremonial which developed was more religious and more elaborate than that in Scotland or Ireland. The first recorded instance in England of a ceremony reflects both its nature and its limitations. In 787 Ecgfrith, son of *Offa of Mercia, was publicly anointed to ensure his succession: in the event he survived for only six months before he was overthrown by a cousin, *Cenwulf. The coronation of *Edgar at Bath in 973 suggests the development of considerable ritual, much of it borrowed from Frankish sources. A ring, sword, and sceptre were delivered as tokens of authority and the anthem 'Zadok the Priest' chanted. *Æthelred, his second son, was crowned at Kingston upon Thames in 978 where the subsequent order of service seems to have been established. *Edward the Confessor was crowned at Winchester in 1043, but all later coronations have taken place at Westminster.

The central features of the ceremony have remained largely unchanged though there have been many alterations in the regalia and the oath. The monarch is first presented, usually by the archbishop of Canterbury; takes a series of oaths; is anointed with holy oil; is crowned, receives the regalia, and accepts homage. A preliminary walk to the abbey was abandoned by Charles I in 1625 and a subsequent banquet in Westminster Hall dropped by William IV in 1831, partly as an economy measure, partly because his brother's banquet in 1821 had ended in unseemly behaviour.

Most of the ancient regalia of the crown was sold off after the execution of Charles I. The spoon and ampulla, in the shape of a golden eagle, survived. The ampulla was believed to contain holy oil, said to have been given by the Virgin Mary to Thomas *Becket and rediscovered in time to assist Henry IV at his coronation in 1399. For good measure the same monarch, who needed all the support he could get, was preceded by four swords, while his predecessors had been content with three. The rest of the regalia now consists of replicas fashioned in 1660 for Charles II, or later additions. A copy of the crown believed to have been worn by Edward the Confessor was made at the Restoration, and a lighter crown produced for Victoria in 1838. The coronation chair was made for Edward I, again on the pattern of Edward the Confessor's, and until 1996 included the stone of *Scone, brought back from Scotland in 1296. Two swords of state were made in 1660, one of which subsequently went missing: a third was made in 1678. The sword of offering was made in 1821. The spurs dated from Henry IV and had to be replaced. Bracelets have made sporadic appearances. The ring was a personal piece of the monarch. Charles I's fell into the hands of the Stuarts in exile, was returned in the 19th cent., and is now in Edinburgh castle. An orb was introduced in the 15th cent. to reinforce the monarch's imperial claims to the throne of France. A bible was added to the ceremony in 1689. Of the ritual, the 'vivat' by

Westminster boys dates from 1625 and *Handel's setting of 'Zadok the Priest' has been used since 1727.

Politically, the alterations to the oath are instructive. The original oaths were fervent but vague, and augmented by the coronation charters. Mistrust of Edward II led in 1308 to a new oath being added, to maintain the laws as chosen by his subjects. Henry VIII wished to modify this and it was much diluted for the coronation of Edward VI. Tampering with the oath in the interests of the royal prerogative was one of the charges against Archbishop *Laud in 1644. After the experience of James II's reign, the oath for William and Mary was intended to bolt the door against catholicism and despotism, obliging the monarchs to observe 'the statutes in parliament agreed on' and to maintain 'the Protestant reformed religion established by law'. A further significant change had the monarch replying 'I solemnly promise' instead of 'I grant.' When George III and George IV pleaded their coronation oaths against catholic emancipation, it was by no means a specious argument or political ploy: George III wrote that the coronation statute was 'understood to bind the crown' not to consent to the repeal of the existing laws for the defence of the protestant religion. Elizabeth II's oath in 1953 included a promise to govern in accordance with the 'respective laws and customs' of the Commonwealth countries over which she reigned.

In practice coronation ceremonies have frequently had difficulty in living up to the solemnity of the occasion. William the Conqueror's coronation was marred by a massacre of his new Saxon subjects, whose shouts of acclamation were mistaken by nervous Norman guards as the signal for a rising. The pageantry of the royal *champion has often caused problems. In 1377 Richard II's champion appeared at the abbey during mass and had to be told to go away. In 1685 James II's champion fell flat on his face, which suggests that it was just as well that the challenge was not taken up. Lord Talbot, in 1761, who accompanied the champion as lord high steward, had trained his horse to back away from the royal presence, but, to the delight of the onlookers, the animal insisted on entering backwards as well. For George IV's coronation, the horse was prudently borrowed from Astley's circus, where he would be used to noisy crowds. After this, the role of the champion was much reduced. In 1559 Elizabeth I complained that the holy oil was greasy and smelled unpleasant. In 1727 Queen *Caroline had to borrow jewels since George I had given the rest to his mistress. A special hazard at the coronation of George IV was the arrival, in the middle of the ceremony, of his estranged wife, demanding to be let in. Victoria's own account tells of the pain she suffered when the archbishop pushed the ring on her wrong finger, and George VI's account of 1937 was that the archbishop juggled so much with the crown that he never did find out if it was on the right way.

The coronation of Scottish monarchs remained much simpler. Until the 13th cent. it was a ceremony of inauguration, usually at Scone, involving the elevation on a stone or chair. Alexander II's aspirations for a crown and anointing met with papal disapproval. Each was granted in 1329 to Robert I by a papal bull and used in 1331 at the coronation of David II. But later ceremony was restrained by the fact that so many Scottish monarchs succeeded as infants or children and could not sustain a demanding role: James III, for example, was inaugurated at Kelso, aged 8, a week after James II's death outside Floors castle in 1460. Charles I's belated Scottish coronation in 1633 added to his difficulties when he insisted on an unpopular Anglican service. The last Scottish coronation, that of Charles II in 1651, was a hasty business in the midst of adversity: Charles was required to swear to the covenant, and anointing was dropped as a superstitious and popish practice. JAC

Cannon, J. A., and Griffiths, R., *The Oxford Illustrated History of the Monarchy* (Oxford, 1988); Rose, T., *The Coronation Ceremony of the Kings and Queens of England and the Crown Jewels* (1992); Schramm, P. E., *A History of the English Coronation* (Oxford, 1937).

Coronel, battle of, 1914. At the outbreak of the First World War, the German Pacific squadron, commanded by Admiral von Spee, steamed across the Pacific with the intention of rounding Cape Horn and returning to Germany. On 1 November 1914 von Spee was intercepted by a British squadron commanded by Rear-Admiral Sir Christopher Craddock off Coronel on the Chilean coast. The Germans had more modern vessels armed with heavier guns and within an hour they had sunk most of Craddock's ships and resumed their voyage. They were themselves sunk at the battle of the *Falkland Islands in December. DF

coroner. The coroner was an official appointed by the king to 'keep' or enrol the pleas of the crown for the county and thus to safeguard the rights of the crown (especially in relation to criminal law). The office was first referred to in 1194 though it probably existed before that time. Under the Norman and Angevin kings the pleas of the crown were noted by the sheriff and any fines due to the king from these offences were collected by him. The coroner was appointed to keep a check on the sheriff so that he did not defraud the crown of its rightful profits of criminal justice. In *Magna Carta the power of the sheriff was further diminished in that he was no longer to hold the pleas of the crown. In addition to keeping the pleas of the crown, the coroner held an inquiry or 'inquest' into certain matters which were of special interest to the king. These included inquiries into the cause of sudden and unexplained death, treasure trove wrecks, and finding of sturgeon as belonging to the crown. The coroner still has an important role, holding inquests in cases of sudden or unexplained death. MM

Corporation Act, 1661. This statute (13 Car. II c. 1) was the first part of the '*Clarendon code' and set out to reassert Anglican supremacy after the Restoration. Persons holding municipal office were obliged to qualify by taking communion with the Church of England. Many nonconformists felt able to do so and the Act did not prevent most dissenters from holding office. It was tightened up by the Act against *Occasional Conformity in 1711 but relaxed during the Walpole period by periodic Acts of indemnity. It remained a bone of contention throughout the 18th cent. and was not repealed until 1828. JAC

corporations. A large number of economic activities are so complex or costly that they can only be undertaken by the combination of the efforts of many individuals. It is not surprising, therefore, that all economic systems have been characterized by the development of large institutions such as the state or the firm. Businesses have always overcome the limitations of individual action by forming partnerships. Early forms of large-scale undertakings were found in the trading *companies whose business took them to the Baltic or Mediterranean. Major companies, trading ever further afield, were granted monopoly rights by the crown. The most famous was the *East India Company, chartered in 1600 for a single voyage, subsequently renewed, and eventually established as a continuous operation in 1657. Such joint-stock companies, as the name suggests, brought together the capital, and sometimes the labour, of many partners. By 1617 the East India Company had 36 ships and 934 stockholders. These large organizations, the precursors of modern corporations, proliferated in the following century with royal charters granted to the *Bank of England in 1694 and, early in the following century, to the *South Sea Company, the *Royal Exchange Company, and the London Assurance. The government took an opportunity in granting charters to secure promises of loans from the beneficiaries. The appearance of the new stock brought opportunities for speculative gain and there was considerable trading in the shares of the companies which increased the value of their stock. This practice was stimulated by the fact that transactions could be conducted on the basis of a partial down-payment, often as little as 5 per cent. These developments mark the beginnings both of a financial market in company shares and of the emergence of large business organizations, whose need for resources was so great that it lay beyond the wealth of the partners and had to draw on a wider pool of funds through the financial institutions. CHL

corresponding societies. The initial welcome to the French Revolution in Britain came largely from middle-class and dissenting groups, but its ideas soon gained wider popularity through the spread of Painite radicalism, disseminated especially by corresponding societies. In 1792 the most famous of all the radical societies of the period—the London Corresponding Society—was founded by Thomas Hardy, a Scottish shoemaker, with the intention of corresponding with provincial radicals in Manchester, Sheffield, Norwich, and elsewhere to promote the cause of parliamentary reform. Unlike other radical reform movements of the 1790s, the corresponding societies were composed mainly of artisans and tradesmen. These 'English Jacobins' were organized in 'divisions' which met regularly in different public houses for discussion, lectures, and fellowship. In 1793–4, as an alternative to petitioning for parliamentary reform, the reformers took up *Paine's suggestion of electing delegates to a national convention on the French model. The government, thoroughly alarmed, arrested the leaders and clamped down heavily on the LCS. By 1797 the corresponding societies had collapsed or been driven underground. They marked the emergence of an articulate political voice from the unenfranchised. At their peak in 1797 there were perhaps over 100 societies, with a nominal membership of 10,000. JFCH

Corrichie, battle of, 1562. When Mary, queen of Scots, returned from France as a widow in 1561, great influence was wielded by her half-brother Lord James Stuart, illegitimate son of James V. He pursued a pro-English and pro-protestant policy. Early in 1562 he was made earl of *Moray, which was also claimed by the 4th earl of *Huntly, a leader of the catholics. Huntly was forced into rebellion and then defeated and captured by Lord James on 28 October at Corrichie, west of Aberdeen. Huntly died that night, being 'gross, corpulent, short of breath'. JAC

Corrupt Practices Act, 1883. Electoral corruption continued to flourish after the Reform Act of 1832 and was not eradicated either by the Corrupt Practices Act of 1854, or by *secret ballot in 1872. The general election of 1880 produced a number of cases of flagrant treating or bribery. The 1883 Act (46 & 47 Vic. c. 51) strengthened the previous Act, which had called for the publication of candidates' expenses, by laying down the limits of electoral expenditure. Corruption was not eliminated but the growing size of the electorate and the disfranchisement of many small boroughs reduced it. Even so, a royal commission reported that at Worcester in 1906 there were 500 voters, 'mainly of the needy and loafing class', who were 'prepared to sell their votes for drink or money'. JAC

Cort, Henry (1740–1800). Cort was born at Lancaster, son of a mason. He became an agent to the navy in the 1760s and his interest in the production of iron developed after the Russians had raised their prices. By 1784 he was able to patent an invention for 'puddling' iron to make it malleable. With Adam Jellicoe he entered into large naval contracts, but Jellicoe's death in 1789 revealed fraud, which brought Cort down. During the last years of his life, he existed on a small pension. During his lifetime, the production of iron in Britain rose from some 30,000 tons to well over 200,000 tons. JAC

Corunna, battle of, 1809. In October 1808 the British, under Sir John *Moore, pushed into northern Spain to ease the pressure on the Spanish army and draw the French from Madrid. Outnumbered and inadequately supplied, they were soon in danger of being cut off. Moore skilfully retreated through the Galician mountains towards the coast, over 250 miles in harsh winter conditions, closely pursued by the French under Marshal Soult. At Corunna on 16 January 1809 Soult attacked with 20,000 men. Moore with 15,000 men uniformly repulsed the French, allowing the British to evacuate safely by sea, but Moore himself was fatally wounded. RAS

Cosgrave, W. T. (1880–1965). President of Executive Council 1922–32, Cosgrave is the least remembered and least colourful of leading politicians of the Irish revolutionary era. He had considerable experience in Dublin corporation before becoming a Sinn Fein MP in 1917, and minister of local government in the Dáil administration of 1919–21. His vote enabled the *Anglo-Irish treaty to be accepted by the Dáil cabinet in December 1921. In August 1922, the darkest hour of the civil war, he replaced Michael *Collins as leader of the Free State and provided much-needed stability. Cosgrave governed along conservative social and economic lines and his party, Cumann na nGaedheal, then Fine Gael, showed no capacity for winning popular nation-wide support. In 1932, defeated by *de Valera and Fianna Fail, he became an ineffective political figure, finally resigning the leadership in 1943. His son Liam, Taoiseach 1973–7, shared many of his father's unheroic characteristics. MAH

Cotman, John Sell (1782–1842). Architect, draughtsman, landscape and water-colour painter. The son of a prosperous silk-mercer in Norwich, he was intended for his father's business, but preferring art, went to London to study in 1798. He exhibited at the Royal Academy 1800–6, before returning to Norwich in 1807 to open a school for drawing and design. He joined the Norwich Society of Artists, becoming president in 1811. In 1834, on the recommendation of *Turner, he became professor of drawing at King's College, London. His later years were clouded by ill-health and depression. His original painting style was not popular, but he is now seen as one of the most original and versatile English artists of the first half of the 19th cent., with the water-colour *Greta Bridge* (1805) probably his masterpiece. JC

Cottenham, Charles Christopher Pepys, 1st earl of (1781–1851). Pepys's grandfather was William Dowdeswell, a pillar of the *Rockingham party in the 1770s, and his father, a master in Chancery, was created a baronet in 1801. After Harrow and Trinity College, Cambridge, Pepys practised law and was brought into Parliament in 1831 on the *Fitzwilliam interest. He succeeded John Campbell as solicitor-general in February 1834, became master of the rolls in September 1834, and was 1st commissioner of the great seal in 1835 when *Melbourne declined to reappoint *Brougham to the lord chancellorship. Pepys was promoted lord chancellor in 1836 and was given a barony, serving until the Whigs went out of office in 1841. On their return in 1846 he resumed the lord chancellorship, resigning in 1850, when he was raised to the earldom. An uncle, Sir Lucas Pepys, was a distinguished physician and a younger brother was a bishop. Cottenham was regarded as sensible and hard-working, but he was not a good speaker, often in poor health, and reserved himself largely for legal matters. JAC

Cottington, Francis, 1st Baron Cottington (*c.*1579–1652). Cottington was a Somerset gentleman who became a leading minister before the Civil War. He was first employed by James I in Spanish matters, knew the country well, and spoke the language. In 1622 he became secretary to Charles, prince of Wales, was given a baronetcy in 1623, and brought into Parliament. A shadow fell over his progress when he quarrelled with *Buckingham, but after the duke's murder Cottingham forged ahead. In 1629 he became chancellor of the Exchequer and held the post until 1642. He was rewarded in 1631 for negotiating peace with Spain with a barony. As master of the Court of *Wards from 1635 he screwed up the income at the cost of much irritation. As soon as the royal government began to falter, Cottington was a marked man and began to divest himself of his offices. When war broke out he joined the king at Oxford, acted as lord high treasurer, and on the surrender in 1646 went into exile. He died a catholic in Spain in June 1652. *Clarendon described him as a good-humoured and entertaining schemer—'he left behind a greater esteem of his parts than love of his person'. JAC

cotton industry. Cotton manufacture was introduced to Britain from the Netherlands in the 16th cent. and was established in a number of areas by 1750, including Lancashire, East Anglia, and the west of Scotland. Mixtures of cotton and linen were particularly in demand, and London was the most important market for these fustians. London bills of exchange were an important element in trading capital, but requirements for fixed capital were modest until the advent of the factory, and met generally from profits. Pure cotton goods were very expensive but highly fashionable and were imported from India by the *East India Company. These oriental products were commonly imitated in cheaper cotton mixtures. Before the industry started to move into factories, an experienced labour force and commercial networks had been created, and in some places concentration of production in large workshops without significant changes in technology had already begun.

Shortly after 1700 the silk industry fathered the water-powered factory, and this organization was transferred to the cotton industry by Richard *Arkwright in the late 1760s. Increasing demand and interruptions to the supply of Indian goods, provoked by wars, encouraged the mechanization of spinning with the introduction of the jenny, water frame, and mule, then improvement of preparation machinery, especially carding, and finally weaving with the power loom. Power was provided at first by horse capstans, windmills, and water-wheels, but James *Watt's rotary steam-engine encouraged location near cheap coal supplies in towns, and the industry tended to concentrate in Lancashire and the west of Scotland. Hand-spinning rapidly declined in the late 18th cent. Hand-loom weaving survived much longer, but growing immiseration was the lot of its practitioners by the 1840s.

Cotton created many opportunities for social and economic mobility. On the supply side the most important feature was the emergence of the southern states of America as the world's leading producer; Liverpool soon after 1800 became the most important port for the cotton trade and superseded London. The rise of Liverpool and the growth of machine-making firms in Oldham and Manchester gave Lancashire cardinal cost advantages. Thus Manchester became the main centre for the cotton trade and manufacture in the 19th cent.

One must not exaggerate the importance of cotton to the British economy. Research suggests that it probably never accounted for more than 8 to 10 per cent of national income. Yet the cotton industry had a wide influence. For instance, it pointed the way for other textile industries; it stimulated civil and mechanical engineering, aided the development of the chemical industry, and was significant in the growth of wholesale and retail trade.

The industry slowly came under pressure in foreign markets because of the rise of competition and the transfer of technology to other countries. Competitive disadvantages were compounded by the hardness of sterling before 1914 and the omnipresence of tariff barriers. Yet Britain was dominant in world cotton markets till 1914. The industry had structural weaknesses which, initially hidden, were exposed in the period 1919–39: an unwillingness or inability or slowness to adopt the latest technology; undue specialization rather than integration combining spinning, weaving, finishing, and the clothing trades; a refusal to acknowledge the weaknesses of **laissez-faire* when faced with economic discrimination; a low wage/low productivity strategy which bedevilled industrial relations; and the rise of man-made fibres, beginning with rayon (artificial silk).

The fall in exports in the inter-war years represented not only the success of competitors and the deficiencies of Britain's industry, but also the problems besetting the world economy. The general acceptance of the need for tariffs and the rationalization of the industry was rapid after 1929, with state intervention reducing capacity under a Spindles Board (1936) and the Cotton Industry (Reorganization) Act (1939), which established a cartel under the Cotton Board. After 1951 decline was swift and would have been worse without high levels of protection and the imposition of import quotas. Yet the progress of artificial fibres and cheap imports, often from the Commonwealth, could not be gainsaid. The state managed further contraction under the Cotton Industry Act (1959), only large integrated multinational firms surviving by 1990. The epic success of the 'industrial revolution' became a horror story from the 1920s. JB

Council, Great. See GREAT COUNCIL.

Council for Wales in the Marches. Edward IV had large estates as earl of March in the Welsh border and in the 1470s established a council at Shrewsbury under the nominal authority of the infant prince of Wales. Henry VII, Welsh by birth, followed the example. After a period in abeyance, the council seems to have been revived by Thomas *Cromwell. The Act of Union with Wales in 1536 brought the whole area under closer royal supervision and a statute of 1543 established a council with wide authority in Wales and in the border counties of Shropshire, Herefordshire, Worcestershire, and Gloucestershire. Much of its business was judicial and petitioners were saved a long and expensive journey to London. Unlike the *Council of the North, the Council in Wales was not abolished by the *Long Parliament, though the English border counties were removed from its remit. Reconstituted in 1660, the council never regained its former importance and was abolished in 1689 by 1 Wm. & Mar. c. 27 on the grounds that the ordinary law courts were quite capable of providing justice. JAC

Council of State, 1649–60. After the execution of Charles I and the abolition of the monarchy, the *Rump Parliament in February 1649 gave executive power to a Council of State of 41 members. It contained three peers, a number of lawyers including *Bradshaw, and senior army officers such as *Cromwell, *Fairfax, and *Skippon. Cromwell dissolved the council in 1653 immediately after he had dismissed the Rump and appointed an interim Council of State in April. When Cromwell became lord protector in December 1653 he was given a council of 21 under the *Instrument of Government. Though it had less power than its predecessor, it was far from negligible and Cromwell complained that he was in toils. In the *Humble Petition and Advice, adopted in 1657, it was referred to as the Privy Council. When the Rump was recalled in 1659, another Council of State was appointed, but it was swept away at the Restoration. Charles II held a meeting of a much truncated Privy Council at Canterbury as soon as he landed in 1660. JAC

Council of the North. The chief arm of government in the turbulent northern shires of Yorkshire, Durham, Cumberland, Westmorland, and Northumberland in the Tudor and early Stuart period. It was responsible for law and order and had wide jurisdiction. As duke of Gloucester in Edward IV's reign, Richard III had shared power in the north with the earl of *Northumberland. Having seized the crown in 1483, he appointed Northumberland warden of the marches but created a separate council at York under his nephew and heir, the earl of *Lincoln. Henry VIII allowed the council to lapse but revived it in 1525 under the nominal control of his natural son Henry *FitzRoy. In 1530 it was made a royal council and after the *Pilgrimage of Grace in 1536, which the council had failed to prevent, it was reorganized once more. Its importance in Elizabeth I's reign is indicated by the fact that, after the dangerous rising of the *northern earls in 1569, the presidency was held by Lord *Huntingdon, the queen's cousin, from 1572 until 1595, and by Lord Burghley, elder brother of Sir Robert *Cecil, from 1599 until 1603. In 1628 Charles I appointed *Strafford to be president. He retained the office while he was lord deputy in Ireland but in 1641 was attainted and executed. The council was abolished by the *Long Parliament shortly afterwards. It was not revived at the Restoration, though Charles II considered doing so in 1664. From the dissolution of the monasteries to its abolition, the council met in the King's Manor at York, the residence of the lord president. JAC

counties. The county (otherwise the shire) has been the main unit of provincial government in England from before the Norman Conquest until modern times. *Domesday Book (1086) describes 32 shires. Five of these were subdivisions of the former kingdom of Wessex. Of these, Hampshire already existed in 757; the others may be as old. Five shires derive from former kingdoms absorbed into the dominions of the house of Wessex (Kent, Sussex, Essex, and East Anglia (divided into Norfolk and Suffolk)). The shires of the midlands were nearly all created in the 10th cent. The only later additions to the system were Westmorland, Cumberland, Lancashire, Durham, Northumberland, and the anomalous Rutland. It is a remarkable fact that the Domesday shires had, to a notable extent, the precise boundaries which they were to retain for many centuries. By 1066 each shire (sometimes pairs of shires) had an official, the *sheriff, responsible for the royal lands and the exercise of aspects of royal authority. The *county court, meeting twice annually, was a principal forum for justice both civil and criminal.

In the generations which followed the Norman Conquest the principal changes were the construction of shire castles as cores of local authority and a great increase in the frequency with which the shire courts met. Although the importance of these courts diminished in the later Middle Ages, the most important new judicial authorities, the *justices of the peace, were organized on a shire basis. The justices acquired many and various powers as time went on; their *quarter sessions were the principal organs of local government until the establishment of *county councils by the Local Government Act of 1888. This Act divided some historic shires for governmental purposes. Their historic boundaries had been modestly rationalized by earlier legislation.

The only major innovation in shire government in the centuries before 1888 (setting on one side the events of the Civil War and Interregnum) was the creation of the office of *lord-lieutenant in 1549. His function was to command the shire levies. From their very earliest days a predominant function of the shires had been military. Shire associations of regular regiments (which sometimes had a long history going back to the Militia Act of 1757) were made standard and universal by an act of 1881. This was an expression of the greater shire-consciousness characteristic of the mid and late 19th cent., expressed also in the associations of archaeological societies, cricket clubs, and agricultural societies. An Act of 1972 brought major changes in county organization. Some historic shires were merged and new ones without historic antecedents created. Further changes were made in 1996. JCa

country houses. The country house was the focal point and symbol of the ascendancy of the gentry and aristocracy in the period between the Glorious Revolution and the First World War. It no longer had military significance. It was not a castle, did not need moats or peel towers, and had no fortifications, unless the owner in the late 18th cent. had a taste for mock Gothic and battlements. It was large enough to accommodate the family and its dependants, and the bevy of servants who supported them. Ideally it could give hospitality to a considerable number of guests since it often served as a political headquarters. It stood in its own park, with a lodge and a drive, partly to give privacy, partly to impress or even overawe visitors. The minimum requirements were a large dining room, good stables, and a reception room: the larger houses ran to long galleries, libraries, orangeries, and lakes. Follies and eye-catchers were optional extras.

Country house does not seem the right term for Tudor residences. The great palaces—*Hatfield, *Longleat, Burghley, *Hardwick—were rather too grand: 'prodigy houses' has been suggested. Many of the rest were modest, often in the middle of a medieval village, squalid rather than picturesque. The fields surrounding the villages were still, for the most part, communally cultivated on a strip system, giving the house little space of its own. One of the objects of *enclosures in the 18th cent. was often to round off a park, eliminate an irritating intrusion, or divert a footpath. Until 1693, the main road from Deptford to Woolwich ran right through the middle of the Queen's House at *Greenwich.

Most of the land released by the *dissolution of the monasteries in the 1540s found its way into the hands of the gentry and nobility and many of the estates were future country houses, betraying their origins as Woburn abbey (Beds.), Newbattle abbey (Lothian), or Hitchin priory (Herts.). The great building period followed the Restoration in 1660 and particularly the Glorious Revolution in 1688. Good examples of the modest 17th-cent. manor house are Washington Old Hall, south of Newcastle upon Tyne, and Woolbridge Manor (Dorset), where Thomas *Hardy made Tess spend her unlucky honeymoon. On a grander scale are Capheaton, Northumberland (1668), Milton, Oxfordshire (1670), and Uppark, Sussex (1685–90). With *Chatsworth, Derbyshire (1687), *Castle Howard, Yorkshire (1699), Stowe, Buckinghamshire (1720), and *Mellerstain, Borders (1725) we are moving towards palaces.

The style of life within the walls depended greatly on the wealth and interests of the owner. After 1688, Parliament met annually, usually in November, and members were not keen to stay in London long after Easter. The country house season was the summer and early autumn. Leading politicians held conclaves—Lord *Temple had a 'grand congress' at Stowe in October 1783 to concert opposition to Fox's *India Bill; county members cultivated their neighbours and freeholders with dinners, balls, and races, the lesser gentry took advantage of the light evenings to visit within a radius of 10 miles or so. Though the vision, particularly for the old, was a country retreat, there were many, especially among the young, who were bored in the country and pined for the London season. The comfort of the house depended greatly on the quality of its servants. Augustus Hervey at Stowe in 1765 'never saw so large a house so well conducted . . . servants all attention and respect'. But Horace *Walpole at Houghton, much neglected, in 1773 found three old servants drunk before breakfast. The problem of finding reliable and cheap servants became acute in the later 19th cent. and was one of the factors undermining the country-house way of life.

The mid-18th cent. was an age of improvement. A large number of country houses were rebuilt in classical style and much money spent on embellishing parks. At Kedleston, Milton, Chippenham (Cambs.), Nuneham Courtenay, and Wimpole, whole villages were removed to give greater privacy. Visiting the new seats and inspecting the improvements became a favourite pastime and housekeepers turned the honest penny by showing tourists round when the family was not in residence. The internal arrangements were remodelled to give much greater privacy and comfort than had existed in the semi-communal house of medieval times, with its great hall. Water closets began to be installed in the late 17th cent. though progress was slow.

Though the 18th cent. was the heyday of the country house, more were built in the 19th cent. than ever before. *Disraeli, who surprisingly became leader of the Tory Party, had no country house of his own and had to borrow money from the Bentincks to buy Hughenden Manor in Buckinghamshire. Sir William *Armstrong, the north-eastern armaments king, built himself an extraordinary country retreat at Cragside in the Northumbrian hills, where elegance gave way to comfort. The Rothschild family covered the vale of Aylesbury with large and ornate country houses—Aston Clinton (1840), Mentmore (1852–4), Tring (1873), Ascott (1874), Waddesdon (1880), and Halton (1884). The spread of the railway network made visiting country houses, particularly for the weekend, easier than ever before.

The decline in the later 19th cent. had a variety of causes. Country gentlemen no longer dominated politics, at Westminster or in the shire, and the country house lost its *raison d' être* as a political centre. The agricultural depression after the 1870s struck the landed interest hard and for decades land ceased to be an attractive investment. The cost of running households and estates escalated just as *death duties and discriminatory taxes were beginning to bite. Though many country houses survive, others have been transformed into hideous parodies of former greatness, and serve as conference centres, reform homes, cult headquarters, and even fun-fairs and amusement parks. JAC

County Councils Act, 1888. The *Municipal Corporations Act of 1835 had given elected corporations to the large towns. Rural administration remained in the hands of the justices of the peace, though the smaller towns had their own local institutions. The 1884 Reform Act, which extended the parliamentary vote to many people in the shires, made the situation anomalous. In the Act of 1888, Lord Salisbury's government created 62 county councils in England and Wales, some of the larger shires being subdivided. Sixty-one towns of over 50,000 inhabitants were given county borough status and London was given its own county council. The franchise was similar to that in the boroughs. Unmarried women could vote for the new councils but not serve on them—a position not remedied until 1907. To the counties' responsibilities for highways, and a share in the police, were soon added powers for education. In England there was great continuity of personnel, many JPs being elected, and several lords-lieutenant becoming chairmen. But in Wales there was a much greater change and nonconformist liberals swept the board at the expense of the gentry. The equivalent Scottish Act was passed in 1889. JAC

county courts. The shire or county courts were the most important of the communal courts which governed all aspects of local life in Anglo-Saxon and Norman England. Each shire held a monthly court or assembly where all local business, legislative, administrative, or judicial, was conducted. The shire court gradually declined with the growth of the common law courts from the *curia regis and with the development of Parliament in the 13th cent., though it remained important as the court in which the itinerant justices sat and as the assembly in which the representatives of the shire to Parliament were chosen. By the 19th cent. there was no legal forum available to the would-be civil litigant whose means were small, hence the gibe that the English courts were open to all 'like the Ritz Hotel'. In 1846, to meet this criticism, the County Courts Act set up a network of new 'county courts' within each area, not necessarily synonymous with the county in which they sat. These courts became and remain civil courts of limited jurisdiction. MM

Courcy, John de (d. 1219). Conqueror of Ulster. De Courcy's parentage is unknown, though he probably came from Somerset. He is said to have visited Ireland in 1171 with Henry II, who promised him Ulster if he could acquire it. Returning in 1176 with a small but well-organized force, he moved north from Dublin and succeeded in gaining the lands east of the Bann. He established a castle and base at Carrickfergus, built other strong points, and strengthened his position in 1180 by a marriage to Affreca, daughter of Gottred, king of Man. From 1185 to 1190 he was justiciar in Ireland. But he had great difficulty in holding his conquests, both against the native Irish and against Hugh de Lacey, a rival Norman colonizer, who was created earl of Ulster by King John in 1205. JAC

court. The institution known as the court has changed its meaning over the centuries. In early medieval times, the court, or household, was the centre of government. The chamberlain and butler performed their personal services for the king but also acted as advisers in broader questions. The monarch, with counsellors and great officers in attendance, would do business, receive petitions, and dispense justice. The king's journeys around the shires enabled some of his subjects to visit him locally, but must have inhibited the social side of court life, since it would not have been easy to accommodate large numbers of unexpected guests: Henry II's movements were notoriously unpredictable. As public business increased, various functions were delegated: much administration was left to the council, and justice to the specialized law courts. But as long as political power remained with the monarch, the division between public and private, government and ceremony, could never be absolute. It has been suggested that, as a result of the 'Tudor revolution in government', the court from the 1530s took on a purely ceremonial role. That is premature. All through the Tudor and early Stuart period, careers could be made or broken at court—*Wolsey, *Leicester, *Essex, *Rochester, *Buckingham. The more routine aspects of government may have been hived off, but the crucial decisions still rested with the monarch and his immediate advisers. But after the Glorious Revolution, as power drained away to Parliament and the cabinet, the importance of the court began to diminish. Charles II's court had been lively, with obliging ladies founding aristocratic families, but money had started to run out. Monarchs also shared with many noblemen the preference for a less public and more domestic home life. By George II's reign, court life was routine and placid, save for a few grand occasions. To some extent this was fortuitous. William III was taciturn, Anne shy, George I inhibited by language difficulties; George II's temper made his receptions distinctly unpredictable, and George III's tastes ran to domestic bliss. Nor could the court any longer afford the patronage that had made Charles I a connoisseur of the arts. Monarchs still wielded considerable influence but in direct consultation with ministers in private or in correspondence rather than through the court. The Edwardian court in the 1900s saw a brief social revival, partly because of the novelty of a visible monarch after Victoria's protracted seclusion, partly because Edward VII enjoyed company. But it was an Indian summer and went down in the trenches of 1917. After the Great War, society did not really recover. There were still people to whom it mattered to be received at court. But to almost all subjects in the late 20th cent. the court meant nothing, politically or socially. Though *The Times* continued dutifully to print a court circular, it is doubtful whether it was as much read as the sports page. JAC

court and country party. Names employed for government and opposition in the late 17th and early 18th cents. The term 'country party' had obvious advantages. It was much broader than Tory or church party and avoided the divisive names of Whig and Tory at a time when many were combining to overthrow *Walpole. It hinted at massive support in the nation at large: 'court and country', wrote one pamphleteer in 1742, 'distinguish the friends and enemies of the people.' It called to mind a golden past when squire and countryman had lived in harmony before the new moneyed interest bore everything down. 'Court', on the other hand, suggested a clique subservient to the monarch, wallowing in patronage and corruption. The basic country programme was a reduction in the number of placemen in Parliament and repeal of the *Septennial Act to bring about more frequent elections and return power to the people. The court party retorted that the country party members were either secret Jacobites or self-seeking careerists, making trouble for their own ends. The court's counter-accusation was strengthened by the fact that so little was done when the opposition took over, particularly in 1742 on the fall of Walpole: the only Place Act was insignificant and the Septennial Act was not repealed. The attitudes and arguments, though not the names, repeated themselves in the 1770s when the *Rockinghams were in protracted opposition to Lord North's administration, prescribed *economical reform, and deplored the excessive influence of the crown. JAC

Courtenay, Edward, 11th earl of Devon (1526–56). Courtenay spent more than half of his life in the Tower. He was son of Henry *Courtenay, marquis of Exeter, and a great-grandson of Edward IV. When Courtenay was 12, he and his parents were sent to the Tower. His father was accused of treason against Henry VIII and executed. Edward Courtenay was attainted in 1539 and not released until Mary succeeded in 1553. His mother was a confidante of the queen and Courtenay had got to know *Gardiner, bishop of Winchester, while they were in the Tower. He was received with great favour, restored to the earldom, and made KB. Handsome, catholic, and of royal blood, he was talked of as a possible husband for Mary. The suggestion was not preposterous: in similar circumstances *Darnley won the throne of Scotland twelve years later. But Mary heard reports of debauchery and turned to Philip of Spain. Courtenay then transferred his hopes to Princess Elizabeth and was implicated in *Wyatt's rising in 1554. He was sent back to the Tower, released in 1555, but died the following year abroad. JAC

Courtenay, Henry, 10th earl of Devon (*c.*1498–1539). Courtenay succeeded his father as earl of Devon in 1511. He was a grandson of Edward IV through his mother and a cousin of Henry VIII. For a time he prospered greatly. Henry gave him the Garter in 1521 and four years later created him marquis of Exeter. He gained from the *dissolution of the monasteries and built up a powerful position in the west country. In 1536 he took part in suppressing the *Pilgrimage of Grace. But his second wife was a catholic and on close terms with Princess Mary and Courtenay himself was at odds with Thomas *Cromwell. His closeness to the throne roused Henry's suspicions and in 1538 he was accused of treason. A flimsy case was constructed against him on the basis of a few loose remarks and he was executed on Tower Hill in January 1539. The Russells succeeded to his position as the leading Devon family. JAC

Courtenay, William (*c.*1342–96). Archbishop of Canterbury. Courtenay's aristocratic connections carried him rapidly up the ladder of preferment. Of the noble Devon family, he graduated in law at Oxford and was chancellor in 1367. In 1370, at the age of 28 or thereabouts, he became bishop of Hereford, transferring to London in 1375. His tenure there saw the *Peasants' Revolt, in which Simon *Sudbury, the archbishop of Canterbury, was murdered. Courtenay replaced him and for a short while held the great seal as chancellor. He opened Parliament with a sermon in English. Hostile to *Wyclif and *John of Gaunt's faction, Courtenay helped to force Wyclif into retirement at Lutterworth. His relations with the young king, Richard II, were turbulent. In 1385 they quarrelled violently when Courtenay attempted to rebuke him for his wild way of life, yet the archbishop supported the statute of *Praemunire (1393), which curbed papal authority. JAC

Court of Session. In the 15th cent. the general jurisdiction of the Scottish royal council was delegated to a committee. In 1532, partly at papal suggestion, James V established a Court of Session, or College of Justice. There were to be fifteen members, 'cunning and wise men', half of whom, including the president, were to be clerics. After the Reformation, the clerical numbers were reduced and the last clerical judge, Archbishop Burnet of Glasgow, served 1664 to 1668. The arrangements were confirmed by the Act of *Union, though the number of justices has been increased to deal with the growth of litigation. The court sits at Parliament House in Edinburgh and there is no appeal in criminal matters to the House of Lords at Westminster. The justices are accorded the courtesy title Lord, though they do not sit in the House of Lords, and the title is not hereditary. JAC

courts leet were originally held as a form of franchise by the lord of the manor. Unlike the seigneurial (feudal) courts, the jurisdiction of the leet did not belong to the lord by right but had to be granted to him by the king. However such a grant entitled the lord to hold the hundred court, dealing with all minor criminal matters within the district, and to receive the fines paid to the court. This passing of hundred courts into private hands was widespread and although Edward I by his 'quo warranto' inquiry clamped down on the holders of franchises, he eventually allowed a lord to hold the court if he could show a specific grant from the crown or that he had held the court from the date of the accession of Richard I (1189). Courts leet declined with the advent of the *justices of the peace but many remained and some became the kernel of a new local government for the growing boroughs which incorporated an existing manor. Courts leet were sometimes combined in one gathering with the court customary (the 'halmote' or 'hallmoot'), presided over by the lord's steward or bailiff. MM

courts martial. Strictly these are courts administering military law, i.e. the special legal rules applicable to members of the armed forces and ancillary personnel. However, the term has also been used to describe courts administering 'martial law'. As early as the Wars of the Roses, powers were exercised by military commanders to try and to punish offenders in areas of conflict. Special courts under such proclamations tried and punished those who transgressed against the orders of the military authority. Proclamations of martial law, issued in times of constitutional struggle, were described as illegal in the *Petition of right in 1628. In so far as there is any such principle as 'martial law', it can only be that necessity may on occasion be a defence to a breach of the law, and the necessity of keeping order and peace may on rare occasions justify conduct which is otherwise unlawful. Trial must still take place in the usual courts after the event. MM

covenanters. As supporters of the Scottish National Covenant (1638) they sought to preserve *presbyterianism in Scotland and oppose royal interference, in particular imposition of the 'Laudian' Prayer Book (1637). After defeating Charles I in the *Bishops' wars (1639–40), they forced him to accept presbyterianism in Scotland. The New Model Army's sectarianism thwarted their attempt by the *Solemn League and Covenant with Parliament (1643) to impose it on England. Though after Charles I's execution Charles II signed the covenant (1650), *Cromwell's victorious army forced the Scots unwillingly to tolerate sectarianism. Revival of Scottish episcopacy (1662) was unpopular and short-lived; presbyterianism was restored (1690). WMM

Covent Garden (London). Anxious to restore his dilapidated estate (land belonging to the convent, or abbey, of Westminster prior to the *dissolution of the monasteries), the 4th earl of Bedford secured a building licence and commissioned Inigo *Jones as architect. Influenced by study in Italy, Jones created a piazza surrounded by St Paul's church and three terraces of tall houses with arcades looking inwards (completed by 1639), the unfamiliar design meeting a mixed reception. The houses became highly sought after, until western developments and the expansion of the fruit, flower and vegetable market (established 1670) made them less fashionable. Shops and coffee-houses proliferated, and its first theatre (now the Royal Opera House) opened in 1732. The area became increasingly unruly and seedy, despite attempted control by the estate authorities and considerable rebuilding. It was eventually sold by the 11th duke (1918), and the market moved to Nine Elms (1974). ASH

Coventry. Cathedral city in Warwickshire. It developed around an important priory, founded in 1043 by Earl *Leofric and Countess Godgifu ('Lady *Godiva' of Coventry folklore). From 1102 to 1539 the priory church had cathedral status, and in the 14th cent. the city rose spectacularly through cloth-manufacturing to become the fourth largest English town. It declined equally spectacularly in the 16th cent., but found renewed industrial prosperity from the 18th cent., and in 1918 became a cathedral city once more. It was heavily bombed in the Second World War, but retains more historic buildings than is often appreciated, including the 14th-cent. St Mary's Hall. DMP

Coventry, diocese of. The modern see, created in 1918, is roughly conterminous with Warwickshire. In Anglo-Saxon and early Norman times the Mercian church had been centred on *Lichfield, then on *Chester, and eventually, after 1102, on Coventry abbey, though the administrative centre remained at Lichfield. Bishops were known as 'bishops of Coventry' until 1228, after which the title 'Coventry and Lichfield' was usual. With the removal of the see's north-western section to form the Chester diocese in 1541 and Coventry abbey's dissolution, Lichfield's administrative importance was acknowledged by the reversal of the title to 'Lichfield and Coventry'. In 1836 Coventry and its neighbourhood were put under the jurisdiction of *Worcester, but the massive increase in population in the midlands necessitated the foundation of the *Birmingham diocese in 1905 and Coventry in 1918. St Michael's parish church at first served as the cathedral, until it was destroyed by bombing in 1940 and retained as a roofless ruin, which is now neatly juxtaposed with the new cathedral, designed by Basil *Spence, the whole being a symbol of death and resurrection. The cathedral's interior is dominated by the great tapestry of *Christ in Glory* by Graham *Sutherland. The twinning of Coventry with Dresden is a powerful symbol of the desire for renewal after destruction, for both dioceses lost their cathedrals in the holocaust of the Second World War. WMM

Coventry, Thomas Coventry, 1st Baron (1578–1640). Coventry was born at Croome d'Abitot in Worcestershire, the son of a judge, and had a rapid rise to legal eminence. By 1616 he was recorder of London, in 1617–21 solicitor-general, and attorney-general 1621–5. From 1625 until his death he was lord keeper and then lord chancellor, receiving his peerage in 1628. He followed the line of royal policy but argued a moderate case and was inclined to reserve himself for legal questions. He advised Charles I to agree to the *Petition of right and defended the imposition of *ship money in general terms. Said to be morose in private, in public he was courteous and civil and Clarendon credited him with 'a strange power of making himself believed'. He died just before the opening of the *Short Parliament in 1640 'in a season most opportune and in which a wise man would have prayed to have finished his course'. Two of his sons had important political careers in Charles II's reign. JAC

Coverdale, Miles (1488–1568). Augustinian friar turned secular priest, popular preacher, and significant figure among early reformers, Coverdale spent most of the time between 1528 and 1548 in exile, producing the first complete translation of the Bible into English, whilst abroad, in 1535. Prior to this, he may have worked with William *Tyndale, upon whose New Testament translation he relied. Five years earlier, Henry VIII deemed an English translation unnecessary, but Thomas *Cromwell obtained royal approval for publication of Coverdale's Bible in England, which encouraged John Rogers's Matthew Bible in 1537. Meanwhile, Cromwell initiated an official translation for use in every parish church, entrusting the improved revision to Coverdale. The 'Great Bible' was published in 1539. Coverdale was appointed bishop of Exeter in Edward VI's reign, deprived, but escaped persecution under Mary Tudor. Christian III of Denmark's intercession enabled him to go abroad again until the more favourable climate of Elizabeth's reign. But he was not restored to his diocese, presumably because his views were too radical. AM

Cowes regatta. Cowes week is held early in August and is the climax of the yachting season. Cowes castle, built by Henry VIII, has been the headquarters of the Royal Yacht Squadron, founded 1815, since 1856. East and West Cowes lie on either side of the estuary of the river Medina in the north of the Isle of Wight. JAC

Cowper, William, Ist Earl Cowper (1664–1724). Politician and lawyer. Called to the bar in 1688, Cowper proved a brilliant lawyer, an attainment which he brought to the Commons in 1695. Despite being a court Whig, he kept a cautious distance from the *Junto. He was appointed lord keeper in 1705, becoming a peer in 1706, and lord chancellor in 1707. In these offices he brought about an improvement of Chancery procedure, and as a true Whig member of the *Godolphin ministry instigated a mass removal of Tories from the magistracy. In 1710 he presided over the trial of Dr *Sacheverell, and later that year resigned with his party. Reappointed lord chancellor by George I in 1714, he promoted the *Riot and *Septennial Acts. By 1718, however, he was voting increasingly with the Tories, disgusted by the powerlust of some of his colleagues, and resigned a month after receiving an earldom. He continued to lead the opposition in the Lords until his death in 1724. AAH

Crabbe, George (1754–1832). Born in Aldeburgh (Suffolk), Crabbe began training as a doctor before taking holy orders. But his love was poetry and, moving to London, he was fortunate enough to be taken up by *Burke, *Johnson, and the Manners family. His poem *The Village* (1783) is a gloomy description of poverty and toil, intended as a contrast to *Goldsmith's idealized *Deserted Village*:

> Here joyless roam a wild amphibious race
> With sullen woe displayed in every face.

It brought Crabbe considerable reputation and much clerical preferment. His other major work was *The Borough* (1810), which described his home town, and included the story of Peter Grimes, a sadistic fisherman, used by Benjamin *Britten. Crabbe's heroic couplets looked back to Pope, but his realism linked him to Wordsworth, and it was unusual to regard the annals of the poor as of much poetic interest. *Hazlitt, while admitting that Crabbe was 'one of the most popular and admired of our living authors', complained of the monotony of Crabbe's response—'he has no delight beyond the walls of a workhouse'. JAC

Craftsman, The: or, The Countryman's Journal. Best-selling newspaper which, from 5 December 1726, spearheaded the opposition to Sir Robert *Walpole. Backed by *Bolingbroke and William *Pulteney, and edited by Nicholas Amhurst under the pseudonym 'Caleb D'Anvers of Gray's-Inn, Esq.', the paper's avowed aim was to expose political craft. 'Country' rhetoric was employed in the attempt to create a political platform strong enough to accommodate the opinions of Tories and dissident Whigs. Bolingbroke was himself a principal contributor, his *Dissertations on Parties* and *Remarks on the History of England* both being reprinted from a series of essays originally published in *The Craftsman*. JAD

Craig, James, 1st Viscount Craigavon (1871–1940). First prime minister of Northern Ireland. Craig, the son of a millionaire whiskey distiller, was elected as Unionist MP for East Down in 1906. With *Carson he led the Ulster Unionist resistance to the third *Home Rule Bill, using his administrative skill and extensive social connections to organize a mass movement: Carson was the charismatic front-man, Craig the tireless manager. He held junior ministerial office as parliamentary secretary to the Ministry of Pensions (1919–20) and as financial secretary at the Admiralty (1920–1): he influenced the Government of *Ireland Act, successfully pressing for a six-county partition scheme. Despite his standing at Westminster, he accepted the premiership of the newly created Northern Ireland in 1921, holding office until his death in 1940. He saw off the IRA challenge to the partition settlement (1921–2), but was unable to address the intractable sectarian and economic problems of the new state. However, Craig had both political imagination and managerial skill. In his later years he was ailing and apparently disengaged from the Northern Irish political scene: the limited powers devolved on *Stormont offered little scope to this once resourceful minister. AJ

Cranfield, Lionel, 1st earl of Middlesex (1575–1645). Cranfield, of relatively humble origins, competent and industrious, became lord treasurer under James I. He was a successful *Merchant Venturer and when in 1613 he was appointed surveyor-general of the customs, it was a case of poacher turned gamekeeper. In 1614 he became a member of Parliament, and attached himself to the royal favourite, George Villiers, later duke of *Buckingham. Under this patronage, Cranfield was appointed to various royal offices, which he performed with great efficiency. In 1621, when he became lord treasurer, he found that reform was needed in 'every particular'. As James I's expenditures exceeded his income, Cranfield made spending cuts, and courtiers lost their pensions and allowances. This was the beginning, though set-back followed, of 'Treasury control'. Cranfield soon fell, brought down by Buckingham, his former patron, and the enemies he had made in the king's service. He was impeached, found guilty of maladministration and corruption, deprived of his offices, fined, and briefly imprisoned in the Tower. He was pardoned in 1625, and for the rest of his life he lived in retirement. MW

Cranmer, Thomas (1489–1556). Archbishop of Canterbury. Cranmer played a greater role than any other single churchman in shaping the Church of England, and above all its liturgy. However, his diffidence in theological controversy has denied him the status of a founding reformer. He was born to a gentry family in Nottinghamshire and studied at Jesus College, Cambridge, where he became a fellow and took orders, becoming a DD in 1526. He rose to sudden prominence in 1529 on the strength of his suggestion that the universities of Europe be asked to provide opinions on the legitimacy of Henry VIII's first marriage. On an embassy to Germany in 1532 he met and married the niece of the Lutheran church leader of Nuremberg, Andreas Osiander, whom he later brought secretly back to England. When Archbishop William *Warham died in August of that year Cranmer was proposed as his successor; despite the stalled divorce negotiations Clement VII provided the papal documents for his consecration early in 1533. Cranmer then presided over the court which annulled Henry and *Catherine's marriage. He was also used, later on, to decree the nullity of Henry's marriage to *Anne Boleyn and to celebrate, and end, the marriage to *Anne of Cleves.

During *c.*1535–8 it is hard to separate Cranmer's role from that of Thomas *Cromwell, or from some other bishops such as Hugh *Latimer, in the shaping of religious policy and documents such as the 'Bishops' Book' of 1537. He was clearly opposed to the Act of *Six Articles in 1539 (which forced him to send his wife away) but, unlike Latimer, did not resign his see in protest. After Cromwell's death he emerged as one of the leading reform-minded privy counsellors. Henry VIII's constant support ensured his survival in the 'Prebendaries' plot' against him at Canterbury in 1543, and gave him the authority to promote his own *English Litany* and *King's Prymer* while suppressing more conservative liturgical projects.

On the accession of Edward VI, Cranmer issued definitively protestant works, above all the first **Book of Homilies*, a set of official model sermons, which were to be amplified and reissued under Elizabeth. In contrast, his first version of the *Book of Common Prayer of 1549 was painfully conservative, to the glee of catholic opponents and the embarrassment of Cranmer's allies. It nevertheless provoked the western rebellion of that year. In 1549 Cranmer welcomed a galaxy of German and Italian protestant stars into England as a refuge from Charles V's campaign against Lutheranism. They helped guide Cranmer into formulating his most explicitly anti-catholic liturgical document, the second version of the Book of Common Prayer (1552) and the Forty-Two Articles of Religion (1553), the basis for the Prayer Book of 1559 and the *Thirty-Nine Articles of 1563 respectively.

Cranmer, like most leading figures in Edward's reign, acquiesced uneasily in the device to divert the succession to Jane *Grey, but offered no resistance to Mary I's accession despite her known catholicism. He and other protestant bishops regarded her coming as a divine test or punishment, and disobeyed passively. An attainder for treason was set aside in favour of a show-disputation at Oxford in April 1554, in which Cranmer defended himself less vigorously than Nicholas *Ridley. He was kept in prison and eventually persuaded to sign recantations in which he accepted key catholic doctrines. He later withdrew these and was burned for heresy on 21 March 1556.

Cranmer's defining quality seems not to have been timidity (the theme of some accusations by historians) but a curiously biddable humility, intense loyalty to the crown, and a preference for very gradual change. The last two might in other circumstances have made a good Lutheran, but the first was most unusual for any 16th-cent. churchman. He wrote relatively little and ranks much less highly as a theologian than many of those he received in England in 1549–53. However, his exceptional gift for framing a poetic liturgical language, which combined the Latinate with the everyday, created a Prayer Book which was appreciated more and more in the centuries which followed. EC

Crashaw, Richard (*c.*1612–49). Poet. Despite his preacher father's puritan zealotry, Crashaw was drawn increasingly to high Anglicanism, aided by education at strongly Anglo-catholic Peterhouse, Cambridge (fellowship, 1635), preaching at the adjoining Little St Mary's (where he embraced Marianism), and friendship with Nicholas Ferrar, founder of the community at Little Gidding. Fleeing Peterhouse (1643) because of the investigative then iconoclastic puritans, he made his way to Paris, where, fully converted to catholicism, he was rescued from poverty by fellow-poet Cowley, who had become cipher-secretary to *Henrietta Maria in France. The queen's intercessions to Rome led merely to the office of attendant to Cardinal Palotta, before a minor cathedral post at Loreto, where he soon died. Remembered for religious rather than secular verse (*Steps to the Temple*, 1646), Crashaw was never more than a minor poet despite his richness of language, but his ecstatic mysticism and unrestrained imagery have been acclaimed as the height of *baroque in English poetry. ASH

Cravant, battle of, 1423. In the summer of 1423, the earl of *Salisbury with his Burgundian allies marched to relieve Cravant on the river Yonne in France, gateway to Dijon and Burgundy. The besiegers, led by *Buchan, constable of France, were caught on 1 August between the garrison, making a sortie, and Salisbury's men, and badly defeated. The victory represented a recovery after the death of *Clarence at *Baugé and the death in 1422 of Henry V while campaigning. JAC

Crécy, battle of, 1346. The first great English land victory of the *Hundred Years War was the high point of a campaign which began with the sack of Caen, and ended with the successful siege of Calais. Edward III landed unexpectedly in Normandy, and was forced by the French strategy of destroying bridges across the Seine to march almost up to Paris. He was able to repair the bridge at Poissy; challenges to meet the French in open battle yielded no results, and the English army marched northwards. The Somme was crossed at Blanche-Taque, and at Crécy in Ponthieu (département Somme) the English prepared for battle. Edward drew up his force on 26 August with knights and men-at-arms dismounted, flanked by archers. The French first sent forward Genoese mercenary crossbowmen, whose weapons, their bowstrings slackened by a shower of rain, proved no match for the English longbows. Cannon, used for the first time in a major battle, helped to terrify the French. The French cavalry charged through their own retreating crossbowmen. The English archers brought down many of the French horses; the dismounted men-at-arms stood firm in the mêlée. Edward III commanded his men from the height of a nearby windmill; his son the Black Prince, in the forefront of the fighting, provided charismatic leadership. The final stages of the battle witnessed moments of pointless chivalric heroism from the French, notably when the blind king of Bohemia was led into the mêlée, his knights bound to him by ropes. All were slain. At the close, the English horses were brought forward, those who were still capable mounted, and the battle turned into a rout. After the victory, Edward laid siege to Calais, which surrendered in August 1347, giving the English a vital line of communication to the continent, which they kept for more than 200 years. MCP

Crediton, diocese of. Carved out of the *Sherborne bishopric in 909, it initially covered all Devon and Cornwall, though from 931 to 1027 *St Germans was the separate see for Cornwall. In 1050 Leofric moved the bishopric to *Exeter, in obedience to Leo IX's command for sees to be in larger towns. Crediton was the birthplace of *Boniface (680), the missionary to Frisia and Germany. WMM

cricket. As with most games, cricket was played in a primitive form many years before rules were drawn up, and some of the most enjoyable cricket is still played in back lanes with a dustbin as wicket. There are suggestions that shepherds in the Sussex weald played some form of the game in forest clearings, presumably with stones, a stick, and a tree stump. Among the games condemned by Edward III for distracting men from archery practice was club-ball. Cricket is not mentioned in James I's *Book of Sports* (1617) but was certainly well developed before the end of the century. An eleven-a-side match for 50 guineas was played in Sussex in 1697 and in 1709 Kent played Surrey at Dartford. Bowling was underarm and the bat was a heavy curved club. In 1744 there was an attempt to formulate agreed rules and the same year an All England XI played the men of Kent at the Artillery Ground, Finsbury. The patronage of the nobility helped to make the game fashionable. *Frederick, prince of Wales, was a keen cricketer in the 1740s and the duke of Dorset in the 1770s, being a member of the Hambledon Club which played on Broadhalfpenny Down (Hants), outside the Bat and Ball Inn, and a patron of the White Conduit Club, which played at Islington Fields. A meeting at the Star and Garter in 1774 drew up new rules, with 22-yard pitches, 4-ball overs, stumping, and no-balling: 'the wicket-keeper should not by any noise incommode the striker.' In 1785 the White Conduits played Kent for 1,000 guineas, winning by 306 after Kent's second innings had collapsed for 28. In 1787 Thomas Lord opened his new ground at Marylebone and in 1788 the Marylebone Cricket Club issued revised rules, prohibiting any attempt to impede a fielder while making a catch. The club moved to its present ground in 1814.

The most important change in the rules in the 19th cent. was the introduction of overarm bowling in 1864 after some vehement controversies. The Gentlemen v. Players match was first held in 1806 and was annual after 1819; Oxford v. Cambridge dates from 1827. By 1864 enough cricket was being played for John Wisden, himself a celebrated bowler (who took all ten wickets playing in 1850 for North v. South), to launch his *Cricketers' Almanack*. The first test match was played at Melbourne in 1877, when Australia won, and when they won again at the Oval in 1882 (England needing 85 in the second innings were all out for 77, Spofforth taking 7–44), the *Sporting Times* declared that the ashes of English cricket would be taken to Australia. Though county teams competed from early days, the county championship did not start until 1889, and was dominated in its early years by Nottinghamshire, Surrey, Yorkshire, and Lancashire. Gloucestershire, for whom the great W. G. *Grace played, had been strong in the 1870s. Grace, probably the best known of all Victorian figures, gave cricket a national following. When he first turned out at 16 for the Gentlemen in 1865 they had lost their last 17 matches to the Players: subsequently they won 35 out of 39. Grace played until well over 50 and took ten wickets on two occasions, in 1873 and 1886—on the second occasion scoring a century as well.

The two main developments of 20th-cent. cricket were the spread of international competition, as the West Indies, India, Pakistan, Sri Lanka, and others came in to join England, Australia, New Zealand, and South Africa, and the introduction after the Second World War of limited-over cricket at the highest level. Limited-over cricket was not quite the innovation sometimes suggested, since village, club, and northern league cricket had always been played on that basis. It was made necessary because gate money could no longer support the traditional county championship in the face of alternative leisure attractions. With limited-over cricket came sponsorship—the Gillette Cup in 1963, the John Player League in 1969, the Benson and Hedges Cup in 1972. It is not difficult to deplore negative bowling, six-hitting flails, complex rules, and often predictable finishes, but cricket has always had its bizarre side. Married women and maidens played at Bury in Sussex in 1793; one-legged Greenwich pensioners v. one-armed Greenwich pensioners in 1796; teetotallers v. whiskey-drinkers at Ballinasloe in 1840; and cricket on the ice at Cambridge in 1870. NJB; JAC

crime is a subject which has, from the 1960s, attracted considerable attention from historians. It is, however, a topic which is fraught with difficulties. A key one is that of defining crime. In any period a variety of forms of behaviour have been criminalized (for example, the prosecution of

Roman catholic recusants in the Elizabethan and Stuart periods), or categorized as deviant. There has also been a tension between social historians studying crime and more traditional legal historians, while it has never proved easy to separate the history of crime from the history of the institutions which attempted to deal with it, and upon whose records students of the subject are largely dependent. Despite these difficulties, considerable work has been carried out on crime in England (the subject has not attracted much attention among historians of Scotland).

Anglo-Saxon law codes suggest a restitutive system, essentially a regulation of the feud. Post-Conquest England experienced a growing criminal justice system, the reign of Henry II (1154–89) providing the most durable elements. Interpreting the level and nature of medieval crime is difficult. There were criminal gangs who at times indulged in outright banditry, but criminal prosecutions in the 14th cent. suggest a more modern criminality in some areas, with theft as the most prominent offence. Certainly, although rates of homicide were high in the Middle Ages, the paradigm of a long-term shift from a 'feudal' criminality characterized by violence to a 'modern' criminality based on property crime remains unproven.

Record survival permits more systematic work from the 1550s, which has centred mainly on the study of felony (a category which includes serious offences such as homicide, burglary, theft, rape, and arson). Prosecution of these offences (especially property offences) reached peaks, according to region, in the late 1590s (a period of bad harvests) and the 1620s, a decade which experienced severe social and economic problems. When the running of criminal courts was resumed after the civil wars, however, levels of prosecuted felonies were low, and remained so until the mid-18th cent., when a resumption of population growth and the economic dislocation which attended the arrival of the industrial revolution caused them to rise.

During the early 19th cent. levels of crime rose alarmingly. Mass demobilization of soldiers and sailors after 1815 caused a crime wave, as had happened at the end of every war in the 18th cent., and this continued as industrialization and urbanization burgeoned. It was in the early 19th cent. that crime was identified as a social problem in the modern sense. The period saw the origins of criminology as a discipline, the introduction of national crime statistics, the emergence of such concepts as juvenile delinquency, and of professional police forces and prison as the standard punishment for serious offenders. With the emergence of some level of economic stability, and especially of improved living standards among the working classes, levels of prosecution dropped slightly in the late Victorian and Edwardian periods. From the 1950s, however, levels of prosecution increased, and continued to do so alarmingly over the 1980s.

JAS

Crimean War, 1853–6. Known to contemporaries as 'the Russian War', this arose from long-term Russian ambitions to expand westward and southward, resisted by Britain as a matter of policy. The immediate cause was a petty struggle between Russia and France over rights in Ottoman Turkey. This produced an ultimatum from Russia to Turkey in March 1853, followed by Russian occupation of the Ottoman Danubian provinces (modern Romania) and a naval victory over Turkey at Sinope on 27 November. Britain and France (later joined by Sardinia as well as Turkey) issued their own ultimatum on 27 March 1854.

The Black Sea theatre dominated contemporary perspectives of the war. Britain supplied a field army of about 28,000, which, with a French contingent of equal size, landed in May 1854 at Varna to defend it against Russian forces crossing the Danube. When this threat failed to materialize, the allied armies were transferred to the Crimean peninsula, landing north of the main Russian naval base of Sebastopol on 14 September. Their first victory, at the *Alma six days later, enabled them to continue south around Sebastopol from the landward side to Balaclava, so establishing a partial siege of the base.

Through the autumn the Russians tried to break the siege of Sebastopol, the two major attacks being at *Balaclava in October and *Inkerman in November. After surviving a bad winter, for which they were not equipped, the allies launched naval expeditions against the smaller Russian bases of Kerch at the eastern end of the Crimea in May and Kinburn (near Odessa) in October 1855. Meanwhile, the Russians made one final attempt to relieve Sebastopol in August at the Tchernaya (in which the British were hardly involved). Repeated British and French attacks on Sebastopol finally led to the base becoming untenable and the Russians abandoned it in October.

Modern historical study pays at least as much attention to the purely naval campaign fought in the Baltic as to the Crimean theatre. The end of the war came about not through the fall of Sebastopol but through the British victory in August 1855 in destroying by bombardment the Russian dockyard at Sweaborg (outside modern Helsinki). Together with Kinburn, this demonstrated the vulnerability of Russian naval bases to British ships, a threat made explicit that winter with the building of the 'Great Armament', a floating siege train of over 360 vessels intended to capture the main Russian naval base in the Baltic at Cronstadt. Rather than face the loss of Cronstadt as well as Sebastopol, the Russians agreed to moderate allied peace terms in the treaty of *Paris of 30 March 1856, with the Black Sea declared neutral and the Danube an open waterway.

The result of the Crimean War has been much debated. By pursuing a realistic limited aim the Allies held Russia in check for a generation, rather than destroying themselves by marching on Moscow. Equally, although British performance in the Crimea was a contemporary byword for incompetence, it is recognized that the army did not perform much worse than at the start of the Napoleonic wars, was as much a victim of government parsimony as of its own faults, and that by the winter of 1855 most of its problems were solved.

SDB

criminal law. In Anglo-Saxon and Norman England, there was no distinction between criminal and civil law. Violence, or the causing of damage or harm to another's person or property, was subject to savage penalties if the offender was caught red-handed, but other cases, including homicide, were dealt with by a system of compensation whereby, according to a tariff, wrongs were recompensed by money payments. Where the offence was serious, in addition to the bot (compensation for injury) or *wergeld (payment to the kin of a murdered person), a payment (the wite) was made to the king.

Certain offences which were especially serious were the 'pleas of the crown', declared by the Anglo-Saxon kings to affect the king's interests especially, such as a breach of the king's peace. The Normans adopted these notions and they and their successors extended the pleas of the crown, as well as introducing the concept of felony. These pleas came to be dealt with by the king's own justice—i.e. by the king or his justices.

In the Assizes of *Clarendon and *Northampton (1166 and 1176), Henry II introduced a system of presentment, under which twelve men of each hundred were to present to the justices of the *curia regis those suspected of serious crime (pleas of the crown). Some see this as the beginning of a true 'criminal law', since it acknowledged that it is the role of government in the person of the king to ensure that crime is dealt with. Those presented might then be put to the ordeal, as directed by the justices, to ascertain their guilt or innocence. When the clergy were forbidden to participate in ordeals by the Lateran Council of the church in 1215, the justices turned to the verdict of a jury to decide guilt or innocence. Presentment soon superseded the appeal of felony as the principal means of bringing criminals to justice.

Lesser offences were presented to the sheriff at the periodic session of the *hundred court (held four times a year), which was known as the 'sheriff's tourn'. Where the lord of the manor held a *court leet, the jurisdiction of the hundred was exercised in that court, and the fines collected were payable to the lord. Later, after the introduction of the *justices of the peace, and especially after their jurisdiction was extended in 1361, lesser offences were tried by the JPs in *petty sessions or *quarter sessions.

The pleas of the crown became the basis of the English criminal law, which was administered in the sheriff's tourn and the court leet, and later in the courts held by the JPs (for minor crimes), and at quarter sessions, and before the judges of *assize, where serious cases were heard with a jury. This system of criminal justice remained until the 19th cent. and was little changed until the 1971 Courts Act. In 1971 the assizes were abolished, as were quarter sessions. Serious criminal cases (indictable offences) are now tried in the crown court with a jury. Less serious cases (summary) are dealt with by magistrates sitting without a jury, or by a stipendiary magistrate. The ancient classification of crimes into treasons, felonies, or misdemeanours was abolished in 1967, and the law now divides crimes into indictable or summary (for purposes of trial) and into arrestable and non-arrestable.

The development of the criminal law and of criminal jurisprudence lagged behind the development of the common law. Indeed, lawyers were very little involved in criminal cases, since until 1837 the accused was not allowed counsel.

The 18th and 19th cents. saw the introduction of large numbers of capital offences, partly in response to fear of revolution among the ruling élite. The so-called 'bloody code' imposed savage penalties for many offences and, even when transportation was introduced as an alternative to the death penalty, punishments remained severe. The severity of the penal system was to some extent modified by the use of fictions, especially the undervaluing of goods stolen at less than a pound; by the use of benefit of clergy to enable a defendant who had been found guilty to evade the death penalty; by the reluctance of juries to convict; and by the very widespread use of the power of pardon. Gradually, under the influence of reformers such as *Bentham, *Romilly, *Mackintosh, and *Peel, the ferocity of the penal code was mitigated.

Appeals against conviction could only be to the Court for Crown Cases Reserved, set up in 1848, and it was not until 1907 that a proper system of criminal appeals was introduced with the creation of the Court of Criminal Appeal. In 1966 the Court of Appeal was divided into the criminal and civil divisions, and there is a right of appeal to that court from the crown court. MM

Cripps, Sir Stafford (1889–1952). Cripps was a successful barrister before he was appointed Labour solicitor-general in 1930. Along with *Lansbury and *Attlee, he became the most important Labour MP to survive the 1931 electoral débâcle. The economic crisis converted Cripps to socialism and he took the leadership of the Socialist League. His energetic advocacy of first the 'Unity Campaign' and later the 'Popular Front' made Cripps prominent but earned him expulsion from the Labour Party in 1939.

During the war, Cripps rose to the fore after the success of his ambassadorship to Russia, although the failure of his subsequent mission to India—perhaps a deliberate ploy by *Churchill to discredit him—checked his advance. In 1945 Attlee appointed Cripps president of the Board of Trade (1945–7) and then chancellor of the Exchequer (1947–50). These jobs he carried out with his characteristic emphasis on self-sacrifice and austerity. His powers of persuasion and sheer moral authority enabled him to arrange a voluntary wage freeze with the unions and a hold on dividends, which was maintained for two years. His dedication and rigorous working schedule forced his resignation in 1950, and he died soon after. LHM

Crofters' Act, 1886. Crofts are smallholdings, particularly found in the Highlands and Islands of Scotland. Clearances in the 18th cent. had pushed numbers of tenants into crofts near the sea, where kelping and fishing eked out a meagre existence. In 1883 *Gladstone, under pressure from the *Highland Land League, appointed a commission under Lord Napier to investigate and report. The Act of 1886 (49 & 50 Vic. c. 29) established fair rents, security of tenure, and compensation for improvements. It also set up a Crofters' Commission, with power to fix rents. A further Act of 1976 made it easier for crofters to buy their holdings outright. JAC

Croker, John Wilson (1780–1857). An Irish lawyer, educated at Trinity College, Dublin, Croker had two separate though related careers as politician and as man of letters. He entered Parliament in 1806 and was taken up by *Canning, becoming a strong Tory supporter, though sympathetic to both *catholic emancipation and a measure of *parliamentary reform. He was on close terms with both *Peel and *Wellington. In 1809 he helped to found the *_Quarterly Review_, in which most of his essays appeared. *Perceval appointed him secretary to the Admiralty in 1809, a well-paid post which he held for 22 years, never quitting his office 'without a kind of uneasiness like a truant boy'. Despite a residual stammer, he was a sharp and effective debater. But his brilliant upwards progress faltered after 1820 when his only child, a 3-year-old son, died. He went out with the Tories in 1830 and played a prominent part in opposing the Whig Reform Act. *Greville, who did not like him, called a $2\frac{1}{2}$-hour speech in reply to *Macaulay in September 1831 'very fine'. But after the passage of the bill, he gave up his seat, to his friends' bewilderment, partly in despair, partly because he was tired and ill. The rest of his life he devoted to his literary work, though staying on close terms with Peel until his conversion over the Corn Laws, which Croker thought had 'ruined the character of public men'. In an age of brutal reviewing, there remains a contrast between Croker's public image as sarcastic and arrogant, and the affection felt for him by his friends and family. Greville wrote at his death: 'While Macaulay is thus ascending to the House of Peers, his old enemy and rival Croker has descended to his grave, very noiselessly and almost without observation, for he had been for some time so withdrawn from the world that he was nearly forgotten. He had lived to see all his predictions of ruin and disaster to the country completely falsified.' JAC

Cromarty, George Mackenzie, 1st earl of [S] (1630–1714). Mackenzie succeeded his father as baronet in 1654 and joined the royalist rising in Scotland the same year. In 1661–4 he was a lord of Session as Lord Tarbat and, after a period out of favour, lord justice general [S] 1678–80 and again 1705–10, lord clerk register [S] 1681–9 and 1692–5. A competent administrator, he was a vigorous supporter of James VII and II, who created him Viscount Tarbat [S] in 1685, but came to terms with William. During Anne's reign, he was secretary of state [S] 1702–5, was advanced to the earldom of Cromarty [S] 1702, and used his influence in favour of the Union. He subsequently served as a representative peer. His grandson, the 3rd earl, was sentenced to death in 1746 for his part in the '45, but pardoned. JAC

Crome, John (1768–1821). Landscape painter, born in Norwich where he spent almost all his life. The son of an innkeeper, Crome had little education and was apprenticed early to a coach- and sign-writer, spending his leisure sketching from nature. He supplemented his income by giving drawing lessons, and became the drawing master at the local grammar school in 1801. In 1803 he helped found the Norwich Society of Artists where he exhibited regularly and of which he became president in 1808. In the company of other British artists, he visited Paris in 1814, to see artworks acquired by Napoleon. Greatly influenced by the Dutch style, and the Romantic concept of landscape, Crome, together with *Cotman, is considered the major artist of the Norwich School. He is well represented at Norwich Castle Museum and in the Tate and National Galleries, London. JC

Crompton, Samuel (1753–1827). Inventor. One of the men who revolutionized the Lancashire textiles industry, Crompton was born near Bolton. His 'spinning mule', invented in 1779, improved upon *Hargreaves's jenny. It was a cross between the jenny and *Arkwright's water frame and produced yarn of high quality, particularly suited to muslins. Like many inventors, Crompton made little out of his discovery and his business ventures failed. He was however given a public grant of £5,000 in 1812. JAC

Cromwell, Henry (1628–74). Oliver's fourth son. Captain of horse at 19, he rose to command his own cavalry regiment in his father's expeditionary force to Ireland in 1650. He stayed on there, returning to sit for Ireland in *Barebone's Parliament. On becoming protector, Oliver sent him back there to investigate the loyalty of the army, whose commander he became. Charles Fleetwood, the lord deputy, returned home, and Henry inherited his authority, though not until 1657 his title. His rule was bedevilled by constant friction with a well-entrenched 'anabaptist' faction, which his thin-skinned, slightly paranoid nature made him too prickly in handling. But he showed real ability in a very difficult task, and gave every support in 1658–9 to his brother Richard *Cromwell, who promoted him to lord-lieutenant and governor-general. Thanks to his fairness to Irish royalists, which *Ormond and *Clarendon attested, he survived the *Restoration to live quietly in Cambridgeshire until his early death. AHW

Cromwell, Oliver (1599–1658). General and Lord Protector. Despite all that has been written about him, it is still difficult to appreciate the unique character of Cromwell's career, and the impact that it made on his contemporaries. No private person until then had taken power to rule a great European kingdom, no subject had taken it upon himself to sit in judgement on his lawful sovereign, condemn him with the formality of a lawful process, and publicly execute him as a criminal. In a country governed by custom, precedent, and the common law, Cromwell completely changed the ancient frame of government, reforming Parliament and imposing a written constitution. By conquest he incorporated the separate kingdoms of Scotland and Ireland into a single commonwealth with England. He remains the only British statesman whose entire career depended on the control and use of military power. Yet his achievement proved to be totally ephemeral. He left no political heirs or legacy. Two centuries were to elapse before his reputation recovered. The New England which his friends created across the Atlantic, and to which he once thought of emigrating, was to flourish: the new regenerate England he tried to create collapsed and vanished completely.

A provincial gentleman of modest means, Cromwell first

became prominent in the second session of the *Long Parliament (1641–2). When the abortive Army plot of royalist officers apparently showed that Charles I intended to renege on his acceptance of the constitutional safeguards enacted in the first session, and a catholic rebellion broke out in Ireland, Cromwell urged Parliament to assume control of both the army destined for Ireland and the home militia. He soon became identified with what has been termed the war party. He believed that the military defeat of the king's forces must precede negotiations for a settlement, whereas a more numerous 'peace party' advocated a defensive strategy while a compromise was negotiated, even if the royal forces continued offensive operations. A 'middle party' also hesitated before becoming committed to all-out war against their sovereign. Cromwell also had to overcome obstruction at the local level from the county committees preoccupied with the defence of their region, making a general offensive strategy impossible. He made the forces maintained by the *Eastern Association the most formidable of the parliamentarian armies, but his practice of commissioning men of determination and ability, regardless of their social status and religious positions, provoked hostility. Cromwell's men contributed decisively to the victory at *Marston Moor (July 1644), but his political associates had to publicize his role to counter their opponents' attribution of the victory to Parliament's Scottish allies.

Cromwell deplored the failure to follow up this victory effectively, and used it to oust irresolute leaders. He denounced his own neighbour and superior officer, Lord *Manchester, and helped pass the *self-denying ordinance. This barred peers and MPs, with exceptions of whom Cromwell was one, from commands and set up a central army, the *New Model, of which he became second in command. This made short work of the royalists. At *Naseby, Cromwell annihilated Charles's field army (June 1645). But once the war became concerned with mopping up royalist fortresses and islands, with Charles I in Scottish hands, a majority of peers and MPs worked to bring the army under direct parliamentary control. They allowed army pay to fall into arrears. Soldiers were refused indemnity to cover wartime actions. The reconquest of Ireland was not to be entrusted to the New Model. Instead its regiments were to be disbanded, the soldiers re-enlisted in new units commanded by a new set of officers nominated by Parliament. A new established church on presbyterian lines would mean restricted toleration for the independents and other sects who were strongly represented in the army. Cromwell shared his men's resentment. He emerged as the chief military politician, eclipsing his superior, Lord *Fairfax. Cromwell took the lead, first in representing army grievances, but soon in a wider sense claiming to speak and act as the embodiment of the 'cause' for which it had fought the war. In June 1647 Cornet Joyce took Charles into the custody of the army. Marching on London the army forced the Commons to send away the most conspicuously anti-army MPs. In July it issued the *Heads of the Proposals, a manifesto for a new constitutional settlement, which it discussed with Charles, whose responses were characteristically ambiguous. The manifesto did not go far enough to satisfy the more radical officers and men. Influenced by *Leveller ideas, the radicals published an *Agreement of the People: this was discussed in the *Putney debates of the army council, a body representing all ranks and units which Cromwell had accepted as a sounding-board for opinions (October–November).

During this period of rapid and frequent change Cromwell developed the techniques which enabled him to keep control over the army for the rest of his life. Historians have condemned him for failing to manage Parliament effectively, but most have overlooked his skill and success in managing the army, manipulating patronage—promotions, appointments, secondments, and dismissals—and using intimidation or persuasion according to circumstances. He could not depend on politicized radicals obeying orders. He had to break up networks of officers that could develop into challenges to his authority, he had to balance the factions—ambitious opportunists (like *Lambert), religious fanatics (*Harrison), professionals (*Monck, Montagu). He learned that neglect of the interests and grievances of ordinary soldiers led to their politicization. Above all he knew that army unity must be maintained—and it was disunity among the officers that brought down the Commonwealth in 1659–60 after Cromwell's death.

In November 1647 Cromwell personally suppressed a potentially infective Leveller-inspired mutiny in a single regiment. Early in 1648 royalist risings broke out in Wales, Kent, and Essex and a Scottish army invaded on Charles's behalf. Cromwell and Fairfax reacted with great speed, annihilating enemy forces. It was clear that Charles had planned these risings at a time when he was negotiating with both Parliament and the army, and trying to widen the breach between them. Despite this a majority in Parliament still wished to continue negotiating with him, whereas opinion in the army now accepted that as a 'man of blood' he had to be punished. Cromwell clearly inspired the action that followed although he personally stayed in the background. Colonel Pride, backed up by armed soldiers, prevented MPs who were unacceptable to the army from entering the Commons. Many were arrested; the purged House that subsequently worked with the army was known as the *Rump. In similar fashion Cromwell did not himself decide that Charles should be put on trial but his was the guiding spirit that led the small group of army officers and their parliamentary associates to make and implement the decision. By killing the king the regicides made any future compromise impossible; they committed treason and their lives were forfeit. Cromwell's body was to be exhumed in 1660 and hung from a gallows in a macabre form of legal retribution—with obvious psychopathic overtones. It also made Cromwell and the regime outcasts in Europe. The survival of each successive form of republican government depended on the physical power of the army, and of the navy in preventing foreign intervention.

In 1649–51 Cromwell was almost continuously on campaign away from Westminster. His militarily successful Irish campaign of 1649–50 has been universally condemned for its ruthlessness, especially for the massacres at *Drogheda and Wexford, and the planned ethnic cleansing of three Irish provinces. Cromwell's methods actually represented a direct revival of those used in Elizabeth's Irish wars and he saw them as a reprisal for atrocities committed by the Irish rebels in 1641. In 1650–1 he was engaged in war against the Scots who crowned Charles II king of Scotland. Cromwell defeated them at *Dunbar and finally *Worcester in successive Septembers, 1650 and 1651. Then in May 1652 the Rump became involved in war against the Dutch. These wars delayed half-hearted attempts to draft a definitive constitutional settlement, and necessitated heavy taxation and expenditure, of which many MPs and officials took corrupt advantage. Absorbed by routine work of government the Rump lost sight of the cause which to Cromwell remained paramount.

Cromwell's second major coup, his ejection of the Rump by force on 20 April 1653, opened the way for an experiment to create a form of government that would be in accord with what he took to be God's will. He and the army council named a constituent body to draft a godly constitution, *Barebone's or the 'Nominated' Parliament. This reflected the influence on Cromwell of the religious radicals, the 'fanatics' or *Fifth Monarchy men. He saw them as fellow-seekers for God's truth who believed that all public as well as private life should be governed by God's providential dispensation. By contrast Cromwell never sympathized with the Levellers because their principles and interests were secular and their leaders mainly deists or atheists. The fanatics in Barebone's Parliament disappointed Cromwell by wanting the abolition of tithe and universities, seeing a salaried and learned ministry as unnecessary. After moderates dissolved the 'Parliament' Cromwell infuriated the fanatics further, and interest groups associated with the Rump, by ending the Dutch War, giving the defeated enemy lenient terms (March 1654). After Barebone's Parliament came a written constitution, the *Instrument of Government (December 1653), introducing a form of government based on a balance of power and duties between a reformed single-chamber parliament elected by a new representative system, an elected council, and the executive, Lord Protector Cromwell. But this constitution was to be superseded in 1657 by the *Humble Petition and Advice which established an upper house in Parliament and empowered the lord protector to designate his successor. Neither constitution gave the impression of a governmental system built to last. This explains Cromwell's reluctant refusal in 1657 to assume the familiar title of king.

In the short term Cromwellian government worked, at a price. He maintained army discipline and unity but he could not eradicate all potential radical activists. Parliaments were called, but known opponents had to be kept out of the 1656 Commons. Quakers as well as catholics and Prayer Book Anglicans were excluded from toleration. The costs of maintaining the army, aggravated by a Spanish war that began in 1655, produced an accumulation of debt that would have ended in an insoluble crisis, the army demanding pay and resisting disbandment, the nation unable or unwilling to provide it. But the greatest change brought about by the institutionalization of the Protectorate was the erosion of the 'cause' which Cromwell embodied, the establishment of a form of government in which the godly, not a monarch, wielded power and guided (or compelled) the nation into ways laid down by God. Previous rulers—even Elizabeth—had failed to undertake and complete all the tasks required of a godly prince. Cromwell's missionary cause was to create a godly nation, but by 1658 few still shared his zeal. His court at Whitehall was full of civilian careerists, the army of mercenaries, ambitious officers, and political radicals biding their time. And the nation generally wanted no more than order, stability, lower taxes, and fewer soldiers, things that the exiled Stuarts could promise, as none of Cromwell's successors could. JRJ

Gregg, P., *Oliver Cromwell* (1988); Morrill, J., *Oliver Cromwell and the English Revolution* (1990); Roots, I., *Cromwell: A Profile* (1973).

Cromwell, Richard (1626–1712). Lord Protector (1658–9). Son of Oliver *Cromwell, he held no important position until 1657. Under the *Heads of the Proposals, the 1656 constitution, Oliver could nominate his successor and probably did so days before he died on 3 September 1658. Despite inexperience, Richard initially provided stability, settling army discontent and calling a Parliament elected on the traditional constituencies, which contained a majority ready to work with him. His eventual failure was caused principally by intractable problems which he inherited. Accumulated debt of £2,500,000 and economic depression worsened by the Spanish War that damaged trade could not be tackled because the main cause of an annual deficit of £300,000 was expenditure on the army and navy. Richard's ability to get practical co-operation from Parliament was frustrated by a determined and brilliantly led republican minority who wanted the return of the Rump. Even more fatal was the revival of radical political activism in the army. In April 1659 Richard tried to use Parliament to gain control over the military: this drove the generals into the radical camp and they forced him to dissolve Parliament, so forfeiting civilian support. Richard was never deposed; his authority was no longer recognized. Thereafter he lived privately, in exile from 1660 to 1680. JRJ

Cromwell, Thomas (*c*.1485–1540). Thomas Cromwell was the second of the great ministers to whom Henry VIII gave much trust and an imposing array of offices; he was the one most personally associated with the programme which made Henry VIII supreme head of the church in England.

1. Early career. Thomas Cromwell was born *c*.1485, the son of a Putney cloth-worker. In his early life he followed the French campaigns in Italy, and somehow acquired a broad education including some knowledge of business and law. He sat in the 1523 Parliament and entered the service of Thomas *Wolsey, assisting in the dissolutions of religious houses used to endow Wolsey's college and school. Though he stayed with Wolsey longer than most after his disgrace, he escaped the wreck to join a group of intellectuals and administrators, including Edward Foxe, Thomas *Audley, and Richard Rich, who were working on plans for Henry VIII to escape from the impasse in his divorce negotiations.

Cromwell became master of the king's jewel house in 1532 and principal royal secretary in 1534. Though he was thereafter to accumulate other offices including chancellor of the Exchequer, master of the rolls, lord privy seal, and great chamberlain, it was on his role as royal secretary, to which he gave unprecedented political importance, that his power rested. Thanks to the survival of vast amounts of his personal papers, seized before his attainder in 1540, his extensive contacts across the entire Tudor state can be documented.

2. Cromwell and the royal supremacy, 1532–1536. It is not certain exactly what role Cromwell played in the birth of Henry VIII's campaign for supremacy over the church. The arguments used to justify this campaign antedated Cromwell's rise to influence. Nevertheless, it seems likely that Cromwell drew the strands together, eliminated the more obviously implausible proofs, and recognized that parliamentary statute—hitherto used only for issues where church affairs bordered on secular concerns—offered the most public and authoritative way to announce and embody the new changes. Cromwell is thought to have been responsible for drafting the Supplication of the Commons against the Ordinaries in 1532. This parliamentary petition resurrected the protests against church courts originally made in 1529 in the attack on Wolsey; it was used to secure the *submission of the clergy, which finally subjected canon law to secular review. Cromwell certainly took charge of the drafting of the Act in Restraint of *Appeals to Rome (1533) and the Act of *Supremacy (1534).

Parliamentary statute was only one of several means Cromwell found to secure consent to the supremacy. Using Berthelet, the royal printer, he saw to the publication of a sheaf of propaganda tracts, written by a range of intellectual clients and allies in both English and Latin, which justified the royal proceedings to readers of every level of education. Just as important was Cromwell's meticulous and ruthless treatment of high-profile opponents of the policy. The long examinations of Sir Thomas *More, and his eventual trial and conviction for treasonably refusing the oath of supremacy, testify to Cromwell's anxiety to be seen to observe the forms of law; this trait can also be seen in his efforts to secure convictions of those implicated in the *Pilgrimage of Grace of 1536.

3. Cromwell and the Reformation. For all his ruthlessness, Cromwell gave away a hostage to fortune by his efforts to propel Henrician religious policy in a moderately protestant direction. As royal vicegerent in spirituals from 1535 Cromwell was responsible for the Ten Articles of 1536 and the royal injunctions of 1536 and 1538, which systematically attacked catholic teaching on works-righteousness, the cult of saints, offerings for the dead, holy relics and shrines, and religious festivals. On a wider front, Cromwell patronized ideas for social reform, especially improvements to poor relief and economic welfare schemes, similar to those being promoted in Europe at the same time. Though largely unsuccessful in the 1530s, these projects anticipated parts of the successful Tudor Poor Law reforms of the 1570s.

4. Cromwell and faction, 1536–1540. Thomas Cromwell never enjoyed the sort of ascendancy in Henry VIII's councils held by Cardinal Wolsey. The last four years of his life were a constant struggle to overcome rivals. Using parliamentary Acts of attainder he secured the judicial killing successively of *Anne Boleyn and her household (1536), and the Courtenay and Pole families (1538). By this period Cromwell was seeking an alliance with pro-protestant princes in Germany who belonged to neither the French nor the Habsburg allegiance. In 1540 he brought about the disastrous marriage of Henry and *Anne of Cleves in pursuit of this policy. He had even intervened to protect preachers at Calais who were almost certainly pushing a harder protestant line than royal policy allowed. In self-defence he tried to accuse the lord deputy of Calais (who knew of his dealings there) of treason. Political and religious enemies led by the duke of *Norfolk and Bishop Stephen *Gardiner momentarily gained the king's ear and convinced Henry that Cromwell was not only a traitor but an ultra-protestant 'sacramentarian' heretic; he was condemned untried by the weapon of parliamentary attainder which he had himself used so often, and executed on 28 July 1540.

5. Assessment. Thomas Cromwell presents the paradox of a statesman of great breadth of vision, who pursued his goals with a degree of judicial brutality only previously seen in times of civil war. Many of his policies display pragmatic calculations of factional advantage as much as, or more than, political principle. His creation of the courts of revenue now looks more like wasteful inflation of his own patronage than modern 'bureaucratic' innovation. The *Privy Council was conjured up to throw a smoke-screen over the Cromwell clique's role in government in 1536, rather than to create an efficient executive committee of the crown. Yet after the bloody backbiting of the 1530s was over, many of his achievements were rediscovered and adopted to become part of the foundations of early modern government. EC

Cropredy Bridge, battle of, 1644. While waiting for news of *Rupert's attempt to relieve York, Charles I's southern army clashed with *Waller at Cropredy bridge, on the Cherwell near Banbury, on 29 June. Waller, seeing the royalist army strung out on the march, hoped to punch a hole between van and rear by taking Cropredy bridge. In turn, he found himself facing a battle on two fronts, when the royalist van turned, and he was fortunate to extricate himself with the loss of some light guns. Though little more than a cavalry skirmish, Cropredy sustained royalist morale until the news from *Marston Moor came through. JAC

croquet may have originated in France, since most of the terms are French in origin, and seems to have been played in England in the 16th cent. Like many games, it became standardized in the Victorian period and an English tournament was organized at Evesham in 1867. Three years later a conference laid down rules, though these have been substantially modified. Simple versions are played in many private gardens, with unexpected hazards, but the national game is administered by the Croquet Association at the Hurlingham Club. JAC

Crotoy, battle of, 1347. In 1346 Edward III laid siege to *Calais with a naval blockade. On 25 June 1347 a French fleet of some 40 vessels bringing relief was scattered at Crotoy, at the mouth of the Somme to the south. Calais surrendered on 3 August and remained in English hands for more than 200 years. JAC

Crowley, Sir Ambrose (1658–1713). Crowley was a remarkable industrial magnate. He came from a quaker family of Worcestershire and his ancestors were blacksmiths, moving up into iron production. Crowley was apprenticed in London and settled there, buying a large house at Greenwich. He built up an enormous iron enterprise, first establishing a foundry at Sunderland, where coal was cheap, transport to London quick, and the Tyneside shipbuilders needed nails. In 1691 he transferred his business to Winlaton, west of Newcastle, and later developed the lower Derwent valley. He was knighted in 1707 while sheriff of London and at his death had just been elected to Parliament for Andover. One daughter married Sir John Hind Cotton, 3rd baronet, of Cambridgeshire, and another Lord St John of Bletsoe. JAC

crown. See MONARCHY.

Cruikshank, George (1792–1878). Caricaturist and book illustrator. Born in London of Scottish parents, apprentice and assistant in his father's print factory, Cruikshank rapidly became *Gillray's successor as leading political caricaturist, but from about 1824 turned to book illustration as humorous artist and social commentator. Immensely productive, incorporating witty anthropomorphism, near-surrealism, and Celtic treatment of the supernatural, he worked with *Thackeray, Ainsworth, and *Dickens, counteracting the strong continental influence upon book illustration and enabling an English school to emerge. But as Regency exuberance yielded to Victorian gentility, his style did not move with public taste, and he began to outlive his popularity. Sprightly and convivial, he espoused total abstinence (1847) as zealously as he had formerly imbibed, to the embarrassment of friends, and lectured indefatigably for both *temperance and Volunteer movements. Despite an active career of 72 years, with little diminution of powers, he struggled to survive. ASH

crusades. The crusades, considered together, constituted the most popular mass movement of the later Middle Ages. They may be defined as a species of holy war, authorized by the pope and proclaimed in the name of Christ; a just war, that is a justifiably defensive reaction to aggression towards Christian people or territory, their participants enjoying a set of privileges offered by the pope and enshrined in canon law. Such a definition, crucially, does not require a crusader to fulfil his vow in the Holy Land, nor does it postulate Muslims as the normative object of crusading. For the fact is that crusades came to be deployed against a considerable variety of opponents and in an equally considerable number of crusading theatres at different times—against Moors in Spain, Mongols in eastern Europe, pagan Slavs in north-eastern Europe, heretics in Bosnia and in southern France, and a variety of papal political opponents within western Europe.

Many of these various applications were controversial at the time and remain so today amongst historians. The same is true of the very notion of crusade, from the time that Pope Urban II made his call to what we now know as the First Crusade at the Council of Clermont in November 1095. In protestant Britain, not surprisingly, the crusade has been harshly judged for centuries. For Thomas Fuller, a 17th-cent. royalist Anglican, as for the 16th-cent. martyrologist John *Foxe, the 'holy war' was fatally tainted by catholicism, while the notion of savage fanaticism was most effectively developed by Edward *Gibbon in the 18th cent., in a general attack on the lamentable consequences of religion and irrationality. This train of thought was famously stated by David *Hume in his condemnation of crusade: 'the most signal and durable monument to human folly that has yet appeared in any age or nation.' This long tradition is still alive, found, for example, in the summing-up by Runciman, whose massive work ends in a ringing denunciation: 'the Holy War itself was nothing more than a long act of intolerance in the name of God, which is the sin against the Holy Ghost.'

Such a tradition has inevitably militated against serious consideration of the significance of the crusades in and for British history. Allowance must also be made for that narrowly insular outlook of so many 19th- and early 20th-cent. historians. Apart from the deeds of Richard I, incongruously a source of English national pride as Richard was not English, nor even Anglo-Norman, the limited English role in the crusading movement was scarcely conducive to extensive historical study. What is more, the very wisdom of English involvement was questionable, especially that of kings. Were the crusades not a terrible distraction, deflecting the king from his primary and proper concerns at home, and resulting in Richard I's case in disastrous consequences for his subjects as well as himself? And it followed that the crusades could also be seen as a deplorable squandering of resources that could have been more usefully employed in England or to England's advantage.

Times and attitudes, as well as historical fashions and historians' interests, have changed. One notable recent trend has been a move towards thorough investigation and assessment of the impact of the crusades upon the societies in which they were preached, and it is now becoming apparent that the crusade affected vast areas of life. It is in these effects, on what might be termed the home front of the crusading movement, that the crusades exerted a most profound influence. It is undoubtedly the case that the heyday of crusading was in the 12th and 13th cents., at least so far as English participation is concerned, but as an institution and as a real force in English life the crusade only finally withered and died in the later 16th cent., as a result of the reordering of values during the turbulence of the Reformation. Every king of England between 1154 and 1327 took the cross, though only one, Richard I, fulfilled it in person. Many of their subjects continued the tradition into the 16th cent. SL

Lloyd, S. D., *English Society and the Crusade 1216–1307* (Oxford, 1988); Runciman, S., *A History of the Crusades* (3 vols., Cambridge, 1954); Tyerman, C. J., *England and the Crusades 1095–1588* (Chicago, 1988).

Crystal Palace. Designed by Sir Joseph Paxton to house the *Great Exhibition in Hyde Park in 1851. It was itself the greatest success of the Exhibition. Paxton based it upon the lily house he had built at *Chatsworth for the duke of Devonshire—a vast glass conservatory, dubbed the Crystal Palace by *Punch*. It was more than three times the length of St Paul's and included 294,000 panes of glass. The astronomer-royal declared that it could not stand, but it survived the 'Hallelujah' chorus at the opening ceremony, several gales, the excitement caused by a lady in bloomers, and the deafening cheers for the duke of *Wellington. Victoria took Paxton's progress from gardener's boy as an example of the social mobility possible. In 1852 the building was removed to Sydenham, where it was totally destroyed by fire in November 1936. JAC

Cubitt, Thomas (1788–1855). Builder. Son of a Norfolk carpenter removed to London, Cubitt set up as master carpenter but abandoned traditional practices of subcontracting for employing his own tradesmen, ensuring their continuous employment and ever considerate for their welfare. After the London Institution (1815) he moved into speculative building, progressing from Highbury villas to Bloomsbury and Belgravia. Active during one of London's great eras of development, and described as 'the Emperor of the building Trade', he appeared before select committees concerned with 'Metropolitan Improvements', advised in town-planning and house-building, was concerned with sewage and smoke nuisance, Battersea Park and the embankment, but was never officially honoured. Cubitt's business acumen and benevolent autocracy—according to Queen Victoria (for whom he altered *Osborne and built the east wing of *Buckingham palace), 'a better, kinder-hearted man never breathed'—led to great wealth, but he was generous to family and employees. ASH

Cuilén (d. 971), king of 'Scotland' (from 966). Son of *Indulf, Cuilén became king following Dub's death fighting the men of Moray. He had challenged Dub unsuccessfully in 965, but had been defeated in battle at Duncrub (7 miles west of Perth). He was killed by Rhydderch son of King Dyfnwal of Strathclyde in a battle fought in Lothian. It is alleged that he had carried off Rhydderch's daughter. Cuilén had a Danish nickname, *Hringr* (ring-giver). This, his father's Danish name, and a brother called Olaf suggest that his family were particularly receptive to Scandinavian influence, and may be linked with the 'hog-back' grave-slabs characteristic of Danish north England found in Fife and Perthshire, perhaps indicating Danish immigration at this time. DEB

Cullen, Paul (1803–78). Archbishop of Dublin, first Irish cardinal (1866). Cullen was born in Kildare, and educated in Ireland and Rome. During his long residence there (1820–49) he was student, and successively vice-rector and rector, of the Irish College and of Propaganda College. He became successively archbishop of Armagh (1849) and primate (1849–78) and archbishop of Dublin (1852). Because political revolution in Rome (1848) made him detest *Fenians and extremists, he prohibited his clergy from participation in politics (1853). A supporter of the crown and constitution, he preferred 'Irishization', advancing Irish to responsible places by constitutional means. He helped found the *Catholic University (1854) and held the first national synod for 200 years (1850). Of immense influence in Ireland and Rome, he was close to Pius IX. He gave the Irish church its characteristically ultramontane tone. WMM

Culloden, battle of, 1746. Fought on Wednesday 16 April about 5 miles south-east of the Highland capital of Inverness. The retreating Jacobites occupied Inverness in February 1746. An attempted night attack on the advancing army of the duke of *Cumberland failed on 15 April, and Charles *Stuart decided to offer battle on the bare boggy Drumossie Moor above Culloden House, despite the view of Lord George *Murray that less suitable ground for Highlanders was difficult to find. The Jacobites could assemble only 5,000 men. Cumberland had 9,000 men including many Scots. Unlike Charles, he had a good, well-served field artillery.

Cumberland's field guns decimated the Jacobite ranks for 20 minutes. Charles, in command for the first time, fatally delayed the order to charge. Lord George launched the Jacobite right and centre, but gallantry could not match discipline, canister shot from the guns, musketry, and ultimately the bayonet's superior reach to the broadsword. The Macdonalds on the Jacobite left rightly pulled back at first in good order, pursued by cavalry. Retreat became rout. BPL

Cumberland consisted of the western part of the Lake District, a surrounding coastal plain, narrow towards the south, broadening towards the north, and two outlying areas, a hilly district to the east towards Alston, and fertile lands north of *Hadrian's Wall towards the Scottish border. The northern part is drained by the Eden, running through Carlisle, and its tributaries the Caldew and the Petteril, running north from Penrith; the Derwent flows from Derwentwater and Bassenthwaite through Cockermouth to Workington; and the southern parts are drained by the Duddon. The great slab of hills in the east is drained by the south Tyne and the Tees, the water finishing in the North Sea. The boundary with Scotland was the river Liddel; with Westmorland the Eamont, flowing out of Ullswater; and with Lancashire, the Duddon. Carlisle grew as a bridge over the Eden, where an important east–west route from Newcastle towards Ireland intersected with two major north–south routes, an ancient road through Tebay, and an old route from Yorkshire across Stainmore via Scotch Corner, Brough, and Appleby.

Cumberland was one of the last shires to take shape and for centuries was disputed between England and Scotland. In Caesar's time it was in the territory of the *Brigantes, but that was a loose confederation and the local tribe were the *Carvetii, inhabiting the Solway region. The Romans were interested in the area for strategic and economic reasons. In the end, their boundary with the Scots settled along the line of Hadrian's Wall, which entered Cumbria at Gilsland and ran to Bowes-on-Solway. Carlisle (Luguvalium) was a major Roman town, protected by a fort at Stanwix, and there were important forts at Hardknott (the worst posting in Roman Britain), and at Maryport, Penrith, Netherby, and Bewcastle. Ravenglass, where the Mite, Irt, and Esk meet, was a superb natural harbour until it silted up. The local mineral resources were also exploited—silver and lead from the Alston region, copper, coal, and iron elsewhere. After the Roman period, the orientation of the region was towards Scotland and Ireland rather than the south. It was a meeting-place of peoples and cultures. The basic stratum was Welsh or British, and the name, Cumberland, means the land of the Cumbri—the Welsh. But the Saxons penetrated across from Yorkshire and from Northumbria and later there were settlers from Ireland and the Isle of Man, who left Norse place-names—Aspatria, Cleator, Ennerdale, and Borrowdale. Carlisle is a case in point, since the Latinized form Luguvalium commemorates a Celtic god; Bede tells us that the Saxons called it Luel; later came the Celtic prefix *caer*, a city; and the Normans added a silent s making Carlisle. Roman and Celtic Christianity also struggled here. St *Ninian's mission at Whithorn was only the other side of Solway Firth and St Kentigern certainly evangelized in the 6th cent. from Strathclyde, judging by the number of churches dedicated to him. After *Æthelfryth's victory at *Degsastan in 603, the region fell under Saxon rule and became part of *Northumbria. The Synod of *Whitby in 664 decided in favour of Roman Christianity and in 685 *Ecgfrith gave Carlisle and district to St *Cuthbert as part of the endowment for the diocese of *Lindisfarne. Bede records how St Herbert left his island in the middle of Derwentwater to meet Cuthbert. *Bewcastle cross also testifies to Northumbrian influence since it commemorates Aldfrith, who ruled 686–705.

But it was hard for any power to keep a firm grip on the area and as Northumbrian influence waned, that of Wessex rose. In 926 *Athelstan, king of Wessex, met the kings of Strathclyde and Scotland at Eamont bridge to dictate terms, and reasserted his authority in 937 with a crushing victory at *Brunanburh. But Wessex control of so distant a territory can only have been fitful and the fact that Athelstan's successor *Edmund ravaged the region in 945 suggests that Dunmail of Strathclyde had regained it. He is probably commemorated in Dunmail raise between Windermere and Keswick. Edmund is said to have ceded the region to Malcolm, king of the Scots, though both the nature of the contract and the extent of the region remain obscure. The arrangement does not seem to have lasted long for in 1000 *Æthelred was once more harrying the region, suggesting that he had lost control, probably to the Norse, since his fleet also attacked the Isle of Man.

By this time the term Cumbria was coming into use. The Normans did not at first occupy the area and neither Cumberland nor Westmorland was included in the *Domesday survey in 1086. But in 1092 William Rufus brought a large force there and began building the castle at Carlisle. In 1133 Henry I established Carlisle as a bishopric. The territory was still regarded as the district of Carlisle rather than as a shire and the Scots had by no means abandoned their claims. David I of Scotland took advantage of the confusion of Stephen's reign to occupy the area and died at Carlisle in 1153. Henry II reconquered it in 1157 and though William the Lion and Alexander II of Scotland made efforts to recapture it, it stayed part of England. Westmorland was hived off to form a separate county and Alston in the east added to Cumberland, though it remained in the diocese of Durham. By the end of the 13th cent. Cumberland, like the other counties, sent two knights of the shire to Parliament.

Though Cumberland was now firmly attached to England, it remained a border county, liable to incursions great and small. The tide of war rolled backwards and forwards. The Scots besieged Carlisle in 1296; Robert I Bruce did homage in the cathedral in 1297; and Edward I died at Burgh campaigning against the Scots in 1307. The region was repeatedly ravaged in the 14th cent. During the Civil War, in 1644–5, Carlisle stood a siege from the Scots who destroyed much of the cathedral. The last serious fighting on English soil occurred in the county during Prince Charles *Stuart's retreat in 1745, when he left a forlorn hope in Carlisle castle. Even in times of peace, the many peel towers were invaluable refuges against reivers and raiders.

Although not a large town, Carlisle dominated the county. Penrith had military importance because of the junction of two major routes, and the market towns of Brampton, Wigton, Cockermouth, and Keswick had local significance. Travellers avoided the area if they could. Celia Fiennes in 1698 described 'villages of sad little huts . . . I took them at first sight for barns to fodder cattle in.' But the character of the county began to change with the industrial revolution, which created an urban fringe to west Cumberland, and the revolution in taste, which brought visitors in search of Romantic scenery of lakes and hills. Local landowners were vigorous in exploiting mineral resources and opening up ports. The Lowthers sponsored Whitehaven, which exported coal to Dublin, the Curwens did the same for Workington. Copper and iron were also mined on an increasing scale. The chief beneficiary or victim of Romanticism was perhaps Keswick, on the shore of Derwentwater, which changed from a small market town into a fashionable Victorian resort and thence into a tourist trap.

By the local government reorganization of 1972 Cumberland was united with Westmorland and the Furness district of Lancashire to form Cumbria. The M6 tears through the county, through Ingelwood Forest—the forest of the English settlers—and at Sellafield on the coast the lights of a nuclear power station twinkle. JAC

Cumberland, Ernest Augustus, duke of (1771–1851). Ernest Augustus, the fifth son of George III, had an eventful life. At 15 he was sent to the University of Göttingen in Hanover and in 1790 was commissioned in the Hanoverian army. A brave cavalry commander, he was severely wounded in 1794, losing one eye. Later he transferred to the British army, finishing as field marshal. In 1799 he was created duke of Cumberland, took his seat in the Lords, and spoke frequently as a protestant Tory. In 1810 he survived a frenzied attack by his valet, though scandal insisted that Cumberland had been the aggressor. In the crisis of 1828–32, Cumberland became the spokesman for those opposed to the repeal of the *Test and Corporation Acts, *catholic emancipation, which he denounced as 'outrageous', and the *Reform Bill. With the death of his elder brother the duke of *York in 1827, he became heir presumptive to the Hanoverian throne, since his niece Princess Victoria could not inherit it. On becoming king of *Hanover in 1837, he at once cancelled the liberal constitution granted in 1833 by his brother William IV, substituting a more limited one three years later. The Hanoverians, delighted to have a resident monarch once more, admired him greatly and he survived the year of revolution in 1848 without difficulty. Politically, his instincts were those of a cavalry officer—to ride straight at the enemy—and his statue in Hanover is very properly an equestrian one. JAC

Cumberland, William Augustus, 1st duke of (1721–65). Cumberland was the second surviving son of the prince of Wales, later George II. Made duke of Cumberland in 1726, he was promoted lieutenant-general in 1744, after fighting at *Dettingen. In 1745 he was proclaimed captain-general of the British army. Shortly afterwards, Marshal Saxe repulsed his attempt to relieve Tournay at *Fontenoy. Recalled in October to deal with the *Jacobite rebellion, he finally crushed it at *Culloden in April 1746. His devastation of the central Highlands was ruthless, but provoked by a refusal to accept terms.

His Anglo-Dutch army back in Flanders was usually outnumbered by that of Saxe, and ill-provided. Mere competence could not bring victory. After the peace of 1748, his stress on disciplinary measures in the army made him unpopular. At the start of the *Seven Years War, he virtually ran the British war effort but was destroyed by defeat against vastly superior French armies in Hanover. The convention of *Kloster-Zeven, which he signed with the French, was repudiated. He retired from the army, but remained a powerful political influence into the early years of George III. Obese and unmarried, he died unexpectedly of a clot on the brain. BPL

Cumbria. The new county of Cumbria was established by the Local Government Act of 1972, which joined the traditional counties of Cumberland and Westmorland, and added that section of north Lancashire to the south of the Lake District, and Sedbergh and Dentdale, taken from the west riding. It includes the whole of the Lake District and is bisected by the London–Glasgow railway and the M6. The county town is Carlisle. JAC

Cum universi, 1192. The papal bull *Cum universi*, issued by Celestine III, confirmed the independence of the Scottish church, declared by the bull **Super anxietatibus* of 1176, resisting in particular the claims of the archbishop of York. It was repeated by Pope Innocent III in 1200 and by Honorius in 1218. The Scottish church was said to be 'subject to the apostolic see, as a special daughter, with no intermediary'. JAC

Cunedda. Leader of the *Votadini tribe of southern Scotland in the late Roman period. Cunedda and the Votadini migrated from southern Scotland to north Wales, as part of the military and social upheavals of this turbulent period, in either the late 4th or the early 5th cent. However it must be remembered that the meagre historical accounts of late Roman Britain are sometimes no more than traditions recorded at a later date. This is particularly so in the case of Cunedda, and the tradition surrounding him has been described as 'folklore'. The contention that the British leader *Vortigern arranged the migration of the Votadini in order to strengthen north Wales against the Irish, thus establishing the royal house of *Gwynedd, must therefore be treated with caution. ES

Cunningham, Andrew, 1st Viscount Cunningham (1883–1963). Sailor. Entering the navy in 1897 as a cadet, Cunningham spent the First World War as captain of the destroyer *Scorpion*. The outbreak of the Second World War found him an acting Admiral as commander-in-chief Mediterranean. This became a post of supreme importance when Italy entered the war in 1940 and an extraordinary situation developed with British convoys moving east–west from Suez to Gibraltar and Italian convoys crossing north–south *en route* for Libya. In November 1940 an air attack on the harbour of *Taranto forced the Italian fleet to withdraw northwards and in March 1941, in a night attack, Cunningham won a decisive victory over an Italian force off Cape *Matapan. He remained in his Mediterranean command during the allied landings in north Africa and Sicily, and in 1943 was appointed 1st sea lord and chief of the naval staff. In 1945 he was given a barony and advanced to viscount the following year. JAC

Cunobelinus succeeded Tasciovanus as king of the *Catuvellauni around AD 5. His coins identify him as the son of Tasciovanus, but whether this was by birth, adoption, or simply political style is uncertain. What is clear is that he continued Tasciovanus' vigorous expansion of the Catuvellaunian kingdom at the expense of neighbouring tribes. By AD 10 he had overrun the kingdom of the *Trinovantes to the east and had moved his own capital from *Verulamium (St Albans) to Camulodunum (*Colchester), from where he now issued most of his coinage. South of the Thames he encroached on the territory of the *Cantiaci, and to the south-west the *Atrebates, whilst to the north and the north-east he pushed into the fringes of the *Coritanian and *Icenian kingdoms. He became the most powerful monarch in Britain and it is hardly surprising that the Roman historian Suetonius described him as 'Britannorum rex'—king of the Britons. He reigned for more than 35 years, dying only a year or two before the Claudian invasion of AD 43. He sired at least three sons, one of whom, Adminius, he banished for unknown reasons around AD 35. His other known sons, Togodumnus and *Caratacus, succeeded him and shared the kingdom between them. Whether, like them, Cunobelinus would have provided Claudius with a pretext for invasion by the expulsion of a Roman ally—Verica of the Atrebates—is open to debate, but many believe he would have avoided such a provocative move. KB

curia regis. See GREAT COUNCIL.

Curragh mutiny. In March 1914 57 officers of the 3rd Cavalry Brigade, stationed at Curragh near Dublin, informed the commander-in-chief that they would accept dismissal rather than undertake operations against Ulstermen to impose the Irish Home Rule Bill. They succeeded in obtaining a written assurance from the chief of staff that they would not be expected to do this. RAS

Curzon, George Nathaniel, 1st Marquis Curzon (1859–1925). Curzon became an authority on the East through travelling extensively in the 1880s, and a passionate advocate of British imperial power. His main contribution to that came when he was sent to India as viceroy in 1899, where he worked hard to further the interests—as he saw them—of both Britain and the natives, and in some splendour. He also quarrelled with his army commander, Lord *Kitchener; and with most of the population of Bengal by partitioning the province in 1905. His resignation later that year was accompanied by bitterness and recrimination, and followed by a period of exclusion from public life, under an unsympathetic Liberal government, until the *First World War resurrected his career in 1916. After the war he was foreign secretary for a while (1919–24), but again quarrelsome; and was disappointed at not becoming prime minister in 1923. His earldom came in 1911, the marquisate in 1921. He had a reputation for arrogance and inflexibility, which some attributed to a painful spinal condition which required him to wear a corset for most of his life. BJP

customs and excise. Monarchs and governments have traditionally levied customs and excise duties, but they became more important as the expense of government increased, particularly during the 17th cent. Customs duty or tariff is an impost on goods crossing a frontier, its purpose being either to raise revenue or to protect home industries. Customs duties, however, were sometimes imposed to supplement or make more effective internal excise duties. Excise, Dr *Johnson's 'hateful tax', has traditionally been levied on a wide variety of home-produced raw materials and manufactures, notably alcoholic drinks, but also including at various times such items as coal, salt, paper, and glass.

Historically, customs and excise duties have been both objects of popular resistance and directly or indirectly the cause of major events. *Ship money, for example, was only one of several imposts introduced by Charles I which caused widespread resentment prior to the civil wars. Later, the 1707 *Union of England and Scotland, though highly contentious, embodied a customs union with equalization of duty on designated items, including an enhanced malt tax, which caused riots in Scotland. With enhanced duties on wines and spirits, *smuggling became widespread during the 18th and early 19th cents., partly because effective policing was impossible and partly because it was socially approved. In the North American colonies, imposition of customs duties on such items as newspapers and Indian tea, though amounting to less than 1 per cent of average colonial income, contributed to the outbreak of the war against the British.

By the late 18th cent. the customs and excise, though still stretched by smuggling and evasion, had become increasingly efficient. Adam *Smith, author of *The *Wealth of Nations*, was a commissioner of customs in Scotland, while the poet Robert *Burns served as an exciseman at Dumfries. In the 19th cent., growing belief in *free trade persuaded governments to reduce customs duties where possible, but increasing international competition towards the end of the century produced a call for protective tariffs which, articulated by Joseph *Chamberlain, split the Conservative Party in 1903. Protectionist arguments made progress after the *First World War, but one of the objects of the *European Economic Community, after the *Second World War, was to reduce customs duties between member states. ID

custos rotulorum. The officer charged in the 14th cent. with keeping the records of the county sessions, though the name did not come into use until the 15th cent. He was always a justice of the quorum and appointed the clerk of the peace. Later the office became identified with the *lord-lieutenancy, though they had separate functions. JAC

Cuthbert, St (d. 687). Known, from two near contemporaries, an anonymous biographer at *Lindisfarne and *Bede, who wrote three accounts, as a man who conversed with angels, struggled against demons, had prophetic vision, and mortified his flesh. Probably of aristocratic Anglo-Saxon origin, and born in Northumbria *c*.635, he was prompted by a vision of the soul of *Aidan to enter the monastery at Melrose, where he trained under Boisil. Almost nothing is known of his life before this. With Abbot Eata, he entered Alchfrith of Deira's new monastery at Ripon (late 650s), but returned after refusing to accept Roman practices. Cuthbert became prior in 664 and undertook teaching tours in Northumbria. He also visited Pictish Christians, with whom he was apparently on friendly terms. After the Synod of *Whitby (664), Eata removed to Lindisfarne. Cuthbert followed and became prior, but had some difficulties managing the monks. He retreated to Farne Island (*c*.676) but was, reluctantly, made bishop of part of Northumbria under Archbishop *Theodore (685). His seat was at Lindisfarne. He retired in 686, in failing health, and died in 687, on Farne. In 698, in promotion of his cult, his remains, buried at Lindisfarne, were exhumed and enshrined, in which process they were found to be incorrupt, and for which the Lindisfarne Gospels may have been produced. Near the royal seat at Bamburgh, Lindisfarne enjoyed royal patronage and prospered and the cult of Cuthbert became a political force. Tenth-cent. West Saxon kings' patronage of Cuthbert in the north, and promotion of his cult in the south, were, partly, attempts to unify their realm and legitimize their authority. Legitimization is the motive behind the tale of Cuthbert promising Alfred, in a vision, rule of all Britain for himself and his descendants, in the *Historia de Sancto Cuthberto*. This was written mainly in the mid-10th cent., at *Chester-le-Street, Scandinavian pressure having caused the community to move. In 995 it reached Durham, where a new shrine was established in 1104. Here Cuthbert attracted many pilgrims, gained a reputation for misogyny, and was perceived as champion of the community. His repose suffered from Henry VIII's commissioners, and again in 1827, when his grave was reopened, likewise in an atmosphere of religious tensions, and some of his relics were dispersed. His 698 decorated coffin survives, in fragments, now displayed with his pectoral cross and some Anglo-Saxon gifts to his shrine in the cathedral.

Cuthbert was no stranger to politics. We see him discussing the royal succession with Abbess Ælfflæd of Whitby (684), as adviser to King *Ecgfrith, and to his widow Iurminburg (685). Becoming bishop involved opposition to *Wilfrid who claimed all Northumbria. His retirement may have discreetly anticipated Wilfrid's forthcoming return. Cuthbert's promotion as saint, and his historiography, are, in part, episodes in the long-running dispute between two parties, each emphasizing its positive contribution to Northumbrian Christianity and its adherence to Roman practice. There is for example a propagandist element in the depiction of St Peter on Cuthbert's coffin.

This makes it hard to discover what Cuthbert was really like and really stood for. His training, some episodes in his career, his asceticism, and some of his miracles (often involving animals and birds) suggest his values were in the Irish tradition, ascetic and contemplative. But his cross suggests that as bishop he cut a more magnificent figure than this might imply. Both biographers give some continental dimension to his traits, behaviour, and values. In Bede's pages Cuthbert harmoniously combines both traditions, as a Northumbrian St Benedict (of Nursia) and embodiment of the episcopal virtues expounded by Pope Gregory I: an exemplar for Bede's contemporaries. AER

Cuthred (d. 756), king of Wessex (*c.*740–56). When Cuthred succeeded, King *Æthelbald of Mercia dominated the southern English kingdoms. In 743 the two kings are recorded as combining against the Welsh, whom Cuthred was fighting again some ten years later. In 750 Cuthred successfully put down the rebellion of Æthelhun, a 'presumptuous ealdorman', who apparently went on to fight for his king in 752, when Cuthred defeated Æthelbald at *Burford, the site of which is uncertain. This victory apparently brought independence to Wessex for a while, but it seems to have reverted to Mercian dependency soon after Cuthred's death in 756. AM

Cutty Sark. The last and most famous full-rigged tea clipper, launched in 1869 from Dumbarton (the figurehead's 'cutty sark'=short chemise). Steamers using the recently opened Suez canal proved too competitive, but she plied the Australian wool trade until 1895. Now restored and rerigged, she lies at Greenwich. ASH

cycling. A primitive wheeled cycle was exhibited at Paris in 1791 but had to be pushed with the feet, as were the hobbyhorses of the 1810s. In the 1860s a front-wheel-drive machine was manufactured—the bone-shaker—and in subsequent decades the front wheel became larger until the penny-farthing had developed. By 1882 speeds of 20 m.p.h. had been attained. The Rover safety model, built at Coventry from 1885, had a rear-wheel chain drive and from 1888 pneumatic tyres could be fitted. Women were able to ride the new models and the industry was established as a major employer in the midlands, turning out 750 bicycles p.a. by the 1890s. Cycle races began early and special tracks were built in the 1880s. The National Cyclists' Union was founded in 1878 and the Cyclists' Touring Club the same year. Time trials began in 1895 and a national championship was introduced in the 1930s. Road racing in Britain was subject to restrictions and did not develop as on the continent. But a Tour of Britain was started in 1951 and became the annual Milk Race. Meanwhile, ordinary cyclists, driven off the road by aggressive motorists, took to the pavements, leaving pedestrians to fend for themselves. JAC

Cynegils (d. 643), king of the West Saxons (*c.*611–643). Cynegils extended his frontier by defeating the Britons at Beandun, probably Bindon, east Devon, but suffered set-backs. In 626, the failed assassination of the Northumbrian king *Edwin, organized by Cynegils's son Cwichelm, was followed by a vengeful attack in which five Wessex princes were killed. The thrust of expansion was slowed by conflict with expanding Mercian neighbours, and although it is recorded that the battle of Cirencester in 628 was followed by an agreement, it seems likely that Wessex lost lands gained in 577, in the lower Severn valley, to *Penda of Mercia. In 635, sponsored by the powerful Northumbrian king Oswald, Cynegils was baptized by the recently arrived missionary Birinus. He became the first Christian king of Wessex and Birinus was established in an episcopal see at *Dorchester-on-Thames. AM

Cynewulf (d. 786), king of Wessex (757–86). Cynewulf deposed his predecessor, Sigeberht. In 757 he attended the Mercian court, witnessing one of *Æthelbald's last charters, suggesting that Wessex was again a Mercian dependency. He witnessed another charter there in 772, but otherwise there seems no evidence of subjection to *Offa. But he appears to have lost lands to Offa after defeat at *Benson (*c.*777). The *Anglo-Saxon Chronicle* account of his death reads like a heroic saga. After a long reign, during which he 'frequently fought great battles against the Welsh', he was attacked and killed by Cyneheard, the deposed Sigeberht's brother, when visiting his mistress. His few attendants fought to the death, refusing freedom under Cyneheard. The next day, Cynewulf's remaining force confronted his killer. Loyal to their lord they refused offers of money and land to accept Cyneheard's succession, slaying him and his followers. AM

Cyprus is the third largest island in the Mediterranean with Turkey and Syria its nearest neighbours. The major agricultural area, the Mesaörian plain, separates the Kyrenia range in the north and the Troodos mountains in the south. The economy of the island is based upon agriculture, manufacturing, and tourism. From AD 647, following occupation by both Roman and Byzantine empires, Cyprus was Arab for 500 years, then an independent Frankish kingdom for about 300 years, before falling briefly into Egyptian hands until 1489, when it was occupied by the Venetians. In 1571 it was conquered by the Ottoman Turks, who encouraged Turkish settlement. In 1878 administration of the island was taken over by Britain as a forward naval base to support Turkey against Russia, but on the outbreak of war with Turkey in 1914 it was annexed. Pressure for independence or union with Greece ('Enosis') developed after the Second World War and in the 1950s EOKA began a guerrilla campaign. Independence was declared in 1960 with Greek Cypriot Archbishop Makarios as president and a Turkish

Cypriot, Dr Küçük, as his deputy. Immediate difficulties arose between Greeks and Turks and a UN peace-keeping force arrived in 1964. In 1974 an EOKA coup to replace Makarios prompted a Turkish invasion and the occupation of northern Cyprus. Despite occasional negotiations, the two communities remain implacably apart. JC

Dafydd ap Gruffydd (d. 1283), prince of Wales (1282–3). The third son of Gruffydd ap Llywelyn of Gwynedd, he was the last prince of Wales. Ambitious, treacherous, and disloyal to his elder brother *Llywelyn, he allowed himself to be manipulated by English kings. Quarrelling with Llywelyn, he did homage to Henry III (1253); after his defeat by Llywelyn at the battle of Bryn Derwin (June 1255), they were reconciled though their relationship was not easy. In 1263 he joined Henry III, though when Llywelyn was recognized as prince of Wales (1267) Dafydd was restored to land and position and swore fealty to Llywelyn. In 1274 he and Powys's princes plotted Llywelyn's death, after which he fled to Edward I. After Llywelyn's defeat (1277), Dafydd was given substantial lands in north-east Wales and England, and married the king's relative, Elizabeth Ferrers. Dissatisfied with this treatment, he attacked Hawarden (21 March 1282) and Llywelyn was drawn into the war. After Llywelyn's death (December), Dafydd held out in Dolbadarn castle and styled himself prince of Wales. He was betrayed by Welshmen, tried at Shrewsbury, and executed for treason (3 October 1283). His children were kept confined for life.
RAG

Dafydd ap Llywelyn (*c.*1208–46), prince of Gwynedd (1240–6). The only son of *Llywelyn ab Iorwerth, prince of Gwynedd, and Joan, daughter of King John, he was declared heir to his father's principality. This was recognized by Henry III (1220) and the pope (1222), and Welsh nobles swore fealty to him (1226, 1238); he did homage to Henry III (1229). Dafydd's marriage to Isabella, daughter of William de *Braose, incorporated Builth into Llywelyn's domain. Dafydd's elevation alienated his illegitimate elder brother Gruffydd, and tension grew as their father aged; in 1239 Dafydd deprived Gruffydd of some lands and imprisoned him. When Llywelyn died (1240), Henry III determined to curb Dafydd's ambitions. At Gloucester (15 May) he was knighted by the king, who received his homage; but Llywelyn's acquisitions outside Gwynedd were withheld and the homage of other Welsh nobles was reserved to the king. These humiliating terms were imposed on Dafydd in agreements at Gwerneigron and London (29 August and 24 October 1241), whilst Gruffydd was handed over to Henry III, who exploited him against Dafydd. After Gruffydd died (1 March 1244) while trying to escape from the Tower of London, Dafydd resolved to resist the king: he gained support from Welsh nobles, sought endorsement from the pope, wrote to the king of France, styled himself prince of Wales, and resumed his father's policy of creating a modern, feudal principality. Henry III launched an expedition against him (1245), but it was Dafydd's sudden death at Aber (25 February 1246) that halted his ambitions. He was buried in Aberconwy abbey. He had no heir and Gruffydd's sons claimed Gwynedd; for the moment, however, the crown's triumph was complete, as the treaty of *Woodstock (30 April 1247) illustrated.
RAG

Dáil Éireann is the Lower House of the Parliament of Eire, the upper house being the Senate. Its first meeting in the Mansion House at Dublin was in January 1919 after *Sinn Fein had won 73 seats at the general election, boycotted the Westminster Parliament, and proclaimed themselves the Parliament of the Irish Republic. There are 166 members elected by proportional representation on a five-year basis. The prime minister is the Taoiseach.
JAC

***Daily Telegraph*.** This newspaper has come to embody the ideology of conservative, middle-class, middle England in popular perception. Its origins were far from this, being a pioneer of 'popular' journalism in 1855, in the wake of the repeal of press taxes, with its selling price of 2 pence later dropping to 1 penny. By 1888, its sales of 300,000 had left *The Times*'s 60,000 far behind. But a decline around the turn of the century was halted only with its purchase by press magnate Lord Camrose, who reshaped it successfully in its middle-class mould and laid the foundations for its unrivalled reputation for wide and authoritative news coverage.
DJA

Dalhousie, James Andrew Broun Ramsay, 1st Marquis and 10th Earl (1812–60). Born at Dalhousie castle, Scotland, he was the son of a commander-in-chief of the Indian army. Politically he was a Peelite and, after serving at the Board of Trade from 1843–5, was appointed governor-general of India in 1848. His period in office was distinguished by its aggressive westernization, which contributed to the *Indian mutiny of 1857. He extended the boundaries of British India, annexing the Punjab (1849) and Pegu in Burma (1852) and declaring a doctrine of 'lapse' to acquire princely states which failed to produce heirs. He centralized authority within the *East India Company state, providing it with a modern system of record-keeping, reporting, and decision-making. He promoted the building of roads, railways, and ports, the extension of western education, and the development of colonial commerce. He resigned exhausted in 1856, the victim of overwork and ill-health. DAW

Dalriada, kingdom of. Dalriada, or Dal Riata, started as an Irish kingdom on the coast of Antrim, but migrated to the west coast of Scotland in the 5th cent., settling Kintyre and Argyll. This brought it into contact with the kingdom of the *Picts to the north-east and *Strathclyde to the south-east. There were three kindreds of Dalriada, based on Islay, Lorn, and Kintyre, the last, the Cenél nGabráin, being predominant at first. *Ædan of Dalriada, consecrated by St *Columba in the later 6th cent., clearly had wide ambitions, raiding in Orkney and Man, and waging war against Picts and Northumbrians. An attack on the Northumbrians *c.*603 ended in severe defeat for Ædan at *Degsastan, joyously reported by *Bede. This, and a further defeat for Ædan's grandson at Strathcarron at the hands of the Strathclyde Britons (*c.*642), weakened the kingdom and led to internal dissensions. Pictish influence increased and the Dalriadan fortress at Dunadd was taken by them *c.*736. Norse pressure to the west in the early 9th cent. might have squeezed Dalriada, but the reverse seems to have happened. The line of advance was apparently perceived as eastwards and in 843 *Kenneth MacAlpin, king of Dalriada, took over Pictland and moved the centre of his combined kingdom to *Dunkeld in Perthshire. Dalriada henceforth merged into the kingdom of *Alba, the nucleus for the later kingdom of Scotland, which took its name from the Latin designation of the Dalriadans, *Scotti*. JAC

Dalrymple, James, 1st Viscount Stair [S] (1619–95). Scottish lawyer and statesman. Born in Ayrshire, Dalrymple was a presbyterian. He was knighted at the Restoration and appointed a lord of Session. By 1681 he was in disfavour, lost his offices, and retired to Holland. He was accused of complicity in plots against Charles II and indicted for treason in 1685. He accompanied William of Orange on his expedition in 1688, was restored as president of the Court of Session, and promoted to the peerage in 1690. In 1681 he published *Institution of the Law of Scotland*, and was regarded by Macaulay as 'the greatest jurist that his country had produced'. JAC

Dalrymple, John, 1st earl of Stair [S] (1648–1707). Lawyer and statesman. Like his father, Dalrymple was in disfavour during the 1680s and was twice imprisoned in Edinburgh castle. But in 1687 James VII appointed him king's advocate [S] and the following year lord justice clerk [S] and a lord of Session. Nevertheless he gave strong support to William of Orange and was reappointed king's advocate 1689–92. From 1690 he was also secretary of state in Scotland. He succeeded his father as 2nd viscount in 1695 but was obliged to resign his offices for his role in authorizing the massacre of *Glencoe. Anne restored him to favour, promoted him to the earldom of Stair in 1703, and he took an active part in bringing about the Union, dying soon after an intervention in debate. His prominent political role attracted the extremes of praise and blame: Burnet wrote that he 'made a better companion than statesman'. JAC

Dalrymple, John, 2nd earl of Stair [S] (1673–1747). Diplomat and soldier. Dalrymple succeeded as 2nd earl at the age of 34 in 1707, having pursued a successful career in the army. He served as a Scottish representative peer 1707–8, 1715–34, and 1744–7, and was given the Thistle in 1710. In 1714–20 he was ambassador in France, where he played an important role in watching the Jacobites and in consolidating the understanding with the Regent d'Orléans. His opposition to Walpole's *Excise scheme in 1733 led to his dismissal from his offices and only after Walpole's fall in 1742 was he restored to favour. In 1742 he served as ambassador at The Hague, was promoted field marshal, and in 1742–3 was commander-in-chief in Flanders, resigning in dudgeon. Walpole's brother Horace thought Stair 'insufferably proud and haughty' and Lord *Hervey described him as of 'a very warm, prompt temper'. JAC

Dalton, John (1766–1844). Chemist, atomist, quaker, and Manchester intellectual, Dalton's first interests were in meteorology and in colour blindness: being colour blind, he made the first scientific study of the phenomenon. From 1794 he worked at the Manchester Literary and Philosophical Society, taking private pupils also to augment his income. In 1803–4 he lectured at the *Royal Institution in London, and met Humphry *Davy; but metropolitan life did not attract him. He wondered why the atmosphere was not a sandwich, with the densest gas at the bottom, and began thinking about the nature of the particles of matter. He concluded that each chemical element has distinct atoms, and began to work out structures of compounds, using simplicity rules. His was the first testable atomic theory, transforming chemistry in subsequent years. DK

dame schools. Before the *Education Act of 1870, many young children were taught by unqualified women in their own homes. The dame schools, which were often in the country, were privately supported and fees were charged. The curriculum was narrow and concentrated on reading and writing. Dame schools acquired a bad reputation yet Samuel *Johnson remembered Dame Anne Oliver, a shoemaker's widow who also sold gingerbread, with affection. PG

Damnonii. A tribe of central Scotland. This Scottish tribe may well have been called the Dumnonii, but the spelling used by Ptolemy is retained here. There is no known connection between them and their namesakes of south-west England. They are known only from Ptolemy's *Geography*, and their location must be determined by the settlements that he attributes to them. These include Colania, Coria, and Alauna which are thought to be identifiable as the Roman forts at Camelon, Barochan Hill, and Ardoch, although only the latter is certain. If these identifications are correct, they place the tribe firmly in the central Lowlands. KB

Dampier, William (1652–1715). Dampier was a seaman whose experiences in the *Anglo-Dutch War of 1674 set him off on his career as a pirate in the West Indies. In 1679 he crossed the Isthmus of Darien to plunder Spain's South American possessions. He returned in 1683 via Cape Horn and then sailed on across the Pacific eventually reaching Australia before returning to Britain. He now showed talent as a writer whose *New Voyage round the World* of 1697 rekindled British interest in the Pacific. The Admiralty hired him to return in a half-rotten ship. He reached the west coast of Australia and in 1700 discovered the islands of New Ireland and New Britain. He was half-way home when the ship finally foundered. Dampier returned to a buccaneering life, including marooning and later rescuing Alexander Selkirk (*'Robinson Crusoe') on Juan Fernández and another circumnavigation of the world. Despite further publications, Dampier died in poverty and bitterness before the large sums of prize money due to him had been paid. RB

Danby, Thomas Osborne, 1st earl of, marquis of Carmarthen, and duke of Leeds (1632–1712). The first minister to construct and manage working majorities in both Houses of Parliament. He did not come from a leading family and at first acted as lieutenant to the 2nd duke of *Buckingham. Appointed lord treasurer in 1673 as a stop-gap to restore royal finances after the collapse of the *cabal he secured himself in office by reversing previous unpopular policies. He made Charles II realize that without money the *Anglo-Dutch War must be abandoned. He rallied the bishops and clergy, out of royal favour since 1663, renewing prosecutions of catholics and dissenters. Danby used patronage to win followers, especially in Parliament and county offices, and installed relations and associates in key positions. He defeated all attempts by *Shaftesbury's country opposition to force the dissolution of Parliament or his dismissal. But Charles retained rivals in court offices and operated a secret alternative policy of co-operation with France. Danby negotiated the marriage of the later William III and Mary II but failed to commit Charles to war against France. By releasing incriminating papers to MPs, Louis XIV drove Danby from office. Under impeachment he was confined in the Tower from 1679 to 1684. During the *Glorious Revolution, Danby seized York and Hull for William. Lord president of the council (1689), he resumed his activities as a political manager and fixer, becoming identified as the leading Tory. But the exposure of his corrupt practices in 1695 ended his active career. JRJ

dance, spontaneous or choreographed, may take a wide variety of forms and serve many functions. As the early Christian church's attitude was ambivalent, many old ritual dances (such as those associated with maypoles) became disguised through new names and contexts, evolving into social dance or absorbed into later theatrical spectacle. The emergence of noble and peasant classes further contributed to the development of social dance: chivalric culture encouraged stately movement, accompanied by instruments such as lutes, while boisterous, rustic figure-dances were accompanied by singing. France's lead in court dance yielded to Renaissance Italy's developments, and the upper classes of early Tudor England were soon familiar with these fashionable new forms; pageants meanwhile developed into *masques, which could range from simple dances with masks to elaborate entertainments with songs and speech. A new liveliness (typified by the jig) then emerged, encouraged by Elizabeth I, and dancing schools so flourished as to prompt ambassadorial comment about 'the dancing English'. Puritan disapproval failed to suppress the popularity of dance, and John Playford's *The English Dancing Master* (1651), which ran to 18 editions in 80 years, eventually included 900 choral dances of rustic origins.

After 1700, *ballet (formalized by the French) became increasingly confined to highly trained specialists, on stage rather than floor, while former open-air choral dances moved indoors, executed by all classes, and seen as contributing to general education and manners. Jane *Austen fully appreciated the role of assemblies and balls in the marriage-market. David Dale's view of dancing—'most favourable for [workers'] spirits, and a strong source of attachment to the works' (1812)—was adopted by *Owen at *New Lanark, where drill, team dancing, and community singing were utilized to control incipient lawlessness. Public ballrooms multiplied in the 19th cent., when the waltz gained international popularity, despite some moral disapproval of such paired dancing. The 20th cent. saw renewed interest in folk dance (morris dancing, now considered a survival from a primitive religious cult; Cecil Sharpe's collections) and search for new forms. England became arbiter of taste for these novelties, Victor Sylvester's *Modern Ballroom Dancing* (1928) a handbook for the dancing world, and dance competitions emerged. The advent of radio and gramophone expanded recreational dancing everywhere, from Scottish reels to jazz-based dances without physical contact, rock 'n' roll, disco, and break-dancing. Ballet meantime had generally dissociated itself from *opera, acquiring less classical themes and experimental choreography. Theatrical dance continues to flourish and influence ice-skating, women's gymnastics, and synchronized swimming. ASH

Danegeld. The term is often wrongly applied to tribute payments made to the *Vikings in the reign of *Æthelred II (978–1016); these payments are known as *gafol* in the **Anglo-Saxon Chronicle*. In 1012 Æthelred introduced an annual land tax, levied throughout the country, to pay for a Scandinavian force led by Thorkell the Tall which he had recruited to fight for him. The levy was continued by *Cnut and his sons to pay for their own standing forces and was only abolished by *Edward the Confessor in 1051. It was this tax which Norman administrative documents called 'Danegeld', though the Anglo-Saxons knew it as *heregeld* ('army tax'). BAEY

Danelaw. When during the 10th cent. the *Viking settlers of eastern England recognized the authority of the English kings, they were allowed to continue to follow some facets of their own traditional laws. By the 11th cent. the term 'Danelaw' was being used in law codes to indicate the geographical area in which customary law was influenced by Danish practice and this is defined in 12th-cent. documents as comprising all of eastern England between the Thames and the Tees. Areas to the south and west were defined as following West Saxon and Mercian law respectively. BAEY

Darby, Abraham (1677–1717). The founder of the great Shropshire iron industry, using local supplies of coal and iron. He was born in Worcestershire of a quaker family, apprenticed in Birmingham, and set up as a brass founder in Bristol. In 1708 he patented a process for casting cheap iron pots in sand and the following year leased a furnace in *Coalbrookdale. Two successive Abraham Darbys developed the business and in 1779 the *Iron Bridge at Broseley advertised the company to the world. JAC

Darcy, Thomas Darcy, 1st Baron (*c*.1467–1537). The Darcy estates were in Yorkshire and Thomas Darcy was descended from the lords Darcy of Knaith (Lincs.). Useful in the reign of Henry VII in the north, Darcy was created a peer in 1504 and given the Garter at the accession of Henry VIII in 1509. But he became increasingly disillusioned with Henry's religious policy, disliked the *dissolution of the monasteries, and began plotting with the imperial ambassador. In the rising of the *Pilgrimage of Grace for the old religion, he played an equivocal role and was accused of treason in surrendering Pontefract castle to the rebels. His explanations that he was trying to steer the rising were brushed aside and he was beheaded on Tower Hill in June 1537. His son was restored to the title in the reign of Edward VI. JAC

Dardanelles campaign. See GALLIPOLI.

Darien venture. Previous Scottish attempts to establish colonies had been small scale, but the Company of Scotland, established in 1695, had grand ideas. It aimed at raising £400,000—perhaps half the capital in Scotland. 'They came in shoals,' wrote an eye-witness: £50,000 was raised on the first day, the remainder in five months. Five ships were equipped, 1,200 men enrolled, and the expedition sailed in July 1698. The destination was a secret even from the captains until they opened their orders on the voyage. The directors had chosen Darien, on the isthmus of Panama, to be called Caledonia. After a difficult voyage of three months, the ships reached Darien, found some friendly Indians, and began building New Edinburgh. But what appeared at first sight an earthly paradise was in reality a fever-ridden swamp. Nor was there much demand for the cargo of wigs and woollen goods which they had brought. On 22 June 1699 the colonists evacuated. A second expedition left the Clyde in August 1699, reached Caledonia, and found deserted huts and hundreds of graves. After four months they surrendered to a Spanish force and were allowed to depart; very few saw Scotland again. The disaster for a small country was shattering. William III, anxious not to be embroiled with Spain at a difficult moment, had warned his subjects not to assist the enterprise. The Scots could therefore blame the English for their misfortunes. In 1705 when an English captain, Thomas Green of the *Worcester*, put in at Leith, he was arrested, falsely accused of piracy, and hanged at the instigation of a howling mob. Paradoxically, the worsening relations between the two countries hastened the *Union of 1707. JAC

'Dark Ages'. A term originally deployed in the 17th and 18th cents. to indicate the intellectual darkness which was believed to have descended on Europe with the ending of the Roman empire until new light was provided by the *Renaissance. Since the achievements of the Middle Ages have come to be properly recognized the term has been in retreat, but it still has a stronghold in what should be more appropriately described as the early Middle Ages (*c*.400–*c*.1000). In the field of British history it is sometimes applied just to the 5th and 6th cents., which many historians would prefer to designate as sub- or post-Roman. BAEY

Darling, Grace (1815–42). One of nine children, Grace Horsley Darling was born on 24 November 1815 at Bamburgh (Northd.). From 1826 her father was lighthouse-keeper of the Longstone Light on the Farne Islands. Although Grace led a secluded existence, receiving little formal education, she was a keen observer of sea-life. By 19 she was resigned to her life on the islands, assisting her father and providing companionship to her mother. She became a national heroine when, with her father, she rescued nine passengers from the steamship *Forfarshire* on its way from Hull to Dundee, when it struck rocks during gales on 7 September 1838. Grace, shy by nature, found the glare of publicity unwelcome. Nevertheless, Grace Darling memorabilia and romanticized depictions of the event were churned out. She continued to live with her parents until her death, from tuberculosis, on 20 October 1842. A Grace Darling memorial and museum are at Bamburgh. SMC

Darnley, Henry Stewart, Lord (1546–67). The son of Matthew Stewart, 4th earl of Lennox, and grandson of *Margaret Tudor, Darnley's place in the English succession was second only to that of Mary Stuart. His father was forfeited for treason in 1544 and Darnley born and brought up in England. In 1564, however, Mary restored Lennox and the arrival of Darnley in Scotland the following year was swiftly followed by their marriage by catholic rite on 29 July 1565. The marriage incensed Elizabeth but provoked in Scotland only a minor rebellion of disaffected protestant nobles, led by *Moray, which she declined to support and which rapidly fizzled out. Within months, stability was restored, Mary was pregnant, and the Stuart dynasty's future seemed assured. But Darnley's good looks, while initially captivating Mary, masked a meretricious personality and his relations with the queen soon soured. Mary's refusal to grant him the crown matrimonial drove him to ally with the disaffected nobles who had opposed the marriage and who carefully implicated him in the *Rizzio murder of March 1566, a protestant demonstration against the prospect of a catholic royal succession which achieved very little. The future James VI was born on 19 June and baptized a catholic on 17 December. The rift between Mary and Darnley, briefly healed following the Rizzio affair, now widened beyond repair. Darnley pointedly missed his son's lavish baptismal celebrations and the political isolation resulting from his betrayal of his fellow Rizzio conspirators was compounded by Mary's increasing dependence on *Bothwell. It remains unclear who precisely murdered Darnley at Kirk o' Field, Edinburgh, on 10 February 1567, or whether Mary was party to the deed. Her precipitate marriage to Bothwell, however, handed the Lennox Stewarts a gift-wrapped opportunity to gild Darnley's memory at Mary's expense. RAM

Dartmouth, George Legge, 1st Baron (1648–91). Legge fought in the second *Anglo-Dutch War, held naval commands in the third Anglo-Dutch War, and had also started to accumulate military and high civil posts, due to his intimate relationship with the duke of York. Created Lord Dartmouth in 1682, he evacuated Tangier in 1683–4. Facing the threat of a Dutch invasion in 1688, James II made this ultimate loyalist commander-in-chief of the navy. Adverse winds made it impossible for him to prevent invasion, and his fleet was rife with disaffection. Dartmouth was appalled by James's determination to send the heir to the throne to France. After James's flight, Dartmouth recognized William of Orange *de facto*. James deserted him, not he James. Committed to the Tower on suspicion of treason in 1691, he died there unexpectedly. No man was less likely to facilitate a French invasion. BPL

Dartmouth, William Legge, 2nd earl of (1731–1801). William Legge was the grandson of the 1st earl, a moderate Hanoverian Tory. Succeeding in 1750, he entered politics after doing the grand tour with Frederick *North, the future prime minister and his half-brother. Dartmouth served as president of the Board of Trade in the Rockingham ministry of 1765–6. In North's administration he was secretary of state for the colonies and president of the Board of Trade from 1772, lord privy seal from 1775. A deeply devout man, with methodistical sympathies, he was known irreverently as 'the psalm singer'. Dartmouth College in Hanover (New Hampshire), chartered in 1769, was named after him. Unhappy with coercion of the American colonies, he supported conciliation proposals in the approach to the American Revolution but by 1776 was convinced that force was the only remedy left. American propaganda painted him as unbalanced and remote from reality. He resigned with North in 1782 and left politics after 1783. BPL

darts evolved from throwing spears or shooting arrows. Hand arrows were a useful weapon, known as 'dartes', and this was one of the few games that medieval and early modern governments did not feel obliged to prohibit. It is possible that the modern dartboard developed from the cross-section of a tree trunk, brought indoors for practice. There were of course many local variations, including the use of blowpipes. The standard clock-face became established in the late 19th cent., and paper flights to fit the darts were patented in 1898. In 1908 a court action at Leeds held that darts was a game of skill rather than chance and could therefore be played in pubs, without offending the laws against gambling. In the 20th cent., two world wars (with much killing of time) followed by the spread of television helped to popularize the game, which has been controlled in Britain by the National Darts Association since 1953. NJB

Darwin, Charles (1809–82). Darwin made evolution scientifically respectable. Intended for medicine, he took courses at Edinburgh, but dropped out unable to bear surgery. He went on to Christ's College, Cambridge, took a pass degree, and became a clergyman, reading W. *Paley with pleasure. There J. S. Henslow and Adam Sedgwick directed his enthusiasm for nature into serious science and in 1831 he was offered a place as companion to the captain on HMS *Beagle* surveying Cape Horn. This was the kind of opportunity that Joseph *Banks had enjoyed; and on the five-year voyage round the world, Darwin became a great descriptive scientist and collector. Thinking about nature's diversity, and reading T. R. *Malthus, he hit upon the idea of natural selection when he got home.

Animals and plants produced more young than could survive: those better adapted to their surroundings would be 'selected' by nature as the stock-breeder selected the woolliest or meatiest sheep, and their offspring would diverge, inheriting characteristics. Unlike earlier theories, his grandfather's or J. B. Lamarck's, this did not involve progressive development in accordance with a plan or law; it was open-ended. Darwin spent over 20 years collecting and marshalling evidence before publishing the **Origin of Species* in 1859. Meanwhile, he had married his cousin Emma Wedgwood, and settled in a remote corner of Kent; his health was poor, and he led a reclusive life, writing the standard work on barnacles. Despite furious controversy, his theory prevailed, and by the end of his life he was universally recognized. DK

David I (*c.*1085–1153), king of Scots (1124–53). An outstanding monarch who 'became a legend in his own lifetime', he was the youngest son of *Malcolm Canmore and Queen (later St) *Margaret, and succeeded his brother *Alexander I. His early career brought him firmly within the English orbit: he was educated at Henry I's court and became earl of Huntingdon in 1113 through his marriage to *Matilda, a great-niece of William the Conqueror. But, once king, he asserted his independence as a sovereign ruler, and drew on his experience of the Anglo-Norman world to bring the Scots kingdom within the mainstream of European development, though recent studies also highlight how far he depended on the strengths and practices of his Celtic inheritance. The 'Davidian revolution' involved the settlement in Scotland of Anglo-Norman nobles, who established powerful local lordships defended with castles and supplied knights to the king's army. The monarchy was also strengthened by the restructuring of law and administration along Anglo-Norman lines, and by an extensive programme of church reform. Thus David created or revived several bishoprics and personally founded ten major monasteries, especially for Cistercian monks (Melrose, Newbattle, Kinloss) and Augustinian canons (Jedburgh, Holyrood, Cambuskenneth). He also developed the economic basis of the kingdom by founding burghs (notably Berwick, Edinburgh, and Aberdeen) and by introducing the first Scottish *coinage.

In all these respects, 'Normanization' followed a very different path from that taken in the rest of the 'Celtic fringe', where both Wales and Ireland experienced Anglo-Norman conquests. In Scotland, by contrast, David's predecessors had already established a sufficiently powerful and unitary monarchy to ensure that change operated on behalf of Scottish interests, not against them. Quintessentially, however, David was as much a conventional Celtic ruler as a new-style 'feudal' monarch. Though he acted decisively to crush the rebellion of the mormaer (provincial ruler) of Moray in 1130, he preferred to work with traditional power structures wherever practicable. He continued to use the ancient centres of royal authority; loyal native lords kept their lands and their prominence as members of the governing élite alongside the Anglo-Norman incomers (all the earls and most of the bishops were native Scots); the existing pattern of administrative offices coexisted with the sheriffs, justiciars, and other new officers; the taxation system remained based on the old levies of cain and conveth ('tribute and hospitality'); and customary methods of military recruitment retained fundamental importance. So, while change was a leading motif, David's reign also exhibited considerable degrees of continuity; indeed, the key to his greatness as a state-builder was the ability to integrate old and new. His Scottish power base was confined largely to the Lowlands; but the reality of growing royal might was firmly demonstrated when he led vast armies (including 200 knights, but mainly comprising native troops from many parts of Scotland) in wars of territorial conquest against the embattled King Stephen, and from 1141 he ruled the 'English' north to the rivers Ribble and Tees as an integral part of an enlarged Scoto-Northumbrian realm. His successes as a war leader help to explain why his modernizing policies were not more strenuously challenged by Celtic lords outside the royal circle. Anglo-Norman adventurers flocked to his court in increasing numbers; and control of the rich silver-mines near Carlisle gave a major boost to the Scottish economy. But in 1152 David's only surviving son Henry predeceased him. When David himself died, he was therefore succeeded not by a mature and experienced heir, but by a boy-king, his grandson Malcolm IV; and in 1157, at Henry II's insistence, the Scots were obliged to withdraw from the north. Yet by 1153 the traditional kingdom of Scots was well on the way to becoming a self-confident, European-style state, and David's reign was arguably the most formative period in medieval Scottish history. KJS

David II (1324–71), king of Scots (1329–71). He succeeded to the throne at the age of 5; and within three years his realm was invaded by Edward *Balliol and Edward III of England. With his young wife *Joan, sister of Edward III, he had to take refuge in France, his kingdom at times on the point of collapse. Not until 1341 was he able to return; and in 1346 he was captured at the battle of *Neville's Cross, near Durham, and spent eleven years in captivity before his release in 1357. As a prisoner, his chief object was to obtain his release. To this end, he was prepared to abandon the steward's right of succession, but not to accept a union with England. He would contemplate the possible succession of *John of Gaunt, a younger son of Edward III, who was not Edward's heir. This proposal, however, was rejected by the Scottish Parliament. In 1357, David was released in return for a large ransom; and proposals for a peace in 1363, on the basis of the succession of Edward III if David had no direct heir, were again rejected, very possibly with the approval of David himself.

After his return to Scotland in 1357, David's government proved efficient. He was able to impose heavy taxation to meet the cost of his ransom; yet royal finances were probably in a better state at the end of his reign than at any other time in the century. He dealt firmly with a baronial revolt in 1363 and with opposition from individual barons. He reacted strongly to disobedience by certain Highland nobles, provoked by increased taxation and an act of revocation of 1367, which bore heavily upon them. As a ruler he was evidently stronger than any of his successors before James I.

His main weakness lay in his personal affairs. His first wife seems to have abandoned him after 1357, returning to England where she died in 1362. David above all required an heir. By 1363 he had formed an attachment to *Margaret Logie, whom he married in that year. When no heir was forthcoming by 1370, he divorced her and was planning to marry Agnes Dunbar, when he himself died unexpectedly, early in 1371. The cause is not given in any source.

David has been accused of lack of patriotism, but there seems little basis for this. Throughout, he tried to maintain the integrity of his kingdom, with success in what were often difficult circumstances. BW

David (Dewi), **St** (d. *c.*601). Bishop of Menevia (St Davids), and patron saint of Wales. All accounts of him are based on the *c.*1090 biography by Rhygyfarch (Ricemarch) which is fanciful and appears to be propaganda to bolster the primacy of St Davids. According to the legend David's birth was predicted by St *Patrick while travelling in the area of Menevia. David was born in Ceredigion to St Non, a nun who had been ravished by Sant (David's father), and there is a tenuous connection to the *Cunedda family. He was educated at Vebus Rubus (Henfynyw, in Cardigan), was later ordained, became a pupil of Paulinus (possibly St Paul of Leon), and is reputed to have worked miracles. Afterwards he travelled through Wales preaching and founding monasteries. He finally settled at Mynyw (St Davids) and began a life of intense austerity. After a pilgrimage to the Holy Land, David attended the Synod of Brefi, where the *Pelagian heresy was condemned and after which, due to his eloquence and holiness, he was elected primate of the Cambrian church with his see at Mynyw. This story is fraught with invention but his cult was well established by the 11th cent. and at least 60 churches were dedicated to him by 1200. David was canonized in 1120 by Pope Calixtus. SMD

Davidson, Randall (1848–1930). Archbishop of Canterbury. Born a Scottish presbyterian in Edinburgh and educated at Trinity College, Oxford, Davidson was successively chaplain to Archbishops *Tait (1877) and *Benson, dean of Windsor (1883), bishop of Rochester (1891) and Winchester (1895), and archbishop (1903–28). An ecclesiastical policy-maker for over 50 years (1877–1928), he was close confidant of two archbishops (1877–95) and an intimate of Queen Victoria, whose death he attended. As a national leader during 25 years of phenomenal change, he gave the primacy substantial prestige. Frequently plagued by ill-health, conciliatory rather than dynamic, Davidson displayed skill and courage with problems domestic, colonial, and international. The first modern archbishop to visit combatant troops at the front (1916), the first to visit America (1904), he was also a keen House of Lords man where his support assisted the passage of the Parliament Bill (1911). Sometimes insufficiently outspoken, he nevertheless courageously opposed the death sentence for Roger *Casement, condemned the *Black and Tans, was even-handed in the *General Strike, supported the *League of Nations, and prevented the patriarch's expulsion from Constantinople. Ecclesiastically he constantly worked to conciliate differing viewpoints. Though the Enabling Act (1919) gave the church some self-government, he resigned after Prayer Book revision failed to gain parliamentary approval. WMM

Davies, Emily (1830–1921). Born in Southampton, brought up in Gateshead where her father had a parish, Emily Davies began by helping Elizabeth Garrett *Anderson to obtain her medical training. In 1862 she joined a committee to lobby for access to university examinations for women and then moved on to help organize a women's college. This opened at Hitchin in 1869 with five students and transferred to Girton, just outside Cambridge, in 1873, with fifteen. Davies served as mistress from 1873 until 1875 and as honorary secretary from 1867 to 1904. She was also a strong advocate of women's suffrage and organized J. S. *Mill's petition to Parliament in 1866. 'Small and plain . . . her face unrevealing between smooth bands of mouse-coloured hair' was a contemporary assessment: 'all at once friendly and formidable' a later comment. JAC

Davies, Sir John (1569–1626). Lawyer and poet. Davies was born in Wiltshire, sent to Queen's College, Oxford, and became a lawyer. In 1597 he was elected to Parliament for Shaftesbury. Appointed solicitor-general in Ireland in 1603 through the patronage of the earl of Devonshire, Davies was knighted and spent much of his life in Ireland, serving as attorney-general from 1606 and as speaker of the Irish House of Commons in 1613. His letters and reports on conditions in Ireland are of great value. He returned to England in 1619 and was appointed chief justice of King's Bench in 1626, but died before he could take up office. His best-known poem, *Nosce teipsum* (1599), dealt with the immortality of the soul, was admired by James I, and was quoted approvingly by *Coleridge in *Biographia literaria*. Davies's wife claimed the gift of prophecy and, predicting his death, irritatingly adopted mourning in advance of the event. JAC

Davies, Richard (*c*.1501–81). Bishop and scholar. Davies was born in north Wales and educated at New Inn Hall, Oxford. He held livings in Buckinghamshire but, as a reformer, took refuge in Geneva during Mary's reign. At the accession of Elizabeth, Davies was made bishop of St Asaph (1560) and moved in 1561 to St Davids. He was on close terms with both Archbishop *Parker and *Cecil, advising them on Welsh matters. Davies collaborated closely with William *Salesbury in producing the Welsh translation of the New Testament in 1567, parts of which he contributed. But a quarrel between them seems to have left the Old Testament to be translated by William *Morgan. JAC

Davis, John (*c*.1550–1605). One of the long line of English navigators who sought the North-West Passage, he obtained some sort of backing from *Walsingham for three expeditions in 1585–7. Following *Frobisher's example, he sailed south and west of Greenland, but then penetrated much further north to about 73° in the strait that bears his name. His men played football with Inuit (Eskimos). Later in his life, Davis sailed to the Magellan Straits, fought the Spanish Armada, and died in a skirmish in the East Indies. He continued to believe that a North-West Passage could be found, expounding the view in books of 1584 and 1595. RB

Davitt, Michael (1846–1906). Irish nationalist. Born in the famine period, evicted at the age of 5, Davitt lost his right arm in an accident in a Lancashire cotton-mill when he was 12. He joined the *Fenians and in 1870 was sentenced to fifteen years in gaol for treason-felony. Released after seven years, he persuaded *Parnell of the potential in a land reform agitation. In October 1879 he formed the *Irish Land League, with Parnell as president. He took a strongly hostile line to Parnell after the divorce scandal and was returned to Parliament in 1895. Though his early belief in violence was moderated, Davitt alienated many potential supporters by his anticlerical views and his collectivist attitude towards land questions. JAC

Davy, Sir Humphry (1778–1829). Cornish chemist and applied scientist. Davy's apprenticeship to an apothecary was interrupted through his meeting with James *Watt's son Gregory, and he was invited to Bristol to a clinic where oxygen and other gases were given to those with tuberculosis. He met S. T. *Coleridge, and with him discovered the properties of laughing gas. In 1801 he was appointed to the *Royal Institution in London, where his eloquence made his lectures fashionable, and where in 1806–7 he proved that chemical affinity is electrical, winning a prize from Napoleon's *Institut*. After marrying a wealthy widow, Jane Apreece, in 1813, he set out for France to collect it, accompanied by his new assistant, Michael *Faraday. On his return in 1815, his help was sought in controlling mine explosions; beginning with laboratory investigation, he came up with the lamp that bears his name. This was a new route to technological innovation. His lamp made him the obvious candidate to succeed Sir Joseph *Banks as president of the *Royal Society in 1820; but his reign was unhappy in a decade of tension between tradition and reform. DK

D-Day, 6 June 1944, and the following days, were decisive in the war on Germany. British and American troops, in roughly equal numbers, including Canadians in the British total, established themselves on the Normandy coast; Rommel, commanding the German side, could not concentrate sufficiently powerful forces to dislodge them. D-Day, though cloudy and windy, justified Eisenhower's decision, as supreme commander, to accept, at the last minute, a comparatively hopeful weather forecast. *Montgomery, in command of ground forces, dispatched five infantry divisions, to five separate beaches, plus three airborne divisions, landing over 150,000 men on the first day. The landings were supported by more than 100 warships, with 4-inch or larger guns, bombarding coastal defences. On one American beach, Omaha, against a good-quality German division and well-prepared German defensive works, casualties were high. The British and American air forces virtually stopped German movement of troops or supplies by day and made impossible a co-ordinated German counter-attack. Allied air forces contributed decisively to the 1st US Army break-out which led to the liberation of France and Belgium in August and September 1944. RACP

deacon. The rank in the Christian ministry below that of bishop and priest or presbyter. The order has its New Testament warrant from Acts 6, the commissioning of Stephen and others to serve the poor, and in 1 Timothy 3, as ministers serving with presbyters. Today the diaconate, open to men and women, has become little more than a preparatory step to priesthood. JRG

dean. The title is most commonly associated with the priest who presides over the life and work of a cathedral. Originally it evolved from the Latin 'decem' (ten) as descriptive of one who had authority over, or the supervision of, a group of ten others. Where a cathedral or collegiate church (e.g. Westminster abbey or St George's, Windsor) had a chapter of canons or prebendaries, the dean was *primus inter pares*, and rarely had (or has) authority to act apart from the capitular body over which he presided. The statutes governing most English cathedrals give the dean and chapter together a considerable degree of independence from episcopal control. The title 'dean' is also held—as 'rural dean'—by a beneficed clergyman in a part-time capacity. The rural dean is appointed by the bishop to act as a channel of communication between himself and the clergy of the parishes which make up his deanery. The office is an ancient one, revived in the 18th and 19th cents. by pastorally minded bishops. JRG

death duties. Death is considered to be a 'taxable event'. The taxation of inheritance (on the acquisition of property from a person who has died) provided a source of government revenue in Roman times. A death tax was introduced in Britain in 1694 but the modern framework dates from 1779–80. Since 1894, when Sir William Harcourt introduced a new system in the teeth of fierce opposition, death duties have mainly been in the form of estate duties (on property left at death), although for a period from 1975 they were replaced by capital transfer tax which applied to transfers of property at any time, including death. Death duties differ from property taxation in that there is only one assessment. Normally some portion or types of assets or bequests are exempt from taxation. It is for this reason that death duties tend to be relatively complicated and seldom either provide a good source of revenue or bring about significant wealth redistribution. KJB

Declaration of Independence, 1776. Conflict in America was well advanced when Congress on 4 July 1776 adopted the Declaration of Independence. Primarily the work of Thomas Jefferson in a five-man committee, a principal objective was to facilitate an understanding with France. The celebrated 'self-evident truths' of life, liberty and the pursuit of happiness were followed by a fierce denunciation of George III—a 27-point indictment, insisting that he was 'a tyrant unfit to be the ruler of a free people'. The drafters understood that hatred is more easily called forth if it can be personified, and though it was doubtful history, it was very effective propaganda. The list of grievances would have been longer had Congress not prudently deleted the accusation that George had vetoed attempts to abolish slavery, 'this execrable commerce'. The declaration concluded that 'all political connection between them and the state of Great Britain is, and ought to be, totally dissolved.' JAC

Declaration of Rights, 1689. In February 1689, the *Convention drew up a Declaration of Rights, which it presented to William and Mary in the Banqueting Hall at Whitehall. It related the misdeeds of James II, begged William and Mary to accept the throne, and laid down an oath of allegiance. William accepted on their behalf and they were proclaimed king and queen. The declaration was given statutory form in the *Bill of Rights in December 1689, which added that no papist, or person married to a papist, could sit on the throne of England. See GLORIOUS REVOLUTION. JAC

Declarations of Indulgence. Charles II disliked the penal laws against protestant and catholic dissenters and in 1672, using his *suspending power, issued a Declaration of Indulgence. The House of Commons protested vehemently: 'we humbly conceive that Your Majesty has been very much misinformed, since no such power was ever claimed or exercised by any of Your Majesty's predecessors.' Faced with a war with the Dutch, Charles climbed down and withdrew it. Learning nothing from the experience of his brother, James II issued another declaration in 1687, repeated it in 1688, and compounded matters with a foolish preface declaring, 'we cannot but heartily wish, as it will easily be believed, that all the people of our dominions were members of the Catholic Church.' He next prosecuted seven bishops for petitioning against the declaration. Several of the judges cast great doubt on the validity of the suspending power and the bishops were acquitted amid widespread rejoicing. The same day the 'immortal seven' (six noblemen and *Compton, bishop of London) sent to William of Orange to rescue them. JAC

Declaratory Act, 1766. This asserted parliamentary sovereignty against the claims of the American assemblies, although in other writings it was made clear that Parliament would not try to tax Americans. It was designed to win the consent of king, Lords, and Commons to the modification, or repeal, of the *Stamp Act. RCS

decolonization. As with many historical processes, the term 'decolonization' was improvised *ex post facto* to indicate a transformation which was not always perceived at the time. Decolonization certainly does not denote the simple loss of authority over an overseas possession—the ending of British rule over the thirteen American colonies in 1783 was not, for example, an act of decolonization, any more than was the loss of Calais in 1558. The origins of British decolonization as an exercise in the devolution of constitutional authority, or even a cast of official mind, may be found in the transition during which responsible government was granted to self-governing settler colonies in the Canadas, Australasia, and southern Africa from the 1840s onwards. But just as responsible government in the 19th cent. was not an enemy to empire, so later policies feeding into decolonization in the 20th cent. were by no means intended as an abrupt abandonment of British preponderance.

There was certainly no decolonization, as such, between the two world wars. Rather, conditions alerted British policy-makers to the wisdom of making alien domination less blatant and, as Lord *Milner put it in his report on Egypt in 1920, to the need to make appearances more acceptable to the indigenous population while retaining imperial reality. The formal empire experiment with the method of dyarchy, especially in India following the 1919 Government of India Act, whereby some branches of public affairs were reserved for the imperial government while others were to be gradually devolved into the hands of elected representatives, reflected the same spirit and aims.

The Second World War may have ultimately proved the prime cause of the disappearance of the British empire, but it cannot be said to have led at the time to any coherent vision of decolonization—if anything the reverse. Although Prime Minister *Churchill joined in the *Atlantic charter (August 1941) which affirmed the right of peoples to determine the governments under which they lived, his subsequent statement that he 'had not become His Majesty's Chief Minister to preside over the liquidation of the British Empire' is just as well known. Some possessions—principally *Malaya and *Burma after December 1941—were overrun, but planning for their reconquest got under way immediately. The British government formally recognized in Parliament during July 1943 a responsibility 'to guide Colonial people along the road to self-government, within the framework of the British Empire', but self-government was not decolonization, and the goal was made contingent on conceptions of social and economic improvements which were clearly decades, perhaps centuries, away.

It was in south Asia after 1945 that decolonization in its characteristic British formulation as the 'transfer of power'—for which phrase there is no French equivalent—took shape. During the events leading up to the independence of *India and *Pakistan (August 1947) the Labour government's essential requirements were that British prestige should not be impaired, that the process should take place on an agreed and ordered basis, and that, so far as possible, no important political, strategic, or economic interest of the United Kingdom should be harmed. Lord Louis *Mountbatten, as the last viceroy, showed how along the way new friends could be made out of old adversaries, as with Jawaharlal *Nehru and his Congress Party, even if it was at the cost of colder relations with such traditional allies as Ali *Jinnah's Muslim League. It was convenient for all concerned in 1947 that the position of the crown remained at first untouched, though in 1949 the expressed wishes of India and Pakistan to become republics were accommodated within a multiracial *Commonwealth, of which the British monarch became head. Meanwhile Burma's statehood (January 1948) outside the Commonwealth, and *Ceylon's independence including a treaty guaranteeing Britain's strategic presence (February 1948), constituted the two poles of British decolonization on the margins of the subcontinent.

The transition in south Asia, however, did not necessarily set any precedents for other parts of the British empire. No British colonial territory became independent during the peacetime premiership of Churchill (October 1951–April 1955). In some cases, most notoriously that of *Cyprus (July 1954), it was stated in Parliament that the principle of self-determination could *never* be applied. Although subsequently *Sudan became the first country in British Africa to attain statehood (January 1956), it did so as part of the unravelling of the old Anglo-Egyptian Condominium, not as symptomatic of a wider shift of colonial policy. Both the Gold Coast (January 1957), renamed *Ghana, and Malaya (August 1957) acquired independence having met certain political and financial requirements, though whether the same tests would be applied to other territories—and, if so, whether they would pass them—remained uncertain.

The second main phase of British decolonization came with the 'acceleration' of colonial policy in Africa following the re-election of Harold *Macmillan's Conservative government in October 1959, and especially his speech before the South African Parliament on 3 February 1960, warning of the 'winds of change'. Macmillan's colonial secretary, Iain Macleod, later claimed that this acceleration was governed by the stark alternative of bloodshed. This was justification for a policy which had more complex causes at a variety of levels. *Nigeria became independent during 1960, Tanganyika (*Tanzania) and *Sierra Leone in 1961, *Uganda in 1962, *Kenya and *Zanzibar in 1963, *Zambia and *Malawi in 1964, the *Gambia in 1965, *Lesotho in 1966, and *Swaziland in 1968. These complicated arrangements were often negotiated at 'Lancaster House conferences' in London which replicated, in narrower compass, the ideal inaugurated in India of a constitutional and amicable separation in which Britain itself seemingly played the leading role. More or less simultaneously the British Caribbean provided a footnote to African decolonization, *Jamaica and *Trinidad opting in August 1962 for independence apart from the ill-fated West Indian Federation, and other Caribbean territories following at intervals. The emergence of the Republic of Cyprus (August 1960), although highly idiosyncratic in the limitations on its external sovereignty, had already signified that smallness was no longer a constraint on the application of self-determination.

If British governments ever pursued a distinct *policy* of decolonization, it was in the Afro-Caribbean world between 1960 and roughly 1966. The very lack of alternatives to this outcome meant that any controversies between, or within, the main British political parties remained limited. More polemic surrounded the scuttle from *Aden (November 1967) and the abandonment of contractual obligations to Gulf rulers—this was the real 'swansong of empire'. Thereafter the process of bringing down the curtain on Britain's imperial history was largely a matter of coping with cases which were *sui generis*. The category of 'Associated State' was invented to meet the needs of the poorer and least viable West Indian islands. By far the most complicated and dangerous 'unfinished business' of decolonization in the later 1960s and 1970s was *Rhodesia, where a white settler rebellion was not quelled and the territory brought back into the mainstream of legitimate independence-making till the emergence of Zimbabwe in April 1980. The final phases of the Rhodesian story showed that it had become the proper acknowledgement of the *forms* of the transfer of power which mattered more to Britain than anything else. Perhaps, if the Galtieri regime in Argentina had understood this point, the status of the *Falkland Islands might not have remained so rigidly frozen in the image of the British population in the wake of the war of 1982.

Since it is the writing of the final page in any historical experience which fixes the record in perpetuity, during the prolonged run-up to the last great British decolonization, that in *Hong Kong (30 June 1997), the preoccupation of the British government and its representative, Governor Patten, has been with establishing beyond dispute the commitment to democracy and the welfare of the local population, which Britain's rulers have always contended lay at the basis of their colonial mission overseas. Whether true or false, the speech before the joint British Houses of Parliament by the greatest living 'freedom-fighter', President Nelson Mandela of South Africa, on 5 July 1996, in which he legitimized Britain's moral statecraft abroad from the ending of colonial slavery through to the granting of African 'freedom' by Harold Macmillan, testified to the final triumph of the British version of decolonization. RH

Darwin, J., *The End of the British Empire: The Historical Debate* (Oxford, 1991); Holland, R. F., *European Decolonization, 1918–81* (1985); Low, D. A., *Eclipse of Empire* (Cambridge, 1991); Porter, A. N., and Stockwell, A. J., *British Imperial Policy and Decolonization, 1938–64* (2 vols., 1987).

Decorated style. See GOTHIC ARCHITECTURE.

Deerhurst. St Mary's priory church at Deerhurst near the Severn in Gloucestershire has a history extending back to the early Anglo-Saxon period, some of its masonry dating from *c.*700. A monastery existed there before 804 when Æthelric granted land to Deerhurst, making it the chief monastery of the kingdom of the *Hwicce. In addition to a fine Saxon tower, there is a tub-font, used for centuries as a farm trough, a remarkable double-headed window from the 9th cent., and several impressive sculptures. Odda's chapel nearby dates from 1056 and was the kitchen of a farmhouse until the late 19th cent. SMD

***De facto* Act,** 1495. The name is rather misleading since the statute, 11 Hen. VII c. 1, does not appear, contrary to much commentary, to distinguish between kings *de facto* and kings *de jure*. Henry VII, victorious at *Bosworth, faced a series of challenges to his throne. To buttress his position, this statute declared that a person performing his duty to the king could be 'in no wise convict of high treason' and that any subsequent legislation to the contrary would be null and void. Whether an Act which could be repealed by a future Parliament gave comfort to any one may be doubted. Perpetual edicts have often had a short life. JAC

Defence, Ministry of. In 1950 there were secretaries of state for war and for air and a 1st lord of the Admiralty. But the exigencies of modern warfare, which demanded ever closer liaison between the armed forces, coupled with severe financial difficulties, which made three separate services appear extravagant, suggested a single command. On taking office in 1940 Winston *Churchill had assumed the title of minister of defence and chaired the defence committee of the cabinet, though there was no corresponding department. This arrangement was continued by his successor Clement *Attlee, but in 1947 a minister of defence was appointed to co-ordinate activities and allocate resources. In 1964 the policy was taken to its logical conclusion and a single Ministry of Defence created, with a secretary of state at its head. JAC

Defenders were Irish catholics who banded together to combat the protestant *Peep o' Day Boys. They began to organize in the 1780s and in the 1790s merged with the *United Irishmen. There were frequent clashes between defenders and the protestants, numerous murders, arming, and drilling: in one encounter at Ballina in 1794 about 70 persons are said to have been killed. The spread of catholic disaffection culminated in the *Irish rising of 1798. JAC

Defoe, Daniel (*c.*1660–1731). Prolific English writer. Educated at Charles Morton's dissenting academy, Defoe was pardoned for fighting for *Monmouth, and gaoled for bankruptcy in 1692, before becoming William III's unofficial apologist in the best-selling *True-Born Englishman* (1701). Imprisoned and pilloried for seditious libel for his satire on high-church bigotry, *The Shortest Way with the Dissenters* (1702), Defoe was recruited as a propagandist and intelligence agent by Robert *Harley, writing the seminal propaganda journal the *Review* (1704–13), and reporting on the passage of the Act of *Union (1707) through the Scottish Parliament. Re-employed by Harley in 1710, Defoe wrote government propaganda until 1714. Having finally made his peace with the Whigs, Defoe published **Robinson Crusoe* (1719), the first of the series of fictional autobiographies, including *A Journal of the Plague Year* (1722), *Moll Flanders* (1722), and *Roxana* (1724), for which he has been confusingly labelled the first English novelist. Crucially significant as sources for early-18th-cent. British society, works like *A Tour thro' the Whole Island of Great Britain* (1724–6) have been intensively quarried by historians. Still hounded by creditors, Defoe, fittingly, died near his birthplace close by the real-life *Grub Street. JAD

Degeangli. Indigenous British tribe of the Iron Age and Roman periods whose territory covered much of northern Wales. They were the northern neighbours of the *Ordovices. Responding to the tribal uprisings instigated by the British chief *Caratacus, the governor P. *Ostorius Scapula attacked the Ordovices and Silures and crushed the first Icenian revolt of AD 47; he then marched north-westwards into lowland Cheshire and on into the territory of the Degeangli. The Degeangli were cut off from the powerful *Brigantes of Yorkshire and subdued. The tribe was incorporated into the province of *Britannia* and became a *civitas* (tribal administrative district). ES

Degsastan, battle of, 603. This was apparently a very severe defeat for *Ædan, king of *Dalriada, at the hands of *Æthelfrith of Northumbria. The site of the battle is usually taken to be at Dawston Rigg, near Saughtree in Liddesdale. *Bede, writing some 130 years afterwards, declared that 'almost all his army was cut to pieces' and that 'no Irish king in Britain' had dared to make war on the English since. JAC

De heretico comburendo, 1401. This statute, 2 Hen. IV c. 15, was directed against the *lollards, 'a certain new sect', who were causing dissension 'under the cover of dissembled holiness'. It threatened them with the stake 'in some conspicuous place'. Strong action against the heresy was pushed by Archbishop *Arundel (1399–1414) and by the new king, Henry IV. The immediate cause was prosecutions against William Sawtre and John Purvey. The church was alarmed at increasing criticism of clerical wealth and the new regime was concerned that heresy might take a political turn. But the statute was not followed up by any sustained campaign to eradicate lollardism. JAC

Deheubarth ('the south part'), a geographical expression also applied to one of Wales's larger medieval kingdoms. Formed during the reign of *Hywel Dda (died 949/50) by combining, through marriage, *Seisyllwg and *Dyfed, it covered the west and south-west of Wales and sometimes extended into *Brycheiniog. Hywel's line ended with *Rhys ap Tewdwr's death (1093) in the early years of Norman advances. The Welsh victory near Cardigan (1136) enabled his son *Gruffydd to recover part of the kingdom; but the invaders were never expelled completely from the south (Dyfed), even by *Rhys ap Gruffydd, the Lord Rhys (d. 1197), under whom Deheubarth was one of the three great kingdoms of 12th-cent. Wales. Its capital, Dinefwr, acquired legendary status, and Rhys's achievements enhanced Deheubarth's traditional significance. It disintegrated after his death, and the princes of *Gwynedd extended their influence over northern Deheubarth until it was replaced (1277–87) by Edward I's new counties of Cardigan and Carmarthen; the marcher lordships of Pembrokeshire and south Carmarthenshire continued to occupy the southern portion. The descendants of Deheubarth's rulers declined into obscurity. The name and concept of Deheubarth has not been revived, unlike Dyfed and Ceredigion. RAG

Deira, kingdom of. Anglo-Saxon kingdom lying north of the Humber and south of the Tees. The origins are obscure, but the name is British and may imply Anglo-Saxon takeover of a British territory. The Deiran dynasty appears well established by the end of the 6th cent. when Ælle was ruling. After his death *Æthelfryth of *Bernicia conquered the province in 604 and expelled Ælle's son *Edwin. Edwin returned in 616 and after killing Æthelfryth ruled both Bernicia and Deira himself. Through his marriage with a Kentish princess, he caused the province to be officially converted to Christianity in 626–7, and *Paulinus from the Gregorian mission in Canterbury was appointed the first bishop of York. After the death of Edwin the royal house was increasingly under threat from its Bernician neighbours. The last member of the Deiran royal house to rule was Oswin (644–51) who was murdered by Oswui of Bernicia who ruthlessly hunted down males of the royal house. Females fared rather better and the monastery of Whitby under a succession of Deiran princess-abbesses was a major ecclesiastical centre. During the reign of *Ecgfrith (670–85) Deira was fully integrated with Bernicia to form the kingdom of *Northumbria. BAEY

deism. A term derived from Latin *deus*, meaning belief in a Supreme Being and used to describe the system of natural religion first developed in the late 17th and 18th cents. The classical exposition of deism was John Toland's *Christianity not Mysterious* (1696), which argued against revelation and the supernatural. Deists asserted the supremacy of reason and denied the validity of miracles, prophecy, and a literal, fundamentalist interpretation of the Bible. They usually coupled this religious unorthodoxy with political radicalism and were condemned as 'infidels' and dangerous subversives. *Paine's *Age of Reason* (1794) spread deism to radical working men, reinforced in the 1820s by Richard *Carlile's publications. In the 1830s and 1840s popular deism was represented by Robert *Owen and the Owenites; and the Owenite legacy was inherited by the secularist movement, led by G. J. *Holyoake and Charles *Bradlaugh. The term deism was not much used after the 18th cent., and those who adopted its tenets in the 19th cent. were known as free thinkers or believers in rational religion. When Victorian liberals felt that they could no longer accept the teachings of Christianity or the institutions of the church, but were nevertheless reluctant to deny the existence of God altogether, they became in effect deists. But deism never had the influence in Britain that it had in France and Germany. JFCH

Delius, Frederick (1862–1934). Composer. Born in Bradford (Yorks.) of German descent, Delius spent most of his life abroad. As a young man he worked in Florida and for many years was domiciled in France, yet his music often evokes a sense of the English landscape. He rejected traditional formalism and as a disciple of Nietzsche believed that the artist's primary duty was to fulfil himself in life and art. His greatest music depicts the beauties of nature and the transience of human life with poetic imagination and a mastery of orchestration. His most popular pieces are short and idyllic, such as *On Hearing the First Cuckoo in Spring* or *Brigg Fair*, but in *Appalachia* and *A Mass of Life* he wrote superbly on a large scale. In his final years he was blind and paralysed but was able to continue composing through the devoted assistance of Eric Fenby, his musical amanuensis. JWD

demesne was a legal term to describe land and property worked for the direct benefit of the owner. During the Middle Ages the importance of such holdings varied: at times it was more valuable for owners to work the land themselves, whilst at others it was more profitable to rent the land to tenants. When demand for agricultural produce was high and profits good, demesnes expanded. For example, during the 13th cent., when a growing population made ever-increasing demands for agricultural produce, many landlords reserved the best land for themselves. In areas such as the Somerset levels, Pevensey marshes by the coasts of Kent and east Sussex, and the Fens in East Anglia, landowners undertook schemes to drain wet lands to increase the available fertile arable, since good yields and the low costs of working the land justified the capital investment in digging ditches and erecting flood defences. Once the costs of production rose, as after the repeated visits of bubonic plague during the 14th cent., many landed magnates leased demesnes to tenants for cash rent, keeping the demesne next to favourite residences to meet the immediate needs of the household. IJEK

Demetae. Indigenous British tribe of the Iron Age and Roman periods whose territory covered Pembrokeshire and much of Carmarthenshire in south-west Wales. The Demetae appear not to have been intensively garrisoned by the Roman army, except along their eastern border, which may have been to protect them from their hostile neighbours the *Silures. The tribe was incorporated into the province of Britannia and thus became a *civitas* (tribal administrative district). The *civitas*-capital has been identified as Carmarthen (Moridunum Demetarum), dating from *c.* AD 75. ES

democracy. The concept of democracy originated in ancient Greece—*demos* means people, *kratos* means rule—and it entails that there is political equality between citizens. However, democracy has taken many different forms, and we may distinguish between seven of its manifestations, beginning with Athenian democracy, which was the first sustained system of rule by an extensive citizenry (up to 45,000 at one point). This was a direct, not a representative, democracy, in which the citizen body met weekly in an assembly to decide all policies, and to make all laws. The quorum was 6,000 citizens, and decision-making was by a majority vote. However, the democratic credentials of Athens were limited: the citizen body only included adult, free-born, non-indigent men—i.e. about 10 per cent of the population. Women had no political rights, nor did resident aliens or slaves (who numbered 100,000 at one point).

The idea of democracy subsequently receded from political thought and practice, partly because of Christianity's shift of focus from man as a political animal to man as subservient to God's will. But with the Renaissance and Reformation political authority acquired some democratic credentials in the Lockian theory of the social contract. This was a representative rather than a direct form of democracy, designed more to protect the individual from an arbitrary government than to ensure that the people themselves determined the laws. This second manifestation of the democratic idea has been designated 'protective democracy'. However, subsequent anxiety about the tyranny of the majority was frequently expressed as a reason for opposing the extension of the suffrage during the 19th cent.

A third, and more radical, notion of democracy was advanced to capture the spirit of the Athenian city-state system within a modern nation state. This was based on Rousseau's principle of self-government, which required that all men (though for Rousseau no women) participated in the sovereign legislative process of lawmaking. In Rousseau's theory this entailed a state small enough for direct democracy to be practicable. But his idea of participatory democracy has since been extended to large states by devices such as referenda and plebiscites, whereby the people's general will decides the laws by which they will be governed.

Rousseau's model has spawned non-liberal and even totalitarian forms of democracy. In principle, the idea of totalitarian democracy (the fourth manifestation of democracy), though paradoxical, is quite coherent. It means that by contrast to liberal democracy, there are no restrictions on what a democratic government may legitimately seek to accomplish. However, in practice, totalitarian regimes have paid only lip service to democracy. Nazism, for example, having gained power through the democratic process, abandoned elections and interpreted the will of the people as the will of the Führer. The fifth manifestation of democracy is élitist democracy, which theorists from J. S. *Mill to Joseph Schumpeter have commended as the means of securing effective leadership and safeguarding essential liberal principles, such as freedom and private property. Schumpeter's influential *Capitalism, Socialism and Democracy* (1942) stated that 'democracy does not mean and cannot mean that the people actually rule in any obvious sense of the terms "people" and "rule". Democracy means only that the people have the opportunity of accepting or refusing the men who are to rule them.' The people do not decide the issues, but only choose the leaders who will decide the issues.

The sixth manifestation of democracy may be termed 'pluralist democracy'. Fashionable in the USA in the 1950s and 1960s, it exemplifies democracy in terms not of competitive élites, but of bargaining between interest groups and pressure groups. Political policies are the result of governments mediating between these different groups—and indeed branches of government are themselves interest groups which form part of the bargaining process. The will of the people is expressed not so much by the formal election process as by the fragmented representation of the interests and opinions by groups, though electoral machinery is still important to ensure that politicians remain 'responsive to the preferences of ordinary citizens' by exposing them to the pressures of competing minority groups. R. A. Dahl defines democracy as 'minorities government'—rule by 'multiple minority oppositions'—rather than rule by the sovereign majority, though he insists that this overall pluralistic framework is consensually endorsed by the majority. In Britain, the pluralist conception of democracy was discredited during the 1970s by the power of organized labour and the overload that it and other competing groups placed on a weakened state authority.

The seventh, and final, manifestation of democracy may be termed 'democratization', to characterize the current movement towards democratic structures that is sweeping across the world in the wake of the breakup of the east European communist regimes, and the ending of the Cold War. The most obvious examples of democratization have occurred in the old Soviet Union, and its satellite countries, but similar patterns can be found in some parts of east Asia, South America, and Africa.

There is also a manifestation of democratization in the workplace—extending the right of decision-making to conditions of employment—which may well be a more effective form of participation for many people than is the electoral system.

The world-wide shift towards democratization has prompted Francis Fukuyama to proclaim the end of history—i.e. the triumph of liberal democracy over all other political systems. Whether this claim is justified or not, time alone will tell: but as the examples of Weimar Germany and, more recently, The Gambia, Nigeria, and Algeria indicate, there is no guarantee that once democracy has been attained in a country it will endure. TSG

Democratic Unionist Party (DUP). Formed in 1971 to challenge the declining position of the Ulster Unionist Party and represent traditional loyalist working-class opinion. Its platform is a mixture of uncompromising, traditional unionism and social and economic populism. Massively dominated by its leader Ian *Paisley, its support extended far beyond the free presbyterian church. In crises, its electoral support has threatened the Official Unionist majority; Paisley in North Antrim and his more pragmatic deputy, Peter Robinson, in East Belfast consistently proved successful vote-winners. The party always opposed peace initiatives: despite support for the Ulster workers' strike 1974, its relations with loyalist paramilitary groups have been uneasy. Its opposition to the *Anglo-Irish agreement 1985 was politically successful, but its rejection of the Downing Street declaration in 1993 has left it isolated. MAH

Denain, battle of, 1712. Marshal Villars, leading a French army of 24,000 troops, many of them heavy infantry, surprised an Anglo-Dutch force of about 10,000 men under the earl of Albemarle in its encampment close to Denain on 24 July. Allied reinforcements under Prince Eugene tried to come to Albemarle's assistance but found that they could not cross the Scheldt river. Pressed by superior numbers, less than 4,000 of Albemarle's men escaped; five allied generals were captured or killed and over 4,000 soldiers taken prisoner. The French suffered about 2,000 casualties. JLP

Denbighshire. A county of north-east Wales created in 1536 at the Act of *Union with England. Its core was Perfeddwlad, the land to the east of the Conwy river, once the Welsh kingdoms of Rhufoniog and Rhos, together with Dyffryn Clwyd. These, after the Norman conquest, constituted the lordships of Denbigh and Ruthin, and to them were added a series of smaller lordships carved out of the northern lands of the Welsh kingdom of *Powys, including St Asaph, Bromfield and Yale, Chirk, and Hope.

Thus constituted, the shire included very varied terrain. At its heart was the vale of Clwyd, but to the east it extended across the Denbigh moors and Mynydd Hiraethog to the Conwy valley. To the south it pushed across the Dee valley to the Berwyn Mountains (Moel Sych, 2,317 feet), whilst eastward it included the Wrexham area to the English border, detaching a section of Flintshire. In 1974 it became part of the county of *Clwyd and the former county was divided into three districts—Colwyn, Glyndŵr, and Wrexham Maelor. In 1996 it was reconstituted as a county, but without Wrexham which became a county in its own right. The population of the three districts in 1991 was 210,408.

Denbighshire's economy was based mainly on agriculture and tourism. Its south-eastern extension prior to 1996 covered the southern part of the North Wales Coalfield. Although mining has ceased, the area is characterized by industrial village settlement and there is a legacy from the past in modern engineering and electronic industries.

Denbighshire straddles north-east Wales from the English border to the Conwy valley. Accordingly it had a characteristic range of Welsh speaking, from 9.9 per cent in Marford and Hoseley to 74.8 per cent in Llangernyw. HC

Denman, Thomas, 1st Baron Denman (1779–1854). Lawyer. Son of a doctor, Denman was sent to Eton and to St John's College, Cambridge. His sympathies were Whig/radical and he defended *Cochrane (1814) and Jeremy Brandreth (1816). In 1818 he entered Parliament for Wareham, transferring to Nottingham in 1820. He was appointed solicitor-general to Queen *Caroline and acquired great popularity in her defence, though his style was considered florid. When the whigs took office in 1830 Denman became attorney-general and took a prominent part in defending the Reform Bill. In 1832 he was appointed chief justice of King's Bench and was given a barony in 1834. In *Stockdale* v. *Hansard* (1837) he maintained that parliamentary privilege could not cover libel, though the decision ultimately went the other way. Much of his later work was concerned with the abolition of the slave trade. Not a profound lawyer, Denman's reputation was as a reformer. JAC

Denmark, relations with. England became part of a Scandinavian empire under Danish kings (*Cnut and his sons) between 1019 and 1042. Although over the next 500 years England's main political and military activities moved elsewhere, trade with the Baltic (especially in naval stores from the 16th cent.) guaranteed interest in Denmark and its Norwegian kingdom at the entrance to the Baltic. In 1801 Danish participation in a league of armed neutrality against the rigorous search for contraband by the Royal Navy unleashed a fierce response with *Nelson triumphing at the battle of *Copenhagen. Six years later the British carried out a pre-emptive strike, fearful that Danish naval power was about to fall under the control of Napoleon. At the end of the Napoleonic wars Britain was involved in the transfer of Norway from Denmark to Sweden. In 1848–52 Britain helped to find a peaceful solution to a disputed succession to the duchies of Schleswig and Holstein in favour of continuing Danish rule. But in 1863–4 *Palmerston was unable to avert a war in which Prussia (assisted by Austria) defeated the Danes. This episode strengthened those in Britain who favoured a lower profile in European affairs. CJB

Denning, Alfred, Lord (b. 1899). From a simple background, Denning obtained a place at Magdalene College,

Cambridge. After a period of service in France during 1917–18, he gained a first in mathematics but returned to Cambridge as the Eldon scholar and gained a first in law. In 1944 he was appointed a High Court judge and gradually worked his way up through the judicial ranking. In 1962 Denning became master of the rolls. He extended the limits of judicial lawmaking as he attempted to free the Court of Appeal from its obligation to follow its own decisions. His dissenting judgments brought many clashes with the House of Lords. Denning became a household name after *Macmillan asked him to conduct an inquiry into the Profumo affair. Often controversial, Denning is acknowledged as perhaps the greatest judge of his age. He retired in 1982, at the age of 83, and has written many books. RAS

dentistry, development of. Practical dental treatment in medieval and early modern Britain was generally restricted to cleaning and extracting teeth, and applying dressings or prescribing mouthwashes to relieve pain. Cleaning by scraping or application of acids was carried out by barbers, who were also legally permitted to extract teeth. Extractions were the due of tooth-drawers, an independent trade group since at least the end of the 13th cent., but were undertaken also by surgeons, blacksmiths, and itinerants at markets and fairs. The emergence of restorative dentistry in mid-17th-cent. London was enhanced by the arrival of skilled immigrant surgeons from the continent and the early stirrings of consumerism, although contemporary satirists saw the provision of artificial teeth as no more than cosmetic vanity. As anatomical and technical knowledge slowly improved throughout the 18th cent., gold or lead fillings appeared, while artificial teeth became increasingly sophisticated, though affordable only by the wealthy. 'Operators for the teeth' gave way to 'dentists', who began to seek business not only in London but in provincial towns. By the mid-19th cent., dentistry was developing into a profession, with scientific journals and professional societies, then qualifications and a register (1878), though still under the control of the General Medical Council. Apprenticeship and informal parental or casual training were superseded by dental schools which had developed out of earlier dental dispensaries and hospitals. The profession was closed by the Dentists Act of 1921, but did not become independent of the GMC until 1957. The inclusion of dental treatment within the *National Health Service (1948) generated an unforeseen demand for treatment, but also revealed a shortfall in practitioners, services, and standards. Expansion of dental schools and reduction in caries rates after the advent of fluoridation have since improved the nation's dental health, but many practitioners have recently returned to independent practice, and the use of auxiliaries is being re-evaluated. ASH

Derby. Described by Disraeli as 'the Blue Riband of the Turf', the Derby is the top event in the flat season's racing calendar. First run on 4 May 1780, the race is named after its founder, the 12th earl of Derby. It is a race for 3-year-olds, run on Epsom downs over 1 mile 4 furlongs. Traditionally run on the first Wednesday in June, from 1995 it moved to Saturday for commercial reasons. RAS

Derby, diocese of. The see, roughly conterminous with Derbyshire, was created in 1927 out of the diocese of *Southwell, where the ecclesiastical union in 1884 of Nottinghamshire and Derbyshire, formerly in the Lincoln and Lichfield dioceses, had not been a success. The cathedral is the former parish church, built in the classical style (1723–5), though the tower is 15th cent. and the reredos dates from 1965. WMM

Derby, Thomas Stanley, 1st earl of. See STANLEY, THOMAS.

Derby, Edward Stanley, 14th earl of (1799–1869). The longest-serving of Conservative leaders. Heir to an ancient title and vast properties (the main estates were in south Lancashire around the family seat Knowsley), Stanley, after Eton and Christ Church, Oxford, was a Whig MP by 1822. After minor office under *Canning, he served in *Grey's cabinet and negotiated with Tory 'waverers' over the Reform Bill. As chief secretary for Ireland he introduced the Irish Church Temporalities Bill and a measure for popular education and as colonial secretary the abolition of colonial slavery, all in 1833. Alienated by *O'Connell and his Irish and by his Whig rival *Russell, Stanley, often spoken of as a future Whig leader, led the resigners from the cabinet in 1834 (the *Derby Dilly) and briefly commanded a following of over 20 MPs, though he declined to join a coalition under *Peel later that year. Over the next few years he and most of his followers moved into the Conservative Party. Colonial secretary in Peel's government of 1841, he had won considerable standing with his party's backbenchers by the time he opted for a peerage and moved to the Lords in 1844. *Lytton saw him as 'frank, haughty, rash, the Rupert of debate'. In 1845 Stanley was the only cabinet minister to hold out against Peel's policy of Corn Law repeal and left the government. He resented surrender to the *Anti-Corn Law League (active in his own territory of Lancashire), any weakening of the aristocratic position and of the interests of land, and also the breaking of party commitments on protection. He saw it as an issue of honour and integrity. Though his efforts to stop repeal failed, he became leader of the protectionist rump of the divided party in July 1846. He attempted to reunite the Conservatives (he resumed the old party name in 1848) and the Peelites, largely unsuccessfully, but he was also cautious about abandoning protection without due cause. He defended the Navigation Acts in 1849 and finally dropped protection only after the election defeat of 1852. By 1849 Stanley had appointed *Disraeli as his subordinate leader in the Commons.

Derby (he inherited the earldom in 1851) was prime minister of three governments (1852, 1858–9, and 1866–8) and twice, in 1851 and 1855, declined to form an administration. Throughout that period the Conservatives remained a minority party in the Commons. In the second ministry Derby attempted a measure of parliamentary reform and displayed a more progressive stance than previously. After the defeat of 1859 he decided to prop up *Palmerston's moderate Liberal government against radical challenges and settled for opposition. He declined to overthrow the government over Schleswig-Holstein in 1864 despite his own caution in foreign policy and doubts about Palmerstonian interventionism. Derby, who voiced concern about the impact of railway developments on working-class housing in London, became chairman of the Lancashire relief fund during the cotton famine and contributed significantly to the success of the period's greatest voluntary relief effort. In 1866 after Palmerston's death the Conservatives overturned Russell's Liberal government over parliamentary reform and Derby became premier again. He determined to pre-empt any further Liberal measure by passing a reform measure of his own; the second Reform Act (he called it 'a leap in the dark') was his initiative, though handled and modified by Disraeli in the Commons. Derby was the only man to have served in the reform cabinets of both 1832 and 1867. He retired because of ill-health in 1868, Disraeli succeeding as premier, but he made a dramatic though unavailing attempt to stop Irish church *disestablishment passing the Lords in 1869. Chancellor of Oxford University since 1852, he had always upheld established churches; his relations with Roman catholicism, particularly in Ireland, had often been uneasy.

A politician of flair and dash and, when roused by the occasion, an impressive parliamentary speaker, Derby never realized the early promise of his career. A great aristocratic figure—shooting and the turf (until he sold his stud in 1863) were among his passions and he was an accomplished classical scholar—he mixed great political talents with a frequent disdain for the drudgery and frustrations of ordinary political life. The restabilizer of Conservative politics after the damage done by Peel, he recognized the importance of party and of reciprocal loyalty between leaders and followers. No ideologue but a pragmatist capable of moving with 'the Spirit of the Age', he also looked to hold the line against destructive change and mixed caution with boldness; like Palmerston he was among the balance-holders of early Victorian politics. Disarmingly (sometimes disconcertingly) open in manner, especially in sporting contexts, he was also acutely aware of his social standing, and aristocratic stiffness handicapped his dealings with middle-class politicians, including the 'fourth estate' of the press and the extra-parliamentary party organization. Resplendent as a political grandee, he was representative of a high point of aristocratic parliamentarianism before later developments undermined it. BIC

Derby, Edward Stanley, 15th earl of (1826–93). Educated at Rugby and Trinity College, Cambridge, and an MP from 1848, Stanley was closer to *Disraeli than was his own father in the 1850s, and a more centrist figure than the elder Derby had become. An uneasy Conservative, sometimes sought by the Whigs or seen as a possible coalitionist, he was also a potential Conservative leader and might have displaced Disraeli but for his poor relations with the party's church interest. He was colonial and Indian secretary in 1858–9 and foreign secretary in 1866–8 and, after inheriting the earldom in 1869, again from 1874. During the Eastern Question crisis he conducted an independent and non-interventionist (some said pro-Russian) policy and, having fallen out with Disraeli, resigned in 1878. In 1880 his support for the Liberals was a factor of some electoral significance in Lancashire. As colonial secretary under *Gladstone from 1882 he was disinclined to a 'forward policy'. In 1886 he broke with Gladstone over *Home Rule and led the *Liberal Unionists in the Lords until 1891. A cool and sceptical politician, though of progressive views, Derby was immune to most of the enthusiasms of his day. He was a notable political diarist. BIC

Derby, James Stanley, 7th earl of (1607–51). Derby was lord-lieutenant of Lancashire, lord of the *Isle of Man, an enormously wealthy landowner, and a leading royalist peer during the *civil wars. In 1642 he raised over 6,000 men in the county for the king. Despite his energetic efforts, however, his army was broken, he quarrelled with his subordinates, and by June 1643 was driven out of his county. He spent most of the next seven years on the Isle of Man, a royalist stronghold, emerging in 1644 to fight at *Marston Moor. His seat at Lathom House was defended against parliamentary siege by his French wife. In 1650 he declared for Charles II and brought a small contingent to the mainland, but was defeated at Wigan Lane (25 August 1651). Having failed to raise Lancashire and Cheshire, he fought at *Worcester (September 1651), was captured, tried by court martial, and condemned to death. He was beheaded at Bolton, a town which he had stormed and sacked in 1644, killing 1,600 civilians. An indifferent military commander, Derby was heavy-handed and conceited. But he acquitted himself courageously on the scaffold, where he was compelled to wait several hours before being executed. IJG

Derby Dilly. *O'Connell's belittling phrase for the moderate Whigs who, led by four cabinet ministers including Edward Stanley, heir to the *Derby earldom, seceded from the reformers in 1834 and began a restructuring of parties. William IV's hopes for a Dilly/Conservative coalition were dashed, but most of the defectors had become Conservatives by 1841. Dilly was slang for a diligence or rapid stage-coach. BIC

Derbyshire is a heart-shaped county in the heart of England, traditionally bordering Leicestershire, Staffordshire, Nottinghamshire, Yorkshire, and Cheshire, but stopping a few miles short of Lancashire and Warwickshire. It has been little altered by boundary changes, but since 1974 borders Greater Manchester.

The Romans, chiefly interested in the county for its lead and the springs at Buxton, established a number of forts and roads. Christianity came with the first religious house in Mercia built at *Repton in 656 (where the Saxon crypt survives), but thereafter Danish invasions placed Derbyshire in the front line of battle until 1013, when *Sweyn conquered the whole country.

Throughout the medieval period Derbyshire remained sparsely populated, but numerous market charters were granted and there is a reference to coal-mining near Ilkeston in 1285. The county suffered grievously from the plague, the final outbreak occurring famously in 1665 when six-sevenths of the population of Eyam died. The Civil War saw Derby occupied by parliamentarians in 1643 and, with the north and west of the county royalist in sentiment, a number of small battles followed, including skirmishes at Hartington and Wirksworth (1643). However, Derbyshire's chief importance to the Stuarts came in 1745, when the young pretender and his army occupied Derby before retreating to Scotland. By the 17th cent., the Cavendishes had established themselves as the premier family, mostly due to Bess of Hardwick (countess of *Shrewsbury) (1520–1608); they owned 14 per cent of Derbyshire at one stage, controlled one of the county's two MPs, built the magnificent *Chatsworth House (1687–1707), and in 1756–7 William Cavendish, 4th duke of *Devonshire, was prime minister.

In addition to the building of great country houses, such as Kedleston and Calke abbey, the 18th cent. saw the development of cotton-mills in Derbyshire (notably by *Arkwright at Cromford, 1771), impressive growth in coal-mining and iron production around Bolsover and Chesterfield, and framework-knitting at Belper, Ilkeston, and Heanor in the east. Though canal-building did occur in the county, it concentrated on the rivers Derwent and Trent (in the south) and to the north of Chesterfield only; more effective in improving communications were the turnpike roads (the first opened in 1725). It was, however, the railways that profoundly changed Derbyshire and, by the mid-19th cent., Derby had become the railway centre of the midlands, hastening the urbanization of the east of the county. Today, although coal has ceased to be of economic significance to Derbyshire, quarrying (especially limestone) is still important, as are textiles and engineering, most famously at *Rolls Royce's aero-engine factory in Derby. In addition, with most of north-west Derbyshire in the Peak District, (Britain's first national park), the county attracts vast numbers of visitors, making leisure and tourism major Derbyshire concerns.

Derby is by far the largest town in the county, with 220,681 inhabitants in 1991, but Derby diocese was only created in 1927 (though the cathedral was founded in the 10th cent.), its city status was conferred as late as 1977, and, culturally, Derby has suffered from its proximity to larger Nottingham. Additionally, the city's southern location reinforces the county's diffuse nature, with the north-east looking to Chesterfield and beyond that to Sheffield, and the north-west looking to Manchester. Furthermore, north Derbyshire is millstone grit and limestone country, with stone walls, sheep farms, and bleak moors, whereas in the south there are hedged dairy and arable farms on clay, sandstone, and alluvium.

The county's administrative headquarters are at Matlock, a fine spa town second only to Buxton, its first bath built in 1698, and its dramatic cliffs drawing visitors ever since. But it was Buxton, in the west of Derbyshire and England's highest market town, that prospered most from its hot waters; its sumptuous Crescent, built by the Cavendishes 1780–6, is said to have cost £120,000 and the town retains a sense of Georgian elegance. Also in the rural west, to the south, lie Bakewell and Ashbourne, both granted charters in the 1250s and boasting magnificent parish churches. In Ashbourne, an ancient Shrovetide football game is still played along attractive Georgian streets, and local villages, notably Tissington, dress their wells with flowers annually.

In the east and north, where iron, cotton, and coal dominated the economy, and where much of Derbyshire's industry is still based, runs the M1 motorway, past Ilkeston and Alfreton. Above them is Chesterfield, with its celebrated twisted spire atop an exceptional Gothic church, and Dronfield, which has almost merged with Sheffield. The north-west tip of Derbyshire is the least populated part and contains the Ladybower reservoir, opened in 1945; its largest town, Glossop, retains the appearance of a Victorian mill town, but has a number of attractive 17th-cent. gabled houses.

The Banham commission proposed in 1995 that the two-tier system should be preserved for the rest of the county but that the city of Derby should be a unitary authority. AIL

Dermot MacMurrough (*c.*1110–71), king of Leinster. Dermot is said to have succeeded his father as king while in his teens and to have been large, violent, and voluble. He plunged at once into fierce fighting but in 1166 was forced into exile and begged Henry II to assist him, promising homage in return. Henry gave him permission to recruit helpers and he was joined in Ireland in 1170 by Richard de *Clare, 'Strongbow'. Together they recaptured Dublin, and Strongbow married Dermot's daughter Eva (Aoife). Dermot died the following year and five months later Henry himself led an expedition which laid the foundation for the Anglo-Norman acquisition of Dublin and the *Pale. JAC

Derry, diocese of. Derry had been a bishopric from 1254 and was continued at the Reformation as a diocese of the Church of Ireland. Among the more remarkable bishops was Frederick Hervey (1768–1803), who succeeded as earl of Bristol in 1779 and played a prominent part in the agitation for parliamentary reform in the 1780s. He was followed by two other noble bishops, sons of Viscount Northland and Baron Ponsonby, who held the see until 1853. The bishopric of Raphoe to the West was joined to Derry in 1834. The medieval cathedral was destroyed by an explosion in 1566. The new cathedral, dedicated to St Columba, was built between 1628 and 1633 and extensively remodelled in Victorian times. The spire was damaged in the siege of 1689; a replacement in 1776 proved too heavy; the third spire, added in 1822, survives. St Eugene's Roman catholic cathedral was completed in 1873 and a spire added in 1903. JAC

deserted villages can be found throughout the British Isles for a variety of reasons. Settlements have been abandoned because their locations proved to be unviable, because populations moved from rural to urban areas, or because a landowner deliberately cleared village sites for a purpose such as sheep pasture.

Villages became deserted in almost every century, although their abandonment has not always been well documented. For example, a great deal is known about those of medieval England through the work of archaeologists and historians of the Deserted Medieval Villages Group which has found and examined sites in great detail. One of the earliest areas to receive the group's attention was Leicestershire, where it was shown that villages were deserted largely because of depopulation caused by the plague. As population declined villagers could no longer maintain isolated communities. A similar process seemed to have occurred at Wharram Percy on the Yorkshire wolds where the population declined to such an extent that its owners initiated the abandonment of the village and its land became grazing for sheep.

An important contemporary account of the use of land was the survey by commissioners in 1517, who gave accounts of the 'pulling down of towns' to create pastures. A similar awareness of such melancholy consequences occurred in the works of Oliver *Goldsmith, in the 18th cent., and the Revd George *Crabbe in the early 19th cent., each of whom wrote on the theme.

One of the most dramatic examples of the enforced abandonment of villages was the 'Highland clearances' of the early 19th cent. when landowners removed people to provide pasture and land for hunting and shooting. Protests were made by the evicted people and in popular songs and poems.

One of the most unusual cases of enforced desertion of a village occurred on Salisbury Plain during the Second World War when the government relocated the entire population of Imber in order to provide for military training, including practice in street fighting. IJEK

Despenser, Henry (*c.*1343–1406). Bishop of Norwich (1370–1406). The younger son of a peer, Despenser studied civil law at Oxford. He became bishop in 1370 after serving in a papal war in Italy. In 1381, he was the first magnate to resort to arms against the rebellious commons, rescuing fenland abbeys from their tenants, restoring order in Cambridge and Norwich, and routing an assembly at North Walsham, Norfolk; he had ringleaders hanged. Parliament decided to send an expedition to support Flemish towns in revolt against their pro-French count in 1383, adopting the pretext that this was a crusade against adherents of a schismatic pope. Despenser was given command of this operation, doomed from the start because the towns had already been defeated. On his return, he was impeached for incompetence and his bishopric sequestrated, until 1385. In 1400 his loyalty to Henry IV was suspect, but he avoided open implication in treason. RLS

Despenser, Hugh, 1st earl of Winchester (1261–1326). Despenser's father had been a leading member of the baronial opposition to Henry III, acted as *justiciar, and was killed with de *Montfort at *Evesham. A coming man under Edward I, Despenser was an ardent supporter of Edward II and his closest companion after the death of *Gaveston. He fought in the defeat at *Bannockburn. He and his son received many estates and incurred great unpopularity. In 1321 Edward was forced to exile him, but the death of his great enemy *Thomas of Lancaster at *Boroughbridge the following year seemed to have secured his position, and Edward created him earl of Winchester. But he was speedily overthrown in 1326. Edward's queen *Isabella led an invasion from France, and Despenser was captured at Bristol and executed. His son was taken a few days later with the king and hanged at Hereford. The king himself was deposed two months later. JAC

Dettingen, battle of, 1743. Britain entered the War of the *Austrian Succession on the side of Maria Theresa and placed an army in the field in Germany under John *Dalrymple, Lord Stair. In June 1743 it was trapped on the river Main near Hanau by a superior French force under Noailles. It succeeded in fighting its way to safety on the 27th mainly because of the musket fire of the infantry. George II led his troops into battle, sword in hand, with remarkable courage. This, the last time a British king fought in person, was a reminder of the original role of the monarch as battle-leader. JAC

Deusdedit, archbishop of Canterbury (655–64), was the sixth man to hold that office and the first Englishman to be appointed; his predecessors were all members of the missions dispatched from Rome by Pope Gregory the Great. He was a West Saxon whose English name seems to have been Frithuwine, but nothing else is known of his early history. Nor is anything recorded of his achievements as archbishop, though we do know that he died on 14 July 664 in the great plague epidemic of that year. BAEY

de Valera, Eamon (1882–1975). The dominant figure in Irish politics for over 40 years despite, or perhaps because of, his aloof, ascetic personality. De Valera was born in New York, reared in Co. Limerick, and was originally a mathematics teacher. He came to advanced nationalism through the Irish Language Movement and Volunteers. His rise to leadership was due to his being the last surviving commandant of the *Easter Rising. Following release from internment in early 1917, he led a broad-based Sinn Fein coalition, and master-minded the move towards a moderate self-determination policy which successfully challenged the Irish Parliamentary Party. Arrested May 1918, de Valera escaped from Lincoln gaol in February 1919, and became president of the Dáil. He spent most of the Anglo-Irish War seeking recognition of the Irish Republic and financial backing in the USA. After the truce in July 1921, de Valera became chief negotiator in Dáil ranks but controversially absented himself from the peace conference, October–December. Opposing the *Anglo-Irish treaty, he advanced external association as an alternative. He strove to avoid the drift to civil war but was rendered impotent by the force of military opposition to the treaty. Marginalized during the civil war, he recovered the leadership amongst republicans after the conflict, aided by being imprisoned until 1924. Splitting from Sinn Fein and the IRA and their Dáil abstentionist policy, he formed Fianna Fail Party, entering the Dáil in 1927. After winning the 1932 election he followed a treaty reform policy, abolishing the oath of allegiance to the British crown and ceasing payment of land annuities to Britain. The constitution of 1937 epitomized his social and cultural conservatism. De Valera followed popular neutrality policy in the *Second World War, despite intense British and American opposition. Defeated in elections 1948 and 1954, but Taoiseach again 1951–4 and 1957–9, he withdrew to the presidency 1959–73. By the 1960s his policies appeared anachronistic in a rapidly evolving modern European state, leading to an increasingly unsympathetic portrayal of his career. J. J. Lee commented that de Valera would have made a leader beyond compare in the pre-industrial world. De Valera himself said: 'I was meant to be a dyed-in-the-wool Tory or even a Bishop, rather than the leader of a Revolution.' MAH

Devon was the third largest of the old counties. Having two sea-coasts, it was orientated in different directions. The northern shore along the Bristol channel runs from east of Lynton to south of Hartland Point: the south shore, along the English channel, runs from east of Seaton, via Exmouth and Torbay, to the Tamar, west of Plymouth. The southern parts are drained by the Tamar, the Dart, the Exe, the Culm, the Otter, and the Axe; the north eastern parts by the Torridge and the Taw, flowing into Barnstaple Bay. The boundary with Cornwall in the west is the Tamar, while the eastern boundary with Somerset is largely the line of hills forming the watershed of the Exe and the Otter. Dartmoor in the south, Exmoor in the north, and the Blackdowns in the east are the highest points, but much of the county is hilly, with deep valleys.

The name first appears in the *Anglo-Saxon Chronicle* in 851 as Defensascir, which appears to be derived from the *Dumnonii, the Celtic tribe inhabiting the area. In Roman times, *Exeter (Isca Dumnoniorum) was an important base and port. The *Fosse Way ran through what is now the south-east of the shire, meeting the Roman road from Dorchester to Exeter.

In post-Roman times, the British kingdom of *Dumnonia embraced both Devon and Cornwall: it survived, perhaps in shrunken form, at least until the early 8th cent., since *Aldhelm in 705 addressed a letter to its king, Geraint. The eastern part of the region had fallen to the Saxons after *Cenwalh's victory at *Penselwood in 658 and much of the western part by the end of the century. It then formed part of the kingdom of *Wessex. *Ine established a bishopric for the area at *Sherborne in 705, moved to *Crediton in 909, and to Exeter itself in 1050. With exposed coast-lines and many creeks, the area was vulnerable to Danish raids and suffered heavily in the 870s and again in 1003, when the monastery at Exeter was destroyed. By the 11th cent. it had taken shape as a shire. In the *Domesday survey of 1086 Exeter was by far the largest town and the only other boroughs mentioned were Totnes, Barnstaple, and Lydford. By the 12th cent. the building of the present cathedral had begun and Exeter was large enough to have problems of water supply.

Though Exeter was the county town and of national importance, it did not dominate in so large a shire as other county towns did. Consequently, Devon developed as a county of seaports—Barnstaple, Bideford, Brixham—and of market towns of largely local significance, Okehampton, Tavistock, Tiverton, Torrington, Newton Abbot, Honiton, and Ashburton. Until the growth of the cloth industry in the later Middle Ages, it was wholly dependent upon agriculture and fishing, with a little mining. *Plymouth developed as a naval base as vessels grew larger and its superb harbour was more needed, replacing Plympton. Charles II built the citadel and William III established the royal dockyard in 1692. Celia Fiennes, who visited the county in 1699, found the hills hard going: 'rarely can you see houses unless you are just descending to them, they always are placed in holes, as it were . . . the lanes full of stones and dirt for the most part.' She was amazed at the bustle of activity in the serge trade at Exeter and for 20 miles round, and at Plymouth left good descriptions of the new dockyard and the first Eddystone lighthouse. Twenty years later, another visitor, *Defoe, was ecstatic, finding the shire 'so full of great towns, and those towns so full of people so universally employed in trade and manufactures, that not only it cannot be equalled in England, but perhaps not in Europe'.

The reputation of the county was for unintelligible speech, turbulence, and independence. In 1549 there was a formidable rising on behalf of the old religion and Exeter was threatened. Later, protestant dissent made much progress. During the Civil War there was heavy fighting. Exeter was held for the king but Plymouth, a fiercely puritan town, resisted throughout the war and proved a thorn in the royalists' side. The county gave some support in 1685 to *Monmouth, who landed at Lyme, and more in 1688 to William of Orange, who came ashore at Brixham in November. There were few great families, though the Edgecumbes owned Mount Edgecumbe at Plymouth, the Courtenays held Powderham near Exeter, and the Russells gained influence after their acquisition of the estates of Tavistock abbey at the *dissolution of the monasteries. The great size of the county made electioneering difficult and was an incentive to avoid contests: in the 100 years from the Glorious Revolution to 1790, there was only one by-election contest, in 1712.

Improvements in roads and the coming of the railway made Devon less inaccessible: Brunel's lines reached Exeter in 1844 and Plymouth in 1848. Exeter grew from 17,000 in 1801 to 47,000 by the end of the century but was surpassed by Plymouth, 16,000 in 1801 and more than 100,000 in 1901. Even more remarkable was the growth of the resorts as the habit of seaside holidays caught on. Ilfracombe, on the north coast, rose from a small town in 1801 to well over 8,000 by 1901: Torquay, a hamlet of only 800 at the beginning of the century, was a town of 33,000 by 1901, and the new borough of Torbay had a population of 122,000 in 1994 against 105,000 in Exeter. Distance from London has given the county some protection, though both Exeter and Plymouth suffered badly from bombing during the *Second World War. The Banham commission on local government reported in 1994 in favour of retaining the two-tier structure but establishing Plymouth and Torbay as unitary authorities. JAC

Devonshire, Spencer Compton Cavendish, 8th duke of, marquis of Hartington (1833–1908). Heir to the Cavendish family's dukedom and a Palmerstonian Whig, Hartington was an MP at 24 and a cabinet minister at 34. Elected Liberal leader in the Commons after *Gladstone's retirement in 1875, he was undermined by the latter's political come-back and, when offered the premiership after the Liberal victory of 1880, recommended Gladstone instead. Firm for the Union (the Cavendishes were great Irish landowners and Hartington's brother, Lord Frederick *Cavendish, had been assassinated by Irish nationalists in 1882), he broke with Gladstone over *Home Rule in 1886 and, as the leader of the *Liberal Unionists with some 78 MPs, maintained *Salisbury's Conservatives in power until 1892, twice declining the premiership himself. In 1895 Devonshire, as he had become, joined Salisbury in a unionist coalition and served as lord president. In 1904 he resigned from *Balfour's government in protest at Joseph *Chamberlain's campaign for imperial preference and argued for continued free trade. Combining a high aristocratic life-style (including devotion to the turf) with moderate Liberal views, Hartington represented the balance point of late Victorian politics. His support for Salisbury's governments helped to restabilize national politics. What a lengthy Hartington leadership would have meant for the Liberal party and politics generally rests with surmise. BIC

Devonshire, William Cavendish, 1st duke of (1641–1707). Devonshire was one of many noblemen who backed the right horse in 1688 and prospered exceedingly, founding one of the great Revolution families. A shrewd marriage to Bess of Hardwick in the 16th cent. gave the Cavendishes prominence in Derbyshire and they obtained a barony in 1605 and an earldom in 1618. William Cavendish was a page at Charles II's coronation, saw naval service, and served as MP for Derby 1661–81, succeeding as 4th earl in 1684. A zealous Whig and keen supporter of *exclusion, he was one of the seven who invited William of Orange over in 1688 and took up arms at Derby. In the new reign, he was at once made lord steward, a knight of the Garter, and, in 1694, a duke. His monumental inscription at Derby, which he wrote himself, praised him as the enemy of tyrants. A gambler, sportsman, gallant, he was turbulent but reputed a good classical scholar. He began the building of *Chatsworth in 1687. 'Of a nice honour in everything but the paying of his tradesmen,' was *Burnet's comment. JAC

Devonshire, William Cavendish, 4th duke of (1720–64). Cavendish came from a highly political Whig family. He entered Parliament at the age of 21 for Derbyshire, when his father was lord-lieutenant of Ireland, and supported the *Pelhams. In 1751 he was called up to the Lords in his father's barony as Lord Cavendish and succeeded as duke in 1755. After serving as master of the horse 1751–5, he was made lord-lieutenant of Ireland. In the crisis of 1756, conciliatory and trusted, he was given the Garter and became 1st lord of the Treasury with *Pitt as the driving force. When Pitt was obliged to come to terms with *Newcastle, Devonshire was moved to be lord chamberlain 1757–62. In the new reign he and his Whig colleagues resented the ascendancy of *Bute. After Newcastle resigned, Devonshire refused to attend councils and in November 1762 was dismissed by George III and his name removed from the Privy Council. Newcastle was scandalized at such treatment of a Whig grandee. Devonshire's early death, caused by a brain tumour, robbed the Whigs of a future leader. JAC

Devoy, John (1842–1928). Irish nationalist. Devoy was born in Kildare and joined the *Fenians as a young man. His task was to foster disaffection in the British army and he was arrested in 1862. Released in 1871 on condition of exile, he spent the rest of his life in America, where he organized the Clan na Gael as a fund-raising group, affiliated to the *Irish Republican Brotherhood. In 1878 he initiated the 'new departure', a proposal for a *rapprochement* between the Fenians and *Parnell's parliamentarians, but it was rejected by the IRB the following year. In 1915 Devoy supported *Casement's mission to Germany to obtain arms, assuring the Germans that Casement had his 'fullest confidence'. After Casement's arrest, Devoy distanced himself. JAC

dialects are popularly defined as regional varieties of a language though, for the linguist, the term also embraces differences which signal social and occupational status.

Place-names and a few runic inscriptions indicate that dialectal varieties of English existed before the 8th cent. Such variation presumably owed much to the differing sources of the Anglo-Saxon settlers, but equally must have been encouraged by the emergence of political and economic groupings within Britain itself. The fuller records of the 8th and 9th cents. show the existence of four major dialects (Northumbrian, Mercian, West Saxon, and Kentish) though our knowledge of them is largely limited to the practices of certain scriptoria. By the later 10th cent. a form based on West Saxon had acquired the status of a standard written language, used alike by scribes at such centres as Winchester, Canterbury, and York, whose own spoken forms differed widely from each other. The adoption of this standard reflected the political and ecclesiastical power of Wessex and the early literary exploitation of the West Saxon dialect by *Alfred.

After the Norman Conquest the grip of this standard written language was broken by the new social order and for the next four centuries all English dialects seem to have had similar status. Increasingly, however, in the 14th cent. writers show themselves sensitive to the fact that language variety was an obstacle to widespread understanding and transmission of their work; Chaucer's envoi to *Troilus and Criseyde* provides one well-known expression of such concerns. But already within Chaucer's period a new written standard was emerging which was based upon the language of London, itself now dominated by the dialectal preferences of the southern and eastern midlands where lay much of the country's wealth. The introduction of printing at the end of the 15th cent. helped further to standardize and spread the use of this form. It was one variety of the language of London also which, from the 15th cent. onwards, acquired the status of a standard spoken language. In this case it was essentially the language of the court but, until the 19th cent., its acquisition depended largely on familiarity with certain circles in the capital; thereafter, through the influence of the public schools, reformed universities, and finally the *British Broadcasting Corporation, it was widely diffused on a basis which was purely social and non-localized. See also ENGLISH LANGUAGE. RNB

Dialogus de Scaccario. The *Dialogue of the Exchequer* is the earliest administrative handbook in English history and a prime source for historians of royal finance. Written in the 1170s it gives an account of Exchequer practice in the form of a dialogue between pupil and master. Its main concern is with the procedures followed when sheriffs brought their accounts to be audited at the Court of the Upper Exchequer. Its author, Richard *FitzNigel (*c.*1130–98), was, like his father Nigel, bishop of Ely, a long-serving treasurer of the Exchequer, rewarded in 1189 by being made bishop of London. JG

Diamond Jubilee, 1897. By 1897 Victoria had surpassed George III as the longest reigning British monarch. The celebrations were restricted by her age and infirmities and the centre-piece, on 22 June, was a short service outside St Paul's, while the queen sat in an open carriage. The emphasis was on the empire—partly to recognize its spectacular growth, partly to avoid the anxiety and expense of entertaining the crowned heads of Europe. A special stand was reserved for survivors of the *Charge of the Light Brigade, 43 years before. The crowds were particularly impressed by the Indian cavalry. 'The cheering was quite deafening,' wrote the queen, 'I was much moved and gratified.' JAC

Diana, princess of Wales (b. 1961). Lady Diana Spencer is the third daughter of the 8th Earl Spencer of Althorp (Northants), by Frances, youngest daughter of the 4th Baron Fermoy. Her father had been equerry to George VI 1950–2 and to Queen Elizabeth 1952–4. Lady Diana was educated at Riddlesworth Hall. Her marriage to Charles, prince of Wales, in 1981 attracted enormous public interest. Her two sons, William and Henry, were born in 1982 and 1984. Soon afterwards there were rumours that the princess was unhappy and in 1992 it was announced that she and Prince Charles were to separate. Divorce followed in 1996. Admiration for the princess's extensive work for many charities was dented when she announced abruptly that she was dropping her patronage of 100 of them. Princess Diana has been the subject and sometimes the victim of massive press coverage, but her attitude towards it has often appeared ambivalent. JAC

Dickens, Charles John Huffam (1812–70). Novelist, born at Portsea, Portsmouth, where his father was serving as a clerk in the navy pay office. His father's transfers to Chatham and ultimately to London were to influence the settings of his work. A fictionalized Chatham, its neighbouring city of Rochester, and the landscapes around them figure prominently in *Pickwick Papers*, *Great Expectations*, and in the unfinished *The Mystery of Edwin Drood*. It was, however, London which became the main focus of Dickens's work as a novelist, journalist, and essayist. It figures as an often confusing, polyphonic and exhilarating setting for the earlier fiction, but, from *Bleak House* (1852–3) onwards, London seems to assume a new darkness, mystery, and drabness. Dickens is the quintessential urban artist, able to transform the multivalency of Victorian city life into a new and flexible kind of fiction. His contemporary success was to some degree assured by his skilful exploitation of monthly-part publication. He used his popularity with readers to campaign in his novels for the reform of British institutions (e.g. the 1834 Poor Law, the prison system, the civil service, the law) which he saw as working against the public good. Thanks to the influence of *Carlyle his two historical novels, *Barnaby Rudge* (1841) and *A Tale of Two Cities* (1859), the first set at the time of the Gordon riots and the second during the French Revolution, suggest that social upheaval is a consequence of injustice rooted in historical conditions. In his *American Notes* (1842) he gave a vivid account of his visit to the USA, which offended many Americans. His disillusion with aspects of American life is also reflected in *Martin Chuzzlewit* (1843–4). ALS

Dictionary of National Biography. The brainchild of the publisher George Smith. The work began in 1882 with Sir Leslie Stephen as editor and the last volume appeared in 1900. Supplements and updates have followed and Oxford University Press have commissioned a new edition. The original contributors included Sidney Lee, C. H. Firth, S. R. Gardiner, Hastings Rashdall, Creighton, Tout, Tait, Round, and Pollard. Though many entries have been overtaken by time and the advance of knowledge, the *DNB* remains an invaluable tool of scholarship. JAC

Dieppe assault, 1942. On 19 August 1942 a raiding force of the 2nd Canadian Division and three British commando units carried out a daylight reconnaissance mission against the German defences at the French port of Dieppe. After a fierce nine-hour battle the force was withdrawn, having sustained 3,670 casualties out of the 7,000-strong force. The costly and much criticized operation provided valuable lessons for the D-Day planners. RAS

Digby, George, 2nd earl of Bristol (1612–77). Digby was a leading opponent of *Strafford but changed sides during his impeachment. He fought at *Edgehill and was appointed secretary of state by the king in 1643. He was a hard-liner, insisting on a dictated peace. *Clarendon thought him ingratiating, but part of his appeal to Charles I was an unquenchable optimism: even after *Marston Moor in 1644 he wrote that 'His Majesty's affairs are in the best posture that they have been at any time since these unhappy wars.' He took over command in the north from *Rupert in 1645, too late to demonstrate whether he had real military talent. Clarendon disliked him and described him as handsome, vain, and unstable: Digby reciprocated the dislike and spent much time after the Restoration in pursuing a vendetta against Clarendon. JAC

Diggers. Small communistic groups, active in 1649–50, sometimes calling themselves True Levellers. Their prophet Gerrard *Winstanley taught that God made the earth to be a common treasury; property and man's subjection to man were results of the Fall. The religious foundations of their beliefs range them nearer to contemporary millenarians than to modern Marxists or Maoists. But unlike the *Fifth Monarchists they eschewed the use of force; their aim was not to dispossess landlords, robbers of their fellow-creatures though they were, but merely to assert the people's right to common land, and to lands recently confiscated by the Commonwealth. A pioneering group began digging the commons on St George's Hill (Surrey), in April 1649. The *Council of State ordered General *Fairfax to disperse them, but it was angry locals who finally destroyed their cabins and crops. They moved on to Cobham, but suffered the same fate. Some evidence survives of nine other short-lived Digger colonies, mainly in the home counties and midlands. AHW

Dilke, Sir Charles (1843–1911). Liberal politician. Dilke is supposed to have ruined his chance of becoming prime minister by his involvement as co-respondent in a famous divorce case (*Crawford* v. *Crawford*) in 1885–6; but he probably would not have made it anyway. Before this happened he was better known as a radical, a close ally of Joseph *Chamberlain, an early propagandist for the *British empire (through his *Greater Britain*, published in 1868), and one of the most boring speakers in the House of Commons. His highest government post was as president of the Local Government Board in *Gladstone's second ministry. After the scandal he was turfed out by his constituency (Chelsea), but found another one shortly afterwards (the Forest of Dean), and devoted the rest of his time in Parliament to championing (boringly) the interests of exploited colonial peoples. BJP

Dillon, John (1851–1927). Irish nationalist. Dillon's father, a lawyer, had been active in the 1848 rising and subsequently served in Parliament. Dillon was born at Blackrock (Co. Dublin) and educated at the *Catholic University. He took a degree in medicine and entered politics as a supporter of John *Mitchel in 1875. In 1880 he was returned to Parliament and served until 1918. He took a prominent part in the *Irish Land League campaign and was gaoled for a year until the *Kilmainham treaty. In 1888 he served another prison sentence and a third in 1891. After the Parnell split he joined the anti-Parnell group, becoming leader when Justin *McCarthy resigned in 1896. Four years later he gave way to *Redmond as leader of the reunited party and represented it at the Buckingham palace conference in 1914. On the death of Redmond in February 1918 Dillon took over the parliamentary leadership, but lost his seat at the general election in December 1918 to *de Valera. He was a man of striking appearance and considerable eloquence. JAC

diplomatic history was likely to rank higher in prestige in the late 19th cent. when Britain was still a major world power and while entry to the Foreign Office remained an ambition for many undergraduates at Oxford and Cambridge. It had the advantage as a subject for study that it looked at evidence from different points of view, demanded some knowledge of languages, and raised interesting problems of causation and contingency. Governments also encouraged the study of diplomatic history by preserving and then making available diplomatic archives, and often subsidizing publication in order to justify policy. Among the leading exponents in Britain of diplomatic history were G. P. Gooch (1873–1968), Charles Webster (1886–1961), author of *The Congress of Vienna* (1919) and a study of Castlereagh (1931), and H. V. Temperley (1879–1939), who produced a celebrated study of Canning (1905) and collaborated with Gooch to edit *British documents on the origin of the war 1898–1914* (11 vols., 1926–38). Its weakness was that it was often taught in isolation from the rest of history as a self-contained study. Its post-1945 decline was in part a consequence of competition from other aspects of the subject, and in part that many found it unsatisfying—'the record of what one clerk said to another clerk', in G. M. Young's comment. The collapse of language teaching in schools also made it difficult to do more than study selected (and pre-packaged?) documents in translation. Though diplomatic history remains an important branch of historical study it seems unlikely to regain its former prominence. JAC

Disestablishment. The 19th cent. saw the questioning of the right and propriety of a church which represented only a minority of Christian believers to be the established church, its clergy supported and maintained by law by parishioners who did not sympathize with or belong to it.

The Irish church, with its two Anglican provinces of Armagh and Dublin, was the first to be disestablished. For some years an alliance of Irish nationalists and Roman catholics had campaigned for the removal of the privileged position of the minority Anglican church, and in 1868 this cause was espoused by *Gladstone. As prime minister in 1869 he introduced a parliamentary bill to disestablish the Church of Ireland, and although strongly opposed by some—including Queen Victoria—it passed into law.

In Wales similar cultural nationalism, allied less with Roman catholicism than with nonconformity (which in the mid-19th cent. held the allegiance of almost 80 per cent of worshippers), produced a similar campaign. The growth of the Liberal Party and the widening of the franchise encouraged the movement, and after 1891 Liberals became formally committed to it. Several parliamentary bills from 1870 onwards either failed or were withdrawn, until one was passed in 1914. The First World War delayed its implementation, but the Act came into force in 1920.

The 1869 Irish disestablishment left the Church of Ireland a shadow of its former self, particularly in the overwhelmingly catholic rural areas—a fact to which the numerous derelict Anglican church buildings still dotting the landscape bear eloquent witness—though it remained strong in some towns and cities. In Wales the long delay saw a different outcome. By 1920 nonconformity was losing its dominant place in Welsh life, and the Church in Wales was able to maintain its widespread presence throughout the principality. JRG

dispensing power was the prerogative or discretion claimed by the monarch of exempting from the operation of statutes in particular cases. It was exercised by medieval and Tudor monarchs but became a bone of contention in the 17th cent. The *Long Parliament, in its *Nineteen Propositions, accused Charles I of making excessive use of it. Charles II employed it to assist catholics who had helped his escape after the battle of *Worcester. James II used it to exempt catholic army officers from the *Test Act and, in a collusive action, *Godden* v. *Hales*, the judges found for the king. After James had fled in 1688, the *Bill of Rights abolished the *suspending power outright and the dispensing power 'as it hath been assumed and exercised of late'. It caused little further trouble. JAC

Disraeli, Benjamin, 1st earl of Beaconsfield (1804–81). Conservative statesman, novelist, and exotic. Of a Christianized Jewish upper middle-class family (his father a distinguished man of letters), Disraeli led an early life that handicapped the political career for which he came to yearn. Egotistical, raffish, self-publicizing, he combined recklessness in financial and sexual matters with a talent for scrambling up available lifelines. Helped by his patron *Lyndhurst, Disraeli, despite radical flirtations, was a Conservative MP from 1837. Desperate for office, he lacked standing and was ignored by Peel in 1841. More notice was gained by his novels, which he wrote partly for money (debt long remained a problem) but which also developed, eclectically rather than consistently, social and political ideas then current. *Coningsby* (1844) explored the nature of aristocratic party politics and *Sybil* (1845), a 'condition of England' novel, deplored the gulf between the 'Two Nations' of rich and poor: *Tancred* (1847) completed the trilogy. Disraeli had belonged to the otherwise aristocratic *Young England group of political romantics and his growing hostility to *Peel, signalled in the novels, expressed itself in the House over *Maynooth and the *Corn Laws in 1845–6. Though the Conservative revolt and split required the weight of Stanley and *Bentinck, Disraeli's coruscating mockery of Peel gave him prominence for the first time. Nearly all the Conservative office-holders having followed Peel, the shortage of talent, particularly after Bentinck's death, on the protectionist front bench made Disraeli indispensable and by 1849 Stanley (the future earl of *Derby) had resigned himself to having this improbable figure as his subordinate leader in the Commons, a position held until Derby himself retired in 1868. Initially a handicap to his party in that his position made reunion with the Peelites harder, Disraeli gained in experience and weight through the long service; he also benefited from the discipline brought by his marriage in 1848 to the wealthy and older Mary Anne, widow of a Conservative MP and determined on political eminence for her new husband. Never a protectionist on principle (his case against Peel had been his contempt for party commitments and loyalty), Disraeli had to be restrained by Derby in his wish to jettison protectionism swiftly (it was abandoned after the 1852 defeat) and in some of his subsequent and wilder flights of political creativity. Hungry for office, he deplored Derby's rejections of opportunities in 1851 and 1855; he was also readier to cultivate the press than Derby was and briefly sustained a newspaper of his own. His biography *Lord George Bentinck* (1852) repaid a considerable personal debt; the Bentincks also provided the money to set Disraeli up as a country gentleman at Hughenden in Buckinghamshire.

Disraeli served as chancellor of the Exchequer (a somewhat improbable role) and leader of the Commons in the three Derby minority ministries of 1852, 1858–9, and 1866–8, though a major triumph came only in 1867 when his skilful and cynically ruthless handling of the details of the government's Reform Bill divided the Liberals and enabled the Conservatives to cling to office long enough to pass a measure. Scarcely 'democratic' in intention, it at least minimized the damage a Liberal measure would have done to Conservative interests. Disraeli succeeded Derby as premier in 1868 ('I have climbed to the top of the greasy pole') and, in opposition after electoral defeat, survived party discontent, helped by the self-doubt of the younger *Derby for the leadership. At this stage he took some interest in party organization and established central office in 1870. By 1872, when he made major speeches at Manchester and Crystal Palace proclaiming a supposedly distinctive Conservative philosophy, *Gladstone's Liberal government was disintegrating and the tide was flowing the Conservative way. The election victory of 1874, the party's first since 1841, owed more to Gladstone than Disraeli, but it gave the latter and his followers the prolonged period of office they sought. Disraeli's platform in 1874—stability and quiet at home and the patriotic assertion of national interests abroad—was pure *Palmerston and a mirror image of what Gladstonian government had apparently provided. Much of Disraeli's policy in his final decade was geared to attracting disenchanted Palmerstonians over from the Liberal side.

Disraeli's name rests mainly upon his ministry of 1874–80. Its social legislation was mainly the work of Richard Cross at the Home Office and had no obvious link with the social theorizing of the premier's Young England past or even with vague references to social reform in the 1872 speeches, though it may have had an element of response to the extent of working-class (and largely anti-Irish) Toryism now evident in Lancashire. Only the trade union legislation of 1875, on which Disraeli backed Cross against cabinet hostility, went markedly beyond what any government might have passed. This phase was over by the time an ageing Disraeli moved to the Lords as earl of Beaconsfield in 1876. More significant than domestic policy was his forwardness in foreign and colonial matters. Disraeli seized the chance to buy a controlling interest in the Suez canal, he sent the flamboyant *Lytton to India as viceroy, and his 1876 *Royal Titles Act proclaimed Victoria empress of India. Over the Eastern Question, the struggle between Russia and Turkey in the Balkans, an equally dramatic confrontation developed between Beaconsfield and the former Liberal leader Gladstone (their mutual antipathy was long established); after much hesitation and at the expense of cabinet resignations, including the foreign secretary Derby, the government decided to intervene to sustain Turkey and found backing in outbreaks of popular patriotism (*'jingoism') in some cities. Beaconsfield's reward was a personal triumph at the Congress of *Berlin, a Balkan settlement that suited Britain ('Peace with Honour'), and the cession of *Cyprus by Turkey. But colonial wars in Afghanistan and southern Africa went less well and gave Gladstone the chance to attack 'Beaconsfieldism' in his *Midlothian campaigns. A new nationalist mood in Ireland and economic (including severe agricultural) depression also contributed, alongside Tory divisions, to the heavy electoral defeat of 1880, which put Gladstone back in office. Though not retiring as party leader, Disraeli was depressed by developments, including the Liberals' Irish land legislation, and his death in 1881 came at a low ebb of party fortunes and morale.

Soon Randolph *Churchill and the *Primrose League were active in cultivating a mythology of Disraelian 'Tory Democracy' and his name was on the way to its 20th-cent. status as a codeword for a leftish and social reforming Conservativism. In fact the substance of Disraeli's politics was far more orthodox than later romance suggested: a matter of upholding the 'aristocratic constitution', the monarchy (his closeness to Victoria, something he exploited politically, helped to draw her back into public life), the Union with Ireland, property rights, and social stability. His foreign policy in the 1870s certainly took Palmerstonism to the point of riskiness and he helped to claim the patriotic and imperial identity for the Conservative Party, though Gladstone made his task easier. In religious matters he upheld established churches as much as he could and had a protestant bent which found both Roman catholicism and Puseyite ritualism within the Church of England distasteful; he backed the 1874 Public Worship Regulation Act to penalize ritualism. But none of this matched the exoticism in rhetoric, wit, and phrase-making that Disraeli brought to politics; he was far more interesting as a political performer than in underlying intentions. What distinguished him most perhaps was his immense stamina and dedication over a long career in party leadership, his great loyalty to the Conservative Party, and his unquenchable thirst for office, power, and patronage. He was a great *arriviste*. BIC

Blake, R., *Disraeli* (1966); Coleman, B., *Conservatism and the Conservative Party in Nineteenth-Century Britain* (1988).

Disruption (1843). On 18 May 1843, a majority of the *Church of Scotland's *General Assembly left St Andrew's church, Edinburgh, for Tanfield Hall, Canonmills, to hold the *Free Church of Scotland's first assembly, under the presidency of Thomas Chalmers (1780–1847). Thus culminated ten years' conflict between those who asserted their church's spiritual independence and those who accepted its apparent subordination to the civil power. The conflict, which focused on whether a minister could be forced on an unwilling congregation, was precipitated by the House of Lords' ruling in the Auchterarder case (1838–9) confirming statute law's supremacy over ecclesiastical courts. Consequently 474 out of 1,203 ministers seceded from the established church, accompanied by a proportionate number of members. CB

dissent (nonconformity). Though dissenting sects could trace some of their doctrines to well before the Reformation, for example to the *lollards, pre-Reformation heterodoxy is usually termed schism or heresy. The term dissent is reserved for those who did not conform to the Church of England and, though this included catholics, it is usually confined to protestant groups. Long before the Civil War there were many puritans but most of them remained in the church, hoping to reform it from within. Elizabeth's Act of *Uniformity of 1559, augmented by royal injunctions to kneel, bow, and wear surplices, did not produce a mass exodus (apart from Mary's bishops) such as accompanied the Act of *Uniformity of 1662 after the Restoration. Thomas *Cartwright (1535–1603), described by John Strype as 'the head and most learned of that sect of dissenters then called puritans', remained shakily within the church all his days, and ended his life as master of the Leicester hospital at Warwick. Robert *Browne (*c.*1550–*c.*1633), described as 'the earliest separatist from the Church of England' and certainly with no fondness for bishops, nevertheless held an Anglican living for the last 40 years of his life.

The seed time for nonconformity was the Civil War. By 1644 Archbishop *Laud was in the Tower, episcopacy abolished, the *Solemn League and Covenant imposed, and the *Book of Common Prayer declared illegal. Perhaps as many as 3,000 Anglican clergy lost their livings and had the *presbyterian form of church government survived, as it ultimately did in Scotland, the Anglicans would have finished up as dissenters. The confused situation during and after the war gave dissenting sects the opportunity to establish themselves. The independents or *congregationalists dissented from the dissenters, disliking the rigour of presbyterian rule and demanding toleration; the *baptists, who had broken away from the Brownists in the early 17th cent. split between the general baptists and the particular baptists, who were closer to *calvinism; George *Fox felt in 1643 the call which led to the foundation of the 'Children of Light', later known as *quakers; Ludowick *Muggleton, who disliked the quakers, organized his own distinctively negative sect in the 1650s; Thomas *Harrison and his men looked for the imminent establishment of Christ's *Fifth Monarchy and the triumph of the saints.

In the declaration of *Breda (April 1660) Charles II offered 'a liberty to tender consciences' in religious matters and the presbyterians at least, powerful in the *Convention that had recalled the king, hoped for an acceptable settlement. They were disappointed. The *Cavalier Parliament, elected in March 1661 to replace the Convention, was much less inclined to forgive and forget: many of its members had suffered imprisonment and sequestration at the hands of the sectaries. The *Savoy conference between twelve bishops and twelve puritans broke down without agreement, and the preface to the revised Anglican Prayer Book condemned 'men of factious, peevish and perverse spirits' who would not accept it. A new Act of Uniformity (1662) led to some 1,000 puritan clergy leaving their livings. The *'Clarendon code' waged war against the nonconformists, forbidding them civic office, prohibiting religious gatherings or conventicles of more than five persons, and demanding that ejected ministers should not live within 5 miles of their former parishes. The *Test Act of 1673 barred dissenters, protestant and catholic, from public office, including membership of Parliament.

The reigns of Charles II and James II were difficult for the dissenters, fierce bursts of persecution alternating with efforts to woo them. The two royal *Declarations of Indulgence (1672, 1687), designed to improve the position of the catholics, placed many dissenters in a dilemma—whether to oppose any concessions to the papists, whom they hated, or to make use of the opportunity. Some, like *Penn the quaker, who had suffered imprisonment for his views, believed the assurances of James II: the majority heeded the warning from *Halifax that 'you are therefore to be hugged now only that you may be the better squeezed at another time'.

After the Glorious Revolution, the *Toleration Act of 1689 was intended to 'exempt their Majesties' protestant subjects, dissenting from the Church of England, from the penalty of certain laws'. While not conceding civil or public rights, or waiving the obligation to pay tithes to the Church of England, it granted freedom of worship, provided that dissenters took a simple oath of allegiance. An echo of the days when they had been regarded as fanatics and malignants was clause 6 which forbade them to lock, bolt, or bar the doors of any chapel. Quakers, unwilling on principle to take oaths, were allowed a 'declaration of fidelity'. At the same time a new schism arose when 400 Anglican clergy decided that they could not swear to the new regime and formed the *non-juring church. The dissenting groups settled down at last to a period of consolidation, though the election of a strongly high-church and Tory Parliament in 1710 produced more hostile legislation in the Act against *Occasional Conformity (1711) and the *Schism Act (1714), both repealed by the subsequent Whig administration. The repeal of the Schism Act allowed the spread of *dissenting academies, whose excellence made up for the exclusion of dissenters from Oxford and Cambridge. At the same time, the acceptance after 1688 of an avowedly presbyterian church order in Scotland, confirmed by the Act of *Union in 1707, was proof that the Church of England no longer had an official monopoly in the British Isles.

Under these comparatively relaxed conditions, the dissenting groups might have been expected to flourish. In practice toleration proved more damaging than persecution. Though exact figures are scarcely possible there is little doubt that dissenters, who had numbered some 300,000 or 5 per cent of the population of England in 1700, lost members in the next 40 years. Some of the more prosperous dissenters conformed for social or political reasons, but the dissenters also suffered from internal convulsions. The 'Happy Union' of congregationalists and baptists formed in 1691 lasted only four years before dissolving amid reciprocal recriminations. A rift in the 1690s among the American quakers spread to Britain when George Keith was expelled for accusing Penn of deistic views, and finished up as an Anglican minister. In 1719 the Salters' Hall controversy revealed the inroads made into presbyterian doctrine by *socinian or *unitarian beliefs. Isaac Watts, the hymn writer and an independent moving towards unitarianism, was afraid that dissent might be found 'nowhere but in books', while Philip Doddridge, a leading presbyterian, feared in 1730 'the echo of our own voices'.

The development of the *methodist movement from the 1730s onwards led in the end to a vast increase in dissent, though during *Wesley's lifetime his followers remained in the Anglican church. By the 1770s the dissenters had arrested their decline and were growing more confident, fortified by the success of nonconformity in America. This led many of them to oppose the American war, bringing them renewed unpopularity. A motion to repeal the Test and Corporation Acts in 1787 received little more support in Parliament than in 1736, and was defeated by 176–98: the prime minister William *Pitt observed that 'there is a natural desire in sectaries to extend the influence of their religion; the dissenters were never backward in this.' The support of many dissenters for the French Revolution in its early stages kindled fresh bitterness and *Priestley's house in *Birmingham was burned in 1791 in church and king riots. In 1828, the long wars safely over, repeal of the Test and Corporation Acts went through with surprising ease. Though nonconformists retained substantial grievances, especially over marriage and tithes, they had at least achieved formal civil equality.

It transpired that they had achieved a good deal more. The early years of the 19th cent. witnessed a remarkable upsurge in support for dissent. 'Old Dissent', particularly in the form of presbyterianism and quakerism, showed little vitality, but 'New Dissent' made many converts. The methodists pointed the way to other sects, and the *evangelicalism of the age embraced dissent, with the congregationalists and the baptists to the fore in foreign missions and the quakers in the anti-slavery movement. The Anglicans were comparatively slow to respond to the rapidly developing urban growth and lost ground. At the time of Wesley's death in 1791 the methodists numbered some 56,000: by 1836 there were 360,000 in the different methodist churches. Congregationalist membership increased from some 20,000 in 1760 to 127,000 by 1838, baptists from 11,000 to 100,000. Organization and liaison improved. The baptists formed a union in 1831, the congregationalists, ever jealous of their autonomy, a looser confederation in 1832.

The effect of these changes was a transformation of the religious scene recorded by the religious census of 1851. Despite some imperfections as a statistical record, the general position was clear. Two things amazed the Victorians. First the census showed that $5\frac{3}{4}$ million people who might have attended church on 30 March—nearly 40 per cent of those eligible—had not done so. This figure, which would have seemed highly satisfactory to churches in the late 20th cent., shocked people in 1851. Secondly, it revealed that Anglican attenders scarcely outnumbered the dissenting sects—3,773,000 against 3,487,000, of whom methodists were 1,463,000, independents 793,000, baptists 587,000, catholics 305,000, unitarians 37,000, and quakers 18,000. Indeed, in the heated exchanges that followed publication of the report, dissenters pointed out that since many of their members attended two or three services, dissenting attendances were higher than Anglican. Dissenters were in a comfortable majority in many northern industrial towns like Sheffield, Leeds, and Bradford, and formed a great majority in Wales.

Anglicans braced themselves for another attack on the established position of the church. Tithes went in 1868; the Irish *church was disestablished in 1869; the Welsh church in 1920. But the Church of England held out until the tide of religious belief was clearly ebbing. Meanwhile the influence of dissent was all-pervasive. The *Municipal Corporations Act of 1835, which set up elected councils in the large towns, had brought hundreds of dissenters into local government. In Leeds, where the old corporation had been Anglican dominated, the *Mercury* reported that only 20 of the 51 new councillors were churchmen and in the next twelve years only 2 of the mayors were not dissenters; in Leicester, of 56 aldermen and councillors, 40 were dissenters, 16 Anglicans. The nonconformist conscience, urged on in the 1830s and 1840s by Jabez Bunting, a methodist, in the 1850s and 1860s by Charles Spurgeon, a baptist, and in the 1880s and 1890s by Hugh Price Hughes, another methodist, was a powerful political force, as Charles *Dilke and *Parnell discovered. The influence of dissent may be seen most clearly in the *Liberal Party. The Whigs had always expected to obtain most of the dissenting vote, but the Liberals relied upon it, and many of their leaders appealed directly to it. *Bright and W. E. *Forster were quakers, Joseph *Chamberlain a unitarian, *Asquith from a congregationalist family, *Lloyd George from a baptist home. The Parliament of 1905, which gave the Liberals their biggest majority ever, contained over 180 protestant dissenters, most of them on the Liberal benches. But both dissent and the Liberal Party were poised for eclipse. The removal of many of their grievances by the Liberals persuaded some dissenters to move to the political right, while the new *Labour Party offered alternative accommodation to those who remained radical.

Dissent itself was also in decline. From 1918 onwards there was a marked falling-off in membership of both the Church of England and the dissenting denominations. This seems to have been caused less by the spread of avowed atheism or agnosticism than by competition from other sources of leisure-time activity, together with a growing dislike of authority in any form. Religious bodies held on with some success to existing members but did less well at recruiting from new generations. There was a dramatic decline in attendance at *Sunday schools, once a mainstay of recruitment, but by 1990 down to 10 per cent of their 1900 numbers. There was increasing difficulty in recruiting clergy. The Church of England had 20,000 clerics in 1900, 10,000 by 1984; the methodists, with 4,700 ministers in 1950, had 2,500 by 1993. In Scotland, there were 3,600 presbyterian ministers in 1900, less than 1,500 in 1990. At the same time, the general population was continuing to grow. Estimates of church and chapel attendance in 1989 suggested that fewer than 10 per cent of the English population attended on any regular basis. The churches responded in a variety of ways—by merging parishes, by abandoning unwanted churches, by institutional amalgamations, and by ordaining women ministers and priests. In 1972 the presbyterian church of England merged with most of the congregational unions to create the United Reform Church, but the decline in membership was not arrested. There were of course other churches whose membership increased notably in the decades after the Second World War—pentecostal churches, Afro-Caribbean churches, Muslim, Hindu, Sikh, and Orthodox churches—but their increase was largely due to immigration and they did not look back to the nonconformity of the 17th and 18th cents. Though religious issues still surfaced in public life, politics was largely secularized. Except in Northern Ireland, there is little positive correlation between religious views and voting behaviour. Many church leaders in the 19th cent., especially in the ranks of dissent, advised their members that it was their duty to take a full part in political questions, but in the late 20th cent. clerics who speak out are likely to be told that religion and politics should not mix. JAC

Bebbington, D. W., *Victorian Nonconformity* (Bangor, 1992); Binfield, C., *So Down to Prayers: Studies in English Nonconformity, 1780–1920* (1977); Brown, K. D., *A Social History of the Nonconformist Ministry in England and Wales, 1800–1930* (Oxford, 1988); Davie, D., *Essays in Dissent: Church, Chapel and the Unitarian Conspiracy* (Manchester, 1995); Ward, W. R., *Religion and Society in England, 1799–1850* (New York, 1973); Watts, M., *The Dissenters* (1977).

dissenting academies. The Act of *Uniformity (1662) excluded dissenting ministers from their posts. Many, out of necessity, became teachers or tutors. Dissenting academies were particularly popular in Devon, Lancashire, London, and Wales, some of the most distinguished being at Tewkesbury, Northampton, and Warrington. They were much used by nonconformists who could not take the oaths at Oxford or Cambridge. Girls' as well as boys' schools were provided and commercial schools for the sons of city merchants set up. The curriculum, at first classically based, developed in the 18th cent. into a utilitarian one. Intellectual freedom was demonstrated by the emphasis on scientific subjects, taught by renowned experts such as Joseph *Priestley. PG

dissolution of the monasteries of England and Wales occurred between 1536 and 1540. Profoundly controversial to contemporaries, and still the subject of lively debate, this was an unparalleled secular spoliation of ecclesiastical property. By the 16th cent. most English monasteries were in some sense in decline. Numbers of religious were falling; the economy of the majority had been seriously disturbed by changes consequent upon 14th-cent. crises; few new communities were being founded, though there were exceptions such as Syon and Sheen; spiritual and literary life were generally insipid, and few new benefactions were being attracted from lay patrons. However, very few houses had been forced into 'liquidation' through religious or economic failure prior to the 1530s, and those that had, disappeared largely because they were 'alien priories', i.e. subject to monasteries in France and hence potentially disloyal. Their property was usually passed to another monastery or, as happened at Cardinal *Wolsey's foundation of Cardinal College (later Christ Church, Oxford), used to finance educational establishments. Nor is there much evidence that lay society was generally hostile to the monasteries: indeed, following their dissolution there was considerable support for them, notably expressed in the *Pilgrimage of Grace (1536) in Lincolnshire and Yorkshire.

But the monasteries remained wealthy communities, and hence tempting to Henry VIII and his chief adviser Thomas *Cromwell. The full-scale valuation of ecclesiastical income, the *Valor ecclesiasticus* (1535), had revealed the extent of monastic revenues. The desire to appropriate these potently combined with the king's continuing onslaught on the ecclesiastical establishment. Royal visitations revealed convenient scandals and corruption and in 1536 all monasteries with an annual income of less than £200 were suppressed. This was followed by the gradual dissolution of individual larger houses and in 1539 all surviving greater monasteries were dissolved. Comparatively few monks raised more than token resistance, those most likely to object having in most cases already been executed for refusing to take the oath of supremacy. Monks were given annual pensions; a number became secular priests. Ex-nuns were more harshly treated and were not permitted to marry till the reign of Edward VI.

Monastic lands, administered through the Court of Augmentations, largely fell into the hands of the aristocracy and gentry, though some were used to endow new bishoprics; buildings were looted for their materials, though some churches were adapted to parochial use; the great artistic treasures accumulated over centuries were destroyed or dispersed. BJG

distraint of knighthood. The post-Conquest military obligations attached to knighthood were not necessarily welcome and increasingly avoided. In theory landowners of a certain status were required to present themselves at coronations to be knighted. Henry III began campaigns to oblige freeholders with estates worth £20 p.a. to take up knighthoods, issuing writs of distraint. At this stage, the motive was primarily military but later monarchs were more interested in the revenue they could raise by allowing subjects to compound or pay fines. By Tudor times the estate value had been raised to £40 p.a., but distraints were little used. Charles I, in his search for extra-parliamentary revenue, ordered the records of the Tower to be inspected to discover devices, and from 1630 began distraining, allowing the victims to compound at less than the cost of a fine. Considerable revenue was raised and even more considerable animosity. When the *Long Parliament met, John *Selden in 1641 carried an Act declaring distraints unlawful and Charles was obliged to give his assent. At the Restoration knight service was abolished. JAC

divine right of kings. It was taken for granted in early modern Europe that monarchs derived their authority from God, but the French wars of religion in the late 16th cent. produced a passionate debate about the limitations, if any, upon royal power. James VI of Scotland, the protestant son of a catholic mother, took part in this as he defended his own authority against the claims of both *presbyterians and *Jesuits. But his insistence that kings were gods in their own right, above the law in theory (though rarely in practice), alarmed his English subjects after 1603, who enjoyed political liberties and property rights embodied in the common law and protected by Parliament. James never, in fact, threatened these, but the less flexible Charles I overrode property rights through prerogative taxation, and political liberties by ruling without Parliament. The divine right of kings apparently died with him but was resuscitated during the later Stuart period. Only after the *Glorious Revolution did it become irrelevant. RL

divorce. Since the Roman catholic church has never recognized divorce, it was not available in Britain until after the *Reformation. Henry VIII was technically never divorced—his marriages to *Catherine of Aragon and *Anne of Cleves were annulled—and thereafter England moved very cautiously indeed. Separation from bed and board was permissible in certain circumstances but without the right to remarry. But after Parliament in 1670 had passed an Act to allow Lord Roos to remarry after the notorious adultery of his wife, a loophole was opened. The number of divorces remained very small. The Church of England retained the ecclesiastical courts from the previous era and the case for ending a marriage had to satisfy canon law. Once the church courts had agreed that the marriage should end, only a private Act of Parliament could give effect to property settlements and issues of succession. Such Acts were expensive, faced a real possibility of failing to pass, and exposed the details of personal family relationships to public knowledge.

With the costs of a private Act so high, it is likely that many unhappy marriages endured or that informal and undocumented separations took place. The wish to divorce appeared to be present at all social levels. For example, there are references in the 16th cent. and later to the curiosity of 'wife sales' amongst the poor, an illegal practice fictionalized in Thomas *Hardy's *The Mayor of Casterbridge*.

Divorce, although still expensive, became more generally accessible with the Matrimonial Causes Act of 1857, which applied to England and Wales. This Act incorporated the recommendations of the Campbell Commission, which had investigated the law relating to marriage. The Act established a Court for Divorce and Matrimonial Causes and allowed divorce on specified grounds. A husband could divorce on the grounds of adultery by a wife, but a wife had to prove that her husband had committed adultery aggravated by desertion, cruelty, incest, rape, sodomy, or bestiality before she could divorce. For those who could not afford to go to the new court, escape from the effects of a violent marriage or desertion was provided by an Act of 1878 which gave magistrates' courts power to recognize formal separation. But by 1913 there were still very few divorces—only 577 in England and Wales.

After the Reformation the situation in Scotland developed differently. Husbands and wives had equal access to divorce and procedures for rescinding a marriage could be initiated in the sheriff court by resident Scots. In the mid-19th cent. the costs of such a divorce were between £20 and £30.

Equality between the sexes was recognized by the Divorce Act of 1923, which made the grounds for divorce the same for both spouses. As a consequence, the number of divorces increased, although remaining relatively small. A major change towards lowering the cost of legal proceedings was incorporated into the Divorce Act of 1937, which also added habitual drunkenness and insanity to the grounds for divorce. Again the number of divorces increased and rose even higher after the Second World War, when those seeking divorce could apply for financial help under the legal aid scheme of 1948.

Until the Divorce Act of 1971 two features characterized divorce proceedings: the guilt of one partner had to be proved, and both partners had to agree to pursuing a divorce. The 1971 Act allowed divorce on the grounds of the irredeemable breakdown of the marriage, and the initiation of divorce proceedings by one partner even against the opposition of the other. The Act also sought to safeguard the welfare of any children of the divorcing couple.

After 1971 the number of divorces rose sharply and continuously so that, by the 1990s, it was estimated that one marriage in three would end in divorce. The Marriage Act of 1996 sought to distinguish between the end of marriages of short duration and those of greater length. The former could be ended very rapidly with few long-term obligations between the partners. The legislation attempted to provide the latter with greater long-term protection in respect of property including resources such as pensions. IJEK

Dobunni. A British tribe and *civitas*. The Dobunni were centred on Gloucestershire, with their pre-Roman capital probably in the fortified settlement at Bagendon. Either by conquest or by the unification and incorporation of smaller tribal groupings, they established by AD 43 a kingdom which seems to have included all of Gloucestershire, most of Somerset, and parts of Herefordshire, Worcestershire, Oxfordshire, and Wiltshire. Their inscribed coinage, however, suggests that their territory was divided, peacefully or otherwise, into two kingdoms each with its own ruler. Trade relations were established with the kingdom of the *Catuvellauni to the east but *Cunobelinus' ambitious plans for expansion may have resulted in some encroachment on Dobunnic territory around AD 40. In any event, according to the Greek historian Dio Cassius, early in the Claudian invasion in AD 43, a part of the Dobunni deserted the British cause and came to terms with the Roman invaders. Subsequently, around AD 70, the tribe were granted *civitas* status and the developing town of *Cirencester (Corinium) became their capital. It grew to be one of the largest towns in Roman Britain, and when Britannia was divided into four provinces early in the 4th cent., Cirencester was chosen as the capital of Britannia Prima. KB

docks and ports. Points of transshipment for goods and passengers at the coast or on inland waterways. Up to *c.*1700, Britain's ports had been largely natural coastal or riverside sites, sometimes with quays and wharfs for lading, and beaching vessels at low tide. In the busiest ports, such as London or Newcastle upon Tyne, where larger vessels were unable to tie up at the quay, smaller lighters were used as intermediaries to carry goods from ship to shore.

The growth of trade from the 16th cent. increased pressures on these natural harbours and stimulated new investment. This created the first wet docks, entered by lock and adding large areas of water to natural harbours, at Rotherhithe (1700) and *Liverpool (1701 and 1715). Development between 1770 and 1830 was remarkable: in 1775, the only commercial docks were in Liverpool, with 14 acres of water; by 1830, there were 397 acres in all, with 42 per cent in London, and the remainder concentrated into Liverpool, *Bristol, *Hull, Grimsby, and Goole. Liverpool was the leading handler of traffic, with 2.5 million tons in 1830, but nationally in 1841 three-fifths of tonnage was still handled without docks.

The coming of the coastal paddle-steamer in the 1830s forced dock rebuilding, and after 1870 the screw-propelled, triple-expansion powered steamship continued the process. Oceanic passenger traffic trebled between 1870 and 1913, as did the volume of goods shipped. From the 1870s, the growth in the scale of ships and their traffic forced the development of deep-water facilities, which led to the rise of *Southampton from the coming of the railway in the 1840s, and as a liner port from the 1890s; *Cardiff, as the 'coal metropolis', its sole credential as capital of Wales from mid-century; and brought *Manchester, after the building of its ship canal (1894), to fourth port in Britain by 1913, by value of goods traded. Heavy investment on Clydeside brought *Glasgow to fifth place.

Britain's loss of shipping supremacy after 1918 reduced the volume of goods handled, and foreign penetration of coastal tramp shipping favoured the revival of small and cheap ports. Shipping technology had significant effects after the Second World War: containerization began at Larne in 1954, and generalized during the 1960s; the shift of trade back towards Europe stimulated the east coast ports; and roll-on/roll-off ferries and hovercraft services developed from the later 1960s. Air travel virtually extinguished the liner ports by 1970, and port and dock employment, which exceeded 120,000 in 1911, fell consistently, collapsing from the 1960s. The full impact of the Channel Tunnel on UK ports has yet to be felt. JCh

Doctors' Commons was the popular name for the labyrinthine complex of law courts just south of St Paul's, London, from 1565 until 1858. The courts of civil law dealt with matrimonial and slander cases, the ecclesiastical courts with clerical discipline, and the Court of Admiralty with maritime disputes. For good measure, marriage licences could also be obtained there. The lawyers who practised there were required to have doctorates in law from Oxford or Cambridge. *Dickens was a clerk there in the early 1830s and made use of his experiences in *Sketches by Boz*, *Pickwick Papers*, *Our Mutual Friend*, and *David Copperfield*. JAC

Dodington, George Bubb, 1st Baron Melcombe Regis (1691–1762). Famous to posterity as the archetypal place-hunter, Dodington, though not heroic, was a politician of some note and a patron of the arts. It was customary to sneer at his ancestry, but he was quite well connected. Born George Bubb, he was related to the Temple family, which eventually inherited his enormous mansion at Eastbury, Dorset (and pulled it down), and his father and grandfather had been MPs. Dodington was sent to Winchester and Exeter College, Oxford, entered Parliament in 1715, and remained in the Commons until made a peer in 1761. He inherited large estates and a considerable electoral influence in 1720 from an uncle, George Dodington, another MP, whose name he took. *Walpole made him a lord of Treasury 1724–40, but he then went over to *Frederick, prince of Wales, who promised to make him a great man in the new reign. Henry *Pelham bought him back in 1744 as treasurer of the navy but he rejoined the prince in opposition in 1749. The prince's early death in 1751 left him stranded. When George III came to the throne, Dodington was too old and too fat for active service, but got his peerage: 'his coronet seems only calculated to adorn his tomb', wrote Horace

Mann, and he was proved right. Dodington's diary, a valuable source, was left to a cousin, whose nephew published it in 1784 with disparaging comments. Dodington summarized his philosophy at the end of his life in his delightful poem 'Shorten Sail':

> Strive thy little bark to steer
> With the tide, but near the shore.

JAC

Doe, John. One of the fictitious characters introduced in a procedure known as ejectment. The writs and remedies available to holders of title in freehold land were not available to leaseholders (i.e. those whose interest in land was limited to a fixed term), who were thus at a disadvantage if they were dispossessed. Through the writ of trespass the common law courts provided leasehold tenants with a remedy, which at first consisted merely of damages against the dispossessor, but later enabled them to recover possession of the leasehold land against the wrongdoer. This remedy, being quick and effective, was attractive to freeholders and, in order to avail themselves of it, they created a fictitious lease involving imaginary characters named John Doe, Richard Roe, and William Stiles. Using this fiction, the two parties to a dispute involving title to freehold land would use ejectment to determine which party had the better right to it. MM

Dogger Bank, battle of the, 1915. The Germans created their high seas fleet as an expression of Germany's great power status and as a political lever to force concessions from Britain. It was not designed to win a war, and faced by a numerically superior enemy, the German admirals had no intention of obliging the British by seeking a naval action until they had reduced the Grand Fleet's numerical superiority by attrition. The battle of the Dogger Bank was fought in the North Sea on 24 January 1915. A raiding force of German battle-cruisers was intercepted and pounded by *Beatty's battle-cruiser squadron. The action only convinced the German Admiralty that they were right to pursue a cautious strategy. DF

Dollar, battle of, *c.*875. The battle, east of Alloa, Scotland, was a crushing defeat for *Constantine I of Alba by the Norsemen, led by Halfdan of York. The whole northern part of Scotland was conceded to the invaders. Though the chronology is very doubtful, the reality of serious warfare is clear. JAC

Domesday Book was the result of the great survey commissioned by William the Conqueror at Gloucester at Christmas 1085. The main manuscript, so-called Great Domesday, written by a single scribe, contains the final version of the surveys of all English counties south of the rivers Ribble and Tees, with the exception of Norfolk, Suffolk, and Essex. These three counties make up Little Domesday, a more detailed, unedited draft text which, for reasons which remain unknown, was not reduced to the final Great Domesday form. Domesday Book's name, given to it in the generations immediately after the survey, shows that it was a source of awe and wonder. During the Middle Ages it continued to be consulted on numerous legal and tenurial matters. It is a fundamental source for all types of historical enquiry and is of importance for geographers, lawyers, and linguists. It is primarily a record of landholders, both in 1086 and in the time of Edward the Confessor, and of the manors and other estates which they held. The detail given for each estate usually consists of geld assessment, numbers of peasantry, ploughs, ploughlands, and some categories of livestock, and estimated value in King Edward's day, in 1086, and sometimes at an intermediate point. Information is often (but not consistently) given about whether title to a particular manor was in dispute and about churches, mills, and woodland. Major towns were supposed to be entered at the start of each county survey, but some important ones, such as London and Winchester, were omitted. The survey's purpose and the method of its compilation are subjects of debate. The current emphasis is on a financial purpose, since it seems to be primarily concerned with resources and assessments. However, its value as a register of title must not be overlooked, even if the disputes which it records were often not resolved. It is clear from chronicle references that the preliminary results were brought to William, perhaps by 1 August 1086 in preparation for the famous *Salisbury Oath, and certainly before he left for Normandy in the autumn. The production of the final Great Domesday text, however, took much longer and was probably not concluded until early 1088. Sets of commissioners toured the kingdom and heard evidence from juries representing shire and hundred courts. The kingdom was divided into circuits, of which there were probably seven. The basic order in which the material was to be set out was predetermined. The most complex modern discussions concern the methods by which this material was collected. While it is clear that some was in existence before the survey was made, the emphasis in recent discussion is on an intense editing process at local level, involving documents of various kinds and the participation of the local representatives. Computer-based studies of Domesday Book's contents are starting to yield impressive results on all kinds of subjects, but the complexities of its terminology and its statistics still baffle investigators. DB

domestic service refers to paid employment as servants in the households of others. The number of such servants depended upon the size of the household and its income. In all periods of history both men and women sought such employment. However, fewer men than women became servants after 1780, when a tax was imposed on all adult male indoor servants. Initially the tax was designed to encourage men into the armed forces or paid work in the expanding non-domestic labour market. Once established it made male domestic workers expensive, so that the typical domestic servant was female.

Domestic service was the most important type of employment for women until after the start of the First World War in 1914, when women took on the jobs of men who joined the services. Simultaneously, many households reduced the number of domestic servants because their incomes were reduced by wartime inflation.

In upper-class households there was often a hierarchy of servants 'below stairs', ranging from the butler to kitchen skivvies. Frequently these servants remained with the household for many years, some holding positions of intimacy and trust. Amongst the lower middle class only a 'maid of all work' was employed, who often endured very long hours and little prestige. Her lot was superior only to the 'daily' helping with the 'rough work'.

After 1918 domestic service never regained its former importance in private households; since 1945, work similar to that of the domestic servant has taken place in public contexts, through employment as cleaners and caterers in hospitals, nursing homes, schools, and universities. The increase in women working outside the home in the late 20th cent. is revivifying domestic service, which is now additionally provided through entrepreneurial small businesses. IJEK

domestic system. The organization of production by entrepreneurs not in a specialized workplace, but in the homes of workers. The method began in the Middle Ages when almost all manufacturing was carried out within the home whether in town or country. However, when markets for products grew rapidly, some production was concentrated in factories. For some products, such as many varieties of textiles, gloves, boots, and shoes, the system of subcontracting into the domestic system remained appropriate. Hand-looms and knitting-machines, such as the Griswold used for stocking- and glove-making, were typical of those installed in workers' homes. In some districts, such as the east midlands, new houses were erected during the 18th cent. with space to accommodate the knitting frames. The spacious room at the top of the house had large windows to capture the maximum daylight for operating the frames accurately.

The domestic or putting-out system had many advantages for the master or capitalist manufacturer. The work was often repetitious and required little training. Workers were paid only for their output, and employers did not have to bear the cost of lighting and heating, nor provide space for the machines which were used. In addition, employers responded to variations in demand by increasing or decreasing the amount of work subcontracted. Most workers paid rents for the machines, whether or not they were in use, and stored in their cottages raw materials or components. The masters employed 'bagmen' to distribute raw materials and to collect finished items. The payments for work done depended on the quality of the product and disputes often arose between agents and workers.

The decline of the domestic system was a consequence of the *industrial revolution. Growth in mass markets, combined with the development of textile machines, gave dominance to factory production of cloth, knitwear, and lace. The domestic system continued in the trades where there were specialized markets or where there were constant changes in the demand for decorative accessories and trimmings for the fashion industry. The pattern also continued in areas such as tailoring, paperbox-making, and even chainmaking.

During the 20th cent. the domestic system or home working survived, usually associated with low-paid work by women. These workers, isolated in their homes, rarely joined trade unions or organized to obtain adequate pay and conditions. The Trade Boards Act of 1909 was designed to cover the 'sweated industries' of the domestic system and established panels, drawn from employers and employees, to determine minimum rates of pay. However, this law provided no effective means of enforcing the statutory wage rates. It was abolished by the Wages Act of 1986.

Home working continues during the late 20th cent. in a wide range of contexts, from the making of exclusive high-fashion knitwear from expensive fibres for the fashion industry to new developments in teleporting and networking from home through computers. IJEK

Dominica is the most northerly of the Windward Islands in the eastern Caribbean. It has been an independent state within the Commonwealth since 1978. Sighted and named by Columbus in 1493, it was disputed in the 18th cent. between France and Britain, changed hands repeatedly, and was finally held by the British when they beat off a French attack in 1805. The economy relies heavily upon bananas, cocoa, and coconuts, but has been severely affected by hurricanes. JAC

Dominicans (or 'black' or 'preaching' *friars) were a mendicant order founded by a Spanish *Augustinian and preacher, St Dominic, to combat the Albigensian heresy in southern France. The order was confirmed by Pope Innocent III in 1215, and its rule, largely based on the Augustinian rule, codified by 1221. Though following ideals of corporate poverty, the order was dedicated to educational activity and quickly established itself at the forefront of intellectual life—Thomas Aquinas was a Dominican—and friaries were found in virtually every university town in the medieval West. Like the *Franciscans there were also strictly enclosed communities of contemplative nuns. Its rule, with its system of representational government under the authority of the master-general, is famous for its organizational sophistication, and partly accounts for its success and appeal both to the ecclesiastical hierarchy, especially the papacy, which used it for administrative, as well as evangelizing, duties, and to the laity.

The Dominicans first settled in England in Oxford and London in 1221 and by their *dissolution in 1538–9 there were over 50 English friaries, constituting the English province, and divided into the four disciplinary 'visitations' of London, Oxford, Cambridge, and York. BJG

dominion status was the term chosen to describe the position of the self-governing member states of the inter-war *Commonwealth. They were to be regarded, proclaimed the 1926 imperial conference, as '*autonomous* communities within the British Empire, *equal* in status, *in no way subordinate* one to another in any aspect of their domestic or external affairs, although united by a common allegiance to the Crown and *freely* associated as members of the British Commonwealth of Nations' (italics added). That was necessary to their self-respect. After 1947, however, when India entered the club, even that was felt to be inadequate, and the word 'dominion' was quietly dropped, as implying—

despite Britain's disavowals—a certain subordination to her. BJP

Donald I (d. 862), 'king of the Picts' (858–62) anachronistically regarded as second king of Scotland. Brother of *Kenneth I, whom he succeeded on the latter's death of a tumour. Little is known of Donald's reign (which may have been untypically peaceful) except that he presided over an assembly of the Gaels at the royal centre of Forteviot (5 miles south of Perth). He died (probably) at 'Rathinveramon'—probably a fort near Scone. A late and debatable source says that he was buried on Iona. He is not known to have had any children, and was succeeded by his nephew *Constantine I—only the second occasion when a family had retained the kingship for more than a generation. DEB

Donald II (d. 900), king of 'Scotland' (889–900). Donald is the first king in contemporary record to be referred to as *'rí Alban'*, 'king of Scotland'. 'Scotland' in this period, however, was only the eastern region north of the Forth. Donald was son of *Constantine I. His family had lost power between 878 and 889, but succeeded in monopolizing the kingship thereafter for 145 years, from Donald's accession to *Malcolm II's death in 1034. Donald's reign, like his father's, was plagued by Scandinavian incursions. He had more success than his father and managed to defeat a Danish force on some unidentified islands. It is likely, however, that he was killed by Scandinavians at Dunnottar (14 miles south of Aberdeen). According to a debatable source he was buried on Iona. DEB

Donald III (d. *c.*1100), king of Scotland (1093–4, 1094–7), known as Donald Bane. He seized the kingship on the death of his brother, *Malcolm III. The children of Malcolm and his English wife, St *Margaret, fled into exile, and Donald expelled Malcolm's English followers who he feared would support them. His first rival, however, was *Duncan II, Malcolm's eldest son by his Orcadian wife Ingibiorg. Duncan had been dubbed knight by William II of England in 1087, and with William's military intervention he dislodged Donald from the kingship in 1094. Duncan was soon defeated, forced to dismiss his Anglo-Norman backers, and before the end of the year was killed in battle and Donald restored to the throne. This time Donald was supported by Malcolm and Margaret's son Edmund whom he probably recognized as his heir. In 1097 William II gave military backing to another of Malcolm and Margaret's sons, *Edgar. Donald was defeated and he and Edmund incarcerated. In 1099 he was blinded by Edgar and died (perhaps as a result). He was buried at Dunkeld, but later reburied on Iona. DEB

Donne, John (1572–1631). Metaphysical poet and churchman. Of catholic stock, his education at Oxford and Lincoln's Inn was directed towards a future state office. Having been a volunteer on the 1596 Cadiz expedition, he became secretary to Sir Thomas Egerton, but marriage to Anne More without parental consent (1601) led to dismissal and a long period of unemployment. Unusually studious throughout his life, he had by then written much of his passionate, witty poetry and begun to reject catholicism. Even as an Anglican, though, his deep, personal religious struggle continued, but since James I refused to appoint him to any position outside the church, he was eventually ordained (1615); preferment was then rapid and he became famous for his powerful and eloquent sermons. Despite uncertain health, he was installed as dean of *St Paul's cathedral (1621), where he was conscientious in his duties and subsequently buried. ASH

Dorchester (Dorset). *Civitas*-capital of the *Durotriges. Lying near the Iron Age hill-fort of *Maiden castle, Durnovaria may have succeeded a base of *legio II Augusta*. A large bath-house lay in the south-eastern part of the town and the amphitheatre lay to the south, reusing the site of a Neolithic henge monument, Maumbury Rings. Earthen defences enclosing an area of *c.*75 acres constructed in the late 2nd cent. were refurbished in stone in the 3rd. Of the 3rd and 4th cents. were well-appointed houses and the large western cemetery at Poundbury, which may have been Christian. ASEC

Dorchester-on-Thames, diocese of. First created in *c.*635 as the see of Birinus for Wessex, it was transferred to *Winchester *c.*663. A Mercian bishopric existed here twice, 675–85, and again following *Leicester's retreat from the 8th-cent. Danish invasions. As the Danelaw was reconquered, Dorchester extended its authority to the Humber; *c.*1072 the see was moved to *Lincoln. WMM

Dorset is one of the oldest and most beautiful shires. But it has been so immortalized in the novels of Thomas *Hardy that to many people it is better known in fiction than in fact—the land of Tess and of Gabriel Oak, of Giles Winterborne and Marty South, of Eustacia Vye, the reddleman, and Michael Henchard—trapped in time, where Mrs Yeobright sits dying on Egdon Heath and the effigy of Henchard swirls round and round the weir-pond outside Casterbridge.

It is not easy to see much geographical unity. The county is largely the basin of the river Frome, which flows through Dorchester and Wareham into Poole harbour, and of the Stour and its tributaries, flowing from Sturminster in the north through Wimborne to Christchurch. For centuries it was the quietest of rural counties, with small market towns like Shaftesbury, Beaminster, and Blandford, and quiet harbours like Wareham, Lyme, and Bridport. The balance of the county was transformed from 1850 onwards by the sudden growth of the coastal towns. In 1801, no town in the shire had above 5,000 people; Poole had 4,800, Weymouth 3,600, Sherborne 3,200, Bridport 3,100, and Shaftesbury, Blandford, and Dorchester were all well under 3,000. But by 1931, when Dorchester had reached 10,000, Poole had grown to 57,000 and Weymouth 22,000. The boundary changes of 1972 reinforced this shift by bringing in Bournemouth and Christchurch from west Hampshire. Bournemouth's growth was amazing. In 1841 it boasted 26 dwellings. But after the coming of the railway in 1870, it gained county borough status by 1895, was well over 100,000 by 1931, and 159,000 by 1991. Since by 1991 Poole had grown to 135,000, nearly half of the county's population was tucked into the south-east corner.

At the time of the Roman invasion in AD 43 the local tribe was the *Durotriges. Their fortress of *Maiden castle was stormed by *Vespasian's second legion, and nearby *Dorchester developed as the Roman town of Durnovaria. In Saxon times it was soon recognized as a distinct area. *Sherborne was established as a bishopric as early as 705, and it remained there until 1075 when it was removed to Old Sarum.

The region formed part of the kingdom of *Wessex: Brithric was buried at Wareham c.802 and Edward the Martyr at Shaftesbury in 979. In the 9th cent. Dorset was repeatedly attacked by the Danes. The *Anglo-Saxon Chronicle* records an encounter in 837 between the men of Dorset and the Danes at Portland and another in 845 when they joined with the men of Somerset to engage the Danes at the mouth of the Parrett. Wareham was taken by the Danes in 876 and Sherborne, Dorchester, and Shaftesbury devastated by *Sweyn in 1002.

By this time Dorset was a recognized county. The *Domesday survey of 1086 identified four boroughs—Shaftesbury, Dorchester, Wareham, and Bridport—the latter having difficulty in sustaining its position because of the vulnerability of its sea defences. Much of the county was owned by the great monastery of Sherborne and by the nunnery at Shaftesbury, reputedly founded by *Alfred.

In the later Middle Ages and Tudor period, the coastal towns suffered greatly from French and Spanish reprisals and from Algerine pirates. The seashore inhabitants gained some recompense by resorting to wrecking, a tradition which lasted well into the 19th cent., and by their own privateering and smuggling. Wareham gradually silted up, losing its prosperity to Poole, which flourished on mackerel, oysters, and the Newfoundland fish trade. Bridport manufactured hempen ropes. The demand for Portland stone increased vastly from the 17th cent. onwards, the *Banqueting Hall, *St Paul's, and *Greenwich palace made of it: as late as 1927, the 87-year-old Thomas Hardy enjoyed watching goods trains carrying stone clattering through Dorchester. Purbeck marble, exported through Swanage, was also much in demand. Inland, cloth manufactures flourished—silk at Sherborne, lace at Blandford, linen at Gillingham, baize at Sturminster. But the mainstay of the county was the sheep on the chalk downs around Dorchester and the cattle in the vale of Blackmoor to the north.

Like most counties, Dorset was divided by the Civil War. Dorchester, Lyme, and Poole were parliamentary strongholds, Sherborne and Corfe castles royalist bastions. The county's position between the parliamentary east and the royalist west, and easy communications with France, made it strategically important. After the royalist victory at *Roundway Down in 1643 much of the shire fell to the king and Lyme, in 1644, survived a royalist siege. In the last years of the war, *club-men were active, and confrontations took place at Sturminster in June 1645 and in August with Cromwell near Shaftesbury.

After 1731 one fortunate result of a disastrous fire at Blandford was a complete rebuilding, making it one of the most charming Georgian towns in the country. Another rebuilding was at Milton Abbas, where Joseph Damer pulled down the old village and employed Capability *Brown to build a new model village. The county remained remote and little known. Visits by George III helped to encourage Weymouth as a resort. In 1796 an Act was passed authorizing a 49-mile canal linking the Stour with the Kennet and Avon but, unsurprisingly, it was never completed. Apart from Bournemouth, not then in the county, the railways did not make much impact, though the Somerset and Dorset passed into folklore as the old Slow-and-Dirty, and the Pines Express, which ran from Bournemouth to Manchester via Bath, Green Park, had a strong claim to be the slowest express ever.

The 20th cent. produced a vast urban build-up between Poole and Bournemouth and a diversification of industry—an atomic energy station on Wynfrith Heath, oil drilling off the coast. The hinterland remains largely unspoiled and boasts villages like Sixpenny Handley, Ryme Intrinsica, Okeford Fitzpaine, Toller Porcorum, and Hazelbury Bryan. The recommendations of the Banham commission in 1994 were to retain the county for ceremonial purposes only, setting up unitary authorities for Bournemouth, Poole, East Dorset, and West Dorset. JAC

Dorset, Henry Grey, 3rd marquis of, duke of Suffolk (1517–54). Dorset succeeded his father at the age of 13, and was lord high constable at the coronation of Edward VI and a knight of the Garter. In 1551 he was made duke of Suffolk. His second wife was the eldest daughter of *Mary Tudor by Charles Brandon, duke of *Suffolk, and he was the father of Lady Jane *Grey. A zealous protestant, he became a close ally of the duke of *Northumberland. He declared his daughter queen on the death of Edward, recanted, and was lucky to save his life. But the following year he was implicated in *Wyatt's rising against Mary's Spanish marriage, was discovered hiding in a hollow tree on one of his Warwickshire estates, and executed. His widow married a ginger-haired groom sixteen years her junior soon after the duke's execution. JAC

Dorset, Thomas Sackville, 1st earl of (c.1536–1608). Thomas Sackville was the son of Sir Richard Sackville, under-treasurer at the Exchequer 1559–66, a wealthy lawyer and administrator, who was *Anne Boleyn's first cousin. A member of the Inner Temple, Sackville was returned to Parliament in 1558 when he was just of age. His interests at that time were literary rather than political. In 1559 he wrote the introduction to *A Mirror for Magistrates* and, with Thomas Norton, was author in 1561 of the tragedy *Gorboduc*, put on at the Inner Temple. In 1567, soon after his father's death, he was made Baron Buckhurst. He served Elizabeth in a number of ambassadorial posts, was given the Garter in 1589, and from 1599 to his death was lord treasurer. James I advanced him in 1604 to the earldom of Dorset. He died at the council table in April 1608. He was granted the reversion of the estate of Knole in Kent, though he did not gain possession until much later, and in the last years of his life began rebuilding the medieval house. JAC

Douglas, Sir Archibald (*c.*1296–1333). Regent of Scotland. Archibald Douglas was younger brother of Sir James *Douglas, the staunch supporter of Robert Bruce. After Bruce's death they stood by his young son, David II. In December 1332 at Annan, Archibald Douglas routed Edward *Balliol, who had claimed the Scottish throne, and in March 1333 he was appointed regent or guardian, after Sir Andrew *Moray had been captured. Edward III of England then besieged Berwick and Douglas marched to relieve it. In July 1333 at *Halidon Hill, the English were victorious and Douglas killed. JAC

Douglas, Archibald Douglas, 3rd earl of [S] (d. 1400), known as 'the Grim'. Douglas rose to prominence as a supporter of David II in a period when the steward and the 1st earl of Douglas were in rebellion (1363). David made him constable of Edinburgh castle (1361), warden of the west marches (1364), and lord of Galloway (1369). He bought the earldom of Wigtown (1372), received Bothwell by marriage, and inherited the earldom of Douglas (1388), creating the Douglas power that dominated Scotland until 1455. He was praised by contemporary chroniclers, particularly for endowment of collegiate churches at Lincluden and Bothwell. From 1399 he supported Robert III's heir, the duke of Rothesay, as governor of Scotland, his death significantly weakening the duke's position. Furthermore, by buying his daughter's marriage to Rothesay (1400), he antagonized the earl of Dunbar, whose daughter was already espoused to the duke. Dunbar persuaded Henry IV to invade in retaliation. RJT

Douglas, Archibald Douglas, 4th earl of [S]**, lord of Galloway and Annandale, duke of Touraine** (*c.*1372–1424). Son and heir of Archibald 'the Grim', 3rd earl of Douglas [S], and later nicknamed 'the Tyneman' (the Loser), perhaps because of his participation in so many battles on the losing side (*Homildon, 1402; *Shrewsbury, 1403; *Verneuil, 1424), in the process losing his liberty, various parts of his anatomy, and ultimately his life. Earl Archibald was none the less a magnate of immense power and influence, the dominating force in southern Scotland and one of the triumvirate (with *Albany and Mar) who controlled the country during the captivity of James I.

Latterly Douglas supported the cause of Charles VII of France against the English, and was thus prudently absent from Scotland on James I's return there in the spring of 1424. Created lieutenant-general of the French army and duke of Touraine, Douglas was killed in battle against John, duke of *Bedford's forces at Verneuil in Perche (August 1424). NATM

Douglas, Archibald Douglas, 5th earl of [S] (*c.*1390–1439). Elder son of Archibald, 4th earl of Douglas, and Margaret Stewart, daughter of Robert III. The future 5th earl took a leading part in Scottish military assistance to France from 1419. As earl of Wigtown, he joined John Stewart, earl of *Buchan [S], in leading Scottish expeditionary forces of 1419 and 1421; in March 1421 Buchan and Wigtown won the spectacular victory of *Baugé in Anjou, killing Henry V's brother Thomas, duke of *Clarence.

Succeeding his father as earl of Douglas following *Verneuil (1424), Archibald had to walk the political tightrope of defending Douglas family interests while maintaining reasonable relations with James I. Despite a brief imprisonment in Lochleven castle (1431), he was broadly successful. Following the king's assassination in February 1437, Douglas was appointed lieutenant-general to lend respectability to the shaky new government. However, he died of plague at Restalrig near Edinburgh. NATM

Douglas, Gavin (*c.*1475–1522). Scottish poet and ecclesiastical politician. A younger son of the 5th earl of *Angus, from an early age Douglas pursued an ambitious ecclesiastical career. His failure to secure the archbishopric of St Andrews was only partially compensated for by his appointment as bishop of Dunkeld in 1516, but as uncle of the 6th earl of *Angus he played a prominent role in Anglo-Scottish affairs following his nephew's marriage to James IV's widow *Margaret Tudor in 1514. His deep but largely unprofitable involvement in political intrigue led to his death (apparently from plague) in English exile, and also prevented him from developing further his considerable poetic gifts. One of the great 'makars' of Renaissance Scotland, Douglas's early work *The Palice of Honour* (1501) was followed by his *Eneados* (1513), a remarkable Scots verse rendering of Virgil's *Aeneid* which is his most enduring memorial. RAM

Douglas, Sir James (d. 1330). One of the most successful leaders in the Scottish Wars of Independence. In 1306, Douglas rallied immediately to Robert Bruce. His forte was the daring surprise attack. Early in 1307, he wiped out the English garrison of his family's castle at Douglas; probably in August 1308 he helped Bruce gain his victory at the pass of Brander by climbing the slopes of Ben Cruachan to attack the enemy unexpectedly in the rear. In 1314, he recovered Roxburgh by a night attack; led one of the brigades at *Bannockburn; and repeatedly thereafter raided into England. His final service was to carry Bruce's heart in a campaign against the Muslims in Spain, in which he himself was killed, though the heart was recovered and brought back to Scotland. The rewards which he received from Bruce during his life established his family as one of the most powerful in Scotland. BW

Douglas, James Douglas, 2nd earl of [S] (*c.*1358–88). Son of William, the 1st earl, whom he succeeded in 1384. To secure his loyalty to the new Stewart dynasty, he was given an annuity of 100 marks, Robert II's fourth daughter Isabella as a wife, and £500 Scots, following his father's brief claim to the throne (1371). Douglas was one of several Scottish earls who took advantage of the expiry of truce, and the domestic troubles of Richard II, to invade England (1388), initially across the Solway Firth to Cockermouth, and later in a smaller invasion in the east. This force eventually met with Henry (Hotspur) *Percy at *Otterburn (August 1388). In the ensuing battle Percy was captured, the English defeated, but Douglas killed. He was commemorated as 'doughty Douglas' in the ballad 'Chevy Chase'. He lacked a legitimate heir, which eventually split the family into 'Black' and 'Red' branches. RJT

Douglas, James Douglas of Balvenie, 7th earl of [S] (*c.*1373–1443), known as 'the Gross'. Second son of Archibald 'the Grim', 3rd earl of Douglas. An able and ruthless man, Balvenie built—or greatly extended—the 'robber baron' castle of Abercorn near Linlithgow and extorted large sums from the burgh custumars during the English captivity of James I. Despite this, Balvenie became a trusted counsellor of the adult James I (1424–37).

Following James's murder, Balvenie was given the earldom of Avandale [S] (November 1437), probably the gift of his nephew, the lieutenant-general. The latter's unexpected death in 1439 was followed by the execution of his sons—probably with Avandale's connivance, as he was justice-general—following the *'Black Dinner' in 1440. Avandale then succeeded, in terms of the Douglas entail of 1342, as 7th earl of Douglas, reunited the vast Douglas estates by marrying his eldest son William to the Galloway heiress Margaret, and died at Abercorn in 1443. NATM

Douglas, James Douglas, 9th earl of [S] (d. 1491). Second son of James 'the Gross', 7th earl of *Douglas. With two companions, James took part in a tournament against three Burgundian champions before James II at Stirling in 1449, and lost. The remainder of his life was one long rearguard action. Succeeding as 9th (and last) earl on his elder brother William, 8th earl of *Douglas's murder by James II (1452), James withdrew his allegiance from the king, then negotiated for a settlement (bond of manrent, 1453), finally fleeing to England before his forfeiture in 1455. As part of the Scottish 'fifth column' in England, Earl James hoped to be restored to his estates with English military aid. With the forfeited duke of *Albany, Douglas finally returned to Scotland, far too late, only to be captured at Lochmaben (1484), and die at Lindores (1491). He had no children by his marriage to Margaret, 'Fair Maid' of Galloway. NATM

Douglas, William Douglas, 8th earl of [S] (*c*.1425–52). Eldest son of James 'the Gross', 7th earl of *Douglas. Knighted while still an infant (1430), together with the royal child who would eventually kill him, he grew up to become by far the most powerful magnate in Scotland. Lieutenant-general for the young James II from 1444, and married to the Galloway heiress Margaret, Douglas and his brothers James (who succeeded him), Archibald (earl of Moray), Hugh (earl of Ormond), and John, Lord Balvenie, defeated all opposition and dominated Scottish politics between 1444 and 1452.

During William's absence abroad, cutting a fine figure in Rome during Jubilee Year 1450, the adult James II plundered the Douglas lands of Wigtown and Selkirk. A hollow reconciliation between king and earl followed in 1451, but the following year a bond between Douglas, Crawford, and Ross provided the excuse for the earl's murder, by James II in person, at Stirling castle. NATM

Douglas cause. On the death of the 1st duke of Douglas in 1761, the estates were disputed on behalf of his cousin, the duke of Hamilton, aged 5, and Archibald Stewart, claiming to be a nephew, aged 13. In 1767 the Court of Session decided against the nephew but in 1769 the House of Lords reversed the verdict. Stewart changed his name to Douglas and was given a barony in 1790. Since Douglas's mother would have been 51 at the time of his birth, the Lords' verdict was received with some surprise. JAC

Dover, treaty of, 1364. This agreement between Edward III and Louis de Mâle, count of Flanders, on 19 October 1364, was intended to lead to the marriage of Edward's fourth son, Edmund, with the count's daughter, Margaret, who stood to inherit not only Flanders but also the counties of Nevers, Rethel, Burgundy, and Artois, and the duchies of Limburg and Brabant. As Edward proposed to settle on his son Calais, Guînes, and Ponthieu, the marriage would have led to English dominance on the northern and eastern fringes of France. Charles V of France thus put pressure on Pope Urban V not to allow a dispensation for the marriage, and was able to negotiate instead Margaret's marriage to his own son Philip. AC

Dover, treaty of, 1670. Louis XIV's attack upon the Dutch in 1667 had been halted by the *Triple Alliance of Holland, Sweden, and England. To prepare for a decisive victory, Louis needed to smash the alliance and in 1669 began negotiations with Charles II. The treaty of May 1670, signed by Charles's sister Henrietta-Anne, pledged the two powers to a joint attack on the Dutch and not to make a separate peace. A secret clause committed Charles to declaring himself a catholic and Louis to providing him with an army if disaffection followed. When, in 1674, Charles assured Parliament that there were no secret clauses in the treaty, it was observed that his hand shook. Suspicions of his sincerity were an important factor in allegations of a *Popish plot in 1678. JAC

Dover castle is the gateway to England. Dover was one of the harbours of the *Saxon Shore and the base for the Roman fleet, **Classis Britannica*. Its Roman lighthouse probably dates from the 1st cent. AD. There was certainly some Saxon fortification there but the present castle was started in the reign of Henry II and ready for use in 1185. Its most remarkable feature is that the large keep is itself protected by further curtain walls. It was one of the last rectangular keeps to be built before castle design moved on to polygonal or circular towers. The keep is similar to that at Newcastle upon Tyne, finished a few years earlier, and by the same master builder, Maurice the Engineer. In 1216 it was held by Hubert de *Burgh for King John against several weeks' siege by Louis, dauphin of France. Its subsequent history was surprisingly peaceful and the heavy fortifications added during the Revolutionary and Napoleonic wars were never called upon. The lord warden of the Cinque ports is also constable of Dover castle. JAC

Dowding, Hugh, 1st Baron Dowding (1882–1970). Air chief marshal. Dowding was born in Dumfriesshire and went to Winchester. He joined the army, served in India, and just before the First World War qualified as an RFC pilot. He finished the war as brigadier-general and transferred to the new RAF. In 1936 he was made commander-in-chief of Fighter Command and though due to retire in 1939 was asked to continue. He thus held a crucial post during the Second World War. In May 1940, in a powerfully argued memo, he begged that no more fighter planes be sent to France, and he was in personal control all through the Battle of *Britain which followed. He was replaced in November 1940, after the German invasion threat had been defeated, and was given a barony in 1943. 'Stuffy' Dowding was austere and could be difficult. But the men under his direct command won one of the vital battles of the war. Churchill called his decision to hold seven squadrons in reserve 'an example of genius in the art of war' and in his victory broadcast of May 1945 paid a special tribute to Dowding. JAC

Dowland, John (*c.*1563–1626). English composer and the leading lutenist of his age. At the age of 17 Dowland travelled in the service of the ambassador Sir Henry Cobham to Paris, where he became a catholic. In 1594–7 he visited Germany and Italy, becoming court lutenist to King Christian IV of Denmark in 1598. Nevertheless Dowland was bitterly disappointed at his failure to achieve an English court position. This eventually came in 1612, but he remained disaffected, his typically Elizabethan tendency to melancholy colouring his most characteristic music, such as the lute-song 'Flow my tears', based on the famous 'Lachrimae' pavan that also appeared in versions for solo lute and for viol consort. Dowland made the lute-song his own, moving from the dance-orientated pieces of *The First Booke of Songes or Ayres* (1597) to the Italianate declamation of 'Sorrow stay' (Book II, 1600) and the deep introspection of 'In darkness let me dwell' (*A Musicall Banquet*, 1610). ECr

Down was one of the six counties of Northern Ireland before the local government reorganization of 1973. Its boundary to the north is the Lagan; to the south, with the Irish Republic, Carlingford Lough; and across to Armagh in the west, with the Newry canal as boundary. The Mountains of Mourne are in the south-west corner. There was a diocese of Down from the early 12th cent., with the headquarters at Downpatrick, where the cathedral dates from 1790. It was united with the see of Dromore in 1842. The chief town is Newry, close to the border, and the seat of the Roman catholic bishopric of Dromore. The land is good grazing, there is fishing from the coast, and Bangor is a seaside resort. The catholic population is largely in the south of the county and at the general election of 1992 the Social Democratic and Labour Party took Down South and Newry and Armagh: Unionist parties took Strangford and Down North. JAC

Down (Dún Lethglaisse), **diocese of.** The Irish bishopric of Down was listed at the Councils of Raithbressail (1111) and Kells-Mellifont (1152) as a diocese in the province of *Armagh. It was united with Connor in 1453. Whereas most of medieval Ulster was Gaelic, Co. Down was English. Since the Reformation both the Catholic and Anglican sees have been known as 'Down and Connor'. In the Anglican church, however, Dromore was united with it (1842). With the separation of Connor (1944), the Anglican see is now known as 'Down and Dromore'. There are cathedrals at both locations. WMM

Downing Street was built by Sir George Downing in the 1680s as a speculation. The site had once been part of *Whitehall palace. Only three of the original houses remain, on the north side—no. 10 used by the prime minister, no. 11 by the chancellor, and no. 12 by the whips. The south side is taken up by Sir George Gilbert *Scott's government offices, built in the 1860s. Behind the modest façade of no. 10 is another large house, fronting the Horse Guards and connected. Sir Robert *Walpole accepted it from George II in 1732 for the prime minister of the day. Its nearness to Parliament was an important consideration. The internal arrangements include work by *Kent, Taylor, and *Soane and are dominated by the staircase, with its collection of engravings and photographs of prime ministers. The cabinet room was redesigned in 1781–3. JAC

Downs, battle of the, 1652. A clash on 18 May which helped to precipitate the first Anglo-Dutch War. Robert *Blake with a force of fifteen vessels was attacked by a superior fleet under Martin Tromp. The encounter was not decisive but the Dutch lost two ships. JAC

Downs, battle of the, 1666. A heavy naval engagement on 11–14 June during the second *Anglo-Dutch War, sometimes known as the Four Days' fight or the Goodwin's fight. Albemarle (*Monck), with a fleet of some 56 vessels, left the Downs and off the North Foreland encountered a large Dutch fleet under de Ruyter, Cornelis Tromp, and de Witt. *Rupert brought up reserves on the fourth day enabling Albemarle to retire into the Thames estuary but the English losses were heavier, and included the *Royal Prince*, a 92-gunner, which ran aground. Both sides suffered severely, but *Pepys wrote 'I do find great reason to think that we are beaten in every respect and that we are the losers.' JAC

Doyle, Sir Arthur Conan (1859–1930). Author. Educated at Edinburgh University, Doyle qualified as a doctor but gave up medicine for writing. He published his first novel, *A Study in Scarlet*, in 1887, which introduced the detective Sherlock Holmes. In 1891 Doyle began to write short stories under the title 'The Adventures of Sherlock Holmes' for the *Strand Magazine*. Doyle's intellectual detective was famous for his powers of analytical reasoning and became associated with his dressing-gown, pipe, violin, and cocaine syringe. His eccentricity was in contrast to the sober nature of his faithful friend Dr Watson, who narrated the stories. In 1893 Doyle killed off Holmes, but such was the public outcry that he eventually resurrected him in 1903. Doyle wrote many other novels of general and historical interest. He was an avid imperialist, serving as a physician during the *Boer War (1899–1902). In later years he was absorbed by the subject of spiritualism. RAS

Drake, Sir Francis (*c.*1543–96). In legend and perhaps in reality, Drake was the greatest of the Elizabethan 'sea-dogs'. A skilled seaman and naval tactician, an inspiring leader of men, he was, nevertheless, capable of greed, disloyalty, injustice towards associates, and poor judgement as a naval strategist. His career was a key part of the process by which England emerged as an oceanic power. Though of yeoman stock, Drake became closely associated with a predatory and aggressive ruling aristocracy ready to sanction piracy and privateering against the French, Portuguese, and above all, the Spanish. The contests with the latter also had a religious edge as Drake was a determined protestant. Yet the Spaniards who knew El Draque admired him.

Originally from Devon, Drake learned seamanship apprenticed on a coastal bark plying from the Thames, but in the 1560s joined a kinsman, *Hawkins, on ventures to Spain and then to west Africa and the Caribbean, procuring and selling slaves in the face of Portuguese and Spanish hostility. By 1569, Drake was in command of a ship. Details of his life are obscure, but he made at least three piratical expeditions to the Caribbean, with that in 1572 capturing 30 tons of silver, part of the Spanish treasure annually brought across the Isthmus of Panama. After an Irish venture, in 1577 Drake embarked on a circumnavigation of the globe financed by the queen and other great people. This was at once further plundering of the Spanish—now on the western coast of the Americas—a search for the Pacific end of the North-West Passage, and an attempt to reach the spice islands by going west. Drake's expedition was the second to circuit the globe and also led to his claiming California for Elizabeth. Just where Drake landed in California and whether a plaque which came to notice in 1937 was actually the one he left there in 1579 remain in dispute. On the return of the 70-foot-long *Golden Hind* in 1580, Drake, rich and famous, was knighted, while England, it has been said, began to think globally.

There followed further raids on Spain and, most notably, assaults on key Spanish positions around the Caribbean in 1585–6 and Cadiz in 1587. These actions, combined with the defeat of the Spanish Armada in 1588 with Drake second in command, ended Spain's unquestioned supremacy at sea, though they did *not* break Spain's naval power. Nor was Drake's role in the defeat of the Armada the key one.

In 1589, Drake led an expedition against Lisbon before settling to active involvement in the life of Plymouth, including becoming its MP. He was encouraged to resume a privateering career in 1595 since Elizabeth's policy favoured predation on Spain as a means of increasing England's stake in world trade. But the attacks in the West Indies failed and Drake died at sea. This disaster was soon forgotten as the legend was elaborated in subsequent years and centuries. RB

drama. See THEATRE.

dreadnought is the name given to a type of battleship introduced into the principal navies after the experiences of the Russo-Japanese War. The chief innovations were higher speed and a main armament of heavy guns of uniform calibre. The first to enter service was HMS *Dreadnought* in December 1906, although other 'dreadnoughts', including the American *Michigan*, had been designed earlier. Although innovative design kept *Dreadnought*'s increases in size and cost moderate, by 1914 'super-dreadnoughts' incorporated further increases in size, armour, and armament, which played a major rôle in the international naval rivalry of the early 20th cent. NMcC

dress may meet practical needs such as protection against climate and labour hazards, but it has also been a powerful tool in the maintenance of hierarchy through its reflection of status, and has served to distinguish occupation and faith as well as rank. It additionally mirrors fashion and permits expression of personal taste. Sumptuous clothes are usually worn by the more privileged classes, to enforce authority, flaunt wealth, or merely dissociate themselves from menial labour: medieval and Tudor monarchs could not wear too many jewels or precious metals; outer clothing was slashed or looped to show underlying layers of expensive fabric; impractical footwear and incapacitating sleeves were signs of leisure, if not symbols of dignity. Sumptuary laws may have been framed to protect home industries by bans on foreign imports (clothes, cloth, wool) and internal trade controls, but they considerably enhanced, then maintained, class distinctions. Because of 'the outragious and excessive apparel of divers peoples against their estate and degree', dress for servants, handicraftsmen and yeomen, esquires and gentlemen, merchants and burgesses, knights, clerks, and ploughmen was firmly regulated in 1363 via quality of cloth and permitted embellishment. Such distinctions were perpetuated in clauses forbidding velvet caps to any below the degree of knight (8 Eliz. c. 11) or demanding the Sunday wearing of woollen 'statute' caps (13 Eliz. c. 19) by all save the nobility, clergy, and London company wardens. Dress, according to Lord *Chesterfield in 1745, was a very foolish thing, 'yet it is a very foolish thing for a man not to be well dressed, according to his rank and way of life'.

In some instances, practicality and symbolic authority merged. The periwig, adopted from French fashion after the Restoration, not only concealed baldness or reduced head-lice (since the natural hair was close-cropped or shaved) but was worn to enhance dignity. Gain in size and artificiality meant that the heavy full-bottomed wig could only be worn on formal or special occasions, or by gentlemen of leisure. Modified for general use, wigs spread slowly throughout the country despite the hazards of inflammability, contagion, moralist attack, and poor durability, but generally decreased in size through the 18th cent. until their demise. Legal wigs, however, as part of traditional professional costume, are only today being slowly abandoned. Combined practicality and authority may also be seen in doctors' white coats and policemen's helmets.

If practical considerations dictated much of working dress, particularly when it remained relatively simple, occupational distinction came through attachment of appropriate emblems (threaded needle, weaver's shuttle), cap or arm badges, apron colour, or the heraldic crest/colours of the family served, while company liveries symbolized competence in a particular skill. Custom grew out of utility, then persisted, partly to prevent workers absconding from their employers, but also from the wearers' desire to maintain their group's recognized trademark. This may be seen today in corporate uniforms (airlines, hotels), identification badges, shoulder-tabs, and arm-bands; regimental and old school ties are merely rose-tinted nostalgia for lost fraternalism. Variations within uniform can denote distinctions of rank, most readily observed within the armed forces.

A prevailing style of dress has become known as being 'in fashion', but fashion has been described as a tyrannically democratic force, enforcing conformity to current social or moral conventions. Attack has come from moralists (frequently men rather than women), medical critics concerned about distorted torsos or incipient pneumonia, politicians and economists, aesthetic critics, animal lovers (against fur and feathers), and caricaturists, but with little long-term effect. Individuals have challenged fashion through aggressive nonconformity—Miss Chudleigh, later countess of Bristol, appeared virtually naked as Iphigenia at a 1749 ball—only to find the shock of the new fading because of growing familiarity, and the focus of attention shifting to another part of the body. Fashionable style moved downwards quite quickly. If Thackeray's duchess of Fitzbattleaxe was emulated by Lady Croesus, then Mrs Broadcloth must follow suit; if her, then also Mrs Seedy, her landlady Miss Letsam, and finally Suky the maid. This might produce vulgarization, but it also spurred the duchess to modifications to restore her lead in fashion. Sumptuary laws had long disappeared (1643 saw the last enactment), and class distinctions had been further blurred by the growing custom for the mistress to give her cast-offs to the lady's maid—such well-dressed servants puzzled many foreign visitors whose own countries still enforced sartorial regulations.

Fashion has frequently reflected overseas influences, despite war or trade restrictions: returning crusaders introduced silks and damasks, emphasis on Germanic puffs and slashes yielded to Spanish *bombast* (padding) and rigid outline as that country's power advanced in the 16th cent., puritan dress had similarities with its Dutch equivalent, and French influence on taste generally was enormous after the Restoration and for most of the 18th cent. The bloomer costume, adopted by some early female emancipators, originated in mid-19th-cent. America, and in the 20th cent., Parisian couture-houses have led the way, even if designs are watered down for high-street shops, though the growing trend towards informality has lessened their importance. ASH

Drogheda is 30 miles north of Dublin at the mouth of the river Boyne. It was the first garrison to be attacked by Oliver *Cromwell when he invaded Ireland in 1649. Its royalist defenders included many English protestants as well as catholic Irish. They were no match for Cromwell's 12,000-strong army and heavy siege guns. When Sir Arthur Aston rebuffed the summons to surrender, Cromwell blasted two holes in the southern wall and on 10 September ordered his men into the breach. Only after the second assault, led by Cromwell himself on foot, did the parliamentarians overrun the town, at which point 'in the heat of action' he ordered 'any that were in arms' put to the sword. Dismayed, some of his soldiers let their prisoners escape. Much of the ensuing massacre, totalling 3,500 soldiers, clergy, and civilians, was carried out in cold blood the next day. Cromwell's intention was that the terrible example of Drogheda would bring Irish catholic resistance to a speedy end. Events proved him wrong. IJG

druids. A priestly caste in British tribal society. The druids acquired a reputation from several Roman writers for inhuman practices perpetrated in the name of their religion. The Greek geographer Strabo accused them of mass human sacrifice, and Diodorus Sicula and Tacitus both claimed that the druids used human entrails cut from sacrificial victims to consult the gods and predict the future. Although they are not specifically identified as the instigators of the slaughter which accompanied the capture of Camulodunum (*Colchester) by *Boudicca's rebels, there can be little doubt that both Tacitus and Dio Cassius held them responsible for the atrocities they reported. These included hanging, burning, crucifixion, and impaling alive. Tacitus and Dio Cassius both emphasize the particular importance of sacred groves as places of worship for the druids. Dio mentions such a grove in the vicinity of Colchester, dedicated to Andate, the goddess of Victory, whilst Tacitus refers to many of them on the Isle of Mona (Anglesey), suggesting that both the druids and their groves were spread the breadth of Britain. Pliny confirms the important role of sacred groves in druidic religion, particularly those of oak trees. It is he who is also responsible for linking the druids to mistletoe, white robes, golden sickles, and herbal medicines, all of which are part of the popular perception of druidism today. What is not clear from the ancient authors is the extent to which druids wielded political power or influence in Britain at the time of the invasion. KB

Drumclog, battle of, 1679. John Graham (*Dundee) of Claverhouse, attempting to disperse a rising of *covenanters on 1 June, was sharply repulsed in a skirmish at Drumclog, near Strathaven. The insurgents went on to occupy Glasgow but were defeated at *Bothwell Bridge by *Monmouth. William *Cleland fought with the covenanting forces and the engagement was described by *Scott in *Old Mortality*. JAC

Drummond, Thomas (1797–1840). Civil servant. Drummond was born in Edinburgh and attended university there. He joined the Royal Engineers and began work on the *Ordnance Survey, where his invention of the 'Drummond light' (a brilliant limelight) greatly facilitated progress. In 1831 he was recruited by *Brougham to provide the statistical data for the Great Reform Bill. In 1835 he moved to become under-secretary at Dublin, where he aimed at the impartial administration of law and order and began the establishment of an efficient police force. His supporters claimed a significant reduction in agrarian crime. Drummond gave great offence to ultra-protestants with his reminder to landlords that they had duties as well as rights. He was subsequently involved in planning a state railway system for Ireland which never materialized. Drummond wore himself out by work and died in harness. JAC

Drury Lane (London) takes its name from Sir Thomas Drury, who had a house there in Elizabeth I's reign. It was a fashionable street in the 17th cent. but rowdy by the 18th. The first theatre opened in 1663. Nell *Gwyn made her début in 1665 and on May Day 1667 *Pepys saw her outside her lodgings 'in her smock-sleeves and bodice, looking upon one—she seemed a mighty pretty creature'. The theatre, burned down in 1672, was rebuilt by *Wren. *Garrick made his début there in 1742, became manager, and passed it on to *Sheridan in 1776. His new theatre, built by Holland in 1794, was burned down in 1809 while Sheridan was at a debate in the Commons. The replacement was by Benjamin Wyatt and, much restored, is the present building. In the 1890s the theatre was famous for Dan Leno's pantomimes and in the 20th cent. for musicals. JAC

Dryden, John (1631–1700). English poet, playwright, and critic. Dryden's influence on contemporary political poetry was marked. Educated at Westminster School and Trinity College, Cambridge, Dryden came from a 'middling' landed family, but made a living from his writing. After commemorating Oliver *Cromwell's death in *Heroic Stanzas* (1658), Dryden turned to celebration of the Restoration of Charles II and the early successes of his reign in a series of poems, *Astraea Redux* (1660), *To His Sacred Majesty* (1661), and *Annus Mirabilis* (1667), as well as writing numerous important and popular tragedies, comedies, and tragi-comedies, and seminal critical works such as *Of Dramatick Poesie* (1668). Appointed poet laureate in 1668 and historiographer-royal in 1670, Dryden continued to support the king, most notably at the height of the *Exclusion crisis with *Absalom and Achitophel* (1681). Other significant poems of this period include the first English mock-heroic, *Mac Flecknoe* (1682), a witty and malicious demolition of his fellow-playwright Thomas Shadwell, and *Religio Laici* (1682), a defence of Anglicanism. However, Dryden converted to catholicism on the accession of James II, writing a religious allegory, *The Hind and the Panther* (1687), as a sort of justification. Stripped of his offices in 1688, he returned with success to the theatre, and began a brilliant series of translations from the classics, particularly Virgil's *Aeneid* and *The Georgics*. Scarcely surprisingly, given his political position, critics have discerned hidden Jacobite meanings in most of Dryden's later writings, including the magnificent *Fables Ancient and Modern*, published in the year of his death. JAD

Dub (d. 966), king of 'Scotland' (962–6). Son of *Malcolm I. He succeeded on the death of *Indulf at the hands of Norwegian raiders. He beat off a challenge for the throne by Indulf's son *Cuilén in 965, at the battle of Duncrub (9 miles south-west of Perth). This may have marked the end of a period of dynastic solidarity which (with the possible exception of Malcolm I's accession in the early 940s) had seen no violent competition for the kingship for 75 years. Dub was not vanquished by dynastic rivalry, however, but by the men of Moray at Forres, an event which apparently coincided with an eclipse of the sun on 20 July 966. It is likely that this defeat undid whatever his father had gained by his victory in Moray. A debatable source claims that Dub was buried on Iona. DEB

Dublin takes its name from the Irish *Duibhlinn*, 'black pool', which may refer to a pool on the river Liffey's tributary, the Poddle. Duibhlinn was an ecclesiastical centre seized by the *Vikings in 841. The city's alternative Irish name, *Áth Cliath*, 'the ford of the hurdles', explains its strategic significance, being one of the region's most important river crossing-points. It quickly became the main Viking military base and trading centre in Ireland and its Hiberno-Norse rulers exercised power over its hinterland (which later developed into County Dublin), though its forces were famously defeated by the *Munster king *Brian Boru at *Clontarf in 1014. Thereafter, Irish rulers established themselves as kings of Dublin and by the time Ireland was invaded by the Anglo-Normans in 1169 Dublin was effectively the country's capital. It fell to Anglo-Norman arms in 1170, was taken by King Henry II into his own hands, and remained the headquarters of the English colony in Ireland, enjoying a period of development and prosperity which continued until the early 14th cent. The subsequent decline lasted well into the 17th cent., considerable growth taking place following the *Restoration in 1660. The 18th cent. was arguably the most colourful era of the city's history, the arts and architecture in particular finding encouragement from the wealthy society of what was now regarded as the second city of the empire. Under the Wide Streets Commissioners (established in 1758), Georgian Dublin flourished and the abolition of its parliament in 1800 did little to lessen the city's expansion. Opposition to the *Union led to the *Easter Rising in the city in 1916 and Dublin featured prominently in the war which led to the establishment of the *Irish Free State in 1921, with Dublin as capital and the home again of an Irish parliament. SD

Dublin (Áth Cliath), **archiepiscopal diocese of.** Originally a Norse city-state, *Dublin was one of the first regular episcopal sees in Ireland subject to *Canterbury. When *Lanfranc claimed primacy of all Britain, he included Ireland and consecrated Patrick, monk of Worcester, as bishop of Dublin (1074). There developed a strong link between Dublin and Canterbury, and 12th-cent. bishops were usually monks from the Canterbury province. Though Dublin was not listed by the Council of Raithbressail (1111), it was to be included in the Glendalough diocese under *Armagh's primacy. Dublin, soon to be the centre of Henry II's colonial administration, became an archbishopric at the Council of Kells-Mellifont (1152), with five dioceses in the south-east of Ireland. Its link with Canterbury was broken. Anglicization came earliest to Dublin and took root there more deeply than elsewhere, so that all five sees of the Dublin province usually had Anglo-French bishops. The archbishopric itself became a reward for administrative service; absenteeism was the inevitable consequence. In 1238 Dublin unsuccessfully challenged the primatial claims of Armagh. It is still the see of both catholic and Anglican archbishops. In 1838 the Anglican province of Dublin absorbed Cashel and is now one of only two Anglican archbishoprics. Uniquely there are two Anglican cathedrals. St Patrick's, the largest in Ireland, is the national cathedral with an Early English interior and massive north-west tower. It holds Dean Jonathan Swift's tomb; the choir was the chapel of the Order of St Patrick (1783–1868). Christ Church is the cathedral for the Dublin diocese. WMM

Dublin, kingdom of. Established by the *Vikings in 841, the kingdom of Dublin survived until the execution of its last Hiberno-Norse king, Asgall Mac Turcaill, by invading Anglo-Normans in 1171. Its earliest rulers may have come from Rogaland in Norway, Olaf the White, famous in Norse tradition, being its first recorded king. In their early years the Dublin Norse faced competition from Vikings of Danish origin, and, although involved in raiding and military alliances in Ireland, much of their attention was devoted to Britain and during the first half of the 10th cent. members of its ruling family were also kings of *York. After the defeat of King *Olaf Cuarán (Sihtricsson) at the battle of Tara in 980 Dublin's kings, now largely integrated into Irish politics and society, came increasingly to feel the domination of the Irish provincial kings, most spectacularly in the defeat of Olaf's son, Sihtric Silkbeard, at the hands of *Brian Boru at *Clontarf in 1014. In 1052 the kingship of Dublin was seized by the *Leinster king, Diarmait mac Maíl na mBó, and from then until the Anglo-Norman invasion Dublin, effectively the country's capital, was largely an appanage claimed by the contenders for the *high kingship of Ireland. SD

Dublin, treaty of, 1646. In the early months of 1646 Charles I's position, militarily and diplomatically, deteriorated sharply. On 28 March 1646 the *Kilkenny Confederates reached an agreement in Dublin with *Ormond, the lord-lieutenant. But when Ormond published the peace terms in July, they were repudiated by the Confederates as giving inadequate recognition to the catholic church. Ormond was accordingly forced to open negotiations with the English Parliament and in June 1647 a parliamentary army reached Dublin. Ormond left for England in July. JAC

Dublin castle. The *Viking town of Dublin was, by the 10th cent., dominated by a fortress which was captured by Anglo-Norman invaders in 1170. In 1204 King John ordered the construction of a castle which was probably located on the site of the earlier fortress. Dublin castle became the administrative headquarters of the English colony in Ireland, housing the main organs of government. Re-edified by Sir Henry *Sidney in 1566–70, and again after a serious fire in 1684, the castle remained a symbol of English power in Ireland until its surrender to the *Irish Free State government on 16 January 1922. SD

Dudley, Dud (1599–1684). The natural son of Edward Sutton de Dudley, the 8th baron. Whilst studying at Balliol College, Oxford, he was appointed by his father to manage the ironworks at Pensnett near Dudley (Worcs.), where the family estates had large reserves of coal and iron ore. He experimented with coal in place of charcoal in the smelting of iron ore. His father secured for him a patent for his process in 1621, renewed in 1638. He demonstrated the quality of his iron for gun-making at the Tower of London. During the Civil War, in 1645, he became the general of ordnance to Prince Maurice, one of the royalist generals. Although sentenced to death in 1648, he survived, but his business had been destroyed in his absence by local ironmasters. In 1665 he published *Metallum Martis* but the commercial viability of a process using coal in place of charcoal for smelting had to await the endeavours of Abraham *Darby in the next century. IJEK

Dudley, Edmund (*c.*1470–1510). Dudley came of Sussex gentry stock and studied law. His first wife was a sister of Andrews, later Lord Windsor, and his second the daughter of Lord Lisle. He was employed with Sir Richard *Empson to raise revenue for Henry VII and was Speaker of the House of Commons in 1504. His work on the king's behalf made him many enemies and at the outset of Henry VIII's reign he was sent to the Tower. He spent his time in prison writing a treatise, *The Tree of Commonwealth*, intended as a handbook for the young king, which argued for a strong monarchy and deplored the deficiencies of aristocratic education. He was executed the following year on an implausible charge of high treason. Dudley's son John, created duke of *Northumberland in 1551, held power during Edward VI's reign, and his grandson Robert was Elizabeth's favourite, the earl of *Leicester. JAC

duelling. The duel, with its formal ritual, developed from trial by combat and its heyday coincided with the period of aristocratic supremacy from the 16th to the 19th cents. The amiable assumption was that the will of God would prevail. The concept of nobility demanded that a warrior would defend his honour, and that of his family, sword in hand. It should be distinguished from private warfare, clan feuds, bloody affrays, or assassinations, and it was a step forward when seconds were limited in numbers, forbidden to take part, but used as witnesses, organizers, and umpires. For obvious reasons, monarchs could not be challenged and had champions to represent them. In practice many monarchs tried to eliminate duelling, which was disruptive, particularly at court or in the armed forces. James I issued an edict forbidding duelling and in 1627 Richelieu in France had Montmorency-Bouteville executed as a grim warning. The change in the 18th cent. from swords to pistols helped to reduce the disadvantage of the novice confronted by an expert. Leading statesmen could expect to be called out. *Pitt fought *Tierney in 1798, *Canning and *Castlereagh exchanged fire in 1809 when both in the same cabinet, and *Wellington and Winchilsea fought in 1829. A peculiarly bloody encounter in 1712 between Lord Mohun, whose aggression bordered on madness, and the duke of Hamilton left both dead. A ludicrous duel, averted in 1782 by the intervention of the Speaker, was between Lord *North, notoriously short-sighted, and Colonel Barré, who had only one eye. It was important to know when to accept challenges as well as when to issue or decline them: the chevalier de Beauvoisis in Stendhal's *Le Rouge et le noir*, mortified to discover that he had fought Julien Sorel, a mere tutor, spread the rumour that his adversary was the natural son of a distinguished nobleman. The decline of the duel in the 19th cent. owed something to the growing concept of the equality of citizens but more to a sense of the duel's unfairness. In Britain duelling came to an end after 1843 when Colonel Fawcett was killed by his brother-in-law Lieutenant Munro, leading the prince consort to insist that the Articles of War be changed to prohibit meetings. Duelling lingered only in the militarized societies of Wilhelmine Germany and tsarist Russia, where a decree as late as 1894 required officers to accept challenges on pain of dismissal. JAC

Duffy, Sir Charles Gavan (1816–1903). Duffy had a strange career. The son of a shopkeeper from Monaghan, he moved to Dublin as a journalist in 1836 and in 1842 launched the *Nation* as the mouthpiece of *Young Ireland. He broke with

*O'Connell in 1846 over the issue of moral force and in 1848 was implicated in the rising. Though put on trial, he was not convicted, and resumed his editorship of the *Nation*, but placing the emphasis on land reform. In 1852 he was elected to Parliament but, despairing of making progress, left for Australia in 1855. There he pursued his second career in Victoria, serving as legislator, minister, and 1871–2 as prime minister. He was knighted in 1873 and acted as Speaker 1876–80. Leaving Australia in that year, he spent most of the remainder of his life in southern Europe. JAC

Dugdale, Sir William (1605–86). Dugdale's father was bursar at St John's College, Oxford, before retiring to Warwickshire. Dugdale married at 18 and spent the rest of his life at Blythe Hall, Shustoke (Warks.), east of Birmingham, devoting himself to history and antiquities. Friends found him a place in the Herald's Office and he became Garter king-at-arms in 1677, and was knighted. A royalist during the civil wars, his property was sequestered and his salary unpaid. In 1655, with Roger Dodsworth, he published the first volume of *Monasticon Anglicanum*, documents relating to the English monasteries. The second and third volumes appeared in 1661 and 1673, and the whole was repeatedly reissued and augmented. In 1656 Dugdale printed his *Antiquities of Warwickshire*, one of the first and greatest of county histories. After the Restoration, Dugdale devoted himself mainly to his heraldic duties, including strict visitations, though he continued to publish important work, particularly the *Baronage*, which came out in 1675 and 1676. In undertakings of this depth, Dugdale relied greatly upon the work of other scholars, not always acknowledged, but a later charge that he was 'that grand plagiary' is ungenerous. He was a fine and dedicated scholar in an age of great scholarship. JAC

duke. The title of duke, derived from the latin 'dux', is the highest in the peerage and until 1448 was restricted to members of the royal family. In that year, Henry VI created William de la *Pole, who had fought in France on many campaigns, duke of Suffolk: he enjoyed the title for less than two years, being murdered in a boat off Dover. Subsequent monarchs were sparing of the title and there were no English non-royal dukes in existence between 1572 and the grant by Charles I to his favourite the duke of *Buckingham in 1623. After the Glorious Revolution, the Whig grandees were promoted to dukedoms in quick succession—Bolton, Shrewsbury, Leeds, Bedford, Devonshire, and Newcastle. George II and III resumed the policy of restraint. Notable 19th-cent. creations included Wellington (1814), Sutherland (1833), and Westminster (1874). The first non-royal Scottish dukedom was Montrose (1488) and the first Irish, Ormond (1661). Along with marquises and earls, dukes are entitled to strawberry leaves on their coronets. The eldest son usually takes the next title and younger sons and daughters are known as Lord Roger or Lady Jane, with the family surname. JAC

Dumfries and Galloway has since 1973 been a local authority region of Scotland comprising the counties of Dumfries, Kirkcudbright, and Wigtown. Till 1996 it shared local government activities with its districts of Annandale and Eskdale, Nithsdale, Stewartry, and Wigtown, but now has sole responsibility. A low-lying, mild, fertile area, agriculture still accounts directly for about 8 per cent of its employment (over five times the Scottish average). The provision and servicing of transport is also a significant industry because proximity to Northern Ireland generates traffic through the port of Stranraer. CML

Dumnonia, kingdom of. After the Roman withdrawal, Cornwall became part of the kingdom of Dumnonia, which also included Devon (the name derived from Dumnonia) and parts of west Somerset. Its domestic history is obscure, though its geographical position enabled it to survive for centuries. Its cultural and religious links were with Wales, Ireland, and Brittany. *Gildas (early 6th cent.) denounced Constantine, 'tyrant whelp of the filthy lioness of Dumnonia', which is fierce but vague. The Britons in Dumnonia were cut off from their allies in south Wales by *Ceawlin's victory at *Dyrham in 577, but since sea-travel was easier than land, the blow may not have been severe. Dumnonia was sufficiently part of the known world for *Aldhelm, bishop of Sherborne, to address a letter, *c.*705, to its king Geraint, putting him right on the date of Easter, and though Geraint was defeated by *Ine of Wessex *c.*710, the kingdom survived. *Egbert of Wessex completed the conquest of the area in 814. Two rebellions, in 825 and 838, were crushed, the second, which had Danish assistance, at *Hingston Down. JAC

Dumnonii. British tribe and *civitas*. The Dumnonii seem to have occupied the whole of the south-west peninsula, and parts of southern Somerset. They issued no coinage, they had no large nucleated settlements which acted as political focuses, and there is no evidence of a dynasty of Dumnonian kings. They were therefore probably a loose confederation of small tribal groups with a common ancestry. They appear to have accepted the Roman conquest without resistance and as a result few garrison forts were placed in their territory. The Romans granted them *civitas* status, and the town of *Exeter (Isca Dumnoniorum) was their administrative centre. KB

Dunbar, battle of, 1296. In 1292 Edward I found in favour of the claim of John *Balliol as king of Scotland. Three years later, relations between the two had broken down and Balliol formed an alliance with France. In the spring of 1296 Edward invaded and captured Berwick. Moving up the coast he laid siege to Dunbar. A relieving army was defeated on 27 April by John de *Warenne and the castle capitulated. Edward then proclaimed himself king of Scotland, called a Scottish Parliament at Berwick, and removed the stone of *Scone to England. JAC

Dunbar, battle of, 1650. Dunbar was *Cromwell's greatest victory, won against severe odds. After the execution of his father, Charles II's hopes rested with his supporters in Scotland, and he arrived there in July 1650. Cromwell followed him three weeks later, advancing up the east coast from Berwick. The royalist army was led by David *Leslie, who had fought alongside Cromwell at *Marston Moor. On 2 September Cromwell's army, weakened by sickness, was bottled up at Dunbar, Leslie, with twice his numbers, having cut off his retreat. Evacuation by sea appeared the wisest move. Cromwell chose to attack the following day and, with very light casualties, destroyed Leslie's force, taking 10,000 prisoners—almost the size of his own army. 'God made them as stubble to our swords,' Cromwell reported to Parliament. JAC

Dunbar, William (*c.*1460–*c.*1520). Widely regarded as the greatest of the late medieval Scottish makars (poets), Dunbar may have been a Franciscan novice and student at St Andrews early in life; but apart from the evidence of his poetry, little is known of the man outside the period 1500–13, when he received an annual pension from James IV, increasing from £10 in 1500 to a generous £80 by 1510.

Dunbar's work covers a vast range—formal court poetry like 'The Thrissell and the Rois' (1503), celebrating the marriage of James IV and *Margaret Tudor; satire, as in his 'Remonstrance to the King' or the lampoons of Damian, alchemist and would-be aviator; and personal meditative poems, above all the grim 'Lament for the Makaris' (1508). Taken as a whole, Dunbar's poetry, embracing heady confidence, complaints about corruption, and bleak despondency, reflects the changing national mood in James IV's Scotland. NATM

Dunblane, diocese of. This see in Perthshire was named after Blane (d. *c.*590), a saint who studied in Ireland and later as bishop preached in Scotland. Dunblane became a bishopric (1162) under David I and the cathedral was built on the site of Blane's monastery. Still with its original 12th-cent. tower, it was largely rebuilt between 1238 and 1258. The roof collapsed at the Reformation and only the choir survives, much restored (1892–1914). Noted for its fine proportions, medieval woodwork, and stained glass, *Ruskin remarked of its west window, 'nothing [is] so perfect in its simplicity and so beautiful'. Robert Leighton (1661–70), whose library of 1,500 volumes was bequeathed to the diocese, was the most celebrated of its bishops. Dunblane is also important for its influential ecumenical centre, Scottish Churches House (1960). The Anglican see was merged with Dunkeld (1776) and with St Andrews (1842). WMM

Duncan I (d. 1040), king of Strathclyde (possibly before 1034) and king of Scotland (1034–40). On the death of *Malcolm II as an old man, the male line of the royal dynasty was extinguished. The vacuum was filled by Duncan, son of Crínán, abbot of Dunkeld (d. 1045), and Bethóc, daughter of Malcolm II. Duncan was possibly already king of *Strathclyde, and may have been appointed by Malcolm II. Far from being Shakespeare's old man, he is likely to have been in his twenties when he died 'at an immature age' according to a contemporary account. He is recorded campaigning both north and south beyond the borders of his kingdom. His prime concern, however, was apparently Northumbria, where he found his wife and where he mounted a disastrous campaign in 1039. This must have weakened him, and gave *Macbeth an opportunity to challenge for the throne. It was Duncan, however, who went on the offensive and led an army into Moray. Battle was joined (probably) at Pitgaveny (2 miles north of Elgin), and Duncan fatally wounded. A debatable source claims he was buried on Iona. DEB

Duncan II (d. 1094), king of Scotland (1094), was the eldest son of *Malcolm III and his first wife, Ingibiorg of Orkney. He was given as a hostage following Malcolm III's submission to William I at Abernethy in 1072, and remained a captive in England until freed and knighted by William II in 1087. William II gave him military backing in a bid to oust his uncle *Donald III from the kingship in 1094. After initial success he was defeated and forced to dismiss his Anglo-Norman supporters. Gravely weakened, he was killed by Mael Petair, *mormaer of the Mearns, at Mondynes (19 miles south of Aberdeen), and his uncle restored to the kingship. Duncan's son William was a key supporter of David I. DEB

Duncan, Adam (1731–1804). Born at Lundie (Dundee), Duncan was a Scot of prodigious strength and height. He entered the merchant service initially, only obtaining his lieutenant's commission when he was 24. A protégé of Keppel, in the Seven Years War Duncan took part in the Belle Île expedition and the successful attack on Havana. In the American War he served under *Rodney at the first relief of Gibraltar 1779 and under *Howe at the second in 1782, attaining the rank of admiral in 1787 when he was 56. Duncan's most celebrated command was in the North Sea in 1797 when, based at Yarmouth, he had to counter the effects upon that command of the *Nore mutiny at a time when the hostile Dutch fleet might put to sea. At one moment he had only two ships with which to watch the Texel, the companies of both his flagship *Venerable* and the *Adamant* being restive. His subsequent defeat of the Dutch off *Camperdown was testimony to the North Sea squadron's fundamental patriotism but, even more, to Duncan's resource and unsurpassed qualities of humane leadership. He was created Viscount Duncan of Camperdown; an earldom was conferred on his heir 30 years after his death. DDA

Dundalk, battle of, 1318. Edward *Bruce's short-lived kingdom of Ireland came to an end in October 1318 when he was defeated and killed at Dundalk by an Anglo-Irish army under John de Bermingham. The victor was created earl of Louth by Edward II. JAC

Dundas, Henry, 1st Viscount Melville (1742–1811). Scottish politician, son of Robert, Lord Arniston, president of the Court of Session. Dundas followed his family tradition by taking up the law, and in 1766 was appointed solicitor-general for Scotland. He was MP for Midlothian 1774–90 and for Edinburgh 1790–1802 when he was created Viscount Melville. A burly figure and a vigorous and forthright speaker with a broad Scots accent, he was appointed to a series of legal and political offices. He became successively lord advocate [S] 1775, joint keeper of the signet [S] 1777, privy counsellor, treasurer of the navy 1782–3 and 1784–1800, home secretary 1791–4, president of the India Board of Control 1793–1801, secretary of state for war 1794–1801, keeper of the privy seal of Scotland 1800, and 1st lord of the Admiralty 1804–5. The list alone testifies to his indispensable value to *Pitt, and Dundas became his right-hand man in the wartime administration as well as his friend and drinking companion. His influence extended far beyond his official duties, for after 1774 he acted as government manager of Scottish affairs and in particular of Scottish elections and MPs. A cynical politician who believed in the power of patronage, he knew almost everyone of importance in Scotland and how to appeal to their self-interest. He was nicknamed 'Henry the ninth of Scotland'. At the height of his influence he secured the return of at least 36 of the 45 Scottish representatives in the Commons and several in the Lords, though it was a moot point whether these men were attached to the administration or to Dundas personally. He kept his grip on Scottish elections even in opposition to the *'Talents' ministry and after his retirement his nephew continued to exercise control of the majority of Scottish members until the Reform Act.

Dundas's success owed much to his command of Indian patronage as president of the Board of Control, which enabled him to bestow lucrative appointments on his Scottish clients. It was said that he sent younger sons 'by loads to the East Indies' and that there was scarcely a family of note in Scotland that was not under some obligation to him.

Dundas resigned with Pitt in 1801 but offered support to *Addington and was given his peerage in 1802. On Pitt's return in 1804 he became 1st lord of the Admiralty but was forced to resign when an inquiry into financial irregularities in the navy pay office implicated him. He was impeached in 1806—the last occasion on which this process was used—and although acquitted was censured for laxity in his financial control. He attended the Lords only occasionally thereafter. EAS

Dundee. Situated on the Firth of Tay, east Scotland, and already a thriving centre with trading connections throughout northern Europe when granted burghal status *c.*1191, Dundee prospered through textiles, guns, and its role as an entrepôt port until the mid-17th cent., despite intermittent assaults by the English. Recovery after *Monck's sack was slow until it became the base for one of Scotland's largest whaling fleets and expanded its textile activities to become 'Juteopolis'. Past renown for shipbuilding, 'jute, jam, and journalism' has yielded to economic and social insecurity, from which it continues to endeavour to emerge. ASH

Dundee, John Graham, 1st Viscount [S] (1648–89). John Graham of Claverhouse was heir to a small estate 10 miles from Dundee. He was educated at the University of St Andrews, and in the 1670s served in the Dutch and French armies. He next accepted a commission in the Scots cavalry. A conservative royalist and episcopalian, he made a career in internal security duties against presbyterian radicals. Politically, he allied with the Drummond brothers and with James, duke of York (later James II). After 1685 the Drummonds ruled Scotland for James, and Claverhouse was made provost of Dundee and a viscount.

After the Glorious Revolution, he rebelled against the provisional government of Scotland in 1689. He could only raise a small army, mainly Highlanders, but his Williamite opponent, the Highlander General Hugh Mackay of Scourie, had few seasoned troops and was routed at *Killiecrankie in Strathtay. Dundee died in the battle. His army failed to break into the Lowlands and disintegrated after defeat. BPL

Dunes, battle of the, 1658. On 14 June Turenne, commanding the French forces with the help of an English contingent under Sir William Lockhart, attacked a Spanish army defending Dunkirk. The Spaniards, under Don John and Condé, were badly beaten, losing 4,000 prisoners. James, duke of York, the future James II, fought on the Spanish side. Dunkirk surrendered soon after and was handed over to the English. JAC

Dunfermline abbey (Fife). On the foundations of a pre-Conquest Celtic church and a small Roman church built by *Malcolm III for Queen *Margaret (*c.*1072), a Benedictine monastery church was erected by David I, dedicated to the Holy Trinity (1150). The burial place of royalty during the 11th–15th cents., its high connections and central position made it one of the richest and most influential abbeys in Scotland, used for meetings of the Scottish Parliament, election of bishops, and even, briefly, as an ecclesiastical prison. Lands and churches were given by royal charter, but although it had 'mitred' abbots as had Aberbrothock, Dunfermline was held increasingly *in commendam* after 1500. By the Reformation considerable land and revenue had already passed into private hands, much to *Knox's anger. After 1587 all remaining properties and revenues were annexed to the crown, with James VI granting it to his bride, Anne of Denmark. The ample monastery guest-house was enlarged as an occasional residence for royalty, and was the birthplace of Charles I (1600). The nave survived despoliation to serve as the parish church until 1821, when a new one was erected over the foundations of the Benedictine choir. ASH

Dungan Hill, battle of, 1647. Michael Jones, sent back to Ireland by a victorious Parliament in 1646 to re-establish English rule, won his first success on 8 August 1647, when an attempt by Thomas Preston to reach Dublin was stopped at Dungan Hill, near Trim, with heavy loss. JAC

Dungeness, battle of, 1652. A sharp naval action during the first *Anglo-Dutch War. Tromp, on convoy duty in the channel, attacked *Blake off Dungeness on 30 November. Blake was obliged to break off the encounter with some losses and the Dutch convoys went through unscathed. JAC

Dunkeld, battle of, 1689. The death of their leader *Dundee deprived the Jacobites of much of the advantage they had gained by the victory at *Killiecrankie in July 1689. Mackay, leading the Williamite forces, was able to regroup. On 21 August, the Jacobites attacked a small force under *Cleland at Dunkeld. Though Cleland was killed in action, his men repulsed the attack with such vigour that the Jacobite force was routed. JAC

Dunkeld, diocese of. The first monastery at Dunkeld ('fort of the Celts') may have been founded by St *Columba. *Kenneth I MacAlpin made it his capital jointly with Scone. The see was revived by *Alexander I (1107–24), a devout son of the church, ruling jointly with his brother

David I (1107–53), who may have founded the cathedral (1127) on the site of the monastery, but a new one was built between 1312 and 1464 in Norman and Gothic styles. It was drastically damaged at the Reformation and again after the battle of *Killiecrankie (1689) when the *Cameronians held out there against the Highlanders. Repairs were carried out in 1691, 1762, 1803, and a full restoration in 1908. The choir, now the Church of Scotland parish church, and ruined nave occupy an idyllic setting near the river Tay. The Anglican see was merged with St Andrews (1842). WMM

Dunkirk. North-eastern French port, whence, and from neighbouring beaches, 27 May to 4 June 1940, 200,000 British troops were brought back to England. On 10 May 1940 German troops attacked the Netherlands, Belgium, Luxembourg, and France. French and British troops moved north to join the Belgian army in resisting the main German attack which they expected to develop north of Namur; instead it came further south on the river Meuse below Sedan. On 20 May German mobile units reached the English Channel, splitting the allied forces. On 25 May Gort, commanding the British Expeditionary Force, deciding that Belgian retreats might expose his rear, gave up attempts to cut the German corridor to the sea, and ordered British retreat to the coast. On 26 May the British government ordered evacuation. French troops, hoping to maintain a bridgehead for counter-attack, played the main role in enabling the British to depart. Coincidentally, the British war cabinet discussed whether Britain could fight on alone. Churchill's view that Britain could and should continue the war against Germany, whatever happened to France, was reinforced by a promising start to the Dunkirk evacuation. Its success, in spite of German confidence that it was impossible, made more difficult any German invasion of England that summer, by increasing the size of the force the German army would need to land. The drama of the evacuation, including the part played by small civilian pleasure boats, raised British morale. RACP

Dunlop, John Boyd (1840–1921). Inventor. Dunlop was a vet from Ayrshire, who moved to Belfast and established a good practice. In 1887 he fixed air tubes to his son's tricycle and the production of tricycles with pneumatic tyres began in 1889. In 1892 he moved to Dublin but the development of his patent, which revolutionized cycling and greatly assisted motor transport, was left largely to others. The Dunlop Rubber Company became one of the industrial giants of the 20th cent. A patent similar to Dunlop's had been claimed in 1846: the key to Dunlop's extraordinary and rapid success was the use of rubber and the fact that cheap mass transport was urgently needed. JAC

Dunnichen Moor, battle of. See NECHTANSMERE.

Dunning's motion. On 6 April 1780 John Dunning carried by 233 votes to 215, in the face of Lord *North's anxious protests, a motion that the influence of the crown had increased, was increasing, and ought to be diminished. This was the high spot of the opposition's campaign for *economical reform. But the *Gordon riots of June 1780 gave North's administration a reprieve. JAC

Duns Scotus, John (*c*.1265–1308). Little is known for certain of Duns Scotus' life. He is said to have been a Franciscan, born at Duns in Berwickshire, and to have studied at Oxford and Paris. His burial was at Cologne. He wrote extensively on grammar, logic, philosophy, and theology. He was concerned primarily with the nature and attributes of God, but distinguished between faith (theology) and reason (philosophy). If his concerns and parameters were still essentially medieval, his methodology was modern. Duns Scotus was greatly admired for the rigour of his thinking, yet, when medieval scholastic philosophy fell into disfavour in the 16th cent. as idle speculation, his name was borrowed to coin the word 'dunce'. JAC

Dunstable, John (*c*.1390–1453). Foremost English composer of the 15th cent., whose music circulated widely at a time when English music was extremely influential on the continent. The contemporary French poet Martin le Franc claimed that Dufay and Binchois had taken from him the new consonant English style (*contenance Angloise*). Very little is known about Dunstable's life and career, although there is evidence that he served John, duke of *Bedford, regent in France and brother of Henry V, and *Joan, dowager queen of Henry IV. By 1438 he seems to have returned to England to serve Humphrey, duke of *Gloucester; two of his motets show links with the abbey of St Albans. Although the attribution of many pieces is uncertain, nearly half his output comprises movements for the ordinary of the mass, including two cyclic settings. The best known of his eleven surviving isorhythmic motets is the four-part *Veni sancte spiritus*, which is typical in its structural principle of progressive diminution in the ratio 3 : 2 : 1. ECr

Dunstan, St (*c*.909–88). Dunstan was born into an aristocratic family related to the royal house of Wessex. His early career owed much to family and royal patronage with special support from King *Edmund, who appointed him abbot of Glastonbury *c*.943, from King *Edred, to whom he became a close adviser, and from his uncle Ælfheah, bishop of Winchester (934–51). Exiled briefly by King *Eadwig to Ghent and Fleury where he came into contact with advanced Cluniac ideas on monastic reform, he returned as Eadwig's half-brother *Edgar took control and was quickly made bishop of Worcester (957), of London (959), and finally archbishop of Canterbury (959–88). Both at Glastonbury and as archbishop Dunstan played a dominant part in the affairs of the English church and state at a critical moment. From his Glastonbury base he was largely instrumental in the introduction of reformed *Benedictine observance into England and for the training and support of prominent figures within the movement, notably *Æthelwold, bishop of Winchester (963–84) and *Oswald, bishop of Worcester (961–92), who was also archbishop of York from 972. As archbishop, Dunstan was immensely influential in secular and ecclesiastical affairs during the reign of Edgar (959–75), in a dominant position to ensure the success of the Benedictine reform and to see to the establishment of monk-bishops so that its influence was felt throughout the English church. At a council held at Winchester in 970 or shortly afterwards, a version of the Benedictine rule, the *Regularis* *concordia*, was drawn up for English usage, placing prominence on royal support for the monks. Æthelwold was responsible for the writing of the *Regularis*, but Dunstan was the inspiration behind it. In 973 he established the *Ordo* for Edgar's coronation at Bath, which remained the basis for English coronation ritual. After Edgar's death Dunstan (possibly because of his age) seemed to fade into the background, but his reputation remained high. Early 'lives' record many personal details, his skill at music and metalwork and miracles of healing (including cures for blindness). Popular opinion quickly accorded him sainthood with a commemorative day on 19 May. In medieval art, the tongs with which he was reputed to have tweaked the nose of the devil were taken as his symbol. HL

Dunwich, diocese of. Felix from Luxueil in Burgundy converted the East Angles in the 630s and established his episcopal seat at Dunwich, then a thriving port on the Suffolk coast. He died in 647. In *c.*673 *Theodore divided the see into two, placing Norfolk under the see of *Elmham. After the Danish invasions in the 9th cent. Dunwich ceased to be active and was not revived. WMM

Dupplin Moor, battle of, 1332. Edward *Balliol, supported by Edward III, claimed the throne of Scotland after the death of Robert I Bruce. On 11 August 1332 he was victorious at Dupplin Moor, on the river Earn outside Perth, over a much larger force led by Donald, earl of *Mar, regent for the young David II. Mar was killed and Balliol was crowned at Scone the following month. JAC

Durham was one of the last shires to be fully incorporated into the English political and legal system, because for centuries it was a *palatinate under the jurisdiction of the bishop. It did not receive parliamentary representation until as late as the 17th cent. But *Cromwell gave it representation in the 1650s and in this rare instance royalists after the Restoration were willing to build with Cromwell's bricks. The county sent two knights to Westminster in 1675 and the city of Durham two burgesses in 1678.

Geographically the county is of two halves and three rivers. The western half is hilly, running up into the Pennines, the eastern half flat with a harsh and somewhat unattractive coastline. It has always been mining country, with iron and lead in the hills and coal in the coastal plain. The northern boundary, dividing it from Northumberland, is the river Tyne and its tributary the Derwent; the southern is the Tees, flowing through Barnard Castle and separating the county from Westmorland and Yorkshire; through the middle flows the Wear, from Bishop Auckland to Durham, and on through Chester-le-Street to Sunderland.

In Roman times the area formed part of the territory of the *Brigantes. After the Saxon occupation, it was part of *Bernicia, the northern half of the great kingdom of *Northumbria. The county owed its distinctiveness and preeminence largely to one man, St *Cuthbert. *Camden noted in the 16th cent. that the shire was often referred to as the Land of St Cuthbert or his patrimony. Cuthbert died in 687 on the Farne Islands and was first buried on Holy Island or *Lindisfarne, of which he had been bishop. In 875 the monks were forced by Viking raids to abandon the place and, taking Cuthbert's coffin with them, established themselves at *Chester-le-Street, which in turn became a bishopric. In 995, in the face of further raids, they fled once more, taking the remains first to Ripon, then to Durham, where it has remained. There it attracted the great wealth on which the power of the later bishops depended. The name—Dunholm, the island on the hill—reflected the nature of the place, a rocky promontory, almost completely surrounded by a loop of the river Wear, and offering an almost ideal defensive position.

The region was not included in the *Domesday survey and offered fierce resistance to the *Norman Conquest. When finally it was subdued, the bishop was given palatinate powers, partly to deal with the local population, partly to resist Scottish incursions. The castle at Durham was begun by William in 1072, blocking the neck of the peninsula: the great cathedral, replacing an earlier 10th-cent. one, was started in 1093.

The palatinate powers exercised by the bishops were formidable. They included full ownership of land; the right to levy taxes; the power to raise troops; full jurisdiction, including capital offences, together with the power of pardon; the claim on property of traitors and outlaws. Such sweeping powers led to repeated clashes. Anthony *Bek, one of the most powerful of the 'prince-bishops', was at odds with Edward I over military obligations against the Scots and with the archbishop of York over ecclesiastical jurisdiction. But by an Act of 1536 in the reign of Henry VIII, the legal powers were removed, and the remaining palatinate privileges were suppressed in 1836 during the episcopate of van Mildert.

Although the coal measures had been worked since the 13th cent., Durham remained thinly populated. Some of the market towns and ports had a local prosperity but none, with the exception of Durham, was given representation in Parliament. Defoe visited the county in the 1720s and was not greatly impressed: Darlington had 'nothing remarkable but dirt', and Chester-le-Street was 'an old dirty, thoroughfare town'. At the first census in 1801, the population was still only 149,000. But the industrial, mining, and shipbuilding developments of the 19th cent. acted as a magnet, and by 1891 the county had well over 1 million people. Though 21st county in size, it was 7th in population. Darlington had grown from a town of 5,000 to 36,000; Gateshead from 8,000 to 85,000; Hartlepool from 1,000 to 15,000; South Shields from 8,000 to 97,000; Stockton from 4,000 to 51,000; and Sunderland, which established itself as a major industrial centre of shipbuilding, pottery, and glass, from 12,000 to 156,000.

The need to find cheaper ways of carrying coal made Durham the birthplace of railways. Well before the 19th cent., the county was networked with rail tracks, usually using wooden rails and horses. The Causey Arch, near Stanley, built by the 'grand alliance' of coal-owners in 1727 to carry their plate-way over a deep ravine, has a claim to be the first railway viaduct. The Stockton and Darlington railway, laid out by George *Stephenson, which opened in 1825 was the first to convey public freight, with passengers an afterthought. Timothy Hackworth's locomotive works at

Shildon opened in 1833 and Stephenson's Locomotion No. 1 is preserved at Darlington. The Brandling Junction Railway between Sunderland and Gateshead opened in 1839 and the main NER line from Darlington to Gateshead via Penshaw and Washington was opened in 1844, with a branch to Durham.

Nineteenth-cent. prosperity was not maintained and the collapse of shipbuilding, mining, and the steel industry led to massive unemployment. The industrial base of the county has diversified, with chemicals at Billingham, car manufacture at Sunderland, and light industry in the Team valley south of Newcastle. In the 1990s the new universities of Northumbria and Sunderland joined the 19th-cent. establishments of Durham and Newcastle upon Tyne.

The county lost areas in the north to Tyne and Wear and in the south-east to Cleveland under the Local Government Act of 1972. In its report of December 1994 the Banham commission proposed that Darlington should be made a unitary authority but that the two-tier system should remain for the rest of the county. JAC

Durham, city of. Though small, Durham is one of the great cities of Britain. It is best seen from the 1857 railway viaduct to the west of the town, which looks down on the great loop of the river Wear, which offered a fine defensive position, and across to the cathedral to the south and the castle to the north on the rocky promontory. The first settlement was probably at Elvet, east of the peninsula, where Pehtwine was consecrated bishop of Whithorn in *c.*762: the church is dedicated to St *Oswald (d. 642), suggesting a 7th- or 8th-cent. foundation. But the arrival of the remains of St *Cuthbert in 995 drew pilgrims to the spot and the diocese was transferred from *Chester-le-Street. A new church was begun at once and Durham seems to have been visited by *Cnut in the early 11th cent. After the Norman Conquest, building of the castle was ordered by William I in 1072 and the foundation stone of the cathedral laid by *William of St Carilef in 1093. The congested peninsula may have prevented much expansion and *Leland commented in the 1530s that 'the town itself within the peninsula is but a small thing'. But it developed into an important regional capital and administrative centre. Many of the houses in the north and south bailey were built or refaced in the 18th cent., and Prebends' bridge dates from the 1770s. The university, after several false starts, was founded in 1832, occupies the castle, and has its administrative headquarters at Old Shire Hall in Elvet. JAC

Durham, diocese of. The bishopric, conterminous with the old county of Durham, was created in 995, when *Aldhelm moved the Northumbrian see there from *Chester-le-Street. The consequent translation of St *Cuthbert's bones to Durham benefited the new see spiritually and financially; no other northern bishopric could compete, so that even the principal see of *Hexham fell into insignificance. Durham initially was not Benedictine, but *William of St Carilef (1081–96), himself a scholarly monk and former abbot of St Vincent, introduced monks on the lines of Canterbury. The Norman kings raised Durham to a palatine earldom as a protection against the Scots and Vikings, with the bishop as earl. *Ranulf Flambard (1099–1128) was William II's adviser. Flambard's notorious reputation amongst contemporaries for rapaciousness led to the see being taken under Henry I's protection for a time. Nevertheless Flambard built the greater part of the cathedral. The prince-bishops of the Middle Ages were people of influence in both church and state, a fact symbolized by the juxtaposition of the massive features of the cathedral and castle. Bishops retained their civil jurisdiction until abolished by the Established Church Act of 1836. Today the bishops of Durham still hold seniority, with London and Winchester, second only to the archbishops of Canterbury and York. In recent centuries bishops have often been scholars of note, including Joseph *Butler (1750–2), the philosopher and theologian, Joseph Lightfoot (1879–89), a leading exponent of New Testament scholarship, and B. F. Westcott (1890–1901). In the 20th cent. H. C. G. Moule (1901–20), Hensley Henson (1920–39), Michael *Ramsey (1952–6), Ian Ramsey (1966–73), John Habgood (1973–84), and David Jenkins (1984–94) have maintained this remarkable tradition of scholarship. The original Anglo-Saxon cathedral of 995 was replaced by the present magnificent Norman cathedral, 'the most impressively situated of the English cathedrals', begun in the Benedictine tradition by Bishop William in 1093 and completed in 1133. High on its rock alongside the castle, it was begun under William I. The cathedral's ribbed cross-vaulting (1104), previously common in Persia and Armenia, was the first seen in the West, probably due to the influence of returning crusaders. The tombs of Cuthbert and *Bede are in the galilee chapel. The bishops live at the historic Bishop Auckland castle. WMM

Durham, John Lambton, 1st earl of (1792–1840). A wealthy Durham landowner and coal-owner, Lambton became one of the county's MPs from 1813, advocating reforms and acquiring the nickname 'Radical Jack'. He was created Baron Durham in 1828. When his father-in-law *Grey became premier in 1830, Durham joined the cabinet and the small committee which drafted the ministry's parliamentary reforms. He was promoted earl of Durham in 1834, when he resigned on grounds of ill-health. While out of office, he campaigned for further reforms, including vote by ballot, household suffrage, and triennial parliaments, embarrassing the Whig ministers. From 1835 to 1837 he was ambassador to Russia. After a rebellion in Canada in 1838, he was sent there on a special mission and produced the *Durham Report, leading to the reorganization of British North America and contributing to the evolution of imperial constitutional conventions. His mission ended in controversy, partly because of his own high-handed conduct. Although talented, he was always a difficult colleague, proud, tactless, short-tempered, and easily offended. NMcC

Durham, treaties of, 1136, 1139. In the struggle between Stephen and Matilda for the throne of England, David I of Scotland supported the latter, his niece. He occupied Northumberland but reached a settlement at Durham with Stephen in 1136 whereby his son Henry did homage for the earldom of Huntingdon. The agreement soon broke down but, despite a sharp defeat in 1138 at the battle of the *Standard, David negotiated similar terms in 1139, retaining Northumberland, save for Newcastle and Bamburgh.

JAC

Durham Report. John Lambton, earl of *Durham, was appointed governor-in-chief of Canada in January 1838 following rebellions in Canada. A dispute with *Melbourne's government quickly ended the mission and Durham prepared an extensive *Report on the Affairs of British North America*, which was leaked to *The Times* in February 1839. He recommended the union of Upper and Lower Canada (now Ontario and Quebec) with local self-government. Durham's *Report* had limited influence at the time, but was hailed by late 19th-cent. enthusiasts as the Magna Carta of the empire. Durham's belief that French-Canadians should be encouraged to speak English remains controversial in Quebec.

GM

Durotriges. British tribe and *civitas*. Centred in Dorset but also occupying the southern parts of Wiltshire and Somerset, the Durotriges seem to have been a loosely knit confederation of small tribal groups or septs at the time of the Roman conquest. Their coinage carries the names of no kings, and there were many occupied hill-forts which were probably the strongholds of locally dominant chieftains. The best known of these is *Maiden castle near Dorchester. In addition, on the south-eastern corner of their territory, they appear to have possessed a major trading centre at Hengistbury Head from which cross-channel trade with Gaul was controlled. This may be the settlement called Dunium by Ptolemy. At the time of the Roman invasion the Durotriges put up spirited if unsuccessful opposition and they were almost certainly one of the two tribes which Suetonius records fighting against *Vespasian and the IInd legion. Archaeological evidence from Maiden castle, Spettisbury Rings, and Hod Hill confirms the Roman assault on Durotrigan hill-forts. Ironically, it was the Emperor Vespasian who created the *civitas* of the Durotriges, with their capital at Durnovaria (Dorchester) in the mid-70s. Later a second Durotrigan *civitas* was created, administered from Lindinis (Ilchester).

KB

Dussindale, battle of, 1549. *Kett's rebellion in Norfolk in 1549 posed a formidable threat to the government of Protector Somerset, since it coincided with widespread disorders in the west country. One relief force under William *Parr, Lord Northampton was driven out of Norwich and Lord Sheffield killed. In August Lord Warwick (*Northumberland) was dispatched with a sizeable force, stiffened by German mercenaries. Warwick avoided being trapped in the alleyways of the city and attacked on 27 August just outside the walls. After heavy fighting and a successful cavalry charge against the rebels, Warwick offered pardon, which most of the peasants accepted.

JAC

Dyfed. County of south-west Wales, extant between 1974 and 1996. The name given to the new county under the Local Government Act of 1972 was derived from that of the post-Roman kingdom which was derived from the tribal territory of the *Demetae. Unlike other Welsh kingdoms there is evidence of a strong Irish influence, attested by a memorial stone at Castell Dwyrain to a possible early ruler Voteporix. The kingdom subsequently became part of the kingdom of *Deheubarth. Norman occupation transformed the area into a series of lordships.

At the statute of *Rhuddlan in 1284, the county of *Cardiganshire was created, and by the Act of *Union with England in 1536, *Pembrokeshire and *Carmarthenshire. It was not until 1972 that these were united as a new county and given the name Dyfed. The Local Government Commission argued that there was a common historical tradition and a 'unity of interest both social and economic, which rests on a geographical basis'. But though there was a tradition of unity, it had been greatly changed by the industrialization of the south-east, and intercommunication was poor. The county had little in the way of contemporary common interest and 400 years had created different loyalties. There was strong identification with the old counties, especially in Pembrokeshire, but little with Dyfed. In April 1996 authority reverted to the former three counties and Dyfed as a formal administrative area ceased to exist.

HC

Dyfed (Demetia)**, kingdom of.** The land of the *Demetae people at the time of the Roman invasions. Throughout its history, this fertile region of south-west Wales has absorbed external influences—Irish, English, Norman, and Flemish—and changed its ethnic character. The kingdom may have been founded by Irish immigrants, the Deisi, in post-Roman times; its royal dynasty lasted until Llywarch ap Hyfaidd's death (904), when his daughter's husband *Hywel Dda, son of the king of neighbouring *Seisyllwg, succeeded; Dyfed then became part of the larger *Deheubarth. Norman raiders arrived from the north-east in 1073–4, and ten years later Pembroke's fortress was built; thereafter, Dyfed was gradually replaced by several marcher lordships. The memory of Dyfed survived, not least in the Welsh prose tales, the *Mabinogi*, which were published in English translation in the 19th cent.

RAG

Dyrham, battle of, 577. The *Anglo-Saxon Chronicle*, with remarkable detail, recorded that at Dyrham, east of Bristol, *Ceawlin, king of Wessex, defeated and killed three British kings, and went on to occupy Bath, Cirencester, and Gloucester. There is little doubt that this was a major victory in the Saxon advance, cutting off the Britons in Wales from those in the south-west, even if Ceawlin was unable to hold all the territory gained.

JAC

Eadgyth (*c.*1022–75), queen of *Edward the Confessor. Eadgyth was the eldest daughter of Earl *Godwine, the most powerful nobleman of his day, and sister of *Harold II. She married Edward in 1045 soon after his succession. There were rumours that the marriage was never consummated and certainly there were no children. She was disgraced with her family in 1051 but restored the following year. Eadgyth seems to have favoured her brother *Tostig against Harold and, after his death at *Stamford Bridge, transferred her support to William of Normandy. She spent the rest of her life in retirement at Winchester, which she held as part of her marriage settlement. JAC

Eadgyth, known as 'Swanneshals' ('Swan-neck'). Mistress of Harold II, Eadgyth probably bore all his children except his posthumous, legitimate son. After Harold was slain, she was given the task of finding his body and delivering it to William the Conqueror for burial. Eadgyth was the likely benefactress of St Benet's abbey, granted Thurgarten in her native Norfolk. AM

Eadwig (d. 959), king of England (955–9). The elder son of King *Edmund, Eadwig succeeded at the age of about 15 on the death of his uncle *Edred. A desire to move away from those who had been influential in the reigns of his father and uncle may explain the confiscation of his grandmother's property, the exile of Abbot *Dunstan, and the retirement to a monastery of senior ealdorman Æthelstan 'Half-King', all in 956. Rivalry at court may also explain opposition to his marriage to Ælfgifu, his third cousin once removed, and their separation in 958 on the grounds of consanguinity. The succession in 957 of his younger brother as king of the Mercians and Northumbrians has been interpreted as revolt against Eadwig's rule, but contemporary sources suggest it was a peaceful, planned event with *Edgar recognizing Eadwig's overriding authority. Ælfgifu's brother Æthelweard in his *Chronicon* says Eadwig was known as 'All-Fair' and that he 'deserved to be loved'. BAEY

Ealdgyth, wife of Harold II. She was daughter of the Mercian earl Ælfgar, and previously married to the Welsh king *Gruffydd, defeated by Harold in 1063, slain by his own men. Harold probably married her to ensure the allegiance of her brothers, the earls of Mercia and Northumbria. Ealdgyth bore him a son after his death. AM

ealdorman in early usage could indicate a patriarch, prince, or ruler. This should nuance the impact of the term in the laws of King *Ine, *c.*700, where the ealdorman appears as a functionary, in charge of a *scir* (shire) and subject to dismissal. In another context such men would probably appear as *subreguli* (under-kings). The shires concerned may already have been the historic shires of Wessex, which the **Anglo-Saxon Chronicle*'s account of the *Vikings showed to have been in existence by the 9th cent., the forces of each led by an ealdorman. A grander usage of the term is its application to King *Alfred's son-in-law, *Æthelred, ealdorman of the Mercians. He was almost a king. In the 10th cent. shire ealdormen disappear. The term is then applied to such great men as Athelstan 'half-king', ealdorman of much of eastern England. From the early 11th cent. the Scandinavian term *'earl' is used for such potentates. But the general sense of 'ealdorman' as indicative of authority gave the term lasting life, in particular in towns. JCa

Ealdred (d. 1069) was a political churchman. Starting as a monk at Winchester, he became successively abbot of Tavistock, bishop of Worcester, and, finally, in 1060 archbishop of York. As bishop of Worcester he took an active role in resisting Welsh encroachments. *Edward the Confessor used him on diplomatic missions to Rome and to the emperor, and in 1058 he made a pilgrimage to Jerusalem. His wish to hold the bishopric of Worcester *in commendam* with the archbishopric of York led to difficulties with the papacy. Ealdred was an active church-builder and tried to improve clerical discipline. He may have crowned *Harold Godwineson and certainly crowned William the Conqueror. He died at York in September 1069 just before the city was burned and devastated by a large Danish raid. JAC

Eardwulf (d. *c.*810), king of Northumbria (796–*c.*810). Before his accession Eardwulf was an *ealdorman and it is not known whether he was of royal descent. He became king at a particularly disturbed period in Northumbrian politics and within four years of his accession had defeated an attempted coup and had two rivals murdered. He attacked *Cenwulf of Mercia in 801 for harbouring his enemies. In 806 or 808 he was forced into exile, but soon returned with help provided by the Frankish king Charles the Great; however, not long afterwards he was succeeded by his son Eanred. Subsequently Eardwulf was venerated as St Hardulf and his remains housed at the Mercian monastery of Breedon-on-the-Hill. His claim to sanctity apparently related to an event in 791 where he was left for dead outside the monastery of Ripon on the orders of King *Æthelred, but made what was regarded as a miraculous recovery. BAEY

earls. Though earl is the oldest peerage title, it has been overtaken by duke and marquis, to which it now ranks third. In early Saxon England it was merely the general name for noble. Administrative responsibility in shires belonged to *ealdormen, particularly charged with leading the shire levies into battle. But the name earl gradually merged with the Danish jarl and, after the reign of *Alfred, earls took over the responsibilities of ealdormen. But since they had responsibility for several shires or provinces, shire administration passed increasingly to the shire reeve. After the Conquest, earldoms tended to become hereditary and, as a consequence, their governmental responsibilities also fell to the sheriff. March earldoms, like Chester and Shrewsbury, retained considerable *palatine powers. In the course of time the connection with a specific county, where the earl had his main estates, grew weaker: the earls of Derby were for centuries strong in Lancashire while the earls of Devonshire were strong in Derbyshire. In the reign of Henry I there were only eight earldoms, but Stephen and Matilda, in their rivalry, created many of their supporters earls. Since the titles of dukes and marquises were restricted, earldoms became, in practice, the senior title. The children of earls are in a curious intermediate position, however. The eldest son normally takes as his courtesy title the family viscountcy. Daughters are treated as duke's daughters and are known as Lady Susan ——; but younger sons are merely known as the Hon. Anthony ——. JAC

Earls Barton. The tower of this Northamptonshire church is one of the best known examples of Late Saxon architecture. There are four pre-Norman stages, separated by string-courses. Each is elaborately decorated with strip-work and long-and-short quoining which all project boldly beyond the plastered face of the tower. There is currently a lively debate as to whether this type of strip-work is primarily decorative or structural in function; what cannot be denied is that the appearance of the tower reflects that of a timber-framed structure and that many of the components appear to have been prefabricated. RNB

Early English architecture. See GOTHIC ARCHITECTURE.

East Anglia, kingdom of. Anglo-Saxon migrants, possibly with some Frisian elements, settled early in East Anglia in the late 5th and early 6th cents. Its difficult western boundary in the Fens ensured a degree of independence and the East Angles preserved in what became the two shires of *Norfolk and *Suffolk their own social and agrarian customs deep into the Middle Ages. Their ruling dynasty, the Wuffingas, appears to have had some affinity with Sweden. The greatest of their early rulers, *Rædwald, who died *c.*625, was probably the king commemorated in the ship-burial at *Sutton Hoo. He had been baptized a Christian, though he still followed pagan practices, and it was not until the generation after his death that the East Angles were converted. Bishoprics were set up at *Dunwich (until the Danish invasions, 870) and at North *Elmham. In the 8th cent. the East Angles fell increasingly under Mercian control, and their young king Æthelbert was murdered on a visit to *Offa's court, a particularly brutal and treacherous act which prompted Offa to penitence, payment to Rome, and the foundation of St Albans abbey. East Anglia played an important part in events that led to the emergence of Wessex against Mercia as the dominant power in England in 825 and 829, but bore the main brunt of the Danish invasions later in the century. Its last king, St *Edmund, was martyred in November 870, and for a period East Anglia was governed by Scandinavian kings, notably by *Guthrum (870–80). On its recovery by *Edward the Elder and *Athelstan, East Anglia was absorbed into the shire system of what was to become a united England, and governed by *ealdormen. HL

Easter—the uniquely English word is derived from the Teutonic goddess Eostre—is the primary Christian feast celebrating Christ's resurrection, an ever-present event to believing Christians. Originally however *pascha*, the Greek form of the Hebrew *pesach* (Jewish passover), signified the Christian equivalent, the redemption or delivery from bondage. Until the 2nd cent. it celebrated the whole redemption event, Christ's passion and resurrection, not just resurrection. Its dating has always presented a problem. While the gentile church, stressing the resurrection element, celebrated it on a Sunday (Resurrection Day), the province of Asia followed the Jewish Passover date in the lunar calendar (Nisan 14). They were tolerated until the Council of Nicaea (325) when Easter was settled as the Sunday following the first full moon after the vernal equinox. Another revision (6th cent.) caused divergence between the remote Celtic church and Rome, thus creating bitter animosity when the 6th/7th-cent. Roman missionaries arrived in Britain. This was resolved at the Synod of *Whitby (664). The eastern church, still following the Julian calendar, has Easter on a different Sunday. Attempts to have a fixed date for Easter in the 20th cent. have failed. WMM

Eastern Association. Consisting of Norfolk, Suffolk, Cambridgeshire, Hertfordshire, and Essex (Lincolnshire was added later), this was the only one of the parliamentary county associations to enjoy any permanence in the Civil War. Its purpose was to break down the reluctance of local levies to venture outside their own counties. Based in Norwich, the association was ordered to raise an army of 20,000 men with *Manchester as commander-in-chief and Oliver *Cromwell as lieutenant-general of the cavalry. While its chief function was to protect the rich and populous eastern counties, the army later ventured further afield, most notably at *Marston Moor (July 1644). This stunning victory heralded the break-up of the association, since it fanned the flames of antagonism between Cromwell and Lawrence Crawford, the Scottish major-general of foot. The quarrel seems to have demoralized Manchester, who became increasingly reluctant to fight after Marston Moor. The public recriminations that erupted between him and Cromwell led to the absorption of the Eastern Association army into the *New Model in the spring of 1645, and the eventual demise of the association itself. IJG

Eastern Question. This was the problem created by the slow collapse of the Ottoman (Turkish) empire, which seemed likely to leave a power vacuum in the Balkans and lead to a general European war. Turkey's weakness became apparent in a series of wars with Russia in the late 18th cent. In 1783 Russia obtained the Crimea. Greece gained her independence, in an agreement brokered by Britain, France, and Russia, after an armed struggle (1821–30). European opinion was divided by anxiety for the balance of power, if Turkey ceased to be a great power, and sympathy for the Christian subjects of a Muslim and decayed empire, reinforced in the case of Greece by memories of her classical glories. The British feared that, if the Turkish empire broke up, Russian power would be enhanced and would become an increasing threat to the British empire in India. Russia gained some territory by the treaty of Adrianople at the end of the Russo-Turkish war of 1828–9 but Russian policy was thereafter governed by the conviction that an intact Turkish empire provided a buffer state which would be preferable to a partition. The *Crimean War of 1854–6, in which Britain, France, and Turkey fought Russia, was the result of miscalculations, arising from France and Russia's over-vigorous championing of the rights of catholic and orthodox Christians respectively, and Britain's misplaced fears that Russia wished to partition the empire and seize Constantinople (Istanbul). Nationalist feelings in the Balkans grew and the problem flared up again in the 1870s. The Bosnians rose in 1875, followed by the Bulgarians in 1876. The Bulgarians were repressed with particular brutality (the 'Bulgarian Horrors'). Russia declared war on Turkey but the other powers thought the peace treaty (treaty of San Stefano, 1877) too favourable to Russia and amended it at the Congress of *Berlin (1878). European opinion wavered over the next 30 years between the comparative stability provided by the Ottoman empire and the volatility of the emerging Balkan states. The situation was complicated by the rival ambitions of the latter. Serbia and Bulgaria, for example, fought each other in 1885. It was also feared that the emergence of Slav states in the Balkans would destabilize the Austrian empire. It can plausibly be argued that the Eastern Question caused the *First World War. Austria angered Serbia by annexing Bosnia in 1908. Russia helped to organize the Balkan League of Serbia, Bulgaria, Macedonia, and Greece, which went to war with Turkey in 1912. Militarily they were successful but they then fought between themselves over the spoils. The situation was still unstable when the heir to the Austrian throne was assassinated in the Bosnian capital, Sarajevo, in 1914. The Austrians blamed the Serbs. Russia, which had been unable to aid the Serbs in 1908, now backed them. Ultimatums, mobilizations, and war followed within weeks. MEC

Easter Rising (1916). The Easter Rising was planned by the *Irish Republican Brotherhood's military council to take advantage of British participation in the world war by staging a nation-wide Irish rebellion. Sir Roger *Casement was sent to Germany to raise a prisoner-of-war force and to win German arms and ammunition. The plans collapsed due to British intelligence discovery of American links and confusion over time of arrival of arms from Germany. The German arms ship was scuttled off the Kerry coast and with it any chance of a successful rebellion in the provinces. Eoin MacNeill, chief of staff of Irish Volunteers, then countermanded the mobilization orders given by *Pearse. The leaders of the IRB military council, including James *Connolly and his citizen army, went ahead with the rebellion by taking over various buildings around the centre of Dublin. Outside the General Post Office, their GHQ, Pearse read out the provisional declaration of an Irish Republic; five days later, after British shelling of centres of resistance, the rebels surrendered. Leaders were executed in stages, and over 2,000 interned in Britain. While there was little overt support for the rising at the time, British actions gave it a retrospective significance. Traditional nationalists have depicted it as a decisive event in awakening Irish nationalist consciousness and have seen it as the realization of Pearse's concept of blood-sacrifice. Lately, historians have criticized the use of violence with only minority support and have questioned whether the rising was central to the achievement of independence. MAH

East India Company. The first English East India Company was formed in 1599 to compete with the Dutch for the trade of the spice islands. However, following the *Amboyna massacre of 1623, it abandoned the East Indies to concentrate on the Indian subcontinent. The Stuarts regularly revoked and reawarded its charter, Charles II no fewer than five times. It was not until the so-called Godolphin Charter of 1709 that the company's institutional structure was consolidated. Thereafter, it prospered greatly from trade with China, over which it also had a monopoly. The company began to acquire a territorial empire in India after the battle of *Plassey in 1757. The defeat of the Maratha empire in 1818 gave it undisputed supremacy. Territorial conquest, however, brought about more direct parliamentary control through the Regulation Act of 1773 and the India Act of 1784. The company was progressively converted from the activities of a merchant to those of a governor. In 1813 and 1833, it lost its monopolies over the India and China trades. It survived somewhat anomalously as a quasi-department of the British state until the *Indian mutiny of 1857, whereafter it was abolished and its powers vested in a secretary of state for India. DAW

Eastland Company. One of the great trading companies, chartered in 1579, and trading with the Baltic. The foreign residence was first at Elbing, then at Danzig. The company imported timber and tar for shipbuilding, flax and linen, and corn, and exported mainly cloth. Dutch competition was fierce and there were the usual complaints of monopoly. The company was thrown open by an Act of 1673 and by the middle of the 18th cent. was moribund. JAC

East Saxons, kingdom of. See ESSEX.

East Sussex. See SUSSEX, EAST.

Ecclesiastical Commission, 1686. The Court of *High Commission, to impose uniformity in the church, was abolished in 1641 by the Long Parliament. The abolition was reaffirmed in 1661 and 'the erection of some such like court by commission' expressly prohibited. Nevertheless, in 1686 James II named seven ecclesiastical commissioners with sweeping disciplinary powers. The commissioners immediately summoned Henry *Compton, bishop of London, to explain why he had not suspended Dr Sharp for preaching what some took to be an anti-catholic sermon. Compton challenged the commission's authority but was himself suspended, and in 1688 was one of the 'seven' who appealed to William of Orange for help. Meanwhile the commission had deprived the vice-chancellor of the University of Cambridge and ordered the expulsion of the fellows of Magdalen College, Oxford, for refusing to elect as president a royal nominee. James's commission was declared 'illegal and pernicious' by the *Bill of Rights in 1689. JFC

ecclesiastical commissioners were established in 1836 as a permanent body to supervise the financial management of the Church of England. In 1948 they were merged with the administrators of *Queen Anne's Bounty and are now known as the church commissioners. They have responsibility for the considerable property of the church, which includes 140,000 acres of agricultural land, and have been under some criticism in recent years for imprudent investments. A large body of nearly 100, many of them honorary members, the commission disbursed £153 million in 1994, of which nearly half went on pensions, and a third on stipends. JFC

ecclesiastical courts have existed alongside secular courts from the Norman Conquest onwards, though their activities were much diminished after the Glorious Revolution of 1688. In addition to supervising clerical discipline and performance, the courts had important jurisdiction over matrimonial disputes, probate, and wills, and a general responsibility for the behaviour and religious observance of the laity. In the 12th cent. the boundaries between royal and ecclesiastical jurisdiction and the extent of *benefit of clergy were hotly disputed and contributed much to the conflict between Henry II and *Becket. Until the Reformation the hierarchy of courts, with appeals to the one above, was archdeacons' courts, bishops' (consistory) courts, archiepiscopal courts, and the papal court. Above the archiepiscopal court for Canterbury was the Court of *Arches: above York, the Chancery Court. After the breach with Rome, a Court of Delegates heard appeals for the archbishops' courts, until in 1833 the duty was given to the Judicial Committee of the Privy Council. In addition, between 1559 and 1641 the Court of *High Commission was very active, and James II established an ill-judged *ecclesiastical commission 1686–8. Until the late 17th cent., the ecclesiastical courts had a high profile, prosecuting for fornication, witchcraft, and absence from church and, for lesser offences, punishing often by public penance. Much of the jurisdiction of the ecclesiastical courts was removed in the 19th cent., particularly over tithes, probate, and matrimonial causes, leaving their authority confined largely to the clergy. In Scotland, the Commissary Court of Edinburgh, set up in 1564, had jurisdiction over matrimony and wills, as well as an appellate role, but was abolished in 1876 by which time many of its functions had been taken over by the *Court of Session. JFC

ecclesiastical history. Traditional teaching of ecclesiastical history, in 19th-cent. seminaries and training colleges, was determined by the need to establish the historical roots of institutions. It began with the patristic foundations, dealt with the great heresies, councils, the papacy, the early reform movement, the great schism of the 16th cent., the Counter-Reformation, and 19th-cent. revival. The contents of the package were determined on confessional lines. In a catholic context the emphasis would be on the destruction of heresies and on the papacy and great councils; in protestant colleges, on the justification of reform and separation.

As a distinctive university discipline, ecclesiastical history developed alongside secular history and the recovery of patristic studies in the 19th cent. Owen Chadwick has described ecclesiastical history as the seed of general history, since historical consciousness first arose within the heritage of Christendom. Ecclesiastical history could be, and was, used by all sides for propaganda and was largely viewed in terms of division, reaction, and rationalization of ecclesiastical separatism. Christianity, being by its very nature historical, meant that some account of that history had to be given, but also had to be imbued with religious meaning.

In the 20th cent. a new context and role has arisen for ecclesiastical history. This role has been enhanced by the rise of serious and scholarly demand for a different kind of denominational history, the social history revolution which has taken church history out of the pulpit and into the pew, and the upsurge of local and family history, which has enabled a more subtle and intimate approach to religious questions. All these, accompanied by the decline in classical languages, have tended to move the focus of interest into the modern and early modern period, towards congregations, social and political interaction, and minority or sectarian interests.

Ecclesiastical history, or the history of Christianity, as it is often tellingly described, is now seen as a significant component in professional historical scholarship, filling a niche alongside other historical disciplines, illuminating our understanding of human society and culture. So much of human experience has been engaged with religion that any history which ignores it is impoverished. Religion, Christianity, and the churches have played a major role in shaping values, institutions, culture, and customs and are therefore worth serious investigation.

However, the religious historian faces a particular difficulty in dealing with religious choices and chances and with the religious impulses of people motivated by a relationship with God. How does the historian account for that relationship and its government of people's lives? The transcendent element, which cannot be ignored, inevitably complicates the ecclesiastical historian's task. JFC

Ecclesiastical Titles Act, 1851. In 1850, Pope Pius IX, encouraged by Nicholas *Wiseman, announced the restoration of a Roman catholic hierarchy in England with English territorial titles, such as archbishop of Westminster. This provocative move, accompanied by comments on 'the Anglican schism', was the consequence of the great numerical increase from Irish immigration of Roman catholics in England in the 1840s and the church's more aggressive attitude to proselytization in England; it caused one of the final bouts of English anti-popery. Lord John *Russell, the prime minister, further encouraged protests by his 'Durham letter' and by passing in 1851 the Ecclesiastical Titles Act, which forbade Roman catholics from using English place-name titles. Opponents of the bill such as *Gladstone pointed out that the episcopalian church in Scotland, which was not established, already did what the Roman catholics proposed to do. The Act was a dead letter from the start and was repealed by Gladstone in 1871. HCGM

Ecgfrith (d. 685), king of Northumbria (670–85). During the reign of Ecgfrith the kingdom of *Northumbria reached the peak of its political power and influence. He extended the range of lordship of his father Oswui, even sending a strong military expedition to Ireland. In his attempts to stabilize his northern frontier he subdued the British kingdom of Strathclyde and the Irish in Argyll, but he overreached himself on campaign against the Picts and was defeated and killed at what proved a decisive battle at *Nechtansmere, in 685. With that disaster all hope of Northumbrian predominance within England disappeared. Even so his achievements were not negligible. Modern scholars point to the secular wealth and dynamism that made possible the great period of the Northumbrian renaissance, the age of Bede (672–735) as it is sometimes called. The foundation of the monastery of *Jarrow/Wearmouth and the activities of Bishop *Wilfrid at York and Ripon were a product of the early, confident days of Ecgfrith's reign. HL

economical reform. Demands for government economy have a long pedigree. Christopher *Wyvill's *Yorkshire Association was launched in 1779 when taxation was biting as a result of the *American War. A programme of retrenchment, with the abolition of sinecures, was bound to have wide appeal and was taken up by the *Rockingham opposition, partly to embarrass *North's ministry, partly to weaken the influence of the crown. The triumph of the campaign was the carrying in April 1780 of *Dunning's motion that the influence of the crown 'ought to be diminished'. The Rockinghams achieved a modest measure of reform when they came to power in 1782: Crewe's Act disfranchised revenue officers; Clerke's Act declared that government contractors could not serve as MPs; Burke's Civil List Act abolished 47 places tenable with a seat in Parliament. Though the campaign faltered after the end of the American War, economical reform was continued by *Pitt, whose maiden speech had been on the subject, largely by administrative action. A further drive by *Liverpool after the Napoleonic wars led some to argue that government had been fatally weakened. But the difficulties caused to ministers by persistent pruning of places was compensated, partly by patronage in other forms, partly by better party discipline. 'Cheap government' continued to be a most popular programme during the 19th and 20th cents. See also PLACE ACTS. JAC

economic history. As the name suggests, economic history is a hybrid discipline fusing together two areas of study with widely divergent interests and methods. The major source of difficulty and debate, according to C. H. Lee, has been the role of quantification in the judgements economic historians make about the past, for example, about the timing and nature of industrialization in Britain during the 18th and early 19th cents. While the problems tackled by economic historians generally require reliable statistics, there has also been a substantial input from other branches of history, like the history of science and technology, and from other disciplines, such as sociology, demography, geography, and politics. Social history has always been closely related and economic and social history, as distinct from political history, together form an important branch of the parent discipline.

R. M. Hartwell identified three phases in the historiography of economic history: the pre-1914 era, when the discipline had a close relationship with economics; an interim period to the 1960s, which was heavily history-orientated, with much study of particular sectors and industries; and the post-1960s, when there was greater recognition of the value of interdisciplinary approaches and, at the same time, a reassertion of the value of economic theory. Of the early practitioners in Hartwell's first two phases, Toynbee, *Tawney, Unwin, Seeley, and Clapham, among others, all made important contributions. Toynbee's study of the *industrial revolution remained a classic for several generations and inspired many of his successors to explore in greater depth, locally and nationally, the impact of industrialization and economic development.

The relationship to theoretical and even to applied economics has always been ambiguous, though it has been greatly strengthened by 'cliometrics', which, introduced from the USA in the 1960s, applied economic modelling to historical problems. Perhaps the most successful instance by an American scholar, Mokyr, was a detailed analysis of the Irish *Famine during the 1840s. An interesting spin-off, again imported from the USA, was the development of counter-factual history which derived its *raison d'être* from the concept of 'social savings' achieved in the economy had developments either been delayed or not taken place at all. Using this method, Hawke was able to show that railways had a more limited impact on the mid-19th-cent. economy than previously supposed, while Von Tunzelmann contradicted the view that the introduction of steam power greatly accelerated British industrialization much before the 1820s. Even the counter-factual horse, as conceived by F. M. L. Thompson, has featured in a debate about transport in the Victorian and Edwardian age.

Social history emerged powerfully in the 1960s with the work of E. J. Hobsbawm, E. P. Thompson, and G. Rudé, who, among others, articulated Marxist or quasi-Marxist views of both social and economic development. Thompson's *Making of the English Working Class* influenced a generation of social historians, not only of 18th- and 19th-cent. Britain, but also of the early modern period, and in much of this work the economic context of social change was closely addressed. There has also been sustained interest in the 20th cent., notably in the impact of war and peace on social change. In the related fields of historical demography and historical sociology, quantification has played a more critical role. P. Laslett in his study of *The World We Have Lost* was one of the most influential of those adopting a sociological approach, while E. A. Wrigley and M. Anderson were among several pioneering computer analysis to produce important studies on the historical demography of Britain during the 18th and 19th cents.

Economic historians have generated and sustained many major debates about the nature and impact of economic change in Britain, including such issues as the origins and timing of agricultural change and of industrialization, the role of various sectors in generating and sustaining economic growth during the era of early industrialization, the impact of industrialization, the standard of living during the industrial revolution, the role of overseas investment and trade on the 19th-cent. economy, the failure of entrepreneurship in later Victorian Britain, the effects of the two world wars on the British economy, and problems of adjustment in the international economy since 1945.

The Economic History Society, established in 1926, is the leading learned society in the field. It publishes the *Economic History Review*, while Scottish and Irish societies produce journals covering the economic and social history of their respective countries. ID

Eden, Anthony, 1st earl of Avon (1897–1977). Prime minister. Eden's career is indissolubly linked with the *Suez crisis. But opinion is divided whether Suez was an aberration brought on by chronic ill-health or whether it confirmed weaknesses present throughout his career. Eden's early rise was distinguished, if conventional, and perhaps too effortless. Born into the gentry, Eden grew up under the shadow of a domineering and eccentric father. After Eton he fought with distinction on the western front. With a first at Oxford in oriental studies he entered Parliament in 1923 for the safe seat of Warwick and Leamington. At this stage Eden showed few signs of distinction or originality. His speeches showed a tendency towards cliché, which he never overcame. None the less, he rose rapidly and as parliamentary private secretary to Austen *Chamberlain 1926–9 began a lifelong association with foreign affairs. He also won the patronage of Stanley *Baldwin, whose brand of consensual Conservatism he much admired.

It was as junior Foreign Office minister after 1931 that Eden's career prospered. Almost miraculously, he managed to distance himself from the deeds of his seniors, whose reputations were damaged as they strove to grapple with the rise of the dictators. In particular, he was seen as the champion of collective security through the *League of Nations, though Eden had a more circumscribed view of the league's potentialities than public opinion imagined. He developed an idealized image among the young and broadened his appeal beyond the Conservative Party. How far Eden differed from the foreign policy of the National Government as a whole remains arguable, but he seems to have kept any reservations as a matter of private dissent.

Eden became lord privy seal in January 1934 and minister for League of Nations affairs in June 1935. In December 1935, after Samuel *Hoare's resignation in the wake of the Hoare–Laval Pact, Eden emerged as foreign secretary, aged 38. Yet many felt that his rise owed more to his charm and good looks than to any intrinsic brilliance. His tenure saw a further deterioration in the position of the democracies, particularly with their failure to resist Hitler's remilitarization of the Rhineland in 1936. Despite calling for accelerated rearmament, there is little evidence that he ruled out an accommodation with Hitler, though he was less ready to appease Mussolini, whom he actively disliked. It was ostensibly over relations with Italy that Eden resigned in February 1938, though the increasing interventions of the new prime minister, Neville *Chamberlain, and the latter's handling of President Roosevelt's recent 'peace initiative' were contributory factors. Nevertheless, his resignation secured his reputation as an anti-appeaser.

With the outbreak of war Eden became dominions secretary and was promoted to the War Office in May 1940. That December Eden returned to the post of foreign secretary where he established an effective, if not always easy, partnership with *Churchill. The latter regarded Anglo-American relations as his own preserve, but Eden was left more scope in relations with the Soviet Union. It was a difficult field for successful diplomacy, but Eden laboured prodigiously, revealing qualities of industry, patience, level-headedness, and attention to detail. He was often called upon to restrain Churchill's fertile but over-exuberant brain. From 1942 Eden was Churchill's designated successor, but his distaste for party politics made him consider seriously Churchill's offer of the Indian viceroyalty. By the end of hostilities Eden was exhausted, ill, and depressed by the loss of his elder son.

After the Conservatives' electoral defeat in 1945, Eden endured a further difficult—and increasingly exasperating—decade as heir apparent. Churchill was frequently absent from Parliament, effectively leaving Eden to act as leader of the opposition. It is often said that Eden neither understood nor interested himself in domestic politics. This is not strictly true, though his contributions were marred by platitudes and he did not go far to translate his vision into detailed reality. He was very much on the progressive left wing of the party and during the war had considered an alliance with congenial socialists such as Ernest *Bevin.

In 1951 Eden returned again to the Foreign Office. By now his relationship with Churchill had markedly deteriorated. Continuing affection was balanced by a growing conviction that Churchill was no longer equal to the demands of the premiership. None the less his final period as foreign secretary was the most distinguished of Eden's career. Britain, through Eden, cut an impressive figure on the world stage which partly belied the decline in her intrinsic power even since 1945. Particular successes were achieved in arrangements for European defence, in ending the conflict in Indo-China, and, apparently, in placing Britain's relations with the emerging states of the Middle East on a new footing. It was once popular to complain that Eden failed in this period to put Britain at the forefront of moves towards European union, but, as the European ideal begins to fade, Eden's reservations in this area appear less culpable. Eden's health collapsed in 1953 and despite—or perhaps because of—three major operations, many considered that he never quite recovered.

Churchill finally retired in April 1955 and Eden began his premiership on a wave of good will. Despite an impressive general election victory in May, the prime ministerial honeymoon was over by the end of the year. Colleagues became increasingly conscious of weaknesses which perhaps made him unsuited for the highest office of state—irritability, vanity, hyper-sensitivity to criticism, and an inability to place sufficient trust in subordinates. Problems with the domestic economy shook the confidence of the Conservative Party and press, while critics on the right felt him too willing to make concessions over Britain's imperial position. Into this unpromising scenario broke the crisis created by Nasser's nationalization of the Suez canal in July 1956. Eden was handicapped by Britain's inability to take immediate military action, and the longer such action was delayed the less likely it was to command domestic and international support. With the illegality of Egypt's actions at least open to debate, Nasser refused to provide Eden with the pretext for military intervention. Yet, ironically, it was when a negotiated solution seemed at last possible that Eden entered into a collusive—and many would say disreputable—pact with France and Israel to invade Egypt. After a secret agreement, which Eden tried desperately to erase from the historical record, Britain and France entered Egypt, ostensibly to separate the Israeli and Egyptian combatants and protect the canal. It was a paper-thin deception. Yet if a prime minister of failing health and judgement had been guilty of underhand collusion to capture the canal and, probably, to topple Nasser, it was a deceit in which several senior cabinet colleagues were active participants. Under the pressure of world opinion, Britain was compelled to accept a cease-fire on 6 November. Above all, Eden had grossly misjudged the response of the USA to Britain's actions.

Despite a period of recuperation, Eden was compelled by his doctors to resign the premiership and withdraw from public life in January 1957. Even without the intervention of renewed ill-health, it seems improbable that he could for long have survived. With the patient care of his second wife, Clarissa, Eden lived for a further 20 years—time to contemplate how a reputation built on integrity, internationalism, and a commitment to peace had ended in such ignominious catastrophe. DJD

Carlton, D., *Anthony Eden* (1981); James, R. R., *Anthony Eden* (1986).

Eden, William, Lord Auckland. See AUCKLAND, 1ST BARON.

Edgar (943–75), king of England (959–75). The reign of Edgar as sole king of England marks an important stage in the development of the English monarchy. His coronation at Bath in 973, when the king was in his 30th year, has strong ecclesiastical as well as secular implications, and indeed the ceremony contained elements that formed the basis for all future coronations. Edgar's early years were not easy. He and his elder brother Edwy were the sons of King *Edmund (939–46), and on the death of their uncle *Edred (946–55) Edwy succeeded to the throne. He proved licentious and incompetent, and a revolt in 957 on the part of the Mercians and the Northumbrians resulted in a partition which left Edwy ruling Wessex, but Edgar (still a boy of only 14) as king in the north. Civil war was averted by the death of Edwy in 959, and Edgar ruled thereafter, with the help of long-serving and competent *ealdormen whom he confirmed in office, a reunited kingdom until his death on 8 July 975. In the secular field he was remembered for his good peace (there was a lull in Viking activity) and for his laws in which, while asserting the unity of all his Christian realm, he recognized the validity of Danish social and legal customs in those parts where they had settled. Late in his reign, *c.*973, he was responsible for inaugurating a massive reform of the coinage, exercising full royal control through the issue of dies, increasing the number of minting places, and initiating a system of recalling and reminting the silver pennies (the sole coins in regular routine mintage). In religious matters he worked closely with St *Dunstan, whom he had appointed first as bishop of Worcester, then of London, and finally as archbishop of Canterbury. Helped by the powerful bishops *Æthelwold of Winchester and *Oswald of Worcester, Dunstan was the inspiration behind the Benedictine reformation which greatly enriched the cultural and educational life of England. King and church worked closely together. Immediately after his coronation, itself a symbol of such co-operation into which some read virtual imperial overtones, Edgar sailed with a naval force to Chester where he received formal pledges of loyalty from a number of rulers (the *Chronicle* says six but later authorities eight) drawn from the Welsh, Scottish, Cumbrian, and Scandinavian communities around Britain. Later historians seize on the importance of this event and tell of a ceremonial rowing on the river Dee from the royal palace to the church of St John and back, with the king at the helm and the other rulers at the oars, a symbolic picture of the political strength of the English king. HL

Edgar (*c.*1074–1107), king of Scotland (1097–1107). Edgar inherited the throne in 1093 when both his father *Malcolm Canmore and his elder brother Edward were killed at *Alnwick. But he was at once driven out by Malcolm's half-brother *Donald Bane. He was, in turn, dispossessed by *Duncan, another of Malcolm's sons, but regained the throne. In 1097, with support from William Rufus, Edgar re-established himself. He relied considerably on his English allies and in 1100 his sister *Matilda married Henry I. He also came to terms with Magnus, king of Norway, not disputing the Norse hold on the Western Isles. He was succeeded by his brothers Alexander I and David I. JAC

Edgar the Atheling (*c.*1052–*c.*1125) was proclaimed king by the English gathered in London after the battle of *Hastings. He was the son of *Edward the Exile, a grandson of *Æthelred the Unready. Still young in 1066, Edgar's claims to the succession were ignored by *Edward the Confessor's death-bed bequest in favour of *Harold Godwineson and brushed aside by William the Conqueror. After 1066, Edgar intermittently played the role of pretender and was deeply involved in the English revolts of 1069–70. Reconciled with

William in 1074, he thereafter lived as a courtier and played a small role in Anglo-Norman politics. He also participated in the First Crusade. Edgar cannot be regarded as anything other than a minor participant in great events. DB

Edgecote, battle of, 1469. In July 1469 Edward IV was in Nottingham to put down a rising in Yorkshire led by 'Robin of Redesdale'; this may have been instigated by the earl of *Warwick. Warwick unmasked his intentions in a manifesto at Calais on 12 July, and then marched on London. Reinforcements for the king led by William Herbert, earl of Pembroke, and Humphrey Stafford, earl of Devon, reached Banbury on 25 July. Here the earls apparently quarrelled over billeting arrangements. Next day, Pembroke's Welsh force, having camped separately, was continuing its march when, 6 miles north-eastward, it was unexpectedly overwhelmed at Edgecote by a small force of Warwick's supporters. Pembroke was captured and beheaded by Warwick's order. On hearing the news, Edward's army deserted and he became Warwick's prisoner. RLS

Edgehill, battle of, 1642. Edgehill was the opening battle of the English Civil War. After raising his standard at Nottingham in August 1642, Charles I embarked on a recruiting march in the west midlands, while Parliament gathered an army under *Essex to face him. Charles began an advance towards London from Shrewsbury, via Bridgnorth and Wolverhampton. Essex shadowed him across from Worcester to Warwick to intercept. The royalists slipped past him but on 23 October turned to fight on the steep slopes of Edgehill, outside Banbury. Each side had about 12,000 men. Prince *Rupert's cavalry had much the better of the exchanges, but the parliamentary infantry stood firm, allowing both sides to claim victory. The road to London was left open for the king but his leisurely advance by way of Oxford gave his opponents time to regroup and look to their defences. JAC

Edinburgh, the capital of Scotland, is an ancient settlement, archaeological evidence pushing its history back over 4,000 years. A fine defensive site, the growth of the city stretched from the castle along glaciated ridges in medieval times to Canongate and the abbey of Holyrood and southwards by Cowgate to Kirk o' Field. The growth of Edinburgh involved the incorporation of districts outside the castle and the development of trade and industry.

The 'Old Town' by 1700 was teeming with people, its population huddled in great tenements. The building of a 'New Town' across the deep troughs, gouged by glaciers centuries before, was a consequence of further population growth. The wealthy were the first to move into a neoclassical grid-square suburb with wide streets and magnificent Georgian houses. By 1801 Edinburgh and Leith housed 83,000 people, but the vibrant 'Old Town' housed the university (1583) and remained the centre of religious, legal, and social activity. Linked by bridges (1772–1857), the 'New Town' became a major shopping area, and financial services—banks and insurance companies—also took root in its spacious squares.

Edinburgh's development in the 19th and 20th cents. involved the absorption of previously isolated industrial and farming communities—for example, Burdiehouse, Cramond, Corstorphine, Colinton, Dean Village, Gilmerton, Leith, Liberton, Portobello, Swanston—and the deliberate relocation of population to large corporation housing estates from the 1930s. By 1951 the city's population numbered 467,000.

From Leith to Sighthill a swathe of industries and factories gave the city considerable economic diversity during these two centuries. Industry was represented by mining, paper-making and printing, tanning and leatherware, rubber, flour- and saw-milling, sugar-refining, ropeworks, cement, brick, tile, soap, glass, and pottery production, brewing, distilling, shipbuilding, and engineering, all served by excellent transport and port facilities; the Union canal (1822), the railways (1836–50), and the improvement of Leith docks reinforced the changing industrial economy.

Employment in the 20th cent. was increasingly dominated by the service sector. The Scottish banks, investment trusts, building societies, and insurance companies provided jobs in financial services; the supreme courts of Scotland—the *Court of Session (1532) and the High Court of *Justiciary—are located in the Old Parliament House (1640), and together with city courts are an important component; the universities (including Heriot-Watt (1964) and Napier (1992)), the merchant company, private and public schools serve a wide constituency. Retailing and the distributive trades, hospitals, and other care institutions added to career opportunities for women. As the capital, Edinburgh was the administrative centre of Scotland, and from the 1930s the departments of the Scottish Office greatly added to service employment. Since the 1950s leisure and tourism have become major civic industries, the International Festival being a particular attraction. By 1981 about 80 per cent of Edinburgh's employment was in service industries.

From 1832 until 1885 the Liberals dominated parliamentary elections; with the split in the Liberals on religious issues and Irish Home Rule politics became more competitive and remained so, although Labour replaced the Liberals as a major force after 1920. JB

Edinburgh, Philip, duke of (b. 1921). The duke of Edinburgh is the son of Prince Andrew of Greece and Denmark, and nephew of Earl *Mountbatten, who was killed in 1979. His grandmother, Victoria of Hesse, was the daughter of Alice, Queen Victoria's second daughter, and married Louis of Battenberg. Prince Louis was first sea lord at the outbreak of the First World War but forced to resign by the clamour against Germans: in 1917, when the royal family adopted the name of Windsor, Prince Louis took the name of Mountbatten and was created marquis of Milford Haven. His daughter married Prince Andrew. After school at Gordonstoun, Prince Philip entered the navy in 1938, served throughout the Second World War, and was mentioned in dispatches at Cape *Matapan. His family connections, particularly through his uncle Louis Mountbatten, brought him into contact with the royal family, and his engagement to Princess Elizabeth was announced in June 1947. Before the marriage in November, he was given the Garter and a dukedom. Since 1952 Prince Philip has filled the difficult role of royal consort. Of the many societies and causes with which he is associated, the duke of Edinburgh's scheme for young people (1956) and his concern for the protection of wild life rank high. He retains much of the briskness and forthrightness of his early naval career. JAC

Edinburgh, St Giles. Founded 854, formally dedicated 1243, rebuilt in stone after burning by Richard II (1385), St Giles was created a collegiate church in 1467, enlarged, and enriched. On *Knox's return from Geneva, it became involved militantly in the new reformed church's activities. Although France and catholicism were surmounted, conflict with monarchs and episcopacy persisted throughout the 17th cent.: Charles I made Edinburgh a bishopric and St Giles a cathedral, before Cromwell's men cut it into four. Subsequently and more quietly under presbyterian rule, 19th-cent. reconstruction of the 'high kirk' has been enhanced by the Thistle chapel (1911). ASH

Edinburgh, treaty of, 1328. The treaty set the seal on the achievements of Robert I Bruce and ended the first War of *Scottish Independence. Negotiations were concluded in March 1328 at Holyrood and ratified by the English Parliament at Northampton in May. Edward III recognized the full independence of Scotland, relinquished his claim to Berwick and the borders, and agreed to a marriage between Robert's young son David and *Joan, daughter of Edward II. Though the treaty was intended as a 'final peace', it unravelled as soon as Robert died the following year. JAC

Edinburgh, treaty of, 1474. The first firm Anglo-Scottish alliance of the century was concluded by commissioners of Edward IV and James III. The Scottish king's son and heir James, duke of Rothesay, was formally betrothed to Edward IV's daughter Cecilia in the Edinburgh Blackfriars, with proxies taking the parts of the infant couple. The alliance has divided opinion amongst historians, some seeing it as a Scottish diplomatic success (which indeed produced five English dowry instalments), others viewing it simply as a device by which Edward neutralized Scotland before his invasion of France (1475). The proposed marriage was never solemnized. NATM

Edinburgh, treaty of, 1560. The treaty has been claimed as a turning-point in Anglo-Scottish relations. Elizabeth had succeeded in England in November 1558. *Mary of Guise, regent for Mary, queen of Scots, faced great opposition in 1559 from the reform party, which begged Elizabeth to intervene on their behalf. By the treaty of *Berwick in February 1560, *Norfolk agreed to protect Scottish liberties, ships and troops were dispatched, and in June 1560 the regent died. At Edinburgh, French and English negotiators agreed on 6 July to withdraw all troops. Though Mary returned to Scotland in 1561 after the death of her husband Francis I in December 1560, the French had no longer the same incentive to support her, and the outbreak of the French wars of religion greatly weakened their position. JAC

Edinburgh castle stands on Castle Rock overlooking the city of Edinburgh and is approached across the Esplanade, the site of the annual military tattoo and other ceremonies. Edinburgh castle has been sacked and rebuilt several times, one of its oldest surviving parts being the tiny St Margaret's chapel dating from the 12th cent. The focus of the layout is the Palace Yard, and on its south side lies the great hall (with its striking hammerbeam roof) built by James IV or James V in the early 16th cent. and subsequently altered in 1887–91 by Hippolyte J. Blanc. Neighbouring buildings in a variety of styles include the semi-circular Half-Moon Battery (1573–88) built by Regent *Morton, the Scottish United Services Museum (1708), the Governor's House (1742), the New Barracks (1796), and the Scottish National War Memorial (1924–7) designed by Sir Robert Lorimer. Edinburgh castle houses the crown jewels (*Honours) of Scotland, and occupies a special place in Scots history: in 1566 Mary, queen of Scots, gave birth there to Prince James, who became King James VI of Scotland in 1567 and James I of England in 1603. PW

Edinburgh Review. The review was founded in 1802 by Henry Erskine and Francis *Jeffrey, the latter as editor for the first 26 years. *Constable in Edinburgh and Longman's in London were the publishers. It followed a somewhat radical Whig line and its contributors included Henry *Brougham, Francis *Horner, Sydney *Smith, *Macaulay, and Thomas *Carlyle. 'To be an *Edinburgh Reviewer*', wrote *Hazlitt, 'is, I suspect, the highest rank in modern literary society.' Though its great days were in the 1830s and 1840s, it survived until 1929. JAC

Edington, battle of, 878. After the disaster at *Chippenham in January 878, Alfred was reduced for some months to guerrilla warfare from the marshes around Athelney. By May he was ready to attack again and encountered *Guthrum's Danes at Edington, near Westbury on the Wiltshire downs. The decisive victory of the Wessex levies forced Guthrum to sue for peace and give hostages. 'Never before', wrote *Asser proudly, 'had they made peace with any one on such terms.' The site of the battle has been disputed and it is sometimes called Ethandun. JAC

Edmund (d. 870), king of East Anglia, known as 'the Martyr'. More famous in legend and because of the grotesque method of his martyrdom than in his life and works, Edmund, the last effective king of the East Angles of native stock, was killed by the Danes, probably under their leaders, Ingware and Ubba, on 20 November 870. Stories quickly grew concerning his sanctity, his refusal to forswear Christianity, and the nature of his death (tied to a tree and shot to death by Danish arrows). His burial place at Bury St Edmunds became a shrine of special veneration, and the great abbey founded there helped to perpetuate his memory. Even in Scandinavia his memory was later held in great esteem. HL

Edmund I (*c.*922–46), king of England (939–46). Edmund succeeded his brother *Athelstan in 939. His prestige as a young warrior-prince who had fought victoriously by the side of his brother at *Brunanburh (937), and the evidence of his law codes, suggests potential greatness as a ruler, but at the age of only 24 or 25 he was murdered by a private enemy at Pucklechurch (Glos.) on 26 May 946. Politically he had to face a revival of Scandinavian ambitions in the north. *Olaf Guthfrithsson, king of Dublin (d. 941), invaded and forced Edmund, after arbitration which involved the archbishops, to yield control of much of northern England including the thriving Anglo-Danish community at York. Edmund found Olaf's cousin and successor *Olaf Sihtricsson easier to deal with. He recovered the territory of the 'five boroughs' (Lincoln, Nottingham, Derby, Stamford, and Leicester) in 942 when the Anglo-Danish inhabitants of that area clearly preferred the rule of the Christian West Saxon king to the more backward rule of the Irish/Scandinavian overlords. By the end of his reign Edmund had regained (temporarily, it is true) York and Northumbria, and had even started to take direct interest in continental affairs on behalf of his nephew, the French king Louis d'Outremer. HL

Edmund II (d. 1016), king of England (1016), known as 'Ironside'. After the death of *Æthelred in April 1016, his vigorous son Edmund, then in his early twenties, was recognized as his successor and took command of the forces resisting *Cnut. A season of hard campaigning resulted in varying fortune. Cnut failed in his efforts to take London, but Edmund, after some successes, was defeated in the autumn at *Ashingdon in Essex. Even so Cnut was content to come to terms and reached an agreement near Deerhurst to partition the kingdom, leaving Edmund in possession of Wessex. However, Edmund himself died on 30 November 1016, and Cnut then was received as king throughout England. Edmund's children went into exile in Hungary, and his grandson *Edgar the Atheling was briefly acclaimed as king in London immediately after the battle of *Hastings. HL

Edmund, son of *Malcolm Canmore by *Margaret, daughter of *Edward the Atheling, is said to have shared the throne of Scotland with his uncle *Donald III from 1094 to 1097, taking the southern part. They were then ousted by Edmund's brother *Edgar, supported by William Rufus. Edmund is reported to have become a monk in England, where his sister *Matilda was queen to Henry I, and to have died in the Cluniac priory at Montacute in Somerset. JAC

Edred (d. 955), king of England (946–55). The third of *Edward the Elder's sons to succeed to the West Saxon kingship, Edred was confronted during the greater part of his reign by an independent Scandinavian kingdom of York, first under *Olaf Sihtricsson and then under *Erik Bloodaxe, son of Harold Fairhair, king of Norway. Only in the last year of his life after the defeat and subsequent death of Eric did Edred rule over a united kingdom of England. Unmarried, possibly deliberately celibate, he brought up his two young nephews, *Eadwig and *Edgar, as his heirs. His health was precarious, and his will, which has fortunately survived, shows him fearful for the depredations of the heathen army. He was a devout Christian, a close friend of Abbot *Dunstan of Glastonbury, to whom he entrusted some of his best treasures and land charters: and he left substantial sums of money to relieve poverty and suffering. He left money, too, to his household officers, and it seems likely, as modern investigation of 10th-cent. charters suggests, that Edred's influence on the developing efficiency of the royal secretariat, possibly under the direct tuition of Dunstan, was more considerable than used to be thought likely. The gloom of a seriously sick man can occasionally be glimpsed. In his will he made provision for the sustenance of alms from his estates with the ominous proviso that this was to continue 'as long as Christianity shall last'. HL

education. In recent years, changes in social and political values have led to increasing public questioning of what is taught, i.e. the selection of knowledge; to whom it is taught, i.e. knowledge for some or knowledge for all; and how it is taught, i.e. the techniques used in education. One way to examine the nature of education is to look at the school curriculum and attempt to explain how changes have come about.

From the early 19th cent., we can broadly delineate two 'traditions' in English education, the elementary and the secondary. Elementary education was equated with mass education, using methods calling for mechanical obedience, appropriate for future workers in factories. The monitorial system introduced at the beginning of the 19th cent. employed the principle of the division of labour: one book, it was claimed, could be used to instruct many children. Cheapness was combined with efficiency. As most schools were financed by religious bodies, one of the main objects was to propagate the ability to read the Bible. Writing was at first discouraged, though computation was considered useful. When the state began to take an interest in education from the 1830s, this narrow approach to the curriculum continued. Until the last decade of the 19th cent., the three Rs provided the staple diet of this sector.

The other tradition was enshrined in the secondary or grammar school curriculum. This stemmed largely from the medieval grammar school which taught the so-called seven liberal arts. The first three—grammar, logic, and rhetoric—formed the trivium, and the other four—music, arithmetic, geometry, and astronomy—made up the quadrivium. Throughout the 19th cent., Latin, Greek, and the arts subjects were considered the hallmarks of a first-class education and retained their supremacy.

Little effort was made to bridge the gap between the two types of curriculum. Indeed, where attempts were made by elementary schools to introduce 'advanced' subjects in the 1880s, they were regarded as over-educating the school board pupil. A test case brought by the district auditor of the School Board for London in 1899 established that it was illegal for certain subjects to be taught in elementary schools.

How to account for the persistence of certain traditions of curriculum practice and why changes take place is complex. The two traditions illustrate one of the crucial factors—the existing ideologies underlying the various types of curriculum. Raymond Williams in his book *The Long Revolution* (1961) identified a number of different ideologies. Élite education, demanded by the landed gentry, was less concerned with utilitarian aspects of the curriculum than with emphasizing culture, athletics, character-building, and service. An alternative ideology which received wide support from the middle classes was that the curriculum should prepare pupils for their future occupations, particularly with the replacement of patronage by examinations in the civil service and in the burgeoning professions. The third ideology was that working-class children should have a utilitarian, restricted curriculum, which would give them practical skills for future manual work. A fourth ideology, appropriate to a democratic society, is that all pupils are entitled to develop their potential regardless of the type of school which they attend. The notion of a common curriculum which evolved from this is now enshrined in the philosophy of the national curriculum. Elements of all four ideologies are to be found, to a greater or lesser degree, in the present-day curriculum.

Other factors must also be taken into account in looking at the nature of the curriculum. There is a direct link between the economic structure of society, demographic changes, and attitudes towards children and schooling. When the need for child-labour diminished as technology improved, the school-leaving age was raised: in 1880 compulsory schooling was to 10 years of age, in 1918 it was raised to 14, and in 1973 to 16. As the school life lengthened, the curriculum was adjusted to accommodate the full age range.

The change from a curriculum determined by religious bodies in the 19th cent. to a more secular one has led to the introduction of 'new' subjects, such as the social sciences, e.g. sociology, psychology, citizenship, and personal and social education. Foreign influences have been relatively small, but the American common school was the basis of the comprehensive school, as the German *gymnasium* had been the model for the new municipal grammar schools established after 1902.

Official commissions have often influenced government attitudes to curriculum policies. The Samuelson Commission on Technical Instruction (1884) expressed concern at the growth of European industrial knowledge in comparison with the United Kingdom and recommended more technical and practical subjects. The Hadow Committee on the Education of the Adolescent (1928), using psychological findings, recommended a reorganization of schooling and curriculum at 11 as pupils' needs became different. As a result, separate primary and secondary schools, with their own curricula, gradually replaced all-through elementary schools. A different view of the curriculum needs of children was postulated by the Norwood Committee on Curriculum and Examinations (1943). It recommended three different kinds of provision at 11—for the academic, the technical, and 'others'—which became the basis of the tripartite system after 1944.

To the factors listed above which determine the curriculum and content of education can be added many more, such as the rise of professional associations, pressure groups, the effect of theory on practice, examinations, differentiation of curriculum between boys and girls, and the effects of war. However, an influential development has been the direct intervention of governments in curriculum matters, either by legislation, particularly the 1988 Education Act which established the national curriculum, or the setting up of quangos in education, such as the School Curriculum and Assessment Authority in 1993. PG

Gordon, P., and Lawton, D., *Curriculum Change in the Nineteenth and Twentieth Centuries* (1978); Lawson, J., and Silver, H., *Social History of Education in England* (1973); Salter, B., and Tapper, T., *Education, Politics and the State* (1981).

Education Acts. Starting in the 19th cent., a series of Education Acts have signalled the reform and reorganization of all aspects of education. Many of the Acts are named after the statesmen who introduced them. The 1870 Act, steered through Parliament by the Liberal W. E. *Forster, was intended to establish a system of efficient elementary schools in England and Wales. Locally elected school boards were to provide schools where there was a deficiency by the denominational bodies, who had previously been the sole providers. This Act was the beginning of the so-called 'dual system' which still exists. The 1880 Act, introduced by the Liberal A. J. Mundella, imposed universal compulsory schooling, making education obligatory for the majority of children under the age of 10.

The 1902 Act, the work of the Conservative A. J. *Balfour, set up a co-ordinated national system of education, administered by a central Board of Education. School boards were abolished and replaced by local education authorities, consisting of elected councils of counties, county boroughs, boroughs, and urban districts, responsible for secular and voluntary schools: county and borough councils were also responsible for secondary and technical education. Grammar schools were established and free places provided for pupils from elementary schools.

The 1944 Act, introduced by Conservative R. A. *Butler, stipulated that public education should be organized in three stages—primary, secondary, and further—and that children were to be educated according to their age, ability, and aptitude. The Board of Education was replaced by a Ministry of Education and provision was made for raising the school-leaving age from 14 to 15. The Act remained in force for the next four decades, but Labour governments from 1964 encouraged comprehensive schooling. PG

Education Board (Ireland). See IRELAND, BOARD OF NATIONAL EDUCATION.

Edward (d. 924), king of England (899–924), known as 'the Elder'. The reign of Edward the Elder falls neatly into two parts. Up to 910 when he won a decisive victory against the Danes at *Tettenhall in Staffordshire, Edward was involved first in suppressing a revolt led by his cousin Æthelwold, who drew support from the Danes settled in East Anglia, and then in efforts to keep the peace with Danish forces active from their bases in Northumbria and East Anglia. After Tettenhall narrative accounts chart a period of almost uninterrupted progress, which left Edward in effective command of all England south of the Humber. In the north of England he was not so successful. A Viking kingdom was set up at York which offered at most a vague recognition of overlordship to him, and a strong element of Irish/Norse colonization was intruded into Cumbria and modern Lancashire. His success was possible partly because of the readiness of Danes, settled into the countryside now for a generation or more, to submit to a strong legitimate king who could offer peace, and partly due to the active co-operation achieved between the West Saxons and the Mercians. Edward worked well first with his brother-in-law *Æthelred, ealdorman of Mercia, and then after his death in 911 with his widow, Edward's own sister *Æthelfleda, the formidable 'lady of the Mercians'. The co-operation had its uneasy moments. The *Anglo-Saxon Chronicle* implies that only after Æthelred's death did Edward take direct control of London and Oxford. On Æthelfleda's death in 918 some local Mercian attempt, quickly suppressed, was made to rally support behind her daughter Ælfwynn. Even at the end of his reign Edward was forced to campaign against the men of Chester who had formed an alliance with the Welsh. But by and large the success of Edward and Æthelfleda in reabsorbing much of the Danelaw did much to cement the Christian English into a common unity under the West Saxon ruling house. An outstanding feature of their campaigns was the implementation of what can best be termed a 'burghal' policy, that is to say the setting up of fortified defences at towns or rudimentary towns manned by forces drawn from surrounding estates according to a fixed system of assessment, each pole ($5\frac{1}{2}$ yards) of wall to be protected by four men. The origins of the system go back to *Alfred's day, and a document dating from Edward's early years, the so-called 'Burghal Hidage', gives details of its implementation for some 30 or so *'burhs', mostly in a great sweep of country defending greater Wessex. Extension now took place and burhs were built or repaired (where existing fortifications already existed) at places such as Hertford, Witham, Buckingham, Bedford, Maldon, Towcester (specially defended by a stone wall), Tempsford, and Colchester by Edward, and at Bridgnorth, Tamworth, Stafford, Warwick, and Runcorn by Æthelfleda, who also took the Danish borough at Derby. The establishment of safe strongholds of this nature, keyed into the landed wealth of the community, were of vital importance to the creation of permanent effective royal administration, essential for the legal and financial as well as the military health of the kingdom. They represent an important stage in the setting up, on the West Saxon model, of the midland shires, based on shire towns such as Hertford, Buckingham, or Stafford.

At various points in his reign Edward also had his overlordship recognized by Welsh princes, Scottish rulers, by the Britons of Strathclyde, and by still independent Northumbrian noblemen exercising authority at Bamburgh, but his major contribution to the ultimate achievement of English unity rested on military and institutional success south of the Humber. HL

Edward (d. 978), king of England (975–8), known as 'the Martyr'. On the sudden death of *Edgar, 8 July 975, succession to the throne was far from clear, and parties formed around his two young sons, Edward, then aged about 13, and Edward's half-brother *Æthelred, who was probably only 7 or 8. Edward was eventually accepted and the two or three years of his reign were marked by a check to the lavish endowments made to monasteries by his father (not necessarily an anti-monastic policy as such). Later authorities speak of the young king as unstable and violent, but all was overshadowed by the manner of his death. On a visit to his young brother and stepmother at Corfe in Dorset on 18 March 978 (just possibly 979) he was treacherously stabbed to death in cold blood by his brother's retainers. It is possible that some of Æthelred's weakness may be attributed to the moral blight thrown on him and his mother Queen Ælfthryth as a result of this murder. Edward was buried without due honour at Wareham, though his body was later translated to Shaftesbury. Popular opinion, encouraged no doubt by the nuns at Shaftesbury, postulated his sanctity and the anniversary of his death, 18 March, was set aside as his commemoration day in the legislation of Æthelred. HL

Edward (*c.*1005–66), king of England (1042–66), known as 'the Confessor'. Edward was born at Islip (Oxon.), the first recorded child of *Æthelred's second marriage. His mother was *Emma (Ælfgifu), the daughter of Richard I, count of Normandy (d. 996), and sister of the powerful Richard II (996–1026). During the Danish conquest of England, Edward took refuge in Normandy, initially in 1013, and then, together with his younger brother *Alfred, on a more permanent basis from 1016. Emma married King *Cnut in 1017, and seems to have been influential in Edward's recall from the long Norman exile in 1041 in the reign of *Harthacnut, her son by Cnut: and in the following year Edward succeeded his half-brother on the throne with general approval. He proved far from the weak and pious nincompoop portrayed by some historians, and should be given full credit for keeping his kingdom intact in troubled times for close on a quarter of a century, for reconciling the English and Danish elements in the aristocracy, and for accustoming England to regular cultural and political contact with continental Europe, especially with Normandy and with the papacy. He intruded some Norman favourites into the English Church and state, but not to excess, apart possibly for a brief period, 1051–2, and generally succeeded in maintaining a balance at his court. It is true nevertheless that the politics of his reign was dominated by his relationship with one of the most extraordinary families in English history, that of Earl *Godwine of Wessex, whose daughter *Eadgyth married Edward in 1045. Godwine's five sons, *Sweyn, *Harold, *Tostig, Leofwine, and Gyrth, all achieved the rank and office of earl, and Harold succeeded his brother-in-law as king in 1066. Much of the credit for the effective military defence of the realm and the pacification of the border with Wales must go to the Godwine family, especially Harold, but the king remained their superior, active in the creation and shuffling of the earldoms and in ecclesiastical matters, and by no means a passive symbol of royalty. Indeed in 1051 as a result of quarrels involving the exercise of both secular and ecclesiastical authority Edward was able to enforce the exile of the whole Godwine family, and although they returned under arms in the autumn of 1052 they did not do so unconditionally. In their absence Edward had indulged in a degree of Normanization. There is evidence, not utterly conclusive but strong, to suggest that Duke William of Normandy, his young kinsman (his mother's great-nephew), may have visited him in England in late 1051 when some loose accord may have been reached over the Norman duke's right to claim succession to the childless Edward. Godwine's return prompted reaction. *Robert of Jumièges, whose promotion to the see of Canterbury in mid-Lent 1051 had caused disaffection, was in turn exiled and replaced by *Stigand, a candidate favoured by the Godwines, but other appointments remained in being, notably that of the influential William, bishop of London, who remained in office until his death in 1075. Earl Godwine himself died in dramatic circumstances at Easter 1053, not long after his return. He is said to have declared on solemn oath that he was guiltless of the death of Edward's brother (murdered in an abortive attempt to lay claim to England in 1036), and then choked to death on the holy wafer taken to confirm his oath. After Godwine's death, Edward affirmed his overlordship in quite spectacular fashion, sending Harold on an embassy, and recalling from Hungary his own nephew and namesake *Edward the Atheling, presumably again as a possible heir. Edward's skill in exploiting doubt over the succession must be ranked among his most formidable diplomatic achievements. Prince Edward died before he could even greet the king, but his children, *Edgar Atheling (who lived on to the 1120s) and *Margaret, queen of Scotland, proved potent pawns deep into the Norman age. The last decade or so of Edward's reign was a period of relative prosperity. The earls, those drawn from the Mercian house of *Leofric and the Northumbrian house of *Siward as well as the Godwines, remained powerful regional commanders but still subject to appointment and removal by king and council. Local government functioned effectively through a network of courts in shires, hundreds, and wapentakes, and urban life flourished, notably in London and Winchester. Tax systems and coinage were advanced, sophisticated, and efficient for the age. In church affairs the appointment of able clerics such as *Wulfstan of Worcester (1062–95), and the influence of *Ealdred, bishop of Worcester (1044–62) and archbishop of York (1061–9), counterbalanced the dubious nature of Stigand at Canterbury. Edward himself remained active almost to the end of his life, planning hunting expeditions in the Bristol channel area in the summer of 1065, and hunting with Tostig in Wiltshire as late as the autumn. An outbreak of rebellion in Northumbria in October, resulting in the exile of Tostig, caused the king much grief and seems to have precipitated his final illness. He had spent much personal energy and treasure on the rebuilding of *Westminster abbey, deeply influenced by similar ventures in characteristic new Romanesque style at Jumièges in Normandy, but was too sick to attend the dedication on 28 December. He died in the first week of 1066, on 4 or 5 January, and was buried in the abbey. His posthumous reputation was distorted by the nature and needs of the Norman Conquest. The Normans pointed back to his reign as a golden age in the recent past, while king Harold was dismissed as a usurper and oath-breaker. William himself claimed direct legitimate succession in kingly office from Edward, and *Domesday Book used 'the time of King Edward' as its standard temporal test for legal rights and tenure. In the 12th cent. Edward became something of a symbol of reconciliation between Norman and English. His reputation as a lawgiver, largely unmerited, became great, and his personal piety (including an unlikely attribution of celibacy within marriage) exaggerated. Westminster abbey had a special interest in him which the monks exploited to the full. In 1161, after earlier attempts had failed, Edward was canonized by Pope Alexander III. The by-name 'the Confessor' persisted, that is to say one who suffered for his faith, though short of martyrdom, even though initially it was given merely to differentiate him from his half-uncle *Edward the Martyr. Henry III fostered his cult, rebuilding Westminster abbey and naming his son and heir Edward. There was every likelihood that he would be adopted as the patron saint of England until more militant elements ousted him in favour of the soldier St *George. HL

Barlow, F., *Edward the Confessor* (1970); Clarke, P. A., *The English Nobility under Edward the Confessor* (Oxford, 1994).

Edward I (1239–1307), king of England (1272–1307). When Edward came to the throne he was already an experienced general and politician. He had played the major role in the defeat of Simon de *Montfort in 1265, the battle of *Evesham being very much his own personal triumph; he was in control of the mopping-up operations that lasted into 1267; and he had taken a leading role in the deliberations of his father's council before departing on crusade in 1270. He returned with a considerable reputation, and for the rest of his life was widely considered as the expected saviour of the Holy Land. His experience of the traumas and the issues of the civil war of the 1260s informed his approach to English affairs when he became king. He appreciated that reform was needed and that Parliament was a necessary institution. The first 20 years of the reign were remarkably successful in this regard, the period marked especially by a great series of statutes which had an enduring significance, and which largely proceeded in response to the grievances of his subjects. These same years also saw Edward's successful scotching of Welsh independence, following his two campaigns of 1277 and 1282–3, symbolically marked by the ten great castles, including *Caernarfon, *Conwy, and *Beaumaris, that he constructed.

The early 1290s proved to be the turning-point in the reign and in Edward's fortunes. Increasing financial problems and domestic political tension, associated with the wars against the French and the Scots, replaced the more relaxed atmosphere of the 1270s and 1280s. It culminated in the crisis of 1297, but it is a measure of Edward's power and authority that although rebellion threatened, none actually rose in revolt—then, or at any other time—something that cannot be said of any of his predecessors since 1066, or of many of his successors.

On his tomb in Westminster abbey Edward is described famously as the 'hammer of the Scots'. But this is far from the truth. He acted as arbitrator between the claimants to the Scottish throne (the *Great Cause of 1291–2), but on the understanding that he be accepted as feudal overlord of the kingdom. The throne was adjudged to John *Balliol, rather than his chief rival, Robert Bruce, and Edward's attempts to secure Balliol and exercise his overlordship proved to be the beginning of the long-drawn-out *Scottish War of Independence. The campaign of 1296 was intended to be as decisive as the conquest of Wales. Edward was victorious, symbolically removed the 'stone of destiny' from *Scone to Westminster abbey, and established his own administration. But it was only a temporary settlement and Edward soon found himself in something of a medieval Vietnam from which he could not withdraw. He lived to see Robert Bruce crowned king in 1306, and it is highly indicative of his dogged determination that he should die leading yet another expedition to Scotland in 1307.

Edward 'Longshanks' was physically impressive and even in old age retained his physical presence. He stood head and shoulders above most men: when his tomb was opened in 1774, the body was measured at 6 feet 2 inches. He met most of the contemporary expectations of a king. He was a very able soldier and general, who possessed considerable courage. He was also a very competent organizer who, like his great-uncle Richard I, appreciated the importance of supply and transport. His military career was notable, although his victories against the Montfortians and the Welsh need to be balanced against defeats by the Scots and French. In most ways he lived up to the chivalric ideals of his age. As a young man, in particular, he was conspicuous for his enthusiasm for tournaments and other chivalric pursuits, and his devotion to the crusading cause is especially notable. (He took the cross again in 1287, but the matter of the Scottish succession and the outbreak of war with France unhinged all plans for departure.) But he could be cruel, as when he imprisoned Bruce's sister Mary, the countess of Buchan, in apparently inhuman conditions in 1306. He may well have sought to make a public example of them, and by then the Scottish war had become extremely savage. His violent temper, shared with his Angevin predecessors, may also have contributed. An account book records the cost of repairs to his daughter Elizabeth's coronet in 1297 after Edward had hurled it into the fire. And on one occasion he even assaulted his eldest son and heir, the future Edward II, tearing out his hair.

Yet, his eldest son apart—at least in Edward I's later years—he was devoted to his family. In particular, his love and fondness for his first queen, *Eleanor of Castile, is legendary and the marriage was plainly both happy and fruitful. (There were probably fourteen children in all.) Indeed, it is possible that the marked change in character of the reign following her death in 1290 owed not a little to Edward's sense of personal loss. He grieved her deeply, and in the famous *Eleanor crosses, twelve in all, one constructed at each stopping-point of the funeral cortège between Harby (Notts.), where she died, and Westminster abbey, where she lies buried, Edward constructed the most elaborate series of monuments ever created for an English queen (or king).

In his considerable achievements, especially in legislation and government, Edward was one of the most notable of English medieval kings, but those achievements have to be set against equally considerable failures, and the poisoned chalice of Anglo-Scottish relations, combined with chronic financial difficulties, which he bequeathed to his son. SL

Prestwich, M. C., *Edward I* (1988); —— *The Three Edwards* (1980); Salzman, L. F., *Edward I* (1968).

Edward II (1284–1327), king of England (1307–27). Tall and good-looking, Edward II had the right physical attributes for kingship, but few other qualifications. Contemporaries ridiculed the pleasure he took in rowing and working with craftsmen; although he was a good horseman he lacked knightly military skills. His predilection for favourites, whether or not based on homosexual attraction, was politically disastrous.

It was not easy to succeed Edward I. Not only was his reputation almost impossible to live up to, but he left a legacy of debt and unfinished war. The political honeymoon at the start of the reign was brief; there were signs of trouble at the time of Edward's marriage to *Isabella of France in January 1308, and at his coronation a new clause was added to the *coronation oath which threatened to limit his authority. The main issue in his first years on the throne was the role of Edward's favourite Piers *Gaveston. The scenes in the dispute were acted out against a backcloth of increasing difficulty in Scotland, and acute financial problems. Gaveston was exiled in 1308, to return in 1309. He was exiled once more by the *Ordainers in 1311. When he returned, the king was unable to protect him from a baronial opposition increasingly dominated by *Thomas of Lancaster. Gaveston was savagely executed in 1312. There was a very real danger of civil war, but neither the king nor his opponents were in a sufficiently strong position to risk fighting. The next twist in the political saga came when the government was discredited by the military disaster of defeat by the Scots at *Bannockburn in 1314. That placed the earl of Lancaster in a dominant position, but he proved no more capable of effective rule than the king. His policy was to try to adhere strictly to the Ordinances of 1311; his inclination was to take as little part in public affairs as he could, while pursuing private profit by questionable means. Lancaster was formally made head of the council in 1316, but soon withdrew from active government, probably in protest at the methods being employed to raise troops for an increasingly hopeless Scottish war.

The earl of *Gloucester had been the most notable casualty at Bannockburn. He left three sisters, and the competition between their husbands for the lion's share of the massive Gloucester inheritance was of major political significance from 1316. Above all, the ambitions of one of them, Hugh *Despenser the Younger, husband of Eleanor, provided a new, threatening, and divisive element in the political equations of the time. A political settlement of sorts was reached in the treaty of *Leake of 1318, which imposed a council on the king, but by 1321 civil war had broken out in the Welsh marches as a result of the blatantly aggressive methods adopted by Despenser to gain yet more lands from his brothers-in-law Hugh Audley and Roger Damory. An alliance was struck between the marcher lords and the earl of Lancaster. Even Bartholomew Badlesmere, hitherto a staunch royalist, joined the coalition. The Despensers, father and son, were forced into a brief exile, but in the autumn of 1321 an astonishingly successful revival of royal and

Despenser power took place. Badlesmere's castle of Leeds in Kent was taken, for Lancaster refused to allow assistance to a man he distrusted. A brief campaign shattered the power of the Welsh marcher lords, and Lancaster marched north from Pontefract, only to be defeated at *Boroughbridge. By the time the battle was fought, most of Lancaster's retainers had abandoned him. The earl of Hereford (*Bohun) was killed attempting to force a crossing of the bridge; Lancaster surrendered, to be executed at Pontefract. An unprecedented bloodbath of his supporters followed.

The royalist triumph at Boroughbridge marked the start of one of the most unpleasant and ultimately ineffectual regimes ever to rule in England. The king, the Despensers, the earl of Arundel, and Robert Baldock, an ambitious cleric, formed a narrowly based clique which controlled the country by means of semi-judicial terror and financial threats. The need for money was a motive force behind a highly successful programme of Exchequer reform, for which the treasurer, Walter Stapledon, was largely responsible. The war with Scotland went badly. An ineffective English march as far as Edinburgh in 1322 was followed by a Scottish raid into England, in which the king himself was nearly captured. Andrew Harclay, royalist hero of Boroughbridge, and newly created earl of Carlisle, was executed for treasonable dealings with the Scots in 1323. Conflict with France over Gascony in the War of Saint-Sardos of 1324–5 further discredited the English. The queen, Isabella, was alienated from Edward by the favour given to the Despensers, and by the way in which she was treated during the French war. She was sent to France to assist in negotiating peace, but went into exile in Paris, where a small but influential group of Englishmen gathered, and where she took as lover Roger *Mortimer, one of the rebels of 1321, who had succeeded in escaping from the Tower.

In the autumn of 1326, Isabella invaded with a small force. She had the backing not of the French monarchy, but of the count of Hainault. The Despenser regime collapsed like a house of cards. London was in uproar, giving full support to the queen. Bishop Stapledon was caught by the mob, and beheaded with a butcher's knife. Edward and his associates fled to Wales, where they were captured. The Despensers and the earl of Arundel were executed with barbaric ritual. Edward's removal from the throne was effected in Parliament in January 1327 by means of a mixture of deposition and abdication. He was murdered in Berkeley castle; a surprisingly circumstantial account that he escaped, to end his days as a hermit in Italy, is unlikely to have been true.

MCP

Fryde, N., *The Tyranny and Fall of Edward II, 1321–1326* (Cambridge, 1979); Maddicott, J. R., *Thomas of Lancaster* (Oxford, 1970); Tout, T. F., *The Place of Edward II in English History* (Manchester, 1936).

Edward III (1312–77), king of England (1327–77), claimant to the French throne (1340–60 and 1369–77). Edward came to the throne in 1327 in most unpropitious circumstances, with the government in the hands of his unscrupulous mother *Isabella and her lover Roger *Mortimer. His reign witnessed demographic disaster with the *Black Death. It did not see major measures of legal reform, such as featured under Henry II or Edward I; concessions to Parliament on a range of issues weakened the theoretical position of the monarchy. Yet Edward must rank as one of the most successful English kings. His war with France saw the great victories of *Crécy and *Poitiers. The king of France and the king of Scots were both captured and held for huge ransoms. The Order of the *Garter epitomized the glittering chivalric glamour of courtly and military circles. Political stability of a type unknown since the 1280s was achieved in the middle years of the reign.

Edward's first independent political action was in 1330, when he led the coup against his mother and Roger Mortimer at Nottingham. In 1333 he took a major gamble, supporting Edward *Balliol's cause in Scotland, and reopening a war which had appeared concluded with the 'shameful peace' in 1328. No doubt Edward in part wished revenge after a disastrously unsuccessful campaign against the Scots in 1327. The battle of *Halidon Hill in 1333 was a signal triumph, but succeeding campaigns achieved little, partly because of French support for the Scots. War with France began in 1337. In part this was similar to previous conflicts, with dispute over the English-held lands in Gascony and commercial rivalry in the Low Countries, but a new element was provided by Edward's claim, through his mother, to the French throne.

The French war dominated Edward's reign. It saw the great triumphs at Crécy in 1346 and Poitiers ten years later, but also the disappointment of the 1359 campaign, which Edward had hoped would culminate in his coronation at Rheims. Instead, it brought an unsatisfactory truce until 1369. The reopening of the war saw the advantage largely gained by the French. The gains may have been mixed with losses, but Edward showed himself to be a great commander. He took great care in the detailed planning of his campaigns, and clearly had the capacity of inspiring his men. He was also an opportunist; the war went through several phases of very different character as chance made new strategies possible. Realization that the initial policy of attacking from the north with the aid of a massive coalition of allies was expensive and ineffective led to intervention in the 1340s in Brittany, followed by the unexpected invasion of Normandy in 1346. How far Edward carefully planned the strategy which led to the great success at Crécy is a matter for debate, but it is at least clear that proper arrangements were made for additional supplies to be brought from England, and that a march northwards was always intended.

The war, particularly in its initial phase, was extremely expensive. By 1339 the king was effectively bankrupt, as were his main creditors, Italian bankers and English merchants. Heavy taxation at home was extremely unpopular, particularly at a time of severe bullion shortage. Political crisis came in Parliament in 1340–1, with the king's former chief councillor and chancellor, John *Stratford, leading opposition to the crown, opposition in which the Commons, unlike the lay nobility, were very active. Edward rolled with the punches; he accepted the new statutes imposed on him in Parliament, only to repeal them once Parliament had been dissolved. He showed himself throughout more ready to compromise with his critics than any of his predecessors on the throne. He was even ready to concede on the question of military service in 1352, readily abandoning innovative concepts of military obligation in the secure knowledge that he would have little difficulty in recruiting troops for his wars by means of contracts with the main commanders. Parliament's demands were also accepted in 1352 over the question of treason. In an attempt to impose order on a lawless society justices had used charges of treason for offences which, though serious, hardly merited such a sledgehammer. Edward willingly accepted a very considerable narrowing of the definition of treason in the interests of political peace. His reign saw the triumph of the Commons in Parliament in a wide range of areas; their power to grant taxes meant that it was impossible to deny them a major voice in public affairs. The king had to abandon useful techniques of raising money by negotiating with merchants' assemblies as a result of the claim that the Commons alone should grant taxes and customs duties. By 1376 the power of the Commons was dramatically displayed in the *Good Parliament, with the impeachment of Lord Latimer, the chamberlain, Richard Lyons, a rich London government financier, many royal officials and servants, and even the king's own mistress, Alice Perrers. Yet, as in 1340–1, Edward knew that once Parliament was dissolved, it would be possible to regain the lost ground. He can be accused of making concessions on a scale that seriously weakened the crown in the long run; at the same time, his concessions achieved many years of political stability and domestic peace, a remarkable achievement following the disastrous reign of Edward II.

Edward was extremely successful in his dealings with his own family, and with the magnates. He was able to provide adequately for his sons, while the war enabled him to provide them with sufficient independent scope, so that he never faced the kind of internal family problems that had beset Henry II. The eldest, *Edward the Black Prince, received the duchy of Cornwall in 1337, and was later given command in Aquitaine; *John of Gaunt received the major duchy of Lancaster in 1362; Ireland was intended to serve as Lionel of Clarence's sphere of activity. The two youngest sons, Edmund (*York) and *Thomas, were less well treated, but they were still young at the end of the reign, and did not present a political problem.

The creation of six new earldoms in 1337, four of them going to important members of the royal household, was a courageous move which could have aroused hostility from the established nobility. In practice, Edward's use of patronage was cleverly judged, and he was consistently able to rely on the support of the magnates in war and in politics. Edward skilfully manipulated the chivalrous feelings of his followers, patronizing tournaments and founding the Order of the *Garter. He did not attempt to curb the authority of his nobles as Edward I had done, and though it can be argued that the crown's control over them was in theory diminished, in practice the results of royal policy prove the wisdom of the king's approach. MCP

Ormrod, W. M., *The Reign of Edward III* (1990); Waugh, S. L., *England in the Reign of Edward III* (Cambridge, 1991).

Edward IV (1442–83), king of England (1461–70, 1471–83). The tall and handsome 'Rose of Rouen', so nicknamed because he was born in that city, the eldest son of Richard, duke of *York, and Cecily Neville, gained the throne of England in March 1461 when he was only 18. Possession confirmed on the field of *Towton a few weeks later, he was crowned in June. His reign, however, was interrupted in 1470 by his deposition and the temporary restoration of Henry VI.

During his first reign Edward was never fully secure on the throne. It took three years for him to eradicate Lancastrian opposition in England, concentrated in Northumberland, and sustained by Scottish and French help. In these early years he owed much to the earl of *Warwick and his kinsmen. No sooner had northern Lancastrian resistance been brought to an end, however, than his secret marriage to *Elizabeth Woodville, the promotion of her family, and a disagreement over foreign policy led to a rift between them. The Lancastrian exiles in France offered a convenient rallying-point for dissidents, the option Warwick finally took in the summer of 1470. When Warwick invaded England, Edward, caught on the wrong foot, fled precipitately to the Netherlands. Here he received the backing of the duke of Burgundy, his brother-in-law, who was also threatened by a Franco-Lancastrian declaration of war. In March 1471 a small fleet put Edward ashore at Ravenspur. Initially claiming only the restoration of his duchy (consciously imitating Henry IV), Edward successfully evaded the forces opposing him in Yorkshire, was reinforced in the midlands, most significantly by his fickle brother George (*Clarence), and defeated Warwick at *Barnet. He then rapidly marched west to intercept and overwhelm a Lancastrian army at *Tewkesbury. With Warwick and *Edward of Lancaster dead, and Henry VI promptly murdered on royal orders, he was now for the first time secure.

Edward began his second reign with a determination to secure reconciliation through war against the king of France, who had instigated his short-lived deposition. For four years he bent every sinew to achieve this end. Parliament, meeting in six sessions in 1472–5, voted generous taxation; a triple alliance with Brittany and Burgundy was forged and a truce with Scotland concluded. In 1475 the largest army to invade France since the days of Edward III crossed the Channel. But at the eleventh hour, after his allies deserted him, Edward came to terms with Louis XI at *Picquigny, accepting a generous pension. For the remainder of his reign Edward sought to enjoy the fruits of success. In 1477, however, he turned on and destroyed his brother Clarence, who was executed in 1478. Two years later, largely through the pressure of his younger brother Richard of Gloucester, he became embroiled in war with Scotland. Moreover, the treaty of Arras, concluded between France and Burgundy in 1483, left his foreign policy in tatters.

Edward died peacefully in his bed after a short illness on 9 April 1483, having apparently secured his dynasty and ended the Wars of the *Roses. Yet immediately his body was buried, a fierce competition for power during the minority of Edward V ensued, leading to the seizure of the throne by his brother Richard, the renewal of civil war, and the ultimate destruction of the dynasty: a pattern of events in stark contrast to the minority of Henry VI. Thus historians have always found it hard to judge his achievement. The earliest admired the manner in which he restored peace and prosperity in his second reign, but admiration gave way to disapproval in the 19th cent. when his personal morals and political failures coloured interpretation. More recently his star has risen again. Impressed by innovations in government, the recovery of royal finances, and the determination with which he imposed his will after 1471, he has been seen as the progenitor of the revival of royal authority, developed further by Henry VII, and known as 'New Monarchy'; the disaster that followed his death has been placed firmly at the feet of Richard III.

But it is a misjudgement to see novelty in Edward's kingship. Indeed it was backward-looking. His reliance on a small circle of trusted intimates, most marked after 1471, has an Arthurian ring to it; and his knights were collectively as reliable and loyal as Arthur's fabled round-tablers. Rule through a band of mighty subjects, however bound to his own person, was no foundation upon which to lay a permanent recovery of the monarchy. The use of members of his household to manage finances and sustain the administration was factional in genesis, the easiest way to survive from day to day in a kingdom over which he did not at first exercise full control. Edward IV aimed low: like Charles II two centuries later, his principal objective after 1471 was never to go on his travels again. In this he succeeded. And had he lived but four years longer his son would have succeeded him without challenge.

Contemporaries attested to Edward's personal charm and ease of manner. He could, when resolved, be decisive, authoritative, even ruthless. He was a brilliant general, victorious in all his battles, who preferred to avoid war against France. In his youth he was callow and inexperienced. He was excessively generous to Warwick; his marriage to Elizabeth Woodville, its manner as much as its fact, was ill judged. Even when he was older and wiser, he was not capable of sustained attention to business. He maintained a magnificent court, influenced by the Burgundians. He was a notorious philanderer, whose last mistress, Jane Shore, was shamefully victimized by Richard III; his over-indulgence in food and drink made him in his later years, like his grandson Henry VIII, 'fat in the loins'. It is probable that his excessive life-style contributed to his early death. He devoted himself to the completion of St George's chapel, Windsor, which he turned into his mausoleum and where he lies buried. AJP

Lander, J. R., *Government and Community: England 1450–1509* (1980); Ross, C. D., *Edward IV* (1974); Scofield, C. L., *The Life and Reign of Edward the Fourth* (2 vols., 1923).

Edward V (1470–*c.*1483), uncrowned king of England (1483). Eldest son of Edward IV and *Elizabeth Woodville, Edward was brought up at Ludlow under his maternal uncle Earl *Rivers. On the death of his father in April 1483, the 12-year-old prince of Wales left Ludlow to be proclaimed king in London, but at Stony Stratford his attendants were arrested by his paternal uncle Richard of Gloucester, claiming a conspiracy to deprive him of the protectorship. Initially lodged at the palace of the bishop of London, hence separated from his mother and siblings, Edward transferred in mid-May to the royal apartments at the Tower as part of the coronation preparations. He was joined by his younger brother Richard in mid-June, when they were seen playing in the garden, but after the execution of *Hastings they were seen more rarely, until, at length, they ceased to appear altogether. The rumours and contested succession that ensued have been followed by continued controversy over the reliability of contemporary accounts, the manner of the presumed death of the princes in the Tower, and the degree of involvement of Richard of Gloucester, who had by then declared himself king as Richard III. The incomplete skeletons of two juveniles unearthed in 1674 in the Tower grounds have been presumed to be those of the princes, but the 1933 exhumation in Westminster abbey merely confirmed the bones to be of human origin, of approximately the correct ages. ASH

Edward VI (1537–53), king of England (1547–53). Since Edward was 9 years old when he succeeded Henry VIII in 1547, he was in tutelage for the greater part of his short reign, with *Somerset as his governor and mentor until 1549 and *Northumberland thereafter. His mother *Jane Seymour died when he was born, his half-sister Mary was 21 years his senior, Elizabeth four years. Edward's chronicle or journal, which he kept from the age of 12, is largely factual and reveals little of character, save perhaps reserve and caution. His main interest was in the sham fights put on to entertain him, the poor state of the currency, and the obstinacy of his sister Mary in refusing to change her religion. From the age of 6 he had learned protestant tutors—Richard Cox, Sir John *Cheke the distinguished humanist, and Sir Anthony Cooke. Contemporaries saw much in him to admire. The Venetian ambassador in 1551 thought him 'handsome, affable, of becoming stature', and in 1552 the imperial ambassador, after a difficult conversation about Mary's religion, reported him 'a likely lad, of quick, ready and well-developed mind'. Less sentimentally, G. R. Elton summed up: 'Edward was naturally haughty and arrogant . . . he had a marked intellectual ability, which an appalling schooling had turned into a precocious passion for protestant theology—a cold-hearted prig.'

The religious policy, the central theme of his reign, must have been that of his two chief ministers, though with Edward's growing approval. The position at Henry's death was an uneasy stalemate: the king's quarrel had been with papal authority rather than the rites and doctrines of the catholic church. But a series of measures during Edward's reign pushed England into the protestant camp. Catholic bishops were replaced by reformers. Persecution of protestants ceased and a number of continental reformers made their way across the Channel. The Act of *Six Articles, which had represented a shift back towards catholicism, was repealed. The *chantries followed the monasteries into dissolution, thus putting even more property into the hands of the gentry and aristocracy. The new *prayer book of 1549, though not going far enough for many protestants, shocked Devon and Cornwall catholics into revolt. The revised prayer book of 1552 and *Cranmer's Forty-Two Articles of 1553 moved the Church of England nearer to calvinism.

Another preoccupation of the reign was the future marriage of the young king. Most promising seemed the suggestion that he should marry Mary, queen of Scots, five years his junior, with the prospect of uniting the two kingdoms. In 1543 the treaty of *Greenwich arranged for the marriage but the Scots were extremely reluctant to endorse it. Henry's savage reprisals in 1544 and 1545 ('the *rough wooing') alienated what support the English had in Scotland and in 1548 Mary was betrothed to the dauphin and sent to France. In 1551 there were negotiations for the hand of Elizabeth, daughter of Henri II of France, but she was even younger than Mary and, in the end, became the third wife of Philip of Spain. In April 1553 the imperial ambassador reported rumours that Edward was to marry Joanna, a daughter of Ferdinand, king of the Romans and brother of the Emperor Charles V.

Further negotiations were not needed. In 1552 the young king had measles and smallpox, from which he seemed to have recovered, but by the beginning of 1553 the signs of pulmonary tuberculosis were evident. Edward's last significant action was an attempt to head off any catholic revival by a 'devise of the crown', switching the succession from Mary. The plan to bring in Lady Jane *Grey, of the blood royal, hastily married to Northumberland's son, was not as hare-brained as the ultimate fiasco made it seem. But the puzzle is why Edward did not try to bring in Elizabeth, popular and protestant. She may have been far too prudent to involve herself in so risky a business or Northumberland might well have thought that she would not prove docile. The last few weeks of Edward's life were grim as the illness took hold and diplomats speculated on his survival in terms of days, then hours. He died at Greenwich palace on 6 July. The settlement of the succession, which had meant so much to him, lasted barely a fortnight. JAC

Jordan, W. K. (ed.), *The Chronicle and Political Papers of King Edward VI* (1966); id., *Edward VI: The Young King* (1968); id., *Edward VI: The Threshold of Power* (1970).

Edward VII (1841–1910), king of Great Britain and Ireland, emperor of India (1901–10). The success of Edward VII's reign would greatly have surprised his parents, who anticipated his accession with ill-concealed foreboding. His uncommon laziness, wrote *Albert when the poor youth was only 18, 'grieves me when one considers that he might be called on at any moment to take over the reins of government'. Victoria doubted her son's discretion and not until 1892, when he was over 50, was he entrusted with the 'golden key' to Albert's dispatch boxes.

His disadvantages were considerable. He was not particularly intelligent, had a short attention span, and was easily bored. His temper was notoriously untrustworthy as a small boy and did not much improve. His mother was irritated by his weak chin and hang-dog appearance. His liaisons were numerous, his taste raffish, and his set fast. While prince of Wales, he was subpoenaed in one divorce case and, even worse, was involved in an unpleasant legal action about cheating at baccarat.

It has often been suggested that his parents were much to blame and could have handled him more tactfully. It is certainly true that Albert and Victoria were earnest, and the queen's manifest disappointment that her son was not more like his beloved father must have been a cross to bear. Yet earnest parents were not unusual in the 19th cent. and some of his problems may have been genetic. His Hanoverian great-uncles had been choleric and eccentric and his son Eddie, who died as duke of *Clarence, was even more sluggish mentally.

Nevertheless, he had certain assets which came to the fore when he became king. He enjoyed company and had a gift for making graceful impromptu little speeches. He could be amusing and considerate when he wished and he looked good in uniform. He had a good memory for names and faces and an excellent command of both French and German. Not least of his assets was his Danish wife *Alexandra, whom he married in 1863. Graceful and slender, with a natural dignity, she was an admirable foil to Edward's flamboyance.

Two incidents at the start of his reign in 1901 indicated that the new king would be his own man. The captain of the vessel bearing him and the queen's coffin from the Isle of Wight was sharply reprimanded for flying the royal standard at half-mast: his stammered explanation 'but the Queen is dead, sir' was met with 'But the King of England lives.' Secondly he announced that he wished to be known, not by his first name Albert, but as Edward—thus frustrating the deepest hopes of his fond parents—though, characteristically, he explained neatly that Albert had been so great that his name should stand alone.

Over the years, Edwardian England has acquired the image of an Indian summer, a golden age of tranquillity before the horrors of the Great War. It was in fact turbulent. There was a marked increase in industrial unrest and in working days lost by strikes. The militant phase of the women's suffrage movement began in 1905 when Sir Edward *Grey was shouted down at Manchester. The rise of the *Labour Party, returned in numbers for the first time at the general election of 1906, heralded a move towards class politics, which the king greatly deplored. The Liberals, after their great election victory, were pushed leftwards by Labour and the Irish, and by the intransigence of their Conservative opponents. The rejection of *Lloyd George's budget in 1909 by the House of Lords and the counter-threats to emasculate the Upper House drew the king into the political arena. Edward made it clear that he was unwilling to create 500 Liberal peers to carry the Parliament Bill, regarding it as a shabby manœuvre, exploiting the royal prerogative of honour for party ends. Whether he could have sustained that position under pressure may be doubted, but he died in the middle of the crisis, leaving *Asquith to wring a grudging promise from his inexperienced son George V.

Internationally, the reign was marked by the abandonment of isolation, splendid or otherwise, which had proved so uncomfortable during the *Boer War. First, an alliance was reached with *Japan in 1902; next, in 1904 the *Entente was formed with France, and lastly an attempt was made to bury differences with France's ally, Russia. By the time of the king's death, Britain was firmly in the Entente camp, ranged against the Triple Alliance of Germany, Austria, and Italy.

The more extravagant claims for Edward's influence may be dismissed. He was credited, in some quarters, with skilful diplomacy and the Kaiser, who was his nephew, thought his uncle a monster of guile. But the encirclement of which the Kaiser complained so frequently was of his own making, and the *rapprochement* between Britain and France owed more to Tirpitz's naval programme than to Edward VII's evident relish for French cuisine and French music-halls.

In two respects, his influence was of some consequence. He took a keen interest in the armed forces, supported *Fisher's naval reforms, and encouraged *Haldane's overhaul of the army, which the humiliations of the Boer War had rendered so necessary. Since the Great War was a close-run thing, it is possible that Edward's interventions were decisive. Secondly, he raised the profile and the publicity of the monarchy. In this he had some luck. Any ruler who succeeded to an 81-year-old widow was bound to have a residue of goodwill to draw on. His great successes on the turf did him no harm at all with the average citizen: he won the Derby three times with Persimmon (1896), Diamond Jubilee (1900), and Minoru (1909), and the Grand National with Ambush II (1900).

Edward was carried off in the middle of the House of Lords crisis by severe bronchial illness, exacerbated by a lifetime devoted to cigars and cigarettes. It is greatly to his credit that his son George V was infinitely better prepared for his royal duties than Edward had been, and mourned him as 'my best friend, the best of fathers'. He was fortunate to die when he did. His reign was brief and he did not overstay his welcome. The great crises of Ireland and the Lords were only beginning to unfold. Though, with the advantages of hindsight, one can see the roots of the Great War growing, the age was not yet in shadow. The crowned heads of Europe—kings, emperors, tsars, and kaisers—still entertained each other at regattas, manœuvres, weddings, and funerals. The king was still head of society and there was society still to be head of. Great shooting parties assembled for long weekends at country houses and partridges by the thousand perished that gentlemen could demonstrate their prowess before the ladies. The landed aristocracy, to which the king was devoted, had not yet gone down before the twin perils of the Great War and penal taxation. Behind the gun-carriage which conveyed Edward to his resting-place at Windsor marched nine kings. JAC

Brook-Shepherd, G., *Uncle of Europe: The Social and Diplomatic Life of Edward VII* (1975); Hibbert, C., *Edward VII: A Portrait* (1976); St Aubyn, G., *Edward VII, Prince and King* (1979).

Edward VIII (1894–1972), king of Great Britain and Ireland, emperor of India (1936). Edward was the eldest son of George, duke of York, later King George V. His parents were strict disciplinarians, and his private tuition was seriously deficient. But an easy-going manner and outward-looking personality more than counterbalanced these disadvantages. A brief period at Oxford was followed by non-combatant but arduous service in the British Expeditionary Force in France. As heir to the throne he was not permitted to serve in the front line, but none the less courted danger—and achieved genuine popularity—in visiting the troops, sharing their cigarettes, and listening to their stories. Edward, much like his grandfather Edward VII, was 'one of the boys', able to communicate with ordinary people at their level—a refreshing antidote to the austere George V and the prudish Queen Mary. In 1919, at *Lloyd George's suggestion, he undertook a tour of Canada and the USA; in 1920 he visited Australia and New Zealand, and toured India and the Far East in 1921–2; in 1925 and 1931 he journeyed to South America. All these voyages were resounding successes, demonstrating that the British monarchy took its imperial role seriously. But Edward had two weaknesses. Each, by itself, need not have been constitutionally fatal: together, they cost him his throne.

Edward was a notorious 'ladies' man', engaging in a succession of sexual liaisons with married women, one of whom, Lady Furness, was to introduce him to Mrs Wallis *Simpson, with whom he became infatuated. He also revelled in his assumed role as the champion of the common man. He made it his business to visit the depressed areas, and his public statements, though they could be construed as nothing more than sympathy for the plight of the deprived, might also be interpreted as critical of current social and economic policy, and thus as political pronouncements. Most famous, or infamous, in this category was a donation of £10 he made to a relief fund set up for the miners after the collapse of the *General Strike (1926) had left them at the mercy of the coal-owners. The donation was made (the covering letter explained), because 'it would be an unsatisfactory end to any dispute that one side should have to give in on account of the sufferings of their dependants'. Never before—or since—has the heir to the throne made such a blatant intervention in a matter of public controversy. The altruism and generosity of the donation may be applauded, but it made Edward many enemies within the Conservative Party (then in office), and marked him out as a future monarch whose judgement (as they saw it) could no more be trusted in matters of constitutional propriety than in matters pertaining to the sanctity of the marriage contract.

Edward's infatuation with Mrs Simpson was not reported in the British press, but within ruling circles was a matter of common knowledge. Wallis came from humble stock in Baltimore. Her first marriage, to an American naval officer, had ended in divorce; she married again, to an English businessman, Ernest Simpson, and lived in London. She lacked beauty, but made good the loss with sophistication, charm, and measured informality. Edward was not content to have her as a mistress. He determined to make her his wife. Mr Simpson let it be known that he was willing to acquiesce in a divorce, which was granted nisi, at Ipswich, at the end of October 1936.

By then Edward had been on the throne for nine months. His brief reign was dominated by 'the King's matter'. Stanley *Baldwin, the prime minister, advised that a marriage to Mrs Simpson would not be popular. Whilst it is impossible to test the truth of this statement, and whilst the king could certainly have married his mistress and insisted on retaining his throne, had he wished, it is equally true that some of those who supported him, such as the *British Union of Fascists, were peripheral elements in British public life, whilst others, such as Winston *Churchill, were mavericks. It was not so much that Mrs Simpson was a commoner: rather, she was an American, twice-divorced commoner. Edward's suggestion that a morganatic marriage be contracted—she would be his wife but not his queen—was counter-productive, since it implied that she was unfit to be queen. Rank-and-file Conservatives regarded the king's morals as an affront to Christian values; but unlike his grandfather, he now proposed to compound sin by marrying the mistress whose bed he shared. They were reminded, too, of his embarrassing political interventions. During a visit to south Wales, in mid-November 1936, the king fuelled this particular prejudice by remarking, in relation to the unemployed, that 'something must be done to find them work'—a comment widely interpreted as an attack on Conservative economic policy.

Baldwin was not prepared to countenance a morganatic marriage; neither was *Attlee, the Labour leader, nor were the dominion prime ministers. On 10 December Edward signed the instrument of abdication, and ceased to be king the following day, when he and Wallis travelled to France, where they were married by a Church of England parson acting without his bishop's authority.

The new king, Edward's younger brother George, agreed to confer on him the title duke of Windsor; but Wallis was not permitted officially to call herself HRH. Relations between Edward and the royal family were, and remained, bitter. It was said that he had brought the monarchy into disrepute, and it was also feared that he would be regarded as a king in exile, and a threat to his brother. Edward's much publicized visit to Hitler (October 1937) was not so much sinister as naïve. None the less, when Edward and Wallis fled to fascist Spain after the fall of France, Churchill, now prime minister, packed them off to the Bahamas, of which Edward became governor. His wartime meetings with American President F. D. Roosevelt caused further embarrassments. But when, following his death in Paris, he was buried in the royal mausoleum at Frogmore, Wallis was permitted to be present at the interment.

Edward was a weak and in some important respects a selfish man. His political judgement was unsound, but there is probably some truth in the view that during the inter-war period he gave the British monarchy the human face so lacking in his austere, class-prejudiced parents. GA

Bloch, M., *The Duke of Windsor's War* (1982); Bolitho, H. H., *King Edward VIII—Duke of Windsor* (1954); Sencourt, R., *The Reign of Edward VIII* (1962); Windsor, duchess of, *The Heart has its Reasons* (1956); Windsor, duke of, *A King's Story* (1951); Ziegler, P., *King Edward VIII: The Official Biography* (1990).

Edward, duke of York. See YORK, DUKE OF.

Edward, prince of Wales (1330–76), known as the 'Black Prince'. He was, both for contemporaries and later generations, one of the great chivalric heroes, though his reputation does not stand up to close inspection in all respects. The eldest son of Edward III, he was made earl of Chester in 1333, duke of Cornwall in 1337, and prince of Wales in 1343. In 1362 he became prince of Aquitaine, becoming a virtually independent ruler there. He was a great soldier. His career began at *Crécy, where he fought bravely, and the notable victories of *Poitiers in France (1356) and *Najerá in Spain (1367) mark him out as one of the best medieval commanders, a man of ability and charisma. The brutal sack of Limoges in southern France (1370) is the one blemish on his military reputation, though it can be excused in strict legal terms. He was less skilled as politician and ruler than as a soldier; his venture into Spain was unwise, and his extravagant and harsh rule in Gascony alienated some of the most influential nobles there. His policies contributed to the reopening of the *Hundred Years War in 1369. In England the administration of his lands was efficiently centralized, but overly harsh. In 1362 he married the celebrated beauty *Joan of Kent in a love match; a more statesmanlike man would no doubt have used marriage as a diplomatic tool. Disease forced him to return to England in 1371, and ruined his last years. In 1376 he predeceased his father, leaving his young son Richard as heir to the throne. MCP

Edward, prince of Wales (1453–71). The heir of Henry VI, Edward spent most of his life in exile in France. In 1470 his prospects were transformed by the restoration of his father. Six months later, he returned to England only to find that Henry VI had been deposed once more by Edward IV. His army was intercepted and defeated at *Tewkesbury on 4 May. He was probably killed in flight from the field. His death sealed the fate of his father. A description of him as eager to display his prowess in the field suggests that he was more like his famous grandfather than his unfortunate father. AJP

Edward, prince of Wales (1473–84), was the only child of Richard III by his marriage to *Anne Neville. He was born at Middleham castle (Yorks.), made earl of Salisbury in 1478, and at Richard's second coronation at York in September 1483 was created prince of Wales. In January 1484 Parliament confirmed his place in the succession. Two months later, he died at Middleham, leaving his parents at Nottingham almost mad with grief, according to the Croyland chronicle. He was buried at Sheriff Hutton in Yorkshire. JAC

Edward the Atheling (d. 1057), known as 'the Exile'. Mystery surrounds the return of Edward the Atheling to England in 1057. The son of King *Edmund Ironside (d. 1016), he was forced into exile as a young boy by *Cnut's conquest of England. Later, not very reliable, sources suggest that Cnut intended that he should be harmed in exile, but in fact he was well treated in Hungary, and married a royal princess, Agatha, connected with the imperial ruling house of Henry II. Negotiations were set on foot for his return by an embassy sent out in 1054, but he died soon after his arrival and was buried at St Paul's in London. One version of the *Anglo-Saxon Chronicle* has the laconic and possibly sinister entry, 'we do not know for what reason it was brought about that he was not allowed to look on (the face?) of his kinsman,

King Edward'. As Edward's nephew, but even more so as Edmund's son, he was next in line by blood to the succession. His children were well treated in England. *Edgar Atheling, his son, was acclaimed king for a brief period at London immediately after the battle of *Hastings, and lived on in a modest role in the Anglo-Norman world into the 1120s. His daughter *Margaret, later St Margaret, was queen of Scotland. HL

Edward Balliol. See BALLIOL, EDWARD.

Edward Bruce. See BRUCE, EDWARD.

Edwin (d. 633), king of Northumbria (617–33). The son of Ælle, king of Deira, Edwin was driven into exile during the reign in Northumbria of *Æthelfryth, head of a rival dynasty. With East Anglian aid he defeated and killed Æthelfryth in 617. His marriage to a Kentish princess in 625 had momentous consequences in a Christian mission to Northumbria led by *Paulinus, who converted Edwin with many of his subjects and founded a church at York. According to *Bede, Edwin gained authority over the whole of Britain, excluding Kent, but including Anglesey and Man. He successfully invaded Wessex in 626. In 633 he was defeated and killed by *Penda, king of Mercia, and *Cadwallon, king of Gwynedd, at *Hatfield Chase. His body was later (allegedly) taken to Whitby abbey, where he was venerated as a saint. JCa

Egbert (d. 839), king of Wessex. After a profitable three-year exile in the kingdom (and then the empire) of Charles the Great, Egbert succeeded to the West Saxon throne in 802. He belonged to the native dynasty, and was descended from Ingild, the brother of King *Ine (688–726). There is little record of the early years of his reign apart from a powerful and successful campaign against Cornwall in 815. In the 820s, however, he took advantage of Mercian dynastic weakness, winning one of the decisive battles in Anglo-Saxon history at *Ellendun (Wroughton to the south of Swindon) in 825, and inflicting further defeat on them in 829. His first victory marks the passing of control of the south-east (and temporarily of East Anglia) from Mercian to West Saxon hands. After his second in 829 the *Anglo-Saxon Chronicle* records that he conquered Mercia and was recognized as a *bretwalda (overlord). The Northumbrians also submitted to him, and for a year (830–1) he was recognized as king throughout England. It is misleading, however, to regard Egbert as the first king of a truly united England. A native prince was quickly restored to Mercia, even if not of the ruling dynasty, and only briefly did Egbert issue coins for Mercia. His own favoured title was 'king of the West Saxons' or 'king of the West Saxons and the Kentishmen'. He set up his son *Æthelwulf as a subking in the south-east, and concentrated personally on the western heartlands of his kingdom, winning a substantial victory in 838 against the Danes and their Cornish allies at *Hingston Down. His permanent memorial proved to be the achievement of West Saxon mastery over England south of the Thames, the making of a true greater Wessex, and with it an end to all hopes of a Mercian nucleus to a united kingdom of England. HL

Egypt. British interest in Egypt arose from concern to protect the route to India. Napoleon's occupation of Egypt in 1798 was terminated by the peace of *Amiens three years later, when control of the country was restored to the Ottoman empire. The opening of the Suez canal in 1869 increased the strategic importance of Egypt to Britain, and British troops occupied the country in 1882 when Anglo-French attempts to sort out the government's debts had led to a revolt by the heavily taxed peasantry. A British protectorate was declared in 1914 when Germany's alliance with the Ottoman empire in the First World War posed a new threat to British interests. Nominal independence, under a constitutional monarch, was restored in 1922, but Britain maintained a military base to control the Suez canal until Gamal Abdel Nasser seized power in 1952 and nationalized the canal. KI

Eikon basilike or King's Book was one of the most successful books ever published and established Charles I's reputation as a martyr. It came out within hours of the king's execution in January 1649 and was a strange mixture of prayer and political commentary. Forty-six editions are said to have been called for within a year. Though purporting to be by the king, authorship was later claimed by John Gauden, appointed bishop of Exeter and then Worcester after the Restoration on the strength of it. Perhaps the greatest impact was made by a woodcut as frontispiece showing Charles at his devotions. JAC

eisteddfod, meaning a session or congress, was a competition of Welsh bards and minstrels under the patronage of the aristocracy. The institution was of great antiquity since the laws of *Hywel Dda (d. 950) describe in some detail arrangements for chairing the bard, the climax of the activities. *Gruffydd ap Cynan, king of Gwynedd, is said to have held an eisteddfod at Caerwys about 1100 and *Rhys ap Gruffydd, king of Deheubarth, at Cardigan in 1176. Another important gathering was at Carmarthen *c.*1450, presided over by Gruffydd ap Nicholas, which laid down the rules of poetic metre. A rather strange commission by Elizabeth in 1568 suggested that the principality was crawling with bards and minstrels and authorized an eisteddfod at Caerwys to restore order—competent bards were to be recognized by experts, 'the rest not worthy to return to some honest labour'. The institution declined in the 17th cent. but in the 18th cent. there was a marked increase of interest in Welsh language and culture, with the Society of Cymmrodorion set up in 1751 and the Gwynnedigion Society in 1771. Revivals of local eisteddfodau soon followed, with meetings at Corwen and Bala in 1789. 'The first of the great modern eisteddfodau' was held at Carmarthen in 1819. The National Eisteddfod Association was formed in 1880 and holds an annual gathering, alternating between north and south Wales. There are also provincial and local eisteddfodau. JAC

El Alamein, battle of, 1942. Fought in Egypt, close to Alexandria, El Alamein was the first decisive, irreversible British victory over German ground forces, which, together with their Italian allies, were forced to retreat 1,500 miles to

Tunisia. Rommel, short of fuel and against British air superiority, could not fight a mobile battle to balance *Montgomery's superiority in combat troops. The 8th Army had nearly 200,000 men, more than half from Britain, the rest from India, Australia, New Zealand, and South Africa, against about 100,000 Italians and Germans. Attrition dominated the battle and British inferiority to the Germans in manœuvre and in co-operation between different ground arms was no handicap. Montgomery has been criticized for sluggish exploitation of his victory and failure to cut off the German retreat. However, the battle caused silenced church bells in Britain to be rung in celebration and made Montgomery a national hero. Together with the much larger-scale victory of the Red Army at Stalingrad, Alamein came to seem the turning-point in the war against Hitler. Cinematographic exploitation followed with *Desert Victory*, the British film which opened by using the dramatic effect of the intense artillery barrage at the start of the battle; a just tribute to the consistent excellence of British field artillery. RACP

Eldon, John Scott, 1st earl of (1751–1838). Lord chancellor. The son of a Newcastle coal merchant, Scott rose rapidly in his profession. He entered Parliament in 1783, and became solicitor-general 1788 and attorney-general 1793. He led for the crown in the 'treason trials' of Thomas *Hardy and other radicals in 1794. He was appointed lord chief justice of Common Pleas in 1799, becoming Baron Eldon, and lord chancellor in 1801. He was a favourite of George III, who called him '*My* Lord Chancellor'. He served in the cabinets of *Addington, *Pitt, *Perceval, and *Liverpool until 1827. He was blamed by liberals for obstructing all reform and by others for the long delays in the Court of Chancery, though these were caused more by his conscientiousness in reaching judgments and the increase of litigation in this period. Eldon came to symbolize political obscurantism and right-wing extremism but was an exceptionally able lawyer and in private life good-natured, even-tempered, and affectionate, fond of a good story and good port. EAS

Eleanor of Aquitaine (*c.*1122–1204), queen of Henry II. Heiress to the vast duchy of Aquitaine, Eleanor first married Louis VII of France in 1137, but they were divorced in 1152, partly because they were temperamentally incompatible, but largely because Eleanor had produced only daughters. Aquitaine accordingly reverted to Eleanor. In 1152 she married Henry of Anjou, soon to be king of England, and over the next fifteen years bore him eight children. Their marital relations deteriorated, however, and this played a part in Eleanor's most significant decision in Henry's reign—to rebel against him in 1173 in support of her sons. Her plans misfired, she was captured by Henry, and until his death in 1189 was kept in close confinement, carefully watched, in England. On Richard I's accession, she was released and renewed her political life with relish, playing an important role during Richard's absence on crusade and then, on his death, crucially securing the loyalty of Aquitaine for John during the succession crisis of 1199–1200. She was very beautiful, very civilized, and a keen patron of the arts. SL

Eleanor of Castile (*c.*1242–90), queen of Edward I. The daughter of Ferdinand III, Eleanor married Edward I in October 1254, when they were both children, bringing with her Gascony. The couple were unusually close and Eleanor accompanied him on several crusades. Much of her time was taken up with raising their fourteen children, including the future Edward II, born in 1284. Although intelligent and cultivated, both she and Edward were regarded as grasping: 'the King he wants to get our gold, the Queen would like our lands to hold,' ran a contemporary jingle. Edward was devoted to her and mourned her death deeply. He commissioned a series of twelve stone crosses, known as the *Eleanor crosses, to mark the stopping-places of her funeral cortège from Lincoln to Westminster abbey. The effigy on her tomb in the abbey shows her beauty and is remarkable for its attention to detail. SMC

Eleanor of Provence (1223–91), queen of Henry III. Daughter of Raymond Berenger IV, count of Provence, Eleanor came from a cultivated and well-connected family. Negotiations for her to marry Henry III began in 1235, the marriage taking place in Canterbury the following year. There were five children, Edward, Edmund, Margaret, Beatrice, and Catherine. The queen and her Provençal relatives were not popular: her uncle William, bishop-elect of Valence, was said to have returned to France with a vast fortune. She raised funds for her husband during the baronial wars and gathered troops on his behalf. Much of her wealth was used up and when she entered a convent after his death in 1272, she was heavily in debt. She died at Amesbury on 25 June 1291 and was given a full burial by Edward I, her son, who paid off her debts. SMC

Eleanor crosses were monuments erected by Edward I at Lincoln, Grantham, Stamford, Geddington, Northampton (at Hardingstone), Stony Stratford, Woburn, Dunstable, St Albans, Waltham, West Cheap in the city of London, and the royal mews at Charing between 1291 and 1294 to commemorate the progress of the funeral cortège of his queen *Eleanor of Castile from Harby where she died to her burial place in Westminster abbey. Those at Waltham, Geddington, and Hardingstone still survive. They represent a personal statement by Edward of grief and loss of a queen of whom 'living we dearly cherished, and whom dead we cannot cease to love'. They are almost certainly modelled on the 'montjoies', crosses erected to mark the progress of Louis IX of France's body from Aigues Mortes to Paris in 1270. LR

electricity industry. As early as the 1830s the researches of Galvani, Volta, Daniell, Davy, Sturgeon, *Faraday and others had provided the scientific basis for the development of the electrical industry. The principles of electrolysis, the arc-lamp, the incandescent lamp, the electric motor, and the dynamo were understood, yet, partly due to the dominance of *gas lighting, electricity was slow to reveal its potential. In the 1840s arc-lighting was used to light a few streets, and chemical batteries and copper wire were used in a rapidly expanding electric telegraph network, which had 3,700 miles of line by 1852.

Despite improvements to the dynamo, it was not until the development of a proven incandescent-filament lamp in 1878 by *Swan in Britain and in 1879 by Edison in the USA that the rapid growth of public electricity supply was feasible. From the early 1880s efficient generators, mainly driven by steam power, and small lamps combined to provide the technical base for the expansion of the industry. A major improvement in generation was provided by *Parsons's steam-turbine, which improved the output of power stations by greatly increasing the speed of rotation of the dynamo. In suitable locations small hydroelectric schemes were promoted, beginning in 1881 in Godalming (Surrey). Other such ventures, including a municipal scheme near Worcester, varied in size and were located as far apart as Greenock and Lynmouth.

During the 1890s the market for electricity widened and power stations were built in many cities and towns by private electricity companies or local authorities. Apart from providing light, they increasingly supplied power for street tramways, and later, in London and Glasgow, for underground railways. Bristol was the first local authority to operate an electricity supply service of any great size. Beginning in 1893 it provided both private and street lighting and soon began to compete effectively with gas. The electricity industry continued to make progress and by 1912 about 25 per cent of power used in British industry was electrical. However, foreign firms dominated, for electrical transport and factory power was mainly provided by American and German expertise.

Before the evolution of the national grid in the late 1920s, the electricity supply industry was in the hands of small stations and relatively small companies. The Electricity Supply Act of 1926 encouraged the regulation of current and greater standardization of the industry. Generating stations increased in capacity as electricity accounted for a growing proportion of power needs. Like coal-mining, the electrical industry was nationalized under the third Labour government.

Subsequently during the 1950s and 1960s, there was considerable expansion to meet industrial and domestic needs, as well as the electrification of the railways. Generation was mainly by coal or nuclear power, and there was also substantial investment in hydroelectric schemes in the Scottish Highlands. Alternative energy sources, mainly wind and tidal power, were explored, but partly on economic grounds, and partly in line with decreasing demand in the wake of the energy crisis in the 1970s, investment was limited to experimental plant. In line with the policies of the Conservative government, denationalization and privatization of both generating and supply took place in the late 1980s. ID

'Eleven Years Tyranny' (1629–40). After the tumultuous end to the 1629 session of Parliament (see ELIOT, SIR JOHN) Charles I broke with convention—though not with law—by ruling without Parliament for eleven years. Financial needs were met through prerogative levies, the most notorious of which was *ship money, and the prerogative court of *Star Chamber supervised the maintenance of order in both state and church. This was hardly a tyranny, for Charles had no police force or standing army to compel obedience. Indeed, despite widespread resentment among the aristocracy and gentry, upon whom royal rule ultimately depended, they never refused to co-operate. In the end, it was Charles's own misjudgement in the *Bishops' wars and not popular anger which brought the 'Eleven Years Tyranny' to an end. RL

Elgar, Edward (1857–1934). Though Elgar was not greatly interested in the revival of English folk-song which gathered pace in his lifetime, his music is soaked in the scenery of his native Worcestershire. He was born at Broadheath, just west of Worcester, where his father kept a music shop, in the shadow of the Malvern hills. Largely self-taught, his early life was spent as a local musician, conducting bands and choirs and teaching the violin. His breakthrough came with the Enigma Variations (1899), commemorating his friends in the area, and heralding a tremendous burst of creative energy until the Great War and the death of his wife Alice. *Sea Pictures* (1899) were followed by *The Dream of Gerontius* (1900), the First Symphony (1908), the Violin Concerto (1910), the Second Symphony (1911) and the darker Cello Concerto (1919). Honours were heaped upon him—a knighthood (1904), the Order of Merit (1911), mastership of the king's musick (1924), and a baronetcy (1931). Standing at the end of the great romantic tradition and on the eve of the Great War, his work is shot through with sunset gleams and his favourite marking was *nobilmente*. His palm-court pieces and the extraordinarily popular 'Pomp and Circumstance' marches gave him a reputation at variance with reality. With the appearance of a retired colonel and often accused of jingo patriotism, Elgar was, in fact, a deeply sensitive man, easily hurt, and haunted by 'the land where corals lie'. Even 'Enigma', to the listener a serene theme, Elgar thought expressed 'the loneliness of the artist'. He is buried in a small catholic cemetery at Little Malvern, overlooking the great plain of the Severn towards Bredon Hill. His statue at Worcester, near the cathedral, surveys a traffic roundabout. JAC

Elgin marbles. These were part of the frieze and pediment of the Parthenon of Athens and other carvings from *c.*440 BC, sent to England by the 7th earl of Elgin. While British ambassador in Constantinople, he obtained authority from the Turks first to study, then to remove some of the antiquities, which were badly looked after. After an eventful journey during which some of the carvings were shipwrecked and the earl detained in France, the sculptures arrived in England to controversy about the wisdom and validity of their purchase by the government. Finally in 1816 Elgin received £35,000, much less than his expenses, and the marbles were placed in the British Museum. The Greek government has at times requested their return. JC

Eliot, George (1819–80). Novelist whose real name was Mary Anne (later Marian) Evans. Born in Warwickshire, she was the daughter of a land agent whose moral qualities are reflected in those of the upright *Adam Bede*. The landscapes and rhythms of daily life in the (fictionalized) towns of the

English midlands are reflected in much of her best work, notably in her two novels set at the time of the first Reform Bill, *Felix Holt, the Radical* (1866) and the masterly *Middlemarch: A Tale of Provincial Life* (1871–2). In 1854 she established a lasting partnership with George Henry Lewes, the 'scandal' of her open liaison obliging her to publish her fiction under an assumed masculine name. Her reading of the works of Feuerbach, Hegel, Comte, and later, *Darwin informs the arguments of her fiction with a decidedly 'historical' base, a *positivist theme being especially noticeable in *Romola* (1863), a novel set in Savonarola's Florence. ALS

Eliot, Sir John (1592–1632). Eliot, a parliamentarian, was initially a client of the royal favourite *Buckingham, but turned against him. In 1626 he took part in the impeachment proceedings against Buckingham, comparing him to Sejanus, the notorious favourite of Tiberius. For this, Charles I imprisoned him in the Tower. Further imprisonment followed in 1627, when Eliot refused to pay the *forced loan. In 1629 he led the Commons' attack on *Arminianism and prerogative taxation, and organized the coup on 2 May when the Speaker was held down in his chair to prevent him foreclosing debate, as the king had ordered. Eliot was again sent to the Tower, where he spent the rest of his life composing a treatise exalting royal authority. His commitment to parliamentary liberties was undoubted, but by preferring the role of demagogue to that of constructive statesman he blocked the way to compromise. RL

Eliot, T. S. (1888–1965). Poet and man of letters. Born in St Louis, after Harvard he studied in Europe, in 1927 becoming a British citizen. With the encouragement of Ezra Pound he produced *The Waste Land* (1922), usually seen as a commentary on the western civilization which collapsed in the Great War, though he preferred to think of it as 'a piece of rhythmical grumbling'. Equally innovative literary criticism helped create the taste by which he was admired, though in 1927 his confirmation in the Anglican church to many seemed an anachronism. For others, the religious poetry of *Ash-Wednesday* (1930) and *Four Quartets* (1943) is his most profound response to the times. Attempts to restore poetic drama to the West End stage had more mixed success, though *Murder in the Cathedral* (1935) has endured. By now very much an establishment figure, he found solace in a late second marriage happier than his first. JNRS

Elizabeth I (1533–1603), queen of England (1558–1603). 'A very strange sort of woman,' wrote the imperial ambassador three weeks after Elizabeth's accession. Much of the pattern of Elizabeth's life and reign was shaped by the circumstances of her birth. Her mother was *Anne Boleyn, Henry VIII's second wife. Elizabeth was born at Greenwich in September 1533 five months after her parents' marriage had been announced. Her father was momentarily disappointed by the birth of a daughter but comforted himself that a son would no doubt follow. *Cranmer's declaration in May 1533 that Henry's previous marriage to *Catherine of Aragon had been invalid meant that Elizabeth took precedence over her half-sister Mary, seventeen years her senior.

Elizabeth's early years were even more turbulent than those of Mary, but with different results. While Mary retreated into her religion, Elizabeth grew up wary and dexterous. Her position as heir was confirmed by the Act of *Succession of 1534 but her favoured situation lasted less than three years. In May 1536 her mother was executed and a new Act of Succession declared Anne's marriage void, Elizabeth illegitimate, and recognized Henry's third marriage to *Jane Seymour as 'without spot, doubt or impediment'. The birth of her half-brother Edward in October 1537 made her chances of succeeding to the throne appear remote. After Henry's three last marriages had failed to produce more children, a third Act of Succession in 1543 reinstated his daughters, declaring that if Edward died without heirs, the throne would pass to Mary and then Elizabeth. The king's will in 1546 confirmed that arrangement and accordingly Edward succeeded in 1547. Elizabeth was then 13.

She had spent most of her girlhood at *Hatfield. She received a high-powered classical education which left her in command of Latin and Greek and speaking French, Spanish, and Italian 'most perfectly'. 'My illustrious mistress shines like a star,' wrote Roger *Ascham, one of her tutors. She was on good terms with *Catherine Parr, Henry's last wife, and when, after his death, Catherine married Lord *Seymour, Somerset's younger brother, Elizabeth moved into the household. The arrangement ended when Seymour made playful advances to Elizabeth which were not totally unwelcome. After Catherine died in childbirth, Seymour suggested marriage to Elizabeth, who replied prudently that such a matter should be laid before the council. Seymour was arrested in 1549 on a charge of treason and Elizabeth closely questioned by Sir Robert Tyrwhitt, who confessed himself baffled that she would not 'cough out' anything: 'she hath a very good wit and nothing is to be got from her but by great policy.'

During the rest of Edward's reign she was in good standing at court and sympathetic towards the religious changes. But there are few mentions of Elizabeth in Edward's journal and they do not seem to have been very close. Consequently, when he was dying in the spring of 1553 and could not bear the thought of a catholic succession, Edward bypassed Elizabeth and named Lady Jane *Grey, *Northumberland's daughter-in-law, as his successor. During the ensuing crisis which placed Mary on the throne, Elizabeth stayed at Hatfield on the plea of illness. She was not well rewarded for her acquiescence in Mary's triumph. Within a month Mary was urging her to attend mass and Elizabeth, in floods of tears, real or simulated, begged for time to study the question. The following month, Mary's first Parliament acknowledged the validity of Catherine of Aragon's marriage, by implication bastardizing Elizabeth once more. Yet Mary did not take the next step of removing her formally from the succession, presumably because, until six months before her death, she hoped for children of her own.

In February 1554 *Wyatt's rising against Mary's Spanish marriage brought Elizabeth to the brink of disaster. Summoned urgently to court as the Kentish rebels advanced upon London, she pleaded more illness, then reluctantly obeyed. In March she was sent to the Tower while the conspirators were racked to provide evidence against her. 'She will have to be executed,' wrote the emperor's envoy Mendoza briskly, 'as while she lives it will be very difficult to make the Prince's [Philip] entry here safe.' But no evidence could be found and after two months she was sent off to Woodstock under house arrest. It was not an experience Elizabeth forgot: twelve years later she told her Parliament, 'I stood in danger of my life, my sister was so incensed against me.' While she was at Woodstock, Soranzo the Venetian ambassador sent a long description of her: 'her figure and face are very handsome, and such an air of dignified majesty pervades all her actions that no one can fail to suppose she is a queen . . . her manners are very modest and affable.' Ultimately she returned to Hatfield, kept her head down, attended mass regularly, and refused all offers of marriage. 'She is too clever to get herself caught,' Renard, the imperial ambassador, told the emperor. Elizabeth received some protection from an unexpected quarter—Philip, who, increasingly aware that his marriage to Mary would be neither fruitful nor lengthy, was thinking of long-term investments. Mary, queen of Scots, the next heir, though a catholic, was betrothed to the dauphin and would certainly carry England, Scotland, and Ireland into the camp of his French enemies.

In the event, Elizabeth's accession, on 17 November 1558, passed off without incident. Even Mary, in her last weeks, had conceded its inevitability. Elizabeth was faced at once with the same problems that had confronted Mary on her accession five years before—the religious question and her own marriage.

The outlines of her religious policy were signalled at an early stage when she pointedly absented herself from the elevation of the host, placed two of Mary's bishops under arrest for intemperate sermons, and in her first Parliament took back the governorship of the church. It would have been surprising had she done anything else. Her mother had sympathized with the reformers, and Elizabeth herself, educated with her brother Edward by protestant tutors, shared his views, though not his zeal. To adopt a catholic posture would have meant accepting her own bastardy and admitting that she had no right to the throne. It might, of course, have been possible in the intricate ecclesiastical politics of 1558 to come to some arrangement with the papacy, but since the pope was at that time a staunch ally of the French, whose new queen, Mary, was a genuine catholic and had just claimed the English throne, it might seem a thin chance. The famous *via media* was to a great extent forced upon her. Catholicism certainly would have meant giving up the headship and possibly the throne as well: calvinism, as James VI of Scotland was to discover, meant being hectored by godly presbyters. By the end of 1559 the whole bench of catholic bishops had been replaced.

The second problem, marriage, had already caused trouble. There has been considerable speculation about the nature of Elizabeth's sexuality. But the romping with Seymour, the long attachment to *Leicester, her sad coquetry with Anjou in the late 1570s, and her appreciation of 'proper men' like *Raleigh and *Essex suggest normal heterosexuality. Nor is there any reason to believe that she could not have borne children. The political objections to marriage were overwhelming and her council and Parliament urged in vain. Any husband would certainly interfere and possibly dominate, and general opinion would support him. A foreign husband would drag the country into continental disputes and reawaken religious animosities: marriage to a subject would be an act of condescension and a formula for faction. Though her reasons for virginity were largely negative, she turned it to her own advantage, declaring that she was married to her people. Elizabeth's decision may have been wrong. But her sister's marriage had scarcely been a success and though Mary, queen of Scots, can hardly be accused of being against matrimony, the results were not encouraging. Elizabeth's cautious attitude extended to naming a successor. No doubt she postponed doing so for the reason that many people postpone making their wills, but essentially it was political—a named successor would create a rival centre of power and an invitation to intrigue. 'I know the inconstancy of the people of England,' she observed privately in 1561, 'how they ever mislike the present government and have their eyes fixed upon that person who is next to succeed.'

Two other decisions could not be delayed—her choice of advisers and her attitude towards the war with France which she had inherited from her sister. On the very first day of her reign she appointed as secretary William Cecil, (*Burghley), whom she had employed as her estates surveyor. He was yoked with *Knollys as vice-chamberlain, Nicholas *Bacon as lord keeper, Clinton as lord high admiral, and *Howard as lord chamberlain. Despite internal rivalries and some very rough treatment from the queen, they stayed in service until they died and, joined in 1559 by Dudley (Leicester) and from 1573 by *Walsingham, formed a remarkable team.

Elizabeth was anxious to wind up the war against France, but dared not risk alienating her ally Philip, lest the nightmare possibility of a grand catholic coalition of Spain, France, and Scotland should come into existence. Nor could she easily reconcile herself to losing *Calais and in the end a face-saving formula had to be devised. No sooner had she escaped from one conflict than another emerged—in Scotland where, with great reluctance, she was persuaded to intervene in 1560 on behalf of the protestant lords against the French. Though the assault on the French-held Leith castle was a dismal failure, the death of Mary of Guise took the heart out of the French resistance and by the treaty of *Edinburgh they agreed to withdraw. Elizabeth's initial reluctance was due in part to natural caution, concern for the cost of the enterprise, but also to the thought that helping subjects to resist their lawful monarch was a bad example. She showed less reluctance in her next adventure, which was an unmitigated fiasco. Religious wars in France in 1562 held out the hope of strengthening the protestant cause there and of regaining Calais. An expedition to assist the Huguenots took possession of Le Havre, to be exchanged for Calais. The French factions then made peace to unite against the English, the English force was decimated by disease, and obliged to surrender.

The next developments in foreign affairs were on a totally different scale—no limited interventions, but the great crisis of her reign. Three problems, only partly related, ran together in the 1570s and 1580s—the international religious question, the problem of Mary, queen of Scots, and the developing rift with Philip over the revolt of the Low Countries. For some time, even after the readoption of the governorship of the church, the reaction of the papacy was restrained, since it was not clear that the breach would be permanent and there were suggestions that Elizabeth was sympathetic to catholicism. But immediately after the failure of the rising of the *northern earls, Pius V, far less moderate than his predecessor Pius IV who had extended an invitation to Elizabeth to send representatives to the Council of Trent, issued in 1570 a bull deposing her and absolving her catholic subjects from allegiance. The result was a series of plots against Elizabeth's life—*Ridolfi 1572, *Throckmorton 1584, Parry 1585, and *Babington 1586. The second element of the worsening storm was the decision of Mary, queen of Scots, after her disastrous marriages to *Darnley and *Bothwell, to flee her country in 1568 and place herself under Elizabeth's protection. She was soon under close arrest. Despair at ever being released led Mary to dabble in plots and each plot produced fresh demands from ardent protestants for her execution to safeguard the regime. For many years Elizabeth resisted but the Babington plot sealed Mary's fate and she was executed in 1587. Elizabeth, characteristically, blamed her secretary Davidson for a misunderstanding but the confusion was largely diplomatic. The third factor was that relations with her erstwhile ally Philip broke down and from 1585 Elizabeth sent help to the Dutch rebels. Philip's retort was to begin planning the invasion of England and in July 1588 the great *Armada left Corunna. At Tilbury, Elizabeth delivered the most famous of all her speeches, 'not doubting that by your obedience to my general, by your concord in the camp, and your valour in the field, we shall shortly have a famous victory over those enemies of my God, of my Kingdom and of my People.'

The defeat of the Armada turned her into a living legend and the most famous of all English monarchs. It was a fame she nurtured carefully, devoting great attention to the presentation of her image. Inevitably the later years were something of an anticlimax. Philip launched more attacks, the plots against her life continued, and the centre of anxiety moved to Ireland, where *Tyrone's rebellion had Spanish support. Many of her counter-measures were unsuccessful and Essex's foolish behaviour in Ireland, followed by his abortive insurrection, darkened her last days. But she died still in charge, capable of putting on performances and, at the end, naming 'our cousin of Scotland', James VI, as her successor.

Though her character was that of her father—a tempestuous personality with sunshine and heavy showers—her policies were more akin to those of her grandfather Henry VII—an attention to money bordering on meanness, reluctance to summon Parliament, and a disinclination to foreign adventure which would not only be inordinately expensive but place her at the mercy of the military. After the usual dip immediately after her death, her reputation soared and as the Stuarts floundered, the great days of Good Queen Bess seemed more and more golden. Lord Cobham at Stowe in the 18th cent. placed her in his temple of British worthies, along with Alfred the Great, Shakespeare, and Newton. The late 20th cent. has seen criticism from historians, to whom admiration does not come easily. 'The defeat of the Spanish Armada in 1588 solved nothing', we are told—a very odd verdict. The love she claimed to have for her people was shallow and insincere; she outstayed her welcome until the gap between image and reality became grotesque; the young men at her court in the 1590s were impatient and ribald; many of her policies were muddled and she made procrastination an art-form; she took little interest in the mechanics of government; her religious policy pleased nobody. In most of these criticisms there is a grain of truth, but collectively they suggest a determination not to be pleased. It is easier to attack her religious policy than to suggest how ardent catholic and zealous calvinist could be reconciled, nor were many of her contemporary rulers conspicuously successful. Images are always inflated—that is their purpose—but it is to her credit that she understood the importance of imagery. Like all sensible rulers she was, of course, interested primarily in her own survival: dead monarchs have no policy. But though her treatment of men was often bad, her judgement of them was usually good. Essex captivated her but Cecil and his son ran the country. Her religious settlement may have been a patchwork of compromises but the Church of England took root and earned respect and affection. It is, of course, perfectly permissible to prefer the wisdom of her predecessor Mary, or the political skills of her successors James and Charles, but it would be a little strange. JAC

Haigh, C., *Elizabeth I* (1988); —— (ed.), *The Reign of Elizabeth I* (1984); Johnson, P., *Elizabeth: A Study in Power and Intellect* (1974); Ridley, J., *Elizabeth I* (1987); Strong, R., *The Cult of Elizabeth: Elizabethan Portraiture and Pageantry* (1977).

Elizabeth II (b. 1926), queen of Great Britain and Northern Ireland (1952–). When Princess Elizabeth was born to the duke and duchess of York in 1926 there was little reason to expect that she would succeed to the throne. Her uncle, the prince of Wales, was only 31 and was being urged to marry: it was also quite possible that her parents would have a son who would take precedence. But the birth of her younger sister Margaret Rose in 1930 closed the family account and the abdication of her uncle in 1936 brought her father to the throne as George VI.

The Yorks were a close-knit and affectionate family and the princess had a secure and uncomplicated childhood. Since she was not sent to school, nurses and governesses bulked large—Clara Knight ('Alla'), Margaret MacDonald ('Bobo'), and Marion Crawford ('Crawfie'). The first two spent the rest of their lives in royal service: the third eventually resigned to marry, broke the convention of confidentiality by writing a book about the two princesses, and was cast into outer darkness. Princess Elizabeth grew up pretty, cheerful, and obedient, though less vivacious than her younger sister. Her strong sense of duty called to mind her grandfather George V and Queen Victoria. As she grew up, Crawfie's instruction was strengthened by teachers brought in for constitutional history and languages and by visits to museums and art galleries. Her education remained unstructured and was further disrupted by the war.

Most of the war was spent at Windsor castle, where the princesses learned the art of rolling out of bed and into air raid shelters when the sirens sounded. At the age of 18, and with the war coming to a close, Elizabeth was allowed to join the ATS as a subaltern and went each day to Aldershot to take a driving and vehicle maintenance course. She was already devoted to her cousin Philip Mountbatten, a naval officer and five years her senior. They regarded themselves as engaged from the summer of 1946 and were married in November 1947. Their first child, Prince Charles, was born a year later. In 1952 she succeeded her father on the throne at the age of 25.

The coronation of 1953, the first to be seen on television, was a great success, a splash of colour and ceremony in a still austere post-war Britain. Excitable journalists wrote fatuously of a New Elizabethan Age to come. In fact criticism developed rather quickly. Though not shy, the queen had reserve and, though nobody could accuse her of taking her duties lightly, she did not seem much to enjoy them, having neither the warmth nor easy manner of her mother. In 1957 when Lord Altrincham complained that she sounded like a 'priggish schoolgirl', he was predictably threatened with horsewhipping and the borough of Altrincham hastened to dissociate itself from so subversive an opinion. Political clouds also rolled in quickly. Britain found it extremely hard to shake off recurrent financial and economic crises and the *Suez fiasco of 1956 was a reminder that the country had neither its former strength, nor perhaps its confidence.

The two themes which dominated the early years of her reign were the painful process of economic recovery and withdrawal from empire. By 1953 the crippled economies of Europe were beginning to recover and Germany, in particular, proved a formidable competitor, especially in car manufacture. This was followed by the rise of the Far Eastern economies, and Japan, Hong Kong, and Korea, which before the war had been synonymous with cheap toys, demonstrated quality and inventiveness in radios, televisions, refrigerators, computers, and shipbuilding. Many of Britain's basic industries—railways, mines, shipyards, cotton mills—were in dire need of re-equipment and investment, yet at the same time there was an urgent demand for houses, schools, and hospitals. Her third prime minister, Harold *Macmillan, wrote rather simply in July 1960, 'the public want them all, but they do not like the idea of paying for them.' Several of her governments ran onto the rocks of balance of payments difficulties, inflation, unemployment, and runs on the pound: traditional industries declined and their replacements were slow to emerge.

The Suez crisis was only one of the more dramatic episodes in the retreat from empire. The withdrawal from India had taken place in 1948 before Elizabeth came to the throne. It was followed into independence by Malaya (1957), Ghana (1957), Nigeria (1960), Sierra Leone (1961), Tanganyika (1961), Uganda (1962), Jamaica (1962), Trinidad (1962), Zambia (1964), and Aden (1967). The withdrawals were effected with relatively little rancour, though there was fighting in Malaya (1948–60), in Aden (1963–73), a protracted crisis over Southern Rhodesia (1965–80), and an unpleasant and tedious campaign in Kenya against *Mau Mau from 1952 to 1955. The queen and the royal family played an active role in efforts to transform the empire into a commonwealth of equal states. But most of the newly independent countries opted to become republics and although the queen remained head of the Commonwealth, her role was largely social. The strength of Commonwealth bonds was weakened by Britain's increasing involvement with Europe. In addition, two of the most influential Commonwealth states seceded for long periods—South Africa between 1961 and 1994, and Pakistan from 1972 until 1989. Royal visits to the former dominions continued but even there difficulties emerged, with severe federal problems in Canada and moves towards republicanism in Australia.

The later years of her reign have seen considerable economic progress, though still subject to sudden mishaps. Macmillan's remark of 1957—'most of our people have never had it so good'—was premature, but despite a decline in Britain's comparative trading position, the gross national product continued to grow, albeit slowly, and her subjects acquired television sets, cars, telephones, washing machines, and spin-driers on a scale quite unknown in 1952. This was partly because the sharp rise in world oil prices which followed the Arab–Israeli war of 1973 and which threatened acute balance of payments problems was offset by the exploitation of North Sea oil from 1975 onwards.

As the empire shrank and economic performance faltered, Britain's relationship with Europe emerged as a major issue. It had implications for the monarchy since the more advanced schemes for a federal Europe would affect sovereignty and therefore the position of the sovereign. A British/European coinage which did not include the monarch's head would be a breach with tradition dating back to *Offa and *Alfred. Britain's first two applications to join the *European Economic Community were vetoed by de Gaulle in 1963 and 1967, before Edward *Heath's government gained acceptance in 1972. In the 1980s, as what was at first envisaged as a trading community moved towards political integration, the question of 'Europe' moved steadily to the front of the political agenda.

Of more immediate concern to the queen was probably the role of the monarchy itself and the vicissitudes of the royal family. The latter were a mixture of bad luck, compounded by the rapidly changing values of society, and the emergence of an intrusive and insistent press, which took pride in its lack of respect. The days when an innocent party in a divorce action could not expect an invitation to royal functions were long past, and the restraint that had kept Edward VIII's infatuation with Mrs *Simpson out of the news until the very last minute would have been unthinkable 40 years later. The first indications that the royal road might be bumpy came in 1953 when the queen's sister wished to marry a distinguished airman, Group Captain Peter Townsend, who was in the process of divorcing his wife. The issue came to a head at the very start of the new reign and the princess was persuaded not to marry him. When she did marry Anthony Armstrong Jones in 1960, it ended in divorce. These were no more than the drops of rain that preceded the deluge. The queen's cousin Lord Harewood was divorced for adultery in 1967. The marriages of all three royal children who embarked on matrimony also ended in divorce. The princess royal's marriage to Captain Mark Phillips was dissolved in 1992; the duke of York divorced Sarah Ferguson in 1995, and the protracted and much-publicized rift between the prince and princess of Wales ended in divorce in 1996. In November 1992 at the Guildhall, the queen referred ruefully to a year which had seen one divorce, two marital breakdowns, and a devastating fire at Windsor castle as 'not a year on which I shall look back with undiluted pleasure . . . an *annus horribilis*'. Many people must have wondered whether the victory of the 'modernizers' in the palace over the 'traditionalists' had been of benefit to the monarchy. The incessant publicity which surrounded the royal family as a result of the activities of the 'royal rat-pack' suggests that it is easier to start the process of reform than to control it, and that lifting the curtain to let in a little light might encourage people to burn the curtain itself.

It is too soon for any informed assessment of the queen's constitutional role. Though her prime ministers have enthusiastically published their memoirs, they have been bland in their references to the sovereign and it is to their advantage to stress the cordiality with which they have been received. There was some criticism of the procedure in 1957 when *Eden was forced by ill-health to resign and was succeeded by Macmillan rather than *Butler. But the lord chancellor and the lord president of the council (Kilmuir and *Salisbury) were asked to sound the cabinet, and its strong preference for Macmillan was confirmed by the chief whip, the chairman of the 1922 committee, the chairman of the Conservative Party, and Sir Winston *Churchill. The queen certainly did not act against advice. Nor did she in 1963 when the choice of Lord *Home to succeed Macmillan caused surprise. She acted on the advice of Macmillan himself, whom she visited in hospital, and who had consulted widely. Changed arrangements in the Conservative Party in 1965 for electing its leader make it unlikely that this royal prerogative will cause awkwardness in future. Nor will many others. At every general election there is earnest discussion of the attitude the queen would take should there be a 'hung Parliament' but the contingency is remote, and the mechanics of consultation seem well established.

There is no doubt that, from the 1980s onwards, there has been increased criticism of the royal family, though not of Elizabeth herself. The urge by some of its members to seek publicity and unburden themselves to the press proved short-sighted and merely fed the monster. The decline in respect is a general phenomenon and applies to many other institutions—to the church, the law, Parliament, and, not least, to the press itself. It is often said that the royal family has become a soap opera. But this element has always been present, centuries before the term 'soap opera' was coined, since spectacle and pageantry, spiced by gossip and anecdote, have always been part of the monarchy's appeal. Not for nothing is the longest running soap opera called *Coronation Street*. Yet a policy of openness, inaugurated perhaps by the film *Royal Family* (1966), has evident dangers. Satire, which in the 1960s was refreshing and witty, may become coarse and spiteful. Newspapers are not slow to understand that fervent admiration sells fewer papers than indignation and envy. 'The Palace' has often had to ponder the balance between over- and under-exposure. That the latter has its risks is demonstrated by the example of Queen Victoria's unpopularity during her seclusion after Albert's death. But the problems caused by under-exposure are more easily remedied. JAC

Bradford, S., *Elizabeth* (1996); Bogdanor, V., *The Monarchy and the Constitution* (Oxford, 1995); Cannon, J. A., and Griffiths, R. A., *The Oxford Illustrated History of the British Monarchy* (Oxford, 1988); Lacey, R., *Majesty: Elizabeth II and the House of Windsor* (1977); Longford, E., *Elizabeth R: A Biography* (1983).

Elizabeth of Bohemia (1596–1662). The lives of Elizabeth and her husband are part of the fabric of European history in the early 17th cent. The eldest daughter of James VI and I and sister of Charles I, she married in 1613 Frederick of the Palatinate. Five years later, the Bohemians elected Frederick as king in defiance of the Habsburgs. In the wars that followed, they were driven out of their new kingdom and the Palatinate overrun. She spent only October 1619–November 1620 at Prague and hence was known as the 'Winter Queen'. Elizabeth's husband died in 1632 and her son Charles Lewis was not restored to part of the Palatinate until the peace of Westphalia in 1648. By then her native land was in turmoil and she was forced to continue abroad: her small court was said to be overrun by rats, mice, and creditors. After the Restoration, she visited her nephew Charles II in England in 1661 but died shortly afterwards. She was the mother of Prince *Rupert and through her daughter Sophia the Hanoverians came to the throne of Britain in 1714. *Pepys, who saw her in 1660, thought her a 'plain lady', but in Sir Henry Wotton's poem 'Ye meaner beauties of the night', written about 1619, she was portrayed as a vision of loveliness. JAC

Elizabeth Bowes-Lyon (b. 1900), queen of George VI and queen mother. Perhaps the most remarkable member of the royal family in modern times, Elizabeth was born at St Paul's Waldenbury (Herts.), daughter of Claude Bowes-Lyon, 14th earl of Strathmore in the Scottish peerage. The earliest title in the family was Lord Glamis (1445). Her mother was a great-granddaughter of the 3rd duke of Portland, prime minister 1783 and 1807–9. She had six brothers, one of whom was killed in the Great War, and three sisters, one of whom died before Elizabeth was born. Her childhood was extremely happy, mainly because of the high spirits of her mother: 'fun, kindness, and a marvellous sense of security' was her own summary. When she was 19 she met Prince Albert (duke of York and future George VI) and in 1923, after some hesitation, agreed to marry him. Their daughters Elizabeth and Margaret Rose were born in 1926 and 1930. The abdication of her brother-in-law Edward VIII in 1936 brought her husband to the throne and made her queen. During the Second World War the royal couple played a prominent role and their decision not to leave London was an important boost to national morale. George VI's death in 1952 at the age of 56 left her facing a long widowhood. She took the title Her Majesty Queen Elizabeth the Queen Mother. Into advanced age she carried out numerous public duties, which she fulfilled with a grace and warmth universally acknowledged. Much of her private time is spent at her London home of Clarence House or at the small castle of Mey in Caithness-shire. JAC

Elizabeth Woodville (*c.*1437–92), queen of Edward IV. Elizabeth was a widow with two children when she married Edward IV secretly at Grafton Regis (Northants) on 1 May 1464. She was the daughter of Earl *Rivers and Jacquetta of Luxembourg. Almost certainly a love match, the unconventional and unwise marriage to a woman whom contemporaries considered beneath the king's dignity caused political tension, and later allowed Richard III to claim that their children were illegitimate. Her reputation has suffered from the hostile propaganda of her enemies, especially Richard III, who accused her of witchcraft. Yet the Croyland chronicler, the best-informed contemporary, described her as benevolent. In truth she was far more sinned against than sinning, by both her unfaithful husband and ambitious brother-in-law. After the disappearance of her son Edward V in 1483, she endeavoured, ineptly, to play one side against the other. After Bosworth, although her daughter *Elizabeth became queen, she was excluded from court and induced to retire to Bermondsey abbey. In her prosperity she was the second founder of Queens' College, Cambridge, where her portrait hangs. AJP

Elizabeth of York (1465–1503), queen of Henry VII. Henry set the seal on his great victory at *Bosworth in August 1485 by his marriage in January 1486 to Elizabeth, daughter and heiress of Edward IV, thus uniting the houses of York and Lancaster. She had spent the first year of Richard III's reign in sanctuary at Westminster and there were rumours that Richard was to marry her after his wife's death in March 1485. She does not seem to have wished for a political role as queen and died soon after the birth of her last child in the Tower on 11 February 1503. She was said to be beautiful, with golden hair and a pleasant manner. She was buried in Henry VII's great new chapel at Westminster abbey. JAC

Ellendun, battle of, 825. *Egbert's victory over Beornwulf at the battle of Ellendun marks the transition of political overlordship within the Anglo-Saxon kingdoms from Mercia to Wessex. Fought just south of Swindon near the modern village of Wroughton, it gave Egbert mastery of the critical strategic area leading into the middle Thames valley and prepared the way for assertion of effective West Saxon control of England south of the Thames and the south-west up to the borders of Cornwall. Beornwulf is a shadowy figure whose political authority rested on a shaky basis and whose connection with the old ruling Mercian dynasty was dubious. Within a twelvemonth of Ellendun he was killed on a campaign against the East Angles. HL

Elmet, kingdom of. British kingdom based in the south-west of Yorkshire, including the area around Leeds; modern place-names with the suffix 'in-Elmet' delineate its eastern border. At the beginning of the 7th cent. its king Gwallog was allied with other British rulers against Hussa and Theodoric of *Bernicia. The last known British king Ceretic was driven out by *Edwin of Deira *c.*616, perhaps in revenge for the death of his nephew Hereric who had been poisoned in the province. Elmet is listed in the Tribal Hidage, but probably before the end of the 7th cent. had been fully incorporated into Deira. BAEY

Elmham, diocese of. The see of Elmham, conterminous with Norfolk, was created *c.*673 by *Theodore's division of the East Anglian bishopric of *Dunwich. The Danish invasions caused an interregnum, but Elmham revived to have oversight of both Norfolk and Suffolk. The see was moved to Thetford in 1072 and soon afterwards to *Norwich. WMM

Eltham palace near Greenwich in Kent was acquired as a manor house by Edward II in 1311 and expanded by Edward III. It remained an important royal residence throughout the 15th cent., Edward IV adding a great hall. Tudor monarchs continued to make use of it but before the Civil War it had fallen into disrepair. The great hall was rescued in the 19th cent. after it had been used for decades as a barn. JAC

Ely, diocese of. The see, now roughly conterminous with Cambridgeshire, was created in 1109. King *Edgar and *Æthelwold founded a monastery here in 970 to replace the double monastery, established in 673, but destroyed by the Danes in 870. The new wealthy monastery was one of the last English strongholds against the Norman invaders (1070). When the see of *Dorchester was transferred to *Lincoln in 1072, the abbot's request for a bishopric was not granted until 1109, when Henry I and *Anselm carved the Ely diocese out of the vast see of Lincoln. Based as it was on a rich abbey, in Domesday second only to *Glastonbury in wealth, Ely was in the first league of wealth and power, supplying several high officers of state throughout the Middle Ages. Together with the archbishops of Canterbury and York and the bishops of *Winchester and *Durham, bishops of Ely had an income equal to the wealthiest barons. The second bishop, Nigel Le Poer (1133–69), emulated his uncle, *Roger of Salisbury, Henry I's justiciar, by becoming treasurer of England and was instrumental in reforming central government under Henry II. William *Longchamp (1189–97) was chancellor and justiciar under Richard I. His successor Eustace (1198–1215), also chancellor from 1197, had to flee after becoming involved in John's dispute with Innocent III. The 13th-cent. arrival of the Franciscans in Cambridge accelerated the university's growth. The bishops of Ely kept a watchful eye on this new development in their diocese. Hugh de Balsham founded the first college, Peterhouse, in 1284 and subsequent bishops retained their right to confirm the chancellorship until 1401. In 1836 the bishops lost their ancient secular jurisdiction over the Isle of Ely, to compensate which, in 1837, the see was enlarged by the addition of Bedfordshire, Huntingdonshire, and parts of Suffolk. In 1914, nevertheless, the diocese lost Bedfordshire to St Albans and west Suffolk to Bury St Edmunds. The town for centuries had a reputation as a squalid and unhealthy place, but the cathedral, begun c.1083, rose majestically above the fens, a landmark for miles. It has a Norman nave and is noted for its 14th-cent. octagonal lantern tower and its unusual northerly Lady Chapel. WMM

Elyot, Sir Thomas (c.1490–1546). Humanist, administrator, and political theorist. Elyot, whose family were Wiltshire lawyer-landowners, was educated at Oxford and the Middle Temple. Clerk to the justices of assize (1511–26) and to Henry VIII's council (c.1523–30), he retired in 1530 to Carlton, near Cambridge, being knighted in the same year and made ambassador to Charles V in 1531–2. In the 1520s Elyot frequented the humanist circles of Richard Pace and Thomas *More. Though remaining a suspect catholic, he benefited materially from the *dissolution of the monasteries. A portrait drawing of him by Holbein (c.1532) is at Windsor castle. Elyot's *Book Named the Governor* (1531, revised edition 1537, and six more by 1580) advocated a monarchical 'public weal' for England and described the education, on Italian humanist lines, necessary to prepare Englishmen to help the king rule it. His use of English for his *Governor* and more than a dozen other works was intended to show how the vernacular, improved by Latin and Greek example, could be effective in encouraging his countrymen to wise private and public conduct. JBT

emigration is the departure of persons from their native country to settle permanently in another. This might be prompted by the 'push' of religious or political persecution or the 'pull' of work opportunities elsewhere. Governments have used emigration as a policy for keeping law and order at home and for populating new 'underpopulated' overseas colonies when empires expanded.

In the British Isles the first of the relatively large-scale emigrations occurred with the opening up of the New World in the late 16th and 17th cents. Many of those who looked for greater political and religious freedom chose to emigrate. For example, the puritans who sailed to North America on the *Mayflower* in 1620 sought the opportunity to practise their religion without interference. Sometimes the emigrants had considerable influence. The quaker William *Penn persuaded Charles II to grant a charter to the colony, later called Pennsylvania, to provide specifically for freedom of worship and expression. At this time the government also wished to populate and provide workers in the expanding overseas colonies in the West Indies. Initially, emigrants were convicted criminals who worked in the sugar, tobacco, and cotton plantations. Similarly during the 18th cent. the demand for cheap labour in Australia stimulated the government to transport convicts from the 1790s until the 1850s. Convicts, freed after completing their sentences, often preferred to remain and make their lives in the colonies.

Individuals also left Britain voluntarily to seek better opportunities overseas. During the 18th cent., Scottish emigrants took service in the Russian army and settlers from all over the British Isles moved to the American colonies (later the USA and Canada) to take up work in agriculture, commerce, and trade in various natural resources such as furs and timber. Among the more prosperous manufactures was shipbuilding in New England for the European market.

During the 19th cent. emigration was on a scale hitherto unknown. The port of Liverpool became the most important departure place for all emigrants and 15 million persons (from the British Isles and northern Europe) were recorded as having left through that port between 1815 and 1914.

Two of the best-documented emigrations were those caused by hardship. In the early 19th cent. the clearances of the Scottish Highlands to make way for alternative land use forced people off the land and large numbers of Highlanders emigrated to Canada and Australia in search of new lives. In the 1840s the Irish potato famine reduced the population by almost half when large numbers settled elsewhere including Britain, the USA, and Australia.

Emigration to all parts of the British empire was encouraged by the government. Commentators such as Gibbon *Wakefield in his book *A Letter from Sydney* argued that emigration could be the solution to the dangers of overpopulation identified by Thomas *Malthus. In addition, colonial governments, such as that of New South Wales, offered free or assisted passages to emigrants and advertised widely in British local newspapers. Encouragement to emigrate was reinforced by those who had settled earlier in the colonies. Not all British emigrants settled in British colonies. Argentina also had a policy of encouraging settlers and descendants of Welsh emigrants to Patagonia continue to keep alive Welsh culture there to this day.

In the 20th cent. emigration continued to the Commonwealth and to the USA, but at a slower rate. Work opportunities declined as a consequence of the world-wide economic depression, as well as the changing links between Britain and her former empire. After 1945 emigration opportunities were increasingly under the control of overseas governments wishing to select only those migrants who had relevant skills. IJEK

Emma of Normandy (d. 1052), queen of *Æthelred II and of *Cnut. Emma played an important role in the confused succession to the English throne between 1016 and 1066. Early in life she became the second wife of Æthelred II, whom she married in 1002. Her first son, *Edward, succeeded to the English throne in 1042: her great-nephew was William the Conqueror. After the death of Æthelred in 1016 she married Cnut. On his death in 1035, Emma tried to obtain the kingdom for their son *Harthacnut, who was then about 16. In 1037 she was obliged to take refuge in Flanders but returned with Harthacnut in 1040. When he died two years later, her first son, from whom she was alienated, took the throne. Much of her property was seized and she lived in retirement at Winchester, where she was buried with her second husband, Cnut. Henry of Huntingdon called her 'the gem of the Normans'. JAC

Emmet, Robert (1778–1803). Irish patriot. Emmet, a middle-class protestant republican, came to prominence after the failure of the 1798 rising. He was influential in reactivating the United Irish movement in 1799, and in 1801 journeyed to Paris in order to revive French support for the Irish republican cause. After March 1803 Emmet and other

United Irish veterans of the 1798 rising began to prepare a second revolt. This occurred in a haphazard fashion on 23 July in Dublin, and although swiftly suppressed, caught Dublin castle ill prepared. Emmet escaped into the Dublin mountains, but was captured in August, and tried for treason. A lengthy state trial was held: Emmet, who readily accepted his guilt, was convicted and hanged. His youth and liaison with Sarah Philpot Curran have encouraged portrayals of the rebellion as a romantic, impulsive, and idealistic gesture. But Emmet had maintained a high standard of secrecy and professionalism in his preparations, and had an élitist conception of Irish independence far removed from that of the catholic democrats who later idealized his actions. AJ

Empson, Sir Richard (d. 1510). Empson and his colleague and neighbour Edmund *Dudley were the first victims of Henry VIII's ruthlessness. Empson came from Towcester in Northamptonshire, took a legal training, represented his shire in the Parliament of 1491, and was elected Speaker. In 1504 he was knighted and appointed chancellor of the duchy of Lancaster. His zeal in collecting taxes and fines on behalf of Henry VII made him extremely unpopular and he was among those servants of the king denounced by Perkin *Warbeck in 1495 as 'caitiffs and villains'. On the second day of Henry VIII's reign he was arrested and sent to the Tower on a trumped-up charge of treason. He was executed with Dudley on Tower Hill. JAC

enclosures. The process of 'enclosing' land into 'private' holdings goes back many centuries, and was a development from the system of open field farming which predominated in much of northern Europe during the medieval period, although in all periods enclosure was frequently of common and waste as well as cultivated land. Enclosure changed agricultural practices which had operated under systems of co-operation in communally administered landholdings, usually in large fields devoid of physically defined territorial boundaries. Instead, agricultural holdings were created which were non-communal, and within man-made boundaries which separated one farm from another. Communal obligations and rights were abolished.

In the 16th cent. landlords tried to enclose their land in order to keep more sheep. This process was condemned by the church and opposed by the government, which passed legislation designed to prevent enclosure. By the 1630s and beyond government opposition was breaking down, and a good deal of 'by agreement' enclosure took place in the period *c.*1630–*c.*1750, with large areas of land, particularly in the midlands, being converted from mixed arable farming to pasture. The extent of 'by agreement' enclosure is still debated, largely because it was not necessarily recorded.

From 1750, and in complete contrast to the 16th-cent. practice, Parliament began to pass bills, on a parish or district basis, to allow for the enclosure of the land under certain clearly defined conditions. As a result, between 1750 and 1830 in England more than 4,000 enclosure Acts were passed, and approximately 6.8 million acres across the country subjected to enclosure. In rough terms 21 per cent of the land area of Britain was enclosed by parliamentary Act in this period. The process varied regionally, the Welsh borders and south-eastern England experiencing very little enclosure, while more than half the land surface was enclosed by Act in Northamptonshire, Cambridgeshire, and Oxfordshire. The process continued through the 19th cent. with another 3 per cent of the land area enclosed by 1914, when there were hardly any open fields remaining. Only in the Nottinghamshire village of Laxton does a common field system continue to operate to this day under the auspices of a manorial court.

Enclosure in Scotland occurred primarily in the 18th cent., in the Lowlands in the 1760s and 1770s and in the uplands at the end of the century. The extent of enclosure was rather less than in England, at least in terms of the acreage involved, but then again the area of land available in Scotland to enclosed farms was relatively small. It also seems likely that enclosure in Scotland was frequently the final deed in a long-drawn-out process of change. JVB

Encyclopaedia Britannica. A typical product of the Enlightenment, when there was a vast amount of new knowledge to be disseminated and a rapidly growing reading public. It was a riposte to the French *Encyclopédie* and was published in three volumes between 1768 and 1771 by a consortium of Edinburgh printers, Andrew Bell, Colin Macfarquhar, and William Smellie. The sequence was alphabetical and the articles lengthy. It is now in its 15th edition (1992). JAC

Engagement, 1647. Charles I gave himself up to the Scots in 1646 and began negotiations. In December 1647, while at Carisbrooke castle, he signed a secret treaty or engagement, buried in a lead casket, whereby *presbyterianism should be established in Scotland, and in England for three years. In exchange, the Scots promised an army to enforce these terms. The result was the second civil war in 1648. But the Scottish army under *Hamilton which invaded England was routed by *Cromwell at *Preston in August 1648. JAC

Engels, Friedrich (1820–95). Engels was the lifelong collaborator of Karl *Marx and systematizer of Marxism. Son of a German textile manufacturer, Engels worked in a family-owned cotton mill in Manchester. He met Marx in 1842, forming a close working partnership with him, and together they wrote the *Communist Manifesto* during the revolutionary unrest of 1848. Engels, who gave Marx generous financial help, was closely involved with all of Marx's writings (their complete works are generally published together), and functioned as the authentic voice of Marxist views after Marx's death. In addition, Engels contributed a distinctive dimension to Marxist ideology—what has been termed 'dialectical materialism'. In his *Socialism, Utopian and Scientific* (1892) he applied the laws of dialectical materialism to history; in *Dialectics of Nature* (post-1927) he applied them to natural science. Whatever Marx himself thought of these crudities, they were incorporated into the official Marxist creed that flourished in the USSR and eastern Europe for most of the 20th cent. TSG

engineering industry. Engineering can take a variety of forms—civil, military, or mechanical—but the term 'engineering industry' is normally used in a more limited sense to describe the industry devoted to the manufacture of engines, machine-tools, and machinery. Up to the 18th cent. such products had traditionally been made by craftsmen such as blacksmiths and millwrights working in their own forges or workshops, but the rapid increase in the processes of industrialization in Britain encouraged the emergence of the modern engineering industry, with power-operated machine-tools brought together in factories, served by forges, foundries, and carpenters' shops preparing metal and wood parts for processing and assembling. The first organized array of these facilities was probably the factory at Soho in Birmingham developed by Matthew *Boulton to manufacture the steam-engines of his partner, James *Watt.

Other manufacturers of steam-engines built up similar establishments, while some engineers entered the business to make textile machines or—like Henry Maudslay in Lambeth—better machine-tools. Maudslay responded to the need for greater precision in lathes, drills, planing machines, and other tools for cutting and shaping metal, and set new standards of excellence. He also trained a generation of engineers, including Richard Roberts, James Nasmyth, and Joseph Whitworth, who further improved reliability.

Whitworth, who became an outstanding figure in British engineering in the middle of the 19th cent. and won prizes at the *Great Exhibition of 1851 for his superb machines, also achieved considerable success in standardizing screws and other basic machine parts. This made possible the development of mass production, whereby machines could be manufactured from sets of identical parts. Such practices had been established at the beginning of the 19th cent. by Marc Brunel and Henry Maudslay in order to create their famous block-manufacturing workshop in the royal dockyard at Portsmouth. But they were adopted with most enthusiasm by the new engineering industry of the USA, so that they became known as the 'American system' of engineering and were widely used in the manufacture of small arms, sewing-machines, and agricultural equipment.

The next stage in the development of the engineering industry was the introduction of systematic assembly techniques based on the moving assembly line, with all the processes linked together in a 'flow' pattern which enabled a complicated product like a motor car to be built quickly and economically. Once this had been achieved it became possible to introduce more and more automation in the performance of the functions of the assembly line. A modern automobile factory, for instance, uses electronically controlled 'robot' machines to perform most of the manufacturing processes, with the human participation reduced in numbers to a small team of controllers and maintenance staff. RAB

England, kingdom of. The kingdom of England was created by its monarchs. Successive rulers, sometimes from ambition, sometimes from fear, strengthened their armed forces, extended their boundaries, imposed law and order on their quarrelling subjects, introduced standardized coinage and administration, and encouraged one religion. Once a nation had been created, the monarchy, its task done, became redundant, save as a symbol of unity and a constitutional device. The afternoon in 1649 when Charles I stood in Westminster Hall and was told that he was indicted by the English people was the moment when Frankenstein's monster destroyed its creator. Though the monarchy was restored, the experience of the Commonwealth suggested that the nation could function without a king: far from falling into anarchy and confusion, Cromwell's England became a powerful force in Europe and the world.

Such an exposition may sound teleological, purposive, and complacent. It is not. There was no predestined goal, no manifest destiny, save perhaps towards a kingdom of the British Isles, which was never quite achieved. It is not a story of steady progress, each ruler improving on the work of his forebears: some rulers were incapable of the task, others lacked interest or had different priorities. There were many moments when the kingdom seemed in danger of being washed away or disintegrating—in the 9th cent. when the Vikings overran most of the country, in the 15th cent. when royal authority faltered in the Wars of the Roses, or during the great Civil War when the nation seemed about to destroy itself.

The evolution of the kingdom of England had, therefore, two foci in its relations with other peoples—Britons, Vikings, French, Scots, Welsh, Irish—and its development as an effective political and military organism. One of the most useful weapons of the monarchy was ideology—respect for kingship, awe at its supernatural origins, belief in its identification with the nation, its past, its triumphs and tribulations. The relationship of monarch and people was symbiotic and changing. The monarch strove to create a nation out of different tribes and peoples: the nation often responded to the monarch, but also advanced claims and demands. If the monarch was, as often asserted, the father of his people, what should be done about a monarch who neglected them, was clearly incompetent, or did not appear to represent their interests?

Many of the characteristics of the English kingdom which emerged derived from the circumstances of the Anglo-Saxon settlements. The settlers came largely from Schleswig-Holstein, where there is a region still called Angeln today. Since the Angles settled mainly in the eastern part of their new land, the Celts were more likely to come into contact with the Saxons, from Holstein. As late as the 18th cent., travellers from England were likely to be greeted with blank incomprehension in Wales and the muttered oath 'Damn Sassenach'. Because of geographical distance, Britain had not been as Romanized as Gaul or Spain. Latin was not widely spoken and English did not have to come to terms with it. Though many Britons remained behind, the fact that much of the north and west of the mainland was mountainous and that the Saxons arrived from the south and east influenced the ultimate division between Saxon and Celt. The mountains of Wales and Scotland provided refuges: they were also less attractive to settlers and less worthwhile to conquer.

England

Bede's account of an English nation in 731 was as much a programme as a description of the immediate reality. The English settlers were still divided into a number of kingdoms, waging constant warfare, the borders vague, the fortunes fluctuating. The enmities between them invited Celtic counter-attack if it could be organized. But the Celts were also divided and, though they were able to inflict sharp defeats on the Saxons, they were not able to drive them out. While the small kingdoms of East Anglia, Kent, Essex, Mercia, Northumbria, and Wessex struggled for supremacy, a kingdom of England remained a long way off. But in the title of 'bretwalda'—overlord of Britain—may be seen aspiration, even if the substance was shadowy and fleeting. Had Northumbria been able to consolidate its 7th-cent. superiority, a more northerly based English kingdom might have come into existence, perhaps centred on York, and with the border much further to the north along the line of the Forth. But with the decline of Northumbria, the struggle was between Mercia and Wessex and the probability was that any English kingdom would be southern. It retained that character throughout its history, despite the personal union with Scotland in 1603. In 1760, though George III gloried in the name of Britain, he not only failed to visit Ireland, Scotland, or Wales, but never penetrated north or midlands England.

From the incessant warfare of the first three centuries of Saxon settlement emerged the kingdom of Mercia. In the later 8th cent., *Offa (d. 796) overran Kent and Essex, including London, pushed back the Welsh, and confined Wessex to south of the Thames. His great dyke remains the rough border between England and Wales. At one stage he took the title Rex Anglorum and Pope Hadrian I recognized him as that. Though Northumbria was not conquered, its king, *Æthelred, married one of Offa's daughters. But Mercia's supremacy depended essentially on Offa's personal prestige and his country was in decline before the Viking raids commenced in the 9th cent. By 878, the north and midlands, including Mercia, had fallen to the Danes, and *Alfred of Wessex was hanging on precariously in the Somerset marshes.

For some time it looked as if Viking raids and settlement would destroy the possibility of an English kingdom and that the British Isles might become part of a grand Scandinavian empire, based on the North Sea. But, in the event, the Vikings promoted the emergence of a kingdom of England. First, by destroying Northumbria and Mercia, they cleared the way for the supremacy of Wessex. Secondly, the effort required to throw back the invaders gave Wessex a new vitality, perhaps a rare instance of Toynbee's dictum of challenge and response. Alfred's counter-attack was so vigorous that he was able to divide the country between Wessex and the Danelaw, and his successors built upon his achievements. *Edward, his son, and *Æthelfleda, his daughter, began the reconquest as far as the Humber, and before his death in 924 Edward had received the submission of northern England. Edward's son *Athelstan went further, receiving the submission of the princes of Wales, the king of the Scots, and the Cornish Britons. In 937 he confirmed his supremacy with a crushing victory at *Brunanburh. Not only had a recognizable kingdom of England been reconstructed from the remnants of Wessex but a vision of a kingdom of Britain began to be entertained. *Edgar was said to have been rowed on the Dee at Chester in 973 by British, Welsh, and Scottish kings, though whether this was alliance or homage is not clear.

Compared with the early Saxon kingdoms of the 7th cent., Athelstan's England was capable of sustained military effort. Strong points or burhs were constructed; control of coinage established; a navy created, and the kingdom divided up into shires and hundreds. The taxation required to resist or buy off the Danes became a permanent feature of the royal finances. The church had gradually built up an ecclesiastical network, with the two archbishoprics of Canterbury (597) and York (625), and bishoprics at London (604), Rochester (604), Winchester (660), Lichfield (669), Hereford (676), Worcester (680), Wells (909), and Durham (995). The strength of the monarchy and the identity of the nation were so well established that the succession of a Danish king, *Cnut, in 1016 no longer threatened disintegration, any more than did the succession of a Dutchman (William III, 1688) or a German (George I, 1714).

It follows therefore that when William and the Normans conquered in 1066 the existence of the kingdom of England was not in jeopardy, though the context in which it was to exist remained doubtful. Though there was an almost total change of top personnel, Norman nobles and bishops replacing Saxon ones, there was no mass settlement and the small number of Normans was bound to be absorbed before long. Some indication of the precariousness of a lone Norman in a largely hostile population can be gauged from William's institution of *Englishry—that a murdered man would be presumed to be Norman, and the hundred fined accordingly, unless it could be proved otherwise. But the ruthless rule of the Norman kings meant that the kingdom was less likely to disintegrate than ever. The main effects were twofold. First, Englishmen and the English language were under a cloud for several generations. Secondly, the country found itself in the wider context of western Europe, as part of an empire which included, at times, most of France.

But rather quickly the kingdom recovered its English character. The Conqueror's youngest son, Henry I, was born in England in 1068, possibly at Selby, brought up in the country, and spoke the language. Within three months of succeeding Rufus in 1100 he had married an English princess, the great-granddaughter of *Edmund Ironside. In just over 100 years from the Conquest, Richard *FitzNigel could write that 'nowadays when English and Norman live close together and marry . . . it can scarce be decided who is of English birth and who Norman'. The English language, which had given way in court circles and administration to Norman French or Latin, took longer to recover, partly because of the international utility of Latin. But in 1362 Parliament was opened with a speech in English and the law courts were instructed to hear cases in the English tongue. There were of course persistent complaints throughout the period of the influence of foreigners, particularly Provençals and Poitevins under Henry III, but they illustrate dominant

Englishness and are paralleled at a much later period by complaints against Scottish, Dutch, and German favourites at court.

Meanwhile the power of the royal government increased. A network of royal castles pinned the country down militarily. One of the greatest of unifying forces was the development in the 13th cent. of Parliament, with representation, usually at Westminster, from most parts of the kingdom. Though in the long run Parliament was to challenge the monarchy, for the first four centuries it was an obedient servant and added greatly to royal power. In the 14th cent., and particularly during the reign of Edward III, came important developments in the legal system—the institution of regular assizes, bringing most of the country under royal justice, and the growing use of justices of the peace to maintain law and order in the localities. In the 16th cent. came further additions—new instruments of government like the prerogative courts and the use of lords-lieutenant for shire administration. Above all, the destruction of papal power by Henry VIII in the 1530s removed a rival source of authority and placed the monarch at the head of the church, with all its resources and powers of persuasion.

The connection with Normandy did not last long and John lost it to Philip Augustus of France in 1204. But the English kings retained Poitou and *Aquitaine. The remaining territories were not lost until 1259 and even then the kings of England, from Edward III to Henry VIII, strove, with varying degrees of success, to regain their former territories. Not until the loss of *Calais in Mary's reign in 1558 did the dream of a French empire finally vanish.

In succeeding to the Anglo-Saxon state, the Normans had succeeded to its neighbours in the British Isles. The north of England had never been fully integrated into the Anglo-Saxon kingdom. William I's answer was the fearsome harrying of the north in 1069 and 1070, following the last great intervention of a Danish force in English affairs. Against Scotland, William achieved a temporary supremacy with a campaign in 1072 as far as the Tay, forcing *Malcolm Canmore to do homage. Of more lasting consequence were the Norman advances against Wales and Ireland, which Saxon England had not been strong enough to attempt. The foundation for the eventual conquest of Wales was laid by the creation of the marcher earldoms and by the colonization and castling of Pembrokeshire and south Wales. The first Norman kings did not attempt anything against Ireland, though a Norman ecclesiastical organization was introduced under the primacy of Canterbury and an archbishopric founded at Armagh. In 1170 Strongbow took advantage of the feuds between the Irish to intervene and in 1171 Henry II landed at Waterford, received the submission of many of the Irish chiefs, and built a palace at Dublin. A foothold had been established.

The transformation of the small Wessex kingdom into a kingdom of Britain was built on these foundations. The conquest of Wales was completed by Edward I. After *Glyndŵr's rising in the early 15th cent., the Welsh were subjected to savage penal laws, but the advent of a Welsh dynasty, the Tudors, in 1485 facilitated an accommodation. The principality was brought into the English political and administrative system in 1536 by the Act of *Union, which gave the Welsh representation at Westminster and divided the country up into shires on the English pattern. The conquest of Ireland proceeded by fits and starts, according to English preoccupations elsewhere. The foothold was never quite lost to counter-attacks. Richard II led two expeditions in 1394 and 1399 to secure the Pale and by *Poynings's law of 1494 the English established control over the Irish Parliament. Henry VIII declared himself king of Ireland in 1541. Later, the Elizabethan settlements, the influx into Ulster from Scotland, and the Cromwellian land redistributions strengthened the English position.

Scotland was a different matter. For centuries the border in the north fluctuated and in 1092 Rufus seized and fortified Cumberland. There were repeated attempts by the English to unite the two countries, by diplomacy or conquest. Edward I's gains were cancelled by the disaster which overtook his son at *Bannockburn in 1314. A plan to marry Edward VI to Mary, queen of Scots, came to nothing when she married the French dauphin instead—potentially a very damaging development for England. But there were already signs that the balance between the two countries was shifting. Between 1329 and 1625 only two of the eleven Scottish rulers succeeded as adults and the repeated minorities were bound to weaken the Scottish monarchy. Three hammer blows in succession—*Flodden in 1513 when James IV was killed, *Solway Moss in 1542 when James V died of grief, and *Pinkie Cleugh in 1547—suggested that the English had gained the upper hand in warfare. Unification came as a consequence of Elizabeth's preference for virginity: the marriage of Henry VIII's sister *Margaret in 1503 paid off 100 years later when her great-grandson, James VI, succeeded as James I of England.

A governmental union of his two kingdoms was top of the agenda for James. A combined flag was designed and the name of Great Britain put forward. To a glum Parliament, James outlined the advantages of union: 'do we not yet remember that this kingdom was divided into seven little kingdoms, besides Wales . . . And hath not the union of Wales to England added a greater strength thereto?' It was to no avail. 'We should lose the ancient name of England, so famous and victorious,' retorted his opponents: 'let us proceed with a leaden foot.' Though Parliament agreed to appoint commissioners, the project foundered.

Where James's arguments failed, Cromwell's sword succeeded. After his victories over the Scots at *Dunbar and the Irish at *Drogheda, the Scottish and Irish parliaments were wound up. The *Instrument of Government in 1653 instituted one Commonwealth Parliament, with 30 MPs each from Scotland and Ireland. The arrangement lapsed at the Restoration, for while the case for union remained strong, Charles II was unwilling to build with Cromwell's bricks.

The issue was raised again in 1669–70 but broke down on the size of Scotland's representation. With the great war against Louis XIV from 1688 onwards and the risk of subversion from a Jacobite Scotland, the matter became urgent. William III pushed the question in 1689 and was still pushing it when he died. More negotiations followed in 1702 and when they broke down, relations between the two countries reached their lowest point since the 1540s, with war discussed as a serious possibility. The Union which came about in 1707 was essentially a Whig move to secure the Hanoverian succession. Scotland obtained access to English markets and to the empire, while preserving its own legal, educational, and ecclesiastical system. England gained a greater measure of military security.

The new state was to be known as Great Britain and strenuous efforts were made to persuade all subjects to abandon old animosities and regard themselves as Britons. For many years such appeals fell upon deaf ears. Londoners, who had jeered at the Welsh in *Pepys's day, jeered at the Scots in *Wilkes's. Parliament was to meet at Westminster and Scotland was given 45 MPs and 16 representative peers. The Union is usually discussed from a Scottish point of view—'the end of an auld song'. But many of the English, including most of the Tories, looked at it sourly. They objected that Scotland was not paying its fair share and mistrusted its retention of a *presbyterian form of church government. Lord Haversham doubted whether a union of 'so many mismatched pieces, such jarring, incongruous ingredients' could hold together and deplored the passing of 'the good old English constitution'.

The push towards British unification continued. True, there was no attempt to bring about a governmental union with *Hanover after 1714: indeed, there were soon proposals to divide the two realms and they parted company in 1837. But the next great crisis, when the new British state faced the French Revolution, brought the Union with Ireland in 1801, and yet another change of name to the United Kingdom.

Wessex, having swallowed its neighbours in England, had now swallowed its neighbours in Britain. But Ireland in particular proved hard to digest. Whereas the unions with Wales and Scotland undoubtedly contributed to British power, that with Ireland was a dubious asset. In 1916, when Britain was fighting for its very existence, it was not possible to apply conscription to Ireland. It is a strange union which the government cannot call upon its people to defend. The breaking away of the *Irish Free State suggested that the process of more than 1,000 years was in reverse. How far it would go remains unanswered.

But even should events push the kingdom of England back whence it came, or, to take the extreme case, Northumbria and Mercia should reappear as more than tourist boards or police authorities, two results of Wessex's supremacy will last for some time. The great imperial expansion of the 17th and 18th cents. produced America, Canada, Australia, and New Zealand and spread the practice of parliamentary government throughout the world. The second was that for centuries to come the language of international diplomacy and communication will remain that of *Hengist and Horsa, *Ælle and Cissa. JAC

Cannon, J. A., and Griffiths, R., *The Oxford Illustrated History of the Monarchy* (Oxford, 1988); Grant, A., and Stringer, K. J. (eds.), *Uniting the Kingdom? The Making of British History* (1995); Kearney, H. F., *The British Isles: A History of Four Nations* (Cambridge, 1990).

Englefield, battle of, 871. No more than a skirmish, the battle at Englefield to the west of Reading in early 871 marks the opening of the bitter struggle between the West Saxons and the Danes. An exploratory raiding party led by two earls, one of whom, Sidroc by name, was killed, was defeated by Æthelwulf, the ealdorman of Berkshire. Four days later, however, Æthelwulf himself was killed in the failure of the West Saxons, commanded by King *Æthelred and his brother *Alfred, to dislodge the Danes from their campaign headquarters at Reading. The failure led directly into the so-called 'year of battles' in the course of which (in mid-April) the king died, to be succeeded by Alfred. HL

English Heritage, the Historic Buildings and Monuments Commission for England, was set up under the National Heritage Act, 1983. Responsible for the care and maintenance of many ancient monuments, historic buildings, and sites, this role includes making grants and giving assistance towards the conservation of privately owned properties, supporting archaeological excavation and research, and giving advice on the listing and scheduling of special sites. A wide variety of sites are in the care of English Heritage and, open to the public, are presented with informative displays, exhibitions, and occasional re-enactments of historic events. AM

English language. This originated in the speech of small groups of Anglo-Saxon settlers in eastern Britain in the 5th and 6th cents. It is now not only the most widely spoken language in the world but also forms the basis for national and international communication between members of other speech communities.

The language of the Anglo-Saxon settlers and their pre-Norman successors is conventionally known as Old English. Closely related to Old Saxon and Old Frisian, it forms part of the Germanic grouping within the Indo-European language system. Little direct evidence of its nature survives from the 5th and 6th cents. but, as fuller records become available with the advent of Christian literacy, it emerges as a highly inflected language realized in four main dialectal varieties: Northumbrian, Mercian, West Saxon, and Kentish. Though Latin was inevitably the main language of learned communication, education, and the church, Old English was used as early as King *Ine (d. 726) as a language of law; King *Alfred's educational reforms of the late 9th cent. built on this precocious official usage and massively expanded its employment in literary and educational texts. As a result, by the 10th cent., the vernacular had acquired a literary prestige attained nowhere else in contemporary Europe.

The Anglo-Saxon period saw two major cultural revolutions: the conversion and the Scandinavian settlement. Both affected the development of the language. The linguistic impact of Christianity is probably exaggerated by the ecclesiastical nature of our sources but there is no doubt that it involved both borrowing from Latin and, more importantly, exploitation of the resources of English through compounding of, and semantic extension to, existing vocabulary to express the concepts of the new religion. The Scandinavian languages of the Viking settlers penetrated much more deeply into English vocabulary, syntax, morphology, and phonology. The influence of this cognate Germanic language clearly operated at the everyday level of communication and even included the transfer of the ancestral forms of the pronouns 'they', 'them', and 'their'—items of a type rarely borrowed from one language to another. More indirectly, the Scandinavian settlement seems to have accelerated the progressive loss of inflexional complexity in English, for it is in the Viking-settled areas that these tendencies are most evident, encouraged no doubt by a desire to remove barriers to inter-intelligibility between the two related languages of Old English and Old Norse.

Paradoxically the extent of Scandinavian influence is not fully apparent until the post-Conquest period. The reason for this is that a standard written language had emerged in the late Anglo-Saxon period which was based upon the dialect of the politically dominant kingdom of Wessex, where also was the heartland of the *Benedictine reform movement. This conservative, southern-based language registered little of the more radical linguistic changes spreading southwards from the Anglo-Scandinavian north. Only with the Norman Conquest, when the introduction of Norman French scribes resulted in the disruption of West Saxon literary conventions, did these changes become apparent. Untrammelled by convention scribes began to write what they heard. As a result the 'Early Middle English' language of their manuscripts differs greatly from that of 'Late Old English' texts, yet all that had happened was that written forms had caught up with spoken developments—which had included simplification of many inflectional distinctions and the absorption of Scandinavian vocabulary.

Under pressure from Latin and French in the post-Conquest period, English lost literary prestige; the 'Middle English' stage of the language between the 12th and 14th cents. is thus a record of geographically limited dialects. By the 14th cent., however, English had risen once more in status though it was only in the late 14th and early 15th that a new standard written language emerged, based upon the language of the capital, London. This standard was later reinforced and spread by the introduction of printing. Linguistic variation in spelling and vocabulary, however, long persisted.

The 14th-cent. language of *Chaucer in the south and the Gawain poet in the north bears the marks of strong French influence in vocabulary and syntax. Detailed analysis of this French impact shows that it did not follow immediately upon the Norman Conquest but effectively began in the 13th cent. under the combined effects of the loss of Normandy in 1204 with a consequent identification of an Anglo-Norman nobility with England, and the European cultural ascendancy of French literary forms.

The flood of new ideas associated with the Renaissance and with Elizabethan and later exploration exposed the English speech community to languages and experience from most of the inhabited world. Terms to express the new concepts of religion, scholarship, and science invaded the language, not least from Latin and Greek; such 'inkhorn terms' were the subject of anguished debate and comedy among contemporary polemicists and satirists. The lack of fixed forms in English, particularly in contrast to the apparent stability of Latin, was also increasingly a matter of concern for those anxious to establish the vernacular as a language of learned discourse. This concern led to the eighteenth-century preoccupation with regularizing, fixing, and recording language of which *Johnson's *Dictionary* and the appearance of prescriptive grammar books represent two complementary facets.

By the 18th cent., however, English was no longer the language of a small part of Britain. In the preceding century settlers had taken it to North America and the West Indies; it was now to spread to Australasia, South Africa, and India. In all of these areas it developed its own forms which proceeded to interact with British English, the more so as communications became easier. The language in its various varieties has continued to evolve, with conservative and innovative forces continually at war within it. One extreme example can illustrate this conflict: alongside the host of new coinages, based on Latin and Greek roots, which have been adopted to express the technology and science of the 19th and 20th cents. there coexisted an extraordinarily archaic, yet highly influential, form of language in the world of religion where the Anglican church continued to use prayer books and bibles published in the period of Elizabeth I, James I, and Charles II which themselves drew heavily upon the language of *Tyndale (d. 1536), *Cranmer (d. 1556), and *Coverdale (d. 1569).

See also DIALECTS. RNB

Barber, C., *The English Language: A Historical Introduction* (Cambridge, 1993); Freeborn, D., *From Old English to Standard English* (1992); Leith, R., *A Social History of English* (1983); Strang, B., *A History of English* (1970).

Englishry. To afford some protection to lone Normans in the tense period after the Conquest, William I declared that if a murdered man could not be proved to be English, he would be presumed to be Norman, and the hundred fined. By the time of Richard I, at the end of the 12th cent. it had fallen into disuse, as the nations merged, though it was not formally abolished until 1341. JAC

entail. The growth of landed estates in England from the mid-16th cent. until the 1880s was partly a product of the system of 'entailing' property which the courts accepted. Until the mid-17th cent., the available forms of entail were quite restricted, but thereafter the courts agreed to permit an owner to tie up his estate to the second and third generation, through a process of 'contingent remainders'. The legal mechanisms were not dismantled until the 1880s and beyond. It was once held that as a result great estates were kept together and acreages increased, but modern research holds that the system of entailing property was introduced partly to protect the financial interests of younger children, that entailed estates could be partially or completely freed through either a common recovery or an Act of Parliament, and that the consolidation of estates must have been due to factors other than the process of entail. As a result, more emphasis is now placed on the ability of landowners to borrow on the security of their property, and to service large mortgages over several generations, with entail seen as a vital element in family strategies. JVB

Entente cordiale. Friendly relations between England and France, stopping short of a formal alliance. The term was coined at Haddo House, the country home of the 4th earl of *Aberdeen, by the French chargé d'affaires, the comte de Jarnac, in 1843. It is sometimes applied retrospectively to the 1830s, when Britain supported the government of Louis-Philippe in the face of the coldness of the conservative powers Austria, Russia, and Prussia, but it applied more properly to 1843–6. It was revived to describe the relationship inaugurated by the agreements of 1904, settling outstanding questions between the two countries, which eventually brought Britain into the *First World War on the side of France and Russia, although no formal obligation existed. MEC

environment briefly describes the surroundings in which we live. We can look at the environment historically in two ways. First, by identifying ways in which the environment has moulded or changed the course of human history. Towns have frequently developed where there were fords or bridges, and ports have grown or declined through the silting-up of themselves or their rivals. Wind and weather have frequently played a decisive role in battles or campaigns. William III in 1688 was assisted by the 'protestant wind' which kept James II's fleet in harbour while allowing the invaders to sail to Devon. The presence of bogs by the river Forth was a vital element in the victory of the Scots over the English at *Bannockburn in 1314.

Secondly, we may consider the effects of human action on the environment itself. From the earliest prehistoric slash-and-burn agriculture to the development of genetically engineered crops, the natural environment of Britain has been modified by its inhabitants. Perhaps the most notable of changes has been the removal of the blanket of trees which once covered virtually all of the British Isles. Clearance for fields, firewood, and building materials had already reduced cover to 15 per cent of England's land by the time of *Domesday Book. By the 16th cent. a timber shortage was developing that encouraged the use of coal, which itself changed the appearance of vast tracts of countryside.

The industrial revolution and the subsequent growth of large towns introduced extensive air pollution and caused acute problems of water supply and sanitation. It was only with legislation such as the Alkali Works Act of 1863 that substantial amelioration of bad conditions was effected. Even so, sooty buildings, smoky chimneys, dead rivers, and grimy canals soon became immortalized in literature set in the industrial north and gave impetus to the Romantic appreciation of 'natural' landscape, and to the development of national cultures, linked to an ideal of rural 'pureness'. Conservation societies were founded from mid-19th cent. onwards.

Calls for conservation accelerated as first railways, then roads, and the inexorable spread of towns, changed the face of the land. Concern has increased about the pollution of rivers and oceans as a result of the indiscriminate dumping of waste. The industrialization of agriculture after the Second World War, with its attendant use of chemicals and uprooting of hedgerows, has destroyed the habitat of many familiar plants and animal species. Many historic town centres have been blighted by insensitive redevelopment, often to accommodate the ever-growing number of cars and lorries. The approaches to most towns now look the same, with the supermarket, the large car park, and the congested roundabout. Sometimes a spectacular disaster has awakened the public conscience. Up to 4,000 people died in the London smog of December 1952: 116 small children were killed in October 1966 at *Aberfan when a slag heap, created by coal waste, slipped down a hillside and buried their school. From the 1960s membership of older conservation groups mushroomed, and new and more radical groups, such as the Friends of the Earth, were founded. The *Green Party, established to campaign specifically on environmental issues, had more success in persuading the other main parties to steal its clothes than in winning electoral support. In cleaning up rivers and reopening canals, much progress has been made: in creeping urbanization it is doubtful whether we have much improved on the 1930s which saw miles of ribbon-development along the new 'arterial' roads. CNL

Eochaid, king of the Picts (877/8–885/889). The limited sources for royal succession in what became *Alba ('Scotland') are very confused, possibly because this was a period of turmoil following the peak of Scandinavian devastation in 875–6. Eochaid, son of Rhun (king of Strathclyde) and a daughter of *Kenneth I, is mentioned only once as king, and even there it is noted that 'others say that *Giric . . . reigned at this time'. The same source claims that Giric may have been Eochaid's guardian, and that both were expelled following an eclipse of the sun on 16 June 885. This, however, contradicts the source's own chronology. Eochaid's ultimate fate is even more obscure than his reign (he perhaps led a warband to north Wales). DEB

Episcopal Church of Scotland. Scotland had no territorial episcopate before the 12th cent. and no archbishoprics before the late 15th cent. Although the church assumed an increasingly *presbyterian accent after the Reformation, bishops remained a lively issue in the conflicts bedevilling church and crown between 1560 and 1690. Thereafter Scotland's remaining episcopalians formed links with English *non-jurors, participating in 1711 in a joint consecration of bishops. An Act of Toleration (1712) gave them legal standing provided their ministers took the oath of allegiance to Queen Anne. Their continued adherence to the Stuarts hindered growth at first, but in 1720 the double election of John Fullarton, to fill the see vacated by the death of Scotland's last diocesan bishop, and as primus (presiding bishop), heralded a consolidation which John Skinner (1744–1816, primus 1788–1816) turned into revival. Skinner's negotiating skills led to the consecration of the United States episcopal church's first bishop (1784), repeal of the Penal Laws (1792), and adoption of the English church's Thirty-Nine Articles. They made possible the Anglican Communion; and reconciliation between non-jurors and the rest was effected at

Laurencekirk (1804). This was the prelude to reconstruction: seven dioceses by 1837, a doubling of churches and clergy by 1857, a Church Council with lay congregational representation since 1876, and a Consultative Council on Church Legislation since 1905, the whole later enhanced by a General Synod and issuing in a theologically and socially alert church. CB

episcopalianism is the form of church polity in which the chief authority is exercised by bishops, as opposed to *presbyterianism, in which it is exercised collegially by ministers and elders, and *congregationalism, in which it is exercised by gathered fellowships of believers. The bishop encapsulates in his diocese the collective powers of the church; he is the local expression of catholic unity, exercising a divinely bestowed authority. The system, normal among Christians by AD 200, became dominant in Christian Europe. Since the Reformation the term has usually been applied to episcopal churches not in communion with the Roman catholic church but, while it might be applied to the Lutheran churches of Scandinavia, the reformed churches in Hungary and Romania, and, by extension, to the methodist episcopal church in the USA and the churches of north and south India, it is particularly applied to the Anglican Communion. It describes the polity of the Churches of England and Ireland and the *Church in Wales. In Scotland the *Episcopal Church developed from the tension between kirk and crown which marked the period 1560–1690, in which bishops were an explosive issue. The Anglican Communion claims to have retained the apostolic succession, as did certain secessions such as the firmly protestant Free Church of England, which broke away in 1844, and the English episcopal churches, which left the Episcopal Church of Scotland in 1842–4, when it dropped the word 'protestant', but which had rejoined that church by 1987. CB

Epstein, Sir Jacob (1880–1959). Sculptor, painter, and draughtsman. Born in New York, he studied in Paris before settling in London in 1905 and becoming a British citizen two years later. From his first commission in 1907/8, eighteen figures for the BMA headquarters in the Strand, which were attacked as obscene, his work was surrounded by controversy. His Oscar Wilde memorial in Père Lachaise cemetery, Paris (1910–11), was at first banned as indecent. His later work was less controversial and his portrait busts of many of the leading figures of the day, for example, *Vaughan Williams, T. S. *Eliot, Einstein, were better appreciated. Examples of Epstein's work can be seen in London at the Tate gallery and Imperial War Museum and also in Walsall, where his widow's bequest is held. Two of the best-known monumental sculptures are *Christ in Majesty* (1954/5) in Llandaff cathedral and *St Michael and the Devil* (1955/8) at Coventry cathedral. He was knighted in 1954. JC

Erik Bloodaxe (d. 954), king of York (947–54). Erik was the last Scandinavian ruler of the short-lived kingdom of *York. Son of Harold Fairhair of Norway, he was a typical battle-leader. Expelled from his native land, he made himself master of York in 947, and was welcomed for the protection he offered against the West Saxon advance, particularly by archbishop Wulfstan. He was soon dispossessed by *Edred but returned in 952. Significantly his coinage for Jorvik (York) shows an unsheathed sword. In 954 he was killed at *Stainmore, possibly making for the Norse kingdom of Dublin or for the Isles. York was then absorbed into the developing kingdom of England. 'Hot-headed, harsh, unfriendly and silent' was a saga description: 'he ruled from York . . . under the helmet of his terror.' JAC

Ermengarde de Beaumont (d. 1233), queen of William I of Scotland. Married to William the Lion at Woodstock, near Oxford, on 5 December 1186, she was chosen for him by Henry II, then overlord of Scotland. Her father was one of Henry's French vassals, Richard, vicomte of Beaumont-sur-Sarthe in Maine, and the marriage emphasized William's subordinate status as Henry's client, though Edinburgh castle, seized under the treaty of *Falaise, was returned to William as a wedding gift. She enjoyed some prominence in public affairs, notably when William fell ill in 1212, and during her long widowhood from 1214 she founded the Cistercian abbey of Balmerino (Fife), where she was buried. KJS

Ermine Street was the Roman precursor of the Great North Road, running from London via Lincoln and the crossing of the Humber estuary to York. It was probably laid out in the late 1st cent. The current name is from the Anglo-Saxon *Earninga Stræt* meaning 'the street of the ?eagle's people'. The similarly named Ermin Street ran from Gloucester through Cirencester. ASEC

Erskine, Thomas (1750–1823). Erskine was the son of the earl of Buchan [S]. After serving in the navy and the army he entered Trinity College, Cambridge, and was called to the bar. After a slow start he became successful in commercial cases and then achieved fame as counsel for the defence in a memorable series of important 'political' trials, such as those of Baillie, Stockdale, Tom *Paine's *The Rights of Man*, and Hardy and others who supported parliamentary reform. He twice served as MP for Portsmouth, was for a time attorney-general to the prince of Wales and, from 1806–7, lord chancellor. He enjoyed immense public popularity when opposing repressive legislation, and again when he defended Queen *Caroline in 1820. Erskine has been described as the supreme advocate in English legal history. His political career was less distinguished than his career at the bar, but his advocacy in some of the great 18th-cent. trials caused him to be hailed as a champion of freedom. MM

escheat was the forfeiture of estates to the crown, or to the lord of the manor, when the owner or tenant died without heirs. It also applied to persons attainted, whose property passed to the crown. It was at times an important source of income, though estates were sometimes granted back to the attainted person's descendants. In Scotland escheat for debt was abolished in 1737. Escheat for felony was abolished in 1870. JAC

espionage. See SECRET SERVICE.

Essex

Essex is one of the larger counties and originated as a kingdom. Its southern boundary is the Thames, the Stour separates it from Suffolk, and the Stort and the Lea from Hertfordshire and Middlesex to the west. For many centuries the marshes along the Lea valley and dense forests around Epping and Waltham protected it from interference. *Cunobelinus moved the capital of the *Catuvellauni from Verulamium to Colchester, subduing the *Trinovantes before Caesar's invasion. The Romans took over the site and made it the provincial capital, Camulodunum, sacked in *Boudicca's rebellion in AD 61. In the 5th cent. the area fell to the Saxons, moving up the coastal creeks, and a kingdom of the East Saxons was in existence by the early 7th cent. It maintained a somewhat precarious existence, sometimes trying to extend its influence into Middlesex, Kent, and Surrey, sometimes trying to hold at bay the superior forces of *Mercia and *Wessex. *Mellitus was appointed bishop of London in 604 with the duty of converting the East Saxons and made some progress, but the area lapsed into paganism until mid-century. By the 9th cent. Essex had become a client state, first of Mercia, then of Wessex. In the late 9th cent. it was overrun by the Danes and allotted to them at the peace of *Wedmore in 878. Danish settlement was not heavy, however, and the region was used mainly as a base, with camps at Maldon and at Mersea. It was reconquered by *Edward the Elder. By the time *Cnut took the whole kingdom, in the early 11th cent., Essex was emerging as a shire, with roughly its present dimensions. The county town was Chelmsford rather than Colchester, perhaps because it was more central.

For centuries Essex remained a rural county and something of a backwater. It had no mineral resources and its harbours were shallow. It was on no great national route, though the roads to Norwich and Ipswich brought some traffic. It could have been of strategic importance in relation to London but few invasion forces ventured up its muddy creeks. Colchester remained a sizeable town, the centre for a vigorous cloth trade, and with a reputation for oysters, but most of the other towns—Saffron Walden, Thaxted, Braintree, Romford, Waltham Abbey, Dunmow, Halstead, and Ongar—were of only local importance. Chelmsford, the shire town, was unusual in having no parliamentary representation, though Maldon, Harwich, and Colchester had two members apiece. Harwich profited from the Hanoverian connection in the 18th cent. to build up its position as a port for the continent. The shire provided London with fresh vegetables, particularly potatoes, but for many years the marshes remained a barrier to urban expansion. As late as 1907, the *Victoria County History* could write that Essex was 'one of the purely agricultural counties of England, depending almost entirely upon tillage for its economic prosperity'.

The chief characteristic of the shire was its religious nonconformity. Proximity to the continent made for easy access to reforming ideas in the early Tudor period and the Essex towns provided a number of protestant martyrs during Mary's reign. Its puritan sympathies made it come down heavily in the 1640s for Parliament against the king and it saw little fighting, save for the siege of Colchester during the second civil war in 1648, which ended with the two royalist commanders being shot after surrendering. In 1698 Celia Fiennes noted that Colchester was 'a town full of dissenters, besides Anabaptists and Quakers'.

Economic transformation of the shire came in the later 19th cent. with the overflowing of London into the old hundred of Becontree, first along the docks of the north bank of the Thames, then following the first railway from Shoreditch to Romford in 1839, which built an important junction and repair works at Stratford. Dockers and railwaymen replaced farmers in the streets of south-west Essex. In 1801, Dagenham, Barking, Ilford, Walthamstow, East and West Ham were still separate villages or small towns. But for a time the increase in population was the fastest in the whole country. West Ham had fewer than 5,000 inhabitants in 1801 but 267,000 in 1901, dwarfing the county town, which had 13,000. While the population of Becontree hundred in the south-west rose from 21,000 to 650,000 that of Dunmow hardly changed and Freshwell hundred in the north actually declined. The taste for sea-bathing gave prosperity to Southend, which became Londoners' favourite resort: from the 1820s paddle-steamers brought day trippers, the pier was opened in 1830, extended in 1889, and the rail link in 1856 brought more: by 1991 its population was 153,000. The arrival of the Ford Motor Company at Dagenham in 1929 created a great new borough. Though suburban growth declined after the Second World War, the new towns at Harlow and Basildon and the airport at Stansted kept numbers increasing, while Epping, Braintree, and Chelmsford became commuter towns, disgorging into Liverpool Street. By 1991, Essex, with a population of 1,400,000, was third only to Hampshire and Kent among counties. In the 1980s the concept of 'Essex man', upwardly mobile, fast-driving, Tory-minded, brought the shire back into national consciousness. The Banham commission on local government reported in 1994 in favour of a unitary authority for Southend.
JAC

Essex, kingdom of. Essex was formed in the 6th cent. by Saxon settlers established to the north of the Thames estuary and east of the river Lea and London. The ruling dynasty claimed descent from an obscure Saxon deity, Seaxneat, rather than from Woden, and there are puzzles about the intensity of settlement with many early place-names but comparatively few archaeological sites and pagan cemetery sites apart from the important settlement at Mucking. In the early 7th cent. London was regarded as part of the kingdom (though subject to Kentish overlordship), and *Mellitus, bishop of London, was forced to flee to the continent during the pagan reaction which followed the death of the East Saxon king Saeberht in 616. Final conversion to Christianity took place in the 650s under Bishop Cedd from Northumbria; the nave of his church at Bradwell-on-sea still survives. After Cedd's death episcopal authority passed to the bishop of London though political control of the city rested in other hands. Indeed, while retaining its own kings until the 9th cent., Essex played a minor role, particularly during the reigns of the powerful Mercian kings in the 8th cent. When dominance passed to the West Saxons after their victories over the Mercians in 825 and 829, the subordinate role of Essex was further emphasized, and from that point onwards it was governed by *ealdormen not by kings. The boundary drawn up by *Alfred and the Danes after 878 left Essex in the Danelaw, though there is no evidence of Danish settlement in depth. Essex was reabsorbed into the English kingdom in the early 10th cent. (Colchester was reoccupied in 917), and played an important part in defence against later Viking attacks; the ealdorman Byrhtnoth was killed in the heroic battle at *Maldon in 991. Ecclesiastical links with London and St Paul's remained strong, and the religious life of Essex was further enriched by the foundation of Waltham abbey (initially served by secular canons) by *Harold Godwineson, late in the Anglo-Saxon period. HL

Essex, Arthur Capel, 1st earl of (1631–83). Capel succeeded his father as baron when he was executed in 1649 as a royalist and at the Restoration was made earl of Essex. In 1670 he was sent to Denmark on a diplomatic mission and from 1672 to 1677 was lord-lieutenant of Ireland. Two years later, after the *Popish plot, he was treasurer for six months, working uneasily with *Shaftesbury. He resigned in November 1679, gave strong support to the *Exclusion Bill and moved closer to *Monmouth. In 1683 Essex was arrested in connection with the *Rye House plot but was reported to have cut his throat in the Tower while awaiting trial, dying in the same room in which his father had been confined. The most recent scholarly inquiry suggests that he may well have been murdered. JAC

Essex, Robert Devereux, 2nd earl of (1566–1601). Courtier. Essex's father, raised to the earldom in 1572, died when his son was 10. Essex served under his stepfather *Leicester at *Zutphen in 1586 and was knighted for gallantry. From 1587 he was Elizabeth's master of horse and was given the Garter in 1588. After his capture of Cadiz in 1596 his success seemed assured. But a second expedition in 1597 was unproductive, his way of life at Essex House was extravagant, and his short spell as lord-lieutenant of Ireland in 1599 was disastrous. Instead of subduing *Tyrone as he had vowed, Essex met him for private negotiations. 'Perilous and contemptible' was the queen's terse verdict on his behaviour, and when Essex returned to England in express defiance of her orders, he was disgraced. His half-hearted attempt at a palace coup in 1600 led to his execution. Though personally brave, he was petulant and totally lacking in judgement—a mere shooting star. JAC

Essex, Robert Devereux, 3rd earl of (1591–1646). Essex was the son of Elizabeth I's favourite, and was 10 when his father was executed. His sympathies being on the parliamentary side, he was appointed commander-in-chief as soon as war came. He fought prudent defensive campaigns at *Edgehill and *Turnham Green in 1642. In September 1643 he succeeded in relieving Gloucester and fought his way back to London at the first battle of *Newbury. In September 1644 he led the ill-advised foray into Cornwall which ended in disaster at *Lostwithiel. Essex resigned in accordance with the self-denying ordinance in 1645 and died the following year. Clarendon praised him for the good discipline of his troops and he seems to have been well liked. But he did not really gain one notable victory and his position depended mainly upon his name and rank. JAC

Essex, William Parr, earl of. See PARR, WILLIAM.

Étaples, treaty of, 1492. In October 1492 Henry VII led an expedition to France in support of the Bretons and to induce Charles VIII of France to repudiate Perkin *Warbeck. He commenced a siege of Boulogne but the French offered terms which he accepted on 3 November. France was to pay substantial financial indemnities and agreed not to assist Warbeck: trade was to be encouraged by moderate customs duties and action against pirates. Henry's campaign of one month proved highly profitable and he was accused of waging war for gain, but the treaty was confirmed by the English Parliament in 1495 and renewed in 1498. AC

Eton College. This public school was founded by Henry VI with the title 'The College of the Blessed Mary of Eton beside Windsor' in 1440. It was modelled on the foundations of *Winchester and New College, Oxford, set up by *William of Wykeham. In the original foundation provision was made for a schoolmaster, 25 'poor and indigent' scholars, as well as choristers, priests, and 25 infirm men. There are two types of scholars, the oppidans who live in houses of some assistant masters, and the collegers who are lodged in the college. PG

European Communities Act, 1972. Act of the British Parliament giving legal effect to the treaties and legislation of the European Communities, effectively confirming Parliament's acceptance of British entry. The primacy of European over British law introduced by the Act was most vividly shown by the ability of the European Court of Justice, in 1991, to overturn provisions made by the British Parliament in the 1988 Merchant Shipping Act on restricting foreign ownership of British registered fishing trawlers, because they infringed article 52 of the treaty of *Rome. CNL

European Economic Community was the full title of the EEC, which Britain joined on 1 January 1973, also known as the Common Market, and later as the European Community; then, after the treaty of *Maastricht, as the European Union.

Britain stayed out of the EEC's forerunner, the European Coal and Steel Community (ECSC), formed in 1952. This was a French initiative designed to ensure continuing influence over the German Ruhr's coal and steel production. This required a supranational high authority and Britain, with its attachment to sovereignty, its economic and psychological links with the Commonwealth, and a special relationship with the USA, could not have joined. The Labour government had also just nationalized Britain's coal industry and faced trade union opposition to 'handing it over to foreign capitalists'. The French had also discouraged Britain from entering the discussions so that they could shape the new entity to fit their interests.

The members of the ECSC agreed at the 1955 Messina conference to explore further economic and atomic co-operation. Britain declined to send a representative and therefore had no influence on the treaty of *Rome that established the EEC. However, it soon became clear that the EEC countries were catching up or surpassing Britain both economically and politically, and this realization led to *Macmillan's formal membership application in July 1961. This was vetoed by French President de Gaulle in 1963, after the Nassau agreement had increased British military dependence on US missile technology. Problems over Commonwealth and EFTA (*European Free Trade Association) trade, and agricultural subsidies would have made agreement difficult, but the challenge posed by British membership to de Gaulle's aspirations as a leader of a 'Third Force Europe' probably condemned the negotiations to failure despite the support of other EEC members. The same factor led to de Gaulle's veto of Britain's second application, made by *Wilson in 1967.

De Gaulle's downfall in 1969, coupled with French economic weakness and increasing German assertiveness under Brandt's leadership, cleared the way for the success of Britain's third application to join, under *Heath in 1970–1. Unfortunately for Britain, the EEC had come to agreements in 1970, detrimental to Britain's future membership, on the Common Agricultural Policy (CAP), and budget contributions.

The application had major consequences for British domestic politics. Labour had opportunistically switched to an anti-EEC policy once in opposition in 1970, but a significant group of committed integrationists, headed by Roy *Jenkins refused to follow, and supported the Heath government's European policy. The split in the Labour Party was only contained by Wilson's promises to renegotiate Britain's terms of membership and to hold a referendum on the results. This took place on 5 June 1975: the cross-party 'Britain in Europe' group managed to highlight the positive benefits of membership and secured 67 per cent of the vote.

Britain failed to use the EEC to her maximum advantage. The ill-will caused by the inept 'renegotiation' of 1974, the disdain shown towards Community institutions by some Labour anti-European ministers; the inability of British politicians and bureaucrats to adapt to the coalition-building necessary to influence EEC policy; and the distractions caused by domestic political problems over devolution and pay policy led to a loss of influence over collective decision-making.

The early *Thatcher years from 1979 were dogged by arguments over Britain's EEC budget contribution. Opinion varies on how far Thatcher's hectoring, aggressive behaviour was responsible for the favourable deal eventually reached at the Fontainebleau European Council in June 1984, but the whole row reinforced Britain's reputation for obstructiveness and consequently undermined her influence.

With the budget row settled, Britain went on to play a positive role in the mid-Thatcher years. A new, more subtle approach to the workings of the Community enabled Britain to work with others to guide the eventual Single Market proposals towards the British aim of trade liberalization with minimal institutional reform. The Single European Act, signed in Luxembourg on 17 February 1985, was the result, coming into force on 1 July 1987. Majority voting in the Council of Ministers was extended to ease the passage of European legislation (directives and regulations) needed to create the single market. British fears of the Greeks vetoing progress towards deregulation proved greater than fears of pooling sovereignty.

However, Thatcher was still regularly to be found in shrill isolation, often due to machiavellian diplomatic machinations, but also because of an inability to recognize good compromises. This was perhaps inevitable given her personal style and perhaps inflated view of the realities of Britain's sovereignty. These underlay her hostility to participation in the Exchange Rate Mechanism (ERM), or European Monetary Union (EMU), which led to the resignation of cabinet ministers Lawson and *Howe. They feared that Britain was not only repeating the mistakes of the 1950s, staying outside institutions rather than influencing them from within, but also deluding itself in believing that national sovereignty was a meaningful concept in an interdependent world without capital or trade barriers. Others ridiculed the idea that national identities were threatened by European integration. Thatcher's opposition to these views was famously articulated in her Bruges speech of 20 September 1988: 'Europe will be stronger precisely because it has France as France, Spain as Spain, Britain as Britain, each with its own customs, traditions and identity . . . We have not successfully rolled back the frontiers of the State in Britain only to see them reimposed at a European level with a European superstate exercising a new dominance from Brussels.' The turmoil in eastern Europe as the Communist system and USSR collapsed encouraged France and Germany to seek reforms to bind the newly unified Germany tighter into European structures. John *Major declared himself happy with the resulting treaty of Maastricht, but the 'no' vote in the Danish ratification referendum (2 June 1992), the ignominious devaluation of the pound and exit from the ERM on 'Black Wednesday' (28 September 1992), emboldened Conservative 'Eurosceptics', who forced Major into a Commons vote of confidence to achieve ratification.

CNL

Dinan, D., *Ever Closer Union?* (Basingstoke, 1994); George, S., *An Awkward Partner* (Oxford, 1994); Kitzinger, U., *Diplomacy and Persuasion: How Britain Joined the Common Market* (1973); Unwin, D. W., *The Community of Europe* (1991).

European Free Trade Association (EFTA). The idea of an intergovernmental organization to reduce tariffs on trade between the non-communist European countries was put forward by Britain in 1956. It hoped to prevent the formation of the EEC, and even after 'the Six' had signed the treaty of *Rome, Britain persisted in attempting to draw the EEC into a wider free trade association. De Gaulle vetoed the idea in 1958. Following this veto, the Swiss government invited those countries who would not join the EEC (Iceland, Norway, Britain, Denmark) or, because of Soviet disapproval of the EEC and considerations of neutrality, could not (Finland, Sweden, Switzerland, Austria) to negotiations which resulted in the Stockholm convention setting up EFTA (3 May 1960). Finland became an associate member and Portugal joined the others as full members, who managed to eliminate mutual tariffs by the end of 1966. Britain's involvement in EFTA was not distinguished by evidence of leadership or team spirit. She applied to join the EEC in 1961, and little consideration was shown to fellow-EFTA members when a 15 per cent import surcharge was imposed in 1964. Britain did, however, insist in her negotiations with the EEC that satisfactory arrangements must be made with EFTA. CNL

Eustace, Prince (*c.*1127–53). Eustace was the second son of King Stephen, but the death of his elder brother Baudouin *c.*1135 made him heir apparent. In 1140 he was married to Constance, daughter of Louis VI of France. Stephen was anxious to have Eustace's claim recognized, but though a council at London acknowledged him as heir, the papacy refused approval. After Eustace's death on 10 August 1153, Stephen came to terms with his great rival *Matilda, accepting her son Henry as his successor. JAC

evangelicalism. A predominantly Anglican movement stemming from the mid-18th cent., originally with links to *Whitefield and *methodism, and led by John Fletcher, Henry Venn, and others, its characteristics have been calvinistic with a literalist interpretation of the Bible, sabbatarianism, conversion-preaching, reform of the heart, human sinfulness, and personal salvation. The second generation was wealthy and close to political power; William *Wilberforce, a Yorkshire county MP, his cousin Henry Thornton, John Venn, vicar of Clapham, and Charles *Simeon formed the *Clapham sect, whose aims were the reformation of manners and the abolition of slavery (see ANTI-SLAVERY). The slave trade was abolished (1807) and slavery itself (1833). Fear of the French Revolution intensified the Clapham sect's attack (1797) on the moral laxity of the privileged as a poor example for the lower orders, and on the weakness of the church and its message. Hannah *More, a great propagandist with her *Thoughts on the Manners of the Great* (1787), and Wilberforce's Proclamation Society called not only for a moral reformation, but respect for government, orderly society, and hard work as part of the moral law. Evangelicalism in achieving increased sobriety by the 1820s anticipated 'Victorianism' and also deflected political radicalism. Evangelicalism offered an anchor of stability in a world of turbulence. World-wide mission was another aim, for which the *Church Missionary Society (1799) and the British and Foreign Bible Society (1804) were founded. With its best disciples leaving to evangelize overseas, evangelicalism's success in thus promoting 19th-cent. foreign mission, associated with Victorian imperialism, enfeebled it at home, so that by the 1920s, unlike *Anglo-catholicism, it lacked its earlier vigour and became narrowly moralistic, conservative, and upper middle class. The Cambridge Christian Union (CICCU), founded 1876 as the watchdog of evangelical orthodoxy, was weak in the 1920s, but revived and spread throughout most universities in the 1930s. Further revival accompanied the visit of the American evangelist Billy Graham (1954). Under John Stott's leadership, its emphasis rather surprisingly changed at Keele (1967) and Nottingham (1977) to embrace ecumenism, increased social responsibility, and greater emphasis on sacramental life. WMM

Evelyn, John (1620–1706). The second great diarist of his time, although his is less self-revelatory than that of Samuel *Pepys. However, it covers a far longer time-span, 1641–1706. Evelyn was a less acute observer and more conventional in his interests and judgements but possessed a wider circle of acquaintances. A fervent royalist, he spent the Civil War years touring in Europe, but after 1660 he was commissioner for sick and wounded in the *Anglo-Dutch War of 1665–7 and for the mint, and member of the Council for *Plantations. Evelyn as a virtuoso or amateur scientist was a founding fellow of the *Royal Society. His *Sylva* (1664) encouraged and educated landowners in forestry, and he wrote a pioneer tract on smoke-abatement for an already smog-enveloped London. JRJ

Evesham, battle of, 1265. After his victory over the forces of Henry III at *Lewes in May 1264, Simon de *Montfort took possession of king and government. But Prince Edward, Henry's son, escaped from Hereford in May 1265 and raised an army in the west. De Montfort entered south Wales to ally with *Llywelyn and then marched to Evesham, hoping to link up with his son *Simon, advancing from Kenilworth. He was intercepted by an overwhelming royalist force and on 4 August, just north of Evesham, de Montfort and his supporters were butchered, 'for battle none it was'. JAC

examinations. The first school examinations were held in the 16th and 17th cents., when diocesan visitations were made. Teachers were questioned on their learning and pupils were tested for attainment. Examinations were required by statute in many schools, including Tonbridge (1564) and St Albans (1570).

From the second half of the 19th cent. the present examination system came into being. In 1853, the College of Preceptors initiated examinations in secondary school subjects. Three years later, the *Royal Society of Arts held examinations for 15-year-old school-leavers. Technological examinations were added in 1873 and were transferred to the City and Guilds of London Institute in 1879. With the introduction of 'payment by results' in the 1860s, all children in elementary schools over the age of 6 were examined in the three Rs. A similar system was employed by the Science and Art Department, though here pupils could be awarded prizes. In both instances, examinations were abolished by the Education Department in 1895.

At secondary school level, Oxford undertook from 1858 the examination of schools through a body of delegates and Cambridge also held examinations in the same year. Only boys were allowed to enter. Universities took up this work, awarding certificates which exempted the holders from university entrance examinations. The Oxford and Cambridge Schools Examination Board was established for this purpose in 1873. The University of London had offered examinations from 1858. In the 20th cent., the School Certificate Examination for 16-year-olds and Higher School Certificate for 18-year-olds operated between 1917 and 1951. They were replaced by the General Certificate of Education (GCE), Ordinary Level, and Advanced Level examinations. Since 1988, the Ordinary Level has been superseded by the General Certificate of Secondary Education (GCSE). PG

Exchequer. Financial institution. The term is derived from the chequered cloth, similar to a chess board, which was placed over a table in order to assist in the counting and computation of sums due to the crown. Its function and organization are first described in the **Dialogus de Scaccario* (*Dialogue of the Exchequer, c.*1179): the Lower Exchequer received and issued money, the Upper Exchequer was essentially a court of account where royal revenue was managed, accounts audited, and disputes dealt with. The Exchequer thus exercised a judicial as well as financial competence. The origins of the Exchequer are not entirely certain, but it seems most likely that its institutional form dates from the reign of Henry I. The first surviving pipe roll for the financial year 1129–30 shows how the sheriffs and other royal officials were summoned to account at the Exchequer twice a year, at Easter and Michaelmas. By the later 12th cent., the Exchequer was no longer itinerant but permanently based at Westminster, the first of the crown's departments to acquire a separate existence, definite organization, and buildings of its own. Although there were reforms in procedures in the mid-13th cent., and other financial bodies, such as the *wardrobe and *chamber, were developed in response to the crown's changing needs, the Exchequer remained the linchpin and apex of the crown's financial administration throughout the Middle Ages. In the 16th and 17th cents., the *Treasury was developed as a separate department, so that the administrative functions of the Exchequer declined. It ceased to be a financial department in 1833 but its judicial functions continued until 1873–80. The Treasury is now a ministerial department headed by the chancellor of the Exchequer, although the prime minister is technically its 1st lord. AC

Excise crisis, 1733. In 1733 Sir Robert *Walpole, George II's first minister, was anxious to conciliate the country gentlemen before the forthcoming general election (1734) by reducing the land tax to 1 shilling in the pound. He had already reimposed a duty on salt (1732), but additional revenue was needed to make up the considerable shortfall. He therefore proposed the substitution of excise duties for customs duties on tobacco and wine, in order to maximize revenue and discourage smuggling. However, commercial anxieties about the scheme were exploited by opposition leaders in Parliament, who saw it as an attempt to expand government bureaucracy, and a full-scale outcry was raised in London and many provincial towns. In the Commons Walpole's majority almost collapsed, and when it seemed that he might lose the king's confidence, he withdrew the measure, immediately re-establishing his sway. AAH

Exclusion crisis. A period of intense political strife during 1679–81 generated by the attempt to bar Charles II's catholic brother James, duke of York, from succession to the throne. Widespread apprehension that James would inaugurate a catholic 'absolutist' monarchy was aroused in 1678 by Titus *Oates's revelations of a *Popish plot against king and government. In the three parliaments called between 1679 and 1681 discontented 'Whig' groups exploited their majority in the Commons to promote 'exclusion' measures, but were each time defeated when the king used his prerogative to close proceedings. The exclusionists' campaign against James represented a radical move by Parliament to dictate the succession in the face of conventional assumptions about the divine nature of monarchical authority, and highlighted the conflict between crown and Parliament which had germinated since the 1660s. Though initially the movement made much impact in the constituencies, it lost momentum as fears of renewed civil war increased, while the king's refusal to summon Parliament again after 1681 took away its main platform. AAH

Exeter (Roman), Isca Dumnoniorum, was successively fortress of *legio II Augusta* from the mid-50s to the mid-70s then *civitas*-capital of the *Dumnonii. The fortress baths were excavated west of the cathedral in the 1970s; little else is known of the base. The civil basilica was constructed over the baths, and a civil bath-house is known. The 2nd-cent. earthen defences enclosed 93 acres and were refurbished in stone in the 3rd cent. Some houses have been excavated, but comfort and degree of Roman culture do not seem to have been high. ASEC

(post-Roman) Exeter was refounded as a fortified town (burh) by *Alfred. It rose to be one of the leading English towns of the 10th–12th cents., apparently through the tin trade, acquired a bishop's see (1050) and, after a rebellion against the Normans, a castle (1068). It declined in the 13th and 14th cents., though this did not prevent a total rebuilding of the cathedral, 'the Decorated cathedral *par excellence*'. The Reformation was unpopular in Exeter, though the city resisted a siege by catholic rebels (1549). From the 15th to the 18th cents. Exeter throve as a cloth-making and cloth-trading town; when the textile industry declined, it became a social and servicing centre instead. It never really industrialized, and has remained a modest-sized regional centre. Since 1942 it has suffered grievously from both air raids and insipid post-war redevelopment. DMP

Exeter, diocese of. The see, now conterminous with Devon, was created when Leofric, bishop of *Crediton, moved his seat to Exeter in 1050, thus becoming one of the first in England to follow Pope Leo IX's injunction to move all sees to major towns. For 800 years it comprised Devon and Cornwall (formerly the sees of Crediton and *St Germans), but in 1877 Cornwall was hived off to form the new diocese of *Truro. Amongst notable bishops was Walter Stapledon (1308–26), who as lord treasurer (1320–1 and 1322–5) was notable in modernizing the royal Exchequer and chamber under Edward II. Miles *Coverdale (1551–3) was important for his own translation of the Bible (1535) and the Great Bible (1539), from which the psalter was incorporated in the Book of Common Prayer. The cathedral, originally the abbey church of St Mary and St Peter, rebuilt between

1260 and 1307, is a fine example of the Decorated period, though with the original Norman towers remaining as transepts. WMM

Exeter, Thomas Beaufort, 1st duke of (*c.*1377–1426). The youngest legitimized son of *John of Gaunt, Beaufort first served his half-brother Henry IV in the Welsh war and at sea. He was chancellor of England when Prince Henry (later Henry V) controlled the king's council, was created earl of Dorset in 1411 and admiral of England for life in 1412. He participated in *Clarence's French expedition and was briefly lieutenant in Gascony. After the capture of *Harfleur, he defended it against French attacks and was rewarded by promotion in 1416 to ducal rank. While visiting north country shrines in 1417, he organized the repulse of a Scottish invasion. From 1418 he had a prominent role in the conquest of Normandy; he was governor of Rouen and Paris. He attended the death-bed of Henry V. Back in England, he was a senior member of Henry VI's council in his own last years. RLS

Exeter, Henry Holand, 2nd duke of (1430–75). As a minor, Holand was the ward of Richard of *York and married to his daughter. Thomas Percy, Lord Egremont, enveigled him into the feud against the Nevilles in 1454, when Holand claimed that he, not his father-in-law, should be protector during the king's insanity. From 1459, he fought against the Yorkists on land and sea. Attainted in 1461, he attended Queen *Margaret in exile, returning with *Warwick to restore Henry VI. After the battle of *Barnet, he was kept prisoner by Edward IV, his brother-in-law. His wife obtained a divorce and married her lover Thomas St Leger in 1472. Holand was taken to France in the king's expedition in 1475 and reportedly fell overboard on the return voyage. RLS

Exeter, John Holand, 1st duke of (1395–1447). Henry V, in his policy of reconciliation, restored Holand in 1416 to the earldom forfeited in 1400 by his father, the 1st duke. He earned restitution by service in the French war from 1415 to 1421, when he was captured at *Baugé. Ransomed for 20,000 marks after five years, his compensation included the king's licence to marry the widow of Edmund *Mortimer, earl of March. Holand was again fighting in France from 1429, a joint warden in the Scottish marches in 1435–6, and finally lieutenant of Gascony for six years from 1439. Henry VI created him duke in 1444 and granted that his son would succeed to his offices of admiral of England and constable of the Tower of London. RLS

exploration. The notion of Europeans discovering other peoples and telling them who they are and where they live is now often suspect, especially as an explorer's discourse is said to be determined by his mind-set rather than any objective reality. Yet descriptions of the surface of the globe and its peoples have been put into a framework of knowledge which has affected historical development. In fact exploration has been linked with the exercise of political and economic power and sometimes religious evangelism. Britain's increasing domination of exploration broadly accompanied the rise of the English and then the British state to world power after 1500. From the late 18th cent., Britain not only organized the most important expeditions but also set the agenda by insisting that exploration be 'scientific'—which meant at the very least that latitudes and longitudes must be established.

More science did not lessen the connections between exploration and other aspects of British life. The state continued to be closely involved, partly for strategic reasons and partly because naval or military personnel so often led expeditions. The upper-class tradition of the *grand tour with travel seen as heightening knowledge and experience had a powerful effect on the organization of exploration and the way it was written up. Another spur to expeditions from the 1790s was the desire of British protestant churches to evangelize overseas. *Livingstone is the perfect example of the missionary becoming a great scientist and associating with aristocratic hunters and travellers before writing a best-selling travel work.

Exploration entered British consciousness in other ways: explorers became the pattern for heroes of boys' adventure stories and the subjects of numerous anthologizers and biographers. *Hakluyt began the anthologies with his *Principall Navigations* . . . of 1589. The great 18th-cent. travel collections continued the tradition and in 1846 William Desborough Cooley founded the Hakluyt Society to publish historical accounts of voyages and travels, as it has done ever since. Biographies abound. We learn that Livingstone was a victim of cyclothymia, or that *Speke had a mother fixation. This sort of writing has had the unfortunate effect of grossly distorting the true significance of explorers in the history both of Britain and of the regions they explored.

Despite Hakluyt, the English contribution to primary exploration in the great age of maritime discovery was rather modest. John and Sebastian *Cabot, English by adoption, contributed to the discovery of the Americas in 1497 and 1509, but most English maritime adventurers in the Tudor period merely followed the Portuguese and Spanish and attempted to steal some of their treasures. This was true of *Drake although his circumnavigation of 1577–8 involved the discovery of California. But the English did try to open up new routes to the Orient—the North-East and North-West Passages with the voyages of *Willoughby and *Chancellor to Russia in 1558 and the contemporary landward travels in central Asia of *Jenkinson matched by the voyages to the west of *Frobisher in 1576 and *Davis in 1585–7. The North-West Passage was to preoccupy Britain for 300 years, no doubt because of its comparative proximity to Canada. *Hudson reached the bay bearing his name in 1607–11 and in the following century attempts on the passage were to be made from the Pacific as well as the Atlantic.

Partly for this reason, the Pacific attracted much British attention in the 18th cent. with *Dampier's *New Voyage round the World* of 1697 and the circumnavigations of *Anson in 1740–4 and Byron of 1764–6 adding interest. The prize would be the trade of the great southern continent believed to exist. *Cook's first voyage of 1768–71 did reveal New Zealand and eastern Australia but the second voyage of 1772–5 effectively disproved the existence of a southern continent. Cook's third voyage was to the northern Pacific, so completing the greatest series of scientific expeditions ever undertaken. *Banks had been on the first voyage and then came to dominate British exploratory activity, sending out more naturalist travellers and being instrumental in founding the African Association in 1788. This aimed to do for the interior of Africa what Cook had done for the Pacific. Mungo *Park reached the upper Niger in 1795–6. Government took over the organization of expeditions by *Clapperton and others and in 1830 *Lander solved the vexed question of where the Niger debouched into the sea. The mantle of the African Association was taken on by the Royal Geographical Society, founded in 1830, which, often in association with government, sent explorers especially to eastern and central Africa and to the Polar regions. Livingstone, *Burton, Speke—who reached the source of the Nile—Cameron, Stanley, and Thomson were the great African explorers, while the old obsession with the North-West Passage led to the expeditions of Parry, and especially of *Franklin whose disappearance after 1845 led to no fewer than 40 search expeditions. In the south polar region, *Ross, Bruce, *Shackleton, and *Scott are the great names.

Scott's failure to be first to the South Pole in 1912 was perhaps a sign that the age of British dominance in exploration was coming to an end. Perhaps the era did end when a British expedition was the first to conquer Everest in 1953, albeit with a New Zealander and a Nepalese actually reaching the summit. RB

extradition. The first recorded instance of extradition procedures was in 1174 with a treaty between Henry II of England and William the Lion of Scotland to exchange criminals who had fled from one country to the other. In 1303 and 1497 similar agreements were made between England and the French and England and the Flemings. In 1794 the Jay treaty inaugurated a formal agreement between Britain and the USA, though it was limited to Canada. The *Ashburton treaty in 1842 also included provision for extradition and was followed by agreements between Britain and France in 1843 and Britain and Denmark in 1862. They did not work well and in 1870 the Extradition Act attempted to improve the mechanisms. Between 1870 and 1904 35 treaties were implemented under the Act which remained in force for 119 years, enlarged by the Extradition Act of 1873, and finally superseded by the Extradition Act of 1989. Extradition does not apply to persons granted political asylum but the definition has often led to disputes. SMD

Eyre. The General Eyre, which probably dates from the reign of Henry I and is believed to derive its name from the Latin *iter*, was a commission issued by the king to officials of the *curia regis, who travelled round the kingdom visiting the different regions every few years. The powers given to the travelling justices under the Commission of the General Eyre were extremely wide. During their visitation they took over the county court and summoned inhabitants to answer questions relating to local affairs and taxation, scrutinized the conduct of the sheriff and other local officials, and thus ensured that the king's interests were protected. The commission was 'Ad omnia placita'—to deal with all kinds of pleas—and in addition to a general local audit, the justices heard pleas of the crown (criminal cases) and common pleas (pleas between subjects). Although not at first oppressive, the General Eyre became feared and unpopular and in the 14th cent. it faded away. MM

Fabian Society. The Society took its name from the Roman dictator Fabius, nicknamed 'Cunctator', or delayer. It was founded in January 1884 by a small group of middle-class intellectuals with the purpose of furthering 'the reconstruction of Society in accordance with the highest moral principles', but *gradually*. Its first pamphlet, or 'Tract', *Why are the Many Poor?*, made it plain that the highest principles were socialist ones. Shortly afterwards Sidney *Webb and Bernard *Shaw, its most famous members, joined. The latter penned some of its most brilliant tracts. The society's main importance thereafter was as an amazingly fecund womb of ideas for the infant and maturing *Labour parties, not all of which were predictable. In 1900, for example, it came out in support of the *British empire, on the grounds that it could be made into a gigantic welfare state, which seemed perverse to other socialists. When Labour came to power, however, the Fabians' willingness to engage with the realities around them was a definite boon. It still survives: the most senior of all Britain's socialist organizations.

BJP

Factory Acts were introduced to protect working people from employers who permitted dangerous practices and environments in workplaces. The first Acts of 1809 and 1823 failed to include effective enforcement clauses. In 1833 Lord Ashley (later earl of *Shaftesbury) introduced the first effective law. It established an inspectorate with powers to enter premises and to require evidence of compliance with restrictions on the employment of women and children. This Act applied only to large textile factories. Acts of 1844, 1847, and 1863 extended the laws to other manufactures and included small workshops. Conditions in mines and quarries, brickfields, railways, shipping, alkali works, aircraft, and shops and warehouses were regulated separately. Concern about workers and the safeguarding of the general public were the subject of many pieces of legislation during the 19th and 20th cents. A coherent law relating to safety at work was not achieved until 1969 when the Health and Safety Executive was set up. IJEK

factory system. The 'factory system' has been an important element in the accelerating processes of industrialization which have become known as the *industrial revolution. As British industrial enterprises expanded in the 18th cent., recruiting more workers and investing in expensive tools and equipment, it became important to develop a more tightly organized and disciplined form of production than the traditional method of employing workers in small workshops or their own homes—as in the *'domestic system' which had operated satisfactorily for several hundred years, for example, in sections of the English woollen cloth industry. The solution to the problem was the construction of large manufacturing establishments, in which the entry and exit of the work-force could be closely controlled and strict conditions of discipline and time-keeping maintained. In this way employers were able to minimize the loss of raw materials and finished goods by theft, and to protect their capital equipment. They were able also to install powerful prime movers (water wheels or steam-engines) to drive all their machines from a single source.

From the employers' point of view, this factory system had such manifest advantages that it was widely adopted, especially in the textile industries, where the Lombe silk factory in Derby was a marvel of the age. It was also used by the heavy iron and steel industries, by manufacturers of pottery, glass, paper, and chemicals, and by processes in the food and drink industries, such as breweries. Indeed, the factory system became the dominant form of industrial organization throughout the 19th cent., and has remained important in the 20th cent., especially in the large complexes of the modern engineering industry. However, the introduction of electricity and road haulage has made possible a significant dispersal of industry, and the 'information revolution' of modern electronics and telecommunications has enabled an increasing number of people to work at home, so that the general trend of recent decades has been for factories to become smaller.

Architecturally, the factory system developed through several phases. Early factories were solidly built to accommodate the necessary machines and sources of power, with the minimum of embellishment. But the hazard of fire in such confined environments compelled entrepreneurs to develop forms of fire-proof construction, using little wood and depending on a solid framework of cast-iron pillars and girders. The need for natural light in some of the processes, moreover, directed attention to improved glazing, and many factories became well-built structures with ample windows and decorative flourishes such as ornate chimneys to carry the furnace flues from the boiler room. Idealistic entrepreneurs, such as Robert *Owen or Titus *Salt, saw their factories as part of a human community, and provided good housing and public amenities for their workers. Modern 'industrial estates' are typically composed of a series of temporary boxes which, while providing good light and a comfortable working environment, have little architectural distinction and can be easily scrapped when they become obsolete. The factory system has thus changed substantially over 200 years, in response to new industrial processes, changing sources of power and transport, and new social needs. But it provides, typically, the modern workplace, symbolizing industrialization and life in industrial society. RAB

Fairfax, Ferdinando Fairfax, 2nd Baron [S] (1584–1648). Parliamentary commander in the Civil War. As soon as fighting began in 1642, Fairfax was put in command of Parliament's forces in Yorkshire, his home county. The early months of 1643 were spent jockeying for position, but in June 1643 he was badly beaten by *Newcastle at *Adwalton Moor and besieged in Hull. With his son Sir Thomas *Fairfax he gained a significant victory at *Selby in April 1644 and he fought at *Marston Moor, where his son Charles was killed. He resigned in accordance with the self-denying ordinance of 1645. JAC

Fairfax, Sir Thomas (1612–71). Fairfax was probably the best commander on the parliamentary side in the civil wars. His career started inauspiciously in March 1643 when he was beaten by *Goring at Seacroft Moor in Yorkshire, but he turned the tables on Goring in May 1643, capturing him at Wakefield. He then gained an impressive string of victories at *Winceby, *Nantwich, *Selby, and *Marston Moor. In the winter of 1644 he was busy training the *New Model Army to unprecedented standards of drill and efficiency. In the spring of 1645 he replaced *Essex as commander-in-chief and his two great victories at *Naseby in June and *Langport in July knocked the heart out of royalist resistance. In the second civil war he besieged and took Colchester. Out of sympathy with events during the Commonwealth and Protectorate, Fairfax helped *Monck in 1660 to bring about the Restoration. *Clarendon paid tribute to his outstanding courage and *Aubrey recorded that his first action on taking Oxford in 1646 was to set a guard on the Bodleian library to prevent looting. JAC

Fairford church (Glos.), dedicated in honour of the Virgin Mary, is first mentioned in the 11th cent. The church was largely rebuilt at the end of the 15th cent. The fabric was completed around 1497 by John Tame, whose tomb stands in the usual position of a founder's tomb on the north side of the chancel. The wonder of the church is its medieval glass, which survives from all twenty-eight windows in the church. The windows are devoted to the life of Christ; the prophets, apostles, evangelists, and doctors; and the Last Judgement. Throughout the scheme the central importance of the Virgin is stressed, as is appropriate in a church dedicated to her. The glass early attracted antiquarian interest, which included speculations that it had been designed by Dürer. Modern study of the glass has confirmed that the designer was indeed a foreigner, probably Master Adrian van den Houte of Mechlin, who was also concerned with the early glass in *King's College Chapel, Cambridge. Because of the affinities of the Fairford glass to other royal projects, and also because of the scale of the undertaking, with four designers and at least twelve glaziers, it is suggested that the glass was actually made under royal patronage after the manor reverted to the crown in 1499, and was probably completed between 1500 and 1517. LR

fairies were thought of as supernatural beings, capable of being helpful and benevolent to humans, or hostile and dangerous, or simply mischievous. Fairy beliefs are of long standing, and over 170 types of fairy have been listed from British sources. Although evidence about fairy beliefs thickens from the 16th cent., most of them were already fixed in the Middle Ages. Fairies were diminutive and could make themselves invisible at will, while fairyland was seen as a timeless realm where the normal problems of human existence were absent. Changelings and fairy lovers were recurrent themes.

The fairies' intermediate position between the human and spirit world had always placed them close to devils. After the Reformation this connection was more readily made and the fairies figured in a number of witchcraft investigations. Belief in the fairies continued among the populace at large, as 19th-cent. folklorists discovered, but belief in them among the educated was long gone by then. Indeed, in that century the supernatural beings of an earlier era were regimented for the purposes of children's storybooks. JAS

fairs, as periodic gatherings for the sale of goods and services including the hiring of labourers, developed in the Middle Ages. They brought together traders from much greater distances than the markets held weekly or more frequently in many towns and villages. Markets dealt in local and seasonal produce; fairs provided the opportunity to buy a wider range of products.

Fairs were held at regular intervals for a fixed number of days. They were licensed by charter, usually from the crown. In turn, they were highly profitable to magnates and corporations through stall rents. Some fairs became famous for their size and their specializations. These fairs drew traders and customers from many parts of the country and even from overseas. Examples include Stourbridge (Cambs.) for dried fish and cloth, St Ives (Cambs.) for wool, hides, and cloth, and Boston (Lincs.) for wine and wool.

Such large, temporary concentrations of strangers challenged the normal mechanisms for maintaining law and order. Special courts of *piepowder (*pieds poudrés*: dusty feet) dispensed rapid justice to breakers of contracts, cheats, or those who behaved rowdily.

Most fairs provided entertainments but these remained only marginal until the major commercial changes of the 18th cent. These changes diminished the trade of fairs because of the expansion of shopping facilities and the regularity of deliveries of goods and services made possible by improved roads and the canal network.

Fairs continued for seasonal agricultural trade in grain, cattle, and sheep into the 19th cent.; and the custom of hiring workers also persisted. However, even these features declined as railways made deliveries of farm produce to major markets reliable and other forms of labour recruitment became the norm.

Only a limited number of fairs remained by the time the royal commission of 1888 examined the role of fairs and markets. Its evidence indicated that fairs had become associated with entertainment and sometimes with disorder. Many fairs with ancient charters continue uninterrupted to the present time, often held in town centres. During the 20th cent. the Showmen's Guild has collaborated with local government to control traffic and ensure public safety.

IJEK

Falaise, treaty of, 1174. Earliest Anglo-Scottish treaty whose terms are known in full. It was imposed by Henry II on the captive William the Lion at Falaise in Normandy early in December 1174, and finally ratified at York on 10 August 1175. To secure his release from custody, William explicitly recognized Henry as feudal overlord of Scotland; Scottish nobles and churchmen followed suit; and the castles of Edinburgh, Roxburgh, and Berwick were surrendered and garrisoned by English troops. These terms were punitive and humiliating, and although Henry refrained from exercising his authority to the full, the treaty remained in force until 1189. KJS

Falkirk, battle of, 1298. *Wallace's victory at *Stirling Bridge in 1297 had shaken the English hold on Scotland. Edward I assembled a large army to restore the situation and on 22 July 1298 attacked William Wallace's men near the river Carron. The Scots had some protection from a marsh but superior archery and cavalry carried the day for Edward. Wallace remained a fugitive until captured in 1305. JAC

Falkirk, battle of, 1746. After the Jacobite retreat from Derby in December 1745, it was not Charles *Stuart's intention to abandon the enterprise but to consolidate in Scotland. *Cumberland handed over the pursuit to General Hawley, whose army of some 8,000 men included many Campbells. On 17 January at Falkirk the Highland charge once more carried the day, inflicting a sharp defeat on the Hanoverians. Cumberland returned from England to Edinburgh to take over. JAC

Falkland, Lucius Cary, 2nd Viscount [S] (1610–43). Falkland was educated in Ireland, where his father was viceroy, but settled at Great Tew, his country house outside Oxford. This became, in the words of *Clarendon, a regular visitor, 'a university bound in a lesser volume', where Falkland and his friends, turning their backs on religious fanaticism and political partisanship, pursued a dispassionate search for unifying truths. Elected to Parliament in 1640, Falkland condemned arbitrary rule in church and state, but opposed radical change. In January 1642 he accepted office as secretary of state, in the vain hope of closing the gap between the king and Parliament. His peace-loving and tolerant nature was revolted by the prospect of civil war, and made him careless of his own life. This 'incomparable young man', as Clarendon called him, found a welcome death in battle in September 1643. RL

Falkland palace. Royal home and hunting lodge, Fife. After Falkland castle (home of the earls of Fife and dukes of Albany) came into the possession of James II, his 1450s extension became the north range of the palace, further chambers being added by his widow *Mary of Gueldres. James IV renovated the north range's great hall (1502) and added the east and south ranges, which were embellished by James V: his French craftsmen transformed them in the 1530s into the first Renaissance building in Scotland, now regarded as among the finest work of its period in Britain and marking the height of the 'Auld Alliance'. The ornamented gatehouse, garden, and royal tennis court (1539) further enhanced this favourite seat of the Scottish monarchs. The north range was burnt, possibly accidentally, when *Cromwell's troops were quartered there (1654), only its foundations now remaining. Still owned by royalty, though no monarch has resided since Charles II, much restoration has been undertaken by the Crichton Stuarts in their role as hereditary constable, captain, and keeper of Falkland; the king's bedroom and Chapel Royal are particularly fine. The National Trust for Scotland has acted as deputy keeper since 1952. ASH

Falklands, battle of the, 1914. After dispatching Craddock's squadron at the battle of *Coronel, von Spee's ships rounded Cape Horn and on 8 December 1914 attacked the British installations at Port Stanley in the Falkland Islands. However, the Germans unexpectedly found themselves fighting a much stronger British squadron. As soon as news of Craddock's defeat had reached London, the Admiralty had dispatched two of its most powerful battle-cruisers to the south Atlantic under Vice-Admiral Sturdee, who now proceeded to sink all but one of von Spee's ships. The battle marked the end of any serious threat to British merchant shipping from German surface cruisers. DF

Falklands War (1982). The Falkland Islands had been under British control since 1833, but Argentina had become increasingly anxious to negotiate their transfer. On 19 March 1982 a group of Argentine scrap metal merchants landed on South Georgia without permission, and this was followed on 2 April by full invasion. The Foreign Office was caught largely unawares and Lord *Carrington described the invasion as a 'great national humiliation'. The government acted swiftly, assembling a task force consisting of 10,000 troops and 44 warships with auxiliary and aircraft support. It was dispatched 8,000 miles to the south Atlantic, using Ascension Island as a forward base.

The USA, anxious to retain good relations with both countries, tried to mediate through Secretary of State Alexander Haig but to no avail. On 25 April marines recaptured South Georgia. On 2 May the Argentine battleship *General Belgrano* was sunk by a British submarine with large loss of life and two days later the British destroyer HMS *Sheffield* was hit by an Exocet missile and sunk.

British troops, under aerial attack, landed on the Falklands at San Carlos on 21 May and established a bridgehead. After fierce fighting the settlements at Darwin and Goose Green were retaken and the capital, Stanley, came under fire. On 14 June the Argentine garrisons surrendered. The war cost the lives of 236 British and 750 Argentine soldiers. It was the turning-point in the fortunes of the Thatcher Conservative government, but in Argentina, General Galtieri's military junta fell from power a year later. RAS

family history refers to the records of those groups comprising parents and their children and all those connected to them by blood or marriage, claiming descent from a common ancestor. In Britain, where property and titles conferring status and privilege were and are inherited according to blood relationships, accurate documentation is of great importance.

From earliest times, tracing ancestors and establishing proof of relationship had practical importance for the wealthy and privileged and, in particular, for the sovereign. Throughout the 15th cent., before, during, and after the Wars of the *Roses, evidence about family relationships formed an essential part of the case advanced by every claimant to the throne of England. Records of the aristocracy and royal families had always been maintained by the earl marshal and, in Scotland, by Lyon King-of-arms. However, in 1484, the *College of Arms was incorporated as a permanent institution comprising heralds, who had the task of investigating descent and establishing incontestable rights to titles and property. At lower levels of society, amongst the gentry and smaller landowners, it was equally important to have knowledge of the family tree. Recognition of property rights guaranteed social status and acceptance. Thus, after the civil wars of the mid-17th cent. and the consequent upheaval and changes in land ownership, both aristocracy and gentry supported the publication of detailed histories of counties in England and Wales, which included family histories, often illustrating coats of arms, houses, and estates. In a formal sense the arrangement of these volumes was territorial, but information about rank, ownership of land, and powers to act as magistrates and to nominate clergy to benefices was given great prominence. These county histories focused on the wealthier residents of each county, giving little information about other levels of society. This pattern was followed by Scottish historians, except that they emphasized the role of the chiefs of Highland clans, particularly those who took peerages.

In the 20th cent. interest in family history has become widespread, particularly since the 1950s with the expansion of popular education, greater resources including more leisure time, and easier access to documentary evidence. Tracing family history has become a popular activity, not as a means of establishing rights to title and property, but as a recognition of the importance of family and ancestry at all social levels. By 1960 county *record offices had been established in all areas of England and Wales, providing readily available sources such as parish records, ancient wills, and, where they existed, family papers. An additional source has been the census enumerators' books, which may only be opened 100 years after their collection and give details about family composition and relationships.

In the 20th cent. social historians have used studies of family histories to illuminate processes of social and geographical mobility in earlier times. This approach to history, combined with popular interest in family history, suggests that we may be moving towards a situation where the common people may be as well documented as the rich and privileged of previous eras. IJEK

famine may be defined as the occurrence of serious food shortages resulting in significant rises in the death rate. Mortality during famines was rarely caused solely by starvation but from related diseases like dysentery, typhoid, and typhus. Hence deaths from food shortages might occur some time after initial harvest failures. Increased migration out of famine-hit areas to towns and cities could also raise death rates since rural refugees often encountered diseases to which they had no immunity, or transmitted epidemics to urban dwellers.

Vulnerability to famine depended on more than the local harvest. Also important were the amount of food imported, the efficiency of distribution and relief systems, and the ability to purchase supplies in the market-place. Famines were more likely to occur when harvests failed successively, when population pressure on resources was extensive, and where populations were over-reliant on one particular crop. Pastoral areas of Britain, often located in more remote upland areas on poorer soils, where animal husbandry took precedence over grain production, were usually more vulnerable to famine than grain-producing regions.

What has been described as the worst famine in England in the last millennium occurred in 1315–18, after a century of rapid population growth, when a succession of disastrous harvests killed between 10 and 15 per cent of the population. Lesser famines had also occurred in 1293–5 and 1310–12. After the arrival of plague in 1348, however, England's agrarian economy was more than able to feed its much reduced population, and famine mortality disappeared until population growth accelerated again in the 16th cent.

When famine returned, the worst crisis took place in 1594–8 with another less serious in 1623–4. Even these were concentrated in England's more remote northern upland pastoral areas, notably Cumberland, and most of the country was unaffected. Famines disappeared from England after 1640. Their end was facilitated by improved agricultural productivity, a well-developed marketing network, and the introduction of England's *Poor Law (1601) which alleviated distress when harvests failed.

England's Celtic neighbours experienced more severe famines for far longer in their history. Scotland suffered spectacularly in 1623–4 when death rates in some areas increased eightfold. Increased specialization on pastoral agriculture in the 18th cent. seems to have increased vulnerability to famine. Scotland suffered severe famine mortality in the 1690s which may have killed 15 per cent of its population, lowland areas were hit by famine mortality in 1740–1, and parts of the Highlands suffered famine late into that century. Famines were experienced in Ireland in the 1620s, 1640s, and 1650s. As its textile industry declined and the diet of its poor increasingly became dominated by the potato, Ireland became more rather than less famine-prone. Serious mortality occurred in 1727–9 and the 1740–1 scourge killed some quarter of a million people. Famines occurred again in 1744–6, 1800–1, and 1817–19 but these were dwarfed by the last Great *Famine in Ireland, caused by potato blight which ravaged the staple potato crop for four successive years, 1845–8. Recent estimates put the number of deaths attributable to this disaster at 1 million. JPB

Famine, Irish (1845–51). The famine originated with the recurrent failure of the potato crop, devastating the Irish cottier and small farmer classes: around 1 million died in Ireland as a result either of starvation or—more commonly—disease. The origin of this demographic cataclysm lay with a fungus, *phytophtora infestans*, which destroyed half the Irish potato crop of 1845, and brought a near total crop failure in 1846. A partial recovery in 1847 was offset by a greatly reduced area under cultivation, so that although there was a good yield per acre sown, the total harvest was poor. The potato crop failed almost totally in 1848.

The social and economic consequences of the famine are disputed. But it is clear that excess mortality effectively doubled for the five years (1846–50). Mortality levels rose from 1846, reaching a peak in 1847–8, though there were social and regional variations. In addition the birth rate fell critically during the famine years. Emigration, a feature of Irish society since the early 18th cent., greatly expanded: between 1845 and 1870 there were at least 3 million Irish emigrants. Ireland emerged from the famine denuded of its cottiers and dominated by the farmer interest.

The political outfall from the famine offers few problems of interpretation. The Conservative administration of Sir Robert *Peel initially tackled the blight with some success, buying and importing Indian meal and establishing food depots. Peel's government fell in June 1846, to be replaced by a more doctrinaire Whig administration. The Whigs relied at first on an extensive scheme of public works, but this was abandoned in 1847, being replaced by soup-kitchens. The limited crop recovery in 1847 persuaded the government that the emergency had ended, and all special relief programmes were abolished. This apparent British complacency, though it had little immediate political impact, fired later 19th-cent. Irish nationalism.

The Great Famine affected all aspects of Irish life and remains one of the most emotive issues in modern Irish historiography. The dominant—'revisionist'—view of the famine, until recently, was that it accelerated existing trends in Irish society: this, in turn, has been challenged by those who, like Cormac O Grada, emphasize the uniqueness of the event, and place less stress on the continuities. AJ

Faraday, Michael (1791–1867). Chemist and pioneer of electromagnetism. As a bookbinder's apprentice, he went to Humphry *Davy's lectures at the *Royal Institution and asked to be taken on as his assistant. Accompanying Davy to Paris and Rome in 1813–15, by 1820 he was himself a prominent chemist, famous for his experimental skill, thinking with his fingers. He isolated benzene in 1825, and when Davy died in 1829 he could escape from his shadow and work on the nature of electricity, magnetism, and light. After his death, this led to the *electrical industry; and by the 1860s with J. C. *Maxwell's work, it had transformed physics with field theory. Faraday was a keen member of the fundamentalist Sandemanian sect. He remained a very private man, refusing titles or (like Robert *Boyle) public offices—a kind of scientific saint. DK

Farington, Joseph (1747–1821). English landscape painter and draughtsman, Farington studied at the Royal Academy from its foundation in 1768, becoming an unofficial but influential part of its government. Until 1921, he was best known for two collections of engravings of the English Lakes, but in that year his copious diary was discovered and revealed Farington as an authority on matters artistic, literary, social, and political. A friend to many in Parliament and well informed on politics in France, Farington's work is rich in anecdote about almost every leading politician of his day. In 1793, with assistance from supporters of the war with France, Farington visited the front at Valenciennes and acting as an early war artist, recorded what he saw. Most of the original diary manuscript is in the Royal Collection at Windsor castle and examples of his drawings are in London at the British and Victoria and Albert museums. JC

farming and estate management. Agriculture was the principal basis of wealth in Britain until its relative importance waned as a consequence of increasing financial returns from commerce and manufacturing industries. Surviving fragments of Anglo-Saxon accounts show that landowners controlled extensive properties but the earliest statements of the principles underlying practices of estate management only survive from the 13th cent. Manuscript treatises on farming and estate management were copied for many larger landowners. For example, *Walter of Henley's Husbandry* gave advice on estate management: appointing and supervising managers and workers, the necessity for surveys of property and assets, keeping accounts, guidelines for estimating likely yields per acre of seeds and of produce from livestock, and conducting audits.

During the 16th and 17th cents. new techniques of farming had implications for the management of estates. Losses of common land to enclosures made possible new practices: creating water meadows and growing new crops such as sainfoin and lucerne to augment supplies of animal winter fodder. Enclosures for permanent pasture enabled sheep flocks to increase in size. In the 17th cent. Dutch techniques for land reclamation, as in the Fens, necessitated enclosures. Landowners protected their interests by studying land law at the Inns of Court and by appointing qualified stewards to manage estates effectively. Encouraging or coercing tenants to adopt new ways of farming challenged tradition, and changes were often achieved only after lengthy legal proceedings.

By the 18th cent. notable advances were made in improving returns to major landowners. Further enclosure in England was achieved by private Acts of Parliament which cost less money and time than the legal procedures of earlier centuries. These Acts became increasingly common after the middle of the century. Estate managers drew up leases specifying minimum standards of good agricultural practices, such as crop rotations, to be used by tenant farmers.

In the Scottish Lowlands landowners faced few legal problems during the 18th cent. and pioneered agricultural innovations. For example, the duke of Richmond brought his experienced estate steward to manage his English estates. In the Scottish Highlands, clan chieftains encouraged their followers to adopt improved farming practices. In contrast, in the early 19th cent. the Highland clearances were undertaken to suit the convenience of landowners, whose priorities often ignored severe hardships imposed on dispossessed tenants.

During the 19th cent. many agricultural innovations were promoted by landowners who wanted to sustain or improve their incomes. This was the period of books and magazines about agriculture and of the agricultural show for disseminating new ideas. In 1839 formal agrarian education for landowners began in England at the Royal Agricultural College at Cirencester. Later in the century local colleges were opened for educating aspiring and working farmers.

In Ireland the history of landownership was characterized by many absentee landlords whose incomes came from the smallholdings of tenant farmers. Traditional farming methods continued into the 19th cent., dominated by the monoculture of the potato. The failure of the potato crop in the 1840s proved calamitous for the rural population. The mass migration precipitated by the famine altered farming practices, changed the social and political relationships of landowners and tenants, and resulted in legislation about tenants' rights.

During the 20th cent. farming has been characterized by innovations: chemical fertilizers, labour-saving machinery for both arable and pastoral farming, hygiene legislation, and interventions in livestock breeding and care. As a consequence estate management has become increasingly like other business management, demanding high capital investment, financial expertise, skills in labour relations, and access to research and development. Sustained government intervention began in the Second World War and still continues. From 1940 subsidies provided much of the finance needed to increase food output and this support continued until Britain joined the Common Market in 1975, when farming began to operate within the framework of the Common Agricultural Policy. IJEK

Fascists, British Union of. See BRITISH UNION OF FASCISTS.

Fashoda crisis, 1898. In 1893 France, irritated by Britain's continued hold over Egypt, decided to go for Fashoda, on the White Nile to the south. An expedition was sent from the west under Colonel Marchand, to French Premier Delcassé's regrets later, because he feared it might provoke a conflict; but by then he could not call it back. Marchand arrived on 10 July 1898. On 18 September a British army under *Kitchener met him there. Europe braced itself for war; but all that happened was that the two men sat down, cracked open a bottle of champagne Marchand had brought with him, swapped stories, and waited for the respective Foreign Offices to patch things up. In the end (3 November) the French gave in. BJP

Faulkner, Brian (1921–77). One of the ablest and most articulate of Northern Irish Unionist prime ministers, Faulkner was from a commercial rather than a landed background. Progressive in economic policies as minister of commerce (1963–9) yet a hard-liner against *O'Neill's attempts to lessen entrenched sectarian divisions, he became the last Northern Irish premier in March 1971 and won British government support for a stiff security policy culminating in internment. The failure of that policy and his vulnerability within his own party led him to change stance abruptly and accept the power-sharing executive following the Sunningdale agreement of 1973. He became chief executive of the new administration, which collapsed after the loyalist strike of 1974. Thereafter Faulkner was left without a political constituency, and died in a hunting accident, a largely forgotten man. Regarded by his own side as too clever to be trusted, he was never forgiven by the catholic minority for his earlier sectarian intransigence. MAH

Fawkes, Guy (Guido) (1570–1606). Fawkes was born in York in a family of protestant ecclesiastical lawyers. His father died when he was 9 and his stepfather seems to have influenced him to become a catholic. At 23 he enlisted in the Spanish army in the Netherlands. In 1604 Catesby and his fellow-conspirators, despairing of obtaining relief for the catholics from James I, brought Fawkes into their plot to blow up the king and Parliament and proclaim the Princess *Elizabeth. Fawkes was put in charge of the house next to Parliament from which a tunnel was to be made, and then of a cellar which they hired directly under the House of Lords. He passed under the name of John Johnson. Parliament was repeatedly adjourned until 5 November 1605. Fawkes's task was to light the slow fuse to ignite the barrels of gunpowder. After a warning letter to Lord Mounteagle, the cellar was searched and Fawkes taken. He faced torture in the Tower with great coolness but confessed after hearing that his fellow-plotters were taken, and was executed at Westminster on 31 January 1606. His dark lantern is in the Ashmolean Museum at Oxford. JAC

fealty derives from the French word *foi* meaning faith or trust. In the Middle Ages those in power demanded *oaths of fealty from those subject to them—kings from their officials and their nobility (as William the Conqueror seems to have demanded at *Salisbury in 1086), prelates from their clergy, manorial lords from their peasants—in order to confirm and strengthen their authority, perhaps at moments of crisis or challenge. Unlike *homage, fealty was a unilateral process: those to whom oaths were given were not obliged to promise anything in return. AC

Felix, St (d. 648). A Burgundian bishop, Felix offered himself to *Honorius, archbishop of Canterbury, for missionary work in England. He was sent to help King *Sigeberht establish the church in East Anglia *c.*631, exemplifying the important partnership between kings and bishops in the evangelization of England. *Bede tells us that he 'reaped a rich harvest of believers', delivering the province from 'its age-old wickedness and infelicity'. He also provided teachers and masters for Sigeberht's school, based on the Canterbury system. His see was established in Dommoc, thought to be *Dunwich (Suffolk), where he remained until his death. AM

feminist history. 'Do women have a history, Professor?' said the French customs officer to a woman claiming to be attending a 1984 UNESCO conference on the history of women. As a question permitting a range of intonation from genuine puzzlement to withering sarcasm, it is richly suggestive of the suspicion and hostility with which the notion of feminist history may be viewed both inside and outside academic circles. Why should 'women's history' have become defined as a separate sphere? For feminist historians, one answer might be that there are two sides to any narrative and that we have heard only one for the last two and a half millennia. Precisely because women outside the ruling classes have been of little interest to historiographers, there has until recently been scant research into the lives and achievements of a wide social range of one half of the historical population.

Many of the protesters in 1960s newsreel footage of women's movement demonstrations were part of the influx of women into higher education in that decade. For those who perceived sexual discrimination as widespread, the male-dominated content of many educational syllabi seemed both part of the problem but also a potential solution. Beginning in the 1960s, a handful of college and university courses across the United States began to redress what was perceived to be a gender imbalance in the study of a range of humanities disciplines. Given that the majority of women in history had found their activities confined to the domestic sphere or a supporting role in politics, it is not surprising that women's history developed alongside social history. So successful have feminist historians been in recovering the history of those marginalized by traditional historiography, that few universities in the Anglo-American world now lack courses focusing on women from the medieval period to the present day.

The academic growth of feminist history has generated a vast critical literature, the authors of which are the heirs of early women writers who protested about the place allocated to them in society in virtue of their sex. Reading Mary Astell's *Serious Proposal To the Ladies* (1694), Mary Wollstonecraft's *A Vindication of the Rights of Woman* (1792), and John Stuart Mill's *Subjection of Women* (1869), we can see that feminist history has finally succeeded in legitimizing a field of enquiry that is at least as old as the history of early modern thought. GR

Fenians. See IRISH REPUBLICAN BROTHERHOOD.

Fens, drainage of. From the 13th cent. the commissioners of sewers in the 1,300 square miles of low-lying fenlands in eastern England were responsible for undertaking works designed to prevent inundation. With James I's declaration in 1621 that he was unwilling to allow waterlogged lands to lie waste and unprofitable, a firmer base was created for action, and this arrived in the form of the Dutch entrepreneur Sir Cornelius Vermuyden who in 1626 began the complex task of draining the fens of Hatfield Chase and the Isle of Axholme. Axholme was drained between 1626 and 1636, but at a price to the fenlanders, and during the civil wars they took the opportunity to undo much of his work. Drainage resumed after the Restoration, but it was the second half of the 18th cent. before much enthusiasm could be generated. In the 1830s and 1840s the introduction of steam pumps ensured that by the later 19th cent. the risk of flooding had virtually disappeared. This, plus the agricultural benefits of cropping the fens, brought resistance to an end. The familiar dikes and drains of the fenland landscape are still a vivid reminder of how vulnerable this area has long been to inundation. See BEDFORD LEVEL. JVB

Ferguson, Harry (1884–1960). Engineer. Born in Co. Down, Ferguson opened a garage in Belfast and in 1909 was the first man in Ireland to fly. During the First World War he developed his interest in farm machinery and in the 1930s produced his ploughing tractor. Between 1939 and 1947 he was in partnership with Henry Ford to mass-produce tractors, and when Ford's successors repudiated the contract, set up on his own. Ford's were forced to settle in 1952 for $9 million in compensation. Ferguson's constant advocacy of reducing prices and holding down incomes became fashionable after his death. JAC

Fermanagh, one of the six counties of Northern Ireland until the local government reorganization of 1973, borders on the Irish Republic. Enniskillen, the chief town, is in the centre of the county. In the north of the county is Lower Lough Erne, to the south Upper Lough Erne. Enniskillen was a protestant settlement in the early 17th cent. and sustained a siege in 1689 which took much of the pressure off the Jacobite attack on *Londonderry. There is a Church of Ireland cathedral, dedicated to St Macartan, and dating from 1841. The area depends upon tourism, cattle, and fishing, with a little light industry. It has a mixed religious population. When Northern Ireland was set up in 1921 the Fermanagh County Council declared its allegiance to the Irish Free State and was dissolved. For parliamentary purposes, Fermanagh is joined with south Tyrone: at the 1992 election, the seat was held by the Ulster Unionists, with the catholic vote split between Social Democratic and Labour Party and Sinn Fein. JAC

Ferrar, Robert (*c.*1504–55). Protestant martyr. Ferrar was born in Yorkshire, took holy orders, and soon adhered to the reforming party. He became chaplain to *Cranmer and took a wife. Under the patronage of *Somerset, he was appointed bishop of St Davids (1548). His chapter brought a series of complaints against him and after the fall of Somerset he was tried and imprisoned. When Mary succeeded in 1553 his fate was sealed. Ferrar was deprived of his see in March 1554 and burned in the market-place of Carmarthen in March 1555. He died with great courage. JAC

Fethanleag, battle of, *c.*584. Fought possibly at Stoke Lyne, near Bicester (Oxon.), between the West Saxons and the Britons. The outcome is not recorded, but although the West Saxon king *Ceawlin is reported to have taken towns and considerable booty, he returned home in anger. It seems likely that he was not wholly victorious and the West Saxons probably suffered a check to their westward expansion. AM

feudal aids. In the English feudal society which followed the Norman Conquest, custom permitted the king, at times of exceptionally heavy expenditure, to take an 'aid' (*auxilium*) from his tenants-in-chief; a lord, similarly, could exact an aid from his free tenants. There was continual conflict about the occasions and amounts of such aids. *Magna Carta (1215) listed three occasions when the king, or a lord, might demand a 'reasonable', but unspecified, amount. These were: the knighting of his eldest son; the marriage of his eldest daughter (once); and the ransom of his own person from captivity. In 1275 in the statute of *Westminster, the king also set a limit on the amounts which could be claimed. MW

feudalism. An abstract term derived from the adjective 'feudal', and commonly used to highlight those features believed to be characteristic of western European society during the Middle Ages. The word was coined in the 19th cent. and is analogous to the earlier French term *feodalité*. It is based on the Latin noun *feudum* (or *feodum*) which is now usually translated as 'fief' and understood to mean property held by a tenant in return for rent in the form of service. This notion of feudal tenure was used by 16th-cent. French legal historians as a key to understanding the origins and development of aristocratic rights and powers in France in the centuries after the fall of Rome. In the 17th cent. Sir Henry Spelman argued that it was imported into England by the Normans. Hence *Maitland's crack that it was Spelman who introduced the feudal system into England. In the 18th cent. historically minded intellectuals such as Montesquieu, Adam *Smith, and David *Hume believed that societies went through a 'feudal' stage—an idea subsequently taken over by Marxist historians who have, however, emphasized the labour services owed by peasants to manorial lords rather than the military or governmental service owed by high-status tenants, which was central to the older tradition. Particularly influential was Montesquieu's hypothesis that when aristocratic fiefs became hereditary in France (which he dated to the 9th cent.), royal government collapsed and 'feudal anarchy' resulted.

Most British historians have remained within the old tradition of thought, partly because if all that is required for a society to be labelled 'feudal' is that tenants of any kind owe service in return for their lands, the term is thought to embrace too wide a range of social structures to be useful, and partly because the whole notion of feudalism originating in France and spreading out from there has become thoroughly entrenched. The view that the Normans brought 'feudalism' to England, and that during the next two centuries French and English invaders and settlers took it to Scotland, Wales, and Ireland remains widely held—and also widely disputed. Since it is clear that, throughout the British Isles, rulers before 1066 expected political and military service from their landed élites, those historians who believe that William the Conqueror feudalized England have had to define feudalism in terms of precisely those features which they believe he introduced: castles, the 'feudal quota' (that is, the obligation of the king's tenants to provide a quota of knights to serve, usually without pay, for 40 days), and the 'feudal incidents' (that is, the king's right to exploit the deaths, marriages, and wardships of his tenants both for profit and as an instrument of political control).

One problem with feudalism is that the 'facts' on which it is said to be based—e.g. that fiefs became hereditary in 9th-cent. France, or that William I introduced 'feudal incidents' and the quota—are themselves highly contentious. So many different definitions of feudalism have been offered—or, worse, simply assumed—that a degree of confusion has been the inevitable result. The adjective 'feudal' is commonly used to denote almost any social system regarded as being oppressive or backward. In these circumstances it is not surprising that some American and British medieval historians believe that both word and concept are past their sell-by date and should be abolished. French historians, more at ease with abstractions than their Anglo-Saxon colleagues, continue to use the term freely and much as Montesquieu did, though now with—thanks to the work of Georges Duby—a new orthodoxy dating the breakdown of public power and hence the 'feudal revolution' to *c.* AD 1000. JG

fidei defensor (Defender of the Faith). A title first given (1521) to Henry VIII by Pope Leo X for writing his *Assertio septem sacramentorum* against Luther. After the break with Rome, Parliament authorized it as a royal title (1544), which it has remained, though for modern multi-cultural Britain Prince Charles has suggested an improved translation, 'Defender of Faith' (i.e. all major religions). WMM

fief (or fee). An estate held by feudal tenure from a lord—in the case of tenants-in-chief the obligation was knight service to the king. In the early Norman period, some 2,500 knights were required. The archbishop of Canterbury was to provide 60, the abbot of Peterborough 60, the abbot of Bury St Edmunds 40: Robert of Gloucester was to provide 100, the honour of Totnes some 75. A five-hide unit was usually regarded as sufficient to maintain a knight, though it varied according to the character of the estate. The tenant-in-chief usually subcontracted to his own vassals and any shortfall in the number of knights needed would be made up by a personal retinue, directly supported by the lord and acting as a bodyguard if necessary. There were also uncommitted knights and mercenaries whom William the Conqueror and his successors employed to augment numbers. As the cost of maintaining horse and armour rose, the complement of the feudal levy declined and the proportion of hired men increased. JAC

Field, John (1782–1837). Field was a piano virtuoso and composer, whose delicate and sentimental nocturnes had considerable influence on Chopin, Mendelssohn, and others. Born in Dublin of a musical family, he made his first public appearance at the age of 9. He was taken to St Petersburg by Clementi, to whom he was apprenticed, and spent most of his life in Russia, coming to England for a visit in 1832. Hamilton *Harty's rather lush arrangement of four pieces as an orchestral suite in 1939 contributed to a popular revival of interest. JAC

Fielden, John (1784–1849). Factory reformer, whose career illustrates the sometimes paradoxical nature of early Victorian radicalism. A wealthy cotton-spinner, whose mills dominated Todmorden (then in Lancs.), Fielden was a friend and admirer of *Cobbett. He held that the welfare of labouring people should be the primary aim of all political endeavour, to be promoted by legislation in Parliament and by local action in the community. As MP for Oldham from 1832 he tirelessly sponsored bills to regulate minimum wages and hours of child labour in mills, and supported *Oastler and the operatives' short time committees. In 1833–4 he collaborated with Robert *Owen in the National Regeneration Society for an eight-hour day. His pamphlet *The Curse of the Factory System* was published in 1836, but it was not until 1847 that his *Ten Hours Bill was finally passed. Fielden fought hard against the New Poor Law and by his encouragement of direct action delayed its introduction into Todmorden. He supported *chartism, though withdrew from a position of leadership in 1839. JFCH

Fielding, Henry (1707–54). English writer and magistrate best known as the intrusive, ironic narrator of his novels. Educated at Eton and Leiden, Fielding wrote numerous plays, including swingeing political satires of *Walpole's government, until the theatrical Licensing Act of 1737. Called to the bar in 1740, Fielding subsequently divided his time between literature and the law, developing his own idiosyncratic theory of fiction as 'comic epics in prose' in *Joseph Andrews* (1742) and his masterpiece, *Tom Jones* (1749), a political allegory set in the midst of the '45. Appointed JP at Bow Street in 1748, Fielding was an energetic advocate of effective measures to reduce crime, corruption, and public disorder in the capital, earning notoriety for insisting on the death penalty in the Bosavern Penlez case. His health undermined by overwork, Fielding travelled to Lisbon after the publication of *Amelia*, his final novel, dying there in 1754. JAD

Field of Cloth of Gold, 1520. This was an extravagant diplomatic spectacle staged by Henry VIII of England and Francis I of France (1515–47) on 7–24 June 1520 at the Val d'Or, half-way between Guines, in the 'pale' round English Calais, and Ardres. An encampment of several hundred luxuriously decorated tents and pavilions was created for the occasion. The two kings and their entourages spent the time jousting, wrestling, and feasting, concluding with a mass and a banquet. Though the meeting was a great cultural spectacle, as a device to foster friendship between England and France following the treaty of *London (1518) it failed dismally. Henry VIII negotiated with the Emperor Charles V both before and after the meeting, and in 1522 and 1523 English troops invaded France. EC

Fields, Gracie (1898–1979). Music-hall artiste and film star. A Lancashire lass, born Grace Stansfield, Fields joined a touring music-hall company (1913) before eight years with Archie Pitt, gaining depth of experience in all aspects of revue work, to become a star overnight in the West End (1924). Talented, versatile, and dedicated, she could control her audience with merely a headscarf for a prop, switching easily from 'Ave Maria' to 'The Biggest Aspidistra in the World'. As music-halls declined, 'Our Gracie' moved successfully into film-making, but when she followed her future second husband into exile in America in 1940 (unjustifiably accused of deserting Britain), public adulation turned to condemnation, and it was many years before she regained British favour. She settled in Capri after the war, but returned periodically for concerts, command performances, media work, and to record, gave generously to charity, and was created Dame (1979). ASH

field systems. From the time that man began to practise agriculture, systems of husbandry were devised and adopted by individual communities which best suited the soil and climate. The precise circumstances in which the systems were adopted, and the external factors influencing particular communities, cannot now be reconstructed, and such were the variations that generalization is hazardous. Perhaps the best-known system was the common, or open field, system of farming in which the land of a particular parish was divided into two, three, four, or even more fields depending on local conditions. The system is usually dated to the Anglo-Saxon era, and emerged with the division of land and livestock among a mass of small occupiers. The need for common folding compelled common management of intermixed parcels of land. The fields were cropped usually on the basis of two crops and a fallow, although with considerable flexibility for individual initiative. Although the system was designed for a mixture of reasons including risk-sharing, plot-splitting (to accommodate sons for example), and the need to restore the fertility of the land, it is now believed that the need to maximize the number of animals may have been critical.

The common field system was found predominantly in midland England, and other systems were nearly as widespread. In upland regions, or on poor-quality soils, and particularly in Scotland, the system of infield-outfield cultivation was found. In Scotland the infield was an area of land under permanent cultivation which was regarded as a vital adjunct of the cattle-keeping sector of the agrarian economy. The 'outfield' land lay in irregular patches at varying distances from the settlement. They were broken up and cropped on a shifting system. Each parcel might be cropped for four or five years and then allowed to rest for five years. Cropping patterns on the infield and the outfield varied. See also ENCLOSURES. JVB

Fife lies on a peninsula between the Forth and Tay estuaries. Its name derives from a Pictish lordship, extending rather further west than the present boundary; the present region is still occasionally called the kingdom of Fife, particularly by those resisting attempts to divide its administration. In the 1973 local government reorganization of Scotland, Fife fought a successful campaign to be a region, and not to be divided between the neighbouring areas (Tayside and Lothian) to which it looks for significant employment, and in the 1996 changes it was Fife, rather than its erstwhile districts (Dunfermline, Kirkcaldy, North East

Fife), which became the all-purpose authority. Though in recent times it has had an in-built Labour majority, Fife continues to display diversity in both political and economic life. It has good agricultural land, partly underlain by coal seams, which formerly provided much employment, and, particularly round its coastline, there is a remarkable concentration of small towns, formerly royal burghs, now mainly inhabited by commuters or retired people. The main population centres are Kirkcaldy (once a major site for linoleum manufacture) and Glenrothes new town (in which the microcomputer industry is an important employer).

CML

Fifteen rising. See JACOBITE RISING.

Fifth Monarchy men. A movement of extreme *millenarians, arising in 1649 and radiating from two centres: London, where Christopher Feake and John Simpson preached, and Wales, where its evangelists were Vavasor Powell and Morgan Llwyd. Fifth Monarchists interpreted the four beasts in Daniel's dream (Dan. 7) as the four great empires of the ancient world. The fourth, the Roman, had been usurped by the papacy, alias Antichrist, or the Beast in Revelation (Rev. 11–20). The fifth monarchy was to be that of Christ, exercised on his behalf by his saints for 1,000 years (Rev. 20: 3–5), until he returned in person to pronounce the Last Judgement. Such beliefs were held by many orthodox puritans; the Fifth Monarchists differed from them in relating the scriptural prophecies very literally to current events, especially the regicide; in setting an early, precise date for the destruction of Antichrist; and in confidently identifying themselves as the saints. Above all, they believed it was their mission to overturn all remnants of 'carnal' government and erect the promised kingdom by their own efforts, though they differed as to its precise form. One accused *Cromwell to his face that he 'tooke the Crowne off from the heade of Christ, and put it upon his owne'. They disagreed over using force, but the militants attempted risings in London in 1657 and 1661. Thereafter they gradually declined.

AHW

Fiji. The republic of Fiji is a group of small islands in the Pacific, 1,000 miles north of New Zealand. They were first explored by Tasman in the 17th cent. but there was little regular contact until the 19th cent. when traders and missionaries arrived. The islands were declared a British colony in 1874 but granted independence in 1970, within the Commonwealth and with a governor-general. In 1987, after coups, Fiji was declared a republic. The capital is Suva, and the principal exports are sugar, coconuts, ginger, and copra.

JAC

film industry. Cinematography, on which many experiments were made in various countries, became feasible after the advent of celluloid film in 1889 and subsequent innovations in the motion film camera and the projector during the early 1890s. Following rapidly on the first public film show in Paris in 1895, the first commercial showing in Britain in 1896 caught public imagination to such an extent that films were soon being shown in halls, music-halls, and theatres. Later many of these buildings were converted into cinemas and by the early 1900s cinematography was becoming widespread. The first major custom-built picture house, the Alpha, opened in St Albans in 1908. A tremendous boom in cinema building and conversion took place during the next few years and continued unabated until the First World War, by which time there were about 3,500. The Cinematograph Act, 1909, sought among other requirements the safety of the audience.

There was a corresponding growth in film-making and for the first decade British producers were very successful, establishing an important export market, particularly to the USA. Nevertheless only 15 per cent of films released in Britain were of British origin, with France and the USA accounting for 36 and 28 per cent respectively in 1910.

The main characteristic of the British film industry in the decade following the war was the dominance of American companies. This had reached such a degree of saturation that by 1926 British films occupied less than 5 per cent of British screen-time. The Cinematograph Films Act of 1927 attempted to counter this situation by setting quotas to combat the 'Hollywood invasion'. The Films Act became the cornerstone of Board of Trade film policy, recognizing the propaganda value of film and its increasing economic importance, and going some way to assisting British film production. A golden era for the film industry began with the arrival of the talkies in 1927–8, and, despite the depression, cinema building accelerated, no fewer than 715 new cinemas being built 1927–32. There was a boom in British production 1933–6, but in attempting to emulate Hollywood's lavish output, costs of film-making escalated dramatically. The international success of Alexander Korda's *The Private Life of Henry VIII* (1933) was exceptional.

The Moyne Committee, reporting in 1936, suggested major reforms, including a Films Commission and a quality test, but the Films Act of 1938, rather than addressing the financial and production problems of the industry, mainly reiterated the quotas of 1927. However, the Films Council was established in 1938. By 1939 the post-war structure of the industry was evolving and the aims and limitations of state intervention were clear. The propaganda value of the medium can readily be appreciated by viewing documentary and feature films of the war years.

After 1945 there were belated efforts to assist the British film industry, mainly through the National Film Finance Corporation, but such success as this brought in the 1950s and early 1960s was consistently overshadowed by American imports. As television became more widely available there was a steady decline in cinema attendances and British film production suffered. After a period of painful rationalization, when even more production and acting talent was lost to the USA, increased government support assisted revival. Despite the overwhelming American challenge many British productions achieved international acclaim and cinema-going recovered dramatically during the 1980s.

The development of film has been promoted by the British Film Institute, founded in 1933, and in Scotland by the Scottish Film Council. The National Film Archive has an extensive international collection of books, periodicals, scripts, stills, posters, and over 200,000 films and television programmes, many of considerable historical interest. The Museum of the Moving Image at the South Bank traces the history of film and television. The Scottish Film Council, based in Glasgow, administers the Scottish Film Archive.

See also CINEMA. ID

financial revolution. This term refers to the extensive changes brought about in the British financial system between the Glorious Revolution of 1688 and the 1720s by the creation of a system whereby a national debt could be accumulated to provide government with spending power beyond the scope of taxation. This became necessary as a result of the extensive military commitments undertaken between 1688 and 1815. War expenditure grew from £49 million in 1688–97 to £1,658 million in 1793–1815 and the national debt soared from £44 million in 1739 to £820 million by 1815. At the same time business, in order to expand, required a secure and reliable means for making payments, as well as a stable system of credit. There were three main elements to this revolution, all of which relied on financial techniques developed in the Netherlands: the use of the bill of exchange for financial transactions, trade in shares of the capital stock of corporations, and perpetual annuities issued by the government and thus free from the risk of default.

In foreign trade, the bill of exchange acted both as a means of payment and as an instrument of credit. Its flexibility was increased by the introduction of serial endorsements in Antwerp in the 16th cent., and was institutionalized in the foundation of the Amsterdam Wisselbank in 1609. This allowed merchant bankers to transfer payments denominated in bank money between them quickly and without great risk. The bill of exchange became the main source of credit for merchants engaged in trade with the American colonies in the 18th cent. By the early years of that century facilities for short-term lending and clearing international payments had been established throughout much of western Europe. In the course of the century London became increasingly integrated with the Amsterdam market and attracted some investment from Holland, principally in government and bank stock.

The bill of exchange was used as follows: a purchaser in country A wishing to pay a debt to his supplier in country B obtained a bill from a merchant banker in the currency of country B which he dispatched to his supplier. This would be accepted by a merchant banker in B and paid in that country's currency, usually at a specific date, often three months after acceptance. Finally the bill was returned to the original drawer to show that payment had been made. A merchant could obtain a bill of exchange as a loan. Legislation at the beginning of the 18th cent. gave the inland bill of exchange the same status as its foreign equivalent, and it acted as a major form of money throughout the century. In 1726 the *Bank of England created a 3 per cent annuity, paying out each year £3 for every £100 purchased, copying the scheme introduced three years earlier by the *South Sea Company.

Another means by which the state raised capital was by the award of monopoly powers to corporations to raise funds on the understanding that they, in turn, would lend to the government. The Bank of England, founded in 1694, sold the £1.2 million of stock in twelve days. Subsequent flotations of the *East India Company and the South Sea Company, together with a further round of subscriptions to the Bank, brought the total capital of the three institutions to £20 million by 1717. Similar monopoly status awarded to the London Assurance Company and Royal Exchange Assurance Company in 1720 was conditional on a government loan of £300,000, which was eventually written off as a bad debt.

The combined effects of these institutional and legal developments had profound economic results. They provided an institutional framework within which economic activity expanded, not only by creating a means by which provincial business could be transacted and linked to the main financial centre in London, but, perhaps more critically, by integrating London with the main European financial centre, Amsterdam, which by the end of the 18th cent. it had superseded. Secondly they provided a conduit through which investment on a hitherto unprecedented scale could be mobilized. Throughout the 18th cent. the principal customer remained the government. The state thus played a major role in stimulating and shaping the development of the financial system. CHL

Finn Barr, St (d. *c.*623). Bishop of Cork. After a reported pilgrimage to Rome, Finn Barr lived as a hermit by Lake Gougane Barra. Attracting numerous followers, he established the monastery of Etargabail, renowned for its school and centre of his cult. More famous was his foundation around which the city of Cork developed and where he is buried. He is believed to have been the first bishop of Cork (*c.*600). According to legend, a vision of Christ prevented Pope Gregory from consecrating Finn Barr in Rome, conferring miraculous, divine consecration in Ireland. Another story alleges that the sun did not set for fifteen days after his death. AM

Finn mac Cumhaill (McCool) is the hero of the 11th-cent. Fionn cycle of Irish tales, father of Oisin, and leader of the élite war-band, the Fianna. He has supernatural powers of prophecy and fighting. His great deeds include saving *Tara from the goblin Aillen, who burns down the stronghold each year on the Feast of Samhain; and successfully challenging Nuadu, god of the Tuatha Dé Danann, for lordship of the sídh of Almu. Finn becomes an outcast after arranging the death of Diarmaid in his jealousy for the love of Gráinne. He dies attempting to leap the Boyne after breaking his 'geis' (bond of honour) by drinking from a horn. SMD

first fruits. A tax, usually of the first year's income, paid to a feudal or ecclesiastical superior. Before the Reformation, first fruits for all clerical benefices went to the pope, together with an annual payment of one-tenth of the income. The Act of *Annates (1532) declared this unlawful, payments were diverted to the crown, and a treasurer and court established to collect them. Mary did not restore the payments to the papacy. In 1649, after the abolition of the monarchy, the *Long Parliament used the first fruits to support preachers and schoolmasters, but at the Restoration it became once more part of royal revenue. Charles II frequently used it for non-ecclesiastical purposes, such as the support of his bastards. In 1704 the revenue was diverted to found *Queen Anne's Bounty, to augment the incomes of poor livings. Since the initial payment, and the accumulation of tenths during vacancies, could be a substantial burden, legislation exempted livings of less than £50 p.a. value. In 1838 the collection was removed from the First Fruits and Tenths Offices and handed over to the Bounty Office. Payment ceased altogether from 1926. JAC

First World War. In August 1914 Britain ostensibly went to war against Germany because of the latter's unprovoked invasion of Belgium. In reality Britain fought the First World War to prevent Germany dominating Europe and, with the help of her Austrian and Turkish allies, threatening the British empire in Asia and Africa. Though from the outset British policy-makers recognized that co-operation with their Russian and French allies would be essential if they were to win the war, they were determined to give that co-operation strictly on their own terms, rendering only enough assistance to their allies to prevent them from collapsing. The men who made British policy during the war had reached maturity and formed their vision of the world in the late 1870s and early 1880s. They had learned to see Russia and France as Britain's most bitter imperial competitors and they did not forget that fact even after the German threat emerged in the decade before 1914. Their misgivings concerning their allies' ambitions played a major role in determining British war aims. They wanted a peace settlement which would reduce Germany's power and also ensure that neither Russia nor France could tilt the European balance against Britain or menace Britain's imperial possessions.

In 1914 the *Asquith government believed that the war would reach its climax in 1917. Britain could achieve her objectives at least cost by allowing her allies to carry the weight of the continental land war with only token British assistance. Meanwhile the Royal Navy would undermine the German economy by blockade and Britain would offer financial help to her allies. *Kitchener formed the New Armies in the belief that by the end of 1916 the armies of the other belligerents would be exhausted. His troops would be unbloodied and in 1917 Britain could intervene decisively in land war, crush Germany and her allies, Turkey, Austria-Hungary, and (after September 1915) Bulgaria, and impose Britain's peace terms on everyone.

This policy collapsed because France and Russia were not willing to fight for three years without British military support. By late 1915 the government had reluctantly accepted that if they failed to give their allies large-scale support on the continent, France and Russia might prefer to make a negotiated peace. But it was equally obvious that the cost of increasing Britain's commitment to the continental land war might be self-defeating. Some argued that if the New Armies were committed to a major allied offensive in France in 1916, losses could only be made good by conscription. But if more men were taken away from the civilian economy, Britain would be bankrupt before the enemy sued for peace. The British offensive on the *Somme in 1916 was an enormous gamble. The government was wagering that the Entente could win the war before Britain went bankrupt.

The attack failed, for although both the British and German armies suffered enormously, the Germans had no intention of asking for peace terms. Instead they tried to starve Britain into submission by launching a campaign of unrestricted U-boat warfare against British shipping. This was the strategic situation which *Lloyd George inherited when he became prime minister in December 1916. His aims were the same as Asquith's, but he was more aware than Asquith that he would have to work hard to sustain popular support for the war, for war-weariness was now rife in Britain. The armed forces were a serious drain on the economy, and nothing was more likely to undermine support for the war than shortages of food, fuel, and housing, especially if such shortages gave rise to the corrosive belief that 'profiteers' were making unfair gains from the war while the rest of the population suffered. But morale depended upon more than adequate supplies of food and fuel. Lloyd George knew that the people had to be convinced that their sacrifices were reaping tangible victories, and if they could not be won on the western front, they had to be gained elsewhere. One reason why he supported offensives at Salonika in Greece, in Palestine, and in northern Italy was his belief that a victory gained on one of those fronts would provide a much-needed stimulus to British morale.

The new government also knew that victory could only be achieved in co-operation with its allies. But in the spring of 1917 the pillars upon which British strategy had rested since the start of the war began to crumble. In March 1917 the British greeted the first Russian Revolution with cautious enthusiasm, hoping that Russia would follow the same path as France in 1794; from the ruins of the tsarist regime would emerge a new military colossus. But news of the crumbling discipline of the Russian army meant that their hopes soon gave way to the fear that Russia would desert the alliance, and that the Germans would move large numbers of troops to the western front and break the allied economic blockade by gaining access to Russian food and fuel. In the mean time a large part of the French army mutinied, and although most French soldiers were ready to defend their trenches, they would not participate in further futile offensives. At sea German U-boats were sinking so many merchant ships that Britain was close to starvation. The only cause for optimism in the Entente camp was that in April 1917 the USA declared war on Germany. But any hope that the Americans would soon be able to throw their weight into the land war in Europe was quickly dashed. The USA had a tiny regular army and would not be able to deploy an appreciable force in France before 1918 or even 1919.

The debate about the future of British strategy in the summer of 1917 therefore concerned one question: what should be the new timetable for administering the knockout blow against Germany which Lloyd George had promised the British people? One option was to follow the French example. After the mutinies they had decided to remain on the defensive in the west for the remainder of 1917, and wait for 1918 and the Americans before trying to drive the Germans back across the Rhine. In the meantime the British might, as Lloyd George urged, divert troops to northern Italy. The Italians had entered the war on Britain's side in May 1915. If they could defeat the Austrians, and persuade them to make peace, they would destroy Germany's ambition of establishing an empire stretching from Hamburg, through Austria-Hungary, Bulgaria, and Turkey, to Baghdad. The alternative was to permit the commander-in-chief, Sir Douglas *Haig, to have his way and mount an offensive in Flanders. If Haig drove the Germans from the Belgian coast he would remove the threat of invasion, inflict a major defeat upon the German army, and take German pressure off France and Russia. Haig believed that he could force the Germans to sue for peace by Christmas 1917. The politicians doubted, but allowed him to try. They expected little military help from the French, but they were afraid that if the British did nothing, France would go the way of the Russians and collapse.

The third battle of Ypres in July 1917 was a failure. Haig then launched a second offensive, using massed tanks, at Cambrai, but that also failed. In October Italy suffered a major defeat at Caporetto and in November the Bolsheviks seized power in Russia and soon signed an armistice. The arrival of the American army was even slower than the British had anticipated. Lloyd George still believed that the war could be won only after the German army had been defeated on the western front but he also believed that, if the British mounted another large-scale offensive in France in 1918, their army would be exhausted, America would dominate the Entente in 1919, and America, not Britain, would dictate the peace treaty. He therefore decided that Britain must preserve her army and economic staying-power in 1918. The knock-out blow against Germany would be delayed until 1919, when the arrival of the Americans would give the Entente a crushing superiority. Only that would ensure that Britain would have enough soldiers left alive at the end of the war to have a major influence over the peace terms.

In January 1918, and despite the opposition of his own generals, Lloyd George persuaded Britain's partners to agree to his new timetable for victory in 1919. In 1918 each partner would increase production of artillery, aircraft, and tanks in order to multiply the fire-power of her dwindling military manpower, and Britain would safeguard her own imperial interests in Egypt and India by defeating the Turks in Palestine. The British were not fighting only to re-establish the balance of power in western Europe, for Turkey's entry into the war on the side of Germany in November 1914 had made the First World War an Asiatic as well as a European war. In 1915–16 the British had mounted expeditions against *Mesopotamia, Palestine, and at the *Dardanelles to protect their Asiatic possessions. The war was a contest for the division of world power. The Germans wanted to replace Britain as a world power by creating a middle European empire. It was a war in which the British assessed victory or defeat by their success or failure in frustrating Germany's ambitions and by their ability to maintain their own security in western Europe and in India and the Middle East.

Lloyd George's timetable for victory in 1919 collapsed because in the spring of 1918 the Germans made their own final attempt to win the war before they became exhausted. Between March and July 1918 the survival of the Entente alliance was in doubt. At one moment the Germans threatened to divide the British army from its French ally. But by June the last German offensive had been stopped, and in July the Entente's armies began a counter-offensive, forcing the Germans back. The way in which the war ended surprised Britain and her allies. As late as August they were still preparing plans to continue fighting into 1919 and even 1920. As late as mid-October Haig did not think that the German army was so badly beaten that the German government would accept the armistice terms which the Entente wanted. When the armistice negotiations began in October the British had to consider several conflicting factors. Should they continue fighting into 1919, to invade Germany and inflict a Carthaginian peace upon the German people? Would such a settlement threaten the future peace of Europe by leaving the French too powerful and by making the Germans vengeful? Were the British people willing to fight for another year? Would the economic and political cost of doing so leave western Europe devastated and dominated by the USA? How could the allies devise armistice terms which would not be so harsh that the Germans would reject them but which would prevent Germany from gaining a breathing space after which it could start fighting again? It was only after weighing these factors they opted for an early peace and the guns fell silent on 11 November 1918, a year earlier than most British policy-makers had anticipated.

DF

Bourne, J. M., *Britain and the Great War, 1914–1918* (1989); Turner, J. (ed.), *Britain and the First World War* (1988); Wilson, T., *The Myriad Faces of War: Britain and the Great War 1914–1918* (Oxford, 1986).

Fishbourne was an exceptionally early, large, and luxurious Roman villa or 'palace'. One mile west of *Chichester, the site at the head of Chichester harbour was first occupied by a supply base of the invasion period. In the Neronian period the first stone civil buildings were constructed. The Flavian 'palace' covered 10 acres with dependencies. It consisted of four carefully planned ranges enclosing a central area with a formal Roman garden. The entrance-hall was in the centre of the east range and box-edged walkways led to the formal reception room in the centre of the raised west range. The north range and the northern part of the east range (now open to the public) were constructed round a series of internal courtyards, perhaps suites for guests or parts of the family. The south range, with a prospect over the sea, was probably the principal residence, though now inaccessible to archaeology. The Mediterranean-style complex and decoration (black-and-white mosaics, stucco-work) were unique in late 1st-cent. Britain. The complex declined through the 2nd and 3rd cents., though still a comfortable villa. It was destroyed by fire in the late 3rd cent. ASEC

Fisher, Geoffrey (1887–1972). Archbishop of Canterbury. Born in Leicestershire of a clerical family and educated at Exeter College, Oxford, Fisher taught at Marlborough. After succeeding William *Temple as headmaster of Repton (1914–32), he was successively bishop of Chester (1932), bishop of London (1939), and archbishop after Temple's sudden death (1945). His considerable administrative skills were evident in London especially during the blitz and at Canterbury where he accomplished the most substantial canon law reform since *Bancroft. As archbishop, he was the first to travel world-wide in the Anglican Communion and the first since the Reformation to visit the pope. Headmasterly in manner, both as bishop and archbishop, he took a central position between Anglo-catholics and evangelicals, thus assuaging earlier antagonisms. On retirement to Trent village in Dorset (1961) he was active as parish curate. WMM

Fisher, John (1469–1535). Bishop. Fisher was educated at Cambridge, became fellow of Michaelhouse, and took priestly orders in 1491. Through the patronage of Lady Margaret *Beaufort, whom he served as confessor, he was made reader in divinity in 1502, and two years later bishop of Rochester. At Cambridge he promoted Renaissance humanist studies, especially at Christ's and St John's Colleges; he recruited teachers of Greek (including Erasmus between 1510 and 1514) and Hebrew. His Renaissance outlook was combined with a profound respect for the church's traditions. He wrote copiously against Martin Luther, his works including the *Assertionis Lutheranae confutatio* (1522/3), the *Defensio regiae assertionis* (1523), and the *Sacri sacerdotii defensio* (1525). When Henry VIII sought to repudiate his first wife, *Catherine of Aragon, Fisher was one of the king's most public and prolific opponents. He led resistance to the attacks on the status of the clergy in the Reformation Parliament and in convocation, and was imprisoned in 1533. In 1534 he refused the oath of supremacy. In 1535, just after his elevation to the cardinalate by Paul III, he was put on trial for treasonably denying the king's supremacy over the church, and was executed on 22 June 1535. He was canonized in 1935. EC

Fisher, Sir John, 1st Baron Fisher (1841–1920). Admiral. 'Jackie' Fisher was the main architect of the fleet with which Britain went to war in 1914. Between 1905 and 1910, when he served as 1st sea lord, he introduced two new classes of warship, the all-big-gun, turbine-propelled Dreadnought class of battleship and the more lightly armoured invincible class of battle-cruiser. They made all existing capital ships obsolete and gained for Britain a brief respite in the Anglo-German naval race. But when the Germans began to launch their own dreadnoughts in 1909, Fisher was determined to out-build them. He succeeded but only at the cost of further souring Anglo-German relations. Recalled to serve as 1st sea lord in October 1914, he resigned amidst great acrimony in May 1915 when he lost patience with his political chief, Winston *Churchill, over the navy's growing commitment to the *Dardanelles. DF

Fishguard invasion, 1797. In one of the more bizarre episodes of the Revolutionary War, the French Directory collected 1,200 men, mainly from gaols, and landed them from three frigates and a lugger near Fishguard on 23 February 1797. They surrendered two days later to the local militia under Lord Cawdor, their commander, an American named Tate, explaining that he thought it 'unnecessary to attempt any military operations as they would tend only to bloodshed'. According to local legend, the invaders mistook the red coats of the Welsh women for cavalry. Though the military threat was negligible, the panic in London was enough to cause a run on the Bank and to drive Britain off the gold standard. JAC

fishing. See ANGLING.

fishing industry. Historically, seafood was an important part of people's diet and fishing was a long-established activity round Britain's coasts, complementing subsistence farming or crofting, and providing livelihoods to sea-going communities. Britain was well favoured for the development of a large-scale fishing trade, located in one of the most prolific sectors of the European continental shelf, with seas of moderate depth readily fished for herring, haddock, pilchard, and cod by small vessels. It was also fortunate that the annual movement of herring round the coast worked greatly to the advantage of fisherfolk, giving opportunities for catches everywhere at some time of the year.

By the 17th cent. fish had become a growing item of trade, especially for the Scots and Irish, but the wealth of the offshore grounds also benefited the Dutch, who were active mainly in the North Sea. Indeed the competition of the Dutch caused much alarm and encouraged government policy to promote native fisheries still further, notably in Scotland under the Board of Trustees for Fisheries and Manufactures, established in 1727. Although bounties (or grants) were offered on vessels fitted out for herring fishing, other legislation on fishing practices and the high duty on salt needed for curing handicapped expansion. The establishment of the British Fisheries Society in 1786 coincided with a new attitude. Bounties were promised on herring catches and on fish exports and the Salt Laws were relaxed soon after in favour of the fisherman.

During the 19th cent. the fishing industry experienced dramatic expansion and by the 1850s the herring fishery on the east coast was the largest in Europe. The fishing population and communities grew accordingly, with Lowestoft, Hull, and Aberdeen the main fishing ports. As with agricultural produce the growth of the market for fresh fish coincided with the development of the railways and of refrigeration and these encouraged the introduction of steam trawling, initially in inshore waters, after 1880. Deep-sea fishing had meantime been pioneered by whalers working out of British ports, including Hull and Dundee.

By 1914 the industry was large scale, capital intensive, and, despite an important domestic market, much dependent on foreign exports. It experienced the same painful adjustment to changing circumstances as other industries during the depression. Falling prices and deteriorating equipment were the main problems, so that by 1939 the industry had shrunk from its peak at the turn of the century. Herring fishing never regained its previous significance, even when revitalization ultimately came after 1945, and white fishing became the mainstay of the industry.

As stocks were progressively exhausted through overfishing, access to fishing grounds became a major source of conflict between Britain and other nations, especially with Iceland to the north and Spain to the south. Relations between Britain and Iceland reached crisis point during a series of 'cod wars' in the 1960s and the fishing of southern waters by Spain was a continuing grievance of the Cornish industry. The European Community and its successor, the European Union, as well as national governments, attempted to regulate catches through quota systems and the Common Fisheries Policy, but not without sustained resistance from the fishing industry. Whaling was abandoned on environmental and conservation grounds. Rising prices made fish-farming in inshore waters more viable and since the 1970s this has became an increasingly important source of supply and export earnings, especially at the luxury end of the market. ID

Fitzgerald, Lord Edward (1763–98). Irish patriot. Fitzgerald was born into one of the wealthiest and most esteemed families of the Irish aristocracy: his father was James, 1st duke of Leinster. He was MP for Athy in the Irish House of Commons (1783), transferring in 1790 to Co. Kildare. An enthusiastic Francophile and more radical than most of his parliamentary contemporaries, he came to regard Parliament as unreformable, and turned instead to the *United Irish Society: after several years of close communication with its leaders, he was inducted into the society in 1796. He narrowly escaped capture when troops raided the meeting-place of the United Irish executive in March 1798. Although this venture enhanced his reputation within the movement and left him as its military leader, he proved to be highly indecisive. He was eventually arrested and mortally wounded on 19 May: his death on 4 June simultaneously freed Dublin castle from its most charismatic opponent, and the United Irish Society from the shackles of caution. AJ

Fitzgerald, Gerald, 8th earl of Kildare [I] (*c.*1457–1513). Fitzgerald's father, the 7th earl, was a prominent Yorkist and deputy to the lord-lieutenant of Ireland on several occasions. Fitzgerald succeeded to the title in 1477 when he was about 20. He was continued as deputy by Edward IV, Richard III, and Henry VII, and since the lord-lieutenant was often a nominal appointment, was effectively ruler of Ireland. In 1487 he and his brother Thomas supported Lambert *Simnel: the earl is said to have crowned him in Dublin and Thomas Fitzgerald was killed fighting for him at *Stoke. Nevertheless, Fitzgerald gained a pardon. In 1494, suspected of conspiracy with *Warbeck, he was attainted, but once more pardoned and reappointed deputy in 1496. In 1505 he was given the Garter, and Henry VIII continued him in his post. Fitzgerald was killed in a skirmish at Lemyvanna, King's County. A member of one of the great Norman/Irish families, much of his time was devoted to subduing the native Irish and the indulgence shown him by Henry VII suggests the strength of the Kildare position in the Pale. JAC

Fitzgerald, Gerald, 9th earl of Kildare [I] (1487–1534). Fitzgerald's father built up a powerful position in Ireland, and served as deputy for many years, dying in 1513. Fitzgerald had been a hostage in England and was well known to Henry VIII, four years his junior. He was appointed to his father's place as deputy and held the office until 1520. He accompanied Henry to the *Field of Cloth of Gold. Reinstated as deputy in 1524 at the expense of his great rival Ormond, he was recalled in 1526 and sent to the Tower. He returned once more to Ireland in 1530 and was reappointed deputy in 1532. When he was recalled again in 1534 and imprisoned in the Tower, his son Thomas led a rising. Fitzgerald, who had been wounded in a skirmish the previous year, died in September 1534. He does not seem to have had the skill his father showed in navigating the turbulent currents of Irish politics and the precariousness of his position suggested that the English crown was growing in strength. JAC

Fitzgerald, Gerald, 14th earl of Desmond [I] (*c.*1533–83). Fitzgerald succeeded his father in the earldom in 1558, in his mid-twenties. In 1565 he was wounded in private warfare with *Ormond and sent to the Tower 1567–70. From 1574 he was in conspiracy against Elizabeth and from 1579 in open rebellion under papal encouragement. He was killed in 1583 and his head stuck on London bridge. 'Dim-witted, barely literate, more a captain than a courtier,' is a modern assessment. JAC

Fitzgerald, James Fitzmaurice (d. 1579). Fitzgerald was nephew of James, 13th earl of Desmond [I], and cousin of Gerald, the 14th earl. In 1569 he claimed the Desmond earldom for himself and launched a catholic crusade. Forced to submit in 1573, he went to the continent, hoping that the king of France or of Spain would claim the throne of Ireland. Pope Gregory XIII encouraged him in an expedition to Ireland and he landed at Dingle in 1579, and began fortifying Smerwick. But he was killed in an affray and the garrison at Smerwick was butchered by Lord *Grey. JAC

Fitzgerald, James, 15th earl of Desmond [I] (*c.*1570–1601). Fitzgerald was about 13 when his father, the 14th earl, was killed in open rebellion. The boy was put into the Tower of London, where he seems to have been in indifferent health. Left there until 1600, he was brought out during the Tyrone rebellion, created earl, and sent to Ireland in the hope that he could bring his compatriots back to submission. But the Irish repudiated him as a protestant and a puppet, and he returned to England, dying shortly afterwards. His period of semi-freedom in adult life lasted just over a year. JAC

Fitzgerald, Thomas, 10th earl of Kildare [I] (1513–37). In 1534 Fitzgerald's father, the 9th earl, was recalled as lord deputy to England and imprisoned in the Tower in disgrace. Fitzgerald, then Lord Offaly, had been appointed deputy by his father. He began with a show of defiance to Henry VIII which developed into open revolt, declaring that the king was a heretic and that all Englishmen were to leave Ireland at once. In the course of the rising the archbishop of Dublin was murdered, probably with Fitzgerald's participation.

Had the revolt received foreign assistance, it could have been formidable. In September 1534 his father died and Fitzgerald succeeded to the earldom. William Skeffington's relief army arrived in October, took Fitzgerald's stronghold at Maynooth, killed the garrison, and shattered the revolt. Fitzgerald surrendered, on promise of life, was sent to London, and there executed in 1537 with five of his uncles. The breach of surrender terms caused anger in Ireland, but the execution of a government official guilty of rebellion and atrocity hardly surprised many Tudor Englishmen. JAC

FitzGibbon, John, 1st earl of Clare [I] (1748–1802). FitzGibbon was the son of a lawyer and Irish MP from Co. Limerick, attended Trinity College, Dublin, and Christ Church, Oxford, and represented Trinity College Dublin 1778–83 and Killmallock 1783–9 in the Irish Parliament. In 1783–9 he was Irish attorney-general and from 1789 until his death he was lord chancellor [I]. Created Baron FitzGibbon [I] in 1789, he was advanced to a viscountcy in 1793 and made earl of Clare [I] in 1795. In 1799, just before the Act of *Union, he was given a British barony. He was one of the leading advocates of the Union, arguing that Ireland would then play her full part in a larger political context. FitzGibbon was a ready speaker and tough politician, a rival to *Grattan, and a most bitter opponent of the catholics. In 1795 he helped to defeat *Fitzwilliam's proposed concessions. After the *Irish rising of 1798 he defended repression in the House of Lords: 'happy would he be if he could go to his bedchamber at home without entering an armoury and could close his eyes without apprehensions of having his throat cut before morning.' JAC

Fitzhamon, Robert (d. 1107). Fitzhamon was one of the leading Norman colonizers of south Wales. He seems to have moved from his holdings in Gloucester to carve out a marcher lordship in Glamorgan, beginning the building of Cardiff castle in 1080. He was generous in his benefactions to Tewkesbury and Gloucester abbeys at the expense of his conquered territories. Fitzhamon was with Rufus in the New Forest when he was killed and gave strong support to Henry I in his struggle for the succession. Fighting in Normandy on his behalf against *Robert of Gloucester, he was captured in 1105 but rescued by the king. At the siege of Falaise he was wounded and on his death in 1107 was buried at Tewkesbury. His daughter married an illegitimate son of Henry I, who created him Robert, earl of Gloucester. JAC

FitzNigel, Richard (d. 1198). Bishop of London (1189–98) and treasurer of England (*c.*1158–98). A member of the outstanding family who developed the sophisticated 12th-cent. English administrative system, he was son of Nigel, bishop of Ely, treasurer, and nephew of Henry II's justiciar, *Roger of Salisbury. He was also successively archdeacon of Ely and dean of Lincoln (*c.*1184), mediated in the furious struggle between *Longchamp and John, and was custodian for Richard's ransom. He is chiefly remembered for writing the **Dialogus de Scaccario* (*Dialogue of the Exchequer*), 'a unique and precious document' on the English governmental system. Written especially for administrative apprentices, it was the first manual anywhere in Europe to explain the mysteries of bureaucratic practice and auditing. WMM

Fitzosbern, William, earl of Hereford (d. 1071). Fitzosbern, steward at the court of Normandy, was one of William the Conqueror's most trusted advisers and fought at his side at Hastings. In reward he was given great estates in the west country, the rank of earl, and palatine powers. Much of his energy went into fighting the Welsh and establishing the Norman position in Glamorgan. He began the building of a number of castles, notably Chepstow, Monmouth, Berkeley, Hereford, and Wigmore. As viceroy in William's absence in 1067 he had to subdue a rising by Edric the Wild in Herefordshire. In 1070 Fitzosbern was sent to Normandy but he was killed in battle the following year, fighting on behalf of the countess of Flanders, whom he had just married. JAC

FitzRoy, Henry, duke of Richmond (1519–36). FitzRoy was Henry VIII's illegitimate son by Elizabeth Blount, a lady-in-waiting to *Catherine of Aragon. Since Henry had no surviving male heir until 1537, and his marriage to Catherine was disputed, the future of FitzRoy produced much comment. In 1525 he was given the Garter and created duke of Richmond, a title held by Henry's father. His appointments as lord high admiral (1525) and lord-lieutenant of Ireland (1529), though nominal, were taken as favours to come. In 1533 he was married to a daughter of the duke of *Norfolk. The second Act of *Succession in 1536 bastardized both Mary and Elizabeth and gave Henry the power, should *Jane Seymour not have children, to name his successor. It was presumed that he would use this on behalf of FitzRoy. Parliament dissolved on 18 July and five days later the young prince died aged 17, of consumption. 'Not a bad thing for the interests of the Princess [Mary]', wrote the imperial ambassador laconically. JAC

Fitzwilliam, William Wentworth, 2nd Earl (1748–1833). Fitzwilliam inherited the wealth and vast estates of his uncle Lord *Rockingham in 1782 and became head of the Whig political interest in Yorkshire. He regularly returned five members to Parliament for his pocket boroughs and in 1807 spent £100,000 to win his son's election for Yorkshire. He was a lifelong friend of *Fox and in 1782 he also succeeded Rockingham as patron of Edmund *Burke. He reluctantly broke with Fox in 1794 and joined *Pitt's cabinet, being sent to Ireland in January 1795 as lord-lieutenant. Under Burke's influence he attempted to establish Whig rule over Ireland and to persuade the cabinet to catholic emancipation, but he was dismissed in March. He rejoined Fox and *Grenville after 1802 and was lord president of the council under Grenville in 1806. He had become lord-lieutenant of the West Riding in 1798 and was efficient and liberal-minded, but he was dismissed from this post in 1819 for chairing a protest meeting against the *'Peterloo massacre'. A humane and genial character and a lifelong defender of aristocracy, he was widely popular and respected. EAS

Five Knights' case, 1627. After the 1626 Parliament had been dissolved without granting subsidies, Charles I raised money by various means, including *forced loans. In 1627

five knights, imprisoned for refusal to contribute, appealed for *habeas corpus. Lord Chief Justice Hyde denied bail: 'if no cause of the commitment be expressed, it is to be presumed to be for matters of state, which we cannot take notice of.' As a means of alienating the propertied classes, Charles's policy was highly successful. JAC

five members, 1642. On 4 January 1642 Charles I, exasperated at the opposition of the House of Commons, which had passed the *Grand Remonstrance, attempted in person to arrest five of its leaders—John *Pym, John *Hampden, Denzil *Holles, Arthur *Haselrig, and William Strode. Forewarned, they made their escape, leaving the king to mutter, 'I see that my birds have flown.' Within a week he had left London, never to return as a free man. JAC

Five Mile Act, 1665. 17 Car. II c. 2 was part of the *'Clarendon code', which aimed at restoring Anglican supremacy. Clergymen and schoolmasters were forbidden to live within 5 miles of any city or parliamentary borough unless they took an oath not to endeavour to alter the government in church and state. Such a loosely framed statute was almost impossible to implement and few prosecutions were undertaken. JAC

fives. The game of fives, in a rough form, certainly dates back to Tudor times, though the derivation of the name is unclear. The essential ingredients are a hard ball, gloves to protect the hands, which are used instead of rackets, and a wall or court. Its modern form derives from versions played at Eton, Rugby, and Winchester, which spread to other schools in the later 19th cent. and then to universities. The first attempt to standardize the rules was in 1877. JAC

Flambard, Ranulf. See RANULF FLAMBARD.

Flamsteed, John (1646–1719). Flamsteed was the first astronomer-royal. He was born near Derby and educated there. Handicapped by ill-health, he began astronomical observations and in 1675 was placed on a panel to investigate claims to ascertain longitude at sea. The same year he took holy orders and was appointed by Charles II to supervise the new royal observatory at Greenwich. In 1677 he was elected to the Royal Society. He was in close touch with the scientists of the age, including *Halley and *Newton, but his health made him irritable and suspicious. In 1707, after many difficulties, Flamsteed's first catalogue of observations was published, but the rest had to wait until after his death. JAC

Flaxman, John (1755–1826). English sculptor, designer, and book illustrator. He studied at the Royal Academy Schools, before working as a designer for Josiah *Wedgwood. In 1787 Flaxman travelled to Italy to study. During the seven years he spent there, he drew illustrations for the *Iliad*, the *Odyssey*, and works of Dante and Aeschylus, which earned him an international reputation. On his return to England he was immediately in demand as a sculptor of monuments and figures; among the best known are those to Lord *Mansfield in Westminster abbey and Lord *Nelson in St Paul's, although his work can be found in many churches, cathedrals, stately homes, and galleries throughout Britain. Appointed RA in 1800, he became the first professor of sculpture in 1812. He continued to draw book illustrations, some of which were engraved by his friend William *Blake, and designs for silverware. Much of his work is held at University College, London. JC

Fleet prison (London) was in use from the time of the Norman Conquest until the reign of Queen Victoria. It held those who owed money to the crown, with prisoners being committed by king's council and the Court of Chancery. A single family, the Levelands, retained control of the prison for 400 years. It closed in 1842. RAS

Fleet Street (London) was for centuries the home of the newspaper industry and the name is still used to describe the national press. It ran from the Fleet river, a noisome ditch, to the Strand—strategically between the city and the court. From Tudor times it was the haunt of booksellers, writers, and printers. The first daily newspaper, the *Daily Courant*, was established there in 1702, and *The Times*, in Printing House Square to the east, followed in 1785, under the name *Daily Universal Register*. In the 1980s there was a wholesale exodus of newspapers to less-congested sites elsewhere. JAC

Fleming, Sir Alexander (1881–1955). Discoverer of penicillin. A farmer's son from Ayrshire, Fleming moved to London at 13 to live with his doctor brother, and then went to St Mary's hospital for training in medicine. He spent his career there. He was assistant to Sir Almroth Wright, working on bacteria, seeking a magic bullet which would be harmless to our cells but fatal to bacteria. In 1928 he noticed that a culture of staphylococcus in his untidy laboratory was being attacked by a mould, which he isolated and grew. He had high hopes of it, but it attracted little attention, and it was not until the Second World War with the work in Oxford of H. W. Florey and E. B. Chain that penicillin was purified to be clinically effective. The three shared a Nobel Prize in 1945. DK

Fletcher, Andrew (1655–1716). Politician. Fletcher of Saltoun was taught by Gilbert *Burnet, minister of his parish, who later described him as 'a most violent republican and extremely passionate'. He represented East Lothian at the convention of estates and in the Scottish Parliament and was in strong opposition to *Lauderdale and James, duke of York (later James II). From 1682 he was in exile in Holland, a supporter of *Monmouth. He accompanied Monmouth in 1685 but left the expedition after shooting one of his own side in a brawl. After the Glorious Revolution he returned to Scotland but was soon in opposition to William III, arguing for limitations on the crown. Returned to Parliament again in 1703, he became a prominent opposition speaker, advocating a Scottish national militia and annual meetings of the Scottish Parliament. He was violently opposed to the Act of *Union, proposing a separation of the crowns instead. An effective speaker and vigorous pamphleteer, Fletcher was hot-headed and uncompromising. *Macaulay wrote that he was 'distinguished by courage, disinterestedness and public spirit, but of an irritable and impracticable temper'. JAC

Flight of the Earls, 1607. *Tyrone and Rory *O'Donnell, who had been in open rebellion against Elizabeth, submitted in 1602. O'Donnell was created 1st earl of Tyrconnel. But increasingly dissatisfied with their position, they fled on 4 September 1607 from Rathmullan on Lough Swilly with some 90 family and retainers and took refuge at Rome. Neither saw Ireland again. Tyrconnel died in 1608, Tyrone in 1616. The result was to deprive the native Irish of a focus for resistance, and colonization from England and Scotland proceeded rapidly until the great rising of 1641. Over the next three centuries, tens of thousands of Irish left their native land. JAC

Flinders, Matthew (1774–1814). Flinders accurately delineated the coasts of Australia and began the practice of using that name for it. After joining the Royal Navy in 1789, Flinders served with *Bligh before surveying the New South Wales coast in detail in 1795. In 1798–9 he and Bass circumnavigated Tasmania, proving its separation from the mainland and impressing naval and scientific opinion in Britain with his qualities as an explorer. A new scientific expedition led by him 1801–3 mapped the coasts of nearly all Australia with great accuracy, completing the basic exploration of the Pacific Ocean section of the world. Flinders became a prisoner of war of the French on his way home but was released from Mauritius in 1809. RB

Flintshire. County of north-east Wales lying along the estuary of the river Dee. The shire was created at the statute of *Rhuddlan in 1284 and was coincident with the Welsh cantref (hundred) of Tregeingl, the most easterly of the four cantrefs of Perfeddwlad. It was subject to Saxon invasion and was largely to the east of Offa's Dike, the 8th-cent. boundary between Welsh and Saxon. Under the Normans, it was soon overrun by the neighbouring earl of Chester, but after the wars of Edward I became crown land. Maelor Saesneg, or English Maelor, to the south was also in crown hands and was, although detached geographically, made part of the shire. The county, with the detached part, remained as such at the Act of *Union in 1536. It was not modified until 1974 when Flintshire became part of *Clwyd and was divided into three districts, Rhuddlan, Delyn, and Alyn and Deeside. The detached part was merged into Wrexham Maelor. In 1996 the county was reconstituted from the three districts.

Flintshire consists of a low coastal strip along the Dee estuary rising to the Halkyn Mountain to the west. The Alyn valley separates it from the Clwydian Range which forms the western border, although the mouth of the river Clwyd is in Flintshire. As in medieval times Flintshire straddles the gateway to north Wales, especially the Dee crossing, the basis of its economic significance. The economy is dominated by tourism, extensively developed on the north coast, and industry. The county includes the central and northern sections of the North Wales Coalfield; the last mine, at Point of Ayr, closed in 1996. Iron and steel production has also ceased, although a range of engineering and electronic industry has succeeded.

The population of the three districts which correspond with Flintshire was 191,706 in 1991. In such a border county, Welsh-speaking proportions are low, ranging from 9.6 per cent in Alyn and Deeside, to 17.8 in Delyn, and 16.2 per cent in Rhuddlan. HC

Flodden, battle of, 1513. While the young king Henry VIII was pursuing military glory against the French, his brother-in-law James IV of Scotland, an ally of France, declared war. He assembled one of the largest armies ever seen in Scotland, crossed the Tweed at Coldstream, and occupied the castles of Norham, Etal, Wark, and Ford. Lord Surrey (*Norfolk), commanding the English forces, marched north from Newcastle to Wooler. His invitation, quaintly anachronistic, to do battle on 9 September was rejected by James, who replied that he would please himself. Nevertheless the armies met on the 9th, on Branxton Hill, near Flodden, having twisted round, the English facing south, the Scots north. Surrey's men fought with the Tweed at their backs. There was little tactical manœuvring, but four hours of desperate hand-to-hand combat, the fortunes fluctuating. The turning-point was when James himself, in the thick of the battle, was cut down. The Scots sustained the heaviest defeat of their history, the flower of their nobility dying with the king. James's body was brought south and for many years the coffin was deposited at Sheen in Surrey in the Carthusian house. The battlefield of Flodden is heavy open land, sombre and desolate. JAC

Foliot, Gilbert (*c.*1108–87). A learned, austere, and ambitious prelate who became *Becket's most outspoken opponent among English churchmen. He protested when Becket was made archbishop of Canterbury at the king's command and then opposed the archbishop at every turn. When Becket quarrelled with the king he became one of the king's principal advisers in church matters. He acted as administrator of the Canterbury estates while Becket was in exile and, not surprisingly, was several times excommunicated by the archbishop. Despite his own highly successful career—prior of Cluny, abbot of Gloucester (1139–48), bishop of Hereford (1148–63), and finally bishop of London (1163–87)—Becket's friends believed that Gilbert had wanted Canterbury for himself. Although many of his letters survive, including some fiercely attacking the archbishop, his character and motives remain enigmatic. JG

folklore. Despite the presence of what might be described as folklorists *avant le mot*, such as William *Camden (1551–1623) and John *Aubrey (1626–97), folklore as a discipline really became established early in the 19th cent. Its immediate origins are in German scholarship, with the works of the brothers Grimm being of central importance, the coining of the English term 'folklore' being attributed to W. J. Thoms (1803–85) in 1846. By the later 19th cent. folklore was an established, and in many ways scholarly, field of study. Its practitioners included enthusiastic amateurs, many of them country parsons and the daughters of the gentry, and such major figures as Andrew Lang (1844–1912), and Cecil Sharp (1850–1924), whose researches into folksong and folk-dance were of lasting significance. The coming of age of folklore in England was symbolized by the founding of the Folk-Lore Society in 1878.

At its widest, folklore was an all embracing discipline, attempting to comprehend the totality of 'traditional' culture. Defining what traditional culture is in this context can be contentious, but, generally, folklorists have concentrated on forms of culture transmitted orally or by imitation. So the folklorist will study such elements of the oral culture as songs, stories, proverbs, and riddles, the broader social phenomena of games, ceremonies, and rituals, and also the products of material culture, including buildings and all sorts of artefacts. The early work was on peasant culture, and folklore still seems to be a discipline which flourishes best when the rural world is being studied: Sharp's work, indeed, is to some extent distorted by an idealization of the English 'peasant'. Work on the folklore of industrial workers and their communities, notably of miners, does, however, indicate some of the broader possibilities of folklore studies.

In its search for the origins of human behaviour and its interest in the 'primitive', 19th-cent. folklore had much in common with the anthropology of the period, and some of the founding fathers of the latter discipline, notably Sir Edward Tylor (1832–1917) and Sir James *Frazer (1854–1941), drew on 'folkloric' sources in their attempts to imagine primitive humans. Yet folklore in England did not become institutionalized as a university discipline in the way that anthropology was, and there are still few British (and more particularly English) universities which offer it as a degree subject.

Folklore's relationship with history remains problematic. Many historians, especially those working on mainstream political or economic history, seem to regard folklore as an ill-defined and unrigorous subject whose eclecticism denies its status as a serious discipline. Yet this seems unduly harsh on a field of study which, despite its appeal to the amateur, has at certain points created high standards of scholarship, for example in the analysis and classification of folk-songs and folk-tales. With the broadening of the subject-matter of history, there are now many historians, particularly cultural historians and those social historians interested in the history of *mentalité*, whose concerns are very similar to those of the folklorist. Both groups study 'culture' defined in a broad, anthropological sense, and concern themselves with customs, orally transmitted culture, the significance of folk-tales, and material culture.

Thus although the grand theory and the search for the origins of human culture in the 'primitive' of the late Victorian folklorists, and the eclecticism of later practitioners, may not be to the taste of modern historians, a dialogue with folklore, or at least the incorporation of elements of human behaviour studied by folklorists, can enter the historian's agenda. JAS

folk-song. The distinction between folk-song and 'art music' is a controversial one, but many writers agree with the main features identified by the international Folk Music Council in 1955: folk-song has evolved through the process of oral transmission, being shaped by (*a*) continuity which links the present with the past; (*b*) variation which springs from the creative impulse of the individual or the group; and (*c*) selection by the community which determines the form in which the music survives. Folk-song is passed down through generations, both words and music undergoing constant evolution in the process, so that it rarely exists in a single identifiable version. Traditionally it has been associated with rural communities and lower socio-economic classes, but in the 20th cent. the pattern of dissemination has changed, with greater emphasis on written transmission and especially on recordings. At the same time many of the original functions of folk-song have been taken over by popular music, another form of 'vernacular' music, although one often involving professional musicians and wide dissemination through the mass media.

Folk-songs are generally functional: examples include those linked to the cycle of the year (whether the rural year as in harvest songs or the church year as in carols), work songs such as sea shanties, children's songs, narrative ballads telling a story—often of a moralistic nature—and songs for dancing. Traditional British folk-songs have generally been performed unaccompanied. The most common verse comprises four-line stanzas, each set to the same basic melody, although the singer will often bend the rhythm or introduce vocal ornaments (this is particularly the case in Ireland). Older English folk-songs frequently have a different tune for each line (ABCD), while more recent ones favour a degree of repetition (ABBA, AABA, ABCA, etc.). Rhythms derive from verse patterns, so that up-beat openings are prevalent and quintuple metre not uncommon. Much English folk-song is modally based, although many Gaelic tunes are pentatonic. Scottish folk-song in fact clearly differentiates between the Gaelic tradition of the Highlands and Hebrides (including the bagpipe-influenced 'pibroch songs'), the Lowland songs and ballads, and the Scandinavian-based songs from Orkney and Shetland.

The boundaries between folk-song and art music are often very indistinct. In the 16th and 17th cents., for example, popular melodies like 'The Western Wynde' provided the framework for masses or motets (composers include Tye and Taverner) and keyboard variations (Bull and *Byrd), while street cries appeared in consort songs (Weelkes and *Gibbons). Eighteenth-cent. ballad operas like *Gay's celebrated *Beggar's Opera* incorporated well-known songs, and the words of broadside ballads were printed and sold on street corners. Interest in collecting folk-songs stems largely from Bishop *Percy's *Reliques of Ancient English Poetry* (1765); the following century saw an increasing number of publications, often of texts without music, especially in Scotland.

The real revival of English folk-song, however, came at the beginning of the 20th cent., primarily due to Cecil Sharp. He travelled around the country collecting over 3,000 tunes and over 200 folk-dances, often publishing them in regional anthologies such as the *Folk-Songs from Somerset*. In 1898 an English Folk Song Society was formed (incorporated in 1932 into the English Folk Dance and Song Society), and similar societies appeared in Wales, Scotland, and Ireland. Folk-songs were used in schools (with totally inauthentic piano accompaniments), while their modal language and undulating melodies became assimilated into a new compositional style. Foremost in this nationalistic movement was *Vaughan Williams, himself a committed collector and arranger of folk-songs. The traditional use of folk-song for social and political protest was revived in the 1960s through the urban genre of folk rock epitomized by Bob Dylan. In Britain this composite style was adopted by groups such as Fairport Convention and Steeleye Span.

ECr

Fontenoy, battle of, 1745. In the War of the *Austrian Succession, the French were besieging Tournai. The duke of *Cumberland, in command of a large army, attacked a superior French force under Marshal Saxe on 11 May. After heavy fighting, the attack was repulsed, the Irish Jacobite brigade particularly distinguishing itself. The fall of Tournai soon after helped to persuade Prince Charles Edward *Stuart to embark on his invasion of Britain. JAC

food and drink are substances and liquids, respectively, which are essential to maintain life and growth. For the most part, historians have been interested in studying the changing patterns of the availability of food and drink together with the social relationships involved in their production, distribution, and consumption. For many centuries difficulties of preserving and transporting food obliged most people to rely upon food and drink produced locally. There were marked inequalities in access to food. However, even the rich, who normally enjoyed better food than others, shared the experience of seasonal swings between plenty and want.

Until the 18th cent. food production depended on the opportunities afforded by agriculture, soil geology, and geographical location near freshwater or sea fisheries. Climate and the seasons imposed further restrictions on the output of food. In the Middle Ages most people had a diet based on grains with a few root crops: meat played a small role because of the costs of production. This pattern began to change in Britain with the growth of towns and industrialization and the associated expansion of trade and transport both within the British Isles and overseas. Improvements in the quantity and quality of food available at relatively low cost developed because of advantageous imperial trade connections. This was marked by caricatures of food habits, for example the images by *Hogarth of 'the roast beef of Old England' in the 18th cent. and, more recently, the self-conscious romanticization of regional and local cuisine.

The changes which accelerated after industrialization had begun with the farming innovations of the 16th and 17th cents. Hops introduced from Europe in the 16th cent. gave longer life and greater variety of flavours to ales frequently known as beers. Some root crops, most notably turnips, once confined to gardens, became part of newly devised elaborate field crop rotations. The cultivation of potatoes spread in the 17th cent. from the gardens of the wealthy to smallholdings of the poor and eventually into the field rotations. In northern and western areas of the British Isles potatoes replaced or equalled grain in the diets of the poor. In southern Britain, potatoes only became part of the staple diet of the poor during the early 19th cent. when the rising cost of wheaten bread obliged people to change.

Until the 19th cent. ensuring a variety and an adequate supply of food throughout the year necessitated using the traditional preserving techniques of drying, salting, and pickling. During the 19th cent. increasing supplies of cheap imported sugar enabled preserves and conserves to move from the pantries of the well-off to a much wider public. A further major innovation was the canning process, made possible by the introduction of safe and cheap thin sheet steel coated with tin. Chemical additives at the same time increased the availability of food and drink. After the mid-19th cent., railways and steamships with refrigerated or controlled atmospheres made possible cheap, regular, and reliable distribution of greater varieties and quantities of food and drink. Exotic fruits such as grapefruit and bananas had become common by the beginning of the 20th cent. These developments in trade and technology removed seasonal restrictions on food availability and choice.

Patterns of food consumption depend greatly on income as well as fashion and taste. Inequalities remained with inadequate diets for the poor. For those with adequate financial resources, the variety and quality of food and drink available became greater than ever previously recorded. Mass media promoted sales of food and drink by using brand names in establishing markets and, in the later 20th cent., freezers and microwave ovens in the home added to the choices of meals available to consumers. IJEK

fools and jesters. Laughter-makers were employed at court in the classical world and in many ancient monarchies. They had various functions—to entertain, to prick solemnity, to defuse awkward situations. They were often allowed considerable licence, though pertness had its dangers. Some were genuinely foolish (John Stultum = 'Stupid') but were tolerated on the principle that there are truths that only madmen know. The heyday of the court fool seems to have been late medieval and early modern, and the jester's costume—green and yellow patchwork garments, cap, bells, and stick—was introduced in the 15th cent. Most fools had their own specialities—singing, dancing, juggling, tumbling, or mimicry. Many of the royal fools are known to us. Martinet of Gascony served Edward I; John Scogan was at Edward IV's court and a jest-book attributed to him came out as late as 1570; Will Somers, said to be a good mimic, served Henry VIII, who also took over Wolsey's fool, Patch; Jeffrey Hudson, dwarf and fool to Charles I, turned cavalry leader during the civil wars. Great noblemen and ecclesiastics also had their fools. Patison, More's fool, was painted by Holbein with his master; the priory of Worcester kept a fool and the prior went in person to order his costume.

Few fools are to be found in the 18th cent. Court life became more dignified and ceremonious; taste changed and buffoonery went out of fashion; the great teeming households full of servants and retainers gave way to a more private existence; card-playing and conversation left little room for full-time jesters; 18th-cent. polite society no longer found dwarfs or little men funny in themselves. Shakespeare's fools—Touchstone and Lear's fool—have a more complex role, singing and diverting, but also acting as chorus on events. Their laughter is often shot through with melancholy and Olivia's clown brings down the curtain in *Twelfth Night* with 'the rain it raineth every day'. JAC

Foot, Michael (b. 1913). Deputy leader (1976–80) and leader (1980–3) of the *Labour Party. A distinguished left-wing author and journalist, Foot, as editor and managing director of *Tribune*, was a leading *Bevanite in the 1950s and after 1958 prominent in the *Campaign for Nuclear Disarmament. An MP from 1945, he accepted office for the first time as employment secretary 1974–6. Between 1976 and 1979 he was lord president of the council and leader of the House of Commons, before succeeding James *Callaghan as party leader. He led a divided party however, and went down to humiliating defeat at the hands of Mrs *Thatcher in 1983 on a manifesto described as 'the longest suicide note in history'. Foot, co-author of a famous polemic (*Guilty Men*, 1940), biographer of Nye Bevan, littérateur, brilliant orator, and devotee of the House of Commons, was a much admired and respected figure both inside and outside the Labour movement. AS

football (soccer). Nobody knows who first kicked an object as if it were a football, though there are descriptions of the practice in early China and in the ancient world. Medieval football was extremely violent, akin to modern hooliganism. Repeated attempts were made by the authorities to suppress it as dangerous, disruptive, and a diversion from archery practice. At Ashbourne (Derbys.) a variant of the old game is still played at Shrovetide.

Modern football developed with the growth of large industrial towns. In the early 19th cent. the game declined in popularity in the face of overcrowded and cramped streets and considerable official disapproval. It survived among public schoolboys and at Cambridge University where, in 1848, a first attempt was made to compile a common set of rules. Previous rules were local and much disputed, with disagreements about charging and hacking, the number of players, the size and shape of the ball, and the duration of the game. The Cambridge rules were adopted by a number of clubs and the game made some progress in the 1850s. A further attempt to produce standard rules, at the Freemasons' Tavern in London in 1863, led to the formation of a Football Association, from which some clubs soon seceded to follow a handling code.

At this stage football was an upper middle-class game and strictly amateur. The new Association launched a cup competition in 1872. Queen's Park, the Glasgow team, entered, but scratched on finding travel costs beyond them. Wanderers beat Royal Engineers 1–0 at the Oval before 2,000 spectators and the following year beat Oxford University 2–0. Gradually the strength of the game moved towards the midlands and the north, where clubs were beginning to pay expenses and retaining fees. A watershed was the 1883 Cup Final, when Blackburn Olympics beat Old Etonians 2–1. In 1885, after protests, professionalism was accepted. Attendances began to edge up. The Cup Final at Manchester in 1893 between Wolves and Everton was watched by 45,000 people, and the attendance at Crystal Palace in 1901 to see Tottenham and Sheffield Wednesday was 111,000. With professional teams dominating the cup competition, an Amateur Cup was instituted in 1893, changed in 1974 to the Challenge Vase.

In 1888 twelve clubs from the midlands and north, including Preston North End, Accrington, and Blackburn Rovers, formed the Football League. The first two seasons were won by Preston. Over the next four years, sixteen more clubs joined, including Nottingham Forest, Sunderland, and Everton, and a second division was added in 1892. There was considerable competition from the Southern League, but by 1914 the Football League had extended south to bring in Chelsea, Arsenal, Tottenham, Fulham, and Bristol City. The Scottish League began in 1890 and an Irish League the same year. Many clubs developed from works teams or from church or chapel. Stoke City and Manchester United both originated with railway workers, Aston Villa was an offshoot of a Wesleyan group. In most large towns in Britain, the Saturday afternoon match became part of the leisure pattern of thousands of working men.

After the First World War, a third division was added to the Football League, divided into north and south. Attendances remained high. When Wembley stadium was opened in 1923, well over 126,000 people crammed in to watch Bolton Wanderers beat West Ham 2–0.

During the Second World War, league competitions were suspended, though exhibition matches, with guest players, remained popular. In the 1948/9 season, more than 40 million people paid to watch football in England. Recognition of the game was accorded by knighthoods to Stanley Matthews, the Stoke and Blackpool winger, to Alf Ramsay, manager of the World Cup victors of 1966, and to Matt Busby, manager of Manchester United. But by the 1980s attendances were falling in the face of rival leisure activities, greater social mobility, and a growing distaste for the coarseness and hooliganism of the terraces. Many of the old grounds seemed vast iron hulks, echoing to depleted crowds, relics of a bygone age.

The first international football match took place at Partick in 1872 between England and Scotland, ending in a 0–0 draw. One of the earliest international games between non-British teams was at Vienna in 1902, when Austria beat Hungary 5–0. FIFA was founded in 1904 but international competition did not make much headway until after the First World War, when the World Cup competition was started in 1930. England did not take part until after the Second World War, and was able to retain a comfortable sense of superiority. This was shattered in 1950 by a 1–0 defeat from the USA, followed three years later by a 6–3 defeat at Wembley from the Hungarians, and was not totally restored by victory in the World Cup at Wembley in 1966. In European competitions, British clubs did well to begin with, Celtic and Manchester United winning the European Cup in 1967 and 1968, and Tottenham the Cup Winners' Cup in 1963, but have struggled in the 1990s. English clubs held the European Cup between 1977 and 1982 inclusive, and Liverpool won in 1977, 1978, 1981, and 1984.

The modern professional game has been dogged by a number of disasters. In 1902, 25 people were killed at Ibrox, home of Glasgow Rangers, when a stand collapsed; 33 were killed at Burnden Park, Bolton Wanderers' ground, when crush barriers gave way in 1946; the young and gifted Manchester United team was almost wiped out in an air crash at Munich in 1958. More recently, fire swept through Bradford City stand in 1985 killing 52 people; the Heysel stadium disaster in Belgium the same year claimed 38 lives; and the death of 93 spectators at Hillsborough in 1989 led to the Taylor inquiry, which made urgent recommendations for improved safety. Recent developments towards premier leagues and super leagues have made life difficult for small and unfashionable clubs and a number of them fell by the wayside in the 1980s. At times the professional game seems in danger of being overwhelmed by television and press coverage, with as much attention given to managers as to football, and by heavy administration. But underpinning the 90 or so professional clubs in the English league are the semi-professional leagues, and the vast number of amateurs, of all shapes, sizes, and talents, who play on windswept recreation grounds in Saturday or Sunday leagues, where attendances are measured in single figures, and it is not unknown for teams to turn up with nine men. NJB

forced loans were non-parliamentary taxes which English monarchs demanded from their richer subjects. The forced loan of 1626 was exceptional in being levied on all taxpayers. This attempt to bypass Parliament provoked intense hostility, and in 1628 such levies were outlawed by the *petition of right. RL

Foreign Office. The Foreign Office was created as a separate department in the general administrative reorganization of 1782. Until the present Foreign Office was built in the 1860s, the department was housed in decrepit buildings in *Downing Street. It was headed by the secretary of state for foreign affairs, a senior cabinet minister, usually second in authority only to the prime minister himself. He was assisted by two under-secretaries. Eventually, the 'parliamentary' under-secretary sat in the Commons, if the foreign secretary was a peer (or in the Lords, if he was an MP), and acted as government spokesman on foreign affairs. The permanent under-secretary was a civil servant. In 1841 the rest of the establishment consisted of a chief clerk, six senior clerks, ten clerks, seven junior clerks, eight other clerks attached to particular duties, a librarian, a sublibrarian, a translator, a private secretary, a précis-writer, and a printer. Translation services were particularly weak. It was expected that communications would be in French and it once took the Office a week to find anyone to read a document in German. The first typist was appointed in 1889. Before that all dispatches were in manuscript and were copied by hand. Telegraphic dispatches began to be received in the 1850s but the first telephone was not installed until 1895. The volume of work increased enormously through the century. The Office handled 4,534 dispatches in 1821, 110,000 in 1905. Originally, the staff was recruited entirely by patronage and even qualifying examinations were not introduced until 1856. Employment in the Office was less prestigious than in the diplomatic service and the two services were quite separate. Only in the years before the First World War did the Office begin to modernize. Limited competition for entry was introduced in 1908 and a higher proportion of recruits, although still from a narrow social élite, now had university degrees. As the Office grew more professional, its influence on policy-making increased. Lord *Palmerston, although he worked his subordinates hard, had regarded them as mere clerks. Even at the end of the century, Lord *Salisbury expected little in the way of 'advice' from the Office. The situation began to change between 1898 and 1914. Sir Edward *Grey's dependence on his permanent officials should not be exaggerated but the fact that the Office, which had been predominantly pro-German in 1900, gradually shifted to being pro-French and suspicious of Germany must be taken into account in assessing the formulation of British foreign policy. MEC

foreign policy. No doubt *Caratacus' resistance to the Roman invasion of AD 43 and his alliance with the *Silures could be regarded as foreign policy, but it scarcely seems a helpful term. As long as monarchs wielded great personal power, it is hardly possible to divorce foreign policy from the individual circumstances and character of each king and treat it as a separate category. Nevertheless, at an early period, certain themes emerged. The connection with France that came about in 1066 was fortuitous in that William the Conqueror took advantage of the fact that Edward the Confessor had no sons in order to claim the throne of England, but it introduced a pattern that survived for 500 years. From the days of William Rufus to those of Henry VIII, English monarchs attempted to retain or extend their French possessions. Not until the loss of Calais in 1558 did this aspiration come to an end, and even then it was another 200 years before they relinquished the title of 'king of France'. This, in turn, had profound effects upon another object of English policy, which pre-dated the Conquest—the ambition to turn a southern English kingdom based upon *Wessex into a kingdom of Britain, which should include the north, Wales, Scotland, and Ireland. So demanding a programme may have been beyond the resources of a small kingdom, yet it should be remembered that one object of these policies was to augment those resources. English possessions in France included some of the most fertile and prosperous regions, while it was a constant complaint of English monarchs that the *Pale in Ireland, far from being a source of profit to the crown, drained men and money. Foreign affairs necessarily interlocked with domestic. Weak rulers like John, who lost Normandy, or Edward II, beaten at *Bannockburn, were heading for disaster, but even successful rulers like Edward I and Edward III could expect opposition at home if their demands were too great.

Even within the limits of so general a context, other patterns of foreign policy may be discerned. The principle of supporting one's enemy's enemy is elementary, yet it had important consequences. The Scots, in their long struggle for independence, soon perceived the advantages of an understanding with France, and the 'Auld Alliance' survived from the treaty of *Paris of 1295 until 1560. This also had domestic consequences. When Philip VI of France was at war with Edward III in 1346 he urged David II to cross the border by way of diversion, which led to his capture at *Neville's Cross. During the *Great Schism from 1378 to 1417 one reason for Scotland's recognition of the Avignon popes was that the English were supporting the rival popes at Rome. Likewise, the desire of James IV of Scotland to take advantage of Henry VIII's absence on campaign in France in 1513 led to his death at *Flodden. England pursued a similar policy, supporting Brittany and Burgundy against France. Balance of power also came into consideration centuries before the phrase was invented. In the 16th and 17th cents., when Spain and France disputed European hegemony, the choice was which side to take—unless England was prepared to run the risk that, by staying aloof, she would facilitate the establishment of a universal monarchy. It was left to the monumental incapacity of Charles I to contrive to be at war with both great powers at the same time.

Two other factors were also of increasing importance. The growth of England's trade, particularly in cloth, gave its rulers concern to protect it, which could not be divorced from foreign policy since embargoes and tariffs were easy diplomatic ploys. A special interest in Flanders and the Low Countries, reinforced by strategic considerations, lasted until the 20th cent. Linked with growing prosperity was the use of England's financial resources to eke out a small population by subsidizing continental allies, a policy operated by Edward III, who supported the small German states and Savoy on France's eastern border, and reaching its climax in the five coalitions needed to overcome Napoleon Bonaparte in the 19th cent.

The rift in Christendom in the 16th cent. introduced a new factor into foreign policy, but one which was rarely decisive. Monarchs certainly supported their co-religionists in other countries when it served their purposes, and some rulers like Philip II of Spain showed more than common zeal, but the co-religionists were well aware that the commitment was a fragile one and that they could find themselves abandoned. Catholic unity did not prevent the long struggle between France and Spain, nor protestant commitment three wars between England and the Dutch in the 17th cent. It is true that the Spaniards gave support to their fellow-catholics in Ireland in the 16th cent., but so did atheistical French revolutionaries in 1798, and *realpolitik* Germans in 1916. Nor, at a later stage, did ideology outweigh national interests. *Burke maintained that the war in the 1790s against revolutionary France was an ideological crusade and quite unlike any previous conflict, but *Pitt, who was in charge of affairs, was more low-keyed and would have made peace with the revolutionaries if they could demonstrate that their regime was stable and that they were sincere. *Churchill, in 1941, reproached with commending the Bolsheviks, is said to have replied that he would speak well of the devil if he would take up arms against the Nazis.

The development of a recognizably modern context for foreign policy dates from the *Glorious Revolution of 1688, when three factors combined to change the context of diplomacy. First was the steady spread of representation at foreign courts, which made policy more of a regular activity and less of a response to occasional crises or particular problems. The change had begun in Italy in the 15th cent. Henry VII had a permanent representative only at the Vatican, and though he added one at Madrid and Henry VIII added a third at Vienna, by 1568 there was only one permanent representative left, at Paris. William III, after 1688, had twelve resident ambassadors as well as envoys and agents. The existence of a network of representatives and the flow of information provided facilitated a more coherent foreign policy. The second factor was the changed importance of Parliament after 1688 which initiated a move away from a personal towards a national foreign policy. The Stuarts had often been at odds with their parliaments over foreign affairs but the annual meetings of Parliament after 1688 made it harder for subsequent monarchs to take an independent line. Monarchs and ministers certainly struggled to prevent Parliament from being informed, pleading that public disclosure could inhibit diplomacy, but in 1701 ministers were impeached for not placing the partition treaties before the council or Parliament. After 1688 ambassadors rarely reported directly to the monarchs and a highly personal policy like Charles II's secret treaty of *Dover would have been difficult to sustain. The process was completed with the creation of the post of foreign secretary in 1782. The third factor was the growth of empire. In 1600 England had no overseas colonies: by 1700, in addition to the twelve American colonies, there were valuable possessions in India, the West Indies, and Africa to be protected.

The importance attached to foreign affairs in the 18th cent. may be gauged from the fact that, until the reorganization of 1782, the two secretaries of state were categorized according to the areas of Europe which they dealt with—north or south. The broad outlines of 18th-cent. foreign policy, for all its complexities and variations, are simple. After the swift collapse of Spanish power and rapid rise of France under Louis XIV, there was no question which was the dominant power in Europe, and the fact that France was also a major colonial competitor helped to bring about what has been called the second Hundred Years War. Between 1689 and 1815 Britain and France were at war for nearly half the time. France's much greater population and resources were a substantial handicap, but to build restraining alliances was far from easy. Spain was no longer an adequate counterweight and for much of the period was in the French camp in a Bourbon alliance. The Dutch, though they had an obvious interest in preventing French aggrandizement, were in rapid decline. The Habsburgs, whose possession of the southern Netherlands placed them in the front line, had very heavy commitments in eastern Europe to consider, and, after the reversal of alliances of 1756, moved temporarily into the French orbit. Russia and Prussia, two emerging powers, were purchasable, but their despotic regimes made them unpredictable. After 1714 there was a further complication that *Hanover, virtually defenceless against a determined French onslaught, had either to be protected or taken out of pawn at the peace settlement. The rivalries and ambitions of the continental powers made the construction of grand coalitions difficult. Napoleon bought off Prussia in 1806 with the offer of Hanover, while at the peace settlement in 1814 Prussia and Russia were near to conflict over the fate of Saxony.

These factors dictated Britain's overall foreign policy. It was an accepted point that she must have a continental ally and, on the one occasion when she did not, she lost the American colonies. Indeed, the 1780s, at the end of the American War, were exceptionally difficult. Britain's gains at the end of the *Seven Years War in 1763 had cast her in the role of overmighty power and made the balance of power operate against her: Spain, France, and Holland, at war with Britain in 1780, were supported by Russia, Denmark, Sweden, Prussia, Portugal, and the empire in the *League of Armed Neutrality. Continental alliances also demanded heavy subsidies and finance ministers from *Newcastle to the Younger Pitt sweated to supply the sinews of war and diplomacy.

The peace which brought the Revolutionary and Napoleonic wars to a conclusion in 1815 was based essentially on balance of power considerations. France was made to disgorge the enormous gains she had made under Napoleon, but there was no attempt to reduce her to a second-rate power and she was speedily welcomed back into the comity of nations. Austria and Prussia both made substantial territorial gains but it was still considered essential that they should balance each other in Germany. Britain retained the Cape of Good Hope, taken from the Dutch, Mauritius, and a number of West Indian islands. In only one respect did the peace clearly fail. The new united kingdom of the Netherlands, intended, with international help, to bolt the door against any future French aggrandizement, lasted only fifteen years before collapsing in the face of Dutch and Belgian hostility.

JAC

Where did Britain stand in the decades after Waterloo? Victorian foreign policy conjures up a vision of a John Bullish Lord *Palmerston in the middle of the century; of Britain dominating world trade by her economic strength; a liberal, constitutional Britain, which supported national and liberal movements on the European continent against the declining forces of despotism; a Britain which, at the end of the century, was to rule the greatest empire in the world, with Queen Victoria reigning over a quarter of the world's population. The picture is not entirely false but it owes too much to the image which clever politicians like Palmerston and *Disraeli wished to project to the British public as they struggled with the problems of controlling a wider electorate. Historical study since the 1930s has revealed a more complex picture. Britain had only firmly established her right to be considered a European great power in the 18th cent. and had come close to forfeiting that status as a result of the American War of Independence. In the French Revolutionary and Napoleonic wars, Britain's naval strength had been of enormous importance but her lack of a large standing army had made the other European powers see her as a minor player on the continent. Even *Wellington's victories in Spain, which dazzled British opinion, were regarded as a side-show until he brought his army over the Pyrenees in 1814. Britain's (justified) fears at that time were that the other powers, Austria, Russia, and Prussia, would conclude a 'continental' peace with France, ignoring British interests. It is a measure of *Castlereagh's stature as a statesman that he not only played a major role in holding the coalition together but that he safeguarded all Britain's vital interests in the settlement at the end of the war.

All those responsible for British foreign policy between 1815 and 1865, Castlereagh, *Canning, Wellington, *Aberdeen, and Palmerston, looked back to William *Pitt the Younger as their mentor. They interpreted the legacy somewhat differently according to temperament and changing circumstances but the similarities were greater than the differences. The *Vienna settlement of 1814–15 followed roughly the lines envisaged by Pitt in 1805 and the powers agreed to meet periodically to maintain the peace settlement, as Pitt had wished. Castlereagh felt obliged to withdraw from the resulting *Congress system because he believed it was being perverted from its original purpose of maintaining international peace to the suppression of any subversion which might threaten authoritarian regimes. As late as 1863 Palmerston refused to join the revisionist Napoleon III in a congress because 'the Treaties of Vienna . . . are still the basis of the existing arrangements of Europe' and chaos would ensue if they were overturned. There was no clear division between Conservatives and Liberals among British foreign secretaries in this period. Where they did differ was in their attitude to Europe. All accepted without question that their first duty was to uphold British interests but whereas Castlereagh, Wellington, and Aberdeen believed that this could best be done by playing a full role in Europe, Canning and Palmerston at least part of the time chose to take a more isolationist position.

The great issues of this period were the Eastern Question—the dangerous vacuum left by the decline of the Ottoman empire—and the rise of liberal and nationalist movements in western and central Europe. In the East, Britain reluctantly followed a policy, in the crises of 1840 and the *Crimean War, of propping up the Ottoman empire to prevent Russian advances. The British public had some genuine sympathy with liberal and national movements, especially in Italy, but the government was always extremely cautious in its approach. In the great revolutionary year of 1848 Palmerston was long on rhetoric but short on action. His rhetoric convinced conservative Europe that he was a dangerous radical. It also won the plaudits of the British radicals, even though Palmerston was a strong Tory in facing the challenges in Britain and Ireland. Henceforth, Palmerston found that he could control the electorate (which in fact he feared) by this John Bull approach.

By the 1860s the balance of forces was changing. The British navy still commanded the seas but Britain's industrial lead was about to be challenged by other powers, especially the USA and Germany. Palmerston's last ministry saw Britain come close to what might have been a disastrous involvement in the American Civil War and Palmerston's bluff over Denmark was called by Bismarck. Britain stood aside from the Austro-Prussian War in 1866. Disraeli put a brave face on it. Britain's abstention, he said, was the result of increased strength, not decline. Britain was no longer 'a mere European Power'.

There was a more real clash of ideologies between Disraeli and *Gladstone than between their predecessors. Gladstone, like Pitt and Castlereagh before him, had a clear vision of how international affairs should be conducted, with all submitting to the rule of law and disputes settled by arbitration, not war. He fought a losing battle for the old self-balancing Vienna system. In Europe he was defeated by Bismarck who created his tight, and dangerous, system of alliances to protect the newly united Germany. Disraeli turned to the empire and made it a Conservative cause.

Britain's acquisition of a new empire in the late 19th cent. is usually seen as defensive, a matter of weakness rather than strength. The old colonies of settlement, Canada, Australia, New Zealand, and South Africa, were becoming increasingly independent. Britain still had a great empire in India and its defence sometimes required further accretions of territory. Ironically, Britain acquired more of Africa, during the Scramble period, under Liberal than under Conservative administrations. The motive was almost always a challenge by another power, usually France or Germany. The rhetoric of Palmerston, Disraeli, and their successors convinced the public of Britain's greatness. Sober statesmen, Lord *Salisbury, *Balfour, or *Grey, knew the dangers of the situation. 'Splendid isolation' was not glorious. It was an uncomfortable reality. In 1902 Britain, embarrassed by world reaction to the *Boer War and feeling that even the Royal Navy was now overextended in view of the growth of other, particularly the German, fleets, concluded an alliance with Japan. Over the next twelve years she shifted from Salisbury's policy of 'leaning' on the Triple Alliance of Germany, Austria, and Italy (the first two, old allies) to close relations (although stopping short of a formal alliance) with her two traditional rivals, France and Russia. The simplest explanation may be correct. Britain could not afford to see Germany defeat France again. She fought Germany in 1914 in defence of a balance of power older than the 19th cent., as she had fought Philip II, Louis XIV, or Napoleon—to stop one power dominating Europe. MEC

After 1918 Britain was a sated and exhausted country. Though she took *mandates under the League of Nations, they proved troublesome: *Iraq became independent as early as 1932 and *Palestine and *Jordan soon after the Second World War. Britain's main concern was the search for security. The alliance which had defeated the central powers had begun to disintegrate even before the Great War ended, as Russia collapsed into revolution and civil war. The USA turned to isolationism, the Anglo-Japanese alliance was not continued after 1922, and France, Britain's main ally, was mistrusted in the 1920s as too belligerent and in the 1930s as too defeatist. The inability of the *League of Nations to deal with the Manchurian crisis was an early warning that collective security might offer little protection and was followed in 1933 by the advent to power in Germany of the Nazis. The policy of *appeasement, which had many facets, was accompanied by a new search for allies. Though Russia was admitted to the League of Nations in 1934, there was massive mistrust on both sides, and in 1939 Stalin preferred to do a deal with Hitler. Much effort was devoted to wooing Italy, whose strength was overrated, and appeasement of Mussolini brought down one foreign minister, *Hoare, in 1935. Under these circumstances, British foreign policy lurched. Having abandoned Czechoslovakia in 1938, Britain gave a guarantee to Poland which could scarcely be honoured.

Many of the same themes re-emerged after the end of the Second World War. Churchill was not alone in wondering before 1939 whether victory, if obtained, would seem much different from defeat. Foreign policy was dogged by economic and financial weakness. In one respect policy was simplified by the pace of de-colonization—Britain shed imperial responsibilities at such speed that protecting the empire soon ceased to be a major consideration. As the shape of the post-war world unfolded, two problems emerged—security in the face of Soviet power and Britain's attitude towards Europe. The first was achieved by the nuclear deterrent, participation in *NATO (1949), and a close understanding with the USA, jeopardized only temporarily by the *Suez crisis. The debate on Europe, which proved so protracted, was governed by three factors. First was that not only was Britain geographically and culturally half-in and half-out of Europe, but her connections with her former colonies gave her a perspective Germany did not share, and France only partly. Though Churchill himself had spoken in favour of some United States of Europe as early as 1945, he did not envisage Britain as part of it: it was well-meaning advice *de haut en bas*. The second was that European unity, which began as the simple determination of European powers never to fight each other again, moved through economic collaboration towards political integration. The debate in Britain was often stultified by refusal to identify what 'Europe' meant at different stages: the phrase 'Common Market', which the British voted to join, masked the political aspirations of many of its continental supporters. The third factor was the timing of Britain's application to join. EFTA (the *European Free Trade Association), Britain's immediate response to 'the six'—a free trade bloc of Sweden, Switzerland, Portugal, Denmark, Norway, Britain, and Austria—was scarcely a formidable economic force, and clearly a holding operation. Britain's application to join the EEC was vetoed by de Gaulle in 1963 and again in 1967 at a time when a federal Europe was hardly on the agenda and Gaullist France would have been very suspicious. But by the time Britain entered the EEC in 1973, the movement towards political integration was gathering pace. Britain acted as a somewhat ineffective brake, usually doing enough to exasperate enthusiasts for European unity while not satisfying the anti-Europeans. It was also paradoxical that at a time when many Scots, Welsh, and others were protesting that decisions were always made in remote London, power should be leaking to remoter Brussels. All too often, the rhetoric of British foreign policy appeared to suggest that Britain should be at the very heart of Europe in order to lead it backwards. JAC

Bartlett, C. J., *British Foreign Policy in the Twentieth Century* (Basingstoke, 1989); Black, J., *A System of Ambition: British Foreign Policy 1660–1793* (1991); Bourne, K., *The Foreign Policy of Victorian*

England, 1830–1902 (Oxford, 1970); Chamberlain, M. E., *Pax Britannica? British Foreign Policy, 1789–1914* (1988); Scott, H. M., *British Foreign Policy in the Age of the American Revolution* (Oxford, 1990); Seton-Watson, R. W., *Britain in Europe, 1789–1914* (Cambridge, 1945).

forest laws. Under the Norman kings, the royal forest grew steadily, probably reaching its greatest extent under Henry II when around 30 per cent of the country was set aside for royal sport. The object of the forest laws was the protection of 'the beasts of the forest' (red, roe, and fallow deer, and wild boar) and the trees and undergrowth which afforded them shelter, known as the vert. Kings frequently granted their tenants the right to take smaller game, such as hares and pheasants, and more extensive hunting privileges were occasionally granted to especially favoured subjects, but generally none but the king and his foresters might hunt the deer or boar. The definitive form to forest law occurred during Henry II's reign, most notably in the Assize of the Forest (also known as the Assize of *Woodstock) in 1184. Its clauses reveal the harsh restrictions which the forest officials enforced. None could carry bows and arrows in the royal forest, and dogs had to have their toes clipped to prevent them pursuing game. Savage penalties for any infringements were often imposed and in 1198, probably reverting to previous custom under Henry I, Richard I declared that those guilty of killing deer were to lose their eyes and testicles. But under Henry II and his sons imprisonment and the exaction of heavy fines were the norm. Discontent with the laws, and the extortions and petty tyranny of forest officials, ensured that the forest became a major political issue in John's reign. It culminated in the Charter of the Forest (1217) which sought to remedy many of the grievances, although it was only partially successful in this. Its clauses provided the framework of forest law throughout the 13th cent., but only in the 14th cent., when large areas were disafforested, did the political issue subside. SL

forma regiminis, or form of government, June 1264, was arrangements after the victory of Simon de *Montfort and his supporters at *Lewes for a provisional government until a general settlement of the dispute with Henry III had been reached. The king was to be advised by a council of nine, three of them always present: the nine were to be nominated by three electors, 'prudent men', of whom de Montfort was one. At the subsequent peace of Canterbury in August, it was declared that the forma regiminis would operate for all of Henry III's reign and for a period of his son Edward's to be negotiated. But when Prince Edward, who had been a hostage, escaped in May 1265, negotiation was at an end, and de Montfort was killed at *Evesham. JAC

Formby, George (1904–61). Comedian. Born in Wigan (Lancs.), Formby followed his father in the old music-hall tradition. His stage character was that of a gormless but good-natured Lancashire lad, with a squeaky voice, toothy grin, and a talent for playing the ukelele. He soon became an established success in provincial theatres and in 1929 began recording his cheerful, cheeky songs such as 'When I'm Cleaning Windows' and 'Chinese Laundry Blues'. He made his first film, *No Limit*, in 1935 and then made an average of two films a year until 1946. He retained the persona of his stage character who, with a mixture of luck and innocent guile, triumphed in the end with his catch-phrase: 'Turned out nice again!' These well-made pictures made Formby the highest-paid entertainer and the top box-office attraction in Britain. He was awarded the OBE in 1946 for entertaining the troops during the Second World War and his films were so popular in Russia he was awarded the Order of Lenin. RAS

Formigny, battle of, 1450. By 1450 Henry VI, beset by disaffection at home, was hard-pressed to defend his French territories. A relief expedition under Sir Thomas Kyriel and Sir Matthew Gough was blocked by the comte de Clermont in Normandy on 15 April and badly defeated. The French use of artillery heralded the crushing victory at *Castillon three years later and the collapse of England's empire in France. JAC

Fornham St Genevieve, battle of, 1173. *Henry the Young King, eldest son of Henry II, rebelled in 1173, complaining of his inheritance. The support of Louis VII of France and William the Lion of Scotland made the revolt formidable. Henry II beat off an attack on Normandy, leaving Richard de *Lucy, justiciar, to defend England. In September Robert, earl of Leicester, landed in Suffolk and joined forces with Hugh, earl of Norfolk. De Lucy abandoned the siege of Leicester castle and marched to intercept the rebels. On 17 October at Fornham St Genevieve, just north of Bury St Edmunds, though outnumbered, he defeated and captured the earl of Leicester. The lucky capture of William the Lion at *Alnwick the following year broke the back of the revolt. JAC

Forster, E. M. (1879–1970). Novelist and man of letters, in *Two Cheers for Democracy* (1951) he described himself as belonging to 'the fag-end of Victorian liberalism'. If his spiritual home was in Cambridge and Bloomsbury, he maintained a certain distance. Emotionally vulnerable, he was critical of their intellectualism. The 'undeveloped heart' of the English, often most debilitating in the English abroad, is his theme. In the early *Where Angels Fear to Tread* (1905) he treats it with a light, dry irony recalling Jane *Austen, digging deeper for his favourite book *The Longest Journey* (1907) and even anticipating D. H. *Lawrence in his 'condition of England' novel *Howards End* (1910). Visits in 1912 and 1922 shaped his richest work, *A Passage to India* (1924), more 'philosophic and poetic' than before. Thereafter, ensconced at King's College as humanist sage, 'the fictional part of me dried up'. His one explicitly homosexual novel, *Maurice* (1914), was published posthumously. JNRS

Forster, William Edward (1818–86). Forster was a hard-working politician whose greatest achievement was the *Education Act of 1870. He was the son of a quaker missionary and began his career in the Yorkshire woollen trade at Bradford. In 1861 he was returned for Bradford as a Liberal. He was given office under *Russell in 1865 and in *Gladstone's first ministry put in charge of education as vice-president of the council, being brought into the cabinet in 1870. His Education Bill proposed state schools where voluntary schools had not been established, to be administered by elected school boards. The religious difficulty was met by the Cowper-Temple clause, whereby the religious instruction was to be of an undenominational character. Forster also guided through *secret ballot in 1872. There was considerable support for him as party leader on the first of Gladstone's retirements in 1875, but many of Forster's fellow-dissenters were bitter at what they regarded as a religious betrayal in 1870, and he withdrew in favour of Hartington (*Devonshire). In 1880 he was appointed chief secretary in Ireland. His Coercion Bill the following year was fiercely contested, with many threats against his life. In 1882 he resigned when Gladstone negotiated the *Kilmainham 'treaty' with *Parnell. His successor, Lord Frederick *Cavendish, was murdered within a few hours of his arrival in Dublin. Forster's offer to return to Ireland was not accepted and though he retained his seat, he did not again hold office. JAC

Fortescue, Sir John (*c*.1394–*c*.1476). Lawyer. Fortescue studied law at Lincoln's Inn, became lord chief justice in 1442, and received his knighthood. A staunch supporter of the Lancastrian cause, he was at *Towton in 1461 and subsequently attainted. In exile in Scotland and Flanders until 1470, he returned and fought on the losing side at *Tewkesbury, being captured. He then made his terms with the triumphant Yorkists. His two most important writings were *De laudibus legum Angliae*, in praise of the laws of England, and *On the Governance of the Kingdom of England*, probably written after 1470. Fortescue was at pains to distinguish between absolute monarchy ('dominum regale' as in France) and limited or constitutional monarchy ('dominum politicum et regale' as in England). The essential difference is that in the first state the king makes the law, in the second the king rules his subjects only by laws 'such as they assent unto'. In his characteristically Lancastrian parliamentary interpretation, Fortescue divided the two types too sharply—the French also had representative institutions. But by doing so he helped to create pride in the liberal character of English government and was much quoted by the opposition to Charles I in the 17th cent. Like *Bagehot, Fortescue helped to create the situation he was describing. JAC

Fortriu was the Gaelic name of a Pictish region. The people of Fortriu first appear in a Latin guise as the Verturiones, a Pictish tribe first mentioned in the 4th cent. along with the more famous *Caledonii. Fortriu, its people, and its kings are frequently mentioned in contemporary sources from the 7th cent. until 904, when they are last heard of led by *Constantine II winning a battle in *Strathearn (Perthshire) against the Danes. Its kings regularly appear in other sources as kings of the Picts, including Bridei son of Bile (d. 693), the victor of the battle of *Nechtansmere (or Dunnichen, 11 miles north of Dundee) in 685 which liberated the Picts from Northumbrian overlordship. It would appear that 'king of Fortriu' was an alternative title for 'king of the Picts'. Fortriu was probably the core area of Pictish kingship and claimed overlordship over all Picts. There is some doubt about its extent. A late source identifies it with the Strathearn and Menteith; but it may have stretched from Menteith to Angus. The last kings of Fortriu mentioned belonged to a Gaelic dynasty which in the 830s, for the first time, retained the kingship without a break for more than a generation. They were, however, wiped out in battle against Scandinavian raiders in 839; and in the turmoil of the following decades Fortriu itself disappeared to be replaced *c*.900 by *Alba, 'Scotland'. DEB

Forty-five rising. See JACOBITE RISINGS.

Fosse Way was the Roman road from Exeter to Lincoln. Exceptional in (*a*) cutting across the grain of the main road-system radiating from London, and (*b*) not deviating more than 6 miles either side of its direct line, it has been proposed as a lateral road along an early frontier line. This would be anachronistic, nor did the campaigns of conquest ever stop on this line. It may have been laid out to link the legions at Exeter and Lincoln after the *Boudiccan revolt. The modern name derives from *fossa*, a Latin loan-word into Anglo-Saxon, perhaps used for a raised earthwork. ASEC

Foster, John, 1st Baron Oriel (1740–1826). Politician. Foster, a lawyer, was returned to the Irish House of Commons when he was 21 and in 1784 became Irish chancellor of the Exchequer. The following year he was elected Speaker and strongly opposed the Act of *Union, presiding over the last meeting of the Irish Parliament. Nevertheless, he was returned to the Westminster Parliament for Louth, and in 1804 resumed office as chancellor of the Exchequer (I), holding it until 1806 and again 1807–11. He was created a baron in 1821 when he was 80. Foster was bitterly opposed to concessions to the Roman catholics and was one of the leading spokesmen for the *Anglo-Irish ascendancy, predicting that Irish catholics would soon tire of the Union and demand first repeal, then separation. Consequently he opposed the Union until it had passed and supported it thereafter. JAC

Fotheringhay, treaty of, 1482. Anglo-Scottish relations deteriorated in 1480. Unruly Scottish lords raided northern England. Counter-raids followed, some by sea in the Firth of Forth. In Fotheringhay castle on 11 June 1482, the exiled brother of James III, Alexander, duke of *Albany, undertook to recognize Edward IV as overlord of Scotland after an English army had set him on its throne. This army, led by Richard of Gloucester (later Richard III), reached Edinburgh, but Albany renounced the treaty after coming to terms with the lords who had imprisoned James. They agreed to surrender the castle of Berwick-on-Tweed, Gloucester's only gain. RLS

Fountains abbey (Yorks.) was founded in Skelldale in 1132 by a group of dissident reforming monks of *Benedictine St Mary's, York, under the direction of Archbishop *Thurstan. In 1133 they adopted the *Cistercian rule. After initial difficulties and in spite of the sack of the abbey, whose abbot, Henry Murdac, had been appointed archbishop of York in 1146, by supporters of William fitzHerbert, a rival claimant, the community flourished, attracting benefactions and recruits from many of the magnates and lords of northern England. It established several daughter houses, as well as

Lysa in Norway. The mismanagement of its largely pastoral economy at the end of the 13th cent. brought Fountains close to ruin. Political unrest and Scottish raids contributed to the crisis, and a falling population led to declining monastic numbers and a switch to a *rentier* economy. Nevertheless, the late Middle Ages saw substantial building works, partly consequent on a relaxation of monastic discipline, and at the *dissolution Fountains was still the wealthiest Cistercian abbey in England. Though much of the abbey was used to build Fountains Hall, the surviving ruins and precincts (landscaped in the 18th cent.) are amongst the most impressive Cistercian remains in Europe. BJG

Fourth Party was the name given facetiously to a parliamentary ginger group in the Conservative Party in 1880 (the other three being Liberals, Conservatives, and Irish). It consisted of Lord Randolph *Churchill, J. E. Gorst, Sir H. D. Wolff, and, at some distance, Arthur *Balfour. The Conservatives had just lost the general election and the contempt of the Fourth Party was as much directed at their own front bench as at Gladstone's administration. Sir Stafford *Northcote was considered particularly supine and nicknamed 'The Goat'. They began with opposition to allowing *Bradlaugh as an atheist to take the oath or affirm and maintained harassing tactics towards the Liberals. When the Conservatives returned to office in 1885, all four were found employment. The main achievement of the group was to launch the spectacular career of Lord Randolph. JAC

Fox, Charles James (1749–1806). A brilliant orator and a man of dazzling charm, Fox never fulfilled his immense potential as a politician. The main reason for this was that his political judgement was erratic. At crucial times in his career he committed errors which proved decisive in denying him the office for which he craved.

Fox was educated at Eton and Oxford and entered the House of Commons while still under age in 1768. He held minor office under *North but fell foul of the king and the prime minister over the *Royal Marriages Act and the admission of reporters to debates in the Commons. Once in opposition Fox was drawn to alliance with the *Rockinghamite Whigs. He became a critic of the influence of the crown, an opponent of British policy towards the American colonists, and the advocate of greater collective responsibility within the cabinet, arguing that cabinets should have a greater say in the choice of prime ministers. He favoured recognizing the independence of the American colonies and made no secret of his belief that the influence of the crown was the cause of British humiliation. He supported parliamentary reform, the repeal of the Test and Corporation Acts, and closer collaboration between parliamentarians and popular reform movements.

When North fell in 1782 Fox became foreign secretary under Rockingham. He wanted to recognize American independence in the hope of securing American goodwill during the peace negotiations but finding himself in disagreement with *Shelburne and other colleagues he resigned office on Rockingham's death. This proved to be a grave misjudgement. He was driven to seek new political allies and entered into alliance with his old foe, North. There was nothing inherently disastrous about this. Coalition was an inescapable fact of political life, but working with North was bound to be risky: many MPs remembered the ferocity with which Fox had denounced North as an agent of corruption. By defeating Shelburne over the draft peace terms, Fox and North forced themselves upon the king. When they tried to reform the administration of the East India Company, George III procured the defeat of the *India Bill in the Lords, dismissed the coalition, and after installing *Pitt as prime minister in December 1783 saw him win a great victory at the 1784 general election. Fox's gamble had failed and he faced the prospect of long years in opposition.

Even when Pitt was defeated over parliamentary reform and Irish free trade, there was little comfort for Fox. When George III became ill in the autumn of 1788 Fox expected that the prince of Wales would call him into office once he had become regent. Fox supported the prince's inherent right to be regent with full powers, but Pitt's advocacy of the need for Parliament to act proved more popular. The king recovered in February 1789 and Fox was blamed by many of his colleagues for mishandling the regency question. His fortunes were again at a low ebb.

When the French Revolution broke out in May 1789 Fox believed that the French were at long last imitating the English Revolution of 1688. But the Foxite party split over the French Revolution, and by 1794 Fox had only 60 supporters in the Commons. Though disgusted by the excesses of the Jacobins, he opposed war with France, arguing the case for a negotiated peace. He bitterly resented the desertion of so many old friends and for a time ceased to attend the Commons.

When *Addington resigned in 1804 George III vetoed Pitt's proposal that Fox should be foreign secretary in a grand coalition. Only after Pitt's death in January 1806 was the king compelled to accept Fox as foreign secretary in Grenville's ministry. But he was now in poor health. Attempts to negotiate a peace with Napoleon collapsed ignominiously. The only consolation for Fox in his last days was the condemnation of the slave trade by the House of Commons. In September 1806 Fox died. He became the inspiration for Whig legend. His advocacy of peace, retrenchment, parliamentary reform, and civil and religious liberty inspired many later reformers. One irony was that the hero of Victorian liberals was so un-Victorian in his private life. In his youth Fox had been a compulsive gambler and womanizer. Though he found happiness with his mistress Elizabeth Armistead, whom he married in 1795, he could never manage his private finances. JWD

Fox, George (1624–91). Founder of the Society of Friends (*quakers). A Leicestershire man of puritan upbringing, Fox was an apprentice shoemaker who, after religious experiences, found no church spiritually satisfying. He began (1647) widespread itinerant preaching, rallying the many small groups of 'Seekers' of similar views. Rejecting organized ecclesiasticism, hierarchical authority, and contemporary social convention, even courtesy, and relying not on sacraments or Scriptures, but on mystical 'Inner Light', his followers were called 'Children of Light' then 'Friends of Truth' and popularly quakers (1654). They only became pacifist and non-political after 1660. Until 1689 they were much persecuted, Fox being imprisoned eight times. By 1660 there were about 30,000–40,000 quakers drawn mainly from rural and urban craftsmen. With the help of Margaret Fell, whom he married in 1669, he gave the movement cohesion. Fox himself travelled all over the British Isles, to the West Indies, and North America. A prolific pamphleteer, his *Journal* was published posthumously (1694). WMM

Fox, Henry (1705–74). Fox entered Parliament in 1735 and quickly found favour with *Walpole. Walpole's successor Henry *Pelham also regarded Fox highly and had him appointed secretary at war in 1746. Fox was a skilled and witty debater, a talented manager of men and money; many believed he would succeed Pelham when he died in 1754. But Pelham's brother the duke of *Newcastle did not trust Fox and would not give him sufficient patronage to control the Commons. Fox was a secretary of state briefly, 1755–6, but his lack of expertise in foreign affairs as the *Seven Years War began told against him. When his greatest rival William *Pitt formed a coalition with Newcastle in 1757, Fox was 'bought off' with the lucrative but uninfluential office of paymaster-general. Fox's opportunity for revenge came in 1762–3 when *Bute and George III employed him to push the peace of *Paris through the Commons. To do so, Fox purged from office most supporters of Newcastle. He was created Lord Holland, but George III regarded his cynical methods with contempt and, politically isolated, his career was over.

One sees Henry Fox most favourably through his love of family. He eloped with a daughter of the duke of Richmond in 1744 and they were a devoted couple, dying within days of one another. He was highly indulgent to his children, particularly his third son, Charles James Fox. His children repaid this indulgence by gambling away most of his vast fortune and Fox's final years were not happy. AIL

Foxe, John (1516–87). Martyrologist. Born in Lincolnshire, educated at Oxford, he was fellow of Magdalen College (1539). Though, as an extreme protestant, he resigned in 1545, he was ordained deacon by Bishop *Ridley of London (1550) and was tutor (1547–53) to the children of the recently executed catholic earl of Surrey. One of these, for whom as 4th duke of *Norfolk he retained affection, he later attended on the scaffold (1572). After exile under Mary, he returned, was ordained priest in 1560, and, despite objecting to the surplice, became vicar of Shipton. Foxe's reputation rests principally on his *Actes and Monuments* (Latin 1554, English 1563) or *Book of Martyrs*, dedicated to Elizabeth, a best seller which reinforced the concept of England as God's elect nation. 'A database for the justification of the Elizabethan "godly" reformation', it was based on massive, but unashamedly biased and often inaccurate protestant scholarship. WMM

Foxe, Richard (*c.*1448–1528). Bishop and statesman. Foxe was born near Grantham and educated at Magdalen College, Oxford. On a visit to Paris he became acquainted with Henry of Richmond who, after gaining the throne as Henry VII, appointed Foxe bishop of Exeter, king's secretary, and lord privy seal. He was greatly employed in diplomatic and matrimonial negotiations. In 1491 he baptized Prince Henry. Foxe was translated to Bath and Wells in 1492, to Durham in 1494, and to Winchester in 1501. From 1507 to 1519 he was master of Pembroke College, Cambridge. His influence waned as that of *Wolsey grew in the reign of Henry VIII and he gave up the privy seal in 1516. In his later years, while growing blind, he founded Corpus Christi College, Oxford, and encouraged the study of Greek. In view of the trust both monarchs placed in him, he would presumably have gained Canterbury were it not for the long tenure of *Warham (1503–32). JAC

fox-hunting. The medieval chase, so much loved by monarchs, was mainly of the deer, either in royal forests or in deer parks. Foxes, regarded as vermin, were killed by farmers and labourers, but without undue ceremony. But by the 17th cent., deer were becoming scarce, as guns took their toll and woodlands diminished. For some time hunters carried on with carted deer, but they were troublesome, expensive, and unsatisfactory. Hares made a good substitute and could be hunted on foot. Organized fox-hunting developed in the late 17th and early 18th cents. The Monsons were hunting foxes in the Burton in Lincolnshire in the 1670s, the Arundells in the 1690s in what became the South and West Wiltshire Hunt: the Puckeridge Hunt dated from 1720, the Belvoir from 1730. Hugo Meynell, who hunted with the Quorn, acquired a national reputation, breeding hounds and horses with great care. The lead was taken by local noblemen, since keeping a pack of hounds was expensive and prestige helped to obtain permission to hunt over other people's fields. Ritual, costume, and terminology developed—'pink', 'brush', 'mask'. By the 19th cent. fox-hunting was becoming a national tradition, with its own sporting writers like Charles Apperley and Surtees, and the walls of countless taverns adorned with paintings and comic prints. An Association of Masters of Foxhounds was set up in 1881. But the same century saw the beginning of serious criticism of hunting and the 20th cent. produced its hunt saboteurs and ugly clashes at meets. Despite the hostility of the *Royal Society for the Prevention of Cruelty to Animals and the League against Cruel Sports, there were 190 packs of foxhounds in the 1970s, more than in Edwardian England. In Scotland, where fox-hunting had never been as popular, there were fewer than a dozen packs. JAC

Fox's martyrs was the satirical description of the 90 or so supporters of the Fox–North coalition who lost their seats in *Pitt's landslide victory at the general election of 1784. It derived its name from John *Foxe's famous book of 1563 of the sufferings of the faithful. JAC

Fox-Talbot, W. H. See TALBOT, W. H. FOX.

Fragment on Government (1776) was Jeremy Bentham's first book, written to refute Sir William *Blackstone's *Commentaries on the Laws of England*. Bentham rejected Blackstone's celebrated treatise which set out the legal basis of

the British constitution, because it perpetuated myths such as the doctrines of 'mixed' government and 'separation' and 'balance' of powers. Moreover, Blackstone confused fact with value, lending spurious legitimacy to whatever laws were in place. Bentham sought to flush out these errors, and 'break loose from the trammels of authority and ancestor-wisdom on the field of law', substituting the rational principle of utility for the irrational practice of tradition.
TSG

France, relations with. From the Norman Conquest of 1066 England was involved in a series of French wars arising out of the continental possessions (and claims) of the Norman and still more of the Angevin kings. The wine trade with Bordeaux was greatly valued. The *Hundred Years War began in 1337, and in 1420 Henry V was recognized as the heir to the French throne. Disaster speedily followed, and by 1453 only *Calais remained in English hands (it was finally lost in 1558). Meanwhile the French used the Auld Alliance with Scotland to add to English embarrassments.

A new era of Anglo-French conflict began in the later 17th cent. when under Louis XIV France emerged as the most formidable kingdom in Europe. In the War of the *Spanish Succession (1701–13) Britain secured Gibraltar, Nova Scotia, and Newfoundland, and confirmed her position as a great power. The War of the *Austrian Succession (1740–8) and the *Seven Years War (1756–63) made Britain the leading European force in North America and India. The French obtained partial revenge when their intervention in the War of *American Independence (1776–83) hastened the loss of the colonies. Despite the fears aroused in Britain by the radical political and social ideas of the French revolutionaries, the wars from 1793 to 1815 were essentially a continuation of those waged over the balance of power in Europe, colonies, and naval supremacy. France was finally defeated in 1814–15, although *Castlereagh was careful to ensure that she remained strong enough to play a major role in the balance of power.

For the rest of the century the British continued to rank France (along with Russia) above all the states which posed a threat to their interests. The two fought on the same side in the *Crimean War, but it needed the resolution of colonial rivalries to bring about the *Entente of 1904, and it was solidly cemented only by the growing fear of Germany. France became the main battleground for the British army in the 1914–18 war. Yet relations soon deteriorated after 1919 in both Europe and the Middle East. Even the advent of Hitler failed to produce a close alliance until 1939. The dramatic fall of France followed in June 1940. At the end of the war Britain was the victorious power most interested in the revival of her neighbour, but the Soviet threat soon aligned Britain much more closely to the USA. The ill-conceived Anglo-French bid to overthrow the Nasser regime in Egypt in 1956 ended in tears, while President de Gaulle vetoed two belated British attempts to join the *European Economic Community (in 1963 and 1967). Even after entry in 1973 Britain remained too semi-detached in her policies to satisfy the French.
CJB

franchise. See SUFFRAGE.

Franciscans (or 'friars minor' or 'grey friars') were a mendicant order founded by St Francis of Assisi (1181/2–1226), the son of a wealthy merchant, in 1209, when he gave his disciples, like him devoted to poverty, care of the sick, and meditation, the 'Regula primitiva', the first rule, heavily influenced by apostolic models. In 1212 a wealthy woman, Clare, joined Francis: she became abbess of a community of Franciscan nuns, like their male counterparts noted for their ascetic poverty. Francis was unwilling to regularize his rapidly growing band of itinerant preachers, and control soon passed from his hands. In 1223 Pope Honorius III confirmed a more institutionalized rule which emphasized total poverty. The friars were to live by their own labour or by begging. Later, following *Dominican example, the Franciscans were organized into provincial and general chapters under the ultimate authority of the minister-general.

Thereafter the order expanded rapidly, appealing particularly to urban benefactors, and the Franciscans settled and preached primarily in towns, though they were also active in missionary work in the East. Tension between those who wished to follow the apostolic ideals of the founder (later known as the 'Spirituals'), however impractical, and those who were prepared to compromise, particularly over the issues of property and corporate poverty (the 'Conventuals'), soon emerged, bringing disunity to the order, particularly in the mid-13th and early 14th cents., when many of the more radical 'Spirituals' were condemned as heretics, while in 1368 a new group, the 'Observants', emerged in Italy demanding a return to the rule of 1223.

The first Franciscans under Agnello of Pisa were sent to England by Francis in 1224 and communities founded at Canterbury, London, and Oxford. Thereafter the Franciscans grew rapidly and there were some 60 houses by 1300. At Oxford the Franciscans soon acquired a reputation for their scholarship, first under Alexander of Hales, and were in the forefront of intellectual activity during the 13th and 14th cents., their number including Roger *Bacon, *Duns Scotus, and *William of Occam. There were also three successful houses of Franciscan nuns, of which the Minories, in London, was the most significant. At the end of the 15th cent. six houses of Observants were established, three being transfers from Conventual friaries. Observant friars were fierce opponents of Henry VIII's policies and many were executed or imprisoned during the 1530s. The English order was dissolved in 1538.
BJG

Franco-Scottish alliance. Also known as the Auld Alliance. An offensive and defensive alliance, aimed at crippling England's attempts to conquer Scotland or France by threatening war on two fronts. First agreed at Paris in 1295, the Franco-Scottish alliance was renewed periodically until renounced by Scotland in 1560.

At its zenith in the 14th cent., after renewal by Robert I at *Corbeil (1326), the alliance was an essential element in Scotland's success in the *Wars of Independence, and was continued in 1371 and 1391. The *Hundred Years War (1337–1453) emphasized the alliance's strengths as successive

English kings found they could not conquer France without defeating Scotland.

The alliance remained an effective way of pressurizing England in the 15th cent., and was reaffirmed in 1428 and 1448. However, Louis XI of France's treaty with England, ignoring Scotland (1463), and James III's alliance with England (1474), illustrated changing Franco-Scottish relations. The alliance was renewed in 1484, 1492, and 1512, although neither nation intended to implement it actively. However, when Henry VIII attacked France (1513), James IV decided to abide by the alliance, resulting in disastrous defeat at *Flodden.

The 16th cent. saw Scotland at the whim of swiftly changing European diplomacy. Alternately courted and abandoned by France, the Scots were reluctant to repeat Flodden on their ally's behalf. With the advent of the *Reformation, many now favoured protestant England. The alliance was renewed by marriage arrangements for James V (1537) and Mary, queen of Scots (1548), but Scotland's refusal to be exploited by France was eventually reflected in the revolution of 1559–60 which saw England embraced, and the Franco-Scottish alliance finally renounced. RJT

Franklin, Sir John (1786–1847). After a distinguished naval career in the wars against Napoleon, Franklin became the most famous British Arctic explorer of his day. Then, like *Livingstone, at the end of his life, he became even more of a national figure by disappearing into the unknown. Although a naval officer trained in 1818 in using large ships to force a way through the ice of the Canadian north to find the North-West Passage and arguably a victim of that policy, Franklin made his greatest discoveries on two overland journeys of 1818–22 and 1825–7 when he explored vast areas of northern mainland Canada and traced the northern coast. After a spell as governor of Tasmania from 1834 to 1843, he was chosen to take the Antarctic ships *Erebus* and *Terror*, which *Ross had used, to the Arctic to force the North-West Passage. It was later learned that, having got through sea passages to the west side of King William Island, the ships had frozen in. Franklin died, but his men survived to perish later of scurvy, starvation, and lead poisoning from their tinned foods. No fewer than 40 official and unofficial expeditions searched for Franklin (and in the process, ironically, showed there was a North-West Passage) but not until 1859 was the nature of the disaster fully established. RB

frankpledge was a form of collective responsibility for good conduct, whereby every member of a tithing, or group of ten, was answerable for the good behaviour of the others, on pain of fine or amercement. Some elements were to be found in Anglo-Saxon and Danish England, but it developed after the Norman Conquest, perhaps to give some security to individual Normans in a hostile land. Sheriffs were instructed to hold twice-yearly meetings to ensure that all persons required to be in tithings had joined them. Individual lords bade for the right to supervise tithings in the view of frankpledge, which added to both their power and profit. There were parts of England where the system never operated, particularly in the north, and by the 15th cent. it was moribund. JAC

Frazer, Sir James (1854–1941). Anthropologist. Frazer was born in Glasgow, where he took his first degree, and was elected to a fellowship at Trinity College, Cambridge, in 1879, which he held for the rest of his life. In 1888 he contributed articles on taboo and totemism to the *Encyclopaedia Britannica*, which laid the foundation for his work on primitive religion. He followed them with *The Golden Bough* (1890), a pioneer work of comparative anthropology, which occupied him until the 1930s. The evolution of society was, Frazer suggested, from magic to religion and then to science. This led him to examine the role of god-kings, scapegoats and sacrifices, and fire festivals. Prodigiously dedicated and hard-working, he amassed a vast pile of evidence, much of it printed in *Anthologia anthropologica* (1938, 1939). He had no field experience and showed little interest in comment and criticisms of his work. His early presbyterian family religion gave way to a vague 'trembling hope' in some 'world of light eternal'. Frazer was knighted in 1914 and given the OM in 1925. JAC

Frederick Lewis, prince of Wales (1707–51). Eldest son of George II and Queen Caroline; father of George III. For most of his life Frederick was at odds with his parents, and by the mid-1730s he had become a willing tool of opposition politicians, hopeful of serving him when he became king. Brought up in Hanover, he came to England in 1728. After his marriage in 1736 to Augusta of Saxe-Coburg, the king's refusal to grant him a fixed income provoked a dramatic rift and he was banned from court. He soon established a rival court at *Leicester House which became an important meeting-ground for *Walpole's leading opponents. After Walpole's fall from power, a period of uneasy reconciliation between father and son lasted until 1747, when Frederick and his Whig followers forged an alliance with the Tories. The 'Leicester House group' made a limited impact in Parliament, and broke up on the prince's sudden death in 1751. AAH

Free Church of Scotland. This issued from the *Disruption of 1843, when those unable to accept the infringements of the *Church of Scotland's right of self-government which the Auchterarder case (1838–9) highlighted seceded under Thomas Chalmers (1780–1847). The result can be regarded as a dramatic tribute to voluntaryism (and Scottish middle-class affluence), or a wasteful duplication of resources: 500 ministers, 600 schools, 700 new churches by 1847; missionary work in India and central Africa; ministerial training renowned for its intellectual rigour. Under a powerful Edinburgh leadership, this church, claiming continuity from the Reformation's Church of Scotland, and retaining the Westminster confession and longer and shorter catechisms, steadily moderated its theological conservatism. It affirmed its political liberalism, developed a centralized financial system new to presbyterianism, and united with other presbyterian secessions: the original seceders (1852), the Reformed Presbyterian Church (1876), and the United Presbyterians (1900), thus forming the United Free Church which joined with the Church of Scotland in 1929. Inevitably each union bred its rump. The Free Presbyterians seceded in 1893, alarmed at the Declaratory Act of 1892, which modified the binding force of the Free Church's original formularies, and a remnant (the 'Wee Frees') has survived the union of 1900, confirmed in its property by the Free Church case (1904), conservative in theology, strong in the Highlands, and active in missions to India and southern Africa. CB

freeholder. Technically any outright owner of land is a freeholder, but the most regular use of the word historically has been in the context of voting rights. Freeholders were those people who owned property worth 40 shillings (£2) a year and were thus entitled to vote in county elections, at least until the franchise extensions of the 19th cent. The 'freeholder' was thought of as an independent voter exercising his legal rights unconstrained by the lure of political parties or threats.

The link with landownership has also led to the term being used in conjunction with social status. Gregory King referred in his social table of 1688 to greater and lesser freeholders, and in this he was followed by later commentators such as Joseph Massie (1760) and Patrick *Colquhoun (1804). Unfortunately, King was not clear what he meant by a freeholder. In his published work he seems to have followed Thomas Wilson in regarding a freeholder as, in effect, a yeoman, but in some of his unpublished estimates he seems to have wavered between including only those who qualified on tenurial grounds, and all of those who were freeholders by virtue of having the right to vote in parliamentary elections. This latter group was rather wider than genuine landed freeholders.

The difficulty both for contemporaries and for historians has been to find a term suitable for describing landowners below the ranks of the *gentry (see also PEASANTRY; YEOMEN). Freeholder has been used because it implies an individual who owned the land he worked, but as our knowledge of the complexity of tenure increases it is apparent that while the term had an effective currency in King's day, this was not so by the 19th cent. A 'freeholder' in the 19th cent. could be anyone who owned a small parcel of land, and the link with independent farming was increasingly detached, partly because so many freeholders were renting land to create a viable holding. JVB

freemasons were originally skilled workers in stone who, in the Middle Ages, travelled from site to site and developed a set of secret signs and passwords for private identification. With the decline in cathedral-building the guilds began to accept honorary members to bolster declining membership, these being similarly required to help all members as brothers. Soon they ceased to have much resemblance to craft guilds and became prosperous social clubs, which claimed to do much charitable and philanthropic work. Freemasonry revived after the expulsion of James II, influenced by Huguenot immigrants such as Desaguliers. Lodges were better organized, with regular meetings after 1691, and admitted broader social ranks; the first grand lodge was founded in 1717. The movement prospered, with many lodges owning their own premises, and in 1802 they established themselves as a national organization, identified with monarchy and protestantism, although freemasonry is not actually a Christian institution. Schemes were developed for mutual help in times of distress and aid for dependents—one of their best-known charitable endowments is the Royal Masonic Hospital. The framework of self-help, particularly to meet privations caused by illness, sudden death, and unemployment, led other organizations such as the Royal and Ancient Order of Buffaloes and the Free Foresters to emulate them. Largely because of their secrecy, freemasons have attracted much criticism, particularly from the Roman catholic church, which believed freemasonry to be a cover for free thinking; others suspected secret political influence or accused members of promoting each other's interest by stealth. IJEK

free trade. The basic tenet of the theory of international trade is that free trade, which is the absence of any artificial restrictions on the level or composition of trade or the price at which commodities are exchanged, represents the superior form of organization in international markets. Free trade, in effect, assumes a state of perfect competition in which producers are price takers and which represents the most efficient form of production. Departure from free trade in the form of protection introduces distortions in the operation of markets which add to costs, fragment production, reduce competition, and allow excess profits.

The fact remains that there are very few historical examples of any country following a free trade policy, Victorian Britain constituting a notable exception. The repeal of the *Corn Laws in 1846 brought a shift in political perceptions, although not an immediate substantive reduction in tariffs, by removing the protection traditionally given to agriculture in favour of securing cheap imported food for the industrial areas. (See PROTECTIONISM.) This established the principle of free trade, the *Navigation Acts were repealed in 1849, and all remaining protectionist regulations disappeared in 1860. The anomaly of the British adoption of free trade, by contemporary international standards, is a reflection of the unusual economic structure of the country. In the Victorian period the British economy was heavily dependent on international trade and finance, especially the latter, as massive overseas investment generated substantial 'invisible earnings' in returns on investment, insurance premiums, and earnings from transport services. No other country, before or since, has diverted such a large share of national income to overseas investment. Furthermore, British industry depended heavily on export markets. It was thus in the interests of the British economy that international trade flourished. Substantial invisible earnings meant that Britain could sustain a trade deficit, the value of exports being less than imports, without experiencing a balance of payments deficit because invisibles added to exports exceeded imports. This free trade policy stimulated world growth by allowing many countries to run a balance of trade surplus with Britain, effectively dumping on the British market.

This structure of trade and the free trade policy could only be sustained for as long as the value of invisible earnings was maintained. In time this advantage would doubtless have been eroded, as other countries provided investment and shipping services. In fact, the First World War severely undermined the British balance of payments as overseas investments were sold to pay for the war and shipping earnings were much reduced as peacetime trade activity went into abeyance. The depressed state of the world economy in the 1920s further eroded the balance of payments as export industries found their markets diminished. The 1929–32 depression marked the end of the fixed exchange rate regime which had, effectively, been based on sterling underpinned by the balance of payments surplus. It also marked the end of free trade. In 1932 a general tariff was introduced imposing a 10 per cent import tax, but allowing preferential treatment to Commonwealth countries in return for concessions on British exports. Thus Britain adjusted to a policy of imperial preference, hoping to create a trading regime with the colonial and imperial territories, exchanging their raw materials for British goods. CHL

French, Sir John (1852–1925). Soldier. After leading a cavalry division during the second *Boer War and serving as chief of the imperial general staff, 'Johnnie' French served as the first commander of the British army in France 1914–15. He was ill suited to this role. French was a charismatic cavalryman but he had little understanding of staff work or diplomacy. His relations with his French allies were frosty and his only solution to the stalemate of trench warfare was to call for ever more shells. By May 1915 that recipe did not work, and he tried to find a scapegoat by secretly encouraging *The Times* and the *Daily Mail* to blame *Kitchener for failing to provide the army with enough shells. French himself barely survived the subsequent scandal and was dismissed in December 1915 following another failure at Loos in September–October 1915. He served 1918–21 as Lord-Lieutenant of Ireland and was given a peerage in 1922 as 1st earl of Ypres. DF

Frere, Sir Henry Bartle Edward (1815–84). Frere was born in Brecknockshire, educated at Haileybury School, and joined the *East India Company service in 1834. He was appointed to the Bombay presidency where, apart from a spell on the viceroy's Council in Calcutta (1859–62), he spent his entire Indian career, finishing as governor (1862–7). He was known as an assiduous administrator and his most notable achievement was the development of the port of Karachi. In 1867–77 he served on the India Council in London but then was posted to South Africa as governor of Cape Colony. His governorship was turbulent and unsuccessful. He faced Sir Theophilus Shepstone's attempt to annex the Transvaal; deepening conflict with the Cape prime minister J. C. Moltene; and the outbreak of a disastrous war with the *Zulus. In 1880, following the defeat of Lord Chelmsford by the Zulus at *Isandhlwana, he was recalled. DAW

friars (from *fratres*, i.e. brothers) belonged to the so-called mendicant (i.e. begging) monastic orders. The four most important were the *Franciscans, *Dominicans, *Carmelites, and *Augustinians. In addition most orders had communities of associated nuns. The friars emerged in the early 13th cent., partly as a response to the spiritual needs of a changing society, particularly increasing urbanization, and the concomitant growth of a literate laity, partly to combat heresy (itself primarily an urban phenomenon) by teaching and example. Ecclesiastical institutions (including the great majority of the foundations of the 'new' monastic orders) were primarily directed to the needs of rural society. Into the vacuum had come evangelizing wandering preachers who represented a potential threat to ecclesiastical authority. Several such groups, e.g. the Waldensians, were condemned as heretical. A few, like the Dominicans and Franciscans, were fortunate enough to gain the conditional support of Pope Innocent III in his struggle against heresy and dissent.

The friars, though frequently following variants of older monastic rules, differed from monks in fundamental respects. Adopting a life of individual and corporate poverty, they refused endowments and property, relying instead on begging; unlike 'traditional' monks they lacked 'stability' but were licensed to travel, moving from place to place at the behest of the order to preach, study, or administer; their *raison d'être* was engagement with, rather than seclusion from, the secular world. The mendicant orders, particularly the Dominicans, developed a supranational organization directed by provincial and general chapters and ultimately subject to the papacy.

As orthodox evangelists they placed much emphasis on learning both within their own communities and in the universities, and it is no coincidence that almost all of the leading intellectuals of late medieval Europe, including Thomas Aquinas and *Duns Scotus, were friars. Though the friars attracted much hostility and satirical comment in the late Middle Ages, there can be little doubt of their continuing appeal to the urban laity until the Reformation. BJG

friendly societies of working men can be traced back to the late 17th cent., but their rapid growth began about 1760. In return for a small weekly or monthly contribution paid into a common fund, they provided sickness and funeral benefits. The members met monthly in a local public house to transact business and have a convivial time. An annual feast was held, and the funerals of deceased members were usually followed by a supper. Ceremony and ritual were essential parts of the societies' life. They held open-air processions with bands, banners, and uniforms. Indoors they conducted initiation rites, using mystical symbols, grandiloquent titles, and regalia, similar to the *freemasons. Originally friendly societies were local institutions with seldom more than 100 members. But in the 1830s and 1840s these were eclipsed by the affiliated orders, with their organization into a unity (headquarters), districts, and lodges: the Oddfellows, Foresters, Druids, Ancient Britons, Antediluvian Buffaloes, and Rechabites. From an estimated 925,000 members in 1815 they grew to about 4 million in 1872—more than any social organization except the churches. By 1892 probably 80 per cent of the 7 million male industrial workers were members of friendly societies. Governments had ambivalent views about friendly societies, on the one hand encouraging and regulating them as instruments of thrift and self-help, on the other suspecting them as independent working-class institutions similar to trade unions (with which in their early days they sometimes overlapped), and regretting the 'waste' of resources on festivities. After 1875 the insurance aspect of the societies became increasingly important; and under the 1911 National Insurance Act the societies were given a new role as agents in the state scheme of national health insurance. JFCH

Friends of the People was an association of radical Whig aristocrats and parliamentarians launched in 1792 by Lord John *Russell, Charles *Grey, and their friends. It advocated moderate parliamentary reform as a means of preserving the constitution. Welcomed at first by other reform bodies, the Friends quickly became distrusted by plebeian and middle-class radicals on the one hand, and by the government and conservative Whigs on the other, and ceased to operate after 1795. Their most important contribution to the reform cause was probably their report on the state of parliamentary representation, corruption, and influence. JFCH

Frobisher, Sir Martin (*c.*1535–94). Although notable as an early English sea trader in west Africa and the eastern Mediterranean in the 1550s and later associated with *Drake in the West Indies expedition of 1585–6 and the defeat of the Spanish Armada in 1588, Frobisher is best remembered as an explorer who made three attempts in the period 1576–8 to find the North-West Passage. The first to penetrate so far, Frobisher discovered Baffin Island and sailed some way into the Hudson Strait, opening the way for later explorers. Frobisher was distracted by thinking he had found gold in the bay which bears his name in Baffin Land, but it was iron pyrites. After more encounters with the Spanish in the 1590s, Frobisher was killed at Brest. RB

Frontinus, Sextus Iulius. Governor of Britain (73/4–77). Of unknown origins, he was probably a legionary legate by 70 and must then have held the consulship before coming to Britain. *Tacitus explicitly credits him with campaigning against the *Silures of south Wales, but otherwise passes over Frontinus' governorship in a sentence. Archaeology strongly suggests that he campaigned well into northern Britain, laying the groundwork for Tacitus' hero *Agricola to build on. After leaving Britain he was consul twice more (98, 100) and *curator aquarum*, in charge of the water supply of Rome itself. His military experiences were memorialized in his book the *Stratagemata*, and his volume *De aquis* remains an invaluable work of reference on the practicalities of Roman water supply. ASEC

Fry, Elizabeth (1780–1845). Reformer. Elizabeth Fry was born into the quaker family of Gurney, bankers of Norwich, and brought up at Earlham Hall. At the age of 20 she married another quaker banker, Joseph Fry, and went on to raise a large family. In 1807 her sister Hannah married Thomas Fowell *Buxton, also of quaker ancestry, and keenly interested in prison reform. Elizabeth Fry began visiting Newgate and in 1817 founded an association to help the female prisoners. In 1818 she gave evidence to a parliamentary committee, insisting on the importance of useful work for prisoners. She became greatly concerned for the plight of women convicts transported to Australia and between 1818 and 1843 is said to have visited more than 100 convict ships. By the 1820s she had acquired an international reputation and the patronage of royalty, though her husband's bankruptcy in 1828 forced her to curtail her activities. In 1842 she was visited by Frederick William IV of Prussia while he was in England. JAC

Fuentes de Onoro, battle of, 1811. On 3 May 1811 Wellington's Anglo-Portuguese army of 37,000 men tried to halt Marshal Masséna's 47,000-strong French army advancing to relieve Almeida. Masséna's attacks on the village of Fuentes de Onoro were repulsed but on 5 May French forces manœuvred around the British flank. Craufurd's Light Division conducted a fighting retreat, buying vital time for *Wellington to redeploy. Masséna wasted his forces in four massive but unsuccessful attacks on Fuentes village, and then broke off the battle. Along with *Albuera, Fuentes de Onoro stalemated the situation along the Portuguese border. GDS

Fulford, battle of, 1066. Eight months after *Harold Godwineson's succession in January 1066, *Harold Hardrada, king of Norway, launched a major attack, in conjunction with *Tostig, Harold's brother, recently deposed as earl of Northumbria. They brought 300 ships, and sailed up the Ouse to Riccall, south of York. On 20 September, Edwin and *Morcar, Harold's brothers-in-law and earls of Mercia and Northumbria, gave battle at Fulford, but were heavily defeated. York fell to the invaders. But Harold led a forced march from London and on 25 September killed both Harold Hardrada and Tostig at *Stamford Bridge. While he was celebrating his victory, Harold received news of William of Normandy's landing in the far south. JAC

funerals are rituals which enable relatives and friends of the dead person to express their feelings and enable mourners to show their grief. The forms of such ceremonies have varied according to the beliefs, religious or other, and the status of the deceased and the wishes of the principal mourners.

Most funerals in Britain before the 19th cent. followed rituals prescribed by Christian churches and varied according to the social standing of the deceased. Before the Reformation, when Britain formed part of catholic Christendom, the funeral included a requiem mass. When a wealthy person died, the funeral ceremonies followed the terms of the will. Often money was left to pay for special clothes for mourners and for distributions of food, drink, clothing, and even money to the poor of the locality, so that the departed soul might benefit from the prayers of those who received charity. Wills often included arrangements for trustees to take income from property in order to build a *chantry chapel and to make charitable gifts such as almshouses, schools, church buildings, and even bridges to the community. Priests received a fee to celebrate a memorial mass in the chantry and further alms were given to those who attended the service.

After the Reformation many wealthy protestants continued earlier traditions by making bequests to support good works such as almshouses and schools. Some left money to buy funeral clothes for mourners, especially servants, although some puritans regarded special clothing as inappropriate.

Before and after the Reformation the families of the deceased commemorated them by erecting tombs bearing brasses or sculptures or placed elaborate gravestones in churchyards. Large numbers of such memorials survive.

State funerals for sovereigns were arranged by the earl marshal. Outstanding statesmen and military commanders were sometimes honoured by a state funeral. For less exalted people funerals were arranged according to local and family traditions. Many people turned to an undertaker, or funeral director, although these terms were not commonly used until the later 19th cent. In most towns and villages a clergyman conducted the religious service including the burial of the body. The sexton had the task of digging the grave in the churchyard. From 1667 until 1814 the law required that bodies should be buried in a woollen shroud. However, fashion and greater affluence made coffins increasingly popular. In the case of pauper deaths, the Poor Law authority paid for a simple funeral.

The accuracy of the records of those buried in the churchyard depended on the diligence of the parish clerk in keeping the parish register and the burial of those with unorthodox religious or social views often went unrecorded. The registration of deaths became a legal obligation only in 1837.

During the 19th cent. many nonconformists held funerals in their own places of worship and, rather than pay fees to be buried in the parish churchyard, established their own burial grounds. Concurrently, many growing towns with overcrowded churchyards took advantage of the Act of 1853 which permitted ratepayers to elect a board with powers to buy land for a cemetery. Land in these burial grounds was divided according to denomination and plots could be purchased for a fixed period or in perpetuity. The costs of funerals were such that poorer people often took out special insurance to meet the bills and saved so that mourners could have an appropriate 'wake'. One of the original provisions of the *'welfare state' established in the 1940s was a burial grant to help meet the cost of a funeral.

General interest in the practice of disposing of the dead by cremation, which was already established amongst groups such as gypsies who believed that the dead and their worldly goods should be burned, grew in the 19th cent. Cremation became legal in 1885 and funerals took place in crematoria which were built by local authorities. Funerals involving cremation of the deceased became more frequent, increasingly without a religious service, during the 20th cent. Since the First World War, there has also been a decline in the elaborate rituals of mourning. With the exception of state funerals, most modern funerals do not involve special clothing or arrangements. Regardless of social standing, mourning has become much more private and the expression of grief more personal. IJEK

furniture, indicator of status, reflector of domestic habits, technological development, and personal taste, has constantly been influenced by architecture and socio-economic change. Until the 14th cent. furniture was scarce, since medieval kings and landowners were peripatetic, and it was customary to transport essential items (including door-locks and window-fittings) from estate to estate. Requirements were therefore basic and minimal, with design subservient to nomadism (folding stools, trestle tables with removable tops, collapsible bed-frames, portable chests); 'fixed' furniture was often built in (stone seating, cupboards recessed within a wall's thickness). Other than chests, medieval furniture was both functional and a reflector of precedence rather than just rank. When most folk used stools and benches, the outstanding symbol of authority was the chair, occasionally upholstered, often on a dais or beneath a canopy. Any bed with seigneurial pretensions (and a probable heirloom) required a canopy too, but other beds were also closed with curtains or set in alcoves for warmth and privacy. Display mattered, but money went on rich hangings, portable and adaptable, rather than on oak fashioned by semi-skilled woodworkers with crude tools.

As a more settled way of life developed, furniture acquired fixed location and function, and specialized items began to appear (lecterns/book-storage in monasteries); emphasis on textiles yielded only slowly to carved decoration influenced by Gothic arches and linenfold panelling. Houses were still sparsely furnished, but changes in furniture construction produced lighter items less inclined to split in damp northern climates, and joiners rather than turners or carpenters became the furniture specialists. Changing social custom affected form: late 16th-cent. tables broadened as host and hostess began to sit at each end rather than on one side with backs to the wall, and the use of upholstery increased. After Flemish immigrants reintroduced board construction in the late 16th cent., producing solid pieces that permitted veneers and elaborate marquetry, joined furniture became restricted to country craftsmen; differences began to appear between urban and rural furniture in both quality and technical approach.

In the 17th cent., increasing shortage of native timbers led to imports of walnut and exotic hardwoods like ebony, letting craftsmen refine their skills and leading to a healthy reciprocal export trade of finished items. The new enthusiasm for collecting boosted showpiece cabinets, while large mirrors increased light in a room and encouraged the integration of furniture with interior decoration. As trade expanded, particularly post-Restoration, overseas influences on design abounded, such as lacquering and cane-seating from the East and *baroque flamboyance from Italy which prompted sculptured/gilded pieces, while France held position as arbiter of fashionable taste. For those unable to afford elaborately carved items or high-quality cabinetry, there was nevertheless much practical, utilitarian furniture. Though convention still dictated sparse furnishing and rigid arrangements (chairs aligned against a wall), associated discomfort prompted 18th-cent. development of private quarters in large country houses, away from deliberately impressive 'state' rooms, subsequently dust-covered; as the middle classes burgeoned, more people owned good furniture, and those in unfurnished lodgings could buy on hire purchase. The introduction c.1720 of mahogany, which gradually displaced walnut, enabled pierced openwork carving, so obsession with fashion generated new styles and the emergence of designer-craftsmen (*Chippendale, *Hepplewhite, *Sheraton); enthusiasm for chinoiserie was renewed, eventually inspiring the royal pavilion at *Brighton. Architects such as William *Kent and neo-classical Robert *Adam produced fully integrated interiors, while Horace *Walpole's neo-Gothic Strawberry Hill innovatively created an environment to express his own personality and taste.

After the Napoleonic wars the demand for expensive furniture fell, but a plethora of styles was still available—Gothic Revival for the dining-room or library, rococo for the drawing-room—though a general diffusion of furniture throughout the population shifted emphasis towards practicality and comfort, while still heavily ornamented. Technological changes led to cheap and partly mechanized furniture, but there was no real factory system in the 19th cent. Sprung upholstery, plywood, and bentwood appeared, metal was used structurally for bed-frames (eliminating bed-bugs) and cast-iron outdoor chairs, and arrangements became more informal. Early Victorian taste favoured opulence and eclecticism, so exhibition showpieces coexisted with simpler, compact items like Windsor chairs. A substantial improvement in the standard of living of ordinary people after 1850, coupled with the spread of mass production, led to the heavily furnished Victorian parlour, with carpet, rugs, fringed tablecloths and antimacassars, and decorated with stuffed birds under glass covers, Staffordshire figures, texts and homilies on the wall, bright fire-irons, and reproductions of Holman Hunt's *Light of the World* (1854), Millais's *Bubbles* (1886), or portraits of the queen. A gradual move to studied simplicity, showing strong Japanese influences, contributed to the aesthetic movement, preceding the rise of art nouveau—Charles Rennie *Mackintosh's black, elongated furniture in the early 20th cent. was both distinctive and scaled to his interiors. As formal living declined and living-spaces shrank after the First World War, the modern movement emphasized function and collaboration with industry, though metal furniture established itself more easily in offices than homes. Technical advances, putting much of the furniture industry on a fully industrial basis, were accompanied by marked stylistic uncertainty, though Scandinavian and Bauhaus influences flourished; the imposition of standardized Utility furniture (1942), to enable sufficient furniture for the bombed-out/newly married, was resented but did much to break down lingering resistance to modern design, and crossed class barriers. Post-war furniture, steered by designer imagination and machine capabilities, has seen technological experimentation (inflatable chairs, granule-filled sacks, expanded plastic foam in fitted covers) and promotion of a 'look'. With portable flat-pack, self-assembly furniture and increase in built-in storage space, the wheel has almost turned full circle. ASH

Fursa, St (d. *c.*649). Successfully establishing a monastery in Ireland, he left to escape the crowds he attracted, and, crossing to East Anglia *c.*633, built one near Yarmouth. When he withdrew again, he lived briefly as a hermit before going to Gaul. His monastery at Lagny, east of Paris, was built *c.*644. He was buried at Peronne, and a foundation developed there known as Perona Scotorum, because it attracted many Irishmen. Fursa's fame, however, rests upon his visions, which informed medieval accounts of the other world. Borne aloft by protecting angels Fursa saw the joys of the blessed, the struggles of evil spirits, the torments of sinners, and the flames destined to consume the world. Touched by a tortured soul, he bore a permanent scar as witness, and it was said that when relating his experience, he sweated profusely, despite bitter winter weather.

AM

fyrd. In theory all freemen of Anglo-Saxon England were under an obligation to serve in the fyrd (army) when called upon. In practice communications were so difficult, crises so sudden, piratical or Viking raids so mobile, and the problems of supply so acute that the national militia was rarely summoned. A major invasion, like that of William of Normandy, was an unusual thing. Local raids were dealt with normally by the fyrd in the shires concerned, led by their *ealdormen. *Alfred in the Athelney marshes called upon the assistance of 'all the men of Somerset and Wiltshire and that part of Hampshire on this side of the sea', and Byrhtnoth 'with his levies' fought against the Danes at the battle of *Maldon in 991. In 1066 Edwin and *Morcar, the local earls, tried to deal with the Norse invasion, but were defeated at *Fulford before Harold could come to their assistance. The local levies would be strengthened if possible by the king and his family, ealdormen, *thegns, and in the 11th cent. *housecarls, with whatever mercenaries were at hand. Hence it has been suggested that there was a great fyrd and a select fyrd, the latter based on the 5-hide unit, and better trained and armed. Though after the Conquest military provision was reorganized on the basis of knight service, the fyrd remained in existence and was called upon by William I and Rufus. In 1138 the local fyrd was a component in the army which defeated the Scottish invasion at the battle of the *Standard. Henry II's Assize of Arms in 1181 gave instructions for its equipment. The growing sophistication of weapons made local forces increasingly ineffective and it is perhaps fortunate that the fyrd's later manifestations, the trained bands, militia, or Home Guard, did not have to face a major invasion. SMD

Gabbard, battle of the, 1653. An important naval battle towards the end of the first *Anglo-Dutch War. *Monck and *Blake with a large fleet encountered Martin Tromp near the Gabbard shoal, east of Harwich. The fighting lasted 12 and 13 June with the Dutch losing seventeen ships. The English followed up their advantage with a blockade of the Dutch coast which did great damage. JAC

Gaelic, one of the Celtic dialects, is of the group known as the Goidelic, comprising Irish, Scottish Gaelic, and Manx. Scottish Gaelic and Manx developed through the migrations of Irish speakers in the late 4th cent. to the Isle of Man and western Scotland. Scottish Gaelic had its origins in the settlement of *Dalriada in Argyll and Bute in the early 6th cent., but the language is not likely to have differed much from Irish Gaelic until the 10th cent. From the original settlement of Dalriada the Gaels spread rapidly northwards and eastwards through Scotland cutting through native Pictish resistance. Following the establishment of the Gaelic church on *Iona by *Columba in the 6th cent., the Gaels acquired the means of spreading both their authority and their language. In the 9th cent., Gaels and Picts were finally united under a Gaelic king, probably of mixed parentage. In the 11th cent., after a period of internal strife, *Malcolm Canmore, son of *Duncan, came to the throne with the aid of English forces and began to introduce Anglo-Norman customs and language into the court of Scotland. His descendants followed this policy and over the next few centuries the Gaelic language was gradually replaced by English in state and church administration, with the Gaeltachd (Gaelic-speaking area) beginning to shrink.

We can accurately chart the decline of Gaelic only from the late 19th cent. to the present. For 1755 it has been estimated that just under a quarter of Scotland's population were Gaelic speakers—i.e. some 290,000. The 1881 census noted that those who were 'habitually' speakers of Gaelic numbered 232,000 out of a total population of 3,735,000—in high contrast to the 1971 census when Gaelic-only speakers numbered no more than 477 out of 5,228,000. Bilingual speakers were first counted in 1891 when they represented 5.2 per cent of the population, which by 1981 had declined to only 1.6 per cent. There was a greater survival rate of Gaelic in North America, especially in Nova Scotia, where it was estimated that there were in 1880 some 80,000 Gaelic speakers out of 100,000 on Cape Breton Island, though these figures have since diminished sharply.

It is not easy to trace the development of the language from the Irish, as the literature of Scotland was consistently written in a standard Early Modern Irish from the 12th to the 17th cent. The 16th-cent. *Book of the Dean of Lismore* is the most important exception. Scottish Gaelic literature made its appearance in the 17th cent., but not until 1767 was the New Testament translated into Gaelic by the *Society for Promoting Christian Knowledge. Support for and promotion of the Gaelic language began in the 19th cent., and in 1882 it became possible to study Gaelic as part of a university degree course. Today children can be educated in Gaelic at the primary level and it can be studied at secondary level. The government has allocated funds for Gaelic education and, along with An Comunn Gaidhealach (the Highland Association, founded 1891), has promoted the use of Gaelic in many areas, such as publishing, broadcasting, and in technological spheres. Since these efforts to save the language have been in place, the number of speakers has increased and the trend seems likely to continue. SMD

Gaelic Athletic Association. Founded in 1884 in Tipperary to encourage Irish sports, particularly Gaelic football and hurling, at the expense of English ones, like soccer, cricket, and tennis. Its first patron was Archbishop Croke of Cashel, and Croke Park, Dublin, became the headquarters of the association. Along with the *Gaelic League it was a powerful stimulus to nationalism, and Douglas Hyde declared that it had done more for Ireland than all the speeches of politicians. JAC

Gaelic League. Founded in Ireland in 1893 with Douglas Hyde as first president. The intention was to revive the Irish language. Ostensibly non-political, the League inevitably attracted Irish nationalists. Patrick *Pearse insisted in 1913 that membership of the League 'ought to have been a preparation for our complete living as Irish nationalists'. The work of the League ensured that Gaelic was declared the national language in 1922 and Douglas Hyde became first president of Eire in 1938. But the decline in the number of Gaelic speakers continued. JAC

Gag Acts. See SIX ACTS.

Gainsborough, Thomas (1727–88). Painter. Gainsborough was born in Sudbury (Suffolk), the youngest of nine children. He showed early promise as a landscape artist and at 13 went to London to study etching and painting. While continuing throughout his life to paint landscapes, which were his first love, he set up as a portrait painter in 1752, first in Ipswich, then, in 1760, in Bath. In 1768 Gainsborough was elected a founder member of the Royal Academy, yet his relations with both the academy and his great rival, its first president, *Reynolds, were always strained. In 1774 the artist settled in London, almost immediately becoming the preferred painter of the royal family. Royal patronage and that of artists, aristocrats and politicians ensured his lasting prosperity. One of his best-known works is the portrait of Jonathan Buttall, known as *The Blue Boy.* His full-length painting of the Hon. Mrs Graham is in the Scottish National Gallery. JC

Gaitskell, Hugh (1906–63). As Labour party leader, Gaitskell exercised a more enduring impact on British politics than might be supposed from his brief ministerial career. After Winchester and Oxford, Gaitskell spent eleven years as an academic before taking up a wartime civil service post at the Ministry of Economic Warfare. Enjoying the patronage of Hugh Dalton, he displayed intellectual penetration and transparent sincerity.

Elected to Parliament in 1945, Gaitskell was among the most impressive of Labour's new intake. Conspicuous success at the Ministry of Fuel and Power ensured rapid promotion and he became minister of state at the Treasury after the 1950 general election. The combined strain imposed by post-war reconstruction, the development of the welfare state, and the outbreak of the *Korean War made this a difficult time to assume responsibility for the national finances. Yet Gaitskell was fortunate in the timing of his ministerial ascent. Many of the leading figures in the cabinet had been continuously in office for a decade. Some were now ageing, ill, or exhausted. Gaitskell, by contrast, seemed to be the coming man of Labour politics. When illness forced the resignation of Stafford *Cripps in October 1950, the 44-year-old Gaitskell was an obvious successor as chancellor.

His only budget in 1951 proved to be controversial to a degree which its provisions scarcely justified. His decision to introduce limited Health Service charges prompted the resignations of Aneurin *Bevan, Harold *Wilson, and John Freeman. In Bevan's case thwarted ambition probably played its part. But the resignations gave notice that a right–left split would emerge once the constraints of office were removed. This happened after October 1951. But Gaitskell consolidated his power base when elected party treasurer in 1954, showing the strength of his following in the trade unions. *Attlee finally retired from the leadership in December 1955 and, to the surprise of many, Gaitskell easily defeated Bevan and Herbert *Morrison for the succession.

His first years as leader were relatively uneventful. He even succeeded in effecting a reconciliation with Bevan. Gaitskell performed effectively in Parliament over the *Suez crisis and confirmed his hold over the party. With the Conservatives badly shaken by Suez, Labour approached the election of 1959 with confidence. If for no other reason, pundits believed that the 'natural swing of the pendulum' would bring them back to power.

The result—a third successive Conservative victory and a substantially increased majority—was a considerable personal blow. With analysts wondering whether Labour was now doomed to permanent opposition, Gaitskell determined to modernize the party to accommodate the aspirations of middle-class voters. To traditionalists, however, this threatened the removal of all socialist content from the party's ideology. Such opposition led to Gaitskell's defeat in 1960 over his attempt to remove clause 4 from the party's constitution. But he restored his authority a year later, resisting the left's attempts to commit Labour to unilateral nuclear disarmament.

Gaitskell died suddenly in 1963, having done much to re-establish Labour as a credible party of government—an achievement which benefited Harold Wilson in October 1964. Whether he would have proved as adroit a party leader in power as Wilson remains an open question. His association with the right seemed to preclude anything like Wilson's capacity to paper over the fundamental divisions in the Labour movement. By the time of his death, Gaitskell could count on a band of devoted followers determined to modernize the party. Many of these had been disappointed by his decision in 1962 to oppose British membership of the Common Market. Even so, the Gaitskellites ensured that Gaitskell's influence survived his death. It is possible to see in this movement some of the origins of the *Social Democratic Party of the 1980s. Many still regard Gaitskell as the lost leader of the Labour Party. DJD

Gallipoli/Dardanelles campaign, 1915–16. In February and March 1915, following a call for help from their Russian ally, the British and French navies mounted an attack against the Turkish defences on the Gallipoli peninsula. They hoped to break through the Dardanelles and capture the Turkish capital of Constantinople. This purely naval attack failed and was therefore followed by two amphibious assaults on the peninsula in April and August 1915. But despite bitter fighting, the British, French, Australian, and New Zealand forces only secured some small beachheads and the passage through the Dardanelles remained closed. Ironically the most successful part of the operation was the evacuation of the allied troops between December 1915 and January 1916. DF

Galsworthy, John (1867–1933). One of the most prolific of Edwardian men of letters, Galsworthy went to Harrow and New College, Oxford. He began as a lawyer but took up writing after meeting Joseph *Conrad. In his plays *The Silver Box* (1906), *Strife* (1909), and *Justice* (1910) he showed how heavily the law could bear upon the poor and defenceless. The first novel of the Forsyte family appeared in 1906 as *The Man of Property,* followed by *In Chancery* (1920) and *To Let* (1921), brought together in 1922 as *The Forsyte Saga.* After that the Forsytes took over and appeared in a string of novels. Galsworthy declined a knighthood in 1918, was awarded the OM in 1929, and the Nobel prize for literature in 1932. His plays lost their topicality, but the novels remained popular and the *Forsyte Saga* had a resounding success when transferred to television in the 1970s. In part this was nostalgia for a bygone age of clubs, cabs, grand hotels, and visits to spas, but it also reflected Galsworthy's gift for creating interesting and living characters. JAC

Gambia. Formerly a British west African protectorate. Britain became interested in the Gambia in the late 16th cent., concentrating upon the river which gave its name to the territory and provided access to trade. French activity nearby meant that British influence never penetrated far from the river and when Britain declared a protectorate in 1894 it was over a long, narrow strip of territory with few trading resources. Groundnuts became the main export crop and the chief source of the country's limited wealth. Though something of a geographical anomaly, Gambia became independent in 1965. KI

game laws. From the later 14th cent. the right to hunt game, and particularly the edible game of deer, pheasants, rabbits, and partridges, was legally restricted to those members of the social order with an income of £40 a year or more. The legal position was reformed and strengthened in 1671 in an effort to try to prevent anyone from hunting hares, partridges, and moor fowl, unless they had freeholds of at least £100 a year, or long leaseholds valued at £150. Wild duck, deer, and rabbits were not included in the legislation because they had a higher legal status as private property and their seizure could therefore be regarded as common theft. Sons and heirs of esquires and others 'of higher degree' were permitted by the 1671 Act to participate, while all lords of manors 'not under the degree of an esquire' were authorized to appoint gamekeepers with the right to seize guns and goods. The 1671 legislation also excluded non-landed wealth from the ranks of sportsmen, and turned the hunting of game into the exclusive pastime of a social minority. Not surprisingly the laws also produced considerable friction in the countryside during the 18th cent. Efforts to repeal the laws began in the 1770s, but came to a successful conclusion only in 1831. However, poaching remained an offence, and as a result an undeclared state of war persisted in the countryside through the 19th cent., although the position was modified by the Ground Game Act of 1881. JVB

Gandhi, Mohandas Karamchand (1869–1948), the 'Mahatma' or Great Soul. Born in an Indian princely state, he read for the bar in London. In 1893 he took up practice in Natal but rapidly turned to politics. He unified opposition among the disparate Indian community to the passing of racially discriminatory laws and pioneered the techniques of *satyagraha* (non-violent resistance), which later were to make him famous. In 1915, he returned to India and, following the 1919 *Amritsar massacre, organized protest on a national scale. In 1920, he won the Indian National Congress over to policies rejecting the *Montagu-Chelmsford constitutional reforms and offering 'non-cooperation' to the British Raj. From the 1920s to early 1940s, he led a series of passive resistance campaigns in pursuit of *Swaraj* (self-rule), which redefined the character of Indian nationalism. As much a religious teacher and social reformer as a politician, he rejected western modernity and demanded a return to the simplicities of the self-sufficient village community. He sought tolerance between Hindus and Muslims and the eradication of caste untouchability. After his final release from gaol in 1944, he became disillusioned at the rise of Hindu–Muslim violence. He refused to celebrate independence in 1947 and rejected the Pakistan partition. In January 1948 he was assassinated by a Hindu fanatic for his pro-Muslim sympathies. DAW

Gandon, James (1742–1823). Best known for the embellishment of Georgian Dublin in the late 18th cent. Born in London of a Huguenot family, he studied architecture under Sir William *Chambers and was awarded the first prize in architecture by the new Royal Academy in 1769. His career took off when he was invited to Dublin in 1781. His first work was the grand Custom House, not completed until 1791. The east and west porticoes of the Parliament House (now the Bank of Ireland) were finished by 1785 and he designed and built Carlisle bridge (now O'Connell bridge). His Four Courts building was opened in 1795. Gandon bought an estate at Lucan near Dublin and spent much of his later years planting and improving. He is buried at Drumcondra near Dublin. JAC

gaol delivery. Henry II, in the Assizes of *Clarendon and *Northampton, instituted the system of presentment by the men of each hundred to the travelling justices of the *curia regis. The commission of gaol delivery issued to the royal justices instructed them to empty the gaols, which they would do by taking the presentments and then, before 1215, deciding whether the accused should be put to the ordeal and, if so, which ordeal. After 1215 they presided at the trial which became trial by jury. After the decline and eventually the end of the General *Eyre in the 14th cent., the commissions of *oyer and terminer and gaol delivery were the usual commissions, under which the justices of assize dealt with charges of serious crime. They were read out at the opening of the assizes until their abolition by the Courts Act 1971. MM

garden cities. Planned estates had been built by Robert *Owen and Titus *Salt in the earlier 19th cent., and by the Cadbury family at Bournville in the 1880s. Garden cities were conceived by Ebenezer *Howard. Impressed by a visit to the 'garden city' of Chicago and influenced by Edward Bellamy's *Looking Backward* (1888), a futuristic look at Boston in the late 20th cent., Howard published *Tomorrow: A Peaceful Path to Real Reform* in 1898 (republished as *Garden Cities of Tomorrow*). Combining the ideologies of 19th-cent. social reformers and philanthropic industrialists, Howard sought to eradicate what he saw as the real cause of poverty, private landownership in the capitalist system. His plan was for limited-size cities built on municipally owned low-cost agricultural land. The centre of each city would be a garden, ringed by civil and cultural amenities, city hall, museum, library, and theatre. Shops and other facilities would be built under glass, with residential and industrial areas on the outer edges of the city. Howard envisaged clusters of garden cities, linked by railways, and powered by new low-pollution electricity. In 1899 the Garden City Association was inaugurated. In 1941 it was renamed the Town and Country Planning Association, having adopted in 1919 the definition: 'a Garden City is a "New" town designed for healthy living and industry; of a size that makes possible a full measure of social life . . . the land being in public ownership or held in trust for the community.' Prototype garden cities were built at Letchworth from 1903 and Welwyn from 1919, greatly influencing the development of garden suburbs and the new towns built after the Second World War. JC

Gardiner, Stephen (*c.*1497–1555). Bishop. One of the most influential courtier-prelates of the early Tudor age, Gardiner sought to reconcile political advancement with principled defence of the rights of the church. He studied and taught at Cambridge until taken up by *Wolsey as a secretary in 1524. Wolsey secured for him the mastership of Trinity Hall in 1525 and several diplomatic missions in 1527–9. On Wolsey's fall Gardiner became principal secretary to Henry VIII, and received the wealthy bishopric of Winchester in 1531. During the establishment of the royal supremacy in 1532–5 Gardiner opposed encroachments on church immunities until they became law, but accepted them once enacted. He acted on Henry VIII's behalf in his divorce suit and wrote *De vera obedientia* ('On True Obedience') in 1535 in defence of the king's actions. On returning from an embassy in France in 1535–8, Gardiner led resistance to Thomas *Cromwell's surreptitiously Lutheran changes in English religion. He promoted the Act of *Six Articles in 1539, and worked for Cromwell's fall the following year. From 1542 to 1547 he was one of Henry's leading ministers, inspiring some conservative religious measures and helping to administer the king's final wars. On Edward VI's accession Gardiner was outspoken in opposition to Protector *Somerset's Reformation: from summer 1548 he was imprisoned in the Tower of London, losing his bishopric and other titles in February 1551. On the accession of Mary I he was at once restored to all his positions and made lord chancellor in August 1553. His last years were clouded by bitter political strife with the Hispanophile minister William, Lord *Paget, who wrecked Gardiner's first attempt to restore papal authority in the Parliament of spring 1554. Gardiner nevertheless married Mary and Philip, welcomed Cardinal Pole to England, and played a minor role in the persecution of leading protestants until his death on 12 November 1555. EC

Garrick, David (1717–79). Actor and manager. Reared in Lichfield, he accompanied *Johnson to London (1737), but soon abandoned law studies for the wine trade; the appeal of acting and overnight success as Richard III (1741) led to further change, since his naturalistic style, expressive eyes, and versatility refreshed audiences weary of attitudinizing. Having purchased a share of Drury Lane's lease, he set about reforming plays, players, and audiences, with modifications to theatre layout, stage design, and eventual introduction of concealed lighting. Despite fluctuating fortunes and accusations of vanity and meanness, he raised his theatre from penury to prosperity. A devotion to Shakespeare induced textual reclamation from the Restoration adaptations, not always creditably, and his cherished Shakespeare Jubilee at Stratford-upon-Avon (1769) was washed out. His own farces and burlesques have faded into obscurity, but this contributor to the 'gaiety of nations' lies buried in Westminster abbey. ASH

Garter, Order of the. This, the oldest and highest order, was instituted in 1348 by Edward III in imitation of King *Arthur and the great deeds of *chivalry. Membership was limited to the sovereign, prince of Wales, and 24 knights. George III's fecundity created a problem since he had seven sons, and in 1786 a statute allowed them supernumerary status. After 1660, very few commoners were honoured, though exceptions were made for Sir Robert *Walpole, Lord *North, and Sir Edward *Grey. The headquarters of the order is at Windsor, where St George's chapel was built by Edward IV. The motto—'honi soit qui mal y pense' (Shame unto those who think evil thoughts)—is said to derive from Edward restoring the countess of Salisbury's garter to her. The significant decorations are the Star, a garter to be worn below the left knee, and a diagonal blue ribbon. JAC

Gascoigne, William (*c.*1350–1419). Chief justice. A member of the Inner Temple, Gascoigne was in practice as an attorney by 1374, a justice of the peace in his native Yorkshire from 1382, and a regular judge in the eastern circuit from 1390. Now a serjeant at law, he was also employed by *John of Gaunt and his son Henry who, when king (as Henry IV), appointed Gascoigne chief justice in 1400. He was probably the judge who secured the conviction of nine friars for treason in 1402. He was believed to have refused to participate in the trial of Archbishop *Scrope. There is no contemporary evidence to this effect, nor for the 16th-cent. legend that an unnamed chief justice imprisoned Prince Henry (later Henry V) for contempt. Gascoigne's age was doubtless the reason for Henry V's decision in 1413 to instal a new chief justice. He remained a JP for the West Riding until his death. His effigy in Harewood church portrays him in judicial splendour. RLS

Gascony. French region lying between the river Garonne and the Pyrenees. In the 11th cent. it was acquired by the dukes of Aquitaine; the 1152 marriage of *Eleanor of Aquitaine to Henry II meant that it passed into the hands of the kings of England. As a result of military defeats suffered in John's reign, from the early 13th cent. onwards the duchy of Aquitaine generally consisted of little but Gascony. Except in the 1290s and 1330s the English spent little time and money on Gascony—Edward I was the last reigning king to visit it—but Gascon appreciation of the value of the English market for the Bordeaux wine trade, and their sense that Paris represented a greater threat to their traditional independence and way of life than did Westminster, meant that the duchy long remained loyal to the English crown. However, the total disarray of Henry VI's government following the sudden collapse of English Normandy in 1450 allowed the triumphant Charles VI of France to walk into Gascony virtually unopposed. An expeditionary force under Talbot (*Shrewsbury) briefly took advantage of Gascon resentment of French rule, but in 1453 his defeat and death at *Castillon marked the end of English Gascony. JG

gas industry. Before the commercial development in the early 19th cent., many observations had been made on the illuminating power of natural gas occurring in coal seams, the first recorded being that of the Revd John Clayton of Wigan, whose discovery that an inflammable gas evolved when coal was heated was reported to the *Royal Society in 1739. Later, George Dixon, a coal-master in Co. Durham, experimented *c.*1760 with an apparatus designed to produce gas from coal.

William *Murdock, an engineer associated with James *Watt, made a significant breakthrough in large-scale production with two important innovations, which allowed coal gas to pass directly into pipes rather than escape, and, by passing the gas through water, washed out suspended matter, such as tar particles, as well as water-soluble components like ammonia. While his research earned him the Rumford medal of the Royal Society, he did not patent his invention, and thus made little direct profit from the expansion of gas lighting in later years. However, his firm, Boulton & Watt, provided a notable display of gas lighting for the national celebrations which accompanied the peace of Paris in 1814.

Meantime others had been less tardy in refining gas production and exploiting the potential of gas lighting. Samuel Clegg, a student of John *Dalton's and an associate of Murdock, developed horizontal retorts, the lime purification process, the hydraulic main, the gasometer or gasholder, and other standard equipment found in 19th-cent. gasworks. Clegg installed gas-making plant and lighting in factories and mills and his son wrote a treatise on the manufacture and distribution of coal gas (1841). A German, F. A. Winsor, gave popular demonstrations of gas lighting in the Lyceum theatre, London, in 1804, and his company provided lighting for Pall Mall in 1807. His 'Gas Light and Coke Company' was formed 1810–12 and within a few years gas lighting was a feature of many London streets.

Despite problems of storing large volumes of gas, its distribution through pipes at high pressure, and the danger of explosions, gas manufacture and lighting spread rapidly to other towns and cities during the 1820s and 1830s. Lamplighters, or 'leeries', immortalized in a poem by Robert Louis *Stevenson, became as familiar figures on the streets of Victorian Britain as constables or 'Peelers'.

The incandescent gas mantle, developed by the German von Welsbach in 1885, greatly increased illuminating power and for a time helped fight off competition from electric lighting. Although electric lighting and power began to make greater inroads into the market after the First World War, distribution problems prior to the development of the national grid meant that gas remained important for lighting and heating, and was only beginning to be seriously challenged in the inter-war period, and in some remoter areas much later.

Following successful exploration and discovery in the late 1960s, natural gas from the North Sea began to be tapped commercially and distribution was rapidly extended nationally, for both industrial and domestic purposes. The last town gasworks using the traditional technology closed in the 1970s. ID

gavelkind was the practice of partible or equal inheritance, as opposed to *primogeniture. It was predominant in Kent but found elsewhere, particularly in Wales and Ireland. The result was the creation of small estates with considerable political independence. It was extinguished in 1922 by 12 & 13 Geo. V c. 16. See also BOROUGH ENGLISH. JAC

Gaveston, Piers (1284–1312). The most notorious favourite of Edward II was the son of a Gascon knight who served in Edward I's household. Whether his relationship with Edward II was sexual is not clear, but it seems likely that it was. It was certainly formed early, in adolescence. Piers was exiled by Edward I in the course of a quarrel with his son; once Edward II came to the throne he showered his waspish 'brother' with many favours, starting with no less than the earldom of Cornwall. Foolish rather than malign, Piers irritated the English nobility by his rudeness, giving them coarse nicknames; he also annoyed them with his skill in tournaments. He controlled royal patronage to an unacceptable degree. He was forced into exile by the king's opponents in 1309, and again in 1311; he returned to surrender at Scarborough in Yorkshire, and died at the hands of his opponents at Blacklow Hill in Warwickshire in 1312. MCP

Gay, John (1685–1732). One of the leading members of the remarkable group of authors in the early 18th cent., Gay was on close terms with *Pope, *Swift, and Arbuthnot. Of Devon dissenting stock, he moved to London, soon abandoned the silk trade, and established himself as a minor poet. Though he had a succession of patrons, he chafed under the system: 'they wonder at each other', he wrote to Swift in 1727, 'for not providing for me, and I wonder at them all.' His enormous success, *The *Beggar's Opera*, was produced at Lincoln's Inn Fields by John Rich in 1728 and was said to have 'made Gay rich and Rich gay'. He followed in 1729 with a sequel, *Polly*, which, though banned from the stage by the Lord Chamberlain, sold well. He wrote the libretto for *Handel's opera *Acis and Galatea*, including the aria 'O ruddier than the cherry'. Gay suffered poor health from asthma and died early. *Johnson wrote of him in the *Lives of the Poets* that he was 'the general favourite of the whole association of wits, but they regarded him as a playfellow rather than a partner, and treated him with more fondness than respect'. JAC

genealogy, the study of ancestry and family descent, is an indispensable handmaiden of history. Its development reflects a gradual process of democratization as interest moved down the social scale. In post-Roman Britain, it was important for monarchs to claim impressive credentials, however unlikely. *Bede insisted that *Hengist and Horsa were descended from Woden: *Nennius traced Britain back to Aeneas through Brutus. Neither claim was closely argued. In the Middle Ages, genealogy was related to heraldry and of concern largely to the monarchy and nobility, to whom the tracing of the succession, estates, and titles was of great importance. As the status of the gentry improved, their own interest in genealogy kindled. Richard III established the *College of Arms in 1484 and from the 15th cent. to 1688 the heralds conducted visitations to confirm or deny claims. The 17th cent. produced in *Camden, *Dugdale, Ashmole, and Cotton distinguished genealogists and antiquarians. Authors of county histories devoted much space to pedigrees of families, since this would induce the gentry to subscribe to their volumes. Status, rank, and patronage opportunities had rarely been of greater importance and even remote family connections could be of real use. Genealogical investigation was also a powerful motive behind the foundation of many 19th-cent. local history societies, with their libraries and card indexes. The Society of Genealogists was founded in 1911. In the later 20th cent. there was a remarkable growth of interest in tracing *family history among ordinary people, using record offices and reference libraries, and assisted by many books and manuals on the subject. As society grew increasingly incoherent and urban life became ever more impersonal, the desire to relate to the past and rediscover one's ancestry grew stronger. JAC

General Assembly of the Church of Scotland. Instituted in 1560 and meeting annually from the 18th cent., but with significant gaps before that, its constitution, statutorily confirmed in 1921, declares it to be the supreme court of a national church. Its national standing is symbolized by the attendance of the lord high commissioner (or the monarch), its freedom of action by that commissioner's place in a gallery outside assembly bounds. The 6 ministers and 35 others of 1560 have become 1,250 commissioners (elders and ministers in equal numbers since 1929) responsible, under an annually elected moderator, for their church's judicial, legislative, and administrative functions. CB

General Council of Estates [S]. The General Council was a meeting of the three estates with smaller membership than that of a parliament and with no judicial powers. It was often an emergency session when circumstances did not permit summoning a full parliament, which required 40 days' notice. Consequently the General Council was frequently not much more than the Privy Council, augmented by commissioners who were available. Later the term *Convention of Estates was more commonly used. JAC

general elections have changed over the years. Until the 17th cent., there was no statutory requirement about their frequency, and the *Triennial Act of 1694, which laid down that a general election must be held every three years at most, was the first effective legal provision. In 1716 the *Septennial Act lengthened the period to seven years, an interval which lasted until the *Parliament Act of 1911 reduced it to five years. These periods were and are maxima and in practice the prime minister usually calls an election before the five years have expired. His right to decide when an election shall be held normally gives a considerable advantage to the party in power.

Many seats were uncontested right up until the end of the 19th cent. Even in 1900, 165 candidates in Great Britain were returned unopposed, and a further 69 in Ireland. Today it is normal for every seat to be contested. At the 1992 election, Conservative and Labour candidates stood in every constituency in Great Britain, and Liberal Democrats in all but two.

In the 17th and 18th cents. general elections scarcely merited the term 'general'. They were essentially struggles between magnates and other interests for local paramountcy, and national factors played little part. Indeed, as late as 1830 it was not clear whether the Whigs or the Tories had won the general election, since many MPs sat loose to party. Elections in the 18th cent. did not choose governments, which, with heavy powers of patronage, could normally expect to carry any election in the country as a whole. The decline of patronage made this increasingly hard and also created a vacuum which was filled by organized parties. Nowadays, general elections are held to choose a government and the choice of MPs is usually incidental to that decision.

Today there are two general election campaigns—one at national level, run by the headquarters of the various parties, and one at local level, run by the constituency associations. Each constituency now returns one member. At the national level the parties publish their manifestos setting out the policies they will implement if they win the election. The larger parties are alloted time on television and radio for their election broadcasts, and locally, candidates and their activist supporters canvass, distribute party literature, and hold (usually poorly attended) public meetings. The campaign proper lasts for three weeks and election expenditure at constituency level is rigorously controlled by law. The ballot is secret. Voting is not, as in some countries, compulsory and the turn-out is usually about 75 per cent.

Britain uses the first past the post formula and the candidate receiving the most votes is elected, regardless of whether or not he has a majority of votes cast. The absence of any element of proportional representation makes it difficult for smaller parties with evenly spread support to breach the two-party domination. Nationally, what is decisive is the number of members elected for each party, not the total number of votes won. Normally one party will win an overall majority in the Commons and the monarch will ask the leader of that party (unless he is already prime minister) to form a government. HB

General Strike, 1926. The strike arose from the problems of the coal industry. Miners were locked out on 30 April; the TUC negotiated with the government, but Baldwin's administration precipitated the strike by breaking off negotiations when the printers at the *Daily Mail* refused to print a leading article. The strike began at midnight on 3 May, with workers in printing, transport, iron and steel, gas, electricity, and building being called out first. A second group of unions, including engineers and shipbuilders, joined the strike on 11 May; about 2,500,000 workers in total were involved. The strike failed because of government preparations which enabled essential supplies and services to be delivered; many, hostile to the unions, were prepared to assist in breaking the strike; the government won the propaganda battle. After nine days the strike was called off, although the miners remained out for many months in the winter of 1926–7. JB

general warrants. Eighteenth-cent. secretaries of state claimed a discretionary power in cases of seditious libel to issue general warrants for the arrest of persons unnamed. In 1763 Lord *Halifax issued one for the apprehension of all connected with printing or publishing No. 45 of the **North Briton*. Forty-nine persons were arrested, including *Wilkes, author of the offending piece. But in December 1763 Chief Justice Pratt (*Camden) in Common Pleas declared general warrants illegal, and he repeated the finding in *Entinck* v. *Carrington* in 1765. The House of Commons confirmed the ruling in 1766, and in 1769 Wilkes won £4,000 damages from Halifax for wrongful arrest. JAC

Gentleman's Magazine. Issued monthly, the *Gentleman's Magazine* was the brainchild of Edward Cave and achieved a spectacular success. The first issue, printed at St John's Gate, Clerkenwell, came out in 1731 and included reviews, essays, songs, births, deaths, and marriages. At an early stage Cave discovered that there was a demand for parliamentary debates and he devoted an increasing share of the magazine to them. From 1741 to 1743 they were written up by Samuel *Johnson. By the late 1730s Cave was claiming to sell 10,000 copies. His success spawned imitations, especially the *London Magazine* and the *Scots Magazine*. In modified form the magazine lasted until 1907 and Cave's premises in Clerkenwell survive. JAC

gentry. Technically the gentry consists of four separately defined groups, socially inferior only to the ranks of the peerage and—within a European definition—part of the nobility, although not entitled to the privileges of the nobility. The senior rank is that of *baronet, a position founded in 1611 by James I (so that he could sell the titles) giving the possessor the hereditary right to be addressed as Sir. The second rank is that of *knight, originally a military honour, but increasingly employed in a secular manner as a reward for service to the crown. Theoretically the number of baronets and knights can be established at different periods, but this is not the case with the third and fourth categories of gentry, esquires and gentlemen. The term 'esquire' originally had connotations with the battlefield. In the 14th cent. it was an honour which could be conferred by the crown, and by the 16th cent. it had a specific Office of Arms definition. Certain offices, including that of *justice of the peace, automatically carried the appellation. Heraldic visitations, which began in 1530, were designed to oblige anyone claiming gentry status to prove their right. Increasingly through the 16th and 17th cents. the heralds found it difficult, if not impossible, to enforce their authority, and numbers proliferated, both of esquires and particularly of the fourth gentry rank, that of gentleman. 'Gentleman' emerged as a separate title in connection with the statute of Additions of 1413 and, like esquire, was originally closely defined.

The inability of the heralds to limit the use of 'esquire' and 'gentleman', particularly after the Restoration when visitations gradually declined, made counting numbers problematic. In 1688 Gregory King estimated the number of gentlemen variously at figures ranging from 12,000 to 39,000, and when in a parliamentary debate during the 1690s one MP suggested a round figure of 100,000 gentlemen, another promptly doubled the estimate. Over time the issue was complicated by the idea of the gentleman, a social construct which could incorporate all members of the peerage and gentry.

The concept of the gentlemanly way of life was current in the 16th cent.—even the king, it was argued, could not make a gentleman—and became increasingly important by the 19th cent. A gentleman was a man who held a social position not purely dependent on the suffix 'gent.', but rather implying a style of living, usually without manual labour, and it also had connotations for the defence of honour. In turn this led to a resurgence of chivalric ideas in the course of the 19th cent.

In terms of wealth, contemporary social commentators such as King and Joseph Massie placed the gentry immediately below the peerage, while Daniel *Defoe argued that £100 a year was the minimum income required for a man to be a gentleman. Certainly this was the qualification figure required for JPs and *land tax commissioners, suggesting that it was widely recognized to be the bottom end of the group. However, such were the vicissitudes of English fortunes that the link with wealth was far more complex than King and Defoe appeared to recognize. Since there were no automatic channels of admission to the peerage, some very wealthy men remained socially as gentry simply because they had no title. This anomaly is clearest by 1883 when John Bateman's survey of landownership revealed that 186 out of 331 landowners with 10,000 acres or more were gentry in this sense. This was the case despite a considerable expansion of the peerage from the late 18th cent. onwards.

Most informed estimates suggest that the gentry historically owned about 50 per cent of the landed wealth of the United Kingdom from the 17th cent. onwards. This position was maintained by the queue of businessmen, merchants, bankers, and industrialists to invest part of their fortune in landed estate. Few of these men attempted to climb to the top of the landownership tree, and many were happy with a villa and a few acres close by a town. Despite some controversy in recent years it is apparent that their numbers were considerable and helped to maintain the overall landholdings of the gentry until land began to lose its social caché in the agricultural depression of the late 19th cent.

The link with landownership, although clearly established from an early date, has to be treated with some care since contemporaries were by no means clear in their understanding. Increasingly a man was a gentleman depending on his style of life, his manners and bearing, and without reference to his ownership (or not) of landed acres. This has given rise among historians to the concept of the town or urban gentry, people who lived in towns but in a genteel manner, enjoying financial independence and a reasonable income but lacking the landed acreage or the mansion associated with the country gentry. Many of these were members of *professions—lawyers, doctors, and clergy—rising in status and in numbers during the 18th cent. As a result, the gentry as a social group has traditionally lacked any cohesion, although today the term seems to apply colloquially to country dwellers with a substantial holding of land, as it did for Gregory King.

Quite separate from the gentry as a social group were a number of honours recognized and invented as carrying gentry titles. Men knighted for service to the state were dubbed 'knight bachelor', to distinguish them from the military service knighthoods. Originally the Order of the *Bath was the most significant of these, exclusively limited to 35 members until the early 19th cent.

From 1814 the number of orders, and the membership of the orders, proliferated. In 1818 the Order of *St Michael and St George was founded for natives of the Ionian Islands and Malta, and this began a wave of new orders, many of them connected with India. In 1843 there were 451 knights bachelor and 787 members of the orders, but these numbers swelled rapidly, and by 1915 there were over 4,000 members of orders. With the decline of the empire in the 20th cent. the position changed, but the number of orders—many of them of antiquated origin in Britain's role as an imperial nation—can still be read twice a year in the New Year and Queen's Birthday honours' lists. JVB

Beckett, J. V., *The Aristocracy in England, 1660–1914* (Oxford, 1986); Heal, F., *The Gentry in England and Wales, 1500–1700* (Basingstoke, 1994); Mingay, G. E., *The Gentry: The Rise and Fall of a Ruling Class* (1976).

Geoffrey (*c.*1153–1212). Archbishop of York. A reluctant archbishop who preferred dogs and horses to books and priests. An illegitimate son of Henry II, his father secured his election as bishop of Lincoln in 1173; he had no wish to be a priest and in 1182 resigned rather than be consecrated. Henry then appointed him chancellor and Geoffrey served him faithfully, as he had during the rebellion of 1173–4, even when the king's other sons turned against him. 'This is my true son, the others are the bastards', the dying king is alleged to have said. Gossip suggested that Geoffrey hoped for the throne, so Richard I forced the reluctant canons of York to elect him archbishop in 1189 and later made him promise not to enter England while the king was on crusade. In 1191 he landed at Dover, taking sanctuary to avoid arrest, but was dragged from the altar. This enabled him to go to York in the heroic guise of a persecuted churchman. His archiepiscopate was filled with quarrels with his cathedral clergy and, from 1207, with King John. He spent his remaining years in exile in Normandy. JG

Geoffrey of Brittany (1158–86). The trouble-making third son of Henry II and Eleanor of Aquitaine. He became duke of Brittany (initially in name only) in 1166 when his father invaded Brittany and forced Duke Conan to resign and agree to Geoffrey's betrothal to his daughter Constance. The wedding took place in 1181 and she was pregnant with *Arthur when he died. In 1185 he issued an assize introducing primogeniture into Brittany. From 1173 onwards, when he joined his mother's revolt against his father, he was in the thick of every Plantagenet family quarrel. He was at Paris plotting with King Philip Augustus of France when he was trampled to death in a tournament accident. Contemporary historians disliked him. According to *Gerald of Wales, he was 'overflowing with words, smooth as oil, a hypocrite in everything, capable by his syrupy eloquence of corrupting two kingdoms with his tongue'. JG

Geoffrey de Mandeville (d. 1144). An English baron whose stormy career caused controversy both in his own day and since. As keeper, like his father and grandfather, of the Tower of London and as possessor of large estates in Essex and East Anglia, he played a central role in the turbulent politics of Stephen's reign. Indeed his allegedly unscrupulous changes of allegiance during the civil war between Stephen and Matilda led to him being represented as 'the great champion of anarchy'. Despite being created earl of Essex by the king in 1140, he joined Matilda in 1141 and was made hereditary sheriff of Essex. Like many others, swiftly disenchanted by her rule, by the late summer of that year he was back in Stephen's camp. He was given a prominent role in the king's counsels, but serious doubts about his loyalty remained. In October 1143 he was arrested on charges of treason and freed only after he had handed over his castles including the Tower. In revenge he seized the abbeys of Ely and Ramsey and, using the fenland as a base, went on the rampage. Until mortally wounded while laying siege to Burwell, he did much of the damage which created the notion of Stephen's reign as 'the anarchy'. JG

Geoffrey of Monmouth (*c.*1100–55). Probably of Breton origin, Geoffrey was raised in Wales. As a young man, he went to Oxford and is thought to have been a canon of St George's church. His consecration as bishop of St Asaph, *c.*1152, may have been no more than a titular appointment. His principal work, earning him fame, was the *History of the Kings of Britain* (*c.*1136). Written in chronicle form, it proved very popular, particularly in Wales, for the portrayal of a long and glorious Welsh past, and for centuries was widely believed. Ultimately recognized as a work of fiction based on old legends, it was nevertheless a great literary work of its time. It also launched the romantic *Arthurian legend in European literature. A separate *Life of Merlin*, based on Welsh traditions of the magician, appeared *c.*1148–50. AM

Geoffrey 'Plantagenet' (1113–51), count of Anjou (1129–51) and duke of Normandy (1144–51), became the husband of Henry I's designated heiress, the Empress *Matilda, on 17 June 1128, in a political marriage which was intended to neutralize Anjou's participation in the wars which troubled Henry's rule in *Normandy. His prospects in England may never have been defined by Henry I and his political ambitions seem always to have been restricted to the traditional aim of the counts of Anjou, the conquest of Normandy. He never visited England during the civil war between his wife and King Stephen, which began in 1135, but his persistent attacks on the duchy between 1135 and 1142 and his eventual conquest of it in 1144 had a huge impact on Britain's history because they laid the foundations from which their son Henry II built the *Angevin empire. DB

George I (1660–1727), king of Great Britain and Ireland (1714–27) and elector of Hanover. George was the eldest son of Ernest Augustus, elector of Hanover (1692–8), and of *Sophia, granddaughter of James I of England, who herself became heir to the British throne by the 1701 Act of *Settlement. She died on 8 June 1714, and George succeeded peacefully to the throne on 1 August upon the death of Queen Anne.

Having established links with the Whig Party before his succession, largely because of their mutual opposition to the Tory peace with France at *Utrecht in 1713, George favoured a Whig administration, though he did employ a handful of senior Tories until the Jacobite Rebellion in 1715 led to the proscription of that party. The Whigs won the general election of 1715, and established their supremacy for the next four and a half decades. Though unpopular, George's position was never seriously threatened either by the rebellion of 1715 or by the Jacobite plots of 1719 and 1722. In fact these episodes served only to strengthen the Hanoverian succession.

George appears to have been diligent in politics, especially in his chosen fields of foreign affairs, diplomacy (he helped to negotiate the *Quadruple Alliance of 1718), and the army, over which he insisted on keeping control. His court was private and he much preferred the company of his German ministers to his British advisers, as well as that of the duchess of Kendal and the countess of Darlington. These two were long thought to have been his mistresses, and indeed Kendal was from 1691, but she may also have later been his morganatic wife (he had divorced his wife *Sophia Dorothea in 1694 for adultery and imprisoned her for life). Darlington, however, was his half-sister.

Contrary to long-established views, George did attend cabinet meetings throughout his reign. The language he commonly used with his ministers was French but he arrived with a smattering of English and knew sufficient to write and converse in it by the end of his reign. However, he rarely attended Parliament and never debates in the House of Lords 'incognito' as had some of his predecessors, such as Charles II and Anne, and this may have been because his English was limited.

Relations between George and his son, the prince of Wales (later George II), were often strained, and in 1717 a violent quarrel erupted. The prince and his wife were expelled from the court (their children were kept by the king) and set up a rival one in *Leicester House. This quarrel coincided with the Whig schism in which *Walpole and *Townshend left the ministry of *Sunderland and *Stanhope. In April 1720 the royal quarrel was patched up as a cover for the reconciliation of the ministry with the schismatic Whigs.

George frequently returned to Hanover in the summer months, leaving the prince of Wales in England as regent. The king's attachment to his electorate and its presumed prominent influence on English foreign policy (as well as the interference of the German ministers at the English court) created a good deal of friction. George, however, was close to some of his English ministers, particularly Stanhope, who looked after foreign policy, and Sunderland. It was the king's attachment to the latter which kept him in power after the bursting of the *South Sea bubble in 1720 (the most serious crisis of the reign) and Stanhope's untimely death in 1721. Sunderland had arranged for fraudulent South Sea shares to be given to the king, and had overseen the distribution of *douceurs* in Parliament to help things along. George and his chief minister had to stick together in the ensuing crisis, and managed to weather the storm. Sunderland's unexpected death in April 1722 forced George to accept Walpole (whose acumen in salvaging the financial disaster had in effect saved the dynasty) and Townshend as his chief ministers, though *Carteret (a protégé of Sunderland) was to remain a serious contender for power for a further two years.

George's reign ended with domestic affairs entering a period of quiet, while abroad Britain was recognized as the major arbiter of the balance of power. He died of a stroke on 20 June 1727 at Osnabrück. CJ

Hatton, R., *George I: Elector and King* (1978).

George II (1683–1760), king of Great Britain and Ireland (1727–60) and elector of Hanover. Despite a reign of 33 years, George II remains a somewhat shadowy figure. He is best remembered for being the last British monarch to lead troops into battle (1743), which is appropriate, given his lifelong love of all things military. However, George was much more than a soldier, and made sensible use of the still considerable political powers accorded to him by the 18th-cent. constitution.

The king could choose his own ministers, but only those with Commons approval were able to do his business. Walpole had served George I for many years and George II soon formed an equally successful relationship with him. Walpole was masterful at holding the favour of both monarch and Parliament, sharing George's distrust of the Tories. He persuaded the king to keep Britain out of the War of Polish Succession and survived the turmoil of the *Excise crisis. Though Walpole fell in 1742, the Whig oligarchy remained and the king gravitated towards *Carteret, the German-speaking former diplomat, but his rivals, the *Pelham brothers (assisted by William *Pitt), rendered him unacceptable to the Commons and he had to resign in November 1744. The Pelhams reinforced their pre-eminence in February 1746 by threatening to resign unless the king took them into his full confidence. He was furious, but was unable to form a viable alternative government. Gradually George came to appreciate the prudence of Henry Pelham, 1st lord of the Treasury until his death in 1754. Thereafter, a period of great instability set in; Pelham's brother, the duke of Newcastle, hitherto foreign affairs minister, became 1st lord, but the Commons was restless, with Pitt and Henry *Fox ridiculing the government (of which they were both members). The king detested Pitt and had long refused to admit him to the higher echelons of government, but there seemed no other option. War and expediency brought Newcastle and Pitt together in 1757, to form one of the greatest ministries in British history. George never came to like Pitt, but they worked effectively together; even in old age and faced with Pitt's dynamic genius, the king remained at the heart of government and had, usually, the final word.

George II was the absolute ruler of a medium-sized German state, Hanover, as well as being the British sovereign. George's affection for and (understandable) desire to visit and protect Hanover was a frequent cause for concern among his British subjects and a significant factor in the development of foreign policy. It gave the king a German-centred view of foreign affairs, shared by Newcastle, but which came into conflict with the colonial vision of Pitt. In addition, his unfettered power to rule in Hanover contrasted with the limitations placed upon the monarch in Britain, which George could find frustrating.

George II's reputation for parsimony was not restricted to his private finances. He was an emotional miser too (he had been separated from his mother as a boy), having few, if any, close friends. This tendency extended to government. He admired Pelham's budget cuts (except when they affected the military) and was notoriously reluctant to 'dilute' the peerage with new creations, despite their political value. The one emotion he displayed liberally was a prodigiously bad temper. He was blunt, rude, and lacked social graces to a surprising degree. He had good health for most of his life, apart from severe piles, and into old age retained full command of his faculties. George had little interest in cultural or intellectual matters (with the exception of his patronage of *Handel). His wife Queen *Caroline, however, was renowned for her intellectual curiosity and quick wit. George loved her deeply, but resented any suggestion that she (and her alleged favourite, Walpole) dictated policy to him. His love did not prevent George from taking a number of mistresses before as well as after her death in 1737. Thereafter, Lady Yarmouth (a German) became the chief object of his not inconsiderable sexual appetite.

The king got along with his daughters fairly well, but towards his sons the difference in attitude was dramatic. His beloved younger son was the duke of *Cumberland; he was very like his father in his devotion to the military with his finest hours coming during the War of *Austrian Succession, including accompanying George at *Dettingen (1743). His ruthless pursuit of the Jacobites after Culloden also met with paternal approval. Cumberland's errors of diplomatic judgement and consequent resignation in 1757 cast a shadow over George's otherwise triumphant final years. The king's pride in Cumberland contrasts with the loathing he (and Queen Caroline) had for their heir, *Frederick, prince of Wales. That George I (whom George II also hated) had liked Frederick may have been the origin of the king's animosity, but it reached such intensity as to be beyond rational explanation. Frederick was often foolish, but he had received little encouragement to show responsibility; despite George II's own contacts with the opposition as prince of Wales, the king was enraged by Frederick's similar behaviour. Frederick's early death in 1751 provided the opportunity for reconciliation between the king and the princess of Wales and his grandson and heir. However, as the future George III grew older, a breach developed here too, so that when the new king acceded to the throne, he had already formulated theories of government notably different from his grandfather's.

During his reign George II demonstrated that his love of the military was not purely ceremonial. His courage in battle was obvious as early as 1708, when as Prince George Augustus of Hanover he fought as a British ally in the War of *Spanish Succession. His courage was required again during the War of Austrian Succession, not just on the battlefield at Dettingen, but in the face of an invasion by Charles Edward *Stuart in 1745. George was certain of victory (unlike some other political figures), even when the Jacobites reached Derby; the minute levels of support the invaders received in England vindicated his instincts and the Jacobites were soon utterly vanquished. The *Seven Years War brought momentous British successes in the colonies and in Europe. George supervised military operations and appointments carefully, though preferring elderly commanders to the more enterprising younger officers advocated by Pitt.

A flamboyant, charismatic, and forceful king may not have been the ideal way for Britain to preserve her balanced constitution in the mid-18th cent. But though George II had his flaws, he was essentially sensible and moderate, and his reign can be judged a success. AIL

Chevenix-Trench, C., *George II* (1973); Davies, G., *A King in Toils* (1938); Owen, J. B., 'George II Reconsidered', in Whiteman, A., Bromley, J. S., and Dickson, P. G. M. (eds.), *Statesmen, Scholars and Merchants* (Oxford, 1973).

George III (1738–1820), king of Great Britain and Ireland (1760–1820), and elector of Hanover. Popular misconceptions about George III are principally of three varieties: first, that he attempted systematically to subvert the traditional constitution; second, that he was personally responsible for the loss of the American colonies; third, that he became mad. None of these assertions has withstood detailed historical analysis. Consequently, the reputation of George III has been revised perhaps to a greater degree than any other British monarch.

He was born in England, the first of the Hanoverian monarchs to be a native of his own kingdom. Upon the death of his father Frederick in 1751, George succeeded as prince of Wales and heir to the throne. The young prince was not on good terms with his grandfather, George II. He came to believe that the old king was the impotent tool of a corrupt clique of politicians. A key influence on the formation of this naïve viewpoint was Lord *Bute, tutor to the prince from 1755. Bute puffed up his protégé with unrealistic expectations of reforming the political system by royal initiative and assumed the character of essential partner in this putative reign of virtue. When George succeeded to the throne in 1760, Bute rapidly rose from courtier to cabinet minister and, in May 1762, became prime minister. Yet, Bute proved a disappointment and resigned within a year. Ministries followed each other in swift succession: there were four different premiers between the fall of Bute and the appointment of *North in 1770. Many contemporaries attributed these fluctuations to the influence, behind the scenes, of Bute. A more balanced assessment is that exaggerated suspicions of him poisoned the political atmosphere, though George III himself rapidly outgrew his youthful dependence. The accusation that the king aimed at increasing the royal prerogative or deliberately connived at secret influence will not bear scrutiny. His view of the constitution accorded with the contemporary interpretation that the monarch possessed the undoubted right to choose his own ministers. One practical constraint, however, was the necessity of managing the House of Commons, the key to both public confidence and national finance.

The advent of the North ministry, led by an able parliamentarian possessing the confidence of the king, inaugurated a lengthy period of political stability. The king, whose actions had never been as innovative as opponents claimed, behaved with impeccable constitutional propriety throughout North's twelve-year premiership. Ministers, not the crown, were responsible for policy. This was particularly the case with regard to America. Colonial propaganda prior to the outbreak of war recognized the realities of political authority in Britain, focusing on the ministerial and parliamentary dimension to the burgeoning conflict. Yet, once war had broken out, it became necessary for the rebels to describe matters differently and the *Declaration of Independence of 1776 enshrined the king as villain of the piece. This was a necessary fiction (justifying recourse to foreign aid) but fundamentally untrue.

George III took a keen interest in the military struggle and stubbornly refused to accept that America was lost, even after the disastrous defeat at *Yorktown in 1781. Bowing to Parliament's refusal to continue the war, the king reluctantly parted with North. The king tried to maintain some freedom of manœuvre by playing upon the rivalry between *Shelburne and *Rockingham, the leading opposition politicians who now formed a ministry. When Rockingham died unexpectedly in July 1782, George III appointed Shelburne as his successor. But Shelburne was unable to secure sufficient support in the Commons and was forced to resign following a concerted attack by the followers of Charles *Fox and Lord North. The king viewed North's actions as personal betrayal, and, in the context of the unprecedented and recent humiliation of the war, remained implacably hostile to the Fox–North coalition. He withheld confidence from his new ministers, refused requests for peerages, and created difficulties over financial provisions for the prince of Wales. The king's obvious dissatisfaction persuaded the younger *Pitt to negotiate secretly for the overthrow of the coalition, which was accomplished during the *India Bill crisis of 1783. There was no constitutional justification for the king's interference in the House of Lords, nor was any public defence attempted. Pitt, at the head of a minority ministry, adroitly distanced himself from recent events and held out until it was safe to call a general election. Although the means had been underhand, the king's choice of Pitt proved excellent. Political stability was re-established and no serious threat arose until the king fell ill in the autumn of 1788. The ensuing *Regency crisis was precipitated by the apparent madness of the king. According to modern diagnosis he was, almost certainly, suffering from acute intermittent porphyria, a hereditary metabolic disorder. This condition, unknown to 18th-cent. medical science, gave rise to rival attempts at a cure, which shared ignorance and brutality in common. The king, in accordance with the pathogeny of the disease, recovered despite the treatment he suffered.

Pitt, having survived in office, continued to dominate parliamentary politics, but found it necessary, in the wake of the French Revolution, to strengthen the ministry by incorporating *Portland and the conservative Whigs. Though an English revolution did not materialize, the king benefited from a groundswell of enthusiasm for monarchy, becoming a personal symbol of the durability of the traditional political system. But the danger of revolution was not negligible, nor was George III universally popular. Indeed, disaffection and rebellion in Ireland convinced ministers of the necessity of parliamentary union. Having achieved this objective, Pitt resigned in 1801 over George III's refusal to countenance the removal of residual penalties against catholics. The king's views were never in doubt, nor had they changed substantially in the previous decade. He considered his coronation oath, with its pledge to uphold the protestant religion, to be absolutely binding and resisted what he regarded as sophistical arguments to the contrary. The fall of Pitt led to a period of factional instability, akin to the early years of the reign, but further complicated by fears for the king's mental state. Some politicians vowed never again to raise the catholic question; and a moderate proposal for relief, by the *Talents ministry in 1807, precipitated a ministerial crisis, during which the king reaffirmed his intransigence.

In 1810 the king suffered a final decline into mental derangement, exacerbated by increasing deafness and blindness. The following year a regency was established under his eldest son, the future George IV. As a hard-working monarch, devoted husband, and sincere Christian, George III compares favourably with his dissolute successor. Although undeniably stubborn, he was prepared to admit some, though not all, of his errors. Three themes from his reign became benchmarks for opposition politicians: his involvement with Bute, his underhand conduct during the India Bill crisis, and his rejection of catholic emancipation. George III was not blameless on any of these counts, but contemporary myth should not be mistaken for historical assessment. DW

Ayling, S., *George the Third* (1972); Brooke, J., *King George III* (1972).

George IV (1762–1830), king of the United Kingdom of Great Britain and Ireland (1820–30), and king of Hanover. Brought up under strict discipline by his parents George III and Queen Charlotte, he was a high-spirited boy and reacted against the regime they imposed in what Horace Walpole called 'the palace of piety'. He and his brother Frederick frequently escaped in their teens to sample the pleasures of the town and their pranks became notorious. In 1780 his father had to buy back the indiscreet letters he had written to the actress Mary 'Perdita' Robinson. Always susceptible to feminine charms, George then fell in love with Maria Fitzherbert, a widow six years his senior, and when she refused to be his mistress forced her to promise marriage by faking suicide. They married secretly in 1785 without his father's consent, so that the marriage was illegal under the *Royal Marriage Act, and as she was a Roman catholic it would have prevented his succession to the throne. It was nevertheless valid in the eyes of the catholic and Anglican churches.

George was fascinated by the arts and had a lifelong mania for building and decorating his residences, at enormous cost. In 1787 he applied to Parliament for additional funds to pay his debts, but to achieve success he had to authorize his friend Charles James *Fox to deny in the House of Commons that he was married. His subsequent disclosure of the truth to Charles *Grey resulted in a breach between him and his Whig political allies, with whom he had been associated since his coming of age in 1783. They made up the quarrel in 1788 when his father suffered his first attack of mental illness, the Whigs proposing that George should be made regent with full use of all the royal prerogatives, hoping that he would change the government in their favour. *Pitt defeated their scheme by proposing statutory limitations on the regent's powers, but the king recovered before the regency came into effect.

When the French Revolutionary War began George appealed to his father for a military command, but was refused. By this time he was again deeply in debt owing to the cost of building and furnishing Carlton House, his London residence, and the pavilion at *Brighton where he disported himself in extravagant style with his cronies and Mrs Fitzherbert. In return for financial help the king insisted that he should marry a protestant princess, to secure the royal succession. The choice fell upon *Caroline of Brunswick-Wolfenbüttel, who was brought over to be his bride in 1795. George, however, took an instant dislike to her lack of cleanliness, coarse language, and flighty manner. He had to be supported, in a state of intoxication, during the ceremony and spent the wedding night asleep on the floor. They separated permanently soon afterwards, though he had managed to father a child, Princess *Charlotte, born nine months after the wedding. She was to provide a further source of contention between her parents over her upbringing, education, and marriage shortly before her premature death in 1817.

During the Napoleonic War of 1803–15 George was again unsuccessful in obtaining a military command and had to content himself with designing elaborate uniforms for himself and his forces. After Fox's death in 1806 he severed his political connection with the Whigs and in 1810, when his father's illness became permanent and he was appointed prince regent, he confirmed the existing Tory ministers in office. During the later war and post-war years he was very unpopular with his subjects, who contrasted his lavish lifestyle and expenditure with the distressed state of the country, and was caricatured and lampooned in the public prints, often in indecent and obscene circumstances. When he became king in 1820 his attempt to divorce his wife by a parliamentary Bill of Pains and Penalties on the grounds of her alleged immoralities aroused a public outcry against him and in favour of Caroline as an unjustly persecuted woman in view of his own infidelities. His popularity sank to its nadir during this period but Caroline's death in 1821 and recovery from the economic recession marked a turning-point. George's love of pageantry, given full rein in the magnificent coronation which he himself designed in 1821, helped to boost his popularity and radical agitation died down.

George IV attempted to exert the royal authority over his ministers and their policies, but he lacked political skill and persistence and he could always be outmanœuvred or outfaced by determined ministers such as *Liverpool and *Wellington. He was compelled to accept the repeal of religious discrimination against dissenters and catholics in 1828–9 and his reign witnessed a further decline in the strength of the 'influence of the crown', which was eroded by financial and political reform.

George IV was a man of some dignity, was affectionate and generous towards his friends, and raised the royal patronage of the arts to greater heights than had been seen since the reign of Charles I. He could be selfish, but though *The Times* remarked, in a famous obituary, that 'there never was an individual less regretted by his fellow-creatures', Wellington more justly declared that he possessed 'a medley of opposite qualities with a great preponderance of good'. EAS

Hibbert, C., *George IV* (1972–3); Richardson, J., *George IV: A Portrait* (1966).

George V (1865–1936), king of the United Kingdom of Great Britain and Ireland and emperor of India (1910–36). The second son of Edward, prince of Wales (later Edward VII), George was not born to be king. His private education was followed by a naval career of great promise, but the death, at the beginning of 1892, of his elder brother, the duke of *Clarence, meant that he was now in direct line of succession after his father. The following year he married Princess Mary of Teck (formerly the fiancée of the duke of Clarence); the couple were, and remained, devoted to each other; there were six children of the marriage. George's naval experience left him with a deep respect for habits of routine and obedience. Mary was a stern disciplinarian. Both Mary and George had what would now be called 'Victorian' moral values, especially in relation to the sanctity of marriage—a sharp contrast to those of George's father and of his son, the future Edward VIII.

When George's father succeeded as king on Victoria's death (22 January 1901), George undertook a strenuous round of international engagements as heir to the throne, visiting Australasia, South Africa, Canada, and Europe. But Edward VII's death in 1910 presented him, as king, with the first of a series of constitutional and political problems, all of which he handled with the utmost propriety.

The refusal of the House of Lords to approve the Liberal government's budget of 1909 had led to a general election (28 January 1910) at which the government had been returned with a reduced but still effective majority. George gave an undertaking that, should it become necessary (which it did not), he would agree to the creation of a large enough number of peers to ensure the budget's passage into law. In December 1910 he authorized a second general election that year in order to test opinion on reform of the powers of the House of Lords; the passage of the *Parliament Act of 1911, destroying the Lords' power of veto over money bills, and severely restricting their ability to delay other bills, owed something to George's own common sense and grasp of *realpolitik*. This crisis was soon followed by another, over the government's intention to grant *Home Rule to Ireland, and the determination of the Ulster protestants, supported by the Conservative opposition, to take up arms unless Ulster remained part of the United Kingdom. The king did not take sides in this quarrel, but he did use his influence with the Conservative leadership in order to moderate the tone of public utterances, and on 21 July 1914 invited representatives of all sides to a round-table discussion at Buckingham palace.

During the Great War, George and Mary shouldered an unenviable burden of morale-raising visits and public appearances; mindful of sensitivities over the German connections of the royal family, he ordered that German names be replaced by English ones: the house of Windsor was inaugurated. In the years 1918–24 the political topography of Great Britain underwent a fundamental change, the Liberal Party being replaced by Labour as the only credible alternative to the Conservatives. George had been deeply shocked by the overthrow of tsarism in Russia, and by the advent there of a Bolshevik government preaching world revolution. The demise of the old ruling dynasties, both in Russia and in Germany and Austria, and the rise to prominence of proletarian movements, might have made a British king suspicious of the Labour Party. In fact, when the first, minority, Labour government of Ramsay *MacDonald took office in January 1924, the king did much to ensure a smooth transition, observing punctiliously the constitutional proprieties, and emerging as a truly national leader, neutral in politics. In 1929, on the occasion of the formation of the second Labour government, he played a similar role. During the crisis of August 1931, which resulted in MacDonald's 'betrayal' of that government and agreement to head a national, all-party administration, the king's role was more controversial. He urged MacDonald to form such an administration, and played a part in persuading the Liberal and Conservative leaders (Herbert *Samuel and Stanley *Baldwin) to agree to serve in it, under MacDonald's leadership. But whether the downfall of the Labour government was a case of murder or simply death from natural causes, the king's hands were clean: in a crisis unprecedented since the advent of constitutional monarchy, he played a moderating and conciliating role; subsequently, as a personal gesture in a period of severe economic recession, he gave up £50,000 from the civil list—i.e. the budget of the royal household.

George was a shy, reserved man, not blessed with an overabundance of intellect, who none the less did his duty in a selfless manner, displaying in the process much common sense. Only once, in a reign lived during an era of international turmoil and great social change, did he ever lose his nerve, during the *General Strike of 1926, when he favoured the use of the military, and was packed off to Sandringham by Prime Minister *Baldwin.

George went out of his way to bring the monarchy closer to the common people, and he succeeded. In 1924 he made the first of a series of radio broadcasts heard throughout the British empire; in 1932 he inaugurated the annual Christmas Day broadcasts by the sovereign. He attended rugby matches at Twickenham, cricket at Lord's, tennis at Wimbledon; but he also presented the trophy at the football Cup Final at Wembley, thereby giving a royal imprimatur to the sport most closely identified with the working man. The fact that Britain escaped revolution in the immediate aftermath of the Great War was due to a mosaic of factors, not least the existence of a rudimentary welfare state and of a parliamentary socialist movement. But some of the credit must go to George V, who gave to the monarchy a quiet, statesmanlike dignity, and in the process made it genuinely national and genuinely popular. GA

Gore, J. F., *King George V* (1941); Nicolson, H. G., *King George the Fifth* (1952); Rose, K., *King George V* (1983); Somervell, D. C., *The Reign of King George V* (1936).

George VI (1895–1952), king of the United Kingdom of Great Britain and Ireland (1936–52), and emperor of India. George was born at Sandringham on 14 December, the second son of the future George V and Queen Mary. It was the same day as the death of Prince *Albert in 1861 and consequently he was christened Albert Frederick Arthur George, to be known as Bertie to the family. As a child Prince Albert lacked close emotional contact with his parents and was often overshadowed by his elder brother, Edward. His subsequent insecurity meant he was intensely shy and developed a stammer.

In 1909–13 he studied at the Naval College at Osborne and then Dartmouth. He was not renowned for intellectual capability but worked hard. Prince Albert then spent time at sea on the battleship *Collingwood* but his active career was not a success. He suffered from chronic seasickness and spent long periods on sick leave for gastric troubles, culminating in an operation on a duodenal ulcer on 29 November 1917. However he was always eager to return to duty, both for his own sake and his father's, and served in the battle of Jutland on 31 May 1916.

In 1919 he spent a year at Trinity College, Cambridge, where he studied history, economics, and civics, and in 1920 he was granted the title of duke of York. By now the duke was occupied with official duties. In 1919 he became president of the Industrial Welfare Society touring industrial areas, showing genuine concern for problems and developing the 'human touch'. He also founded the Duke of York's camp in 1921 to promote better relations between boys of different class backgrounds.

It was at this time he fell in love with Lady Elizabeth Bowes-Lyon, young, spirited, and attractive. She finally agreed to marry him in 1923 and the wedding took place on 26 April at Westminster abbey. She was to be the stabilizing influence in his life and provide him with the love and support he had often been without. They had two daughters: Elizabeth Alexandra Mary born on 21 April 1926 and Margaret Rose born on 21 August 1930. They were devoted parents and formed a close family unit.

The duke and duchess toured the empire, visiting Ireland and East Africa in 1924, and New Zealand and Australia in 1925, opening the new parliament building in Canberra on 9 May. His stammer was still evident and made it difficult to make public speeches. In 1925 he was put in touch with

Lionel Rogue, a speech therapist, who over the years helped him become a more assured speaker.

On 20 January 1936 George V died and by the end of the year Edward VIII had abdicated. The duke dreaded the prospect of becoming king, a role he was unprepared for, but reluctantly resigned himself to the task. At the coronation on 12 May 1937 he was crowned George VI in an effort to restore a sense of continuity and stability.

George VI supported *Chamberlain in his policy of appeasement before 1939 but with the outbreak of war was determined to retain the integrity of both nation and empire. Although initially sceptical of *Churchill, they soon developed a close working partnership and the king remained well informed on most matters, including D-Day and the atomic bomb.

The king and queen refused to leave London during the Blitz, although Buckingham palace was bombed nine times in all. Thus the royal family shared a sense of common danger with the nation. They toured devastated areas, met civilian workers, and the king devised the *George Cross medal for civilian gallantry. He also shared the grief of loss when his youngest brother George, duke of Kent, was killed in action. He visited troops abroad: in North Africa (1943), in Italy (1944), and on the Normandy beaches just ten days after D-Day. The actions of the king and queen during wartime were a great boost to national morale.

The post-war period was stressful for the king who fretted constantly. With Labour victory in 1945, he was worried at the scope and speed of the new legislative programme. Yet despite being a traditionalist, the king was not averse to social reform when necessary. He watched with great regret the dissolution of the Indian empire. In 1947 he toured South Africa in an attempt to strengthen ties to the Commonwealth, the future of which he was anxious to secure.

The strains of war and the post-war period took their toll on his health. On 12 March 1949 he had an operation to remove a thrombosis on his right leg and on 23 September 1951 he had the whole of his left lung removed. Both operations were a success but he fought a losing battle to regain his health, and died in his sleep at Sandringham on 6 February 1952.

He enjoyed hunting and gardening, was an accomplished sportsman, and a devoted family man. Like his father, he was scrupulous in his attention to detail and formality. George VI was a man of simple tastes and understanding, but displayed a passionate devotion to duty that earned him both the respect and affection of his people. RAS

Judd, D., *George VI* (1982); Wheeler-Bennett, J., *King George VI: His Life and Reign* (1958).

George, St. Little is known for certain about St George, patron saint of England and of several other countries. He is said to have been martyred at Lydda in Palestine in the 4th cent. and began to attract reverence in the 6th cent. Ælfric included him in his homilies and saints' lives *c.*1000. The story of the dragon appears as late as the 12th cent. and is presumably a reminiscence of Perseus and Theseus. His adoption as patron saint of England is post-Conquest though a church in Doncaster was dedicated to him in 1061. Crusaders may have brought back accounts of the respect paid him in the Middle East and the red cross may have come from the same source. The Synod of Oxford in 1222 made St George's Day, 23 April, a lesser holy day. The cult probably gathered pace after the foundation of the Order of the *Garter in 1348, with the emphasis on chivalry and St George as patron. *Caxton printed the 13th-cent. *Golden Legend* in 1483 and in 1515 Alexander Barclay published a translation of Spagnuoli's *Georgius*. The saint was still holding his own in late Victorian England, when *Elgar wrote *The Banner of St George* for Victoria's *Diamond Jubilee in 1897. He is often confused with George of Cappadocia, a 4th-cent. Aryan bishop of Alexandria. JAC

George of Denmark, Prince (1653–1708), consort of Queen Anne. The younger son of Frederick III of Denmark, George was affable but dull. 'I have tried him drunk,' Charles II once remarked, 'and I have tried him sober and there is nothing in him.' Trained in science and warfare, he saw action against the Swedes in the late 1670s. His marriage to Anne (his second cousin once removed) in 1683 sealed a diplomatic concord between their respective kingdoms against the Dutch. A highly devout Lutheran protestant, he was a most devoted husband. He deserted his father-in-law James II at the 1688 revolution, but was never on good terms with William III. At his wife's accession in 1702 he was made titular head of the Royal Navy as lord high admiral. Though dogged by ill-health, he was the queen's mainstay throughout her many personal and political tribulations. AAH

George Cross and Medal. The award was instituted by George VI in September 1940 for acts of outstanding heroism, particularly among the civilian population dealing with the *Blitz—firemen, police, ambulance men, and civil defence personnel. The cross, which ranks second only to the *Victoria Cross, replaced the Empire Gallantry Medal. The silver cross has a representation of St George slaying a dragon, with a dark blue ribbon. The George Medal has a red ribbon with blue stripes. JAC

Gerald of Wales (1146–1223). Gerald was born at Manorbier in Pembrokeshire with a Norman father and a Welsh mother—consequently, he reflected, he was not accepted by either side. After education at Gloucester and at Paris, a promising career in the church (he was archdeacon of Brecon by 1175) ran into difficulties and he consoled himself with his writing. He failed to become bishop of St Davids (a see which an uncle had held) because the strong support given to him by Welsh princes may have alarmed the English. His best-known works were his accounts of Ireland and Wales—*Topography of Ireland* (1188), *Conquest of Ireland* (1189), *Journey through Wales* (1191), and *Description of Wales* (1194). 'Incurably egotistic' is one comment, but he took trouble with his writing and was a keen observer. He was said to be tall, handsome, with bushy eyebrows and vast energy. JAC

Geraldine League is the name given to the political alliance formed in 1538 in Ireland to seek the reinstatement of Gerald *Fitzgerald as earl of Kildare, resist the protestant

Reformation, and secure the recall of the Lord Deputy *Grey. The instigator was Manus O'Donnell, chief of Tyrconnel, who was joined by Con *O'Neill, James FitzJohn earl of Desmond, O'Connor of Sligo, and O'Brien of Thomond. In August 1539 they raided the Pale but were defeated by Grey at Bellahoe. Grey's successor, Sir Anthony *St Leger, worked out a deal with the league which amounted to an ambitious new policy. The Irish chiefs were to recognize Henry VIII as king of Ireland, to surrender their lands and have them regranted, to be accorded full constitutional rights, and to be granted peerages as appropriate. It would have been an important step towards the Anglicization of Ireland, introducing English law and language. St Leger's scheme made some headway and he even succeeded in raising some troops for service abroad. But the death of Henry in 1547 and the decision of Edward VI's council to pursue a vigorous protestant policy produced fresh mistrust. JAC

Gerard, John (1564–1637). Jesuit. Gerard was from a Lancashire catholic gentry family and was sent to Douai. He was ordained priest at Rome in 1586 and joined the Jesuits in 1588. Captured on a mission to England, he made a daring escape from the Tower in 1597. He was on the fringes of the Gunpowder plot, aware that something was afoot, but ignorant of the details. He managed to make his escape in 1606 and spent the rest of his life in catholic teaching institutions on the continent. His autobiography throws much light on English catholicism under James I. JAC

Germain, Lord George (1716–85), formerly Sackville. After a promising early career, both as politician and army officer, Sackville was court-martialled for disobeying orders at *Minden in 1759. Stripped of his rank and forbidden the court, he did not rehabilitate himself until the 1760s, eventually becoming American secretary in 1775. It was expected that Germain (as he was now called) would invigorate the war effort against the American colonies, but difficulties of slow communication militated against effective direction from Britain. Germain, moreover, never achieved complete control, since fellow cabinet members jealously guarded their own authority. A flawed strategist, he must share responsibility for the defeat at *Saratoga (1777), having authorized two separate offensives, mistakenly hoping that each might succeed independently. He continued to hope, despite contrary evidence, that each fresh campaign would tap latent American loyalism, and was predisposed to favour the more ambitious *Cornwallis over Commander-in-Chief *Clinton. Germain's attitude exacerbated defects in the command structure during the prelude to *Yorktown (1781). Despite this disastrous defeat, he opposed abandoning the war and resigned in 1782. He was created Viscount Sackville on his retirement. DW

Germanus of Auxerre, St. Soldier, bishop, and church emissary who visited Britain in AD 429 to counter heresy. In the early 5th cent. the teachings of *Pelagius were proving popular in Britain. In 429 the Roman ecclesiastical authorities in Gaul dispatched Germanus to Britain to combat Pelagianism by preaching the true faith—Divine Grace—in British churches and the countryside. Although lacking in specific details, Constantius of Lyons's account of Germanus's visit is significant because of the incidental light it sheds on early 'post-Roman' Britain; Germanus apparently encountered organized town life, suggesting that Britain remained strongly 'Romanized' in character. Before becoming a bishop Germanus had been a soldier, and he defeated *Picts and *Saxons in a battle where he gave his troops the battle-cry 'Alleluia'. Germanus may have visited Britain for a second time in 435–7, and he probably died in 437. ES

Germany, relations with. The German empire as established in 1871 was at first seen by Britain as a satiated power. Such views changed rapidly from 1905, when an attempt to break the *Entente with France excited fears that Germany was bidding for hegemony in Europe. By 1909 the bulk of the British navy was concentrated in home waters to meet the challenge from the new German fleet. Not surprisingly Britain speedily entered the war against Germany (4 August 1914), and soon became committed to the total defeat of German militarism. This did not preclude discussion of Germany's future role in the balance of power, and although victory was purchased at a bitter price, emphasis on revenge was soon qualified by doubts concerning the wisdom of what was widely considered to be the excessively punitive peace of *Versailles.

Many saw Germany as a necessary economic partner in the 1920s, but efforts at conciliation had made little progress when Hitler came to power in 1933. Although the possibility of revisionist policies under the Nazis was recognized, and small increases in Britain's armed forces followed, the *National Government regarded war as a last resort. Controversy over efforts to conciliate Hitler reached serious proportions only from the Sudeten crisis in the autumn of 1938. Neville *Chamberlain himself until late in the day was persuaded that he could negotiate a satisfactory settlement with Hitler. Only when Germany persisted with the attack on Poland did Britain declare war on 3 September 1939.

Hitler, it seems, had some hopes of peace with Britain after the fall of France in June 1940, but soon turned to other objectives when no speedy victory proved possible. Britain, while not an immediate major threat to Germany, was well placed to help with the later provision of western aid to the USSR, just as it was the indispensable base for American operations against Germany. Victory left the British burdened with an expensive occupation zone in Germany, and unsure of what sort of Germany they wanted in the future. Fear of the USSR, however, soon persuaded them that there would be no stability in Europe if western Germany were to slip into the Soviet orbit. The British supported the USA in the Berlin Airlift (1948–9), and assisted in the creation of the German Federal Republic. Despite initial reservations, they also played a major part in devising a satisfactory structure within which West Germany could be rearmed, and included in *NATO in 1955. From the formation of the *European Economic Community Britain was often troubled by Franco-German co-operation, and Mrs Thatcher was not alone in her reservations when the two

Germanies were reunited at the end of the Cold War in 1990. CJB

Ghana. Formerly the Gold Coast, British west African colony and protectorate. British traders became interested in the Gold Coast in the second half of the 17th cent., attracted by the trade in gold and, increasingly, in slaves for the Americas. As the campaign against the slave trade strengthened in the 19th cent., British policy towards the Gold Coast vacillated until, in the face of competition from other European countries, it was decided to establish a crown colony in 1874. Friction between the ethnic groups within the colony and those in the interior induced Britain to declare a protectorate over the hinterland in 1901. The development of cocoa as an export crop brought prosperity to the country and made possible the expansion of European education there. The Gold Coast then became the leader in the nationalist movement in the British African dependencies and gained its independence, as Ghana, in 1957. KI

Ghent, treaty of, 1815. Peace talks to end the *War of 1812 between Britain and the USA began at Ghent (modern Belgium) in August 1814. A treaty was signed on 24 December and ratified the following year. It resolved none of the proclaimed causes of the war. Neutral rights, an American grievance, ceased to be controversial as war had ended in Europe, while disputed boundaries were referred to arbitration. Because of slow communications, a major battle was fought after the conclusion of the treaty, at New Orleans in January 1815. GM

gibbeting was the exhibiting of the corpses of executed criminals in public. It was normally reserved for criminals convicted of unusually heinous crimes, or others of whom the authorities wished to make examples. Their bodies were hung either in a much frequented location on the borders of a town or at the place where the crime was committed. They were left to rot, suspended from a pole with their body supported by iron hoops. The first definite case of gibbeting involved a Scot executed in London in 1306, the last a murderer named James Cook in 1832. JAS

Gibbon, Edward (1737–94). Historian. After fourteen months at Magdalen College, Oxford, which the laziness of the dons made 'the most idle and unprofitable of my whole life', Gibbon converted to catholicism and had to leave. This was fortunate since it probably prevented him from becoming an obscure academic. His enraged father sent him to Lausanne (Switzerland), under a Calvinist tutor, where he learned French, reverted to protestantism, and determined to write some great work. He spent 1760–2 as a captain of the Hampshire militia—a strange inhabitant of the officers' mess. In 1773 he began serious work on *Decline and Fall of the Roman Empire*, the inspiration of which was a visit to Rome in 1764, described in his *Memoirs*. The following year he entered Parliament, was given minor office by Lord North, but never spoke: 'the great speakers', he wrote memorably, 'fill me with despair, the bad ones with terror'. The first volume came out in 1776 and established him at once: the work was completed in 1788. Gibbon was fortunate that his study touched on contemporary anxieties—the enervating effect of luxury, the fragility of civilization. But the intrinsic merits of his book, its scholarship, silky style, and philosophic detachment, made it an enduring classic. Gibbon spent his last ten years back in Lausanne. Unmarried, very short, plump early in life, fat later, overdressed, vain, and watchful, Gibbon was easy to make fun of, and though he belonged to Johnson's Club, he was not a clubbable man. His 'cheerful temper' and urbane, balanced prose masked, but did not hide, strong and disturbing feelings. JAC

Gibbons, Grinling (1648–1721). Woodcarver and sculptor. Born in Rotterdam and probably trained in Holland, he was in England by 1668. Writing in 1671, the diarist John *Evelyn refers to introducing Gibbons, 'whom I had lately found in an Obscure place', to Charles II and Christopher *Wren. Gibbons's decoration appears in Windsor castle and Hampton Court and also in St Paul's cathedral on the choir-stalls and organ screen. One of the most skilful woodcarvers ever, his garlands of fruit, flowers, small animals, and cherubs led Horace Walpole to say, 'There is no instance of a man before Gibbons who gave to wood the loose and airy lightness of flowers.' He was less at home with bronze and marble. The bronze of James II outside the National Gallery in London, attributed to Gibbons and for which he was paid, was probably the work of his partner Artus Quellin. Other examples of woodcarving are in the Victoria and Albert Museum and many country houses throughout Britain. JC

Gibbons, Orlando (1583–1625). Jacobean composer and keyboard player who contributed to most musical genres of the time. A chorister at King's College, Cambridge, in 1596, by 1605 Gibbons was a gentleman of the Chapel Royal, later serving as joint organist. He was also organist at Westminster abbey from 1623. Gibbons's madrigals favoured the serious approach of the moralistic 'Silver Swan': 'More geese than swans now live, more fools than wise.' His Anglican church music includes full anthems such as the exuberant 'Hosanna to the Son of David', but his most significant contribution was to the verse anthem. These works, including the popular 'This is the Record of John', alternate sections for soloist/s and organ or instrumental consort with choral passages. Gibbons's instrumental fantasias display the same skilful counterpoint, and in his day he was chiefly famous as an organist and virginalist, being described by one listener as 'the best finger of that age'. ECr

Gibbs, James (1682–1754). As an architect Gibbs was unusual for his time, not because he was Scottish-born or even because he was Roman catholic, but because he spent six years in Rome and studied under Carlo Fontana (1703–9). Although Gibbs shared with the *Palladians an admiration for Palladio, his thought was unblushingly *baroque. He was predictably patronized by Tory magnates, but his own Toryism did not preclude him from a governorship of St Bartholomew's hospital (1723), for which he planned a rebuild; in 1728 the Whig duke of *Argyll accepted Gibbs's dedication of his *Book of Architecture*. Appointed as surveyor for the '50 new churches' legislated for London in 1711, Gibbs built St Mary-le-Strand (1714), but he lost the 'political' surveyorship in 1715. It appears to have been through his sheer professional competence that he was appointed architect for the unbaroque St Martin-in-the-Fields (1722–6). Probably his best-known secular building is Oxford's Radcliffe library, the 'Camera', completed 1748; at Cambridge, he built the Senate House and Gibbs's Building at King's. DDA

Gibraltar. At the southern tip of Spain, with an area of $2\frac{1}{2}$ square miles and 1,270 feet at its highest point, 'The Rock' commands the western entrance to the Mediterranean. The name derives from Djebel Tarik (Mountain of Tarik) after Tarik ibn Ziyad, the general leading the Moorish invasion of Spain in 711. Gibraltar was subject to numerous sieges as Christian rulers attempted to eject the Moors. Finally, in 1462 it was recaptured and became the evacuation point for Jews and Moors expelled from Spain. Queen Isabella of Spain in the 16th cent. laid it as a solemn charge in her will that her successors retain and hold the city. For almost 200 years few people, apart from privateers, showed much interest in Gibraltar until in 1704, during the War of the Spanish Succession, it was captured by an Anglo-Dutch fleet under Sir George *Rooke and ceded to Britain by the treaty of Utrecht (1713). It has remained in British hands ever since. During the Great Siege of 1779–83, the garrison under General Elliott (Lord *Heathfield) resisted all attempts to bombard or starve them out. During the Second World War, fighting in north Africa and Italy gave Gibraltar a crucial role. Spain resumed pressure after the war ended but in a referendum of 1967 the colony voted to retain its connection with Britain. Spain closed the border for sixteen years from 1969 and the Rock remains a bone of contention. JC

Gibson, Edmund (1669–1748). Bishop of London, scholar and prelate. Educated at Oxford, Gibson produced several translations of major historical works, including *Camden's *Britannia*, before being ordained in 1697. In the convocation controversy he vigorously defended the archbishop's prerogatives, and in 1703 was made canon of Chichester and rector of Lambeth. His extensive researches in ecclesiastical law resulted in 1713 in the publication of his monumental *Codex juris*. A high-church Whig, he was appointed bishop of Lincoln in 1716, and in 1723 translated to the see of London. In the early years of his administration *Walpole relied heavily on him in church affairs and patronage, and their partnership went far in replacing the old Tory hierarchy of Queen Anne's day with a Whiggish one firmly yoked to the Hanoverian dynasty. Nevertheless, Walpole resisted Gibson's calls for ecclesiastical reform, anxious to keep the church off the political agenda. Their association, long under strain, ended in 1736 over Walpole's support for the Quakers' Bill which Gibson had advised his fellow bishops to oppose. Gibson was passed over for Canterbury in 1737. AAH

Gielgud, John (b. 1904). Actor, director, and producer. Great-nephew of Ellen *Terry, sharing her passion for *Shakespeare and the Terry mellifluence of voice, Gielgud has devoted himself wholly to the theatre and maintenance of a classical tradition, as one of his generation's greatest stage and screen actors. Joining the Old Vic, his portrayal of Hamlet (1929) preceded a series of impressive performances where stagecraft and sensibility of speech and silence illumined a desire to serve his author while entertaining an audience. Ambition to direct was realized in the 1930s (Queen's and Haymarket theatres), followed by wartime productions in Britain and abroad. In the 1950s he seemed happier in classical revivals and solo Shakespeare recitals than new drama—he was knighted in 1953—but his versatility led to acclaim in contemporary works later. Enjoyment of film-making (Academy award, 1982) and television has continued, with cameo roles into his nineties. ASH

Giffard, Walter (d. 1279). Archbishop of York and chancellor. A Wiltshire man, Giffard was successively archdeacon of Wells, bishop of Bath and Wells (1265–6), and archbishop. A royalist, he was consecrated bishop in Paris (1265) by the Savoyard bishop of Hereford, Peter Aquablanca, during Simon de *Montfort's rule. After the battle of *Evesham (1265) he became chancellor, actively engaging with the papal legate in restoring Henry III's authority and arbitrating the dictum of *Kenilworth (1266). He subsequently became archbishop of York by papal provision, tutor to Prince Edward's sons, and, with *Mortimer and *Burnell, a strenuously active regent during Edward I's absences abroad (1272–4 and 1275). He was in dispute with Archbishop Boniface of Canterbury and his successor *Kilwardby, over his rights in the south. WMM

Gilbert, Sir Humphrey (*c.*1537–83). A half-brother of *Ralegh, Gilbert was able to get official support for his interests in overseas activities. In the 1560s, he began to argue against England's current interest in the North-East Passage, recommending in a treatise circulated then, although not published until 1576, the merits of the North-West route to Cathay. After service in Ireland, and as an MP, he was knighted and began practical expeditions with a patent from the queen to plant colonies in North America. A venture in concert with Ralegh in 1578–9 apparently failed, but in 1583 Gilbert annexed *Newfoundland, though no settlers were left. He and his ship were lost on the return voyage. His treatise was an important influence on the long English obsession with the North-West Passage. RB

Gilbert, Thomas (1720–98). Poor Law reformer. The son of a Staffordshire gentleman, Gilbert was called to the bar in 1744 but worked as land agent for Lord Gower. He was MP for Newcastle under Lyme (1763–8) and Lichfield (1768–95). Among the reform measures he introduced into the Commons, the two which bear his name are the Act of 1782 which permitted two or more parishes to unite to administer the poor law, and the Act of 1793 which permitted the commissioners of *Queen Anne's Bounty to lend money to build parsonages to facilitate a resident clergy. He also secured an Act in 1793 to encourage with parochial funds the formation of *friendly societies. He unsuccessfully advocated a 25 per cent tax on government places and pensions during the American War (1776), restrictions on alehouses, and taxes on dogs. ER

Gilbert, William Schwenck (1836–1911). Gilbert is one of the rare examples where the librettist is as well known as the composer, and rightly so. His achievement in his partnership with *Sullivan was threefold. Like all good librettists, he interested and stimulated his composer and helped him to produce colourful and sparkling music. Secondly, Gilbert spiced his plots with contemporary satire, which helped to sell tickets, had a cutting edge, and has lasted remarkably well. Finally, like all great writers, he created his own world, a world of gentle cynicism, honest simplicity, and legal quibbling, and he peopled it with memorable characters—the reluctant policemen; the decent, patriotic pirates; the philosophical sentry; the modern major-general; the skittish judge in *Trial by Jury*; the duke of Plaza-Toro, who led his regiment from behind; the three little maids who, all unwary, came from a ladies' seminary; Little Buttercup and Sir Joseph Porter, KCB. Though occasionally the humour degenerates into facetiousness, the verbal dexterity of the verse is superb.

Gilbert was born in London and educated at King's College. He spent his early years as an 'impecunious party' practising the law, before turning, with great success, to literature. He met Sullivan in 1871 and *Trial by Jury*, their first success, was produced in 1875. They worked together until 1896 when *The Grand Duke* was a comparative failure. Gilbert's many publications brought him considerable wealth, he was knighted in 1907, and he died after rescuing a woman from drowning in the lake at his home. JAC

Gilbert and Ellis islands. See KIRIBATI.

Gilbert of Sempringham, St (*c.*1083–1189). Founder of the *Gilbertines, a purely English order. A wealthy Norman knight's son, Gilbert became incumbent at Sempringham (Lincs.), where (*c.*1131) he allowed a group of devout women to use a building next to the church. On the abbot of Rievaulx's advice he added lay sisters and brothers, in Cistercian fashion, to care for their physical needs. Failing to persuade the general chapter of Cîteaux to oversee the order, he was confirmed as administrator by Pope Eugenius III (1147), himself a Cistercian. Gilbert then added secular canons—like Augustinians—to act as chaplains. Growth was so rapid that by his death there were 1,500–2,000 members and, in addition to many leper-hospitals and orphanages, he had founded more than a dozen monasteries. His longevity appears well documented. He was canonized in 1202. WMM

Gilbertines. St *Gilbert, parish priest of Sempringham (Lincs.), became spiritual adviser to a group of seven anchoresses *c.*1131. His following increased and in 1147, after his unsuccessful attempts to persuade the *Cistercians to take over responsibility for his communities, they were organized as an order. It was intended for nuns (who followed the *Benedictine rule), *Augustinian canons, lay brothers, observing a version of the Cistercian rule, and lay sisters. They lived in double houses: however, following early scandal and dissension, they were rigidly segregated. Though these were ultimately virtually indistinguishable from other nunneries and while the canons gradually came to dominate, the order represented one of the best-articulated attempts to organize communities of religious men and women in medieval Europe. It enjoyed considerable success in eastern England, and by Gilbert's death in 1189 there were nine double houses and four for canons only. However, the order never successfully spread outside England and disappeared following the *dissolution of its 24 communities in 1538–9. BJG

Gildas (fl. some time between *c.*475 and *c.*550). An important British cleric, Gildas is chiefly known for his tract *On the Ruin of Britain*. This work outlines some of the history of 4th- and 5th-cent. Britain as a study in divine judgement, which he expected to come to bear on the evil rulers of his own day. He is the only early author to provide an account of the first Saxon settlements in Britain. As such he has attracted much exegesis, often fruitless. The most certain thing his book shows is that he was a well-educated man with a sophisticated style. JCa

Gillray, James (1756–1815). Caricaturist. Abandoning the discipline of reproductive engraving for pungently witty etching, and stimulated by the political satires of James Sayers but concealing his own views, Gillray played a key role in the evolution of pictorial journalism by his development of recognizable caricature and rapid response to events. Using brightly coloured, almost grotesque distortion of an individual's salient features, to conjure amusement or contempt, Gillray targeted the royal family, politicians, society figures, exquisites, and charlatans. Fashionable London both approved and feared. From 1791 he settled down to etch almost exclusively for the printseller Hannah Humphrey, lodging over her West End shop, and briefly in receipt of a Tory pension, but generally retaining his independence. Failing eyesight (probably stemming from his meticulous craftsmanship) and increasing insanity from 1810 hastened his decline. ASH

Gin Act, 1751. Repeated attempts during George II's reign to curb the growing consumption of cheap gin proved fruitless. In January 1751 Henry *Fielding in his *Inquiry into the Late Increase of Robbers* called for further legislation against this 'diabolical liquor' and his appeal was reinforced by *Hogarth's print comparing the pleasures of Beer Street with the miseries of Gin Lane. The Act 24 Geo. II c. 40 curtailed the 'immoderate drinking of distilled spirituous liquor by persons of the meanest and lowest sort' by forbidding distillers to retail directly, restricting sales to taverns worth £10 p.a., and declaring debts of less than 20 shillings to be irrecoverable. JAC

Giric, king of Picts (877/8–885/9). The sources for the succession in what (*c.*900) became the kingship of the Scots are meagre and confused following the peak of Scandinavian devastation in 875–6. The descendants of *Kenneth I in the male line lost the kingship between 878 and 889. Two names of possible kings in this period are *Eochaid and Giric. Giric is very obscure; he may have been Eochaid's guardian; and he may have lost power following a solar eclipse on 16 June 885. By the 12th cent., however, he mysteriously acquired legendary status as liberator of the Scottish church from Pictish oppression and (fantastically) conqueror of Ireland and most of England. As a result, Giric was later known as 'Gregory the Great'. DEB

Girl Guides. Female branch of the Scouting movement founded in 1910. At the first big rally of the *Boy Scouts at Crystal Palace in September 1909 there appeared a large contingent of girls dressed in the Scout hat and scarf and parading with the boys. *Baden-Powell was not in favour of incorporating girls into his organization as he believed it would discourage boys from joining. The following year his sister Agnes established the Girl Guides with £100 at her disposal and together they wrote the Guide Handbook *How Girls Can Help Build up the Empire*. The initial reaction was enthusiastic with around 8,000 girls joining. However the movement began to stagnate due to Agnes's poor organization and an uninspiring programme. The Girl Guides were also viewed with suspicion by some who thought it was a part of the women's suffrage movement, which was particularly active in this period.

In 1915 Baden-Powell made himself chairman of the Girl Guides and brought younger women into the organization, including his wife Olave. He also rewrote the Guide Handbook, *Girl Guiding*, in 1918. The Brownies were formed in 1914 for 8–11-year-olds. They were originally called Rosebuds, but the name Brownie was adopted in 1918. It derived from a book of 1870 by Juliana Ewing where Brownies were little elf-like creatures who, at night, finished the housework for humans. In 1988 the Rainbow Guides were introduced for 5–7-year-olds.

The first international Guide conference was held at Oxford in 1920. At the sixth conference, in 1930, Lady Baden-Powell became World Chief Guide, a post she held for 40 years. Today there are estimated to be around 8.5 million Guides in over 100 countries. RAS

Gladstone, William Ewart (1809–98). Statesman and author. Gladstone was one of the longest serving of British politicians and one of the most controversial. He was in office every decade from the 1830s to the 1890s, starting as a Tory, ending as a Liberal-radical prime minister. He was born in Liverpool on 29 December 1809, the son of Anne and John Gladstone, a merchant from Scotland who made his family's fortune in the Baltic and American corn trade. Gladstone was educated at Eton and Christ Church, Oxford, and from the start was marked out for success in public life. Intensely religious, initially in the evangelical tradition taught him by his mother, he at first felt drawn to ordination in the Church of England, but not sufficiently to go against his father's objections. While president of the Oxford Union, he strongly opposed the Whigs' proposals for parliamentary reform and was elected to the Commons as a Tory in December 1832. Influenced by both *Coleridge and the *Oxford movement, he published *The State in its Relations with the Church* (1838) and *Church Principles* (1840) arguing that the Church of England should be the moral conscience of the state; *Macaulay, in a savage refutation of Gladstone's arguments, called him 'the rising hope of those stern and unbending tories'. In *Peel's government 1841–5 he was vice-president and then president of the Board of Trade. This experience made him a firm free trader. He resigned in 1845 over the *Maynooth grant, returning in 1846 to be briefly colonial secretary and to support repeal of the Corn Laws (though he was not during that year in the Commons) and to become a leader of the Peelite group. In the 1840s Gladstone thus left the Tory Party and reorientated his political and religious position.

In 1839 he married Catherine Glynne, of an old north Wales family; between 1840 and 1854 they had eight children.

In 1852, as a member of the *Aberdeen coalition, he began the first of his four terms as chancellor of the Exchequer (the others were 1859–66, 1873–4, and 1880–2); his greatest budgets were those of 1853 and 1860. Gladstonian finance emphasized a balanced budget (i.e. with no deficit), minimum central government spending, the abolition of all protective tariffs, and a fair balance between direct and indirect taxes (Gladstone hoped to abolish income tax, which he disliked, and to replace it with other direct taxes). In his 1853 budget he repealed about 140 duties; in 1860 he repealed duties on 371 articles, many of them as a consequence of the treaty with France which he planned and Richard *Cobden negotiated. His plan for phased abolition of income tax was ruined by the costs of the *Crimean War.

Gladstone saw the budget as the chief moment of the parliamentary year—a national commitment to sound finance. Finance was, he said, 'the stomach of the country, from which all other organs take their tone'. He deliberately made the presentation of the budget a dramatic and controversial political event. His budgetary strategy was accompanied by the imposition of Treasury control on a more professional civil service (deriving from the Northcote–Trevelyan Report which Gladstone commissioned) and financial accountability through the Public Accounts Committee which he set up. Gladstone had an explosive political character, which occasionally spilled over into outburst; but his reputation for sound finance gave him a firm political bedrock.

In the 1850s and 1860s Gladstone emerged as a politician of clear national standing with a reputation for oratory. Though MP for Oxford University from 1847 to 1866, and though initially supporting the South in the American Civil War, he began to take increasingly radical positions, especially on questions like parliamentary reform, and his statement in 1864, that 'any man who is not presumably incapacitated . . . is morally entitled to come within the pale of the constitution', seemed to mark him out as the future leader of the party of progress. However, the modest Reform Bill proposed by Gladstone and *Russell in 1866 led to the temporary disintegration of the Liberal Party and the resignation of the government. Gladstone responded with increasingly radical demands on other questions, such as the abolition of compulsory church rates and disestablishment of the Irish church. Campaigning on these questions, he led the Liberals to win the 1868 election and became prime minister in December 1868: on receiving the queen's telegram of summons he remarked, 'My mission is to pacify Ireland'. In his first government, one of the greatest of British reforming administrations, he disestablished the Irish church (1869), passed an important Irish Land Bill (1870), but failed with his Irish University Bill (1873, when the government resigned, only for *Disraeli to refuse to take office). This government also abolished purchase of commissions in the army and religious tests in the universities; it established the *secret ballot and, for the first time, a national education system in England, Wales, and Scotland (1870–2). However, a series of scandals in 1873–4 damaged the government's standing. Gladstone called and lost a snap general election in January 1874 with a quixotic plan to abolish income tax; he then announced his retirement (often previously contemplated) from the party leadership.

Gladstone, 64 in 1874, expected a retirement of writing and scholarship. He was already an established if idiosyncratic authority on Homer with his *Studies on Homer and the Homeric Age* (1858) and a frequent book reviewer. In his lifetime he published over 30 books and pamphlets and about 200 articles, chiefly on classical, theological, literary, and contemporary political topics. His articles provided a useful source of income when out of office and enabled him to retain the centre of the political stage even when in opposition. Gladstone had that rare gift of being thought to be controversial even when at his most anodyne; no public figure has more easily kept a place in the limelight.

In his pamphlets of 1851–2 and a stream of subsequent works, Gladstone opposed the 'temporal power' of the papacy. He opposed the declaration of papal infallibility in 1870 and denounced 'Vaticanism' in 1874–5. He nurtured links between Orthodoxy and Anglicanism as an antidote to Roman catholicism's hegemonic claims. Not surprisingly, therefore, he was swiftly drawn into the Bulgarian atrocities campaign in 1876. A series of speeches and pamphlets broadened into a general attack on 'Beaconsfieldism' and having fought the *Midlothian campaign 1879–80 he was elected MP for Midlothian. He thus had a Scottish constituency, a Welsh home (his wife Catherine's house, Hawarden castle), and widespread English connections. He had become that very rare phenomenon, a fully 'British' politician. He again became prime minister in 1880. His second government passed an important Irish Land Act (1881) and, after initial rejection by the Lords, the Reform Act of 1884; but it failed to establish elected local government for Ireland or for Great Britain.

Since the 1860s, Gladstone had tried to pacify Ireland by accommodating Irish demands. He accompanied the concessionary *Land Act (1881) with coercion, imprisoning C. S. *Parnell, and breaking the power of the *Irish Land League. From 1882, disregarding the set-back of the *Phoenix Park murders, he sought to encourage the constitutional character of the *Home Rule movement. His government resigned in 1885, unable to agree on local government for Ireland. Gladstone encouraged Parnell to bring forward a Home Rule proposal and fought the general election of November 1885 on a manifesto which carefully did not exclude it. In January 1886, his son Herbert having flown the *'Hawarden Kite' and Lord *Salisbury having turned down Gladstone's proposal that the Tory government introduce a Home Rule measure with bipartisan support, Gladstone formed his third cabinet with ministers pledged to inquire into Home Rule. He had come to see devolution as the best means of maintaining Ireland within the United Kingdom, as well as having substantial advantages for the United Kingdom as a whole. He drew up a Home Rule Bill, providing for a legislature with two Houses in Dublin and with a generous financial settlement for the Irish, and he proposed to accompany it with a substantial Land Purchase Bill (to buy out the Anglo-Irish landowners). This bold settlement was too bold for his party and the Government of Ireland Bill was defeated in the Commons in June 1886, many *Liberal Unionists defecting and eventually forming their own party. The government did, however, pass the *Crofters' Act for Scotland, one of the few significant land-tenure reforms ever passed for the mainland. Gladstone called a general election and resigned on losing it. The 1886 proposal was probably the best chance the British had for a constitutional settlement which retained Ireland within the Union.

In foreign policy, Gladstone stood for an international order governed by morality and based on an updated Concert of Europe. To achieve this he was, unlike many free traders, ready to intervene diplomatically or if necessary militarily. His first government submitted the **Alabama* dispute to international arbitration and paid the consequent hefty fine, thus clearing the way for good relations with the USA. In the Midlothian campaign, Gladstone laid out 'six principles' of foreign policy, which recognized the equal rights of nations and the blessings of peace—these principles were extremely influential in world-wide liberal thought, and especially on President Woodrow Wilson and the liberals planning the *League of Nations. In office in the 1880s, however, Gladstone found himself intervening in unpalatable ways; to maintain order, as he came to see it, in *Egypt, he bombarded Alexandria in 1882 and then invaded Egypt in what was intended as a brief occupation to remove 'extreme' nationalists. Egypt proved, however, to be the 'nest egg' of Britain's north and central African empire. In 1882, war against the Boers in South Africa included the public-relations disaster of *Majuba Hill. Order had also to be established in the *Sudan and Gladstone, despite misgivings, failed to prevent Lord Hartington and others sending Charles *Gordon to a Sudanese imbroglio partly of Gordon's own making; Gordon's death in 1885 was a further embarrassment to a beleaguered government. Gladstone always opposed imperial expansion and annexation, arguing—in a vein now common among economic historians—that expansion into tropical areas was a dangerous deflection from Britain's true economic and strategic interests (he was, however, a keen proponent of development of the 'white' empire). But he always lost the decision (if not the argument) and was an unwilling party to major imperial expansion in Africa and the Pacific.

Gladstone was aged 75 when his first Government of Ireland Bill was defeated. Now committed to campaigning for another attempt, he led the Liberal Party in opposition 1886–92 (his first period as formal opposition leader), winning the general election of 1892 despite the set-back of the split of the Home Rule party in 1890. In 1892 he formed his fourth and last government. In 1893 he successfully piloted his second Government of Ireland Bill through the Commons after 82 sittings; the Lords then brusquely rejected it, as they did many of the government's other proposals. Throughout his life Gladstone had battled to keep down defence expenditure. Already defeated in his attempt in 1892 to withdraw from *Uganda, his final political struggle was an unsuccessful dispute with his own cabinet over naval expansion in 1893–4. His eyesight deteriorating, he finally resigned the premiership in March 1894, aged 84. He completed his edition of the works of Joseph *Butler, the 18th-cent. theologian, and died on Ascension Day, 19 May 1898.

Gladstone stood 5 feet 10½ inches, with a large head and a powerful voice. He was always spry, his fitness maintained by long walks and his legendary tree-felling. Intense sexuality competed in his character with equally intense religious belief, and he had difficulty maintaining the two in balance when he undertook his 'rescue' work with prostitutes. These inner struggles combined with outward confidence to make him a very characteristic Victorian. His enduring governmental monument was the establishment of a tight code of financial principles, which remained influential long after the type of economy they were intended to serve had passed away. In British politics Gladstone was the most successful of non-Tory political leaders. Among executive politicians he has had few rivals in range and staying power, or in the capacity to meet new challenges with fresh policies. His use of speech-making and political meetings to bring great political questions before the people helped to integrate the mass electorate after 1867 and set a style which has influenced democratic countries ever since. HCGM

Hammond, J. L., *Gladstone and the Irish Nation* (1938); Matthew, H. C. G., *Gladstone 1809–1874* (Oxford, 1986); id., *Gladstone 1875–1898* (Oxford, 1995); Morley, J., *Life of Gladstone* (3 vols., 1903); Ramm, A., *William Ewart Gladstone* (Cardiff, 1989); Vincent, J., *The Formation of the Liberal Party 1857–68* (1966).

Glamorgan. County of south Wales. It was part of the Welsh kingdom of Glywysing, but in the 10th cent., under Morgan Hen, became known as Gwlad Morgan, from which the later name is derived. Under the Normans it was converted to the lordship of Glamorgan, and remained a lordship of the march until 1536, when it was made into a shire at the Act of *Union with England, with the addition of the lordship of Gower (Gŵyr). In 1974 it was divided into three—South, Mid, and West *Glamorgan.

The county consists of three main elements. Blaenau Morgannwg is the coalfield upland, deeply segmented by valleys, of which the Taff and its tributary, the Rhondda, are best known. In contrast, the southern section called Bro Morgannwg, or the vale of Glamorgan, is a low, level plateau of some 200 feet. The third element is the Gower peninsula.

The county was best known for the coalfield and the mining villages strung out along the valleys. The iron and steel industry of the late 18th and 19th cents. developed on the northern outcrop in places such as Merthyr Tydfil, but exhaustion of local iron ores led to a shift to the coast. The British Steel plant at Margam in West Glamorgan is the contemporary successor. Coal-mining has virtually ceased. There is only one deep mine operative, but there are extensive opencast operations. Modern industry has collected about the M4 motorway, which crosses the vale, and north of *Cardiff, which grew as a port and is now the capital of Wales. The coalfield communities have suffered greatly from unemployment and contain some of the most deprived areas in the UK (e.g. the Cynon valley).

The total population in 1991 was 1,256,462, nearly half the population of Wales. Welsh speaking increased east to west—3.6 per cent in Trowbridge, a ward of South Glamorgan, to 79.1 in Gwaun-cae Gurwen in the west—and also up-valley, south to north—6.3 per cent at Llantwit Major on the coast to 19.3 in Rhigos, a ward on the northern boundary. HC

Glamorgan, Edward Somerset, 1st earl of, 2nd marquis of Worcester (1603–67). Somerset, known until 1645 as Lord Herbert, was born at Raglan and in 1642–5 held south Wales for the king, though taking little part in the military skirmishes. After *Naseby, when the king's position was quite desperate, Herbert was made earl of Glamorgan (though the patent was not subsequently recognized) and sent to Ireland to treat with his fellow-catholics in the *Kilkenny Confederation. His private instructions were to obtain Irish troops at all costs. Once in Ireland, he floundered in a confused situation, victim of Charles I's tricky diplomacy. Glamorgan's secret treaty made such sweeping concessions to the catholics, in exchange for the promise of 10,000 men, that, when it became known, the king was obliged to repudiate it. After the wars, Glamorgan made his terms with the Commonwealth and recovered his estates at the Restoration. His private interest was engineering and in 1663 he published a celebrated book, *Century of Inventions*: the 'water-commanding engine' which he exhibited at Vauxhall seems to have been an irrigation-pump rather than any form of steam-engine. JAC

Glamorgan, kingdom of. A medieval Welsh kingdom which emerged from an earlier kingdom called *Morgannwg that covered most of south-east Wales. It may be equated with the post-Roman kingdom of Glywysing, whose line of kings from Meurig ap Tewdrig lasted until the late 11th cent.; these kings extended their power in the 8th cent. to *Gwent and Ergyng (Archenfield) to create Morgannwg, probably named after Morgan ab Arthrwys (died *c.*665) or Morgan ab Owain (Morgan Hen, d. 974). Prior to the Norman invasions, there were uneasy relations with *Deheubarth and *Gwynedd. From the 1090s Robert *Fitzhamon and the Normans occupied the lowlands and established a marcher lordship between the rivers Neath and Rhymni called Glamorgan; manors, knights' fees, and feudal sublordships replaced earlier Welsh divisions. The conquest accentuated the division between upland and vale, for descendants of native Welsh dynasties continued in the hills until the early 14th cent., acknowledging the overlordship of Deheubarth and, then, of Gwynedd. RAG

Glamorgan, Mid, South, and West. These three counties were created by the Local Government Act of 1972 and came into operation in 1974. They were in being for only 22

years before being replaced by a new set of unitary authorities in 1996. The problem facing local government reorganization in Wales in the 1960s was the great imbalance in population. At the 1971 census, Glamorgan, including the county boroughs of Cardiff, Merthyr Tydfil, and Swansea, accounted for 46 per cent of the whole population of Wales. Any reform necessarily involved the subdivision of Glamorgan to ensure some parity, but the nature of that division was controversial. The first proposals simply eliminated the small county borough of Merthyr and transferred the Rhymni valley to Gwent. But that accomplished little and, in any case, the county borough was not to be retained. A Consultative Document in 1971 proposed a simple twofold division into East and West Glamorgan, but in 1972 the Local Government Act set up a threefold division into: West Glamorgan, the Afan, Neath, and Tawe valleys and centred in Swansea; South Glamorgan, or Cardiff and its immediate hinterland; Mid Glamorgan, the coalfield valleys but extending across the vale of Glamorgan, via the drainage of the river Ogmore, to the coast. This was an incoherent area, the administrative centre of which remained in Cardiff, which was not part of it. The populations in 1991 were West Glamorgan 361,428, South Glamorgan 392,780, and Mid Glamorgan 534,101 respectively.

The lowered and balanced populations are evident and more in line with those of the other counties, but the late separation of South Glamorgan was widely regarded as politically motivated, an attempt by a Conservative government to retain the possibility of control of one local authority in south Wales.

The counties were replaced in April 1996 by eight unitary authorities. They are, with approximate populations in brackets, Swansea (232,000), Neath and Port Talbot (140,000), Bridgend (130,000), Vale of Glamorgan (119,000), Rhondda, Cynon, Taff (238,000), Merthyr Tydfil (60,000), Caerphilly (171,000), Cardiff (302,000). There were minor boundary adjustments made in creating these authorities. HC

Glanvill, Ranulf (d. 1190). One of Henry II's most influential legal and administrative experts, though what was once his greatest claim to fame has been stripped from him as he is no longer regarded as the author of *The Laws and Customs of the Kingdom of England*, the first systematic treatise on English common law and a work still commonly referred to as 'Glanvill'. Younger son of a Suffolk baron, he became sheriff of Yorkshire in 1164, made his name as a soldier when he captured King William of Scotland at *Alnwick in 1174, and then rose rapidly in Henry II's service. From 1180 he was chief *justiciar at a time of significant development for the English legal system. According to a well-informed contemporary, Roger of Howden, 'by his wisdom the laws which we call English were established'. But he was notorious for corruption and was dismissed by Richard I. He went on crusade and died in 1190 at the siege of Acre. JG

Glasgow, an ancient burgh (1175–8), first developed as an ecclesiastical centre on a hill near the cathedral. Having a grammar school from the early 14th cent., in 1451 the burgh acquired its university by papal bull and became an archbishopric in 1492. An attractive residential market town with its annual summer fair, Glasgow, little affected by the Reformation, was remarkable for its amenities.

From the mid-17th cent. Glasgow began to develop its overseas trade with Europe and the American colonies. By 1668 Port Glasgow had been established by Glasgow merchants. After the *Union of 1707 Glasgow dominated the tobacco trade because of natural advantages reinforced by superior organization, and the city with about 12,000 inhabitants in 1700 began to grow as a manufacturing centre with its merchants controlling fine linen production over a wide area and developing other industries.

By 1776 Glasgow merchants imported more than half of Britain's tobacco and had lucrative re-export markets in Europe. The improvement of Glasgow harbour and the development of a diversified industrial economy had also progressed; the problems posed by the American War led to the formation of the Glasgow Chamber of Commerce (1783) and the growth of the West Indies trade. Cotton imports became significant, and Glasgow by 1850 had become a manufacturing city with a population of 345,000.

The importance of cotton diminished in the late 19th cent., but this was offset by the rise of heavy industry. Situated in a region rich in coal and iron, Glasgow became a major shipbuilding and engineering centre, the Clyde leading the world for tonnage launched and railway rolling stock and machinery produced. These industries were supplied by engineering firms which competed in world markets. By 1911 Glasgow had become the second city of the empire with a population of just over 1 million. A city with massive housing and other social problems, Glasgow was economically successful up to 1920.

The 20th cent. witnessed the decline of heavy industries. They were vulnerable to the vagaries of world markets, lacked adequate capital investment, and their record in labour relations was poor. Glasgow acquired the reputation of a politically radical city, Labour taking more and more political control, and the corporation embarking upon a public housing programme from the 1920s. Service industries gradually provided more employment, and consumer industries became more significant. Glasgow has gone full circle, important for its amenities—education, leisure, entertainment—and white-collar employment. JB

Glasgow cathedral. The earliest church, dedicated to the Holy Trinity, was part of a monastic foundation established by St Kentigern (more popularly, St Mungo, d. 603) on ground consecrated by St *Ninian in the 5th cent., where Kentigern had buried the holy man Fergus. This site is now covered by the Blacader aisle. The diocese of Glasgow was re-established by David I and the first stone building consecrated in 1136 in his presence; despite later major rebuilding under Bishops Jocelin (after fire damage) and Bondington, there is a generally unified appearance. Its importance as a place of pilgrimage was underlined by a papal decree of 1451 declaring that journeys to Glasgow and Rome were of comparable merit; Edward I made three visits to the tomb of St Kentigern and his shrine in 1301.

Although furnishings were stripped or damaged, the cathedral survived the Scottish Reformation in 1560, before being adapted to house three separate congregations. By 1835, it became possible to open up the interior again, but the fabric escaped the proposed restoration 'improvements' by Kemp, although the western towers were demolished. It is now crown property, worshipped in by the *Church of Scotland in the reformed tradition, under presbyterian government. ASH

Glastonbury, a Somerset market town *c.*30 miles south of Bristol, is distinguished by a conical hill, Glastonbury Tor, rising out of the Somerset levels. Noted for its Iron Age lake village settlements, its magnificent medieval Benedictine abbey was a centre of pilgrimage, inspired by a complex of legends about *Arthur, Joseph of Arimathea, the young Jesus, and the Holy Grail. A monastery existed here at least from the 6th cent., and in the 10th cent. under *Dunstan was the centre of vigorous monastic reform. In 1184 fire destroyed the abbey. The monks, by skilful use of the legends and newly discovered relics, raised funds to rebuild on a glorious scale. At the abbey's dissolution (1539), Abbot Whiting was hanged on the Tor. WMM

glebe was a portion of land allocated to support a priest. Though originally it was intended as the sole support, it soon required substantial augmentation, usually through tithes. At the Norman Conquest, the glebe was twice the holding of a villein: in the 18th cent. many glebes were enlarged, either in compensation for enclosures or in lieu of tithes. JAC

Glencairn, William Cunningham, 9th earl of [S] (*c.*1610–64). Glencairn succeeded his father as earl in 1631. In 1647 Parliament appointed him lord justice general [S] but he entered into the *Engagement in 1648 and was deprived of his post. In 1653 he headed a Scottish rising against the Cromwellian regime but was forced to come to terms. After the Restoration he was appointed chancellor [S] but was on uneasy terms with *Lauderdale. JAC

Glencoe massacre. The massacre, on 13 February 1692, has remained one of the most potent 'myths' in Scottish history. As part of the pacification of the Highlands after the collapse of the Jacobite rising of 1689–90 a royal order required all clan chieftains to take an oath of allegiance to William and Mary. The chief of the Macdonalds who lived in Glencoe, 10 miles from Fort William on the north-west coast of Scotland, did so, but only after the time limit of 1 January. The Scottish secretary, Sir John *Dalrymple, and the administration in Edinburgh used his lateness as a pretext to send a force to Glencoe to exact the submission of a clan known to be Jacobite in its sympathies. The officers and men of this force were Campbells, hereditary enemies of the Macdonalds, who had raided Campbell land as recently as 1690. After being given traditional Highland hospitality the soldiers turned on and massacred some 40 of their hosts, and many of those who escaped soon died in winter storms. William had not authorized the action, but he did not punish those held to be responsible by a 1695 commission of inquiry. His failure was vociferously exploited by Jacobite propaganda. JRJ

Glenfruin, battle of, 1603. The clan Gregor in Scotland had long been lawless and troublesome. After their attack on the Colquhouns on 7 February 1603 at Glenfruin near Loch Lomond, they were subjected to draconian measures, designed to extirpate or subdue them. JAC

Glenlivet, battle of, 1594. Throughout the 1580s and 1590s, the catholic lords in Scotland were in touch with Philip II of Spain about an invasion to restore catholicism. In October 1594 *Huntly and Erroll joined forces and on the 3rd defeated at Glenlivet, south of Elgin, a larger royalist force led by the inexperienced Argyll. But the rebels did not pursue their victory, Spanish troops were not forthcoming, and they were forced into temporary exile. JAC

Glenshiel, battle of, 1719. A small Spanish force landed at Loch Alsh in April 1719 to support the Jacobite cause. But the other part of the invasion was aborted, they received little local support, and Wightman advanced against them from Inverness. On 10 June the two groups, each about 1,000 strong, met at Glenshiel. After a short engagement, the Scottish Jacobites fled and the Spaniards surrendered. JAC

gliding. Repeated attempts to glide by fitting wings ended in failure. But Sir George Cayley in 1852 at Brompton Hall, North Riding, sent his coachman a distance of 500 yards and in 1891 Otto Liliethal successfully launched himself in a hang-glider. As a sport, gliding developed after the *First World War and at an international meeting in Sussex in 1922 a flight of 3 hours 21 minutes was achieved. Thermal soaring enabled long flights to be made and by 1939 the world records were 465 miles and 22,500 feet in height. Considerable use was made of gliders during the invasion of Normandy in 1944. Hang-gliding, the pioneer of the sport, made a come-back in the 1970s. JAC

Globe theatre. Built 1598/9 on Bankside in Southwark, by Richard *Burbage the actor and his brother Cuthbert, its sign showed Hercules carrying the globe on his shoulders. The company used it during the summer since it was not roofed. Burned down in 1613 during an over-ambitious performance of *Henry VIII*, it was rebuilt but closed by the puritans in 1642 and demolished. Admission was a penny for the pit, twopence for the gallery, and threepence for seats. *Shakespeare was both a shareholder and an actor and several of his plays, including *Romeo and Juliet*, *Othello*, *Lear*, and *Macbeth*, were first performed there. A replica of the first theatre was opened in 1996. JAC

Glorious First of June, 1794. An Anglo-French naval battle fought some 400 miles out in the Atlantic from the Breton peninsula, which shelters the French naval base of Brest. Though the opposing fleets were of similar strength, the French under Villaret de Joyeuse were rather more concentrated than Lord *Howe's better-found and manned ships: Howe's strategy was to watch Brest from Torbay, giving cover to Britain's Atlantic traffic, and to her West Indies possessions. The battle's immediate cause was Villaret de Joyeuse's evasion of Howe in order to cover a 117-strong convoy bound for Brest from America with 67,000 barrels of wheat flour for the critically under-provided French capital.

Hence the French fleet putting to sea had been a political imperative. By a brilliant chase in foggy conditions, Howe intercepted the French, taking six ships prize and sinking another. As against 1,500 French killed there were only 300 British, with no ships lost. But the convoy from America reached Brest unscathed on 15 June. Though in some circles seen as a partial and overdue success for Howe, popularly his action was deemed a triumph over French republicanism. DDA

Glorious Revolution. Title given to the revolution of 1688–9, which resulted in the 'abdication' of James II and the succession of William III and Mary II. Participants had differing objectives. Tories and Anglican clergy wanted to stop James undermining the church. Whigs aimed to depose James and limit the powers of the crown. Ordinary people detested James for his catholicism. William needed to remove a potential ally of Louis XIV and lead England into the war against France that had just begun. Louis left James unassisted, calculating that William's army would be tied down in an English campaign.

William had earlier established clandestine connections with leading politicians and army and navy officers hostile to James's policies. In June 1688 he instigated an invitation from two Tories, four Whigs, and Bishop *Compton to intervene in order to prevent James continuing to favour catholics, expand and purge the army, and manipulate elections for a parliament that was to sit in November. The birth that month of an infant prince to James had transformed the political future: he would succeed James in place of Mary (his eldest, protestant daughter, married to William). But most people were persuaded that the infant was 'supposititious', somebody else's baby smuggled in to give the appearance of a royal birth. William's intervention was necessitated by the size of James's professional army. However, William was promised that most of its officers would defect. When this happened soon after William landed at Torbay on 5 November James found that he could not fight a battle. William moved on London unopposed while his adherents took over provincial centres. Demoralized, James tried to fly the country but was stopped. A second successful escape to France was the direct result of William's pressure. This left a vacuum. Tories wanted his return as a limited king, or for a regent to rule for him, or for Mary to reign as queen. Instead the *Bill of Rights (1689) followed the Whig formula, construing James's flight as abdication, declaring the throne vacant, and William and Mary as joint sovereigns. But the limits it imposed on the crown were less than the Whigs desired. It made illegal royal claims to suspend laws and maintain an army without parliamentary approval. It barred catholics from succeeding. In Scotland the Revolution went further. James was deposed. Bishops were abolished, presbyterianism restored. Civil war resulted. JRJ

Gloucester (Roman) was successively a Roman legionary fortress and the *colonia* of *Glevum*. The earliest Roman military site, of *c.* AD 50, was at Kingsholm by an old channel of the Severn. The move to the present site took place in the mid-60s with the building of a legionary fortress (garrison uncertain). This was turned into a *colonia* for legionary veterans under Nerva (96–8). As at *Colchester the military buildings were converted to civil use: the headquarters building became the forum, and barracks became housing. The *colonia* retained the legionary defences, fronted in stone as a mark of status. This gave a defended area about half that for towns of comparable rank, but there were extensive suburbs, in one of which has been found a tilery with products bearing stamps, some referring to the municipality and its magistrates. Another fronted a major Severn-side quay. As elsewhere, well-appointed houses became more common at Gloucester in the 3rd and 4th cents. Some were occupied into the early 5th cent., but there is no evidence that the town was still in being when it fell to the Anglo-Saxons after the battle of *Dyrham in 577. ASEC

(post-Roman) Gloucester revived as a royal and ecclesiastical centre in the 7th cent., and as a fortified and planned town (burh) in the 9th. Situated at the lowest point bridgeable on the Severn (until 1966), it was long an important inland port. The medieval town was dominated by St Peter's abbey (created the cathedral in 1541) and the Norman castle: the Norman kings wore their crown at Gloucester annually and the town then ranked among the ten richest in England. It remained prosperous until the 15th cent., but in Tudor and Stuart times suffered an economic decline and developed a radical tradition. It held out for Parliament in a siege of 1643, perhaps the turning-point in the first civil war, and was punished for it after 1660. In 1780 Robert Raikes started the national Sunday school movement there. From the 1820s there was rapid industrial growth, lasting until the mid-20th cent. DMP

Gloucester, diocese of. The see, roughly conterminous with Gloucestershire, was founded in 1541 by Henry VIII from part of the *Worcester diocese. From 1836 to 1897 it was united with Bristol in a combined new diocese to allow new sees for Ripon and Manchester without increasing the total episcopal bench. Its first bishop was John Wakeman, abbot of Tewkesbury. John *Hooper (1551–5), notable for his close association with extreme continental reform, in particular Zwingli and Laski, was a vigorous reformer within the diocese, but was burned at the stake for heresy in 1555 under Mary. Consequently there was within the diocese a strong tradition of puritanism, which became a target for both James I and *Laud. James Monk (1830–56) was a vigorous bishop, who did much to improve the finances of livings. The Norman cathedral, previously St Peter's Benedictine abbey church, was partly transformed in perpendicular style, reputedly the earliest example, by the inflow of money from pilgrims to the shrine of Edward II. The tomb of *Robert of Normandy, William I's eldest son, who died in Cardiff castle, is also there. The 14th-cent. fan-vaulted cloisters are among the finest in England. WMM

Gloucester, Gilbert de Clare, 4th earl of (d. 1230). Gloucester, who inherited the title in 1217, had been one of the barons in opposition to John and was among the 25 appointed in 1215 to see that *Magna Carta was carried out. Consequently he was excommunicated by Innocent III when John did his deal with the papacy. After John's death,

Gloucester supported the dauphin's attempt on the throne and was captured at the battle of *Lincoln in 1217. In later years he campaigned against the Welsh. He is buried in Tewkesbury abbey, to which he had been a great benefactor. His widow married *Richard of Cornwall, younger brother to Henry III. JAC

Gloucester, Gilbert de Clare, 6th earl of (1243–95). On his entrance into public life on succeeding his father in 1262, Gloucester joined de *Montfort's party in opposition to Henry III and fought at *Lewes in 1264 capturing the king. But he soon changed sides, joined Prince Edward, and was prominent in the defeat of de Montfort at *Evesham in 1265. By 1267 he was once more at odds with the king, occupied London, and negotiated terms on behalf of the 'dispossessed', de Montfort's former supporters. Much of his time was devoted to holding back the Welsh under *Llewelyn and he was responsible for the building of the great castle at *Caerphilly. Next he saw service against the Scots and from 1292–3 was in Ireland. His second wife, married 1290, was Joan, a daughter of Edward I. He was buried at Tewkesbury. JAC

Gloucester, Gilbert de Clare, 7th earl of (1291–1314). Son of the 6th earl by his second wife, de Clare was therefore nephew to Edward II and was brought up with the young king, who was seven years older. He inherited the title at the age of 4. He seems to have tried to moderate the animosity caused by Edward's favourite, Piers *Gaveston, who had married his sister. He acted as guardian or regent in 1311 and again in 1313. His political future seemed to be assured but he was much employed in warfare against the Scots and was killed in the thick of the fighting at *Bannockburn. JAC

Gloucester, Humphrey, 1st duke of (1390–1447). The youngest son of Henry IV and brother of Henry V. Created duke of Gloucester in 1414, Humphrey played a prominent role, both in France and at home, during his brother's reign. He became protector of England following Henry's death in 1422, surrendering the office in 1429 when Henry VI was crowned, but continued as president of the minority council until 1437. These years were dominated by his quarrel with Cardinal *Beaufort, which caused disruption in 1425–6, 1432, and 1440. Fiercely loyal to the memory of his dead brother, Gloucester emerged in the 1430s as the principal opponent of moves towards peace. As a result, after the king came of age, he was edged from influence. The scandal of his duchess's trial for witchcraft finally discredited him in 1442. But still perceived as a threat to the court faction, in 1447 he was accused of treason, imprisoned at Bury St Edmunds, and died in suspicious circumstances before he came to trial. Posthumously he acquired the reputation of Good Duke Humphrey. He commissioned the first official history of Henry V, patronized John *Lydgate, England's leading poet, and sponsored English humanist scholars. He bequeathed his substantial library to the University of Oxford, where it forms the nucleus of the Bodleian collection. He died childless. AJP

Gloucester, Richard de Clare, 5th earl of (1222–62). Succeeding his father in the earldom at the age of 8, he became a ward of Hubert de *Burgh, whose daughter he married. His estates were on the Welsh border and in Ireland. His political course appears fluctuating. In 1258 he joined the barons trying to restrain the conduct of Henry III but he died before the civil war began and was buried at Tewkesbury. Matthew of Paris lamented that his great talents were ruined by avarice. JAC

Gloucester, statute of, 1278. This was an important attempt by Edward I to tighten up royal authority. Writs of *quo warranto were to be issued to anyone claiming territorial franchises. The decision was much resented by the older nobility and the Earl *Warenne was said to have protested sword in hand. But, in practice, most franchises for which no warrant or charter could be produced were confirmed on payment of a fine. JAC

Gloucester, Thomas, duke of (1355–97). Also known as Thomas of Woodstock, from his birthplace. He was the youngest son of Edward III, brother of *John of Gaunt, and uncle to Richard II. In 1376 he was declared constable of England and acted as such at his nephew's coronation. On that occasion he was created earl of Buckingham and in 1380 received the Garter. He added the earldom of Essex in 1380. After serving in France and against the Scots, he was created duke of Gloucester in 1385. He took a prominent part against the royal favourite Michael de la *Pole. In 1387 he defeated de Vere (*Oxford) at *Radcot Bridge, occupied London, seized the king, and used the *Merciless Parliament against his adversaries. For some years there was an uneasy *rapprochement* with Richard, but in 1397 Gloucester was seized, at the king's orders, and taken to Calais, where he died, having apparently been smothered under a feather bed. JAC

Gloucestershire falls naturally into three parts: the eastern hills of Cotswold limestone from Winchcombe down to Bath, spilling towards Oxfordshire at Stowe and Fairford; the central heavy clay valley of the Severn from Tewkesbury down to Avonmouth; and the old red sandstone, wooded Forest of Dean in the west, for centuries a community cut off from its neighbours. At Gloucester itself, until the opening of the Severn bridge in 1966, was the highest road bridge over the river, giving it a critical strategic position between south Wales and the west of England. Gloucestershire is one of the bigger counties, even after losing part of its southern fringe to *Avon in the local government reorganization of 1972. From Chipping Campden in the north to Marshfield in the south is over 50 miles, and from Coleford to Lechlade, west to east, is nearly as far. The balance of the county has been much affected by two great towns. *Bristol was a major city with a mint well before the Conquest and in 1373 was given status as a county in its own right, the first town to be granted such a privilege. Consequently it was outside county government, though remaining in the economic and cultural orbit. Cheltenham was a mushroom development of the late 18th and early 19th cent., after the celebrated visit by George III in 1789 had helped to spread the fame of its waters. In 1801 it had 3,000 inhabitants to Gloucester's 8,000. But within ten years it had overtaken its neighbour, and by 1901 was a town of 45,000.

Roman Gloucestershire was prosperous. A military base was soon established at *Gloucester (Glevum); *Cirencester (Corinium) became the second largest town in Roman Britain; great villas at *Woodchester and at *Chedworth testify to the wealth of some of the inhabitants; a network of roads, including Ermine Way, *Fosse Way, and *Akeman Street gave easy communication with the rest of the province, and another road ran to the Forest of Dean to enable the iron to be exploited. The local inhabitants were the *Dobunni tribe. After the withdrawal of the legions, much of Gloucestershire fell to the Saxons in 577, when *Ceawlin of Wessex defeated British chiefs near Cirencester. But Wessex did not long retain the area. In 628, *Penda, pagan king of *Mercia, defeated the Wessex levies, also at Cirencester, and took possession. The eastern part became the kingdom of the *Hwicce under Mercian overlordship: the western fringes of the Forest of Dean formed part of the autonomous kingdom of the *Magonsaetans. This division was reflected in the ecclesiastical organization. The Hwicce territories became part of the see of *Worcester, while the Magonsaetans fell under the jurisdiction of *Hereford, founded in 676. *Æthelfleda, lady of the Mercians, fortified Winchcombe and Gloucester against Danish inroads in the early 10th cent., and was buried at Gloucester. The area then changed hands again, falling once more to Wessex: *Athelstan pushed back the Welsh, with the boundary becoming the Wye rather than the Severn, and died at Gloucester in 940.

After the Norman Conquest, Gloucestershire, first named as a county in 1016, was still a frontier region, and the earl of Gloucester was given *palatine powers. William of Malmesbury, in the early 12th cent., described the region in idyllic terms: the soil was so fertile that it bore fruit 'of its own accord'; the vineyards were prolific; 'the villages are thick, the churches handsome, the towns populous and many.' By *Camden's time, in Elizabeth's reign, the vineyards had all gone, which he blamed on the sloth of the inhabitants, but the Cotswold pastures had proved ideal for sheep, and a flourishing cloth industry had established itself around Stroud and Dursley. The establishment of a bishopric at Gloucester in 1541, after the *dissolution of the monasteries, gave a shot in the arm to the county town. In the 17th cent. tobacco growing flourished for some years before the government closed it down to give protection to the new American colonies.

In the 18th cent. Gloucestershire was divided politically between the Beauforts and the Berkeleys, who, after an expensive election contest in 1776, reached agreement to share the county seats. Increasingly the county was knit together by improvements in transport. The Thames and Severn canal through Sapperton tunnel in 1789 never fulfilled the high hopes, and the Hereford and Gloucester canal linked two towns of only moderate importance. But the Gloucester and Berkeley canal in 1827 shortened the line of the Severn and enabled Gloucester to remain a busy port. Railways arrived in the 1840s—first the narrow gauge line from Birmingham to Gloucester, then broad gauge lines to Gloucester from Bristol and from Kemble. The change of gauge at Gloucester was for many years a major obstacle until the Great Western gave up the struggle in 1872. The Worcester to Oxford line, passing through the county via Moreton-in-Marsh, opened in the 1850s, but remained more picturesque than profitable, until in the late 20th cent. it found a new lease of life serving commuter traffic to Oxford. The western parts of the county were opened up by the railway bridge at Sharpness in 1879 and by the Severn tunnel in 1885.

As the cloth industry in the east and mining in the west went into decline, the county's industries diversified—wagon works at Gloucester, aeronautics at Bristol, piano-making, printing, furniture, chemicals, and tourism in the Cotswold valleys. In the 1960s the county was criss-crossed by the M4 running east–west and by the M5 running north–south: the interchange at Almondsbury was briefly a traffic sensation. Even more important was the Severn bridge in 1966 which brought to an end the old Beachley–Aust ferries: queueing for the ferry had once been a regular bank-holiday activity, and generations of Gloucestershire people had watched the last ferry disappear into the sunset before starting wearily on the 60-mile diversion via Gloucester. JAC

Glyndŵr (Glendower), **Owain** (*c*.1359–*c*.1415), self-styled prince of Wales. A wealthy landowner in north-east Wales, his father was descended from princes of *Powys and his mother from princes of *Deheubarth. His rising (1400–10) was a serious and costly threat to the usurper Henry IV. Owain was a well-to-do gentleman, trained at the Inns of Court, serving in Richard II's armies against the Scots (1384–5), and becoming a retainer (by 1387) of the lord of Chirk, Richard Fitzalan, earl of Arundel. He married Margaret, daughter of Sir Edward Hanmer, a distinguished judge. By 1400 conditions in Wales were ripe for rebellion: there was racial tension between Welsh and English fanned by poets and propagandists; economic and social dislocation after the Black Death was made worse by the crown and English nobles exploiting their Welsh resources more harshly; and the Welsh church was dominated by an English hierarchy at the expense of Welsh priests. French meddling and encouragement from Scotland and Irish lords fed the resentment, and risings before 1400 (especially by Owain Lawgoch in the 1370s) were a foretaste of widespread unrest.

Glyndŵr took the lead partly because of personal grievances against Lord Grey of Ruthin and Henry IV. He was proclaimed prince of Wales by friends and relatives at Glyndyfrdwy (Merioneth) on 16 September 1400, and attacked Grey's estates and towns close to the English border. He relied on his kinsmen, especially the Tudors of Anglesey who captured *Conwy castle (April 1401). Owain advanced into central and south Wales following a victory in the Plynlimmon mountains (1401); his capture of Lord Grey (April) and the uncle of Edmund *Mortimer, earl of March and claimant to the English throne (22 June), was a political coup, especially when the captive Mortimer married

Owain's daughter. Expeditions led by Henry IV (1400–3) achieved little, and Parliament (1401–2) panicked into passing legislation to curb the rights of Welshmen. Owain sought allies among other rebels, especially the Percy family and the earl of March's supporters, though Henry IV's victory at *Shrewsbury (21 July 1403) was a set-back. Owain focused on south Wales, capturing several castles, as well as Aberystwyth and Harlech (1404). He negotiated the treaty of Paris with Charles VI of France (14 July 1404), and he 'and his hill-men' held assemblies at Machynlleth, Harlech, and Pennal (1404–6) where ambitious plans were laid for an independent principality. These included support for the Avignon pope, a Welsh church, university, and civil service, and a principality extending into the English midlands. Although French troops landed in Milford Sound to assist him, 1405–6 saw significant reverses, and his French and Percy allies faded away. Aberystwyth and Harlech capitulated in 1408, and Owain's wife and two daughters were captured. Following a raid in Shropshire in 1410, Owain disappeared; he refused a pardon from Henry V in 1415 and may have died soon afterwards. RAG

Goderich, Frederick John Robinson, 1st Viscount (1782–1859). Prime minister. Educated at Harrow and St John's College, Oxford, Goderich entered Lincoln's Inn in 1802 but was never called to the bar. In 1806 he sat as a moderate Tory for the borough of Carlow and a year later for Ripon, a seat he held for over twenty years. From 1813 to 1817 he acted as joint paymaster-general of the forces and accompanied *Castlereagh to the continent for the Vienna peace negotiations. In 1815 he introduced 'with great reluctance' the notorious measure to prohibit the importation of wheat until the average price in England was 80 shillings per quarter. From 1823 to 1827 Goderich served as chancellor of the Exchequer. Along with *Huskisson at the Board of Trade he introduced sweeping fiscal reforms to reduce customs duties and tax. The economic improvement led *Cobbett to nickname him 'Prosperity Robinson'. He was created viscount in 1827 and became leader of the Lords. Despite being a popular man in the Commons, Goderich was less effective in the Lords. In August 1827 he became prime minister after *Canning's death. Although able, Goderich was unsuited to the task due to lack of resolution. He resigned in January of the following year and became secretary for war and the colonies in the *Grey administration of 1830. In 1833 he was created earl of Ripon and made lord privy seal. 'A transient and embarrassed phantom', was Disraeli's description in *Endymion* of Goderich's premiership. RAS

Godfrey, Sir Edmund Berry (1621–78). On 17 October 1678, in the middle of lurid allegations by Titus *Oates of a *popish plot to assassinate Charles II, the body of Godfrey, the magistrate who had taken Oates's evidence, was found on Primrose Hill (London). He had been missing for five days. Godfrey, a tall, stooping man, was a prosperous London wood merchant, educated at Christ Church, Oxford, and knighted for his exertions during the plague year. Money and jewellery had been left untouched and Godfrey had been run through with his own sword, though death appeared to have been by strangulation. It was readily assumed that he had been done to death by papists and a catholic silversmith, Miles Prance, was taken up and confessed. Three fellow-conspirators were then hanged. But in 1686, after the accession of James II, Prance was convicted of perjury and pilloried. Godfrey had predicted prior to his disappearance that he would be knocked on the head. Suicide seems improbable. Murder by Oates's friends to fan the flames of suspicion is possible. Pollock suggested that Godfrey had been murdered by catholics to suppress secrets that he knew, through his friendship with Edward Coleman, about the future king. A last possibility is that the murder was not political or connected with the plot at all. JAC

Godiva (Godgifu) (d. between 1057 and 1086). Wife of Earl *Leofric of Mercia. To obtain her request that Coventry be relieved of a heavy toll, she is alleged to have ridden naked through the market. The legend obscures her reputation as founder and benefactress of religious establishments. A number of monasteries were recipients of her own and Leofric's generosity. Together they founded and richly endowed the Benedictine monastery and church at Coventry in 1043, where relics included an arm of St Augustine of Hippo bought by *Æthelnoth, archbishop of Canterbury. The church was said to be resplendent with Godiva's gifts of gold and precious stones, and on her death she left a jewelled rosary to be placed on the image of the Virgin Mary, to whom she was especially devoted. She and Leofric were both buried in their Coventry church. Roger of Wendover in the 13th cent. first related her ride; 18th-cent. writers embellished it with picturesque detail like 'Peeping Tom'. AM

Gododdin, kingdom of the. A British kingdom of the 6th cent. in south-east Scotland. Ptolemy recorded that the area was occupied in Roman times by the *Votadini, whose capital was at Traprain Law, near Haddington. In the 5th cent. they seem to have moved their capital west to Edinburgh and re-emerge as the Gododdin. *Aneurin's heroic poem in Welsh tells of a carefully planned raid by the Gododdin on the Anglo-Saxon kingdoms of *Bernicia and *Deira, and of the battle at *Catterick (*c.*600). The Gododdin were utterly routed: 'of three hundred, save one man, none returned.' The Anglo-Saxons continued their advance into Lothian and after they had taken Edinburgh in 638, the kingdom of the Gododdin disappeared. JAC

Godolphin, Sidney Godolphin, 1st earl of (1645–1712). Prime minister. MP for Helston (1668–79) and St Mawes (1679–81), Godolphin was created baron (1684) and earl (1706). A Tory by inclination, he was the archetypal bureaucratic politician, described as 'never in the way and never out of it', who held the offices of a lord of the Treasury (1679), secretary of state for the northern department (1684), 1st lord of the Treasury (1684–5, 1690–6, 1700–1), chamberlain to Queen Mary of Modena, and a commissioner of the Treasury (1687). From the accession of Anne, he and *Marlborough (the 'duumvirate'), and from 1704 to 1708 with Robert *Harley (the 'triumvirate'), as political managers, ran the government, Godolphin being lord treasurer and, effectively, prime minister (1702–10). His forte was in financial affairs, and he was responsible for raising the money which enabled England to fight 20 years of continental wars. He found himself increasingly unable to withstand political pressure from the Whig Junto and the duchess of Marlborough, and from 1706 the Whigs began to take over the ministry, leading to Harley's resignation in 1708. Harley intrigued with the queen and took his revenge in 1710 when Godolphin was dismissed. CJ

Godwin, William (1756–1836). English writer and novelist. In 1793 Godwin published his anarchist masterpiece *Enquiry Concerning Political Justice*, which caught the public imagination and made his reputation. He argued against the use of coercion of any kind, whether political, ecclesiastical, or military, not because it violated natural rights, but because it was corrupting and counter-productive. Godwin was an extreme determinist, rejecting the idea of free will: indeed he asserted that the 'assassin can no more help the murder he commits than the knife in his hand'. He claimed that the ills of society were due to the bad influences exerted on people, largely by governments, and that the path to improvement lay in the power of reason, not coercion. In the ideal society there would be no government and no punishment: individuals would live in harmony because of their mutual grasp of reason. TSG

Godwine, earl of Wessex (d. 1053). Godwine rose to prominence in the reign of *Cnut, as one of his chief advisers, and has traditionally been held responsible for the brutal death of Æthelred the Unready's exiled son *Alfred in 1036. When the Danish line ended (1042), Godwine supported the accession of Alfred's brother Edward, who married Godwine's daughter. When his sons were established in earldoms, his area of influence was vast. In 1051, he defied Edward's order to harry Dover after an affray with men of Boulogne, and mustered a great force, bringing England to the brink of civil war. But the earls of Mercia and Northumbria supported the king, the matter was referred to the *witan, and the Godwines were exiled. Resentment of an increasing foreign entourage around the king may account for the support Godwine gathered when he returned the next year, obtaining reinstatement and the dismissal of many Normans. Within a few months Godwine died, his enemies said choking while protesting his innocence of Alfred's murder. Wessex passed to his son *Harold, who died at the hands of William of Normandy in 1066. AM

Gold Coast. see GHANA.

Golden Jubilee, 1887. The fiftieth anniversary of Victoria's accession saw a well-orchestrated outburst of loyalty. Lord *Rosebery assured the queen that the previous fifty years would be considered 'the golden age of English history'. The Round Tower at Windsor was illuminated by electrical light, prisoners amnestied, medals struck, statues erected, the fleet reviewed at Spithead, and a thanksgiving service held at Westminster abbey with music by the late Prince Albert. 'And *all* was the most perfect success,' wrote Victoria afterwards. It set the pattern for the *Diamond Jubilee of 1897 and subsequent royal celebrations. JAC

Goldsmith, Oliver (1728–74). Man of letters. Born in Ireland, the son of an Anglican clergyman, Goldsmith attended Trinity College, Dublin, before briefly studying medicine in Edinburgh and Leyden. On settling in London from 1756, he supported himself partly as a physician, partly as a hack-writer, and partly by borrowing from friends. But he gradually pulled himself out of Grub Street and began to acquire a reputation. His poem *The Traveller* (1764) was well received; a novel *The Vicar of Wakefield* (1766) has remained a minor classic; *The Good-Natured Man*, a comedy (1768) had a respectable stage run; *The Deserted Village* (1770) touched the chord of nostalgia and was much admired; the *History of England* (1771), though derivative, sold well; *She Stoops to Conquer* (1773), which Goldsmith claimed was based upon personal experience, was a great success. Goldsmith was a strange man, feckless, naïve, unworldly, generous. *Boswell, a fellow-member of the Club, treated him as a butt and buffoon, but *Johnson admired him as 'a very great man'. He died heavily in debt, and Horace *Walpole wrote of him, not unfairly, that 'he had sometimes parts, though never common sense'. JC

golf. Though the Dutch game of *kolf* has been claimed as the origin, the first undoubted reference to golf was in 1457 when the Scottish Parliament deplored its popularity, along with that of football, since it took young men away from archery practice. James VI and I is said to have taken golf clubs with him when he moved south in 1603. But the great development of the game was in the later 19th cent. The handful of golf clubs in the early decades had risen to a dozen by 1870 and well over 1,000 by 1914. The first British open championship was held at Prestwick in 1860 and, since professionals dominated, an amateur championship at Hoylake in 1885. The main developments have been the standardization of the number of holes; the evolution of balls from the original wooden or feather-filled balls to cheaper gutta-percha balls in the 1840s and more aerodynamic rubber balls in the early 20th cent.; and the introduction of specialist clubs, up to a maximum of fourteen. The British governing body is the Royal and Ancient Club at St Andrews, founded in 1754. JAC

Good Parliament (1376). This Parliament saw the first use of *impeachment by the Commons, and the emergence of the office of Speaker. There was widespread discontent with an ineffective and apparently corrupt government. Charges were brought against the chamberlain, William Latimer; a London merchant much involved in government finance, Richard Lyons; the king's mistress Alice Perrers; the steward of the royal household, John Neville, and others. It appears to have been the knights of the shire who led the attack, though it may be relevant that Peter de la Mare, the Speaker, was the earl of March's steward. The Commons' triumph did not last long; the government, guided by *John of Gaunt, undid most of their work in the following year. Those who had been found guilty received royal pardons, and Peter de la Mare was imprisoned. MCP

Gordon, Charles George (1833–85). British soldier and Christian mystic. After serving with distinction in the *Crimean War (1853–6), Gordon gained public acclaim by his exploits in China (1860–5) where he showed his great talents as a military engineer and as commander of irregular troops in the defence of Shanghai during the Taiping rebellion. Seconded to the service of the khedive of Egypt as governor of Equatoria (1873–6) and then as governor-general of the Sudan until 1880, Gordon mapped the upper reaches of the White Nile, successfully combated the slave trade which used the river, and established firm administrative control over the whole region. He returned to the Sudan in 1884 to evacuate Egyptian troops threatened by the forces of the Mahdi, a Muslim revivalist who had declared a holy war against the Egyptian government. A relief force failed to arrive in time and Gordon was killed in Khartoum in January 1885. KI

Gordon, Lord George (1751–93). Soon after his election to Parliament in 1774 Lord George, third son of the 3rd duke of Gordon, began to exhibit signs of mental derangement and religious mania. His frequent lectures to the House of Commons were not much appreciated: 'the noble lord has got a twist in his head,' remarked one sympathetic member, 'a certain whirligig which runs away with him if anything relative to religion is mentioned'. Gordon's reply was that he and his supporters 'had not yet determined to murder the king and put him to death, they only considered that they were absolved from their allegiance'. On 2 June 1780, as president of the Protestant Association, he presented a monster petition denouncing concessions to the catholics. Six days of rioting and looting followed and Gordon was tried for treason. It was argued on his behalf that he had not intended violence and had tried to discourage it, and he was acquitted. He subsequently converted to Judaism and, convicted of libel, spent the last five years of his life in comfortable confinement in Newgate prison. See also GORDON RIOTS. JAC

Gordon riots, 1780. The greatest outburst of civil disorder in modern British history. They lasted for six days from 2 to 8 June and did enormous damage in London. They began with the presentation by Lord George *Gordon of a petition to Parliament against recent concessions to the catholics, but violent and criminal elements soon took over. Prisons were attacked and the inmates released, catholic chapels destroyed, breweries, taverns, and distilleries plundered, and the houses of catholics and magistrates set on fire. Order was with difficulty restored after troops had been called out. Many members of the mob lost their lives, shot by the military, engulfed by flames, or buried in rubble. In all, 135 were put on trial, 59 capitally convicted, and 26 hanged, including a Jew, a negress, a one-armed man, and 'a poor, drunken cobbler'. The riots were used by Dickens as the backcloth to *Barnaby Rudge*. JAC

Gore, Charles (1853–1932). Bishop of Worcester, Birmingham, and Oxford. Born at Wimbledon, educated at Balliol College, Oxford, Gore was an *Anglo-catholic of liberal views and strong social conscience. As fellow of Trinity College (1875) and first principal of Pusey House (1884–93) he probably had more effect on Oxford University religious life than anyone save *Newman. He founded the Community of the Resurrection (1892) for celibate priests, established at Mirfield 1898, of which he was superior until 1901. His controversial essay in *Lux mundi* on 'The Holy Spirit and Inspiration' (1889) and *The Incarnation of the Son of God* (1891) displayed his liberal theology. As bishop of Worcester (1902), he promoted the carving of a new Birmingham diocese out of Worcester. He made a powerful impact as Birmingham's first bishop (1905), and moved with reluctance to Oxford (1911), where he was involved in incessant controversy. He travelled widely, to India, America, the Near East, and the front during the war. Resigning his see to write, preach, and travel, he lived ascetically in London. WMM

Gorham judgment, 1850. George Gorham (1787–1857) was an Anglican minister with a taste for antiquarian and theological pursuits and a leaning towards calvinist views on baptism. In 1847 Lord Chancellor *Cottenham wished to present him to the living of Brampsford Speke in the diocese of Exeter, but the bishop, Henry Philpotts, refused. A protracted legal action then ensued, the Privy Council deciding in 1850 in favour of Gorham, whose supporters presented him with a silver tea service. JAC

Goring, George (1608–57). Royalist commander in the Civil War. Despite being universally disliked, George, Lord Goring, rose high in the king's service. He was first under *Newcastle in Yorkshire and gained a notable victory over Sir Thomas *Fairfax at Seacroft Moor in March 1643. At *Marston Moor, in 1644, he commanded the left wing of the royalist army. After driving Fairfax's cavalry from the field, his men returned in disorder, and were routed by *Cromwell's cavalry. Goring's ambition divided the royalists and the outrageous behaviour of his troops towards civilians discredited their cause. After *Naseby, Goring was forced to give up the siege of Taunton by the approach of Sir Thomas Fairfax's victorious army. Despite the tactical brilliance with which Goring deployed his men at *Langport, they were easily vanquished in July 1645. Goring then fled the country and joined the service of Spain, where he died. *Clarendon, no friend, recognized Goring's wit and courage, but declared that he could 'without hesitation, have broken any trust, or done any act of treachery'. IJG

Goschen, George Joachim, 1st Viscount (1831–1907). A front-rank and long-serving politician in his day, Goschen is now remembered chiefly in one phrase. He was the grandson of a Leipzig publisher: his father settled in London as a merchant in 1814. Goschen was sent to Rugby and Oxford to get an English education, took first-class honours in classics, and was president of the Union. By 1858 he was a director of the Bank of England, entered the Commons in 1863 as the Liberal member for London, and remained in Parliament all his life. Given junior office by *Russell in 1865, he was brought into the cabinet the following year as chancellor of the duchy of Lancaster, and served as president of the Poor Law Board 1868–71, 1st lord of the Admiralty 1871–4 and 1895–1900, and chancellor of the Exchequer 1887–92. Given a viscountcy in 1900, he was chancellor of the University of Oxford from 1903. A financial expert, useful speaker, good administrator, Goschen was a safe pair of hands. 'A violent moderate' was his own description and he became increasingly uneasy at the Liberals' drift towards radicalism, refusing to serve in Gladstone's second ministry. After the Home Rule crisis of 1886, he joined *Hartington in leading the *Liberal Unionists. When Lord Randolph *Churchill resigned dramatically from Salisbury's government in 1886, expecting to be recalled, his place was filled by Goschen, and not a dog barked. 'I forgot Goschen,' explained Lord Randolph ruefully. JAC

Gothic architecture. The main medieval style in western Europe, characterized by the pointed arch, slender columns and shafts, buttresses, pinnacles, and increasingly complex ceiling vaulting and window tracery. Courtly and sophisticated, often with chivalric connotations and redolent of theological symbolism, it found its fullest expression in the great cathedrals and churches of the Middle Ages; in Britain it flourished until the 16th cent., a time when many parts of Europe had adopted Renaissance forms.

Higher, lighter, and more delicate than the heavy, massive Romanesque or Norman style which it superseded, Gothic has been memorably described by Gombrich as the epitome of the 'church triumphant' rather than the earlier 'church militant'. The origins of Gothic are obscure—the adoption of the pointed arch may well have stemmed from contact with the Saracens during the crusades—but probably lie in northern France during the late 12th and early 13th cents.

Before long, the English were making a major contribution, as in the nave of Wells cathedral or the western choir of Lincoln, both designed shortly before 1200. Another good example is Salisbury cathedral, unusual in being largely the product of a single building programme (*c*.1220–84), and where the usual emphasis on verticality occurs even more in the slightly later tower and spire than in the interior. Many English cathedrals combine Gothic with earlier Norman work and were built and rebuilt over several centuries, which seems to accentuate their distinctive, even occasionally eccentric, character. For example, the early Gothic western façade of Peterborough cathedral (*c*.1193–1230) is far wider than the (Norman) nave hidden behind, as is that at Wells (*c*.1230–60), where, above tiny entrance portals, the effect is one of a screen of sculptured figures. At Lincoln, the western towers and upper portions of the façade (13th and 14th cents.) are grafted onto an earlier Norman structure and, typically, but in complete contrast to the French prototype, the cathedral has double transepts and a squared-off east end. Of English examples, Canterbury cathedral, its choir (1175–8) designed by a Frenchman, William of Sens, and Westminster abbey (basically 13th cent.) are the most French in character.

In Britain, Gothic is traditionally classified into three main phases, although there were periods of overlap and transition between them and with earlier Norman architecture. These are, with approximate datings: 'Early English' (*c*.1180–1270); 'Decorated' (*c*.1270–1370); *'Perpendicular' (*c*.1350–1550). The first of these has an austere purity, as in the examples of early Gothic mentioned above, and utilizes the simple, 'lancet' window type (e.g. the 'five sisters' window in the north transept of York minster, *c*.1250). The 'Decorated' is marked by intricate vaulting and window tracery (as in the nave of Exeter cathedral, 1328–42, and the early 14th-cent. east window at Carlisle); and the uniquely English 'Perpendicular' by even more elaborate vaulting, and ever-larger window apertures almost like a screen of glass. The great east window of Gloucester cathedral (*c*.1337–50) is a classic early example.

During the Civil War and after, systematic damage was inflicted upon the Gothic heritage by Cromwellian iconoclasts, but the *Gothic revival of the 18th and 19th cents. reasserted its significance. TEF

Gothic Revival. There is some truth in the suggestion that Gothic architecture in Britain never entirely died out, especially in the hands of local craftsmen in remote, rural areas, although too much can be made of this. Certainly, even during the 17th and early 18th cents., a period dominated by classicism, the style had major patrons such as John Cosin, bishop of Durham between 1660 and 1672; and both *Wren and *Hawksmoor sometimes adopted it, although almost invariably for works intended to blend in with existing structures, as with the latter architect's additions to All Souls College, Oxford, begun 1715.

Thus, it is not until the mid-18th cent. that we have the first really self-conscious revival of Gothic, when, for example, Horace *Walpole (1717–97) began to enlarge his villa, Strawberry Hill, Twickenham (near London), during the 1750s, and the amateur architect Sanderson Miller (1717–80) remodelled Lacock abbey (Wilts.) (1754–5). Arbury Hall (War.) (altered from about 1750 by Henry Keene), is another early example of the 'Gothic' taste. This architecture often seems whimsical, an intellectually fashionable alternative to *Palladianism, although 'Gothick' buildings often retained Palladian proportions and soon many leading architects, such as James Wyatt (1748–1817), designed in both styles.

'Gothic' was at first an essentially literary movement, inspired by the new interest in medieval and Elizabethan poetry and the increasingly antiquarian spirit of the time. Later in the century, the Gothic Revival, always more English than British, became associated with Romantic ideas of the Sublime and Picturesque. For the eccentric millionaire William Beckford, Wyatt built the gigantic, rambling Fonthill abbey (Wilts.), from 1796 (now demolished). The Picturesque movement encouraged this new kind of asymmetry in architecture and its greater integration with landscape. Gothic was often combined with castellated forms and merged into the 'Tudor-Gothic' of the early 19th cent.

By this time, however, the fanatical medievalist Augustus *Pugin (1812–52) gave the revival a new moral and stylistic authority through his writings and designs. A Roman catholic, he argued that Gothic was truthful and Christian: a comprehensive English national style. His ideas coincided with the upsurge of church building after the *Catholic Emancipation Act of 1829 and influenced many Anglicans associated with the *Oxford movement. John *Ruskin (1819–1900) was also a great champion of the Gothic Revival, and the 'high Victorian' period (*c*.1850–80) saw its widespread adoption for large public buildings and monuments in the growing cities and towns. Examples include Manchester town hall (by Alfred Waterhouse, 1869–77) and, in London, the Midland hotel, St Pancras station (by G. G. *Scott, 1865–71), the Law Courts, Strand (by G. E. Street, 1874–82), and the Albert memorial (again by Scott, begun 1863). In church architecture, the revival continued until at least the early 20th cent. TEF

Gower, John (*c.*1330–1408). Poet. A contemporary and friend of *Chaucer, Gower was probably born in Kent and then lived in Southwark. He wrote in French, Latin, and English. His main work, *Confessio Amantis* (*c.*1386), contained 141 examples and stories of love in a conversation between a lover, Amans, and a priest of Venus, Genius. He drew on the classics and on medieval romances. By the time the lover had understood the nature of love, he was too old and tired to care. Of Gower's political works, *Vox clamantis* (*c.*1382) recorded the upheaval of the *Peasants' Revolt and his hope that Richard II's reign would prove a blessing: when it did not, he transferred hope to Henry IV in *Cronica tripertita*. Highly thought of in the Tudor period, Gower's lack of humour led to Chaucer overshadowing him. JAC

Gowrie, William Ruthven, 1st earl of [S] (*c.*1541–84). The Ruthven estates were in Perthshire and the family, protestant by religion, formed part of the English interest. Gowrie's father, the 3rd Lord Ruthven, took a leading part in the murder of *Rizzio in 1566, but died almost immediately after. Gowrie was also involved, and at Lochleven in 1568 helped to obtain Mary's abdication in favour of her young son. From 1571 he was treasurer of Scotland and in 1581 was created earl of Gowrie. He was the leader in 1582, with Mar and Angus, of the *Ruthven raid and held the king prisoner for ten months, demanding the withdrawal of *Lennox from the kingdom. An ill-judged reconciliation with *Arran in 1584 led to his downfall and he was executed at Stirling. His sons were involved in the *Gowrie conspiracy in 1600, both being killed. JAC

Gowrie conspiracy, 1600. James VI of Scotland mistrusted the Gowrie family. The 3rd Lord Ruthven had murdered *Rizzio and the 1st earl of *Gowrie had held James captive after the *Ruthven raid in 1582. On 5 August 1600, while hunting, James was urgently invited by Alexander Ruthven to Gowrie House in Perth, according to the king to investigate a mysterious stranger with a pot of gold. James dined at the house but no stranger materialized and after the meal James repaired to an upper turret with Ruthven. James's version was that Ruthven then reproached him with the execution of the 1st earl and told him to prepare to die: James wrestled free and cried 'Treason' from a window, whereupon his followers rescued him and killed both Ruthven and his elder brother, Lord Gowrie. It has never been clear who was plotting against whom. James owed the Ruthvens a good deal of money, but the suggestion that he deliberately acted as a decoy seems most unlikely, given the king's notorious cowardice. James's story of the pot of gold is so feeble that it might even be true, since it would not be hard to invent a better tale. Yet if the brothers were conspirators, looking for a repeat of the Ruthven raid, they are among the most incompetent in Scottish history. Since Alexander Ruthven was 20, and James's fondness for handsome young men is well established, it is not difficult to think of alternative explanations. JAC

Grace, W. G. (1848–1915). Grace was probably the greatest sporting hero of late Victorian and Edwardian Britain, his bulky form and black beard instantly recognizable. He was by profession a Bristol surgeon with four brothers. Before he was 17 he had appeared for the Gentlemen against the Players at the Oval and at Lord's. In 1866 he made 224 not out for England against Surrey and his volume of runs was unprecedented. In 1870 he launched the Gloucestershire side. In all he made 126 centuries and took 2,876 wickets, playing his last first-class game in 1908, at the age of 60. JAC

Grafton, Augustus Henry Fitzroy, 3rd duke of (1735–1811). Prime minister. Grafton came from an aristocratic Whig background and opposed Lord *Bute in the early years of George III's reign. He became secretary of state in the first *Rockingham administration, but his admiration for the elder *Pitt caused a breach with his colleagues, and he resigned in April 1766 after the failure to negotiate Pitt's entry into the ministry. Grafton returned to office in July, when Pitt (now earl of Chatham) succeeded Rockingham as prime minister. Although Grafton became 1st lord of the Treasury, Chatham headed the ministry as lord privy seal. This unusual arrangement (devised to free Chatham from a heavy departmental work-load) did not achieve its object of preserving Chatham's precarious health. Grafton gradually emerged as *de facto* prime minister during 1767 and officially led the ministry after Chatham finally resigned in October 1768. The Grafton ministry was plagued with serious problems, such as the *Wilkes case and the *Townshend duties crisis; Grafton himself was ridiculed in the press by *Junius. Unable to withstand the pressure (the final straw being a parliamentary attack by Chatham, who had recently recovered from illness), Grafton resigned in January 1770. He never returned to the front rank of politics, but served as lord privy seal in 1771–5 and 1782–3. Grafton is often accused of lacking political stamina and preferring the aristocratic good life to the burdens of office. Whilst partially true, it was a formidable assault by three former premiers (*Grenville, Rockingham, and Chatham) which prompted Grafton's resignation. Furthermore, the emergence of *North removed any necessity for the king to rely on Grafton. DW

Graham, Sir James (1792–1861). Heir to an important border landed estate, Graham was educated at Westminster School and Oxford. He succeeded his father in 1824, and implemented extensive estate improvement. He joined the Whig opposition in Parliament, supporting *catholic emancipation and parliamentary reform. In 1830 he became 1st lord of the Admiralty in *Grey's cabinet, and was one of the four ministers who drafted the Great Reform Act. At the Admiralty he introduced administrative reform, before resigning in 1834 over proposals for reforming the established

Irish church. He refused to join *Peel's minority government of 1834–5 but moved into opposition to the succeeding Whig ministry. He became home secretary and Peel's right-hand man in the 1841–6 ministry, supporting him in Corn Law repeal and resigning with him in 1846. After Peel's death, Graham remained a prominent Peelite politician, returning to the Admiralty in *Aberdeen's coalition ministry of 1853–5. NMcC

grammar schools. In Roman times schools of grammar taught language and literature. This type of school and its curriculum was adopted by early Christian educators, such as *Alcuin. In 826 Pope Eugenius required bishops to ensure that grammar schools were founded in their dioceses.

The term was first used in England in the 14th cent. Grammar schools were under ecclesiastical supervision, but endowments were made by other institutions, such as guilds, charities, and hospitals. The grammar school was recognized as providing a training for future churchmen: Henry VI founded *Eton College (1440), and Cardinal *Wolsey Ipswich Grammar School (1528). From Tudor times, merchants, traders, and a number of women founded schools—Peter Blundell at Tiverton (1599) and Lady Alice Owen at Islington (1613).

After the Restoration, the grammar schools declined: they were described by Lord Chief Justice Kenyon in 1795 as 'empty walls without scholars, and everything neglected but the receipt of salaries and emoluments'. Attempts to widen the curriculum to allow mathematics and modern languages to be taught were rejected in the Eldon judgment 1805; but in 1840 a Grammar School Act allowed a wider range of subjects. Some of the schools had developed into non-local boarding schools: from these emerged the *public school. The Endowed Schools Act 1869 helped to reform grammar schools, following the report of the Taunton Commission in 1868, including provision for girls. The 1902 Education Act established a system of municipal and county schools alongside the older grammar schools, which were popularly known as grammar schools. Because of the spread of comprehensive education from the mid-1960s, by 1990 only about 7 per cent of local authorities had retained grammar schools. PG

Grampian (named because the eastern Grampian mountains lie within it) was from 1973 to 1996 a local authority region of Scotland. It was formed from the counties of Aberdeen, Kincardine, and Banff and most of Morayshire, and certain administrative functions were the responsibility of five districts. From April 1996 the new all-purpose local authorities for the former Grampian region are: Aberdeen; Aberdeenshire (comprising the former Banff/Buchan, Gordon, and Kincardine/Deeside districts); and Moray. Over 40 per cent of the region's population live in *Aberdeen, Scotland's third largest city. Oil and gas deposits were first discovered in the northern North Sea in the early 1970s, with production starting in 1975; thanks to its location, Aberdeen has become the oil capital of Europe. Its prosperity since the mid-1970s engendered a diversification of much of the Grampian economy, to which agriculture and fishing are now much less important, with oil-related activity representing over 10 per cent of employment; the oil boom brought about increases in income, population, and employment well above all other parts of Scotland, with consequent boosts to services and to the tourist industry, already established by its castles and 'Royal' Deeside. CML

Granby, John Manners, marquis of (1721–70). Granby, heir to the dukedom of Rutland, became a national hero after brilliant cavalry actions at *Minden (1759) and Warburg (1760), during the *Seven Years War. He was elected to Parliament before he was 21 and remained in the Commons all his life. From 1763 to 1770 he was master of the ordnance, and commander-in-chief from 1766. He spent lavishly, drank heavily, gambled on the turf, and was always in debt. He was less at home in politics than on the field of battle. A newspaper attack upon Granby in *Junius' first letter in 1769—'nature has been sparing of her gifts to this noble lord'—led to Sir William Draper defending him and provoked the Junius series. In January 1770 he resigned office, having changed his mind on the *Wilkes issue: 'he recanted a vote he had not understood,' wrote Horace *Walpole, 'for reasons he understood as little.' He died unexpectedly at the age of 49, leaving Chatham to declare, extravagantly, that his loss was 'irreparable'. *Reynolds painted his florid, bald, ruddy countenance many times, and for decades less distinguished portraits swung outside countless taverns. JAC

grand jury. The Assize of *Clarendon provided that twelve men of each hundred were to present on oath, to the travelling justices, often the justices in *Eyre, those suspected of serious crimes. They acted from their own local knowledge. After the Eyres ceased, the grand jury consisted of 24 persons, summoned by the sheriff from the county generally, to make presentments to the justices of *oyer and terminer and *gaol delivery. From the late 14th cent. the grand jury had the task of scrutinizing indictments to examine whether or not the accused should be sent for trial. In 1933 the grand jury was abolished; its function as a preliminary 'sifter' of indictments was superfluous in the light of the preliminary hearings of all indictable offences by examining magistrates. MM

Grandmontines. This monastic order was founded by the hermit St Stephen (*c.*1054–1124) of Muret, near Limoges. It was an ascetic community of choir and lay brothers which, after Stephen's death, established itself at Grandmont and followed a strict version of the *Benedictine rule. Its temporal affairs were almost entirely controlled by the lay brothers ('conversi'), an arrangement which gave rise to much internal dissension. Three small priories were founded in England where the order enjoyed the patronage of the Angevin kings. Only one of these (Grosmont, Yorks.) survived till the *dissolution. In the later Middle Ages, the monks were often styled 'Bons Hommes'. BJG

Grand National. The most famous jumping race in the world. First run in 1839, it is a handicap for horses six years old and upwards, run near the end of March at Aintree, Liverpool. The course of 4 miles and 856 yards includes 30 jumps, such as the Canal Turn Fence, Valentine's Brook, and the notorious Becher's Brook, making it a severe test for both horse and jockey. Red Rum holds the record for the most wins, finishing first in 1967, 1973, and 1977. In 1993 the race had to be abandoned after a chaotic false start, and in 1997 it was disrupted by an *IRA bomb hoax. RAS

Grand National Consolidated Trade Union. Founded in 1834 by delegates of societies nation-wide in response to calls of Derby artisans and labourers 'locked out' for belonging to 'combinations'. It was associated with Robert *Owen, who became president only after the trial of the *Tolpuddle martyrs in March. The GNCTU's attempt to co-ordinate unions on a general (rather than trade-specific) basis was innovative, aiming to provide financial support by imposing levies on affiliates and practical help by establishing co-operatives for strikers. Hitherto unorganized groups of workers, including agricultural labourers and some women, were amongst the 500,000 members. Handicapped from the outset by meagre funds (only a tiny fraction of fees were paid), the GNCTU's demise was precipitated when the treasurer absconded with its finances in December 1834. The collapse of this short-lived movement was symptomatic of the fate of trade unionism prior to the 1850s. SC

Grand Remonstrance, 1641. This lengthy petition was part of *Pym's campaign to retain the initiative in his parliamentary struggle against Charles I. It was given added urgency by the news of the Irish catholic revolt. A long indictment of the misdeeds of the reign, attributing them largely to popish advisers, was carried on 18 November by 159 votes to 148. It demanded, on threat of withholding supply, that in future the king should employ such counsellors as Parliament 'may have cause to confide in'. Charles replied that in the 'choice of our counsellors . . . it is the undoubted right of the crown of England to call such persons . . . as we shall think fit'. JAC

grand tour. A standard part of the education of the English aristocracy between the Restoration and the outbreak of the Revolutionary and Napoleonic wars in 1789, though since it could take two or three years, it was extremely expensive and only a few could afford it. It therefore tended to be limited to elder sons. It had several objectives—to broaden the mind, to introduce the tourist to classical civilization, to encourage social grace, to improve the command of languages, to establish useful personal and diplomatic links, and to enable wild oats to be sown at a discreet distance. It was usually undertaken between the ages of 17 and 22, under the supervision as 'bear-leader' of a prudent clergyman, if one could be found. The tourist was frequently required to write long letters home reporting progress, and often resorted to copying from guide books to eke out inspiration: a stream of advice, exhortation, and often reproach flowed in the opposite direction. The basic tour was to Paris and on to Rome, though many variations were possible, and Holland, Germany, and the Habsburg dominions were often included. Greece and Spain were much less popular and only a few intrepid souls penetrated to Stockholm, St Petersburg, and the Ottoman empire. Many commentators, such as *Smollett, *Johnson, and *Gibbon, disapproved, arguing that the tour encouraged habits of dissipation and that the noblemen were too young to have much appreciation of what they saw. Others were concerned that tourists might come to admire Roman catholicism, but Anglican clergy were at hand to point out superstition, and bugs and brigandage were sufficiently common to impress most travellers with the delights of home. The English 'milord', tutor in tow, was a well-known sight on the continent and was not popular, save among innkeepers, since he was often arrogant and complaining. 'I find everything here so extremely inferior', wrote J. C. Villiers from France in 1778, 'that I glow with pride and rapture when I think that I am an Englishman.' Some tourists came to grief. George Damer's sexual proclivities got him into a scrape in Rome in which a coachman was killed and money had to be distributed to get him off: Viscount Morpeth caught venereal disease and died at the age of 22. The advent of railways in the early 19th cent. meant that the journeys could be made in a few weeks and the tour did not survive in its traditional form. JAC

Grantham, Thomas Robinson, 1st Baron (1695–1770). Robinson's father was baronet of Newby Hall, east of Ripon. His first parliamentary seat in 1727 was Thirsk. At Westminster School he formed a friendship with Henry *Pelham and the duke of *Newcastle, who looked after him for the rest of his life. Until the conclusion of the peace of *Aix-la-Chapelle in 1748 his career was diplomatic, with seven years in Paris and eighteen at Vienna. From 1749 to 1754 he held minor government posts. He was thrust into prominence in 1754 when Henry Pelham died unexpectedly and Newcastle needed a spokesman in the House of Commons. But his months as secretary of state were a torment, assailed by *Fox and *Pitt, often in tandem: 'the Duke might as well send his jackboot to govern us,' remarked Pitt. In 1755 he was replaced by Fox and held only minor office subsequently. But his compensation as a discard was substantial—a handsome pension and a barony in 1761, when even his minor post was needed for someone else. Fox, while paying tribute to his honesty and good nature, called Robinson 'an instance of men to whom fortune has been constant . . . by mere chance made Secretary of State; by mere chance brought out of it with a pension . . . by mere chance made a peer . . . He needed all this luck, for he was a very dull man.' JAC

Granville, Granville George Leveson-Gower, 2nd Earl (1815–91). Politician. Son of the 1st Earl Granville and the grandson, on his mother's side, of the 5th duke of Devonshire, he was educated at Eton and Oxford. A lifelong Whig, he was MP for Morpeth (1836–41) and Lichfield (1841–6) before succeeding to the title. He was under-secretary for foreign affairs 1840–1 and, after holding various minor offices, succeeded Lord *Palmerston as foreign secretary 1851–2. Granville was considered a possible prime minister in 1859 and 1865 but tended to hold honorific offices until he became colonial secretary (1868–70), foreign secretary (1870–4, 1880–5), and colonial secretary (1886) under *Gladstone. An urbane and well-liked man, he was not an energetic politician. He was at the Colonial Office during the transfer of the Hudson Bay territories to Canada and the *Red River rebellion of 1869. His greatest test in foreign affairs was the Franco-Prussian War of 1870–1, when he maintained British neutrality. He had little understanding of the new forces of imperialism during his third term at the Foreign Office, which saw the British occupation of Egypt and the death of General *Gordon at Khartoum. MEC

Grattan, Henry (1746–1820). Statesman. Grattan was educated at Trinity College, Dublin, and called to the Irish bar in 1772. Returned to the Irish Parliament in 1775 for Charlemont, he rapidly gained a reputation as an orator and became a leader of the patriot group, pressing for Irish legislative independence, granted in 1782. He was later given £50,000 by the Irish Parliament for his services to the nation and the period 1782–99, the high-water mark of the protestant ascendancy, was known as Grattan's Parliament. In 1790 he founded the Irish Whig club and was elected for Dublin, denouncing parliamentary corruption and advocating concessions to the catholics. He was in England for the 1798 rebellion but was elected to the Dublin Parliament in 1800 in time to protest against the Act of *Union: what the minister proposed to buy could not be sold—liberty. In 1805 he was persuaded to enter the Westminster Parliament for *Fitzwilliam's borough of Malton and from 1806 to 1820 represented his old seat in Dublin. He declined office and strove continuously for *catholic emancipation, his hopes remaining unrealized. A brilliant orator, a man of integrity and political consistency, Grattan died in London and was buried in Westminster abbey. 'What Irishman', wrote Sydney *Smith, 'does not feel proud that he has lived in the days of Grattan . . . he thought only of Ireland, lived for no other object.' RAS

Gravelines, battle of, 1558. In August 1557 the Spaniards gained a major victory over the French at Saint-Quentin. A French counter-stroke in January 1558 gained them *Calais at the expense of the English. In July 1558 the Spaniards gained another victory at Gravelines, assisted by an English naval force, sent by Mary to help her husband Philip of Spain. The French were obliged to make peace in 1559 at Cateau-Cambrésis. But they did not restore Calais. JAC

Gray, Patrick Gray, 6th Baron [S] (1558–1611). Known for most of his life as the master of Gray (he did not inherit the barony until he was 50), he was an adroit politician. The family estates were in Forfarshire and Gray's wife was from the house of Ruthven. He spent much of the early 1580s in France amid pro-Mary catholic groups. On his return to Scotland, personable and polished, he became a favourite of James VI, who appointed him gentleman of the bedchamber and master of the wardrobe in 1584. Sent to England as ambassador by *Arran, he plotted to overthrow him. He betrayed Mary to Elizabeth and his protests against her execution were muted. From 1587 to 1589 he was in exile but remained a favourite with James on his return, though with diminished influence. *Camden thought him 'a quaint young gentleman, and one that thought himself able for the weightiest business'. But he seems at times to have lost himself in meaningless treachery. JAC

Gray, Thomas (1716–71). Gray led a sheltered existence: 'a life so barren of events as mine', he wrote to a friend. Educated at Eton, he went to Peterhouse, Cambridge, and returned after a grand tour as a fellow-commoner. In 1756 he transferred across the road to Pembroke College, having found his Peterhouse neighbours boisterous and noisy. He did not greatly like Cambridge but remained there for the rest of his life. In 1768 he was made professor of history and, characteristically, did not lecture but worried about it. His poetic fame came in 1750 when, through Horace Walpole, his 'Elegy in a Country Churchyard' was published. It touched many of the themes that tormented the 18th cent., particularly the vanity of human wishes: 'the paths of Glory lead but to the grave.' Gray was offered the poet laureateship in 1757 in succession to Cibber, but declined. His poetic output was small but crafted. *Johnson, whose assessment of Gray in the *Lives of the Poets* is very cool, admitted that 'in the character of his Elegy I rejoice to concur with the common reader'. JAC

Great Britain. The geographical term Great Britain was used to distinguish the largest of the British Isles from Brittany, or Little Britain. As early as the reign of Edward IV, when a marriage alliance with the future James IV was in negotiation, the advantages of a union of England and Scotland as Great Britain were pointed out. When James I succeeded Elizabeth in 1603 he hastened to propose that the union of the crowns should be followed by a governmental union and he suggested the name Great Britain. Though the English Parliament could not be brought to agree, James adopted the name by proclamation and used it on his coinage. It was given statutory authority by the Act of *Union with Scotland in 1707, article 1 of which stated that henceforth the two countries were 'united into one kingdom by the name of Great Britain'. This usage lasted until the Act of Union with Ireland in 1801, which substituted the term 'United Kingdom of Great Britain and Ireland'. After southern Ireland established its independence, the name was again modified to the 'United Kingdom of Great Britain and Northern Ireland'. The Channel Islands and the Isle of Man are not part of the United Kingdom but direct crown dependencies. The constitutional evolution is reflected in the cheerful complexity of the *Union Jack, adopted in 1801 when the cross of St Patrick was superimposed on those of St Andrew and St George. JAC

Great Britain was the second of three highly innovative steamships designed by I. K. *Brunel. It was intended by the Great Western Steamship Company as a sister ship to Brunel's *Great Western*, which had been launched in Bristol as a wooden-hulled paddle steamer in 1837 and became the first steamship to enter commercial trans-Atlantic service. But Brunel conceived a much bigger vessel, the first large iron ship and the first large screw-propelled ship. Launched in Bristol by the Prince Consort on 19 July 1843 (gross register 3,270 tons, compared with 1,340 for the previous ship), the *Great Britain* entered service between Liverpool and New

York in 1845 and, despite a severe accident the following year when she went aground off Ireland at the start of her fifth voyage, she went on to have a long working life on the route to Australia. She was eventually abandoned in the Falkland Islands in 1886, but survived to be brought home to Bristol in 1970, where she is on show. RAB

Great Cause. The disputed Scottish succession which arose when Alexander III died in 1286 leaving only a young granddaughter, the Maid of Norway, who herself died in Orkney on her journey to Scotland in 1290. Edward I had already been consulted before the Maid's death and was called in again to adjudicate between the twelve 'competitors', chief of whom were John *Comyn, John *Balliol, and Robert Bruce (Robert I). The complex proceedings culminated in Edward claiming the throne of Scotland for himself. Though Bruce's grandson succeeded in resisting the English claim, the dispute poisoned relations between the two countries for generations. JAC

Great Contract, 1610. By the time James I ascended the throne of England the royal finances had been undermined by inflation. In 1610, therefore, Lord Treasurer Robert *Cecil proposed that Parliament should vote the king a regular annual income. In return, the crown would abandon its deeply resented right to make wards of under-age heirs of landowners and sell control of their estates to the highest bidder. The Commons were allergic to the idea of permanent taxation, particularly for the benefit of the spendthrift James, but eventually accepted Cecil's proposal, though they offered far less than he had hoped for. The contract was duly formalized, but during the parliamentary recess members were made aware that their constituents were implacably opposed to it. Since James had become convinced that it would leave him no better off, the contract was abandoned, amid general recriminations. RL

great council and king's council. It can hardly be claimed that scholarship has yet entirely clarified the problem of medieval councils. The discussion is haunted by difficulties of nomenclature, the fluidity of the situation, and the fact that many developments were on an *ad hoc* basis. It is not even clear whether one can speak of more than one council, or whether they should be regarded as aspects of, or variants on, one body.

Elementary prudence dictated that medieval monarchs should seek the advice of their greatest subjects and should be seen to have their support. Anglo-Saxon monarchs had the *witan. Norman and Plantagenet monarchs had their council, under various names. As business became more complex, councils tended to divide into specialized bodies, though with much overlapping of personnel. Two bodies have been suggested, the great council and the king's council (curia regis). The great council began as a meeting of the tenants-in-chief and barons and was largely advisory. The three traditional crown-wearings, at Christmas, Easter, and Whitsun, were good opportunities to consult the great men of the realm, but such infrequent meetings could not deal with day-to-day administration or requests for justice. Nor would great magnates necessarily wish, or be able, to devote much of their time to routine matters. Consequently a smaller and more specialized council developed, consisting of household officers, sometimes in attendance on the king in his progresses, sometimes at Westminster. This was the king's council, though it was not formally an institution with defined functions until the later 13th cent.

At times the great council attempted to take a more detailed role in government—against Henry III in 1258—but such arrangements were rarely successful for long. The growth of Parliament was bound to encroach upon its importance by offering another body which could claim to speak for the nation. By the early modern period, the great council was but an echo. In the desperate crisis of 1640, Charles I summoned a great council to York, after a lapse of centuries, but the peers who responded merely suggested calling a Parliament. In 1688, James II having fled, another assembly of peers advised William of Orange to summon a Convention or Parliament.

The king's council, on the other hand, survived and coped with an ever-increasing volume of business. In the 16th cent. it threw off the *Star Chamber to take over more judicial work, and in Henry VIII's reign developed into the *Privy Council, with a small membership of hard-pressed administrators, meeting most days. For a hundred years it was the main engine of executive government, but after the Civil War and Restoration, it began to lose ground to the cabinet council and the *cabinet. JAC

***Great Eastern*.** After the *Great Western* and the **Great Britain*, I. K. *Brunel went on to design his third and largest steamship, the *Great Eastern*. This was a huge vessel of 18,915 tons gross register, the largest ship built before the 20th cent., with a cellular double hull and two sets of steam-engines, one driving paddle wheels and the other a screw. The construction of the ship, which took place on the Isle of Dogs opposite Greenwich, caused novel and formidable problems for Brunel and his partner—with whom he quarrelled severely—the shipbuilder John Scott Russell. She was launched sideways into the Thames in January 1858 and set out on her first trial voyage in September 1859. The *Great Eastern* failed to establish herself as a successful passenger ship, but she performed a valuable service in laying the trans-oceanic cables across the Atlantic and Indian Oceans. She was broken up at Birkenhead in 1888. RAB

Great Exhibition, 1851. Master-minded by *Albert, consort to Queen Victoria, the Great Exhibition was the largest trade show the world had ever seen. Joseph Paxton's *Crystal Palace, spanning 19 acres within Hyde Park (London), was accepted after 233 other plans had been rejected. Some 6 million people between 1 May and 11 October 1851, many of them on railway excursions, visited 100,000 exhibits (Raw Materials, Machinery and Invention, Manufacture, and Sculpture and Plastic Arts). Entrance fees ranged from 1 shilling to 3 guineas, with refreshments provided by the entrepreneurial Messrs Schweppes. Queen Victoria, always keen on her husband's achievements, visited 34 times. It was a paean to progress, though trade did not immediately pick up. But profits secured land in Kensington, future sites for the Victoria and Albert Museum, the Science Museum, and the Natural History Museum. Mayhew wrote that the crowds on the opening day were so dense that they formed a kind of road, paved with heads: 'on they went, fathers with their wives, and children skipping jauntily along, and youths with their sweethearts in lovely coloured shawls and ribbons.' On the last day Victoria wrote in her diary: 'To think that this great and bright time is past, like a dream, and all its success and triumph, and that all the labour and anxiety it caused for nearly 2 years should likewise now be only remembered as "a has been" seems incredible and melancholy.' SMC

Great Reform Act, 1832. The first major reform of the representative system since the time of *Cromwell. The demand for reform at the end of the 18th cent. had been tainted by association with the French Revolution and it was not until the Whigs came to power in 1830 that there was any prospect of successful legislation. Lord *Grey saw reform as a means of satisfying the desire of the respectable middle classes for greater representation and the character of the Act was accordingly moderate. Only the mechanics of the system were changed. The principal changes were:

1. Redistribution of constituencies. Boroughs with a population of less than 4,000 were either disfranchised, or reduced to one member instead of two. Some seats were added to the rural counties and others to towns such as Birmingham and Manchester, where industries or trade had developed since the 16th cent.

2. Changes in the electoral qualifications: long leaseholders were added to the '40*s*. freeholders' in the counties and in the boroughs a uniform franchise, vested in householders occupying property valued at £10 or more for local rates, was established. All voters were to be resident adult males.

3. Rules were established for the conduct of elections.

The Act satisfied the middle classes in general but agitation for more radical reform continued among the working classes, though no further general changes were made until 1867. EAS

Great Schism, 1378–1417. After the papacy's stay from 1309 at Avignon, an enclave in southern France, the Roman populace in 1378 demanded an Italian pope and the conclave, intimidated, elected Urban VI. Within three months, his conduct had alienated many supporters, who elected Clement VII. The rival pope established himself once more at Avignon. The rift perpetuated itself and the Council of Pisa in 1409, summoned to restore church unity, merely succeeded in electing a third pope, Alexander V. Not until the Council of Constance in 1417 was unity restored with the election of Martin V. The response of governments to the schism was almost purely political. The king of France supported the Avignon popes, who were more likely to be under French influence. The English, bitterly opposed to France, recognized the Roman popes. The Scots, allied to France, joined in acknowledging Avignon. An Irish synod at Roscommon in 1383 also supported Avignon. The rival popes, greatly weakened, were obliged to make substantial concessions. Scotland received from the Avignon popes its first cardinal and its first university at *St Andrews, granted by Benedict XIII in 1414. The Scots even stayed with Benedict after Martin V had been elected until the Faculty of Arts of the new university carried the day to abandon its benefactor. In 1406 Owain *Glyndŵr, in rebellion against Henry IV, offered submission to Benedict if he would confer archiepiscopal status on St Davids, establish a university for Wales, and declare Henry IV a usurper. JAC

great seal. The seal originated in the reign of Edward the Confessor as an imitation of the emperor's seal and was about 3 inches in diameter. The king is depicted in majesty, bearing sceptre and orb. The Norman rulers continued its use and the custody of the seal was given to the *chancellor. William the Lion's seal in Scotland seems to have been based on the English one. The seal is broken at the start of a new reign and a fresh one made. Since the great seal was heavy, the practice developed of employing a privy seal and later a signet. In the Tudor period, the great seal was in the hands of the chancellor or the *lord keeper but from the accession of George III the office of lord keeper has disappeared. The possession of the great seal was a matter of political importance. It was a charge against Cardinal *Wolsey at his downfall that he had illegally taken the great seal out of the kingdom to Calais in 1521. When Charles I left for York in 1642 at the start of the Civil War, Parliament had its own great seal made, and another had to be produced for the Republic in 1649. James II flung the great seal into the Thames when he fled in 1688, hoping to bring government to a standstill, but it was retrieved by a fisherman. Burglars stole the great seal from the home of Lord Chancellor *Thurlow in 1784. Since an election was imminent, craftsmen worked all night to make a new seal and jokes passed at the expense of the Foxite opposition. The great seal is used for proclamations, writs, letters patent, and treaties. A separate seal for Scotland, authorized by the Act of *Union in 1707, is in the custody of the secretary of state for Scotland. JAC

great seal and great seal register [S]. A mark of sovereign authority, the great seal was appended to crown charters as a means of authentication. The appendage marked the final stage of a long bureaucratic process known as 'passing the seals'. The register of the great seal is a record of crown charters granted under the great seal, and is printed in eleven volumes dating from 1306 to 1668. Unfortunately, it is an incomplete record. Crown charters were originally recorded on charter rolls, many of which have since been lost or destroyed. Many more charters were simply not recorded. PER

Great Yarmouth, on the Yare estuary in Norfolk, developed in the 11th cent. as a fishing town, especially for North Sea herring. From then until the First World War it was a major port, one of the largest towns in England, with stone defences which largely survive, a huge medieval parish church, and a unique pattern of 'Rows' or parallel alleys, which were largely destroyed in the Second World War. In Victoria's reign the town more than doubled in size and turned round to face the sea, becoming a very popular holiday resort. DMP

Greece, relations with. Although Greece was included in a number of *grand tours, the extra distance and primitive conditions meant that it was less well known to British travellers than Italy. When the Greeks rose in revolt against their Turkish rulers in 1821, British opinion was divided. There was sympathy for struggling nations and for Greek culture, but the policy of supporting the Ottoman empire lest Russia become overmighty was already well established. For a while the British government solved its dilemma by urging the Turks, not for the first time, to institute reform. The revolt dragged on, with appalling atrocities on both sides, and in 1827 Britain, France, and Russia by the treaty of *London offered mediation: the Greeks accepted, the Turks declined. At *Navarino, *Codrington with an allied naval force intended to separate the combatants destroyed the Turkish fleet. In 1830 the three powers guaranteed Greek independence. Codrington's action, though unintended and for which the British government apologized to the Turks, was important, though France and Russia played a greater role in establishing Greece.

Britain did not always find the new Greek regime easy to deal with, but the Don *Pacifico affair in 1850, though it had important consequences for *Palmerston, was not a serious rift. Greece made substantial territorial gains. In 1864 Britain ceded the Ionian Islands (including Corfu) which had been acquired in 1815. In 1881 Greece added Thessaly and, after the Balkan War of 1913, Macedonia and Crete. In 1914, under great pressure from both sides, Greece remained neutral, even after the Turks and Bulgarians had entered the war on the side of Germany (November 1914, October 1915). The country was badly split and on the verge of civil war, but joined the allies in 1917 when they landed troops to support Venizelos, the former prime minister. At the peace conference, Greece made large demands, including Thrace and Smyrna, which the Turks refused to hand over. Even with British support, Greece had to be content at *Lausanne in 1923 with western Thrace.

In the Second World War Greece was invaded by the Germans in April 1941 and though the British sent troops, they were unable to stem the attack. But at the end of the war, *Churchill succeeded at *Yalta in keeping Greece out of the Soviet sphere of influence. It soon became clear that Britain had no longer the military or economic strength to offer protection, but the intervention of the USA by the Truman doctrine of 1947 kept Greece outside the iron curtain. JAC

Green, Thomas Hill (1836–82). Philosopher. Born in Yorkshire, educated at Rugby and Balliol College, Oxford, Green became Whyte's professor of moral philosophy at Oxford in 1878. He made a lasting contribution to moral and political philosophy by attacking the prevailing materialism and empiricism of utilitarian thinkers, arguing for a Hegelian sense of duty to promote the common good. His ideal was human self-perfection—a condition in which people voluntarily chose to develop their potential as active citizens in pursuit of the good life. In his essay 'Liberal Legislation and Freedom of Contract' (1881) Green claimed that the inequality of power between employer and worker vitiated freedom in the labour contract and prevented workers from achieving perfection. But Green was no ivory tower academic; he took an active interest in politics and social affairs, participating in the work of a royal commission on education in 1865–6, taking a leading part in the *temperance movement, and becoming in 1876 a member of Oxford City Council. TSG

Greene, Graham (1904–91). One of the most versatile, prolific, and popular writers of the mid-20th cent., Greene was born at Berkhamsted (Herts.), where his father was headmaster of the public school, and educated at Balliol College, Oxford. He converted to catholicism at the time of his marriage in 1927. Greene published a book of verse, *Babbling April*, in 1925, and followed with a historical novel, *The Man Within*, in 1929. Next he produced a series of thrillers ('entertainments') starting with *Stamboul Train* (1932) and continuing to *The Third Man* (1950), made into a remarkable film. Increasingly Greene explored the world of catholic guilt in *Brighton Rock* (1938), *The Power and the Glory* (1940), *The Heart of the Matter* (1948), and *The End of the Affair* (1951). He also wrote verse, travel books, short stories, children's stories, and plays. His autobiography is *A Sort of Life* (1971) and *Ways of Escape* (1980). His themes of ambiguity, moral confusion, betrayal, and seediness reflected and appealed to his own times. JAC

Green Party. The British Green Party started life in 1973 as an environmental pressure group called 'People'. Two years later it became the Ecology Party dedicated to 'policies which preserve the planet and its people; decentralised decision-making in all areas of government, industry and commerce; a recognition that the human spirit is integral to a political system; and the realisation that all our policies are connected and none can be designed in isolation'. In the 1983 general election the party fielded 108 candidates but mustered barely 1 per cent of the vote. In 1985 it changed its name to the Green Party in line with similar international environmental movements. However it never managed to emulate the success of its continental counterparts. Its biggest success came in winning 15 per cent of the vote in the European elections in June 1989. But in the 1992 general election the Greens again managed to gain only 1 per cent of the vote. Although the party is hampered by an unconventional decentralized organization and internal disputes, it has been instrumental in putting environmental issues on the political agenda. RAS

Green Ribbon Club. An important Whig venue in London, formed in the mid-1670s and so-called from the colours its members wore in their hats. Based at the King's Head in Chancery Lane, it played a major part in staging rowdy pope-burning processions and other demonstrations during the *Exclusion crisis. AAH

Greenwich, treaty of, 1543. On 1 July 1543, after their defeat at *Solway Moss the previous year, the Scots made peace and agreed to a marriage between the infant Queen Mary and Prince Edward, Henry VIII's heir, which would lead to a union of the kingdoms. The terms were repudiated by the Scottish Parliament in December and fighting resumed the following year. Meanwhile, Henry VIII's last campaign against the French faltered. JAC

Greenwich palace began life as Bella Court, built by Humphrey, duke of *Gloucester, brother of Henry V, whose library housed the great collection which finished up in the Bodleian, Oxford. After passing to *Margaret of Anjou, the palace came to Henry VII, who built extensively. Its position on the Thames made it convenient for receptions and it became a major Tudor palace: Henry VIII and his daughters Mary and Elizabeth were born there. James I gave it to his wife Anne of Denmark, who employed Inigo *Jones to begin building the Queen's House. It passed next to *Henrietta Maria, but during the civil wars fell into decay and at one time was a biscuit factory. Charles II began a major reconstruction, but did not complete it, though the observatory on the hill dates from 1676/7. William III decided in 1694 to employ *Wren to build a great new hospital for seamen, which took many years to finish. George I stayed there in September 1714 on his way from Hanover. It subsequently became a naval college and home to the National Maritime Museum. The existing palace is probably the grandest of royal buildings and the Queen's House, colonnaded in the early 19th cent., and recently restored, is a jewel of cool classicism. JAC

Gregory, Lady Augusta (1852–1932). Though her plays and other writings fill many volumes, she is most often remembered in connection with W. B. *Yeats. Her translations from the Gaelic influenced his work and in verse he celebrated Coole Park, her Co. Galway house, and the 'powerful character' which made her collaboration valuable. Her son, Major Robert Gregory, he elegized as embodiment of the artist as man of action. Though from the protestant ascendancy and sometimes at odds with nationalist opinion, she was committed to the Republic and Coole survived the civil war. Into her seventies she was active on the board of the Abbey theatre and her plays show a gift for comedy lacking in Yeats. Attempts to secure a Dublin home for her nephew Hugh Lane's picture collection were less successful, but her place as a moving spirit in the Irish renaissance is assured. JNRS

Grenada, the southernmost of the Windward Islands in the Caribbean, became independent in 1974. It is a constitutional monarchy with the queen as head of state, within the Commonwealth. It was sighted by Columbus in 1498 and colonized by the French. In 1762 it was captured by *Rodney and ceded to Britain in 1763. In October 1983, after a military coup, American troops intervened and returned power to the governor-general. Cocoa, bananas, and copra are exported, but tourism is important to the economy. JAC

Grenville, George (1712–70). Prime minister. After training as a lawyer, Grenville entered Parliament in 1741 and held a number of junior posts from 1744. Although he soon gained respect for his abilities as a parliamentarian, he was not offered high office until October 1761, when Lord *Bute suggested him for a secretaryship of state. Grenville declined, partly out of fear of his brother-in-law *Pitt, whose resignation had created the vacancy. He was, however, prepared to defy Pitt by accepting the leadership of the Commons. Soon afterwards he accepted cabinet office, becoming northern secretary in May 1762, but was moved to the Admiralty in October after clashing with Bute over patronage and policy. Grenville, therefore, was not a leading candidate for the premiership after Bute's resignation in April 1763, but when Henry *Fox, the front-runner, declined he became 1st lord of the Treasury virtually by default. As prime minister he was responsible for the *Stamp Act of 1765, which provoked serious rioting in America, marking a preliminary stage in the American Revolution. Despite its undoubtedly serious repercussions, it would be wrong to see the Stamp Act as part of an ideologically driven programme of legislation. Grenville, in fact, inherited some key facets of colonial policy, such as the intention to curb western expansion and the decision to maintain a larger peacetime army in America than had previously existed. Moreover, the Currency Act (1764) forbidding paper currency in the southern colonies and the Mutiny Act (1765) permitting limited quartering of troops did not form part of a preconceived strategy: the first was hastily devised to block an independent proposal for even harsher restrictions, whereas the second responded to complaints from the commander-in-chief in America. Grenville was, however, responsible for the American Duties Act (sometimes called the Sugar Act) of 1764, which *inter alia* halved the prohibitive 100 per cent duty on foreign molasses and created a new Vice-Admiralty Court at Halifax (Nova Scotia). This signalled two clear intentions: to raise revenue via customs duties and to deny smugglers the benefit of lenient local juries. Grenville's colonial policy as evidenced by the Sugar Act and the Stamp Act reflected his adherence to financial and legal rectitude. In Britain there was no significant opposition to this legislation until after the Stamp Act crisis. Grenville understandably favoured enforcement of the Act, but was unable to prevent repeal because he had already been dismissed. American affairs had played no part in Grenville's fall in July 1765. The prevailing atmosphere of political suspicion left by Bute's resignation, exacerbated by Grenville's propensity to lecture the king, jeopardized political stability. Having narrowly avoided dismissal in the spring of 1765, Grenville determined to extort public proof of his mastery, insisting upon the removal of Bute's brother from the Scottish privy seal, thereby forcing the king to break his promise of granting the office for life. Unable immediately to retaliate, the king rid himself of Grenville at the first opportunity. Grenville spent the remainder of his political career in opposition, consistently defending both his conduct as prime minister and his policy towards America. DW

Grenville, Sir Richard (1542–91). Of a landed family, Grenville was born at Buckland abbey, between Tavistock and Plymouth, which he sold to Francis *Drake in 1581 (hence it became a Grenville–Drake shrine). Having campaigned against the Turks as a soldier, and in Ireland, in 1576 Grenville became sheriff of Cornwall and was knighted. A relative of *Ralegh, Grenville was much involved, both as MP and man of action, in transatlantic settlement, especially during 1585–6 at Roanoke Island (North Carolina). In 1588 he fitted out ships against the Spanish Armada, and in 1591, under Lord Thomas *Howard's command, Grenville sailed to the Azores to intercept the Spanish treasure fleet. Detained at Flores, with many sick, Grenville, in *Revenge*, a ship of proven fighting qualities, confronted alone a force of over 50 Spanish warships. Sinking one and damaging others before surrendering, Grenville died of his wounds; *Revenge* foundered in a gale shortly afterwards. Grenville's last fight became a legend. DDA

Grenville, William Wyndham, 1st Lord (1759–1834). Prime minister. The third son of George *Grenville, prime minister 1763–5, he was educated at Eton and Christ Church, Oxford, where he became a distinguished classical scholar, an interest he retained throughout life. He entered Parliament in 1782 and cast in his lot with his cousin the young William *Pitt. *Shelburne appointed him chief secretary in Ireland in 1782 and under Pitt he was paymaster of the forces 1783–9, an office he held together with membership of the India Board of Control and of the Board of Trade after 1784. A diligent administrator, he contributed to the major financial and economic achievements of Pitt's peacetime ministry. In 1787 he was sent on diplomatic missions to The Hague and Versailles and sounded out the possibilities of an agreement with the French to end the African slave trade, a cause which remained close to his heart until he was able as prime minister in 1807 to accomplish it.

In January 1789 Grenville agreed to become Speaker of the House of Commons in order to help Pitt in the midst of the *Regency crisis, but he craved a cabinet post and when the crisis was over was appointed home secretary. By this time he was recognized as Pitt's 'second in command' and in 1790 was elevated to the Lords to oversee the government's business there. He was translated to the foreign secretaryship in 1791 and for ten years was responsible for British policy in the French Revolutionary War. Grenville found the post uncongenial and his successes were few. In 1801 he resigned with Pitt over the king's refusal to grant catholic relief, but unlike Pitt he determined not to take office again unless the king withdrew his veto. Accordingly he did not return with Pitt in 1804 but formed an alliance with the Foxite Whigs, with whom he served in the 'Ministry of all the *Talents' in 1806–7.

As prime minister, Grenville achieved little beyond the abolition of the slave trade. The ministry was inharmonious and foreign policy was confused and ineffective, partly due to Grenville's own hesitancy and lack of firm leadership. The government collapsed when George III thwarted their attempt to smuggle concessions to the Irish catholics past his protestant conscience. For the next ten years Grenville and *Grey, Fox's successor, led the opposition to *Portland, *Perceval, and *Liverpool but neither found the position agreeable. The alliance ended in 1817 when they disagreed over the government's suspension of *habeas corpus to deal with radical agitation. Grenville then retired from political life, devoting his remaining years to classical scholarship and to his duties as chancellor of Oxford University.

Grenville was a diligent administrator and a conscientious politician but the glittering prizes eluded him. He lacked warmth, imagination, and leadership qualities. His forbidding manner earned him the nickname of 'Bogey' and he seemed remote and insensitive except to his circle of family and friends. EAS

Gresham, Thomas (1519–79). Second son of Sir Richard Gresham, he became a banker, merchant, and royal agent or king's factor. Born in London and educated at Gonville Hall, Cambridge, from 1551 to 1574 he was based in Antwerp, where he successfully negotiated royal loans with Flemish merchants to buy military supplies. As adviser to Queen Elizabeth I he was an advocate of sound monetary policy, seeking the restoration of base money, a reduction in debt, and prompt payment by the crown. He is credited with 'Gresham's Law', that 'bad money drives out good', arguing that if coins of different metal content but of equal legal tender are in circulation, those with lower value metal content will be used for exchange whilst the rest will be hoarded. He founded the *Royal Exchange in London to function along the lines of the Bourse in Antwerp, gave Gresham College to London, as well as establishing paper mills at Osterley and a number of almshouses. JRP

Greville, Charles (1794–1865). Greville's journal, kept from 1814 to 1860, is an invaluable source for the politics and society of his period. Originally published in part nine years after his death, his candid comments caused consternation and 'social outrage'. Greville, a grandson of the duke of *Portland, prime minister 1807–9, and of the 1st earl of Warwick, went to Eton and to Christ Church, Oxford. Two sinecures given to him as a boy provided for him and his passion was horse-racing. His entrée into high society, where he was known as 'Punch', gave him the chance to hear political and social gossip, but he wrote well and with some impartiality. His memoirs were published in full in 1938. Greville finished as a deaf bachelor with a reputation for testiness. *Disraeli thought him the vainest man he had ever met, not excluding Bulwer-*Lytton. JAC

Grey, Charles, 2nd Earl Grey (1764–1845). Prime minister. Son of General Sir Charles Grey of Fallodon, Northumberland, a distinguished soldier in the wars of the later 18th cent., Grey entered Parliament in 1786 as a member for Northumberland through the efforts of his uncle Sir Henry Grey of Howick. Grey inherited Howick in 1808 and made it his beloved home from which he could rarely be tempted to attend to his duties as leader of the Whig Party after *Fox's death.

A headstrong young man, Grey was attracted to Fox and his circle of drinking and gambling cronies and joined the opposition to *Pitt almost immediately on entering the Commons. He had a notorious affair with Georgiana, duchess of Devonshire, by whom he had a daughter in 1792. In 1794 he married Mary Ponsonby, by whom he had fifteen children.

Grey distinguished himself from the outset as a brilliant orator in the House of Commons, and quickly formed the ambition to be the next leader of the Whig Party after Fox, but in 1792 he committed himself to parliamentary reform, helping to found the Association of the *Friends of the People. He hoped to use the reform movement to advance his career but the step split the Whigs, aristocratic grandees like the duke of *Portland and Earl *Fitzwilliam being frightened by the prospect of the spread of the French Revolution. They joined Pitt in 1794, while Fox and Grey led the rump of the party in opposition. In 1798 they seceded from the Commons in protest against Pitt's repressive measures.

After the peace of *Amiens and the subsequent resumption of war against Napoleon the Whigs formed a coalition with the group led by Lord *Grenville, but their conservatism meant that Grey had to give up active support of reform. In the 'Ministry of all the *Talents' (1806–7) Grey served as 1st lord of the Admiralty and after Fox's death succeeded him as foreign secretary. He abandoned Fox's attempt to make peace with France, believing that the war was now a defensive one against Napoleonic aggression, but he was heavily criticized by some of Fox's followers as well as by the London radicals, who accused him of abandoning the cause of reform. After the fall of the 'Talents', Grey tried to steer a middle course between radicalism and conservatism but with little practical success.

In 1807 Grey inherited the peerage which, to his dismay, *Addington had conferred on his father in 1802. For the remainder of his life he sat in the House of Lords, where his oratorical gifts were less effective, and this added to the despondency which often characterized his later career. Though he never quite abandoned the position of leader of the Whig opposition, the party suffered from a lack of positive direction. He consistently advocated *catholic emancipation and gave important assistance to *Wellington in achieving it in 1829. He was widely expected to join Wellington's cabinet as foreign secretary, but George IV refused to allow an offer to be made. His dislike of Grey dated back to the time when Grey had refused to help him, when prince of Wales, in the affair of his illegal marriage to Mrs Fitzherbert, and Grey had also supported Queen *Caroline against the king's attempt to divorce her in 1820.

In 1830 George IV's death removed the royal veto and at the same time the demand for parliamentary reform revived in the country. Wellington's refusal to consider it broke up his administration and William IV sent for Grey, at the age of 66, to form the ministry which was to pass the *Great Reform Act.

The Reform Act was Grey's major achievement. He proposed it on the same principles which he had professed in 1792, the need to settle the disturbed state of the country by satisfying the demand of the respectable classes for greater representation while denying power to the mass of the people who, he believed, were not ready to be trusted with it. He saw the Act as a means of preserving the essential elements of the existing constitution by removing abuses but perpetuating aristocratic leadership. He was able to persuade William IV to maintain a reluctant support for the measure and, finally, to promise to create enough new peers, if necessary, to force the bill through the House of Lords. The Reform Act bears the stamp of Grey's character—pragmatic, moderate, and fundamentally conservative—and its ultimate passage owes much to his ability to manage the king and his divided colleagues. His cabinet was a coalition of interests rather than a united party, and in 1834 when its divisions over the Irish church question became public Grey resigned, with relief at the ending of his burdensome duties. He spent the rest of his life in retirement at Howick.

Grey's early ambition was overt and headstrong, and gained him few friends, though Fox admired his talents. Later in life he became more circumspect, but his lack of personal warmth hindered his effectiveness as a party leader. His genuine belief in the necessity of political reform was tempered by his conservative instincts and aristocratic outlook. He was not a charismatic leader like Fox and he was never idolized by his followers or the public, but his achievement in piloting the Reform Bill through Parliament helped to preserve the traditional institutions of the country and to set the pattern for future peaceful development.

EAS

Derry, J. W., *Charles Grey, Aristocratic Reformer* (Oxford, 1992); Smith, E. A., *Lord Grey, 1764–1845* (Oxford, 1990).

Grey, Sir Edward (1862–1933). Foreign secretary. Grey has been described as curiously 'suspended between the world of high politics and rural isolation', a man who sought refuge from the toils of office in fishing and ornithology. Behind the reserve lay a very determined and tough politician. He was among those Liberals who supported the *Boer War, and was involved in the attempt to compel *Campbell-Bannerman to move to the Lords on becoming prime minister in 1905. But it was as foreign secretary (December 1905–December 1916, the longest continuous tenure of that office) that he has attracted the interest of historians. He has been variously portrayed as unduly rigid in his dealings with Germany; as missing opportunities to convince Berlin that Britain would fight on the side of France in the event of war; as one who might have done more to act as a mediator in European affairs; or as one who at best had little opportunity to alter the course of events leading to war. What is most evident is his conviction that there could be no return to the policy of the 'free hand' as practised by Salisbury.

He gained his first experience in the Foreign Office under Lord *Rosebery in the mid-1890s. As foreign secretary himself Grey quickly dispelled fears that a Liberal government might weaken Britain's role in the world. In the Moroccan crisis with Germany (1905–6), he went further than his predecessor by agreeing to precautionary military staff talks with France. He also overcame the doubts of some cabinet colleagues to push through the entente of 1907 with Russia. This led some contemporary radical critics to ask why, if he could negotiate with tsarist Russia, he could not do the same with the more progressive state of Germany. But Grey's overtures on the question of the Anglo-German naval race always fell foul of Berlin's insistence on British neutrality in the event of a European war. Limited progress on other issues did not narrow the fundamental divide.

As Europe stumbled towards war in July 1914 cabinet divisions prevented Grey from unambiguously signalling that Britain would fight in defence of France. Berlin would have preferred British neutrality, but chose to risk war. Grey himself threatened to resign rather than abandon France, but it was German infringement of Belgian neutrality which ensured that most of the cabinet opted for war on 4 August. Grey did much in the first two years of the conflict to prevent serious differences with the USA, especially over American complaints arising from the British blockade of Germany. Horrified by the war, he became a supporter of the *League of Nations, but failed in his bid for ongoing Anglo-American co-operation. CJB

Grey, Ford Grey, 3rd Baron (1655–1701). Grey had a turbulent but dexterous political career. He inherited his barony at the age of 19 and was an ardent exclusionist, voting Lord *Stafford guilty in 1680. In 1682 he was tried for abducting his wife's sister but the matter was compromised after he had been found guilty. In 1683 he was again on trial for a riot at the Guildhall and was later implicated in the *Rye House plot. Sent to the Tower, he escaped and joined *Monmouth. He commanded Monmouth's cavalry without much skill in the western rising, was captured, and saved his life by testifying against his companions. Though reinstated by James II in 1686, he adhered to William of Orange, was created earl of Tankerville in 1695 and held office as 1st lord of the Treasury and lord privy seal 1699–1701. 'A cowardly and incestuous traitor' was *Complete Peerage*'s terse dismissal. JAC

Grey, Lady Jane (1537–54). Jane was the eldest daughter of Henry Grey, marquis of *Dorset, later duke of Suffolk, and a cousin of Edward VI. An intelligent and well-educated girl, she joined the household of *Catherine Parr. After Catherine's death in 1548 she became a ward of Catherine's fourth husband, Thomas *Seymour of Sudeley, who hoped for a marriage between her and Edward VI. After Seymour's execution in 1549, Jane returned to live with her parents. The duke of *Northumberland then planned to use her to seize the succession when Edward should die. Against her own wishes, she was married on 21 May 1553 to Guilford Dudley, fourth son of Northumberland. After Edward's death on 6 July 1553, she was proclaimed queen and Guilford declared himself king. Mary Tudor's supporters rallied and on 19 July Jane's father admitted defeat and recognized Mary's succession. Lady Jane's reign had lasted a mere nine days. She hoped to return to private life but was held in the Tower and executed on 12 February 1554. She was the innocent victim of her family's heartless ambitions. SMC

Grey, Leonard, 1st Viscount Grane [I] (1490–1541). Grey was one of many who perished in the mire of Tudor Ireland. He was a younger son of the 1st marquis of Dorset. His grandmother was *Elizabeth, queen of Edward IV, and his nephew's daughter was Lady Jane *Grey. A tough soldier, he was sent to command in Ireland in 1535, where Thomas *Fitzgerald, son of Gerald *Fitzgerald, 9th earl of Kildare, was in rebellion. The rising was crushed and Fitzgerald and five of his uncles sent to England and executed. Grey was appointed lord deputy in 1536 and given an Irish peerage. He presided over the Dublin Parliament which effected the Reformation, including dissolution of the monasteries. But his rough manner made many enemies and the 9th earl of Kildare's young son, in flight, was his nephew. Despite considerable military success, Grey was accused of treason. In a long submission, the council charged him with not doing all he could to apprehend his nephew and of overbearing behaviour: 'when contradicted in the council, he falleth in fury with menacing words and great oaths, laying his hand on his dagger or sword.' Though he sounds brutish, the charges seem to fall far short of treason. Nevertheless, he was found guilty and executed in July 1541. JAC

greyhound racing as an organized sport developed in the USA, though greyhounds had been bred and raced for centuries. The sport owed its appeal to the oval course, which makes for tactical running, and to betting. In England the first track was opened at Belle Vue (Manchester) in 1926. The National Greyhound Racing Club was established in 1928. The major national event is the Greyhound Derby at the White City, London, which is usually televised. JAC

Griffith, Arthur (1871–1922). A printer from Dublin, Griffith was active in the Celtic Literary Society, the *Gaelic League, and the *Irish Republican Brotherhood. He spent 1896–9 in South Africa, returning to Ireland to commence vigorous journalism, urging that Ireland could emulate Hungary and acquire substantial autonomy. In 1906 he launched *Sinn Fein, preaching abstention from British politics, and was involved in the Howth gun-running in 1914. Twice imprisoned during the First World War, Griffith did not take part in the *Easter Rising, but was returned for East Cavan at a by-election in 1918. He was again imprisoned but emerged to lead the Irish delegation at the negotiations in 1921 which resulted in the *Irish Free State. He succeeded *de Valera as president of the Dáil in January 1922 but died from a stroke seven months later, just as the civil war between pro- and anti-treaty factions was beginning. JAC

Grindal, Edmund (1519–83). Archbishop of Canterbury (1575–83). Born in Cumberland, Grindal was educated at Pembroke Hall, Cambridge, where he was later master (1559–61). As chaplain to Bishop *Ridley of London, he supported the protestant changes under Edward VI. After exile in Germany under Mary, he was successively bishop of London (1559–70), despite reservations over vestments, and archbishop of York (1570) and Canterbury. Though prominent in framing the *Thirty-Nine Articles, he was too calvinistic to help *Parker re-establish Anglicanism. His ruthlessness towards catholics and reluctance to bring puritan London clergy into line persuaded Parker to recommend him for the less puritan see of York (1570) where dissidence was mainly catholic. Later *Cecil suggested his translation to Canterbury (1575) where he was soon in conflict with Elizabeth for refusing to suppress puritan 'prophesyings' (1576), and was suspended from the temporalities of his see 1577–82. WMM

Griqualand, East and West. Griqualand West, an arid region occupied by the Griqua people, was annexed to Cape Colony in 1871 after diamonds had been found there. It is south of the Kalahari desert. The chief town is Kimberley. It now forms part of Cape Province (South Africa). Griqualand East was annexed to Cape Colony in 1880, but is now divided between the Transkei and Natal. JAC

Grocyn, William (*c.*1449–1519). Cleric and Greek scholar. Grocyn came up from Winchester to Oxford in 1465, and taught in the university in the 1470s–1480s. In March 1488 he went to Florence to improve his Latin and Greek, along with William Latimer and Thomas *Linacre; he also got to know the great Venetian scholar and printer Aldus Manutius. From 1491 Grocyn taught Greek in Oxford. From 1496 he spent more time in his living of St Lawrence Jewry, London; and from 1506 in Maidstone as rector of the College of All Hallows, dying at Maidstone after having been incapacitated by a stroke in 1518. A letter to Aldus is Grocyn's only known publication, but his scholarship was much admired by contemporaries, including Erasmus, who lodged with him. His Oxford Greek lectures were the first given by an Englishman, and he collected a remarkable Latin and Greek library, which reflects forward-looking humanist tastes as well as knowledge of medieval authorities. It is known from Linacre's catalogue of it and from many volumes now in Corpus Christi College, Oxford. JBT

Grosmont (Gwent). Though no more than a pretty village today, Grosmont, just west of the Monnow, was an important part of the Anglo-Norman defences against Welsh incursions, protecting Hereford and the lush valley of the Severn. Glamorgan fell early to the Norman advance into north Wales, and Monmouth and Chepstow castles were begun immediately after the Conquest. White Castle, Skenfrith, and Grosmont, 15 miles west, formed a defensive triangle and belonged in the 1200s to the formidable justiciar Hubert de *Burgh, who began converting them to stone castles and improving the living accommodation. Grosmont was given borough status which it retained until 1857, when the last mayor was elected, and the church of St Nicholas was larger than the township required. The castle's last military activity was in March 1405 when a raid by *Glyndŵr's son was beaten off by a relief force sent from Hereford by Prince Henry. By Tudor times it was in ruins but much survives, including a fine 14th-cent. octagonal chimney, crested by a coronet. Grosmont was briefly one of the Monmouth contributory boroughs when Wales was given parliamentary representation in the 16th cent. The three castles belonged to the crown, through the duchy of Lancaster, from 1267 to 1825, when they were sold to the Beauforts. They resold in 1902, giving the town hall, substantially rebuilt in 1832, to the community. JAC

Grosseteste, Robert (*c.*1170–1253). Scholar and bishop. Of a humble Suffolk family, Grosseteste went to Cambridge and later lectured at Oxford. He held archdeaconries for Wiltshire, Northampton, and Leicester before election in 1235 to the vast diocese of Lincoln. He plunged into reforming the discipline of the see and into the quarrels that preoccupied him for the rest of his life. From 1239 he was in collision with the chapter at Lincoln in a flurry of excommunications, until Innocent IV found in his favour in 1245. While this quarrel continued, he engaged in others, including several with Henry III. In 1253 he resisted the pope's attempt to place his nephew in a canonry at Lincoln. A man of great learning, Grosseteste wrote innumerable translations and commentaries. He was on close terms with Simon de *Montfort and acted in his later years as tutor to his sons, which led Stubbs to identify him as a great constitutional statesman. Southern called him an 'enigma', adding that he was 'genial and courteous but a tyrant'. The combination of pugnacity and piety, more common in the 13th cent. than today, persuaded Powicke to classify him as the 'church militant'. JAC

Grote, George (1794–1871). Grote, whose family came from Exeter, was a banker, politician, and historian. After attending Charterhouse, he joined the family bank at 16. Greatly influenced by *Bentham and James *Mill, he took an active part in the foundation of the University of London, keenly supporting the admission of women. From 1832 until 1841 he was a radical MP for London and in April 1833 moved for the first time for *secret ballot, a cause with which he is associated: he was defeated by 211 to 106. He did not stand for re-election in 1841 and gave up his banking interest to devote his time to finishing his *History of Greece*. Volumes i and ii came out in 1846 and the twelfth and final volume in 1856. He followed it with three volumes on Plato in 1865. From 1868 he was president of University College London, to which he left endowments and his brain. JAC

Grove, Sir George (1820–1900). Civil engineer and writer on music. After embarking on a career building lighthouses in the West Indies, Grove became secretary to the Society of Arts (1850) and the Crystal Palace (1852), for whose concerts he wrote numerous programme notes. Interested in biblical studies, he co-founded the Palestine Exploration Fund and co-edited Smith's *Dictionary of the Bible*; he also wrote on many other subjects including geography and was editor of *Macmillan's Magazine*. He became the first director of the *Royal College of Music in 1883. His *Dictionary of Music and Musicians* (1879–89), has remained the foremost English-language musical dictionary. Its most recent sixth edition, published in 20 volumes as *The New Grove Dictionary of Music and Musicians* (1980), was rewritten under the editorship of Stanley Sadie. Grove also published *Beethoven and his Nine Symphonies* (1896). ECr

Grub Street is a derogatory term for bad writing. Its figurative use was commonplace by the early 18th cent. and Jonathan *Swift referred to a paper he was involved with as 'a little upon the Grub-Street'. In his *Dictionary* of 1755 Samuel *Johnson commented: 'originally the name of a street in Moorfields in London [now under the Barbican development], much inhabited by writers of small histories, dictionaries, and temporary poems; whence any mean production is called grubstreet.' JAD

Gruffydd ap Cynan (*c.*1055–1137), king of Gwynedd (1081–1137). He was the son of Cynan ab Iago, a descendant of *Rhodri Mawr but an exile in Ireland, and Ragnhildr, daughter of the Scandinavian ruler of Dublin. With skill and persistence, he turned himself from an adventurer into a ruler of *Gwynedd, contending with Viking-Irish, Anglo-Normans, and volatile Welsh along the way. With Viking and Norman aid, he returned to re-establish Rhodri's line in Gwynedd (1075), but then attacked Rhuddlan and failed to overcome rivals. In his second foray (1081), again with Viking aid, he allied with *Rhys ap Tewdwr in *Deheubarth, but he was betrayed to the Normans and imprisoned at Chester. He took part in the major uprising of 1094, but by 1098 was again in Ireland. Only with Norman agreement did he return permanently (1099) and rule in Anglesey, whence he extended his dominion to the east and south, consolidated his control of Gwynedd, and created a stable, prosperous kingdom. His court poet, Meilyr Brydydd, and the *History of Gruffydd ap Cynan* commissioned by his son Owain (in Latin, later translated into Welsh), suggest a cultural vitality, perhaps under Irish influence, that extolled his achievements. RAG

Gruffydd ap Llywelyn (d. 1063), king of Gwynedd and Powys (1039–63). The son of Llywelyn ap Seisyll, king of *Gwynedd, and Angharad, the king of Deheubarth's daughter, Gruffydd created a personal dominion over much of Wales in alliance with English and Scandinavians. He was later said to be slow and listless as a youth, but he grew into an ambitious warlord who won Gwynedd and *Powys in battle (1039) and defeated the Mercians on the river Severn. His conquests in *Deheubarth took longer (1040–55), during which he slew two of its kings. His alliance with Earl Ælfgar of Mercia, whose daughter he married, sustained a long struggle with *Harold Godwineson (later Harold II), and Bishop Leofgar of Hereford also led an army against him (1056). To a Welsh chronicler he was 'the head and shield and defender of the Britons'. Harold's attack on Gruffydd's court at Rhuddlan (1062) caused him to flee, and soon afterwards (5 August 1063) he was killed by his own men; his territorial dominion collapsed at the same time. RAG

Gruffydd ap Rhys (*c.*1090–1137), pretender to the kingdom of *Deheubarth. Following the death of his father, *Rhys ap Tewdwr, in 1093, Gruffydd was taken to Ireland for safety. In 1113 he returned with kinsmen and 'young hot-heads' to claim his inheritance, but others declined to support him. His rising against Norman settlers in 1116 was seen as 'repairing and renewing the Brittanic kingdom' in the spirit of the struggle between British and invader. Gruffydd ravaged south-west Wales but failed to capture the new castles or make permanent conquests. He had to be content with lands in the Tywi valley. He married Gwenllian, daughter of *Gruffydd ap Cynan, king of *Gwynedd; in the general uprising after Henry I's death (1135), Gruffydd took part in the Welsh victory near Cardigan in 1136, while Gwenllian led his army against Kidwelly castle and was killed there. He died soon afterwards and his four sons inherited his claims in Deheubarth. RAG

***Guardian*.** Newspaper which has come to embody the ideology of liberal, middle-class, regional, and metropolitan England in popular perception. From its founding as the weekly *Manchester Guardian* by John Edward Taylor in 1821, it was a radical voice, demanding liberal economic and political reform. It became a daily from 1855, but did not drop its 'Manchester' prefix until 1959. It is notable today as the only national daily which has a strong regional input to supplement its London base, and which has escaped the ownership of any press magnate, preserving the democratic Scott Trust structure which has run the paper from 1936. DJA

Guildford, diocese of. The see, created in 1927, comprises most of Surrey. Because the area is poor agriculturally, economic development was weak and the population small, until road improvements in the 17th and 18th cents. and the advent of the railways knit Surrey closely to London. Because of this only half the parish churches date from before 1830, but Chertsey abbey, founded *c.*960, was significant enough in medieval times to be Henry VI's original burial place before his final interment at Windsor (1484). John Wesley preached his last sermon at Leatherhead in 1791. The massive increase in commuter population in the early 20th cent. necessitated the creation of a new bishopric which, simultaneously with *Portsmouth, was carved out of the *Winchester diocese (1927). The cathedral, designed by Sir Edward Maufe and built between 1936 and 1961, is in a simplified Gothic style. WMM

Guilford courthouse, battle of, 1781. As late as the spring of 1781 British forces in America were capable of inflicting sharp defeats on the rebels. To follow up his victory at *Camden in August 1780, *Cornwallis moved northwards towards Virginia, impeded by Nathaniel Greene's forces. At Guilford courthouse on 15 March Greene gave battle. Cornwallis had scarcely 2,000 men and was heavily outnumbered, but carried the day, capturing the American guns. But his own losses were heavy and his army now tiny. JAC

guilds. The guild was one of the most characteristic organizations of the later medieval period and an instrument of local urban monopoly control operated by a particular craft or by the market guild, which was the commercial guise of the local administration. Major towns had specialized guilds for different trades and London had a great variety of both mercantile guilds, such as grocers, goldsmiths, and vintners, and manufacturers like tailors and saddlers. The purpose of the guild was to regulate the local market. This took the form of control of the price and quality of goods. In Leicester, where the local wool trade was particularly important, guild restrictions were intended to retain as much of the business as possible in the hands of local merchants. Outsiders could not buy wool in the town and could only sell to members of the guild. Weavers were prevented from working at night since poor lighting would diminish the quality of workmanship. The guild also limited production and ensured that each individual member secured a fair share of the available business. Recruitment and employment were also limited through entry fines, a preference for the sons of existing members, or apprenticeships which could last for seven years. Membership conferred substantial advantages. Members of Southampton's guild were exempt from local tolls and customs and enjoyed the right of the first option to purchase goods brought to the town. Non-members were prevented from buying certain commodities including honey, herring, oil, or skins, from keeping a tavern, and could only sell cloth on market or fair days. Guilds were characteristic of an economic system, under threat from population decline and competition from unregulated rural industry, in which established interests sought to protect themselves through the maintenance of a monopoly. CHL

Guild Socialists advocated workers' control of industry by transforming trade unions into monopolistic producers' guilds. These guilds would form one part of a pluralist power structure with the state, which would represent the individual as consumer on equal terms. These ideas, developed in the monthly *New Age* by A. R. Orage and S. G. Hobson, and later by G. D. H. Cole, had a degree of influence on the left until the mid-1920s.

Guild Socialism developed partly as a reaction to *Fabian 'state socialism'. Hilaire Belloc feared that state intervention would make workers 'well fed instruments of production' whilst maintaining 'wage slavery'; as capitalist power lay in the economic field it was argued that parliamentary means would achieve little. Peaceful change was advocated by the gradual encroachment on the role of employers by union representatives. But the practical achievements of Guild Socialists were meagre. In 1915 an attempt to capture the Fabian Society for the idea failed. The Building Guilds established in 1920 by *Hobson collapsed in 1923 due to the ending of government subsidies, the slump, building employer hostility, and Hobson's mismanagement. Guild Socialist ideas did, however, experience brief resurgences in the 1930s and 1960s. LHM

Guinness, Edward (1847–1927). Born at Clontarf, Co. Dublin, son of the proprietor of Guinness brewery, he was educated at Trinity College, Dublin. Eventually he became chairman of the company which, in 1886, became a public company, known as Arthur Guinness & Son. He retired in 1889 and devoted himself to various public services. His many benefactions began with housing schemes to replace slums in Dublin and London. He endowed the Lister Institute for Tropical Medicine in London and, during the Boer War, equipped a field hospital for Irish troops. He made various gifts to Dublin hospitals. Although a unionist, the nationalist majority of Dublin corporation offered him the lord mayoralty, which honour he declined. He became successively Baron Iveagh in 1891, viscount in 1905, and earl in 1919. Among his bequests was his celebrated collection of paintings, which included some *Gainsboroughs and *Romneys, to the British nation. IJEK

Gulf War, 1990–1. On 2 August 1990 Iraq invaded the tiny neighbouring state of Kuwait, giving the Iraqi dictator Saddam Hussein control of about 15 per cent of the world's oil, with a threat to a further 25 per cent. The almost defunct Soviet Union (which collapsed in December 1991) did not block a strong American response, which employed the United Nations Security Council to denounce Iraq's action and won Saudi Arabian agreement to receive large American forces. In response, on 8 August, Iraq announced the incorporation of Kuwait into Iraq, an act of direct conquest unprecedented among United Nations members.

President George Bush portrayed American military action as the start of a 'New World Order' following the end of the *Cold War. Bush assembled a coalition of twenty-nine countries against Iraq, although with its immense armed forces and technological superiority the USA dominated the coalition in all respects. Britain's policy was to support the USA completely, to demonstrate both her reliability as an ally and her importance as a second-ranking power. By stripping her armed forces Britain contributed small but significant naval, air, and ground units to the war, all closely subordinated to American command.

The coalition forces took several months to assemble in Saudi Arabia. Iraqi strategy was to prevent a coalition forming by playing on pan-Arab sentiment, in particular over past American support for Israel. On 29 November the United Nations Security Council set a deadline of 15 January 1991 for Iraqi withdrawal from Kuwait, authorizing the use of force ('all necessary means') to support this.

Early on 17 January 1991, the coalition began with a massive air bombing attack against Iraq, which responded by attacking Israel (which was not a coalition member and had taken no military action) with long-range missiles. Critically for coalition solidarity, Israel refused to retaliate. The coalition launched its ground offensive to clear Kuwait on 24 February. This revealed that the Americans had greatly overestimated the Iraqi army, which virtually disintegrated, offering only token resistance. On 28 February, having achieved the objective of liberating Kuwait, Bush called a unilateral cease-fire, and a permanent cease-fire came into effect on 11 April.

With the liberation of Kuwait dissident groups within Iraq, notably the Kurds of the north, rose in rebellion. Over the next year Saddam gradually reasserted his rule, and survived in power. Ironically, Prime Minister Margaret *Thatcher, who had first committed Britain to the coalition, was forced from office in November 1990, and Bush failed to gain re-election in 1992. Although the Gulf War secured oil supplies for the West, effectively destroyed Saddam's ambitions for Iraq as a regional power, and upheld the rule of law through the United Nations, it failed to deliver the promised 'New World Order'. SDB

Gulliver's Travels, Jonathan *Swift's best seller, appeared on 28 October 1726. Purporting to be an autobiographical account of Gulliver's 'Travels into Several Remote Nations of the World', and read as a 'general' satire on political and social institutions, contemporaries also interpreted Swift's work as a 'particular' political allegory on the administration of Sir Robert *Walpole. Attempts to identify a close allegory have been unconvincing, however. Although Swift's scathing portrait of the bestial Yahoos outraged Victorian sensibilities, *Gulliver's Travels* endured as a children's classic. It appeals to modern readers as a general political allegory and a savage indictment of human folly. JAD

Gundulf (*c.*1024–1108). Bishop of Rochester. Born in Normandy, Gundulf became a monk at Bec, where he formed friendships with both *Lanfranc and *Anselm. Anselm called him 'first among my friends' and wrote that 'thy spirit and mine can never bear to be absent from each other'. In 1070 when Lanfranc became archbishop of Canterbury, he brought over Gundulf as an administrator and had him elected to the bishopric of Rochester in 1076. Gundulf changed it from a secular to a monastic church and began rebuilding the cathedral. William the Conqueror employed him to supervise the construction of the White Tower. In 1093 he wrote to the monks at Bec urging them not to oppose Anselm's appointment as archbishop of Canterbury. Gundulf remained on good terms with both Rufus and Henry I and had sufficient authority to beseech Rufus in 1093 to lead a better life, though he received a ribald answer. He was one of the most saintly and respected of post-Conquest bishops. JAC

Gunpowder plot, 1605. Soon after becoming king of England in 1603, James I discreetly relaxed the penal laws which subjected catholics to fines, imprisonment, and even death. However, the ensuing uproar in Parliament persuaded him to backtrack, leaving the catholics feeling betrayed and hopeless, particularly since the conclusion of peace with Spain in 1604 had deprived them of help from that quarter. A band of young catholic hotheads decided to seize the initiative by destroying the entire English government. They smuggled barrels of gunpowder into the cellars of Parliament, and Guy *Fawkes stood ready to ignite these on 5 November 1605, when the king, Lords, and Commons were assembled for the opening of the new session. The plot was betrayed, however, and the conspirators captured, tried, and executed. The plot etched itself upon the collective English memory, and bonfires and 'burning the guy' have remained traditional features of Bonfire Night celebrations. RL

Gurkhas or Gorkhas were the ruling clan of the Kathmandu valley who, in the 18th cent., expanded their empire over much of Nepal and encroached into sub-Himalayan India. They were defeated in 1814–16 by Lord *Hastings. However, their valour and fighting qualities—especially with the *kukri* knife—earned much respect. The king of Nepal was invited to supply Gurkha contingents to the British Indian army. Gurkha batallions served with distinction in many colonial engagements, including the *Indian mutiny, and in the First and Second World Wars. They are still represented in both the British and the Indian armies. DAW

Guthlac, St (*c.*674–715). Of Mercian royal stock, a native of Middle Anglia (around Leicestershire), Guthlac, baptized as a baby, for nine years led a war-band, before entering at 24 the monastery at *Repton and at 26 occupying a (robbed) burial mound on the Lincolnshire island of Crowland (possibly territory of north Gyrwe), on the Middle–East Anglian border. His biography, by Felix, bears resemblances to the poem **Beowulf*. Guthlac's life as a hermit, fighting demons, exemplifies the combination of Germanic heroism, Mediterranean influence, and genuine faith which characterized aristocratic Anglo-Saxon Christianity. Guthlac was politically influential, his visitors including Bishop Hedda, Ecburh, daughter of Aldwulf of East Anglia, and *Æthelbald, future king of Mercia, whose accession Guthlac prophesied. Guthlac's support was exploited in Æthelbald's promotion of his cult. Crowland abbey developed from his hermitage. Vernacular lives were composed later and his cult flourished particularly in the 12th cent. AER

Guthrum (d. 890). Viking leader, king in East Anglia, and major opponent of King *Alfred. Guthrum probably first appeared in England as the leader of the 'great summer army' which joined the forces commanded by Halfdan at Reading in 871. When the army split up in 875, Guthrum returned with his contingent to Wessex. In 878 he was nearly successful in capturing Alfred when the latter was taken by surprise at *Chippenham and received the submission of many West Saxons, but was defeated by Alfred at the battle of *Edington later the same year. Guthrum was subsequently baptized with Alfred as his godfather and took the new name of Athelstan. He retired with his forces to rule East Anglia and issued coins there in his baptismal name. The text of a treaty survives which Guthrum made with Alfred at some point between 878 and his death in 890. BAEY

Guyana, an independent republic within the Commonwealth since 1970, was the only British colony on the South American mainland. The population is about 800,000 and the chief exports are sugar, rice, and bauxite. The first European settlements were made by the Dutch. During the Revolutionary and Napoleonic wars they changed hands repeatedly, but in 1803 Essequiba, Berbice, and Demerara were finally taken by the British. In 1831 they were united as British Guiana and became a crown colony in 1928. The capital is Georgetown. JAC

Gwent. County of the south-east Wales border, which has had a singularly complex administrative history. Its basis was the Welsh kingdom of Gwent, which emerged on the lower Wye river in the 7th cent. It was quickly seized by the Anglo-Normans moving west after 1066 and a series of lordships created in both upper (Gwent Uwchcoed) and lower (Gwent Iscoed) Gwent. These were merged in 1536 to form the new county of Monmouthshire, which took its name from the royal lordship. The anomalous position of the county was evident when, after the Act of Great Sessions of 1542, it was not included in a Welsh judicial circuit. But after the Local Government Act of 1972, Wales was defined formally to include Monmouthshire, which, with some minor territorial adjustments, was renamed Gwent. The county town was moved from Monmouth to Cwmbran. In 1996, in yet another reorganization, Gwent was divided into four new unitary authorities, Blaenau Gwent, Torfaen, Monmouthshire (reviving the old name), and Newport. As might be expected from its location, Gwent was highly Anglicized and only 2.4 per cent of its population spoke Welsh. In 1991 the population was 442,212, and the estimated population of the new authorities is Blaenau Gwent 73,000, Torfaen 91,000, Monmouthshire 81,000, Newport 137,000. It will be interesting to see if this tug of war, which has lasted a mere 900 years, continues in the future. See also MONMOUTHSHIRE. HC

Gwent, kingdom of. A post-Roman kingdom situated between the rivers Wye and Usk that took its name from the Roman town of *Caerwent, and lasted until Norman incursions in the late 11th cent., though it had been incorporated with Glywysing in the kingdom of *Morgannwg from the 8th cent. From 1070 the Norman conquerors quickly created several marcher lordships in more accessible parts; native dynasties survived elsewhere, even acknowledging the overlordship of the lord *Rhys of *Deheubarth and, in the 13th cent., of the princes of *Gwynedd. The new county of Monmouth (1536) was old Gwent together with the marcher lordship of Newport (formerly Gwynllwg); it took its name from one of the larger lordships and survived until 1974, when Gwent reappeared with only minor border adjustments. RAG

Gwyn, Nell (1650–87). Born in 1650 in Hereford, Nell first worked as a barmaid in her mother's drinking-house and then as an orange-seller outside the Theatre Royal, Drury Lane (London), before attracting the attention of Charles II, by which time she was a popular actress at the Theatre Royal itself. She became his mistress though sharing his affections with Louise de Kéroualle (duchess of *Portsmouth) and others. Charles was infatuated not only by her physical appeal but also by her natural wit, boldness, and sparkle. The birth of two sons, Charles Beauclerk, later earl of Burford and duke of St Albans, on 8 May 1670 and James, on 25 December 1671, ensured that she remained in favour. But Charles's intention of creating her countess of Greenwich never materialized, emphasizing the social distinction made between the treatment of Nell and other royal mistresses. She remained, despite everything, 'the darling strumpet of the crowd'. Following Charles's death in 1685, she was given Bestwood Park near Nottingham, where she lived until her own death following a stroke on 16 November 1687. She was buried at St Martin-in-the-Fields, London. SMC

Gwynedd. A county of north-west Wales created by the Local Government Act of 1972 and extant in its initial form from 1974 to 1996, when it was modified by the removal of *Anglesey (Ynys Môn), which became a separate unitary authority. It was based upon the post-Roman and medieval kingdom of Gwynedd which, after conquest by Edward I, had been divided by the statute of *Rhuddlan in 1284 into the counties of Anglesey, Caernarfonshire, and Merionethshire. The name was revived in 1972 when new counties were created. Initially the proposal was to include all the counties of north Wales in a county to be called Gwynedd, a name acceptable because of its 'historical associations as well as . . . shortness and pronounceability'. But a Consultative Document in 1971 accepted a twofold division, defining Gwynedd as Anglesey, Caernarfonshire, and Merioneth, though there were minor changes by which the Conwy valley was included in Gwynedd and the Edeirnion rural district moved to Clwyd.

In 1996 further changes occurred with the establishment of unitary authorities. Ynys Môn was separated and reconstituted as the county of Anglesey and a new authority, Caernarfonshire and Merionethshire, proposed, again with some minor additions from the former Glyndŵr district. That new authority, however, opted to retain the name of Gwynedd. HC

Gwynedd, kingdom of. The name was derived from the district called in Latin, Venedotia, and the kingdom was based upon Snowdonia and Anglesey, extending at its height to include territory to the east of the Conwy. It was one of the immediate post-Roman kingdoms of the 6th cent., ruled by Maelgwn (Maelgwn Gwynedd), said to be a descendant of *Cunedda, who, about AD 440, moved, or was moved, with the *Votadini from Strathclyde to meet a threat from the Irish. From the outset Gwynedd was one of the most significant of the Welsh kingdoms, with claims to overlordship, and pursuing an expansionary policy. Under rulers such as *Rhodri Mawr (d. 878), *Gruffydd ap Llywelyn (d. 1063), *Owain Gwynedd (d. 1170), *Llywelyn the Great (d. 1240), and *Llywelyn ap Gruffydd (d. 1282), much of Wales was brought under its hegemony, and titles such as 'king of the Britons' and 'prince of Wales' were employed. Under Gwynedd there was certainly a move towards statehood in Wales. Its downfall came from overambition on limited resources. Gwynedd took advantage of English divisions during the reign of Henry III to reassert itself and the treaty of *Montgomery in 1267 gave it substantial territorial gains. But after the campaigns of Edward I in 1277 and 1282–3 it became part of the principality under the control of the English crown and was eliminated as a political entity, being divided by the statute of *Rhuddlan in 1284 into the counties of Anglesey, Caernarfonshire, and Merionethshire. HC

gypsies and tinkers had different origins although the terms are sometimes interchangeable. Gypsies came from northern India and adopted a wandering life-style, keeping their Romany language and traditions. They arrived in the British Isles during the 15th cent. and their foreignness led to the presumption that they were Egyptians, corrupted to 'Gypsy'. They earned their livings by dealing in horses and making small household goods. Some of the women told fortunes and sold charms, which added to their air of mystery and magic, although it brought the dangers of being associated with witchcraft.

In Scotland and Ireland gypsies were often called tinkers because of their similar wandering life-style. A 'tinker' was an itinerant metalworker, who sharpened cutting tools and made or repaired items for household or farm use.

Despite the idyllic life described by George Borrow and other romantics of the 19th cent., tinkers and gypsies had a reputation for fecklessness and theft. They attracted hostility largely because of their refusal to accept a settled way of life. They were often treated harshly. Gypsies from Germany, expelled by laws forbidding their traditional life-style, were denied refuge in the British Isles early in the 20th cent. Recently local authorities have attempted to control travellers' movements by designating approved sites, and powers to move them on were enhanced during the 1980s. IJEK

habeas corpus. Before Magna Carta, the writ of habeas corpus constituted a command in the king's name to have a defendant brought physically before the court. It had then no libertarian function. In the 15th and 16th cents. it was used to remove a case from an inferior court to the central courts. By the mid-15th cent. it tested the legality of detention and the common law courts used it to release litigants who had been imprisoned by the Court of Chancery. In the 17th cent. it was employed to challenge arbitrary arrests by the royal government and, as such, played a crucial role in the constitutional disputes. In Darnel's case in 1627, which arose out of a forced loan, the judges refused to allow bail to a person detained 'at the special command of the king'. The *petition of right (1628) protested at the practice, but opponents of the crown such as Sir John *Eliot and John *Selden (1629) continued to be committed for political purposes.

When the king lost control of the situation in 1640, his adversaries moved to defend habeas corpus. The Act of 1641 which abolished *Star Chamber declared that the writ could ensure that a person imprisoned by king and council should be brought before the court without delay with the cause of imprisonment shown, the court should pronounce on the legality of the detention, and should bail, discharge, or remand the prisoner.

After the Restoration, the struggle was resumed, since many loopholes in the law remained. In Bushell's case (1670) habeas corpus was used to release a juryman who had been gaoled for returning what the court regarded as a perverse verdict. After several attempts, the Habeas Corpus Act of 1679 blocked up many of the loopholes and improved the mechanism of enforcement. Though habeas corpus was suspended at many times subsequently, the suspension had to be justified and aroused concern for civil liberty. In Scotland, the equivalent to habeas corpus was obtained by an Act for Preventing Wrongous Imprisonments in 1701. There was considerable agitation throughout the 18th cent. for the extension of habeas corpus to Ireland, but governments insisted that the situation was too volatile. It was one of the concessions gained in 1781 by the Irish *Volunteer movement. JAC

Habsburgs, relations with. The addition of the Low Countries to the Habsburg empire in 1482 made the latter a force in northern Europe. Henry VIII was at times allied with the Habsburgs against France, but the divorce of *Catherine of Aragon turned her nephew, the Emperor Charles V, into an obdurate opponent. The central European parts of Charles's empire did not greatly interest the English until, with the accession of William III, the Habsburgs joined the Austro-Dutch alliance against Louis XIV. Notable successes were achieved in the War of the *Spanish Succession, including the remarkable co-operation of *Marlborough and Prince Eugene of Savoy at the battle of *Blenheim (1704). Their alliance in the War of the *Austrian Succession (1740–8) was, however, marred by mutual recriminations. A renewed threat from France and a common interest in the exclusion of that power from the Low Countries brought the two together again from 1793. Years of frustration and fractiousness followed until 1814 when *Castlereagh and Metternich began an eight-year partnership to preserve the balance of power in Europe against Russia as well as France. Britain's subsequent relations with Austria were frequently upset by the latter's determination to uphold autocracy, notably during the revolutions of 1848–9. Although *Palmerston saw the Habsburg empire as an essential component of the European balance, he began to treat its presence in northern Italy as injurious to the Italians and itself. Both Britain and Austria were fearful of Russian ambitions in the Near East in 1854–6, 1878, and again in 1887–97 when the two powers were loosely bound by the Mediterranean agreements. The *First World War ranged them on opposite sides, but even so the British, until late in the war, showed some interest in the survival of at least part of the Habsburg empire as a component of the balance of power. CJB

Haddington, Thomas Hamilton, 1st earl of [S] (1563–1637). Hamilton's father was a lord of Session as Lord Priestfield. Hamilton studied law at Paris and at 29 became a lord of Session himself as Lord Drumcairn. He was appointed by James VI one of the *Octavians to control royal finances and in 1596 became king's advocate. Knighted in 1603, he was created Lord Binning (1613), earl of Melrose (1619), and earl of Haddington (1627). He was secretary of state [S] 1612–26, president of the Court of Session from 1616 until 1626, and lord privy seal [S] 1627–37. For many years Haddington was one of James VI's chief administrators in Scotland, attempting to restrain the king's zeal for his episcopal policy. James's nickname for him—taken from the Edinburgh street—was 'Tam o' the Cowgate'. The king found him an ideal servant—learned, reliable, and, above all, not terrifying. JAC

Haddington, treaty of, 1548. The response of *Mary of Guise and the pro-French party to intimidation by the English *'rough wooing' of 1544–8 was the treaty of Haddington of 7 July 1548. Mary, queen of Scots, then aged 5, was to marry the dauphin, though Scottish independence was guaranteed. The following month Mary was sent to France to be brought up. The marriage took place in April 1558. JAC

Hadrian. Roman emperor 117–38. Publius Aelius Hadrianus was born in 76, probably at Italica near Seville. Related by marriage to Trajan, he became a ward of the future emperor on the death of his father. During Trajan's reign he progressed through a series of military and civil offices, succeeding Trajan in 117. In the early part of his reign he toured his empire, coming to Britain in 122. Here he commanded the building of the wall which bears his name. The forum at *Wroxeter was dedicated in his reign and other public buildings are dated to this period, though it is far from certain that he consciously encouraged civil development in the province. An over-life-size bronze head of Hadrian from the Thames suggests a colossal statue or a temple to him in London, perhaps after his deification by the Senate at the urging of his successor, Antoninus Pius. ASEC

Hadrian IV. See ADRIAN IV.

Hadrian's Wall was a Roman frontier work of the early 2nd cent. running 70 miles from the Tyne near Newcastle to the Solway west of Carlisle. Commenced at the behest of *Hadrian on his visit to Britain in 122, the wall was originally to consist of a running barrier fronted by a ditch (except on the crags of the central sector), with a gateway defended by a fortlet every mile (milecastle) and two watchtowers (turrets) between each pair of milecastles. The troops remained based in forts along the Tyne–Solway road, the Stanegate. The eastern three-fifths of the wall were in stone, the western two-fifths in turf, later rebuilt in stone. With the construction of the wall well advanced, the decision was taken to place the garrison forts actually on the line of the wall and to extend the eastern terminal from Newcastle to Wallsend. The final addition was the 'vallum' to the rear of the wall, a ditch flanked by two mounds with causeways only at the forts. The western terminal of the wall was at Bowness-on-Solway, but fortlets (milefortlets) and watchtowers (towers) continued down the Cumberland coast. The entire complex was built by the three legions in Britain, though garrisoned by the more mobile auxiliary troops. Apparently a frontier, it was designed to be permeable, to supervise not to deny movement. The line could not have been held against a concerted attack; in the event of a crossing Roman forces would concentrate to the south to expel invaders. North of the wall were further forts monitoring Northumberland and the Lowlands. The psychological and propaganda effect of this enormous feat of construction and of the garrison along it must have been immense, not to mention the demographic and economic impact of the thousands of troops stationed along its line. ASEC

Haig, Sir Douglas, 1st Earl Haig (1861–1928). Soldier. Before 1914 Haig was recognized as one of the outstanding soldiers of his generation. In December 1915 he replaced Sir John *French as commander-in-chief of the British armies in France. He fought two of the most costly and controversial battles in British history, the *Somme (1916) and third Ypres (1917), because he was convinced that the German army would run out of soldiers if he continued to attack. His reputation never recovered from the casualties his own army suffered and these battles have overshadowed the far more successful campaign he waged between August and November 1918 which finally broke the German army's resistance. Haig remains a figure of great controversy. Despite attempts by some historians to portray him as an 'educated soldier', his popular image remains that of a callous butcher. In reality, he was a man of limited professional ability, sustained by a deep religious faith. DF

Hailsham, Quintin Hogg, 2nd Baron (b. 1907). Conservative politician and lawyer. Hogg entered Parliament at the Oxford by-election of 1938, a supporter of appeasement. He turned against *Chamberlain before the latter's fall in 1940. Hogg rose to prominence in the Tory Reform Group, seeking to commit the party to a vigorous policy of social reform. Elevated to the Lords in 1950 on his father's death, he anticipated a career as a barrister. But Hailsham was recalled to government by *Eden and enjoyed high office under *Macmillan, including a successful period as party chairman. He renounced his peerage in 1963 to contest—unsuccessfully—the party leadership, returning to the Commons. He anticipated becoming home secretary under *Heath in 1970 but, ennobled with a life peerage, served instead as lord chancellor, as his father had done. Hailsham showed his adaptability by retaining frontbench status under Margaret *Thatcher, becoming lord chancellor again in 1979. By the time he retired in 1987, he was the longest-serving cabinet minister since the war. DJD

Hakluyt, Revd Richard (*c.*1551–1616). In 1589, 'for the honour and benefit of this commonwealth wherein I live and breathe', Hakluyt published the *Principall Navigations, Voiages, Traffiques and Discoveries of the English Nation*. He wished to persuade the English to abandon the depressed trades to the continent and embark on enterprises in the wider world. Christ Church, Oxford, had introduced him to 'the sweet study of the history of cosmography' and then as chaplain to the English embassy in Paris from 1583 to 1588 he had come to realize how far behind France, Spain, and Portugal was England in the pursuit of wealth from non-European regions. Later a canon at Westminster, he became a publicist for the North-West Passage idea and other projects, and adviser to the new *East India Company in 1600. The 1598–1600 three-volume extended edition of *Principall Voyages*, a 'prose epic' as well as a record of English explorations, is his chief memorial. RB

Haldane, Richard Burdon, 1st Viscount Haldane (1856–1928). Haldane was the son of a Perthshire landowner and was perhaps most famous for the report to which he gave his name when secretary for war. After a Scottish education, he became a successful Chancery barrister in London, though he had little skill in advocacy. In 1885 he was elected to Parliament for East Lothian and remained an MP until he left the Commons for the Lords in 1911. Haldane took office in *Asquith's 1905 Liberal government as secretary for war. His reforms of the army earned him considerable respect. In 1911 he was created viscount and he became lord chancellor in 1912. In 1914 he returned to the War Office but his affinity with and affection for Germany and German philosophy caused public suspicion and criticism. He was dismissed by Asquith in 1915. He served briefly as lord chancellor in the first Labour government under Ramsay *MacDonald. MM

Hale, Sir Matthew (1609–76). Hale was one of the great authorities on English law (particularly on the criminal law), and had a distinguished judicial career. He took office as chief justice of Common Pleas under the Commonwealth and after the Restoration became the chief baron of the Exchequer and in 1671 chief justice of Common Pleas. However his fame rests primarily on his writings, among them his *History of the Common Law, The Jurisdiction of the Lords' House, The Prerogatives of the King*, and above all his *History of the Pleas of the Crown*, which has continued to be an important source of the criminal law, and was quoted as recently as 1991 in the case of *R.* v. *R.* where Hale's statement that there could be no rape committed by a husband on his wife was finally overruled by the House of Lords. Hale was remarkable for his scholarship and for his personal qualities of integrity and humanity. MM

Halidon Hill, battle of, 1333. For years after the great victory of *Bannockburn in 1314 Scotland was in a powerful position, confirmed by the treaty of *Edinburgh–Northampton in 1328. But the death of Robert Bruce in 1329, leaving a young son David II, encouraged Edward III to intervene once more, supporting the claims of Edward *Balliol. In the spring of 1333 Edward besieged Berwick in person. Sir Archibald *Douglas led a large Scottish army to the rescue. At Halidon Hill, just north-west of Berwick, the armies met on 19 July. The Scots had to attack up the hill and suffered severely from English arrows. Their heavy losses included Douglas. Balliol was reinstated as king of Scotland and Berwick passed into English possession permanently. JAC

Halifax, George Montagu Dunk, 2nd earl of (1716–71). Halifax was a hard-working and useful administrator. He inherited the title at the age of 23 and two years later made a lucrative marriage to the heiress of a London merchant, taking the name of Dunk. He began in opposition as a supporter of the prince of Wales and from 1742 to 1744 was a lord of the bedchamber to the prince. But in 1744 he joined the Pelhams and began his governmental career as master of the buckhounds 1744–6 and as 1st lord of Trade 1748–61. He worked hard on colonial questions and in 1749 the town of Halifax in Nova Scotia was named after him. In 1761–3 he was lord-lieutenant of Ireland, next served with Grenville as secretary of state for the north, and then the south, 1762–5. He was given the Garter in 1764. As secretary in 1763, he signed the *general warrant under which John *Wilkes was apprehended and seven years later, after general warrants had been declared illegal, had to pay £4,000 damages. Despite his marriage, he was usually short of money, building heavily at Horton in Northamptonshire, running an expensive mistress, and facing ruin after a costly election contest at Northampton in 1768. This may have persuaded him to accept office again under his nephew Lord *North in 1770, though Horace *Walpole commented that he was 'too old to learn'. In 1770–1 he was lord privy seal and for a few months before his death resumed his old office as secretary for the north. George III mourned him politely as 'an amiable man'. JAC

Halifax, Charles Montagu, 1st earl of (1661–1715). Though of aristocratic background, Montagu achieved political recognition and advancement through matchless powers of oratory and a measure of machiavellian trickery rather than under a patron. Entering Parliament in 1689, he soon achieved prominence as a court spokesman and manager, becoming a Treasury commissioner in 1692, chancellor of the Exchequer in 1694, and 1st lord of the Treasury in 1697. Ambitious for the exalted office of lord treasurer, accusations of malversation forced his resignation in 1699, but in the year following he was created baron. An attempt to impeach him in 1701 failed. Throughout Anne's reign he was a *Junto leader in the Lords, and at George I's accession (1714) was reappointed 1st lord and made an earl. He is chiefly remembered for the financial reforms he undertook in the 1690s, most notably the establishment of the national debt (1693) and the foundation of the *Bank of England (1694), which greatly helped to rationalize the existing system of government finance. AAH

Halifax, George Savile, 1st marquis of (1633–95). Politician and essayist. Halifax both epitomized and advocated the 'middle path' in politics, but in the shifting partisan atmosphere of the post-Restoration era he was regarded as an oddity, with whom few politicians could work easily. A wealthy Yorkshire baronet, and of royalist background, he entered politics in the 1660s and was made a viscount in 1668. But successive administrations felt the edge of his finely tuned intellect. Initially hostile towards *Clarendon, he was then critical of the pro-catholic policies of the *cabal, and then of the Anglican reaction of *Danby. He emerged by 1679 as a firm opponent of *'exclusion', was reappointed to the Privy Council and in 1682 was created a marquis. As lord privy seal, however, he was increasingly unhappy in the enclaves of high Toryism. In 1685 James II dismissed him. Although in 1688 he threw aside his neutrality and supported William of Orange, he soon found himself out of favour with other power-politicians and retired in 1690. See TRIMMER. AAH

Halifax, Edward Wood, 1st earl of (1881–1959). A Conservative politician, Halifax made some progress as viceroy of India (1926–31) towards constitutional change in talks with the nationalist leader Mahatma *Gandhi. A devout high churchman, he was at first out of his depth in dealings with Nazi Germany. As foreign secretary (1938–41) he continued the search for an accommodation until September 1939, but he displayed mixed feelings during the Munich crisis (1938), and argued early in 1939 for tougher policies, including faster rearmament. In the leadership crisis of May 1940 he was favoured by some to succeed *Chamberlain as prime minister. Briefly, while the Dunkirk evacuation hung in the balance, he showed interest in exploratory talks to end the war. Between 1941 and 1946 this tall, aloof aristocrat served with surprising success as ambassador in Washington. CJB

Hall, Edward (*c.*1497–1547). Hall published posthumously in 1548 his *Union of the Two Noble and Illustre Famelies of Lancastre and Yorke,* tracing royal history from Henry IV to Henry VIII. He was a keen spokesman for the Tudors, whom he saw as restorers of order after decades of anarchy, greatly admired Henry VIII, disliked *Wolsey and the clergy, and supported the Reformation. His book was consequently burned in Mary's reign for its anticlerical tone. Hall was born in London, educated at Eton and King's College, Cambridge, became a Gray's Inn lawyer, and served as a member of Parliament. He was made common serjeant of London in 1533 and under-sheriff from 1535. His early history owed much to Polydore Vergil but, as he approached his own times, he added eye-witness accounts, particularly of the London scene. *Shakespeare's use of his works in his historical plays helped to popularize Hall's view of the past. JAC

Hall, Sir Edward Marshall (1858–1929). Hall was one of the greatest English advocates and a legend in his own time and since. He enjoyed, at the height of his powers, the sort of reputation and glamour in the eyes of the public later enjoyed by actors and film stars. His most famous cases were criminal trials, such as the trial of Marie Hermann in 1894, where, as was frequently the case, he obtained an acquittal for his client by his eloquence, his striking presence and voice, and his magnetic personality. It has been suggested that his knowledge of law was poor and he was frequently criticized by judges, but his success, especially as counsel for the defence, was undeniable. MM

Hallé, Sir Charles (1819–95). Conductor and pianist. Born in Hagen (Germany), Carl Hallé was a child prodigy, giving piano recitals and conducting operas at the age of 11. After a period in Paris, he settled in Manchester and in 1849 became conductor of the Gentlemen's Concerts. On 30 January 1858 the reconstituted Hallé Orchestra inaugurated a new series of concerts which soon became the centre-piece of Manchester's musical life. Hallé conducted the orchestra until his death; he also appeared frequently as soloist and gave regular London recitals, gaining special acclaim for his interpretations of Beethoven's sonatas. Although a conductor of determination, he was a man of charm and humour. In 1893 he was appointed principal of the new Royal Manchester College of Music. The Hallé Orchestra has continued to the present day, gaining particular renown under the conductorship of Sir John Barbirolli (1943–70). ECr

Halley, Edmond (1656–1742). Astronomer, remembered because his name is attached to a comet. Leaving Queen's College, Oxford, without a degree in 1676, he went to St Helena to map the southern stars. After a famous meeting with *Wren and *Hooke, he visited *Newton in Cambridge, and hearing about his work on gravitation, persuaded him to publish it; he was thus the catalyst making the *Principia* (1687) possible, seeing it through the press and providing a financial guarantee against failure. In 1703 he became professor of astronomy at Oxford, and in 1720 astronomer-royal. He computed the orbits of several comets, and deduced that those of 1456, 1531, 1607, and 1682 were periodic returns of the same body: some comets at least thus moved in vast elliptical orbits, their regularity proving how empty space must be. DK

Halsbury, Hardinge Gifford, 1st earl of (1823–1921). Conservative lawyer. Son of the editor of the Conservative *Standard* newspaper, Gifford was trained up to both the law and party politics. With an early reputation for relentless determination and formidable memory as a barrister, he was solicitor-general under *Disraeli in 1875 even before he had become an MP. He was prominent in the Conservative harassment of *Bradlaugh. Lord chancellor in all Conservative or Unionist governments from 1885 to 1905—seventeen years in all—Halsbury made many political appointments to the judicial bench and intensified the sense of confrontation between the judiciary and trade unionism. Few holders of his office have been so partisan. A hard-liner in opposition, he was one of the 'die-hard' peers who fought to the end to prevent the 1911 *Parliament Bill removing the Lords' absolute veto. A productive legal reformer, Halsbury oversaw the production of the digest of *The Laws of England* (1905–16) which bears his name. BIC

Hamilton, William Douglas, duke of [S] (1634–94). A younger son of the 1st marquis of Douglas [S], he was created earl of Selkirk in 1646, at the age of 12, when his father was campaigning with *Montrose. In 1656 he married the daughter of the 1st duke of *Hamilton, who had been executed in 1649, and who was duchess in her own right. At the Restoration, he was created duke for life. Favourable to *presbyterianism, Hamilton spent much of Charles II's reign in rivalry with *Lauderdale. James II favoured him. He was given the Garter in 1682, made a commissioner of the Treasury [S] 1686–9, and appointed to the English Privy Council in 1687. But he joined the Williamite cause in 1688 and presided over the Convention which met at Edinburgh in 1689 and offered the throne to William and Mary. He was again commissioner to the Scottish Parliament in 1692. *Burnet called him 'rough and sullen, with a boisterous temper'. JAC

Hamilton, James Hamilton, 1st duke of [S] (1606–49). Charles I's adviser on Scottish affairs during the civil wars. Educated at Exeter College, Oxford, Hamilton became a privy counsellor under Charles I and fought for the protestant cause in Germany during the 1630s. Successful neither as a general nor a politician, he was deficient in both intelligence and moral principle. He failed to pacify the Scottish religious disturbances of the late 1630s, or to wrest control of Aberdeen from the *covenanters in 1639. His attempts in the early 1640s to find an accommodation with *Argyll and the presbyterians brought royalist accusations of treachery, especially when he subverted *Montrose's plan to attack Argyll's party. Fleeing Scotland in 1644 for the king's court in Oxford, he was arrested and imprisoned. Freed in 1646 he laboured to persuade the Scots to support a royalist-presbyterian uprising in England. When the rising did occur in the spring of 1648, Hamilton was unprepared and did not arrive with his promised army until July. Indecisive, and unable to prevent his cavalry from stringing out in a thin line more than 20 miles long, he was easy prey for Cromwell's hardy veterans, who dashed his army to pieces at *Preston (August 1648). Hamilton surrendered at Uttoxeter, was condemned for treason by Parliament, and executed on 9 March 1649, five weeks after his king. IJG

Hamilton, James Hamilton, 4th duke of [S] (1658–1712). Hamilton played an important but equivocal part in the Union of Scotland and England in 1707. His grandfather had been executed in 1649 as a royalist and his great-uncle had been killed fighting for Charles II at *Worcester. His mother, duchess in her own right, surrendered her title to him in 1698. Though his father supported William of Orange at the Glorious Revolution, Hamilton stayed with James II and was long suspected of Jacobitism. After taking his seat in the Scottish Parliament in 1700, he became leader of the party which brought about the confrontation with England caused by the Act of *Security of 1703. But, to the indignation of his followers, he switched in 1705, moving that the queen should appoint the commissioners to treat for Union. He was not included in the commission and opposed the terms of Union vehemently. After the Union, he served as a representative peer 1708–12 and was given the dukedom of Brandon [GB] in 1711. The House of Lords refused to allow him to take his seat. In 1712 his fortunes seemed to have recovered: he was appointed master-general of the ordnance and given the Garter, but perished in a duel in Hyde Park (in which his opponent Lord Mohun was also killed). Hamilton was a good and persuasive speaker. *Rosebery suggested that he was unduly influenced by honours, but irresolution seems to have been equally present. JAC

Hamilton, William Hamilton, 2nd duke of [S] (1616–51). Scottish royalist leader in civil wars. Hamilton was educated at the University of Glasgow, created earl of Lanark in 1639, and made secretary of state for Scotland the following year. He had little influence on policy and was regarded with suspicion by English royalists on account of his links with the *covenanters. In 1646 he regained the king's confidence and worked throughout 1647 for a treaty with the Scots, the *Engagement, to restore the king to his throne in exchange for establishing presbyterianism in England. He played a leading part in preparing the invasion of England in 1648, led by his brother, the 1st duke, though he did not take part himself. After inheriting his brother's title in 1649, he joined the second invasion of England in 1651. 'To go with a handful of men into England', he wrote, seems 'very desperate'. He was right. Wounded at *Worcester, he died a few days later and was buried in the cathedral. *Burnet said of him that he was franker, more passionate, more enterprising, and more religious than his brother. IJG

Hamilton, Emma (1765–1815). Born in the Wirral as Amy Lyon, Emma's earliest employers *c.*1778 had links with London artistic circles, and her sensational beauty became celebrated through the art of an early mentor, George *Romney (1734–1802). Mistress of Sir Harry Fetherstonhaugh, and then in 1782 of the more worthy Charles Greville, Emma was much indebted to Greville and fell deeply in love with him. But his ultimate ambitions excluded her, and in 1786 he cynically passed Emma on to his widower uncle Sir William Hamilton (1730–1803), British representative at the court of Naples and Sicily. Hamilton delighted in Emma's ear for languages and music, and her theatrical flair, and in 1791 he contentedly married her. An intimate of Queen Maria Carolina, Emma was able to bring timely sustenance to Nelson's ships before the Nile battle in August 1798. From this time on Nelson's infatuation with her, reciprocated by Emma with boisterous panache, moulded her future and dramatized Nelson's. Defiant in self-induced adversity, after her mother's death in 1810 Emma Hamilton degenerated beyond redemption. She died in Calais. DDA

Hamilton, Sir James, of Finnart (*c.*1500–40). An illegitimate son of the 1st earl of Arran and brother of the archbishop of St Andrews, Hamilton became a successful architect. As a youth he was impetuous and aggressive, taking part in many affrays. He was a close companion of the young king James V, and was employed in the renovation of the palaces of *Falkland and *Linlithgow. In 1540 he was suddenly accused of plotting to murder the king and executed in haste. It has been suggested that the king may have been anxious to take possession of the great wealth which Hamilton had accumulated. JAC

Hamilton, John (*c.*1511–71). Archbishop of St Andrews. Hamilton was an illegitimate son of the 1st earl of Arran and brother of Sir James *Hamilton of Finnart. He became a Benedictine monk as a boy. After study at Paris, he used his influence with his half-brother, the Regent *Arran, on behalf of the old religion and was appointed lord privy seal in 1543. He was made bishop of Dunkeld in 1544 and three years later, after the murder of Cardinal *Beaton, was translated to the archbishopric of St Andrews and primacy. He was a strong persecutor of protestant heresy. After 1560 he lost much of his power though Mary, whose cause he supported, restored his consistorial authority in 1566. Captured in Dumbarton castle in 1571 after Mary's cause had collapsed, he was accused of complicity in the murders of *Darnley and of *Moray, and hanged at Stirling. JAC

Hamilton, Sir Thomas. See HADDINGTON, 1ST EARL OF.

Hampden, John (1594–1643). Hampden, a parliamentarian, sat in every Parliament from 1621 until his death. He was imprisoned in 1627 for refusing the *forced loan and became a close friend of Sir John *Eliot. He rose to national fame by providing the test case of the legality of *ship money

(1637–8), and in the Short and Long Parliaments his reputation was second only to *Pym's. But he was more moderate than Pym—he would not vote for *Strafford's attainder, and defused an explosive confrontation over the *Grand Remonstrance—and his great influence stemmed partly from his conciliatory spirit. He had no doubts, however, over Parliament's cause in the Civil War. He raised his own foot regiment in his native Buckinghamshire, fought at *Edgehill, and fell mortally wounded in a skirmish with *Rupert's horse at *Chalgrove Field. Compared with Pym, his great standing derived less from sheer oratory and managerial skill than from his human touch in debate and his evidently charismatic moral authority. AHW

Hampden clubs (1812–17), named after the 17th-cent. parliamentarian, marked a new era of agitation for parliamentary reform after the radicalism of the 1790s. Founded by Major *Cartwright, the clubs were at first gentry-dominated, but spread rapidly in the provinces among the working classes. Each club was nominally a separate unit in order to circumvent the 1799 ban imposed on such organizations. They met for discussion, lectures, and adult education, as well as to further demands for reform. A national convention was held in 1817; whereupon the clubs were immediately suppressed by government legislation. JFCH

Hampden Park (Glasgow) is the home of the Scottish national football team and of Queen's Park FC. It was begun in 1903 under the supervision of Archibald Leitch, who also built Ibrox and Parkhead stadiums. The ground capacity was increased in 1910 to 125,000 and to 149,000 in 1937, but has since been reduced to 64,000. After years of post-war neglect, a programme of renovation has begun. JAC

Hampshire was essentially the hinterland of the great port of *Southampton from which it took its name, plus the *Isle of Wight. The central parts are drained by the rivers Test and Itchen, the western by the Avon, and the eastern by the Hamble and the Meon. The shire is bordered by Dorset, Wiltshire, Berkshire, Surrey, and Sussex.

At the time of the Roman occupation, the region was inhabited by the *Regni in the south-east, the *Belgae towards the south-west, and the *Atrebates in the north. The Roman advance, undertaken by *Vespasian, was early and occupation thorough. There were two major towns, each probably of pre-Roman origins—Silchester (Calleva Atrebatum) in the north, *Winchester (Venta Belgae) in the south. Of the many villas in the area, the best known is probably Brading on the Isle of Wight. Portchester, near Fareham, was a Roman fort, erected by *Carausius in the 3rd cent.

Saxon settlement was relatively easy and Winchester became the capital of *Wessex, though Silchester was abandoned. Birinus visited the region in 634 on a mission. His bishopric was established at *Dorchester-on-Thames to the north and he was buried there, but the see was soon transferred to Winchester and the building of a cathedral started. The Isle of Wight and the eastern valley of the Meon were areas of Jutish settlement and for a while formed part of the kingdom of *Sussex. By the 8th cent., a harbour of Hampton had developed near the site of the small Roman port of Bitterne Clausentum. Under 755, the *Anglo-Saxon Chronicle* referred to Hampton-shire, though we cannot be sure what area was intended. As Wessex flourished, Winchester became the capital of England: *Edward the Confessor was crowned there and many kings, including *Alfred and *Cnut, buried there. The area suffered severely from Viking raids. In 860 a host stormed Winchester and during *Æthelred's reign another army sacked Southampton in 981 and wintered there in 994, living off the countryside.

By the time of the Norman Conquest, Hampshire was an established shire. In the course of the 12th cent., the capital was removed from Winchester to Westminster, but Winchester retained importance as a bishopric: the new cathedral, the longest in Europe, was begun in 1079. The connection with Normandy and the continent enhanced Southampton's trade, particularly in wine from Gascony and Aquitaine. In the west of the county, the New Forest was appropriated by William I as a game reserve and it was while hunting there in 1100 that his son William Rufus met his death, and was taken to Winchester for burial.

In the *Domesday survey of 1086, Winchester and Southampton were clearly important towns, and Basingstoke, Christchurch, and Stockbridge were of local significance. *Portsmouth is not mentioned by Domesday but was granted a charter in 1194. Its prosperity rose with the establishment of the Royal Navy. The Tudors spent a good deal on fortifications and in Stuart times it became a major naval base. By 1801 it was the ninth largest town in England with more than four times the population of Southampton. Andover developed as a centre for the north-west of the shire and Basingstoke for the north-east: each was far enough from Southampton and Portsmouth to have its own sphere of influence. But, with the exception of the coastal fringe, Hampshire remained a predominantly rural county, growing corn and rearing cattle, providing timber for the navy, and supporting a domestic cloth industry.

During the Civil War, Hampshire was parliamentary territory, and attempts by the royalists to retain Southampton, Winchester, and Portsmouth were unsuccessful. But Basing House was held for the king by the marquis of Winchester throughout the whole war and surrendered only to Cromwell, who destroyed it. *Hopton and *Waller skirmished in the county in 1643 and the following year Hopton's men were badly mauled at *Cheriton, near Alresford. After Charles I's escape from Hampton Court, he spent a year at *Carisbrooke castle on the Isle of Wight and three weeks at Hurst castle on the mainland before being taken to Windsor for his trial.

Gilbert *White was born in 1720 at Selborne, south of Alton, where he wrote his *Natural History.* Edward *Gibbon, the historian, had an estate at Buriton, near Petersfield, and served as a captain in the Hampshire militia. Jane *Austen was born at Steventon, near Basingstoke, and spent the later years of her life at Southampton and at Chawton, near Alton. She died at Winchester and is buried in the cathedral. William *Cobbett, the radical, had a farm at Botley, between Southampton and Portsmouth and in *Rural Rides* wrote with enthusiasm of the downland country of north Hampshire.

Though relatively little touched by the industrial revolution, the shire changed considerably in the 19th and 20th cents. The popularity of seaside holidays in the Victorian period produced the extraordinary growth of Bournemouth. The Isle of Wight also profited, partly no doubt because of the publicity given to *Osborne House: Ryde, Ventnor, and Shanklin in turn waxed and Cowes achieved social cachet in the Edwardian period. An equally spectacular growth was in the north-east of the county. The army began building barracks at Aldershot in 1854, transforming a hamlet into a sizeable town, and Basingstoke, chosen for urban development in 1963, grew from 25,000 to nearly 150,000. The Isle of Wight was given its own county council in 1890. By the local government reorganization of 1972 Bournemouth and Christchurch in the west were transferred to Dorset. The Banham commission on local government recommended further changes in 1994—that Southampton, Portsmouth, and New Forest become unitary authorities. JAC

Hampton Court conference, 1604. Although Elizabeth I established a protestant church in England in 1559, it offended *puritan opinion by retaining many catholic practices. In 1603 the accession of James I provided the puritans with an opportunity to state their case by presenting him with the *millenary petition. James, who relished theological debate, responded by summoning a conference of puritans and bishops to Hampton Court in January 1604. Discussions produced considerable convergence on minor matters, but the only major achievement was the authorization of a new translation of the Bible—the 'King James version'. Puritans were disappointed at the outcome, especially when a number of hard-line ministers were expelled from their parishes. But James was no persecutor and during his reign all but a tiny minority of puritans retained their commitment to the established church. RL

Hampton Court palace (Middx.). Royal residence, situated on the banks of the Thames, 15 miles south-west of London. Started by Cardinal *Wolsey in 1514, Hampton Court was confiscated in 1529 by Henry VIII who subsequently added the great hall, and a new court where the present Fountain Court is, and remodelled the Chapel Royal and the Clock Court. The palace was used by Mary, Elizabeth, James I, and Charles I, but little further building was done until William III appeared. From 1689 Sir Christopher *Wren started work on the new Fountain Court, with its east and south frontages to the garden, and on a new range of the Clock Court. Wren's buildings are classical essays in brick and stone. William Talman completed interior apartments (1699–1702) and helped to lay out the gardens in Home Park and Bushey Park in which Hampton Court is set. Influenced by Le Nôtre in France, Charles II had made a *patte d'oie* (radiating avenues), and a long canal flanked by double avenues of limes, and King William (aided by Wise and *Bridgeman) added the Great Fountain Garden, the Privy Garden, the Great Terrace, and the Chestnut Avenue. Much of this 17th- and 18th-cent. layout remains, together with the magnificent wrought-iron gates made by Jean Tijou in 1689–99 for the Fountain Garden. Externally, Hampton Court is the finest British parallel to a French palace set in a formal garden; internally, the state apartments, with their original decorations and art collections, offer an unrivalled perspective on English royalty from Tudor times to the present. PW

Handel, George Frideric (1685–1759). German-born composer who took English nationality. Initially cathedral organist in his native Halle, Handel played violin and harpsichord at the Hamburg opera-house, where his first two operas were produced in 1705. In 1706–10 he travelled around Italy, assimilating the latest musical styles, meeting leading composers, and writing some fine church music, including 'Dixit Dominus' (1707), over 100 Italian cantatas, two oratorios, and two operas.

In 1710 Handel was appointed Kapellmeister to the elector of Hanover (later George I of England), although within a few months he was in London. Here the colourful arias and magnificent stage effects of his opera *Rinaldo* (1711) created a sensation, and by 1712 he had settled permanently in England, acting 1717–19 as resident composer to the future duke of Chandos at Cannons (near Edgware). Handel's first love was the theatre, and the Royal Academy of Music (1720–8), formed to promote Italian opera, commissioned several masterpieces including *Giulio Cesare* and *Tamerlano* (1724).

Although Handel continued composing operas until 1741, increasing financial pressures and poor audiences encouraged him to turn to a new dramatic medium, the English oratorio. *Esther* (1732) initiated a series of oratorios, operatic in concept and performed in theatres but using English texts and singers and incorporating frequent choruses. The oratorio gradually displaced opera in the public's interest, forming the basis after Handel's death for a lasting English choral tradition centring especially on **Messiah* (1742).

Handel wrote in every contemporary genre, also creating the organ concerto to display his own virtuosity in the intervals of oratorio performances and publishing two fine sets of concerti grossi. His music, drawing elements from various national styles, was enormously influential, both in England and abroad; 'Zadok the Priest', for example, has been sung at every English coronation since 1727. Nevertheless, some of his best music, especially for the stage, is still shamefully neglected. ECr

Handley, Tommy (1892–1949). Comedian. Handley's heyday was the Second World War when, with much entertainment suspended or curtailed, radio predominated. Born in Liverpool, Handley began as a commercial traveller and singer in variety shows, with modest success until the launch of the radio programme *ITMA* (*It's That Man Again*) in 1939. The weekly programme attracted vast audiences to the gallery of comic characters—Mrs Mopp, Colonel Chinstrap, Mona Lott, Funf—and repetitive catch-phrases. The show was still running when Handley died at 57. The *Spectator* called the end of *ITMA* 'something like a national calamity' and the *New Statesman* wrote that 'our little world, shared weekly by millions of ordinary people, has collapsed as completely as the Third Reich which indirectly brought it into being'. Though Handley received no honours in his lifetime, the king sent a message of condolence to his widow and there was a service in St Paul's. By later standards much of the humour was unsophisticated but it contained a satirical and surrealist element that was developed by later programmes: the *Goon Show* was first broadcast in 1951 and *Hancock's Half Hour* in 1954. JAC

Hanover was in personal union with Britain from 1714, when George I succeeded Queen Anne under the terms of the Act of *Settlement, until 1837 when the Salic Law prevented Victoria from retaining Hanover and it passed to her uncle, Ernest Augustus, duke of *Cumberland.

The line of Brunswick-Lüneburg or Hanover had been chosen in 1701 because Sophia, electress of Hanover, was a granddaughter of James I, through her mother *Elizabeth, queen of Bohemia, and the nearest protestant heir. In 1692 Hanover had been granted electoral status within the Holy Roman empire and in 1705 it was reunited with the larger state of Celle, making it the leading second-line German power.

In 1714 it had a population of just over 500,000 and, with some 7,000 square miles, was rather bigger than Yorkshire. The chief town, Hanover, had about 10,000 inhabitants. In 1719, the acquisition of Bremen and Verden at the expense of Sweden gave the electorate access to the North Sea. George I had more authority as elector of Hanover than as king of England, but he did not rule Hanover autocratically. Most of the component territories had retained their assemblies, usually acting through committees, though executive power was firmly in the hands of the Privy Council, instructed by the *Regierungsreglement* promulgated by George before he left the country.

The connection with Hanover was regarded by most Britons with distaste or at best as a necessary evil. The Act of Settlement had indicated a marked distrust. The new monarch could not appoint Germans to any post in Britain, could not declare war to help Hanover without parliamentary consent, and could not even visit his native land without parliamentary approval. Though the last condition was soon dropped, as personally offensive to the sovereign, suspicion remained. Britons were afraid that the connection would mean continental entanglements and resented the evident pleasure their kings took in visiting their electorate. In December 1742, William *Pitt gained great popularity by declaring that 'this great, this powerful, this formidable kingdom is considered only as a province of a despicable electorate'.

But the main problem was strategic. Hanover was almost defenceless against French or Prussian attack and, if overrun, would have to be rescued at the end of the war by concessions elsewhere. In the War of the *Austrian Succession, with France and Prussia in alliance, the situation was particularly tense. Britain put into the field the Pragmatic Army, under William, duke of *Cumberland, the hero of *Culloden. To avoid reproach, Hanoverian troops for the alliance were placed under Austrian command but paid for by British subsidies. With Prussia concerned mainly with Austria, and France bogged down in Holland, Hanover survived.

During the *Seven Years War, Hanover's defence was easier, since Prussia had become a British ally. Indeed, the search for protection for Hanover had been an important factor in bringing about the reversal of alliances which preceded and precipitated the conflict. Cumberland, attacked in 1757 by superior French forces, was forced into the humiliating capitulation of *Kloster-Zeven and Hanover occupied by the French. But the armistice was repudiated and the Army of Observation, under Ferdinand of Brunswick, succeeded in holding the French at bay, and even won a victory at *Minden in 1759.

After 1760, British hostility to Hanover declined. The declaration by the new king, George III, that 'born and educated in this country, I glory in the name of Britain' played the nationalist card to some effect, and the swarms of Scots who clustered around *Bute gave the English new people to hate. George III never visited Hanover, though at moments of crisis he mused on retiring there.

It was not possible for Hanover to escape the maelstrom of the Napoleonic wars. It gained Osnabrück in 1803 in one of the many reorganizations of Germany, but was occupied first by Prussia, then in 1806 by the French. Napoleon took the northern parts into his swollen French empire, giving the rest to a new kingdom of Westphalia, ruled by his younger brother Jerome. At the peace settlement in 1814, Hanover was given the status of a kingdom and gained important territories, including East Friesland, Hildesheim, and Lingen. The reign of Ernest Augustus from 1837 was turbulent. But his son, the blind George V, took the side of Austria in the war of 1866 and paid the penalty. Hanover was annexed to the new German empire.

The connection with Britain for well over a century left few traces. There was little attempt to develop trade between the two countries and little contact between the inhabitants, save for diplomats and soldiers. Though the University of Göttingen, founded by George II in 1737, soon acquired a fine reputation, few Britons went there. Though the British complained more fiercely, it is arguable that the Hanoverians suffered more. They were dragged into British struggles and had to put up with an absentee ruler and a diminished court at Herrenhausen. As a consequence, they welcomed Cumberland with joy in 1837, and his equestrian statue with an inscription 'Dem Landes Vater sein treues Volk' still stands outside the main railway station at Hanover. JAC

Hansard, Thomas Curson (1776–1833). Hansard's father Luke came from Norwich, set up as a printer in London, and from 1774 onwards published the *Journals of the House of Commons*. Hansard entered his father's business and in 1803 began printing the parliamentary debates for William *Cobbett. In 1810 he was tried as the printer of Cobbett's *Political Register* for an article protesting at flogging in the army: Cobbett was sent to prison for two years, Hansard for three months. Cobbett's acute financial difficulties while in gaol forced him to sell the debates to Hansard and from 1813 the volumes appeared 'under the superintendence of T. C. Hansard'. The Hansard family retained the enterprise for most of the 19th cent. but had considerable trouble achieving an acceptable standard of reporting. In 1909 the House of Commons decided to issue an official report of proceedings prepared by the Stationery Office. The term 'Hansard' remains in general use and the name still appears in brackets on the cover. JAC

Hanseatic League. The league was a trading alliance which, at its height, included 200 towns, of which the most important were Lübeck, Hamburg, Bremen, Cologne, and Danzig. Founded in the 13th cent., it survived until the 17th and exercised great naval and diplomatic, as well as economic, power. The German word *hanse* meant a guild or company. Its London base, the Steelyard, was just west of London bridge, until closed by Elizabeth I in 1598. Other *kontore* were at Bergen, Novgorod, and Bruges. There was a vigorous trade with Scotland and the east coast ports: Boston imported furs and timber and exported cloth, and a Hanseatic warehouse survives at King's Lynn. The decline of the Hanse in the 16th cent. was caused partly by internal rivalries, by the growth in power of Prussia, Russia, Sweden, and Denmark, and by strong economic competition from the Dutch. JAC

Hanway, Jonas (1712–86). Philanthropist. Hanway was born at Portsmouth into a family with naval connections. He went into overseas trade, spent twelve years in Lisbon, joined the *Russia Company, and from 1743 until 1750 was in Russia, travelling as far as Persia. He published an account of his journeys. In 1756 he became a supporter of the Foundling Hospital and was later elected a governor. His Marine Society, founded at the start of the Seven Years War in 1756, started boys on careers in the navy, and in 1758 he helped to establish the Magdalen hospital for penitent prostitutes. An indefatigable pamphleteer, Hanway campaigned on behalf of climbing-boys and parish children, in favour of Sunday schools, and against the 'pernicious' effects of drinking tea. The last crusade brought him into a literary conflict with Samuel *Johnson. *Carlyle, with some justice, called Hanway a 'dull, worthy man' and his writings, though well intended, are not sprightly. JAC

Harcourt, Simon Harcourt, 1st Viscount (1661–1727). Of an Oxfordshire gentry family at Stanton Harcourt, Simon Harcourt studied law and, returned for Abingdon in 1690, supported the Tories. His fortunes closely followed those of his schoolfriend Robert *Harley. In 1702–8 he was solicitor-general and then attorney-general, resigning with Harley. In 1710 he defended *Sacheverell at his impeachment, speaking to great acclaim. During the subsequent Tory ministry, he was lord keeper and then lord chancellor, obtaining a barony in 1711. On George I's arrival, he was dismissed. He then seems to have acted as political go-between, joining *Walpole in 1720 and raised a step in the peerage in 1721. But he spoke in favour of Harley (Oxford) and took a part in persuading Walpole to allow *Bolingbroke's return in 1723. He was on close terms with *Pope, *Swift, *Gay, and Prior. Though his legal knowledge was said to be moderate, his oratorial ability was outstanding. JAC

Harcourt, Sir William Vernon (1827–1904). Liberal politician. Harcourt probably regarded himself as a failure. He was a brilliant lawyer, politician, and polemicist, who rose to be home secretary (1880–5) and chancellor of the Exchequer (1886, 1892–5), and expected to succeed *Gladstone as premier, but was passed over when the latter retired (1894) in favour of *Rosebery. He blamed the queen; but Harcourt also had enemies within his own party, among both the Whigs, who disliked the radicalism of his pronouncements, and the radicals, who distrusted their sincerity. His personal rift with Rosebery, not all his fault, did great damage to the Liberal Party in its wilderness years of 1895–1905. Harcourt's main contribution to British history was his introduction of death duties in the budget of 1894, and the claim 'We are all socialists now' that went with it. BJP

Hardie, James Keir (1856–1915). Socialist politician. Born in Lanarkshire, Hardie grew up in extreme poverty. While working as a journalist he was instrumental in organizing the Lanarkshire and Ayrshire miners, becoming secretary of the Scottish Miners' Federation in 1886 and, in 1887, chairman of the Scottish Labour Party. In 1892 he was elected as an independent Labour MP for South West Ham; the following year he established the Independent Labour Party. Hardie was a thoroughly class-conscious socialist (outraging Westminster opinion by wearing a cloth-cap and tweed jacket in the Commons), but was also acutely aware of the moderate nature of the British trade union movement, and he deliberately downplayed his socialist creed in order to persuade the Trades Union Congress of the need for the foundation (1900) of the Labour Representation Committee, forerunner of the Labour Party. Hardie believed that international working-class solidarity would prevent war in 1914, and never recovered from the realization of the strength of nationalism amongst the working classes. GA

Hardknott was the Roman fort of Mediobogdum on the road over the Hardknott and Wrynose passes from the Lake District to Maryport on the coast. It was built in the reign of *Hadrian and garrisoned by *cohors IV Dalmatarum* until its abandonment at the end of the 2nd cent. Constructed in stone, the fort contained the usual complement of buildings (many now on display) and to the east was a levelled parade-ground. ASEC

Hardwicke, Philip Yorke, 1st earl of (1690–1764). As the longest-serving lord chancellor of the 18th cent., Hardwicke had significant legal achievements to his credit, particularly in clarifying the laws of equity, and great political importance too. He was solicitor-general at the age of 29, chief justice and a peer at 42 and lord chancellor at 46 (1737); this rise being more extraordinary given (for a court Whig) his humble background. He was committed to maintaining order in society with stern sanctions for those who broke it. He presided at the trials of the Jacobite peers and designed the proscriptive measures against the Scottish Highlanders following the 1745 rebellion. An austere man, he had the lifelong friendship of the duke of *Newcastle and was a steadying hand on the governments of the 1740s and 1750s. Although resigning as lord chancellor in 1756, he remained a member of the 'effective cabinet' until 1762. AIL

Hardwick Hall (Derbys.), west of Mansfield, was the creation of the celebrated Bess of Hardwick, countess of *Shrewsbury, four times married, who stamped her initials on walls and on parterres. It has a magnificent position on cliffs overlooking the valley of the river Doe Lee, through which snakes the busy M1. It is one of the grandest of Elizabethan houses, with a vast expanse of window glass. In front of the building is the Old Hall which, though in ruins, has surprisingly been allowed to remain. One of the most impressive rooms is the long gallery, used for recreation and for exhibiting family portraits and purchases, and a remarkable innovation was that the architect, Robert Smythson, turned the hall 90 degrees, so that it runs from front to back. JAC

Hardy, Thomas (1840–1928). Novelist and poet, Hardy initially trained as an architect. He left his native Dorset, the 'Wessex' of his books, for London where he lost his faith under the influence of *Darwin and *Huxley. His famous pessimism developed early and coloured everything to come. In the 1870s he caught the taste of an increasingly urbanized England for accounts of a vanishing world with *Under the Greenwood Tree* (1872) and *Far from the Madding Crowd* (1874). Yet he was no sentimentalist of rural life, and his interest in the past had little of the nostalgia of *Tennyson or *Arnold. An unrivalled observer of the countryside, he found no Wordsworthian solace there, nor in his own unhappy marriage. His major novels tackled the social issues of the day, the double standard in *Tess of the D'Urbervilles* (1891), the unfairness of the divorce laws in *Jude the Obscure* (1895), the hostile reception they encountered prompting a return to his first love, poetry. Some of the best came with his first wife's death in 1912, as buried emotion resurfaced, though he had already produced *The Dynasts* (1908), his epic drama on the Napoleonic wars, the most ambitious but probably least read of his works. JNRS

Harfleur, siege of, 1415. In August 1415 Henry V laid siege to Harfleur at the mouth of the Seine. After a heavy cannonade, the town surrendered on 22 September. But Henry's forces had suffered serious losses from dysentery and when he marched northwards towards the safety of *Calais, he found his way blocked at *Agincourt by a superior French force. Henry's intention was to encourage English settlement and turn Harfleur into a second Calais, but it was recaptured by the French during the reign of his son. JAC

Hargreaves, James (1720–78). Inventor. Hargreaves was a largely self-taught weaver from Lancashire, who invented the spinning jenny in 1764 and patented it in 1770. *Kay's flying-shuttle had greatly speeded up the process of weaving and Hargreaves's jenny, using several spindles at once, enabled spinning to keep up. He experienced many of the difficulties that Kay had faced. In 1768 his house was attacked by a mob from Blackburn and he was involved in extensive litigation in an attempt to protect his patent. JAC

Harington, Sir John (1560–1612). Epigrammatist. Son of two of Elizabeth's loyal servitors, thereby her godson, 'Boye Jacke' was educated at Eton and Cambridge. Witty and well-read, he divided his time between the court and his estate at Kelston, near Bath, according to the queen's smiles or frowns. In 1599 he accompanied *Essex to Ireland, where he was knighted, but weathered Elizabeth's displeasure on his return. Ever loyal to her, he nevertheless favoured James's accession to the English throne but failed to obtain his favour, despite preparing manuscripts for the young Prince *Henry. Irrepressible, extravagant, and disarmingly candid, Harington has been dismissed as a Rabelaisian trifler, but his miscellaneous writings demonstrate keen observation and a more tolerant attitude towards the Irish than many of his contemporaries. If it is true that he installed the first water-closet at Kelston in 1596, he was a great benefactor to the human race. ASH

Harland, Edward James (1831–95). Co-founder of the Belfast shipyard Harland & Wolff. Harland, a Yorkshireman, was trained in the shipyards of Newcastle and Glasgow. In 1854 he moved to Belfast in order to manage Robert Hickson & Co. In 1858 he bought the firm with the assistance of the Liverpool capitalist G. C. Schwabe, and in 1861 went into partnership with Schwabe's nephew G. W. *Wolff. A gifted and inventive engineer, Harland turned a small-time concern into an internationally successful business. He retired from active involvement in the yard in 1889, and devoted himself to Conservative and Unionist politics until his death. He was mayor of Belfast (1885–6), and Conservative MP for North Belfast (1889–95). He was granted a baronetcy in 1885. AJ

Harlaw, battle of, 1411. Donald, lord of the Isles, engaged in a dispute over the earldom of Ross, which he claimed by right of his wife, raised considerable forces, occupied Inverness, and advanced towards Aberdeen. On 24 July he was met near Inverurie, 20 miles north-west of Aberdeen, by the earl of Mar, supported by townsfolk from Aberdeen. The result of the encounter was variously reported, but Donald failed to obtain the earldom. JAC

Harlech castle was built for Edward I as one of a series of fortifications intended to secure his conquest of north Wales. Begun in May 1283, it was largely completed in seven years and is one of the greatest achievements of its architect, Master James of St George. It combines powerful defences, which enhance the natural strength of the site, with elaborate and well-planned accommodation for the king and his court. In the Welsh rising of 1400–13, Harlech fell to Owain *Glyndŵr, became the residence of his court and his family, and may have been the place where he was formally crowned as prince of Wales. In the Wars of the *Roses the castle was held for the Lancastrians, as a chronicler remarked: 'Kyng Edward was possessed of alle Englonde, excepte a castelle in Northe Wales called Harlake.' It was eventually surrendered in 1468; traditionally it is this defence which gave rise to the song 'Men of Harlech'. Harlech was the last castle to fall to Parliament in March 1647 and its loss marked the end of the war. Parliament ordered its destruction but this was not carried out, so, despite the passage of time, the walls still stand to virtually their full height, making it one of the most impressive ruins in Britain. LR

Harley, Robert, 1st earl of Oxford and earl Mortimer (1661–1724). Prime minister and bibliophile. From a puritan Herefordshire family, Harley was MP for Tregony (1689–90) and New Radnor Boroughs (1690–1711), and in the 1690s a leader of the new country party (which attacked the royal prerogative and a standing army), as well as twice being chosen Speaker of the Commons. He was again Speaker (1702–5), and in 1704 was appointed secretary of state for the northern department in the *Godolphin ministry. His growing Toryism and reputation for deviousness and (in the eyes of the Junto Whigs, *Marlborough and Godolphin) untrustworthiness led to his resignation from the ministry in 1708. His revenge was to gain the confidence of Queen Anne and to engineer the fall of the ministry in 1710, becoming chief minister for the next four years, first as chancellor of the Exchequer and then in 1711 as lord treasurer (when he was raised to the peerage by a grateful queen after he had recovered from an assassination attempt).

Though the leader of an essentially Tory ministry, Harley wanted to establish a government above party. His failure was as a result of increased extremism in the Tory Party (which won decisively in the general elections of 1710 and 1713), the problems of the peace with France (which the Whigs strenuously opposed), and the rivalry with *Bolingbroke. One week before she died, Anne dismissed Harley from office. He was impeached in 1715, largely for his part in the peace of *Utrecht which George I had opposed, and remained in the Tower until 1717 when proceedings were dropped. His main political achievement was to develop a 'party of the crown' in Parliament, which was later taken up and refined by *Walpole. His extensive collection of books and manuscripts later formed the basis of the British Museum library. CJ

Harmsworth, Alfred, 1st Viscount Northcliffe (1865–1922). Newspaper proprietor. The eldest son of a Dublin barrister who moved to London in 1867, Northcliffe was largely self-educated. Attracted to journalism, he discovered that he had a natural aptitude for the profession. In 1887 he formed his own publishing house, which he ran with his brother *Harold. The business acquired first the *Evening News*, later the *Daily Mail*, the *Daily Mirror*, the *Observer*, and, in 1908, *The Times*. He was created baron (1905) and viscount (1918). If Northcliffe injected into *The Times* a refreshing element of commercialism, it was even truer that he used his newspaper empire as a political weapon, denouncing government ministers and their policies whenever the fancy took him. Northcliffe was frequently accused of exercising power without responsibility; but the support of *The Times* was a factor in bringing about the Irish peace treaty of 1921, and his personal efforts as head of the British mission to the USA in 1917 were widely and rightly applauded. GA

Harmsworth, Harold, 1st Viscount Rothermere (1868–1940). Newspaper proprietor. Younger brother of Alfred *Harmsworth, Viscount Northcliffe. Harold Harmsworth accepted Alfred's offer to provide financial management for the publishing venture which eventually became the Amalgamated Press. Neither a journalist by profession nor a politician by inclination, Harold eschewed the public limelight enjoyed by Alfred, but in 1917 accepted *Lloyd George's invitation to take charge of the Air Ministry. Meanwhile he had increased the scope of his own newspaper proprietorship, producing the *Sunday Pictorial*, London's first Sunday picture newspaper, in 1915. Created baron (1914), he was advanced to viscount (1918). On his brother's death in 1922 Harold assumed control of Associated Newspapers, and used this opportunity to write forceful articles for the *Daily Mail* in praise of Hitler and Mussolini; he was initially sympathetic to the *British Union of Fascists, and used the *Daily Mail* in an ill-judged and unsuccessful campaign (1930) against Stanley *Baldwin on the issue of empire free trade. GA

Harold I (*c.*1016–40), king of England (*c.*1035–40), known as 'Harefoot', was a son of *Cnut, by Ælfgifu of Northampton, his first wife. In 1035, on Cnut's death, he claimed the throne of England in opposition to his half-brother *Harthacnut, whose mother was *Emma, Cnut's second wife. Since the sons were young, the probability is that they were pawns in the hands of formidable mothers. They agreed to divide England, Harold taking the northern part and acting as regent for the rest, but by 1037 he had established himself as king of the whole realm. Harthacnut prepared to invade but Harold's death at Oxford in 1040 allowed a peaceful succession. When Harthacnut in turn died after a reign of only two years, Emma's other son, by *Æthelred II, succeeded as *Edward the Confessor. JAC

Harold II (Harold Godwineson) (*c.*1022–66), king of England (1066), the last Old English ruler before the *Norman Conquest, was defeated and killed by William the Conqueror at the battle of *Hastings. Along with the rest of his family, Harold rose to increasing prominence in England during the reign of *Edward the Confessor, receiving the earldom of East Anglia in 1044 and succeeding his father *Godwine as earl of Wessex in 1053. He was subsequently the most powerful man in the kingdom after the king. His role in the complex politics of the English kingdom in Edward the Confessor's reign, and, in particular, his attitude to the succession, can never be entirely clear, because there is no record of his personal motives and because the attitude of the childless Edward cannot be conclusively unravelled. Despite his great power, there is nothing to suggest that Harold was being groomed for the succession or that he coveted it, until he was designated as his successor by the dying Edward. Harold's career passed through a number of periods of crisis. In 1051–2, for example, he was temporarily banished from England along with the rest of his family when they quarrelled with the king. He was in some way involved in the mysterious return to England in 1057 of *Edward the Exile, the father of *Edgar the Atheling. In 1064 or 1065 (so Norman sources tell us), he visited Normandy to confirm Edward the Confessor's earlier promise of the succession to Duke William, swearing there the fateful oath which enabled William in 1066 to portray him as a perjurer.

Late in 1065, he failed to assist his brother *Tostig in the (probably) impossible task of crushing a rebellion against Tostig's authority in Northumbria; the embittered Tostig thereafter became his brother's enemy and fought and died with the army of King *Harold Sigurdsson (Hardrada) at the battle of *Stamford Bridge. The most probable explanation of Harold's career between 1053 and 1066 is that, while remaining essentially the loyal subject of Edward the Confessor, he was also a careful politician who did not take any risks likely to jeopardize his own situation. He obeyed orders and kept his own counsel. Edward's death-bed bequest of succession to the English kingdom was probably a recognition that Harold was the only successor likely to be accepted with anything resembling unanimity by the English. After his coronation on the day immediately following Edward's death, Harold's efforts to defend his kingship against his rivals were effective and courageous; he kept an army and navy in readiness for several months in southern England and the main institutions of government appear to have continued to function. The support he received during the great campaigns of 1066 must indicate that he was widely accepted as king, much preferred by the English to any of the alternatives. His march north to win the battle of Stamford Bridge was a remarkable military feat, as was the return to confront William the Conqueror. His generalship can, however, be criticized. He could have delayed confronting William in order to assemble a larger and fresher army and he concentrated his forces too close to William's, perhaps allowing the latter to attack him before the English army was ready. The length and hard-fought character of the battle of Hastings none the less suggests that the English were both well led and well organized. Harold's death occurred late in the battle. Its manner will always be controversial. Was he, or was he not, killed by an arrow through the eye? Interpretations of the crucial scene on the *Bayeux Tapestry will always differ. DB

Harold Sigurdsson (d. 1066), king of Norway. Harold, the half-brother of St Olaf, was the last great Viking invader of England. Nicknamed 'Hardrada'—stern in council—and a man of great stature and strength, he joined forces in 1066 with *Tostig, *Harold II Godwineson's exiled brother. Harold Hardrada claimed the throne of England and Tostig was to be restored to his earldom of Northumbria. He may have been misled by Tostig into counting on more support in England than he found. His great fleet touched at the Orkneys, moved south to the Tyne to join with Tostig, and then entered the Humber, menacing York. The local earls, Edwin and *Morcar, were defeated at *Fulford, just outside York, but five days later the victorious Norsemen were attacked at *Stamford Bridge by Harold, who had led a forced march from the south. After bloody fighting, Harold Hardrada and Tostig were killed. Three days after the victory, William of Normandy landed near Hastings. JAC

Harrington, James (1611–77). Political philosopher. His *Commonwealth of Oceana* (1656), though dedicated to *Cromwell, implicitly censured the *Protectorate. Its central doctrine was that the distribution of property in a state determines its form of government. Where one ruler disposes of all the land, absolute monarchy results; where an aristocracy holds most of it, mixed monarchy is the natural form; but where property is widely distributed, only a republic can provide stable government. To maintain its stability, Harrington prescribed an upper limit to any individual's holding of land and an obligation on all property-owners to serve in arms, the wealthier as cavalry, the less affluent as infantry. A two-chamber legislature was to be elected by these local militias: a senate of 300 (all cavalry) to initiate laws, and an assembly of 1,050 (mixed horse and foot) to ballot silently for or against them. A third of their members were to retire each year. Officers of state and magistrates were to be similarly subject to election (by ballot) and rotation. AHW

Harrington, William Stanhope, 1st earl of (*c.*1683–1756). Stanhope was a younger son who, with moderate abilities but good connections, built an extremely distinguished career. Queen Anne complained of his 'insipid sloth', Lord *Hervey of his 'infinite laziness', and Horace *Walpole admitted that he had no talent for speaking in Parliament. But the earls of Chesterfield were distant cousins and James *Stanhope, commander in Spain and briefly first minister, was another cousin. William Stanhope served in the army in Spain under his cousin, was soon given a regiment, and continued to hold rank, rising to full general. In 1715 he was returned to Parliament for Derby and began a diplomatic career as envoy and then ambassador to Spain. In 1730 he joined *Walpole's cabinet as secretary of state, receiving a barony. His connections were with the duke of *Newcastle and he survived Walpole's fall, gaining promotion to an earldom in 1742 and serving as lord president of the council 1742–5. In 1744 he resumed as secretary of state and finished his career as lord-lieutenant of Ireland between 1746 and 1750. There the agitation of Charles Lucas and the radicals made for a turbulent ending to his public life. JAC

Harris, Sir Arthur Travers (1892–1984). Marshal of the Royal Air Force, famous as commander-in-chief, RAF Bomber Command, 1942–5. This force absorbed much British productive capacity and high-quality manpower. Early in the war it showed itself incapable of daylight attacks on Germany and highly inaccurate at night. Under Harris, it became effective at 'area bombing', seeking to destroy civilian housing, injure morale, and reduce production. Harris repeatedly claimed that wrecking large German towns would win the war. British 'strategic bombing' killed and maimed civilians, destroyed beautiful buildings, and sacrificed many bomber crews (an RAF rear-gunner was unlikely to survive) but did not win the war. Harris resisted 'precision bombing' but his favoured methods failed to reduce war production as he planned. He was not engaged in 'genocide', nor was he a 'war criminal'; he did not inflict casualties for reasons other than shortening the war. Nevertheless, he did not get a peerage and there were hostile demonstrations when a statue to him was erected in London in 1992. RACP

Harris, Howell (1714–73). A founder of Welsh calvinistic methodism. Born at Trefecca, Talgarth, near Brecon, and educated locally, Harris hoped for Anglican ordination, but started teaching (1730). Following a conversion experience, he began studies at Oxford (1735) but soon returned home. Though an Anglican until his death, he began itinerant open-air preaching (1737) several times a day so effectively that by 1739 he had aroused much of Wales. After parting from his colleague Daniel Rowlands (1751), he founded a protestant monastery at Trefecca (1752) which soon had 120 inhabitants. Fear of French catholicism encouraged him to join the militia and gave him a chance to preach in many parts of England. He had close contacts with Selina, countess of *Huntingdon, and *Whitefield. WMM

Harrison, Thomas (1606–60). Soldier and regicide. A butcher's son, born at Newcastle under Lyme, and trained as a lawyer, Harrison enlisted in *Essex's bodyguard in 1642, fighting at *Marston Moor as a major in Fleetwood's horse and subsequently at *Naseby, *Langport, and the sieges of Winchester and Basing. Thereafter his political and military lives were interwoven. Elected MP for Wendover (1646), he served in Ireland (1647), and escorted Charles I from Hurst castle to London, later signing his death-warrant. Intimate with *Cromwell, he held the chief command in England during Cromwell's absence (1650–1). He helped expel the *Rump in 1653 and was prominent in *Barebone's Parliament. Then his influence waned and his health failed. He had developed *Fifth Monarchist views, lost his commission under the *Instrument of Government, and was imprisoned in 1655–6 and again in 1658–9. One of the first to be arrested at the Restoration, Harrison was tried in October 1660 and defended himself stoutly: 'this thing [the king's execution] was not done in a corner.' He was hanged at Charing Cross looking, according to *Pepys, 'as cheerfully as any man could do in that condition . . . the first blood shed in revenge for the blood of the king.' CB; JAC

Harrowby, Dudley Ryder, 1st earl of (1762–1847). Harrowby's grandfather was an eminent lawyer, who became attorney-general and died just before his peerage took effect. Harrowby was elected on the family interest at Tiverton in 1784 at the age of 21, supported *Pitt, and worked his way up the ladder. He was made under-secretary at the Foreign Office in 1789, served as paymaster 1791–1800, was foreign secretary 1804–5, and chancellor of the duchy of Lancaster 1805–6. He succeeded his father as 2nd baron in 1803 and was raised to the earldom in 1809. From 1812 until 1827 he served under Liverpool as lord president of the council and in December 1827 was offered the premiership, which he declined on grounds of ill-health. He played an important role during the reform crisis of 1831–2 as a leader of the waverers, who ultimately voted for the bill. Harrowby was more respected than liked. *Greville, while admitting his integrity, found him irritable and dismissed him as 'the top of the second-rate men'. His younger brother Richard held the family seat 1795–1830 and served as home secretary under *Perceval. JAC

Harrow School was founded by John Lyon, a yeoman in the neighbouring village of Preston, in 1571 as a free grammar school for the education of 30 poor children. It was not opened until 1611. 'Foreigners', i.e. children from other parishes who paid for their education, were allowed in from 1660 and the school prospered. After a period of decline, the school's fortunes were restored largely by the effort of the eminent headmaster Dr Charles Vaughan (1816–97). Amongst its old boys are four 19th-cent. prime ministers—*Peel, *Palmerston, *Aberdeen, and *Goderich—and a 20th-cent. one, Winston *Churchill. PG

Harthacnut (*c.*1019–42), king of England (1040–2), was a son of *Cnut by his second wife *Emma of Normandy, widow of *Æthelred II. At his father's death in 1035 he was in Denmark, but his mother put forward his claim to the throne of England against his half-brother *Harold Harefoot. On the latter's death in 1040 Harthacnut succeeded. He was said to have desecrated his brother's grave and the *Anglo-Saxon Chronicle* observed that 'he never did anything worthy of a king while he reigned'. In 1042, at the wedding-feast of his standard-bearer Tofig the Proud, he 'died as he stood at his drink and suddenly fell to the ground with a horrible convulsion'. He was succeeded by his half-brother *Edward the Confessor. JAC

Harty, Sir Hamilton (1879–1941). Irish composer, conductor, and pianist. After holding organist's posts at Belfast and Dublin, Harty moved to London in 1900, where his Comedy Overture was performed at the Promenade Concerts (1907) and his Violin Concerto premièred by Szigeti (1909). Having gained a reputation as a conductor through concerts with the London Symphony and Hallé Orchestras, he was appointed permanent conductor to the Hallé from 1920 to 1933. Under his leadership the orchestra became one of the finest in the country, performing many new works (including his own *Irish Symphony*) and giving memorable English premières of Mahler's ninth and Shostakovich's first Symphonies. A witty and sometimes controversial figure, he is probably best known today for his full orchestral arrangements of Handel's *Water Music* and *Fireworks Music*. ECr

harvesting—the gathering of crops at the end of growing seasons—was a crucial time for our ancestors because the size and quality of crops determined whether there was to follow a time of feast or famine: life itself was at stake. As late as the 1840s the failure of the Irish potato crop brought death to tens of thousands. Although the cycle of the seasons had its role, each season varied from year to year and over long periods of time climatic variations had resulted in the warm summers of the early 13th cent. and the little ice age of the 17th cent. Adapting to these longer-term shifts limited the cultivation of wheat in northern Britain since 90 frost-free days were required. Similarly, vineyards declined in the later Middle Ages and were revived for commercial farming only in the 20th cent.

Celebrations of harvests safely gathered in formed part of many rural traditions for centuries. The feast of Michaelmas (29 September) marked the end of the farming year when annual accounts were rendered. However, 'harvest festivals' in churches with special services and elaborate decorations only became formally part of many Christian church calendars during the 19th cent.

Yields of crops have increased since the Middle Ages arising from the selective breeding of plants and animals particularly since the early 18th cent. From the mid-19th cent. manufactured fertilizers and various technologies have enabled expansion of output. For example, yields of wheat from seed sown in the early 14th cent. were seldom more than eightfold whereas in the later 20th cent. yields reached fortyfold. In the 20th cent. mechanization has reduced sharply the numbers of people needed to harvest most crops, and bringing in the harvest no longer concerns most city-dwellers. IJEK

Harvey, William (1578–1657). Physician. After Cambridge, Harvey went to the great medical school at Padua. His teacher Fabricius had identified valves in veins, and was interested in animal generation; these became Harvey's great concerns also. Back in England, he settled down to successful practice in London, becoming physician to Charles I and a staunch royalist. The structure of the heart and vein valves convinced him that, contrary to received physiological opinion, blood must circulate round the body (rather than ebb and flow), which he determined to confirm 'by sense and experience' (animal dissection, vivisection), but *De Motu Cordis* (1628) initially met with considerable controversy. He then turned to embryology, inferring that all animals start from an egg. DK

Haselrig, Sir Arthur (*c.*1600–61). Haselrig, a Leicestershire baronet, was a leader of the parliamentary cause throughout the civil wars. A staunch puritan, educated at Cambridge and Gray's Inn, he was a close associate of *Pym and brother-in-law of Lord Brooke. He served for his native county in the *Short and *Long Parliaments and his strong opposition to *Strafford and *Laud led to his being one of the *five members 'named' by Charles I in January 1642. He was an active cavalry commander during the first civil war, at the head of his regiment of 'lobsters', and was made governor of Newcastle upon Tyne in 1647. He refused to serve on the High Court which tried the king and quarrelled with *Cromwell when the *Rump Parliament was dismissed. He declined to serve in Cromwell's 'other house', attacking it as a new House of Lords. In 1659 when the Rump was recalled, Haselrig was briefly influential, serving on the *Council of State. But after quarrelling with *Lambert, he threw in his lot with *Monck. At the Restoration he was stranded and though Monck saved his life, he spent his last months in the Tower. An uncompromising and rigid republican, he was called by *Clarendon 'an absurd bold man', and by *Ludlow, who knew him well, 'a man of a disobliging carriage, sour and morose of temper'. JAC

Hastenbeck, battle of, 1757. *Cumberland, the hero of *Culloden, commanded the Army of Observation in the *Seven Years War, charged with the protection of Hanover. Frederick the Great, Britain's ally, was too hard pressed himself to offer assistance. On 26 July, on the Weser near Hameln, Cumberland was attacked by a superior French force under Marshal d'Estrées, and though at one stage the French were preparing to retire, Cumberland was forced to retreat. Acting on private instructions from his father George II, he retired in good order to Stade, where he negotiated the convention of *Kloster-Zeven, disbanding his forces. The British government repudiated the convention. JAC

Hastings, battle of, 1066. Fought on 14 October at what is now Battle (Sussex), where William the Conqueror ordered the construction of an abbey to commemorate his decisive victory over King *Harold Godwineson. Much is obscure about the course of the battle, although several crucial features can be deduced from the *Bayeux Tapestry and other contemporary sources. The core of Harold's army had marched south in under three weeks after its victory at *Stamford Bridge. It must have been tired and was undoubtedly surprised by the speed at which William advanced to force battle. The two armies were probably almost evenly matched numerically, but William's contained cavalry, whereas Harold's did not. An apparent lack of archers made the English excessively passive. A mixture of genuine and feigned retreats by William's army appears to have disrupted the packed English forces by drawing them down from their defensive position on the ridge where the town of Battle now stands. King Harold's death, late in the day as the Normans poured through the English ranks, ensured that the battle would be decisive, despite attempts to organize English resistance around the young *Edgar the Atheling. DB

Hastings, William Hastings, 1st Lord (*c.*1430–83). Hastings was the lifelong confidant of Edward IV, and, according to contemporary gossip, shared both the adversities and mistresses of his master. The son of a Yorkist retainer, he came into prominence at the beginning of the reign as chamberlain of the household. He recruited on Edward's behalf a well-documented body of indentured retainers in the north midlands. In the last years of the reign he was one of the half-dozen powerful men on whom the king relied. Unquestionably loyal to the dynasty, he gave his total support to the young Edward V in the early summer of 1483. Because of his antipathy towards the Woodvilles, he was prepared initially to support Richard of Gloucester in his bid for power. But he himself became a victim when he was suddenly seized and executed on 13 June. The manner of his death has secured for him a reputation for unimpeachable probity, but he too was a courtier in pursuit of his own ends. AJP

Hastings, Francis Rawdon-Hastings, 1st Marquis, and 4th Baron Moira (1754–1826). Hastings was born in Ireland and educated at Harrow and Oxford. In 1771 he joined the army and served in the American War of Independence 1776–81. Thereafter he held appointments mainly at home until he was made governor-general of India in 1813. His period in office was marked by major military conquests, which consolidated British power. In 1814–16 he successfully prosecuted the Gurkha and Pindari wars. In 1818, he inflicted a final defeat on the peshwa of Poona to dismantle the Maratha empire, which once had been the *East

India Company's principal rival for supremacy in India. His last years, however, were marred by financial scandals in Hyderabad involving Palmer & Company. He retired from India in 1823 and was appointed governor of Malta 1824–6. DAW

Hastings, Warren (1732–1818). Hastings joined the *East India Company in 1750. He rose quickly in its service, being a member of the Bengal Council by 1757 when Robert *Clive achieved his first military victories. He was at the heart of the subsequent intrigues surrounding the nawabi of Bengal. In 1764 he retired to England with a large fortune which he rapidly lost. He returned to India in 1769 and, three years later, was appointed governor of Bengal. In 1773, he became the first governor-general of India. In office, he reformed the company's revenue and commercial systems and extended its influence across the Ganges valley. He retired with a second fortune after the establishment of a parliamentary Board of Control for east India affairs, which subsequently impeached him for murder and extortion. The prosecution was led by Edmund *Burke and the proceedings lasted from 1788 until 1795, when Hastings was acquitted, but left impoverished and discredited. DAW

Hatfield, Council of, 680. The council arose out of concern over the Monothelite heresy, significant in the East, and finally condemned at the Council of Constantinople, 680–1. To test the soundness of the West, synods were held by metropolitans in their provinces and the pope in Rome. Any possible fears that the Cilician *Theodore, archbishop of Canterbury, might have introduced Greek customs to England would have been unfounded. At Hatfield, the bishops and teachers summoned by him united in their declaration of the orthodox catholic faith. AM

Hatfield House. Soon after his arrival in England, James I suggested to Sir Robert *Cecil that they exchange Theobalds and Hatfield in Hertfordshire. At Hatfield there was a palace that had belonged to the bishops of Ely; Cecil began building a new house in 1607, using materials from the palace. It is therefore thirty years later than *Longleat and fifteen years later than *Hardwick Hall. It is a large house on the traditional E plan, with a remarkable grand staircase. The house remains in the Cecil family and was one of the first to be lighted by electricity, since Lord *Salisbury, prime minister in the 1890s, was an amateur scientist and rigged up a power supply from the river Lea. He also introduced an early and erratic telephone system. JAC

Hatton, Sir Christopher (1540–91). Lord chancellor. Of Northamptonshire gentry stock, and not wholly studious at the Inner Temple, his good looks and graceful dancing brought him to Queen Elizabeth's attention. Despite total dedication and devotion to her, his governmental career was slow to develop, though he early on became her recognized spokesman in the House of Commons. Vice-chamberlain and a privy counsellor by 1577, member of the commissions which tried *Babington and Mary, queen of Scots (1586), and regarded as most likely to know Elizabeth's real mind, he was appointed lord chancellor in 1587, when any shortfall in legal training was outweighed by impartiality, common sense and Star Chamber experience; his moderate attitude that 'neither fire nor steel' should be used in settling religious matters helped maintain internal quiet. A lover of literature, occasionally a patron, he died unmarried and was buried in St Paul's cathedral. ASH

Havelock, Sir Henry (1795–1857). Havelock was born in Sunderland and trained for the bar but took an army commission in 1815. He served with distinction in the first *Burmese War (1824–6), the first *Afghan War (1838–42), and the first *Sikh War (1845–6). However, promotion was slow until he was appointed quartermaster of the Indian army in 1854 and adjutant to the queen's troops in India in 1855. He was a member of Sir James Outram's expedition to Persia in 1857 but returned to India after the outbreak of the *Indian mutiny. He commanded the first attempts to reconquer the Ganges valley. However, although winning several victories, he failed to hold *Cawnpore or lift the siege of *Lucknow. He had to await the arrival of Sir Colin *Campbell's army, brought back from China, before success could be achieved. He died of dysentery at Lucknow in November 1857, shortly after its relief. DAW

'Hawarden Kite'. After the general election of 1885 Gladstone's Liberals with 333 seats were balanced by 251 Tories who had an understanding with *Parnell's 86 Irish MPs. Gladstone suggested that the Conservative government should sponsor a *Home Rule measure, which it was not keen to do. In December 1885 Gladstone's son Herbert leaked to the press that his father had a scheme for Home Rule. The Conservative government was defeated and resigned, and Gladstone formed his third administration, splitting his party on the Irish question. The satirical name given to Herbert Gladstone's initiative was taken from Hawarden in Flintshire, where Gladstone had made his home. There is no evidence that Gladstone knew of his son's intention, though few of his political opponents gave him the benefit of that doubt. JAC

Hawke, Sir Edward (1710–81). The son of a barrister. His early naval career was in time of peace but he was captain at 24 and rear-admiral at 37. His chance came towards the end of the War of the *Austrian Succession when the commander of the Channel fleet, Sir Peter Warren, fell ill and Hawke took over. Off *Cape Finisterre in October 1747 he won a decisive victory, taking seven out of nine enemy vessels. He was created KB and returned as MP for Portsmouth. Hawke was again employed in the *Seven Years War. An expedition against Rochefort in 1757 was a dismal failure but in 1759 he blockaded Brest and in November his brilliant victory at *Quiberon Bay ended all chance of a French invasion: *Newcastle described it as 'the most glorious event at sea this century'. After the war, Hawke was promoted admiral of the fleet and served as 1st lord of the Admiralty 1766–71, though his health was giving way. His barony in 1776 was somewhat belated and not excessive compared with honours given to others. JAC

Hawkins, Sir John (1532–95). Hawkins began his career as an overseas navigator and trader as an ally of the Spanish, to whose West Indies and South American colonies he carried west African slaves in expeditions between 1562 and 1569. *Drake was with him when relations with Spain became hostile on the last expedition. He was subsequently an MP and comptroller of the Navy, which he significantly developed. Further active commands followed—against the Armada, on an expedition to Portugal in the following year, and the disastrous association with Drake on the West Indies anti-Spanish expedition of 1595, when he died off Puerto Rico. Although as originator of England's long involvement in the slave trade his reputation must be to some degree dubious, Hawkins was one of the most important of the men who brought about the close involvement of the English state with overseas activity. RB

Hawksmoor, Nicholas (*c.*1661–1736). 250 years after his death some late 20th-century critical opinion hails Hawksmoor as the most interesting and daringly original architect England has produced, if not the greatest. The process resulting in this reappraisal has been one of informed deduction made the more complex because of the problems in distinguishing the collaborative work of Hawksmoor from that of his chief *partners*, rather than masters, *Wren and *Vanbrugh. Hawksmoor, self-schooled in the architecture of the classical world (though he never went abroad), ultimately, and above all in his seven London churches built during the twelve years 1712–24, revealed a profoundly original control of mass, if not of the play of light, over complementary broken surfaces. St Anne, Limehouse, St George-in-the-East, and Christ Church, Spitalfields, are all examples of a rare genius. For all Hawksmoor's indebtedness to contemporaries, a modernity stemming from primal forms seems to link him with the explosive, revolutionary imaginations of Ledoux and Boullée (active in France *c.*1760–1800). DDA

Haydon, Benjamin Robert (1786–1846). A historical painter, born in Plymouth, the son of a painter and publisher, Haydon was encouraged to sketch while at school. From an early age he showed great determination to succeed, yet his life ended in imprisonment for debt and suicide. For much of his life he painted large canvases of historical or religious subjects rather than more marketable works. A stubborn man, invariably in opposition to the establishment, he campaigned strenuously for patronage for the arts, the foundation of schools of design, decoration of public buildings, in particular the Houses of Parliament, and to save the *Elgin marbles for the nation. He also became involved in radical politics. Despite his pugnacious character he had many admirers among the Romantic movement in literature, especially *Wordsworth and *Keats, whose portraits he painted. He is now chiefly remembered for his *Autobiography and Memoirs*, published in 1853. JC

Hazlitt, William (1778–1830). Hazlitt was the son of a unitarian minister and grew up in Wem (Shropshire), where he met *Coleridge. Religious doubts preventing him following his father's profession, he started as a painter, and then began literary work for newspapers and periodicals. He was an idiosyncratic radical and had some success as a lecturer. But he was cantankerous—'I have quarrelled with almost all of my old friends'—his two marriages failed, and he was frequently in financial distress. Hazlitt is at his best as an occasional essayist—his piece on the bare-knuckle fight between Neate and the Gas-man is in many anthologies. To historians, his early biography of Thomas Holcroft is of value, as are the *Political Essays* of 1819: the late life of Napoleon (1828–30), intended as his *magnum opus*, was derivative if not plagiarized, and too hagiographical to win much approval when published. His best work is *The Spirit of the Age* (1825), with vivid and caustic sketches of contemporaries such as *Godwin, *Bentham, *Southey, *Scott, *Byron, and *Wordsworth. Of his love of history he wrote: 'I cannot solve the mystery of the past, nor exhaust my pleasure in it.' JAC

Heads of the Proposals, 1647. In June 1647 the army had taken custody of Charles I and, in the course of July, *Lambert and *Ireton worked out a basis for negotiation on behalf of the army council. The monarchy was to continue and to retain its veto; episcopacy was confirmed, though the bishops were to lose their coercive authority; there were to be guarantees of religious toleration; the militia was to be under the control of Parliament for ten years; parliaments were to be biennial and were to be elected on a reformed system that related representation to taxation; there was to be a council of state. Though these proposals were remarkably conciliatory in the aftermath of civil war, Charles rejected them out of hand. JAC

health. Efforts to attain and maintain good health have a long history as the concern of individuals and of society. A plea for good health remained an important theme for prayers from ancient times until the present day, and was often the occasion for pilgrimages. The alleged curative powers of springs precipitated the establishment of spas where wealthy visitors came to take the waters and which may be considered the forerunners of modern health farms. Poorer people sought good health through folk medicine, using herbal remedies and techniques such as the laying-on of hands. Until the 19th cent. many believed the king's *touch would cure scrofula. Caring for the sick had the blessing of the Christian churches, which urged their members both to be charitable and to care for those suffering. State intervention on a large scale in the 19th and 20th cents. aimed to promote good health amongst the population. This period also saw the development of professions and occupations, such as medicine, nursing, paramedical services, and environmental health, specifically intended to promote good health.

The general health of people during the Middle Ages was discussed only obliquely in historical accounts and it was taken for granted that everyone suffered from the effects of seasonal food shortages. However, recent studies have suggested that larger towns were especially unhealthy because of poor sanitation and that their growth often depended on continuous migration from rural areas. Even the well-off in towns did not escape from health problems. Life expectation was relatively short. More has been recorded about the outbreak of spectacularly lethal diseases such as bubonic plague (known as the *Black Death) during the mid-14th cent. and the Great Plague in 1665.

The first systematic attempt to devise indicators of the health of some groups of the population, particularly the upper and middle classes, was made by life assurance companies in the 18th cent. Measuring the size of these populations and their composition had commercial significance because life assurance companies needed data to ensure that they made good profits. Statistics about the entire population began with the establishment of the nation-wide decennial *census in 1801. Censuses became increasingly sophisticated in the range of data collected. The compulsory registration of births, marriages, and deaths in 1837 made it possible to identify and analyse important overall trends in the population. For example, the government gained information about the total number of men available for national service and it was possible to start to analyse the increase in the total population.

The population of Great Britain rose from about 10 million in 1801 to over 56 million in 1991. Within these totals the distributions of age groups varied. During the 19th cent. children under the age of 15 years accounted for more than a third of the population whereas during the later 20th cent. they formed only a quarter of the total. Throughout the 19th cent. about a twentieth of the population was aged over 65 years whereas by the late 20th cent. they accounted for almost one-fifth of the total. These changes, particularly the greater life expectation, arose for several reasons: rising incomes, environmental improvements, and healthier diets.

One of the most sensitive indicators of a nation's health is that of infant mortality, the death rate of children under 1 year of age. Infant mortality rates remained well over 100 in every 1,000 live births for almost the whole of the 19th cent. By the late 20th cent. the rate had declined to about 12 in 1,000 births. Within the British Isles there were geographical variations, with the highest mortality rates in the most densely populated areas. There were differences between social class with the highest rates amongst children whose fathers were in unskilled work and the lowest amongst the children of fathers in professional occupations. Relevant factors in explaining these rates appear to have been incomes, quality and quantity of food, heating, clothing, and housing.

Public health became a matter for government intervention during the 19th cent., partly precipitated by an outbreak of *cholera in 1831 whose virulence paid no respect to social class. Interventions were based on theories about the link between health, clean water supplies, and adequate sanitation. The *Public Health Act of 1848 required districts with above-average death rates to have a public health board with powers to raise loans and levy rates to pay for pure water supplies, drains, and sewers. These powers were extended subsequently to all parts of the country. Advances in the biological sciences with regard to the transmission of disease and the need for high standards of hygiene were incorporated into legislation after the middle of the 19th cent. Then, as now, such developments were controversial. Nineteenth-cent. debates about compulsory vaccination, immunization, and drug-taking can be compared with modern debates about fluoridization and smoking.

Efforts to improve the health of the school population began at the end of the 19th cent. They started with 'drill' and evolved later into physical education, emphasizing gymnastics, swimming, athletics, and games. From the end of the 19th cent., the curriculum for girls included cookery, later domestic science, and more recently home economics, whose purposes included imparting some basic knowledge of personal and household hygiene as well as dietary information. With the establishment of the national curriculum in the early 1990s, health studies became an optional subject for all.

During the 19th cent. there was an expansion in medical knowledge and in the variety and range of occupations devoted to the care of the sick. In the 20th cent. the care of the sick became increasingly likely to take place in hospital rather than at home. The establishment of the *welfare state, in particular the *National Health Service in 1948, indicated the political will to find resources for public health.

Evidence indicates that the health of the population has improved through the control of infectious diseases, public health provisions, such as clean water and sanitation, and effective legislation about the quality of food and drink. There has also been an expansion of medical services. A major controversy about the evidence of improved health of the general population is whether medical interventions, including public health measures, contributed as much as adequate nutrition, shelter, clothing, and heating. IJEK

McKeown, T., *The Rise of Modern Population* (1976); Oddy, D. J., 'The Health of the People', in Barker, T. and Drake, M. (eds.), *Population and Society in Britain 1850–1980* (1982); Porter, R., *Disease, Medicine and Society in England* (2nd edn. 1993); Smith, F. B., *The People's Health, 1830–1910* (1979).

Healy, Timothy (1855–1931). Healy was born in Bantry (Co. Cork) but moved to Newcastle upon Tyne in 1871 to work as a railway clerk. He was largely self-taught, assisted by a prodigious memory. He became a devoted disciple of *Parnell, writing in his support in the *Nation*. He was elected to Parliament in 1880 for Wexford and at once established himself as a clever debater. In 1883 he served a six-month sentence for incitement to violence and in 1884 was called to the bar. In 1890, when the Parnell divorce scandal broke, Healy attacked him vehemently: his interjection in Committee Room 15, 'who is to be the mistress of the party?', still reverberates. He was in the anti-Parnell group until the Irish party reunited in 1900, but remained on uneasy terms with *Redmond and the leadership, and moved towards *Sinn Fein. Healy did not stand in the 1918 election which swept Sinn Fein to victory, but in 1922 became the first governor-general of the Irish Free State, serving until 1928. JAC

Heath, Sir Edward (b. 1916). Prime minister. Heath rose from humble beginnings to Balliol College, Oxford, where he secured an organ scholarship and became president of the Union. Music remained a lifelong passion. His first taste of national politics came in Oxford's famous by-election in 1938, when he campaigned against the Conservative Quintin Hogg (Lord *Hailsham).

The *Second World War deepened Heath's conviction that European reconstruction and unity represented the greatest challenge facing his generation. He was among the impressive new Conservative MPs elected in 1950, joining the 'One Nation' group of Tories who took a particular interest in social policy. It was a style of progressive Conservatism to which Heath clung tenaciously throughout his career, even though the group's ideas revealed a more radical approach to welfare spending than Heath might now wish to concede. His maiden speech was on the subject of Europe—the most consistent theme in his career. Less than a year after entering Parliament, however, Heath was made a junior whip. This effectively silenced him as a parliamentarian. Appointed chief whip in 1955, Heath had to hold the party together during the Suez crisis in 1956. This he did with firmness and more charm than he tended to display in later years.

Heath enjoyed good relations with both *Eden and *Macmillan; under the latter his career prospered. After the 1959 general election he became minister of labour. In 1960, however, Macmillan decided to make Lord *Home foreign secretary with a second cabinet minister (Heath) in the Commons. This proved a turning-point in Heath's career. In 1961 the government determined to seek membership of the Common Market and Heath had the delicate task of negotiating the terms of entry. Though the mission was doomed, Heath won widespread applause for his handling of the discussions.

The choice of Home as a short-term leader in 1963 suited Heath since he was himself not yet ready to stake a claim. In the last year of Conservative government, Heath, as president of the Board of Trade, surprised many by introducing controversial legislation to abolish retail price maintenance. It served, however, to underline his credentials as the most dynamic figure in the new generation of Conservative politicians.

As shadow chancellor in 1965 Heath further impressed. With his energy and commitment to the tasks of opposition he stood in marked contrast to his leading rival for the succession, Reginald Maudling. When Home suddenly resigned in July, Heath secured a narrow victory over Maudling—the first leader elected by a simple vote of Conservative MPs. Heath owed his election to the conviction that he was the man to take on Labour's Harold *Wilson on his own terms.

Such expectations proved wide of the mark. Heath never had the subtlety or political skills to compete effectively with Wilson. His popularity lagged behind that of the prime minister even when the Conservatives were running well ahead. None the less Heath prepared assiduously for government. His approach was based on intelligence rather than intellect, pragmatism rather than ideology. A major policy review emerged in the document 'Putting Britain Right Ahead'. Its themes survived largely unchanged through the rest of the decade. It spoke of encouraging a competitive economy, moving from direct to indirect taxation, greater selectivity in the social services, and taking Britain into Europe. Such objectives inevitably encourage comparisons with the Thatcherism of later years. But for Heath the new policies represented a practical approach to the modernization of British society with little if any ideological underpinning.

Heath's defeat in the 1966 election had been widely expected. But his comfortable victory in June 1970 surprised most commentators. Whatever Heath's true intentions, his government seemed more right-wing than any since the war. In particular it espoused an industrial policy which would break the post-war consensus of planning and intervention. The government was certainly beset by bad luck. The chancellor, Iain Macleod, died within a month of the election; Northern Ireland provided unlooked-for difficulties; world economic problems, especially the quadrupling of Arab oil prices in 1973, distorted domestic politics and fuelled inflation. None the less, it is hard to escape the conclusion that Heath's government was a failure. Its one lasting achievement was to take Britain into the EEC, though on terms which ensured that this would remain a contentious issue.

Rising unemployment initiated an abrupt change in policy by the end of 1971. Heath's government now became one of the most interventionist since the war. By 1972 he had re-embraced the notion of an incomes policy. Industrial relations policy proved a disaster. The much heralded *Industrial Relations Act, designed to introduce a framework of legislation into the workplace, proved inoperable. The government finally collapsed in the wake of the miners' strike of 1973–4, to which Heath responded with a three-day week and finally a general election. The campaign was mishandled. Heath's inability to convey his sincerity, which had long worried many Conservatives, proved decisive. A minority Labour government took office after Heath failed to negotiate a deal with the Liberals.

Further defeat followed in a second election in October. By now Heath had succeeded—through electoral failure and personal tactlessness—in alienating many of his own backbenchers. Senior Conservatives began to question the overall approach of his policies. Challenged by Margaret *Thatcher, he withdrew from the leadership contest after failing to win the first ballot in February 1975.

Heath never reconciled himself to these events, his anguish intensified by being replaced by a colleague for whom he had never had much regard. Time failed to heal or even soothe his wounds. He found it difficult to find anything creditable in Mrs Thatcher's Conservatism, especially when it was claimed that she was implementing the policies upon which he had been elected in 1970. Heath remained an MP throughout her premiership, increasingly surly and devoid of his earlier charm. He greeted her fall in 1990 with undisguised glee and sought unconvincingly to find merit in the government of John *Major, even though this owed far more to Mrs Thatcher's legacy than to his own.

He remained to the end an unqualified enthusiast for the European ideal. Overall, however, Heath's career leaves a feeling of disappointment. A man of great energy and considerable ability, his performance was marred by major character flaws. DJD

Campbell, J., *Edward Heath* (1993).

Heathfield (Haeth felth, Hatfield Chase), **battle of,** 633. Here on the Lindsey–Elmet border, north of the Idle on Hatfield Chase, or possibly near Cuckney (Notts.), died *Edwin of *Deira, king of Northumbria, in circumstances which enabled his promotion as a saint. He was defeated on 12 October by the allies *Penda of Mercia (pagan) and *Cadwallon of Gwynedd (Christian), both threatened by Northumbrian expansion, and perhaps supported by *Bernician royal exiles. Union of Deira and Bernicia was broken, and the progress of Northumbrian Christianity temporarily halted (the next kings reverting to paganism and Bishop *Paulinus fleeing), to be resumed, under *Oswald, under Irish rather than, as formerly, Roman influence. AER

Heathfield, George Augustus Eliott, 1st Baron (1717–90). Eliott, a younger son of a Scottish baronet of Roxburghshire, attended the University of Leiden and served in the Prussian army before joining the Horse Grenadiers, his uncle's regiment, in 1739. He fought at *Dettingen and *Fontenoy, and in the *Seven Years War served in Germany, and was second in command at the capture of Havana in 1763. He was promoted lieutenant-general in 1765, served as commander-in-chief in Ireland 1774–5, and became general 1778. In 1776 he was appointed governor of *Gibraltar, a post he held for the rest of his life. During the War of *American Independence, Gibraltar resisted a four-year siege, 1779–83, against Spanish and French forces. Eliott inflicted enormous losses on the Spanish floating batteries in September 1782 with red-hot shot and the following month *Howe raised the blockade. Eliott was knighted in 1783 and given his barony in 1787. *Reynolds's magnificent portrait was painted in 1788. JAC

Heavenfield, battle of, 634. Fought near Hexham, *Oswald of Northumbria defeated and killed *Cadwallon of Gwynedd, who had been ravaging the province after slaying Osric of Deira and Eanfrith of Bernicia (brother of Oswald) the year before. Through this victory Oswald secured his own position as king of both Bernicia and Deira and ensured that Northumbria would return to Christianity after a year of apostasy. The battle takes its name from the place where Oswald erected a wooden cross and prayed for victory before the engagement; the monastery of Hexham subsequently erected a church on the site and splinters from the cross were famed for miracles of healing. BAEY

Hebrides. See WESTERN ISLANDS.

Hedgeley Moor, battle of, 1464. Despite her crushing defeat at *Towton in 1461, Queen *Margaret retained a following in the north of England and was given assistance by the Scots. In the spring of 1464 they raised a substantial force under the duke of Somerset and Sir Ralph Percy. Montagu, *Warwick's younger brother, was sent to deal with it and on 25 April defeated it at Hedgeley Moor, between Alnwick and Wooler. Sir Ralph Percy was killed but the duke of Somerset survived to offer battle three weeks later at *Hexham. JAC

Heligoland. A small island in the North Sea off the mouth of the Elbe. It was taken from Denmark by the British in 1807 and used by British commerce, during the Napoleonic wars, as a base from which to smuggle goods into continental ports closed by the Berlin and Milan decrees. Heligoland was formally ceded to the British in 1814, but in 1890 was given to Germany in exchange for territories in east Africa, and subsequently used as a naval base. After the First World War, article 115 of the treaty of Versailles declared that the island should be demilitarized but remain under German sovereignty. RAS

Heligoland Bight, battle of, 1914. In a confused naval encounter on 28 August 1914, *Beatty's battle-cruisers sank three German light cruisers and one destroyer. The action, though fierce, was limited, but any victory when the Germans were still advancing on Paris was welcome. JAC

Henderson, Arthur (1863–1935). Labour politician. Brought up on Tyneside and apprenticed as an ironfounder, Henderson, then a fervent Gladstonian Liberal, moved slowly to the view that the political future of the manual working classes lay in separation from Liberalism. Elected as MP for Barnard Castle under the auspices of the Labour Representation Committee in 1903, Henderson succeeded to the secretaryship of its successor, the Labour Party, in 1911. Unlike Ramsay *MacDonald, Henderson approved of the British war effort in 1914; he succeeded MacDonald as leader of the parliamentary Labour party, and in 1915 agreed to serve in Asquith's government, becoming a member of Lloyd George's war cabinet the following year. In 1917 he resigned from the government over his support for a negotiated peace, and while playing a major part in the constitutional restructuring of the Labour Party in 1918 he devoted himself increasingly to international reconciliation and support for the *League of Nations; he was foreign secretary in the second Labour government. GA

Hengist and Horsa. Reputed founders of the kingdom of *Kent and its royal house. *Bede was the first to identify the two brothers as the leaders of Germanic forces invited to Britain by *Vortigern in 449; fuller accounts are provided in the 9th-cent. **Anglo-Saxon Chronicle* and *Historia Brittonum*. The stories concerning them should be seen as part of Kentish foundation legends rather than as records of actual events. 'Stallion' and 'Horse' are more likely to have been horse-deities than genuine ancestors and with their alliterating names recall other legendary founding pairs of the Indo-European world such as Romulus and Remus. BAEY

Henley Royal Regatta was established in 1839 and from 1851, under the patronage of Prince Albert, took the prefix Royal. It is held on the Thames with races over 1 mile 550 yards. The two chief events are the Grand Challenge Cup (1839) and the Diamond Challenge Sculls (1844). The four-day event is held in the first week in July. JAC

Henrietta Maria (1609–69), queen of Charles I. Charles married Henrietta Maria, youngest daughter of Henri IV of France, in May 1625 after his Spanish marriage plans had come to naught. She was aged 15, small and vivacious, with dark curly hair, large brown eyes, and protruding teeth. She danced and sang well, surrounded herself with her French catholic servants, and found her first years in England trying. Her husband was rather solemn and there was a very sharp quarrel in 1626 when he sent all her servants packing. But her relations with her husband became close, particularly after the death of *Buckingham in 1628. Their first child, the future Charles II, was born in May 1630. The 1630s she looked back on as halcyon days but increasingly Charles's political troubles darkened their lives. She fled to Holland in February 1642 with the crown jewels to raise men and money. Returning in July 1643 she joined Charles at Oxford, spending her time at Merton College. Heavily pregnant, she fled once more in 1644, giving birth to her youngest daughter at Exeter in June *en route* for France. She never saw her husband again. During the Cromwellian years she remained in France, returning to England at the Restoration in 1660, when Pepys noted her as 'a very little plain old woman'. She left England for good in 1665. *Clarendon thought her meddlesome and historians have blamed her for many of Charles's misfortunes. She appears to have urged the disastrous attempt to arrest the *five members, which she also inadvertently betrayed. But her influence has probably been exaggerated and Charles was quite capable of making his own mistakes. SMC

Henry I (1069–1135), king of England (1100–35) and duke of Normandy (1106–35), was the youngest son of William the Conqueror. In 1087, on his death-bed, William had given Henry a large sum of money, which he used to purchase land in Normandy. He played an intermittent role in the struggle between his elder brothers *Robert Curthose and William Rufus for control of the Anglo-Norman realm and seized the opportunity provided by the latter's (probably) accidental death in 1100 to take over the English kingdom while Robert was still on his return journey from the First Crusade. Henry moved quickly to consolidate his coup, issuing a coronation charter which promised to renounce the supposed abuses of William II's rule, recalling Archbishop *Anselm from exile, and marrying *Matilda, the niece of *Edgar the Atheling and the daughter of *Malcolm Canmore, to create a dynastic link with the Old English ruling house and an alliance with the kingdom of Scots. By 1101 he was sufficiently powerful to resist Robert's invasion of England and to agree terms with him which confirmed Henry's kingship in England. Thus established, Henry then proceeded to disinherit a number of powerful magnates known to be supporters of Robert's cause and to undermine his brother's already precarious authority in Normandy. In 1105–6 he invaded Normandy and completed his conquest of the duchy by defeating Robert in 1106 at the battle of *Tinchebrai, thereby recreating William the Conqueror's Anglo-Norman realm. Henry ruled both England and Normandy for the rest of his life, but his control over Normandy was always threatened until the death of Robert's son William Clito in 1128 by alliances between William, the French king Louis VI, territorial princes such as the counts of Flanders and Anjou, and a group of Norman nobles with few landed interests in England. Henry suffered set-backs such as a military defeat at Alençon in 1119, but was successful in defeating invasions of Normandy in 1118–19 and 1123–4. Marriage alliances were used to secure useful allies, such as the one between his nephew, the future King Stephen, and *Matilda, the heiress to the county of Boulogne. The death of his only legitimate son in the **White Ship* disaster increased Henry's problems and his failure to obtain an heir through his second marriage to *Adela of Louvain eventually forced him to the apparently desperate measure of marrying his daughter, the Empress *Matilda, to Count *Geoffrey Plantagenet of Anjou in 1128, thereby neutralizing one of his most powerful opponents at the cost of the prospect of an Angevin succession to England and Normandy after Henry's death.

The frequent warfare in northern France had an impact on England because Henry was obliged to raise money to finance the wars. His administration, supervised by Bishop *Roger of Salisbury, had a reputation for efficiency and has on occasion been regarded by historians as being notably innovative. The developments should, however, be seen as taking place within the existing institutional framework. The most obvious, the *Exchequer, involved a centralized audit of royal revenue and expenditure under Bishop Roger's supervision, for which there were precedents in the 11th cent. Other developments, such as the more frequent interventions of royal justices in the localities, can also be regarded as opportunist centralization because they relied fundamentally on the existing structure of shire courts and were not regular visitations after the pattern later established in Henry II's reign. Henry's regime is also notable for the advance of individuals of lower aristocratic status to positions of administrative prominence, but, with the important exception of Bishop Roger, their power came nowhere near rivalling that of the great magnates. The general character of Henry's rule was one of expedient centralization within a socially conservative framework. The basis of his rule in both England and Normandy, like his father's, was a group of powerful cross-channel families into which Henry advanced a small number of his own relatives, most notably his nephew, the future King Stephen, and his illegitimate son, Earl *Robert of Gloucester. Despite enduring problems, Henry was without doubt a very successful ruler. England was at peace after the early years of his reign and Normandy was kept secure. He dominated Wales as no predecessor had done and good relations were maintained with his nephew, David I of Scotland. He experienced problems with the church in his early years, most notably when Archbishop Anselm of Canterbury took a stand over the practice of lay investiture of bishops and went into exile in 1103. Henry and the papacy reached a settlement in 1107 and thereafter Henry's relations with the church were generally good, even if some contemporaries regarded his attitude to religion as being more calculated than sincere. He was a great patron of monasteries, most notably of Reading abbey, in which he was buried. His last years were difficult because of the continuing insecurity of the succession, and because he was reluctant to provide his designated heir Matilda and her husband with lands and castles to assist their succession. At the time of his death at Lyons-la-Forêt on 1 December 1135, he was involved in another quarrel with Matilda, which facilitated the coup carried out by Stephen. Despite his many successes in war, diplomacy, and government, Henry

I's legacy was a disputed succession and almost inevitable civil war. DB

Bates, D., 'Normandy and England after 1066', *English Historical Review*, 104 (1989), 851–80; Green, J. A., *The Government of England under Henry I* (Cambridge, 1986); Hollister, C. W., *Monarchy, Magnates and Institutions in the Anglo-Norman World* (1986); Southern, R. W., 'The Place of Henry I in English History', *Proceedings of the British Academy*, 47 (1962), 127–70.

Henry II (1133–89), king of England (1154–89). The first of the *Plantagenet kings of England was also one of the most able and successful of all of this country's monarchs. His achievements are the more remarkable since his responsibilities encompassed not just England, but also two-thirds of France as well, for Henry was also duke of Normandy, count of Anjou, and, by right of his wife Eleanor, duke of *Aquitaine. England was but part of the vast *Angevin empire, each constituent dominion requiring Henry's attention. The consequence was that Henry was frequently absent from England, as he was from his other lordships. Twice, indeed, he was absent for more than four years at a time, and it has been calculated that in the entire course of the reign he was in France for some 21 years.

The problem of government, and the maintenance of peace and stability, were among the greatest challenges facing Henry when he succeeded in 1154. Nowhere was this more so than in England, since Henry inherited a realm severely affected by the disorder and political disintegration that had occurred in Stephen's reign. He proceeded to restore, and then further develop, the governmental structure inherited from his grandfather Henry I, one which assumed an absentee ruler, authority being delegated to one or more chief *justiciars who acted as viceregal figures. But to restore the crown's overall position, including the recovery of lands, offices, and castles lost in Stephen's reign, Henry needed at least the tacit co-operation of the greater magnates. Equally, it was from this same group of men that Henry demanded the restoration of the crown's rights—a seemingly impossible task. But through a skilful mixture of policies, and using both carrot and stick, Henry attained his end. While bending the magnates to his will, he also succeeded in placating them and finding a place for them in his regime. Hence the remarkable general political stability of England during Henry's reign. Only in 1173–4 did serious unrest occur, in connection with the so-called Great Rebellion in England and France, and even then only a handful of English nobles were involved. Henry had clearly found the means to deter defiance effectively.

This political settlement helped provide the necessary stable context for a notable extension of the crown's activities in other spheres, especially through the introduction of the famous assizes. A far greater positive role was being taken by the crown than hitherto, whereby the king's law was becoming truly national in scope, affecting the lives of royal subjects in a new way. Some concerned trade and commerce, such as the assizes of wine, ale, bread, and measures, whilst the *Assize of Arms dealt with matters connected with the defence of the realm. But the most significant assizes were those which transformed both civil and criminal law. The grand jury, established by the Assize of *Clarendon, would be fundamental in the prosecution of crime until the establishment of the director of public prosecutions in 1879, whilst the civil law reforms established essential procedures and principles that endured for centuries. National in scope, applicable to all freemen of the realm regardless of their feudal position, enshrining uniform rules and procedures, these various reforms marked the opening up of the royal courts as courts of first instance, to the inevitable detriment of the seigneurial courts. It is perhaps ironic that the 'grandfather of English common law' was a Frenchman.

It is fortunate that Henry's reign coincided with a great flowering in English historical writing and that men close to Henry penned descriptions of him. Stocky, of medium height, he was robust in his prime but was becoming fat in his later years, not through over-indulgence, because he was moderate in his eating and drinking. In the 1180s, it seems, he was aged beyond his actual years, worn out by the constant travelling and exertions needed to govern the Angevin empire. His remarkable energy and vitality struck everyone, a man who plainly demanded to be in the thick of the action all of the time. (Louis VII of France, indeed, was said to be so astonished by his movements that he was convinced that Henry could fly.) When not on the move around his dominions, he seldom sat still for long, except to eat or play chess. He was a fidget. Even at mass, he scribbled memoranda or whispered on business to courtiers. And like all noblemen, he was addicted to hunting and hawking. Henry lived in the saddle.

He was a man of violent passions, easily moved to anger and outbursts of his famous temper, at times uncontrollable. He was also capable of hatred, most notoriously revealed in his struggle with Thomas *Becket. But it seems that much of the threatening side of his nature was deliberately cultivated, stage-managed to get his own way. This was an aspect of his personal statecraft, and he knew how to bind men to him, in respect tinged with fear if not in love. But there was another side to his character, simple, good-hearted fun. He was also quite well educated, applying his intellect to practical matters in the art of government, analysing a problem, and then formulating solutions in association with his advisers. The reforms in the legal system are a case in point.

But one problem he never satisfactorily resolved—the partition of the Angevin empire between his sons. The issue blighted the last 20 years of his life, and poisoned relations within the family. Indeed, he died vanquished, defeated by his son Richard and Philip II of France over that very issue. SL

Gillingham, J. B., *The Angevin Empire* (1984); Warren, W. L., *Henry II* (1973); id., *The Governance of Norman and Angevin England 1086–1272* (1987).

Henry III (1207–72), king of England (1216–72). Henry was one of the most cultured monarchs ever to sit on the English throne. He seems to have been inspired by artistic beauty for its own sake, judging by his recorded payments for a wide range of objects—silver, gold, and enamel work, hangings and embroideries, and frescos for the royal palaces. Equally, it is plain that he chose to sink large sums into works of art to give visual expression to his heightened conception of monarchy and dynasty. Nowhere is this more apparent than *Westminster abbey, which he established as the royal necropolis. Huge sums were spent on its rebuilding after 1245, despite an ever-worsening overall financial position. Henry also brought a new mystique and theatricality to English monarchy. He loved display and liturgical ceremony, as when he processed to Westminster abbey in 1247 personally bearing his newly acquired relic of the Holy Blood. He increased the number of occasions when the *Laudes regiae*, the liturgy in praise of the ruler, were to be chanted; and he deliberately promoted the cult of Edward the Confessor, his beloved patron saint, having his own tomb in Westminster abbey placed within the aura of sanctity of Edward's tomb.

It is not surprising to find that his conception of monarchy looked back to the period before *Magna Carta when kingship was untrammelled and unlimited, in theory if not in practice, and he may well have sought to counter the dramatic growth in constitutional ideas by deliberately emphasizing the aura of kingship. The traumatic experiences of his early years—the bringing down of his father, French invasion and civil war, tutelage by baronial regency council—probably propelled him in this direction as well. He certainly had consistently a definite set of views which held as axiomatic that a king is free in his sovereignty to do as he will, be it appointment or removal of ministers and officials, or conduct of foreign policy. In so doing, Henry was ignoring the new realities following Magna Carta and this contributed to that series of crises which characterize his reign after his personal rule began in 1232. It culminated in the demand for radical reform in 1258 and the imposition of the provisions of *Oxford, the prelude to the so-called Barons' War that tore the country apart until the defeat of Simon de *Montfort at the battle of *Evesham (1265). But it was by no means only, even chiefly, constitutional issues that were at stake, in 1258 or before. Recent research has shown how much friction was generated by very real political issues, of patronage, for example, and Henry's protection of his kinsmen and favourites from justice. Protest against his hated half-brothers, the Lusignans, who came to England after 1247, lay at the heart of the sworn baronial confederacy of 1258.

Henry was particularly vulnerable in 1258 because he faced imminent excommunication if he did not meet the gigantic debt he owed to the papacy, incurred when he accepted the grant of the kingdom of Sicily to his son Edmund in 1254. This was the culmination of a foreign policy that became ever more grandiose. At first, Henry's chief goal was the recovery of those parts of the *Angevin empire lost under John. This was entirely reasonable. It was not inevitable that they would never be recovered, and as an Angevin Henry was dynastically impelled to seek to regain his inheritance and restore the honour of his lineage. But for a variety of reasons none of the expeditions dispatched to France succeeded, and the odds stacked against Henry steadily rose as the power of Louis IX of France and his brothers, installed in the former Angevin territories, increased. His failure led him into a wider European strategy that involved a network of foreign allies, including Emperor Frederick II, who married Henry's sister Isabella in 1236, and the Savoyards, the powerful kinsmen of *Eleanor of Provence, whom Henry himself married in 1236. When Frederick was deposed by Pope Innocent IV in 1245, Henry was drawn into an attempt to secure the different parts of the imperial inheritance. He accepted the crown of Sicily for Edmund, he encouraged his brother *Richard of Cornwall to accept the kingdom of Germany in 1257, and there are signs that he briefly toyed with the idea of extending his influence to the east Mediterranean through a marriage alliance involving Edmund and the Lusignan rulers of Cyprus, who also had claims to Jerusalem.

None of these schemes came to anything, and the huge costs incurred in the pursuit of Sicily, by stimulating the events of 1258, forced him to abandon them. In 1259, too, he finally accepted reality and agreed to the treaty of *Paris, whereby he renounced his French claims as well. Henry's capacity to play for very high stakes, and yet lose, is truly remarkable. SL

Carpenter, D. A., 'King, Magnates and Society: The Personal Rule of King Henry III, 1234–1258', *Speculum*, 60 (1985), 39–70; Clanchy, M. T., *England and its Rulers 1066–1272* (Glasgow, 1983); Powicke, F. M., *King Henry III and the Lord Edward* (2 vols., Oxford, 1947).

Henry IV (1367–1413), king of England (1399–1413). The eldest son and heir of *John of Gaunt, duke of Lancaster, he was born at Bolingbroke (Lincs.) in the same year as his cousin Richard II, whom he deposed in 1399. Returning from exile with the declared intent only to recover his inheritance seized by Richard, within three months he usurped the throne. It is not certain that he intended to do so when he landed; it is likely that he made the decision only after he had secured control of the person of the king. Although descended from Edward III, his claim to the throne was weak. He might have judged that only by taking the crown did he have a chance of securing his long-term future; if so, he was successful.

The first seven years of Henry's reign were years of continuous crisis. He faced his first rebellion in January 1400 from a group of Richard II's excluded courtiers. Its principal victim was Richard himself, who died in custody at Pontefract shortly afterwards. Other baronial rebellions followed, especially those of the Percys who had been his principal supporters in 1399. In 1403 *Hotspur, heir to the earl of *Northumberland, was defeated and killed at *Shrewsbury. In 1405 the earl himself fled to Scotland after a failed rising; he was finally killed in an abortive invasion in 1408. More serious to king and kingdom was the rebellion of the Welsh under Owain *Glyndŵr in 1400, which, despite annual English campaigns, led to the complete liberation of Wales by 1405. In addition war with Scotland, a running war at sea, and constant threats to the remaining English possessions in France left Henry beleaguered. The cost of defending the throne and the realm (exacerbated by his own profligacy and indifference to financial management) led to frequent parliaments, frequent requests for taxation, and a hostile reaction from the Commons, especially in 1401, 1404, and 1406.

That Henry survived these torrid years was due to several factors; his own determination, decisiveness, and energy; the strength, commitment, and ability of his own supporters (whose loyalty he wisely sustained by lavish rewards); and his own pragmatism (he would have agreed with Harold Wilson that a week was a long time in politics). But he was also helped by the divisions in the ranks of his enemies, especially the development of civil war in France. As a result, by the end of 1406 the worst of his difficulties were over: the French were no longer a threat, the reconquest of Wales was under way (completed in 1409), and a reformed government began to bring order to royal finances.

But the strain ruined his health. In the spring of 1406 Henry had what was probably the first of a series of strokes, which by 1410 left him incapacitated and unable to play much more than a token part in public affairs. While the later years of the reign saw the return of domestic peace and greater security, they also saw the emergence of factions at court, one led by the prince of Wales, the future Henry V, the other led by the prince's younger brother (and father's favourite) *Thomas of Lancaster. Yet at no time was Henry's throne threatened, and when he died in 1413 there was no challenge to the succession of his charismatic son.

In the 19th cent. Henry was credited with an experiment in government by limited monarchy. His usurpation was justified on the grounds of Richard II's tyranny; he had been one of the *appellants who had sought to impose conciliar government on Richard; and after 1399 he had himself willingly accepted rule through a council answerable to Parliament. In reality he sought to maintain the prerogatives of the crown, but was vulnerable and accepted the need to make concessions to a political nation unwilling to bear the open-ended cost of his usurpation. Moreover he was conciliatory by nature, a man who had been the head of a baronial council and knew the value of working with rather than against his leading subjects. To this extent he represented a different type of kingship from the 'absolutism' of Richard II, something akin to the participatory style of Edward III. It is indeed arguable that he had opposed Richard II out of principle as well as self-interest.

Henry was an able, accomplished, and much-admired man. As a youth he was renowned for his chivalry, the leading jouster of his generation, and a crusader. His piety was deep and sincere; he made a pilgrimage to Jerusalem in 1393. He was well fitted for kingship. But he was a usurper. A tradition grew up that he was later racked by guilt, for the execution of Archbishop *Scrope of York in 1405 as well as his usurpation. It was early speculated that this guilt hastened the collapse of his health. Moreover, although he established his dynasty on the throne, he created a precedent which was subsequently used against his grandson Henry VI. No longer after 1399 was the crown of England sacrosanct. AJP

Kirby, J. L., *Henry IV of England* (1970); McFarlane, K. B., *Lancastrian Kings and Lollard Knights* (Oxford, 1972); Wylie, J. H., *History of England under Henry the Fourth* (4 vols., 1884–98).

Henry V (1386/7–1422), king of England (1413–22). Eldest son of Henry IV and his first wife Mary Bohun, Henry was born at Monmouth. The exact date is unknown, but was most probably 9 August or 16 September 1386 or 1387. The young Henry was thrust into prominence by his father's successful usurpation of the throne in 1399. He carried the sword 'Curtana' at the coronation on 13 October and two days later was created earl of Chester, duke of Cornwall, and prince of Wales, and subsequently duke of Aquitaine and of Lancaster. From then on Henry took a prominent part in affairs as befitted the heir to the throne. Between 1400 and 1408 he was mostly in the west, concerned with the war against the Welsh, initially as a figurehead but increasingly as an effective leader. On 21 July 1403 he was with his father at the battle of *Shrewsbury, where the English rebels under Henry *Percy, 'Hotspur', and their Welsh allies were defeated. Henry took a prominent part in the battle, but the story that he killed Hotspur himself is without foundation. Between 1410 and 1413 there seems to have been tension between the king and the prince. Henry IV's health began to fail and at first Prince Henry took an increasingly prominent role in the king's council, supported by the chancellor, Thomas *Beaufort. This led to factions in the council with divergent policies being pursued, especially with regard to France. In 1412 the prince's faction seems to have been defeated, because Beaufort resigned the chancellorship, and Prince Henry withdrew from the council. It is possible that the king was asked to abdicate in favour of the prince on the grounds of ill-health, but refused to do so and successfully reasserted his authority, supported by his son Thomas, who was made duke of *Clarence. The story of the prince taking his father's crown from a cushion beside his bed as dramatized by Shakespeare may represent the actual disagreements between the prince and his father at this time. In the last fifteen months of the reign the prince seems to have taken little active part in government. Henry succeeded his father on 20 March 1413 and was crowned at Westminster on Passion Sunday, 9 April.

The start of Henry's reign was seen by contemporaries as a new beginning. Thomas Walsingham, a monk of St Albans, claiming that with the new king winter was past and the rain over and gone. Commentators were eager for the new reign and saw in Henry a man 'young in years but old in experience', who had dealt successfully with protracted Welsh rebellion and had been a prominent member of the king's council, well able to rule. The stories of Henry's wild youth and amazing 'conversion', as dramatized by *Shakespeare, have some contemporary justification. The chronicler Elmham says that Henry 'was in his youth a diligent follower of idle practices, much given to instruments of music, and fired with the torches of Venus herself' and that on the night of his father's death, Henry visited a recluse at Westminster, made confession of his former life, and promised to amend. But the famous story of Henry's dispute with Lord Chief Justice Gascoigne, alluded to and embroidered by Shakespeare, is first recorded only in 1531 and has no foundation in fact. Perhaps it does not really matter whether these stories about Henry are true or not. They should be seen as symbolizing a break with the past, that is the failure of Richard II's and Henry IV's reigns, and a new beginning.

Henry lived up to these expectations and enjoyed considerable popularity during his reign. He provided good and dynamic leadership that fired widespread enthusiasm. He seems to have appealed to feelings of nationalism and nationhood; Christopher Allmand wrote that 'It was as a very English Englishman that Henry caught something of the mood of the day.' Henry encouraged the keeping of the festivals of English saints and promoted the use of English. He gave active encouragement to translators and began the use of English rather than French in government. From 1417 his signet letters to his English subjects were written in English. He used the war with France to promote the idea that England was a nation blessed by God and favoured because their king was also favoured. The general enthusiasm for the war is evidenced by the large number of the nobility who followed him to France, and by the generous grants of taxation made by Parliament before the first campaign. The contemporary *Agincourt carol commemorated the battle as a famous English victory. The *Gesta Henrici Quinti* describes the reception of the king after he returned to England after Agincourt. The Londoners staged a triumphal entry with music and pageants attended by great masses of people, the civic dignitaries escorting the king from Blackheath.

A desire to create unity and nationalistic fervour were not the only reasons for Henry's aggressive policy towards France. He seems truly to have been persuaded of the justice of his claims, which required action. He did not at first claim the French throne but began by pressing hard for the full implementation of the treaty of *Calais of 1360 in which the French had ceded Aquitaine and other lands, and to which he added further claims to Normandy, Touraine, and Maine. It is not clear whether Henry really expected to gain his ends by diplomacy, for he had made extensive preparations for war before the negotiations broke down in June 1415. The subsequent campaigns for the conquest of France were thoroughly well organized and carried through. Henry's diplomacy secured the early neutrality of John, duke of Burgundy; and after Agincourt the whole-hearted support of the Emperor Sigismund, with whom he signed the treaty of Canterbury in 1416. Militarily his main objective was the systematic reduction of the main centres of northern France. These, when provided with permanent garrisons, would become the centres from which the countryside could be subdued and governed. Henry's idea was that, once the initial conquests had been made, further warfare would pay for itself in the form of taxes from his new lands. The initial invasion was financed by borrowing and through generous parliamentary grants. The first campaign brought the capture of *Harfleur in September 1415, and victory at Agincourt on 25 October 1415. Further campaigns were aimed at the effective conquest of Normandy, during which Rouen fell in January 1419. Henry's success forced the French to agree to the treaty of *Troyes in May 1420, by which Henry was recognized as heir to the throne of France. The treaty was cemented by Henry's marriage to the Princess *Catherine, which took place on 2 June. After this Henry continued his campaigns to reduce areas of the country still loyal to the deposed dauphin, Charles. During the sieges of Melun and Meaux his health began to fail and he died, probably of dysentery, at Bois de Vincennes on 31 August 1422, leaving, as his heir to both crowns, his son Henry, less than a year old.

Even before Henry's death the initial enthusiasm for the war was waning in England. There were complaints about the high levels of taxation needed, and in 1421 the Norfolk gentry refused to join Henry in France. There was widespread resistance to Henry in France and, even in Normandy, English rule was not as welcome as Henry had assumed that it would be. It has been argued that the treaty of Troyes, which appeared to have been such a triumph, was in fact a mistake and that Henry would have been better advised to restrict himself to securing Normandy. Henry's interest in Europe was not limited to the war with France, however, and he had notable success at the Council of Constance, where, in collaboration with the Emperor Sigismund, he helped to resolve the *Great Schism. It is possible that all Henry's efforts with regard to France and the papacy were ultimately directed towards his plans for a crusade, which he never undertook. LR

Allmand, C., *Henry V* (1992); Seward, D., *Henry V as Warlord* (1987); Taylor, F., and Roskell, J. S. (eds.), *Gesta Henrici Quinti: The Deeds of Henry V* (Oxford, 1975); Wylie, J. H., and Waugh, W. T. (eds.), *The Reign of Henry V* (3 vols., Cambridge, 1914–29).

Henry VI (1421–71), king of England (1422–61 and 1470–1). Henry VI was the youngest king of England ever to ascend the throne; the only king never to know what it was like not to be king; the only one ever to be crowned king of France; and arguably the worst, who inherited two kingdoms and lost both. His reign is divided into three parts by modern historians as well as by Shakespeare. The first is his minority (1422–37); the second is his active majority (1437–53); and the third is the period of his mental incapacity (1453 until his death). Given the inherent dangers, Henry's minority was remarkably successful. Those who inherited power in 1422 in the name of the infant king were the same lords and retainers who had served the house of Lancaster from the time of *John of Gaunt. They shared the overriding objective of preserving for the time he came of age the inheritances won by his grandfather and father in England and France. Fifteen years later not only was Henry still on the throne (he was crowned king of England in 1429, king of France in 1431), but his kingdom was not unduly lawless, the crown was solvent, and a substantial part of Henry V's conquests in France remained in Lancastrian hands. In 1437, when the king began to play a part in affairs, the old guard had discharged its duty as well as could be expected.

It was a cruel trick of fate to provide Henry V with a son who was the very antithesis of the martial and regal traditions of the house of Lancaster. Henry VI proved to be improvident, malleable, vacillating, partisan, uninterested in the arts of government, and, above all, antipathetic to the chivalric world his ancestors had adorned. As soon as he came of age he turned his back on the war in France. The defining moment came in 1440 when at 18 he had the opportunity to take the field in Normandy. Instead he sent his cousin the duke of *York as his lieutenant, devoting himself to the foundation of *Eton College. Within ten years the government of the kingdom had fallen into the hands of an unscrupulous court faction led by William de la *Pole, duke of Suffolk, royal debts were mounting, and Normandy was lost. In 1450 the regime was shaken by *Cade's revolt, the most widespread and sustained popular rising since 1381. It says much for the residual strength of the dynasty that it survived these shocks. Indeed when Henry suffered his devastating mental collapse in 1453, the reign appeared to be set on a more stable course.

Henry VI fell into a coma in August 1453. He recovered his senses just before Christmas 1454, but was permanently impaired. In some respects his recovery was politically more destabilizing than his collapse. While comatose Henry could be treated as a child again, a protectorate was established, and government entrusted to a council; after his partial recovery, he became a puppet tossed this way and that by faction. By 1459 royal government was almost totally powerless, the administration of the law had virtually collapsed, and the crown was bankrupt. In the civil war that erupted Henry was but a passive onlooker. In 1461 he became the victim when he was deposed by the victorious Edward IV. But his life was spared. There was no sentiment in this. Throughout the 1460s the hope of his cause was carried by his only son and heir *Edward, in exile in France; killing Henry would only have promoted a more plausible Lancastrian claimant. In 1470 he was restored to the throne for six months. Coming out of the Tower for rare public appearances, he was a pitiful sight. But the death of the prince of Wales at *Tewkesbury in 1471 sealed his own fate, and a few days later he was done to death.

Henry was a more effective force after his death than ever he was in his life. There soon developed a cult surrounding his saintliness, miracles were reported, and Edward IV was obliged to repress it. Richard III moved his body from Waltham, which had become a place of pilgrimage, to Windsor, the better to control the phenomenon. After 1485 Henry VII endeavoured, unsuccessfully, to secure his canonization. It was at this time that John Blacman was commissioned to produce his *Recollections*, which have fixed the image of the saintly king. But Blacman's portrait of a prudish, unworldly man inhabiting a court more like a convent drew upon memories of Henry after 1453. Before then he had been a man of the world, maintaining a court as splendid as any in Europe. The sad truth is that between 1437 and 1453, between the ages of 16 and 32, Henry had been, as king in deed and as well as name, one of the most incompetent ever to rule England. In another age, and another society, a man who turned his back on vainglorious war, and whose greatest achievements were in the promotion of education (through the foundations of Eton and *King's College, Cambridge), might have been more highly regarded. But in 15th-cent. England a king like Henry VI was a public disaster. AJP

Griffiths, R. A., *The Reign of Henry VI* (1981); Storey, R. L., *The End of the House of Lancaster* (1966); Wolffe, B. P., *Henry VI* (1981).

Henry VII (1457–1509), king of England (1485–1509). Though the belief that Henry VII was a new kind of ruler at the head of a new kind of monarchy has long been abandoned by historians, he was certainly an unusual ruler. Despite the fact that he was a competent soldier and personally brave, he did not hanker after military glory, even against the French, as many of his predecessors had. Secondly, he seemed to take positive pleasure in the detail of government and administration, while many monarchs left the hard work to ministers. Thirdly—and this may have distinguished him from most rulers, then and now—he seems to have wished to amass money rather than spend it. Consequently, he left his successor, if not a fortune, at least a healthy competence, and though Henry VIII reverted to type, disliking business and pining for glory, it took him some time to undo his father's good work.

The weakness of Henry's claim to the throne has been rather exaggerated: 'up to June 1483 Henry Tudor was hardly any more plausible as a king of England than Lambert *Simnel or Perkin *Warbeck were to be later.' That is absurd. Simnel and Warbeck were commoners pretending to be someone. Henry's father was a half-brother of King Henry VI; his grandmother had been queen to Henry V and a princess of France; his great-great-grandfather was John of Gaunt, son of Edward III. Once Edward IV's sons had been murdered, only *Clarence's son *Warwick had an obviously better claim to the throne, and across that lay the shadow of Clarence's attainder. Nevertheless, Henry's early life was inauspicious. His father Edmund Tudor, earl of Richmond, died three months before Henry was born at Pembroke castle. His young mother Lady Margaret *Beaufort remarried. His grandfather Owen *Tudor was beheaded at Hereford after the Lancastrian defeat at *Mortimer's Cross in 1461, and his uncle Jasper *Tudor, earl of Pembroke, was forced to flee. Custody of the boy was then given to the new Yorkist earl of Pembroke and he was brought up mainly at Raglan. On the brief restoration of Henry VI in 1470 he was reunited with his uncle, but after the crushing defeat at *Tewkesbury, they both fled to Brittany. Not until Richard usurped the throne in 1483 did Henry's prospects brighten, his cause sustained largely by his redoubtable mother. In secret negotiations with Edward IV's widow, it was agreed that Henry should marry her daughter *Elizabeth, thus uniting the houses of Lancaster and York. But an attempt on the throne in 1483 proved premature. His ally *Buckingham was captured and beheaded, and Henry's own expedition to the south coast was scattered by gales. In 1484 Richard put pressure on Brittany to hand over Henry, who escaped to France in the nick of time. Thence he sailed with 2,000 men to Milford Haven on the journey that brought him to *Bosworth and the throne.

It is sometimes said that Henry is a ruler of whom we know little. That is not quite true. We have excellent representations of him, a bust by Torrigiano, a portrait by Sittow, a remarkable death mask, coinage likenesses, and a realistic tomb effigy. There are descriptions by foreign diplomats and by Polydore Vergil, who knew him in later years. It is more that people do not always admire what is known about him. He was clearly reserved and rarely affable: he had little of Henry VIII's false heartiness nor of Elizabeth I's adroit condescensions. 'His appearance', wrote Vergil, 'was remarkably attractive and his face cheerful, especially when speaking; his eyes were small and blue, his teeth few, poor and blackish; his hair was thin and white; his complexion sallow.' His 'most cheerful countenance' was noted in 1498 by a Spanish envoy. He was more than commonly dutiful in his religious observance and, while aspiring neither to scholar nor saint, founded many religious houses and left as his main architectural memorial the chapel in Westminster abbey. His relations with his mother and wife were good, perhaps close. His application to business was proverbial, though his attention to accounts is often held against him as unworthy of a monarch. His reputation suffered from Francis *Bacon's very readable *Life*, which exhibited him as close and mean—'a sad, serious prince, full of thoughts'. But it should be remembered that although Bacon is sometimes quoted as though a contemporary, he wrote 137 years after the battle of Bosworth, and his artistry often led him to caricature. 'For his pleasures,' wrote Bacon, 'there is no news of them.' In fact there is plenty of news had Bacon wished to find it. Henry enjoyed hunting and hawking, music and dancing, tennis, dice, archery, and cards—often, unlike many kings, losing and, characteristically, recording his debts.

He needed to learn very quickly since his nomadic existence before Bosworth had left him short of experience in government. He was undoubtedly circumspect, as anyone who hoped to survive at the top of Tudor politics needed to be. He learned early not to be too trusting. Lord *Lincoln, who had fought against him at Bosworth, was at once forgiven, taken into employment, and attended the council to decide how to deal with Lambert Simnel—before riding off to join the rebels. But Henry became a good judge of men, and was well served by John *Morton, archbishop of Canterbury from 1486, and by Richard *Foxe, who finished as bishop of Winchester.

His main political objectives were to secure his own position, to found a dynasty, and to establish a stable government. Of his four predecessors as kings, two had been murdered, one had died in battle, and the fourth (Edward IV) had been driven ignominiously from the kingdom in the middle of his reign. The foundation of Henry's success was the marriage to Elizabeth of York, and though not all Yorkists were reconciled, his political opponents were divided. Lincoln proved implacable, but Lord Surrey (*Norfolk), who had fought alongside Richard at Bosworth and been attainted, worked his way back into favour, was increasingly employed by Henry, and had a military career of great renown under Henry VIII. The first challenge from Yorkist irreconcilables came as soon as April 1486, was headed by Lord Lovel and the Hastings brothers, and was put down without difficulty. It was followed by the Simnel plot in 1487. Simnel claimed to be Edward, earl of Warwick, despite the fact that Warwick was in the Tower, and was crowned in Dublin as Edward VI. His supporters, strengthened by German mercenaries, were subdued at *Stoke near Newark only after hard fighting. Simnel, a mere boy, was given a place in the royal kitchens and lived out a long life in safe obscurity. Perkin Warbeck, claiming to be Richard, duke of York, was received by James IV of Scotland as Richard IV, captured in 1498, but executed with Warwick the following year. Even then Henry had to face the claims of the de la Pole brothers and only for the last three years of his reign, with Edmund de la *Pole in the Tower, was he totally secure. His dynasty by then hung on a single thread, since two of his sons, Arthur and Edmund, had died, leaving Henry as the sole surviving male heir. The marriage of Henry VII's daughter *Margaret to James IV of Scotland reaped long-term dividends in 1603 when their great-grandson James VI united the two kingdoms.

Under these circumstances, Henry's foreign policy could hardly be very ambitious and he played a marginal role in the struggle between the French and the imperialists. He was unable to save Brittany from annexation to France but the task was impossible once the duchess of Brittany herself had married the French king, and Henry escaped creditably from his brief 1492 campaign. The short war with Scotland 1496–7 was not of Henry's making but arose from James IV's support for Warbeck. Henry stood on the defensive and used the large parliamentary subsidy to emerge with a handsome profit. By the end of his reign, England's standing in Europe had been greatly enhanced. At home the nobility was kept in check less by legislation against livery and maintenance than by large financial bonds hanging over them. Financial security, which had the advantage of allowing Henry to do without parliaments for much of his reign, was built up by the patient exploitation of the opportunities and dues open to the crown. Crown lands which brought in only £3,000 p.a. between 1487 and 1489 were worth £40,000 p.a. by 1502–5; wardships provided only £343 in 1491 but £1,588 three years later and had doubled again by 1504; bonds, bringing in £3,000 p.a. in 1493–4, had increased to £35,000 p.a. by 1504–5. Their zeal on Henry's behalf made his servants *Empson and *Dudley the most hated men in the kingdom and they were instant victims of Henry VIII's new reign in 1509.

The historical controversy about Henry's place in government derived in part from a desire to divide the past too categorically into medieval and modern. But both sides shared a somewhat simple misunderstanding—that innovation in government is everything. The first group credited Henry with new policies and new expedients, to which the second group replied by tracing many of them to his predecessors, and particularly to Edward IV—action against maintenance, use of loyalty bonds, and the establishment of councils. But it was of more consequence that Henry pursued his policies, whether new or old, with rigour, system, and tenacity. Many rulers begin with economy drives, but are blown off course. Henry was not and, as Bacon put it, 'what he minded, he compassed'—though, again, it sounds more grim than appealing. JAC

Chrimes, S. B., *Henry VII* (1972); Grant, A., *Henry VII* (1985); Lockyer, R., *Henry VII* (2nd edn. 1983); Storey, R. L., *The Reign of Henry VII* (1968).

Henry VIII (1491–1547), king of England (1509–47). Henry VIII was born on 23 June 1491 at Greenwich, the third child and second son of Henry VII and Elizabeth of York. On the death of his elder brother *Arthur in April 1502 he became heir apparent; a few days after the death of his (by then) deeply unpopular father, he was proclaimed king on 23 April 1509.

1. The early years to *c*.1514. Despite being only 17, Henry acted as king in his own right at once. Shortly after his accession he solemnized his fateful marriage to *Catherine, daughter of Ferdinand and Isabella of Spain and widow of his brother Arthur. In these first years Henry reversed many of his father's more obnoxious policies: he relaxed control over the aristocracy and allowed revenue to decline through neglect. However, apart from sacrificing Richard *Empson and Edmund *Dudley, his father's two most detested apparitors, he made few changes among his leading advisers. He began to play the European game of military alliances almost at once: a disastrous campaign in the Pyrenees in 1512 was followed in 1513 by the more successful seizure of Tournai and Thérouanne and the earl of Surrey's demolition of the Scottish aristocracy at *Flodden. Peace was made in 1514.

2. The ascendancy of Wolsey *c*.1514–*c*.1527. The political scene was transformed by the arrival of a clergyman-academic turned administrator, Thomas *Wolsey, who used his position as royal chaplain and almoner to build up a formidable collection of church and government posts, becoming lord chancellor in 1515 and papal cardinal-legate *a latere* in 1518. He and Henry communicated via their secretaries; Henry attended to business fitfully and occasionally intervened in details, but mostly left Wolsey to find the means to carry out the royal designs. With the accession of Francis I of France (1515–47) Henry found a rival whom he both disliked and imitated. For several years he manœuvred in the diplomatic game, until in 1518 he and Wolsey stage-managed the great European peace treaty of *London (1518). The next year another charismatic leader, Charles V of Austria, Burgundy, and Spain, became Holy Roman emperor, and Henry began meddling in the endless duel between Charles and Francis. He attacked France in 1522–3, but withdrew from the alliance just too soon to profit from Francis's defeat and capture at Pavia (1525); in that year he renounced the imperial connection and began to court French support. Within England, the power-play plunged the crown deep into debt and forced highly unpopular increases in taxation, culminating in the taxpayers' strike against an illegal benevolence, the 'Amicable Grant', in 1525.

3. The marriage question, 1527–1532. During the 1520s Henry's marriage to Catherine had deteriorated for reasons both personal and diplomatic. After bearing a princess (the future Mary I) in 1516, the queen had suffered a series of miscarriages and still-births which reawakened Henry's early misgivings about the marriage and raised the spectre of his dying without a male heir. When Charles V dropped his plan to marry Mary in 1525, the Aragonese-cum-Habsburg alliance lost its political rationale. By early 1527 an annulment of the marriage was openly discussed. However, in that year Charles V's troops sacked Rome and forced Pope Clement VII to seek protection from Charles V. While in the emperor's hands, the pope would not shame his captor's aunt by annulling her marriage and thereby freeing Henry, it was supposed, to marry a French princess. Wolsey tried unsuccessfully to persuade the pope to allow him to resolve the issue in England. When the final failure of this effort became apparent, Wolsey was stripped of his offices; after negotiating unofficially with foreign powers he only escaped treason charges by his own death (1530).

Henry was now adrift among rival groups of advisers: some, like Thomas *More, urged him to abandon the divorce and take back the queen; others carefully nurtured in him the belief that papal authority was, in any case, an illegitimate usurpation and might be rejected unilaterally. Henry subjected the English bishops and clergy to costly ritual humiliations, ostensibly because their support for Wolsey's legatine status had infringed English law; this tactic may have paved the way for forcing them to oppose papal authority. By May 1532 the king seems to have chosen an anti-papal solution to the marriage crisis, and several of his leading pro-Aragonese advisers resigned.

4. The supremacy and the 'Henrician Reformation', 1533–1540. The king's belief in his status as God's representative, supreme over all his subjects, now became a very potent political factor. It was exploited by a group of political theorists managed by the new rising minister, a former client of Wolsey, Thomas *Cromwell (1485–1540). They devised an argument against papal authority which, unlike those advanced by the Lutherans in Germany, rested not on reformed theology but on a rewriting of the history of Anglo-papal relations. In the Act in Restraint of *Appeals (24 Hen. VIII c. 12, 1533), the preamble enunciated Henry's claim to 'imperial' authority, without earthly superior, over clergy and laity alike; the text merely rejected appeals to Rome in matrimonial, testamentary, and other lawsuits. Henry secretly married *Anne Boleyn in January 1533, and was formally separated from Catherine the following May. Having then been excommunicated by the pope, however, Henry's regime enacted further statutes up to 1536, which cut all fiscal, legal, and spiritual ties to Rome and left the English church in schism.

The English church having now broken with the papacy, the question of its doctrine could not be evaded. Henry had a queen, Anne Boleyn, an archbishop of Canterbury, Thomas *Cranmer, and a leading minister, Cromwell, all of whom were in varying degrees Lutheran sympathizers. Many others at court, however, were either zealous conservatives or, like one nobleman, boasted of never having read the Bible and never intending to. Henry's personal detestation of Luther, with whom he had exchanged polemics in the 1520s, and his horror of what he called 'sacramentarian' heresy made the two forms of emerging protestantism unacceptable, and left religious policy the plaything of factions. Nevertheless, enough innovations, both religious and fiscal, were introduced to enrage the population of the northern counties of England and bring about the complex of revolts known as the *'Pilgrimage of Grace' in autumn 1536. The regime survived these by biding its time and retaining the loyalty of the nobility and the south. Up to 1537 Henry accepted and endorsed cautious moves, disguised as 'humanist' purifications of religion, to abolish parts of the old cult. An official English Bible was authorized in 1538 and issued in 1539. However, the Act of *Six Articles of 1539 marked a reaffirmation of certain traditional shibboleths and a hunt for 'heretics'. Meanwhile, and without overt religious logic, the regime plundered the church, taxing the seculars heavily while abolishing the regular orders entirely and confiscating their wealth (1536–40).

Instability in official doctrine was matched by increasingly sanguinary feuds at court. In May 1536, after the birth of a daughter (the future Elizabeth I) and a miscarriage, the temperamental Anne Boleyn, with her brother and several of her attendants, were executed for alleged acts of treasonable adultery, which varied from the implausible to the impossible. By the end of the month the king had married *Jane Seymour, who bore him his only son, the future Edward VI, on 12 October 1537 and died twelve days afterwards. Cromwell, having disposed of religious and political opponents of the supremacy, embarked on legal purges of those families he regarded as suspect or a threat, notably the Poles and Courtenays. Court rivalry and religious instability combined in the king's search for a fourth wife. Despite the reactionary strain then evident in religious policy, Henry was cajoled into a marriage-contract with *Anne, sister of the duke of Cleves, a reforming sympathizer. Henry accepted her on the strength of a flattering portrait, and married her, with already too evident distaste, on 6 January 1540. Thomas Cromwell survived this disastrous marriage for a few months, but when he tried a pre-emptive strike against several conservatives, he was swiftly attainted of treason and executed.

5. The years of faction and failing powers. Henry seems to have regretted the execution of Cromwell soon afterwards, and thereafter no minister wielded the same sort of authority. Government became more 'conciliar': the Privy Council, adumbrated as early as 1536 and filled with opponents of Cromwell, began to work more effectively as an executive cabinet from 1540. In his final years the king became more unpredictable and vulnerable. *Catherine Howard, niece of the duke of Norfolk, whom Henry had married on the day of Cromwell's execution, proved unfaithful and indiscreet. Her fall and execution on 13 February 1542 left the king devastated. He threw himself once more into diplomacy and war. A successful campaign in 1542 by Lord Wharton in Scotland left Scotland's army broken and accelerated the death of its king: but Henry did not follow up the victory. Instead he made fresh overtures to Charles V and in June 1544 invaded France again, capturing Boulogne at huge cost shortly before Charles V made a separate peace with Francis I. A retaliatory attack by the French on the south coast in 1545 saw an embarrassing spectacle when the second largest ship in the fleet, the **Mary Rose*, sank spontaneously before the king's eyes; but a reasonable peace was made in 1546. In these final years Henry wavered between a campaign against 'heresy', which reached peaks in 1543 (when it threatened Cranmer) and 1546 (when it briefly threatened Henry's last queen, *Catherine Parr), and periods when Henry allowed Cranmer to embark on cautious, partial reform of the so far barely altered old liturgy. In the dying months of the reign the reformers, led by the earl of Hertford (*Somerset) and the Seymour family, secured the near-total defeat of the conservative Howards; the duke of *Norfolk was awaiting execution when the king himself died on 28 January 1547. The education of the young Edward VI had been committed to reforming humanist tutors, so the old king's conservative legacy would not last into the new reign.

6. Assessment. Few kings of England set so consciously to glorify the style and splendour of the monarchy. Henry was the first to be addressed as 'Majesty' and the first defender of the faith and supreme head of the church. He presided over a spectacular court and built *Nonsuch palace in Surrey in 'the highest point of ostentation'. He had great athletic strength, a real talent for music, and an enthusiasm for theology (although his tendency to regard doctrines as unconnected building-blocks led to confusion and inconsistency). He enjoyed the windfall of the largely unchallenged plunder of the church and the service of talented and energetic ministers. In this light, the overwhelming impression is of advantages squandered. He came to the throne rich and bequeathed debts, a corrupt coinage, and roaring inflation; much of the newly acquired land was sold to the gentry and aristocracy by his death. Few monarchs before and none after were so ready to listen to, or to concoct, spurious charges of treason to get rid of unhelpful ministers or discarded wives. He showed little sign of that gift for managing the squabbles of courtier-politicians displayed by his daughter Elizabeth. His impact on the history of his time was colossal; yet nearly every part of his legacy was either disowned or significantly reinvented under his successors. EC

Scarisbrick, J., *Henry VIII* (1968); Smith, L. B., *Henry VIII: The Mask of Royalty* (1971); Starkey, D., *The Reign of Henry VIII* (1985).

Henry, prince of Wales (1594–1612). Eldest son of James VI and I and Anne of Denmark, born at Stirling but immediately entrusted to the earl of Mar's guardianship. Following his father to England in June 1603, he impressed the crowds by his fine horsemanship and erect bearing. He had absorbed the precepts laid down in his father's *Basilikon doron*, which not only stressed the patriarchal nature of kingship but encouraged self-restraint and modesty, only to find himself critical of its author's own behaviour. His promise and popularity, despite an element of priggishness, occasioned jealousy in James; championship of *Ralegh, dislike of the royal favourite *Carr, and naval and military interests further increased tension. Marriage plans were overtaken by his sudden death from typhoid fever, leaving his less-gifted brother Charles as heir. Though he has been seen as the hope of England, this is mere speculation. ASH

Henry, the Young King (1155–83), was the eldest surviving son of Henry II and *Eleanor of Aquitaine. At Montmirail (Maine) in January 1169 Henry II announced his intentions for the division of his vast dominions, the Young Henry, as eldest son, to receive England, Normandy, and Anjou, Henry II's own inheritance. In May 1170 the young king was duly crowned joint king of England, but like his brothers remained essentially powerless since Henry II had no intention of abdicating, and would not hand over territory or power until his sons had proved themselves worthy. Young Henry, though, was ever feckless and irresponsible, concerned to cut a fine chivalric figure but utterly uninterested in the serious business of government. This, combined with his father's very close monitoring of his activities and purse, led Young Henry into revolt in 1173. Relations between father and son never fully recovered thereafter and he rebelled again in 1183, shortly before his death. SL

Henry of Blois (d. 1171). Prince-bishop of the English church. Nephew of Henry I, he was made abbot of Glastonbury in 1126 and bishop of Winchester in 1129; by holding on to both he remained for over 40 years the richest prelate in England. Although brought up as a monk at Cluny, he became a great builder of castles and palaces (notably Wolvesey palace) and an art connoisseur who brought back pagan statues from Rome. Not surprisingly the ascetic St Bernard of Clairvaux branded him 'whore of Winchester' and 'old wizard'. In 1135 he helped his brother Stephen of Blois to obtain the throne and played a prominent political and military role throughout the reign. In 1139–43, when the conflict between Stephen and *Matilda was at its height, he used his authority as papal legate to hold councils in unsuccessful but highly publicized attempts to settle the affairs of the realm. At Henry II's accession he withdrew for a while to Cluny, but returned as the elder statesman of the English church. JG

Henry of Grosmont (*c.*1300–61) was a cousin of Edward III and the king's right-hand man. His father was earl of Lancaster and Leicester. He was born in *Grosmont, created earl of Derby in 1337, and succeeded his father as earl of Lancaster in 1345. In 1349 he was created earl of Lincoln and in 1351 duke of Lancaster. He was also created earl of Moray in Scotland in 1359. When the order of the *Garter was instituted, he was next to the prince of Wales. Henry fought constantly against the French and the Scots and was with the king at the naval victory of *Sluys in 1340 and at the surrender of *Calais in 1347. He was also much employed on diplomatic missions. His life was spent on campaigns, his reputation for chivalry widely recognized, and he was never tempted into treason or insurrection. His palace at the Savoy was sumptuous. He died at Leicester of the plague and was buried there in the presence of the king. His younger daughter and ultimate heir married *John of Gaunt, for whom the dukedom of Lancaster was revived. JAC

Henry Stewart. See DARNLEY, LORD.

Henryson, Robert (d. *ante* 1505). Scottish poet. Very little is known of him, but he must have been born before 1450. He is usually said to have taught at the grammar school at Dunfermline abbey, and is probably the Robert Henryson recorded at Glasgow University in 1462. By 1478 he was a notary public at Dunfermline. His poetry was very popular with contemporaries, and by 1599 large quantities of his *Testament of Cresseid* had been printed in Scotland, and many manuscripts survive. In poems such as *Orpheus and Eurydice*, *The Fables*, and his finest poem, *Cresseid*, he blends medieval and humanist elements with great technical mastery. *The Lion and the Mouse* links a moral fable to a criticism of the kingship of James III—the lion a ruler who does not govern, the mice the 'commonty' who as a result rebel. He is now recognized as one of Scotland's finest poets. RJT

Hepplewhite, George (d. 1786). Cabinet-maker and furniture designer, Hepplewhite linked the ornate style of *Chippendale and the severer lines of *Sheraton. He was apprenticed to Robert Gillow of Lancaster, then opened a business in London about 1760. Little of his life is known and none of his furniture survives. No great innovator, more practical than novel, Hepplewhite adapted the designs of others, particularly Robert *Adam, to suit both cabinet-maker and customer. His reputation rests with *The Cabinet-Maker and Upholsterer's Guide* published two years after his death. This catalogue, with 300 illustrations, which Sheraton said had 'already caught the decline', aimed to provide designs 'of every article of household furniture in the newest and most approved taste'. Hepplewhite is most associated with pierced and shield-back chairs often with wheels, lyres, or Prince of Wales feathers, and painted or japanned work of gold on black. JC

heptarchy. The description of 7th-cent. England as a 'heptarchy' probably derives, ultimately, from the historian Henry of Huntingdon, writing in the earlier 12th cent. It came into printed prominence in the works of historians of the late 16th and early 17th cents., beginning, probably, in Lambarde's work on Kent (1576). The idea was that there were seven kingdoms, Northumbria, Mercia, East Anglia, Essex, Kent, Sussex, and Wessex. Reality was more complicated. But the formulation was a useful one and had a long life as a term of art. JCa

heraldry. The use of personal distinguishing marks on shields and banners seems to have developed in England and Scotland in the second half of the 12th cent. and in Wales in the 13th cent., initially as a way of telling men apart in battle and tournament. Such devices rapidly became consistent and hereditary, and were used in a wide range of contexts, such as seals, surcoats, architectural features, and stained glass. The original purpose of identification was never lost, but the bearing of arms developed a further, social significance in denoting those of noble or gentle birth and status; by the later Middle Ages merchants and men who had never seen military service had coats of arms. By the mid-13th cent. armorial bearings had developed complex systems of description—preserving the (by then) rather archaic forms of Anglo-Norman French—and of differencing (i.e. modification in design to denote a family or feudal relationship), cadency (i.e. to distinguish younger sons), and marshalling (i.e. combining arms, often as a result of marriage). Such a complicated and socially sensitive subject required increasing scrutiny; this was provided by heralds, who make their first official appearance in English royal records under Edward I. Their duties expanded and became more fully defined over the course of the next two centuries. The office of Lord Lyon in Scotland appears in 1318, and that of Garter king-of-arms in 1417, with the full incorporation of the *College of Arms by Richard III in 1484. Tudor and Stuart heralds embarked upon visitations of counties 'to remove all false arms', and 'to take note of descents'. Arms are still granted today by the College of Arms (for England, Wales, and Northern Ireland), and by Lord Lyon Court (for Scotland). AC

Herbert, Arthur (1647–1716). Created earl of Torrington by William III in June 1689, following an indecisive action with French transports in Bantry Bay, south-west Ireland, Herbert is a controversial if not disreputable figure in English naval history. A member of the Pembroke family, he early saw service in the third Dutch War and then the Mediterranean, where from 1680 he served as a flag officer, having lost an eye in action with Algerine corsairs. He was vigorously attacked for the extensiveness of his illicit trading at Tangier 1680–3, but back home in 1685 James II appointed him master of the robes. In March 1687 he refused to support James II's suspending of the Test Act, and so became ranked with the king's opponents, in June 1688 personally carrying to Holland the invitation to William to intervene in the nation's affairs. He commanded the Dutch invasion fleet, and became 1st lord of the Admiralty in February 1689. In June 1690 Torrington commanded an outnumbered Anglo-Dutch fleet off *Beachy Head in an engagement with the French, which saw the Dutch badly mauled. His court-martial for a tactical withdrawal of his fleet to the Gunfleet Sand off Essex led to his acquittal, but he never served again. DDA

Herbert, Edward, 1st Baron Herbert (1583–1648). Herbert was of a younger branch of the earls of Pembroke which had settled in Montgomery castle. After attending University College, Oxford, he was knighted at the coronation of James I in 1603. From 1619 to 1624 he served as ambassador in Paris and was given an Irish barony, followed by an English one in 1629. He waited in vain for further employment and during the Civil War kept a low profile at Montgomery. He made no resistance when parliamentary troops occupied the castle in 1644, being anxious to preserve his books. Herbert's many publications include *De veritate* (1624), an early deist exposition, and an admiring *Life of Henry VIII* (1649). But he is best known for his *Autobiography*, first published by Horace *Walpole in 1764. Herbert was not inhibited by false modesty and pays warm tribute to his own valour, appearance ('I could tell how much my person was commended'), irresistible sex appeal, and good breath. George Saintsbury, a strong-minded critic, dismissed him as 'not a very bad poet, a very great coxcomb, and a hero chiefly by his own report'. He was the elder brother of George *Herbert. JAC

Herbert, George (1593–1633). Poet. Younger brother of Edward *Herbert, grounded in classics at Westminster School, then graduate of Trinity College, Cambridge, Herbert successfully sought the post of university orator (held 1620–7) as a preliminary to public service. But by 1625 his 'Court-hopes' had faded with his patrons' deaths, so, ill-health increasingly recurrent, he abandoned ambition and turned to the church, finally being ordained in 1630 and inducted at Bemerton, near Salisbury. Additionally chaplain to Lord Pembroke, he became friends with Nicholas Ferrar at Little Gidding and, with saint-like devotion, concentrated his remaining few years on the parish and church repair—'Holy Mr Herbert' was a contemporary assessment. Herbert is best known for his sacred poetry (*The Temple*, posthumously 1633), portraying his spiritual conflicts, but so well crafted and full of simple dignity that he not only influenced others like *Crashaw and *Vaughan but is now regarded as a major metaphysical poet. ASH

Herbert, Sidney, 1st Baron Herbert of Lea (1810–61). Politician. Herbert was educated at Harrow and Oxford. He entered the Commons as a Conservative in 1832, being in office in 1834–5 and 1841–6. In 1845–6 and 1852–5 he was secretary of war, being less blamed than others by the Roebuck Commission of 1855 for the poor organization of the army during the Crimean War, during which he supported Florence *Nightingale's nursing reforms. He returned to the War Office in 1859 and began an energetic programme of reform; overwork and Bright's disease caused his early death. He was talked of as a future prime minister, Lord Houghton saying of him, 'He was just the man to rule England: birth, wealth, grace, tact and not too much principle.' HCGM

Herbert, William, 3rd earl of Pembroke (1580–1630). Herbert succeeded to the earldom at the age of 21 in 1601. He was under a cloud at Elizabeth's court for getting Mary Fitton, one of the maids of honour, pregnant. He fared better with James I, was awarded the Garter in 1603, and from 1615 served as lord chamberlain. In 1626 he became lord steward. He was often at odds with royal policy and on bad terms with *Buckingham, favourite to both James I and Charles I. Nevertheless, his wealth and amiability gave him standing, he was chancellor of the University of Oxford, and Pembroke College was refounded in his honour. A patron of authors, including *Donne, *Jonson, and *Shakespeare, the attempt to identify him with the W.H. of the sonnets is implausible. *Clarendon praised him as 'the most universally loved and esteemed of any man of that age', while admitting that Pembroke was 'immoderately given up to women'. JAC

Hereford, diocese of. Around 679 *Theodore created the bishopric, conterminous with Herefordshire and south Shropshire, for the *Magonsaetan tribe, out of the Mercian see. Despite the Danish invasions its westerly position enabled it to maintain continuity of bishops. Hereford was, by contrast, vulnerable to the Welsh, who sacked the cathedral in 1055 and killed the bishop, Leofgar. William I strengthened the region's defences by making it (until 1076) a Norman palatine earldom. Notable bishops include Thomas de Cantilupe (1275–82), canonized in 1320, chancellor of England during baronial rule in 1265 and adviser to Edward I; Herbert Croft (1662–91), stabilizer of the see after the Restoration; and James Beauclerk (1746–87), Charles II's aristocratic grandson, a conscientious 18th-cent. bishop. The cathedral, dedicated jointly to the Virgin Mary and Æthelbert, the martyred East Anglian king (753), is mostly Norman and its 15th-cent. College of Vicars is still intact. There are many fine Norman churches on the borders of Wales. The diocese was famed liturgically for 'the Hereford use' which rivalled Sarum before the Reformation. In 1716/17 Thomas Bisse, brother of Philip Bisse (bishop 1713–21), founded the *Three Choirs Festival (with Worcester and Gloucester). WMM

Hereford and Worcester. This was a new county, formed under the Local Government Act of 1972. It included the county borough of Worcester, the old county of Hereford, and all of Worcestershire, save for Dudley, Halesowen, and Stourbridge, hived off to West Midlands. There was considerable opposition from Herefordshire, the smaller of the counties, complaining that it had little in common with the industrialized parts of north Worcestershire. A Hereford bull was paraded in Whitehall in protest. The debate turned largely on the extent to which the Malverns formed a natural barrier. But the Banham commission in 1994 proposed to separate the counties once more, with Herefordshire as a unitary authority and Worcestershire as a two-tier structure. JAC

Herefordshire is a small border county, full of castles, running from the Black Mountains in the west to the Malverns in the east. Hereford itself was for centuries a stronghold against the Welsh, holding the crossing of the Wye, not far from its junction with the Frome and the Lugg. The name denotes an army-ford. Almost all the towns were on the east side, out of reach of the Welsh—Hereford, Leominster, Bromyard, Ross, Ledbury: in the western part is only Kington, 4 miles from the Radnorshire border, and with a population of no more than 2,000.

In the pre-Roman period, Herefordshire was part of the territory of the *Silures, to whom *Caratacus appealed in his fight against the Romans. In the mid-7th cent., it fell to *Penda, pagan king of the Mercians. Soon after his death in battle, Hereford was founded as a diocese (676). A hundred years later Offa's Dike marked the limit of Mercian expansion, running through the west of the county from Kington, through Hay, to White Castle.

In the reign of *Athelstan Welsh princes did homage at Hereford, but the next 500 years were turbulent. Hereford itself was sacked by *Gruffydd ap Llywelyn in 1055 and the new cathedral destroyed. The next bishop of Hereford was a fighting man, Leofgar, who, according to the *Anglo-Saxon Chronicle*, 'after his consecration, forsook his chrism and his cross, his spiritual weapons, and seized his spear and his sword, and thus armed joined the levies against Gruffydd, the Welsh king'. But Leofgar lasted a mere eleven weeks before he was slain. The Normans took the border in hand. William *Fitzosbern was given palatine status as earl of Hereford and began the building of a formidable castle there—'one of the fairest, largest and strongest in all England', according to *Leland. Even so, the county remained vulnerable. It was only just held against *Llywelyn the Great in the early 13th cent. and threatened again by *Glyndŵr in the early 15th.

Tudor rule brought peace to the county. *Camden's *Britannia* in 1586 described Herefordshire as 'of an excellent soil, both for feeding cattle and produce of corn'. His account of the Golden Valley in the west was idyllic: 'the hills that encompass it on both sides are clothed with woods, under the woods lie corn-fields on each hand, and under those fields, lovely and gallant meadows. In the middle, between them, glides a clear and crystal river.' Edmund *Gibson, editing Camden in 1695, drew attention to the 'vast quantities of cider, as not only serve their own families, for 'tis their general drink, but also to furnish London and other parts of England; their Red Streak, (from a sort of apple they call so), being extremely valued.'

The county saw yet more fighting during the Civil War. The line of communication was important since the king drew heavily upon Wales for recruitment. The shire was royalist in sympathy but harassed in the south by parliamentary troops from Gloucester, and in the north by forays from Bryan Brampton, the Harley estate. Hereford changed hands several times, stood a siege from the Scots in 1645, and was a centre of *club-men activity.

The industrial revolution touched Herefordshire lightly and it remains a quiet rural county. In the local government reorganization of 1972, Herefordshire, the fourth smallest county in population, was merged, despite much protest, with its larger eastern neighbour, Worcestershire. But the final report of the Banham commission on local government in December 1994 favoured separating the two counties, reconstituting Herefordshire as a unitary authority. JAC

heresy is the holding of religious views regarded or defined as unacceptable by the church and, if persisted in, carried the punishment of burning. The first notable British heretics were *Pelagius and Celestius, who taught in Rome in the early 5th cent., and argued, against Augustine, that man's own efforts could steer him towards salvation. Condemned by Pope Innocent I, pelagianism continued to find support in Britain and St *Germanus was sent over in 429 specifically to deal with it. Accusations of heresy were rarely made against lay people, who neither preached nor published, and whose grasp of Christian doctrine was often, as their pastors complained, distressingly approximate. The assumption was that they were ignorant of the truth and seldom persisted in error when it was pointed out to them. Heresy was hardly a problem in the Anglo-Saxon church or in the immediate post-Conquest period, and only a handful of cases can be identified. Nevertheless the church remained on its guard. A group of weavers, possibly Cathars, arrived in 1165 from Flanders or Germany and settled in Worcester: they were branded and not allowed to remain. Concern over heresy dates from *Wyclif's challenge to the doctrine of transubstantiation and his attacks upon the wealth of the church, which, coming in the 1370s at a time of economic unrest, gained him considerable support. Though Henry IV's act **De heretico comburendo* passed in 1401 it was only after Oldcastle's *lollard rebellion in 1414 that systematic persecution of heresy began. In Scotland, James Resby, a follower of Wyclif, was burned at Perth in 1407, and a Hussite at St Andrews in 1432. There was a marked revival of lollardy in the late 15th and early 16th cents., which merged with the Lutheran heresy. Henry VIII repealed *De heretico comburendo* in 1533 but retained the right to burn heretics. Edward VI then repealed all statutes against heresy, though it remained an offence at common law. Mary at once revived the previous statutes and Elizabeth abolished them again in 1558. *Anabaptists continued to suffer since they were regarded as totally subversive of the social order, James ordering a burning in 1612. In Scotland the laws against heresy were repealed by the Reformation Parliament of 1560. In Charles II's reign, an Act of 1677 abolished the writ *De heretico comburendo*, but reiterated the right of ecclesiastical courts to punish heresy, short of death.

Though persecution of laymen for heresy ceased, the careers of clerics and academics (in holy orders) could still be jeopardized by charges of heresy, and the offence of *blasphemy remained dangerous. James Nayler, a quaker, was whipped, branded, and had his tongue bored for blasphemy in 1656/7, and Thomas Aikenhead, a mere youth, was executed in Edinburgh in 1697. William Whiston, Newton's successor at Cambridge, was deprived of his chair in 1710 for arianism; John Simon, professor of divinity at Glasgow, was suspended in 1729 on the same charge; Thomas Woolston, a fellow of Sidney Sussex College, Cambridge, lost his fellowship in 1721, was prosecuted for blasphemy in 1729, and died in prison. Later prosecutions included the publishers of *Paine's *The Age of Reason* (1797, 1812, 1819), the publisher of *Shelley's *Queen Mab* (1821), and George *Holyoake for a lecture (1842). In 1977 Mary Whitehouse brought a successful private action against *Gay News* for printing a poem portraying Christ as a homosexual. Existing legislation against blasphemy protects Christianity only and there has been pressure to extend it to cover Islam and other religions.

JAC

Hereward (11th cent.), known as 'the Wake' ('the watchful one') was the leading figure in the fenland revolt against William the Conqueror. In 1070, the appearance of a Danish fleet in the waters of Ely raised hopes of resistance among Englishmen of that district, many of whom had Danish blood. Hereward, leading a band of outlaws and Danish allies, sacked and plundered the monastery at Peterborough, but soon afterwards the Danes agreed terms with William and sailed away. Hereward was joined by other English leaders and their men in the defence of the Isle of Ely. In 1071 William attacked with ships, constructing a causeway for his main force. The outlaw's deeds are legendary. The alleged treachery of the abbot and monks of Ely after William seized monastic lands is blamed for the ultimate surrender. Hereward escaped by water, after which nothing certain is known of him, although there are legends of subsequent adventures. His fame is as a symbol of English resistance to Norman oppression. AM

heriot is derived from the Anglo-Saxon word for 'war-gear' (in Scotland, *hereyeld*). This was a feudal obligation due to a lord on the death of a tenant. Originally the tenant's heir returned armour and weapons lent to him, but it developed into a claim by the lord to the best beast or chattel, and even more. It was, in effect, a kind of death duty, though its incidence varied widely. By the 14th cent. it was becoming common for the heriot to be commuted to a money payment. JAC

Heriot, George (1563–1624). Heriot was a prosperous Edinburgh goldsmith who became jeweller to James VI and goldsmith to the queen. He moved down to London after the king and advanced large loans to the royal couple. Impressed by the success of Christ's Hospital in London, Heriot left the bulk of his fortune to establish a school in Edinburgh, to be administered by the town council. The school opened in 1659. As 'Jingling Geordie' he appears in Scott's *The Fortunes of Nigel* and he is also commemorated in Heriot-Watt University. JAC

heritable jurisdictions. In the Scottish legal system before 1747, many of the king's subjects were not under the jurisdiction of royal courts either at local or at central level. Instead, they were answerable to a complex of hereditary or franchise jurisdictions in the hands of the feudal nobility. The basic heritable jurisdiction was the barony, which was universal. Towns could be burghs of barony under a feudal superior. Though there was an appeal from the barony to the royal sheriff court, this was not true of baronies in the regalities. These units, some as small as a town, some like Argyll 500 square miles in extent, were autonomous jurisdictions with their own supreme courts. High treason alone justified royal intervention.

Though resented by the crown, the system provided cheap, quick local justice, as its extensive records show. It was abolished after the 1745 *Jacobite rising by the Heritable Jurisdictions (Scotland) Act of 1747. Compensation was paid. Only baron courts survived though with curtailed powers. BPL

Herrick, Robert (1591–1674). Poet. Son of a Cheapside goldsmith, initially apprenticed to the trade but graduating at Cambridge (1617), Herrick was ordained in 1623. Returning to London and in contact with other writers (especially Ben *Jonson), musicians, and court wits, he established himself as a poet, but, having accompanied the duke of *Buckingham to La Rochelle (1627), was admitted to the living of Dean Prior (Devon). Here he spent most of the rest of his life, although, as an Anglican with strong royalist sympathies, he was ejected from the living in 1647 (retiring happily to Westminster); he was restored in 1662. Herrick's poetry was widely appreciated, appeared in miscellanies, and was set to music. From epigrams to epithalamions, though influenced by English folklore and covering a wide range of subjects, it was carefully polished yet retained much charm. A collected edition of his poems was published as *Hesperides* (1648). ASH

Herrings, battle of the, 1429. In October 1428 the duke of *Bedford invested Orléans. On 12 February 1429 Sir John Fastolf, bringing supplies of herrings and lentils to the besiegers, was attacked at Rouvray by a superior force under the comte de Clermont. The attackers were driven off with heavy loss and the supplies got through, but Orléans was relieved by Joan of Arc in April. JAC

Herschel, John (1792–1871). The most eminent physicist of early Victorian Britain. His father *William was a famous astronomer, and John went to Cambridge where with Charles *Babbage he reformed the mathematics course. After toying with law, he turned to physics, working on optics as the new wave theory was coming in, and to astronomy. In 1830, he just failed to be elected president of the *Royal Society, and published his *Preliminary Discourse on the Study of Natural Philosophy*, an extremely influential account of scientific method. In 1833 he sailed to the Cape to observe the southern stars (results published 1847). He became a great pundit, widely consulted and involved in numerous scientific projects: he is remembered as a pioneer in *photography, and also in geophysics; for editing the admiralty *Manual of Scientific Enquiry* (1850); and for his essays and poems. DK

Herschel, William (1738–1822). An astronomer, he added the planet Uranus to the list known since antiquity. He came to England from Hanover as a musician, and in 1766 became an organist in Bath. Taking to astronomy, he made his own reflecting telescope: with it in 1781 he saw the planet, which he had at first thought a comet. He named it *Georgium Sidus*, after George III who, as Galileo's patron had done in similar circumstances, duly appointed him court astronomer. He inferred that the sun was moving with respect to the fixed stars; found that some double stars were orbiting each other under gravity; and, helped by his sister Caroline, estimated the form of our galaxy, the Milky Way. DK

Herstmonceux castle (Sussex) was built mid-15th cent. by Sir Roger de Fiennes. Despite moat, battlements, and turrets, it was a defensible country home rather than a strong castle. One of the largest houses of its time, the stately, rose-hued Herstmonceux was an early and fine example of brickwork, a novel building material in England then. Neglected for some years, parts were dismantled in 1777. The castle remained a ruin until 1913 when some work was done, then extensive restoration undertaken by Sir Paul Latham in 1933, with the architect Walter Godfrey. The only radical change made was to have one large courtyard instead of four of differing sizes. The Royal Observatory in 1948 moved from Greenwich to Herstmonceux where it remained for some forty years. AM

Hertford, Synod of, 672. Convened by *Theodore, archbishop of Canterbury, to reorganize the church following the Synod of *Whitby (664), when Celtic Christianity gave way to Roman traditions, the synod was the first general assembly representing the whole English church. The Roman dating of Easter was affirmed. The precedence of one bishop over another was determined by seniority of consecration. Bishops' activities were confined to their own dioceses and monasteries exempted from episcopal interference. Monks and clergy were forbidden to travel without permission from their superiors. Pronouncements on marriage included the forbidding of incest and divorce, except for adultery. Theodore wanted to increase the number of bishops, dividing the larger dioceses, but as no decision was reached, he was doubtless opposed. It was agreed that annual meetings would take place at the unidentified Clofesho. AM

Hertfordshire, though a small county, has little geographical unity. The southern parts are within the orbit of London and discharge commuters into Euston, St Pancras, King's Cross, and Liverpool Street. The north retains quiet spots like Gaddesden in the west and Wyddial in the east. The magnetic attraction of London has meant that, since Roman times, communications have run north–south, with *Akeman Street, *Watling Street, and *Ermine Street as the main thoroughfares. East–west communications have always been difficult. The *Icknield Way, the great pre-Roman route, is too far north to unite the shire. Even today it is doubtful how often people from Tring find themselves in Bishop's Stortford, save to play football.

The divisions within the county run deep within its natural and political history. It consists of two river basins, with the natural watershed forming the northern boundary. The Lea rises just outside the county near Luton and leaves it in the south-east to join the Thames near Blackwall Tunnel: with its tributaries the Mimram, Beane, Rib, Ash, and Stort, it drains the eastern half. The western parts drain into the Ver, Colne, Chess, and Gade, which meet near Watford and join the Thames at Staines. The north-west of the county, adjoining the Chilterns, is gentle, wooded chalk country; the north-east is downland and bare wide fields; the south-east is flat clay, running down to desolate marshes at Cheshunt, bordering Essex.

In the immediate pre-Roman period, the area was part of the territory of the *Catuvellauni, whose chief, *Cassivellaunus, opposed Caesar's expeditions. His grandson *Cunobelinus seems to have moved his capital from *Verulamium, near St Albans, to Colchester, ruling over the *Trinovantes. *Caratacus, his son, led a protracted resistance to the Roman invasion of AD 43, was driven west, captured, and died a prisoner in Rome. The area was soon brought under Roman control, but Colchester, Verulamium, and London were all sacked during *Boudicca's revolt of AD 61. Braughing is on the site of a Roman settlement of some importance.

The area was one of the earliest to be occupied by the Saxons and formed at first part of the diocese of London, established in the early 7th cent. to minister to the East Saxons. There was subsequently an ecclesiastical reorganization since, until the foundation of the new diocese of St Albans in 1877, most of Hertfordshire was in the vast diocese of Lincoln, only the eastern part staying with London. In the 8th cent. the region formed part of the kingdom of Mercia, and *Offa is said to have died in 796 while building the great abbey on the site of St Alban's martyrdom. In the 9th and 10th cents., Danes and Saxons fought for control. The boundary between the territories of *Alfred of Wessex and *Guthrum was settled by the treaty of *Wedmore in 878 as the line of the river Lea. The truce was temporary, for in

896 the Danes are reported to have sailed up the Lea to near Ware and to have been stranded when Alfred ordered ditches to be dug to drain the stream. *Edward the Elder, in his counter-attack in 913, fortified Hertford as a strong point and it became the nucleus of the emerging county. The first reference to Hertfordshire by name is in the *Anglo-Saxon Chronicle* for AD 1011 and by the time of the *Domesday survey it had been divided up into $8\frac{1}{2}$ hundreds. In the 13th cent. Hertford and St Albans established their right to parliamentary representation and were joined, on and off, by Bishop's Stortford and Berkhamsted. In 1586 Camden admired the county enormously: it was 'well furnished with corn-fields, pasture-ground, meadows, little woods and small, but very clear, streams'. Hertford, slightly off centre, never dominated the shire as some county towns did, and a considerable number of small market towns grew up, serving their immediate locality—Ashwell, Buntingford, Royston, Baldock, Hitchin, and Hoddesdon. St Albans was always bigger than Hertford and when the first county council was set up in 1889, it met alternately in the two towns.

The modern history of Hertfordshire is one of slow encroachment by London, *Cobbett's 'Great Wen'. The pull of London had been felt from the earliest days, particularly in the south-east, where the river Lea gave easy access to east London. Efforts to improve the river began centuries before the river Lea navigation was completed. Competition was fierce. Neighbours, who depended on sending corn and malt to London by cart, smashed banks and destroyed locks on the river, as well as hinting that barge cargoes picked up moisture and weighed heavily. Hertford and Ware had a long-standing feud, with the Ware men stringing barges across the river to stop Hertford traffic. In the west of the county, the opening in 1800 of the Grand Junction canal, through Tring and Rickmansworth, assisted the growth of industry, especially paper-making and printing. Yet despite these developments, the county remained rural until late. There were plenty of open fields surviving well into Victoria's reign, estates in the county were much sought after by gentlemen with business in London, and tributes to the beauty of the shire continued to pour in. Charles Lamb, in a famous essay, sang the delights of 'Mackerye End in Hertfordshire'. In 1801 no town in the county had as many as 4,000 inhabitants. By 1851, though Hertford had scarcely grown at all, St Albans was over 8,000, Hitchin and Hemel Hempstead over 7,000, and Watford over 6,000.

But by 1901 the shape of the 20th cent. was becoming clear. Watford had increased to 32,000, twice the size of the next town, St Albans; and Cheshunt (12,000) and Barnet (7,000), on the fringes of London, had moved up. Two years later, a development which cast a long shadow, took place. The first garden city was started on a 4,000-acre site at Letchworth, chosen in the main for its nearness to London. It was joined after the First World War by the second garden city at Welwyn. In the first half of the 20th cent. the county population increase was five times the national average. The success of the garden cities prompted governments to look to Hertfordshire for sites for the new towns. Stevenage was the first to be set up after the Second World War, followed by Hatfield and Hemel Hempstead, and Welwyn was taken over as a new town. Whatever the merits of new towns as such, the effect upon a small county of five in such close proximity was predictable. Increasingly it is reduced to quiet pockets and enclaves. Within the network of motorways and junctions, fragments of an old county survive. But few of the motorists using the M25 between junctions 24 and 25 have time to reflect that, beneath them, is the estate of Theobalds, where James I once nearly drowned in Sir Hugh Myddleton's *New River. JAC

Hervey, John, Lord (1696–1743). The second son of the 1st earl of Bristol, Hervey was elected to represent Bury St Edmunds (1723), supported Walpole, and was rewarded with the posts of vice-chamberlain and privy counsellor. His quarrel with *Pulteney, formerly a friend but prominent in opposition, led to a duel. A favoured companion of Queen *Caroline, Hervey had considerable influence at the court of George II, where life and intrigue furnished ready material for his cynical and witty *Memoirs*, a superb and sustained piece of writing. His epicene beauty and use of cosmetics to cover hypochondriacal pallor prompted *Pope's spiteful brilliance of 'Let Sporus tremble'. Hervey, a fluent writer, skilled pamphleteer, and more than useful debater, was elevated to the House of Lords in his father's barony in 1733 to strengthen Walpole's position after the Excise crisis. He was briefly lord privy seal 1740–2. ASH

Heseltine, Michael (b. 1933). Conservative politician. Heseltine entered politics after making his fortune in publishing. He believes in a combination of entrepreneurial enterprise and partnership between government and industry. As environment secretary (1979–83) he pioneered the sale of council houses, rate-capping of local authorities, and development corporations to regenerate inner cities. Popular with party grass roots and noted for his rousing conference speeches, Heseltine was never fully trusted by Mrs *Thatcher. In January 1986 he walked out of cabinet, resigning as defence secretary (1983–6), over the fate of the Westland Helicopter Company. In November 1990 Heseltine precipitated Thatcher's retirement in a leadership challenge. His own ambition to be prime minister was thwarted by losing to John *Major in the second ballot. For his loyalty to Major in the 1995 July leadership contest he was created deputy prime minister and 1st secretary of state. As chairman of numerous cabinet committees he had an input on all important policy issues. RAS

Hexham, battle of, 1469. The duke of Somerset, campaigning on behalf of Henry VI, was defeated at *Hedgeley Moor in April 1469, but rallied his forces at Hexham the following month. They were trapped by Montagu, *Warwick's younger brother, and cut to pieces on 15 May, 3 miles south of the town near West Dipton wood. Somerset was executed after the battle. JAC

Hexham, diocese of. The see was created in 678 for part of Northumbria. *Theodore unsuccessfully tried to persuade *Cuthbert to be bishop, who, though consecrated, refused. The most notable bishop was St John of Beverley

(686–705; York 705–18). The bishopric collapsed under the Danish invasions (*c*.821) and was not revived. WMM

Hexham abbey was founded around 673 by St *Wilfrid in Northumberland on land granted to him by Queen Æthelthryth. It was created a bishopric in 678 but after 821 the see was merged with *Lindisfarne. In 875 the abbey was burned by the Danes and its inhabitants dispersed. In 1113 Archbishop Thomas II of York reconstituted the church as a priory of Augustinian canons. The abbey is noted for its Early English choir, the crypt and the night stair in the south transept, a broad flight of steps leading to the dormitory, used by monks attending night services. RAS

hides. The difficult study of the 'hide' is essential for understanding the history of the English state and, by connection and analogy, that of much of western Europe. In *Domesday Book (1086), every village and estate in southern and western England is assessed in terms of hides. (In large areas of the north and east the corresponding unit was the 'carucate'.) The system of assessment was comprehensive, related to the levy of tax and military and naval service, and elaborately patterned. It was normal, in some shires, for almost every village to be assessed at 5 hides. In others, somewhat larger areas were assessed at, say, 20 hides. The system was remarkable in its completeness and complexity, and was very old. The very earliest land grants, late 7th cent., denote the estates concerned in Latin terms which must be intended to translate the vernacular *hid*. The etymology of this word indicates a connection with the idea of a household. This is echoed in *Bede's description of a land such as that of the southern Mercians as 'of seven thousand families'. The extensive use of hidation for such wide areas is demonstrated by the 'Tribal Hidage', which may be a tribute list of the 7th or the 8th cent. and gives hidages for some entire kingdoms, also for lesser areas. The Burghal Hidage (*c*.900), shows how hidage assessments were used to allocate responsibility for fortress maintenance. Domesday and related evidence indicate that there could be extensive revision of hidages. Hidage assessment determined national taxation for a period after the Conquest. By the 13th cent. its use was residual and local. The hide was essentially a unit of assessment. Its relationship to real area and value varied, though commonly there was one. In much of England the hide was reckoned as of 120 acres, in Wessex generally as of 40 or 48. JCa

high church. Within the Church of England, the high-church party stresses continuity with the pre-Reformation church and holds a 'high' concept of the authority of the church, bishops, and sacraments. Originating in the resistance of certain churchmen to the protestantizing determination of Elizabethan and early Stuart puritanism, the term was first coined in the later 17th cent. High churchmen flourished under the later Stuarts because of their insistence on the *divine right of kings. Despite successful political campaigns into the early 18th cent., they were doomed to disappear along with the *Jacobite cause. Their theological and ecclesiastical opinions survived, to be rediscovered by the *Oxford movement of the 1830s. Separated from the politics of succession, 19th-cent. high churchmanship emphasized the spiritual nature of the Church of England and its role in society. High-church influence on the Church of England encouraged a recovery of its intellectual life, especially the study of patristic and medieval history, liturgy, and ecclesiology. By the end of the 19th cent. high churchmanship was the dominant orthodoxy, despite court battles over the ritualist movement, which represented one aspect of it. Its success also contributed to bitter divisions between the high church or catholic grouping and the *low church or *evangelicals. JFC

High Commission, Court of. Known as such from *c*.1570, it emanated from earlier ecclesiastical commissions (after 1547), was given statutory authority (1559), reconstructed (1583), and exercised the ecclesiastical appellate and original jurisdiction of the crown as supreme governor. Originally a visitatorial commission supervising clerical discipline, it became a full-blown court for various lay offences, often political. Extensively used by *Whitgift, *Bancroft, and *Laud, its inquisitorial methods, swift and secret in action, demanding the oath ex officio rather than trial by indictment and jury, were more efficient than diocesan courts and likened by *Burghley to the Romish inquisition. Savagely attacked by *Coke and 17th-cent. common lawyers, its powers were enhanced (1611). Feared and detested universally, its abolition with *Star Chamber (1641) was not revoked (1661), though James II revived it briefly in modified form (1686–8), when it suspended Bishop *Compton of London and imposed a catholic president on Magdalen College, Oxford. WMM

high kings of Ireland. See IRELAND, HIGH KINGS OF.

Highland. An administrative region of Scotland, created in 1973 from the counties of Caithness, Nairn, Sutherland, Inverness (except the Outer Hebrides), Ross and Cromarty (except Lewis), and a northern part of Argyll. Between 1973 and 1996 it was a region, sharing local government activities with its eight districts, but now exercises all local government functions. It is a very large and very sparsely populated area, of which large tracts are mountainous. Many parts of the region lost population through the 19th-cent. clearances, when agricultural communities were shifted to make way for sheep-farming. Most of the present population is in the eastern part of the region around Inverness, where there is small-scale manufacturing and food-processing, established particularly with the support of the local economic development agency. Farming by crofting is still significant in the north and west and the islands, and tourism for the whole region. CML

Highland clearances were evictions which eliminated the bulk of the Gaelic-speaking population from the Highlands and Islands of Scotland. Between 1763 and 1775 thousands of Highlanders migrated to colonial British North America motivated by resentment at higher rents and consolidation of farms, and led by tacksmen, former clan gentry who were leasees of land, but were being eliminated as unnecessary middlemen.

Next, large-scale sheep-farming came to the Highlands, based on the replacement of the small indigenous sheep by commercial breeds such as the black-faced Linton. With Lowland sheep came Lowland farmer-capitalists and often Lowland shepherds, though some former tacksmen contrived to thrive. By the early 19th cent. this revolution had reached the vast Sutherland estates north of Inverness. Tenants were resettled on the coastal areas to combine fishing with farming and ancillary activity such as gathering kelp on the beaches to make commercial alkali.

The collapse of kelping due to cheaper imports after 1815 was followed by the decline of wool prices due to the arrival of cheap Australian and then New Zealand wool, and in 1848–9 by widespread famine conditions. After 1860, tenants were cleared to create deer forests, treeless shooting estates which, by 1914, covered $3\frac{1}{2}$ million acres in the Highlands. By 1886 a residual crofting population clung to the margins of the region with legal security of tenure. BPL

Highland games were originally meetings of clans. They developed into more formal gatherings under the influence of the revival of interest in Scottish antiquity fostered by *Scott and others in the 1810s. At Invergarry in the 1820s the games included not only piping, tossing the caber, hammer-throwing, wrestling, and running, but twisting the four legs off a cow. A sanitized version at Braemar in 1850 was attended by Queen Victoria, whose ghillie, Duncan, 'an active, good-looking young man', won the race up and down Craig Cheunnich, finished 'spitting blood', and was never the same man again. Modern gatherings are held in various places, usually in late summer. JAC

Highland Land League. Scottish crofters in the 1870s watched the success of the Irish in obtaining concessions, had 'a mind to turn rebels themselves', and concluded that the *Irish Land League might be copied. The Highland Land League was formed in 1882 and returned four sympathetic MPs at the election of 1885. Results were gratifyingly swift. *Gladstone's *Crofters' Act of 1886 gave security of tenure and *Salisbury, the same year, established a separate secretary of state for Scotland. These concessions dampened the agitation, though the Highland Land League stayed in existence, becoming the Scottish National League in 1921 and eventually merging with the *Scottish National Party. JAC

highwaymen are more picturesque in fiction and retrospect than they were in reality. The heyday of the highwayman was from the Restoration, when coaches began to appear on the roads in large enough numbers to make the occupation profitable, to the end of the 18th cent., when stage-coaches travelled with armed guards and policing was better. There was usually a flurry of highway robbery after each great war, with demobilized soldiers turning their hands to it. Because of the density of traffic, the outskirts of London were particularly frequented by robbers, and Finchley Common, Hounslow Heath, Bagshot Heath, and Blackheath all acquired a bad reputation. The Newmarket road was also hazardous, especially near Epping Forest. Highwaymen soon became popular heroes, accorded the sneaking admiration reserved in the 20th cent. for the great train robbers. The exploits of Claude Duval (a ladies' man), William Nevinson, James Whitney, Jack Sheppard (an escapologist), Dick *Turpin, and 'Sixteen-string' Jack Rann, often turned into execrable verse, sold in broadsheets and ballads, usually accompanied by a woodcut of the final gallows scene. Highwaymen were expected to die game. JAC

Hilda, St (614–80). Baptized in 627 with her kinsman, the Northumbrian king *Edwin, at 33 Hilda became a nun, joining a community on the banks of the Wear. A year later she became abbess at Hartlepool, and in 657 founded the double monastery at Streanaeshalch (Whitby). Renowned for her high standards, no fewer than five bishops were trained under her rule. Hilda encouraged the poetic Whitby cowherd *Cædmon, taking him into the monastery to ensure sound doctrine in his vernacular verses. Kings and princes sought her advice, and, representing Celtic traditions, she was an important figure at the Synod of *Whitby. News of her death is said to have reached a neighbouring monastery through a vision of angels transporting her soul to heaven. AM

Hill, Octavia (1838–1912). Social reformer. Early influence from her grandfather, the sanitary reformer Dr Southwood Smith, and work with the *Christian socialists, led to conviction of the need for better housing for the poor. A loan from John *Ruskin (1865) enabled purchase of squalid property in Paradise Place, Marylebone (London), for which, ever strict and businesslike, she encouraged both prompt rent payments and cleanliness, with profits directed to repairs and improvements. The experiment was so successful that the scheme spread, more houses were purchased or put under her charge, and other workers trained in her methods; her system of housing management was eventually introduced into Europe and America. Concerned with improving the quality of life generally, though not politically inclined despite appointment to a royal commission, she actively supported the Charity Organization and Kyrle societies, while her passionate belief in preserving open spaces for public use led to co-founding the *National Trust (1895). ASH

Hill, Rowland, 1st Viscount Hill (1772–1842). Soldier. Hill was a younger son of Sir John Hill, baronet, of Shropshire and one of five brothers to join the army. He was wounded near *Alexandria in 1801 while serving under Abercromby and was promoted major-general in 1805. Later he served in Portugal and was again wounded at *Talavera (1809). In 1812 he was knighted. He was with *Wellington in the advance into France 1813–14 and was given a barony. On Napoleon's return from Elba, Hill hastened to Brussels and was in action at *Waterloo, where he had a horse killed under him. From 1828 until 1842 he was general commanding-in-chief and was raised to a viscountcy just before his death. Melbourne confided to the young Queen Victoria that Hill was 'a very dull man'. There is a large monument to him at Shrewsbury. JAC

Hill, Sir Rowland (1795–1879). Inventor of penny postage. Hill was born in Kidderminster, son of a schoolmaster and pioneer of shorthand. He took over his father's school and instituted a novel system of discipline, involving the boys as assessors. After 1828 he abandoned teaching, experimented with a number of inventions, and in 1835 became secretary to a commission to colonize south Australia. He then became interested in the postal service, which was so prohibitively expensive that the revenue of the Post Office was falling in a period of rapid population growth and commercial expansion. Hill suggested pre-payment, a standard delivery charge irrespective of distance, and the use of an adhesive stamp. A pamphlet of 1837 attracted attention and penny postage was adopted in 1839. Hill was put in charge but met with vast obstruction from within the Post Office and was dismissed in 1842. Reinstated by *Russell in 1846, he held office until 1864. He was knighted in 1860 and *Gladstone said of his reform that it had 'run like wildfire through the civilized world'. Anthony *Trollope, who worked at the Post Office with Hill, was less flattering: 'a hard taskmaster who had little understanding of the ways of men . . . it was a pleasure for me to differ from him on all occasions.' JAC

Hillary, Sir Edmund (1919–95). A New Zealander, Hillary's reputation as a mountaineer and, in particular, his experience of Himalayan climbing led to an invitation to join the Everest expedition of 1953. The leader, Sir John Hunt, selected him and Sherpa Tenzing to make the actual assault on the summit, and in May 1953 they became the first two men to reach the top of the world's highest mountain. News of the success became known as Queen Elizabeth was crowned, adding to the excitement of that occasion. Hillary also explored the Antarctic, reaching the South Pole in 1958. He made further Himalayan expeditions and was involved in development and welfare schemes for the Sherpas. RB

Hilliard, Nicholas (1547–1619). The greatest of English miniaturists. In 1570 he was appointed to the court, where his jeweller's skills suited Elizabeth I's desire for a painted image of splendour, handled with delicacy and elegance. About 1600, he wrote a treatise *The Arte of Limning* (published in 1912) in which he records that his method of painting without the use of shadow was in agreement with the queen's taste, 'for the lyne without shadowe showeth all to a good Iugment'. Her patronage, and later that of James I, brought Hilliard other important sitters and a reputation in France, but did not prevent his financial problems, which, at one stage, resulted in his imprisonment for debt. In London there are examples of Hilliard's exquisitely detailed work in the Victoria and Albert Museum and National Portrait Gallery. A large-scale portrait of Elizabeth I hangs in Liverpool's Walker Gallery. The queen and the duke of Buccleuch have large collections of his work. JC

Hingston Down, battle of, 838. For decades the Britons of Cornwall (*Dumnonia) had been resisting the growing pressure of *Wessex. In 838 they joined with a Viking force, possibly from Ireland, but were defeated at Hingston Down, between Callington and the Tamar, by *Egbert. Cornwall was then incorporated into the Wessex empire. JAC

historical novels. Most novels are set in the past, however recent. Fielding habitually described himself as a historian, and *Tom Jones* (1749) covers the same period as *Waverley* (1814), but *Scott can claim to be the first historical novelist because his characters are caught up in history, defined as much by historical forces as by the whim of the author. The emerging nationalism of the Romantic period brought a new interest in history, seen first in the 18th-cent. taste for the Gothic and the Picturesque, but deepening to a more profound awareness of social change. The French historian Thierry praised *Ivanhoe* (1819) not for the romantic plot but for the study of 'two peoples, two languages; customs that contrasted and struggled against each other'. Socialist realism learnt from the genre, and the Marxist critic Georg Lukács saluted Scott's understanding of historical necessity.

The form has been seen as fundamentally unstable, the fiction detracting from the history and vice versa. This is what Manzoni came to feel, though his *I promessi sposi* (1825) is one of many 19th-cent. novels to acknowledge Scott's example. Bulwer-*Lytton's painstakingly researched forays into the past are out of fashion now, but he brought a new seriousness to the problem of 'how to produce the greatest amount of dramatic effect at the least expense of historical truth'. *Dickens was less punctilious, but *Barnaby Rudge* (1842) perhaps deepened the social concerns of the fiction he wrote when he returned to his own century, and *A Tale of Two Cities* (1859) has given generations of readers their first picture of the French Revolution. The title of *Thackeray's 'novel without a hero' suggests his basically moralistic approach, though *Vanity Fair* (1848) has a sharper and tarter flavour than Lytton manages, while the Victorian taste for religious polemic prompted Charles *Kingsley's *Hypatia* (1853). George *Eliot, Elizabeth Gaskell, and Thomas *Hardy continued the tradition, and even a proto-modernist like Ford Madox Ford (1873–1939) based his trilogy *The Fifth Queen* (1908) on the Tudor period. In our own day the 'non-fiction novel' and 'drama-documentary' testify to an enduring appetite for the mingling of fact and fiction. JNRS

HMI (Her Majesty's Inspectors). The first two inspectors, Seymour Tremenheere and the Revd John Allen, were appointed in 1839 to supervise the proper spending of £30,000 for the education of the poor. Dr J. P. *Kay-Shuttleworth, the secretary of the Committee of the Privy Council for Education, determined that inspectors should be independent, ensured that they were appointed by order in council. Kay-Shuttleworth emphasized the inspecting rather than the examining role of HMI, stating that 'inspection is not intended as a means of exercising control, but of affording assistance'. However, with the introduction of the revised code (or 'payment by results') in 1862, whereby teachers' salaries depended on pupils' attainment in the three Rs, the role of HMI was seriously distorted; from this time they became hated and feared in elementary schools. With the advent of Liberal governments in the later 19th cent., this rigid system was modified. By 1895, payment by results came to an end. After the 1902 Education Act, the inspectorate was restructured into elementary, secondary, and technological branches. The Education (Schools) Act 1992 established the Office for Standards in Education (OFSTED), which took over many of HMI's functions.

PG

Hoadly, Benjamin (1676–1761). Bishop of Winchester. Born in Kent and educated at Catherine Hall, Cambridge, Hoadly held livings in London and successively the bishoprics of Bangor (1716), Hereford (1721), Salisbury (1723), and Winchester (1734). A Whig polemicist in conflict with *Atterbury and his high-church colleagues after 1705, he was rewarded by becoming George I's chaplain, but his appointment to Bangor shocked even supporters. His sermon (1717) advocating private judgement and sincere conscience in preference to ecclesiastical authority challenged both high churchmen and the established church. It thus provoked the furiously bitter *Bangorian controversy and consequent suspension of *convocation. Later, writing as 'Britannicus' (1722), he tore Atterbury's defences to pieces. Traditionally cast as the archetypal Hanoverian absentee prelate, modern research shows that, though a cripple with inability to travel much, he nevertheless attended to his dioceses as best he could or made sure others covered his work. He was genuinely concerned with the spiritual issues of his day and used his 'razor-sharp, if acerbic, intellect' in support of his ideals.

WMM

Hoare, Samuel, 1st Viscount Templewood (1880–1959). Hoare came from a Norfolk family and was educated at Harrow and New College, Oxford. He entered Parliament in 1910 as a Conservative and sat for Chelsea until given his peerage in 1944. He took office under Bonar *Law in 1922 as secretary of state for air and held the same office under *Baldwin. In 1931 he became secretary of state for India in the National Government and carried the Government of India Bill, advancing towards self-government. Baldwin, in 1935, moved him to the Foreign Office. 'Your stay at the Foreign Office will be memorable,' wrote *Beaverbrook in congratulation. It was. Hoare was plunged straight into the crisis over Italy's designs on *Abyssinia. In December 1935 he drew up with Pierre Laval, French foreign minister, a plan which would have dismembered Abyssinia. The public outcry forced his resignation, though Hoare defended his deal as the best he could do for Abyssinia unless governments were prepared to fight Mussolini. Though he was brought back as a minister in 1936, and served as 1st lord of the Admiralty, home secretary, lord privy seal, and secretary of state for air, his career limped. After resigning with *Chamberlain in 1940, he served for four years as ambassador to Spain, at a very critical juncture. Hoare had held high public office almost continuously for more than twenty years. He was unlucky about the Hoare–Laval pact. He was ill at the time and much of the abuse he suffered for 'betraying the League of Nations' was from people who would never have supported war. But there is no reason to believe that the episode brought down a future prime minister.

JAC

Hobbes, Thomas (1588–1679). Philosopher. Hobbes is without doubt the greatest political philosopher to have written in the English language. After graduating from Oxford, he devoted his very long life to private tutoring and study. He fled to France in 1640, fearful for his life under the Long Parliament because of his perceived endorsement of royal absolutism. In 1651 he published in English **Leviathan*, his masterpiece of political philosophy, in which he set out systematically an ingenious social contractarian case for an authoritarian government. Hobbes argued that the state of nature (i.e. the pre-political condition) was a condition of 'war of all against all', since humans are by nature moved by competitiveness, fear, and pride to coerce others. They would contract together to establish an absolute ruler, since that was the only way in which their security could be guaranteed. Hobbes was thought by many to be an atheist, and there was an attempt in Parliament to investigate *Leviathan* as a possible cause of God's wrath in visiting London with the Great Plague in 1665 and the Great Fire in 1666. But the attempt failed, and Hobbes breathed a sigh of relief. He is remembered today for his brilliant defence of political absolutism from individualistic premisses.

TSG

Hobson, John Atkinson (1858–1940). An economist with views that were unconventional for his time, and led him—he claimed—to be blackballed from academic posts. He earned his living therefore through part-time lecturing, journalism, and writing too many books. Two of those books however launched revolutions: *The Physiology of Industry* (1889), written in collaboration with the mountaineer A. F. Mummery, which undermined *laissez-faire* economics by arguing that its tendency was to over-produce; and *Imperialism: A Study* (1902), which attributed the militaristic colonial expansionism of that time to the resultant surpluses of goods and capital. In this way he can be said to have sown the seeds of two of the most powerful ideologies of the 20th cent.: Keynesian economics, and the Leninist interpretation of imperialism. He also contributed importantly to contemporary politics, especially the evolution of a 'New' kind of Liberalism around 1900 to replace the old. Later he dedicated himself to the cause of internationalism.

BJP

hockey claims a very ancient pedigree since there are tomb-drawings and classical reliefs showing men hitting a ball with curved sticks. Variations were certainly played in the medieval period but, like most games, it was formalized and regulated in the 19th cent. Blackheath had a hockey club before 1861 and Teddington introduced the hard ball into the game in the 1870s. The National Association was formed in 1886, mainly by London clubs, and the first women's hockey club was founded at Wimbledon in 1889. Wales played Ireland in 1895 and men's hockey entered the Olympics in 1908. The game was introduced into India by British army officers and flourished exceedingly. The Federation of International Hockey was established in 1924.

JAC

Hogarth, William (1697–1764). Artist. London-born, disinclined to scholarship, but frustrated with armorial engraving, Hogarth set up as an illustrator, largely self-taught, before producing 'conversation pieces', engraving scenes of contemporary life, and history painting. Pugnacious, provocative, and a passionate believer that honest naturalism was preferable to the sterility of formal training, he suffered for his attempts to ridicule the deeply entrenched, Renaissance-based theories of good taste, and sought vainly to encourage a native English school of art. Underrated as a painter, he is best remembered for his moral and satirical engravings (*Rake's Progress, Marriage à la Mode, Gin Lane*) which provide a forthright dissection of the times; promoting industriousness and respectability, the prints were deliberately cheap to facilitate wide distribution. A chauvinistic Englishman, Hogarth was actively interested in philanthropic projects, especially Thomas *Coram's Foundling hospital, was appointed sergeant-painter to the king (1757), quarrelled with *Wilkes, and declined in acrimony. ASH

Hogg, James (1772–1835). Poet and novelist. 'The Ettrick Shepherd' had a long career as a minor poet and novelist before publishing anonymously an extraordinary masterpiece. *The Memoirs and Confessions of a Justified Sinner* (1824) dealt with psychological disorder and antinomian presbyterianism with a disturbing realism which has its roots in the psychology of the Scottish Enlightenment. Largely self-educated, Hogg acquired a taste for the vernacular culture of the borders and began to see himself as a new *Burns. His early verse attracted *Scott and gave rise to a complicated but enduring friendship which taxed them both. He made his way in Edinburgh as a literary journalist and as a historical poet, *The Queen's Wake* (1813) being much admired. His historical novels ape Scott's but are now attracting scholarly attention. A man with a highly developed taste for self-dramatization, he cultivated the role of the professional Scot in his popular contributions to the Tory *Blackwood's Magazine*. NTP

Hogue, La, battle of. See LA HOGUE, BATTLE OF.

Holbein, Hans (*c.*1497–1543). Painter. It is hardly an exaggeration to suggest that our visual image of Henry VIII and his courtiers is derived from Holbein's portraits. Born the son of an Augsburg artist of the same name, Holbein paid two visits to England, a short one 1526–7 and a longer one 1532–43. On the first occasion he brought with him introductions from Erasmus, whom he painted frequently, to Sir Thomas *More, painted a celebrated More family portrait, and may have carried out decoration work at court. On his next visit his patron More was in disfavour, but Holbein received many commissions, and entered the service of the king, for whom he painted a family reconstruction, showing Henry, his parents, and *Jane Seymour. Holbein was also employed to travel abroad and paint prospective brides for the king: his too-flattering portrait of *Anne of Cleves caused considerable embarrassment. The largest group of Holbein's work in Britain is in the Royal Collection. His magnificent portraits include More (1527), Archbishop *Warham (1527), Thomas *Cromwell (1534), Henry VIII (1536), Jane Seymour (1536), the duke of *Norfolk (1540), the duke of *Suffolk (1541), and the young Edward, prince of Wales (1543). An early commentator wrote of Holbein: 'he is not a poet but an historian.' JC

holidays in their modern secular sense of days free from the demands of paid labour, but not necessarily channelled or confined by the demands of religious observance, are in many ways a product of industrial society, and the concomitant precise demarcation between work time and leisure time. Many older calendar customs survived into urban and industrial society, especially where craft industries persisted for a long time alongside the factories in the 19th cent. and migration flows were predominantly short-distance, as in the textile-manufacturing districts of Lancashire and the West Riding of Yorkshire. Thus the Lancashire Wakes and the Yorkshire Tides and Feasts, along with similar customary holidays in the Black Country and the Potteries, survived through into the second half of the 20th cent., although increasingly removed from their origins as celebrations of the saint's day or anniversary of the foundation of the local parish church. National religious festivals, especially Christmas, Easter, and Whitsuntide, also survived erosion from the apostles of economic rationality, order, and propriety between the late 18th and mid-19th cents. Christmas was remade in more secular and commercial form, with an array of imported and invented traditions such as the Christmas tree, greeting cards, robins, and Father Christmas, while many northern towns introduced the Whit walks at which religious congregations paraded the streets in competitive finery. The more political festival of Bonfire Night (5 November), part of the politico-religious calendar since the 17th cent., also continued as a widely observed red-letter day, although aspects of its celebration were toned down by local authorities anxious to uphold public order in the mid-Victorian years. Meanwhile, the secular and unofficial holiday of 'St Monday', abstention from work on the day following the weekend, was particularly popular among the better-paid craft workers and miners, and although it was systematically attacked by employers and moral reformers, playing havoc as it did with work schedules and family budgets, it proved difficult to extirpate, especially among workers in heavy, hot industries who were paid well by the shift, and it survived strongly in coal-mining in the late 20th cent.

Holidays in the sense of extended periods away from home in pursuit of health and pleasure in enjoyably different surroundings were emerging as a regular practice among the better-off by the later 17th cent. *Bath led the way among the spa towns, and the emergence of seaside resorts from the 1730s encouraged an opening-out of the market, as London shopkeepers flocked to Margate cheaply by sailing vessel and also found their way to Brighton. Fashions for cultural and scenic tourism emerged in the late 18th cent. and began to percolate down the social scale. But the holiday away from home as a popular and commercial phenomenon (as opposed to such activities as returning to one's home village to help with the harvest) was mainly a product of the railway age. At working-class level such holidays were almost always unpaid, and they emerged first as a genuinely popular phenomenon in northern England, where the customary Wakes holidays (especially in the Lancashire cotton towns) were adapted for extended seaside visits from the 1850s and especially the 1870s, and families saved through the year in special clubs to be able to afford them. The Bank Holiday Acts of 1871 and 1875, which came to guarantee four free Mondays in the year including the first Monday in August, were of no importance here, although they did help to open out summer holiday opportunities in parts of the country where the older holidays had not survived. Paid holidays for manual workers before the First World War were offered by only a few paternalistic or enlightened employers, and although they spread gradually through the inter-war years a compulsory Holidays with Pay Act was not passed until 1938, and did not become effective until after the Second World War, when English seaside resorts had a particularly prosperous couple of decades, before generally failing to meet the challenge of new opportunities and new destinations. JKW

Holinshed, Raphael (*c.*1520–*c.*1581). Holinshed was the author and compiler of *Chronicles of England, Scotlande and Irelande*, published in 1577. A second and enlarged edition in 1587 was edited by John Vowell and took the story into recent times. Holinshed had little method or sceptical approach but his eclecticism made him a valuable quarry for historical playwrights. *Shakespeare made use of the *Chronicles* in several plays, including *Lear, Macbeth*, and *Cymbeline* and the later historical plays. Though he made considerable changes to Holinshed's version of Macbeth, the episode of the witches is reproduced almost verbatim—'All haile, Makbeth, that hereafter shalt be king': the taking of the crown in *2 Henry IV* comes straight from Holinshed. Of his life, very little is known for certain. He may have been from Cheshire, is said to have been at Cambridge, and could have been in holy orders. He worked for the printer Reyner Wolfe. His will was proved in April 1582, when he was described as steward to Thomas Burdet of Bramcote (War.). JAC

Holkham Hall (Norfolk), 2 miles west of Wells-next-the-Sea, is a slightly forbidding house, built in a rather hard and unlovable local yellow brick. But the grand hall and staircase is majestic and the interior decoration sumptuous. It was built for Thomas Coke, earl of Leicester, in the mid-18th cent. and designed largely by William *Kent and Lord *Burlington, close friends of Coke. It passed to Thomas *Coke, the agricultural improver, for whom the earldom of Leicester was revived in 1837. Lancelot *Brown is believed to have worked on the gardens, but the park, flat and near the sea, offered modest capabilities, even to him. JAC

Holland, Henry Richard Vassall Fox, 3rd Baron (1773–1840). The nephew of Charles James *Fox, whom he idolized and who formed his literary tastes and political principles, Holland travelled extensively in Europe, spoke several languages, and cherished wide connections in European 'liberal' circles. He ran away with the formidable Elizabeth, wife of Sir Godfrey Webster, and after her divorce they established at Holland House in Kensington a salon which became the centre of early 19th-cent. Whig society. He held office in 1806–7 as lord privy seal and 1830–4 as lord president of the council but was unfitted for a departmental post. He was a man of leisure, a noted *bon viveur*, and suffered badly from gout. Holland did much to smooth relationships in Whig society by his urbanity, and devoted himself to preserving the memory of his uncle, the defence of whose principles and reputation was the cornerstone of his life. EAS

Holland, relations with. English interest in the revolt of the Dutch protestants against Philip II of Spain led to direct intervention (1585), but only after all else had failed. Both the Dutch and English profited from their alliance against Spain, yet at times in the next century the Dutch threatened to eclipse the English as the two peoples competed and fought for trade, colonies, and command of the seas. Lord *Shaftesbury commented in 1663 that the Dutch were 'England's eternal enemy, both by interest and inclination'. Cromwell's navy had the better of the first *Anglo-Dutch War (1652–4), but the Dutch were able to destroy much of the English fleet in the Medway in 1667. A third war (1672–4) was inconclusive. The political crisis in England of 1688 brought a Dutch prince, William of Orange, to the English throne, and the English and Dutch were allied in two wars against Louis XIV between 1689 and 1713. In due course the British emerged as much the stronger power. Holland was under French control for most of the Revolutionary and Napoleonic wars. Even *Trafalgar failed to provide Britain with a lasting sense of security against the French presence in the Low Countries, and at Vienna in 1814–15 *Castlereagh set out to create a strong north-eastern barrier against France, engineering what proved to be the short-lived union of Holland and Belgium. Of the Dutch colonies captured during war, only the *Cape of Good Hope was retained. Britain tried in vain to assist the Dutch in their defence of the East Indies against Japan in 1942, but contributed to the short-lived restoration of their colonial rule after 1945. CJB

Holles, Denzil (1599–1680). Holles, a parliamentarian, achieved notoriety on 2 May 1629 when, acting in concert with *Eliot, he held down the Commons' Speaker. Punished by a brief spell in prison, he was re-elected to Parliament in 1640. Though included by Charles I among the five members threatened with impeachment in January 1642, Holles advocated a negotiated settlement. This brought him into collision with the army, and in December 1648 he fled to France. *Cromwell permitted him to return to England in 1654, but he took no part in political life until the restoration of Charles II, who made him a baron. His increasing distrust of Charles's catholic tendencies drew him into opposition, but he rejected the call to exclude James, duke of York, from the succession. In 1680 as in 1640 what Holles wanted was a law-abiding, unequivocally protestant king, but he died before finding one. RL

Holst, Gustav (1874–1934). Of German/Swedish ancestry (Gustavus Theodore von Holst), he was one of the most original English composers of his day and an influential teacher, particularly of amateurs. Holst studied composition with *Stanford at London's *Royal College of Music alongside his lifelong friend *Vaughan Williams, with whom he shared a passionate interest in folk-song. Other influences included plainsong and Hindu culture, the latter apparent in his own translations of Sanskrit texts for the *Choral Hymns* *from the Rig Veda* (four groups, 1908–12) and in his libretto for the much underrated chamber opera *Sāvitri* (1908–9, first performed 1916). The sparse economy of his later works, together with their adventurous harmonies and use of bi-tonality, was regarded by many contemporaries as unnecessarily cerebral. *The Planets* (1914–16, first performed 1919), however, was an immediate and lasting success, not least for its masterly orchestration, the pounding 5/4 rhythms of 'Mars', and the haunting female voices in the final movement 'Neptune'. ECr

Holt, John (1642–1710). Holt was the son of a serjeant at law, who enrolled him at Gray's Inn at the age of 10. After a riotous year at Oxford, he was called to the bar in 1663. He showed his independence and fearlessness in state trials by defending Pilkington and others in 1675 and the 'popish lords' in 1679. In 1686 he became recorder of London and was subsequently knighted and received the coif as king's serjeant, but resigned after refusing to condemn to death a soldier who deserted in peacetime. After the flight of James II he was returned to the 1689 Convention Parliament and in that year he was appointed chief justice of King's Bench, which office he filled for 21 years. His judgments were famous, especially in the case of the *Aylesbury voters (1703–4). He also had an important influence on the development of commercial law. MM

'Holy Alliance' was the derisive name given to the declaration at Paris in September 1815 by Alexander I of Russia, Frederick William III of Prussia, and Francis I of Austria that they would govern and collaborate in accordance with Christian principles. The driving spirit was the tsar in the midst of a devout phase. Orthodox, protestants, and catholics should bury their differences and the other European monarchs (except the sultan) were invited to adhere. Britain, pleading her constitutional position, did not sign, though the prince regent expressed personal approval. *Castlereagh, then foreign secretary, dismissed it privately as 'a piece of sublime mysticism and nonsense', but defended it publicly in the Commons in February 1816 against *Brougham, who denounced it as a mask for autocracy and pointed out that the same three powers had preceded their partition of Poland in 1793 with a similar declaration of high principle. Castlereagh replied that 'it was certainly couched in language unusual in diplomatic documents but should be regarded solely as a pledge of peace'. No mechanism was included in the declaration and disagreements between the signatories soon appeared. JAC

Holyoake, George Jacob (1817–1906). Secularist, Liberal journalist, and co-operator. Born in Birmingham, the son of an artisan, he entered radical politics as an *Owenite socialist lecturer in 1840 and gained early notoriety when imprisoned for blasphemy in 1842–3. He edited a number of papers in support of socialism, atheism, and republicanism, notably the *Reasoner* (1846–61), and was last secretary of the chartist National Charter Association in 1852. In the 1850s he rallied the scattered forces of radical free thought under the name of *secularism, but was a poor public speaker and lost the leadership to Charles *Bradlaugh in the 1860s. His influence came as a writer, journalist, and political lobbyist. In later life he was closely associated with propaganda for the *Co-operative movement, and advocated co-partnership schemes, supported Gladstonian Liberalism, and in 1899 was first chairman of the Rationalist Press Association. ER

Holyrood (Edinburgh). The palace of Holyroodhouse, with Holyrood abbey in its grounds, stands at the foot of the Canongate in the Old Town of Edinburgh, in the lee of Arthur's Seat. Holyrood abbey was built for *Augustinian canons, and the ruins of its 12th- and 13th-cent. nave have inspired many travellers, including Felix Mendelssohn on his Scottish tour in 1829. The palace of Holyroodhouse, the official residence in Scotland of the reigning monarch, was started in the reign of James IV of Scotland and extended by James V. In 1671–9 it was enlarged and remodelled for Charles II to the designs of Sir William Bruce (*c.*1630–1710), assisted by Robert Mylne (1633–1711), the king's master mason. It is set around the four sides of a courtyard, and although the interiors are in an Anglo-Dutch style, the character of the exteriors is French. After a period of change and neglect, royalty came back to Holyroodhouse in 1745 in the person of Prince Charles Edward *Stuart (Bonnie Prince Charlie), but it was not until after George IV's visit in 1822 that it was rejuvenated. Improvements were carried out 1824–35 by the architect Robert Reid (1774–1856), and subsequent alterations by Queen Victoria completed the transformation of Holyroodhouse from a Restoration to a Victorian palace. PW

homage was the formal and public acknowledgement by a vassal of his allegiance and obligations to a lord of whom he held land or whose overlordship he accepted. Thus English kings paid homage, albeit usually reluctantly, to the kings of France for their tenure of *Aquitaine, and in turn claimed homage from Welsh princes and Scottish kings. Simple homage accepted that the land was held of a lord but did not oblige the vassal to pay the full range of feudal services. Liege homage involved the vassal admitting his obligation to pay all services, including the provision of military assistance. By making an act of homage, the vassal's own rights were deemed to be confirmed by his lord. The ceremony of homage involved the vassal kneeling before his lord, the clasping of hands, the uttering of certain key words which acknowledged lordship, and the kissing which symbolized accord. An oath of *fealty might also be paid. In theory the reciprocal bond created by an act of homage lasted for the lifetime of both parties but was broken if either failed to maintain his side of the agreement. Homage by the peers of the realm remains part of the *coronation service. AC

Home, Sir Alec Douglas-Home, 14th earl of [S] (1903–95). Prime minister. Douglas-Home succeeded to the earldom in 1951 but relinquished it in 1963 to re-enter the Commons as prime minister, in succession to Harold *Macmillan. In 1974 he returned to the House of Lords as Lord Home of the Hirsel. He was first elected in 1931 and served as private secretary to Neville *Chamberlain (1937–40), minister of state at the Scottish Office (1951–5), Commonwealth secretary (1955–60), and foreign secretary (1960–3). He also served as deputy leader (1956–7), then leader of the House of Lords and lord president of the council (1959–60). Between 1964 and 1965 he was leader of the opposition.

As foreign secretary Lord Home was a convinced anti-communist. He had spent the years 1940–2 flat on his back as a result of an injury and had read widely on current affairs. In particular, he had studied the theory and practice of communism and retained a deep suspicion and hostility towards the Soviets. Nor was he worried about nuclear weapons, telling an audience in April 1963: 'The great advantage of the nuclear bomb is that at last ordinary decent men have been given a weapon which can stop the wicked from achieving their ends by war.' On the other hand, he was deeply involved in the negotiations which led to the Test Ban treaty that same year.

An immensely sincere and straightforward figure, he appeared to be almost out of touch with political realities as prime minister. A poor public speaker and television performer (he confessed to 'counting with matchsticks' during a TV discussion on economics), he was unfortunate to encounter Harold *Wilson's brilliance as leader of the opposition. His upper-class, 'grouse moor' image was another political drawback, while the refusal of both Iain Macleod and Enoch *Powell to serve under him undermined his political credibility. They objected to the way in which Sir Alec had emerged as prime minister, believing that the cabinet favourite for the job, R. A. *Butler, should have become premier. Both believed that Sir Alec had ruled himself out as a candidate. Yet, as Macleod was to write in a famous article in the *Spectator*, the 'magic circle' of Tory grandees had manœuvred Sir Alec into the job. It was a charge which the new prime minister deeply resented. He also clearly resented the attacks on his upbringing. In a famous speech, he pointed out that if he was the 14th earl of Home, Mr Wilson was 'the fourteenth Mr Wilson'.

None the less, after a year of almost non-stop electioneering, Sir Alec, who concentrated on foreign and defence affairs, lost the 1964 election to Labour by the most slender of margins. Given the legacy of economic problems and scandals he had inherited from Macmillan, this was no small testament to his character. The British public clearly recognized him as a 'true gent', someone who could be trusted, but doubted his competence to modernize the economy or accept social change.

Given the controversy aroused by the way in which he had become prime minister, given that the queen could not choose a Tory leader while the party was in opposition, and given the need for a new leader after the party's defeat, Sir Alec arranged that his successor as party leader should be elected. This turned out to be Edward *Heath under whom he served as foreign secretary between 1970 and 1974. Relations between them were smooth, unlike those between Heath and his successor a decade later. As foreign secretary, Sir Alec was one of those who helped take Britain into the Common Market in 1973. All in all, he was a decent, if not a notably successful, political figure. AS

Home, John (1722–1808). Scottish dramatist and man of letters. Home was the author of *Douglas: A Tragedy* (1756), one of the most popular plays of the age with one of Sarah *Siddons's favourite parts. It also encouraged a Scottish fan to yell, 'Whaur's yer Wullie Shakespeare noo?' at the first London performance. Born in Leith, educated for the kirk, Home fought for the government during the '45. A member of the moderate wing of the kirk, he was greatly distrusted by the orthodox. One of *Bute's Scottish coterie of advisers and a royal pensioner, he was an active campaigner for a Scottish militia and a reasonably prolific playwright, who never managed to repeat the success of *Douglas*. His last work, a *History of the Rebellion of 1745*, lacks the panache and historical acumen one might have expected of a leading member of the Edinburgh literati. Home was a gregarious man who lived well and failed to live up to expectations. NTP

Home Guard. A volunteer organization founded by Anthony *Eden, the secretary of state for war, in May 1940. Originally called the Local Defence Volunteers, its task was to assist in the defence of Britain against a possible German invasion. When this threat had diminished, it manned anti-aircraft guns and coastal defences. By 1943 over 2 million men served in the Home Guard in their spare time. It was composed of civilians exempt from military service because of their age or occupation. During their first year in operation they possessed few weapons, often parading with broom handles instead of rifles. Nevertheless they acted as a boost to British morale. The Home Guard was disbanded on 31 December 1944 but was immortalized in the television series *Dad's Army*. RAS

Home Office. Until 1782 the two secretaries of state divided their responsibilities into southern and northern Europe, dealing with the catholic and protestant powers. Domestic duties needed little attention: the justices of the peace looked after most problems of law and order and the secretary at war was at hand if troops needed to be called in. In 1782, when the Rockinghams took office, a new division was agreed: one secretary took domestic and colonial affairs, the other foreign affairs. In 1801 the secretary of state for war took on the colonies, leaving the home secretary free to concentrate on domestic matters. The first home secretary, Lord *Shelburne, had two under-secretaries, a chief clerk, and ten other civil servants. But in the 19th cent. business increased dramatically as the office picked up responsibility for aliens, prisons, and police supervision. In 1833 the Home Secretary was empowered to appoint factory inspectors. The marked increase in the number of lobbies and protest movements meant difficult decisions about permitting or banning meetings and marches: Spencer Walpole was forced to resign in 1866 over his handling of the *Hyde Park reform riots. Another area of delicacy was in advising the monarch on the prerogative of mercy, especially before the abolition of capital punishment. By the 20th cent. the post of home secretary had become one of the most senior and difficult in the government. Until 1885 the home secretary was responsible for Scotland; then a secretary for Scotland was appointed, whose office included a home department. JAC

Home Rule. See IRISH HOME RULE.

Homildon Hill, battle of, 1402. The clash at *Otterburn in 1388 was followed by a ten-year truce on the Anglo-Scottish border. In June 1402 *Hotspur and March got the better of a small skirmish at Nisbet Moor, in Berwickshire. *Glyndŵr's rising in Wales gave the Scots a chance of revenge and in September 1402 a large force under *Douglas pillaged Northumberland. Hotspur cut off their retreat near Wooler, and Douglas fought at Homildon Hill. The Scots were badly deployed, the English archers kept up a hail of fire, and Douglas was captured. JAC

Hong Kong island, which possesses the only safe deep-water anchorage between Shanghai and Haiphong, was used by the British as a staging-post for the opium trade and was taken by them as a free port during the *Opium War (1839–42). Their occupancy was ratified by the treaty of *Nanking. In 1860 the Kowloon peninsula was added to the port and in 1898 the New Territories were received from China on a 99-year lease. At its fullest extent, the colony reached 398 square miles. It developed as a commercial entrepôt and in 1917 was granted letters patent to be administered by a governor, and executive and legislative councils. Growth was particularly rapid during the 1930s when many Chinese fled the civil wars and Japanese invasion on the mainland and the population doubled to 1.6 million. Hong Kong itself surrendered to the Japanese on Christmas Day 1941 and was not liberated until 30 August 1945. During the 1960s, the colony became a major manufacturing centre and its population further expanded, reaching over 4 million in 1991. The lease for the New Territories ended in 1997, whereupon the whole colony reverted to the People's Republic of China. DAW

Honorius (d. 653). Archbishop of Canterbury. Honorius was the fifth and last of the archbishops to be appointed from the missionaries dispatched to convert the Anglo-Saxons by Pope Gregory the Great. Little is known of Honorius' activities, but *Bede reproduced a letter sent to him by Pope Honorius after his appointment and recorded support he provided for the evangelization of the East Angles. Following his death in 653 there was an interregnum of eighteen months before the appointment of the West Saxon *Deusdedit. Honorius was buried at Canterbury and subsequently revered as a saint. BAEY

Honours of Scotland. The Scottish crown jewels, consisting of a sceptre given to James IV (1488–1513) by Pope Alexander VI (1494), a sword from Pope Julius II (1507), and a crown made for James V (1513–42) in 1540. Representing royal authority, following the Union of the crowns (1603) they came strongly to symbolize Scotland's nationhood, because of an absentee monarchy. Buried in Kinneff kirk (1652–60) to avoid Oliver *Cromwell's attentions, the Honours were feared lost following the Union (1707). They were found hidden in Edinburgh castle by Sir Walter *Scott (1818), and remain there today. RJT

honours system. Although the honours system is routinely denounced every January and June, when awards are published, there is, in fact, very little system. Like many things, it is a patchwork of accretions over the centuries. Consequently it reflects, to a considerable extent, the political evolution of the nation, from governing monarchy, through oligarchy and aristocracy, to parliamentary democracy. At each stage those who wield power award honours to themselves and their friends. The slow increase in the influence of ordinary people, as they have been brought into the political system, may be traced in the way in which, once totally excluded from honours, they are now accorded recognition as postmen, traffic wardens, and lollipop ladies. The declining power of the monarchy may also be traced as monarchs fought, with little success, to retain control of honours, sometimes refusing recommendations, sometimes creating new honours out of reach of the prime minister of the day.

In the early Middle Ages the highest honours were reserved for the royal family and their immediate favourites. The Order of the *Garter, founded by Edward III in 1348, was jealously restricted: *Pitt, *Peel, and *Gladstone were never included, and *Disraeli only after he had become earl of Beaconsfield. The Scottish Order of the *Thistle, refounded by James II, was restricted to peers until 1876 when Sir William Stirling-Maxwell, a mere baronet, was admitted. The knights of St Patrick, instituted by George III in 1783, were equally exclusive. Particular favourites might receive rapid advancement: Edward II made his friend *Gaveston earl of Cornwall in 1307 to the indignation of the rest of the nobility; Richard II created Michael de la *Pole earl of Suffolk in 1385. These were rare instances. The title of duke, highest in the land, was carefully restricted. Between 1572 and 1603 there were no English dukes at all, and between 1553 and 1660 the title was given to only one non-royal, Charles I's favourite *Buckingham. Titles were, of course, augmented by other honours—lavish grants of estates (particularly at the expense of vanquished opponents), places of profit at court, functions at the coronation ceremony. Though there were always complaints that unworthy persons were being honoured, the circle remained very small indeed. At the end of Henry VII's reign, there were no more than 44 peers, and by 1603 it had increased only to 55.

The process of extending honours, which began in the 17th cent., had a number of causes. The penury of the Stuarts forced them to sell honours, and in addition to a sharp increase in titles, new orders of baronetcies—hereditary knights—were introduced. The victory of the nobility in 1688 opened the gates for Whig grandees to be promoted—no fewer than 23 were created dukes between 1688 and 1720. The parliamentary system meant that, more than ever, honours became an indispensable part of government, particularly since the crown had far fewer estates to give away. Promotions in the peerage eked out creations. Superannuated politicians like Sir Thomas Robinson were pacified by peerages, borough patrons like Sir James Lowther bought over. It was a powerful blow to the Fox–North coalition in 1783 when George III made it clear that he would not grant peerages at its request, since it advertised that supporting the coalition was not the way to win royal favour. The award of honours for conspicuous gallantry came rather late, with the *Victoria Cross during the Crimean War. The Order of *Merit in 1902 was an attempt to create an order for men of letters that the politicians would not seize, but even then George V failed to carry a nomination against Lloyd George's disapproval. The great breakthrough for democracy came in 1917 with the establishment of the Order of the *British Empire—significantly at the same time that the dynasty changed its name to *Windsor to get closer to the people. Though the order was still ranked, it reached further into the people than ever before, and included substantial numbers of women. Even so, there was unease among some when the *Beatles were given an MBE in 1965. Since, in an egalitarian society, there are few opportunities to wear crosses and ribands, the Order of the British Empire has begun to sell ties.

There is considerable debate about the nature and role of honours in a democratic society. The present confusion may be illustrated with reference to the peerage. By origin peerages were not necessarily hereditary and it was an early object of noble ambition to make them so. Eventually the principle was established and when in 1856 the crown attempted to create life peerages for judges, they were declared unlawful. By the time life peerages were brought in in 1958, governments had lost the confidence to recommend hereditary titles. None were created until William Whitelaw was made a viscount on Mrs *Thatcher's advice in 1983. How long the royal prerogative to create hereditary peers can remain valid if not employed is an interesting question.
JAC

Hood, Alexander (1726–1814). Admiral. The younger brother of Samuel *Hood, Alexander had an active naval career of 54 years, first commissioned in 1746 and still commanding at the blockade of Brest in 1800. In 1755 he served under Saunders in North America, in 1759 was at *Quiberon Bay with *Hawke, and in 1761, off Belle Île, retook the *Warwick* from the French in a fierce contest. Made treasurer of Greenwich in 1766, he nurtured his relations with the Chatham family. He served under Keppel at Ushant in 1778, attained knighthood and admiral rank, and took part in the second relief of Gibraltar in 1782. In 1794, at the Glorious First of June action, he was second in command to *Howe, and was subsequently created Lord Bridport in the Irish peerage. Made a British peer in 1796 and a viscount in 1800 he commanded the Channel fleet for the rest of his active service and was at Portsmouth during the Spithead mutiny. Hood was scorchingly critical of the Admiralty's mishandling of the mutiny and his part in the peaceful resolution may remain underestimated. Through the marriage of his daughter to *Nelson's elder brother, the 1st Earl Nelson, the Sicilian dukedom of Brontë passed to the Bridports.
DDA

Hood, Samuel (1724–1816). Admiral. Born of Dorset clerical stock, Hood and his brother Alexander entered the navy at the same time and prospered under the patronage of the Lyttelton family and its relatives the Grenvilles and Pitts. Given a commission in 1746, Hood served throughout the Seven Years War and was present at *Quiberon Bay in 1759. In 1767, still a captain, he was appointed commander-in-chief in North America; subsequently from 1771 to 1780 he was stationed at Portsmouth, where, in 1778, George III entrusted to him the naval grounding of the future William IV. A baronet (1778) and rear-admiral (1780), Hood was *Rodney's second at the battle of the *Saints (April 1782), and was severely critical of Rodney's failure to pursue the French. An Irish peer in 1782, he was returned to Parliament in 1784 for Westminster after a celebrated and fierce contest. Ten years later he conducted, with considerable address, the combined operations which led to the capture of Toulon. Raised to a British viscountcy in 1796, Samuel Hood stood high in the navy's esteem and was outspoken about the primitive conditions under which the lower deck served.
DDA

Hooke, Robert (1635–1703). Hooke made the microscope well known as a scientific instrument, publishing his *Micrographia* in 1665. Its splendid engraving of the flea made a tremendous impression, and the book opened up a new world below the level of naked-eye observation. Previously, Hooke had worked with Robert *Boyle on the air pump, and in 1662 had been appointed curator to the *Royal Society, with the duty of performing experiments at the meetings. He was referee of Isaac *Newton's first optical paper, and his critical comments made Newton his enemy. Hooke lectured on earthquakes, worked on pendulum clocks, toyed with something like a wave theory of light, and was a great, versatile, and controversial figure in the *scientific revolution in England.
DK

Hooker, Richard (1554–1600). Theologian and political theorist. Educated at Oxford, Hooker became a fellow of Corpus Christi College and master of the Temple before 'retiring' to a country living to write his masterly defence of the Elizabethan system of government *The *Laws of Ecclesiastical Polity.* His intention was to show how in England there was an essential unity between church and state, which were different aspects of a single community, both subject to the authority of the monarch. However, Hooker insisted that the monarch's authority, though supreme, was not arbitrary. It was limited both by being founded on the consent of the people, and by being subject to the rule of law, a body of civil and ecclesiastical statutes originating in Parliament. In this work, Hooker supplied the most effective statement of the theoretical foundations of Anglicanism that has ever been written, and greatly influenced the ideas of later political theorists such as John *Locke and Edmund *Burke.
TSG

hooliganism is public behaviour, usually by a group of young men, which the supporters of law and order find threatening and disruptive. The term came into use at the end of the 19th cent. when a gang in south-east London, allegedly drawn from Irish immigrants, destroyed much property. Their conduct made no explicit political and social point, which was in some ways more disturbing.

Such rowdy, ruffianly, and apparently motiveless violence has a much longer history than the term hooligan. In

*Pepys's day, gangs of youths, known successively as Hectors, Scourers, and Mohawks, roamed the streets, leering at young ladies and pushing old gentlemen. In 1838 the younger members of the hunting fraternity at Melton Mowbray, a quiet provincial town, 'painted the town red'. Public concern at this behaviour spurts up at intervals. In the 1950s there was considerable anxiety about Teddy Boys, though they were in fact little inclined to violence, which would ruin their clothes and disturb their hair styles. They were replaced in the 1960s by Mods and Rockers, who 'beat up' seaside towns on their motor-cycles. Attention then moved to sporting events. Gangs of teenagers at soccer matches, or on their way to and from events, threw missiles, fought running battles with rival supporters, relieved themselves in front gardens, and became a source of considerable irritation to football clubs, the police, and owners of property near football grounds. The phenomenon became sufficiently disturbing during the 1970s to attract research into the causes of such behaviour and the means of effective control. It is not likely that the phenomenon will be totally eradicated in the 21st cent., and may perhaps be regarded as the price society pays for not sending its young men to be killed every thirty years. IJEK; JAC

Hooper, John (d. 1555). Bishop of Gloucester and Worcester. Born in Somerset and educated at Oxford, Hooper probably took Cistercian vows at Gloucester. After the *dissolution he returned to Oxford to study reformed theology, but fled abroad in disguise and eventually settled in Zurich (1547–9), where he knew the reformer Bullinger. A radical extremist of 'blazing sincerity' and 'intolerable obstinacy', too militant for *Cranmer, he returned to London as Protector *Somerset's chaplain. When offered the see of Gloucester (1550), his disagreement with Cranmer over vestments led to brief imprisonment before he agreed to consecration fully robed (1551). A zealous reforming bishop, he set to work, but with the merger of Gloucester and Worcester (1552) he was retitled bishop of Worcester. In Mary's reign he was imprisoned, deprived (1554), and burned at Gloucester. His actions and writings were a potent force in spreading puritanism in England. WMM

Hopton, Sir Ralph (1596–1652). One of the most successful royalist commanders during the Civil War, Hopton was given a barony in 1643. Educated at Lincoln College, Oxford, he had fought in Bohemia for the protestants during the Thirty Years War. In the *Long Parliament, he initially opposed the king, voting for *Strafford's attainder in 1641. The following year he joined the royalist cause, having on his battle standard the motto 'I will strive to serve my sovereign king.' A west countryman by birth, he spent almost all his time campaigning in that region. He had a good record of success, winning at *Braddock Down (January 1643), *Stratton (May 1643), *Lansdowne (July 1643, where he was badly wounded), *Roundway Down (July 1643), before being beaten by his old friend and opponent *Waller at *Cheriton in March 1644. Beaten again by *Fairfax at *Torrington (February 1646), he was forced to capitulate at Truro in March and went into exile. *Clarendon called him 'the soldiers' darling . . . the soul of that army'. IJG

Horner, Francis (1778–1817). As *Bagehot pointed out in 'The First Edinburgh Reviewers', Horner had an influence and standing out of all proportion to his career or achievements. It was not just a case of the Whigs buttering up each other: tributes at his death came from all sides of the House. Born and educated in Edinburgh, he was called to the bar in 1800. Two years later he joined *Jeffrey and *Smith in launching the **Edinburgh Review* as a radical Whig journal. He was brought into Parliament in 1806 and made a reputation as a financial expert, chairing an important committee on bullion. After a diffident start, he became a useful and experienced member of the Whig opposition, speaking particularly against the Corn Laws and in favour of catholic relief. He left England at the end of 1816 in search of better health and died in Italy aged 38. Smith related how, during a previous illness, Horner was told to read amusing books: on searching his library it appeared he had no amusing books—the nearest being *The India Trader's Complete Guide.* JAC

Horne Tooke, John (1736–1812). A man of many parts (clergyman, philologist, conversationalist, and wit) who carried the radicalism of the 1760s into the early 19th cent. His legal and organizational talents were first apparent in his vigorous championing of *Wilkes. His subsequent support for the American colonists led to a prison sentence. In 1781 he joined the *Society for Constitutional Information, which he soon dominated; and in 1792 assisted in the formation of the London *Corresponding Society. He was tried for high treason in 1794 and acquitted. Although twice unsuccessful, his contest of the Westminster elections helped to prepare the way for the radical triumphs of 1807. Tooke's radicalism, like that of *Cartwright and others, was based on belief in an ancient constitution which had become corrupted, thus denying the traditional rights and freedoms of Englishmen. JFCH

horse-racing consists of flat racing or jumping, 'over the sticks'. Racing became popular during the 16th cent. and the first race-course with an annual fixture was established on the Roodee at Chester in 1540. Racing received support from successive monarchs. James I established a hunting stable at Newmarket where he bred horses and Charles I offered a gold cup as a prize for a race in 1634. Noblemen founded stables and became interested in breeding thoroughbred racehorses. Old Bald Meg (*c.*1659) is the oldest recorded mare in the *General Studbook* and it is argued that every thoroughbred has descended from her.

Racing expanded with courses springing up at Doncaster (1595), York (1709), Ascot (1711), Epsom (1730), Goodwood (1801), and Aintree (1827). In 1750 the Jockey Club was founded to regulate the sport. The first Racing Calendar was introduced in 1773 and stud books and jockeys' colours followed. Lord George *Bentinck (1802–48), an influential horse breeder-owner, devised the flag start, race card, paddock parade, and much of modern race-course practice. Highlights of the flat season include the *Derby, Oaks, and St Leger.

Steeple-chasing derived from horses racing each other cross-country to the nearest church steeple. The concept of a course with artificial fences originated at the Newmarket Craven meeting in 1794. A Grand Annual Steeplechase began at Cheltenham around 1815. In 1866 the Grand National Hunt Steeplechase Committee was formed to establish rules and the first Calendar appeared in 1867. It became the National Hunt Committee in 1889 and merged with the Jockey Club eighty years later. Highlights include the *Grand National and the *Cheltenham Gold Cup.

Horse-racing has become synonymous with betting. The on-course Totalizator introduced in 1929 and the Horserace Betting Levy Board founded in 1961 both aimed to distribute betting revenue for the good of the sport. A Joint Racing Board was established in 1968 to facilitate policy discussion between the Turf Authorities and the Levy Board. RAS

hosiery trade. The trade had its origins in antiquity and remained a handicraft industry until the 16th cent. when William Lee, a Nottinghamshire clergyman, invented the framework-knitting machine. Many regions of the British Isles had maintained or developed the making of specialized hand-knitted wear, not just for family use but for sale elsewhere. The widespread use of frames had developed by the later 17th cent. making use of long staple wool yarns. The east midland counties of Leicestershire and Nottinghamshire became centres for framework-knitting during the 18th cent. The processes took place in the homes of the workers. Working with frames required light as well as space and so houses were built with large windows in the upper storey. Specialized products included stockings, gloves, caps, and many other types of garment. To a considerable extent, then as now, the prosperity of the industry was determined by the dictates of fashion.

Steam-powered frames were developed only in the second half of the 19th cent., accompanied by other inventions such as William Cotton's patents of 1864 which made possible the knitting of fully fashioned garments. The industry still plays a vital role in the economy of the east midlands, producing a great diversity of textiles. The sophistication of modern machines includes the use of computers to design and control production, superseding Jacquard controls. An important innovation of the 1970s was the lock-stitch, invented by Gordon Wray, which enabled new ways of processing and using textiles.

Until the 19th cent. wool fibres dominated knitting but other textile fibres came into use. In the later 20th cent. not only did man-made fibres for garments become common, but industrial uses of knitting processes utilized other materials such as fibre glass.

It was usual practice for the finishing trades of the bleachers and dyers to develop alongside hosiery. Similarly suppliers of frames and needles became established in the same geographical areas. IJEK

Hospitallers. Originally established at the end of the 11th cent. to care for Jerusalem pilgrims, following the success of the First Crusade the Hospitallers' role expanded, with papal support, to include care of the sick and armed protection of pilgrims. They followed the *Augustinian rule, and were divided into three groups, the knights, the infirmarians, and the chaplains. During the 12th cent. the order spread rapidly both in the crusading states and in western Europe. The first English priory was founded *c.*1144 at Clerkenwell and other smaller preceptories or commanderies followed, administering the order's estates, training its knights, and dispensing hospitality. Following the suppression of the *Templars (1312) most of their possessions passed to the Hospitallers, whose headquarters had been transferred to Rhodes in 1309 following the fall of *Acre (1291). After the Turkish capture of Rhodes (1522) the order moved to Malta until the island's capture by Napoleon. Its English properties were confiscated in 1540. BJG

hospitals. Since Christian tradition emphasized care for one's neighbours rather than their isolation because of disease, monastic infirmaries functioned alongside lay endowments founded on earth to buy grace in heaven; medieval hospices provided care and hospitality for the aged, infirm, and travellers, and were not necessarily devoted just to the sick. The *dissolution of the monasteries (1538–40) not only ended hospital building in England for almost two centuries but transferred responsibility for much health care from the church to secular hands. St Bartholomew's, St Thomas's, and Bethlem were sold to the city of London, which claimed that the sick poor would suffer if the hospitals ceased to exist but also had regard to their endowments. Despite subsequent growth in London's population, however, it still had only two hospitals of significant size.

With expansion of both population and the middle classes in the 18th cent. came a surge of new establishments, initially in the older towns, then the manufacturing centres. The Westminster was established in 1719, to be followed by Guy's (1721) and St George's (1733); Edinburgh Royal Infirmary (1729) was deliberately planned to accommodate students. Still set in the context of charity, social rather than medical criteria determined admission to these voluntary hospitals. Benefactors, whose names were published, were given rights to admit patients according to their contribution, and often sought to exclude the socially 'undeserving' (drunkards and prostitutes). Incurables, fever cases, and venereal patients were excluded from the general hospitals and sent to peripheral town sites such as lock hospitals. Treatment was free, but patients had to conform to strict rules and assist when convalescent. As towns grew, the number and size of hospitals increased, while less-established practitioners set up new institutions such as dispensaries. Entrepreneurs challenged traditional patterns with specialized establishments (Royal National Orthopaedic Hospital, Moorfields Eye Hospital), supported by new explanations of disease; the initial hostility of the general hospitals lessened as they themselves set up specialist departments.

The introduction of general anaesthesia in the 1840s increased the practice and scope of surgery, but high infection rates and deaths from 'hospital diseases' undermined confidence; the medical profession, unsurprisingly, opposed any ideas of hospital disbandment in order to reduce mortality. Florence *Nightingale's advocacy of good ventilation led to pavilion-plan buildings on elevated sites, but *Lister's antiseptic approach had more impact in transforming both surgery and hospitals. As medical science progressed, hospital complexity was promoted by an increasing range of diagnostic sciences and techniques such as bacteriology, pathology, and radiology. Hospitals themselves began to lose their charity status and were more attractive: patient demand came increasingly from the better off, workhouse infirmaries took away the poorest patients, whilst the image of nursing was being transformed. Cottage hospitals, established for rural patients, gave the general practitioner access to beds as well as retaining fees that would otherwise have been lost, insurance schemes increased entitlement to admission, while nursing-homes were essentially small private hospitals for the middle classes. Playing a central role in health care by the 1920s, hospitals were under the firm control of the medical staff, but developed financial crises as staffing and medical technology costs rose. The idea of scientific management, to increase institutional efficiency, had been introduced in the late 19th cent., but change was slow.

Despite reluctance at being taken into state service, hospitals formed an important arm of the newly formed *National Health Service in 1948, emphasis on their role having continued as recent changes seek to establish an internal market again and move more treatment back into the community. Interventionist and invasive, but now perceived as essential centres for medical education and advances, and prestigious for ambitious staff, hospitals are increasingly criticized and very costly, but generally remain high in public regard, and are a popular subject for television drama and documentaries. ASH

hotels are largely a 19th-cent. development. Until the railway age, travellers stayed mainly at inns and those who visited seaside resorts rented rooms or houses. What hotels existed were small family businesses. But the advantages of a hotel attached to a railway station were obvious and the London and Birmingham railway built one at its Euston terminus in 1839. The Great Western hotel at Paddington in 1852 was on a much grander scale and the Midland railway's hotel at St Pancras in 1873 bigger still. Rail travel also opened up the seaside resorts: Scarborough's Grand hotel was built in 1867. The first large London hotel not owned by a railway was the Westminster Palace hotel in 1860. There followed a period of intense competition, hotels competing with distinguished chefs, palm courts, turkish baths, and smart liveried staff. The Grand hotel in Northumberland Avenue in 1881 allowed non-residents to dine. The Savoy was built in 1903–4, the Ritz 1903–6, the Hotel Russell 1907–11, the Dorchester 1930. Post-Second World War hotels have clustered round airports and motorways, and the elaborate dining-rooms have given way to conference suites. Railway hotels are for connoisseurs of departed grandeur. JAC

Hotspur. See PERCY, HENRY.

housecarls were the immediate bodyguard of Danish and late Saxon kings, the nucleus of the army. They were introduced by *Cnut and were similar to Saxon thegns. They were men of some rank, with a strong code of honour and service. Though by 1066 they did not necessarily reside at court, they were ready at short notice. *Harold's housecarls at Hastings are said to have died in heaps around their fallen king. Modern scholarship has questioned the extent to which the housecarls formed an élite corps. JAC

household. Originally not merely the domestic residence of the monarch but the place from which the kingdom was governed. No very rigid distinction was made between its different functions. But as administration grew more complex and requests for justice more common, offices became more specialized and departments were hived off to undertake particular tasks. By the time of the *Constitutio domus regis* in 1135, there were many separate officers, with the chancellor at the head, followed by the *treasurer, *lord high steward, *chamberlain, *butler, and *constable, down to the turnspits, carters, scullions, and watchmen. Early to develop was the *chamber, which dealt with revenue, and out of which evolved the *Exchequer and the courts of law. The *Chancery also developed in England since the size of the kingdom meant more need for writs and instructions, which the scriptorium or secretariat provided. At first the whole household moved from place to place, with only a skeleton staff left behind: when the king was absent in Normandy officers left in England had to possess some discretionary authority. The peripatetic nature of the household became increasingly inconvenient and in clause 17 of *Magna Carta in 1215 it was declared that *common pleas would be heard in one place. At length the household and its offshoots settled at Westminster, with other royal palaces in reasonable proximity. A permanent headquarters allowed more comfort and more ceremonial and the household developed into the *court. JAC

households. The study of British households from census-type listings was pioneered by Peter Laslett and his colleagues at the Cambridge Population Group in the 1960s, and was essentially designed to test widely held assumptions about the nature of family life in the past. It was supposed that most people in the past had lived in large households, with several generations under the same roof, often containing relatives. In practice, mean household size was relatively small. The average size of household in England before 1750 was just 4.44 persons, rising to 4.81 in the following 70 years. It fell thereafter and by the end of the Second World War was just 3.67 persons. Households in the 1990s are historically the smallest they have ever been, at only 2.4 persons. Laslett's analysis of household listings, dating from the 16th cent. to 1820, demonstrated that they were also relatively simple in their structure. The predominant form was *nuclear,* that is they consisted of one married couple, with or without children. Relatives other than unmarried children were found in only about 11 per cent of households, and only a handful, some 4 per cent, consisted of more than one married couple. Although some historians disagree and comparable data is lacking, most historians think that this form of household structure has predominated since at least the early medieval period.

The experience of living in households in the past differed from that of today in important respects. To begin with, they frequently contained servants and lodgers. Between 1650 and 1821 between 11 and 14 per cent of the total population were servants (either domestic or working as live-in labourers) and a further 5–6 per cent were lodgers in other people's households. In 1970 just 1 per cent of the population could be so classified. Again, the proportion of households containing relatives was at its greatest in 1947 (when it was three times more common than in the 100 years before 1750), caused largely it seems by the temporary post-war housing shortage, which forced many newly-weds to start married life in a parental household. Living alone has dramatically increased, particularly since 1960. In 1981 those in their 60s and early 70s were five times more likely to live alone than before 1790. There are also some striking similarities. Single parenthood today is only as common as it was in the 16th and 17th cents., although divorce, rather than death, is now the chief cause. JPB

housing refers both to shelter in houses and to the provision of houses. It is the latter which has attracted historians, who have been particularly interested in tracing the provision of accommodation in response to population increases in towns and, above all, in cities.

During the industrial revolution large increases in urban populations occurred because of migrations from the countryside and the reduction of the death rate. Housing was initially left to the open market. The provision of accommodation rested on a balance between the cost of building and what households could afford to spend on rents. Speculative builders often borrowed capital for construction from solicitors, who loaned them the money clients had deposited with them for returns which were said to be 'as safe as houses'. A limited number of houses were built by owner-occupiers who had borrowed money from the newly formed building societies. Not all housing was of good quality and some landlords built cheap and often badly constructed buildings, which rapidly became slums because of overcrowding. These slums attracted the attention of Parliament, municipalities, and social reformers. The sanitary laws of the second half of the 19th cent. stipulated minimum standards for new dwellings. Liverpool corporation erected the first council housing in 1867. However the provision of housing at public expense did not become government policy until the 20th cent. The slum clearance law of 1876 did not require local authorities to rehouse the homeless, although in towns where railways took powers to clear sites for stations and sidings they were compelled to provide alternative new houses elsewhere. Some philanthropic attempts were made to provide good housing for the poor, one of the most active being the Peabody Trust which erected flats in London.

Some industrial developments, for example, coal-mining and some manufacturing using water power, occurred in places where there was no previous settlement. Entrepreneurs provided accommodation for their workers. The quality varied greatly. High standards were adopted by *Arkwright at Belper (Derbys.), in the 1780s and by Peter Greg at Styal (Ches.). In the 19th cent. model housing was provided by several industrialists, for example Titus *Salt at Saltaire, Cadbury at Bournville (Birmingham), and in the 20th cent. Lever Brothers at Port Sunlight on Merseyside.

During the 20th cent. successive governments intervened in housing by making loan funds available to local authorities, by subsidies to builders, and by giving tax concessions to owner-occupiers purchasing their homes through mortgages. Little house-building took place in the First World War and by 1918 there was a great unsatisfied demand. The election slogan of 1918 'Homes Fit for Heroes' proved difficult to translate into reality. Few houses were built under the terms of the Addison Act of 1919 because of high interest rates and shortages of materials. Subsidies for housing became available to local authorities by the Wheatley Act of 1924 and for private enterprise by the Chamberlain Act of 1925. The financial crisis of 1931 ended these forms of assistance. However, since the cost of borrowing money dropped, local authorities and building societies were able to advance mortgages to owner-occupiers during the 1930s.

After the Second World War the housing shortage remained acute for some years because no houses were built during the war and much accommodation had been destroyed by bombing. From 1945 to 1955 the greater part of house-building was undertaken by local authorities which built homes for rent. Between 1955 and 1980, largely because of a change in conditions which were more favourable to borrowing, there was a major shift from rent to owner-occupation. By 1980 owner-occupiers held about two-thirds of housing, most of the rest being in the hands of local authorities. During the 1980s legislation gave tenants of local authorities the option of buying their houses at very advantageous prices so that rented 'council housing' took a declining share of the market. By the late 1980s, owner-occupation, albeit with a rising level of repossession due to mortgage arrears, continued to be the most prevalent pattern of housing. In the rented sector, housing associations emerged as the main providers, their finance coming from the government and mortgage lenders. IJEK

Housman, A. E. (1859–1939). Poet and classicist, whose failure at Oxford only delayed a career taking him to chairs of Latin at London and, in 1911, Cambridge. Labour expended on editions of Juvenal, Lucan, and Manilius made him the leading classical scholar of his generation and a formidable reviewer. His emotional life went into his poetry, *A Shropshire Lad* (1896) and *Last Poems* (1922). Shropshire, over the border from his native Worcestershire, became 'the land of lost content', where the beauty of nature is no defence against betrayal and death. He acknowledged affinities with *Blake and Heine, and his relentless pessimism recalls *Hardy, though expressed with more elegance and wit. His poems have inspired fine musical settings, and his stoic pastorals are some of the most sheerly beautiful in the late Romantic tradition. He is buried at Ludlow. JNRS

Howard, Charles, 2nd Baron Howard of Effingham and 1st earl of Nottingham (*c.*1536–1624). Howard took advantage of his high birth to sustain a long and distinguished career. *Anne Boleyn was his first cousin. He was a grandson of the 2nd duke of *Norfolk, the hero of *Flodden, and son of Lord William *Howard, created 1st Baron Howard of Effingham in 1554: he went on to serve Mary as lord high admiral and Elizabeth as lord chamberlain. In 1563 Charles Howard married a daughter of Lord *Hunsdon, cousin and confidant to Queen Elizabeth: his wife was a lady of the bedchamber for many years. In 1569 he accompanied Hunsdon on the campaign which crushed the northern rebellion and in 1575 was given the Garter. In 1585 he was appointed lord high admiral for life, holding the position until he was 83: he held supreme command when the *Armada was destroyed in 1588. In 1596, with *Essex, he stormed Cadiz to forestall another Armada. The following year he was created earl of Nottingham and served as lord high steward until 1615. He remained in busy employment, acting as commissioner for peace with Spain in 1604 and commissioner to treat with the Scots for a union. Of the great naval action in 1588, he wrote to *Walsingham that the Spaniards were very strong 'yet we pluck their feathers by little and little'. He was accused of being too circumspect, but *Ralegh wrote that Howard was 'better advised than a great many malignant fools that found fault with his demeanour'. In the aftermath of victory he was greatly concerned for the care of his men. JAC

Howard, Charles. See CARLISLE, 1ST EARL OF.

Howard, Ebenezer (1850–1928). Howard, born in London, made a modest living as a shorthand writer and his importance was as a pioneer of the garden city movement. He believed that unrestricted private development of towns must lead to squalor and the communities which he advocated in his book *Garden Cities of Tomorrow* (1898, 1902) were to be owned by trustees, carefully planned, and surrounded by a green belt. He founded the Garden City Association in 1899 and the planning and development of Letchworth in Hertfordshire began in 1903. In 1919 he followed it with the purchase of an estate nearby at Welwyn. The examples had a vast influence on the planning of new towns in Britain and abroad, particularly after the Second World War. Howard spent the last years of his life on the Welwyn estate and was knighted in 1927. JAC

Howard, Henry, 1st earl of Northampton (1540–1614). Howard's father Lord Surrey was executed when he was 7. In Edward VI's reign, he was tutored by John *Foxe, the protestant martyrologist, but at Mary's accession a catholic bishop took over. The indiscretions of his elder brother the 4th duke of *Norfolk blighted his prospects in the 1570s. Howard seems also to have entertained thoughts of a marriage to Mary, queen of Scots, and continued a correspondence with her. He was several times questioned and admitted to catholic sympathies. Not until 1600 did Elizabeth consent to receive him at court. By that time, he was cultivating James VI of Scotland and advising him by correspondence. It paid off handsomely. In 1604 he was created earl of Northampton, given the Garter in 1605, and became lord privy seal in 1608. He joined in the attack upon *Ralegh and was believed to have been involved in the murder of Sir Thomas Overbury in the Tower. Northampton was reputed a man of much learning, but thought to be a flatterer and a schemer. JAC

Howard, John (1726–90). Prison reformer. Howard was born in London and owned a small property at Cardington (Beds.), where he spent the last 30 years of his life. He was an independent in religion, worshipping at the chapel *Bunyan had served, a teetotaller, vegetarian, and a man of austere habits. In 1773 he was appointed sheriff of Bedfordshire and discovered that prisoners who had been acquitted were unable to leave gaol unless they could pay the gaoler's fee. His colleagues on the bench rejected his suggestion that the gaoler should be paid a salary, leading Howard to embark upon an extraordinary life of prison visits throughout the British Isles and ultimately most of Europe. His *State of the Prisons in England and Wales* (1777) exposed the squalor and brutality of many gaols. He died of typhus while on a visit to Russia and was buried there, though a statue was erected to him in St Paul's. Almost single-handedly, Howard placed the question of prison reform on the agenda. JAC

Howard, Thomas, 1st Baron Howard de Walden and earl of Suffolk (1561–1626). Howard's father, the 4th duke of Norfolk, was executed in 1572 when Thomas was 11 for conspiring to rescue Mary, queen of Scots. His mother was heiress to Baron *Audley of Walden, Henry VIII's lord chancellor, and he inherited *Audley End. In 1584 he was restored in blood and four years later was knighted for gallantry against the Armada. He served at sea in the 1590s and was given the Garter in 1597. The same year, when he was believed to be on his death-bed, he was summoned to Parliament as Baron Howard de Walden. He was in favour with James I, who made him earl of Suffolk and employed him as lord chamberlain 1603–14. From 1614 to 1618 he was lord high treasurer. His daughter Frances married the favourite *Somerset and Howard was nearly brought down over the murder of Sir Thomas Overbury. His building programme at Audley End was on a lavish scale and pushed him heavily into debt. In 1619 he was imprisoned in the Tower and fined £30,000 for peculation. Though he was restored to favour in 1620 and the fine reduced, he never recaptured his former influence at court. JAC

Howard, William, 1st Baron Howard of Effingham (*c.*1510–73). Howard was a younger son of Thomas, 2nd duke of *Norfolk, who died in 1524. He was great-uncle to princess Elizabeth. In the 1530s he served as ambassador to Scotland and to France but was in danger in 1542 when his niece *Catherine Howard was executed. Howard was convicted of misprision of treason but pardoned in 1544. In 1552–3 he was governor of Calais. For the last 20 years of his life he held high office continuously as lord high admiral 1553–8, lord chamberlain 1558–72, and lord privy seal 1572–3. He took an active part in repelling *Wyatt from London in 1554, after his half-brother's forces had been badly beaten, and was rewarded by Mary with the Garter and a barony. He gained some displeasure by protecting the Princess Elizabeth, Froude writing that she owed her life to him. On her succession in 1558 he was in high favour. His son Charles commanded the fleet against the Spanish Armada.

JAC

Howe, Sir Geoffrey (b. 1926). Howe served in *Heath's government (1970–4) first as solicitor-general and then as minister for trade and consumer affairs. When the Tories lost the 1974 elections he became opposition spokesman first for social services and then for the economy. In 1979 he became chancellor of the Exchequer under Mrs *Thatcher, before moving to the Foreign Office after the 1983 election. However, his growing antagonism towards the prime minister over the exchange rate mechanism led her to remove him from that post in 1989. He then became leader of the House of Commons before dramatically resigning in 1990. A grey personality whose rhetoric has been likened 'to being savaged by a dead sheep', he will be remembered chiefly for his part in Mrs Thatcher's downfall. As chancellor he succeeded in bringing inflation down from the high level of the Labour government but at the cost of eliminating a large part of the country's manufacturing base.

AS

Howe, Richard (1726–99). Descended through his mother from a half-sister of George I, Howe was commissioned in the navy in 1745, seeing active service through to 1758, when he succeeded his elder brother as 4th viscount in the Irish peerage, becoming also MP for Dartmouth until 1782. He was already known as 'the Sailor's Friend'. Promoted admiral in 1770, Howe's professional standing, influence, and conciliatory disposition saw him given wide powers in 1776 to try to negotiate peace in America. After two indecisive years and lacking the ministerial support he expected, Howe gave up the task in disillusion. Raised to a British peerage in 1782, he relieved Gibraltar that October, and from 1783 to 1788, when he became an earl, was 1st lord of the Admiralty. Imperturbable in demeanour and high professionalism, Howe was notably lacking in lucidity of expression. But his standing as a leader was further enhanced by the *'Glorious First of June' victory (1794), and his reputation proved incalculably important in quelling the *Spithead mutiny in spring 1797, in which year he received the Garter. Howe largely perfected a code of signalling.

DDA

Howe, William (1729–1814). Younger brother of Richard *Howe, William served in the army in Flanders 1747–8, and with distinction in Canada and Cuba 1759–62. Between 1758 and 1780 he was MP for Nottingham, where there was a family interest. Having previously refused to serve in America at the outbreak of rebellion, he arrived in Boston in May 1775, and after *Bunker Hill was appointed KB. The following May, alongside his brother, William Howe was deputed to offer conciliation to the colonists; but after two years they resigned this joint commission, and *Clinton succeeded Major-General Howe. Promoted full general in 1793, Howe became governor of Berwick-on-Tweed and, in 1805, of Plymouth, where he died. In 1799 he had succeeded, on Richard's death, to the Irish barony first conferred on their great-grandfather by George I. Lord *Melbourne, in his breezy way, told the young Victoria that Howe was 'as brave as a lion, but no more of a commander than a pig'.

DDA

Hudibras. Popular satire in mock-heroic style by Samuel *Butler, in three parts (1662, 1663, 1677). Inspired by a west country knight (a parliamentary army colonel) and his clerk (an independent), with whom Butler had lodgings in Holborn, the two main protagonists are Hudibras, an Aristotelian knight whose intellectual accomplishments have no practical relevance, and Ralpho, his squire, proud of his ignorance and claiming to be divinely inspired. It delighted the royalists but was less an attack on the puritans than a criticism of antiquated thinking and contemporary morals, and a parody of old-fashioned literary form. ASH

Hudson, George (1800–71). Born near York and apprenticed to a linen draper, Hudson became a prominent York merchant. Inheriting £30,000 from a relative in 1828, he entered local politics and the developing world of railways. After several years on the city council, he became lord mayor in 1837. Hudson played a leading part from 1837 onwards in creating the railway network in the north. By 1844 he controlled 1,016 miles of railway and had been nicknamed 'the Railway King'. This facilitated his election as Conservative MP for Sunderland in 1845. He was deputy lieutenant of Durham and magistrate in three counties, acquiring estates and houses which became centres of high society. The financial basis of his empire was precarious and he was in trouble by late 1847. By 1849 he was stripped of his railway chairmanships and investigations disclosed much 'cooking' of railway accounts. He never recovered from this catastrophe. NMcC

Hudson, Henry (d. 1611). Though clearly a very accomplished navigator, Hudson's life is obscure. However, by 1607 he was employed by the *Muscovy Company in whose service he reached Svalbad (Spitsbergen). After another northern expedition, he was recruited by the Dutch, for whom he explored Chesapeake and Delaware bays before entering New York harbour and following the Hudson river as far inland as Albany in a vain search for the North-West Passage. Hence the Dutch empire in North America until the 1660s. Meanwhile, Hudson returned to English service in 1610, again to search for the passage to India, entered the bay now bearing his name, and sailed to its southern end. But he and his son were cast adrift by a mutinous crew, who returned home without them. RB

Hudson's Bay Company. The company was founded on 2 May 1670 under the patronage of Prince *Rupert after a voyage in 1668 had proved that access to the fur trade could be established through Hudson Bay. The company fought the French for control of the bay until 1713. Reliance on native peoples to supply furs (criticized as 'sleeping by a frozen sea') was challenged by long-distance competition from Montreal, forcing the company from 1774 to establish posts inland. In 1821, the company absorbed its Montreal rivals. Its territorial rights were sold to the dominion of Canada in 1869, but the company continued to trade.

GM

hue and cry. Early English common law process of pursuing felons 'with horn and with voice' (*hutesium et clamor*), also a proclamation for capture of a criminal or recovery of stolen goods. The outcry could be raised by peace-officer or private citizen, whereupon everyone was duty bound to search and pursue on horse or foot, from town to town and county to county; both constables of the vill or hundred and citizens could make the arrest. Seizure while in possession of incriminating evidence boded ill. The main statutes and amendments (1285, 1585, 1735) were repealed in 1827, though the element of 'citizen's arrest' has persisted. ASH

Hugh of Lincoln, St (1140–1200). Bishop. Born in Burgundy and educated in a convent at Villard-Benoît, Hugh was ordained deacon at 19 and subsequently made prior of a smallholding at Saint-Maximin. He became a *Carthusian in 1160 after visiting the Grand Chartreuse. Known for his holiness, in 1175 he was asked by King Henry II to become abbot of the first Carthusian monastery in England at Witham (Som.) (built as part of his penance for the murder of Thomas *Becket). He reproached Henry for keeping sees vacant to enrich royal coffers and as a result, in 1186, Hugh was elected to the see of Lincoln, vacant for some time. In 1192 Hugh undertook the rebuilding of the cathedral at Lincoln, a project which continued long after his death. He is said to have had remarkable concern for lepers, tending them with his own hands and often sharing a meal from the same dish. Hugh condemned the persecution of the Jews which spread throughout England in 1190–1. He had a sharp clash with Henry over ecclesiastical patronage, and later refused to help Richard I fund his war with Philip Augustus in 1198 (the first time an English king had been refused a levy). Hugh died in 1200 after undertaking a diplomatic mission to France for King John, and his funeral was attended by the primate of all England, 14 bishops, 100 abbots, an archbishop from Ireland, and another from Dalmatia, *Gruffydd ap Rhys from south Wales, King William the Lion of Scotland, and King John of England. Twenty years after his death he was canonized by Pope Honorius III, the first Carthusian saint. SMD

Hugh de Puisset. See PUISSET, HUGH DE.

Huguenots, a term of uncertain origin, were French-speaking (and some Walloon-speaking) protestants of *calvinistic temper, who fled from two centuries of persecution to seek asylum and freedom of worship in countries more sympathetic to Reformation practices. After the St Bartholomew's Day massacre (1572), the first wave of refugees to Britain were received at already established French churches in London, Canterbury, and Norwich, but hopes that their exile would be short soon faded. Relative quiet in France lasted only until 1661, when there commenced a steady erosion of privileges, culminating in the Revocation of the Edict of Nantes (1685), after which the trickle of emigrés became a flood, then a raging torrent. Some 40,000–50,000 Huguenots are estimated to have settled in England, the majority in London (those associated with the silk trade around Spitalfields, professional families in Leicester Fields/Soho) but other communities in East Anglia, the south/south-west, and at Edinburgh; 10,000 are estimated to have settled in Ireland.

A distinct minority element, but deriving much support from their close-knit communities and their faith, they proved highly-motivated, productive, and a considerable economic asset to their new host nation, though sympathetic acceptance was not universal, since their craft innovations and competition were sometimes resented. Involvement in clothing and textiles (especially silks), luxury trades like goldsmithing, watchmaking, glassware, and cabinetry, and the introduction of white paper were complemented by professional expertise in law, banking and insurance, education, and the armed forces, and contributions to the arts and sciences, and freemasonry. Integration and assimilation generally took several generations, though a few refugees migrated on to America. Today only one French church remains in London, but Huguenot names such as Courtauld and *Olivier are familiar to all, and Huguenot descendants retain great respect for their forebears. ASH

Hull, Kingston upon. See KINGSTON UPON HULL.

'humanism' is the term conventionally used to describe a set of moral and literary values and techniques chiefly associated with the *Renaissance of the 15th and 16th cents. It embraced enthusiasm for the Greek and Latin classics in their purest, most original forms; preference for rhetoric over logic as the means to persuade; the belief that good literary education would produce better people; and optimism about mankind's dignity and worth. However, this value-system was neither watertight nor exclusive: 'humanists' varied in their attachment to any of these elements, and often combined them with traditional learning.

Renaissance 'humanism' originated in Italy: even the word 'humanist' in this sense was derived from the Italian for a teacher of grammar. It was through literary and church contacts with Italy that humanism spread to England in the first half of the 15th cent. At first, some English patrons employed Italian secretaries and scribes to prepare for them manuscripts of ancient and more recent texts in the round, open, clear characters favoured by Renaissance book-collectors. Humphrey, duke of *Gloucester (1390–1447), youngest brother of Henry V, employed such writers as Tito Livio Frulovisi, Antonio Beccaria, Lionardo Bruni, and Pier Candido Decembrio to prepare texts for him. John *Tiptoft, earl of Worcester (d. 1470), collected books in Italy and patronized English scholars working there. The majority of the early English enthusiasts for humanism, however, were not noblemen but academics and churchmen, especially royal representatives at the papal curia such as George Neville, bishop of Exeter, or James Goldwell, bishop of Norwich.

By *c.*1500 the teaching of rhetoric, poetry, and those classical writers neglected in the Middle Ages had become appreciated at both Oxford and Cambridge universities. Humanist propaganda often depicted the campaign for 'good letters' as a gladiatorial struggle against the 'barbarism' of Gothic Latin and medieval school-logic. The reality, in England as elsewhere, was rather that humanistic studies developed alongside older styles of scholarship, within the traditional institutions. William *Grocyn (c.1449–1519) introduced Greek studies to Oxford on his return from Italy in 1491. The royal physician and Oxford academic Thomas *Linacre (c.1460–1524), pupil of Angelo Poliziano, wrote works on Latin composition and also encouraged good medical practice. In 1511–14 John *Fisher recruited the famous Netherlands humanist Desiderius Erasmus (c.1466–1536) to teach Greek at Cambridge, and fostered the inclusion of humanist courses within the university curriculum.

The apogee of English humanism as a conscious movement was reached in the first four decades of the 16th cent. John *Colet (1467–1519) learned Greek in Italy and taught at Oxford from c.1497; as dean of St Paul's from 1504 he refounded St Paul's School with a curriculum based on the new classical learning. His pessimism about human nature and emphasis on mordant criticism of failings among the clergy, however, were not typical of all humanists. Thomas *More (1478–1535), unusually for humanists a lay lawyer rather than an ecclesiastic, cultivated the friendship of Erasmus and produced the most bewildering literary fantasy of the movement, **Utopia* (1516). Sir Thomas *Elyot (c.1490–1546) in *The Boke Named the Governour* produced an English equivalent of the many treatises on education and politics current in Europe at the time.

As in France, Germany, and Italy, the advent of the Lutheran movement provoked a crisis in English humanism. The older generation of scholars, who had previously mocked or bemoaned the state of the church, rallied zealously to its defence when dogma was threatened. Both Thomas More and John Fisher deployed their rhetorical techniques to lambast reformers such as Luther, Oecolampadius, or *Tyndale without mercy. Younger scholars such as Thomas Starkey (c.1495–1538) were pulled between two poles of attraction: the household of Thomas *Cromwell, who encouraged humanist writers to produce work defending the royal divorce, the supremacy, and the changes to religious practice; and the group around the expatriate English Cardinal Reginald *Pole in Italy, which wavered on the royal marriage before c.1535, was moderate in theological controversy, but stayed loyal to the papacy.

By the mid-16th cent. it becomes impossible to speak of 'humanism' as a distinct entity, because its influence was spread so widely. Renaissance techniques for learning classical languages and editing classical texts became generally accepted. Erasmus' *Colloquies* were repeatedly printed in England well into the 17th cent. Humanist opinions on such issues as structured poor relief, proper family relationships, even maternal breast-feeding became standard elements in the teaching of English protestants. The belief that exposure to vast quantities of Greek and Latin literature, combined with vigorous physical exercise, would produce healthy, moral young men survived in the public school system until about a generation ago.

EC

humanitarians. The word 'humanitarian' was a 19th-cent. invention and usually had a contemptuous flavour, denoting a tedious, self-advertising busybody. But the roots of humanitarianism run deep. A feeling of concern for one's fellow-creatures is presumably as old as humanity itself, even if it has often been confined to one's own family, tribe, clan, or neighbours. The duty of giving alms and the need for good works was an integral part of the Christian message, though donations were often private in character or local in scale—almshouses, schools, bequests, and charities. In the 18th cent. this stream of philanthropy was reinforced and modified in two ways. First, many of the problems facing a rapidly changing and teeming society could only be attacked on a grander scale, calling for communal or national effort. The early Georgian period saw the establishment of a large number of hospitals, London and provincial, and although often associated with individuals like Thomas Guy or Captain *Coram, they looked to a wider community for support and maintenance. They appointed management committees, elected trustees, issued appeals to the public, organized concerts to raise funds, sought patronage. This impulse was joined by a stream from the Enlightenment which, for all its occasional fatuities, had generous aspirations—to eradicate serfdom and slavery, to banish torture and barbaric punishments, to improve the lot of debtors in prison and lunatics in madhouses, to protect women and children from exploitation. Indeed, the *philosophes* have been called 'the party of humanity' and, though they were thin on the ground in England (less so in Scotland), reformers were plentiful. Oglethorpe strove to help debtors, *Howard campaigned for prison reform, *Gilbert tried to improve poor relief, *Wilberforce worked for the abolition of the slave trade, and Jonas *Hanway—once memorably described as the greatest bore in British history—worked on behalf of orphans and chimney sweeps.

The French Revolution and the atrocities that accompanied it discredited enlightened thinking and for a time *Canning's 'Friend of Humanity' in the **Anti-Jacobin* was a stock figure of ridicule, a self-important do-gooder. But the tide was too strong to be held back and, once the dark days had gone, humanitarianism reasserted itself. *Romilly attempted to reduce the great number of capital offences, Elizabeth *Fry campaigned for women in prison, *Shaftesbury for children in mines and factories, *Plimsoll for merchant seamen in peril on unseaworthy vessels. There were improvements in the treatment of the mentally ill, beating and confinement giving way to patience and understanding. *Gibbeting, slavery, the press-gang, public executions vanished. Flogging in the armed forces disappeared, the stigma of illegitimacy was gradually removed. The advance of democracy meant that, in the 20th cent., humanitarianism became the creed of governments, expected to reform and protect. Crofters were assisted to purchase their plots, industrial workers were protected by safety legislation, the disabled helped and encouraged. The balance to be struck between mollycoddling and indifference has always been debated. The motives of humanitarians have always been mixed. In the 18th cent. the trustees of the Foundling hospital pointed out that every abandoned infant saved was one more adversary against the French, and much of the public concern in the 1900s about the condition of the people was because of the poor quality of recruits for the *Boer War. But as a force, particularly in its international role, humanitarianism is neither discredited, nor perhaps exhaustible. 'Do-gooder' is still a term of reproach, as humanitarian was in 1830, but there are worse things to be. JAC

Humberside was a new county established by the Local Government Act of 1972. It was built around the county boroughs of Hull and Grimsby, with a substantial hinterland taken from the East Riding of Yorkshire, from parts of Lindsey in Lincolnshire, and Goole, previously part of the West Riding. There was much opposition to the change, particularly from people in north Lincolnshire, who voted by more than 2 : 1 against the proposal. The Humber bridge, intended to knit the two parts together, was opened in 1981. The administrative centre was Beverley. It was abolished in 1996. JAC

Humble Petition and Advice. The second written constitution of the *Protectorate, formulated by its second Parliament early in 1657. Originally, its main purpose was to make *Cromwell king, but it also proposed a new second chamber ('the other house'), to be nominated by him. Other innovations were that no member of either House could be excluded (as many MPs had been in 1656) except by that House's own decision, that the appointment and removal of privy counsellors were subject to Parliament's approval, and that the regular revenue was precisely stated (£1,900,000 was finally agreed). The established church was to have a confession of faith, and the bounds of toleration outside it were more strictly defined.

Cromwell was much drawn to a constitution bearing Parliament's authority, the *Instrument of Government having only the army's, but he was asked to accept all of it or none, and he did not want the crown. Skilfully, he protracted negotiations for six weeks, until Parliament agreed to let him have the new constitution with the old title. The succession problem was settled by empowering him to name his own successor. AHW

Hume, David (1711–76). Philosopher and historian, the younger son of a strict presbyterian laird, Hume lost whatever Christian belief he had at Edinburgh University in the 1720s. His *Treatise of Human Nature* (1739–40) provided a devastating critique of contemporary metaphysics, which cleared the ground for a genuinely empirical account of human understanding. He devoted the 1740s to clarifying the principles of his philosophy and applying them to contemporary political issues. His massive *History of England* (1754–63) is a neglected masterpiece, which remained a best seller for more than a century. His analysis of party is still one of the most acute investigations of that difficult subject. His account of the rise and fall of the feudal system is now attracting the attention it deserves. In general Hume wanted to reconstruct the political culture of his age and to recommend a 'sceptical Whiggery' to his contemporaries as the best antidote to party zealotry and the best ally of commerce. In spite of long absences in England and France and in spite of constant friction with the kirk, Hume remained a loyal and much-loved member of the Scottish literati, whose influence on its thought can be traced in its historical, literary, and scientific thinking as well as in its philosophy. He died in 1776, probably of cancer of the bowel. NTP

Hume, Joseph (1777–1855). The archetypal middle-class parliamentary radical. A confirmed *Benthamite, Hume was an indefatigable speaker in Parliament and organizer of committees, pressure groups, and alliances designed to promote advanced liberal causes. Among these were repeal of the Combination Acts, catholic emancipation, Poor Law reform, disestablishment of the Church of England, repeal of the Corn Laws, free trade, extension of the suffrage, retrenchment in government spending, reform of municipal corporations, and the establishment of London University. He entered Parliament in 1812 as Tory MP for Weymouth after making a fortune as a surgeon in India. By 1818 he was a radical and represented a succession of Scottish boroughs. Hume was a friend and ally of Daniel *O'Connell and such *philosophic radicals as John Arthur *Roebuck, George *Grote, and Sir William Molesworth. JFCH

hundreds were the principal subdivisions of most English shires from before the Conquest and for many centuries afterwards. Their approximate equivalents in Northumberland, Durham, and Cumberland were called 'wards', in six Danelaw shires 'wapentakes'. Hundreds are first mentioned by name in the laws of *Edmund (*c.*940); it is likely that they derive from a somewhat earlier reorganization of local government. The adoption of the new term 'hundred' suggests recognition of the Carolingian *centena* as something of a model. The late Anglo-Saxon hundred was simultaneously a jurisdictional, a fiscal, and a military unit. Through most of the Middle Ages, the jurisdictional function was predominant. The hundred court usually met every three weeks, was attended by a variable number of freemen from the component villages, and exercised petty civil jurisdiction. On two of these occasions each year the sheriff attended to regulate the *frankpledge system and then criminal justice was done. Hundred courts had a long decline until Victorian legislation (especially an Act of 1867) dismantled them. A few hundred courts were important through serving developing but unchartered industrial areas, e.g. Salford. Many more hundreds kept significance as recognized areas of authority, for *petty sessional divisions or, ultimately, rural district councils. JCa

Hundred Years War. This term for the Anglo-French hostilities of 1337–1453 was coined in the 1860s but has enjoyed universal acceptance ever since. When the last descendant of the main Capetian line died in 1328, Edward III had a claim to the French throne through his mother. The war which broke out in 1337, like earlier conflicts, arose largely out of Edward's tenure of *Aquitaine as a fief of the French crown, but was fuelled by dynastic ambition and by English annoyance at French involvement in Scottish affairs. Only in January 1340, however, did Edward adopt the title king of France, initially, it seems, to win Flemish rebels to his cause. He proved militarily successful in France but the seriousness of his claim to the throne is thrown into doubt by his agreement to a territorial settlement in 1360. When war resumed in 1369, the French had the upper hand until Henry V's victories (1415–19) coincided with civil war and the insanity of the French king, Charles VI. Although Henry's main aim seems to have been to secure territory rather than the French crown, the murder of the duke of Burgundy by the Armagnac faction in September 1419 enabled him to negotiate the treaty of *Troyes whereby he became both heir and regent to Charles VI. From 1420 to 1435 the English controlled much of northern France, and Henry VI was crowned king in Paris in 1431. The successes of Joan of Arc and the defection of the duke of Burgundy after the Congress of *Arras weakened the English position, forcing them to accept a truce in 1444 and leading to their expulsion from Normandy in 1450 and Gascony in 1453. *Calais remained English until 1558, but English kings continued to call themselves kings of France until 1802. The 'Hundred Years War' is a misleading term in that it disguises the different phases and variety of causes of the conflict, but it does remind us of the longevity and intensity of Anglo-French hostilities in the 14th and 15th cents.: neither warfare nor diplomacy could produce a permanent solution. As both protagonists sought allies, the war was fought on many fronts, on land and sea. It was costly and at times politically destabilizing for both countries, and contributed much to the enhancement of a sense of nationalism in England and France. AC

Hunsdon, Henry Carey, 1st Baron (1526–96). Hunsdon's mother was Mary Boleyn and he was therefore Elizabeth I's first cousin. Since Mary Boleyn was Henry VIII's mistress for a time, it was suggested that he was also Elizabeth's half-brother. He was MP for Buckingham 1547 and 1554. At Elizabeth's succession he was given a barony, followed by the Garter in 1561. Appointed governor of Berwick in 1568, he won an important victory the following year near Carlisle over Sir Leonard Dacres, one of the leaders of the rising of the *northern earls. The queen acknowledged his services in her own hand in warm and affectionate terms. In 1581 he was made captain-general of the forces on the border, and lord chamberlain in 1585. Much of his time was spent on his duties in the north, which deprived him of some influence. At the crisis of the Armada in 1588 he commanded the troops at Tilbury. He was said to be unpolished and excitable and his capacity for swearing was awesome. JAC

Hunt, Henry (1773–1835). Radical reformer. 'Orator' Hunt was a Wiltshire gentleman farmer, whose radicalization followed his imprisonment in 1800 for challenging a colonel of yeomanry and the social ostracism following his adultery. He became convinced of the need for a thorough reform of the existing political system, based on universal suffrage, annual parliaments, and the ballot. In 1816–17 he headed three huge anti-government demonstrations in Spa Fields, London, which established his reputation as a great radical orator (or, as his critics alleged, demagogue). He was arrested for his part at *Peterloo and imprisoned for 2½ years in Ilchester gaol. Hunt's tactics were those of the mass platform, i.e. extra-parliamentary pressure, legitimized through the constitutional right to meet, demonstrate, and petition. After several unsuccessful parliamentary contests, he was returned for Preston in 1830. He opposed the 1832 Reform Bill as a half-measure which did nothing for the working class. JFCH

Hunt, William Holman (1827–1910). Painter. The eldest son of a warehouseman, one of his early jobs was as a clerk in the London agency of Richard *Cobden, the manufacturer and MP. He entered the Royal Academy Schools in 1844, where he met *Millais and *Rossetti, with whom he founded the *Pre-Raphaelite Brotherhood. Hunt devised the technique of the brotherhood, using bright colours with no strong contrasts of light and shade. He travelled extensively in Egypt and the Holy Land to paint biblical and moral subjects in authentic settings. Among his best-known works were *The Light of the World* and *The Hireling Shepherd*, which were reproduced in great numbers in Victorian Britain. In 1905, the year he was awarded the OM, he published a memoir, *Pre-Raphaelitism and the Pre-Raphaelite Brotherhood*. JC

Hunter, William (1718–83) **and John** (1728–93). Scottish anatomists. Intended for the church, William turned to medicine, studying at Edinburgh and London before establishing a private anatomy school in Covent Garden (1746) with dissection on the Paris model. Abandoning surgery for obstetrics, he became physician to Queen Charlotte and delivered all her children. A hard worker, clear lecturer, cultured though frugal, William formed a notable anatomical and pathological collection, and published *On the Human Gravid Uterus* (1774). John, blunt and irascible, no book-lover but a passionate though disciplined enquirer, joined his elder brother in London (1748) before receiving surgical tuition from Cheselden and Pott. After army service in Portugal, he practised surgery with distinction while continuing investigations and experimentation into human and comparative anatomy; granted a royal appointment (1776), he has become regarded as 'the founder of scientific surgery'. The brothers' importance rests not only upon their anatomical discoveries but on their teaching methods which so influenced the early 19th-cent. teaching hospital entrepreneurs, linking structure with function and underpinning diagnostic accuracy by knowledge of physiology and pathology. Their personal estrangement is mirrored by William's collections now resting at Glasgow University, John's at the Royal College of Surgeons (London). ASH

hunting. See BEAGLING; FOX-HUNTING.

Huntingdon, earldom of. In the 12th and early 13th cents., an earldom acquired and held, though not continuously, by members of the Scottish royal house. Their association with it, which placed them in the front rank of the English nobility, stemmed from the marriage in 1113 between David (later David I) and the heiress Matilda, daughter of Earl Waltheof. Its lands, the 'honour of Huntingdon', sprawled across a dozen shires, but lay mainly in Bedfordshire, Huntingdonshire, and Northamptonshire, and a significant number of tenants—notably the Bruces, Lindsays, and Olifards (Oliphants)—were able to develop Scottish interests and careers. An important weapon in Anglo-Scottish diplomacy, it made Scots kings and princes vassals of the English crown; but it also enabled them to challenge English claims to the overlordship of Scotland itself, by insisting that homage was due for English lands alone. KJS

Huntingdon, Henry Hastings, 3rd earl of (1536–95). Huntingdon was of royal blood and briefly within reach of the throne. His great-grandmother, countess of *Salisbury in her own right, was a daughter of the duke of *Clarence and a niece of Edward IV. Huntingdon was summoned to Parliament in 1559 in his father's barony and succeeded him in 1560. Two years later, when the queen was believed to be dying of smallpox, Huntingdon, as a protestant, was discussed as a monarch to keep out Mary, queen of Scots. Elizabeth recovered and Huntingdon became a trusted servant, given the Garter in 1570 and acting as lord president of the north from 1572 until his death. JAC

Huntingdon, Lady (1707–91). Foundress of the countess of Huntingdon's Connexion, Selina Shirley, daughter of the 2nd Earl Ferrers, married the 9th earl of Huntingdon (d. 1746) in 1728. Despite her aristocratic background, her fortune was slender and her marriage a love match. Small in stature but characterful in the extreme, she was converted by her sister-in-law, Lady Margaret Hastings, and joined the methodist society in Fetter Lane in 1739. Coming to know the *Wesleys, the Welsh evangelist Howell *Harris, and George *Whitefield, whose side she took in his dispute with the Wesleys in 1749, she built a number of chapels in such places as Brighton (1761), Bath (1765), Tunbridge Wells (1769), Worcester (1773), and Spa Fields, London (1779), served by ministers trained after 1768 at the college which she instituted at Trevecca, near Talgarth. Thwarted in 1770 by a ruling that her rank did not entitle her to appoint as many Anglican clergymen to be her chaplains as she wished, she registered her chapels as dissenting places of worship under the *Toleration Act, forming them into an association in 1790. Many of her sixty chapels, like her college, long survived her. Opinion towards her among the nobility varied greatly. The duchess of Buckingham rebuked her sternly for sentiments 'so much at variance with high rank and good breeding', and Horace *Walpole tried out a variety of jokes at her expense as 'Lady St Huntingdon' and 'Pope Joan of Methodism'. George Lyttelton thought her 'a gentle angel', and George III gave her an audience in 1772, wishing there were a Lady Huntingdon in every diocese. CB; JAC

Huntingdonshire was the third smallest of English counties in population until merged with Cambridgeshire by the Local Government Act of 1972. In pre-Roman days it was on the borders between the *Iceni of East Anglia and the *Catuvellauni of Hertfordshire. The origins of the county almost certainly derive from the establishment of a Roman settlement at the point where two roads, from Cambridge and Sandy, joined Ermine Street, just before it crossed the river Ouse. Godmanchester, which arose on that site, was for centuries part mother, part rival to the town of Huntingdon, which developed just north of the bridge and no more than half a mile away. The area passed into the kingdom of the East Angles but was taken over by Mercia, forming part of the first Mercian diocese. In the later 9th cent. it was overrun by the Danes, who seem to have fortified Huntingdon as part of their defensive network of the five boroughs. Reconquered in 920 by *Edward the Elder, king of Wessex, it was fortified by him and had both a mint and a market by the mid-10th cent. The earliest mention of the shire is in the *Anglo-Saxon Chronicle* for 1011, when it was once more overrun by the Danes. By the time of the *Domesday survey, Huntingdon was one of the largest towns in the kingdom. Many of the manors in the county belonged to the church, particularly to the great abbey of Ramsey, and to Thorney and Peterborough.

Huntingdon received a charter from John in 1206 and was granted parliamentary representation in the 13th cent., with two seats for the borough and two for the county. The main weight of property was in the estates at Hinchingbroke, just outside Huntingdon, and Kimbolton in the west. Since the two cousins, the earls of *Manchester and of *Sandwich, both supported Parliament, and *Cromwell himself sat for the borough, the county was firmly in the Eastern Association during the Civil War. Charles I led a forlorn hope into Huntingdon after the battle of *Naseby but was soon obliged to withdraw.

The county remained overwhelmingly rural. Drained by the Ouse, the western parts were good arable land, the eastern good grazing land. *Cobbett in 1822 echoed *Camden in the 1580s in admiring the meadows around Huntingdon—'the most beautiful that I ever saw in my life—it would be very difficult to find a more delightful spot in the world'. The main line from King's Cross to Edinburgh passes through the middle of the shire without causing much disturbance. Godmanchester and Kimbolton slowly stagnated, but the existence of several other flourishing market towns seems to have inhibited the growth of Huntingdon—St Ives and St Neots remain comparable in size, and Ramsey, in the north-east, is considerably bigger. Just before the merger in the 1970s, the population of the county was a little over 80,000. JAC

Huntly, George Gordon, 4th earl of [S] (1513–62). Gordon's mother was an illegitimate daughter of James IV of Scotland. His father died when he was an infant and Gordon inherited the earldom from his grandfather when he was 11. He won a success against the English at Hadden Rigg in 1542, was a regent after the death of James V, but was defeated and captured by *Somerset at *Pinkie Cleugh in 1547. In 1546–9 he was chancellor [S] and again in 1561, but lost favour with Mary after her return from France. When she gave the earldom of Moray, which he claimed, to her illegitimate brother Lord James *Stewart, Huntly rose in rebellion. His troops were defeated at *Corrichie and he died immediately after the battle, being 'gross, corpulent and of short breath'. His son was restored to favour, served as chancellor [S] 1565–7, and died 1576. JAC

Huntly, George Gordon, 1st marquis of [S] (1563–1636). Huntly played an important but erratic role in Scotland during the reign of James VI. He succeeded to the earldom at the age of 13 and in 1588 married the daughter of Esmé Stuart, duke of *Lennox. In the same year he was involved in a rising with Spanish help but was soon restored to James's favour. In 1592 he was responsible for the murder of James Stewart, earl of *Moray, and in 1594 was once more in rebellion, defeating a royal force at *Glenlivet. But he retained James's favour and in 1599 was created marquis. His influence declined sharply after the death of James. After a good deal of religious temporizing he died a catholic. JAC

Huntly, George Gordon, 2nd marquis of [S] (1592–1649). Huntly played a curiously ineffective role in Scotland during the Civil War. He spent much of his early life at the court of James I and then in France. In 1632 he was created Viscount Aboyne [S] and succeeded his father as 2nd marquis in 1636. His vast influence in the north-east made Charles I appoint him king's lieutenant in the north. But he was proud, moody, and irresolute. In the skirmishes of 1639 he was overwhelmed by *Montrose, then acting for the *covenanters. The hatred Huntly entertained for Montrose seriously weakened the royal cause in Scotland. Though his sons George and Lewis fought alongside Montrose when he waged his great campaign, and George was killed at *Alford, Huntly remained aloof. He was arrested in 1647 and beheaded in March 1649. His son Lewis was restored to the family honours by Charles II in 1651 and his grandson was created duke of Gordon [S] in 1684. JAC

Huntsman, Benjamin (1704–76). Huntsman was born in Lincolnshire, a quaker in religion, and set up as a clock-maker in Doncaster. Dissatisfied with the quality of the steel for springs and pendulums, he began about 1740 a series of experiments near Sheffield to improve cast steel. He experienced great difficulties—technical problems, industrial espionage, and the hostility of the Sheffield manufacturers, who complained that his steel was too dear and hard to handle. For some years he was forced to export mainly to France. But in 1770 he established a successful foundry at Attercliffe, where he is buried. The business was continued by his son and helped to make Sheffield for decades the steel capital of the world. JAC

Hurd, Douglas (b. 1930). Former Conservative cabinet minister. After attending Eton and Trinity College, Cambridge, Hurd entered the diplomatic service. He served in Peking (1954–6), at the United Nations (1956–60), and in Rome (1963–6) before leaving to enter politics. In 1966 he joined the Conservative research department and later served as Edward *Heath's private secretary (1968–74). In 1974 Hurd became MP for Mid-Oxon and managed to make a smooth transition from Heath to *Thatcher. Considered a moderate, he held various cabinet appointments including Northern Ireland (1984–5) and the Home Office (1985–9) before becoming foreign secretary (1989–95). He is the first former official of the Foreign Office subsequently to become its head. Hurd stood in the leadership contest of November 1990 but came third behind John *Major and Michael *Heseltine. He retired in 1995 to take a position in the city. Hurd also has a sideline as a writer of thriller novels. RAS

Huskisson, William (1770–1830). Huskisson's father was a country gentleman from Staffordshire, in moderate circumstances, and Huskisson had a career to make. He was in France at the outbreak of the Revolution and became acquainted with Lord Gower, the ambassador and a Staffordshire man. On their return to England in 1792, Huskisson was employed to help French refugees and became known to *Canning, *Pitt, and *Dundas. In 1795 he was made under-secretary for war with Dundas as his chief and was brought into Parliament in 1796. Though not a ready speaker, he built a reputation as an administrator, particularly in financial matters. He went out of office with Canning in 1809 and returned in 1814 to the comparatively humble post of commissioner of woods and forests, which he held until 1823. Next he became president of the Board of Trade, and on Canning's death *Goderich made him colonial secretary, with the leadership of the Commons. Huskisson was now a leader of the liberal Tories, with close links to *Melbourne and *Palmerston, and an advocate of retrenchment and of modification to the Corn Laws. He stayed in office under *Wellington, but with increasing friction, especially over parliamentary reform, and his offer of resignation in May 1828 was eagerly accepted. He was in poor health for his last two years and though he could have expected office under *Grey, he was no longer a rising sun. In September 1830, at the opening of the Liverpool to Manchester railway, he was run down and killed, 'seeming like a man bewildered', by the engine *Rocket*. A shy, awkward man, shambling and devoid of social graces, Huskisson was a strange fish in what was still an aristocratic pond—a man of business of more than common talent. JAC

Hutcheson, Francis (1694–1746). Scots-Irish philosopher. Educated for the kirk at Glasgow University, he returned to Ireland, taught at a dissenting academy in Dublin, and became the most prominent member of Viscount Molesworth's radical Whig circle. He made his reputation by publishing three metaphysical treatises between 1725 and 1728 attacking Mandeville's sceptical *The Fable of the Bees*, and attempting to prove that the roots of human sociability lay in a moral sense which would make men and women sociable and virtuous. Professor of moral philosophy at Glasgow from 1729 to 1746, he revolutionized the university's moral philosophy curriculum and attempted to justify toleration and a radical interpretation of the British constitution in terms of the principles of human nature. Distrusted by orthodox presbyterians, he was regarded by *Hume and Adam *Smith as an inspirational if misguided student of human nature. His political thought was much admired in colonial America. NTP

Hutchinson, Lucy (b. 1620). Author. Studious daughter of Sir Allen Apsley, lieutenant of the Tower, Lucy married John Hutchinson (the regicide) in 1638. Apart from translating Lucretius and writing two religious treatises, she is best known for her *Memoirs of the Life of Colonel Hutchinson* (penned for her own consolation and their children's information, unpublished until 1806), which depicted the life of a puritan family, vividly narrated the progress of the Civil War in Nottinghamshire, and recorded her husband's career with a partisan attempt to justify his political activities. Probably the stronger in character but believing utterly in women's subjection, her devotion led to energetic campaigning to save his life in 1660—Lucy wrote a letter to the Speaker pleading for pardon (later claiming that this was the only occasion she disobeyed her husband)—and tending him during his final months in the Tower and Sandown castle, Kent (1663–4). ASH

Hutton, James (1726–97). Geologist. The son of an Edinburgh merchant, Hutton went to his local university where he studied first chemistry, then medicine. From 1754 he took up farming but maintained his scientific interests, being on close terms with Joseph *Black. A paper he printed in the transactions of the Royal Society of Edinburgh foreshadowed his major work, *The Theory of the Earth* (1795), which laid the foundations of the modern study of geology. Though overladen with quotations, it offered a coherent and plausible account of the evolution of the earth's crust and insisted that the present could be used to explain what had happened in the past. It explained the steady destruction and reformation of rocks, the origin of fossil deposits at the bottom of great oceans, the effect of volcanic action, and offered a new concept of evolutionary time, which 'is to nature endless'. Of the process of change, he could 'find no traces of a beginning, no prospect of an end'. JAC

Huxley, T. H. (1825–95). Biologist, *Darwin's bulldog, essayist, public figure, and sage, Huxley was one of the most prominent Victorian scientists. After sketchy schooling, he studied medicine in London on a scholarship, and became a naval surgeon. Serving on HMS *Rattlesnake* surveying in Australian waters, he dredged, described, and classified marine invertebrates. Leaving the navy, he sought academic posts, and was appointed to the School of Mines, an ancestor of Imperial College, London. After 1859, he became famous defending Darwin's **Origin of Species*. He coined the word *agnostic* to describe his attitude to science and to religion, and with John Tyndall and others formed the X-club, promoting professional science free from establishment interference. His lectures to working men were noteworthy, as was his introduction of German laboratory methods into Britain. DK

Hwicce, kingdom of the. An Anglo-Saxon kingdom conterminous with the diocese of Worcester. Archaeology suggests both Anglian and Saxon settlement in the region and there seems to have been competition between Mercia and Wessex to control it in the early 7th cent., settled by *Penda of Mercia's victory at the battle of Cirencester in 628. The royal house of the Hwicce, whose earliest recorded kings Eanhere and his brother Eanfrid belong to the second half of the 7th cent., may have been established with Mercian help. Five generations of rulers are known, with several instances of joint rule by brothers. The Hwicce seem to have come increasingly under Mercian domination and the last independent Hwiccian rulers appear as subordinates in the charters of *Æthelbald and *Offa of Mercia. By the end of the 8th cent. the province was controlled by Mercian ealdormen and seems to have been closely associated with the family of *Cenwulf, who became king of Mercia in 796. BAEY

Hyde, Anne (1637–71). Though she did not survive to become queen herself, two of Anne Hyde's daughters, Mary (b. 1662) and Anne (b. 1665), became queen. The daughter of Edward Hyde, earl of *Clarendon, staunch royalist and lord chancellor to Charles II, Anne met James, duke of York, while she was maid of honour to Mary, princess royal and princess of Orange. Marriage did not take place until September 1660, when Anne was eight months pregnant with a son, who died an infant. After considerable hesitation, not least by her father who feared that his daughter's marriage to the heir presumptive would make him unpopular, the couple were accepted at court. Though Pepys thought the new duchess very plain and she rapidly grew fat, it was said from over-eating, by 1668 he remarked that 'the duke of York, in all things but in his codpiece, is led by the nose by his wife'. She converted to catholicism in 1670 though this did not become public until her death from cancer in March 1671. A patron of the arts and with some talent for sketching, she was repeatedly painted by *Lely. SMC

Hyde Park riots, 1866. Soon after the death of *Palmerston, Lord *Russell's government introduced a second Reform Bill, extending the franchise. Opposition by discontented Liberals led to the fall of the government in June 1866 and a minority Conservative administration took office under Lord *Derby. On 23 July a large *Reform League meeting called for Hyde Park found it closed. The crowd broke down the railings and clashed with police in reserve inside the park. Lord Stanley, a member of the cabinet, commented that there was 'more mischief than malice, and more of mere larking than either', though a policeman was killed. Nevertheless, when there were further disturbances in 1867 the home secretary, Spencer Walpole, was forced to resign. Matthew *Arnold awarded the riots a significance they scarcely possessed when in *Culture and Anarchy* he took them as a symbol of the collapse of civilized values in the face of mob rule: 'all over the country . . . [men] are beginning to assert and put in practice an Englishman's right to do what he likes, his right to march where he likes, threaten as he likes, smash as he likes. All this, I say, tends to anarchy.' JAC

hydrogen bomb. See NUCLEAR ENERGY.

hymns. In the sense in which most people understand the word, hymns are overwhelmingly a product of the 18th cent. They have been described as sacred poetry set to music, and have always been part of the Christian tradition, and the Jewish from which it derived. The psalms and specially composed sacred songs were certainly widespread in Christian worship by the 4th cent., and there is evidence to suggest that some passages in the New Testament, e.g. Ephesians 5, are actually quotations from hymns already in use within a generation or two of the lifetime of Christ.

Hymns in the early and medieval church were less expressions of personal or corporate devotion, than associated with the daily offices sung by members of monastic communities. In England the Reformation saw their virtual disappearance from public worship. There was a deep-seated prejudice against the use of non-scriptural language among many protestants, but the 16th and 17th cents. saw the composition of metrical versions of the psalms, notably by Sterhold and Hopkins (1557) and Tate and Brady (1696). These attained widespread popularity and were bound in with many editions of the *Book of Common Prayer.

The work of Isaac Watts and John and Charles *Wesley revived the popularity of congregational hymn-singing, and Wesley's *Collection* of 1737 is widely regarded as the first hymnal as we understand it. Suspicion of hymnody remained among many Anglicans, who associated it with evangelical 'enthusiasm', and not until *Hymns Ancient and Modern*, a fruit of the *tractarian movement and *Anglo-catholic revival, appeared in 1861 was this finally overcome.

Since then the writing of hymns and the publishing of collections has gone on apace among Christians of all traditions, though the appearance of many repetitive 'choruses' alongside hymns expressive of doctrine or personal devotion in recent years, whilst embraced enthusiastically by some, has been viewed with distaste by others. JRG

Hyndman, Henry Mayers (1842–1921). Socialist. Born into riches—the West Indian fortune of his grandfather—Hyndman was converted to Marxism by reading *Das Kapital* on board an Atlantic steamer on a business trip. In 1881 he published a kind of précis of it under the title *England for All*, which he distributed to delegates at the first *(Social) Democratic Federation conference in order to convert them to socialism. This irritated Marx, because Hyndman had not mentioned him by name. From 1884 he edited the leading British Marxist journal *Justice*. A committed anti-imperialist, he opposed the *Boer War, but then supported the First World War, which estranged him from most of his fellow-socialists. He also apparently alienated working people by his extremism, and his habit of quoting from Virgil in Latin in his speeches to them. He is probably the only western Marxist leader ever to have played county cricket for Sussex; but that was before he saw the light. BJP

Hywel (d. 949/50), king of much of Wales (*c.*904–49/50), known as Hywel Dda ('the Good'). The grandson of *Rhodri Mawr, king of *Gwynedd, he and his brother inherited *Seisyllwg from their father Cadell. After his brother died (920), he became sole ruler. He extended his authority into *Dyfed *c.*904, when he married Elen, probably the daughter of its last king; Gwynedd and *Powys fell into his grasp when their king was killed by the English in 942. Faced with Viking threats, Hywel acknowledged the English kings *Edward the Elder (918) and *Athelstan (927) as his overlords; he visited their courts, witnessed their charters, and called his son Edwin. Like King *Alfred he visited Rome (928), and Alfred's example may have inspired the codification of Welsh law which tradition attributes to Hywel. The earliest surviving texts of 'The Laws of Hywel Dda' date from the early 13th cent., but parts seem older and may have been codified by Hywel. A silver penny inscribed *Rex Houel* is said to have been minted by him; though if true, it would have been minted at Chester rather than in Wales. His dominion disintegrated after his death, but Hywel's reputation as 'the head and glory of all the Britons' flourished and in the early 12th cent. he was described as 'the Good'. RAG

ice hockey was pioneered by McGill University in 1880 and spread rapidly throughout Canada and the USA. A small English league was formed in 1903 and the first Scottish game was played in 1908. A British Ice Hockey Association was formed in 1914 and the sport was introduced into the Olympics in 1920. JAC

Iceni. British tribe and *civitas*. The tribal coinage, which carries the name ECEN or ECENI, suggests that the tribe were restricted in their geographical extent to Norfolk and parts of Suffolk and Cambridgeshire. Their first appearance in written history is probably in Caesar's account of his British expeditions, where he refers to a tribe called the Cenimagni. They appear to have been a wealthy and powerful tribe in the 1st and 2nd cents. BC, for from their territory come the finest hoards of gold torcs found in Iron Age Britain. Other hoards of elaborately decorated bronze chariot fittings also point to a love of conspicuous display by the nobles of the Iceni. This wealth may well have continued through the period of the Roman occupation, for some of the finest hoards of Roman gold- and silverware have also been found in or close to Icenian territory. Initially their contacts with the Roman invaders were not unfriendly, and the Icenian king Prasutagus became a client-king of Rome. On his death, however, his kingdom was incorporated into the Roman province and this, and other alleged abuses, led to the Icenian revolt, led by Prasutagus' widow *Boudicca. No doubt this set back plans for the Iceni to be given self-governing status as a *civitas*, but eventually that was accorded the tribe and their capital was established at *Caistor St Edmund (Venta Icenorum). Strangely, despite the tribe's apparent wealth, the town remained unusually small (under 35 acres) and poorly developed for a *civitas*-capital. KB

ice-skating in its simplest form dates back many centuries, with skates made out of animal bones. It became fashionable in the 18th cent. and a London Skating Club was founded in 1842. Speed skating held its first international competition at Hamburg in 1885 and was admitted to the Olympics in 1924. Ice rinks were built in large numbers after one was opened in Manchester in 1877. Figure skating had its first world championship at St Petersburg in 1896 and pair skating in 1908. The popularity of the sport was much increased by Sonja Henie of Norway, who won ten consecutive world championships for figure skating between 1927 and 1936 and appeared in a number of films. In the 1980s Jayne Torvill and Christopher Dean achieved vast popularity, winning world, Olympic, and European ice-dance titles in 1984 before turning professional. JAC

Icknield Way. A trackway which runs from the central Thames, through the Chilterns, and northwards to the Wash near Hunstanton. Though claims are made for a prehistoric origin, it is doubtful that such long-distance trackways existed, at least as a single entity, until the Iron Age at the earliest. At Baldock, the Icknield Way was certainly being formalized in the early 1st cent. AD by the digging of side ditches, but an earlier Iron Age date may be claimed from the dikes which cut across its line in the Chilterns. JRC

iconoclasm. Image-destruction has been a constant possibility in Christian history, for while for some artistic expression in sculpture, painting, or stained glass expresses the soaring upthrust of the soul to the divine, for others it is a distraction, 'obnoxious lumber' to be abhorred and discarded. For John of Damascus, what the written word was to the lettered 'the icon is to the unlettered'. The Byzantine iconoclastic controversy (7th–9th cents.), driven by the astringent impact of Monophysitism, Manicheism, and Islam, created widespread devastation and led many to retreat, for instance, to the caves of Cappadocia. Medieval Cistercians, preferring their own stark abbeys, abhorred contemporary Cluniac embellishment. The 16th-cent. Reformation unleashed another iconoclastic trail of destruction, approved by Zwingli, though himself a lover of art and music, but shocking to Luther. Though Calvin was no extreme iconoclast, his followers wreaked havoc in 16th-cent. France and Scotland and 17th-cent. England, where in the Cromwellian period much of her heritage of medieval stained glass and statues was destroyed and wall-paintings whitewashed. Bible and sermon replaced imagery. WMM

Ida (d. *c.*559), king of Bernicia (*c.*547–*c.*559). Founder of the *Bernician royal house from whom all subsequent Bernician and, after the reign of *Oswui, Northumbrian kings with genealogies surviving claimed descent. One written tradition records that his grandfather Oesa was the first of the family to come to Britain. *Bede believed that Ida came to the throne in 547 and ruled twelve years. His calculation appears to have been made by working backwards through a regnal list, but it is not certain that all the early Bernician kings ruled concurrently or have had their regnal years recorded accurately. In Northumbrian tradition Ida is associated with the conquest of the area around *Bamburgh.

BAEY

Idle, River, battle of the. See RIVER IDLE, BATTLE OF THE.

immigration refers to settlement in a country not one's own. It has been a characteristic of the British Isles from earliest times, often through invasion and subsequent colonization, as well as through peaceful movements of individuals and groups. Historians are able to trace patterns of immigration from archaeological remains, and from the persistence of languages and place-names, as well as from historical records.

Celtic peoples came to the British Isles from the European mainland centuries before the Roman invasion of the 1st cent. AD. Celtic languages, Erse, *Gaelic, Manx, and Welsh, continue to be spoken in Ireland, Scotland, Isle of Man, and Wales. In Cornwall, the Celtic language was spoken until the 18th cent. and even now is preserved in Celtic literature. Within the areas where these languages were spoken there were often separate legal traditions, particularly concerning landownership, which remained important until the 18th cent.

In those areas of the British Isles which formed part of the Roman empire immigrants settled alongside the indigenous people. After the Roman empire collapsed in the 5th cent., Angles, Saxons, and Jutes from continental Europe moved into most of what had been the Roman provinces. They were followed between the 9th and 11th cents. by Scandinavian immigrants, many of whom settled in the *Danelaw, those parts which became Derbyshire, Leicestershire, Lincolnshire, and Nottinghamshire as well as further north, particularly Yorkshire.

The Norman Conquest of 1066 brought settlers from various parts of northern continental Europe. Many continued to use the French language and maintained cultural and dynastic ties with their former homelands. Initially their prestige and military power set them apart. However, by the 14th cent. they had mingled with the indigenous population to such an extent that Anglo-Saxon and French had blended to form the English language and, in various arts, including architecture, distinctive English styles had emerged.

Some groups of immigrants remained identifiable. For example the *Jews, who arrived in Britain after the Normans, kept their religious and ethnic differences, but were dependent on royal protection to keep them from persecution. In addition Jews were forbidden to hold land and undertake a variety of trades and often they made their living by money-lending, an activity nominally forbidden for Christians. In 1297 Edward I expelled the Jews officially, after he had exploited their financial resources. Although it is not known whether all Jews left the country, there are records of Jews active as doctors in England during the reign of Elizabeth I. However, they did not receive religious toleration until the Protectorate of Oliver *Cromwell in the mid-17th cent. After that time there were further immigrations as a result of persecutions, particularly in the Russian empire during the 19th cent., and the Nazi regime in Germany during the 1930s. Other minorities have also settled in the British Isles. *Gypsies first came to Britain in the 15th cent., and in the 16th and 17th cents. small numbers of protestant Christians came to England fleeing from persecution by Roman catholics in Europe. Amongst these the largest identifiable group was the *Huguenots, who left France because of the hostility of Louis XIV. They brought with them economically important craft skills relating to silk textiles and created for themselves positions of wealth and prestige in their adopted country. Starting in the 17th and continuing into the 18th cent. black slaves were brought to Britain. Their number is unknown and their history has only recently attracted any attention.

To a considerable extent immigration during the later 19th and 20th cents. has been characterized by the recruitment of workers with skills which were in demand. For example, a shortage of clerical labour in London gave rise to the recruitment of German clerks, as well as well-educated Germans who could develop applications of science and technology in industrial chemicals. Similarly in the 20th cent. after the Second World War labour shortages at all levels prompted the recruitment of workers from the Commonwealth and former empire, such as the West Indies, the Indian subcontinent, and western Africa. These workers were recruited to vacancies in a range of occupations in the health service, in public transport, in local government, as well as in textiles and heavy engineering.

Since the 1960s the right of immigrants to settle in Britain has been subject to ever stricter political control focused on the definition of citizenship. The period after the Second World War was also marked by the immigration of refugees and others from communist-dominated societies in eastern and central Europe.

IJEK

impeachment was a trial by the House of Lords at the instigation of the House of Commons, which presented articles and arranged the management. The first clear example was the presentation in 1386 of Michael de la *Pole, earl of Suffolk, but the practice became common in the 17th cent. with the struggle between crown and Parliament, when a number of royal ministers—*Bacon, Middlesex (*Cranfield), *Strafford, and *Danby—were impeached. In 1710 the Whig government attempted to use impeachment against its critics by prosecuting Dr *Sacheverell, but it misfired badly. The impeachment of Warren *Hastings, which went on for seven years and ended in acquittal, helped to discredit the process and the impeachment of Henry *Dundas, Viscount Melville, in 1806 for peculation was the last. Impeachments were normally held in Westminster Hall with the lord high steward or the lord chancellor presiding

JAC

imperial conferences. The development of the white dominions from Canada onwards (1867) implied some structure for liaison and consultation within the empire. In 1884 the Imperial Federation League was set up to lobby for closer union, and the first conference met in 1887 when the leaders were in London for Victoria's *Golden Jubilee, the main discussion being imperial defence. A second conference at Ottawa in 1894 discussed cable laying in the Pacific, and a third met in London in 1897 to coincide with the *Diamond Jubilee, when it was agreed to hold regular meetings. The autonomous character of the dominions was reaffirmed by the statute of *Westminster in 1931. After the Second World War, the name was changed to Commonwealth conferences and the number of participants increased considerably. In 1949 the conference accepted that India could be a republic yet remain in the Commonwealth and in 1961 the conference insisted on a declaration against apartheid, which drove out South Africa. After 1969 it was agreed that London would not necessarily be the venue and that conferences should be held every other year. In 1996 there were 51 countries entitled to send their heads of government to the meetings. JAC

imperialism was not used in its modern sense until the later 19th cent. Before then it usually referred to the aggression of Napoleon Bonaparte. That does not mean of course that it cannot be used retrospectively, to describe the origins and growth of the *British empire in Stuart and Hanoverian times, for example; but the convention is to call these 'colonization', and to restrict the word 'imperialism' to the later period. It has also taken on a wider meaning. It usually refers to territorial acquisitions, but can also cover extensions of power or influence which fell short of that. 'Economic imperialism', for example, means the process by which an economy extends its financial control over others. *Missionary endeavours have been labelled 'cultural imperialism'. Sometimes all these different kinds of British expansion in the world are lumped together as 'informal imperialism'. That confuses the picture somewhat.

It has been explained in various ways. Missionaries used to attribute Britain's imperial successes to the will of God. 'Social Darwinists' thought they proved the British race was 'fittest' to survive. An Austrian sociologist called Joseph Schumpeter saw imperialists as a throwback to feudal times. Dr Ronald Hyam of Magdalene College, Cambridge, thinks that the male sex drive had a lot to do with it. The favourite theories, however, are economic. At the root of imperialism lay Britain's phenomenal commercial expansion following her industrial revolution. That gave her world-wide material interests, which needed to be secured. Later, according to J. A. *Hobson, the Marxists, and some capitalists (like *Rhodes), that need grew desperate, as capitalism began 'over-producing', and the industrialized countries began competing with each other for outlets. That, however, is controversial.

At its height, around 1900, imperialism also took on a domestic character. Britons forgot the old Napoleonic connotations, and took pride in their imperialism. At its crudest, this pride manifested itself in *jingoism; but it also had a more responsible side. All the main political parties—even Labour—sprouted imperialist wings. Keeping up the empire, they insisted, had implications nearer home. It could not be done with a weak, stunted, fickle population, especially in the competitive world of that time. That led some of them to advocate state intervention in order to strengthen people's bodies and loyalties, known as '*social* imperialism'. That had an impact on the Liberal government's reforms of 1906–14. Later it created an unlikely bond between Tory imperialists and more conventional kinds of socialists, which kept free marketism at bay in Britain for many years.

By 1902 it was clear that the empire was stretched about as tight as it could be without bursting, and imperialists turned away from expansion to consolidation. That added yet another meaning to the word. An imperialist became someone who wished to federate the empire: economically (through *imperial preference), militarily, and even politically. Many of these imperialists were highly idealistic, and even liberal in their vision of a great multiracial empire, which would bring peace and civilization to the world. Some of them hoped that the post-Second World War *Commonwealth might achieve all this, only to be disappointed in the longer run.

*Decolonization did not bring an end to imperialism, especially in the more 'informal' sense of the word. British capitalism still lords it over other economies. Conversely, Britain could be said to be an economic colony of her own creditors. The 1982 *Falklands War was widely taken to represent a reversion to an imperialism of a more traditional kind. For many foreigners, especially, it proved that Britain was still infected by the virus. That may have been unfair. BJP

imperial preference. This was a favourite nostrum of late 19th- and early 20th-cent. imperialists to bind the empire together by levying lower tariffs on colonial imports than on others. The colonies were supposed to reciprocate. Joseph *Chamberlain championed it from 1903. But there was a snag. Britain still adhered to *free trade. You cannot grant more preferential tariffs than none at all. Chamberlain wanted a tax on imported corn, to make this possible, but that was rejected at the election of 1906 because it would mean dearer bread. So the imperialists had to wait until 1932, when food import tariffs were introduced generally again, and a series of bilateral agreements negotiated with the dominions and colonies to favour them. Imperial trade increased thereafter, though that may not have been wholly due to this. After the Second World War the policy slowly declined, as a result of American pressure, the General Agreement on Tariffs and Trade (1947), and Britain's adhesion to a rival trading unit—the *European Economic Community—in 1973. BJP

Imphal, battle of, 1944. In March 1944 the Japanese 15th Army under Mutaguchi advanced over the river Chindwin into India towards Imphal and Kohima. *Slim's 14th Army was taken by surprise, but three divisions were able to take up defensive positions around the town of Imphal on 4 April. The Japanese besieged Imphal on the following day, the British garrison being sustained by an airlift of men and materials. Imphal was relieved on 22 June after bitter close-quarter fighting. Japanese offensive power was severely damaged at Imphal and Kohima, and they were forced to fall back to Burma. GDS

impositions. Tudor sovereigns received lifetime parliamentary grants of customs duties called *tonnage and poundage, but as inflation reduced the royal revenue they had recourse to impositions—additional prerogative levies on imports, first collected under Mary I. Impositions were the subject of a legal challenge in 1606, but the court upheld the crown's right, thereby enabling James I's treasurer, Robert *Cecil, greatly to expand their range and yield. The Commons never accepted the validity of these non-parliamentary levies, and they were a cause of constant friction with both James I and Charles I. They were finally declared illegal by the Tonnage and Poundage Act of 1641. RL

impropriations. Impropriation was the assignment of a benefice to a lay proprietor, as distinct from appropriation to a monastery. In either case medieval benefices were served by poorly paid vicars or curates, while the rectors, who received the income, were often licensed, privileged absentee pluralists, yet valuable members of the community as royal civil servants. When the monasteries were dissolved, many appropriated monastic benefices were impropriated, causing Matthew *Parker, for instance, great difficulty as primate in curbing Elizabeth's rapacious courtiers. Lay impropriators, as *Tenison noted (1713), were known for seeking cheap and often indifferent curates. An effective Whig 1830s reform insisted on incumbents being resident. WMM

Inchiquin, Murrough O'Brien, 1st earl of [I] (*c.*1614–74). Inchiquin, a protestant, was one of several commanders who played a semi-independent role in the confused situation that followed the Irish rising of 1641. He had succeeded to the barony of Inchiquin in 1624 when he was about 10. He took up arms against the catholic Confederation and inflicted several defeats upon it in Munster. Passed over by Charles I for the presidency of Munster, which he expected, he joined the parliamentary side in July 1644 and working with *Monck won an important victory over the Confederation troops at Knockmanus near Mallow in 1647. But the following year he rejoined the royalists. Driven into exile when *Cromwell landed, he was raised to the earldom by Charles II in 1654, converted to catholicism, and fought for the French. At the Restoration he was given back his Irish estates with substantial compensation. Though the complex situation does much to explain his tergiversations and he could never be entirely sure of his army, his political and religious shifts do not suggest steadiness of purpose. JAC

income tax was introduced in 1799 by William *Pitt's government to fund the war against the French. Proposing the legislation Pitt pointed to evasion of existing assessed taxes and claimed that the levies on income were equitable if not 'perfectly free from the objection of inequality'. The final form of the income tax system was embodied in the Act of 1803, the creation of *Addington, prime minister and chancellor of the Exchequer.

The need for a new tax arose from unprecedentedly high expenditure on the British armed forces and on subsidies to the allies. Simultaneously, interest payments on the national debt had increased because the government continued to finance some expenditure by raising further loans. Many supposed that income tax would be a temporary expedient of war and in fact Parliament repealed the tax in 1816 and ordered the commissioners for the affairs of taxes to destroy their records. Although this was done, duplicates remained with the king's remembrancer.

Raising revenues continued to present problems to chancellors of the Exchequer. Moves towards free trade had led to the abolition of many indirect taxes on goods and services, and in addition the introduction of the penny post in 1840 reduced revenues from the postal services. In 1842 Sir Robert *Peel proposed that 'for a time to be limited, the income of the country shall be called upon to contribute to remedying this growing evil [the deficit]'. No chancellor since 1842 has removed income tax.

The 1842 income tax followed closely the administrative mechanisms established in the Act of 1806. There were only two differences: the minimum income taxed was £150 instead of £50, and the assessment of taxes on incomes from commercial activity was subject to the scrutiny of special commissioners to prevent fraud and evasion. Incomes were taxed under five Schedules: A, income from land and buildings; B, farming profits; C, funds and annuities from public revenues; D, profits and interest; E, income from employments, annuities, and pensions. These schedules remain until the present time with the exception of A, which was abolished in 1963.

Although *Disraeli proposed, in 1853, the abolition of income tax by 1860, the expense of the *Crimean War encouraged *Gladstone to keep it. Government expenditures on defence continued to rise and after 1906 the cost of defence and social welfare increased rapidly. David *Lloyd George's 'People's Budget' of 1909 imposed, for the first time, income tax with rates varying according to the ability to pay. Thus income tax became more than a device for raising revenue and was a step towards redistribution of income. During the First World War alterations in the rates of tax on incomes offset some costs of warfare. The highest personal rate was known popularly as 'supertax' and the prosperity of firms involved in wartime activities incurred Excess Profits Duty. Higher personal taxes remained after the war ended, a Corporation Profits Tax replacing the Excess Profits Duty.

Although changes in the rates of income tax occurred between the two world wars, the *Second World War required both more revenue and limits on demand inflation. This latter threat arose from higher wages seeking inadequate quantities of goods and services. The year 1941 saw the introduction of a new type of levy, reimbursable post-war credits, at the rate of 10*s.* (50p) in the pound, to enforce savings. Repayment was slow; many taxpayers waited as long as 20 years for their money. Simultaneously the surtax rate increased to 19*s.* 6*d.* in the pound.

Since 1945 reductions in the standard rate have occurred, although rates have always remained above those of peacetime in earlier periods. IJEK

Indemnity and Oblivion, Act of, 1660. Restorations after long exiles usually disappoint the loyalists since there are so many claims to be rewarded. In the declaration of *Breda, Charles II had promised a general amnesty and the Act of 12 Car. II c. 11 put it into effect, 'to bury all seeds of future discords'. Fifty persons who had signed the death warrant of Charles I and those who had been involved in the Irish rising of 1641 were expressly excluded. But the many changes in landownership which had taken place during the Commonwealth were ignored, leading royalists who had suffered severely to jeer that it was indemnity for enemies, oblivion for friends. JAC

Independent Irish Party. The forerunner of the *Irish National Party put together by Isaac *Butt and *Parnell. It was formed by about 40 Irish MPs in 1852 to assist the *Tenant League campaign and to obtain the repeal of the *Ecclesiastical Titles Act. But it split badly between catholics and protestants, sympathizers of the Liberals and of the Conservatives, and those who gave priority to land reform over the religious question. The latter were known to their admirers as 'the Irish brigade', to their detractors as 'the Pope's brass band'. It collapsed within a few years, one of its founders, Charles Gavan *Duffy, emigrating to Australia. JAC

Independent Labour Party (ILP). The party was established in 1893 at a conference in Bradford, composed of 120 delegates largely drawn from the industrial north and Scotland and chaired by Keir *Hardie. By 1910 it had a membership of 28,000. Although the word 'Socialist' was deliberately excluded from its title, the ILP was still attacked by Liberal trade unionists. Chronic lack of union funding and modest successes at local and parliamentary elections led the ILP to take the initiative in forming the Labour Representation Committee in 1900. With the outbreak of war, a significant number of ILP members including Ramsay *Macdonald adopted a pacifist stance. Some became involved in the *Union of Democratic Control, thereby strengthening contact between Labour and left-wing Liberals.

The end of the war saw the ILP lose its seat on the NEC and much of its influence, as individuals could now join a Labour Party constituency association. However, under the skilful Clifford Allen, the ILP developed into a significant socialist pressure group. Its most important document was *Socialism in our Time*, which anticipated many of the later *Attlee government reforms.

Disappointment over the second Labour government (1929–31) accelerated the leftward drift of the ILP and made many of its members rebellious in Parliament. As a result the party, under the Clydeside firebrand Jimmy *Maxton, disaffiliated from Labour in 1932. The consequences of disaffiliation were far reaching. By 1935 the ILP, which assumed a neo-Marxist character, had less than 5,000 members, only a quarter of the previous figure. However, the party still played an important role in the Unity Campaign, hunger marches, and anti-fascist activities. In 1939 the party opposed an 'imperialist war' and its decline continued after 1945. Yet the ILP continued to exist and rejoined the Labour Party in 1975. LHM

India, or Hindustan, was named by the Greeks after the Indus valley. Its dominant civilization was Hindu and Buddhist but, from the 11th cent., it was subject to successive waves of conquest from the Islamic north. The most famous of its conquerors were the Mughals, who established their empire in 1526. In the age of exploration, the first Europeans to arrive were the Portuguese who developed a seaborne empire centred on Goa. In the early 17th cent., the Dutch displaced the Portuguese, but India was peripheral to their principal interests in Java. The English *East India Company established its presence from the 1610s and concentrated on the textile trade. The French arrived in the 1660s. From the 1720s, the power of the Mughal empire started to decline. A series of regional successor states replaced it, in all but name, and extended war-frontiers against each other. In Europe, France and England also found themselves at war in this period and their respective companies carried on the conflict by constructing alliances with the successor states. Both were also drawn deeper into Indian politics by the prospects of wealth made from banking, monopolies, and trade with China. At first, the French under Dupleix had the upper hand. But, from the late 1740s, the English company's fortunes began to turn as Robert *Clive won a series of military victories. The major threat posed by the French was eliminated after the battle of *Wandewash in 1760. However, even before that, Clive had begun to lay the foundations for empire at the battle of Panipat in 1757, which made him the 'kingmaker' in Bengal, India's richest province. For the next thirty years, there was some hesitancy in British circles at building on these foundations. But, during the Revolutionary and Napoleonic wars, the opportunity was seized and by 1818, with the defeat of the Maratha empire, the East India Company had gained supremacy. After the *Indian mutiny of 1857, however, the company was abolished and sovereignty passed to the British crown. In the 19th cent., India was undoubtedly Britain's most important colony. It provided a free army, a field for capital investment and a captive market for British goods. After the First World War, both its military and economic status began to decline and a mass nationalist movement emerged under the leadership of Mahatma *Gandhi. As early as 1920, the British began to clear the way for 'responsible self-government' and, by 1935, had drawn up plans for India's eventual conversion into a dominion. However, the Second World War cut short this programme of devolution and promoted an extremely hasty retreat. 'Communal' problems also arose between Hindus and Muslims to complicate withdrawal. British India was partitioned into the separate states of Pakistan and India, which became independent on 15 August 1947. DAW

India Bill, 1783. An abortive reform of the *East India Company, drafted largely by Edmund *Burke and introduced by the Fox–North coalition. Opponents expressed exaggerated fears that the patronage thus created would give the coalition a stranglehold on power. The actual cause of the bill's defeat in the Lords in December 1783 was the resentment of George III against his ministers and the underhand pressure he brought to bear by letting it be known, via Lord Temple, that anyone voting for the bill would henceforth be treated as a personal enemy. Secret and prior negotiations with *Pitt allowed the king summarily to dismiss the coalition. DW

Indian mutiny. On 10 May 1857, sepoys of the Bengal army shot their British officers and marched on Delhi to restore the aged Mughal emperor, Bahadur Shah, to power. The mutiny spread down the Ganges valley—to Agra, *Cawnpore, and *Lucknow—and into central India. It encouraged a widespread civil revolt against the institutions of British rule. Existing 'loyalist' forces were unable to quell the rebellion and reinforcements had to be called from China. It took until December 1857 for Sir Colin *Campbell's army to reoccupy the key strategic points along the Ganges valley and the last vestiges of armed resistance were not stamped out before the spring of 1859. The causes of the mutiny (by no means the first in British Indian military history) lay in attempts to impose British-style army discipline onto Indian warrior traditions—the celebrated issue of cartridges greased with animal fat being symptomatic of wider problems. The vehemence of the civil rebellion reflected the anxieties of aristocracies and peasant communities at threats posed to them by aggressive policies of westernization, especially under Lord *Dalhousie. The events of 1857 marked a watershed in Indo-British relations. Afterwards, the British came to doubt the possibilities of a rapid social transformation and treated their Indian subjects with increasing suspicion. The army was reorganized to improve British surveillance. State policy became more conservative and politically defensive. DAW

Indulf (d. 962), king of 'Scotland' (954–62). His father was Constantine II and his mother was (probably) Danish, which would account for his Danish name. He succeeded Malcolm I, and extended the kingdom's territory south across the Firth of Forth to include Edinburgh. His reign witnessed a resurgence of Scandinavian incursions. A fleet of Vikings was defeated in Buchan, and Indulf himself perished in battle against a Norwegian force at 'Invercullen' (either Cullen, 55 miles north-west of Aberdeen, or Cowie, 15 miles south of Aberdeen). A debatable source says that he was buried on Iona. A 17th-cent. collection of annals records that he expelled Bishop Fothad of St Andrews (d. 963), but the circumstances are unknown. DEB

indulgences. Arising in crusading times—first in 1063—from Roman law concepts, they became an integral part of every late medieval crusader's—and pilgrim's—commitment. After sacramental confession, absolution, and penance, the church, on God's behalf also, from the treasury of merit built up by Christ and the saints, granted the sinner remission of 'temporal penalties' still inevitable after sin. Later, widespread abuse, often financial, made religious commitment mechanistic, and indulgences vulnerable to attack from 16th-cent. reformers. The Thirty-Nine Articles condemned 'the Romish doctrine concerning Purgatory, Pardons' as unscriptural. The Council of Trent (1545–63) and second Vatican Council (1961–5), while condemning their abuse, commended their continued use as 'beneficial to Christians'. WMM

industrial archaeology, a term invented by Professor Donald Dudley and used in print for the first time by Michael Rix, is the study and recording of the industrial heritage. Conservation in a few cases may be justified, but generally, the purpose of practitioners is to illuminate industrial and social history by using physical evidence. Field surveys have occasionally been used by historians; for the industrial archaeologist they are essential. An interdisciplinary study, industrial archaeology has attracted a popular audience in Britain since 1960; there are many local societies, groups, and periodicals and a national society, the Association for Industrial Archaeology, which publishes *Industrial Archaeology Review.*

Industrial archaeologists employ techniques used by other historians, including evaluating the evidence provided by documents, maps, and plans and the critical use of printed sources. Oral evidence may also be important. To these are added others: measuring, surveying, and photographing a site so that an accurate record can be produced. In a few situations excavation is essential. These latter techniques reveal affinity with archaeology.

Apart from involving more people in the local study of industrial and social history as a recreational activity, industrial archaeology has a number of other purposes. Economic change has been so rapid that there is a grave risk that industries and crafts as well as machinery and plant will disappear before any adequate record is made, thereby reducing the prospects for future historians. The scale of local operations can only be appreciated by fieldwork, and a wider comparison be made only if similar work is undertaken in other places. An enlightened preservation policy can only be produced from knowledge of what survives and which is the best of the survivors. Churches and castles have long had this recognition; industrial artefacts such as mills, pumping stations, mines, and railway stations, require similar treatment. Industrial remains are simply part of that evidence to be used in complementing other sources. The disappearance of some processes may be offset by an adequate technical record taken on site from those who worked in obsolescent industries. The record and analysis of human endeavour demands an open outlook to new perspectives; the use of industrial archaeology can elucidate forgotten elements of human experience. JB

Industrial Relations Act, 1971. The Act, designed to weaken the bargaining powers of trade unions by a newly elected Conservative government (which abandoned incomes policy), had its origins in the problems encountered by earlier administrations, such as excessive wage demands, unofficial strikes, and inter-union disputes. Unions had to register to keep their legal privileges; before a strike, they had to hold secret ballots of their members, effectively a cooling-off period; a National Industrial Relations Court was to ensure that these provisions were kept, and the

Commission for Industrial Relations, established by Labour (1969), was to iron out inter-union conflicts. JB

industrial revolution. In 1837 Louis-Auguste Blanqui used the phrase to describe the changes Britain had undergone during the previous half-century in its social and economic life. Widespread use of the term followed from Arnold Toynbee's *Lectures on the Industrial Revolution of the Eighteenth Century in England* published in 1884. 'Industrial revolution' became the commonplace characterization of the complex developments in Britain during the later 18th and first half of the 19th cents. Debates about the precise period and its meaning reflected efforts to identify what brought about the transformation from a predominantly rural society, whose major source of livelihoods derived from the land, to a rapidly urbanizing country whose wealth came from commerce and manufacturing.

Symbolic of the industrial revolution was the use of coal as a source of energy. The conversion of coal to coke made cheaper iron ore smelting possible and simultaneously produced town gas, used from the early 19th cent. for lighting. Coal-fuelled boilers provided steam-power for mines drainage, factory machinery, and locomotives, making speed and repetitive activities less arduous and greatly augmenting output. Particularly associated with such changes were cotton textiles, made cheaply in large quantities. Inventions of processes and discoveries of new materials increased the sophistication of products available. Examples of these occurred in metallurgy in the uses of iron and in chemicals. Organizational developments as well as large-scale capital investments gave impetus to the construction of well-built roads run by turnpike trusts and to the making of a nationwide canal network. The better distribution of raw materials and finished products expanded the domestic economy and made exporting easier.

Social changes occurred simultaneously. Many new jobs were created between the later 18th and the mid-19th cent. from the ever widening applications of technical innovations such as in gas-making, in the chemical industry, in canal and railway transport, and in textiles. In the case of textiles, increased output depended on water- or steam-powered machinery installed in purpose-built factories. Although the total number of jobs in textiles rose, much unemployment was experienced in areas where factory products undercut the prices of the old domestic system of production. New methods of industrial production also required many people to move to urban locations. Some existing towns such as *Manchester expanded very rapidly, whilst new towns emerged, such as St Helens (Merseyside). Rapid urban growth posed many unforeseen problems of overcrowded houses, inadequate sanitation, and law and order.

Marx's ideas about the making of capitalist society had their origins in his observation of British industrialization, particularly in Manchester during the 1830s. Marxists went on to argue that the triumph of capitalist organization of production and trade was exemplified most completely in the history of Britain between the accession of George III and the accession of William IV. This process was accomplished by the emergence of the middle class and the creation of an industrial working class from the landless labourers and smaller peasant farmers.

In 1958 W. W. Rostow in his *Stages of Economic Growth* proposed a model of economic and social change to challenge the Marxist analysis. This 'non-communist' manifesto identified five stages in the growth of economies. The crucial third stage was 'take-off' which, in the case of Britain, corresponded to the onset of rapid industrialization in the late 18th cent. and lasted until the early years of Victoria's reign when the economy became 'mature'. The fourth stage involved having a variety of heavy industries and commercial institutions and imperial ambitions. Rostow claimed for his model predictive capabilities which could be applied world-wide.

Many historians, geographers, and political economists have sought to explain the origins of the changes during the second half of the 18th cent. and why they should have occurred in Britain. The search for one main underlying cause has led to elaborate and careful studies of both economic activities and social developments, including geographical determination, religious discrimination against nonconformists, technological innovations in sources of power, and the rise of literacy.

In contrast other historians have challenged the very concept of an industrial revolution. For example, econometric techniques applied by N. F. R. Crafts and others to data available about national incomes and production indicate slow rates of change in British economic life. Innovations in technology and in organization occurred piecemeal in different parts of the economy, suggesting that the image of revolution seems inappropriate. Others have pointed to important economic changes both earlier and later than the period usually identified. For example, E. M. Carus-Wilson identified an industrial revolution in the 13th cent. associated with using water-powered fulling mills in woollen cloth-making. J. U. Nef used the term to describe developments between 1540 and 1640 when the greater use made of coal and metallic ores was accompanied by innovations in agriculture and the growth of overseas trade.

The debate will continue. However, any argument has to explain the causes of the development of Britain as the first industrial nation. IJEK

Clarkson, L. A., *Proto-industrialization: The First Phase of Industrialization?* (1985); Crafts, N. F. R., *British Economic Growth during the Industrial Revolution* (Oxford, 1985); Hudson, P., *Britain's Industrial Revolution* (1992); Nef, J. U., *The Rise of the British Coal Industry* (1932).

Ine (d. 726), king of Wessex (688–726). The reputation of Ine rests on two foundations, legal and ecclesiastical. There is little known about his political and military achievements, though by inference they cannot have been inconsiderable. He reigned from 688 for a very long period, 37 years, and was confident enough to resign his throne to younger men, making his way as a pilgrim to Rome where he died. His laws were impressive. Alfred (871–99), who was descended from Ine's brother, used Ine's decrees when he drew up his own statement of just law, and added Ine's code (drafted between 688 and 694, and much concerned with theft and the agrarian routine) as a supplement to his own pronouncements. In the ecclesiastical field Ine himself presided over the first synods known to have been held among the West Saxons, and founded the bishopric at *Sherborne to serve his people west of Selwood. Internal evidence within the law code betrays a deep concern with ecclesiastical law. Heavy penalties were imposed on failure to see that a child was baptized or to pay proper dues to the church. In this sense his reign marks the legal consolidation of the total conversion of the West Saxon peoples to Christianity. His laws also show a significant concern with the status of Welshmen assimilated to the kingdom. A Welshman was accorded the substantial blood-price (*wergeld) of 120 shillings if he possessed one hide of land, 80 shillings if half a hide, and 60 shillings if none at all. He also had rights in basic legal procedures of accusing by oath in cases concerning stolen cattle. There was discrimination: a penally enslaved Welshman was to be flogged if oaths assessed at 12 hides were sworn against him, an Englishman in such a plight needed an oath of 34 hides (probably a misprint for 24). There was still an independent British king, Geraint by name, operating in Devon as late as 710. The Welshmen of the code of laws clearly referred to the British inhabitants of the west country taken over and governed according to Germanic law by the West Saxon king. Ine was also from time to time busy in the south-east. In 694 he compelled the Kentishmen to pay an immense compensation for the murder of the West Saxon prince Mul, the brother of Ine's own predecessor. He was regarded at times as king in both Surrey and Sussex though both communities were acting independently at the end of his reign. But his main efforts and achievement lay in the heartlands of Wessex and the south-west. Scholarship flourished under the inspiration of *Aldhelm, abbot of Malmesbury, and then first bishop of Sherborne (705–9). Exeter, where St *Boniface received his early training, possessed a monastery ruled by an English abbot in the 680s. It seems right to recognize Ine's master achievement as the completion of the political conquest of Devon, following on a generation or so of steady Saxon migration and agrarian settlement under arms in the fertile valleys of the south-west. HL

infangthief (in-caught-thief) and **outfangthief** were early medieval jurisdictions. The first gave the right to deal with a thief (including hanging) caught red-handed on the lord's manor or estate, provided he was the lord's own man. Such jurisdiction was prestigious and occasionally profitable, since the thief's chattels were forfeit. Outfangthief was much rarer and more complex. It seems to have started as the right to bring one's own man back for sentencing in one's own court for a theft committed elsewhere. But *Bracton interpreted it as the right to try someone else's man, caught red-handed, in one's own court. That seems unlikely since it would conflict with another lord's outfangthief rights and be bound to cause dissension. Whether the custom had changed or whether there was legal confusion is not clear. These private jurisdictions were whittled away by the growth of royal justice in the 13th cent. JAC

Inkerman, battle of, 1854. In November 1854 an Anglo-French force was besieging Sebastopol in the Crimea. On 5 November a Russian army under Menshikov attacked at Inkerman, hoping to drive from the field forces supporting the besiegers. Despite having superior numbers, perhaps 50,000 to 15,000 allies, the Russian attacks were badly co-ordinated. The appalling nature of the terrain, and thick fog, ensured that Inkerman was a 'soldier's battle', with attacks and counter-attacks launched in an *ad hoc* and haphazard fashion. The arrival of allied reinforcements eventually forced the Russians to withdraw, having lost about 12,000 men to the allies' 3,400. GDS

inns. The most prosperous period for inns was the 200 years from the middle of the 17th cent., when the first regular stage coaches began, to the 1840s when the railways began to put them out of business. During those years they were a vital part of the network of communication—as important for the changing and care of horses as for the welfare of passengers. In the Victorian period, they gave way to railway dining-rooms and hotels, and in the late 20th cent. to motels and service stations.

In the later Middle Ages there were numerous inns, but monasteries also provided accommodation for travellers. Inns were to be found mainly in London, at busy ports, bridges, and ferries, in county towns where there was business to transact, and along the great pilgrim routes to *Canterbury and *Walsingham. *Chaucer's pilgrims set out from the Tabard at Southwark. Few genuinely medieval inns survive, though there are cellars, staircases, windows, and bays. One of the oldest is the Angel at Grantham, where in 1483 Richard III signed the death warrant for *Buckingham: it had originally belonged to the *Hospitallers and was probably a much earlier hostelry. Another is the George at Glastonbury, built by the abbot in 1475 and previously known as the Pilgrim's Inn. More of the great Tudor and Stuart inns are still in business: the Feathers at Ledbury (*c.*1560), the Feathers at Ludlow (1603), the George at Southwark (rebuilt 1676), and the Bell at Tewkesbury (1696). The basic pattern was a courtyard, with galleries on the first floor, and extensive stabling. The many fine classical inns include the George at Stamford, in existence by 1568 and given its frontage in 1724; that most aristocratic of inns, the Duke's Head, at King's Lynn, built by Henry Bell *c.*1680 as a private house, and converted; and the George, Penrith, where Prince Charles Edward lodged in 1745.

By the 1840s many of the old inns were losing their struggle against the growing railway network, and in the 1960s and 1970s most of the remainder were bypassed by the *motorways, leaving them to varying fates. JAC

Inns of Court. Legal institutions of medieval origin situated in London and responsible for the education of barristers. By the 14th cent. the bar was organized, like the guilds, as an association of the members of the Inns of Court. They were first used as accommodation and were a cross between the college, the club, and the trade union. Originally around twenty Inns were known to have existed of which only four survive: Inner Temple, Middle Temple, Gray's Inn, and Lincoln's Inn. The Temple was the London residence of the knights *Templar until their dissolution and was let to lawyers in the mid-14th cent. Gray's Inn was formerly the town house of the Lords Gray of Wilton and Lincoln's Inn is thought to have belonged to Henry de Lacy, earl of Lincoln. In the 15th cent. the Inns gradually assumed responsibility for the education of students and today anyone wishing to become a barrister must first join one of the Inns. They are unincorporated bodies controlled by their senior members known as masters of the bench or benchers. When students are considered qualified for the profession they are 'called' to the bar by their Inn and entitled to practise in the higher courts of law. RAS

inoculation. See VACCINATION.

Instrument of Government. The written constitution under which Oliver *Cromwell became lord *protector on 16 December 1653. Its author was Major-General *Lambert, who had never approved of *Barebone's Parliament and helped to engineer its abdication on 12 December. Like the army's earlier *Heads of the Proposals, which he had helped to draft, the Instrument was a prescription for limited monarchy, and it originally named Cromwell as king. Cromwell declined the crown, but eventually accepted authority as protector under the instrument's terms.

These were that he should govern by the advice of a council, whose members it named and who were not dismissible at pleasure. On his death the council was to elect his successor. Legislative power was vested in a single-chamber parliament representing England, Wales, Scotland, and Ireland and elected at least every three years on a property franchise. Bills must be submitted to the protector for his consent, but could become law without it if they did not contravene the instrument itself. He was to have sufficient revenue for the navy, an army of 30,000, and £200,000 a year for civil government, but for any more he must come to Parliament. A national church was to be maintained, but with freedom of worship for protestant dissenters. AHW

insurance means securing payment of a sum of money in the event of loss or damage to property or life (in the latter case sometimes referred to as assurance) by payment of a premium. An embryonic form of life assurance existed during the Middle Ages in monastic institutions as a way of raising money. A wealthy person could purchase a corrody, which provided for either care in the monastic community or cash at agreed intervals. The sums paid depended on the donor and were not a calculated life risk.

Property insurance developed in response to the hazards faced by medieval exporters, for example losses from shipwreck, piracy, or theft. The rules of the Lombards, Italian merchants, formed the basis for spreading risks. They devised a system of partnerships which sent their produce in several ships with all partners undertaking to bear a portion of any loss but sharing in the profits of the venture.

Such insurance provided for particular combinations for specific ventures. More general cover emerged in the late 17th cent. when the expansion of overseas trade encouraged the development of a market in insurance. At this time Edward *Lloyd's coffee-house became a meeting-place for marine insurers, although they accepted other risks. As other insurers of the time, members of Lloyd's offered insurance on terms of the unlimited liability of 'names', each name meeting the full cost of any loss personally. Most insurers moved towards limited liability by forming companies under the companies Acts of the mid-19th cent. However, Lloyd's names continued with unlimited liability until 1993 when, because of unprecedented losses, their council admitted limited liability companies into syndicates to underwrite risks. Insurers invested premiums in loans and mortgages, for example, to landowners enclosing land in the 18th cent. and, more recently, in stocks and shares and in property developments.

Calculating risks required the systematic collection and analysis of appropriate data. Early in this field were life assurance companies selling annuities. Particularly successful was the Equitable Company, founded in 1762, which drew upon an analysis of mortality rates for Northampton. Profitability depended on accurate data and life assurance companies were active supporters of population censuses initiated by the government. In contrast with the commercial insurance companies, many assurance companies were organized as mutual societies, distributing all profits to members after administrative costs had been met. Commercial insurance against fire and other risks also came to be based on systematic knowledge of the incidence of loss. In towns and cities largely built of wood the risks of fire were high. The Great Fire of *London (1666) hastened the development of insurance against fire. The first company to offer fire insurance was that of Nicholas Barbon's Insurance Office for Houses in London, established in 1681. By the early 18th cent. other companies insured housing and business premises. These companies encouraged positive precautions to prevent fires by the design and construction of buildings, and to deal rapidly with conflagrations. Companies such as the Sun Insurance Office, founded in 1710, had private fire brigades in the largest towns, and its badges can still be seen on some old buildings.

During the 19th cent. insurance cover became available to a larger proportion of the population. Friendly societies and industrial assurance companies collected premiums weekly from mainly artisan subscribers. They paid out sums to meet losses of earnings and health care expenses arising from sickness or injury at work. It was also possible to insure against the cost of funerals and to provide for the subscriber's family.

Insurance has increased during the 20th cent. to meet an ever widening range of risk. Two major areas of insurance are outstanding. First is insurance associated with travel and vehicles. Their importance is demonstrated by the fact that insurance against third party risk became a legal requirement in 1930. Second is the growth of a competitive market in pension provision and a shift from occupational to personal pensions. IJEK

intercursus magnus and intercursus malus were treaties between Henry VII and the Archduke Philip of Burgundy, primarily for the encouragement of trade between England and the Low Countries. By the first (1496) Philip agreed not to support Perkin *Warbeck, pretender to the English throne, to limit tolls, and to provide for speedy redress for merchants. Difficulties continued and the second treaty in 1506 allowed English cloth exports without duty. It was not ratified and a third treaty, in 1507, returned to the terms of the 1496 agreement. The names are those which, according to Bacon, the Flemings attached to the treaties. JAC

interdict is a papal prohibition which could operate at various levels. A general interdict could be imposed only by the pope. Pope Alexander III placed Scotland under an interdict when William the Lion rejected the papal nominee to the see of St Andrews in 1178, and Innocent III issued an interdict against England when John in 1206 refused to accept Stephen *Langton as archbishop of Canterbury. The Scottish interdict ended in a compromise after ten years, when the royal nominee died and the pope's accepted the see of Dunkeld instead. Innocent's interdict forbade all ceremonies save baptism of infants and confessions for the dying: it operated from 1208 and John was excommunicated in 1209. John resisted strongly but in 1213, beset by baronial opposition, he surrendered completely, agreeing to hold his kingdom as the pope's vassal. The interdict was lifted in 1214. JAC

Interregnum is the name sometimes used for the period between the abolition of the monarchy in February 1649 and the Restoration of Charles II in May 1660. Royalists insisted that Charles II had become king as soon as his father was executed and his statutes were dated from 1649. The republican period is divided into the *Commonwealth from 1649 to 1653, when power was exercised by the *Rump Parliament and its *Council of State, and the *Protectorate from 1653 until 1659, when Oliver *Cromwell and his son Richard were lords protector.

In Scotland, two interregna followed the death of Queen *Margaret, the Maid of Norway, in September 1290. The first lasted until the nomination of John *Balliol in November 1292. The second followed his deposition by Edward I in July 1296 and lasted until the coronation of Robert I, the Bruce, in March 1306. The disputed succession gave Edward I the chance to intervene and from 1296 to 1306 he governed Scotland himself. JAC

'Intolerable Acts', 1774. These Acts were the British government's response to the *Boston Tea Party and an attempt to isolate and suppress the allegedly contagious radicalism of Massachusetts. The Boston Port Act, the Massachusetts Government Act, and the Massachusetts Justice Act temporarily closed the port of Boston, replaced an elective council by a crown-nominated one, and allowed capital trials of soldiers and officials to be transferred outside Massachusetts. These Acts received overwhelming parliamentary support. In America, together with the *Quebec Act and a new Quartering Act, they were seen as proof of Britain's wish to destroy American freedoms. RCS

inventories. Detailed lists of household and personal effects possessed by those recently deceased or attainted, insisted upon by probate courts (to be attached to will or letters of administration) from *c.*1526 but rarely after 1782 unless on request of an interested party. With valuations carried out by local men under oath, including leases and debts owed, inventories covered cottages and farms to mansions; their itemization (despite some limitations) has enriched social and economic history, particularly of the early modern period, through reflection of living patterns and standards, old crafts and industries, regional farming practices, wealth distribution, and economic growth. ASH

Invergordon mutiny. Severe pay cuts imposed by the National Government in 1931 led sailors of the British Atlantic fleet at the naval port of Cromarty Firth, Scotland, to refuse to go on duty. The cuts were revised slightly, but this led to financial difficulties for the government. The mutiny ringleaders were discharged from the navy. RAS

Inverlochy, battle of, 1645. *Montrose's victory at *Aberdeen in September 1644 was but a raid and he was soon on the move again, pursued by superior forces under *Argyll himself. When the covenanters retired for the winter, Montrose was persuaded to an insolent incursion into the heart of Campbell country around Inverary. On 2 February 1645, under the shadow of Ben Nevis, Argyll's forces were cut to pieces at Inverlochy, while their hapless chief watched from the safety of a galley on the loch. To the king, Montrose wrote jubilantly that he would soon lead his army south to the rescue. JAC

Inverness, treaty of, 1312. By the treaty of *Perth of 1266, Magnus VI of Norway ceded the Hebrides and the Isle of Man to the Scots in exchange for a permanent annual payment of 100 marks. But the Norwegian presence in Orkney and Shetland led to continued friction.

Robert I Bruce, whose sister Isabella had married Eric II of Norway, was anxious to improve relations. On 29 October 1312 at Inverness, he and Haakon V adjudicated the disputes and repeated the terms of the Perth treaty. JAC

Inverurie, battle of, 1308. A decisive victory of Robert I, king of Scots, over John *Comyn, earl of Buchan, probably on 23 May. After his escape at *Slioch, Robert was able to capture strong points on the coastal plain of Moray and in the Black Isle before returning to Buchan, where, near Inverurie, he routed the earl's forces. He then ravaged the whole of Buchan. Comyn fled to England, leaving Robert to exploit his victory by forcing the earl of Ross to make peace and submit on 31 October 1308. The battle thus gave Robert control of the north. BW

Investiture contest. Name given by historians to the conflicts which ensued when 11th-cent. church reformers, popes like Gregory VII (1073–85) at their head, tried to free the church from its customary subordination to the secular world. To reformers that subordination was symbolized by the investiture ceremony in which a new bishop or abbot received the staff or ring of office from the hands of the lay ruler, who had in practice appointed him. On the other side, rulers wanted to be sure of the loyalty of churchmen who controlled rich estates. In Germany and Italy the quarrels took on the dimensions of a great 50-year struggle between empire and papacy. In England the contest between kings and church reformers such as *Anselm was a relatively brief one and was ended in 1107 by a compromise. Henry I renounced his right of investiture but, as before, prelates continued to be chosen in accordance with royal wishes and swore homage to the king. By focusing attention on a ceremony it proved possible to find a formal solution to a dispute which—as *Becket was to show—was probably insoluble when raised to the level of high principle. JG

Invincibles. A terror gang in Ireland in the 19th cent. After failing to assassinate W. E. *Forster, chief secretary, they murdered his successor, Lord Frederick *Cavendish, and T. H. Burke in Phoenix Park in 1882. James Carey turned queen's evidence at his trial, was pursued on board a ship bound for South Africa, and shot. The murders were a severe embarrassment to *Gladstone and *Parnell who had just reached the *Kilmainham agreement. JAC

Iona. The monastery founded by St *Columba in 563 soon became the centre for Celtic Christianity, sending out missionaries to Scotland and Northumbria. Although the ravages of Viking raids before and after 800 made Iona a more dangerous place to live, its prestige continued well into the 9th cent. Following a massacre of its monks in 806, work began apace on the Irish midland monastery of Kells, which was gradually to become the focus of the Columban communities in Ireland. Kells was finished in 814, and not long after (*c.*818), a new Columban monastery in central Scotland was founded, *Dunkeld. It is generally held that in 849 the relics of St Columba were split between the two new monasteries, confirming shifts in patronage and power centres which had been under way for some time. From the end of the 9th cent., we find the head of the Columban communities, the *comarba Choluim Chille*, based in Kells, and the headship remained there until the 12th cent.

None the less, Iona's importance as a religious centre continued, and began to attract the newly converted Norse settlers of the Hebrides. Two Norse cross slabs are now housed in the Iona museum, one bearing an inscription in Norse runes, another bearing a scene from Norse legend. In 980, the powerful king of Viking Dublin, Olaf Cuarán, died on pilgrimage to the island. This was an up-and-down relationship, however, as six years later, a raiding party from the Northern Isles slaughtered the elders of the monastery and the abbot.

The wider influence of Iona monks can be seen as far afield as Carolingian Europe. Dicuil, a cosmographer who wrote a description of the world *c.*825 in the court of Charles the Bald, probably came from Iona, and he describes other Iona monks ranging as far north as the Faroes and as far south as Egypt. The martyrdom of Blathmac, son of Flann, defending the relics of Columba from Viking raiders in 825 caught the imagination of Walahfrid Strabo, based in the monastery of Reichenau on Lake Constance. One of the 10th-cent. heads of the Columban communities, Mugrón (965–81), who appears to have been partially based in Scotland, was a devotional writer of some skill.

The 11th cent. was marred by such incidents as the loss of some of Columba's relics on a journey back to Ireland from Iona (in 1034), and slaying of the abbot by a rival, the son of a former abbot of Kells in 1070. None the less, Scottish kings, according to tradition, continued to be buried there, and *Margaret, wife of Malcolm III, king of the Scots, held the monastery in favour.

In the next century, it again became the religious hub of a new island-centred power-base. *Somerled mac Gille-Brigde, the powerful Argyll sea-lord whose descendants became the Lords of the *Isles, attempted in 1164 to lure the head of the Columban communities back to Iona. He failed, but the building of a new Benedictine monastery in 1204, followed by an Augustinian nunnery, spelled the return of Iona's fortunes. Closely linked to the Lords of the Isles from the 14th cent. onwards, and the seat intermittently of the bishop of the Isles, Iona in the later Middle Ages was a great centre of sculpture. The present church on the island dates substantially to the 15th-cent. renewal programme, and displays the skills and patronage then available. Only with the forfeiture of the lordship in 1493 and the Reformation did Iona's decline set in in earnest. TOC

Ipswich. Suffolk town, on the Orwell estuary. It was one of the earliest post-Roman towns in Britain, originating in the 7th cent. as a trading port (wic) and industrial town. Large and wealthy from *c.*650 to 850, it was less important in the high and later Middle Ages. Thomas *Wolsey, a major benefactor, was born there in 1471. Under the Tudors and Stuarts it enjoyed a second heyday as a port and cloth town, and was one of the half-dozen largest and wealthiest English provincial towns. Since the 18th cent. it has been of regional rather than national importance. DMP

Iraq, which formed part of the Turkish empire, was the scene of heavy fighting in the First World War, the British capturing Baghdad in 1917. At the end of the war the territory became a *mandate under the *League of Nations, though there was a substantial nationalist rising in 1920. From 1921 until 1958, when Faisal II was assassinated, the country was a monarchy. The second Labour government gave notice in 1929 that it would relinquish the mandate in 1932 and in that year Iraq entered the League of Nations as an independent country. The mandate was replaced by an Anglo-Iraq treaty which gave Britain military bases, held until after the Second World War. The attack on Kuwait in 1990 by Saddam Hussein, who had come to power in 1979, led to the *Gulf War, in which Britain sent troops under United Nations auspices. JAC

Ireland, Board of National Education. By the end of the Napoleonic wars, there was an urgent need in Ireland to provide national education for the children of the poor. Large grants to separate denominational bodies, such as the *Kildare Place Society, had proved unsuccessful. In September 1831 Thomas Wyse, an Irish MP, introduced a bill to educate catholics and protestants in the same school. Although the bill never became law, at the end of 1831 a Board of Education was established to institute an elementary school system. Members of the board, consisting of moderate catholics and protestants, administered an annual grant to local schools, supervised their work, supplied textbooks, and trained teachers. Although secular instruction was given in common, denominational religious teaching was conducted separately. Grants were given to schools on condition that part of the money needed was raised locally. Whilst the question of religious instruction caused many difficulties, by the 1840s the board had made much headway, providing over 3,500 schools attended by 400,000 children. PG

Ireland, Government of, Act, 1920–1. The first major constitutional reform since the Act of *Union 1800–1 resulted from the need for an alternative to the third Home Rule Bill, suspended 1914, which no longer had the backing of Southern Irish nationalist opinion. It aimed to establish two devolved governments for the six counties of the north-east and the twenty-six counties of south and west. Essential powers were to be retained at Westminster, proportional representation was to be used at elections, and a Council of Ireland was to be established for the administration of agreed all-Ireland matters. It was intended to meet demands for self-determination and to hold out hope for eventual Irish unity. The Dáil rejected the Act, which was supplanted by the *Anglo-Irish treaty of 1921. Any prospect of a Council of Ireland collapsed in 1925. For 70 years the Act has provided the legal basis for Northern Ireland's existence. Following the Downing Street declaration of 1993, debate has concerned possible changes to the Act in response to the Irish Republic government's potential flexibility on its claim to Northern Ireland. MAH

Ireland, high kings of. Despite the popular perception of the importance of the 'high kingship' of Ireland, it is clear that early medieval Ireland did not possess a monarch whose rule was effective over the entire island, since the early law tracts (7th–8th cent.) specify only three grades of kingship, the most senior of which is a province king. Nevertheless, the most powerful dynasty in the country, the Uí Néill, who dominated the northern half of the island, were often able to compel most, if not all, of the other province kings to submit to them, so that by the mid-9th cent. at the latest the concept of the high kingship had taken root. *Brian Boru, however, destroyed the Uí Néill monopoly of the title and the 11th and 12th cents. were ones in which Ireland generally only had a high king 'with opposition', the last of whom was Rory *O'Connor, high king at the time of the Anglo-Norman invasion in 1169. SD

Ireland, lordship of. Ireland first emerges into the light of history with the introduction of Christianity in the 5th cent. in documents ascribed to the British missionary, St *Patrick. Thereafter it developed a highly literate society, which has left us a substantial corpus of Latin and vernacular literature, allowing us to form a mental picture of Dark Age Ireland that is clearer and far more detailed than that available for almost any other European country. The 7th–8th cent. law tracts, heavily influenced by the Scriptures, portray a society that was intensely hierarchical, where status and honour meant much, and where sharp distinctions were made between the various grades of society, principally between those regarded as 'sacred' (including kings, clerics, and poets) and those who were not, and between the free and the unfree.

At the highest rung of the ladder stood the kings, around whom society revolved. Ireland was a land of many kings, the law tracts defining three grades: kings of petty local kingdoms, overkings ruling several of these, and 'kings of overkings' who effectively ruled a whole province. Although the laws rarely refer to a *high king of all Ireland, it is clear that for several centuries until the early 11th cent. the leading dynasty, the Uí Néill (based in the northern half of the country, having their capital at *Tara), did claim, and were occasionally able to enforce, supremacy throughout the island. Their primacy was smashed by the upstart *Munster king *Brian Boru (d. 1014) and throughout the 11th and 12th cents. power revolved around a half-dozen or so leading province kings, each seeking to force his rivals into submission and assert himself as high king.

It is difficult to assess the extent to which these changes were the result of the *Viking incursions which began in the late 8th cent., and which for a time in the 9th cent. seemed likely to overwhelm the country. Certainly, the Vikings increased the intensity of warfare in an already violent society, and by developing towns at *Dublin, Waterford, Limerick, Wexford, and Cork, and trading networks overseas, they added to the wealth of what was otherwise a largely pastoral economy. In time, the Viking enclaves were assimilated into the Irish political superstructure, and those Irish kings who succeeded in asserting dominance over them, in some cases establishing the Viking town as their capital, gained an advantage over their rivals in the race for the high kingship. This was especially true in the case of Dublin, overlordship of which was, by the late 10th cent., generally asserted by successful claimants to the high kingship and which, by the mid-11th cent., was directly ruled by Irish kings, in effect replacing Tara as the country's symbolic capital.

What appears to have been the evolution of a national monarchy was cut short in the mid-12th cent. by the Anglo-Norman invasion, spearheaded by men from the Welsh borderlands, at the instigation of the *Leinster king, *Dermot MacMurrough, who had been expelled by the reigning high king, *Rory O'Connor. The invaders were led by Richard de Clare, earl of *Pembroke, better known as Strongbow, who married MacMurrough's daughter and succeeded to Leinster himself. At this point, late in 1171, Henry II (who had received a papal licence to invade Ireland in order, it was claimed, to aid in the process of reform then under way in the Irish church) came to Ireland himself, the first English king ever to do so, and established the English lordship. A widespread process of colonization then began, which involved the introduction to Ireland of English common law and institutions. Early attempts to reach an accommodation with Rory O'Connor were soon abandoned in favour of a policy of all-out conquest which at first proved remarkably successful, to the extent that, by the end of the 13th cent., English rule was effective over perhaps two-thirds of the island.

At this point a gradual decline began to take place in the fortunes of the English colony, exacerbated by a Scottish invasion led by Robert Bruce's brother *Edward in 1315–18, and worsening economic conditions throughout much of the 14th cent. This was accompanied by a dramatic revival in the power of the native Irish lords, whose culture many of the settlers had begun to adopt, in spite of frequent attempts by the Irish *Parliament to legislate against it. Costly military campaigns in the second half of the 14th cent., two led by Richard II, the first English king to visit his lordship since King John's expedition in 1210, failed to turn the tide. A preoccupation with the war with France and a series of cash-starved Lancastrian administrations meant a curtailment in the English commitment to the government of Ireland in the 15th cent., resources being channelled into the preservation of peace in a cordoned enclave surrounding Dublin known as the *Pale, with responsibility for the government of the rest of the lordship being devolved on the resident Anglo-Irish magnates, principally the earls of Ormond, Desmond, and Kildare.

A growing separatist tendency among the Anglo-Irish community, culminating in a declaration of parliamentary independence in 1460 (though checked by the passage of *Poynings's Law in 1494, forbidding the holding of parliaments without the king's licence), led to the emergence of the earls of Kildare as effective masters of the Pale and of much of the country, though nominally the king's deputy. The Kildare ascendancy continued until the rebellion by Thomas *FitzGerald, son of the 9th earl, in 1534, which was used by Henry VIII as a pretext for destroying Kildare power, the males of the family being put to death and their lands confiscated. The fall of the Geraldines left much of Ireland ungoverned and served to reinforce the view that a reconquest of the country was needed. The Irish 'Reformation Parliament' convened in 1536 declared Henry supreme head of the church, while that of 1541 gave the English monarch for the first time the title of king (as opposed to lord) of Ireland, in the process bringing the medieval lordship to an end. SD

Duffy, S., *Ireland in the Middle Ages* (1996); Frame, R., *Colonial Ireland, 1169–1369* (Dublin, 1981); Ó Corráin, D., *Ireland before the Normans* (Dublin, 1972); Ó Cróinin, D., *Early Medieval Ireland, 400–1200* (1995).

Ireland Act, 1949. Following the Irish Free State government's declaration of a republic in September 1948, the Act regulated relations with Ireland in clause 1(1)B, and gave guarantees that the constitutional status of Northern Ireland would not be changed without the consent of the Parliament of Northern Ireland. That assurance has been reiterated at frequent intervals during the Ulster crisis since 1969 although rephrased as: no change without the consent of a majority of the electorate—in the Sunningdale agreement 1973, Anglo-Irish agreement 1985, and Downing Street declaration 1993. It has, however, never completely managed to reassure Unionist opinion, constantly fearful of a British sell-out. Opinion on all sides is now aware that there will probably be a catholic majority in the six counties early in the 21st cent. MAH

Ireton, Henry (1611–51). Ireton was plunged into the Civil War, since he was appointed by Parliament to command the horse at Nottingham two months before Charles I raised his standard in the same town. He fought at *Edgehill and in the first battle of *Newbury, where he was wounded and temporarily captured, and rapidly became one of *Cromwell's most trusted lieutenants. In 1646 he married Cromwell's daughter Bridget. *Whitelocke described him as an excellent man of business with a great influence over Cromwell. In 1647 he was mainly responsible for the Representation of the Army and the *Heads of the Proposals, which set forth a constitutional settlement, including reform of Parliament. At this stage Ireton was a moderate and had not despaired of coming to terms with the king. He took a prominent part in the *Putney army debates of November 1647, ardently defending the rights of property against radical and egalitarian proposals. The second civil war, in which he served at the siege of *Colchester, persuaded him that no deal with Charles was possible and in January 1649 he signed the king's death warrant. He accompanied Cromwell to Ireland and remained in charge when Cromwell returned to England in May 1650. The following year he died of fever and was buried with an elaborate funeral in Westminster abbey. At the Restoration he was one of the regicides whose body was exhumed and hanged. A strong, determined, and capable man, Ireton might have been a possible successor to Cromwell had he not died at the age of 40. JAC

Irish Citizen Army. Ulster responded to the introduction of the third Home Rule Bill in 1912 with the *'Ulster covenant' and prepared for armed resistance. A section of the nationalists retorted with a Citizen Army in November 1913, which began drilling. Led by James *Connolly, it was one of a number of nationalist paramilitary groups, not always on good terms with each other. But it took part in the occupation of the General Post Office during the *Easter week rising of 1916 and made a raid on Dublin castle. JAC

Irish Constabulary/Royal Irish Constabulary (after 1867). The Irish Constabulary was created in 1836 with an initial strength of around 7,500: this figure rose to 12,358 in 1850, before settling at around 10,000. The force was distinct from its English counterparts: it conformed more closely to continental models, being armed and centrally controlled. The prefix 'Royal' was granted in 1867 in recognition of the constabulary's conduct during the *Fenian rising. However, pay remained low, while the administrative burden and unpopularity of the force grew: morale was therefore vulnerable, as evidenced by the police strike of August 1882, and by police disaffection during the Belfast dockers' strike of 1907. The RIC bore the burden of the *Irish Republican Army onslaught of 1919–21, sustaining around 416 killed and just under 700 wounded. The force was disbanded in 1922 after the ratification of the *Anglo-Irish treaty in London and Dublin. AJ

Irish famine. See FAMINE, IRISH.

Irish Free State, 1922–48. The state was formed by the *Anglo-Irish treaty of December 1921, which granted dominion status, with defence safeguards, to twenty-six counties of the south and west of Ireland. Its first months,

December 1922–April 1923, saw the completion of a bitter civil war; that conflict established political authority over the military challenge, but the tactics used by the Free State government, especially executions, ensured long-term acrimony. Thereafter the Free State proved remarkably stable, thanks to an overwhelmingly catholic agrarian population and the exclusion of the north-eastern counties. Once stability was established, the fundamental conservatism in social and economic affairs asserted itself. Both Cumann na nGaedheal (1922–32) and Fianna Fail (from 1932) governments adopted protectionist economic policies and catholic hierarchy-approved social policies. British forms ironically were major models for the governmental institutions. Heavy emphasis was put on Gaelic revivalism. Issues unresolved from the revolutionary period—partition and relations with Britain—dominated party politics. *De Valera's government of the 1930s successfully widened the treaty settlement by abolishing the oath to the crown and removing the governor-general. The constitution of 1937 established a virtual republic and independence in international affairs was confirmed by neutrality during the *Second World War; those achievements at the cost of becoming isolated. A republic was finally declared by the coalition government at a press conference in Ottawa in September 1948. Recently historians have emphasized the poor performance of the Free State economy, resulting in appalling levels of emigration and a sluggish, parochial character. The pro-treaty leader Kevin O'Higgins had been correct to observe: 'we were probably the most conservative-minded revolutionaries that ever put through a successful revolution.' MAH

Irish Free State/Republic, relations with. Given the background of bitterness and the controversial circumstances behind the *Anglo-Irish treaty of December 1921, relations were bound to be tense. The treaty left many issues unresolved: the precise definition of the South's constitutional connection with Britain; its autonomy in foreign affairs; potential changes in the border with Northern Ireland. The British government during the civil war doubted the integrity of Irish support for the treaty and frequently showed old colonial arrogance towards the Free State government. A majority in the South accepted the treaty without enthusiasm, but a minority supported the republican side in the civil war and did not agree to compromise at the end of the conflict. Partition and the constitutional status dominated Irish politics in the 1920s and 1930s: the agreement between the British and Irish governments not to change the border in 1925 hardened anti-British resentment. The two main parties in the South, Cumann na nGaedheal/Fine Gael and Fianna Fail, are best distinguished by their relative position over Britain. *De Valera consolidated his electoral popularity by abolishing the oath to the crown and by refusing to pay land annuities; the British response resulted in a trade war, only settled in 1938 with an agreement favourable for Ireland, in which Britain agreed to vacate the so-called Treaty Ports. Relations soon deteriorated over Irish neutrality during the Second World War and refusal to bow to pressure to hand back the ports.

The coalition government's declaration of a republic in 1948 was made without consultation with Britain and caused the constitutional position of Northern Ireland to be reinforced by the *Ireland Act a year later. Not until the 1970s, which saw Ireland and Britain in the *European Economic Community and revision of the traditional nationalist ideology in the South did communications improve. In the early years of the Northern Ireland crisis, relations were put back on a footing reminiscent of the early 1920s: the Irish government talked of establishing field hospitals on the border and elements in it helped to finance the Provisional IRA in its early stages; the British embassy in Dublin was burnt down after Derry's Bloody Sunday, February 1972. As the northern conflict wore on, southern attitudes became increasingly pragmatic, particularly when Garret FitzGerald was Taoiseach (June 1981–March 1982, December 1982–March 1987). Increasing criticism within the South of the old irredentist outlook and appreciation of the need to change a conservative social framework were both part of a *rapprochement* with Britain. The British government came to recognize that Dublin must play an important part in any settlement of the northern question. Such developments culminated in the *Anglo-Irish agreement 1985, which had disappointing results in the North, but dramatically improved Anglo-Irish communications, and was belatedly accepted by Charles Haughey, Fianna Fail Taoiseach (1987–92). With the worsening northern security situation, increasing concern in Ireland and Britain about the level of expenditure, and agreement between leaders of Sinn Fein and the IRA, British and Irish prime ministers John *Major and Albert Reynolds redefined their countries' aims in December 1993 in the Downing Street declaration. Never as cold as they superficially appeared, Anglo-Irish relations since the 1960s have become progressively warmer, but many fundamental differences have yet to be settled over Northern Ireland before the past can be buried. MAH

Irish Home Rule. From the formation of the Home Government Association, led by Isaac *Butt in 1870, Home Rule became the ill-defined term representing the demands of the constitutional nationalists. Its origins lay in Daniel *O'Connell's Repeal Movement of the 1840s: like O'Connell, Home Rulers between 1870 and 1918 never made clear precisely what form amendment of the Act of *Union 1800–1 should take, whether it would mean a reversion to the legislative independence of 1782, whether some Irish representation would be retained at Westminster, or whether the desired aim should be a truly independent Irish state. There was agreement that the movement's tactics should be based on winning concessions from the British Parliament by influencing British MPs and by building up effective Irish representation in the Commons. Butt's embryonic party and his leadership, however, proved ineffective during the 1870s. From 1881 the movement entered upon its most successful period under the charismatic and autocratic leadership of Charles Stewart *Parnell. Through his leadership of the *Irish Land League, Parnell was able to provide mass popular backing for Irish MPs, organizing a disciplined parliamentary party with Home Rule as its priority demand. Parnell took advantage of *Gladstone's dependence on the Irish Party for the survival of his government to influence him to introduce the first Home Rule Bill 1886. The bill allowed for only limited devolution: the British government was to retain control over security, foreign policy, and financial institutions. Though the bill divided the Liberal Party and failed to pass the Commons, it represented a triumph for Irish nationalism and an acknowledgement that Ireland could govern itself. Neither Parnell nor Gladstone allowed for resistance from Ulster protestants. From 1886 and with the advent of a new Conservative government, Parnell's party lost much influence and unity collapsed over Parnell's involvement in the O'Shea divorce case in 1890. In 1893 Gladstone introduced a second Home Rule Bill, which was soundly defeated in the House of Lords. The Home Rule Movement did not recover the appeal it had possessed in the 1880s for most elements of the Irish population. Between 1893 and 1910 more limited forms of self-government were considered by Tory and Liberal governments and the growth of cultural nationalism in Ireland challenged the hegemony of the parliamentary party, particularly amongst the young. A constitutional crisis, caused by reform of the House of Lords 1910–11, resulted again in a minority Liberal government, dependent on the Irish Parliamentary Party, and led to the introduction of a third Home Rule Bill, with the expectation that it would become law within two years. The years 1912–14 produced a great test for the Home Rule cause in British politics, with fierce Ulster resistance, backed up by the Tory Party and by large elements of the British establishment. By 1914 and the final stages of the bill, civil war threatened in Britain and Ireland with the option of partition, temporary or permanent, as the only alternative. When the First World War intervened, the Home Rule Bill was on the statute book, but was suspended for the duration of the war, with temporary exclusion for Ulster. Following the *Easter Rising, *Lloyd George made another attempt to achieve a Home Rule settlement, which again foundered on the partition question. By the end of 1918 the situation was transformed by the collapse of the Irish Parliamentary Party and Sinn Fein's demand for a settlement considerably in advance of Home Rule. The Government of *Ireland Act 1920–1 attempted a Home Rule settlement, with separate north-east and southern parliaments: ironically it was the loyalist Northerners who accepted the offer. Home Rule's demise was a failure for Liberal moderation in Britain and for constitutional nationalism in Ireland. British methods of conciliation and compromise had not worked in the Irish context. The consequences of Home Rule's failure are still felt on both sides of the Irish Sea. MAH

Irish Land League, 1879–82. The league was formed during the agrarian depression to demand tenant rights, including fair rents and security of tenure. It spread through much of the south and west of Ireland, unifying the interests of large and small farmers, provincial town and countryside. Aided by developments in communications and literacy, it became the most popular organization in 19th-cent. Ireland. Its adoption of the boycott tactic towards rack-renting landlords and other forms of exploitation pressurized *Gladstone to introduce his *Land Act in 1881, granting many of its demands. Following this Act, divisions occurred between large and small farmers/labourers and between militants and moderates. *Parnell, president of the league, in accepting a revised Land Act and rejecting further agitation by the *Kilmainham treaty 1882 effectively terminated the movement. MAH

Irish National Party (Irish Parliamentary Party). Beginning from 1870 under Isaac *Butt's Home Government Association, it only became a disciplined successful party under *Parnell 1880–90. In the 1880s Parnell took advantage of the extension of the franchise, improved literacy and communications, and favourable circumstances at Westminster to build up a highly organized modern party which pressed the issue of Home Rule on British politicians. It increased popular support by its association with the land reform agitation. It split into contending factions over Parnell's fall 1890–1 and unity was only restored in 1900 under John *Redmond. But the party never recovered the wide popularity enjoyed under Parnell and was overtaken by the appeal of new nationalism to the young. Appearing close to success when the third Home Rule Bill was introduced in 1912, it suffered from the effective opposition in Ulster and in the Conservative Party to that bill. By supporting the British government in the First World War, it was blamed for the war's increasing unpopularity. It declined rapidly in the two years after the *Easter Rising following the final failure of Home Rule settlement in 1916 and its apparent weakening over partition, and was obliterated by Sinn Fein in the 1918 general election. It suffered from being a single party for so long, for being associated with a single issue, and for being so dependent on British politicians. MAH

Irish rebellions, 1641, 1848, 1867, 1916. See KILKENNY, CONFEDERATION OF; O'BRIEN, WILLIAM SMITH; IRISH REPUBLICAN BROTHERHOOD; EASTER RISING.

Irish rebellion, 1798. The 1798 rising occurred in the summer, and involved between 30,000 and 50,000 insurgents and around 76,000 government troops. The intellectual leadership came from the Francophile *United Irish movement (1791), originally middle class and urban and in favour of constitutional reform; but after 1795–6 there was an overlap between the United Irishmen and a rural protest organization, the catholic *Defenders. As the possibility of nonviolent reform diminished in the 1790s, the militancy of the United Irish movement and of popular protest developed: the prospect of French military aid after an abortive invasion at Bantry Bay (1796) also encouraged rebel preparations. The revolt was precipitated by the government's brutal efforts, especially in April–May 1798, to suppress sedition and conspiracy. There were two main centres of rebellion: in eastern Ulster, where the insurgents were decisively defeated at Antrim and at Ballynahinch; and in south Leinster, where the critical rebel defeat occurred at *Vinegar Hill (Co. Wexford) on 21 June. A French landing, at Killala (Co. Mayo) in August, came too late to assist the Irish insurgents, and was defeated at Ballinamuck (Co. Longford) within a week of arriving. The rising cost perhaps 30,000 lives. It further discredited the Irish government with William *Pitt, and reinforced his sympathy for a constitutional union between Britain and Ireland. As the first expression of popular militant republicanism, the rising, though a failure, had a lasting symbolic significance for physical-force nationalists. AJ

Irish Republican Army (IRA). The Irish Volunteers, formed in 1913/14 and reorganized along conventional military command lines after the *Easter Rising, became known as the IRA from 1919. During the Anglo-Irish War, 1919–21, it became the dominant military arm of the Dáil government, and fought a limited successful guerrilla war until stalemate was acknowledged by the truce of July 1921. Divided over the *Anglo-Irish treaty of December 1921, the minority formed the Provisional Government/Free State Army, while the majority armed against the new state in the civil war 1922–3. Guerrilla warfare tactics were then less successful, and defeat was implicit in the cease-fire of April 1923. The *raison d'être* of the organization remained because of partition and the allegiance to the British crown. For four decades, the IRA was undecided whether to concentrate on a campaign against the border, or against British and Free State/Republic government, or to focus on social and economic issues. It waged an unsuccessful border campaign 1956–61, and shifted into being a Marxist pressure group. The outbreak of violence in Derry and Belfast from 1969 found the movement wanting in its traditional protective role for the catholic minority: graffiti claimed IRA stood for 'I ran away'. A split occurred between the Belfast-based traditional nationalist Provisional IRA and the Marxist Official IRA, with the latter shrinking and splintering into smaller republican organizations. The Provisional IRA waged a high-profile terror campaign, which was instrumental in the collapse of *Stormont in 1972 and in power-sharing initiatives, but it lost support and momentum as a result of an unsuccessful truce 1974/5, though continuing operations in the province and in Britain. Gaining considerable support from the hunger strike crisis of 1981, the movement adopted a more political strategy with Sinn Fein Armalite and ballot policy. The use of cell organization in the 1980s gave greater secrecy and effectiveness, but made widespread acceptance of political strategy difficult and caused protracted debate leading to the cease-fire of August 1994–January 1996. MAH

Irish Republican Brotherhood. Better known as the *Fenian movement. A secret society, organized along cell lines, it became the long-term agency for the planning of Irish insurrections. It was behind the abortive uprising in Ireland in 1867 and the equally unsuccessful 'invasions' of Canada between 1867 and 1870. From the 1870s, its supreme council—consisting of Irish, British, and American-based representatives—claimed to be the existing government of the Irish Republic. Revived after 1910, it infiltrated the Volunteer movement and regarded the British involvement in the First World War as its great opportunity. Its military council planned the *Easter Rising; many advanced nationalists blamed the IRB for the rising's failure and argued that its usefulness was over. Others, however, notably Michael *Collins, continued to regard it as a crucial élite and the means by which to defeat British intelligence and secure arms contacts. Like all other nationalist institutions, the IRB divided over the *Anglo-Irish treaty and did not survive the effects of the civil war. MAH

Irish Volunteers. See VOLUNTEER MOVEMENT.

Ironbridge (Shropshire). The valley of the Severn below the Cistercian abbey of Buildwas developed in the early 18th cent. as a great iron manufacturing area under the *Coalbrookdale Company, run by the *Darby family. The bridge itself was designed and built by Abraham Darby the third and opened in 1779. Much of the ironwork was made by John *Wilkinson, who followed up the success with an iron barge, launched in 1787. The intricate iron tracery gives the bridge a delicate, almost fragile appearance. It was one of the wonders of its age and is now the focal point of a superb museum complex. JAC

iron industry. Iron has been used in the British Isles since the prehistoric Iron Age. Its importance has continued until the present day. Archaeological evidence of iron production has been found on many sites over most of Britain, wherever iron ores could be extracted with comparative ease and there was adequate fuel for smelting. Most villages employed a smith and it became the most common surname in England.

Iron production depended on the availability of smeltable ores and refining and casting techniques. For many centuries the highest-quality ore was haematite and the heat source for smelting was charcoal. Thus, for example, the weald of Sussex and the Cumbrian area, which both possessed the necessary resources, remained important centres of high-quality British production from the Middle Ages until the early 19th cent. However, mining of lower-quality ores supported the industry elsewhere.

When many areas became denuded of trees, efforts were made to find other fuels, notably coal, for smelting ores. Coal had only been used in fashioning iron previously. Experiments were undertaken by many ironmasters, including Dud *Dudley in the 17th cent., but it was not until the early 18th cent. that Abraham *Darby succeeded. The technique took many years to become economically worthwhile and only towards the end of the 18th cent. was coal usually used to smelt iron ores. The consequent quantity production at lower prices encouraged many developments in the uses of both wrought and cast iron.

The most famous centre of ironworking using coal was founded by Darby at *Coalbrookdale (Shropshire). The adjacent iron bridge across the river Severn, designed and built by John *Wilkinson, stands to this day. Wilkinson's pioneering efforts encouraged many innovators so that by the 1780s mills were erected with stressed iron members allowing height and scale in buildings, utilizing the principles of what came to be skyscraper engineering. One of the most spectacular buildings of iron was the *Crystal Palace for the *Great Exhibition of 1851.

Although unusual uses of iron for building purposes in the early 19th cent. impressed the public (iron-framed churches and wrought-iron Regency balconies), the more significant demands on the industry were supplying households with kitchen ranges, firebacks, and cooking utensils. During the 1830s and 1840s significant demand came from railways. These required iron for their tracks, locomotives, and as components for many kinds of equipment. The relationship of railways with the iron industry was close and continuous. However, such was the variety of demand for iron that the industry was never dominated by railway demands even at the heights of the mania in the 1840s.

Before 1850 manufacturers of many kinds of engineering products demonstrated the versatility of iron, either wrought or cast. During the 1820s, steam-engines made of iron and driving paddles gave an impetus to shipbuilding. In the middle of the century the Royal Navy received HMS *Warrior*, its first iron-clad warship. This was soon superseded by all-iron vessels of much greater size and mobility. From the mid-19th cent. the merchant navy ordered many iron ships, with greater speed and larger cargo capacity.

In the 1840s sheet iron plated with tin was invented. This gave rise to an industry, concentrated in south Wales and the west midlands, providing the basic material for many utensils for the kitchen, food-processing, and storage. The cutlery trade used iron for many products, reserving steel, a semi-precious metal, for cutting edges. The *Bessemer process, patented in 1855, made mild steel a cheap and superior rival for wrought and cast iron in some products.

Iron continued to be in demand as the basic raw material for steel-making. However, steel had structural advantages and durability which iron lacked, and the railways adopted steel for their tracks. Research in steel manufacture produced metals for special purposes. Amongst these was stainless steel and, from the late 19th cent., a succession of armour plates evolved for warships, armoured cars, and tanks.

Iron continues to have a role in its own right for many engineering uses, ranging from building supplies to the structural beds for many machines, where its weight and strength make it ideal. Its cheapness keeps it in use. In the late 20th cent., challenges come not from other metals but from plastics. IJEK

Ironsides was a nickname given to Oliver *Cromwell by Prince *Rupert after the battle of *Marston Moor (July 1644). The title was derived, according to a contemporary writer, 'from the impenetrable strength of his troops, which could by no means be broken or divided'. Later the term was extended to the soldiers themselves—the double regiment of cavalry which Cromwell had raised and trained in East Anglia at the outbreak of the Civil War, and known both for its rigid discipline and its religious radicalism. At the founding of the *New Model Army in 1645 the regiment was divided, half being assigned to General Thomas *Fairfax and the other half to Colonel Edward Whalley. IJG

Irvine agreement, 1297. In 1296 Edward I led a large army into Scotland, deposed John *Balliol, and removed the stone of *Scone. At Irvine in July 1297 a number of Scottish barons, including possibly Robert Bruce (later Robert I), submitted. But Scottish resistance flared and in September *Wallace's great victory at *Stirling put English supremacy in doubt once more. JAC

Irving, Edward (1792–1834). Religious leader. Born in Annan, educated at Edinburgh University, Irving was successively master of Kirkcaldy Academy, assistant at St John's, Glasgow, and minister at Hatton Garden chapel, London (1822), where his extravagant preaching moved many, but made him pretentious. He published his naïve *Argument for Judgement to Come* (1823) and moved to a large new church in Regent Square (1827) where his congregation grew to 1,000. Convinced of Christ's imminent second coming, he encouraged 'speaking with tongues' and translated a Spanish Jesuit's *The Coming of the Messiah in Glory and Majesty* (1827). After returning to Scotland (1828) where he was greeted with crowded churches, he was charged with heresy for his tract *The Orthodox and Catholic Doctrine of our Lord's Human Nature* (1830) and removed from Regent Square (1832). His congregation mostly followed him to found the *Catholic Apostolic Church (or Irvingites). The Church of Scotland deprived him of his orders (1833). WMM

Irving, Henry (1838–1905). Actor and theatre manager. Born John Henry Brodribb, but abandoning a merchant's clerkship for ten years' apprenticeship with theatrical stock companies in the provinces, Irving emerged as a leading actor, with a gift for the macabre, in 1871. On becoming lessee and manager of the Lyceum theatre (London), he mounted elaborate, sumptuous productions, paying much attention to detail and hiring leading designers and composers; the company made several successful American tours, and he became the first actor to be knighted (1895). Though a charismatic 'intellectual' rather than 'emotional' actor, described by Ellen *Terry (his professional partner for 24 years) as 'an egotist of the great type', but criticized for mannerisms in delivery and gait, Irving ignored new drama from *Shaw and Ibsen. After heavy losses in a fire and serious illness (1898), the struggle to maintain the Lyceum company ended in 1902. ASH

Isabella of Angoulême (*c.*1188–1246), queen of King John. Isabella was the second wife of King John and was about 12 at the time of their marriage in August 1200. The alliance seems to have been a mixture of passion and diplomacy on John's part, since Angoulême lay in the heart of *Aquitaine, which John was seeking to retain. She was crowned in Westminster abbey in October 1200 and appeared with John at Canterbury for a crown-wearing at Easter 1201. The spite and malice of the chroniclers make it difficult to be sure of her personality. Matthew Paris insisted that she and her husband were vicious and adulterous and that John threatened to hang her gallants over her bed. But their fifth child, Eleanor, was born in 1215, the year before John's death, which suggests that their relations were normal, if not close. Their first child, the future Henry III, was born in 1207. After John's death, Isabella returned to France and in 1220 married Hugh de Lusignan, comte de la Marche, to whom she had previously been betrothed. From then on she was engaged in the dynastic politics of that region. Her son Henry erected a tomb over her grave at Fontevraud. SMC

Isabella of France (1292–1358), queen of Edward II. The daughter of Philip IV of France, Isabella married Edward II at Boulogne in January 1308, soon after his accession. Infatuated by Piers *Gaveston, Edward neglected her. Nevertheless, they produced four children. The future Edward III was born in 1312 and their last child, a daughter, in June 1321. The influence of the *Despensers estranged her from her husband and in 1325 she took refuge in France, supported by her brother Charles IV. In 1326 she joined her lover, Roger *Mortimer, in an invasion which easily swept away Edward's power. London rose in her favour, the Despensers were executed, Edward deposed in January 1327 and murdered at Berkeley castle in September 1327. For three years she and Mortimer ruled the country on behalf of the young Edward III. But in 1330 they were overthrown by a coup at Nottingham which had the king's support. Mortimer was at once executed, Isabella lived in comfortable retirement before entering a convent for her last years. She died at Hertford. As an adulterous queen, Isabella achieved a notoriety she scarcely deserved and remained for centuries material for saucy lampoons or parallels directed at later royal couples. SMC

Isabella of France (1389–1409), queen of Richard II. The second daughter of Charles VI of France, Isabella became second wife of Richard II in November 1396 as the basis for a *rapprochement* between England and France. She was only 7 at the time but commented: 'they tell me that I shall be a great lady.' Richard showered his child-bride with gifts and seemed to be genuinely fond of her, making some effort to learn French. But in May 1399 he left for Ireland and on his return was deposed by Henry of Bolingbroke. Richard's successor, as Henry IV, had some idea of marrying Isabella to Henry, prince of Wales, partly to avoid paying back her dowry, but she was returned to France in 1401. She married her cousin Charles, count of Angoulême, in 1406 but died in childbirth in September 1409 and was buried at Blois. SMC

Isabella of Gloucester (d. 1217), queen of King John. Isabella, also known as Avice or Hawisa, was the youngest daughter and co-heiress of William, 2nd earl of Gloucester. She was betrothed to John, son of Henry II, in 1176 when he was only 9, presumably to provide him with estates. The marriage did not take place until 1189, when John's brother Richard had succeeded. It is doubtful whether they ever lived together. There were no children by the marriage and John's natural children date from this period. Isabella was not crowned when John became king in 1199 and the following year they were divorced on the grounds that, as cousins, they were within the prohibited relationships. John married his second wife, *Isabella of Angoulême, almost at once. Isabella of Gloucester remained a wealthy heiress and seems to have lived in honourable confinement. But in 1214 she was given as a bride to *Geoffrey de Mandeville, presumably as a favour, and on his death in a tournament in 1216 she married, very shortly before her death, Hubert de *Burgh. SMC

Isandhlwana. Hill, located 75 miles north of Pietermaritzburg (South Africa), site of an important battle in the *Zulu War. Part of the centre column of a three-pronged British invasion of Zululand, having underestimated its opponents, was surprised by a Zulu army on 22 January 1879. Disciplined rifle fire enabled the column to hold its own until it ran short of ammunition. Then it was overrun and almost completely wiped out. The Zulus did not follow up their victory because their ruler, Cetshwayo, anxious not to appear to be acting provocatively, had given orders that his forces should not cross into British territory. KI

Isle of Man. The Isle of Man in the Irish Sea is 48 miles from Anglesey, 38 miles from the Irish coast, and only 20 miles from Scotland. It is some 30 miles from north to south and 10 east to west—i.e. rather smaller than Anglesey but larger than the Isle of Wight. The population in 1991 was 70,000, many of them retired people. There is no evidence of Roman settlement, though they must have known it since Ravenglass, an important Roman port, was less than 40 miles away. A handful of Roman coins, probably from traders, have been found. From AD 800 it formed part of the Norse empire, though the control of the king of Norway was fitful. The representative institutions reflect the Norse influence. In 1266 it was ceded to Scotland after the battle of *Largs, but did not stay long in Scottish possession. The island was disputed between Scots and English until 1333, when Edward III annexed and retained it. The bishopric of *Sodor and Man, founded in 1134, continued under the supervision of the archbishopric of Trondhjem but was placed in the archdiocese of York in the 15th cent. From 1406 the island belonged to the Stanleys, earls of Derby, who ruled it as lords of Man, and held it until 1736. It then passed to the dukes of Atholl, but in order to curtail smuggling the British government purchased it in 1765 and took full control in 1828.

The island is a crown possession with wide independent powers under a lieutenant governor. There is a two-chamber assembly, the *Tynwald, the lower house of which is the House of *Keys. The emblem of the island—the three legs of Man—is an ancient design, possibly going back to the Norse period. The Manx language, basically Celtic, was widely spoken until the 19th cent., but is now an acquired tongue. With the decline of fishing and mining, tourism provides the main income, with regular sailings in the season to Douglas from Heysham, Fleetwood, Liverpool, Stranraer, Belfast, and Dublin. The largest town and capital is Douglas (22,000), followed by Ramsey (6,500), Peel (3,800) and Castletown, the old capital (3,000). JAC

Isle of Wight. Known to the Romans as Vectis, the Isle of Wight is largely chalk, some 22 miles across by 13 north–south, and almost bisected north–south by the river Medina. At the end of the Roman period it was settled by the *Jutes and for a time had its own kings. But it was difficult to stand against the kingdoms of Sussex, Mercia, and Wessex. *Cædwalla of Wessex took it *c.*687 and gave a quarter of the land to St *Wilfrid for the church. It was used as a base by the Danes in 998, and in 1371 Newport was sacked by the French. In the 1840s the building of *Osborne House for the queen and the establishment of the Royal Yacht Squadron at Cowes nearby in 1856 did much to popularize the island. The population grew from just over 20,000 in 1801 to over 80,000 by Victoria's death in 1901, and to 125,000 by 1992. From Saxon times the island formed part of the county of *Hampshire and fell under the authority of the bishop of *Winchester. The island was given a county council in 1890. The Banham commission on local government recommended in 1993 that the county be made a unitary authority. JAC

Isles, kingdom of the. The origins of the kingdom of the Isles can be sought as far back as the 840s. It was apparently the successor kingdom in western Scotland to *Dalriada (last mentioned in the Irish annals in 839). It developed in the power vacuum left by the departure of *Kenneth MacAlpin, king of Dalriada and 'conqueror' of the Picts, to *Fortriu in 842. Kenneth may have had a hand in its inception, because its first king appears to have been his ally, and possible father-in-law, Gofraid mac Fherghusa (an ancestor of the Clan Donald), described on his death in 851 as *Toisech* or *Rí Innse Gall*, 'king of the Isles'. The extent of the kingdom is unclear, but by the late 10th cent. it included the *Isle of Man.

The inhabitants of this new kingdom were of mixed Gaelic and Norse origin, there having been heavy Norse settlement between *c.*795 and *c.*825, a 30-year period of unparalleled turmoil in western Scotland, which saw the Isle of Skye overwhelmed and *Iona attacked at least five times. In the 850s the mixed population of the Isles made an appearance in Ireland. They were called *Gall-Gaidheil*, 'Scandinavian Gaels', and were led by Caittil Find, presumably Gofraid's successor as *Rí Innse Gall*. Like early gallowglasses, they were supporting Mael Sechnaill, king of Tara, against the Scandinavians of Dublin and his Irish rivals. They may have joined forces with Ireland's most powerful king because they felt threatened by the formidable Norwegian warrior-king Olaf, who had become king of *Dublin in 853.

After a period of complete obscurity, from the 930s a close relationship developed between the Isles and Dublin. In 937, a *Rí Innse Gall* called Gébennach was slain at the battle of *Brunanburh, fighting against *Athelstan, the Anglo-Saxon king, apparently as a subordinate of *Olaf Godfreyson (or Guthfrithsson), king of Dublin, described by Florence of Worcester as 'king of the Irish and the many islands'.

Under Maccus and Godfrey, the sons of Harald and members of a side branch of the Uí Imar, the Dublin royal family, the kingdom of the Isles began to impinge violently upon its neighbours. Maccus ravaged Penmon in Wales in 971 and attended a meeting of kings at Chester in 973, where he was called 'king of the very many islands', whilst Godfrey raided Wales in 972, 980, 982, and 987, when he took 2,000 captives from Angelsey. Both these kings appear to have made Man their base. With the death of Godfrey's son Ragnall in 1005, this lineage seems to have come to an end.

In addition to a continuing close relationship between the Isles and Dublin, the kingship of both being held on occasion by the same figure, the 11th cent. apparently saw a conquest of the Isles by *Thorfinn the Mighty, jarl of Orkney, from the 1040s until his death *c.*1065. However, the most important event for the future history of the Isles was the reign of Godfrey Crovan, probably from Islay. Godfrey, also related to the Uí Imar, was a capable warrior who had taken part in the battle of *Stamford Bridge as a mercenary. He conquered Man with a force of Hebrideans and took the kingship *c.*1079. In 1091 he also seized control of Dublin. However, in 1094 his Irish venture was brought to an end, when he was driven from Dublin by Muirchertach Ua Briain, king of Ireland. He died in Islay in 1095. His descendants were the kings of Man and the Isles for the next 200 years. By the treaty of *Perth (1266) Man and the Isles, which had fallen under a shaky Norwegian overlordship, became part of the kingdom of Scotland. The lordship of the Isles was vested in the Scottish crown in James IV's reign in the 15th cent. AJe

Islip, Simon (d. 1366). Archbishop of Canterbury. Born near Oxford and a fellow of Merton, Islip was an ecclesiastical lawyer who became the bishop of Lincoln's vicar-general, archdeacon of Canterbury (1343), and dean of Arches. As Edward III's keeper of the privy seal, he was sent on embassies abroad or acted as adviser to regents in the king's absence. Elected archbishop (1349) at the king's request and consecrated at St Paul's, he was at odds with the monks of Canterbury for not being consecrated there. During his primacy he agreed to the archbishop of York carrying his cross in the southern province and the statutes of *Provisors and *Praemunire were passed. To improve the standards of clergy after the *Black Death, he founded (1361) at Oxford a mixed college for monks and seculars, a bold experiment, which *Wolsey absorbed into Cardinal College (later Christ Church). WMM

Italy, relations with. Medieval English kings were several times involved in fierce disputes with the *papacy concerning church–state relations. The papal refusal to grant a divorce to Henry VIII precipitated the English Reformation. Rome supported the Jacobite cause from 1688, and continued to excite the hostility of British liberals as well as protestants far into the 19th cent. The Italian Renaissance, in contrast, attracted growing admiration, and until the mid-19th cent. the Italian language was second only to French in popularity in Britain. Italy became one of the highlights of the *grand tour for the sons of wealthy families. Trade was also important, with Italian merchants proving very influential in London in the Middle Ages.

In the 18th cent. Savoy-Piedmont attracted much interest politically and strategically, as a possible barrier against France and a restraint on Austrian influence. By 1814–15 *Castlereagh, however, was so impressed by the success of French arms since the 1790s in the politically divided and relatively backward peninsula that he looked primarily to the Habsburgs to police and protect Italy. *Palmerston, in contrast, as early as 1848–9, was considering alternatives to Austrian rule. Only ten years later, he led a government which gained significant credit during the unification of much of Italy (1859–60)—although British policy had been by no means consistent or far-sighted. Approval of unification was assured only once it became evident that the new Italy would not become a dependency of France. Anglo-Italian relations continued to be much influenced by relations with that power. For ten years from 1887 the two states subscribed to the Mediterranean agreements in order to maintain the status quo in that region.

In 1915 Italy finally opted to fight beside Britain and her allies in the *First World War, but Italian patriots were disappointed when their country's services were not more amply rewarded in 1919. In the 1930s the fascist regime of Mussolini was increasingly tempted to manœuvre between Nazi Germany on the one side and Britain and France on the other in search of territorial gains. The British responded ambivalently to Mussolini's war against Abyssinia in 1935–6, and only succeeded in driving *Il Duce* closer to Hitler. Italian involvement on the side of Franco in the Spanish Civil War led to further difficulties. Mussolini, however, did not enter the *Second World War until France was on the verge of defeat. The Mediterranean became a major war theatre to which Churchill enthusiastically assigned forces in the belief that southern Europe was the 'soft underbelly of the axis'. But Italy's surrender in 1943 left the allies confronted by strong German opposition, and they became increasingly conscious of the difficulties of the terrain rather than of an easy route into the heart of Europe. CJB

Ithamar (d. 655/64). Bishop of Rochester. Ithamar was a Kentishman and the first native bishop of the English church from *c.*644. Nothing else is known of him. It is remarkable that for 47 years after the coming of Augustine every bishop in England had been either Italian or Irish. His name may sound vaguely Germanic but is in fact biblical. JCa

Jacobins were originally a faction or group in Paris who met in the old Dominican convent at the church of St Jacques, and opposed the more moderate Girondin group. The name was soon borrowed in England and applied, not merely to admirers of the French Revolution, but indiscriminately to radicals and reformers. It was exploited by *Canning and his friends in their *jeu d'esprit* the **Anti-Jacobin*, which came out in 1798/9. JAC

Jacobite risings were attempts after 1689 to reverse the expulsion of the senior branch of the Stuart family from its thrones. Supporters of the exiled dynasty were known as Jacobites from the Latin form of the name James which is *Jacobus*. James VII and II fled from England in December 1688. He landed in Ireland in March 1689, with French troops, but left when defeated at the *Boyne in 1690. Military emigration after the last Jacobite army surrendered at Limerick in October 1691 ensured that future Irish Jacobitism was exilic.

The first Jacobite rising was in Scotland in 1689 led by Viscount *Dundee and Lord Balcarres. They withdrew from the Scots Estates or Parliament, and launched a military assault on its provisional government. A coalition of conservative episcopalians and the smaller clans of the central and western Highlands, the rising had as little active support as the Williamites. Large clans and great magnates were inactive, apart from the Campbells, whose chief, *Argyll, was restored by the events of 1688–9. Dundee died in victory at the battle of *Killiecrankie in July 1689, and the Jacobite army was finally routed at the Haughs of Cromdale in May 1690.

Until the French lost control of the sea at *La Hogue in 1692 James was more interested in returning with a French army than in promoting risings. However, the exclusively presbyterian settlement in the kirk in 1690 alienated many Scots, as did such tyrannical misgovernment as the massacre of *Glencoe in 1692. Nevertheless, despite the stresses of war, it was not until the passage of the *Union of 1707 that outraged Scottish national sentiment made another rising thinkable. Louis XIV planned a Jacobite seizure of Scotland. In March 1708 James Francis Edward *Stuart, after his father's death in 1701 the Jacobite claimant, was off the coast of Fife with a French expedition, but the French fled north at the sight of Royal Navy ships. Designed to recover only Scotland, the plan aborted.

Queen Anne's death in 1714 was followed by the smooth accession of the protestant Hanoverian dynasty. The outbreak of the 1715 rising surprised the exiled Stuarts. It was the only rising entirely explicable in domestic terms. The Whig coup at the accession of George I drove many Tories to despair, some to rebellion. After failing to get a job from George I, the earl of *Mar started a Scottish national rising. There was also a small English rising in Northumberland, supported mostly by catholic and high Anglican squires who were bankrupt. The Scottish rising failed due to the action of *Argyll, who blocked the path south at Stirling, and Mar's incompetence. An attempt by an Anglo-Scottish Jacobite force to raise the Lancashire catholics was foiled at *Preston on the same day (14 November) that Mar failed to sweep Argyll aside at *Sheriffmuir. The late arrival of James Stuart, and surreptitious Spanish aid, failed to avert the collapse of the rising in early 1716.

Forfeitures, plus measures such as the *Septennial and *Riot Acts, seemed to entrench Whig power permanently. The next Jacobite rebellion was a fiasco cynically sponsored by a Spanish government which was quarrelling with the British over Mediterranean issues. The main invasion force was intended to strike at the west of England, but was scattered by storms. A purely diversionary force, including the exiled Scots Jacobite Lords Tullibardine and Seaforth, did invade the north-west Highlands, only to be crushed by General Wightman at *Glenshiel in June 1719.

The rise of an Anglo-French entente, the strength of *Walpole's regime, and the disrepute which the failure of the Jacobite claimant's marriage brought ruled out another rising. By 1744, however, war had broken out between France and Britain, and the French brought Prince Charles *Stuart, elder son of James Stuart, to France to front an invasion. Then they dropped the idea. The arrival of Charles in the west Highlands in the late summer of 1745 was designed to reverse the French decision by seizing a poorly defended Scotland and then invading England to provoke French intervention. With the help of the Camerons and smaller central Highland clans, and some marginal members of the Scots aristocracy, Charles occupied Edinburgh before shattering government forces under Cope at *Prestonpans. The invasion of England in late 1745 was agreed to reluctantly by many Jacobite Scots. Even the field commander, Lord George *Murray, regarded it as a reconnaissance to test English willingness to restore the Stuarts.

By Derby, it was clear there was none, and retreat in the face of superior armies was brilliantly executed. A final victory over the pursuing Hanoverian army under General Hawley at *Falkirk in January 1746 merely postponed the day of reckoning which came on 16 April at *Culloden east of Inverness, where the Jacobites were totally routed by the duke of *Cumberland, a younger son of George II. Devastation, confiscation, and disillusionment with both Charles and France effectively destroyed all danger of another rising. The risings underlined the unpopularity of governments which were seen as corrupt and betraying their own principles, but also showed the unacceptability of the Stuart alternative, and their failures reinforced the Hanoverian regime. BPL

Jacobitism was a series of political movements which supported the restoration of the exiled house of Stuart after James II had been ousted from the throne at the Glorious Revolution in 1688 and had fled to France. Jacobites continued to support the claims to the throne of James's son James Francis Edward *Stuart (the Old Pretender or 'James III') and his two grandsons Charles Edward *Stuart (the Young Pretender or 'Charles III') and Henry *Stuart (the cardinal duke of York or 'Henry IX').

There has been much recent controversy over Jacobitism, particularly who were or were not Jacobite MPs. One school of thought claims that as many as a third or more of Tory MPs were Jacobites, along with the major party leaders; while another believes that the bulk of the party were Hanoverian Tories who supported the new dynasty after 1714, despite the proscription of the party after the 1715 Rebellion. The problem lies with the definition of a Jacobite, with the sparseness of the evidence (engaged in treasonable activity Jacobites took care not to leave too much evidence behind), with the often ambiguous or even downright misleading evidence that has survived, with the use of the term Jacobite as rhetoric and as a smearword to damn one's political opponents, and with the emotional advocacy with which the topic has become charged. Some historians believe that once a Jacobite always a Jacobite, whereas it seems clear that, though there was a hard core of lifelong Jacobites, most drifted in and out of Jacobitism as circumstances or mood dictated. Some politicians thought by contemporaries and later historians to favour Jacobitism only worked with Jacobites in opposition because they were one of the few groups to hand (such as Earl *Cowper in the new opposition grouping of dissident Whigs, Hanoverian Tories, and Jacobites in 1721–3); while others used Jacobites for their own (largely) political ends and discarded them when their objective had been achieved (such as the earl of *Sunderland in 1721–2 when he negotiated with Jacobite MPs and peers to stave off impeachment proceedings over his involvement in the South Sea scandal).

Jacobitism had a religious, as well as a political, dimension. James II and his son and grandsons were catholics, whose refusal to convert to protestantism made their restoration virtually impossible other than by armed invasion with foreign assistance. However, most of their supporters were protestants, and a great many were non-jurors, who had refused the oaths of loyalty to William and Mary (who had replaced James on the throne in 1689), and consequently had lost their secular or religious offices. Some who were prepared to take the oaths in 1689, and later to Anne, refused to recognize the Hanoverian succession and turned to Jacobitism. In Scotland, where Jacobitism was strongest, the episcopalian church had been disestablished at the Glorious Revolution, and subsequently many (though not all) episcopalians became Jacobites. Jacobitism in Scotland also became a refuge for many who opposed the Union with England in 1707. There is also evidence that Jacobitism appealed to the lower, even the criminal, elements of society, as a form of social protest.

That Scotland was central to Jacobitism is shown by the two main risings which took place in 1715 and 1745. Many Highland chiefs and clansmen, who did battle for the Stuart cause, paid for their loyalty with the loss of life and property. Few English Jacobites came out in support of either rebellion. Jacobitism was largely crushed as a political force after the retreat from Derby by the forces of the Young Pretender and the defeat at *Culloden in 1746. Thereafter the romantic and cultural aspect of the movements, which had always been a potent factor in attracting supporters, became dominant. CJ

Jamaica, immediately to the south of Cuba, is the third largest of the Caribbean islands. It was sighted by Columbus in 1494 but the name is of Amerindian origin. Becoming independent in 1962, it is a constitutional monarchy with the queen as head of state, and a member of the Commonwealth. Under Spanish occupation, the Arawak population was decimated. During *Cromwell's regime, it was seized by the English under William *Penn in 1655. In the 18th cent. the sugar plantations were extremely lucrative and the *Beckfords were only one of many families which owed their fortunes to Jamaican slave labour. Coffee and bananas were introduced as alternative crops. A serious rising in 1865 led to the recall of Governor Eyre and a vigorous debate on colonial policy. The modern progress of Jamaica's economy has been much retarded by periodic hurricanes. JAC

James I (1394–1437), king of Scots (1406–37). Contemporary views of the style and kingship of James I were sharply divided. Abbot Bower described James as 'our lawgiver king'; Sir Robert Graham saw him as 'a tyrant, the greatest enemy the Scots or Scotland might have'; and the pope's emissary, the bishop of Urbino, claimed that the murdered king had died a martyr.

James was the third son of Robert III (1390–1406) and his queen Annabella Drummond (d. 1401), and was born in July 1394. By the age of 7, he was the sole surviving male and heir to the throne. An elder brother Robert was dead; his eldest brother, David, duke of Rothesay, ran the kingdom as lieutenant-general for the ailing Robert III between 1399 and 1402, being arrested in the latter year and incarcerated in Falkland castle at the instance of his uncle and greatest rival, the chamberlain, Robert Stewart, duke of *Albany. Rothesay's death in a matter of weeks provoked fears as to Albany's ambitions; and by the winter of 1405–6 the country was racked by civil war, with the rump of Robert III loyalists supporting the young Prince James against a formidable Albany/Douglas faction. Early in 1406 events came to a head when James fled for safety to the Bass Rock, took ship for France, only to be captured at sea (22 March) and delivered to Henry IV of England. Less than a fortnight later Robert III died (4 April), and James became king at the age of 12, uncrowned and in English hands for the next 18 years.

These were the formative years of James I's life, instilling in him an admiration for English royal government, the most centralized in western Europe, and in particular for the aggressive Henry V, in whose armies James served in the French campaigns of 1420–1. Already suspicious of the Albany Stewarts, James had his fears of Albany ambitions further fuelled by the release of Duke Robert's son and heir Murdac (*Albany) from English captivity in 1416. The king had to wait a further eight years for his own release, and then it was to return to a Scotland in which Duke Murdac had succeeded his father as governor.

James re-entered Scotland in April 1424, in his 30th year, bringing with him an English wife, *Joan Beaufort, and a desire to emulate Henry V of England in a country which had no tradition of the intensive and masterful rule he sought to introduce. Having taken part in English wars in France, on occasion against his Scottish subjects, he can hardly have been popular; and he was saddled with a ransom (euphemistically described as 'expenses') of £40,000 sterling, which would necessitate the raising of taxation in Parliament and the sending south of noble hostages as security.

Despite this inauspicious start, James possessed virtues which earned him praise in his own day. Abbot Bower describes his many accomplishments, including prowess in sports, music, and literary pursuits: the king was the author of the autobiographical love poem 'The *Kingis Quair'. He was, untypically for the Stewarts, a faithful husband, and Queen Joan responded loyally by producing twin sons and a string of daughters, whose marriages abroad would greatly enhance the prestige of the dynasty in the next reign. And James's zeal for law and order was real enough, even if it had an obvious fiscal motive and despite the fact that he was very selective in its application—for example, James *Douglas of Balvenie, a blatant extortioner of burgh customs before 1424, was not punished but employed as a trusted counsellor of the king.

In his efforts to increase the authority, resources, and security of the crown, James launched pre-emptive strikes against members of his nobility. The Albany Stewarts were all but annihilated in 1425, though the charges brought against them are obscure, and contemporaries muttered about the king's acquisitiveness. At Inverness in 1428 the story was the same; Highlanders arriving for a 'parliament' were arrested while the king composed Latin poetry. The earl of *Douglas was suddenly arrested in 1431, the earl of March in 1434. Furthermore, the king had abandoned efforts to redeem the hostages in England, instead investing the ransom money collected in building projects like his unfortified palace at *Linlithgow and the Charterhouse at Perth, and in artillery and luxuries for the court.

James's failure at the siege of Roxburgh (August 1436), amid rumours of a possible assassination plot, was followed by Sir Robert Graham's abortive attempt to arrest him during a general council, and his murder at Perth (20–1 February 1437) as part of a coup (which ultimately failed) by Walter Stewart, earl of *Atholl, using Graham and former Albany Stewart retainers to do the deed. Ultimately the king was the victim of his own methods; Atholl, seeing his influence in Strathearn threatened by the king, responded with his own pre-emptive strike. If James I was a mixture of Bower's lawgiver and Graham's tyrant, perhaps his martyrdom can be understood in terms of his efforts to impose strong monarchical government on a country which initially rejected it; but he had set the agenda for his successor. NATM

Balfour-Melville, E. W. M., *James I, King of Scots* (1936); Brown, M., *James I* (Edinburgh, 1994); Donaldson, G., *Scottish Kings* (1967); Nicholson, R., *Scotland: The Later Middle Ages* (Edinburgh, 1974).

James II (1430–60), king of Scots (1437–60). James II is the first Scottish king of whose appearance we can be fairly certain. An Austrian visitor to the Scottish court in 1458, Jörg von Ehingen, had a portrait made of the king, presumably for the edification of James's sister Eleanor of Austria. King James is portrayed as a confident young man, his hands on a dagger at his belt, with the whole of the left side of his face from forehead to chin disfigured by the livid vermilion birthmark described by the French poet François Villon and the contemporary Scottish 'Auchinleck chronicler'. The confidence and ruthlessness suggested by this face are an accurate reflection of the king's character and policies. In a short life—he died at 29—and extremely short period of personal rule, he followed the path taken by his father, broke the power of the greatest magnate house, the Black Douglases, secured a sizeable increase in royal power at home and a formidable reputation abroad.

James was the younger of twin sons born to James I and *Joan Beaufort at Holyrood in October 1430. (The elder twin, Alexander, died in infancy.) His father's assassination at Perth in 1437 thrust James into the kingship aged only 6 and necessitated a long minority (1437–49), in the first part of which he was controlled by the rump of his father's supporters, headed by the queen. He was crowned (March 1437) by Michael Ochiltree, bishop of Dunblane, a close associate of James I but hardly the premier ecclesiastic in Scotland. The disappearance of many major noble families, either through forfeiture and execution or failure of heirs in the male line, meant that by 1437 there were very few earls left in Scotland; and the political imbalance which resulted from this caused an enormous concentration of power in the hands of the Black Douglas family, with its head, the young William, 8th earl of *Douglas, becoming lieutenant-general for James II (probably in 1444) and—together with the Livingston of Callander—using the office to acquire earldoms and other honours for his brothers and allies.

In July 1449 James II married *Mary of Gueldres, only daughter of Duke Arnold of Gueldres and niece of Philip the Good of Burgundy (who paid his niece's dowry in instalments). Four of James's sisters had already made prestigious European marriages—Margaret to the Dauphin Louis in 1436, Isabella to Francis of Brittany in 1442, Mary to the Lord of Veere in 1444, and Eleanor to Sigismund of Austria in 1449. Thus the Scottish king threw off the frustration of being under tutelage with confidence and ruthlessness. He arrested and forfeited the Livingstons in 1449–50, driving the young earl of Ross (who was James Livingston's son-in-law) into rebellion in 1451.

However, James II's real target was the Black Douglases. Various motives have been suggested for his attack on the family—royal financial difficulties, linked to the king's determination, from 1451, to secure the Douglas earldom of Wigtown; James II's perception of Douglas weakness in Galloway as a result of the *'Black Dinner' of 1440; the bond (probably of friendship) between Douglas, Crawford, and the rebel Ross of 1451–2, bringing together former rivals in a potentially dangerous combination; or simply the issue of authority, with Douglas's predominance at court (in spite of his having relinquished the lieutenant-generalship by 1450) unacceptable to an adult Stewart king. The outcome was an attack on Douglas estates by James II, a policy apparently urged by Chancellor Crichton, Admiral Crichton, and Bishop Turnbull of Glasgow during Earl William's absence in Rome in Jubilee Year 1450. There followed a temporary reconciliation (indicating royal weakness), and the great crime of the reign, James's murder of Douglas at Stirling castle on 22 February 1452, following a two-day conference which Douglas attended under a royal safe conduct.

Civil war followed, with the 9th earl of *Douglas pitted against a determined James II. The king was lucky to escape from Stirling with his life when the Douglases arrived to confront him a month after the murder. Thereafter the situation improved. A male heir was born to Mary of Gueldres at St Andrews (May 1452); a royalist Parliament justified the Douglas murder; and the king walked the political tightrope of satisfying his own supporters and negotiating with the Douglases until he was strong enough to deliver the killer punch. Events in England—the outbreak of the Wars of the Roses—assisted James by depriving the Douglases of the possibility of armed support. In 1455 the king's sieges of Abercorn and Threave, and a skirmish at *Arkinholm on the river Esk, completed the ruin of the Black Douglases.

James II's five remaining years reveal no let-up in the king's energy and aggressiveness—organizing an abortive attack on the Isle of Man; leading border raids; playing off Lancaster against York; restocking the Scottish peerage with earls, including royal Stewarts; adopting an astonishingly high-handed attitude towards the Danes in his demand for a marriage alliance for his son ceding Orkney and Shetland to Scotland; and receiving from Philip of Burgundy the gift of the huge cannon 'Mons Meg' in 1457. James II died as he had lived, the eternal warrior, mortally wounded by the explosion of one of his own guns at the siege of Roxburgh castle in August 1460. NATM

Donaldson, G., *Scottish Kings* (1967); Grant, A., *Independence and Nationhood: Scotland 1306–1469* (1984); McGladdery, C., *James II* (Edinburgh, 1990); Nicholson, R., *Scotland: The Later Middle Ages* (Edinburgh, 1974).

James III (1452–88), king of Scots (1460–88). Perhaps because he inherited fewer problems than his two immediate predecessors, James III presented to the world a different face of Stewart kingship. There can be little doubt that he had a dangerously exalted view of his kingly role, an attitude which was reflected in his adoption of concepts of imperialism in the first Parliament of his personal rule (1469), and in the minting of the earliest Renaissance coin portrait outside Italy, showing James III wearing an imperial crown, in the very last silver coinage of the reign (1488).

The eldest of the three sons of James II and *Mary of Gueldres, James was born at St Andrews late in May 1452. His father's death at the siege of Roxburgh (August 1460) was swiftly followed by the Scots' winning of the castle and the coronation of the 8-year-old James III at nearby Kelso abbey. The ensuing minority (1460–9) had its difficulties, but under the wise guidance of Mary of Gueldres (d. 1463) the Scots secured the cession of Berwick from the refugee Lancastrians (1461), and then swiftly changed horses to back the victorious Yorkists. The late king's marital and territorial schemes finally came to fruition in the 1468 treaty of Copenhagen, by which James III was to marry *Margaret, daughter of Christian I of Denmark-Norway. Christian's inability to afford his daughter's dowry resulted in his pawning first the earldom of *Orkney, then the lordship of *Shetland; and both were annexed to the Scottish crown by 1472. Thus, by the early years of James III's personal rule, the Scottish kingdom had reached its widest territorial extent.

The view of James III which has come down to us is largely that of late 16th-cent. writers. These portray the king as something of a recluse who ignored or despised the counsel of his nobility in favour of that of low-born familiars; he disliked war (to prove the point, the chronicler Pitscottie has him fall off his horse at the fatal battle of *Sauchie Burn); and he was a committed patron of the arts.

This later legend is broadly unconvincing. The unwarlike king is difficult to discern in a ruler who proposed annexations or invasions of Brittany, Gueldres, and Saintonge between 1471 and 1473, and this view may draw its relevance only from James's alternative policy of peace and alliance with Yorkist England, which he pursued obsessively—excepting one disastrous interlude (1480–2)—from 1474 to the end of the reign. Again, complaints of neglect of his magnates may reflect James's failure to reward support, as in the classic case of the earl of Huntly in 1476, whose invasion of Ross and capture of Dingwall castle for the king merited only a gift of 100 marks' worth of land. This breath-taking royal meanness no doubt weighed heavily with Huntly twelve years later, when his role as a committed neutral may have cost James III his life.

The king's patronage of the arts—excepting the Trinity College, Edinburgh altarpiece, which he may or may not have commissioned—is rather elusive, as is the contribution of his English musician familiar William Roger; and although James III's most exotic friend, Anselm Adornes of

Bruges, spread the king's name and fame as far afield as Tunis, James as a Scottish Renaissance patron remains an enigmatic figure. Perhaps significantly, his most despised familiars, William Scheves, archbishop of St Andrews, and Thomas Cochrane, were respectively a powerful court 'fixer' and a royal troubleshooter in the north-east. And the elusive royal whore 'Daesie' is surely the figment of a later imagination.

In fact, James III's failure may be explained largely without reference to the later legend. He was a static king, rarely moving out of Edinburgh during his adulthood, and thereby neglecting to travel on justice ayres, visiting far-flung areas of the country to settle feuds and make the royal presence felt. Successive parliaments criticized him repeatedly for this failing, as they did also for his attempts to tax and granting of remissions for serious crimes. Furthermore, James may have been unfortunate to have adult brothers as potential rivals, though his treatment of them was appalling. Alexander, duke of *Albany, fled to France in 1479—and significantly an assize of Parliament would not forfeit him—while John, earl of Mar, was arrested later that year and died mysteriously in custody shortly afterwards. The return of Albany in 1482, backed by an English army sent by Edward IV, prompted a great Stewart family crisis, with the seizure of James III at Lauder, the permanent loss of Berwick to the English, Albany's temporary acquisition of the office of lieutenant-general, the king's incarceration in Edinburgh castle, and his subsequent release and recovery of power through the timely intervention of loyal north-eastern nobility.

However, crown–magnate mistrust persisted, and the king's wide-ranging Treasons Act (1484) showed that he had learned nothing from the warning of 1482. When his eldest son James, duke of Rothesay, a youth of 15, moved against him in the spring of 1488, with extensive support from a huge array of disaffected magnates, no armed assistance was forthcoming from the former loyalists of the north; and on 11 June James III, bearing Robert Bruce's sword and a black box full of money and jewels, succumbed to his son's army on the 'field of Stirling' (Sauchie Burn). NATM

Donaldson, G., *Scottish Kings* (1967); Macdougall, N., *James III: A Political Study* (Edinburgh, 1982); id., *James IV* (Edinburgh, 1989); Nicholson, R., *Scotland: The Later Middle Ages* (Edinburgh, 1974).

James IV (1473–1513), king of Scots (1488–1513). James IV was the most successful of all the Stewart rulers of Scotland. Two decades after James's death, Sir David Lindsay of the Mount, who as a young man had known the king well, described him as 'the glory of all princely governing', a view which is largely substantiated by contemporary witnesses, most strikingly by the Spanish ambassador, Don Pedro de Ayala, in 1498. A combination of luck, military prowess, skilful use of royal patronage, and shrewd diplomatic manœuvring explains King James's success.

The eldest son of James III and *Margaret of Denmark, James IV was born at *Stirling castle on 17 March 1473. The successful rising against his father in 1488 associated his name with an act of regicide and patricide, and he undertook elaborate penances to atone for his role in James III's death for the remainder of his life—the iron belt worn round his waist was no invention of later chroniclers. Yet the young king benefited greatly from the manner of his accession, for he was assisted by a very wide spectrum of magnates who had found his father's rule unacceptable, and who had no choice but to support him. By the end of James IV's reign, the royal council displayed a much broader territorial representation than had ever been known under the king's three predecessors, embracing the crown's greatest subjects, including Hepburn, Hume, Angus, Argyll, Lennox, Arran, and Huntly. And at the outset of James IV's personal rule, in the spring of 1495, there was no violent political upheaval, but a smooth transition—the king, a late developer, was already 22.

In almost every respect, King James's government affords a sharp contrast with that of his father. The king was a tireless traveller, driving the justice ayres in the south and north-east, intervening in major feuds, for example those in Cunningham and Strathearn; and he placed himself at the centre of a glittering court. His expenditure on building, especially on *Holyrood palace and the King's House and great hall at Stirling castle, was large, his lavishing of money on a royal navy (probably more than £100,000 Scots) spectacular. An insight into James's court is provided not only by the treasurer's accounts (which survive in some quantity from this reign), but also by the poetry of William *Dunbar and Robert Carver's astonishing nineteen-part motet 'O bone Jesu'.

An ambitious programme of Renaissance patronage in the manner of his more powerful European neighbours cost James vast sums of money. Yet his father's methods of attempting to acquire funds (with some success) through forfeitures, taxation, and debasement of the coinage carried grave political dangers. Recognizing that parliaments were often a focus for criticism (or worse) of the crown, James IV called only three in the seventeen years of his adult rule. The money he needed for his navy, his building programmes, above all for his wars, was acquired through rigorous exploitation of feudal casualties, by income from profits of justice, by taxation of a loyal clergy, by the imposition of two Acts of revocation (1498 and 1504), and perhaps above all by setting royal lands in feu-farm in the later years of the reign. These devices raised annual royal revenue from around £13,000 in the 1490s to a total in excess of £40,000 Scots by 1513.

In foreign affairs, James IV adopted a high-risk policy which proved broadly successful. His invasions of Northumberland (1496–7), ostensibly in support of the Yorkist pretender Perkin *Warbeck but in fact to utilize the military talents of the Scottish nobility and put pressure on Henry VII, provoked the English king into furious retaliation. But the Cornish rising of 1497, born partly out of resentment at the imposition of heavy taxation to support the Scottish war, put an end to Henry's efforts to chastise the Scots; and the eventual alternative was the treaty of *Perpetual Peace of 1502, as a result of which James IV married Henry's daughter *Margaret Tudor (August 1503).

This union of the Thistle and the Rose, celebrated in Dunbar's poetry and much lauded by later historians, did little to improve Anglo-Scottish relations. The real Scottish understanding was with Louis XII of France, who from 1502 to 1513 provided James IV with shipwrights, soldiers, ships, money, and munitions. Significantly James's fleet started taking shape late in 1502, the year of the English treaty; and in the war of 1513, it was to be paid for by the king of France. A naval race with the English resulted in the construction of the Scottish *Margaret* followed by the English **Mary Rose*; and in October 1511 James attended the launch at Newhaven of the *Michael*, briefly the largest warship in northern Europe. When the young Henry VIII sought to renew the *Hundred Years War in 1512–13, James made a formal treaty with Louis XII, employed crusading language to justify his cause, accepted excommunication with equanimity, invaded England, and took Norham castle by storm (while the Scottish fleet attacked Carrickfergus in Ulster *en route* to France). However, on 9 September 1513 James rashly committed himself to battle against the earl of *Surrey at *Flodden and was killed, together with no less than nine of his earls, a striking if tragic reflection of his popularity in Scotland. NATM

Donaldson, G., *Scottish Kings* (1967); Macdougall, N., *James IV* (Edinburgh, 1989); Mackie, R. L., *King James IV of Scotland* (Edinburgh, 1958); Nicholson, R., *Scotland: The Later Middle Ages* (Edinburgh, 1974).

James V (1512–42), king of Scots (1513–42). A fine exponent of Renaissance kingship, James V's death aged only 30 cut short a reign characterized by the pursuit of royal aggrandizement both at home and abroad.

Born on 10 April 1512, James inherited the throne when barely 18 months old on the death of his father James IV at *Flodden on 9 September 1513. The protracted regency which ensued witnessed the kind of magnatial power struggle which had dominated the minorities of successive Stewart monarchs. In this case, however, the conflict between James Hamilton, 1st earl of *Arran, and Archibald Douglas, 6th earl of *Angus, was aggravated by the latter's marriage in 1514 to the queen mother, *Margaret Tudor, sister of Henry VIII, and the involvement of the king's French-born kinsman John Stewart, duke of *Albany. While Albany was regent from 1515 to 1524, it was Angus who came to dominate the regime and from whose clutches the 16-year-old king engineered his own escape in May 1528.

The vindictive pursuit of his former Douglas captors is often seen as the leitmotif of James's personal rule. However, while Angus was forced into English exile in 1529, and his sister Lady Glamis was executed for treason in 1537, the king's justifiable suspicion of the Douglases hardly amounted to a relentless vendetta. Likewise, the charge that a paranoid fear of his nobility led to the ruthless expropriation of their lands and goods is exaggerated. Certainly, James wished to assert the crown's authority and his punitive expeditions to the borders in 1530 and to the Western Isles in 1540 vividly demonstrate his concern that the royal writ should run even in the outlying reaches of his kingdom. His attitude to the nobility was informed by a similar desire to assert royal authority, and James exploited the full repertoire of legal devices in order to recover and augment crown lands and revenues. Some noblemen undoubtedly suffered as a result. Yet the aggressive pursuit of crown interests was nothing new and, if it was particularly effective in James V's reign, the reason probably lies less in the king's alleged paranoia than in the expertise of a cadre of lay lawyers (such as his influential secretary, the Pavia-trained Sir Thomas Erskine) who played an increasingly prominent role in the royal bureaucracy.

Lawyers like Erskine may well have lent juridical weight to the authoritarian style of kingship suggested by James's fascination with the most potent contemporary symbol of royal power: the closed 'imperial' crown. If so, the clergy had as much—probably more—reason to fear the king as the nobility. Although James's former tutor, Gavin Dunbar, archbishop of Glasgow, remained chancellor throughout the reign, the clergy's monopoly of legal and administrative expertise was being steadily eroded, while the spread of reforming opinion in the 1530s threw them further on the defensive. James exploited to the full both the weakness of his own ecclesiastical hierarchy and the papacy's fear that he might follow his uncle Henry VIII in repudiating Rome altogether. Thus, with papal blessing, he was able to consolidate royal control over appointments to major benefices, milk the revenues of the wealthiest religious houses, and levy the heaviest tax on clerical income which the *ecclesia Scoticana* had ever experienced. James may well have been personally pious and was certainly aware of the growing pressure for ecclesiastical reform; but neither factor was allowed to stand in the way of replenishing the royal coffers from the church's vast resources. Determined to establish a court-life befitting a Renaissance prince, the king spent lavishly on maintaining a large royal household and on creating the architectural settings at *Falkland, *Linlithgow, and *Stirling in which the full majesty of his kingship could best be displayed.

Even with greatly augmented revenues, however, James was hardly in a position to compete with contemporary princes like Henry VIII, Charles V, or Francis I. Nevertheless, the intense rivalry between France, England, and the empire, compounded by heightened religious tensions and the nervousness of Rome, lent the Scottish king unwonted diplomatic weight. His shrewd exploitation of the marriage market led to his securing first the hand of Francis I's eldest surviving daughter *Madeleine, and then on her death that of *Mary of Guise. Despite Henry VIII's attempts to sever them, Scotland's traditional ties with France and Rome remained intact, the bargain sweetened by two generous dowries and lucrative papal concessions. Yet the alliance with France came at the price of war with England—and a military reversal from which the king's reputation has never recovered. Although a Scottish army was beaten at *Solway Moss on 24 November 1542, it was neither a personal humiliation for the king (who was not there) nor the result of noble disaffection. In fact, James had substantial support for his war policy and, when he died on 14 December 1542, preparations were already in train for a further English campaign.

As this suggests, the king's death was hardly the result of shame or despair at military defeat. Nor, despite the sudden death of his two male heirs in April 1541, is it likely to have been caused by disappointment at the birth of a daughter on 8 December 1542. More probably, and prosaically, it was the plague or cholera which brought his vigorous rule to a premature end. RAM

Bingham, C., *James V* (1971); Donaldson, G., *Scottish Kings* (1967); Marshall, R. K., *Mary of Guise* (1977); Wormald, J., *Court, Kirk and Community: Scotland 1470–1625* (1981).

James VI (1566–1625), king of Scotland (1567–1625) and, as **James I,** king of England (1603–25), was the son of Mary, queen of Scots, whose enforced abdication brought him to the throne when he was not 2 years of age. A lonely but intelligent child, James was educated by a succession of formidable tutors, including George *Buchanan, whose insistence that kings were servants of their people provoked his pupil into believing the opposite. Royal authority had been brought to a low ebb by Mary, and during James's minority the factious nobility lived in a state of civil war. James's assumption of power in 1585 marked a turning-point, for he brought the nobles to heel at the same time as he involved them in government. His main adversary was the presbyterian church, or kirk, which claimed that its authority, deriving directly from God, was superior to his own. James skilfully outflanked the kirk's leaders by encouraging the moderates and reviving the office of bishop. He also used his learning and forensic skills to buttress his position. *The Trew Law* and the **Basilikon doron*, both written in the 1590s, proclaimed that kings were the images of God upon earth and should be venerated as such.

James, deprived of female company during his formative years, found an outlet for his deepest emotional needs in male favourites, of whom Esmé Stuart, created duke of *Lennox by the boy king in 1581, was the first of a long line. But James was also capable of relations with the opposite sex, as he showed in 1589 when he crossed the seas to Norway to bring back *Anne of Denmark as his wife. The marriage began well and produced a number of children, of whom two sons, *Henry and Charles (later Charles I), and a daughter, *Elizabeth, survived into adult life.

In 1586 James concluded a treaty with Elizabeth I which provided him with a substantial pension and acknowledged his right to succeed to the English throne. This enticing prospect may have kept James from protesting when his mother was executed by Elizabeth's government in 1587, but Mary was virtually a stranger to him, and her steadfast commitment to catholicism was at odds with his deeply held protestant convictions. When, in early 1603, news came of Elizabeth's death, James was impatient to quit his impoverished kingdom, but he was not ashamed of his Scottishness. On the contrary, his major objective once he was established in England was to complete the union of crowns by a union of states. This could only be done with the support of the two parliaments, but while he could ensure the co-operation of the Scottish assembly, the English one proved recalcitrant. Debates on the union, the principal business of the Parliament which James summoned in 1604, revealed the depth of English prejudice against the Scots. They also revealed that James's subjects were acutely suspicious of his intentions. In his writings and speeches alike, he used the language of absolutism, and he was not familiar with the very different English political tradition based on *Magna Carta and the common law. James, who had worked harmoniously with the Scottish Parliament, found the larger and more formal English institution alien and intractable.

James's open-handed generosity, particularly towards his Scottish companions, won him few friends among the English. Nor did the spread of corruption in public life, including the sale of titles and offices, much of which was generated by royal favourites such as *Carr and *Buckingham. Conviction that James would squander any money grants, plus fear that without dependence upon parliamentary supply he would develop into an absolute monarch on the European pattern, brought about the collapse of the *Great Contract. James's resort to non-parliamentary taxes like *impositions made matters worse and led to the failure of the *'Addled' Parliament. It took time before James realized that, while he was much richer than he had been in Scotland, he still needed to exercise restraint. Matters improved considerably after 1620, when he appointed a merchant-financier, Lionel *Cranfield, to the Treasury, but by then the damage was done.

In the sphere of religion James was far more successful, not least because his protestantism was unquestionable. After the *Hampton Court conference he came to realize that English *puritans were far less dangerous than Scottish presbyterians, and in 1610 he pleased them by appointing the low-church George *Abbot as archbishop. James also remained tolerant towards his catholic subjects, even after the *Gunpowder plot, and drew up an oath of allegiance designed to enable them to express their loyalty without offending their conscience. The problem for James was that religion and politics were inextricably intertwined. In hopes of acting as a European peacemaker, he married his daughter to a leading protestant prince and planned a match between his son and the daughter of the king of Spain, the archetypal catholic ruler. This ecumenical approach to international politics baffled and outraged his subjects, who believed that England's place was at the head of a protestant crusade. When, in 1621, James forbade the Commons to discuss the Spanish marriage on the grounds that such matters were his concern, not theirs, they drew up a protestation asserting their right to debate all 'urgent affairs'. James responded by sending for the Commons' journal and ripping the offending protestation out. The next Parliament, the last of the reign, which met in 1624, was more harmonious, but only because James was no longer in full control. A powerful alliance between his son and heir Charles, his favourite Buckingham, and the parliamentary leaders forced him to acknowledge, however reluctantly, the possibility not merely of breaking off relations with Spain but even of fighting her.

Fortunately for James, he died in March 1625, before war broke out. He was not deeply mourned in either England or Scotland; undignified and conceited, long-winded and short-tempered, he caused offence without realizing it. But he cannot be written off as a failure. He kept his kingdoms in peace at home and abroad, he preserved the powers of the crown, and he held the church firmly to a middle course. It was no accident that while James's mother and son both met violent ends, he died peacefully in his bed. RL

Akrigg, G. P. V. (ed.), *Letters of James VI & I* (1984); Lee, M., *Great Britain's Solomon: James VI & I in his Three Kingdoms* (Urbana, Ill., 1990); Peck, L. L. (ed.), *The Mental World of the Jacobean Court* (1991).

James VII (1633–1701), king of Scotland and, as **James II,** of England (1685–8). James's formative years before 1660 were spent in the French and Spanish armies. His experiences in exile permanently distanced him in mentality and sympathies from most Englishmen. As duke of York under his brother Charles II he developed a career as lord admiral, defeating the Dutch off *Lowestoft (1665) and commanding at Sole Bay (*Southwold) (1672). He showed himself honest, straightforward, and brave, but not a good strategist. James advocated wars against the Dutch with the objective of strengthening royal power, particularly by reducing its dependence on Parliament and the militia. His association with the ministers who formed the *cabal represented a reversal of his earlier connection with the constitutional royalism of *Clarendon, whose daughter Anne *Hyde he married: she produced two future sovereigns, Mary and Anne.

After 1667 James constantly worked for an alliance with France, seeing this as the prerequisite to free the crown from Parliament. Around 1672 James became a catholic, refusing in 1673 to take the Anglican sacrament as required by the *Test Act and resigning as lord admiral. He had urged Charles to veto the Test, to dissolve Parliament, and continue the third Dutch War in alliance with France. When he remarried to a catholic Italian, *Mary of Modena, suggested by the French, opposition politicians began to exploit a growing impression that James was unfit to succeed Charles. In 1678 'revelations' of a *popish plot to murder Charles so as to place James on the throne led *Shaftesbury and the Whigs to lead a parliamentary and popular movement to exclude James from the succession. This issue dominated three parliaments in 1679, 1680, and 1681. James feared that Charles would abandon his right, especially when he was exiled in 1679 and 1680, but the king resisted all Whig pressure and after concluding a subsidy treaty with France ruled for his last four years without Parliament. James succeeded without opposition in February 1685.

A Tory Parliament voted revenues which, with foreign trade expanding, freed James from his predecessors' dependence on parliamentary grants. The Whigs were discredited. *Monmouth's rebellion was easily crushed. Anglicans generally acquiesced in non-enforcement of the penal laws against catholics. But James aimed to free the crown from any dependence on its subjects. He ended the parliamentary session when votes of money were linked to representations about the illegal commissioning of catholics in the army. The *Ecclesiastical Commission, set up to discipline Anglican clergy who attacked catholicism, suspended the bishop of London. James used his *dispensing power to put catholics in offices. The militia was run down, the professional army expanded. James ineffectively canvassed peers and MPs to pass legislation granting catholics equality of civil and religious rights. Their refusal led him to suspend discriminatory statutes by the *Declaration of Indulgence (April 1687), provoking fears that this asserted and dubious royal power could be used to terminate any law that restricted the actions of the crown. Sweeping changes in Ireland, where catholics replaced protestants in government, army, law, professions, and corporations, seemed to indicate such an intention. In England James initiated a political campaign to manipulate elections to a future parliament. This involved purging the justices and deputies in the counties and the urban corporations. Several thousand persons were displaced for refusing to promise that if elected they would legislate as James directed, or would vote for such pre-engaged candidates. James also encouraged a catholic mission to convert the nation which had limited success. Open opposition to his policies was impossible: the army, camped outside London, prevented disturbances.

Some Whig and Tory notables established clandestine contacts with William of Orange, but most people believed that James could not live long. His protestant daughter Mary, married to William, would then reverse James's policies. The queen's pregnancy and the birth of a prince (June 1688) dashed these hopes, while James demonstrated his intention to persist with his policies by reissuing the Declaration of Indulgence and (unsuccessfully) prosecuting the *seven bishops who contested its legality. These developments led to the invitation sent to William by Whig and Tory leaders to intervene (30 June). Although James uncharacteristically abandoned all his unpopular policies in October he could not persuade his subjects to help him resist William. Army and navy officers defected, the provinces declared for William, and even the Anglican clergy stood neutral. Broken psychologically, James fled to France. Louis XIV sent him to Ireland under French supervision. Defeated at the *Boyne (July 1690) he lived as Louis's client at Saint-Germain praying for another restoration. JRJ

Miller, J., *James II: A Study in Kingship* (1978).

Jameson Raid, 1895. At the time (29 December 1895) this was presented as a brave attempt by a troop of part-time cavalry led by Dr Leander Starr Jameson, the British South Africa Company's representative in *Rhodesia, to rescue English women and children persecuted by a wicked Boer government in the *Transvaal. It turned out, however, to be a sordid conspiracy by Cecil *Rhodes, almost certainly with the British colonial secretary Joseph *Chamberlain's prior knowledge, to seize the Transvaal for the *British empire on that pretext. It failed ignominiously, and sullied Rhodes's, Chamberlain's, and the empire's reputations thereafter. BJP

Jane Seymour (*c.*1509–37), 3rd queen of Henry VIII. Jane Seymour was a lady-in-waiting to *Anne Boleyn in 1534 when she began to attract Henry's attention. From a Wiltshire gentry family at Wolf Hall, which the king visited in September 1535, she was said to be quiet and amiable, while Anne was growing more highly strung and imperious. By May 1536 Anne was under arrest and Jane's marriage took place soon after her execution and before the month was out. Honours were showered upon her family. Her elder brother Edward (the future Protector *Somerset) was created Viscount Beauchamp in June and earl of Hertford in October 1537: another brother, Thomas, became a gentleman of the privy chamber. A new Act of *Succession disinherited the Princesses Mary and Elizabeth in favour of Jane's offspring. In October 1537 she gave birth to the future Edward VI but died twelve days later. Henry seems to have felt genuine grief and ten years later was buried at Windsor at her side. JAC

Japan, relations with. Britain was among the powers to follow up the American initiative which opened Japan to the West from the 1850s, and to provide models upon which the Japanese based their modernization from 1868 (especially the development of their navy). The British were pioneers in the renegotiation of the unequal treaties which governed Japan's relations with the West, an agreement being reached in 1894. In January 1902 Britain and Japan became allies, the Admiralty being especially anxious for assistance in offsetting Russian and French naval power in the Far East. Japan's victory in the war against Russia in 1904–5 added temporarily to British security at sea and on the north-west frontier of India, but increasing Anglo-Japanese trade competition soon developed in China. The alliance from 1911 was largely designed by Britain to restrain Japan and to facilitate the navy's concentration in home waters against Germany. Japan's assistance to Britain in 1914–18 was balanced by her advancing influence in China. Yet the alliance was given up in 1921–2 only in response to American pressure and in the context of efforts to regulate competition in the Far East. British interests, however, were dangerously exposed when Japan embarked upon an increasingly aggressive policy from 1931. German successes in Europe made the British empire ever more vulnerable as Japan advanced into south-east Asia. War broke out in December 1941. The loss of Malaya and Singapore soon followed, defeats often seen as a turning-point in the history of the empire. Commonwealth forces later took the offensive, but it was the USA which was primarily responsible for Japan's defeat in 1945. By the 1980s and 1990s it seemed as if the wheel was coming full circle with Japanese industry and investment helping to revitalize the British economy. CJB

Jarrow, on the south bank of the Tyne, was founded in 682 by *Benedict Biscop and thereafter formed a single monastery with *Monkwearmouth. Largely through the work of *Bede this foundation had an enormous impact on medieval European learning. One of Biscop's churches still survives as the present chancel; the larger basilica, dedicated in 685, lay to its west and was destroyed in the 18th cent. As at Wearmouth, these churches and the surrounding excavated monastic structures reflect Gaulish tastes. The present standing buildings lying to the south of the church are of post-Conquest date, some associated with Aldwine's attempt to revive monasticism on the site in the 1070s. RNB

Jeffrey, Francis, Lord Jeffrey (1773–1850). Scottish law lord and literary critic, Jeffrey was called to the Scottish bar in 1794, but unable to attract work because of his switch of allegiance from his father's high Toryism to Whiggism, turned to literature and edited the newly founded **Edinburgh Review* for 27 years. He was an outstanding editor, and the *Edinburgh Review* became the most influential medium of critical opinion in Britain. Jeffrey's appointment as lord advocate in 1830 on his resignation from the *Edinburgh Review* was both a reward for his political services to the Whig Party, and a recognition of his legal qualities. He entered Parliament in 1831, but in 1834 became a judge of the Court of Session. However, it is as a literary critic that Jeffrey's fame rests: *Carlyle even compared him to Voltaire. TSG

Jeffreys, George (1648–89). Notorious as the judge who presided at the *Bloody Assizes, Jeffreys was a career lawyer who became conspicuous as an aggressive prosecutor and partisan judge. At political trials his success in harassing defendants and intimidating juries earned him royal approval for upholding the interests of the crown. In 1684 he ordered the execution of Sir Thomas Armstrong without trial, as an outlaw. Attached to James II since 1677, he became lord chancellor in 1685 and as Baron Wem acted as Speaker of the Lords. In dealing with his peers his bullying manner proved counter-productive. The other judges involved in the Bloody Assizes allowed Jeffreys to incur responsibility for the brutal treatment of Monmouth's rebels. Consequently Jeffreys was cast as scapegoat after the *Glorious Revolution, but died soon after being arrested. Whig historians subsequently created the legendary figure of a unique judicial monster. JRJ

Jehovah's witnesses. An exclusive millennialist sect developed out of Charles Russell's International Bible Students Association (founded in Pittsburgh, 1872), now world-wide. Russell's successor, Judge Rutherford, sought to affirm Jehovah as the true God and developed the concept of a 'theocratic Kingdom' which will emerge after Armageddon. Date setting and prophecy have lessened, but they refuse any association with other denominations and regard civil authorities and secular governments as allies of Satan. Baptized by immersion, witnesses insist on high moral probity, oppose blood transfusions on scriptural grounds, write and publish prolifically and anonymously (chief periodicals: *The Watchtower* and *Awake!*) and, after training, preach enthusiastically on doorsteps, so attracting the disaffected through their subversive message. The British headquarters functions as The Watch Tower Bible and Tract Society. ASH

Jellicoe, Sir John (1859–1935). Admiral. As commander-in-chief of the Grand Fleet until December 1916, Jellicoe knew that a single wrong decision could cost Britain the war by losing command of the seas. Confronted by a growing threat to his battleships from German mines and submarines, he was determined not to risk his ships unless he was certain of destroying the German high seas fleet. His handling of the Grand Fleet at *Jutland was marked by excessive caution and he forfeited any chance of decisively defeating the Germans. He was a tired man in December 1916 when he was transferred to the Admiralty as 1st sea lord. Jellicoe lacked the political skills necessary to prosper in

Whitehall. His natural pessimism, coupled with a reluctance to employ convoys to counter the German U-boat offensive against allied merchant shipping, cost him *Lloyd George's confidence. He was dismissed in December 1917. He received his earldom, rather belatedly, in 1925. DF

Jenkins, Roy (b. 1920). Chancellor of the University of Oxford; previously deputy leader (1970–2) of the Labour Party and leader (1982–3) of the *Social Democratic Party. Author, bon viveur, and quintessential establishment figure, he became Lord Jenkins of Hillhead in 1987. His political appointments included minister of aviation (1964–5), home secretary (1965–7, 1974–6), chancellor of the Exchequer (1967–70), and he was easily the most successful of *Wilson's cabinet ministers. From 1977 to 1981 he was president of the European Commission. One of the 'Gang of Four' who broke with the Labour Party in 1981 to form the *SDP, he was replaced as leader after 1983 by David *Owen. His main political achievements were to facilitate the 'moral revolution of the 1960s' as home secretary (defending the 'permissive society' as 'the civilized society'), to give strong support to the move into Europe, and to help keep the Labour Party out of power in the 1980s and 1990s. AS

Jenkins's Ear, War of. Although Captain Jenkins's ear was cut off by the Spanish in a skirmish in 1731, the war between Spain and Britain that bears his name did not begin until October 1739. American colonial trade was at the heart of the conflict and, initially, Britain made gains. Defeats followed, which had virtually destroyed her Caribbean army by spring 1741, though the navy remained potent. Domestic pressure for war with Spain marked the beginning of the end for *Walpole's premiership. From December 1740 the War of Jenkins's Ear was subsumed into the War of the *Austrian Succession. AIL

Jenkinson, Anthony (d. 1611). Jenkinson, a member of the Mercers' Company, made a series of remarkable voyages to Russia and the Near East in the reign of Ivan the Terrible. His first, via Norway (1557–60), took him to Moscow, where he met the tsar, and on to Bokhara. The second (1561–3) was to Persia to negotiate with the shah. A third (1566–7) and a last (1571–2) were to Moscow. He then settled down to trade at home. His voyages were related in *Hakluyt's *Principal Navigations*, first published in 1589. JAC

Jenner, Edward (1749–1823). Vaccination pioneer. As John *Hunter's first house-pupil and dresser at St George's hospital (London), Jenner shared Hunter's disciplined observation and belief in experimentation, but chose to practise at home at Berkeley (Glos.), where he joined local medical groups and continued his interests in heart disease and natural history. He became obsessed with the idea that inoculation of cowpox matter (a mild contagious disease) was a better protection against the scourge of smallpox than using exudate from smallpox lesions. An initial paper having been rejected, he published privately *An Inquiry into Cow-pox* (1798), and very slowly the idea of 'vaccination' was popularized, though not without problems of controversy, contamination, and chicanery. World-wide recognition and honours ensued, but Jenner lost rather than gained financially, as he spent the remainder of his life in an ever-widening campaign to eradicate smallpox from the world. This was finally achieved in 1978. ASH

Jervis, John, 1st earl of St Vincent (1735–1823). Promoted earl following his triumph over the Spanish fleet in February 1797, Jervis, son of a crooked Staffordshire lawyer, had an inauspicious and impoverished start in life. But these circumstances formed an unflinching character of firmness and integrity; and as a hard yet humane disciplinarian Jervis attained a standing in the navy which was all his own. A symbol of professionalism, he was commanding in the Western Approaches in his 71st year. Jervis served with *Wolfe at Quebec in 1759, and subsequent service in the North Sea and Mediterranean endorsed his talents as a seaman. In the 1770s he spent a year in France, familiarized himself with France's Biscay bases, and visited all the ports of the Baltic. He was present at *Keppel's indecisive action off *Ushant in July 1778, while at home he became MP for Launceston, Yarmouth (Walpole interest), and Wycombe 1783–90. Promoted admiral in 1787 he combined well with the army in the West Indies in 1793, but it was his command in the Mediterranean 1795–9 which established his fame, together with his affectionate tutelage of his mercurial subordinate *Nelson. In 1801, as 1st lord of the Admiralty, St Vincent energetically prosecuted an inquiry into waste and theft in the dockyards which contributed to Lord *Melville's impeachment in 1806 for malversation of funds. In 1810 *Sheridan saluted St Vincent's 'triple laurels over the enemy, the mutineer, and the corrupt'. DDA

Jesuits. The Society of Jesus was founded by Ignatius Loyola and approved by Pope Paul III in 1540. It offered total obedience to the papacy and was prominent in the effort to recover ground lost to the church by the Reformation. Mary Tudor, though a devoted catholic, mistrusted the order and did not invite it to England, though a number of Englishmen went abroad to join it. But the deterioration of relations between Elizabeth and the papacy, culminating in the bull of excommunication of 1570, changed the situation. William *Allen had already founded a seminary at Douai and about 100 catholic priests had made their way back to England by 1580, living an undercover existence, hiding in priest holes, and protected by the old catholic gentry. In that year, two Jesuit priests landed—*Campion and *Parsons—accompanied by a lay brother. Their mission lasted only a few months but gave an important boost to the morale of English catholics. Campion was soon apprehended and executed in December 1581: Parsons left for the continent and never returned. Elizabeth's ministers were at pains to convict the Jesuits of duplicity and indeed their interpretation of the papal bull—that catholics were not bound by it 'things being as they are'—was disingenuous. The events of the rest of the decade—powerful French and catholic influence in Scotland, plots against the queen's life, the threat of the Armada—combined to strengthen anti-catholic feeling in England, much of it concentrated on the Jesuits. But the culminating disaster for English catholics was the *Gunpowder plot of 1605, which resulted in the capture of Henry Garnett, Jesuit superior in England for nearly twenty years.

Though he claimed that he knew of the plot only through the confessional, others doubted, and he was executed as a traitor. For decades, 'Jesuitical' became a term of abuse, signifying mental reservation, prevarication, and casuistry. The prominence of Jesuits throughout Europe as teachers and confessors encouraged the belief that they practised relentless and insidious indoctrination. The fires of fear and hatred were stoked again by suspicions that Charles I (with a catholic wife) and Archbishop *Laud were crypto-papists, and in 1679 by the lurid allegations of the *Popish plot. Titus *Oates purported to be a repentant Jesuit and his revelations of a Jesuit scheme to murder Charles II and place James, duke of York, on the throne brought nine Jesuits to the scaffold. But, in the long run, the Enlightenment proved more damaging to the order than downright persecution. The Jesuits were accused of accommodation and undue pliability in their zeal to proselytize and the order was wound up by Pope Clement XIV in 1773 after France, Spain, and Portugal had all moved against it. Surprisingly, it continued in Russia and Prussia, where there were many Jesuit teachers, and where Catherine the Great and Frederick the Great paid little attention to papal bulls. Though reconstituted in 1814 by Pope Pius VII, the circumstances which had made Jesuits so hated were no longer in existence. The French Revolution, in which the catholic church had been persecuted, first by de-Christianizers and then by Napoleon, had brought about a realignment, and French refugee clergy had been welcomed and given assistance in Britain. The English province of the order was re-established in 1829, with the Jesuits in Scotland, who had never been strong, tucked into that organization. Although fierce bursts of anti-catholic feeling were still possible, particularly at the time of 'papal aggression' in 1850, the role of the Society of Jesus was no longer a national bugbear. JAC

Jevons, W. S. (1835–82). Distinguished neo-classical economist. Jevons was born in Liverpool, and educated in Liverpool and London. After studying chemistry at University College, London, and working as an assayer in Australia, he returned to University College in 1859 to study political economy, philosophy, and mathematics. From 1863 he was tutor, lecturer, and then professor at Owens College, Manchester, moving, in 1876, to a chair at University College, London (until 1880). He married the daughter of the founder of the *Manchester Guardian*, and drowned in the sea near Hastings. Jevons had wide interests in political economy, from currency and finance to the relation of sunspots to business cycles. His principal contribution, however, is his work on the marginal utility theory of value (*Theory of Political Economy*, 1872), the introduction of marginal analysis marking 'the true dividing line between classical theory and modern economics'. MW

Jewel, John (1522–71). Bishop. Born in Devonshire and educated at Merton College, Oxford, Jewel became a fellow of Corpus Christi College, Oxford, but was deprived at the accession of Mary and fled to the continent. He returned in 1559 after Elizabeth's accession and was made bishop of Salisbury. In 1562 his *Apologia pro Ecclesia Anglicana* defended the Church of England from the charge of heresy. At the same time, Jewel resisted *calvinist demands for further changes. One of his disciples was Richard *Hooker, who produced the most famous justification of Elizabeth's church settlement as a *via media*. JAC

Jews. Though there must have been individual Jews in Anglo-Saxon England, there is no evidence of settled communities. But after the Norman Conquest, some hundreds of Jews entered the country, mainly from Normandy where there had been settlements. Since Christians were not allowed to practise usury, Jews quickly established themselves as financiers and money-lenders. Their position was extremely precarious, exploited ruthlessly by monarchs in constant need of funds and hated by the native population. As their numbers increased and they moved outside London into provincial towns, tensions rose. As early as 1144 the accusation of ritual murder was made against them, with the charge that they had killed a small boy in Norwich, 'St William'. Severe restrictions were placed upon them. They were confined to Jewries, from 1218 were obliged to wear badges steadily increased in size, and in 1232 a *domus conversorum* was opened in London for proselytizing. Fresh hostility came with the crusading movement. At the accession of Richard I in 1189—a notable crusader—there were attacks on Jews in London, which spread to the provinces, and culminated in the slaughter of 150 Jews in the castle at York. Religious zeal was reinforced by greed and envy. Some of the jews were already very wealthy—Aaron of Lincoln in the 1170s dealt with kings, archbishops, municipalities, and monasteries.

The difficulties of the Jews continued in the 13th cent. John's financial worries made him severe and the baronial opposition to Henry III disliked Jews who could assist the crown. The story of William of Norwich was repeated in 1255 with the account of Hugh of Lincoln—another boy said to have been butchered, and again given saintly status. In 1275 Edward I in a statute forbade Jews to practise usury, allowing them to trade and own property. But if this was meant as an attempt at integration, it was followed in 1278 by a savage attack in which hundreds of Jews were hanged. In 1290, in exchange for a large subsidy from Parliament, all Jews were expelled from the kingdom and given three months to leave. They were given safe conducts though inevitably numbers were set upon and robbed.

Between 1290 and the 1650s there were no Jewish communities of any size, though individuals slipped through, sometimes professing conversion. In Elizabeth's reign, there were Spanish and Portuguese Jews in the country though they practised their religion with circumspection. When approached in the 1650s, *Cromwell was more sympathetic than his council, perhaps because he had made use of some Jews in espionage and diplomacy. There was no dramatic reversal of policy but Jews were allowed in once more. Their numbers and status built up and the financial and commercial revolutions of the early 18th cent. gave them enhanced possibilities. Sir Samuel Gideon was prominent in assisting the government with loans in the crisis of 1745, and his son was given an Irish peerage in 1789, though he had to change both name and religion. But old hatreds died hard and when the Pelhams brought in a modest measure to facilitate naturalization in 1753, the public outcry was so great that they were forced to repeal it.

Catholic emancipation in 1829 left the Jews as the only religious group suffering under severe disabilities. Repeated attempts at concessions were thwarted in the House of Lords but the progress of Jews in society was unmistakable. David Salomons was made sheriff of London in 1835 and lord mayor in 1855; Francis Goldsmid was the first practising Jew to be given a baronetcy in 1841. When first Lionel *Rothschild (1847) and then Salomons (1851) were elected to Parliament, only to be kept out by their inability to take the oath as a Christian, the plight of the Jews was dramatized, and the law was changed in 1858. The first government minister of Jewish faith was appointed in 1871, the first judge in 1873. Powerful prejudices remained and were strengthened by an influx of poorer Jews from eastern Europe in the later 19th cent. The obstacles facing Jews remained substantial, but they were personal and social rather than legal. JAC

Jex-Blake, Sophia (1840–1912). Pioneer of women in medicine. Ever concerned with women's education, Sophia Jex-Blake was mathematics tutor at Queen's College, London (1858), but an American friendship drew her to medical studies, initially in New York but then in Edinburgh, until increasing hostility prevented clinical training. The cause of women's medical education now publicly aired, she responded by founding the London School of Medicine for Women (1874), negotiating clinical work at the Royal Free Hospital. Gaining MD, Berne, then the Dublin licentiate (registrable in Britain), but too stormy for the LSMW (who appointed Elizabeth Garrett *Anderson as dean), she returned hurt to Edinburgh, where she founded her own medical school for women (1886). Like many of her schemes, this did excellent work but foundered through her domineering personality and intransigence. Impetuous trail-blazer, concerned with tuition and legal qualification but difficult to work with, Jex-Blake finally admitted defeat (1898) and retired to Sussex. ASH

jingoism. The word comes from a music-hall song popular at the time of the 1876–8 Eastern crisis: 'We don't want to fight, but by jingo if we do . . .'. Later it was used to describe other manifestations of popular bellicosity during foreign wars. The most famous example was on *Mafeking night, 18 May 1900, when crowds took to the streets to celebrate the relief of a British garrison during the second *Boer War, although there is controversy over how widespread or solid the feeling was. It also erupted later, notably during the *Falklands War of 1982, stoked up—as it generally is—by the gutter press. BJP

Jinnah, Mohammed Ali (1876–1948). Jinnah, 'the father of Pakistan', was born in Karachi and trained as a barrister. Initially, he was sympathetic to the Indian National Congress and did not join the Muslim League until 1913, when it became more critical of colonialism. He helped to organize the Lucknow pact (1916) and the Khilafat movement (1919–22), by which the Muslim League ran campaigns of anti-British resistance parallel to those of the Congress. However, he became suspicious that, especially under *Gandhi's leadership, the Congress was being taken over by a narrow Hindu nationalism. His concern was heightened by the Nehru Report (1928) in which Congress proposals for Indian self-government denied Muslim claims for protected minority rights. In 1934 he became president of the Muslim League and chaired its 1940 conference at Lahore when the demand for a separate Pakistan state was first made. In the 1946–7 negotiations, he stubbornly resisted proposals, favoured by both the British and the Congress, that India should be granted independence as a unitary nation state. Eventually, both the other parties came to accept partition as the price of a rapid British withdrawal. Pakistan proclaimed its independence on 15 August 1947 with Jinnah as its first governor-general. DAW

Joan (Joanna) (1210–38), queen of Alexander II of Scotland. Eldest daughter of King John and sister of Henry III, her marriage to Alexander at York on 19 June 1221 helped to reinforce the Anglo-Scottish peace which lasted from 1217 to 1296. Said to have been 'of comely beauty', she was overshadowed in Scotland by her mother-in-law, the queen-dowager *Ermengarde, and she disappointed her husband's dynastic hopes by failing to have children. She died in London during a visit to Henry III's court, and was buried in the Cistercian nunnery of Tarrant Keynes (Dorset). KJS

Joan, Princess (d. 1237). An illegitimate daughter of King John, Joan was married 1205/6 to *Llywelyn ab Iorwerth of Gwynedd, prince of North Wales. Thereafter, she was a wise counsellor to her husband and a peacemaker in the fluid and often belligerent relations between England and Wales. In 1211, when John attacked Wales, Joan pleaded her husband's cause. The following year she warned her father of the hostile plans of his barons. She continued to act as a mediator during the reign of John and of his successor Henry III. In 1226 Pope Honorius III removed the stigma of her illegitimacy. Llywelyn remained indebted to his wife for her support, forgiving her an affair in 1228. He founded a Franciscan monastery to her memory at Llanfaes (Anglesey), where she is buried. JC

Joan Beaufort (*c.*1400–45), queen of James I of Scotland. Daughter of John Beaufort, earl of Somerset, Joan was married to James I of Scotland at Southwark in February 1424, a match celebrated in James's poem 'The *Kingis Quair'. She was by James I the mother of twin sons, Alexander and James (later James II), and six daughters, and took some part in the business of government. A target for King James's assassins in 1437, the wounded queen escaped to head her infant son's administration. Following her second marriage (1439), to Sir James Stewart of Lorne, Joan lost support, and died at Dunbar castle in July 1445. NATM

Joan of Kent, princess of Wales (*c.*1328–85). Joan was a daughter of Edmund, earl of Kent (d. 1330), and succeeded as countess in 1353. While considerably under age, she secretly married Thomas Holand. In his absence in Prussia, she soon contracted a second marriage with the earl of Salisbury; this was annulled nine years later, in 1349. Within a year of Holand's death, this reputed beauty married *Edward the Black Prince and accompanied him to Gascony, where their sons Edward (d. 1370) and Richard (II) were born. Widowed again in 1376, Joan had charge of Richard's upbringing until his accession, and is believed to have remained a restraining influence upon him. A popular figure, she was well received by turbulent Londoners and humble rebels, while *John of Gaunt and John *Wyclif benefited from her kindly intervention. RLS

Joan of Navarre (*c.*1370–1437), queen of Henry IV. A daughter of Charles the Bad, king of Navarre, Joan married John IV, duke of Brittany, in 1386; they had eight children. After his death in 1399, she acted as regent for Duke John V until his inauguration in 1401. Henry (IV) had visited the Breton court during his exile, which may partially account for his suit. Joan came to England and was crowned in 1403; the marriage was childless. She chose to remain in England after Henry's death. Relations with her stepson Henry V were amicable until 1419, when she was accused of plotting his death by witchcraft. She was confined without trial until 1422, and her revenues seized but restored by Henry's deathbed wish. She was buried with Henry IV, under their effigies in Canterbury cathedral. RLS

Joanna of the Tower (1321–62), queen of David II of Scotland, was the youngest daughter of Edward II and born in the Tower of London. In 1328 when she was 7 she was married to David Bruce, son and heir of Robert I of Scotland, who succeeded in 1329. In 1334 when Edward *Balliol invaded, the young couple were sent to France and did not return until 1341. Five years later, David was captured by the English at *Neville's Cross and taken to London. Joanna visited him and for a while resided at Hertford castle. Soon after his release in 1357 she left him, and spent the rest of her life in refuge at the court of her brother Edward III. JAC

John (1167–1216), king of England (1199–1216). As every schoolboy knows, John was a monster and a tyrant. It is a reputation with very deep historical roots, culminating in the judgements of Victorian historians such as J. R. Green, whose hugely influential popular history of England decisively shaped attitudes. His image of John is grisly: ' "Foul as it is, hell itself is defiled by the fouler presence of John." The terrible view of his contemporaries has passed into the sober judgment of history . . . in his inner soul John was the worst outcome of the Angevins. He united into one mass of wickedness, their insolence, their selfishness, their unbridled lust, their cruelty and tyranny, their shamelessness, their superstition, their cynical indifference to honour or truth.' Precisely because of these characteristics, it is no wonder that John lost the support of his subjects, that he lost the *Angevin empire in France, and that he was brought to book at Runnymede in 1215.

The Victorian view of John stemmed from a perspective on history from the high moral ground, and it drew its support almost entirely from contemporary chroniclers. At the time of John's death, there was already plenty of material and many charges that might be used to condemn him, but his legend was by no means complete and not even agreed by all. That process only occurred in the next 40 years, critically as a result of the deliberate fabrication of an image of John by Roger of Wendover and *Matthew Paris, successive historians of St Albans. (It is Paris whom Green cites in the quotation above.) It is to them that so many of the notorious anecdotes concerning John are due, anecdotes that acted as a vehicle for savage denunciation of the inner being as well as the policies of the king, the better to justify the stance made against him in 1215, and to emphasize the need for *Magna Carta. By *c.*1250, the elements of the legend, descending down the centuries, had crystallized.

In this century, the unreliability and ulterior purposes of many of these chronicle sources has been sharply exposed, serving partly to rehabilitate John. More importantly, through close analysis of the considerable body of record evidence for the reign, John has come to appear in a new light as a very capable administrator with great powers of organization and application. Other talents have also come to be stressed, and none would now doubt that John was a very intelligent and able man. The system of continental alliances that he built up against Philip II of France prior to the disaster at *Bouvines (1214) reveals great diplomatic skill and a sure grasp of strategy. His surrender of England as a papal fief in 1213 was a brilliant piece of manœuvring, at a stroke dividing the pope from the conspiracy developing against John in France and England. Again, his actions in 1215–16 show both considerable ingenuity and a sure tactical sense, both political and military.

Another approach has stressed the continuity between the regimes of Henry II and his sons, placing John firmly in his dynastic context rather than isolating him. Many of John's alleged acts of tyranny appear as continuations of the policies of his predecessors as a result, although it is agreed that he bore down ever more heavily upon his subjects. And he did this, it is argued, not out of any innate wickedness, but because he had no option. His English subjects would have to be exploited, because only with English resources would he be enabled to regain his lost French lands, his overriding policy goal after 1204 when the Angevin empire collapsed.

From these perspectives, John has been rescued from the excessive moralizings of Victorian historians and their predecessors. None, properly informed, would now consider him to be of superhuman wickedness. Yet modern scholarship has also strengthened some of the traditional charges against him. Perhaps the most infamous charge, that he murdered—or caused to be murdered—his own nephew, *Arthur of Brittany, now seems virtually certain. Other acts of cruelty are also proven, his hanging of 28 hostages, sons of rebel Welsh chieftains, in 1212, or his pursuit of the Braose family and the starving to death of William de *Braose's wife and son in a royal prison. The consensus has grown that although men of his age, and of others, could be excessively cruel, John overstepped the mark, that thin line between what his age accepted as justifiable and what not. Here, he does stand out.

In a similar vein, he did not live up to contemporary expectations of a king. In contrast to his brother Richard I, he seemed incompetent in warfare. Particularly damaging was the epithet 'Softsword' applied to him as early as 1200. Yet he could be capable of decisive military action. Again, he took the business of dispensing justice seriously, but all too often his subjects could complain that the judgment rendered was unjust and partial. And in pressing ever harder upon his subjects out of financial necessity, if nothing else, he laid himself open to the charge of introducing evil customs and unlawful innovations.

Had John succeeded in regaining his lost lands, Magna Carta would almost certainly not have occurred and the legend about him would never have developed. But he lost, and paid a posthumous penalty as well. And one of the chief reasons that he lost lay in his appalling handling of his greater subjects. Whatever John's technical competence as a ruler, it was constantly compromised by his secretive and suspicious nature towards them, his jealousy, unpredictability, and caprice, most notoriously shown in the handling of William de Braose. None could live easily with such a ruler, his conviction that they were untrustworthy serving only to alienate them. Rule by fear might keep them in check in the short term, but in the long run, John's regime was dangerously unstable. He and his greater subjects confronted each other in a closed system of self-fulfilling preconceptions. John remains baffling and enigmatic. As Lewis Warren put it so succinctly, 'He had the mental abilities of a great king but the inclinations of a petty tyrant.' SL

Holt, J. C., *King John* (Historical Association pamphlet, 1963); Painter, S., *The Reign of King John* (Baltimore, 1949); Turner, R. V., *King John* (1994); Warren, W. L., *King John* (2nd edn. 1978).

John, Augustus Edwin (1878–1961). British painter. John was born in Tenby (Wales), the son of a solicitor. A brilliant student, he trained at the Slade School, then went to Liverpool as an art instructor. In the first decade of the 20th cent. he was at the height of his powers, expressing in art and life an independent and rebellious nature. Although he had been rejected for military service, he served in Paris as an official war artist for a few months. Between the two world wars, he became the leading society portraitist. He was elected ARA in 1921 and a full academician seven years later. Following an argument over the rejection of another artist's work, he resigned from the academy in 1938 but was re-elected in 1940 and awarded the OM in 1942. JC

John, lord of the Isles. See MACDONALD, JOHN.

John Balliol. See BALLIOL, JOHN.

John Bull. The character of John Bull was invented by John Arbuthnot in a series of pamphlets, *Law is a Bottomless Pit*, published in 1712. Bull's sturdy honesty contrasted with the wily Frenchman Lewis Baboon. He became popular with cartoonists in the early 19th cent. and acquired the Pickwickian squat top hat and the Union Jack waistcoat. His heyday was the later Victorian period, when he appeared in countless *Punch* cartoons. A popular magazine, taking the name, was founded in 1906 by Horatio Bottomley. JAC

John of Gaunt, 1st duke of Lancaster (1340–99). The third surviving son of Edward III, born in Ghent, and England's greatest territorial magnate following the death of his father-in-law *Henry of Grosmont. As earl of Richmond (1342–72), he was engaged in the French war from 1355, eventually leading major operations, the most notable the *chevauchée* from Calais to Bordeaux in 1373. He also had commands on the Scottish border. His wealth enabled him to form the largest baronial retinue of knights and esquires; their badge was his collar of linked SS. Gaunt's contingent was a quarter of the army raised by contract for Richard II's Scottish campaign in 1385. From 1372 he assumed the title of king of Castile in right of his second wife, which he renounced—profitably—after campaigning there in 1386–7. In Edward's dotage, Gaunt was virtually regent, incurring widespread odium for military failures and government corruption and for opposing criticism in the *Good Parliament. His patronage of *Wyclif and hostility to the bishop of London roused riots; his Savoy palace was sacked in 1381. Lords feared his wisdom as well as his might; they resented his 'poaching' their retainers. In response to *Northumberland's opposition in the north, he advanced his Neville followers; Ralph Neville was made earl of *Westmorland and married Gaunt's daughter Anne Beaufort, who with her brothers was legitimized in 1397. Despite allegations of treason by hostile courtiers, Gaunt's backing was invaluable to Richard; while Richard was childless, it is doubtful if this loyalty was disinterested. His son seized the throne in 1399 and reigned as Henry IV. RLS

John of Salisbury (*c.*1120–80). Scholar and clerical author. His letters and books drew on his own experience in church politics and reflected the immense range of his classical and Christian scholarship. Born at Salisbury, a student at Paris (1136–46) in the days of Abelard, in his *Metalogicon* he defended the value of logic as an intellectual discipline. As political secretary to Archbishop *Theobald (1147–61) of Canterbury he used his friendship with *Adrian IV to promote Canterbury's interests at the papal curia and then used his insider knowledge to discuss both the theory of church–state relations and contemporary history in his *Policraticus* and the *Memoirs of the Papal Court*. He acted as adviser to *Becket during his quarrel with Henry II and then became an active hagiographer, promoting the cult of the murdered archbishop. In 1176 he was elected bishop of Chartres. JG

Johnson, Samuel (1709–84). Johnson was the son of a bookseller in Lichfield (Staffs.). He attended local schools before spending just one year at Pembroke College, Oxford, 1728–9. His early attempts at teaching failed, but he married the widow Elizabeth Porter at this time (1735). The hard life of Grub Street in London beckoned him next, but it was some years before he was regularly commissioned by Edward Cave, proprietor of the **Gentleman's Magazine*, to report parliamentary debates and undertake book translations. Johnson wrote his fine poem *London* at this time (1738), containing the line, 'Slow rises worth, by poverty depressed.' In 1746–55 Johnson worked on his *Dictionary*, the first full collation of the English language and a masterpiece of prose. He composed *The Vanity of Human Wishes* in 1749 and lost his wife three years later. To pay for his mother's funeral, Johnson wrote *Rasselas* (1759) in one week; it is possibly his finest work, a profound novel upon 'the choice of life'. Between the larger works Johnson composed periodical moral essays under the title of the *Rambler*, the *Idler*, and the *Adventurer*. In 1762, Lord *Bute bestowed upon Johnson a pension of £300 a year, ending his financial difficulties. He met *Boswell in the following year, received a doctorate from Dublin in 1765, and met George III in 1767. After receiving his pension Johnson's literary output was smaller, but he produced his masterly edition of Shakespeare (1765), *Journey to the Western Islands of Scotland* (1775), undertaken with Boswell, and *Lives of the Poets* (1779–81). In addition, he wrote a number of political pamphlets in defence of the government, most notably its policy towards the American revolutionaries. Johnson's religious writings were published posthumously as *Prayers and Meditations* (1785), underlining his reputation as a devout Christian.

Much of Johnson's fame comes from his personality and conversation. To list his friends is to list many of the leading cultural figures of the 18th cent., painter Sir Joshua *Reynolds, novelist Oliver *Goldsmith, politician Edmund *Burke, and actor David *Garrick. All of these were members of the celebrated Literary Club, of which Johnson was a founder; many of the splendid discussions that took place there were recorded by Boswell in his incomparable *Life of Johnson* (1791). Johnson was a ferocious opponent in debate, but kind and understanding in daily life, loyal to friends, and sympathetic to their shortcomings. His house in London was filled with the needy and upon his death he bequeathed it to his black servant Frank Barber. Johnson was plagued by depression, loneliness, and ill-health, but fought valiantly against them, aided by Hester Thrale, perhaps his closest friend. Politically, he was a Tory, but despite declaring, 'the first Whig was the Devil,' he had many Whig friends. To many Samuel Johnson has become the personification of the 18th cent. AIL

Jones, Inigo (1573–1652). Masque designer, architect, and courtier, Jones's architectural legacy only fructified in the early 18th cent. through the neo-Palladian movement. So infectious did his derivations from the functional architecture of Andrea Palladio (1508–80) then become that until the early 19th cent. English townscapes were arguably Jonesian in their lineaments. Yet Jones personally remains frustratingly elusive, for all his arrogance and engrossing power as surveyor of the king's works (1615–44). Palladio's *Four Books of Architecture* were not exclusively influential, for two visits to Italy, the second with the greatest Italophile of the age, Thomas Howard, earl of *Arundel, brought other influences to bear, such as Serlio and Scamozzi (architectural) and Peruzzi and Parmigianino (painters and draughtsmen). Apart from entrancing scenic and costume designs, only seven of Jones's 45 architectural works survive: the most notable are the Whitehall *Banqueting House, Queen's chapel at St James's, Queen's House at *Greenwich, and, by no means least because of its Carolean town-planning context, St Paul's church, *Covent Garden. DDA

Jones, Sir William (1746–94). Oriental scholar. Educated at Harrow and University College, Oxford, Jones was a gifted linguist, eventually mastering 13 languages and knowing 28 others. His opposition to the American War and the slave trade probably cost him the chair of Arabic at Oxford in 1781. Called to the bar in 1774, he was knighted and appointed a judge in the High Court of Calcutta in 1783. He remained in India until his premature death, founding the Bengal Asiatic Society (1784) and developing an appreciation of Indian law and culture unusual in a European. Having mastered Sanskrit, he translated parts of Indian classics including the scriptures (the Veda) and laid the foundations for comparative philology. His writings were a useful counter in Britain to the developing forces of Christian cultural imperialism. He was elected fellow of the *Royal Society in 1772. ER

Jonson, Ben (1572–1637). English Renaissance poet and playwright, the most forthright and politically conservative of his contemporaries. His writing—poetry, drama, and opinions—is a curious blend of disciplined classicism and carnival grotesque. He was imprisoned twice, once for his part in the scurrilous play *Isle of Dogs* and once for killing an actor in a duel. He converted to Roman catholicism whilst in jail. Along with John Marston (with whom he exchanged dramatic fire in the 'war of the theatres', 1599–1600) and Thomas Middleton, he created 'Jacobean city comedy'. His best-known plays are *Volpone* (1605), *The Alchemist* (1610), and *Bartholomew Fair* (1614). Socially and culturally aspirant, Jonson attracted royal patronage, creating a series of court masques (in collaboration with Inigo *Jones) and receiving a life pension from James I. Unlike most of his fellow-playwrights, he carefully supervised the publication of his plays for his grandiosely named *Workes* in 1616. The latter part of his career was less successful, though he continued to be lionized, notably by a group of young royalist writers known as the 'tribe of Ben', who later formed the nucleus of the 'Cavalier poets'. He died in 1637 and was buried in Westminster abbey. GAM

Jordan, previously known as Trans-Jordan, was part of the Turkish empire in 1914 but after the First World War became a British *mandate under the *League of Nations. In 1946 the independence of Jordan was declared and a kingdom established under the Amir Abdullah. After Abdullah's assassination in 1951, his son Talal was briefly king, before giving way in 1953 to his son Hussein. In 1967 Israel occupied the territory west of the Jordan and annexed east Jerusalem, sending a million Palestine refugees into Jordan. In 1988 the Jordanians conceded their west bank rights to the Palestine Liberation Organization. During the *Gulf War of 1990 Jordan maintained a precarious neutrality. JAC

Jowett, Benjamin (1817–93). Scholar. Jowett held the regius chair of Greek at Oxford for nearly 40 years and was master of Balliol College for more than 20 years. He was born in London, went to St Paul's school, and won a scholarship in 1836 to Balliol—'a little puny, boyish, chubby-faced youth'. Two years later he was elected a fellow while still an undergraduate and the following year, presumably to everyone's relief, gained a first. He became professor of Greek in 1855 and began a successful series of lectures in Greek philosophy, while devoting much time to individual students.

Elected to the mastership in 1870, his four-volume translation of Plato appeared in 1871, followed by Thucydides (1881) and Aristotle's *Politics* (1885). Waterhouse's rebuilding of the Broad Street front of Balliol was finished during Jowett's mastership and under his influence the college became pre-eminent in the university. It was said that in the late 1890s more than 40 MPs were Balliol men. Among his many *bons mots* one has certainly not lost point with the passing of years: to a young lady he remarked, 'You must believe in God, my dear, despite what the clergymen say.' JAC

Joyce, James (1882–1941). High priest of modernism and most uncompromising of novelists. The short stories of *Dubliners* (1914) chapter the moral history of his country 'in a style of scrupulous meanness'. In *A Portrait of the Artist as a Young Man* (1916) he set an ironical distance between himself and the catholicism and aestheticism of his youth before escaping to a life of cunning and exile on the continent. The major work, *Ulysses* (1922), chronicles a single day in June 1904 but was eight years in the writing and passed the censors only in 1933. An encyclopedic obsession with language in all its aspects does not exclude comedy, warmth, and humanity, but in the still more experimental *Finnegans Wake* he goes where few readers follow. Though he died in Zurich, in his writing he had never really left his native Dublin. JNRS

Judicature Acts, 1873–5. These Acts brought about a much needed reorganization of the courts in England and Wales. Before the Acts there were a number of common law courts, all with overlapping jurisdiction—Common Pleas, *King's Bench, and *Exchequer. There was also the Court of *Chancery, which administered the rules and remedies of equity, separately from the rules of common law, and which had become a scandal through its delays and expense. Finally there were courts administering family and probate matters, which had inherited their jurisdiction from the *ecclesiastical courts, and the Court of *Admiralty. The Judicature Acts abolished these separate courts and instead set up the Supreme Court of Judicature, consisting of a Court of Appeal, to hear appeals on civil matters, and a single High Court, having several divisions corresponding to the previous separate courts; there were now the King's Bench, Common Pleas, Exchequer, and Chancery divisions of the High Court, and the remaining jurisdictions were combined in a Division for Probate, Divorce, and Admiralty. MM

Julian of Norwich (1342–*c*.1416). Anchoress and mystic. Probably educated by Benedictine nuns, her claim that she was 'unlettered' probably means that she knew no Latin. After nearly dying (1373) she had a series of sixteen religious experiences, 'shewings', and decided to become a recluse and spiritual counsellor in an anchorage attached to St Julian's church, from which she took her name. Twenty years later, she wrote *The Revelations of Divine Love*, meditations on her 'shewings', the first book known to have been written by a woman in English. She describes God as all-loving, despite contemporary suffering. Her saying 'All shall be well', and her vision of all creation in 'a little thing, the size of a hazel-nut, lying in the palm of my hand . . . for God loves it' are well known. A positive thinker in an age of suffering, uncertainty, and change, her meditations are attractive in the late 20th cent. WMM

Junius was the pseudonym adopted by the unknown author of 69 letters to the *Public Advertiser* between 1769 and 1772. After an unspectacular start, they became a political sensation, boosting the sales of the paper and being widely reproduced. Junius moved from an exchange with Sir William Draper to repeated attacks upon the first minister, the duke of *Grafton, and at length to a celebrated and offensive letter to the king himself. Junius' staple diet was political and legal commentary, but the letters were enjoyed for their scandalous insolence, for the secrecy surrounding the author, and for the inside knowledge he appeared to possess. They are a remarkable example of the growing importance of the newspaper press. Dozens of people have been suggested as possible authors and many volumes devoted to unravelling the mystery, but the evidence points strongly to Philip Francis, then a senior clerk in the War Office. JAC

Junto was the name given to the Whig allies in the later part of William III's reign and that of Anne. They were particularly strong in the Lords, where the leaders included *Somers, *Halifax, *Orford, *Sunderland, and Wharton. Their luck turned when George I succeeded in August 1714. JAC

jury system. The origins of the jury system are disputed. The name means a body of persons sworn to make a statement on a matter. Although it has been suggested that the jury has Germanic-Anglo-Saxon origins, it is more likely that the institution of a body of men giving an answer, under oath, to a specific question put to them by the ruler originated in the Frankish inquest. The first juries in the common law were juries instituted by Henry II to make presentment of serious crimes to the travelling justices, and the juries under the Grand Assize and the petty or possessory assizes, who replied under oath to inquiries by the sheriff or the justices on questions relating to right to land or questions of disseisin of land.

The 'trial jury' originated when, in 1215, the Lateran Council of the church forbade clergy to participate in ordeals, which were, at that time, the means of deciding guilt where a person had been presented to the justices as suspected of crime. Deprived of the ordeal, the justices resorted to the use of sworn bodies of neighbours to decide whether the accused person was guilty. Gradually the 'trial jury' of twelve developed after a number of experiments. This jury became common in both civil and criminal law through the action of trespass and became one of the most marked features of the common law. Gradually juries ceased to speak from their own knowledge and instead were supposed to have an open mind and to decide questions by listening to evidence.

The jury was one of the attractive features, for litigants, of the common law, though there were periods of unrest (e.g. the 15th cent.) when it was discredited because of interference with its verdicts by the rich and powerful. In 1670 it was decided in Bushell's case that a jury could no longer be attainted for reaching a verdict contrary to the evidence or the wish of the court. This, coupled with the decisions in the period of constitutional strife in the 17th cent., led to the jury's being regarded as the 'bulwark of liberty' and trial by jury as a protection for the rights of the subject against tyrannical prosecution. Majority voting was introduced in the 20th cent. and the complexity and length of some trials, particularly in matters of fraud, led to suggestions that the use of juries should be reviewed. MM

justice Eyre. See EYRE.

justices of the peace. The forerunners of the justices of the peace were the conservators of the peace, first appointed in the reign of Richard I. In the 13th cent. conservators of the peace, consisting of knights and gentry of the county, served on the commissions of *assize, *oyer and terminer, and *gaol delivery and were also given other peacekeeping duties, extended from time to time by legislation until, in the reign of Edward III, they were given powers to punish offenders and in 1344 to hear and determine criminal cases. A new function was entrusted to the conservators when, after the *Black Death had decimated the population, the statutes of *Labourers provided for the fixing of wages by the justices. In 1361 it was provided by statute that in every English county there should be 'one lord and with him three or four of the most worthy in the county with some learned in the law' to 'keep the peace, to arrest and imprison offenders, to imprison or take surety of suspected persons and to hear and determine felonies and trespasses done in the county', and in 1363 a further statute provided for the holding of sessions four times a year (the *quarter sessions). They were now the 'justices of the peace' and were and still are appointed by the crown to the commission of peace for the county.

From that time onwards, the legislature increasingly extended the role of the justices of the peace. Their judicial function remained a vital part of the administration of criminal justice, though the calibre of the justices was variable—they were at first noblemen or country gentry, later prosperous burgesses or clergy, and until 1906 were subject to a property qualification. Literature provides us with numerous examples of justices, many of whom were scarcely admirable in performing their duties, especially when dealing with the poor and indigent.

The justices of the peace have been called the maids of all work of the English legal system. In addition to their judicial and peace-keeping duties, they were used to administer the *Poor Laws and, through the quarter sessions, to oversee the whole of local government. These duties are no longer performed by the justices, but they retain a role in the keeping of the peace—they issue warrants in certain circumstances—and although quarter sessions were abolished in 1971, the magistrates' courts remain a vital part of the administration of criminal justice in England and Wales, trying most criminal cases. They also hear and decide applications for the licensing of premises for the sale of alcohol or for gambling. MM

justiciar. The frequent absences of Norman kings on the continent necessitated a competent viceroy or regent in England. This function became associated with the justiciar, who acted as chief minister, performing a great variety of duties, including campaigning, as well as presiding over the *curia regis. *Ranulf Flambard and *Roger of Salisbury acted in this capacity under William Rufus and Henry I, without having the title: later the office was held by men of the calibre of Richard de *Lucy, Ranulf *Glanvill, Hubert *Walter, Peter des *Roches, and Hubert de *Burgh. After de Burgh's overthrow by Henry III in 1232, the office lapsed, though the baronial opposition in the 1250s attempted to revive it. The legal duties were taken over by the chancellor or the lord chief justice. In Ireland the justiciar was the king's chief representative in the 13th cent. until superseded by the king's lieutenant, the lord deputy, and the lord-lieutenant. In Scotland the justiciar was the supreme law officer until replaced in the 15th cent. by the lord justice general. JAC

Justiciary Court (Scotland). The High Court of Justiciary is the supreme criminal court in Scotland. It was established in 1672, and consisted of the lord justice general, the lord justice clerk, and five of the lords of Session. From 1887 all lords of Session have been lords commissioners of Justiciary. The court has jurisdiction over serious crimes in Scotland and also acts as a court of appeal. Since 1836 the lord president of the Court of Session has also held the office of lord justice general and presides. JAC

Justus, St (d. *c.*627). Sent, according to Bede, by Pope Gregory I with *Mellitus to Kent in 601, and consecrated bishop in Rochester by *Augustine in 604, Justus was associated with Archbishop *Laurentius' exhortations to bishops and abbots in Ireland, and to British priests, to follow Roman practices. The accession of pagan kings in Kent and over the East Saxons prompted all three to decide to return to Rome, but after a year awaiting developments in Gaul, Justus and Mellitus, whom Justus succeeded as fourth archbishop of Canterbury in 624, were recalled. Justus consecrated Romanus to replace him at Rochester, and died on 10 November in, probably, 627, certainly no later than 631. As bishop he played some part in the conversion of Eadbald of Kent, he consecrated *Paulinus to carry the torch to Northumbria, probably in 625, and maintained links with the papacy. AER

Jutes. Bede's account of the Jutes is highly specific—that they were a Germanic people who inhabited a region north of the Angles and that their settlements in England had been in Kent, the Isle of Wight, and on the mainland just north of the Solent. Their leaders had been *Hengist and Horsa. Modern research has modified these suggestions, holding that the differences between Angles, Saxons, and Jutes was smaller than assumed and that the Jutes are less likely to have come from south Schleswig than from Frisia or even the mouth of the Rhine. The pattern of settlement has also been queried. There is evidence from burial practices and place-names of a variety of cultures in Kent, including strong Romano-British survival, and the settlements in the west are seen as secondary migrations rather than direct from the continent. The Jutish territories around the present city of Southampton were seized by *Cædwalla, king of Wessex, *c.*686, presumably to acquire excellent harbours and access to the sea. Nevertheless, as late as 1100 Florence of Worcester could write that the New Forest was known in the English tongue as 'Ytene' (Jutes). Kent retained many distinctive characteristics, including the practice of partible inheritance or *gavelkind, which made for a more equal society. The kingdom of Kent, prominent in the early 7th cent., found it hard to cope with powerful neighbours and during the 8th cent. was taken over by Mercia and in the 9th by Wessex. JAC

Jutland, battle of, 1916. The war in the North Sea was a frustrating experience for the Royal Navy. The Grand Fleet never gained the overwhelming victory over the German High Seas Fleet for which it yearned. The Germans, aware of their numerical inferiority, usually preferred to remain in port. The best opportunity the British had to fight a second Trafalgar was on 31 May 1916 when *Beatty succeeded in luring the High Seas Fleet under the guns of the Grand Fleet. But the outcome only served to demonstrate the weakness of the British fleet. The Grand Fleet's range-finders were deficient, its target-plotting machinery prone to error, and its gunnery computers, staff work, and armoured protection defective. The British suffered greater losses of both ships and men, proof of the excellence of German gunnery and ship construction.

But although Jutland was a tactical victory for the Germans, it was a strategic victory for the British. The British were able to repair their damaged ships faster than the Germans, so after the battle *Jellicoe still had more capital ships than his enemy. And crucially, the allied naval blockade of Germany, which was doing so much to strangle its economy, remained unbroken. Although the High Seas Fleet ventured out of harbour on several occasions after June 1916, it never again sought a fleet action with the British, and when it was ordered to make a final attack in October 1918, its crews mutinied. DF

Juxon, William (1582–1663). Juxon, a bishop and statesman, came to prominence through the favour of *Laud, who persuaded Charles I to make him bishop of London in 1633 and, three years later, lord treasurer. As the first ecclesiastic to hold this key government post for 170 years, Juxon's appointment intensified fears of a return to clerical rule, but although a conscientious administrator, he preferred persuasion to compulsion. Juxon's unwavering commitment to Anglican values brought him close to the king, and he acted as Charles's spiritual adviser until the very end, standing beside him on the scaffold. Thereafter he lived quietly in the countryside until the restoration of Charles II in 1660, when he was appointed archbishop of Canterbury, but old age and infirmity made him little more than a figurehead. He had the rare distinction, in an age of bitter passions, of being widely loved and respected. RL

Kames, Henry Home, Lord (1696–1782). Judge and man of letters. Son of a petty laird, educated for the Scottish bar, Kames became a lord of Session in 1752. He was a prominent member of the Edinburgh literati and an important patron whose protégés included Adam *Smith and John *Millar. A prolific and often acute essayist, Kames's interests ranged from metaphysics to manners, morals, jurisprudence, *belles-lettres*, and agricultural improvement. A friend and relative of David *Hume, he provided an early and intelligent reply to his kinsman's sceptical metaphysics. A jurist, Kames was one of the first Scots to have been interested in 'conjectural history' of the Scottish Enlightenment. His *Elements of Criticism* (1762) was an early and influential textbook, widely acclaimed in the Anglo-Saxon world. He was a gregarious if overbearing man. NTP

Kay, John (1704–*c*.1780). Engineer and inventor. Born in 1704 near Bury (Lancs.), Kay patented his flying-shuttle for a loom in 1733. It produced a great speeding-up in the process of weaving. Kay experienced considerable difficulty in exploiting his invention. His house was destroyed in 1753 by a mob, concerned about unemployment in the industry, while the Leeds manufacturers banded together to indemnify each other against legal proceedings to enforce Kay's patent. Kay took refuge in France, where he tried to carry on, but died in obscurity. JAC

Kay-Shuttleworth, Sir James Phillips (1804–77). Administrator and founder of the English education system. Educated at Edinburgh University, he studied medicine and graduated as a doctor in 1827. Working in Manchester, Kay (Shuttleworth was added after his marriage) quickly became aware of the suffering of the poor and interested himself in sanitary and educational reform. He was appointed assistant Poor Law commissioner in 1835 in the eastern counties and London area, writing valuable reports on the training of pauper children. Kay-Shuttleworth's opportunity to develop national education came in 1839 when he was appointed secretary to the Committee of the Privy Council. For the next ten years, until his health broke down, he worked with great zeal to establish a public system of elementary education, supervised by a national body of inspectors. He was responsible for the first training college for teachers at Battersea in 1840, with students from Norwood Pauper School. PG

Kean, Edmund (1787–1833). Actor. Son of an itinerant actress, Kean was exploited as an infant prodigy in London before being forced onto various provincial circuits, undergoing years of hardship but eventually playing most of the major parts. The impassioned delivery of his reappearance at Drury Lane (1814) as Shylock was so remarkable that the theatre's coffers were rapidly replenished. Barely average height, his flashing, sometimes demoniac approach, which so contrasted with the measured Kemble school, made him one of the most controversial of the early 19th-cent. actors, generating as much abusive criticism as admiration. Described by Talma as 'a magnificent uncut gem', and famous for his tragic roles of Richard III, Shylock, and Othello, he briefly visited France and America. Youthful irresponsibility quickly evolved into recklessness, vanity, intolerance of rivals, and drunken debauch, so, by 1827, loss of respectability had been joined by visible physical disintegration. ASH

Keats, John (1795–1821). Poet and sometime surgeon's apprentice, his early work suffered by association with Leigh Hunt and the 'Cockney School', though he was never, as *Byron gibed, 'snuffed out by an article'. Most richly sensuous of Romantic poets, with a Schubertian sensitivity to love and death, the 'indescribable gusto' which *Arnold found in his writing continues to attract. 'O for a life of sensations rather than thoughts!' he exclaimed, but a keen intelligence is inseparable from the rapid development of his brief career. A severe self-critic, he introduced *Endymion* (1818) with apologies and abandoned the over-Miltonic *Hyperion* the following year. Nursing his dying brother he was torn between the 'realms of gold' he encountered in literature and the world 'where men sit and hear each other groan'. His best work, the *Odes* of 1819, dramatizes this conflict. By now ill himself with tuberculosis, a visit to Italy came too late to save him. JNRS

Keble, John (1792–1866). Credited with launching the *Oxford movement with his Assize Sermon of 1833, Keble spent most of his life as a country parson. The sermon was provoked by the moderate reform of the Irish Church Temporalities Act, which to Keble represented a sacrilegious interference with church order by the secular power. He was heeded as a man of deep spirituality and the author of the much-loved volume of religious verse, *The Christian Year* (1827), and struck a chord with the growing *high-church party seeking a more spiritual view of the Church of England. Keble was brought up in a clerical family near Fairford in Gloucestershire in the high-church tradition of the Caroline divines. At Oxford he was regarded as a brilliant intellect and was professor of poetry (1831–5) until he married and left Oxford for the parish of Hursley in Hampshire, where he spent the rest of his life. JFC

Keith, James (1696–1758). Keith was the younger brother of the 9th Earl *Marischal. They took part together in the '15 and fought at *Sheriffmuir. Keith next joined the Spanish expedition which ended at *Glenshiel in 1719, whence he escaped with difficulty. The rest of his life was spent as a highly successful soldier of fortune. For nine years he served the Spaniards, taking part in the siege of Gibraltar in 1727. He next joined the Russian service and distinguished himself in the war against Sweden 1741–3. In 1747, weary of Russian court politics, he transferred to the service of Frederick II of Prussia, who made him a field marshal. He was killed in October 1758 at Hochkirk, the most outstanding of Scottish mercenaries. JAC

Kells, Book of. A Latin copy of the four Gospels and some preliminaries, possibly late 8th cent., but first recorded at the monastery at Kells (Co. Meath) in 1007 after its theft and loss of covers. The unrestrained decoration and unusually large size suggest that it was an altar-book, for liturgical reading and ceremonial pomp; full-page illuminations and lavish embellishment render distinction amongst similar 'insular' manuscripts. In 1654 the town governor sent it to Dublin for safety from Cromwellian iconoclasm, following which it was presented to Trinity College by Henry Jones, post-Restoration bishop of Meath. ASH

Kelvin, William Thomson, 1st Baron (1824–1907). Pioneer of thermodynamics and one of the greatest of classical physicists. Educated in Belfast, Glasgow, and Cambridge, he was in 1846 chosen professor of natural philosophy at Glasgow. He remained there for 50 years, and on retirement signed on as a research student. He said that one word characterized his work, 'failure'. He was not serious: in fact, he had done fundamental research on electromagnetism and light, on telegraphy, and on heat, where he had come up with the idea of an absolute zero of temperature—the scale based on this is named after him. He was happy to turn his talents to practical use, over telegraph cables, liquefaction of gases, and the construction of instruments. The leading physical scientist in Britain, he was made a peer in 1892. DK

Kemble, Charles (1775–1854). Actor and manager. Youngest son of actor-manager Roger Kemble, Charles abandoned the post office for the stage, first appearing in the provinces (1792), then Drury Lane, London (1794). Often performing with his brother John Philip and sister Sarah (Mrs *Siddons), he had an extensive repertoire but excelled in comedy (Doricourt, Mercutio) and was noted for secondary Shakespeare roles (Malcolm, Cassio). His management of Covent Garden commenced 1822/3, but it was saved from bankruptcy only by the début in 1829 of his daughter Fanny; their teamwork proved as successful in America as in Britain. Increasing deafness led to nominal retirement from the stage but appointment as examiner of plays (1836), until he resigned this post to his philological son John Mitchell (1840) and ceased his Shakespeare readings. Though perpetuating the family's declamatory and stilted style and favouring melodrama, Kemble introduced the use of historically 'authentic' costumes and stage-sets. ASH

Kemp, John (d. 1454). Archbishop of York and Canterbury. Like *Chichele, Kemp was an Oxford DCL who began his career in church courts, becoming dean of Arches in 1414. After an embassy to Aragon, he was a member of Henry V's council in France, as chancellor of Normandy and keeper of the privy seal. He was one of Henry *Beaufort's supporters in the council of Henry VI's minority and appointed chancellor of England in 1426. By now he had risen through the episcopate as bishop successively of Rochester (1419), Chichester (1421), and London (1421), to the archbishopric of York (1426). Duke Humphrey of *Gloucester removed Kemp from Chancery in 1432, but he remained a councillor, occasionally an ambassador. When the regime of William de la *Pole, duke of Suffolk collapsed in 1450, this veteran was recalled to be chancellor. From 1452 he was archbishop of Canterbury. An uncompromising champion of royal authority, he was sympathetic to victims of its abuse by corrupt courtiers. His death, while Henry was insane, was a loss from which the Lancastrian government never recovered. Kemp was created a titular cardinal in 1439, recognition of his political stature; he rarely visited York diocese. He founded a collegiate church and grammar school at Wye (Kent), his birthplace. RLS

Kempe, Margery (*c.*1373–*c.*1440). The manuscript of her memories, which she had dictated in the later years of her life, was discovered in 1934, first published in 1947, and is now considered to be the earliest English autobiography. After the birth of her first child, Kempe, daughter of a prosperous burgess of King's Lynn (Norfolk), suffered a spiritual crisis and was subsequently redeemed by a vision of Christ. In later life she became deeply religious and undertook many pilgrimages to the Holy Land, Rome, and Santiago de Compostella, amongst others. Her devotion manifested itself in excessive lamentation, for which she was ridiculed and imprisoned, and even denounced as a heretic, 'for some said that she had a devil within her'. A mystic of remarkable courage, she is often likened to *Julian of Norwich, whom she knew. Her story inspired admiration and pity for all she suffered in her search for God. SMD

Ken, Thomas (1637–1711). Bishop of Bath and Wells. Educated at Winchester and New College, Oxford, Ken was chaplain to Morley, bishop of Winchester (1665), and to Princess Mary (later Mary II) at The Hague (1679–80). He became bishop of Bath and Wells (1684) and attended *Monmouth on the scaffold (1685). As one of the seven bishops petitioning James II to withdraw the *Declaration of Indulgence he was imprisoned in the Tower (1688), but acquitted. Nevertheless, a man of conscience, he refused to recognize James's abdication or William's accession, was deprived of his see (April 1691), and lived at Longleat until his death. Refusing to acknowledge Richard Kidder as his successor, he retained his episcopal signature until his friend George Hooper succeeded (1703). A man of great sanctity, caring for the poor in his diocese, he was a notable poet and hymn-writer. WMM

Kenilworth, dictum of, 1266. Simon de *Montfort's death at *Evesham in August 1265 brought to an end the protracted civil war of Henry III's reign, though young Simon de *Montfort escaped to France, and Kenilworth castle held out for another year. The dictum of Kenilworth of 31 October 1266 was an attempt at a reconciliation, offering a general amnesty, but reasserting in full the king's rights. JAC

Kenilworth castle (War.) combined strong fortifications with palatial residential accommodation. From the first the castle seems to have included extensive water defences and these were enlarged during John's reign when it was in royal hands. The effectiveness of the defences was demonstrated when supporters of Simon de *Montfort held the castle for a year against Henry III after the battle of *Evesham and were able to surrender on terms in December 1266. The future Edward I was present at the siege and it has been suggested that the importance of water defences in his later castles was taken from Kenilworth. In the later Middle Ages the castle belonged to the duchy of Lancaster and was developed as a palace by *John of Gaunt and later by Henry V, who had a pleasure garden with a small harbour created across the mere. Robert Dudley, earl of *Leicester, also undertook major building work at the castle, to which Elizabeth was a visitor; one such visit is vividly described in *Scott's *Kenilworth*. LR

Kennedy, James (d. 1465). Provided to the bishopric of Dunkeld by his uncle, James I (1437). Support of Queen *Joan in James II's minority, and opposition to the Basle conciliarists, enabled his promotion to bishop of St Andrews (1440). His foundation of St Salvator's College at St Andrews (1450) is his most enduring legacy. His political career was less successful than many historians have believed. He supported the wrong faction in the 1440s, and in the 1450s, despite receiving considerable patronage, particularly the 'Golden Charter' (1452), he held no governmental office. Abroad on James II's death (1460), Kennedy was overlooked in *Mary of Gueldres's distribution of minority government offices. He was upset, and managed to undermine the queen's policies by a campaign of black propaganda and misogyny, based on his parliamentary popularity. He finally gained possession of James III on her death (December 1463), and acted as royal guardian until his death in May 1465. RJT

Kenneth II (d. 995), king of 'Scotland' (971–95). His father was *Malcolm I and his brother King *Dub. He succeeded *Cuilén to the kingship, but faced competition from Cuilén's brother Olaf, whom he killed in 977. His reign was untypically long and, like his father's, characterized by aggression beyond the kingdom's borders. He repeatedly raided northern England and attacked the Britons of *Strathclyde, who defeated him at 'Moin Uacornar' (unidentified). His rule over *Lothian was recognized *c.*975 by *Edgar, king of England. It is likely, however, that Lothian was lost to the earls of Northumbria in the last year of his reign. He met his end at Fettercairn (30 miles south of Aberdeen), assassinated by the daughter of the earl of Angus in revenge for killing her only son. It is possible that his wife was a daughter of one of the Uí Dúnlainge kings of *Leinster. He founded (or refounded) a monastery at Brechin, probably the community of **céli Dé* ('clients of God') attested in later record. In some accounts Kenneth is included among the British kings who submitted to King Edgar at Chester in 973, but this is not corroborated by other sources which are more contemporary. DEB

Kenneth III (d. 1005), king of 'Scotland' (997–1005). He was son of King *Dub and became king by killing *Constantine III in battle at 'Rathinveramon' (probably a couple of miles north of Perth). This engagement represented the final victory of Kenneth's branch of the royal dynasty over its rivals, the descendants of *Æd (d. 878). Kenneth faced competition for the kingship from his own branch of the dynasty, however, and was killed in battle at Monzievaird (15 miles west of Perth) by *Malcolm II, his first cousin. A debatable source says that he was buried on Iona. Later king-lists credit Kenneth's reign to a son called *Giric, but this conflicts with contemporary evidence. DEB

Kenneth I MacAlpin (d. 858), king of Dal Riata (*c.*840/1–58) and 'king of the Picts' (842/3–58). Kenneth is anachronistically regarded as first king of Scotland because he is deemed to have unified the *Picts (north of the Firth of Forth) with the Gaels (in Latin, *Scoti*) of *Dalriada (Argyll). 'Scotland' (*Alba in Gaelic) does not emerge until 900, however, and is likely to have begun as a much smaller area than the united territories of the Picts and Dalriada.

It is typical of the 'Dark Ages' of documentary history that so little information survives to illuminate Kenneth's career. There are no contemporary sources which can confirm or explain his alleged unification of Picts and *Scoti*. From as early as the late 10th cent. it was commonly thought that Kenneth founded the kingship of the Scots by conquering the Picts. It is possible, however, that Kenneth's role as founding father was devised by the dynasty descended from him who monopolized the kingship from 889 to 1034 and who, in 900, presided over the abandoning of Pictish identity and the creation of the new kingdom of Alba.

Kenneth's ancestors were probably kings of Dalriada and his father Alpin may have been king before him. Both Dalriada and the Picts were suffering from the first large-scale Scandinavian incursions which, in 839, wiped out the Gaelic dynasty which had ruled the key Pictish region of *Fortriu since 789. The confusion in Fortriu which followed is reflected in two king-lists which espouse different successions in the 840s. By 849, however, all are agreed that Kenneth had secured his grasp on the kingship. Whatever his attitude to the Picts may have been, he clearly looked to Gaeldom for support, and in 849 erected a church in *Dunkeld which housed relics of St *Columba, implying that Kenneth sought to cultivate the enormous influence of the Columban network of monasteries as a power base. Such a policy was not new, however, and had probably been anticipated by the Gaelic king of Fortriu, *Constantín son of Fergus (789–820).

Kenneth raided Northumbria repeatedly, but his kingdom suffered assaults from the Britons of *Strathclyde as well as Scandinavians. He died of a tumour on 13 February 858, at Forteviot (5 miles south-west of Perth). His brother *Donald I succeeded him. DEB

Kensington palace is architecturally one of the more modest royal residences, but historically it is full of interest. It began life as a private residence of the Finch family and was purchased by William III in 1689 since it provided fresh air but was near to London. *Wren, surveyor of the works, was employed to rebuild extensively, but the scale was moderate, partly because speed was essential, partly because there was lavish building at *Hampton Court. The delightful orangery by *Vanbrugh was added during Anne's reign. Much of the later internal decoration, including the king's staircase, was by William *Kent, and the gardens were laid out and redeveloped by George London, Henry Wise, and Charles *Bridgeman. The Round Pond and the Serpentine were finished during the reign of George I. The palace was popular with the royal family until George III began developing Buckingham House. William and Mary died at Kensington; Anne had her celebrated quarrel with the duchess of *Marlborough in a small ante-room, and later died in the palace. George II and Caroline were fond of the place and there are two admirable terracotta busts by Michael *Rysbrack. George III made over apartments to his royal brothers and the young Victoria, daughter of the duke of Kent, was brought up there. At Kensington she held her first Privy Council on the day of her accession in 1837. It is still used as a royal residence and Princess Margaret and the princess of Wales have suites there. It is open to the public and includes a permanent exhibition of court dress. JAC

Kent is one of the oldest counties, having been a kingdom in Saxon times. (See KENT, KINGDOM OF.) It has always been of great importance because of its strategic position as gateway to the continent. It is comparatively little known, since the millions who pass through it hurl themselves towards the ferries or the tunnel.

The shire was defined by the Thames and its estuary to the north and by the coast to the south and east. The border with Sussex followed the rivers Teise and Rother, and the western border with Surrey was largely the watersheds of the rivers Ravensbourne, Darent, and Medway. The north downs running from west to east end in the chalk cliffs of Dover. There has been considerable silting of the coast: the Isles of Grain, Sheppey, and Thanet are now united to the mainland, while many once flourishing ports and harbours such as Lydd in the south-west are now miles from the sea.

In pre-Roman times, the inhabitants were the *Cantiaci, a group of tribes who offered serious resistance to *Caesar's two expeditions. The name Cantium goes back at least to the 4th cent. BC and seems to be of Celtic origin, meaning border or coastal land. The main Roman port was Richborough (Rutupiae), where the AD 43 expedition landed, and where there remains a remarkable Roman lighthouse. A major road ran from the port to *Canterbury (Durovernum) and crossed the Medway at Rochester (Durobrivae), before reaching London. It was later known as *Watling Street.

In the middle of the 5th cent., the area was overrun by *Jutish settlers and a kingdom established. *Æthelbert pushed Kentish power to its height, occupying London and taking control of the East Saxons. He converted to Christianity and founded the sees of Canterbury (597) and *Rochester (604). Later kings of Kent found it difficult to sustain their independence against powerful neighbours and fell under the domination, first of *Mercia, then of *Wessex. Kent became a subkingdom or province and, at length, a county. In the 9th cent. the region suffered severely from Viking raids but there was little Scandinavian settlement.

Kentish society had a number of unusual features. The shire was divided into five large divisions or lathes and then into more than 60 small hundreds. The local custom of *gavelkind supported equal inheritance and Kentish men had a reputation for independence. How dangerous this could be to governments was demonstrated in the *Peasants' Revolt (1381), *Cade's rising (1450), and *Wyatt's rebellion (1554). As late as the 1720s, *Defoe commended the sturdy Kentish yeomen, 'the graycoats', who could turn any election and were treated by the gentlemen with great respect. The east–west division of the shire, hinted at by the establishment of two bishoprics, continued strongly. There was a convention that representation in Parliament should be shared between east and west and JPs normally exercised their authority only in their own half. Quarter sessions were at Canterbury for east Kent, Maidstone for west Kent.

By *Domesday in 1086, Dover had developed as an important borough, along with Canterbury and Rochester. Also of significance were Romney, Hythe, and Sandwich, subsequently recognized among the *Cinque ports, and given special privileges in exchange for heavy defence responsibilities. The close association with the continent after the *Norman Conquest brought the shire considerable prosperity, and more came with the development of the royal dockyards. By 1801 the largest towns in the shire were Deptford (17,000), Greenwich (14,000), and Chatham (10,000). Production for the ever-growing London market encouraged orchards, market gardens, hop-fields, and the rearing of sheep and cattle. Whitstable was renowned for its oysters. But as the remorseless growth of London continued, the balance of population in the county shifted to the north-west. Lewisham with 4,000 people in 1801 had 174,000 in 1921; Deptford had risen to 119,000, Plumstead to 76,000, Bromley to 68,000. Another rapid development was Gillingham with 95,000. In 1888 Kent lost a slice of London suburbia to the new London County Council, and in 1965 Erith, Bromley, Bexley, Chislehurst, and Orpington were moved out into the Greater London Council. Neither the Local Government Act of 1972 nor the Banham commission report of 1994 proposed any changes in the county. JAC

Kent, kingdom of. Kent was founded, according to tradition, in the middle of the 5th cent. by two brothers of Jutish origin, *Hengist and Horsa, who came to Britain to protect the native inhabitants against the Picts and Scots, turned against their paymasters, and won a kingdom for themselves. Archaeology and evidence from place-names (the name Kent itself, Dover, and the first element of Canterbury) and from later institutions tell a more complicated story involving some Romano-British survival and considerable variety of Germanic invaders from high-status leaders with splendid jewellery among their grave goods to poor and backward Germanic peoples. Kingship was not always unitary, and there were two clear-cut divisions within Kent along the Medway, the men of Kent and the Kentishmen. There are also vestiges of survival of Roman administrative divisions. Contact with the continent was never lost, and was intensified in the later 6th cent., especially after the marriage of *Æthelbert (before 589) to a Frankish princess, *Bertha. Under Æthelbert (d. 616), who was recognized as overlord by all the Germanic settlers south of the Humber, Kent reached the height of its political power, falling back later in the 7th cent. as overlordship passed briefly to East Anglia, and then to Northumbria. Æthelbert's chief claim to fame is his acceptance of Christianity, and with the help of the mission led by St *Augustine he framed laws to accommodate the new church and also to lay down rules of social behaviour. Later Kentish kings followed this lawgiving precedent, especially Wihtred (*c.*690–725), whose laws had a very high social content, showing deep concern over marriage law, and rules concerning Christian oaths, an indication of the completeness of the conversion of Kent to the new faith. But politically Kent had no high aspirations, and was overshadowed in the 8th cent. by Mercia, and after 825 by Wessex. The West Saxon kings used Kent (and Surrey and Sussex) as a sort of appanage to be ruled as subkingdoms by West Saxon princes. There were no independent kings in Kent after 825, though Canterbury preserved its special prestige as the see of an archbishop. HL

Kent, William (1685–1748). Architect, painter, furniture designer, and landscape architect. In 1719 Kent was brought back to London from Rome by Lord *Burlington, and together they became the leading proponents of *Palladianism in England. In 1727, with Burlington's support, Kent published *The Designs of Inigo Jones* (though most of the designs were by Webb). Although Kent, as a member of the Board of Works, designed the Horse Guards, the Royal Mews, and the Treasury buildings, most of his architecture was for private clients. A notable instance of this was his collaboration with Burlington at *Holkham Hall, Norfolk (1734 onwards, executed by Brettingham), with its 'staccato' elevations with Venetian windows, and its dramatic apsidal entrance hall with columns, coffered ceiling, and grand staircase. Here, as in other places, Kent's elegant furniture and rich decoration anticipated the interiors of Robert *Adam. Significant too are Kent's illustrations for Gay's *Fables* (1727), Thomson's *The Seasons* (1730), and Spenser's *Faerie Queene* (1751), and his garden buildings and progressive landscaping at Chiswick, Rousham, Stowe, Claremont, and elsewhere. In Horace *Walpole's words, as *Bridgeman's successor, Kent 'leapt the fence, and saw that all nature was a garden'. PW

Kentish Knock, battle of, 1652. Naval encounter on 28 September during the first *Anglo-Dutch War between Robert *Blake and a Dutch fleet under de Ruyter and de With. The Dutch suffered considerable losses and were forced to retire. JAC

Kenya. Former British protectorate and colony in eastern Africa. British interest in the region in the 19th cent.—missionary, anti-slave trade, then legitimate trade—saw Kenya only as a route to the more remote interior. A British protectorate was declared in 1895. The development of the agricultural resources of the area by white settlers was made possible by the administration's need of a quick means of generating income and by the construction of the Uganda railway from 1897. So influential did the settlers become that the country was declared a colony in 1920. Although African resentment of the advantages enjoyed by the whites became more vocal, and despite Britain's having declared a policy of trusteeship for Africans in 1923, the economy remained under settler control. The change in Britain's attitude towards colonial dependencies in the 1950s led to Kenyan independence under African rule in 1963. KI

Kenyatta, Jomo (*c.*1894–1978). Kenyan nationalist statesman. Kenyatta's involvement in politics began in 1922 when he campaigned for the restoration of land lost by his Kikuyu tribe to white settlers. In 1929 he went to London to plead the case of the Kikuyu and stayed in Europe, studying, writing, and lecturing. Returning to Kenya in 1946 he was elected president of the Kenya African Union in 1947. In 1952 he was accused and found guilty of master-minding the *Mau Mau rebellion although the evidence was far from conclusive. When the government gave the vote to Africans he was elected president of the newly founded Kenya African National Union while still in detention. He was released in 1961 and became prime minister in 1963 when the country achieved independence, then president in 1964 when Kenya became a republic. His sympathies inclined towards the western powers and he displayed remarkable magnanimity towards his former white opponents. KI

Keppel, Arnold Joost van, 1st earl of Albemarle (*c.*1670–1718). Dutch confidant of William III. Born in Holland, Keppel attended William of Orange to England in 1688 as a page of honour. He rose quickly in the king's favour, and was appointed groom of the bedchamber in 1691 and master of the robes in 1695. He spent much time with the king on state business, and also accompanied him on campaign. With Keppel's youthful, slightly effeminate good looks and charm, gossips inevitably spoke of an improper relationship, while in parliamentary opinion he (together with *Portland) was regarded as a sinister Dutch influence on the king. Notwithstanding, William lavished handsome gifts upon him including, in 1697, an earldom and the rank of major-general. After the king's death in 1702 he returned to Holland and was a commander of the Dutch forces in the allied campaigns against Louis XIV. AAH

Kett, Robert (d. 1549). Kett showed more organizational skill than is usually found in the leaders of peasant risings. He was a tanner and small landowner, holding the manor of Wymondham (Norfolk). Residual resentment over the *dissolution of the monasteries, local feuds, and anger over enclosures sparked a riot in the town in the summer of 1549 which developed into a major rising. The insurgents set up camp for six weeks on Mousehold Heath, notable for the discipline which Kett imposed, electing a governing council and maintaining law and order. After he had occupied Norwich, the second town in the kingdom, the royal government gathered a force under Lord Northampton, which the rebels routed. Three weeks later, a second force, stiffened by mercenaries, cut the insurgents to pieces at *Dussindale. Kett was hanged at Norwich, his brother William at Wymondham. The coincidence of Kett's rebellion with the *Prayer Book rising in Devon and Cornwall caused Protector *Somerset's government great anxiety. JAC

Kew Gardens (Surrey). Location of the Royal Botanical Gardens, which contain a vast collection of herbs, trees, and shrubs gathered from all over the world. Kew Gardens evolved from two adjoining 18th-cent. royal estates: Richmond Gardens, belonging to George II and Queen Caroline, and Kew House, the residence of their son Frederick, prince of Wales, and his consort Princess Augusta. Charles *Bridgeman assisted in the laying out of Richmond Gardens, where William *Kent designed the Hermitage (1730) and Merlin's Cave (1735). After George III inherited Richmond in 1760, he had the parkland re-landscaped by Capability *Brown (1764–73). At adjacent Kew, following the death of Frederick in 1751, the Dowager Princess Augusta employed Sir William *Chambers to lay out the grounds and to embellish them with a variety of temples and garden buildings, some classical and others oriental in style, including the orangery (1757–61), the Alhambra (1758), the Temple of the Sun (1761), and the pagoda (1761–2). These were publicized in Chambers's book *Plans, Elevations, Sections and Perspective Views of the Gardens and Buildings at Kew in Surrey* (1763). Two other major buildings at Kew—both pioneering structures largely in glass and cast iron—are the Palm House (1845–8) by Decimus Burton and Richard Turner, and Burton's Temperate House (1859–62, wings added 1895–7, restored 1977–82). In 1844–8 the area around the Royal Botanic Gardens was landscaped by William Andrews Nesfield (1793–1881), with the Palm House the pivot of his layout. PW

Keynes, John Maynard (1883–1946). Arguably the foremost economist of the 20th cent., Keynes was born in Cambridge and able to combine a successful academic career with that of civil servant and government adviser. His early work in economics evolved out of the *Marshall tradition in Cambridge, but through the 1920s and 1930s he increasingly broke new ground. His *Treatise on Money* (1930) and *The General Theory of Employment, Interest and Money* (1936), particularly the latter, heralded the Keynesian revolution, which regarded government control of spending as the key to providing full employment. But his influence stretched beyond macro-economic policy. He was critical of the 1919 treaty with Germany and a main architect of the international monetary system created at Bretton Woods in 1944. As a prolific writer in newspapers and popular journals, occasional broadcaster, and speaker, he had a major impact upon the cultural and intellectual life of his time. JRP

Keys, House of. The elected chamber of the *Tynwald, parliament of the *Isle of Man. Dating back to Nordic times, when the island was the centre of a western sea empire including the Hebrides and the inner islands, it claims to be the oldest parliament in continuous existence. From early times there have been 24 members, self-chosen until 1866. Propertied women were given the vote in 1881, nearly 40 years before the rest of Britain. The House sits with the Council to form the Tynwald. The name is probably an English imitation of the Manx Yn Kiare-as-feed, the *four and twenty*. JAC

Khartoum. Capital city of the *Sudan. Khartoum became Egypt's foremost military base in the Sudan in the mid-19th cent., but when Britain occupied Egypt in 1882 the British government was reluctant to become involved in the area, where the mahdi had proclaimed a religious war against Egypt a year earlier. It did, reluctantly, allow General Charles *Gordon to take charge of the evacuation of the city but was slow to respond to his request for reinforcements. The city fell in January 1885 when Gordon was killed but was reoccupied by *Kitchener in 1898 and became the seat of the Anglo-Egyptian government of the Sudan until 1956. KI

Kildare Place Society. The society for promoting the education of the poor in Ireland (commonly known as the Kildare Place Society) was founded in 1811, pledged to avoid sectarian distinctions. It was given a substantial parliamentary grant. Harmony did not last long. By 1820 *O'Connell and the catholics, complaining that the society proselytized for protestants, withdrew from membership. It was replaced in 1831 by a national education system, also devised to be non-sectarian, and also denounced by both sides. JAC

Kilkenny, Confederation of, 1642. The Irish rebellion of 1641 was not a spontaneous peasant rising but a planned insurrection, though the attempt to seize Dublin failed. The rebels, while protesting their loyalty to Charles I, took steps to organize the large areas under their control. An assembly or parliament summoned at Kilkenny in October 1642 adopted a provisional constitution, with a general assembly choosing a supreme council. The new Confederation raised armies for the four provinces, imposed taxes, confirmed the privileges of the catholic church, and appointed a number of envoys to foreign powers. The situation was extremely complex. *Ormond represented the king at Dublin, the Scots had sent an army into Ulster under Monro, and other leaders had declared for the English Parliament. Charles I's policy was to offer terms to the Confederation that would enable an army to be sent over to England to turn the scales in the Civil War, and as his position worsened, the terms improved. Ormond negotiated a truce or cessation in September 1643, which was repeatedly extended. But the negotiations proved difficult and protracted. Many of the confederates were prepared to wait until Charles was forced to offer not merely relaxation of the penal laws against catholics but their total removal, and they were strengthened when the papal nuncio, Rinuccini, who arrived in November 1645, took an intransigent line. Charles's diplomacy was characteristically convoluted. He dispatched the earl of *Glamorgan on a special mission with powers to offer concessions far greater than Ormond could suggest—the next lord-lieutenant should be a catholic, and catholic bishops should sit in the Irish House of Lords. For good measure, *Henrietta Maria conducted her own diplomacy in exile. When details of Glamorgan's proposals became known, Ormond's position was undermined and Charles had to repudiate the mission. It was, in any case, of no avail, for though Glamorgan succeeded in collecting a force together, Chester surrendered in February 1646 and there was nowhere left for them to land. The confederates now found the English Parliament a much more formidable opponent than Charles had been. The agreement they reached with Ormond in 1649, which marked the end of the Confederation, was too late to be of consequence, and their joint forces were routed at *Rathmines by Michael Jones. *Cromwell's campaigns of 1649 and 1650 restored English supremacy. JAC

Kilkenny, convention of, 1341. The English crown was too preoccupied with Wales and Scotland in the reign of Edward I, and too insecure in the reign of Edward II, to give much attention to the government of the English Pale in Ireland. Edward III was forced to pay attention in 1341 by a Parliament which began in Dublin and adjourned to Kilkenny when the royal ministers lost control. The Anglo-Irish protested vigorously against the decision to revoke and reconsider all grants since 1307, demanded action against English ministers who knew nothing of the country and thought only of making money, and warned that much territory had been lost to the native Irish. Edward returned a conciliatory answer and dismissed most of the ministers. The condition of the Pale continued to give concern. In 1361 the king's second son, Lionel, duke of Clarence, was sent as lieutenant and in 1394 Richard II himself visited Ireland to restore English authority. JAC

Kilkenny, statutes of, 1366. Lionel, duke of Clarence, second son of Edward III, was appointed the king's lieutenant in Ireland in 1361. In 1366 he summoned a parliament at Kilkenny, which passed a number of statutes intended to buttress the position of the English. They were not to use the Irish language, or intermarry with the Irish; they were not to sell horses or armour to the Irish; they were forbidden to play hurling but told to practise archery; the Irish were excluded from cathedrals, abbeys, or benefices in the English sector. The preamble referred significantly to the king's 'Irish enemies'. The statutes, though frequently repeated, did not prevent the Anglo-Irish from becoming Irish-speaking. Draconian though they appear, the provisions were for the most part not new; they applied only to the one-third of the country under Anglo-Irish control; and they were subsequently widely disregarded, either by default or by licence. JAC

Killiecrankie, battle of, 1689. *Dundee's campaign for James VII in Scotland in the spring of 1689 led to a chase through the glens between his small force and a slightly larger Williamite army under Hugh Mackay. On 27 July Mackay's men were caught in the pass of Killiecrankie, near Pitlochry, and badly beaten. But Dundee was shot in the side and killed. The Jacobite campaign lost impetus and disintegrated after the check at *Dunkeld in August. JAC

Kilmainham 'treaty', 1882. In October 1881, Charles Stewart *Parnell was arrested and imprisoned in Kilmainham gaol (Dublin) under the government's emergency measures 'on reasonable suspicion' of encouraging violence. In April 1882 Gladstone opened negotiations with him. In exchange for his release and a government promise to help with tenants' arrears of rent, Parnell agreed to denounce violence and appeal for law and order. The Irish chief secretary, W. E. *Forster, resigned in protest. His replacement, Lord Frederick *Cavendish, was murdered in Phoenix Park the day he arrived. JAC

Kilmore (Cell Mór), **diocese of.** This Irish see, in *Armagh province, was first named Ardagh and then Kells at the Council of Kells-Mellifont (1152). The northern part of Co. Meath was absorbed into the Meath diocese (1152) and later, when the bishop of Kells was expelled (*c.*1185) by the bishop of Meath, the see of Kells was abolished. The territorial struggles between lordships confused loyalties so that in *c.*1453 the pope agreed to the obscure parish church of Kilmore on the borders being raised to cathedral status. Later the see was merged with Elphin and Ardagh (1841). It is still a diocese in both catholic and Anglican churches. The Anglican cathedral is 19th cent. with a fine Romanesque doorway. William Bedell (Anglican bishop 1629–42) reputedly made the first translation of the Bible into Irish. WMM

Kilsyth, battle of, 1645. Six days after Baillie had been beaten by *Montrose at *Alford, outside Aberdeen, in July 1645, a covenanting parliament assembled at Stirling. Montrose moved southwards to harass it, with a force of 5,000 men. Baillie was confirmed in his command and faced him at Kilsyth, south of Stirling on 15 August, with an army of 7,000. The covenanters were caught while still deploying and suffered very heavy casualties. But it was the last of Montrose's victories. JAC

Kilvert, Robert Francis (1840–79). Kilvert, a young Victorian curate, kept a diary in the 1870s when he served at Clyro, near Hay-on-Wye, and assisted his father at Langley Burrell, near Chippenham. He was born at Hardenhuish (Wilts.), where his father was vicar, and educated at Wadham College, Oxford, taking an undistinguished fourth in law and history. His simple and direct style and his keen interest in the country people he met on his walks and visits make his diary a vivid and moving account of the period—the mysterious family at Mouse castle, the dissenting ministers boating on Llangorse Lake, the curate of Cusop's extraordinary misfortune. Kilvert died of peritonitis four weeks after his marriage, and is buried at Bredwardine, his last living. The diary was first published in 1938. JAC

Kilwardby, Robert (*c*.1210–79). Dominican scholar, archbishop of Canterbury, and cardinal. Educated at Paris, Kilwardby taught grammar and logic before becoming a Dominican friar (*c*.1240). Later by upholding traditional scholasticism against the new Aristotelianism he was Aquinas's foremost opponent, though a fellow-Dominican. As occupant of the Oxford Dominican chair (1248–61) and provincial prior of the English Dominicans, he was energetic, establishing eleven new priories. Appointed archbishop by the pope in 1272, he was the first English friar to hold high office, but, little involved politically, he was on good terms with Edward I. Of moderate temper, his primacy was overshadowed by clerical grievances over crusading taxation. He made regular provincial visitations and held frequent synods. He 'visited' Oxford (1277) and, like *Peckham, denounced its Thomism. To move him from Canterbury, the pope elevated him to the curia as cardinal-bishop of Porto (1278). He died at Viterbo. WMM

Kimberley, John Wodehouse, 1st earl of (1826–1902). A Whig politician, Kimberley served in all of Gladstone's ministries. A distinguished scholar at both Eton and Oxford, he never quite fulfilled his early promise. At the Colonial and India Offices he acquired the reputation of an 'imperial handyman'. Some thought him irresolute during the first *Boer War in 1880–1, but he finally concluded that a military victory would not give Britain real control of the Transvaal. Self-government under British suzerainty followed. He also accepted the need for *Irish Home Rule. As foreign secretary in 1894–5 he recognized that Britain could not respond to popular demands for intervention against the savage Turkish repression of an Armenian uprising. Inaction, however, during the Sino-Japanese War of 1894–5 meant that Britain did not share the odium incurred in Tokyo by Russia and other powers when they deprived Japan of some of her gains. CJB

Kimberley, siege of. Episode during the second *Boer War (1899–1902). Kimberley was a diamond town of 50,000 inhabitants on the westernmost railway line in South Africa. From November 1899 it was defended by about 1,000 troops under Colonel R. G. Kekewitch with 3,800 irregulars (largely De Beers's employees), and besieged in a haphazard fashion by about 7,500 Boers. The presence of Cecil *Rhodes in the town made British attempts to relieve the siege urgent, resulting in disasters at Modder River on 28 November and *Magersfontein on 11 December (part of 'Black Week'). The relief of Kimberley was finally accomplished in spectacular fashion by the cavalry division under Major-General John *French on 15 February 1900. In 124 days Kimberley had lost 35 soldiers and 5 civilians killed, 99 soldiers and 24 civilians wounded, with many more dead of disease. Rhodes, who had fallen out with Kekewitch, obtained his dismissal. SDB

'Kingis Quair'. A poem now generally accepted to have been written by James I of Scotland following his return from imprisonment in England (1424), perhaps in the mid-1430s. Written in Scots, with English influences, it is an autobiographical account of the king's incarceration, his love for his future queen, and their eventual marriage. This is linked to an allegorical account of the king's journey from ignorance to reason, through meetings with Minerva, Venus, and Fortune. Skilfully written, and influenced by *Chaucer, *Gower, and Boethius, the poem gives a fascinating insight into a different side of an often ruthless king. RJT

King's Bench, Court of. One of the three courts of common law. The Court of King's Bench evolved from the *curia regis, the itinerant royal court which dealt with the administration of the realm. The court was held 'before the lord king wheresoever he should be in England'. Its origins have been traced back to 1178 when Abbot Benedict of Peterborough recorded that Henry II ordered five judges of the Curia Regis to sit permanently to hear complaints from his subjects. However, it was another century before a distinct court emerged. In 1268 King's Bench was appointed its first chief justice and the court also kept its own records, the *coram rege* rolls. Gradually it separated from the king and the royal council. Under Edward III the court became free of the obligation to follow the king and during 1305–18 settled at Westminster Hall. It had unlimited criminal jurisdiction throughout the realm and was similar, though superior in dignity, to the other common law courts from which it heard appeals. During the Interregnum, the court was renamed Upper Bench due to the absence of the monarch. The Judicature Act of 1873 unified the courts system and transferred jurisdiction to a single High Court of Justice. The Queen's Bench Division became the sole representative of the old courts of common law. RAS

King's Bench prison (London) took its name from the court it originally served from the 14th cent. In the 16th cent. it was one of the prisons used to hold political and religious prisoners during the swings of persecution. It later became a flourishing debtors' prison infamous for the privilege it offered the wealthy. The better-off could pay the warders for comfortable rooms, to entertain and often be joined by their families: a celebrated inmate in 1769 was John *Wilkes. The poor remained in squalid and overcrowded conditions, a prey to disease. In 1842 the name changed to Queen's Bench and began receiving prisoners from *Marshalsea and the *Fleet after changes in law virtually abolished imprisonment for debt. The prison was finally demolished in 1880. RAS

King's College chapel (Cambridge). Eton and King's College, Cambridge, were founded by Henry VI to celebrate his majority (aged 15) in 1437, before his reign had disintegrated into defeat in France and civil war at home. King's began in 1441 as the College of St Nicholas and the name was changed in 1443. Henry laid the foundation stone of the chapel on 25 July 1446. His personal interest is demonstrated by his 'will' or testament in 1448, which included a detailed plan. As early as 1451 Parliament was complaining that the king's endowments were 'over-chargefull'. The chapel was not completed until 1515 and for many years afterwards totally dominated the site, since Gibbs's building, which helps to balance it, was not started until 1723 and the King's Parade neo-Gothic façade by Wilkins was only begun in 1824.

The chapel was started with magnesium limestone from Thevesdale and Huddleston, west of Tadcaster (Yorks.), and finished with stone from the Northamptonshire limestone belt. Though Henry had expressed a distaste for elaborate ornamentation, much embellishment was added over the years. The fan-vaulting (the most striking feature of the interior), the stained glass, and the screen all date from the reign of Henry VIII. Henry VI's original establishment of a choir to sing daily services has been internationalized by the broadcasting of the service of Nine Lessons and Carols at Christmas, introduced at King's in 1918 by Milner-White, then dean. JAC

king's counsel. See QUEEN'S COUNSEL.

king's evil, touching for. See TOUCHING FOR THE KING'S EVIL.

king's friends. The term gained credence with *Burke's *Thoughts on the Present Discontents* (1770), which explained the lack of success of the Rockingham party by the machinations of royalists, manipulating policy through a 'double cabinet'. No such organized, sinister, and servile corps existed. But George III's desire for a non-party administration appealed to many, the advent of a young monarch with long expectations could hardly fail to strengthen royal influence, and the abandonment by the Tories of fruitless opposition meant a corresponding stiffening of governmental resolve. The growth of militant and radical movements at home and abroad, with *Wilkes and *America, helped to promote a countermove towards authority. JAC

King's Inns. The Society of King's Inns in Dublin was the Irish equivalent of the English *Inns of Court. Its site on the north bank of the Liffey was taken in 1786 for the new Four Courts and the Society moved to Henrietta Street. Its new premises were designed by James *Gandon. JAC

Kingsley, Charles (1819–75). Vicar of Eversley (Hants), social reformer, novelist, and 'muscular Christian'. Influenced by F. D. *Maurice and Thomas *Carlyle, Kingsley became a leading spirit in the *Christian socialist movement of 1848–54, and under the pseudonym 'Parson Lot' contributed to *Politics for the People* (1848) and *The Christian Socialist* (1850–1). His novels *Yeast* (1848) and *Alton Locke* (1850) were sympathetic middle-class descriptions of working-class life. Kingsley looked to co-operation, education, and sanitary reform rather than radical politics for amelioration of the working classes. He was paternalistic and averse to monasticism, clerical celibacy, and all forms of asceticism, emphasizing instead the virtues of manliness, sport, and a 'muscular' type of Christianity. Kingsley was not an intellectual (despite his ludicrous appointment as professor of modern history at Cambridge, 1860–9) and was no match for John Henry *Newman, whom he rashly accused of lying and whose reply led to the publication of the latter's *Apologia* (1864). JFCH

King's Lynn, on the estuary of the Great Ouse (Norfolk), was for centuries one of England's major ports. It was developed by the first bishop of Norwich in the 1090s, and enlarged by the third bishop, each sector with its own church and market. It was Bishop's Lynn from the 11th cent. to 1536, when Henry VIII acquired it and renamed it. Its trade was international in the Middle Ages, but mainly domestic from the 16th cent. Since the 1950s it has expanded, fortunately without much damaging its historic core, which is still grouped around its medieval guildhall, churches, and market-places. DMP

Kingston, treaty of, 1217. Immediately after the defeat of his supporters at *Lincoln in May 1217, Louis, dauphin of France, began peace negotiations. They broke down in the summer but a further naval defeat at *Sandwich persuaded him to agree terms. In exchange for a large indemnity, he renounced his claim to the crown of England against the young Henry III. Supporters on each side were to be restored to their estates and *Magna Carta was confirmed. In September 1217 Louis returned to France. (See also LAMBETH, TREATY OF.) JAC

Kingston upon Hull. Yorkshire port at the junction of the river Hull with the Humber, usually called just 'Hull'. It originated as a monastic wool-exporting port, but was acquired and renamed by Edward I (1293). Its huge Holy Trinity church, and its Trinity House for mariners, testify to its late medieval importance. Henry VIII made it a fortified base, crucial enough for its control to become the flashpoint for civil war in 1642. Hull's MPs included Andrew *Marvell in the 17th cent. and William *Wilberforce in the 18th. By 1800 it was the third British port (measured by volume of trade) after London and Liverpool. The city (as it became in 1897) was hard hit by Second World War bombing, and by the collapse of its fishing industry in the 1970s. DMP

Kinnock, Neil G. (b. 1943). Formerly leader of the Labour Party (1983–92), European commissioner from 1995. Having lost two general elections in a row to the Conservatives (1987, 1992), Kinnock disarmingly confessed to being a failure. His left-wing views (particularly support for the *Campaign for Nuclear Disarmament) alienated many voters, while his rhetorical style was considered verbose even by many of his own supporters. His opponents labelled him 'the Welsh windbag'. His poor record at university, his lack of much professional experience before entering Parliament, and his lack of experience in government were all factors which reinforced the impression that he lacked the *gravitas* required of a potential prime minister. Though he demonstrated courage in facing up to left-wing extremists in his party, dropped unpopular policies, and began the process of modernizing Labour, ironically, the end-result was that few knew what he stood for. AS

Kinsale, battle of, 1601. Around 4,000 Spanish troops sent to assist Hugh *O'Neill, earl of Tyrone, against Elizabeth I landed in September 1601 on the south coast of Ireland at Kinsale, where they were besieged by Lord *Mountjoy, who had taken over from *Essex. On 24 December an attempt to relieve the town failed and the Spaniards surrendered on terms. Tyrone's power was broken and the Tudor conquest of Ireland completed. JAC

Kipling, Rudyard (1865–1936). Kipling is often thought of primarily as the trumpet of empire, but his writings were more varied than that suggests and he was far from triumphalist in tone. His parents were methodists. Kipling was born in Bombay, where his father had a chair in architecture. His first name is derived from Rudyard Lake, near Leek (Staffs.), where his parents had met. Stanley *Baldwin was his first cousin. Kipling hurt his eyes reading as a boy and wore spectacles from his schooldays. After United Services College in Devon, he returned to India as a journalist and rapidly acquired a reputation. At 24 he settled in London, though continuing to travel widely, particularly in America and South Africa. *Life's Handicap* (1891) launched him as a London figure and he followed with *The Jungle Book* (1894/5). His poem 'Recessional' for the *Diamond Jubilee of 1897—'lest we forget'—made him a national figure. *Stalky and Co.* (1899) drew on his schooldays and *Kim* (1901) on India. He published the *Just-So Stories*, one of the few children's books that children enjoy, in 1902 when he moved into Bateman's in Sussex, and *Puck of Pook's Hill*, set in the post-Roman period, in 1906. His poem 'The Way through the Woods'—a lovely example of controlled nostalgia—was in *Rewards and Fairies* (1910). Kipling declined national honours but was awarded the Nobel prize for literature in 1907. His only son was killed in the Great War in 1915. Kipling's reputation after his death sank even more quickly than that of most authors: the new generation did not respond to calls to shoulder 'the white man's burden', and whimsy was out of fashion. It is true that Kipling published too much and his work is uneven, but at his best he coined haunting phrases—'the Captains and the Kings depart'; 'and there's no discharge in the war'; 'and the dawn comes up like thunder out of China cross the bay'. JAC

Kiribati, formerly the Gilbert Islands, is an independent republic within the Commonwealth. It lies to the north-east of Fiji, and became independent in 1979. The islands were visited by various navigators in the later 18th cent., including Captain Thomas Gilbert in 1788. The inhabitants were then cannibals. The Gilbert Islands became a British protectorate in 1892 and were occupied by the Japanese during the Second World War. They rely upon fishing and agriculture and export coconuts, copra, and bananas. JAC

Kirkcaldy, Sir William (*c.*1520–73). Kirkcaldy had a tempestuous life in turbulent times. His father Sir James had been lord high treasurer to James V of Scotland, an opponent of Cardinal *Beaton and privy to his murder. William was present and took an active part. He adhered first to the pro-English party, escaped from captivity in France in 1550, and served Edward VI. In Mary I's reign he transferred his allegiance to the king of France. Returning to Scotland in 1557, he resumed his English policy, taking up arms against the French troops there. But when Mary, queen of Scots, arrived back in her kingdom in 1561, Kirkcaldy entered her service until she married *Darnley. He then changed sides again, leading the opposition at *Carberry Hill. When she escaped from Lochleven, he led the forces against her at *Langside. He then changed sides for the last time and attempted to hold Edinburgh castle for her in 1572–3 against the Regent *Morton. When the castle was forced to surrender, Morton hanged him. Kirkcaldy was brave and capable but the verdict of *DNB* that he won for himself 'a place of honour in Scottish history' seems over-enthusiastic. JAC

Kitchener, Horatio Herbert, 1st Earl (1850–1916). Soldier and imperial statesman. Kitchener saw extensive service as a soldier and imperial administrator in Egypt, South Africa, and India. Amongst his achievements were the reconquest of the Sudan (1898) and the imposition of British peace terms on the Boer republics (1902). He was given a viscountcy in 1902 and promoted earl in 1914. But his greatest service to the British empire was between 1914 and 1916, when he served as secretary of state for war. Far from being merely a great poster, as *Lloyd George claimed, he was a prescient strategist. He recognized that a conflict between the European great powers would not end quickly but would degenerate into a long war of attrition. To ensure that Britain emerged victorious he expanded the small regular army by raising a huge new army of volunteers. He was drowned when HMS *Hampshire*, the cruiser carrying him to a conference in Russia, was sunk off Orkney by a German mine. DF

Kit Kat Club. An early 18th-cent. London dining club which took its name from Christopher Cat, who kept the tavern in which it first met. Although not a political club, its members were prominent in the Whig Party and as well as the writers *Congreve, *Addison, and *Pope, and artists *Vanbrugh and *Kneller, included Robert *Walpole, *Newcastle, and John Churchill (*Marlborough). Kneller was commissioned to paint portraits of the members. All but one of the 42 pictures, now in the National Portrait Gallery, measure 36 inches by 28 inches and the term kit-cat came to refer to a canvas or portrait of this size. JC

Kloster-Zeven, convention of, 1757. After *Cumberland's defeat at *Hastenbeck in July, he withdrew to Stade and opened negotiations with the French. He interpreted his orders from his father, George II, as authority to preserve his army at all costs and on 8 September signed the convention of Kloster-Zeven, arranging for it to be disbanded. Though George II had been thinking of Hanoverian neutrality in the *Seven Years War, he repudiated the convention. Cumberland, hastening to Kensington palace, was greeted with 'Here is my son who has ruined me and disgraced himself.' He resigned all his military offices in protest and never held command again. JAC

Kneller, Sir Godfrey (*c.*1646–1723). A native of Lübeck who had studied under Rembrandt, Kneller came to England *c.*1676. He became court portraitist to William and Mary, Anne, and George I, enjoying a reputation which evidently eclipsed *Van Dyck's. In fact, like all portraitists he was at his best with sitters to whom he warmed; otherwise a stereotyped baroque grandiloquence and a thronged studio obscured his real talents as a designer and handler of paint. In high favour with William III, Kneller was knighted in 1692 (created a baronet by George I), and was integrally of the 'protestant establishment'. Kneller's more notable works include the eight 'Hampton Court Beauties' commissioned by Mary II, and his *'Kit Kat Club' portraits, executed between 1697 and 1721. There are at least 40 of these, all painted to a standard size and often revelatory of the versatile men who comprised this Whig dining club. DDA

knights. In continental Europe from the 10th cent. onwards, the term *miles* (knight) was applied to a mounted warrior usually dependent on a greater lord. *Domesday evidence suggests that this definition is appropriate for the knights of Norman England. Few held much land, and many were maintained within their lords' households. Their importance was thus derived from their military function, as had been that of the *cnichts* of Anglo-Saxon England. Over the next two centuries, knights were enfeoffed with land, becoming more fully involved in landed society and royal administration in the localities. Although the term never lost its military connotation, it had become by the late 14th cent. a social rank below the nobility, but above the squirearchy. It has been estimated that there were 4,000–5,000 knights in mid-12th-cent. England, but that the number declined to about 2,000 by 1250. The escalation of warfare from the reign of Edward I onwards may have helped to keep numbers up and even to revivify the military significance of the knight (680 English knights, for instance, served in the French campaign of 1359), but a major decline is evidenced after the end of the reign of Edward III. By the mid-15th cent., knights numbered only a few hundred. The decline has usually been explained in terms of personal preference: men of the requisite wealth and social standing resisted the crown's attempts to force them, by *distraint of knighthood, to take up the rank because they feared the additional expense and burden of responsibility. It seems that the rank of esquire became socially acceptable as an alternative indicator of gentility: it too had developed within a military context from the late 13th cent. onwards, and had adopted many of the trappings of knighthood, such as armorial bearings, military effigies, chivalric concepts, and administrative functions. Most knights were knights bachelor; the title was personal, not hereditary, nor did it give noble status, so that knights were represented in Parliament in the Commons not the Lords. The knight *banneret emerged in the early 13th cent. as a senior rank, probably relating, in its initial stages, to special military significance. Some bannerets were summoned to attend the Lords, and their titles were passed on to their sons, so that they became, by the early 15th cent., indistinguishable from barons. The creation of baronetcies, which were hereditary, in the early 17th cent. brought about a further decline in the status of knighthood. Though the link with military service did not totally disappear and successful admirals were often knighted, 18th-cent. knights were just as likely to be diplomats, lord mayors of London, or wealthy merchants. AC

Knollys, Sir Francis (1512–96). Knollys was a prominent courtier and parliamentarian during Elizabeth I's reign. His father was a minor courtier, usher of the Privy Chamber. A zealous protestant, Knollys became gentleman pensioner to Henry VIII and escorted *Anne of Cleves to her marriage. Knollys's career took off after he married the daughter of Mary Boleyn, first cousin to Princess Elizabeth. Most of Queen Mary's reign he spent abroad, but on Elizabeth's accession he was made a privy counsellor and vice-chamberlain. His accumulation of estates and a large family gave him a powerful electoral interest: six of his seven sons sat in Parliament and Knollys was a leading government spokesman in all the Elizabethan parliaments. In 1567 he became treasurer of the chamber, in 1570 treasurer of the household, and in 1593 was given the Garter. His daughter Lettice married the 1st earl of Essex and then *Leicester, and his grandson, the 2nd earl of *Essex, was a rising sun at court in the 1590s. His second, but surviving son, was created Baron Knollys (1603), Viscount Wallingford (1616), and earl of Banbury (1626). Though Elizabeth was sparing with peerages, it is surprising that Knollys did not receive one: perhaps he was too useful in the Commons. His religious views, shading into puritanism, may have alienated the queen and his rebukes may have grown tedious. JAC

Knox, John (*c.*1514–72). Scottish protestant preacher. Born at Haddington (East Lothian) and educated at St Andrews University, Knox was ordained a catholic priest before being called to the protestant ministry in 1547. In 1549, following two years' imprisonment on a French galley, he settled in England, where his powerful preaching and extreme reliance on biblical authority (typified by his opposition to kneeling at communion) established his radical credentials. Driven into continental exile by Mary Tudor's accession in 1553, his radicalism developed a powerful political edge, culminating in his infamous diatribe against female rule, *The First Blast of the Trumpet against the Monstrous Regiment of Women* (1558). On Elizabeth's accession later that year, Knox was barred from England and returned instead to Scotland where in 1559 his iconoclastic preaching triggered a protestant rebellion against the regent, *Mary of Guise. The reformed settlement of 1560, however, was jeopardized by the return to Scotland in 1561 of the catholic Mary Stuart. While Knox denounced her idolatry from his Edinburgh pulpit, politically he was marginalized and played no significant role in Mary's subsequent downfall. Dogged by failing health, he devoted his later years to compiling his biased but invaluable *History of the Reformation in Scotland*. RAM

Korean War, 1950–3. On 25 June 1950 the communist North Korean army, supplied with Russian equipment, attacked the Republic of South Korea, crossing the 38th Parallel, which acted as the artificial boundary. The army of the South was caught by surprise and forced to retreat. On 27 June the United Nations voted to provide military aid and the USA led a fifteen-nation task force to the peninsula. The South fell back on the key south-east port of Pusan and dug in, halting the communist advance. On 15 September the UN gained the initiative by launching an amphibious assault on Inchon and breaking out of Pusan. They pushed north capturing Pyongyang, the North Korean capital, on 20 October. However, by January 1951 the communists, massively reinforced by China, were marching south again. The UN secured a line 75 miles below the 38th Parallel and on 25 January counter-attacked. Communist counter-offensives on 22–3 April and 15–16 May were checked and by 15 June the UN held a line 20 miles north of the 38th Parallel. A cease-fire came into effect on 10 July.

After protracted negotiations and the repatriation of prisoners on 20 and 26 April 1953, an armistice was signed on 27 July. The UN listed 1 million men killed, injured, or missing. Communist casualties were estimated at 520,000 for North Korea and 900,000 for China. RAS

Kruger, Paul (1825–1904). Boer (Afrikaner) statesman and devout calvinist. Kruger spent most of his life trying to escape British rule. As a boy he accompanied his parents on the Great Trek of Boers away from Britain's Cape Colony. He was present at the signing of the *Sand River convention in 1852 and was a founder of the South African Republic (Transvaal) in 1856. When Britain annexed the republic in 1877, he led the resistance to British administration which culminated in the first Anglo-Boer War (1880–1). His diplomacy resulted in two Conventions (*Pretoria 1881 and London 1884) which recognized the internal autonomy of the Transvaal and in 1883 he became president of the republic, though regarding himself as essentially God's vicegerent rather than as head of state. Renewed British designs on the Transvaal, instigated by Alfred *Milner, led to the second Anglo-Boer War (1899–1902). The elderly Kruger sought help in Europe and died there in 1904. KI

labour aristocracy. Top 10–15 per cent of manual wage earners in the 19th cent., characterized by relatively high and regular earnings, membership of a trade union, and respectable life-style. This élite of skilled artisans—engineers, cabinet-makers, printers, cotton-spinners, and the like—set the tone of working-class leadership between the 1840s and the 1890s. The gulf between the labour aristocracy and the mass of unskilled or semi-skilled workers was precise and virtually unbridgeable; but at the upper end of the social stratum the labour aristocracy merged with the lower middle class. The strength of the labour aristocracy rested partly on its control of entry to a trade (usually through apprenticeship) and the custom of subcontracting. Some historians have suggested that a labour aristocracy with a conservative ideology and a stake in the status quo may help to account for the social stability of mid-Victorian Britain; and Marxists have used the concept of a labour aristocracy as a partial explanation of the non-revolutionary character of the British working class. However, the labour aristocracy maintained a distinctive working-class ideology through its unions, and also provided the leadership in some radical reform movements. JFCH

Labourers, statute of, 1351. The statute was an early attempt at a wage freeze, rarely a popular policy. The scourge of the *Black Death led to an acute shortage of labour and in June 1349 the council issued an emergency ordinance (23 Edw. III s. 1) imposing restraint. When Parliament met in 1351 there were complaints that 'out of singular covetise' the ordinance had been disregarded, and the statute (25 Edw. III s. 1) was passed. Men were to work at pre-1349 wage levels, which were laid down, and masters were forbidden to offer more. Persons below the age of 60 not in employment were not to refuse offers of work. Prices were merely to be 'reasonable'. Despite determined efforts to impose the policy and the appointment of special justices of labourers, it proved difficult to enforce. Even the carpenter at Knightsbridge who made the stocks to hold offenders had to be paid over the odds. But resentment played a part in the grievances leading to the *Peasants' Revolt in 1381. JAC

labour history is an important specialism which has greatly extended its scope in the last fifty years. Scholars' perspectives, apart from exceptions such as J. L. and B. Hammond, concentrated on institutions and activists within them or the very poor. Moreover, it was widely believed that sentiment clouded scholarly judgement when in other branches of history researchers were attempting to adopt and adapt techniques pioneered in the social sciences. Labour history has come to terms with these techniques and recognized the importance of work undertaken by social anthropologists, labour economists, historical demographers, and business historians. Consequently, subjects for investigation have changed, and methods of analysis have become more rigorous and less open to the charge of subjectivity and political bias.

There has also been a marriage between the 'old' labour history and the 'new'. Union histories often tend to follow the narrative style set by the *Webbs in their *History of Trade Unionism* (1894) but are more analytical in their treatment of issues such as wage movements, labour productivity, and labour markets (which were either ignored in earlier work or passed over quickly). The past is not interpreted by sole reference to the trade union officials or activists at local level as it would have been earlier; rather, labour history has become concerned with the whole experience of workers.

Treatment is uneven and patchy; urban workers and their experience have received more attention than workers in factory villages and small towns. However, it might be reasonably argued that the big battalions are more representative and more important. Some subjects have prompted massive debate and swamped the periodical literature, notably the standard of living between 1790 and 1850; more work needs to be done on other periods. In most periods the majority of the labour force has not been unionized; good work has been done on female, seasonal, and casual labour for some areas of Britain, but geographical and occupational unevenness is a problem. For instance, the very important category (up to 1914) of domestic servants has increasingly attracted scholarly attention, but female clerical workers in the 20th cent. have been neglected.

On the positive side, excellent new work has been done on working-class agitations and movements. *Chartism, for example, which in the 1950s seemed to demonstrate only two characteristics—moral and physical force and a national homogeneity—has been exposed as essentially a diverse local and regional movement. Structural changes in the demand for labour have been clearly analysed, taking account of labour productivity, and the history of groups such as hand-loom weavers has been much improved. Machine-breaking was simply seen as a blind reaction to industrial capitalism; recent work emphasizes its role in the process of industrial relations. Employers' strategies were commonly discussed when newly-won trade union rights were challenged in the courts. The latest work emphasizes workplace experience of workers and employers' responses at the factory or industrial level.

Excellent new work is available on workers' consumption. This discusses the physique, diets, and health of workers and their families. Child labour and its regulation has always attracted the attention of historians, but only recently has it been understood how old and how widespread this was. More energy has been expended on female labour, often analysing census data, parliamentary papers, and business records in a more systematic fashion than was possible earlier. The family and housing have received more attention. Migration, immigration, and emigration have been studied in greater depth, and the incidence of poverty, which *Booth, *Rowntree, and their imitators examined locally over 100 years ago, has been examined over a wider area. Labour history prospers and has a healthy specialist periodical literature. JB

Labour Party. Labour has been the principal progressive alternative to the Conservative Party since the 1920s, forming governments in 1924, 1929–31, 1945–51, 1964–70, and 1974–9. The Labour Representation Committee was established in 1900 by a conference of trade unionists and socialists orchestrated by Keir *Hardie. Although it won only two seats in the 1900 'khaki' election, the secret electoral pact with the Liberal Party negotiated by Ramsay *MacDonald in 1903 helped the rechristened Labour Party enjoy a tally of 30 MPs after the 1906 election.

Thereafter, advance was patchy, but the First World War (despite the divisions it caused) proved to be Labour's turning-point. Arthur *Henderson (parliamentary chairman after MacDonald's resignation on the outbreak of war) entered the cabinet on the formation of the wartime coalition in 1915 and from August 1917 worked with Sidney *Webb in devising a new constitution. In 1918 Labour became formally committed to the socialist objective of 'public ownership of the means of production' (clause 4); although this served to underline Labour's independence from the Liberals, it strengthened the trade union domination of the party's organization.

Under conditions of manhood suffrage, the 1918 'Coupon' election awarded Labour 63 seats for 2.4 million votes. In 1922 Labour gained 4.2 million votes and 142 seats to become the official opposition. Following the inconclusive 1923 election, Labour briefly formed the government with 191 MPs between January and October 1924, which demonstrated Labour's competence. However the second MacDonald government exposed the financial orthodoxy of ministers in the face of mounting unemployment and the financial crisis of 1931. The resignation of the Labour cabinet in August and the subsequent formation of the *National (coalition) Government by MacDonald (with the support of only a handful of Labour figures such as *Snowden and Thomas) caused lasting bitterness within the Labour Party. After the disastrous 1931 election (which reduced Labour from 288 to 52 seats) and the disaffiliation of the *ILP the following year, Labour began a gradual recovery and won 154 seats in 1935 on 38 per cent of the vote. The unassuming Clement *Attlee was elected leader before this election. The participation of Labour in *Churchill's coalition government from May 1940 rebuilt its image with voters and *Bevin, *Morrison, and *Cripps played highly visible and constructive roles on the 'home front', while Attlee's administrative talents found expression as deputy prime minister. The year 1945 heralded an unexpected landslide victory for Labour, which won 393 seats with 48 per cent of the vote. This strong administration, with Bevin at the Foreign Office, Dalton and then Cripps as chancellor, and 'Nye' *Bevan at Health, was Labour's 'finest hour'. Despite economic headaches, notably the 1949 devaluation of sterling, by 1950 the 'Attlee consensus' of a mixed economy with a welfare state was firmly established.

Despite achieving its highest ever poll (fractionally under 14 million votes) in 1951, Labour began thirteen years of opposition. The period witnessed faction fighting between left-wing 'Bevanites' and right-wing followers of Hugh *Gaitskell, elected leader in 1955. In response to three successive (and widening) election defeats, Gaitskell unsuccessfully attempted to persuade the conference to abandon 'clause 4' in 1959. The following year, Labour's anti-war tradition resurfaced in conference support for unilateral nuclear disarmament (reversed in 1961).

However, a tottering economy together with Harold *Wilson's invigorating leadership allowed Labour to squeeze back into office in October 1964 by a four-seat majority. An easy victory in the 1966 'follow-up' election was Labour's last electoral triumph. Despite positive achievements in the field of education and liberalizing social legislation in particular, Wilson's government struggled to cope with the legacy of Britain's relative economic decline and was humbled by the 1967 devaluation of sterling and consequent policy U-turns. Relations with the wider Labour movement deteriorated as a result of Barbara Castle's bold attempt at industrial relations reform, 'In Place of Strife'.

In opposition again after 1970, Labour divided over Britain's entry into the EEC and the left's call for more extensive public ownership. Wilson's two further narrow election victories in 1974 obscured a weakening of Labour's appeal since the 1960s. Left-wing alienation from the government's (under *Callaghan from 1976) deflationary response to mounting unemployment and inflation came to a head after Labour began a further lengthy spell in opposition after 1979.

In 1980 and 1981 Tony Benn's supporters won constitutional changes which precipitated the defection of right-wingers to form the *Social Democratic Party. Subsequently, Michael *Foot led Labour to heavy defeat in the 1983 election. Under Neil *Kinnock (1983–92) and John *Smith (1992–4) a slow revival of Labour's fortunes occurred as the party shifted back towards the 'centre' and purged itself of militant infiltration. Tony Blair's 'New Labour' strategy from 1994 accelerated this trend, and secured a massive win at the 1997 general election. SC

Hinton, J., *Labour and Socialism* (1983); Morgan, K. O., *Labour*

People: Leaders and Lieutenants (1987); Pelling, H., *Short History of the Labour Party* (10th edn. 1993).

labour services were tasks undertaken by tenants as part of their obligations to landowners for the right to farm or use land. These duties came to be seen as part of the rent paid by tenants under the *'manorial system' during the Middle Ages. One of the definitions of villein status was performing labour services at the will of the lord because, in theory, the obligations were unrestricted. In practice, the levying of labour services depended on the farming regime of the lord of the manor. When cash crops were especially profitable, as during the 13th cent., lords of the manor increased their directly farmed demesne land and used labour services to take advantage of good weather conditions: for spreading manure, ploughing the arable, repairing and maintaining boundaries and ditches, gathering crops of hay and grain, and carrying them to barns or markets.

Precise statements of labour services owed by landholders to the lord of the manor were set out in 'custumals', documents produced in manorial courts under oath. Villeins, tenants of the lord of the manor, resisted attempts to extend labour services. During the 14th cent. landowners found it profitable to commute labour services for fixed cash payments. Declining demesne farming by landowners after the middle of the 14th cent. reduced labour services and they ceased to be a determinant of social status by the 16th cent. A few labour services survived in economically underdeveloped areas until the early 18th cent., as in parts of rural west Lancashire. IJEK

Ladysmith. Town in northern Natal, scene of a siege by Afrikaner forces during the second Anglo-Boer War. Ladysmith became the main British military supply base in Natal in 1897 and when the Boers advanced into the colony at the outbreak of war in 1899 the British commander in Natal, Sir George White, expected an easy victory. Instead, his army was heavily defeated and White found himself surrounded in Ladysmith, a strategically unsuitable site for a beleaguered force to occupy. Fortunately for White, the Boer commander, Joubert, did not exploit his success and the town was relieved at the end of February 1900. KI

Lagos, battle of, 1693. On 17 June 1693 off Lagos in southern Portugal, Sir George *Rooke, escorting a convoy of 400 vessels to the Mediterranean, was attacked by the French admiral de Tourville with a vastly superior force. One hundred English and Dutch merchantmen were lost. The defeat was attributed to poor intelligence. JAC

Lagos, battle of, 1759. In the summer of 1759 the nucleus of a French invasion fleet under de la Clue left Toulon and slipped past Edward *Boscawen's squadron at Gibraltar. A running fight developed and on 18 August four French vessels sought refuge in Lagos Bay in southern Portugal. They were attacked, two captured and two burned, and de la Clue killed. The Portuguese protested at the violation of their neutrality. JAC

La Hogue, battle of, 1692. Control of the Channel, lost by the defeat off *Beachy Head in 1690, was restored in May 1692 by the victory of La Hogue, or La Hougue, near Barfleur. De Tourville, the French admiral, had orders to engage while still awaiting reinforcements from the Mediterranean. This gave Edward Russell (*Orford), who had replaced Torrington (*Byng) as commander-in-chief of the Channel fleet, an advantage of nearly two to one. The French were badly beaten and when they sought shelter were assailed by fireships and boarding parties. James II, on shore with a French invasion force, watched the destruction of his hopes. The *Soleil Royal*, flagship and pride of the French navy, was among the vessels burned. Russell was raised to the peerage as earl of Orford. JAC

lairds. The Scots word 'laird' is a shortened form of 'laverd', an older Scots word deriving from an Anglo-Saxon term meaning lord. It implied ownership of landed property in the form of an estate. By the 15th cent. it was widely used of lesser landowners holding directly of the crown and therefore entitled to go to Parliament, but lairds were clearly distinguished from the higher aristocracy or lords of Parliament. In the 16th and 17th cents. it was commonly applied to the chief of a Highland clan with no other title, as in 'the laird of McGregor'.

The feuing movement which peaked at the time of the 16th-cent. Reformation enabled tenants to buy for a steep price feu charters which apart from a small ongoing feu duty bestowed virtual ownership. Some of these tenants, really small proprietors, were known as 'bonnet lairds', but the term is jocular, and it is best to equate the rank of laird with the possession of a barony held either of the crown or of a great lord of regality such as *Argyll, who had the right to create his own baronage.

Lairds were therefore a numerous class in rural Scotland, though decreasing relative to the higher nobility over time. Baronial jurisdiction was extensive, though subject to appeal to the royal sheriff court or the regality court. The lairdly particle was the word 'of', as in 'Irvine of Drum' or 'Ferguson of Kilkerran'. The number of lairds is difficult to state before the 18th cent., but allowing for the large number of baronies directly in crown or noble hands, equating the laird class with all others, and remembering that in a Fife parish such as Creich there were at one stage three baronies, a figure in the lowish thousands seems the maximum. They were not a homogeneous class: Orkney and Shetland produced merchant-lairds. When great landlords, defined as those with a rental over £2,000 Scots (£166 13*s*. 4*d*. sterling), already held by 1770 half the agrarian wealth of Scotland and were consolidating their ascendancy, businessmen were buying into the laird class around the larger cities. As baronies survived after 1747, it is still possible to buy laird status with an estate which is a barony. BPL

laissez-faire. The transition from the medieval to the modern economy was characterized by the progressive removal of restrictions on individuals and groups in favour of the operation of market forces. The balance between complete unrestriction based on the assumption that the best social organization is that which allows the individual maximum freedom, *laissez-faire*, and some control is still strenuously debated. In reality the state of complete *laissez-faire* has never existed. The classical economists believed that natural law required that the influence of government should be limited in favour of individual liberty. Strong supporters of this notion argue either that the actions of individuals pursuing their own ends are complementary, best reflected through the operation of a free market where individuals negotiate as equal partners, or that society is no more than the artificial aggregation of individuals so that no reference to a greater good is permissible. Beyond this extreme the main issue is to find a balance between complete *laissez-faire* and too great a degree of control. John Stuart *Mill defined what has become accepted as the minimum level of state intervention. Amongst such interventions for the greater good, he included the power to enforce contracts and secure property rights, the administration of justice, the right to tax in order to provide public goods such as transport systems, sanitation and public health, and state-supported education. Typical *laissez-faire* constraints on 19th-cent. government were the fixed exchange rate and a minimalist attitude towards taxation. Ideas of social justice combined with individual freedom found a compromise in 19th-cent. *Poor Law legislation, designed to provide help for the truly needy, while ensuring that the idle should be excluded.

While the notion of *laissez-faire* is usually associated with the decline of the medieval and mercantilist economic regimes, it has an enduring modern counterpart, or legacy, in the views of the neo-classical and new classical economists, who may use different terminology, but whose essential view is that individual freedom to function within untrammelled markets, with little involvement from government, represents the best type of economic organization. Variations of this position are found in monetarism, public choice theory, and the belief of some new classical economists that involuntary unemployment does not exist. All these strands of thought assert the right of the individual and depict state involvement in the economy as ineffectual or malign.

CHL

Lamb, Charles (1775–1834). The mild and gentle character of Lamb is fresh air among the abrasive and arrogant men of letters of the early 19th cent. He was born in London, spent his 'joyful schooldays' at Christ's Hospital, and earned his living as a clerk in the East India House. Much of his life was devoted to caring for his sister Mary, who killed their mother in a fit of madness. Lamb himself, with his stammer and desperate punning, ran close to the edge at times. His most successful works were the *Tales from Shakespeare* (1807) for young readers, and the *Essays of Elia* (1823, 1833). Less interested in politics than many of his friends, much of his work was frankly nostalgic—'The Old Familiar Faces', 'Dream Children'—and shot through with love of Hertfordshire, where he spent much of his boyhood. JAC

Lambert, John (1619–83). Lambert had a strange life, missing his footing on the steps of power. He was a good cavalry commander under the *Fairfaxes in the first civil war, and a leading general in the second, serving with *Cromwell at *Preston. He added to his military reputation at *Dunbar in 1650 and at *Worcester in 1651, becoming, in *Clarendon's phrase, 'first in the affection of the army'. He was largely responsible for the *Instrument of Government setting up the Protectorate in 1653, became a major-general for the northern counties, and was widely tipped as Cromwell's successor. In 1657 however he went too far in opposing the *Humble Petition and Advice and was stripped of his military and civil appointments. Triumphantly reinstated when the army overturned Richard Cromwell in 1659, he helped to restore the *Rump Parliament. But he soon quarrelled with the Rump and defied its attempt to cashier him by leading a military coup in October. At this stage he looked like a *Monck in the making and there were rumours that Charles II would marry his daughter. But his position collapsed speedily. When Monck in Scotland threatened to intervene on the Rump's behalf, Lambert marched north to face him, but his troops melted away. He was captured and put in the Tower. He escaped in April 1660 to lead a last desperate rising for the Commonwealth, but few supporters came in to his rendezvous at Edgehill. Lambert spent the remaining 23 years of his life in captivity, mainly in the Channel Islands, watched by the government as a dangerous man. As late as the *Popish plot in 1678, Charles's ministers were worried what Lambert might do, though his mind had long been clouded over. AHW; JAC

Lambeth, treaty of, 1217. After John's death in 1216, the supporters of his young son Henry III defeated Louis of France's men at *Lincoln. On 20 September 1217 the treaty of Lambeth ratified terms agreed at *Kingston upon Thames. Louis abandoned all claims to the English throne and retired to France but was given 10,000 marks in compensation. The king's supporters, chief of whom was William *Marshal, earl of Pembroke, agreed to maintain the liberties of the subject as defined in *Magna Carta. JAC

Lambeth palace. Originally approached by boat, Lambeth and its manor house was bought by *Baldwin (*c.*1185). Known as Lambeth House until 1658, it is conveniently near the administrative centres of Westminster and Whitehall for archbishops as 'Primates of all England'. The Old Palace, Canterbury, is their diocesan residence. The chapel was the venue of *Parker's historic consecration, the only archbishop to be buried there. The first Lambeth conference (1867) was held in the 14th-cent. guard room; later conferences (1878–1958) were held in the hall. The chapel undercroft dates from *Langton, the chapel itself originally from *c.*1230. The great hall, with its hammer-beam roof, has an exterior rebuilt, possibly by *Wren (*c.*1660–3), after destruction during the Commonwealth. From *c.*1830 it has housed the library, now of *c.*200,000 books and 4,000 manuscripts, a collection founded by *Bancroft (1610). The residential section was rebuilt in Tudor style (*c.*1830). The entrance is by *Morton's tower (*c.*1495). Second World War bombing destroyed the chapel and severely devastated the hall and residence, but all was restored (1955). The chapel and its undercroft were refurbished with murals and stalls for each primate world-wide (1988). The historic private garden, London's oldest and second largest, was restored and revitalized (1988). WMM

Lancashire. Isolated by dense forests and scarcely marked by the Romans, this north-western area of England remained remote and desolate even at *Domesday; the coastline of dunes, marshes, and mosses had discouraged intensive settlement from across the Irish Sea, although combined Norse/Anglian place-names still persist. Fully recognized as one of the English shires by 1194 and a county *palatine since 1351, the palatine rights were subsequently vested in the sovereign as duke of Lancaster. Its relative remoteness later sheltered recusancy and Jacobitism.

Cloth-manufacturing was initially a subsidiary employment in the upland farms, encouraged by the soft water and mild, moist climate, since the Pennine hills entrap east-moving clouds; linen (west) and wool (east) had become increasingly important by the 17th cent. The invention of machines for spinning (*Hargreaves's spinning jenny, *Arkwright's water frame, *Crompton's mule) and development of steam-power in the later 18th cent. encouraged exploitation of the coalfield and a move from a domestic to a factory system, with increasing concentration on the more easily worked cotton. Aided by improved communications and transport (canals, then railways), and growth of *Manchester as a business centre and *Liverpool as an Atlantic port, the expansion in cotton was such that Lancashire came to dominate the British textile industry. Commerce, cotton, chemicals, and engineering generated industrial development, massive growth in population, and local wealth but at the expense of scarring of the valleys, the health of the work-force, and child labour, despite growing trade unionism. Church-building was matched by equally rapid growth of nonconformist chapels.

The gradual loss of vitality of Lancashire since 1880 has been attributed less to 'entrepreneurial failure', aggravated by economic depression between the world wars, than to a reduction in export demand as rival overseas industries developed. Glass, soap, and shipping still prospered, but as textiles and mining declined, unemployment, urban decay, and out-migration accelerated. Museums have replaced mills. However, arable farming with some reversal of enclosures has made a significant return in the north and west, since the drained mosses yielded rich soils, while market gardens flourish; coastal towns such as Blackpool have become tourist resorts. Cricket and association and rugby league football retain passionate support, but, despite its regional distinctiveness, the county (shorn in 1972 of Merseyside, Greater Manchester, and its southern Lakeland fringe) continues to drift back to its former position on the periphery. ASH

Lancaster, duchy of. The duchy of Lancaster originated in the desire of Henry III to provide for his youngest son Edmund Crouchback, after the failure of a scheme to make him king of Sicily. He was granted many of the estates of Simon de *Montfort, killed at *Evesham, and in 1267 was given all the royal estates in Lancashire, assuming the title of earl. Edmund's grandson, *Henry of Grosmont, was created duke by Edward III in 1351, with considerable *palatine powers, including the right to hold his own chancery with his own justices, and to appoint his own sheriff. Henry left a daughter who married *John of Gaunt, Edward III's younger brother. When John's son Henry seized the throne as Henry IV in 1399, the dukedom of Lancaster was merged with the crown. But a separate administration was maintained, possibly in case the new regime did not prosper, but more probably to give the king an independent source of income. The chancellorship of the duchy of Lancaster has been used in recent centuries as a supernumerary post, often in the cabinet, for an elder statesman. Queen Victoria used the title countess of Lancaster when she wished to travel semi-privately on the continent. JAC

Lancaster, Joseph (1778–1838). Founder of the Lancasterian system of education. The son of a nonconformist, Lancaster opened a school at Borough Road, south London, in 1798, offering free education to those unable to pay. He divided it into small classes each under a monitor; a group of these classes was supervised by a head monitor. In this way, and by using mechanical methods of learning, he could accommodate 1,000 boys. Recognition came in 1805 when George III met Lancaster and promised his support. However, Lancaster opposed the notion that education should be Anglican and encountered rivalry from a Church of England clergyman, Andrew *Bell. A Royal Lancasterian Society, later the *British and Foreign School Society, was set up in 1808, but Lancaster quarrelled with the trustees and emigrated to America. He died in a street accident in New York in 1838. PG

Lancastrians. The three kings of England between 1399 and 1461 (Henry IV, Henry V, and Henry VI) were so named because they were descended from *John of Gaunt, duke of Lancaster. The term is also applied to their retainers, identifiable in many effigies by the wearing of the Lancastrian collar of SS, and to those who supported Henry VI in the Wars of the *Roses. It would be wrong to liken them to a political party, although in its heyday the Lancastrian affinity was a powerful force, which played a crucial role in sustaining the dynasty on the throne during the first quarter of the 15th cent. AJP

Land Acts is a collective term applied to a series of Irish land reforms enacted between the end of the 19th and early 20th cents. This legislation was partly an attempt to defuse the increasingly assertive peasant nationalism which, fuelled by rural grievance, was threatening the stability of British rule in Ireland. Though often very different in detail, the legislation generally had two aspects: first, the immediate improvement of the tenant's contractual position, and, second, the gradual encouragement of a peasant proprietorship. *Gladstone's Land Act of 1870 sought to give legal force to the *Ulster custom, and to give tenants enhanced security of tenure; his more comprehensive measure of 1881 offered more decisive relief in the same areas, establishing in effect the principle of joint-proprietorship: rents might be fixed by judicial arbitration, and the tenant was given both the right to free sale, and enhanced protection against unjust eviction. Conservative legislation developed these Gladstonian precedents, although the principle of land purchase (a secondary feature of the Act of 1870) was much more prominent: the 'Ashbourne' Land Purchase Act (1885) provided £5 million in order to fund sales of property to occupying tenants. This measure, even when boosted by subsequent funding, had a restricted impact, but it provided a precedent for the much more lavishly funded and successful Wyndham Land Act (1903): this built upon an earlier political agreement between landlords and tenants (the land conference of December 1902), and offered a range of inducements to both classes. Although watered down by the Birrell Land Act (1909), Wyndham's measure facilitated a massive transfer of land from the old Anglo-Irish proprietors to their tenants. This legislation, together with its predecessors, effected a social revolution in Ireland long before the Anglo-Irish War of 1919–21. AJ

Landen, battle of. See NEERWINDEN.

Lander, Richard Lemon (1804–34). Originally from Cornwall, Lander was a servant of *Clapperton to whom he showed great loyalty on the expedition to what is now northern Nigeria. After Clapperton's death in 1827, he returned to London and was soon commissioned by the government to return to west Africa in 1830, this time penetrating from the Guinea Coast to Bussa on the Niger. Lander then followed the river down to its outlet on the coast, solving the age-old problem of the great river's course and termination. He died on a later expedition to west Africa. RB

landscape gardening. The 18th-cent. English landscape garden or park was a major, and highly influential, contribution to European art. It replaced the earlier fashion for highly formal gardens (most of which were destroyed during this period) as adjuncts to country houses and ultimately presented an effect of natural, rolling grassland coming right up to the house, with distant clumps of trees; so much so, in fact, that the architect Sir William *Chambers found the landscapes of the celebrated Lancelot 'Capability' *Brown (1716–83) to 'differ very little from common fields, so closely is common nature copied in most of them'.

Among Brown's numerous works were the landscapes at *Alnwick castle, Northumberland (*c*.1760), *Blenheim palace, Oxfordshire (1763), Bowood, Wiltshire (*c*.1761–6), *Holkham Hall, Norfolk (1762), *Kew Gardens and Richmond Park, London (from 1764), and Prior Park, near Bath (*c*.1764). The naturalness and expansiveness of such landscapes undoubtedly encouraged a sense of surveillance and possession in the minds of their aristocratic owners, although they were also held to demonstrate the spirit of British libertarianism. Certainly they were associated with the general trend towards enlarging estates through the enclosure of common land; sometimes whole villages were moved to create the desired effect, as at Kedleston (Derbys.) or Milton Abbas (Dorset).

Pioneers of the new taste in gardening, favoured by the poet Alexander *Pope, were Stephen Switzer (1682–1745), Charles *Bridgeman (fl. 1709–38), the latter credited with the invention of the 'ha-ha', a hidden ditch which halted the movement of animals without interrupting the view, and William *Kent (1685–1748). Their landscape gardens were more intricate and contrived, with wooded areas, glades, temples, and monuments. At Rousham in Oxfordshire, William Kent, from 1738, modified the original garden plan by Bridgeman of *c*.1715–20, adding cascades, ponds, walks, statues, and a pyramid. (Brown emphasized aquatic features but made little use of architectural elements.) Kent also designed the gardens at Chiswick House, Middlesex (*c*.1727–36). Such schemes often had complex, symbolic 'programmes' based on literary or political allusion, as at Stowe (Bucks.). The extensive gardens there were laid out mainly from 1713 by Viscount Cobham and his successor Earl Temple. Again, the scheme was initiated by Bridgeman and developed by Kent (mainly 1730s); a process of simplification and enlargement was begun by Brown, *c*.1749.

The final phase of the English landscape garden began late in the century, Picturesque theorists having rejected what they saw as the repetitive, over-formulaic approach of Brown. Thus Humphry *Repton (1752–1818) adopted a more complex and varied approach, involving the effect of 'accidents' of nature and a more organic relationship between buildings and landscape. TEF

Landseer, Sir Edwin (1802–73). English painter, sculptor, and engraver of animal subjects, Landseer was the son and pupil of an engraver. Of precocious talent, he first exhibited at the Royal Academy when he was 13, became ARA at 24, and an academician five years later. In 1865 he declined the presidency of the academy. Engravings of his paintings were made by his brother Thomas and prints from these were widely available, making Landseer the most popular artist of his day. Capitalizing on an upsurge of Scottish Romanticism and a demand for sporting pictures, Landseer painted many Highland subjects, notably *The Stag at Bay* and *The Monarch of the Glen*. He also sculpted the lions at the foot of Nelson's Column in London. He was the favourite painter of Queen Victoria, from whom he received a knighthood in 1850, having refused the honour eight years earlier. In 1869 he began to suffer bouts of madness and by his death had become quite insane. JC

land tax is an indirect tax levied on the value of land and often forms part of wider property taxation. In Roman times the provinces relied upon land taxes for a considerable part of their revenue and their importance continued into medieval times. Local government relied upon land taxes (in the form of rates) for much of their revenue from the mid-17th cent. until the 1980s. Throughout the whole of the 18th cent. the land tax was the main source of government revenue. Introduced in 1693 to pay for the French wars of William III's reign, it sufficed until 1799 when the cost of the Revolutionary War forced *Pitt to the even more drastic expedient of income tax. It was an object of *Walpole's government in particular to avoid involvement in war so that the land tax could be kept down and the gentry content.

Land tax may be on the capital value of land or on an imputed rental value. Its physical fixity and productive potential, together with the difficulties of avoidance, means land has been seen to form a good tax base. Philosophical arguments have also been advanced since feudal times that landholding is a privilege conferred by the state and that holders are liable to tax in perpetuity. Economic thinkers such as John *Locke and Adam *Smith have favoured shifting much of the burden of taxation to land for these reasons. There are practical difficulties however in assessing the value of land to be taxed and in ensuring that there are no disincentive impacts on its productive use. Land taxes are *in rem* and unlinked to the circumstances of owners, which can lead to undesirable distributional consequences. KJB

land tenure. Land could be held in a number of ways. Theoretically all land was owned ultimately by the crown, but most of it has been 'sold' to private individuals or public bodies. Since the disappearance of feudal tenure in the Middle Ages, most land has been 'let' to tenants, in a variety of different forms. Of these the best known is 'rack rent', in which land and buildings are let by the owner to a tenant for what is agreed by both parties to be a fair economic rent, reflecting its real value. However, this has been universal in England only since the abolition of copyhold in 1926, and prior to that time various other forms of tenure existed, usually based on time (three lives, 99 years, lifeleasehold)—or type of holding (copyhold, customaryhold). Under both systems the tenant paid a nominal rent but ensured the continuance of the holding through fines and other dues, enjoying virtual security of tenure as a result. These tenancies were particularly suited to non-inflationary periods and to estates over which the landlord wished to exercise little or no supervision. By the 18th and 19th cents. they were gradually being abolished, usually by the landlord refusing to insert new lives in a lease, or to accept payment of the traditional renewal fine. However, they remained in place through much of northern and western England well into the 19th cent., and on the estates of institutions such as Oxbridge colleges.

In Scotland, two forms of land-leasing were common: co-joint tenancy in which all the tenants on a farm were responsible for its cultivation and rent payment; and an alternative system in which several cultivators of a single farm each had a separate lease (or 'standing') for which they were responsible. The latter was the multiple tenancy farm. The early 18th cent. saw a decisive move, particularly in the Lowlands, towards the single tenancy which made enclosure and related innovations easier to obtain. JVB

Lanfranc (*c*.1010–89), archbishop of Canterbury (1070–89), was an Italian from Pavia, who moved to northern France in the 1030s, and rose in *Normandy before 1066 to be William the Conqueror's chief ecclesiastical adviser. A theologian and teacher of European renown, Lanfranc's presence gave the church in Normandy a prestige which it otherwise lacked; a fact which contributed considerably to the support given by the papacy to the *Norman Conquest. Lanfranc originally came to northern France to seek pupils and, around the year 1040, he passed through a spiritual crisis and sought seclusion in the then impoverished abbey of Le Bec. He emerged in the late 1040s and was thereafter always close to the centre of affairs. After 1070 his influence was widely pervasive throughout the Normanized church in England. Among other things, he controversially asserted Canterbury's primacy over York and, as a result, was able to preside over synods of the entire English church which gave a central direction to the efforts of the new Norman bishops. He circulated an abridged, but authoritative, collection of canon law throughout the English church and, through his *Monastic Constitutions*, he helped several English monasteries to adopt more up-to-date continental customs. His letters reveal a quiet disciplinarian who was also a pragmatist. His close and harmonious co-operation with William the Conqueror assisted the Norman settlement of England and contrasted with the attitudes of his pupil and successor St *Anselm, who placed a much greater emphasis on obedience to the papacy and to the rigorist policies of the *Investiture contest popes. DB

Lang, Cosmo Gordon (1864–1945). Archbishop of Canterbury. Lang was a native of Scotland. After a short ministry at the university church in Oxford, he became (1896) vicar of Portsea, an important and populous parish, where he trained and deployed a large team of assistant curates. At the age of only 37 he was nominated as suffragan bishop of Stepney, in London's East End, and then promoted (1908) to be archbishop of York. Here he proved a marked contrast to the more conservative, cautious, and diplomatic Randall *Davidson, his fellow-Scot who was archbishop of Canterbury. The contrast is well illustrated by their attitudes to the Prayer Book reform of 1928. Davidson did not want it, and Lang wanted a return to the more catholic Prayer Book of 1549. Lang succeeded Davidson at Canterbury in 1928, but his work as primate was overshadowed by criticism for his part in the *abdication crisis of 1936, and the outbreak of war in 1939. He resigned in 1942 and died three years later. JRG

Langham, Simon (d. 1376). Archbishop of Canterbury, chancellor, and curial cardinal. Born in Rutland, Langham entered the Benedictine monastery at Westminster (*c*.1335), and was successively prior and then abbot (1349), then treasurer of England (1360), bishop of Ely (1362), chancellor (1363), and archbishop (1366–8). As chancellor, his speeches at the opening of parliaments were the first in English. After a brief spell as archbishop, Edward III forced him to resign, whereupon he accepted a cardinalate without royal permission, thus becoming a valued diplomat in the papal curia at Avignon (1368). Regaining Edward's favour, he held various English dignities in plurality. When the Canterbury monks re-elected him archbishop (1374), the pope would not spare him, though, when the papacy was to move to Rome (1376), he was given permission to return to England, only to die in Avignon before setting out. Langham was a skilful administrator and a great benefactor of Westminster. WMM

Langland, William (1330s–90s). Author of **Piers Plowman*. Almost nothing is known about Langland beyond what can be surmised from his great allegorical poem: that he was a cleric in minor orders, married to one Kit, that he originated in the south-west, had connections with Malvern, and lived for a period in London. DCW

Langport, battle of, 1645. After his defeat at *Naseby in June 1645, Charles had few resources left in England. He managed to raise another army, largely of Welsh recruits, and *Goring was still pursuing a rather desultory siege of Taunton. *Fairfax moved against him and at Langport, on 10 July, inflicted a severe defeat. Goring lost 2,000 prisoners, and was forced back to Bridgwater and then to Barnstaple. News of the surrender of Carlisle and of *Montrose's defeat at *Philiphaugh completed a disastrous summer for the royalists. JAC

Langside, battle of, 1568. On 2 May 1568 Mary, queen of Scots, imprisoned for nearly a year in Lochleven castle, made her escape and raised support. Marching west to join forces with the Hamiltons, her troops, under the earl of *Argyll, confronted a smaller force under the regent, *Moray, on 13 May near Glasgow. The issue was decided by a cavalry charge and Mary's supporters broke. She fled to the south-west and made her way to Carlisle, where she appealed for help to Elizabeth I of England. She never saw Scotland again. JAC

Langton, Stephen (*c*.1156–1228). Biblical scholar and ecclesiastical politician who helped in the making of *Magna Carta. Educated at Paris, Langton stayed on to teach theology there. As a theologian he is most famous for his practical work in revising the order of the books of the Bible and arranging them into chapters. Pope Innocent III made him a cardinal in 1206 and next year consecrated him as archbishop of Canterbury against the wishes of King John. John's refusal to allow Langton into England led to a quarrel between king and pope that lasted until John submitted in 1213. Once in England, Langton's concern for lawful government made him an important mediator between the king and his baronial enemies, and he played a key role in the negotiations which led up to Magna Carta. Once this had been sealed, he remained fully committed to its principles. But this brought him into conflict with Innocent III since the pope thoroughly approved of a king who had submitted to him and, at John's request, declared Magna Carta null and void. Langton was suspended from office in September 1215 and went to Rome. He returned to England in 1218 but it was not until he had paid another visit to Rome in 1220–1 to secure the recall of an all too influential papal legate that he was free to play an active role in English affairs. During the minority of Henry III his moderating presence and co-operation with Hubert de *Burgh did much to keep the peace, until he withdrew from politics in the year before his death. JG

Lansbury, George (1859–1940). Christian socialist and pacifist. Lansbury came from working-class stock, and after flirting with Liberalism in London's East End in the 1880s identified himself with socialist politics, more especially in the context of local government. In 1921 he and other members of Poplar Borough Council suffered imprisonment rather than authorize the payment, to the London County Council, of monies which they claimed impoverished London boroughs could not afford. Perhaps for this reason, Lansbury was excluded from the 1924 Labour government, but in 1929 he became first commissioner of works. In 1931 he managed to retain his parliamentary seat at Bow and Bromley, and was elected Labour leader in the Commons. His obsession with pacifism in the early 1930s led him to oppose sanctions against Italy following Mussolini's invasion of Abyssinia, and in a dramatic but empty gesture he resigned the leadership at the 1935 Labour conference, striding defiantly out of the conference hall after being denied access to the microphone. GA

Lansdowne, battle of, 1643. This Civil War encounter was part of the early manœuvring for control of the west country, and fought between two old friends, Sir William *Waller and Sir Ralph *Hopton, who exchanged letters before the fight, lamenting 'this war without an enemy'. Hopton's royalists attacked Waller on 5 July, trying to drive him from the Lansdowne ridge, 5 miles north of Bath. In hand-to-hand fighting, Hopton's men pushed their way up the wooded slopes and, during the night, Waller made an orderly retreat. A week later his forces were badly beaten at *Roundway Down, just outside Devizes. There is a memorial on the field of battle to Sir Bevil Grenville, the Cornish leader killed in the attack. JAC

Lansdowne, William Petty, marquis of. See SHELBURNE, 2ND EARL OF.

Lansdowne, Henry Petty-Fitzmaurice, 3rd marquis of (1780–1863). Statesman. Lansdowne was a Whig grandee and for decades Bowood in Wiltshire and Lansdowne House in London were headquarters of Whiggism. His father, better known as *Shelburne, was prime minister 1782–3. Lansdowne succeeded his half-brother as marquis in 1809, having been chancellor of the Exchequer in the Ministry of All the *Talents at the age of 26. He supported *Canning's brief ministry in 1827, which caused a temporary breach with his less flexible Whig friends, and was home secretary in *Goderich's administration 1827–8. He served as lord president of the council in Whig ministries 1830–4, 1835–41, and 1846–52, and remained in the cabinet without portfolio 1852–8, as guardian of the Foxite tradition. He was given the Garter in 1836 and refused a dukedom in 1857. Lansdowne was several times within reach of the premiership but lacked ambition and was perhaps disinclined to ministerial toil. By 1857 he was, according to Greville, the first of the cabinet to fall asleep. JAC

Lansdowne, Henry Petty-Fitzmaurice, 5th marquis of (1845–1927). A Liberal politician, Lansdowne resigned from *Gladstone's government over Irish land reform in 1880. After serving as governor-general of Canada and viceroy of India, he joined *Salisbury's 1895 cabinet. As foreign secretary from 1900, he did much to satisfy those who believed that Britain could no longer afford the so-called policy of *'splendid isolation'. In 1901 he resolved Britain's outstanding disputes with the USA. An alliance with Japan followed in 1902. His effort to negotiate with Germany in 1903 over the Berlin–Baghdad railway was thwarted by Joseph *Chamberlain, but an entente with France in 1904 resolved various imperial differences—notably over Morocco and Egypt. Although he stood firmly with the French in the Moroccan crisis of 1905, he hoped that this was no more than a temporary rift with Germany. As leader of the Unionist peers from 1903 to 1916, he was much criticized for his conduct in opposition to *Asquith's Liberal government. Initially a strong supporter of the war against Germany, he wrote a highly controversial letter to the *Daily Telegraph* in November 1917 putting the case for a compromise peace. CJB

Largs, battle of, 1263. Though the fighting was little more than skirmishing, the consequences were significant. Throughout the reign of Alexander III of Scotland there were disputes about the Western Isles, under the sovereignty of Norway. In the autumn of 1263 Haakon IV of Norway assembled a large fleet, raiding and raising revenue. Early in October, some of his ships were driven ashore near Largs and others sent to protect them were attacked by the Scots. It was not clear who had the better of the fighting, but after Haakon had returned to Kirkwall, where he died, negotiations began for the Isles to be ceded to Scotland. Orkney and Shetland did not, however, become Scottish until 200 years later. JAC

Larkin, James (1876–1947). Larkin was the nearest thing to a revolutionary leader that the modern trade union movement has thrown up. He wished, on *syndicalist lines, to use trade union power not merely to obtain concessions but as a battering ram to destroy capitalism. Born in Liverpool of Irish parents, he became involved in union activity and went to Ireland to organize the dock workers. His first task was to persuade protestants and catholics to work together. In 1908 he founded the Irish Transport and General Workers' Union, supporting it from 1911 in the *Irish Worker*. In the autumn of 1913 a strike on the Dublin trams led to a long confrontation with the employers and gave Larkin his finest hour. Threatened with arrest, he whipped off a false beard on the balcony of the Imperial hotel, O'Connell Street, to encourage his men. But he alienated British trade union support and the rest was anticlimax. The strike dribbled away with little gained and there were other matters to preoccupy Ireland. Larkin spent the war years in America, where he was gaoled and then deported, and returned a convinced Marxist with an admiration for Bolshevik Russia. His militancy led to expulsion from the union he had founded. Elected to the Dáil in 1927 he was unseated as a bankrupt, but elected again in 1937. A large man, with a powerful voice and powerful emotions, Larkin has been called 'lion-hearted and erratic'. *The Times'* obituary remarked that 'of late he had not been much in the public eye'. JAC

Larkin, Philip (1922–85). Poet, librarian, novelist, and, it has been said, 'unofficial laureate of post-1945 England'. Wartime Oxford prompted his first novel, *Jill* (1946), but the early poetry was strongly influenced by *Yeats and *Auden. The discovery of *Hardy's poems helped him find his own distinctive voice, first heard in *The Less Deceived* (1956). Though an admirer of *Lawrence, he had little time for modernism, 'whether perpetrated by Parker, Pound or Picasso', and his taste in jazz drew the line at 1945. With the responsibility for a large university library at Hull, writing was pushed to the margins and only two more collections followed: *The Whitsun Weddings* (1964) and *High Windows* (1974). A reclusive figure, he alternated between self-deprecation and self-dislike. Since his death, the letters and biography have perhaps damaged his reputation; if often very funny, he was seldom politically correct. Even so, it is not clear that anyone since the war has written better poems. JNRS

Latimer, Hugh (*c.*1485–1555). Bishop. One of the 'Oxford martyrs', Latimer was also one of the most celebrated and effective preachers of the Tudor church in the early years of the Reformation. The son of a Leicestershire yeoman, he was educated at Cambridge, ordained priest, and in 1522 licensed as one of the university's preachers. Some time between then and 1525 he came under the influence of reforming ideas, reputedly through contact with Thomas Bilney. Inhibited from preaching by the bishop of Ely, Latimer regained his licence on appeal to Cardinal *Wolsey. He briefly preached at court around 1530, then moved to a Wiltshire living, where his preaching was once again censured in 1532. In 1535, after the break with Rome, he was appointed bishop of Worcester. As bishop he demonstrated the concern for the poor and the skill in humorous invective for which he was later well known. He resigned his see in 1539 in protest against the Act of *Six Articles and was twice imprisoned in the 1540s. On Edward VI's accession he was released, resuming his career of energetic and fashionable preaching. His sermon 'Of the Plough', preached at Paul's Cross in 1548, contains a classic combination of practical theology with social insights and concerns. On Mary I's accession he was summoned to London, declining opportunities to escape into exile. He confronted catholic spokesmen in the Oxford disputation of April 1554; after two examinations for heresy in 1555, in which he refused to submit to catholic teachings on the real presence and the sacrifice of the mass, he was burned at Oxford on 16 October 1555, alongside the former bishop of London, Nicholas *Ridley. Less a theologian than a preacher and communicator, he did more than most to instil practical protestantism in the minds of those lay people who stood by it in the reign of Mary Tudor and thereafter. EC

Latin America, relations with. English activities in Latin America began in 1562–8 when Sir John *Hawkins carried three cargoes of slaves from Africa to Spanish possessions in the New World. The third of these voyages precipitated a series of clashes with Spanish forces, sometimes authorized by London and sometimes not, as the English battled for trade and gold. Charles II's commercial treaty with Spain in 1667 finally placed English trade with the colonies on a better footing—although English merchants remained far from satisfied. The treaty of *Utrecht (1713) officially opened the colonies to British slave traders, but further incidents led to the so-called 'War of *Jenkins's Ear' in 1739. Spain's alliance with Napoleon tempted the British to try to seize Buenos Aires in 1806–7. They failed, but Napoleon's intervention in Spain in 1808 was followed by growing unrest in Spain's

American colonies. The British tried to strike a balance between the colonists and those Spanish elements which were allied with them against Napoleon in the Peninsula. Later, as Spain's hold on its American colonies weakened, the British, eager to build up their trade and to ensure that the USA did not acquire too much influence and esteem, moved towards *de facto* and finally *de jure* recognition in the 1820s. The new states themselves recognized that the British navy was their best defence (rather than the Monroe doctrine) whenever there were suggestions that other European powers might be disposed to assist Spain to recover her colonies.

Britain retained her leading role in trade and investment in much of Latin America until the First World War. Meanwhile *Canning in the early 1820s had assisted in the peaceful separation of Brazil from Portuguese colonial rule. Anglo-American rivalry persisted mostly in central America, partly because of British interest in the Mosquito Shore, and partly because both were interested in any project to build a trans-isthmian canal. Their relations were eased in part by the Clayton–Bulwer treaty of 1850 and further negotiations in 1856–60. Later in the century the British were forced to recognize that the balance of power was shifting decisively in favour of the USA. They were rudely reminded of this by US intervention in 1895 in a British frontier dispute with Venezuela. The Hay–Pauncefote treaty of 1901 yielded control of any canal to the USA. But later British retreats and concessions to the Americans did not prevent friction between London and Washington as, for instance, on policy towards Fidel Castro's Cuba in the 1960s. On the other hand, the USA, after some hesitation, supported the British in the war to recover the *Falkland Islands after their seizure by Argentina in 1982. Sovereignty over the islands had been in dispute with Argentina since 1833. CJB

latitudinarianism was a reaction against the theological controversies and civil wars of the 17th cent. It drew upon the ideas of Cudworth and the Cambridge Platonists, placing little emphasis on precise points of doctrine and arguing for toleration. The spirit was evident soon after the Restoration, with *Pepys noting in 1669 that Dr *Wilkins, bishop of Chester, was 'a mighty, rising man, as being a Latitudinarian'. *Tillotson, archbishop of Canterbury after the Glorious Revolution, preached a celebrated sermon on 'His commandments are not grievous.' Their high-church opponents retorted that tolerance could slide into deism, as it did with *Locke, or into downright indifference, their charge against *Hoadly. Latitudinarianism has often been seen as the prevailing characteristic of the Hanoverian church. But there were powerful counter-currents, and *methodism and *evangelicalism, while agreeing to avoid doctrinal disputes, laid great emphasis on Christianity as a profound spiritual experience. JAC

Laud, William (1573–1645). Archbishop of Canterbury. Laud has always been a controversial character. Born at Reading, a graduate of St John's College, Oxford (1594), he was successively chaplain to the earl of Devonshire (1603), president of St John's (1611–21), dean of Gloucester (1616), bishop of St Davids (1621–6), Bath and Wells (1626–8), and London (1628–33), and archbishop (1633–45). Traditionally, but incorrectly, historians have regarded his use of the Court of *High Commission and especially his supposed attempt to enforce the English Prayer Book on Scotland (1637) as the watershed of the reign. Impeached by the *Long Parliament (December 1640), committed to the Tower (1641), and tried (1644), Laud was beheaded on 10 January 1645. Past historians have evaluated him either as a secret papist who corrupted the church or as the martyr of true Anglicanism. One recent historian described him as 'the greatest calamity ever visited upon the Church of England', and another as 'an ayatollah of rigid theological views and liturgical preferences', who intensified suspicions that arminianism was popish so powerfully that civil war was inevitable. Modern research, however, based on his own writings reveals a different picture; Laud aimed not to provoke, but to heal, controversy. Not a theologian, he was unconcerned by doctrinal minutiae; far from encouraging popery his one known theological work was a stout defence of the church against catholicism. His diary (17 August 1633) records that he 'would not suffer [reconciliation] till Rome were other than it is'. The church was the community of the 'commonweal', within whose compromises calvinism and arminianism could coexist without schism. Thus he aimed to promote unity and uniformity of worship, as enshrined in the Elizabethan settlement (1559), requesting decency of worship and restoration of decayed churches. This required reactivation of emasculated episcopal authority, a return to the 1559 situation which seemed so novel in 1630 that it was vilified by puritans. By emphasizing the differences in the three kingdoms, Charles blew apart the Jacobean compromise which relied on the ambiguity and flexibility of the Elizabethan settlement. Charles's use of the royal prerogative to impose new canons and the Prayer Book on Scotland was unwise and probably unconstitutional; Laud saw the dangers. The Scottish Prayer Book, revised without ambiguities, was not the work of Laud, but of the Scottish bishops, backed by Charles. Laud enforced arminianism neither through the High Commission nor through influencing Oxford to create an arminian clergy. He stoutly supported the Anglican church as the purified form of traditional catholicism. If the altar controversy bulked large to Charles, to Laud it was a matter of 'indifference'. Though tolerant himself over doctrine, his rigorous drive for liturgical uniformity was his undoing. At Oxford he is gratefully remembered for establishing chairs of Hebrew and Arabic, for university reform, and for his large MS donation to the Bodleian library. WMM

Laudabiliter, *c.*1155–60. The authenticity of this papal bull, granted by Adrian IV and recognizing Henry II as lord of Ireland, has been much debated. 'Laudably and profitably does your magnificence contemplate extending your glorious name on earth . . .' The balance of scholarly opinion finds in its favour, but there is, in any case, little doubt that the papacy supported Henry's pretensions. Alexander III, Adrian's successor, praised Henry's attempt to subjugate 'this barbarous and uncouth race which is ignorant of divine law'. JAC

Lauder, Sir Harry (1870–1950). Entertainer. A genial if thrifty Lowland Scot, initially a miner, Lauder progressed from amateur concerts to travelling concert parties and small music-halls before appearing at Birkenhead (near Liverpool) as an Irish comedian. Risking Scottish songs in London (1900), he soon became one of vaudeville's greatest box-office attractions, toured successfully in America and the empire, and tirelessly entertained the troops in both world wars (earning a knighthood, 1919). 'The Laird of the Halls' interspersed songs with patter, drawing on traditional airs to produce simple attractive lilts ('I love a lassie'), and could carry his audience easily from trifles to more serious ballads. Lauder's exploitation of 'quaint old Caledonia' which prompted a nostalgic glow in expatriates was resented by young nationalists in later years, but in the Second World War he was president of the Scottish Regional Committee of ENSA. ASH

Lauderdale, John Maitland, 2nd earl of [S] (1616–82). Born to a Lowland territorial base, Lauderdale subscribed to the Scottish National *Covenant in 1638 and usually adhered to the nationalist and monarchic persuasions which underlay it. His record through the Civil War—he was prominent in negotiating the *'Engagement' with Charles I in December 1647 and in persuading Charles II to go to Scotland in 1650—demonstrated Lauderdale's Scottish royalism; and he suffered imprisonment in England and severe material loss during the Republic. His strangely enduring hold upon Charles II ensured a dominant role in Scottish government throughout the 1660s and 1670s, earning him the fear and detestation of compatriots. But he could never bring the king round to an absolutist-structured government in Scotland through which England might be coerced. Elevated to a dukedom and the Garter in 1672, Lauderdale's second marriage to his paramour the countess of Dysart saw his insolence, avariciousness, and brutality freed from all inhibition. Yet this unattractive couple were discerning patrons of the arts, and Lauderdale's formidable learning was never contested. DDA

Lauffeld, battle of, 1747. After subduing the Jacobites in 1746, William, duke of *Cumberland, was placed in charge of an allied army in the Low Countries, commanding English, Hanoverian, Dutch, and Austrian troops. On 2 July 1747 he was attacked at Lauffeld, just west of Maastricht, by a large French army under Marshal de Saxe. After heavy fighting, Cumberland was forced to retreat but a brilliant cavalry charge by Sir John Ligonier enabled him to do so in good order, and the French losses were heavier. Peace negotiations to conclude the War of the *Austrian Succession began soon afterwards. JAC

Laurentius (Lawrence) (d. 619). Second archbishop of Canterbury. Named Lawrence 'the priest', he landed in Kent with *Augustine in 597. At Augustine's request he returned to Rome (601) with 'Peter the monk' to fetch a new body of missionaries and the pallium, the archiepiscopal insignia, for Augustine. Before his death Augustine consecrated him as his successor (*c.*604). Presumably he was not recognized at Rome, for he never received the pallium, but he worked closely with his fellow-bishops *Mellitus and *Justus. Little is known of his episcopate, but he tried unsuccessfully to bring the Celtic church into conformity, the Irish bishop, Dagan, being especially hostile. Lawrence completed and consecrated the monastery of SS Peter and Paul (613), founded by Augustine. When *Æthelbert of Kent died (616), there was likelihood of reversion to paganism under Eadbald, but, unlike Mellitus and Justus, Laurentius stayed and converted him. WMM

Lausanne conference, November 1922–July 1923. The conference was held to negotiate a treaty with Turkey to replace the unratified and disputed treaty of Sèvres (1920) imposed following the First World War. Turkey renounced all claims to territories of the former Ottoman empire occupied by non-Turks but recovered eastern Thrace in Europe. Freedom of navigation in the Straits was assured and the demilitarized zones of the Dardanelles confirmed. The question of minorities was resolved by an exchange of populations. Over 1 million Christian Greeks were expelled from Turkey and 350,000 Muslim Turks returned from Greece. The Lausanne treaty was signed on 24 July 1923. RAS

Law, Andrew Bonar (1858–1923). Prime minister. Described on his death as the 'Unknown Prime Minister', Bonar Law was a modest and melancholy figure, who appeared content to remain as second in command to *Lloyd George from 1916 to 1921. The first Tory leader to be indubitably bourgeois and provincial, he made no attempt to play the usual role of a party leader; he had no country house, avoided entertaining, and took no pleasure in food and drink. Even *Asquith professed disdain for the 'gilded tradesman' who 'has the mind of a Glasgow Baillie'. Law in fact represented a half-way stage in the evolution of the modern Conservative Party. Politically, his identification with the cause of Ulster and the Union with Ireland made him a Victorian survival, but in social terms he proved to be the harbinger of the middle-class men who dominated the 20th-cent. leadership.

Law's Ulster-Scottish parentage and stern presbyterian upbringing reinforced his rather dour personality. He joined the family ironmasters' business in Glasgow and worked for the Clydesdale Bank. This meant that as an MP from 1900 onwards he possessed—unusually—a personal understanding of business. His excellent memory and aggressive style soon made him a useful orator at a time when tariff reform was becoming central to the party's policy.

But Law did not appear to be heading for the top until, after *Balfour's enforced resignation in 1911, the Tory Party split evenly between Walter *Long and Austen *Chamberlain. Energetically promoted by Max Aitken (*Beaverbrook), Law emerged as a compromise candidate, acceptable to the protectionists but also loyal enough to the party for the traditionalists. 'The fools have stumbled on the right man by accident,' commented Lloyd George. Certainly Law's sharp House of Commons style seemed an improvement on Balfour's ambiguities, and the party's morale rose. However, he was a weak leader because he had almost no experience of government, enjoyed few powers of patronage, and led a party subject to bitter divisions over tariffs. As a result he encouraged his own extremists to pursue their attack on *Irish Home Rule in the belief that this was best calculated to restore party unity. In this he lent respectability to violent resistance to the government's Home Rule Bill.

While the outbreak of war in August 1914 resolved one dilemma, it created another. Law found himself under pressure both to maintain the party truce and to follow his backbenchers and the press in attacking the Liberals' conduct of the war. In May 1915 he partly resolved the problem by a private agreement with Asquith to join a coalition. Remarkably Law failed to insist on a major position for himself and accepted the Colonial Office. Before long the ubiquitous Aitken had involved him in collaboration with Lloyd George, and in December 1916 they presented Asquith with proposals for the reorganization of the machinery of war. When this led to Asquith's resignation, Law had an opportunity to seize the premiership. But he felt that he would have neither a parliamentary majority nor sufficient support in the country. Instead he served under Lloyd George as chancellor and member of the war cabinet. A remarkable period of co-operation ensued. The two men shared a modest social background, but very different temperaments; the dour, industrious Law was the perfect foil for the prime minister's brilliant, mercurial personality. As leader of the House he played a vital role in keeping the coalition majority intact.

In 1918 Law judged that the Conservatives' best interests lay in keeping the coalition in being and fighting the election under Lloyd George's leadership. Eventually ill-health forced him to retire in March 1921. However, by this time many Conservatives were restless, and at a meeting in October 1922 they voted to sever relations with Lloyd George. Law played a crucial role in this simply by indicating his willingness to return as party leader. As a result he succeeded at last to the premiership and won an immediate general election. Though obliged by poor health to withdraw after a few months, he had the satisfaction of having guided his party through a dangerous period and detached it from Lloyd George before it suffered serious damage. MDP

law, development of. Every society develops rules of law which govern it and its members. Legal rules are different from purely moral rules or rules of etiquette in that they carry within them the authority of the community. The distinction may be made between criminal laws, which deal with the prevention of conduct contrary to and unacceptable to the community—transgression of which will lead to retribution—and civil law, which is concerned with the solving, through courts or similar tribunals, of disputes between individuals. In some societies there may be little distinction between criminal and civil law (e.g. in Anglo-Saxon England where murder, rape, or robbery would result in a payment being made to the injured person or their kin).

The way in which law develops and the meaning of the very term 'law' have been the subject of philosophical discussion and historical analysis for many centuries and the science or subject of jurisprudence is devoted to such discussions. Customary law develops in most societies and may be written down in codes or superseded by them.

The great legal codes of the world, dating back to the laws of Hammurabi, the ruler of Babylonia in 2000 BC, have been an important source of law. Other famous lawmakers have been Draco, Lycurgas, Manu, Moses, Muhammad, and Solon of Athens. One of the most famous and far-reaching systems of law was Roman law, one of the most admirable and important features of the Roman state, and also one precious legacy which Rome the colonizer gave to the peoples whom it conquered. Roman law, contained especially in the *Institutes* of Gaius and Justinian, modified and interpreted by the medieval scholars of Europe, has provided the basis for the laws of most European countries as far as the shores of the eastern Mediterranean.

In England, however, despite the Roman conquest, little Roman influence remained after they left Britain, and during the period known as 'the Dark Ages' such law as existed in England was apparently customary. The invasions of Germanic peoples brought strong traditions of customary law to these shores. Under the Anglo-Saxon and Danish kings of England these customs were recognized, declared, and enforced in local assemblies such as the shire court. The unification of the several Anglo-Saxon kingdoms into a unitary state brought about a synthesis of many of these legal customs, often confirmed by 'Dooms' or codes of law declared by the kings, usually with the advice of the leaders of the Christian church in England. After the Danish conquest of parts of England, especially of the east and north-east, separate laws of Danish origin were recognized in these regions—known by the collective name of 'the *Danelaw'.

In 1066 William the Conqueror promised the English people that he would preserve 'the laws of Edward the Confessor' and apart from the introduction of a new and strict system of feudal landholding he did not change the laws of the English. However the combination of this new brand of 'military feudalism', the centralization of power and government, and the development of the king's *curia regis led to the development of royal justice and hence of the common law, which gradually unified and through the decisions of the courts built up a body of laws common to all the kingdom, including Wales, after its conquest by Edward I.

English law continued to develop, primarily through the decisions of the courts, modified or altered by Parliament, which is ultimately sovereign and can change or repeal any rule of common law. Increasingly, in the 19th and 20th cents., the law is made by Parliament in the form of Acts of Parliament or subordinate legislation. MM

Law, Edward, 1st Baron Ellenborough (1750–1818). Lawyer. Law was called to the bar in 1780 and practised successfully on the northern circuit. He was leading defence counsel in the impeachment of Warren *Hastings and through his success acquired a lucrative London practice. In 1793–4 he acted as counsel for the crown in the 'treason trials' of prominent radicals. He accepted office as attorney-general under *Addington and entered Parliament in 1801, becoming lord chief justice of Common Pleas a year later. He spoke forcefully in the Lords and in 1806 he was brought into the cabinet to strengthen Addington's numbers, but the appointment was objected to on the grounds that it violated the independence of the judiciary. He presided over several important political trials and led the opposition in the Lords to criminal law reform. The collapse of his health obliged him to resign from the bench in November 1818 and he died a month later. He was 'a remorseless cross-examiner', too severe and intolerant to be popular, but in private an entertaining table companion. EAS

Law, Edward, 1st earl of Ellenborough (1790–1871). Law succeeded his father, a distinguished lord chief justice and 1st baron, in 1818. Elected to Parliament in 1813 as a Tory, he had a long and varied political career. He held the privy seal in *Wellington's government 1828–9; was president of the Board of Control for India 1828–30, and on three later occasions for short periods; governor-general of India 1841–4; and 1st lord of the Admiralty in 1846. He was raised to the earldom in 1844 when he returned from India. His term of office as governor-general was dominated by the first *China War, the winding-up of the ill-fated *Afghan campaign, and the annexation of Sind. A forceful and effective speaker, Ellenborough was thought to be extravagant, theatrical, and overbearing, and his career in office ended in 1858 during *Derby's ministry when, as president of the Board of Control, he dispatched an indiscreet letter censuring the governor-general, Lord *Canning, and was forced to resign. JAC

Law, John (1671–1729). Law, a Scottish financial genius, banker, and gambler, believed that an increase in the quantity of money would stimulate production. In 1716 the French regent gave him permission to set up his own bank in France, which was suffering from Louis XIV's wars and deeply in debt. Law issued paper money, lent both to the state and to private entrepreneurs, business revived, and industry expanded. In 1719 his Mississippi Company absorbed other trading companies and gained the monopoly of all French overseas trade. Its stock was placed on the market, demand was high, prices soared, speculators made fortunes. In the mean time Law had become director-general of the Banque Royale (previously his Banque Générale) and issued paper notes, in ever-increasing amounts, to match the share issues of the company. The proceeds of the sales of stock, however, went not to develop the company, but as loans to the government, which spent them. Recipients of this money bought more stocks, the government received more money, paid it out, and so on. Holders of paper money began exchanging it for coin, of which there was insufficient to redeem all paper; a decree to halve the notes' value led to loss of confidence, panic, and crash (1720). Law fled and spent the remaining years of his life in England and Italy, where he died. Galbraith called him 'perhaps the most innovative financial scoundrel of all time'. MW

Law, William (1686–1761). Law was one of the most influential religious writers of his age. He came from a modest family at King's Cliffe, near Stamford, and was elected to a fellowship at Emmanuel College, Cambridge. But in 1714 he refused to take the oaths of loyalty to George I and was deprived of his fellowship. He then became tutor to *Gibbon's father. His most famous work, *A Serious Call to a Devout and Holy Life*, came out in 1728 and preached a quiet and meditative Christianity, restrained, humble, and charitable. *Johnson spoke of the great effect it had upon him as a student and *Wesley and *Whitefield were also much influenced. In 1732 he published *The Case of Reason*, arguing faith against deistical scepticism. From 1740 he established at King's Cliffe a devout household, including the widow of Archibald Hutcheson, MP, and Gibbon's aunt Hester. Most of their income went on schools, almshouses, and the poor, and their charity attracted so many beggars that there was bad feeling in the village. When Miss Gibbon died in 1790 at the age of 84, her nephew wrote, disrespectfully: 'aunt Hester is gone to sing Hallelujahs, a glory she did not seem very impatient to possess. I received the news of this dire event with much philosophic composure.' JAC

lawn tennis evolved from real (royal) tennis in the 1870s. Among the pioneers was Major Walter Wingfield who introduced Christmas guests in 1873 to Sphairistike, which contained the ingredients of tennis, though with a narrow net. The MCC tried to draw up standard rules in 1875 and championships were first staged at Wimbledon in 1877, the crowd at the final numbering 200. The scoring system, which is of crucial importance, probably derived from clock quarters. The game's remarkable popularity was partly due to the fact that it could be played by women, and mixed doubles were soon established. The Lawn Tennis Association was formed in 1888 and the sport was included in the Olympics as early as 1896. It has since been played on a variety of surfaces, including clay, sand, and asphalt. JAC

Lawrence, D. H. (1885–1930). Nottinghamshire miner's son destined for notoriety as the author of *Lady Chatterley's Lover* (1928). His autobiographical *Sons and Lovers* (1913) sketches the background and the Oedipal tensions from which he escaped, a scholarship boy, first to London and then the continent. With him went Frieda von Richthofen, their early struggles recorded in his poem sequence *Look! We Have Come Through!* (1917). He had found his true subject, the relationship between men and women, and he wrote 'to make English folk alter and have more sense'. The frankness of his approach led to prosecution of *The Rainbow* (1915), and the war years were a time of trial, though he was unfit for military service. Even so, *Women in Love* (1920) rivals Joyce's *Ulysses* as the greatest novel of the century. His subsequent wanderings took him as far as Australia and New Mexico in search of better health and the ideal society, but he found neither. JNRS

Lawrence, Sir Henry (1806–57). Soldier. Henry Lawrence was the elder brother of John *Lawrence, later viceroy of India, and younger brother of General Sir George Lawrence. All three made their careers in India. Henry was commissioned in 1822 as a lieutenant in the Bengal artillery, took part in the expedition to Kabul in 1842 after the disastrous retreat, and fought in the *Sikh War of 1846. He was knighted in 1848. From 1849 he administered the Punjab but resigned in 1853 after a disagreement with his brother John. He was moved to Oudh and was in *Lucknow when the Indian mutiny broke out in May 1857. In June Lucknow fell to the mutineers and Lawrence was forced back to the residency. There he was struck by shell-fire and died after two days. His eldest son was given a baronetcy in his honour. The residency was relieved by *Havelock in September 1857. Henry Lawrence, prematurely aged and with a hot temper, was respected as a man of honesty. JAC

Lawrence, John Laird Mair, 1st Baron (1811–79). Lawrence was born in Yorkshire, educated at Haileybury School, and joined the East India Company service in 1830. He achieved celebrity during and after the *Sikh wars (1845–6 and 1848–9) which brought the company possession of the Punjab. As the first commissioner of Jullundur district, he laid the foundations of 'the Punjab school' of administration which identified closely with the interests of the peasantry and sought to preserve traditional forms of society and law. In this, he clashed fiercely both with his brother and fellow Punjab commissioner, Henry, who favoured the Indian aristocracy, and with prevailing government policies which, under Lord *Dalhousie, strongly promoted westernization. However, he proved his point during the 1857 *Indian mutiny when he kept the Punjab 'loyal' and was able to send troops to relieve Delhi. Subsequently, the Punjab became the principal recruiting base for the Indian army and the influence of his 'school' was established. He was viceroy of India from 1864 to 1869, and was given his barony on leaving office. DAW

Lawrence, Sir Thomas (1769–1830). Painter. Lawrence was born in Bristol, the son of an innkeeper, and almost completely self-taught. In 1791 he was elected ARA, made a full academician three years later, and president in 1820. A portrait of Queen Charlotte, painted in 1790, led to enormous success and his appointment as painter to the king on the death of *Reynolds in 1792. Knighted in 1815, three years later he was commissioned by the prince regent to paint the portraits of all the principals involved in the struggle against Napoleon. This group hangs in the Waterloo chamber in Windsor castle. Lawrence made probably the finest collection of old master drawings in England, which he offered to the nation in his will. This was refused and the collection dispersed on his death. Fellow-artist Benjamin *Haydon, less successful, said of him, 'Lawrence . . . was suited to the age, and the age to him. He flattered its vanities, pampered its weaknesses, and met its meretricious taste.' JC

Lawrence, T. E. (1888–1935), generally known as 'Lawrence of Arabia'. Born in north Wales of Anglo-Irish stock, educated at Oxford High School and Jesus College, Oxford, Lawrence's interest in medieval military architecture led to a travelling fellowship to excavate in the Middle East, enabling familiarization with its language and people. In 1914 his rare expertise in Arab affairs resulted in intelligence work in Egypt, where he sought to undermine Germany's ally Turkey, and met Faisal (later ruler of *Iraq). He was not the only British officer involved in the Arab rebellion, but his guerrilla attacks, particularly on communications (bridges, railways), distracted and contained Turkish troops remarkably effectively. Demobilized as a colonel, he was appointed adviser on Arab affairs to *Churchill in the Colonial Office (1921), and worked on his war memoir *Seven Pillars of Wisdom*. An extremely complex individual, Lawrence then enlisted as a lowly RAF aircraftsman, changing his name to Ross, then Shaw by deed-poll (1927), and spent several years developing high-speed watercraft, before discharge in 1935 and almost immediate death in a motorcycling accident. ASH

Laws of Ecclesiastical Polity, The (1594, 1597, 1648, 1662). Richard *Hooker set out to expound the Anglican philosophy of government, in both civil and spiritual matters. The essence of Anglicanism lay in the state establishment of the Church of England under the supreme authority of the monarch. Hooker's book, the most outstanding work of 16th-cent. political thought written in English—not least because of its beautiful prose—is a classic expression of conservatism, defending the Elizabethan polity as a middle way both between puritanism and papism, and between traditionalism and rationalism. TSG

lead-mining took place in Britain before the Roman invasion and archaeological remains of mining occur in the Mendip Hills in Somerset, Devon, Cornwall, the Pennines, and Wales. Demand for lead grew during the Roman occupation when the metal was used for various purposes including making water-pipes. Lead-mining continued after the Romans left and lead's value was recognized during the Middle Ages when it was used for many purposes such as roofing churches and castles, fixing decorative glass in windows, and in the manufacture of pewterware and paint.

Most lead-mines were located in relatively remote areas which lacked high-value agricultural land. In consequence the value of lead and the skills needed to mine the ores enabled miners to sustain their social independence from the attempts of feudal magnates to control them. Miners secured separate special jurisdictions and regulated their mining activities and social life. These legal privileges remained in being until most of them were superseded by the formation of commercial mining companies during the 16th cent. or later. These organizations became necessary to pay for the equipment needed for extracting ores at greater depths and to meet the costs of installing furnaces making use of water-powered bellows in smelting processes. Capital from outside the lead-mining areas came first during the 16th cent. when lead prices rose as the metal was used more extensively, including for making weapons. Lead-mining intensified during the late 18th cent. as a consequence of increased demand. But mining in Britain became less worthwhile once cheaper supplies of lead from overseas became available and British mining dwindled rapidly in importance after 1850. IJEK

League of Armed Neutrality. The league was founded in 1780 during the American War of Independence to resist Britain's blockade of the rebels. The founding members, Sweden, Denmark, and Russia, were joined by the Dutch, the Holy Roman empire, Prussia, and Portugal. At issue was the right to search neutral vessels and the league retorted by arming convoys. One consequence was war between Holland and the British. A second league was formed in 1800 during the Napoleonic War and included Denmark, Sweden, Russia, and Prussia. The British response was the attack upon the Danish fleet at Copenhagen by Lord *Nelson, and the Russians withdrew after the assassination of Paul I. In January 1801 a maritime convention in St Petersburg attempted to resolve the problems but the right of search continued to cause difficulties for many years.

JAC

League of Nations. The League of Nations was formally established on 10 January 1920 with a permanent headquarters at Geneva. It was very much the brainchild of President Woodrow Wilson, who insisted that it should be included in the peace treaties at the end of the First World War, and supported by the other allied statesmen, notably *Lloyd George, with rather less enthusiasm. There was an assembly, at which all members were represented, and a council which included four permanent members (Britain, France, Italy, and Japan, joined by Germany in 1926) and a number of other members elected by the assembly. It supervised the transfer of German and Turkish colonies to the victorious allies under the *mandate system. As a peace-keeping body, the League suffered from two handicaps which proved insuperable. First, some of the most important world powers were not members: Germany was excluded until 1926, the Bolshevik government in Russia denounced it as a capitalist club and did not join until 1934; worst of all, Wilson failed to persuade the US Senate to ratify the treaty and the most powerful nation of the world was therefore absent. Secondly, the League had no armed force of its own and member states were reluctant to provide troops: it was therefore obliged to rely upon economic sanctions, which were difficult to enforce and slow to take effect.

The League had some modest successes in its early days. Its specialized agencies did much to encourage international co-operation against slavery, drugs, and disease, and the Permanent Court of International Justice, set up by the League in 1920, resolved a number of minor disputes. In December 1925 at *Locarno, Britain, France, Germany, Belgium, and Italy reaffirmed their commitment to peace and accepted their western boundaries, a prelude to Germany's entry into the League in 1926. In 1928 the Kellogg–Briand pact, signed by most powers, announced their aim to repudiate war and settle all disputes peacefully. No more than a declaration, at least the USA was involved. Cynics pointed out that it merely repeated matters to which League members were already fully pledged.

The League's first major test came in 1931 when the Japanese invaded Manchuria. The League retorted with an investigation followed by a condemnation of Japan's violation of the covenant, and the Japanese promptly withdrew from the League in March 1933. A second challenge came in October 1935, when Mussolini's Italy invaded Ethiopia. This time the League did attempt to enforce economic sanctions, though there were vast gaps, particularly oil, and the invasion was completed before sanctions could bite. But, in any case, the rise of Nazi Germany presented a challenge on a far larger scale. Hitler had always made clear his contempt for the League of Nations as a talking shop and a tool for the Versailles victors. He lost no time in withdrawing Germany. The remilitarization of the Rhineland, the Anschluss with Austria, the dismemberment of Czechoslovakia, and the invasion of Poland followed in quick succession, with the League helpless. The council met only once after the outbreak of the Second World War, on 8 April 1946 when it handed over its powers to the new *United Nations. JAC

Leake, treaty of, 1318. The negotiation at Leake, south of Nottingham, on 9 August was yet another round in the struggle to control Edward II. The king and his leading adversary, his cousin *Thomas of Lancaster, agreed to a council and to unite their forces against the Scots. The disastrous campaign of 1319, with its abortive attack upon Berwick, reopened the wounds and led to renewed conflict. Lancaster was executed after his defeat at *Boroughbridge in 1322. JAC

Lear, Edward (1812–88). Artist. Commencing his career as an illustrator for others, particularly of birds, he depicted the earl of Derby's private menagerie at Knowsley in 1832–7, when he entertained his patron's grandchildren with humorous verses, tales, and sketches. These subsequently developed into the engaging books of nonsense for which he is today chiefly remembered, though their word colour and quirkiness is suffused with melancholy. Despite an affinity with children, he remained unmarried, and, owing to his poor health, spent most of his life abroad. Travelling widely in Mediterranean countries, indefatigable and productive, yet remaining careful and accurate, he earned a living as a topographical landscape painter in both water-colour and oils, and published illustrated travel journals. On one visit to England, he gave lessons in drawing to Queen Victoria. He died quietly at San Remo (Italy), where he is buried. ASH

Leeds. The earliest mention of Leeds is in Bede's *Ecclesiastical History* as the region of Loidis in the 7th cent. The derivation of the name is unclear. It is mentioned in *Domesday but not as a place of particular importance. But by 1207 it had been granted a charter by the lord of the manor and it developed with the cloth trade from the 14th cent. onwards, less as a manufacturing centre than as a market for the surrounding villages. A bridge across the Aire is first mentioned in 1384 but may have existed much earlier. Charles I gave Leeds a charter in 1626 and its assessment for ship money in the 1630s suggests a town of importance—£200 as against £520 for York and £140 for Hull. *Cromwell gave the town parliamentary representation but Leeds lost it again at the Restoration and until 1832 had to be content with the influence it exerted in the elections for the county. In 1698 Celia Fiennes found Leeds 'esteemed an excellent town of its bigness in the count(r)y, its manufactures in the woollen cloth, the Yorkshire cloth in which they are all employed, and are esteemed very rich and very proud'. Before *Defoe visited the town in the 1720s, improvements to the rivers Aire and Calder had encouraged export through Hull of cloth and coal: 'large, wealthy and populous' was his comment; 'the cloth market not to be equalled in the world.' Communications were further improved by the opening of the Leeds and Liverpool canal, in stages, between 1770 and 1816. The first railway, in a complex network, was the Leeds to Selby line in 1834, followed by lines to Derby (1840), Manchester (1841), and Thirsk (1849). By 1801 Leeds was the fifth largest provincial town with a population of 53,000 and its prodigious expansion in the 19th cent. took it into fourth place by 1861, having overtaken Bristol. The Kirkgate covered market, opened in 1857, housed Marks's Penny Bazaar in the 1880s—the forerunner of Marks & Spencer's. In the 20th cent., as the cloth trade moved to *Bradford, Leeds diversified, with engineering, chemicals, banking, and services becoming important. The construction of the M1 and M62 motorways in the 1970s, when canals and railways had faded, preserved its importance as a great commercial centre, the crossroads of the north–south and east–west highways. JAC

Leeds, Francis Godolphin Osborne, 5th duke of (1751–99). Leeds was known as Lord Carmarthen till 1790, but sat in the Lords as Baron Osborne from 1776. Carmarthen was a supporter of Lord *North, but shifted to opposition and was punished, in 1780, with dismissal from his lord-lieutenancy (Yorkshire, East Riding). Although reinstated in 1782, he was never a Rockinghamite and supported *Shelburne after Charles *Fox's resignation. Shortage of available talent led to his appointment as foreign secretary under William *Pitt in December 1783. An active, but never illustrious, foreign secretary, Leeds resigned in April 1791, when Pitt refused to back his aggressive policy towards Russia. Thereafter he had little political influence, but suffered occasional delusions of grandeur, as in the summer of 1792, when convinced that he could unite Pitt and Fox by acting as a neutral 1st lord of the Treasury. An embarrassing interview with George III disabused him. This episode confirms contemporary characterizations of him as a vain man, puffed up by an immediate circle of sycophants. DW

Leeds castle, east of Maidstone in Kent, is one of the most spectacular of later medieval fortresses, with three islands in a lake formed by damming the river Len. The castle passed into royal possession in 1272 and Edward I strengthened it considerably in the 1280s. From then until Tudor times it formed part of the queens' dower. It has been heavily restored. Maiden's Tower is Tudor and the main building part of an extensive early 19th-cent. reconstruction. The castle is much used for conferences. JAC

Leeward Islands. The Leeward Islands in the Caribbean form part of the Lesser Antilles, lying to the east of the Dominican republic. They include the *Virgin Islands, *St Kitts and Nevis, *Antigua and Barbuda, *Montserrat, and Guadeloupe. The largest of the islands, Guadeloupe, is a *département* of France. JAC

Legh, Rowland (d. 1543). Bishop. Legh came from Northumberland and was educated at Cambridge. After he had taken holy orders he was fortunate to come under the patronage of two powerful men, *Wolsey and Thomas *Cromwell. He was much employed in the early visitations of monasteries and priories and in negotiations about Henry VIII's divorce. In 1534 he was made bishop of Coventry and Lichfield and a little later was appointed president of the Council in the Marches of Wales. It was a task which he approached with vigour and which preoccupied him for the rest of his life. He survived the fall of Thomas Cromwell in 1540 and died in harness at Shrewsbury. JAC

legions, Roman. See ROMAN LEGIONS.

Le Goulet, peace of, 1200. On Richard I's death in 1199 a struggle over the succession to his lands broke out between King John and his nephew *Arthur of Brittany. Philip II 'Augustus' of France lent Arthur support and invaded Normandy and Maine, but following defections he was obliged to retreat and consider peace. For his part, John needed breathing space to establish himself securely. The two met at Le Goulet (near Vernon, southern Normandy) and sealed a treaty (22 May 1200). Philip recognized John as Richard's successor, receiving his homage, and abandoned Arthur. But John had to pay a heavy price. In particular, he consented to pay the enormous sum of 20,000 marks as relief (succession duty) to Philip as his overlord, something which his predecessors had never agreed to. SL

Leicester (Roman) was the Romano-British *civitas*-capital of Ratae Corieltavorum (formerly Coritanorum). Possibly succeeding a major late Iron Age settlement, there was a brief period of military occupation before the new town started to develop in the late 1st cent. In the reign of *Hadrian a forum/basilica complex was constructed, and slightly later a set of public baths in the *insula* (block) to the east of the forum. Part of the wall dividing the baths from their exercise hall survives today as the Jewry Wall. In the *insula* north of the baths was a *macellum* or covered market. Leicester does not appear to have had the later 2nd-cent. earthwork defences common at other towns of its status; in the 3rd cent. stone walls were built enclosing a roughly square area of about 105 acres. Relatively little is known of the development of private buildings in the town, but in the *insula* north of the forum was a major 2nd-cent. private house with exceptional wall-paintings. There were also shops of this date in the town; 3rd- and 4th-cent. residences and commercial premises have been identified. ASEC

(post-Roman) Next a Mercian town, Leicester became one of the Danish five boroughs until captured by the English in 918. Under the Normans it was a seigneurial town, its lords the earls of Leicester based in the castle (Simon de *Montfort was a benefactor still remembered there). Lordship then passed to the earls and dukes of Lancaster, and in 1399 to the crown: the end of the castle as a ducal residence was a blow to Leicester's prosperity. The town revived through hosiery from the 17th cent. and later through footwear; by 1901 it was the fifteenth largest English town, a city from 1919 and a diocesan see from 1926. More than most industrial cities, it has a very visible past: 'the castle, St Mary and the Newarke, St Nicholas and the Roman baths, and St Martin and the Guildhall are monuments the patriotic citizen of Leicester might proudly take any visitor to' (Pevsner). DMP

Leicester, diocese of. The modern see, created out of the *Peterborough diocese in 1926, comprises Leicestershire without Rutland. The ancient bishopric's origins are obscure. *Theodore intended to establish a Mercian see at Leicester and a bishop, Cuthwine, may have been consecrated in 679. *Wilfrid in his third exile administered the area from 692 to 703 at *Æthelred of Mercia's request. Certainty of the see's existence begins in 737, when it was one of six, planned by *Offa for his projected archbishopric of *Lichfield. But when the 9th-cent. Danish invasions made Leicester untenable, the diocese was moved to *Dorchester (*c.*870), while Leicester became one of the Danish five boroughs. The cathedral is the mainly 15th-cent. parish church of St Martin. WMM

Leicester, Robert Dudley, 1st earl of (*c.*1532–88). Son of John Dudley, duke of *Northumberland, Dudley became one of Elizabeth I's most prominent courtiers. Until his death in 1588, he was master of the queen's horse and a privy counsellor (from or just before 1563); he was created earl in 1564 in part to make him a more acceptable match for Mary, queen of Scots. Following the example of his brother Ambrose, he was appointed general of the English forces in the Netherlands in 1585.

Leicester was a controversial figure. He was involved in his father's plan to crown Lady Jane *Grey and was sentenced to death in January 1554, but pardoned in October of that year. His reputation as Elizabeth's favourite—an aristocratic and arrogant courtier—has been encouraged by historians but contemporaries were also gripped by rumours that the suspicious death of his first wife Amy Robsart was linked with his marriage designs on Elizabeth. In the 'factional' model of Elizabethan politics he has been seen as the rival of *Burghley. Burghley certainly produced in 1566–7 a rather damning list of Leicester's qualities (or lack of them), questioning his knowledge ('meet for a courtier') and reputation ('hated of many'). Leicester's career was probably less conspiratorial. He was certainly part of Elizabeth's new court in November 1558 and was appointed to organize the stables the day after her accession. But Burghley and he collaborated in Privy Council business and, judging from their correspondence, had a fairly easy relationship. Like many of the early Elizabethan councillors, courtiers, and diplomats, who made their names at Cambridge in the 1530s and under Edward VI, Leicester had his own Edwardian connections. As master of the horse he emulated his brother Ambrose, earl of Warwick, who had held the office in 1553. He seems also to have used his religious patronage to benefit Edwin Sandys, bishop of Worcester, and John Aylmer, later bishop of London. His parliamentary influence was considerable and he promoted men to the Commons, as a privy counsellor keen on having 'discreet and wise men' in the House. SA

Leicester House opposition. Leicester House, built in the 1630s, was leased in 1718 by George, prince of Wales, and became a focus of opposition to his father's ministers. Twenty-five years later, his own son *Frederick, prince of Wales, set up in opposition there and, after his death, the tradition was continued by his widow Princess Augusta, and his son, the future George III. Though Leicester House politics was often factious, it was free from the taint of Jacobitism and helped make the concept of opposition acceptable. George III sold Leicester House in 1764 and, after serving as a private museum, it was demolished in 1791. Thomas Pennant described it neatly as 'the pouting place of princes'. JAC

Leicestershire was one of the most regularly shaped shires, with Leicester itself almost exactly in the middle, on the river Soar. The western boundary with Warwickshire ran along the line of *Watling Street, the north-west between Derbyshire and Nottinghamshire was the angle formed by the Soar joining the Trent, and the southern border with Northamptonshire followed the rivers Avon and Welland.

Leicester was not far from the intersection of two great Roman roads, Watling Street and the *Fosse Way. It became an important town of some 2,000–3,000 people, Ratae Corieltavorum, the tribal capital of the *Coritani. In the course of the 6th cent. the area was occupied by Anglo-Saxon settlers. It became part of the kingdom of Mercia in the 7th cent., under the episcopal jurisdiction of Lichfield. *Breedon-on-the-hill, where there are magnificent Saxon carvings, was founded as a monastery about the year 675. For a while there were bishops of Leicester, but the see did not survive the Danish occupation, and when it was recovered was placed under the diocese of Lincoln. Leicester became one of the five boroughs when the Danes overran the region in the late 9th cent., and though it was reconquered by *Æthelfleda on behalf of Mercia in 918, Danish influence remained substantial. The shire was divided into wapentakes rather than hundreds, and many of the place-names—Ingarsby, Scraptoft, and Barkby Thorpe—are of Scandinavian origin. The name Leicester made its appearance in the *Anglo-Saxon Chronicle* for 917 as Ligera ceastre: this has been variously explained, but seems to be the fort of the people of the river Legra—possibly a tributary of the Soar.

Throughout the medieval period, Leicester remained an important town, granted a charter during John's reign. The de *Montfort family in the 13th cent. took its earldom from the shire. *Wyclif, the morning star of the Reformation, was vicar of Lutterworth in the later 14th cent.: in 1428, many years after his death, his bones were dug up as those of a heretic and thrown into the river Swift. Parliament met at Leicester in 1414 and 1426 and it was to Leicester that Richard III summoned his troops in August 1485 before marching out to fight his last battle at Bosworth.

The north-west of the shire around Charnwood Forest was still heavily wooded, but the open country to the east of the Soar was ideal for rearing sheep. Local wool became the basis of a flourishing textile industry, and though the county was rather thinly populated, Loughborough, Melton

Mowbray, Market Harborough, Hinckley, and Ashby de la Zouch developed as small market towns. *Camden, in Elizabeth's reign, described Leicestershire as 'champain country, rich in corn and grain', though he had no great opinion of the inhabitants of Market Harborough, complaining of their 'harsh and ungrateful manner of speech'.

The shire was hotly disputed during the Civil War. Leicester itself was held for Parliament, Ashby and Belvoir for the king, which made for harassing sorties. The royalists achieved almost their last success in May 1645 when *Rupert stormed Leicester and sacked it, but the victory was cancelled by the shattering defeat at *Naseby the following month. The war damaged the Hastings family, which had been predominant, and marked the rise of the Manners at Belvoir, though their county interest was always shared with the country gentlemen.

*Defoe visited the shire in the 1720s and thought the sheep the best in England for wool, and commented that 'the whole county seems to be taken up in country business'. It was still isolated. In Market Bosworth, where Samuel *Johnson spent a few miserable months as a schoolteacher, the inhabitants were said to set their dogs on strangers. But the character of parts of the county began to change in the later 18th cent. Attempts to overcome the liability that the main river, the Soar, was not navigable had been made since the early 17th cent. But improvements in turnpike roads, canals, and then railways fastened the shire into a national network of communications. The Soar navigation, or Loughborough canal, linked Leicester with the Trent and Mersey canal in the 1790s, and was followed by the Oakham canal (1802), the Ashby canal (1804), and the Grand Union (1814) which, with a branch to Market Harborough, linked the county to the Grand Junction near Rugby, and thence to London, Birmingham, and the north. The dramatic reduction in the cost of conveying coal led to the opening of a number of pits in the north-west. The first steam railway was the Leicester to Swannington, largely a mineral line but carrying passengers. At the opening, in May 1832, George *Stephenson drove his *Comet*, whose chimney hit the roof of Glenfield tunnel. The first major link was the Midland Counties railway, which joined the London to Birmingham at Rugby in 1840.

The growth of industry and population in this period was extraordinary. The domestic system of textiles production gave way rapidly to a factory system. Leicester itself, some 17,000 in 1801, was 60,000 by 1861, and 211,000 by 1901: it continues to dominate the shire, with nearly half the population in 1951. Coalville was an almost overnight growth. In 1801 it was not in existence. The opening of the Whitwick colliery in 1824 led to 1,200 people by 1846, 15,000 by 1901, and 25,000 by 1951. Hinckley and Loughborough also grew rapidly. By the local government reorganization of 1972 Leicestershire took over the neighbouring county of Rutland. In 1994 the Banham commission proposed a further reorganization with Rutland to be restored as a separate county and the city of Leicester to be established as a unitary authority. JAC

Leighton, Frederic (1830–96). Painter. Born in Scarborough, the son of a doctor, Leighton studied art in Frankfurt, Rome, and Paris. Talented and personable, he soon had several wealthy patrons. In 1854 Thackeray warned *Millais: 'look to your laurels: there is a young fellow in Rome called Leighton, who will one day be President of the Royal Academy.' The following year he exhibited at the academy *Cimabue's Madonna Carried in Procession through the Streets of Florence*. It was purchased by Queen Victoria: 'Albert was enchanted with it and made me buy it.' Leighton was elected ARA in 1864 and duly made president in 1878. Among his best paintings are a portrait of Sir Richard *Burton (1875) and *The Garden of the Hesperides* (1892). He suffered increasingly from poor health and was given a barony on his death-bed: this unique peerage lasted only one day. Sir Walter Armstrong, writing in the *DNB*, admitted Leighton's technical skill, but observed disparagingly that, as a painter, 'he had nothing particular to say'. JC

Leinster, which takes its name from a people known as the Laigin, was, in the early medieval period, dominated by two dynasties, the Uí Dúnlainge, in the plains of Kildare, and the Uí Chennselaig, whose capital was at Ferns, Co. Wexford. By the time of the Anglo-Norman invasion the latter, who had come to exercise overlordship of the Viking town of *Dublin, were dominant, and were led by *Dermot MacMurrough, who initiated the invasion in an effort to recover his kingship. Dermot's daughter married the leader of the invaders, Strongbow (*Pembroke), who succeeded to Leinster after him, making it the heartland of the new Anglo-Norman colony in Ireland, with Dublin as its capital. Leinster became the most heavily Anglicized part of Ireland, but by the late 13th cent. even the Dublin hinterland was under threat from the resurgent Irish of the Wicklow mountains. In the late medieval period it was dominated by the Anglo-Irish earls of Ormond and Kildare, the latter being masters of the English *Pale. The 16th cent. saw renewed English plantation, notably of Laois and Offaly in the 1550s, though a more widespread transference in landownership to English protestants only followed from *Cromwell's response to the *1641 rebellion. The province, particularly Co. Wexford, was the focus of the failed *1798 rebellion which led to the Act of *Union. SD

leisure may be defined as the amusements, entertainments, and creative pursuits enjoyed by people in their non-working hours. Our modern understanding of leisure is different from the classical ideal of the worthwhile pursuit of the arts by a leisured class freed from the necessity of work. Contrary to its innocuous image, leisure is in fact one of the most controversial and contested areas of British social and cultural history, with a tradition of class-related disputes over how leisure time should be spent and how far it should be controlled.

An underlying ruling-class fear has often been that the boisterous leisure activities of the people might spill over into political riot; witness the frequent banning of early town ball games and similar sports. At the same time, a policy of 'bread and circuses' was a familiar and much-used weapon in the ruling-class armoury for winning the consent of an unruly populace. Organizations sponsored by paternalistic employers, such as *brass bands in north of England towns and workplaces, can be seen as part of this hegemonic strategy; while works outings, holidays, and sports events were often more than just the disinterested acts of generous employers. In reply, the working class would either accept the opportunities on offer—sometimes renegotiated to gain some level of control—or carve out their own areas of leisure, free from ruling-class respectability, such as dog-fighting and badger-baiting.

There is little evidence of a nation-wide 'social control conspiracy' within the ruling class to use leisure as a pressure valve to defuse class tensions. Indeed there were more often conflicts within the ruling class over how to approach the issue of leisure. Some held to the classical ideal that leisure should be used for self-improvement, allowing the working class to educate themselves into their role in society. From this ideology came the Victorian 'rational recreation' movement, encouraging public libraries, *museums, *mechanics' institutes, and 'pleasant Sunday afternoons'.

An alternative element in the ruling class was the entrepreneurs, who saw leisure as a commodity, and the working class as a new mass of consumers to be exploited. Thus much leisure activity in late Victorian times moved from participation to spectator status, with the boom in *music-halls, variety theatres, *pubs, holiday resorts, spectator sports, and the *mass media of press, magazines, and eventually *cinema.

These splits in the ruling class were echoed within the working class. Some adopted the aim of respectability, advocating self-improving leisure, sabbatarianism, teetotalism, and the like—a puritanical streak which became a pillar of the trade union and labour movement. The vast majority of the working class preferred a hedonistic approach, using the increasing leisure time of the 20th cent. (with the spread of paid holidays from work) for the simple, commodified, 'packaged' enjoyments of sport, gambling, holidays, music, dancing, hobbies, and mass media. By the end of the 20th cent. the leisure 'industry' has become one of Britain's economic mainstays. DJA

Leland, John (*c.*1506–52). Leland, a distinguished antiquarian, was born in London, and educated at St Paul's and at Christ's College, Cambridge. He took holy orders, served the duke of Norfolk, and was appointed royal librarian by Henry VIII, composing elegant and complimentary Latin verses. In 1533 he was made king's antiquary and spent much of the next ten years on a remarkable tour of cathedrals and churches. He was particularly concerned at the dispersal of many archives and books by the *dissolution of the monasteries. He was given considerable encouragement and preferment, but became insane before his collections could appear in print. His notes were scattered but were used by John *Stow in his work on London and by William *Camden in his *Britannia* (1586). The *Itinerary* was not published until 1710, when Thomas Hearne produced an edition at Oxford. An ardent patriot, Leland was hostile to papal pretensions and his zeal led him to insist that King *Arthur was far from a legendary figure. The *Itinerary* is in note form and a mine of information rather than a polished work, but Leland made a significant contribution to Tudor scholarship. JAC

Lely, Peter (1618–80). Portrait painter. Born Pieter van der Faes, 'Lely' was a nickname borrowed from his family home at The Hague. He seems to have come to England in the early 1640s as an aspiring landscape artist. His natural enterprise procured him patronage from the Commonwealth government, and by the time of Charles II's restoration Lely enjoyed high repute as a portraitist. Within two years he had become naturalized and in receipt of a royal pension. A wonderfully fluent technician, who moved in virtuosi circles, Lely recorded the worlds of politics and fashion alike, and sometimes revealed undoubted powers of character penetration. Above all he revelled in a sensuous treatment of the human form and of costume, and his popularity obliged him to employ numerous studio assistants to the detriment of his overall output. Lely was knighted in January 1680. DDA

Lennox, Esmé Stewart, 1st duke of [S] (1542–83). Lennox was a comet who blazed across the Scottish sky and was gone. His father was a brother of Matthew Stewart, earl of *Lennox and regent 1570–1. He held the seigniory of Aubigny in France, to which his son succeeded in 1567. In 1579 Lennox arrived in Scotland, an exotic visitor from the court of France, and captivated the 13-year-old James VI with his worldliness and sophistication. He was created earl of Lennox, his uncle resigning the title for him, and in 1581 was promoted to duke. Meanwhile he had announced his conversion to protestantism and brought down the regent, *Morton. It has been presumed that his ulterior motive was the restoration of Mary, queen of Scots, but others have seen him as purely self-seeking. In 1582 James was seized by *Gowrie and other lords in the *Ruthven raid and forced to order Lennox to leave the kingdom. He died shortly afterwards. His young son was brought up in Scotland, given an English peerage as earl of Richmond in 1613, and raised to the dukedom in 1623. JAC

Lennox, Margaret Stewart, countess of (1515–78). The daughter of Lady *Margaret Tudor by her second husband Archibald, earl of *Angus, Lady Margaret was niece to Henry VIII. If Elizabeth was bastardized, the countess was near the throne. In 1544, at St James's, Westminster, she married Matthew, earl of *Lennox, a great-grandson of James II of Scotland. During Mary's reign, as a catholic, the countess was in high favour and given precedence over Elizabeth, who subsequently bore her 'little love and affection': she was chief mourner at Mary's funeral. By 1562 Elizabeth was concerned at her plan to marry her son, Lord *Darnley, to Mary, queen of Scots, and when it was accomplished in 1565, the countess was sent to the Tower. She managed to effect a partial reconciliation but was in trouble again in 1574 when her second son Charles married a daughter of Bess of Hardwick: the queen's suspicions were aroused by the fact that Bess's husband, the earl of *Shrewsbury, was custodian of Mary, queen of Scots. Lady Lennox played for high stakes. According to *Cecil's reports, prophecies at the death of her first infant son declared that a future son would unite the thrones of England and Scotland. In the shape of her grandson James VI and I, Lady Lennox gained a posthumous victory. JAC

Lennox, Matthew Stewart, 13th earl of [S] (1516–71). Lennox succeeded to the earldom at the age of 10 when his father was murdered: his great-grandmother was a daughter of James II of Scotland and his grandfather had been killed at Flodden. Lennox spent some years in France and was hostile to the English interest until Henry VIII gave him his niece Lady Margaret Douglas in marriage in 1544. The double royal connection made him a person of some consequence and he was handsome and personable, but largely under the influence of his wife. After the marriage he was forfeited in Scotland and spent much of his life in England. During Mary's reign, he and his wife, both catholics, were in high favour, but Elizabeth regarded them with suspicion. He was confined to the Tower in 1562 and was again in disgrace after 1565 when his son Lord *Darnley married Mary, queen of Scots. Elizabeth allowed him to return to Scotland but he lost influence after his son was murdered in 1567. In 1570 Elizabeth had him elected regent for his grandson, but took the precaution of keeping the countess in England. Civil war in Scotland ensued and in 1571 he was stabbed in Edinburgh by a partisan of Mary. JAC

Leofric, earl of Mercia (d. 1057). Leofric rose to power in the reign of *Cnut, as one of three great earls involved in governing England. Loyal and temperate, with *Siward, earl of Northumbria, he appears to counterbalance the powerful and ambitious Earl *Godwine of Wessex. In the division over the succession after Cnut's death in 1035, Leofric's proposal of the first son *Harold's regency on behalf of the absent heir *Harthacnut, in Denmark, was a compromise accepted by the *witan, despite Godwine's opposition. In 1051, when Godwine defied Edward the Confessor and raised an army against him, Leofric and Siward supported the king with matching strength, civil war was avoided, and the dispute referred to the witan. Credited with wisdom in secular and religious matters, a number of foundations were enriched by his gifts, not least the monastery and church he built with his famous wife Godgifu (*Godiva). AM

Leslie, Alexander (*c.*1580–1661). Leslie was a good professional soldier, who served for many years with great distinction in the Swedish army and fought alongside Gustav Adolf at Lützen in 1632. When the Scottish presbyterians began armed resistance in 1639, Leslie was placed in command of the covenanting army. In 1640 he brushed aside royalist resistance at *Newburn and occupied Newcastle. During the armed truce before the outbreak of the Civil War, he was created earl of Leven [S] in 1641. He remained at the head of the Scottish forces in alliance with the English Parliament and fought at *Marston Moor. When Charles II, after the execution of his father, reached an understanding with the Scottish presbyterians, Leslie once more commanded their forces, but was badly beaten by *Cromwell at *Dunbar in 1650. Captured in 1651, he spent some time in the Tower of London. Leslie was a competent experienced man with unusual gifts of conciliation and tact. JAC

Leslie, David (*c.*1600–82). Like his namesake Alexander *Leslie, David Leslie also fought alongside Gustav Adolf of Sweden. He returned to Scotland in 1640 to help the covenanters and commanded the Scottish cavalry at *Marston Moor in 1644. He was then recalled to Scotland to deal with *Montrose, whom he defeated at *Philiphaugh in September 1645. When Charles II accepted the covenant in 1650, David Leslie had effective control, under Alexander Leslie, of the Scottish forces resisting *Cromwell, but they were heavily defeated at *Dunbar. Outmanœuvred in the subsequent campaign, he commanded the royalist advance into England, was beaten at *Worcester, and subsequently captured. He remained a prisoner until the Restoration, when he was created Lord Newark [S]. As a commander he was careful and patient rather than inspired. JAC

Lesotho, kingdom of. Former British crown colony of Basutoland. Threatened by the Boers of the *Orange Free State, Mshweshwe, the ruler of the Basuto, sought British protection in 1843 and in 1869 agreed to the annexation of his country. Britain handed the administration of Basutoland to Cape Colony in 1871, but so badly did the colony's government fulfil its obligations that the Basuto rebelled. At the request of Cape Colony, and with the agreement of the Basuto, Britain reluctantly declared the territory to be a crown colony in 1885. Basutoland was administered by its traditional rulers under British supervision until it became independent in 1965. KI

Levant Company. The company, granted a charter by Elizabeth in 1581, had the sole right to trade with the Ottoman empire. A new charter in 1592 increased the number of traders and added Venice to its sphere. It was commonly known as the Turkey Company. The main imports were spices, perfumes, and currants: it exported mainly cloth. Entry into the company was made easier by an Act of 1754 and its charter was finally surrendered in 1825. JAC

Levellers. A popular democratic movement which emerged fully in 1647, though its leading pamphleteers, John *Lilburne, Richard Overton, and William Walwyn, had campaigned earlier for specific rights and reforms. The Levellers' basic principle was that all men and women are born equal, and are rightfully subject to no authority except by agreement and consent. Their so-called 'Large Petition' of March 1647 confronted Parliament with a wide range of grievances, but was burned by the common hangman in May. By then the *New Model Army was defying Parliament's threat to disband it, so the Levellers set about indoctrinating its newly elected agitators. They made some converts, notably Edward Sexby, but most soldiers remained loyal to their commanders. They therefore persuaded six cavalry regiments to adopt new agents or agitators, and through them brought a revolutionary *'Agreement of the People' before the army's general council in the famous *Putney debates. Implying the abolition of monarchy and the House of Lords, the agreement proposed that biennial, popularly elected parliaments should wield supreme authority, subject only to certain 'native rights' such as liberty of conscience and equality before the law, which the sovereign people reserved to themselves. Unwisely, they accompanied their agitation among the soldiery with incitements to mutiny. They suspended their opposition during the second civil war, but when the *Commonwealth was established their leaders (Walwyn excepted) denounced it virulently in *Englands New Chains Discovered* and other tracts. They also raised a new and more serious mutiny in the army. After its suppression they lost coherence as an organized movement, and some of them later intrigued with the royalists against Cromwell's *Protectorate.

The Levellers' claim to be true democrats has been challenged, because they later qualified their demands for manhood suffrage by excluding those who subsisted by alms or worked as servants in a master's household; but this modification was tactical rather than principled. It was their principle, however, to preserve property, and not 'level men's estates'; here they differed from the self-styled True Levellers, or *Diggers. AHW

Lever, William Hesketh, 1st Viscount Leverhulme of the Western Isles (1851–1925). Lever was born in Bolton (Lancs.). A congregationalist, he believed in self-help and free trade. He began work as a grocer. He later established a soap factory and expanded by purchasing firms in the same trade. His marketing strategies included the use of brand names, such as Sunlight, which was packaged and promoted by skilful advertising. In 1890 he founded Port Sunlight, situated on the Cheshire side of the Mersey, to provide well-designed works, housing, and facilities for his employees. His company acquired plantations for supplying raw materials in west Africa, the Belgian Congo, and the Solomon Islands. Efforts to form a soap monopoly were thwarted. In the 20th cent. the firm diversified to produce margarine, broadening its range by taking over Wall's, producers of ice cream and other foods, and establishing Macfisheries to sell the catch of the Western Isles of Scotland. In 1929, after his death, the company merged with the Dutch firm Jurgens to form Unilever. IJEK

Leviathan (1651) was the masterpiece on political philosophy written by Thomas *Hobbes to justify absolute sovereignty. Hobbes held that the greatest threat to human security was the anarchy of the 'State of Nature', and that to avoid that horrific condition, where life was 'solitary, poor, nasty, brutish, and short', men must contract to establish a sovereign power with sufficient authority to enforce laws and maintain order. Hobbes claimed that the recent civil wars in England would never have occurred if men had followed the path of reason and worked out the necessary truths of political obligation. TSG

Lewes, battle of, 1264. In the early hours of 14 May 1264, before sunrise, the army of Simon de *Montfort advanced on Lewes (Sussex), where Henry III's forces lay. Battle was joined between the town walls and some point on the slope, leading up to the ridge of the south downs, beginning half a mile west of the castle. Although outnumbered, Montfort won a complete victory, able through his surprise advance to attack his enemies at a place and time of his choosing. The cause of the provisions of *Oxford was saved and Montfort's protectorate, which lasted until his death at Evesham (1265), established. SL

Lewes, mise of. The mise of Lewes was drawn up between Henry III and Simon de *Montfort following the battle of *Lewes (14 May 1264). No text survives, but it plainly dealt with the surrender of hostages against Henry's good behaviour, the release of prisoners taken by both sides and the establishment of arbitrators. SL

Lewis, C. S. (1898–1963). Lewis was a fellow of Magdalen College, Oxford, from 1925 to 1954, and then took the chair of medieval and Renaissance English at Cambridge until a few months before his death. He was attached to Magdalene College, but his spiritual and literal home remained Oxford and he went there most weekends. Lewis was born in Belfast, the son of a solicitor, was wounded in the First World War, attended University College, Oxford, as a classicist, but made his career in English literature. His most significant scholarly book was *English Literature in the Sixteenth Century* (1954). His influence with the wider public came from broadcasts during the war, from his Christian apologetics *The Problem of Pain* (1940) and *The Screwtape Letters* (1942), and from his heavily allegorical and highly successful Narnia books for children, beginning with *The Lion, the Witch and the Wardrobe* (1950). JAC

Lexington, battle of, 1775. The first serious encounter in the American conflict occurred when General Gage, surveying the drift towards war, dispatched on 18 April a force of 700 men from Boston to Concord, some 20 miles, to recover arms and ammunition. To effect surprise, the troops set off on a night march. Just over half-way, at Lexington, they clashed with a small force of rebel militia. By the time they reached Concord to conduct a search, the Americans were in arms and heavier fighting took place. On the retreat back to Lexington, the British forces were harassed by snipers, but were met in the town by a sizeable relief party under Lord Algernon Percy. They had suffered well over 200 casualties and tasted a new kind of warfare. JAC

Lhuyd, Edward (1660–1709). Scholar. After attending Oswestry Grammar School and Jesus College, Oxford, Lhuyd became under-keeper, and in 1690 keeper, of the newly opened Ashmolean Museum at Oxford. At first his interest was mainly in fossils. But in 1695 he helped Edmund *Gibson with the revised edition of Camden's *Britannia*, contributing 'the whole business of Wales'. A student of Celtic civilization, he learned Cornish and visited Brittany, and in 1707 published by subscription the first volume of a study of the Celtic language. No second volume was called for. His notes on Celtic antiquity were dispersed at his death, though the Irish portions found their way to Trinity College, Dublin. JAC

Libel Act, 1792. Prior to 1792 the jury in a libel case only had power to determine the facts of publication and was not permitted to decide whether the matter in question was libellous—that decision being reserved to the judge. In May

1791 Charles *Fox argued that civil liberty and freedom of debate would be safeguarded by extending the jury's competence to the whole question of libel, whilst reserving to the judge a discretional right to direct the jury in points of law. The measure was not opposed by the prime minister, William *Pitt, and duly became law the following year. DW

Liberal Democrats. British political party founded in 1988 from the merging of the *Social Democratic Party (SDP) and *Liberal Party, following the disappointing performance of the two parties' alliance at the 1987 general election. The tortuous and mismanaged negotiations, the failure to agree on a party name, and the existence of a rump 'continuing SDP' led by David *Owen ensured that the early years of the party were dogged by low opinion poll ratings and bad local, European, and by-election results. The 6.4 per cent vote achieved at the 1989 European election was worse than any Liberal showing since 1959.

The increasing popularity of party leader Paddy Ashdown (especially following television performances during the *Gulf War) enabled the Liberal Democrats to recoup much of the support that had been lost. About 18 per cent voted Liberal Democrat at the 1992 general election. The promise to raise income tax by 1 penny specifically for education was particularly prominent in their 1997 campaign. In general, policies sought compromise between Labour and Tory views, but on issues of constitutional and electoral reform, environment, and European integration the party developed a more radical, distinctive agenda. CNL

Liberal Imperialists were a faction of the Liberal Party around 1900, who disagreed with their leaders' lukewarm line over the *Boer War. Their leaders were *Rosebery, *Grey, and *Haldane. At one time they threatened to secede formally, but did not, partly because of Rosebery's dithering. That was probably fortunate, because once the war was ended they found they had more in common with other Liberals than they thought. All wanted the empire run more benevolently than under the Conservatives. It also meant that they were able to benefit from the Liberals' election landslide victory of 1906, and play their full part in the government that followed. Opponents sometimes shortened their title to 'Limps'. BJP

Liberal League. A political organization within the Liberal Party, founded in February 1902 with Lord *Rosebery as president and including H. H. *Asquith and Sir Edward *Grey among its vice-presidents. Membership included Liberal Imperialist MPs, a number of Fabians, Liberal landowners, imperialistically minded journalists, and nonconformist ministers. Its aims were vague but 'moderate'. It succeeded in retaining within the Liberal Party some who considered leaving it over the party's cautious attitude to the Boer War. The league supported the 'national efficiency' campaign and a 'step-by-step' progression towards Irish Home Rule. It was well represented in the Liberal government of 1905 (though not by its president). Rosebery tried with little success to use the league to oppose that government's policies, including the 1909 budget, and it was dissolved in acrimony in May 1910. HCGM

Liberal Party. Before 1868 the Liberal Party had been an uneasy coalition of Whigs and radicals. The Whigs, led by some of the richest aristocratic magnates in the land, dominated Liberal cabinets and imposed a veto on radical legislation. The broadening of the suffrage in the boroughs in the *Reform Act of 1867 strengthened the radicals and the *Gladstone government of 1868–74 ranks as one of the great reforming administrations of modern times. Whig disquiet grew, especially during the second Gladstone government of 1880–5. There was a slow drift of Whigs to the Conservatives but Gladstone's *Home Rule Bill of 1886 was the catalyst for the realignment of parties which had long been prophesied. The bill saw a mass defection of Whigs, or moderate Liberals, to the Conservatives. Ninety-three Liberal MPs voted against its second reading in June 1886. Many of these rebels were Whigs for whom Home Rule afforded not only an incentive to leave the Liberal Party, but an excuse. The rebels, however, also included a contingent of radicals, led by Joseph *Chamberlain, until then the most prominent and articulate of the radical leaders. Despite the loss of Chamberlain and his closest colleagues, the effect of the schism was to radicalize the Liberal Party: it also fractionalized it.

More important than the Whig secession was the change in the character of radicalism. Until 1868 radicalism was an individualist creed. The mid-century Liberal slogan—'Peace, Retrenchment and Reform'—summed up radical aspirations. Most radicals opposed armaments, belligerence in foreign affairs, and imperial expansion: the reforms they did espouse were political not social—the extension of the franchise, curtailment of the powers of the House of Lords, the equalization of constituency electorates, not factory legislation or the development of social services. The mid-century radicals were conspicuous champions of **laissez-faire*. The radical programme was negative in character. It called for the disestablishment of the Church of England and for the redress of other nonconformist grievances. It sought to limit the power of government and demanded that government should not intervene in economic and social affairs. As late as 1888, Labouchère and *Bradlaugh, two of the most advanced radicals, voted against a measure to provide one half-day holiday for shop assistants. Such legislation, they averred, 'would strike a blow at the self-reliance of the individual'.

After 1868 there was a gradual but major change in the nature of radicalism. Increasingly it was defined in collectivist terms. Radicals, perhaps seeking support from the now partly enfranchised working class, began to address the problems of industrial society. Thus, Joseph Chamberlain, while pressing the cause of disestablishment, as mayor of Birmingham embarked on a major programme of social reform in that city. Nationally, he declared for free and compulsory education and even, at one stage, urged redistributive taxation.

The events of 1886 and the exodus of the Whigs from the party has tended to obscure the significance of the transformation that was taking place. By the 1890s it was largely complete. Radicalism was now collectivist radicalism. It stopped a long way short of socialism but, even if it had no blueprint for a new society, was prepared to use the power of the state in a positive way to help the poorest sections of the nation.

The loss of the stabilizing power of the Whigs, however, meant that the way was open for every minor section of the party—the 'faddists' and 'crotcheteers' as they were called—to invoke their own demands. All parties are institutionalized log-rolls, but the Liberal Party after 1886 set a new standard for factionalism. The Welsh insisted on the disestablishment of the Church of England in Wales; the *temperance lobby on the strictest control of the liquor trade; the coal-miners wanted the eight-hour day; rural Liberals agitated for parish councils and smallholdings.

In the 1890s a new cleavage developed. Individual radicals had been Little Englanders, hostile to the growth of empire and fervent for a pacific foreign policy. The Unionist Party, as the conservatives were now called, became the party of imperialism, of strong defence, and of *realpolitik* abroad. Many Liberals still clung to the anti-imperial prejudices of the past. But after Gladstone gave up the leadership, some of the most prominent Liberals, such as *Rosebery, his successor as prime minister, demanded a reorientation of party attitudes. The Liberal Party must show that it could be trusted with the administration of a great empire. *Liberal Imperialism ranged itself against Little Englandism. *Asquith, *Grey, and *Haldane, all to hold high office in Liberal governments after 1906, were among the leaders of the new organization, the *Liberal League. The onset of the *Boer War dramatized and made more acute the division of the party. Liberal critics of the war were called pro-Boers, and for a time the party seemed irrevocably split. *Campbell-Bannerman, chosen in 1899 because there was no one else, strove to hold Liberals together.

In the end, the mistakes of the Unionists restored the unity of the Liberal Party. The *Education Act of 1902 upset the religious balance achieved by the Liberal Education Act of 1870. Nonconformists were outraged and many of those who had deserted the party in 1886 came back. More important, in 1903, Chamberlain, now one of the leading figures in the Unionist government, repudiated free trade, an article of faith to both parties for over 50 years. A minority of Unionists still believed in free trade: *Balfour, the prime minister, tried to trim by adhering to a qualified *protectionism, but the bulk of the party followed Chamberlain and the tariff reformers, as the protectionists were called. The Education Act and tariff reform healed the rift in the Liberal Party which, in 1906, won a landslide victory.

Liberal hegemony lasted until 1915. During those nine years the party largely completed the unfinished agenda of Victorian radicalism, restricting the powers of the Lords, introducing *Irish Home Rule, and disestablishing the Church of England in Wales. At the same time it looked forward, with the introduction of old-age pensions in 1908, the Trade Boards Act of 1909, and the National Insurance Act of 1911, to the collectivist agenda of the 20th cent.

There were two general elections in 1910, both bound up with the problem of the House of Lords. The Liberals, now led by Asquith, lost their overall majority and their continuance in office depended on the recently founded *Labour Party and on the Irish nationalists. The next few years were a period of bitter political conflict over Irish Home Rule and a dangerous division between the two main parties was averted only by the outbreak of the First World War in 1914. A coalition government under Asquith was formed in 1915; dissatisfaction with Asquith's leadership led to the formation of a new coalition with Asquith's rival, *Lloyd George, as premier. Asquith, still party leader, went into opposition, with the Conservatives and a section of the Liberals following Lloyd George. This alignment was a paradox: Lloyd George had been one of the leaders of the radical wing of the party before the war, while Asquith had been a prominent Liberal Imperialist. At the general election at the end of the war in 1918, Lloyd George and his Liberals allied with the Conservatives against Asquith's independent Liberals and Labour. The election saw a huge increase in the suffrage, with the right to vote given to women over 30 and many more male voters on the register. Many of these new voters may have had no firm party allegiance. The result was a triumph for Lloyd George and a disaster for the Liberals. Even the two wings added together could muster only 170 MPs.

The early post-war years provided the most encouraging backcloth that Labour could have had. Heavy unemployment and other hardships contributed to the unpopularity of the governing coalition which Labour, with more MPs than the Asquithians, could exploit. In 1922 the Conservatives broke with Lloyd George: a purely Conservative government was formed and called an early general election. The Liberals fought as rival sections, sometimes standing against each other. Their combined total fell to 115 while Labour more than doubled its representation to 142. This was a decisive victory, for Labour now became the official opposition in Parliament and henceforth the alternative to the Conservatives. Two years and two elections later, the reshaping of the party system was confirmed. In 1924 the Liberals, though reunited, were reduced to 40 MPs.

The Liberal Party split again in 1930 over the question of supporting the minority Labour government, a split made permanent in 1932 when more than half the party's MPs decided to support the *National Government, under the title of National Liberal. The independent Liberals soldiered on but elected only nineteen MPs at the general election of 1935: after the Second World War the decline continued, in a seemingly inexorable way, until the party was reduced to five MPs in 1957.

There then began the first of the post-war Liberal revivals. Those of 1958 and 1962 soon petered out; but another revival in the early 1970s was followed by a remarkable Liberal performance in the two elections of 1974, when in October, for example, the party polled one-fifth of the votes and elected 13 members. The schism in the Labour Party in 1981 led to the formation of the Liberal-SDP alliance: in 1983 it won 25 per cent of the votes (2 per cent behind Labour) and elected 23 MPs, the best showing for the Liberals since

1929. Strains within the alliance led to a merger of the two parties in 1987 under the name *Liberal Democrats. In policy the party's collectivist borrowings are more evident than its individualist roots: it shares, however, the commitment of 19th-cent. Liberals to constitutional reform and the devolution of power. It, and its predecessor the Liberal Party, has been the most consistently pro-European of all three parties.

The history of the Liberal Party in the 20th cent. illustrates the impact of the 'first past the post' electoral system on small parties. The problem the Liberals have faced, ever since the early 1920s, has been that their support, while substantial, is evenly spread. Never was this so starkly shown as in 1983: Liberal-SDP alliance 25 per cent with 23 seats, Labour 27 per cent with 209 seats. All the learned explanations of Liberal decline fade into nothing when set against the penalties which the electoral formula imposes on evenly spread minority parties. By the mid-1990s, the party's hope of a breakthrough, despite its strong showing in local government, still seemed to depend upon the introduction of proportional representation, or, short of that, a willingness among British electors to buck the electoral system by tactical voting. HB

Cook, C., *A Short History of the Liberal Party, 1900–1988* (3rd edn. Basingstoke, 1989); Douglas, R., *The History of the Liberal Party, 1895–1970* (1971); Searle, G. R., *The Liberal Party: Triumph and Disintegration, 1886–1929* (1992); Vincent, J. R., *The Formation of the British Liberal Party, 1857–68* (Harmondsworth, 1972).

Liberal Unionists The Liberal government's proposal for Irish Home Rule and land reform in 1886 caused substantial opposition within the party and the fall of the government in June 1886. The opponents of Gladstone's Irish settlement, known to themselves as Liberal Unionists, and to other Liberals as Dissentient Liberals, believed Home Rule would lead to separation. They were of three chief sorts: (*a*) Lord Hartington and other Whigs who were important numerically and because of the loss of their money and their numbers in the House of Lords; (*b*) many Liberals in Lowland Scotland and Ulster (those in Ulster forming their own organization) who had become Unionists; (*c*) Joseph *Chamberlain and his group of Birmingham MPs. After the 1886 election, when about 55 Liberal Unionists were elected, and the failure of talks in 1887, several returned to the Liberal Party.

In the 1890s the Liberal Unionists became more closely linked with the Unionists, Chamberlain and *Devonshire (as Hartington had become) entering *Salisbury's government in 1895. They split over tariff reform in the 1900s, some following Chamberlain into protection, others forming, with some Tories, the Unionist Free Food League. The Chamberlain family maintained control of the Liberal Unionist Council. The Liberal Unionists fused with the Conservative Party in 1912 and their members were admitted to the *Carlton Club. HCGM

Lib-Labs were working-class MPs who, whilst prepared to speak out on 'labour' issues, accepted the Liberal whip. In 1874, Thomas Burt (Morpeth) and Alexander Macdonald (Stafford) became the first two such MPs. In constituencies where union members (chiefly miners) predominated, Liberal associations were often coaxed into nominating them, although William Abraham ('Mabon') at Rhondda in 1885 had first to defeat a Liberal employer. That election produced 11 Lib-Labs, but their numbers stagnated thereafter, except at the 1906 'Liberal landslide' when 24 were elected. The appointment of Henry Broadhurst to the 1886 government reflected Gladstone's appreciation of the Lib-Labs' loyalty; however the leadership during the 1890s was frustrated by the reluctance of impoverished local associations to adopt Lib-Lab candidates. The decision of the miners to join the *Labour Party in 1908 dealt a fatal blow to the Lib-Lab creed, notwithstanding the handful of Liberal working-class MPs who persisted until 1918. SC

libraries. Before printing, collections of MS volumes were held in some monasteries and cathedrals, notably at Canterbury, Wearmouth, and Jarrow: the Benedictine rule prescribed reading as one of the duties of a monk. They were largely commentaries on the church fathers and philosophical and legal works and in the later Middle Ages were usually kept in the cloister. Though occasionally loaned to scholars, they could not be generally available. With the foundation of Oxford and Cambridge colleges from the 13th cent. onwards, more collections were started. Thomas Cobham, bishop of Worcester, built a small library at Oxford *c.*1320; Archbishop *Chichele gave 49 books to his new college of All Souls in 1438, and Duke Humphrey of *Gloucester, a great patron of learning, made handsome bequests to the university in the same period. The libraries were small and the books often kept in chests or chained to avoid the need for a librarian: chained libraries are extant at Merton College, Oxford, and in Hereford cathedral. In addition, a few noblemen or ecclesiastics had their own collections—*Richard de Bury, bishop of Durham (d. 1345), and John *Tiptoft, earl of Worcester (d. 1470).

The invention of printing in the 15th cent. allowed the development of modern libraries. A great many MS volumes and books were dispersed at the dissolution of the monasteries (*c.*1540) and, though Archbishop *Parker, Sir Robert Cotton, and Sir Thomas *Bodley recovered some, many perished. The Duke Humphrey library at Oxford was devoid of books and given over to other uses. But the number of scholarly libraries was increasing. Cambridge University library began in a modest fashion, the books kept in chests, but in the 1470s Archbishop *Rotherham endowed a new library building in Old Schools. Edinburgh began collecting a library in the 1580s before the university was established. The Bodleian at Oxford, incorporating the Duke Humphrey, dates from about 1610, and the library of Trinity College, Dublin, is from the same period. The libraries of the Inns of Court date from the mid-16th cent. to the 17th cent. Over the next 200 years, some of the college libraries were rebuilt on a magnificent scale. *Wren's library at Trinity College, Cambridge, by the banks of the Cam, was built between 1676 and 1695: Queen's at Oxford between 1692 and 1695. *Hawksmoor's great Codrington library at All Souls was started in 1715 but not completed until 1751; the Radcliffe library by James *Gibbs opened in 1749; Christ

Church's library took even longer to finish than the Codrington, being begun in 1717 and completed in 1772. The first move towards a national library was the foundation of the *British Museum in 1753, housing the Harleian, Cotton, and Sloane collections and augmented by gifts from George II and George III: Smirke's great classical building was opened in 1847. *Playfair's library for the University of Edinburgh, another splendid piece of cool classicism, was finished in 1837. The Faculty of Advocates library in Edinburgh, dating from the 1680s, had acted as a Scottish national library and was entitled to the privilege of one copy of every book published, under the Copyright Act of 1709. It was not officially transformed into the National Library of Scotland until 1925, and opened its new building in 1956.

These were libraries for scholars and a high proportion of books were still in Latin. There was little provision for ordinary people unless their parish church had a small collection, though many homes had a few prized books. Grantham had a library as early as 1598 and Humphry Chetham left money in 1653 for libraries in Manchester and Bolton. In the course of the 18th cent. the situation began to change. The literacy rate started to rise. Circulating libraries were established in a number of towns, catering for the new novel reader—often a woman. By the end of the century, literary and philosophical societies and *mechanics' institutes were being formed, most of which had libraries attached. Subscription libraries appeared in the 19th cent., the best known being perhaps the London library, founded by Thomas *Carlyle in 1841, exasperated at the service in the British Museum. In 1849 a parliamentary select committee on library provision deplored the low standard, and a cautious Act of 1850 allowed towns of more than 10,000 people to spend a halfpenny rate (raised in 1855 to a penny) on library provisions (though not on books). Winchester, Manchester, Liverpool, Birmingham, and Leeds had all established libraries by 1870. Municipal undertakings were assisted by donations in the late 19th cent. from Andrew *Carnegie, Passmore Edwards, John Rylands, and others. In 1919 a further Act lifted the rate restriction and a county library service, to cope with the rural areas, was begun. The proliferation of universities and colleges from 1860 onwards saw dozens of new libraries established. By the late 20th cent. libraries were focal points in most towns, with particular emphasis on children's sections, and a diversification of activities into lectures, evening classes, and music and video provision. JAC

Licensing Act, 1662. A feature of the Commonwealth period was the unprecedented proliferation of pamphlets and broadsheets. In 1662 Charles II's government moved to curb them, 13 & 14 Car. II c. 33 condemning 'the general licentiousness of the late times', and the 'heretical, schismatical, blasphemous, seditious and treasonable books, pamphlets and papers' which had appeared. Henceforth, publications were to carry the name of printer and author and were to be submitted for approval to a licenser. From 1663 until the Glorious Revolution, the office was held by Sir Roger L'Estrange, who used his powers in favour of the Tory/royalist cause. After 1688 the matter became even more contentious. A Whig licenser, Fraser, was forced to resign: a Tory licenser, Bohun, was dismissed. In 1693 the Act was continued for two years only and in 1695 it was not renewed at all. Macaulay remarked that while the decision owed more to practical objections than to high principle it did 'more for liberty and civilization than the Great Charter or the Bill of Rights'. That is excessive, since many controls continued and Parliament refused to allow the publication of its debates until the 1770s. Nevertheless, within a decade of the Act lapsing, the London and provincial newspaper press had established itself. JAC

Lichfield, diocese of. There were Celtic bishops from 656, but no formal see until *c.*669, owing allegiance to *Lindisfarne, not Canterbury. Though the modern diocese comprises only Staffordshire and north Shropshire, the Mercian see also included Derbyshire and most of Warwickshire. *Theodore of Canterbury nominated *Chad as first bishop (d. 672). Lichfield became briefly (788–803) an archiepiscopal see, while *Offa, as *bretwalda, was in conflict with Canterbury. After the Norman Conquest, the see was nominally moved to *Chester *c.*1075, only to be moved again in 1102 to Coventry abbey. The bishopric had the title 'Coventry and Lichfield', reflecting the continuance of administration in Lichfield despite the see's peregrinations. Serious disputes over episcopal elections ensued between the monastic chapter of Coventry and the secular canons of Lichfield. The creation of the separate Chester diocese in 1541 reduced Lichfield's significance, though the dissolution of Coventry abbey enabled the Lichfield chapter's sole right to elect to be recognized in the reversed title 'Lichfield and Coventry'. In 1836 Coventry came under the *Worcester diocese, further reducing Lichfield's significance. The 12th–13th-cent. cathedral of red sandstone with three spires was badly damaged in the Civil War, restored in the 1660s, and again in the 19th cent. WMM

Lichfield House compact. This was an agreement in the London house of Lord Lichfield on 18 February 1835 between the Whigs, radicals, and Irish to work together in the forthcoming parliamentary session. *Peel's Conservative government, which had been in office only three months, was defeated the following day, and in April Lord *Melbourne formed his second administration. JAC

Lilburne, John (1615–57). Leveller leader. Of minor Durham gentry stock, he was apprenticed to a London clothier. In 1638 he was hauled before *Star Chamber, flogged, pilloried, and imprisoned for distributing illegal anti-episcopal literature. *Cromwell secured his release in 1640, and he rose to lieutenant-colonel in Cromwell's Eastern Association cavalry, but left the service in 1645. Thenceforth he was in and out of prison, offending both Lords and Commons with his voluminous, unlicensed pamphlets and his claims for the rights of free-born Englishmen. Combative, indomitable, and self-dramatizing, he was the leading spirit of the *Leveller movement from 1647 onward, and broke with Cromwell. In 1649 he denounced the newly established

*Commonwealth in *Englands New Chains Discovered*, fostered a serious army mutiny, and publicly demanded Cromwell's impeachment. A London jury acquitted him of treason, but the *Rump banished him in December 1651. He returned without leave in 1653 to a life of captivity, which was eased latterly. He died a quaker. AHW

'Lillibullero', which 'sang a prince out of three kingdoms', was a doggerel ballad, attributed to Lord Wharton, with a tune by *Purcell. It purported to be the native Irish welcoming James II's lord-lieutenant *Tyrconnel in 1687 to 'cut the Englishmen's throats'. The refrain 'Lillibullero' is probably a nonsense-jingle. According to *Burnet, this 'foolish ballad' swept Britain 'the whole army and at last the people, both in the city and country, singing it perpetually'. JAC

Limerick (Luimnech), **diocese of.** The Irish see of Limerick was first named as such at the Council of Raithbressail (1111), though its first bishop Gilli was elected in 1106. As Limerick was originally a Norse settlement and thus important for Anglo-Norman colonization, Gilli had strong contact with *Canterbury, was papal legate for 28 years, and presided over the Council of Raithbressail (1111). Though situated in western Ireland, Limerick's association with Canterbury enabled it to have Anglo-French bishops from the early 13th cent. It is now the seat of both Catholic and Anglican bishops. There are two cathedrals. St Mary's (Anglican) has much 15th-cent. work and a 12th-cent. west doorway. Its oak choir-stalls with misericords are unusual in Ireland. St John's catholic cathedral is 19th cent. WMM

Limerick, treaty of, 1691. The treaty concluded the siege of Limerick and the Jacobite war and was signed on 3 October. The military articles were generous, allowing the besieged army to migrate in French and English ships to join the forces of Louis XIV, thereby securing a French career for *Sarsfield. The civil articles were confirmed by William III. Their intention was to protect former Jacobite officers from confiscation if they remained, and to give catholics the freedom to practise their religion which they had had under Charles II. The first aim was honoured, but did not protect many other catholic landowners. The Irish Parliament, which reluctantly ratified the treaty only in 1697 in a maimed form, later wholly defied its spirit of toleration by passing penal laws. BPL

Limited Liability Act. This legislation was introduced in the United Kingdom in the 1850s and consolidated in an Act of 1862. Prior to this anyone owning a share in a commercial activity was responsible for any debts incurred in the case of bankruptcy without limit and this was an obvious deterrent to potential investors. The legislation limited the extent of this liability to the amount initially invested. But as a restraint on uncontrolled expansion, companies claiming limited liability were required to have 15 per cent of their nominal capital paid up, to have at least 25 shareholders, and to have 25 per cent of the capital fully subscribed. CHL

Linacre, Thomas (*c.*1460–1524). Linacre is believed to have come from Canterbury and was educated at Oxford, where he was elected a fellow of All Souls in 1484. He then went to Italy, graduating as MD from Padua. He returned to Oxford, where his contemporaries included *Grocyn and *Colet, with a fine reputation as a Greek scholar. In 1509 he was appointed physician to Henry VIII. Linacre was largely instrumental in founding the College of Physicians in 1518 and served as its first president. He left funds for the establishment of lectureships in medicine at both Oxford and Cambridge. His last years were spent in holy orders. Linacre College, Oxford, was founded in 1962 as a postgraduate institute. JAC

Lincoln (Roman) was a legionary fortress, then the *colonia* of Lindum, where the river Witham flows east through the ridge of the Lincoln Edge. The earliest known fortress, under the later town, was constructed by *legio IX Hispana* *c.*60, but there may have been earlier military occupation south of the river. In the early 70s *IX Hispana* was replaced by *legio II Adiutrix* which left the fortress in the late 70s, and the *colonia* was probably founded in the 80s. As at Gloucester, the legionary defences, on the hilltop, were maintained and fronted in stone, but at Lincoln the defensive circuit was extended down to the river as earthwork in the later 2nd cent., later fronted in stone. This brought the defended area to *c.*100 acres. The gates, including the surviving Newport Arch, were impressive. The principal public buildings were in the 'upper' *colonia*, including a forum/basilica incorporating the extant Mint Wall, baths supplied by an aqueduct which crossed the Roaring Meg stream on arches, and a sewer system. The evidence of houses, mosaics, sculpture, and burials suggests a considerable degree of prosperity and Mediterranean-style culture. In the 4th cent. Lincoln may have become a provincial capital; a bishop may have attended the Council of Arles in 314. ASEC

(post-Roman) After five centuries of near-desertion Lincoln was revived by the Vikings as a river port. The Normans planted a castle and cathedral in the upper city (the Roman site); the commercial centre spread downhill, where it still is. Lincoln's heyday was the 12th and 13th cents., when it was one of the six largest English towns, with 47 parish churches and a thriving textile industry. Its importance and strategic position made it the scene of decisive civil war battles (1141, 1217) and a second coronation of Henry II (1157). It declined spectacularly in the 14th and 15th cents., a decline which grants of privileges from the crown (culminating in county status in 1409) could not avert. Lincoln revived only modestly as a social centre in the 18th cent. and as an industrial town in the 19th; it has thus been able to preserve much of its historic fabric. Jewels in Lincoln's crown include the cathedral (called by Ruskin 'the most precious piece of architecture in the British Isles'), the only Roman gateway in Britain still used by traffic, and the only medieval bridge in Britain still lined by shops and houses. DMP

Lincoln, battle of, 1141. Stephen, besieging Lincoln castle, held by supporters of *Matilda, the rival claimant to the throne, was himself attacked by a relief force under *Robert, earl of Gloucester, Matilda's half-brother, and Ranulf, earl of Chester, Gloucester's son-in-law. After heavy fighting in the streets on 2 February, Stephen was captured and taken to Bristol for imprisonment. JAC

Lincoln, battle of, 1217. The opponents of King John called in Louis, dauphin of France, to assist them. He continued his campaign in 1217 after John's death. On 20 May 1217 his supporters besieging Lincoln castle were themselves attacked by a relief force under William *Marshal, earl of Pembroke and regent for John's young son Henry III. The comte de la Perche, commanding the French troops, was killed and resistance melted away. The ironic nickname 'The Fair of Lincoln' suggested that the rebels did not fight with undue tenacity. JAC

Lincoln, diocese of. Now merely conterminous with Lincolnshire, this was one of the largest medieval sees, founded *c.*1072. Lincoln itself, originally in the short-lived Anglo-Saxon see of *Lindsey, came under the episcopal oversight successively of *Lichfield, *Leicester, *Dorchester (and for a short while, *Winchester), as pressure from the Danes increased. After the reconquest of the Danelaw (10th cent.) the see of Dorchester extended from the Thames to the Humber. In 1072 it was moved to Lincoln. Though princely secular bishops became the norm, two major exceptions were the saintly *Hugh of Lincoln (1186–1200), canonized in 1220, and Robert *Grosseteste (1235–53), a scholar, ardent reformer, patron of the Franciscans, and friend of Simon de *Montfort. The vast diocese was reduced in size by the creation of the sees of *Ely (1109), *Peterborough (1541), and *Oxford (1542). Nevertheless it continued to have notable incumbents, like Thomas *Tenison (1692–5) and William *Wake (1705–16), future archbishops of Canterbury, and Edmund *Gibson (1716–23), later Walpole's ecclesiastical lieutenant. The saintly Anglo-catholic Edward King (1885–1910) was prosecuted for his 'Romanizing' practices in 1890. The cathedral, begun in 1192 by St Hugh, stands magnificently on its hill, a superb example, the epitome perhaps, of 13th-cent. cathedral-building. WMM

Lincoln, John de la Pole, 1st earl of (*c.*1462–87). Pole's mother was Edward IV's sister Elizabeth: his father, John de la *Pole, 2nd duke of Suffolk. He was given a peerage in his own right at the age of 5 and married a niece of the king. Under Richard III he was in high favour. Though there is no evidence that Richard recognized him as heir after the death of the prince of Wales in 1484, he was next in line if his young cousin *Warwick's claim was disregarded on the grounds that his father *Clarence had been attainted. He served Richard as president of the Council of the North and fought for him at *Bosworth. Lincoln and his father submitted to Henry VII but, with Warwick in the Tower and a boy of 10, he was the strongest Yorkist claimant. In 1487 he suddenly fled the country and returned with an invading force supporting Lambert *Simnel's claim to be Warwick. Lincoln's motives can only be conjectured, but presumably, had the rising succeeded, Simnel would have been pushed aside and Lincoln enthroned. As it was, he was killed at the battle of *Stoke. JAC

Lincoln judgment, 1890. Edward King, bishop of Lincoln, was prosecuted by the Church Association for alleged illegal practices during worship, such as mixing water with sacramental wine and using lighted candles on the holy table. In his judgment, delivered on 21 November, the archbishop of Canterbury supported the bishop and decided not to take the matter further. RAS

Lincolnshire is the second largest English county but one of the most thinly populated. From the Humber in the north, which formed the border with Yorkshire, to the Welland in the south, running through *Stamford, is more than 70 miles. The greater part of the county is flat but there are three parallel north–south ridges. *Lincoln stands at the gap in the western ridge, the Lincolnshire edge, Louth at the gap of the eastern. The northern parts drain into the Humber via the Trent and the Ancholme, the southern into the Wash via the Witham, Glen, and Welland.

At the time of the Roman invasion, the region formed part of the territory of the *Coritani. The Romans established a legionary base and then a *colonia* at Lincoln (Lindum) where the Fosse Way and Ermine Street intersected. The name derives from the Celtic *Linn*, a pool—presumably the Brayford pool—with the suffix *coln*, derived from *colonia*. The Roman north gate survives and is still used by traffic. Caistor was another Roman town of significance, possibly a spa. The Foss dike, a Roman canal, joined the Trent with the Witham.

There were few obstacles to early Saxon settlement except in the south where salt marshes rendered the land impenetrable. *Lindsey, in the northern part, may have formed a subkingdom, disputed between Mercia to the west and Northumbria to the north. *Bede records the evangelizing visit to Lincoln of *Paulinus in the 620s and a diocese of Lindsey was established from 678, though it fell victim to Danish raids in the 9th cent.

From the 870s onwards, the area formed part of the *Danelaw, Lincoln and Stamford being two of the five boroughs. The Danes left a great impression on the area. Many of the place-names are of Danish origin—Grimsby, Saxby, Beckby, Swinthorp. The area was divided into three trithings—Lindsey, Kesteven, and Holland—and the largest, Lindsey, was further divided into three ridings. The smaller divisions known elsewhere as hundreds were in Lincolnshire called wapentakes, the brandishing of arms by assemblies of warriors. The shire itself seems to have been formed after 1016, when the southern divisions of Kesteven and Holland, previously orientated towards the east midlands and East Anglia, were united with Lindsey. The *Domesday survey treated it as one unit.

In 1066 Lincoln was one of the leading towns in the country, with a population of about 5,000. Torksey, at the junction of the Trent and the Foss Dike, Stamford, Grantham, Barton, and Grimsby were also important. Castles were built at Lincoln and Stamford and in 1072 the diocese was transferred from Dorchester to Lincoln. The building of the cathedral began almost at once. The new diocese was enormous and in the 13th cent. Lincoln itself was said to have more than forty churches. Barton did not long retain its importance, partly because the Great North Road diverted to the west from Ermine Street, bypassing the shire completely, partly because *Hull took much of its river traffic.

Boston, however, not mentioned in Domesday, developed rapidly and by 1204 was second only to London in subsidy payment. Lincoln soon complained of the competition, particularly after the wool staple was transferred in 1369. Louth and Sleaford, under the jurisdiction of the bishop, were just outside Lincoln's pull at 26 and 17 miles, and developed as local centres. The main activity of the shire was sheep-rearing on the wolds, cattle on the flatlands, and fishing: reclamation of fenland went on steadily.

In the later Middle Ages a slow decline began. Stamford and Lincoln suffered much from the *Black Death in 1349. Other areas in the west, such as Wiltshire and the Cotswolds, developed their own cloth industries. A number of small harbours suffered from silting up of the coast. The Foss Dike was out of action frequently and Grimsby and Boston each found silting hard to deal with. With the growth of colonies in the New World the whole axis of trade shifted towards western ports. *Camden in 1586 wrote of the county largely in terms of past glories. Torksey was 'now a little mean town, but heretofore very noted': of Lincoln itself ''Tis incredible how much it hath sunk and decayed, under the weight of time and antiquity.'

Tudor and Stuart Lincolnshire was little known or visited—a quiet county of small market towns, left to its own devices. Its participation in the *Pilgrimage of Grace in 1536 provoked Henry VIII to denounce its inhabitants as 'the most brute and beastly of the whole realm'. Celia Fiennes in the 1690s noted that Lincoln's waterways were choked up, and twenty years later *Defoe, while admiring the minster and the countryside, dismissed the town as 'an ancient, ragged, decay'd and still decaying city'—if, indeed, it could be called a city. His crossing of the Humber from Barton, which he shared with fifteen horses and twelve cows, took four hours and made him very sick. Isolation encouraged insularity. Mary Yorke, wife of a dean, remarked in 1769 that 'the people in general of Lincoln have the least curiosity for anything out of their own circle that ever I met with'.

The industrial developments of the 19th cent., while leaving the character of the shire basically unchanged, helped to diversify it. The improvements in transport—turnpikes, canals, railways—helped to knit the shire together but did comparatively little to integrate it with the rest of the nation. The bridge at Gainsborough opened in 1790—the only one north of Newark—improved communications with the north-west. Schemes for a main railway line north through Lincoln came to nothing and in the end the main line followed the Great North Road, almost bypassing the county. But the growth of an agricultural industry brought employment to Lincoln, Gainsborough, and Grantham. Grimsby opened its new dock in 1800 but its spectacular expansion followed the arrival of the railway in 1848, which benefited the fish trade. By 1901 it had overtaken Lincoln as the largest town in the shire. The discovery of iron in the north-west of the county led to the development of a steel industry and the town of Scunthorpe came into existence from a group of small villages: by 1961 it was the third largest town with 67,000 people. Rail transport and the cult of seaside holidays produced Cleethorpes, Skegness, and Mablethorpe with holiday camps and caravan sites. The balance of town and country shifted steadily. In 1801 only 21 per cent of the shire lived in the twelve largest towns; by 1901 it was 34 per cent, by 1931 50 per cent, and by 1961 53 per cent.

The ancient divisions of the shire were acknowledged in 1888 when separate county councils were established for Lindsey (Lincoln), Kesteven (Sleaford), and Holland (Boston). The Local Government Act of 1972 brought them together again but hived off Grimsby, Cleethorpes, Brigg, and their surrounding villages to form the new county of Humberside, which was to be welded together by the Humber bridge, opened to traffic in 1981. Though Humberside was abolished in 1996, the towns were not returned to Lincolnshire, but made into the unitary authorities of North Lincolnshire and North-East Lincolnshire. The Banham commission on local government reported in 1994 in favour of maintaining the existing two-tier system for the rest of the county. JAC

Lindemann, Frederick, 1st Viscount Cherwell (1886–1957). Lindemann is one of the comparatively small band who have combined science and politics. His father came from Alsace but settled in Britain and prospered. Lindemann was educated in Germany, took his doctorate in 1910, and stayed on to do research in low-temperature physics. In 1919 he was elected to a chair at Oxford, reorganized the Clarendon laboratory, and was attached to Wadham College, though living in Christ Church. A strange creature in the aristocratic world which his wealth allowed him to frequent, he was known as 'the Prof.' His experience of flying during the First World War and his friendship with Winston *Churchill led him to an interest in air defence in the 1930s but he was an awkward colleague. When war broke out, Churchill leaned upon his scientific knowledge, got him a barony in 1941, and made him paymaster-general. His report of March 1942 that German morale would collapse if housing in 58 German towns could be destroyed was impeccably argued, coolly scientific, and based on a report of bombing in Hull which had reached totally opposite conclusions. In 1951, when Churchill formed his second administration, the Prof. was promoted viscount and resumed as paymaster until 1953. Confident and overbearing, as a wartime adviser he was a doubtful asset. JAC

Lindisfarne (Holy Island) is a small island off the coast of Northumbria south of Berwick-on-Tweed. It is connected to the mainland by a causeway which is inaccessible at high tide. The island is home to several species of birds, who find the bleak landscape ideal for breeding. It was the seat of sixteen bishops from 635 to 883, the most famous of them being St *Aidan, who was brought from *Iona by *Oswald to Christianize the north, and later St *Cuthbert, who took charge of the Romanized see after the Synod of *Whitby. After the island had been ravaged in the 8th and 9th cents. by Vikings, the religious community removed to seek a new sanctuary, eventually settling at Durham. The priory was rebuilt *c.*1070 but was abandoned *c.*1541 and some of the stones used on the construction of the fort, rebuilt by *Lutyens as a small castle in the 1900s. The island has retained its religious significance and has been the site of many pilgrimages through the centuries. SMD

Lindisfarne, diocese of. The bishopric, originally based on the island monastery founded by *Aidan (*c.*635), became the spiritual springboard of Celtic Christian mission in England. *Cuthbert became bishop in 685, but died in 687. After the island had been sacked twice by the Danes in 793 and 875, the monks fled with Cuthbert's relics and the *Lindisfarne Gospels to *Chester-le-Street and then to *Durham. The see and monastery were not revived. WMM

Lindisfarne Gospels, now British Library, Cotton MS Nero D.iv. A Latin text of the Gospels, with a later Anglo-Saxon translation or gloss, which was made at the monastery of Lindisfarne, in the north-east of England, by Eadfrith, who was bishop of Lindisfarne 698–721. It is an elaborately decorated book. Each Gospel is preceded by three fully decorated pages: an author portrait, a carpet page, and an initial. Matthew's Gospel has a second initial page (1: 18), to mark the beginning of the story of the Incarnation. It is likely that the manuscript was made for the elevation of the relics of St *Cuthbert in 698. The Gospels remained closely associated with the saint during the Middle Ages, travelling with the body to Chester-le-Street and then to Durham. When Cuthbert's shrine was pillaged at the Reformation, the Gospels were taken to London. They became part of Sir Robert Cotton's library and subsequently part of the national collections in the British library. LR

Lindsay of the Mount, Sir David (*c.*1486–1555). The most important Scottish Renaissance poet, Lindsay was extremely popular in the 16th cent. A Fife laird, from 1508 he was a courtier closely associated with the future James V (1513–42), a herald from 1530, and Lyon king-of-arms from 1542. His numerous works deal extensively with the need for good government and religious reform. In *The Testament of the Papyngo* (1530) Lindsay provides moral advice to James V and his court, and attacks clerical abuses. *Ane Satyre of the Thrie Estatis* (1552) calls for the estates to serve the commonweal during the minority of Mary, queen of Scots (1542–67). *The Monarche* (1554) develops earlier calls for religious reform into strong anti-papalism through a description of corruption at the papal court. Such themes make Lindsay an important source for the political, religious, and cultural issues of Renaissance and Reformation Scotland. RJT

Lindsey, diocese of. *Theodore carved this bishopric out of the Northumbrian diocese of *York *c.*677 to serve part of modern Lincolnshire, then an area disputed between Mercia and Northumbria. It collapsed under the Danish invasions *c.*873 and was not revived. The region later came under *Dorchester-on-Thames and then *Lincoln. WMM

Lindsey, kingdom of. Lindsey was one of the smaller kingdoms of early Anglo-Saxon England and its existence must always have been rather precarious. Bordered in the north by the Humber and the east by the North Sea, it followed the Trent in the west, taking in the Isle of Axholme, and the Witham in the south, including Lincoln itself. The name—the island of Lincoln—reflects its character, surrounded by sea, marshes, and fens. A list of the kings of Lindsey has survived, though Stenton called it 'the obscurest of English dynasties'. It starts, conventionally, with Woden and ends with Aldfrith, probably in the 8th cent. In the 7th cent. Lindsey was disputed between Mercia and Northumbria, changed hands repeatedly, and seems to have been more of a subkingdom than an independent state. Converted by Paulinus *c.*630, Lindsey had its own bishopric from 678 which did not survive the Danish invasions of the 9th cent. An area of heavy Scandinavian settlement, it became one of the ridings of the later county of Lincolnshire and was itself divided up into ridings. These divisions lasted and Lindsey was given its own county council in 1888, the county town being Lincoln. JAC

linen. Historically, the linen industry was widespread throughout much of Britain, though the major areas of production were in the north of England, the Scottish Lowlands, and Ireland. Flax cultivation and linen production were of considerable economic importance by the end of the 17th cent., thanks to parliamentary encouragement and to skills and techniques introduced by immigrants from the Low Countries. The industry expanded dramatically during the 18th cent. In Ulster, bounties contributed to the growth of the export trade to the colonies, while in Scotland the Board of Trustees, using capital derived from the Equivalent (union compensation fund), encouraged the industry by giving grants for flax cultivation and processing, as well as enhancing skills in spinning, weaving, and bleaching.

A proto-industrial phase saw the introduction of limited mechanization. Scutching mills, using water-power and operating on the same principle as the threshing-machine, greatly raised productivity in the preparatory stages. The poet Robert *Burns worked in such a mill at Irvine in Ayrshire. Later stages of production, spinning and weaving, were highly labour-intensive domestic activities, co-ordinated by entrepreneurs, whose networks, in many instances, radiated throughout the surrounding countryside from centres like Nottingham, Leeds, Manchester, *Belfast, Glasgow, and *Dundee.

With the adoption of machinery, initially developed for the *cotton industry, spinning became increasingly factory-based and, with greater use of steam-power, more concentrated in urban centres. Technological lags retarded the mechanization of weaving, but when it caught up in the early 19th cent., it led to the demise of hand-loom weaving. Reorganization led to even greater localization around Belfast, Paisley, and Dundee and to increased specialization, with fine linen being produced mainly in Ulster and the west of Scotland, and coarser linen in the east of Scotland. Bleaching, which had become a specialized trade, was also mechanized and became more efficient following the development of chemical bleaching. Belfast became the major centre of production with a large proportion destined for overseas markets. Paisley specialized in fine linen and linen thread, its famous 'Paisley pattern' prints derived from imported Indian designs. A significant spin-off in Dundee was the development of the jute industry, which expanded rapidly during the 19th cent. to create 'Juteopolis', as the city became known.

During the 20th cent. linen, like other textile industries, contracted in the face of foreign competition. Having experienced painful rationalization and modernization following the depression and the Second World War, it continued production on a reduced scale in its long-established locations, most notably in Ulster. ID

Linlithgow, Victor Alexander John Hope, 2nd Marquis (1887–1952). Linlithgow was born in Scotland and educated at Eton. He was a member of the Conservative Party who served at the Admiralty under *Baldwin. His connection with India developed through his chairmanship of the Royal Commission on Agriculture in India (1926–8) and the Select Committee on Indian Constitutional Reform (1930–2). He was appointed viceroy of India in 1936. His period in office witnessed the growth of mass support for the Indian National Congress, the withdrawal of Congress co-operation for the Second World War, and the Quit India movement of 1942. An unbending imperialist without sympathy for the Indian national cause, he exacerbated rather than eased political tensions and showed a strong preference for repression over negotiation. His harsh response to the Quit India movement helped to spread guerrilla resistance to British rule, which harmed the war effort against Japan. He resigned in 1943. DAW

Linlithgow palace (Lothian). Initially a royal manor house beside the loch, and lodging for Edward I who strengthened it (1301–3), it was rebuilt in stone by James I of Scotland after the 1424 fire; the great hall and royal apartments were augmented by his successors to close off the open west side and transform it into a fashionable residence. Birthplace of James V (1512), it remained empty after the death of James IV at Flodden (1513) until the 1530s, when work was resumed reflecting James V's tastes, as at Falkland. Birthplace also of Mary, queen of Scots (1542), and set aside for the queen mother, *Mary of Guise, the palace fell into disrepair after the accession of the infant James VI (1567). The ruinous north range was rebuilt 1618–24 with one of the finest Renaissance façades in Scotland, but was never used by James after his accession to the English throne. Charles I was the last monarch to sleep there (1633), *Cromwell wintered there (1650), while the earl of Linlithgow forfeited his titles and hereditary keepership by supporting the 'old pretender'. Roofless since a bad fire in 1746, it is currently cared for by the Scottish Development Department. ASH

Lister, Joseph (1827–1912). Surgeon and pioneer of antisepsis. Having qualified at London, then teaching at Edinburgh, he was appointed (1860) as regius professor of clinical surgery at Glasgow, where, interested in inflammation and concerned at high hospital mortality from 'septic diseases', he was one of the few to pursue the implications of Pasteur's recent work on fermentation and the beginnings of the germ theory. An open-minded, patient investigator, he laid the foundations of antiseptic management of wounds and surgical intervention, initially using carbolic sprays and gauzes, thereby reducing mortality and revolutionizing hospital practice and the art of surgery. Like most pioneers, he encountered criticism and professional opposition, but recognition led to chairs at Edinburgh and London, honours such as presidency of the *Royal Society, and a barony (1897). His work improved public confidence in both hospitals and surgery, and stimulated the infant science of bacteriology. ASH

literacy, the ability to read and write, is the measure usually taken as a key indicator of a country's economic and social advancement. Efforts by historians to pinpoint the exact level of literacy in Britain at any time have proved notoriously difficult, with estimates requiring further qualification by regional, gender, class, and rural/urban divisions, and by what level of literacy is meant. Estimates for mid-17th-cent. basic literacy, for example, range from 10 to 30 per cent of the population, with differences such as 15–20 per cent in the rural north, against 40–60 per cent in southern urban centres. The gender division is illustrated by one set of figures comparing 1841 and 1870, when a rise in male literacy of 67 per cent to 80 per cent was matched by a female rise from 51 per cent to 73 per cent.

The main early spurs to 'useful literacy' were religious or, later, economic, bringing strong associations with the protestant work ethic and the rise of industrial capitalism, whereby individuals sought literacy for their self-advancement, and capital (and eventually the state) encouraged it to create an educated literate work-force. These needs of the British capitalist nation state made education one of the first areas where the move from **laissez-faire* to intervention became evident. Through providing government assistance to voluntary institutions from the 1830s–1860s, and then intervening directly from 1870 with a series of *Education Acts, the state mopped up most of the last traces of illiteracy.

While the agencies of the state made this undoubted contribution to the rise in literacy through education (serving also, according to the left, to extend a fair degree of 'social control'), the role of working-class self-help should not be ignored. For every paternalistic Society for the Diffusion of Useful Knowledge, there was a working-class equivalent Society for the Diffusion of *Really* Useful Knowledge, challenging the reformist ideologies of the *mechanics' institutes, adult schools, working men's colleges, people's palaces, and religious, scientific, and philosophical societies, with a contrasting co-operative, trade union, chartist, socialist (and latterly Marxist) ideology.

Consequently, some historians have estimated that of the 1840 population—before compulsory state schooling—most adults had some form of education (allowing for class and regional variations), with 75 per cent able to do some reading and 60 per cent some writing. Through the 20th cent., the expansion of the audio-visual media has led to demands for education to concentrate on *visual* literacy as much as its traditional task of ensuring written literacy. DJA

Liverpool, created a borough by royal will (1207) as a convenient place of embarkation for Irish campaigns, fluctuated in prosperity until the early 17th cent. when Irish industries developed and Chester declined (from silting). Of protestant temper, its value as a point of contact between Ireland and the northern royalists accounted for its importance in the Civil War, being twice besieged. Continuing to control the larger share of the Irish trade, Liverpool gained impetus from lucrative commerce with the *plantations (sugar, tobacco, cotton) and the rapid development of Manchester's textile industries. Both legitimate and illegitimate trade with the West Indies and South America enabled gain at the expense of Bristol and London, and led traders into the even more lucrative African traffic. Involvement in the slave trade brought riches and an unsavoury reputation, but the money improved transport and communication with the highly profitable Lancashire industries. When trade with the East Indies and Spanish America was thrown open and the American midwest began to expand, Liverpool's dominance of Atlantic trade and as an emigration port produced a cosmopolitan but overcrowded, unhealthy, politically corrupt, and turbulent city. Systematic attempts to reconstruct led to steady and sustained improvement, growth being accompanied by high levels of immigration (especially from Ireland), and continued establishment of new local industries. Despite extensive reconstruction of the business quarters after severe bomb damage in the Second World War, the subsequent de-industrialization of Liverpool has led to its being better known for its football teams, pop music groups, and comedians, yet it still exerts economic and cultural dominance over the surrounding metropolitan region. ASH

Liverpool, Charles Jenkinson, 1st earl of (1729–1808). Tory politician. Jenkinson was a 'man of business', serving Lord *Bute as private secretary and under-secretary of state, 1761–2, and holding similar second-rank offices through to 1782. He was 'a born bureaucrat, of restricted sympathies . . . rigid in his ideas and authoritarian in his outlook', according to the *History of Parliament*. During Lord *North's administration and particularly throughout the American War of Independence he was believed to be influential 'behind the scenes' and the secret agent of George III in the ministry. He was a close adviser of Lord North and supplied the king with information about the state of the government. He left office on the fall of North but returned under *Pitt in 1784, becoming president of the Board of Trade 1786–1804 and chancellor of the duchy of Lancaster 1786–1803. He was made Lord Hawkesbury in 1791 and promoted earl of Liverpool in 1796. EAS

Liverpool, Robert Banks Jenkinson, 2nd earl of (1770–1828). Liverpool was a capable and intelligent statesman, whose skill in building up his party, leading the country to victory in the war against Napoleon, and laying the foundations for prosperity outweighed his unpopularity in the immediate post-Waterloo years. The son of a distinguished MP, Liverpool was educated at Charterhouse and Oxford. He was present at the fall of the Bastille in 1789 and never lost a dread of public tumult and mob violence. He entered the Commons while under age in 1790 and supported the war with France after 1793. After gaining experience at the India Board, he served *Addington as foreign secretary, had two spells as home secretary, and between 1809 and 1812 proved himself as an efficient war secretary. When he became prime minister in 1812 the prospects for his ministry were uncertain but Liverpool soon showed that he was in command. The war against Napoleon was turning in favour of the allies. Napoleon suffered serious reverses in Russia and Spain in 1812. Liverpool had the ability to get the best out of his colleagues, to support them diligently, to restrain them when they became restless, and to work patiently towards broadening the ministry's support in Parliament and in the country. He was adroit in handling the prince regent: by 1820 he had the advantage of knowing that his colleagues would follow him out of office if he had to resign. He was a good chairman but much more than a good listener. It was Liverpool who insisted that the prince regent could not accede to the *Holy Alliance in a personal capacity. Within the Commons Liverpool cultivated the support of the country gentlemen. When their support was lost, as over the income tax in 1816, the consequences were embarrassing. Liverpool was protective towards the landed interest, but though he favoured a corn law he was compelled to accept a fixed duty in 1815 because his supporters were not prepared to accept a sliding scale. Liverpool was responsive to the commercial and manufacturing interests, grafting new economic ideas onto an essentially traditional outlook. He opposed parliamentary reform, but was eager to find some compromise on the catholic question short of full emancipation. He knew that the catholic issue had to remain an 'open question', for any attempt to impose uniformity upon his colleagues would precipitate the collapse of his ministry. Liverpool was determined to maintain public order but had no desire to strengthen the powers of central government. Lacking a police force he had to rely on the local magistrates for law and order. He reacted to events rather than anticipating them. At the time of the *Peterloo affair in 1819 Liverpool criticized the Manchester magistrates in private but defended them in public. The *Six Acts of 1819 were a response to the demands of nervous backbenchers for action. After 1820 the situation improved. The *Cato Street conspiracy was the last gasp of expiring *Jacobinism. The economy revived and Liverpool allowed his ministers greater freedom in reducing duties and stimulating trade. He appointed *Canning as foreign secretary and gave more scope to *Peel, *Huskisson, and Robinson (*Goderich). In his last five years as premier Liverpool accomplished much by way of cautious reform. The extent to which the government depended upon him was revealed when a stroke compelled his retirement in 1827. By the time of Liverpool's death in December 1828 the disintegration of the Tory Party was all too evident. In retrospect Liverpool had a remarkable ability to win widespread confidence and to impose cohesion on his ministry. He rose to the challenge of events with unfussy self-control. In war and peace he served the country well. JWD

Liverpool cathedrals. Giles Gilbert Scott (1880–1960) was only 22 when his design in a Romantic Gothic style on an immense scale won the competition for the proposed Anglican cathedral, commenced under the inspiration of Bishop

Chavasse. The foundation stone was laid in 1904 by Edward VII, and the first section to be completed was the ornate Lady Chapel, with Bodley as co-architect. After Bodley's death, Scott simplified the whole design of the main part of the cathedral which was being built in the local red sandstone. Consecrated in 1924, when George V knighted Scott, the cathedral was finally completed in 1978, generally as intended, apart from an economically enforced new west front. Set on raised ground, and having the highest interior of all English cathedrals, it dominates the Merseyside skyline and awes worshippers.

The metropolitan cathedral, linked to its Anglican counterpart by a street named Hope, was originally designed by Edwin *Lutyens but only the crypt completed. Frederick Gibberd's prize-winning design (1959) has resulted in a circular building whose radial buttresses and glass-walled central tower have prompted a number of affectionate nicknames. Dedicated to Christ the King, it was consecrated in May 1967. ASH

livery and maintenance. See BASTARD FEUDALISM.

livery companies were organizations of master tradesmen which developed in the city of London during the Middle Ages. Their purpose was to control the numbers and character of new entrants. Originally livery referred to the special clothing of retainers and servants, but later the term became associated with distinctive costumes for grand occasions worn by high-ranking members of the companies. Prosperous companies erected their own guildhalls and endowed churches dedicated to the patron saint of their crafts, with chapels for their use. Most companies provided benefits for members and their dependants such as widows and children. The influence of the companies grew as their wealth increased: most of them made loans to the crown in exchange for privileges for their members. Such privileges ranged from the right to wear livery to having a role in the government of the city of London.

Livery companies lost control of specific trades by the 19th cent., but being a freeman conferred prestige. The companies continued to have political influence, only slightly modified by Victorian local government reforms. They have retained their independence to the extent that, currently, members of a company have the status of freemen of the city of London. They serve with the aldermen, sheriffs, and the lord mayor on the Court of Common Hall and participate in the selection of the lord mayor for each year. By 1979 there were 84 livery companies. Over time new companies have emerged, one of the most recent being the Guild of Air Pilots and Air Navigators. IJEK

Livingstone, David (1813–73). Scottish missionary and explorer. Livingstone arrived in South Africa in 1841 to assist in the work of the *London Missionary Society. He was soon attracted northward in the hope of spreading the gospel in the more densely populated regions of central Africa. His travels took him first to the Atlantic coast and then across the continent to the Indian Ocean. His encounter with the Arab-controlled slave trade led him to conceive a plan to open Africa to the civilizing influences of Christianity and legitimate commerce. His discoveries brought him fame in Britain and won him the support of the Royal Geographical Society. A second exploratory journey between 1858 and 1864 laid the foundation for Britain's involvement in Nyasaland (Malawi) and the circumstances of his death in the interior of Africa in 1873, during a final journey, proved to be the decisive factor in stimulating British action against the east African slave trade. KI

Llandaff, diocese of. Llandaff cathedral looks to the 6th-cent. saints *Teilo and Euddogwy as its founders, and the shrine of the former was a place of pilgrimage until the Reformation. Work on the building of the present cathedral, and the definition of the territorial boundaries of the see, were however the responsibility of the first Norman bishop, Urban, early in the 12th cent. The cathedral still contains several richly ornamented doorways and arches from this time. The diocese, the most populous in Wales, originally encompassed most of the counties of Glamorgan and Monmouth (Gwent), though the latter became a separate bishopric in 1921. None the less it has been calculated that half of the population of Wales lives within 25 miles of the cathedral, today in a suburb of Cardiff. The cathedral has had a chequered history. In the 17th and 18th cents. it fell into ruin, and was completely restored in the 19th, only to be partially destroyed again by German bombs in 1941. Restored by the architect George Pace, the cathedral now contains numerous works of art, including examples by Dante *Rossetti, Jacob *Epstein (his controversial *Majestas*), and Frank Roper. JRG

Lloyd, Marie (1870–1922). Music-hall artiste. Born Matilda Wood, but quickly rejecting the stage-name 'Bella Delmare' for 'Marie Lloyd' when first appearing in music-hall aged 15, she was soon performing in London's West End. Despite some pantomime roles, her forte was music-hall, where she specialized in character songs imbued with vitality, sauce, and skilled gesture and expression ('Oh, Mister Porter', 'Wink the Other Eye'), highly rated by Beerbohm, Sarah Bernhardt, and Ellen *Terry. A meteoric rise to fame was followed by world-wide tours. Talented, ever-popular, and incapable of hypocrisy, her reputation for salaciousness and irregular private life meant that by the official moral standards of the time 'the Queen of the Halls' was socially unacceptable; lavish generosity to the poor and war work could not prevent exclusion from royal command performances or near-deportation from New York. Latterly unhappy, overwork and domestic violence broke her health and hastened her final collapse. ASH

Lloyd, Selwyn (1904–78). Despite high office, Lloyd never fully emerged as a public figure of the first rank. A successful lawyer, he entered Parliament as a Conservative in 1945. Appointed to junior office in 1951, he rose steadily and was a surprise choice as foreign secretary in December 1955. Many, however, viewed his elevation as indicative of Anthony *Eden's intention to take personal control of foreign policy—an impression not dispelled by Lloyd's role in the Suez crisis of 1956. He came near to achieving a negotiated settlement with Egypt in October. Though consistently loyal to Eden, Lloyd never seemed at ease about collusion with France and Israel. After *Macmillan replaced Eden in January 1957, Lloyd retained the Foreign Office—a gesture of defiance on Macmillan's part over Suez. He moved to the Exchequer in 1960 where his tenure marked the high-water mark of Conservative economic planning in the post-war era. A victim of Macmillan's 'Night of the Long Knives' (1962), Lloyd's career enjoyed a renaissance as leader of the Commons (1963–4) and Speaker (1971–6). DJD

Lloyd George, David, 1st earl Lloyd-George (1863–1945). Prime minister. Lloyd George made a greater impact on British public life than any other 20th-cent. statesman. He laid the foundations of what later became the *welfare state, and put a progressive income tax system at the centre of government finance. He also left his mark on the system of government by enlarging the scope of the prime minister's role. He was acclaimed, not without reason, as the 'Man Who Won the War'. Yet until the appearance of a spate of sympathetic books in the 1970s his reputation remained remarkably low. This is partly attributable to the way in which his later career was clouded by financial scandal and by stories of his infidelities. But above all he was blamed by many Liberals for destroying their party in 1918, hated in the Labour movement for his handling of industrial issues after 1918, and disparaged by Conservatives for his radicalism. No one, it seemed, had an interest in defending him.

He grew up in a modest, but not poor, home in north Wales. Once he and his brother had qualified as solicitors, he was able to use the firm's income as the base on which to build his political career. In 1890 he rather luckily won a by-election in the marginal Conservative seat of Caernarfon Boroughs which he retained until 1945. However, a parliamentary career imposed a strain upon his marriage to Margaret Owen. While he found Westminster fascinating, she hated London and insisted on staying with the family in Criccieth. Left alone he found alternative company. His most prolonged extramarital relationship was with Frances Stevenson from 1911 until his death. Formally his secretary, Frances gave him vital support in his political work, and became, in many ways, a second wife; they had a daughter in the 1930s, and married in 1943.

After nearly a decade as a lively backbench rebel, Lloyd George became a national figure as a result of his courageous opposition to the South African War (1899–1902). In this he risked his seat and a certain amount of mob violence, notably in connection with a speech at Birmingham in 1901 when he was obliged to escape disguised as a policeman. In December 1905 his talents were recognized by *Campbell-Bannerman, the new Liberal premier, who made him president of the Board of Trade. Here he revealed unexpected skills in getting his legislation enacted.

Lloyd George's real breakthrough came in 1908 when *Asquith promoted him as chancellor of the Exchequer. His unorthodox methods often caused irritation; he bypassed civil servants, read little, and preferred to make policy by discussion, especially on the golf course. Moreover, as he felt politically disadvantaged by his lack of a large private income, he was always apt to grab an opportunity to make a quick profit; hence his rash involvement in the *Marconi scandal. But Asquith had correctly seen that Lloyd George possessed the necessary political flair to be chancellor. His famous 'People's Budget' of 1909 solved the government's problems by levying extra taxes on a few large incomes and on items of conspicuous consumption like motor cars. This enabled them to pay for both *old-age pensions *and* *dreadnought battleships. When his budget was rejected by the peers Lloyd George quickly grasped the opportunity to attack the Conservatives for selfishly trying to preserve a privileged élite. He derided the peers as 'five hundred men, ordinary men, chosen accidentally from among the unemployed'. This restored the initiative to the Liberals and enabled them to retain their working-class vote in two general elections in 1910. Subsequently Lloyd George maintained his radical credentials with the 1911 *National Insurance Act which introduced both health and unemployment insurance for millions of people. During 1913–14 he again seized the initiative with the Land campaign which promised minimum wages for agricultural labourers and a rural house-building programme.

After the outbreak of war he stood out as the only minister whose reputation rose significantly. This was largely attributable to his success in meeting a new challenge as minister of munitions from May 1915. The need to improvise and the freedom from departmental conventions meant that he was in his element in this job. However, his brief spell as secretary of state for war proved less happy precisely because he found himself trapped by the conservative thinking of the military men. His frustration led him to join with Bonar *Law in putting pressure on Asquith to streamline the war machine. The result—largely unintended—was Asquith's resignation in December 1916. Following the king's invitation Lloyd George managed to put together a government based on Conservative support plus a majority of the Labour members and a minority of the Liberals.

He made an immediate impact on the war effort by instituting a five-man war cabinet serviced by a cabinet secretariat under Sir Maurice Hankey. He also developed a personal secretariat of advisers. New ministries were created—Food, Shipping, Air, National Service, Pensions, Labour—to deal with the problems thrown up by the war, and non-party experts and businessmen such as Sir Eric Geddes were often appointed to them.

None the less, Lloyd George's premiership remained a precarious affair because he depended heavily on the Conservatives for his majority. Most Tories neither liked nor trusted him, but thought that the alternatives were worse. The sudden military victory in November 1918 gave Lloyd George immense prestige and, thus, a degree of bargaining power. Instead of returning to the Liberal Party he decided to organize his own Lloyd George Liberals and to fight the election in co-operation with the Conservatives.

As a result of his government's overwhelming victory in 1918 he retained office until 1922. Although restricted by the numerical dominance of the Conservatives he had many major achievements to his credit: the parliamentary reform of 1918 which enfranchised women, the 1918 Education Act, the 1919 Housing Act, the settlement of the Irish question in 1921, and, of course, the treaty of *Versailles. But in time both Liberal and Tory followers grew dissatisfied. Controversy over the huge funds the prime minister accumulated by the sale of honours undermined him; knighthoods were freely offered for £12,000 and baronetcies for £30,000. Finally at a meeting in October 1922 the Conservatives voted to cut their links with Lloyd George. He resigned immediately and never took office again.

Though he spent much of the 1920s engaged in Liberal Party infighting, he still made a major constructive impact on politics by means of his collaboration with J. M. *Keynes and others over a detailed strategy for tackling unemployment. The Liberal Yellow Book, entitled *Britain's Industrial Future* (1928), formed the basis of the Liberal revival before the 1929 election. However, the electoral system prevented the party from translating its extra votes into seats, and Lloyd George was reduced to attempts to collaborate with the new premier, *MacDonald. He was too ill to join the National Government in 1931. Though widely expected to serve in Churchill's coalition after 1940, Lloyd George was not keen to do so, and the invitation never came. MDP

Gilbert, B. B., *David Lloyd George: A Political Life* (1987); Morgan, K. O., *Lloyd George* (1974); Pugh, M., *Lloyd George* (1988); Rowland, P., *Lloyd George* (1975).

Lloyd's of London. From the late 1600s to the late 1700s London coffee-houses were the centre of social and business life. From the 1690s merchants, bankers, and seafarers met in Edward Lloyd's coffee-house in Lombard Street, where they exchanged information and undertook shipping business. Merchants prepared to take a share of a marine risk would write their names on a policy one beneath the other, becoming 'underwriters'. Lloyd's was incorporated in 1871; in 1911 an Act allowed its underwriters to do insurance business 'of every description'. Still dominant in marine insurance, they also took on unlimited liability for unusual or specialized risks and reinsurance business. From the late 1970s Lloyd's experienced turbulent times: claims, particularly from natural disasters, have got much larger, and there has been incompetence, fraud, theft, suspensions, and resignations; a new regulatory framework is planned. MW

Llywelyn ap Gruffydd (d. 1282), prince of Wales (1246–82). Known as Llywelyn 'the Last', his ambition to create a permanent, independent Welsh principality came close to realization. The second son of Gruffydd, son of *Llywelyn ab Iorwerth, he may have been designated the heir of his uncle *Dafydd ap Llywelyn. After Dafydd's death (1246) and the treaty of *Woodstock with Henry III (1247), Llywelyn and his elder brother Owain were restricted to *Gwynedd west of the river Conwy. By 1255 Llywelyn had defeated his brothers and restored his uncle's dominion: he advanced east of the Conwy, exploited divisions in England, and raided to south Wales. Most Welsh lords regarded him as overlord (1258) and Llywelyn took the title of prince of Wales. At *Pipton (1265) Simon de *Montfort acknowledged his status and allowed Llywelyn to marry his daughter (though the marriage did not take place until 1278). At *Montgomery (1267) Henry III conceded recognition. But in Gwynedd, Llywelyn's rule alienated churchmen and his brother *Dafydd, who deserted him in 1274; there was an attempt to assassinate Llywelyn in Powys. He also misjudged Edward I in refusing to fulfil his obligations as the king's vassal. The war of 1276–7 was a disaster for Llywelyn, who was confined once more to west Gwynedd by the treaty of *Aberconwy (1277); he kept his title but only five Welsh barons were acknowledged to be his vassals. The uneasy peace was shattered by Dafydd's impulsive assault on Hawarden (1282) and, in the renewed struggle with Edward, Llywelyn was killed near Builth on 11 December. His infant heiress Gwenllian was placed in a nunnery, whilst Dafydd failed to revive his family's fortunes. RAG

Llywelyn ab Iorwerth (1173–1240), prince of Gwynedd (1195–1240), known as 'the Great'. The son of Iorwerth 'Flatnose' and Margaret, princess of *Powys, Llywelyn spent most of his life restoring and enhancing the hegemony of his grandfather *Owain Gwynedd. A striking youth and a successful warrior at an early age, he acquired (from 1194) lands at the expense of his kinsmen, enabling him to master *Gwynedd by 1203. Good relations with King John brought recognition and his marriage to John's natural daughter *Joan. But his aggression towards Powys made John retaliate (1210–11) and Llywelyn then allied with the French. He aided the rebel barons and exploited the civil war in England to extend his power to modern Carmarthenshire and Cardiganshire and east towards Montgomery, making himself lord of Powys by 1216. Henry III's regime recognized all this (1218), and despite hostilities with marcher lords like the Marshalls, he sustained his position by marriage alliances with other lords like the Braoses. He planned to perpetuate his principality by securing recognition from king and pope (1220–2) of his son *Dafydd as his sole heir, even though this breached Welsh custom and alienated his elder son, the bastard Gruffydd. He took the evocative title of prince of Aberffraw and lord of Snowdon (1230), which seemed to imply suzerainty over other Welsh lords, and he compared himself to the king of Scots; but Llywelyn did not deny his own homage to Henry III. Llywelyn probably suffered a stroke in 1237 and after his death (11 April 1240) he was buried at Aberconwy abbey which he had patronized, leaving Dafydd to assert the position his father had bequeathed to him. RAG

local government, the administration of units smaller than the state, has a long but shadowy early history. Not only do many books on the subject begin only in 1835, but the purposes of local government are different, and the sources different, as one goes further back in time. In very early periods 'central' and 'local' government are difficult to separate, since many areas of Britain had independent or semi-independent rulers; and for centuries the primary purposes of local officials, as of central government, were seen to be defence, law, and order, rather than social services.

Britain before the Romans consisted of many tribal units. Those areas conquered by Rome were welded into a single province of Britannia (though in the 3rd and 4th cents. it was subdivided into two, and later into four and five, provinces). Within that province, however, most of the tribal units survived as *civitates* (city-states), with the larger towns governed separately as *coloniae* and *municipiae*. In the 5th and 6th cents. the pattern dissolved, and Britain became a patchwork of small states of both natives and invaders. As smaller states were absorbed into larger ones, old units often survived within them as administrative areas. By the 9th cent. Wessex was organized into shires, and as the kings of Wessex conquered the rest of England, they imposed the shire-system on it. By 1066 most of England, at least south of the Humber, was divided into shires, which in turn were divided into hundreds or (in the former Danish areas) into *wapentakes (from *vápnatak*, the brandishing of weapons to show assent). Wales, however, was divided into independent principalities, each subdivided into commotes and hundreds (*cantrefs*).

Each English shire (often called by the French name of county after 1066) was controlled by a royal official called a *sheriff (shire reeve), whose powers and duties were greatly increased by the Norman kings; while in Lowland Scotland the kings created a similar pattern in the 12th cent., with sheriffdoms and thanages (under sheriffs and thanes respectively). Similarly, when Edward I conquered independent Wales in 1276–83, he reorganized his conquests into shires on the English model, though he left alone the marcher lordships of south and east Wales. However, in none of the three countries was there a tidy and uniform system of administration. Some of the larger English towns, for example, acquired the status of counties corporate and excluded the county sheriffs altogether; while in both counties and towns there were numerous islands of exempt jurisdiction (immunities or 'liberties'). It should also be remembered that all of these arrangements applied only to secular administration; the church had its own administrative and judicial structure, with extensive powers over laity as well as clergy.

In late medieval England kings increasingly entrusted local government to resident gentry and burgesses, many of them acting under crown commissions, especially in the new offices of *justices of the peace. In the 16th cent. the sheriffs lost further control of their counties with the institution of *lords-lieutenant, and with increasing powers and responsibilities laid on the county justices. The parish became, after the Reformation, the basic unit of secular as well as ecclesiastical administration, and new parochial officials were introduced to deal with highway maintenance and poor relief. This English pattern was imposed on the whole of Wales in 1536–43, but in independent Scotland there were differences. Sheriffdoms began to evolve into counties only in the 16th cent., and their jurisdiction did not become completely coextensive with counties until 1747, when private jurisdiction of baronies and regalities, and traditional Highland clan jurisdiction, were abolished.

With this Scottish exception, central government interfered very little with existing local government structures between 1688 and the 1830s. However, during that 'long 18th century' those structures became increasingly inadequate, and Parliament had to alleviate problems by delegating many responsibilities to groups of improvement commissioners, and from 1834 to Poor Law unions. In 1835 the *Municipal Corporations Act transformed local government in England and Wales, creating standardized urban local authorities elected by ratepayers, and in 1872 sanitary districts were added. In 1888–9 the whole of British local government was reorganized, with *county councils taking over most of the country, though some large towns were made all-purpose authorities outside the county structure. Within the counties, the sanitary districts were made into urban and rural districts (1894). In Scotland the Scottish Office, established in 1885, has since acted as an intermediary stage of government, taking over some of the functions exercised by local authorities in England and Wales. Otherwise the broad pattern persisted until 1974, when another reorganization divided England and Wales into counties and districts, and 1975, when a more drastic rearrangement produced new regional and district councils in Scotland.

From 1992–5 the Banham commission undertook another major review of local government in England, proposing the restoration of Rutland, the separation of Herefordshire and Worcestershire, and the abolition for all but ceremonial purposes of the eight counties of Avon, Bedfordshire, Berkshire, Buckinghamshire, Cleveland, Dorset, Humberside, and Somerset. Local government in Wales was reorganized by the Local Government (Wales) Act of 1994 and in Scotland by the Local Government (Scotland) Act of 1994.

DMP

local history in medieval England chiefly took the form of histories of particular monasteries and their estates. A good example is the *Abingdon Chronicle*, *c.*1160. More comprehensive local history was provided by William of Malmesbury, whose *Gesta pontificum* (*c.*1125) has the earliest (though brief) historical/topographical accounts of a number of English places. In the mid-15th cent. William of Worcester made fuller descriptions of many more.

The *Itineraries* of John *Leland (not published until 1710) were a similar but grander enterprise, part of the Tudor 'discovery of England'. He failed in his intention to complete a history of England arranged by shire, but William *Camden's *Britannia* (1586) did provide such an account. An English translation (1610) and extended editions by *Gibson (1695) and Gough (1789 and 1806) gave *Britannia* a long and useful life. William Lambarde's *A Perambulation of Kent* (1576) began the long and noble series of English county histories. The title is significant. Writing a county's history and describing its present state ('chorography') went hand in hand. William *Dugdale's *Warwickshire* (1656) set a new standard for county histories. Characteristic of such works was a commanding interest in the genealogies and lands of the *gentry who patronized, and often wrote, them.

Such major histories followed as Francis Blomefield's *Norfolk* (1739–75) and Edward Hasted's *Kent* (1778–99). Characteristically neither work was completed without a mighty struggle and financial peril. Plans for most such works from the 16th cent. to the 19th have left nothing behind, but at best a book covering part of the shire, more frequently a collection (often extensive) of manuscript materials, sometimes just a prospectus.

Parallel to the county histories were those of towns. The true founder of urban history in England is John *Stow. His *Survey* of London (1598) retains the value of great learning and close observation. Such other studies followed as, for example, William Somner's of Canterbury (1640). In this field also, major research such as that of John Kirkpatrick (*c.*1686–1728) on Norwich remained unpublished. On a lesser level, White Kennet's history of Ambrosden (1695) was innovatory as a study of 'parochial antiquities'.

In the 19th cent. there was far more local history of most kinds, at various levels. No doubt this was broadly in consequence of increases in population, wealth, and literacy and decreases in printing costs. More specifically much was done by new local societies concerned with history and historical publication. The Society of Antiquaries of Newcastle upon Tyne was a pioneer. Its journal, *Archaeologia Aeliana*, has been in continuous publication since 1822. From the 1840s many comparable societies were founded, usually on a county basis. Their journals impress. For example, *Norfolk Archaeology* (1847 on) demonstrates not only the learning of its contributors but also the excellence of Norwich printing and illustration. Such a provincial production more closely resembles a modern historical periodical than any produced nationally until the *English Historical Review* (1886). Local learning could now draw on the sources made available by the Record Commission (1802–37), the Rolls Series (1857–96), and, from the 1850s, via the new Public Record Office. Some 19th-cent. societies were concerned to publish records relating to their counties but the main movement for the foundation of county record societies came in the next century, Lincolnshire (founded 1910) and Northamptonshire (1920), providing important models. The clergy of the Church of England were important in all this, not least because of the force of the new interest in the medieval church and its buildings.

In the *Victoria County History*, inaugurated in 1899, old and new worlds married fruitfully. The project was to write history of the whole of England, county by county, and, within the county framework, parish by parish. This was the near institutionalization of the collective ambition of local historians over 300 or so years. A new element was the presence of such contributors as John Horace Round, men of a new breed in having been trained in history at a university. One of these, Frank Merry Stenton, was appointed, at Reading, to a post of an unprecedented kind: 'Research Fellow in Local History'. Like his predecessor of 1160 he devoted himself to the early history of the abbey of Abingdon. In the 20th cent. the pursuit of local history was transformed by its study in universities. Particularly from the 1960s a flood of studies of all kinds appeared. The most influential of the university historians was William George Hoskins. His *The Making of the English Landscape* (1955) changed the understanding of our past. Hoskins was an English original: learned, opinionated, radical, conservative. His contributions were the introduction of a sense of landscape, for which shire-historians had found no place, fox-hunters though they sometimes were, and the capacity to see local history as a yeoman looking up, rather than a squire looking down. Much of his academic life was spent at Leicester, where he founded a school of local history.

Though local history became increasingly professionalized, the 20th cent. saw an enormous development in 'amateur' interest also. This was partly because local records became more readily available with the provision of professionally staffed county *record offices. Such provision began to be made in the 1920s and 1930s. Fast development came in the decades after the war of 1939–45. This was the period in which local studies came to play a part in the school teaching of history. The most numerous users of the new record offices were in search of their own ancestors. The magnetism of *genealogy is as strong in the 20th cent. as it was in the 17th and draws far more people. JCa

Currie, C. R. J., and Lewis, C. P. (eds.), *English County Histories, a Guide: A Tribute to C. R. Elrington* (1994); Finberg, H. P. R., *The Local Historian and his Theme* (Leicester, 1952); Simmons, J., *English County Historians* (East Ardsley, 1978).

Locarno, treaties of, 1925. These treaties (1 December 1925) briefly raised hopes that Europe was at last settling down after the First World War. They confirmed the inviolability of the frontiers between France, Belgium, and Germany, and the demilitarization of the Rhineland. Britain, intent on European peace and security at the lowest cost to herself, refused to make any engagements to reinforce French commitments in eastern Europe. German entry to the *League of Nations followed in 1926, while the key negotiators—Briand (France), Stresemann (Germany), and Austen *Chamberlain (Britain)—continued to meet at the 'Geneva tea-parties' (1926–9). Locarno was at best a form of 'limited détente'. CJB

Locke, John (1632–1704). Arguably the most influential English-language philosopher and political theorist, Locke is regarded as the founding thinker and author of liberalism. However, his influence on contemporaries was restricted by the political conditions of Charles II's last years. Locke lived in the household of *Shaftesbury the Whig leader and like him had to go into exile. Locke's important works could not be published until after 1688, although written earlier. He advocated religious toleration, including it in the constitution he drafted for Shaftesbury's Carolina colony. His *Letter Concerning Toleration* (1689) contains two fundamental assumptions: that religion is a matter for each individual, and that churches are voluntary associations. These rule out religious coercion and uniformity, but political considerations led Locke to deny toleration to the intolerant (catholics, he argued) and atheists. His arguments lead logically to the principle and practice of separation of church and state, but Locke did not say so. The *Two Treatises of Government* bases government on the consent of the governed, who need an authority to defend their property. A ruler who turns himself into a tyrant, as Charles II and James II had been doing, forfeits his authority and may be resisted. *An Essay Concerning Human Understanding*, Locke's main philosophical work, appeared in 1690. It and *The Reasonableness of Christianity* (1695) provoked more controversy than the political works. JRJ

Lockhart, Sir George (*c.*1630–89). Lawyer. Lockhart's father was a Scottish judge and his elder brother William a soldier and diplomat. George Lockhart served as advocate to *Cromwell when he was protector, was pardoned at the Restoration, and became one of the leading advocates at the Scottish bar, defending *Argyll at his trial for treason in 1681. In 1685 James VII appointed him lord president of the Court of Session. He was shot in March 1689 by an aggrieved private suitor. His elder son George, an active Jacobite, was killed in a duel in 1731: his younger son Philip was shot after the Jacobite surrender at *Preston in 1715. JAC

lollardy. Described recently as 'the premature reformation', lollardy developed originally from *Wyclif's teaching. Lollards (from middle Dutch *lollaerd*—a mumbler) were a motley group lacking theological coherence. Though few lollards emulated Wyclif's intellectualism, Oxford lollardy lingered on with a resurgence in the 1400s under William Taylor and Peter Payne. Though Archbishop *Arundel dealt the death blow to academic Wyclifism at the Council of Oxford (1411), the last academic, Richard Wyche, was not put to death until 1440. Lollardy also attracted influential men, close to the court, some driven by genuine puritanism, some anticlerical, some selfishly cynical with eyes on clerical wealth. These included the archbishop of York's brother William Neville, and even Arundel's relatives had lollard friends. Providing havens for writing and copying texts, they patronized lollard preachers, which alarmed the government, who enacted the statute *De heretico comburendo (1401) to arrest unlicensed preachers and sometimes hand them over for public burning. After Sir John Oldcastle's abortive revolt (1414) and death (1417), aristocratic lollardy was a spent force. Chased from university and aristocracy, lollardy became geographically disparate, embracing local artisans and yeomen farmers, who held negative, often simplistic, views. They banned organ music and church bells, but caused greater concern by criticizing transubstantiation, confession, indulgences, and pilgrimages. Though the authorities feared lollards as dangerously articulate with a backbone of literacy, their negative ideas had little popular appeal except for emphasis on Bible-reading. A small Wyclifite group produced the lollard Bible, the first full translation from the Vulgate (1390), a 'very literal almost unreadable version' which the Church unsuccessfully banned (1407). By leaving biblical translation in the hands of this radical group, ecclesiastical authority damaged the case for authorized Bible translation, which existed on the continent. Though lollardy went underground, its extremism made the mass of lower orders, already conservative, more so. Modern historians feel that Wyclif 'did little or nothing to inspire [the Reformation] and in effect [unintentionally] did every thing possible to delay' it by discrediting even moderate reform. WMM

London (Roman). Londinium was the provincial capital of Roman Britain from *c.* AD 60 onwards. Roman remains have been located at the confluence of the rivers Thames and Fleet. The precise legal status of Roman London is much debated. It was probably a *colonia*, though it appears to have been something of a special case; the main impetus for its development probably came from the existence of a trading association of Roman citizens (the *conventus civium Romanorum*) taking advantage of London's superb geographical location at the hub of the network of Roman roads and on the banks of the navigable Thames. London's status appears to have been enhanced after *Colchester (the original provincial capital of Roman Britain) was destroyed during the Boudiccan revolt of AD 60. A tombstone of the new procurator, Gaius Julius Classicianus, dating to the aftermath of the revolt, suggests that London had now become the seat of administration. Possibly London had been less severely damaged than Colchester. This would explain London's rapid development in the later 1st cent., when building projects included the first forum and basilica, the governor's palace, the public baths at Cheapside, and, dating to *c.* AD 100, a fort and adjacent amphitheatre. ES

London, diocese of. The senior see after the two archbishoprics, it comprises Greater London and part of Surrey north of the Thames. Though a British bishop from London attended the Council of Arles in 314, *Augustine did not establish a diocese for the East Saxons until 604, but pagan reaction soon forced *Mellitus, the first bishop, to flee. The set-back and popular veneration for Canterbury thwarted Pope Gregory's intention that London should be the metropolitan see. The true succession of London bishops restarts with Wine in 666, for Cedd, Celtic bishop of the East Saxons (654–64), was never based in the city. Many bishops of London have been translated to Canterbury, but, of those who were not, significant ones include Gilbert *Foliot (1163–87), opponent of Becket; Edmund *Bonner (1539–50 and 1553–9), papalist; Nicholas *Ridley (1550–3), reformer, burned at the stake; Henry *Compton (1676–1714), opponent of James II; Edmund *Gibson (1723–48), Walpole's ecclesiastical manager; Mandell Creighton (1897–1901), the historian. *St Paul's cathedral dates from the earliest years of the see, when significantly *Æthelbert, king of Kent, not the king of the East Saxons, founded it for Mellitus. The medieval St Paul's, mostly 12th and 13th cent., was destroyed in the Great Fire of 1666. The present cathedral (1675–1710) by Christopher *Wren is in Renaissance style and miraculously survived the London Blitz (1940–1). WMM

London, fire of, 1666. The dangers of fire in any early town with close-packed wooden buildings were always considerable, but the blaze that started in Thomas Farriner's bakehouse in Pudding Lane, near London Bridge, in the early hours of Sunday, 2 September, has become known as the 'Great Fire'. *Pepys saw it early, shrugged his shoulders, and returned to bed. But a driving east wind fanned the flames across firebreaks, and, despite the efforts of ward and parish officials and the lord mayor, they soon became uncontrollable. Residents gathered up what valuables they could and fled, many believing that the Dutch and French had started the conflagration. The wind persisted until Tuesday night, but it was not until Friday that the firefighters and county militia could assess the devastation. The Tower of London (to the east) had survived, but Old St Paul's cathedral, the Guildhall, Royal Exchange, 87 parish churches, 52 company halls, markets, gaols, and 13,200 houses had succumbed; the area damaged (463 acres) was greater than that in the 1939–45 Blitz, with losses estimated at the then almost incomprehensible sum of over £10 million. Charles II, who had placed his brother in control of the city to maintain order and discourage looting, rapidly introduced measures for recovery. Some of the rebuilding schemes submitted were too hurried to be practical, but under six commissioners a new city was built on the old plan though with improved access and hygiene, and in brick rather than wood. To commemorate events, the Monument was erected near the site of the outbreak (1677); to the inscription on the north panel the words 'But Popish frenzy, which wrought such horrors, is not yet quenched' were added in 1681 but removed in 1830. ASH

London, government and politics. The exceptional size and resources of London gave it military significance in addition to its political importance as the capital. William the Conqueror granted London a charter, confirming its previous privileges, but also began building the White Tower, nucleus of the *Tower of London, as a strong point. London did not replace the old Wessex capital of *Winchester until the 12th cent. Indeed, as long as the king and his household were continuously on the move, the concept of a capital could scarcely develop, but Edward the Confessor's decision to build his great abbey at *Westminster, reinforced by William Rufus's building of *Westminster Hall, and the beginning in 1176 of a stone *London bridge, pointed the way. Before the Conquest, Saxon rulers had granted London remarkable privileges—a folk moot which met three times a year; the husting (Danish: *hus-ting* (house assembly)) which met every week; aldermen to supervise justice in the ward moots. In 1018 London had paid one-seventh of the national tribute to *Cnut and in the decades before the Conquest the *witan had met there more often than anywhere else. Londoners added to their privileges in subsequent centuries in a long series of charters. Henry I granted them the right to elect two sheriffs who should also act for Middlesex, and in Richard I's reign they gained a mayor. During the convulsions of John's reign, they gained further concessions and the mayor of London was the only commoner to serve on the committee of 25 appointed to enforce *Magna Carta. When representatives of the boroughs began to be summoned to Parliament in the late 13th and early 14th cents., London usually returned four members rather than the standard two—though even that grossly under-reflected its population and wealth.

The government of the city, as it developed, consisted of a Court of Aldermen, chosen for life; a Common Council of some 200 members, chosen annually by the wards; a Common Hall of some thousands, representing the liverymen; and ward moots or parish meetings. The wards were further divided into precincts—small neighbourhood units of 50 to 100 houses—which also met regularly. The Court of Common Hall elected the two sheriffs and nominated two members for the mayoralty, the Court of Aldermen choosing one. The executive was the mayor (after 1283 increasingly referred to as the lord mayor), the two sheriffs, a large number of paid officers, of whom the recorder and town clerk were the most important; and a host of lesser officials, paid and unpaid, down to precinct level, including scavengers, constables, night-watchmen, and rate-collectors. The wealth of the city from tolls and dues enabled each level of government to entertain itself well and award contracts to its friends and supporters. The lord mayor presided over the Court of Common Council, in which the aldermen also sat, and which acted as a kind of executive committee. There was a constant struggle for power between the component parts, the Common Council and even more the Common Hall tending to radical disenchantment with the national government, the aldermen, consisting of the senior and wealthy merchants, often on close terms with the government of the day. Seldom did the city speak with one voice on any political issue. Great influence was also exerted by the *livery companies which developed from the medieval guilds: the Weavers' charter was granted in 1155, Fishmongers' 1272, Goldsmiths', Merchant Taylors', and Skinners' 1327, Drapers' 1364, Mercers' 1394, and Grocers' 1428. London's wealth and its closeness to the court meant that its representations had to be taken seriously, and its privileges included the right of direct access to the sovereign, which could be used to present irritating petitions and unwelcome advice.

On several occasions London was in the hands of rebels—Wat *Tyler in 1381, Jack *Cade in 1450, Thomas *Wyatt in 1554—attempting to seize or intimidate the government. These incursions were rarely successful, partly because there was little government to seize, partly because it was difficult for rebel leaders to control their men once they had entered the city. Nor were Londoners—extremely conscious of their own privileges—greatly inclined to welcome peasants, Cornishmen, or Highlanders. Of more consequence in national affairs were the occasions when the city itself acted with unity and resolution. Londoners, with their close financial and trading links with the Low Countries, were very receptive towards reformed doctrines in the early Tudor period and London became the spearhead of the English *Reformation. One hundred years later, it was in the forefront of the opposition to Charles I, and the Civil War may, in one sense, be seen as London versus the rest. The resources of the capital in men and money were the mainstay of the parliamentary cause and the pattern of the conflict was dictated by Charles's efforts to fight his way back into London after he had fled the capital in 1642. London gave strong support to *Shaftesbury during the *Exclusion crisis and forfeited its charter temporarily as a consequence, and for much of the 18th cent. was a thorn in the side of Whiggish aristocratic governments. The tensions between a Whig Court of Aldermen and a Tory/Jacobite Common Council led *Walpole in 1725 to push through the City Election Act to strengthen aldermanic control. But radical London was not subdued. William *Beckford and John *Wilkes used London as their power base for attacks upon George III's ministers, the former even offering the king a well-publicized rebuke at an audience in 1770. In the 1790s the *London Corresponding Society pressed for reform of Parliament and London played an important part in the *chartist agitation of the 1840s. Later in the century London radicalism was less evident, partly because new towns like Birmingham, Manchester, and Sheffield had taken up much of the running, partly because London's enormous size made it difficult for politicians to organize it.

The growth of London also placed great strain on its governmental institutions. London itself had long before expanded beyond the city limits, taking in Southwark in 1550. By 1811, only one-tenth of the capital's population lived within the city's jurisdiction and the corporation had little desire to acquire responsibility for the remaining nine-tenths. What administration there was outside the city was left largely to parishes and vestries, supported by a patchwork of trusts, commissions, and charities. A leap forward in co-ordination came in 1829 with the Metropolitan Police Act but, significantly, it did not apply to the city proper, which set up its own police force ten years later. The *Municipal Corporations Act of 1835 did not include London, whose government continued unchanged while some of the new councils like Birmingham acquired a reputation for municipal enlightenment. Not until 1888 was the London County Council established, taking in an area from Woolwich to Hampstead and from Wandsworth to Hackney. A second tier of 28 borough councils operated beneath, sharing responsibilities. The London County Hall, on the south bank of the Thames, was opened in 1922 as a symbol and headquarters for the new authority. It was controlled first by the Liberals, from 1907 by the Conservatives (Municipal Reformers), and from 1934 by Labour. Herbert *Morrison's leadership in the 1930s was intended to make Labour London a flagship for municipal socialism, particularly in housing and environmental matters. But London was once more reorganized in 1965, partly for party advantage, partly because Greater London had outgrown the LCC area. The Greater London Council supervised 31 boroughs and the cities of London and Westminster. The Conservatives held power at first but lost control to Labour in 1973. Dislike of its left-wing politics and jealousy of any rival source of authority caused the Thatcher government to abolish the GLC in 1986, leaving London as the only capital city with no overarching authority. The problem of local government for London is real enough, but it is not easy to believe that the response of national governments in the last two centuries has been constructive or thoughtful. JAC

Beier, A. L., and Finlay, R. (eds.), *London 1500–1700: The Making of the Metropolis* (1986); Brigden, S., *London and the Reformation* (Oxford, 1989); Pearl, V., *London and the Outbreak of the Puritan Revolution: City Government and National Politics, 1625–43* (Oxford, 1961); Rudé, G., *Hanoverian London, 1714–1808* (1971); Stevenson, J. (ed.), *London in the Age of Reform* (Oxford, 1977); Webb, S., and Webb, B., *English Local Government: The Manor and the Borough*, Part II (1908); Williams, G., *Medieval London: From Commune to Capital* (1963).

London, growth of. Describing London's growth is hampered by two problems. First, there are no reliable estimates of its population before the middle of the 16th cent. and secondly there is the contentious issue as to what geographical area 'London' covered. Before the 19th cent., 'London' is sometimes taken to mean the effective jurisdiction of the lord mayor, the city within and without the walls and the so-called 'liberties'. Others, however, take the limits of the London bills of *mortality, as finally determined in 1636, to define the boundaries of the capital. In the 19th cent. the geographical area covered by the London County Council (1889–1965), sometimes called 'inner London', is referred to; elsewhere London can include that rapidly growing suburban area known as 'outer London' included within the jurisdiction of the short-lived Greater London Council (1965–86). London here refers to the widest definitions.

There is little doubt that London's growth is a historical phenomenon of startling proportions. It was Britain's biggest settlement as early as the 7th cent. It began a phase of rapid growth in the late 10th cent., in 1100 its population may have numbered 25,000, and by 1200 perhaps 40,000. Recent research suggests that the city numbered between 80,000 and 100,000 people by 1300. London's population contracted after the famine of 1315–18 and the *Black Death (1348): its population still numbered only about 50,000 in 1500.

Sixteenth-cent. London grew more rapidly than England. The first well-grounded estimates suggest a population of about 75,000 in 1550, 200,000 in 1600, 400,000 in 1650, and over half a million by 1700. The 18th cent. saw an initial slowdown of metropolitan growth but the first *census in 1801 revealed the population of London to be about 1,117,000. Before 1800 most of this growth had been fuelled by immigration since more people died in the capital than were born there, but thereafter London's expansion was by natural increase. Its population doubled again by 1851, when it contained 2,685,000 people and by 1901 it comprised a metropolis of some 6,586,000 inhabitants. London's growth peaked at about 8,700,000 on the eve of the Second World War. Since then out-migration to more distant suburban areas has seen the population of 'Greater London' fall, and in 1988 it contained just 6,700,000.

London's early growth owed much to its development as a seat of government in the 13th and 14th cents., and to its increasing share of the nation's overseas trade. Disproportionate growth thereafter also occurred because it was a world city, not merely a national capital. The development of its financial institutions in the late 17th cent., its role as a colonial and then imperial capital in the 18th and 19th cents. are vital in explaining its phenomenal expansion. JPB

London, treaty of, 1357. David II of Scotland was captured at *Neville's Cross in 1346 and taken to the Tower of London. Protracted negotiations for his release came to nothing until the treaty of London of May 1357. The Scots paid a large ransom and gave hostages, but the question of the succession in Scotland was left to one side. The treaty was confirmed at *Berwick in October. JAC

London, treaty of, 1358. Draft treaty. Edward III's diplomatic hand was considerably strengthened by the capture of John II of France at *Poitiers. This treaty, to which the latter seems to have agreed, would have given Edward Aquitaine, Poitou, Ponthieu, and Calais in full sovereignty, as well as a ransom payment of 4 million *écus*, yet without obliging him to drop his claim to the French throne. It was never ratified, and Edward subsequently increased his demands in a second treaty (March 1359), to include Normandy, Anjou, and Maine. It may be that he had set his demands deliberately high so that the inevitable French refusal would justify the renewal of war. He invaded again in October 1359 with his largest ever army, aiming, it seems, for a coronation at Rheims. AC

London, treaty of, 1423. Anglo-Scottish agreement finalizing the terms of James I's release from English custody. King James was to pay 60,000 marks in English coin, 10,000 of which would be remitted as the dowry of his queen, *Joan Beaufort. A seven-year truce was subsequently made at Durham (March 1424). NATM

London, treaty of, 1474. In 1473 Edward IV was preparing an attack upon Louis XI of France but having difficulty mustering allies. In July 1474, by the treaty of London, Charles of Burgundy agreed to recognize Edward as king of France and join his campaign, in exchange for territorial concessions. But in 1475 Burgundy gave little help, Edward's campaign was inconclusive, and an Anglo-French settlement was reached at *Picquigny. JAC

London, treaty of, 1518. The victory of Francis I, the young king of France, over the Swiss at Marignano in 1515 threatened the balance of power in western Europe. *Wolsey and Henry VIII began constructing an anti-French alliance which soon collapsed. In 1518 they switched policy to a *rapprochement* with Francis and the treaty of London followed. Tournai, captured by the English in 1513, was to be handed back for compensation; Mary, Henry's 2-year-old daughter, was to marry the dauphin; France was not to support the anti-English party in Scotland; there was to be a treaty of universal peace and a crusade against the Turks. Though endorsed by the meeting of Francis and Henry in 1520 at the *Field of Cloth of Gold, the peace did not hold and the *rapprochement* did not prosper. By 1521 Wolsey was negotiating for a marriage between Mary and Charles V, the Habsburg emperor, and a visit by Charles in 1522 agreed plans for an attack upon France. JAC

London, treaty of, 1604. When James I succeeded Elizabeth, he found his new kingdom at war with Spain in support of the Dutch. After lengthy negotiations in London, a suspension of hostilities was converted into peace. James refused to recall 'volunteers' in the Dutch service but agreed that they should not be recruited in his dominions. The vexed question of trade with regions claimed by Spain was left unresolved. Spanish ships in distress were to be permitted to seek refuge in English ports. Englishmen in Spain would not be harassed by the Inquisition provided that they caused no public scandal. Though James reserved the right to represent the Dutch case should they wish to open negotiations, the treaty was widely regarded as abandoning them. Reconciliation with Spain remained a major objective with James for the rest of his reign. JAC

London, treaty of, 1827. This was an attempt by Canning in company with Russia and France to protect British interests during the Greek revolt against Turkish rule by a partnership with Russia. It followed an earlier protocol (April 1826) which aimed at securing internal autonomy for a tribute-paying Greece. The three powers demanded an immediate armistice, and an allied fleet under Admiral *Codrington was sent with vague instructions to prevent further fighting. In the event the Ottoman navies were destroyed at *Navarino in October 1827. The treaty was a step on the road to an independent Greece in 1832. CJB

London, treaty of, 1831. The settlement of the Belgian question was the first test for *Palmerston on becoming foreign secretary in Lord *Grey's administration. Belgium, previously the Austrian Netherlands, had been reunited with Holland in 1815 to form a barrier to French expansion, but had rebelled in August 1830 and declared itself independent. Under threat from the Dutch, the Belgians looked to France for assistance, provoking fears of renewed French aggrandizement. A conference of the great powers in London in February 1831 recognized Belgian independence and, when the Dutch refused to submit, French troops marched in. When they proved reluctant to leave, Palmerston dropped hints of war. By the treaty of November 1831 Belgian independence and neutrality were guaranteed. The Dutch refused to accept until 1839 when a second treaty of London repeated the assurances. Palmerston had prevented any French territorial acquisitions and helped to establish a constitutional state, under Leopold of Saxe-Coburg. In accordance with the guarantee of 1839, aimed at protecting Belgium from France, Britain declared war in 1914 when Belgium was invaded by the Germans. JAC

London, treaty of, 1840. This was concluded with Russia, Austria, and Prussia to secure the ultimate return of Syria from Egypt to Turkey. While it provided for the closing of the Straits to all warships (to Britain's disadvantage), it ended whatever unilateral advantages Russia had enjoyed under the treaty of Unkiar-Skelessi (1833). *Palmerston finally persuaded sceptical cabinet colleagues that France, which was backing Egypt, would not risk war. Allied forces speedily restored Syria to Turkish rule. The settlement was confirmed by all the powers, including France, by the Straits Convention of 13 July 1841. CJB

London, treaty of, 1871. The treaty of Paris, at the end of the Crimean War, declared the Black Sea to be neutral and demilitarized. In 1870, during the Franco-Prussian War, Russia took the opportunity to repudiate the clause. Since there was nothing a conference in London could do but acquiesce, it passed a pious resolution that states could 'rid themselves of their treaty engagements' only with the consent of the other signatories. JAC

London bridge, for centuries the sole thread across the Thames, saw both ceremonial entries into the city and rebellious challenges; the gruesome custom of displaying traitors' heads above the gatehouse, commenced with William *Wallace (1305), was discontinued in 1661. *Rennie's 1831 stone bridge was recently sold and re-erected in Arizona. ASH

Londonderry was until 1973 one of the six counties of Northern Ireland. Its border with Antrim to the east is the river Bann, the river Foyle marks it off from Donegal in the Irish Republic to the west, and the border with Tyrone to the south runs through the Sperrin Mountains. It is dominated by Londonderry itself, near the mouth of the Foyle, with a population of nearly 100,000. As *Derry, it was a see from 1254; there is also a Roman catholic bishopric. In 1610 the city of London took over the area for colonization and began building the walls. In 1689, as a protestant bastion, it withstood the famous siege by James II's troops. Later it became a centre for linen manufacture and in the 20th cent. diversified into chemicals and light industry. The naval facilities of Lough Foyle were of great importance during the Second World War since the Irish Republic had reneged on its treaty obligations. Civil rights demonstrations and disorder in the city in 1969 were the beginning of the renewed troubles that have haunted Northern Ireland for many years. The county is divided between catholic and protestant. In 1992 the Foyle division returned a Social Democratic and Labour Party member to Westminster, and Londonderry East an Ulster Unionist Party member. JAC

Londonderry, siege of, 1689. When William of Orange landed at Brixham, Lord-Lieutenant *Tyrconnel, to furnish Irish troops for England, had weakened his Ulster garrisons. In December both Londonderry and Enniskillen shut their doors against fresh garrisons, and, after the rout of the Ulster protestants at Dromore in March 1689, became crowded with refugees. In April James II himself advanced against Londonderry. Governor Robert Lundy was prepared to surrender, but was overthrown by a popular rebellion and replaced by Major Henry Baker and the Revd George *Walker.

The besiegers lacked artillery, and their communications were harassed by the aggressive Enniskillen men. Londonderry, however, was ill provided and had 30,000 mouths to feed. It was in extremes before a Williamite supply ship broke the besiegers' boom on Lough Foyle on 28 July, terminating the siege. Apart from securing the Williamite bridgehead in Ulster, the siege became a symbol of populist defiance and distrust of official leadership in protestant Ulster. BPL

London Gazette. Published as the *Oxford Gazette* prior to 5 February 1666, this bi-weekly was an immediate success, despite its dullness, since it carried all the official news. Competition from new, livelier publications after 1695 and the Stamp Act (1712) led to a decline in importance and sales, though not demise. ASH

London Missionary Society. Founded in 1795 as a non-denominational body to proclaim 'the glorious gospel of the blessed God' abroad, it adopted the name London Missionary Society (1818) and became mainly *congregationalist. The first mission to Tahiti (1797) only became successful under John Williams (1817), translator of the New Testament into Rarotongan (1834), who was killed and eaten (1839). Brief success in Sierra Leone was followed by lasting success in South Africa under John Philip, where its most celebrated missionaries were Robert Moffat and David *Livingstone. There were also missions to India and under Robert Morrison to Guangzhou, China (1807–34), the first protestant missionaries there. Since 1973 it has been known as the Council for World Mission. WMM

London University was founded largely on the initiative of Lord *Brougham. Opening in 1828, University College had no religious entrance requirements and became known as 'the godless institution of Gower Street'. In the following year, in contrast, King's College was founded to promote 'the doctrines and duties of Christianity'. By a charter of 1836, the university, consisting of King's, University College, and some medical schools, became an examining body, offering degrees to students who had studied elsewhere. From 1858, matriculation examinations were added, which required candidates to pass five subjects at the same examination. Women were admitted to examinations from 1867 and three colleges were opened for them in 1870 and the 1880s.

The Selborne royal commission (1889–90) recommended that teaching powers were needed for London. The Gresham royal commission (1892–4) favoured a single university authority. These changes were implemented in 1900 and a federal structure adopted. London has a vice-chancellor and a principal, and consists of schools of the university, medical schools, postgraduate medical schools, and senate institutes. Senate House and a nucleus of colleges were built in Bloomsbury in the late 1930s. PG

Long, Walter (1854–1924). Conservative statesman. After holding junior office, Long entered the cabinet in 1895 and held a variety of middle-rank ministerial positions until the Conservative electoral disaster of January 1906. Between 1906 and 1910 he consolidated his position within the first rank of Conservative politics, emerging as a moderate tariff reformer and as an enthusiastic patron of Irish unionism. He was a contender for the Conservative leadership in November 1911, but—with Austen *Chamberlain—withdrew in favour of Bonar *Law. It is doubtful whether he had either the equanimity or the political subtlety to lead the Conservatives, though he certainly represented an antidote to Balfourian sophistication. He was appointed president of the Local Government Board at the formation of the first wartime coalition in May 1915, and became colonial secretary when the Lloyd George coalition was formed in December 1916. He was 1st lord of the Admiralty, his last ministerial post, between January 1917 and February 1921: he received a viscountcy after his retirement. A conscientious though unimaginative administrator, who held a representative significance as a leader of landed Toryism, Long is often depicted as a dull-witted squire, but was ferociously ambitious and strategically alert. AJ

Longchamp, William (d. 1197). Bishop and statesman. Longchamp was born in Normandy and was taken up by Richard, heir to Henry II, who appointed him chancellor of Aquitaine. When Richard succeeded in 1189, Longchamp was made chancellor of England, given the see of Ely, and became a papal legate. In the long absences of Richard, he was the most powerful man in the kingdom. With the bishop of Durham, he was appointed joint *justiciar in 1189 and sole justiciar the following year. A recent arrival, with little or no English and a domineering manner, he was far from popular. Richard's brother John acted as a rallying-point for opposition to Longchamp; his seizure of *Geoffrey, archbishop of York, scandalized many; and in 1191 he was besieged in the Tower and forced into exile on the continent. Richard continued to employ him on diplomatic and financial matters and he made two more brief visits to England in 1193 and 1194. He died at Poitiers on a mission to Rome. The hatred of most chroniclers, particularly *Gerald of Wales, makes it hard to know the truth, but Longchamp was said to be stunted, lame, and uncouth. JAC

Longleat near Warminster in Wiltshire was one of the earliest of the great Elizabethan show or prodigy houses, started before Wollaston (1580s) or *Hardwick (1590s). It was begun by Sir John Thynne, who had done well out of the *dissolution of the monasteries. The advising architect was Robert Smythson, later employed at Wollaston and Hardwick. Its main feature is the great expanse of windows. *Brown and *Repton were both employed in the 18th cent. on the great park. The Thynne family, subsequently viscounts Weymouth and marquises of Bath, were among the earliest to perceive the commercial potential of aristocracy, and the lions of Longleat are probably better known than the architecture. JAC

Long Melford church (Suffolk), dedicated in honour of the Holy Trinity, was completely rebuilt in the second half of the 15th cent. Surviving inscriptions, glass, and wall-painting testify to the prominence of the Clopton and Martin families, among others, in this rebuilding. Very unusually, some idea of what the interior of the late medieval building looked like can be got from a description by Roger Martin, who was a recusant in the reign of Elizabeth I, and who wrote down all he could remember of the furnishings of his parish church. He also gave details of the ceremonies that made up the liturgical year, which included bonfires, feasts, and processions. LR

Long Parliament, 1640–60. Charles I's defeat by the Scots in the *Bishops' wars diminished both his reputation and his financial resources, leaving him with no option but to summon Parliament in November 1640. But the initiative was seized by his critics, who impeached his chief minister, *Strafford, and pushed through a bill forbidding the dissolution of Parliament without its own consent. Further Acts, in mid-1641, abolished the instruments of prerogative rule, such as *Star Chamber, outlawed prerogative taxation, and provided for triennial parliaments, thereby restoring the traditional constitution. Members of both Houses were broadly united behind these measures, but when their leaders, distrusting Charles, proposed to take away his right to appoint ministers or control the army, they alienated the conservatives and opened the way to civil war. Even after victory had been secured there were continuing divisions between radicals and moderates over the shape of the post-war settlement, and these were only resolved by a radical coup in December 1648, when Colonel *Pride 'purged' the Commons of its moderate members.

England was now governed by the *'Rump' of the Long Parliament, which executed the king, abolished the monarchy and House of Lords, and declared a republic. But this was the limit of its radicalism, and army leaders like *Cromwell, who had been looking to the Rump to take the lead in reforming both state and church, became angered and frustrated. Faced with the prospect of continuing stalemate, Cromwell called in troops to expel the Rump in February 1653 and set up a new regime. The Long Parliament remained in abeyance until 1659, when the army generals who seized power after Cromwell's death briefly recalled the Rump. But not until early 1660, when *Monck ordered the readmission of the excluded members, did the full house reassemble. By this time, however, the need for new elections was overwhelming, and in March 1660 the Long Parliament voted to dissolve itself. RL

lord advocate. The post dates from the 15th cent. when the lord advocate quickly became a prominent officer of the Scottish crown. He had a legal and political role, becoming public prosecutor with a seat in Parliament. From 1746 the lord advocate was largely responsible for the management of the Scottish administration until the department of the secretary for Scotland was established in 1885. Today the lord advocate advises the government on Scottish legal matters and has complete discretion over criminal prosecution in Scotland. He is often an MP and a member of the Privy Council. The post is political and changes with the government. RAS

lord chamberlain. See CHAMBERLAIN, LORD GREAT.

lord chancellor. *Edward the Confessor first created the post of chancellor, which has always remained one of the leading offices of state. The chancellor was keeper of the great seal and acted as chief secretary to the king, drawing up charters and writs. When the office of *justiciar ended in the mid-13th cent. the chancellor became the most important man in the country after the king. He was a leading adviser and presided over meetings of the *great council. In the 14th cent. the chancellor entered the legal system when he began to hear appeals from subjects unable to obtain justice from the common law courts. From this it evolved that the chancellor became a judge in his own court, the Court of *Chancery, operating in accordance with the 'principles of equity'. The modern role of the lord chancellor thus straddles both political and legal spheres. He presides over the highest court of appeal in the country, the House of Lords. He is also part of the legislature, acting as Speaker in the Lords. Finally, the lord chancellor is a government cabinet minister responsible for the operation of the English judicial system. RAS

lord chancellor of Ireland. The earliest chancellor of Ireland was Stephen Ridel, appointed in 1189. An Irish Chancery was established in 1232 and granted to the chancellor of England, who normally executed the duties by deputy. Later the office was held by English lawyers. As a result, the development of the Irish Chancery followed closely that of the English equity system. Since 1922 there has been one lord chancellor for the whole of the United Kingdom, who is always chosen from the English bench or bar. RAS

lord chief justice. The second highest post in the judicial ranking. Since the days of Sir Edward *Coke, the chief justice of King's Bench has informally used the title of lord chief justice. It is only since 1875 that it has been the statutory title of the president of the Queen's Bench Division of the High Court of Justice. With the creation of the High Court, in 1875, it was decided there was no necessity to retain three separate common law divisions. However it was important to avoid the demotion, or compulsory retirement, of the senior judges as this would have broken the constitutional principle that judges were irremovable. In 1880 the deaths of Sir Alexander Cockburn (chief justice of Queen's Bench) and Sir Fitzroy Kelly (chief baron of the Exchequer) meant that the offices of chief justice of Common Pleas and chief baron of the Exchequer could be abolished. The Exchequer and Common Pleas were merged with the Queen's Bench Division and Lord Coleridge, former chief justice of Common Pleas, became lord chief justice of England. Unlike the lord chancellor, the lord chief justice has no political role and remains in office after a change of government. RAS

lord high steward. Originally purely a household officer, the task of the steward, or seneschal, was to place dishes on the royal table, but like many comparable offices it gathered other duties and rose in prestige. Eventually, as lord high steward, he performed at coronations and presided over the trial of peers. The lord steward, at first the deputy, retains the household responsibilities and remains an officer of the court. In the 12th cent. the office of lord high steward belonged to the Bigods, earls of Norfolk, but was taken over by de *Montfort as earl of Leicester. After his death at *Evesham, the office was given to Edmund Crouchback, Henry III's son, and then merged with the crown. It therefore became necessary to make temporary appointments for particular occasions. At the trial of Lord *Stafford in 1680, Lord Chancellor *Finch was created lord high steward so that he could preside; in 1760, at the trial of Lord Ferrers for murder, Sir Robert Henley was hastily given a peerage and appointed. In Scotland, the office became hereditary in the 12th cent. in the Stewart family, who became monarchs in the 14th cent. JAC

lord justice clerk. Scottish legal post. Originally the lord justice clerk of Scotland was clerk and assessor to the *Justiciar's Court. The court, usually presided over by peers, had professional lawyers as clerks. Gradually the post increased in importance and by the late 16th cent. the holder was always a member of the Privy Council. By the late 17th cent. he had become one of the judges in the court itself. Reforms in 1672 created the High Court of Judiciary, the central criminal court of Scotland. The lord justice clerk was usually working head of the court, although he ranked second to the lord justice-general. In the *Court of Session he ranked equally with the other judges until the reorganization of 1808 when he was made president of the second division of that court. Today the lord justice clerk is the holder of the second highest judicial office in Scotland. RAS

lord justice-general. Scottish legal post. From the 15th cent. the lord justice-general was recognized as the supreme judge of criminal cases in Scotland, superseding the post of *justiciar. The office, usually held by peers, was hereditary in the Argyll family from 1514 until 1628. Though the office continued to be held by noblemen after the reorganization of courts in 1672, the effective work was done by the *lord justice clerk in the High Court of Judiciary. In 1830 the Court of Session Act declared that after the death of the existing office-holder, the 3rd duke of Montrose, the office of lord justice-general would be merged with that of the lord president of the *Court of Session. RAS

lord keeper. The great seal of England was normally in the custody of the *lord chancellor. But an office of vice-chancellor or sealbearer in the 12th cent. developed into the separate office of lord keeper. The lord keepership seems to have been used when the holder did not have the standing necessary for the chancellorship and in 1562, by an Act 5 Eliz. c. 18, it was confirmed that the lord keepership carried the full authority of the chancellorship. Bishop *Williams, the last clerical holder of the seal, was lord keeper 1621–5, Sir Nathan Wright from 1700, and Sir Robert Henley from 1757, though he was subsequently made chancellor. When no adequate candidate was available, the seal could be put into commission, last done in 1835. JAC

lord president of the council. A regular member of the cabinet for much the same reasons as the *lord privy seal—it is useful to the prime minister to have ministers whose duties are small and who can be asked to undertake special responsibilities or fill the role of elder statesmen. The office originated in Tudor times when the *Privy Council was evolving from the medieval council. The earliest certain holder of the post was the duke of *Suffolk, brother-in-law to Henry VIII, from 1530. An Act of 1529, 21 Hen. VIII c. 20, gave the president precedence below the *treasurer and the *chancellor but above the *lord privy seal. The lord president's responsibilities are now residual. Lord *Harrowby held the post for a remarkable fifteen years 1812–27; *Balfour held it 1919–22 and 1925–9, and Stanley *Baldwin 1931–5. JAC

lord privy seal. The privy seal developed early in the 13th cent. when the use of the *great seal was too cumbersome or the king was travelling. From 1275 there was a keeper of the privy seal and the office was upgraded in 1487 when Bishop *Foxe was designated lord privy seal. By the end of his long tenure, the office had established itself as one of the most important in the realm. Though the privy seal, in turn, became too formal an authorization and was superseded by the signet, the lord privy seal found new tasks, presiding over the Court of *Requests, set up in the Tudor period to provide justice for poor men. The use of the privy seal was finally abolished in 1884 but by that time the lord privy seal had long established his position as a member of the cabinet. Being without portfolio, he is now available to take on special governmental responsibilities. JAC

Lords, House of. The upper chamber of the British Parliament. Originally part of the *great council or the king's council of the Norman and Plantagenet monarchs, the Lords became separated from the Commons in the reign of Edward III. It has been in continuous existence since, except between 1649, at the end of the English Civil War, when it was abolished by a unanimous vote of the Commons, and 1660, when it reassembled at the Restoration of Charles II. Its membership today consists of the 'lords spiritual' (the bishops) and the 'lords temporal' (the hereditary and life peers). Before the Reformation the spiritual lords (who then included abbots and priors) were in a majority. Since 1529, when the abbots and priors were removed, the House has been dominated by the peers, whose numbers have expanded enormously, particularly since the late 19th cent. With the introduction of life peerages in 1958 (which also allowed peeresses in their own right to sit for the first time), the hereditary element in the House (while still a theoretical majority) has declined in its daily attendance.

The numerical strength of the lords spiritual was fixed at the Reformation to include the archbishops of Canterbury and York and the 24 bishops (an increase of 5 bishops on the pre-Reformation period). Upon the expansion of English sees, which began with the creation of the bishopric of Manchester in 1847, it was enacted that the number of bishops sitting in the Lords should not be increased. The current lords spiritual consist of the archbishops, the three senior bishops of London, Durham, and Winchester, and the 21 next in seniority of consecration.

Since the Anglo-Scottish Union in 1707, the Scots peerage had assembled in Edinburgh (or by sending a proxy or signed list) to elect sixteen *representative peers at each general election to sit in the House. By-elections were held when necessary. By votes of the House in 1709 and 1711, Scottish peers who held British titles (i.e. titles conferred after the Union) were not allowed to vote in Scottish peerage elections, nor to sit in the Lords. These votes were reversed in 1782. In 1963 the Act which allowed peers to renounce their titles on their succession also abolished the election of Scottish representative peers (the last election took place in 1959), giving all peers of Scotland rights of membership.

At the Union with Ireland in 1801, the Irish peers met in the Irish House of Lords in Dublin and elected 28 representative peers for life. All subsequent elections to fill a vacancy were conducted by post. The last election took place in 1919, and no vacancies were filled after the creation of the Irish Free State in 1922, although those peers already elected remained members of the Lords. The last Irish representative peer died in 1961. The Irish Act of Union also allowed for the election of four representative bishops of the Anglican Church of Ireland.

The House of Lords is the highest court of appeal, a function developed since the late 13th cent. when Parliament was regarded as the highest court of royal justice, though the control by the House of appeals from the English courts of common law may be traced back to the king's great council. This control was later extended to the Courts of *Chancery or equity in England (1677), and to the courts of Scotland (by the Union) and Ireland (by an Act of 1720). The appeals were heard by the whole House and any member could take part. An increased work-load led to the problem of finding judicial personnel, and eventually (after a failed attempt in 1856 to create a judicial life peer) led to the creation in 1876 by the Appellate Jurisdiction Act of the modern judicial powers and practice of the House. These included salaried 'lords of appeal in ordinary' (who were to hold peerages only during their terms of office), though the Act did not disqualify any peer from taking part in judicial proceedings. A further Act of 1887 allowed the lords of appeal to retain their peerages for life.

Over the years the powers of the House of Lords *vis-à-vis* the House of Commons have been severely curtailed. This process probably began in 1407 when Henry IV agreed that money grants were to be initiated in the Commons. By resolutions of 1671 and 1678 the Commons asserted their exclusive right to control taxation. The custom was that the Lords could reject, but not amend, a money bill, but rejection was rarely used as it invariably led to a crisis between the Houses. The rejection by the Lords of the Finance Bill in 1909, which contained *Lloyd George's 'People's Budget', including such important social measures as old-age pensions, led to a major constitutional crisis which was resolved by two general elections and the promise of a massive creation of peers given by King George V to Prime Minister *Asquith. The Lords backed down and the resulting Parliament Act of 1911 drastically reduced the powers of the Lords to those of limited delay. A money bill could receive the royal assent after one month even though the consent of the Lords had been withheld, while other public bills could only be delayed by two years (reduced to one year by the Parliament Act of 1949). Upon the massive Labour victory in 1945 the marquis of *Salisbury, the leader of a permanent inbuilt Conservative majority in the House, established an understanding that the Lords would not delay legislation that had appeared in the winning party's election manifesto. Designed to avoid conflict with the *Attlee government, this understanding has sometimes led to the House being more critical of Conservative than Labour legislation.

Until 1801, when an increase in membership resulting from the Union with Ireland necessitated a larger venue, the Lords had met in the white chamber of the old palace of Westminster. It then moved to the white or lesser hall. After the fire of 1834 which destroyed large parts of the old palace, the Lords occupied the painted chamber until they moved in 1847 into their present chamber in the new palace. Between 1941 (when the Commons' chamber was destroyed by German bombing) and 1950 the Commons met in the House of Lords, while the Lords met in the royal robing room.

Graves, M. A. R., *The House of Lords in the Parliaments of Edward VI and Mary I: An Institutional Study* (Cambridge, 1981); Jones, C. (ed.), *A Pillar of the Constitution: The House of Lords in British Politics, 1640–1784* (1989); Jones, C., and Jones, D. L. (eds.), *Peers, Politics and Power: The House of Lords, 1603–1911* (1986); Powell, J. E., and Wallis, K., *The House of Lords in the Middle Ages: A History of the English House of Lords to 1540* (1968).

CJ

Lord's cricket ground, home of the Marylebone Cricket Club and of the Middlesex County Cricket Club, was opened in 1787 by Thomas Lord from Yorkshire in Dorset

Square, near Regent's Park. The first match was between Middlesex and Essex. In 1809 he was obliged to move to St John's Wood, a little to the north. The first test match on the ground was between England and Australia in 1884. JAC

lords of Articles. See COMMITTEE OF ARTICLES.

lords-lieutenant came into existence at a time of considerable unrest after the death of Henry VIII. Protector *Somerset appointed the earl of Shrewsbury in 1547 to be his lieutenant in the counties of Yorkshire, Lancashire, Cheshire, Derby, Shropshire, and Nottinghamshire and to muster the levies: other lieutenants were appointed a little later. The system was extended in 1549 when there was widespread rioting. Subsequent monarchs found it a useful office and the lord-lieutenant became the chief royal representative in each shire, usually, though not invariably, a leading nobleman. He suggested to the *lord chancellor persons fit to serve on the bench and acquired, in the course of time, considerable electoral influence. The growth of a standing army and the reforms of 1871 deprived the lord-lieutenant of most of his military responsibilities, but social prestige remained. JAC

Losecoat Field, battle of, 1470. Soon after his capture by *Warwick's supporters after the defeat of his troops at *Edgecote, Edward IV succeeded in regaining some freedom of action. In the spring of the following year, Warwick gave covert support to a Lancastrian rising in Lincolnshire, led by Sir Robert *Welles. Edward defeated the rebels without much difficulty on 12 March 1470 near Empingham, 5 miles west of Stamford. In the rout the rebels tore off their incriminating coats and badges. Welles and his father were beheaded. JAC

Losinga, Herbert de (*c.*1054–1119). First bishop of Norwich (*c.*1094–1119). Possibly a Lotharingian by descent but English-born, Losinga was educated at Fécamp (Normandy), where he became prior, before moving to Ramsey (Hunts.), as abbot (*c.*1088) and buying the bishopric of Thetford (1091). Sensitivity forced him to Rome (1094) to resign on grounds of simony, but Pope Urban reinstated him. Losinga moved the see to flourishing Norwich (1094), where he started building the impressive cathedral (1096) and monastery on the lines of Canterbury and Durham, but using the Fécamp custumary. Fatherly to his Norwich monks, an energetic, enterprising bishop and reputable scholar, he was superior to most contemporaries. Like his predecessors, he unsuccessfully tried to subvert the prestigious independence of Bury St Edmunds abbey. He contributed to the literature over lay investiture and Henry I sent him to Rome to back his case. WMM

Lostwithiel campaign, 1644. Charles I's stunning success at Lostwithiel rescued the royalist cause when almost at its last gasp. *Marston Moor in early July 1644 had been a devastating blow to the king. He was given respite through *Essex's ill-conceived excursion into Cornwall. The people were hostile, liaison with the fleet bound to be difficult, and it was not clear what strategic advantage the county would afford, even if it could be held. Unsurprisingly, Charles took the opportunity to pursue Essex and cut off his retreat. Essex was bottled up in the Fowey peninsula, heavily outnumbered and desperately short of supplies. His cavalry managed to break out, and Essex himself abandoned his troops, but 6,000 of the infantry were forced to surrender on 2 September. Since the royalists could neither feed them nor guard them with safety, they were disarmed and allowed to leave. JAC

Lothian is the name applied to the tract of land bounded by the Forth and Tweed rivers, which was absorbed into *Northumbria in the 7th cent. and became firmly part of Scotland in the 10th cent. Its name was perpetuated in the counties of East, West, and Midlothian and, from 1973 to 1996, in an administrative region of Scotland, comprising the city of Edinburgh and the counties of East Lothian, West Lothian (except Bo'ness), and Midlothian (except Heriot and Stow). The region was dominated by Edinburgh, the capital of Scotland, with a population of about 435,000, whose employment was derived mainly from administrative, financial, professional, and tourism services; for the remainder of the region's 750,000 people, including those in Livingston new town, manufacturing, including electronics, was more important. The region was abolished in 1996 and its territory divided between four all-purpose councils, Edinburgh, East Lothian, Midlothian, and West Lothian. Whatever the administrative structure, the number and strength of the institutions based in Edinburgh—notably, the banks, the Church of Scotland, the Scottish Office—cannot fail to ensure that the area round Edinburgh retains a large part of the leadership which it acquired when medieval kings of Scotland made it their capital and when ships at the quayside at Leith unloaded French claret and calvinist theology. CML

Loudoun, John Campbell, 1st earl of [S] (1598–1662). Loudoun played a dexterous part in the tortuous politics of mid-17th-cent. Scotland. The foundation of his career was his marriage to the granddaughter of the master of Loudoun, a baroness in her own right. Loudoun was raised to the earldom in May 1633 but, since he opposed Charles I's policies, the promotion was not confirmed until 1641. In the meantime, he had become a prominent member of the *covenanting party. In 1640 he was sent briefly to the Tower on a charge of treasonably urging Louis XIII of France to intervene, though he claimed that only friendly mediation was intended. Nevertheless, bereft of friends, Charles I was obliged to appoint him chancellor of Scotland and 1st commissioner of the Treasury in 1641. He supported Scottish intervention in the Civil War and was a member of the team which negotiated with the king at *Uxbridge in 1645 and *Carisbrooke in 1647. In 1650 he issued a fierce denunciation of *Montrose at his trial. He was on the losing side at *Dunbar, took part in Charles II's coronation at Scone in 1651, but surrendered to *Monck in 1655. At the Restoration, he was deprived of the chancellorship and fined. Though Clarendon accused him of a 'loose and vicious life', Loudoun seems to have been devoted to a *presbyterian form of church government. JAC

Loudoun Hill, battle of, 1307. After the defeat at *Methven in 1306, Robert I Bruce fled and his followers were savagely treated. He resumed campaigning the following spring and on 10 May inflicted a sharp defeat on a superior force under Aymer de *Valence at Loudoun Hill, near Kilmarnock. The initiative Bruce had regained was reinforced when Edward I died in July 1307. JAC

Louisbourg on *Cape Breton Island was the keystone of 18th-cent. French strategy in the North Atlantic. Massive fortifications were commenced in 1719–20, and completed shortly before a British and American colonial force captured the 'Dunkirk of North America' in 1745. Restored to France in 1748, Louisbourg was a thriving fishing and trading port as well as the key to the French colony in the St Lawrence valley. Captured again after heavy bombardment in 1758, Louisbourg was razed by the British in 1760. Since 1961, the fortress has been partly rebuilt as a regional development and heritage project. GM

Louviers, treaty of, 1196. When Richard I left the Third Crusade and was imprisoned in Germany, Philip Augustus of France launched an attack on Normandy. Once Richard was released he began a successful counter-attack. At Louviers, in January 1196, Richard recovered most of the territory that had been lost. But after John's accession, the whole of the duchy of Normandy was lost in 1204. JAC

Lovett, William (1800–77). Chartist. Born in Newlyn, Lovett migrated in 1821 to London, where he became a cabinet-maker and soon immersed himself in radical reform movements, such as *Owenite co-operation, the National Union of the Working Classes, and the National Political Union. In 1836 he founded the London Working Men's Association, from which emerged the *chartist movement. Helped by Francis *Place and J. A. *Roebuck, Lovett drafted the People's Charter, and from 1838 was a national chartist leader, though he soon quarrelled with *O'Connor, whom he denounced as 'the great I am'. Lovett was arrested in 1839 following riots in Birmingham and spent a year in gaol. On his release he concentrated on 'knowledge chartism', emphasizing education, self-help, and alliance with the middle class. But from 1842 he became increasingly marginalized from chartism; and in his later years turned to teaching, writing, and the support of liberal-radical causes, including *temperance, international peace, and the abolition of slavery. JFCH

low church. As against the *high-church view of the Church of England, low churchmen minimized continuity with the medieval past and the role of bishops and sacraments. Their views owed more to the reform of the 16th cent. but were often described in the late 17th and 18th cents. as *'latitudinarian'. Politically, they favoured the revolution settlement and were generally Whig in sympathy. Therefore, the accession of the Hanoverians brought them into the ascendancy and also into the political machine. Theologically they represented a liberal arminian view, opposed to calvinism which developed in one direction in Wesleyan methodism. The term passed out of use until the 19th cent. when it was recovered in contrast to the high-church views of the *Oxford movement. By then it had taken on some of the characteristics of the *evangelical revival and shed its lukewarm latitudinarianism. To counter the tractarian influence, low churchmen and evangelicals often made common cause with the increasingly popular protestant nonconformist congregations. Whereas the high-church emphasis was on salvation within the divinely appointed church through a sacramental system, the low church emphasized personal salvation through individual conversion and close attention to Scripture as the inspired word of God. Low-church worship was consciously anti-ritualist and held fast to the *Book of Common Prayer. JFC

Lowe, Robert (1811–92). Liberal politician. An albino and a sharply sarcastic debater, Lowe cut a distinctive political figure. Of Anglican clerical family and educated at Winchester and Oxford, he went to New South Wales and made his name on the legislative council and money from legal practice and property transactions. Back as a Liberal MP (later London University's first member), he gained a reputation for free market and anti-democratic views, the latter apparently sharpened by Australian experience. As vice-president of the Privy Council and responsible for popular education, he introduced the 1862 'revised code' linking government grants to examination results in basic subjects, antagonizing the religious denominations and the teachers. Out of office Lowe fronted the Whig *'Adullamite' revolt against the 1866 Reform Bill, bringing down *Russell's government and putting the Conservatives in office. When they passed a comparably 'democratic' measure, Lowe concluded it was necessary 'to compel our future masters to learn their letters'. Chancellor of the Exchequer in *Gladstone's 1868 government, Lowe, after early success, had to withdraw his 1871 budget and was moved to the Home Office in 1873 under a cloud of departmental mismanagement. A public speech criticizing the queen in 1876 led to withdrawal and apology in the Commons, but failing eyesight and personal unpopularity also weakened Lowe's position. He was created Viscount Sherbrooke in 1880. A notable administrative and educational reformer, Lowe suffers in reputation from the sharpness of his anti-popular language. BIC

Lowestoft, battle of, 1665. A heavy engagement in the second Anglo-Dutch War between the English fleet, commanded by James, duke of York (later James II), *Sandwich, and Prince *Rupert, and a Dutch fleet under Jacob van Opdam, on 3 June. Pepys wrote that the noise of the gunfire could be heard in the streets of London. Opdam was killed when his flagship blew up and the Dutch losses were severe. 'A great victory, never known in the world,' was Pepys's summary. JAC

Lucan, George Charles Bingham, 3rd earl of (1800–88). Born into an aristocratic family, George Bingham became an officer in the British army by purchase in 1816. After ten years of further purchase, he gained command of the 17th Lancers. Bingham had a reputation for personal bravery but was also ruthless and harsh. He relinquished his command in 1837, succeeding to the title of Lord Lucan two years later. Despite his lack of recent military experience, in 1854 Lucan was appointed to command a cavalry division for service against the Russians. Landing in the Crimea in September, the cavalry accompanied the rest of the army in an advance on Sebastopol; on 25 October, during the battle of *Balaclava, Lucan's poor relations with his brother-in-law Lord *Cardigan contributed to the ill-fated *'Charge of the Light Brigade' under Cardigan's command. Lucan rose to the rank of field marshal in 1887. JLP

Lucknow or Luknau was the capital of Awadh annexed by the British in 1856. During the *Indian mutiny, the British residency was subjected to a long siege beginning in June 1857. Sir Henry *Lawrence, the chief commissioner, was killed in August and the town's relief was not accomplished until 16 November. DAW

Lucy, Richard de (d. 1179). Justiciar. De Lucy was one of the chief props of Henry II's reign. He came from the knightly class. He originally supported Stephen and by the treaty of *Winchester of 1153, which arranged the succession, he was put in charge of the Tower. He was joint justiciar with the earl of Leicester until 1168 and sole justiciar until 1178. He supported the king against Thomas *Becket, who excommunicated him in 1166 and again in 1169 as 'a promoter of royal tyranny'. In the great crisis of Henry's reign in 1173–4, when the king was campaigning against rebels on the continent, de Lucy was the mainstay at home, driving back William the Lion of Scotland and defeating the rebel earl of Leicester at *Fornham St Genevieve. He held the office of justiciar for well over twenty years and was known as 'the loyal'. JAC

Luddites. Machine-breakers, so called after a mythical leader, General Ludd. In 1811–16 textile workers in the east midlands, south Lancashire, and west Yorkshire met secretly in public houses or on the moors, took oaths, and smashed the machinery of mill-owners who refused their demands. The attacks were for specific industrial objectives: the destruction of shearing frames and gig mills (Yorkshire), power looms (Lancashire), and resistance to the breakdown of custom in the midlands framework-knitting industry. These were economic grievances which sprang from structural and technical changes in the industry, aggravated by trade depression, unemployment, and high prices. At a time when trade unions were illegal, Luddism may be interpreted as collective bargaining by riot: frame-breaking in the east midlands was an attempt to coerce employers rather than hostility to machines as such. Some Luddites may have harboured revolutionary intentions: the organization was so shrouded in secrecy, and so difficult to penetrate, as to support fears of an underground movement aiming at armed insurrection. Despite the deployment of spies and informers and 12,000 troops in the north and midlands, the government experienced great difficulty in dealing with the Luddites who, after their nightly attacks, disappeared into sympathetic local communities. Eventually the Luddite bands were tracked down and the reputed leaders executed or transported. The background to Luddism in Yorkshire is vividly described in Charlotte Brontë's novel *Shirley*. JFCH

Ludford Bridge, battle of, 1459. After *Salisbury's victory at *Blore Heath, he marched to Ludlow to join his allies *Warwick and *York. They were confronted by a large Lancastrian force led by Henry VI himself. After a skirmish on 12 October near the bridge over the Teme, the Yorkist leaders fled, leaving their troops to surrender. JAC

Ludlow, Edmund (*c.*1617–92). Ludlow was one of a group of austere republicans that included *Vane and *Haselrig. His father Sir Henry Ludlow, a Wiltshire landowner, represented the county in the *Long Parliament and was a fierce opponent of the king's policies. Ludlow himself joined *Essex's army in 1642 and fought throughout the war, mainly in Haselrig's cavalry. Returned for Wiltshire in 1646, he signed the king's death warrant in 1649. In 1651–5 he served in Ireland, though disapproving *Cromwell's Protectorate. Returning to Parliament in 1659, he opposed Richard *Cromwell and, after his fall, joined Haselrig in the *Council of State. He was about to join *Lambert's rising when it collapsed and at the Restoration in 1660 he escaped to the continent. Charles II's supporters hunted for him with considerable zeal. He took refuge in Switzerland and survived plots against his life. In 1689 he misjudged the situation in England, returned to London, and was obliged to flee again when a proclamation was issued for his arrest. His memoirs, first issued in 1698/9, are an important source for the Commonwealth period. JAC

Ludlow castle (Shropshire), standing on a cliff above the river Teme, has long been regarded as a romantic and picturesque ruin, attractive to artists and writers. As early as 1772 public walks were laid out round the castle. Founded soon after the Conquest by the de Lacy family as a strong point in the turbulent march area, the castle and town remained important throughout the Middle Ages. In 1473, when Edward IV sent his son to Ludlow, the castle became the headquarters of the nascent *Council of the Marches, which between 1534 and 1641 was the focus of government for the Welsh border. The castle was often the residence of the princes of Wales. Edward V was there when he succeeded in 1483 and Prince *Arthur and *Catherine lived there briefly after their marriage until the prince's death in 1502. The political importance of Ludlow made it also a cultural centre. In 1634 John *Milton wrote the masque *Comus* for John, earl of Bridgwater, then president of the council, and it was performed in the castle by members of his family on 29 September. LR

Lugard, Sir Frederick, Baron Lugard (1858–1945). Colonial administrator. Lugard started as a soldier and adventurer, then got drawn into east Africa's religious wars (protestant converts v. catholic converts), until the area (*Uganda) was formally annexed by Britain in 1894. Then he helped the Royal Niger Company in the west, and when its charter ran out became British commissioner in northern Nigeria. While there he devised a new way of governing 'natives', called 'indirect rule', or ruling them according to their own customs rather than by imposing alien ones. He later justified this philosophically, in a seminal book called *The Dual Mandate in British Tropical Africa* (1922); but it clearly had practical advantages too. The *Dual Mandate*'s other message was that colonies should be run for the benefit of both their subjects and the world as a whole. That made Lugard an obvious choice for the League of Nations Permanent Mandates Commission, on which he sat from 1922 to 1936. BJP

Lulach (d. 1058), king of 'Scotland' and Moray (1057–8). His mother Gruoch belonged to the royal dynasty which failed in the male line in 1034. She married *Macbeth after the death of Lulach's father Gille Comgáin, king of *Moray, in 1032 at Macbeth's hands. He probably allied with *Malcolm Canmore against Macbeth, and became king of Scotland when Malcolm killed Macbeth in 1057. Four and a half months later Lulach was himself Malcolm's victim, slain 'by treachery' at Essie (38 miles west of Aberdeen), probably on 17 March 1058. According to a debatable source his body was taken to Iona for burial. He is the last king of Moray recognized as king of Scotland in Scottish king-lists. DEB

Lullingstone was a Romano-British villa in the Darent valley, Kent. Originating in the late 1st cent., by the late 2nd cent. the residence contained a sunken *nymphaeum*, later housing two fine marble busts. The house was extensively remodelled at the beginning of the 4th cent., including a mosaic of Europa and the Bull. The northern end was partitioned off to form a Christian chapel whose wall-paintings included the *chi-rho* (the Christogram) and praying figures, preserved by having collapsed into the former *nymphaeum*. Nearby were a circular shrine and a temple-mausoleum, as well as agricultural buildings. ASEC

Lumphanan, battle of, 1057. On 15 August 1057 *Malcolm Canmore defeated and killed *Macbeth. The version given in Shakespeare's play runs together several encounters in different places. Dunsinane (Dunsinnan) is about 6 miles north of Perth: Lumphanan, whither, according to *Holinshed, Macbeth fled, is due west of Aberdeen. JAC

lunacy. A term describing insanity, once considered to have been due to changes of the moon, now used legally and colloquially but not by clinicians. In the middle ages, the symptoms and behaviour of those with mental disorders or defects was often ascribed to demonology or witchcraft, and some sufferers were cared for by monastic orders: *Bedlam hospital, first used for 'distracted' persons 1377, was attached to the Priory of St Mary Bethlehem. Many were allowed their liberty if not dangerous, but increasingly they were deliberately segregated, often in company with vagabonds and malefactors, undergoing callous or barbarous treatment (ducking, whipping, chaining to the wall), and becoming a public spectacle for entertainment.

It was not until the latter half of the 18th cent. that a more enlightened approach was adopted (York Retreat, 1796) and the mid-19th cent. that an extensive programme of mental hospital construction was undertaken. Lord *Shaftesbury, long interested in the problem and appointed a lunacy commissioner in 1828, secured passage of the Lunacy Act (1845) which distinguished through medical certification 'persons of unsound mind' from social rejects. Optimism about curability was misplaced despite the emerging science of psychiatry, and hospital crowding led to a lapse to custodianship again. Subsequent psychotherapeutic, physical and pharmacological approaches, if sometimes controversial, have generally proved beneficial, but de-institutionalization of patients and their return to the community in the second half of the 20th cent. has not been without problems. At law, lunacy is regarded as mental unsoundness that relieves a person of criminal responsibility for their conduct, but all legal tests for insanity put forward have attracted criticism, and many think the issue of responsibility less important than identification and treatment of the disturbed. ASH

lutheranism. While the views of Calvin were largely expounded in one treatise, his *Institutes*, those of Martin Luther (1483–1546) had to be gleaned from a number of tracts and sermons, and developed over time. The most definitive statement was the Formula of Concord, drawn up thirty years after his death by reforming scholars and published, with additions, in the *Book of Concord* (1580). Luther took the Bible as the ultimate authority for Christians and his main belief was justification by faith alone: it was therefore essential for Christians to understand the Bible and Luther made his own celebrated translation into German. He recognized three sacraments: baptism, the eucharist in both kinds, and penitence. He was as committed to predestination as Calvin, finding no freedom for the human will. He disapproved of the mass, came to mistrust monasticism, advocated (and practised) clerical marriage, and taught the doctrine of the real presence in the eucharist. As his quarrel with the papacy developed, he was led to emphasize the supremacy of the secular ruler in religious matters and most of the Lutheran churches accepted the authority of bishops.

Lutheranism's greatest success was in north Germany and in Scandinavia. In England, his reputation was marred by a sharp theological exchange with Henry VIII, to whose *Defence of the Seven Sacraments* (1521), which had won from the papacy the title 'Defender of the Faith' for the king, Luther replied with *Against Henry King of England* (1522). The sequel was unfortunate for Luther. He was persuaded in 1525 to offer a humble apology for the 'hasty and speedy' printing of his book: Henry's retort was contempt for the man and his views, which were 'abominable and odious.' Many English churchmen thought it wise to distance themselves from Luther and to insist that the English Reformation, though having much in common with the German, was autonomous and independent. After Luther's death, the influence of Calvin and Geneva on the English clergy, and certainly on the Scottish, was much greater than that of lutheranism. JAC

Lutyens, Sir Edwin Landseer (1869–1944). English architect who embraced both classicism and Arts and Crafts ideals. Starting in 1896 with Munstead Wood (Surrey) for the gardener Gertrude Jekyll (1843–1942), Lutyens's early houses include Deanery Gardens, Sonning, Berks. (1899–1902), Tigbourne Court, Witley, Surrey (1899–1901), and Folly Farm, Sulhamstead, Berks. (1905). All demonstrate his ingenious planning and his imagination, sensitivity, and wit in the use of brick, tile, stone, and other traditional materials. In contrast, Heathcote, Ilkley (1905–7), and Gledstone Hall (1922–6), both Yorkshire houses, are grand and formal. Lutyens's commitment to classicism is best seen in such London office buildings as Britannic House (1920–4) and the Midland Bank (1924–37), and in his design for the Roman catholic cathedral, Liverpool (1929–44), whilst his free and whimsical interpretation of historical styles was finely expressed in his Viceroy's House, New Delhi (1912–31). Lutyens's Cenotaph in Whitehall (1919–20), noble though it is, lacks the eerie grandeur of his memorial to the missing of the Somme at Thiepval, near Arras, France (1927–32). PW

Lydgate, John (*c.*1370–*c.*1450). Poet. Born in Lydgate, a village in Suffolk south of Newmarket, he became a Benedictine monk at Bury St Edmunds. In 1421 he was made prior of Hatfield Broad Oak in Essex, but from 1432 spent the rest of his life back at Bury. Lydgate's enormous output—twice the size of Shakespeare's—was written under the patronage of Humphrey, duke of *Gloucester, and Henry V, but has not been greatly admired. His main work is a long poem describing the siege of Troy. *The Falls of Princes*, a paraphrase and translation of Boccaccio, established that discord was dangerous in a state—a truth which could have been conveyed in less than 36,000 lines. Joseph Ritson, an 18th-cent. commentator, thought him a 'voluminous, prosaick and drivelling monk': a less savage critic referred to his 'prosodic incompetence and long-winded prolixity'—serious defects in a poet. JAC

Lyndhurst, John Singleton Copley, 1st Baron (1772–1863). Lord chancellor. Born in Boston (Mass.), son of J. S. Copley the elder, the portrait painter, he came to England, attended Cambridge University, and was called to the bar in 1804. He was appointed solicitor-general in 1819 and prosecuted the *Cato Street conspirators and in the 'trial' of Queen Caroline. He became attorney-general in 1824, master of the rolls 1826, and Tory lord chancellor 1827–30, 1834–5, and 1841–6. A leading opponent of the Reform Bill, and a tower of strength to the Conservative Party in the Lords after 1830, he was a vigorous and effective speaker even in his later years. In 1856 at the age of 84 he was instrumental in defeating the government's plan to create life peerages. Benjamin *Haydon wrote in 1845 that he looked like 'a superannuated Mephistopheles'. EAS

Lynedoch, Thomas Graham, 1st Baron (1748–1843). General. On 3 September 1785 Graham participated in the first cricket match to be played in Scotland. After the death of his wife (whose portrait by Gainsborough hangs in the Scottish National Gallery) in 1791, Graham turned from managing his estate to a political and military career. In 1794 he became Whig MP for Perthshire and raised the Perthshire Volunteers. He distinguished himself at the capture of Minorca in 1798 and obtained permanent military rank through the influence of Sir John *Moore. Lynedoch subsequently became Moore's aide-de-camp during the *Corunna campaign. After commanding a brigade in the ill-fated *Walcheren expedition (1809), Lynedoch returned to the Peninsular War and defeated the French in March 1811 at *Barrosa. He then joined *Wellington, assisting in the capture of *Ciudad Rodrigo (January 1812) and commanding the left wing at *Vitoria (June 1813). The following year he was created a peer and in 1817 co-founded the United Service Club. RAS

Lytton, Edward Robert Bulwer-Lytton, 1st Earl (1831–91). Lytton was educated at Harrow and privately on the continent. He enjoyed a successful career in the diplomatic service and became attached to the Conservative Party interest. He was also a poet and friend of the Brownings. He was appointed viceroy of India in 1875 by *Disraeli and organized the great 'durbah' proclaiming Victoria queen-empress in 1877. His administration was principally distinguished for its aggressive external policies which, in 1878, brought about the second *Afghan War. His army set off for Kabul. However, a change of government at home saw him recalled and Lord *Ripon, his Liberal successor, sued for peace. In 1887 Lytton was appointed ambassador to Paris by Lord *Salisbury. DAW

Maastricht, treaty of. Popular name for the treaty on European Union, signed on 7 February 1992 at Maastricht in the Netherlands by the twelve EEC members. The treaty amended the treaty of *Rome and Single European Act, making institutional changes, increasing the competence of the European Union (EEC), and giving the European Council (meetings of heads of government) greater powers in the fields of defence and immigration. John Major, the British prime minister, obtained opt-outs for the social chapter and single currency and claimed the negotiations as a victory. This satisfied neither those who wanted full participation, nor Euro-sceptics who feared a loss of sovereignty. CNL

Mabinogi (*Mabinogion*). A cycle of early Welsh tales preserved in two 14th-cent. manuscripts: the White Book of Rhydderch (Llyfr Gwyn Rhydderch) and the Red Book of Hergest (Llyfr Coch Hergest). The *Mabinogi* comprises the four branches of Pwyll, Branwen, Manawydan, and Math. These four branches are found with seven other tales and together they are known as the *Mabinogion* (a misnomer first applied to the tales by Lady Charlotte Guest), one of which, the tale of Culhwch and Olwen, is the earliest Welsh *Arthurian tale. The content is mythological and imaginative, an example of the Celtic genius at its best. SMD

McAdam, John Loudoun (1756–1836). Road surveyor. Returning as a loyalist from New York in 1783, McAdam settled in Ayrshire, and managed the British Tar Company; selling his modest estate in 1795 to discharge debt, he re-emerged at Falmouth from 1798 as a naval prize-monger. His travels turned interest into profession, as he covered nearly 19,000 miles in 1,900 days on the road, 1798–1814, making the observations that formed his 'principles': employing small stones direct onto the subsoil as the method of making effective roads largely impermeable to water. These were presented to the House of Commons in 1811, and further observations (1819–20) came in dispute with *Telford, whose roads proved more durable but expensive. McAdam secured appointment as surveyor-general of the Bristol roads from 1816, and unpopularly consolidated his dynasty across Britain: McAdam, three sons, four grandsons, and a brother-in-law held 136 surveyorships in England and 8 in Scotland, 1816–61, with a total of around 3,700 miles of turnpike road. His fame led to the use of the term 'macadamize' as early as 1824, and was revived in Hooley's patent *Tar Macadam* (1901). JCh

Macartney, George, 1st Earl Macartney (1737–1806). Born in Ireland and educated at Trinity College, Dublin, Macartney had a varied career. He was envoy to St Petersburg (1764–7); a chief secretary for Ireland (1769–72); and captain-general of the Caribbee Islands (1775–9). In 1780 he was appointed governor of *Madras. He arrived at Fort St George during a time of great troubles. The Madras Council was riddled with corruption and Hyder Ali, the sultan of Mysore, stood at the gates of the fort threatening, with French naval help, to drive the English into the sea. Macartney re-established some semblance of internal order and engaged Mysore in a truce. After returning to England in 1786, his most important office was as first British ambassador to the court of Peking (1792–4), where his relations with the imperial court soon became strained. His final office was that of governor of the Cape of Good Hope (1796–9). DAW

Macaulay, Thomas Babington, 1st Baron (1800–59). Poet, historian, and politician. Of Scottish presbyterian ancestry, he was the son of Zachary Macaulay, the evangelical anti-slaver and co-founder of the *Clapham sect. A child prodigy, educated at Trinity College, Cambridge, he acquired an early reputation as a Whig orator and a later reputation as a formidable contributor to the **Edinburgh Review*, where he first published most of his greatest essays. A Whig MP for Calne, Leeds, and Edinburgh, he became secretary at war, paymaster-general, and was involved in drafting a new penal code for India. His *Lays of Ancient Rome* appeared in 1842, four years after he had projected the future *History of England*. The *History* was published between 1848 and 1862. Originally intended as a history of England since 1688, Macaulay had only reached 1702 by the time of his death. The *History* can be regarded as a triumphant reply to David *Hume's *History of England* and its attack on the Whig historiographical tradition, setting the terms of a new Whig historiography which survived until the middle of the 20th cent. NTP

Macbeth (d. 1057), king of Moray (1032–57) and king of 'Scotland' (1040–57). Macbeth's reputation as a tyrannous usurper is, of course, anachronistic. His career is none the less the stuff of drama. He lived during unprecedented uncertainty for both the kingship of *Moray and the Scottish royal succession. Nevertheless, he became the only person from northern Scotland to rule the Scottish kingdom for more than a few months, and the only king of Scotland to visit Rome (in 1050) where, we are told, 'he scattered money like seed to the poor'. He was also the first to bring Norman knights to Scotland. So strong was his position that he retained the Scottish throne in 1054, despite defeat at the battle of Dunsinnan (6 miles north of Perth).

Macbeth's family was riven by a feud that claimed the life of Macbeth's father in 1020, which Macbeth avenged in 1032 by burning his cousin Gille Comgáin, king of Moray. He married Gille Comgáin's widow Gruoch, perhaps in an attempt at reconciliation, but probably also because she belonged to the Scottish royal kindred. Macbeth, whose mother may have been a daughter of *Malcolm II, only benefited from the opportunity afforded by the royal dynasty's extinction in 1034 when he killed *Duncan I (probably) at Pitgaveny (near Elgin) in 1040. In 1045 he reached his zenith when he crushed Duncan's father. After Dunsinnan, however, he was forced to accept the return of Duncan's son *Malcolm Canmore from exile, and in 1057 was killed at *Lumphanan (25 miles west of Aberdeen) by Malcolm, probably in collusion with Gille Comgáin's son *Lulach. A debatable source says he was buried on Iona. DEB

McCarthy, Justin (1830–1912). Irish politician and writer. McCarthy was a journalist who was elected as Home Rule MP for Co. Longford in 1879. He moved to represent Derry City in 1886, but returned as MP for North Longford (1892–1900). As vice-chairman of the Irish Parliamentary Party he acted as mediator between *Parnell and the Liberal government in November 1890, at the time of the O'Shea divorce: when Parnell was rejected by the majority of his parliamentary party, McCarthy assumed the chairmanship, a position which he held until 1896. He pursued a second career as a popular historian and novelist, producing in 1877 a successful *History of Our Own Times*. He retired from politics in 1900, but remained a prolific author until his death. He was awarded a civil list pension in 1903. His reputation remains burdened by Parnell's brutal observation that 'he was a nice old gent for a tea party'. AJ

Macclesfield, Thomas Parker, 1st earl of (1667–1732). Parker was the son of a Staffordshire attorney and educated at Trinity College, Cambridge. Returned for Derby as a Whig MP in 1705, he took a leading part in the prosecution of Dr *Sacheverell in 1710. From 1710 to 1718 he was lord chief justice of Queen's Bench and was made Baron Parker in 1716. He removed to the lord chancellorship in 1718 and became earl of Macclesfield in 1721. In 1725 he was accused of peculation and forced to resign. Though he was a favourite with George I, he had never been close to Sir Robert *Walpole, who did nothing to save him. After a unanimous verdict of guilty at the impeachment, he was fined £30,000. Macclesfield admitted privately that he had accepted gifts from masters in Chancery on taking office but pleaded that it was the common practice. He took no further part in public life. JAC

McCormack, John (1884–1945). Irish tenor who took American citizenship in 1917. After studying in Italy, McCormack made his British operatic début at Covent Garden in 1907, reappearing every year, sometimes alongside *Melba, until 1914. In 1909 he made his New York début, gaining popularity during the next decade with the Metropolitan, Boston, and Chicago opera companies. His acknowledged limitations as an actor, however, led him to abandon the stage for a concert and recording career. He was a particularly fine interpreter of Handel, Mozart, Verdi, German *Lieder*, and Irish folk-songs, with a sweetness of tone and a stylish technique, although his later career reached a wider public through a preponderance of popular sentimental ballads, sometimes of dubious quality. ECr

MacCormick, John MacDonald (1904–61). A Glasgow lawyer and son of a sea-captain, MacCormick was a leading founder of the National Party of Scotland in 1928. A presbyterian by religion, he had originally been a supporter of the *Independent Labour Party. In 1934 the National Party merged with the Scottish Party to form the *Scottish National Party. MacCormick lost control of the party in 1942 to more radical leaders, who opposed the war. He then formed a Scottish Convention which summoned a 'Scottish National Assembly' in 1947 to call for devolution. The Labour Party's strong opposition persuaded MacCormick to launch a new covenant in 1949, which called for a Scottish Parliament and attracted 2 million signatures, but made little headway. MacCormick stood repeatedly for Parliament under a variety of banners; for Glasgow, Camlachie (1929) as SNP; Inverness-shire (1931 and 1935) as SNP; Glasgow, Hillhead (1937) as SNP; Inverness-shire (1945) as a Liberal; Paisley (1948) as 'National', losing to Labour in a straight fight; Borders (1959) as a Liberal. His consolation was election as rector of Glasgow University 1950–3. MacCormick surveyed his political career in *The Flag in the Wind* (1955). JAC

MacDonald, Flora (1722–90). Born on South Uist, but educated in Edinburgh, Flora's help was enlisted during a visit to the island of Benbecula for Charles Edward *Stuart's escape to Skye, after *Culloden. Reluctant, but persuaded to succour one in distress, she sought a passport from her stepfather (in charge of the militia) to enable her to cross the Minch with a manservant and 'an Irish spinning maid, Betty Burke'; the party then travelled from Kilbride to Portree for a boat to take Charles to Raasay. When the escape became known, she remained self-possessed throughout her arrest and subsequent brief detention in the Tower of London. Once Jacobitism had become a safe lost cause, her actions were heavily romanticized. Described by *Johnson as 'a woman of soft features, gentle manners, and elegant presence' on meeting her in Kingsburgh (1773), Flora MacDonald emigrated to North Carolina the following year, but later returned to Skye. ASH

MacDonald, James Ramsay (1866–1937). Prime minister. Between 1900 and 1929 Ramsay MacDonald contributed more than any other individual to building the Labour Party into a credible, national party of government. Throughout his career he retained a clear and consistent vision of a democratic socialist movement which would unite middle-class radicalism with working-class votes and achieve its goals by parliamentary means. As prime minister and foreign secretary in the first Labour government of 1924 he went a long way to demonstrating Labour's fitness to govern. Yet under pressure, defects of temperament undermined his effectiveness as an executive leader. Basically a shy and insecure man, despite his achievements, MacDonald depended greatly upon the support of his wife Margaret Gladstone; her early death in 1911 dealt him a blow from which he never recovered. His loneliness made him vulnerable to friendships in aristocratic circles later in life. But to his critics his fondness for the marchioness of Londonderry looked like social climbing and a desire for acceptance by the establishment. This was all the more natural when the failures of his second government led to his participation in the *National Government in 1931. This decision immediately destroyed his standing on the left; and he has been regarded as a traitor ever since, though recent scholarship has gone some way to restoring his reputation for consistency if not for competence.

Born into poverty in Lossiemouth on the north-east coast of Scotland, MacDonald was the illegitimate child of a servant girl and a farm labourer. His early career in the 1880s took him back and forth across the borders of Liberal and Labour politics. He joined the Rainbow Circle, worked as secretary to a Liberal MP, and could well have emerged as a Liberal politician had he managed to get elected to Parliament earlier. But by the 1890s he had become a leading figure in the new *Independent Labour Party. He fought several elections without success, handicapped by the lack of a trade union base and his own poverty. He supported himself by journalism and, from 1896, his wife's personal income. By 1900 he was sufficiently well known and respected to be invited to serve as secretary to the new Labour Representation Committee which became the Labour Party in 1906. In this capacity he was directly responsible for what proved to be the crucial breakthrough for the party. In 1903 he negotiated an electoral pact with Herbert Gladstone, the Liberal chief whip, which meant that the Liberals would refrain from running candidates in 29 of the 50 constituencies contested by Labour at the 1906 general election. In 24 of the 29 seats Labour candidates subsequently proved successful, including MacDonald himself, elected for Leicester.

As an MP his oratorical powers and capacity for mastering legislative detail made him the outstanding parliamentarian on the Labour bench. In 1911 he became chairman of the parliamentary party. In this period he suffered attack from socialists such as Ben *Tillett and Victor Grayson for excessive loyalty towards the Liberal government. He also encountered much resistance from local ILP activists who wished to field candidates in Liberal constituencies in by-elections. However, up to 1914, it appears that he intended to maintain the pact.

The First World War interrupted both this strategy and MacDonald's steady rise. By opposing British entry into the war he put himself in a minority and gave up the party chairmanship. Instead he founded the *Union of Democratic Control, a pressure group which advocated a negotiated peace and a *League of Nations. As a result he was vilified by the right-wing press, which even published a copy of his birth certificate. In the chauvinistic mood of the 1918 election MacDonald suffered a heavy defeat at Leicester.

He achieved his come-back in 1922 when he became the member for Aberavon. Now that opinion had turned against the pre-war arms race and wartime casualties, he gained much credit for the principled stand he had taken in 1914. Consequently many left-wing MPs were willing to support him in the contest for the party leadership in which he narrowly defeated J. R. Clynes. For some years MacDonald stood out as a popular hero to socialists; but as leader he took care to smother radical policies, such as the capital levy, which he thought likely to lose votes.

MacDonald deserves great credit for the skill with which he played a difficult hand in the aftermath of the 1923 election. With only 191 MPs he was invited to form a government. He deliberately avoided any deal with the Liberals, so as to prevent a return to the client relationship Labour had enjoyed before 1914. He strengthened his administration with former Liberal and Conservative ministers, avoided controversial economic policies, and, as foreign secretary, played a constructive role in reducing German reparations. Although the government was defeated in Parliament after nine months, MacDonald had largely succeeded in his object of establishing Labour as a competent governing party.

During the next five years the inability of the *Baldwin government to tackle unemployment helped Labour to a further advance in public support. In 1929 they won 288 seats, not far short of a majority. But this time MacDonald's conventional economic policy proved inadequate; the commitment to the gold standard, an over-valued pound, and the restoration of British export markets proved fatal. As unemployment mounted the prime minister seemed indecisive and self-pitying—the 'Boneless Wonder' in *Churchill's derisive phrase. By August 1931 the balance of payments deficit obliged the cabinet to attempt to restore confidence by balancing its budget. But it split decisively over proposed cuts in unemployment benefit. MacDonald astonished his colleagues by accepting the king's invitation to lead a *National Government with the Liberals and Tories. Though originally seen as a temporary expedient, the National Government rapidly assumed a permanent form by holding a general election in October 1931. MacDonald thus retained the premiership until 1935 and continued in office until 1937. An isolated and ineffectual figure, he presided over a disastrous phase in foreign policy in which the *League of Nations collapsed in the face of aggression by the fascist dictators; he clung to office largely because he had nothing else to live for. MDP

Elton, G., *The Life of James Ramsay MacDonald* (1939); Marquand, D., *Ramsay MacDonald* (1977); Morgan, A., *J. Ramsay MacDonald* (Manchester, 1987).

MacDonald, John, 4th lord of the Isles (1434–1503). According to a MacDonald chronicler of the 17th cent., John, 4th lord, was 'a meek, modest man . . . and a scholar, more fit to be a churchman than to command so many irregular tribes of people'. He succeeded his father Alexander, 3rd lord, in 1449, aged 15, and was almost immediately involved in efforts to defend his huge inheritance—which included not only the Hebrides and western coastline from Lewis to Kintyre, but also the earldom of Ross—from predatory neighbours (especially the earl of Huntly), discontented lordship families, and a hostile crown.

MacDonald's rebellion of 1451, and his bond with Crawford and Douglas (1451/2), put him on the wrong side in the James II–Black Douglas civil wars of the 1450s. In 1462 he made the treaty of *Westminster-Ardtornish with Edward IV of England, an abortive pact which envisaged the tripartite division of Scotland among MacDonald, his cousin Donald Balloch, and the forfeited 9th earl of *Douglas. Summoned for treason, MacDonald finally forfeited his earldom of Ross in 1476, and lost his credibility in the Isles at the same time, with his illegitimate son Angus and—much later—his grandson Donald Dubh seeking to provide the focus for a reunited MacDonald lordship. The forfeiture of the lordship (1493) left John MacDonald a pathetic pensioner of the crown until his death at Dundee in January 1503. The Achilles' heel of the lordship had always been Ross, control of which fell to Alexander Gordon, earl of Huntly. NATM

Macintosh, Charles (1766–1843). Industrial chemist. Macintosh, born in Glasgow, was an extremely inventive scientist, who experimented with the production of dyestuffs, alum, steel, and bleaching powder. His work on possible uses for coal naphtha, a by-product of the gas industry, led to a patent in 1823 for producing waterproof clothing, using India rubber dissolved in naphtha. His factory at Manchester was taken over by the North British Rubber Company. JAC

Mackenzie, Sir Alexander (*c.*1764–1820). Probably from Inverness, Mackenzie joined a fur-trading company beginning to operate from Lake Athabasca in what is now Canada. In 1789, seeking a waterway along which the furs might be carried to the Pacific, he reached the Great Slave Lake and from there followed the Mackenzie river down to what, disappointingly for him, but an exploratory feat, turned out to be the Arctic Ocean. Four years later, he set out again westwards along the Peace river and then through the Rocky Mountains to reach the Pacific coast at Dean Channel north of Vancouver, so becoming the first known man to cross the North American continent north of Mexico. He returned to Britain to publish an account of his travels and was knighted in 1802. RB

Mackenzie, Sir George (1636–91). 'Bloody Mackenzie' was a nephew of the 2nd earl of Seaforth [S], briefly secretary of state [S] to Charles II in exile. A lawyer by profession, he opposed the rule of *Lauderdale at first but in 1677 was appointed king's advocate [S]. In this capacity he harassed the *covenanters, particularly after the skirmish at *Bothwell Bridge in 1679. He rated his services to the crown highly and is reported to have boasted that he deserved a statue riding behind Charles II's in Parliament Square. His use of torture and his legal ingenuity earned him his nickname and the 1680s were known in covenanting circles as 'the killing time'. He took no part in public life after the Glorious Revolution. JAC

Mackenzie, Sir George. See CROMARTY, 1ST EARL OF.

Mackenzie, Henry (1745–1831). Novelist and man of letters, once described by *Scott as 'the Scottish Addison'. Son of an Edinburgh physician, he was educated for the law in Edinburgh and London. His first novel *The Man of Feeling* (1771) established him as a sentimental novelist in the tradition of Marivaux and *Sterne. He was the moving spirit in a group of Edinburgh men of letters who published the *Mirror* (1779–80) and *Lounger* (1785–7), the last popular imitations of *Addison and *Steele's *Spectator.* Mackenzie was the first critic to recognize the importance of *Burns. A Tory loyalist and close associate of Henry *Dundas, he became controller of customs in 1804. Unfortunately, his novels have not worn well. NTP

Mackenzie, William Lyon (1795–1861). Mackenzie was born in Dundee and emigrated to Upper Canada (now Ontario) in 1820, where he became a newspaperman and radical politician. Stung by his abuse, in 1826 Toronto Tories smashed Mackenzie's printing presses. In 1831 Mackenzie's attacks provoked Tories to expel him from the Assembly, an overreaction which the British government countermanded. In 1834 Mackenzie became first mayor of Toronto, but in 1836 reformers were routed in Assembly elections. During 1837 Mackenzie organized armed demonstrations and threatened revolt, but lost control of events. Rebellion broke out on 4 December. Mackenzie escaped to the USA, but an amnesty enabled him to return to Canada in 1849. GM

Mackintosh, Charles Rennie (1868–1928). Scottish architect and designer, a leading exponent of the Glasgow School of art nouveau. He designed a number of houses in and around Glasgow at the turn of the century but his best work was the designs for the Glasgow School of Art, its library, and extensions made between 1897 and 1909, which show bold lines and minimal decoration. His furniture and interior designs, often made in collaboration with his wife Margaret Macdonald, are characteristically art nouveau while avoiding florid excess. Especially fine were those for the Willow Tearooms in the centre of Glasgow. His work was highly influential in Europe but less so in Britain. He moved to London in 1923 but his practice folded soon after and he retired to the south of France where he concentrated on painting in water-colour. JC

Mackintosh, Sir James (1765–1832). Scottish philosopher, historian, lawyer, and politician. A man of many talents, Mackintosh read philosophy at Aberdeen University, qualified in medicine at Edinburgh in 1787, and was called to the bar in London in 1795. He contributed to literary journals, and wrote a celebrated critique of *Burke's *Reflections on the Revolution in France*, entitled *Vindiciae Gallicae* (1791)—which however he subsequently regretted. Mackintosh became recorder of Bombay in 1804, a post which carried a knighthood, and he returned to England to take up a parliamentary seat in 1813, speaking in defence of civil liberty against the authoritarian policies introduced by the post-war Tory administration. He also became professor of law and general politics at Haileybury (1818–24). His main writings were *Dissertation on the Progress of Ethical Philosophy* and *History of England from Earliest Times*, both published in 1830. TSG

Maclise, Daniel (1806–70). Historical and portrait painter and caricaturist. Born in Cork, the son of a Scottish soldier, Maclise became a student of Cork Academy when it opened in 1822, and of the Royal Academy Schools in London in 1828. Between 1830 and 1838, *Fraser's Magazine* published a series of his character drawings of literary men of the day, under the pseudonym Alfred Croquis. One of these was of his friend Charles *Dickens for whom he also did book illustrations. In 1840 he was elected RA but later declined the presidency and a knighthood. Between 1857 and 1866 he was occupied with his best-known work: two frescos for the royal gallery of the new House of Lords, *Wellington and Blücher at Waterloo* and *The Death of Nelson*, of which *Rossetti said, 'These are such "historical" pictures as the world perhaps had never seen before.' JC

Macmillan, Harold (1894–1986). Prime minister. Anglo-American by birth, Macmillan proceeded from Eton to Balliol College, Oxford, where he secured a first in classical moderations shortly before the outbreak of the *First World War. During the war he was badly injured and spent the last stages of the conflict hospitalized. After the war he served as ADC to the governor-general of Canada before going into the family publishing firm.

Macmillan was elected as member for Stockton at his second attempt in 1924. He was not a conventional Conservative and had earlier toyed with Liberalism. In Parliament he associated himself with a group of progressive Tories, styled the YMCA, but his career suffered a blow when he lost his seat in the 1929 general election. He won it back in 1931, but his unconventional views seemed to preclude a ministerial career. In domestic politics he was greatly influenced by the poverty of the north-east and was attracted by the ideas of the Cambridge economist J. M. *Keynes to stimulate recovery from the depression. The publication of *The Middle Way* in 1938 showed Macmillan's commitment to a mixed economy and considerable government intervention. Such ideas became commonplace in the post-1945 Conservative Party; a decade earlier they marked Macmillan out as an intellectual rebel. Macmillan was also at odds with the foreign policy of the National Government and resigned the Conservative whip for the last year of *Baldwin's premiership. A critic of the Munich agreement of 1938, he was overshadowed in the public mind by the more elegant though intellectually less able Anthony *Eden.

When *Churchill became premier in May 1940 Macmillan's ministerial rewards were initially small. But in 1942 he made his first major political advance with his appointment as minister of state for north Africa. Macmillan took easily to his new authority and struck up a good working relationship with General Eisenhower.

Macmillan lost his Stockton seat again in the general election of 1945, but was soon returned to Parliament following a by-election in Bromley. He rose steadily in the Conservative Party, but lacked popular appeal and still trailed Eden and R. A. *Butler among the coming generation. He showed an interest in European integration, though perhaps not to the extent he later claimed. As minister of housing after 1951 Macmillan achieved credit as the man who fulfilled the Conservative pledge to build 300,000 houses in a single year. He served briefly as minister of defence, but became foreign secretary when Eden succeeded to the premiership in 1955. Too forceful in this post for Eden's liking, he was transferred to the Exchequer after six months. Relations with the prime minister were never fully restored.

An ardent proponent of the Suez adventure in 1956, its failure provided Macmillan with his opportunity. Though it was he who pressed the financial necessity of bringing the operation to an end, his earlier enthusiasm ensured the backing of the Conservative right. To the surprise of many he was preferred to Butler when ill-health forced Eden's resignation in January 1957.

As prime minister Macmillan displayed political skills which few had anticipated. Against the odds, he restored party morale after Suez and led the Conservatives to a third successive electoral victory in 1959. In the meantime he repaired the special relationship with America, badly damaged by Suez, using his wartime friendship with Eisenhower to advantage. His calm self-assurance stood him in good stead, especially when the whole of his Treasury team resigned in 1958. By 1960 Macmillan stood at the height of his power. The nickname 'Supermac' encapsulated the public's acclaim. His progressive views of the 1930s still dominated his thinking as he strove to maintain full employment (at the cost, it has been argued, of stoking up inflation) and speeded up the process of decolonization. But then problems arose. The collapse of the summit conference of 1960 was a particular blow and one which helped persuade Macmillan to seek British admission to the European Common Market. This quest ultimately met with the veto of General de Gaulle. Meanwhile difficulties mounted on the domestic front. Many sensed panic when Macmillan dismissed a third of his cabinet, including the chancellor, in the famous 'Night of the Long Knives' in July 1962. Thereafter the government was beset by a series of sex and spy scandals in which Macmillan's image as an Edwardian patrician, once an asset, now suggested someone out of touch with the modern world. Illness precipitated Macmillan's resignation at the time of the Conservative Party conference in October 1963. He left the Commons a year later, somewhat discredited. In his long retirement, however, Macmillan's reputation enjoyed a considerable renaissance, especially after his elevation to the peerage as earl of Stockton in 1984 at the age of 90.

Macmillan was a complex individual. An external self-confidence was matched by inner doubts and moods of depression, exacerbated no doubt by his wife's long-standing affair with Robert Boothby. The years of his premiership remain controversial. For some they represent a period of unprecedented prosperity; for others a time when a blind eye was turned to underlying problems in the British economy. DJD

Aldous, R., and Lee, S. (eds.), *Harold Macmillan and Britain's*

World Role (Basingstoke, 1991); Horne, A., *Macmillan* (2 vols., 1988–9); Turner, J., *Macmillan* (1994).

MacPherson, James (1738–93). Man of letters, and the moving force behind the discovery of the *Poems of *Ossian*. Taken up by the Edinburgh literati in 1760 as a Gaelic speaker with a taste for bardic verse, he was sent to the Highlands to search for more substantial works. These were quickly discovered, translated, and published 1762–5, prefaced by long and influential essays by MacPherson and the critic Hugh Blair. MacPherson was immediately accused of forgery, a charge which he resented, but never tried to rebut. His literary career faltered although his free version of the *Illiad* (1773) is not without interest and his *History of Great Britain from the Restoration to the Accession of the House of Hanover* (1775) achieved a limited success. He died in 1790, having made a living as a government propagandist and a fortune as agent of the nabob of Arcot. NTP

Macready, William (1793–1873). Actor. Macready had a long and successful career in the age of Mrs Siddons and Kean. The son of an Irish actor settled in London, he took up the stage when his father's ventures collapsed, appearing at Birmingham in 1810 as Romeo. He first appeared on the London stage at Covent Garden in 1816, but not until his Richard III in 1819 was his popularity firmly established. He transferred to Drury Lane in 1833 and went into management in 1837. A boisterous American tour in 1849/50 led to serious rioting, and he retired in 1851. Scholarly in his approach to his parts and with considerable versatility, Macready was also difficult, moody, and, at times, violent. His own favourite role was Macbeth. JAC

McTaggart, William (1835–1910). Painter. McTaggart was born in Kintyre (Strathclyde), in a poor labouring family. He studied in Glasgow and Edinburgh, meeting his expenses by painting portraits, and first exhibited in 1856. He became a regular exhibitor at the Royal Academy and Royal Scottish Academy, but refused to work in London, saying, 'I would rather be first in my own country than second in any other.' He decided early on to concentrate on landscapes, undertaking portraits only when he needed money. By the 1870s the sea and boats were the most recurrent themes of his work. Following public reports on the Highland clearances in the 1880s, McTaggart painted a series of works showing emigrants leaving Scotland. In 1897, to celebrate the thirteenth centenary of the death, on Iona, of St *Columba, McTaggart painted incidents from the life of the saint. He was elected ARSA in 1859 and RSA in 1870. JC

Madeleine of France (1520–37), queen of James V of Scotland. The eldest surviving daughter of Francis I of France, Madeleine married James V in Paris on 1 January 1537. The French king, at war with the Emperor Charles V and facing renewed hostilities with England, paid a high price for maintaining Scottish friendship. James was originally offered the daughter of the duke of Vendôme, but on travelling to France to negotiate the marriage found her 'hunch-backed and misshapen'. He held out for Madeleine and a dowry of 100,000 *livres*, plus the annual rent on a further sum of 125,000 *livres*. Madeleine herself favoured the match, despite warnings that her fragile health would not survive the Scottish climate, and sailed for Scotland in May 1537. She died only weeks later on 7 July. The following year the Franco-Scottish alliance was renewed through the marriage of James V to *Mary of Guise. RAM

Madog ap Maredudd (d. 1160), prince of Powys (1132–60). The Welsh princes took advantage of the civil war in England during the reign of Stephen to rebuild their position after the reign of Henry I. Madog inherited Powys from his father Maredudd ap Bleddyn in 1132 and had to deal with the expansionary ambitions of *Owain, prince of Gwynedd, on his northern border. Around 1150 he joined with Ralph, earl of Chester, in an attack but was defeated. He maintained a watchful neutrality in 1157 when Henry II fought Owain. After his death, Powys was divided into north and south lordships (Powys Fadog and Powys Wenwynwyn). JAC

Madog ab Owain Gwynedd. Legendary hero. Madog was reputed to have sailed westwards *c.*1180, never reappeared, and was supposed to have discovered America. In 1790 John Evans set off to find the lost Welsh tribes but was disappointed: Robert *Southey wrote a poem 'Madoc' in 1805. The first mention of the story is in Tudor times, 400 years after the event, and it is merely one of countless heroic myths. But John Dee in 1577 used the legend of Madog to argue that a great Welsh colony had been established in America by King *Arthur, and he coined the term 'British empire'. JAC

Madras was founded by Francis Day of the English *East India Company in 1639. It stood north of the Portuguese settlement of São Tomé on a strip of the Coromandel coast famous for its textiles. A fortification (named after St George) was built and became the headquarters of company activities. However, in the 18th cent. the Coromandel cloth trade declined and Madras was overtaken by *Calcutta in company esteem. Fort St George was seized by the French in 1746 although subsequently returned. The city became the capital of a presidency in the 19th cent. but suffered economic stagnation. Its population in 1901 was 400,000. DAW

madrigals. A term originating in 14th-cent. Italy but later applied to Italian and English secular vocal music of the 16th and 17th cents. The 16th-cent. Italian madrigal grew up around 1520, reaching England through Italian-trained court musicians and imported manuscripts. Anthologies of Italian madrigals with English translations, such as Nicholas Yonge's *Musica transalpina* (1588) and Thomas Watson's *Italian Madrigalls Englished* (1590), provided a model for the native English madrigal, which began with Thomas Morley's *Canzonets or Little Short Songs to Three Voyces* (1593) and flourished briefly until *c.*1620.

Morley, the most prolific English madrigalist, favoured a light-hearted style and frivolous pastoral verse, writing canzonets and strophic balletts (the latter modelled on works by Gastoldi with their 'fa-la' refrains) as well as true madrigals. He also edited *The Triumphes of Oriana* (1601), a collection of madrigals by 21 Englishmen in praise of Elizabeth I; each ends with the phrase 'Long live fair Oriana', although in fact both Elizabeth and Morley died soon afterwards. Other composers, such as Wilbye, Weelkes, and Ward, wrote in a more serious vein, expressive Italianate chromaticisms and dissonances reflecting imagery in the text. After 1600 the madrigal lost ground to the lute ayre, and many publications blur the boundary between the madrigal and other genres. Its popularity with amateur singers has continued until the present day. ECr

Mael Snechta (d. 1085), king of Moray (*c*.1058–*c*.1078). A son of *Lulach, it is likely that he succeeded his father as king of *Moray after his death at the hands of *Malcolm III. Mael Snechta himself suffered a serious defeat by Malcolm III which may have broken his power. He died peacefully in 1085; there is a suspicion that he may have retired to a monastery. He is credited in a near-contemporary Irish source as being king of Scotland. Although his name does not appear in medieval Scottish king-lists, it is possible that his reign has been suppressed or, what is more likely, that he was initially recognized as Malcolm III's successor. DEB

Mafeking is a small town in the north-east corner of Cape Province (South Africa), where a British garrison was besieged for seven months during the second *Boer War, before being relieved on 17 May 1900. That gave rise to the most notorious displays of *jingoism back in Britain, for which a new word—'mafficking'—was coined; and made the reputation of the commander of the garrison, *Baden-Powell. BJP

Magersfontein, battle of, 1899. As Lord Methuen, commanding a British division, advanced to relieve the Boer siege of *Kimberley, he crossed the Modder river and approached the Magersfontein heights. A Boer force of 9,000 men under General Cronje lay in wait, and when Methuen's Highland Brigade tried to turn the enemy flank at night on 11 December, the Boers inflicted heavy punishment. Unable to advance further, the British withdrew, having suffered over 1,000 casualties. Simultaneous British disasters at Stormberg and Colenso led to the period being dubbed 'Black Week' by the press. JLP

magic is a phenomenon whose reality has been accepted in most societies. Differentiating it entirely from *witchcraft is difficult, the generally accepted distinction being that whereas the ability to perform witchcraft is innate or inherited, magic involves the use of techniques and skills which can be learned.

Magical beliefs and practices existed at all social levels in the medieval and early modern periods, and were enmeshed in medical and scientific thought and techniques. The acceptance of *astrology and *alchemy as serious intellectual activities, the influence of hermetic writings and Neoplatonism, all of them accepting the reality of mystic forces, were symptomatic of widespread magical beliefs. It is instructive that, during the 15th cent., both the Scottish and English royal houses thought themselves to be threatened by plots involving the use of occult powers.

The interconnection between magic and what the modern mind accepts as legitimate intellectual activity is demonstrated by the career of John Dee (1527–1608). Dee was a mathematician of European repute, who while still young was offered the professorship of mathematics at the University of Paris. Later he travelled to eastern Europe, and resided in Prague, then an important intellectual centre. In between, he became virtual astrologer-royal to Elizabeth I. His advice was called for when fears arose of a plot to kill her by witchcraft and when the court was debating the deeper significance of the appearance of a new comet in 1577. From 1584, however, he became increasingly involved in attempts to make contacts with the angels, and raise spirits. It is little wonder that he was popularly regarded as a witch, although Dee and others like him regarded their activities as lawful.

That body of intellectual changes which is known as the *scientific revolution downgraded magic as a serious area of study or means of explanation among the educated, although the interest of *Newton and *Boyle in alchemy demonstrates that the process was not a straightforward one. Among the lower orders, however, belief in magic continued well into the 19th cent. The medical advice and other services offered by cunning men and women were more readily and cheaply available than those of middle-class professionals, were more culturally familiar, were frequently as effective, and provided psychological comfort. JAS

Magna Carta was sealed by King John on 15 June 1215 at Runnymede (Berks.). It followed a period of intense political and military activity after John's ignominious return to England in October 1214 following the decisive battle of *Bouvines which ended his hopes of recovering his lost French lands. Shortly after, in late 1214 or early 1215, the rebels decided to demand from John a charter of liberties, their initial grievances and demands expressed in the so-called 'Unknown' Charter (January–June 1215) and the Articles of the Barons (early June). Magna Carta was the product of long and hard negotiation. It was designed to be a negotiated peace, bridging the extreme rebels on the one hand, and John and his supporters on the other, for political society was split down the middle in 1215. But in this it was a total failure for John had no intention of adhering to Magna Carta, agreeing to it only to gain time, and without goodwill and trust on both sides the charter was unworkable as a basis for government and peace. In September 1215 civil war began in earnest. The charter's achievement and significance lie elsewhere, for it laid down standards to be observed in the future by the crown and its agents, for the first time in written law establishing defined limitations to royal rights. It was the abuse of unwritten custom by John and his predecessors and their exploitation of the vaguenesses of the feudal relationship which Magna Carta sought to remedy. But this could only occur once the charter was brought back to life as a royalist manifesto after John's death by the regency government of Henry III. With the reissues of 1216 and 1217, and the definitive version of 1225 (much briefer than the original), the charter became a statement of law, confirmed and interpreted in Parliament and enforced in the law courts. Some of its chapters still remain on the statute book, a measure of its remarkable and enduring significance for the law of the UK, USA, and elsewhere. SL

Magnentius, a usurping emperor 350–3, was at his elevation an army commander in Britain. The hostile surviving sources make it difficult to reconstruct his life. He was probably born at Amiens. In 350 he was proclaimed emperor by the Gallic cabal which deposed Constans. He crossed to the continent and was defeated by Constantius II at the costly battle of Mursa in Pannonia in 351. It was two years before Constantius could press home his advantage and kill Magnentius at the battle of Mons Seleucus in Gaul. After Magnentius' death, vicious reprisals were visited on his supporters in Britain. ASEC

Magnus, St (*c.*1075–*c.*1117). Magnus was the victim of his ambitious cousin Haakon, who intrigued with the Norwegian king Magnus Barefoot to bring about the downfall of their fathers, ruling earls of the Orkney Islands. The king installed his own son in their place. Magnus was seized, compelled to take part in coastal raids, but refused to fight against the Welsh at Anglesey. He finally escaped, taking refuge first at the Scottish court, then in a bishop's house in Britain, living a life of prayer and penitence. When the Norwegian king died, Haakon returned to rule the Orkneys. Magnus claimed his share of the earldom, but within a few years Haakon determined to dispose of his political rival. Magnus, with a few retainers, was invited to meet and confirm a covenant of peace, but was confronted by Haakon and a large armed retinue. Offering no resistance, he accepted his death, absolving the man ordered to kill him. Kirkwall cathedral is dedicated to him. AM

Magnus Maximus. Army commander and usurper of the late Roman period. In AD 383 the British commander Magnus Maximus led an uprising which resulted in the assassination of the western *Augustus* (emperor) Gratian, son of Valentinian I. Frontier problems were occupying the eastern *Augustus*, Theodosius I, and he was unable to send help in time to rescue Gratian. Indeed he even recognized Magnus Maximus' claims to the throne for a while. Magnus Maximus gained control of the western Roman empire, ruling from Trier. Theodosius finally avenged Gratian in 388, defeating and killing Magnus Maximus after the usurper moved against Italy. ES

Magonsaete, kingdom of the. Although the Anglo-Saxon kingdom which was conterminous with the diocese of Hereford is usually referred to as the kingdom of the Magonsaete, the name is not recorded until the 9th cent. The people of the province may originally have been known as the West Angles and be the 'Westerna' of the Tribal Hidage. The first element of 'Magonsaete' is possibly derived from Magnis, the Roman town of Kentchester, and the royal family, recorded for the late 7th and early 8th cents., seems to have been based in its vicinity. The earliest recorded king is Merewalh, who is described in a late 11th-cent. source as a son of *Penda of Mercia. Other evidence supports the idea of kinship with the Mercian royal house, including the burial of Merewalh at *Repton. Merewalh is said to have married Eormenburga, a Kentish princess, and sources connected with their daughter St Mildburga, for whom the monastery of Much Wenlock was founded, provide information for the family and the early history of the province. The last known ruler Mildfrith, son of Merewalh, died *c.*735 and it would appear that the province became a Mercian ealdormanry after that date. BAEY

Maiden castle is perhaps the most spectacular Iron Age hill-fort in Britain. However, this 50-acre hilltop 3 miles south of Dorchester has a longer history stretching back to the neolithic, when a causewayed enclosure was constructed on its eastern end. Subsequently around 3500 BC a bank barrow 600 yards long was built along its central spine.

The Iron Age fort, initially enclosing 25 acres, was built over the neolithic camp around 600–500 BC. Its double eastern gateway, subsequently elaborated by the addition of stone revetting and outworks, already hinted at a special status compared to other neighbouring sites, and this was confirmed around 400–300 BC when the defended site was doubled in size. The defences were gradually elaborated by the addition of further ramparts, finally achieving their present form around 100 BC. Wheeler argued that the multivallate ramparts were for defence in depth against sling warfare, and certainly it was defended against Roman attack around AD 43–5, as skeletons with wounds from sword cuts and ballista bolts were found buried in the east entrance. In the 4th cent. AD a small Romano-Gallic temple was constructed in the interior. JRC

Maidstone, battle of, 1648. Although the Kentish royalists in 1648 had assembled an army of 11,000 men, they dispersed them among several towns, leaving only 2,000 in Maidstone. Sir Thomas *Fairfax, after assembling a 4,000-strong parliamentary force, attacked the town on 1 June. Though heavily outnumbered, the defenders resisted fiercely, using their cannon to deadly effect in the town's narrow streets. Under heavy rain they were eventually overpowered. This defeat prompted most of the Kentish royalists to desert, while the remainder—fewer than 3,000—fled north to Chelmsford and Colchester. IJG

Main plot, 1603. Regarded by the government as the principal conspiracy to distinguish it from the *Bye plot. The Spaniards were said to have encouraged a scheme to replace James I by his cousin Arabella *Stuart in the hope of obtaining peace. *Ralegh, already out of favour with the new monarch, was implicated on the dubious evidence of Lord Cobham. They both spent almost all their remaining days in the Tower. JAC

Maitland, Frederick William (1850–1906). Historian. By common consent, Maitland was one of the great British historians, with remarkable influence after a comparatively short academic career. Educated at Eton and Trinity College, Cambridge, he began as a lawyer but switched to history. He performed a vast amount of editorial work on medieval records, most of it for the Selden Society, but his most famous book was a *History of English Law* (1895) of which his co-author, Sir Frederick Pollock, wrote only a fraction. Maitland was elected professor of the laws of England at Cambridge in 1898, which he held at Downing.

'A model of critical method, a model of style and a model of intellectual temper,' was A. L. Smith's comment. JAC

Maitland, John Maitland, 1st Baron [S] (*c.*1545–95). Maitland succeeded his father in 1567 as keeper of the privy seal [S]. He and his elder brother Sir William *Maitland were strong supporters of Mary, queen of Scots. He was forfeited in 1571 and took refuge with his brother in Edinburgh castle. He was lucky to escape with his life when in 1573 the castle was forced to surrender. But when James VI came of age, Maitland found himself in favour. In 1584 he was knighted and made secretary of state for life, and from 1587 until his death he was lord chancellor [S]. On the occasion of the coronation of Anne of Denmark in 1590, he was made a peer as Maitland of Thirlestane. His influence was used to support the presbyterian party and he favoured good relations with England. Maitland's son was created earl of Lauderdale. JAC

Maitland, Sir William (*c.*1528–73). Maitland of Lethington began his career in the service of *Mary of Guise, regent for Mary, queen of Scots, but in 1559 denounced the French alliance and urged an understanding with the English. His embassy to Elizabeth resulted in the treaty of *Berwick in 1560. Mary's return from France placed him in jeopardy but he was employed to persuade Elizabeth to recognize Mary as heir. Though unsuccessful, he continued to be employed in English negotiations, informing Elizabeth of Mary's intention to marry *Darnley. He had complicity in the murders of *Rizzio and Darnley, opposed *Bothwell, and encouraged a marriage between Mary and *Norfolk. He was now one of Mary's leading supporters and, surrounded by enemies, took refuge in Edinburgh castle in 1571. Two years later the castle was besieged, largely by English troops. Maitland was forced to surrender and, already ill, died shortly afterwards. He had a high reputation as a diplomat and was an accomplished man of letters, but it is not easy to perceive much consistency in his policy. Maitland's younger brother John exercised great influence with James VI in the 1580s. JAC

Major, John (b. 1943). Prime minister. Major entered the House of Commons in 1979 after a career in banking and during the next decade had a meteoric rise to power. His parliamentary career began in the whips' office (1983–5) which clearly left its mark on him, and then in the Department of Health and Social Services (1985–7). He became chief secretary to the Treasury in 1987 but two years later, still a political unknown, was chosen by Mrs *Thatcher to replace first Sir Geoffrey *Howe as foreign secretary, then Nigel Lawson as chancellor of the Exchequer. Unable to make a mark at the Foreign Office, he made his reputation as chancellor by persuading a reluctant Mrs Thatcher to enter the exchange rate mechanism at a rate of his choosing, which events proved to be too high. In 1990, on Mrs Thatcher's resignation, Major defeated Douglas *Hurd and Michael *Heseltine for the leadership, attracting support as Thatcher's political heir. As prime minister he stuck to the ERM policy until the pound was forced out of the system in September 1992 by market forces. This disaster cost him much credibility since recovery, when it came, was based on a floating pound and reduced interest rates, the opposite of his campaign platform in 1992, when he had won the general election against the odds.

Relations with Europe were at the heart of Major's difficulties as prime minister. The Tory Party was split on the issue, yet in 1992 he agreed to sign the treaty on European unity at *Maastricht, which laid down a timetable for a single currency and established majority voting in almost every area of policy. It even foresaw a European army and police force and made all British subjects citizens of a new state, the European Union. The concessions Major gained in the negotiations appeared cosmetic and it was not easy to understand how he could claim to have won 'game, set and match'. Lady Thatcher opposed ratification, and the treaty was pushed through the House of Commons only by brutal government whipping.

Major's popularity, based in part on the contrast he offered to his predecessor, declined sharply. The run on the pound had been extremely expensive and produced record unemployment, record deficits, and record tax increases. A 'back-to-basics' initiative, intended to improve the moral climate of the nation, foundered amid Tory scandal and sleaze. The government's policy towards the *National Health Service alienated many voters. In 1994 Major attempted to recapture the initiative by tackling the Irish problem, although it involved, contrary to previous assurances, negotiating with the *Irish Republican Army. But Major's declaration that the British government had no 'selfish, economic or strategic interest' in Northern Ireland confirmed Ulster's fears of further betrayal, and although a cease-fire brought welcome relief, it did not last. In spite of a considerable economic recovery, Tory divisions over Europe continued to fester, although in 1995 Major beat off a challenge to his leadership from John Redwood, representing the anti-Europe sceptics. Further difficulties were caused by the protracted scare over British beef, which killed its export market and imposed severe financial strains on both government and industry. Major showed little enthusiasm to face the electorate and postponed a general election until the last possible moment. In May 1997 his party suffered a severe defeat and he resigned immediately. Though widely regarded as honest and well-intentioned, and considerably more popular than his party, Major's years as leader were dogged by misfortune and he rarely seemed in advance of events. AS

major-generals, rule of the. The division of England into twelve military districts, each under the direct rule of a major-general, was in part a consequence of the breakdown of the *Instrument of Government, in part *Cromwell's response to *Penruddock's rising in March 1655. The emergency measure was deeply resented by many of the local gentry, the natural rulers of the shires, and the major-generals were bitterly attacked as men of low birth. Others disliked the attempt to impose laws against immorality and irreligion. As soon as a Parliament was called in January 1657, it refused to provide funds for the scheme and a search for a new government settlement began. Though the regime of the major-generals was neither as ruthless nor as effective as has been suggested, it stayed in the national mind as a dire warning against army rule and religious fanaticism. JAC

Majuba Hill, battle of, 1881. Majuba Hill was the only major battle of the first *Boer War (1880–1), which arose from the British annexation of the Republic of the *Transvaal in 1877. In December 1880 the Boers rose in revolt, laying siege to isolated British garrisons. A relief column of 1,100 soldiers and sailors led by Major-General Sir George Pomeroy-Colley was checked at Laing's Nek (pass) in January 1881. The area is dominated by Majuba Hill, rising 1,100 feet above it. At night, on 26 February, Pomeroy-Colley led a force of about 400 men onto the hill, failing to reach the summit by dawn. The defending Boer force of 3,000 men also sent contingents onto the hill, and in the ensuing fight the British were driven off with 287 casualties compared to 7 Boers. Pomeroy-Colley was killed, and (the future General Sir) Ian Hamilton lost the use of his hand. By the convention of *Pretoria of 5 April the Transvaal regained its independence. SDB

Malachy, St (*c.*1094–1148). Malachy was a great reforming bishop in Ireland, when hereditary succession linked church with clan, sacraments were neglected, and old customs frequently prevailed over canon law. His own nomination as archbishop of *Armagh, 1129, was strongly opposed by his predecessor's kin and took several years to resolve. Journeying to Rome, 1139, Malachy stayed with Bernard of Clairvaux. They became firm friends, and with monks trained under Bernard, Malachy established a Cistercian monastery at Mellifont (Co. Louth). Appointed papal legate to Ireland, his wish to remain at Clairvaux was denied, but it became his final resting place when he died there *en route* to Rome. AM

Malawi. Former British central African protectorate of Nyasaland. The missionary explorer David *Livingstone led the first group of Britons to the region in 1859 and after initial set-backs Nyasaland became a thriving centre of missionary activity. A British protectorate was declared in 1893. Early hopes of economic development rested upon the introduction of white settlers although cotton-growing by the indigenous people was later encouraged. Economic motives also led to the creation of the Central African Federation of the Rhodesias and Nyasaland in 1953, but African opposition resulted in its dissolution in 1963. Nyasaland became independent as Malawi in 1964 and a republic in 1966. KI

Malaysia, or the Malay archipelago, was long famous for its trade. In the 15th cent., an important sultanate arose at Malacca and the region was subject to Islamic conversion. The Portuguese took Malacca in 1511 and, subsequently, the Dutch exercised a pervasive hegemony. English interest began in 1786 with the foundation of Penang and increased in the 1820s with the development of the Straits Settlement. The settlement became a crown colony in 1867. It was amalgamated with other sultanates, previously held as protectorates, to form the Federation of Malaya in 1948. In 1957 the Malaysian Federation became independent. DAW

Malcolm I (d. 954), son of *Donald I, was king of 'Scotland', but the sources are confused whether he became king in 940, 943, or 945. This may simply be due to copying errors, or may also reflect a period of political uncertainty as Malcolm attempted to oust the aged *Constantine II, who resigned the kingship and retired to monastic life. Malcolm was evidently aggressive and ambitious, and succeeded in extending the power (if not necessarily the territory) of his kingdom both north and south. He led a victorious army into *Moray, raided northern England as far as the Tees, and in 945 won *Edmund, king of Wessex's recognition that the kingdom of *Strathclyde/Cumbria lay within his sphere of influence. His only recorded set-back outside his kingdom was as part of an alliance with Britons and Saxons (probably against *Erik Bloodaxe in York) defeated in 952 by a Scandinavian force. He was killed by the men of the Mearns at Fetteresso (15 miles south of Aberdeen) and, according to a debatable source, was buried on Iona. DEB

Malcolm II (d. 1034), king of 'Scotland' (1005–34). Son of *Kenneth II, Malcolm was known to later generations as 'the most victorious', and at his death was described by an Irish chronicler as 'the honour of all the west of Europe'. His career was not always so, however. He became king in 1005 by killing his first cousin Kenneth III in battle at Monzievaird (15 miles west of Perth), and in the following year invaded northern England as far as Durham, but was thoroughly defeated. Despite this reverse he successfully re-established control over *Lothian by a famous victory at *Carham (16 miles west of Berwick) in 1018 which was to prove decisive in bringing Northumbria as far south as the Tweed under the rule of the king of Scots. He apparently controlled the kingdom of *Strathclyde after the death of its king in 1018, and possibly appointed his grandson *Duncan (I) to rule over it. He could not escape the power of *Cnut, however, and submitted to him in 1031/2. His last year saw more dynastic violence, killing another cousin in 1033, before himself dying in old age (perhaps assassinated). He was the last direct male descendant of *Kenneth I to hold the kingship. A debatable source claims that he was buried on Iona. DEB

Malcolm III (d. 1093), king of 'Scotland' (1058–93). Malcolm 'Canmore' ('big head' or 'great leader') was the son of *Duncan I and his mother was probably Northumbrian. He was still a child when his father was killed by *Macbeth in 1040. Malcolm found refuge in England, and was backed by *Siward, the Anglo-Danish earl of Northumbria, who led an army into Scotland in 1054 which defeated Macbeth at the battle of Dunsinnan (6 miles north of Perth). Despite this victory Malcolm won only the recovery of his lands. On 15 August 1057 Malcolm defeated and killed Macbeth at *Lumphanan (25 miles west of Aberdeen), but *Lulach, Macbeth's stepson and cousin, won the kingship. It is possible, however, that Malcolm and Lulach were allies against Macbeth, whose rise to power probably involved killing Lulach's father as well as Malcolm's. After only eighteen weeks on the throne Lulach was killed 'by treachery' by Malcolm at Essie (38 miles west of Aberdeen). Malcolm's grip on the kingship was only secure, however, after he defeated Lulach's son Mael Snechta, king of *Moray, in 1078.

Malcolm's struggle against *Mael Snechta made him an ally of Moray's traditional foe, the earl of Orkney, whose close relative Ingibiorg he married. Malcolm was already a widower, however, when the Anglo-Saxon royal family fled to Scotland in 1070, and he took *Edgar Atheling's sister *Margaret as his second wife. Malcolm supported her zeal for ecclesiastical reform. His attention now focused on Northumbria, which he raided repeatedly despite submitting to William the Conqueror in 1072 at *Abernethy (6 miles south-east of Perth). In August 1093 he laid the foundation stone of Durham cathedral; two months later he was killed on a raid at *Alnwick. DEB

Malcolm IV (*c.*1141–65), king of Scots (1153–65), later known as 'the Maiden'. Grandson and successor of David I, his uncontested enthronement in 1153 at the age of 12 reflects the contemporary strength and prestige of the Scottish monarchy. He and his advisers continued to implement David I's Normanizing policies, despite mounting native opposition led by Fergus of Galloway and *Somerled of Argyll. Whether interpreted as a conservative Celtic reaction against modernization or viewed merely as hostility to the spread of royal power, this resistance had been contained by 1164—a fact of crucial importance for Scotland's future development. In other respects, Malcolm was less successful. After the crisis of Stephen's reign, Henry II swiftly restored English royal might, and at Chester in 1157 Malcolm had to surrender the northern English counties in return for the earldom of Huntingdon. Another indication that the balance of power had shifted back in England's favour was his presence on Henry's expedition to Toulouse in 1159, when Henry knighted him. The epithet 'the Maiden' was first applied in the 15th cent., in recognition of Malcolm's well-attested reputation for chastity. KJS

Maldives. The Maldive islands lie 400 miles south-west of Sri Lanka. Their population was converted to Islam in the 12th cent., and in the 14th cent. the sultanate was secured by the ad-Din family who ruled for the next 600 years. The Portuguese briefly established a settlement 1518–28 but the islands were left as a dependency of the prevailing power in Sri Lanka. In 1887 the British government placed them under a direct protectorate. The sultanate was overthrown for a republic in 1952 but restored in 1954. From 1956 to 1986 the RAF maintained an important air base at Gan. DAW

Maldon, battle of, 991. In August 991 Byrhtnoth, ealdorman of Essex, was defeated and killed by a Danish force led by Guthmund and Olaf Tryggvason at Maldon on the river Blackwater in Essex. Byrhtnoth's heroic death was commemorated in one of the greatest Anglo-Saxon battle poems, *The Battle of Maldon*. JAC

Malmesbury abbey (Wilts.) grew from a community established by an Irish hermit in the mid-7th cent. This was soon expanded by *Aldhelm, later bishop of Sherborne. It received the patronage of Wessex kings, especially *Athelstan, who was buried there. The community was reformed as a *Benedictine house during *Edgar's reign. A substantial library was built up during the abbacy of Godfrey (*c.*1090–1105) and a monk, William of Malmesbury (*c.*1095–*c.*1143), was the greatest historian of 12th-cent. England. The abbey continued to flourish till the *dissolution, when it had a net income of *c.*£800. BJG

Malory, Sir Thomas (d. 1471). The identity of Malory, author of *Le Morte Darthur*, is not certain. The author referred to himself as a 'knight-prisoner'. The most likely suggestion is Sir Thomas Malory of Newbold Revel (War.), who had been in prison for crimes of violence. If it is correct, he had been knighted in 1445, served in Parliament for Warwickshire the same year, and was a follower of *Warwick the Kingmaker. Of several other candidates who have been proposed, only Thomas Malory of Papworth (Cambs.) and Thomas Malory of Hutton Conyers (Yorks.) seem worth serious study, though neither of them appears to have been knighted. Malory's famous volume was a compilation from various sources, mainly French, and was printed by Caxton in 1485. JAC

Malplaquet, battle of, 1709. As allied (British–imperialist) forces under the duke of *Marlborough and Prince Eugene laid siege to Mons, a French army under Marshal Villars moved towards them from the south-west. Unable to leave Mons until reinforcements arrived, the allies allowed Villars to build entrenchments to the north-east of Malplaquet. When the allies finally advanced on 11 September they faced heavy opposition, and although the French were forced to retreat, the costs to both sides were horrific. At least 12,000 French were lost, while allied casualties may have been more. JLP

Malta. The island of Malta, of great strategic significance, lies 60 miles south of Sicily: it is 17 miles in length and 9 across. Malta was acquired by Britain at the end of the Napoleonic wars in 1814, having belonged to the Knights of St John from 1530. From 1940, when Italy entered the Second World War, it was subjected to constant bombing until 1943 and received the George Cross as a tribute. It became independent in 1964 and was declared a republic in 1974. The grand harbour in Valletta is capacious but the main resource today is tourism. JAC

Malthus, Thomas Robert (1766–1834). Though Malthus's views were extremely controversial, his character was pleasant and his life uneventful. He was born near Guildford, his father having private means. After attending Jesus College, Cambridge, he was elected to a fellowship (1793), took holy orders, and became a curate in Surrey, and from 1805 taught at the East India Company College at Haileybury. His most celebrated work, the *Essay on Population* (1798), was directed at the facile optimism of Condorcet and *Godwin. Malthus argued that while population, unchecked, would increase geometrically, subsistence would increase only arithmetically. Consequently any improvement in the standard of living would soon be wiped out. This, Malthus admitted in his preface, had a 'melancholy hue'. He produced a revised and much enlarged edition in 1803, and appealed for 'restraint'—by which he meant late marriage—to prevent population outstripping support. His theory was seized upon by those who wished to argue that progress or amelioration must be an illusion, and his condemnation of the Poor Laws for encouraging breeding had important consequences. But the simplicity of Malthus's basic proposition reveals its naïvety, and it had little statistical support. As the standard of living improved, people did not breed to the maximum but took steps to limit the number of their children. JAC

Man, Isle of. See ISLE OF MAN.

Manchester. Sited where natural routes crossed and bridges could be maintained, the Roman military station Mamucium or Mancunium controlled the *Brigantes, while acting as a supply base. In medieval times it was a dependency of the capital manor of Salford, becoming a trading centre within an agricultural community, and during the Civil War was strongly parliamentarian, although some prominent local families remained stubbornly catholic. Encouraged by the moist atmosphere, soft water, and nearby coal supplies, local textile industries so flourished that Manchester became their chief commercial centre as well as a manufacturing and finishing site. New production methods and transport facilities (e.g. Bridgwater canal) greatly increased output, and the merchants and manufacturers began to organize a factory system. Population expansion from immigrants attracted by employment opportunities resulted in social and political problems because of the conflict between a still feudally run market town (enfranchised only in 1832) and a burgeoning industrial centre. Crowded, makeshift dwellings and dangerous sanitary conditions underlay a strong working-class radical movement and the so-called *'Peterloo massacre' (1819), but unemployment and *Luddism were tempered by the rise of trade unionism and methodism. Belief in free trade prompted *Cobden and *Bright to push for the repeal of the Corn Laws, and the city's political temper began to harden into Liberalism. Prosperous, confident, and progressive, the merchant princes of Victorian Manchester invested in bricks and mortar, railways, and the ship canal, but the smoke pushed residents into the suburbs; its commercialization attracted accusations of philistinism, and poverty and squalor persisted. Home of the *Manchester Guardian*, Victoria University, and the Hallé Orchestra, it was a city of enormous vitality in its cultural and intellectual life. After the decline of cotton, the huge variety of engineering projects and distributive trades helped maintain it as a regional and metropolitan centre, with less air pollution, but service industries are replacing these in their turn, and it remains a city in transition. The metropolitan area as a whole has become a magnet for Commonwealth immigrants into Britain. ASH

Manchester, diocese of. The rapid population expansion of the industrial north led the ecclesiastical commissioners of 1835 to recommend that Chester diocese be relieved by the creation of two new sees of Ripon and Manchester. The order in council (1838) to constitute the latter foundered on the sensitive issue of increasing the number of bishops in the House of Lords and the accompanying proposal to fuse Bangor and St Asaph. Manchester diocese was eventually established in 1847, with the constitutional innovation that bishops' seats in the Lords were occupied in order of consecration. Covering Lancashire, except for Liverpool district, Furness, and Cartmel (transferred to Carlisle), the initial archdeaconries of Manchester and Lancashire were augmented by those of Blackburn (1877) and Rochdale (1910); Blackburn became a separate diocese in 1926. Suffragan bishops were appointed at Burnley (1901), Whalley (1905), Hulme (1924), and Middleton (1926).

A grandiose scheme to build a new cathedral worthy of the see was realistically replaced by restoration of the dilapidated parish church of St Mary, St George, and St Denys, a collegiate church since 1422, with fourteen carved minstrel angels supporting the nave roof. No other English cathedral except Coventry suffered so severely in the Second World War. ASH

Manchester, Edward Montagu, 2nd earl of (1602–71). Parliamentary commander during the Civil War. Manchester (Mandeville until inheriting the earldom in 1642) was sympathetic towards *presbyterianism and a leading opponent of the king in the years before the outbreak of war. He fought in the opening battle at *Edgehill and was in command at *Marston Moor and at the second battle of *Newbury. Clarendon remarked that he was 'universally acceptable and beloved' and he seems to have been sweet-tempered and conciliatory. Praise from opponents did not endear him to zealots on his own side and in November 1644 *Cromwell launched a fierce attack upon him in Parliament, accusing him of lethargy and of hankering after compromise. He was forced to resign by the *self-denying ordinance in the spring of 1645. He survived to help bring about the restoration of Charles II, was made a knight of the Garter in 1661, and held high court office for the rest of his life. JAC

Manchester, Greater. A term first used in 1914 to describe a commercial rather than municipal focus in north-west England, but now applied to the major conurbation which was created a metropolitan county after local government reform (1972). Although smaller than the 'Selnec' (SE Lancs./NE Ches.) area proposed by the Maud Commission (1969), it nevertheless has ten constituent districts and includes the crescent of industrial towns to its north and dormitory areas in Cheshire. Of the six such counties created, it is the only one to be named after its central city, and had its own county council until 1986. ASH

Manchester martyrs, 1867. On 18 September an attempt was made to rescue *Fenian leaders Thomas Kelly and Timothy Deasy from police custody in Manchester. During the attempt, Police Sergeant Charles Brett was killed, causing strong anti-Irish feeling. Three Fenians, William Allen, Michael Larkin, and Michael O'Brien, were executed for the murder on 23 November. There was widespread indignation in Ireland and the 'martyrs', as they became known, were given a public funeral attended by over 60,000 people. The incident did much to raise recruitment to the *Irish Republican Brotherhood and increase distrust of the British authorities. RAS

Manchester School. This provided a convenient label to identify many of the 19th-cent. advocates of **laissez-faire* and, in particular, *free trade. Widespread support for free trade developed amongst the manufacturers of the cotton industry in Lancashire and Cheshire. The intellectual focus for this movement included Richard *Cobden and John *Bright whose economic philosophies dominated the Liberal Party for much of the period. The initial case for removing mercantilist regulations of trade had been made by Adam *Smith in *The *Wealth of Nations* (1774). In Lancashire and elsewhere support grew rapidly in the early 19th cent. with the aim of making exports and imports as easy as possible without the restraints of taxation or protective laws, such as *Navigation Acts. Associated with the free trade movement was the Manchester Statistical Society, founded to publish research which could advance their cause. IJEK

mandates. After the First World War, the colonial territories of the defeated powers were distributed to the victorious allies, under the general supervision of the *League of Nations, which set up a Permanent Mandates Commission. It was insisted that the mandated territories would move towards self-government. Britain acquired Iraq, Trans-Jordan, and Palestine from Turkey, and Tanganyika, West Togoland, and South Cameroons from Germany. South Africa took German South West Africa, Australia became responsible for New Guinea, and New Zealand for Western Samoa. Iraq became independent in 1932. After the Second World War, a United Nations trusteeship replaced the mandate scheme and the territories moved rapidly towards independence. Britain relinquished its mandate for Trans-Jordan in 1946 and for Palestine in 1948; West Togoland joined Ghana in 1957; South Cameroons joined East Cameroons (a former French mandate) to form an independent state in 1961. Tanganyika became independent in 1961 and joined with Zanzibar in 1964 as Tanzania. Western Samoa became independent in 1962 and Papua New Guinea in 1973. The independence of former German South West Africa was retarded by South Africa's refusal to obey United Nations rulings and a guerrilla war developed. The territory achieved independence under the name of Namibia in 1990. JAC

Mann, Tom (1856–1941). Socialist and trade union leader. Born near Coventry and apprenticed as an engineer in Birmingham, Mann moved to London in 1877 and was active in the *Social Democratic Federation from 1885. He achieved notoriety as a leader of the London dock strike of 1889, was elected first secretary of the *Independent Labour Party in 1893, stood unsuccessfully for Parliament on three occasions in the 1890s, and founded the Workers' Union in 1898. In 1901 he visited New Zealand and Australia, where he started what became the Socialist Party of Australia. Returning in 1910, he founded the Industrial Syndicalist Education League and led the Liverpool transport workers' strike of 1911. In 1916 he joined the British Socialist Party and in 1919 became first secretary of the Amalgamated Engineering Union. Between the wars he was a leading member of the *Communist Party. Unlike some of his contemporaries, he never lost his working-class roots or subsided into conservatism in old age. ER

Manners, Society for the Reformation of. These societies, which sprang up in the 1690s in London and the larger provincial towns, were a mixture of evangelicalism and social control. The early signs of the *commercial revolution, accompanied by great anxiety about the spread of free thinking, persuaded many conservatives that vice, drunkenness, and luxury were rotting the fabric of society. The church courts were no longer keen to enforce morality and sabbath observance. The societies brought prosecutions against vice and protested against lewd plays and lascivious entertainments, such as masquerades. By the early years of George I's reign, they were bringing more than 2,000 prosecutions a year. They acquired considerable unpopularity. Magistrates found them tediously zealous and as early as 1698 *Defoe commented that 'we do not find a rich drunkard carried before my Lord Mayor'. Their support collapsed in the 1730s, despite the efforts of Bishop *Gibson. *Wesley and the methodists revived them in the 1750s but by 1766 Wesley wrote that this 'excellent design is at a full stop'. The disappointing results of the crusades did not prevent the establishment of a Society for the Suppression of Vice in 1802. JAC

Manning, Henry Edward (1808–92). Cardinal. Manning was born in Hertfordshire, son of a wealthy banker and MP. Educated at Harrow and at Balliol College, Oxford, he was president of the Union in 1829. An enigmatic and complex figure, he was an Oxford high churchman and gained ecclesiastical preferment rapidly, becoming archdeacon of Chichester in 1840, where he remained until his conversion to catholicism ten years later. The strong ideas expressed in *The Unity of the Church* (1842) helped him into a powerful position in English catholicism. He voiced strong support for the papal states and was the chief proponent of papal infallibility at the first Vatican Council (1869–70). From 1865 Manning was the second cardinal-archbishop of Westminster. He was, and remains, a contentious figure, accused by some of scheming and power-mongering. Yet he was much loved as a champion of Irish Home Rule and as the hero of the working classes in London. His intervention in the bitter London dock strike of 1889 has been called 'the crowning act of his archiepiscopate'. JFC

manor houses were the habitat of the gentry, the headquarters of the squire. In medieval England they were both governmental and economic units. The lord of the manor dispensed justice through his court and could call upon the villagers for labour and financial assistance. It is not clear to what extent Roman *villas fulfilled these functions or how widespread the development was in Saxon times. There was always considerable diversity. Some wealthy men owned many manors, others but one: some villages had no resident lord of the manor, others had two. Manors and villages did not necessarily coincide. Though the growth of royal justice and the development of a freer economy undermined the position of the lords of the manor in the later medieval period, their social prestige remained high and their increasing functions as *justices of the peace went some way to compensating, since most could expect to be on the bench, unless excluded by party animosity or personal idiosyncrasy.

The essential feature of medieval manor houses was the great hall, the living and sleeping quarters of the lord's followers and servants, as well as his family. The fireplace was normally in the middle, the gentry often had a dais or table at one end (as in a college hall), and there was little privacy. Some defence was afforded by moats, which also supplied fish, or stockades, though the manor house must be distinguished from the castle, which was the preserve of the mighty. At Boothby Pagnell, Lincolnshire (*c.*1200), and Donington, Leicestershire (*c.*1280), the hall was on the first floor, for comfort and security. Lower Brockhampton (Herefordshire) had a moat, though more ornamental than formidable, and Stokesay in Shropshire had a great hall, to which towers were subsequently added: each of them acquired a free-standing half-timbered gatehouse in the Tudor period. Gradually, with greater attention to privacy, manor houses became less public and more comfortable, with windows, carpets, and more furniture. The old great hall was sometimes partitioned to make smaller rooms. A remarkably ornate late Tudor house is Little Morton Manor in Cheshire, which retained the great hall, but added a long gallery at the top for recreation or receptions. Other houses were rebuilt, or sometimes moved, to take them out of village mud or poultry. By the Stuart period the withdrawal from communal living had gathered pace. Though the stately homes had vast reception rooms and bedrooms for many guests, the average manor house catered for the immediate family and its servants. After the Restoration, the retreat from the public gaze accelerated, with walls erected, lodges built, drives constructed, roads diverted, and the parks planted and embellished. Milton Manor (Oxon.), built soon after the Restoration, is severely classical: the moat has given way to an elegant pond, the great hall has gone, and in the following century a library was added. At Ramsbury Manor in Wiltshire, built in the 1680s, the great hall has dwindled into an imposing entrance hall. We must not exaggerate the grandeur of manor houses. Many remained little more than farm-houses and others stayed in their villages. The manor house at Woolsthorpe in Lincolnshire, where *Newton was born in 1642, was only 20 years old, and a very modest dwelling in the middle of the hamlet, hardly distinguishable from other good residences. Capability *Brown, having made his fortune improving aristocratic parks, bought himself a small manor house at Fenstanton in 1768, near the church and in the town. The prestige of the gentry remained high, since they often owned the *advowson and had a cousin or an uncle in the rectory as well. Their influence declined markedly in the 19th cent. as they lost their local powers to elected councils, but the position of the squire remained important in Victorian times and is still significant in some villages today. JAC

manorial courts. After the Norman Conquest the system of feudal landholding required the lord of the manor to provide a court for his tenants. Such 'seigneurial' courts were the court of the honour and the court baron, for free tenants, and the court customary for unfree tenants or villeins. The court of the honour, the principal manorial court, soon fell into disuse. The court baron was attended by all free tenants who were both its suitors and its judges. It decided questions of tenure, the fulfilment or non-fulfilment of feudal services, the payment of feudal dues, and disputes between free tenants of the same lord. The court customary (or hallmoot) was the court for unfree tenants or villeins and was presided over by the lord's steward or bailiff. It decided matters relating to performance or non-performance of feudal services and also disputes between unfree tenants (e.g. debts and minor assaults) and tenants who held by unfree tenure. It also ensured that the agricultural services and land use necessary to the proper upkeep of the manor were duly performed. The lord would frequently have the franchise to hold the local hundred court to take the view of *frankpledge and to hear minor criminal cases, such as assaults, nuisances, and breaches of the Assizes of Bread and Ale. This *court leet was also therefore a 'manorial' court, though its jurisdiction arose not from the feudal relationship *per se*, but from royal grant.

Eventually the distinctions between the seigneurial courts and the courts leet became blurred; the court baron faded into oblivion and the court customary survived as a court for free and unfree tenants alike. This court and the court leet were both held by the lord's steward in the same place, traditionally the hall of the manor. The manorial courts had declined by the 15th cent., but many of the courts leet survived as the basis of new towns and local government. MM

manorial system. A term used by historians to describe the method of estate management of landowners in the Middle Ages and in Tudor and Stuart times. Landowners whose estates embraced the major part of a village or a whole cluster of small villages found it convenient to administer such property by establishing a manor. In some places where a large village was divided in ownership among several landowners, there were several manors. It seems probable that manors existed in Anglo-Saxon times but that the structure of control changed according to the needs of the landowners.

By the 13th cent. most manorial lords had established two courts, *leet and baron, which met at the same place and whose proceedings followed one another. These had a senior officer of the lord or even the lord in the chair and all tenants were required to attend these meetings (known as suit of court) whether they were free or bond in status. Between them these courts dealt with all matters relating to the maintenance of boundaries, preservation of property, and changes in tenure. They regulated the pattern of agriculture, for example the rotation of crops in the common fields, and the manorial market. Enforcement of decisions rested on the officials appointed by the court. Where the lord of the manor had a demesne farm, the court appointed a *reeve to supervise the farming activities, using labour services and collecting rents. Usually at Michaelmas the reeve presented an annual account to the lord or senior administrator. When demesne farming dwindled or disappeared, the reeve remained as a rent collector.

So long as *villeinage (serfdom) had importance, the courts reinforced status by requiring some labour services over and above that fixed by custom and practice. Those who wished to leave the manor had to seek permission or be penalized by a fine.

Where urban communities developed within manorial boundaries, appointments of constables and other local officers such as street masters provided some of the necessary organization for town government. Their duties usually included fire precautions, and coping with dangerous structures and nuisances, such as dumping rubbish in the street. These functions continued well into the 19th cent. in some places. IJEK

Mansel, John (d. 1265). Mansel was a clerical counsellor to Henry III and greatly employed as administrator, diplomat, and soldier. In exchange he was given a large number of benefices. He began with a post in the Exchequer in 1234 and held the great seal 1246–7 and 1248–9. He represented the king's interest on the committee and council set up under the Provisions of *Oxford in 1258 and under pressure the king was obliged to dismiss him in 1261. When the civil war began in 1263, Mansel took refuge in the Tower before escaping to France to try to raise troops. He was again a royal representative at the mise of *Amiens in January 1264, which led to civil war, but died before the great royal victory at *Evesham in 1265. Defending him in 1262, Henry wrote: 'he was trained under my wing. I have tested his ability, his character and merits since his boyhood.' JAC

Mansfield, William Murray, 1st earl of (1705–93). Judge. In 1742 Mansfield became solicitor-general with a seat in Parliament for Boroughbridge. He was an effective debater, second only to *Pitt. *Newcastle relied heavily on Mansfield and was reluctant to see him become chief justice of King's Bench in 1756. However Mansfield remained in the cabinet until 1763 and was attacked by *Junius for being a 'political judge'. He set about reforming the slow practices of the court, developed and clarified commercial law, and, when the occasion arose, adapted the law to the needs of his day. He twice refused the lord chancellorship, preferring the security of a non-political post. Mansfield hated religious persecution and his house was burned during the *Gordon riots (1780). He retired in 1788 with a reputation as the greatest judge of the 18th cent. RAS

Maori wars, 1844–72. The treaty of *Waitangi in 1840 was not accepted by all chiefs, nor was the confirmation of Maori land rights easy to implement. The Maoris were a warlike people and clashes continued between Maoris and settlers, and between Maori tribes. The first period of warfare began in 1844 at Kororareka and remained small scale, since most Maori tribes held aloof. A small British force took casualties but regained control by 1847. The second conflict developed after repeated incidents in Taranaki, beginning in 1860 and continuing as a guerrilla war, flaring up and dying down, until 1872. One thousand settlers and colonial troops lost their lives, and perhaps twice that number of Maoris. Three million acres of Maori land were confiscated, some restored, but the sale and loss of Maori territory continued. JAC

Mar, John Erskine, earl of [S] (*c.*1510–72). Mar's grandfather died at Flodden. Mar commenced a clerical career but abandoned it when his two elder brothers died. He succeeded his father as Lord Erskine in 1555 and was recognized as the rightful earl of Mar in 1565. A member of the reforming party, he had custody of the infant James VI and was active against Mary. In 1571–2 he was regent, though real power was in the hands of *Morton, and after his death his widow remained governess of the king until 1578. His son John was one of the leaders of the *Ruthven raid in 1582 in which the young king was kidnapped, and was disgraced in 1584. But, unlike *Gowrie, he worked his way back into favour and became one of James's closest friends. He followed the king to England in 1603 and was given the Garter. From 1616 to 1630 he was treasurer [S]. JAC

Mar, John Erskine, 11th earl of [S] (1675–1732). Debts being his inheritance, Mar entered politics in 1696 as placeman in the court party in Scotland, led by the duke of *Queensberry until his fall in 1704. Mar rejoined him in office in 1705, helping him push the Act of *Union through the Scots Parliament in 1707. Elected to Westminster as a representative Scots peer, by 1713 he was supporting a motion for repeal of the Union.

Having failed to attract the favour of George I, he sailed for Scotland to raise the standard of Jacobite rebellion on the Braes of Mar. The national response was spectacular, but he ruined the enterprise by sheer incompetence. After 1716 he lived in exile, until 1725 in association with the exiled dynasty, though after 1719 as a double agent currying favour with the Westminster government. He pottered with plans for economic improvement after 1725, but died unrestored to his estates. BPL

Mar, John Stewart, earl of [S] (*c.*1459–80). Fourth son of James II, created earl of Mar 1459. Although a royal brother, Mar took almost no part in the affairs of state, and little is known of his life apart from his execution, by early 1480, and subsequent forfeiture. A contemporary explanation of Mar's execution as punishment for association with witches and warlocks may be the result of royal propaganda following an execution that seems to have had little provocation. It is most likely that he was executed covertly to avoid parliamentary opposition, and for little reason apart from James III's paranoia, possible opposition to the king's indictment of Alexander Stewart, duke of *Albany, in October 1479, and fear of a new focus for extensive dissatisfaction. Mar's death is prominently, and often luridly, described in later chronicles, and was probably exploited by the 1488 rebels as part justification for their actions. RJT

marches of Scotland. The Anglo-Scottish border. The border lands of both England and Scotland were divided into two or three marches. Northumberland with Berwick-on-Tweed was the east march 'towards Scotland' and Cumberland and Westmorland the west march. Adjacent Scottish shires were likewise arranged. In both kingdoms, wardens were commissioned by their sovereigns to protect and restrain inhabitants of their marches from cross-border crime in times of truce, and to mobilize and direct them in wartime. War in the 1380s caused the English wardenships to be given a dangerous character for the following century. Instead of several commissioners, a single warden was appointed for each march. He was engaged by indenture for one year, later for more, at an annual rate of payment which would be doubled (at least) in wartime; with these large sums he was to employ as many soldiers as he considered necessary. Magnates with lands in the marches, and therefore tenants, were normally appointed. Percy and Neville wardens were to lead their private armies of marchmen against the king and each other. Tudor wardens were not great magnates and less well paid. Most of Northumberland was put under a warden for the middle march. The wardenships were abolished in 1603, when the two kingdoms came under the personal union of James VI and I. RLS

marches of Wales. See WALES, MARCH OF.

Marchmont, Patrick Hume, 1st earl of [S] (1641–1724). Hume succeeded his father as baronet at the age of 7. A strong presbyterian, he represented Berwick in the Convention of Estates in 1665 and 1667, and was MP for Berwickshire 1669–74 and 1689–90. His opposition to *Lauderdale in the 1670s led to two spells of imprisonment. He was implicated in the *Rye House plot and in 1685 joined *Argyll's abortive rising on behalf of *Monmouth. Next he threw in his lot with William of Orange, accompanying his expedition in 1688. He was created Lord Polwarth [S] in 1690, with an orange in his coat of arms, and advanced to an earldom in 1697. From 1696 until 1702 he was chancellor [S] and in that capacity used his casting vote for the immediate execution of Aikenhead, an 18-year-old youth charged with blasphemy—'the worst action of his bad life', in *Macaulay's words. At the accession of Anne, his influence waned, though he exerted himself to carry the Union. Macky remarked that he was 'a lover of set speeches' and Macaulay ridiculed his loquacity: *Complete Peerage*, more tersely, called him a 'turbulent scoundrel'. His son, the 2nd earl, was a vigorous opponent of Sir Robert *Walpole in the 1730s. JAC

Marconi scandal. An Edwardian political-financial controversy. The scandal arose out of a contract for the construction of a chain of wireless stations between the English Marconi Company and the British government represented by the postmaster-general, Herbert *Samuel, who was a wholly innocent party. One of the company's directors, Godfrey Isaacs, was also a director of the American Marconi Company which had no holdings in the English company but stood to benefit indirectly from its success. In April 1912 Godfrey offered shares in the American company to his brother Rufus Isaacs (attorney-general), *Lloyd George (chancellor of the Exchequer), and Alexander Murray (Liberal chief whip). Lloyd George unhesitatingly bought 1,000 shares at £2 each before they went on sale to the public at a price of £3.50.

In July rumours of ministerial speculation surfaced, notably in *Eye Witness*, a journal edited by Cecil Chesterton, which coined the phrase 'Marconi scandal'. This was taken up by the opposition and led to the appointment of a House of Commons select committee. Though this exonerated the ministers, its verdict was essentially a party political one, for Murray had purchased additional shares for Liberal Party funds and subsequently disappeared to Bogotá in South America. MDP

Margaret (1283–90), queen of Scots (1286–90), known as 'the Maid of Norway'. Daughter of Eric II of Norway, she succeeded her grandfather Alexander III, whose children had all predeceased him, at the age of 3 in 1286, and her premature death four years later was one of the most significant events in medieval British history. Her betrothal to Edward of Caernarfon (the future Edward II), agreed by the treaty of *Birgham, was intended to perpetuate Anglo-Scottish peace through dynastic union. But she died at Kirkwall in Orkney on her way from Bergen to Scotland. This tragedy led to a disputed succession in Scotland, to Edward I's ill-judged interventions in Scottish affairs, and to the *Scottish Wars of Independence. KJS

Margaret, St (*c.*1045–93), queen of Malcolm III of Scotland. Mother of Kings Edgar, Alexander, and David. Her father *Edward, son of *Edmund Ironside, was exiled from England by *Cnut, and ultimately found refuge in Hungary, where Margaret was born. Hungary had only recently converted to Christianity, and it has been suggested that Margaret owed her religious zeal to the atmosphere of the Hungarian royal court. She returned with her father to England where he died soon after. The Norman conquest of England in 1066 left Margaret's brother *Edgar as the last hope of the English royal dynasty; but, following an unsuccessful rising in 1070, he and his family took refuge in Scotland, where Margaret was soon espoused to Malcolm III. Her commitment to piety is testified by her support for pilgrims to St Andrews, her help for *Iona, her patronage of ascetics, and her foundation at *Dunfermline of a cell of three monks from Canterbury—the first Benedictine community in Scotland.

Her sanctity was celebrated soon after her death in a biography written for her daughter Queen *Matilda of England. This work may, naturally, have exaggerated her role in reforming the church in Scotland. Her posthumous significance, however, was chiefly that she gave inspiration as well as prestige to the Scottish royal dynasty which, by the time of her canonization in 1250, had made the Scottish throne its own by following her lead in 'Europeanizing' its realm. DEB

Margaret of Anjou (1430–82), queen of Henry VI. The daughter of René of Anjou, her marriage to Henry VI was part of the terms of the truce of *Tours. Virtually dowerless, and quickly compromised by the cession of Maine to her father, she was never popular in England. Her life was made more difficult by her husband, whose mental health failed in 1453 when she was pregnant with her only child. After his birth she began to play an active part in politics and by 1456 was the leader of the court faction. She was a formidable woman, who, convinced that the duke of *York represented a threat to her son's inheritance, set out to destroy him. In the event the thing she most feared came about when Edward IV usurped the throne. Portrayed by Yorkist propaganda as a ruthless virago, her reputation has suffered because of the fatal combination of being French and on the losing side. She fled to France with her son in 1461 and schemed for her husband's restoration, succeeding in 1470, only for her hopes to be dashed when her son was killed at *Tewkesbury on 4 May 1471 and her husband murdered a fortnight later. She spent the rest of her life in obscure retirement in France. She was the first founder of Queens' College, Cambridge. AJP

Margaret of Burgundy (1446–1503) was a sister of Edward IV. After considerable negotiation, she was married in 1468 to Charles, duke of Burgundy, amid lavish celebrations. The marriage had great diplomatic significance in creating an alliance against Louis XI of France, and the duke gave assistance to Edward IV in 1470 when he was driven into exile. Margaret's husband was killed at the battle of Nancy in 1477 fighting against the Swiss. After Henry VII took the throne of England, she continued to support the Yorkist cause, giving refuge to both Lambert *Simnel and Perkin *Warbeck. *Caxton was in her service 1470–6. JAC

Margaret of Denmark (1457–86), queen of James III of Scotland. Daughter of Christian I of Denmark-Norway (1448–81). The royal marriage took place at Holyrood in July 1469. The queen bore her husband three sons, James (IV), James (duke of *Ross), and John (earl of Mar). Her near-contemporary Italian biographer Sabadino described Margaret as having more skill than her husband in running the kingdom. Certainly she played some part in politics following James's incarceration in Edinburgh castle in 1482, and the two may have become estranged. Margaret had charge of her sons at Stirling castle, where she died in July 1486. NATM

Margaret of England (1240–75), queen of Alexander III of Scotland. Eldest daughter of Henry III, she married Alexander III at York on 26 December 1251. Her early married life was disrupted by the factional quarrels of Alexander's minority (1249–60), and Henry III was frequently concerned for her welfare, himself coming to Scotland to see her in 1255—and to back a new government by Scottish nobles who had his confidence. She later made several visits to the English court, and in 1261 gave birth at Windsor to her eldest child Margaret (married to Eric II of Norway in 1281). Her sons Alexander and David were born in 1264 and 1273 respectively. Apparently a beauty and deeply pious, she was buried in Dunfermline abbey. By 1284 her three children were also dead, which left as heir to the Scots throne her granddaughter Margaret, 'the Maid of Norway'. KJS

Margaret of France (*c.*1282–1318), queen of Edward I. Edward's second wife, whom he married in 1299, has attracted little attention from historians. She was some 40 years younger than her husband, and there is no evidence to suggest that she was as close to him as his first queen *Eleanor of Castile had been. The marriage was the result of diplomatic moves in the aftermath of the war of 1294–7 between England and France; Margaret was a daughter of Philip III of France by his second marriage. The ceremony was an occasion for considerable celebration, but Margaret was never crowned queen. She bore Edward a son, Thomas, in admirably short order. A second son, Edmund, and a daughter, Eleanor, followed. Margaret performed the traditional queenly function of interceding with the king to obtain pardons more extensively than had her predecessor Eleanor, and used her influence to help reconcile the king with his eldest son Edward when the two quarrelled bitterly in 1305. Edward did not grant her a generous landed endowment, and there are indications that she suffered some financial problems. Her widowhood was uneventful. She was notably pious, and patronized the Franciscans, in whose London church she was buried in 1318, rather than at Westminster beside her husband. MCP

Margaret Logie (d. *c.*1375), queen of David II of Scotland. Daughter of Sir Malcolm Drummond and widow of Sir John Logie. After the death of David II's first wife in 1362, Margaret Logie was openly recognized by the king as his 'beloved'. The relationship seems to have been among the causes of a revolt in the early part of 1363. On its suppression, the two were married. Margaret had, by her first marriage, at least one son, who received generous grants from David, favours which may have aroused hostility. There were however no children of her marriage to David and in 1370 the king divorced her, probably to leave him free to marry again. Margaret fled the country and appealed to the pope. David died in 1371, but the process was still dragging on when Margaret herself died some four years later. BW

Margaret Tudor (1489–1541), queen of James IV of Scotland. Elder daughter of Henry VII of England, Margaret was married to James at Holyrood on 8 August 1503, and bore her husband six children—four sons and two daughters—of whom only one, Prince James (James V), born in April 1512, survived. Perhaps significantly, Margaret's second son was christened Arthur, recalling the recently deceased heir to the English throne, Prince *Arthur, and reflecting the Scottish king's claim to Henry VIII's throne if the Tudor line should fail.

After James IV's death at *Flodden (1513), Margaret threw her energies into politics during the magnate struggles of her son's minority (1513–28). She married Archibald Douglas, earl of *Angus (1514), but divorced him in 1526 to marry Henry Stewart, Lord Methven. She took a prominent part in James V's coup of June 1528, and died at Methven (1541). NATM

Marischal, George Keith, 10th Earl [S] (*c.*1693–1778). Marischal was the son of a Jacobite sympathizer and succeeded to the earldom in 1712. The title carried with it the hereditary marshalship of Scotland. In 1715 he joined in the earl of *Mar's rising on behalf of the pretender, fought at *Sheriffmuir, and was attainted. With his brother James he embarked on the abortive rising of '19 and was wounded at *Glenshiel. Thereafter their lives were spent largely abroad, mainly in the service of Frederick the Great. The younger brother became a Prussian field marshal and was killed at Hochkirchen in 1758. The earl served as ambassador to France 1751–4 and to Spain 1759–61. He passed on useful information about the family compact between France and Spain to George II and was pardoned in 1759, though not restored to his title. In 1763 he returned to his native Scotland and recovered many of the family estates, but found the climate disagreeable, preferring that of Prussia, to which he returned. In later years he spoke bitterly of the selfishness and ingratitude of the Stuart family. *Boswell, in his European tour of 1763/4, was befriended by Marischal and Rousseau also describes him in the *Confessions*. JAC

market gardening. There was little need for market gardening in medieval society since towns were small, and monasteries and large estates supplied most of their own needs. But in London gardeners petitioned in 1345 for permission to sell their own produce in public. The growth of the new industry dates from Tudor and Stuart times. Henry VIII's gardener, Richard Harris, had an orchard in Teynham (Kent) producing cherries, pears, and pippins (eating apples), said to have been 'the chief mother for all the other orchards of those kind of fruits'. A rash of market gardens developed in the small villages of Middlesex, Surrey, Kent, and Hertfordshire, sending their produce in by carts, which brought back the night soil and manure on which productivity depended. Samuel Hartlib, writing in the 1650s, suggested that market gardening began to 'creep into England' from Holland and Flanders about 1600 and that old men could remember the first gardeners in Fulham, growing cabbages, cauliflowers, turnips, carrots, and parsnips 'all of which at that time were great rarities'. The Gardeners' Company, still in existence, was founded in 1605 and Fulham parsnips, Hackney turnips, and Sandwich carrots were already sought after. Stocks Market, on the site of the Mansion House, had been in existence for some centuries but was increasingly challenged by *Covent Garden, started as a few sheds and stalls. Celia Fiennes, in her travels in the 1690s, noted at Gravesend (Kent) many gardens 'convenient for to convey the cherries to London' by water. As the larger provincial towns like Bristol and Norwich grew in size, they acquired their own market garden hinterland. The development of the railway network in the 19th cent., providing quick and cheap transport, changed market gardening from a strictly local to a national business. The Great Western railway brought the Thames valley as far as Wiltshire into the London orbit. The Great Northern opened up parts of Bedfordshire, most villages sending produce down to London, but Sandy supplying Yorkshire, Tyneside, and even Scotland. Evesham, too distant at first from London, exploited rail links to Birmingham and then Manchester. Diversification into market gardening enabled farmers to face increasing competition in corn and meat from overseas in the 1870s, and with improved rail and road communications, specialist areas began to appear. The Channel Islands went over increasingly to early potatoes, while the Scilly Isles sent their first early spring flowers to London in 1865. A short-lived but intensive development was in the Lea valley in Hertfordshire just north of London, where glass-houses and greenhouses proliferated, producing tomatoes and cucumbers, from the 1880s, dominated the area, and had vanished by 1960. Tomatoes were a rare and unusual delicacy when Rochfords of Turnford opened one greenhouse in 1883 and were followed by a number of Danish entrepreneurs—Larsens, Jensens, Hansens, Rasmussens. Cheshunt was said in 1898 to have more acres under glass than the rest of England outside Middlesex and Kent. By 1960 the nurseries had moved out to the south coast around Worthing or had sold up for Greater London overspill housing. In the 1970s the spread of supermarkets offered tempting contracts to some gardens operating on a large scale, but also brought increasing foreign competition. A number of market gardens turned themselves into garden centres, selling garden furniture, grass seed, tropical fish, and gnomes—one of the redoubtable growth areas of the late 20th-cent. economy. JAC

markets provide public opportunities for buying and selling at a fixed time and place. For centuries they have played a vital role in the economy. During the Middle Ages lords of manors established markets at the centre of settlements on their estates or on their lands at crossing points on major routes. Until the industrial revolution and the development of permanent shops, markets were the usual way of trading in everyday goods and services; exceptional items were bought at fairs or in very large towns.

Manorial lords levied a rent on each stall-holder in exchange for the right to trade on a particular day of the week throughout the year. Markets usually served the population within about 10 or 12 miles, which was about as far as a laden horse-drawn cart could journey to and from home in a day, whilst allowing time to trade. However, some markets became famous for the sales of special produce, drawing merchants from further afield.

Markets usually took place in the main streets where traders erected their stalls or pens for animals or other livestock. Such streets often show their function by their spaciousness and were given names such as Market Place, Market Street. Other places carried names such as Butter and Hen Cross, Cattle Market, Haymarket, or Lace Market. In larger towns, markets were held in different locations on different days. During the Middle Ages, the naves of many parish churches frequently served as covered markets. However, the unseemly conduct of some traders led to the discontinuation of this practice and the erection of special market halls.

By the 20th cent. markets had become associated with the sale of either fresh local produce or cheap mass-produced goods. IJEK

Marks, Simon (1888–1964). Marks was the son of Michael, a Russian Jewish refugee, who began penny bazaars in Leeds market. Born in Leeds, Simon attended Manchester Grammar School, where he formed a lifelong friendship with Israel Sieff, subsequently brother-in-law and business partner. Michael, with Thomas Spencer as partner, expanded the penny bazaars into the clothing and textile retail chain of Marks & Spencer. It was not until after the First World War that Simon consolidated the Marks family control and with Sieff adopted policies to expand the company. They established stores with a distinctive style, emphasizing light and hygienic surroundings, value for money to customers through quality and standard of design, together with a strong policy of welfare for staff. Between the world wars, Marks and Spencer diversified into food. However clothing and textiles remained important and in 1960 the firm supplied 10 per cent of all such purchases in Britain. IJEK

Marlborough, John Churchill, 1st duke of (1650–1722). The most successful general of his age, Marlborough was from 1704 until 1710 the leading European statesman, eclipsing even Louis XIV. Son of an impoverished royalist squire he owed the start of his dual career as courtier and soldier to the future James II. He gained military experience in Tangier and under Turenne in the French service. From page he became confidential emissary to James, and in 1685 after playing a decisive part in defeating *Monmouth's rebel army he became a major-general. After 1683 he and his wife Sarah also developed an intimate and lasting connection with the future queen Anne.

Churchill made a massive contribution to the success of the *Glorious Revolution by organizing a network of officers who defected to William, so preventing James from making William fight a Bosworth-style battle. As reward he became earl of Marlborough. He organized and led a combined operation that took Cork and Kinsale in southern Ireland (1690), but by championing Anne against her sister Mary he provoked his dismissal from all posts (1692). Alienated, he made promises to Jacobite agents but this was principally an insurance policy against James's possible restoration.

After 1700, faced with an impending European war and broken in health, William designated Marlborough to command the British forces in the Low Countries, disregarding both his past behaviour and his inexperience as a general. William's purpose was to ensure the continuation of his policy of containing and reducing French power, and the Dutch alliance, when Anne succeeded. In 1702 Marlborough, commanding Dutch forces also, manœuvred the French out of territories bordering on the Dutch Republic. Anne made him duke. In 1703 the Dutch generals obstructed his offensive plans, fearing to risk everything on a major battle. But in 1704 French armies in Bavaria threatened to force the German allied princes to capitulate, isolating Britain's other major ally, the Emperor. However, these French armies put themselves in a strategically and logistically untenable position. Superb organization enabled Marlborough to march his army to the Danube where at *Blenheim (13 August) he inflicted the greatest defeat the French had suffered for 150 years. Blenheim was fought in partnership with Eugene, the Emperor's general, with whom Marlborough worked harmoniously. Skill as a diplomat was vitally important since success depended on Marlborough holding the alliance together, a task that became more difficult as French defeats made the allies less fearful of Louis XIV. Marlborough pioneered personal diplomacy, travelling to Vienna, Berlin, and Hanover, and corresponding continually with allied sovereigns and ministers. In 1707 he diverted Charles XII of Sweden from attacking the emperor, and so disrupting the alliance.

In 1705 Marlborough failed in an invasion of France up the Moselle valley, but in 1706 he won a second massive victory at *Ramillies and overran most of the Spanish Netherlands. This achievement was soured when the Dutch reaction made him decline the Emperor's offer of the lucrative governor-generalship of these provinces. In 1708 he totally defeated a French counter-offensive at *Oudenarde, took the fortress of Lille, and planned a final invasion of France. The excessively expensive victory of *Malplaquet (September 1709) prevented this and convinced a war-weary Britain that Marlborough and the Godolphin ministry were committed to an endless war. *Swift pilloried him as motivated purely by greed. Dismissed by the Tory government in December 1711 Marlborough exiled himself. Reinstated by George I as captain-general, he supervised suppression of the Jacobite rebellion in 1715. JRJ

Marlborough, statute of, 1267. Called by Powicke 'the one great statute' of Henry III's later years, it arose from the king's quarrels with the baronial opposition and was based upon the provisions of *Oxford (1258) and the provisions of *Westminster (1259). The preamble declared that it would end 'the many tribulations and unprofitable dissensions' of the past and guarantee the 'peace and tranquillity of the people'. It confirmed *Magna Carta but its primary purpose was to regulate wardship and to protect persons outside the lord's jurisdiction being forced to attend his court. JAC

Marlowe, Christopher (1564–93). English playwright, poet, and spy, reportedly an atheist and probably homosexual. Born in Canterbury (Kent), he was educated at Corpus Christi College, Cambridge, possibly beginning his brief career as a spy on the continent while still enrolled there, and receiving his degree only after intervention by the Privy Council. His plays, beginning with *Dido, Queen of Carthage* (*c.*1587), are energetic, restless, generically daring explorations of selfhood. Success came with his two-part epic of ambition and war, *Tamburlaine* (1587–8), and between 1588 and 1593 he wrote four more plays: *The Massacre at Paris, The Jew of Malta, Doctor Faustus,* and *Edward II*. The last two are generally considered his masterpieces, the former a deceptively simple tale of aspiration and damnation, which reconfigures the morality play tradition for the early modern stage, the latter a remarkably frank account both of a homosexual king's relations with his favourite and of the bleak outworkings of *realpolitik*. Shortly after a warrant for his arrest was issued in May 1593 on charges of atheism (and before he had completed his narrative poem *Hero and Leander*), Marlowe was killed, apparently in a pub brawl. GAM

Marprelate tracts. In 1588–9, six books and a broadside, published under the pseudonym of Martin Marprelate, were a severe indictment of the episcopal hierarchy and associated press censorship. Their rollicking irreverence made them the most popular prose satires of the period, but predictably incensed Elizabeth, the Privy Council, and the establishment. Some suspects were racked in order to identify the author, printers, and distributors, and writers such as Lyly and Gabriel Harvey commissioned to produce counterblasts. Despite the execution of *Penry and the death in prison of *Udall, the most probable author is now regarded as the puritan extremist Job Throckmorton.

ASH

marquis. The title of marquis, second to duke in rank, was the last to be introduced into the peerage and was slow to catch on. The first marquis, Robert de Vere, earl of *Oxford, was made marquis of Dublin in 1385 by Richard II, but within a year had been promoted duke of Ireland. The next, John Beaufort, earl of Somerset, was promoted marquis of Dorset in 1397, degraded in 1399, and offered reinstatement in 1402: he declined, explaining that the title had a foreign flavour. In 1714 there were still only 2 marquises in the English peerage, compared with 22 dukes and 74 earls. The eldest son usually takes his father's earldom as his courtesy title: younger sons and daughters are referred to as Lord James or Lady Mary, with the family surname.

JAC

marriage, the act of marrying and the ceremony by which persons are made husband and wife, establishes links between the families of the bride and groom and guarantees the legitimacy of any children born in wedlock. Traditionally, two major values underpinned marriage: moral commitment of the partners to each other; and contractual commitment in relation to rights of property and succession.

The institution of marriage was an integral part of both church and state, with the state accepting the jurisdiction of the church in the licensing of marriage and in regulating the conditions in which it could take place. Although it was not a sacrament, in the mid-12th cent. Pope Alexander III ruled that for all Christendom the vows partners made to each other should be in the presence of witnesses, preferably, but not essentially, at the parish church door. Within the protestant churches of Great Britain this pre-Reformation tradition remained the legal requirement for marriage until Hardwicke's *Marriage Act (1753), which compelled all marriage ceremonies to take place before a minister within the parish church building. Since the Council of Trent (1545 to 1563) had declared marriage one of the sacraments of the Roman church, catholics received this from their priest. The Marriage Act (1836) formalized many of the customs of previous eras. A superintendent registrar of births, marriages, and deaths had the duty of registering all marriages. The superintendent registrar was also empowered to license religious premises, other than Anglican churches, for the conduct of marriages, so that nonconformists and catholics could marry in their own places of worship. Additionally, register offices were set up in all cities and towns, for the marriages of those not wishing to have a religious ceremony. The Marriage Act of 1995 extended the range of places which could be licensed for the conduct of marriage to any location which was appropriately seemly and dignified.

Until recently, when the importance of romantic love and individual choice became a higher priority, the selection of a marriage partner was usually the prerogative of the family of the bride or groom. At all levels of society marriage partners were usually chosen from within the same social and religious group. Amongst the nobility dynastic considerations, particularly the potential succession to title and property, guided the selection of a suitable spouse. In addition, male relatives had the responsibility of finding suitable marriage partners for their female dependents, with its attendant dangers of the choice being made to benefit the guardian rather than the woman. There was also the problem of forced marriage, recognized by *Magna Carta (1215), which included protection for wards and widows. In the Middle Ages there was no minimum age for entering into marriage, so that betrothal promises, which also had legal force, and marriage vows were sometimes exchanged by immature children. Such arrangements were recorded amongst aristocratic families, where their purpose was to secure dynastic alliances with a likely succession to title and property. The validity of such marriages was challengeable in the courts, where the marriage contract could be annulled if it could be established that the marriage had not been consummated. The testimony of witnesses present at the bedding of the married pair could be taken as evidence of consummation.

The establishment of a minimum age for legal sexual relations was relevant to the determination of who might enter into marriage. During the 19th cent. the ages of consent were fixed at 14 years for males and 16 for females and the ages were later raised to 16 years for both sexes, although marriage at such ages was very infrequent. In contrast, the age of majority for entry into all other legal contracts was 21 years, reduced to 18 years in 1968. It continues to be the case that all minors must seek parental permission to marry, and, for those without parents, permission must be obtained from a guardian, magistrate, or a person of standing.

The registration of marriages and the issuing of 'marriage lines' to be held by one of the spouses, usually the wife, were important procedures for establishing status and the legitimacy of children. Children born out of wedlock suffered discrimination, in that they could not inherit property or status as of right. In contrast to the rest of Britain, Scottish common law marriages, that is marriages which had not taken place in church, could be registered in the Sheriff Court office and subsequently had the standing of licensed marriages. Such documentation of the existence of a marriage became of greater importance for more and more people during the 19th cent. as growing numbers held property and as geographical and social mobility increased. In the 20th cent. such documentation was important for establishing the right to concessions on personal taxation. The promise to marry continued to have legal force and breach of promise cases could be brought by a fiancée whose reputation was deemed to have been tarnished by a broken engagement. Legal proceedings were costly and that, together with growing equality in the commitment to marriage in the 20th cent., meant that breach of promise cases were very infrequent.

Until the later 19th cent. husbands had virtually complete control over their wives and their property. The marriage contract was not an equal one. On marriage wives brought to their husbands total rights to their property and earnings, unless the wife's family had entered into a marriage settlement which limited what a husband might do with the wife's dowry. However, only far-sighted families with the money to pay for legal services made such arrangements. Wives' rights over their own property, earnings, and children began to be recognized by the *Married Women's Property Acts of the later 19th cent. The rights of a wife to manage her own financial affairs and to be wholly responsible for them were achieved in 1988 with legislation to assess husbands and wives as separate individuals, rather than as a married pair for taxation purposes.

In spite of access to divorce and the removal of the social stigma of living together out of wedlock, marriage and remarriage after divorce remain highly valued, to the extent that marriage, often associated with expensive wedding ceremonies, continues to be part of the experience of the great majority of the population. IJEK

Brooke, C. N. L., *The Medieval Idea of Marriage* (Oxford, 1989); Gillis, J., *For Better, for Worse: British Marriages, 1600 to the Present* (New York, 1985); Stone, L., *The Family, Sex and Marriage in England, 1500–1800* (1977); id., *Uncertain Unions: Marriage in England, 1660–1753* (Oxford, 1992).

Marriage Act, 1753. Sometimes known as Lord Hardwicke's Act (26 Geo. II c. 33), this was a fundamental reform of English marriage law. Before 1753 a free exchange of vows between a couple could create a perfectly valid marriage. This led to much abuse, notably the practice whereby most Londoners married secretly, and often drunkenly, in private chapels near the Fleet prison. The Act stated that only weddings conducted in church, according to the rubric of the English Book of Common Prayer, and with banns called, were valid. Since only *Jews and *Quakers were exempted from the scope of the Act, dissenting marriages were disallowed. Not until the Dissenters' Marriage Act of 1836 were they permitted to marry in their own chapels or by a civil contract. JPB

Married Women's Property Acts, 1870, 1882. Prior to these a woman's property became her husband's upon marriage. Reformers sought the same rights for married women over their property as those enjoyed by men and unmarried women. Whilst recognizing the principle that, in certain circumstances, women should retain and control their own property, the 1870 Act was regarded as a 'feeble compromise' and the Married Women's Property Committee pressed for greater reform. The 1882 Act, allowing wives to acquire, hold, use, and dispose of their separate property, with recourse to the same legal protection as if unmarried, was a major victory. AM

marshal. One of the great medieval offices of state. The marshal developed as deputy to the *constable and had responsibility for the horses. He then picked up a number of additional duties, including keeping records of military service and adjusting disputes over precedence. From these duties derived the supervision of heraldry and of the *College of Arms, and the organization of coronations, which remain among the duties of the earl marshal. In the reign of Henry I, the position was held by the Fitzgilberts. The fourth holder, William *Marshal, was created earl of Pembroke and became so great a man in John's reign that the office increased in importance. It then descended via the Bigods and the Mowbrays to the Howards, and from 1483 has stayed with the dukes of Norfolk, save for the period 1572 to 1672. In Scotland, the comparable office developed in the 12th cent. and became hereditary in the Keith family from *c.*1290. From 1458 they possessed the title earl marischal. The last Earl *Marischal supported the Jacobite cause, fought at Sheriffmuir, and was deprived of all his honours in 1716. JAC

Marshal, William (*c.*1147–1219). William the Marshal began life as the fourth son of a minor lord who was hereditary royal master marshal. From such modest beginnings, he rose to become earl of Pembroke (from 1189), through marriage to the heiress Isabella, and ultimately regent of England (1216–19) at the time of Henry III's minority, a spectacular example of the open-endedness of English aristocratic society at this point. The secret of his success lies in his service to Henry II and his sons, their patronage propelling him to great wealth and power. His martial prowess, quick wit, and integrity led Henry to appoint him as tutor in chivalry to his son, Henry the younger, in 1170. Thereafter, he rose rapidly in royal service, but great wealth came only with his marriage of 1189. From then on, he was one of the crown's greatest subjects. He acted as an associate justiciar during Richard I's absence on crusade and fought for him in Normandy and elsewhere on his return. He was estranged from John, but rallied to his cause during the civil war that followed Magna Carta. After John's death, William, more than any other perhaps, saved England for the Plantagenets following French invasion. SL

Marshall, Alfred (1842–1924). Born in Bermondsey (London), and educated at St John's College, Cambridge, Marshall took the mathematics tripos (1862–5). By 1868 he was college lecturer in moral sciences at St John's College, with particular responsibility for teaching political economy. His reputation as the greatest British economist of his time was founded upon his *magnum opus, Principles of Economics* (1890). He dominated economics at Cambridge University almost to his death with many disciples, including A. C. Pigou, the young J. M. *Keynes, and D. H. Robertson. Many believed that, where economics was concerned, 'it's all in Marshall'. His major contributions related to the economics of the stationary state, welfare economics, and partial equilibrium analysis; although claims could be made on his behalf for much that became part of economics textbooks over generations, including innovations relating to utility theory, economies of scale, and supply curves. JRP

Marshalsea prison, Southwark (London). It was established in the 13th cent. to act as a state prison serving the

Marshalsea Court, which dealt with cases involving the royal household. It came under attack from Wat *Tyler's rebels in 1381 and Jack *Cade's men in 1450. After the Restoration, Marshalsea became a debtors' prison and as such featured prominently in Dickens's novel *Little Dorrit*. It was closed in 1849. RAS

Marston Moor, battle of, 1644. In the early summer of 1644 Charles I's forces in the north were pressed between the Scots under Alexander *Leslie, Lord Leven, and parliamentary armies under *Fairfax and *Manchester, moving into south Yorkshire. The marquis of *Newcastle fell back upon York, heavily fortified. In June *Rupert set out from Lancashire to relieve the city. On 1 July, crossing the Ure at Boroughbridge, he outflanked his opponents massed west of York to intercept him, and made contact with the defenders. The following day he gave battle at Marston Moor, in flat pasture land 7 miles west of the city, with roughly 18,000 men against 27,000. *Cromwell, with his first major command, was in charge of the cavalry on Fairfax's left wing. Rupert's defeat was severe and he was said to have been forced to hide in a bean-field. Though the full significance was masked by Charles I's success at *Lostwithiel two months later, the north was lost to the royalist cause and Newcastle fled at once to the continent. JAC

Martello towers. On 8 February 1794 the English, with great difficulty, took a small fort at Cape Mortella on Corsica. It was little more than a pill-box but the British government was greatly impressed with its defensive potential and in 1804, when facing an invasion threat from Napoleon, began a building programme of similar forts on the south coast. They were designed to mount one gun and to have a garrison of 1 officer and 24 men. Seventy-four were erected in Kent and Sussex. Since, like the pill-boxes hastily erected in 1940, they were never put to the test, we shall never know how effective they would have proved. Surviving examples are at Folkestone, Sandgate, and Dymchurch in Kent. JAC

Marten, Henry (1602–80). Regicide. Educated at University College, Oxford, Marten trained as a lawyer. A republican member of the *Long Parliament, he was expelled (1643–6) for his outrageous speaking against king and Lords and imprisoned in the Tower. After his release he led the extreme party associated with the *Levellers and sided with the army against Parliament. He left the House in the second civil war to raise his own cavalry regiment. Closely involved in the king's trial, he was in the *Council of State for the Commonwealth, though, as *Cromwell's power increased, relations between them grew frigid. At the Restoration he surrendered himself and was tried, but his life was spared. Charles II, he declared, was king 'upon the best title under heaven, for he was called in by the representative body of England'. He spent the rest of his life in prison at Chepstow. WMM

martial law. The term has been used in two senses which may cause confusion:

1. The rules which apply to military discipline and related matters. The discipline exercised over the army, particularly a standing army, required special rules and special measures. These rules are now more accurately called military law.

2. The rules and discipline which exist at times of public emergency, and displace the ordinary principles of the law. This notion has been of greater constitutional importance. A proclamation of martial law would therefore suspend or alter the usual operation of the law and people may be punished and, on occasion, even executed by order of special tribunals set up in this way. This was one of the grievances objected to in the *Petition of right and the *Bill of Rights.

The prevailing legal opinion is that there is no such thing as 'martial law' except in so far as the crown must have certain powers to act in the case of emergency, e.g. to put down a rebellion. This is not a special code of law but rather an example of the principle of necessity. MM

Marvell, Andrew (1621–78). Satirist and poet. Son of a Yorkshire clergyman, Cambridge-educated with linguistic skills acquired from four years in Europe, Marvell tutored Lord *Fairfax's daughter (when he wrote his best poetry) and a ward of *Cromwell's before being eventually appointed (1657) as assistant in the Latin secretaryship to *Milton, whom he later defended vigorously. Despite having served the Protectorate, he was able to accept the Restoration, though his forceful political tracts (some prudently anonymous) criticized corrupt and profligate government and railed at religious intolerance. He was elected MP for Hull in 1659 but, despite being moderately active in Parliament, was ineffective in the country party, though he continued to watch his constituents' interests until death from inappropriate treatment for an ague. Regarded by contemporaries as a political satirist, Marvell is now generally remembered as a metaphysical poet, eclectic but lyrical and delighting in nature (*Miscellaneous Poems*, posthumously 1681). ASH

Marx, Karl (1818–83). German revolutionary socialist. Born in the Rhineland to Jewish parents who became Lutheran, Marx was educated in law, history, and philosophy at the Universities of Bonn and Berlin before obtaining his doctorate on Greek philosophy at Jena in 1841. A radical young Hegelian, Marx's left-wing and atheist views ruled out a university post, and he turned to journalism, editing the liberal *Rheinische Zeitung* in Cologne until it was suppressed by the Prussian authorities in 1843. From then on Marx became virtually an exile, fleeing first to Paris where he began his lifelong partnership with Friedrich *Engels, then to Brussels to meet workers' groups, where he and Engels wrote the *Communist Manifesto* (1848) as a rallying call for the proletarian class to overthrow the bourgeoisie. Expelled from Brussels during the revolutionary fervour that swept through Europe in 1848, Marx returned to Cologne to edit the *Neue Rheinische Zeitung* during a short-lived period of democracy. In 1849 he was tried for sedition, and though found not guilty, he was exiled once more, and made his home in London, where he stayed for the rest of his life, studying and writing in the British Museum, and living off Engels's generous allowances. Apart from his involvement with the First International—the International Working

Men's Association—in which he took the leading part from its inception in 1864 until its ignominious demise in 1872 because of his struggle against the anarcho-communist Michael Bakunin, Marx's entire bequest to the communist movement consisted of writing. His most important book was *Capital* in which he set out to expose the flaws in classical political economy by showing how capitalism was not a neutral economic system, founded on timeless laws of supply and demand, but a highly exploitative system, characterized by contradictions that would eventually undermine and destroy it. A new era of socialism—the dictatorship of the proletariat—would be ushered in, followed by communism—a stateless, egalitarian, and co-operative society, founded on the principle of providing for everyone according to their needs, not their wealth.

Marx's practical influence has of course been vast, in the establishment of communist regimes in eastern Europe, east Asia, and elsewhere during the 20th cent. However, the demise of communism in eastern Europe suggests that the enduring influence of Marx may lie more in theoretical terms—i.e. in his seminal contribution to our understanding of society as a system of relationships, ultimately reflecting its economic substructure (i.e. 'mode of production'). In other words, Marx as a sociologist may be of longer-lasting significance than Marx as a revolutionary. TSG

Mary (1542–87), queen of Scots (1542–67). The most thoroughly mythologized of the Stewart monarchs of Scotland, the key to Mary's career lies in her unique dynastic situation and her ultimately fatal attempts to exploit it. The sole legitimate heir to James V, she inherited the throne on 14 December 1542 when only 6 days old. The ensuing minority was dominated by the conflict between France and England for control of Scotland through the promise of the infant queen in marriage. Initially betrothed to Henry VIII's son Edward Tudor, the Scots' rejection of the match led to war with England and Mary's removal in 1548 to France and an eventual marriage to the Dauphin Francis.

The maintenance of French catholic interests in Scotland was the prime aim of the queen mother, *Mary of Guise, whose increasing importance was recognized in 1554 when she replaced *Arran as regent. Her daughter's marriage to Francis in April 1558, followed by the bestowal of the title of a king on her son-in-law, bound Scotland to a French monarchy heavily influenced by the militant catholicism and dynastic ambition of the young queen's Guise relatives. In catholic eyes Elizabeth Tudor was illegitimate and her accession to the English throne in November 1558 a usurpation of Mary Stuart's lawful right to succeed. When Henri II died on 10 July 1559, the new French monarchs, Francis II and Mary, united a dynastic inheritance encompassing potentially not just France and Scotland but also England and Ireland.

The potential was never realized, however, for the death of Francis on 5 December 1560 left Mary a childless widow with no obvious place at the French court. Her decision to return to Scotland in August 1561, where in 1559–60 a protestant revolution had seen the defeat and death of Mary of Guise and the establishment of an English-backed administration led by Mary's half-brother Lord James Stewart, was driven by the desire to pursue her dynastic ambitions within Britain. Spurning the opportunity to lead a catholic counter-revolution, Mary chose instead to deal with her half-brother, whose close links with Elizabeth held out the hope of official recognition in the English succession. While maintaining her own catholic household—thus leaving open communications with France and the papacy—Mary made no move against the newly reformed Scottish kirk.

Yet the stability of Mary's rule depended on a delicate balancing act which the explosive issue of her marriage was always likely to upset. Neither the threat of a foreign catholic match nor the tireless efforts of Lord James—now earl of *Moray—persuaded Elizabeth to recognize Mary as her heir. If Mary's catholic marriage to *Darnley on 29 July 1565 was a love-match, the rehabilitation of the Lennox Stewarts, whose claim to the English throne was second only to that of Mary, was also a calculated diplomatic snub. Mary easily rode out the ensuing storm—an abortive rebellion by Moray which Elizabeth was impotent to support—but the problems posed by the rapid breakdown of relations with Darnley proved insoluble. Embittered by the now pregnant queen's refusal to grant him the crown matrimonial, Darnley joined the *Rizzio conspiracy of March 1566, a protestant demonstration against the possibility of a catholic succession which proved futile. Mary gave birth to a son on 19 June 1566 and the future James VI was baptized a catholic on 17 December.

Mary's complicity in Darnley's murder on 10 February 1567 cannot now be established with certainty. However, her marriage on 15 May to the leading suspect, the earl of *Bothwell, jeopardized her claim to innocence and handed her opponents the chance to destroy her. Moves to 'liberate' her from Bothwell led in July 1567 to her enforced abdication and the appointment of Moray as regent. Moray's regime was far from secure, however, and Mary mustered extensive support on her escape from confinement in May 1568. Although defeated at *Langside, it was her ill-considered flight to England which sealed her fate. Characteristically, Elizabeth prevaricated endlessly over signing her dynastic rival's death-warrant. But Mary's incessant plotting and involvement in a series of catholic intrigues led finally to her execution at Fotheringhay on 8 February 1587.

RAM

Mary I (1516–58), queen of England (1553–8). Few lives can have been sadder nor few reigns more disastrous than that of Mary Tudor, victim of the dynastic and religious tensions in her family. Her birth to Catherine of Aragon and Henry VIII after three miscarriages and a dead infant son was the occasion for great rejoicing and it was presumed that a brother would follow. He did not, and Catherine's only other daughter in 1518 was dead at birth. Though Henry was proud of Princess Mary, his marriage was breaking down and Catherine took refuge increasingly in her religion and her Spanish ladies-in-waiting. Mary seems to have been a lively little girl, 'promising to become a handsome lady', according to one observer in 1522. From birth she was a pawn in the diplomatic game and in 1518, at the age of 2, was betrothed to the dauphin of France. Before she was 3 she accosted the admiral of France at a reception: 'are you the Dauphin? if you are, I wish to kiss you.' But two years later there was a marriage treaty with the Emperor Charles V and by 1523 rumours that she was to marry James V of Scotland. By this time the shadow of a possible divorce was falling across her: Henry had a healthy son by a mistress, the five years Catherine was his senior were all too apparent, and remarriage was increasingly discussed.

The effect of the annulment of her parents' marriage in 1533 was shattering. All her sympathies were with her mother, whom she was allowed to see only rarely until her death in January 1536. Unless the plea was conceded that she had been conceived *in bona fide parentum*, Mary was illegitimate, losing any claim to the throne and precedence at court. In the hard dynastic world of 16th-cent. Europe, her matrimonial prospects plummeted. Worse followed. The execution of *Anne Boleyn and her father's remarriage to *Jane Seymour brought no respite, since the king continued to demand that she acknowledge that her mother's marriage had been invalid and recognize his own ecclesiastical supremacy. Desperate plans to flee to the continent and seek the protection of the emperor were mooted. But in June 1537, with the assistance of Thomas *Cromwell, she submitted, was granted her own household again, and restored to precarious favour. The birth of a half-brother Edward in October 1537 appeared to remove any chance that she would ever be queen.

The remaining years of Henry's life were quieter for Mary and she was on good terms with his last wife, *Catherine Parr. But her troubles had taken a heavy toll. She had lost much of her youthful vivacity, was often unwell, and in 1542 her life was said to be in danger. But she hunted, danced, was fond of dress, and enjoyed music, and the carousel of marriage plans never stopped. In 1541 her old governess of many years, Margaret, countess of *Salisbury, went to the block, but in 1543 a statute restored Mary to the succession, after Prince Edward and any children Catherine Parr might have. From 1547 Edward VI's reign brought new trials. The king's two chief advisers, *Somerset and *Northumberland, promoted protestant doctrines and the young king grew up an eager reformer. When the Act of *Uniformity of 1549 forbade the use of the mass, Mary continued to hear it and was warned. She replied that, in her conscience, 'it is not worthy to have the name of law'. Charles V gave her powerful support and the overthrow of Protector Somerset afforded temporary relief, but Edward, as he grew older, appeared even more determined than his ministers to bring her to heel. In March 1551 he summoned her before the council, declared that he 'could not bear it', and was told in reply that 'her soul was God's and her faith she would not change'. Her release from this stalemate came with the first signs of the illness that killed Edward on 6 July 1553.

Even then, Mary's succession was by no means certain. Edward had declared Lady Jane *Grey his heir and on 9 July she was proclaimed queen. Mary had already fled to Kenninghall in East Anglia, where she had estates and much support, and on 10 July proclaimed herself queen. Northumberland's support collapsed within days and on 7 August Mary entered London to begin her reign. She was 37.

She had triumphed against all odds and it is not surprising that she attributed it to her steadfastness in her faith and to the help she had received from her co-religionists in Europe. She may have misjudged the widespread support she received at home for enthusiasm for the old religion, whereas it is more probable that it was recognition that, despite all the twists and turns of policy and fortune, she was Henry VIII's obvious heir, by birth and by his last will.

Mary had, as the imperial ambassador Renard pointed out, no experience of government at all. Until the spring of 1553 it did not look at all likely that she would ever be called to reign and, even then, the general assumption was that she would be guided by a husband. She turned at once to Renard for advice. The twin objectives of her reign were to restore the catholic faith and to negotiate a marriage which would hold out some hope that the succession would not pass to her half-sister the Princess Elizabeth. Roles were now reversed. In the dark days for catholics in the reign of Edward VI, Mary's known resistance was a beacon of hope: now Elizabeth played the same part for reformers in Mary's reign, though, characteristically, she played it with more finesse and pliancy.

Healing the breach with Rome was not simple. The mass could be celebrated and certain bishops were soon suspended—*Cranmer, *Hooper, *Latimer, *Ridley—while *Gardiner and *Bonner, who had spent most of the previous reign in prison, were restored to their sees of Winchester and London. But many of the ecclesiastical changes had been introduced by statute and would require a parliament to abrogate them. Mary's first Parliament in the autumn of 1553 made a beginning by declaring her mother's marriage legal and by repealing most of Edward VI's religious legislation. But the gentry and aristocracy showed little enthusiasm for disgorging the monastic estates they had acquired, even when urged to do so voluntarily.

In view of her age and the need for an heir, marriage had to be arranged at once. Mary had a sentimental regard for her cousin Reginald *Pole, whom she cannot have seen since she was 15, but he was committed to his life in the church. The claims of Edward *Courtenay flickered for a moment and died. A young catholic, he had spent fifteen years in the Tower, was released and created earl of Devon, but proved, on closer acquaintance, a sore disappointment. When the Emperor Charles V suggested his son Philip, who had just become a widower, Mary was attracted by the Spanish connection and agreed readily. *Wyatt's risingagainst the Spanish marriage—part of a wider conspiracy which misfired—threatened for a moment, but Mary stood firm and it collapsed. Princess Elizabeth was sent to the Tower under suspicion of complicity, but no evidence against her could be found. Philip himself arrived in the summer of 1554. Though he behaved with courtesy, his Spanish courtiers were in private disparaging: 'the queen is not at all beautiful,' wrote one, 'small and rather flabby than fat . . . a perfect saint and dresses badly.' Another, more pointedly, observed that he did not envy Philip his duty: 'to speak frankly it will take a great God to drink this cup.' At first the marriage seemed to have fulfilled its main purpose. Later in 1554 Mary announced herself pregnant. In the summer of 1555 an ornate cradle was prepared and rockers appointed. But no child arrived and in August 1555 Philip left for urgent business in the Low Countries.

Meanwhile the work of reconciliation to Rome went on. It was a joyful day for Mary in November 1554 when Pole returned at last from the continent and pronounced absolution from the sin of schism, and in March 1556 he succeeded Cranmer as archbishop of Canterbury. The supreme headship of the church was revoked by Parliament in December 1554 and acknowledgement made of the authority of the pope, who had sent Pole 'to call us home again into the right way from whence we have all this long while wandered'. Three statutes against heresy were revived. Mary's instincts at first had been for patience towards protestants and the overwhelming advice she received was not to drive too fast. But as opposition developed, her attitude stiffened. A first victim, John *Rogers, a London preacher, went to the stake at Smithfield in February 1555, and was followed by John Hooper, former bishop, at Gloucester, and by Robert *Ferrar, deposed bishop of St David's, at Carmarthen in March. Latimer, Ridley, Cranmer, and some 300 others followed. Moderate catholics were dismayed: 'haste in religious matters', wrote Renard to Philip, 'ought to be avoided. Cruel punishments are not the best way.' But Renard's influence was in decline. There has been much discussion of the responsibility for the burnings, and Gardiner, Bonner, Philip, Pole, and Mary have been named in turn. Of these Mary was probably the gentlest, but she bears the main responsibility since she alone could certainly have stopped them.

In 1554 one of the Spanish entourage wrote that Philip 'fully realises that the marriage was concluded for no fleshly considerations but in order to . . . preserve the Low Countries'. Though the articles of marriage forbade England going to war to assist Spain, that was the intention, and in June 1557 Mary declared war on France. By an ironic twist, the emperor and Philip had quarrelled violently with the new pope, Paul IV. Mary found herself denounced by the pope as 'the wife of a schismatic', Cardinal Pole's legation was revoked, and he was summoned to Rome to answer charges of heresy. In January 1558 the French seized the initiative and besieged Calais. The great outpost of empire, English for more than 200 years, surrendered within a week.

There was little comfort in the short time remaining to Mary. Philip's second and last visit in 1557 had lasted a bare three months. But in January 1558 Philip was told by Mary that she was once more pregnant and the arrival of the child imminent. This time she deceived nobody but herself. On 30 March she made her will 'thinking myself to be with child' and conscious of the dangers of childbirth. That was no danger but there were others. Philip urged her to come to terms with her sister Elizabeth, an improving asset. Mary begged him to let the matter wait until he returned and not to be angry, 'for I have already begun to taste your anger all too often, to my great sorrow'. By the summer she was obviously ill and more and more people were paying their respects to Elizabeth. In October Mary added a sad codicil to her will, 'as I then thought myself to be with child'. She died on 17 November 1558, twelve hours before Cardinal Pole, telling her ladies that while she dozed fitfully she had seen 'many little children like angels, playing before her'. Her husband wrote politely, 'I felt a reasonable regret at her death' and the first act of her sister's first Parliament was to reclaim the governorship of the church which Mary had so enthusiastically abandoned.

Among Mary's first words as a toddler had been 'priest' and she was buried, not in royal finery, but in the plain garb of a religious order. Her failure was total and she died with no earthly hope. Modern historians have pointed to the constructive achievements of her reign—reform of the currency, attention to the navy, reorganization of the customs. Mary herself would have counted them as nothing against the collapse of her grand design. Her reign had begun full of promise, with a spontaneous rising on her behalf and a joyous welcome. The loss of Calais might have been redeemed, though contemporaries were too close to see it, as later commentators did, as a blessing in disguise. But the burnings discredited the church she loved, sowed a harvest of hatred, and dogged the catholic cause for centuries to come. Mary did more than anyone else to make England a protestant nation. JAC

Loades, D., *Mary Tudor: A Life* (Oxford, 1989); Marshall, R. K., *Mary I* (1993); Prescott, H. F. M., *Spanish Tudor: The Life of Bloody Mary* (1940); Ridley, J., *The Life and Times of Mary Tudor* (1973); Tittler, R., *The Reign of Mary I* (1983).

Mary II (1662–94), queen of Great Britain and Ireland (1689–94). Mary was the elder daughter of James, duke of York, by his first wife *Anne Hyde, daughter of the earl of *Clarendon, Charles II's first lord chancellor. Her parents did not convert to catholicism until the end of the 1660s, and she and her sister Anne (born 1665) were brought up as protestants, one of their preceptors being Henry *Compton, their lifelong adherent. Their protestant faith remained central to the sisters' lives. Mary was tall, of striking beauty and winning charm, and without Anne's vindictive tendencies. Her marriage to her cousin William of Orange in 1677, of such profound political consequence, initially filled Mary with misgivings; and it proved childless. But she overcame her reservations, and though William was unfaithful to her they shared a taste for simple domesticity, however ambitious their building and garden projects in Holland and Britain alike. Mary was soon at home in Holland, and her return to England as queen in February 1689 was her first since marriage.

Mary's willing submission to William ensured that he held the executive power in the joint monarchy; but her strong awareness of her hereditary right made Mary share in the widespread scepticism about the legitimacy of her half-brother James Francis Edward, born to James II on 10 June 1688, so assuring a catholic succession to the crown. Mary's relations with Anne were cool owing to Anne's intense resentment at William being joint monarch. Mary acted as regent during William's prolonged absences in Ireland and on the continent 1690–4, and he implicitly trusted her application and judgement. Her death from smallpox in

December 1694 was widely mourned, not least by the king himself. DDA

Mary Bohun (*c.*1370–94), queen of Henry IV. Mary, Henry's first wife, was the younger daughter and co-heiress of Humphrey Bohun, earl of Hereford, Essex, and Northampton (d. 1373). In 1380 she married Henry, earl of Derby, who thus became earl of Hereford and an important magnate in the lifetime of his father *John of Gaunt. Their surviving children, born between 1386 (or 1387) and 1394, were Henry (later Henry V), Thomas, John, and Humphrey (later dukes of *Clarence, *Bedford, and *Gloucester), Blanche, who married Lewis (IV), later elector of the Rhine Palatinate, and Philippa, who married King Eric VII of Denmark. Mary died in childbirth. RLS

Mary of Gueldres (d. 1463), queen of James II of Scotland. Daughter of Duke Arnold of Gueldres and niece of Philip the Good of Burgundy, Mary became James's queen in July 1449, and bore him at least seven children, of whom five survived—Mary, James (later James III), Alexander (duke of *Albany), John (earl of Mar), and Margaret. After a decade of producing children, Mary took control of government after her husband's death at Roxburgh (August 1460), and showed herself an able diplomat, negotiating first with the Lancastrians (to obtain Berwick in 1461), and then switching sides to the victorious Yorkists. Mary founded Trinity College, Edinburgh, and built Ravenscraig castle, Fife. NATM

Mary of Guise (1515–60), queen of James V of Scotland. The daughter of Claude, duke of Guise, and thus a member of one of France's most militantly catholic families, Mary married James in June 1538. By him she bore two sons, who both died in infancy, and a daughter, Mary, who was barely a week old when her father died on 14 December 1542. In the ensuing minority, the dowager queen staunchly upheld French catholic interests in Scotland. In 1548 her daughter was contracted to marry the Dauphin Francis and in 1554 Mary was formally appointed regent. While this marked a tightening of French control, Mary pursued a conciliatory religious policy to ensure the acquiescence of the protestant nobility in the French marriage. With this achieved in April 1558, the need for conciliation lessened and the onset of more repressive policies sparked an inconclusive protestant rebellion in May 1559, whose outcome was determined by external factors. Rocked by the Tumult of Amboise in March 1560, France was unable to counter England's intervention on the protestants' behalf. Her forces besieged at Leith, Mary fell ill and took refuge in Edinburgh castle, where she died on 11 June. RAM

Mary of Modena (1658–1718), queen of James II. Mary of Modena was the second wife of James II, whose first wife *Anne Hyde died in 1671. Since Charles II, James's brother, was unlikely to have further legitimate children, James's remarriage was imperative and a hunt for suitable partners began. Louis XIV urged the claims of Mary, an Italian princess who was tall, good-looking, and an ardent catholic. But her ambition was to enter a nunnery and she had to be persuaded that matrimony was an even more noble sacrifice. Consequently she reinforced James's catholic zeal, and after a shaky start, when she burst into tears at the sight of James, the marriage developed into one of affection, especially after James substituted piety for mistresses. Up to 1684 none of her five children survived and she had had several miscarriages. But after a visit to Bath in 1687, she gave birth to a son in June 1688. Protestants regarded the birth with suspicion and despair, and it was a factor in precipitating their appeal to William of Orange. There is no evidence to support the rumour of a suppositious child and Mary gave birth to a healthy daughter in 1692. In December 1688 she and her infant son fled to France, and were followed by James. Mary remained at Saint-Germain after his death in 1701. She does not seem to have had great influence on policy, though concern for her safety in 1688 undoubtedly helped to bring about James's ill-judged flight. JAC

Mary of Teck (1867–1953), queen of George V. Mary of Teck, known before her marriage as Princess May, had a difficult task as queen in following *Alexandra, who had been extremely popular. But her natural dignity, verging on stiffness, and a strong sense of duty, made her fill the role well. She dressed all her life as an Edwardian lady, which her husband liked, and as the decades unfolded seemed increasingly like a visitor from a bygone age. She was the only daughter of the duke of Teck, her mother being a granddaughter of George III and first cousin to Queen Victoria. By royal standards the family was not wealthy and faced a certain amount of condescension. At the age of 25 she was engaged to Albert Victor, duke of *Clarence ('Eddie'), and after his sudden death married in 1893 his younger brother George, created duke of York. Their preference was for a quiet life at Sandringham: Mary was not boisterous, and took no interest in shooting and hunting, preferring reading and the collection of antiques and *objets d'art*. Despite a natural reserve, she took an active part in public visiting with her husband and, assisted by photography and later film, became a familiar and reassuring figure. During her long widowhood, she continued to appear in public while in no way overshadowing George VI or his wife Elizabeth. JAC

Mary Tudor (1495–1533), queen of France and duchess of Suffolk. Mary Tudor was Henry VIII's younger sister and from her descended the claim of Lady Jane and Lady Catherine *Grey to the throne. Her mother *Elizabeth of York died when she was 7 and the same year her elder sister *Margaret married James IV of Scotland. In 1508, when she was 13, she went through a marriage contract with the future Emperor Charles V. But in 1514, as the result of a diplomatic *bouleversement*, she was married to the elderly king of France, Louis XII. 'She is very beautiful', wrote a Venetian merchant, 'and has not her match in all England—tall, fair and of a light complexion, affable and graceful.' Her ailing husband claimed to have performed valiantly on the wedding night but the court wondered whether the marriage had been consummated. She was queen of France for three months, her husband dying on 1 January 1515. She had previously claimed from Henry the right to choose for herself should she be widowed and within a few weeks had made a private marriage to Charles Brandon, duke of *Suffolk, sent to France to congratulate the new ruler. A public marriage at Greenwich followed in May 1515. The haste of the marriage seems to have been on Mary's side, agitated that she would be used as a pawn in French diplomacy and impressed by Suffolk's prowess at jousting. Her brother's wrath was assuaged by gifts of money and jewels. Her daughter Frances, born in 1517, married the marquis of *Dorset and was the mother of Lady Jane Grey, proclaimed queen in 1553. JAC

Marylebone Cricket Club. The world's premier cricket club. The MCC was founded in 1787 by a group of noblemen headed by the earl of Winchilsea, Lord Charles Lennox, the duke of York, and the duke of Dorset and based at Thomas *Lord's ground in Dorset Square, London. It replaced the Hambledon Cricket Club as the country's leading club and governed the game for 182 years until control passed to the Cricket Council in 1969. During its rule the MCC set up bodies to administer county, test, and worldwide cricket affairs. Its importance as a playing club declined and from 1877 Middlesex Cricket Club shared its ground. RAS

Mary Rose. Built between 1512 and 1514, the *Mary Rose* was one of the finest vessels of Henry VIII's navy. On 19 July 1545, under the command of Sir George Carew, and watched by the king and by Lady Carew, she sailed from Portsmouth to join in an engagement with the French fleet. Not far from the shore, while setting sail, she sank with the loss of hundreds of men, including the vice-admiral. Although not in deep water, attempts to salvage her failed. But the Mary Rose Trust, founded in 1979 with the support of the prince of Wales, succeeded in recovering the hull on 11 October 1982. It is now on public exhibition at Portsmouth. JAC

Maserfield, battle of, 642.*Penda of Mercia defeated and killed *Oswald of Northumbria. Penda is said by *Bede to have removed Oswald's head and hands and to have hung them on stakes, perhaps as an offering to a pagan god of war. Penda's actions helped facilitate the cult of Oswald and miracles were credited not just to his relics, but also to the place where he was killed. The site of the battle, which in British sources is called Cocboy, is uncertain. It has sometimes been identified as Oswestry ('Oswald's tree') in Shropshire, but somewhere closer to the Northumbrian–Mercian border, the location of many other 7th-cent. engagements between Mercia and Northumbria, is more likely. BAEY

masques were a form of English courtly entertainment, involving dancing, speech, song, and instrumental music, that flourished from the later 16th cent. until 1640. In the later 17th and 18th cents. the term was also applied to self-contained musical entertainments, normally accompanying a spoken play. During the reigns of James I and Charles I the masque became an opulent affair, its allegorical or mythological plot symbolizing the monarch's political power and wealth. The most celebrated works involved the collaboration of the first poet laureate Ben *Jonson and the architect Inigo *Jones, who designed not only the spectacular stage effects and costumes but also the *Banqueting House at Whitehall where the works were often performed. The songs, dances, and incidental instrumental music were normally written by different composers. The main characters or 'masquers' were courtiers who were joined by members of the audience for the 'revels'. Professionals were, however, increasingly used, particularly for the 'antimasques': grotesque or comic scenes first introduced in Jonson's *The Masque of Queens* (1609). The only masque whose music survives complete is *Cupid and Death* (1653 and 1659), which—unusually—experimented with Italianate recitative. After the Restoration the masque transferred to the professional theatre, where its tradition continued in *Purcell's semi-operas. ECr

Massachusetts Bay Company. The company received a crown charter in 1629 for the settlement of a New England territorial grant. Its leading members were puritan gentry, divines, and merchants, who agreed that the charter should be transferred from London to Massachusetts. After extra-legal alterations, including restricting voting rights and office-holding to church members and the creation of law courts, the charter became the Massachusetts frame of government, until its vacation in 1684 and the imposition of a second charter (1691). Criticized for creating a semi-independent godly commonwealth by its enemies, it was cherished for this reason by the colony's political and religious leadership. RCS

mass media signifies the means by which communications—either factual or fictional—are transmitted to a mass audience through a variety of printing or audio-visual technologies. The purposes of communication have always remained the same: artists wish to entertain and stimulate; entrepreneurs aim to make money; governments and interest groups hope to inform or persuade; advertisers help to sell goods and ideas. What have changed are the technologies used, which, with the developments of industrial capitalism and mass urban populations, have become increasingly complex, sophisticated, and all-embracing, causing continuing concern about the role and power of the mass media in the 'global village'.

Earliest advances in mass communications were in the written print technologies, where the printing innovations of *Caxton in the 15th cent. developed eventually into the newspaper and magazine industry of the industrial era—first the broadsheet 'quality' press and periodicals of the early 19th cent., then the tabloid 'popular' press, magazines, and comics of the late 19th cent. New means of reproduction for drawings and photographs created more visual mass communications. When the illusion of movement was created by projecting still images at 16 frames per second in the 1890s, the powerful mass medium of *cinema was created.

With the developing electrical technologies of the 19th cent., a realistic reproduction of the human voice was created, first in the gramophone and the telephone, which began to replace telegraphy from the 1870s. Experiments in wire-less telegraphy by Marconi in the 1890s confirmed that messages could be transmitted on sound waves, and with the human voice carried on these waves, the influential medium of *radio was developed through the early years of the 20th cent. When a similar means of transmitting visual images was developed, *television was launched in the 1930s, and when sound was married to cinema's silent images from the late 1920s, the inter-war range of innovative audio-visual media was complete. The quickening pace of technological change after the Second World War—with microchips, digitization, laser, and fibre optics bringing video, satellite, cable, CD-ROM, and the Internet—has meant that the media can now be used to transmit messages instantly on a world stage to the biggest mass audiences imaginable.

Accompanying each stage of the mass media's development has been a series of struggles and debates over who owns and controls these vital means of communication, who can get access to them, and what messages should or should not be allowed. In Britain, there has been a tradition of strong government regulation, compared with the generally *laissez-faire* approach of free enterprise USA. Stamp duty and other taxes on the early press were meant to keep potentially seditious literature out of the hands of the masses—though the working classes developed their own means of communication in the underground radical press. Ironically a more efficient way of controlling the masses' reading was developed when the government 'deregulated' the system with the abolition of stamp duty in 1855, and a flood of non-political popular papers arrived to divert the energies of the working class.

Television and radio have always been highly regulated—both the official 'voice of the nation' the *British Broadcasting Corporation, and commercial 'independent' TV and radio stations. Where there is no direct government Act or royal charter to set standards, self-regulation has been encouraged, such as the film industry-sponsored British Board of Film Censors (now Classification) set up in 1912; press control bodies like the Press Council (now the Press Complaints Commission); broadcasting control bodies like the Independent Broadcasting Authority (now Independent Television Commission), the Radio Authority, the Broadcasting Complaints Commission, and the Broadcasting Standards Council. The problems of regulating a worldwide medium like satellite TV are major causes of concern to British politicians of the late 20th cent.

The phenomenon of the 'moral panic' has regularly followed the development of each new mass medium, with establishment fears that the young, the working class, the outsiders of society will be corrupted by the media products and contribute to the decline of society—whether it be Victorian 'penny dreadfuls', early cinema adventures, American comics in the 1950s, or the 'video nasty' scares of the 1980s. Fears have also been regularly expressed about the swamping of British culture by brash American media-led values—Hollywood cinema, American comics, rock and roll music, and 'trashy' television.

From the left, the main concerns have centred round questions of ownership and control, with power concentrated in the hands of a series of media tycoons, from the early 20th-cent. newspaper magnates like Northcliffe, Rothermere (the *Harmsworth brothers), and *Beaverbrook to the late 20th-cent. multi-media owners such as Maxwell and Murdoch. Further concerns about the role of the media in transmitting ideology—both obviously in non-fictional news and propaganda, but also more innocuously in the form of apparently 'value free' entertainment—will ensure that the mass media remain a constant subject of controversy and debate. DJA

master of the king's (queen's) **music.** The title of the director of the monarch's private musicians. Inaugurated by Charles I in 1625 and first held by Nicholas Lanier, the post developed during the Restoration to include the direction of Charles II's band of 24 violins. Nowadays, however, the duties merely involve composing occasional works for state or royal events. Holders of the title have included John Eccles (1700–35), Maurice Greene (1735–55), William Boyce (1755–79), John Stanley (1779–86), William Shield (1817–29), Edward *Elgar (1924–34), Arnold Bax (1942–52), Arthur Bliss (1953–75), and, since 1975, Malcolm Williamson. ECr

master of the rolls. One of the senior judges whose responsibilities include preserving the records of Chancery and who was custodian of the Public Records until 1958, when they were transferred to the *lord chancellor. He also serves as president of the civil division of the Court of Appeal. The master admits solicitors to the Supreme Court and is responsible, through a tribunal, for their professional discipline. JAC

Matapan, battle of, 1941. At a time when Britain was standing alone against the axis powers, victories were scarce. In the Mediterranean, however, the Italian fleet was poorly led and badly deployed. On 28 March 1941, a British fleet under Vice-Admiral Pridham-Wippell, comprising three battleships, four cruisers, and an aircraft carrier, encountered the Italians off Cape Matapan. In an action characterized by the use of carrier-borne aircraft and radar, the British sank three of Italy's latest cruisers and two destroyers, while damaging a battleship—all for the loss of just two aircraft. JLP

Mathew, Theobald (1790–1856). Irish temperance apostle. Born in Tipperary, educated at Maynooth, he joined the Capuchins in Dublin. After ordination (1814) he took charge of the Little Friary among the destitute in Cork, where he opened free schools and founded a charitable society in St Vincent de Paul's tradition. Asked by Cork nonconformists to head their *temperance movement (1838), he signed the pledge. Within nine months 250,000 followed him. As provincial of his order (1822–51), he addressed temperance meetings throughout Ireland. Travelling to London (1843), he held temperance meetings, met *Peel, won public subscriptions, and warned the government of the incipient potato famine. His nomination by Cork clergy as their bishop was not ratified by the Vatican. He travelled in America preaching to catholic congregations and addressing temperance meetings (1849–51) despite ill-health, which caused him to refuse a bishopric on his return. He died at Queenstown. WMM

Matilda (*c.*1030–83), queen of William I and duchess of Normandy. The Daughter of Count Baldwin V of Flanders, her marriage to William *c.*1050 was initially prohibited by the papacy on grounds of (unspecified) consanguinity. The couple made amends by founding two abbeys at Caen. The marriage seems to have been an exceptionally successful one, not just because it guaranteed the succession by producing nine known children, but also because Matilda was admirably suited to the role of deputy and supporter which medieval society required of aristocratic women. She frequently acted as regent during William's absences from Normandy and seems to have been a unifying force in an increasingly disunited family, maintaining some sort of mutual tolerance between her husband and their eldest son *Robert Curthose up until her death. DB

Matilda (*c.*1080–1118), queen of Henry I and duchess of Normandy. First wife of Henry I and daughter of *Malcolm Canmore, king of Scotland, and his queen St *Margaret, sister of *Edgar the Atheling. Her marriage to Henry in 1100 was clearly intended to reinforce the legitimacy of his kingship by establishing a link with the old English royal house; Henry's determination to marry her was such that he had to await a definitive ruling from the archbishop of Canterbury, St *Anselm, whether she had once been a nun, which would have automatically prevented the marriage. Matilda appears to have performed competently the expected queenly role of supporting her husband's rule and frequently acted as regent in England when he was in *Normandy. She is said to have kept a splendid, but pious, court and was a generous patron of artists and musicians. DB

Matilda (Maud) (d. 1131), queen of David I of Scotland. Widow of Simon de Senlis and daughter of Earl Waltheof of Northumbria and his wife Judith, William the Conqueror's niece, she married the future David I in 1113. This marriage, arranged by Henry I, was of profound significance for Scottish history. It brought the Scottish royal house the earldom of Huntingdon (Waltheof's other earldom), dependent status as tenants-in-chief of the English crown for English lands, and a deep involvement in English society which facilitated the processes of modernization in 12th-cent. Scotland. Matilda was a benefactor of several religious houses, including Elstow abbey (Beds.), and the mother of two Scottish princes, both of whom predeceased David. KJS

Matilda (Maud), **Empress** (1102–67). Matilda was the daughter of Henry I. When she was just 8 years old she left England for Germany to marry the Emperor Henry V, the ceremony occurring in 1114, and she only returned on his death in 1125. Matilda was designated as Henry I's successor in England and Normandy in 1127 since she was now his sole surviving legitimate offspring, Prince William having died in the wreck of the **White Ship* (1120). Her second husband, whom she married in June 1128, was *Geoffrey of Anjou, only 14 years old, who inherited the county shortly afterwards. It was a very unhappy marriage, but the awaited heir, the future Henry II, on whom Henry I's hopes depended, was born in 1133, the first of three sons. But when Henry I died in 1135, his nephew Stephen of Blois staged a coup and took the English throne. Matilda landed in England in 1139 in pursuit of her right. She came closest to success in 1141, when Stephen was captured, but the crown eluded her, partly because of her mismanagement of the situation. It gradually became apparent that her task lay in maintaining her position in England and preparing the way for her son (later Henry II), altogether more acceptable to the English magnates and approaching manhood. In 1148 she retired to Normandy, but not entirely from political life. She occasionally acted as Henry II's viceregent and he relied on her counsels in a number of important matters. An impetuous, indomitable, haughty woman, Matilda was greatest in her offspring, but he owed much to her determination to fight for England. SL

Matilda of Boulogne (*c.*1103–52), queen of Stephen. Matilda was a doughty supporter of Stephen's cause in the civil war against the Empress *Matilda. Heiress to the lands of the counts of Boulogne in France and England, she provided her husband with substantial resources and a power base in the home counties which facilitated his seizure of the kingdom in 1135. After 1135 she made a considerable contribution to his cause, playing a central role in disrupting the empress's plans during Stephen's imprisonment in 1141–2, and arranging an important marriage between their son *Eustace and the daughter of the French king Louis VII in 1140, which gave her husband a useful ally. Stephen's cause declined quite rapidly after her death. DB

Matthew Paris (*c.*1200–59) is one of the greatest of all historians, partly because of his astonishing output, partly because of the remarkable comprehensiveness of his work, partly because of his historical method, and partly because of his extensive range of interests. He entered the monastery of St Albans in 1217 and spent most of his life there writing history. He wrote a series of saints' lives. He composed the *Gesta abbatum*, recording the history of his monastic house. His greatest work, the monumental *Chronica majora*, for which he is renowned, was the most comprehensive history yet written in England, and concerned not just with English affairs but with those of the entire known world from the Creation to Paris's own day. He also wrote the *Historia Anglorum*, a chronicle from 1066 to 1253, and two shorter histories, the *Abbreviatio chronicorum* and the *Flores historiarum*. Paris was also a significant artist, as shown by the compelling illustrations to his various texts, and an important cartographer. SL

Matthews, Sir Stanley (b. 1915). Footballer. Born at Hanley in the Potteries, Matthews made his début for Stoke City in 1932 and his first appearance for England in 1934, when he scored one of his comparatively rare goals. From 1947 to 1961 he played for Blackpool, returned to Stoke from 1961, and retired at the age of 50. He played for England on 54 occasions, and was Footballer of the Year in 1948 and again in 1963. He was knighted on his retirement. Matthews played on the right wing, providing crosses of pin-point accuracy for his strikers. His most famous game was the Cup Final of 1953, when Blackpool were trailing 1–3. In the last 20 minutes, Matthews turned on an extraordinary exhibition of wing play, mesmerizing opponents, to defeat Bolton Wanderers 4–3. His brilliant ball control was matched by his physical fitness and sportsmanship. JAC

Mauchte, St (d. *c.*535). Born in Britain, taken to Ireland by Christian parents, Mauchte became a disciple of St *Patrick. When in Rome, he was allegedly consecrated by Pope Leo I. He returned to Ireland with twelve followers, eventually settling to build a monastery at Louth, and is claimed as its first bishop. The enormous community was said to include 200 bishops. Probably 90 when he died, one of many legends attached to him claims he lived for 300 years, a sentence pronounced on him by St Patrick for questioning the ages attributed to Old Testament patriarchs. AM

Mau Mau rebellion. The violent, grass-roots resistance movement launched by the Kikuyu and related ethnic groups against the British colonial government in Kenya in the 1950s. It had its origins in the sense of deprivation felt by the Kikuyu, who had lost much of their land to white settlers. However strong their resentment towards white domination, most educated Kikuyu were anxious to avoid military confrontation. The movement consequently lacked high-quality leadership and failed to win support from other ethnic groups within the colony. Its defeat when confronted by trained soldiers and police, though protracted, was inevitable. KI

Maurice, Frederick Denison (1805–72). Anglican theologian and social reformer. Son of a unitarian minister, Maurice was ordained in the Church of England and became professor of theology at King's College, London, but was forced to resign in 1853 because of his unorthodox views on eternal punishment. Maurice rejected the narrow moralism of his day and called for a wider understanding of the kingdom of God. He was deeply moved by the political events of 1848 and declared himself a *Christian socialist. In 1854 he founded the Working Men's College in London and became increasingly recognized as a leader of Christian social reform. Contemporaries like John Stuart *Mill criticized Maurice as muddled and obscure; but to his friends he was a saintly and prophetic figure. His writings supported the tenets of the *broad-church school of Anglicans (modernists) and also influenced the Christian socialist revival of 1877–1914. JFCH

Mauritius was long known to the Arabs. It was discovered by the Portuguese but settled by the Dutch who named it after Maurice of Nassau. The French East India Company took possession in 1715 and, under Mahe de la Bourdonnais, developed sugar, cotton, spice, and indigo plantations. The British captured it in 1810 and kept it as their own crown colony. When slavery was abolished, Indian indentured labour was imported to work the plantations. Representative government was established in 1947 and Mauritius became independent within the Commonwealth in 1968. In 1992 it adopted a republican constitution. DAW

Maxton, James (1885–1946). Socialist agitator. The son of a Glasgow schoolteacher, and initially a teacher himself, Maxton joined the *Independent Labour Party (ILP) in 1904 and acquired a well-deserved reputation as a fiery but witty orator in the socialist cause. In 1916 he suffered imprisonment for calling a general strike on Clydeside in protest against the deportation of engineers who were opposed to wartime measures permitting the 'dilution of labour'—that is, the employment of those who had not served regular apprenticeships. In 1919 Maxton became an ILP organizer, succeeding to the chairmanship of the party in 1926; meanwhile he had been elected as ILP MP for Glasgow Bridgeton (1922–46). Jimmie Maxton was ever a rebel, the leading member of the Clydesiders whose unshakeable faith in Marxist socialism became a feature of parliamentary politics in the inter-war period. But he was also a perfect gentleman, much admired (if unloved) on all sides in the Commons. GA

Maxwell, James Clerk (1831–79). Maxwell was a mathematical physicist particularly eminent for his work on electromagnetism, and on the theory of gases. Educated in Edinburgh and Cambridge, his earliest work was on the stability of Saturn's rings. After holding chairs in Aberdeen and in London, and managing the family estates in Scotland, he was in 1871 appointed to the professorship at Cambridge founded in memory of Henry *Cavendish. He oversaw the building of the Cavendish Laboratory, where J. J. *Thomson and Lord *Rutherford were to work. He gave mathematical form to Michael *Faraday's discoveries, leading to a new understanding of light and to the discovery of radio, and introduced statistical explanation into physics with his work on gases. He was an intellectual giant, who also wrote playful verse, and his early death was a great loss. DK

***Mayflower*.** The *Mayflower*, an unremarkable ship of about 180 tons, has been immortalized, since it carried the first Pilgrims to New England and because the Mayflower Compact of 21 November 1620 was agreed on board. This was a covenant by the adult males, many of whom were not previously known to, and were distrusted by, the Pilgrim leaders, to obey agreed laws and ordinances. It allowed the election of officials and the suppression of disorder, in the absence of a formal charter. An early exercise in self-government, it was later followed by the formal election of a governor and assembly. RCS

Maynard, Sir John (1604–90). Lawyer. Maynard was born in Tavistock and educated at Exeter College, Oxford. He soon built up a successful practice on the western circuit and entered Parliament for Totnes in 1640. A zealous presbyterian, he was an implacable opponent of the king and prominent in the attacks upon *Strafford and *Laud. He continued his legal practice under the Commonwealth, served Richard *Cromwell as solicitor-general, and was in the *Council of State in 1660. Nevertheless, he prospered under the Restoration, was appointed king's serjeant, and knighted, though Pepys reported that he was far from popular. He remained in the House of Commons for the rest of his life, prosecuted Lord *Stafford in the Popish plot, but was at hand to welcome William III. For fifteen months 1689–90, though very old, he served as commissioner for the great seal. Maynard was recognized as a good lawyer, a fine speaker, and an imposing man, willing to serve all regimes. 'In legal murder none so deeply read,' remarked Strafford's nephew mordantly in 1681. JAC

Mayne, Cuthbert (*c*.1543–77). Catholic martyr. Mayne was born near Barnstaple and became an Anglican minister early in life, being admitted BA at St John's College, Oxford, in 1566. Through the influence of *Campion he converted to catholicism, attended the seminary at Douai, and was ordained priest in 1575. In April 1576 he was sent to Cornwall but was captured within three months. It suggests considerable unawareness of his danger that, when taken, he was wearing an Agnus Dei and in possession of a papal bull. His case went to the council, which was greatly alarmed at reports of the spread of catholicism, and determined on severity. Mayne was executed as a traitor at Launceston in November 1577, being the first seminary priest to suffer martyrdom. His skull is preserved in the Carmelite monastery at Lanherne (Corn.) and he was canonized in 1970. JAC

Maynooth seminary. When catholic seminaries in France were closed by the Revolution, the Irish hierarchy asked to open one in Ireland. The British government approved, since it might remove young Irish priests from the contamination of foreign revolutionary doctrines, and *Camden, the lord-lieutenant, laid the foundation stone of St Patrick's College, Maynooth, in 1796. The government provided an annual grant which the Ministry of All the *Talents in 1806 wished to increase. In 1845 *Peel, as part of his reorganization of Irish higher education, increased the grant again, leading *Gladstone to resign from the cabinet, though his reasons for doing so remained a mystery, particularly after he had explained them. Peel's action was seen by the unbending Tories as yet another betrayal and there was massive petitioning against the bill. But when Gladstone found himself prime minister in 1868 he re-endowed the college as compensation for stopping the grant. JAC

mayors have been familiar urban officials in England and America (but not Scotland) for so long that it is easy to forget their exotic origin. The word (*major*='greater') was used in the post-Roman West for officials with supervisory responsibilities for others, and was taken up by the elected heads of revolutionary town governments in northern France. In imitation of them, the Londoners elected a mayor when they formed a sworn association about 1190, and King John recognized the London mayoralty in 1215. In the later Middle Ages most leading English towns followed London's example, with an annually elected mayor as their chief official. The more important mayors were treated with great respect, and processed publicly with attendants such as a sword-bearer or mace-bearer; from the 15th cent. those of London and York came to be called lords mayor. Until the 19th cent. mayors exercised considerable power by both charter and by-laws, presiding over courts and having powers of arrest. Municipal reform since 1835 has allowed the multiplication of towns with mayors and lords mayor but has diminished their real power: they have become simply chairmen or chairwomen of their councils, and are expected to devote much time to ornamental and ceremonial functions. The London Lord Mayor's Show, originating with the medieval ceremony of the mayor going to Westminster to be presented to the barons of the Exchequer, has survived and grown to be one of the most famous civic pageants in the world. DMP

maypoles. Ancient fertility emblems, brought in ceremonially from the woods on May Day, erected on village greens, and decorated with flowers as central features during festivities. Permanent poles were usually very tall. According to *Stow, one London pole in Aldgate ward outtopped the adjacent church's steeple, hence St Andrew the Apostle being renamed St Andrew Undershaft; after the 1517 apprentice riot it remained hooked under house eaves along Shaft Alley until residents burned it in response to a sermon denouncing it as an idol (1549). Reviled by puritans because of associations with paganism and immorality, maypoles were forbidden in 1644, but reappeared after the Restoration for May Day or Oak Apple Day (29 May) celebrations. The shorter poles used today for plaited-ribbon dances are a late 19th-cent. import. ASH

Meath (Mide), **diocese of.** The Irish see of Meath in *Armagh province was created in 1216 by the amalgamation of the dioceses of Clonard, Kells, and Duleek, after a confused period of 12th-cent. ecclesiastical history in the Clonmacnoise region. Though there was an Anglo-French bishop in John's reign, this was not regularly the case until after 1327. By the 15th cent. it was in the region of the Armagh province known as *inter Anglicos*, Meath being part of the 30-mile strip behind Dublin and Kildare, the English administrative centre. There are still dioceses of Meath in both the Catholic and Anglican churches, though the Anglican diocese was transferred from Armagh to the Dublin province in 1976. There are cathedrals at Trim and Kildare. WMM

Meath, kingdom of. Meath (Mide, 'middle province') became the fifth province of Ireland along with Ulster (Ulaid), Leinster (Laigin), Munster (Mumu), and Connacht (Connachta) after the Uí Néill established their supremacy over central and north Ireland in the 5th cent. It is not mentioned in the *Táin Bó Cuailnge* and must have come into existence afterwards. The dynasty was founded by Níall Noígiallach, a Goidel, with Tara as the centre of power and sanctuary. However, in the 8th cent. the kingdom of Meath collapsed and a separate kingdom of Brega was formed, taking in the present county of Meath, south Louth, and north Dublin. Though the two were reunited in the 11th cent. when Brega came to an end, Meath never regained its former importance. SMD

mechanics' institutes. Following the foundation of the London Mechanics' Institute (later Birkbeck College) in 1823, these adult education institutions spread rapidly, especially in the industrial areas of the north and midlands. Their original aim of providing science for artisans, however, proved impracticable and by 1840 they had become centres for 'rational recreation' and the 'diffusion of useful knowledge', frequented by lower middle-class clerks and tradesmen and a few better-off artisans. The membership nationally rose from 7,000 in 1831 to 200,000 in 1860. Mechanics' institutes were favoured by middle-class liberals as promoting self-help, respectability, and 'intellectual and moral improvement'. From the 1860s mechanics' institutes acquired a new role as night schools and examination centres for the Society of Arts and the Science and Art Department, thus becoming forerunners of technical colleges.

JFCH

medicine, development of. The wort-cunning of the Anglo-Saxon leeches, allied to nursing skill, became displaced by the introduction of Salernitan doctrine into England as the great medieval schools at Montpellier, Paris, Bologna, and Padua were founded. Ancient and hence medieval medical knowledge had fused around the writings of the Hippocratic corpus and Galen, and was predominantly found in monasteries, where Christian tradition encouraged care for one's neighbour. Such knowledge became institutionalized within the medieval universities of Oxford and Cambridge, which conferred the right to practise. But the bulk of the population had little access to physicians, seeking instead barber-surgeons, apothecaries, empirics such as bonesetters and tooth-drawers, or wise women. In principle subordinate to the medical faculties, these groups in practice had considerable autonomy; separation between the book-learned physicians and the practically-orientated surgeons grew as each developed their own professional structure, while the guilds sought to keep their own practice exclusive. The 16th-cent. attack on the doctrine of the humours (which emphasized symptoms rather than causes of disease) by the turbulent Paracelsus, and his rejection of authority, led to a split with the Galenists; the Paracelsians, or chemical physicians, became particularly prominent in northern Europe and England as they attempted a more rational approach to diagnosis and treatment, favouring metallic rather than herbal remedies. The College of Physicians (established 1518) suffered serious crises in the 17th cent. because of its continued identification with Galenic theory and its links with patronage, heightened by a resurgence of empiricism and knowledge based on experience rather than scholarship. As the natural sciences advanced and old Aristotelian ideas were discarded, observation and experiment gradually replaced theory and guesswork: William *Harvey's explanation of the circulation of the blood was confirmed by Malpighi's microscopic identification of the capillary vessels, while Thomas Sydenham encouraged detailed bedside observation.

As the power of the guilds declined, unregulated groups of medical practitioners emerged, whose training and practice were controlled more by the growth of a cash economy, resulting in a highly competitive 'health-for-sale' market. The establishment of voluntary hospitals and new medical schools, with increased clinical training at the bedside, broke the monopoly of the medieval universities, while, outside the official schools, private courses in anatomy and midwifery could be purchased. Educated lay people had long had access to medical knowledge, but once microscopic anatomy, pathology, and the stethoscope were developed, and greater rigour demanded, such learning became increasingly exclusive to the professionals. The introduction of inoculation and then vaccination made slow inroads upon the scourge of smallpox, surgery began to acquire some respectability, obstetrics was increasingly in the hands of the man-midwives, specialities began to emerge through new explanations of disease, and public health and hygiene received more attention.

The 19th cent. was characterized by a rise in scientific medicine, convergence between the separate disciplines of physic and surgery, and commencement of regulation throughout the profession. The structure of the body being known, attention turned to its detailed function; the concept of the cell as the centre of all pathological changes finally destroyed the view that an imbalance in the humours underlay disease. General anaesthesia (1840s) increased the scope and practice of surgery, most noticeably after *Lister's antiseptic principle had been introduced (1860s), dramatically reducing infections and mortality, especially in hospitals and after childbirth. Verification of the germ theory transformed pathology, though maintenance of health was becoming as important a concern. The overall standard of medical education improved and medical societies burgeoned, but the existence of 21 separate licensing bodies stimulated the 1858 Medical Act, which created a central governing body and established a register of practitioners. Attempts to have a single portal of entry to the profession were thwarted though, and many unqualified practitioners persisted. Radiology, psychiatry, and tropical medicine having been established, the 20th cent. continued to change the face of medicine beyond recognition. Life expectancy increased steadily, particularly after commercial production of antibiotics and vaccines. Developments in immunology have enabled organ transplants and genetic disorders are slowly yielding their secrets, but heart disease and malignancies remain disturbingly prevalent. Improved communication and teamwork have replaced isolated study, with widespread advances in medical technology furthering claims to professional monopoly, if not élitism, at the same time as affecting medical education and generating funding crises. The introduction of the *National Health Service in 1948 markedly altered the pattern of provision of health care, but morale within the profession has declined as, increasingly challenged, it struggles to adjust to changing cultural values and expectations.

ASH

Medina del Campo, treaty of, 1489. In 1489 Henry VII was attempting to prop up Brittany against French encroachment and also pursuing a marriage between his heir *Arthur and the infant Catherine, daughter of Ferdinand of Aragon and Spain. In March 1489 the treaty of Medina del Campo confirmed the marriage arrangements and concluded an alliance against France. Though the treaty was not formally ratified, it served as the foundation of Henry's foreign policy. But in 1491 the duchess of Brittany married Charles VIII of France and the realms were united. The marriage of Catherine and Arthur was postponed until 1501 and within five months Arthur had died.

JAC

Medway, battle of, AD 43. A major battle of the Roman invasion campaign, it is identified only as having taken place at a river between the beachhead and the Thames, almost certainly the Medway. Unusually for the ancient world, it lasted two days. On the first day auxiliary troops swam across and killed the British chariot horses, and legionaries under the future emperor *Vespasian also forced a crossing. The decisive combat took place on the second day, when the Roman general Hosidius Geta distinguished himself after nearly being captured. ASEC

Medway, Dutch attack in the, 1667. One of the most brilliant of all naval exploits, the Dutch attack upon the Medway anchorage was on 10–14 June, as the English were attempting to recover from the Plague and the Great Fire of London. Anticipating peace negotiations, Charles II had laid up many vessels. The Medway was protected by difficult access, sunken ships, and a boom, but the Dutch penetrated the defences and caused consternation. The *Royal Charles* was towed away to Holland, and the *Royal James*, the *Loyal London*, and the *Royal Oak* sunk. Peace was signed at *Breda the following month. Part of the stern of the *Royal Charles* may still be seen in the National Museum in Amsterdam. JAC

Melba, Nellie (1859–1931). Opera singer. Born of Scottish parents as Helen Porter Mitchell, near Melbourne (Australia), it was only after marriage to Charles Armstrong that her gifts were developed. She came to England largely by her own efforts, but her potential was not recognized and *Sullivan refused her work. After study in Paris came a brilliant début in Brussels (1887) as 'Mme Melba', clearly derived from her birthplace. World-wide acclaim followed. She eventually had many operas in her repertoire but was identified predominantly with early Verdi, Gounod, and Donizetti—*The Times* referred to 'the exquisite voice and the perfect use of it'—and sensibly avoided Wagner. She studied roles with Verdi and (later) Puccini, subsequently making *La Bohème* her own. Immensely popular and honoured as 'Dame' because of her work for war charities, she bade farewell at Covent Garden in 1926, though her last charity concert appearance was 1929. ASH

Melbourne, William Lamb, 2nd Viscount (1779–1848). Prime minister. Melbourne was such an agreeable man—perhaps the most pleasant prime minister since Lord *North—that it is not easy to form a detached judgement. In some respects he was an essentially 18th-cent. figure: his idea of government was static, if not negative—the maintenance of law and order, conduct of foreign relations (usually with tiresome powers), and the implementation of those changes that could neither be postponed nor avoided.

To appearances he was an archetypal old-fashioned Whig—lounging, aristocratic, amiable, amateurish. But appearances were deceptive. He was not of the old nobility. His grandfather was a clever attorney who had acquired a baronetcy and obtained Melbourne Hall by marriage: his father, an obscure MP and follower of the prince of Wales, added an Irish and then an English peerage. Though Melbourne's attitude of ironic unconcern was not a pose, he was capable of hard and sustained application. 'I am sorry to hurt any man's feelings,' wrote Sydney *Smith, another ironist, 'and to brush away the magnificent fabric of levity and gaiety he has reared, but I accuse our minister of honesty and diligence.' But near the core of Melbourne was a sadness: 'the man was mournful in his heart of hearts,' wrote W. M. Praed, in a poetical assessment. His mother was pretty and charming but, as Melbourne was overheard muttering in old age, 'not chaste, not chaste': consequently it is uncertain who his real father was and the earl of Egremont is as good a bet as any. At the age of 26 he was unlucky enough to marry Lady Caroline Ponsonby, whose indiscretions, scenes, and tantrums reinforced Melbourne's horror of unpleasantness and confrontation, which she adored. Their only child was retarded. Politically Melbourne turned all this to advantage in that he was a sensible and conciliatory man among Whig prima donnas—*Grey, *Brougham, *Durham, and *Russell. But it also meant a reluctance to face disagreeable reality, and to some extent Melbourne was a Wilsonian figure, the very man to hold the party together, but less well equipped to tackle the urgent problems of a great nation.

He grew up in a large, high-spirited cliquish family, went to Eton and Trinity College, Cambridge, and spent a year at Glasgow under Professor John *Millar. With few pretensions to scholarship, he finished with a lifelong love of books and a well-stocked mind. His fortunes changed abruptly in 1805 when the death of his elder brother left him as heir to the peerage. He abandoned the legal career upon which he had started and began a political one. He joined the Whig opposition but was on the right of the party, and had much in common with *Peel, *Huskisson, and the liberal Tories. His rise was slow, and, indeed, coping with Lady Caroline was a full-time job. He was 48 before, in 1827, he held office in *Canning's ministry as chief secretary for Ireland, and within a year he was out again, resigning with the Huskissons.

This limited service was of consequence since the Whigs, when they took office in 1830, were short of experience and Melbourne became home secretary in Grey's government. He showed unexpected firmness in dealing with the *Swing riots in 1831 and the *Tolpuddle martyrs in 1834. He was the obvious choice to succeed Grey in 1834. It was to his advantage that, after six years of reform, the country was not averse to a pause. But his colleagues were unusually quarrelsome, William IV mistrusted the government, and Grey scrutinized every action, looking for backsliding. After six months, the king turned out the ministry and brought in the Tories. Peel dissolved, failed to win a majority, and Melbourne returned, taking the opportunity to drop Brougham, one of the more impossible ministers.

It cannot be said that Melbourne's second administration made much of a mark. It was dependent upon Irish and radical votes and the Tory House of Lords killed off several of its measures. Melbourne soldiered on, swearing, jesting, despairing. But the succession of Victoria in 1837 changed everything. He experienced an Indian summer in which he basked in royal favour, the young queen hanging on every word, enjoying every joke. *Greville wrote kindly: 'he is passionately fond of her as he might be of his daughter if he had one, and the more because he is a man with capacity for loving without having anything in the world to love.' He talked less and less about retirement and though his attitude to his opponents was generous, it merely confirmed to Victoria that they were horrid, horrid Tories. She and Melbourne were hissed at the races and 'Mrs Melbourne' was a vulgar taunt. The *Bedchamber crisis of 1839, when Peel failed to form a ministry in the face of the queen's evident hostility, gave Melbourne's government two more years. It lost by-elections with regularity though surviving a sharp foreign crisis over Mehemet Ali with some skill. But in 1841 he went to the country and was defeated. The parting with Victoria was painful, even though an irresistible competitor in the shape of Albert had arrived. Melbourne kept in touch in a series of confidential letters of an unconstitutional nature. But in 1842 he suffered a stroke and well before his death in 1848 he was a figure from the past. 'Not a good or firm minister,' was Victoria's cool judgement on a man she had once adored.

As a prime minister, Melbourne does not rank high. He had no great achievements to his credit, no grand principles to enunciate. But he was kind, honest, and not self-seeking—he refused both the Garter and promotion in the peerage—and these are not inconsiderable virtues. JAC

Mellitus. Bishop of London (604–19), archbishop of Canterbury (619–24). Mellitus was one of the missionaries sent from Rome in 601 to reinforce *Augustine's original mission of 597. He was the recipient of a famous letter from Pope Gregory I urging that the English mission should, within the limits of orthodoxy, accommodate itself to practices of the pagans. He is the only missionary known to have made a return visit to Rome, attending a synod there in 610. In 617, when the Christian king of Essex was succeeded by pagan sons, Mellitus was driven from London. (Though they refused baptism they demanded the white communion bread.) A (temporarily) pagan king succeeded in Kent at much the same time, and Mellitus was exiled in Gaul before returning to become archbishop. *Bede provides a detail or so about him: he was of noble birth; he suffered from gout. JCa

Melrose abbey (Roxburgh) was the first Scottish *Cistercian abbey. A religious community had been established nearby (at Old Melrose) from Iona in the 7th cent. but by 1074 it was deserted and the site came into the hands of Durham cathedral. About 1136 David I of Scotland obtained the property by exchange and colonized his foundation from *Rievaulx. David's stepson Waltheof became its second abbot and enjoyed a reputation for sanctity. With four daughter houses and an income in the mid-16th cent. of over £5,000, Melrose was the most influential of the Scottish Cistercian houses. It attracted considerable royal support: Alexander II was buried here in 1249, as was the heart of Robert I Bruce. However, its position near the Anglo-Scottish border made it vulnerable and it was sacked several times in the 14th cent. and again in 1545, and never fully recovered. It fell under lay commendation from 1541. The surviving ruins (celebrated by *Scott) are amongst the finest Cistercian remains in Scotland. BJG

Melun, treaty of, 1593. Elizabeth and Henri IV of France pledged themselves at Melun not to make a separate peace with Spain. When Henri concluded a settlement in 1598 at Vervins, Elizabeth was indignant. JAC

Melville, Andrew (1545–1622). Scottish presbyterian leader and academic. Born in Forfar (Tayside), educated at St Andrews and Paris, Melville was professor at Geneva in close contact with Beza. As principal of Glasgow University (1574) he introduced significant academic reforms there, at Aberdeen (1575), and at St Andrews (1579), where he became principal of St Mary's College (1580). Ecclesiastically more extreme than *Knox, he attacked residual episcopacy and, as moderator of the General Assembly (1578) which enthusiastically adopted *The Second Book of Discipline* with its Bezan ethos, drove the church's organization into extreme non-Erastian *presbyterianism. The Scottish Privy Council threatened him with imprisonment (1584) but, though royal supremacy over the church was re-established (1585) and bishops' jurisdiction restored, Parliament endorsed the presbyterian system (1592). When the tide turned again, James VI regained his ecclesiastical powers (1597) and Melville was deprived of his rectorship at St Andrews (1597). After deriding Anglican worship in London, he was summoned before the English Privy Council (1606), disputed with *Bancroft, and was sent to the Tower without trial (1607–11). On release he went to Sedan University, France, where he died. WMM

Melville, George Melville, 1st earl of [S] (1636–1707). Melville succeeded to his father's barony when he was 7. An ardent presbyterian from Fife, he was implicated in the *Rye House plot and gave support to the *Monmouth rising. In exile he joined William of Orange. He was prevented by illness from taking part in the expedition of 1688 but followed soon after. He was raised to the earldom in 1690 and his family had great influence in Scotland during William's reign. Melville himself was secretary of state [S] 1689–90, lord privy seal [S] 1690–6, and lord president of the council [S] 1696–1702. His eldest son Lord Raith was treasurer depute [S] 1688–9 but predeceased his father; his second son Lord Leven was governor of Edinburgh castle 1689–1702 and commander-in-chief [S] 1706. An advanced Whig, Melville was dismissed by Anne in 1702. *Macaulay characterized him as prudent and circumspect rather than talented: 'a very mean figure in his person, being low, thin, with a great head, a long chin, and little eyes' was Macky's unkind description. JAC

mercantilism. This general term, coined in 1763 by Mirabeau, is usually applied to the system of economic thought and policy which flourished between the 16th and 18th cents. Mercantilists were concerned to increase and sustain the power of the nation state by competition with hostile rival nations. Most characteristic were their ideas about trade and gold. Wealth was defined exclusively in terms of gold bullion reserves, so that a positive trade balance became a prime aim of policy to increase the currency reserves. Conversely a trade deficit represented disaster, through the loss of gold reserves in payment for the excess of imports over exports. Such notions supported the acquisition of colonies to provide necessary imports or exotic commodities like sugar and tobacco which, otherwise, would have to be bought from rivals in exchange for bullion. The *Navigation Acts introduced in the 17th cent. by the English government represented a typically mercantilist attempt to manipulate the costs of trade by stipulating that goods in the colonial trade must be carried in English ships. Another characteristic mercantilist strategy lay in the granting of legal monopolies by the state, such as the franchise given to the *East India Company to trade exclusively with specified territories. Mercantilist doctrine also favoured control of the domestic economy by the state. Advocates agreed that low wages and a growing population were necessary to sustain national prosperity. Workers should be kept on the brink of poverty because any surplus above the level of subsistence, it was feared, would be frittered away in indulgence and idleness.

Modern economic thought gives little support to the basic ideas of mercantilism. Few today, except perhaps the mandarins in the Treasury, would subscribe to the view that national wealth should be defined exclusively in terms of gold reserves. Current theory regards the restriction of trade as damaging to economic growth. Similarly monopolistic control and the regulation of economic activity are perceived as sources of inefficiency. While historical evolution has rendered mercantilism unfashionable, and the evolution of economics has exposed some of its theoretical limitations, it had a rationale in the context of the power struggle of the early modern period, and provides important insights into the ideas which motivated policy at that time. CHL

merchant navy. In the medieval period there was no absolute distinction between merchant ships and warships. In time of war ships were commandeered from ports, particularly on the south coast. When commandeered, they were largely floating platforms for archers and men-at-arms and tactics consisted of little more than grappling and boarding. Their routine employment was in exporting cloth, lead, tin, and coal, fishing, and conveying passengers. The stern rudder had been introduced by the 13th cent. and a few of the vessels were of 200 tons, though most were much smaller. They were clinker built, with a single square sail. They were vulnerable not only to the elements, but to pirates and privateers, and to the hostility of sailors from rival ports. The poor state of the roads meant a considerable amount of river and coastal traffic, mainly in barges or cogs.

In 1545, when Henry VIII assembled a fleet against the French, 56 of the 181 ships were royal. The *Great Harry*, built at Deptford in 1513, was of over 1,000 tons, others of 400 tons, but most smaller. Drake's *Golden Hind*, which circumnavigated the globe, was 160 tons, and the *Squirrel* of 8 tons crossed the Atlantic in 1580. Of the 177 ships called to give battle to the Armada, 34 were naval vessels: the remainder included craft only fit to make up the numbers.

The 17th cent. saw a considerable increase in the size of ships, particularly those belonging to the *East India Company, founded in 1600. The *Trades Increase*, the Company's first vessel, was almost 1,000 tons and was wrecked in Java on its first voyage, and though its size was exceptional, 800-ton Indiamen were not. The great expansion of empire made enormous calls on shipping, the *Navigation Act of 1651 helped to fight off the challenge of the Dutch, and the total tonnage of English merchant shipping increased fivefold between 1586 and 1686. Many of the vessels were engaged in the slave trade, which brought prosperity to Bristol, Liverpool, and, along with the tobacco trade, to Glasgow. Newcastle, Sunderland, Whitby, and Hull grew in importance as shipbuilding ports.

The 19th cent. saw the British merchant navy at its strongest before international competition had bitten deep. Steamships came in during the 1820s, at first for short-haul ferry services, where the problems of storing coal were not so acute. *Brunel's *Great Western*, a paddle steamer, crossed the Atlantic in 1838 and inaugurated a regular service. His second vessel, the **Great Britain*, launched in 1843, was made of iron, and screw-propelled. By 1847 the P. & O. line was running a regular steamship service to India. The great tea clipper races of the 1860s were between vessels of a dying breed. By 1890 over half the tonnage of the merchant fleet were steamers, most of the remaining sailing ships being small coastal vessels. At that time Britain owned half of the world's tonnage.

From then onwards, the impetus faltered. Though the total British tonnage continued to increase, as a proportion of the world's shipping it fell steadily. By 1914 it was down to 39 per cent, with Germany, the USA, Norway, France, and Japan coming up fast. The size of ships had again increased enormously. The *Mauretania*, launched on the Tyne for Cunard in 1907 and built by Swan Hunter, was 31,938 tons; the *Olympic*, built in Belfast for White Star in 1911, was 45,324 tons; its sister ship the *Titanic* in 1912 was 46,392 tons.

The effect of two world wars accelerated Britain's decline. Between 1914 and 1918, 9 million tons of British shipping were lost, mainly to German U-boats, and building could not keep pace. Britain's share of world tonnage continued to slide, from 33 per cent in 1921 to 26 per cent in 1939. The Second World War repeated the pattern, 2,426 ships totalling 11 million tons being sunk, with the loss of 28,000 seamen.

After a pause in the immediate post-war period, the decline was resumed. Great passenger liners gave way to oil tankers of more than 200,000 tons, and cargo vessels to roll-on roll-off container ships. New countries put British shipbuilding yards out of business; flags of convenience, particularly from Liberia or Panama, took away registrations; over-fishing in the coastal waters produced unpleasant confrontations with Iceland, Denmark, and Spain, and cut fishing fleets drastically. In 1948 Britain still retained 22 per cent of the world's registered tonnage: by 1970 it was down to 8 per cent, and by 1986 to less than 3 per cent. Only some 30,000 are now employed as seamen, many of them on short-distance ferries. JAC

Merchants, statute of, 1285. This statute made at Westminster (13 Edw. I s. 3) strengthened the provisions in the statute of *Acton Burnell for the swift recovery of debts in the interest of promoting trade. Proceedings could be instituted in more towns, to be named, debtors could be at once imprisoned on default, and were liable to lose all their lands. The statute did not apply to Jews. JAC

Merchant Venturers. One of the greatest trading companies. Privileged trading concessions can be traced back to the 13th cent. and the duke of Brabant granted a charter in 1296 to English merchants in Antwerp. Though a number of companies and merchants traded with different places, the Netherlands gradually predominated, particularly for the export of cloth. The London Merchant Venturers were closely associated with the Mercers' Company, sharing Mercers Hall until the Great Fire in 1666, and rivals of the Staplers' Company, which specialized in wool export. Henry VII granted them a charter in 1505, establishing a governor and 24 councillors. The company had links or affiliations with other towns, such as York, Newcastle, Exeter, and Bristol. They defended their cloth monopoly against numerous rivals and enemies at home and abroad. They complained frequently of the activities of interlopers and their relations with affiliated companies were far from cordial. Abroad they struggled against the *Hanseatic League and against the vagaries of foreign diplomacy. They switched their trading base repeatedly to retain or enhance their privileges, moving from Antwerp to Emden and then to Hamburg. During Elizabeth's reign they succeeded in seeing off the challenge of the Hanse, but protests against their monopoly persisted and the advocates of free trade gained ground. In 1689, immediately after the *Glorious Revolution, the export of cloth was opened up by statute to all subjects, thus depriving the Merchant Venturers of their monopoly. They continued to trade until the Napoleonic wars. JAC

Mercia, kingdom of. Mercia dominated Anglo-Saxon politics in the late 7th and 8th cents. The name 'Mercians' means 'the borderers' and is thought to derive from their position between the Anglo-Saxon settlements of the east coast and British kingdoms of the west. The middle Trent valley seems to have been the heartland of the Mercian kingdom, which included the modern counties of Staffordshire, Leicestershire, Nottinghamshire, southern Derbyshire, and north Warwickshire. Within this area lie the Mercian episcopal centre of *Lichfield (founded 669 and briefly an archbishopric during the reign of *Offa) and the important royal centres of *Repton and Tamworth. The Tribal Hidage, which may be a Mercian tribute-list of the late 7th cent. (though there are many problems in its dating and interpretation), appears to show this core area surrounded by other provinces, including those of the Pecsaete (Peak District) and *Lindsey to the north, the Wreocensaete (Wrekin) and *Hwicce to the west, and numerous small peoples of the Middle Angles to the south and east.

No detailed foundation traditions survive for the Mercian royal house and the first king who is reliably attested is Cearl, whose daughter Cwenburh married *Edwin of Deira in the early 7th cent., but it is not known how or whether he was related to any subsequent Mercian kings. It is usually assumed that it was *Penda (*c.*626–55) who established Mercia as a major Anglo-Saxon kingdom. He and his son *Wulfhere (658–75) followed an aggressive military policy which enabled them to collect tribute from the southern Anglo-Saxon kingdoms, Northumbria, and probably some British kingdoms as well. Rivalry with Northumbria was intense for much of the 7th cent. and led to the deaths of several kings of both nations in battles, including those of *Heathfield, *Winwaed, and *Trent, as well as by more underhand means. But although military force was the basis of their power, Penda and Wulfhere also established relationships with kings of other provinces, including those of the Hwicce, *South Saxons, and *East Saxons, to their mutual advantage.

The 8th cent. was dominated by two very powerful kings *Æthelbald (716–57) and Offa (757–96), both of whom claimed descent from Penda's brother Eowa. During their reigns many of the peripheral midland peoples were absorbed into Mercia and they attempted to extend Mercian control, as opposed to mere tribute-collecting overlordship, to eastern parts of Wales, East Anglia, and provinces south of the Thames. *Kent and *Sussex became Mercian provinces and their native rulers were deposed. *Wessex remained independent, but lost territory south of the rivers Thames and Avon to Mercia. Unfortunately we have few written records produced in Mercia itself from this period, but surviving remains which reflect the wealth and power of the 8th-cent. Mercian kings include Offa's Dike and the churches of *Brixworth and Repton. The extended boundaries of Mercia were maintained by *Cenwulf (796–821), but increasing discontent with Mercian dominance in Kent, East Anglia, and Wessex and rivalry within Mercia between different collateral lines weakened Mercian hegemony. When *Egbert of Wessex defeated Beornwulf of Mercia at the battle of *Ellendun, near Wroughton in Wiltshire, in 825 he was able to permanently detach Kent, Sussex, Surrey, and the East Saxons from Mercian control. The only Mercian possession south of the Thames was Berkshire which seems to have been ceded to the West Saxons by Burgred (852–74).

However, West Saxon successes did not really threaten the main Mercian province. It was the 'great Danish army' led by the sons of Ragnar Lothbrok which shattered the kingdom in 874. Burgred was expelled, but Ceolwulf II (874–9) was allowed to rule in western Mercia (centred on the former Hwiccian province). The area became increasingly dependent on Wessex for survival and *Æthelfleda of Wessex, a daughter of Alfred who had married Ceolwulf's successor *Æthelred, was ruler of the province in the early 10th cent. When Æthelfleda died in 918, her brother *Edward the Elder, who was already winning parts of eastern Mercia from Viking control, annexed western Mercia as well. Although the Mercians continued to have some distinctive identity and in 957–9 had Edgar as their own subking, for most practical purposes they were controlled through ealdormanries and shires as part of the kingdom of England. Although most Mercian shires are mentioned for the first time in 10th-cent. records, it is likely that their boundaries were influenced by earlier Mercian administrative arrangements, many of which in turn depended upon the bounds of once independent peoples who had been integrated into the Mercian province. BAEY

'Merciless' Parliament, 1388. The lords *appellant, having defeated their opponents at *Radcot Bridge in December 1387, dominated the Parliament which met from February to June 1388. Suffolk (Michael de la *Pole) and *Oxford had escaped to France, but many of their supporters, including Sir Robert *Tresilian, lord chief justice of King's Bench, and Sir Nicholas Brembre, lord mayor of London, were put to death. Richard II reasserted his power the following year. JAC

Merionethshire (Meirionydd). County of north Wales deriving its name from Meirion, one of the sons of *Cunedda, who supposedly moved from Strathclyde in late post-Roman times with his people, the *Votadini, in order to offset the threat of Irish invasion. It was probably an early kingdom but became part of the kingdom of *Gwynedd. The annexation of the lands of the last *Llywelyn by the crown under Edward I led to the creation of the shire in 1284. The coastal commote of Ardudwy to the north, and of Penllyn and Edeyrnion in the interior, taken by Llywelyn Fawr from Powys, were added. At the Act of *Union in 1536 the lordship of Mawddwy was added to the county.

The county is predominantly heavily glaciated mountains and uplands with a coast of cliffs and bays. Cadair Idris is its highest point (2,927 feet) and it also includes the Aran and Rhiniog mountains, as well as the Harlech dome. Bala Lake or Llyn Tegid is the largest natural lake in Wales. Much of the county is within the Snowdonia National Park.

The vulcanism, which forms much of the highland, fancifully known as 'the Ordovician ring of fire', produced metamorphosed rocks, and slate has been widely quarried, at Blaenau Ffestiniog to the north and Corris to the south. Sheep-farming and tourism are the main supports of the economy. But there is a Magnox nuclear power station at Trawsfynydd, now being decommissioned. The drowning of Tryweryn 1957–63 to form Llyn Celyn to supply water for Manchester led to massive protest. Merionethshire has 65.4 per cent of its population able to speak Welsh. Merioneth was once again linked to Gwynedd in 1974 when it became part of that new county, and with *Caernarfonshire constituted a reformed Gwynedd in 1996. In 1991 the total population was 31,963. HC

Merit, Order of. The order was established by Edward VII in June 1902, limited to 24 persons in the armed forces or of distinction in art, science, or literature. It was based upon Frederick the Great's *Pour la mérite* and is in the personal gift of the sovereign. The founding members included Lord *Kitchener, G. F. Watts the painter, and Lecky the historian. *Elgar was given the order in 1911 and the first woman to receive it was Florence *Nightingale in 1907 at the age of 87. JAC

Merlin was famous in myth and tradition as the soothsayer and magician at King *Arthur's court. Fragmentary evidence of early oral traditions suggests Merlin's earliest incarnation was as the mythical Welsh poet-madman Myrddin. This figure's transformation into Merlin was probably the work of *Geoffrey of Monmouth (*c.*1100–54), who welded Merlin onto the Arthurian myth. This process was consolidated in *Malory's *Morte Darthur* (published 1485), and revived with the Victorian reinvention of the Arthurian legend. In the interim, Merlin was regarded as the prototype magician, and his 'prophecies' were frequently reworked and republished in the 16th and 17th cents. JAS

Merseyside. Conurbation in north-west England, centred on Liverpool, made a metropolitan county after local government reform in 1972. Encompassing the dormitory areas for Liverpool, Birkenhead, and Bootle, it thus included much of the Wirral peninsula (formerly Cheshire) and the west Lancashire coastal strip to Southport; divided into five districts, it had its own administrative metropolitan county council 1974–86. Integrated transport (rail and two road tunnels beneath the river Mersey, though nearly defunct ferries) aimed to assist commuters. A distinctive local dialect ('scouse') and wry humour contribute to a regional identity, with Liverpool as the main cultural focus. The metropolitan council was abolished by the Local Government Act of 1985 but the term 'Merseyside' remains in use as a geographical expression. ASH

Merton, statute of, 1236. As much a discussion document as a statute, it arose from an assembly at Merton (Surrey) in January 1236 in Henry III's reign, and was an attempt to clarify a number of miscellaneous points of law. Among the many issues, including rights of widows, heirs, and pasturage, was a difference between canon law and common law: canon law held that a subsequent marriage legitimated natural children, common law did not. Despite an earnest appeal by Robert *Grosseteste, the barons refused to change the laws of England. Another difference of opinion was between the barons, who wanted authority to deal with malefactors in parks and common pasture land, and the king, who was reluctant to grant it. Powicke called the statute 'the first striking example of a changing attitude to law'. It was regarded as important, and copies were sent to all sheriffs and communicated to the king's representatives in Ireland. JAC

Merton, Walter de (d. 1277). Clerical statesman. Educated at Oxford, Walter became a clerk in Chancery and amassed a large number of livings. He was employed by Henry III to negotiate from the pope recognition of Edmund, the king's son, as king of Sicily. In 1261–3 he was chancellor but was forced out by de *Montfort's party and not reinstated after the royal victory at *Evesham. But he acted as chancellor once more 1272–4 after Henry's death and while Edward I was absent on crusade, and was thanked on the new king's return. For the last three years of his life he was bishop of Rochester. The careful rules he laid down for the governance of his foundation Merton College, Oxford, in 1264 were copied at Peterhouse, the oldest of the Cambridge colleges, and greatly influenced the development of both universities. JAC

Mesopotamian campaign, 1914–18. Following Turkey's entry into the *First World War in November 1914, a small Anglo-Indian force landed in Mesopotamia. The purpose of the expedition was to protect the nearby Persian oilfields and to deny the Turks and their German allies access to the head of the Persian Gulf, from whence they might threaten British India. Encouraged by early victories, but inadequately supplied, the British advanced towards Baghdad, but were halted by the Turks in November 1915. A considerable British force was besieged at Kut and surrendered in April 1916. Prestige demanded that this defeat be avenged and in March 1917, with fresh troops and a new commander, the British finally occupied Baghdad. They then pressed slowly forward until, following an armistice with the Turks in October 1918, they had occupied the strategically important oilfields around Mosul in northern Mesopotamia.

DF

Messiah, Handel's most famous and frequently performed oratorio, was written in just over three weeks and first performed in Dublin on 13 April 1742. It was a great success, raising £400 for charity, and Handel revived it many times, often adding different arias for new soloists. Charles Jennens's libretto selects biblical texts concerning the birth, death, and resurrection of Christ, and this subject-matter, together with the unusually high proportion of choruses, has contributed to the work's lasting popularity with choral societies. The gentle lyricism of arias like 'I know that my redeemer liveth' and the jubilant grandeur of the 'Hallelujah' chorus have survived countless rearrangements and doubtful performances. ECr

Metcalf, John (1717–1810). Road-builder, known as 'Blind Jack of Knaresborough'. Blinded by smallpox at the age of 6, Metcalf proved extraordinarily adaptable, and became successively travelling fiddler and horse-dealer, recruiting for *Cumberland's army in 1745, and was present at both *Falkirk and *Culloden, trading thereafter in Aberdeen stockings. He set up a stage-wagon to York (1754), and traded in horses and provender, before securing his first road-building contract in 1765, eventually constructing 180 miles in northern England, and employing at peak 400 men. He was perhaps the first to apply coherent principles to construction, based upon the excavation of firm foundations, ditch drainage, and convex section. Metcalf retired in 1792, and set down his achievements in his autobiography (1795). JCh

methodism began as a religious revival in the 18th cent. and grew to become the largest of the nonconformist churches. Under the leadership of John *Wesley, societies for cultivating religious fellowship were set up, intended originally as auxiliary to the established church, but soon forced into independence by the hostility of the clergy. The movement grew rapidly from the 1740s and developed distinctive institutions, notably the weekly class meeting of 10–12 members and an itinerant body of lay preachers, who visited the societies, preaching in the homes of members and in the open air. At Wesley's death in 1791, there were 72,000 members of methodist societies and perhaps nearly half a million adherents. By 1850 membership was about half a million and an estimated 2 million persons (one-tenth of the total population) were under direct methodist influence. In Yorkshire one-sixth and in Cornwall one-third of the total population attended methodist services in 1851. During Wesley's lifetime there was no open breach with the Church of England, but after his death the methodists became a separate denomination with their own chapels. Schismatic tendencies led to the establishment of a number of different methodist churches ('connexions'). Later in the 19th cent. a process of reunion began and was completed in 1932.

Theologically, methodism differed little from the evangelical wing of the Church of England, stressing personal conversion and salvation by faith in the atoning death of Christ. But socially methodism was a transforming force. Most of the 18th-cent. 'people called methodists' were of humble origin without advantages of education, wealth, or social position. However, their puritan virtues brought them worldly prosperity and, by the 1830s and 1840s, the big Wesleyan chapels in northern towns were dominated by wealthy mill-owners and businessmen. Official methodism in the 19th cent. was middle class and socially conservative. Yet underneath there was a more liberal and democratic spirit. Methodism in the 18th cent. was a popular movement, and most of the schisms which rent the central Wesleyan body until 1849 were attempts in one form or another to reassert this basic characteristic. The breakaway churches (such as the methodist New Connexion, primitive methodists, *Bible Christians, protestant methodists, Barkerites, Wesleyan reformers) were characterized by differences of organization and personalities, not doctrine. Methodism, unlike the Church of England, was essentially a layman's religion. In addition to the full-time ministers (who had the superintendence of a number of chapels in a circuit), there was an army of active lay helpers, numbering in 1850 some 20,000 local preachers, over 50,000 class leaders, together with trustees, stewards, prayer leaders, and Sunday school teachers. Around the chapel there developed an intense world of personal and social relationships, which lasted into modern times. Friendship, marriage partners, help and support in time of need, a sense of security and personal worth were assured to methodists, who were exhorted to 'watch over one another in love'.

Methodism made an important contribution to the leadership of working-class movements like *trade unionism and *chartism by providing opportunities for self-education and training in leadership and organization in running the chapel. The general culture of methodism was toward respectability through living a temperate, thrifty, hard-working life; and early government fears that methodism was potentially disruptive gave place to the realization that it was more a force for stability than conflict in a working-class community. Indeed, historians have argued (somewhat exaggeratedly) that it was methodism that prevented revolution in Britain during the revolutionary decades 1789–1848.

Methodism has been criticized as providing a useful work-discipline for Victorian employers, and also as a religion which encouraged pessimism, repression, guilt feelings, and psychic inhibitions. Certainly some of its manifestations were crude, emotional, narrow, and self-righteous. But to thousands of ordinary men and women, methodism offered a view of human nature which harmonized with and interpreted their own experiences. In a world full of disease, early death, injustice, and all kinds of insecurity, methodism brought joy and hope. When a miner or farm labourer or domestic servant 'found Jesus', their life was transformed. Methodism gave them a cheerful conviction that in God's providence there was a place for everyone, however humble. JFCH

Methuen treaty, 1703. The long-standing trading links between England and Portugal were reinforced in 1662 by the marriage of Charles II to *Catherine of Braganza. When the War of the *Spanish Succession broke out in 1701, the assistance of Portugal was essential. The political alliance was followed in December 1703 by a commercial treaty, negotiated by John Methuen. The Portuguese agreed to allow in English woollen goods while the English offered a preferential duty on Portuguese wines. The treaty stayed in force until 1836 and helped to replace consumption of French burgundy in England by port. JAC

Methven, battle of, 1306. On 19 June 1306 a small force under Robert I Bruce was surprised and routed at Methven, near Perth, by an army commanded by Aymer de *Valence, earl of Pembroke, acting for Edward I. Bruce fled, his wife and young daughter were captured, and his brother Neil subsequently taken prisoner and hanged at Berwick. But within a year Bruce regained the initiative. JAC

Middle Angles, kingdom of. In Book 1 of his *Ecclesiastical History* *Bede includes the Middle Angles among the major peoples of Anglo-Saxon England, but elsewhere in his work they appear only under Mercian control. The only known king of the whole Middle Angles is *Peada of Mercia, who was appointed by his father *Penda *c.*653. It was during his rulership that the Middle Angles were officially converted to Christianity through a mission from *Northumbria, although the regular succession of bishops of the Middle Angles based at *Leicester only began in 737. In the Tribal Hidage, which may be a Mercian tribute-list of the late 7th cent., the Middle Angles are not listed as such and seem to have been represented by a number of smaller units in the east and south midlands. These include the Faerpingas who may be identical with the Feppingas whom Bede identifies as a Middle Anglian district (*regio*) and whose territory seems to have included Charlbury in Oxfordshire. Another likely Middle Anglian group the South Gyrwe, probably based in the fenland around Ely, had their own ruler *princeps* Tondbert who married Princess *Æthelthryth of the East Angles. The existence of these subgroups within Middle Anglian territory and the lack of any corporate history before their domination by Mercia had led some historians to doubt whether the Middle Angles had any prior political unity and to see them instead as a Mercian administrative creation. However, that does not seem to be what Bede believed and a similar substructure of *regiones* can be found in other 7th-cent. Anglo-Saxon kingdoms. BAEY

middle class. The middle class has been an influential and often enigmatic presence in British history since the early 19th cent. It first gained sustained recognition as a group through the language of class used in the campaign for parliamentary reform in 1832. The use of the 'middle classes' (plural) recognized the vast range of status and wealth denoted by the term, from prosperous merchants and manufacturers to shopkeepers and master craftsmen. The theoretical identity of the middle classes was related to the control of property and capital, directly through ownership or indirectly through professional skills and accumulated savings. The increasing impact of this group on national life was identified with dissenting religion and with rapid changes in manufacturing and industry, especially in the coalfield areas. This account has been questioned in recent years. Historians have abandoned the notion of the *'industrial revolution' as a sharp break in continuity. Provincial manufacturers have been shown to be relatively poor compared to London-based merchants and aristocratic landowners. Dissenters had dominance and numerical superiority in a very limited number of areas. Indeed, the presence of a 'middling sort' since the late 17th cent. made an impact through patterns of consumption and urban life. However, middle-class formation requires not only middle status occupations, but also a self-aware social group, which can act and is identified in some sense as a unit. Dissent, manufacturing, and specific regional economic experiences may well have produced dynamic elements in middle-class development, such as the Manchester-based campaign for *free trade and the development of municipal trading and government in Birmingham and Glasgow. Claims which base middle-class formation in economic change are countered by historians who see middle-class formation as a political and cultural development.

The British middle class never produced a formal class political movement. Few middle-class MPs entered Parliament immediately after the 1832 reform and middle-class politicians did not dominate the highest ranks of government until the 1860s. Middle-class formation and influence operated through two major social processes, which although not new became more important in the early 19th cent. The middle classes created an increasingly active public life of voluntary societies and pressure groups. These often had a major influence on the aristocratic-led government, such as the *anti-slavery and *anti-Corn Law movements. Others, like the school societies and voluntary hospitals, became incorporated in the activities of the state. This associational culture created and spread middle-class values beyond the formal boundaries of the group.

Middle-class influence was also expressed through a domestic culture based upon gender subordination, increasing standards of material consumption, a desire for order and security, and for the separation of home and work. The residential suburbs which grew rapidly in the last thirty years of the 19th cent. were an important expression of this.

There is considerable debate over the outcome of the turbulent years before 1850. Some see a victory for the middle class and its values of respectability, of rational negotiation in social relationships, and of freedom for profit-seeking within the regulation and support of the state. Others see the failure of an entrepreneurial spirit in the face of gentlemanly aristocratic-led capitalism, a failure responsible for the slow-down in British economic growth after 1870. Part of the problem lay in the lack of a coherent middle-class set of values. Ideologists of both right and left look for an aggressive profit-seeking middle class central to the conflict between capital and labour. In practice, such values and actions were tempered by a paternalistic sense of obligation, often guided by the dictates of evangelical religion.

The years after 1870 saw an increasing number of low-paid, salaried, and professional people included in the middle class, notably schoolteachers and clerks. Increasing feelings of insecurity, growing ambitions for children, and a desire to sustain higher standards of consumption led to new strategies based upon smaller families, birth control, and saving through insurance policies. The opening of the civil service to competitive examination and the growing importance of professional and scientific knowledge after 1870 increased the value and need for middle-class education.

In the 20th cent. the relationships of the middle class to property and to the rest of society changed. The number of salaried and professional people increased, especially in the state sector and in the managerial structures of large manufacturing and commercial corporations. Even small firms were owned through private limited liability companies rather than directly. Middle-class property and privilege increasingly relied upon owner-occupied housing, distinctive forms of education, and superior pension rights. Older privileges were eroded by universal suffrage, by narrowing income differentials, and by the growth of a mass commercial culture.

See also CLASS; PROFESSIONS. RJM

Middlesex was one of the smallest, oldest, and strangest of counties. The southern border was the Thames, from Staines to the Isle of Dogs. It was divided from Buckinghamshire in the west by the river Colne and from Essex in the east by the river Lea. Much of the western part was drained by the river Crane and its tributaries from Pinner to Isleworth and by the river Brent, starting near Barnet. The northern boundary with Hertfordshire ran roughly along the ridge of the watersheds of the Colne and Brent, adjusted in the Middle Ages to take account of manorial ownership.

In Roman times it formed part of the territory of the *Trinovantes and their competitors the *Cassivellauni. Very soon after the Roman arrival, Londinium developed as by far the largest town and the seat of government and this dictated the subsequent history of the area. *Watling Street, the great road to the north-west, bisected the county from Tyburn to Elstree: *Ermine Street, the road to York, ran just inside the eastern border, from Tottenham to Cheshunt. Since, until the opening of the M25, all the great routes radiated to and from London, crossing the county was not easy, and Palmer's Green in the east had little contact with Staines in the west, nor Enfield with Uxbridge.

That part of the territory which survived as Middlesex was probably too small to sustain an independent kingdom, unlike *Sussex, *Essex, and *Wessex. But the existence of Surrey (the south land) suggests a brief Middle Saxon kingdom straddling the Thames. The importance of London meant that there was strong competition from neighbouring kingdoms. By the 6th cent. the area seems to have formed a province of Essex, and by the 8th it had been taken over by Mercia. In the later 9th cent., after the struggle between Alfred and the Danes, the region became part of Wessex. By then it was a recognized shire.

The development of Middlesex as a county was stunted by the influence of London in the south-east. It fell naturally into the diocese of London, founded in 604. In the 12th cent. the city of London was given the right to appoint the sheriff of Middlesex and the assizes were held at the Old Bailey. Though the original area was thinly populated, with forests in Enfield Chase, marshes in the east, and poor thin soil in the west, in the course of time it became one of the most densely populated areas in the world. The influence of London was so overwhelming that few Middlesex towns grew to any size. Apart from Westminster, none had their own parliamentary representation. Economically too, the shire was totally dependent upon London, and from an early period became a scene of market gardens and gentlemen's parks, of which Hampton Court (royal), Sion House (Northumberland), Osterley (Child), and Cannons (Chandos) were the most celebrated.

By 1700, London had half a million inhabitants, by 1800 nearly a million. At that time, setting aside towns like Edmonton, Chelsea, and Hammersmith, which were already London suburbs, the largest towns in the shire were Enfield with 6,000 people and Isleworth with 4,000, Uxbridge 2,100, Hendon 1,900, Staines 1,700, and Brentford 1,400. Of the six hundreds into which the county was divided, Spelthorne, Elthorne, Gore, Edmonton, and Isleworth had a total of 55,000 inhabitants, while the sixth, Ossulston, where the growth of London had taken place, had well over 750,000.

The political absorption of the county by London gathered pace in the 19th cent. The growth of the railway network brought another leap forward by the capital. In 1888 a considerable portion of south-east Middlesex, including Highbury, Hampstead, and Hammersmith, was sliced off to form part of the new county of London. In 1965, in another reorganization, the county disappeared altogether, most going to Greater London, but Staines and Sunbury moving to Surrey and Potters Bar to Hertfordshire. JAC

Middleton, Charles Middleton, 2nd earl of [S] (*c.*1650–1719). Middleton's father came from Kincardineshire, fought against *Montrose and the royalists, but changed sides and was with Charles II at the battle of *Worcester in 1651. At the Restoration he was created earl of Middleton [S]. His son succeeded to the peerage in 1673, was secretary of state in Scotland 1682–4 and in England 1684–8, despite adhering to protestant views. One of James II's chief supporters, he joined him in exile at Saint-Germain in 1693 and was then attainted. He retained much of his influence at the Jacobite court until 1713, and was given a Jacobite English peerage as earl of Monmouth in 1701. *Burnet described him as pleasant and conciliatory and in December 1688 he attempted to dissuade James II from fleeing the country. After 1688 he was one of the leading Compounders, who urged compromise on James. But James's declaration of April 1693 offering assurances to his erring subjects was received with suspicion. *Macaulay called Middleton 'one of the wisest and most moderate of the Jacobites'. JAC

Middleton, John Middleton, 1st earl of [S] (*c.*1608–73). From Kincardineshire, Middleton was a soldier of fortune. He began his military career in France but joined the Scottish covenanting army in 1639. He transferred to the service of the English Parliament and was active during the Civil War, particularly in the south-west. Returning to Scotland, he fought against *Montrose at *Philiphaugh. Next he changed sides and fought for the king at *Preston, where he was taken prisoner, and at *Worcester (1651), where he was wounded. In 1654 he joined with *Glencairn in the unsuccessful Scottish royal rising but was defeated by *Monck at Lochgarry. He escaped from the Tower of London to join Charles II in exile. At the Restoration he was created earl and served in Scotland as commander-in-chief and as commissioner to the Parliament. But his political career was less successful and in 1663 he was dismissed at the instigation of *Lauderdale. In 1668 he was made governor of Tangiers, where he died. *Clarendon thought him the best of the Scottish generals. By the time *Pepys met him in the 1660s, though a legendary figure, he was over the hill—'a dull, heavy man . . . a good soldier but a debauched man, a drinking man'. JAC

Midlothian campaign, 1879–80. Unhappy in his Greenwich constituency, and retired from the Liberal Party's leadership, *Gladstone accepted the Midlothian Liberal Association's invitation of May 1878 to contest the constituency of Edinburghshire (as Midlothian, the county around the Scottish capital, was technically known) at the 1880 election against Lord Dalkeith, the Tory candidate and son of the powerful duke of Buccleuch. With less than 3,500 electors the constituency was open to manipulation and both Buccleuch and Lord *Rosebery for the Liberals spent heavily. Gladstone made a series of long and highly effective nationally reported speeches—six major speeches in 1879 and fifteen in 1880—attacking what he dubbed 'Beaconsfieldism' (the policies of Disraeli's government), especially its foreign, imperial, and financial politics. He denounced 'a catalogue of expedients' and 'a new method government', exposed the Tories' loss of moral equilibrium, and put forward 'six principles' of foreign policy. Political speech-making was by no means new to British politics, but the Midlothian campaign was the apogee of the popular presentation of politics through 'the platform' and established Gladstone as the dominant orator of the century. He easily won the seat and the campaign played a part in winning the great Liberal majority in the Commons (though present-day historians accord it a less significant role than contemporaries). It re-established him as the unavoidable leader of the Liberal Party. Lords *Granville and Hartington (*Devonshire) (the official party leaders) felt unable, despite strong pressure from Queen Victoria, to form a government, and Gladstone began his second administration. HCGM

military history. The study of war and its effects has a long and distinguished history, dating back to at least 2500 BC, when the Chinese philosopher Sun Tzu wrote his treatise on *The Art of War.* European theorists came later, but the tradition which began with Julius Caesar's *Commentaries* nearly 2,000 years ago created a rich vein, culminating in the 1830s with Carl von Clausewitz's masterpiece *On War.* In all cases, practical experience and deep thought combined to ensure that the study of military history was both analytical and fruitful.

Such a tradition was largely absent from Britain, where military history was seen as the stuff of amateurs and armchair generals. The reason for this is not difficult to find: until the early 20th cent. Britain's wars tended to be fought at great distance from home, away from public gaze, while in times of significant threat, such as during the French Revolutionary and Napoleonic wars (1793–1815), naval rather than military affairs took precedence. Individual military historians emerged—William Napier's epic six-volume *History of the War in the Peninsula* began to appear in 1828—but they displayed a preference for straight narrative rather than insight. Indeed, this became a strong theme running throughout British military history and one that continues today. Exciting accounts of military deeds, designed to engage the reader's attention and reinforce national pride, clearly have their place, but they do not offer deep analysis. More serious military history, using the events of the past to enhance understanding of war and prepare both the army and the people for future conflicts, only began to emerge in Britain after the traumas of the First World War. Historians such as Major-General J. F. C. Fuller and Captain Basil Liddell Hart used their experiences of the trench deadlock on the western front to speculate on the ways in which warfare might be changed to avoid horrendous casualties in the future. Their views on the use of the tank and aircraft to restore mobility to the battlefield may have found more favour in Germany than Britain during the inter-war period, but their use of military history laid a new emphasis on analysis and informed speculation.

This has continued to the present day and is seen as an integral part of the process of evolving and establishing war-fighting doctrine within the British army. Other factors may come into play, not least the influence of American thinking on war, but the British experience of conflict has been unique. It is reflected in the use of military history to support a doctrine which, while emphasizing large-scale conventional war, looks back just as much to the low-level counter-insurgency campaigns that form such an integral part of British army history. Moreover, the growing seriousness with which military history is being viewed in the British academic world provides a backcloth against which meaningful study can be made. JLP

militia. The British regionally-based volunteer armed forces (from the Latin *miles*, a soldier). Of Anglo-Saxon origin or earlier, the militia was established as an obligation for all freemen by the Assize of *Arms of 1181. In 1558 Mary I created the new post of *lord-lieutenant to command the militia in a county structure, and Charles II in three Militia Acts (1661–3) established its legal basis. Although militarily negligible throughout its existence, the militia was intended to repel any invasion, to secure order locally, and as a regional 'constitutional force' to balance royal control of the standing army. Service in the militia (and its mounted equivalent, the *yeomanry) evolved to be essentially voluntary except in times of emergency, such as the 1757 Militia Act, which used a ballot. During the Napoleonic wars, the militia was supplemented by various 'fencibles', and after 1859 by the Rifle Volunteers. The 1852 Militia Act finally placed it under the secretary for war, and in 1881 militia regiments were attached to regular county infantry regiments. The 1907 *Territorial and Reserve Forces Act abolished the militia by amalgamating all volunteer forces into the Territorial Force, renamed the Territorial Army in 1921, which continues in existence. SDB

Mill, James (1773–1836). Utilitarian philosopher. Son of a Scottish shoemaker, educated at Edinburgh University, Mill became an itinerant preacher but lost his faith and came to London in 1802 to work as a hack journalist. He fell under the influence of Jeremy *Bentham and developed his ideas into a coherent philosophy, substituting strict puritanical morality for Bentham's hedonism. Mill rather than Bentham formulated the distinctive *'philosophical radicalism' of the 19th-cent. British utilitarians. He contributed ideas on education, political economy, psychology, penology, law, history, and political theory, which he set out in five books and over 1,000 essays. His best-known political work, the *Essay on Government* (1820), argued the case for representative democracy against monarchy and aristocracy and declared that the purpose of all government was to achieve the happiness of the whole community. EAS

Mill, John Stuart (1806–73). Utilitarian and liberal philosopher. The son of James *Mill, a disciple of Jeremy *Bentham, Mill was converted to Benthamite utilitarianism at the age of 15, but later rejected its egoistic psychology and mechanical concept of pleasure. He was employed for 35 years by the East India Company, afterwards serving as an independent member of Parliament for Westminster (1865–8), arguing for radical measures such as votes for women. In *Principles of Political Economy* (1848), Mill adopted a modified **laissez-faire* position, believing in the efficiency of free enterprise, but aware of the frequent failure of the market to maximize utility. In *Utilitarianism* (1861) Mill revised Benthamism, distinguishing between higher and lower pleasures, and affirming a moral duty to promote happiness. In *On Liberty* (1859) Mill wrote the most celebrated defence of individual freedom to appear in the English language, based on utilitarian values, not natural right. In *Considerations on Representative Government* (1861) he defended democratic participation, but only under strict conditions designed to protect the position of the virtuous élite. Finally, in *Subjection of Women* (1869) Mill defended the rights of women on equal terms with men—a landmark in the history of feminist writing. Mill's legacy as a founding father of liberal thought is unrivalled. TSG

Millais, John Everett (1829–96). Painter and book illustrator. A scion of an old Norman family, settled in Jersey since the Conquest, Millais was a prodigy. He entered the Royal Academy Schools in 1840 and first exhibited there at 16. In 1848, with Holman *Hunt and D. G. *Rossetti, he founded the *Pre-Raphaelite Brotherhood, of which he was the most technically brilliant. Great hostility was shown to his *Christ in the House of his Parents* (1850). He was attacked in *Blackwood's Magazine*, which called the work 'ugly, graceless and unpleasant', and by Charles *Dickens, later a friend, who thought it 'mean, odious, revolting and repulsive'. He was defended by John *Ruskin, whose former wife he married in 1855. After moving away from the Pre-Raphaelite style, he became a fashionable painter of portraits and costume history and is best known for *Ophelia* (1852), *The Blind Girl* (1856), and *Bubbles* (1886). Elected ARA in 1853, a full academician in 1863, and president of the RA just before his death in 1896, Millais was created baronet in 1885. JC

Millar, John (1735–1801). Millar was born in Lanarkshire, son of a minister. Educated at Hamilton Grammar School and Glasgow University, he became a lawyer and in 1761 accepted the regius chair at Glasgow, which he held for the rest of his life. The Glasgow Law School flourished under his supervision and his pupils included Lauderdale and *Melbourne. Though in early life a friend of *Hume, Millar was an advanced Whig, an advocate of parliamentary reform, and sympathetic to the French Revolution. *Historical View of the English Government* (1787) was a Whiggish analysis, dedicated to Charles *Fox: the Stuarts were roundly condemned as devoted to arbitrary principles. More influential was his *The Origin of the Distinction of Ranks* (1771). Heavily influenced by Montesquieu and Hume, it was a pioneering work in comparative sociology. Millar doubted the suggestion that a cold climate stimulates activity and encourages progress, and argued that commercial prosperity, by instilling a 'contemptuous and insolent behaviour to persons of superior rank and station', must undermine traditional authority. JAC

millenarianism. Belief in a future millennium (1,000 years) either preceding (premillennialism) or following (postmillennialism) the second coming of Christ, when he will reign on earth in a kingdom of his saints. Unlike postmillennialists, who anticipated a gradual progress towards the millennium through Christian, human agencies, premillennialists (or millenarians) looked for a sudden change through divine, cataclysmic action. Contemporary events were interpreted by reference to biblical prophecies or divine revelations concerning the immediate arrival of Christ on earth. Millenarian hopes and visions surfaced at the time of the *Peasants' Revolt (1381) and again among 17th-cent. sects such as the *ranters, *Muggletonians, *Fifth Monarchy men, and some early *quakers. Prophets and prophesyings continued into the 18th cent., and the French Revolution occasioned an outburst of both popular millenarianism (as among the followers of Joanna *Southcott) and scholarly exegesis of the millennium by orthodox churchmen. Because of its concern with imminent change, millenarianism appealed to radical reformers and could be secularized into utopianism. It appeared as a strand in some of the revolutionary rhetoric of the 1790s and provided a vocabulary for Robert *Owen and some of his followers. Later millenarian sects included *Seventh day adventists, *Plymouth brethren, and *Jehovah's witnesses. JFCH

millenary petition, 1603. Elizabeth I, having authorized the establishment of a protestant church in England at the beginning of her reign, stood firm against any further changes. This angered those of *puritan inclination, who believed that it preserved too many catholic vestiges in its structure and worship. They took advantage of the accession of a new monarch in 1603 to present James I with a petition, said to have 1,000 signatories, setting out their position. James responded by summoning the *Hampton Court conference and using the millenary petition as its agenda. RL

Milner, Alfred (1854–1925). British administrator and ardent imperialist. After serving in Egypt (1889–92) and as chairman of the Inland Board of Revenue (1892–7), knighted 1895, Milner became high commissioner in southern Africa and governor of Cape Colony in 1897. Convincing himself of the incompetence of the government of the neighbouring Boer South African Republic (Transvaal), and of its unjust treatment of British residents, he undertook a campaign of criticism which led directly to the second Anglo-Boer War (1899–1902). He was created baron in 1901 and viscount in 1902. After the war he was mainly responsible for the revival of the all-important gold-mining industry and for initiating the move towards a closer union of the South African colonies and former republics, but his intense desire to retain Britain's overall control reinforced his unpopularity among the Boers. Returning to England in 1905 he took office again as a member of Lloyd George's war cabinet (1916–21). KI

Milton, John (1608–74). Milton was intended for the ministry by his father, a well-to-do London scrivener, and was educated at St Paul's School and Christ's College, Cambridge. He became increasingly dedicated to poetry, however, and after graduating he spent long years in private study, nurturing a vocation to write a great Christian epic. But he put this aside soon after the *Long Parliament met, because he believed that England was on the brink of a great new reformation and that he must serve it with his pen, in prose. His first five tracts (1641–2) were directed mainly against the bishops. **Areopagitica* (1644), a plea for a free press, presented a vision of England as 'a noble and puissant Nation rousing herself like a strong man after sleep, and shaking her invincible locks'. Neither his optimism nor his faith in his fellow-countrymen were to last. A series of tracts in favour of divorce (1643–5) brought him under the lash of the presbyterian clergy, and his sonnet to *Fairfax (1648) breathed disillusion. The establishment of the *Commonwealth brought him fresh hope, however, and his *Tenure of Kings and Magistrates* eloquently justified the trial of Charles I. Gratefully, the *Council of State appointed him as its secretary for foreign tongues. Besides various diplomatic duties, this entailed writing (with the last of his eyesight) lengthy defences of the Commonwealth in both English and Latin. He eulogized Cromwell's *Protectorate too, but gradually turned against its ecclesiastical policies and monarchical tendencies. By 1659–60 he was a thoroughgoing republican, and risked his life by publishing a virulently anti-monarchical tract on the eve of the Restoration. He was briefly imprisoned, but was spared to complete the epic masterpieces **Paradise Lost*, *Paradise Regained*, and *Samson Agonistes*, whose composition he had postponed for so long. He was not an original political thinker and his polemical manners were deplorable, but he defended his ideals of Christian liberty and republican virtue with noble rhetoric and stoic courage. AHW

Minden, battle of, 1759. Ferdinand of Brunswick, commanding a force of 54,000 Hanoverian, British, and Prussian soldiers, manœuvred to tempt a French army, 64,000 strong, out of seemingly impregnable positions at Minden. The French commander, the marquis de Contades, obliged on 1 August. A brigade of British and Hanoverian infantry, misinterpreting orders, launched a frontal assault on French cavalry in the centre and, against all odds, held firm when counter-attacked. Unfortunately the British cavalry, commanded by Lord George Sackville (*Germain), failed to move forward to exploit, and the French, having lost over 7,000, retreated. JLP

Mines Act, 1842. Parliament had already intervened in 1774 and 1799 to improve the position of Scottish miners, whose bonds were described as akin to serfdom. In the 1830s a number of investigations into coal-mines revealed the extent of *truck payments, employment of women and children, and disregard of safety. The first report on the employment of children in 1842, graphically illustrated, caused a sensation. Lord Ashley (*Shaftesbury) took advantage of the indignation to steer through the Mines Act (5 & 6 Vic. c. 99) which forbade the employment of women underground, and of boys below the age of 10. Though inspection remained inadequate, it was an important breakthrough in protective legislation. JAC

Minorca is a Balearic island in the western Mediterranean of strategic importance, with Port Mahon a fine harbour. It was taken by the British in 1708 and retained at the treaty of *Utrecht in 1713. At the outbreak of the *Seven Years War in 1756, Admiral *Byng's failure to prevent the French from capturing it brought down *Newcastle's ministry and led to his own court martial and execution. It was returned to Britain again in 1763 by the treaty of *Paris. Lost to a combined French and Spanish force in 1782 it was ceded to Spain in 1783, and though the British once more took the island in 1798, it was given back to Spain at the peace of *Amiens in 1802. JAC

minstrelsy. The term minstrel signified those employed, by the crown, nobility, or urban corporations, as players of musical instruments. As the Middle Ages progressed there was an increasing demand for professional performers to play at special events such as weddings and banquets: entertainment of this sort was an integral part of aristocratic lifestyle. At the dubbing of Edward of Caernarfon in 1306, the crown paid 27 minstrels, playing various stringed, wind, and percussion instruments. Many of these were permanent members of the royal household, others were specially employed for the occasion. Documents suggest that the term often covered acrobats, jugglers, and other kinds of entertainers, such as, in 1306, Matilda Makejoy, 'saltatrix' (a female acrobat). Minstrels might also be employed as messengers and in sounding the curfew. They accompanied the late medieval English kings on military campaigns at home and abroad, being required to compose and perform works which celebrated great deeds and victories. This is thought to be the context within which the poem *The Siege of Cælaverock* was written. The nobility had their own personal troops of minstrels who performed similar duties. Rates of pay seem to have been generous in both royal and aristocratic circles, and minstrels also received clothing from their masters in the form of liveries. AC

Minto, Gilbert Elliot-Murray-Kynynmound, 1st Earl (1751–1814). Minto was educated in Paris under the supervision of David *Hume and at Oxford. He was called to the bar in 1774 and entered Parliament in 1776 in the Whig interest. He was a close friend of Edmund *Burke and assisted him in the impeachment proceedings against Warren *Hastings. He was appointed governor of Corsica in 1794, envoy to the court of Vienna from 1799 to 1801, and president of the Board of Control for East India Affairs in 1805. In 1806 he became governor-general of India. His period in office saw the consolidation of British power in the subcontinent and, in prosecution of the Napoleonic wars, the extension of influence into south-east Asia. He dealt with the threat of Ranjit Singh's Sikh kingdom and captured Java and the Moluccas from the Dutch—although the latter were subsequently returned. He retired in 1813. DAW

Minto, Gilbert John Elliot-Murray-Kynynmound, 4th Earl (1845–1914). Minto was educated at Eton and Cambridge and joined the Scots Guards in 1867. He was famous for riding racehorses until he broke his neck in the 1876 Grand National. Thereafter, he became a newspaper correspondent in Spain, Turkey, and Canada and observer of the wars in Afghanistan and Egypt. A Liberal, he was appointed governor-general of Canada 1898–1904, and in 1905 became viceroy of India. His period in office was principally distinguished by his work with Secretary of State John *Morley to pass constitutional reforms which introduced (albeit in a very restricted form) the principles of elected representation to the government of India. However, his relations with Morley were strained by his conservatism, which included reintroducing deportation without trial for nationalist 'agitators'. The Morley–Minto reforms are also remembered for introducing separate Hindu and Muslim 'communal' electorates. He retired in 1910. DAW

missionary activity. Along with evangelical zeal, an element often present in missionary work has been rivalry between Christian sects. Perhaps the first missionary to post-Roman Britain was *Germanus, sent over in 429 by Pope Celestine I to combat the *Pelagian heresy. Nor was rivalry long in appearing in *Augustine's mission of 597 to reinvigorate Christianity: he was soon involved in a dispute with the *Celtic church, whose own missionaries had made much progress in Scotland and north and west England. But within a century the English church was well enough established to send out missionaries of its own, *Willibrord to the Frisians, *Boniface to the Germans. During the Middle Ages, missionary enterprise was to some extent replaced by *crusades. A mission from Pope Innocent IV in 1246 to the Mongol great khan was politely received but the message back invited the pope to submit or 'I shall make you understand.'

The Reformation renewed rivalries by formalizing the divisions of Christianity and the earliest post-Reformation missionaries were the *Jesuit priests from Douai who strove to maintain or if possible extend the faith in Elizabethan England. Protestant counter-activity took at first the form of hunting them down, but later in the 17th cent. the considerable success of the Jesuits in America, India, Japan, and China stimulated protestant missions. In 1698 Thomas Bray, an Anglican clergyman, drew up plans for the *Society for Promoting Christian Knowledge to supply libraries and missionaries to the colonies, and three years later the missionary work was handed over to the *Society for the Propagation of the Gospel. In 1710 the SPG gave top priority to converting the American Indians but the other colonists wiped them out so fast that little progress could be made. Bray's links with Oglethorpe were partly instrumental in the foundation of the colony of Georgia as a haven for debtors, where the *Wesleys and *Whitefield worked in the 1730s. As the methodists gathered strength, they also turned to missionary work, particularly after the French Revolution had encouraged evangelicalism. The Methodist Missionary Society was set up in 1786 and the Baptist Missionary Society in 1792. The first baptist missionary to India was William Carey, victim in 1808 of Sydney *Smith's savage ridicule in the *Edinburgh Review*: missionaries, wrote Smith, an Anglican clergyman, were 'insane and ungovernable' and would lose Britain its Indian empire if not stopped. The *London Missionary Society was established in 1795, the *Church Missionary Society in 1799, and the British and Foreign Bible Society in 1804. Later in the century, there was much missionary interest in Africa, partly as a consequence of the fame of David *Livingstone, who began working for the LMS in 1841. The LMS was avowedly undenominational, leaving the form of church governments for converts to decide. Elsewhere rivalries persisted. A mission to the Maoris in New Zealand made little immediate progress and when Bishop Selwyn, an Anglican, arrived in mid-century he warned the Maoris that the Wesleyans were to be shunned as schismatics. Slowly the attitude of missionaries and their supporters changed. It was increasingly argued that missions should be self-destroying in the sense that they should lead to a self-governing autonomous local church. An ecumenical landmark was the holding of a World Missionary Conference in Edinburgh in 1910 which established an International Missionary Council. This, in 1961, was integrated with the World Council of Churches, started in 1948. JAC

Mitchel, John (1815–75). Irish nationalist. Mitchel's father had taken part in the '98 rising. Mitchel, a protestant, educated at Trinity College, Dublin, became a solicitor. A militant supporter of *Young Ireland, he joined the staff of the *Nation*. An inflammatory article, pointing out how easy it was to cut the railway network around Dublin, led to a breach with *O'Connell, anxious that his *Repeal Association should not be smeared by violence. Mitchel founded a weekly paper, the *United Irishman*, in February 1848 and began publishing articles on drilling and the use of the pike. In March 1848 he was charged with 'treason-felony', sentenced to fourteen years transportation, and was on board boat when the abortive 1848 rising occurred. He was sent to Bermuda for a year and then to Tasmania, where he broke parole and escaped to America. There he founded a newspaper in New York, the *Citizen*, preaching hatred of Britain. In the Civil War he supported the South. Mitchel returned to Ireland in 1875, was elected MP for Tipperary, disqualified, and died. His *Jail Journal* (1854) has been called 'the bible of republicanism'. JAC

'Model' Parliament was the name given by Stubbs to Edward I's assembly at Westminster in November 1295 on the grounds that it was the first to include both knights of the shire and burgesses. But the phrase is inappropriate. Writs found later demonstrate that previous parliaments had a similar composition. Nor was the 1295 composition subsequently followed, since the lesser clergy gradually ceased to be summoned and made do with *convocation. But though the 1295 Parliament was less significant than Stubbs believed, it was a very large body. Almost 100 clergy (including 67 abbots), 8 earls, 41 barons, 73 knights, well over 200 burgesses, and 39 royal officials and judges meant that the number summoned certainly exceeded 400. JAC

monarchy. Since heroic origins added to the prestige of monarchy, early Saxon chroniclers claimed descent for their dynasties from Woden, god of war. Later writers traced their monarchs to *Brutus, great-grandson of Aeneas of Troy. *Geoffrey of Monmouth was highly specific, explaining that Brutus landed at Totnes, overthrowing the race of giants, chief of whom was Gogmagog. Geoffrey's account, with Merlin's prophecy that Britain would be united, was used to claim supremacy over the Scots. Scottish chroniclers, not to be outdone, traced their monarchy's descent from Pharaoh of Egypt, whose daughter Scota had settled in their land.

More sober claims traced English monarchs back to Cerdic, king of Wessex in the early 6th cent. Even this was difficult to sustain, the royal blood running thin in places. Eighth-cent. Wessex kings are particularly badly documented and the link with Cerdic has largely to be taken on trust. Harold II had no royal blood at all, and William the Conqueror's claim was merely that his grandfather's sister, *Emma of Normandy, had been married first to *Æthelred, then to *Cnut. But lineage was of such consequence that rulers whose claims looked shaky hastened to buttress them. The Conqueror's son Henry I married a Saxon princess, great-granddaughter of *Edmund Ironside.

If we accept Cerdic as founder, the English monarchy dates back to about 519. The Scottish monarchy may be dated from *c.*843, when *Kenneth MacAlpin of *Dalriada united Picts and Scots to form the kingdom of *Alba. The role of the monarch was essentially that of battle-leader. As a consequence, strict primogeniture was slow to establish itself, since it could result in a child or a simpleton on the throne. Few monarchs lasted long enough for old age to be a problem. In the earlier period, the king was chosen from the extended royal family and was often a brother or a cousin of his predecessor. With expectation of life short, it was unlikely that the eldest son would be old enough for the task. *Edgar's eldest son Edward was only 13 when chosen in 975 but the innovation was hardly encouraging since he was murdered within three years. As royal power grew, kings increasingly chose their sons or were succeeded by them. The earlier convention increased the chances of having an effective ruler, but added to the risk of disputes, and many early kings were overthrown, exiled, or killed by their kin.

Apart from waging war—admittedly at times a demanding business—early kings had little to do. They attempted very few of the activities of the modern state. Justice was dispensed by landowners themselves; the king did not make law, though he might declare what it was; there was little revenue to collect, though he was entitled to support and hospitality. There was no economic or education policy to supervise. One doubts whether the army spent much time drilling, an occupation which fascinated later rulers. Foreign relations consisted of sending envoys to neighbouring kings, arranging alliances, and negotiating marriages. The most sophisticated organization was the church and sensible rulers devoted care to choice of archbishops and bishops.

But the great effort needed to push back the Danes in the 9th and 10th cents. produced important developments in the institutions of Wessex. Burhs, erected as strong points, had to be built and garrisoned, naval vessels commissioned and manned, and all had to be paid for. At *Winchester, the capital of Wessex and then of England until the 12th cent., more than 3,000 yards of walls necessitated a garrison of 2,400 men. There were well over 50 burhs and they included places of great importance—Worcester, Bedford, Oxford, Colchester, Nottingham, Exeter, Derby, Stafford, Bath, Chichester, and Manchester. Even if the garrisons were not permanent nor necessarily efficient, a remarkable organizational effort was required, and the Burghal Hidage shows a systematic attempt to ensure adequate support. By the reign of *Athelstan a much more complex governmental structure is apparent and the kingdom of England has emerged. Indeed, by the reign of Edgar, one can see the outlines of a claim to British sovereignty, with the monarch rowed on the Dee in 973 by kings from Scotland, from Wales, and of the British.

The monarchy was still, and for centuries remained, dependent upon the personal ability of the ruler. The 11th-cent. Saxon kingdom was unable to sustain the momentum. The return of Viking raids at the end of the 10th cent. proved almost too much for Æthelred and at his death the kingdom passed rapidly to Cnut. Though his rule was firm, he was no great innovator. The royal bodyguard and a navy were maintained and the revenue to support them raised. But his Scandinavian and imperial ambitions left him little time to ponder English problems, and the law code for which he is famous was largely derived from Edgar. Nor was *Edward the Confessor, the last Saxon king, the man to invigorate government. The main development was the increasing use of the sheriff, a direct royal officer, to implement decisions in the shires.

With the Conquest in 1066 the kingdom was once more in alien hands, though to subjects accustomed to Scandinavian rule only a generation before, this may not have seemed novel, however unwelcome. By adding yet another people to be assimilated, the Conquest multiplied domestic problems, though the resentment felt by most of the English may have served to unify them. The first three Norman rulers were powerful. Their significance is seen more in relations with the other rulers in the British Isles than in domestic reform. Scotland felt the change quickly. William I paralleled the expedition by Cnut in 1031 with his own march to the Tay in 1072, which brought about the submission of Malcolm Canmore. His son William Rufus reoccupied Cumberland in 1092. Into Wales, the incursion of Norman lords began, particularly in the south, as early as one year after *Hastings and William visited St Davids in 1081. The Norman attack upon Ireland was postponed until the 12th cent. and the reign of Henry II.

Since medieval government centred on the king, its efficacy varied greatly. Under strong rulers, the monarchy advanced, royal justice was extended, revenue increased, local government reorganized. Under weak rulers, control became slack and important concessions were made to subjects—*Magna Carta in 1215, even if the immediate beneficiaries were the barons. Monarchs were frequently in danger since they were still expected to lead in battle: Edward II, Richard II, and Henry VI were deposed and killed, Edward V murdered, Richard III killed on the battlefield. The institution of monarchy was not in itself in danger—indeed, brutality often led to the survival of the fittest. Success in war, on the other hand, gave the king a strong, if not impregnable, position—William I, Edward I, Edward III, Henry V.

The prestige and standing of the monarchy was enhanced in a variety of ways. The *coronation ceremony became more elaborate and more dignified. Some early coronations were so hasty that rehearsals could hardly have been possible. Harold was crowned the day after Edward's death, and Henry I apologized to *Anselm for his coronation three days after succeeding Rufus, explaining that 'enemies would have risen up against me'. Monarchs were competitive. The kings of France were proud that, at the coronation of Clovis, an angel had appeared bearing holy oil: fortunately the balance was more than restored when the Virgin Mary herself presented *Becket with holy oil, which was quickly incorporated into the English coronation ceremony. Scottish kings in the 13th cent. petitioned the pope for permission to include anointing, but the English kings protested and the Scots were forced to wait until 1329. Similarly, hearing that the kings of France practised the royal *touch, English monarchs from Edward I onwards began stroking and continued until the *Glorious Revolution.

It was also of value to a monarch to be associated with great buildings and great deeds. The Confessor built Westminster abbey, consecrated just before his death, and Henry III rebuilt it. Rufus built Westminster Hall and Richard II embellished it. Henry VI sponsored Eton and King's College, Cambridge. David I of Scotland founded the abbeys of Holyrood and Dunfermline, later turned into royal residences. Edward III's institution of the Order of the *Garter was supported by a new chapel at Windsor, completed by Edward IV, and deliberately echoed the legendary deeds of King *Arthur.

Cheaper was glory through the proliferation of titles. Edward I created his son prince of Wales in 1301; for decades the title of duke, first used in 1337, was reserved for members of the royal family. In 1483 the use of cloth of gold and purple was by statute limited to the king and his close relatives. By the 16th cent., the usual form of address had moved from 'Your Grace' or 'Your Highness' to 'Your Majesty'. By the 1530s the breach with Rome had added to the monarch's authority his headship over the church.

By the 16th cent., the traditional role of the monarch as battle-leader was declining, though George II still led his men at *Dettingen as late as 1743. But as warfare became more professional and since guns were no respecters of persons, royal valour diminished in importance. Though Henry VIII pined for military glory, he was usually kept at a safe distance from the action, and the greatest victory of his reign at *Flodden was achieved not by the king but by Lord Surrey (*Norfolk). Circumstance in both England and Scotland facilitated the change. In England Edward VI was too young, Mary and Elizabeth ruled out by sex, though Elizabeth's heroic speech at Tilbury was an effective substitute. In Scotland, James IV died fighting at Flodden in 1513; James V was too ill to take the field at *Solway Moss; Mary, queen of Scots, could not fight in person, though she urged her men on; and the inclinations of James VI and I did not run towards martial glory. Charles I was with his troops all through the Civil War, but as supreme commander rather than a fighting man—a role subsequently played by William III.

The Tudor period is usually regarded as the apogee of the English monarchy. Certainly it was stronger than in the 15th cent., when the Wars of the *Roses produced frequent changes of ruler. None of the Tudor rulers was to be trifled with. Yet lawlessness and rebellion were not easily stamped out. Henry VII faced risings on behalf of the pretenders *Simnel and *Warbeck, Henry VIII the *Pilgrimage of Grace, Edward VI's government *Kett's rebellion, Mary the Lady Jane *Grey episode and the *Wyatt rebellion, Elizabeth the rising of the *northern earls and innumerable plots against her life. Several of their policies returned to haunt their successors. The take-over of church powers added greatly to the patronage of the monarch but also involved him more directly in religious disputation at a time when the waves of controversy were beginning to run high. The pope was no longer a lightning conductor for disgruntled critics, and James I's attempts to hold the line—'no bishop, no king'—plunged his son into further difficulty. The Civil War, after all, began with Charles I's dispute over religion with his Scottish subjects. The vast proceeds of the *dissolution of the monasteries were not merely squandered by the crown but finished up with the nobility, helping to strengthen its position. The house of Russell, which gained enormously from the dissolution, was prominent in its opposition to the crown in the 17th cent. Henry VIII's use of Parliament to effect the *Reformation, and Mary and Elizabeth's use to adjust it, gave it confidence to challenge the monarchy in the following century.

Though at one level the Civil War was disastrous for monarchy—the king beheaded, the institution abolished—in the end it may have helped its survival. The role of the army in the 1650s and the social upheaval of the Commonwealth period sobered the gentry and nobility and prepared the ground for the peaceful restoration of Charles II in 1660. The complex negotiations of the early 1640s, in which Charles I, with what sincerity one knows not, had described the role of the crown as a balancing one, pointed the way to a compromise between crown and Parliament. From the melodrama of James II's reign, the monarchy emerged strengthened—limited certainly in its formal powers and prerogatives, but more in touch with the wishes of the nation.

From 1688 onwards, though the monarchy retained fundamental powers, it was in slow constitutional retreat. The *Bill of Rights removed the suspending power and the dispensing power as it had been employed. The prolonged warfare under William and Anne meant that the crown could no longer avoid annual sessions of Parliament and the timing of a dissolution became a matter for ministers, in practice if not in form. The right of veto fell into abeyance after Anne's reign. Though the choice of ministers remained an important prerogative it was increasingly limited by the growth of party loyalty, and the fiasco of Lord *Bute at the start of George III's reign suggested that royal favourites would no longer serve. During George IV's reign the debility of the monarchy was apparent. The king could no longer prevent *catholic emancipation, though he regarded it, with some justice, as a breach of his coronation oath. In 1827 he contemplated leaving the choice of prime minister to the cabinet. Even the granting of honours fell largely into the hands of the prime minister and new orders had to be invented so that the monarch could retain some personal control.

But there were compensations in the changing role. It was not necessarily to the advantage of the monarch to be involved in the dust and reproach of day-to-day government, and the crown's retreat opened the way for a more national role. After the first three Georges, who had revealed little desire to show themselves to their subjects, George IV introduced a new note, with well-publicized visits to Scotland and Ireland. Victoria and *Albert, a more appealing spectacle than a florid and elderly gentleman, were able to exploit the new railway age and built on George's foundations. Though Victoria was not a battle-leader, she undoubtedly became a symbol of the nation and of the empire, as her *Golden and *Diamond Jubilees in 1887 and 1897 demonstrated.

The 20th-cent. British monarchy survived when most others were swept away because it came to terms with democracy. The dangers that awaited it were, in the end, not red revolution or republican egalitarianism, but the more insidious difficulty of knowing what image to present in an age of rapidly changing standards, and how to do it. Like the church, the monarchy, once regarded as a rock of stability and certainty in a confusing world, came to seem, by the end of the century, as confused as its subjects. Royal advisers tended to be modernizers or traditionalists. The abdication of Edward VIII in 1936 appears in retrospect less a grave constitutional issue than an early warning of the problems that would arise if the monarch, or members of the royal family, were not prepared to do their duty. Though few people still regarded the monarchy as a sacred institution, they expected, as *Baldwin pointed out, high standards from it in exchange for its social privileges. The monarchy was not helped by the growth of a vulgar, censorious, and meretricious press. Universal education produced a nation of critics, less respectful than their 7th-cent. ancestors. An increasing number of subjects felt that members of the royal family wished to be ordinary people when it suited them, royal when it did not. The monarchy had survived 1,500 years by a process of adaptation to change, but the pace and nature of change at the end of the 20th cent. were so rapid that the monarchy was in danger, not merely of being left behind, but of seeming increasingly irrelevant. JAC

Cannon, J. A., *The Modern British Monarchy: A Study in Adaptation* (Reading, 1987); id. and Griffiths, R., *The Oxford Illustrated History of the Monarchy* (Oxford, 1988); Golby, J. M., and Purdue, A. W., *The Monarchy and the British People: 1760 to the Present* (1988).

monasteries, or religious communities of men or women living apart from secular society, had their origin in the early church in Egypt where hermits (the word monk is derived from the Greek *monos*, one alone) came together to live a common life of contemplation and work under the direction of an abbot (from Aramaic *abba*, father), such as Pachomius, generally regarded as monasticism's founder. Pachomius' codification of the monastic way of life (or 'rule') was followed by several others including those of Basil (most influential in the eastern church), Augustine of Hippo, Caesarius of Arles, and Benedict of Nursia or Monte Cassino. His rule later became dominant in the West. Monastic communities spread rapidly with the expansion of Christianity following the conversion of Constantine. The first monasteries in the British Isles were established in the 5th cent. in Ireland, probably from Gaul, where the most influential figure was Martin of Tours (d. 397). Thereafter communities spread throughout Celtic Britain, notable centres being at *Iona under St *Columba, at *St Davids, and later at *Lindisfarne (or Holy Island). Monasticism was introduced into Anglo-Saxon England by *Augustine of Canterbury, himself a monk, the first community being St Augustine's, Canterbury (*c.*598). By *c.*650 many monasteries had been founded throughout Britain: some were communities of men and women, the most famous being *Whitby ruled by its abbess, *Hilda. They followed a wide variety of rules and customs. Attempts to standardize these under the rule of Benedict were made by *Wilfrid of Ripon and Hexham, *Benedict Biscop of Jarrow-Monkwearmouth, *Theodore of Canterbury, and others, but were not wholly successful. The Viking raids that began in 787 and continued for over a century destroyed all the northern and eastern houses, while in areas less affected most fell under the control of secular lords, who appropriated their property and appointed members of their family as lay abbots. Recovery accompanied Anglo-Saxon political recovery under the Wessex dynasty. Monasteries were founded, or refounded, often with support from the continent, particularly from Flanders and Lorraine, where there was a new reformed monasticism that looked for a more rigorous communal life, greater austerity, and freedom from secular authority, though operating in association with lay patrons and advocates. The nature and extent of the 10th-cent. reform, led by three monk-bishops, *Dunstan of Canterbury, *Æthelwold of Winchester, and *Oswald of Worcester, who produced (*c.*970) with the support of King *Edgar a new codification of the rule, the *Regularis concordia*, remains controversial, as does the state of Anglo-Saxon monasticism prior to the Norman Conquest. By 1066 there were some 35 male houses and 10 nunneries. Many, especially the former, were wealthy landholders, such as Winchester, St Albans, Bury St Edmunds, or Worcester, while the nunneries included great aristocratic institutions at Shaftesbury and Wilton. Virtually all were concentrated in the old kingdom of Wessex, the west midlands, and the Fens.

The Norman Conquest resulted in the seizure of some monastic lands by the invaders, but generally set-backs were temporary and monasticism was invigorated by new foundations such as Chester, Shrewsbury, St Mary's York, and Durham, as well as by the reforms of *Lanfranc of Canterbury, whose *Constitutions* were widely adapted. These reflected contemporary good practice in Norman monasticism, and were influenced by *Cluny, whence a number of priories were also established. The late 11th and 12th cents. also saw an increase in the number of houses for women, some of which belonged to new orders, such as the *Gilbertines and that of Fontevraud. In 1128 the first *Cistercian community in Britain was established at Waverley (Surrey). Cistercian monasteries and, to an even greater extent, *Augustinian priories constituted the most numerous foundations of the 12th cent.

Thereafter monastic foundations declined markedly: few patrons had the necessary resources to endow a new community, though they might continue to support an existing one linked to their family or by tenurial relationship, while the crown became increasingly concerned at the loss of services and control occasioned by grants of land (in 'mortmain') to the church. Ecclesiastical patronage was especially directed at the new mendicant orders of *friars, and *chantries, frequently established in cathedrals and other churches to pray for the souls of donors and their families, tended to replace monasteries in the pious affections of the laity. Nevertheless the economy of most monasteries, some of which like Winchester and Christ Church, Canterbury, led the way in agricultural and administrative innovation, prospered during the 13th cent. The next century, however, saw serious structural crises consequent upon the *Black Death, exacerbated in some instances by the Anglo-Scottish wars. The spiritual and intellectual condition of the late medieval monasteries is more controversial, but there is little doubt that there was decline from the 'golden age' of the 12th and 13th cents., as friars took the lead in theological debate and universities began to replace monasteries as educational centres. By the time of the *dissolution (1536–40) many monasteries were finding it difficult to attract sufficient recruits, though the *Valor Ecclesiasticus* (1535) revealed that many communities still enjoyed considerable revenues.

A few monasteries, notably Douai, were established on the continent by English Benedictine monks early in the 17th cent. and the Douai community returned to England after the French Revolution, a time when other continental monasteries transferred to England, forming the nucleus for the re-emergence of Roman catholic monasticism in England, while a number of Anglican communities were founded through the influence of the *Oxford movement. BJG

Burton, J., *Monastic and Religious Orders in Britain, 1000–1300* (Cambridge, 1994); Knowles, D., *The Monastic Order in England* (2nd edn. Cambridge, 1963); id., *The Religious Orders in England* (3 vols., Cambridge, 1948–59); Lawrence, C. H., *Medieval Monasticism: Forms of Religious Life in Western Europe in the Middle Ages* (1989).

Monck, George, 1st duke of Albemarle (1608–70). Monck, a stolid and taciturn soldier, played a crucial part in bringing about the *Restoration of 1660. The younger son of a Devon gentry family, he had his career to make. In the 1630s he was in the Dutch service but at the outbreak of the Civil War joined the king. After a year in Ireland fighting against the rebels, he was captured at *Nantwich in 1644 and sent to the Tower. At the end of the war, he returned to Ireland on the parliamentary side, fought a difficult campaign, and was captured by royalist forces in 1649. When released, *Cromwell took him to Scotland, where he commanded the regiment that became the Coldstream Guards. When Cromwell pursued Charles II south to *Worcester, Monck was left as commander-in-chief Scotland. In 1653 he was given naval command and had considerable success against the Dutch. Cromwell relied greatly upon him as a 'simple-hearted man' and nominated him to the 'other house' in 1657. On Cromwell's death, Monck's potential role as king-maker was obvious to all. The royalists began wooing him. When *Lambert's troops in London expelled the *Rump Parliament, Monck marched his men across the Tweed, brushing aside Lambert's forces. Parliament soon fell out with its deliverer and was forced to dissolve itself. Monck reopened negotiations with Charles II, effected his restoration, and met him on the beach at Dover. Next day he received the Garter and a week later his dukedom. He was again at sea in the second *Anglo-Dutch War and served as a figurehead lord of the Treasury from 1667. His lack of ideology made him a consummate politician, moving with events. His wife, reputed a washerwoman, had great influence on him. *Pepys found him 'a very heavy, dull man' and his devoted duchess 'a plain, homely dowdy'. JAC

Mond, Alfred, 1st Baron Melchett (1868–1930). Industrialist and politician. Son of a German Jew who came to Britain in 1862 and built up a large chemical firm, Mond began as a lawyer but moved into the family business, which, in 1926, became the nucleus of ICI. An advocate of the advantages of size in industry, Mond sought to reconcile capital and labour by profit-sharing and employee shareholding. He entered Parliament in 1906 as a Liberal, was 1st commissioner of works 1916–21 and minister of health 1921–2 in *Lloyd George's coalition government. In the 1920s he converted to imperial preference and took the Conservative whip. He was a convinced Zionist. His barony came in 1928. *The Times* obituary wrote that he had triumphed over 'a bad voice, a bad delivery, and a presence unimpressive to all but the caricaturists'. JAC

Monkwearmouth, at the mouth of the Wear, was founded in 674 by a Northumbrian nobleman, *Benedict Biscop. All that now remains above ground of his monastery is the west wall of St Peter's church, begun with the aid of Gallic masons in 675, to which the surviving porch was added before 716. These fragments, together with documentary evidence, surviving sculpture, and the results of recent excavations, show that Biscop's work consciously evoked the buildings and culture of the Italian and Merovingian monasteries he had visited in his earlier continental travels. With the donation of *Jarrow to Biscop in 682 Monkwearmouth became part of 'one monastery in two places' and by 716 there were 600 brethren at the two sites. Monastic life seems to have died in the 9th cent., though the early 11th-cent. tower shows that some ecclesiastical activity continued. Late in the same century the site became a dependent cell of the Durham Benedictines. RNB

Monmouth, diocese of. The diocese was created out of the ancient see of Llandaff in 1921, and is virtually conterminous with the county of *Gwent. It is the smallest in the Church in Wales, few parishes being more than 25 miles from the cathedral. When the diocese was formed, there was no obvious choice for a cathedral. The ancient priory churches at Abergavenny and Chepstow were considered, as was the parish church at Monmouth. There was even a suggestion that the ruins of Tintern abbey be restored. In the event, the parish church of St Woolo in Newport, the most populous town, was chosen as the pro-cathedral, but its status was not confirmed until 1949. Since then this fine Romanesque church has been (in the 1960s) much enlarged. Of the eight bishops since the formation of the see, several have been notable scholars, including the canon lawyer C. A. H. Green (1921–8), the educationalist Derrick Childs (1972–86), and the theologians Edwin Morris (1945–68) and Rowan Williams (1992–). The rural character of much of the diocese is now changing. Within its borders are Cwmbran new town and an expanding industrial belt along the Severn estuary, between Caldicot and Newport. JRG

Monmouth, James Scott, 1st duke of (1649–85). Charles II's eldest and most favoured illegitimate son, Monmouth gained experience with the French army in 1672–4. Becoming an English general in 1678, he defeated the Scottish rebels in 1679. In that year his political ambitions began to soar when *Shaftesbury, in his campaign to exclude the future James II from the succession, exploited the story that Charles had been secretly married to Monmouth's long-dead mother, Lucy Walter. Charles tried to discourage Monmouth's pretensions by exiling him, but an unauthorized return committed him to the opposition Whigs. They procured popularity for him as the 'protestant duke' but John *Dryden pilloried him in his satirical poem *Absolom and Achitophel*. Implicated in the Whig *Rye House plot to assassinate Charles and James he fled to Holland, from where he launched his disastrous invasion and rebellion after James succeeded Charles. After defeat he was executed under an Act of attainder. JRJ

Monmouth rising. While in exile in Holland radical Whigs persuaded the duke of *Monmouth to invade England while *Argyll invaded Scotland. Landing at Lyme in Dorset on 11 June 1685 with 80 followers only, but arms for 2,000, Monmouth depended on the Whigs rallying to him. The gentry were unwilling or (being in preventive detention) unable to do so. Promised diversionary risings in London and Cheshire failed to occur. However Whig rank-and-file supporters, mostly artisans in the depressed textile industry who, as dissenters, were also suffering religious repression, joined and formed an army of about 3,000 untrained infantry. Aware that this force was no match for the royal professionals, Monmouth conducted an irresolute campaign, failing to move quickly on Bristol, a potential source of mass support. He issued a declaration proposing radical political changes, but then proclaimed himself king in place of James II. Having lost the initiative, he gambled on a night attack (5–6 July) on the royal army camped at *Sedgemoor, outside Bridgwater in Somerset. His men were routed. Monmouth was captured (8th) and executed in London a week later. He had never expected to lead what proved to be the last popular rebellion in England and did not know how to do so. JRJ

Monmouthshire was the most border of all counties, straddling England and Wales throughout its 400 years' history. It was bisected by the Usk, the Monnow, from which its name derived, forming the northern boundary, the Wye its eastern, and the Rhymney the western. The coastal plain and gentle hills of the south-east gave way to rugged mountains and valleys in the north-west.

In pre-Roman times, the area was part of the territory of the *Silures. It was rapidly brought under Roman control, the remains at *Caerleon and *Caerwent being among the most impressive in the country. It stayed British after the Romans left, for some time formed an independent kingdom of *Gwent, and at others was part of the kingdom of *Deheubarth.

The Normans began systematic colonization after 1066, constructing castles at *Chepstow, *Raglan, Usk, Monmouth, White Castle, Skenfrith, *Grosmont, and Abergavenny, as well as protected boroughs like Newport. The region was divided up into marcher lordships, which defended it as best they could from Welsh attacks: even so, Grosmont, Abergavenny, and Newport were burned in *Glyndŵr's rebellion in the early 15th cent. The remote region was known mainly for the excellence of its archers and for the woollen Monmouth caps which were popular. Henry V was born in Monmouth, where his statue adorns the town hall. The advent of the Tudors, a Welsh dynasty, changed the status of the area. By the Act of *Union of 1536, the territory was incorporated into England, joining with land to the west of the Usk to form the new county of Monmouthshire. Its peculiar position was reflected by the fact that, like English counties, it was given two knights of the shire, but Monmouth had only one member and shared the representation with six contributory boroughs on the Welsh pattern. The most enduring interests were those of the Herberts, earls of Pembroke, who eventually concentrated on their Wiltshire properties; the Somersets, earls of Worcester and future dukes of Beaufort, who owned Troy House and Raglan castle; and the Morgans of Tredegar. The Somerset family dominated the borough of Monmouth, while the county was usually shared. The Somerset interest was powerful enough to secure the county for the king during the Civil War, though it was harassed by parliamentary forays from Gloucester. Charles I stayed at Raglan late in the war and it was the last royalist stronghold to surrender, in August 1646, when the garrison marched out with full honours. Along with Monmouth and Abergavenny castles, Raglan was then slighted.

The western parts of the county were little developed, though *Camden noted in 1586 that they were 'not unserviceable to the industrious husbandman'. The large-scale exploitation of the coal and iron resources of Monmouthshire began in the early 19th cent., transforming the economic and political balance. Monmouth, the largest town in 1801 with 3,300 inhabitants, was by 1871 outstripped by Abergavenny, Pontypool, Blaenavon, Tredegar, and Newport. The last had grown from about 1,400 persons in 1801 to 40,000 by 1871 and more than 100,000 by 1961. Politically the county became first a Liberal, then a Labour stronghold. In 1831 Samuel Lewis wrote that there were churches in the shire where the services were in English, others in Welsh, and still others where the language alternated: 'the antipathy of the people to the introduction of the language and manners of the English is still inveterately strong . . . they stigmatise every thing assimilating to what is English with the epithet of *Saxon*.' By the mid-20th cent. the Welsh language had retreated and the opening of the Severn bridge in 1966, replacing the old Beachley–Aust ferry, suggested that Monmouth was being pulled back into the English economic orbit. The Local Government Act of 1972 moved the county back into Wales, restoring the name of Gwent, and Monmouth, which had always been on the eastern extremity of the county, lost its position to Cwmbran, a new town just north of Newport. Even this was not the last throw, for in 1996 a further reorganization of local government divided Gwent into four unitary authorities, one of which was to be called Monmouthshire. A better example of the importance which people attach to names could scarcely be found.

JAC

monopolies. Strictly, monopolies exist when there is a single supplier in a market and a monopsony when there is only one buyer. More common is the notion of monopoly power where one actor can exert a strong influence over the way a market functions. Natural monopoly power is often associated with the existence of economies of scale but legal monopolies have been common in the provision of many forms of public goods and services. Adam *Smith, in the **Wealth of Nations*, provided a sustained attack on monopolies but thought of them more as multi-firmed industries with statutory protection along the lines of the medieval guilds.

Attitudes towards monopolies have changed over time. Monopolies granted to courtiers by Elizabeth I and James I caused bitter resentment and there were fierce protests in Parliament. Monopolies were also introduced as a means of indirectly controlling supply, e.g. guilds and, recently, professional associations have codes of conduct which remove the need for direct controls. Conferring monopoly power has also been a traditional way of stimulating investment—the *turnpike system for roads. Legal monopolies may also be created to prevent inefficient duplication of supply. At the international level, monopoly trading power formed a key element in colonial development with singular powers being conferred on bodies such as the *East India Company (1600) to conduct business in designated parts of the empire.

Modern concerns about the implications for consumers from the exploitation of monopoly power have led to state regulation of monopolies—through price controls or profit limits. Mergers which create monopolies are also subjected to scrutiny. The large-scale state ownership of monopolies is a relatively modern phenomenon stemming back to the nationalization programme of the Labour government of 1945–50. More recently (since 1979), following a questioning of the economic efficiency of public ownership, there has been a return to regulated private monopolies. KJB

Monro, Alexander (1697–1767). Scottish surgeon and anatomist. John Monro (1670–1740) had been so impressed by the system of medical education experienced at Leiden that he determined to introduce the same into Edinburgh, educating his son Alexander to play the principal role. After apprenticeship to his father and studies in London (under Cheselden), Paris, and Leiden (under Boerhaave), Alexander returned home to be admitted to the Incorporation of Surgeons by examination (1719). Rapidly appointed by the town council as 'Professor of Anatomy in this city and college', a public riot against body-snatching in 1725 encouraged him to move from Surgeons' Hall to within the university walls. A brilliant extempore speaker, his lectures (in English, not Latin) covered anatomy, surgery, bandaging, and physiology, and he claimed 4,400 students passing through his hands. Thriving in practice as a surgeon-apothecary, his third son Alexander (1733–1817, later known as *secundus*) was educated to follow him, both being conjoint professors of anatomy by 1754. Awarded an MD (1756), Monro *primus* disenfranchised himself from the incorporation, modified his title to 'Professor of Medicine and Anatomy', and was received into the medical faculty of the university, thus essentially completing it as a medical school. ASH

Montagu–Chelmsford Report. The First World War both increased Britain's need for Indian men and *matériel* and presented the Indian national movement with an opportunity to demand constitutional reform. Edwin Montagu, the secretary of state, was sent to India in 1917 and, together with Viceroy Lord Chelmsford, prepared the report which was to lead the country towards 'responsible self-government'. It was enacted by Parliament in 1919. However, the reforms, which were extremely cautious, proved a grave disappointment to Indian national opinion. *Gandhi moved to leadership of the Congress by proposing a boycott of the first elections and 'non-cooperation' with the new constitution. DAW

Montfort III, Simon de (*c.*1170–1218). Simon is best known as the ruthless leader of the notorious Albigensian Crusade against the Cathar heretics of southern France. He first participated in the crusade in 1209, and this venture remained the centre-piece of his career thereafter. As with other participants, Simon's motives are often considered to have been entirely cynical, but it should be remembered that he had previously gone on the equally notorious Fourth Crusade in 1202, significantly withdrawing from the army and going to the Holy Land when it became apparent that the crusade was being diverted from its intended goal, something which suggests genuine piety and a conscience. His significance for English history lies in his claim to the earldom of Leicester through his mother. King John initially accepted the claim but in 1207 seized all his English estates, only committing them through the earl of Chester for Simon's use in 1215. His son, the more famous *Simon IV, duly recovered them from Henry III. SL

Montfort IV, Simon de, earl of Leicester (1208–65). Earl Simon was no stranger to controversy in his lifetime, and has been the subject of extraordinary controversy ever since his death at the battle of *Evesham (1265). Then, the victorious royalists dismembered his body in revengeful exultation; a detested traitor had met his end. But his followers found solace in the rapid emergence of a cult. Evesham abbey, where his mutilated remains were buried, became the centre of a pilgrimage, and the cult took hold so fast that the attempt was made to suppress it. But so strong was popular canonization that it defied suppression and, within thirteen years of his death, over 200 miracles had reputedly occurred. Songs were also composed comparing him to both *Becket and Christ in his preparedness to sacrifice himself for both church and realm. A 'political' saint was born.

It is as a supposed martyr for justice and the liberties of the realm that Simon has largely attracted both denigration and adulation ever since. Nineteenth-cent. scholars saw the *baronial movement for reform, which Simon came to lead, as a formative phase in the making of the English constitution, his famous Parliament of 1265, to which knights and burgesses as well as barons and clergymen were summoned, being a crucial step on the road to democracy. A popular, creative statesman, the champion of oppressed classes, had emerged. The view of Earl Simon as a liberal statesman has been carried into our own times, most notably by Treharne, but Powicke reacted sharply, considering Simon to be a fanatic, a moral and political crusader, whose arrogance and stubbornness played the greater part in wrecking the early promise of the reform movement enshrined in the provisions of *Oxford (1258). Recent work, particularly on the early history of Parliament, has tended to diminish Simon's reputation so far as his longer-term historical significance is concerned. But lively controversy continues to surround the events of his life, his role in the baronial movement of 1258–65, and his motives. What does seem clear is that Simon was no great radical or social reformer. Rather, he accepted the social order of his day and took support from whatever quarter he could once it became apparent that he could not unite the magnates behind him. But that does not necessarily mean that he was purely a cynical manipulator and self-seeker. Popular veneration suggests otherwise. SL

Montgomery, Bernard (1887–1979). General and then field marshal (August 1944), Montgomery was the most controversial general of the Second World War. Arrogant, confident, and self-centred, he did not endear himself to equals or superiors, but 'Monty' won the confidence of subordinates and ordinary soldiers. After capable service in France and Belgium in 1939–40 and in southern England, he rose to fame as commander-in-chief, 8th Army, in north Africa in 1942. With stronger forces and unequalled knowledge of his enemy's weaknesses, he directed the victory of *El Alamein, forcing Italian and German withdrawal back to Tunisia. He was criticized for failure to cut off the retreating enemy. In Sicily and the south of Italy, he was alleged to show indifference to the needs of formations not under his command. The climax of his career was the command of ground forces in the attack on Normandy in 1944 until September. He aroused controversy after D-Day when his progress in capturing Caen was thought perilously slow. Montgomery undermined his reputation, then and since, by insisting that in battle everything followed his 'master plan', including the enemy. He showed high qualities in making cautious, 'balanced' provision for the unexpected: he claimed, however, that for him nothing was unexpected. After Eisenhower took over command, Montgomery continued to insist that he should control active operations. He delayed the clearance of the approaches to Antwerp for his unsuccessful *Arnhem gamble. His boastfulness after the battle of the *Bulge, when he was given temporary command, helped to reduce his influence in 1945. He became a viscount. RACP

Montgomery, treaty of, 1267. After the defeat of his ally Simon de *Montfort in 1265, *Llywelyn came to terms with Henry III at Montgomery. He was recognized as prince of

Wales in exchange for homage and 25,000 marks. The treaty was the highest point of Llywelyn's power. JAC

Montgomeryshire (Sir Drefaldwyn). Border county of mid-Wales. It was created at the Act of *Union with England in 1536 and was coincident with the Welsh kingdom of southern *Powys. Powys, which covered much of mid- and north-east Wales, was split at the end of the 12th cent. and the south (Powys Wenwynwyn), separated from the north (Powys Fadog), was the basis for the county in the form of the Norman lordship of Powys, together with the crown lordships of Montgomery, Cydewain, Ceri, and Caus. The English name comes from the French home of the early conqueror, Roger de Montgomery.

Montgomeryshire comprises the eastern sloping plateaux of the Cambrian mountains, broken by a series of valley lowlands along the river systems of the river Severn and its tributaries, the Banwy, Vyrnwy, and Clywedog. However, it extends across the mountain massif to include part of the western flowing Dyfi drainage. The deeper upper parts of the valley systems have been used to create reservoirs for water supply for north-west England, notably Lake Vyrnwy (1880–90) for Manchester. The more recent Llyn Clywedog (1968) is a regulator of river flow for downstream extraction. There was an early woollen industry in the towns of the Severn valley, and its demise, together with the closure of lead-mines and greater capitalization of agriculture, led to extensive depopulation. In response, Newtown was developed under the New Towns Act and has a range of light industry.

Montgomery is pre-eminently border terrain; every aspect registers an east to west transition whether it be landscape, farming, or culture. Welsh is spoken by 23.3 per cent of the population but characteristically ranges from 4.6 per cent at Church Stoke on the border to 68.3 per cent at Llanbrynmair in the extreme west. In 1974 Montgomeryshire became a district in the county of Powys and was incorporated in the unitary authority of Powys in 1996. The population in 1991 was 51,527. HC

Montrose, James Graham, 1st marquis of [S] (1612–50). Though his activities were necessarily on a small scale, Montrose was the most brilliant commander on the royalist side during the Civil War and a ray of hope for a sinking cause. He inherited the earldom in 1626 when he was 14 and spent the years 1633–6 in continental travel. In 1639 he joined the covenanters but changed sides, and spent several months in 1641 in confinement in Edinburgh castle. He joined the king at Oxford, was raised to marquis in 1644, and appointed to command the king's forces in Scotland, such as they were. Montrose rode north from Carlisle with two companions and put together a scratch force, never many more than 4,000 men, composed mainly of Irish and Macdonalds. His speed of movement, courage, and tactical skill won him a series of remarkable victories against the odds—at *Tippermuir (September 1644), *Aberdeen (September 1644), *Inverlochy (February 1645), *Auldearn (May 1645), *Alford (July 1645), and *Kilsyth (August 1645). After Inverlochy, where his great enemy *Argyll watched in discomfort, Montrose wrote to the king: 'I doubt not before the end of this summer I shall be able to come to Your Majesty's assistance with a brave army.' It was an illusion. No man could defy the odds for ever. At *Philiphaugh in September 1645 he was surprised and beaten, and forced to flee abroad. Returning in 1650 with a forlorn hope, he was defeated at *Carbisdale, betrayed, and hanged at Edinburgh in May. JAC

Montserrat is one of the Leeward Islands and a British colony. It was sighted by Columbus in 1493, disputed between France and Britain, and finally confirmed to Britain by the treaty of *Versailles in 1783. It relies mainly upon tourism, cotton, and light industry. JAC

Moore, Henry (1898–1986). One of the greatest sculptors of the 20th cent. Drawing inspiration from primitive sculptures and Italian frescos, he intended his work to have 'a pent-up energy, an intense life of its own'. Moore taught at the Royal College of Art 1925–32 and at the Chelsea School of Art 1932–9. At about the same time as his first public commission, the *North Wind* relief on the London Transport Building (1928), Moore produced his first reclining figure. This theme, together with that of mother and child, was repeated throughout his life. During the 1930s, Moore's style tended to the abstract and was disliked by traditionalists. But his series of drawings *Shelter*, of people sleeping in London Underground stations during the Second World War, brought him popular recognition. *Madonna* (1944) for St Matthew's church, Northampton, and *Three Standing Figures* (1947–8) in Battersea Park (London), resulted in many further commissions. He was given the OM in 1963. JC

Moore, Sir John (1761–1809). Soldier and military reformer. Moore was educated mainly on the continent before entering the army in 1776, where he saw active service in many theatres of war. In Corsica, on 10 August 1794, he led the storming party at the siege of Calvi. After an expedition against St Lucia in 1796 he was appointed governor of the island for a time. Moore distinguished himself in Egypt during the night-time landing operation at Aboukir on 22 March 1801. As a military reformer, Moore successfully developed light infantry tactics and training methods. In 1808 he assumed command of the British forces in the Peninsular War, but was killed at *Corunna (16 January 1809) after conducting a hazardous but successful retreat. Napoleon commented: 'His talents and firmness alone saved the British army [in Spain] from destruction; he was a brave soldier, an excellent officer, and a man of talent.' RAS

Moray, kingdom of. Morayshire, the county centred on Elgin from the 12th cent. to 1975, was only a small part of the kingdom of Moray, which originally extended from the west coast facing the Isle of Skye across to the river Spey in the east, and from probably the river Oykell in the north to the central highlands in the south. The kingdom was created by the Gaels of northern Argyll, who advanced up the Great Glen and, with the Norse from Orkney, overcame the Picts in northern Scotland in the 9th cent. Throughout their history the kings of Moray were faced by powerful enemies to the north and south. In the north they struggled to resist the Norse earls of *Orkney, eager to control the rich woodlands of northern Scotland as a supply of timber for their ships. In the south they strenuously resisted the ambitions of Scottish kings, who sought to make Moray part of their realm. The most famous king was *Macbeth, who successfully turned the tables on the Scottish kings in the south and became king of Scots after killing *Duncan I in 1040. Even though Duncan's son *Malcolm (III) killed Macbeth in 1057, it was *Lulach of the Moray dynasty who became king of Scots. Malcolm slew Lulach the following year, but seemingly had to recognize Lulach's son *Mael Snechta, king of Moray, as heir to the Scottish throne. Only when Malcolm defeated Mael Snechta in 1078 can it be said that Moray's chances of dominating the Scottish kingdom were brought to a halt. Moray's hopes of regaining power were not extinguished, however. In 1130 Angus, Lulach's grandson, led an army south, only to be defeated decisively at Stracathro (25 miles north-east of Dundee). Despite conquest, colonization, and expulsion, the leading families of Moray continued to resist the kings of Scots until 1230. The days were over, however, when Scotland was a patchwork of regional kings. The king of Scots, the greatest regional power in northern Britain, brought all of the mainland north of the Tweed and Solway within his realm, and Moray was dominated by a Fleming family, introduced by David I (1124–53) to pacify the area, who took Moray as their name. DEB

Moray, Thomas Randolph, 1st earl of [S] (d. 1332). Randolph was a nephew of Robert I Bruce and a stalwart of his regime. Captured fighting for Bruce at *Methven in 1306, he changed sides but was captured again, this time by Bruce's men. He rejoined Bruce and, after this unpromising start, became one of his trusted allies and most reliable commanders. He was created earl in 1312.

In March 1314 he seized Edinburgh castle from the English in a brilliant night attack and fought prominently at *Bannockburn. Next he campaigned in Ireland with Edward *Bruce. He won more victories over the English at *Myton in 1319 and at *Byland in 1322. He was chief negotiator for the treaty of *Corbeil in 1326 which laid the foundations for the 'Auld Alliance'. On the death of Bruce he acted as regent 1329–32 for the young David II. His standing is shown by the fact that his was the second name to appear on the declaration of *Arbroath in 1320. JAC

Moray, Alexander Stewart, 5th earl of [S] (1634–1701). Moray was a descendant of Regent *Moray, himself an illegitimate son of James V. He rose to high office after the Restoration, campaigning against the covenanters. From 1675–6 he was justice-general [S], a lord of the Treasury in 1678, and served as secretary of state [S] from 1680 to 1689. During the reign of James VII he was appointed commissioner to the Parliament summoned in 1686 to give relief to the catholics and he subsequently announced his own conversion. In 1687 he received the Thistle. He was deprived of all his offices after the Glorious Revolution and was fined in 1693 for not attending Parliament. JAC

Moray, James Stewart, 1st earl of [S] (1531–70). Illegitimate son of James V and thus half-brother of Mary Stuart. As Lord James Stewart, he played a key role in the protestant rebellion of 1559–60, subsequently dominating the provisional government which negotiated Mary's peaceful return to Scotland in 1561. Rewarded in 1562 with the earldom of Moray, his policy of 'amity' with England was destroyed by Mary's marriage to *Darnley in 1565, which pushed Moray into rebellion and temporary exile in England. Restored to favour the following year, he was judiciously absent abroad during the crisis triggered by Mary's marriage to *Bothwell. On his return in August 1567, he was made regent for the infant James VI. His defeat of Mary at *Langside in May 1568 lent his regime some credibility, but support for the Marian cause remained strong. In January 1570 he was assassinated by the Hamiltons, staunch supporters of the exiled queen. RAM

Moray, James Stewart, 2nd earl of [S] (*c.*1566–92). Regent *Moray, assassinated in 1570, left a young daughter who was recognized as the countess of Moray. In 1581 she married the son of Lord Doune [S], who was in turn recognized as earl of Moray. He succeeded to the barony in 1590. He was murdered in a fray by his rival *Huntly. The ballad 'The Bonny Earl of Moray' suggests that he was too much the favourite at court of *Anne, James VI's new queen. JAC

Moray, Sir Robert (*c.*1609–73). Moray, the son of a Scottish laird from Perthshire, was soldier, scientist, and politician. He spent many years in the French service, acting as go-between for Charles I, who knighted him in 1643. He took part in *Glencairn's rising in Scotland in 1654 before returning again to the continent, where he practised music and chemistry. After the Restoration, Moray took a prominent part in the foundation of the *Royal Society, acted as president, and looked after Charles II's private laboratory in Whitehall. Until 1670 he also collaborated with *Lauderdale in the government of Scotland where, sympathetic towards the presbyterians, he exercised a moderating influence on government policy. But most of his time was spent in London at the court. *Burnet, *Pepys, and *Evelyn wrote of him with affection and respect, and John *Aubrey paid a glowing tribute to his disinterestedness: 'he was far from the rough humour of the camp breeding, for he was a person the most obliging about the court, and the only man that would doe a kindnesse *gratis* upon an account of friendship . . . as free from covetousness as a Carthusian.' JAC

Morcar, earl of Northumbria (*c.*1040–*c.*1090). Morcar was from the Mercian nobility, grandson of *Leofric and his wife 'Lady *Godiva', and son of Ælfric, earl of East Anglia. The family was in rivalry with the Godwines. In 1065 Morcar and his brother Edwin joined a rebellion in Northumbria against Harold Godwineson's brother *Tostig, and Morcar replaced him as earl of Northumbria. When Tostig returned with *Harold Hardrada in 1066, Edwin and Morcar gave battle but were defeated at *Fulford, near York. Harold retrieved the situation by killing Tostig and Harold Hardrada at *Stamford Bridge, but Morcar and Edwin did not march south with him to *Hastings, possibly because their forces were shattered. On Harold's death, the brothers tried to lead a resistance, failed, and submitted to William. In 1068 they rebelled and were again obliged to submit. After a further unsuccessful revolt in 1071 Morcar took refuge in the Isle of Ely, surrendered, and was imprisoned in Normandy. He was alive at the Conqueror's death in 1087 but Rufus returned him to prison and no more was heard of him. His elder brother Edwin was killed by his own men in 1071. JAC

More, Hannah (1745–1833). One of the best-known and most prolific polemicists of her day, Hannah More was born at Stapleton, near Bristol, and joined her sisters in running a school. She became acquainted with London literary circles and was a particular favourite with Dr *Johnson. A poem *Sir Eldred* was well received (1776) and her play *Percy* had a good run at Covent Garden in 1777, thanks to David *Garrick's support. Her growing evangelical interest was evident in *Thoughts on the Importance of the Manners of the Great to General Society* (1788). From her cottage at Cowslip Green, near Blagdon, south of Bristol, she started in the 1790s Sunday schools for the Mendip villages: 'I allow of no writing for the poor,' she told *Wilberforce in a memorable phrase. Meanwhile the outbreak of the French Revolution gave her a chance to write simple and didactic tracts, in which the poor were invited to count their blessings, and which sold and were distributed in vast quantities. She died a wealthy woman, leaving her money to religious institutions and charities. JAC

More, Sir Thomas (1478–1535). More, lawyer, humanist, and amateur theologian, held great intellectual and moral ascendancy over Henrician England, until his defence of the Roman catholic cause brought about his downfall. He practised common law in the 1500s, and married in 1505 despite previous plans to take holy orders. His legal and political career prospered in the 1510s and 1520s: he became undersheriff of London (1510), master of requests (1518), and Speaker of the Commons (1523). He was knighted in 1521, and succeeded *Wolsey as lord chancellor in 1529. Meanwhile, More became a celebrated enthusiast of humanism, and friend not only of other English scholars but also of Desiderius Erasmus. His **Utopia*, which described an imaginary land whose inhabitants shaped their lives by natural reason, made his literary reputation, though scholarship has never been able to agree on the book's real intention. More's later religious writings had no ambiguities. He advised on Henry VIII's *The Assertion of the Seven Sacraments* against Martin Luther and rebutted Luther's refutation (1523). Licensed from 1528 to read heretical books and refute them, he wrote long, fervent catholic ripostes against William *Tyndale and Simon Fish. The king's first marriage-crisis placed More in a quandary. He tried to persuade Henry to take *Catherine back, and to persecute heretics, until failure forced his resignation from office in May 1532. When required to swear an oath to the new royal succession in 1534, More refused, but claimed that his silence over his reasons could not be construed as 'malicious' denial of royal claims. He was imprisoned and interrogated until one witness, Richard Rich, convinced himself that More had really denied the royal supremacy. Swiftly tried and condemned on perjured evidence (as he claimed), More finally spoke out in defence of the papacy, and was executed on 6 July 1535. He was canonized in 1935. EC

Morgan, Sir Henry (*c.*1635–88). Morgan was a buccaneer and adventurer in the Spanish main. He came from Glamorgan and was a nephew of Colonel Edward Morgan, lieutenant-governor of Jamaica, who was killed in 1665. The Caribbean was a scene of permanent warfare between the English and Spaniards. Morgan joined an expedition in 1666 led by a buccaneer, Edward Mansfield: when he was killed in action, Morgan was 'chosen' to lead the raiders. They captured Porto Bello, slaughtered the Spanish garrison, and ransacked the town—on the pretext that the Spaniards were preparing an invasion of Jamaica. Next Morgan plundered parts of Cuba, including the town of Maracaybo, and was appointed naval commander in the area, to be paid in plunder. He proceeded to capture Panama despite a pitched battle by its defenders. His atrocities caused his recall to England, but he gained favour with Charles II, was made lieutenant-governor of Jamaica in 1674, and knighted. He spent the rest of his life there as a stern defender of law and order. Ferocious and fearless, Morgan was a brilliant guerrilla leader and a scourge to the Spaniards. JAC

Morgan, William (*c.*1545–1604). Bishop and Welsh scholar. Morgan was born in Cardiganshire and sent to St John's College, Cambridge. In 1575 he was made vicar of Welshpool, moving in 1578 to Llanrhaidadr Mochnant. He then undertook to complete the translation of the Bible into Welsh, begun by William *Salesbury. The edition, including a revision of Salesbury's New Testament, appeared in 1588. Morgan was made bishop of Llandaff in 1595 and promoted to the slightly wealthier see of St Asaph in 1601. JAC

Morgannwg, kingdom of. The immediate post-Roman kingdom in south-east Wales was Glywysing, ruled over in AD 600 by Meurig ap Tewdrig. At a later period, it gave way to the kingdom of Morgannwg, which excluded Gwent, and may have been named after Morgan Hen ('Morgan the Old'), who died 974. The area was quickly penetrated by the Normans after 1066 and Robert *Fitzhamon established the lordship of Glamorgan, beginning his castle at Cardiff *c.*1080. JAC

Morley, John (1838–1923). Journalist and politician. The son of a north country surgeon, and educated at Oxford, Morley used free-lance journalism as a stepping-stone to the editorship of the *Fortnightly Review* (1867–82), which under his direction became a major vehicle for the propagation of a new species of radical Liberalism, campaigning against jingoism, imperial adventures, repression in Ireland; it was Morley, together with Joseph *Chamberlain and Charles *Dilke, who formulated the so-called Radical Programme (1885). Elected to Parliament in 1883, Morley, now a Home Ruler, broke with Chamberlain over Ireland, serving as Irish secretary in Gladstone's last ministry (1892–4) and under Rosebery (1894–5). Morley denounced British policy in South Africa at the time of the Boer War, but virtually retired to write a much-acclaimed life of *Gladstone. As a member of the Liberal governments of 1905–14 he was responsible for the reform of the British administration of India, resigning in 1914 over the issue of war with Germany. GA

mormaers were provincial rulers in the Gaelic kingdom of Scotland from the 10th to the 12th cents. The original area of the kingdom of Scotland, stretching east of the Grampians from the Forth in the south to the Spey in the north, was divided into a patchwork of provinces ruled by a mormaer. They raised the men of their province for the defence of the kingdom, collected tribute from the province's peasants, and administered justice, assisted by the lawman of the province. The provinces were not large. Modern Perthshire included the provinces of Strathearn, Atholl, most of Menteith, and the Gowrie; Aberdeenshire included Mar and Buchan; the province of Fife was (at least by *c.*1100) confined to east Fife. South of the Spey only Angus and the Mearns corresponded to later counties. Outside the kingdom's core area the mormaers of Ross in the north of Scotland and the Lennox in the south (focused on Dumbarton and Loch Lomond) may have been created in the 12th cent.; while the ruler of *Moray, an abnormally large province, stretching from Glenelg on the west coast to the Spey in the east, called himself a king, and was only referred to as a mormaer by the king of Scots or his allies. Mormaers are first mentioned in 918, soon after the emergence of the new kingdom of the *Scots. With the exception of Atholl, none of the provinces is referred to earlier than 918. Some, such as Angus, Strathearn, and the Gowrie, are almost certainly no older than the 10th cent. It might be supposed, therefore, that the position of mormaer was a creation of the new Gaelic kingdom of the Scots. A linguistic case, however, has been put for regarding *mormaer* as a Pictish word meaning 'great steward', and that it belonged to a Pictish system of local administration. The argument is complicated by *mormaer*'s later philological development in Gaelic which can more readily be explained if *mormaer* was originally Gaelic 'sea steward', rather than a borrowing from a Pictish word meaning 'great steward'. It is true that mormaers are found inland, but an analogy may be made with Carolingian border officials 'margrave' and 'marquis' which became titles for members of the nobility far away from a frontier. It is possible, therefore, that mormaers were created *c.*900 as guardians against Scandinavian raids. In the 12th cent., chiefly by virtue of adopting primogeniture and 'military feudalism', mormaers developed into provincial earls. In this guise they remained a key feature of the political geography of the kingdom of the Scots until the disappearance of provincial earls in the late 14th and early 15th cents. DEB

Mormons, or the Church of Jesus Christ of Latter Day Saints, result from visions experienced in Manchester, NY, during the 1820s by Joseph Smith (1805–44), enabling him to locate and translate *The Book of Mormon* (1827), a history of American religion from Babel to the 5th cent. AD, written on gold tablets in 'reformed Egyptian' and deciphered by sacred crystals which Smith had to return to the angel Moroni on completion. There followed seventeen years of sectarian vagabondage: founded in 1830, the sect settled in Kirtland, Ohio (1831–7), Jackson, Missouri, and Nauvoo, Illinois (1839), reaching Great Salt Lake Valley, Utah, in 1847. In that time twelve apostles were appointed, Smith became first president, received his revelation about plural marriages (1843), and was killed in prison. Mormonism's survival, therefore, owes most to Smith's successor Brigham Young (1801–77), who shaped Utah into a model state (polygamy was abolished in 1890). Mormonism had a recognizably evangelical core (acceptance of Scripture, faith in God and Christ, repentance, baptism as preparation for the gift of the Spirit), with a millennialist skin—belief in the Second Coming and the charismatic signs of the primitive church. *The Book of Mormon*, however, adds another dimension: baptism for the dead, securing heaven for the ancestors of Mormons; marriage binding beyond death; God as an exalted man, and Christ as a forerunner of Joseph Smith. The whole was expressed in lives of strenuous simplicity and aggressive missionary endeavour. The first Mormon missionaries reached England in 1837. Their methods were foolproof. Utilizing existing networks, they reached respectable artisans through sympathetic *baptist or *congregational ministers. Since the imminent Second Coming would be in America, converts made their way to Utah rather than form local congregations. Consequently few British Mormon churches can be traced to these early meetings and most have been founded since 1945. CB

Morris, William (1834–96). Poet, artist, craftsman, and socialist, Morris was educated at Marlborough and Oxford. At first intended for the church, he changed to study architecture and then became a painter under the influence of *Rossetti. He quickly realized he had no great talent for painting but that he could design, and in 1861 founded Morris & Co. to produce wallpapers, furnishings, and stained-glass windows. He raised the standards of English design and craftsmanship and through his Kelmscott Press, founded 1890, had a similar effect on book design and printing. A founding member of the Socialist League, many of his later writings were anti-industrialist, supporting a return to handicraft. In 1877, Morris founded the Society for the Protection of Ancient Buildings. JC

Morrison, Herbert (1888–1965). Labour Party politician and statesman. After he became secretary in 1915, Morrison's organizational skills accelerated the steady rise of the London Labour Party. Mayor of Hackney 1920–1, London county councillor from 1922, and MP for South Hackney in 1923–4, 1929–31, 1935–45 (and Lewisham 1945–59), Morrison led Labour to victory in the 1934 LCC elections. The culmination of his London-based successes was the 1951 Festival of Britain. After a brief spell as minister of supply (May–October 1940), for most of the wartime coalition he served as Churchill's high-profile and popular home secretary (1940–5). In the post-war Labour government, Morrison played a key co-ordinating role as lord president and leader of the Commons (1945–51) before an unhappy tenure as foreign secretary (March–October 1951). His 1931 London Passenger Transport Bill (whilst minister of transport 1929–31) provided the 'public corporation' model of nationalization adopted by the *Attlee government; however after 1947 he urged 'consolidation'. Despite serving as Attlee's deputy for a decade (and having a sounder judgement over the timing of the 1950 and 1951 elections), Morrison was defeated in the Labour leadership contest in 1955, as he had been in 1935. SC

mortality, bills of. Weekly official returns of the deaths (later, also baptisms) in 109 London parishes, published by the Company of Parish-Clerks from 1592, probably prompted by the plague but limited to Anglicans in parish burial-grounds. Diseases and casualties for both sexes were distinguished by 1629, but the ignorance of the searchers, unreliable and venal 'antient matrons' who reported the cause of death to the parish clerks, occasioned notoriously imprecise diagnoses and distinctions. The figures nevertheless enabled John Graunt to compile the first known life table (1662). A national civil vital registration system was not established until 1837. ASH

Mortimer, Edmund, 3rd earl of March (1352–81). March inherited at the age of 8 and married a daughter of Lionel, duke of Clarence, second son of Edward III, who brought him vast possessions, particularly in Ireland. In 1377, when Richard II succeeded as a child, March was a member of the Regency Council and was influential both in Parliament and in the field, especially in Scottish matters. From 1379 he served as king's lieutenant in Ireland but died in Cork. Through his marriage, March established a family claim to the throne. His great-grandson was Richard, duke of *York, whose son gained the throne as Edward IV. JAC

Mortimer, Edmund, 5th earl of March and Ulster (1391–1425). Mortimer was the king's ward after the death of his father Earl Roger in 1398; he was kept in Henry IV's family circle. Potentially a valuable pawn because of his royal blood, he was apparently too amiable and unambitious to worry the Lancastrian establishment. He disclosed to Henry V the treasonable schemes of his brother-in-law Richard, earl of *Cambridge. Until Henry's death, Mortimer was regularly employed, without distinction, in the French war. In 1424, Henry VI's council appointed him lieutenant of Ireland, where he soon died. Richard, duke of *York, was his heir. RLS

Mortimer, Roger, 6th Baron Wigmore (*c.*1231–82). Mortimer was one of the most powerful marcher barons of Henry III's reign and preoccupied with resisting Welsh advance. His mother was a daughter of *Llywelyn ab Iorwerth and he also inherited great estates through his marriage to a daughter of William de Braose. He succeeded to the title in 1246. At the outset of the political struggle in 1258, Mortimer stood with the baronial opposition to Henry III. But de *Montfort's *rapprochement* with *Llywelyn ap Gruffydd, with whom Mortimer was constantly at feud, caused him to change sides. He fought with the losing royal army at *Lewes in 1264 and subsequently helped Prince Edward to escape captivity and take refuge at Wigmore. He took a leading part in de Montfort's defeat at *Evesham in 1265, sending his head as a grisly trophy to his wife at Wigmore. Thereafter Mortimer worked closely with Edward, as prince and king, much involved in sometimes desperate campaigning against Llywelyn in the 1270s. JAC

Mortimer, Roger, 1st earl of March (*c.*1287–1330). A lord of the Welsh march, with major interests in Ireland, Roger Mortimer was one of the rebels who surrendered to Edward II in 1321. He made a dramatic escape from the Tower of London in 1324, and went into exile in Paris; it is probably there that he became Queen *Isabella's lover. He was at her side during the invasion of 1326, and after the deposition of Edward II early in 1327 he, with the queen, dominated government until 1330. He became earl of March in 1328, and had no reservations in displaying his power, wealth, and position. This regime proved to be as corrupt and incompetent as that of the *Despensers which it succeeded, and in 1330 in a remarkable coup the young king, Edward III, with a small group of followers seized Mortimer at Nottingham. His execution followed trial in Parliament. MCP

Mortimer, Roger, 4th earl of March and Ulster (1374–98). Mortimer was a great-grandson of Edward III through his mother Philippa, sole heiress of Edward's second surviving son Lionel, duke of Clarence, whose wife was heiress to the earldom of Ulster. As his father died in 1381, Mortimer spent many years in wardship. He won a reputation for knightly courage, liberality, and religious and moral laxity. He was killed in Ireland while acting as the king's lieutenant. The legend that in 1385 Richard II recognized Mortimer as his heir to the throne comes from tainted sources and is otherwise improbable. RLS

Mortimer's Cross, battle of, 1461. The young earl of March (the future Edward IV) was at Gloucester when his father was defeated and killed at *Wakefield. He marched north to intercept a strong Lancastrian force under the earl of Wiltshire and Jasper *Tudor, earl of Pembroke, whom he defeated on 2 February at Mortimer's Cross, 4 miles south of Wigmore. On the morning of the battle, the Yorkists claimed three suns in the sky as a good omen. This was Edward's first important victory. Owen *Tudor, Pembroke's father and grandfather of the future Henry VII, was taken prisoner in the fight and beheaded in Hereford market-place. JAC

Mortmain, statute of, 1279. Mortmain refers to property held by a 'dead hand' and therefore inalienable. Kings and barons objected to persons granting their land to a religious institution and receiving it back again, having shed, in the process, their military and other feudal obligations. The provisions of *Westminster (1259) declared against alienation of land without the lord's permission. Edward I's statute of 1279 forbade such transfers on pain of forfeiture, to the chagrin of the clergy. Loopholes in the statute were found and repeated efforts were made to block them. After the Reformation, bequests were more likely to be made to charities or educational establishments, and exceptions to the prohibition of mortmain were made in favour of Oxford and Cambridge colleges, and trusts like the British Museum. JAC

Morton, James Douglas, 1st earl of [S] (d. 1493). Made earl of Morton by James II (1458). Although married to

Joanna, sister of James II, Morton took little part in affairs of state. However he was briefly associated with the Kennedy faction, which controlled the minority government of James III between 1463 and 1466. He was also on the assize that forfeited Robert, Lord *Boyd, and his rival faction in 1469, and possibly gave support in their fall. Morton frequently attended Parliament, but was hardly ever at court. He was one of the few magnates to remain loyal to James III in both the crisis of 1482 and that of 1488, although his son John, later 2nd earl, was involved with the treasons of Alexander, duke of *Albany, in 1482. He showed no ill-will towards the regime of James IV, attending Parliament almost annually until his death. RJT

Morton, James Douglas, 4th earl of [S] (*c.*1516–81). The position of regent to young James VI of Scotland was not an enviable one. *Moray, the first, was shot in 1570; *Lennox was stabbed in 1571; *Mar lasted a year before dying unexpectedly, with poison rumoured; Morton was the fourth and last, and had exercised effective power during the two previous regencies. He succeeded to the earldom in 1548, having married a daughter of the 3rd earl in 1543. In 1548 he was captured by the English and held in the Tower until 1550. He made useful contacts and his subsequent policy favoured an English alliance and support for the reformed religion in its English episcopal form. After Mary's return from France in 1561, Morton played an increasingly important role, first as chancellor [S] 1562–6 and again 1567–73. He took a leading part in the murder of *Rizzio, an equivocal one in the murder of *Darnley, but in 1567 led the opposition to Mary and *Bothwell, defeating their supporters in 1568 at *Langside. He succeeded Mar as regent in 1572 and consolidated his position when Mary's supporters in Edinburgh castle were forced to surrender in 1573. His strong policy antagonized nobles and kirk alike, and in 1578 he was overthrown by *Atholl and *Argyll. Elizabeth's intervention afforded him a shaky return to office, though scarcely to power, until in 1580 he was charged with Darnley's murder and beheaded in 1581. A formidable man, Morton collected superlatives—greedy, grim, lewd, cruel—but his few years in power gave Scotland a little stability in the difficult early years of James VI, and he made a determined attempt to stamp out border raiding. JAC

Morton, John (*c.*1420–1500). Cardinal. Morton was one of the greatest ecclesiastical statesmen of the 15th cent. He came from Dorset and went to Balliol College, Oxford. A useful ecclesiastical lawyer, he advanced rapidly under the patronage of Archbishop *Bourchier but, as an adherent of the Lancastrians, fell into disfavour after *Towton in 1461. He escaped to the continent, returned with *Warwick in 1470, and after the Lancastrian disaster at *Tewkesbury in 1471 made his peace with Edward IV. In 1473 he was appointed master of the rolls and in 1479 bishop of Ely. During the short reign of Richard III, Morton moved into opposition and was again forced to flee the country, returning after Henry VII's triumph at *Bosworth. Henceforth Morton was the mainstay of the new regime, becoming archbishop of Canterbury in 1486 and lord chancellor in 1487. In 1493 Henry obtained for him a cardinal's hat from Pope Alexander VI. The story of 'Morton's fork', which came from *Bacon, credited him with financial rapacity, but he seems not to have had specific financial responsibilities. His extraordinary domination prompts comparison with *Wolsey twenty years later. 'The very mother and mistress of wisdom', was Thomas *More's assessment. JAC

Morton, William Douglas, 6th earl of [S] (1540–1606). Douglas was son of Sir Robert Douglas of Lochleven and, by his mother, a half-brother of the Regent *Moray. He inherited the earldom of Morton in 1588 from a distant cousin. He was involved in the murder of *Rizzio and in 1567–8 was in charge of Mary at Lochleven castle, from which she escaped with the help of his younger brother George. He fought with the anti-Mary forces at *Langside in 1568 and remained a close supporter of his kinsman, the Regent *Morton. A favourite at the court of James VI, he was commissioner to the Scottish Parliament in 1592 and 1593. JAC

mortuary. Formerly a gift of the second-best beast of a deceased parishioner to the incumbent of the parish church, later the second best of the moveable goods from the estate. Subsequently merely a payment, the 'Corse presente' was limited by statute to a maximum of 10 shillings (1529), with many exemptions, while remaining lawful to certain Welsh bishops and the archdeacon of Chester on the death of a priest within their respective jurisdictions. The custom persisted sporadically into the 18th cent.; the term now applies more usually to a place for the temporary reception of the dead. ASH

Mosley, Sir Oswald (1896–1980). Labour politician, orator, and fascist. Born into the landed aristocracy and educated at Winchester, Mosley served with distinction during the Great War. From 1918 to 1924 he sat as MP for Harrow, first as a Conservative and then as an Independent. In 1924 he joined the Independent Labour Party, and was Labour MP for Smethwick 1924–31. Mosley epitomized the impatience of post-1918 youth with conventional party politics, which he felt was incapable of dealing with social and economic problems. In Labour he affected to see 'the forces of progress' as opposed to 'the powers of reaction', but as a member of the Labour government of 1929 he became disillusioned with its unwillingness to challenge Treasury orthodoxies, and was lured by the attractions of fascism as an ideology and of anti-Semitism as a device. His British Union of Fascists (formed 1932) failed to win a parliamentary seat, and was proscribed in 1940, when Mosley himself was interned. GA

Mothers' Union. Church of England women's organization, founded in 1876 by Mary Sumner, wife of a Hampshire rector, originally as a parochial body aiming to uphold 'the sanctity of marriage' and to nurture young families in a Christian environment. Having developed into a diocesan organization by 1885, it spread rapidly, launched its own journal, formed a central council (1895), and was granted a royal charter (1926); the first overseas branch was founded in 1897. It now operates throughout the Anglican Communion, admitting spinsters, men, and divorcees, and continues to promote stable family life, with active involvement in many social concerns. ASH

motor-cycle racing. Daimler's motor-bicycle of 1885 could reach 12 m.p.h. Britain lagged behind France and Germany in the development of racing at first but in 1907 Brooklands was opened and the first Tourist Trophy race in the Isle of Man was held. International competition was organized by the Fédération Internationale des Clubs Motor-cyclistes (FIM). Speedway racing was introduced into Britain from America in the 1920s and a league started in 1929. After considerable vicissitudes, it is now re-established and organized by the Speedway Control Board. JAC

motor industry. Manufacturing in Britain began during the 1890s in small workshops often in association with bicycle production. Business grew rapidly so that by 1913 British firms produced annually 34,000 vehicles. Rolls at the top end of the market and Morris at the other were already established. Specialist firms supplied many components for vehicle-building, including batteries, castings and sparking plugs, upholstery, tyres for wheels, and glass for windscreens and windows.

During the 1914–18 war technological developments made possible supplies of powerful and more reliable vehicles. After the war motor vehicles took an ever-growing share of road transport. The first mass-production car-builder in Britain was Ford's, which initially assembled imported kits from the USA. However the company soon found it advantageous to manufacture in Britain cars, vans, and lorries specially designed for the British market. Assembly-line methods for quantity production were adopted in the late 1920s by Herbert *Austin and later by other British companies. During the 1930s the motor industry became the leading source of growth in the economy. In 1939 the world war gave additional impetus by the demand for military transport and fighting vehicles (including aircraft) and agricultural tractors.

Between 1945 and 1955 motor manufacturing had a pivotal role in the British economy. For example, by 1950 it contributed to the balance of trade by exporting 52 per cent of output. This position of world leader was lost to overseas competitors whose investment was matched by attention to design, quality, and sales and marketing skills. Simultaneously the British industry suffered from managerial and labour relations problems; over-manning was accompanied by inadequate attention to delivery at home and abroad.

The British-owned motor industry responded to its difficulties with a variety of strategies. Mergers and amalgamations created the British Motor Corporation formerly *Austin and Morris (*Nuffield) in 1952, but its organizational difficulties had not been resolved fully when the company merged with Leyland in 1968. Leyland itself evolved from being a commercial vehicle producer by mergers with Standard Triumph and Rover. The Rootes group suffered difficulties and was acquired by the American Chrysler company in 1967 but subsequently it joined Talbot, a part of the French Peugeot group. Competition from German and Japanese companies in home and overseas markets was increasing. Managerial and investment problems precipitated the nationalization of British Leyland in 1977. It was privatized, and renamed Rover after its sale to British Aerospace. During the 1980s the motor industry was characterized by investments by overseas companies. By 1994 mass-production car-makers in Britain included BMW-Rover, Ford, General Motors, Honda, Nissan, Peugeot, and Toyota.

The few firms remaining in British ownership specialize in high-performance or quality cars, for example, Aston Martin and Morgan. The most famous of these is Rolls Royce, whose engine design and manufacturing standards are still world renowned. IJEK

motor racing began soon after Karl Benz invented the petrol-driven car in 1885. The first race took place on 11–13 June 1895 from Paris to Bordeaux. Road racing was popular on the continent but in Britain it was banned, leading to the development of closed circuits on private land. In 1906 H. F. Locke King built a 2.75-mile concrete track at his Surrey estate called Brooklands. It featured long, steeply banked turns to allow cars to corner at speed. The first Grand Prix was held at Le Mans in 1906 and thereafter racing became more professional.

New courses sprang up in Britain: Donnington Park near Derby (1933), Silverstone in Northamptonshire (1948), Brands Hatch in Kent (1949), and Oulton Park in Cheshire (1953). The British Grand Prix was first held in 1948. Britain made little impact on the sport, apart from the famous Bentley victories between the wars. It was not until the introduction of the World Drivers' Championship in 1950, which provided a focus for the sport, that Britain made her mark. That year saw the launch of British Racing Motors (BRM) in an attempt to match the European competition. In 1958 Stirling Moss, driving a Cooper, won the Argentine GP. Cooper-Bristols pioneered the lightweight mid-engined car and the victory was seen as a triumph for the small, entrepreneurial British engineering companies. British racing engines, first the Coventry Climax and then the Cosworth, powered cars designed by John Surtees, Ken Tyrrell, Colin Chapman, and Frank Williams. Chapman, the innovative Lotus designer, developed and refined the rear-engined car.

In the 1950s Stirling Moss and Mike Hawthorn became household names. Graham Hill won the Drivers' Championship in 1962 and 1968, Jim Clark in 1963 and 1965, and Jackie Stewart in 1969, 1971, and 1973. James Hunt and Nigel Mansell followed suit in 1976 and 1992, and Damon Hill in 1996. RAS

motorways are segregated roads devoted to trunk motor traffic. Conceptualized by Lord Montagu of Beaulieu in 1906, and proposed by private member's bill in 1924, they were evaluated by a parliamentary delegation to Germany in 1937, and a toll-financed route from London to Birmingham was surveyed in 1938, but became a casualty of rearmament. This reservation for specific users broke the principles of open access to the king's highway, and required permissive legislation in the Special Roads Act of 1949, a little-known feature of the *Attlee government's integrated transport policy. The first true motorway was the Preston bypass of 1958, precursor to the opening of the first part of the M1 in 1959. The network grew slowly: by April 1963, only 194 miles were open, reaching 957 by 1973, 1,731 in 1984, and 1,969 in 1994.

Motorways cut journey times, halving the coach journey from Birmingham to London in 1960, and reduced fatal accidents to less than half the level of ordinary roads. They spread the commuting zone, especially around London, and shifted industrial location to such as the 'M4 corridor', and in the cities divided communities in ways unknown since the railway. Urban routes led to protest, starting in London's western suburbs over the M4, visible in the destruction of southern Leeds in the 1970s, and developing with the green movement in the 1980s. Space and resource requirements for motorways, their access roads, and service areas were high, around £2 million per mile in 1970, and attracted increasing public criticism as the road transport lobby demanded further investment. In the 1990s, toll- and traffic-charged private finance has been employed to escape the constraints of 'public expenditure', a return to the project of 1938. JCh

Mount Badon, battle of, *c.* AD 500. *Gildas, the chronicler of the decline of Roman Britain, attached great significance to this British victory, which he saw as giving 40 years of respite from the Saxon advance. The most likely sites are Badbury near Swindon, or Baydon near Lambourn, both on the Wiltshire downs. Gildas associated the victory with the resistance led by *Ambrosius Aurelianus: *Nennius in the early 9th cent. introduced the name of King *Arthur and dated it 516. JAC

Mountbatten, Louis Francis Albert Victor Nicholas, 1st Earl Mountbatten of Burma (1900–79). Naval commander and statesman. Mountbatten was born to a family closely related to the house of Windsor. After a spectacular career in the navy and in London high society, in April 1942 he was made commander of combined operations against occupied Europe. In August 1943 he became supreme allied commander for south-east Asia and led the campaign to recover Burma and Malaya from the Japanese. After the war, he showed himself particularly sympathetic to the causes of indigenous nationalism. In December 1946 he was appointed the last viceroy of India to oversee the transfer of power, which took place on 15 August 1947. In 1949 he resumed his naval career and was at the Admiralty, as 1st sea lord, at the time of *Suez, over which he clashed sharply with the *Eden government. He was chief of the defence staff from 1959 to 1965. He was murdered in Ireland by the IRA. DAW

Mountjoy, Charles Blount, 8th Baron (*c.*1562–1606). The Blounts were a Derbyshire family, ennobled by Edward IV as Yorkist supporters in 1465. Charles Blount succeeded his brother in 1594. He had fought in the Low Countries under *Leicester, who had knighted him in 1587, and commanded a ship in the defeat of the Armada. He seems to have made a good impression on Elizabeth and was given the Garter in 1597. His big chance came in 1600 after *Essex, a political ally, had so signally failed to subdue *Tyrone in Ireland. Mountjoy was appointed lord deputy and won a crucial victory in 1601 at *Kinsale when the arrival of a Spanish expedition forced Tyrone to abandon the guerrilla tactics that had been so successful and give battle. By 1603 Tyrone had surrendered. James I reappointed Mountjoy lord-lieutenant of Ireland, made him master of the ordnance, and promoted him earl of Devonshire. A patron of authors, Blount appeared a coming man, but died of inflammation of the lungs at the age of 44. Since the legality of his marriage to Essex's sister was disputed, he left no legitimate heirs. JAC

Mugabe, Robert (b. 1924). Zimbabwean nationalist statesman. Mugabe was a founder-member of the Zimbabwe African National Union (ZANU) in 1963, but was arrested and imprisoned in 1964. He was released in 1975, having become leader of ZANU the previous year. Almost immediately, as joint leader with Joshua *Nkomo of the Patriotic Front, he took up arms against the white-minority government led by Ian *Smith. He played a decisive role in the peace negotiation held in London in 1979, and after the elections held in the following year became Zimbabwe's first African prime minister. His relations with his rival Nkomo followed an uncertain pattern until 1987, when they agreed to form a coalition government with Mugabe as executive president. A convinced Marxist, he hoped to establish a one-party state; however, with the collapse of communism in Eastern Europe he agreed to abandon his plan in 1991 but insisted on redistributing land to benefit Africans. KI

Muggletonians, or 'believers in the third commission', were the followers of Ludowicke Muggleton (1609–98) and his cousin John Reeve (1608–58), the recipients in 1651–2 of revelations for which Reeve was to be the messenger and Muggleton the mouthpiece. Their denial of the Trinity, their claim to be the two witnesses of Revelation 11, and such beliefs as that heaven's government was left to Elijah during the incarnation led to Muggleton's conviction for blasphemy in 1653–4 and again in 1677, and to the controversies with *quakers reflected in William Penn's *New Witnesses Proved Old Heretics* (1672). Their followers survived into the 19th cent. with a reading room in London, but neither preachers nor worship beyond readings of the founder's writings. CB

Munich agreement. 'Munich' has entered the English language as a synonym for betrayal and weakness, and historians continue to debate whether it would have been wiser as well as more honourable for Britain to have risked war rather than to require Czechoslovakia to surrender the Sudetenland to Hitler. At the time (30 September 1938), the commonest feeling in Britain was one of relief. Perhaps the most realistic verdict—given the national unpreparedness for war—was that it was a 'necessary defeat'. Neville *Chamberlain, however, was not negotiating primarily to buy time for rearmament but in the belief that peace was possible. CJB

Municipal Corporations Act, 1835. A corollary to the 1832 parliamentary reform was local government reform. As with the Poor Law, the Whigs prepared the way with a royal commission to investigate the existing municipalities. This apparent willingness to precede reform by systematic inquiry was less than complete. The well-paid post as secretary to the royal commission went to the government's principal electoral manipulator, Joseph *Parkes, whose conduct of the inquiry was partisan. The subsequent Act swept away the existing heterogeneous borough constitutions and replaced them by a standard form of councils consisting of mayor, aldermen, and councillors elected by ratepayers. Provision was made for the establishment of the same system in urban areas like Manchester and Birmingham which were without proper municipal institutions, if local ratepayers approved. The powers of the new councils were narrowly limited and few of them showed much inclination to spend ratepayers' money in expensive schemes of local improvement. NMcC

Munster was ruled by the Eóganacht dynasty from the 7th to the mid-10th cent., who were then overshadowed by Dál Cais, to whom *Brian Boru (d. 1014) belonged. By the 12th cent. Brian's descendants, the O'Briens, were ruling north Munster (Thomond) from their capital at Limerick, while the main branch of the Eóganacht, the MacCarthys, were ruling south Munster (Desmond) from Cork. The province was directly affected by the Anglo-Norman invasion of 1169 which saw widespread colonization, the O'Briens and MacCarthys being confined in the far west. Munster was gradually shired in the 13th cent., and was dominated by powerful Anglo-Irish families such as the Poers (in Waterford), Barrys, Roches (in Cork), the Butler earls of Ormond (Tipperary), and the Geraldine earls of Desmond (north Kerry and Limerick), who became increasingly integrated into Irish society. The establishment of the presidency of Munster in 1570 helped restore English government there, but a Desmond revolt in 1579 led to its plantation by English protestant settlers, and the defeat of the Irish forces at the battle of *Kinsale in 1601 meant the collapse of the Gaelic ascendancy throughout Ireland. The 18th cent. was marked by agrarian disturbances, especially those by the *'Whiteboys', while Ballingarry, Co. Tipperary, was the scene of a futile rebellion by the *Young Irelanders during the Great Famine in 1848. Munster was the focus of much of the guerrilla warfare that characterized the War of Independence, 1919–21. SMD

Murdock, William (1754–1839). Inventor. Murdock was born in Ayrshire and spent almost all his life in the employment of *Boulton and *Watt's firm at Soho. For many years he represented them in Cornwall, where they had sold many pumping-engines, which he maintained. While at Redruth he succeeded in lighting his house by coal-gas and in 1802 there was a great gas illumination at Soho to celebrate the peace of *Amiens. There were difficulties in obtaining a steady light with no objectionable smell but during the 1800s gas lighting was installed in a number of factories and Murdock read a paper on the subject in 1808 to the *Royal Society. He was also interested in the possibility of steam locomotion, though his employers were far from encouraging, and he experimented with compressed air and steam guns. There is a bust of Murdock by *Chantrey in Handsworth church (Birmingham), along with busts of James Watt and Matthew Boulton. JAC

Murphy, Father John (*c.*1753–98). Irish rebel. Murphy was a leader of the Wexford insurgents during the Irish rising of 1798. A local man, he studied in Spain, became a catholic priest, returned to Ireland in 1785, and became an assistant in the parish of Boulavogue. In May 1798 he raised rebellion, defeated some local militia, and advanced to Enniscorthy. Having established a camp on Vinegar Hill, just outside the town, the rebels occupied Wexford, defeating a small government detachment under Colonel Walpole. But an attempt on Arklow was beaten off and Vinegar Hill stormed. Murphy escaped to continue the struggle, hoping to find support among the colliers at Castlecomer in Kilkenny. His fate is not known for certain. He may have been killed in battle on Kilcomney Hill, but it is more likely that he was captured and hanged. JAC

Murray, Andrew (d. 1297). An undeservedly unsung hero of the *Scottish Wars of Independence, he came to the fore in 1297, when most prominent Scots had submitted to Edward I. He master-minded widespread risings in northern Scotland, advanced south with his supporters, and joined forces with William *Wallace. Together they brilliantly exploited English tactical errors at the battle of *Stirling Bridge (11 September 1297) by waiting until the enemy had begun to cross the bridge over the river Forth, and then pouncing to massacre the vanguard while the rest watched helplessly from the other bank. This was the first full-scale defeat inflicted by the Scots in battle with the English since the early 11th cent., and vital in keeping the cause of Scottish independence alive. Wallace went on to invade northern England, but Murray was soon dead, apparently from wounds sustained at Stirling. KJS

Murray, Sir Andrew (1298–1338). Guardian of Scotland, 1332 and 1335–8. A member of the powerful family of de Moravia, he became prominent in 1326 when he married the sister of Robert I. After the death of the earl of Mar at the battle of *Dupplin (1332) Murray succeeded as guardian, but was captured by the English towards the end of the year. Released and returned to office in 1335, he rapidly showed his ability by relieving Kildrummy castle and defeating and killing David of Strathbogie at the battle of Culblean (30 November 1335); recovering Gowrie and the Mearns in 1336; and recapturing his ancestral castle of Bothwell in 1337. His leadership put heart into the Scottish resistance, which was somewhat demoralized by his early death in 1338. He was a guerrilla leader of genius, though criticized for the destruction inevitable in this kind of warfare. BW

Murray, Lord George (1694–1760). Jacobite general. A younger son of the 1st duke of Atholl, a Whig, but an opponent of the 1707 *Union, Lord George returned from France to fight for the Jacobites in the '15 under the leadership of his eldest brother, the marquis of Tullibardine. Escaping to France after failing to secure an indemnity, he returned to Scotland with the Jacobite invasion of 1719. After further exile and service with the Sardinian army, he obtained a pardon and went back to Scotland.

He joined Prince Charles at Perth in August 1745. As lieutenant-general, he was the real Jacobite commander.

To him goes the credit for victory at *Prestonpans, for the retreat from England in the face of superior cavalry, and for the victories at Clifton and *Falkirk. He fought bravely at *Culloden, while disapproving of offering battle. He died in the Netherlands. BPL

Murray, James. See ATHOLL, MARQUIS OF.

Muscovy Company. See RUSSIA COMPANY.

museums. The foundation of museums was an offshoot of the great explosion of knowledge in the early modern period which stemmed from the invention of printing, the voyages of discovery, the new interest in the classical world, and the increase in literacy, and it forms part of the Enlightenment. It is the counterpart of the attempt to classify and explain phenomena which stimulated the publication of encyclopedias and dictionaries, and for years the term *museum* was used to signify a study or library.

It was not unusual for 16th-cent. rulers to have collections, often of a miscellaneous character, partly because they exchanged so many gifts. In Britain the royal family rarely took the lead, but a number of private citizens were avid collectors. Sir Robert Cotton (d. 1631) concentrated largely on manuscripts but also collected coins and fossils. Sir Walter Cope, his contemporary, had an Indian canoe, an Egyptian mummy, and an African necklace made of teeth. John Tradescant opened his 'Ark' at Lambeth, charging sixpence admission, and his son published a catalogue of the curiosities in 1656, claiming a dodo and many non-European plants. A rival commercial collection was Robert Hubert's, near St Paul's, who claimed 'thousands of other rarities of nature'. This collection, though primarily a museum of oddities, was purchased by the *Royal Society, which could not look after it and eventually gave it to the *British Museum. Museums long retained their quirky and unusual character and *Johnson defined them in the 1750s as 'repositories of learned curiosities'. Tradescant junior bequeathed his collection to Elias Ashmole, who left it to Oxford University. The Ashmolean Museum opened in 1683 in what is now the Museum of the History of Science, and the general public was admitted on payment. The Balfour collection in Scotland, handed over in 1697 to the University of Edinburgh had a less happy fate, and was neglected and dispersed.

The change from private cabinets to public museums, initiated by the Ashmolean, was continued in 1753 by the foundation of the British Museum. Sir Hans Sloane (d. 1753) had a collection of more than 100,000 specimens, many of them plants from the West Indies, which he had visited. He left it to the nation, and the new museum, supported by a lottery, also incorporated the Harleian and Cottonian collections. Although the public was admitted, it was on a very restricted scale, and the principal librarian in the 19th cent. defended Saturday and Sunday closing on the grounds that it kept out 'sailors and girls whom they might bring with them'.

A great increase in museums, national and provincial, followed. The National Museum of Antiquities of Scotland was founded in 1780, the Royal Scottish Museum in 1854, the two amalgamating in 1985. The Ulster Museum began in 1831, becoming the national museum in 1961. The National Museum of Wales opened in 1907. The *Victoria and Albert Museum (1852) and the *Science Museum at south Kensington were part of a great complex triggered by the *Great Exhibition of 1851. Most of the national museums have branches: the Science Museum runs the railway museum at York and the Museum of Photography, Film, and TV at Bradford. In addition to the great national museums, municipal museums were founded, assisted by friendly legislation: an Act for encouraging the establishment of museums in large towns (1845) permitted the raising of a halfpenny rate. The Liverpool Museum opened in 1851, the Birmingham Museum in 1885. In the 20th cent. the emphasis has been on specialist collections—the National Maritime Museum (1934), the Royal Air Force Museum (1963), and a host of smaller museums devoted to motor cycles, trams, cider, musical instruments, costume, and teddy bears. Museum complexes such as the Ironbridge Trust at Coalbrookdale and open-air museums like Beamish in Co. Durham have proved very successful. After 1945 there was a determined effort to make museums less forbidding, to remove the glass cases and drawers, and to use displays, films, and hands-on working models. Many villages have their own splendidly idiosyncratic local collections, even if they are housed in huts and open only on Tuesday afternoons. JAC

music, development of. The history of British music is inevitably coloured by geographical, political, and social factors. Continental influences loom large, although at times, as in the 15th cent., a distinctive English voice can be heard and the influence becomes reciprocal. The traditional perception of British music—that of a Tudor golden age followed after the death of *Purcell by near-terminal decline only halted by an 'English Renaissance' at the end of the 19th cent.—is unjust, stemming from a fruitless search for individual composers to rank beside Purcell, *Elgar, or *Britten rather than a willingness to value more general 18th- and 19th-cent. developments.

Early musical history in Britain is largely a matter for conjecture, for no music has survived. There is evidence from the 7th cent. onward that the harp was popular throughout Britain, remaining to this day the traditional Welsh instrument. It was a common form of accompaniment for *minstrels, allowing the singer his own flexible accompaniment. Part-singing clearly existed by the 12th cent., when *Gerald of Wales observed that the Welsh sang not in unison, as in other countries, but in 'as many parts as there are singers'. *Bede tells of the use of Roman chant in the 7th cent., although the earliest extant liturgical manuscripts of polyphony are the two 11th-cent. Winchester tropers, containing two-part *organum* in which a free part is added note-against-note to an original plainsong. The organ was also used liturgically at this time, alongside solo and choral singing, whilst the most famous piece of English medieval music, the six-part canonic 'Sumer is icumen in', also has an alternative Latin text.

The Old Hall Manuscript, the earliest of several important 15th-cent. English manuscripts, contains primarily mass movements. Many pieces are, unusually, attributed to specific composers, including Leonel Power, *Dunstable, and 'Roy Henry', probably Henry V. Note-against-note technique is again prominent, although canon and isorhythm (a structural principle applying the same rhythmic pattern to repetitions of a plainsong melody) are also employed. Around 1500 the Eton Choirbook, a collection of polyphonic antiphons and Magnificats for the chapel at Eton College, looms large in every sense, as its 23-inch by 17-inch format allowed it to be read from a lectern by the choir. As with the Old Hall music, consonance and sonority are all-important, but now textures are more complex, with intricate ornamental rhythms and a greater number of parts allowing a much wider pitch range. A similar massive style can be seen in contemporary Scottish music, most notably the five masses by Robert Carver with their granite-like blocks of harmony, while in secular music the carol was popular for its memorable, simple melodies and repeated refrains.

At the Reformation, Henry VIII's suppression of the monasteries and collegiate churches meant that cathedral choirs and the Chapel Royal became the main musical centres. The imposition of the *Book of Common Prayer in 1549 was accompanied by the publication of various metrical psalters, whose simple four-part harmonizations of psalm tunes allowed the vernacular texts to be heard easily. Nevertheless, Elizabeth I's catholic sympathies allowed composers such as *Byrd to write much Latin church music, including three fine masses, alongside complex Anglican services. Imitation between the voices now becomes a basic structural principle, while many works, particularly those in Latin such as *Tallis's *Lamentations*, are powerfully expressive.

This high-point in British music coincided with a rise in music printing, something that also contributed to the popularity of the English *madrigal, a genre originally imported from Italy. Instigated by Yonge's *Musica transalpina* (1588), it flourished for the next couple of decades with works by Morley, Weelkes, Wilbye, and *Gibbons (composers who were all primarily church musicians). The rise in amateur music-making is also reflected in the importance of instrumental music, many works of the period being published as 'apt for Viols and Voyces', allowing some or all the voices to be replaced or doubled by instruments. Music specifically for viol consorts became increasingly sophisticated, with elaborate contrapuntal fantasias or 'Fancies'. Complex solo lute and keyboard works became virtuoso showpieces, culminating in the brilliant sets of variations in the *Fitzwilliam Virginal Book*. John *Dowland, the leading lutenist of his day, also raised the lute song to unsurpassed heights.

As with the Reformation, so the Civil War and the Restoration had a profound impact on music. Cathedral choirs were disbanded and organs dismantled, although, ironically, the puritan closure of public theatres in 1642 seems to have encouraged composers to experiment briefly with all-sung opera rather than the traditional mixture of spoken dialogue and music found in the Stuart *masque. During his exile Charles II had acquired French tastes, and his Restoration encouraged strong continental influences in music. Pelham Humfrey and Purcell brought a new, incisive style of string music to the Chapel Royal anthem as violins replaced the old viols, much to the horror of John *Evelyn, who felt it 'better suiting a tavern or a Play-house than a church'. Solo 'verse' sections exploited the virtuosity of singers, something also featured in the ode—celebratory music for court occasions or for St Cecilia's Day.

Continental music continued to loom large into the 18th cent., both in the opera-house, where *Handel's success created a vogue for Italian opera, and in instrumental music, where the popularity of Corelli's sonatas and concertos influenced numerous composers, including Handel and Geminiani in England and John Clerk in Scotland. Amateur interest in music steadily increased. Instrumental tutors were published and glees (simple part-songs for male voices) became popular. Handel's oratorios appealed to an increasingly middle-class audience, and England led the way in the field of public concerts, held in both halls and pleasure gardens. The Bach–Abel concerts ran from 1764 to 1782, while the impresario Salomon brought Haydn to London in the 1790s and commissioned his last twelve symphonies.

Music flourished in the provinces as well as in London, with the establishment of the *Three Choirs (*c.*1715), Birmingham (1768), and Norwich (1770) festivals, and the Edinburgh Musical Society (1720). A flourishing tradition of amateur choral singing built on the popularity of Handel's oratorios, especially **Messiah*; the Huddersfield Choral Society was founded in 1836, while the première of Mendelssohn's *Elijah* (Birmingham, 1846) typified the trend for British commissions from leading European composers. John Curwen's tonic sol-fa method for sight-singing was much used in schools and by choirs, especially Welsh male-voice choirs. This lasting tradition was fostered by the *Eisteddfod, a festival held annually since 1880 but whose origins go back to the medieval bards, which has provided a focus for a national cultural identity. Many other British competitive festivals grew up, some involving the new vogue for *brass bands.

The upsurge in music publishing at the beginning of the 19th cent. and the mass production of pianos by firms like Broadwood coincided with the presence of many foreign pianists in London (including Clementi, Dussek, Cramer, and *Field). The piano became the main domestic instrument of Victorian Britain, where it was also used to accompany the singing of drawing-room ballads. In the opera-house, British composers remained overshadowed by their European contemporaries; the title 'The Royal Italian Opera' indicates the dominance of the Italian language into which even works by Mozart and Wagner were translated. Apart from the brilliant success of *Gilbert and *Sullivan's operettas, a true native style is difficult to identify. Outside the theatre, *Parry, *Stanford, and even that most 'English' of composers, Elgar, still spoke a predominantly Germanic musical language. The revival of interest in folk-song, spearheaded by Cecil Sharp, and in Tudor music, encouraged by the many editions from E. H. Fellowes, nevertheless fostered a new sense of 'nationalism' particularly in the work of *Vaughan Williams and other English songwriters.

The 1945 première of Britten's *Peter Grimes* marked a new era. With a flair, unmatched since Purcell, for setting the English language, Britten's blend of traditional techniques with real dramatic understanding helped re-establish English opera, alongside the grittier, psychologically orientated works of *Tippett. The founding of several fine orchestras, including the London Philharmonic, Royal Philharmonic, and three BBC orchestras in the 1930s and 1940s, established Britain's leading role in concerts and recordings. The British Broadcasting Corporation took over the Henry Wood *Promenade Concerts in 1927 and has played a leading role in commissioning new works and encouraging new artists. The excellence of British orchestras, opera companies, and international festivals such as those at Edinburgh and Aldeburgh has become increasingly threatened by low state subsidies; the present disregard for the Arts Council bodes ill for music in 21st-cent. Britain.

See also FOLK-SONG; OPERA. ECr

Caldwell, J., *The Oxford History of English Music: From the Beginnings to c.1715* (Oxford, 1991); Meckerness, E. D., *A Social History of English Music* (London, 1964); Young, P. M., *A History of British Music* (1967).

music-halls flourished in the second half of the 19th cent., but were under competition before 1914 from picture houses and after 1922 from radio. They have been subjected to deadening Marxist analysis as 'the dominant form of cultural production in the context of a modernizing capitalist society' and were indeed socially conditioned, since they provided mass entertainment in the new large industrial towns. They developed from a variety of sources—from the music and acrobatics offered at pleasure gardens like *Vauxhall and *Ranelagh and from sing-songs at local taverns. The Eagle, in City Road, London (commemorated in 'Pop goes the weasel'), was an early concert hall and in 1838 the Rotunda in Southwark advertised itself as a music-hall. The first music-halls served food and drink at tables: only gradually was drink eliminated and the audience placed in rows of seats. Since the halls were of doubtful respectability and had frequent brushes with authority, the audience was predominantly working class or lower middle class, though middle-class patrons and even respectable ladies were more in evidence towards the end of the century.

The 'father of the music-hall' was Charles Morton, who opened the Canterbury at Lambeth in 1851 and transferred to the Oxford in 1861. By 1875 there were more than 300 music-halls in London and they were well established in the larger provincial towns: indeed, the Star at Bolton in 1832 has some claim to have been the first music-hall. They produced their own stars. Dan Leno's career began in the 1860s almost as soon as he could walk, and he died in 1904 at the age of 43. Marie *Lloyd made her début at the Eagle in 1885 with a repertoire that included 'The boy I love is up in the gallery'. She too burned out and died relatively young in 1922. The careers of Harry *Lauder and Gracie *Fields were taking off as Leno's came to an end. The final blow to the music-hall tradition came with the spread of television in the 1950s, though *The Good Old Days*, from Leeds, had a long nostalgic run as a TV programme in the 1970s. JAC

Mutiny Act. Before the *Glorious Revolution, James II had collected a large army on Hounslow Heath to intimidate London. The *Bill of Rights in 1689 declared that a standing army in peacetime was illegal without parliamentary consent and the procedure was adopted of passing an annual Mutiny Act which authorized the imposition of military discipline. The navy had been under statutory authority since 1661 and was less politically delicate since the fleet could hardly be used to threaten public liberties. In 1784 the Fox–North coalition toyed with the idea of rejecting the Mutiny Bill as a means of getting rid of William *Pitt's minority government, but flinched from so drastic an action. The system was reorganized by the Army Discipline and Regulation Act of 1879. JAC

Myddleton, Sir Hugh (*c.*1560–1631). The sixth son of Richard Myddleton, governor of Denbigh castle, and younger brother of Thomas, the much-married lord mayor of London, Hugh Myddleton was sent to London to train as a goldsmith/banker. Nevertheless he retained his connections with Denbigh and represented the borough in Parliament six times between 1603 and 1628. Interested in cloth-making, engineering, and sea trade, he is best remembered for his entrepreneurial feat of constructing the *New River, an artificial waterway created to improve London's water supply. Faced with difficulties from recalcitrant landowners and political opponents, the scheme eventually necessitated financial rescue by the king himself. It was completed by 1613, but the New River Company paid no dividends until 1633, and prospered only after 1640. In recognition of Myddleton's engineering skill and enterprise, James I confirmed his lease of the mines royal in Cardiganshire, and created him a baronet in 1622. ASH

Mynydd Carn, battle of, 1081. After 1066 Norman pressure began on north and south Wales, and a period of confused fighting among the Welsh princes ensued. But at Mynydd Carn, near St Davids, *Gruffydd ap Cynan and *Rhys ap Tewdwr defeated and killed their rivals Trahaearn, Caradog ap Gruffydd, and Meilys ap Rhiwallon of Powys, and established the supremacy of *Gwynedd and *Deheubarth. JAC

mystery plays. Best preserved of the vernacular religious drama which flourished in England, as on the continent, in the high Middle Ages, the mystery plays were known as 'the play of Corpus Christi', since originally performed at that festival. They versify and dramatize the biblical and apocryphal narrative of man's fall and salvation from Creation to Doomsday, with emphasis on Christ's trial, death, resurrection, and harrowing of hell. The plays offered religious instruction, entertainment, and a boost to civic pride and commercial interests. Their dramatic impact was enhanced by music, special effects, and moments of comedy, and their contemporary relevance by the presentation, for instance, of high priests as bishops, and shepherds as medieval Yorkshiremen.

Major cycles survive from York (51 short plays) and Chester (25), together with documentation about their performance by trade guilds or 'mysteries' on wagons in the streets.

The 32 'Towneley' plays are plausibly associated with Wakefield, and the 42 N-Town plays (formerly 'Hegge' plays or, misleadingly, *Ludus Coventriae*) tentatively with Lincoln or Norwich. One or two plays each survive from Coventry, Newcastle, Norwich, and Northampton, and records, but no texts, from several towns from Aberdeen to Canterbury. Suppressed by the protestant hierarchy around the 1570s, performance of the plays has enjoyed a revival since 1951. DCW

Myton, battle of, 1319. While Edward II was besieging Berwick in 1319, Robert I Bruce sent Sir James *Douglas and the earl of *Moray on a diversionary raid, deep into Yorkshire. They were confronted at Myton-on-Swale, just east of Boroughbridge, by a scratch army hastily collected by William Melton, archbishop of York. The Scots routed their opponents and Edward abandoned the siege. So many clerics joined the archbishop that the episode was known sardonically as the Chapter of Myton. JAC

nabobs, a corruption of the Urdu *nawab*, a governor or nobleman, was the fashionable term for men who had returned from India with ample fortunes, and often a taste for lavish living and political advancement. They were satirized by Samuel Foote in a highly successful play, *The Nabob*, put on at the Haymarket in 1772. Well-known nabobs included *Clive, Sir Robert Fletcher, General Richard Smith, Sir Francis Sykes, and Paul Benfield. JAC

Najerá, battle of, 1367. This engagement, fought in northern Spain, contributed much to the renown of *Edward, the Black Prince. He had intervened in Castile to assist Peter II (the Cruel), deposed by his half-brother, Henry of Trastamara. The victory on 3 April restored Peter to power. Within two years, however, Trastamara had regained the throne, this time with French help, and the Black Prince, having never received the financial reward Peter had promised, was forced to increase taxation in his principality of Aquitaine to cover the cost of his Spanish expedition. The battle is also known as Navarrete. AC

Namibia. After much missionary activity, South West Africa was annexed by Germany in 1884. After the First World War, the territory was administered as a mandate by South Africa. In 1966 the United Nations ended the mandate but South Africa retained control in the face of an increasing guerrilla war, waged by the South West Africa People's Organization. In 1990 the territory became independent and a SWAPO government was established. Much of the area is barren and the population is sparse. The main economic activity is the extraction of diamonds, uranium, and copper. JAC

Nanking, treaty of, 1842. The first *Chinese War 1839–42 originated when the Chinese authorities seized and destroyed large quantities of opium, which British merchants were importing. After sporadic military and naval actions, the Chinese emperor agreed to open up trade, pay compensation for the loss of the opium, and cede *Hong Kong. Queen Victoria wrote that 'Albert is very much amused at my having got the island of Hong Kong.' JAC

Nantwich, battle of, 1644. Throughout the Civil War, Charles I entertained excessive hopes of assistance from Ireland. In the summer of 1643 he negotiated an armistice with the catholic Confederacy, permitting a number of Irish royalists to cross to England. Lord *Byron, holding Chester for the king, sought to organize them and in January 1644 was laying siege to Nantwich. He was attacked on 24 January by Sir Thomas *Fairfax and Sir William Brereton, and though he got his cavalry away, lost most of his new infantry, killed or captured. JAC

Napier, Sir Charles James (1782–1853). Soldier. Napier was commissioned into the army at the age of 12 thanks to the patronage of his cousin and namesake, Charles James *Fox. He served in the Peninsular War (1808–11) and in the American War (1812–14). From 1819 to 1830 he was a military resident in Greece and was offered command of the Greek liberation army, which he declined for reasons of penury. In 1839 he was appointed military commander of the north of England during the chartist revolt. In 1841 he accepted a lucrative Indian staff appointment and, amidst considerable controversy, provoked the conquest of Sindh from which he made £50,000 in loot. He announced his victory with the famous signal 'Peccavi' ('I have sinned'). He left India in 1847 but returned in 1849 as commander-in-chief of the Indian army. However, he clashed with the governor-general, Lord *Dalhousie, and resigned in 1851. DAW

Napier, John (1550–1617). Mathematician. Napier invented logarithms, greatly simplifying calculations involving multiplying and dividing. As Kepler put it, he doubled the life of astronomers (by halving the time they took number-crunching). He was 8th laird of Merchiston. Educated in France and then at St Andrews, he published his *Mirifici logarithmorum canonis descriptio* in 1614, with tables and explanations. The basic principle was to reduce multiplication to addition by using powers: thus $10^2 \times 10^3 = 10^5$. In the course of 20 years' work, he came up with the base 10 for logarithms, so that the examples above would be 2, 3, and 5. In 1617, he published *Rabdologia*, describing 'Napier's bones', or rods calibrated logarithmically; as developed into the slide rule, this was essential in science and engineering until the electronic calculator was invented. DK

Napier, Robert, 1st Baron Napier (1810–90). Soldier. Napier was born in Ceylon and almost all his career was in India. Entering the Bengal Engineers in 1826, he was twice wounded in the 1840s in the *Sikh wars, and was wounded for a third time while defending *Lucknow in the *Indian mutiny of 1857. He was knighted in 1858. He served in the *China War and in 1867 commanded an expedition to Abyssinia where the eccentric King Theodore was holding English representatives prisoner. Napier defeated the royal troops at Magdala, the new capital, and King Theodore shot himself. Napier was given a barony in 1868, was commander-in-chief in India 1870–6, served as governor of Gibraltar 1876–82, and finished as a field marshal in 1883. JAC

Naseby, battle of, 1645. The battle in the first civil war that extinguished royalist hopes which, after the defeat at *Marston Moor, had rested largely on *Montrose's brilliant Scottish campaign. In May 1645 Prince *Rupert captured Leicester, forcing the parliamentarians to raise the siege of Oxford. The armies met on 14 June 1645 at Naseby, 12 miles east of Rugby. After initial success, the royalists were heavily defeated by superior forces. Even more damaging than the casualties was the loss of Charles's private correspondence, published by Parliament to the world as proof of his duplicity. Though fighting continued for a further year, the king was never able to put another major army into the field. JAC

Nash, John (1752–1835). Born in London, the son of a millwright, Nash was the most successful English architect of the early 19th cent. After a short apprenticeship, he enjoyed early success on his own account before money troubles forced him to retire to Wales, where he rapidly recovered financially, designing houses for the local gentry. His first public commission was Carmarthen county gaol. Returning to London, Nash quickly built up a large practice, at first in partnership with Humphry *Repton, the landscape designer, then on his own, producing designs in an enormous range of styles. For most of his life he worked on grand projects for the prince regent, in particular on a most imaginative scheme for a garden city in the heart of London. Much of the work was completed by Nash's death, but now only Regent's Park remains as envisaged. Buildings as varied as All Souls', Langham Place, Marble Arch, and the Pavilion at Brighton point to Nash's imagination and eclecticism. JC

Nash, Paul (1889–1946). Painter and graphic artist. Originally intended for the navy, Nash failed to qualify and went to study art at the Slade School. Wounded during the 1914–18 war, he was appointed an official war artist and examples of his work from this time, *We are Making a New World* and *The Menin Road*, are in the Imperial War Museum. In the 1920s and 1930s Nash became established as one of the most individual painters of his day. Essentially a landscape artist, who saw himself as a successor to *Blake and *Turner, and influenced by modern European movements, his work was imbued with deep, sometimes prophetic symbolism. In the Second World War, he was again an official war artist; his *Totes Meer* (Dead Sea) and *Bomber in the Corn* hang in the Tate Gallery. He was also highly successful as a fabric and scenery designer, photographer, writer, and book illustrator. JC

Nash, Richard (1674–1762), later known as 'Beau' Nash. Son of a Swansea glass-maker, and briefly lured by the scarlet, Nash entered the Inner Temple (1693), but his self-assurance, good manners, and dress concealed penury, hence his resort to preposterous wagers. Addiction to gaming drew him to Bath (1705), which, although fashionable, had few arrangements for comfort or entertainment. Good organizational skill and energy led to a position as master of ceremonies (later, additionally, at Tunbridge Wells), where, mixing kindness, generosity, conceit, and cynicism, he crusaded against overcharging, duelling, and informality. Although 'arbiter elegantarium', he was primarily a professional gamester, so the 1739 and 1745 Acts against organized gambling undermined successively his income, display, and then authority. Despite his contributions to Bath's prosperity and the establishment of its Mineral Water Hospital, the corporation coldly watched its uncrowned king slide into poverty, but interred him in Bath abbey. ASH

Natal. Former British colony in South Africa. British traders and missionaries settled at Port Natal (Durban) in 1824. A British colony was declared in 1843 to check the spread of Afrikaner influence in the region and British settlers were officially encouraged though their numbers were never large in comparison with the black population. Sheep-farming and, at the coast, sugar-growing were the main sources of wealth. The dismemberment of Zululand in the 1880s and 1890s extended the boundaries of the colony and in 1910 the colonists reluctantly accepted the inclusion of their country within the South African Union. KI

national anthem. First published in recognizable form in 1744 (ambiguously as 'God save our Lord the King') but performed at Drury Lane, September 1745, specifically naming King George in response to the Jacobite threat, it was essentially a compilation of loyal phrases set to a recast Tudor galliard, and merely a patriotic song. Rapidly gaining widespread popularity, it was known as the national anthem by 1819 despite its anti-Scots references (still balefully resented by some north of the border). Subsequent political parodies, 'improvements', church use, translations, and overseas adoptions have made it one of the world's best-known tunes. ASH

national debt. Throughout history governments have had difficulty in maintaining the balance between income and expenditure, since the former relies on the raising of taxation which is seldom popular. The national debt is the excess of expenditure over revenue, often accumulated over many years and financed by borrowing. This debt grew markedly in the 18th cent. as a result of involvement in numerous wars. (See FINANCIAL REVOLUTION.) The Napoleonic wars lasted for a quarter of a century and were especially expensive. Public expenditure fell to a more modest scale throughout the 19th cent. and the national debt actually fell. It escalated in the 20th cent. as a result of war and the increasing state obligations for welfare payments such as social security and pensions. At the beginning of the century, public spending stood at about 10 per cent of national income, but since the Second World War it has varied in the 40–50 per cent range. But the rapid inflation in the 1970s created a large imbalance between taxation and expenditure and thus increased the deficit. The national debt, now more usually known as the public sector borrowing requirement, has recently ranged between 6 and 8 per cent of national income. CHL

National Front. Established from several small extremist right-wing organizations in 1967, the National Front came to prominence in the 1970s after capitalizing on fears of increasing numbers of immigrants, whipped up by politicians like Enoch Powell. Although never close to winning a seat in Parliament, it had strong support in parts of London, the midlands, and some northern cities. After reaching a peak in early 1977, support declined, with a poor showing in the 1978 local elections. The decline was exacerbated by growing public criticism of its leadership, the adoption of restrictive policies on immigration by the Conservatives, and the growth of an active anti-fascist movement. The 1979 general election saw the National Front receive only 1.3 per cent of the vote. In 1982 the chairman, John Tyndall, left to form the British National Party, which has since supplanted the National Front on the extreme right. LHM

national galleries. Towards the end of the 18th cent., after most of the principal national galleries of Europe had opened, the idea of a National Gallery in London began to be discussed. During the 1820s two notable collections, of Sir George Beaumont and the Revd W. Holwell Carr, were promised to the nation and the Treasury was persuaded to purchase 38 paintings from the estate of city broker John Julius Angerstein. This growing national collection soon outgrew its first home in the Angerstein house in Pall Mall and in 1838 a new building housing the Royal Academy (until 1869) and the National Gallery opened in Trafalgar Square. Treasury grants, generous gifts, loans, and bequests allowed the collection to grow and the gallery to become one of the best and most representative in the world.

The National Gallery of Scotland opened in Edinburgh in 1859, with pictures from the Royal Institution, the Royal Scottish Academy, and the University of Edinburgh. Despite receiving no Treasury aid before 1906, the collection grew by discerning purchase, loans, and bequests. Assistance from the National Heritage Memorial Fund and the National Art Collections Fund has enabled some exceptional and controversial acquisitions, most notably the joint purchase with the Victoria and Albert Museum in London of Canova's sculpture *The Three Graces* in 1995. In 1960 a separate Scottish National Gallery of Modern Art was established for painting, sculpture, and graphic art of the 20th cent.

In Dublin, there was talk of a national art collection in the 1760s, yet it was not until 1864, following a successful exhibition paid for by railway owner William Dargan, that a National Gallery, Library, and Museum was opened. As in London and Edinburgh, the collection grew by Treasury funds, private donation, and gifts. A most generous bequest was that of Sir Hugh Lane, director of the Gallery, who died in the sinking of the liner *Lusitania* in 1915. His will gave almost his entire estate to the gallery. JC

National Government. The Labour government of Ramsay *MacDonald in 1931 faced a severe economic crisis with more than 2 million unemployed and a run on the pound. It fell in August when the cabinet split on a proposal to cut unemployment benefit. MacDonald consulted *Baldwin, leader of the Conservative Party, and Sir Herbert *Samuel, leading the Liberals during the illness of Lloyd George. Samuel urged a coalition and Baldwin agreed to serve under MacDonald. Intended as a temporary measure, the coalition stayed in power until the Second World War when *Churchill in 1940 formed a wartime national government. MacDonald's new cabinet contained four Conservative ministers, four Labour, and two Liberals, but the great majority of the parliamentary Labour party repudiated the deal and expelled MacDonald. In the general election which followed in October 1931, the National Government won a landslide victory with 473 Conservative seats, 35 National Liberals, and 13 National Labour, against a Labour opposition reduced to 52 seats. Baldwin replaced MacDonald as prime minister in June 1935, dissolved in November, and won a handsome majority, though Labour went up to 154 seats. Baldwin gave way to Neville *Chamberlain in 1937. In Labour demonology, MacDonald was the arch class and political traitor and the National Government a Tory sham. The poor showing of National Labour in the 1931 election (when MacDonald was himself beaten at Seaham) gave support to the second opinion, but MacDonald was under the impression that he was putting country before party and probably committing political suicide. A majority of his Labour cabinet had, after all, supported the unemployment benefit cut. George V's role has also been criticized. He urged MacDonald to remain as prime minister. But monarchs are often disposed to favour governments of national unity and the king had acted on the advice of the three party leaders. JAC

National Health Service. Established in 1948, the NHS grew out of the Second World War's reconstruction planning of social and medical services, after long debate over health-care provision (Dawson Report, 1920; Cathcart Report, 1936; Sankey Commission, 1937). The 1942 *Beveridge Report assumed that a satisfactory social security scheme depended on 'comprehensive health and rehabilitation services for prevention and cure of disease and restoration of the capacity to work', available to all the community. The subsequent deadlock arising from self-interested opposition was broken by Aneurin *Bevan, who established a tripartite administration: local authorities (for existing clinics and new health centres), panel practice, and nationalized hospitals (conceding some private practice for consultants, and giving teaching hospitals special status). Since the new service was entirely free to patients, funding had to come from taxation, but Beveridge's view that costs would lessen as the nation's health slowly improved had not allowed for the massive backlog of unmet need nor for technological advances such as joint replacements. The introduction of charges for prescriptions, dental, and ophthalmic treatment (1951) led to Bevan's resignation on grounds of principle. Accusations of extravagance proved unfounded (Guillebaud Report, 1956), and hospital-building, application of medical advances, and staff expansion continued to be sustained by economic growth. Under the aims of improved management and services, the 1960s saw recommendations for the abolition of tripartite administration (new structure implemented 1974), with such reorganization being associated with more professional management. But implementation of policies formulated in a more confident economic climate led to increasing criticism of the use of business theory to solve the NHS's financial problems. Total spending continued to rise. As resources were shifted away from patient care into administration, justifications for internal markets to produce savings were unconvincing to many commentators; economies from ward/hospital closures or sale of assets seemed illusory, while the morale of many NHS employees plummeted. The opting-out of newly formed hospital trusts from local health board control and introduction of fund-holding for general practitioners threatened to recreate earlier inequality and fragmentation, despite the perceived need for better community and preventive medicine. Though the widespread consensus of earlier decades had been shattered by the strains of 1980s' confrontational government (despite assurances that the NHS remained in safe hands), public confidence in the service continued high. ASH

national hunt. See HORSE-RACING.

National Insurance. In 1911 the *Asquith government, reflecting changes in public attitudes towards the causes and cures for poverty, passed the National Insurance Act—Health and Unemployment, which introduced sickness and unemployment benefits to be paid for out of employers' and employees' contributions. This was the beginning of the contributory, non-means-tested half of the British social security system; in 1925 state insurance for contributory old-age pensions was added.

The 1946 National Insurance Act, based on the principles of the *Beveridge Report (1942), established a comprehensive national social insurance scheme: employers, employees, and the self-employed were to make contributions, which would make the insured and their families eligible to receive categorical benefits when they suffered the contingencies insured against—unemployment, sickness and invalidity, widowhood and old age. Though the original intention was to create a fund of income-producing assets, the system was unfunded, based on the pay-as-you-go principle, with current contributors paying for the benefits of current recipients. MW

nationalism is a sense of shared identity and loyalty, based upon common history, language, culture, and traditions. Though it has much in common with religious and local loyalties, it may be distinguished since it almost invariably aims to be the basis of government. Its origins and development have been much disputed, since different attributes may appear at different times, and progress towards national self-determination is unlikely to be regular and uneventful. Within the same nation there often exist severe disagreements and deep enmities. To separate nationalism from regionalism or particularism is difficult and may well depend upon the eye of the observer. Yorkshire is clearly not a nation, though it has 5 million people and well-defined characteristics: Denmark and Catalonia, with 5 and 6 million, clearly are nations.

The tendency of recent scholarship has been to see the roots of European nationalisms deep in the past rather than regarding them as essentially 19th-cent. phenomena. A sense of English nationalism seems to have developed during the campaigns to drive back the Danes, though for centuries mistrust between Northumbria, Wessex, Mercia, and East Anglia persisted. It was reinforced after 1066 by resentment of Norman-French domination. But ironically the Normans did much to create a powerful state, which the English succeeded in recapturing in the 13th and 14th cents. The thrust of Norman advance into other regions of the British Isles stimulated rival nationalisms in turn. The military campaigns led by *Wallace and Robert I Bruce, culminating in the declaration of *Arbroath (1320), and those in Wales led by *Llywelyn ap Gruffydd and *Glyndŵr gained wide popular support because they convinced many people that they fought to liberate Scotsmen and Welshmen from English oppression.

From the personal union of England and Scotland in 1603, and more particularly from the governmental union in 1707, strenuous efforts were made to encourage a sense of British nationalism. Though an artificial concept, it was not ignoble and attracted much support. While accompanied by military success, imperial achievement, and economic growth, it flourished. In the 20th cent., and especially after 1945, as economic and political problems multiplied, the concept of British nationalism faltered and Celtic nationalist parties began to have some success. Ironically, the Conservative Party, which has always drawn most of its support from England, has strongly endorsed British nationalism, with its identification with the monarchy and its use of the Union Jack. Conversely, a completely independent Scotland and Wales (with no representation at Westminster) could well be a fatal blow to the electoral chances of the Labour Party.

Ireland always presented particular problems for the idea of a British people to parallel a British state. The link between protestantism and Britishness made governments reluctant to let the catholic majority in Ireland share the rights upon which popular Britishness became based, while the willingness of some catholics to look to Spain, France, or Germany for assistance encouraged the English to regard them as potential traitors. In addition, many members of the protestant ascendancy developed an Irish identity of their own and campaigns for increased powers for the Irish Parliament were led in the 18th cent. by protestants like *Grattan and Wolfe *Tone. They were inhibited however from playing the Irish card too strongly by their ambivalence towards the catholic Irish and by their need for English assistance should there be another catholic revolt, as there had been in 1641.

Concessions to the Irish catholics after the Act of *Union of 1801 ('too little, too late' is the easy cliché) failed to prevent the growth of a more militant Irish nationalism, which in turn led to the development of protestant resistance to *Home Rule ('loyalism') and ultimately to the partition of

Ireland in 1921. Since the protestant minority in the south was small, Eire was able to transform its ethno-religious nationalism into a more secular civic form, though the catholic church retains a special position in the constitution. In Northern Ireland, the existence of a large catholic minority, with powerful friends, meant that ethnic nationalism remained the basis of politics, the protestant majority justifying discrimination on the grounds that the catholics were dangerous aliens. But since the claims of Ulster protestants to be British were based on views of religion and history that had waning appeal on the mainland, they were frequently disappointed in the support they could expect and constantly haunted by fear of a British betrayal.

In Wales, the survival of the Welsh language has given a cultural focus to nationalism. In the 19th cent. dissatisfaction with the power of Anglicized landlords and the privileged position of the Anglican church was used by the Liberal Party to mobilize a Welsh-speaking population, already undergoing a cultural revival. But the take-over of the Welsh Liberal Party by Lloyd George's nationalist cultural-political Cymru Fydd movement was halted by English-speaking south Wales Liberals in 1896, demonstrating, as events in the 20th cent. were to prove, that nationalist appeals based upon language tended to alienate the English-speaking majority in Wales. Consequently, the close links between the Welsh nationalist party, *Plaid Cymru, and language preservation groups has inhibited its political potential. Its first by-election victory was in Carmarthen in 1966, and by the 1992 general election its strength in Welsh-speaking areas returned four MPs, but support in English-speaking south Wales has been low.

Nationalism in modern Scotland emerged as the autonomy of civil society and local government obtained by the Act of Union of 1707 began to be eroded by the increased speed of communications, the integration of the British economy, and the expansion of the Westminster government's powers of intervention. The resentment of Whitehall, found in many regions, could take a nationalist form in Scotland. But although agitation secured the re-establishment of a Scottish secretary in the cabinet (1885) and led to the foundation of a Scottish Home Rule Association (1886), Scottish nationalism did not mobilize the masses. Scotland in the early 20th cent. turned increasingly to Labour, which had powerful reasons for not pursuing Scottish nationalism *à l'outrance*. Conservative and Labour lack of interest in Home Rule led to the foundation of the National Party of Scotland (1928), which metamorphosed into the *Scottish National Party (SNP) in 1934.

The decline in class-based voting in the 1960s, coupled with increasing dislike of economic and political centralization, and optimism that North Sea oil could provide a rosy future, led the SNP to shock by-election victories at Hamilton (1967) and Govan (1973). At the October 1974 general election, the SNP took 30 per cent of the Scottish vote and eleven seats. Although the SNP's challenge declined after the inconclusive devolution referendum in 1979, the Thatcher years were widely seen in Scotland as government by an English nationalist. Labour and the Liberals increasingly appropriated Scottish nationalist rhetoric, creating a climate where the SNP and the idea of Scottish independence increased in popularity.

The tactical dilemma for those who, for whatever reasons, do not wish to see the breakup of Britain remains much as it was during the debates on Home Rule for Ireland in the 19th cent. Would devolution or some form of Home Rule defuse or stimulate demands for total independence? And if Northern Ireland, Scotland, and Wales were to go down the path of independence or devolution, what about Cornwall and the north of England? In the 1970s the Wessex nationalists were a joke, but in the light of events in eastern Europe since 1989, with small nations asserting their own rights to self-determination, Wessex may make a come-back. English nationalists are faced with a war on two fronts. While their influence on the Celtic fringes is being challenged, the influence upon their own sovereignty of Brussels and the European Community increases. This squeeze suggests that, in the 21st cent., the problem of the definition and rights of nationalism will still be with us.

CNL; JAC

nationalization. Although the 1945 Labour government was chiefly responsible for enlarging the public sector of the British economy to over 20 per cent of GDP, coal, railway, and even land nationalization had been advocated by Edwardian socialists and radicals. The First World War boosted the credibility of state intervention in industry and in 1918 the Labour Party committed itself to 'common ownership of the means of production'. However, it was Conservative-dominated governments which founded the Central Electricity Board (1926) and London Passenger Transport Board (1933) and 'nationalized' the BBC (1927) and British Overseas Airways Corporation (1939) as semi-autonomous 'public corporations'. Prior to the First World War, it was assumed that nationalization would take the form of a government department (like the Post Office) but in the inter-war period the Labour Party gradually accepted the 'Morrisonian model', which gave no concessions to either workers' control or direct administration by civil servants.

The Second World War gave further impetus to calls for public ownership; the succeeding Labour government followed its 1945 manifesto 'Let Us Face the Future' and nationalized the Bank of England, Cable & Wireless, coal (1946), inland transport, electricity (1947), gas (1948), and iron and steel (1949), generously compensating shareholders. Party-political strife over iron and steel (denationalized in 1953 but renationalized by Labour in 1967) scarcely detracted from the acceptance of Attlee's 'mixed economy' by the Conservatives. The latter even established the Atomic Energy Authority (1954) and nationalized Rolls Royce, after it faced bankruptcy, in 1971. Further 'lame-duck' industries were nationalized by Labour in the 1970s, notably British Leyland (1975) and shipbuilding (1977). However, the *Thatcher governments halted the process and began a 'privatization' programme in 1981; by 1996 the public sector of the economy had been virtually eliminated. SC

national parks. Proposals for national parks were first heard in the 19th cent. as industrial towns grew ever bigger and suburbs swelled. But advocates found it difficult to decide whether the parks should be places to which people could resort for relaxation and pleasure, or whether the public should be excluded as far as possible. The *National Trust was founded in 1895, the Society for the Protection of Nature Reserves in 1912, and the Council for the Protection of Rural England in 1926. The CPRE obtained from *MacDonald in 1929 an inquiry into the need for national parks, which reported in favour and recommended a National Parks Authority. Economic and political crisis then intervened, but the Forestry Commission was persuaded to create a number of national forest parks. The issue was taken up again after the Second World War and a National Parks Commission established in 1949, with power to designate national parks, and to identify areas of outstanding natural beauty, outside the parks, but in need of protection. The commission did not apply to Scotland. It would not own the parks, nor have direct administrative responsibility, but would operate through the county councils. The first parks, established in 1951, were Dartmoor, Snowdonia, the Peak District, and the Lake District, followed by the Pembrokeshire coast (1952), the north Yorkshire moors (1952), Exmoor (1954), the Yorkshire Dales (1954), Northumberland (1956), and the Brecon Beacons (1957). The New Forest and the Norfolk Broads were given 'equivalent status'. Forty areas of outstanding natural beauty have been recognized, including the Chilterns, Cotswolds, Gower, the Malverns, the Long Mynd and Wenlock Edge, and the Wye valley. In 1968 responsibility was transferred to the Countryside Commission, and a Countryside Council for Wales. There are no national parks or areas of outstanding natural beauty in Scotland, but national scenic areas have been designated and afforded some protection. The original predicament continues to cause problems and policy has to balance the interests of visitors and residents, which not infrequently clash over industrial and mining development. JAC

national portrait galleries. The English National Portrait Gallery was founded in 1856 at the urging of the 5th earl of Stanhope, supported among others by Prince Albert. The present building, opened in 1896 in London, was largely funded by a single benefactor, W. H. Alexander. The collection contains portraits of celebrated Britons in every medium including photography. In fulfilling the aim of the gallery to illustrate the nation's history, selections are made on the importance of the sitter rather than the quality of the artist, so there is great variation in the works. The National Trust properties of Montacute in Somerset and Beningbrough in Yorkshire also house a number of portraits from the NPG.

The Scottish National Portrait Gallery in Edinburgh was founded in 1882 with endowments from the owner of the *_Scotsman_ newspaper, J. R. Findlay. The building on Queen Street houses portraits of eminent Scots, antiquities, and the national photography collection. A permanent exhibition portrays the history of the royal house of Stewart in portrait and artefact and includes a pastel of Prince Charles Edward (Bonnie Prince Charlie) by de la Tour acquired in 1994 with help from the National Art Collections Fund. Since 1983, with a painting of Queen*Elizabeth, the queen mother, the gallery has commissioned works direct. JC

National Schools Society. Because of the success of Joseph *Lancaster in establishing non-sectarian schools, leading to the founding of the *British and Foreign School Society, the bishops of the Church of England were anxious to promote a rival body. In October 1811 the National Society for Promoting the Education of the Poor in the Principles of the Established Church was formed. Dr Andrew *Bell was engaged to organize monitorial schools, teaching both secular and religious subjects. From its inception, the society published a number of textbooks which were 'suitable' for its schools. A central branch for training teachers was established in Holborn, but later five other colleges were erected, including St Mark's and Whitelands, Chelsea, and St John's, Battersea. Starting with 52 schools attended by 8,620 pupils in 1811, the society rapidly expanded its activities; by the following year there were 230 schools with 40,484 pupils. In 1833 government grants were first given towards building the schools and in 1853 towards their maintenance. By 1888 the society's schools were educating 2,300,000 children.

After the 1902 Education Act, some local education authorities objected to contributing towards schools which were outside their control. The National Schools Society fought this issue in the law courts and obtained equal treatment for their schools. PG

National Society for the Prevention of Cruelty to Children. Despite late 18th-cent. *humanitarianism and philanthropy, there was scant concern about neglect and abuse of children before 1870. Piecemeal legislation (work-practices, baby-farming) and local rather than national experiments in child welfare lagged behind growing concern for animals, but pioneer work in America observed by the Liverpool banker Thomas Agnew (1881) led to the formation of several provincial societies for the prevention of child cruelty 1883–5. Through the untiring efforts of a London congregational minister, Benjamin Waugh, the London society amalgamated with some provincial counterparts to form the NSPCC, which then co-ordinated efforts to promote legislation (1889). Initially contentious, since this 'Children's Charter' appeared to challenge parental rights, its enforcement via the society led to eloquent testimony to their work and strengthened amplified legislation. The NSPCC was incorporated in 1895, since when concern about criminal neglect has extended to general physical welfare, and national consciousness has been raised about children's civil rights. ASH

National Theatre. First proposed by Effingham Wilson (1848), but bedevilled by false starts, conflicts of interest, and two world wars, the idea of a state theatre received parliamentary approval (1949) but the promised funding was not forthcoming. The National Theatre company was finally incorporated in 1963, with Laurence *Olivier as director and the Old Vic providing a nucleus of actors, but it was not until 1976, after financial difficulties and criticism, that the company moved into its permanent home, a three-theatre complex on the South Bank (London), partly state subsidized. Since 1988 the prefix 'Royal' has been permitted. ASH

National Trust. The National Trust was founded in 1895, largely by Octavia *Hill, Sir Robert Hunter, and Canon H. D. Rawnsley of Westmorland. Its object was to preserve buildings or land of historic interest and beauty. The trust was incorporated by Act of Parliament in 1907 and a separate trust for Scotland established in 1931. The first acquisition was cliffs overlooking Cardigan Bay and the first large appeal in 1901 was to buy Friar's Crag at Derwentwater. The trust is now custodian for more than 350 stately homes and places, and the National Trust for Scotland for another 100, including the battlefields of Bannockburn and Culloden, Cliveden, Cragside, Culzean castle, Knole, Petworth, Powys castle, Wallington, and West Wycombe. JAC

NATO is the acronym for the North Atlantic Treaty Organization, established in Washington, DC, on 4 April 1949 by the USA, Canada, UK, France, and other west European countries. This was the culmination of diplomatic efforts by those, including the British government, who saw a defence alliance as vital to safeguard western Europe against possible threats by the USSR. The signing of the Brussels treaty a year later was part of a strategy to convince US public opinion that American involvement was desirable. The treaty's anti-communist orientation was made clear in its preamble, which declared the parties 'determined to safeguard the freedom, common heritage and civilization of their peoples, founded on principles of democracy, individual liberty and the rule of law'. The signatories committed themselves to taking 'necessary action' to aid any member facing attack. The *Korean War induced the formation of an integrated military command for NATO, which apart from occasional disputes over nuclear deterrence strategies and 'out of area' problems functioned well until the end of the Cold War. Britain however sought additional security through the possession of an independent nuclear deterrent and the cultivation of a 'Special Relationship' with the USA. Both its length of existence and its role in seeing off the Soviet challenge give NATO a claim to be among the most successful alliances in history. CNL

Nauru is a small Polynesian island, east of New Guinea, whose economy is based largely upon phosphate. Visited first in 1798, it became a German colony and was occupied by the Australians in 1914. After the First World War, it was administered as a mandate by Britain, Australia, and New Zealand and occupied during the Second World War by the Japanese. It became an independent republic in 1968 and is an associate member of the Commonwealth. JAC

naval history. In about 1436 Adam de Moleyns in *The Libelle of English Policy* wrote: 'Flemings to our blame, Stop us, take us, and so make fade the flowers of English state.' This may be the earliest polemic in English urging a system of mercantile protection, at a time when the fleet of Henry V had been dismantled. Nearly 150 years later Richard *Hakluyt could view a more spacious world, and in a new dimension. In 1580, securing the translation of the Breton explorer Jacques Cartier's account of North American shores, Hakluyt insisted that the English should be throwing off 'their sluggish security and continual neglect' of opportunities the French were so actively seizing. The foothold gained, however tenuously, in Newfoundland (1583) and the founding of Virginia (1607–19), events occurring before and after the Spanish Armada of 1588, may have helped to assuage the proselytizing zeal of Hakluyt. But he, and such forwarders of enquiry as Lord *Burghley, who confessed to 'fantasising of cosmography', encouraged the beginnings of naval history as a scholarly discipline, separable from the demands of canvassing causes. Canvassing of course continued—how could it not, given such issues as the state of the early 17th-cent. navy, the self-perpetuating problems of timber supply, and manning? But the triumphs over the Dutch and Spanish 60 years after the Armada afforded the English an awareness of the implications of maritime superiority.

No man in his time was better equipped to write a comprehensive naval history than Samuel *Pepys, and by 1680 he had accumulated material for such a work which, he rightly believed, would 'consort mightily with my genius'. Unfortunately for future scholars, Pepys did not complete his history; the one written by a successor in the Admiralty secretaryship, Josiah Burchett (1720), is of value only for the period 1689–1713 of which Burchett had intimate knowledge. But in 1735 Thomas Lediard's two-volume history was of an altogether different calibre, and was usefully supplemented by John Campbell's *The Lives of the Admirals* (1742–5), which brought the personalities of past commanders into focus. It is questionable how far John Charnock's *Biografia navalis* (1794–8) advanced on Campbell, though his enquiries were pertinacious. In 1806 Charles Derrick, of the Navy Office, brought out the first valuable treatment of the navy's administrative history.

Possibly the first 'modern' panoramic treatment of the navy's history was W. L. Clowes's seven-volume work 1897–1903, but an arguably more estimable contemporary was Sir John Knox Laughton, an indefatigable researcher and effective founder, in 1893, of the Navy Records Society. That year Derrick found a successor in the industrious M. M. Oppenheim, who brought out an administrative history of 1509–1660 (the volume designed to follow it never appeared). Coincidental with Britain's naval race with Germany, the great age of naval history scholarship had now arrived, and was dominated by Sir Julian Corbett (1854–1921) and Admiral Sir Herbert Richmond (1871–1946). The definitive history of the navy in the First World War *From the Dreadnought to Scapa Flow* (1961–70) was in fact written by an American, Arthur G. Marder, the Second World War being covered in S. W. Roskill's *The War at Sea* (1954–61). Both these distinguished historians, but especially Marder, enjoyed the inestimable benefit of perspective: today's historians have fewer bearings in a world where sea-borne missiles can destroy inland cities and where, irrespective of financial constraint, there are complex dilemmas in forward planning. Above all, British seafarers, the ultimate makers of naval history, are in drastic numerical decline. DDA

Navarino, battle of, 1827. An accidental encounter fought on 20 October between a Turco-Egyptian fleet of 70 vessels, and a British, French, and Russian fleet of 28 ships, heavier than most of their adversaries. Navarino Bay is a commodious anchorage in the Morea (Greece), sheltered to the west by the island of Sphacteria and with only one navigable entrance. The Turkish government had prevaricated in acceding to an armistice with its insurgent Greek subjects negotiated by the tripartite powers. The allied fleet under Sir Edward *Codrington put into Navarino with the formal intention of escorting the Egyptian ships to Alexandria and the Turkish to Constantinople. However, a distrustful Turkish commander opened fire, and in the ensuing engagement, in which the quality of allied gunnery much exceeded that of the Turks, the fleet of the latter was virtually destroyed. In 1830 Britain endorsed the Greek proclamation of independence of 1822. DDA

Navarrete, battle of. See NAJERÁ.

Navigation Acts were intended to protect English (later British) commerce from foreign competition. They originated in Tudor times and were based on ideas usually called *mercantilist. This assumed that the volume of world trade was finite and that any gain by one country could only be at the expense of another. The great Act of 1651 was aimed at the Dutch carrying trade. It required that all imports should be carried in ships either owned by English subjects or owned by the nationals of the country from which the goods came. Exports were similarly restricted. The Acts had the concurrent purpose of fostering the *merchant navy, which retained an important defensive role. The Navigation Acts were abolished in 1849, a final step towards making Britain a free trade economy. IJEK

navy. 'For the regulating and better government of H.M.'s, ships of war and forces by sea, wherein, under the good Providence of God, the wealth, safety, and strength of the Kingdom is so much concerned' (Preamble to *Naval Discipline Act*, 1661); 'Fishermen, yachtsmen . . . river boatmen . . . manned their craft with volunteer crews and rushed them to the assembly point, although they did not then know for what purpose they were required' (Admiralty communiqué, *The Times*, 4 June 1940). Separated by three centuries, these records of mid-17th-cent. aspiration in the wake of Cromwellian successes against Dutch and Spaniards, and mid-20th-cent. summons of all seafarers from Sussex to East Anglia to rescue at Dunkirk the only army the nation possessed, proclaim the importance of naval power for an island. The first is a perception of state interest which dates back well beyond the *Armada to the reign of Elizabeth I's grandfather Henry VII, and has never ceased to apply, while the second invokes the duty owed the realm by the subject best equipped to discharge it. That obligation can be traced back to *Æthelred II's plight under Danish attacks at Sandwich in 1006, and probably to *Alfred's native-found ships at Poole, again resisting the Danes, in 897. Yet few aspects of the crown's prerogative power were more strenuously questioned through the 17th, 18th, and 19th cents. than that to impress the subject for sea service. Not until 1853, when fixed terms of service in the navy and pension rights were made statutory, did age-old constraints cease to be obnoxious. There seems poetic justice that the first *Victoria Cross was won by a non-commissioned seaman in the *Crimean War.

Britain's place in the 'Viking World' was rendered most definitive through the person of *Cnut (1016–35). King, or overlord, also in Denmark (1019) and Norway (1028), no English monarch had such distant dominions again until Charles II in the later 17th cent. Cnut's navy seems not to have been a personal apanage but an auxiliary, its periods of service specifically fixed by financial provision. In 1051 it was dispensed with by *Edward the Confessor out of economy, though this Norman-raised king may also have intended to ease the succession to his crown of the rich and ecclesiastically regenerated *Normandy. William I had continuous trans-channel ferry needs during his reign, after the first crucial shipment of an army to Pevensey in September 1066; and he, William II, and Henry I may have made some 40 Channel crossings in all. *Portsmouth, a nascent naval base by the reign of John (1199–1216), or *Southampton were their usual destinations. But did they pretend to naval power beyond such dictates, or occasionally commandeering the resources of English merchants trading with Scandinavian, Flemish, or, later, Gascon ports? By the end of the 12th cent. the *Cinque ports had long enjoyed privileges from the crown in return for an annual provision of ships and men. Through the 13th cent. these ports, joined by Winchelsea and Rye, provided the 'drive' for assembling royal fleets, though under Henry III (*c.*1255) they so resisted his weak authority that Henry had to look to the east coast shipbuilding ports. By this time the oared single sail 'long ship' or galley, while still predominant in northern waters and the Mediterranean, was ceding place to wider-beamed and higher-sided vessels, furnished with fore and stern castles. These were more difficult to manœuvre than galleys, but they could carry bowmen and projectiles in their castles and were more suitable for boarding an enemy, even if oar-power remained the handiest means finally to position a warship. Edward III's victory over the French at *Sluys in 1340 must have featured such ships; and before the 14th cent. was out there was vital sail evolution through the development of the three-masted ship. The age-old side rudder also gave place to the stern-post rudder aligned on the keel, facilitating steering a few points off the wind.

The evolution of the navy in the 15th and even the 16th cent. has to be seen in the context of an ever-increasing volume of trading voyages, to Iceland, the Baltic ports, to the Basque coast and Portugal, and then the Newfoundland Banks. The east coast coal trade needed many ships, and Hanseatic competition in the shipment of English cloth to the processors in the Low Countries had to be countered. More distant trades made big ships economic: in 1400–25, 68 per cent of crown-hired ships were of less than 100 tons burthen, but by 1451 that percentage had dropped to 52. The three great ships of Henry V were each over 550 tons; the *Grace Dieu* of 1420, whose timbers yet lie in the Hamble river, was of over 1,000, though she may never have put to sea. These ships were unique, and possibly uniquely unserviceable. Around 170 years later, when England faced the Armada in 1588, only 14 of the 177 private ships enlisted for service were over 200 tons, and only 5 of the 34 'Queen's Ships' exceeded 500 tons. The late medieval small ship had a durable progeny in the navy of the Tudors, the dynasty which truly founded the navy with its yards at Portsmouth, *Chatham, Deptford, and Woolwich, and which fostered native gun-founding. In 1546, Henry VIII's last year, the Navy Board was formed from the navy's principal officers: it was destined to serve as the executant of the fleet's construction, maintenance, and supply, the country's largest industrial undertaking until the 19th cent. The names of *Hawkins, *Pepys, and *Barham are inseparable from its record, strained though the board's relations with the policy-making Board of Admiralty often were. The critical change in warship design came during the 40 years before 1588, the removal of the medieval 'castles' in favour of a lower superstructure, with ships' sides pierced for guns on wheeled carriages, which made for some ease of movement between decks and allowed for recoil. Through to the coming of the steam-powered 'ironclad' this was the basic character of the warship; the teamwork, ensuring high rates of fire, inculcated in motley crews described in the 18th cent. as of 'naturally generous dispositions though turbulent, fearless, or, rather, thoughtless of consequences', made a singular contribution to Britain's awesome repute at sea in the century of *Vernon, *Hawke, *Rodney, and *Nelson.

When in June 1808 Sir Arthur Wellesley (the future *Wellington) spoke in Parliament of the navy as 'the characteristic and constitutional force of Britain', he was expressing a national sense of obligation to a service which, resolutely administered by Middleton (Barham) since 1778, and liberally provided for by *Pitt in the 1780s, had earlier withstood the unprecedented challenges of the *American War and had next reaped the laurels of victory under exceptional commanders. In the years to come the navy played a crucial role in supporting Wellington in the *Peninsula. Wellington's logistical back-up had been prefigured, however modestly, by the first wintering of a British fleet in the Mediterranean in 1694–5; but few developments in Britain's Atlantic economy were more spectacular than the doubling of her exports to the Caribbean after 1808, following the Anglo-Spanish entente. At long last, and following *Trafalgar, the book was closed on one of the most abiding and distracting of Britain's strategic preoccupations: the security of the West Indies possessions had exercised the minds of all thinking naval officers, as well as commercial lobbies, since the age of William III. This concern lay close to the beginnings of Britain's *commercial* empire in the 16th and 17th cents.—the *Levant Company 1592, the Virginia Adventurers 1609, the *Royal Africa Company 1660, above all the *East India Company 1600—all undertakings calling for ships which must dwarf the warships of Elizabeth I. Some traces of her fleet's tonnage possibly survived even in the great battle fleets sent out under Cromwell; but by the time of Pepys's '30 ship' building programme of 1677, '*your* ships' as he defensively reminded Parliament, there may have been an average burthen tonnage of 1,200 for ships of over 70 guns as against 940 in 1660. The navy finally became 'royal' in name under Charles II, and it was of incalculable importance for its future self-identity that there was, deliberately, no discrimination against that religious dissent among seamen which had afforded the Cromwellian navy its special pugnacity.

The first steam-powered vessels in the navy were the paddle-driven frigates/sloops of the 1820s, but the navy's ships in the Crimean War did not look much different from those of 75 years before. Even *Warrior*, Britain's first screw-driven ironclad (1860), retained sail-power after modifications in 1887. Within the period 1867–90 there was a breath-taking acceleration in the power of warships, but seamen of all ranks lacked the training to exploit these advances. During the incipient naval race with Germany in the 1890s there emerged, in the fascinating and powerfully prophetic educator John Arbuthnot *Fisher, the man who drove the navy into the 20th cent. What has to be understood about his 18,000-tons displacement **Dreadnought*, with her 21-knot speed (keel laid October 1905, launched February 1906), is that such a ship was *waiting* to be built: turbine and not reciprocated engine driven, and with a provision of *uniformly* heavy guns ensuring straddling salvoes of the highest possible accuracy. Yet *Dreadnought* was rapidly overtaken by more powerful and faster sisters, and she herself played little part in the First World War. Though included in the 1922 scrapping programme, *Dreadnought* had served her turn through her very launching and her specifications became common currency across the world. But at the end of his life (1920) Fisher was convinced that air power was inseparable from sea power in any future conflict, and that the capital ship, in spite of all, had had her day—a glimpse of what was to happen in the Second World War to the *Prince of Wales*, *Repulse*, and *Hood*. The mine, the torpedo, and the submarine had already set the pace of change; and at the Coronation Review of 1953 only one British battleship remained, the 42,000-ton *Vanguard*, which had never seen action. Accompanied though she was at Spithead by five major aircraft carriers, these great ships lay among a myriad of smaller vessels of a versatility of purpose which would have won the approbation of a Fisher—and a Nelson. DDA

Grove, E., *Vanguard to Trident* (1987); Hattendorf, J. B., and Knight, J. B. (eds.), *British Naval Documents 1204–1960* (Aldershot, 1993); Lewis, M., *The Navy of Britain* (1949).

Nechtansmere, battle of, 685. Fought at Dunnichen, near Forfar, it was an unmitigated disaster for Northumbria, which probably held the territory south of the Forth and had established overlordship of the Picts to the north. King *Ecgfrith fiercely attacked the Picts against all advice, including that of *Cuthbert, bishop of Lindisfarne, who had foreseen the king's early death. Lured into a narrow mountain pass, Ecgfrith and his army were slain. The defeat marked the beginning of decline in Northumbrian power. The Picts were freed from overlordship, and although *Bede records that Ecgfrith's successor Aldfrith 'restored the shattered fortunes of the kingdom', it was 'within smaller boundaries'. AM

Neerwinden, battle of, 1693. Sometimes known as Landen. On 29 July Marshal Luxembourg with 80,000 men attacked William III with 50,000 near Liège. William suffered severe losses of men and guns, but retreated in good order and saved Brussels. But he admitted 'great chastisements'.

JAC

Nehru, Jawaharlal (1889–1964). Independent India's first prime minister. The son of Motilal Nehru, a prominent lawyer and leader of the Indian National Congress, Nehru was educated at Harrow and Cambridge and trained for the bar. He became politically active during *Gandhi's first non-cooperation movement (1920–2). A socialist by conviction, he frequently clashed with Gandhi over tactics and policy. However, he was spellbound by the mahatma and remained personally loyal to him. In 1939 he was Gandhi's choice to displace fellow-socialist S. C. Bose as Congress president. Nehru played a leading role in the negotiations for independence in 1946–7 and was prime minister in India's first interim government. He was confirmed in office at three subsequent general elections. He was much impressed by the material achievements of the Soviet Union and sought to lead India in a similar direction. But he was also a democrat and had to modify many of his ideals accordingly.

DAW

Nelson, Horatio (1758–1805). Emphasis should always be placed on Nelson's East Anglian background. Through both his parents (via his mother Catherine née Suckling he was a great-great-nephew of Sir Robert *Walpole) his roots were tenaciously regional, and his father's pastoral duties in his living at Burnham Thorpe, where Nelson was born on 29 September 1758, brought Edmund Nelson's eight surviving children into daily contact with parishioners whose livelihood was wrung from field, marsh, and coast. All his life Nelson was profoundly aware of the drudgery of toil, whether on the furrow or the lower deck, and humanely responsive to the concerns of the least privileged. And the influence of his strong-minded mother, who died when he was only 9, always remained with him. By 1801 only two of her six sons survived, and this year, probably the most testing of his life, when he parted from a blameless wife, became the father of two daughters by Emma *Hamilton, and, after *Copenhagen, assumed against his will a most challenging anti-invasion command reaching from Harwich down to Dover, stretched his highly strung temperament to its limits. A natural recklessness, which had underlain past feats and past censure, was snuffed out before the defences of Boulogne in August 1801, and fame itself was tasting sour for Nelson: a plan to quit England with Emma for the Sicilian dukedom of Brontë, given to him by a grateful king of the Two Sicilies in August 1799, had not been abandoned. But within eighteen months, by the time Nelson assumed the Mediterranean command in May 1803, he had found composure, and for this Emma Hamilton (then widowed) may claim some credit. The devotion shown him by the fleet also helped the serenity of the last three years, a potent contribution to Nelson's 'legend' in its ultimate form; and in May 1804 late proof of his mother's benign legacy breaks through in one of his innumerable letters: 'the thought of former days brings all my mother into my heart, which shows itself in my eyes.'

Nothing is known for certain about Nelson's earliest acquaintance with the sea, but he took so readily to navigation in Thames and Medway, and later through tropical shoals and rivers, to the grand moments at the Nile and Copenhagen that there may have been childhood experiences of north Norfolk's creeks, even if only by punt when angling. His entry to the navy in 1770 was through patronage, that of his uncle Maurice Suckling, comptroller of the navy 1775–8. For all his natural intolerance of regulation, Nelson was unfeignedly sincere in sustaining lifelong friendships with his seniors: Captains Lutwidge, no discourager of initiative, and Locker, a profoundly educative influence and no supporter of outmoded sea-fighting; Sir Peter Parker, who in June 1779 eased Nelson's promotion to a post-captaincy and so placed his feet on the ladder to becoming an admiral; Sir Samuel (Lord) *Hood, and Sir John *Jervis (earl of St Vincent). Through 'pull' in the right quarters Nelson made early voyages to the West Indies and the Arctic, followed by a spell in the East Indies during which he escaped death by malaria only through the care of Captain James Pigot. Examined for lieutenant in April 1777, Nelson immediately returned to the West Indies, and his years there, to July 1788 when he was within four months of being placed on half-pay back in England, formed him as a naval officer. A ten-month break at home and in France, June 1783 to the following spring, caused him briefly to consider standing for Parliament.

Before Maurice Suckling died he had predicted admiralship for his nephew (attained February 1797), while Hood, a friend of Suckling's, noted the young captain's exceptional dedication. Prince William Henry, the future William IV, to whom Nelson became a trusted councillor in the Leeward Islands, thought him 'no common being', and many from other walks of life were struck by his flair and address: we can yet recover something of Nelson's flavour through reading even a random sample of his 5,000 surviving letters, incisively lucid, often humorous, and with insights unexpected in a man apparently prone to self-absorption. His grasp of the essentials in commanding men was allied to administrative exactitude; and the latter quality prompted him to take issue with illicit American trade in the West Indies which, though a justifiable policy, placed his professional future at risk. The attraction he felt towards women—on at least one occasion, in Canada, he was close to disobeying orders until rescued by a friend—suggests strong emotional cravings. Perhaps it was some self-knowledge which brought him to a marriage, grounded only in 'esteem', with Frances Nisbet (née Woolward) in March 1787. The match involved a serious misjudgement of Frances's likely capacities as a naval officer's wife: dutifully loyal to the navy, the maintenance of the same quality towards his spouse became a burden for Nelson, before ever he met Emma Hamilton.

If Frances Nelson could not comprehend her husband's professional zeal, neither could she share in his attachment to north Norfolk during his years of unemployment until, in

January 1793, he was at length appointed to the 64-gun *Agamemnon* at Chatham. Nelson assured his wife he would 'come laughing back one day', and although no finality was intended, a marriage which had proved childless was even less likely to bring him back involuntarily. The seven years which ensued in the Mediterranean, broken only by sick leave September 1797 to March 1798, under the commands of Hood, Hotham, Jervis, and, least happily, Keith, saw Nelson become a surpassing commander for those who served under him, and a hero to his countrymen and -women. But they were costly, his wounds, as he drily commented, being 'tolerable for one war': a right eye lost at Calvi (Corsica) July 1794, an internal rupture at St Vincent February 1797, loss of his right arm in a foolhardy assault on Tenerife the following July, a head wound at the Nile in August 1798, which almost certainly affected his mental balance and increased his fear of blindness. This may be a charitable explanation, but it is a not unconvincing one, for the intensity of his passion for Emma Hamilton, his intoxication with the honours which fell to him from George III, Naples, Constantinople, Malta, his maladroit and insensate involvement in Neapolitan politics 1799–1800, and his flagrant disregard of a superior's orders. A national hero, yet a flawed one, the last three years 1803–5, which included a further spell in the Mediterranean and the untiring, frustrating chase after Villeneuve to the West Indies and back in the summer before *Trafalgar, confirmed Nelson's renown as a leader of men with an almost spiritual power to articulate the national will to resist Napoleon. He was given a barony after his victory of the *Nile and advanced to viscount after the battle of *Copenhagen. DDA

Nicholas, N. H. (ed.), *The Letters and Despatches of Vice-Admiral Lord Nelson* (7 vols., 1844–6); Oman, C., *Nelson* (1947); Pocock, T., *Horatio Nelson* (1987).

Nennius. Author of the *Historia Brittonum*, *c.* AD 800, a principal source for the post-Roman period. Much of the *Historia* attributed to Nennius has been described as having 'all the historical reliability of fairy-stories'. Nennius' reference to *Arthur may well fall into this category. However, Nennius also included some short passages derived from reputable earlier authors, such as Constantius of Lyons on St *Germanus. Nennius himself wrote in his preface: 'coacervavi omne quod inveni' ('I have made a heap of everything I have found'). The result of Nennius' efforts is a well-intentioned but sometimes bizarre account of Britain in the 5th and 6th cents. which cannot be relied upon, although some scholars argue that Nennius preserved useful titbits of information. ES

neo-classical architecture was part of a European-wide movement, *c.*1760–1830, affecting also the fine and decorative arts, to which Britain made a substantial contribution. It was directly inspired by, or imitative of, classical antiquity (i.e. the art and architecture of Greece and Rome) and associated with rationalist principles and Enlightenment ideals of the perfectibility of the human spirit through such means as civic 'improvements' and exposure to noble monuments.

Consequently, this imposing and severe style was frequently adopted for public buildings such as courts of justice, hospitals, museums, and schools; Edinburgh is a city particularly rich in neo-classical architecture, W. H. *Playfair (1790–1857) being one of its leading exponents.

The first stirrings of the neo-classical mentality can be seen around 1760, when Robert *Adam (1728–92) initiated a style based more on the direct inspiration of Roman antiquity than on Italian Renaissance, especially Palladian, architecture. Thus his south front of Kedleston Hall, Derbys. (1760–8), suggests the form of a triumphal arch. James Wyatt (1748–1813), who also studied in Italy, was said by his contemporaries to have further refined the Adamesque style, which, particularly for interiors, tended to be decorative. Sir John *Soane (1753–1837) developed a personal neo-classical style founded on a deeply felt interpretation of the antique, exploiting the effect of domes and of simplified, pared-down ornament.

By *c.*1800, an interest in Greek antiquity, based on first-hand archaeological study, had largely supplanted the earlier Roman taste. Symptomatic of this was the acquisition of the 'Elgin marbles' from the Parthenon at Athens. Earlier, the first volume of James Stuart and Nicholas Revett's *The Antiquities of Athens* (1762) had become a source book for the Greek Revival, a movement further encouraged by the important connoisseur and patron Thomas Hope (1769–1831). Neither Stuart nor Revett achieved much success as an architect. However, the former's redesign of the interior of Greenwich hospital chapel (1780–8) was influential, and it became obligatory for the new generation of neo-classical architects such as C. R. Cockerell (1788–1863), Sir Robert Smirke (1780–1867), and William Wilkins (1778–1839) to make extensive study tours of Greece. The aristocratic amateur Sir Charles Monck also visited Greece, a fact reflected in his design for his own house, Belsay Hall, Northumberland (1807–17). Externally, this austere and seminal work made emphatic use of the Greek Doric order as did William Wilkins's characteristic Grange Park, Hampshire (begun 1809). Wilkins, a Cambridge graduate himself, also designed the new Grecian-style buildings of Downing College, Cambridge (1807–20).

An extreme example of the Greek Revival, this time employing the Ionic order, is the church of St Pancras, Euston Road, London (1819–22), by William and his son H. W. Inwood. It embodies features adapted from the Erechtheion, an Athenian temple which the younger Inwood (1794–1843) had studied at first hand. By the 1830s taste was changing in favour of different types of classicism, particularly Sir Charles *Barry's neo-Renaissance style. TEF

Nepal, a kingdom in the Himalayas, was formed in the 18th cent. out of the expansion of the Gurkha clans of the Kathmandu valley. It is extremely diverse—embracing mountains and valleys and Indo-Aryan- and Tibetan-Burman-speaking peoples. In 1814–16 the kingdom was defeated by Lord *Hastings and brought into tributary relations with British India. Its dynasty, a sacral Hindu kingship, has survived and has only recently accepted constitutional forms of monarchy. The country is among the poorest in the world and has long been dependent on the earnings of its famous Gurkha soldiers from service in British-Indian armies. DAW

netball is derived from basketball, which was invented in America in 1891, and introduced into Britain in 1895. It made rapid progress since it was particularly suitable for girls at a time of expanding female education. The national game is controlled by the All-England Women's Netball Association, founded in 1926. The International Federation of Women's Netball Associations was established in 1960. One of the best advertisements for the game is the lunchtime contests by office staff in Lincoln's Inn Fields, London. JAC

Neville's Cross, battle of, 1346. In 1346 Edward III resumed campaigning in France and in August won his great victory of *Crécy. The French urged their Scottish allies to put pressure on England and in October David II led a large force across the border. On 17 October he had reached Durham and was confronted by local English forces at Neville's Cross, just to the west of the city. His adversaries were led by the archbishop of York, Ralph, Lord Neville, and Henry, Lord Percy. The Scots suffered severe losses and David II was captured. He remained a prisoner until 1357. JAC

New Brunswick was detached from *Nova Scotia to form a separate colony when 14,000 loyalist refugees arrived from the USA in 1784. The economy boomed from 1809 after Napoleon had blocked timber supplies from the Baltic. Self-government was introduced in 1848 and in 1865–6 New Brunswick was the crucial battleground between supporters and opponents of the union of British North America. British Prime Minister Andrew Bonar *Law and newspaper magnate Lord *Beaverbrook were New Brunswickers. French-speaking Acadians make up one-third of the population: in 1969, New Brunswick became Canada's only officially bilingual province. In 1987 the incumbent Conservative government lost all 58 seats in the legislature. GM

Newburn, battle of, 1640. Though the battle of Newburn was little more than a skirmish, it helped to bring Charles I to the scaffold. His attempt to impose upon the Scots, many of whom were *presbyterian, a new prayer book led to armed resistance. The first *Bishops' War in 1639 ended in negotiation, but the following year a large Scottish army, led by Alexander *Leslie, crossed the border and was confronted by Lord Conway's troops, trying to hold the line of the Tyne. At the ford at Newburn, 5 miles west of Newcastle, on 28 August 1640, the Scots crossed with little difficulty, occupied Newcastle, and dictated such financial terms to the king that the calling of another Parliament was inevitable. The *Long Parliament, the following year, executed *Strafford and declared itself irremovable, save with its own consent. JAC

Newbury, battle of, 1643. After relieving Gloucester in September 1643, *Essex was shadowed on his return journey to London by Charles's army. The royalists reached Newbury a few hours before their opponents, cutting off the retreat, and took up defensive positions just west of the town. The king's army was some 10,000 men, Essex's perhaps a little less. On 20 September battle commenced with an artillery exchange but the fighting, though heavy, was inconclusive. Charles, running short of ammunition, was obliged to withdraw to Oxford, leaving Essex free to return to the capital. A royalist victim in the battle was Viscount *Falkland, their *chevalier sans peur et sans reproche* who, despairing of the war, rode deliberately to his death in a hail of bullets. JAC

Newbury, battle of, 1644. Charles I's staggering victory at *Lostwithiel in September 1644, when most of *Essex's infantry had been forced to surrender, enabled him to take the initiative once more. While the parliamentarians regrouped and re-equipped, Charles moved to relieve Banbury, Donnington castle near Newbury, and Basing House. On 27 October he dug in at Newbury to face a superior force under senior command of *Manchester. The parliamentary army was large enough to permit an enveloping move, but the east–west attack was badly co-ordinated and beaten off. Under cover of darkness, the royalists retreated to Oxford, but they had shown more enterprise than their opponents and boosted morale. JAC

Newcastle, William Cavendish, 1st duke of (1593–1676). Newcastle was one of the leading royalist commanders during the Civil War. A man of vast estates in Nottinghamshire and Derbyshire, he made spectacular progress up the peerage ladder, moving from viscount (1620), to earl (1628), marquis (1643), and finally duke in 1665. As lord-lieutenant of Nottinghamshire from 1626 to 1642, he entertained Charles I lavishly at Welbeck in 1633 and at Bolsover in 1634. He was an almost automatic choice as commander in the north when war came and had considerable success, gaining control of most of Yorkshire through his victory at *Adwalton Moor in June 1643. In 1644 he was forced back to York by the advance of the Scottish army and Rupert's attempt at relief ended in the shattering defeat of *Marston Moor, where Newcastle watched his own regiment of Whitecoats cut to pieces. He left at once for the continent and did not return until the Restoration. *Clarendon thought his conduct inexcusable and, though granting him 'invincible courage', wrote severely: 'he liked the pomp and absolute authority of a general well, but the substantial part and fatigue of a general, he did not in any degree understand.' A cultivated man, Newcastle wrote books and treatises, corresponded with Thomas *Hobbes, and was the subject of a memorable biography by his wife, published nine years before he died. JAC

Newcastle, Thomas Pelham-Holles, 1st duke of (1693–1768). Newcastle held important offices of state for over forty years. His record is decidedly mixed, but the attention devoted to his many personal idiosyncrasies, such as his incessant chattering and fear of damp beds, can lead to some of the more successful aspects of his career being overlooked.

Created a duke in 1715, Newcastle rose quickly to high office, becoming lord chamberlain in 1717 and secretary of state for the southern department in 1724. He was very much subordinate to fellow-secretary *Townshend, but his prominence increased when *Walpole edged Townshend out in 1730, though Walpole was to direct policy. As Walpole's grip on power loosened, Newcastle's loyalty loosened with it, and he successfully advocated war with Spain despite Walpole's misgivings. Walpole's fall in 1742 led to *Carteret being promoted secretary for the northern department and he quickly won favour with George II. Newcastle and his brother Henry *Pelham used the power of parliamentary support to overwhelm Carteret's purely personal power and forced George II to dismiss him in 1744. In 1746 the Pelhams won full control over the government, after resigning and obliging the king to invite them back.

Newcastle and Pelham, together with Newcastle's lifelong friend *Hardwicke, ran the government 1746–54 upon a *'broad-bottomed' principle, including as many political factions as possible within it to avoid parliamentary opposition. In this they were successful, both brothers being masters of patronage and electoral strategy, but it made for a lacklustre administration. Though Henry Pelham as 1st lord of the Treasury quickly became the 'prime' minister, Newcastle retained very wide powers over foreign affairs and patronage, particularly in the Church of England. Newcastle showed his limitations very clearly during the War of the *Austrian Succession; his grasp of military matters was poor, and his desire to conduct the war through subsidies to potentially friendly countries was expensive and unsuccessful.

The death of Henry Pelham in 1754 dealt Newcastle a heavy blow and the previously peaceful political situation immediately dissolved into bitter rivalry. Newcastle took the post of 1st lord, but could not bring himself to give a minister in the Commons real power and *Pitt and Henry *Fox subjected the government to heavy attack because of this. War with France commenced to a string of military disasters which led Newcastle to resign in 1756 after two highly inept years. In an astonishingly short time, however, he returned as 1st lord in one of the most successful modern ministries, the Pitt–Newcastle coalition, 1757–61. Pitt brilliantly directed the war effort whilst Newcastle dealt with patronage and financial matters. The accession of George III in 1760 with new attitudes changed the political situation dramatically, and Newcastle (and his loyal followers) soon followed Pitt out of office as the *Seven Years War drew to a close in 1762.

The move to opposition was not easy for Newcastle. He was the link between the old Whigs of the Walpole era and the new Whigs guided by *Rockingham, but although Newcastle served as lord privy seal in the Rockingham government 1765–6, he was increasingly marginalized. Throughout his career, Newcastle was most effective as deputy to a man of greater ability, be this Walpole, Pelham, or Pitt. Newcastle was a foolish man in many ways, but loyal to his royal masters, a devoted husband, and a good friend. AIL

Newcastle Programme, 1891. The split in the *Irish Home Rule party in 1890 weakened the likelihood of a successful Home Rule Bill, and *Gladstone did not attend that year's meeting of the National Liberal Federation. At the 1891 meeting in Newcastle upon Tyne he reaffirmed on 2 October the primacy of Home Rule, but associated it with reforms on the mainland by adopting various (but not all) of the proposals of the NLF Council, in particular: land reform; reform of the Lords; shorter parliaments; district and parish councils; registration reform and abolition of plural voting; local veto on drink sales; employers' liability for workers' accidents; Scottish and Welsh disestablishment. So detailed a 'shopping list' from an opposition leader was innovatory in British politics. HCGM

Newcastle propositions, 1646. At the end of the first civil war, Charles I fled from Oxford and surrendered to the Scots, who removed him to Newcastle. Negotiations for a settlement then began. In July, Parliament's commissioners demanded that the king should accept the *covenant, institute a *presbyterian form of church government, hand over control of the army for 20 years, and abandon leading royalists to punishment. Though Charles continued discussions for several months, the terms were totally unacceptable to him and his mind turned increasingly to escape. After six months, the Scots handed him back to Parliament. JAC

Newcastle upon Tyne. A city and river port in Northumberland, and the administrative and commercial centre of north-east England. Its urban history starts abruptly with a 'New Castle' begun by *Robert, the Conqueror's son, in 1080, and a borough planted at its gate. Newcastle, like most of Northumberland, was held by the Scots in Stephen's reign, but retaken by Henry II. It was one of the most successful Norman 'new towns', rising to become the eleventh largest English town by 1377 and one of the top half-dozen in Tudor and Stuart times. Its growing importance was based on coal exports, controlled by the wealthy and powerful Company of Hostmen. The town was captured by the Scots in 1644, and Charles I was held there in 1646–7. Coal-exporting rose further in the 18th cent., followed by shipbuilding and engineering in the 19th; in the 20th it has become part of a huge conurbation straddling the river Tyne. The medieval centre, though it retains much of its walls, was largely replaced between 1825 and 1840 by the architect John Dobson and the visionary speculator Richard Grainger, making Newcastle 'the only major city in England with a planned commercial centre of that date' (Pevsner). DMP

Newcastle upon Tyne, diocese of. The see was created in 1882 out of the *Durham diocese simultaneously with *Wakefield, *Southwell, and *Liverpool, to provide further pastoral care for the rapidly increasing population of industrial Newcastle. The diocese, conterminous with the former county of Northumberland, is an area of major contrasts from highly industrial Tyneside to sparsely inhabited border territory. It contains *Lindisfarne, the historic springboard of the Celtic mission to northern England in the 7th and 8th cents. The cathedral is the former 14th- and 15th-cent. church of St Nicholas with its Scottish-style buttressed lantern tower. WMM

Newcomen, Thomas (1663–1729). Dartmouth ironmonger and inventor of the atmospheric steam-engine. He combined *Savery's independent boiler with the piston in his first 'fire engine' of 1712 at Dudley, applying atmospheric pressure to the top of the cylinder in which steam was condensed to create a partial vacuum and drive down the piston linked by chain to the beam that transmitted the stroke to pumps. Its use was confined to pumping water from mines or to supply networks; diffusion was limited by under-boilering and the extension of Savery's generic patent to 1733, but extended to Wales, the midlands, and the Newcastle collieries; up to 60 had been installed by 1733, the best producing a *duty* (pounds of water raised one foot by a bushel of coals) of 3.75 million, but a lift of under 45 yards. *Smeaton's improvements allowed such engines to supply most of horsepower *c.*1800, and Thompson's patent (1792), effective rotary motion. JCh

New Delhi displaced *Calcutta as the capital of British India in 1912. It was selected to stand adjacent to Old Delhi, an erstwhile capital of the Mughal empire, to emphasize continuity between the two imperial traditions. Many of its public buildings and avenues were designed by Sir Edwin *Lutyens to provide a sense of grandeur and majesty, suggestive of power and permanence. But the impression was illusory—within 35 years the British had gone. New Delhi remains the capital and seat of government of the Republic of India and contains the diplomatic enclaves of all foreign governments. DAW

New England was the name given by Captain John Smith in 1614 to the coastline of America north of the Hudson river, between the 41st and 45th degrees. Two years later he published a *Description of New England*, claiming at least 25 fine harbours. The **Mayflower* settlers landed at Plymouth in 1620 and the name New England was applied to the colony at Plymouth (later absorbed by Massachusetts), New Haven (later part of Connecticut), Massachusetts, Connecticut, Rhode Island, New Hampshire, and Maine. A New England Confederation, or United Colonies of New England, in 1643, to co-ordinate defence, though ineffective, was an early example of inter-colony collaboration. The New England colonies, with their strong puritan tradition, ultimately became the core of American resistance in the War of Independence and it was to cut them off from their neighbours in 1777 that *Burgoyne began his march south from Canada down the Hudson river, which ended with his capitulation at *Saratoga. JAC

Newfoundland was probably 'discovered' by John *Cabot in 1497. Europeans soon exploited its cod fishery. Although Newfoundland was claimed for England in 1583 by Sir Humphrey *Gilbert, sovereignty was disputed until 1713, and France retained rights of access to the coasts until 1904. Settlement was discouraged by the harsh environment and by British governments, which regarded the fishery as a source of personnel for the navy. Population reached 50,000 in the 1820s, drawn from the west of England and southern Ireland, the mix creating a rich culture, distinctive speech, and sectarian division. The last native Beothuk died in 1829. An assembly was introduced in 1832 and self-government in 1855. Newfoundlanders rejected union with Canada in 1869. The economy depended on fishing and most Newfoundlanders were poor. Facing bankruptcy, Newfoundland agreed in 1934 to rule by a commission of government appointed by Britain. Military bases in the Second World War brought prosperity and in 1948 Newfoundlanders voted by 52 to 48 per cent to become Canada's tenth province, formally joining in 1949. While population had almost doubled to 586,000 by 1986, Newfoundland relied on Canadian subsidies to survive. In 1992, even survival seemed threatened when international plundering of cod stocks forced the closure of the fishery. GM

Newgate prison was founded during the reign of Henry I in the west gatehouse of the city of London. It was extensively modified in 1423 following a bequest from the mayor of London, Richard *Whittington. Warders were corrupt, as their offices could be bought and sold: drinking, gambling, and prostitution were commonplace in a harsh and squalid environment. It housed mainly serious criminals and from 1783 replaced *Tyburn as the place for public executions. The prison was destroyed and rebuilt twice, once following the Great Fire of *London in 1666 and again after the *Gordon riots of 1780. Newgate, the most famous and forbidding prison in the land, finally closed in 1902. RAS

New Guinea. See PAPUA NEW GUINEA.

New Hebrides. See VANUATU.

New Lanark (Strathclyde), a factory village, was built by David Dale to exploit the water-power provided by the Clyde in 1784–5. Dale erected four cotton-mills and housing for over 200 families by 1793, the population consisting of Highlanders and pauper apprentices. In 1799 Dale sold New Lanark to Robert *Owen, his son-in-law, and the village acquired a reputation as a profitable and contented community. Owen built schools and an Institution for the Formation of Character, demonstrating his commitment to environmental psychology and improving his work-force. After Owen, the village went through several changes of ownership and is now a museum conservation area. JB

Newman, John Henry (1801–90). Cardinal. The greatest catholic theologian and spiritual writer of the last 200 years, and likely to be officially declared a saint, Newman was the leading convert of the *Oxford movement. His published writings, including *An Essay on the Development of Christian Doctrine* (1845), sermons, and *Letters and Diaries*, profoundly influenced the second Vatican Council (1962–5), often called 'Newman's Council'. His writings on the Christian church brought ecclesiastical censure and, after a period of withdrawal and reflection, he became a catholic in 1845. Theological controversy pursued him through his life of pastoral ministry at the Birmingham Oratory, which he founded. Sensitive to the alleged and often real rebuffs of friends, but also to the demands of ecclesiastical authority, he was often at its mercy. He was delated to Rome for his writings on the laity and the shadow of suspicion was not lifted until he was made cardinal in 1878.

Newman was the son of a London banker and educated at Trinity College, Oxford. He became a fellow of Oriel

College and held the living of St Clements, Oxford, which he resigned in 1843 before joining the catholic church. *Apologia pro vita sua* (1864) explained his spiritual and religious views. *The Idea of a University* (1852) was a plea for universities to offer a liberal education, for the cultivation of the mind. JFC

Newmarket (Suffolk and Cambs.) is the headquarters of flat racing, run on the downs since the reign of Charles II, who founded the Newmarket Town Plate and after whom the 'Old Rowley' mile course is named. It is the home of the Jockey Club, which built a coffee-house at the course in 1752. The best-known races include the 2,000 and 1,000 guineas, the Cambridgeshire, and the Cesarewitch. Newmarket is home to a large number of racing stables and to the National Stud. JAC

New Model Army. Created by the Long Parliament early in 1645 out of the three existing armies of *Essex, *Manchester, and Sir William *Waller. Although run on administratively similar lines, the new army represented the triumph of Oliver *Cromwell in his political struggle against Essex and Manchester. Purged of the old aristocratic and parliamentary leadership, the New Model, under the excellent generalship of Sir Thomas *Fairfax, vanquished the king's forces at *Naseby (June 1645). This battle was followed by an unbroken chain of victories ending in the surrender of the king in June 1646. There then ensued a political struggle with Parliament, now under the sway of the presbyterian peace party of Denzil *Holles and Essex. This conflict, interrupted by the second civil war, culminated in the army's purging of Parliament (6 December 1648), and the subsequent trial of Charles I by a court dominated by New Model Army officers and their parliamentary allies. Having established undisputed mastery in England, the army went on to invade and eventually conquer Ireland (1649) and Scotland (1650). IJG

Newport, treaty of, 1648. The end of the second civil war found Charles I still at Carisbrooke in the Isle of Wight. In September, Parliament, alarmed at the growth of radicalism in the army, resumed negotiations with the king in the town hall at Newport. Charles made substantial concessions over episcopacy and control of the militia, but admitted privately that he negotiated 'merely in order for my escape'. When the negotiations foundered in November, the army seized power and the king was moved to Hurst castle on the mainland, as a preliminary to bringing him to trial. JAC

'Newport rising', 1839. Parliament's rejection of the first *chartist petition in July 1839 placed the chartist leadership in a quandary. There was not enough support for a 'sacred month' (general strike), while to begin an even bigger petition seemed daunting. The physical force men argued for direct action. In the Welsh valleys, the situation was enflamed by the imprisonment of Henry Vincent in Monmouth gaol. But the march on Newport led by John Frost on 3 November can hardly have been intended as more than a mass demonstration. Troops had been moved into the Westgate hotel, where some local chartists were held captive, and opened fire, killing at least fifteen. Frost and two others were tried for treason, condemned, and sent for transportation. To rescue Vincent, they were in the wrong place, and even if Newport had been seized, it would scarcely have brought the government to its knees. The 'rising' was a show of strength that went wrong. JAC

New River. As Elizabethan London grew, the demand for water outstripped supply, prompting Sir Hugh *Myddleton to construct an artificial waterway from Ware in Hertfordshire (1609–13). Fed by the Chadwell spring, thirteen wells, and small tributaries, its 39-mile meander terminated at the New River Head, near King's Cross Road; it included over 40 sluices and two long aqueducts made from timber troughs lined with lead. Water distribution in the city was via some 400 miles of wooden pipes, some of which, despite leakage, were still in use about 1800. Subsequently straightened and shortened, it now ends at Stoke Newington waterworks. ASH

New Ross, battle of, 1798. On 5 June 1798 some 30,000 rebels from Wexford (Ireland), led by Bagenal Harvey and Father Philip Roche, launched an attack on New Ross, where there was an important bridge over the river Barrow. The defence, numbering 1,500 men under General Henry Johnston, was disciplined and determined. Government artillery inflicted heavy casualties and, after desperate hand-to-hand fighting, the rebels were driven off. The king noted Johnston's exemplary conduct: *Cornwallis wrote privately that Johnston, though a blockhead, was now considered 'the saviour of the south'. JAC

New South Wales, a member state of the federal Commonwealth of Australia, was founded 26 January 1788 as a penal colony when Britain annexed over two-thirds of the Australian continent. NSW was later separated into Tasmania (1825, settled 1803), South Australia (1834, settled 1836), Victoria (1851, settled 1834), Northern Territory (1863, incorporated as a federal territory in 1910, yet to achieve full statehood), Queensland (1859, settled 1824), and the Australian Capital Territory (1911). With an area of 310,372 square miles and 6,115,100 inhabitants (1995), of whom 3,736,000 reside in its state capital, Sydney, NSW is the most populous state. For a long time dominated by its convict past, NSW eventually became a thriving self-governing colony, utilizing its savannah grasslands to establish one of the world's largest wool-producing industries, and its coal, mineral, and forest resources to found manufacturing industries; and, with the advent of inland railways (1870–1900), extensive wheat-farming.

With its convict heritage, large unionized industrial population, and somewhat left-of-centre political attitudes, as well as its leading role in the export of wheat and wool, and Sydney's position as Australia's major stock exchange and growing importance as a company headquarters city, NSW is politically and economically Australia's most powerful state. Sydney's pre-eminence has been achieved against strong competition from Melbourne (1995 population 3,197,800), which long regarded itself as the more important financial and company centre. Sydney, with its famous bridge, ocean beaches (Bondi and Manly), and even more famous opera-house, provides Australia with its most readily identified international images. MJW

newspapers. It was well over 100 years from the invention of printing to the appearance of the first newspapers. A number of *corantos*, based on German and Dutch models, were published in the 1620s, but they were confined to London, carried very little English news, appeared erratically, and had print-runs of only a few hundreds. The Civil War stimulated the demand for news and in the 1640s the royalist *Mercurius Aulicus* waged ideological warfare from Oxford against the parliamentary *Mercurius Britannicus* in London. The authorities, republican or royalist, mistrusted newssheets and in 1663 Sir Roger l'Estrange was given wide licensing powers as surveyor of the press. Two years later, the **London Gazette* was started to provide official news. This thin government diet proved unpalatable and the broadsheets which continued to appear were devoted more to mayhem and bawdy than to political information. The excitement of the *Popish plot in the 1670s persuaded many printers to risk prosecution by producing unlicensed papers, and there were also several manuscript news-letters, expensive to produce, and distributed to a limited number of subscribers.

The growth of a newspaper press in a modern form dates from the failure to renew the *Licensing Act in 1695. Several newspapers were quickly off the mark, including the tri-weekly *Post Boy, Post Man*, and *Flying Post*, all of which survived until well into the 18th cent. In April 1702 they were joined by the first daily paper, the *Daily Courant*, and though its circulation was modest, it stayed until 1735. At the same time the provincial press made its appearance with the *Norwich Post* (1701), followed by the *Bristol Post Boy* (1702), *Exeter Post-Man* (1704), and the *Worcester Post-Man* (1709). Though casualties among newspapers were heavy, the general progress through the 18th cent. was remarkable. By 1760 there were four London dailies and by 1790 fourteen. Provincial papers multiplied even quicker: by 1760 there were 35 in existence, 50 by 1780, and 150 by 1821. Stamp duty, introduced in 1715 to curb papers, brought in £911 in its first year but by 1781 was yielding more than £40,000 p.a. to the revenue. Circulation was much larger, comment less restrained. *Mist's Weekly Journal* pursued *Walpole in the 1730s, the *Middlesex Journal* attacked *North in the 1770s, and *Cobbett's **Political Register*, claiming a staggering 60,000 copies in the 1800s, sustained a long campaign for reform of Parliament. From cautious beginnings, the press had become a major political force. Parliament was obliged in the 1770s to abandon its attempt to suppress publication of its debates, and though prosecution of editors continued and the stamp duty was raised during the Napoleonic wars, public appetite grew. The stamped papers were expensive, but an unstamped press flourished, and papers could be read by the less wealthy in coffee-houses, pubs, and barbers' shops.

Sunday newspapers, at first much opposed, began in 1779 with the launch of the *Sunday Monitor*, joined in 1791 by the *Observer*, whose great days were well ahead in the 1920s. By mid-century the Sunday papers were outselling the dailies and had already acquired a reputation for sensational journalism. The *News of the World* began its career in 1843. Among the dailies, the prodigious success was that of *The *Times*, started in 1785 as the *Daily Universal Register*, changing its name in 1788, and forging ahead in the 19th cent. with the introduction of steam printing and a news service so good that government ministers begged to know what was taking place. By 1850 it was selling four times the number of the *Morning Chronicle*, *Morning Herald*, and *Morning Post* combined, and claiming (1852) that it stood 'upon the breach between the present and the future, extending its survey to the horizons of the world'. Three years later, the abolition of the stamp duty enabled the **Daily Telegraph* to launch itself as a rival to *The Times* and by 1880 it was claiming 250,000 copies.

The 'newspaper revolution' of the late 19th and early 20th cents., which ushered in the 'popular press', was progression rather than a sudden change. Ever since newspapers began, the authorities had been anxious about their effect on the masses. The broadsheets of the 1640s had revelled in sex, violence, and the bizarre. George Reynolds in the 1840s mined a rich seam with *Reynolds Magazine*, offering articles and stories which sounded more lurid than they were—'Wagner, the were-wolf', 'Varney the Vampire', and 'Maniac of the Deep'. W. T. Stead's campaign in the *Pall Mall Gazette* in 1885 against the prostitution of young girls (for which he went to well-publicized gaol for two months) anticipated later crusades, not least in its ambiguity. What was changing was the growth of a vast new reading public, benefiting from the introduction of compulsory elementary education in 1880, able to afford a paper, yet unprepared for long and strenuous reading. First to exploit the new market was George Newnes, whose *Tit-Bits* (1881) rocketed to success, with odd news items, tips and hints, and competitions. T. P. O'Connor followed with the *Star*, a London evening paper, in January 1888, and was selling 125,000 within the month, mainly to rail commuters. Next came Alfred *Harmsworth, literally the first of the newspaper barons, with *Answers* (1888), *Comic Cuts* (1890), and *Home Chat* (1895), before launching the *Daily Mail* in 1896, selling at a halfpenny, and reaching 989,000 copies by 1900. Earnest citizens could not decide whether it was splendid that the masses were now reading, or shocking that they were reading trash.

In the post-1918 period, the national dailies increased their market share, largely at the expense of the provincial papers. The competition, even with an expanding readership, was fierce. The *Mail* was followed by the *Daily Express* (1900), the *Daily Mirror* (1903) which was selling more than a million copies daily by 1914, and the *Daily Herald* (1919), organ of the new *Labour Party. Reliance on advertising revenue meant that circulation figures were of crucial importance and give-away offers—pens, insurance, books, holidays—became common. Though the *Herald* peaked in the 1930s, it was handicapped because its readership had poor purchasing power and was unattractive to advertisers: when it closed in 1964 it still had nearly 5 million readers, but of the wrong mix. After the customary wartime boom from 1939 to 1945, the press faced new problems—sharply rising labour costs, and in the 1970s competition for advertisements from television. Ownership of the press passed from proprietors or families to large consortia with the resources to re-equip and compete. After a series of damaging confrontations with the unions in the 1970s (*The Times* was out of production for eleven months 1978/9), the papers began moving out of *Fleet Street, with which they had been associated since the 17th cent., into purpose-built premises well away from the city of London. The quality papers continued to do well and at the bottom end of the market the competition in vulgarity would have won the approval of their 1640s predecessors. In 1994/5 the readership claimed for the *Sun* was 10.1 million, followed by the *Mirror* (6.5), *Mail* (4.4), *Express* (3.2), *Telegraph* (2.8), *Star* (2.0), *Today* (1.7), *The Times* (1.7), **Guardian* (1.3), and *Independent* (0.9). Among the Sundays, the *News of the World* still outsold its rivals with a claimed readership of 12.5 million (1992 figures), followed by the *Sunday Mirror* (8.8), *People* (6.1), *Mail on Sunday* (5.8), *Sunday Express* (4.9), *Sunday Times* (3.5), *Sunday Telegraph* (1.8), *Observer* (1.7), and *Independent on Sunday* (1.3). JAC

Black, J., *The English Press in the Eighteenth Century* (1987); Boyce, G., Curran, J., and Wingate, P. (eds.), *Newspaper History from the Seventeenth Century to the Present Day* (1978); Brown, L., *Victorian News and Newspapers* (Oxford, 1985); Cranfield, G. A., *The Development of the Provincial Newspaper 1700–1800* (Oxford, 1962); id., *The Press and Society* (1978).

Newton, Sir Isaac (1642–1727). Newton was born near Grantham after his father's death, on Christmas Day; his mother soon remarried, and he had a lonely upbringing. He went to Trinity College, Cambridge, in 1661; during the plague year, 1665–6, the undergraduates were sent home, and he is supposed to have thought of the nature of light, differential calculus, and the theory of gravity. In fact, all these things needed much further work over succeeding years. In 1669 he was appointed to the Lucasian chair of mathematics at Cambridge, where he divided his time between mathematical sciences, alchemy, and biblical study. He became a closet *socinian, denying the doctrine of the Trinity; this made him even more secretive. In 1672 his first paper went to the *Royal Society, containing his 'crucial experiment' to prove that white light is a mixture of all the colours. Because he believed that refraction inevitably produced coloured fringes, he advocated reflecting telescopes, and made one. His paper was criticized by Robert *Hooke, to whom it had been referred, and Newton took umbrage. He did not publish his book, *Opticks*, until 1704, after Hooke was dead. It was the standard work for a century.

In 1684 Edmond *Halley came to see him after discussing planetary orbits with Hooke and Christopher *Wren, and found that Newton had worked out the laws of motion and of gravity which would account for them. With Halley as midwife, Newton's *Principia* was published in 1687. It begins with setting out the nature of space, time, and motion; then come the laws of mechanics, a proof that whirlpools of ether cannot explain the phenomena, and, finally, the demonstration that gravity and inertia fit the facts. He showed that attraction between planets will produce wobbles in their orbits, which were indeed observed. Nevertheless, attraction across void space seemed a mystery, and some of his eminent contemporaries were unwilling to accept his physics. He represented the university in Parliament, and in 1696 was appointed warden (later master) of the mint in London, where he supervised recoinage. By the time of his death, he was regarded with awe in Britain, and soon after came to stand as the symbol of enlightenment: a mind for ever voyaging through strange seas of thought, alone. DK

Newtown Butler, battle of, 1689. In the summer of 1689 Enniskillen, second only to Derry in importance in Northern Ireland, still held out against the Jacobite advance, a rallying-point and a great nuisance to their lines of communication. But when Mountcashel was ordered to pinch out the town, its defenders got their blow in first, attacking his troops at Newtown Butler on 31 July. Though heavily outnumbered, the Williamite forces carried the day, taking all the Jacobite guns and capturing their commander. It was the start of the turn of the tide. JAC

new towns. See GARDEN CITIES.

New Zealand. The two main islands of New Zealand, lying more than 1,000 miles to the east of Australia, have a land area of nearly 104,000 square miles, and are larger than the United Kingdom (94,000). South Island is rather bigger than North Island, but contains only a quarter of the people. In the mid-1990s the population was $3\frac{1}{2}$ million, most of them living in towns. The capital, Wellington, with 329,000 people, is in North Island: Auckland has nearly 1 million people, and Christchurch 318,000. Mount Cook in the Southern Alps rises to more than 12,000 feet and in North Island there are geysers and hot springs. The economy is still largely based on cattle- and sheep-rearing, with Australia, Japan, USA, and UK the main markets, but New Zealand wine flourishes, industry increases, and tourism expanded rapidly after the spread of fast air travel.

The first inhabitants were Polynesian people, ancestors of the Maoris, who settled by the 8th cent. Abel Tasman, the Dutch explorer, sighted the west coast of South Island in December 1642, but four of his men were killed by the Maoris and he did not land. The Dutch named the land New Zealand but showed no further interest in it. The first encounter confirmed the warlike nature of the natives. Captain *Cook, in the 18th cent., guessed that there were 100,000 of them, but he had no means of knowing and the figure was probably a substantial underestimate. They lived mainly in North Island, expectation of life was little more than thirty years, and cannibalism was practised.

Not until 1769 was Tasman's initiative followed up when, on his first voyage, Cook circumnavigated both islands. Again, his landing found a hostile reception and several Maoris were shot in skirmishes. He revisited the country on his second and third voyages, reporting that it would sustain an industrious people and that the natives would be too divided to offer much opposition. Thereafter contacts increased, with whalers and sealers calling in for supplies. In 1814 a small Christian mission was established, with little success at first, but progress by mid-century. For fifty years, the situation was close to a state of nature. Increased contact brought diseases to which the Maoris were extremely vulnerable and the acquisition of guns allowed them to try to exterminate each other. The native population declined sharply. By 1838 there were some 2,000 Europeans living and trading in New Zealand—the English, in *Darwin's opinion, 'the very refuse of society'. Disputes over land deals and violent clashes led many settlers to demand British protection. A New Zealand Association in 1837, supported by Lord *Durham and E. G. *Wakefield, was founded in London to encourage mass emigration. In 1839 an unenthusiastic British government sent Captain William Hobson to propose annexation to the Maoris to protect them from indiscriminate expropriation and in 1840 the treaty of *Waitangi was signed, ceding sovereignty to the British in exchange for promises of security. The new colony was placed under *New South Wales but in 1841 established in its own right.

The economic development of New Zealand was boosted by the discovery of gold in South Island in the 1850s, and, more enduringly, by the development of refrigeration in the 1880s, which enabled it to export cheese, butter, and meat to Britain. Constitutionally it progressed at remarkable speed, despite the protracted *Maori wars which continued until 1872. As early as 1846 responsible government was granted, though suspended by the governor, Sir George Grey. A federal constitution was granted in 1852, with the country divided into six provinces, and was followed in 1856 by full representative government. The capital was moved from Auckland to Wellington in 1867. Though it took part in the negotiations, New Zealand did not join the Commonwealth of Australia in 1901 and in 1907 became a self-governing dominion. New Zealand sent a high proportion of its men to fight in the First World War and was given *Western Samoa, a former German colony, as a *mandate under the League of Nations at the end of the war: it became an independent state in 1962.

The population of New Zealand rose undramatically at first. The Maori population in 1896 was put as low as 42,000 and extinction seemed a possibility: it increased throughout the 20th cent. and by the 1990s was more than 400,000. The total population of New Zealand in 1907 was still less than 1 million, grew slowly in the 1920s, partly as a result of high wartime casualties, and had risen to 1.7 million by 1945. After that it rose quickly, reaching more than 3 million by 1975, before flattening out. As in South Africa, sport has been a bond of the emerging nation—the All Blacks' attempts to terrify their opponents with the Maori haka, the prominence of Maoris in rugby teams, and the development of the Western Samoans as formidable opponents. The New Zealanders have, with some truth, been described as 'genteel Aussies'. JAC

Nigeria. Former British colony and protectorate in West Africa. British missionaries arrived in Nigeria in the 1840s and in 1853 Lagos was annexed as a British colony as part of the campaign to halt the West African slave trade. When the activities of legitimate British traders in the Niger delta region were threatened by French rivals, the British government took responsibility for the conquest of the interior in 1900. The presence of powerful Muslim emirates in the north and of disparate systems of tribal organization in the south resulted in the division of Nigeria by the British into three distinct administrative regions, amalgamated under one central authority in 1914. Cocoa and palm-oil products brought a measure of wealth to the two southern regions but the populous north remained poor. The religious and economic differences between north and south resulted in the creation of an uneasy federal system of government when Nigeria became independent in 1960. KI

Nightingale, Florence (1820–1910). Nursing reformer. Named after the city of her birth, liberally educated, she chafed at the restricted opportunities for women of her station but eventually found purpose in relieving suffering. She learned nursing skills from the deaconesses at Kaiserwerth, but her real talents lay in administration, where she could manipulate and assert her will. Invited to go out to Crimea (1854), her success in mitigating Scutari's appalling conditions stemmed from organization, discipline, hard work, and being outside the army structure. On return, exploiting the legend of the Lady with the Lamp and chronically unwell, perhaps as a result of brucellosis (for 40 years), she undertook reform of the army medical services, then hospital architecture, nursing education, and sanitary reform in India. A person of considerable complexity, she raised nursing from disrepute to an honourable vocation, but was a lukewarm supporter of women's emancipation. ASH

Nijmegen, treaties of, 1678–9. Though England was not directly involved in the protracted Nijmegen negotiations, since the third *Anglo-Dutch War (1672–4) had been wound up by the treaty of *Westminster, her interests were much at stake. Louis XIV had clearly failed in his original intention of crushing the Dutch, yet he was still able to make significant territorial gains, including fifteen frontier towns and Franche-Comté. It was becoming obvious that France had replaced Spain as Europe's overmighty power and the shape of the coalition to restrain Louis 1688–1714 began to appear. JAC

Nile, battle of the, 1798. The site of this annihilating encounter between thirteen British ships of the line under *Nelson, and thirteen French under Brueys, is at the western end of Aboukir Bay. This extends some 18 miles southwest/north-east 20 miles east of Alexandria, close to Rosetta on the Nile delta. In the evening of 1 August 1798, after a chase of over two months, Nelson sighted Brueys's ships there, Napoleon having disembarked the 'Army of Egypt' at Alexandria a month before. Brueys had moored his ships in line about 3 miles offshore, but at intervals which prevented them from mutual support if attacked: their moorings betrayed their situation, since each ship was moored only at the bows, showing that each had room to swing to either side and yet be clear of shoals. In a night action five British ships attacked from the landward side where the French were least prepared for action, and seven from seaward, led by Nelson in *Vanguard*. By midday on 2 August all but two of Brueys's ships had surrendered, at no British loss. In consequence French land forces were both marooned and blockaded. Nelson was rewarded with a barony. DDA

Nineteen Propositions. In the summer of 1642, Charles I withdrew from London and prepared for war. On 1 June, Parliament sent to him at York nineteen propositions, which were more of a manifesto than a negotiating draft. They demanded complete political and military control. The king's answer, drafted by Colepeper and *Falkland, was a skilful exposition of the case for a balanced constitution. The propositions would 'destroy all rights and properties, all distinctions of families and merit, and by this means this splendid and excellently distinguished form of government [would] end in a dark, equal chaos of confusion'. Though mainly a tactical manœuvre for the middle ground, the answer was not forgotten and was much discussed as the basis for some form of limited or constitutional monarchy. JAC

Nine Years War, 1689–97. Also known as 'King William's War' or the 'War of the English Succession'. William of Orange accepted England's throne in 1688 in the hope that the nation's superior sea power and financial strength could be used in his struggle against Louis XIV's ambitions in the Netherlands and Germany. The French king's support for the exiled James II in Ireland and his harassment of the English fleet early in 1689 made war inevitable, and in May William formed a Grand Alliance which included England, the United Provinces, and the Empire. What was initially envisaged as a short struggle to compel French recognition of the English succession developed into a prolonged conflict of unprecedented scale and financial commitment. As William indicated to his English ministers, saving the nation from French invasion and the restoration of James II required nothing less than the annihilation of French might. In Ireland James's Franco-Irish army was soon defeated at the *Boyne in July 1690 and the rebels finally suppressed in 1691. But England's naval mastery of the English Channel was initially weakened by the French fleet and several times invasion was threatened until in May 1692 the allies overwhelmed the French off *La Hogue. Meanwhile, William was enmeshed in a desperate war in the Netherlands. In the slow, yearly grind of siege warfare he suffered a series of costly defeats before capturing the key fortress town of Namur in 1695, but his only real achievement was in preventing the French from completely overrunning Flanders. The war ended in September 1697 when the exhausted protagonists signed the treaty of *Ryswick. AAH

Ninian, St, properly Nynia, first apostle of the Scots. A very obscure figure mentioned by *Bede and subject of a much later life by Ailred of Rievaulx. Bede says he was a Briton and he appears to have lived around the time of the ending of Roman Britain, probably in the 5th cent. He is linked with south-western Scotland outside the Roman wall by his association with Whithorn (Dumfries and Galloway), in the territory of the Novantae. Known to Bede in Latin as Candida Casa, the white house, its Anglo-Saxon name Hwitærn means the same. Recent excavations at Whithorn have revealed an important early medieval ecclesiastical complex, perhaps going back to the postulated time of Ninian. ASEC

nisi prius. The statute of Westminster II, chapter 30, established this system which was an important factor in the growth of the *common law. The Court of *Common Pleas was established at Westminster palace after *Magna Carta (1215), but the disadvantage of bringing cases before the justices there was that the jury, which had to come from the litigant's own locality, had to travel to Westminster to give its verdict. In order to avoid the inconvenience of this system, Edward I's legislation provided that the jury verdict should be given at Westminster 'unless before' the date arranged, the travelling justices visited the area and took the jury's verdict in their own local court. It was then ensured that justices should invariably visit the locality before the specified date, thus speeding and making more convenient the process of litigation in the common law court. MM

Nkomo, Joshua (b. 1917). Pioneer Zimbabwean African nationalist. After studying in South Africa, Nkomo returned to work on the Rhodesian Railways and became president of the black railway workers' union in 1951. He was elected president of the African National Congress (ANC) in 1957 and was founder and president of the National Democratic Party in 1960 and the Zimbabwe African People's Union (ZAPU) in 1961 as each of the earlier parties was banned. Nkomo was detained by the white-controlled government from 1964 to 1974 and then led ZAPU, in alliance with Robert *Mugabe's ZANU, in a guerrilla war against the government. In the peace negotiations held in London in 1979 he was overshadowed by Mugabe, and when the latter became prime minister of Zimbabwe in 1980, relations between the two remained uneasy. In 1987 ZANU and ZAPU united and, when Mugabe became the country's executive president, Nkomo was appointed vice-president. KI

Nkrumah, Kwame (1909–72). Africa's most influential nationalist leader. After university education in the USA, Nkrumah helped to organize the fifth Pan-African Congress in Britain in 1945. Returning to the Gold Coast in 1947 he parted from the moderate leaders of the campaign for self-government to found the populist Convention Peoples' Party in 1949. Imprisoned after organizing a campaign of non-cooperation with the British colonial government in 1950, he was elected to Parliament in 1951 and was released from detention, becoming prime minister of the Gold Coast in 1952. He remained in office when the country, renamed *Ghana, gained its independence in 1957, and became president of the Republic of Ghana in 1960. He worked hard to promote the political unification of Africa as a defence against neo-colonialism, but his financial extravagance and his increasingly authoritarian rule at home led to his overthrow in 1966. He subsequently lived in exile in Guinea. KI

nobility. See ARISTOCRACY.

Nollekens, Joseph (1737–1823). An English sculptor, Nollekens was the son of an Antwerp painter settled in England. Between 1760 and 1770, in Rome, he laid the foundations of his financial and artistic success. He made a fine, if not always honest, living, dealing in antique fragments and sculpture. Several portrait busts he carved at this time ensured that his reputation preceded him, and on his return to London he established a successful practice. Nollekens's sitters included royalty, literary men, and numerous politicians; William *Pitt refused to sit for him, yet casts of the excellent bust which Nollekens made from a death mask and a portrait were extremely popular. Many of his monuments and busts are in Westminster abbey. Nollekens was established as notoriously mean in the biography written by his pupil J. T. Smith (1828). JC

Nominated Parliament. See BAREBONE'S PARLIAMENT.

nonconformists. See DISSENT.

non-jurors were the high churchmen of the late 17th-cent. Church of England, who refused the oath of allegiance to William and Mary after their accession in 1688. They held to the doctrine of the *divine right of kings and believed, therefore, that the Stuarts remained the legitimate monarchs. Eight bishops (including *Sancroft of Canterbury), 400 priests, and a few laymen refused the oath. They were dispossessed and tried to keep an alternative church in existence with illegal services in their churches, but were divided among themselves over the correctness of this. Their links with the Stuarts and the fears of restoration made them unpopular in early Hanoverian England. They were linked in belief and religious principles to the Caroline divines of the 17th cent. and the *Oxford movement of the 19th cent. JFC

non-residence. Residence in one's place of ministry has been compulsory since early times for all bishops and beneficed clergy, but absence became a substantial abuse in the later Middle Ages. Notable examples were *Wyclif who, though he attacked the abuse, was himself not resident, and *Wolsey who successively held several sees *in commendam* with the archbishopric of York. Non-residence was a major target of the reformers. The Council of Trent specifically banned it, as did the Anglican canons of 1604 and 1964–9. Nevertheless it was commonplace in the 18th cent. since many livings were too poor in themselves to support a priest; 60 per cent of incumbents were non-resident in 1808. WMM

non-resistance. 'For who can stretch forth his hand against the Lord's anointed and be guiltless?' The doctrine of non-resistance flourished in the aftermath of the Civil War, holding that monarchs had total jurisdiction and that their subjects owed them total obedience. Sir Robert Filmer's *Patriarcha*, published in 1680 some 40 years after it was written, declared that the idea that 'the multitude may correct or depose their prince' was a 'damnable conclusion'. After the Restoration, the *Corporation Act (1661) and the Act of *Uniformity (1662) insisted on an oath that 'it is not lawful on any pretence whatsoever to take up arms against the king'. But James II's attack upon the Church of England placed many Tories in an acute dilemma and the majority abandoned non-resistance to support the invasion of William of Orange. In 1689, the statute 1 Wm. & Mar. c. 8 specifically declared that the previous oath against the lawfulness of resistance 'shall not from henceforth be required'. The last great debate on the subject took place during the impeachment of Henry *Sacheverell in 1710. After 1714, with a Hanoverian on the throne and the Whigs firmly entrenched in power, the doctrine of non-resistance seemed less appealing to the Tories. JAC

Nonsuch, treaty of, 1585. After years of characteristic hesitation, in August 1585 Elizabeth took a momentous decision. The fall of Antwerp persuaded her that, without aid, the Dutch rebels would be crushed by Philip II of Spain. Putting aside the temptation of sovereignty, she agreed, at Nonsuch palace, to place 7,000 men in the field at her own cost. *Leicester was put in charge. Philip's response was the preparation of a great *Armada. JAC

Nonsuch palace near Cheam in Surrey was built on a grand scale round two courtyards by Henry VIII from 1538 onwards, sold by Mary, and repurchased in 1592 by Elizabeth. In the 17th cent. it belonged to *Henrietta Maria, who reoccupied it at the Restoration. After her death Charles II gave it to his mistress the duchess of Cleveland, who had it demolished in 1682. JAC

Nore naval mutiny, 1797. Unlike *Spithead, the Nore, at the mouth of the Medway, was not a fleet station but an assembly point. This helps to explain the mutiny's uncoordinated nature, though its causes were fundamentally the same as Spithead's and it lasted for a similar period, from 12 May to 16 June. The noisome conditions in the depot/flag ship *Sandwich*, with her complement swollen by articulate 'Quota Men' (provided by counties and ports under the Acts of 1795) such as the mutiny's apparent leader Richard Parker, sparked an agitation which was disseminated through the anchorage, since the Spithead royal pardon did not obtain there. The coherent pattern of the Spithead outbreak was lacking at the Nore, but Sheerness was nevertheless cowed, Thames traffic halted, and from there up to Yarmouth the navy's guard against the hostile Dutch fleet lowered. Starvation, and a popularly supported governmental attrition, smothered the mutiny; Parker, and 29 of his erstwhile confederates, were hanged. DDA

Norfolk was the fourth largest of the traditional counties. From Yarmouth in the east to Sutton bridge in the west is over 70 miles. The county is separated from Suffolk in the south by the rivers Waveney and Little Ouse, and from Cambridgeshire to the west by the river Nene. Much of the eastern half is drained by the river Wensum, which rises west of Fakenham and flows through Norwich to join the Yare, which is joined by the Bure just before it enters the sea at Yarmouth: the western rivers Wissey and Nar are tributaries of the Great Ouse, which flows into the Wash at Lynn. From Yarmouth round to the Wash is coast, lashed by what *Camden called that 'great, roaring ocean': the coast was so dangerous that when *Defoe visited Cromer in the 1720s he noticed no barn, shed, or pigsty which was not 'built of old planks, beams, wales and timbers, the wrecks of ships and ruins of mariners' and merchants' fortunes'. The shire is mainly flat, a county of vast horizons and of nippy salt breezes blowing off the sea.

The county takes its name from the North-folk of the Saxon settlement. In Roman times it was in *Iceni territory. It then became part of the Saxon kingdom of *East Anglia, which retained some independence until the 9th cent., when it fell under Danish control. The difference between Norfolk and Suffolk was acknowledged early: the whole area was under the diocese of *Dunwich until 673, when a new diocese was establish at North *Elmham, near East Dereham. Despite severe depredations—Thetford and *Norwich were sacked by the Danes in 1004—the region grew in population and prosperity. Thetford, Yarmouth, and Norwich were flourishing towns by the time of the *Domesday survey in 1086. Thetford gained a temporary advantage in 1072 when the bishopric was moved there from North Elmham, but in 1094 it was transferred again, this time to Norwich, where it stayed. The great cathedral was started in 1096. Bishop's Lynn, which became King's Lynn at the time of the Reformation in 1536, may have existed before the Norman Conquest, probably as a place where salt was made, but its development as a major port was in the late 11th and 12th cents.

Norfolk's prosperity owed much to its geographical position. The long coastline, though hazardous, promised abundant fish. Yarmouth bloaters soon acquired a national reputation and the town remained in the top ten until the later 18th cent. After the Danish attacks had ceased the county was free from marauders. Unlike Northumberland or Herefordshire, it did not have to face Scottish or Welsh border raids, and during the Civil War, though there was skirmishing and King's Lynn suffered a month's siege in 1643, there was no fighting on the scale that Gloucestershire, Somerset, or Worcestershire saw. *Kett's rising in 1549, mainly a protest against *enclosures, did little permanent damage, though Norwich was taken and retaken. In the south-west of the county, schemes of improved drainage in the 17th and 18th cents. turned thousands of acres of fen into good agricultural land. Norwich became one of the great centres of the cloth industry and by Tudor times was the second town in the kingdom. Norfolk's nearness to London gave it great opportunities as the capital grew to unprecedented proportions and East Anglia became London's larder.

Defoe's visit in 1723 came when Norfolk's prosperity was still at its height. He was amazed at the 'prodigious number' of turkeys and geese driven up to London in vast droves of 1,000 or 2,000 birds. At Norwich, the clothiers 'employ all the country round in spinning yarn for them': nobody was unemployed who wished to work. At Yarmouth, so many vessels were crammed in by the quayside that 'one may walk from ship to ship as on a floating bridge'.

By 1800, the county's relative prosperity was over. As colonies were established, the ports of the west coast—*Bristol, *Liverpool, and *Glasgow—had the advantage, and, in population, Norwich was surpassed by the new industrial towns of *Manchester, *Sheffield, and *Leeds. Competition from the Yorkshire woollen industry and then from Lancashire cotton was severe.

In the 19th cent., Norfolk became something of a backwater, though connected by rail to London in the 1840s via Cambridge or Colchester. The growth of seaside holidays brought modest prosperity to Hunstanton, Cromer, and Sheringham and the Broads developed from the 1870s as a playground. *Pevsner wrote in 1962 that parts of Norfolk remained curiously secluded, 'with many stretches and patches so remote that one cannot believe one is only one hundred miles from London'. But in more recent decades the pace has quickened as industry diversified—Colman's mustard, Matthews's turkeys, the Norwich Union—and the flight from London gathered pace. Population growth is well above the national average and Norfolk once more faces the problems of areas of outstanding beauty and tranquillity in a teeming nation. JAC

Norfolk, Roger Bigod, 4th earl of. See BIGOD, ROGER.

Norfolk, Roger Bigod, 5th earl of. See BIGOD, ROGER.

Norfolk, Charles Howard, 11th duke of (1746–1815). Known as Lord Surrey until he succeeded to the dukedom in 1786, Howard renounced the catholic faith in 1780 and embarked upon a political career as an advanced Whig. He served as MP for Carlisle 1780–6, spoke often in the Commons, was a keen advocate of parliamentary reform, and held office in the coalition ministry as a lord of the Treasury. Though he built up an electoral empire of eleven seats, his political standing was scarcely commensurate. But in 1798 he offered a toast to the 'Majesty of the People' at a public dinner at the Crown and Anchor tavern to celebrate Fox's birthday. Despite an apology to the king for 'unguarded expressions' he was dismissed his post as lord-lieutenant of the West Riding and lost his colonelcy in the militia. He was replaced as lord-lieutenant by *Fitzwilliam, who was also dismissed in 1819 for condemning the massacre at *Peterloo. Norfolk received partial restoration in 1807 when he was appointed lord-lieutenant of Sussex. *Boswell found him a 'lively, affable, talking man' but some of his conviviality seems to have been due to drink. JAC

Norfolk, John Howard, 1st duke of (d. 1485). As grandson of the 1st duke, Howard was an heir general to the Mowbray titles and estates. From the death of his father in 1436, he was merely lord of the manor of Stoke Neyland (Suffolk). He was a retainer of the 3rd duke and perhaps on his nomination the first Yorkist sheriff of Norfolk in 1461, shortly before Edward IV knighted him on the battlefield of *Towton. Thereafter he was one of the king's most valuable servants, in office at court and in East Anglia, in diplomacy and war on land and sea; he was enriched by generous rewards and his own enterprise, which included ownership of fourteen ships. He became Lord Howard in 1470, but Edward excluded him from the Mowbray inheritance by a parliamentary Act of dubious legality; this allowed its retention by the king's younger son Richard, in right of his late wife, sole heiress of the 4th duke. In 1483 Howard supported the usurpation of Richard III, who created him duke of Norfolk; that the title was at the king's disposal suggests that Prince Richard had died in the Tower of London, of which Howard was constable. That he was the only magnate killed fighting for Richard at *Bosworth seems to confirm his complicity. RLS

Norfolk, Thomas Howard, 2nd duke of (1443–1524). Norfolk had a remarkable political and military career at the highest level, despite a bad start. His father was a prominent Yorkist, who fought at *Towton, was created duke by Richard III, and died fighting at his side at *Bosworth. The son was wounded at *Barnet in 1471 and taken prisoner at Bosworth. He spent some years in the Tower before Henry VII restored his title as earl of Surrey and in 1489 made him chief justice in Eyre north of Trent, with heavy law and order responsibilities. From 1501 to 1522 he was lord high treasurer. In 1510 Henry VIII made him earl marshal for life and in 1513 he annihilated the Scots at the battle of *Flodden, showing himself a capable and determined commander, even at 70. His reward was the dukedom of Norfolk. In the king's absence in France at the *Field of Cloth of Gold in 1520, Norfolk acted as guardian of England. For a man who started on the wrong side, this was a crowning achievement. JAC

Norfolk, Thomas Howard, 3rd duke of (1473–1554). Norfolk picked a precarious path through the hazards of Tudor politics. He was closely related to the royal family. His first wife was a daughter of Edward IV; his second wife's grandmother was sister to Edward IV's queen; he was uncle to both *Anne Boleyn and *Catherine Howard. He was given the Garter in 1510 and after fighting under his father at the great victory of *Flodden was created earl of Surrey when his father was made duke of Norfolk. From 1513 to 1525 he served as lord high admiral, was lord-lieutenant of Ireland 1520–2 and lord high treasurer 1522–47. He helped to bring down *Wolsey and in 1534 presided over the trial of his niece Anne Boleyn. In 1537 he put down the rising of the *Pilgrimage of Grace with severity. In 1540 he succeeded in ousting Thomas *Cromwell. The disgrace of Catherine Howard rocked his position but he survived and held commands against the French and the Scots. The imprudence of his son Lord *Surrey, in sporting the royal arms, brought a conviction for treason in 1546 and Norfolk escaped execution only because Henry VIII died. Throughout Edward VI's reign, Norfolk remained in the Tower but, as a catholic, was released by Mary, restored to his honours, and served against *Wyatt's rebellion in January 1554, which was defeated largely by the zeal of his half-brother Lord William *Howard. He died the same year at the age of 80. JAC

Norfolk, Thomas Howard, 4th duke of (1538–72). Norfolk was grandson of the 3rd duke. His father Lord Surrey was executed when he was 8. He and his grandfather were restored to their honours at the accession of Mary in 1553 and he succeeded as duke the following year. Elizabeth gave him the Garter in 1559 and employed him in Scotland to oust the French party. This proved his undoing. After the death of his third wife in 1567, he conceived a plan to marry Mary, queen of Scots, still a possible successor to Elizabeth. They had not actually met but went in for a good deal of literary swooning. In October 1569 he was committed to the Tower and in November his brother-in-law the earl of *Westmorland led the rising of the *northern earls, on behalf of Mary and the old religion. Norfolk was released in 1570 and assured Elizabeth that the marriage had been abandoned, but allowed himself to be drawn into the *Ridolfi plot to replace Elizabeth by Mary. Norfolk's role was to liaise with a Spanish expedition which was to land at Harwich. He was again put in the Tower and executed in June 1572. His personal popularity was considerable but he was vain, vacillating, and timorous. The dukedom was restored to his great-great-grandson in 1660. JAC

Norfolk, John Mowbray, 3rd duke of (1415–61). After coming of age in 1436, Norfolk had a brief career in public service, in the relief of Calais from siege, as warden of the east march, and as an ambassador in Anglo-French negotiations. He allowed himself, however, to be implicated in the lawless activities of his steward Sir Robert Wingfield, which led to their detention in the Tower of London in 1440. Norfolk next quarrelled with Wingfield, assaulting his house with cannon, and consequently returned to the Tower in 1448. His ambition to dominate the shire of Norfolk was frustrated by the more potent 'good lordship' of William de la *Pole, duke of Suffolk. After Suffolk's fall, Norfolk expected to have a free hand. He joined forces with Richard of *York in demonstrations against the new court clique in 1450. It compelled him, however, to dismiss his own councillors who favoured York, a purge which occasioned the anarchy reported in the *Paston letters for 1453, after which Norfolk again veered towards York in a half-hearted way. The first battle of *St Albans had been fought before his arrival. He agreed to York's attainder in 1459, but joined him after the battle of *Northampton. He escaped to London from the Yorkist defeat at *St Albans in 1461, was in the junta which recognized Edward IV as king, and fought in his victory at *Towton. His last military exploit was the seizure of Caister castle from John Paston. Norfolk's foremost interest remained his own regional aggrandizement; he was unreliable as both political ally and noble patron. RLS

Norfolk, Thomas Mowbray, 1st duke of (1366–99). Mowbray was created earl of Nottingham on succeeding to his elder brother's lands in 1383, and received the title of earl marshal in 1386. He was one of the lords *appellant who prosecuted Richard II's favourites in 1387–8. Subsequently he assisted Richard's despotic ambitions. In 1397 he arrested the duke of *Gloucester and murdered him at Calais, and was one of the eight lords who indicted the king's victims in Parliament. His ducal title in 1397 was a reward, as was a share of the forfeitures. Soon afterwards Norfolk was accused of treason by Henry (later Henry IV), duke of Hereford; in consequence, both dukes were exiled. Norfolk died in Venice. RLS

Norham, treaty of, 1209. In August 1209, after some years of strained relations with the Scots, King John brought a large army to Norham, 7 miles west of Berwick-on-Tweed. In return for peace, William the Lion promised to pay £10,000 and handed over his two elder daughters for marriage into the English royal house. In February 1212 John secured a renewal of this treaty and, apparently, the right to arrange the marriage of William's son and heir, the future Alexander II. Although John failed to secure acknowledgement as feudal overlord of Scotland, these agreements emphasized William's submission and his dependence on English goodwill. KJS

Norham adjudication, 1291–2. Edward I's adjudication of the claims put forward by John *Balliol and twelve others to the vacant Scottish throne, which began at Norham, near Berwick-on-Tweed, on 10 May 1291. On the death of *Margaret 'the Maid of Norway' (1290), the Scottish royal house had failed in the main line. Edward insisted on intervening in the succession dispute, or *'Great Cause', not as an impartial arbitrator, but as feudal overlord of Scotland; and his standing as such was recognized by the claimants, though not by the rest of the Scottish political community, in June 1291. Their claims were scrutinized by a court of 104 'auditors' (assessors), and after the proceedings had resumed at Berwick, judgment was given on 17 November 1292 in favour of John Balliol, who was enthroned at Scone on 30 November. When on 26 December Edward extracted homage from Balliol as king of Scots, he was thereby unambiguously acknowledged as overlord of Scotland. KJS

Norman architecture. A version of the European Romanesque style of the early Middle Ages, introduced into England by the Normans after 1066. Used extensively for ecclesiastical and military purposes until the rise of Gothic during the early 13th cent., it is characterized by heavy, load-bearing masonry construction, comparatively modest window apertures, deeply recessed doorways, massive columns or piers, and the use of the round arch and its derivatives, the groin- and barrel-vaults. Ornament was usually restricted to repetitive, geometric mouldings such as those of the lozenge, chevron, or zigzag type. In comparison to practice on the continent, sculpture was very sparingly used.

The numerous monasteries, cathedrals (many of monastic origin), and castles which the Normans built symbolized their authority, the Norman castle in particular, with its 'shell' or rectangular keep, being an essential element of the subjugation process. In ecclesiastical buildings, the triforium, a windowless gallery above the main arcade, was of great importance, largely for structural reasons, in contrast to the enlarged clerestory of Gothic architecture. This can be seen in the nave (begun 1099) of Durham cathedral, an outstanding example of Norman work. Other Norman examples include the cathedrals of Chichester (nave 1114–48), Ely (nave begun *c.*1090), Norwich (nave, transepts, and choir 1096–1145), and Peterborough (nave, transepts, and choir 1118–*c.*1190), the church of St Bartholomew the Great, Smithfield, London (choir begun early 12th cent.), the keep and chapel ('White Tower') of the *Tower of London (1078–90), Colchester castle (begun *c.*1071) and Castle Hedingham (*c.*1140), both in Essex, Oakham castle (late 12th cent.), and portions of Durham castle, especially the undercroft chapel (possibly as early as 1070–80). TEF

Norman Conquest. William the Conqueror's victory at the battle of *Hastings in October 1066 was followed by six years of campaigning, which irrevocably established the new king's grip on England. In the succeeding decades, the Norman kings and their followers expanded their power into Wales and Lowland Scotland. The sequence of events which led up to William's victory is uncertain, because of the existence of accounts which are contradictory and irreconcilable. It is undeniable that at some point, probably in the year 1051, an arrangement was made which William believed entitled him to claim the English succession as *Edward the Confessor's legitimate heir. From William's point of view, it was irrelevant that Edward had made a similar promise on his death-bed to *Harold Godwineson, since Harold had visited Normandy in 1064 or 1065 as Edward's ambassador and sworn an oath to accept William's succession. However, since this story is told exclusively in Norman sources and since later English sources cast doubt on both the purpose and the nature of the visit, it may not be the whole truth. The massive support which Harold enjoyed in 1066 shows that the English regarded him as a popular and rightly chosen king. William's belief in the legitimacy of his kingship, which was buttressed by the support which the papacy gave in and after 1066, conditioned many of the developments which followed the battle of Hastings; not only was William's kingship legal, but so also was the settlement of thousands of Normans, Flemings, Bretons, and other Frenchmen which he sanctioned. A massive take-over of English land and resources accomplished within a framework of notional legality and through the agency of existing institutions was largely complete by 1086, the year when *Domesday Book was made.

On a longer-term perspective, it is arguable that the Conquest was the last in a series of conquests of lowland Britain and itself had relatively little impact on a broader evolutionary process of economy, society, landscape, and language. The newcomers were after all a small military élite who were gradually assimilated into Britain and whose connections with the continent were severed with the loss of Normandy in 1204. On the other hand, it is not unreasonable to think of the Norman Conquest as a decisive shift within this broader process; the England and the Britain which emerged from the Norman military take-over were surely significantly different from the one which would have developed if Harold had won on 14 October 1066. There can be no doubt that William and his successors governed through mechanisms which were essentially those of the late Old English kingdom. The new aristocracy claimed to exercise the same rights and powers over their peasants as their English predecessors had done. Not everyone, however, would accept this appearance of continuity at face value. William I, William II, and Henry I all intervened with increasing frequency in the shires; it is far from certain that Harold and his successors would have made the same use of the existing structures. At a local level, many estates were reorganized, apparently in the short term depressing the fortunes of the peasantry. It was also the case that the Conquest's creation of the cross-channel Anglo-Norman realm sucked England into the feuds between the territorial rulers of northern France and can be linked over centuries to the outbreak of the *Hundred Years War. The new connection with France also established cultural connections which arguably ensured that England's place in the so-called 12th-cent. renaissance was much more closely linked to developments in France than it would otherwise have been. The Conquest definitively extracted England from the Scandinavian political orbit which had brought about the earlier conquest by *Sweyn Forkbeard and *Cnut and *Harold Hardrada's invasion, defeated in 1066 by Harold Godwineson at the battle of *Stamford Bridge. It is doubtful whether Wales, Scotland, and—ultimately—Ireland would have been as intensively colonized from England but for the presence there of a new aggressive aristocracy. To ask what would have happened had Harold won the battle of Hastings is to pose an unanswerable question. For some historians, much about England after 1066 was a continuation of what had existed before. For others, the Conquest created a dynamic which brought about major change. DB

Normandy, duchy of. The origins of the duchy of Normandy lie in a grant of territory around Rouen and the Seine valley made early in the 10th cent. by the king of the west Franks to a Viking chieftain named Rollo. This initial grant was supplemented by others and the whole was forged into a coherent political entity during the 10th cent. by Rollo's descendants and their aristocracy. The respective roles within the duchy's development of sustained Scandinavian connections and culture, as opposed to adaptation and assimilation into the territory's Frankish environment, is a controversial subject; while many aspects of Normandy's Scandinavian heritage remain very evident into the early 11th cent., the essentially Frankish and Christian character of its government and society surely indicates a process of assimilation to, and exploitation of, existing forms, which began early in the territory's history. By the first years of the 11th cent. Normandy still retained political and economic connections with Scandinavia and Scandinavian settlers in Britain and Ireland. But monasteries were being refounded, bishoprics were recovering, government was conducted according to patterns which were Frankish, and society was taking on a feudal structure typical of neighbouring regions. At the same time, Normandy became the centre of an extensive movement of conquest and colonization into southern Europe and Britain which lasted for much of the 11th cent. Why this should have happened is difficult to explain; internal turbulence and a dynamic inherited from the Viking past may play a part, but it is notable that northern French society as a whole was in a period of expansion. The great conquests in the Mediterranean and Britain are best interpreted as a Norman-led movement which absorbed the energies of a large number of enterprising individuals from many regions of northern France; the *Norman conquest of Britain, for example, was a relatively short-lived migration involving Bretons, Flemings, and others, as well as Normans, led by a great war-leader William the Conqueror, a stereotypical—if outstandingly successful—ruler of a French territorial principality. Normandy's place at the centre of a colonizing movement came to an end by the early decades of the 12th cent., though its far-flung connections endured much longer. Its history is thereafter dominated by wars with other French principalities, which in certain fundamental respects are no more than a continuation of the volatile politics of northern France throughout the period of the duchy's existence; the province had after all struggled to survive in its earliest years. Henry I had to work hard to defend it, it was absorbed into the *Angevin empire after its conquest by *Geoffrey Plantagenet in 1144 and, subsequently and definitively, into the French kingdom in 1204 after its conquest by Philip Augustus. Its three centuries of independent existence supported some of the more remarkable exploits of the medieval period. Yet ultimately its history must be analysed in the context of the history of the French kingdom; its expansion was part of the expansion of Francia, its rise and fall was an element in the politics of that region, and its final conquest was brought about by the French king, to whom the dukes owed fealty. In the 12th cent. its internal history is characterized by a lack of enterprise and innovation once the great days of expansion had passed, a state of affairs evident in government, architecture, and learning. Many among its aristocracy possessed lands in Normandy and England, but others resided principally in the duchy; their actions assisted the drift to the status of a province of France. After 1204 many Anglo-Norman magnates abandoned their smaller Norman estates. This was followed by an extensive colonization of Normandy from France. DB

'Norman Yoke'. The belief that Anglo-Saxon institutions had been essentially democratic until replaced by autocracy under the Normans, despite its implausibility, was held by many radicals in the 17th and 18th cents. One of its most powerful advocates was Edward *Coke, who assured Queen Elizabeth that the Anglo-Saxons had had a parliament composed of two chambers, with boroughs and shires represented. The advantage of the theory to the opponents of Charles I was that they could shake off the charge that they were dangerous innovators and insist that they merely desired the restoration of ancient rights. The theory was so useful that it had a long run for its money. Major John *Cartwright, the indefatigable exponent of parliamentary reform, was urging it in 1818, it was resuscitated by some of the chartists, and last heard when the House of Lords' resistance to *Lloyd George's 'People's Budget' in 1909 was denounced as 'Normanism'. JAC

North, Frederick, Lord, 2nd earl of Guilford (1732–92). North is one of several prime ministers—*Walpole, *Pitt, *Asquith, and *Chamberlain are others—whose careers were distorted by war. For the first five years of his ministry, he established a stable government, defused domestic problems, and introduced useful financial reforms. From 1775 onwards, he was increasingly overwhelmed by the American troubles, which not only brought him down, but established his popular reputation as a weak and ineffective minister.

North was the eldest son of Francis, 1st earl of Guilford, but in some ways his life resembled that of a younger son with a career to make. The family was not wealthy, nor his father generous, and since he lived to be 86, North inherited only two years before his own death. He did not use his position to enrich his family and ran into debt: when the king gave him £18,000 to clear it, it established a personal obligation that made it difficult for North to resign, though he admitted openly that he was not the man to wage war.

He was returned to the House of Commons in 1754 for the family seat at Banbury, at the age of 22, and soon began moving up the ladder. He was a useful man of business, hard-working, fat, and cheerful. Almost the whole of his life he spent in the Commons, defended its privileges with tenacity, gauged its temper skilfully, and, according to Gibbon, became 'a consummate master of debate'. He was brought onto the Treasury Board in 1759 by his cousin the duke of *Newcastle. He remained in office when Newcastle went out in 1762, mainly because he needed the money, but stayed on friendly terms. He went out with *Grenville in 1765, declined to serve with the Rockinghams, and came back into junior office in *Grafton's administration in 1766. His great chance came in 1767 with the sudden death of Charles *Townshend, whom he succeeded as chancellor of the Exchequer. He was now the main spokesman for the government in the Commons and conducted the difficult debates on the Middlesex election issue. When Grafton resigned in January 1770, North took over as 1st lord of the Treasury at the urgent entreaty of the king. He was 37.

His first few years in office were impressive. Government majorities were restored, the Wilkes issue receded, North's reputation climbed. His relations with the king were excellent—he was given the Garter in 1772—and his mastery of the Commons undisputed. An acknowledged expert in finance, his budgets were received with scarcely a dissentient voice. He handled his first test—the dispute with Spain over the Falkland Islands—with skill and judgement. In his Indian legislation, he tried to co-ordinate activities under a governor-general, and it has been called 'a revolution in policy'. His *Quebec Act in 1774 was an important concession to the catholics and helped to persuade Canadians in 1776 not to throw in their lot with the American rebels. Horace Walpole, no easy critic, wrote in June 1770 that North was 'sensible and moderate' and in 1773 that opposition was almost at a standstill. The American question, which ultimately brought him down, had its roots deep in the past. (See AMERICAN WAR OF INDEPENDENCE.) Once the French had been expelled from Canada during the Seven Years War it was not hard to perceive the possibility of American independence. The British, heavily burdened after the war, resented the colonists' refusal to pay taxes. Grenville's *Stamp Act and Townshend's duties brought in little revenue. North's first action was conciliatory—to abandon all of Townshend's duties save that on tea, retained more as a token of authority than a source of revenue. It is doubtful whether any prime minister could have gone further. The American response was the seizure of the revenue cutter *Gaspée*, the intimidation of customs officers, and the *Boston Tea Party. Coercive measures against the colonists were inevitable. But once fighting began, North was marginalized and the military men took over. His conciliation proposals came too late to affect the issue. Repeatedly he begged to resign and warned the king that a stronger minister was needed: time after time the king refused, understanding the value of North's parliamentary skill in presenting government policy. Only after the surrender at *Yorktown in 1781, with his majority down to single figures, was North allowed to go.

The last ten years of his life were largely a postscript. He returned to office as home secretary in the spring of 1783 in the coalition with Charles *Fox, but was unwell for several months and content to let his more vigorous colleagues make the running. Dismissed in December 1783, he slid gracefully into the role of a premature elder statesman, defending the Church of England from dissenting attacks and the constitution from dangerous innovation. His parliamentary following dwindled with the years and from 1786 he was blind and had to be led into the House. Too unimaginative to be a great statesman, North's significance is as an extraordinary parliamentarian, whose sure touch in the House stayed with him to the end. JAC

Cannon, J. A., *Lord North: The Noble Lord in the Blue Ribbon* (1970); Thomas, P. D. G., *Lord North* (1976).

Northampton, Assize of, 1176. The Assize of Northampton was an important stage in the development and enforcement of English law in the reign of Henry II. In the form of instructions to royal justices, it tightened up the provisions of the Assize of *Clarendon ten years earlier and has been seen as the response to a crime wave. The offences of arson and forgery were added to those into which the justices were to inquire and severe punishments included the loss of the right hand. Trial was still ordeal by water. JAC

Northampton, battle of, 1264. When Simon de *Montfort and his supporters took up arms in the spring of 1264, his second son Simon was besieged in Northampton by the king, Henry III. Despite de Montfort's march to relieve it, the castle surrendered on 6 April and young Simon was taken prisoner. This set-back to the baronial cause was cancelled by their victory at *Lewes in May, when the king was in turn taken captive. JAC

Northampton, battle of, 1460. The Yorkist leadership fled abroad after its ignominious and precipitate flight from *Ludford Bridge in 1459, but returned in the summer of 1460. On 10 July *Warwick and the future Edward IV encountered Henry VI's army just south of Northampton, under the duke of Buckingham. The battle was decided quickly when Lord Grey of Ruthyn deserted the king. Henry was captured and his leading supporters, including Buckingham, executed. JAC

Northampton, treaty of, 1328. On 4 May 1328 Edward III, or more precisely his mother *Isabella and Roger *Mortimer who then controlled the government, recognized Robert I (Bruce) as king of Scotland and did not demand homage from him. This was a volte-face from the line which English kings had adopted since the mid-1290s in denying Scottish sovereignty, and reveals the weak position of the English in the wake of the deposition of Edward II and the abortive campaign against the Scots in Weardale in 1327. Edward III was subsequently determined to overturn this 'turpis pax', as the Meaux chronicler called it, and, encouraged by the success of Edward *Balliol against Robert's heir, invaded Scotland in 1333 to restore English lordship. AC

Northamptonshire is one of the quieter English counties, less affected by the industrial revolution than its western neighbours. The shire is traversed by the river Nene, which rises near Daventry and leaves near Peterborough. *Camden called it 'a noble river and a continual blessing to this province'. In the north, the Welland marks the border with Rutland and Leicestershire, and in the west the Cherwell separates the county from Oxfordshire. Northamptonshire covered a great swathe of central England: Brackley in the west seems like a Cotswold town, Eye, east of Peterborough, is a fenland village.

In Roman times the region was in the territory of the *Coritani. Towcester on *Watling Street was a small Roman town and the Nene valley at Castor, on *Ermine Street, was an important pottery centre. In Saxon times the shire was part of the kingdom of *Mercia. *Peada, son of *Penda, founded a great monastery about 657 at Peterborough, which survived sacking by the Danes in 870. The first mention of Northampton is when a Danish army seized it in 917 and dominated the surrounding countryside. When the area was recovered by *Edward the Elder a little later, the Danish territory seems to have been the basis for the emergent county. Two remarkable Saxon churches are at *Brixworth and *Earls Barton. Hamtun, the chief settlement on the Nene, became Northampton after the Norman Conquest to distinguish it from Southampton.

In the medieval period the shire was fertile and prosperous. Northampton was a town of importance. The massive castle was not finally destroyed until the railway station was built in Victorian times. Its charter dated from 1189 and parliaments were frequently summoned there. In 1460 it was the site of a bloody Yorkist victory and in 1645 the last major battle of the Civil War took place at *Naseby, after Rupert's ephemeral victory at Leicester. In 1675 the greater part of Northampton was destroyed by fire. The rebuilding, possibly supervised by Henry Bell of King's Lynn, was much approved. *Defoe commented in the 1720s that 'the great inn, at the George, the corner of the High Street, looks more like a palace than an inn'. The county produced corn and cattle and, according to Camden, was 'overrun with sheep'. Northampton horse fair was of national importance. Among the great landed estates were Althorp, Deene, Easton Neston, De la Pré, Boughton, and Burghley, though the parliamentary representation was dominated by the country gentlemen.

Although the industrial revolution came to Northamptonshire, it was gentler than elsewhere and its effects muted. Northampton was slow to tie into the growing canal network, but after the Grand Junction branch opened in 1815, connecting with London and Birmingham, it began to grow into a manufacturing town, specializing in boots. But the London to Birmingham railway bypassed it in 1838, largely for technical reasons, and a loop line to Birmingham was only established in 1872. Peterborough, promoted to a bishopric in Henry VIII's reign, profited from the coming of the railways, became a major junction, and developed heavy engineering. Wellingborough, Kettering, and Rushden all profited from rail links to become boot centres, the latter trebling in population between 1881 and 1901. Corby, no more than a village in 1801, developed as a steel town, exploiting the local iron resources. Stewart and Lloyd's factory was established in 1934 and Corby was given new town status in 1950. Though it has grown to more than 50,000, its planned development was stunted by the decision in 1980 to abandon steel-making.

The county has suffered considerable boundary changes. In 1888 the soke of Peterborough, which retained special jurisdictions, was given its own county council, and in 1965 was merged with Huntingdonshire, before finding its way in 1972 into a substantially enlarged Cambridgeshire. The rest of Northamptonshire was not affected by the local government reorganization, and the Banham commission recommended in 1994 that the two-tier system should continue. JAC

North Briton was the satirical name John *Wilkes gave to his weekly periodical, launched in June 1762 in opposition to *Smollett's the *Briton*, published in support of *Bute's administration. It included severe attacks on the peace of *Paris and general abuse of Scots. Issue no. 12 led to a duel between Wilkes and Lord Talbot, and when the government resolved in April 1763 to prosecute no. 45 as seditious libel, it let 'Wilkes and Liberty' out of the bottle. JAC

Northbrook, Thomas George Baring, 1st earl of (1826–1904). Baring's father was grandson of the founder of the banking firm, served as chancellor of the Exchequer under Melbourne 1839–41, was created baron in 1866, and died eight months later. Thomas Baring sat in the Commons as a Liberal 1857–66, and held a number of minor posts before serving as viceroy of India 1872–6, retiring after *Salisbury had taken over as secretary of state for India in *Disraeli's government. In India he succeeded Lord Mayo, who had been assassinated. Much of his time was devoted to attempting to deal with the Bengal famine, which he succeeded in holding in check. His desire to keep taxation down would, in any case, have ruled out expansionist policies. He was given an earldom on his retirement and served as 1st lord of the Admiralty in *Gladstone's second administration 1880–5. He left the Liberals over Home Rule in 1886 and did not hold office again. A cautious, reserved, and conservative man, Northbrook was a typical Whig, committed to public service without much enthusiasm. JAC

Northcliffe, Viscount. See HARMSWORTH, ALFRED.

Northcote, Sir Stafford, 8th baronet, 1st earl of Iddesleigh (1818–87). Of a Devon gentry family and educated at Eton and Balliol College, Oxford, Northcote, a civil servant in the early 1840s, was *Gladstone's secretary at the Board of Trade, then joint secretary to the 1851 *Great Exhibition and co-author of the Northcote–Trevelyan Report on the *civil service. A Peelite free trader and high churchman, he remained close to Gladstone in the 1850s. An MP from 1855, he was recruited by *Disraeli to the Conservative ministry in 1859 and served in the cabinets of 1866–8. He became chairman of the *Hudson's Bay Company and helped to negotiate the 1871 *Washington treaty with the USA. Chancellor of the Exchequer in 1874–80, Northcote succeeded Disraeli as leader in the Commons in 1876, though his unease with the premier's policy over the Eastern Question became evident. He was joint leader of the Conservatives with *Salisbury from 1881, but his emollient centrism, designed to attract moderate Whigs, brought criticism from his own side, particularly the *Fourth Party *frondeurs*. In 1885 Salisbury, now premier, removed Northcote from the Commons leadership and gave him an earldom and the 1st lordship of the Treasury. Briefly foreign secretary in 1886, Iddesleigh died suddenly as Salisbury was replacing him. BIC

northern earls, rising of the, 1569. This was one of the most serious risings on behalf of the old religion during the Tudor period. Between November and December 1569, Thomas, earl of *Northumberland, and Charles, earl of *Westmorland, mustered a rebel army in the northern counties and gained initial success. The rebels carried the catholic banner of the five wounds of Christ, which had been used during the *Pilgrimage of Grace, destroyed English bibles and Elizabethan Books of Common Prayer, restored traditional altars, and celebrated mass in Durham cathedral. In addition to the religious settlement, the earls complained of the queen's choice of 'divers disordered and evil-disposed persons', whose 'subtle and crafty dealing' had 'disordered the realm and now lastly seek the destruction of the nobility'. The rising was suppressed by troops under Lord *Sussex. The political underpinning for the rising was the proposed marriage between the duke of *Norfolk and Mary Stuart, a catholic match supported by the earls. The plan was discovered and led to Norfolk's disgrace and execution. Westmorland escaped into exile but Northumberland, who fled to Scotland, was handed back and beheaded. SA

Northern Ireland was formed by the Government of *Ireland Act 1920–1. It comprises the six counties of the north-east of the island: Antrim, Down, Armagh, Londonderry, Fermanagh, and Tyrone. To ensure a comfortable protestant majority for the foreseeable future, the nine counties of the historic province of Ulster were rejected as the boundary. Fermanagh and Tyrone, though possessing small catholic majorities, were included to provide a credible geographical entity. The British government had preferred an all-Ulster option, hoping that partition would therefore be temporary. Initially, loyalist opinion was opposed to the establishment of a separate province; but once Northern Ireland had been set up, it was seen as the crucial bulwark against Irish unification.

The artificial character of the province is demonstrated by the awkwardness of its title: parts of Donegal in the Free State/Republic are further north. It is frequently referred to as 'the six counties', *'Stormont', or 'the Northern Statelet', terms revealing the bias of the observer. The decision to draw the boundary according to county lines made little social, economic, or geographical sense. The natural hinterland of the city of Derry is Co. Donegal; Newry was cut off from much of its locale; isolated enclaves of catholics or protestants were created; border areas such as south Armagh saw no justification for being included in the new province; the erratic border itself divided farms, towns, and communities.

The circumstances of the province's formation dictated its turbulent subsequent history. The catholic minority, always over 30 per cent of the population, never accepted partition and usually boycotted the Belfast Parliament. The emerging Free State refused to recognize Northern Ireland. An *IRA offensive in early 1922 threatened to destabilize the nascent province. In the *Anglo-Irish treaty of December 1921, provision was made for a boundary commission, holding out hope of a substantial alteration of frontier. The commission did not meet until 1925 and no changes were finally made. Not surprisingly, the province established itself along the lines of a protestant state for a protestant people, with a heavy emphasis on security considerations.

After 1925, the province's future seemed more assured but still few concessions were made to the minority. Economic development was retarded by over-dependence on the British Treasury and by over-reliance on declining traditional industries. The government was dominated by narrow landed and commercial interests; all were members of the *Orange order and preoccupied with appeasing their protestant constituents. Sir James *Craig was prime minister 1921–40, Lord *Brooke 1943–63. Unionist confidence was increased by their contribution in supplying bases and ports for Atlantic convoys, contrasting with the Free State's neutrality. However, lack of foresight and general incompetence in government circles caused the effects of German bombing of Belfast to be severe; embarrassingly, fire services had to be secretly begged from Dublin.

The declaration of an Irish republic in 1948 caused the constitutional status of the province to be clarified in the *Ireland Act of 1949. Dependence on Britain was increased by the new welfare state; unemployment became the worst in the UK; the disparity between west and east of the province grew wider. But the abject failure of the IRA offensive 1956–62 appeared to remove any immediate threat and increased catholic acceptance of the province. Terence *O'Neill's attempts, as premier from 1963, to modernize the economy and reform the sectarian basis of the province highlighted all inherent tensions. Unionists divided over his reforms and the catholic minority demanded more substantial changes, mounting their first effective challenge via the civil rights movement from 1967. Police and special constabulary's reaction to civil rights demonstrations, together with the unionist backlash, resulted in major riots in Derry city and Belfast, and the belated intervention of British troops to restore order and ensure more fundamental reforms. The security situation deteriorated rapidly in 1969–72, resulting in further polarization of the two communities, the alienation of the catholic population from the British army, and the formation of the Provisional IRA. The British government's declaration of direct rule from Westminster in 1972 was followed by the establishment of a power-sharing executive in January 1974, which was brought down as a consequence of the loyalist strike within five months.

The 1970s and 1980s saw a continuous, if limited, IRA offensive against both the security forces and the economy;

the growth of loyalist paramilitary retaliation; spates of sectarian assassinations and bombings in the province, in Britain, and occasionally in the Republic. Abortive attempts to restore some form of devolved government only revealed the extent to which violence had hardened divisions. Demands for political status for republican prisoners in 1981 led to further catholic alienation and support for *Sinn Fein. While direct rule saw a considerable diminution in governmental discriminatory practices, little progress was made on economic performance. Unionist suspicions concerning British government intentions increased and the British taxpayer was progressively alarmed about the expense of continued involvement.

By 1985 and the *Anglo-Irish agreement, attention turned to co-operation between the Republic and the British government on security and political matters as a potential base for settlement. The level of violence, particularly by protestant paramilitaries, increased. A sense of exhaustion after 25 years of conflict, better Anglo-Irish government communications, European and American concern, and, finally, negotiations between the *SDLP and Sinn Fein leaders, John Hume and Gerry Adams, all contributed to the Downing Street declaration of December 1993, the IRA cease-fire of August 1994, and the loyalist paramilitary one two months later. There is little evidence of any consensus between the communities over any political settlement. It is difficult to conceive of a long-term settlement being achieved in a purely Northern Ireland context. James Craig was moved to comment: 'Czechoslovakia and Ulster are born to trouble as the sparks fly upwards.' MAH

Buckland, P., *A History of Northern Ireland* (Dublin, 1981); Wichert, S., *Northern Ireland since 1945* (1991).

Northern Ireland Labour Party (NILP). Founded in 1924, as a socialist alternative to the largely sectarian politics of Ulster. It strove to remain neutral on the partition question, but in 1949—after the declaration of an Irish republic—it came out in favour of the constitutional link between Northern Ireland and Britain. This helped its position in protestant working-class areas, while constraining its appeal to catholics. Nevertheless, with unemployment rising in the late 1950s and early 1960s the NILP increased its vote, winning four Belfast constituencies in the Stormont elections of 1958 and 1962. Thereafter, the party faced greater challenges. A new Unionist prime minister, Terence *O'Neill, proved to be an energetic champion of the local economy, and—with the establishment of new industries—unemployment fell. The renewal of communal violence in 1969 heightened sectarianism and put further pressure on the NILP electoral base. The establishment of new parties in 1970–1 (the *Social Democratic and Labour Party, *Alliance) eroded different aspects of NILP support. The party polled well in the Westminster general election of June 1970 but thereafter rapidly declined: it survived with a minimal electoral following until 1987. AJ

Northern Rhodesia. See ZAMBIA.

North Foreland, battle of, 1666. A major engagement in the second Anglo-Dutch War, sometimes known as the St James's Day fight, was fought on 4 and 5 August in the Thames estuary and off the Suffolk coast. This was a continuation of the battle of the *Downs after each side had repaired and resupplied. Albemarle (*Monck) and Prince *Rupert with 89 warships were confronted by a Dutch fleet of 88 vessels under Cornelis Tromp and de Ruyter. The English had the better of the exchanges but the Dutch made harbour. *Pepys's laconic comment was: 'we keep the sea which denotes a victory, or at least that we are not beaten. But no great matter to brag on.' JAC

Northumberland is a large county of ancient origins as an independent kingdom and one of the earliest centres of British Christianity. A great border region, it is full of peel houses and castles, like Dunstanburgh, *Alnwick, Prudhoe, *Bamburgh, and Warkworth. The industrial development of Tyneside, largely a 19th-cent. phenomenon, is confined to the south-east corner. The rest is a shire of high fells and deep valleys, thinly populated, with small market towns like Corbridge, Haltwhistle, Morpeth, Hexham, Rothbury, Wooler, and Alnwick. *Berwick-on-Tweed is part of Northumberland geographically, though a county in its own right. The southern boundary is the Tyne, the northern the Tweed.

The main northern tribe in pre-Roman times was the *Brigantes, though *Camden placed the county under the Ottadini or *Votadini. The crossing of the Tyne at the Pons Aelium must soon have become a settlement, the nucleus of Newcastle itself. Hadrian's Wall, which runs east–west across the county, was for decades the limit of the Roman empire. In early Saxon times, the area formed part of the kingdom of *Bernicia, which joined with *Deira to the south in 651 to constitute *Northumbria (the land north of the Humber), which for centuries disputed supremacy with *Mercia and *Wessex. The conversion of King *Edwin in the early 7th cent. led to the foundation of a famous monastery on *Lindisfarne or Holy Island, and the decision of the Synod of *Whitby in 664 to follow the Roman practice of worship pulled Northumbria into a southerly orbit. In the late 8th cent. the area began to suffer from Danish raids and in the following century was in conflict with the Viking kingdom of *York. In 920 it submitted to *Edward, king of Wessex, at Bakewell, and subsequent attempts to recover its independence were of no avail. After the defeat at *Carham in 1016 the lands north of the Tweed were ceded to the kingdom of Scotland.

Northumbrian resistance to the Normans after Hastings led to William I's despoiling of the area in 1069. It was not included in the *Domesday survey, having yet to recover from the devastation. In the later Middle Ages it was the first line of defence against the Scots, the border region being divided up into marches. Vast power was wielded by the local lords, particularly the Percies of Alnwick. England's weakness under Stephen led to the Scottish king David I occupying the county and pushing his border south to the Tees. It was retaken by Henry II, though Berwick, in the far north, changed hands repeatedly. The remoter parts of the county like Redesdale, Coquetdale, and Allendale were under fitful control, border raiding was common, and bloody encounters, like *Otterburn in 1388 when Percy fought Douglas, were not uncommon. Even in the reign of Elizabeth I, feudal loyalties remained strong, and more than 5,000 men turned out to support the catholic rising of the *northern earls, *Northumberland and *Westmorland, in 1569. The union with Scotland in 1603 gave some respite from cattle-raiding. The last spasm of lawlessness was produced by the Jacobite movement. Sir John Fenwick, a former member for the county, was executed in 1697 for conspiracy against William III, and Thomas Forster, another member, was supported by a number of shire gentlemen in the '15, though they did little save proclaim the old pretender at Warkworth and occupy Holy Island for one day.

Camden, in 1586, drew a picture of a county that was still wild and untamed: 'the county itself is mostly rough and barren, and seems to have hardened the very carcasses of its inhabitants.' One hundred years later, things were changing. Regular services plied the Great North Road, and Edmund *Gibson wrote in 1695 that strangers were no novelty to the shire, nor had cause to be apprehensive: 'a roundlet of red wine is a greater rarity in a countryman's house in Middlesex than on the borders of Northumberland . . . the gentry are generally persons of address and breeding, the peasants are as knowing a people, and as courteous to strangers, as a man shall readily meet with in any other part.'

In so large a county, administration was bound to be decentralized. The assizes were held in Newcastle, but the elections for the shire at Alnwick. Quarter sessions were held at Newcastle, Alnwick, Morpeth, and Hexham in turn. But Newcastle had always been by far the most important town and in the 19th cent. it grew disproportionately to its neighbours. From a base of about 28,000 in 1801, it was 87,000 by 1851, and by 1914, having swallowed its surrounding villages, had reached 271,000. The explosion was due, in the main, to coal-mining and shipbuilding. In 1857, 4 million tons of coal was being exported from the Tyne: by 1888 it had reached 10 million tons, and by 1900 17 million tons. By the 20th cent. there were far more miners in the county than farm labourers. The long-established tradition of shipbuilding was transformed after 1850. Armstrong's works at Elswick were opened in 1847, *Parsons' at Heaton in 1889. The political effect of this economic development was acknowledged in 1974 with the creation of a new county of Tyne and Wear, and although the new authority was itself abolished in 1986, the areas north of the Tyne did not return to Northumberland. The decision of a Roman commander to cross the Tyne at Pons Aelium had lengthy consequences. JAC

Northumberland, Henry, earl of (*c.*1115–52). The only son and heir to David I of Scotland and grandson of *Waltheof, earl of Northumberland (d. 1076). His father intervened against King Stephen but reached an understanding in 1136, resigning the earldom of Huntingdon to his son, who did homage to Stephen. The following year another settlement gave him the earldom of Northumberland, excluding Newcastle and Bamburgh. There is testimony to his bravery and piety. His sons Malcolm IV and William the Lion succeeded on the Scottish throne. JAC

Northumberland, John Dudley, 1st duke of (*c.*1505–53). Dudley had a brilliant but brief career at the very top of Tudor politics. His father, Henry VII's financier Edmund *Dudley, was executed in 1510 when John Dudley was a small boy. His mother Elizabeth Grey, daughter of Viscount Lisle, remarried in 1511. Her second husband, Arthur Plantagenet, was an illegitimate son of Edward IV and therefore an uncle of Henry VIII. Dudley's early career was made under the protection of his stepfather, who was in high favour, created Viscount Lisle in 1523, given the Garter in 1524, and made governor of Calais in 1533. John Dudley began as a soldier, made a reputation for jousting, was knighted in 1523, helped to put down the *Pilgrimage of Grace, and became deputy governor of Calais in 1538. His stepfather's disgrace and death did not affect Dudley's upward progress: in 1542 he was made warden of the Scottish marches, served as lord admiral, was created Viscount Lisle in turn, and in 1544 captured Boulogne from the French. After the death of Henry VIII, he worked closely with *Somerset, Edward VI's uncle, and was advanced to the earldom of Warwick. He fought alongside Somerset at the battle of *Pinkie Cleugh against the Scots and crushed the Norfolk rebels in 1549 at *Dussindale. From October 1549 he supplanted Somerset and for the rest of Edward's short reign held power as lord president of the council. In 1551 he was created duke of Northumberland, the title vacant as a consequence of Sir Thomas Percy's involvement in the Pilgrimage of Grace. But Northumberland's position was rendered precarious by the growing ill-health of the young king and in 1553 he turned to desperate measures to retain power. Edward issued letters patent setting aside the claims to succession of his half-sisters Mary and Elizabeth and nominating Lady Jane *Grey. Northumberland then arranged a marriage between his son Lord Guildford Dudley and Lady Jane and on Edward's death declared her queen. The coup failed miserably and Northumberland surrendered at Cambridge to Mary's supporters. He was executed in August 1553 where his father had been. But his support for the reformed religion was of critical importance in moving England from the caesaro-papism of Henry VIII's last days to a protestant settlement. JAC

Northumberland, John Neville, 1st earl of (*c.*1431–71). The third son of Richard Neville, earl of Salisbury, John led family retainers in a private war with Percy followers headed by Thomas, Lord Egremont, which concluded with the Neville victory at Stamford Bridge (Yorks.) in 1454. He fought alongside his father at *Blore Heath and was attainted in 1459, but was restored, created Baron Montagu, and appointed Henry VI's chamberlain after the Yorkists won control of government in 1460. Taken prisoner in the second battle of *St Albans, he was freed after Edward IV's victory at *Towton. Thereafter he was Edward's chief lieutenant in the north. He broke the Scottish siege of Carlisle in 1463 and was warden of the east march from 1463, defeating Lancastrian forces at *Hedgeley Moor and *Hexham in 1464. In reward, and to support his responsibilities, he was granted the forfeited title and estates of the Percy earls of Northumberland. Although John did not take part in his brother

*Warwick's machinations in 1469–70, Edward's design to reduce the Nevilles' power included restoring a Percy as earl of Northumberland and warden of the east march. John was created marquis of Montagu, a hollow promotion which threatened impoverishment. He consequently supported Warwick's restoration of Henry VI and was killed at the battle of *Barnet. RLS

Northumberland, Henry Percy, 1st earl of (1341–1408). Heir to the 3rd Lord Percy of Alnwick, Percy's military career began in France under Dukes Henry and John of Lancaster; he remained a political associate of the latter, *John of Gaunt. He was created earl at Richard II's coronation in 1377. In 1381 his (second) marriage to the heiress of Thomas Lucy of Cockermouth (Cumberland) made him the predominant magnate in the border counties. Gaunt's appointment as lieutenant in the marches led to a breach, from which Northumberland emerged as sole warden in both marches in 1384, after which either he or his son Hotspur (Henry *Percy) usually held one of the wardenships. They won both in 1399 as one of many rewards for their key role in Henry IV's usurpation. Fearing this regional hegemony was threatened, they revolted in 1403. Prevented from joining Hotspur, Northumberland survived to instigate Archbishop *Scrope's rebellion; on its collapse he fled to Scotland and was deemed forfeit. He was killed in a skirmish at *Bramham Moor (Yorks.). RLS

Northumberland, Henry Percy, 3rd earl of (1421–61). Percy was warden of the east march from 1440. He was entitled Lord Poynings following his wife's succession to that Sussex barony. The feud with the Nevilles and the death of his father, the 2nd earl, in the first battle of *St Albans made him a Lancastrian partisan. He continued as warden despite being owed wages for several years. He helped to defeat Richard of *York at *Wakefield in 1460. The unruly conduct of his army of northerners alarmed the citizens of London; their success at the second battle of *St Albans thus failed to win the capital. Northumberland was killed in the battle of *Towton. RLS

Northumberland, Henry Percy, 4th earl of (*c.*1449–89). Edward IV kept Percy in detention after the death of his father, the 3rd earl, in 1461. He was restored to the earldom in 1470 and appointed warden of the east march to replace John Neville. Tension with Richard, duke of Gloucester (later Richard III), who had replaced *Warwick in his northern lands and offices, was allayed by Northumberland being retained by the duke in 1474. He supported Richard's usurpation in 1483, but apparently resented the king's continuing interest in the north. He obeyed the call to arms against Henry Tudor but remained inactive at *Bosworth Field. Henry VII soon realized that he needed Northumberland's services in the east march. He was killed in an anti-tax demonstration in Yorkshire. RLS

Northumberland, Henry Percy, 8th earl of (*c.*1532–85). Percy's brother, the 7th earl, was involved in the 1569 rising and executed in 1572. Henry Percy, who had made a reputation in border fighting in the 1550s, remained loyal to the queen and held Tynemouth castle on her behalf. The queen wrote acknowledging his fidelity during the rebellion and he succeeded to his brother's title under the special remainder. But he spent some time in the Tower 1571–2 under suspicion of plotting with Mary, queen of Scots, and was fined and released. He was once more arrested in 1583 in connection with the *Throckmorton plot to welcome a Spanish invasion. In June 1585 he was found dead in the Tower from a pistol-shot, which the coroner declared had been self-inflicted. JAC

Northumberland, Henry Percy, 9th earl of (1564–1632). Northumberland inherited the title at the age of 21 in 1585 when his father, confined to the Tower, was found shot. He was given the Garter in 1593 and performed some military services. But his opportunity came with the death of Queen Elizabeth. He had corresponded with James I, urging him to make concessions to the catholics, accompanied him on the journey south, and was made captain of the gentlemen pensioners. But *Cecil was a secret enemy and Northumberland did not find court life much to his taste. In November 1605 he was arrested on suspicion of complicity in the *Gunpowder plot. Thomas Percy, one of the conspirators, was a distant cousin, had been employed by Northumberland as constable of Alnwick castle, and had been made a gentleman pensioner. He had dined at Sion House with Northumberland the night Guy *Fawkes was arrested. Northumberland protested his innocence, claiming that he was known to live a retired life, building and gardening. Nevertheless, he was kept in the Tower until 1621. A fellow-prisoner for much of the time was Sir Walter *Ralegh. The earl played chess, entertained well, had a good library, a laboratory, and patronized scholars. His scientific interests earned him a nickname, 'the wizard earl'. He was a difficult man and when his release was granted after sixteen years was reluctant to leave the Tower. He spent most of his remaining eleven years at Petworth. JAC

Northumberland, Thomas Percy, 7th earl of (1528–72). Percy's uncle, the 6th earl of Northumberland, died in June 1537 at the age of 35, it was said of grief at the execution of Anne Boleyn; his father Sir Thomas Percy died the same month, executed for his part in the *Pilgrimage of Grace. Thomas Percy was restored in blood in 1549, and in 1557, after helping to suppress a rising in the north, was created earl of Northumberland by Mary. He was made warden of the east march in 1558 and given the Garter in 1563. But in 1569 he joined with the earl of *Westmorland in the rising of the *northern earls, which captured Durham and celebrated mass in the cathedral. On the collapse of the rebellion, he fled to Scotland but was handed back and beheaded at York in 1572. JAC

Northumbria, kingdom of. From the middle of the 6th cent. to the 870s when the Danes took over control at York, the Anglo-Saxons who dwelt north of the river Humber achieved their own often turbulent institutional life, ruled by kings. The borders of the territories over which they exercised authority fluctuated widely, as did their degree of dependence (or in the 7th cent. overlordship) in relation to rulers further south in Mercia, East Anglia, and Wessex. At its greatest extent the kingdom of Northumbria embraced the lands which stretched from the Humber and the Mersey in the south to the Clyde and the Forth in the north, straddling the old Roman frontier on Hadrian's Wall, and especially strong in what was to become south-east Scotland as far as Edinburgh. The political roots of the kingdom grew from two principal sources, the northern kingdom of *Bernicia based on the gaunt fortress rock of *Bamburgh, and the kingdom of *Deira in the fertile vale of York. Rivalry between the two dynasties, both of which traced their origins to 6th-cent. rulers, bedevilled the politics of Northumbria, as did also their divergent interests, Bernicia concerned with threats from the north from Picts and Scots, and Deira more entangled with the problems of the Mercian frontier. Even so in the 7th cent. under a succession of powerful rulers, *Æthelfryth of Bernicia (d. 616), *Edwin of Deira (616–32), the brothers, again with Bernician origins, St *Oswald (633–41) and *Oswui (641–70), Northumbria was a dominant force in English political life. Edwin was said by *Bede to have ruled over all the inhabitants of Britain, English and Britons alike, except for Kent; and Oswui went even further in overwhelming and making tributary the Picts and the Scots of northern Britain. After the defeat and death of Oswui's son *Ecgfrith at the hands of the Picts in 685 Northumbria lost aspirations to overlordship and the 8th and 9th cents. provide a sorry tale of unrest and violence at the royal level. Many kings were exiled or murdered after a short reign. Yet some feeling for the integrity of the kingdom and the mystique of the blood royal persisted, and in the cultural and religious spheres the kingdom continued to flourish and produce great work well into the 8th cent. The age of *Bede (672–735) saw the flowering of the so-called Northumbrian renaissance when some of the finest literary and artistic work of the early Middle Ages was produced in the northern kingdom in the shape of the writings of the Venerable Bede and the great Gospel Books, of which the *Lindisfarne Gospels is a supreme example. The monastery of *Jarrow/Wearmouth and the prestigious school at York were focal points, together with Lindisfarne, for such enterprises, and in spite of political violence the school of York with its great library continued to flourish deep into the 8th cent. and was responsible for training one of the most influential and prolific scholars of the Carolingian age in the person of *Alcuin (735–804). Towards the end of the century a fresh and ultimately disastrous new element was introduced into the political life of the kingdom with the first *Viking attacks. In June 793 they brutally sacked the monastery at Lindisfarne, an event which sent shock waves throughout western Christendom. Alcuin, writing from the Frankish court, laid some blame squarely on the shoulders of the Northumbrian rulers whose kingdom had almost perished because of internal dissensions. Alcuin warned that the evil was not yet at an end; and his warning proved true. Scandinavian control of communications over the North Sea put Northumbria in the front line. Political mastery within Anglo-Saxon England had already passed south, first to Mercia and then in the 9th cent. to Wessex. When the Danes in the reign of *Alfred (871–99) made their serious attempt to conquer England, the Northumbrian kingdom collapsed, leaving Danish kings after 878 in firm control of York and only vestiges of native English authority under ealdormen in the more northerly parts of the kingdom. The Danes remained in political control of York until 954, a period of significant Scandinavian migration. Thereafter no attempt was made, nor was it possible, to revive the kingship of Northumbria which was integrated, though with occasional manifestations of independence, in the kingdom of England. HL

North Yorkshire. See YORKSHIRE, NORTH.

Norton, Caroline (1808–77). Author and reformer. Caroline, a society beauty and granddaughter of Richard Brinsley *Sheridan, married at the age of 19 in 1827 the Hon. George Norton, brother of Lord Grantley. Her husband, an unpleasant bully, brought an action in 1836 for crim. con. (adultery) against Lord *Melbourne, then prime minister, which was laughed out of court and formed the basis for *Dickens's *Bardell* v. *Pickwick*. Norton continued to ill-treat his wife, preventing her access to her own children and trying to seize her literary earnings as poet and novelist. In her defence, Mrs Norton published, claiming the rights of mothers to custody and of wives to independent property. The Custody of Infants Act (2 & 3 Vic. c. 54) of 1839 gave the courts discretion to award custody of children up to the age of 7 to their mothers. The right of wives to independent property was introduced by successive Married Women's Property Acts in 1870, 1882, and 1893. Though Mrs Norton's literary reputation has faded, her position as a pioneer of women's rights is secure. JAC

Norwich. County town of Norfolk, situated on the river Wensum, and a cathedral city since 1094. It is not recorded before 900, yet by 1066 it was one of the three or four most important towns in England, a position it retained until late Georgian times. It may have begun as a wic or trading port under the Vikings before rising rapidly to become a major town, in a way that still lacks explanation. The Normans transformed the city by building a castle and cathedral, and laying out a new French borough. From the 1140s to 1290 Norwich housed an important Jewry, and from 1194 the citizens accumulated privileges of self-government, while between 1297 and 1344 they built stone walls which enclosed an area of a full square mile (as much as London's). By this time it was the wealthiest provincial town, possessing a major Benedictine priory, 6 friaries, and 57 parish churches. In the 14th and 15th cents. textile manufacture became the dominant industry, especially of cloths called worsteds after a local village. In the 16th and 17th cents. it overtook its rivals to be once more the largest and wealthiest English town after London, its economy sustained partly by a massive immigration of refugees from the Spanish Netherlands who introduced the New Draperies. It also became a social centre for the East Anglian gentry. In the late 18th and early 19th cents. the textile industry declined in the face of Yorkshire competition, and Norwich reverted to its traditional function as a marketing and trading town with only modest industries. The city centre is still dominated by its cathedral, castle keep, and 32 medieval churches (more than in any other British town); the most notable modern accent is perhaps the city hall of 1932–8, inspired by Stockholm's town hall, and a reminder of Norwich's tradition of municipal socialism. DMP

Norwich, diocese of. The see, conterminous with Norfolk, was founded in 1094. Herfast (1070–85) moved the East Anglian see of *Elmham to *Thetford *c.*1072 to comply with the Council of London, but Herbert *Losinga (1091–1119), monk of Fécamp and former abbot of Ramsey, moved it again *c.*1094 to Norwich, where he established a Benedictine monastic community. The abbey of St Edmundsbury (Suffolk) was another rich and powerful force in the medieval diocese. It was not until 1914, with the creation of the diocese of *Bury St Edmunds and Ipswich, that Suffolk regained its own see for the first time since the Danish invasions. Norwich cathedral, monastic in origin, begun by Herbert Losinga in 1096, is a fine Norman building, but with 15th-cent. lierne vaulted roofs and spire. The diocese is renowned for its numerous beautiful parish churches. WMM

Norwich Crusade, 1383. Led by Henry Despenser, bishop of Norwich (1370–1404), this 'crusade' had scandalously mixed ecclesiastical, commercial, and political motives—with disastrous results. Supported by Pope Urban VI (Rome) in his move against Pope Clement VII (Avignon) and backed by Parliament, it was cheaper than *John of Gaunt's planned 'crusade' against Castile—the cost being borne by ordinary people's alms, with the added advantage of releasing Philip of Burgundy's stranglehold on the Flemish wool trade. Plenary indulgences were liberally granted in return for enthusiastically given valuables. Despite military experience, Despenser was no strategist. Landing in May, he took coastal towns, invaded Urbanist Flanders instead of Clementinist France, and besieged Ypres, but hastily abandoned all at Philip's approach. No Clementinists were converted, the route from Calais remained closed, and access to Flemish markets denied to English traders; the church and Despenser were discredited by the gross abuse of indulgences. Despenser was impeached. WMM

Nottingham. County town of Nottinghamshire, situated on the river Trent, and a city since 1897. It is first recorded as one of the 'five boroughs' of the Danes, succeeded by an English fortified town (burh) after 921. It quickly became a county town, and was extended after 1066 with a new 'French borough' and a major castle. In the 12th and 13th cents. it became a regional centre with self-government, town walls, and a major fair. The castle remained a royal stronghold, and it was at Nottingham that Charles I raised his standard in 1642. After the Restoration the town became a social centre for the county gentry, and the duke of Newcastle built a mansion on the site of the castle. Industry developed after 1700 with framework-knitting, and later lace-making, and the town grew rapidly. The burgesses, however, refused to enclose the surrounding open fields, and overcrowding became desperate. Not surprisingly, the Lords' rejection of the second Reform Bill in 1831 provoked riots, and the castle (the duke of Newcastle's mansion) was burned. By the time the fields were enclosed in 1845, the damage was done, and not until the 20th cent. did slum clearance remove Nottingham's notorious courts and alleys. DMP

Nottingham, Daniel Finch, 2nd earl of (1647–1730). A Tory politician, the sober and principled Lord Nottingham was the chief standard-bearer of 'high-church' politics during the reigns of William III and Anne. He disapproved of James II's pro-catholic measures, but only when James fled in 1688 did he align with William of Orange, and even then never accepted the latter as king *de jure*. Appointed secretary of state, Nottingham's *Toleration Act (1689) ensured the preservation of Anglican supremacy after the revolution, though his plan to include presbyterians and other nonconformists in a broadened church proved unacceptable. He lost office in 1693. During his second term as secretary, 1702–4, his independent-mindedness again made him a difficult colleague and his campaign for a bill against *occasional conformity endangered the ministry's war measures in Parliament. A leader of the Hanoverian Tories, and excluded from the 1710–14 Tory ministry, he was made lord president by George I in 1714 but quarrelled with the Whig ministers in 1716 and was dismissed. AAH

Nottingham, Heneage Finch, 1st earl of (1621–82). Finch was a barrister, son of one Speaker of the House of Commons and nephew of another, Sir John Finch. He avoided public life during the Commonwealth but after the Restoration his rise was rapid. He was returned as MP for Canterbury in 1660, transferring to Oxford University in 1661. As solicitor-general in 1660 he prosecuted the regicides, was promoted attorney-general in 1670, granted a barony in 1674, and from 1675 to his death was lord chancellor. In 1681, sixteen days after the death of the previous holder of the title, he was created earl of Nottingham. A skilful, hard-working, and conciliatory lawyer, he steered a shrewd course amidst the rapids of Charles II's reign. His house at Kensington, with fine gardens, was purchased after the Glorious Revolution by William III and became *Kensington palace. *Pepys admired his eloquence greatly but *Burnet seems to have found it old-fashioned and florid. JAC

Nottingham, Thomas Mowbray, 2nd earl of (1385–1405). Mowbray's father was created duke of *Norfolk in 1397 by Richard II but the grant was annulled by Henry IV's first Parliament. A minor when his father died in 1399, Mowbray seems to have inherited his father's hatred of Henry IV. In 1405 he joined Archbishop *Scrope in rebellion and shared his fate. RLS

Nottinghamshire is the county of the river Trent, which flows through it from south-west to north-east, forming the border with Lincolnshire for the last 20 miles: the Erewash divides the county from Derbyshire to the west and the Soar from Leicestershire to the south-west. Nottingham was an important river crossing. The Great North Road crossed the Trent at Newark and ran up the eastern side of the county through Tuxford and East Retford to Bawtry. The *Fosse Way ran south-west to north-east, crossing at

Newark on its way to Lincoln. *Camden's *Britannia* placed the county in the territory of the *Coritani and divided it into a sandy northern part, much of it covered by Sherwood Forest, and a heavier clay south-east. Sherwood Forest, though much diminished by Tudor times, 'still feeds an infinite number of deer and branchy-headed stags'. The area was disputed between *Mercia, *Lindsey, and *Northumbria, and formed part of the diocese of *Lichfield and then of *York, until the separate see of *Southwell was created in 1884.

The shire developed in Saxon times around Nottingham itself, where the rock made a strong defensive position. Various derivations of the name have been suggested but the earliest usage was Snotengaham, the settlement of Snot's people: the opening S, being difficult for the Normans to pronounce, was dropped after the Conquest. In 868 a large Danish army took possession of the town and was attacked by the men of Mercia and Wessex, but by the treaty of *Wedmore of 878 it was retained by the Danes and formed one of their five boroughs. Though Danish rule lasted less than 50 years, Danish settlement was strong: there are many Scandinavian place-names—Fiskerton, Gunthorpe, Thoresby, Granby—and the shire was divided, not into hundreds, but into *wapentakes. In the early 920s *Edward the Elder recovered the town, and built fortifications and a connecting bridge. It was ravaged by *Cnut in 1016 and when William I moved north in 1067 to deal with his recalcitrant subjects, he began the building of Nottingham castle.

Nottingham retained its importance throughout the medieval period, its goose fair in October attracting traders from all over the country. In the 17th cent. it developed as a social centre. Celia Fiennes, visiting in 1697, was impressed: 'the neatest town I have seen, built of stone and delicate large and long streets, much like London, and the houses loftily and well built.' She found Nottingham ale particularly agreeable. East Retford, Newark, Mansfield, and Worksop developed as market towns, but the area remained thinly populated. The *dissolution of the monasteries strengthened the influence of the gentry and nobility and the shire became famous for its landed estates. The Stanhopes gained 20 villages that had belonged to Shelford priory; Welbeck abbey found its way to the Cavendish family, Rufford priory to the Saviles, and Newstead abbey to the Byrons. As the gentry moved up the social scale, the north of the shire became known as the Dukeries, Newcastle having Clumber, Portland Welbeck, and Rutland Kelham. The duke of Kingston's estate was at Holme Pierrepoint, east of Nottingham. 'The idea I gave Lord Rockingham of this county', wrote Sir George Savile in 1769, 'was four dukes, two lords, and three rabbit warrens, which I believe, takes in half the county in point of space.' The nobility arranged the county representation among themselves and there was no contest between 1722 and the 1832 Reform Act.

Nottinghamshire had taken an important part in the civil wars of the 17th cent. Charles I raised his standard at Nottingham in 1642, though the response had been disappointing. Seven brothers of the Byron family fought for the king. Newark sustained several sieges on behalf of the king and was rewarded for its loyalty after the Restoration with two parliamentary seats. It was at the Saracen's Head in Southwell that Charles surrendered to the Scots after his strange journey from Oxford.

The agricultural character of the shire began to change in the later 18th cent. The Trent had always been a busy thoroughfare, but was augmented in the 1770s by the Trent and Mersey canal, one of the earliest to be built, and by *Brindley; by the Chesterfield canal in 1777 serving Worksop and East Retford; and by the Grantham canal, opened in 1793. The development of a canal network made the transport of coal much cheaper and led to a great expansion of the Nottinghamshire coalfield. The same period saw the development of the textile industry, *Hargreaves and *Arkwright setting up factories in Nottingham. But a severe recession after the Napoleonic wars caused great distress and gave a radical tinge to local politics. Brandreth's *Pentrich rising of 1817, though little more than a skirmish on the march to Nottingham, was in part the product of unemployment and low wages; in the reform crisis of 1831 the duke of Newcastle's mansion at Nottingham was burned; and Nottingham was the first town to return a chartist MP when it chose *O'Connor in 1847. In the later 19th cent., prosperity returned and there was a diversification of local industries. *Boot's Pure Drug Company was established in 1883; the Raleigh bicycle company had 800 employees by 1896; and Player's tobacco company employed more than 1,000 by 1898. Coaching towns like Tuxford and Blyth stood still as the railways passed them by, but Mansfield and Worksop expanded at roughly the same rate as Nottingham, and the balance remained the same. Nottinghamshire was hardly affected by the local government reorganization of 1972, save for the loss of some acres in the north to South Yorkshire. But the Banham commission on local government reported in 1994 in favour of a unitary authority for the city of Nottingham, while maintaining the two-tier structure in the rest of the county. JAC

Nova Scotia owes its name to a 17th-cent. Scottish attempt at colonization. France ceded its claims to Britain in 1713. Halifax was founded in 1749, and an assembly introduced in 1758. British garrisons discouraged temptations to join the American Revolution. In the 19th cent. Nova Scotians exploited their timber resources and Atlantic orientation to create a trading economy based on the sailing ship. Self-government was achieved in 1848. After heated controversy, Nova Scotia joined the dominion of Canada in 1867. Historians attribute subsequent sluggish development to the decline of the 'wood, wind, and water' economy. Nova Scotians, who retain a pronounced 'Bluenose' patriotism, blame the indifference of Canadian governments. GM

nuclear energy is obtained by releasing the binding energy which holds together atomic nuclei, for example, in uranium. This fission process was used in the development of the atomic bomb during the Second World War, but by the mid-1950s scientists had been able to control it within the reactor cores of experimental power stations to produce utilizable energy. The nuclear reactor releases energy in the form of heat which is used to generate steam, and the steam to generate electricity. Plutonium, a highly fissile material used in the manufacture of nuclear bombs, is a by-product.

The Atomic Energy Authority oversaw the development of the nuclear industry, which from the outset proved controversial on strategic, cost, and environmental grounds. When in 1956 power was switched from the first generator at Calder Hall to the National Grid it was hailed as a great achievement but scant attention was paid to the real purpose of the programme, to breed plutonium for Britain's nuclear deterrent. An experimental fast reactor, built at Dounreay in the north of Scotland, began operation in 1959, and paved the way for the first fast-breeder reactor power station.

From the standpoint of the 1950s, discounting the perceived need for a nuclear deterrent during the Cold War, nuclear power seemed an excellent investment, given the likelihood that unit costs could be as little as a fifth that of fossil-fuel electricity. In the ensuing years the industry expanded, though the balance of cost advantage remained uncertain. But the upsurge of oil prices in the 1970s, coupled with uneasy labour relations in the coal-mines, added to the comparative economic attraction of nuclear power, which began to accelerate dramatically, as did the nuclear component of electricity output.

Successive British governments since the 1950s wanted to lessen dependence on petroleum-exporting countries, but with the development of North Sea oil and gas, this was less pressing. Energy requirements in general began to be adjusted as a response to the energy crisis, and this brought about a reassessment of the high-energy role of nuclear power. While in its early stages of development nuclear energy appeared environmentally inoffensive to the general public, increased concern was voiced about its safety following major disasters at power plants internationally during the 1980s, and about the twin problems of waste disposal and decommissioning of redundant plant. ID

Nuffield, William Morris, 1st Viscount (1877–1963). Born in Worcester, Nuffield attended school at Cowley where he became a cycle repairer and, by 1896, a manufacturer. By 1901 his partnership with Joseph Cooper produced motor-cycles from components bought from midland suppliers. By 1903 he was repairing motor cars, and, in 1909 he was running the Morris Garage which sold various car models and had a hire department. In 1912 he established WRM Motors to sell his own Morris Oxford cars for £150, in 1914 producing 1,000 cars. The Cowley works made cars for the man in the street with all profits reinvested in the firm. In the early 1930s assembly-line production was introduced for the Morris 8 and by 1938 annual output reached 100,000 vehicles. In 1951 the firm merged with *Austin to become the British Motor Corporation. Lord Nuffield endowed educational and medical activities through the British United Provident Association, the Nuffield Foundation, and Nuffield College of Oxford University. IJEK

nunneries. In the early Anglo-Saxon period, monastic life for women was almost always in double houses, of which *Theodore disapproved. In most of these, monks and nuns shared a church, though at Wimborne (Dorset) each group had its own church. An abbess ruled over the community. She was often of royal or noble birth and for centuries nunneries remained places for aristocratic women. *Hilda of Whitby was related to King *Oswui of Northumbria and Wimborne was founded by two sisters of King *Ine. The first double monastery was probably at Hartlepool, since Hilda is said to have modelled her foundation at Whitby upon it, *c.*650. In the largest of these houses at Wimborne, there were said to have been 500 nuns in the early 8th cent., and Shaftesbury, Wilton, Winchester, Romsey, and Amesbury were all flourishing foundations.

A number of double monasteries were destroyed during the Viking incursions, and when the monastic revival developed in the 10th cent. single houses were in favour. The second Council of Nicaea in 787 forbade the foundation of double monasteries. By 1275 there were ten Saxon nunneries surviving in England and Wales, and another 118 had been founded since the Conquest. After 1275 only another ten nunneries were established, including the famous one by the Thames at Syon, endowed by Henry V in 1414. Of the total of 138 nunneries between 1275 and 1535, well over half were *Benedictine; there were 28 *Cistercian nunneries, 18 *Augustinian, 4 *Franciscan, 2 *Cluniac, and 2 *Premonstratensian. In Scotland there were a dozen or so nunneries, mainly Cistercian, and in Ireland about ten of the 140 monasteries were nunneries, all of them for regular canonesses. By the time of the dissolution, there were some 125 English nunneries still in existence, sheltering about 2,000 women. Three nunneries had closed after the *Black Death; another went in 1496 to help found Jesus College, Cambridge; two more were dissolved in 1524 to help St John's College, Cambridge; and three more were suppressed by *Wolsey to support his great Cardinal College, later Christ Church, Oxford. SMD

nursery rhymes are one of the more enduring forms of oral culture. Although taken for granted, some of them are of considerable longevity, dating from the 17th cent. or earlier. The origins of these rhymes vary enormously. Some lie in riddles, others in singing games. Many, however, originated from printed ballads and song books, genres which were firmly established by 1700, while others can be traced back to plays or folk-songs (there was, of course, considerable interchange between these genres).

It has been argued that many of these rhymes originally referred to historical events or personalities, although attempts to prove such arguments in individual cases are rarely convincing. There is a risk of over-interpretation: the analysis of nursery rhymes in John Bettenden Ker's *An Essay on the Archaeology of Popular English Phrases and Nursery Rhymes*, published in three volumes between 1834 and 1840, is, according to one modern authority, 'probably the most extraordinary example of misdirected labour in the history of English letters' which has 'given delight to students of mania ever since'. Sometimes historical origins to nursery rhymes can be traced: thus 'Ring o' Roses' refers (albeit disputedly) to the plague of the 17th cent., while 'The Grand Old Duke of York' was almost certainly Frederick Augustus, son of George III, who led a less than successful campaign against the French in the Low Countries in 1793–5.

Most connections are hard to sustain. Thus there is no way of proving the early 18th-cent. notion that Old King Cole of the nursery rhyme can be identified with the mythical founder of Colchester. The 'fine lady' riding her horse to Banbury Cross (a structure destroyed by the local puritans around 1600) has been variously identified as Queen Elizabeth I, Lady *Godiva (there is a version of the rhyme referring to Coventry Cross), and the traveller Celia Fiennes (1662–1741), 'Fiennes' being corrupted as 'fine'. Such identifications of 'origins' are highly speculative.

It is far more profitable to use these rhymes, and the publications in which they were collected, as evidence of changing attitudes towards children and childhood. That so many of them had their origins in the 'adult' milieux of the theatre and the song book before coming to the nursery (many fairy-tales made a similar transition) is suggestive of a certain relationship between the adult world and that of children, while the proliferation of nursery rhyme books around the middle of the 18th cent. might support the suggestion that new sensibilities towards children were developing then. This is a contentious area, and tracing changes in sensibility is always difficult. But the content and illustrations in books of nursery rhymes (the first of any substance published in 1744) would repay serious investigation, and would throw much illumination on the history of childhood. JAS

nursing did not develop as an organized profession until the mid-19th cent., despite the establishment of voluntary hospitals in the 18th. Until then, caring for the sick had been undertaken mainly at home by relatives and neighbours, whose knowledge and experience was variable though not always as minimal as detractors have claimed. The medieval religious orders had had infirmaries, where non-liturgical nursing duties were undertaken by lay brethren in charge of maintenance and catering, but after the *dissolution of the monasteries the able-bodied poor were often used or required to tend their sick counterparts. The early voluntary hospitals, whose nurses were drawn mainly from the domestic servant class and not thought to require any special training, frequently insisted that convalescent patients helped out on the wards (with reprimands for non-compliance), and also refused to admit those with fevers, incurable, or venereal disease; such patients were dumped in workhouses, to be tended by healthier though often infirm paupers, since there were no special arrangements for the sick. John *Howard, the prison reformer, commented on the poor state of hospital care in the 1780s, but it was not until 1840 that Elizabeth *Fry established an Institute of Nursing Sisters at Bishopsgate, though the scale was small. Florence *Nightingale's great contribution was twofold: the work in the Crimea of her 40 nurses, sent out by public subscription, dramatized the problem, and after the war she began systematically organizing nursing services with her Nightingale School attached to St Thomas's Hospital, offering a year's course; her best pupils became matrons of other hospitals, which started their own courses. A parallel development was the district nursing scheme, initiated by William Rathbone of Liverpool, and developed through the Metropolitan Nursing Association, and then the Queen Victoria Institute for Nurses. Although the British Nurses' Association, founded in 1887, began to press for state registration of nurses, opposition to this did not lessen until a precedent was set by the far-reaching Midwives Act (1902); the College of Nursing was established in 1916, but the Nurses Registration Act (1919) and the General Nursing Council (1920) developed out of the government's own bill rather than either of the two feuding bills submitted. Nurses are now seen as important in the culture of a hospital; their training may come through a three-year course in hospital, specialized college, or degree course in a higher education institution. JAC

Nyasaland. See MALAWI.

Oakboys in Ireland were the northern and protestant equivalent of the *Whiteboys in 1771, protesting against compulsory service as road-menders. The campaign of intimidation was less violent than in Munster and lasted only a few months. JAC

Oastler, Richard (1789–1861). Factory reformer and anti-Poor Law agitator. Born in Leeds, the son of a leading Wesleyan, Oastler was educated by the Moravians at Fulneck, but became Church of England when he succeeded his father in 1820 as steward for Thomas Thornhill, the absentee landlord of Fixby Hall near Halifax. He was a romantic Tory, defending old values against utilitarian radicalism and political economy, attacking the vicar of Halifax over tithes in 1827, criticizing the employment of children in Bradford worsted mills in 1830, leading the *Ten Hours campaign for factory reform, and denouncing the New *Poor Law of 1834. His extreme language and immense popularity alienated his employer who had him imprisoned for debt (1840–4). As a staunch protestant, he opposed *catholic emancipation but supported the movement to restore *convocation for the government of the Church of England. His motto was 'Altar, Throne and Cottage'. ER

Oates, Lawrence Edward Grace (1880–1912). Having entered the army in 1898, Oates saw service in the South African War. His interest in sailing, hunting, and kindred pursuits led him to apply for a post on *Scott's 1910 expedition to the Antarctic. He was in charge of the ponies and was chosen as one of the party of five which reached the South Pole in January 1912. On the return journey, Oates, unable to walk properly because of severely frost-bitten feet, decided that he was lessening his companions' chances of survival and on 17 March 1912 walked out into a blizzard saying, 'I am just going outside and may be some time.' His body was never found. RB

Oates, Titus (1649–1705). Perjurer and fabricator of the *'Popish plot'. Despite his status as an Anglican priest, Oates's penchant was for lies and petty crime. Recognizing by the mid-1670s that the surest way to advancement was to feed the public taste for catholic scare-mongering, he wormed his way into catholic counsels, learning their secrets, and became a member of the faith himself in 1677. In 1678, he unveiled to the government his highly wrought tale of a conspiracy to overturn the protestant establishment for which corroborative evidence soon came to light. A wave of hysteria swept the country, the political impact of which was the *Exclusion crisis, and Oates's accusations resulted in the execution of 35, including 9 Jesuit priests. From 1681, however, his testimony was increasingly discredited and he lost the court's protection. Tried in 1685 for perjury and condemned to life imprisonment, he was pardoned in 1689. AAH

oaths. From early days the taking of solemn religious oaths was regarded as an essential part of the political and social order. Monarchs swore oaths at their *coronations, vassals swore oaths on doing homage, jurors swore oaths on being empanelled. Difficulties began at the Reformation when oaths were devised to make it impossible for catholics to take them: the Elizabethan Act of *Supremacy in 1559 demanded an oath from all ministers, judges, graduates, or mayors that they acknowledged the queen as supreme governor of the church. The next century saw torment by oaths. Right-thinking persons in 1644 were required to take an oath to support the *Solemn League and Covenant and in 1662 to repudiate it. *Quakers were in the most disagreeable of all positions since their refusal to take oaths on principle was regarded as utterly subversive, and they suffered imprisonment and loss of property. James II, when duke of York, was forced to resign as lord high admiral because the oath of office under the *Test Act contained a declaration against transubstantiation which, as a catholic, he could not take. The first group to obtain concessions was the quakers, who lobbied hard after the Glorious Revolution. In 1689 they were allowed to make a solemn declaration of loyalty, in 1696 they were permitted to affirm in civil cases, and in 1749 to affirm whenever an oath was required by statute, though they were still excluded from public office. A collision of oaths kept catholics out of Parliament until 1829, since George III insisted that any concession would damage the protestant constitution and breach his coronation oath. Jews remained ineligible for Parliament after 1829 since the oath was on the true faith of a Christian, and were not admitted until 1858. Atheists had to wait until after the *Bradlaugh case. In 1888 the Oath Act cleared up the whole matter by permitting a solemn affirmation in all cases. JAC

O'Brien, James (Bronterre) (1805–64). Dubbed 'the schoolmaster of chartism'. An Irish barrister, O'Brien was the most theoretical of the chartists and might have rivalled *O'Connor for the leadership but for his unstable personality. An admirer of the French Jacobins and also of Robert *Owen, he advocated revolutionary action, including physical force if necessary. But after imprisonment in 1840 for seditious speaking, O'Brien concluded that the use of force was impracticable, and supported a tactical alliance with middle-class radicals. He broke with O'Connor and elaborated plans for socialism and land nationalization through a National *Reform League (1850). His influence was greatest in the early 1830s through his editorship of the *Poor Man's Guardian* and as a contributor to other radical journals. JFCH

O'Brien, Murrough. See INCHIQUIN, EARL OF.

O'Brien, William (1852–1928). Irish nationalist. A journalist from Co. Cork, O'Brien became editor of *United Ireland* in 1881 and was imprisoned for his *Irish Land League agitation until released under the *Kilmainham treaty. In 1883 he was returned to the Westminster Parliament in which he served until 1918. He was again imprisoned for six months in 1887 for supporting a rent strike and for a third time in 1890. In the Parnell split he was a moderate and worked for the reunification of the Irish Parliamentary Party in 1900. But he pursued an increasingly independent line and finished up leading his own small breakaway group. His passionate opposition to partition led him towards *Sinn Fein. He did not stand for re-election in 1918 and declined nomination to the Senate of the Irish Free State, since he refused to accept the treaty and the partition it introduced. JAC

O'Brien, William Smith (1803–64). Smith O'Brien was an unlikely, unwilling, and unsuccessful Irish rebel. The younger son of a protestant baronet from Co. Clare, with family links to the earls of Thomond, he was educated at Harrow and Trinity College, Cambridge. He served in Parliament 1828–31 and from 1835 when he was returned for Co. Limerick. He moved steadily into a nationalist stance, much influenced by *Young Ireland, and in 1843 declared for repeal of the Union. He also moved from advocating peaceful agitation to toying with armed protest. In May 1848 he was prosecuted in Dublin for an inflammatory speech but no verdict was returned. A rising planned for August dwindled into a farcical riot at Ballingarry, Co. Tipperary, where O'Brien explained that he had no food to give his followers and did not intend any violence to property. An attack upon 46 policemen, holed up in Widow McCormack's cottage, was unsuccessful. O'Brien was sentenced to death, but pardoned against his will and transported. After six years in Tasmania he was released but took no further part in politics. He himself described the rising of 1848 as an 'escapade'. JAC

O'Casey, Sean (1880–1964). Irish playwright and author. His real name was John Casey, but was later changed to the more Gaelic Sean O'Casey. Self-educated, he had a natural talent for the theatre. He worked as a casual labourer until the age of 30 when he became involved in Irish politics as a member of the *Gaelic League, the *Irish Republican Brotherhood, Jim *Larkin's Union, the *Irish Citizen Army, and the Irish Socialist Party respectively. In 1916 he turned to writing plays, but it was not until 1923 that one of his plays was staged. His three early plays, *The Shadow of a Gunman* (1923), *Juno and the Paycock* (1924), and *The Plough and the Stars* (1926), dealt with the impact of the Troubles on ordinary people. He was awarded the Hawthornden prize in 1926 for *Juno*, after which he moved to England, where he spent the rest of his life. His career began to wane after the production of the play *Within the Gates* (1934), which was set in London's Hyde Park, and he spent the rest of his life attempting to recapture his former popularity. His genius was particular to his Irish roots and subject-matter, and his inspiration faded once he cut himself off from them. O'Casey died in Torquay. SMD

Occasional Conformity Act, 1711. This Act prevented nonconformists from taking communion in an Anglican church to qualify for national and municipal office according to the *Corporation and *Test Acts. Three previous attempts (1702, 1703, and 1704) had failed because the large Tory majority in the Commons (who aimed at depriving the Whigs of the electoral support of the nonconformists) had been frustrated by the Whig majority in the Lords. The less severe 1711 bill passed because the Whigs agreed to it in exchange for the support of the Tory earl of *Nottingham (the instigator of all four bills) against the Harley ministry's peace policy. The Act was repealed in 1719. CJ

O'Connell, Daniel (1775–1847). Irish catholic politician. Born into the catholic aristocracy and called to the Irish bar in 1798, he built up a successful practice as a barrister and by 1815 was the recognized leader of the movement for *catholic emancipation. In 1823 he started the *Catholic Association to mobilize catholic peasant opinion for emancipation, repeal of the Union, land reform, an end to tithes, and a democratic suffrage. In 1828 he stood successfully for Co. Clare in a parliamentary by-election, although as a catholic he was disqualified. Faced with civil war,*Wellington's government conceded emancipation in 1829. O'Connell's campaign became a model for mass pressure-group politics and influenced both the *Birmingham Political Union, formed later in 1829, and the *chartist movement whose charter he endorsed in 1838. Though a democrat, his acceptance of the 1834 *Poor Law, opposition to trade unions, and support of the Whig government (1835–41) meant he was mistrusted by many British radicals, but he continued to hold the loyalty of most Irishmen through his National Repeal Association (founded 1841) until *Young Ireland, with its more revolutionary version of Irish nationalism, broke away in 1846. His hopes shattered by the *Famine, he died on pilgrimage to Rome the following year. ER

O'Connor, Arthur (1763–1852). Irish republican. Born in Mitchelstown (Co. Cork), into a landed family, his background was protestant but he was a sceptic. He sat in the Dublin Parliament as a follower of *Grattan (1791–5), speaking in favour of *catholic emancipation, but in 1796 joined the *United Irishmen and conducted negotiations for the French invasion of that year. Imprisoned in Dublin for six months for seditious libel in 1797, he was arrested again on his way to France in February 1798. Tried for high treason and acquitted, he was detained on lesser charges but released into exile in France in 1803. In 1807 he married Condorcet's daughter and settled on an estate near Nemours which had once been Mirabeau's. He became a French citizen in 1818. His rationalism and capacity for organization marked him out as one of the ablest of Irish leaders. ER

O'Connor, Feargus (1794–1855). Chartist. An Irish barrister, O'Connor was MP (and follower of Daniel *O'Connell) for Cork in 1832 and for Nottingham (as a chartist) in 1847. He was the greatest of the chartist leaders, the champion, as he said, of the 'unshorn chins, blistered hands, and fustian jackets'; and for ten years he was at the head of the movement. His influence came from his charismatic, flamboyant style of oratory, and his ownership of the chief chartist newspaper, the *Northern Star*. He was imprisoned in 1840 for seditious libel. Contemporaries like *Lovett and some historians later attributed the failure of chartism to O'Connor's demagoguery and his promotion of the National Land Company (1845–51), designed to settle working people on agricultural smallholdings. O'Connor's appearance at the last great chartist demonstration on Kennington Common on 10 April 1848 marked the end of the mass platform as a pattern of popular radicalism. JFCH

O'Connor, Rory (Ruaidrí Ua Conchobair) (d. 1198), last *high king of Ireland, became king of *Connacht in 1156, and high king in 1166, and is widely perceived as a weak ruler. He banished overseas the *Leinster king, *Dermot MacMurrough, who returned with Anglo-Norman aid in 1167. Rory, initially conciliatory, reacted strongly to the arrival of the main body of Anglo-Norman forces in 1169, and made two failed attempts to eject them from Dublin. He did not submit to Henry II during his expedition to Ireland in 1171–2, but reached an accommodation under the short-lived 'treaty' of *Windsor in 1175, which secured Rory's rule over the unconquered parts of the country. O'Connor's position was, however, gradually eroded and he suffered mounting opposition from within his own family, temporarily abdicating in favour of his son in 1183. He never recovered his former status and died at Cong in 1198, being buried in Clonmacnoise. SD

Octavians. A group of eight ministers, appointed by James VI in 1596 to bring order into the Scottish royal finances, possibly at the suggestion of Lord Drumcairn. The king promised not to override them. Their economies provoked protests and they were opposed by another court faction, the Cubiculars (bedchamber servants). Since they were in power for only a year and the task was daunting, progress was limited. James waxed 'very merry', explaining that he would not have one great man but servants he could hang if necessary, but there remains a hint of a non-royal independent bureaucracy. JAC

Octennial Act, 1768. Until 1768 the Irish Parliament existed for the lifetime of the king and general elections were therefore infrequent. A radical campaign in the 1760s demanded a Septennial Act and the institution of *habeas corpus. In 1768 the English government gave way and accepted an Octennial Act, though refusing habeas corpus. Though the Act contributed to the vigour of Irish parliamentary life in the later 18th cent., its effect was mitigated by the unreformed electoral system and, with the Act of *Union of 1801, it ceased to apply. JAC

October Club. A ginger group of Tory MPs formed after the election victory of 1710 to watch *Harley and the moderates and hound the Whigs. They took their name from October ale, beloved of country gentlemen, and met regularly at the Bell Tavern, Westminster. At its peak, the club numbered 150 and its greatest triumph was the expulsion of *Walpole in 1712 on charges of corruption. But it was weakened by the defection of the March Club, even more hostile to the ministers, and it did not long survive the electoral disaster of 1715. JAC

Oda (d. 958). Archbishop of Canterbury, known as 'the Good'. A remarkable, saintly Dane, whom *Athelstan made bishop of Ramsbury (*c.*927), he proved useful to kings in their dealings with people of his race and speech; Athelstan sent him to Paris to treat with Hugh Capet (*c.*936) and later, with Archbishop *Wulfstan of York, he arranged a treaty with *Olaf Guthfrithsson after his invasion of northern England. As archbishop from 942, he ordered bishops to repair ruined churches and issued canons to improve clerical and lay standards. His contribution to 10th-cent. monastic reform has been underestimated. Deeply influenced by the recently reformed abbey of Fleury-sur-Loire, he took Benedictine vows and wore Fleury's habit on becoming archbishop. He sent for training there his nephew *Oswald, future reforming bishop of Worcester. WMM

Odo of Bayeux (*c.*1036–97) was half-brother to Duke William II of Normandy (later William I of England). He was destined for an ecclesiastical career from an early age, receiving the bishopric of Bayeux from William in about 1049, when he was perhaps 13 years old, the first of many acts of patronage that were as much political as fraternal, since William intended Odo to strengthen ducal authority in Lower Normandy. He participated in the invasion of England in 1066, the *Bayeux Tapestry, almost certainly produced for Odo, exaggerating his role. In 1067, he received Dover castle and the earldom of Kent, his particular remit being defence of the coast and ports in this vital strategic area. Thereafter, he acted occasionally as the Conqueror's viceregent and accumulated enormous wealth in England, second only to the king. In 1082, William stripped him of his English lands and incarcerated him for reasons that remain obscure. Released in 1087, he joined the rebellion against William II 'Rufus' in 1088. This time he was exiled from England for ever and returned to Normandy. In 1096 he joined the First Crusade, but died *en route* at Palermo in 1097. SL

O'Donnell, Hugh Roe (*c.*1571–1602). O'Donnell was married to a daughter of *Tyrone. From 1587 to 1591 he was held in captivity in Dublin but escaped and built up a powerful position in Connacht. He drifted into open rebellion against Elizabeth, sharing Tyrone's victory at *Yellow Ford in 1598. On hearing of the Spanish expedition to *Kinsale in 1601, he moved south to join forces with Tyrone. They were routed by *Mountjoy and O'Donnell left at once for Spain, where he died eight months later. His younger brother Rory *O'Donnell took over the chieftainship. JAC

O'Donnell, Rory, 1st earl of Tyrconnel [I] (1575–1608). The second son of the chief of the O'Donnells, Rory joined his brother Hugh Roe and *Tyrone in rebellion against Elizabeth from 1598 until 1602. After the disaster at *Kinsale, Hugh Roe fled to Spain and died in September 1602. Rory assumed the chieftainship and submitted to Elizabeth's lieutenant *Mountjoy. After a visit to James I in June 1603 O'Donnell was created earl of Tyrconnel but became increasingly dissatisfied. Learning that a plan to seize Dublin castle had been betrayed and fearing arrest, he joined Tyrone in the *Flight of the Earls in September 1607. He spent his remaining months in Rome, where he died in July 1608, amid suspicions of poison. His son served in an Irish regiment in the Spanish army: a daughter, born after the flight, developed a taste for adventure in men's clothing and lived in poverty in Rome. JAC

Offa (d. 796), king of Mercia (757–96), came to the throne after a disputed succession with Beornred following the murder of King *Æthelbald. He continued the expansion of Mercia from its midland base through incorporation of neighbouring kingdoms. By the end of his reign Offa had added the provinces of the *Hwicce, the *South Saxons, and *Kent and had expelled their royal houses or reduced them to the status of ealdormen. But he also had to deal with strong opposition. Although he had gained control in Kent in 764, the Kentishmen recovered their independence after the battle of *Otford in 776 and retained it until 785. *Cynewulf of Wessex fought Offa at *Benson *c.*779 and although he lost some parts of northern Wessex to Offa, remained an independent ruler. Offa may have had more influence in Wessex during the reign of Beorhtric, who married his daughter Eadburh in 786. Æthelbert of the East Angles presumably offered resistance as well since in 794 Offa had him beheaded. Offa's Dike still stands as testimony to the seriousness of his campaigns against the Welsh and also to his ability to exact military services from his subjects and co-ordinate a major building campaign.

Offa was considered sufficiently powerful by his contemporary Charles the Great to warrant bringing into his sphere of influence by the bestowal of gifts. The two kings corresponded on trade between their kingdoms, and marriage between their children appears to have been considered. Offa introduced the 'penny' coinage circulating in Francia and copied Frankish usage in including his portrait in the style of a Roman emperor. He may also have been influenced by Frankish example to attend to the moral and spiritual welfare of his people and drew praise from Charles's Northumbrian advisor *Alcuin for encouraging 'good, moderate and chaste customs'. But, as is often the case with early medieval rulers, his interest in the church had political connotations as well. His presidency of a synod of the southern church in 786 attended by two papal legates helped stress that he was the dominant king of southern England. His wooing of the pope resulted in a grant of archiepiscopal status for the Mercian see of *Lichfield in 787 and the consecration there of Offa's son Ecgfrith as king of the Mercians later the same year. Archbishop Jaenbert of Canterbury, who was part of the Kentish opposition to Offa, seems to have refused to carry out the ceremony. It appears to have been opposed in Mercia as well. Alcuin was not surprised that Ecgfrith only survived his father by 141 days for it was a judgement on the blood Offa had shed to secure his succession; perhaps a reference to the culling of rival royal claimants. BAEY

Official Secrets Act, 1911. The first Official Secrets Act (1889) was ineffective. It required the government to *prove* a suspect was a spy, even where it was obvious. The 1911 Act put this right, and extended the law further. It was passed in a panic, during an anti-German spy scare, and on a hot summer's day when many MPs had gone home. Section I dealt with espionage; section II, however, forbade the unauthorized revelation of any government information, however innocuous to national security. In 1985 Clive Ponting, a civil servant, was acquitted under it, against the evidence, because the jury felt he had acted in the public interest. That led to a third Official Secrets Act in 1989, which narrowed the range of information it covered, but made it impossible to plead 'public interest' as a defence. BJP

oil. See PETROLEUM INDUSTRY.

Olaf Guthfrithsson (d. 941), king of Dublin. Olaf succeeded to the throne in 934. His first years as ruler were spent in establishing his position in Ireland, where in 935 he raided the monastery of Clonmacnoise and in 937 overran Limerick. This freed him for an attempt to regain the Viking kingdom of *York, from which his father had been expelled in 927 by *Athelstan. But Olaf's grand coalition, which included the king of the Scots and the king of Strathclyde, was cut to pieces by Athelstan at *Brunanburh, Olaf escaping in flight (937). After Athelstan's death in 939, Olaf renewed the struggle, occupied York, harried Mercia, sacked Tamworth, and forced *Edmund to concede all the lands north-east of Watling Street. He was killed the following year at Tyningham, near Dunbar, and his successors were unable to hold the territories he had won back. JAC

Olaf Sihtricsson (d. 981), king of Deira (941–3, 949–52), king of Dublin (945–81). Olaf's father was *Sihtric, king of *Deira, whose second wife was *Athelstan's sister. On Sihtric's death in 927, his brother Guthfrith took the throne (Olaf being a child), but was at once dispossessed by Athelstan. *Olaf Guthfrithsson regained it in 939 and on his death in 941 was succeeded by Olaf Sihtricsson, who had married a daughter of *Constantine, king of the Scots. He could not hold the territories regained from *Edmund, Athelstan's successor, and was driven out of his capital, York, in 943. He did, however, recover the throne of the Norse kingdom of Dublin in 945, may have briefly been restored in York in 949, and was again dispossessed by *Erik Bloodaxe in 952. He managed to hold his kingdom of Dublin in the face of incessant warfare against the Irish, but at the end of his life suffered a severe defeat at Tara (980), abdicated, and spent his last months on Iona. JAC

old-age pensions were first paid to persons over 70 years of age on 1 January 1909. Their introduction had been debated for many years, raising questions about the redistribution of incomes and reducing the burden of poverty on people who had not sufficient resources to provide for themselves. A regular weekly payment by the state from taxation was preferred to any contributory scheme because of the high administrative cost. Only those with an annual income of less than £31 10*s*. a year, who had no criminal convictions, and who had never received support from the Poor Law were eligible for an old-age pension. Almost half a million people qualified. Later amendments increased payments to cope with inflation and after 1925 the age for support was lowered to 65 years. Pension entitlement began under the National Health and Insurance Act (1925) when worker, employer, and the state each contributed. Retirement pensions superseded the old-age pension in 1946 for all except those who had no contribution record after 1946. IJEK

Old Bailey. This is the popular name given to the Central Criminal Court in London, set up in 1834. It is the successor of the Old Bailey sessions of gaol delivery for *Newgate prison and of *oyer and terminer for the city of London and the county of Middlesex. The sheriffs of London were also sheriffs of Middlesex, and the lord mayor of London was included in the commissions of oyer and terminer and is still ex officio a judge of the Central Criminal Court. The jurisdiction of the Central Criminal Court extends throughout the whole metropolis. MM

Old Sarum was the original site of the city of Salisbury, abandoned in 1220 for the situation closer to the river Avon. By Tudor times it was totally deserted. It continued to return two members of Parliament until 1832 and became a symbol of the old regime, having, by the 18th cent., no more than a handful of voters and not knowing a contest between 1728 and its abolition in Schedule A of the *Great Reform Act. JAC

'Oliver the Spy' became the mythic villain of generations of English radicals after allegedly egging on the *Pentrich rebels in June 1817, and then betraying them. Three were executed as a result. Oliver's real name may have been William Richards, but no one knows for certain, because he vanished afterwards. BJP

Olivier, Sir Laurence (1907–89). Actor and director. Praised by Ellen *Terry in a school play, Olivier became one of his generation's leading actors, and achieved a respectable film career. Commencing in repertory, he established a reputation with Shakespearian roles and joined the Old Vic; after starring in film versions of *Wuthering Heights* and *Rebecca* in America, he returned to England to serve in the Fleet Air Arm, before helping rebuild the Old Vic after the Second World War. Handsome, charismatic, often generating a sense of risk, then youngest stage knight (1947), he directed and acted under his own management from 1950, revolutionized the art of filming Shakespeare (*Henry V*, *Hamlet*, *Richard III*), became director of the newly formed National Theatre Company (1962–73), and was the first actor to receive a life peerage. The outstanding success of Olivier's later career, before ill-health supervened, was as Archie Rice in John Osborne's *The Entertainer* (1957). One of the Royal National Theatre's stages is named in his honour. ASH

Omdurman. Town in central *Sudan which came to prominence when the mahdi, a religious leader who led a holy war against the Egyptian government, made it his capital in 1885. Although British forces had occupied Egypt in 1882 the British government showed little interest in extending its influence further south until France cast covetous eyes on the region. In 1898 an Anglo-Egyptian army led by Sir Herbert *Kitchener advanced into the Sudan. Early in September the battle for Omdurman took place, the town was occupied by Kitchener's forces, and the army of the mahdi was completely destroyed. KI

O'Neill, Con, 1st earl of Tyrone [I] (*c*.1484–1559). Con O'Neill's life was turbulent and his political course fluctuating. He became chief of Tyrone in 1519. He clashed repeatedly with successive lord deputies—*Surrey, Skeffington, *Grey, and *St Leger—but came to terms in 1540, visiting Henry VIII at Greenwich, and being created by him earl of Tyrone in 1542, with remainder to his illegitimate son Matthew. From 1551 his authority was disputed by his legitimate son *Shane, and he was driven to take refuge in the English *Pale. JAC

O'Neill, Daniel (1612–64). Daniel O'Neill was an Ulster protestant and made a living in the 1630s as a volunteer soldier fighting for the Dutch. He returned to England when the *Bishops' wars commenced and was captured at *Newburn in 1640 fighting for the king. He dabbled in royalist conspiracy, was confined by Parliament to the Tower, but made his escape in women's clothes. He joined Charles's army in 1642 and in 1644 was sent to Ireland to raise troops. He returned to fight at *Marston Moor, *Lostwithiel, the second battle of *Newbury, and *Naseby. From 1645 to 1650 he was in Ireland trying to rescue the king's cause. He next joined Charles II in Holland, fought alongside him at *Worcester in 1651, and escaped to The Hague. At the Restoration he became an MP, was given a pension and property, and in 1663 appointed postmaster-general. He died in 1664 causing Charles to regret 'as honest a man as ever lived and a good servant'. Clarendon admired his dexterity and adroitness. JAC

O'Neill, Hugh, 3rd earl of Tyrone [I] (1550–1616). O'Neill was brought up in England in the charge of Sir Henry *Sidney and *Leicester. On the death of his brother Brien in 1562 he succeeded to the earldom, though his title was not recognized by Elizabeth until 1585. He was sent to Ireland in 1568 after the death of Shane *O'Neill as a counterweight to the influence of Turlough O'Neill, who claimed the headship of the family. But no sooner had he established his supremacy, by 1595, than he was in full-scale rebellion against Elizabeth, greatly encouraged by the catholic powers of Europe. He defeated and slew Sir Henry Bagenal at *Yellow Ford in 1598, outmanœuvred *Essex without great difficulty at their famous meeting in September 1599, and maintained resistance until crushed by Mountjoy in 1602.

He was reconciled to James I but in September 1607 fled abroad with the earl of Tyrconnel. He died in exile in Rome, blind and powerless. JAC

O'Neill, Owen Roe (*c.*1590–1649). O'Neill was the military linchpin of the Confederation, which struggled for control of Ireland after the rising of 1641. He was a nephew of Hugh *O'Neill, 3rd earl of Tyrone, and spent his early years in the Spanish service. He was not in Ireland at the start of the rising but arrived in July 1642 and took over command of the Ulster army from Sir Phelim *O'Neill. He managed to keep an army together through all the extraordinary political vicissitudes of the next few years and in 1646 gained a significant victory at *Benburb over Monro and the Scottish army. But the end of the Civil War in England enabled Parliament to strengthen its position in Ireland. The Confederation split badly on political tactics and O'Neill was declared a traitor in 1648 for supporting the intransigent line of Rinuccini, the papal nuncio. Early in 1649 he reached an agreement with *Monck, who commanded the parliamentary forces in Ulster. It is doubtful whether he could have put up much resistance to Cromwell, who landed in August 1649, but he died in November of the same year. JAC

O'Neill, Sir Phelim (*c.*1604–53). O'Neill was one of the commanders of the Irish rebels or Confederation. In 1641 he captured Charlemont castle on the Blackwater and was put in charge of the army of the Ulster rebels. He claimed to be acting on behalf of Charles I but had great difficulty in maintaining his position until assisted by the arrival of Owen Roe *O'Neill, with whom he subsequently quarrelled. He continued to fight for the Confederation and took part in the victory at *Benburb in 1646, but was forced to capitulate to parliamentary forces in 1650. He failed to make good his escape and was put on trial in 1653. Refusing to purchase a pardon by implicating Charles I, he was executed in Dublin as a traitor. JAC

O'Neill, Shane (*c.*1530–67). The legitimate son of Con *O'Neill, he was passed over in 1542 when his father was created earl of Tyrone, presumably because of his youth, and remainder given to an illegitimate son, Matthew. As soon as he grew up he claimed the inheritance, insisting that Matthew's claim was entirely spurious, and by 1557 had driven his father and Matthew O'Neill to take refuge in the *Pale. In 1558 he killed Matthew, but at her succession Elizabeth offered to recognize him if he submitted to the lord deputy, *Sussex. The negotiations broke down amid mutual mistrust, but O'Neill held his own against Sussex and in 1562 visited Elizabeth in London, where he and his followers (who spoke mostly Irish) created a sensation. On his return to Ireland, he resumed his warfare with gusto, particularly against the Macdonnells. Fresh attempts by Sussex and then Sir Henry *Sidney to subdue him failed, but O'Neill, appealing to his old enemies the Macdonnells for support, was assassinated in June 1567. JAC

O'Neill, Terence, Lord O'Neill of the Maine (1914–90). Prime minister of Northern Ireland (1963–9). O'Neill, who saw himself as a modernizer, was keen to promote economic development within Northern Ireland, and to address the traditional hostility between unionist and nationalist, and between Belfast and Dublin: he welcomed Sean Lemass, the taoiseach (prime minister) of the Republic of Ireland, to Belfast in January 1965, the first such official visit since partition. However, he simultaneously alienated hard-line loyalists without offering substantive concessions to the increasingly alienated Ulster catholics. The rise of the Northern Ireland Civil Rights Association (founded in January 1967) brought further pressure on O'Neill. In November 1968 he conceded a five-point reform programme, but this satisfied neither the NICRA activists nor many of his unionist colleagues. He held an election in February 1969 in order to test his strength, but inadvertently intensified the divisions within his party. On 28 April 1969, against the background of a splintering unionism and relentless NICRA pressure, he resigned. O'Neill was a well-intentioned, if paternalistic, leader, who could also be crude in his political judgement and style. Like Harold Wilson he was strong on the rhetoric of modernization; like Wilson he was susceptible to conspiratorial fantasies. AJ

On Liberty (1859) was John Stuart *Mill's influential justification of individual freedom. In this book, Mill set out to establish a 'simple principle'—that the only legitimate reason for interfering with someone's action was to protect someone else; the good of the agent himself/herself was not sufficient warrant. Mill based his defence of liberty on utilitarian grounds, not on a natural right to freedom; arguing that on balance people were happier when left to choose their life-styles for themselves. He also believed that social well-being and scientific progress depended on the greatest possible freedom of expression and publication. His attack was directed not only at governmental paternalism but also at social conformity. TSG

opera. The general term, taken from the Italian *opera* meaning work, describes a staged drama in which the actors sing some or all of their parts. Opera involves a union of music, drama, and spectacle in varying degrees; although the first Florentine operas around 1600 emphasized the text through recitative—a form of heightened speech—music soon became the dominant partner. While all-sung opera has always been the norm in Italy, the strong British tradition of spoken drama favoured the *masque, and spoken drama with music remained the pattern for dramatic works in English. Full-length, all-sung English operas were a rarity until the 20th cent.; for the previous 200 years the British operatic scene was dominated by Italian imports. Only since the outstanding success of *Britten's *Peter Grimes* in 1945 has Britain played a major role on the international operatic stage—ironically at a time when opera-houses have become 'museums', relying on revivals of well-known works in preference to commissioning new operas.

Music featured in Shakespeare's works and in Elizabethan choirboy plays, and the Stuart masques drew on this tradition. Even at the end of the 17th cent., *Purcell's dramatic music for the professional stage fell into the category of 'semi-opera': spoken plays reworked to include a series of masques for subsidiary characters. French influence is apparent in both the staging, with elaborate sets, machinery, and costumes, and the music, including choruses and dances. Purcell's finest semi-opera *The Fairy Queen* (1692), an arrangement of *A Midsummer Night's Dream*, sets none of Shakespeare's text to music; nevertheless allegorical figures such as the Four Seasons are skilfully characterized by contrasting vocal styles and orchestration. Purcell's only 'true' opera, *Dido and Aeneas*, was performed at a girls' school in Chelsea (London) in 1689 and is modelled on Blow's court masque *Venus and Adonis*.

Davenant's *The Siege of Rhodes* (1656) was the first full-length, all-sung English opera, set 'in recitative musick' by several composers to overcome the Commonwealth ban on spoken drama. It included probably the first woman to appear on the public stage in London; the music is now lost. Its occasional successors did not catch on, and the early 18th-cent. London public turned to imported Italian opera. *Handel's *Rinaldo* (1711), with its spectacular magic effects, was a stunning success, and for the next thirty years he produced a string of fine works, emphasizing the arias by reducing the amount of recitative in his *opera seria* librettos. Handel and the rival Opera of the Nobility imported leading Italian stars, including the famous castrati Senesino and Farinelli.

John *Gay's enormously popular *The Beggar's Opera* (1728) began a brief vogue for ballad opera, with simple, popular tunes sung by actors interspersed with spoken English dialogue. The satirical treatment of London's low life appealed to a wider social range than the aristocratic *opera seria*, and the following decades spawned many short English works. These were often presented as afterpieces following spoken plays, such as Arne's patriotic *Thomas and Sally* (1760), while both serious and comic Italian opera, particularly the pasticcio using arias by various composers, remained dominant until the end of the 19th cent. Five Rossini and two Verdi operas were performed in the first Royal Italian Opera season at Covent Garden in 1847; even works by Mozart and Wagner were translated into Italian, although a German *Ring* was produced in 1882. Some English dialogue operas were successful—Balfe's *The Bohemian Girl* (1843) remained in the repertoire for nearly a century—and works such as Macfarren's *Robin Hood* (1860), MacCunn's *Jeanie Deans* (1894), and *Stanford's *Shamus O'Brien* (1896) cultivated romantic nationalism in their choice of plots and use of folk-song. The most outstanding English works, however, were the brilliant operettas of *Gilbert and *Sullivan, achieving lasting popularity through their blend of W. S. Gilbert's satirical texts with Arthur Sullivan's tuneful music.

In the early 20th cent., Stanford, Ethel Smyth, and *Delius produced all-sung works that were strongly Germanic, although *Vaughan Williams and *Holst used folk-song to impart an English flavour. The reopening of London's Sadler's Wells theatre in 1945 with Britten's *Peter Grimes* heralded a renaissance in English opera, presenting a powerful drama full of well-drawn characters. Britten's setting of the English language (influenced by Purcell) and his large-scale motivic and tonal planning gave his operas an unrivalled power and direct appeal. His choice of plots with a strong social dimension is shared by Michael *Tippett, whose Jungian symbolism and complex contrapuntal musical style are exemplified in his psychoanalytical *The Knot Garden* (1970). Other recent operatic composers include Peter Maxwell Davies and Harrison Birtwistle. ECr

Opium War. See CHINA WARS.

Oporto, battle of, 1809. On 12 May 1809 British forces in the Peninsula under Wellesley faced Soult's French army of 11,000 across the Douro opposite Oporto. Believing a frontal assault to be impossible, Soult was taken by surprise when the British used four wine barges to ferry troops across the river. The British occupied a convent which they held against French counter-attacks. When the French withdrew from the waterfront, the citizens of Oporto took many more vessels across to the British to speed up the crossing. Soult was forced to retreat, and by 19 May the French had been driven out of Portugal. GDS

opposition. The concept of a loyal parliamentary opposition grew slowly for two reasons. As long as the monarch played an active part in government, opposition was bound to be tainted with disloyalty: though the opposition to Charles I in the 1640s claimed to be loyal and conservative, it ended by cutting his head off and abolishing the monarchy. Secondly, the existence from 1688 until 1760 of an active Jacobite cause retarded the concept since some of the Tories in opposition undoubtedly wished to overthrow the regime itself. Nevertheless, the concept made progress in the 18th cent. and was helped by the fact that successive princes of Wales, who could scarcely be accused of treason, went into opposition to their father's government. Monarchs continued to find the concept suspect and the protestations of loyalty insincere: George III observed in 1778 that 'men who have been active in opposition rarely make useful servants to the crown'—a phrase which reveals a slightly old-fashioned attitude. Charles *Fox, on the other hand, declared in 1783 that a 'systematic opposition to a dangerous government is, in my opinion, a noble employment for the brightest faculties'. The phrase 'His Majesty's Opposition' was first used jocularly by Hobhouse in 1826 and was so useful that it took root. The validity of the concept was subsequently recognized in a variety of ways. From 1937 the leader of the opposition received an official salary and is now provided with an official car and chauffeur: the chief opposition whip and two assistant whips also receive salaries. He is accorded prominence in public ceremonies, such as the Armistice Day commemoration. All parliamentary parties have since 1975 received some public funding. Governments sometimes offer confidential information to opposition spokesmen, who are frequently wary lest it blunt their attacks. The concept of opposition is close to the heart of parliamentary democracy, not merely in curbing government, resisting encroachments upon liberty, and keeping ministers on their toes, but as a stabilizing factor by offering to the most embittered of citizens hope that governments do not last forever. JAC

Orange Free State. Former British colony in South Africa. Founded as a republic by Boers (Afrikaners) fleeing British rule in Cape Colony in the mid-19th cent., the Orange Free State retained its independent status until 1900 because of the absence of any resources which might attract the cupidity of foreigners and because its government pursued a policy of friendship with its neighbours. When the Transvaal declared war on Britain in 1899, the Free State's leaders felt bound by treaty to assist. The Boers were defeated and the country became the Orange River Colony in 1900. It was incorporated into the Union of South Africa in 1910. KI

Orange order. An Irish protestant organization run along masonic lines and dedicated to the preservation of the protestant constitution and the 'glorious and immortal memory' of King William III, the victor of the *Boyne (1690). The order was founded in Loughgall (Co. Armagh) in September 1795 by the protestant veterans of a sectarian clash, the battle of the Diamond. It infiltrated the army and yeomanry, and was associated with the bloody suppression of the 1798 rising. Although it experienced a rapid initial growth, both geographically and socially, the order came under parliamentary scrutiny in 1835: the select committee report into its activities was couched in such critical terms that it went into voluntary dissolution. In the later 19th cent. the order enjoyed a revival: it was the vehicle by which the populist demagogue William Johnston mounted an assault on the Party Processions Act in 1867; and it was one of the organizational foundations of popular unionism in the early and mid-1880s. Since 1905 the order has been formally connected with the *Ulster Unionist Party, although this relationship is at present under review. The order continues to attract a large Ulster protestant membership (perhaps 80,000–100,000). AJ

Ordainers. The initial political crises of Edward II's reign culminated in 1310, when the king was forced to agree to the appointment of 21 Ordainers, chosen by a complex system of election. An initial six Ordinances were followed in September 1311 by the main Ordinances, an elaborate programme for reform of government which included a request for the exiling of the king's favourite, Piers *Gaveston. Royal finance and the administration of justice were the subject of many clauses. The Ordainers included men of very different political attitudes. At one extreme was Edward I's former opponent Archbishop *Winchelsey, and at the other the moderate earl of Gloucester, who was married to the king's niece and brother-in-law to Gaveston. The Ordinances were repealed in the statute of *York of 1322. MCP

Orderic Vitalis (1075–*c.*1142), the great historian of the Normans, was born near Shrewsbury of mixed English and French parentage, but from 1085 lived his entire life at the abbey of Saint-Evroult in southern *Normandy. His greatest historical work, the massive *Ecclesiastical History*, was composed from 1123 onwards and came to include material on many of the major events of his lifetime, most notably the expansion of Norman power throughout Europe and the *Norman Conquest of England. Orderic's historical writing derives its importance from his insatiable curiosity and powers of observation; the vast array of information he assembled is invaluable for our understanding of the social history and religious life of his times. He continued the history up almost to the moment of his death and concluded it with a deeply moving autobiographical epilogue. DB

orders in council. In November 1806 Napoleon's Berlin Decree attempted to exclude British trade from the continent. The British government replied with the orders in council, using the emergency powers of the sovereign, approved by the Privy Council. The orders of November and December 1807 declared a blockade of any harbour that excluded British commerce and insisted that neutral vessels must visit British harbours and pay transit fees. The USA protested strongly and its resentment was one of the causes of the *War of 1812. JAC

Ordnance Survey. One of the beneficial results of the '45 rebellion. The difficulties of both the campaign and the measures after Culloden persuaded Lieutenant-General Watson, deputy quartermaster-general, that better maps of the Highlands were needed. Much of the work, later extended to the Lowlands, was done by William Roy. In 1765 Roy was appointed to survey coastal areas of Britain and to report to the master-general of the ordnance. At the same time the newly formed *Royal Society of Arts offered rewards for county maps. After Roy's death in 1790, the duke of Richmond, master-general of the ordnance, appointed a small team in 1791, the effective work falling upon William Mudge. Working from the headquarters of the Ordnance in the Tower, they issued in 1801 the first of a series of one-inch maps, the county of Kent. A survey of Ireland was started in 1825. JAC

Ordovices. Indigenous British tribe of the Iron Age and Roman periods whose territory covered much of mid-Wales. The Ordovices were the northern neighbours of the *Silures and the southern neighbours of the *Degeangli. After the Claudian invasion the Ordovices and the Silures were stirred into rebellion by *Caratacus. Between AD 47 and 51 the governor P. *Ostorius Scapula temporarily subdued the revolting tribes in Wales and elsewhere. His successor Aulus Didius Gallus also struggled against the Welsh tribes. *Agricola finally defeated the Ordovices in 77–8. The tribe was incorporated into the province of Britannia and thus became a *civitas* (tribal administrative district). ES

Oregon treaty, 1846. The disputed eastern boundary between Canada and the USA was settled by the *Ashburton treaty of 1842. The vast area between the Rockies and the Pacific known as the Oregon Territory was covered by a convention, extended from 1818, whereby subjects of both states had access. In 1845 James J. Polk was elected president on the slogan of '54' 50 or fight' and in his inaugural speech he insisted that America's claim was 'clear and unquestionable' and would be pursued by force if necessary. The *Peel government, then in its last months, negotiated a settlement on the line of the 49th parallel, which required only minor revision in 1872. JAC

Orford, Edward Russell, 1st earl of (1652–1727). Russell was nephew of the 1st duke of Bedford, entered the navy in 1671, saw much service in the second *Anglo-Dutch War, and made rapid progress in his profession. Alienated from the court by the execution of his cousin Lord *Russell, he signed the invitation to William of Orange in 1688 and landed with him at Brixham. He was promoted admiral in 1689 and gained the victory of *La Hogue over the French in 1692. Though the victory was both important and decisive there was some disappointment that Russell's superiority of numbers had not told more emphatically. Russell commanded in the Mediterranean 1694–5 and in the Channel in 1696. The following year he was created earl of Orford. He served as 1st lord of the Admiralty 1694–9 and again 1709–10. He was impeached by the Tories in 1701 for involvement in the *partition treaties but unanimously acquitted. Under George I, he resumed as 1st lord until 1717. He died without issue and in 1742 the title of Orford was revived for Sir Robert *Walpole. JAC

Origin of Species, The. Charles *Darwin's book of 1859 setting out the development of new kinds of creatures through natural selection, and inheritance with variability. After 20 years' work on a great tome, *Natural Selection*, he received in 1858 a letter from A. R. Wallace in Malaysia setting out that very theory. His friends published this and Darwin's earlier sketch, but nobody took any notice. So the *Origin* was meant to be a lengthy abstract, without notes or bibliography, of the full work; hence it looks deceptively accessible. Its readability, and basis in an immense bulk of varied evidence, carried the day, and made evolution scientifically respectable. DK

Orkney. A group of islands lying at the north-east tip of Scotland. The islands are rich in archaeological monuments. Skara Brae is a well-preserved prehistoric village, Maes Howe the best of a series of impressive prehistoric burial cairns, and numerous brochs and settlements attest to the islands' Pictish and Viking periods. Orkney, together with Shetland, became part of Scotland in consequence of the marriage of *Margaret of Denmark-Norway to James III of Scotland in 1469; the marriage settlement provided for a temporary transfer of the islands until a cash payment was completed, but the cash was never forthcoming and Orkney and Shetland remained Scottish. Orkney is mainly low lying and fertile, with agriculture, fishing, and food-processing, and now oil-related activity, significant sources of employment. It constitutes a county of Scotland, which remained a unitary local administrative authority throughout the Scottish 1973 and 1996 local government reorganizations. CML

Orkney, jarldom of. From the late 9th cent. the fertile Orkney islands were the locus for a Norse jarldom, for centuries the dominant power in northern Scotland. Orkney had been the seat of a Pictish subkingdom in the 6th cent., according to *Adomnán. However, there is no evidence of continuity between the two, although the possibility should not be ignored.

Despite the origins of the jarldom being shrouded in obscurity, it is clear that the first jarl was Røgnvald, also jarl of Møre in western Norway. He passed on the jarldom to Sigurd the Mighty, his brother. Sigurd, in partnership with Thorsteinn the Red from the Hebrides, turned his attention to the Scottish mainland. Together they are credited, in Icelandic tradition, with conquering Caithness, Sutherland, Moray, and Ross. Sigurd died (*c.*892) on one of his forays south, and may have been buried at Cyder Hall, on the banks of the river Oykell.

The jarls had sole possession of the archipelago, apart from periods when the king of Norway or his family attempted to establish a claim to authority, as, for example, in *c.*947, when the joint jarls, Arnkel and Erlend, were visited by the exiled *Erik Bloodaxe, ex-king of Norway. They accompanied him to York, where he became king. They were still in his retinue at the battle of *Stainmore in 954, where he and they were killed.

The jarldom entered its period of greatest power and influence during the late 10th to mid-11th cents., under Sigurd the Stout and his son by a daughter of the 'king of Scots', *Thorfinn the Mighty. During this period, the authority of the jarls spread south down the western searoute towards Dublin. The beginning of this expansion is perhaps to be seen in the attack on *Iona in 986, when the abbot and fifteen elders of the monastery were slain by a force of unidentified 'Danes'. It is unclear whether Sigurd's presence in the Hebrides amounted to conquest, but Icelandic tradition claims he gathered tribute from Man and the Isles. He was definitely a powerful player in the politics of the Irish sea province, as his presence, and death, at the battle of *Clontarf in 1014 make clear. With Thorfinn, there is more solid evidence for his conquest of the Hebrides. He was remembered by the Icelandic historian Snorri Sturluson as 'the ablest jarl of these islands, and has had the greatest dominion of all Orkney jarls'. Thorfinn was also an administrator. He is credited with the establishment of a bishopric and with building Orkney's first documented church. However, his political achievements were transitory. After his death in 1065, his conquest fell apart. AJe

Orléans, siege of, 1428–9. On 12 October 1428, Thomas, earl of *Salisbury, laid siege to Orléans as part of a strategy to advance across the Loire. He died from gunshot wounds on 3 November, but the siege continued, with an attack on the English supply lines (the battle of the *Herrings) being unsuccessful. The English were already weakened and deserted by their Burgundian allies, however, by the time Joan of Arc arrived on 29 April and were forced to raise the siege on 8 May. AC

Ormond, James Butler, 1st duke of (1610–88). Ormond, a protestant and a leading member of the Anglo-Irish ascendancy, succeeded to the earldom in 1633. After the departure of *Strafford from Ireland in 1640, Ormond became the mainstay of royal authority, first as commander-in-chief, then as lord-lieutenant. He struggled with considerable success after 1641 to keep a footing in the shifting sands of Irish politics. He was able to check the Irish rebels at Kilrush in March 1642 and again in 1643 at Ross, but the king, hard pressed, constantly urged him to negotiate, in the hope of obtaining troops to turn the scales in the Civil War. Ormond agreed a 'cessation' in September 1643 but by the time a permanent settlement was reached in 1646, the position in England had been lost. The following year, Ormond left Ireland, handing over Dublin to Michael Jones, representing the English Parliament. When he returned with royalist troops late in the second civil war, he was defeated by Jones at *Rathmines and left the country in 1650. In exile until the Restoration, Ormond resumed his position in Ireland under Charles II, acting as lord-lieutenant from 1662 to 1669 and again from 1677 to 1685. He was given an Irish dukedom in 1661 and an English dukedom in 1682. At James II's accession, he retired from public life. Like Strafford, Ormond did not receive from the Stuarts the loyalty he gave. JAC

Ormond, James Butler, 2nd duke of (1665–1745). Butler, born in Dublin, was heir of the earl of Ossory. Succeeding in 1680, he lived with his grandfather, the 1st duke, in Ireland until 1682. He fought for James II against *Monmouth's rising in 1685. Succeeding his grandfather in July 1688, he supported the petition to James for a free parliament, then accepted William of Orange, for whom he fought in Ireland and Flanders. A pillar of the Tory Party and Anglican church, he commanded unsuccessfully the 1702 expedition against Cadiz, and was twice a controversial lord-lieutenant of Ireland. He replaced *Marlborough in 1712, restraining his troops in the field to facilitate Tory negotiations with France. Dismissed in 1714, despite his role in proclaiming George I, he was threatened with impeachment by the Whigs. Panicking, he fled to the Jacobite court. Jacobite failures to invade England deprived him of chances to display his military incompetence again, and he died exiled and insignificant. BPL

Ormond, Thomas Butler, 10th earl of [I] (1531–1614). 'Black Tom' Ormond inherited the title from his father at the age of 15 and was brought up as a protestant at the English court. From 1559 he was treasurer of Ireland and in 1588 was given the Garter, for zeal in tracking down the survivors of the Spanish Armada. Much of his life was spent campaigning in Ireland, in the 1560s and the 1580s against the earls of Desmond (*Fitzgerald), his family's rivals, and in the 1590s with *Essex against *Tyrone. He died aged 83 having been blind for many years. JAC

Orthez, battle of, 1814. *Wellington's troops crossed the Bidassoa into France in October 1813 but Soult's army continued to resist strongly, falling back on a series of river lines. On 27 February 1814, with a slight numerical superiority, Soult tried to hold the line of the Gave de Pau at Orthez, but was badly beaten. On 12 April 1814 Wellington occupied Toulouse, where he received the news of Napoleon's abdication. JAC

orthodox church. The eastern orthodox church dating from earliest Christian times has its centre at Constantinople (Istanbul), the residence of the ecumenical patriarch, who has primacy of honour over much of the 'intricate tapestry' of the Christian East, including the Greeks, Serbs, Bulgars, Georgians, and Russians. In 1995 there were *c.*190 million adherents world-wide. The earlier rupture with Syriac monophysite churches was followed by the break with Rome and the West (1054), which the crusades intensified. Orthodoxy has always been closely associated with temporal power. Priests are usually married, though bishops are always celibate. Icons are central to devotion, but at the heart of orthodox life is the mystery of the liturgy with its chanting and ceremonial in icon-lined churches—an experience of 'heaven on earth'. Orthodoxy's greatest contribution to the West has been its mystical writings, ranging from 7th-cent. Symeon the New Theologian to the 18th-cent. *Philokalia*, and its practice of silent, contemplative prayer. British contacts with orthodoxy began with 16th-cent. merchants and Peter the Great's visit to England (1698). Since the 1950s orthodoxy has flourished in England with *c.*287,000 members (1995). WMM

Orwell, George (1903–50). Orwell, whose real name was Eric Blair, was one of the best-known British writers, embodying the hopes and aspirations of the left in the 1930s, and the subsequent post-war disillusionment. His career began as a policeman in Burma, but in 1927 he returned to England determined to be a writer. The experience of poverty enabled him to write the highly informative *Down and Out in Paris and London* (1930); *Burmese Days* (1931) followed. Based on personal experiences, it was critical of the British empire. But Orwell's breakthrough came when he was commissioned by Gollancz of the Left Book Club to write a study of poverty in England. The *Road to Wigan Pier* (1937) was a brilliantly incisive and emotive impression of working-class life.

The experience of fighting with the POUM militia against fascists in Spain, which almost led to his death, cemented Orwell's socialist ideas. *Homage to Catalonia* (1938), which aroused great hostility, was an honest and graphic description of the Spanish revolution. *Animal Farm* (1945), the result of these experiences, launched an acerbic satirical attack on Stalinism. His final book, written in solitude on the Isle of Jura, was *1984* (1949), a grim yet believable warning of the dangers of totalitarianism. Over the course of his life Orwell developed a distinctive and quintessentially English revolutionary libertarian socialism of his own, which continued to influence and inspire long after his life was cut prematurely short by tuberculosis in 1950. LHM

Osborne House (Isle of Wight). Soon after their marriage, Victoria and *Albert looked around for a private residence, where their growing family could enjoy seaside holidays. In 1845 they purchased the Osborne estate near Cowes. Albert, with the assistance of Thomas *Cubitt, builder of Belgravia, designed a large house in the Italian style. Victoria was devoted to it: 'we can walk about anywhere by ourselves without being followed and mobbed,' she wrote. She died there in 1901. Her son Edward VII was less enchanted, perhaps because he had been sent there as a youth to study. In defiance of his mother's wishes, he turned it into a naval college and convalescent home. It is now open to the public and contains many Victorian memorabilia. JAC

Osborne judgment, 1909. Osborne, a Liberal, went to law to stop his union, the Railway Servants, contributing to the Labour Party. The case reached the House of Lords; their judgment was that unions could not use their funds to support a political party, a severe blow to the Labour Party. JB

Ossian, son of Fingal, father of Oscar, whose death—so James *MacPherson claimed—marked the end of Celtic civilization in Scotland. MacPherson asserted Ossian's Scottish ancestry in spite of stiff and compelling counter-claims by the Irish and in spite of the fact that many thought that his translations of Ossian's 'poems' (1762–5) were forgeries. Nevertheless, the poems caused a literary sensation. They were translated into most European languages and even into Gaelic. In the event they turned out to be a mixture of genuine verses handed down by oral tradition and imaginative translation and pastiche by their editor. However, the Scottish tourist industry has every reason to be grateful for them. NTP

Ostorius Scapula. Second governor of Roman Britain, AD 47–52. Publius Ostorius Scapula's career before his arrival in Britain is unknown, though he had served as consul, probably in 45. On his arrival he expelled invaders from provincial territory. He may have ordered the disarming of Britain south-east of the Trent–Severn line, provoking the first revolt of the *Iceni, quickly dealt with. He tried to cut off the tribes of Wales under *Caratacus from supporters amongst the *Brigantes of the north by advancing into the Cheshire Gap, but this provoked trouble. So Ostorius attacked Wales directly, first the *Silures in the south, then the *Ordovices of the centre. In 51 he brought Caratacus to bay in a hill-fort (possibly Llanymynech) and defeated him. Caratacus fled to Brigantia but was handed over by *Cartimandua. The Silures continued to harry Roman forces and Ostorius died in 52 'worn out by the cares of his office'. ASEC

Oswald, St (*c.*604–42), king of Northumbria (634–42). Son of *Æthelfryth and Acha, Oswald spent *Edwin's reign in exile amongst the Irish, becoming a Christian. Defeating *Cadwallon of Gwynedd, at *Heavenfield (634), brought him *Bernicia and *Deira. With *Aidan (from Iona) he restored Northumbrian Christianity. Oswald established an overlordship over Wessex (under *Cynegils) and perhaps other English kingdoms, and probably the southern Picts and Scottish *Dalriada, and is one of the so-called *bretwaldas. *Bede's portrait, influenced by the Old Testament, presents Oswald as an exemplar for kings, demonstrating that piety would strengthen power. Killed in a campaign against the pagan *Penda of Mercia, at Maserfield, his cult was promoted by his niece Osthryth, queen of Mercia, who moved his remains to Bardney (where *Offa was to adorn his tomb), and by *Wilfrid, and taken by pilgrim-exiles and missionaries, including *Willibrord, to Ireland and Germany. In 909 *Æthelfleda of Mercia transferred his remains to Gloucester. His skull came to be preserved in the coffin of St *Cuthbert. His hands and arms stayed in *Bamburgh. AER

Oswald, St (d. 992). Archbishop of York. One of the three great monastic bishops of the 10th-cent. reformation, Oswald came from an East Anglian family of Danish origin who specialized in careers in the church. Archbishop *Oda of Canterbury was his uncle and another kinsman Oscytel was Oswald's predecessor at York. Oswald was first a priest at Winchester and then lived for a time in the reformed Benedictine monastery of Fleury-sur-Loire, before joining the household of Archbishop Oscytel. In 961 he was created bishop of Worcester (where he also seems to have had family connections) and continued to hold that see after he was appointed to York in 971. Oswald gradually introduced monks into the Worcester chapter, and founded or refounded monasteries at Westbury-on-Trym, Winchcombe, and Pershore, as well as at Ramsey in his native East Anglia. He was buried at Worcester. BAEY

Oswin (d. 651), king of Deira (644–51). *Bede describes Oswin as handsome, pleasantly spoken, and courteous, a good and generous lord who ruled prosperously and was much loved. Humility was his greatest virtue. Bede tells how the king gave *Aidan a good horse for difficult journeys, and was offended when the bishop gave it to a beggar. When Aidan asked if he valued the horse more than a child of God, Oswin knelt before him and begged his forgiveness. Aidan, moved to tears, predicted Oswin's early death as his subjects were unworthy of such a king. Conflict arose between Oswin and *Oswui, king of Bernicia. The two Northumbrian armies gathered, but Oswin, realizing Oswui's greater strength, sent his men home. With one companion, he took refuge in the house of a friend who betrayed his trust. Oswui had him murdered. AM

Oswui (d. 670), king of Northumbria (642–70). Ruling *Bernicia, Oswui was responsible for the death of the Deiran king *Oswin (651), his wife's kinsman. He seems to have gained nothing, and appeased his wife by founding a monastery at Gilling (Yorks.). Oswin's successor allied with the powerful Mercian king *Penda, who, refusing to be bought off, attacked in 655, but was defeated and killed at the battle of *Winwaed, near Leeds. Oswui fulfilled his promise that, if victorious, he would grant twelve estates for monasteries and dedicate his infant daughter to God's service. The triumph gained Oswui control of Deira and undisputed overlordship of the southern kingdom for a time. He used his influence to convert the Mercian prince *Peada, and revive East Saxon Christianity. Oswui is distinguished for his decision to conform with Roman traditions at the Synod of *Whitby. Death thwarted his ambition to go to Rome, but he was one of few early kings to die naturally. AM

Otford, battle of, *c.*776. In the later 8th cent., *Kent was struggling to retain its independence against the growing power of *Mercia. In the 770s Kent's rulers were resisting their demotion to subkings. According to Henry of Huntingdon, the Mercians were victorious at this battle near Sevenoaks. But Stenton argues that *Egbert of Kent defeated *Offa and that Kentish independence was restored for some years. But after Offa's victory over *Wessex at *Benson, pressure was resumed and Kent subdued and absorbed into Mercia. JAC

O'Toole, St Laurence (Lorcan Ua Tuathail) (*c.*1130–80). Archbishop of Dublin. An ascetic, born in Kildare, O'Toole became leader (*coarb*) of the Glendalough community, but reluctantly accepted the archbishopric of Dublin from Pope Gelasius in 1162. He attended a meeting (1167) called by the *Ard Ri* (high king), Rory *O'Connor, king of Connacht, to improve religion and good government. Some historians have vilified him as a collaborator for mediating with O'Connor's rival *Dermot MacMurrough, and Strongbow before the capture of Dublin (1170), for submitting to Henry II (1171), and negotiating terms in the treaty of *Windsor (1175) after O'Connor's own submission. After attending the Lateran Council (1179) where Pope Alexander III confirmed Dublin's archiepiscopal rights and made him papal legate, he ruled strictly, trying to improve clerical discipline. Sent again by O'Connor to Henry II (1180), he was forbidden to return to Ireland. Following Henry to France, he died at Eu. He was canonized (1226). WMM

Otterburn, battle of, 1388. Though little more than a routine border skirmish, Otterburn was rendered remarkable by the number of ballads it inspired, including 'Chevy Chase', and by the ferocity of the encounter, which caused Froissart to describe it as 'one of the sorest and best fought, without cowards or faint hearts'. A large Scottish gathering near Jedburgh in the summer of 1388 resolved on a two-pronged campaign, one attack west towards Carlisle, the other across Carter Bar into Redesdale. The eastern army, under James, earl of *Douglas, having ravaged as far as Durham, was pursued in retreat by Henry *Percy ('Hotspur') and his brother Ralph. Late on 15 August the English caught up at Otterburn and went straight into the attack. As night fell, the battle developed into a series of hand-to-hand single combats. Both the Percies were captured but Douglas himself was killed. A second English force under the bishop of Durham arrived the following day but did not choose to attack. The dead from the battlefield were buried nearby at Elsdon. JAC

Oudenarde, battle of, 1708. As French forces under the duke of Burgundy and Marshal Vendôme laid siege to Oudenarde, the duke of *Marlborough marched against them at the head of some 78,000 English, Dutch, and German troops. The French offered battle on 11 July, but were badly deployed. Allied units on the left and right, commanded by Marshal Overkirk and Prince Eugene respectively, pressed in on the flanks, while Marlborough's infantry advanced in the centre. As the French right flank collapsed, over 6,000 French soldiers fell. A further 7,000 were captured. JLP

outfangthief. See INFANGTHIEF AND OUTFANGTHIEF.

outlawry originated as the community's way of dealing with a violent or dangerous wrongdoer. A declaration of outlawry deprived the outlaw of the protection of the king and the law; his property was forfeit to the king and he could be killed with impunity. By the 12th cent. outlawry had become a part of legal process as a sanction to compel a person to submit to the court's authority, especially in actions of trespass before the king's courts, and it was extended through this action to other civil actions. Outlawry was formally abolished in 1879 in civil cases. It was never formally abolished in criminal matters, though it became obsolete. MM

overseas trade. Overseas, as opposed to internal trade, played a modest but expanding role in the pre-industrial economy. Primary products such as wool, tin, and lead were the mainstays of the English export trade, but the expansion of manufacturing is reflected in the growing proportion of wool exported as cloth, which had reached 50 per cent by the mid-15th cent. and was over 85 per cent by 1540. The major market for these products was north-western Europe, though there was also some trade to the Mediterranean. The main imports were textiles, wine, salt, and a wide range of luxury goods. The principal exports of Scotland and Ireland were wool, hides, fish, and grain, destined either for English or nearby European markets in the Low Countries and the Baltic.

The concentration on the Low Countries began to weaken during the latter half of the 16th cent. when English merchants began to exploit more distant markets in Russia and the Levant. As exploration proceeded, trading was extended during the 17th cent. to Africa, India, the Caribbean, and North America. However, the development of overseas trade during the late 16th and 17th cents. provoked conflict with other European trading powers, notably the Dutch, Spanish, and French.

By the end of the 17th cent., when exports were roughly 5 per cent of the national income of England and Wales, the composition of trade was beginning to reflect an advancing economy. Imports consisted mostly of raw materials and food, and exports of manufactures. There was both a substantial increase in overseas trade and a change in direction, which set the pattern for subsequent growth during the 18th and much of the 19th cents., with India, Africa, and the North American colonies becoming significant. The *East India Company, packed with Scots, secured a virtual monopoly over the trade to India and the East Indies via the Cape of Good Hope. At the same time the Navigation Acts were designed to give England a monopoly in the shipment of goods to and from the colonies. Though evasion was widespread, this legislation proved a major cause of friction with the Scots, who attempted their own colonial schemes in *Nova Scotia and at *Darien, until the Union in 1707 brought legitimate access to colonial markets. Irish merchants were also excluded until the free trade concessions of 1780. More critically, the restrictions contributed to rebellion in the North American colonies themselves.

Overseas markets for manufactures and as sources of supply of raw materials were central factors in British industrialization. By 1800, exports represented 13 per cent of the national income of England and Wales, and with the abandonment of protection in the 1840s expanded still more, reaching their peak in the 1870s at around 22 per cent. Trade cycles brought periodic booms and slumps, but the British economy was becoming more dependent on overseas trade, including 'invisible' earnings from finance, insurance, and shipping. Though the volume of international trade had expanded dramatically, Britain's share began to contract in the face of foreign competition from the USA, Germany, France, and other industrializing countries. The empire took a growing proportion of exports, but imperial trade, rather than a benefit, is increasingly regarded as having been a burden. This was obvious to contemporaries as early as the 18th cent. when Jamaican sugar sold for a higher price in Britain than on the world market, thanks primarily to the West Indian sugar lobby.

Uncompetitive imperial preference was less of a problem than the underlying weaknesses of an export economy heavily dependent on traditional industries, the disruption caused by two world wars and the depression, and the painful adjustments of modernization after 1945. In the face of continuing international competition, the industrialization of the Third World, and the loss of empire, Britain was forced into the European Community, with which a growing proportion of trade was conducted. ID

Owain ap Gruffydd (Owain Cyfeiliog) (*c.*1130–97), prince of southern Powys. He was the nephew of *Madog ap Maredudd, prince of *Powys, whom he served (from 1149) in the commote of Cyfeiliog, from which he took his name. He resisted advances by *Owain Gwynedd and *Rhys ap Gruffydd of *Deheubarth (though he married a daughter of each in turn); after Madog's death and the murder of Madog's eldest son (1160), he came to terms with fellow-princes of Powys and Henry II to establish his rule in southern Powys, probably from Welshpool. Having submitted to Rhys ap Gruffydd (1171), he married his daughter. Owain declined to aid Archbishop *Baldwin and *Gerald of Wales in preaching the crusade (1188) and was excommunicated as a result, but this did not prevent Gerald from lauding him as a capable soldier and wise ruler. A patron of poets, he composed at least one poem (about warriors in a prince's service, 'The Shepherds of the Severn') and his court poet was Cynddelw Brydydd Mawr. There was no better way of acquiring an enduring reputation. RAG

Owain Gwynedd (*c.*1100–70), king of Gwynedd (1132–70). Noted by contemporaries for his wisdom, prowess, and prudence, his creation of a large feudal principality in *Gwynedd was an inspiration to his successors, skilfully propagated by his court poets. The second son of *Gruffydd ap Cynan (d. 1137), king of Gwynedd, he and his brother Cadwallon helped their father to expand Gwynedd's power (1120s). As king (Cadwallon died in 1132), he strengthened his hold on church and state in Gwynedd, exploited the anarchy in England to advance south (he was at the Welsh victory near Cardigan, 1136), and he took his authority eastwards to the Dee (by 1165) despite hostility from the earl of Chester and *Powys's rulers. His only major (and temporary) reverse was at Henry II's hands (1157), after which Owain wisely acknowledged English suzerainty. By his death (28 November 1170) he was the pre-eminent ruler in Wales; he was buried in Bangor cathedral. RAG

Owen, David (b. 1938). Former leader of the *Social Democratic Party (SDP). After qualifying as a doctor Owen entered politics as a Labour MP. He rose swiftly, becoming foreign secretary in 1977 at the age of just 38. With the party's swing to the left, Owen became increasingly disaffected and helped to found the SDP as one of the 'gang of four'. He became leader of the party in 1983 and envisaged a multi-party system with proportional representation. He worked hard to maintain the political integrity of the SDP and remained aloof from the merger with the Liberal Party after the 1987 general election. Owen continued to preside over a rump SDP until the party was wound up in 1990. He retired from the Commons in 1992 and was created baron of the city of Plymouth, the seat he represented for over twenty-five years. He has since acted as European Community Peace Envoy to the former Yugoslavia (1992–5). RAS

Owen, Robert (1771–1858). Cotton magnate and utopian socialist. Born in Newtown (Powys), Owen became a partner in cotton firms in Lancashire and at *New Lanark (Strathclyde), where he managed the mills and village (1800–25), gaining a reputation as a successful and humanitarian businessman. His experience led him to publish *A New View of Society* (1814–18), in which he advanced propositions that character was formed by environment, and that a system of villages of co-operation rather than unplanned large industrial towns was conducive to social progress. Attacked for his secularism and millenarianism, he accepted the labour theory of value and favoured state intervention to offset the effects of depressions in his *Report to the County of Lanark* (1820); he espoused factory reform, the legalization of trade unions, a national system of education, and co-operation. Described as the 'Father of British Socialism', Owen could be regarded also as a protagonist of scientific management. JB

Owen, Wilfred (1893–1918). Most gifted of the poets who died in battle, though it was the war which transformed him from a minor follower of *Keats and *Shelley into a writer of the first rank. He joined up in 1915 but a meeting with Siegfried Sassoon at Craiglockhart military hospital two years later was crucial to his development: 'You have fixed my life—however short.' The poems he produced over the next twelve months go beyond Sassoon's more straightforward assault on complacency at home, but he was not primarily interested in technical innovation: 'I am not concerned with Poetry', he wrote, 'The Poetry is in the pity.' Describing himself as a 'conscientious objector with a very seared conscience', solidarity with the men under his command took him back to the front. In October 1918 he won the Military Cross and the following November he was killed in action on the Sambre canal, a week before the Armistice. JNRS

Oxford, diocese of. The see, now conterminous with Oxfordshire, Berkshire, and Buckinghamshire, was carved out of the vast *Lincoln diocese by Henry VIII in 1542. Originally planned as the see of Osney and Thame with the cathedral at Osney, it was refounded in 1546 as the see of Oxford. The last abbot of Osney, Robert King, was the first bishop. Because initially the diocese was small, consisting only of Oxfordshire, and relatively poor, most late 17th- and 18th-cent. bishops were eager for preferment elsewhere. They were thus easy prey to politicians, keen to manipulate episcopal patronage. In 1845, however, the see was greatly enlarged by the addition of Berkshire (from *Salisbury) and Buckinghamshire (from Lincoln). Some Oxford bishops were, nevertheless, notable: John Fell (1675–86), also renowned in the university as dean of Christ Church; John Potter (1715–37) and Thomas Secker (1737–58), both future archbishops; Richard Bagot (1829–45), who had to cope with the complexities of the *tractarian movement; and Samuel

Wilberforce (1845–70), a great administrator and pioneer in modern standards of episcopal life and work. Other distinguished bishops were William Stubbs (1889–1901), the historian, and Charles *Gore (1911–19), the Anglo-catholic leader, previously the first bishop of *Birmingham. The cathedral, formerly St Frideswide's Augustinian priory church (1158–85), in Norman style with a 15th-cent. choir vault, is an integral part of Christ Church college. WMM

Oxford, provisions of, 1258. The struggle between Henry III and the baronial opposition culminated in civil war 1264–5. In 1258 the main grievance was Henry's attempt to acquire the kingdom of Sicily for his second son Edmund, and the influence of his Poitevin advisers: famine and lack of success in Wales added to the king's difficulties. A committee of 24 was appointed to meet at Oxford and limit the king's actions. The *justiciarship was revived, a standing council of fifteen appointed, and Parliament was to be summoned three times a year. Though baronial control soon disintegrated, the provisions, and those of *Westminster which followed in 1259, were a clear attempt to limit royal authority and listen to the opinions of the community. JAC

Oxford, Robert de Vere, 9th earl of (1362–92). According to a chronicler, the 9th earl was one of the young men brought up with Richard II who plotted the death of *John of Gaunt in 1384. Oxford's inheritance was meagre for his rank, but Richard's favour enriched him; he was also raised in the peerage, to marquis of Dublin in 1385 and duke of Ireland in 1386. *Thomas of Woodstock and other critics of the king were incensed by Oxford's conspicuous enjoyment of royal patronage. When Richard was planning to regain control of government in 1387, Oxford raised forces in Cheshire; they were defeated at *Radcot Bridge (Oxon.). He was one of the royal favourites indicted in the *Merciless Parliament of 1388, but had fled and remained in exile until his death at Louvain. RLS

Oxford, St Mary the Virgin. University and parish church. Adopted as the centre of the fledgling medieval university, St Mary's was the seat of its government, academic disputation, and award of degrees until the mid-17th cent.; the attached Old Congregation House (*c.*1320) contained the first university library. Considerably rebuilt in the perpendicular style, it hosted the trials of the Oxford martyrs (*Latimer, *Ridley, *Cranmer) in 1554–6, gained the Laudian 'Virgin porch' whose Marian statue so incensed the puritans, heard *Wesley and *Newman preach, and saw the launch of the *'Oxford' or 'tractarian' movement for the revival of catholic spirituality. ASH

Oxford Group. Founded by Frank Buchman (1878–1961), an American who had experienced new conversion (1908). Evangelizing (1920s) at Cambridge and especially Oxford, where his undergraduate following was strong—hence the name—its influence rapidly spread through English professional classes. Vehemently anti-communist—Hitler was briefly respected (1936)—Buchman launched the Moral Re-armament movement (1938) which at its peak (1950s) claimed to effect international and industrial reconciliation. Though he held world conferences and had headquarters in USA and Switzerland, the thrill of 1920s group evangelism had moderated to MRA's 'undoctrinal moralism'. Criticized for shallow conversions, it nevertheless touched many outside the churches. WMM

Oxford movement. Founded by a group of clerical Oxford dons in the 1830s and 1840s, who sought to renew the Church of England through rediscovering its catholic inheritance. It was a response to the perceived decline of the Church of England into dangerous liberalism and excessive control by Parliament, which produced a desire to emphasize the spiritual and divine institution of the Church of England. Its starting-point is usually taken as *Keble's Assize Sermon of 1833. The end of the first phase came with the reception of *Newman into the Roman catholic church in 1845. Between 1833 and 1841 its leaders produced the *Tracts for the Times*, hence the alternative name of *'tractarianism'. JFC

Oxford Parliament, 1258. The Oxford Parliament of June 1258 was summoned while there was much discontent with the rule of Henry III and irritation at the rapacity of his Poitevin relatives. By the provisions of *Oxford, de *Montfort and his supporters set up a council to control the king and supervise government. The experiment failed and led in 1264 to civil war. JAC

Oxford Parliament, 1681. The Oxford Parliament was the denouement of the great *Exclusion crisis and established Charles II's supremacy for the last four years of his reign. The Shaftesbury Whigs who opposed him had won three general elections between 1679 and 1681. In April 1681 Charles summoned a parliament to Oxford where the influence of the London radicals would be less. Nevertheless, the Whigs expected royal capitulation and proposed another bill to exclude James, duke of York, from the succession. But a secret deal with Louis XIV to supply money enabled Charles to dissolve the Parliament after only one week. The Whigs offered no resistance. Three months later, *Shaftesbury was arrested and the power of the Whigs broken. JAC

Oxfordshire. In Roman times the region belonged to the *Dobunni tribe. Until 1972 the southern boundary of the county was the Thames, flowing past Kelmscott to Henley, a distance of some 70 miles: to the north, east, and west, the boundary was roughly the watersheds of the rivers Windrush, Evenlode, Cherwell, Ray, and Thame. Since they came together near Oxford, the shire had a pinched waist. It covered the area between the Cotswolds at Chipping Norton and the Chilterns at Watlington and, until modern times, much of it was heavily wooded.

The town of Oxford owed its existence to a ford and later a ferry, providing a north–south crossing at Hinksey. It developed early as an important Saxon centre. Councils were held there in the early 11th cent. and in 1066 it was the sixth largest town in the kingdom. The Normans began building Oxford castle in 1071. As late as 1901, the population of 50,000 was almost double that of all the other towns in the county combined: Banbury had 7,300, Chipping

Norton 3,700, Henley 3,500, Thame 2,900, Witney 2,800, and Bicester 2,700.

In the 7th and 8th cent. the area was disputed between *Wessex, south of the Thames, and *Mercia the midlands kingdom. Wessex seems to have held the region in the earlier part of the 7th cent., but surrendered it to Mercia. After *Cuthred's victory at *Burford in 752 it reverted to Wessex, only to be retaken by *Offa after *Benson in 777, together with some land south of the river. Wessex regained it after *Ellendun in 825. It became a shire in the early 11th cent. when *Edward and *Æthelfleda were reorganizing Wessex's defences against the Danes, who burned Oxford in 1009. The county was therefore based upon a central strong point, like its neighbours Gloucestershire, Warwickshire, Northamptonshire, Worcestershire, and Buckinghamshire.

Ecclesiastical organization fluctuated in similar fashion. An early bishopric was established at Dorchester in 634, possibly because, along with Bicester, it had been a Roman town. But after 680 it was placed under Sherborne, a Wessex diocese. When Mercia regained control, the see was moved to Leicester. Dorchester recovered its position *c.*870, probably because Leicester had been overrun by the Danes. The bishopric stayed at Dorchester until after the Conquest but was transferred to Lincoln in 1072. For five centuries the shire remained a rather remote part of the vast Lincoln diocese, until a new see was created at Oxford itself in 1542, with the cathedral at Osney abbey, one of the recently suppressed monasteries. The last abbot became the first bishop. Three years later it was amalgamated with Christ Church.

Despite the intellectual and ecclesiastical importance of Oxford, the shire remained rural and secluded. *Camden, in the reign of Elizabeth I, thought it rich and fertile: 'the lower parts cultivated into pleasant fields and meadows, the hills covered with great store of woods'. Those industries which did develop were agriculturally derived and small in scale—cloth manufacture of different kinds at Witney, Chipping Norton, and Banbury, saddles at Burford, lace and slippers at Bicester, leather at Bampton, brewing at Henley, glove-making at Oxford and Woodstock. As late as the 1830s, the shire could be described as having 'no manufactures of any account, being chiefly agricultural'. The *Victoria County History* in 1907 seemed to find this deplorable: 'the county is prevented, as if by fate, from ever attaining to the position of a great industrial centre'. The University Press, with 650 employees, was the largest industrial enterprise in Oxfordshire. Unknown to *VCH*, fate had already intervened in the shape of William *Morris, who had opened a bicycle-repair shop at Oxford in 1901—the forerunner of the great car factory at Cowley.

The Thames crossing remained for centuries of great strategic importance. In the civil wars of Stephen's reign, Oxford changed hands, *Matilda being besieged in the castle for three months in 1142. During Richard II's reign, de Vere, earl of *Oxford, was defeated at *Radcot Bridge.

In the Civil War of the 17th cent., Oxford was the king's capital. The royalist Parliament met there and it was a forward base against London. The parks and quads became encampments, trees and shrubs were cut down, and attendance at lectures languished. One of the first actions of the war was at *Chalgrove Field near Watlington, where *Hampden was mortally wounded and took himself off to die at Thame; and a much-needed royalist victory in the summer of 1644 was at *Cropredy Bridge, north of Banbury. Oxford surrendered in 1646 a few weeks after Charles I had fled, disguised as a servant. Politically city and county continued to be royalist in sympathy. In 1681 Charles II summoned Parliament there and routed his Whig opponents. The county representation was in the hands of Tory country gentlemen and though the election of 1754 was one of the fiercest contests of the century, it was uncharacteristic, since there was no other contest between 1710 and 1826.

The Oxford canal, opened in 1790, and the network of railways which developed in the county in the 19th cent. speeded up internal communication, but did little to promote any great industrial growth. The Local Government Act of 1972 extended the shire south of the Thames, bringing in Abingdon, Wallingford, and Wantage—yet another victory for Mercia over Wessex. The M40 bisects the county from south-east to north-west, from Aston Rowant to Banbury. But north Oxfordshire remains peaceful and unspoiled, and *Blenheim, once a Whig bastion in a Tory countryside, is one of the finest of all landscaped parks.

JAC

Oxford University. When the quarrel between Henry II and Philip Augustus in 1167 made it impossible for English students to attend the University of Paris, the opportunity for developing a similar institution arose at Oxford. The town was already the residence of kings and by 1186 *Gerald of Wales was lecturing to doctors, masters, and scholars. By the beginning of the 13th cent. there was a sufficient body of scholars to cause an encounter with the townspeople in 1209, leading to the long-running 'town versus gown' dispute.

Dominican friars established their main house of study there on arrival in England in 1221 and were followed in 1224 by the Franciscans. Divinity was constituted as a superior faculty and students were admitted who already possessed an arts degree. Until the *dissolution of the monasteries, Oxford came within the diocese of Lincoln, with the chancellor appointed by the bishop. The first recorded chancellor was the great scholar Robert *Grosseteste.

University colleges, endowed by patrons, were gradually formed where students resided during their long courses of study. Though the claim that University College was founded by *Alfred the Great is no longer seriously entertained, the donation by William of Durham on which it was founded came in 1249. John *Balliol left money which his widow applied to founding Balliol College in 1282. Earlier, in 1264, Walter de *Merton, chancellor of England, devoted most of his fortune to establishing Merton College. Clerical patrons were particularly prominent and included *William of Wykeham, who founded New College (1379), Richard *Foxe, who founded Corpus Christi College (1517), and Cardinal *Wolsey, whose great college became Christ Church in 1546. Undergraduates were admitted for the first time about 1500. By Elizabeth's reign, there were fifteen colleges, including Oriel (1324), All Souls (1438), and Brasenose, refounded 1502 by William Smyth, bishop of Lincoln. As at Cambridge, they increasingly attracted the sons of wealthy or aristocratic families rather than poor scholars.

The Oxford statutes were revised in 1636 by Archbishop *Laud, a great benefactor to the university. Oxford became associated with high-church views, reinforced after the 1640s when the city was the headquarters of the royalist army during the Civil War. In the early Hanoverian period it was reputed a nest of *Jacobitism, though such disloyalty as there was caused the authorities little more than momentary irritation. More than two-thirds of its graduates entered the Church of England, and the *Oxford movement in the 19th cent. reflected their concerns about priesthood.

The 19th cent. saw the beginnings of change. Degrees were no longer awarded without written examination. Honours degrees in both classics and mathematics were introduced in 1801, creating the 'double first', and a similar provision was made for science and law in 1890. Further reforms followed the Oxford University Act of 1854, pushed through by *Gladstone and instituting a new and less oligarchical constitution, and in 1871 the requirement that dons should be in holy orders was abandoned.

From the last quarter of the 19th cent. the number of Oxford colleges began to increase. The first two colleges for women were Lady Margaret Hall and Somerville (1879), and since 1937 colleges for postgraduate study, such as Nuffield, St Antony's, Linacre, and Wolfson, have been founded. PG

oyer and terminer. After the Assizes of *Clarendon and *Northampton, the commission of oyer and terminer was issued to the travelling justices to visit the shire and to receive the presentments of those suspected of crime in each hundred. They were instructed to hear and determine (oyer and terminer) each case. Before 1215 they decided whether those presented should be released or put to *trial by ordeal. After 1215 when the Lateran Council of the Church forbade the participation of the clergy in ordeals, the justices presided over trial by *jury. Until the assizes were abolished in the 1971 Courts Act, the commission was issued to the judges of assize and read out at the beginning of each assize session. MM

Pacifico, David (1784–1854). The case of 'Don Pacifico' provided *Palmerston with a great oratorical triumph. A Portuguese Jew, Pacifico was born in Gibraltar and was therefore a British subject. In 1847, while a merchant in Athens, his house was destroyed in an anti-Jewish riot. The Greek government refused compensation, believing that his claim was inflated, whereupon Palmerston sent a naval squadron to the Piraeus and seized all Greek vessels. The House of Lords censured Palmerston's actions by 169 votes to 132 but in the House of Commons, 29 June 1850, Palmerston carried the day by 310 votes to 264. His speech of $4\frac{1}{2}$ hours concluded that as a Roman could say 'Civis Romanus sum', 'so also a British subject, in whatever land he may be, shall feel confident that the watchful eye and the strong arm of England will protect him against injustice and wrong'. Palmerston's stand earned him vast popularity and established his domination of politics for the rest of his life.

JAC

paganism. In the late Roman world a *paganus* was a 'rustic', and the word's shift to mean 'non-Christian' reflects a period when Christianity had spread among the upper classes and within towns, but not to the rural peasantry. In the Middle Ages the term was applied indiscriminately to any religious beliefs or practices which were felt to be incompatible with Christianity. Pagans need not share any common ground, but in the case of Britain the Anglo-Saxons and Vikings recognized the same major gods and goddesses, but with slight variations in name (e.g. Woden/Odin), and although the native British had different deities these had responsibility for similar aspects of life such as warfare and fertility. The Romans had no trouble in assimilating the deities of either group with their own pantheon.

It is impossible to reconstruct fully the pagan beliefs and practices of either Celts or Germans as these were not written down. We have to rely either on the accounts of foreign observers such as *Caesar or *Tacitus, or on collections of legends recorded sometime after conversion to Christianity such as the Irish mythological literature or the Prose Edda of the Icelandic writer Snorri Sturluson. Occasionally parallels can be found between the written myths and archaeological evidence from periods of pagan practice; Scandinavian-influenced sculptures from Britain, for instance, appear to depict tales recorded by Snorri such as Odin's battle with the wolf Fenrir.

However, one should not envisage either Celtic or Germanic paganism as having structures or doctrines comparable to those of the Christian church. The building of temples and existence of a professional class of priests seems to have been more a feature of Celtic than Germanic practice which, when these are to be found, seem to have been associated with kings or other secular leaders who may have had cultic functions. What may have mattered far more to the majority of people were localized guardian spirits who might be honoured at natural sites such as a spring, a grove of trees, or a hilltop. However, the need to ensure the support of deities with a wider remit for fertility or good weather would lead to some commonality of practice at key points of the agricultural and calendar year.

Christianity saw off the major pantheons of gods and goddesses without too much difficulty and major festivals of the pagan year such as midwinter could be replaced with appropriate Christian celebrations like Christmas. What was harder to eradicate was the attachment to local holy places, though healing springs, for instance, were sometimes absorbed into local saints' cults. What came to be described as superstitious or magical practices by which people tried to control their destinies, heal illnesses, or see into the future persisted longest of all and have faint echoes today when we touch wood or throw a coin into a wishing-well.

BAEY

Paget, William, 1st Baron Paget (1505–63). Paget, founder of a distinguished aristocratic family, was of modest origins. He was educated at Trinity Hall, Cambridge, where Stephen *Gardiner, later bishop of Winchester, was master, and began his career in Gardiner's service. He acted as secretary to *Jane Seymour and *Anne of Cleves, as ambassador to France, and then as secretary of state 1543–7. After Henry VIII's death, Paget allied with Protector *Somerset, was given the Garter, and served as chancellor of the duchy of Lancaster and as comptroller of the household. He was in disgrace in 1552 and degraded from the Garter, but restored to favour by Mary, whom he served as lord privy seal 1556–8. He retired from public life at the accession of Elizabeth.

JAC

Paine, Thomas (1737–1809). Radical writer and revolutionary activist. Paine led an uneventful life as a stay-maker and exciseman before emigrating to Philadelphia in 1774, where he became involved in the American independence movement. In *Common Sense* (1776), he argued for American severance from the British empire, and for isolationism in American policy towards Europe. As revolutionary forces in France began to gather strength, Paine went to Paris to give his support, publishing *The *Rights of Man* (Part I 1791; Part II 1792), defending the Revolution against the attack launched by *Burke in his **Reflections on the Revolution in France*. The popularity of the book in Britain was a source of considerable concern to *Pitt's government. The French revolutionaries made Paine an honorary citizen of France, and he was elected to the French National Convention in 1792. However, Paine did not subscribe to the atheism of the revolutionaries, and in his *Age of Reason* (Part I 1794; Part II 1795), while attacking Christianity, he argued for the existence of the deity as a first cause. Nor did Paine support the execution of Louis XVI, and his plea for the king's life to be spared led to his dismissal from the Convention. Narrowly escaping execution in the Luxembourg prison, Paine found life in France under Napoleon intolerable and returned to his adopted America in 1802, passing his last years as a newspaper columnist. TSG

painting. The coming of Christianity with the building and decoration of churches marks a good point from which to look at recorded painting in Britain. Pope Gregory (late 6th cent.) agreed that paintings in church would assist the understanding of Christianity. Painting was done on manuscripts, walls, wood panels, glass, and tiles. The Anglo-Saxon artistic tradition was a mix of Roman and native British styles. One of the finest manuscripts, the *Lindisfarne Gospels (*c.*698), illustrates this mixture. Illuminated manuscripts were painted on animal skins and richly decorated with subjects, including portraits of saints, stylized animals, and geometric designs.

Manuscript and panel painting continued throughout the Middle Ages, not always by monks, and covering subjects outside religion. Bestiaries were popular. The artists, who often travelled widely, rarely painted from life even when representing a living person. Sometimes, however, they needed a life model for a new experience, as the monk *Matthew Paris did when he copied an elephant for a painting presented to Henry III (*c.*1255). There is small evidence in English painting of the 13th and 14th cents. of the skills shown in Italy and France at the same time, with little attempt to make the figures proportional or lifelike.

The Reformation brought a crisis to painting in Britain with protestants objecting to images of saints in church and home. Not only did religious commissions cease, except briefly under Mary I, but waves of iconoclasm during the reign of Edward VI, and intermittently until the final destructions in the Civil War, resulted in many examples of painting, sculpture, and glass being destroyed. The increased wealth of the nobility in the 16th and 17th cents. produced a vigorous demand for family portraits and most great houses contained a long gallery. But English artists did not have the prestige of foreign painters, which explains why William *Hogarth is the first native artist represented in the National Gallery. The arrival in England of Hans *Holbein momentarily changed the way in which portraits were painted. But although he was appointed court painter by Henry VIII, his skill as a painter was never fully exploited and his influence was minimal. After his death, his simple and direct style was replaced by more mannered paintings like the *Hilliard miniature *Portrait of a Young Man* or the cult portraits of Elizabeth. Charles I was an important and knowledgeable collector of art and a patron of *Van Dyck. The safe option of portrait painting got artists through the Civil War with the Restoration seeing the Stuart court looking abroad for portraitists. The Dutch artist *Lely spanned both Commonwealth and Restoration portraiture, as did Samuel *Cooper, the miniaturist.

The 18th cent. was the great age of country house building and decoration. Fashionable gentlemen linked painting with taste and bought old masters or used foreign portrait painters. Hogarth campaigned on behalf of English artists, but his greatest success was not in portraiture but in social and moral commentary, like *The Rake's Progress* (1735), highly successful as prints. But in the next generation, British painters came into their own with *Reynolds, *Gainsborough, and *Ramsay offering dignified and beautiful portraits. At court, the German *Zoffany painted informal family groups called conversation pieces, a genre repeated for Queen Victoria by *Landseer and Winterhalter. The foundation of the *Royal Academy in 1768 acknowledged the improved position of the artist in society. Growing interest in art and new markets among the middle classes, who had less need for portraits, changed the rules of taste. New subjects, for example contemporary history in *West's *Death of Wolfe* (1771), personal experience such as *Blake's visions, and the portrayal of everyday life by *Wilkie, signalled a change in attitude towards painting which led in turn to a reassessment of landscape painting. *Turner and *Constable represented very different interpretations of this genre, the latter breaking with tradition in attempting to paint only what he saw.

Breaks with tradition echoed the speed of change in the outside world. Artists wanted to be free to experiment while customers wanted to buy what they knew. Many 19th-cent. artists were underrated in their lifetime: the *Pre-Raphaelites and later *Whistler disregarded the conventions of their day and faced a barrage of criticism.

The spirit of modernism informed the whole of the 20th cent., with artists experimenting with ideas and media. Some find modern art difficult to understand, or even repellent, but artists of the standing of Paul *Nash and Graham *Sutherland gave a deep insight into war, L. S. Lowry recorded the bleak factory spaces of an industrial society, and David Hockney introduced humour into painting. Though in many ways modern art has become overspecialized and divorced from everyday life, in another sense all are consumers of painting, which is everywhere—in advertising, in magazines, in greeting-card designs, on the street, and always variable. JC

Paisley, Revd Ian (b. 1926). The voice of intransigent Ulster unionism and anti-catholicism, Paisley's massive physical presence and booming voice is in the 19th-cent. Ulster evangelical tradition. He co-founded the Free Presbyterian Church (1951), and vigorously campaigned against the ecumenical movement. He led the resistance to the reforms of the *O'Neill government from 1963 onwards, and rallied traditional loyalist support against the civil rights movement from 1967. Paisley launched the virulently anti-catholic, anti-communist *Protestant Telegraph* and Ulster Constitution Defence Committee 1966. He stood against O'Neill in the 1969 Stormont election, was narrowly defeated, but was instrumental in O'Neill's fall. He became MP in 1970 and formed the *Democratic Unionist Party in 1971, trumping competition from the Vanguard Unionist Progressive Party to represent working-class loyalism. His support was well beyond the confines of his church and he challenged the position of the middle-class *Unionist Party. Paisley supported the Ulster workers' strike in 1974 which destroyed the power-sharing executive; opposed the Sunningdale agreement 1973, the *Anglo-Irish agreement 1985, the Downing Street declaration 1993. A member of the European Parliament since 1979, Paisley is the most successful electoral vote-winner in the province. He is a more calculating politician than his rhetoric suggests, but, following the republican and loyalist cease-fires in 1994–6, he appeared at times outmoded and isolated. MAH

Pakistan was created, and achieved its independence, on 15 August 1947 as the result of a partition of British India. It consisted of the former provinces of Sindh, Baluchistan, and the North-West Frontier together with the east of Bengal and the west of Punjab. These were all regions with a Muslim-majority population. Although Hindu–Muslim religious conflict had intensified during the 19th cent., it was not until the 1930s that the idea of a separate Muslim-majority state gained any currency. Not until the 1940s did the majority areas themselves, where the Hindu 'threat' was limited, show enthusiasm. M. A. *Jinnah, the leader of the Muslim League, was the principal advocate of Pakistan. However, it is unclear that the Pakistan that emerged was at all what he demanded. The country, as it came into existence, was bereft of Kashmir, truncated between western and eastern halves, and disruptive of long-standing cultural, economic, and communications linkages with regions still in India. Chaotic conditions at the time of partition also led to at least half a million people being killed in ferocious 'communal' violence. The precise form that partition took, and the severity of loss of life, owed most to the precipitate withdrawal of the British under Lord *Mountbatten. Since independence Pakistan has enjoyed a chequered history. Tensions with India have remained high and have led to three wars. East Pakistan seceded in 1971, amidst much bloodshed, to form the independent state of *Bangladesh. Full general elections were not held until 1970 and democratic institutions have remained at risk from military coups. DAW

palatinates were border regions where the demands of security dictated that the local rulers should have special powers, particularly to raise troops and to administer justice to all levels. The earldom of Chester, created in 1071, gradually acquired palatinate privileges, its tenants-in-chief holding directly of the earl and paying all taxes to him. But after 1237 the earldom was taken into the crown and became in due course part of the territories of the princes of Wales. Not until 1543 however were Chester and Cheshire given representation at Westminster and the palatine courts survived until 1830. The privileges of Durham, the other great palatinate, go back beyond the Conquest to an independent *Northumbria. The palatine powers were exercised by the bishops. Durham was not brought into the Westminster Parliament until the later 17th cent. and its privileges were not totally extinguished until 1836. The county of Lancaster was granted palatine status in 1351, though its privileges were less than those of Cheshire or Durham, and it was represented at Westminster from the outset. The palatine status remained with *John of Gaunt and then descended through Henry IV with the crown. Certain palatine powers were claimed for the earldoms of Kent and Shropshire, for the viceroys of Ireland, and for the proprietors of some of the American colonies. Though the palatinates have often been described as 'imperia in imperio', where 'the king's writ did not run', many of the privileges were shared at a lower level with other landowners. The monarch, after all, appointed the bishop of Durham and could dispose of the earldoms. The earls and bishops palatine were powerful men, but subjects they remained. JAC

Pale, The. Originally implying a fence, and by inference the area enclosed by it, this was the name given to an area in Ireland in the late Middle Ages similar to the English Pale which developed in the 15th cent. in Calais and its hinterland, the last area left to the English in France. Its first recorded usage in Ireland is in a document that dates from 1446–7, when it clearly refers to that part of Ireland to which effective English government had shrunk. While the rest of the island was divided into large semi-autonomous lordships held by Anglo-Irish lords, or remained in the hands of native Irish lords, the Pale was the area surrounding *Dublin in which the king's writ ran, and which a determined effort was made to defend. Its exact geographical dimensions, running from Dundalk to Dalkey, and including much of modern counties Louth, Meath, Kildare, and Dublin, were defined by the Irish Parliament in 1488 and at succeeding parliaments, while the famous 1494–5 Parliament held by Sir Edward Poynings passed an Act ordering the construction of a 6-foot bank and ditch around the whole district, parts of which still survive, although it was almost certainly never completed. SD

Palestine, awarded by the *League of Nations to Britain as a *mandate in 1922, proved an uncomfortable responsibility. *Balfour's declaration in 1917 tried to square the circle by insisting that Britain would support a national home for the Jewish people while doing nothing to prejudice the position of the non-Jewish peoples of Palestine. Persistent Jewish immigration provoked fierce Arab resistance. The advent of the Nazis to power in Germany in the 1930s gave a strong boost to greater Jewish immigration which, in turn, led to Arab armed resistance. After the war, British control was shaken by her economic difficulties, by Zionist terror groups, and by international sympathy towards Jewish settlement. The United Nations' scheme for a partition of Palestine had little chance of acceptance and civil war had broken out before the British left in May 1948. A Jewish state of Israel was declared at once and immediately recognized by the USA. JAC

Paley, William (1743–1805). Paley wrote standard works on the evidences for Christianity. Senior wrangler at Cambridge, he was ordained and after tutoring at Cambridge moved to clerical posts in Carlisle diocese, and then to Monkwearmouth (Sunderland). His *Evidences* was published in 1794, and his *Natural Theology* in 1802. Extremely successful, with more than 20 editions, they were required reading for undergraduates at Cambridge and at the infant university of Durham. Charles *Darwin was most impressed by *Natural Theology*, and the **Origin of Species* can be seen as a riposte to it. Paley argued that the world and the creatures in it are like watches, and must have had a Watchmaker: it is a classic expression of the Design argument for the existence of God, well organized, cumulative, and beautifully written. A clumsy man with a broad northern accent, Paley delighted in fishing. DK

Palladianism. A simple, harmonious, classical style of architecture derived from the works of Andrea Palladio, the Italian Renaissance architect. The first British architect to employ this style was Inigo *Jones, designer to James I and Charles I. Little of his work survived the Civil War, but the Queen's House at Greenwich and the *Banqueting House in Whitehall remained as ideals of classicism. The great revival of British Palladianism came during the first half of the 18th cent. with Colen Campbell, Richard Boyle (Lord *Burlington), and William *Kent. Campbell, the architect of Houghton Hall (Norfolk), the home of Robert *Walpole, published his *Vitruvius Britannicus* in 1715, in reaction to the baroque style of *Vanbrugh and *Hawksmoor. He inspired Lord Burlington, described by Horace *Walpole as 'The Apollo of arts', who commissioned Campbell to remodel Burlington House in London (1718–19). With William Kent, his protégé, friend, and collaborator, Burlington was responsible, as architect, patron, and arbiter of taste, for the development of English neo-classicism in the 18th cent. His designs include Chiswick House (London) with interiors by Kent and his masterpiece, the Assembly Rooms in York. JC

Palmer, Samuel (1805–81). English landscape painter and etcher. The son of a nonconformist bookseller, Palmer's was a learned and religious childhood. He first exhibited at the Royal Academy at 14 and through the painter John Linnell (later his father-in-law) met William *Blake. In Blake's work, Palmer saw the means to express his own mystical tendencies and he became the most outstanding of Blake's followers. In 1826 Palmer moved to Shoreham (Kent). During his seven years there he produced his most exciting and visionary work (*In a Shoreham Garden*, *The Magic Apple Tree*). Following his return to London he married, then spent two years in Italy. From that point, what he described as his 'primitive and infantine feeling' faded and his work became more conventional. Examples of his painting may be seen in London at the Tate and Victoria and Albert Museum; in Oxford, Cambridge, and Manchester. JC

Palmerston, Henry John Temple, 3rd Viscount (1784–1865), Prime minister. A pupil of Dugald *Stewart at Edinburgh, he went on to Cambridge University and shortly afterwards stood unsuccessfully as a parliamentary candidate there—his peerage being an Irish one, he was eligible to sit in the House of Commons. He was elected in 1807 for a pocket borough in the Isle of Wight and subsequently represented Cambridge University 1811–31, Bletchingley 1831–2, Hampshire South 1832–4, and Tiverton 1835–65.

Palmerston was perhaps the most famous foreign secretary of the 19th cent. He began his long official career as a lord of Admiralty 1807–9 and then served in the relatively junior office of secretary at war from 1809 to 1828. He declined a seat in the cabinet not so much from modesty, as he claimed, as from doubt whether *Perceval's government would last, an early example of his pragmatic attitude. In the Commons he largely confined himself to the necessary business of his office and, a later colleague recollected, 'he slept much in the House of Commons, and never omitted, if he could get away by twelve o'clock, to trot home in his cabriolet, and dress himself, and go to some party'. He kept racehorses and was much liked by the ladies. This carefully cultivated image as a man about town however belied the industry which he brought to his office, laying the foundation for his later success as a hard-working and knowledgeable foreign secretary.

Palmerston became a follower of *Canning, and resigned with his fellow-Canningites from *Wellington's administration in 1828 over the question of parliamentary reform. He was not an enthusiastic reformer, however, and when he decided to join *Grey's ministry rather than return to Wellington in 1830 it was another example of his ability to spot the winning side. He was a somewhat reluctant supporter of Grey's Reform Bill though he was a loyal colleague.

Palmerston modelled his foreign policy on Canning's. He was foreign secretary from 1830 to 1841, excepting only the brief interlude of *Peel's 'hundred days', and again from 1846 to 1851. His principles were to defend British political, strategic, and economic interests in Europe and overseas, to remain aloof as much as possible from long-term commitments, to mediate in European disputes to preserve peace, which was in Britain's interests, and to assert British power when necessary. His first great success was his settlement of the Netherlands crisis of 1830–9, when as chairman of the London conference of great powers he secured the independence of Belgium under international guarantee and with a monarch, Leopold of Saxe-Coburg, who was friendly to Britain. This prevented the Low Countries from falling under French control, a long-established objective of British policy. He saw France as Britain's major potential enemy and was always concerned to preserve the *Vienna settlement of 1815 which placed restrictions on future French expansion. Thus he also tried to prevent the Spanish and Portuguese thrones from falling under French influence, though without full success. He generally supported 'liberal' constitutional movements in Europe, as being more likely to be friendly to Britain than absolutist regimes, but his attitude was wholly pragmatic and non-ideological. Britain's interests were paramount. He opposed Russia not because of the tsar's absolutism but because of the threat to British interests in southern Europe and Asia; yet he was willing to co-operate with Russia to thwart French ambitions in the Middle East for the sake of British commercial expansion there. British trade with Turkey increased eightfold between 1830 and 1850. He was less successful in Afghanistan but he followed a policy of extending British control in north-west India. All these policies were popular with the British public and Palmerston followed Canning in cultivating public opinion as a source of support. His prosecution of the *'Opium War' against China, designed to force the Chinese to open some of their markets to British trade, was received with moral disapproval in some quarters, but was beneficial in economic terms.

Palmerston as foreign secretary was outstandingly successful. Peace was maintained, the cost of military and naval establishments reduced, and yet British power, prestige, and trade were enhanced. Palmerston's popularity as 'John Bull' was sealed by his robust if somewhat disingenuous defence in 1850 of a Portuguese merchant named Don *Pacifico who claimed British citizenship and who appeared to have been victimized by the Greek government. Palmerston's appeal to patriotic sentiment and his bullying attitude towards weaker nations came to be seen as the hallmarks of his 'gunboat diplomacy'. His confidence led him too far in 1851, however, when he sent congratulations to Louis Napoleon on his *coup d'état* in Paris without first consulting the queen or his colleagues and he was dismissed. He remained in the government as home secretary but became prime minister by popular demand when *Aberdeen's ministry collapsed during the *Crimean War.

Palmerston's foreign policy gave the Liberal Party a somewhat incongruous electoral appeal but in domestic affairs his attitudes were never particularly 'liberal'. He strenuously opposed further electoral reform, which failed to make any headway until after his death. In Europe, his support for 'liberal' movements such as Italian independence, or in the European revolutions of 1848, was always secondary to his concern for national interests which required stability in Europe.

Palmerston was tall and handsome; he had many affairs and was nicknamed 'Cupid' but he did not marry until he was 55, chiefly because of his attachment to Emily Lamb, wife of Lord Cowper, which began in 1813 and lasted until his death. They had at least four children out of wedlock and he also had children by other women. In 1839, two years after Cowper's death, they married and enjoyed another twenty-five years of 'unfamiliar married bliss'. EAS

Bourne, K., *Palmerston: The Early Years 1784–1841* (1982); Ridley, J., *Lord Palmerston* (1970); Southgate, D. G., *The Most English Minister* (1966).

Pandulf (d. 1226). Bishop of Norwich. Born in Rome, Pandulf was sent by Innocent III to negotiate an end to the dispute with King John, which had brought England under *interdict. He arrived in 1211 and demanded the restoration of Archbishop *Langton. John refused and Pandulf departed. He was sent back in 1213 by which time John's position had weakened and he sued for terms, doing homage to the pope for his kingdom. Henceforward Pandulf advised John and was created bishop of Norwich in 1215, though he was not consecrated until 1222. After John's death, Pandulf took a prominent part in the government of the country during the minority of Henry III, forming a triumvirate with Hubert de *Burgh and Peter des *Roches. He did much to restore the royal position after the vicissitudes of John's reign. But Langton's return from Rome resulted in Pandulf's legatine authority being cancelled in 1221 and his installation as bishop followed. He died in Rome but was buried in his cathedral at Norwich. JAC

Pankhurst, Emmeline (1858–1928). *Suffragette leader. A superb platform speaker with a fine physical presence, Emmeline Pankhurst came to symbolize the women's struggle for the parliamentary vote. Her personal experience of hunger strikes and forcible feeding in prison inspired many women to support the women's cause.

Emmeline acquired radical views from her father Robert Goulden, a Manchester cotton-manufacturer. In 1874 she married the Liberal lawyer Dr Richard Pankhurst and followed him into the *Fabian Society and the *Independent Labour Party. She won election as a Poor Law guardian in 1894 and as a school board member in 1900. Following Richard's death in 1898 Emmeline fell under the influence of her eldest daughter Christabel, who became increasingly impatient with the failure of the ILP to give priority to women's suffrage. As a result they established the Women's Social and Political Union in 1903, moved to London, and adopted militant tactics. She received her first term of imprisonment in February 1908 for entering the lobby of the House of Commons. Subsequently she decided to vary her methods by attacking property: 'the argument of the broken pane of glass is the most valuable argument in modern politics.' After a spate of window-breaking in the West End in March 1912 she was charged with conspiracy to commit damage and awarded a nine-month sentence. In February 1913 she accepted responsibility for a bomb which exploded at *Lloyd George's house at Walton Heath and was sentenced to three years' penal servitude. Under the terms of the *'Cat and Mouse Act' she was rearrested twelve times.

On the outbreak of the First World War, Emmeline abandoned militancy to devote herself to assisting recruitment. After 1918, when women finally received the vote, she supported herself by means of lecturing tours in the USA and Canada. She returned to Britain in 1926 and became the Conservative candidate for Whitechapel. MDP

papacy, relations with. *Augustine of Canterbury was the somewhat reluctant papal missionary to the Anglo-Saxons, sent by Gregory the Great in 596–7. According to *Bede, 'Lawrence the priest and Peter the monk were sent to acquaint Pope Gregory that the nation of the English had received the faith of Christ and that he himself was made their bishop.' As Roman order spread over the western church, English ecclesiastical contacts with the papacy grew. As early as 605, *Mellitus, bishop of London, conferred in Rome with Pope Boniface on matters concerning the English church. The encouragement of pilgrimage and papal investiture of bishops with the pallium (the symbol of office), as recorded enthusiastically by Bede, were among the means used to secure the 'Romanizing' of Christianity.

Kings were among the first English and Celtic visitors to Rome. *Cædwalla of Wessex was baptized as an adult by the pope in 689. He died soon after and was buried in St Peter's. *Ine of Wessex spent time in Rome and helped to create the English pilgrims' hospice. Concen, king of Powys, died there in 854 and *Alfred the Great was taken to Rome as a child of 5 by his father. Papal authority over the church in Britain also extended through churchmen like *Benedict Biscop who made five visits in all during his career. By the 10th cent. Rome was the recognized source of ecclesiastical authority and it was established practice for archbishops of Canterbury to go for investiture by the pope—despite the fact that Alsine froze to death on the Alps in 958 on his way to Rome for that purpose.

The Norman Conquest strengthened ties between England and continental Europe but the Norman kings deliberately kept themselves apart from Rome. Indeed they hindered communication with Rome and would not allow subjects to travel there without permission. This began a battle over control of the church in England, culminating in the dispute between Henry II and Thomas *Becket, vigorously supported by the pope, Alexander III. Becket's murder in 1170 shocked Christian Europe, which hailed him as a martyr for the freedom of the church from royal power, and his relics were enshrined in Rome as well as in Canterbury.

Traffic increased between Rome and the English church as ecclesiastical government became more complex and centralized. There was a continuous presence of Englishmen in the medieval Roman curia. The heyday for papal employment of the English was probably under Urban VI and Boniface IX (1378–1404), after which it declined, despite England's broadly pro-papal attitudes. Diplomatic and royal links had become stronger and between 1417 and 1467 the English took to keeping a king's proctor in the curia to deal with ecclesiastical appointments. Yet at the same time, archbishops of Canterbury had ceased to attend Rome to receive the pallium. None of the five archbishops of the 15th cent. was consecrated in Rome and only one went there for any purpose. English cardinals ceased to live in or visit Rome. Even *Wolsey, a strong candidate for papal election in 1521 and 1522, did not attend either conclave.

By the early 16th cent. royal links with Rome were more important than strictly ecclesiastical ones. Under Henry VIII the English pilgrim hospice in Rome became known as the King's Hospice. Tudor enthusiasm for the papacy led to the appointment of a cardinal-protector for England in 1492—the first in Europe. The Roman residence of the English ambassador, the Palazzo Torlonia, was a gift from the English cardinal-protector to Henry VIII, who in turn gave it to the papal legate Lorenzo Campeggio. His role in Anglo-papal relations was unique, for despite being the trusted ally of Henry and Wolsey, his judgment on the marriage case in 1528 went against the king and led to the final breach with Rome.

As royal–papal relations disintegrated and authority over the English church was seized by the Tudors, it became vital for the catholic resistance to retain links with the papacy. In 1538 the King's Hospice in Rome was taken under papal control and Cardinal Reginald *Pole appointed as warden. Pole, whose career was dedicated to trying to reconcile the Roman and English factions, returned to England when Mary Tudor appointed him archbishop of Canterbury. He died within hours of the queen herself in 1558.

Particularly after the excommunication of Elizabeth I in 1570, relations with the papacy were at a low ebb. Catholics retained semi-covert contacts through the hospice which from 1579 became a seminary training English priests. During the reigns of Elizabeth I and James I, protestants could only visit Rome in defiance of a government ban. Gradually, as some of the heat went out of Anglo-papal conflicts under Charles I and his catholic queen *Henrietta Maria, it became possible to re-establish quasi-diplomatic relations between Rome and the English court. Three papal envoys were appointed to London, before the Civil War dashed Roman hopes.

The short-lived and disastrous attempt by James II to restore catholicism to England put paid to any restoration of relations with the papacy for all but the small recusant catholic community. After the fall of the Stuarts, diplomatic relations were strained by papal support for the *Jacobite court, which settled in Rome from 1717. The chill began to lift after the death of James III (the old pretender) in 1766 when the papacy refused recognition of the royal claims of Charles Edward *Stuart and later of his brother *Henry, cardinal duke of York. By the end of the 18th cent. the cardinal duke of York, who had impoverished himself supporting Pius VI against Napoleon, was in receipt of a royal pension given by George III. By 1806 Britain found herself in an unlikely alliance with the papal states resisting Napoleonic bullying and fire-power. Cardinal Ercole Consalvi, Pius VII's secretary of state, became the first Roman cardinal since the 16th cent. to set foot in England, when he arrived on diplomatic business concerning the treaty of *Vienna in 1815.

Nineteenth-cent. contacts were prickly as the papacy became more insistent on retaining temporal power over the papal states and English catholicism reasserted itself. Unofficial or semi-official government envoys were sent to Rome—Lord Minto in the 1840s before the catholic hierarchy was restored, and Odo Russell in the 1860s during the Risorgimento. British government policy from the 1850s favoured Italian unification and opposed the pope's intransigence over the papal states. Yet Queen Victoria sent Pius IX a letter of condolence on the loss of his lands. *Gladstone heatedly opposed the decrees of the first Vatican Council in 1869–70, fearing that the definition of papal infallibility would lead to papal interference in civil governments. Not until the creation of the British legation in 1915 were formal diplomatic relations re-established with Rome. In the meantime the papacy gained a greater emotional power and ecclesiastical authority in the hearts and minds of English catholics, encouraged by Cardinals *Wiseman and *Manning. The office and person of the pope took on an almost mystical power and ecclesiastical government was dominated by constant recourse to Roman judgement. Thus while English catholics became 'more Roman than Rome', deeply rooted protestant anti-papalism, based on folk memory, continued to be difficult to eradicate. JFC

Brooke, Z. M., *The English Church and the Papacy from the Conquest to the Reign of John* (1989); Buschkuhl, M., *Great Britain and the Holy See 1746–1870* (1982); Harvey, M., *England, Rome and the Papacy 1417–1464* (1993); Robinson, J. M., *Ercole Consalvi 1757–1824* (1993).

Papineau, Louis-Joseph (1786–1871). Papineau was leader of the *patriote* party in Lower Canada (modern Quebec), and the voice of a vocal nationalism, which by 1834 confronted the British government with demands for effective control of the province. In response, the House of Commons in March 1837 authorized the governor to ignore the Assembly, which was refusing to vote taxes. Lower Canada simmered with protest until November, when an attempt to arrest Papineau triggered open rebellion. British forces suppressed the uprising with much loss of life. Papineau went into exile, returning to Canada in 1845 and later campaigning against the abolition of the seigneurial system. GM

Papua New Guinea is an independent monarchy within the Commonwealth with the queen as head of state. It is formed by the eastern half of the large island of New Guinea together with a number of adjacent islands to the east and north. The western part of the island was claimed by the Dutch and is now part of Indonesia. In the 19th cent. the Germans and British took increasing interest in eastern New Guinea. In 1906 British sovereignty was transferred to Australia and in 1914 Australian troops occupied the German settlement. It was handed to Australia as a *mandate in 1921. During the Second World War there was heavy fighting after the Japanese invaded. Its economy depends upon coffee, tea, bananas, and the mining of gold and copper. JAC

Paradise Lost. Epic poem by John *Milton (1667) concerning mankind's disobedience and consequent expulsion from Paradise through Satan's agency. Derived principally from the biblical account of the fall of man but illuminated by Milton's breadth of scholarship and shaped by his involvement in the Commonwealth cause, it has become the blind poet's best-known work through its panoramic vistas and mastery of language. *Dryden's acknowledgement ('that Poet has cutt us all out') was later echoed by *Hazlitt's commendation that its musicality was unsurpassed. The sequel *Paradise Regained* (1671) is concerned with Christ's temptation in the wilderness, his resistance atoning for Eve's frailty. ASH

Paris, treaty of, 1259. By this Anglo-French treaty of 13 October Henry III surrendered his claim to the Plantagenet lands of northern France which his father John had lost in the first decade of the century. In return, his possession of Aquitaine in south-west France was confirmed by Louis IX of France. The treaty clearly stated that Henry should pay liege homage to Louis for his French lands. The subsequent exercise of French sovereignty, combined with the reluctance of English rulers to demean themselves by paying homage, and continuing controversies over the extent of English landholdings in France, led to a series of wars from the 1290s. AC

Paris, treaty of, 1295. In 1292 Edward I placed John *Balliol on the throne of Scotland. Two years later, when war broke out between Edward and Philip IV of France, Edward called on Balliol to give him support. But a number of Scottish barons sent to France and on 23 October 1295 signed a treaty of mutual assistance which became the basis for the long-lasting *Franco-Scottish alliance, the 'Auld Alliance'. Balliol threw in his lot with the pro-French party, refused a summons to join Edward at Newcastle and in 1296 was defeated and deposed. But the *Scottish Wars of Independence were only beginning. JAC

Paris, treaty of, 1303. The treaty of 1259 did not end friction over England's possession of Gascony, and war between Philip IV of France and Edward I broke out again in 1294. After complex negotiations, the treaty of Paris in 1303 confirmed Edward's fealty to Philip for the territory and arranged for the marriage of Prince Edward to the French princess *Isabella. Edward I was free to turn his attention to his last campaign in Scotland. JAC

Paris, treaty of, 1727. Philip V of Spain was far from reconciled to the loss of *Minorca and *Gibraltar to Britain after the War of the *Spanish Succession. In 1725 a Spanish–Austrian *rapprochement* forced Britain, France, and the Dutch into a defensive treaty of Hanover and in February 1727 the Spaniards began a siege of Gibraltar. It was beaten off, Austria gave Spain little support, and in May 1727 a preliminary settlement was agreed at Paris. A major European war was avoided but Anglo-Spanish tension remained. JAC

Paris, treaty of, 1763. Though the treaty of Paris, which brought to an end the Seven Years War, gave Britain great gains, including Canada, supremacy in India, Grenada, St Vincent, Dominica, Tobago, Senegal, and Minorca, it was denounced by the opposition as wholly inadequate and the duke of *Bedford, chief negotiator, was accused of betraying his country. *Pitt complained that we had abandoned our ally Frederick of Prussia and that the treaty 'obscured all the glories of the war and surrendered the dearest interests of the nation'. A more plausible view is that it was so triumphant that it invited Spanish and French revenge and European jealousy, which was given its opportunity in the War of *American Independence. JAC

Paris, treaty of, 1814. The treaty was concluded between France and the victorious allies (Austria, Great Britain, Portugal, Prussia, Russia, Spain, and Sweden) on 30 May. Napoleon Bonaparte had abdicated on 6 April and the allies wished to offer a generous peace to help the restored king, Louis XVIII. France was allowed to keep her frontiers as on 1 January 1792, thus retaining some of the gains of the revolutionary period. With some exceptions, she regained her colonies. She was to return archives but not the looted art treasures to the countries she had conquered. By a secret clause, the former Austrian Netherlands (Belgium) were to be united with Holland, under the Dutch king. Switzerland was to be neutral. Germany and Italy, which had been reconquered from the French, were to be reconstituted as mosaics of separate states. Details of the territorial settlement were to be determined at a congress to meet shortly in Vienna. MEC

Paris, treaty of, 1815. This treaty (20 November), after Napoleon's Hundred Days and defeat at the battle of Waterloo, was more severe than the first treaty of 1814. With a few exceptions, France had to withdraw to the frontiers of 1790. She also had to pay an indemnity of 700,000,000 francs and agree to an allied army of occupation in certain frontier regions for a period of up to five years. It had previously been agreed that France would restore the looted works of art to their owners. MEC

Paris, treaty of, 1856. This treaty was signed at the end of the *Crimean War by Austria, France, Great Britain, Prussia, Russia, Sardinia, and Turkey. It was meant to strengthen the security of the Ottoman (Turkish) empire and limit the power of Russia. The other powers undertook to respect the integrity of Turkey and admitted her to the Concert of Europe: in return the sultan promised good treatment of his Christian subjects. The Black Sea was to be neutralized, its waters open to the merchant ships of all nations, but closed to warships. This meant the dismantling of the Russian Black Sea fleet. The free navigation of the Danube was guaranteed and, in return, Russia ceded some territory, mainly in Bessarabia, to Turkey. In 1870 Russia unilaterally abrogated the Black Sea clauses. MEC

parish churches. There are parish churches of all sizes, ages, and architectural styles, with internal fittings equally diverse. What is common to all of them is that they are buildings at the centres of their communities, that is of the 'community of the parish'. As such they embody the history of groups of people often otherwise poorly documented, in an area of importance in their lives; a history which in some cases stretches back for over 1,000 years. In the past religion played a much more important role than it does for the majority today. The rights and wrongs of how God should be worshipped aroused great passions, and parish churches have been built and rebuilt, furnished and refurnished throughout their history in conformity with these shifting and often conflicting ideals of worship. The abiding interest of parish churches is their diversity and the light they can throw on the practice of religion in thousands of communities over hundreds of years.

A parish is a territorial area, with a church at its centre, served by a priest having the 'cure of souls'. The parochial system developed piecemeal from the 10th cent., but was in place by the 13th. From then until the early 19th cent. the parish and priest was supported by a landed endowment, the *glebe; by a tax payable by the parishioners, the *tithe; and by various, semi-voluntary, offerings like *mortuaries. It was within the community of the parish that ordinary people received Christian teaching and the sacraments of the church; baptism, confirmation, marriage, and burial. The parishioners supported their priest through their tithe payments, but their obligations did not end there. By the early 13th cent. at the latest it was established that the rector could only be expected to maintain the fabric of the chancel of the church from his income, the parishioners being responsible for the upkeep of the nave of the church and for the books and vestments needed for the services held within it. The imposition of this collective responsibility resulted in the emergence of a real sense of community in the later Middle Ages, with the people taking a dominant role in the organization of parish life and the form and development of the church building and its contents, through their elected representatives, the *churchwardens.

There are examples of parish church buildings from all periods, like the Saxon church of Escomb (Co. Durham), the Romanesque church of Kilpeck (Herefordshire), or the great Decorated church of St Mary Redcliffe (*Bristol). But the majority of surviving medieval churches were added to piecemeal, by the people who used them and worshipped in them. The entire community might contribute to the rebuilding of the whole or a part of the fabric, as happened at Bodmin (Corn.), but generally additions were made by individuals or groups within the parish, the individual patron, or the trade and religious guilds. Two generations of the Canynges family, merchants of Bristol, contributed substantially to the rebuilding of St Mary Redcliffe; whilst the trade guilds attached to St Michael's, Coventry, built a series of guild chapels leading off the aisles of the church, and the Palmers' Guild of Ludlow, a society dedicated to assisting pilgrims, had a large chapel built in the parish church of St Laurence. The Reformation brought an end to the extensive rebuilding of the later Middle Ages and there are comparatively few churches built between the mid-16th and early 19th cents. The churches built by *Wren after the Great Fire of *London are an exception, and there are fine Hanoverian churches at Stoke Edith (1740–2) and Shobdon (1752–6) in Herefordshire. The 19th cent. saw another massive church-building programme as the Church of England tried to provide for the growing population; in 1815 about $8\frac{1}{2}$ million, by 1850 over 17 million, and by 1901 $32\frac{1}{2}$ million. About half of all those parish churches which remain in use were built after 1815: these include Victorian rebuildings of older churches but more often represent the foundation of new parishes in the expanding industrial centres. These churches are often in the Gothic or, more particularly, the 13th-cent. Gothic style. Victorian churchmen perceived in the Middle Ages a Christian ideal which they sought to emulate.

Parish churches may not often have been rebuilt after the 16th cent. but their interiors were often remodelled. The numerous altars, and images of the saints in stone, wood, glass, paint, and needlework, were swept away in the Reformation and its aftermath. In the 19th cent. church interiors were completely remodelled along the lines advocated by the Victorian reformers to provide space for the proper celebration of the liturgy. Thus, whereas parish churches are of very diverse architectural styles, their interior arrangements are generally 19th cent., and reflect a desire for both processional space and a focus on the altar. The interior space was unified by creating level floors for the nave and aisles. The sanctuary was screened off and raised above the floor of the nave by steps, the altar was returned to its medieval position near the east wall, railed off and raised on further steps, so that space was created for the parish choir and organ within the east end. An unrestored interior like Holy Trinity, Goodramgate (York), shows by contrast the chaotic nature of a medieval interior, with its varying floor levels and with its added 18th-cent. pulpit and box pews; St Mary, Whitby has also kept its box pews. LR

Anderson, M. D., *Looking for History in British Churches* (1951); Cox, J. C., and Ford, C. B., *The Parish Churches of England* (5th edn. 1946–7); Duffy, E., *The Stripping of the Altars* (1992); Randall, G., *The English Parish Church* (1982); Smith, E., *English Parish Churches* (1976).

Parish Councils Act, 1894 (more properly the Local Government Act). The Act completed the great reform of *local government in the 19th cent. Towns had been given elected councils by the *Municipal Corporations Act of 1835 and *county councils had been established in 1888. There had been considerable pressure in the Liberal Party for parish councils to develop grass-roots democracy and they were included in the *Newcastle programme of 1891. *Gladstone's legislation introduced urban and rural districts, parish councils for villages of over 300 inhabitants, and parish meetings for hamlets. The Act gave women, whether married or not, the right both to vote and serve. Its passage in the Commons and Lords was strongly contested and the severe limits placed on the revenue-raising powers of the new councils meant that few of them had much room for action. The urban and rural districts were swept away by the Local Government Act of 1972, but parish councils survived, save in Wales, where community councils were established. JAC

parishes, origins of. Traditional theories that the English parish system was the brainchild of Archbishop *Theodore of Tarsus (668–90) are no longer held. English dioceses, geographically much larger than Italian counterparts, could not be administered from the centre and needed more local oversight, but origins of the parochial system remain obscure. *Paulinus, bishop of York (627–34), built some local churches and so did the 7th-cent. Celtic mission to Northumbria. *Bede (d. 735) mentions houses of prayer. His advice to Archbishop Egbert (734) shows that no organized system then existed; he advised him to seek aid from others by 'ordaining priests and instituting teachers who may devote themselves to preaching the word of God in the individual villages, and to celebrating the celestial mysteries and especially to performing the sacred rites of baptism'. Some of the injunctions of the Synod of Clofesho (746) speak of bishops' instituting priests to local churches. Thus the parish system gradually and unobtrusively evolved in the 8th cent. probably by a two-way process, from the diocesan centre outwards and from local private churches towards the centre. Soon after the conversion period the only 'parish' was that surrounding the bishop's cathedral or 'head-minster', with his clergy journeying out to convert and minister to the flock. Distances demanded the development of more remote local centres, 'ordinary minsters' (large collegiate churches) subsidiary to the cathedral, whose districts were the size of the modern rural deanery. In turn from these there spread groups of 'field-churches', usually already built by thegns as chapels to their private halls. These were the centres of embryo parishes. Some may have been pagan temples newly blessed as the thegn was converted or replaced. Little is known about these, because the thegn had no formal charter from the king and his church was simple and wooden, thus leaving no trace. It was his own property, served by a poor priest in return for glebe land of 2 virgates, twice as much as a ceorl. In addition the priest was allowed fees for baptisms, marriages, or supervising ordeals. Private churches became normal appurtenances for thegns. Other 'field-churches' developed like the minsters as royal or episcopal foundations within minsters' districts, especially on newly cultivated territory. Yet others, founded by kings or bishops as their own, were later known as 'peculiars', withdrawn from ordinary diocesan jurisdiction. Founders could sell or bequeath the church at will. The parish system developed as churches continued to be built in villages throughout the Anglo-Saxon period and by the Norman Conquest it was for the most part fully developed. The tension, however, between the lord's dominance of his priest and the rightful desire by the bishop for oversight had to be partly alleviated by the third Lateran Council's injunction (1179), giving the bishop the right of institution to the benefice. In the course of time, governments found the parish a very useful administrative unit, particularly for dealing with poor relief. It then became even more necessary to ascertain and establish the exact boundaries of parishes, and the annual perambulation, or 'beating the bounds', usually done on Rogation Day, became an important event. Nevertheless, until well into the 19th cent. the pattern of the 10,000 parishes remained chaotic, with separated pockets, disputed areas, and countless idiosyncrasies. WMM

parish registers. Records of baptisms, burials, and weddings were kept in England following an order of Thomas *Cromwell in 1538. Registers began in Scotland in the 1550s and 1560s, although few survive before the 17th cent. Irish parish registers, too, do not normally start before that century and those that do usually cover only the protestant Church of Ireland; few registers recording the majority catholic population start until the 18th cent. Register-keeping in England was poor during periods of religious conflict, such as the reigns of Edward VI or Mary I, or during periods of civil unrest such as the Civil War and Interregnum (1642–60). The form and content of English parish registers was altered by a brief dalliance with civil registration under the *Protectorate (1653–60) and also by Hardwicke's *Marriage Act (1753) and Rose's Act (1813).

Before civil registration in 1837 parish registers provide historical demographers with the best means of calculating population statistics. Their techniques involve the counting of monthly totals of events in parish registers (aggregative analysis) and the reconstruction of individual families by linking together baptisms, burials, and marriages (family reconstitution). The reliability of their results, however, depends on overcoming the many deficiencies of Anglican parochial registration, since registers record church ceremonies, rather than births, deaths, and marriages. Many babies died before baptism, and, over time, an increasing proportion of the population deserted the Church of England so that by the 1810s English registers contain only about two-thirds of the nation's births and deaths. JPB

Parisi. British tribe and *civitas*. The Parisi as their name suggests seem to have ancestral links, betrayed in particular by their unusual 'chariot-burials', to a Gallic tribe of the same name. Overshadowed by their far more powerful neighbours, the *Brigantes, it is possible that they acquiesced in the Roman occupation of their territory, which lay in the East Riding of Yorkshire. The geographer Ptolemy ascribes one town to them, Petuaria (Brough on Humber), and it is from here that an inscription survives which appears to confirm the existence of the *civitas*. It is likely that Petuaria served as the tribal capital. KB

Park, Mungo (1771–1806). A child of the *Scottish Enlightenment, Park's Edinburgh medical and botanical training and Sumatran experience led *Banks to choose him to explore the interior of west Africa for the African Association in 1795. From the Gambian coast he reached the Niger near Segu, ending long controversy by proving that the river flowed eastwards. A more ambitious expedition for the British government ended in disaster in 1806 when Park was killed at Bussa much further down the Niger. His fate remained a mystery for 20 years, as did the termination of the Niger. Park's *Travels* of 1799 have remained in print ever since. RB

Parker, Matthew (1504–75). Archbishop of Canterbury. Born in Norwich and educated at Corpus Christi College, Cambridge, Parker was successively chaplain to *Anne Boleyn, master of Corpus Christi (1544), vice-chancellor (1545 and 1549), dean of Lincoln (1552), and archbishop. Close to Bucer and a supporter of Lady Jane *Grey, he was deprived under Mary and lived in obscurity. As a diffident, scholarly man, he reluctantly agreed to the primacy at Elizabeth's request. His consecration in Lambeth palace in 1559 by four former Edwardine bishops was unusually significant, for it claimed to transmit valid succession to the Anglican episcopate despite catholic denials. Though earlier associated with Cambridge reformers, his patristic studies gave him independence, and a distaste for extreme protestantism. The major architect of the Elizabethan settlement, Parker courageously promoted theological comprehension within liturgical conformity, a middle road between Rome and calvinism. For this he revived convocation, revised the Thirty-Nine Articles (1563), initiated a new translation of the Bible, the 'Bishops' Bible' (1568), and published his 'Advertisements' (1566), enjoining the use of cope and surplice. WMM

Parkes, Joseph (1796–1865). Parkes was an early example of the kind of man needed by the politics of lobbying—the parliamentary agent. He was born in Warwick, was much influenced by *Bentham, became a solicitor, and married a daughter of Joseph *Priestley. In 1828 he was secretary to a committee which lobbied successfully for the transfer of East Retford's parliamentary seats to Birmingham, and in the reform crisis of 1832 he acted as go-between for the Whig ministers in their dealings with the *Birmingham Political Union. Though Parkes was not inclined to underestimate his services, it was tactically useful to the Whigs to have radical pressure. Parkes's reward in 1833 was to be made secretary to the committee looking into municipal corporations, which, not surprisingly, reported that there was vast dissatisfaction and substantial reform of local government was needed. Next, under the patronage of Lord *Durham, he threw himself into the registration of voters in the Reform Association, which spawned the *Reform Club in 1836. He continued to work for the Whigs in election matters until 1847, when he was appointed taxing master in Chancery. JAC

parks and recreation grounds. There was little need for public parks until the great urbanization of Victorian Britain, since before then most towns were small and green fields not far away. London, by far the largest town, had the royal parks, particularly St James's, Green Park, Hyde Park, Greenwich, Richmond, and, later, Regent's Park. But access to the parks was severely limited. They had walls, with lodges and janitors, and only respectable citizens were allowed in. Railings did not replace walls until the mid-19th cent. The great pleasure gardens, *Vauxhall and *Ranelagh, were far too expensive for ordinary people. Outside London, some large towns were fortunate: Bristol had its incomparable downs, Edinburgh its meadows, and Newcastle upon Tyne its Town Moor, protected by an early Act of 1774. But as the industrial towns doubled and redoubled in size, the need for action to provide open spaces and to preserve existing commons became obvious. Robert Slaney, MP for Shrewsbury, obtained a select committee in 1833 and, though a very modest affair, it opened up the subject, reporting that provision in Manchester, Birmingham, Sheffield, Leeds, Hull, Wolverhampton, and Blackburn was bad. It also drew attention to the urgent need to preserve Primrose Hill in London and Parliament responded by purchasing the site in 1836 for £300. In 1841 Parliament voted £10,000 for public parks on a matching financial basis, but by 1849 only five towns—Dundee, Arbroath, Manchester, Portsmouth, and Preston—had taken advantage of the offer. The Public Health Act of 1848 allowed corporations to raise funds for 'public walks and pleasure grounds'. A further Act of 1855 extended permission to London, with Finsbury Park the first to be created. These cautious approaches had been reinforced by many examples of philanthropy or self-help. Victoria Park (Bath), west of Royal Crescent, was started in 1829 to revive the fading glories of the spa; Joseph Strutt gave Derby its arboretum in 1840; Birkenhead, Manchester, and Liverpool all opened parks in the 1840s. In the later 19th and early 20th cents. the pace quickened, assisted by another Public Health Act of 1907. Manchester was said to have 57 parks by 1920. The late 20th cent. has seen retrogression. Few new parks have been created, though a good deal of landscaping has been carried out, particularly in new towns and on motorways. But roundabouts, car parks, motorways, and sports centres have all encroached on parks, public and private. Desperate town-planners have often seemed less enlightened than their Victorian forebears, and no jewel, not even Petworth, is safe. The combination of rising maintenance costs, straitened budgets, and persistent vandalism has made some parks dismal places, the pavilion roofless, the bandstand gutted, and the lavatories boarded up. JAC

Parliament

English Parliament. Parliament is a servant which became a master. It originated with three royal needs; the need of monarchs to obtain advice and information; the realization that subjects were more likely to pay taxes if they knew what they were for; and the need to find some way of dealing with complaints, grievances, and petitions from all over the realm. The third function of Parliament gradually atrophied as, in the Middle Ages, an elaborate network of local and national courts was established, though the concept of the High Court of Parliament survives in the appellate jurisdiction of the House of Lords and petitions are still submitted. Two other characteristics which have survived are that the advice is not always palatable, nor the taxation paid cheerfully even after explanation given. Representative institutions developed for similar reasons in many other European countries, though they varied in composition and powers according to local circumstances.

In a general sense, Parliament may be traced back to the Saxon *witan and the Norman *council, each of which included the chief men of the realm, lay and clerical. But the development of Parliament as a wider, national body, with a representative element, reflects the incessant demands of government for more money, and a change in the distribution of wealth brought about by the spread of commerce and the growth of towns. Feudal dues were intended to be exceptional—for the king's marriage, his ransom, or the knighting of his son—but chronic warfare, particularly against France, demanded ever-increasing taxation and made it impossible for the king to 'live of his own'. Consequently, Parliament developed at moments of crisis, usually associated with a disputed succession, or domestic or foreign war.

Any institution which survives over eight centuries must have adapted and changed its functions. In Saxon and Norman times, a good deal of public business was done at crown-wearings, ceremonial occasions at Christmas, Easter, and Whitsun. Since the great men were expected to attend to show respect, it was easy to consult them. Charters often referred to the consent of the barons, since it was to the king's advantage that his policies should be known to have the support of all important subjects. In the course of the 13th cent., these meetings came to be referred to as discussions—*colloquia* or *parliamenta*. But though their purpose was to assist the king, they could also be turned against an unpopular or unsuccessful monarch. In December 1203 John left Normandy to seek urgent help from his barons at Oxford in saving the duchy: they promised obedience but demanded 'the rights of the kingdom inviolate'. In 1234, the council at Gloucester forced Henry III to dismiss his unpopular foreign adviser Peter des *Roches. In 1257, when the king was absent fighting in Gascony, his regents called another council to appeal for money. Though they augmented the barons with representatives of the lower clergy and two knights from each shire, the money was not forthcoming. During the conflict between Simon de *Montfort's party and the king, each side used Parliament in turn: de Montfort's Parliament in January 1265 included both knights and members from certain boroughs.

By this time, Parliament was becoming a familiar institution, usually, but not invariably, meeting at Westminster. But its composition still varied considerably. The lesser clergy, summoned for the first time in 1257, attended irregularly thereafter, and then dropped out, using *convocation instead. Edward I's *'Model' Parliament of 1295, called to provide funds for war against the Scots, included 2 archbishops, 18 bishops, 67 abbots, 3 heads of religious orders, 48 lay barons, the lower clergy, 2 knights from each shire, and 2 burgesses from 110 boroughs—a total of more than 400 members. Though not a model in the sense that its composition was subsequently adhered to, it was very different from a small council of 40 to 50 members. For some years, composition and procedures remained flexible. In 1305 all members not of the council were sent home early, though the Parliament continued. In 1372, the burgesses were held back after the knights had been dismissed to see whether they would make a separate grant.

The next important step in the evolution of Parliament was the separation into houses. Previously there had been only one chamber, with groups of committees breaking off for discussions: the burgesses had a largely silent role as spectators. At first the knights of the shire tended to identify with the barons as the landed or aristocratic interest, but in the course of the 14th cent. they sat increasingly with the burgesses. The lay lords and the greater clergy then came to form the upper house.

We must not however exaggerate the importance of Parliament at this stage in the regular business of government. Attendances were not always good, partly because travel was difficult, partly because involvement was not always welcome. Sessions were short—sometimes no more than a week, often a month or so. But the Commons were beginning to assert themselves. Taxation, which had been voted jointly, was said in the reign of Henry IV to be by the Commons 'with the assent of the Lords'—a significant change.

The early part of the 15th cent. saw further advances. The *Hundred Years War against France led to incessant demands for supply, and in the Wars of the *Roses which followed, each side made use of parliaments as an instrument and to demonstrate support. With the return of more stable conditions, the use of parliaments diminished. Edward IV summoned only one parliament in the last five years of his reign and Henry VII only one in the last twelve years of his.

The Tudor period saw a great leap forward, the power of Parliament and that of the monarchy advancing together. Henry VIII's use of Parliament to regulate the succession and to reform the church strengthened its authority and the elimination of the abbots from the Upper House left the lay lords in a strong majority. In 1536, the Act of *Union brought the principality of Wales into Parliament's range. Yet, by and large, it remained under royal control. During Elizabeth's reign there were signs of restiveness, but in the last ten years of her reign, Parliament was in existence for only some seven months.

In the course of the 17th cent., Parliament made a decisive breakthrough. The ineptitude of James I and Charles I lost them control and lack of trust led in 1642 to civil war. But the result was stalemate. The restoration of the monarchy in 1660 could be seen as proof that, as kings had always argued, it was the bulwark against anarchy or despotism. Few vital royal prerogatives were lost. Yet Parliament in 1660 was far from discredited. It had demonstrated a remarkable capacity to improvise in government and to wage war, and an important part of Charles II's appeal from exile had been his promise to summon a free parliament: none of his predecessors, he assured the speaker rather excessively, had greater esteem for parliaments than he had. Even so, relations with parliaments during the rest of his reign were often fraught. The balance tipped in 1688. After James II's flight, the House of Commons took advantage of the situation to improve its position in relation to the new monarchs. The financial settlement given William III was deliberately ungenerous: 'when princes have not needed money,' declared Sir Joseph Williamson, with great candour, 'they have not needed us.' Twenty-five years of almost continuous warfare, on a scale never before seen, guaranteed annual sessions and assured Parliament of a regular and inescapable place in the machinery of government. Ministers like *Harley and *Walpole learned how to control Parliament through patronage and cajolery and made reputations as managers. The 'corruption' of Hanoverian politics, which used to be greatly deplored, is no more than a testimony to Parliament's enhanced position, since no one bribes when they can ignore or intimidate. They were helped in their task by the Act of *Union with Scotland in 1707 since the 45 MPs and 16 representative peers who arrived at Westminster were, by and large, penurious and purchasable.

In many ways, Parliament after the revolution was at its zenith. The government of aristocracy and gentry, who had a near monopoly of wealth, leisure, and education, seemed natural and inevitable and could boast of notable achievements. The constitution was greatly admired, at home and abroad. The standard of debate was high, with orators like *Pulteney, *Murray, *Chatham, *North, *Fox, *Burke, *Sheridan, *Pitt the Younger, and *Canning. In 1801, the Act of *Union with Ireland meant that, for the first time, Parliament could claim total sovereignty over the British Isles, though the result was not an unmixed blessing.

Yet even when Parliament was at its strongest, there were tremors. The breakaway of the Americans in 1776 foreshadowed the time when Canada, Australia, India, New Zealand, Ireland, and the colonies would follow suit. At the same time, Parliament, with great reluctance, allowed reports of its proceedings to appear in newspapers. 'This', Pulteney had once declared, 'looks very like making us accountable without doors for what we say within.' He was right and through that gap public opinion forced an entrance. The movement of population, the growth of great unrepresented towns, and the development of a more critical, utilitarian attitude gnawed at the foundations of aristocratic rule. In 1832 the first great reform took place. As its opponents gloomily forecast, it led, by stages, to full democracy, though not at the speed which they had envisaged. A continuous series of adjustments, many of them piecemeal, changed the nature of Parliament—the abolition of religious tests, more equal electoral areas, payment for MPs, extension of the franchise through to 1948. Though the *Parliament Act of 1911 stripped the House of Lords of much of its remaining power, the introduction of life peerages in 1958 gave it an unexpected and new lease of life. The institution of *referenda—on the *European Economic Community and on devolution—took some powers away from Parliament itself, handing them directly to the electors, and critics of the EEC argued that the very sovereignty of Parliament had been surrendered.

There is still much criticism of Parliament as an institution, though perhaps less than in the 1930s. The domination of party is deplored by many people who would never dream of voting for an independent: the last genuine independents, other than members who had quarrelled with their party, went out in 1950. The introduction of TV does not seem to have much effect in improving decorum. But the familiar accusation that Parliament is a talking-shop is based upon a misunderstanding. It is not, and never has been, a governing body, but a check upon government. Whether it does that well is much debated. In the prime minister, the Commons found a master more powerful than kings in the past, even if his ultimate deterrent, a dissolution, is little more than a threat of mass suicide. But events in many countries remind us that there are worse things than talking-shops: there are civil wars. JAC

Irish Parliament. The Irish Parliament was instituted at much the same time as the English, Sir John Wogan summoning an assembly in 1295 to Kilkenny, which included the lords and two knights from certain counties. Burgesses were added in 1311. The native Irish were excluded as 'not fit to be trusted with the counsel of the realm'. Though an Act of 1542 allowed the native Irish to take part, Parliament remained an Anglo-Irish institution. Control was exercised through *Poynings's law (1494), which subjected the Irish Parliament to the English Privy Council. More counties and boroughs were brought in during the 17th cent., and after the Glorious Revolution the Commons consisted of 64 knights, 234 burgesses, and 2 representatives from Trinity College, Dublin. There were some 80 peers in the House of Lords.

Though the Irish Parliament had a splendid building on College Green, begun in 1729, real power was in the hands of the lord-lieutenant and the English government. Debates were often eloquent and the castle government paid much attention to management, but they did not engage directly on the levers of power. Until the *Octennial Act of 1768 parliaments lasted the length of the reign: there was no parliament between 1666 and 1692 (save for James II's Assembly of 1689), and the first Parliament of George II in 1727 lasted until 1760. Sessions were held every other year.

Throughout much of the 18th cent. there were repeated attempts to wriggle free from English control and complaints of the way in which Englishmen were parked on the Irish pensions list. Not until England began to run into difficulties after the *Seven Years War were concessions forthcoming. The granting of the Octennial Act in 1768 came at a time when the English were anxious to increase the Irish army to cut military expense, and the repeal of Poynings's law in 1782 came when the *Volunteers carried a clear threat in the midst of the American War.

The grant of legislative independence ushered in the final phase of the Irish Parliament, which has been bathed in a golden light as *'Grattan's Parliament'. *Pitt's commercial propositions had to be withdrawn in 1785 and the Irish Parliament cut loose during the Regency crisis of 1789. But in the end the decisive factor was that law and order broke down in the great rising of 1798. Without a union, Ireland would, wrote the lord-lieutenant *Camden, be 'dreadfully vulnerable in all future wars', and Pitt seems to have resolved on a union the very day he ordered 5,000 more troops to Ireland to put down the rebellion. By the Act of Union of 1801 the Irish Parliament was suppressed and representation transferred to Westminster. The new parliament house in Dublin, no longer required, became the Bank of Ireland. JAC

Scottish Parliament. The Scottish Parliament differed significantly from its English counterpart. No equivalent of the Houses of Commons and Lords ever existed; instead, the three estates—clergy, barons, and burgh commissioners—assembled in one chamber. Legislation, from the early 15th cent., was drafted by the *lords of the Articles, a smaller committee elected by the estates, before being passed in full Parliament. Likewise many judicial matters were delegated to a committee of lords auditors. Parliament was supplemented by the institutions of general council, until the late 15th cent., and from the 16th cent. by the *Convention of Estates, effectively parliaments without judicial powers. In the past these bodies were accused of making the Scottish Parliament constitutionally defective—simply a 'rubber stamp' for royal decisions. This opinion is now substantially discredited.

Evolving from the king's council of bishops and earls, Parliament is first recorded in 1235, referred to as a *colloquium*, already with a political and judicial role. In the early 14th cent. the presence of knights and freeholders became important, and from 1326 burgh commissioners attended, because of the need to secure their consent for taxation. In the 15th cent. Parliament was often willing to defy the king, repeatedly opposing taxes for James I (1406–37), and frequently openly critical of James III (1460–88). By refusing to forfeit the duke of *Albany (d. 1485) between 1479 and 1481, it seriously undermined the king's authority. Called in this period on average more than once a year, Parliament was expected to provide support for many crown policies. However, it could be a dangerous place for a monarch, and James IV (1488–1513) avoided meetings after 1509.

The composition of Parliament remained the same in the 16th cent., although following the *Reformation many opposed the presence of the clergy, particularly as they were essentially crown nominees. Shire commissioners attended Parliament from 1594, again as a result of the need to collect tax. By James VI's reign (1567–1625), the Committee of the Articles was heavily dominated by crown supporters, creating parliamentary weakness.

With the Scottish constitutional settlement (1640–1), the royal prerogative was curtailed, and Parliament took control of the executive, a precedent for the English Long Parliament. The *Interregnum saw a union of parliaments (1657), but the Scottish Parliament returned strongly after the Restoration (1660). In 1689 the attendance of clergy was abolished, followed by the Committee of the Articles (1690). Parliament's strength was such that the crown turned to corruption to undermine its autonomy. Bribery and parliamentary division, rather than dominant unionism, best explain the crown's ability to secure a parliamentary majority in favour of incorporating union with England (16 January 1707). Finally dissolved on 28 April 1707, the Scottish Parliament has remained important to Scottish national identity, and by the mid-1990s, three of the four main Scottish political parties supported its return in some form. RJT

Welsh Parliament. Though there is no evidence of a Welsh parliament as a regular part of the machinery of government, there was a tradition of consultation. *Llywelyn called an assembly of magnates at Aberdovey in 1216 to decide on the territorial divisions of south Wales. *Glyndŵr is said to have summoned two parliaments—at Machynlleth in 1404 and at Harlech in 1405—to the second of which four influential men from each commote (hundred) were summoned. Since Glyndŵr was anxious to assume the trappings of monarchy, there is no reason to disbelieve the reports. Some representatives from Wales were summoned to the English Parliament in 1322 and 1327 but Wales was not included in the regular representation until after 1536. JAC

Butt, R., *A History of Parliament: The Middle Ages* (1989); Davies, R. G., and Denton, J. H. (eds.), *The English Parliament in the Middle Ages* (Manchester, 1981); Donaldson, G., *Scotland: James V to James VII* (Edinburgh, 1965); Ferguson, W., *Scotland: 1689 to the Present* (Edinburgh, 1968); Graves, M. A. R., *The Tudor Parliament* (1985); id., *Early Tudor Parliaments 1485–1558* (1990); Johnston, E. M., *Great Britain and Ireland, 1760–1800* (1963); Nicholson, R., *Scotland: The Later Middle Ages* (Edinburgh, 1974); Porritt, E. and A. G., *The Unreformed House of Commons* (2 vols., 1903); Rait, R., *The Parliaments of Scotland* (Glasgow, 1924); Richardson, H. G., and Sayles, G. O., *The English Parliament in the Middle Ages* (1981).

Parliament, Acts of. The procedure whereby a bill becomes an Act of Parliament is lengthy and has evolved over many centuries. The main stages of a bill in the House of Commons are first reading, second reading, committee, report, and third reading. The first reading is purely formal with the title of the bill read out. If the bill is controversial, the second reading debate is likely to occupy a full parliamentary sitting. The debate is about the policy or principle embodied in the bill, not its detail. At the end of the debate, a division is likely to be called, which the government will usually win. However, most bills, in number though not in significance, are uncontroversial and not subject to a division.

After second reading, most bills are sent to a standing committee for detailed discussion. The standing committee consists of between 16 and 50 members, chosen to reflect the party balance and for their knowledge or experience of the bill's subject-matter. The bill (unless guillotined) is considered clause by clause, amendment by amendment. The minister may respond to criticism by bringing in amendments to his own bill, or by promising to consider amendments when the bill is reported back to the full House. The inbuilt government majority will ensure that most opposition amendments are defeated, but there are occasional revolts by government supporters, and governments are sometimes outvoted in committee. Some very important bills, especially those of constitutional significance, will go for their committee stage not to a standing committee but to the committee of the whole—i.e. the full House, sitting under rather more flexible procedure.

The bill, as amended, goes back to the full House for its report stage: this is a rather less thorough and less time-consuming version of the committee stage, but taken on the floor of the House. The government's majority in the House as a whole is usually more reliable than in committee, and the minister may take the opportunity to reverse defeats in committee.

The last stage is the third reading, when the House once again debates the principle of the bill. If, as is likely, it passes at this stage, the bill will go to the House of Lords to undergo a similar process. The main difference is that the committee stage in the Lords will be taken (normally) in the full House. The bill may be amended by the Lords and, exceptionally, rejected. If passed with amendments, the bill goes back to the Commons to consider the changes. For the bill to become law in that session, the two Houses will have to agree on the full text. The bill is then sent to the monarch for royal assent, which is invariably given.

The procedure outlined is that for public bills. Private bills, those relating to a particular corporation, individual, or company, go through a distinct, complex, and semi-judicial process. Private bills should not be confused with private members' bills, which are simply public bills introduced by a backbench MP. HB

Parliament, Houses of (London). The competition for the Houses of Parliament was won in 1836 by Sir Charles *Barry in the required 'Gothic or Elizabethan' style. Construction started in 1840, but the building was incomplete when Barry died 20 years later and was finished 1860–70 by his son Edward Middleton Barry (1830–80). The plan is clear and formal, with the House of Commons and House of Lords on either side of an axis. Yet the external composition is medieval, not to say picturesque, partly due to the Victoria Tower and the Clock Tower (Big Ben), and to the turrets and central *flèche* which disguise heating and ventilation ducts. Much of the detail, including the richly embellished interiors, is by A. W. N. *Pugin. The House of Commons and adjacent areas were destroyed in the Second World War but rebuilt by Sir Giles Gilbert Scott and Adrian Scott in a Gothic manner. PW

Parliament Act, 1911. Though the immediate cause of the Parliament Act was the House of Lords' rejection of *Lloyd George's budget in 1909, the deeper cause was the late 19th-cent. disintegration of the Whig Party which carried the Liberal Unionists into the ranks of the Conservatives, thus confirming a permanent Conservative majority in the Upper House and placing Liberal legislation at the mercy of the peers. The Act declared that a money bill could be presented for royal assent after one month, even without the Lords' consent, and other public bills after two years. The duration of Parliament was changed from seven to five years. It was carried in the Lords by 131 : 114 only after *Asquith, prime minister, had extracted from a reluctant George V a pledge to create enough Liberal peers if necessary to carry the measure. The most immediate consequence was that the House of Lords could no longer veto *Irish Home Rule. By the Parliament Act of 1949 the delaying power of the Lords was reduced to one year. JAC

parliamentarians was the polite name given to the opponents of Charles I in the civil wars. The pejorative term was roundheads. Charles's decision not to summon his own Parliament at Oxford until 1644 and his evident mistrust of it gave his adversaries some advantage. But *Cromwell also found great difficulty in dealing with parliaments during the Commonwealth. JAC

parliamentary reform is a general term covering a variety of proposals and changes which need to be carefully distinguished. Alterations to the composition, powers, procedure, and structure of Parliament have continued since the first parliaments were summoned in the 13th cent., but a sustained campaign for parliamentary reform did not develop until the 18th cent. After the *Septennial Act of 1716 there were intermittent calls for shorter parliaments, for a reduction in the number of placemen to lessen the growing power of the executive, and for the abolition of some rotten boroughs to give more representation to the counties. These were modest proposals that would have increased the already overwhelming influence of the aristocracy and gentry. More radical suggestions were put forward during the *Wilkes agitation in the 1770s when the case for manhood suffrage was deployed for the first time since the Civil War period. A comprehensive reform programme was put forward by the Westminster Committee, affiliated to the *Yorkshire Association in 1780, calling for manhood suffrage, equal electoral areas, annual parliaments, secret ballot, payment of members, and the abolition of the property qualification for MPs—the six points of the *Charter sixty years later.

Legislative response was at first slow. A few small boroughs were reformed in the 1770s and 1780s for gross corruption but no review of the entire electoral system was undertaken. Statutes against bribery were largely ineffective. But a series of major changes came 1828–32. Repeal of the *Test and Corporations Acts in 1828 allowed protestant dissenters to become MPs and the following year the same concession was extended to Roman catholics; the *Great Reform Act of 1832 abolished 56 of the smallest boroughs and brought great new towns like Manchester, Birmingham, Sheffield, and Leeds into the representation, introducing a standard franchise for the boroughs. Further legislation in 1867, 1884, 1918, 1928, and 1969 extended the right to vote eventually to all men and women over 18. Religious disabilities were removed when Jews were allowed to become MPs in 1858 and atheists in 1886. The longstanding problem of bribery and intimidation at elections was dealt with by *secret ballot in 1872, reinforced by the *Corrupt Practices Act of 1883. JAC

Modern consideration of reform of Parliament has been concerned with different aspects. In earlier centuries, the term 'parliamentary reform' connoted measures to make Parliament more *representative* and more *independent* of the executive. Today, making Parliament more representative is usually associated with *electoral reform*: parliamentary reform is concerned with the organization of the House of Commons.

The advent of mass democracy brought renewed fears of growing parliamentary subservience to the executive. At first such fears focused on the powers of the party whips, and these anxieties reached their zenith soon after the Second World War. More recently, discussion has centred on the procedures of the House. The way the Commons did its business almost insensibly strengthened the power of the executive: ministers, backed by the resources and experience of their departments, had a near monopoly of knowledge. The problem is that so much of the business of the House is transacted on the floor of the House itself. Until the procedural reforms of the 1960s and 1970s, the role of committees in the House was limited. The legislative standing committees were appointed to consider the committee stage or detailed amendments to bills, the principle of the bill having been already approved at the second reading. These standing committees had a fluctuating membership and no subject specialism. In the American Congress, by contrast, the Agriculture Committee or the Foreign Relations Committee of Senate are specialized and their composition relatively permanent. The British standing committees are designated by letters of the alphabet, Standing Committee A, Standing Committee B, and so on. The only element of specialization is that members are chosen in the light of their knowledge of the subject-matter of a particular bill: thus, former teachers and members of education authorities may be appointed to standing committees dealing with education bills.

The consequences of non-specialization and fluctuating composition are twofold. Members do not gather the sort of informed authority that a long-serving member of a specialist committee will have, and cannot challenge the government in the same way. Nor can the committees develop a corporate identity that can compete with the overriding loyalty of party.

What these arrangements do is to reinforce, almost insensibly, the claims of party allegiance. Most of the debates take place in a chamber that is, at best, half-full: when the division bell rings, members appear as if by magic, asking 'which is our lobby?' It is not that members vote against their consciences: on most issues their consciences have nothing to say. It is only on the great issues of the day—a Suez affair, for example—that members are likely to feel the tug of conscience. Thus, what has been called the Prussian discipline of the two great parliamentary parties owes as much to the mundane arrangements of the House as to the power of the whips.

For some fifteen years after the end of the Second World War, the House went on its way complacently, ignorant of the often radically different procedures of other legislatures. A proposal in 1959 to set up a select committee on the colonies was denounced as a radical constitutional innovation which would detract from the sovereignty of the full House. Not until the 1960s did discussion switch from the (alleged) power of the party machines to the institutional arrangements of the House. Bernard Crick's seminal *Reform of Parliament* (1964) saw in the House's lack of information its major weakness. The elections of 1964 and 1966 brought into the House a new generation of backbenchers hungry to play a more active role in its work. The Wilson government responded with the establishment of a few select committees with powers to inquire into the workings of particular activities of government, such as science and technology. This experiment, though tentative, set the pattern for more extensive change. The *Heath government continued on similar lines. Margaret *Thatcher's arrival in office saw the setting up of the modern select committee system, with committees which broadly paralleled the various government departments. The task of these committees is not to legislate but to *inquire*, by questioning ministers and civil servants about the reasons for particular decisions. This takes place in a setting which discourages, if it does not wholly prevent, the easy evasions of question time.

The departmental select committees have now become part of the accepted practice of the House. Their scope remains limited for they have no power to consider particular bills, which are still referred to the standing committees. On the other hand, their reports present information with a detail and on a scale not hitherto normally available.

These procedural changes have been accompanied by a loosening of party ties in floor votes. Backbenchers are now more willing to cast occasional votes against their party. This assertion of greater freedom began in the 1966 Parliament and seems to have continued. Yet the change must not be exaggerated; party loyalty remains overwhelmingly the chief determinant, or at least the chief correlate, of voting. Parliamentary reform and the greater independence of backbenchers have dented, but not greatly impaired, the supremacy of party in the House of Commons. HB

Parnell, Charles Stewart (1846–91). The most effective and charismatic, if enigmatic, Irish constitutional nationalist leader. Born in Co. Wicklow into an Anglo-Irish protestant family, Parnell inherited the Avondale estate, and became MP for Meath in 1875. He quickly associated with the obstructionist wing of the Home Government Association. He led the 'New Departure' of 1878–9, bringing together ex-Fenians, Irish-American nationalists, and advocates of land reform. He became president of the *Irish Land League in

1879, and forced *Gladstone to grant major changes in the 1881 Land Act. To preserve control of an increasingly radical movement, Parnell initially resisted the Act's implementation and was imprisoned. In the *'Kilmainham treaty', 1882, he agreed to an amended Land Act and to keep to parliamentary opposition only. For the next three years, Parnell concentrated on developing a disciplined parliamentary party, enabling advantage to be taken of the favourable electoral circumstances in 1885–6. Skilful manœuvring of support between Conservatives and Liberals culminated in Gladstone's Home Rule Bill 1886, the summit of Parnell's career. Following the bill's defeat, his effectiveness and flexibility were compromised by the Liberal alliance and his remoteness from Ireland. Accused of association with Fenian violence in *The Times* in 1887, he was proved innocent in February 1889, only to be ruined by being cited as co-respondent in O'Shea's divorce in 1889/90. Deserted by an unholy alliance of the nonconformist Liberal conscience with the catholic hierarchy, Parnell was forced to choose between resignation or alliance with the Liberals. After his party split, he led unsuccessful polemical campaigns in by-elections in early 1891. Parnell wed Katharine O'Shea in June 1891, but died that autumn, probably from complications of chronic kidney disease. The melodramatic circumstances of his fall encouraged a romantic myth which obscured his essential conservatism and the limitations of his achievement. His long-term aim to reconcile declining landlordism with advancing nationalism failed totally. MAH

Parr, William, 1st marquis of Northampton (1513–71). Parr was the son of Sir Thomas Parr of Kendal and the younger brother of *Catherine Parr, Henry VIII's last wife. He took part in suppressing the *Pilgrimage of Grace in 1536 and was created Baron Parr of Kendal in 1539. The following year he became captain of the gentlemen pensioners and in April 1543 was appointed warden of the Scottish marches and given the Garter. In July 1543 his sister became queen and her relatives began to prosper. Parr's uncle was made Baron Parr of Horton and the same day he was advanced to the earldom of Essex. He fought in the French campaigns of 1544 and at the accession of Edward VI was made marquis of Northampton. He was influential during Edward's reign as a leading protestant, though his campaign against the Norfolk rebels in 1549 finished in humiliating defeat. In 1550 he was appointed lord chamberlain. On the death of Edward, Northampton backed Lady Jane *Grey and when her cause collapsed was sent to the Tower for execution. Surprisingly he was pardoned, though he lost his titles and most of his estates. But his fortunes rose again when Mary died. Elizabeth restored him to his titles and gave him back the Garter. He remained in favour for the rest of his life and the queen paid for his funeral at St Mary's, Warwick. Though neither a prominent statesman nor a brilliant general, Northampton was cultivated and believed to be honest. JAC

Parry, Sir Hubert (1848–1918). Together with Charles *Stanford, whose music he detested, Parry inspired what is called the 'English musical renaissance' of the later 19th cent. This was despite an unpromising educational background—philistine *Eton—and a talent which was not in the very highest class. That talent none the less produced some fine second-rank works, of which his Fourth Symphony, Piano Quartet, and shorter choral settings are perhaps the best. He is best known for the ripping tune he wrote for *Blake's 'Jerusalem', which was first performed at a patriotic concert in 1916, much to his unease, for he was not a tub-thumper. Later he was delighted when Millicent Fawcett asked if it could be adopted as the suffragist anthem. His radicalism did not, however, prevent his rising to the top of the British musical establishment, from which position he was able to help *Elgar, who *was* a tub-thumper, and also, of course, the greater composer of the two. BJP

Parsons, Sir Charles (1854–1931). Engineer. A son of the 3rd earl of Rosse [I], Parsons grew up at Birr castle in Ireland before going to Trinity College, Dublin, and St John's College, Cambridge. His father was a distinguished chemist and astronomer and Parsons's education was scientific. After Cambridge, he took an apprenticeship at the Elswick works in Newcastle of Sir William *Armstrong, of whom he spoke later with great admiration. He began working on electricity supply and by 1884 had constructed a turbo-dynamo. In 1889 he founded Parsons of Heaton on the Tyne and a power station at Newcastle was operating by turbo-generation by 1890. Parsons then applied turbines to ships, building the *Turbinia*, by far the fastest vessel afloat, and preserved in the Newcastle Discovery museum. Turbines were adopted for both warships and passenger liners, helping *Mauretania* (1906) to hold the blue riband of the Atlantic for many years. Parsons was given a knighthood in 1911 and the Order of Merit in 1927. He has been called the most original engineer in Britain after James *Watt. A shy, quiet man, his relaxation was fishing. JAC

Parsons, Robert (1546–1610). Jesuit missionary. Born in Somerset to protestant parents, he resigned his Balliol fellowship and was received into the Roman church at Louvain, before offering himself to the Society of Jesus (1575). A workaholic with a powerful personality, he was sent to England with *Campion in 1579, enjoined to stay apolitical, but his sole aim soon became its return, by persuasion or force, to Rome. For nearly 20 years he was one of the most ardent promoters of the Spanish invasion, his diplomatic and language skills enabling him to deal easily with kings and popes. After failure of the *Armada, he concentrated on his order's internal affairs, but, as a controversialist (one of the best writers of his day), made as many enemies amongst catholics as protestants because of his traitorous activities, especially after publication of his *Conference about the Next Succession* (1594), which supported the Infanta Isabella as the most suitable for the English throne. His missionary zeal combined with political intrigue have contributed much to the popular image of Jesuitry. ASH

partition treaties, 1698, 1700. The imminent death of Carlos II of Spain, without children, so soon after the end of the *Nine Years War persuaded European powers to try to settle the Spanish Succession without bloodshed. By the first treaty, signed in October 1698 by Louis XIV and William III, the Spanish inheritance was to go to Joseph Ferdinand, electoral prince of Bavaria, with compensation to the dauphin of Naples and Sicily and to the Archduke Charles of Milan and Luxembourg. The prince of Bavaria died within a few weeks. By a second treaty in 1700, the Archduke Charles was to take the lion's share, with France receiving Naples, Sicily, and Milan, to be exchanged for Lorraine. But when Carlos II died in October 1700, leaving by will Philip of Anjou, Louis's grandson, as sole heir, Louis abandoned his treaty obligations and accepted. The War of the *Spanish Succession followed. JAC

party system. Though parties have existed in Parliament since the later 17th cent., many MPs prided themselves on their independence, and party ties were loose and often personal. There was little supporting organization in the country, save for *ad hoc* committees at election time, and little of the paraphernalia of discipline and propaganda which characterizes modern parties. In the later 18th cent., as public opinion became more vocal, there were indications that parties were improving their organization and encouraging coordinated effort, particularly for electoral purposes, but the influence of individual patrons remained great. Mass parties were a late 19th-cent. development, reflecting the growth of the electorate, and the need for an army of enthusiastic helpers in the larger constituencies. The National Liberal Federation, founded in 1877, was a body separate from the traditional and informal Liberal party organization within the House of Commons. The two were eventually grafted together, and a similar process occurred on the Conservative side. In contrast, the Labour Party was founded as a body outside Parliament, whose task was to elect Labour members to the House of Commons.

The general election of 1992 was contested by more than 90 parties, but few had much chance, under the existing electoral system, of returning an MP. It is difficult to believe that the Jolly Small Brewers Party (polled 343 at Worcester) or the Forward to Mars Party (91 at Huntingdon) threatened the supremacy of the main parties. The tiny parties, however valuable they may be in representing opinion, do not really form part of the party system.

That system, as it has developed, fulfils four important functions in a democratic state. First, the parties raise finance and mobilize a massive voluntary organizational effort, especially when their role in local government is taken into account. Running the party machine, particularly if the party is in power in a large city, demands much time and trouble, but leaves the parties with some independence from the state. Secondly, the parties act as a valuable conduit for public opinion, with procedures for formulating party policy, conferences for giving their approval, and manifestos on which the party will fight a general election. Thirdly, the parties have their own mechanisms for choosing local and parliamentary candidates and some method of electing their party leader, who becomes prime minister if their party wins a majority of seats. They offer a valuable training in democratic politics and many cabinet ministers have begun their careers as local chairmen, treasurers, and councillors. Lastly, but most important, the system offers alternatives to the voters and provides a safety valve or stabilizing mechanism against frustration and disappointment. We should therefore carefully distinguish democratic parties from the political parties found in many authoritarian forms of government, which are merely an extension of state power. The party system in a democratic society is a means both of contributing to government and of containing it. HB; JAC

Passaro, Cape, battle of. See CAPE PASSARO, BATTLE OF.

Passchendaele, battle of, 1917. The British army tried to advance from the Ypres salient in southern Belgium towards the Belgian ports of Ostend and Zeebrugge for several reasons. *Haig believed that he could defeat the German army and win the war in 1917. The navy supported him because they wanted to drive the Germans away from the Channel ports where they menaced Britain's communications with the continent. *Lloyd George did not think that the Germans could finally be defeated until 1918, but allowed Haig to continue because he feared that, if the British were not seen to be actively fighting, the French might go the way of tsarist Russia and collapse into revolution. The battle began on 31 July 1917, but fierce German resistance, heavy rain, and the destruction of the drainage system of the Flanders plain by the artillery meant that the advance literally bogged down in the mud. Haig continued the operation until mid-November, at a cost of some 260,000 British casualties, but failed to reach the coast. DF

Paston letters. Private correspondence (15th–17th cents.) of a Norfolk family, that of the 15th cent. in particular providing significant insights into the social history of the pre-Reformation period. Not only a family saga (Margery's clandestine marriage to their estate manager in 1469 caused consternation), business affairs, property matters, and associated litigation trace the progress of 'new' gentry, despite some archival fragmentation. Although property was confined mainly to East Anglia, their interests were far from parochial, so accounts of national events leaven those of regional politics and matrimonial negotiations, all reflecting social attitudes, culture, and the state of the English language. ASH

Patay, battle of, 1429. After Joan of Arc had relieved Orléans, the English fell back to bridgeheads on the Loire at Meung, Jargeau, and Beaugency. The first two were soon lost, and in attempting to relieve the third, the troops of Lords Talbot (*Shrewsbury) and Scales were overwhelmed on 18 June by the French, in whose company was Joan. Talbot was captured and imprisoned until 1433. Sir John Fastolf, in command of the rear, escaped but was subsequently charged with having acted dishonourably. The battle put paid to English expansionist ambitions and facilitated Charles VII's advance to Rheims for his coronation. AC

Paterson, William (1658–1719). Founder of the *Bank of England. Paterson was born in Dumfries but brought up in

England. He made a rapid fortune in trade in America and the Low Countries. A supporter of the Glorious Revolution, he was engaged during the *Nine Years War in government finance and pressed upon the government the establishment of a national bank to help finance the war. In 1694 when the bank was founded, Paterson became a director. He withdrew the following year and became involved in schemes to improve London's water supply. He was one of the leading protagonists of the *Darien venture and worked for the Company of Scotland raising investment. He was lucky to survive the first expedition in 1698, in which his wife and only son perished, but continued to be consulted by the government, urging a union with Scotland. When negotiations began, Paterson advised on the financial and economic aspects of the treaty. A prominent example of the *commercial revolution of the period, Paterson was one of the first to advocate the systematic study of economics.
JAC

Patrick, St (*c*.389–*c*.461). Patron saint of Ireland. Born in Britain, in his youth he was seized by raiders and taken to Ireland. In slavery for six years, he was sustained by prayer and a deepening faith. Told in a dream of his impending return home, he made his way to the coast and joined a merchant ship, facing many dangers before rejoining his family. In clerical training, he seems to have spent some years in France at the monastery of Lerins and at Auxerre, where he was probably consecrated by St *Germanus before embarking on his evangelistic work in Ireland. Despite hostile druids, he apparently impressed the high king Laoghaire and was favoured by many chieftains. Often at risk, he was fearlessly determined to destroy paganism. Through his tireless efforts, countless numbers were baptized and confirmed, many clergy ordained, and his see established at *Armagh, whence he began to organize the emerging church on Roman diocesan lines. In popular legend, the saint who expelled snakes from Ireland was a miracle-worker. Patrick's own 'Confession', and letter to Coroticus, reveal a deeply caring man, not well educated, but with a complete trust in God which enabled him to make so significant a contribution to the conversion of Ireland.
AM

patriot king. The concept of a patriot king was largely an opposition device of the early Hanoverian period. It hinted that the first two Georges were more interested in Hanover than in Britain and deplored the exclusive confidence they placed in the Whigs. The concept was most fully worked out in *Bolingbroke's treatise *The Idea of a Patriot King*, written in 1738 for *Frederick, prince of Wales, who was then heading the opposition to *Walpole. The 'essential character' of a patriot king was 'to espouse no party but to govern like the common father of his people'. When the young George III in 1760 gloried in the name of Britain and declared war on parties, the patriot programme seemed to be fulfilled, though harmony did not noticeably follow. There is no evidence that George III read Bolingbroke and the ideas were commonplace in court circles. But they helped to persuade Horace *Walpole and *Burke that George had been brought up on prerogative notions and contributed to the interpretation of his reign as a reassertion of royal authority.
JAC

patriots. The name was appropriated by the opponents to *Walpole since it implied that the interests of the nation were neglected by a supine and corrupt government. William *Pitt, in particular, beat the patriotic drum when he inveighed against Britain's subservience to Hanover, a 'despicable electorate'. Ministers, in reply, were scornful of patriotic rhetoric: 'it is but refusing to gratify an unreasonable or insolent demand,' declared Walpole, 'and up starts a patriot.' The phrase was so overworked that it became pejorative, indicating factious and self-seeking opposition—hence Johnson's famous (and much misunderstood) remark in 1775, 'Patriotism is the last refuge of a scoundrel.' JAC

patronage, artistic. Patronage goes beyond the act of purchasing art. Traditionally a patron offered the means of support to the artist, a home, a pension or place, as well as specific payments. The monarchy, church, and aristocracy were the great patrons of medieval architecture, art, and music: Edward the Confessor built Westminster abbey, Henry III rebuilt it, and Henry VII added the east chapel; Henry VI endowed Eton College, Christ's College and King's College, Cambridge. Many of the Oxford and Cambridge colleges were founded by clerics: Peterhouse, Cambridge, by Hugh de Balsham, bishop of Ely (1284), New College, Oxford, by *William of Wykeham, bishop of Winchester (1379), Corpus Christi College, Oxford, by Richard *Foxe, bishop of Winchester (1517), Christ Church, Oxford, by Cardinal *Wolsey (1525). Among the many aristocratic patrons were Humphrey, duke of *Gloucester (d. 1447), and John *Tiptoft, earl of Worcester (d. 1470), whose gifts of books formed the basis for the Bodleian Library, Oxford.

The tradition of religious patronage declined after the Reformation, as much of the wealth of the church was alienated and clerics ceased to dominate political life as *Morton and Wolsey had done. Elizabeth I encouraged the cult of majesty, patronizing artists like *Hilliard and Hans Eworth to convey her image of royal splendour. Inigo *Jones was involved in architecture, decoration, and the design of *masques for the courts of James I and Charles I, and the first poet laureate was Ben *Jonson in James I's reign. Thomas, earl of *Arundel, patron to several painters including Rubens, introduced *Van Dyck to Charles I, the last great royal patron of arts. The Civil War put many artists out of work or into exile, yet patronage continued. Peter *Lely prospered under Charles I and II, as well as under *Cromwell, who, along with other parliamentarians, sat for portraits by Robert Walker. Cromwell also loved music and retained a small group of domestic musicians. The Restoration brought back the Stuarts but not intensive royal patronage. Charles II recognized his duty to the arts but salaries or pensions were often erratically paid. He was, though, an enthusiastic patron of the theatre and horse-racing, while many of the noblemen who followed him out of exile both practised and patronized literature.

The beginnings of the 18th cent. saw increasing political patronage of the arts. The *Kit Kat Club, a group of influential Whigs, whose members included the writers *Congreve and *Addison, artists *Vanbrugh and *Kneller, and politicians *Walpole and *Newcastle, extended patronage over all aspects of art and music. Among traditional patrons, returning grand tourists commissioned or rebuilt great houses, and filled them with decoration, paintings, sculpture, silverware, and furniture. Chandos was patron to *Handel and the duke of Richmond patron to Canaletto, who spent nine years in England. Lord *Burlington befriended William *Kent, financed his publications, and collaborated on several of his Palladian designs. George I and George II enjoyed music and patronized Handel and the opera, and employed the sculptors *Rysbrack and *Roubiliac.

Increasing prosperity meant a role in patronage for the general public. The *Three Choirs Festival of Worcester, Gloucester, and Hereford was founded in 1713; books were published by subscription; prints and engravings and later caricatures from artists like *Hogarth and *Rowlandson sold in large numbers. New money from industry went into the arts: *Wedgwood the potter was patron of George *Stubbs and Joseph *Wright of Derby. In the 19th cent. the *Pre-Raphaelites found support among the industrialists of the midlands and north of England, and throughout the century wealthy art lovers like Angerstein, Tate, and Wallace made generous gifts to public galleries. At a lower level, the newly formed borough and county councils filled their foyers with sculptures and their corridors with portraits of chairmen, mayors, and aldermen.

Patronage of art is now institutionalized. Few individuals in a century of heavy taxation have the wealth to support the arts but royalty still sits for portraits, even if the commissioning organization pays the artist. New town corporations place lonely sculptures on wind-swept grassy banks. But in the main it is orchestras or bodies like the BBC who commission new music, and universities which find funds for painters or poets in residence. Funding comes from a diversity of sources, from the Arts Council to the National Lottery. An artist is unlikely to have a home provided by a patron. He will be paid but not by a long-term stipend. He may receive the freedom of a city but not a government office. He retains his independence, which Dr *Johnson valued more than a patron, 'who supports with insolence and is paid with flattery'. JC

Paulinus, St (d. 644). First bishop of the Northumbrians. A Roman monk, tall, dark, thin-faced with an aquiline nose, according to *Bede one of *Mellitus' party sent in 601 by Pope Gregory I to help *Augustine in Kent. He was consecrated by *Justus, apparently on 21 July 625, to accompany the Princess *Æthelburg to Northumbria to marry *Edwin, but the dating is controversial. Paulinus may have met Edwin previously, at the court of *Raedwald of East Anglia, and baptized him at York, his episcopal seat, in 627. He preached at Yeavering, Catterick, Lincoln (where he consecrated *Honorius to succeed Archbishop Justus), and elsewhere, and introduced the building of churches in stone. His duties may have included reading the works of Gregory to Edwin. After Edwin's death (633) at *Heathfield Chase, Paulinus fled to Kent and took up the see of *Rochester, where he was buried in the church of St Andrew. AER

Pax Romana was the peace and consequent potential development brought by inclusion in the Roman empire. The *lex Iulia de Vi Publica* outlawing the carrying of weapons except when hunting or travelling was probably enforced in Britain. This did not abolish brigandage or invasion, but helped create stability. ASEC

Peacock, Thomas Love (1785–1866). Peacock had modest private means but earned his living as an official in the East India Company. He wrote essays, poetry, plays, and pamphlets, but is best known for his novels, *Headlong Hall* (1816), *Melincourt* (1817), *Nightmare Abbey* (1818), *Crotchet Castle* (1831), and *Gryll Grange* (1860–1). Peacock was a friend of *Shelley in his youth and radical in politics, but he grew increasingly independent, and his satirical victims included ardent Romantics as well as 'march of mind' men like Henry *Brougham. The novels are quirky and an acquired taste, with little plot and much conversation, but offer vignettes of Peacock's contemporaries—*Repton (Milestone in *Headlong Hall*), *Malthus (Fax in *Melincourt*), *Coleridge (Flosky in *Nightmare Abbey*), Shelley (Foster in *Headlong Hall*). JAC

Peada (d. 656), king of the *Middle Angles (*c.*653–6), was a son of King *Penda of Mercia, who appointed him king. Shortly afterwards Peada married Alhflaed, daughter of *Oswui of Northumbria, and as a condition of marriage agreed to become a Christian and to allow evangelization by a mission from *Lindisfarne. After Oswui defeated Penda at the battle of *Winwaed in 655, he appointed Peada king of the southern Mercians, keeping control of the northern Mercians himself, but, according to *Bede, Peada was murdered the following Easter through the treachery of Alhflaed. BAEY

Pearse, Patrick (1879–1916). Pearse was the son of an English-born stonemason, a non-practising lawyer, dramatist, and headmaster of St Enda's School (Dublin), which he ran on Gaelic Revivalist lines. A leading member of the *Gaelic League, he was a supporter of *Home Rule up to 1912: the Ulster crisis caused him to advocate a militant nationalism and to join the *Irish Republican Brotherhood. He became a dominant voice in the Irish Volunteers and a member of the IRB military council which planned the *Easter Rising. His philosophy of blood-sacrifice appeared to anticipate and justify the course of events during and after the rising. Pearse read the declaration of the Provisional Irish Republic outside the General Post Office on 24 April 1916; gave orders for surrender five days later; and was executed on 3 May. The traditional view of him as a heroic voice of Irish nationalism has recently been questioned, but while impractical and unstable, he was, nevertheless, inspirational. MAH

peasantry. Although widely used, in a British context the term 'peasant' has no obvious contemporary definition which fits the way it is employed today. Medievalists have questioned whether Britain ever had a social group to which the word peasant was applicable, and would certainly question the continued existence of such a group beyond the Middle Ages. Even the famous *'Peasants' Revolt' of 1381 was referred to by the chronicler as a rustic rather than a peasant tragedy. In literary sources the term was occasionally used of labourers, implying someone of low birth and inferior standing, rather than a small owner and/or occupier in the countryside. This link with rural labour can be found through the 18th and into the 19th cents. The term also acquired romantic overtones, with the peasantry depicted as the humble members of a fast-disappearing rural society, a Hardy-esque chorus.

By the later 19th cent. historians writing of England from a European perspective often saw peasants as small freeholders, copyholders, and even farmers. Modern anthropological definitions of peasant societies allow the term to be employed for what has been called 'analytical simplicity', largely because it is widely used (as in the French term *paysan*) to mean simply a countryman. As a result, it has been employed as a useful shorthand term without specific definition. Most historians use the term to mean small landowners and/or small farmers, but it can also be used loosely to include the cottager, the commoner, and the squatter; in other words, of the social group which depended on common rights (at least prior to *enclosure) and stitched together an income from farming, labouring, and a range of other activities. As such, 'peasant' refers to some of the least identifiable rural dwellers, simply because they do not appear in the written record.

The term has also become a useful catch-all for the social group largely displaced through the economic conditions prevailing in the post-Restoration period, or at enclosure. Some have argued that, as a result, the term is inappropriate after 1750 because by then England had no peasantry in the continental sense of the word. However, it is accepted that peasants survived in Ireland and in thinly populated parts of Wales and Scotland, and even in some of the pastoral upland counties of northern and western England. Recent scholarship asserting a stronger survival of 'peasant-type' rural dwellers than has often been accepted suggests the term still has a currency. JVB

Peasants' Revolt. This rebellion in 1381 was the first large-scale popular uprising in England. It began in Essex, in the village of Fobbing. Kent soon followed, and the rebels moved rapidly to London. There were also significant risings in East Anglia, Bury St Edmunds, and St Albans. The rapidly changing economy, in the aftermath of the *Black Death, provides one explanation for the rising; the inadequacy of the government, the church, and the failure of the war with France another. The spark to the revolt was provided by the third *poll tax, which was to be levied uniformly at 1 shilling a head, and so bore particularly hard on the poor. Commissions to investigate the low level of returns provoked the Essex uprising. The rebellion took a dramatic and strongly political turn in London, where the rebels took and executed the archbishop of Canterbury, the treasurer, and others. Radical demands were made by Wat *Tyler, one of the peasant leaders, at Smithfield: serfdom was to be abolished; there was to be no law save the law of Winchester (an obscure request); outlawry was to be abandoned; lordship was to be divided between all men. There should be only one bishop, and one prelate; the wealth of the church should be distributed among the people. Wat Tyler was killed at this meeting. Resistance elsewhere in the country was short-lived. Perhaps the one lasting achievement of the revolt was that very few poll taxes were levied again in England for some 600 years. MCP

Peckham, John (*c.*1220–92). Archbishop of Canterbury. Born in Sussex and educated at Oxford, Peckham became a Franciscan. After teaching in Paris (*c.*1250) as a distinguished Augustinian scholar, like *Kilwardby often in conflict with Aquinas, he returned to Oxford (*c.*1270), and became provincial minister of the English Franciscans (*c.*1275). After lecturing in Rome (1277–9), he reluctantly accepted papal nomination to Canterbury (1279). Scholarly, austere, living in humility, a friar at heart, and yet outspoken and combative, he had a high idea of archiepiscopal authority, vigorously exerting it through penetrating provincial visitations and, with 'garrulous frankness', resisting Edward I's encroachment on ecclesiastical authority. At his Reading council (1279), he excommunicated all pluralists and those impeding church courts, which Edward answered by compelling him to withdraw and by limiting church acquisition of lay property by the statute *De religiosis*. WMM

Pecock, Reginald (*c.*1395–*c.*1460). Bishop of Chichester (1450–9). A Welshman, educated at Oriel College, Oxford, Pecock was fellow there (1414–24) and under Humphrey, duke of *Gloucester's patronage became master of Whittington College, London (1431–44), bishop of St Asaph (1444), of Chichester (1450), and a privy counsellor (1454–7). A rationalist himself, he tried to win over *lollards by vigorous argument—'by cleere witt [to] drawe men into consente of trewe faith'—rather than by burning, which involved him in controversy with conservatives. A sermon at St Paul's Cross (1447), defending non-preaching bishops, offended reformers. His works include *Repressor of Over Much Blaming of the Clergy* (1455), the first theological treatise in English since 1066, his *Book of Faith* (1456) promoting the authority of reason, and *The Provoker* questioning the authorship of the Apostles' Creed. As a Lancastrian and arraigned for heresy (1457), he was expelled from the Privy Council and forced to resign his see (1459) after public recantation. He was confined in Thorney abbey (Cambs.), where he died. WMM

peculiar people. Evangelical sect, also known as 'Plumstead peculiars' or 'Banyardites', founded in Rochford by the ex-Wesleyan James Banyard (1800–63), in 1838, and confined to south-east Essex and nearby parts of London and Kent. After Banyard's deposition (1855), their ablest leader was a Southend credit-draper, William Heddle (1846–1948). Distinctive in name, appearance, and habits, their men clean-shaven and their women black-bonneted, they developed an order of bishops, elders, and helps, serving circuits or dioceses. Taking the Bible as their rule, their emphases on divine healing, the imminence of the Second Coming, and pacifism led to well-publicized court cases, since they refused conventional medicine and became conscientious objectors in 1916. Renamed the Union of Evangelical Churches, they associated themselves with the Fellowship of Independent Evangelical Churches in 1956. CB

Peel, Sir Robert (1788–1850). Prime minister. Peel was born into a family which had recently become wealthy and distinguished through cotton manufacture. His father became a baronet in 1800, and Peel was destined for a political career without direct involvement in industry. He was educated at Harrow and Oxford, where his contemporaries mainly came from established governing groups. Like his father, a traditional church and king Tory, Peel was a loyal supporter of *Pitt's wartime government. When he was 21, his father bought him a parliamentary seat for the Irish borough of Cashel. He was widely seen as an able young man and in June 1809 became under-secretary for war and colonies, gaining experience in the routine of administration. He also quickly earned a reputation as a fine parliamentary orator. In 1812 he became chief secretary for Ireland, described as 'one of the most difficult and laborious offices under the government'. During his six years there he developed administrative skills and acquired a defensive armour of apparent aloofness. He had a strong physique but by 1818 overwork had impaired his health and he resigned. But he retained close links with ministers and was responsible for piloting through the return to cash payments in 1819. In 1822 Peel became home secretary in *Liverpool's government. He introduced several important measures, including far-reaching reform of the criminal law and the creation of the Metropolitan Police, exhibiting both administrative competence and political dexterity. He also distinguished himself as a leading opponent of *catholic emancipation, increasing his status with many Tories in and out of Parliament. He left office in 1827, refusing to serve under *Canning, who supported catholic emancipation, but returned after Canning's early death. When *Wellington felt obliged to concede emancipation in 1829, Peel resigned but then yielded to Wellington's pleas to return to office and skilfully piloted emancipation through the Commons. This earned him the enmity of many of his old admirers and raised doubts as to his trustworthiness. After the Tory government fell in 1830, Peel increasingly emerged as leader of the opposition to the new Whig ministry. He opposed the *Great Reform Act, but tried to keep within bounds the enmity of right-wing Tories towards the Whigs.

Peel began to establish a national reputation for moderation, exemplified by his *Tamworth manifesto, in which he accepted the Reform Act and committed his Conservative Party to a policy of cautious reform, while pledging to conserve all vital national interests. This was a successful ploy, although its vagueness held the seeds of future trouble since it was easy to disagree as to what vital national interests were. The manifesto was issued for the general election after William IV dismissed his Whig ministers late in 1834. Peel became prime minister with a minority of seats. In the following election his party gained about 100 seats, but not a majority. The Whigs forced Peel's resignation and returned to office, but the following years saw them weaken both in Parliament and in the country. The 1837 election brought further Conservative gains. Peel's moderation and obvious ability attracted many supporters, though this involved a dangerously broad range of political opinion, from reactionary Tories to moderate reformers. Deepening economic and political troubles and failures in budgetary policy brought the Whigs in 1841 to propose a more radical financial policy which involved reductions in tariffs, including the *Corn Laws which protected agriculture. Peel then defeated ministers on a no-confidence motion, took office, and dissolved. In the ensuing election Peel won decisively. He had projected an image of strength and responsibility, while the Whigs had seemed to many voters both financially inept and culpably weak in face of *chartist agitation. Although the country was suffering grave social and economic troubles, he chose to use the winter of 1841–2 to mature plans for recovery and in the 1842 budget scored a major success. He slashed tariffs seen as impediments to commerce and revised the Corn Laws downwards. Unlike the Whigs, he was strong enough to balance this loss of revenue by enacting direct taxation on incomes. Ensuing years saw further moves towards free trade, including a second comprehensive tariff-cutting budget in 1845, and growing restiveness in some Conservative quarters, as Peel's commitment to the preservation of the Corn Laws became doubtful. To him, agricultural protection was now no more than a commercial expedient, but to many Conservatives this bulwark of the landed interest was a vital national concern. The *Anti-Corn Law League's agitation increased right-wing anxiety. From 1842 onwards, Peel's Conservative critics had warned that free trade policies would fail, but economic recovery by 1845 seemed to confound them. By then Peel was at heart a free trader, although he knew that to attack the Corn Laws was politically perilous. In 1845 the potato crop failed, bringing catastrophe to Ireland. Peel determined to take the opportunity to repeal the Corn Laws. He was unable to persuade his cabinet to back him, and resigned, but when the Whigs failed to form a ministry late in 1845, he returned to office. He had lost some right-wing ministers and alienated many backbenchers and supporters outside Parliament. He introduced his repeal measures cleverly, offering concessions to the landed interest in addition, but this device failed to preserve his position when the aristocratic Lord George *Bentinck and the political adventurer Benjamin *Disraeli succeeded in organizing protectionist opposition. With his own following among the Conservatives and support from Whigs and radicals, Peel succeeded in repealing the Corn Laws in 1846. At the same time, disaffected Conservatives were bitter enough to join the opposition in defeating an Irish Coercion Bill, in order to bring Peel down. He resigned immediately after this defeat and never held office again. For the remainder of his life he possessed great influence, since the political scene was fragmented after the Conservative rift, and enjoyed great prestige in the country, as the numerous memorials erected after his death in 1850 demonstrate. His status owed much to the widespread belief that as a minister he had preferred the public good to his own retention of power. The conviction that under Peel a legislature dominated by the landed interest had sacrificed the Corn Laws to the need to feed the people played a part in ensuring that subsequent change in 19th-cent. Britain was evolutionary rather than revolutionary. NMcC

Gash, N., *Mr. Secretary Peel* (1961); id., *Sir Robert Peel* (1971).

peel towers were temporary refuges, often attached to manor houses, farms, or churches, and commonly built in the 15th and 16th cents. They were normally two storeys, the lower one for cattle, with slit windows, if any, in thick stone walls, and a narrow stair or ladder leading to the upper storey. Of little use against regular forces, they offered some protection against border raiders and were mainly to be found either side of the Anglo-Scottish border. There are good examples at Corbridge and Elsdon in Northumberland. On the Welsh border, strong church towers, like those at Ewyas Harold and Rowlstone, probably served a similar purpose. JAC

Peep o' Day Boys was the name adopted by Ulster presbyterians in the 1780s and 1790s to confront the catholic *Defenders. On 1 September 1795 they routed their adversaries in a pitched battle at the Diamond, near Armagh, killing many of them. They then joined in the foundation of the *Orange order. JAC

peerage. The formal body of aristocracy, distinguished by titles and by the right to sit in the House of Lords. Though the rank of earl preceded the Conquest, it was hardly necessary to define the peerage closely until the House of Lords developed as a regular element in Parliament in the 13th cent. To the ranks of baron and earl were added duke (1337), marquis (1385), and viscount (1440). The number of peers remained small until the end of Elizabeth's reign, when there were just over fifty English peers, but the impecuniosity of the early Stuarts led them to sell titles and by 1641 there were more than 130 peers. Apart from attendance in Parliament, their main privileges were access to the monarch and the right to trial by the House of Lords. By the Act of *Union of 1707 the Scottish peerage was closed, sixteen representative peers elected to the House of Lords at Westminster, and a new peerage of Great Britain instituted. After 1801, the Irish peerage was severely limited, 28 representative peers elected, and a new peerage of the United Kingdom established. Over the next two centuries, the number of peers increased greatly as bankers, industrialists, scientists, and men of letters were ennobled to augment the landed aristocracy. The greatest change however was the introduction of life peerages from 1958. By 1993 there were more than 1,000 peers, 758 of them hereditary and 382 life peers. Those bishops who sit in the Lords do so, not as peers, but as lords of Parliament. JAC

Peerage Bill. This bill, introduced into the Lords in March 1719 by the *Sunderland/*Stanhope ministry and dropped in April due to the uncertain position of the Commons, had three aims: to protect the chief ministers against impeachment should the prince of Wales, who opposed them, succeed to the throne; to settle the unsatisfactory Scottish representation in the Lords; and to maintain the existing peerage's social position, by limiting creations. The bill laid down that (excluding royal princes) the king could create only six more peerages, then further peers only on the extinction of titles; the 16 Scottish elected peers were to be replaced by 25 hereditary ones. The bill was reintroduced in December 1719, easily passed the Lords, but was defeated in the Commons largely due to the opposition of Robert *Walpole. CJ

peine forte et dure. After the Lateran Council of the church in 1215 forbade the clergy to take part in ordeals, the king's justices had no means of trying the guilt or innocence of suspected criminals. After a number of experiments they developed the trial *jury of twelve men to decide. Since this jury was an innovation and not part of the Englishman's customary rights, the accused was always asked if he was willing to be tried by jury—to 'put himself upon the county'—and if he refused, jury trial would not be proceeded with. Under the statute of *Westminster I (1275), Parliament provided that anyone who refused to accept jury trial should be put into a 'prison forte et dure' until he agreed to it. By some error this section came to be interpreted as '*peine* forte et dure', which in turn came to be literally interpreted as the placing of weights upon the hapless prisoner, increasing to a stage where he either consented to jury trial or perished. In 1772 the peine forte et dure was abolished. MM

Pelagius. Early 5th-cent. Christian theologian of British or Irish extraction. Pelagius travelled to Rome as a monk *c.* AD 400 and was deeply disappointed by the lax moral standards there. He preached that strenuous efforts were needed to avoid sin and attain individual salvation. The theologian *Augustine was appalled by this insistence on the effectiveness of free will, and Jerome called Pelagius 'a fat hound weighed down by Scotch porridge'. Pelagius twice suffered excommunication, and where and when he died is unknown. After his death the Gallic monks remained sympathetic to Pelagius' views, but the new sect of Pelagianism was denounced by the Roman ecclesiastical authorities as a heresy. St *Germanus was sent to Britain in 429 to counter its influence in the British church. ES

Pelham, Henry (*c.*1696–1754). Prime minister. Pelham was 1st lord of the Treasury for over ten years (1743–54) and highly regarded by his contemporaries. But time has faded his reputation between the vividly coloured careers of *Walpole and *Pitt the Elder. Pelham's career began under the wing of his elder brother, the duke of *Newcastle, who brought him into Parliament (MP for Seaford 1717–22 and Sussex 1722–54). The brothers quickly realized that Walpole was becoming the man to support. Pelham became secretary at war in 1724 and paymaster-general in 1730, though his status, certainly in the 1730s, was higher than his offices suggest.

After Walpole's fall in 1742 he recommended Pelham as his successor to George II, who favoured *Carteret, the new secretary of state for the northern department. However, in obtaining the Treasury in 1743 Pelham had a firm power base and by the end of 1744 Carteret had resigned. In February 1746, following the retreat of the Jacobites, the king considered replacing his ministers. The Pelham brothers and their many followers resigned, forcing the king to accept them back on their own terms. This 'storming of the closet' was of great constitutional significance, demonstrating that government could only work with ministers of whom Parliament approved.

Though Pelham was now thought of as 'prime' minister, the government was really a triumvirate of Pelham, Newcastle, and *Hardwicke. Newcastle shaped foreign policy, but Pelham controlled the purse strings. Hardwicke often had to mediate between the brothers, who, though extremely fond of each other, were not temperamentally suited; his advice was respected and usually heeded. Pelham pursued a policy of including as many political factions in government as possible, leading to an era of undoubted calm. Central to maintaining this calm was the smooth operation of the government's vast patronage system, which Pelham ensured with his bland affability, eye for detail, and, crucially, his presence in the Commons. He also had the respect of talented young politicians such as *Pitt and Henry *Fox, which Newcastle did not.

Pelham's common sense and restrained style was important in preventing excessive reprisals against the Highlanders following the Jacobite rising of 1745, in restraining Newcastle's policy of subsidy payments to allied countries during the War of the *Austrian Succession, and in damping down the popular clamour that followed the bill to naturalize Jews in 1753. But these were essentially reactions to events. Pelham instituted useful Treasury reforms and piloted Hardwicke's 1753 *Marriage Act through the Commons, but it was not part of his political philosophy nor his personal inclination to encourage change.

Pelham's death in 1754 surprised his colleagues and marked a decided change of pace in British politics. George II's declaration upon hearing of it, 'Now I shall have no more peace,' would have seemed to Henry Pelham the highest compliment a politician could receive. AIL

Pembroke, Richard de Clare, earl of (*c*.1130–76), commonly known as 'Strongbow'. A member of the aristocratic Clare family—according to *Gerald of Wales 'his blood was better than his brains'—he inherited his father's earldom of Pembroke in 1148 but, being a supporter of Stephen, forfeited it when Henry II came to the throne. In 1166, still out of favour, he decided to accept *Dermot MacMurrough's offer of his daughter Eva (Aoife) in marriage and the succession to the kingdom of Leinster in return for military assistance against Dermot's Irish enemies. In 1170, in defiance of Henry's wishes, he took a force to Ireland and occupied Dublin and Waterford, where he married Aoife. In 1171 he succeeded Dermot as king. Alarmed by this Henry II invaded Ireland, forcing most Irish kings to recognize him. But by the time he left in 1172 he had recognized Richard both as earl and as his representative in Ireland. Strongbow's gamble had succeeded and the English invasion of Ireland had begun. JG

Pembroke, Thomas Herbert, 8th earl of (1656–1733). Pembroke had a long and distinguished political career, was sword-bearer at five coronations, and was a keen patron of the arts. He succeeded to the title in 1683 and was appointed lord-lieutenant of Wiltshire, but fell into disfavour with James II after refusing to discipline boroughs and was dismissed in 1687. He supported William of Orange, though, as a Tory, he favoured a regency. He was 1st lord of the Admiralty 1690–2, lord privy seal 1692–9, lord president of the council 1699–1708, viceroy of Ireland 1707–8, and lord high admiral 1708–9. He served frequently as a lord justice (regent), was a commissioner to negotiate union with Scotland, and a strong supporter of the Hanoverian succession. Holmes described him as 'a man of mild Tory sympathies and the centre of any coalition ministry'. *Locke dedicated to him the *Essay Concerning Human Understanding* (1690), and *Berkeley his *Principles of Human Knowledge* (1710). JAC

Pembroke, William Herbert, 1st earl of (*c*.1507–70). William Herbert's grandfather was a Yorkist earl of Pembroke, executed at Northampton in 1469, but his father was illegitimate. The family estate was at Ewyas Harold, north-east of Abergavenny. *Aubrey describes him as 'a mad, young, fighting fellow', who could neither read nor write. He held minor court office but his great chance came in 1543 when his sister-in-law *Catherine Parr married Henry VIII. He was knighted, given the estates of the abbey of Wilton, and appointed a gentleman of the bedchamber. In 1549 he helped to suppress the western rising and was given the Garter. After backing the duke of *Northumberland against his rival *Somerset, he took many of the executed duke's estates and in 1551 was created earl of Pembroke. He did homage to Lady Jane *Grey in 1553, but changed step nimbly and retained Mary's favour. He commanded her forces against *Wyatt in 1554, stayed at court under Elizabeth, and was lord steward for the last two years of his life. Aubrey wrote of him as founder of the house of Herbert at Wilton: 'from a private gentleman, and of no estate, but only a soldier of fortune . . . at the dissolution of the abbeys, in few years from nothing slipt into a prodigious estate.' JAC

Pembrokeshire. County of south-west Wales. The county was created at the Act of *Union with England in 1536. The peninsula, part of the Welsh kingdom of *Deheubarth, was conquered by Arnulf de Montgomery, who established the lordship of Pembroke in the south. This was later to become the palatine earldom of Pembroke, which included the lordship of Tenby and the baronies of Daugleddau, Carew, and Walwynscastle. To that basis was added the smaller lordships of the north of the peninsula, Cemaes and Cilgerran, together with the episcopal lands of St Davids (Pebidiog, or Dewisland), the cathedral city of the patron saint of Wales, as well as those of the centre, Haverfordwest and Narberth, and the barony of Llawhaden which belonged to the bishops of St Davids. Henry I reinforced the occupation of the south by promoting a Flemish immigration. The result was that the county had a distinctive dual character, markedly English to the south, Welsh to the north. So clear was the dividing line that it acquired a name—the Landsker. In 1974 the county became part of *Dyfed, but, reflecting the basic internal contrast, it was divided into two districts, South Pembrokeshire and Preseli.

To a degree the divide marks a physical contrast between the low coastal plateau of the south and the Preseli mountains of the north.

Pembrokeshire has been pre-eminently an agricultural county, the southern section being one of the few areas of arable land in Wales, its mild maritime climate giving rise to early vegetable- and flower-growing. A further distinctive feature is its fine coast and offshore islands (Skomer, Skokholm, and Ramsey). The whole coast is designated a heritage coast and makes up the Pembrokeshire National Park. Tourism is in consequence a major economic aspect. The coast is broken by the major sea inlet (ria) of Milford Haven. Once a major fishing port, it is now dominated by oil refineries, developed for supertankers.

North–south contrasts dominate the county, 68.8 per cent speaking Welsh at Crymych in the north but only 4.6 at Manorbier in the south. The district percentages in 1991 were 8.2 in South Pembrokeshire and 24.4 in Preseli. The population in 1991 was 109,534. In 1996 the county was reconstituted as a unitary authority. HC

penal laws. The general name given to the enactments against Roman catholicism made between the accession of Elizabeth I and 1700. They enforced the Elizabethan religious settlement and tried to protect political activity from the influence of the pope and catholic Europe. The overall effect was to drive catholicism underground and to create recusancy. Catholics were placed beyond the political pale and evolved an informal and illegal network of religious and social connections.

Rejection of papal authority was imposed by an oath of allegiance in 1563, stating that 'no foreign prince, person, prelate, state or potentate hath or ought to have any jurisdiction, power, superiority, pre-eminence or authority, ecclesiastical or spiritual within this realm'. Refusal of the oath was treasonable. After the excommunication of Elizabeth I in 1570, the purpose of legislation changed from securing royal supremacy to defeating the new recusant missionary campaign. Priests were tried and executed for treason, particularly after the Acts of 1584–5 which made it treasonable for a priest to enter England. In 1581 an Act to retain the Queen's Majesty's subjects in their due obedience was passed, declaring it treasonable to pervert people from their religious or political allegiance.

James I reinforced the legislation and further regulations limited the freedom of catholics in movement, professional activity, and inheritance of property. The laws of the Restoration period, especially the *Test and *Corporation Acts, kept the catholic community on the margins. Catholics suffered for the disastrous reign of the last catholic king James II under laws barring them from carrying arms, inheriting or buying property, sending children abroad for education or teaching in a school, and offering a £100 reward for the prosecution of a priest.

Had this massive penal code been enforced, it could have eradicated English catholicism, but catholics survived and even flourished in its shadow. Local imposition was sporadic and the Hanoverian mind found religious persecution distasteful. The *Jacobite threat disappeared and repeal of the penal laws became possible. This happened in three main relief Acts of 1778, 1791, and 1829. JFC

Penda (d. 655), king of Mercia, can in many ways be seen as the anti-hero of *Bede's *Ecclesiastical History*—a resolute pagan, responsible for the deaths of many Christian kings in battle, including that of St *Oswald at *Maserfield. However, Bede also admitted that he allowed Christian missionaries to preach in areas under his control and that he was *vir strenuissimus* 'a man exceptionally gifted as a warrior'. Penda first appears in recorded history in 626 battling with rulers of the West Saxons for control of the province of the *Hwicce. The *Northumbrians apparently first encountered him in alliance with *Cadwallon of Gwynedd at the battle of *Heathfield in 633 and he also fought at least two major battles with the *East Angles. Penda's energetic campaigns from his midland base greatly increased the territory under Mercian control and enabled him to establish a wide-ranging overlordship, recognized in Northumbria and parts of Wales as well as in the southern English kingdoms. It was *Oswui of Bernicia's challenge to his authority as overlord which led to Penda's death at the battle of *Winwaed in 655, where he had come with 30 *duces regii*, probably commanders leading military contingents from his subject provinces. BAEY

Peninsular War, 1808–14. Provoked by Napoleon's intervention in Portugal and his imposition of his brother Joseph on the throne of Spain, the war in the Iberian peninsula marked a turning point in the Napoleonic War. By closing Spanish and Portuguese ports to British trade Napoleon had hoped to compel Britain to sue for peace, but his intervention aroused massive popular hostility in Spain and Portugal. Although they were often defeated, the Spanish armies continued to defy the French, while Spanish guerrillas held down large numbers of French troops. When the Spaniards asked Britain for assistance the decision to commit an expeditionary force was a bold one. Initially British opinion exaggerated the likelihood of early success, and only in 1809 did the British accept that the war would be long and arduous. Under *Wellington the British collaborated effectively with the Portuguese, whose army was retrained by British officers. In the winter of 1810–11 Masséna's attempt to drive the British into the sea was thwarted by the lines of *Torres Vedras, a masterpiece of military engineering and a tribute to Anglo-Portuguese co-operation. Thereafter Wellington regularly challenged the French, knowing that his Portuguese base was secure. In 1812 he won the dramatic battle of *Salamanca, and in 1813 he exploited British sea power to conduct a brilliant campaign in northern Spain which reached its climax at the battle of *Vitoria. After expelling the French from Spain, Wellington invaded southern France in 1814. Throughout the Peninsular War, Wellington used the 'reverse slope defence' to establish the superiority of the line over the column. Choosing his ground carefully, he drew up his main force behind a ridge, while light infantry impeded the French advance. The French were handicapped by their lack of artillery and cavalry, which had ensured the success of the column elsewhere. The war in Spain sapped the energies of the French military machine and encouraged the Russians, Prussians, and Austrians in their resistance to Napoleon. It established Wellington's renown as a general and restored the reputation of the British army in the field. JWD

Penn, William (1644–1718). Penn, son of Admiral Sir William Penn, educated at Oxford and Lincoln's Inn, exhibited an early religious sensibility, rejecting a conventional career to join the *quakers. Their leading legal spokesman, international propagandist, and public witness, his advocacy of liberty of conscience and religious toleration found some support from Charles II and James, duke of York, and Penn's wealth aided his efforts. Although a prolific pamphleteer, he rejected the violence of English politics at the *Exclusion crisis. He suffered for his royal friendships at the Glorious Revolution. Penn gained an extensive American proprietary in 1681, drafting a constitution for Pennsylvania embodying his very liberal political ideas. The colony lost rather than (as he hoped) gained him a fortune; he faced growing opposition there and in England. One of the few colonial proprietors who actually visited America, he died in penury and self-pity. RCS

penny post. See HILL, SIR ROWLAND; POST OFFICE.

Penruddock's rising, 1655. Soon after Charles II's flight into exile after the defeat at *Worcester in 1651, his supporters began to plan a general rising in England. The schemes, taken up by the royalist conspiracy of the Sealed Knot, were soon known to *Cromwell's government, which took vigorous counter-measures. On 8 March 1655 only 100 supporters turned up to a rendezvous at Marston Moor which was to have seized York, and even fewer near Morpeth for an attack on Newcastle upon Tyne. A small Wiltshire rising under John Penruddock, a local gentleman, got off the ground four days late, but never numbered more than a few hundred. The rebels held Salisbury for some hours, marched to Blandford, and then retreated into Devon, pursued by Commonwealth troops. At South Molton they were rounded up by a small cavalry force. Penruddock was executed at Exeter in May 1655. Cromwell's response to the disorders was to introduce the rule of the *major-generals. JAC

Penry, John (1563–93). Puritan writer. A *de facto* clergyman though never taking holy orders, and regarded by some as pioneering Welsh nonconformity, Penry's concern about the lack of preaching ministers in his native Wales so displeased Archbishop *Whitgift that he was briefly imprisoned and the offending *Treatise* seized (1587). As his attacks on the established church coincided with appearance of the *Marprelate tracts, he was ineluctably drawn into the controversy; friendship with *Udall and Job Throckmorton, and close association with Robert Waldegrave's secret printing press, made him a prime suspect for 'Martin Marprelate', though he was merely sympathetic collaborator and co-ordinator rather than author. He fled to Edinburgh (1589) but returned to London in 1592, allying himself to Henry *Barrow and the separatists, only to be captured the following March and imprisoned. Despite slender evidence when tried at the Queen's Bench, he was indicted, convicted, and hanged. ASH

Penselwood, battle of, 1016. An encounter in the struggle for the crown between *Edmund Ironside and *Cnut after the death of *Æthelred. The place is given in the *Anglo-Saxon Chronicle* as Peonnan near Gillingham and has consequently been identified as in Kent or at Penselwood on the Dorset–Somerset border. A case can be made out for each. Penenden Heath in Kent (pronounced 'Pennendn') is $4\frac{1}{2}$ miles south of Gillingham. Cnut certainly besieged London in the course of 1016, while the battle of *Sherston, later in the summer, was in Wiltshire. The result at Penselwood was inconclusive but the Danish victory at *Ashingdon, closely followed by Edmund's death in November 1016, left Cnut master of the kingdom. JAC

pensions, old-age. See OLD-AGE PENSIONS.

Pentecostal churches believe that the Pentecost experience remains accessible. Consequently they stress baptism in the Spirit, which they distinguish from conversion or water baptism. This conveys power to practise the gifts of the Spirit: speaking in tongues, prophecy, healing, exorcism. Although similar beliefs are discernible among 2nd-cent. Montanists, 16th-cent. *anabaptists, 19th-cent. *Irvingites, and later offshoots of revivalism, 20th-cent. pentecostalism began at the Asuza Street mission, Los Angeles, 9 April 1906, when members started to speak in tongues. The movement reached England via Norway in 1907, when an ex-methodist, T. B. Barratt, influenced the rector of Monkwearmouth, spread to Wales, where the Jeffreys family of Maesteg founded the Elim foursquare gospel alliance, and thence to Ireland. The largest British churches are the assemblies of God (formed in the United States in 1914), the apostolic faith church, the Elim churches (their foursquare gospel can be encapsulated in Christ—saviour, healer, baptizer in the Spirit, and coming king), and the New Testament Church of God, with its strength among West Indian communities. Their worship is spontaneous, with emphasis on extempore prayer, believer's baptism, and the Lord's supper. Their doctrines are those of world-denying conservative protestantism. Their rapid 20th-cent. growth, especially in Latin America and Africa, has attracted the label of Christendom's 'Third Force', after Roman catholicism and protestantism. CB

Pentland rising, 1666. Support for the *covenant was strong in south-west Scotland and clandestine conventicles continued after the Restoration, the covenanters fined for not attending their parish churches. In November 1666 an incident at Dalry, near New Galloway, sparked off a rising. The covenanters occupied Dumfries and advanced upon Edinburgh by way of Lanark. But their numbers dwindled in the face of heavy rain and fewer than 1,000 of them were intercepted and dispersed at Rullion Green, near Penicuik in the Pentland Hills. Retaliation was severe with 30 executions and many transportations. JAC

Pentrich rising, 1817. Demobilization, rapid industrialization, and agricultural recession made the post-war years miserable. In November 1816 the *Spa Fields riots culminated in an attack upon the Tower and were followed by the suspension of habeas corpus. The march of the *Blanketeers from Manchester followed in March 1817. The east midlands had its own problems of unemployment among textile workers. In the summer of 1817, *Oliver, the government spy, reported the likelihood of risings. On 8 June several hundred men assembled at Pentrich and Ripley and began the 14-mile march to Nottingham, where, their leader Jeremiah Brandreth assured them, they would find mass support. They found none and in heavy rain were easily dispersed by the hussars. Brandreth, who had killed a man on the march, was executed with two others, and 30 rioters were transported. The subsequent revelation of the role of Oliver as *provocateur* embarrassed the government. JAC

Pepys, Samuel (1633–1703). Diarist, naval official, bibliophile, musician, member of Parliament, president of the Royal Society, twice master of Trinity House, Pepys lived through an epoch of increasing sophistication in government, when capacity and drive could help a man rise high, especially if assisted by patronage. Pepys's patron was his cousin Edward Montagu, a naval commander under the republic who promoted Charles II's restoration and became earl of *Sandwich. Pepys was appointed clerk of the acts (secretary) to the Navy Board in 1660 when that body effectively ran the navy under James, duke of York. The young secretary's assiduity rapidly won him esteem, and some dislike. But, weathering the disasters of the second Dutch War, Pepys was appointed the first secretary of the Admiralty in 1673. Though out of office 1679–84, a victim of the *'Exclusion' agitation, his return saw Pepys become the crown's minister for the navy until the Glorious Revolution. Then he was forced from office as too closely associated with James II.

For all his contributions to the navy's well-being, however, Pepys has become much the best-known Englishman of the 17th cent. through his diary, or 'Journal', kept in shorthand and complete secrecy between January 1660 and May 1669, and first transcribed in 1822. Sometimes priggish, it is guileless in self-revelation. 'Traits of actual speech fleck its pattern' and mark the author as a journalist of genius, in his own words 'ever with child to see any strange thing'. Pepys's scholarly discrimination is plain from his library, scrupulously preserved in Magdalene College, Cambridge. DDA

Perceval, Spencer (1762–1812). Prime minister. Perceval was the seventh son of John, earl of Egmont. At Trinity College, Cambridge, he became associated with the evangelical group led by Isaac Milner. He was studious and earnest, modest and timid, but known as a fun-loving companion. Having to make his own way in the world, he trained for the bar and practised on the midland circuit. His appointment as a commissioner of bankrupts in 1790 enabled him to marry Jane, daughter of Sir Thomas Wilson, MP for Sussex, but they had to live in lodgings over a carpet shop in Bedford Row until he increased his income at the bar. He came to notice as a junior counsel for the crown in the trials of the radicals Tom *Paine and Horne *Tooke but he declined *Pitt's offer of the chief secretaryship in Ireland in 1795 because the salary would not support his increasing family. His connections from the midland bar helped to secure him election as MP for Northampton, where he was deputy recorder, in 1796.

Perceval was a conscientious and popular member, giving handsomely to local charities. *Wilberforce thought him the most generous of evangelical Christians: he gave away all that he could spare to the poor, disapproved strongly of gambling and hunting (though he was a steward of Northamptonshire races), and would have made adultery a criminal offence. He refused to transact business on Sundays, held regular family prayers, and was a student of biblical prophecy. A thoroughly orthodox Anglican, he was accused of religious bigotry, but he objected not to the practice of religion by catholics and nonconformists, but to their being allowed political power. He considered the primacy of the Church of England as essential to the security of the state and he was a most determined opponent of *catholic emancipation. Nevertheless, he was conscious of the existence of abuses in the Anglican church and supported efforts to end pluralities and non-residence of the clergy and to increase low clerical incomes. He supported missionary work, especially in India, popular education through the Anglican *National Schools Society, and the abolition of slavery and the slave trade.

Perceval's forensic skills made him an effective parliamentary speaker and he rose quickly up the political ladder, becoming solicitor-general under *Addington in 1801 and attorney-general in 1802. He agreed to stay on under *Pitt in 1804 only on condition that there should be no concessions to the catholics. On Pitt's death in 1806 he was seen as one of the contenders for leadership of the Tories, together with *Castlereagh, *Canning, and Hawkesbury (*Liverpool) and he helped to bring about the defeat of the Whigs in the general election of 1807 by campaigning against the catholics. In *Portland's ministry of 1807–9 he became chancellor of the Exchequer and was given the chancellorship of the duchy of Lancaster as well, to increase his income. He reluctantly accepted the leadership of the House of Commons as a compromise candidate and, after the duel between Castlereagh and Canning brought about Portland's resignation, he was appointed prime minister in October 1809, with the king's enthusiastic approval.

Perceval was by no means an ineffective prime minister. He survived the crises of the inquiry into the *Walcheren expedition and the *Burdett riots in London in 1810 and doggedly supported the expedition to the Peninsula which, against all expectation, was to play a major part in the eventual defeat of Napoleon. He modelled his financial policies on Pitt's and at least kept the war effort going. On George III's final relapse into insanity in 1810 he was confirmed in office by the prince regent but his career was brought to a sudden and tragic end on 11 May 1812 when he was assassinated in the lobby of the House of Commons by an aggrieved and deranged Russia merchant named John Bellingham, who mistook him for Castlereagh.

Perceval was small in stature—he was nicknamed 'Little P.'—pale in complexion, and usually dressed in black. Lord

*Holland likened him to Robespierre in appearance. He was a staunch conservative, a devout evangelical Christian, and a tireless campaigner against inhumanity. His spotless private life and his integrity in public life were in total contrast to the lives of most politicians of his age. EAS

Percy, Henry (1364–1403), known as 'Hotspur'. Eldest son of the earl of *Northumberland, Percy was first appointed sole warden of the east march in 1385; Scottish borderers were soon calling him 'Haatspore'. On an evening in early August 1388, he was captured at *Otterburn while pursuing a Scottish army, a battle immortalized in verse as 'Chevy Chase'. Soon ransomed, he was warden of the west march for five years from 1390, and from 1396 succeeded his father in the eastern wardenship, continuing there after Henry IV's usurpation, which he had assisted. Father and son defeated a Scottish invasion at *Homildon Hill in 1402; the king's order against the ransom of their prisoners was one reason for their rebellion. Its objective may have been the coronation of Edmund *Mortimer, the nephew of Hotspur's wife. Percy was making for Wales to join Owain *Glyndŵr when the king intercepted him near *Shrewsbury; he was killed in the battle. RLS

Percy, Henry, 1st Baron Percy (1273–1314). Percy's father Sir Henry, who died seven months before his son was born, fought for Henry III at *Lewes and married the daughter of John de *Warenne, earl of Surrey, by the king's half-sister. Young Percy accompanied his grandfather on the *Dunbar campaign in 1296, was knighted, and subsequently summoned to Parliament as a baron. Most of the rest of his life was devoted to warfare against the Scots. In 1310 he joined the *Ordainers in their opposition to Edward II and was present at the capture of *Gaveston, though not party to his murder. He was summoned for the campaign which ended at *Bannockburn, but it is not certain that he attended, and he was dead four months later. He is said to have excelled at knightly arts, purchased the estate of Alnwick, and laid the foundations of the great border family. His son Henry fought with success at *Neville's Cross in 1346 when David II of Scotland was captured. JAC

Percy, Thomas (1729–1812). Percy was the son of a grocer from Bridgnorth in Shropshire and educated at Christ Church, Oxford. He took orders, from 1757 to 1782 held the living at Easton Maudit in Northamptonshire, and for the rest of his life was bishop of Dromore in Co. Down. A scholar and antiquarian, he began early in life collecting ancient ballads, having rescued from a friend in Shifnal an old manuscript folio of verse which the maids were using to light the fire. Negotiations with printers were difficult, but he received encouragement from Shenstone and from Samuel *Johnson, who wrote the dedication. The *Reliques of Ancient English Poetry* came out in 1765 and was a leap forward in the preservation and understanding of medieval *ballads. Johnson's ridicule and well-known parodies were directed, not at Percy's ballads, but at contemporary imitations. Percy's scholarly interests were increasingly hampered by his episcopal duties and by failing eyesight. JAC

periodicals, popularly known as magazines, is the branch of the press industry which publishes on a regular, or periodic, basis, usually every week or month. In terms of numbers, the trade or technical press dominates Britain's periodical publishing, but in terms of mass readership, it is the consumer magazine which is of most interest.

Even more than newspapers, periodicals are aimed at a very specific market, gathering together articles of interest to a particular gender, age, class, region, or special interest group. Where a more general periodical has been a success, it has often been due to the novel and authoritative slant it has put on current affairs to supplement newspaper coverage, such as the *Illustrated London News* or **Punch* in the 19th cent., or *Picture Post* in the 20th cent.

The most prominent specialist groups served by periodicals in British history have been adherents of various political positions; the 'cultured' social classes; women; and children. The longest tradition has been political commentary, with the growth of 'courants', 'diurnalls', and 'mercuries' in the early 17th cent. conveying the latest news and comment. After being suppressed at the *Restoration, they flourished in the early 18th cent. with writers like *Defoe (*Review*), *Steele and *Addison (*Tatler* and *Spectator*), and *Swift (*Examiner*). The 18th-cent. 'taxes on knowledge', which attempted to restrict the press, helped create a literature of dissent, which particularly flourished in the early 19th-cent. radical press (*Poor Man's Guardian*, **Political Register*, *Black Dwarf*, *Northern Star*, and *Reynold's News*). While most political comment became confined to the daily and Sunday press in the 19th and 20th cents., the occasional political magazine has flourished, such as the *Spectator* (1828), *The Economist* (1843), and the *New Statesman* (1913), or satirical scandal sheets such as *John Bull* and *Private Eye*.

General cultural periodicals, appealing to the top ranks of society, first appeared in the late 17th cent. in titles such as the *Gentleman's Journal* and the *Athenian Gazette*, continuing in the 18th cent. with the **Gentleman's Magazine*, the *Scots Magazine*, and in the 19th cent. with the **Edinburgh Review*, the **Quarterly Review*, and *Blackwood's*. Lower middle-class equivalents appeared with the printing revolution of the 19th cent., such as *Tit Bits*, the *Strand Magazine*, and *Pearson's Weekly*.

Magazines for women have appeared in unbroken tradition from the late 17th cent., with the *Ladies' Mercury* (1693). Titles of the 18th and 19th cents. such as the *Ladies' Magazine*, the *Englishwoman's Domestic Magazine*, and the *Lady* appealed to the leisured classes, and constructed the identity of domesticity that has come to be associated with women's magazines. Only the rare periodical, such as *The Female Friend* (1846), raised any issues of women's rights, a task similarly undertaken in the 1970s by the feminist *Spare Rib* challenge to the dominance of *Woman*, *Woman's Own*, and *Woman's Realm* with their domestic ideology.

Magazines for children—with an ideology of improvement, as opposed to comic amusement—have a tradition stretching from the late 18th-cent. *Juvenile Magazine* (1788) to the classic Victorian *Boy's Own Paper* (1879) and *Girl's Own*

Paper (1880). Unlike women's magazines, this market has tended to decline in the 20th cent., with comics becoming the dominant periodical fare of children. DJA

Perkin, William Henry (1860–1929). Chemist. Perkin's father was a distinguished chemist, who discovered a new dyeing process producing mauve from coal-tar, and maintained his own private laboratory. After studying in Germany, Perkin was appointed in 1887 to the chair of chemistry at Heriot-Watt College, Edinburgh. In 1892 he moved to Owen's College, Manchester, holding the chair of organic chemistry. Next he moved to the Waynflete chair at Oxford in 1912, where a new laboratory was opened in South Parks. His renown was as a practical experimental chemist and as a remarkable research supervisor. JAC

Perpendicular architecture was the last, great, culminating phase of *Gothic architecture in England, so called because of the vertical lines of its window tracery and the similar effect of panelling, executed in stone, covering wall surfaces. Complex and decorative, it also makes use of the 'four-centred' arch, allowing extended, sometimes enormous, window apertures. Ever more intricate 'stellar', 'fan', and ultimately 'pendant' vaulting systems are also typical. So distinctively English was this style, and of such longevity (*c.*1350–1550), that the term 'Perpendicular' fails to convey its true importance; as John Harvey suggested it was, in effect, the national style of English Gothic and as such a major contribution to European art.

No complete English cathedral dates from the Perpendicular period, but many 14th- and 15th-cent. parish churches, especially in wool-rich East Anglia, exemplify the richness of this architecture; so too do the royal chapels of St George, Windsor (1475–1528), and of Henry VII, Westminster abbey (begun 1503), and, on a smaller scale, the numerous late Gothic chantries and tombs often inserted into earlier ecclesiastical buildings. The Divinity School, Oxford (1424–83), with its remarkable pendant-vaulted roof, is another excellent example. Quintessentially Perpendicular is *King's College chapel, Cambridge (1447–1515), where the new, more open concept of space and light is seen to advantage in a building almost like an elaborate cage of glass and stone. This had later parallels in the development of domestic architecture during the Tudor period, as at *Hardwick Hall, Derbyshire ('more glass than wall').

The Perpendicular style seems to have originated in the remodelling of the choir and east end of Gloucester cathedral (carried out *c.*1337–67) by the king's master mason, William Ramsey (d. 1349). Here the aisles are disguised and thus the spatial concept is remarkably unified, accentuated by panelling, tracery, vaulting, and, above all, the light pouring in through the gigantic east window itself. Ramsey reminds us of the increased importance and status of named architects (or designer-masons) at this time, a process initiated during the earlier periods of Gothic architecture. There was, for example, John Wastell, responsible for the completion of King's College Chapel, Cambridge, the central tower of Canterbury cathedral (1493–7), and probably for the retrochoir at Peterborough cathedral (*c.*1496–1508), and, above all, the prolific royal masons William Wynford (*c.*1320–1405) and Henry *Yevele (*c.*1320–1400). Wynford redesigned the nave of Winchester cathedral (from 1394) and the influential Yevele, who was the king's master mason from 1360 until his death, was responsible for the nave and south transept of Canterbury cathedral (begun 1379). One of the last great works of Perpendicular Gothic was *Bath abbey (1501–39), designed by Robert and William Vertue. TEF

'perpetual peace', treaty of, 1502. James IV of Scotland gave considerable assistance to Perkin *Warbeck, the Yorkist pretender against Henry VII in the 1490s. But in a change of policy after Warbeck's death he negotiated in 1502 a treaty of perpetual peace with England, guaranteed by the papacy and sealed in 1503 by James's marriage to Henry's eldest daughter *Margaret—*Dunbar's 'Marriage of the Thistle and the Rose'. The treaty itself lasted no longer than most perpetual treaties. By 1513 the two countries were at war and James was slain at *Flodden. But the longer consequences were remarkable. A series of unforeseeable contingencies brought the great-grandson of the marriage to the throne of England in 1603 as James VI and I. JAC

Perrot, Sir John (*c.*1527–92). Lord deputy of Ireland. Perrot was one of many who came to grief in the bogs of Tudor Irish politics. A Pembrokeshire man, he established his reputation as a jouster and was knighted at Edward VI's coronation. As a protestant he was in some difficulty during Mary's reign but Elizabeth chose him to help carry the canopy of state at her coronation. From 1570 to 1573 he was governor of Munster, spending most of his time dealing with James *Fitzgerald. After some years mainly employed as vice-admiral of the Welsh seas, he was sent back to Ireland in 1584 as lord deputy. His first action was to subdue the Macdonnells in Ulster. But he found the Dublin Parliament difficult to deal with, quarrelled violently with colleagues, and was recalled in 1588. In 1591 he was sent to the Tower on a charge of treason, accused of speaking against Elizabeth and plotting with Philip of Spain. He died while under sentence of death. JAC

Pershore abbey (Worcs.). A religious community established here in the late 7th cent. became a *Benedictine house in the reign of *Edgar (957–75) through the influence of Bishop *Oswald of Worcester. Many of its endowments were later granted to Westminster abbey by *Edward the Confessor, patronage which caused considerable friction between the two abbeys in the 13th cent. Two disastrous fires, in 1233 and 1288, combined with reduced agricultural revenues, brought considerable indebtedness, from which Pershore never recovered, and by the time of its dissolution in 1539, though it had an assessed income of nearly £650, the abbey was experiencing major economic and disciplinary problems. BJG

Persian War, 1856. The Crimean War ended in March 1856 but a new war with Persia followed in November after the shah had seized Herat, a disputed city in the north-west of Afghanistan. Sir James Outram led a punitive expedition of 6,000 in January 1857. Peace was signed on 4 March whereby the shah withdrew from Herat and promised not to intervene in Afghanistan. JAC

Perth, James Drummond, 4th earl of [S] (1648–1716). Perth, who inherited the title when he was 27, became James VII and II's chief adviser in Scotland. In 1682–4 he was justice-general [S] and from 1684 until 1688 chancellor [S]. He began as a presbyterian, moved to the Church of England, and as soon as James succeeded declared himself a catholic. His brother Lord Melfort was secretary of state [S] and governor of Edinburgh castle. Both men were given the Thistle in 1687. At the revolution, Perth tried to escape by boat, but was brought back to Kircaldy and imprisoned until 1693 at Stirling. He was then sent into exile. James created him duke of Perth in 1690 and he spent the rest of his life at Saint-Germain. His brother was made duke of Melfort in 1692. Perth's son, the 2nd Jacobite duke, fought at *Sheriffmuir in 1715 and his grandson, the 3rd duke, at *Culloden in 1746. JAC

Perth, treaty of, 1266. The failure of Haakon IV's great expedition at *Largs in October 1263 led to a vigorous Scottish counter-attack, which subdued the Inner Hebrides. On 2 July 1266 Magnus IV of Norway, Haakon's successor, signed the treaty of Perth with Alexander III of Scotland. In return for four payments of 4,000 marks and a tribute of 100 marks in perpetuity, the Norwegians surrendered sovereignty over all the Western Islands and the *Isle of Man. They retained possession of *Orkney and Shetland. The Isle of Man had to be subdued and at length fell under English rule, but the Western Islands remained Scottish. JAC

Peterborough, Charles Mordaunt, 3rd earl of (1658–1735). Politician, soldier, and diplomatist. Known until 1697 by his earlier title of earl of Monmouth, Peterborough's cleverness ran to dishonesty and to any ministry was a liability and a worry. An opponent of James II, he mixed with Whig radicals and was an early associate of William of Orange. In 1689 he was given the senior Treasury post of 1st commissioner, for which he was totally unsuited, and resigned a year later. He remained an assertive influence at William III's court, however, quarrelling and plotting against those whom he believed were thwarting his own ambitions. In 1696, when he accused *Shrewsbury and *Marlborough of involvement in the Fenwick conspiracy, he was sent to the Tower. In their propaganda the Tories claimed him as their hero after the expeditionary force he commanded captured Barcelona and overran Valencia in 1705, but his unreliability cost him any further advancement, and he was fortunate to escape parliamentary censure. AAH

Peterborough, diocese of. The see, now comprising Northamptonshire and parts of Cambridgeshire and Leicestershire, was founded by Henry VIII in 1541 out of the *Lincoln diocese. In the 7th cent. *Penda's son *Peada founded a monastery here which was rebuilt and dedicated to St Peter in 970, hence the town's name. In 1837 Leicestershire was transferred to the see from Lincoln. Distinguished bishops include the historian Mandell Creighton (1891–7), author of *The History of the Papacy.* The cathedral was built between 1118 and 1237 as the Benedictine abbey church. It has a dignified Norman nave, a 13th-cent. west front, and 15th-cent. fan-vaulted retrochoir. *Catherine of Aragon was buried there. WMM

Peterloo. The massacre which was derisively dubbed 'Peterloo' took place in St Peter's Fields (Manchester) on 16 August 1819. A radical reform meeting of 60,000–100,000 people was violently broken up by the local yeomanry who were ordered by the magistrates to arrest the speaker, Henry *Hunt. Eleven people were killed and over 400 wounded. The government promptly congratulated the magistrates and rushed through the *Six Acts. There was an immediate national outcry from liberals and reformers of every shade, angrily portrayed in *Shelley's *The Masque of Anarchy* and *England in 1819*. To middle-class reformers and Whigs, Peterloo was a warning of the aspirations of the unenfranchised. To working-class reformers Peterloo became a symbol. It was condemned at mass meetings throughout the country and was commemorated for many years afterwards. 'Remember the Bloody Deeds of Peterloo' proclaimed chartist banners 20 years later. JFCH

Peter's Pence or Rome-scot began in Saxon times as an annual tribute of 1 penny from each household to the papacy. After the Conquest, it became a total payment of about £200 p.a., collected by the bishops. Attempts to increase it were strongly resisted. Though the amount of revenue involved was insignificant, the claim of tribute was of symbolic importance. Monarchs could put pressure on the papacy by withholding payment and by Henry VIII's statute of 1533 (25 Hen. VIII c. 21) it was abolished altogether. JAC

Petillius Cerialis was governor of Britain 71–73/4. Probably originating from Umbria, Cerialis is first attested in Britain as legate of *legio IX Hispana* during the *Boudiccan revolt. Attempting to stem the rising after the sack of Colchester he was defeated, and spent the rest of the revolt besieged. Subsequently he probably married the daughter of the future emperor *Vespasian. When Vespasian came to power in 70 Cerialis was appointed joint commander of the large force to suppress the revolt of Civilis in the lower Rhineland. From there he was posted to Britain. His governorship saw the resumption of military expansion following the deposition of *Cartimandua of the *Brigantes. The areas of modern Lancashire and Yorkshire were annexed and forces may have penetrated further north. Cerialis probably held the consulship before governing Britain, and again in 74 and possibly also in 83. ASEC

petition of right, 1628. Charles I's levy of a *forced loan in 1626–7 and his imprisonment of non-contributors led the Commons in 1628 to frame a petition outlawing non-parliamentary taxes and arbitrary imprisonment. Charles, concerned to preserve his prerogative, gave an ambiguous reply, to which the Commons responded by withholding their offer of a much-needed money grant. The king, with ill grace, therefore authorized a second, conventional, reply which turned the petition into law. When it was printed, Charles included only his first response, thereby arousing fears that he would renege on his promises, but in the event he scrupulously adhered to the letter cf the petition. RL

Petroc, St (6th cent.). Particularly associated with Cornwall, Petroc allegedly renounced royal responsibilities in Wales for a religious life. With his followers, he went to Cornwall where he founded monasteries at Padstow and Little Petherick. Later accounts of his life include stories of travels and numerous miracles, portraying him as a typical Celtic saint, alternating between community life and solitude. He died at Treravel and was buried at Padstow, the original centre of his cult, later replaced by Bodmin, where his shrine and relics were taken. Renowned in Cornwall, his cult became widespread in Devon and Wales and in Brittany, where his stolen relics were taken in the late 12th cent. Henry II intervened for their return to England and *Walter of Coutances provided a fine ivory head reliquary, which was hidden during the Reformation and rediscovered over the porch of Bodmin parish church in the 18th cent. AM

petroleum industry. The industry came to maturity in the 20th cent. but it has a longer history. One of the curiosities of the *Ironbridge Gorge was a spring of natural bitumen discovered in 1786. In 1847 a petroleum seepage was discovered in a Derbyshire coal-mine; this yielded 300 gallons per day and required refining. James 'Paraffin' Young (1811–83), a technical chemist, developed the technology. He wrongly imagined that the petroleum had been condensed from the coal and began to distil oil-bearing coals and shales. The best was Torbanite, found near Bathgate (Scotland); Young patented his process in 1850 and founded the Scottish shale-oil industry. His technology was transferred to the petroleum industry.

In 1890 petroleum was discovered in Sumatra, and the Royal Dutch Company was formed. Marcus Samuel, an overseas merchant, began shipping Russian kerosene in 1892; he formed the Tank Syndicate the following year, the ancestor of Shell Transport and Trading Company (1897). By 1914 America controlled 65 per cent of the world's output.

In 1900 William Knox D'Arcy, a successful English speculator in Australian gold-mining, accepted an oil concession in Persia and formed the Anglo-Persian Oil Company. This was the origin of British Petroleum. In 1903 Admiral 'Jackie' *Fisher decided that, as an experiment, fuel oil should be tried in two battleships, and this proved to be economic without impairing performance. In 1905 Burmah Oil Company contracted to supply fuel for the navy, but the naval race with Germany encouraged Winston *Churchill and Fisher to secure strategic supplies of petroleum. Burmah and the government became the leading shareholders in Anglo-Persian, and in 1914 the navy's requirement for 277,000 tons of fuel oil was met.

Despite disarmament, the inter-war years witnessed an expansion of markets: the first mass-produced British cars and the development of aviation increased the demand for petrol. Major refineries were built in Britain at Llandarcy and Grangemouth as the potential of the petrochemical industry was recognized. Oil became the fuel of the world's merchant marine and important in electricity generation and domestic heating.

These developments became more significant after 1945. Petroleum was the fastest-growing component in the energy sector until 1973. For strategic reasons and to save imports the government favoured home-based refining. Capacity was increased, and new plant was built at Stanlow (1947) and Fawley (1951); in 1953 29 million tons were refined, and in 1980 133 million tons. Some refineries were very large by 1980: all but 3 per cent of output was refined in plants with a capacity of over 1 million tons, and three, Fawley (Esso), Kent (BP), and Shell Haven (Shell), were at 10 million tons or more.

In the 1970s the petroleum industry was affected by two major shocks. The first was increased prices engineered by OPEC, a cartel of the leading exporting countries, and this was followed by the Arab–Israeli War (1973). Prices, which had remained stable between 1950 and 1972 at £7/8 per ton despite inflation, increased more than fourfold by 1974 and thereafter to over £60 by 1979. Oil consumption fell, and the search for alternative oilfields grew apace. Viable oilfields were discovered in the North Sea off Scotland in 1971 and by November 1975 the Forties field was on stream. North Sea production, largely pioneered by American investment and technology, in 1981 exceeded home demand. Capital formation between 1976 and 1979 averaged over £2 billion. This expansion brought new jobs, new government revenue, compensated for the decline in manufacturing in the 1980s, and assisted the balance of payments. JB

pets. The keeping of animals and birds for companionship is probably as old as human society, and there is medieval evidence for cherished lap-dogs and hunting-dogs which were kept for more than utilitarian motives. The cats and toads which were adduced as witches' familiars provide evidence from lower down the social scale. Pet-keeping as an activity with wider economic and social significance emerges as part of the rise of 'consumer society' in post-Restoration England, with the development of selective breeding to emphasize approved characteristics (for dogs as well as cattle and sheep) and the introduction of new species which could display the purchasing power and discernment of the owner (as with the rapid diffusion of goldfish). A full-scale pet industry emerged in Victorian Britain, as the élite trends of earlier years found echoes in a growing middle-class public, and the competitive display of newly defined breeds found formal expression in the proliferation of shows and clubs of fanciers. Working-class pet-keeping was decried by those who complained of uncontrolled mongrels roaming the streets and regarded expenditure on pets as a feckless waste of scarce resources, but the demand for commercially produced pet foods, clothing, and other accoutrements which built up firms like Spratts, whose advertisements helped to sustain the specialist press, came from higher up the scale. Commercial, practical, and recreational motives were often combined with affective ones, as book titles like *Cats for Pleasure and Profit* (1908) confirmed, and the romantic anthropomorphism which was exhibited (for example) in some of Wordsworth's poetry in the early 19th cent. was widely diffused a century later. By the Edwardian years the full range of attitudes to pets which still endured at the end of the 20th cent. could already be identified, and the pet supply and servicing industries had become big business. JKW

Petty, Sir William (1623–87). Born in Romsey (Hants), his education took him to the Jesuit College, Caen, and later to Leiden, Utrecht, Amsterdam, Oxford, and London, where his studies focused upon medicine. With doctorates in both physics and medicine, he became professor of medicine, then anatomy, at Oxford University (1648), taking a chair in music in 1651 at Gresham College, London, and at the same time acting as medical officer to the English army in Ireland. In this latter connection he undertook a topographical survey of land in Ireland later assigned to Cromwell's soldiers (as well as to himself). Hence his work covered many subject areas. His best-known and most influential publications were *Political Arithmetic* (1678) and *Treatise of Taxes and Contributions* (1662), two texts in economics. They both placed emphasis upon the use of economic statistics in determining economic policy. Two years before his death he became adviser to James II. JRP

petty sessions. These were the regular courts held by the *justices of the peace to try minor criminal offences summarily—i.e. without a jury. The office of *justice of the peace dates back to the conservators of the peace, appointed by Richard I, but the most important legislation instituting the office was passed in the 14th cent., notably the Justices of the Peace Act, 1361. The first courts held by the justices were the *quarter sessions, but by statute and practice justices were also empowered to hear cases 'on examination' or summarily. These petty sessions (from French *petit* or lesser) were first so called in the first half of the 19th cent. They dealt with most criminal offences and, as the magistrates' courts, they continue to do so. MM

Petworth House in Sussex is on the edge of the small market town, though it manages to create its own serene world. The property belonged originally to the Percy family, from whom it passed to the Wyndhams, earls of Egremont, via the 6th duke of *Somerset. Somerset rebuilt the house in the 1690s, the architect remaining unknown. The long west front gives directly onto the park, landscaped by Capability *Brown, with the south downs in the distant background. The 3rd earl of Egremont gave hospitality to *Turner, many of whose paintings are preserved at Petworth, along with others by *Reynolds, *Gainsborough, Wilson, *Zoffany, and Opie. JAC

Pevensey, battle of, 491. The *Anglo-Saxon Chronicle*, in remarkable and suspicious detail, records a Saxon attack in 491 led by *Ælle and his son Cissa on Britons entrenched in the old Roman fort of Anderida or Andredes-cester, near Pevensey. The place was stormed and 'there was not even one Briton left there'. It sounds a very plausible episode in the establishment of the kingdom of *Sussex. Cissa gave his name to the chief town of the region, Chichester. JAC

Pevsner, Sir Nikolaus Bernhard Leon (1902–83). A German-born art historian, Pevsner came to Britain in 1934 as a refugee from Nazism. He lectured and wrote widely on art and architecture, was a founder member of the William Morris and Victorian societies, and Slade professor of fine art at Oxford and Cambridge, as well as professor of the history of art at Birkbeck College, London. Of his many publications, including the Pelican *History of Art* (begun 1953), the best known is *The Buildings of England*, which he began in 1949 and worked on for 21 years. Through these county guides he aimed to record every notable architectural object from the distant past to the present day to provide books of interest to travellers and to tell the story of England through her buildings. He achieved the status of 'Look in Pevsner', was made CBE in 1953, and knighted in 1969. JC

Philip II of Spain (1527–98), consort of Mary Tudor. Philip's marriage to Mary in July 1554 was a diplomatic part of Spain's long struggle against the French. The son of the Emperor Charles V and Isabella of Portugal, he was regent of Spain between 1542 and 1548 and king from 1556 until his death. Although he was not crowned, Philip took the style of king of England. Mary was overjoyed with her young husband and bitterly disappointed when the marriage produced no heir. From Philip's point of view the marriage served its purpose by drawing England into the conflict with France, the effects of which were summed up by Armigail Waad in 1558—it had 'consumed our captains, men, money, victuals' and lost *Calais, England's last continental possession.

After Mary's death in 1558, Philip offered himself as a husband to Elizabeth. Though she refused, England needed Spain as a counterbalance to France. But by 1565 many councillors were convinced that Philip intended to overthrow Elizabeth, place Mary Stuart on the throne, and restore catholicism. There was a sharp anti-Spanish turn in policy in 1569 which set the pattern for the rest of Elizabeth's reign. Philip was involved in plots against her—*Ridolfi and *Babington—and formal invasion plans—the great Armada in 1588, and further scares in 1595, 1596, and 1597. Elizabeth, for her part, sent an army into the Spanish Netherlands in 1585 and offered to support Philip's Morisco subjects against the Spanish government in the late 1580s. SA

Philiphaugh, battle of, 1645. *Montrose's brilliant Scottish campaign, which had begun in August 1644 when he met up with a small force from Ireland, received its first check at Philiphaugh, near Selkirk, when he left the Highlands and came down towards the borders. Severely weakened by desertions, his troops were surprised on 13 September 1645 and outnumbered by *Leslie. Though most of the cavalry escaped, the survivors of the Irish infantry surrendered, only to be massacred in cold blood. JAC

Philippa of Hainault (*c.*1314–69), queen of Edward III. Edward married Philippa in 1328. Her main achievement was to provide him with at least twelve children, of whom nine survived infancy. Chroniclers praised her, and she was probably an important influence on the king, though her personality is difficult to recapture. She spent more time in the company of her husband than did most queens, even on occasion accompanying him in France. She is probably best known for her intervention in 1347, when she is said to have pleaded with Edward not to execute the six 'Burghers of Calais' when they surrendered the keys of the town to him. In 1352 there were complaints about disorder on her estates, and the role of her officials. She could be extravagant, and this may explain the amalgamation of her household with that of the king in her final years. MCP

philosophical radicals is a loose term for the group of reformers in the early 19th cent. who based their approach to government and society largely on the *utilitarian theories of Jeremy *Bentham, though they were also influenced by *Malthus, *Ricardo, and Hartley. The leading proponents were James and John Stuart *Mill, George *Grote, and John *Roebuck, supported by the *Morning Chronicle*, *Westminster Review*, and *London Review*. Their immediate objectives were an extension of the franchise, frequent parliaments, secret ballot, law reform, and the dismantling of the system of aristocratic government. Their efforts to construct a radical party in Parliament after 1832 did not succeed: 'they did very little to promote any opinions,' wrote J. S. Mill, 'they had little enterprise, little activity.' But the general influence of utilitarian ideas permeated politics and, particularly in the period 1820 to 1850, produced an 'age of reform'. The term 'philosophical radicals' was popularized by J. S. Mill in his *Autobiography* (1873) and introduced into history by the French historian Halévy in *The Growth of Philosophical Radicalism* (1904; trans. 1928). JAC

Phoenix Park murders. Late in the afternoon of 6 May 1882 Lord Frederick *Cavendish, newly appointed chief secretary for Ireland, and Thomas Burke, his under-secretary, were walking in Phoenix Park (Dublin) when four men leapt from a cab and stabbed them to death. Soon afterwards newspaper offices in Dublin received black-edged cards, claiming the outrage for a nationalist group called the 'Irish *Invincibles'. They were never caught. The immediate political effect was a new bout of 'coercion' in Ireland, against Prime Minister *Gladstone's more conciliatory instincts. In 1888 *The Times* claimed it had proof that *Parnell had been implicated; but it turned out to have been fooled—not for the last time—by a forgery. BJP

photography. In an age of film, television, and holiday snapshots, it is hard to remember that until comparatively recently people had little idea what their rulers or celebrities looked like, nor much impression of foreign parts, save for the odd painting or engraving. Some rulers turned this to advantage. The Tudors gave much thought to the public image their portraits presented and Elizabeth ordered the destruction of unflattering reproductions. Occasionally the situation produced embarrassment. Rushing to meet his new bride, *Anne of Cleves, Henry VIII complained that she was not at all like *Holbein's portrait and that he would not go through with the marriage were it not for offending her brother.

The origins of modern photography are to be found in the camera obscura (darkened room), described in the 16th cent., in which a shaft of light produced an inverted image. This could be improved if a lens was used and the inversion corrected by a mirror. The problem was to capture and reproduce the image. The German physicist Schulze demonstrated in 1727 that a mixture of chalk, nitric acid, and silver could retain an image. Thomas Wedgwood, son of the potter, experimented in the early 19th cent., but his pictures faded on exposure to light. In 1837 the French painter Daguerre produced a photograph of part of his studio and exhibited it in Paris in 1839. But since the exposure time was protracted, daguerreotype was unsuitable at first for portraits, nor could it be reproduced. Fox *Talbot had already begun his own experiments at Lacock abbey in Wiltshire, using a negative, and on hearing of Daguerre's work arranged a public demonstration the same month at the *Royal Institution in London. His technique was called calotype (beautiful image). By the 1850s photography was a commercial success. We have no photographs of *Melbourne or Sir Robert *Peel but several of Prince *Albert and *Palmerston. Two early and celebrated portraits are of Isambard Kingdom *Brunel, taken by Robert Howlett in 1857, and of Alice Liddell (the original 'Alice') by Charles Dodgson in 1859. Roger Fenton's photographs from the Crimea, reproduced in the *Illustrated London News*, gave readers their first impressions of the scenes of war, followed in America in the 1860s by pictures of the Civil War. The census of 1851 showed that already 51 persons gave their occupations as photographers: by 1901 there were more than 17,000. At the end of the 19th cent. newspapers regularly carried photographs and the Kodak No. 1 box camera, marketed from 1888 by George Eastman, catered for the amateur photographer. The development in the 1900s of the cinema and the spread of television just before and after the Second World War meant a breadth of visual experience never known to people before. JAC

Picton, Sir Thomas (1758–1815). Soldier. Born in Pembrokeshire, he joined the army at 13, but was put on half-pay at the peace in 1783. In 1794 he volunteered for service in the West Indies and fought with distinction, being appointed governor of Trinidad, captured from the Spaniards, in 1797. Accusations of cruelty forced his resignation in 1803 and legal actions continued until 1810 when he was cleared on the grounds that Spanish law still operated. By that time he was in Portugal with *Wellington and fought gallantly in the *Peninsular campaign. In 1813 he was knighted and promoted lieutenant-general. As soon as Napoleon left Elba, Picton rejoined Wellington, was wounded at Quatre-Bras, but took his post at Waterloo two days later. He was killed by a bullet at the head of his men, roaring them on. There is a statue of Picton at Carmarthen and the top hat he wore at Waterloo is preserved at Sandhurst. JAC

Picquigny, treaty of, 1475. Edward IV's great campaign in northern France in 1475 was something of a non-event. Greatly dissatisfied with the help he had received from his Burgundian allies, the king was very willing to make terms at Picquigny near Amiens, on 29 August. There was to be a seven-year truce; free commercial exchange; provision for arbitration of disputes; a marriage between the dauphin and *Elizabeth of York; and a regular payment by Louis XI of France to Edward. In England the payments were seen as tribute, in France as a bribe or retainer. The *rapprochement* did not last long and the marriage never took place. JAC

Picts. An indigenous tribe or group of tribes in Scotland during the Roman and post-Roman periods. They are first mentioned in AD 297 by Eumenius who calls them 'half-naked enemies' of the Britons. 'Picts' is probably a Latinized word meaning 'painted people'. Classical writers, among them Julius *Caesar, refer to the British habit of body-painting with materials such as woad. The Picts, along with other Britons, may even have been tattooed.

Because our historical sources give us only brief glimpses of the Picts, it is difficult to determine whether they had a substantive ethnic identity or if 'Picti' was merely a convenient label given by classical writers to all tribal peoples in Scotland in the later Roman period. A Roman poet observes in AD 310 that the Emperor Constantius chose not to acquire the woods and marshes of the 'Caledones and other Picti'. The *Caledonians were certainly one major tribe north of the Forth–Clyde frontier, whereas it would seem that 'Picti' were a whole group of tribes, possibly a new federation.

An important historical attestation of the Picts is provided by Ammianus Marcellinus. He records attacks on Roman Britain by Picts, Scots, Irish, and Saxons culminating in the 'Picts' War' of AD 367–8. Count Theodosius was sent to recover the situation and he restored the province after a major campaign. St *Patrick refers to the Picts of the 5th cent. as 'most shameful, wicked and apostate' after they bought some of his Christian converts from slave dealers. *Gildas refers to 'marauding Picts', savages with more hair on their faces than clothes on their bodies, who came by sea from the north and raided post-Roman Britain. In the 8th cent. Bede believed that at the time of St *Columba's mission the Picts were divided into northern and southern groups, the latter having been converted to Christianity by St *Ninian. According to legend, the last king of the Picts was killed at the instigation of *Kenneth MacAlpin *c.* AD 842.

Archaeologically, the Picts are possibly represented by a number of carved standing 'Pictish symbol stones' found throughout Scotland. These probably date from the 6th–10th cents. AD and are incised with a wide corpus of symbols inspired by Celtic, Anglo-Saxon, and Christian iconography. It is debatable whether these stones are indeed a correlate of a Pictish culture. ES

piepowder courts were the courts attached to fairs and markets and were probably so called because of the dusty feet (*pieds poudrés*) of the travelling merchants. When the king gave a town or community the franchise to hold a fair or market, he also granted the right to hold a court to decide disputes between merchants at the fair and to deal with criminal offences occurring during the fair. The judges in these courts were merchants. Piepowder courts were popular with the mercantile community, being quick, effective, and not unduly hampered by procedural technicalities. However they gradually declined, especially after statutes limited their jurisdiction in the 15th cent., and by the end of the 16th cent. most had fallen into disuse. MM

Piers Plowman. Late 14th-cent. poem by William *Langland. Over 50 manuscripts survive, representing progressive revisions known as the 'Z', 'A', 'B', and 'C' texts, of which 'B', comprising a prologue and twenty passus, is the most frequently read.

Cast in the familiar medieval form of a quest, the poem uses a series of dream-visions to trace the tortuous progress of 'Will' from intellectual wrangling to spiritual understanding as he searches for Truth and then for Do-Wel, Do-Bet, and Do-Best. The climax presents Christ's mortal 'joust' and triumph over hell with extraordinary power; yet the close brings another departure, as Conscience, frustrated by corruption within Christendom, sets out to walk the world in search of Piers Plowman. Piers, who has appeared as type of the virtuous poor, ideal Christian, and almost Christ himself, has by now fused into St Peter as archetypal pope. Throughout the poem, personified abstractions such as the comically depraved Seven Deadly Sins interact, and overlap, with contemporary caricatures including the self-indulgent Master of Divinity and the besmirched pilgrim Haukyn the Active Man. Langland's passionate commitment to spiritual and social reform finds expression in his restless and emphatic alliterative lines, and in a complex battery of literary devices including allegory, recurrent metaphors, word-play, and Latin quotation. DCW

pigeon-fancying. Pigeon clubs are usually confined to small areas to ensure equality of weather conditions, but the birds may fly up to 500 miles. The pigeons, which used to be transported by rail, are now taken to the starting-point in specially constructed road vehicles. The performance of each pigeon is very carefully monitored and recorded, and breeding and feeding rigorously controlled. The speed of the birds varies with wind conditions but they average 40 m.p.h. and speeds up to 90 m.p.h. have been recorded. They are descended from the rock doves (*columba livia*) and have been used since ancient times for carrying messages: Reuters, the international news agency, founded in 1850, relied at first on pigeons. The modern sport developed in the later 19th cent., as the railway network spread, particularly in Belgium and Britain. The Royal National Homing Union of Great Britain was founded in 1896 and the international body, the Fédération Colombophile Internationale (FCI), in the 1950s. It is one of the most demanding of sports, for breeders and for pigeons. In bad weather a large proportion of the birds do not survive. JAC

Pilgrimage of Grace, 1536–7. The Pilgrimage was a widespread northern rising against Henry VIII's religious policies and the greatest challenge to his position during his reign. It seems to have been triggered by the *dissolution of the smaller monasteries, began at Louth in Lincolnshire, spreading to Yorkshire and then to Cumberland and Westmorland. The rebels, who took the badge of the five wounds of Christ and called themselves pilgrims, were led by Robert *Aske and for some weeks commanded overwhelming numbers. Henry's response was to temporize, to offer pardons, and to attempt to split gentry from commoners. By the spring of 1537 most of the rebels had dispersed and he was able to take a bloody revenge on the pilgrims. Aske was executed at York and Lord *Darcy, who had surrendered Pontefract castle to the rebels, was beheaded on Tower Hill. The weakness of royal control which the rising had demonstrated led at once to the establishment of the *Council of the North in October 1537 to reassert authority. JAC

pilgrimages, visits to shrines or holy places, were undertaken for a variety of reasons—from piety, as thanksgiving or penance, in hope of a cure, or as a form of holiday. The great and mighty could visit Rome, Jerusalem, or Compostella: *Ine of Wessex went to Rome to die *c.*726; the real *Macbeth visited Rome in 1050; Henry IV died before he could fulfil his intention to see Jerusalem. Other people visited the great national shrines—*Becket's at Canterbury, *Cuthbert's at Durham, or the Virgin Mary's at *Walsingham. But there were many other shrines with regional or local fame—St *Hugh at Lincoln, St *Guthlac at Crowland, St Joseph at Glastonbury, St *Ninian at Whithorn, St *Chad at Lichfield, St *David in west Wales. Rather unlikely candidates for veneration included Simon de *Montfort, *Thomas of Lancaster at Pontefract, and Edward II at Gloucester. The possession of sacred relics was of great spiritual and financial value to religious communities, and to their towns: Walsingham was said by Erasmus to have 'scarcely any means of support except for the tourist trade'. Monks promoted the cult of their own saints and could write disparagingly of others. The church encouraged the practice of pilgrimages through the imposition of penances and the granting of indulgences, and substitutes could even be sent. As early as the 5th cent., St Augustine of Hippo complained of dubious relics and Erasmus in 1526 launched a strong attack on the vulgarity and commercialism of pilgrimages. Though protestant reformers disapproved strongly of pilgrimages, the concept of life as a pilgrimage survived in *Bunyan's **Pilgrim's Progress*. Among catholics, pilgrimages continue, particularly since 1858 to Lourdes and since 1879 to Knock, in Co. Mayo, Eire. JAC

Pilgrim Fathers. The leaders of the Plymouth settlement on Cape Cod, made under a Virginia Company grant in late 1620. Religious dissidents from Scrooby (Notts.) had exiled themselves to Leiden in Holland, but decided their Englishness could better be preserved in English America. After a terrible early mortality and with Indian help, the colonists, not all of whom were associated with the Leiden group, survived and increased. The first Thanksgiving was celebrated in November 1621. The Pilgrims' fortitude and their religious and communal values, rather than the chaotic individualism of early Virginia, have been traditionally commemorated by later generations. RCS

Pilgrim's Progress. Religious allegory by John *Bunyan, published in two parts (1678, 1684). Widely regarded as a classic in puritan literature, it renders Bunyan's own spiritual progress (recounted in *Grace Abounding*) into a more objective universalized myth, embodied by the solitary pilgrim Christian's search for the Celestial City. Allegorical figures (Giant Despair, Hopeful), satirical portraits of hypocrites or backsliders (Mr Worldly-Wiseman), and realism enliven an episodic series of adventures, though each reflects a step in the puritan stages of conversion. Part II, centred around Christian's wife, is more concerned with problems in nonconformist communities than with the individual. ASH

pillory. Social corrective combining public humiliation and discomfort, occasionally death. The offender's hands and neck were immobilized within a hinged pair of planks attached to an upright post on a platform, erected in open spaces, usually for an hour on market-day. Generally a sentence for acts that aroused common resentment and hostility (e.g. dishonest commerce), it also forewarned potential victims by public identification. The spectators' mood could vary. *Defoe found them kind (1703), but taunts and pelting with eggs, vegetables, and vermin were more common; if real anger prevailed, stones could prove fatal. The practice was abolished in 1837. ASH

Pinkie Cleugh, battle of, 1547. One of the first decisions taken by *Somerset when he became protector for Edward VI in 1547 was to settle the long-running war against Scotland with a decisive blow. The Scots had rejected proposals for a marriage between the young king of England and the infant Mary, queen of Scots, and had formed an alliance with France. The Scottish army, under *Huntly and *Arran, had a numerical advantage on 10 September when the two sides met at Pinkie Cleugh, east of Edinburgh, near Musselburgh. The Scots had the better of the early exchanges, but superior cavalry and the help of some warships gave Somerset a crushing victory. He went on to occupy Edinburgh but was unable to sustain his position. JAC

pipe rolls. The great rolls of the *Exchequer are preserved in the Public Record Office from the reign of Henry II to that of William IV. Their nickname is taken from their tubular appearance. Since they include the accounts of the sheriffs and deal with crown revenue and crown lands, they are a very valuable historical source. A society for the publication of pipe rolls was founded in 1883 and has published nearly 100 volumes. A useful survey of the system of the Exchequer is to be found in volume i of the society's new series (1925). JAC

Pipton-on-Wye, treaty of, 1265. An agreement between *Llywelyn ap Gruffydd and Simon de *Montfort, the baronial leader who had Henry III in custody. On 19 June Llywelyn capitalized on civil war in England to secure advantageous terms from the barons, consolidating his control of the central marches of Wales. In return for £20,000 over ten years, Simon recognized Llywelyn's title as prince of Wales and vassal of the king, and his suzerainty over the Welsh nobility; he also promised Llywelyn further lands and castles on the English border. Although Simon was soon dead at *Evesham (4 August), Henry III concluded a similar peace with Llywelyn at *Montgomery (25 September 1267), confirming his title and status of prince, and his right to the allegiance of Welsh nobles. Llywelyn's power was at its height. RAG

piracy. The oldest profession of the sea, piracy in British coastal waters by Saxon or north German seafarers may have become common by *c.* AD 400; with the Viking era, from *c.* AD 800, depredations by Norse adventurers became seasonal events. Essentially, however, piracy was pursued without the sanction of any higher authority unless, as was not infrequently the case, it had a measure of official connivance. This may partly explain why early sea laws in the west, which by implication place piracy 'without the law', do not seem to do so explicitly. In England, before the emergence of the Court of Admiralty in the 14th cent. the crown accorded substantial 'self-regulation' to the ports of the realm, but it did not do so lightly: in 1343 Edward III forthrightly condemned piracy in Dartmouth, for such abuse of foreign ships injured the royal preserve of relations with other states. An expanding sea-borne commerce, which in volume of shipping seems to have reached its first peak in England in about 1570, made piracy in waters which individual governments might pretend to control difficult if not impossible to counter. The quintessence of this situation lay in the Caribbean archipelagos of Spain's transatlantic empire, where a theoretical dominion was frequently challenged, and sometimes (Britain's treaty with Spain of 1670 is a case in point) with the active concurrence of Madrid. If there was a European precedent for the Spanish monopolistic approach it was in the *Hanseatic League, with its self-protective commercial overlordship of northern waters in the 14th and 15th cents. Hanseatic power explains why English piracy flourished in the south-west, whence it reached into Biscay, the chief medieval source of salt and wine, rather than upon the coasts fronting the North Sea.

For all the dexterity and legalism of Elizabeth I's responses to Spanish allegations of piracy, it is inescapable that piracy there was; and that if government was a circumspect backer of *Hawkins and *Drake it was transparently a gainer from their daring. Elizabethan piracy was essentially a business venture, even if the force of a protestantism determined to challenge the papal award of the western hemisphere to Spain and the eastern to Portugal in 1494 should not be underrated. With the 17th cent. came piracy's great age in the West Indies. The Spanish need to purchase West African slaves from English and other slavers, Spain's extended communications which themselves invited rootless seafarers to prey upon cargoes of fabulous wealth, combined with the loose proprietorial hold on those islands Spain virtually conceded to Britain, such as New Providence in the Bahamas, or had lost to her through war, preeminently *Jamaica. The heyday of *Morgan, Teach (Blackbeard), Avery, Roberts, Kidd, though of hardly more than 50 years' duration, was symptomatic of Spain's equivocal self-defence in central America. Through her reforms at home, and a series of better-structured commercial treaties, institutional piracy did not recur in the later 18th cent., and had little place in South America's 19th-cent. independence movements.

The 'internationalism' in modern maritime law may stem from such 17th-cent. jurists as Grotius, but marine technology has so varied that law as to blur 'old law and custom'. The submarine as a weapon of war in the early 20th cent., independent in operation as well as invisible, unable to afford assistance to torpedoed ships' companies, was plainly seen in some British circles as piracy re-emerging in a fresh and terrible guise. Only in 1917, with Germany's unrestricted U-boat war, did Britain cross the Rubicon and respond in kind. DDA

Pitt, William, 1st earl of Chatham (1708–78), known as Pitt the Elder. In 1735 Pitt launched his belligerent political career by insulting King George II over his son's marriage and was dismissed from the army commission he had held since 1731. Thereafter Pitt quickly established himself as a leading speaker against *Walpole's ministry and its policy of support for *Hanover.

Walpole's fall did not immediately bring Pitt into the government, but after turning his oratorical fire on *Carteret, he was given the post of paymaster-general in 1746. He refused to make money from this lucrative post. The king's enmity ensured, however, that he remained outside the cabinet. Pitt dextrously altered his attitude towards support for Hanover during the War of the *Austrian Succession, one of a series of shifts on this and other issues marking his change from opposition to government. Henry *Pelham, the prime minister, kept Pitt quiet and on the sidelines, but upon Pelham's death in 1754, Pitt entered the great struggle between leading politicians. The new minister, the duke of *Newcastle, would not give power to a serious rival in the Commons; consequently Pitt and Henry *Fox joined forces to ridicule Newcastle's minions to devastating effect. Fox was the first to break ranks and join Newcastle, but when the *Seven Years War began with the loss of *Minorca and defeats in America, Pitt came to be seen by many as the country's only hope. With great reluctance George II invited him to form a government with the duke of *Devonshire nominally at its head in December 1756. It soon became apparent that no government would have the combination of skill and numerical strength in Parliament necessary to prosecute the war unless Pitt and Newcastle acted together; thus, in July 1757, Newcastle was appointed 1st lord with Pitt as secretary of state for the southern department.

Pitt unquestionably acted as leader of the war effort. He had the backing of independent MPs (notably through his encouragement of the Militia Bill), dominated the cabinet, showing singleness of purpose and an immense capacity for detail. He inspired the military and the country at large and won the confidence of Britain's major ally, Prussia. Once again he found it necessary to alter his position to one of support for large-scale engagements in Europe, but excused this by declaring that 'America has been conquered in Germany.' Pitt's goal was colonial expansion, and by 1761 Britain had driven the French from Canada, India, and most of the Caribbean. It was also a period of significant economic growth despite tax rises and a swelling national debt which Pitt was prepared to sanction.

Pitt had won George II's respect, though never his affection, by the time of the king's death in 1760, but when George III's reign commenced his position was less secure. The new king, encouraged by his tutor *Bute, wanted peace. Pitt disagreed, and after another year of military success, he resigned over the cabinet's refusal to permit attacks upon the Spanish in October 1761, stating, 'I . . . will be responsible for nothing that I do not direct.' War with Spain soon followed. In the Commons, Pitt condemned the peace settlement but Fox's managerial skills ensured that the treaty was overwhelmingly approved.

The 1760s was a decade of political instability due in no small measure to Pitt himself. He refused to ally with any political faction, uniformly support the king, or retire. His strongest feelings were reserved for America and he bitterly attacked his brother-in-law Prime Minister *Grenville for passing the *Stamp Act. However, he would not agree with the *Rockingham faction either, who repealed the Act.

The king persuaded Pitt to form a ministry in July 1766. Pitt (hitherto popularly known as 'the Great Commoner') took the title of earl of Chatham and the office of lord privy seal (with the duke of Grafton as 1st lord). Within months he had plunged into a state of virtual insanity and without him his ministers displayed their second-rate status, falling into disarray. Chatham officially resigned in October 1768, but did not regain his senses until late 1769. The final decade of Chatham's life was divided between illness and dramatic appearances in the Lords to attack *North's American policies. He was against American independence, but believed, as late as 1778, that an imperial settlement could be reached. In April 1778 Chatham was escorted to the Lords by his favourite son, William *Pitt the Younger, but during debate collapsed and died on 11 May.

The complexity of Pitt's character added to the mystery, fear, and reverence that surrounded him. He was a skilled orator and yet a three-hour speech (not uncommon) left his listeners with memories of just a few sentences. He is said to have required his under-secretaries to stand in his presence, yet could declare, 'he should be prouder to be an alderman than a peer'. He despised the concept of party and yet arranged posts for his followers. He had a romantic, deferential view of monarchy but demanded personal control of policy. Pitt had few friends, no sense of humour, and found it difficult to treat people as equals, but he was a devoted father and husband. He spared his sons the Etonian thrashings he had suffered, educating them and his daughters at home, rigorously but lovingly. His wife Hester supported him diligently during his lifelong bouts of gout and mental disorder. For a man with so many problems, in office for such brief periods, to be regarded as one of the country's greatest premiers testifies to the scale of his achievements. AIL

Ayling, S., *The Elder Pitt, Earl of Chatham* (1976); Black, J., *Pitt the Elder* (Cambridge, 1992); Williams, B., *The Life of William Pitt, Earl of Chatham* (2 vols., 1913).

Pitt, William (1759–1806), known as Pitt the Younger. Prime minister. The second son of William *Pitt, earl of Chatham, was an intellectually precocious but physically delicate boy. He was educated privately and at Cambridge. From an early age, his father supervised his upbringing, paying particular attention to skill in public speaking. He also introduced him to politics and although the younger Pitt qualified as a lawyer there was never any doubt that he would follow a political career. He entered Parliament in 1781 and soon made his mark in the Commons. He was a critic of *North, whom he blamed for the loss of America, and advocated both economical and parliamentary reform. Pitt's basic political convictions mirrored those of his father. He upheld the king's right to choose and dismiss ministers; he detested party, and he believed that the secret of British prosperity lay in the maintenance of the balance between king, Lords, and Commons established after 1688. He was keenly interested in financial and commercial questions and knew the writings of Adam *Smith and Richard Price. When North fell in 1782, Pitt refused a merely subordinate station in *Rockingham's ministry. After Rockingham's death, Pitt became chancellor of the Exchequer under *Shelburne. He deeply resented *Fox's alliance with North, seeing the Fox–North coalition as a conspiracy to impose a ministry upon the king. Yet Pitt was wise enough to refuse George III's invitation to head a ministry after the fall of Shelburne, preferring to bide his time until a more propitious moment. The crisis over Fox's *India Bill gave George III and Pitt their chance. Pitt agreed to become prime minister provided that a public demonstration of George III's hostility towards the Fox–North ministry indicated where the king's confidence lay.

When Pitt took office in December 1783 few thought his ministry would survive. He faced an opposition majority in the Commons. But several factors worked in his favour. He had the unflinching confidence of the king; the Fox–North coalition was unpopular; and he was able to win over opinion in the Commons. He called the opposition's bluff over their threat to refuse supplies and he was able to distance himself from the unpopular Shelburne. At the general election of 1784 Pitt won a decisive victory.

During his peacetime administration he achieved much in the fields of fiscal, economical, and commercial reform. He cut customs duties and stimulated trade, set up a sinking fund in the hope of paying off the national debt, and put government loans and contracts out to tender. Having established his mastery in public finance he negotiated a commercial treaty with France and ended Britain's diplomatic isolation by entering into alliance with Prussia and Holland in the aftermath of the Dutch crisis of 1787. But there were frustrations and disappointments. Pitt's proposals for a moderate reform of Parliament were defeated; he was compelled to drop his scheme for free trade with Ireland; plans to improve the defences of Portsmouth and Plymouth had to be abandoned; the abolition of the slave trade had to remain an open question within the government. These setbacks reflected Pitt's acceptance of conventional ideas about the role of the crown and the functioning of the cabinet, and his vulnerability to shifts of opinion among the country gentlemen in the Commons. Pitt did not see himself as a party leader and neglected to build up a party within Parliament. This made him all the more dependent on the support of the king and unable to overcome opposition on controversial questions within the cabinet. His position was threatened in 1788 when the illness of George III presaged a change of government. But Pitt saw off the Foxite challenge. He studied precedent, stood forth as the defender of the rights of the king and the privileges of Parliament, and insisted that Parliament had the right to decide who should be regent and on what terms. When the king recovered in 1789 Pitt seemed invincible. He knew when to yield to political pressure, as over the impeachment of *Hastings, and was adept at turning the ideas of others into practicable policies. By 1789 the confidence and prosperity of the country had been restored after the humiliation of the loss of the American colonies.

When the French Revolution broke out in 1789 Pitt was sympathetic to reform in France but was determined to stay out of European complications if possible. As late as February 1792 he affirmed his expectations for fifteen years of peace in Europe. But with the collapse of the French monarchy and the aggressive policies pursued so energetically by the French republic his hopes for peace were shattered. He was under pressure from those who feared radical movements in Britain and Ireland, especially when these were seen to be inspired by Jacobinical ideas. The outbreak of war in 1793 was a disaster for Pitt. His hopes for further reform were indefinitely postponed and he became transformed into 'the pilot who weathered the storm', a symbol of the nation's resistance to the French republic and empire. The war was long, arduous, and inconclusive. Though loyalism was the dominant feeling in Britain there was much economic distress and rebellion broke out in Ireland in 1798. Pitt had tried to appease Ireland by granting civil rights to Irish catholics and enfranchising the catholic freeholders in the Irish counties. Though the rebellion was crushed, Pitt was convinced that the credibility of the Dublin Parliament was destroyed. He carried an Act of Union with Ireland, hoping to follow it with catholic emancipation and other reforms. He was thwarted on the catholic question, partly by the opposition of George III, partly by hostility within his own government, and partly by the unpopularity of catholic relief in Britain. He resigned in 1801, giving general support to *Addington's ministry from the back benches and approving the peace of *Amiens when it was signed in 1802.

During his years out of office he was criticized for failing to build up his party. He had recognized that a more dominant role for the prime minister was a desirable accompaniment of cabinet government, but when Addington left office in 1804, Pitt once again felt the constraints of the contemporary system. Despite their differences Pitt wanted to bring Fox into a coalition as foreign secretary. George III vetoed this appointment. As a result, the Foxites and Grenvillites refused to serve. Pitt's health was now in decline and the strains of office wore him out. He built up a coalition to defeat Napoleon, but hopes of a decisive end to the war were dashed by Napoleon's victory at Austerlitz in 1805. On 23 January 1806 Pitt died. He left behind him a band of younger men whose talents he had recognized and fostered and a legend which shaped popular Toryism in the early 19th cent. Yet, to the end of his life, Pitt regarded himself as an independent Whig. With a little ingenuity Victorian conservatives and liberals could claim to stand within the Pittite tradition when it was expedient for them to do so. In this sense Pitt became part of a national mythology. JWD

Ehrman, J., *The Younger Pitt: The Years of Acclaim* (1969); id., *The Younger Pitt: The Reluctant Transition* (1983); id., *The Younger Pitt: The Consuming Struggle* (1996); Rose, J. H., *Life of William Pitt* (1923).

Place, Francis (1771–1854). The 'radical tailor of Charing Cross' was associated, either directly or indirectly, with virtually every reform movement from the *corresponding societies to *chartism. He rose from being a journeyman breeches-maker into a prosperous shopkeeper and employer, from Jacobinism to respectability, and became a disciple of *Bentham and *Mill. His skill as a backroom organizer was demonstrated in the London Corresponding Society, the Westminster elections, the repeal of the Combination Acts, the 1832 Reform Bill agitation, and chartism. Place believed in working-class advancement through self-help, education, and extension of the franchise. He eschewed violence and advocated alliance with the middle classes. Place accumulated a huge collection of books, pamphlets, and papers of all kinds (now in the British Library) on which historians have relied heavily, without always appreciating the extent to which the record is coloured by Place's partisan views. JFCH

place Acts. As soon as parliaments were established as annual events after the *Glorious Revolution, ministers began to consider how to use patronage to obtain reliable majorities. Oppositions countered by proposing place bills to preserve the independence of the House of Commons from encroachment by the executive by disqualifying members under government influence. A fierce struggle raged in William III's reign, with bills defeated in the Lords or vetoed by the king. Nevertheless, statutes were passed excluding commissioners of the excise and of the customs. The grandest attempt was in the Act of *Settlement of 1701, which forbade membership of the Commons to any person holding an office or place of profit under the crown: if implemented, it would have divorced executive and legislature on the American pattern. But the provision was circumvented by the device of re-election on taking office, which lasted until 1926. Subsequent campaigns were ragged and ineffective. After the fall of *Walpole, an act to exclude commissioners of the navy was carried and a place measure became part of the *Rockinghams' campaign for *economical reform in the 1770s. Clerke's Act in 1782 excluded government contractors. But the cumulative effect was slight, government influence being more than sustained by the vast growth of the civil service, army, and navy. JAC

place-names provide a rich source of historical information, often for areas and subjects which are otherwise not well documented. The initial stages of their study are the province of the linguist because the original meaning of the majority of names is no longer immediately intelligible from their present form. The evolution of the name 'Eboracum' through 'Everog' and 'Eoforwic' to 'Iorvik' and thus to modern 'York' provides a good example of the complexities involved. Though the explanation of this sequence is a linguistic matter, it clearly has important implications for any historian concerned with settlement continuity and the changing control of this major centre.

England's place-names have been intensively explored by the English Place-Name Society and its publications provide the basic data for most of the country. They show that the majority of English names were formed in the Germanic languages of the Anglo-Saxon and Scandinavian settlers of pre-Norman Britain. It is to the Anglo-Saxons that we owe names ending in *-ham* and *-tun*, both indicating a village or farm, whilst the Scandinavian settlers spawned the numerous names in the north and east of the country which contain the elements *-by* ('farm'), *-thorpe* ('secondary settlement'), and *-thwaite* ('clearing'). The relative dating and interpretation of all of these elements is still, however, a controversial issue. Other language groups are less well represented in the onomastic palimpsest; the relative paucity of Celtic names, together with the survival of only a small number of Romano-British names, is, for example, particularly marked and is obviously of relevance to studies of settlement and social change in the 5th and 6th cents. Similarly the advent of a Norman aristocracy added only a few French names, though the representation of their scribal system changed the spelling (and later, by extension, the pronunciation) of many English names. In the post-medieval period, names have continued to be coined; to this group belong most street-names and field-names which are valuable sources on changing patterns of industry, trade, and agriculture.

Scotland's names are linguistically equally complex, though they have been less intensively studied than those south of the border. There is an early stratum of P- Celtic elements (Gallo-Brythonic) which appear to represent the Pictish language: the *c.*300 names in *pit-* ('piece of land'), such as Pitlochry, or the *-pevr* ('radiant') of Strathpeffer provide good examples of a group whose distribution is markedly north-eastern. Old English and Scandinavian forms to the south of the Forth–Clyde line reflect various extensions of Northumbrian and English power after the 7th cent. whilst the distribution of Scandinavian elements like *setr* ('dwelling') and *stathir* ('dwelling'; 'farm') is the result of Norse activity in the northern and western isles and adjacent coastlands. It is, however, the Gaelic names which give Scottish maps their distinctive appearance. Within these can be seen forms like *sliabh* ('mountain'), largely limited to Dalriada and Galloway, which represent a pre-7th-cent. phase. These contrast with the more widespread distribution of other names such as those containing *baile* ('hamlet'; 'farm') which show the extent of Gaelic usage before the 17th cent. and the language's decline in the Lowlands.

Place-names in Wales are more readily intelligible to native speakers than those elsewhere in Britain for they have shared the general development of the Celtic language. But even here the linguistic make-up is far from straightforward, with interesting forms of Anglicization (e.g. Prestatyn—'village of the priests') and traces of Scandinavian naming (e.g., Swansea—'Sveinn's island') around the coast. RNB

plague. Bubonic plague is a disease of rats, spread to humans by fleas deserting dead or dying rat hosts. The bacillus *Yersinia pestis* is either transmitted by direct flea bite or via flea faeces entering the bloodstream. Occurring primarily in the summer, it causes fever, vomiting, and inflammation of the lymphatic glands to give the characteristic swellings or buboes. Bubonic plague kills between 60 and 80 per cent of those infected. Still more lethal is *pneumonic* plague, which occurs when the bacillus enters the lungs and is then transmitted by droplet infection. Although it might have helped to cause the exceptional mortality of the *Black Death in 1348–9, the pneumonic variety played only a minor role in plague epidemics after the early 15th cent.

Plague arrived in England in 1348 as part of a European pandemic that lasted until the early 18th cent. No subsequent plague epidemic had the same ferocious impact as the Black Death. Recent estimates put the death toll at something like 47 per cent of the entire population. The disease returned, albeit with diminished force, in secondary national epidemics in 1360–2, 1368–9, 1375, and 1390–1. After the late 14th cent. plague tended to occur on a regional rather than a national level, although 1413, 1434, 1439, and 1464 were country-wide. It remained a frequent scourge: in one 15th-cent. Canterbury priory 16 per cent of all monks died of plague, and it usually visited that institution at least once a decade.

The overall impact of plague on the national death rate, however, diminished progressively. From the late 15th cent., plague increasingly became a disease of towns and cities, where man and rat lived in closest proximity, or hit villages located on lines of communication. Between 1544 and the 1660s, no plague epidemic ever affected more than one in five English parishes. Our historical perceptions are coloured by the experiences of those minority of communities which were devastated by plague. Norwich lost a third of its population in 1579. London accounted for one third of *all* plague deaths that occurred in England between 1570 and 1670. The capital lost at least 25 per cent of its inhabitants in 1563, and a further 20 per cent or so perished in 1603 and again in 1625. The last 'Great Plague' in London in 1665, recorded in *Pepys, killed about 56,000 people.

Plague was interpreted as God's punishment on sinful man. Epidemics therefore provoked penitential acts of worship, fastings, and exhortations to moral and religious improvement. In the 17th cent., the increasing identification of the poor as carriers and chief victims of plague reinforced attempts by their social superiors to control and reform their behaviour. The disease disappeared from Britain after the mid-17th cent. Scotland's last serious outbreak was 1645–9, England's was 1665–6. Why the plague disappeared is still debated, but it was probably due to the much more efficient quarantining of ships, which prevented the initial importation of the disease, and to increased use of brick rather than wood in houses, which reduced the contact between humans and rats. JPB

Plaid Cymru (Welsh Nationalist Party). Plaid Cymru was established in 1925 mainly to campaign for the protection of Welsh language and culture. After the Second World War the organization took on the functions of a political party to tread the parliamentary road to Welsh independence. During the 1960s its policies became more economically motivated, aimed at reducing unemployment, halting the migration of Welsh youth, and replacing declining traditional industries. It had little success until 1966 when it won a by-election at Carmarthen. In the election of February 1974 two seats were gained—Caernarfon and Merioneth. Plaid Cymru exploited the minority position of the Labour government (1974–9) to force discussion on constitutional change. However, the March 1979 devolution referendum was a blow to the party. From a turn-out of 58.3 per cent, only 11.8 per cent voted for a Welsh assembly.

After this set-back, Plaid Cymru attempted to build on its traditional support in northern rural Welsh-speaking areas by wooing the southern English-speaking majority. In 1983 it began publishing a quarterly English-language journal called *Radical Wales*. It has increased awareness of Welsh issues at Westminster and gained recognition of the need for Welsh-language education. In the 1987 general election Plaid Cymru won Ynys Môn (Anglesey) and in 1992 gained Ceredigion and Pembroke North, taking its number of seats to four. Its grass-roots support remains healthy, with Plaid Cymru having the second highest number of local councillors in Wales, though it still lags far behind the Labour Party. RAS

Plantagenets. The Plantagenet dynasty took its name from the *Planta Genesta*, or broom, traditionally an emblem of the counts of Anjou. Members of this dynasty ruled England from 1154 to 1399. However, in conventional historical usage, Henry II (son of Count *Geoffrey of Anjou) and his sons Richard I and John are normally termed the Angevin kings, and their successors, up to Richard II, the Plantagenets. The term Plantagenet was not used until about 1450, when Richard, duke of *York, called himself by it in order to emphasize his royal descent from Edward III's fifth son, Edmund of Langley. MCP

plantations was the name employed for colonial settlements and the supervising body of the first British empire was known as the Board of *Trade and Plantations. One of the earliest attempts was Sir Humphrey *Gilbert's expedition to *Newfoundland which failed and cost him his life (1583). His half-brother Sir Walter *Ralegh sponsored the equally ill-fated attempt on Roanoke Island (Virginia), which began in 1585 and was deserted by 1589. American settlement resumed in James I's reign with Virginia (1607), Plymouth (1620), followed by Massachusetts Bay (1628), Maryland (1634), Connecticut (1635), Rhode Island (1636), and New Haven (1638). Gilbert and Ralegh were also much involved in the Tudor plantations of Ireland. After the initial expedition by *Pembroke (Strongbow) in the 12th cent., the English *Pale had led a precarious existence. A new series of plantations began in the reign of Mary and Philip (Queen's County and King's County), was continued by Elizabeth, and urged on by James I and Charles I, who encouraged English and Scottish settlement in Ulster. During the Commonwealth, many of *Cromwell's soldiers were given vast estates in Ireland. Native Irish resistance to expropriation was a factor in the risings of 1598 and 1641 and in the support given to James II after 1688. The effect of the Tudor and Stuart plantations was to set the pattern of Irish politics for the next 400 years. JAC

Plassey, battle of, 1757. Aware that the French-supported nawab Siraj-ud-Daula was intent on further rebellion against East India Company rule, Robert *Clive led a force of about 1,000 European and 2,000 Indian soldiers to confront him. He found Siraj on 23 June at Plassey, on the banks of the Bhagirathi river, at the head of 50,000 men. However, a rainstorm soaked Siraj's artillery powder and Clive, who had kept his powder dry, opened a devastating fire when the nawab's cavalry tried to charge. Siraj fled, leaving Clive in control of Bengal. JLP

Playfair, John (1748–1819). Mathematician and natural philosopher. Playfair was the son of a presbyterian minister, educated for the kirk, a professor of mathematics and, later, natural philosophy at Edinburgh 1785–1819, and author of a standard edition of Euclid (1795). A friend of the great geologist James *Hutton, Playfair developed into a geologist of note by virtue of a lucid and attractive commentary on Hutton's dense and brilliant theory of the earth. The *Illustrations of the Huttonian Theory* (1802) did much to popularize and clarify the business of Victorian geology. Playfair was a popularizer of the best sort. His *Dissertation on the Progress of Mathematical and Physical Science since the Revival of Letters in Europe*, a supplement to the *Encyclopaedia Britannica* (1816), was one of the best histories of that subject. NTP

Playfair, Lyon (1818–98). Playfair was a chemist and statesman, and one of the organizers of the *Great Exhibition of 1851. Educated at Edinburgh and then at Giessen, where Justus Liebig had built up a great research school, Playfair worked in textiles in Manchester, and met John *Dalton. In 1845 he moved to London, to the School of Mines, an ancestor of Imperial College; he realized that although the *Crystal Palace seemed to show Britain as the workshop of the world, in fact other countries were overtaking her. In lectures, and from 1868 as a Liberal MP and minister, and after 1892 as Baron Playfair, he promoted awareness of the importance of science for the prosperity of the country. He became a great spokesman for technical and scientific education; with his wide circle of friends in high places, including Prince *Albert, he has been compared to Joseph *Banks as an influential figure. DK

Playfair, William Henry (1790–1857). Scottish architect who perhaps studied under Wyatt and Smirke in London. He returned to Scotland in 1816 to complete Robert *Adam's building for Edinburgh University, and thereafter made his mark on the Scottish capital with his public buildings, notably those on the Mound—the Doric Royal Institution (now the Royal Scottish Academy, 1822–6, enlarged 1832–5), and the Ionic National Gallery of Scotland (1850–7), overlooked by the Gothic towers of Free Church College (now New College, 1846–50). On Calton Hill he designed monuments to his uncle John *Playfair and Dugald *Stewart (1831), as well as the City Observatory (1818), and the National Monument, in collaboration with C. R. Cockerell (1824–9, unfinished). Non-Grecian buildings by Playfair in Edinburgh include Donaldson's hospital (1842–54), in a

Jacobean style, and St Stephen's church (1827–8, later altered), which calls to mind the London churches of *Hawksmoor. PW

pleas of the crown. The notion of the pleas of the crown can be traced back to Anglo-Saxon times to describe those wrongs which were the particular concern of the king and for which the king was entitled to take a fine (wite). Later under the Norman kings and their successors the term came to mean those pleas or cases which concerned the king as distinct from pleas between subjects—common pleas. Although these pleas were principally what we would now regard as crimes, some were to develop as torts (civil wrongs), notably trespass, which was a plea of the crown because the writ alleged that it was a wrong 'vi et armis et contra pacem regis' ('by force of arms and against the king's peace'). Increasingly the pleas of the crown became the substance of the criminal law—indeed the great classic of the criminal law was Hale's *Pleas of the Crown*. MM

pleasure gardens for the public, with entertainments and light refreshments, began in the 17th cent., but their heyday was the Georgian period, with more leisure and surplus income. They aimed at enchantment and elegant relaxation—coloured lights in the trees, flowers and arbours, music, fountains and fireworks, breakfasts and supper parties, masquerades and dancing, flirtation, and, above all, the pleasure of seeing and being seen. In London, *Vauxhall and *Ranelagh were augmented by less ambitious gardens at Marylebone, Hampstead, Sadler's Wells, Islington, and elsewhere. Bath had its own Vauxhall in Bathwick meadows by 1742 and Bristol its Vauxhall gardens near the Hotwells. Celia Fiennes noted 'a sort of spring garden' at Newcastle upon Tyne in 1698 and a new Ranelagh garden opened there in 1760. They did much to improve public taste and discourage boorishness but fell victim, in the end, to changing demand: the *ton* found them increasingly vulgar, the *hoi polloi* too tame. JAC

Plimsoll, Samuel (1824–98). Radical MP. Born in Bristol, a congregationalist, Plimsoll was successively a solicitor's clerk, manager of a brewery, and honorary secretary for the *Great Exhibition of 1851. In 1853 he became a coal merchant in London, gaining an extensive knowledge of coastal shipping. Elected to Parliament for Derby in 1868, he proposed a compulsory load line to prevent shipping accidents and obtained a royal commission on the subject in 1873. His anger at the greed of shipowners who resisted his plans led to his temporary exclusion from the Commons in 1875, but his persistence was rewarded with the Merchant Shipping Act of 1876 and the load line soon came to bear his name. Out of Parliament after 1880, he retained his interest in shipping, publishing a pamphlet on cattle ships in 1890, and became president of the Sailors' Union the same year. ER

Plunket, St Oliver (1629–81). Catholic archbishop of Armagh and primate of Ireland (1670–81). Born in Meath, educated in Rome, Plunket was successively professor of theology there (1657–69) and archbishop of Armagh after consecration in Ghent. He was on good terms with successive viceroys. Diligent in his diocese, he also went on mission to the Hebrides (1671). An ultramontane, he established firm ecclesiastical discipline and raised standards, and, though in dispute with Archbishop Talbot of Dublin over precedence, presided at the synod (1670). Threatened with expulsion after the English Test Act he went into hiding (1674), but was arrested in Dublin (1678) and falsely accused of involvement in the *Popish plot. Tried in London on a trumped-up charge of conspiring to bring a French army to Ireland, Plunket was convicted of treason and, despite general agreement of his innocence, was hanged, drawn, and quartered at Tyburn. His relics are in Downside abbey (Som.). He was canonized in 1975. WMM

Plunket, William, 1st Baron Plunket (1764–1854). Lawyer. The son of a presbyterian minister at Enniskillen, Plunket was educated at Trinity College, Dublin, and studied law at Lincoln's Inn. He was elected to the Irish Parliament in 1798 and opposed the Act of Union. In 1807 and 1812–27 he sat at Westminster, pursuing a *Grenvillite line, and was given a peerage in 1827. He became solicitor-general [I] 1803–5, attorney-general [I] 1805–7 and 1822–7, and lord chief justice of Common Pleas 1827–30. Lord Grey then appointed him lord chancellor [I] and he served with one short interruption from 1830 until 1841. A wealthy and successful lawyer, Plunket (though a protestant) was an ardent advocate of catholic emancipation. *Greville commended his speech in favour of the Reform Bill in October 1831, and five years after his death bracketed Plunket with *Grattan and *Burke as great parliamentary orators. JAC

Plunkett, Sir Horace (1854–1932). Plunkett was a lifelong advocate of agricultural co-operation. A younger son of the 16th Lord Dunsany [I], he was born in Gloucestershire, but spent his early years rearing cattle in America. In 1889 he settled in Ireland and began preaching co-operative farming. He became a member of the *Congested Districts Board in 1891 and entered Parliament the following year as a Unionist. The Irish Agricultural Organization Society (1894) led to a Department of Agriculture for Ireland in 1899, in which Plunkett served for seven years as vice-president, despite losing his parliamentary seat in 1900. But like many moderates, his political hopes foundered on growing militancy in Ireland. Reluctantly converted to *Home Rule, he urged Ulster not to stay out. When it did, he became in 1922 a member of the Senate of the Irish Free State, but returned to England after his house had been burned down in 1923. In January 1920 Plunkett was reported dead by mistake and had the dubious pleasure of reading his own obituary notices. JAC

pluralism is the holding of more than one ecclesiastical benefice with cure of souls simultaneously. Although consistently denounced by the church, there was never a time, certainly from the Middle Ages onwards, when pluralism did not take place. There were many reasons for its continuance. The poverty of many benefices often made the holding of more than one a necessity. Shortage of clergy—increasingly a problem in the 20th cent.—was another reason. Today many Anglican clergy in rural areas are technically pluralists, holding three or more grouped benefices simultaneously—though now with official approbation and authority. The Church of England from the 16th cent. onward made efforts to reduce or regulate the incidence of pluralism, but not until the passage of the Pluralities Act of 1838 was there any real success. Even that Act protected the position of most of those already in possession of more than one benefice, and not until the last quarter of the century did its provisions come fully into force. JRG

Plymouth owes its importance to the magnificent estuary into which drain the rivers Plym and Tamar. The original settlement was at Sutton, the name Plymouth being attached to the harbour. Sutton Prior was a borough in the 13th cent. and Plymouth developed from a small fishing village. By *Leland's time, in the 1530s, it was 'very large' with 'a goodly rode for great shippes'. The war against Spain in Elizabeth's reign brought Plymouth into national prominence. *Drake and his colleagues sailed from the Hoe to defeat the Armada and *Essex left in 1596 with his expedition against Cadiz. During the civil wars, Plymouth was of great strategic importance as a parliamentary bastion in a predominantly royalist region and resisted repeated attempts to subdue it. After the Restoration it increased with the growth of the navy. The royal citadel, to strengthen the defences, was begun in 1666 and the dockyard at Devonport was developed in William's reign. In the course of the 18th cent., it passed *Exeter in population, though Plymouth, Stonehouse, and Devonport were brought under one administration as late as 1914. As a vital naval base, within easy bombing range from occupied France, Plymouth suffered heavily in the Second World War, and the subsequent replanning did not command total enthusiasm. The population in 1992 was 258,000. JAC

Plymouth brethren, Christian brethren, or Darbyites, began in Dublin in the mid-1820s when groups of young men, several from *Trinity College, met for communion regardless of denomination. With no intention of starting a separate movement, they did exactly that, thanks to J. N. Darby (1800–82), a non-practising barrister who had recently resigned his Anglican orders. Growth in the 1830s was followed by predictable tensions in the 1840s, especially in Bristol and Plymouth. These culminated in the 'Bethesda Question' (1848), which divided brethren into open and exclusive sections. Henry Craik (1804–66), of Bethesda, Bristol, believed that all Christians should be welcome at the breaking of bread. Darby did not; for him, believers were called from the ruined church to witness against the errors of the last days. Thereafter Darby led the exclusives while men like A. N. Groves (1795–1853), the Exeter dentist who became a missionary to Baghdad and India, were associated with the open. Despite this division they remained similar in beliefs and structure: a world-denying pietism; the Bible as their supreme rule; an interest in prophecy and the Second Coming; believers' baptism; weekly breaking of bread; no set liturgy; no ordained ministry, though many full-time evangelists; a congregational polity with no co-ordinating organization. Despite their fissiparous tendencies, they spread steadily. In England and Ireland they attracted an educated membership with rather an aristocratic veneer. In Scotland, where they benefited from the revival of 1859–60, they spread in industrial and fishing communities, especially in the north-east. They also spread in Europe and the empire with missions ('Christian Missions in Many Lands') in central Africa, India, and Latin America. Popularly stamped with the exclusive image, reinforced in the 1960s when one exclusive section withdrew its members from universities and professional activities, their ideal atmosphere is better seen as one of spiritual and intellectual liberty set in a context of brotherly love. CB

poaching. The punishment for poaching in the king's forest in Norman times was severe: Richard I's assize of 1198 threatened deer-stealers with blinding and castration. Though the royal forests were exceptional, and savage punishments were relaxed, poaching, in its various forms, continued as a major irritant until rural society gave way to town life in the later 19th cent. G. M. Trevelyan wrote that 'there never was a truce in the poaching war'. One of the earliest poems, *The Parlement of the Thre Ages* (*c*.1350), begins with a magnificent account of the shooting of a hart with a crossbow at night. The *Peasants' Revolt of 1381 was one of the first insurrections in which demands for the relaxation or abolition of the game laws were made. In the jittery period that followed, Parliament complained (1389) that servants and labourers absented themselves from church to go hunting with dogs in 'parks, warrens and coneyries', and enacted that the right to hunt should be restricted to owners of property worth at least 40 shillings a year. Although in popular mythology the poacher is a solitary operator, organized gangs made an early appearance. Having just won the battle of *Bosworth (1485) Henry VII was called upon by his Parliament to tackle the problems of malefactors in Kent, Surrey, and Sussex who 'in great number, some with painted faces, some with visors' roamed the woods at night. Such behaviour was declared a felony. During the civil wars of the 17th cent., the relaxation of law and order gave poachers much freedom and after the Restoration, in 1671, there was an effort to tighten up. Game was reserved for freeholders of property worth £100 p.a., copyholders worth £150, and the son and heir of esquires and above: these persons could hunt over other people's land and appoint gamekeepers with right to search. In a desperate attempt to reduce poaching, an Act of 1755 totally forbade the sale of game, which led to a thriving black market. At the same time, improvements in guns prompted landowners to breed game in greater numbers. Poaching was then no longer a question of pinching rabbits from a common or trout from a stream but organized attacks upon private property. The poaching war of the later 18th and early 19th cents. saw bloody affrays, with the landowners defending their game with spring-guns and man-traps. *Blackwood's Magazine* wrote in 1827 that there was 'a war raging against the aristocracy', and poaching was an important element in the *Swing riots of 1830. Even in the midst of the reform crisis, Parliament found time to legislate. The Game Reform Act of 1831 repealed 27 previous acts, declared a close season for hunting, allowed tenants to hunt and shoot on their own land, and introduced a system of certificates which gave permission to kill game, subject to the law of trespass. But any improvement in relations was temporary, for further improvements in guns led to vast *battues*, in which 1,000 birds might be shot in one day. Breeding enough birds became a large industry and the crops consumed by the birds caused bitter resentment. Confrontation between gamekeepers and poachers continued. But after the Great War the ruling class was less keen on mass slaughter and poaching became incidental rather than endemic. JAC

pocket boroughs or nomination boroughs were constituencies where the patron could usually control the return of the members of Parliament. They were often, though not invariably, burgage or corporation boroughs with small electorates. The Frankland family of Thirkleby commanded two seats at Thirsk between 1688 and 1832 without once facing a contest: Sir James Lowther returned nine members in 1784. The number of seats under patronage has been put at over 250 in 1761 out of a total of 558. JAC

poet laureate. James I awarded Ben *Jonson a pension in 1616 and he and Sir William Davenant (1637) were widely recognized as laureates. But the first court appointment of a laureate was in 1668 when Charles II chose *Dryden. In the 18th cent. the laureate was expected to produce birthday odes and wedding verses. Among the more distinguished laureates were *Wordsworth (1843) and *Tennyson (1850): less distinguished were Whitehead (1757), Pye (1790), and Alfred Austin (1896). The present poet laureate (1984) is Ted Hughes. JAC

Poitiers, battle of, 1356. *Edward, the Black Prince's blooding had been at Crécy in 1346 and he spent much of the next ten years campaigning in France. In August 1356 he was before Bourges but threatened by a much larger army under John II of France. The English attempted to retreat towards Bordeaux but found their way blocked at Poitiers. The Black Prince offered terms, hoping to avoid battle, but on 19 September the French attacked. Archers, lying in ditches and behind hedges, broke up the first assaults, and in their last attack the French were taken in the flank. The large number of prisoners included the French king. Since King David of Scotland, captured at *Neville's Cross in 1346, was still a prisoner, Edward III now had two kings on his hands. JAC

Poland, relations with. Poland excited little interest in Britain before the partitions of that country between 1772 and 1795. Although widely regarded as a crime, the first partition was not seen as a threat to the balance of power, though in the early 1790s difficulties with Russia encouraged the British to look to Poland as an alternative economic partner (including naval stores) in the east. During the second and third partitions Britain was preoccupied with the war with revolutionary France, and in 1814–15 Russian military control denied Britain any effective say in the future of Poland. This story was repeated during the uprisings by the Poles against their Russian overlords in 1830–1 and 1863. *Palmerston recognized in the second instance that nothing could be done without France, and he feared that Napoleon III might seize the opportunity to make other major territorial changes in Europe.

The upheavals at the end of the First World War enabled Poland to re-emerge as an independent state, but British ministers often thought the Polish leaders reckless and ambitious. The guarantee of Poland in March 1939 owed much to the fear that German expansion in eastern Europe might be the prelude to war in the west. It was still hoped, however, that Hitler could be persuaded to negotiate. Although the German invasion brought Britain into the war in September 1939, it was assumed that Poland could not be saved and that its reconstitution was dependent on an allied victory in the west. Churchill tried to mediate between Stalin and the Polish government in exile in London later in the war, but their aims were incompatible, and diplomacy could not prevent a communist take-over by 1947. The British sympathized strongly with the reform movement (Solidarity) from 1980, but their trading interests conflicted with American efforts to impose sanctions a year later. CJB

Pole, Edmund de la, 3rd duke of Suffolk (*c.*1472–1513). Pole's mother was Elizabeth, sister to Edward IV and Richard III: Henry VIII's mother was his first cousin. Pole was therefore close to the throne, a dangerous position in Tudor times. He succeeded his father as duke in 1492 but because the family had lost estates was recognized as earl only. His elder brother John, earl of *Lincoln, had perished in rebellion at *Stoke in 1487. Henry VII gave him the Garter around 1496 but in 1501 he resumed the title of duke, went abroad, and set up as Yorkist claimant. He was attainted, handed back to Henry VII and placed in the Tower. Henry VIII had him executed in May 1513. JAC

Pole, John de la, 2nd duke of Suffolk (1442–92). Pole was originally married to his father's ward Margaret *Beaufort, daughter and heir of John, duke of Somerset (d. 1444). The marriage was annulled and he married Richard of *York's daughter Elizabeth. He was demoted to earl in the proscription of Yorkists in 1459, but earned reinstatement as duke by serving in Yorkist armies in 1461. His rewards from Edward IV, his brother-in-law, were insubstantial. He was apparently a political lightweight, never a royal councillor, loyal enough to support Edward against *Warwick, but an embarrassment through his high-handed efforts to dominate East Anglia. Suffolk survived by acquiescing to the accessions of both Richard III and Henry VII, even having some favour from the latter after the rebellion of his son, the earl of *Lincoln, in 1487. RLS

Pole, Margaret de la. See SALISBURY, COUNTESS OF.

Pole, Michael de la (*c.*1330–89). Son of William de la Pole (d. 1366), merchant of Hull and a major financier of Edward III's campaigns in France, Michael served the crown in various military and diplomatic capacities before becoming chancellor of England in 1383. He enjoyed the favour of Richard II, being created earl of Suffolk in 1385. When Richard lost control of the government in 1386, Pole was impeached for supposed malpractices concerning the French war which was going badly. In 1387 the king declared the impeachment void, but further attacks by the *appellants led to Pole's flight in December 1387 and he was declared guilty of treason. Stripped of all his lands and honours he died in exile in Paris in September 1389. AC

Pole, Reginald (1500–58). Cardinal and archbishop of Canterbury. Pole was a younger son of Margaret, countess of *Salisbury, daughter of George, duke of *Clarence: he was therefore of the blood royal and his mother was governess and companion of Princess Mary. Intended from the beginning for the church, he spent 1521–7 on the continent in study. On his return he was made dean of Windsor and on *Wolsey's death seems to have declined the archbishopric of York. Increasingly opposed to the king's divorce policy, he went abroad again in 1532. Asked for his opinion by the king, Pole produced in 1536 a strong counter-statement, placing his relatives in England in acute danger. His nomination as cardinal increased their peril: his eldest brother was executed, his nephew died in the Tower, his mother was beheaded in 1541. Pole remained on the continent in constant fear of assassination. On Mary's accession in 1553 he was anxious to return to England at once and found it hard to understand why there should be delay. He came back as legate in November 1554 and in March 1556 succeeded *Cranmer as archbishop of Canterbury. But the return of England to the faith—the object of Pole's life—was fraught with problems. The burning of protestants caused great outrage; the nobility were most reluctant to return church lands; Mary's husband *Philip found himself at war with the papacy and Pole's legatine authority was revoked. He died on the same day as Mary in November 1558. Pole's dedication to his church was beyond question, but his long absence from England and the terrible fate that had overcome his family rendered his judgement questionable. JAC

Pole, William de la, earl, marquis, and 1st duke of Suffolk (1396–1450). Suffolk had a chequered career in the French war from 1417 to 1437. As an associate of Cardinal *Beaufort, he became steward of Henry VI's household in 1432. This position enabled him to make himself the king's chief councillor after Beaufort's death, create a household faction, and monopolize royal patronage, so that he prospered while crown revenues dwindled. He was made duke in 1448. He continued Beaufort's quest for peace by negotiation. In 1444 he headed two embassies to France which arranged Henry's marriage to the dowerless *Margaret of Anjou but only a short truce; its extension to 1449 had to be bought by the surrender of Maine. The failure of Suffolk's diplomacy was exploited by enemies, including the duke of *Norfolk and Lord Cromwell, who had suffered by his manipulation of royal favour and legal procedures. Impeachment by Parliament led to his banishment and murder at sea. RLS

police. For years Britons resisted having a proper police force, because they associated it with repression, especially of the French kind. They also feared it would raise their rates. This was despite rampant crime in the 18th cent., which in the absence of police was dealt with by draconian penalties, especially death, designed to deter. In the more humane 19th cent., however, the sight of poor folk being strangulated for minor offences became less acceptable, and other methods of crime prevention were sought. The middle classes also worried about public order, in an era (*c.*1790–1820) of serious riot and rebellion. Their only recourse was the army, backed up by even tougher sanctions. That could be counter-productive. *Peterloo, for example, and the *Cato Street executions set people against the government. A gentler means of public control was required.

This was where Sir Robert *Peel came in. He devised his first police bill while chief secretary for Ireland, leading to the creation of the Irish Constabulary in 1822. In 1829 he persuaded Parliament to accept something similar (though not so militaristic) for London, to be called the Metropolitan Police. For its first years it was clearly on trial. Its commissioners, therefore, proceeded cautiously. All policemen were put in a distinctive uniform, so that they could not be taken for 'spies'. They were unarmed, except for short batons. Rules of conduct were demanding. Of its first 2,800 recruits, 2,238 were dismissed from the force, sometimes for simply taking a drink or a nap. But it worked. The police became accepted by a suspicious middle class, and eventually by large numbers of the working classes too. They may have deterred crime (though figures are unreliable; and other factors, like rising prosperity, were active). They developed methods of dealing with public demonstrations which were subtle but effective. Other areas of the country called the 'Met' in to help. After 1833 they were permitted to set up their own forces, on the London model. Most did. Those which did not were finally made to by Acts of 1856 (England and Wales) and 1857 (Scotland).

All except the Irish and London forces were locally accountable. (The latter came directly under the home secretary: initially because London had no unitary government for it to be accountable to, later because of the national role it was thought to play.) That set the freedom-loving Victorians' minds at rest. Subsequently there have been pressures to centralize the police more, which achieved some successes in the 1980s.

Another later development was the growth of a plain clothes detective branch. That began in London in 1842, but consisted initially of only eight men. They tended to be distrusted. In 1877 that distrust seemed to be vindicated by a scandal which implicated three of the detective branch's four inspectors in a turf fraud they were supposed to be investigating. That provoked a shake-up, out of which the present-day Criminal Investigation Department was born in 1878. In the 1880s the latter spawned the police's first political arm: a 'Special Branch' formed initially to look after Irish-American *Fenian bombers, but later extended to *anarchists, *suffragettes, and other sources of irritation to the government. The same period saw the police taking on other duties: regulating vice, drink, and gambling, for example, and watching out for foreign spies.

The police's most controversial role has always been its public order one. Its problem was that keeping order in times of civil unrest could be interpreted as acting for the state against the democracy. Strikes were the most difficult case. The 1890s, 1920s, and 1980s saw the police brought into the political arena in this way. In 1918 they had a strike of their own, which created another kind of concern. In general, however, the British police have successfully maintained their image of being 'consensual', at least in happier times. BJP

Political Register. The best-known radical newspaper in the early 19th cent. It was launched by William *Cobbett in January 1802 as a weekly, supported by William *Windham, and pursued a fiercely right-wing anti-French stance. But Cobbett soon moved to a radical position, condemning the Whigs as mere temporizers and calling constantly for reform of Parliament. In 1816 he brought out a cheap edition—the famous 'Twopenny Trash'—which sold in tens of thousands. It ceased publication in 1836, the year after Cobbett's death. JAC

poll tax. A fixed amount of tax per head, or poll. Poll taxes first came to prominence in the late 14th cent. when they were imposed to pay for the war in France (the *Hundred Years War). The taxes of 1377, the 'tallage of groats' (4 pence per person over 14 years, 'except real beggars'), and 1379, 'the evil subsidy', were at higher rates than usual; and the *Peasants' Revolt of 1381 arose from that year's tax of 1 shilling per head. Violence against collectors and justices turned to rebellion and the rebels converged on London where Wat *Tyler and John *Ball became their leaders. Poll taxes were very occasionally used in the 15th to 17th cents., the last time being 1698. However at the end of the 20th cent., Margaret *Thatcher's Conservative government reintroduced the tax, under the name community charge (1990–3, 1989–93 in Scotland), to replace domestic rates for the finance of local government. As in the 14th cent., evasion and riots ensued; and the tax was, in part, the cause of Mrs Thatcher's downfall. MW

polo is derived from the Tibetan word for a willow stick and originated in the East, probably among the horsemen of central Asia. It was very popular in Persia and variants were played in India, Japan, and China. British tea-planters and cavalry officers adopted it in India and inter-regimental competitions were organized. The first game in Britain was held in London in 1871 and the Hurlingham Club, at Fulham, founded in 1875, established itself as the governing body of the sport. It was included in the Olympic Games between 1908 and 1936. Since it involves the ownership or hire of several ponies for each player, it is unlikely to sweep the country, but it still has a considerable following in Argentina and in Britain is played mainly by army officers. JAC

poor. 'A decent provision for the poor', declared Samuel *Johnson, 'is the true test of civilization.' But identifying the poor with any precision has proved difficult for those wishing to help them and for historians wishing to study them. In general terms the poor are those who, compared with others in the same society and in the same historical period, are judged to have no or few material possessions, and are without the resources to obtain the comforts and necessities of life.

Efforts to identify the poor using systematic measurements were attempted from the later 18th cent. onwards and were part of the debate about the extent of poverty in Britain. The destitution of orphans, the aged, and the sick was accepted as a suitable condition for public support, but the extent of poverty among physically fit adults was disputed. Sir Frederick Eden attempted in 1797 to document the lives of the poor in terms of expenditure on food, fuel, clothing, and shelter, but his studies were criticized as unsystematic and unrelated to the basic minima needed to maintain a healthy life. Similar shortcomings were found in the anecdotal account *London Labour and the London Poor* published by Henry Mayhew in 1851. Investigators of the London Statistical Society (later the Royal Statistical Society of London) and the Manchester Statistical Society attempted to be more scientific by initiating studies of intakes per head of various commodities of food and drink, but it was not until 1886 that a survey of the budgets and consumption of necessities of a large sample of the London poor was undertaken by Charles *Booth.

Booth's calculations rested on assumptions about the level of expenditure needed to maintain a healthy life. He allowed no expenditure for entertainments or pleasure. Even with disciplined expenditure on necessities only, his survey showed that almost 30 per cent of the population of London lived below 'the poverty line'. Using similar criteria to Booth's, Seebohm *Rowntree undertook a survey of the poor in York in 1900 and identified a similar proportion of the population living in poverty. Medical examinations of the men volunteering for military service in the Boer War and those serving in the two world wars provided evidence of the effects of long-term poverty. Many of the poor were rejected as unfit, probably because they had suffered from inadequate diet and care during their childhood and youth. Such evidence was used to support the arguments in favour of comprehensive social welfare and of the 'welfare state' established during the 1940s.

Debates about the extent and condition of the poor and the limits of state *welfare continue. However, in spite of popular hostility to scroungers, the evidence suggests that the proportion of the poor in modern Britain is similar to that of the past. IJEK

poor laws relate to the support of the poor at public expense. They have their origins in the church's canon law but were developed within the framework of the state.

During the Middle Ages, canon law required each member of the parish to pay a tax of one-tenth, a tithe, of their income to the church. From this income the rector was required to set aside one-third each year for the relief of the poor. The money was intended to provide for the regular needs of the poor in the parish, such as orphans, the old, and the infirm. It was not intended to remove the duty of Christian charity to give help in times of crisis and emergency.

This parochial system for the support of the poor was undermined when tithe incomes began to be appropriated for other uses. For example, papal licences permitted tithe revenues to be claimed by other institutions within the church. In England some of the richer abbeys acquired tithe income in this way. The situation worsened when tithes became a fixed levy rather than a true tenth of incomes within a parish. By the beginning of the reign of Richard II in 1377, about one-third of parishes no longer had any tithes available for the support of the poor and others had depleted resources.

The state intervened to make good the shortcomings in the parochial system with the parliamentary Acts of 1388 and 1391. These Acts legitimized begging and stipulated that the able-bodied poor should look to their birth parish or the parish where they usually lived for support. Poor relief through the allocation of tithe income, where it existed, and begging elsewhere, continued until the Poor Law of 1536. This required the better-off members of each parish to collect money to support the 'impotent', who were defined as the infirm and children. Those who were fit but unemployed could expect no direct help. However, parish funds, where available, could be used to provide employment for them. Initially, giving to the parish collection was a matter of strong moral obligation, but in 1563 it became a legal requirement. Justices of the peace (magistrates) were given the task of determining what should be paid by each householder and an Act of 1572 required that the basis of payment should be reviewed regularly.

Such piecemeal legislation was replaced by a coherent system for England and Wales by the provisions of the Poor Law Act of 1601. This Act required each parish to be responsible for its own poor. Justices of the peace had the duty of setting up a framework for the administration of the law in their parish and they, together with the minister of the parish and those householders designated as members of the parish meeting or vestry, had the task of organizing poor relief. The vestry had the authority to raise the necessary money by collecting a rate, the level of which depended on the estimated value of each property in the parish. In practice, some parishes, mainly in large towns, came under the control of a small group of powerful ratepayers including the magistrates and minister, who formed a select vestry. The decisions of all vestries were enforced, on a day-to-day basis, by the parish constable and, where appropriate, by paid officials, who collected rates and acted as overseers of the poor.

Care of the poor varied from place to place. Some parishes bought cottages to house the homeless or built a house where the poor might live. In small rural parishes relief, in money and in kind, was sometimes provided for the poor in their own home. Such a system assumed a settled agrarian society with few itinerants seeking help. In an effort to control the consequences of increasing population movements following the civil wars of the mid-17th cent., the Act of Settlement of 1662 obliged parish authorities to give poor relief only to those either long resident or born in the parish. All others seeking assistance had to return to their place of origin.

During the 18th cent. there were changes in response to increasing numbers of poor amongst those who had migrated to work in expanding industrial areas. The earlier system continued, but the law was amended to allow Poor Law authorities to attempt novel solutions to the problem of the increasing numbers of those seeking relief. Some parishes combined to form a union, which built a workhouse and required those who were poor but able to work to live within it. The poor who entered the workhouse had to wear a uniform and were referred to as paupers. It was hoped, not always justifiably, that the work undertaken in the workhouse would cover its costs. At the end of the 18th cent. rural poverty in southern England grew so persistently that the Berkshire magistrates met at *Speenhamland and devised a system of poor relief in cash which supplemented inadequate wages. This system was taken up by other authorities and persisted in some places until the Poor Law Amendment Act of 1834.

The Act of 1834 put into practice a system which had operated in the previous decade in the parish of Southwell (Notts.). Relief was given only to those poor who agreed to accept the strict regime of the workhouse, where the conditions provided were funded from the rates at a level which was below that affordable by a person in work. In addition, the new Act created a commission to supervise the establishment of unions of parishes in England and Wales. These unions were to be administered by boards of guardians comprising magistrates and parish ministers of the Church of England, ex officio, and representatives of parishes elected by ratepayers.

All the evidence from official reports and popular literature shows that the Act and its implementation were loathed by the poor. However, although the Act was amended on several occasions to make it more appropriate to meet the needs of large urban areas and to respond to the problems of trade depressions and the special needs of children, the basic system remained in place until 1929 when provision for the poor was transferred to county and county borough councils. IJEK

pop art began in Britain in the mid-1950s and then spread to America. The movement was based upon the assumption that all aspects of modern life, including advertising, cinema, popular music, and consumer goods, were in themselves art-forms. The term was coined by art critic Lawrence Alloway, one of a number of artists, architects, and critics, known as the Independent Group, who met at the Institute of Contemporary Art in London. Among the more important names associated with British pop art were Eduardo Paolozzi, Richard Hamilton, Peter Blake, and David Hockney. JC

Pope, Alexander (1688–1744). English poet and master of the heroic couplet. Largely self-educated, the son of a Roman catholic draper, and crippled by a tubercular condition during his adolescence, Pope was always an outsider, although his precocious poetic talents quickly brought him to the attention of the literati. He made his reputation with his *Pastorals* (1709), the verse *Essay on Criticism* (1711), and the heroi-comical *Rape of the Lock* (1712, 1714). *Windsor-Forest* (1713), at once a paean to peace and a celebration of British imperialism, led to his vital association with *Swift, *Gay, and the Scriblerus Club, and his later involvement in political satire, particularly at the expense of *Walpole, beginning with *The Dunciad* (1728). While the *Moral Essays* (1731–5) and *An Essay on Man* (1733–4) employed moral and philosophical themes to expose contemporary failings, the more strident criticism of the *Imitations of Horace* prepared the way for the apocalyptic revised *Dunciad* of 1743. Although suspected of Jacobite sympathies because of his opposition to Walpole and George II, Pope's party allegiances are difficult to establish with confidence. Financially independent as a consequence of his translations of Homer, Pope moved in 1718 to Twickenham, where he spent the rest of his life, indulging his passion for gardening. JAD

pop groups. A term normally relating to popular music since the 1960s, when a new form of British pop music emphasized small groups of musicians playing guitars and drums, rather than star soloists. Centring on Liverpool, it drew elements from rock and roll, rhythm 'n' blues, and skiffle into a strong rhythmic style. The most famous group of this period, the *Beatles, produced their first record in 1962, while their 1967 album *Sergeant Pepper's Lonely Hearts Club Band* exemplifies their musical range and the strong psychedelic influence typical at this time. In the late 1960s groups like Pink Floyd developed 'progressive rock', with complex compositions exploiting electro-acoustic sounds. The Rolling Stones and the Who were more aggressive, fostering a style that led in 1976 to punk rock with its noise, antisocial dress, and offensive behaviour. In the 1970s many groups adopted the Caribbean rhythms of reggae, an influence continued in the 1980s through the rhythmic speech of rap. ECr

Popish plot, 1678. Comprised of 43 articles deposed by two skilful fabricators, Titus *Oates and Israel Tonge, before a London magistrate in September 1678, the 'plot' was a tissue of lies. It purported to reveal a Jesuit conspiracy to assassinate Charles II, assuring the succession to the catholic James, duke of York, through a French invasion of Ireland and a Jesuit-directed government in London. The ground had been prepared for the story's reception at least since 1672, owing to doubts over Charles's Anglican orthodoxy and his manipulation of a parliament he had kept in being since 1661. Immediately the plot compelled the king to dissolve Parliament; in the longer term it precipitated judicial murder and unprecedented party strife over excluding James from the succession. DDA

population. Despite the work of John Graunt, whose *Observations* on the London bills of *mortality came out in 1662, and his friend Sir William *Petty, whose *Political Arithmetick* was published in 1690, little was known for certain in the 18th cent. of the size of the population of Britain or even whether it was increasing or diminishing. Dr Richard Price in 1779, at a time when population growth was accelerating, argued that the population of England and Wales had decreased since the Glorious Revolution. Since the country was at war with France and Price concluded that the French population was rising, this caused much alarm. In the absence of accurate statistics, the debate which followed was bound to be inconclusive. In Parliament it was argued that a census would provide Britain's enemies with valuable information but John Rickman in the 1790s lobbied with success and the first census for England, Wales, and Scotland was held in 1801. In 1821 the first complete census for Ireland was made. Though the census methods were crude by modern standards, the institution of decennial censuses offered a systematic basis for estimates and one which Rickman helped to refine and improve. The publication of *Malthus's *Essay on Population* in 1798, revised and expanded in 1803, ensured that the subject received great attention for many years. The study of population in all its aspects has become an important branch of historical investigation, particularly since the Second World War, with the foundation of the journal *Population Studies* in 1947 and the establishment of the Cambridge Group for the History of Population and Social Structure in 1964.

Three broad generalizations may be offered. First, that the population history of the four peoples of the British Isles has been different and that there have been marked divergencies and changes within each group. Second, that until the late 18th cent. the population was small, with considerable fluctuations dependent upon the birth and death rates, harvests and famines, plague and warfare, immigration and emigration. From the late 18th cent., there was a sudden acceleration of growth until parts of England, the central region of Scotland, and parts of south Wales became among the most densely populated areas of Europe. Third, that in England, the growth of London from Tudor times was so rapid that it forms, in itself, a special factor.

Very few conclusions have been agreed about the population of the British Isles before the Norman Conquest. Large-scale migrations of Angles, Saxons, Jutes, Danes, and Norsemen, and substantial movements between Ireland, Scotland, and Wales, make estimates very hazardous. The population of Roman Britain remains highly conjectural with a disturbing divergence of scholarly opinion between 1 million and 6 million for the later 2nd cent. It has been suggested that London may have had 30,000 inhabitants, Colchester and Cirencester 15,000, Lincoln and Gloucester 5,000, and the remaining towns between 2,000 and 3,000. A figure of 20,000 has been proposed for Wales, though there is no way of checking it. Nor is it easier to offer figures for the subsequent Saxon period, since we cannot be sure to what extent devastation and warfare were offset by new arrivals. The consensus puts the figure for England towards the end of the Saxon period at about $1\frac{1}{2}$ million, which would suggest a substantial decrease from later Roman times, and the towns significantly smaller—London at 12,000, York 8,000, Norwich and Lincoln 5,000. The most prudent historians of Ireland and Scotland refuse to suggest or endorse any estimates for those countries.

There is little disagreement that the population of England increased greatly between 1066 and the plague disasters of the mid-14th cent., though much less agreement about the exact figures. If the estimates for William I's reign, based on Domesday Book returns, are correct, the population was about $1\frac{1}{2}$ million and had more than doubled by 1300 to about 4 million. This was part of a general European pattern, assisted in England after the Conquest by the absence of major invasions and a lessening of internal conflict. The increase had almost certainly slowed by the time the *Black

Death struck, since the early 14th cent. saw adverse climatic changes and a pressure on subsistence which produced periodic famine. Plague then struck four times between 1349 and 1375 with devastating consequences. Estimates of mortality may be inferred from the death of clerics, which is recorded, and by information from particular villages or estates. But each source of evidence is open to hazard. The clergy as a profession might be unduly at risk from their obligation to visit and succour victims and therefore the 50 per cent death rate in the dioceses of Exeter, Winchester, Norwich, and Ely may not have been replicated in the country at large. Similarly, though all twelve of the bishop's villeins at Cuxham in Oxfordshire perished from plague in 1349, there were other villages and areas comparatively little affected. In short, it seems that over 40 per cent of the population died, with profound political and economic consequences. The Black Death also visited Ireland, Wales, and Scotland at much the same time. Only in Scotland does the mortality seem to have been significantly lower, perhaps because the plague was at its most deadly in crowded towns and ports.

Recovery from the Black Death and its later visitations was slow. The population of England may have been reduced to about 2½ million. The poll-tax returns for 1377 have been employed to suggest total numbers, with the usual difficulties, but at least offer evidence on population distribution: East Anglia and the east midlands were most densely populated, the north and west much less so. Not until the middle of the 15th cent. did the rate of increase pick up and even then it was patchy. But during Tudor times, the population reached its pre-plague position and by the end of the 16th cent. stood at just over 4 million. Rickman, in an analysis of parish register returns, printed a preface to the 1841 census suggesting a figure of 4.3 million for 1600. The population of Ireland was about 1 million, that of Scotland perhaps a little less, with more than half of the inhabitants north of the Tay. Wales was still very thinly populated with about 350,000 people: Carmarthen, the largest town, had no more than 2,000 people—less than one-hundredth of the size of London—and followed by Brecon with 1,750. Elsewhere the size of towns was beginning to increase. At over 200,000 London was already the largest town in western Europe and outstripping all its rivals. The population of Norwich was about 15,000, Bristol and York about 12,000, Newcastle and Exeter, around 10,000—all of them important provincial centres and with good water communications.

From the 17th cent. the sources for demographic study improve, though their use remains complex. Thomas *Cromwell ordered the keeping of parish registers from 1538, but many incumbents did not at first do so, and some registers have been destroyed by fire, flood, wars, and mice. They are augmented from 1629 onwards by the regular London bills of mortality. The high Tudor growth rate was not sustained throughout the whole 17th cent., when emigration, civil war, and plague dampened the increase. The population of England and Wales rose to about 5.4 million by 1656 and then steadied, or even declined slightly. The population of Wales cannot have increased greatly and by 1700 may have been 400,000. Scotland was affected by plague in the 1640s, heavy emigration to Ulster, and by severe famine in the 1690s. Its population in 1700 was probably little higher than in 1600: Edinburgh, by far the largest town, had between 30,000 and 40,000 people. Despite heavy warfare, the Irish population may have doubled by 1687 and reached well over 2 million by 1700, with Dublin beginning to grow rapidly. London continued to grow disproportionately, had reached half a million by 1700, and was larger than all the other urban centres together. Of great political importance for the future was the expansion of the American colonies, at about 250,000 by 1700, of whom some 10 per cent were negroes: New York, Boston, and Philadelphia were already sizeable towns, edging towards 10,000.

There were few indications at the beginning of the 18th cent. that the British Isles were on the threshhold of a population explosion. Population increase had, if anything, slowed down, though the country had recovered from the ravages of the Black Death. The causes of the acceleration to come have been extensively debated. The establishment of voluntary hospitals and improved methods of combating smallpox were bound to be slow in their effect since they did not operate much outside urban areas. Plague at last disappeared, though contemporaries could not be certain that it would not return. Agricultural yields were improving and the development of turnpike roads and canals later in the century enabled food to be transported more quickly to areas of shortage. But any explanation must have a European dimension since the increase was a general one. The early view that the population rise was largely due to a falling death rate has been increasingly challenged, partly because the increase accompanied widespread urbanization and 18th-cent. cities were by no means healthy places. More emphasis is now placed upon a significant rise in fertility rates, as a result of people marrying earlier, and because a smaller proportion of the population remained unmarried. The move to towns may have freed young men to marry, since their labour was no longer needed on the family farm which could not support several households—a phenomenon still evident in small hill-farms in the later 20th cent.

Though the causes of the great acceleration are still far from agreed, the consequences are clear. From the 1740s onwards, the population began to rise, not to fall again as it had so often in the past, but a sustained and incremental growth. From 5.7 million in 1750, the population of England reached 8.6 million by 1800 and 16.5 million by 1850. The Scottish population also grew, particularly in the industrial and trading towns of the central region, though less rapidly than that of England—from 1.2 million in 1750 to 1.6 million by 1800 and 2.8 million by 1850. But the most startling increase was in Ireland, where from about 3 million in 1750, it reached 5 million by 1800, and in 1845, on the brink of the famine, stood at well over 8 million, dangerously dependent on the potato harvest.

The Irish *Famine, from 1845 to 1848, was a unique event in modern European demography and its effects comparable to those of the Black Death. One million people died of starvation and disease, the birth rate fell, and there was a large-scale exodus, mainly of younger people, in the decades after the disaster. Well over a million people left Ireland in the 1840s, another million in the 1850s, and 850,000 in the 1860s—mainly for North America, and especially from Munster and Ulster. Co. Clare, with 286,000 people in 1841, had 85,000 100 years later. The Irish population was down to 6.5 million by 1851, 5.8 million by 1861, 4.4 million by 1901. A hundred years after the famine, it stood at 4.3 million, just over half what it had been in 1845.

In the rest of Britain, the sustained growth was felt in every part of public life. Internationally, it changed Britain's relative position. In 1550 the population of Spain and Portugal was double that of the British Isles: by 1914 the position was reversed. Just before 1914 the population of the United Kingdom passed that of France. But of greater long-term significance was the transformation brought about from the 17th cent. onwards by emigration, which brought into being the USA, Canada, Australia, and New Zealand and effected a fundamental shift in world power. At home, despite Malthus's fears of extra mouths to feed, agricultural improvements meant that fewer and fewer farm labourers could support more and more factory workers. The increase provided labour for the industrial expansion and purchasing power to sustain it. The internal balance of England shifted as the great industrial towns of the north developed. In Scotland, Glasgow rose from a town of 10,000 in 1688 to a conurbation of a million in 1901: in Wales, the balance of population moved to the mining areas of the south and Cardiff, a town of 1,800 people in 1801, had 128,000 inhabitants by 1901. The old electoral system, with its little Wiltshire and Cornish boroughs, looked increasingly absurd after 1801, when the census revealed that three of the six largest English towns—Manchester, Birmingham, and Leeds—had no MPs at all. The shift of power to the north after the *Reform Act of 1832 and the *Municipal Corporations Act of 1835 gave vast influence to the *dissenters, who dominated towns like Bradford, Leeds, Manchester, and Halifax. The churches found their urban parishes swelling out of control, and there were massive building efforts by the dissenters in the earlier 19th cent. and the Anglicans in the later.

The population of England and Wales continued to rise in the 20th cent., though at a reduced rate. By 1996, England and Wales totalled 50 million, Scotland 5 million, Northern Ireland 1½ million, and Eire 3½ million. England became by far the most densely populated of the major European powers—four times the density of France, and on a par with Holland and Belgium. From this stemmed many social problems: of law and order, bearing in mind that a second-division football match in the 1990s might well attract a crowd twice the size of the second largest city of Stuart England; of traffic jams, road rage, and general transport policy; of noise pollution and broader environmental questions. The slowing down of the birth rate after the Second World War meant an ageing population, with heavy demands on medical care and for pensions. The general movement out of older towns led to the problem of decaying city centres. Substantial immigration from the Commonwealth in the 1950s and 1960s produced suburbs and, in some cases, whole towns where the character of the community had changed. Though demography is a rarefied and demanding discipline, its implications are profound. JAC

Connell, K. H., *The Population of Ireland, 1750–1845* (1950); Flinn, M. W. (ed.), *Scottish Population from the Seventeenth Century to the 1930s* (Cambridge, 1977); Houston, R. A., *The Population History of Britain and Ireland, 1500–1750* (1992); Razzell, P., *Essays in English Population History* (1994); Vaughan, W. E., and Fitzpatrick, A. J. (eds.), *Irish Historical Statistics: Population 1821–1971* (Dublin, 1978); Wrigley, E. A., and Schofield, R. S., *The Population History of England, 1541–1871* (Cambridge, Mass., 1981).

Porson, Richard (1759–1808). Scholar. Of comparatively humble family in Norfolk, Porson's youthful promise was so obvious that means were found to send him to Eton. Further contributions sent him to Trinity College, Cambridge, where he was elected to a fellowship. In July 1792, being unwilling to take holy orders, he lost the fellowship, but five months later was elected to the regius chair of Greek. He did not lecture, rarely visited the university, but studied in London, producing a celebrated edition of Euripides. The London Institution elected him librarian, at a good salary, but his attendance was hardly adequate. His health deteriorated quickly, partly as a result of drink. A reclusive scholar, unpredictable, eccentric, and untidy, his life was textual commentary. In his last illness, he finished up, speechless, in St Martin's workhouse, which advertised to see if anyone could identify 'a tall man, apparently about 45 years of age, . . . and having in his pocket a memorandum book, the leaves of which were filled with Greek lines, written in pencil'. JAC

Portal, Charles, 1st Viscount Portal (1893–1971). Portal came from a Berkshire gentry family of Huguenot ancestry. After Winchester and Christ Church, Oxford, he joined the army at the outbreak of war in 1914 but in 1915 transferred to the *Royal Flying Corps, and flew more than 900 sorties before 1918. Promoted air marshal in 1939 he took over Bomber Command in 1940, but after six months became chief of the air staff, which he retained until the end of the war. Tall, hawk-like, and able, he protected *Tedder and, like most people, found 'Bomber' *Harris difficult to work with. After the war he served as controller of the atomic energy establishment at Harwell (1946–51) and as chairman of the British Aircraft Corporation (1960–8). Eisenhower thought Portal the finest of all the war leaders, 'greater than Churchill', and *Churchill himself remarked that Portal 'had everything'. JAC

Porteous riots, 1736. In Edinburgh on 14 April 1736 the hanging of a smuggler sparked an angry reaction from the watching crowd, and as the body was cut down stones were thrown at the town guard. The troops then opened fire, though Captain John Porteous always denied that he gave the order. Six were killed and about a dozen more injured. The provost feared the mood of the populace and had Porteous arrested; he was tried by the Court of Judiciary and sentenced to be executed. But the government, concerned that the partiality of these proceedings had compromised its authority in the city, granted Porteous a temporary reprieve. Resentment was widespread, and on 7 September a mob of 4,000 stormed the Tolbooth prison, seized the captain, and hanged him. A parliamentary inquiry in 1737 resulted in punitive measures against the city, but the episode cost *Walpole much Scottish support in Parliament, which played an important part in his downfall in 1742. AAH

Portland, battle of, 1653. Naval engagement in the first Anglo-Dutch War, which developed into a running fight up the Channel from 18–20 February. A large fleet under *Blake encountered Martin Tromp's fleet off Portland Bill escorting a convoy. Tromp lost twelve warships but saved most of the convoy. JAC

Portland, Hans Willem van Bentinck, 1st earl of (*c.*1649–1709). Dutch confidant of William III. Entering the household of William of Orange in the early 1660s, Bentinck went on to become the prince's close friend and right-hand man, playing an important diplomatic role in the preparations for William's invasion of England in 1688. On becoming king, William rewarded Bentinck handsomely with English lands and honours, and in April 1689 he was given an earldom. A general in both the English and Dutch armies, he attended the king throughout his campaigns in Ireland and Flanders, and his informal negotiations with the French in 1697 opened the way for peace. But his vast wealth and close proximity to William made him deeply unpopular. He was impeached in 1701 for keeping English ministers in ignorance of his negotiations with France over the partition of Spain, but was never put on trial. He retired from court following William's death in 1702. AAH

Portland, William Cavendish-Bentinck, 3rd duke of (1738–1809). Portland began his career as a follower of *Newcastle and rose to the status of second in command to *Rockingham, succeeding the latter as official head of the Whig opposition in 1782. He shared the leadership with the party's principal Commons spokesman, Charles *Fox, whose charismatic personality has obscured Portland's underrated role. As nominal premier during the short-lived Fox–North coalition ministry, Portland conducted a series of difficult negotiations with the king, which belie his reputation for weakness and indecision. The *India Bill crisis, which precipitated the fall of the coalition, set the pattern of politics for a decade, with Portland and Fox the twin leaders of an increasingly organized Whig opposition. Although Portland was a hard-working party organizer, the limitations of his leadership were revealed both during the *Regency crisis and, more seriously, by the repercussions of the French Revolution, heralded by *Burke's jeremiads. The duke long resisted the pressure to break with Fox, but in 1794 led the conservative Whigs into coalition with Pitt. As home secretary (1794–1801) Portland favoured the use of surveillance and repression to counter the threat of radicalism. He was also a prime mover in the recall of *Fitzwilliam from Ireland in 1795 over the question of catholic emancipation—though the assertion that this amounted to a betrayal is not borne out by the surviving evidence. The Fitzwilliam episode contributed to the decline of the Portland Whigs as a distinct group within the ministry and by the early 19th cent. Portland had ceased to be a party leader, but had become an elder statesman, respected by the king. For this reason the aged and infirm duke became the figurehead prime minister (1807–9) in a ministry that contained the germs of the Toryism that was later to flourish under *Liverpool. Portland's career ended on a sour note with the unseemly duel between two of his cabinet colleagues, *Canning and *Castlereagh, an event for which the duke's misguided prevarication must be held partly responsible. DW

Portland, Richard Weston, 1st earl of (1577–1635). Of an Essex family, Weston trained at the Middle Temple and sat in the House of Commons for various constituencies until raised to the peerage. After administrative and diplomatic posts, he was appointed chancellor of the Exchequer in 1621 and held the post until 1628 when he became lord treasurer. In 1628 he was given a barony, appointed to the Garter in 1630, and advanced to the earldom in 1633. After *Buckingham's murder, he was the most influential of Charles I's ministers. A catholic, he was sympathetic to Spain and determined to avoid war, partly to reduce reliance upon Parliament. *Clarendon's long account is hostile, claiming that he was imperious, unpopular, and ambitious. But his policies appear moderate and Charles's difficulties began soon after Portland's death. JAC

Portsmouth is not mentioned in *Domesday Book (1086) but began to develop on Portsea Island as Portchester, on a Roman site, started to silt up. It was granted a charter by Richard I in 1194 and the growth of the navy in the 16th cent. established it as a major town. Henry VII began a dry dock there in 1495, the **Mary Rose* sank off Portsmouth harbour in 1545, and the duke of *Buckingham was stabbed to death in the Greyhound Inn in 1628 when leaving for the expedition to La Rochelle. From the time of Charles II, Portsmouth became the chief naval base. The Royal Naval College was founded in 1720, the **Royal George* went down in the harbour in 1782, and on 15 September 1805 *Nelson hoisted sail in **Victory* for *Trafalgar. His flagship is preserved at Portsmouth today. By 1801 the town had a population of 32,000, 94,000 by 1861, and 189,000 by 1993. The naval presence has diminished but Portsmouth has developed engineering and tourism. There are ferry sailings to the Isle of Wight and to France and northern Spain. JAC

Portsmouth, diocese of. The see, comprising south-east Hampshire and the Isle of Wight, was carved, with *Guildford, out of the *Winchester diocese in 1927. It has a close association with the Royal Navy. The cathedral, the former parish church of St Thomas of Canterbury, originally built *c.*1190, has an Early English east end and a late 17th-cent. nave and tower (1683–95). Further extensions were completed in 1992. WMM

Portsmouth, Louise de Kéroualle, duchess of (1649–1734). Of Breton lineage, Louise de Kéroualle accompanied Henrietta Anne, sister of Charles II, to England in 1670; Charles's despair at Henrietta's sudden death and obvious infatuation with Louise encouraged Louis XIV to send her back to England. Her baby-faced charms led Charles to call her 'Fubbs' (fubsy = chubby), though her emotional outbursts prompted 'the weeping willow' from

Nell *Gwyn, and she rapidly rose to become 'the most absolute of the king's mistresses'. Her son by Charles (1672) was created duke of Richmond and she herself made duchess of Portsmouth in 1673. Universally unpopular as Frenchwoman and catholic, she was mercenary, recklessly extravagant, and haughty to inferiors; her Whitehall apartment, extended and altered 1672–4 (further rebuilt 1678), was so luxuriously furnished and full of silver plate as to surfeit *Evelyn. James II offered reassurances of protection, but after the 1691 fire she returned to France. ASH

Portugal, relations with. The first treaty with 'England's oldest ally' dates from 1373. *John of Gaunt led English forces in the mid-1380s on the side of Portugal against Castile, and the alliance was confirmed by the treaty of Windsor in 1386. The modern connection dates from a treaty concluded by *Cromwell in 1654 which gave the English considerable trading advantages. Ties were further strengthened by Charles II's marriage to *Catherine of Braganza in 1662. The *Methuen treaty of 1703 was another milestone. The complementary character of the English and Portuguese economies, the importance of Portuguese independence and its colonies to Britain, the value of its ports (notably Lisbon and the Tagus estuary) to the Royal Navy in many parts of the world, and Portugal's need for a defender against its larger neighbour, together made for a strong but uneven connection. In 1808 the British initiated military operations in Portugal which developed into the ultimately victorious Peninsular campaign. *Wellington for a time was forced to hold out around Lisbon behind the famous *Torres Vedras lines. In 1826 a small British force arrived in Lisbon to defend the constitutional regime from reactionary groups assisted by Spain. In the early 1830s the British gave further indirect aid against the reactionary forces of Dom Miguel, and, with France, warned against meddling by the absolutist great powers. Britain under *Palmerston continued to show a sometimes controversial interest in the independence and political stability of Portugal. With the fall of the autocratic regime of Dr Caetano in 1974 Britain (with other European states) provided support to parliamentary groups at a time when a communist takeover was considered possible. CJB

positivism was the philosophical system originated by Henri, comte de Saint-Simon, and developed by Auguste Comte. Positivists hold that science is the only valid form of knowledge, and that 'positive' facts—the sole subject-matter of science—are the only valid objects of knowledge. We must accept the natural world as we experience it, and not attempt to go behind nature in search of some ultimate reality or metaphysics. For positivists all aspects of human life, including politics, ethics, and even religion, could be established on a scientific basis, since human values were themselves simply facts. According to Comte, there have been three phases of intellectual development. The first was the theological stage, in which events in the physical world were explained in terms of external miraculous powers. The second was the metaphysical stage, in which natural events were assumed to be caused by some intrinsic quality or vital spirit within natural phenomena. Only in the third, the scientific or positive stage, has mankind advanced beyond pseudo-explanation to genuine knowledge. Progress depends upon scientific development, and the ultimate society is one ruled by a sociocracy, a scientific élite, dedicated to the worship of humanity (the positivist divinity which replaces God). Comte had few British disciples, though Buckle was attracted by positivism. But he influenced many scientists, philosophers, and sociologists, and positivism became part of the western scientific attitude in the 20th cent. TSG

Post Office. Before the 17th cent., royal ministers had their own king's messengers, but private persons sent letters through servants or friends. Henry VIII had a master of the posts in 1512 but he served only the government. The first attempt at a public system was in 1635 when a service was established to important towns, carrying letters at 2 pence per sheet per 80 miles. Under the Commonwealth, *Thurloe was appointed postmaster-general in 1657 and the arrangement was continued at the Restoration. In 1680 a London penny post was started and soon taken over by the government; penny posts were established in large provincial towns in the later 18th cent. Members of both Houses of Parliament had the privilege of free postage (save for the penny post) and gave large numbers of franks to friends, constituents, or even business colleagues: the privilege was not abolished until 1840. Two 18th-cent. developments were Ralph Allen's scheme of cross-country services, followed by John Palmer's introduction of scheduled mail coaches. Rowland *Hill's plan of penny postage was adopted in 1840 in the teeth of powerful opposition: prepayment through stamps was introduced and there was no extra charge for mileage. It was followed in the 1850s by the introduction of pillar boxes (a suggestion of Anthony *Trollope), which put an end to the bellmen who had rung for final collections. The services offered by post offices proliferated—the introduction of telegrams delivered by messenger boys; the establishment by *Gladstone in 1861 of the Post Office Savings Bank; and the beginning of parcel post in 1883. Penny post was a casualty of the First World War, the rate going up to 1½ pence in June 1918, and after the Second World War inflation brought constant increases. The start of the use of post offices for a variety of welfare payments was the decision in 1908 to deliver *old-age pensions through them. JAC

Potsdam conference, 16 July–2 August 1945. This overlapped a British general election, *Churchill and *Eden being replaced midway by *Attlee and *Bevin (Labour). The Americans and Russians, however, observed no significant change in British policy, with both struck by Bevin's pugnacity. A compromise was reached on German reparations—the Treasury having earlier expressed its concern at the cost of the British occupation zone unless reparations were restricted and Germany treated as one economic unit. Churchill hoped that the acquisition of the atomic bomb by the USA would increase the bargaining power of the West with the USSR as well as hasten the end of the war with Japan. CJB

Potter, Beatrix (1866–1943). Writer and illustrator of children's books. Born in London, taught by governesses, she combined her early love of drawing with a keen interest in natural history, copying flowers and drawing small animals kept as pets or found on summer holidays in Scotland and the Lakes. Illustrated anecdotes about her pet rabbit, sent to amuse a convalescing child, inspired her first published book, *The Tale of Peter Rabbit*, in 1901. It was soon followed by *The Tale of Squirrel Nutkin*, *The Tailor of Gloucester*, and others. Immediately successful, they remain nursery classics with Mrs Tiggywinkle, Jeremy Fisher, and Jemima Puddleduck among many favourite characters. In 1905 she bought Hilltop Farm in the Lake District and in 1913 married William Heelis, a solicitor. Ultimately a successful sheep-breeder and landowner, actively concerned with the preservation of the Lake District, she left her extensive property to the National Trust. AM

Powell, J. Enoch (b. 1912). The key to what might appear Powell's maverick political career is belief in Britain. Educated at King Edward's School, Birmingham, he began as a classicist, was a fellow of Trinity College, Cambridge, and then professor of Greek at Sydney. During the war he rose to brigadier. Elected to Parliament in 1950, he was a keen advocate of monetarism and resigned as financial secretary to the Treasury in the *Macmillan government in 1957, though returning as minister of health in 1960. He declined to serve under *Home in 1963 and never held office again. His outspoken hostility to coloured immigration led *Heath to sack him from the shadow cabinet in 1968, though his proposals for repatriation had considerable popular support. He was at odds with his party once more over Europe, bitterly denouncing the loss of British sovereignty, and he retired in February 1974 advising his supporters to vote Labour. Miraculously reborn as an Ulster Unionist in October 1974, he won the Down South seat and held it until 1987, tenaciously defending Ulster's position against encroachment and concession. Like many intellectuals, his logic guided him into passionate and uncompromising positions. JAC

Powys. County of the middle Welsh borderland. The name derives from the Welsh kingdom of post-Roman times. With Norman control it was divided into a series of marcher lordships which were themselves integrated in 1536 into the counties of Denbighshire and Montgomeryshire. It was not until the Local Government Act of 1972 that the name was revived and given, not completely appropriately, to the new county formed by the merging of Montgomeryshire, Radnorshire, and Breconshire. The White Paper 'Local Government in Wales' referred to it as 'a reasonably homogeneous area, even though its resources are poor'. The adverb 'reasonably' hides considerable diversity, but it was because of limited size (Radnorshire has a population of only 23,360) and resources that no changes were made in 1994 and in spite of active campaigning by Montgomeryshire, Powys was retained in 1996 as a unitary authority, with only minor adjustments. HC

Powys, kingdom of. A Welsh kingdom that survived the English conquest as part of the march of Wales. Although its origins are unclear, the name may come from *pagus* (or *pagenses*), the Roman term for the hinterland of the *Cornovii; but the first reference to Powys dates from the 9th cent. Its kings claimed descent from northern Britons, a royal centre at 'Pengwern' (unidentified), and a role in resisting early English invaders. There does seem to have been a kingdom covering central Wales and modern Shropshire whose eastern part was overrun by Mercians from the mid-7th cent. Powys withstood encroachments from England and *Gwynedd throughout its existence, although the Welsh custom of partible inheritance caused rivalries among the ruling family. The most powerful prince, *Madog ap Maredudd, was the last to rule over all Powys. After his death (1160) it was divided, Powys Wenwynwyn (the south) being named after his nephew's son, with a centre at Welshpool, and Powys Fadog (the north) after his grandson, with its centre at Dinas Brân. By 1300 both were absorbed into the polity of the marcher lordships. The name survived in Welsh tradition and in the castle and barony of Powis; in the local government reorganization of 1972 it was given to the combined counties of Brecon, Radnor, and Montgomery, much of which had never been part of earlier Powys. RAG

Poynings's law, 1494. Sir Edward Poynings served as lord deputy in Ireland from 1494 to 1496. A parliament summoned at Drogheda in December 1494 declared that the English Privy Council must approve the summoning of any Irish parliament and agree to legislation, and that English laws applied to Ireland. Despite Irish protests, the position was reaffirmed by 6 Geo. I c. 5 in 1719 which stated that Ireland 'is and of right ought to be subordinate unto and dependent upon the imperial crown of Great Britain' and that the Irish House of Lords had no appellate jurisdiction. Poynings's Act was not repealed until 1782, when the *Rockinghams conceded Irish legislative independence. JAC

Praemunire statutes. The statutes of Praemunire, the first dating from 1351, were passed to prevent the pope from interfering with the king's rights in relation to clergy benefices in England. The statutes imposed penalties on anyone who invoked papal authority to oust the jurisdiction of the king's courts. In 1363 a statute provided that any persons who offended against the statutes must answer for their action before the king's *council. This was to be of great significance in the Reformation period and was one of the principal grounds for arraigning before the council those who sought to appeal to Rome, or to accept the authority of the pope after Henry VIII's break with Rome. MM

Pragmatic Sanction. An edict of 1713 attempted to ensure the undisputed and undivided succession of the Habsburg lands when Charles VI should die by setting aside the claims of his elder brother's daughters in favour of any daughters he should have. The cause of great diplomatic activity in the 1720s and 1730s, it did not suffice to prevent Maria Theresa being attacked in 1740 by Prussia, France, Spain, Saxony, and

Bavaria. Britain came to her assistance and helped to place a pragmatic army in the field. JAC

Prayer Book. See BOOK OF COMMON PRAYER.

Prayer Book rising, 1549. The regime of Protector *Somerset at the accession of Edward VI moved sharply towards protestantism and in January 1549 Parliament ordered the new *Book of Common Prayer in English to be used. The day after it was introduced at *Sampford Courtenay in Devon the villagers demanded that their priest should say the old mass, complaining that the new service was like some 'Christmas game' and in a language they could not comprehend. Joined by insurgents from Cornwall, they besieged Exeter. Protector Somerset, with *Kett's rising in Norfolk to deal with as well, moved cautiously, but on 17 August at Sampford Courtenay, Lord Russell (*Bedford) subdued the rebels. Somerset's hesitancy helped to undermine his position. Lord Russell was rewarded by promotion to the earldom of Bedford. JAC

Premonstratensians (also known as the 'white canons' or 'Norbertines') were founded at Prémontré (near Laon in north-eastern France) in 1120 by St Norbert who, after his conversion, was a canon at Xanten (his birthplace) before becoming a wandering preacher. In 1126 he was appointed archbishop of Magdeburg. The early community was strongly eremitical in tone and followed an austere interpretation of the *Augustinian rule, heavily influenced, however, by the *Cistercians. Originally the order included double houses of canons and nuns, but these were suppressed in 1140, the nuns being housed in separate nunneries, of which there were initially four in England. The first house of canons was established in England in 1143 at Newhouse and by the dissolution there were 35 English communities, one in Wales, and several in Scotland, including Dryburgh. Foundations were never very prosperous, perhaps reflecting the relatively modest status of most of their patrons and benefactors: the wealthiest abbey at the dissolution was Torre (Devon) with a net annual income of nearly £400. They were equally widespread on the continent, particularly in central and eastern Europe, where they were extensively employed in the conversion of territories east of the Rhine. BJG

Pre-Raphaelites (1848–*c.*1854). The Pre-Raphaelite Brotherhood, also known by the initials PRB, was a short-lived, essentially English, association of seven artists, including Holman *Hunt, *Millais, and Dante Gabriel *Rossetti. Disliking what they felt was the superficiality of 16th-cent. Italian art, they sought to recapture the direct religious sincerity of pre-Renaissance painting. The movement was very literary, painting deeply symbolic historical, poetic, or religious subjects with great attention to detail, using pure, bright colours. 'The Pre-Raphaelites had but one idea—to present on canvas what they saw in Nature' (Millais).

The work of the Brotherhood was, at first, well received. Only when the meaning of the initials PRB, on their paintings, became understood was there a protest, the brothers accused of blasphemy and of setting themselves up as better than Raphael. The influential art critic John *Ruskin intervened on their behalf in 1851, and their reputation began to improve. Other artists adopted the brotherhood technique so that many paintings thought of as typically Pre-Raphaelite were not in fact painted by the founders. By the early 1850s the brotherhood was in decline and had dissolved by 1855. Rossetti founded a second brotherhood at Oxford with Edward Burne-Jones and William *Morris (*c.*1860s–90s). JC

Prerogative. See ROYAL PREROGATIVE.

presbyterians were supporters of *calvinism, preaching the doctrine of the elect and advocating church government by a hierarchy of courts—the kirk session, the presbytery in a locality, the synod in a region, and the general assembly, consisting of ministers and elders, governing the whole church. Ultimate authority was the Bible and services gave great prominence to preaching. The leading exponent of presbyterianism in the Elizabethan church was Thomas *Cartwright, responsible for the *millenary petition to James I in 1603, which objected to surplices, bowing at the name of Jesus, and other ceremonies. They were in strong opposition to the regime of Archbishop *Laud, and after his imprisonment dominated the *Westminster Assembly called by Parliament in 1643 to reform the church. The Westminster Confession which they put forward and which was accepted by Parliament in 1648 was a presbyterian statement and the basis for their domination during the *Commonwealth and *Protectorate. Bishops were abolished, statues and pictures removed, ceremonies cleansed. In Scotland, presbyterianism, brought by John *Knox from Geneva in 1559, made rapid progress and was the core of the *solemn league and covenant, adopted in 1643.

After the Restoration, the fortunes of English and Scottish presbyterianism diverged. In England, hopes of a compromise with the Church of England faded fast and many of the 2,000 ministers forced out by the Act of *Uniformity in 1662 were presbyterians. Thereafter, presbyterianism formed a declining dissenting sect, vulnerable to *socinian and *unitarian arguments in the early 18th cent. and outdistanced by the *Methodists in the later 18th cent. The Presbyterian Church in England, re-established in 1844, was reported to have only 76 places of worship in 1851—one-fifth the number of *Quaker meeting-houses. After severe persecution in the reigns of Charles II and James II, the Scottish presbyterians emerged triumphant in 1690, when their church was recognized as the established *Church of Scotland. Its special position was guaranteed by the Act of *Union of 1707. The large number of presbyterian churches in Northern Ireland are largely the result of Scottish emigration, and Scots and Irish took presbyterianism to flourish in North America. JAC

press-gangs. The British crown possessed an ancient right to seize for naval service 'seamen, seafaring men and persons whose occupations or callings are to work upon vessels and boats upon rivers'. The 18th-cent. jurist *Blackstone stated that 'The power of impressing men for the sea service by the royal commission . . . is of very ancient date, and has been uniformly continued by a regular series of precedents.' The power was implicitly recognized in statutes from the late 14th cent. onwards. The term 'impress' derives from the 'imprest' money paid to recruits for the armed forces. Several attempts to replace this system of arbitrary conscription failed. A 1696 scheme for registering seamen for limited periods of service was abandoned in 1711. Pitt's Quota Acts of 1795 also failed to remove the need for impressment. Press-gangs hunting seamen came either from individual warships or from the Impress Service which developed within the navy in the later 18th cent. and reached its peak of sophistication during the Napoleonic War. In 1809 the service employed 24 captains and 56 lieutenants. With death rates in the navy very high, particularly in the West Indies, seizure by a press-gang was no light matter. Impressment fell into disuse after 1815, as social changes made its harshness unacceptable, but no satisfactory alternative for manning the navy was developed until much later in the 19th cent. NMcC

Preston, battle of, 1648. The first civil war ended in 1646 when Charles I gave himself up to the Scots at Southwell. Late the following year, he signed an *'Engagement' with the Scots, agreeing to a presbyterian church order for three years. In the spring of 1648 a series of uncoordinated risings heralded the second civil war. In July a sizeable Scottish army under *Hamilton crossed the border near Carlisle, shadowed by *Lambert. *Cromwell wound up his operations in Wales and hastened to join Lambert. Hamilton missed his chance to crush Lambert before the junction could be effected at Knaresborough. The parliamentary force then crossed the Pennines to cut off Hamilton's retreat to Scotland. Hamilton had substantially more men, but they were badly strung out and were caught still disorganized outside Preston on 17 August. When the royalists withdrew south during the night, a running fight developed. Hamilton's infantry surrendered at Warrington: he and his cavalry were eventually rounded up at Uttoxeter. The defeat at Preston spelled Charles's doom since the army leaders now regarded him as a man of blood, impossible to deal with. The king was executed in January 1649 and Hamilton six weeks later. JAC

Preston, battle of, 1715. The Jacobite rising in Northumberland was under the command of Thomas Forster, member of Parliament for the county. He occupied Holy Island for one day, failed to take Newcastle, and joined with Scottish Jacobites at Rothbury. The rebels then made for Lancashire, where they hoped to find support, moving through Brampton, Penrith, and Kendal. At Preston they were bottled up by Hanoverian forces led by Carpenter and Wills, and capitulated on 14 November. Forster subsequently made a daring escape from Newgate and joined the pretender abroad. JAC

Prestonpans, battle of, 1745. Charles Edward *Stuart's first and critically important victory in the '45 rising was gained on 21 September at Prestonpans, on the coast east of Edinburgh. The Hanoverian army of some 2,300 men, under the command of Sir John Cope, had been ferried from Inverness to Dunbar to cut off the rebels' advance south. The issue was decided within a few minutes by a fierce Highland charge at dawn. Cope, forced to flee to Coldstream and Berwick, was much ridiculed, but his dispositions were perfectly sound and he was exonerated by a court martial. JAC

Pretoria, convention of, 1881. This convention brought to an end the first *Boer War, which followed the British annexation of the Transvaal in 1877. The Boers were given self-government, but the British retained suzerainty and the conduct of foreign relations. This shaky compromise was undermined by the discovery of gold on the Witwatersrand south of Pretoria in 1886. JAC

prices reflect the payments made by consumers for the goods and services that they buy. Prices relate not only to the final goods bought in shops but also to factor inputs. Inputs prices reflect the payments required to attract factors of production into the market—i.e. wages, rent, interest, and profit for labour, land, capital, and entrepreneurship respectively. While monetary prices are the norm today, in earlier times prices were represented by the relative worth of goods used in trade. Indeed, there are still many goods and services which have no money prices attached to them because they are outside the market process.

Prices for individual commodities vary as market conditions of supply and demand fluctuate. If demand rises then, without a commensurate increase in supply, prices will also rise. Equally, a contraction in supply will, other things unchanged, result in higher prices. In the past, for instance, the price of foodstuffs fluctuated considerably according to the nature of the harvest—poor harvests in the 1840s, for example, pushing up the price of wheat and potatoes. Speculation about future market conditions can also result in price changes with, for instance, anticipation of shortages pushing up prices. There may also be price rises if the currency is debased (e.g. the gold content of coins reduced) or confidence is lost in its acceptability. This essentially means the value of the commodity being used as the numeraire has fallen relative to other goods.

A general rise in prices across all commodities is inflation and a fall in prices is deflation. The rate of inflation in Britain has fluctuated considerably although never to the same extent as experienced in countries such as Germany, which suffered hyperinflation in the late 1920s. Britain was affected by the severe inflation experienced across the Roman empire under Diocletian in the 3rd cent. but price data do not exist for England until the Middle Ages. The medieval period saw only modest overall general price rises although there were periods of rising prices—e.g. after the *Black Death had swept Europe (1348/9)—interspersed with periods of falling prices. This trend continued through the next centuries but with bouts of rapid price rises. These periods of high inflation were often associated with wars and the pressures to finance them. Wars increase the demand for goods but reduce the available resources to produce them. Prices rose, for instance during the Revolutionary and Napoleonic wars (1793–1815). There have also been times, most notably in the Tudor period, when the currency has been debased, reducing its value and creating general price rises. Since the deflation of the Great Depression of the 1930s, however, Britain, in line with other industrial countries, has experienced consistently gradually rising prices. The price increases have generally been low, 2–4 per cent a year, but have included a period of quite rapid inflation—over 10 per cent p.a.—in the early 1980s.

The underlying causes of general price rises are disputed but, since high levels of inflation are seen as socially inequitable and can reduce confidence in a country's economy, understanding them is important for policy-making. Traditionally, classical economists supported the quantity theory of money as explaining price levels. The idea, in its simple form, was that any increase in money supply directly pushes up prices. To contain inflation, advocates of this school look to controlling the money supply. The more recent Keynesian theories focus on aggregate demand and market distortions—demand pull theories of inflation. They emphasize the role of price controls and the regulation of total expenditure.

The state has periodically attempted directly to regulate prices. At the firm level, there is a long history of price controls over monopoly suppliers. When markets are perfectly competitive, no individual actor has sufficient influence to affect prices—they are determined by Adam *Smith's 'invisible hand'. Where markets are imperfect, those with monopoly (or monopsony) power can withhold supply and increase prices beyond the competitive level. Action is then taken either to limit prices by reducing the monopoly power of the supplier or by acting directly on the prices permitted.

At various times in recent history there have also been efforts by government to control the general prices (e.g. price and incomes policies) especially during wartime and as a counter-inflation strategy. In some instances (e.g. for periods of rationing during the world wars) the price mechanism has been abandoned over parts of the economy. Macro-efforts at price control have, however, in general, proved to be singularly unsuccessful as long-term policies, producing political difficulties and tending to run against the natural tide of market forces. KJB

Pride's Purge was a military *coup* by *Fairfax's army, organized by Commissary-General *Ireton and executed on 6–7 December 1648 by Colonel Thomas Pride. Its purpose was to prevent the conclusion of the so-called treaty of *Newport between the Long Parliament and Charles I, whom it would have reinstated on terms that the army considered unsafe and unjust. Ireton had intended to dissolve the Parliament, but was persuaded by friendly members to purge it instead, upon their promise that it would soon dissolve itself. Pride prevented 231 known supporters of the treaty from entering the House, and imprisoned 45 of them. What was left became known as the *Rump. AHW

Priestley, Joseph (1733–1804). Chemist, clergyman, and political theorist. Priestley was born in Yorkshire and educated at Batley Grammar School and at Daventry dissenting academy. An amateur scientist of great renown, his discovery of 'dephlogisticated air', later named oxygen by Lavoisier, transformed the study of chemistry. As a theologian, Priestley moved from *presbyterianism via arianism to a unitarian position. He argued against the atonement; questioned traditional views of the person of Christ; and rejected the doctrine of Christ's perfection. He was a lively polemicist. His *Essay on the Principles of Government* (1768) was a strong plea for liberty, and he campaigned for the repeal of the Test and Corporation Acts and for the abolition of the slave trade. An incautious phrase in his *Letter to Edward Burn* (1790) caused him to be satirized as 'Gunpowder Priestley', plotting to blow up the British constitution, and brought down upon him the wrath of the Birmingham 'church and king' mob. In July 1791 it burned his house, wrecked his laboratory, and destroyed most of his papers. Priestley left England and spent the rest of his life in Pennsylvania. TSG

prime minister. The modern office of prime minister developed over several centuries. Medieval and early modern monarchs often had chief ministers and advisers on whom they greatly relied and who wielded vast power—men such as Cardinal *Morton in Henry VII's reign, *Burghley under Queen Elizabeth, and *Buckingham for James I and Charles I. But they depended totally upon the favour of the monarch, as the fate of *Wolsey, Thomas *Cromwell, and *Clarendon demonstrated. The crucial change came after 1688 when it became necessary to summon Parliament every year, and the ability to manage it, and particularly the House of Commons which held the purse-strings, became a vital political qualification. Robert *Harley, later earl of Oxford, in Anne's reign, had some of the attributes of a prime minister, including a keen understanding of the growing power of the press, but the title of first prime minister is usually given to Sir Robert *Walpole, though the term was derogatory and he denied it. His 21 years in office (still a record) reflected political judgement, financial acumen, debating ability, but also his standing at court, and he nearly lost power in 1727 on the death of George I. The subsequent development of the office, which was of course subject to personal fluctuation, depended upon the gradual development of party, which limited the king's choice of minister; on the growing complexity of public business, which demanded a co-ordinating hand; on the slow decline in the influence of the monarch, whose personal approbation remained useful but, by the 19th cent., was no longer essential, as the long careers of *Liverpool, *Palmerston, and *Gladstone demonstrated; and on the development of an organized public opinion, expressed through a reformed electoral system, which substituted the choice of the voters for the choice of the monarch.

Lord *North during the American War was still inclined, particularly in moments of crisis, to shuffle off responsibility: in 1778 he told the Commons that 'he did not think our constitution authorized such a character as that animal called a prime minister'. But William *Pitt, a stronger man, took a more determined view of the office, in both theory and practice, observing in 1803 that 'there should be an avowed and real minister, possessing the chief weight in the council, and the principal place in the confidence of the king . . . There can be no rivality or division of power. That power must rest in the person generally called the First Minister, and that minister ought, he thinks, to be the person at the head of the finances.'

As the office grew in stature, the prime minister gradually took over many of the powers of the monarch—the granting and timing of a dissolution of Parliament, the appointment and replacement of ministerial colleagues, and, above all, the granting of honours. Monarchs fought rearguard actions and occasionally won successes, resisting suggestions, proposing their own candidates, doubting policy, but the general drift was against them. Two heavy blows came in quick succession. In 1832 William IV, with great reluctance, agreed to create enough Whig peers if needed to carry Lord *Grey's reform bill, thus allowing a vital royal prerogative to fall into the hands of a determined prime minister: three years later, when he dismissed Lord *Melbourne, he was obliged to recall him after *Peel had failed to win a majority at the general election. Even at court, the monarch was often on the defensive. As early as 1755 George II complained that *Newcastle 'meddled with the bedchamber', and in 1839 Victoria fought another rearguard action in defence of her 'ladies'.

Though the power of the office was clearly established by the mid-19th cent., it retained something of its disreputable flavour and was slow to be acknowledged. But in 1865 *Bagehot wrote bluntly that 'the Queen is only at the head of the dignified part of the constitution. The prime minister is at the head of the efficient part.' In 1878 at the Congress of *Berlin, Beaconsfield (*Disraeli) was referred to as 'Prime Minister of Her Britannic Majesty', and in 1905 a royal warrant gave the prime minister precedence after the archbishop of York. JAC

The development of the office of prime minister has been closely linked to the growth of the party system. For all but ten years of the 20th cent. the prime minister has been the leader of the majority party in the House of Commons. The three exceptions were *Lloyd George (1916–22), *MacDonald (1931–5), and, for a few months in 1940, Winston *Churchill. Lloyd George was first appointed during the First World War, and MacDonald held office as head of an ostensibly coalition government after the 1931 financial crisis. Churchill became prime minister in 1940 without at the time being party leader, but within five months he had assumed that role. The office depends on the holder being able to command the continuing support of a majority of the House of Commons.

The powers of the prime minister, though not closely defined, are extensive. He appoints all the other ministers, including junior ministers, can transfer them to different offices, or dismiss them altogether. He chairs the meetings of the cabinet and appoints ministers to the numerous cabinet committees. Although he lacks a department of his own, he controls the cabinet office, and his personal policy unit. Honours, such as knighthoods, peerages, and other decorations, are awarded on his recommendation. As leader of the government, he exercises a general if not always clearly articulated authority over policy.

The impact of a prime minister on national policy varies with both the forcefulness of his or her own personality, and the setting in which he or she works. Thus Margaret *Thatcher took care to appoint numerous opponents (the so-called Wets) within the party hierarchy to her first cabinet. After two years she felt strong enough to purge the government of the leading Wets; and after her sweeping election victory of 1983, she dismissed her foreign secretary, Francis Pym. However, in later years she felt constrained to appoint men who had served their apprenticeships under her arch-rival, Edward *Heath.

In spite of their great powers, prime ministers have been inhibited by fear of losing office. Labour leaders used to be elected by their colleagues in the parliamentary party. Since 1981 they have been chosen by an electoral college, consisting of all Labour MPs and delegates from trade unions and constituency Labour parties. Until 1965 Conservative leaders used to 'evolve'. Sometimes, though not often, there was a recognized heir apparent. More frequently, when the party was in office, a candidate was presented to the monarch after consultations had taken place among the party's grandees (the 'Magic Circle', as one ex-minister sourly put it). Since 1965, the party leader, whether in or out of office, has been elected by the Conservative MPs, and since 1974 the leader has had to run the gauntlet of re-election each year.

The provision for annual re-election makes the leader, even when prime minister, highly vulnerable. Margaret Thatcher resigned in 1990 after she had narrowly failed to win outright on the first ballot and when it became clear that she was likely to lose on the second. For years she had dominated the political landscape. She went down to defeat for two reasons: accumulating evidence that, though she had won three elections in a row, she had become an electoral liability, and resentment of her high-handed and to some arrogant style of leadership.

Yet even before the introduction of the annual re-election of the leader, there were obvious limitations to a prime minister's power. *Baldwin, *Eden, and *Macmillan suffered severe criticism, though the first held on until the age of 70, and the other two left office because of ill-health. *Chamberlain resigned in 1940 after losing the support of a section of his party and Churchill was edged out as his abilities lessened with age. It follows that the apparently vast powers of the prime minister are often subject to stringent limits. His overriding need is to have the support, preferably the united support, of his party in the Commons.

In recent years it has become fashionable to describe the office of prime minister as presidential. The official doctrine is that the prime minister is simply the first among equals, and the rule of collective responsibility emphasizes the collegial character of the cabinet or government. The office was conceived as being on the model of a team leader rather than an autocrat. Whenever the post is held by a strong and self-willed prime minister, the assertion that it has become presidential is propounded, and a contrast is drawn between the office in the 19th cent. and today. The comparison has some force. The urgency of many decisions in the modern world, the increased importance of foreign affairs, media emphasis on the personality of the prime minister, have all tended to enhance the office at the expense of departmental ministers. Yet it is easy to exaggerate the change. The gladiatorial contests between *Gladstone and *Disraeli anticipated the modern concentration on the rival party leaders. Similarly, crucial decisions were sometimes taken by the prime minister and a few colleagues, with the cabinet sidelined. Most of the Liberal cabinet in 1914 were unaware of the extent of the Anglo-French conversations relating to a possible war with Germany.

The rule of a prime minister such as Thatcher will always give colour to the image of the prime minister as all-powerful. But though it may be conceded that there is a long-term trend towards the enhancement of the office, there are frequent fluctuations, as dominating prime ministers are followed by more diffident successors. Thus a Thatcher is succeeded by a *Major, a Macmillan by a Douglas-*Home. The bitter price Thatcher paid for her overbearing style suggests than an excessively presidential attitude may exact its own penalties. HB

Barber, J., *The Prime Minister since 1945* (Oxford, 1991); Blake, R., *The Office of Prime Minister* (Oxford, 1975); King, A. (ed.), *The British Prime Minister* (2nd edn. 1985); Van Thal, H. (ed.), *The Prime Ministers* (2 vols., 1974–5).

primitive methodists broke away from the main Wesleyan body and formed their own connexion in 1811, led by Hugh Bourne, a carpenter, and William Clowes, a potter, who had been expelled for holding American-style camp-meetings at Mow Cop (Staffs.). Condemned by the middle-class churches as ranters, the primitive methodists provided a form of evangelism attuned to the needs of labouring people. In a crowded cottage or plain village chapel, listening to a local preacher who was a working man or woman, they felt at home in a way they seldom did in the parish church. The 'prims' were noted for their open-air, hell-fire style of preaching, their revivalist, tented camp-meetings, their acceptance of women preachers, and their teetotalism. Until the 1840s they re-enacted the religious 'enthusiasm' of *Wesley's early preachers and suffered similar persecution. Thereafter the primitive methodists became more respectable and conservative, evolving from a sect into a denomination. Authority in the church became more centralized, though the power of the laity at local level was greater than in other methodist connexions. By the 1850s the primitive methodists had over 100,000 members, concentrated particularly in the Potteries, the Durham and Northumberland coalfields, Yorkshire, Lincolnshire, and Norfolk. In 1932 they joined the United Methodist Church. JFCH

primogeniture. The character of the inheritance custom has a great bearing on the social and political evolution of a country. Primogeniture, inheritance by the eldest son, developed in England after the Norman Conquest and had military implications—that the *fief should not be subdivided lest it become incapable of fulfilling its feudal obligation. There were always regions where the custom did not apply—*gavelkind was widespread in Kent and in parts of Wales giving partible inheritance, and the custom of *borough English in some places gave inheritance to the younger son. One consequence of primogeniture, especially when buttressed by *entail, as it was in the 17th and 18th cents., was to encourage the accumulation of large estates and restrict the proliferation of small proprietorships or peasant holdings. Since it applied also to titles, it meant that the English nobility was a small group contrasting with thousands of impoverished noblemen to be found in many parts of the continent. But the custom had its critics and the plight of younger sons, forced to seek their fortunes because they had poor expectations, is a commonplace of 18th-cent. novels and drama. Primogeniture was abolished by legislation in 1926 in England and in 1964 in Scotland. JAC

Primrose League. Victorian Conservative organization. Founded in 1883 by Lord Randolph *Churchill and John Gorst, the Primrose League was intended to enable the Conservatives to adapt to the extension of democracy. The Tory leaders feared that any popular organization would eventually challenge their authority. However, the league avoided this problem because it was not officially part of the Conservative Party, and because it made no claim to influence the party's policy.

The key to its success lay in combining political propaganda, often in the form of lantern slides, with a regular programme of social activities. These included music-hall, dances, teas, summer fêtes, train excursions, and cycling clubs, all available very cheaply. Though derided by opponents as a 'matrimonial agency', the league benefited greatly from its social role. By 1886, 200,000 members had been enrolled, and by 1891 over a million, of whom half were women. This made the league the largest political organization in Britain in its heyday—the late 1880s and 1890s. Thereafter it suffered a steady decline and after 1918 its membership was largely absorbed into the official party structure. MDP

Prince Edward Island was ceded by France in 1763, becoming a separate colony in 1769. The island was granted to absentee proprietors in 1767. It was called St John's Island until 1799. Most settlers came direct from the British Isles, bringing sectarian conflict. Attempts by tenants to dispossess landlords provided models for land legislation in Ireland. Although the dominion of Canada was planned at a conference in Charlottetown, the island's capital, in 1864, Prince Edward Island remained aloof until 1873. L. M. Montgomery's *Anne of Green Gables* (1908) was set on 'the only island there is'. GM

prince of Wales. The title 'prince of Wales' was not of great antiquity when it was bestowed by Edward I on his 16-year-old son Edward in 1301. *Llywelyn ab Iorwerth had called himself 'prince of Aberffraw and Lord of Snowdon'. *Dafydd ap Llywelyn had taken the title prince of Wales in 1244, though he failed to gain papal recognition, but Henry III was forced to acknowledge *Llywelyn ap Gruffydd in the 1260s. Llywelyn was killed in 1282. The adoption in 1301 was presumably a gesture of conciliation by Edward I, though the tradition that his infant son, born in *Caernarfon castle, had been shown to the people is a later invention. The title has since been reserved for the heir apparent and is held with the dukedom of *Cornwall. Of the 21 holders of the title since 1301, 14 have succeeded to the throne. JAC

printing with movable types, or letterpress, as opposed to printing using carved wooden blocks, was invented by Johannes Gutenberg of Mainz *c.*1440, though there is evidence that a Dutchman, Coster of Harlem, made a similar breakthrough about the same time. One of Gutenberg's associates, Peter Schoffer, produced a psalter in 1457, the first known book with a printed date. In 1462 the sack of Mainz dispersed printers and their equipment, the process being introduced to England by William *Caxton in 1476. It did not reach Scotland until 1507 when the first printing press was set up in Edinburgh by Walter Chapman and Andrew Myllar.

Early printers used a wooden press, types, paper, and ink. The primitive press, constructed of wood and iron, was a screw press resembling a wine or cloth press. The plate, or 'platen', was applied by a vertical screw, hand operated by a lever, to the printing surface, or 'forme', placed horizontally on the bed of the press. Ink was applied to the type by dabbers, known as ink balls, a technique which survived until the development of the ink roller at the beginning of the 19th cent. Printers at first made their own types, but typefounding, an early instance of mass production, soon became a separate trade. Although many improvements were made, the process remained essentially the same until the early 19th cent.

Printing and publishing, which were closely allied, grew slowly until the latter half of the 18th cent. This was partly due to censorship, which intermittently constrained publication, and partly to the high cost of paper, which was also heavily taxed. While censorship continued until the early 19th cent., paper became cheaper and could be produced in continuous sheets following the introduction of paper-making machines developed in France by Nicholas Louis Robert (1798) and Henri Fourdrinier (1806). John Dickinson, an English paper-maker, patented the first cylinder machine in 1809. Paper could thus be produced in larger sizes and greater quantities than by hand.

The 19th cent. also brought significant developments in the industrialization of printing itself. Lord Stanhope developed the first all-metal platen press in 1804. At the same time the screw mechanism was improved, resulting in greater and more even pressure on the forme, and the ink roller greatly increased the speed of production. The improved Stanhope press doubled the output of the traditional wooden press. Even greater gains in productivity were made following the introduction of the first practical mechanized printing press developed by Friedrich Koening in 1811. It was designed to feed single sheets of paper through a cylinder press and in 1814 was modified for *The Times*, to become a two-feeder machine printing on both sides of the paper at once. The first power-driven platen press was developed about 1822.

The Times continued to lead the field with a steam press, producing 5,000 copies per hour, in 1827. Another important breakthrough was the rotary press with types fastened round a cylinder, introduced in 1848, and, after a further period of development, the continuously running rotary press, where a stereotyped printing surface was attached to the cylinder, pioneered at *The Times* in 1868. With subsequent refinements, this remained the standard method of newspaper-printing for over a century.

Pictorial reproduction was greatly influenced by the development of photography. Wood blocks and wood engravings, the commonest means of illustration, were gradually replaced by the photo-engraved line block and later by the half-tone block in which gradations of tone were simulated by typographic dot-formations of varying pattern and size. The monochrome half-tone process, introduced in 1872, was refined by the end of the 19th cent. to allow full colour reproduction. Similar technology was adopted in the book-printing trade.

Composing methods, using movable type, underwent a parallel revolution with the development, initially in the USA during the 1880s, of composing and casting machinery operated from keyboards. For nearly a century, the text to be printed was cast in hot metal, using monotype to set single characters or linotype to set text line by line. Thus, despite mechanization, printing remained a skilled occupation and historically a highly unionized craft, notably in the newspaper industry, which expanded dramatically in the early 20th cent.

Consequently the print unions had a long history of confrontation with the press barons. The printers' solidarity was threatened and ultimately undermined during the 1970s and 1980s by a move away from hot metal to computerized typesetting using high-speed optical methods and electronic page make-up systems. The introduction of new technology led to dramatic rationalization and to redundancies in printing and related trades. In London, bitter strikes and lock-outs resulted from the movement of newspaper printing from its traditional heartland in *Fleet Street to new production units in the East End. Elsewhere in newspaper-printing, notably in Manchester and Glasgow, similar effects were felt. Book-printing, like publishing, was also transformed by the new technology. Printing has always had important backward linkages to paper manufacture and the metal trades, and, with increasing mechanization during the 19th cent., to engineering. It was also closely linked after the mid-18th cent. to the development of *publishing, of both books and newspapers. ID

prisons. The first use of prisons in England was to detain an accused until trial or to keep a convicted criminal until execution. Under the Anglo-Saxons and the Normans, and throughout the Middle Ages, criminals were punished by fines and, for serious crime, death or mutilation. Minor criminals might also be punished in the village or manor by whipping, the stocks, or the *pillory.

With the advent of the system of presentment of those suspected of serious crimes, introduced by the Assizes of *Clarendon and *Northampton by Henry II, it became necessary to keep suspects until the royal justices arrived to receive the presentments made by twelve men of each hundred. The first prisons were therefore the local lock-up or the castle keep. In addition the church had its own prisons, reputedly less uncomfortable than those of the secular powers.

In the sphere of civil law, each central court of common law had its prison (such as the *Marshalsea for the Court of *King's Bench). Imprisonment for contempt of court was and still is possible and the Court of *Chancery became notorious for imprisoning those who were deemed to be in contempt. Imprisonment for debt was also common and was not abolished until late in the 19th cent.

The development of imprisonment as a penal sanction took place comparatively late in English history. Prison as we know it had a number of predecessors; convicted criminals might be locked up in gaols but this practice was not widespread. At different periods society provided workhouses, *'Bridewells' or houses of correction, and, in the 18th and 19th cents., the 'hulks' or convict ships, depicted in *Dickens, used for convicts as well as for prisoners of war.

Before the 19th cent. prisons might be 'farmed out' to private individuals, who would charge prisoners for their accommodation and food. During the 19th cent. prison became an important penal sanction though it was not until the 1850s that it became the prevailing form of punishment, especially after the end of *transportation. The condition of English prisons was deplorable; males and females could be and were crowded into cells together. Overcrowding, dirt, and low hygiene as well as a miserable diet made the prisons breeding places for disease such as typhoid—indeed an illness known as 'gaol fever' was common, and many inmates died in prison.

In the 18th cent. certain reformers became aware of the appalling conditions in English prisons—two of the most famous being John *Howard, the great prison reformer who gave his name to the Howard League for penal reform, and Elizabeth *Fry who worked for the improvement of the lot of women in prison.

In 1865 the principle was introduced of work for prisoners. In 1895 the Gladstone Committee was set up to review the prisons and reform followed. Gradually during the 20th cent. corporal punishment, penal servitude, and hard labour were abolished for prisoners and the rehabilitative aspect of prison re-emphasized, but the prison system remains an object of controversy up to the present day. MM

privateering was a device for commerce raiding in time of war whereby a privately owned, manned, and armed ship could operate on the high seas as a conventional warship, yet, in the event of making captures, was entitled to a very substantial share of their adjudicated value. The share was always capable of variation as between the sanctioning authority, usually the crown, and the proposer, prior to a voyage; and in every instance the agreement was encapsulated in the 'letter of marque', carried by the privateer as her warrant. In England privateering can be dated back to the late 13th cent., but the late 17th cent. and the whole of the 18th witnessed the apogee of the practice, pursued with especial vehemence by the French and the Dutch, and also by the seaboard colonies of North America during the *American War of Independence. Privateering was abolished by the convention of Paris (1856). DDA

Privy Council. The fate of most councils or committees is to grow too large to be effective and to be replaced by an executive or inner caucus, like a series of Russian dolls. The *council of late medieval times became too big and in the late 1530s a smaller Privy Council was set up. To a considerable extent this was the work of Thomas *Cromwell, though how much *Wolsey contributed and how much was left to Cromwell's successors is debated. In 1540 the Privy Council, with some twenty members, acquired a clerk and a minute book. It became the work-horse of late Tudor government. As such it made many enemies. The Long Parliament replaced it in 1649 by a *Council of State, but Richard *Cromwell restored it, and it was continued by Charles II after 1660. But its great days were by then over. The emergence of the cabal in the 1670s and James II's use of an inner cabinet in the 1680s heralded its fate, and it began to lose importance, first to the cabinet council, then to the cabinet. Its defenders offered a rearguard action and the Act of *Settlement of 1701 declared that government business should be transacted in the Privy Council and that all counsellors should sign their advice. The clause was repealed by 4 Anne c. 8 s. 24 in 1705 before it could take effect. As the Privy Council continued to grow, its duties became almost purely formal, though the *lord president of the council is invariably a cabinet minister and supervises a number of functions in relation to education, science, and charters. Its judicial committee of legal experts acts as a court of appeal for British dependencies, the Isle of Man, and the Channel Islands. By 1994 the membership of the Privy Council had risen to more than 400.

The Scottish Privy Council dated from the late 15th cent. After the union of the crowns in 1603, though the crucial decisions were taken in London, the Scottish Privy Council had considerable influence as the day-to-day executive. It was abolished immediately after the Act of *Union of 1707. JAC

pro-Boer was the misleading name given to those who opposed the government's policy of fighting the *Boer War of 1899–1902. Few of them actually sympathized with their country's enemies. Most were either old-fashioned Gladstonian Liberals, or socialists. Some were physically assaulted by *jingoists. *Lloyd George and J. A. *Hobson both forged their reputations as pro-Boers. BJP

proclamations were part of the royal prerogative to deal with emergencies or to make enactments while Parliament was not in being. They were therefore normally only temporary measures and it was accepted that they could not touch life, limb, or property. Nevertheless, under the Tudors they dealt with a large variety of matters—the sale of meat, courtesy to the French ambassador, exile for anabaptists, reduced access to Windsor castle, prohibition of the export of leather, and discouragement from playing dice, cards, or tennis. The statute of Proclamations of 1539 reminded subjects that proclamations had the force of statutes, 'as though they were made by act of parliament'. The Act was repealed in 1547 but James I's use of proclamations led to a protest in the petition of grievances of 1610 that they were encroaching upon statute and could 'bring a new form of arbitrary government upon the realm'. James was unusually conciliatory and accepted *Coke's view that proclamations could not create new offences. Charles I made considerable use of them, but they were too necessary to government to be abolished, though their employment after the Restoration ceased to be controversial and they were often exhortatory in nature. JAC

professions. In English, the word 'profession' has since the 16th cent. been applied to a limited number of occupations in which a specific body of knowledge is used to solve problems for clients. By the 18th cent. these involved a social status well above that of trade and handicrafts and included the upper ranks of law, medicine, the church, and maybe the military. The authority of knowledge was often linked to the status of gentleman, which many had by birth, and others gained by achievement.

Social and economic change in the first half of the 19th cent. brought many challenges to the authority of the 'traditional' professions. The medical men faced rising expectations, the failure of urban public health, and public anger over body-snatching and dissection. The lawyers met the demands of the rational law reformers and the ridicule of people like Charles *Dickens in his account of *Chancery in *Bleak House*. The authority of the church was already compromised by the disputes between establishment and dissent. The military met mid-century condemnation for the incompetence of the *Crimean War.

Response centred upon the reform and creation of a series of qualifying associations. There were 7 in 1800, 20 more by 1880, to which 39 were added by 1914. They sought to control entry, to set standards, and ultimately to supervise training and the development of professional knowledge. The British Medical Association was formed in 1856 and its authority gained legislative backing in 1858. It had developed from the Provincial Medical and Surgical Association (1834) which itself had recognized that the old division between physicians, surgeons, and apothecaries had been replaced in functional terms by the general practitioner. The Law Society, founded in 1825, came to supervise examinations in the 1870s. New areas of knowledge and knowledge application also organized. The Institute of Civil Engineers, founded in 1818, came to supervise examinations in the 1890s. Other groups, such as schoolteachers, did not gain full control of entry and work conditions but a variety of organizations worked to raise standards and improve public perception of their work. By 1900, an increasing amount of professional training was taking place in universities and colleges, rather than through the personal relationship of apprenticeships.

The 20th cent. not only saw a rapid increase in the areas of work and knowledge regarded as professional but fundamental changes in the workplace relationships of many professions. In the 19th cent., doctors, lawyers, and self-employed schoolteachers collected fees directly from clients. A few like the poor law surgeon from the 1830s and the school board teacher (1870/2) had begun to work for salaries. After 1900, this trend accelerated. Professional people worked for a growing number of state agencies and private sector corporate bodies. Here they joined a new group of career salaried managers, who applied new management 'science' to industrial organization and created their own professional organizations. Professional and managerial occupations accounted for less than 10 per cent of the occupied male population in 1900 but grew to around 20 per cent by the 1970s. They were distinguished from wage labour by a greater degree of workplace autonomy, by better working conditions, and often by career progression, sick pay, holidays with pay, and pensions. In some senses the emphasis on service and standards, and on status derived from knowledge and training, challenged profit and capital accumulation in the value system of British society. At the same time the experience and often the ideological views of professionals in the public sector were very different from those in the private sector, where the market and profits still dominated, although usually mediated by professionals like accountants. RJM

Promenade Concerts. London's leading concert series. The Queen's Hall Promenade Concerts were established by impresario Robert Newman and conductor Henry *Wood in 1895. Initially they were all given by Wood and the Queen's Hall Orchestra, which was replaced by the BBC Symphony Orchestra in 1930 following the BBC's adoption of the series, but later various orchestras and conductors were involved. After the Queen's Hall was bombed in 1941, the series moved to the Royal Albert Hall, becoming the Henry Wood Promenade Concerts on Wood's death in 1944. William Glock's tenure as head of music at the BBC (1959–72) saw a broadening of repertoire, ranging from medieval music to Stockhausen and including 'semi-staged' operas. The concerts have fostered many new British works, while their unique, vibrant atmosphere culminates in the exuberant 'Last Night of the Proms'. ECr

prophecies were, during the medieval and early modern periods, a source of interest and concern throughout the political and social hierarchies. They could involve exact predictions, but were also frequently ambiguous statements, often taking the form of an 'ancient' piece of verse or quasi-proverbial wisdom, usually attributed to a past person, either real or mythical (prophecies attributed to *Merlin surfaced regularly). The genre was wide ranging, and acquired added credibility from its association with biblical prophecy. Prophecies were numerous, and (like proverbs) could be reworded or reinterpreted to suit changing circumstances or local conditions.

Prophecies assumed a serious political dimension under the Tudors, when they were frequently interpreted by central government as bearing on political or dynastic changes. Henry VIII, Mary Tudor, and Elizabeth I all included prophecies as a species of seditious words in their treason legislation, while the closing months of Edward VI's reign saw intense anxiety over prophecies as the regime crumbled.

The political instability of the 1640s and 1650s gave new life to political prophecies, but, as with so many aspects of the 'magical' world, interest in prophecies among the educated had dwindled by 1700, although prophecy still retained its hold among the less educated. JAS

prorogation is the royal power, now exercised by the prime minister, to suspend the session of Parliament. Since 1854 the sovereign has not appeared in person but has delegated the task to commissioners. Prorogation suspends all parliamentary activity save impeachment and the judicial work of the House of Lords. Bills must be reintroduced. Clearly the prerogative of prorogation, like dissolution, could be used tactically, to allow time for negotiation or for tempers to cool. Charles I prorogued Parliament in June 1628 rather than listen to more remonstrances against tonnage and poundage. When he prorogued the 1629 Parliament, the Speaker was held down in his chair to allow protests against innovations in religion. The prorogation was followed by a dissolution and eleven years elapsed before another parliament sat. JAC

prostitution, the sale of sex for money or material gain, predominantly by females with male clients and frequently associated with criminal activity, has always been affected by cultural values. Brothels first sprang up in Southwark where Roman soldiers guarded the Thames crossing, to develop into the Bankside stews that became part of the bishop of Winchester's liberty in the early 12th cent. and were regulated by Henry II (1162); the church took a pragmatic view since the revenue was highly profitable to both bishop and king. After the outbreak of virulent syphilis throughout early 16th-cent. Europe, stricter controls were imposed and brothels briefly closed. With the Reformation, moral rather than health concerns began to prevail, so prostitutes were publicly humiliated and imprisoned for 'correction'. Puritanism merely hardened existing attitudes. Whereas the upper-class prostitutes of the demi-monde were involved in sexual liaisons outside marriage in order to gain influence and social advantage, most whores were regarded as social lepers. During the 19th cent. governments made efforts to regulate the practice, particularly around naval and military garrisons (a third of all sick cases among soldiers were venereal in origin by 1864). Female prostitutes were subject to humiliation and callous treatment under the Contagious Diseases Acts of the 1860s, only repealed in 1886 after the campaigns of Josephine *Butler. The close link between venereal infection and guilt may possibly underlie the 1888–9 Whitechapel murders by Jack the Ripper and the 1892 strychnine poisonings in Lambeth by Neil Cream. Female prostitution is now legally tolerated, though with prohibition of open solicitation, but young women are still forced into the practice by poverty, homelessness, or lack of skills for self-support. Homosexual male prostitution, particularly in large cities, is increasing. IJEK

protectionism. While international trade has been recognized as a major influence on the growth of the world economy throughout history, virtually all countries at all times have sought to protect either the whole economy, or at least some part of it, from the rigours of international competition by imposing barriers. The protection of industries perceived as vital to the national interest in terms of future growth, current employment, or military security have all been identified as worthy of protective support. This has usually taken the form of a tariff, or government levy, on imported goods to bring their price up to or even above the price of home-produced goods. Thus domestic producers are protected against the impact of foreign imports. Besides tariffs, quotas, and other forms of overt discrimination, there exist less obvious non-tariff barriers to trade, such as technical specifications written to favour domestic producers, differential tax regimes, and customs delays together with a variety of bureaucratic regulations. A familiar modern example of protection is the support given to agriculture in the *European Economic Community. This has been so successful that, far from being swamped by a massive tide of cheap food imports as was feared when the Common Agricultural Policy (CAP) was originally devised, farmers in the European Union have become large-scale exporters to the rest of the world. Support of domestic industry can also take the form of subsidies to help exports, a payment allowing exporters to offer competitive prices in international markets without having to reduce their costs by an equivalent amount.

Protective barriers distort trade patterns, and bring about redistribution of income. A tariff imposed on imports raises domestic prices so that consumers are worse off. The government gains tax revenue from the tariff and producers gain from the price increase. The redistribution of welfare benefits between different groups in society frequently leads to political disputes. The repeal of the *Corn Laws in 1846 redistributed income away from wealthy agriculturalists to manufacturers, although not to any great extent. The repeal also redistributed income to consumers through the fall in food prices, although the scale of this is uncertain. (See FREE TRADE.) *Chamberlain's tariff campaign of 1903 was intended to redistribute income to industrialists by protecting sectors like the steel industry from the effects of cheap imports. More recently, the CAP has effected substantial redistribution to the advantage of producers and the detriment of consumers and taxpayers. Since the distribution of agriculture is uneven throughout the European Community, some countries have enjoyed a substantial welfare gain from these policies, notably Ireland and Denmark, while others, like Germany and the United Kingdom, have lost. Protection always entails some loss of efficiency, as compared to free trade, because the lowest price obtainable through competition is replaced by a higher subsidized price. The result is over-production in the home market by suppliers who are less efficient than they would be if exposed to world-wide competition, consumer loss through higher prices, and an increase in government revenues from tariffs. A reduction in the level of protection will have the opposite effects: a fall in prices from which consumers gain, increased competitive pressure on producers, and a loss in government tariff revenue. CHL

Protectorate. The Protectorate was established on 16 December 1653 when Oliver *Cromwell became head of state as lord protector. Since his power rested on a formidable army, whose officers had devised the Protectorate's constitution, the *Instrument of Government, his regime has often been called a military dictatorship. The description needs to be qualified. The constitutional restraints imposed by the Instrument were considerable, and Cromwell welcomed them. Serving officers were always outnumbered by civilians on his council, and formed only a tiny minority among the justices of the peace, to whom local government had been restored. The size of the army was progressively reduced; the numbers stationed in England and Wales varied between 11,000 and 14,400. With rare exceptions, the rule of law was well respected, and political prisoners were extremely few. Religious liberty officially stopped short of 'popery or prelacy', but in practice was broad.

Cromwell's first Parliament refused to ratify the constitution and proceeded to frame one of its own; he dissolved it in January 1655. Shortly afterwards, *Penruddock's rising and other royalist designs gave his military councillors a temporary ascendancy, and the result was the regime of the *major-generals. These officers did not supersede the local magistracy in their eleven districts, but their duties went far beyond suppressing royalist conspiracy and they were much resented, not least for their inferior birth. Their regime was running down, however, long before Parliament terminated it by refusing to legitimize the levy on the royalist gentry (the 'decimation') which paid for it.

This second Protectorate Parliament (1656–8), from which the council excluded over 100 elected members, reflected a growing division in the effective (i.e. non-royalist) political nation between conservative civilians and supporters of the military. Led by the former, it presented Cromwell with a new constitution, the *Humble Petition and Advice, naming him as king and restoring other more traditional ways. His senior officers strongly opposed it, but despite them Cromwell accepted it, though without changing his title of Protector. Their influence thereafter diminished, and *Lambert, author of the Instrument of Government, was forced into retirement after refusing the new councillor's oath. Cromwell resumed his policy of healing old wounds, but died on 3 September 1658. His son *Richard's Protectorate lasted only eight months, not so much because he was personally inadequate—his one Parliament gave his government more support than either of Oliver's had done—as because the disgruntled military 'grandees' were bent on recovering their old political influence. By bringing Richard down, they wrecked the 'Good Old Cause' that they professed to serve. AHW

protestantism. The term originated with the protest of the reforming minority at the diet of Spires in 1529 against the catholic majority. As a general description of the anti-catholic position, it was adopted with some caution: several of the churches into which the new movement dissolved were strongly opposed to each other, while conservatives were not anxious to stress the role of individual conscience in religious matters. The common protestant ground was rejection of papal authority, emphasis on the Bible, devotion to preaching, clerical marriage, and a more austere ceremonial. The main divisions of protestantism were *calvinism, *lutheranism, and zwinglianism, with the Church of England claiming an autonomous and independent position.

In Scotland, a protestant regime in its *presbyterian form was established in 1560 and survived, amid great vicissitudes, to become the national religion in 1690. Protestantism also made much headway in northern Ireland, where Scottish influence was strong, but much less in the south which remained predominantly catholic. In England, the consolidation of the protestant Church of England owed much to the misjudgements of catholic monarchs Mary and James II, and to the upsurge of national enthusiasm produced by the long struggle against catholic Spain.

Catholic polemicists in the 16th cent. argued that the appeal to private conscience must, in the end, lead to religious anarchy. Protestantism was not long in dividing—indeed it was born divided—over the nature of the eucharist, the role of bishops, the importance of good works, and the method of baptism. The fissiparous nature of the movement continued to the 20th cent., with splits, secessions, and schisms in most denominations. Even the *methodists, one of the more sober sects and themselves a split from Anglicanism, divided into Wesleyan Methodists, Calvinistic Methodists, Methodist New Connexion, Primitive Methodists, Wesleyan Methodist Reformers, Bible Christians, and Wesleyan Methodist Association, while the religious census of 1851 identified Wesleyan Christian Union, Benevolent Methodists and Temperance Wesleyans. In the late 20th cent., falling membership, financial problems, and a more ecumenical spirit prompted a number of protestant reunions—the *Free Church of Scotland rejoined the *Church of Scotland in 1929, the Presbyterian Church of England merged with the Congregational Church to form the United Reform Church in 1972—but though relations between protestants and catholics are much warmer than in the 19th cent., re-unification has yet to come about. JAC

provincial council of church [S]. Ordained to be annual meetings of a metropolitan and his suffragans; bishops in Scotland received special permission to hold provincial councils in a papal bull dated 1225, despite having no archbishop until 1472. These councils were to deal with clerical excesses and the reformation of morals, to ensure canonical laws were read and observed, and, generally, to act as the governing body of the Church in Scotland. The provincial councils of 1549, 1552, and 1559, for example, passed numerous statutes for the internal reform of the church, designed to counter the criticisms and growth of the reform movement in Scotland. PER

Provisors, statute of, 1351. The papal practice of appointing to benefices (provisions), or granting reversions, was much resented, particularly since many of the clerics were foreign. Edward III was anxious to assert his own rights against both cathedral chapters and papacy. The Parliament of 1351 legislated against the practice (25 Edw. III s. 4), declaring the nominations invalid, and the restrictions were repeated and strengthened by a second Act in 1390. But Richard II, who needed papal support, reached a concordat with the papacy in 1398 which conceded much of the ground gained. JAC

Prussia, relations with. Regular diplomatic contact between Britain and Prussia dates essentially from the Hanoverian succession. The two states were closely allied for most of the *Seven Years War (1756–63), an alliance which allowed Britain to devote many of her resources to overseas expansion while Prussia preoccupied large French forces in Europe. Prussia and Britain were briefly allied against France in 1793–5, but their most significant collaboration occurred in 1815 when their armies defeated Napoleon at *Waterloo. The British did not share the Prussian desire for a harsh peace against France in 1814–15, and *Castlereagh briefly aligned Britain with Austria and France to reduce Prussian demands for Saxon territory. Rather he wanted a balance in Germany between the Prussians and the Habsburgs, hoping that together they might help to restrain France and Russia. He thus favoured a Prussian presence on the Rhine. Thereafter Prussia's association with the reactionary powers (Russia and Austria) usually discouraged friendship, although Prussia contributed to the isolation of France in the Near Eastern crisis of 1840. Britain's role in the Schleswig-Holstein question (1848–64) was understandably unpopular in Prussia, although from 1847 *Palmerston intermittently showed interest in the emergence of a strong north German power which he hoped would improve the balance in continental Europe as a whole. His successors, despite periods of distrust of Bismarckian methods and Prussian militarism, broadly welcomed German unification in 1870–1 in the belief that this would make for stability in the heart of Europe. CJB

Prynne, William (1600–69). Puritan lawyer, antiquarian, and politician. Educated at Oriel College, Oxford, and Lincoln's Inn, Prynne was hauled before the Court of *Star Chamber in 1634 for publishing the *Histriomastix*. This work, a 1,000-page denunciation of female actors and of theatre in general, was interpreted as an attack on Charles I and *Henrietta Maria. Prynne was rewarded with the loss of his ears. His attacks on the bishops landed him a second time before Star Chamber in 1637, where he was sentenced to lose what remained of his ears. After his release by the *Long Parliament in 1640, Prynne was instrumental in securing the conviction and death of his enemy Archbishop *Laud. He next turned his fire against religious radicals and the *New Model Army. The army cordially returned his hostility, and had him arrested at *Pride's Purge (6 December 1648). He continued to write long-winded pamphlets against the republic, popery, and quakerism during the 1650s. When the Long Parliament was recalled, Prynne introduced the bill in March 1660 for its dissolution. As a member of both Convention and Cavalier parliaments, he remained a presbyterian and resumed his attacks on bishops. IJG

Public Health Act, 1848. An Act of Parliament for England and Wales (11 & 12 Vic. c. 63) was carried following an agitation organized by Edwin *Chadwick and the Health of Towns Association. It created a General Board of Health in London and local boards of health with wide powers to enforce standards of public hygiene where the death rate exceeded 23 per 1,000 or where 10 per cent of ratepayers petitioned for a local board. Though the General Board was disbanded in 1858, over 700 local boards had been set up in England and Wales by 1871 and the Act was extended to Scotland in 1867. A consolidating measure created medical districts for the whole of Britain in 1875. ER

Public Record Office. See RECORD OFFICES.

public schools. During the Middle Ages, the *grammar school provided education for poor scholars intended for the church and for the sons of noblemen. This included such schools as *Eton and *Winchester. By the 18th cent. a number of 'Great Schools' had emerged, including *Harrow, *Rugby, Sherborne, and Canterbury.

Other changes during the early 19th cent. stimulated the demand for public schools. These included the spread of railways which enabled wealthy parents to send their children to board at far-off schools; the increase in political power of the middle classes after the 1832 Reform Act; and the rise of the *professions. Reforms in public schools were introduced by heads such as Samuel Butler at Shrewsbury (1793–1836), and Dr Thomas *Arnold at Rugby (1828–42), who were clerics. The school chapel became the focal point of life, discipline was enforced through prefects and team games emphasized. Proprietary schools, such as Marlborough (1843) and Haileybury (1864), often more progressive than the older public schools, were established to meet the demand from the middle classes. At first day schools, they later accepted boarders.

Criticism of some of the public schools, such as *Westminster and Charterhouse, was so persistent that a royal commission was appointed in 1861, under Lord *Clarendon, to investigate conditions in the nine large public schools Winchester, Eton, Westminster, Charterhouse, Harrow, Rugby, Shrewsbury, St Paul's, and Merchant Taylors'. Whilst broadly satisfied, the commissioners made a number of recommendations which were embodied in the Public Schools Act (1868). Governing bodies were reformed and schools such as Harrow developed a modern side. The Endowed Schools Bill (1869) threatened further intervention by the state into the affairs of schools, especially limiting the powers of headmasters. Edward Thring, headmaster of Uppingham, organized a meeting of thirteen heads at the school in December 1869 to oppose these contentious clauses. The meeting eventually became the annual headmasters' conference, membership of which denoted public school status.

Attempts have been made in the 20th cent. to bridge the gap between public schools and the state-provided sector. The Fleming Report (1944) and the first report of the Public Schools Commission (1968) (Newsom) were impracticable. The second report (1970) (Donnison) was more positive, but the advent of a Conservative government avoided further threats. The term public school has now been superseded by independent school. PG

publishing. Publishing, in the modern sense, dates from the 19th cent. when the book publisher became distinct from the bookseller and printer. Monasteries and then universities had the virtual monopoly of book production before the introduction of *printing, which made possible publication for a wider readership. Broadsheets and pamphlets, often with woodcuts or engravings, and produced mainly for propaganda purposes, were among the earliest publications designed for a popular audience.

The first *Copyright Act was passed in 1709. It freed author and publisher from printers' monopolies and gave them the right to negotiate for royalties and other terms. It also gave the public free access to an author's work after a given time. During the 18th cent. the bookseller supplanted the printer in dominance of the book trade. This coincided with increased demand for books from circulating libraries and the more affluent members of the public. Religious, philosophical, and topographical works were published in large numbers, though eventually overtaken in popularity by the novel.

The earliest publishers were booksellers who sold authors' works direct to the public. Among the first were Longman's, established in 1724, and John Murray, founded in 1765. The subsequent development of publishing during the 19th cent. was a consequence of higher levels of literacy and improved printing technology. The Publishers' Association was established in 1896. Apart from newspapers, publication for a mass market was pioneered during the 19th cent. in periodicals serializing novels, like those of *Dickens, with the complete novel produced later in inexpensive format. J. M. Dent's Everyman's Library, established to make available cheap editions for a popular market in 1906, was a forerunner of Allen Lane's paperback Penguin imprint, launched in 1935, which revolutionized the industry and public reading habits.

While many publishers produced books on a wide range of subjects, some specialized in particular fields, for example, legal, medical, scientific, and management studies. University presses, including those of Oxford, Cambridge, Manchester, Wales, and Edinburgh, were established to publish academic works. Another specialist branch, cartographic publishing, producing charts, maps, and atlases, grew in importance during the late 18th and 19th cents., pioneers being John Bartholomew, William Lizar, and the *Ordnance and Geological Surveys.

Outside London, the nucleus of the industry, Edinburgh became an important centre of publishing and printing, especially after the success of Sir Walter *Scott's novels, but the publishing industry there, after flourishing during the 19th and first half of the 20th cents., was a victim of progressive metropolitan take-overs. Publishing in Glasgow, though never on the scale of Edinburgh, suffered a similar fate. Nevertheless Scottish publishing, in common with that in Wales, has experienced a revival since the 1960s. ID

pubs. The term 'public house', denoting premises licensed for the sale of alcohol, became current in the late 17th cent. and was increasingly applied to what had hitherto been known as inns and taverns. It became a standard term for a drinking-place in the early 19th cent., only for matters to be complicated by the Beer Act of 1830, which allowed so-called beerhouses to be set up on payment of a derisory annual fee to the Excise, opening the floodgates to a spectacular proliferation of decidedly down-market drinking-dens, most of them in the front rooms of terraced houses. Publicans, as such, were licensed by the magistrates, and were angry that these new competitors were exempted from this surveillance; but they could sell wines and spirits as well as beer, and in practice their bigger premises and more respectable image helped them to survive and flourish during an extended Victorian heyday. Pubs at this time offered transport, information about job opportunities, facilities for changing money, meeting-rooms for a variety of societies, and increasingly entertainment, as the informal singalong became more formalized as the 'free and easy' and in some cases grew into the *music-hall, with purpose-built premises attached to the pub, which might eventually take on a separate life of their own. Pubs also became centres for popular sport, offering refuges for pedestrianism when it was driven from the streets and for cock-fighting and dog-fighting when they became formally illegal. In the 1860s and 1870s publicans were among the most important patrons of emerging football teams, the same man being behind the foundation of both Everton and Liverpool. As licensing laws were tightened up from the late 1860s and early 1870s it became more difficult for pub provision to keep pace with urban expansion, and late Victorian and subsequent residential areas (even working-class ones) have fewer and larger pubs than older districts. More capital was expected of pub providers, and architectural display became more elaborate as a marker of respectability, while breweries took over increasing numbers of pubs as tied houses, and 'landlords' increasingly became tenants or even managers in all but name. Disreputable pubs in older areas were already being sacrificed in exchange for new licences before the First World War, which saw even stricter regulation of licensing hours and introduced the afternoon 'gap' which has only recently been restored. During the inter-war years new 'roadhouses' in what came to be known as 'bypass Tudor' appeared in favoured suburban locations, while simply furnished old-fashioned rural pubs, patronizingly idealized by the likes of G. K. *Chesterton, fell into decline. The most drastic changes in pub architecture and internal arrangements have been left for the late 20th cent., with theme pubs, fake Victoriana, and a range of new entertainments, coupled with the restoration of women and children to the centre of pub life, the provision of better food, and the impact of restrictions on drink and driving. The remaking of the pub during the last quarter of the 20th cent. has involved the most sudden and dramatic changes in the whole history of this venerable institution. JKW

Pugin, Augustus Welby (1812–52). Architect and pioneer of the Victorian Gothic Revival. Before Pugin, 'Gothick' architecture had been largely a romantic plaything of rich dilettantes. He saw something deeper in it. According to Pugin, Gothic was the only Christian—by which he meant

Roman catholic—style. His book *Contrasts* (1836) set drawings of medieval buildings beside drawings of their modern—square, crude, simple—equivalents, in order to show how much more attractive the former were. It was grossly unfair, but influential. Pugin was commissioned to put his set-square where his mouth was all over the country. Alton Towers (1836), Scarisbrick Hall (1837), the catholic cathedrals of Birmingham (1841) and Newcastle (1844), and the lush Perpendicular-style detailing of the new Houses of Parliament (1840–52)—the classicist Charles *Barry did the main plan—are some of the results. They are not the greatest examples of the genre; but Pugin should really be judged by the inspiration he gave to better architects (like *Scott and *Butterfield) after him. Besides, he died very young, after religious fanaticism turned to certifiable madness in his late thirties. His son, E. W. Pugin (1834–75), another short-liver, carried on his work. BJP

Puisset, Hugh de (*c.*1125–95). Bishop of Durham. Puisset was a great aristocratic churchman, who held the wealthy see of Durham, with palatine powers, for more than forty years. He was a nephew of King Stephen and received his first preferment (an archdeaconry) from Stephen's brother *Henry of Blois, bishop of Winchester. Next, another relative, William Fitzherbert, archbishop of York, gave him the post of treasurer in the diocese. In 1153, probably before he was 30, he was made bishop of Durham. Politically he seems to have been circumspect. He stayed out of the *Becket controversy and played an equivocal role in the rebellion of 1173. For years he maintained resistance to the authority of Geoffrey, archbishop of York. A hint at his essentially secular attitude came at the start of Richard I's reign, when the king was raising funds for the crusade. Hugh purchased the earldom of Northumberland and the *justiciarship. He was ousted from the justiciarship by William *Longchamp and surrendered the earldom in 1193. He lived in great style, built lavishly, patronized learning, and fought his corner. JAC

Pulteney, William, 1st earl of Bath (1684–1764). Pulteney was Whig MP for Hedon (1705–34) and Middlesex (1734–42), becoming secretary at war in 1714. He supported *Walpole and *Townshend in opposition during the Whig schism from 1717 to 1720, but felt insulted when not offered a post in the reunited Whig administration. Thereafter he became alienated from Walpole and in 1725 made a final break with him, joining *Bolingbroke in attacking the ministry in print via the **Craftsman*. On the accession of George II in 1727 he was disappointed not to replace Walpole. His greatest triumphs in opposition were the destruction of the *excise scheme in 1733 and his agitation for war with Spain, which eventually brought down Walpole in 1742. But Pulteney refused to take office and was created earl of Bath. Disappointed once more at not being made first minister in 1743, he tried to overthrow Henry *Pelham in 1746 but failed to form a government. Thereafter he played no part in public affairs. Pulteney was one of the first politicians to head a sustained appeal to public opinion, only to raise hopes which he dashed. With a great reputation as a debater, he was increasingly mistrusted by his allies among the 'patriots'. His failure to effect reform or root out corruption after Walpole's fall was thought by many to reveal factiousness and self-seeking and he was accused of avarice. 'A paltry fellow', was the disillusioned *Johnson's terse dismissal. CJ

Punch, a satirical weekly periodical, was founded in 1841 under the editorship of Henry Mayhew and Mark Lemon, early contributors including *Thackeray, Hood, and Tenniel. Famous for its cartoons, and a former stand-by in professional waiting-rooms, it closed in 1992 due to debt, but reappeared in 1996 under new ownership. ASH

Purcell, Henry (1658–95). The outstanding musician and composer of his time in Britain. Like other 17th-cent. musicians, Purcell's career began in the church, first as a chorister at the Chapel Royal, then as organist at Westminster abbey composing anthems. At court he enjoyed the favour of successive monarchs composing odes on special occasions, but his works for Mary II are the best known, composed when Purcell was reaching the height of his powers, just before his premature death. The music he composed for her funeral is of a truly majestic solemnity and profundity. He also composed for the theatre, particularly for works by John *Dryden, and his own operas achieved considerable success. However what is now most often heard, and regarded as his masterpiece, *Dido and Aeneas*, was originally written for performance by schoolgirls in 1689 and only became appreciated over a decade later. Unlike most of his contemporaries Purcell was influenced by Italian as well as French styles, but what distinguishes his work is the personal element. Like Christopher *Wren in architecture he took from a variety of sources what he wanted, but added a distinctive, personal contribution, the product of his genius. JRJ

puritans. During the reign of the catholic Mary Tudor (1553–8) many hundreds of English protestants went into exile on the continent, where they experienced forms of worship which were 'purer' than those prescribed in the 1552 *Prayer Book because they contained virtually no trace of catholicism. Returning to England at the beginning of Elizabeth I's reign, they hoped to create an established church closer to continental models, but the queen insisted on a comprehensive settlement. The Elizabethan church therefore retained a number of 'impure' ceremonial practices, which a minority of hard-line clergy refused to accept. They were harried by the government, under the name of 'puritans'. The conforming majority, both clerical and lay, shared many of their reservations but were willing, albeit reluctantly, to obey the orders of their royal governor. They were helped by the fact that in its theology, if not its practice, the established church was *calvinist. This remained the case under James I, despite the failure of the *Hampton Court conference, but the accession of Charles I in 1625 brought the high-church *arminians to power. By insisting that they alone constituted the true Church of England, and by calling all its low-church adherents puritans, the arminians drove the conforming majority into opposition. This opened the way to the destruction of the established church after the collapse of Charles's rule, but the victorious puritans were divided about how to replace it. The *presbyterians wanted a state church similar but not identical to that in Scotland, whereas the independents insisted on autonomy for individual congregations. Matters were complicated by the proliferation of sects demanding freedom to worship as they pleased. Continuing puritan divisions throughout the Interregnum created a backlash which found expression in the re-establishment of the Church of England after the restoration of the monarchy in 1660. The legislation known as the *Clarendon code imposed severe penalties upon nonconformists, and sporadic persecution of puritans continued until the *Glorious Revolution. Only in 1689 did the Toleration Act permit protestant nonconformists to worship freely, but even so they remained officially barred from public life. RL

purveyancing was the means of supplying the king and his court on progress with the provisions and services they needed at prices to be fixed by royal officers. Consequently the subject was lucky to be paid inadequately, if at all. Purveyancing for war supplies was an even heavier burden and a major grievance during the protracted warfare of Edward I's reign. Since the king could not have palaces and stores everywhere, purveyancing was the only way he could travel his realm. *Magna Carta attempted to regulate it; *Speculum regis* of *c.*1331 declared it a cursed prerogative; the *Ordainers of 1310 moved against it, and it was still a matter of loud complaint in the reigns of James I and Charles I. It was finally abolished during the Civil War. JAC

Pusey, Edward Bouverie (1800–82). A leader of the *Oxford movement, Pusey contributed to the series which led to the alternative description of *'tractarians'. He also gave the movement another nickname by maintaining the tradition of the tractarians within the Church of England after *Newman's secession to Roman catholicism. Pusey fought a rearguard action to prevent others following and his supporters, dedicated to restrained and respectable high churchmanship, became known as 'Puseyites'. He refused to be drawn into the ritualism which for many was the natural consequence of the Oxford movement, but supported the revival of Anglican monastic life, particularly for women. He was unique in England in his deep knowledge of contemporary German theology and was also a prodigious scholar of Syriac, Arabic, and Hebrew. A prime mover in making the writings of the church fathers more widely known, he was appointed regius professor of Hebrew in Oxford at the age of 28. JFC

Putney debates. These occupied the general council of the army from 28 October to 1 November 1647, and were recorded almost verbatim by its secretary William Clarke. The council included two officers and two soldiers ('agitators') elected by each regiment, and the central question was whether to continue seeking a negotiated settlement with the king. Representatives of the *Levellers put before it a revolutionary alternative, an *Agreement of the People, and the ensuing arguments for and against manhood suffrage were memorably eloquent. The outcome was inconclusive, for with mutiny threatening in several regiments the general council agreed on 8 November to its own suspension. AHW

Pym, John (1584–1643). Parliamentarian. One of the few members of the Commons who realized that poverty was driving Charles I into arbitrary rule, Pym consistently, but vainly, argued the case for restoring the crown's finances. But his attitude towards the king hardened with the conviction that Charles, by patronizing the *arminians, was opening the door to catholicism, and in 1628 he led the impeachment of a royal chaplain who had publicly affirmed the king's right to impose non-parliamentary taxation. Pym was by then a political client of the earl of *Bedford, and drafted the petition calling on the king to summon Parliament which was drawn up at Bedford's London house in September 1640. When the *Long Parliament met in November, Pym was the driving force behind the impeachment of Charles's chief minister *Strafford, but he also supported Bedford's plan to reach an accommodation with the king. Had it succeeded, Pym would have been appointed chancellor of the Exchequer, with responsibility for the royal finances. The revolt of the Irish catholics in 1641 confirmed Pym in his belief that the king was involved in a 'popish plot' to destroy English religion and liberties, and in order to compel him to co-operate with Parliament he pushed through the *Grand Remonstrance. Not surprisingly, he was one of the *five members whom the king sought to arrest in January 1642. Pym's major contribution to the parliamentary cause came in 1643 when he persuaded members to impose an excise to meet the costs of war and to accept the *Solemn League and Covenant as the price of Scottish support. RL

Pyrenees, battle of the, 1813. Following *Wellington's offensive in the spring of 1813, Marshal Soult's army of 88,000 men attempted to lift the siege of the French-held towns of San Sebastián and Pamplona in northern Spain. The series of actions that resulted are known as the battle of the Pyrenees. Soult achieved surprise and forced small British forces to retire from the key mountain passes at Maya and Roncesvalles on 25 July. Wellington met Soult at Sorauren near Pamplona on 28 and again on 30 July and won hard-fought victories. On 2 August the French retreated, ceding the initiative to Wellington. GDS

Quadruple Alliance. 1. 1718. After the War of the Spanish Succession, Philip V of Spain was anxious to regain territory. France, Britain, and the Dutch formed a defensive *Triple Alliance in 1717, which the Emperor Charles VI joined in 1718. The other allies agreed to support the Hanoverian succession in Britain. The emperor was to be given Sicily, and Sardinia was to go to Savoy. A British naval squadron defeated the Spanish fleet off *Cape Passaro immediately after the treaty had been signed in 1718, and a French invasion of Spain in 1719 forced Philip to come to terms.

2. 1815. At the end of the Revolutionary and Napoleonic wars in 1815, the victorious powers—Britain, Russia, Prussia, and Austria—formed a Quadruple Alliance to maintain the peace and to hold periodic conferences to consider matters of common interest—the so-called *Congress system. Meetings were held at Aix-la-Chapelle (1818), Troppau (1820–1), and Verona (1822), but differences between the allies were soon apparent. See HOLY ALLIANCE.

3. 1834. In the 1830s, the young queens of Portugal and of Spain were challenged by their uncles. Britain and France formed a Quadruple Alliance with Spain and Portugal in 1834 to protect them, as constitutional rulers, against intervention by Metternich. 'All my own doing' was *Palmerston's claim, and he saw the alliance as a counter-balance to the despotic powers of Eastern Europe. But the alliance was short-lived and the liberalism of the queens suspect. JAC

quakers, or Society of Friends, are said to have derived their name either from ecstatic shuddering or from George *Fox's advice to Justice Bennet in 1650 to tremble at the word of the Lord. They originated during the religious tumult of the 1650s, had no formal ministry or service, and professed the principle of the 'inner light', a sense of the direct working of Christ. Their refusal to pay tithes, insistence upon addressing everyone as thou, refusal to doff hats to authority, and the extravagant behaviour of some of their members, shocked a hierarchical society, and they were fiercely persecuted before and after the Restoration. The earlier excesses of the movement were soon abandoned and they acquired a reputation for sobriety and peaceableness. Quaker organization was based on a monthly meeting, quarterly county meetings, and an annual meeting in London. They benefited from the *Toleration Act of 1689 and in 1696 were allowed to affirm rather than take an oath. There was considerable emigration to Pennsylvania, founded on quaker principles. They were not enthusiastic evangelists and did not share in the rapid growth of dissent in the early 19th cent., having 413 meeting-houses in 1800 and 371 in 1851. Quakers refuse military service but are often prominent in ambulance and medical corps. JAC

Quarterly Review. This was the Tory riposte to the very successful *Edinburgh Review*, which had been launched in 1802. It was started in 1809 by Sir Walter *Scott, George Ellis, and John Wilson *Croker, with William Gifford as editor. The early contributors included *Canning and Robert *Southey. By the middle of the century the taste for magisterial, learned, and lengthy reviews was beginning to decline. JAC

quarter sessions. The office of *justice of the peace can be traced back to the 'keepers of the peace' in 1195 and 'conservators of the peace' during the reigns of Henry III and Edward I, but the principal statutory provisions establishing the justices of the peace were those of the 14th cent., especially the Justices of the Peace Act, 1361. By a statute of 1362, the justices of each county were to meet four times a year and these sessions were therefore known as 'quarter sessions'. At these sessions presentments of those suspected of crime were made to the justices and other matters, outside the realm of the purely judicial, referred to them. Between them the *assizes and quarter sessions dealt with all serious crime. From time to time, the commission issued to the justices put certain limits on the range of crimes which could be dealt with at quarter sessions, but in 1590 it was finally settled that they had jurisdiction to try all offences, though it was provided that certain justices should be present where cases were difficult, and some cases were reserved for the assizes.

During the 18th cent. the practice arose of reserving the many capital cases for the assizes, and by the Quarter Sessions Act 1842 the jurisdiction of quarter sessions over such offences as treason, murder, felonies punishable with penal servitude for life, and certain other offences was removed. In 1914 quarter sessions were given appellate jurisdiction over petty sessions in certain circumstances. Quarter sessions were abolished by the Courts Act 1971. MM

Quatre Bras, battle of, 1815. After resuming control of France in 1815 on his return from Elba, Napoleon advanced into Belgium, striking with his main force against the Prussians at Ligny. A subsidiary force under Marshal Ney headed towards the vital crossroads at Quatre Bras. Although initially outnumbered, elements of the Anglo-Dutch army defended stoutly until reinforcements, and *Wellington himself, arrived. A French corps spent the day marching between Quatre Bras and Ligny, and participated in neither battle. By nightfall, Wellington had 36,000 men to Ney's 20,000, and was able to fall back to the position at *Waterloo, having won an important strategic victory. GDS

Quebec, capture of, 1759. This ended French sovereignty in Canada. British sea power reduced the fortress of Louisbourg (1758), opening up the St Lawrence. Despite fears that the strongly entrenched French, under the brilliant Montcalm, could be dislodged only by a long siege, *Wolfe's troops, with a surprise night manœuvre, followed by a pitched battle, achieved an epic victory. While Quebec's capture formed the summit of British imperial success, problems of taking Canada into British control and the lessening of colonial anxieties about French power contributed to the circumstances leading to the revolt of the thirteen colonies. RCS

Quebec Act, 1774. This followed but was not part of the *Intolerable Acts. It settled matters relating to the British acquisition of French Canada by recognizing the catholic church, allowing the exercise of French law, denying Quebec an elected assembly, and extending its boundaries to the Ohio. Opposed by only a few parliamentarians and by virulent British anti-catholics, it was fervently condemned in the thirteen colonies, as an attack on protestant and constitutional liberties and on their territorial expansion and as confirmation of the malign intentions of Lord *North's ministry and of the British crown and Parliament towards America. RCS

Queen Anne's Bounty was a product of the strong Anglican resurgence during her reign, caused partly by concern at the apparent progress of dissent since the Glorious Revolution. In 1703 the queen announced that she would devote the income from *first fruits, which had been appropriated from the papacy at the Reformation, to the relief of poor clergy, and trustees were appointed to administer the scheme. In 1710 Parliament made funds available for the building of 50 new parish churches in London. JAC

Queensberry, James Douglas, 2nd duke of [S] (1662–1711). Queensberry's father was promoted marquis in 1682, duke in 1684, and 1682–6 was lord high treasurer [S]. Nevertheless, he came to terms with William quickly after the Revolution. Douglas (Drumlanrig until he succeeded in 1695) was one of the first to join William, was a gentleman of the bedchamber 1689–1702, lord privy seal [S] 1696–1702, and received the Garter in 1701. As commissioner to the Scottish Parliament, Queensberry played a crucial role in carrying the *Union in Anne's reign. After losing control of the Parliament in 1704, and suspected of Jacobite intrigues, he was briefly replaced by *Tweeddale. A spell in opposition demonstrated his usefulness and he was reappointed commissioner and resumed as lord privy seal [S] in 1705. Handsomely rewarded for his part in effecting the Act of Union, he was granted a large pension, served 1707–8 as a representative peer, and in 1708 was created duke of Dover in the British peerage. From 1709 he was in charge of Scottish affairs but died early. Vilified by the Jacobites as an arch-traitor, Queensberry seems to have been moderate, persuasive, and personally agreeable. JAC

Queensberry, John Sholto Douglas, 9th marquis of [S] (1844–1900). Douglas inherited the title at the age of 14. He was a representative peer of Scotland from 1872 until 1880, when he lost re-election, largely for his outspoken support for *Bradlaugh. A keen amateur boxer, he helped in 1867 to draw up the Queensberry rules, which governed boxing. His life was turbulent. His first wife obtained a divorce and his second marriage was annulled. A younger brother died climbing the Matterhorn. His first son died in a shooting accident in 1894. His third son, Lord Alfred Douglas ('Bosie'), formed a friendship with Oscar *Wilde, of which his father violently disapproved. Queensberry's notorious card, left at Wilde's club, provoked Wilde to the action for criminal libel which ruined him. JAC

Queensberry, William Douglas, 5th duke of [S] (1725–1810). Son of William Douglas, earl of March [S], whom he succeeded at the age of 6, Douglas became duke in 1778 when his cousin's sons died young. From 1760 until 1789 he was a lord of the bedchamber to George III and received the Thistle in 1763. From 1761 to 1786 he was a Scottish representative peer and was then created a British peer as Baron Douglas. After wobbling in the *Regency crisis of 1789, he was deprived of his position in the bedchamber. A small, irritable, and foul-mouthed man of stupendous wealth, he was well known in gambling and racing circles and as a man about town. In his declining years, as Old Q, toothless and deaf, he was constantly to be seen on the balcony of his house in Piccadilly, watching life go by, an antiquated beau. JAC

queen's counsel (king's counsel). These were barristers appointed in the late 16th cent. to assist the law officers of the crown in the conduct of legal affairs. Unlike the *serjeants at law they belonged to the *Inns of Court. During the 18th cent. they ceased to be closely connected with the crown and the title came to be merely a mark of honour for distinguished barristers. They are said to 'take silk' on appointment, as they then wear a silk gown instead of a 'stuff' gown. To some extent they replaced the serjeants at law whose office died out in the 19th cent. in that they became the senior members of their profession. MM

Queenston Heights, battle of, 1812. The first major battle of the *War of 1812 occurred when 1,000 New York State militia crossed the Niagara river and unexpectedly scaled the river cliffs. The British commander, Sir Isaac Brock, was killed leading a charge. British reinforcements and Indian allies eventually forced the surrender of over 900 Americans at a cost of 28 British fatalities. It was believed that Brock's last words were, 'Push on, brave York volunteers', addressed to colonial troops. Queenston Heights thus became a symbolic Canadian rejection of the USA. Brock and his second-in-command, militia officer John Macdonell, were ceremonially reburied on the battlefield in 1824, and a memorial column was erected in 1853. GM

Queen's University, Belfast, was founded as Queen's College, Belfast, under Sir Robert *Peel's Colleges Act (1845): in common with the two other colleges created by the Act (at Cork and Galway), Queen's Belfast first admitted students in 1849. The colleges were at first constituent parts of the Queen's University in Ireland (1850), and later, alongside University College, Dublin, more loosely associated with a new Royal University of Ireland (1880). The Irish Universities Act (1908) created both a National University of Ireland (binding the colleges of Cork, Galway, and Dublin) and a new Queen's University of Belfast out of the former Queen's College. Since 1908 the social character of the university has been transformed: once a small and largely presbyterian body (the college had only 195 students in the session 1849–50), Queen's now reflects, if still inadequately, the greater political and economic strength of the catholic minority in Northern Ireland. AJ

quia emptores, also known as the statute of *Westminster 1290. This statute of Edward I brought to an end the practice of subinfeudation. Before then it was possible for a tenant to grant land to another tenant, who would owe him service, thus creating a further subtenancy and extending the feudal ladder. The statute *quia emptores* provided that where a tenant of land alienated that land, he could not create a new relationship of lord and tenant with the purchaser, who would instead 'stand in the shoes' of the seller. The effect was to preserve order, to prevent extending the feudal 'ladder', and to safeguard the lords' interests in their tenants' services. The end of subinfeudation, coupled with the vicissitudes of *escheat, forfeiture, and the failure of heirs led to the crown acquiring the overlordship of much land by the reign of Henry VIII. MM

Quiberon Bay, battle of, 1759. This bay lies on the Biscay coast of France between Lorient and Saint-Nazaire. Here, on 20 November 1759, was fought one of the most brilliant engagements in the annals of naval warfare. Britain stood in danger of invasion by France, and by November Sir Edward *Hawke had blockaded the fleet of Conflans in Brest since the previous May. When the weather blew Hawke off station, Conflans was able to break out, but early on the 20th Hawke, a little superior in strength, had news that Conflans's 24 ships had entered Quiberon. He risked everything by following the French into this barely known anchorage in fading light and heavy squalls, and did indeed lose two ships through weather, though their crews were saved. But six French ships were destroyed in the ensuing action, and many of the remainder suffered irreparable damage in flight. Hawke considered that 'all that could possibly be done has been done', and the French admiringly conceded his achievement. DDA

***quo warranto* proceedings.** The *quo warranto* inquiry was instituted by Edward I when he succeeded to the throne in 1272. Among other measures he instituted proceedings whereby his royal justices investigated the claim of every lord who claimed to have a franchise of a hundred court—a *court leet—inquiring 'by what warrant' the lord made such a claim. The lord had to prove that such jurisdiction had been granted, usually by royal charter. However, Edward allowed lords to show that they had acquired the franchise by prescription 'from time immemorial'; in practice that they had exercised such jurisdiction since 1189, the accession of Richard I. MM

R 101 airship. The larger of two rigid airships commissioned by the government in 1924. Designed by Barnes Wallis, it was built to carry up to 50 passengers on the long-haul route to India. It set out on its maiden voyage on 1 October 1930 with an official party on board, including the secretary of state for air. At 2 a.m. the following morning it touched the ground on its approach to Beauvais, caught fire, and exploded. Only four people survived. The disaster put an end to the use of airships in Britain. RAS

race relations. A thorough survey of race relations in Britain would demand a history of the British Isles, since one of its persistent themes has been the interplay of the native peoples, the intervention of Romans, Saxons, Danes, and Normans, and the reception of Jews, Palatines, Huguenots, and, after the Second World War, citizens from the Commonwealth. It would also include a study of the rise and fall of the first and second British empires. Before the 20th cent., governments did not often intervene to protect newcomers or promote racial harmony. *Cnut was anxious to hold a balance between his Danish and English subjects; Henry VIII in 1535 complained that 'rude and ignorant' people were stirring up 'discord, division and murmur' between his Welsh and English subjects; and James I took the earliest opportunity to recommend 'mutual love' between his Scottish and his new English subjects. Racial questions were usually complicated by other considerations, particularly religion and employment. French Huguenots in the 17th cent., because of their religion, were on the whole welcomed: Jews and Irish catholics less so. In its modern form, race relations developed mainly through the *anti-slavery campaign in the late 18th and early 19th cents. Opponents of emancipation justified slavery on arguments of racial inferiority, offensively expressed by Thomas *Carlyle in an essay on 'The Nigger Question' in *Frazer's Magazine* for 1849. Immigration from the Commonwealth in the 1950s and 1960s, particularly from India and the West Indies, placed the question on the political agenda. The 1965 Race Relations Act, passed by the Wilson government, prohibited discrimination in places of public resort, such as hotels or restaurants, made the promotion of hatred on grounds of 'colour, race, or ethnic or national origins' an offence, and established a Race Relations Board to hear complaints. The measure was extended by further Acts in 1968 and 1976, the last providing for a Race Relations Commission to promote 'equality of opportunity and good relations'. JAC

Radcot Bridge, battle of, 1387. The accession of a 10-year-old king, Richard II, in 1377 led to baronial rivalry. In 1386 five noblemen, Arundel, Derby (the future Henry IV), *Gloucester, *Nottingham, and Warwick, formed an alliance, the lords *appellant, to remove two royal favourites, Michael de la *Pole, duke of Suffolk and *Oxford (created duke of Ireland in 1386). Suffolk was impeached and forced to flee. De Vere, earl of Oxford, raised an army in Cheshire in December 1387 and marched south to join the king. He was intercepted at Radcot Bridge, just east of Lechlade, on 20 December and trapped between armies led by Derby in front and Gloucester behind. Oxford fled and joined Suffolk in France. JAC

radicalism seeks a fundamental change in political structures through a programme of far-reaching but constitutional reform. Its features include some or all of individualism, democracy, minimal government, a market economy, freedom of speech and publication, and opposition to tradition, hereditary privilege, and religious influences.

There was never a single radical party in Britain, though three loose groupings may be identified. The *philosophical radicals were the *utilitarian followers of Jeremy *Bentham (1748–1832) who formed a small but influential reforming group in the 1830s, including George *Grote and Joseph *Hume within the Commons, and Edwin *Chadwick, Joseph *Parkes, and James and John Stuart *Mill outside Parliament. Their ideas were publicized through the *Westminster Review.* Secondly, from the later 1830s, the *Manchester School radicals, led by *Cobden and *Bright, campaigned for *free trade and against aristocratic privilege through organizations such as the *Anti-Corn Law League. They were supported by nonconformist religious opinion opposed to the established church. Thirdly, outside Parliament, admirers of Thomas *Paine's **Rights of Man* (1791–2) formed a loose alliance of democratic agitators which gave leadership to the *chartist movement (1838–52). These extremists were often in conflict with the other, more middle-class radicals. To a large extent they coalesced in the later 1850s into the radical wing of the *Liberal Party under *Gladstone's leadership. Notable parliamentary radicals in the 1870s and 1880s were Charles *Dilke, Joseph *Chamberlain, and Charles *Bradlaugh. Radicalism declined as the most advanced school of progressive political opinion with the rise of socialist ideas at the end of the 19th cent. ER

radio was the dominant sound medium of the first half of the 20th cent., and—though now less popular than television—still has a residual power in areas such as news and music. The solution to the technical problem of how to send telegraph and telephone messages without connecting cables was found in the late 19th cent. when wire-less means of communication became viable with the discovery by Hertz of electromagnetic waves. In Britain, Italian inventor Marconi developed the first wireless telegraph in 1896, sending airwave messages in Morse code over the Atlantic in 1901. The development of the thermionic valve in America by Lee de Forest and in Britain by John A. Fleming allowed speech to be turned into radio waves, and the First World War brought rapid developments in this means of transmitting messages on the airwaves.

After the war, electrical companies such as Marconi's experimented with transmitting entertainment items to the many amateur radio receivers throughout Britain. After initial attempts to ban such activities, the government decided to license the experiments, leading to the creation in 1922 of the *British Broadcasting Company as a monopoly private consortium of radio companies, responsible to the postmaster-general and supported by a licence fee.

With its elevation to a corporation in 1927, the BBC set the tone for radio in Britain over the next 40 years—a paternalistic diet of information and education, with some concessions to entertainment in the form of light musical and variety items. Challenges from the more populist fare of other radio stations—Radio Luxembourg from 1933, American Forces Radio in the Second World War, and offshore pirate radio stations in the 1960s—brought gradual revision to programming policy. The biggest changes to British radio however came in the early 1970s with government legislation to permit commercial radio, under the name of Independent Local Radio (ILR). Capital and LBC in 1973 were the first of a network of stations that grew up throughout the country over the next few years, under the guidance of the Independent Broadcasting Authority (now the Radio Authority). ILR's populist fare often proved more successful than the BBC national and local radio in certain areas, and under Conservative free enterprise policy in the 1980s and 1990s, the expansion of commercial radio was cemented with licences to new national, regional, local, community, and ethnic stations. The pattern of radio consumption has been irrevocably changed, and the BBC looks set to enter the 21st cent. with fundamental questions about its position in British culture and society still to be answered. DJA

Radnorshire (Sir Faesyfed). County of mid-Wales created at the Act of *Union with England in 1536. It was part of the Welsh kingdom of *Powys but was subject to Saxon attack both before and after the construction of *Offa's Dike. It was rapidly overrun by the Normans, and the north, the Welsh cantref of Maelienydd, became Mortimer land, whilst the south, the Welsh cantref of Efael, was taken by the Braoses. These two areas were eventually formed into the new county, the smallest of the Welsh shires. Incorporated into Powys as a district in 1974, it became part of the Powys unitary authority in 1996.

Radnorshire was both the smallest and the poorest of the pre-1974 counties. It was mainly made up of the high moorlands of Radnor Forest (2,660 feet) and the drainage system of the upper Wye and its tributaries, the Claerwen, Elan, Irfon, and Ithon.

Given its physical character, sheep-farming is the dominant agricultural enterprise, but in the 19th cent. the exploitation of mineral springs gave rise to small spas which are now tourist centres. Water resources have also been developed mainly to supply the English midlands. The Elan valley reservoirs were constructed between 1892 and 1906. Forestry is another activity and the complex of upland, lakes, forests, and former spas underpins tourism.

As a consequence of its early Anglicization Radnorshire has a low proportion of Welsh speakers. Even in 1901 only 6.2 per cent spoke Welsh, a figure lowered by construction workers on the dam sites. In 1991 the percentage was 8.3. The total population in 1991 was only 22,982. HC

Raeburn, Sir Henry (1756–1823). Raeburn was born and worked all his life in Edinburgh. He was the leading Scottish portrait painter of his day, recording many of the personalities of the city and a number of Highland chieftains before the time of depopulation and emigration. Largely self-taught, he visited London in 1784 on his way to study in Italy and met *Reynolds, whose style influenced him in a way that his Italian experience did not. Having married a wealthy widow in 1780, he added to their fortune by buying land on the outskirts of Edinburgh which he developed speculatively. In 1812 he was elected ARA and a full RA three years later. In 1822, when George IV visited Edinburgh, he knighted Raeburn, creating him king's limner and painter for Scotland the following year. Raeburn's portraits of Mrs Scott-Moncrieff and of the Revd Robert Walker skating on Duddingston Loch are among many of his works in the National Gallery of Scotland. JC

Raedwald (early 7th cent.), king of the East Angles. Baptized under the influence of King *Æthelbert of Kent, he compromised with his heathen wife and subjects, adding a Christian altar in his temple alongside those to pagan gods. Sheltering the Deiran royal exile *Edwin, *c.*616, he was under pressure from the Northumbrian king *Æthelfryth to kill him or hand him over. His wife persuaded him that to betray a guest was unworthy of so great a king. At this time, Raedwald was probably asserting his overlordship in the south. Pre-empting Æthelfryth's threats, he attacked, defeated, and killed him by the *river Idle (Lincs.), securing the Northumbrian kingdom for Edwin. Raedwald's name is often linked with the famous ship-burial at *Sutton Hoo. Whether or not it is his grave, it represents the wealth, contacts, and power of such a man. AM

Raffles, Sir Thomas Stamford (1781–1826). Raffles was born off the coast of Jamaica on board his father's merchantman. He joined the *East India Company in 1795 and was appointed to Penang where he rapidly rose to be secretary to the council. In 1810 he was made agent to the Malay states to prepare an invasion of Java, then under the control of the Batavian Republic. He governed Java between 1811 and 1816, instituting far-reaching economic reforms. When the island was restored to the Dutch, he returned to England and was made a fellow of the Royal Society. In 1818 he became lieutenant-governor of Fort Marlborough (Sumatra). Fearing Dutch influence over the region, he persuaded the company to found a settlement at Singapore. He raised the flag there on 2 June 1819 and, by the time of his final return to England in 1824, had established it as an important port. DAW

ragged schools were elementary schools for street children pioneered at the beginning of the 19th cent. by John Pounds, a Portsmouth cobbler, 'to chase away ignorance, to relieve distress, and to teach the Gospel'. The Ragged School Union, with the 7th earl of *Shaftesbury as president, was formed in 1844 to further this object. Within a few years, most large towns had ragged schools. Other urgent needs were also supplied: food, clothing, and footwear. In 1851 the shoeblack brigades were formed as a means of giving employment to their pupils. Schemes of emigration to the colonies were also introduced. After 1870 the union concentrated on Sunday schools. PG

Raglan, Fitzroy James Henry Somerset, 1st Baron (1788–1855). Lord Fitzroy Somerset, eighth son of the duke of Beaufort, was appointed aide-de-camp to Lieutenant-General Sir Arthur Wellesley, the future duke of *Wellington, in 1808. He accompanied the duke throughout his campaigns in the Iberian Peninsula (1808–14) and was badly wounded at *Waterloo on 18 June 1815. Despite this, he remained on Wellington's staff. In 1852—the year of the duke's death—Somerset was created Baron Raglan, and two years later given command of British forces in the war against Russia. When those forces invaded the Crimea in September 1854, it soon became apparent that Raglan was not suited to high command, for although promoted to field marshal, he was widely criticized for orders leading to the *'Charge of the Light Brigade' at *Balaclava on 25 October. He died of dysentery in the Crimea on 25 June 1855. JLP

Raglan castle (Gwent), half-way between Monmouth and Abergavenny, was probably first built in the 1070s as one of a number of castles intended to support the Norman invasion of south Wales. In the early 15th cent. the castle came by marriage to William ap Thomas, whose son Sir William Herbert rose to prominence under Edward IV as the first earl of Pembroke. The castle became the centre of an important lordship and home of one of the wealthiest men in the kingdom. It was completely rebuilt incorporating the latest defensive features, including a great tower designed for the use of cannon, as well as sumptuous domestic accommodation for Pembroke's family and household. It was probably at Raglan that the young Henry Tudor, the future Henry VII, was housed under the supervision of Pembroke's wife Anne Devereux. In 1492 the Herbert barony passed by marriage to Sir Charles Somerset, lord chamberlain to both Henry VII and Henry VIII, created earl of Worcester in 1514. During the Civil War Raglan was garrisoned for the king. After a protracted siege the castle surrendered in August 1647 and was slighted. After the Restoration, Henry Somerset, first duke of Beaufort, built a new house at Badminton transferring some fittings from Raglan. LR

rail system. Means of conveyance by wheeled vehicles guided on fixed tracks, especially when propelled by locomotive. English usage of the flanged wheel and long-distance horse-drawn links between mines and water transport distinguished the wagon-way from the European *hund* (truck). It is first recorded at Woolaton (Notts.) *c.*1604 and Broseley (Shropshire), and was introduced by Huntingdon Beaumont to Northumberland by 1605. Diffusion of 'wagon-ways' was widespread and systematic around the rivers Tyne and Wear in the century after 1660, and lesser systems appeared in Shropshire, Yorkshire, Cumberland, and Fife. Charles Brandling's wagon-way built to supply Leeds with his coal was the first to employ the private act to secure wayleave (1758), and to apply steam commercially in the Murray and Blenkinsop locomotive (1812). The wagon-way was an integral element of most canals, advanced with the introduction of iron rails from the 1790s, and attained its ultimate development in the Stockton and Darlington railway (1825).

The Liverpool and Manchester railway (completed 1830) was the effective transition to the rail system, being designed for steam haulage throughout; for communication between two major towns; and to convey passengers as a principal element of the business. Secondary consequences followed: the effective exclusion of public access on grounds of safety; by this the establishment of monopoly; and transport at speeds beyond that of a horse transformed the psychology of travel. It was followed by the Grand Junction from Crewe to Birmingham (1837) and the London and Birmingham railway (1838). England thus established a long-distance link between the capital and the industrial north-west. The companies founded in or before the 'railway manias' of 1836–7 and 1844–7 had largely completed the rail system by 1854, with more than 6,000 route miles open, and a further 3,200 authorized. The third mania of 1863–6 concentrated upon branch and subsidiary lines, and London suburban development, bringing route mileage to over 15,500 by 1870.

Subsequent development continued the pattern: the bridging of the Scottish estuaries of the Tay (1878 and replacement 1887) and Forth (1890) completed the direct line to Aberdeen, and the Severn tunnel (1886) cut journey times into south Wales and released capacity for routes to the north-east, but no major additional trunk routes were added after 1870. The Midland railway attempted to abandon the last navvy-built trunk line, the Settle–Carlisle (opened 1876), in 1868–9, but was forced to complete, and the Great Central's entry to London at Marylebone (1894) was a highly engineered superfluity. Mileage in Britain reached 21,000 by 1914 and was maintained until 1938, before falling to below 19,000 at the end of the 1950s and 12,000 in 1970, of which passenger mileage was around 9,000.

Remarkable traffic growth before 1914 was accompanied by rising costs and falling levels of profit. Freight rose from *c.*38 million tons in 1850, to 167 million in 1870, and 513 million in 1912, of which 60 per cent was coal and coke, and passenger journeys grew from 73 million in 1850 to 337 million in 1870, and 1,580 million in 1912 (*c.*2,000 million including London). Competition in services and facilities, the rising ratio of running costs to gross receipts, and falling labour productivity characterized much of the period 1870–1914. Railway direct employment peaked at just under 750,000 in 1921. The railway system was correspondingly more important to the British economy in 1914 than in 1870, measured by its estimated specific contribution to economic growth, or 'social saving'.

Passengers gained accordingly in the quality and volume of services: sleeping cars were introduced in 1873, as were the first lavatories outside royal trains; the 'express' from the 1870s; the Pullman in 1874; dining cars in 1878; and corridor stock in the early 1890s. All were costly in terms of passengers carried per ton hauled: the best corridor stock before 1914 carried 2.4 passengers per ton, 30 per cent better than the ratio for 1875, but comparing poorly with suburban carrying capacity of 3.5. This growing weight of trains demanded increasing investment in more powerful locomotives.

The system had been the creation of individual joint-stock companies, perhaps Britain's first experience of large-scale business, which provided the core securities traded in the new provincial stock exchanges. There were 366 railway companies in the mid-1860s, and still around 100 in 1914, and the system was unplanned by comparison with that of Belgium or France. Government competition policy inhibited amalgamations, but 'end-on' linkages such as the LNWR (1846), the NER (1854), and territorial monopolies such as the Great Eastern (1854) did emerge, and left the system dominated by four English and three Scottish units at the grouping into four companies in 1923. London's Underground Electric Railways Company, formed by Charles Tyson Yerkes in 1900 to establish a coherent system, soon neared bankruptcy and merged into the London General Omnibus Company in 1912, taking in the remaining tube lines in 1913. Most joined the London Passenger Transport Board in 1933, and London Transport on its formation in 1948.

The excess pressures of the First World War left the system severely run down, and the grouping of 1923, a compromise between public and private ownership, failed to eliminate wasteful competition in cities such as Birmingham and Leeds, and coincided with the downturn of traffic and the rise of road competition. In response, only the Southern railway electrified extensively, at a cost of £21 million, and was able to improve services to its short-haul passenger base at reduced fares: for the system as a whole, investment proved insufficient to redress falling income, and operating ratios remained poor. Nationalization in 1948 found an exhausted system, beset by the structural and competitive weaknesses of pre-war years, in urgent need of modernization, rationalization, and the standardization of its equipment. Subsequent experience of shifting government policy, uneven conditions of competition with road and air travel, and uncertainty about the balance to be struck between commercial and service objectives left a still under-capitalized system to be privatized in the 1990s in a dutch auction of subsidies, and Railtrack in possession of a potential property bonanza. JCh

Dyos, H. J., and Aldcroft, D. H., *British Transport: An Economic Survey from the Seventeenth Century to the Twentieth* (Leicester, 1969); Freeman, M. J., and Aldcroft, D. H. (eds.), *Transport in Victorian Britain* (Manchester, 1988); Gourvish, T. R., *British Railways, 1948–73: A Business History* (Cambridge, 1986); Munby, D. L., and Watson, A. H., *Inland Transport Statistics, Great Britain, 1900–1970* (Oxford, 1978); Simmons, J., *The Railway in England and Wales, 1830–1914*, vol. i: *The System and its Working* (Leicester, 1978); Simmons, J., and Biddle, G., *The Oxford Companion to British Railway History* (Oxford, 1997).

railway stations had no distinctive history until the Liverpool and Manchester railway of 1830, with the opening of Manchester Liverpool Road and Liverpool Crown Street: the light passenger traffic on the Stockton and Darlington had run in a horse-drawn coach from inns. Both consisted of two-storey classical town houses, controlling access to a departure platform, the model for the first phase of British railway development. No intermediate stations were built.

Initially, stations were located on the fringes of the urban area to ease access and economize on land costs. Facilities shared by different railway companies normally proved unworkable and led to their proliferation. Some early developments were able to trace a route to central locations through undeveloped land: London Bridge (1836); and in the 1840s, the Great Western's route to Paddington ran to the fringe of London's built-up area. Curzon Street (Birmingham), Oldham Road (Manchester), and Bridge Street (Glasgow) were similarly approached through uncongested lands in the 1830s and 1840s.

Competition intensified the pressure to attain more central termini, and made the first mile for every railway by far the most expensive. Town-centre land values were consistently expensive: the London and Birmingham's entry from Camden Town to its new Euston terminus in 1838 cost an additional £380,000, and the imposition of a supplementary fare, in addition to a renewed call on the shareholders. Routes of entry were selected to affect the minimum number of most co-operative landowners. The new Hunt's Bank (Victoria) terminus for the Manchester and Leeds (1839) affected more than 250 properties, but most lay in the hands of two owners, the earl of Derby and Lord Ducie, who also controlled the line for the link to Liverpool (1842). Only at Birmingham New Street did civic support create an equivalent to the grand central station of many European cities.

This was precluded for London in 1846, when the Royal Commission on Metropolis Railway Termini recommended the exclusion of termini from the city north of the river, creating the 'London quadrilateral'. Development was thus concentrated upon New Road in the north; east of the City; south of the river; and west of Park Lane. Seven of the fifteen termini London acquired by 1894 broke these precepts. Other cities too saw the wasteful proliferation of termini, with, by 1900, five in Glasgow, three each in Liverpool and Leeds, and four in Manchester. With sidings and other facilities, railway stations both defined the central business districts of Victorian cities and occupied up to 9 per cent of inner urban land.

The characteristic elements of British station design emerged early: the open-box 'U-shaped' terminal of platforms fronted by service buildings at Nine Elms (1838); the 'train shed' of ribbed iron supporting glass at Newcastle Central (1846); and the railway hotel at Euston in 1839. Hotels were first integrated at the U-planned Paddington station in 1854. Railways led the adoption of Greenwich time nationally, promoted through the station clock, standardized by telegraph to the Royal Observatory from 1852. Architecture rapidly became an element in competition by 'quality', and aped the classical temple (Euston, Newcastle, Huddersfield) and the Italian villa, popular for country stations but employed at Chester General (1848); it reached its creative height with the Midland Grand Hotel at St Pancras (1876); and admitted nationalist aspiration in the Scottish baronial style adopted at Dundee West (1889). Intermediate stations employed local materials, echoing the regional vernacular, with a characteristic corporate style: Italianate villas for the London, Brighton, and South Coast railway; French Renaissance châteaux (GWR); or Swiss chalets (Furness railway).

Separate goods stations were modelled on the integrated warehouse and trans-shipment operations of the canal companies: the Camden depot of the London and Birmingham (1830s) developed into the separate goods station and wholesale market, as at King's Cross (1852 and 1864), and the two-tier goods and passenger station at Broad Street (1865). In the smaller towns these tended to displace livestock and provisions markets, and by the 1880s auction markets at railheads were extinguishing the long-distance droving trades. Redundant passenger stations, such as Birmingham's Curzon Street, were converted to goods use.

Stations as interchanges for sea travel or river crossings effectively served new ports: Lowestoft by the Great Eastern, from 1844; Penarth by the Taff Vale for coal (1865); and Hartlepool (1840). Before dining cars (King's Cross to Leeds, 1878), there were designated refreshment stops: by contract until 1895, all Great Western trains stopped at Swindon for a ten-minute refreshment break, leading to its nickname 'Swindleum'; and Normanton's grand suite of rooms provided dinner for the Midland's Scottish route.

New station developments took place with the creation of the London Metropolitan railway in 1863, the completion of the Circle Line (1884), and the beginnings of deep 'tube' services in the capital (Monument to Stockwell, 1890). Suburban stations proliferated around London and other cities as passenger facilities were generally improved.

Evidence on numbers is lacking before 1947, when passenger and passenger/freight stations peaked at 6,701, and all stations, including freight units only, at 8,448 in 1950, before falling to 4,877 and 7,283 respectively in 1960, and 2,446 and 2,868 in 1970. Post-war contraction concentrated upon freight units, which collapsed in the Beeching cuts from 1963, and less than a quarter of stations were engaged with freight by 1970. This facilitated some station redevelopments, as in the rebuild of Birmingham New Street incorporating a shopping mall (1972), but the performance of British Railways' portfolio compared poorly with that of the general property market in the 1970s. Since 1970, some new development has occurred in 'park-and-ride' stations, of which the first, Bristol Parkway (1972), remains the distinctive success, followed in the 1980s by new commuter station developments or reopenings under the initiative of local Passenger Transport Executives. JCh

Gourvish, T. R., *British Railways, 1948–73: A Business History* (Cambridge, 1986); Kellett, J. R., *The Impact of Railways on Victorian Cities* (1969); Richards, J., and MacKenzie, J. M., *The Railway Station: A Social History* (Oxford, 1986); Simmons, J., *The Victorian Railway* (1991).

Ralegh, Sir Walter (*c*.1554–1618). Ralegh's spectacular career was broken by the mistrust of James I. Of Devon gentry stock, Ralegh was half-brother of Sir Humphrey *Gilbert, with whom in 1578 he shared a short expedition at the expense of the Spaniards. He spent 1580–1 in Ireland and on his return rose rapidly in court favour under the patronage of *Leicester. Knighted in 1584 and returned to Parliament, he became warden of the stannaries, captain of the queen's guard, lord-lieutenant of Cornwall, and was granted vast estates in Ireland. His attempts to promote the colonization of Virginia ended in failure, though they introduced tobacco and potatoes into England. He did not take part in the naval action against the Armada in 1588 but was greatly employed in the land operations. But as the star of *Essex rose at court, Ralegh's began to wane and he fell into disgrace with the queen after an affair with one of her maids of honour, Elizabeth Throckmorton, despite their subsequent marriage. In 1595 he led an expedition to the Orinoco in search of gold and in 1596 took part in the attack on Cadiz. His prospects were further undermined by the correspondence which Henry *Howard, earl of Northampton, established with James VI of Scotland, which succeeded in discrediting Ralegh. As soon as James succeeded in 1603, Ralegh was stripped of all his offices, was tried for treason, condemned to death, and imprisoned in the Tower. Not until 1617 could he obtain release to lead a second Orinoco expedition, which proved a disaster. He brought back no gold and his son was killed. James then had him executed on the original charge. During his long years in the Tower, Ralegh wrote his *History of the World*, brooding much on time and vicissitudes. It has grand passages and became popular, but Ralegh only reached 130 BC and as a work of history it was old-fashioned before it appeared. John *Aubrey included Ralegh in his *Brief Lives*. Ralegh's 'graceful presence was no mean recommendation' to Queen Elizabeth, who liked 'proper men'. Ralegh was a 'tall, handsome and bold man, but damnable proud . . . he spake broad Devonshire to his dying day.' JAC

Ramillies, battle of, 1706. *Marlborough's second major victory in the War of the Spanish Succession, in the Spanish Netherlands (modern Belgium) north of Namur, is regarded as his masterpiece. A bold advance by a French army of about 70,000 under Villeroi was intercepted by a roughly equal number of allied forces (British–Dutch–Danish) under Marlborough, and routed in a battle dominated by tactical subtleties. French losses were over 13,000, allied losses about 3,500. As a result France was forced permanently onto the defensive in the war, any French threat to the United Netherlands was ended, and Brussels, Antwerp, and most of the Spanish Netherlands came under allied control. SDB

Ramsay, Allan (1713–84). Portrait painter, born in Edinburgh, son of the poet Allan Ramsay. He studied in Edinburgh, London, Rome, and Naples, settling in London in 1739 and quickly establishing himself as the leading portraitist of the capital. He was particularly successful in painting women. 'Mr. Ramsay is formed to paint them,' said Horace *Walpole, and Ramsay was a serious rival to *Reynolds. He became a favourite painter of the royal family and was appointed principal painter in ordinary to George III in 1767. His employment at court and his career as a portrait painter ended in 1773 when he suffered an accident to his right arm. The rest of his life was spent in travel, writing, and conversation. His friends included David *Hume, for whom he painted Rousseau, Adam *Smith, and Samuel *Johnson, who said of him, 'You will not find a man in whose conversation there is more instruction, more information, and more elegance, than in Ramsay's.' JC

Ramsay, Sir William (1852–1916). Chemist. Ramsay was born in Glasgow and educated at Glasgow University. He developed an interest in chemistry, the profession of his grandfather, a manufacturer of dyestuffs, and studied in Germany. Appointed to the staff at Glasgow in 1874, he moved to Bristol in 1880 to take the chair of chemistry and became principal in 1881. From 1887 until his retirement in 1912 he was professor at University College, London. Ramsay's greatest discoveries were of the inert gases argon, helium, neon, krypton, and xenon, and his demonstration that radium produces helium when disintegrating and that this source of energy might be harnessed. He was knighted in 1902 and received the Nobel prize for chemistry in 1904. JAC

Ramsbury, diocese of. Founded in 909 by *Edward the Elder in his reorganization of the *Winchester diocese, Ramsbury comprised Wiltshire and Berkshire. In 1058 it was merged with *Sherborne, which in 1075 was moved to *Salisbury (Old Sarum). WMM

Ramsey, Michael (1904–88). Archbishop of Canterbury. Ramsey was born in Cambridge, the son of a congregationalist minister, and was educated at Repton, where the headmaster was Geoffrey *Fisher, the man he ultimately succeeded as archbishop. In 1928 he was ordained as a curate in Liverpool, but soon returned to academic life (1930) when he joined the staff of Bishop's Hostel, Lincoln, training men for the ordained ministry. It was as an academic theologian, and as a spiritual writer and director, that he made a major contribution to the life of the church. At the age of 35 he became divinity professor at Durham, and after the war returned to his native Cambridge as regius professor of divinity. In 1952 he was consecrated as bishop of Durham, becoming archbishop of York in 1956 and finally of Canterbury in 1961. Ramsey made notable contributions to debates on moral, social, and political concerns, and was an enthusiastic ecumenist, whose personal relationship with Pope Paul VI was close, but who at the same time was deeply saddened by the failure of moves to reunite the Anglican and methodist churches. As primate he travelled widely throughout the Anglican Communion. He retired in 1974, and devoted his latter years to writing and to teaching on prayer and spirituality. He died in 1988. JRG

Ranelagh was the chief rival as a pleasure garden to *Vauxhall and claimed to be a cut above its competitor. It opened in April 1742 in the grounds of a house built in the 1690s for Lord Ranelagh. The chief attraction was the great Rotunda, demolished in 1803 when the gardens closed. *Johnson thought Ranelagh the finest thing he had ever seen but used it as yet another example of the vanity of human wishes: 'it went to my heart to consider that there was not one in all that brilliant circle that was not afraid to go home and think.' Mozart performed there in 1764 at the age of 8. The site was adjacent to Chelsea hospital, where new gardens, still extant, were laid out in the 1860s. JAC

ranters. An anarchic quasi-religious movement which emerged in 1648 and horrified orthodox puritans. Ranters were never an organized sect, and their writings were so heterogeneous that their very existence as a movement has recently been denied. Contemporaries, however, had no doubt that they existed. Ranters typically believed in an immanent God, present in all his creatures, man above all; men and women who attuned themselves to the godhead within them were free of sin, since all God's work is good. Groups of them scandalized the godly by their unbridled dancing, drinking, smoking, swearing, and sharing of sexual partners. Through lack of organization and the extreme hostility of magistrates and ministers, their heyday was short. AHW

Ranulf Flambard (*c.*1060–1128). A Norman cleric whose nickname—Flambard meaning incendiary—probably reflects the burning and destructive eloquence which he turned against the king's enemies. His role as political and financial adviser to William Rufus—in 1097 Flambard was managing, to his own and his king's profit, no less than sixteen vacant bishoprics and abbeys—made him notorious in the church circles in which most contemporary historians moved. In 1099 he was made bishop of Durham. In 1100 Henry I, in a gesture calculated to win support, threw Flambard into the Tower. Within six months he escaped and made his way to Normandy. He helped to plan Duke Robert's 1101 invasion, yet soon afterwards was back in Henry

I's favour and restored to Durham. Here, though his lifestyle scandalized the monks, he won applause as an effective defender of the rights of the see, a generous patron, and a great builder. JG

rapes. *Domesday Book shows Sussex in 1086 divided into five secular 'rapes', strips running from north to south, each named after its Norman lord, and containing a castle and a harbour. Each had a sheriff and they seem to have been, in effect, miniature shires. The names and nature of the rapes suggest that they were a post-Conquest creation. But the word 'rape' is Old English and a pre-Conquest origin is also suspected. In any case rape arrangements were altered post-Conquest. Battle abbey gained jurisdiction equivalent to that of a rape; and a new rape (of Chichester) was created before 1275. JCa

rates are taxes on the occupiers of land and buildings. Various Acts in the 16th cent. provided for a poor rate for the relief of the sick and destitute, but in England 'the rates' date back formally to the Poor Relief Act of 1601, which made the parish the administrative unit for rating and gave 'overseers' (churchwardens and substantial householders) the power to tax. In 1647 an ordinance consolidated the church rate with the poor rate. As local authorities provided new services, additional rates were levied.

The Rating and Valuation Act (1925) brought in the general rate and made county boroughs, boroughs, etc. the rating authorities (in place of the overseer) and the units of rating (in place of the parish). The rates were unpopular because they were mildly regressive and paid by only part of a local electorate. In the 1970s and 1980s various investigations, the Layfield Report (*Local Government Finance*, 1976) and two Green Papers ('Alternatives to Domestic Rates', 1981, and 'Paying for Local Government', 1986) set out alternative local taxes. Domestic rates, but not business rates, were abolished in 1989–93, in Scotland, and in 1990–3, in England and Wales, when they were replaced by the community charge or *poll tax. MW

Rathmines, battle of, 1649. In June 1649 Michael Jones and the parliamentary forces were besieged in Dublin by *Ormond. Reinforcements from England enabled him on 2 August to make a sortie and destroy Ormond's camp at Rathmines. JAC

Ray, John (1607–1705). Naturalist. The son of an Essex blacksmith, Ray was enabled to study at Cambridge, where he subsequently taught for thirteen years. Although ordained episcopally in 1660, he declined to subscribe to the Act of Uniformity, so lost his fellowship in 1662. Supported by prosperous friends, he then pursued his career as a naturalist, attempting a systematic description of all living things. His expeditions around Europe as well as Britain recorded antiquities, local customs, and institutions in addition to flora and fauna. Botany remained his first love, however, and he laid the foundation for a system of classification based on all structural characteristics, setting out many of the natural orders now employed by botanists. His three-volume masterwork *Historia plantarum* (1686–1704) and his precision of terminology have led to him being regarded as the father of natural history in Britain. ASH

Reading. County town of Berkshire, situated where the river Kennet joins the Thames. A small borough by 1086, it grew partly thanks to Henry I's foundation of a major Cluniac abbey (1121), where he was buried. The abbey dominated the town until the dissolution (1539), and not until 1542 did Reading become an autonomous borough. From the 14th to the 17th cents. it flourished through cloth-making: it was temporarily the eleventh wealthiest English town under Henry VIII, and Archbishop Laud was the son of a Reading clothier. The town suffered badly in the Civil War; was only of modest importance in the 18th cent.; but revived as an industrial town in the 19th ('Biscuitopolis'). DMP

Reading, Rufus David Isaacs, 1st marquis of (1860–1935). After a bumpy start, Isaacs had an unusually varied and distinguished career. The son of a Jewish fruit merchant from the East End of London, he left school at 14 to join the family business. He next turned to stockbroking but was 'hammered' in 1884. His third start was reading law. He was called to the bar in 1887 and quickly established himself. Entering Parliament as a Liberal for Reading in 1904, he was solicitor-general by 1910 and attorney-general the following year. Though singed in the *Marconi scandal of 1912, he was appointed lord chief justice in 1913 and given a barony. After successfully negotiating a government loan from America, he was promoted viscount in 1916 and earl in 1917. Next, from January 1918 until 1919 he was ambassador to the USA at a critical time of the war. Reading resumed his legal career, but in 1921 was sent to India as viceroy, remaining there during a tense period until 1926. His third promotion in the peerage came on leaving office. Even then he was not finished and crowned his remarkable performance by acting from August to November 1931 as foreign secretary while the *National Government was being formed. JAC

Rebecca riots, 1838–44. These riots in west Wales took place over a long period and, coinciding with the *chartist agitation, caused the government much concern. They originated as protests against *turnpikes which, because of the many small trusts, imposed heavy burdens on farmers and local people. They took the form of night attacks on toll-houses and -gates, the rioters often well organized, with blackened faces and wearing women's clothes. Their name came from the biblical reference—'the seed of Rebecca shall possess the gates of her enemies' (Gen. 24: 60). But they extended also to attacks upon workhouses, protests against tithes, and personal grudges. Workhouses were destroyed at Narbeth in 1839 and at Carmarthen in 1843. The government employed troops, police, and spies to control the situation, but the eventual remedy was an Act of 1844 (7 & 8 Vic. c. 91) to ease and reduce tolls. JAC

record offices. Article 24 of the Act of Union of 1707 guaranteed that Scottish records would remain in Scotland. The Register House in Princes Street, Edinburgh, designed by

Robert *Adam, was begun in 1771 and completed in 1827. It is said to be the first building erected to house national archives. New Register House (1859–63) holds records of Scottish births, deaths, and marriages.

After a select committee report and a Public Records Act of 1838, the Public Records Office was opened in Chancery Lane, London. The Victorian building was begun in 1851 with Sir James Pennethorne as architect and has been several times extended. A further Record Office was opened in Kew in 1977. The archives were the responsibility of the master of the rolls until 1959 when the lord Chancellor took over. The enormous miscellany of records includes *Domesday Book and *Magna Carta, Guy Fawkes's signature, Dick Turpin's indictment, Nelson's will, and Edward VIII's abdication document. Wills are held in Somerset House, London, parliamentary archives by the House of Lords Record Office at Westminster, and births, deaths, and marriages since 1837 by the General Registry Office. The Public Record Office for Northern Ireland was set up in Belfast in 1923.

The great majority of county record offices have been established since the Second World War, often beginning with one archivist in a picturesque but unsuitable building before moving to purpose-built but duller premises in the 1960s. The Bedfordshire County Record Office dates from 1913 and claims to be the oldest archives department. It was followed before the Second World War by Surrey (1928), Warwickshire (1931), Kent (1933), Oxfordshire and Somerset (1935), Gloucestershire (1936), Buckinghamshire and Essex (1938), and Hertfordshire (1939). Fifteen more record offices were opened in the 1940s. In addition, archives are held by many colleges, societies, libraries, museums, diocesan offices, and by city and town record offices. The most complete list is in *British Archives*. Non-public records are catalogued in the National Register of Archives, kept by the Royal Commission on Historical Manuscripts (est. 1869); the Scottish register is kept by Register House. JAC

recruiters. In 1641 Charles I gave his consent to a bill which declared that the *Long Parliament could not be dissolved save by its own consent. That Parliament sat until 1653 when *Cromwell forcibly dissolved it. Out of just over 500 original members, about 200 joined the king and many others died or were killed: the small size of the House of Commons became a political embarrassment. After 1645 the absentees were replaced by 'recruiters', returned at by-elections, and by March 1647 244 new members had been brought in. By the time of its dissolution, fewer than 100 members of the pre-war House of Commons were in attendance. JAC

Reculver was a fort of the *Saxon Shore on the north coast of Kent. In the Roman period the Wantsum channel separating the Isle of Thanet from Kent was open water. Reculver was built to a traditional fort design at the north-east of the channel in the early 3rd cent. Regulbium is listed in the *Notitia dignitatum* as garrisoned by *cohors I Baetasiorum*. Marine erosion since the Roman period has removed about two-fifths of the northern part of the site. ASEC

recusants were catholics who refused to attend church as required by law (1559). Though initially tolerated, Mary, queen of Scots' arrival (1568), the rising of the *northern earls (1569), Elizabeth's excommunication (1570), and the *Ridolfi plot (1571) hardened the government's attitude. Obeying the excommunication bull's provisions became treasonable. Because the Spanish (and the 17th-cent. French) threat made recusancy seem synonymous with treason, persecution increased. The mission of English priests from Douai (1574) and of Jesuits, such as *Campion and *Parsons (1580), strengthened catholicism—there were 400 priests in England by 1603. Recusants thus faced further penalties; saying or hearing mass was punishable by fine and imprisonment (1581), the recusancy fine was increased to £20 a month, and being a priest was punishable by death (1585). Between 1581 and 1603 180 recusants, including 120 priests, were executed. Nevertheless the catholic aristocracy, strong in the north and west, who preferred a quietist approach continued to practise; others, 'church papists', nominally attended church, while secretly practising catholicism. After temporary alleviation under the *Declarations of Indulgence (1672, 1687, 1688), they were not included officially in the Toleration Act, though afterwards authorities normally turned a blind eye to their worship. Civil disabilities were not removed until the *Catholic Emancipation Act (1829). WMM

Redmond, John (1856–1918). Redmond, a lawyer, was born in Co. Wexford. He became clerk of the House of Commons in 1880, and an Irish Parliamentary Party MP from 1881. He led the Parnellites from 1891 and the entire party from 1900. His great opportunity appeared to come with the introduction of the third Home Rule Bill in 1912, but when opposition in Ulster and in the Tory Party mounted, Redmond seemed increasingly weak and over-dependent on the Liberal alliance. He underrated the depth of Ulster resistance. He sought to undercut opposition to his leadership by taking over the leadership of the Irish Volunteers and ensured that the war's increasing unpopularity would reflect on his party. Redmond failed to react effectively to the British execution of the *Easter Rising's leaders in 1916, and weakened on the partition issue during *Lloyd George's Home Rule negotiations. In 1917, his leadership of Irish nationalism collapsed under Sinn Fein challenge. He died before the final defeat of his party in the 1918 general election, but events had overtaken his youthful radicalism, and he had failed to reconcile his nationalism with his respect for the British Parliament. MAH

Red River rebellion, 1869. In 1869 the Hudson's Bay Company sold its territorial rights to the new dominion of Canada. Both parties largely ignored the Métis of the Red River, a French-speaking community of part Indian descent. Led by Louis Riel, they established a provisional government in December 1869. While the Canadian government negotiated, through fur-trader Donald A. Smith, Riel ordered the shooting of Ulsterman Thomas Scott to uphold his authority. An expeditionary force, commanded by Garnet *Wolseley, reached the settlement in August 1870, after Riel had escaped. The Red River became the province of Manitoba in

1870. Riel was hanged in 1885 after leading a second western rebellion. GM

reeve (Anglo-Saxon *gerefa*). Reeve was the general medieval term for a supervising official and is found in a number of different contexts. The shire-reeve (*scire-gerefa*), appointed by the king, was for centuries the chief royal representative in the counties: the right to elect one's own sheriff was a valuable privilege, granted sparingly. The sheriff lost many of his judicial functions to the royal justices and the JPs and was superseded in the 16th cent. by the lord-lieutenant, though the post remains prestigious. The sheriff's deputy was the hundred-reeve, who held the hundred court. The term was also used for the chief officer of a town—a port-reeve or burh-reeve—until overshadowed in the larger towns by the office of mayor or lord mayor. The manorial reeve was one of the most familiar officials for most peasants. He was elected by the tenants but sometimes nominated by the lord, and was responsible for the organization of communal tasks, usually working with the lord's bailiff, and under the supervision of the lord's steward, who might have oversight of several manors. A notable description of the functions and duties of a manorial reeve before the Norman Conquest is to be found in 'Gerefa', a postscript to the tract *Rectitudines singularum personarum* ('Rights and Ranks of People'). JAC

referenda. Although there have been many calls to hold referenda, by *Balfour on tariff reform in 1910, and *Churchill on extending the life of Parliament in 1945 for example, little use has been made of them in the UK. The constitutional importance of parliamentary sovereignty, and the fear by established parties of losing control of the political agenda, have meant that referenda have been used only to rescue governing parties from insoluble problems and ideological splits. In this they succeeded, but referenda results have failed to provide final settlements of issues. The 1973 Northern Ireland referendum on continued UK membership was boycotted by catholics and solved nothing. The 1975 UK-wide referendum on *European Economic Community membership confirmed that Britain was 'in' for good, but did not prevent calls for further referenda as the powers of the European Community increased. The 1979 Scottish devolution referendum produced a simple majority in favour, but not the 40 per cent of the total electorate required, and in both the Welsh and Scottish cases, the 1979 referenda could be seen as rejections of inadequate devolution proposals by an unpopular government, rather than outright and permanent rejections of the principle of devolution, which soon returned to the political agenda. The timing and wording of referenda is of crucial importance. CNL

Reflections on the Revolution in France (1790) by Edmund *Burke exemplified the ideology of conservatism. Part I refuted the claim of Dr Richard Price that the French revolutionaries were following the English revolutionaries of 1688, in demanding a right to determine their own constitutional system. On the contrary, the English Whigs had sought to protect the established Anglican constitution from subversion by James II, a Roman catholic. In Part II, Burke enumerated the false principles of the revolutionaries in France, including libertinism, egalitarianism, disrespect for private property, atheism, and, above all, rationalism. He feared that the spirit of *Jacobinism, unless challenged, would sweep through Europe undermining all traditional institutions. TSG

Reform Acts. The transition from the unreformed system of 1830 to full democracy in the 20th cent. was effected by seven franchise measures—the Acts of 1832, 1867, 1884, 1918, 1928, 1948, and 1969—supported by a number of other reforms.

It is not possible to form an exact estimate of the size of the electorate before 1830, since there was no registration, assessments are unreliable, and we cannot be certain of the number of votes uncast. In addition, though registration of voters was introduced by the Act of 1832, it was at first very imperfect until party managers realized how many votes were going to waste. *Grey's Reform Act introduced a standard franchise of £10 householders in the towns and augmented the franchise in the counties by allowing tenants at will to vote—the Chandos clause. The biggest increase was certainly in Scotland, where the electorate jumped from 4,500 to 65,000; in Ireland the electorate nearly doubled, from 49,000 to 90,000, and in England and Wales the increase has been put at from 435,000 to 653,000. Most of the new voters were middle-class citizens and many of the working classes were disappointed to find themselves excluded. Though as a debating ploy the Whigs insisted that the Act was a final settlement, agitation for an extension of the franchise soon recommenced and was an important ingredient in the *chartist programme of the late 1830s. By the second Reform Act of 1867, introduced by *Disraeli after Lord John *Russell's measure had foundered on party disunity, the vote was extended to working-class urban electors on the basis of household suffrage, adding some 938,000 to the existing electorate of 1,056,000. By 1884 natural increase had raised the UK electorate to some 3 million. *Gladstone's Act of that year raised it to 5 million, bringing in large numbers of county voters. With the majority of adult males now enfranchised, the total exclusion of women became more prominent and by 1897 a majority of MPs had been converted to the general principle of enfranchising women. The First World War did not so much change attitudes as enable politicians to climb down with some dignity and the 1918 measure went through with little disagreement. Even so, the vote was restricted to women over 30, so that they should not form a majority in the electorate, bearing in mind the heavy male casualties during the war. The electorate was increased by some 7 million to more than 21 million (13 million men, 8.5 million women). Three more measures brought about almost complete adult suffrage. In 1928 the age limit for women voters was brought down to 21, giving the vote to 5 million extra 'flappers'. The Labour government's Act of 1948 ended plural voting by taking away the business vote and the special university representation. In 1969, with little controversy, the voting age was lowered to 18, bringing in another 3 million voters. At almost every extension, apprehension was expressed that the new voters would prove fickle and irresponsible: in every instance they behaved very much like the older voters they had joined.

Of equal importance were accompanying redistribution measures, legislation against undue influence and corruption, and the introduction of democracy into local government. The redistributive clauses of the Great Reform Act of 1832 were probably its most dramatic feature, with the total abolition of 56 'Schedule A' boroughs, including Old Sarum, Gatton, Dunwich, and Hindon, and the award for the first time of parliamentary representation to great industrial towns like Manchester, Birmingham, Leeds, Sheffield, Bolton, Blackburn, Bradford, and Wolverhampton. Further redistribution was effected by the 1867 Act, which deprived 38 small boroughs like Honiton, Stamford, and Dorchester of one of their two seats; brought in Burnley, Middlesbrough, Gravesend, and 7 other boroughs with one seat (two for Chelsea); and gave an extra third seat to Birmingham, Liverpool, Leeds, and Manchester. An even more drastic redistribution accompanied the 1884 Act. Seventy-nine towns with less than 15,000 population lost both members, and a further 36 with less than 50,000 lost one: the Act moved a long way towards single-member constituencies, which predominated in the 20th cent.

The struggle for purity of elections was laborious throughout the 19th cent. The introduction of the secret ballot in 1872 did not solve the problem. The *Corrupt Practices Act of 1883 made more impact by tightening up control of election expenses, though isolated instances of bribery continued to be revealed.

Local government reform was effected by the *Municipal Corporations Act of 1834, which set up elected councils in the larger towns; by the *County Councils Act of 1888, which replaced the old government in the shires by justices of the peace by 62 elected councils; and by the *Parish Councils Act of 1894, hailed as a great measure of local democracy, but hamstrung by financial limits and watered down by 20th-cent. legislation. JAC

Reformation. Although 'reform' means many things, 'the Reformation' always denotes the 16th-cent. division of Latin Christendom into protestant and catholic. *Protestantism rejected the catholic belief that salvation comes through grace received in the sacraments and other rites of the traditional church; it restricted the church's role to one of proclaiming the unmerited gift of divine forgiveness. The *Church of England, established by statute in 1559, was unambiguously protestant. However, hindsight, and the diversity of later Anglicanism, has led many to argue that the Church of England stands somehow midway between catholic and reformed traditions.

1. Before the Reformation. The church in England *c.*1500 was devoutly catholic and loyally papalist. Many parish churches were extravagantly rebuilt, and lavished with vessels and ornaments which foreign visitors thought worthy of a cathedral. Kings and popes usually got on well: royal orators and cardinals-protector handled the nation's business at the curia, and royal nominees were accepted for major church posts. The 'English heresy', *lollardy, always threatened the church more in theory than practice: while it called for disendowment of the hierarchy, it had little effect on church wealth, privileges, or even attendance.

2. The early English reformers. The fame of the German Reformation leader Martin Luther (1483–1546) caught the imagination of some English followers in the 1520s. Churchmen including Thomas Bilney (*c.*1495–1531), Robert *Barnes (d. 1540), and the Bible translator and controversialist William *Tyndale (*c.*1494–1536) reinterpreted the Reformation message. However, their support was confined to young university students and those with foreign connections. They posed no threat, though Thomas *Wolsey burned heretic books publicly, and Thomas *More wrote against Tyndale.

3. The royal marriage and the 'humanist' phase. Henry VIII's failure to secure papal annulment of his first marriage led to the break with the papacy during 1532–6. This policy required theoretical justification if the king was to carry such a profoundly catholic nation into schism. Thomas *Cromwell recruited a number of young humanist writers, whose propaganda pieces criticized both the papacy and some aspects of the old cults, such as papal indulgences. The Ten Articles of 1536 and the two sets of Injunctions of 1536 and 1538, together with the 'Bishops' Book' of 1537, sought to strip away many of the festivals, relic-cults, shrines, and even parts of the service for the dead. Nevertheless, these moves were not avowedly 'protestant': Henry VIII detested Luther and loathed the Swiss heresies against the presence of Christ in the sacrament. Though Thomas Cromwell's commissioners who toured the doomed monasteries in 1535–6 mocked spurious relics and hunted dissolute monks, the ensuing abolition of the monastic order had no declared religious rationale. During 1539–43 conservative tendencies stopped the embryonic protestantism of Henrician England in its tracks: certain catholic beliefs and practices were reaffirmed, 'sacramentarian' heretics burned, and Bible-reading restricted by statute. Nevertheless, Henry never ceased to trust his reform-minded archbishop Thomas *Cranmer, and even suggested to a bemused ambassador in 1546 that he and the French king might together abolish the mass.

4. Public protestantism under Edward VI. All ambiguity was swept away in the next reign. Revision of the mass-book began almost at once, leading in 1549 to the publication of Cranmer's first, very cautious, *Book of Common Prayer. Meanwhile royal commissioners ruthlessly stripped parish churches of most of the ornaments and furniture associated with the old cult. Distinguished continental reformers such as Martin Bucer and Pier Martire Vermigli settled in the universities and influenced further changes in worship. In 1552 a revision of the Prayer Book simplified the apparatus of worship to the barest protestant essentials, and its abusive anti-papal rhetoric left no room for doubt. The Forty-Two Articles of Doctrine in 1553 set out reformed beliefs.

5. Catholicism restored, 1553–1558. Mary I inherited religious legislation, in her eyes *ultra vires* and void, which took some eighteen months to reverse. Nevertheless, priests and laity restored the mass at the mere breath of royal suggestion. In 1554 most 'scandalously' married priests accepted their humiliation and went back to saying mass. Once owners of monastic lands were assured of their titles, papal authority was received back with some enthusiasm. Protestantism remained confined to cells mostly in southern and eastern England. The impact of the campaign which burned *c.*280 heretics between 1555 and 1558 was greater in hindsight (helped by *Foxe's martyrology) than at the time. Many counties saw no burnings or only a few; latterly they took place in London at dawn, attended only by groups of demonstrators from the clandestine congregation.

6. A precarious settlement, 1558–1563. Elizabeth, daughter of *Anne Boleyn and legatee of the schism, found the catholic hierarchy much more stubborn than in 1531–3. Re-establishment of the royal supremacy and abolition of the mass required an almost clean sweep of the episcopate, and careful management of Parliament, which wrecked the proposals several times. It is now generally accepted that catholic resistance was the chief reason for the delay, caution, and occasional ambiguity of the Elizabethan church settlement. The anti-papal abuse of the 1552 Prayer Book was excised from the 1559 version; ineffectual efforts were made to restore some vestments and restrain priestly marriage. Even the *Thirty-Nine Articles approved by convocation in 1563 were altered by the queen herself, probably to placate conservatives.

7. The making of a protestant people. The new bishops chosen by Elizabeth from leading reformed clergy in 1559, and most protestant zealots, assumed that the concessions made to tradition were temporary sops, to be discarded once the regime was secure. To their increasing horror and bewilderment, they found that the queen obstinately refused to strip away the veneer of ritual, and tried to stick it back where it was removed illegally. She feared that combative, doctrinaire protestant preaching still risked alienating parts of the kingdom and sparking a religious war: the restoration of the mass during the *northern earls' revolt of 1569, and her excommunication by the pope in 1570, lent these fears substance. In the 'puritan' controversies of the 1570s Elizabeth found and nurtured a faction of clerics led by John *Whitgift (archbishop of Canterbury 1583–1604) which believed with equal zeal in protestant dogma, episcopal church government, and traditionalist ceremonial. So was the peculiar hybrid 'Anglican' church, founded both on Foxe's *Martyrs* and on *Hooker's *Ecclesiastical Polity*, brought to birth by the end of the 16th cent. EC

Cameron, E., *The European Reformation* (Oxford, 1991); Cowan, I. B., *The Scottish Reformation: Church and Society in Sixteenth-Century Scotland* (New York, 1982); Dickens, A. G., *The English Reformation* (1964); Donaldson, G., *The Scottish Reformation* (Cambridge, 1960); Haigh, C. (ed.), *The English Reformation Revised* (Cambridge, 1987); Sheils, W. J., *The English Reformation, 1530–1570* (1989).

Reform Club. Founded in 1836, the Reform Club was a radical initiative, drawing in Whig support. It was a riposte to the Tory *Carlton Club and reflected the desire for better organization, particularly of electoral registration, after the Great Reform Act. The founders included Lord *Durham, Joseph *Parkes, and Molesworth. It drew together the Westminster Club and the Reform Association, and *Barry's premises at 104 Pall Mall opened in 1841. The success of the club was as much gastronomic as ideological, since it employed an outstanding French chef, Alexis Soyer. JAC

Reform League, 1865–9. The Reform League was established in 1865 to press for manhood suffrage and the ballot. The president was Edmond Beales and the secretary George Howell, and more than 400 branches were formed. It collaborated with the more moderate and middle-class Reform Union and its parliamentary spokesmen included *Gladstone and John *Bright. It gave strong support to *Russell's bill in 1866 and the *Hyde Park riots, a by-product of the mass protest meetings in July 1866, helped to push through *Disraeli's second Reform Act. The League ran parliamentary candidates at the general election of 1868 but with little success and was dissolved in March 1869. Historians dispute whether popular pressure was decisive or whether the second Reform Act was the outcome of high political manœuvring. JAC

regalia. The English coronation regalia is kept in the jewel house of the Tower of London. The collection of a regalia for coronation purposes added to the solemnity and antiquity of the occasion and seems to have been begun by the monks of Westminster abbey. But almost everything was destroyed during the *Commonwealth as items of superstition. Only a 12th-cent. anointing spoon survived: an ampulla, in the shape of a golden eagle, to hold the holy oil, was made for the coronation of Charles II in 1661. On the same occasion, a copy was made of St Edward's crown: a second, imperial, crown was made for Victoria in 1838. An orb, signifying authority, was also made in 1661, and two sceptres, with a dove and a cross. Bracelets were occasionally used and in 1953 the dominions gave Elizabeth II a pair. Two swords of justice and a sword of mercy (Curtana) date from the early 17th cent.: a fourth sword, the sword of state, was made in 1678. A sword of offering was made for the coronation of George IV in 1821. For the Scottish royal regalia, see HONOURS OF SCOTLAND. JAC

Regency. Though there have been several regencies in British history, the term is usually confined to the period 1810–20 when George, prince of Wales, acted as regent on behalf of George III, who had gone mad. The Whigs confidently expected that the regent would bring in his old friends and began cabinet-making. He did not, and the Tories remained in office throughout the period. It was a time of acute contrasts. Until *Waterloo in 1815 the country was still at war, with bread shortages, *Luddite riots, and severe distress. The post-war years were no better: agricultural depression, widespread unemployment, and the dislocation of early industrialization fuelled radical protest, exemplified at *Peterloo. The fashionable world retained its poise. Beau *Brummell, the prince's friend, was the arbiter of elegance. Harriette, Amy, and Fanny Wilson entertained the gentlemen. The prince regent pressed on with his Pavilion at *Brighton until the prime minister, Lord *Liverpool, pointed out what offence it gave at a time of national distress and warned that the cabinet would not find a penny more. The radicals—*Cobbett, *Hunt, *Hazlitt, and *Shelley—and the caricaturists—*Cruikshank and *Rowlandson—had plenty to aim at. The prevailing taste in architecture, costume, and furniture was severely classical, aiming at balance and restraint, and rarely lapsing into extravagance. The finest monument to the period is the Regent Street and Regent's Park complex, built by John *Nash. JAC

Regency crisis, 1788–9. In October 1788 George III appeared to have gone mad. It was expected that the prince of Wales would become regent, dismiss *Pitt, and call on *Portland and *Fox to form a ministry. Although a regency bill was prepared, it was not enacted because of the unexpected recovery of the king in February 1789. DW

regicides. After the second civil war in 1648, most army leaders despaired of reaching an agreement with the king that would be honoured and resolved to put him on trial. Fifty-nine signed Charles's death warrant in January 1649. At the Restoration, the remains of *Cromwell, *Ireton, and *Bradshaw were taken from Westminster abbey and hanged at Tyburn. Of the 41 regicides still alive, 9 were put to death. Thomas *Harrison, one of Cromwell's major-generals, told the court, 'This was not a thing done in a corner.' JAC

Register House (Princes Street, Edinburgh) contains the Scottish national archives. It was built by Robert *Adam and was in use by 1778, though completion took many years. One of the finest features is the magnificent dome. The equestrian statue of the duke of *Wellington, facing North bridge, is by Sir John Steele and was erected in 1852. JAC

regium donum (royal gift) originated as a grant of £600 p.a. by Charles II to augment the salaries of Irish presbyterian ministers in 1672 when he was trying to win support for his *Declaration of Indulgence. It was revived by William III, who increased it to £1,200 p.a., but was much disliked by high Anglicans as breaching the principle that only the Church of England should have support from the state. By the end of Anne's reign it was paid irregularly. George I increased it to £1,600 p.a. and in 1723 extended the principle to England by giving £500 p.a. for the widows of dissenting clergy. The regium donum became a significant precedent when *Pitt's government decided in 1795 to support the training of Irish catholic priests. The English grant was abolished in 1851, the Irish in 1869 when the Irish church was disestablished, though with compensation for the presbyterians. JAC

Regni. A British *civitas*. The *civitas* of the Regni appears to be an artificial creation of the Roman government. It seems to have been based on a kingdom created by them in AD 43 for their client-king *Cogidubnus from the southern part of the territory of the *Atrebates. During the invasion period, *Chichester harbour was used by the Roman general *Vespasian as a safe base to supply his troops campaigning in south-west England. Cogidubnus subsequently built his palace over the Roman camp. The special status of Cogidubnus and his kingdom is perhaps reflected in the choice of the name Regni, or Regneses, which means simply 'the people of the kingdom'. Only when Cogidubnus died, perhaps around AD 80, did the kingdom disappear and the *civitas* take its place. The boundaries of the *civitas* were marked by the river Meon in the west and the river Wey to the north, and probably ran just beyond Beachy Head to the east, thus encompassing much of the Sussex and Hampshire downland. The capital of the new canton, however, was located at its south-western corner, where the major Iron Age stronghold at Chichester was succeeded by the Roman town of Noviomagus. KB

Reith, John, 1st Baron Reith (1889–1971). Reith stamped his image on the first 40 years of the *British Broadcasting Corporation. The son of a minister of the Free Church of Scotland, 'famous for his impassioned advocacy of righteousness in every department of human activity' (as his son put it), he was born at Stonehaven in Kincardineshire. He began as a railway engineer and was badly wounded in the First World War. In 1922, at something of a loose end, he saw an advertisement for general manager of the new BBC and was appointed. Reith created his own vision of an austere, sober, and responsible corporation, with important educational and religious obligations. He stayed until 1938 and then went to Imperial Airways, but at the outbreak of war was brought into Parliament, serving as minister of information, minister of transport, and minister of works. He and *Churchill disliked each other and he was abruptly dismissed in February 1942. Though after the war he held a number of important commercial posts, the draft title for his post-1938 memoirs was 'Adrift'. A tall, gaunt, impressive, and fierce man, he had no concept of compromise and his diaries are full of unpleasant and savage remarks about colleagues. His conceit bordered on megalomania: with Churchill as prime minister, Reith deplored the lack of leadership—'and I might have given it—a lot of it'. He was knighted in 1927 and given his barony in 1940. JAC

reivers or moss-troopers were the names given to border raiders. There was little protection against them, save the building of *peel towers and bastle-houses as temporary refuges. Liddesdale on the Scottish side and Redesdale on the English were notorious nests for reivers. Repeated agreements were made between the monarchs of England and Scotland to permit the border wardens to bring offenders to justice and a special code of border law operated. Even after the personal union of the kingdoms in 1603 it remained difficult to put down raids. JAC

religious toleration, a principle accepted without question by most people in the late 20th cent., came about more by a process of exhaustion than by the triumph of reasoned argument. Few people in the 16th cent. doubted that state and church had not only the right but the duty to put down religious *dissent. They assumed that religious truth was God-given and absolute; that a country divided in religion would be fatally weakened; that nonconformists were potential traitors who would make common cause with co-religionists in other countries; that the exercise of private judgement must, in the end, undermine all authority and produce a shattered and anarchic society, in which everything was permissible.

The *Reformation brought about toleration neither by design nor directly, but as a by-product. None of the great reformers—Luther, Calvin, Zwingli—were tolerant of their opponents. In defence of his own position, Luther was first obliged to challenge papal authority, then to expound the right of the secular ruler to declare the religious policy of his state. That formula was accepted in the Augsburg peace of 1555 after years of bloodshed in Germany—*cuius regio, eius religio* (the ruler shall decide religion). Only *catholicism or *lutheranism were permitted choices and there was no provision for toleration. But in practice political considerations sometimes made rulers embrace toleration. Countries like Prussia, which were chronically short of labour, might find it imprudent to drive out subjects and might welcome refugees from less tolerant states: the Hohenzollerns who, as *calvinists, were of a different faith from the vast majority of their lutheran subjects, might think twice before insisting on their formal rights. Augsburg even contained a slight measure of practical toleration in that, in a vastly divided Germany, subjects might move to a more friendly state.

Nevertheless, for decades the dream of a reunited Christendom dominated, either by force or by theological compromise. Force failed. The Emperor Charles V was unable to reconquer northern Europe in the 1550s and the Thirty Years War ended in 1648 with the religious boundaries largely unchanged. Well-meaning men arranged conferences and debates where rival theologians could agree on fundamentals and reach common ground. They failed at Marburg in 1529, at Worms and Regensburg in 1541, at Regensburg again in 1546. Even conferences to unite the protestants failed. James I summoned anglicans and puritans to *Hampton Court in 1604 without success: Charles II called the *Savoy Conference between anglicans and presbyterians in 1661. It failed. Under these dispiriting circumstances, the few voices calling for toleration were accorded increased attention. Could we not have, asked *Milton, 'a little generous prudence, a little forebearance of one another, and some grain of charity?'

In England there had been little need for a hunt after heretics until the late 14th cent., when *Wyclif's teaching combined with social unrest to produce *lollardy. The authorities responded with the act of 1401 **De heretico comburendo*—on the burning of heretics. In the 16th cent., Henry VIII executed catholics for treason, reformers for heresy; Mary burned reformers; Elizabeth executed catholic priests. *Anabaptists, regarded with peculiar horror, were hunted down by rulers in almost all countries. The seed-time for toleration in England was after the civil war, when sects multiplied and the victorious parliamentary army demanded from the presbyterians toleration for *baptists, *congregationalists, and independents. *Cromwell lent his vast prestige to the cause of toleration, readmitting *Jews to England after a gap of nearly four hundred years.

The Restoration in 1660 saw a lurch backwards, with Parliament passing severe legislation against catholics and dissenters. But, again, the exigencies of politics called for tactical behaviour and Charles II and James II both issued *Declarations of Indulgence. In the crisis of 1688, when the dissenters held the balance between the anglicans and the king, they supported the revolution, and reaped the reward from William III in 1689 in the *Toleration Act, which at least permitted freedom of worship, provided doors were unlocked. It was far from complete. Toleration did not apply to catholics, who faced a battery of *penal laws, nor to anti-Trinitarians. In Scotland, *episcopalians were persecuted as crypto-Jacobites. Even protestant dissenters did not have full civil rights and could neither sit in Parliament nor on corporations unless their consciences were flexible. But the narrow basis was gradually broadened, with concessions to the *quakers over oath-taking and to the Scottish episcopalians over lay patronage. Underpinning the shift in policy was the start of a change in attitude. In his *Letter on Toleration*, published in 1689, *Locke caught a new mood of calm reason: persecution created, not converts, but hypocrites, 'for no man can, if he would, conform his faith to the dictates of another . . . All the life and power of true religion consists in the inward and full persuasion of the mind.'

There remained the problem of civil equality. No catholic and few dissenters could be MPs. But once the catholics had demonstrated their loyalty in the 1745 invasion, small concessions were made, and in Ireland catholics were given the vote in 1793. Though full emancipation was held up in 1801 by the refusal of George III to sanction it, it was granted in 1829. Dissenters were allowed into Parliament in 1828 and more concessions on tithes and on marriages followed. In 1858 Jews were allowed into Parliament. At length, in 1886, after the *Bradlaugh case, even atheists were admitted to Westminster. From the beginning of the Reformation, it had taken a mere 350 years. JAC

Remonstrants. See RESOLUTIONS.

Renaissance (rebirth) primarily characterizes the impulse, initiated in Italy and expanding into western Europe, towards improving the contemporary world by discovering and applying the achievement of classical antiquity. The movement was at its strongest from the time of Petrarch (1304–74) through the 'long 16th cent.' (1450–1625). 'Renaissance' is now generally used to describe the politics, beliefs, philosophy, science, scholarship, discourse, literature, handwriting, printing, painting, engraving, sculpture, architecture, and music judged to characterize that period. The 20th cent. identified stages of this renaissance (pre- or proto-, early, high, and late), as well as earlier revivals of classical studies (Carolingian, Byzantine, 12th-cent.), and unrelated other renaissances (American, Bengal, black).

'Renaissance' is first used alone in the 19th cent., though Giorgio Vasari (1550) saw a 'rinascità delle arti' in his own time, and Voltaire two centuries later a 'renaissance des lettres et des beaux-arts' in Medicean Florence. 'Renaissance' *tout court*, current French in the 1830s and employed in 1842 by Queen Victoria to define a style, was influentially used by Jules Michelet as title for a volume of his *Histoire de France* (1855). Michelet's concept of an epoch marked by 'the discovery of the world and of man' was taken up most importantly in Jakob Burckhardt's *Kultur der Renaissance in Italien* (1860). For Burckhardt the defining emphasis of the Renaissance was secular and individual; the new attitudes he detected in the Italy of that epoch to nature, morality, religion, affairs, art, and literature made him see it as inaugurating the modern era. Some later historians intensified Burckhardt's stress on paganism. Others reacted against it both by indicating continuities with medieval Christianity and by positing earlier renaissances. Post-Burckhardtian valuation of social, economic, and political factors has led to stress on difference in continuity, with classical learning, defence of the active life and of the virtue of possessions seen as coexistent with earlier knowledge and ideals.

The Renaissance discovery of classical antiquity was essentially a revival of learning, which Petrarch believed had dispelled the darkness and ignorance which had prevailed since late antiquity. Petrarch's mode of studying and transmitting the Latin classics became the province of the 15th-cent. *(h)umanista*, or teacher of Latin and Greek (hence 'humanist' and, but not until the 19th cent. *'humanism'). From the 15th cent. onwards, humanist activity spread to other countries. At the turn of the 15th–16th cents. German imperial scholarship claimed a *translatio studii* parallel with the Carolingian *translatio imperii*. Later German humanists such as Melanchthon were usually advocates of the *Reformation. Greek studies flourished especially in 16th-cent. France.

The English Renaissance was influenced by the Italian indirectly, through France, Burgundy, and the Netherlands, as well as directly. In its earliest phase, the patronage and book collections of Humphrey, duke of *Gloucester (1390–1447), were important; later, under Henry VII, William *Grocyn and Thomas *Linacre, after Italian experience, won a reputation for Greek. From about 1500, however, the chief force in English humanism was the concept of *pietas literata*, or evangelical humanism, associated with Erasmus. The friendship of Erasmus with John *Colet and with Thomas *More was particularly significant. Colet's St Paul's School was influenced by Erasmus; he and More translated Greek together; his *Praise of Folly* (1511) was dedicated to More, who supported him in controversy.

England produced no humanist scholar of the first rank during the Renaissance, More's *Utopia* being the finest Latin achievement of its early Tudor phase. Many classical and humanist works were translated into the vernacular, however. A pattern of civility on the Italian model was offered by Sir Thomas *Elyot (*Book Named the Governor*, 1531) and Sir Thomas Hoby (translation of Castiglione's *Courtier*, 1561). In spite of opposition to things Italian, Machiavelli's *Prince*, known in the 1530s, was printed in Italian at London in the 1580s, as were works by the philosopher Giordano Bruno. Greek studies were notable, from the 1520s especially in association with the Reformation. Erasmus' Greek New Testament with Latin translation (1516–19) was used by Martin Luther for his German New Testament (1521): William *Tyndale used both for his English version (1526–34); later reformed English versions, including the Authorized (1611), kept much of Tyndale's language.

A protestant Renaissance poetic tradition embodied by Edmund *Spenser, who was also, like John *Donne, influenced by Italian Renaissance poetry, poetics, and Neoplatonism, extends to Andrew *Marvell and John *Milton. Sir Thomas Wyatt and Henry Howard, earl of *Surrey, had earlier introduced Italian lyric forms. In drama, *Shakespeare, Christopher *Marlowe, and Ben *Jonson were much indebted to the Italo-classic tradition.

The visual arts and architecture of Renaissance England remained predominantly traditional, in spite of the presence of Italian sculptors and of north European painters such as Hans *Holbein the Younger, Rubens, and *Van Dyck. The first English architect and designer of international stature was Inigo *Jones, the Palladian (1573–1652). Music similarly remained traditional until the flowering of the Italian fashion (1575–1625).

The Renaissance in Scotland was notable for logical and theological studies, and for its connections with French humanism. Its earlier stages produced three of the finest poets of their time in Robert *Henryson (d. 1490), William *Dunbar (d. *c.*1515), and Gavin *Douglas (d. 1522); Douglas was also the first translator of the whole of Virgil's *Aeneid* into any British vernacular. George *Buchanan (1506–82) won a lasting European reputation as humanist, poet, and historian; he was also tutor to the young James VI and I. JBT

Hale, J. R., *The Civilization of Europe in the Renaissance, 1450–1620* (1993); Kraye, J. (ed.), *The Cambridge Companion to Renaissance Humanism* (Cambridge, 1996); Panofsky, E., *Renaissance and Renascences in Western Art* (Stockholm, 1960); Rice, E. F., Jr., and Grafton, A., *The Foundations of Early Modern Europe, 1460–1559* (2nd edn. New York, 1994); Skinner, Q., *The Foundations of Modern Political Thought*, i: *The Renaissance*; ii: *The Reformation* (Cambridge, 1978).

Rennie, John (1761–1821). Millwright and civil engineer from Phantassie (Lothian). Rennie learned millwrighting from Andrew Meikle, but added an academic education at Edinburgh, consulting in Scotland before his first major project, *Watt's Albion Mills in London (1784–8). He continued to advise on mills, but became primarily a civil engineer, of canals (notably two east–west links, the Kennet and Avon (completed 1810) and Rochdale (1804), the first Pennine crossing); bridges (famously Waterloo (1817), Southwark (1819), and London (1831), excelling in the design of the elliptical arch and use of ironwork); Bell Rock lighthouse (1810) and numerous dock and harbour works (London (1805), Holyhead (completed 1824), and the massive breakwater at Plymouth (from 1811)); and urban water supplies, including Edinburgh, Manchester, and Leeds. Rennie also developed engineering technologies, with iron mill works (1784), the diving bell (at Ramsgate, 1813), and the steam bucket-dredger, critical to his work at Hull (1803–9), and advised the Admiralty to adopt the steam tug, seen in the *Comet* (1819). JCh

Renunciation Act, 1783. Pressure from the Irish *Volunteers during the American War forced the British government in 1782 to repeal the Declaratory Act of 1719 (6 Geo. I c. 5) which had affirmed the authority of the British Parliament over Ireland. After a few weeks, Henry Flood launched a new agitation, insisting that the concession was inadequate. To 'remove all doubts' a Renunciation Act (23 Geo. III c. 28) was hastily passed in 1783 explaining that the Irish people were subject only to laws passed by the Irish Parliament. But as long as the lord-lieutenant was a British cabinet minister, Britain remained in control. JAC

Repeal Association, 1840–8. *O'Connell's *Catholic Association was suppressed when catholic emancipation was carried in 1829 but agitation for the repeal of the Union soon recommenced. For some years O'Connell preferred to work with the Whig governments but in 1840, faced with the prospect of a Tory government under *Peel, he responded by organizing the Repeal Association, supported by the 'repeal rent', collected mainly by catholic priests. It drew up petitions, arranged candidates, sponsored monster meetings, claimed 3 million supporters, and employed 50 headquarters staff. In 1843 the government banned a meeting at Clontarf and four months later O'Connell was sent to gaol for conspiracy. The association was weakened by splits over tactics of violence, O'Connell's death in 1847, and the impact of the Famine. It was replaced in 1848 by a short-lived Irish League. JAC

representative peers. At the time of the negotiations for Union in 1707, there were more than 130 Scottish peers to 170 English ones. To unite them in one House would have given the Scots disproportionate influence. By the Act of *Union, Scotland was awarded 16 representative peers, to be elected by their colleagues before each session. Since the Scottish peerage was not replenished, the constituency was constantly shrinking until by 1800 there were fewer than 70 electors. The practice soon developed of circulating government and opposition lists and, under normal circumstances, the Scottish representative peers were useful allies of government in the House of Lords. A similar formula was adopted at the Union with Ireland in 1801. There were then some 260 English peers and 170 Irish. The Act gave Ireland 28 representative peers and four spiritual peers. But the lay Irish peers, unlike the Scots, were elected for life and those who were not chosen could sit in the House of Commons. The four bishops lost their seats when the Church of Ireland was disestablished in 1869 and no elections for Irish peers were held after the creation of the Irish Free State in 1922. The last Irish representative peer, Lord Kilmorey, died in 1961. By the Peerage Act of 1963 all the remaining Scottish peers were declared members of the House of Lords. Irish peers were still excluded but were made eligible to sit in the Commons for any constituency. JAC

Repton. A 'double monastery', founded in the late 7th cent., it had close associations with the Mercian royal house. The Mercian prince St *Guthlac began his monastic career at Repton, and several Mercian kings and princes were buried there including Merewalh, *Æthelbald (d. 757), and *Wiglaf (d. 840). It was also the burial place of Wiglaf's grandson Wigstan, murdered in 849 and shortly afterwards recognized as a saint. The crypt of the present church may have been originally a free-standing mausoleum in which Wiglaf and Wigstan were buried. In 873–4 Repton was used as a winter fortress by the Viking great army. Recent excavations have revealed details of the fortifications and a mass burial, probably of those who died of disease during the occupation. The church was a significant minster in the later Saxon period and was created an Augustinian priory in 1153. BAEY

Repton, Humphry (1752–1818). The leading landscape gardener after Lancelot 'Capability' *Brown and a contemporary of Sir Uvedale Price (1747–1829) and Richard Payne Knight (1750–1824). Knight attacked Brown's smooth and artificial style in his poem *The Landscape* (1794), to which Price added *An Essay on the Picturesque* defining the Picturesque as an aesthetic category as distinct from *Burke's Sublime and Beautiful. Generally Repton followed Brown, but introduced formal parterres, terraces, and steps near the house, and used arbours, conservatories, lodges, and cottages. Although Repton undertook a few architectural commissions on his own, and some in a brief partnership with *Nash, most were largely left to his sons John Adey (1775–1860) and George Stanley (1786–1858). Repton's celebrated technique of explaining his designs involved using 'Red Books' with sliding panels indicating the effects 'before' and 'after' improvement. Examples of Repton's work executed between 1800 and 1810 are Cassiobury (Herts.), Harewood (Yorks.), West Wycombe (Bucks.), and Woburn abbey (Beds.). Repton's *Sketches and Hints on Landscape Gardening* of 1795 lists 57 Red Books already prepared by that date, and this and his other publications were brought together by John Claudius Loudoun (1783–1843) in *The Landscape Gardening and Landscape Architecture of the Late Humphrey Repton, Esq* (1840). PW

republicanism. After the only British experience of a republic, the *Commonwealth of 1649–60, republicanism did not have its own party nor was it a major constituent of the programme of other parties or movements. Unlike most of Europe and America, where republicanism was regarded as a prerequisite of democracy, the extension of popular government in Britain was attained without revolution or overthrow of the monarchy. Nevertheless, republican sentiment was common among British radicals and reformers in the late 18th and 19th cents. Supporters of the American and French revolutions and admirers of Thomas *Paine were usually republicans, as also were the plebeian radicals of the 1820s and 1830s, notably the followers of Richard *Carlile, who published the *Republican* from 1819 to 1826. Some chartists were openly republican, as witness two late chartist journals, C. G. Harding's *Republican* (1848) and W. J. Linton's *English Republic* (1851–5). Chartists were also happy to invoke Commonwealth heroes in articles and speeches. Periods of monarchical unpopularity stimulated republicanism. This was so during the Regency and again in the late 1860s and early 1870s, when a group of Liberal MPs, including Sir Charles *Dilke and Joseph *Chamberlain, revived the republican cause, fuelled by Queen Victoria's withdrawal from public life after the death of the prince consort, the cost of the royal family, and the scandals associated with the prince of Wales. At the same time popular republicanism was spread by Charles *Bradlaugh and the secularist movement; and a short-lived journal, the *Republican*, appeared in

1870. Republican clubs were formed in London and throughout the country during 1870–2. The labour and socialist movements of the 1880s and 1890s were republican in principle. But, as with earlier radical and reform movements, republicanism was only one of the constituents and not a major part of the programme. British republicanism has been a matter of principle or sentiment rather than an issue of practical politics. JFCH

Requests, Court of. A minor court of equity. It was originally a committee of the king's *council, set up in the reign of Henry VII to hear 'poor men's causes' and causes involving the king's servants. Unlike other conciliar courts, it was not abolished in 1641 but faded away during the 17th cent. The masters of requests were often civilian lawyers who practised in the *ecclesiastical courts and the Court of *Admiralty. In the 18th and 19th cents. attempts were made to supply the deficiency of cheap and accessible justice by the establishment of local courts of limited jurisdiction called courts of requests. These were superseded in 1846 by the *county courts. MM

resolutions, 1650. Efforts to rally Scottish resistance after *Cromwell's crushing victory at *Dunbar in September 1650 were handicapped by the kirk's insistence that only godly men were fit to uphold the cause. The remonstrants—zealous presbyterians mainly from the south-west—complained that Charles II was not to be trusted: their moderate opponents retorted with 'resolutions' that qualification for service in the army be relaxed. Though the remonstrants protested that crypto-royalists were being recruited, the army was still not strong enough to do battle. Instead, it marched south into England and was cut to pieces at *Worcester. JAC

Restoration. The restoration of the monarchy in 1660 was due more to the failure of alternative republican regimes than to the efforts of loyalists. An army junta dispersed the *Rump Parliament in October 1659 but failed to rally civilian support. Dissident garrison soldiers restored the Rump and General *Monck invaded England with the army of occupation in Scotland. He quickly realized that the Rump no longer possessed the consent of the nation; he therefore restored the MPs who had been excluded from the Commons in 1648, on condition that they dissolved Parliament so that new elections could be held. The resulting *Convention—so called because it had not been summoned by the crown—invited Charles II to return. Suggestions that conditions should be attached came to nothing.

Restoration meant the return of legality, ending arbitrary or 'sword' government and changes enforced by a politicized army. Arbitrary high courts disappeared and Charles I's prerogative courts were not revived. Parliaments were again to be elected on the traditional franchises and by the old constituencies. The Lords returned. Levels of taxation fell sharply as most of the army was disbanded. An amateur militia replaced it. An Indemnity Act pardoned all except the regicides. The Convention contained a majority of former parliamentarians but old cavaliers in the 1661 Parliament tried to modify what had been done. Charles successfully resisted their attempts to exclude from office all who had fought his father and to restore estates to cavaliers who had lost them. This Parliament strengthened the crown with new treason laws, a *Licensing Act establishing censorship, and a purge of urban corporations. It also enacted the *Clarendon code restoring the church and it was this narrow settlement that provoked bitterness and lasting division. JRJ

retail trade. Until the 19th cent. selling directly to consumers was largely associated with the production of goods or rendering a service from domestic premises or market stall. Items sold were mostly local and seasonal, farm produce or locally made artefacts. In England places with a market were usually not more than 15 miles apart; this distance enabled a horse and cart to travel to a market and return the same day. Only at fairs did vendors come from long distances to sell goods or services not readily available.

In most towns the principal thoroughfares were the favoured locations for shops with living accommodation. Purpose-built shops, separate from the producer's home, with extensive displays and facilities for customers, emerged only in the later 18th cent. The 'Wedgwood Room' concept of space set aside to sell specialist items to better-off customers was a major innovation.

During the 19th cent. increasing population was accompanied by more purchasing power. This had consequences for the organization and development of retailing. Markets and fairs became less important as a wide range of products, carried by regular and reliable transport at diminishing costs, became available in established shops in cities, towns, and villages. Most towns by the middle of the century supported at least one shop specializing in the sale of 'ironmongery'. Some of these businesses became the core of department stores.

Department stores with purpose-built premises are said to have started with Joseph Whiteley's in Bayswater (London). All cities saw the development of similar shops which met the needs of various social classes. From its beginnings, Harrods (1849) sought upper-class trade whilst others such as Marshall & Snellgrove concentrated on middle-class customers. Many of these department stores developed into chains and all large cities had several of these stores in the main shopping streets by the end of the 19th cent.

Consumers seeking an alternative to commercial retailing supported the self-help model pioneered in *Rochdale (Lancs.) of a retail co-operative shop. Beginning in 1844 the concept spread rapidly throughout the British Isles. Co-operatives sold quality-guaranteed produce at affordable prices mainly to the urban working class. Commercial shops selling a limited range of groceries of low price and standard quality were begun by David Greig and Thomas Lipton in Glasgow. Their chains spread rapidly after the mid-1870s to most towns. They were so successful that other firms imitated their methods, not only in groceries but in butchery and other products. Shops, such as F. W. Woolworth and Marks & Spencer, which sold a variety of products were further examples of retailing success in the 20th cent.

In recent decades, consumer choice has expanded with

the goods available unconstrained by locality or season. At the same time the independently owned retail outlets have declined. Private car ownership stimulated the development of supermarkets from the late 1950s. Supermarkets and hypermarkets on the edges of towns also depended on readily available transport and added to the retail competition in food, home improvement equipment, and household goods and furniture. Since the early 1980s some stores have been relocated in purpose-built shopping malls and, whilst providing choice for consumers, they have caused a decline of the traditional urban shopping centre. IJEK

retainers. See BASTARD FEUDALISM.

Revocation Act, 1625. When Charles I succeeded his father he already had difficult relations with the Scottish kirk. He increased these in 1625 by a prerogative Act of Revocation, whereby church or royal property which had been alienated since 1540 was taken back by the crown. This greatly alarmed the nobility and raised the spectre of a wholesale attack upon property rights. Charles then compounded his blunder by sending a Roman catholic adviser, Lord Nithsdale, to enforce the measure. Though the matter was compromised, it was an inauspicious start to the new reign—'the ground stone of all the mischeiffe that followed after'. JAC

Revolutionary and Napoleonic wars (1793–1815). Following its defeat of the Prussians at Valmy in September 1792, revolutionary France announced its expansion to its 'natural frontiers' and war against the states of the *ancien régime*. In response Britain sent an army under the duke of *York to Flanders in February 1793, joining the Dutch and Austrians in the 'War of the First Coalition'. After an inept campaign the defeated Dutch made peace and the remnants of York's army were evacuated from Breda in March 1795. Expeditions against French colonies in the West Indies 1793–6 met with mixed success, although in 1795 the British seized Cape Town (in modern South Africa) and Ceylon (modern Sri Lanka) from their former Dutch allies. Naval victories over the French in 1794 ('the *Glorious First of June'), the Spanish at *Cape St Vincent in February 1797, and the Dutch at *Camperdown in October 1797 confirmed Britain's mastery of the seas.

The British government responded to radicalism and possible revolt at home with repression, suspending *habeas corpus in 1794. A French-backed rebellion in Ireland 1797–8 was also violently suppressed, as were naval mutinies at *Spithead and the *Nore in 1797. The cost of the war, including the creation of an army of 220,000 and 80,000 militia, forced Britain off the gold standard in 1797. A programme of barracks-building was started in 1798 deliberately to isolate soldiers from radicalism.

In 1795 Prussia and Spain made peace with France, and in 1796 Spain re-entered the war on the French side. The defeat of Austria, which made peace by the treaty of Campo Formio in October 1797, ended the first coalition. This was followed by Napoleon's expedition to Egypt in 1798, intended to support Britain's enemies in India, which came to nothing with the destruction of the French fleet at the *Nile in August 1798, the defeat of Tipu of Mysore by an Anglo-Indian army under Arthur Wellesley (*Wellington) in May 1799, and the elimination of the French in Egypt by Abercrombie at *Alexandria in March 1801.

Britain formed the 'second coalition', including Austria, Russia, Portugal, Naples, and Ottoman Turkey, in autumn 1798, but a renewed expedition to the Netherlands by an Anglo-Russian force under York in 1799 again achieved little. Austria was defeated by Napoleon at Marengo in June 1800, and made peace by the treaty of Lunéville in February 1801. Russia also made peace, joining with Sweden, Denmark, and Prussia to form the *League of Armed Neutrality in 1800. This collapsed after the assassination of Tsar Paul and the destruction of the Danish fleet by the British at *Copenhagen in April 1801.

The treaty of *Amiens in March 1802 between Britain and France ended the 'War of the Second Coalition'. But continued French expansion in southern Europe, together with support for Britain's enemies in India, brought a renewed declaration of war from Britain by May 1803, followed by another abortive French-backed rebellion in Ireland in July. The Indian threat was ended by Wellesley's defeat of the Mahratta Confederacy at Assaye in September 1803, leading to a negotiated peace in India by 1806.

On 2 December 1804 Napoleon proclaimed himself emperor of the French, leading to British treaties with Russia, Austria, and Sweden in the 'War of the Third Coalition'. Despite the failure of Napoleon's plans to invade Britain and the destruction of his fleet by Nelson at *Trafalgar in October 1805, he drove Austria out of the war with victories at Ulm and at Austerlitz (also against the Russians), leading to the treaty of Pressburg in December. This was followed by Napoleon's humiliating defeat of Prussia at Jena in October 1806. Russia was also defeated at Eylau and Friedland, and accepted the treaty of Tilsit of July 1807, leaving France dominant in central Europe.

Against Britain, his remaining enemy, Napoleon resorted to economic warfare ('the Continental System'), one by-product of which was the Anglo-American *War of 1812–15, little more than a distraction to the British. Unsuccessful British expeditions were mounted against Buenos Aires 1806–7, Naples 1806 (despite the victory at Maida), and *Walcheren island in the Netherlands 1809–10. A French campaign against Portugal, begun in November 1807, was complicated by a Spanish revolt in May 1808, followed by the arrival of a British army under Wellesley in August (the start of the *'Peninsular War'). The convention of *Cintra (also in August) allowed the French to withdraw, and a failed offensive under Sir John *Moore in October led to retreat and evacuation through *Corunna in January 1809 after Moore's death. In April Wellesley returned to the Peninsula, which became the main British theatre of the war, with victories over the French at *Talavera in July 1809 (for which he was made Viscount Wellington), *Fuentes de Onoro in May 1811, Badajoz and *Salamanca in April and July 1812, and *Vitoria in June 1813.

In June 1812 Napoleon attacked Russia, winning at Borodino in September and reaching Moscow. Thereafter he suffered his worst defeat as his army disintegrated through supply problems, disease, Russian attacks, and finally winter. Austria and Prussia rose in revolt, and at Leipzig ('the battle of the Nations') in October 1813 Napoleon was again defeated by a combined Russian-Austrian-Prussian force. In February 1814 Wellington crossed into France from Spain, by March the Prussians had reached Paris, and on 20 April Napoleon abdicated, being exiled to Elba.

The final flourish of the Napoleonic wars was the 'Hundred Days', Napoleon's escape from Elba on 1 March 1815 and return to power in France, which culminated in his decisive defeat by a coalition army under Wellington at *Waterloo on 18 June 1815, and his exile to St Helena. SDB

Barnett, C., *Bonaparte* (New York, 1978); Chandler, D., *The Campaigns of Napoleon* (1966); Duffy, M., *Soldiers, Sugar and Sea Power* (Oxford, 1987); Hall, C. D., *British Strategy in the Napoleonic Wars 1803–1815* (Manchester, 1992); Pimlott, J., *The Guinness History of the British Army* (1994).

Reynolds, Sir Joshua (1723–92). Portrait painter, born in Devon to a scholarly and clerical family. Educated at his father's school, Reynolds showed early skill in drawing and portraiture and by 1743 was in practice on his own. His portraits already included classical allusions which gained him many patrons among the grand tourist gentry. In 1749 he travelled to Europe, spending two years in Italy studying the old masters and making many influential friends. On his return to London his great success allowed him to move in circles of intellect and wealth. Almost every person of note in the second half of the 18th cent. had their portrait painted by Reynolds. In 1764 he formed the Club, whose members included Samuel *Johnson, Edmund *Burke, Oliver *Goldsmith, and Adam *Smith. In 1768, on the founding of the Royal Academy, Reynolds was the obvious choice for president, although the patron, George III, did not like his pictures. In 1769 he was knighted and awarded an honorary doctorate at Oxford. Among Reynolds's finest portraits are those of the courtesan Nelly O'Brien (1760–2), of his fellow-club members Goldsmith (1770), Baretti (1774), and *Gibbon (1780), and the grand painting of *Heathfield, defender of Gibraltar (1788). Between 1769 and 1790 he wrote and delivered an influential series of *Discourses* on art. JC

Rheged, kingdom of. A 6th-cent. British kingdom round the Solway Firth and southern Galloway, its capital was possibly Carlisle. In Roman times the inhabitants of the area had been the Novantae. Its best-known ruler, Urien, much praised by *Taliesin, was said to have attacked the *Bernicians *c.*580 and to have been killed some ten years later besieging *Bamburgh. Rheged disappeared in the 7th cent., but *Oswui's first wife was said to have been a descendant of Urien, which might have facilitated a Northumbrian takeover. JAC

Rhodes, Cecil (1853–1902). Imperialist and capitalist, probably in that order. In 1870 Rhodes went to *Natal to help his brother grow cotton, but amassed a huge fortune in diamonds and gold. The early appearance of the heart and lung ailments that were eventually to kill him prompted him to make a series of wills from his 25th year onwards, devoting his money to expanding the British empire, so that eventually it would even reabsorb the USA. On a more practical level he became prime minister of the Cape in 1890; opened up the country north of the Limpopo, modestly naming it *Rhodesia; and was involved in the *Jameson Raid. When he died, his final will provided for a series of scholarships to Oxford open to young colonials, Germans (because of the racial affinity), and Americans (in preparation for re-entry). BJP

Rhodesia was the name given to an irregularly shaped region of southern Africa, bounded by Bechuanaland, the Congo, German east Africa (Tanganyika), and Mozambique, first exploited by *Rhodes's British South Africa Company in the 1890s. In 1964 the northern part became the independent nation of *Zambia, leaving the white minority in Southern Rhodesia (now just plain 'Rhodesia') to mount a rearguard action against black rule, through a 'Unilateral Declaration of Independence'—independence, that is, from British suzerainty—issued in 1965. That caused constant trouble for successive British governments, especially from other *Commonwealth countries, who expected them to put the rebellion down by force. Eventually the native peoples won their own battle, helped by international sanctions; and Rhodesia achieved legal independence as the majority-ruled state of Zimbabwe in 1980. BJP

Rhodri (d. 878), king of Gwynedd, Powys, and Deheubarth (844–78), known as Rhodri Mawr ('the Great'). The son of Merfyn Frych ('the Freckled'), king of *Gwynedd, and Nest of *Powys, Rhodri assembled a dominion that inspired others to attempt the same; the later dynasties of Gwynedd and *Deheubarth were proud of their descent from two of his sons. Rhodri acquired Gwynedd when his father died (844), Powys through his mother and uncle (855), and *Seisyllwg (modern Carmarthenshire and Cardiganshire) after his wife's brother died. He contended with the Vikings, defeating them in battle (856), but 20 years later they forced him into exile. After his return, he was killed by Mercians and his dominion collapsed; it was not forgotten. RAG

Rhuddlan, statute of, 1284. Sometimes known as the statute of Wales, this was in fact a royal ordinance, not issued by Parliament. It was intended to settle the government of Wales after the execution of *Dafydd ap Gruffydd in 1283. English criminal law was to be introduced, under a justice of Snowdon, but Welsh custom and law were to operate in civil proceedings, and especially property matters where partible inheritance was common. Six sheriffdoms were established in Anglesey, Caernarfon, Merioneth, Flint, Carmarthen, and Cardiganshire. The statute was followed in 1301 by the creation of Edward I's son as *prince of Wales. JAC

Rhys ap Gruffydd (1132–97), king of Deheubarth (1155–97), known as 'the Lord Rhys'. The younger son of *Gruffydd ap Rhys, king of *Deheubarth, and Gwenllian, daughter of *Gruffydd ap Cynan, king of *Gwynedd, he married Gwenllian, daughter of *Madog ap Maredudd, king of *Powys. He did not unite the three kingdoms, but after *Owain Gwynedd's death (1170) he was regarded as 'the unconquered head of all Wales'. He helped his brother Maredudd to combat the Anglo-Normans and when Maredudd died (1155) he became king. He acknowledged the overlordship of Henry II (1158), who tried to limit his dominion; but Rhys rebelled and in 1164–5 seized Cardigan and surrounding territory. Henry II respected his power and after Anglo-Norman lords were diverted to Ireland (1169) they came to terms, and Rhys was receptive to Anglo-Norman culture and organization. He rebuilt Cardigan and Dinefwr castles, extended his power in *Dyfed, exploited his resources effectively, and encouraged the new religious orders; he even held an *eisteddfod at Cardigan (1176) and may have codified Welsh law. Richard I was less sympathetic and hostilities marred the years before Rhys's death on 28 April 1197 (and burial in St David's cathedral). In the hands of his quarrelsome sons, his kingdom disintegrated. RAG

Rhys ap Tewdwr (d. 1093), king of *Deheubarth (*c.*1078–93), known later as Rhys the Great. A descendant of *Hywel Dda, he came to power in 1075, though only at the battle of *Mynydd Carn (1081), and with *Gruffydd ap Cynan's aid, did he defeat his rivals and relatives. By then the Norman advances in Wales had begun. William I travelled to St Davids in 1081, probably to assert his authority over Rhys, who may have acknowledged the king's overlordship. Rhys's power was resented by other Welsh rulers, and in 1088 those in Powys forced him into exile in Ireland; the Scandinavians of Dublin helped him to return. He also defeated his rivals in Deheubarth (1091). After William I's death (1087), Rhys tried to stop further Norman incursions, but was killed near Brecon. His son *Gruffydd was taken to Ireland for safety; when he returned, he failed to recreate his father's dominion. RAG

Ribbonmen were members of Irish catholic secret societies between the Napoleonic wars and the rise of the *Fenians. They wore white ribbons in their hats to aid identification at night. The aims of their loosely structured organization were nationalist but vague and they have been compared with the Mafia. JAC

Ricardo, David (1772–1823). Born in London of Dutch parents, Ricardo's career 1793–1814 was as a stockjobber, initially in the family firm. Accruing a reasonable fortune, he bought the country estate of Gatcombe Park in 1814; by 1819 he was elected member of Parliament. Much of his time was devoted to the study of mathematics, sciences, and political economy; this led to *On Principles of Political Economy and Taxation* (1817), where the influence of Adam *Smith's *Wealth of Nations* is to be seen. His work was highly significant, with great originality in theoretical economics across a broad subject area, covering the theory of value and distribution and particularly the law of rent. He is credited also with the theory of comparative advantage which proposed international specialization in traded products and was the foundation of the *free trade argument. JRP

Rich, St Edmund (*c.*1170–1240). Archbishop of Canterbury. Born at Abingdon, he studied at Oxford and Paris where he was a renowned teacher of logic (*c.*1185–90). A 'saintly man of courage and candour', he was an ascetic, though remaining a secular. While treasurer of Salisbury (*c.*1222–34) Rich preached the crusade at the pope's request (*c.*1227). As primate (from 1234), he maintained *Langton's ideals by resisting both royal and papal power. He threatened to excommunicate Henry III for not dismissing his ministers and rebuked him for inviting Otto, papal legate, into England (1237). Differences with king, papacy, and his Canterbury monks were such (1240) that he retired to Pontigny, where he died. His 'brief . . . poignant and dramatic' primacy was lived out in the thick of controversy, but after his death his memory was treasured by all, kings and friars, rich and poor. He was canonized (1247) and his shrine at Pontigny visited by Henry III and Edward I. WMM

Richard I (1157–99), king of England (1189–99). Richard has attracted legends and romance in a way that bees are proverbially attracted to the honey-pot. The process began in his own lifetime. Already, by 1199, the epithet Cœur de Lion/Lionheart was being applied, and within another 50 years certain episodes in his life, still fondly retained today, had taken on a legendary significance. The legend and myth-making has continued ever since with inevitable distortions and misunderstandings of the historical Richard.

In the popular imagination today, so far as his reputation remains, Richard is a national English hero, the valorous warrior and glorious crusader who struggled against all the odds (and especially the treacherous French) to come within an ace of recapturing Jerusalem from the equally legendary Saladin on the Third Crusade. On returning from crusade, he was shipwrecked and captured by Duke Leopold of Austria, who shamelessly sold him on to Emperor Henry VI. This allowed John, Richard's evil brother, to scheme with Philip II of France. But Richard so impressed his imperial captor by his courtesy, dignity, bearing, and self-possession that he was soon released—to turn the tables on his enemies at home. The massive bronze statue of Richard in Westminster Palace Yard, between the abbey and the Houses of Parliament, captures superbly the Ricardian qualities admired for centuries. A powerfully muscular Richard, imposing and magnificent, sits on horseback, in full armour and wearing a crown, his sword triumphantly raised aloft. Significantly, the statue lies at a symbolic centre of English history; no less significantly, it was first displayed at the *Great Exhibition (1851).

Yet English Richard was not, nor even Anglo-Norman. Although born in Oxford, he briefly visited England just twice before his accession in 1189. As king, he spent a mere six months in England. He was born of French parents, Henry II and Eleanor of Aquitaine, and only from Edith (*Matilda), his great-grandmother, wife of King Henry I, did he derive any 'English' blood. Richard spoke no English; his vernacular tongue was the French of Poitou, in which he composed troubadour poetry. He willed his body for burial in Fontevraud abbey (Poitou), his heart for interment in Rouen cathedral (Normandy). He was French through and through.

Yet despite this, most modern historians have judged him from an Anglocentric viewpoint. He might have been a warrior second to none, they argue, but he was an utterly irresponsible king of England, who plundered English wealth in pursuit of his own glory in France and the Holy Land, and who recklessly endangered the security and stability of his island realm. In lighter vein, but just as telling, are the words of Sellar and Yeatman: 'he went roaring about the Desert making ferocious attacks on the Saladins and the Paladins, and was thus a very romantic king. Whenever he returned to England he always set out again immediately for the Mediterranean and was therefore known as Richard Gare de Lyon.'

Since 1948 another legend has grown up. This was when J. H. Harvey, in his book *The Plantagenets*, sought to prove that Richard was homosexual. His claims have come to be widely accepted, and it is as a homosexual that Richard appears in many modern novels, films, and plays, and even in *Encyclopaedia Britannica*. Gillingham has effectively demolished Harvey's claims, but, as with so many legends concerning Richard, this one has taken deep root.

Modern scholarship is at last beginning to reveal another Richard, one free from the excessive adulation or denunciation of the past, more balanced and credible. This has only become possible by considering him as *not* first and foremost an English king, but rather the lord of the French-based *Angevin empire which he inherited as a whole in 1189; by allowing for the international pull of the crusade and the duty to participate therein, an imperative acknowledged by contemporary western princes; and by examining carefully Richard's political and diplomatic skills. His military reputation remains intact. Indeed, it has been enhanced. The inspired battlefield commander of tradition, and brilliant tactician—as evidenced, for example, by the march from *Acre to Jaffa and the battle of *Arsuf (1191)—is also coming increasingly to be seen as a master of planning and logistics. His crusade, in particular, involving the raising, fitting out, and dispatch of a fleet from northern waters to the east Mediterranean, is a superb example of administrative efficiency. His campaigns in France on his return, to undo the damage wrought by his treacherous brother John in concert with Philip II, reveal not just military competence of the highest order, but also a very sure sense of strategy backed up by effective diplomacy. For Richard set about constructing an international coalition against Philip, designed to enable him to concentrate on the struggle in the crucial heartland of the Angevin empire.

It has also become apparent that had Richard not been shipwrecked and captured, he would have returned home to find the governmental structure of the Angevin empire intact as he had established it before departure for the crusade in 1190. Far from setting out on crusade without a care for the security and stability of his various dominions, England included—one of the traditional charges against him—Richard did what he could in the short time available to him.

Of course Richard had his faults. But there now seems little doubt that he was in fact one of the ablest men to have sat on the throne of England. SL

Gillingham, J. B., *Richard the Lionheart* (2nd edn. 1989); id., *Richard Coeur de Lion: Kingship, Chivalry and War in the Twelfth Century* (1994).

Richard II (1367–1400), king of England (1377–99). Richard's failures have attracted more interest than the successes of greater rulers. His reign was characterized by aristocratic opposition and political ineptitude.

Richard became king in 1377 aged 9. There was no formal regency, but the government during his early years was dominated by his uncle *John of Gaunt. The French war was going badly, and royal finances were in an unsatisfactory state. The imposition of the third *poll tax was a major cause of the outbreak of the *Peasants' Revolt in 1381; this was the occasion of Richard's first independent political action, when he faced the rebels at Smithfield, witnessed the slaying of Wat *Tyler, and saved the situation by his own intervention. The king's subsequent moves to play a greater political role led to escalating crises. In 1386 the chancellor, Michael de la *Pole, was impeached; Richard infuriated Parliament by declaring that he would not dismiss even a kitchen boy at its request. He provocatively appointed his favourite, Robert de Vere, earl of *Oxford, to be duke of Ireland.

There has been much debate whether Richard had high, possibly novel, concepts of the nature of monarchy. In the summer of 1387 he asked the justices questions about the constitutional position and the right of Parliament to act as it had done in 1386, which suggests that he was very conscious of the problems he faced. The issues were settled less by legal argument than by force, for the defeat of de Vere at *Radcot Bridge in the autumn of 1387 left Richard defenceless in the face of his aristocratic opponents. He may even have been deposed for a brief period after Christmas 1387, until his opponents fell out over the question of who should replace him. The so-called *Merciless Parliament of 1388 conducted a purge of government, using the weapons of appeal and impeachment against a range of royal ministers and favourites, including de la Pole and de Vere. Richard was clearly deeply angered by what took place, considering that his opponents had acted treasonably. His desire for revenge provides one explanation for some of the later events of the reign.

The return of John of Gaunt from Spain in 1389 brought a renewed sense of purpose and direction to government, although relations between John and the king were not always easy. The work of the Merciless Parliament was undone, as far as was possible, in 1389, and Richard wisely did not revert to the excesses which had led to crisis in 1387. He was prepared to allow some control of affairs by the council; the regime was relatively financially stable, and significant efforts were made to deal with problems of lawlessness. There was barely any overt opposition to Richard between 1388 and 1397, although from 1393 discontent began to develop once again, partly as a result of hostility to the king's policy of negotiating a peace with France, and also because of resistance to his plans for re-establishing strong English rule in Ireland. In 1397 the refusal of the earls of *Gloucester and Arundel to attend a council made their displeasure at royal policy all too evident, and the final crisis of the reign began.

In September 1397 Richard moved against those he regarded as his enemies in a carefully managed Parliament, at which the threatening presence of his Cheshire archers ensured that all would go his way. Archbishop *Arundel was impeached and exiled. Royalist magnates brought appeals against the earls of Gloucester, Arundel, and Warwick. Arundel was executed, Warwick exiled, and Gloucester almost certainly murdered. Forfeited lands were granted out to Richard's supporters, and five new dukes created. The Arundel lands in north Wales were combined with the earldom of Chester, and a powerful new principality and royal power base was created. Charters were extracted at Shrewsbury early in 1398 from representatives of the southern counties, giving the king virtually unlimited powers. The grant of the principal customs revenues for life in 1398 gave Richard's regime new financial strength. The 1397 Parliament had dealt with the senior appellants of 1388; in 1398 a dispute between Henry Bolingbroke, duke of Hereford (John of Gaunt's son, later Henry IV), and the duke of *Norfolk led to the exiling of the two men, after Richard prohibited a judicial duel between them at Coventry. In March 1399 Bolingbroke's Lancastrian inheritance was confiscated. In May the king embarked on a new expedition to Ireland. This was a disastrous move for, in June, Bolingbroke, now duke of Lancaster after his father's death, invaded England. In the king's absence, there was little resistance. On his return from Ireland, Richard was taken in north Wales, and on 30 September, a broken man, he agreed to abdicate, and was deposed in Parliament. Since 1397 his regime had been narrowly based, with men such as the knights Bushy, Bagot, and Green playing a dominant part. Government was conducted by means of threats and fear, with a high-handed use of legal form. Richard certainly thought the law should be on his side. Suggestions that he had an elevated and clearly articulated theory of royal government are not convincing; arguments which see Richard as reacting to the humiliations he had suffered during the years up to 1388 are more plausible. Richard did not long survive his deposition; he died at Pontefract, probably early in 1400. MCP

Steel, A., *Richard II* (Cambridge, 1941); Tuck, J. A., *Richard II and the English Nobility* (1973).

Richard III (1452–85), king of England (1483–5). Richard is one of England's most controversial figures, immortalized as evil personified by *Shakespeare, sanctified by a society dedicated to clearing his name. Born at Fotheringhay (Northants), he was the youngest son of Richard of *York and Cecily Neville. He was still a child when his brother Edward IV became king. He entered the political world in 1469 in the midst of crisis. Stalwartly loyal to his brother, he shared in the triumph of 1471, distinguishing himself on the field of *Barnet. He was handsomely rewarded by Edward IV who granted him the Neville estates and royal offices in the north of England. With these, and *Warwick's daughter *Anne as his duchess, he made himself even more powerful in the north than the Kingmaker. In 1480 he led the war against Scotland, secured the recovery of Berwick in 1482, and was rewarded early in 1483 with the grant of a county palatine in Cumberland.

In April 1483 Richard's future was put in doubt by the death of his brother. By a series of palace coups, he seized power, first at the end of April to secure himself as protector of the realm in the minority of his nephew Edward V and secondly in June to make himself king. He was crowned on 6 July. In September his enemies in the southern counties raised rebellion in the name of Henry Tudor. Even though they were joined by the duke of *Buckingham they were easily dispersed. Richard reigned for two further years in a climate of intensifying crisis as, with French support, Henry Tudor planned to invade England. The two finally came to blows on 22 August 1485 near Bosworth in Leicestershire. Although he fought courageously, Richard was overwhelmed and killed in the mêlée. He was buried at the Greyfriars, Leicester. Fifty years later, when the friary was dissolved, his remains were discarded.

Almost every aspect of Richard's dramatic career is controversial. Loyal to Edward IV before 1483, he is seen by many to have devoted his energies to the well-being of the north. But it has also been argued that he was single-mindedly pursuing his own aggrandizement. The coup of 1483 is interpreted as justifiable self-preservation, or a calculated and skilfully executed usurpation, or a sequence of ill-considered impulsive reactions. Some maintain he was shocked to discover his nephews were bastards; others that he made up the story to justify his usurpation. His reign has been seen alternatively as a valiant attempt to administer justice impartially, or as tyranny in which his northern retainers occupied the south. On the one hand he was genuinely pious, on the other hand he was a cynical hypocrite. Even Bosworth does not escape dispute: was he betrayed or was the battle lost by his own folly?

But above all looms the controversy over his crimes. He is probably to be found not guilty of the murder of *Edward at Tewkesbury, of manipulating the destruction of *Clarence, of poisoning his queen; probably a party to the murder of Henry VI; and not proven on the princes in the Tower. Henry VII and the duke of Buckingham have been proposed as alternative culprits. Yet the fact remains that the boys were widely believed to be dead by the middle of September 1483 and Richard himself was believed by contemporaries to have been responsible. This perception that he had destroyed innocent children may have had a bearing on his failure to hold the throne.

It is almost impossible to get to the bottom of all these controversies; partly because insufficient evidence has survived; partly because so much is coloured by propaganda (that put out by Richard himself as much as that generated by Henry VII); partly because he divided opinion sharply in his day; and partly because over 500 years the stories of Richard III have taken on their own independent life. Thus Richard III has become a literary figure. This was so from the very beginning, for the supposed peculiarities of his birth and the hunchback, for which he is renowned, were but inventions to signify evil. Indeed were it not for the fascination of the stories, the only failed usurper of the 15th cent., who reigned but for two years and a bit, would have scarcely troubled the scorers. AJP

Horrox, R. E., *Richard III* (Cambridge, 1989); Pollard, A. J., *Richard III and the Princes in the Tower* (Stroud, 1991); Ross, C. D., *Richard III* (1981).

Richard, earl of Cornwall (1209–72), king of the Romans (1257–72). The younger brother of Henry III, he was granted vast estates by his brother, notably the earldom of Cornwall (with its tin-mines), which made him the richest man in England after the king, who frequently turned to Richard for loans. Although he exerted great influence over Henry, and at times of crisis dominated his policies, he was by no means always in agreement with his brother. In particular, he led the baronial opposition to Henry in the late 1230s. But he remained solidly loyal in the years of baronial reform and rebellion (1258–65), for his pains suffering the indignity of being captured in a windmill, after the battle of *Lewes (1264). In 1257 he was elected king of Germany, the only Englishman to wear that crown, but he never fully established his authority over the country before his death. SL

Richard de Bury (1281–1345). Bishop of Durham. From Bury St Edmunds, Richard studied at Oxford and became a Benedictine monk at Durham. He was appointed tutor to Prince Edward and, after his succession in 1327 as Edward III, was given great preferment. In 1333 he was made bishop of Durham and in 1334–5 was chancellor. A patron of learning, he was said to have more books than all the other bishops combined. His own treatise *Philobiblon*, a guide to library practice, was first printed in 1473. He endowed a library at Oxford attached to Durham College, laying down careful rules for its management. After the Reformation, the college was absorbed into Trinity College. JAC

Richard of Chichester (*c.*1197–1253). Bishop of Chichester. Born of an ordinary family at Wych (Droitwich), he studied in poverty at all three famous European *studia*, Oxford, where he became chancellor (1235), Paris, and Bologna. One of an outstanding group of dedicated 13th-cent. men led by *Grosseteste, he belonged to Edmund *Rich's household, went into exile with him, and was present at his death. In spite of Henry III's opposition, he became bishop of Chichester in 1245 by the active support of Archbishop Boniface and Pope Innocent IV, by whom he was consecrated at Lyons. A saintly man, he showed 'immense pastoral concern' for his diocese and raised clerical standards. He was canonized in 1262. WMM

Richardson, Samuel (1689–1761). Novelist. Born in Derbyshire, Richardson settled in London and became a master printer. His first novel *Pamela or Virtue Rewarded* (1740–2) was published when he was 51. *Clarissa Harlowe* and *Sir Charles Grandison* followed in 1744 and 1753. They were instant successes. They dealt with the manners and morals of relatively ordinary people attempting to survive in a naughty world with some degree of happiness and self-respect. They were salacious enough to make excellent reading. As such they caught a taste for a contemporary interest in manners and morals started by *Addison and *Steele's *Tatler* and *Spectator*. They established the value of epistolary writing as a vehicle for fiction. Richardson was much read in France where Marivaux had already established sentimental fiction; Rousseau's *Nouvelle Héloïse* is indebted to him. Such literature provided endless material for speculation by philosophers interested in the workings of the sentiments and the formation of the human personality. NTP

Richborough, site of the Claudian invasion, major port, and supply base, was later a fort of the *Saxon Shore. Lying at the southern entrance to the Wantsum channel between the mainland and the Isle of Thanet, Richborough was the site of the Roman invasion in 43. Excavation in the 1930s revealed the double ditches and a gate of the beachhead defences. In the Flavian period a monumental four-way arch commemorated the acquisition of Britain. In the later 1st and 2nd cents. Rutupiae was a cross-channel port and a major military supply base. In the mid-3rd cent. the arch base was surrounded by triple-ditched earthwork defences. These were replaced in the later 3rd cent. by the stone defences of a square 8-acre fort of late Roman type. In the *Notitia dignitatum* the garrison is listed as *legio II Augusta*. The fort probably had a church in its north-western corner. A civil settlement with possible amphitheatre lay to the south. ASEC

Richmond castle (Yorks.) was the centre in the Middle Ages of the great honour of Richmond. The lands which made up the honour were held before the Norman invasion by Edwin, earl of Mercia, who seems to have retained them until 1068 when he rose in revolt. The honour was then granted to Alan the Red, son of Eudes, count of Penthièvre, who was related to the dukes of Brittany. This connection meant that his successors to the honour were often subjects of both the kings of England and of France, which in the disturbed relations between the kingdoms in the Middle Ages often meant that the honour was forfeit to the crown. The centres of the Anglo-Saxon estate were at Gilling and Catterick, but Earl Alan seems to have preferred Richmond as the site for his castle, which is a naturally strong one, and building started in the 1070s. This castle is of 'ringwork' type, with the domestic range, of which the 11th-cent. Scolland's hall survives, placed above the river cliff opposite the gate. The defences of the castle were strengthened during Henry II's reign by the addition of a keep, built over the original gate passage. LR

Richmond palace began as a manor house at Sheen (Surrey) and was much used by Edward III, who died there. Henry V restored it and, after a disastrous fire in 1497, Henry VII rebuilt it on the grand scale, giving it his own title of Richmond. Mary used it frequently and Elizabeth died there, but during the civil wars it fell into decay. Only the lodge remained, used in the 18th cent. by George II and Caroline, *Frederick and Augusta, and George III and Charlotte. Ambitious plans by George III to build a new Gothic palace, employing James Wyatt, were abandoned after his death. The present Kew palace, built privately in 1631, was known as the Dutch House. It was used as a royal nursery and private retreat and Charlotte died there in 1818. JAC

riding is a term indicating a third part. By 1086 Yorkshire was divided into North, West, and East Ridings, all three converging on York. The arrangement may well be of Scandinavian origin. For a time ridings had courts; their jurisdiction is uncertain. It appears that in the 11th cent. the term was also applied to the divisions of Lincolnshire: Lindsey, Holland, and Kesteven. Furthermore, medieval Lindsey was divided into North, South, and West Ridings. The Yorkshire ridings became independent counties by the Act of 1888; the arrangements being much altered by local government legislation of 1972 and 1996. JCa

Ridley, Nicholas (*c.*1500–55). One of the celebrated 'Oxford martyrs', Ridley played a significant role in shaping the protestant Church of England under Edward VI. A Northumbrian by birth, he studied at Newcastle, Cambridge, Paris, and Louvain, and around 1524 became a fellow of Pembroke College, Cambridge. In 1537 Archbishop *Cranmer chose him as a chaplain; in 1540 he returned to Pembroke as master. Soon after the accession of Edward VI, he was made bishop of Rochester. He played a role in the drafting of the first, moderate but controversial 1549 version of the *Book of Common Prayer. In 1550 he was translated to London when the then bishop, the staunchly catholic Edmund *Bonner, was deposed and imprisoned. At London he introduced some of the explicitly protestant liturgical innovations which were adopted nationally in the second Book of Common Prayer (1552). He was implicated in the duke of *Northumberland's plot to divert the succession to Lady Jane *Grey; however, it was for heresy rather than treason that Mary I pursued him. Ranged against catholic antagonists at the Oxford disputation of 1554, he defended himself ably and bravely. He was degraded on 30 September 1555, and executed by burning at Oxford on 16 October, alongside the former bishop of Worcester, Hugh *Latimer. EC

Ridolfi plot, 1571. Organized by the Italian banker Roberto Ridolfi, this was one of many conspiracies to free Mary, queen of Scots, and promote the catholic cause. Ridolfi was questioned by English authorities in October 1569 but the following year began to plan Mary's escape, with Thomas, duke of *Norfolk, Philip II of Spain, the Spanish ambassador, and the pope. The plot was uncovered by the agents of William Cecil, Lord *Burghley, and led to the execution of Norfolk for treason in 1572. Ridolfi escaped. SA

Rievaulx abbey (Yorks.) was founded in 1131 in the Rie valley by Walter Espec, lord of nearby Helmsley, in consultation with St Bernard, abbot of Clairvaux, and Archbishop *Thurstan of York. It was the second *Cistercian abbey to be established in England. Under the abbacy of St Ailred, who had joined the abbey as a monk soon after its foundation, it flourished, becoming the largest Cistercian community in England. At Ailred's death (1166) it was said to contain 140 monks. Its lands were concentrated in north Yorkshire and the basis of its economy was pastoral farming, particularly wool production. It attained its greatest prosperity in the first half of the 13th cent. and though it had declined somewhat by the end of the century, it still possessed some 12,000 sheep. However, it was never one of the wealthiest Cistercian abbeys: in 1322 it was sacked by the Scots, a disaster from which it never fully recovered. At the dissolution Rievaulx had a net income of *c.* £278. The extensive ruins of the abbey constitute perhaps the finest surviving buildings of any English Cistercian house, and the east end of the abbey church, rebuilt *c.*1225, is a masterpiece of English Gothic architecture. BJG

Rights of Man, The (Part I 1791; Part II 1792). Thomas *Paine's defence of the principles of the French Revolution against the attack launched by Edmund *Burke in his **Reflections on the Revolution in France* (1790). Part I traced the origins of the Revolution and explicated the Declaration of the Rights of Man made by the National Assembly. Part II denounced the hereditary system, prophesied the immediate overthrow of the monarchy, argued that the only defensible form of government was representative democracy, and sketched the outlines of a system of state welfare. For these views Paine was indicted for treason by the British government, and hurriedly left England for France to take up his seat in the National Convention as the elected member for the *département* of Calais. TSG

Ripon, diocese of. Though the modern bishopric, in north-west Yorkshire, was not carved out of the *York diocese until 1836, Ripon's early ecclesiastical history is inextricably associated with *Wilfrid. About 650 Celtic monks from Melrose and Iona founded a monastery here, but in 661 Wilfrid, by then in Roman orders, became abbot and introduced the Benedictine rule. Consecrated bishop of York while in Gaul and finding on his return that *Chad had already been appointed to York, he initially used Ripon as his seat. On Chad's move to *Lichfield in 669, Wilfrid was restored to York, but for a short spell following 678 Ripon remained a bishopric under Eadhaed. Later, after exile, Wilfrid spent his last days in Ripon, though he held the see of *Hexham from 705 to 709. Growth of industrial population, especially round Leeds, in the 19th cent. led to the creation of the modern diocese, simultaneously with *Manchester. The present cathedral is the former late 12th-cent. Augustinian minster, transitional in style, though the nave is early 16th cent. The Saxon crypt is all that remains of the stone church, built *c.*678 by Wilfrid. WMM

Ripon, George Frederick Robinson, 1st Marquis (1827–1909). Ripon was the son of the 1st earl of Ripon (*Goderich). He was returned to the House of Commons as a Liberal in 1852 but succeeded to his father's title in 1859. He was a loyal *Gladstonite, serving as under-secretary and then secretary of state for war and for India. In 1880, upon Gladstone's re-election, he was appointed viceroy of India to reverse the belligerent Afghan policies of his predecessor, Lord *Lytton. His time in India proved highly controversial among the Anglo-Indian community. He advanced the causes of Indian education and local self-government. He also introduced the notorious Ilbert Bill which attempted to enforce non-racial principles of justice. He retired from India with the defeat of Gladstone's government in 1885 but remained politically active into old age. He was colonial secretary in 1892 and lord privy seal 1905–8. DAW

Ripon, treaty of, 1640. The treaty of Ripon brought to an end the second *Bishops' War between Charles I and the

Scottish *covenanters. The Scottish army occupied Newcastle and in September 1640 the royalist garrison of Edinburgh castle surrendered. Charles had little to negotiate with. By the terms of the armistice, the Scots were left in occupation of the six northern counties and were to receive expenses of £860 a day. The final peace settlement was to be concluded in consultation with the English Parliament. The king had lost control of the situation. JAC

Riot Act, 1715. The Riot Act (1 Geo. I s. 2 c. 5) was hastily passed in July 1715 by a Whig Parliament to deal with the threat of Jacobite insurrection. It provided that, if twelve or more persons, tumultuously assembled, refused to disperse within one hour of a magistrate reading a proclamation, they would be guilty of a felony and could face the death penalty. Persons assisting the dispersal were indemnified. But a secondary motive was to clarify the law of riot, which the case of Dammaree in 1710 had shown to be defective. Daniel Dammaree, a London waterman, had been involved in the *Sacheverell riots and had helped to destroy dissenting meeting houses. He was charged with constructive treason in levying war against the queen. Though found guilty, he had been pardoned, since the interpretation seemed strained. But if the Act was intended to stiffen magistrates, it was a doubtful success. The procedure which became known as 'reading the Riot Act' was difficult to carry out and the proffered indemnities offered little protection: magistrates were reluctant to read the proclamation and troops even more reluctant to open fire. The proclamation was read for the last time in 1919 but the Act was not repealed until 1967. JAC

Ritchie, William (1781–1831). Founder of the **Scotsman*. Ritchie was a solicitor from Fife. In 1817, irritated by the refusal of the Edinburgh papers to print his criticisms of the Royal Infirmary, he joined with Charles Maclaren and others to launch the *Scotsman*. It began as a weekly, became bi-weekly in 1823, and was first issued as a daily in 1855. His elder brother John (1778–1870) began life as a weaver and draper, but took over the paper after William's death and became sole proprietor. JAC

River Idle, battle of the, 616. According to *Bede, *Edwin, young son of Aelle, king of *Deira, was driven out of the kingdom by Æthelfric, king of *Bernicia, and at length took refuge with *Rædwald, king of East Anglia. Rædwald resisted demands by *Æthelfryth, successor to Æthelfric, to surrender Edwin and accompanied him to the river Idle, west of Gainsborough, where they won a great victory. Edwin took both Deira and Bernicia and the united *Northumbria made a vigorous effort at domination, Edwin claiming the *bretwalda-ship. JAC

River Plate, battle of the, 1939. A German 'pocket battleship', *Graf Spee*, heavily armoured, with 11-inch guns, sinking British merchant ships in the South Atlantic, was attacked on 13 December 1939 by three British cruisers, *Exeter* (8-inch guns), *Ajax*, and *Achilles* (both 6-inch guns). Though putting *Exeter* out of action, *Graf Spee* withdrew to Montevideo in the Plate estuary. Captain Langsdorff then blew up and sank *Graf Spee* rather than fight the superior British force he expected and shot himself. Early in 1940 HMS *Cossack* entered Norwegian waters and liberated merchant seamen taken prisoner by the *Graf Spee* and transferred to the *Altmark*. British confidence in the skill and daring of the Royal Navy was confirmed. RACP

rivers. In the late 20th cent. motorways stride so effortlessly across great rivers that it is easy to overlook the part they have played in British history. We can distinguish a number of different aspects.

(*a*) They were potentially defensible barriers and often formed the boundaries between early kingdoms or later shires. When *Ostorius set out to subdue Britain, he conquered, according to *Tacitus, the heartland between Severn and Trent. For centuries the Trent and the Humber were the border between north and south England; and the border between England and Scotland, which fluctuated considerably, eventually settled on the Tweed. The Severn, likewise, was at one time the border between England and Wales, until the English pushed it west to the Wye. In the south, the Thames was the effective border between Mercia and Wessex, and neither side found it easy to consolidate gains across the river. Even small rivers were important markers. When *Alfred divided the kingdom at *Wedmore in 878 with the Danish leader *Guthrum, they took the lands east and west of the river Lea. When England was divided up into shires in the 11th cent. rivers were frequently the boundaries—the Tamar, Somerset Avon, Colne, Stour, Ouse, Welland, Dove, Teme, Tyne, Tees, and Mersey.

(*b*) Loops and angles of rivers often provided the opportunity for a defensible settlement. The most spectacular example is perhaps at Durham, where the river Wear curls round the rocky promontory on which castle and cathedral are built. But there are many others. Shrewsbury is on a loop of the Severn; Bristol grew where the Frome joined the Avon, York where the Foss joined the Ouse; Malmesbury where the Tetbury and Sherston branches of the Avon converged.

(*c*) River crossings, by ford or bridge, were of critical importance in both peace and war. They were the natural sites for castles—at Worcester, Oxford, Hereford, Bedford, Cambridge, Carlisle—and the stream of carts and horsemen invited taverns and inns, smiths and stables. Ipswich, Exeter, Gloucester, London, Newcastle all grew up at the first point where the river or estuary could be crossed. Many of the battles in British history were fought at or near river crossings—to prevent escapes, cut off reinforcements, or obstruct junctions. Simon de *Montfort was trapped at *Evesham in 1265 in the bend of the Avon; *Thomas of Lancaster was caught at *Boroughbridge in 1322 at the crossing of the Ure; *Percy (Hotspur) in 1403, trying to reach his ally *Glyndŵr in Wales, found that the king had taken possession of the crossing at Shrewsbury; the English Civil War began in 1642 with a cavalry skirmish at Powicke bridge, south of Worcester, on the river Teme.

(*d*) Rivers facilitated communication and, until the introduction of turnpikes and macadamization in the 18th cent., transport by water was quicker and less fraught than by road or footpath. Towns on estuaries which provided harbours—Plymouth, Hull, Southampton—were particularly well placed, but inland navigation was also important. Few great towns were to be found far from rivers. With the development of river improvements and then canals in the 17th and 18th cents., inland ports—Bewdley, Gainsborough, Rotherham, Reading—flourished. The smallest barge had a capacity vastly greater than the sturdiest packhorse. Even small rivers, if improved, could be turned to good use. *Defoe commented in the 1720s that Leominster's prosperity was due to the river Lugg, 'lately made navigable to the very great profit of the trading part of this country, who have now a very great trade for their corn, wool and other products of this place into the river Wye, and from the Wye into the Severn, and so to Bristol'.

(*e*) The water supply, provided that it was not too contaminated, enabled settlements to grow into thriving towns. There can be little doubt that one reason for the abandonment of Old Sarum in the early 13th cent. for Salisbury was that the old borough on its chalk hill (chosen for its defensive strength) had little water, while the new site to the south was at the confluence of the Avon, Nadder, and Bourne.

(*f*) Rivers became valuable sources of power as soon as water-mills were introduced during the 9th cent. By the time of Domesday there were said to be more than 5,000 mills. In the later Middle Ages, power began to be applied to industry, notably to cloth manufacture, first in fulling, then to other processes. This gave a great advantage to areas with good rivers like west Wiltshire, the Cotswolds, and the Yorkshire dales. JAC

Rivers, Anthony Woodville, 2nd Earl (1442–83). The eldest brother of *Elizabeth Woodville, he benefited from the marriage of his sister to Edward IV. He fled into exile with Edward IV in 1470, returning in triumph in 1471. He was thereafter entrusted with the upbringing of the prince of Wales and given extensive power in the principality and marches as the president of the prince's council. Shortly after Edward IV's death, he was seized at Stony Stratford by Richard of Gloucester, whom he had taken to be his ally. On 22 June he was summarily executed at Pontefract. Rivers enjoyed a high reputation among his contemporaries for his chivalry, piety, and learning. After his death he was found to have been wearing a hair shirt. But he was no naïve idealist; he was on the contrary a shrewd and alert politician, outwitted by another. AJP

Rivers, Richard Woodville, 1st Earl (*c.*1410–69). Father of Elizabeth, queen of Edward IV. He was raised to the peerage in 1448 on account of his marriage to *Bedford's wealthy widow. Following distinguished service in France, he remained attached to the Lancastrian court, fighting on the losing side at *Towton. However, he had made his peace with Edward IV by 1463. After his daughter became queen, he rose rapidly in favour, incurring the hatred of the earl of *Warwick. He was one of the first victims when the Kingmaker rebelled in 1469, being killed at *Edgecote Field. AJP

Rizzio, David (*c.*1533–66). Servant of Mary Stuart, brutally murdered in the presence of the pregnant queen by a group of conspirators including Mary's husband *Darnley. Born in Turin, and arriving in Scotland in 1561 in the entourage of the Savoyard ambassador, Rizzio drew Mary's attention through his musicianship, but later acted as her secretary. Contemporary suggestions that he was a papal agent and the father of the queen's unborn child are palpably false. He was the victim of the protestant nobility's growing insecurity and Darnley's search for a scapegoat following the queen's refusal to grant him the crown matrimonial. RAM

roads. Medieval Britain inherited around 10,000 miles of Roman road, combined with an extensive network of trackways following less clearly defined routes. Difficult terrain and hills led to multiple pathways being employed, many still visible to aerial photography, recognized by the statute of *Winchester (1285), which prescribed a 400-foot clear tract for main roads as a preventive to brigands. Such largely 'soft' roads were capable of bearing extensive traffic, including from the 14th cent. enhanced use of carts, their tracks leading to fords and bridges. These, and customary uses, were recorded in place-names, such as Saltersford. Early maps show Britain's trunk roads: *Matthew Paris (*c.*1250) mapped the route from Dover via London to Berwick; and the Gough map (*c.*1360) records around 3,000 miles of roads, 40 per cent on the Roman lines, and the local networks in Yorkshire and Lincolnshire.

From the 16th cent., traffic growth combined with closer definition of property boundaries to channel roads more precisely. Concentrated usage from the 1560s by wagons impacted adversely on this strip, and legislation introduced four days a year of 'statute labour' for all householders (1555, extended to six days in 1563) with their equipment, in place of common obligation, and from 1662 this could be commuted to rates. Continuing pressures after 1600 led to county initiatives to create paved causeways for packhorses, to adopt and erect bridges, and to signpost the way (directed by statute in 1697). Road books began with Ogilby's *Britannia* (1675), and became pocket-sized with Bowen (1720). The increasing employment of vehicles, even in the Pennines, enforced the realignment of roads to less demanding gradients, changes further developed by *turnpikes. Legislation was passed to preserve road surfaces by restricting the size and draft teams of vehicles (1621, 1662, 1741) and the breadth of wheels (1718, 1753). Higher standards of engineering on *Telford or *McAdam principles after 1810 reduced the need for such restraints, but weight-related tolls priced the economical steam carriages available from the later 1820s off the turnpike.

The dualism of road management lasted to 1894, when the parish repair was eliminated: turnpike debts had soared as long-distance traffic was lost to the railways from the late 1830s, but despite some consolidation into unitary trusts—London (1826) and south Wales (1844)—and dissolution by the Local Government Board from 1872, most turnpike trusts lasted until the new county councils (1888), and the last to 1895. By then, road usage had already revived for feeder services to and from railways; into the growing towns; for the safety bicycle after 1880, and steam and motor vehicles. By 1900 as in 1830, there were 120,000 miles of public roads in England and Wales. Rising traffic and the heavy dust created by automobiles led to the improvement of surfaces by tarring from 1904, replacing one environmental hazard with another, as the run-off from roads poisoned fish. The 'Red Flag' and 4 m.p.h. legislation of 1865, intended to restrict road steam locomotives, had restrained all traffic growth, and only in 1896 were speed limits raised to 14 m.p.h. (reduced by the Local Government Board to 12 m.p.h.), raised to 20 m.p.h. in 1903, and abolished outside built-up areas in 1930.

Road use grew rapidly from the mid-1920s, with around 3 million commercial vehicles, motor-cycles, and cars registered in 1938, and the 1930s were a 'golden age' for all but casualties: 120,000 were killed on British roads, 1918–39. The period thus saw the introduction of new speed limits, the driving test, and Hore-Belisha's pedestrian crossings (1934); the transfer to county authorities of responsibility for major roads (1929); and of 4,500 miles of 'trunk' roads to the ministry (1936). Road-building was a favoured object of unemployment relief schemes. The concept of a segregated motorway was discussed, evaluated by a delegation to Germany in 1937, and the London to Birmingham route surveyed (1938). Post-war, passenger miles by road quadrupled between the 1950s and the 1990s, and ton miles of goods rose rather more, with by 1990 more than nine-tenths of all traffic on roads. Their full economic and environmental costs were more slowly appreciated, but the success of roads has made them a central item of the public policy debate in the 1990s. See MOTORWAYS. JCh

Robert I (Robert Bruce) (1274–1329), earl of Carrick (1292–1306), king of Scots as Robert I (1306–29). Grandson of Robert *Bruce, the competitor for the Scottish throne in 1291, Bruce never lost sight of his claim to the throne, but after John *Balliol's enthronement in 1292 had little prospect of attaining it. After John's resignation in 1296, Edward I starkly refused any consideration of the Bruce claim. Despite the Scots' continued loyalty to their deposed king Bruce was deeply involved in the rising of 1297, and continued in resistance even after the defeat at *Falkirk (22 July 1298). He served as joint guardian from 1298 probably to early 1300, and remained on the Scottish side till 1302.

Then however he made his peace with Edward. His position needs to be understood. He still nursed hopes of the crown; but he had little chance in Scotland while Balliol was still being treated as the legitimate sovereign. He was also regularly at odds with the Comyn family who were Balliol's leading supporters. Bruce's desertion certainly reduced the chances of Balliol's restoration; and resistance to Edward collapsed in 1304.

Bruce's next move, the coup of 1306, remains very hard to explain. We know that in 1304 he made a secret pact with Bishop Lamberton of St Andrews, who was to be a future ally. We know also that he tried to negotiate with John *Comyn of Badenoch just before he revolted openly early in 1306, and that the result was a quarrel in which Comyn was murdered. But Bruce's decision to seize the throne was clearly already taken, since his actions after Comyn's death were carefully planned and rapidly executed. Barrow has suggested that Bruce had been biding his time till Edward was close to death, and that in 1306 he judged the time ripe. Events proved him right, though only just.

Bruce was crowned as Robert I on 25 March 1306; but though Edward was sick he was not to be trifled with. Robert himself was defeated at *Methven (19 June 1306) by Edward's newly appointed lieutenant Aymer de *Valence; and, probably in July, at Dalry in Perthshire, by a Scot, John Macdougall of Argyll. Kildrummy castle was captured by Valence in September. Robert's supporters and relatives were hunted down and executed; he himself had to go into hiding.

He reappeared in Ayrshire in the spring of 1307, and Edward I died in July. Edward II had little energy to spare for Scotland for some years, and this enabled Robert to overcome his internal enemies. The power of the Comyns was destroyed at the battle of *Inverurie and in the 'herschip' (harrying) of Buchan that followed. Others, such as the earl of Ross, were won over. The king's brother Edward *Bruce gradually reduced English authority in the south-west, while Robert himself concentrated on the western Highlands and Islands. By 1314, effective English power was limited to Lothian.

The years from 1308 also saw King Robert's grip over government tightened. In a parliament at St Andrews in 1309, declarations were issued in the name of the nobles and the clergy, asserting Robert's right to the throne as the lawful successor of Alexander III, and denouncing the aggression of Edward I in terms which set the pattern of Scottish national propaganda for centuries to come. Robert I was now widely accepted in Scotland as the rightful king. His authority was confirmed by the decisive victory of *Bannockburn (24 June 1314), following on the recapture of Edinburgh and Roxburgh castles earlier in the year. Only Berwick and a few other border strongholds remained in English hands; and the rest of the war was fought by raids into the north of England. Berwick itself was recaptured in 1318.

In the rest of his reign, Robert I showed himself a masterful king. He was willing to be reconciled with his former enemies, and readily accepted the loyal service of those who were willing to submit; those who would not were exiled, but the vast majority of the nobility served him well. His two chief problems were to secure the succession (his lack of a direct male heir till the birth of his son David in 1324 required three successive 'tailzies' (entails) of the crown in the parliaments of 1315, 1318, and 1326); and to secure his recognition by other rulers. He fell foul of the papacy by his refusal to comply with a papal truce in 1317, as a result of which he was eventually excommunicated in 1320. An earlier excommunication for the sacrilegious murder of John Comyn may have been lifted in 1308. That of 1320 was respited as a result of the appeal usually known as the 'declaration of *Arbroath' and its accompanying letters; from then on, the pope was prepared at least to give King Robert his proper title. English recognition was more difficult. Edward II would not concede it; and it came only after his deposition. At last in 1328, by the treaty of *Edinburgh/*Northampton, the English government admitted that

Robert was king, and agreed to a marriage between his heir and a sister of the young Edward III as an earnest of a settled peace between what it recognized were two separate and independent nations.

Robert died, perhaps of leprosy, on 7 June 1329, having secured both his own position and the independence of his country. It was hardly his fault that Edward III overturned the settlement of 1328 only five years later. Robert I did not create the sense of an independent identity for Scotland: that had roots that went back long before the death of Alexander III and the conflicts that followed; but ever since his death, he has been the great hero of the Wars of Independence, the man who foiled Edward I's attempt to assert his authority over Scotland, and who defeated all efforts by Edward II to recover the position which Edward I had lost in 1306. BW

Barrow, G. W. S., *Robert Bruce and the Community of the Realm of Scotland* (3rd edn. Edinburgh, 1988); Duncan, A. A. M., 'The War of the Scots, 1306–1323', *Transactions of the Royal Historical Society*, 6th ser. (1992), 125–51; Nicholson, R., *Scotland: The Later Middle Ages* (Edinburgh, 1974).

Robert II (1316–90), steward of Scotland (1326–71), earl of Strathearn (1357–69 and 1370–1), the first Stewart king of Scots (1371–90). Grandson of Robert I of Scotland and heir presumptive to the throne by the 'tailzie' (entail) of 1318. The birth of a son to Robert I in 1324 left Robert only as heir presumptive failing a direct heir to David II. He was several times king's lieutenant during David's minority and captivity, but showed himself inactive against the English and ineffective in government, admittedly in very difficult circumstances.

Robert was 55 when he eventually succeeded the childless David. For a time he proved more capable than his earlier career would have suggested. Too old to take the field himself, he made good use of the younger nobles, who dominated the borders, to exploit the weakness of English authority during the senility of Edward III and the minority of Richard II. Payment of David's ransom was stopped in 1377; and by the early 1380s most of the lands in English occupation had been recovered. By that time, however, Richard II was emerging as a determined ruler, while Robert II's age was telling. In 1384, as more open war was breaking out, a general council, apparently with his consent, deprived Robert of control of justice, which was given to his son John, earl of Carrick, the future Robert III. He was in turn succeeded in 1388 by the king's second son Robert, earl of Fife, and future duke of *Albany. Robert II died in April 1390, at the age of 74.

The 15th-cent. chronicler Walter Bower stressed the prosperity of Scotland at the time, the maintenance of peace and order, and the fact that Robert left Scotland almost entirely free of English control. Later writers have been less flattering, though it seems that at least till 1384 he was an effective and successful ruler. Unfortunately he left a large number of descendants from his two marriages, and rivalries between the various lines tracing descent from him repeatedly disturbed the peace of Scotland, at least until the death of James I. BW

Robert III (*c.*1337–1406), earl of Carrick (1368–90), king of Scots (1390–1406). Eldest son of Robert, steward of Scotland, later Robert II. His baptismal name was John, but he took the name Robert when he became king. In his own alleged words, Robert III was 'the worst of kings and the most wretched of men!' His reign was marked by disorder and by violent quarrels among his relatives and leading nobles, which the elderly king proved unable to stem.

From 1384, the incapacity of his father left John responsible for the administration of justice; but in 1388 he himself was incapacitated by a kick from a horse, and his brother Robert, earl of Fife, was made guardian, an office which he continued to hold for a year or two after John's accession in 1390 as Robert III. Neither the earl of Fife nor the king himself proved able to contain the flood of disorder and violence, particularly in the north, where Forres was sacked in 1390, and Elgin in 1391 by another of the king's brothers, Alexander, earl of *Buchan, notorious as the 'Wolf of Badenoch'.

Robert was faced in 1398 with a struggle for power between the earl of Fife, created duke of *Albany in that year, and the king's 20-year-old son David, created at the same time duke of Rothesay, and appointed in his turn lieutenant for a period of three years. Rothesay proved energetic, but his energy aroused hostility. In 1402 he was removed from office in a coup evidently organized by Albany and the earl of *Douglas, and died in captivity shortly after. Robert III could do nothing to check the power of these nobles, despite the disastrous result of a battle which they provoked against the English at *Homildon Hill (14 September 1402). In 1406 he tried to send his remaining son James (b. 1394) to safety in France, but he was captured by 'pirates' off Flamborough Head and sent to captivity in England. Robert's death followed almost immediately on the shock of the news. BW

Robert, earl of Gloucester (*c.*1090–1147), was Henry I's favourite from among his many illegitimate sons and was advanced by him to be one of the leading magnates of the Anglo-Norman realm. In 1135 Robert apparently accepted King Stephen's succession, but in 1138 he declared his support for his half-sister *Matilda, and was thereafter the empress's most powerful supporter. His large estates in the west of England and Normandy provided a base for her campaigns. His importance to her cause is illustrated by the way in which he was exchanged in 1142 after his capture at Stockbridge for the captive King Stephen, himself taken at the battle of *Lincoln in 1141, and by the fact that Matilda left England very soon after his death. In 1142 he brought the future Henry II to England for the first time. DB

Robert of Bellême, earl of Shrewsbury (b. *c.*1054). Soldier. The eldest son of one of William the Conqueror's closest aides, Roger of Montgomery, he inherited his father's French estates, including Bellême, in 1094. He was notable for his consistent loyalty to *Robert Curthose, supporting him in 1077 against his father, in 1087–8 against Rufus, and in 1101–6 against Henry I. When Curthose granted Normandy to Rufus for the duration of his crusade, Robert served as one of Rufus' principal commanders, winning a great reputation for his military skill—and possession of the earldom of Shrewsbury, when his own younger brother Hugh died in 1098. But he also became notorious for cruelty and some—though not all—contemporaries seem to have thought that this justified Henry I arresting him in 1112 while under safe conduct and keeping him in prison until he died at an unknown date. JG

Robert Curthose, duke of Normandy (*c.*1050–1134), the eldest son of William the Conqueror, was designated as heir to *Normandy before 1066 and succeeded his father there, despite a series of quarrels and two periods of exile. Any hopes Robert may have had of obtaining England were, however, dashed by his father's death-bed bequest in 1087. Two attempts in 1088 and 1101 to wrest the kingdom from his brothers William II and Henry I failed and in 1106 he was himself ousted from the duchy by Henry after the battle of *Tinchebrai. He was thereafter kept in prison until his death. Contemporary sources portray Robert as brave, but ineffective; a harsh verdict given that his difficulties in Normandy and Maine can be interpreted as the consequence of a reaction against his father's oppressive rule and that his two brothers unquestionably commanded greater resources. His heroic contribution to the First Crusade shows him as a redoubtable warrior capable of prospering in a great military enterprise. His nickname, literally 'Short Boots', is said to have been conferred by his father. DB

Robert of Jumièges (d. *c.*1052). Archbishop. Born in Normandy, Robert Champart became abbot of Jumièges in 1037 and made the acquaintance of the future Edward the Confessor. He followed Edward to England and was made bishop of London in 1044. In great favour with the king, he was hostile to the powerful *Godwine family. In 1051 the king appointed him archbishop of Canterbury, but he was not popular as a Norman, and his attacks upon the Godwines precipitated a sharp crisis. The Godwines were driven into brief exile, but when they returned in strength in 1052, Robert fled to the continent. Though he gained papal support, he was unable to recover his see and *Stigand, an ally of Earl Godwine, was appointed in his place. The inability of the king to save his friend and adviser suggests the power of the Godwine family, and William the Conqueror used Robert's deposition as propaganda in his descent upon England in 1066. JAC

Roberts, Frederick Sleigh (1832–1914). Field marshal. Roberts first demonstrated his talents as an army officer during the Indian mutiny (1857–8). During the second *Afghan War (1878–80) he defeated Ayub Khan's army at the battle of Kandahar and was created baron of Kandahar in 1892. From 1885 to 1893 he was commander-in-chief in India and came to prominence once again during the second Anglo-Boer War (1899–1902). The British forces had suffered several humiliating defeats before Roberts arrived in South Africa to take command, when his strategy led to the capture of the two Boer (Afrikaner) republican capitals, Bloemfontein and Pretoria. Wrongly assuming that all that remained was a straightforward tidying-up operation, Roberts handed over command to his deputy, who was left to conduct a prolonged guerrilla war. Created viscount and then earl in 1901, Roberts served as C.-in-C. of the British army from 1901 to 1904. KI

Robertson, William (1721–93). Historian. Son of a presbyterian minister, educated for the kirk at Edinburgh University, Robertson became the leader of a group of moderate presbyterian clergy who took control of the General Assembly of the kirk in 1752 and dominated its politics until 1805. Their power base lay in the universities and in the support they received from government. Robertson became the greatest of Edinburgh University's principals in 1762; it was under his leadership that the university became the most admired of the enlightened world. His *History of Scotland* (1759), *History of the Reign of Charles V* (1769), and the *History of America* (1777) constituted a vast history of the modern world set in the context of a general history of the progress of civilization, notable for the elegance and sophistication with which Robertson employed the so-called 'conjectural history' of the Scottish Enlightenment as a context for the history of great events. They established Robertson as a historian of the first rank, regarded as the equal of Voltaire and *Hume, and much admired by *Burke and *Gibbon. NTP

Robin Hood. Along with King *Arthur, Robin Hood is one of the most enduring of legendary heroes. In part this is because the details are so vague that the stories can be added to and adapted to the interests of different generations. The early versions emphasized Robin's skill with a bow, the later ones that he robbed the rich to help the poor. Maid Marian, who provides the love interest, was a 16th-cent. addition to the story. The earliest reference is in Langland's *Piers Plowman* (*c.*1377), in which one character remarks that he knows the rhymes of Robin Hood. The earliest detailed written source has been dated to about 1400 and a Scottish source was in existence by 1420. The stories are set in the 1190s, with King Richard away on crusade and his shifty brother John misgoverning the country. Though many genuine references to persons with the correct or similar name have been found, some even outlaws, it is most unlikely that the stories were based on one person. The area of the greenwood is usually taken as Sherwood Forest in Nottinghamshire, or Barnsdale near Wentbridge in Yorkshire, but Barnsdale in Rutland is also a possibility. The many Robin Hood wells and caves are subsequent namings: Robin Hood's Bay, south of Whitby, is first mentioned in 1544. Though authority in the shape of the sheriff is mocked, the satire has been steadily sanitized. In the original versions Robin, though an outlaw, was loyal to Richard and ultimately pardoned. The 16th and 17th cents. promoted him to be the rightful earl of Huntingdon, and the egregious Stukeley in the 18th cent. produced a pedigree, giving him royal blood and tracing his ancestry back to *Waltheof, earl of Northumberland in the 11th cent. The original poems were intended for minstrel performance but plays, novels, films, and cartoons eventually followed. JAC

Robinson, John (1650–1723). Diplomat and bishop of London. A Yorkshireman of humble origins, educated at Brasenose College, Oxford, he became chaplain to the English embassy to Sweden (*c.*1680) while still an Oxford don (1675–86), and, remaining abroad until *c.*1709, won a reputation as a competent envoy to Sweden; he accompanied Charles XII to Narva. Later he was successively dean of Windsor (1709), bishop of Bristol (1710) and of London. As lord privy seal under *Harley (1711) and joint plenipotentiary, he represented Britain at the peace negotiations at *Utrecht (1712–13). Partly responsible for Britain's advantageous terms, he was made bishop of London in 1713. A Tory, but opposed to *Bolingbroke, he backed Harley and the Hanoverian succession. More of a professional diplomat than a cleric, Robinson was the last ecclesiastic to hold high political office. WMM

Robinson Crusoe. This fictional autobiography, published anonymously in 1719 by Daniel *Defoe, has attained the status of myth. Although its indebtedness to the true story of the experiences of Alexander Selkirk has been greatly exaggerated, Crusoe's shipwreck and subsequent desert-island experience is central whether it is approached as traveller's tale, religious allegory, or proto-novel. Modern critics tend to follow Marx in discounting its religious burden, viewing it as an allegory either for the growth of capitalism or of western imperialism. Defoe cashed in on the original's tremendous success, publishing *Farther Adventures* (1719) and *Serious Reflections* (1720). The many imitations are known as *Robinsonades*. JAD

Rochdale Pioneers is the name given to William Cooper, Charles Howarth, and the other 26 founders of the *Co-operative movement, whose retail shop opened in Toad Lane in 1844. They had been encouraged by a lecture from George *Holyoake the previous year on self-help. It began on a very small scale, opened only on Saturday and Monday evenings with the members serving in the shop. The principle on which they acted was that profits should be redistributed to purchasers by means of a dividend. By 1851 there were 130 similar shops and by 1862 450 co-operative enterprises. As the volume of business expanded, the original social, political, and educational objectives were pushed into the background by commercial considerations. JAC

Roches, Peter des (*c.*1175–1238). A cleric from the Touraine, he entered royal service in the 1190s and was rewarded with the bishopric of Winchester in 1205. He remained loyal to the king throughout John's quarrel with the papacy and was appointed *justiciar in 1213 and then guardian of the young Henry III in 1216. He was a key figure in the minority government, his military skill helping to win the 1217 battle of *Lincoln. Ousted by his rival Hubert de *Burgh in 1227, he went on crusade—and did much to enhance his reputation—before returning to England and, for a while (1232–4), regaining his dominant position at court. Although certainly not indifferent to religion, his career priorities laid him open to criticism—'sharp at accounting, slack at scripture' said one satirist. The most prominent of the foreigners active in English politics, labelled 'the Poitevins' by their opponents, Peter was an easy target. JG

Rochester, diocese of. Now comprising west Kent, Rochester is the second oldest English see, founded by King *Æthelbert of Kent in 604, with *Justus as first bishop. *Paulinus, the former missionary to Northumbria, expelled in 632, was bishop of Rochester (635–44). Despite its vulnerability to the 9th-cent. Danish invasions, it survived intact. The diocese consisted only of west Kent until the addition of Essex and most of Hertfordshire from *London in 1845; this proved unsuccessful and they were removed to form the *St Albans diocese in 1877. In compensation Rochester was given eastern and mid-Surrey from *Winchester, which proved equally unsuccessful. In 1905 the Surrey area was taken to form part of the new *Southwark diocese (1905). The medieval bishopric had a small population compared with those of the midlands and north, but in the 19th and 20th cents. it became densely inhabited. Notable bishops include John *Fisher (1504–35), executed with Thomas *More for refusing to recognize Henry VIII's supremacy and later canonized. A noted 18th-cent. bishop was Francis *Atterbury (1713–23), deprived of his bishopric for Jacobite sympathies. The cathedral, alongside the 12th-cent. castle, has an impressive late Norman nave, completed in 1130 with additions (1179–1240). WMM

Rochester, Laurence Hyde, 1st earl of (1642–1711). Laurence Hyde was the second son of the historian and lord chancellor and younger brother of the 2nd earl of *Clarendon, lord privy seal and lord-lieutenant of Ireland in James II's reign. His sister *Anne married the duke of York (later James II) in 1660 and died in 1671. Hyde served in the House of Commons 1660–81, was employed on diplomatic missions, and was made 1st lord of the Treasury 1679–84 (not the post it later became). He was rewarded with a viscountcy in 1681 and an earldom the following year. When James succeeded in 1685, Rochester and Clarendon, brothers-in-law to the king, carried all before them. Rochester was given the Garter, appointed lord president of the council 1684–5, and then lord treasurer. But James dismissed him, though with a generous pension, in 1686 when he refused to convert to catholicism. A fierce high Tory, he accepted William and Mary after the Revolution, was lord-lieutenant of Ireland 1700–3 and lord president of the council again 1710–11. *Burnet thought him 'of far greater parts' than his brother and for years he and *Nottingham were regarded as the pillars of high Toryism. A capable and experienced politician, Rochester was said to be handicapped by a quick temper: 'when he was in a rage,' wrote Macaulay, 'and he very often was in a rage, he swore like a porter.' JAC

Rochester, John Wilmot, 2nd earl of (1647–80). Poet and courtier. Wilmot's father fought for the king in the Civil War, was created a baron in 1643, and advanced to the earldom in 1652. Wilmot inherited the title at the age of 11, spent a year at Wadham College, Oxford, fought as a volunteer in the naval battle off *Lowestoft in 1665, and was appointed a groom of the bedchamber the following year. Sympathizers say that he was then corrupted by the court, but it seems to have had good material to work on. In 1667 he married an heiress, whom he had attempted to abduct. He was a crony of *Buckingham, with a reputation as a wit, debauchee, drunkard, and patron. Some of his poems circulated in manuscript during his lifetime: the collected poems came out in 1680 and 1691. Much of the output is tediously coarse, but there are occasional jewels. His epigram on Charles II is justly famous—'who never said a foolish thing, nor ever did a wise one'. *Johnson, in the *Lives of the Poets*, while deploring Rochester's depravity, praised 'a mind which study might have carried to excellence'. JAC

Rochester castle (Kent) stands above the river Medway whose crossing it controlled. The first castle on the site was an enclosure within the Roman city walls. The present castle, also originally a 'ringwork', was begun by *Gundulf, bishop of Rochester, for William Rufus 1087–9. The castle was transformed by the addition of a tower keep built 1127–40, after Henry I had granted the castle to the archbishop of Canterbury and his successors. The keep, which is 70 feet square and rises to the height of 113 feet to the parapet, was designed to be the defensive heart of the castle and also to contain the best residential accommodation, which is arranged on three floors above a basement. The grandest suite, presumably intended for the archbishop himself, is on the second floor and has its own chapel. The defensive strength of the castle was demonstrated in 1215 when rebel barons held it against King John. The royal forces took the castle only after they managed to dig a mine under the south-east angle tower, which caused the tower to collapse. LR

Rockingham, Charles Watson-Wentworth, 2nd marquis of (1730–82). An often underrated politician, Rockingham contributed significantly to the emergence of a distinct Whig ideology out of the factional politics of the 1760s. Although his two periods as prime minister (1765–6 and 1782) were brief and unhappy, Rockingham achieved a great deal as a party leader, despite a profound aversion to public speaking and recurrent bouts of ill-health. Having held a court appointment from 1751, Rockingham resigned in November 1762 and joined the opposition to Lord *Bute. He was appointed 1st lord of the Treasury in 1765 and successfully orchestrated the repeal of the *Stamp Act in 1766. Rockingham, nevertheless, believed in the necessary subservience of the colonies and repeal was accompanied by a *Declaratory Act, asserting British legislative supremacy. Dismissed in March 1766 because of his continuing suspicions of Bute's influence, he remained in opposition for the next sixteen years. The Bute myth was integral to Rockinghamite ideology in the 1760s, but was gradually transcended by a more sophisticated interpretation which abandoned Bute as the target, but remained focused on secret influence. Rockingham and his followers constantly reiterated that they were the only true Whigs and, by force of repetition, a diffuse and platitudinous term was reclaimed: the Rockinghamites gradually developed a near monopoly of the title 'Whig Party'. This ideology was unashamedly élitist: one central belief was that the country's natural leaders, the Whig aristocracy, had been excluded from power by George III. Much was made of the supposedly increased power of the crown and it was suggested that the political advantages derived from granting places and contracts ought to be reduced. *Economical reform, as this was called, was favoured rather than parliamentary reform. Rockingham was at best ambivalent towards the latter and, upon his regaining office in 1782, economical reform was adjudged sufficient for immediate circumstances. Rockingham's return to power, in the wake of Lord *North's fall, was irresistible, since his party was the largest in opposition. Rockingham insisted on becoming 1st lord of the Treasury, but his premiership was undermined by the king's insistence on cabinet office for *Shelburne, whom Rockingham rightly mistrusted. Ministers were soon at loggerheads and Rockingham's unexpected death in July 1782 may have simply hastened a looming political crisis. Rockingham's party survived his death, led jointly by Charles *Fox and *Portland, confirming that this had become more than just a personal faction. DW

Rockingham, Council of, 1095. This was an important episode in the medieval relations of church and state. *Anselm had become archbishop of Canterbury in 1093 at a time when there were rival popes, Urban II and Clement III. He asked William Rufus for permission to seek the pallium from Urban, and was refused. On 25 February 1095 a council at Rockingham attempted to resolve the question of divided allegiance and urged Anselm to conform to the royal will. Though the conflict was compromised and Rufus recognized Urban, the pope refused to depose Anselm. The archbishop spent the years 1097 to 1100 abroad, returning only after Rufus' sudden death. But his relations with Rufus' successor Henry I were also difficult. JAC

Rodney, George Brydges (1719–92). Admiral. Rodney's family was distantly connected to the fabulously rich and influential James Brydges, duke of Chandos, and this may account for Rodney's rise to a naval captaincy at the age of 23. Yet he was born to straitened circumstances, and a certain resentment in his complex character may not have been helped by a reputed education at Harrow School. Always solicitous towards the concerns of the lower deck, Rodney conspicuously failed in his relations with brother officers, and his ill-starred quest for wealth could prejudice his commands out of a greed for prize money. His service spanned the mid-18th-cent. wars and he became well acquainted with the West Indies theatre; at home he was an assiduous applicant for parliamentary seats. Promotion to rear-admiral in 1759 did not afford future financial security, and during 1775–8 Rodney was effectively bankrupt and self-exiled. Yet the special exigencies of the American War proved his salvation, and with his relief of Gibraltar (1779) and his saving of Jamaica through his defeat of de Grasse at 'the *Saints' on 12 April 1782, Rodney's lasting fame, though significantly not his fortune, was assured. Created a peer, his closing years were dogged by sickness and litigation. DDA

Roe, Richard. One of the fictitious individuals used in the old procedure of ejectment. Ejectment was a writ which developed from trespass *de ejectione firmae* to enable a leaseholder to recover his leasehold land. Since it was speedy and effective, the procedure was attractive to freeholders, who in order to avail themselves of the writ pretended that a lease had been granted to a fictitious individual—John Doe—who became the plaintiff. The defendant's lessee—

also fictitious—would be Richard Roe (or William Styles). The action was abolished in 1852 but these fictitious names are still used in the common law, especially in the USA, to disguise a real litigant. MM

Roebuck, John (1718–94). An entrepreneur and inventor, Roebuck was born in Sheffield, studied in Edinburgh, and took a medical degree at Leiden. His early efforts in Birmingham led to a partnership with Samuel Garbett to produce sulphuric acid. He then set up a factory at Prestonpans to make sulphuric acid, then pottery, and finally cast iron. In 1760 he opened the Carron ironworks near Stirling, using pit-coal rather than charcoal, and specializing in ordnance. For many years Carron was the largest British foundry. Roebuck's later venture into coal-mining proved disastrous, despite collaboration with James *Watt to try to prevent flooding. His grandson was the radical MP John Arthur *Roebuck. JAC

Roebuck, John Arthur (1801–79). Radical MP for Bath (1832–7, 1841–7) and Sheffield (1849–68, 1874–9). Born in Madras, raised in Canada, and qualified as a barrister, Roebuck was nicknamed 'Tear 'Em' for his fierce attacks on aristocracy, privilege, and inefficiency. As a *Benthamite and friend of J. S. *Mill, Roebuck proposed a system of state education, supported the New Poor Law, and helped *Lovett draft the Charter. In 1855 he moved for a committee of inquiry into the conduct of the Crimean War, which resulted in the fall of *Aberdeen's government. From the exposure of military inefficiency, Roebuck went on to campaign for administrative (civil service) reform. He believed in *laissez-faire*, and opposed sabbatarianism, factory legislation, and trade unions. As he grew older, Roebuck became increasingly interested in foreign causes and his radicalism became nationalistic. He advocated overseas colonization and supported the South in the American Civil War. JFCH

Roger (*c.*1065–1139). Bishop of Salisbury. Roger joined the future Henry I's entourage in the 1090s and rose rapidly after Henry seized the English throne in 1100, becoming bishop of Salisbury in 1102. His role was to preside over the administration of the king's English finance and justice. In particular he was closely associated with the development of the accounting techniques of the *Exchequer, which was first referred to in 1109. He was the chief of a small administrative group who supported members of Henry's family, such as Queen *Matilda, when they acted as regents during Henry's lengthy absences in *Normandy, and who operated as itinerant royal justices. Roger was himself regent 1123–6. He remained in office after Henry's death, but in 1139 incurred King Stephen's distrust for reasons which are not entirely clear, and was arrested and deprived of his power. DB

Rogers, John (*c.*1500–55). Martyr. Born in Birmingham and educated at Pembroke College, Cambridge, Rogers took holy orders but became a reformer under the influence of *Tindal, whose English edition of the Bible he prepared for the press. He spent much of his time on the continent and married a Flemish wife. In Edward VI's reign, Rogers was in favour and given London preferments, and immediately after the king's death preached at St Paul's Cross, by order of Lady Jane *Grey's council, warning the people against popery. By January 1554, after Mary had established her claim to the throne, Rogers was in prison and in February 1555 he was burned at Smithfield—the first of the protestant martyrs. The French ambassador wrote that Rogers died with such composure that it might have been a wedding. JAC

Rolls, Charles Stewart (1877–1910). Rolls was the third son of a wealthy Monmouthshire landowner, who served as Conservative MP for Monmouth 1880–5 and was created Lord Llangattock in 1892. He studied mechanical engineering at Trinity College, Cambridge, where he was a bicycling enthusiast. In 1895 he imported a Peugeot car from France and was stopped outside Victoria station by a policeman who pointed out that he needed a man with a red flag to precede him: his journey back to Cambridge took just under 12 hours. In 1900 he won a gold medal for a motor race from London to Edinburgh. In 1905 he joined forces with another engineer, F. H. *Royce, and with Claude Johnson to establish a company producing cars at Derby: the *Motor Trader* warned that 'we cannot help thinking that the promoters have made a very weak appeal to the investing public'. Rolls concentrated on sales and publicity. Greatly interested in aviation, he made many balloon flights, and in June 1910 crossed the Channel and back non-stop in a Wright brothers aeroplane, completing the journey in $1\frac{1}{2}$ hours. The following month he was killed in a flying accident at Bournemouth and buried at Llangattock-Vibon-Avel, near Monmouth. A good statue of Rolls, holding a model aeroplane, stands in Agincourt Square, Monmouth. RAB; JAC

Roman Britain. Britain was the Roman province Britannia, AD 43–410. Although there had been increasing contact between Britain and the classical world during the late Iron Age, the first official Roman presence in Britain was that of Julius *Caesar in 55–54 BC. In AD 43 Emperor *Claudius, desiring the prestige of military triumph, invaded Britain on the pretext of dealing with troublesome tribal princes and druids. The island was subsequently occupied by the Romans who took advantage of Britain's mineral and agricultural wealth. The process of the incorporation of the province into the social and economic systems of the Roman empire is known as 'romanization', and the speed and manner with which the Britons became Romanized is currently the subject of academic debate. For example, the recent discovery that agricultural innovations—tools, techniques, and crops—were at their most significant in Britain in the late Iron Age and the late Roman period is a demonstration of the complexity of such patterns of cultural development.

Within a generation the British landscape had changed considerably. The Roman army built legionary fortresses, forts, camps, and roads, and assisted with the construction of buildings in towns. A number of important military installations, notably the legionary fortresses, were built close to pre-existing tribal centres (*oppida*) which then became the focus of important Romano-British towns, such as

*Colchester. The earliest phases of towns, dating to the mid-1st cent., reveal timber strip buildings—houses and shops—as well as stone public buildings such as Roman temples and administrative headquarters. The Romans also brought their particular style of architecture to the countryside in the form of *villas. Some very large early villas are known, such as Eccles in Kent and *Fishbourne in Sussex. The latter is often assumed to be the palace of the pro-Roman British king *Cogidubnus, although this is impossible to prove.

*Tacitus tells us that the Romans experienced a number of tribal revolts in the 1st cent. and used the long-established practice of combining treaties with decisive military action to quell unrest. Rome created three client kingdoms: the *Iceni, the *Brigantes, and the *Atrebates. In AD 60 the Iceni rose up under the leadership of *Boudicca, destroying the Roman towns of Colchester, London, and St Albans. The crushing of the Boudiccan revolt was followed by a period of expansion of the Roman province, including the subjugation of south Wales. Between AD 77 and 83 the new governor *Agricola led a series of campaigns which enlarged the province significantly, taking in all Wales, Anglesey, northern England, and southern Scotland. Agricola was however recalled by the Emperor Domitian and subsequently Roman military attention was turned to the Danube; as a result Roman troops were withdrawn from Scotland. Rome thus lost its chance to conquer the whole of the island of Britain, and the 'natural' northern border of Roman Britain was apparently seen as the Tyne–Solway isthmus.

There has been much debate about the date of the introduction of a 'true' money economy into Roman Britain. It is now generally accepted that although the Roman troops brought their cash wages and purchasing power with them into Britain, they did not change the socially embedded economic structures of Britain overnight. However, by the late 1st/early 2nd cents. AD the imposition of taxation and the increasing availability of and desire for Roman consumer goods—such as imported fine ware pottery—led to a wide-scale use of coins as currency, even on the humbler farmsteads of the province where the majority of the native population lived.

The 2nd cent. also saw important military and urban developments, particularly under the Emperor *Hadrian. He visited Britain following military disturbances, and in AD 122 ordered the construction of *Hadrian's Wall between the Tyne and the Solway. It was built ostensibly to separate the Roman province from the barbarian north, but probably also acted as an effective customs barrier and a visual testament to the power of Rome. In AD 139–42 the Emperor Antoninus Pius abandoned Hadrian's Wall and constructed a new frontier defence system between the Forth and the Clyde—the *Antonine Wall—but its use was short-lived and Hadrian's Wall was again the main northern frontier by AD 164.

Roman towns fell into one of three main types: *coloniae*, *municipia*, and *civitates*. The *coloniae* of Roman Britain were Colchester, *Lincoln, *Gloucester, *York, and possibly *London, and their inhabitants were Roman citizens. The only certain *municipium* was *Verulamium (St Albans), a self-governing community with certain legal privileges. The *civitates*, towns of non-citizens, included the bulk of Britain's administrative centres, such as the tribal capitals of *Silchester, *Winchester, and *Canterbury. Roman towns were grid-planned and their character created by a combination of official Roman involvement and acts of public munificence by wealthy locals desirous of increasing their chances of attaining public office. Towns usually contained temples, public baths, aqueducts, and an amphitheatre, most acquiring such a range of facilities by the mid-2nd cent.

On the evidence of the relative quantities of inscriptions associated with the construction of public buildings, it has been mooted that whereas towns flourished in 2nd-cent. Britain the 3rd cent. saw a decline in their fortunes. Such negative evidence must however be interpreted carefully. The 3rd cent. may well have been simply a period of consolidation after a long period of growth. During the 2nd and the 3rd cents. larger and more elaborate town houses appeared, probably inhabited by the indigenous urban élite. Urban earthworks of the 2nd and 3rd cents. were often adorned with elaborate stone gateways and external towers and represent a substantial investment of resources in the development of defences which would have been a symbol of civic pride.

By the 4th cent. the towns were dominated by stone-built 'mansions', and there were also profound changes in the countryside. Villas grew in size and became more enclosed, exemplified by 'courtyard villas' such as *Chedworth. It was in the early 4th cent. that the majority of British villas were embellished with their mosaics, an apparent investment in the agricultural basis of the province's wealth in this period.

The impression of the religious life of the province is one of complexity and harmony. Romans and incomers from other provinces introduced their own religious customs, such as the worship of Isis and Bacchus, without destroying indigenous Celtic beliefs. This religious integration was facilitated by fundamental similarities between Celtic and classical cults. The evidence for Christianity in Roman Britain reflects this amalgam of beliefs; the great 4th-cent. silver hoards from Mildenhall, *Canterbury, Traprain Law, and *Corbridge all combine pagan and Christian motifs.

Epigraphic and literary evidence suggests that the Britons adopted Latinized names (e.g. Tiberius Claudius Cogidubnus) and that the élite (at least) spoke and wrote Latin. The indigenous Gaelic or 'Celtic' language of the Roman province Britannia also continued to be spoken; it survives today as Welsh and Cornish.

The end of Roman Britain followed a protracted series of empire-wide crises, and in particular barbarian raids and settlements in north-western Europe such as the 'Picts' War' of AD 367–8. In AD 401–2 troops were withdrawn from Britain by Stilicho to defend Italy, and in AD 408–9 Britain was attacked by Saxons. In AD 410 the Emperor Honorius told the cities of Britain to look to their own defence.

The year AD 410 does not however mark a sudden and dislocating end to Roman Britain. The reported accounts of contemporary figures such as St *Patrick and St *Germanus, coupled with archaeological evidence from sites such as the Roman town of *Wroxeter, suggest strongly that Romanized life in Britain continued well into the 5th cent. ES

Frere, S., *Britannia: A History of Roman Britain* (3rd edn. 1987); Millett, M., *Roman Britain* (1995); Potter, T. W., and Johns, C., *Roman Britain* (1992).

Roman catholicism. See CATHOLICISM.

Romanesque architecture. See NORMAN ARCHITECTURE.

Roman legions formed the core of the Roman army. Each legion of heavily armed infantry consisted of some 5,000 Roman citizen men. The legionary soldier was recruited aged 18–20 for a period of 25 years. Good promotion prospects and a pension of a land grant ensured a constant supply of recruits. The rest of the army—infantry and cavalry—was made up of auxiliaries (the *auxilia*, or 'aids') who did not have to be Roman citizens. Auxiliaries were sometimes provincial specialists, such as the famed Syrian archers.

The legions which invaded Britain in AD 43 under the command of *Aulus Plautius were the *II Augusta*, *IX Hispana*, *XIV Gemina*, and *XX Valeria*. With auxiliaries, the force totalled some 40,000 men. The *II Adiutrix* replaced the *XIV Gemina* during a major reorganization of military dispositions in the 60s/70s AD. Each legion was based in a legionary fortress. The *II Augusta*, for example, was based variously at fortresses in *Exeter, *Gloucester, and *Caerleon.

Extensively excavated forts include those of *Hadrian's Wall, notably Birdoswald, Vindolanda, Chesters, and Housesteads. Such research indicates that the Roman army which invaded Britain in AD 43 was very different in structure from that which abandoned the province in AD 410. ES

Romanticism was a European phenomenon, at its height in Britain from 1785 to 1825, a movement of all the arts, though in England literature and painting predominantly. In its modern sense, the term seems to have originated in Germany, by association with romance languages and the characteristics of medieval romance. For Goethe and Schiller it signalled our alienation from the order and harmony of an earlier classical world, the resultant melancholy one of its most representative tones.

*Coleridge used the word in recalling his aims for *Lyrical Ballads* in 1798. He was to procure a 'willing suspension of disbelief' for 'persons and characters supernatural'. A taste for supernatural terrors had already been exploited by the novelists Horace *Walpole and Matthew Lewis. The poets learned from them. *Wordsworth's contribution to *Lyrical Ballads* illustrates another aspect of the Romantic impulse. In the 1800 preface, the manifesto of English Romanticism, he investigated the relationship between language and nature as Herder had done before him, though the German took his inspiration from the supposedly more 'natural' genius of the early English writers. Later, *Constable was to recommend that the painter seek perfection 'at its PRIMITIVE SOURCE, NATURE'. The appeal of the ballad, stimulated by *Percy's *Reliques* (1765), lay in its folk form; the sophisticated Wordsworth imitated its simplicity, but his interest in 'low and rustic life' was more than aesthetic. Poetry and politics went hand in hand. *Hazlitt was to say that 'this school of poetry had its origins in the French Revolution, or rather in the sentiments and opinions which produced that revolution'. *Blake shared his friend Tom *Paine's antipathy to 'Priestcraft and Tyranny', and where direct action was suppressed, it surfaced in verse.

In claiming that 'passion speaks truer than reason' Hazlitt echoed Rousseau, founding father of the movement with its new emphasis on subjectivity and emotion. 'The way to all mysteries heads inward', wrote Brandes in the year Wordsworth chose the growth of his own mind as a subject for epic. In his notebook, Coleridge recorded that 'in looking at objects of nature . . . I seem to be seeking a symbolical language for something within me that already and forever exists'.

Increasingly the 18th cent. was dismissed as an age of prose, or at best of thoughts translated into the language of poetry. Blake's quarrel with Sir Joshua *Reynolds lent an edge to his work as an engraver, his 'wiry bounding line' challenging the ideals of the Academy. *Turner followed Wordsworth to the Alps, while his extraordinary *Rain, Steam and Speed* looks to the future. In arguing that 'if poetry comes not as naturally as the leaves to the tree it had better not come at all', *Keats illustrates the cult of spontaneity and of organic metaphor.

The displacement of reason by imagination as the faculty by which the truth is apprehended is a commonplace of the period. Coleridge's famous definition of it as 'the living power and prime agent of all human perception' owes a good deal to Kant and Schelling, but there was always a certain native resistance to German metaphysics. The second generation of Romantics had other priorities; Keats questioned Wordsworth's cultivation of 'the egotistical sublime', while for *Shelley Wordsworth had betrayed the hopes of the Revolution. As that Revolution receded, and young radicals became old Tories, the dynamism of the movement was dispersed or transmuted, though its currents can be felt into the present century. JNRS

Rome, treaty of. Signed by France, Belgium, Italy, the Federal Republic of Germany, the Netherlands, and Luxembourg on 25 March 1957, it established both the *European Economic Community (EEC) and European Atomic Energy Community (Euratom) from 1 January 1958. The EEC treaty set out objectives (such as eliminating mutual tariff barriers, establishing a common external tariff, and formulating a Common Agricultural Policy) to be achieved within twelve years and outlined the communities' institutions and rules. Britain stayed aloof, disliking the shared sovereignty implicit in the treaty's supranational institutions and expecting that the negotiations would fail. CNL

Romilly, Sir Samuel (1757–1818). Legal reformer. Born of a Huguenot family in London, he abandoned religion in favour of Rousseau and continental reformers, including Dumont (later editor of *Bentham's works), Beccaria (the Italian legal reformer), and Mirabeau (the French revolutionary leader). An initial enthusiast for the French Revolution, he successfully defended John Binns, the Irish radical, on a sedition charge in 1797. In 1800 he became a king's counsel in Chancery and in 1806 Whig solicitor-general. He sat as MP for Queenborough (1806), Wareham (1808), Arundel (1812), and Westminster (1818), opposing the *Corn Law in 1815 and the suspension of *habeas corpus in 1817, and supporting the abolition of slavery and *catholic emancipation. Romilly wished to reduce the number of capital crimes but most of his time was spent powerless in opposition. He committed suicide four days after the death of his wife in 1818. ER

Romney, George (1734–1802). Painter, mainly of portraits. He was born in Lancashire and worked in the north of England until 1762, when he abandoned his wife and children to go to London, where he attracted a fashionable clientele. Between 1773 and 1775 he was in Italy, which inspired him to plan a number of literary and historical works that rarely went beyond the sketching stage. About 1781 he became infatuated with Emma *Hamilton and is probably best known for his many portraits of her. A fast and prolific painter who, according to John *Wesley, 'struck off an exact likeness at once, and did more in an hour than Sir Joshua [*Reynolds] did in ten', Romney rarely exhibited and never at the Royal Academy. In his later years he became insane and returned to his wife to die. JC

Rooke, George (1650–1709). Admiral. One of the most successful naval commanders of his day, promoted admiral in 1690, Rooke was unusual among his naval contemporaries in being a Tory and was linked, through two of his three marriages, with the prominent Tory earl of *Nottingham, William III's secretary of state (north) and *de facto* navy minister 1689–94. Rooke was at Bantry Bay (1689), *Beachy Head (1690), and *La Hogue (May/June 1692), where he distinguished himself and gained his knighthood. A year later he commanded the ill-fated 300-ship Smyrna convoy, but escaped blame for this débâcle which was largely due to lack of vigilance by others. An MP for Portsmouth 1698–1708, Rooke held a command with the Dutch at the Copenhagen Sound in 1700 which called for prudent diplomacy between Denmark and Sweden. In 1702 he burnt a Franco-Spanish fleet at *Vigo, and in August 1704 commanded at the capture of Gibraltar, subsequently fighting a bitter though drawn battle with the French Toulon fleet off Malaga. His success invited the jealousy of the Marlborough faction and this command proved his last. DDA

root and branch petition, 1640. Charles I's opponents made most of the running in the *Short and *Long Parliaments of 1640. On 11 December, the Commons received a petition from Londoners demanding the destruction of episcopacy, 'root and branch'. A bill to implement it and to substitute a *presbyterian form of church government was introduced in 1641 but made no progress. But when the king's position deteriorated rapidly after the attempt to arrest the *five members in 1642, he was obliged in February to consent to 17 Car. I c. 27, whereby the bishops were excluded from the House of Lords. JAC

Rorke's Drift, battle of, 1879. Ford across the Buffalo river, 70 miles north of Pietermaritzburg, South Africa; site of a battle in the *Zulu War. On 22 January 1879 a force of 139 British troops left to guard the ford was attacked by between 3,000 and 4,000 Zulus, who had not been directly involved in the Zulu victory earlier in the day at *Isandhlwana. The British had hastily prepared a strong, defensive position, and the Zulus' tactics proved ineffective when confronted by the courage and disciplined rifle fire of the British troops. All their attacks having been repulsed with heavy losses, the Zulus withdrew at dawn the following day. No fewer than eight VCs were awarded among the survivors. KI

Rosebery, Archibald Philip Primrose, 5th earl of (1847–1929). Prime minister. From an early age Rosebery seemed destined for a glittering public career. He enjoyed outstanding oratorical powers, considerable wealth, much enhanced by his marriage to Hannah Rothschild in 1878, and inherited his peerage in 1868. But faults of temperament severely hampered him. He was sent down from Oxford without a degree because he insisted on running his horse in the Derby. This lifelong passion for the turf—his horses won the Derby three times—complicated his relations with strait-laced Liberal nonconformity. Without the steadying influence of his wife, who died in 1890, Rosebery seemed to lose what little taste he had for the mundane business of party management and legislation. He said, with some truth, that he had been drawn into politics by force of circumstances and always hated it. Thus, despite his advantages, Rosebery largely failed as prime minister, and his career yielded no substantial achievements.

It was a sign of Rosebery's diffidence that he refused office from *Gladstone in 1872 and 1880, served from 1881 to 1883 when he resigned, and then declined the Scottish Office in the same year. Yet his political reputation steadily rose, partly through his role as Gladstone's impresario in the *Midlothian campaign of 1879. The departure of many Whigs over the *Home Rule issue in 1886 made Rosebery a vital figure in the House of Lords, and he thus became a young foreign secretary in that year.

For a time he enjoyed remarkably wide acclaim. On the one hand he had the confidence of the queen, who chose him as Gladstone's successor in 1894. On the other hand he seemed to many radical Liberals to be better attuned to social problems than Gladstone. One sign of this was his election as first chairman of the London County Council in 1889.

But his chief interest was foreign and imperial affairs. He developed a Liberal vision of the British empire as a 'Commonwealth of Nations', and as chairman of the Imperial Federation League he advocated a more cohesive structure involving regular colonial conferences and formal colonial representation on the Privy Council. As foreign secretary (1892–4) he resisted party pressure to withdraw from *Uganda and imposed a protectorate on that territory.

On his succession to the premiership in 1894, Rosebery's career collapsed under the strain. He fell out with colleagues over the death duties in *Harcourt's budget and his wish to drop Irish Home Rule. On the defeat of his government in the Commons in 1895 he promptly resigned, forcing the Liberals into a disastrous election. A year later he quit as leader. Subsequently he attacked the Liberal position over the South African War and promoted a separate organization of *Liberal Imperialists. In a famous speech at Chesterfield in 1901 he called for a 'clean slate', by which he meant dropping traditional Gladstonian causes like Home Rule. However, Rosebery was easily outmanœuvred by *Campbell-Bannerman, and the rest of his career was spent as a crossbencher increasingly out of sympathy with the radical reformism of Edwardian Liberalism. MDP

Roses, Wars of the. Once applied to the whole of the 15th cent., the name is now given to the sequence of plots, rebellions, and battles that took place between 1455 and 1487. They are so called because of the notion that, fought between the dynasties of Lancaster and York, Lancaster was represented by a red rose, York by a white. In fact the idea of the warring roses was invented by Henry VII after he seized the throne in 1485. He claimed to be the heir of Lancaster and represented his marriage to *Elizabeth of York, the heiress of Edward IV, as the union of the red and white roses, bringing peace, order, and prosperity after the war, anarchy, and ruin of the preceding decades. While the actual phrase 'Wars of the Roses' did not appear until the 19th cent., the idea of the warring roses was rooted in Tudor propaganda.

There were three distinct phases of civil war: between 1455 and 1464; 1469 and 1471; and 1483 and 1487. In the first two fighting for the control of royal government led to outright war for possession of the crown; the third was dynastic from the start. There was also a strong element of baronial feuding and rivalry for local dominance, especially in northern England between the Percies and the Nevilles. The scale of the fighting and the extent of disorder were much exaggerated by Tudor writers. The most intense period was between July 1460 and March 1461, but as a whole there were barely more than two years' military activity throughout the thirty-year period. Civilian casualties and physical destruction were light; even at its worst most were able to go about their normal affairs.

Nevertheless, especially in 1459–61 and 1469–71, there was considerable political upheaval and instability as the houses of Lancaster and York competed for the throne. In 1455 the duke of *York led his supporters in a successful rebellion against Henry VI. In 1459 they rebelled again, were at first defeated, but were victorious at *Northampton in July 1460. Four months later York claimed the throne for himself. Although he was defeated and killed at the battle of *Wakefield, his heir Edward seized the throne and won a decisive victory at *Towton. In 1469 Edward in his turn faced rebellion from *Warwick the Kingmaker. Warwick too endeavoured to rule the kingdom by force, but also found it impossible. Thus he resorted to the restoration of Henry VI. Edward IV, however, had the last word, defeating Warwick at *Barnet and a Lancastrian army at *Tewkesbury. The virtual destruction of the Lancastrians seemed to have brought the wars to an end. They were reopened when Edward's brother Richard III made himself king in 1483. It was then that Henry Tudor emerged as a claimant to the throne. Leading an alliance of die-hard Lancastrians and supporters of the deposed Edward V, he swept to power at *Bosworth in August 1485. He brought the wars effectively to an end when he defeated a Yorkist invasion at *Stoke (by Newark, Notts.) in 1487.

In the later 20th cent., historians have much debated the origins and causes of the wars. Some, arguing that in 15th-cent. politics everything rested on the fitness of the king to rule, have put the entire blame on the shoulders of Henry VI. But there were deeper causes in the social, economic, and political trends of the later Middle Ages, which suggest that any monarch would have faced severe problems. Nevertheless the recovery of royal authority under the Tudors was rapid. No great political or social change resulted: the old feudal nobility did not destroy itself, nor did the Tudors represent a new middle class. The most lasting impact of the Wars of the Roses has been on the historical imagination. Lewis *Carroll used his schoolboy knowledge of them as a recurring motif in *Alice in Wonderland*. And they have come to be a byword for anarchy: the last months of the Callaghan administration in 1979 were dubbed with telling effect 'the Winter of Discontent' from the opening line of Shakespeare's *Richard III*. AJP

Rosicrucians. Members of a world-wide fraternity who claim to continue the old Rosicrucian tradition. Its origins are obscure, since the order was reputedly founded by a Christian Rosenkreuz (who had acquired the Arabs' secret wisdom) in 1418 but first mentioned only *c.*1614. There is still debate whether or not this esoteric brotherhood of magician-scientists ever actually existed. Wide interest was aroused, and new societies with alchemical interests came under the umbrella of its name, since elements of occultism were reflected in claims of ability to prolong life and transmute metals. The London physician Robert Fludd (1574–1637) spread Rosicrucian ideas in several medico-theosophical books. A Rosicrucian society arose in mid-19th-cent. England, as an offshoot of masonry (the twin emblems of a rose and a cross were venerated by freemasons as symbolic of Christ's resurrection and redemption), but there is no historical continuity with any earlier group. ASH

Ross, James Stewart, 1st duke of [S] (*c.*1477–1504). Second son of James III. As marquis of Ormond he received more favour from his father than the duke of Rothesay, the future James IV. In particular James III proposed him as part of a marriage alliance with England, but not his elder brother (1486); and made him duke of Ross, an act that precipitated Rothesay into the open rebellion that ended with James III's death at *Sauchie Burn (1488). Potential trouble continued. Ross had links with James III's councillor Archbishop William Scheves, and Henry VII's spy John Ramsay (1496). James IV solved this problem by making Ross archbishop of St Andrews (1497). Thus Ross was removed as focus for opposition, the king could reclaim his secular estates, and his substantial ecclesiastical revenues went to the crown. Chancellor, in name only, from 1501,

Ross died shortly before reaching the canonical age for consecration, 27. RJT

Ross, Sir James Clark (1800–62). Ross was involved in eight Arctic and Antarctic expeditions after joining the navy in 1812. Those of 1818 and 1829–33 were with his uncle John *Ross, those of 1819–20, 1821–3, and 1824 with Sir William Parry. With Ross he discovered the Magnetic Pole, while with Parry he reached 110 degrees west in Melville Sound. His first Arctic command in 1836 was followed by appointment to lead the navy's first full-scale Antarctic expedition which was also a terrestrial magnetism investigation. In specially strengthened ships, the *Erebus* and *Terror*, Ross reached further south than anyone hitherto and got through the pack ice to the continent itself where an ice shelf and an island were later named after him. He called the mainland Victoria Land and it became the locus of all the major British Antarctic forays of the 20th cent. The final venture of Ross was to return to the Arctic in 1848–9 to search for *Franklin. RB

Ross, Sir John (1777–1856). Originally with the East India Company, Ross joined the navy in 1805 and became an Arctic explorer. He led the 1818 expedition which sailed into Lancaster Sound from Baffin Bay but inexplicably turned back. The error was retrieved in his most important venture when, in 1829–33, he headed a privately financed expedition employing very inefficient steam vessels for the first time in the Arctic. The ships went under sail through the Strait to explore the Boothia Peninsula and King William Island. Here, in 1831, Ross's nephew James Clark Ross located the North Magnetic Pole. After service as British consul in Stockholm, Ross made an unsuccessful return to the Arctic to search for *Franklin in 1850. RB

Rossetti, Dante Gabriel (1828–82). Poet and painter. Rossetti was born in London, the son of an Italian refugee. Taught drawing by *Cotman, he also worked with Ford Madox Brown, before coming under the guidance of Holman *Hunt in 1848. His first major work, *The Girlhood of Mary Virgin*, was also the first to bear the initials PRB (*Pre-Raphaelite Brotherhood). He soon moved away from brotherhood principles to follow what *Millais called 'his own peculiar fancies', his best painting being done during his association with the model Elizabeth Siddal, whom he married in 1860. In 1857, following a suggestion by John *Ruskin, Rossetti and others including William *Morris and William Burne-Jones were involved in the decoration of the Oxford Union. Technical difficulties caused the paintings to degrade quickly. At the end of his life, which was marred by ill-health, Rossetti lived virtually as a recluse. JC

Rotary clubs. The first Rotary club was founded in 1905 by Paul P. Harris, a Chicago attorney, to promote service and fellowship among the business community. There was to be a member from each profession or branch of business and meetings were to be held in their rooms in rotation. In 1912 an international association was formed, changed in 1922 into the Rotary International. The clubs sponsor scholarships for study abroad. JAC

Rotherham, Thomas (1423–1500). Archbishop of York and chancellor. Born in Yorkshire and educated at King's College, Cambridge, Rotherham was chaplain to the earl of Oxford (1461), where he met *Elizabeth Woodville, Edward IV's future wife. This contact helped him to become keeper of the privy seal (1467–74), bishop of Rochester (1468–72), bishop of Lincoln (1472–80), chancellor (1474–83 and 1485), and archbishop (1480–1500). Involved diplomatically with France and Burgundy, he was present at Edward IV's meeting with Louis XI at *Picquigny (1475). In Gloucester's coup following Edward's death (1483), Rotherham was suspected of being pro-Woodville, surrendered the great seal, and was imprisoned until after Gloucester's coronation as Richard III. Henceforth he had little political involvement except briefly as chancellor under Henry VII. He established a school in Rotherham and was a benefactor of Lincoln College, Oxford. WMM

Rothermere, Viscount. See HARMSWORTH, HAROLD.

Rothes, John Leslie, 1st duke of [S] (1630–81). Leslie's father, the 6th earl, was in high favour with Charles I but died in 1641 at the age of 41. Leslie marched south with Charles II in 1651 and was taken prisoner at *Worcester. At the Restoration, honours were showered upon him. He became president of the council [S] 1660, lord high treasurer [S] 1663, captain-general of the forces [S] 1664. In 1667, through *Lauderdale's influence, he was dismissed from office but made lord chancellor [S] for life, despite his protests that he had no legal knowledge nor learning. In 1680, when the duke of York was in Scotland, Rothes was created duke [S] but died the following year, his health undermined by good living. Rothes's letters in *The Lauderdale Papers* (Camden Series) are idiosyncratic and ungrammatical. JAC

Rothschild, Lionel (1808–79). Banker and politician. Rothschild's father, of an international family of German Jews, came to England in 1797 to conduct business and was greatly employed in financing the Napoleonic wars. Lionel succeeded to the English business in 1836, supplied loans for the *Crimean War, and provided *Disraeli with £4 million in 1876 for the purchase of the *Suez canal shares. Returned to Parliament in 1847 for London as a Liberal, Rothschild could not take the required oath as a Christian and was not allowed to sit. Though re-elected in 1849, 1852, and 1857, it was not until the law was changed in 1858 that he could take his seat. His son Nathan was created Baron Rothschild through *Gladstone in 1885, the first practising Jew to be ennobled. Disraeli offered an idealized portrait of Rothschild in *Coningsby* (1844) as Sidonia, a man of profound wisdom, though it is not clear what it was: a less flattering portrait was given by *Trollope, who is said to have drawn on Rothschild for elements of Melmotte, the great fraudulent financier in *The Way We Live Now* (1874). JAC

rotten boroughs was the term used before 1832 to describe parliamentary constituencies where the voters had almost disappeared. A classic example was Old Sarum, which had been deserted since the inhabitants moved down the valley to Salisbury in 1220. But it was close run by other boroughs, such as Gatton in Surrey, which was down to 20 voters at the Restoration and only two 100 years later, or Dunwich, a once thriving port, which had long since crumbled into the sea. They were defended as affording opportunities for new non-landed interests—brewers, bankers, nabobs—to obtain representation. Chatham (*Pitt) denounced them in 1766 as the rotten part of the constitution and declared they would not last the century. Most of them finished up in Schedule A of the *Great Reform Act. JAC

Roubiliac, Louis François (*c.*1705–62). French sculptor. Roubiliac settled in Britain about 1732 and made his reputation with a statue of *Handel, now in the Victoria and Albert Museum. He taught at St Martin's Lane Academy, the forerunner of the *Royal Academy, and worked as a modeller for the Chelsea china factory. His busts show great vividness and energy, conveying character and age. He is often compared to his rival *Rysbrack, whose work was more restrained. There are several Roubiliac busts at Trinity College, Cambridge (including one of Sir Isaac *Newton), in the *National Portrait Gallery, and in the Royal Academy. Roubiliac also made several monumental sculptures for Westminster abbey, which include another of Handel and the particularly popular and dramatic monument of 1761 to Lady Elizabeth Nightingale. JC

Rouen, treaty of, 1517. The defeat at *Flodden left Scotland with an infant king, James V. The duke of *Albany became regent in 1515 and on 26 August 1517 negotiated the treaty of *Rouen with Francis I of France. Mutual support against England was to be cemented by a French marriage for the young king. The treaty was not ratified until 1522. Albany then launched an attack upon northern England which was a fiasco. The marriage of James to *Madeleine, daughter of Francis, did not take place until 1537. JAC

rough music was a component of folkloric rituals classified under the generic continental term of *charivari*, or such English ones as skimmington, riding the stang, or simply riding. These rituals probably emerged in the later 16th cent., and usually involved satirical representations by sections of the community of conduct they regarded as reprehensible. At first they were directed against wives who offered violence or insubordination to their husbands, but later they might be directed against wife-beating husbands, or even employers in industrial disputes. The 'rough music' was the discordant beating of pots and pans that usually accompanied these ceremonies. JAS

'rough wooing', 1544–8. The birth of Mary, queen of Scots, in December 1542, only a week after her father's death, seemed an ideal opportunity to unite the thrones of England and Scotland. Prince Edward, Henry VIII's heir, was 5 years old and the English pressed for a marriage agreement. By the treaty of *Greenwich in July 1543 Mary was to be betrothed before she was 10 and thereafter brought up in England. When the Scottish Parliament in December 1543 rejected the treaty, preferring to stay with the French alliance, Henry retorted with a punitive expedition led by Lord Hertford (*Somerset), devastating the south-east border—ironically dubbed the 'rough wooing'. The Scots split and rival parliaments were summoned at Edinburgh and Stirling. A second expedition in 1545 devastated Melrose but the Scottish victory at *Ancrum Moor in February put heart into the resistance and Hertford led another raid at harvest-time. In September 1547, after Henry's death, Hertford, now Protector Somerset, led an army to victory at *Pinkie Cleugh, but consolidation proved hard. The Scottish reply, by the treaty of *Haddington, was to accept a proposed marriage between Mary and the dauphin and she was taken to France in July 1548. With justice, Henry's policy has been described as 'never very sophisticated' and 'incredibly stupid as well as brutal'. JAC

roundheads. Scornful nickname coined to describe first the soldiers, and then the whole party which supported Parliament during the Civil War. It arose, explained Lucy *Hutchinson, 'from the puritans' custom of wearing their hair cut close round their heads', like apprentices, who shortened their hair to demonstrate their contempt for lovelocks. This was in contrast to the flowing tresses of the royalist cavaliers. The people against whom the nickname was directed did not hesitate to embrace it. A roundhead, averred one pamphleteer, was 'a good, honest, zealous, and true protestant', called by God to do his work. 'A Roundhead's use is of many sorts and kinds', another writer told the troops, 'but all for good; and first to set forth the splendid glory of God.' This sense of being God's chosen people was an important ingredient in the morale of the parliamentary armies. By the late 1640s, after the roundheads' military triumph against the king, the word seems to have fallen into disuse. IJG

Roundway Down, battle of, 1643. After Charles I's march on London at the outset of the Civil War in 1642 had been halted, the following year developed into a war of manœuvre. After savage fighting on *Lansdowne on 5 July, both sides were badly mauled. *Hopton made off to Devizes, where he was penned into the town and bombarded by *Waller with superior numbers. But reinforcements from Oxford enabled Hopton on 13 July to counter-attack his opponents in rolling chalk downland just outside the town. Waller's cavalry suffered severely on steep grassy slopes and he lost all his guns and 1,400 men. JAC

rowing. Organized competitive rowing, like most sports, developed in the 19th cent., though the Irish comedian Doggett founded his sculling race on the Thames for the Coat and Badge in 1715. The Oxford and Cambridge *Boat Race was first rowed in 1829. *Henley regatta was established in 1839, the main events being the Grand Challenge Cup for eights and the Diamond Sculls for single oarsmen. Rowing was recognized as an Olympic sport in 1908. Professional contests were common and popular in the 19th cent., with heavy betting on the result, but died out in the 20th cent. JAC

Rowlandson, Thomas (1756/7–1827). Artist. Social commentator rather than caricaturist, sardonic rather than angry, Rowlandson's eye for life's comedies and absurdities led him to favour types rather than individuals, burlesque rather than biting satire. A Royal Academy student and fascinated by physiognomy, his prodigious output of pen-drawings, water-colours, and prints, demonstrating mastery of line and billowing rococo shapes, were so full of gusto that he has been seen as a personification of his age. If inclined to the characteristic excesses of the period (hard drinking, gambling, promiscuity), his view of the world depicted its manners, vices, politics, and incidents, but without censoriousness; his native London, the English countryside, and European cities provided both inspiration and backgrounds. A friend of *Gillray, he worked for the publisher Ackermann, creating 'Dr Syntax', but technique and vision suffered after 1800 in consequence of his productivity, and he founded no school. ASH

Rowntree, Benjamin Seebohm (1871–1954). Rowntree, of the York, Liberal, quaker, chocolate-manufacturing family, conducted a local survey of poverty, the first of three during his life, published as *Poverty: A Study of Town Life* (1901). He classified poverty in two categories: families endured primary poverty when the four basic requirements of food, fuel, shelter, and clothing were not met from income, no matter how carefully managed; secondary poverty occurred when families had the income to cover the basic necessities, but did not have money for other essentials such as medicine. Rowntree concluded that 9.91 per cent of York's population were living in primary poverty and 17.93 in secondary poverty. These combined figures were so close to *Booth's earlier calculations for London as to demonstrate that the problem of poverty was general, although its incidence might vary with the trade cycle and within a family cycle determined by the wage-earning capacity of all its members. JB

Rowton Heath, battle of, 1645. After *Naseby, Charles I's hopes were of reinforcements from Ireland or of a junction with the victorious *Montrose in Scotland. Chester, held by a royalist garrison, was the key to both strategies. In September, Charles moved northwards through north Wales to Chester, unaware that Montrose's brilliant run of success had already come to an end at *Philiphaugh. On 23 September Charles relieved the garrison but the following day Langdale's cavalry was badly cut up by Poyntz's horsemen at Rowton Heath, just south of the city. JAC

Roxburgh, John Ker, 1st duke of [S] (*c.*1680–1741). Ker succeeded his brother as earl of Roxburgh at the age of 16. When in his twenties he was secretary of state [S] 1704–5, along with *Tweeddale. A warm advocate of the Union, he was created duke in 1707 and served as a representative peer in the parliaments of 1707, 1708, 1715, and 1727. In 1714–16 he was keeper of the privy seal [S] and fought bravely for the Hanoverians at *Sheriffmuir in 1715. From 1715 until 1725 he was again secretary of state [S]. Awarded the Garter in 1722, he lost favour in 1725 when he was suspected of encouraging the Shawfield riots against the malt tax and of favouring *Carteret against *Walpole. He spent the rest of his life in retirement at Floors. Roxburgh was said to be a ready speaker and a cultivated and agreeable man. JAC

Royal Academy of Arts (London). In 1768 the artist Benjamin *West, with the architect William *Chambers, approached George III for his approval of a national academy to foster a school of art, set standards of good taste, and provide for the free exhibition of works of excellence. The first president was Sir Joshua *Reynolds, whose famous *Discourses*, delivered over a period of 20 years, laid down the basic concepts of the academy which was to form 'a repository for the great examples of the Art', an important function before the establishment of the National Gallery in 1824. During the 19th cent. the academy was slow to accept innovation and its reputation declined. Since the mid-20th cent., policy has been more liberal and the annual summer exhibition a popular event, although whether it fulfils the function of exhibiting the best contemporary work is open to question. JC

Royal Africa Company. A number of short-lived charters in particular areas had been granted in the late 16th and early 17th cents., but the Royal Africa Company was not established until 1672. It traded with west Africa for gold and ivory but its main concern was to supply slaves to the West Indian islands. The company defended its charter with the argument that it was obliged to provide forts to protect warehouses, and it survived after reorganization in 1750 until 1821. JAC

Royal Air Force. The RAF was formed in April 1918 when the *Royal Flying Corps and the *Royal Naval Air Service were amalgamated to improve co-ordination. The new service was given its own minister and its own ranks: the other two services were amused at airmen who did not fly and at the plethora of marshals. After the armistice the new force was drastically reduced, falling to less than 50 aircraft in 1922 for home defence. It also struggled for its independent existence against the army and navy, defended by Lord *Trenchard. Even so, the RNAS was resurrected in 1924 as the Fleet Air Arm, jointly administered until 1937 when it was handed over to the navy. A cadet college was opened at Cranwell in 1920 and a staff college at Andover in 1922. The basic problem was how to obtain adequate resources from governments in acute financial difficulties and often committed to the cause of disarmament. Strategically, it was a question of striking a balance between offence and defence—bombers and fighters. Trenchard was a strong believer in the smallest possible fighter force—just enough to keep the civilians quiet. For many years the doctrine that the bomber would always get through, especially when supported by the prime minister, *Baldwin, suggested that defence was useless. But the invention of radar in 1935 and the successful flights of the Hurricane (1935) and Spitfire (1936) tipped the balance back to defence.

It is not easy to compute exact figures for aircraft at the outbreak of the Second World War in 1939 since some were trainers, some unserviceable, and some obsolescent. The Germans had substantial but not overwhelming numerical superiority with some 4,000 planes to Britain's 2,000: the French air force, in poor shape, had some 1,500. But while the British figures included sedate Gloster Gladiators and Hawker Furies (not very furious with a top speed of 223 m.p.h. and introduced in 1931), the Luftwaffe had been completely re-equipped after Hitler's rise to power.

A major problem for the Royal Air Force was the spread of its commitments, especially after the entry of Italy (1940)

and Japan (1941) extended the war to north Africa and the Pacific. But it received vital help from the Dominions' air forces, which provided about a quarter of the squadrons. From the fall of France in May 1940 the role of the RAF was essentially defensive, save for raids on enemy airfields and occasional bombing attacks to boost morale. During the Battle of Britain its resources were severely stretched, even more in trained aircrew than in machines, with the life expectation for fighter pilots down to four or five weeks. On 8 August 1940, Goering issued an order to 'wipe the British Air Force from the sky'. But his first surprise was that the Stuka dive-bombers, which had spread such terror in Poland and France, proved slow and vulnerable to Spitfires and Hurricanes. The Luftwaffe, operating over enemy territory and using bombers, suffered disproportionate losses in aircrew. The number of planes lost is a matter of dispute, since both sides issued exaggerated claims for kills, but the Germans lost about twice the number of machines. What is not in dispute is that the Royal Air Force was not destroyed, that Goering switched to softer targets with raids on British cities, and that operation Sealion, the invasion of Britain, was called off.

Meanwhile Coastal Command struggled against the U-boat menace. More than 120 merchant ships were sunk in the month of March 1943 alone. But by May 1943 better-organized convoys, improved weapons of attack, and the introduction of new long-range aircraft like the Sunderland, Catalina, and Liberator, which could bridge the 'Atlantic gap', gave Britain the edge.

The counter-offensive could now develop. The strategic issue became whether a massive bombing campaign could pound Germany into surrender without the need for a bloody invasion. The great proponent of that view was 'Bomber' *Harris. In June 1942 he mustered a scratch force of just over 1,000 aircraft (including training personnel) for a demonstration onslaught on Cologne, and followed up his success with a memo against 'the disastrous policy of military intervention in land campaigns of Europe'. But the evidence is dubious. *Churchill pointed out that civilian morale is often surprisingly resilient under intolerable suffering, mass bombing was less destructive of the German war effort than had been hoped, and aircraft losses were very heavy. Bomber Command lost 55,000 men during the war—more, it has been said, than all the officers killed in the First World War. Until the end of 1944 German production of tanks, guns, and fighter aircraft continued to increase, with factories camouflaged and dispersed. Allied air power was also needed to cover the Normandy landings in June 1944, to deal with the V1 flying bombs which began to arrive in Britain a week after D-Day, and to attack launching sites for V2 rockets from September 1944 onwards.

Since the end of the Second World War, the Royal Air Force has taken part in a number of campaigns—the Berlin Airlift of 1948/9 when 147 planes flew more than 63,000 sorties; the *Suez operation in 1956 when Egyptian airfields were bombed; the *Falklands War of 1982 when the possession of Ascension Island was critical and air cover was provided largely by ship-borne Harriers; and the *Gulf War of 1990 when the Tornado squadron in its low-level attacks had a bad first week. But its main tasks since the 1950s were to carry the British nuclear deterrent in the V-bomber force and to retain operational efficiency in the face of shrinking resources. JAC

Raleigh, W. A., and Jones, H. A., *The War in the Air: Being the Story of the Part Played in the Great War by the Royal Air Force* (6 vols., Oxford, 1922–); Terraine, J., *The Right of the Line: The Royal Air Force in the European War 1939–1945* (1985).

Royal British Legion. Essentially a product of the Great War, the legion emerged from amalgamation of rival voluntary societies in 1921 as a non-party association of ex-servicemen, in response to demobilization confusion and disillusion in a time of industrial unrest. Disbursements to alleviate distress (sickness, unemployment), employment offices and schemes, disabled retraining, and increasing preoccupation with pensions followed. Poppy Day (derived from the emblem of Flanders's fields) started cautiously in 1921, to become the best known and most productive of appeals. A royal charter came in 1925, then royal patronage. In the Second World War, legionaries everywhere contributed to national and civil defence (air-raid duties, Home Guard), and remembrance festivals were revived. While interest grew in provision for the aged and incapacitated, and war-grave pilgrimages, the Legion's principal service to 'second-generation' ex-servicemen concerned pensions. The 50th anniversaries of VE- and VJ-Days reminded many of this national institution's work. ASH

Royal College of Music. London music conservatoire for the training of performers, composers, and teachers. Founded in 1883 and based on the former National Training School of Music, it opened with 50 scholars and 42 fee-paying students under the directorship of George *Grove. *Stanford was an influential founding professor there (1883–1924), as was *Parry (1883–1918), who succeeded Grove as director in 1894. The Britten Opera theatre was opened in 1986. The college owns valuable collections of musical instruments and archival material. ECr

royal commissions. Though there was an element of investigation in each, it is scarcely helpful to suggest, as some writers do, that the *Domesday survey of 1086 or the inquiry into the state of the monasteries in the 1530s should be regarded as early examples of royal commissions. In neither case were they panels of persons appointed to investigate and advise. The preferred 18th-cent. method of proceeding—apart from leaving things alone—was the select parliamentary committee. This had some disadvantages: composed of MPs it was likely to be partisan; few MPs had the time to devote to a thorough inquiry; and it was almost impossible to take the committee round the country to gather evidence. From 1800 onwards, with increasing concern for social questions, royal commissions multiplied—11 in the first decade, 46 in the fourth, 75 in the sixth. The period immediately after the Great Reform Act saw a number of extremely influential reports—on the Poor Law (1834), municipal corporations (1835), employment of children in mines (1842), and the state of the large towns (1844). The defects of royal commissions are not inconsiderable. They are expensive, slow, and there is no guarantee that action will follow. Indeed, cynics regard them as an admirable way of disposing of awkward issues until after the next general election. JAC

Royal Exchange. The first Royal Exchange building was erected by Sir Thomas *Gresham in 1565–7 as a bourse where merchants and bankers could meet. Modelled on the Antwerp Bourse, it lay in the city of London between Threadneedle Street and Cornhill. Elizabeth I proclaimed it the Royal Exchange on her visit in 1570. In the 19th cent. it housed the foreign exchange market. It was twice destroyed by fire (1666 and 1838) and twice rebuilt. In 1982 its central glass-domed courtyard was refurbished and occupied by the financial futures market. MW

Royal Flying Corps. The Royal Engineers experimented with balloons in the 1870s and a small factory was established at Chatham in 1883. Several balloons were used for observations during the *Boer War. Blériot's flight across the Channel in 1909 and the German Zeppelin programme persuaded the army to set up an Air Batallion in 1911 and the RFC was established in April 1912, with a Central Flying School at Upavon on Salisbury Plain. In 1914, 4 squadrons went to France with 63 aeroplanes, most of them BE2 biplanes (Blériot Experimental), made at the Royal Aircraft Factory at Farnborough. The first reconnaissance was carried out on 19 August. The early role of the corps was scouting, with the odd hand-grenade tossed over the side of the cockpit, but the buildup of forces and the invention of the synchronized machine-gun, firing through the propeller, led to frequent dog-fights. Albert Ball, flying an SE5, shot down 43 German planes before he was killed in May 1917: the total was surpassed by the Canadian William Bishop (72) and Edward Mannock (73). The corps's defensive capabilities were demonstrated on 3 September 1916 when William Leefe Robinson shot down Zeppelin SL 11 while it was raiding London. In 1918 air warfare was reorganized to assist co-ordination. The RFC amalgamated with the Royal Naval Air Service to form the *Royal Air Force, with its own minister. JAC

***Royal George*.** On 29 August 1782 Admiral Kempenfelt at Spithead was preparing his flagship, the *Royal George*, to sail to the relief of Gibraltar. It was an old vessel and patched up for service. When her guns were run over to one side to give the ship a list and enable repairs to the hull to be made, she sank at once, drowning the admiral and up to 800 crew and families. The vessel was never recovered and was eventually blown up. JAC

Royal Institution. Founded in 1799 to apply science and technology to the improvement of the lives of the poor. The leading members included *Banks, Count Rumford, Thomas Bernard, Henry *Cavendish, and *Wilberforce. It received a royal charter the following year and moved into the premises in Albemarle Street which it still occupies. Its main activity has been to popularize science through public lectures and its success was assured by Humphry *Davy and then Michael *Faraday, who had started as Davy's assistant in 1813. Subsequent lecturers have included John *Tyndall, Sir James Dewar, T. H. *Huxley, *Rutherford, and Julian Huxley. Though it is doubtful whether the institution has had much effect on the condition of the poor, it has done a great deal for the diffusion of scientific knowledge. JAC

Royal Irish Academy. The academy was founded in Dublin in 1785 and was given royal recognition the following year. Its aims were the exploration and preservation of Irish culture, collecting manuscripts, and publishing transactions on a variety of topics. Its first president was Lord *Charlemont and the founder members included *Grattan and *Gandon. JAC

Royal Irish Constabulary. See IRISH CONSTABULARY.

royalists. See CAVALIERS.

Royal Marriages Act, 1772. Prompted by the unsanctioned marriage of George III's brother Henry, duke of Cumberland, an Act was passed in 1772 making it illegal in future for any member of the royal family under the age of 25 to marry without the previous consent of the crown: all such marriages to be declared null and void. The Act created problems for the future George IV when he married Mrs Fitzherbert in 1785 at the age of 23, and is still in force. DW

Royal Naval Air Service. When the *Royal Flying Corps was founded in 1912 it had a military and naval wing. The latter soon adopted the name Royal Naval Air Service, which was officially recognized in July 1914. It then possessed 39 aircraft, 52 seaplanes, and 7 airships. Their main responsibility was defence against submarines, including bombing of their bases, observation for the fleet, and coastal defence against Zeppelins. Seaplanes could be carried on cruisers, but not until August 1915 did an adapted seaplane take off from *Campania* and it was two years later that a seaplane relanded on its carrier. The RNAS was amalgamated with the RFC in 1918 to form the *Royal Air Force. But the special requirements of the navy led to the creation of the Fleet Air Arm, jointly administered until 1937 when it was placed under naval control. JAC

Royal Navy. See NAVY.

Royal Opera House (Covent Garden, London). The original Covent Garden theatre was opened by John Rich in 1732; *Handel used it for operas and oratorios, including the first London performance of **Messiah*, while the second half of the century saw both plays and English operas. In 1808 the theatre was destroyed by fire, reopening the following year and from 1847 housing the Royal Italian Opera in direct rivalry with Her Majesty's theatre. It burned down again in 1856; the present building designed by E. M. Barry opened in 1858. Many German and French operas were translated into Italian, although in 1892 'Italian' was dropped from the Royal Opera's title and *The Ring* was given in German under Mahler. Patti was London's first Aida (1876), while *Melba sang there many times. The dominant conductor during the first part of the 20th cent. was *Beecham, while more recent musical directors include Solti and Davis. After the Second World War the theatre became home to the permanent Covent Garden Opera Company and Sadler's Wells Ballet (later known as the

Royal Opera and Royal Ballet). Covent Garden has seen the premières of works by *Holst, *Walton, *Britten, and especially *Tippett. ECr

Royal Philharmonic Society. London concert society formed by professional musicians in 1813 to promote primarily orchestral and instrumental music. For the first Philharmonic Society concert, the orchestra was led by the violinist Salomon and directed from the piano by Clementi. Spohr claimed to be the first director to use a baton in 1820, while later famous conductors included Mendelssohn, Sterndale Bennett, *Sullivan, Tchaikovsky, Nikisch, *Wood, *Beecham, and, for a single disastrous season, Wagner. New commissioned works included Beethoven's 'Choral' Symphony (1825) and Mendelssohn's 'Italian' Symphony (1833). The society was granted its 'Royal' title in 1913 and has awarded a prestigious gold medal since 1871. ECr

royal prerogative is a term which has changed its meaning considerably. In modern times it mainly refers to a reserve or discretionary power entrusted to the monarch, though it is far from clear what that power is. In the medieval period the term was used largely to describe feudal rights. There was no implication of reserve power since the medieval monarch had massive immediate power, making all important appointments, granting honours, estates, and charters, issuing proclamations, dispensing justice, and declaring war and peace, limited mainly by custom and prudence. In the later medieval and early modern period, the meaning began to change again to signify powers peculiarly close to the monarch—honours, foreign policy, marriage, and succession. The most lofty assertions of royal prerogative came from Richard II and James I—perhaps when the monarchy was under pressure and as a defensive reaction. Too many definitions of prerogative are theoretical rather than factual. James I wrote that 'it is presumption and sedition in a subject to dispute what a king may do'—a case of whistling in the dark; while *Blackstone's observation in his *Commentaries* (1765) that 'the king has the sole prerogative of making war and peace', while nominally correct, was fundamentally misleading.

Many of the constitutional conflicts in the reigns of John, Henry III, and Edward II turned on aspects of the prerogative—e.g. the king's right to *tallage. Even more basic royal powers were under fire in the 1370s when the Commons began to impeach royal ministers and in 1395 when they asserted their right to approve taxation. But the great struggle over the prerogative was decided largely in the 17th cent. At the end of her reign Elizabeth ran into criticism for granting *monopolies by prerogative and promised redress while reasserting her right: James I was obliged to give way completely on that issue, the statute of Monopolies of 1624 declaring that they were 'altogether contrary to the laws of this realm'. The House of Commons recorded mournfully in its *Apology of 1604 that 'the prerogatives of princes may easily and do daily grow . . . the privileges of the subject being once lost are not recovered but with much disquiet'. Eighty years of disquiet reversed that situation. First Parliament attempted to safeguard its own position since, as long as the monarch could dismiss and summon it at will, its power was precarious: an Act of 1641 demanded *triennial parliaments and, though it was modified after the Restoration, it was made effective in 1694. *Purveyancing—the right of the crown to buy at its own prices—for centuries a bone of contention, was formally abolished in 1660, along with *benevolences, *forced loans, and the surviving *feudal dues. *Habeas corpus in 1679 protected subjects from imprisonment without trial. More prerogatives were removed by the *Bill of Rights after the revolution of 1688—the power to suspend laws, and the power to dispense with laws in individual cases 'as it hath been assumed and exercised of late'. Two other measures help to bolt the door—the prohibition of a standing army in peacetime without the consent of Parliament; and the strengthening of the independence of the judges by appointing them on good behaviour (not at will), a practice adopted by William III and confirmed by the Act of *Settlement of 1701.

After 1688 the monarchy retained formidable powers, but over the next 150 years most of its prerogatives either fell into abeyance or were appropriated by the prime minister. The right to veto legislation was not exercised after 1708 and is presumably defunct. The power to call a general election is now exercised on the advice of the prime minister. Choice of ministers remained a tug-of-war throughout the 18th and early 19th cents. but is now a matter for the prime minister. Except for some special orders, honours are now given on the advice of the prime minister: the crown lost an important prerogative when William IV agreed in 1832 to create peers to carry the *Great Reform Bill if necessary. It is not easy to know what prerogatives are left to the monarch in the late 20th cent. In a crisis, he or she retains a certain power of initiative: George V begged the warring politicians in 1910 and again in 1914 to negotiate but the results were not encouraging. Though the monarch retains some reserve power in the choice of prime minister, he or she acts carefully on advice, and changes to the method of selecting the party leaders have greatly reduced the area of uncertainty. As *Churchill once declared, 'the prerogatives of the crown have become the privileges of the people'. JAC

Royal Scottish Academy. In the 18th cent. the opportunities in Edinburgh for exhibition did not stop the flow of Scottish painters to London where there was greater demand as well as the possibility of becoming a Royal Academician. On the initiative of the artists themselves, the Scottish Academy was founded in 1826 and received its royal charter in 1838. Membership became an important factor in fostering the idea of a separate Scottish School and the annual exhibitions at the RSA became popular with English as well as Scots artists. JC

Royal Society. The oldest surviving scientific body in the world, the Royal Society was founded in 1660 and obtained its first charter in 1662, for the promotion of natural knowledge. Religion and politics were excluded; and the charter brought respectability, and the right to publish. In 1665 Henry Oldenburg, the secretary, began a journal, *Philosophical Transactions*, which evolved from letters to papers, and still continues. Earlier groups had flourished and collapsed, but the Royal Society with its elected president, secretary, treasurer, and council could go on indefinitely. Unlike the Paris Academy of Sciences founded soon after, it was and is a kind of club, and it was not until Humphry *Davy was president in the 1820s that a majority on council had published any science. Joseph *Banks reigned for over forty years, 1778–1820; but since the mid-19th cent. terms of office have been limited, and entry strictly controlled. Instead of a group of mostly amateur enthusiasts, the society by the 1870s had become a body of distinguished professional scientists, so specialized that in the 1880s the *Philosophical Transactions* was divided into 'physical' and 'biological' parts. Since the mid-19th cent. the society has received a parliamentary grant to support research, and increasingly it has advised governments about science, so that it has come to function more like an academy. It has a splendid library, but has never had a laboratory. DK

Royal Society for the Prevention of Cruelty to Animals. The RSPCA, the largest animal welfare organization, grew out of the humane movement's concern about abuse of working animals, entertainments (cock-fighting), and slaughterhouse conditions. Early bills were defeated, but the group formed by Revd Arthur Broome to enforce Martin's Cattle Cruelty Act (1822) pursued both prosecution and propaganda. Princess Victoria's patronage, royal endorsement (1840), and burgeoning auxiliary societies outside London increased the society's prestige and prosperity, and its influence began to spread overseas. A network of local branches and animal shelters evolved, and the crusade continues against transit offences and illegal sports, and for wild mammals' protection. ASH

Royal Society of Arts. Founded in 1754 by William Shipley, a drawing-master from Northampton, supported by Viscount Folkestone and Lord Romney. Its objective was to 'encourage Arts, Manufactures and Commerce' and the method was to raise funds by subscription in order to award prizes for useful talents and inventions. The early members included *Johnson, *Goldsmith, *Hogarth, *Gibbon, *Pitt, *Chippendale, and *Banks. In 1774 it moved into the premises in the Adelphi, built by the *Adam brothers, which it has occupied ever since. The society was largely instrumental, with its patron Prince *Albert, in planning the *Great Exhibition of 1851. It holds meetings nationally and locally and publishes a journal. JAC

Royal Titles Act, 1876. After the Indian mutiny in 1857, sovereignty in India was transferred to the crown and the governor-general became a viceroy. The elevation of Wilhelm I to be Emperor (of Germany) seems to have upset Victoria, who asked her private secretary in 1873, 'why have I never officially assumed this title?' The change of prime minister in 1874 from *Gladstone to *Disraeli enabled the measure to go ahead, despite objections that the title was un-English. By the Royal Titles Act (39 & 40 Vic. c. 10) the queen became Empress of India. JAC

Royal Ulster Constabulary. Created under the terms of the Constabulary Act (1922) as a police force for Northern Ireland, the RUC was modelled on the Royal Irish Constabulary (which was disbanded in 1922), being armed and centrally controlled. The initial establishment was 3,000 men, and it was the original intention to allocate one-third of this total to catholic recruits: however this quota was never filled. The RUC lost 6 men and had 30 wounded during the *Irish Republican Army border campaign (1956–62); just under 200 full-time RUC men and over 100 RUC Reserve were killed between 1969 and 1994, while a total of over 7,000 were injured in the same period. The 'troubles' brought radical change to the force: it was restructured along English lines in 1970, following the Hunt Report, and was enlarged from 3,500 members in March 1970 to almost 8,500 members by November 1991. AJ

Royal Victorian Order. The order was founded in 1896 for members of the royal household and is at the personal disposal of the monarch. The classes are Knights Grand Cross, Knights Commander, Commander, and Member. The chapel of the order is at the Queen's Chapel, Savoy (London). The Royal Victorian medal is associated with the order. JAC

Royce, Sir (Frederick) Henry (1863–1933). Royce was an engineer whose first large commission was to install a system of electric street lighting in Liverpool. That was in 1882, and two years later he moved to Manchester and established his own electrical engineering firm. With the advent of the automobile he was drawn into this new field of engineering and in 1904 produced his first motor car. His early vehicles so impressed the automobile enthusiast C. S. *Rolls with their smooth running and reliability that the two men entered into partnership in 1906 as Rolls-Royce Ltd. Royce provided the engineering talent, and developed the superb marque of large, 40–50 horsepower motorcars of which the Silver Ghost was the first, to be followed by the Phantom and Wraith models in the 1920s. Rolls was killed in an aeroplane accident in 1910, and Royce suffered a severe illness in the following year as a result of overwork. In the *First World War he responded to pleas from the British government by manufacturing the Eagle aeroplane engine, and he went on to design other aero-engines, some of which won the Schneider trophy in 1929 and 1931. Royce was created a baronet in 1930. RAB

rugby football. William Webb Ellis is credited with inventing rugby in 1823 by picking up the ball while playing football at Rugby School and running with it. The claim is much disputed but there is little doubt that rugby developed at public schools out of a large-scale, few-rules, mauling scrum game. Other schools played with different shapes and sizes of ball until the oval ball gained favour to facilitate handling and passing. Definition of the code began in 1863 when the Football Association was formed and outlawed handling and hacking. Richmond, Blackheath, and some London clubs stayed with the handling code and in 1871, at the Pall Mall restaurant, the Rugby Football Union was formed. The Scottish Rugby Union followed in 1873, the Irish in 1874, and the Welsh in 1881. As in soccer, the balance moved in favour of northern clubs and there were accusations of professionalism, under the pretence of expenses and broken-time payments. In 1895 St Helens, Wigan, and a number of northern clubs formed a breakaway union, which became the Rugby Football League in 1922. The number of players was reduced from fifteen to thirteen and scrums restricted to produce a fast handling game, which would attract spectators. Rugby league also gave rise to a large number of amateur clubs.

The first rugby union international match was played at Raeburn Place (Edinburgh) in 1871 between Scotland and England, and the Calcutta Cup was introduced in 1879. The spread of the game to the former dominions and some unlikely spots such as Romania allowed the introduction of World Cup competitions in the 1980s. Rugby league made little progress in southern England but spread to Australia, New Zealand, and France, allowing international 'test' competitions.

The two codes, amateur and professional, treated each other with disdain for many years and those union players who turned professional, often with marked success, were at once banned from the amateur game. But the advent of television and the growth of commercial values after the Second World War led to a gradual thaw. Rugby union introduced a league system, with promotion and relegation, expenses became ever more substantial, and the ban on players returning after playing rugby league was lifted in 1995. Full professionalism followed. In 1996, in two exhibition matches between the two codes, Wigan outplayed Bath 82–6 at Maine Road (Manchester) in the league game; at Twickenham, in the return match under union rules, Bath won 44–19. NJB

Rugby School is a boys' public school founded by Laurence Sheriff, a merchant grocer of London, in 1567. Originally built opposite the parish church, the school became unfit for use in 1748 and was rebuilt on its present site consisting of a school house, quad, chapel, and a magnificent playing field. In 1797 the 'Great Rebellion', a mutiny by the pupils, was dealt with by soldiers with fixed bayonets and drovers with horsewhips. The game of rugby takes its name from the school where the sport is said to have originated. The subsequent high reputation of the school stems from the headmastership of Thomas *Arnold. PG

'Rule, Britannia!' A song with chorus from the final scene of Thomas Arne's masque *Alfred* (words by James Thomson and David Mallett), first performed at the prince of Wales's residence Cliveden in 1740. It was published shortly afterwards as 'The celebrated ODE, in Honour of Great BRITAIN call'd Rule BRITANNIA'. It has been quoted by various composers, including Beethoven in a set of piano variations and his 'Battle' Symphony. It has become a second British national anthem and is traditionally sung at the last night of London's *Promenade Concerts, frequently by a redoubtable mezzo-soprano. ECr

Rump Parliament. What remained of the Long Parliament's House of Commons after *Pride's Purge. Claiming to be the representative of the sovereign people, it assumed full legislative authority, and its early acts (January–May 1649) set up the tribunal that sentenced Charles I to death, abolished the monarchy and the House of Lords, and declared England to be a commonwealth. Regarded by the army as a mere caretaker government, it soon readmitted many more than its original 70 or so members, forgot its promises of early elections, took on a more conservative temper, and settled down to surviving. It only came under serious pressure to make way for a successor when *Cromwell and his officers returned from the wars in Scotland and Ireland in 1651, and even then it sought to hold elections only to the many vacant seats. Eventually it introduced a bill for a genuinely new parliament, but the army remained unsatisfied, and Cromwell forcibly expelled the Rump on 20 April 1653. The army reinstated it in May 1659 after a coup against Richard *Cromwell, but interrupted it again from 13 October to 26 December. Its independent existence finally ended when General *Monck readmitted the members 'secluded' in Pride's Purge on 21 February 1660. AHW

Runcie, Robert (b. 1921). Archbishop of Canterbury. After war service as a tank commander, winning the MC, Runcie graduated from Brasenose College, Oxford. He was successively principal of Cuddesdon Theological College (1960), bishop of St Albans (1970), and archbishop (1980). A liberal catholic, witty and intelligent, he developed Canterbury's quasi-patriarchal role by frequent visits overseas, including at least seven to Africa, two to China, and several to eastern Europe and in 1988 to the USSR. To 'Europeanize Canterbury' he fostered relations with other west European churches, whether catholic or protestant. As the first archbishop to propose 'an ecumenical primacy' for Rome, he welcomed Pope John Paul II on the first ever papal visit to Canterbury cathedral (1982). Vilified by the media for compassion towards bereaved Argentinians after the *Falklands War (1982) and also for *Faith in the City* (1985), a report exposing poor urban conditions, Runcie also faced controversy over women's ordination. The first women deacons were ordained in his primacy (1987). He retired in 1991. WMM

Rupert, Prince (1619–82). Prince Rupert had two military careers, as an army officer until 1646 and as a naval commander thereafter. Son of *Elizabeth, queen of Bohemia, a grandson of James I, and first cousin to Charles II, he was born in Prague just before his parents were driven out at the start of the Thirty Years War. In his teens he gained military experience in Holland, but was taken prisoner by the Austrians in 1638 and spent nearly three years in captivity. Within months of his release, he travelled to Nottingham and placed himself at the service of his uncle Charles I. For the next four years he was the toast of the royalists, the terror of the roundheads, and the mainstay of the king's war effort, more sober than *Goring, more resourceful than *Hopton. His forte was the cavalry raid, surprising outposts, sweeping down on garrisons, catching the enemy off guard. He fought in the first skirmish of the war at Powick Bridge, commanded the right wing at *Edgehill, led the daring raid which culminated in *Chalgrove Field, and harassed *Essex at the first battle of *Newbury. His relief of York in 1644 was a tactical masterpiece and his subsequent defeat at *Marston Moor was probably due to his understanding that the king had given him 'peremptory' orders to engage, though heavily outnumbered. He took overall command of the royal forces in November 1644 when it was too late and was defeated at *Naseby in June 1645. Sent to hold Bristol, he surrendered in September 1645, causing a bitter breach with the king, who reproached him for 'so mean an action'. Rupert left the country in July 1646.

The next few years were spent commanding small naval squadrons. He took a fleet to Ireland in 1649 but was outgunned by *Blake, and from 1650 to 1652 cruised in the Mediterranean and West Indies, preying on parliamentary shipping and attempting by privateering to improve royal finances. His chance to exercise high naval command came after the Restoration, when he returned to England and shared responsibility in the second and third *Anglo-Dutch wars with *Monck (Albemarle) and James, duke of York. Confronted by tough and experienced Dutch admirals, his triumphs were less heady than on land, though the action off *Lowestoft in 1665 was an important victory.

After the Restoration, Rupert was prominent at the court of Charles II. He retained his reputation as a dashing leader of men, yet he was already a figure from the past, solemn among the wits and gallants of the new generation. He suffered from a head wound gained fighting for the French against the Spaniards in 1647 and survived two operations for trepanning. The combination of high rank, strong views, and a life spent in camps and on board ships made him forthright, though he was not devoid of political judgement. A lifelong servant of the Stuart cause, he is buried in Westminster abbey. JAC

Ruskin, John (1819–1900). Ruskin was the most influential art critic of his time as well as a talented draughtsman and water-colourist. The son of a wealthy wine merchant, he was able to travel extensively after Oxford, developing his artistic knowledge. His large written output gave him enormous influence over public opinion; he successfully defended the *Pre-Raphaelites and championed *Turner. While continuing to write prolifically on art, after 1860 he also wrote on social, political, and economic matters. These writings emphasized his view of the moral function of the arts as a 'visible sign of national virtue'. Ruskin disliked the effects of the industrial revolution, but also resisted plans to improve mass design in industry, as commercially tainted. In 1870 he was appointed Slade professor at Oxford and endowed the Drawing School there. His last years were marred by mental illness and he died in the Lake District having rarely spoken for several years. JC

Russell, Bertrand, 3rd Earl Russell (1872–1970). In his long and complex life, Russell took many roles. He was a grandson of the Lord John *Russell who had introduced the *Great Reform Bill in 1831. After a distinguished mathematics and philosophy course at Trinity College, Cambridge, he was elected to a fellowship. His major early work was *Principles of Mathematics*, written by 1910 but not published until 1930. It was followed by *Principia mathematica* (1911) and *The Problems of Philosophy* (1912). During the First World War Russell's pacifist activities resulted in the loss of his fellowship. In the inter-war years he lectured and wrote copiously, was increasingly tempted to set up as sage, and produced facile, readable essays. In 1938 he took an academic post in America and stayed there for most of the Second World War. His *History of Western Philosophy* (1945) sold well and removed his financial troubles. He was given the OM (1949) and the Nobel prize for literature (1950). His private life continued to be as demanding as ever, with four marriages, and innumerable affairs. From 1954 onwards he took a prominent part in the *Campaign for Nuclear Disarmament, instantly recognizable in public demonstrations against the bomb. His judgement became foolish and he declared that Harold *Macmillan was worse than Hitler. By his supporters he was regarded as a man of vast moral authority, by his opponents as a rather dotty peer. JAC

Russell, Lord John, 1st Earl Russell (1792–1878). Prime minister. A small, cocky man, with an abrasive and resilient personality, Russell was the third son of the duke of Bedford and was educated at Westminster and Edinburgh University. He entered Parliament in 1818, sitting for several constituencies until returned for the City of London in 1841, which he represented until his elevation to the peerage as Earl Russell. He first made his mark in taking a leading role in the repeal of the *Test and Corporation Acts as they affected protestant dissenters in 1828 and he supported *catholic emancipation in 1829. In *Grey's administration he helped to draft the Reform Bill, introduced it in the Commons, and was prominent in securing its passage through Parliament. Russell used the argument of 'finality' with such enthusiasm that he earned the nickname 'Finality Jack'. Ironically his later career demonstrated that the reform carried in 1832 was not the final step but the first in taking Britain down the road to democracy. Russell was never an advocate of universal suffrage, however. In the 1860s he favoured reducing the franchise qualification but not the total abolition of a property level. In the abortive Reform Bill introduced during his second premiership in 1865–6 he sought to lower the household franchise in the boroughs from £10 to £7. During his long career Russell served in many offices of state. He was home secretary and colonial secretary under *Melbourne, leader of the House under *Aberdeen, foreign secretary under first Aberdeen and later *Palmerston. He was twice prime minister: from 1846 to 1852 and again in 1865 to 1866. Russell never disguised his convictions. This made him a wayward colleague. In 1845 he became a convert to the repeal of the *Corn Laws. Outraged by what he saw as papal aggression he denounced the revival of catholic bishoprics in England in 1850 and introduced the controversial *Ecclesiastical Titles Bill in 1851. He had strong sympathies with Italian nationalism. During the American Civil War he kept Britain neutral but refused to accept responsibility for the damage inflicted on Federal commerce by the Confederate raider the **Alabama*, which had been built on the Mersey. He sympathized with the Poles and the Danes but could do little to help them. Though associated in the public mind with Palmerston, Russell's relationship with his famous colleague was often stormy. Russell had been happy to see Palmerston go after the approval he had given to Louis Napoleon's coup in December 1851. In turn he fell victim to Palmerston's desire for revenge when in 1852 his government was defeated on its militia proposals. Russell was almost as difficult a premier as he was a colleague. He often failed to consult colleagues and, though he was quick to identify crucial issues and to see the need to act, he was less successful in carrying his colleagues with him. In his second premiership he was determined to take the lead in introducing parliamentary reform, which he believed had been thwarted by Palmerston for too long. But he could not manage shifting opinions within the Commons and had the mortification of going out of office and seeing *Disraeli carry a Reform Bill which was more advanced than that which Russell had proposed. Russell has never had as much attention from historians as several of his contemporaries but he was closely involved in many major political controversies and was often central to the conduct of events. He did not lack intelligence but his judgement was questionable. As a Whig, standing within the Foxite tradition, he edited the correspondence of Charles James *Fox for publication, but his enthusiasm for his subject outran his skills as an editor.

JWD

Russell, Lord William (1639–83). Russell, son of the earl of Bedford, entered Parliament in 1660 for the family borough of Tavistock and became a leader of the *Shaftesbury Whigs. In 1678 he moved an address asking Charles II to remove his brother James, duke of York, from his counsels and in 1680 he joined in presenting the duke as a notorious papist. He was a strong advocate of the bill to exclude James from the throne. But the court took its revenge. In 1683 Russell was accused of complicity in the *Rye House plot to assassinate James and Charles and was beheaded in Lincoln's Inn Fields. After the Glorious Revolution, his services to the Whig cause were recognized in the dukedom granted to his father, the patent of which described Russell as 'the ornament of his age'. The *Complete Peerage*, by contrast, called him a 'canonised ruffian'. JAC

Russia, relations with. The search for the North-East Passage to Asia in the 1550s opened up a direct route to Russia, and led to a mutually advantageous trade until the 1620s. But once Russia became the leading power in the Baltic from 1709, Britain (with her huge demand for naval stores from that region) had to take considerable account of this new force. In 1780 Catherine the Great organized the Armed Neutrality coalition in response to Britain's naval blockade methods during the *American War of Independence. By the end of the century Britain was also beginning to fear Russian expansion at the expense of the Ottoman empire. The two powers co-operated in the overthrow of Napoleon (1814–15), but only for each to feel that the other had profited excessively from the war. Competition was soon renewed over the Ottoman empire and to some extent in Persia. Fear of Russia in central Asia was the cause of two British bids to turn *Afghanistan into a client state (1839–42 and 1878–80).

Meanwhile in Europe Russia was distrusted as an ultra-reactionary power which seemed all too anxious to interfere in the affairs of other states, though first *Canning (1826–7) and then *Palmerston (1839–41) worked briefly with Russia in Near Eastern crises. Later fears of Russian ambitions at the expense of the Ottoman empire and outrage among British progressives against Russia as the defender of autocracy led to the *Crimean War (1854–6). Russia and Britain nearly came to blows again in the Near East in 1878 as well as over Penj-deh (Afghanistan) in 1885. Only defeat by Japan and revolution at home in 1905 forced Russia to conclude an *entente with Britain in August 1907. The two were rarely comfortable partners, even during the First World War.

The Bolshevik triumph in November 1917 was followed by civil war in which Britain gave some support to the counter-revolutionaries (the Whites). Anglo-Soviet relations in the inter-war years were at best distant and usually frigid. Despite the rise of Nazi Germany from 1933 it was not until the British guaranteed Poland in March 1939 that they saw the need for some sort of agreement with the USSR. The half-heartedness of British approaches was only partly responsible for Moscow's final decision to opt for the Nazi–Soviet pact in August 1939. From June 1941 Britain and the USSR were allies in the war against Germany, the Anglo-American landings in northern France in June 1944 being dependent on the Soviet pressure on Germany in the east. But British worries soon began to accumulate concerning the scale and implications of post-war Soviet and communist influence in Europe. For 40 years from the late 1940s Britain was deeply involved in the *Cold War struggle with the USSR, though the governments of *Churchill, *Eden, and *Macmillan in particular helped to pioneer the search for greater restraint in the conduct of East–West rivalries.

CJB

Russia Company. The pioneers of a North-East Passage to Russia were rewarded by the English government in 1555 with a trading charter with exclusive rights. The tsar also granted them special privileges. The charter was confirmed by an Act of 1566. Fur and timber were imported, cloth exported. Dutch competition and the tsar's hostility to a republican regime made difficulties during the Commonwealth and the company ceased to trade corporately. The monopoly was opened up by an Act of 1699 and trade with Russia flourished in the 18th cent. JAC

Rutherford, Ernest (1871–1937). Rutherford's work in radioactivity and nuclear physics changed our views of matter. He was born in New Zealand, and on graduating won a scholarship to go to Cambridge to work with J. J. *Thomson. In 1898 he went to McGill University in Canada, where he proved that radioactivity was subatomic chemical change: one element was turning into another spontaneously, but at a definite rate. This new alchemy made his reputation. In 1907 he moved to Manchester, and in 1919 succeeded Thomson at the Cavendish Laboratory in Cambridge, where he built up one of the greatest research schools in the history of science, far more than the sum of its parts. Artificial nuclear fission, and the existence of neutrons, were among the facts demonstrated there. The bluff Rutherford was especially good at devising relatively simple and decisive experiments. He was made a peer in 1931.

DK

Ruthven raid, 1582. This was an episode in the faction fighting during the minority of James VI of Scotland. Resentful of the influence of the king's cousin Esmé Stuart, who led the pro-French and pro-catholic party and had been created earl in 1580 and duke of *Lennox in 1581, a protestant group, led by the 1st earl of *Gowrie, seized the 16-year-old king and held him captive for ten months. Stuart was forced to return to France but James escaped in June 1583 and took refuge in St Andrews. An insincere reconciliation was followed in 1584 by Gowrie's execution. JAC

Ruthwell cross (Dumfries and Galloway). Though now heavily restored, this carving epitomizes the classical tastes of early Anglo-Saxon monastic art. Originally some 17 feet high, it is elaborately decorated on all four sides. The narrow faces carry full-length panels of vine-scroll; around their borders is a runic text of part of the Old English poem *The Dream of the Rood*. The broader faces are divided into a series of deeply cut figural panels whose iconography, and accompanying Latin inscriptions, focus on the recognition of Christ's divine power, particularly as expressed in the eucharist. The carving probably dates to the first half of the 8th cent. RNB

Rutland was for more than seven centuries a tiny county, some 17 miles across, and only one-fortieth the size of Yorkshire. It had no clear geographical definition but was pleasant, gentle, wooded countryside, hunted from the 1720s by the Cottesmore. There were only two towns, Oakham, the county town, and Uppingham, famous for its school, founded in 1584.

In the early Saxon period, Rutland formed part of the kingdom of the *Middle Angles, and then of *Mercia. The existence close at hand of Stamford, one of the five Danish boroughs, must have meant considerable Viking influence, at least in the eastern half. It had not acquired county status by the time of the Norman Conquest, but was given as their personal property to successive queens. When John granted it to *Isabella in 1204, it was described as a county, and at the end of the century was given two knights of the shire, like the other counties. In the absence of much middle-class element, Rutland was totally under the domination of the gentry and nobility, particularly the owners of Exton, Burley-on-the-Hill, Normanton, Whissendine, and the Cecils of Burghley, near Stamford. Elections were very rarely contested, and the Noel family held one seat from 1727 until 1883, save for 1841–7. The county lost one of its two seats in 1885.

During the Civil War, Rutland was under parliamentary control and formed part of the Midland Association, though there was skirmishing and raiding. The population in the 1970s was no more than 25,000, of whom 5,000 lived in Oakham. By the Local Government Act of 1972 the county was merged with Leicestershire, though a vigorous protest movement continued. The protestors triumphed in 1994 when the Banham commission on local government recommended the restoration of Rutland's county status, as a unitary authority. JAC

Rye House plot, 1683. This quasi-republican plot, the plans for which were never finalized, was directed against the persons if not the lives of Charles II and James, duke of York. Disclosed to the crown in June 1683, it would have involved intercepting the royal brothers at the Rye House (near Hoddesdon, Herts.) on their return from Newmarket. This return had in fact been brought forward owing to a fire at Newmarket, and hence the plot was forestalled. Charles II could now be quite relentless in upholding James's succession rights after *'Exclusion's' failure, and such opponents as *Russell and *Sidney suffered through a wide application of treason law. DDA

Rysbrack, John Michael (1694–1770). Flemish-born sculptor, who settled in England about 1720 and was soon making portrait busts for most of the leading men of his day, often using a classical style new to Britain, as in his statue of Sir Robert *Walpole as a Roman senator, in Houghton Hall (Norfolk). A prolific artist, especially skilful in handling equestrian subjects, for instance his William III in Bristol, his approach was simple and dignified. Although *Roubiliac overtook him in popularity, Rysbrack remained a formidable rival. There are numerous monuments in Westminster abbey and other examples of Rysbrack's work in the Royal Collection, cathedrals, noble houses, and galleries throughout Britain. JC

Ryswick, treaty of, 1697. In July 1697 the treaty brought to an end the *Nine Years War, in which Louis XIV's France faced a grand coalition of England, the emperor, the Dutch, and Spain. Louis agreed to return most of his territorial acquisitions or *réunions* made since *Nijmegen, but retained the important fortress town of Strasbourg. He recognized William III as king of England while refusing to order James II to leave French territory. The Dutch were allowed to garrison *barrier fortresses in the Spanish Netherlands. The treaty, negotiated with much difficulty, lasted only four years before the *War of the Spanish Succession broke out. JAC

sabbatarianism. Strict observance of the sabbath (Hebrew *shabath*—to rest) as a rest-day in accordance with the fourth commandment 'Remember the sabbath day, to keep it holy'. Christians transferred commemoration from the traditional seventh day to Sunday to honour Christ's resurrection—by worship rather than absence of work. Nevertheless Constantine decreed limits of Sunday work (321). Sabbatarianism was uniquely enforced by 17th-cent. English and Scottish presbyterians, especially in the *Interregnum. For puritans sabbath-keeping had to be total. Puritan magistrates' inflexible enforcement led James I to issue his *book of sports (1618, reissued in 1633), allowing sabbath participation in morris-dancing, maypole, and rush-bearing. Vehemently opposed as 'iniquity established by law', this prompted many to emigrate to America. Eighteenth-cent. church courts were still hearing cases of sabbath-breaking by work, 'tippling', or games. The evangelical revival made sabbatarianism fashionable, so that on a Victorian Sunday there was no sport or pleasure, not even reading of serious secular literature. In the 20th cent. there has been progressive relaxation until Sunday trading is freely allowed (1990s). WMM

sac and soc. Medieval legal phrase, possibly of Danish origin, referring to manorial jurisdiction. It was at the expense of the hundred court, though not the county court. Though each word had its original and precise meaning, it became what Stubbs called 'a mere alliterative jingle', which did not bear close analysis. The phrase survived in the privilege of the soke of Peterborough, where special jurisdiction over eight hundreds was granted to the abbey of Peterborough. JAC

Sacheverell riots, 1710. These erupted in London's West End on the night of 1/2 March 1710 following the third day of the impeachment of Dr Henry Sacheverell. This outspoken high Anglican Oxford don was on trial at Westminster Hall for publishing a sermon condemning the Whig government for undermining the fabric of church and state through its favouritism towards dissenters. Rioters from a broad cross-section of London society, inspirited with church fervour and anti-government hatred, demonstrated their sympathy for the doctor by sacking and burning six prominent dissenting chapels. The trial and the riots heralded the collapse of the *Godolphin ministry in August. AAH

Sacket's harbour, battle of, 1813. During the *War of 1812, British and American forces struggled for control of Lake Ontario. In May 1813 Sir George Prevost, governor-general of Canada, launched an attack upon the American base at Sacket's harbour, at the east end of the lake, but was repulsed. Initial success was cancelled by Prevost's caution. JAC

Sadler, Sir Ralph (1507–87). Sadler spent much of his life among the Scots, a nation he thought 'unreasonable, rude, beastly and inconsistent'. But at least he was rewarded and died a wealthy man. His career began under the patronage of Thomas *Cromwell. He was made a gentleman of the privy chamber in 1536, knighted in 1538, and appointed a secretary of state in 1540. Though he served in most of the parliaments during his lifetime, he was not of the first rank as a speaker. He was employed in several missions to James V of Scotland and after his death in 1542 returned to try to negotiate a future marriage between Prince Edward and Mary, queen of Scots. When this went wrong and resulted in war, Sadler took the field. A strong protestant, he was under a cloud in Mary Tudor's reign but on Elizabeth's accession was sent back to Scotland to foster the reforming party. In 1568 he negotiated with the Scots over Mary and forwarded the incriminating Casket Letters. In 1569 he helped to suppress the rising of the *northern earls. His last active service was to have charge of Mary, 1584–5. From 1568 he was chancellor of the duchy of Lancaster. Small in stature, he was reputed competent and honest. JAC

sailing covers a great range of activity from ocean racing to 12-foot dinghy competitions, or merely messing around in boats. At the top end of the sport is the America's Cup, preserve of millionaires and syndicates, and named after the famous yacht which caused such a sensation when it visited Cowes in 1851. The Fastnet race, started in 1925, is from Cowes to Ireland and back to Plymouth. Yachting was admitted to the Olympics in 1908. The governing body is the Royal Yachting Association, which organizes Cowes week in August. There is a Dinghy Cruising Association, and large numbers of local competitions are arranged by clubs, in rivers and estuaries, gravel pits and reservoirs. JAC

St Albans, battle of, 1455. The first battle of St Albans on 22 May was little more than a hand-to-hand skirmish in the streets of the town. But since it ushered in the Wars of the

*Roses, the consequences were important. Richard, duke of *York, had marched south, demanding from Henry VI the dismissal of his rival the duke of *Somerset. The Yorkist victory was largely owing to Richard, earl of *Warwick ('the Kingmaker'). Somerset and his supporters Northumberland and Clifford were killed, Henry VI captured, watching the proceedings. JAC

St Albans, battle of, 1461. The second battle of St Albans took place on 17 February 1461. Queen *Margaret hastened south to exploit her crushing victory at *Wakefield and rescue her husband Henry VI, held captive by *Warwick. The Yorkists were again defeated, despite some novel netting traps and devices, but Warwick salvaged some troops and joined the future Edward IV from Wales. Henry VI was released by his queen, who failed to follow up her advantage and allowed Edward to beat her to London. JAC

St Albans, diocese of. Now conterminous with Bedfordshire and Hertfordshire, the see was founded in 1877 from parts of the *Rochester diocese (Herts., Essex and north Woolwich). This was a failure, and Essex and north Woolwich were removed in 1914 to form the new see of *Chelmsford; in return St Albans gained Bedfordshire from *Ely, a more natural liaison. The city, well known for its early history as *Verulamium, a principal Romano-British city, was where St *Alban, the first British martyr, reputedly met his death. Because of this Pope Hadrian IV gave its wealthy Benedictine abbey, founded by *Offa of Mercia *c.*794, special precedence over all other English monasteries. Its abbot headed his colleagues in 14th-cent. parliaments. *Matthew Paris, the medieval chronicler, was a St Albans monk from 1217 to 1259. The cathedral is the former abbey church, which served the parish after the *dissolution. Built between 1077 and 1088 to replace the original Saxon church of Offa, it is basically Norman with 13th-cent. additions. Its exterior is the second longest (521 feet) in Europe, after *Winchester. Recently a new chapter house has been completed (1982) and St Alban's shrine restored (1993). WMM

St Andrews is a city, royal burgh, and university town in the north-east of the county of Fife in Scotland, some 55 miles north of Edinburgh. It developed from a royal fortress of the Picts situated on the site later built over by St Andrews castle. Celtic clergy were attracted to nearby Kilrymont. Never technically part of the medieval burgh, this area fostered the cult of St *Andrew, which became national. Between 1160 and 1318 was built the cathedral which with its 357-foot long nave was the largest church in Scotland.

A municipality was erected under Bishop Robert around 1140. In 1412–13 Bishop Wardlaw and Pope Benedict XIII incorporated and chartered St Andrews University, the nation's first. An important medieval town, and from 1472 the seat of an archbishop, St Andrews was a cockpit of the Reformation. John *Knox retired there, while Andrew *Melville, father of Scots presbyterianism and bane of King James VI and I, was head of St Mary's College. Still the university of Scotland's aristocracy in the 17th cent., it declined in the 18th due to Jacobite associations, reviving in the 20th. Uniquely good golfing facilities helped the town to become a residential and resort centre from the mid-19th cent. BPL

St Asaph, diocese of. It is claimed that the church at St Asaph (Llanelwy) was founded by St Kentigern (Mungo), a fugitive from Strathclyde, in the 6th cent. The cathedral, however, bears the name of his successor, Asaph. Later, as a territorial diocese, the see approximated to the native Welsh principality of Powys, extending from the Conwy in the west to the Dee in the east, and as far south as Newtown in Montgomeryshire. The area of the diocese remains little changed today, and is made up of contrasting regions. Many of the popular north Wales coastal resorts, the industrial heartland of Deeside, the populous town of Wrexham, and the largely Welsh-speaking upland farming districts of Merionethshire come within its borders. The ancient Welsh *clas* (monastic community) at St Asaph seems to have survived into the 12th cent., for the Norman diocese dates only from 1143, and serious work on the cathedral—the smallest in England and Wales—does not seem to have begun before 1230. Most of the church dates from the 14th cent. Severely damaged in the Owain *Glyndŵr revolt, and again under the Commonwealth, it was subject to a major restoration by Gilbert *Scott between 1867 and 1875. JRG

St Brice's Day massacre, 13 November 1002. Considered a cardinal blunder committed by King *Æthelred, who is said to have ordered the killing of all Danes in England on that day. This is scarcely credible, considering the numbers involved. Yet some action was taken, probably provoked by Pallig, the Dane who, after taking Æthelred's gifts, broke his pledge of loyalty by joining raiders ravaging the south coast. The murder of Pallig's wife Gunnhild, sister of the Danish king *Sweyn, may well have provoked Sweyn's invasion in 1003, which was followed by continual onslaught, until in 1017 a Danish king was on the English throne. AM

St Christopher and Nevis are part of the *Leeward Islands in the eastern Caribbean and form an independent republic within the Commonwealth. The islands were visited by Columbus and for some time disputed between Spain, France, and Britain. They were confirmed as a British colony at *Utrecht in 1714. The principal resources are sugar and tourism. JAC

St Davids, diocese of. The cathedral of St *David, which still houses the bones of the patron saint of Wales, is one of the outstanding buildings in the principality. On the site of David's monastery, famous as a centre of learning and for the austerity of its community life, the present cathedral dates from the early 12th cent. and the episcopate of Bishop Bernard. Bernard persuaded Pope Calixtus II to canonize David, and also to decree that two pilgrimages to St Davids were equal to one to Rome, a decision which ensured the popularity of the shrine until the Reformation. Bernard's church was entirely rebuilt by Peter de Leia (1176–97) and enlarged in the 14th and 15th cents. The diocese originally covered the greater part of south-west and mid-Wales, until 1923 when the newly created see of Swansea and Brecon removed Breconshire, Radnorshire, and parts of west Glamorgan from its jurisdiction. It is largely rural, and much of the population bilingual, with few large towns other than Llanelli. In the years since Bernard there have been many notable bishops, including the protestant martyr Robert *Ferrar, William *Laud, and the distinguished patristic scholar George Bull. JRG

Saint-Germain, treaty of, 1919. Peace treaty with Austria after the First World War, signed on 10 September 1919. Austria lost all the non-German parts of her former empire. South Tyrol went to Italy; Slovenia, Bosnia-Herzegovina, and Dalmatia to Yugoslavia; Bohemia and Moravia to Czechoslovakia; Galicia to Poland; and the Bukovina to Romania. The union of Austria and Germany was forbidden and the Austrian army was restricted to 30,000 men. Austria was made liable for reparations and a note attached to the treaty declared that Austria must take her share of responsibility for the war. RAS

St Germans, diocese of. *Athelstan created this specifically Cornish see by dividing the see of *Crediton in 931, though the Celtic church, *Canterbury, and Crediton had in turn provided episcopal oversight for the region. Poverty enforced its reunion with Crediton in 1027. The combined see moved to *Exeter in 1050. WMM

St Helena, a volcanic island in the South Atlantic, is 1,200 miles from Africa and 1,800 from South America. With a length and breadth of 10 miles by 6, it is roughly the size of Jersey. The *East India Company took possession of it in 1659 as a port of call and it has been a British colony ever since. The capital is Jamestown and the population more than 5,000. The British government, much exercised after *Waterloo to know what to do with their unwelcome guest the Emperor Napoleon, found it more secure than Elba, from which he had escaped without difficulty. Lord *Liverpool described it as 'particularly healthy' and 'the safest station that could be found'. Bonaparte spent the last six years of his life at Longwood, under the anxious supervision of the governor, Sir Hudson Lowe. JAC

St James's palace, though still nominally the headquarters of the British monarchy, since ambassadors are accredited to the court there, is not well known and has been much patched. Originally it was the leper hospital of St James's. Henry VIII purchased the property, still in the fields outside London, in 1532 and began building round four courtyards. The basic pattern is still red-brick Tudor. His daughter Mary liked the place and her heart and bowels were buried at the Chapel Royal. Prince *Henry and his younger brother Prince Charles held court there and Charles II, when prince of Wales, escaped from custody there in 1648. During the Commonwealth, it was used as a barracks. At the Restoration, Charles began its renovation and the park, with its lake, was laid out. Nearby Pall Mall was the pitch for the fashionable croquet-like game which the royal princes brought back from their exile in France. The palace was greatly used during the next 100 years, since *Greenwich had been given up and *Whitehall was burned in 1698. The 'warming-pan baby', later to become the old pretender, was born there in June 1688, when the palace was the residence of James II's wife *Mary of Modena. Queen Anne spent most of her time there and at Kensington palace, and the $2\frac{1}{2}$-year-old Samuel *Johnson was taken to St James's to be *touched for the evil by the queen in 1712. George II and Caroline spent much time there and it was to St James's that Frederick, prince of Wales, hustled his wife, in labour, in 1737. Damaged in a fire in 1809, the palace was still much used by Victoria, who was married in 1840 in the Chapel Royal. But gradually *Buckingham palace replaced it for most state occasions, and St James's is now given over to grace-and-favour residences and used only occasionally for grand receptions. JAC

St Kitts. See ST CHRISTOPHER.

St Leger, Sir Anthony (*c.*1496–1569). Lord deputy of Ireland. Of a Kentish family, St Leger married the niece and heiress of *Warham, archbishop of Canterbury, and rose under the patronage of Thomas *Cromwell. In 1537 he was leader of a commission to report on Irish affairs and was knighted in 1539. In 1540 he succeeded *Grey as deputy of Ireland, with a policy of reasserting royal authority, a first step being Henry VIII's adoption of the title king of Ireland. Several of the Irish chiefs, and particularly *O'Neill, were brought to submit. St Leger was given the Garter. He was retained in office on Henry's death in 1547 but returned to England in 1548. When his successor died shortly afterwards, St Leger was sent out again but recalled in 1551 on suspicion of being too conciliatory towards Irish catholics. Mary's reign saw him reinstated for the third time (1553) and he served until 1556, when accusations of peculation were brought against him. His long term of office gave some coherence to English policy and he was credited with a cautious and moderate approach. JAC

St Lucia is one of the *Windward Islands in the eastern Caribbean and an independent member of the Commonwealth with the queen as head of state. It became a French colony in the 17th cent., and changed hands frequently in the 18th cent. before being ceded to Britain in 1814. It relies upon bananas and tourism. JAC

St Michael and St George, Order of. The order was founded by the prince regent in 1818 and is reserved mainly for diplomats. Originally it commemorated British rule over Malta and the Ionian Islands, but the scope has been widened. There are three classes—Knight Grand Cross, Knight Commander, and Companion, with the equivalent female rank of Dame. The order's chapel is in St Paul's. JAC

St Paul's cathedral. The first cathedral was founded by *Æthelbert, king of Kent, on the site of a former Roman temple (604); destroyed by fire, it was rebuilt in stone (675–85) by Bishop Earconweald, whose shrine attracted many medieval pilgrims, but was destroyed by Vikings (962). The third building burned down in 1087, and its replacement, known as 'Old St Paul's', outshone anything previously seen in London. Initially in Norman style, it developed into a great Gothic cathedral with a towering spire, the largest church in England and third largest in Europe. The spacious walled precincts contained Paul's Cross, an open-air pulpit, whence papal bulls, royal proclamations, and impassioned sermons, while the cathedral itself was used for royal ceremonies and thanksgivings. Deprived of much of its revenue by the Reformation, structural decay set in; houses and shops were erected against its walls, and the nave became a common thoroughfare ('Paul's Walk') and place for conducting business. Repairs were makeshift until Inigo *Jones altered the west front and attempted to strengthen the entire fabric (1634–43), but the parliamentarians turned the nave into cavalry barracks and appropriated the rest of the repair fund. A 'loathsome Golgotha' by 1660, *Wren offered a design to the 1663 royal commission, but, although it had been hoped that the cathedral would escape the conflagration, the only thing to survive the Great Fire was John *Donne's effigy. Wren's 'Warrant Design' was approved in 1675, fortunately permitting 'variations, rather ornamental than essential', of which he took full advantage; progress was slow, but it was completed within his lifetime. A resting-place for naval and military commanders (*Nelson, *Wellington) as well as Wren himself, it has continued as a focus for state services, surviving the Blitz and retaining a close relationship with the city, although its skyline dominance has lessened from recent office-building. ASH

Saints, battle of the, 1782. This was the last important naval action in the *American War of Independence. The loss of naval superiority in the western Atlantic in 1781 forced *Cornwallis to surrender at *Yorktown. The French and Spanish then began picking off British West Indian islands and an invasion of Jamaica was expected. *Rodney left Plymouth in January 1782 with reinforcements and on 10 April 1782 won an important victory over de Grasse at the battle of the Saints in the Leeward Islands. The British had a slight superiority in capital ships. The French lost seven vessels, de Grasse was captured, and the threat to Jamaica removed. Though too late to affect the war with the American colonies, Rodney's victory enabled Britain to make a respectable peace with France and Spain, and he received the thanks of Parliament and a peerage. JAC

St Vincent and the Grenadines form part of the *Windward Islands in the eastern Caribbean and are an independent state within the Commonwealth. They are believed to have been named by Columbus but became a French colony until ceded to Britain by the peace of *Paris in 1763. The chief exports are arrowroot, sugar, and bananas. JAC

Salamanca, battle of, 1812. In July 1812 the French, under Marshal Marmont, with 42,000 men manœuvred to cut *Wellington off from his base in Salamanca. Wellington, with 46,000 men, gave ground and appeared to retreat. On 22 July, 6 miles south of the city, Marmont sent his leading division to harass the British. However Wellington was already in position, quickly overcame the division, and then attacked Marmont's centre with a deadly rifle volley and bayonet charge. Marmont was wounded and the French were driven from the field with losses of 13,000. Wellington had destroyed the main French army in Spain and Joseph Bonaparte, the French puppet king, was forced to evacuate Madrid. RAS

Salesbury, William (*c*.1520–*c*.1584). Welsh scholar. Born in Denbighshire and educated at Oxford, Salesbury studied law. He converted to protestantism and began writing in the Welsh language. His collection of Welsh proverbs, published in 1546, is said to have been the first book printed in Welsh. Salesbury followed it with a Welsh–English dictionary in 1547. In 1563 he was commissioned to translate the Bible and Book of Common Prayer into Welsh, within four years. By 1567 only the New Testament was ready. Salesbury did not complete his translation of the Old Testament and his New Testament was replaced by a revised version, issued by William *Morgan in 1588. JAC

Salisbury (Sarum). Cathedral city in Wiltshire. It originated with an Iron Age hill-fort which housed successively a Roman, Anglo-Saxon, and Norman town. In the 1070s it acquired a cathedral, which in the 12th cent. was a major intellectual centre. In 1219 the bishop moved to a new, level site 1½ miles south; a large cathedral was built in uniform style *c*.1220–1320, its tower crowned by the tallest surviving medieval spire in Europe. The bishop also laid out a new town on a grid plan, the best-known planted town of medieval England. The city flourished through the cloth industry, becoming the fourth largest English town in the 15th cent.; acquired independence from the bishops in 1612; and lost its cloth industry in the 18th cent. The original town (*'Old Sarum') had long been deserted, and was the most notorious of the *'rotten boroughs' until disfranchised in 1832. DMP

Salisbury, diocese of. Now roughly conterminous with Wiltshire and Dorset, the see was founded *c*.1075 when the West Saxon bishopric of *Sherborne, united with *Ramsbury in 1058, was moved to Old Sarum. From 1496 to 1499 the Channel Islands, previously under Coutances, were temporarily attached to Salisbury before passing on to *Winchester. In 1542 Dorset and some Wiltshire parishes were incongruously assigned to the new Bristol diocese until 1836, when Salisbury regained Dorset. Bristol retains the north Wiltshire deaneries. Some medieval bishops were significant as officers of the crown. Most distinguished of all, perhaps, was *Roger of Salisbury (1107–39), responsible, as Henry I's justiciar, for major developments in royal administration. Others include Hubert *Walter (1189–93), later archbishop and justiciar under Richard I and John; Richard Poore (1217–28), scholar and noted ecclesiastical administrator; John Waltham (1388–95), treasurer of England in the turbulence of Richard II's reign; Gilbert *Burnet (1689–1715), historian and Whig supporter of William III. The Norman cathedral, built next to the castle by Osmund the first bishop, at Old Sarum, north of the modern city, is now a ruin, but replaced on lower ground by the present magnificent cathedral, conceived by Herbert Poore (1197–1217), begun by his brother Richard in 1220, and completed *c*.1258. The exterior is a splendid example of Early English architecture with its slender 14th-cent. spire, the tallest in England, rising 404 feet above the water-meadows. Liturgically important was the Sarum Rite, largely compiled by Richard Poore, widely used in the late Middle Ages and an important source for the 16th-cent. English Prayer Book. WMM

Salisbury, Robert Gascoyne-Cecil, 3rd marquis of (1830–1903). Prime minister. Salisbury was an unlikely candidate for such a long tenure of the premiership. A younger son of an ancient Tory house, he was intellectual, withdrawn (with little taste for aristocratic sports) and unsociable, seriously high church, sharp-edged in political controversy. From 1863, at odds with his family over his happy but non-aristocratic marriage, he supplemented his allowance by regular journalism (over 600 *Saturday Review* articles and 33 for the *Quarterly Review*), so that we have more of his thinking in print than that of any other prime minister, though none of it dates from his premierships. Though he was an MP for a family borough from 1853 and in *Derby's cabinet in 1866, his prickliness and rigidity made him an awkward colleague and a natural resigner. Anti-democratic and anti-populist in both instinct and argument and long distrustful of *Disraeli as a political mountebank, Cranborne (as he then was) resigned with two cabinet colleagues in early 1867 over the borough franchise proposals in the government's Reform Bill. Out of office he remained a trenchant critic of Disraeli and a standing threat to his leadership. In 1869 he succeeded to the marquisate and the great house at *Hatfield, and succeeded Derby as chancellor of Oxford University and a foremost defender of its Anglican character. He agreed reluctantly to join the government of 1874, clashed with Disraeli over the Public Worship Regulation Bill and was clearly a potential dissident in the Eastern Question crisis. Disraeli had, however, worked to cultivate Salisbury, to whose India Office brief the issue had relevance, and when Derby and *Carnarvon resigned in the critical moment in early 1878 Salisbury threw in his lot with Disraeli and accepted the Foreign Office. His motives seem to have included a desire to effect a desperately needed settlement (which he helped Beaconsfield to do at the Congress of *Berlin) and a distrust of colleagues, a realization of the importance of the Conservatives' hold on office and of resisting *Gladstone's campaign in the country, and an ambition to succeed the ageing Beaconsfield. When the latter died in 1881, Salisbury became party leader in the Lords and co-leader of the whole party with *Northcote. Angered by Liberal land legislation for Ireland, he played a leading role in the obstruction of Liberal measures in the Lords, including the 1884 Franchise Bill which was held up until accompanied by a Redistribution Bill, and began to elaborate a theory of the governmental mandate to regulate relations between the two Houses. Helped by *Churchill's insubordination in the Commons, Salisbury got the better of his rival Northcote, a more centrist and emollient figure, and in 1885 he was the premier in the Conservative caretaker government. He maintained a tactical ambiguity in Irish policy to assist an informal electoral alliance with the Irish party, but, once Gladstone had declared for *Home Rule after the election, Salisbury mounted a resolute defence of the Union and, by polarizing the issue, skilfully exploited Liberal divisions. By summer 1886 Salisbury was back in office, though still without a Conservative majority and dependent on the support of the *Liberal Unionists. This uncomfortable position lasted until 1892 and Salisbury had to make various policy concessions (over Irish land purchase, education, and county councils, for example) to conciliate his allies, particularly the demanding *Chamberlain. This relationship made Salisburian government look more progressive than it would otherwise have done. By 1887 Salisbury had disposed of both Northcote and Churchill and in 1891 he installed his nephew *Balfour, who had made his name with a policy of resolute coercion in Ireland, as leader in the Commons. (Nepotism became a feature of Salisbury's ministries and was resented by those outside the Hatfield circle.) For most of his time as premier Salisbury held the Foreign Office rather than the 1st lordship of the Treasury, though the arrangement reflected no lack of interest in domestic politics. In diplomacy he displayed a skill and caution which kept policy on a steady track and away from the alternating extremes of Gladstone and Disraeli earlier; he saw bi-partisanship as the ideal. He also kept Britain clear of entangling alliances (the ironic description *'splendid isolation' has stuck to this policy), though he was a successful negotiator in reconciling differences over colonial claims.

In opposition Salisbury led the Lords in its overwhelming rejection—by 419 : 41—of Gladstone's second Home Rule Bill in 1893. He was also ruthless in exploiting the queen's Unionist preferences; some of his confidential dealings with her from opposition went beyond accepted constitutional bounds. After the Liberal resignation in 1895 Salisbury brought the Liberal Unionists under Hartington into a formal coalition with the Conservatives and this Unionist government won the election and another in 1900 (the 'khaki' election) when the opportunity of the *Boer War was seized. By now Salisbury's vigour was declining—the approach to war had seen Chamberlain rather than the premier in control of policy—and his policies both at home and abroad were looking dated to younger politicians. He resigned the Foreign Office in 1900 and the premiership in 1902, opening the way for new departures in policy. He did not live to see the sharp divisions caused within Unionism by Chamberlain's tariff reform campaign.

Though Salisbury spent a notable proportion of his later career in office, his governments were either minorities or Unionist coalitions, so that, outside diplomacy, he never had the command of policy to which he aspired. Over the church, which remained dear to his heart, his governments disappointed him. Though a high aristocrat at a time when events were moving against the aristocracy, he recognized the importance of cultivating middle-class and urban opinion, particularly after the 1885 Redistribution Act, and gave firmer support to central office and extra-parliamentary organizations, overseen by the party agent 'Captain' Middleton, than his predecessors had done. He was a free-market ideologue, reflecting the spread of **laissez-faire* ideas from the Liberals to the political right, and an upholder of property rights at a time when bourgeois property, alarmed by Irish developments, trade unionism, and intellectual socialism, was moving rightwards. The Conservative Party became more responsive to business interests (the city of London swung its way) and more hostile to trade unionism; the *Taff Vale case came at the end of Salisbury's premiership. His success owed much to Gladstone's talent for wreaking havoc upon the Liberal Party, and upon the Liberal Unionist Hartington's support from 1886 onwards. In his later years Salisbury could become more relaxed about the simplistic fears of veiled class war—the have-nots plundering the haves—which he had expressed in his early writings. Much of Salisbury's politics had dated by the end of the century and 20th-cent. Conservatives have tended until recently to make little of him in comparison with more presentable figures like *Peel and Disraeli. Salisbury was too much the anti-democrat, too much the free marketeer, for his party's comfort in an age of democracy and welfare economics. Only in the *Thatcher era did his reputation improve and his politics find reappraisal. The toughness and ruthlessness he displayed in his party's interests as well as his own do not easily date. BIC

Blake, R., and Cecil, H. (eds.), *Salisbury: The Man and his Policies* (1987); Marsh, P. T., *The Discipline of Popular Government: Lord Salisbury's Domestic Statecraft, 1881–1902* (Hassocks, 1978).

Salisbury, Robert Gascoyne-Cecil, 5th marquis of (1893–1972). Conservative politician. Cecil entered Parliament in 1929 and served as junior minister at the Foreign Office. He resigned in February 1938 in support of *Eden's opposition to opening talks with Mussolini. Returning to government under *Churchill, he was spoken of as a possible foreign secretary. His peerage—after elevation to the Lords in 1941—was felt to be a handicap for such an office. He continued to prosper after the war, particularly as a result of his close friendship with Eden, and he was one of the more prominent cabinet members during the Suez crisis of 1956. On domestic issues, however, he found himself at odds with the thrust of post-war Conservatism and soon lost sympathy with the premiership of Harold *Macmillan. The occasion of his second resignation was the freeing of the Cypriot leader Makarios from imprisonment in 1957. In his later years he became a focal point for right-wing dissatisfaction, especially through his association with the Monday Club and his support for the white regime in Southern Rhodesia. DJD

Salisbury, Thomas Montagu, 4th earl of (1388–1428). Like John Holand (*Exeter), Salisbury was restored by Henry V to estates forfeited by his father. He amply earned this favour by outstanding service in the French war from 1415 onward. He held Normandy after *Clarence's defeat and death in 1421. He remained there after Henry's death and was *Bedford's principal field commander. He defeated the French at *Cravant, took part in Bedford's victory at *Verneuil, and captured Le Mans. Salisbury began the siege of *Orléans but died, an irreparable loss, before Joan of Arc's campaign. RLS

Salisbury, Richard Neville, 5th earl of (1400–60). Neville was the first son of the (second) marriage of Ralph, 1st earl of *Westmorland, and *John of Gaunt's daughter Anne Beaufort. From 1420 to 1436 he was warden of the west march. Here he built Penrith castle after he inherited his father's estates in Cumberland and Yorkshire in 1425, in accordance with a settlement which impoverished the 2nd earl of Westmorland. Royal offices increased his north country dominance. He gained the earldom of Salisbury by marriage to its heiress. He served in France in 1431–2 and 1436–7. Warden again from 1443, he remained a member of the Beaufort faction controlling the king's council, to his profit both financially and as a source of patronage to his retainers. Percy opposition to his regional preponderance led to violence in which his son John was a ringleader, and became a reason for Salisbury's breach with the court after 1453 and his alliance with Richard of *York. He was chancellor in York's first protectorate and fought with him at *St Albans; in 1459, at *Blore Heath (Staffs.), he defeated royalist forces opposing his junction with York. Following the Yorkist collapse, he was attainted and took refuge at Calais, returning with his son *Warwick to defeat the royalists at *Northampton. He was murdered after the battle of *Wakefield, probably by Percy retainers. RLS

Salisbury, Margaret Pole, countess of (1473–1541). Margaret Plantagenet was a daughter of George, duke of *Clarence, and a niece of Richard III. She married Sir Richard Pole who died in 1505. After the execution of her brother the earl of *Warwick in 1499, she was sole heiress to the dukedom of Clarence and the earldoms of Salisbury and of Warwick, and was granted the title countess of Salisbury in 1513. From 1520 until 1533 she was governess to Princess Mary and subsequently offered to continue at her own expense. But after her son Reginald *Pole was made a cardinal in 1536, Henry VIII moved against the Pole family. Her eldest son Lord Montagu was executed in 1539 and her younger son Geoffrey sentenced to death. The countess was attainted in 1539 and executed in the Tower two years later, the executioner bungling the beheading. She was the last of the Plantagenets. JAC

Salisbury, oath of, 1086. In August 1086 William I summoned 'landowning men of any account' to attend at Salisbury and swear allegiance to him and to be faithful against all other men. The oath was demanded at a time of crisis when the Conqueror was facing revolt and invasion. It has been much discussed and has been seen as an attempt to limit the fissiparous nature of feudal obligations: others have argued that the intention was to reinforce feudal duties. There seems little doubt that it was intended as a practical assurance and reminder rather than as a constitutional statement. JAC

Salisbury, treaty of, 1289. When Alexander III of Scotland died in a fall from his horse at Kinghorn in March 1286, he left no children, but a granddaughter, *Margaret, 'the Maid of Norway', aged 3. A regency was established. In November 1289 commissioners from Norway, England, and Scotland reached agreement at Salisbury, later confirmed by the Scots at *Birgham. The young queen was to be brought to Scotland within a year and was not to be married without Edward I's consent. His intention was to marry the Maid to his son Edward and unite the two kingdoms. But the death of the young queen in September 1290 on the voyage threw all arrangements into confusion. JAC

Salt, Sir Titus (1803–76). Salt, a worsted manufacturer and creator of the model village of Saltaire, entered the wool trade as a stapler and then moved into spinning (1834). By clever technical adaptation, he exploited supplies of imported fine wools such as mohair and alpaca, manufacturing excellent worsteds for the women's fashion market. A radical Liberal, Salt was a paternalist, who wanted to provide a good environment for his workers; he moved from central Bradford and created Saltaire between 1850 and 1875. He rationalized production, previously in several plants, in one great mill (1853), designed in the Tuscan Renaissance style by Lockwood and Mawson of Bradford and built between the Midland railway line and the river Aire. Housing and community facilities at Saltaire were excellent. Knighted in 1869, Salt contributed to many charities and despite an introverted nature served the city of Bradford in almost every capacity, including MP (1859–61). JB

Salvation Army. In 1865 William *Booth and his wife launched the 'Christian Mission to the Heathen of our Own Country' in Whitechapel (London), and this mission expanded into the Salvation Army (1878). It was both a religious community and an evangelistic agency. Its doctrines were those of evangelical revivalism: sin, conversion, justification by faith, hell, and heaven. At the 'holiness meetings' of the army, the emotional scenes and sudden conversions were reminiscent of early methodist revivals. The aim was to reach out beyond the established churches to working-class non-worshippers at their own cultural level. The officers and soldiers (i.e. members) of the army were themselves working men and women, who had experienced conversion and practised self-denial. At their open-air meetings, with bands and banners and sales of the *War Cry*, they sometimes met with violent opposition. From the late 1880s the army turned to social action, establishing slum posts, night shelters, and schemes for assisting the unemployed. The military organization of the Salvation Army ensured strict discipline of the members under the dictatorship of Booth and (later) his family. A tribute to the success of the Salvation Army was the foundation in 1882 by the Church of England of its own *Church Army. JFCH

Sampford Courtenay, battle of, 1549. The Cornish rebels against the Prayer Book in English in the summer of 1549 declared that they would not accept the new service which was 'but like a Christmas game'. Later in June they crossed the Tamar and laid siege to Exeter. The protector to the young King Edward VI, *Somerset, was in a difficult position, with widespread risings in Norfolk and other parts of the country. Early in August a punitive force under Lord Russell (*Bedford) drove the insurgents from Clyst St Mary with heavy loss and relieved Exeter. The remainder were routed on 17 August at Sampford Courtenay, near Okehampton. The Norfolk rising was suppressed at the end of the month. JAC

Samson (1135–1211). Abbot of Bury St Edmunds. A Norfolk man, educated in Paris, Samson taught at the abbey, took vows (1166) and was elected abbot in 1182. A shrewd, hard-headed businessman typical of his age, he speedily restored abbey finances after years of mismanagement. Not a great spiritual leader, still less a saint, he was an upright, God-fearing, just, and enthusiastic administrator with qualities essential for running a 13th-cent. abbey with its numerous estates and buildings; he rebuilt part of the abbey and founded a hospital and a school. Though previously unknown to the papacy, he was drawn into public service by being appointed papal judge-delegate. He led his knights in the siege of Windsor (1193) and travelled to Germany to visit the imprisoned Richard. His powerful local influence, if unpopular, was beneficial in a turbulent age. A man of affairs, he nevertheless wrote an account of the miracles associated with St Edmund's shrine. WMM

Samson, St (*c.*485–*c.*565). Born in Wales, educated and ordained at Llantwit (South Glamorgan), Samson's missionary endeavours established his renown in Cornwall, the Channel Islands, and Brittany, where he spent his last years. Establishing the monastery at Dol (Brittany), with which he is linked, he is said to have founded many more in the province. After negotiations with King Childebert in Paris, for Brittany's rightful heir (555), he gained royal approval for a foundation at Pental (Normandy), and seems to have been a signatory at the Council of Paris, *c.*557. Chief among Breton saints, Samson died at Dol. AM

Samuel, Sir Herbert, 1st Viscount Samuel (1870–1963). Samuel's father, who died when Samuel was 7, was a Jewish banker. After taking a first in history at Balliol College, Oxford, he entered Parliament as a Liberal in 1902. In the Liberal government of 1906 he served as under-secretary for the Home Office and entered the cabinet in 1909 as chancellor of the duchy of Lancaster, transferring to the postmaster-generalship the following year. He was home secretary when *Asquith resigned in 1916, followed him into opposition, and lost his seat at the 'Coupon' election of 1918. In 1920–5 he served as high commissioner in *Palestine and in 1926 presided over a commission on the coal industry which, by recommending a cut in wages, helped to provoke the *General Strike. Samuel returned to Parliament in 1929 and was acting leader of the party (in the absence of *Lloyd George) at the time of the crisis of 1931. He joined *MacDonald's *National Government as home secretary but resigned the following year when it moved towards protection. He was given a peerage in 1937. Respected rather than outstanding, Samuel's career rose and fell with the fortunes of his party. JAC

Sancroft, William (1617–93). Archbishop of Canterbury. Sancroft was a graduate and fellow of Emmanuel College, Cambridge (1637), but during the Interregnum moved to Suffolk (1651) and then to Europe (1657). He became master of Emmanuel (1662), dean of York, then of St Paul's (December 1664), where he worked closely with *Wren on the new cathedral, consequently refusing the bishopric of Chester (1668). As archbishop (1678), he hoped to refurbish clerical learning and Anglican discipline, especially through the church courts. He crowned James II (1685), but refused to sit on his Court of *Ecclesiastical Commission. Leader of the seven bishops petitioning the king against the *Declaration of Indulgence (1688), he was committed to the Tower, tried, but acquitted. After James's departure, Sancroft refused to swear allegiance to William, was deprived of his see (1690), and, as the leading non-juror, lived in Suffolk until his death. WMM

sanctions. The economic boycott of a country refusing to follow international conventions. Sanctions were the chief coercive method of the *League of Nations under article xvi of the covenant. In October 1935 they were imposed on Italy after her invasion of Abyssinia. However, vital materials such as oil, steel, and iron were excluded and Italian trade with non-league members was not disrupted. This undermined the effectiveness of the sanctions, which were lifted in July 1936. More recently, United Nations mandatory sanctions include trade restrictions placed on *Rhodesia after the unilateral declaration of independence in 1965, on South Africa in the 1980s due to apartheid, and on Iraq following the invasion of Kuwait in 1990. The effectiveness of trade sanctions is questionable as they are easily circumvented. Mrs *Thatcher stood against other Commonwealth nations in opposing the adoption of sanctions against South Africa as she believed they would have little practical effect and damage the British economy. Deliberate evasion of sanctions, or 'sanctions-busting', by individual companies often proves difficult to eradicate. For instance, the Bingham Report of 1978 discovered that Shell-BP and Total continued to supply oil to Rhodesia despite the embargo. RAS

sanctuary. Originally open land where the divine was present, but later associated with a religious building or part of it, its sacred character afforded protection where no blood was to be shed. Recognized first in Roman law (4th cent.) and by the church (Council of Orléans 511), Christian sanctuaries were later protected under English common law whereby a fugitive charged with any offence except sacrilege or treason could delay punishment by reaching sanctuary, often by grasping the ring or knocker of any church door. He had the choice of submitting to trial or, clad in sackcloth, confessing crime to a coroner and swearing to leave the kingdom after 40 days, in which case he became an outlaw, forfeiting all his goods and his wife, who was then regarded as a widow. If he did neither, he was starved into submission. Often abused, sanctuary became a source of dispute between church and state. Chief Justice *Tresilian was seized from sanctuary and executed (1388). Archbishop *Bourchier threatened to excommunicate lay officers who breached sanctuary (1463). It was even more abused by political fugitives in the Yorkist–Lancastrian struggles, especially in Westminster and St Martin-le-Grand, London, by debtors, and 'a rabble of theues, murtherers and malicious heyghnous Traitours'. Pope Innocent VIII (1487) and Henry VIII (1540) limited the privilege, the latter to seven cities. Sanctuary was abolished for criminals (1623) and for civil cases (1723). WMM

Sandringham House (Norfolk) is the private country estate of her majesty the queen. Sandringham has been owned by four generations of monarchs, starting with Edward VII who bought it in 1860 when prince of Wales. At first he made only minor alterations, but in 1870 he and Princess *Alexandra started to rebuild the house to the designs of the architect Albert Jenkins Humbert (1822–77), a royal favourite whose work includes the mausoleum at Frogmore and Whippingham church, near Osborne on the Isle of Wight. The style adopted at Sandringham was Elizabethan, the materials a harsh red brick and stone dressings. After Humbert's death, Sir Robert William Edis (1839–1927) acted as the architect for a ballroom in 1883 and further additions in 1891 following a fire. The elaborate main entrance-gates in wrought and cast iron are by Thomas Jeckyll and were shown at the International Exhibition in London of 1862. Sandringham House contains royal portraits and collections of porcelain, jade, quartz, and enamelled Russian silver, whilst royal memorabilia are displayed in the museum in the grounds. King George VI was born at York Cottage, Sandringham, and died in 1952 at the house. PW

Sand River convention, 1852. Appointed governor of Cape Colony and high commissioner in southern Africa in 1847, Sir Harry Smith tried at first to reimpose British authority over the people of Dutch descent—Boers (Afrikaners)—who, dissatisfied with British rule, had quitted the colony some years earlier. The realization that such a policy might lead to endless strife forced Smith to reconsider his plan and to approve the Sand river convention which recognized the independence of Boers living north of the Vaal river. A similar convention was signed with the Boers residing north of the Orange river two years later. KI

Sandwich, battle of, 1217. After suffering considerable losses at the battle of *Lincoln (May 1217), Prince Louis of France sent home for further reinforcements in his bid to become king of England. King Henry III's regency council realized that it was imperative to prevent these troops landing and a great sea-battle took place off Sandwich on 24 August 1217. The English sailed to windward of the French and engaged their flagship. Knights and sailors were tormented and blinded by powdered lime thrown from the English ships and carried by the wind. The flagship was boarded and overpowered. The other troopships managed to sail back to France, but the ships carrying stores were largely seized by the English. It was a decisive engagement, ending Louis's hopes in England. SL

Sandwich, Edward Montagu, 1st earl of (1625–72). Montagu's cousin, the 2nd earl of *Manchester, was a leader on the parliamentary side during the Civil War. Montagu joined him as a young man and fought at *Marston Moor and *Naseby. He sat in all the Commonwealth parliaments, was a member of the *Council of State in 1653, and took his seat in Cromwell's 'other house' in 1658. He also saw considerable naval action. Early in 1660 he was reappointed general of the fleet and took it over to Charles II's cause, carrying back the king in his flagship. He was rewarded by the Garter and the earldom of Sandwich. From 1660 to 1670 he was master of the great wardrobe. He was often in employment, bringing over *Catherine of Braganza in 1662 and serving as ambassador to Spain 1666–8. In the second *Anglo-Dutch War, he was victorious at the battle of *Lowestoft, but lost his life in the third war in the action off *Southwold Bay in 1672. His body was identified by the

Garter star he was wearing. Sandwich was on close terms with both *Pepys and *Evelyn. JAC

Sandwich, John Montagu, 4th earl of (1718–92). A politician of considerable achievements and a discerning patron of the arts, particularly music, Lord Sandwich is most frequently recalled as the inventor of the sandwich—popularly supposed to have sustained him during lengthy spells at the gaming table, but perhaps more attributable to his known practice of working long hours in the office. Sandwich's political ambitions were focused on the Admiralty, where he thrice served as 1st lord (1748–51, 1763, 1771–82), demonstrating both administrative ability and a pragmatic approach to reform. The longer-term benefits of Sandwich's initiatives were reduced by the exigencies of war and he was unjustly blamed for the failings in naval preparedness revealed by the *American War of Independence. It is, however, now appreciated that Sandwich deserves credit for the improved naval situation in the latter stages of the war, which enhanced British bargaining power during the peace negotiations. DW

sanitation. See HEALTH.

Saragossa, battle of, 1710. A mixed force of Austrians, Dutch, British, and Portuguese, under the Archduke Charles, attacked on 19 August 1710 the Spaniards defending Saragossa. *Stanhope commanded the British troops on the left. After a decisive victory, they went on to occupy Saragossa and advanced on Madrid. JAC

Saratoga, surrender of, 1777. *Burgoyne's 1777 expedition was ill defined, over-ambitious, and badly executed. The plan to drive south from Canada along the Hudson river to Albany, isolating the New England colonies, sounded plausible. But it was not clear, in an area of dense forest, how the New Englanders would be isolated, what Burgoyne would do when he got to Albany, or even whether he could obtain the supplies and ammunition to get there. Above all, the strategy depended upon a degree of co-ordination almost impossible to attain with armies hundreds of miles apart and communication hazardous. Burgoyne left Canada towards the end of June and had an initial success when the enemy abandoned Fort Ticonderoga. But in August a large foraging party was annihilated at *Bennington. The march was slow and painful, supplies inadequate, and the enemy vigilant. On 19 September Burgoyne encountered Gates at Bemis Heights and lost more men he could not replace. He fell back on Saratoga and was surrounded. An attempt to break out on 7 October was repulsed and on 17 October Burgoyne and nearly 6,000 men surrendered on terms. The disaster helped to bring the French into the war as allies of the American rebels. JAC

Sarawak (north-west Borneo) long had trading links with Siam and China and, in the 15th cent., fell under the influence of the sultanate of *Brunei. In 1841 the sultan offered it as a rajadom to Sir James *Brooke, who had helped to put down a revolt of the local Dayaks and Malays. Sarawak was recognized as an independent state by the USA in 1850 and by Great Britain in 1864. It was overrun by the Japanese in 1942 and, after the war, became a British crown colony. Representative government was established in 1963 and Sarawak joined the *Malaysian Federation. DAW

Sargent, John Singer (1856–1925). American painter who settled in England and became the outstanding portraitist of his time. Born in Italy, Sargent studied there and in Paris, where he became a good friend of Monet. A scandal surrounding his portrait *Madame Gautreau* caused him to leave Paris in 1884/5. He settled in London where he remained until his death, although he visited the USA frequently and retained his citizenship. His portraits of high society brought him great success and he was elected ARA in 1894, RA in 1897. After about 1907, he took few commissions; he travelled and concentrated on water-colour landscapes as well as some mural paintings in America. He was an official war artist during the First World War and his powerful *Gassed* hangs in the Imperial War Museum. JC

Sark, battle of, 1448. Renewed border skirmishing saw Henry Percy, future 3rd earl of *Northumberland, defeated by Hugh Douglas, earl of Ormond, on 23 October 1448. The encounter took place on the river Sark, near Gretna. Percy was taken prisoner and had to be ransomed. The following year the English burned Dumfries and Dunbar, and the Scots Alnwick and Warkworth. JAC

Sarsfield, Patrick (*c.*1650–93). Jacobite earl of Lucan. Born to a catholic family of mixed Anglo-Norman and Gaelic ancestry, Sarsfield entered the Irish army in 1678. He then served in the English regiments which Charles II detached to fight in the army of Louis XIV of France, but returned to England at the succession of James II in 1685, and helped to crush *Monmouth's rising. When James and *Tyrconnel radically catholicized the Irish army Sarsfield was a beneficiary, commanding Irish troops in England in 1688. He fled to France with James, returning with him to Ireland in 1689.

In the war that followed Sarsfield rose rapidly to major-general. After fighting at the *Boyne, he emerged as the voice of the Gaelic nobility to whom Tyrconnel's exclusively Anglo-Norman counter-revolution offered nothing. His attacks on Williamite supply lines forced the raising of the first siege of *Limerick but, after defeat at *Aughrim, he concluded the second siege of Limerick on terms which allowed him to sail for France. Louis XIV made him a French general, James II a peer in 1691. He was mortally wounded at the battle of *Landen. BPL

Sauchie Burn, battle of, 1488. In the summer of 1488, James III of Scotland was faced with a large rebellion, led by Archibald Douglas, earl of *Angus, and supported by the heir to the throne, the 15-year-old Prince James. The king gathered supporters from the north and east and advanced through Stirling to the site of Bannockburn. On 11 June his army was routed and he was killed, possibly while in flight. JAC

Saunderson, Edward James (1837–1906). Orangeman. Saunderson was a protestant of Irish gentry descent in Cavan, with hunting, sailing, and the militia as his great interests. From 1865 to 1874 he served in Parliament as a Liberal, but was defeated by a Home Ruler. *Parnell's rise caused a hardening of attitude and from 1881 until his death he was a Conservative MP. He developed into a lively and aggressive opponent of the nationalists and a leading member of the *Orange order. Vehemently opposed to *Gladstone's Home Rule Bill in 1884, he warned that Orangemen would take up arms if it went through, and in 1892 he declared that though Parliament could pass a Home Rule bill 'you have not the power to make us obey it'. Rebuked on 2 February 1893 in the House for calling Father MacFadden 'a murderous ruffian', he changed it to an 'excited politician'. JAC

Savery, Thomas (*c.*1650–1715). Savery was a military engineer who attained the rank of trench master by 1696, and acquired the title of 'Captain'. His inventiveness was perhaps stimulated by his knowledge of tin- and copper-mining in his native Devon. Savery's outstanding achievement was the invention of a machine for raising water by steam pressure, for which he took out a patent (No. 356) in 1698, calling it 'the miner's friend'. The device was essentially a pressure vessel which raised water partly by the direct pressure of steam, and partly by condensing the steam to create a vacuum, thus allowing the water to be raised by atmospheric pressure. The second part of this cycle was subsequently adopted by Thomas *Newcomen in his radically different and much more successful atmospheric engine of 1712, but he was obliged to co-operate with Savery under the terms of the latter's patent. While it is possible that he borrowed ideas from other inventors, Savery was the first person to demonstrate a workable steam-engine. RAB

Savoy conference, 1661. This was an attempt to reach a compromise at the Restoration between the presbyterians and the Anglicans. Twelve clerics from each side met at the Savoy hospital in April 1661 under the chairmanship of *Sheldon, bishop of London and a future archbishop of Canterbury. The negotiations broke down and in July the delegates reported that 'they could not come to any harmony'. The revised Prayer Book did little to ease puritan consciences, the bishops were reinstated in the House of Lords, and a thousand presbyterian ministers resigned or were ejected from their livings. The dream of a comprehensive church had faded. JAC

Saxons. See ANGLO-SAXONS.

Saxon Shore. A coastal network of late Roman forts stretching from Brancaster to Portchester intended to repel attacks by Saxons. The name 'Saxon Shore' (*litoris Saxonici*) appears only in the *Notitia dignitatum*, a document drawn up *c.* AD 408. The *Notitia* is an administrative handbook, concerned with the organization of late Roman military units. Interpretation of the functioning of the Saxon Shore is notoriously difficult, but the *Notitia* appears to list units stationed at sites in south-eastern Britain. The nine forts listed in Latin have been identified with late forts surviving in varying states of preservation at Brancaster (Branodunum), Burgh castle (Gariannonum), Bradwell (Othona), Reculver (Regulbium), Richborough (Rutupiae), Dover (Dubris), Lympne (Lemanis), Pevensey (Anderita), and Portchester (Portus Adurni). A possible further 'lost fort' may be at Walton castle. The overall commander of the military network was the *comes*, normally translated as 'the Count of the Saxon Shore'.

For a long time the Saxon Shore was regarded as being an entirely new creation of the 4th cent. AD. Seven of the listed units are new to the army of Britain as known in the principate (the Roman system of government 27 BC–AD 284). The appearance and style of the Saxon Shore forts themselves is new and different; they had high thick walls, massive rounded external towers, and more readily defensible secure gates. However, a closer examination of the evidence indicates continuity between the **classis Britannica* (the Roman fleet in the Channel) of the principate and the military dispositions discernible in the late empire. Archaeology has revealed an impressively large *classis Britannica* fort at Dover, and there is epigraphic evidence, in the form of stamped CL.BR tiles, for *classis Britannica* structures of the 2nd and 3rd cents. at Lympne, Portchester, and Pevensey. At Reculver there are archaeological indications of a 1st-cent. fortlet.

The name 'Saxon Shore' may have meant either of two things: the coast being attacked by Saxons, or the coast settled by Saxons. Most scholars prefer the former meaning, given the date of the *Notitia* and the fact that the string of forts was clearly employed during the 4th cent. against attack from the sea. ES

Saye and Sele, William Fiennes, 1st Viscount (1582–1662). Saye and Sele was a leading member of the radical, win-the-war faction in the House of Lords during the 1640s. As early as the 1620s he was a critic of arbitrary government and illegal taxation. During the 1630s he gave himself to puritan colonization schemes in the New World. Saye refused to pay *ship money, and declined the military oath imposed by Charles on the nobility at the outbreak of the *Bishops' wars with Scotland. In the *Long Parliament he continued to work with the radical opponents of the regime despite being appointed to the Privy Council. He backed both the *self-denying ordinance of 1645, which excluded the aristocracy from the leadership of the parliamentary armies, and the creation of the *New Model Army. In 1647, as the leading political Independent in the House of Peers, he worked closely with *Ireton and the council of the army in drafting the *Heads of the Proposals. This projected settlement was the most generous ever offered the king during the course of the civil wars. Politically inactive after 1649, Saye devoted himself to religion. In 1654 he published *Vindiciae veritatis*, arguing for a minimal role for the magistrate in regulating men's beliefs. Upon Charles II's return in 1660 he was again appointed to the Privy Council. IJG

Scapa Flow in the Orkneys is a magnificent natural harbour and naval base, commanding the approaches to both the North Atlantic and the North Sea. It was developed immediately before the First World War when the fleet increased in numbers and the vessels in size. The German high seas fleet was escorted to Scapa in 1918 and on 21 June

1919 the 74 vessels were scuttled. At the start of the Second World War, a brilliant U-boat action torpedoed the *Royal Oak* at anchor with the loss of over 800 lives. The naval base was closed in 1956. JAC

Scarlett, James, 1st Baron Abinger (1769–1844). Born in Jamaica and educated at Trinity College, Cambridge, Scarlett became an extremely successful lawyer and in 1819 was brought into Parliament by *Fitzwilliam as a Whig. His maiden speech went off well and *Tierney wrote that he had 'a better parliamentary manner than any lawyer I recollect'. But Scarlett could not quite sustain this brilliant début and all through the 1820s the Whigs were in opposition. In 1827 he took office with *Canning as attorney-general, resigned in 1828, and resumed in 1829. The following year he gave strong opposition to the Whig Reform Bill and was obliged to change patrons, coming in for one of Lord Lonsdale's boroughs. He seemed to have switched allegiance at the wrong moment and on the death of Lord Tenterden in 1832 was passed over for lord chief justice. But *Peel's brief minority government in 1834 made him lord chief baron of the Exchequer with a peerage. Scarlett was more successful as an advocate than either a parliamentarian or a judge. JAC

Scheveningen, battle of, 1653. Naval battle off the Dutch coast during the first *Anglo-Dutch War. Martin Tromp was ordered to sea to try to break the English blockade under *Monck. Tromp was killed early in the action on 10 August and the Dutch lost eleven vessels. It is sometimes known as the battle of Texel. JAC

Schism Act, 1714. An extreme Tory measure designed to stamp out *dissent by preventing nonconformists and catholics educating their children in their own schools. Teachers (except in the universities and those who taught the young at home) had to apply for licences, which would only be granted if they had taken the Anglican sacrament within the previous year, had sworn the oaths of allegiance, abjuration, and supremacy, and had made the declaration against transubstantiation. A licensed teacher who subsequently attended non-Anglican worship was to be disqualified. On the day the Act was due to take effect, Queen Anne died, and her successor, George I, took no steps to enforce it. It was repealed in 1719. CJ

Schomberg, Frederick Herman, 1st duke of (1615–90). Schomberg was one of the greatest soldiers of the 17th cent. His father had been ambassador for Frederick of the Palatinate to James I and his mother was a daughter of the 5th Lord Dudley. Born in Heidelberg, he pursued a military career with the Swedes and Dutch before entering French service in 1652 and rising to be a marshal of France. A Huguenot by religion, he left France in 1685 at the revocation of the edict of Nantes and accompanied William of Orange to England in November 1688. After the success of the Glorious Revolution, he became a naturalized Englishman in 1689, was given the Garter, and created duke of Schomberg. In the summer of 1689 he took over William's forces in Ireland and was killed at the battle of the *Boyne encouraging his troops: 'allons, Messieurs, voilà vos persécuteurs.' His son, the 3rd duke, had a distinguished military career under William III. JAC

schools. The earliest elementary schools date from the Middle Ages. They consisted of song schools and reading schools, the former to train boys as choristers, the latter to teach youths to read and write. Education was free and the schools were usually endowed. From the time of the Reformation, there was a variety of private, petty, and parish schools, usually taught by people who had other occupations. The *charity schools, particularly those provided by the *Society for Promoting Christian Knowledge, provided widespread elementary schooling for the poor. As urban and industrial changes took place in the later 18th cent., *Sunday schools provided part-time schooling for working children. Rival religious bodies supplied the monitorial schools at the beginning of the 19th cent., the *British and Foreign School Society (1808) and the *National Schools Society (1811). The need for universal elementary education was recognized by 1870, when school boards were established to provide buildings where necessary. During the 20th cent., as the need for a more child-centred education was recognized, the elementary school became the primary school, catering for children up to the age of 11. Infant and junior departments, separate or combined, were established.

The distinctive feature of secondary schools from the earliest time was the predominance of Latin. To teach this the *grammar school was established throughout England, varying in size and social intake. Alongside these, from Tudor times, were the private schools, usually kept by clergymen, with boarding facilities. In the following century, modern schools or academies, offering a literary and scientific education, flourished. These often catered for specific occupations, such as the army, business, or trade. Girls were almost exclusively educated at home, by parents or by tutors. The leading grammar schools during the course of the 19th cent. developed into more exclusive *public schools. A new type of public school, the proprietary school, established by non-profit-making church and secular companies, received recognition in towns where alternative education was frequently not available.

Secondary schooling was reformed after the Endowed Schools Act of 1869 and provision made for the first time for the daughters of the middle classes. After the 1902 *Education Act, the rise of the municipal grammar school increased the provision of secondary education. Comprehensive secondary schools replaced the majority of grammar schools from the 1960s. There are now other types of schools at this level, including sixth-form colleges, grant-maintained, and city technology colleges. PG

Schools Act (Scotland), 1696. In 1616 the Scottish Privy Council decreed that in Scotland a school should be established in every parish. This was ratified by the Scottish Parliament in 1633 and a further Act for Founding Schools passed in 1646. These statutes were re-enacted by the Scottish Parliament in an Act for Settling Schools in 1696. A uniform system of parish schools came into being; the salary of the schoolmaster was paid by the heritors (landowners) and the schools were supported out of the rates. It was a further 200 years before a similar system was established in England. PG

Schooneveld, battle of, 1673. In May 1673, during the third *Anglo-Dutch War, it was resolved to attack the Dutch in the Schooneveld, off the island of Walcheren. *Rupert was joined by a French squadron, which gave him some superiority over a Dutch fleet under de Ruyter and Cornelis Tromp. The first engagement on 7 June was inconclusive. On 14 June the Dutch attacked in turn and a running fight developed. Once more the result was inconclusive—'a grand skirmish rather than a straight fight' was the French commander's comment—though the Dutch had prevented a threatened landing. JAC

Science Museums (Kensington). The museums are the fruit of the *Great Exhibition of 1851. It made a profit, and land was bought in Kensington Gore; Prince *Albert hoped to establish there a great cultural centre, but to many people it seemed remote from central London. In 1862 the next exhibition was staged there; in 1864 the underground railway station was authorized; and the Department of Science and Arts ran what grew into the Science Museum. Richard Owen, superintendent of natural history at the British Museum, campaigned from 1861 to have 'his' exhibits moved to a new building, and in 1881 the Natural History Museum opened its doors. DK

scientific revolution. Herbert Butterfield, scourge of Whig historians, called attention in 1948 to the tremendous intellectual change he saw taking place during the 17th cent., when the modern scientific world-view was propounded by Francis *Bacon, Galileo, Descartes, and their disciples. This change was reflected in institutions, notably the *Royal Society and the Paris Academy of Sciences, and in publications—especially journals. It meant a break with the servile attitude to Aristotelian philosophy, and also with Platonic toying with *magic. The science which had made the running was astronomy: the heavens had been demystified, and the power of mathematics demonstrated. Bacon's view that experiments must be fruitful made science seem a matter of organized common sense, accessible not only to a highly educated élite but to craftsmen: having been something for a few soloists, science now acquired a chorus.

Butterfield's thesis went with the self-image of the great thinkers of the 17th cent., and made history and philosophy of science fashionable. It has been criticized by medievalists who have seen little really new in the New Philosophy; by historians of medicine, where magical and Aristotelian ideas (in Paracelsus, and in William *Harvey) went with progress; and by students of *astrology, *alchemy, and apocalyptic, who have shown how important these were to people we would like to think of as 'modern'. Research into rhetoric has indicated how important that was for virtuosi anxious to promote their world-view: the plain style, sometimes verbose, was chosen deliberately to carry conviction. To be too ready to see modernity among the fellows of the Royal Society is to write Whig history.

Butterfield had seen one revolution: but it might be that, like the French, science has had several. Thomas Kuhn in 1962 came to see things this way. A science came into being when a mass of facts was ordered by someone, whose work became paradigmatic and led to a period, usually prolonged, of normal science, which has something in common with painting by numbers or solving puzzles. It is dogmatic, and deals with questions difficult to answer; but there comes a time for questions difficult to ask, when anomalies have blurred the picture, and a revolution and new paradigm are needed. This will be incommensurable with the old one, and the change is like a religious conversion, a leap of faith; the revolutionary has to work to make converts, and the middle-aged will probably refuse to shift. Thus we have revolutions associated with Galileo, Isaac *Newton, Charles *Darwin, and perhaps Michael *Faraday or J. J. *Thomson. This idea has stimulated historians, who have been moving forward into the more recent past.

A. L. Lavoisier succeeded before his death in the Terror in 1794 in changing the language of chemistry in accordance with his new theory of combustion. His great book came out in 1789, and he was self-consciously bringing about an intellectual revolution, using that frightening word—which previously had evoked feelings of a return to the good old days. He and his contemporaries were Kuhnians before Kuhn, though no doubt he believed that like Newton his paradigm would last for ever, and that only one revolution per science was required. Nineteenth-cent. chemists had a great respect for tradition, and liked to look back through their 'fathers in science' to Lavoisier's time; but there were other claimants for his title, including Humphry *Davy with electrochemistry, John *Dalton with his testable atomic theory, and Marcellin Berthelot with chemical synthesis.

Studies of the 19th cent. indicate how many elements of modern science we owe to that epoch rather than to an earlier period, and may make us wonder if it was not the Age of Science, or the period when science began to revolutionize everyday life. Formal courses in physical sciences began with the revolutionary École Polytechnique, where the teachers also undertook research, and were then taken up in the German universities. At Giessen, Justus Liebig began laboratory instruction and then independent research for the PhD degree from 1825; and his pupil A. W. Hofmann came to Britain in 1845 at Prince *Albert's instigation to start the Royal College of Chemistry, subsequently part of Imperial College, London. Science was no longer a matter of informal apprenticeship.

The Royal Society was joined in 1831 by the more open and democratic *British Association for the Advancement of Science, promoting public awareness and local pride. It had earlier been joined by specialized societies, dedicated to natural history, geology, and astronomy; and later to chemistry, statistics, and physics. John *Herschel decided not to specialize, but for most people this was not possible. Education began to divide the scientists (a word coined by William *Whewell in 1833, but not popular) from humanists; and as the former divided into chemists and physicists, and then further into organic or physical chemists, so the latter began taking degrees in history or English. Scientific societies with narrower and narrower scope were founded, with journals addressed to experts only.

Science also became a profession. Davy was one of the first in Britain to make his way by research and lecturing in a great London institution; with an expanding educational system, this became more possible as the 19th cent. went on. The earliest scientific societies (outside medicine) had been learned ones; but during the 19th cent., as science at last really became useful, they were joined by societies promoting the interests of qualified engineers and applied scientists.

Exponential growth also became evident in the 19th cent., so the question whether there was one scientific revolution or many, or evolution, is open. Butterfield founded an industry. Clearly, science has been developing in ways that Bacon could only have dreamed of, and it has transformed the way we see the world, although we rely upon authority for our world-view quite as much as our ancestors ever did. Whereas Bacon and Galileo hoped that science would bring certainty, where the church and the ancients had failed as authorities, and T. H. *Huxley thought that science had never done anybody any harm, we are now sadder and wiser. DK

Butterfield, H., *The Origins of Modern Science* (1949); Cohen, I. B., *Revolution in Science* (Cambridge, Mass., 1985); Hall, A. R., *The Scientific Revolution, 1500–1800* (1954); Knight, D. M., *A Companion to the Physical Sciences* (1989); Lindberg, D. C., and Westman, R. S. (eds.), *Reappraisals of the Scientific Revolution* (Cambridge, 1990); Shea, W. R. (ed.), *Revolutions in Science: Their Meaning and Relevance* (Canton, Mass., 1988).

Scilly Isles. A group of 50 granite islands, five of them inhabited, lying 30 miles off Land's End in Cornwall. The largest islands are St Mary's and Tresco. Belonging to the abbey of Tavistock in the Middle Ages, they passed to the Godolphin family and in 1933 to the crown. Piracy, wrecking, and smuggling were not unknown before market gardening and tourism took over. The population is just over 2,000. JAC

Scone, stone of. A block of sandstone, long associated with the inauguration of early Scottish kings at Scone (Perthshire) but seized by Edward I in 1296; since 1308 every anointed English sovereign has been crowned on the special coronation chair built to contain it, thereby claiming overlordship of Scotland. It was transferred briefly to Westminster Hall for *Cromwell's investiture as lord protector (1657). Buried for safety in the Islip chapel 1939–45, it was stolen by Scottish Nationalists on Christmas morning 1950, but was yielded up to Arbroath abbey the following April before being returned to Westminster abbey. In 1996, 700 years after its seizure, Elizabeth II authorized the stone's return to Scotland. ASH

scot and lot was a contribution towards municipal expenses, largely poor relief, scot being the amount and lot the share. In 37 parliamentary boroughs in the period before 1832, including Westminster with 12,000 voters, the right to vote was restricted to scot and lot payers, excluding the poorest inhabitants. The franchise led to frequent disputes about the exact character of the payments made and who made them. JAC

Scots, kingdom of. In the 9th cent. a new kingdom emerged out of the ashes of the kingdom of *Fortriu and in succeeding centuries became established as the dominant political force in north Britain. It was born out of the wreckage wrought by repeated Scandinavian incursions in eastern Scotland. In 839 the Gaelic dynasty which had almost monopolized the kingship of Fortriu for half a century was annihilated in battle. Fortriu's heartland in eastern Perthshire was repeatedly devastated, reaching a nadir of desperation in 875 when Danes inflicted another crushing defeat at the battle of *Dollar (9 miles east of Stirling) and drove the defenders back to the highlands of Perthshire. These Scandinavian attacks were not, however, followed by attempts to colonize eastern Scotland; the aggressors were often involved in struggles to control *York and *Dublin, the chief Scandinavian centres of power in Britain and Ireland, and used eastern Scotland as a staging post for attack or a haven for retreat. It may be assumed that in eastern Scotland, as in other parts of Europe devastated by Scandinavian attacks, the raiders' immediate legacy was political and social dislocation. What brought misfortune to many could, however, also offer the opportunity for a few to fill the vacuum and refashion political relationships to their own advantage. By the beginning of the 10th cent. a Gaelic lineage—the descendants of *Kenneth MacAlpin—had succeeded in entrenching itself as the rulers of eastern Scotland. For the first time in eastern Scotland kingship was monopolized by a single dynasty. With this new kind of kingship came a new identity for the kingdom and its people. From 900 the kingdom was no longer 'Fortriu' (or 'Pictland'), but *Alba, the Gaelic word for Scotland; and its people were no longer referred to as 'men of Fortriu' (or 'Picts'), but now became *Albanaig*, the Gaelic for 'Scots' (literally 'inhabitants of Alba'). The medieval kingdom of the Scots was born.

Alba had originally been the Gaelic word for Britain. It is hard to believe, however, that this term for the new kingship was adopted *c.*900 because of any claim to rule all Britain. In truth, the territory which the first kings of Scots held firmly in their grasp was probably little larger than an 11th-cent. English earldom. Until as late as the early 13th cent. Alba, 'Scotland' (or Albania/Scotia in Latin), was used to refer to the area east of the Grampian mountains stretching north from the river Forth to (approximately) the border with *Moray. This puzzling phenomenon could be explained if the original kingdom of Alba in reality extended only across this area. In the 13th cent. 'Scotland' came to be used regularly by Scots themselves to refer to the whole of what is now mainland Scotland.

The survival of this new kingdom can be attributed largely to the long reign of *Constantine II. He succeeded his cousin *Donald II, the first recorded 'king of Scotland (Alba)', in 900, and reigned for at least four decades, enabling the fledgeling kingship to consolidate. The emergence of 'Scotland' in this period can, therefore, be compared with other new countries of a similar size, such as Flanders and

Normandy, which rose out of the ashes of Scandinavian devastation and established their place on the map of medieval Europe.

Constantine II's reign was also crucial to the kingdom's survival because he halted the Scandinavian tide of destruction. In 904 a Danish army led by the sons of Ivarr was defeated in battle in Strathearn (southern Perthshire). The kingdom was not attacked again by Vikings for more than fifty years. Constantine's success at keeping the Danes at bay was, however, achieved principally by a policy of *rapprochement*. His daughter married the Danish king of Dublin, while Constantine himself may have had a Danish wife: his son *Indulf bore a Scandinavian name. The culmination of this new relationship with the Danes was a grand alliance of Scots, Danes, and Britons of *Strathclyde against *Athelstan, king of England. In 937 a campaign was launched backing *Olaf Guthfrithsson's claim to be king of York, but the army of the allies was destroyed at *Brunanburh. The threat of Scandinavian aggression returned briefly during the reign of Constantine's son Indulf (954–62), who was killed defending the kingdom from a Norwegian raid. This was the last occasion, however, when a king of Scots lost his life during a Scandinavian incursion. The possibility of raids from the north remained, but they no longer threatened to overwhelm the kingdom.

When the new kingdom of 'Scotland' emerged in the 10th cent. from its grim struggle for survival it was well placed to expand and dominate north Britain. It was based initially on the fertile lands of Strathmore and Strathearn. Its natural rival in the north was the kingdom of Moray which harnessed the resources of the rich Lowlands surrounding the Moray Firth. The kings of Moray, however, faced constant pressure from the Scandinavian earls of *Orkney, and as a result their ability to challenge the kings of Scots was seriously weakened. They served, indeed, as a buffer protecting the kingdom of the Scots from the full power of the earls of Orkney. But the greatest danger to the long-term success of the kingdom would have arisen from a rejuvenated *Northumbria stretching from Edinburgh to York. In the 7th cent. Northumbria had established itself as the dominant force in north Britain, but had since imploded into internal chaos and had been largely conquered and settled by Danes. The Danish kings of *York, however, constantly looked west to *Dublin in an attempt to establish pre-eminence among the Scandinavians in Britain and Ireland, and in turn were targeted by kings of Dublin. This left northern Northumbria—*Lothian and the Merse—as a buffer zone between the kingdom of Scotland and York, which the Scottish kings endeavoured to bring under their control. In Indulf's reign Edinburgh was captured, and later *Edgar, king of the English, recognized *Kenneth II's claim to Lothian. In the late 10th cent. Northumbria south of the Tweed was revived as an earldom and was at times able to match the kings of Scots. It is likely that Kenneth II was driven out of Lothian by the earl of Northumbria in 994/5, but Scottish rule as far as the Tweed was decisively reasserted by *Malcolm II at the battle of *Carham (16 miles south-west of Berwick) in 1018. By this time the king of the Britons of Strathclyde (or king of the Cumbrians) had become a client of the king of Scots, and after the accession of *Duncan I, king of the Cumbrians, to the Scottish kingship in 1034 it appears that the two kingdoms were ruled by one line of kings. When *Macbeth, king of Moray, became king of Scots in 1040, Moray, too, became bound into the kingdom of the Scots, though it remained a springboard for dynastic rivals to the Scottish kingship until 1230. By the mid-11th cent., therefore, the kingdom had begun to assume a form recognizable as the Scottish kingdom of the Middle Ages and beyond. With the Norman conquest of Northumbria in 1070 the north of England was left without the strong regional leadership provided by the native earls, and the kings of Scots sought to exploit this to their advantage. Their ambition to expand into northern England was only relinquished in 1237.

The success of the kingdom of the Scots in this period was second only to that of the kings of *Wessex, who during the 10th cent. brought most of what is now England under their rule. The new English realm was undoubtedly more powerful than its northern counterpart. This was already evident in the 930s, which saw on the one hand an English army penetrate deep into Scotland and, on the other hand, the destruction of a combined Scottish, Danish, and British force in England. English kings, however, made no sustained effort to conquer Scotland, and attempted merely to neutralize kings of Scots through agreements or submissions which were rarely of enduring significance. These agreements included English recognition that Strathclyde (in 945) and Lothian (*c.*975) fell within the king of Scots' sphere of influence. Britain's division into two power blocks had begun, and would eventually crystallize into the kingdoms of England and Scotland.

Britain's nascent geographical polarity was not, however, reflected culturally. The territories ruled by the king of Scots included regions which were predominantly Welsh (in the south-west) and English (in the south-east), as well as Anglo-Danish settlers in the kingdom's heartland. Gaelic was the predominant language, and Gaelic institutions such as professional castes of poets and judges, or churches founded on the cults of Gaelic saints such as *Columba and *Brigit, were at the apex of the kingdom's culture and society. Gaelic saints, cultural institutions, and language were not, however, exclusively Scottish, but showed how the Scottish kingdom was but one region of a homogeneous Gaelic high culture which stretched from Munster to Moray. This Gaelic high culture was not isolated or backward, as some have supposed, but identified itself firmly as part of contemporary Christendom. A number of leading Gaelic kings and churchmen went on pilgrimage to Rome, including Macbeth. Neither was the Scottish kingdom closed to English and Scandinavian influence, as is suggested by the existence of 'shires' before 1100 and the custom of 'fencing' a court of law. Its cultural receptivity has, indeed, been immortalized in a string of church towers in the midlands built *c.*1100: two, at Abernethy and Brechin, are Irish round towers; others, however, as at Dunblane, Muthill, and Dunning, are northern English in style.

As far as the kingdom's core north of the Forth was concerned, cultural diversity did not mean that it suffered a lack of cohesion. The church was led by a chief bishop (at St *Andrews); and the area between the Forth and the Spey was bound together by a network of provincial rulers (*mormaers) and local officials (thanes) who kept order and mustered the able-bodied for defence. This is not to say that internal strife was unknown; but it could be withstood, even when it involved protracted rivalry for the kingship itself, following the failure of the royal dynasty in 1034. The solidity of the kingdom's core proved a firm foundation for the expansion of royal power after 1100. DEB

Barrow, G. W. S., *Kingship and Unity: Scotland 1100–1306* (1981); Broun, D., 'The Origin of Scottish Identity in its European Context', in Crawford, B. E. (ed.), *Scotland in Dark Age Europe* (St Andrews, 1994); Duncan, A. A. M., *Scotland: The Making of the Kingdom* (Edinburgh, 1975); Smyth, A. P., *Warlords and Holy Men: Scotland 80–1000* (1984).

Scotsman. One of the two daily newspapers which has laid claim to be Scotland's 'national' newspaper, the other being the *Herald* (formerly *Glasgow Herald*). Their competitiveness has symbolized the Edinburgh–Glasgow rivalry for pre-eminence in Scotland. Both have followed a broadly similar trajectory—founded as weeklies (the *Herald* as the *Glasgow Advertiser* in 1783, the *Scotsman* in 1817), becoming dailies in the 1850s; and politically turning from an early Liberalism to Unionism and a broad Conservatism over Gladstone's Irish Home Rule policies. Both were latterly acquired by press magnates—the *Scotsman* by Lord Thomson in 1953, and the *Herald* by Sir Hugh Fraser in 1964, then Tiny Rowland in 1979. DJA

Scott, Sir George Gilbert (1811–78). Architect. Scott was the most famous and successful of Victorian Gothic master builders; and also the most correct stylistically, except when it came to railway stations. The most famous of those is St Pancras in London (1865), a kind of Disneyland castle in bright orange brick. A few years earlier he had submitted a similar design for the new Foreign Office in Whitehall, only to have it vetoed by *Palmerston on the grounds that Scott would 'Gothicize the whole country' if given his head. This was called the 'battle of the styles'. Scott lost it, but not the commission itself, if he promised to carry it out in an Italian Renaissance style, which he did. The result probably vindicates Palmerston's pig-headedness. Scott was also a restorer—even an over-restorer—of hundreds of ancient churches. His talent was inherited by his grandson, Sir Giles Gilbert Scott (1880–1960), who built Liverpool's Anglican cathedral in his grandfather's favourite style, and Battersea power station in a more modern one. BJP

Scott, Sir Robert Falcon (1868–1912). Scott had entered the navy as a boy in 1880 and by 1897 was a lieutenant and torpedo officer. He was noticed by Sir Clements Markham whose influence led to his appointment as leader of the Royal Geographical Society and Royal Society Antarctic Expedition of 1901–4. He proved a capable captain of the *Discovery* and leader of the personnel who carried out much scientific and exploratory work in the Ross Sea and Victoria Land region. Scott himself, with *Shackleton, made a sledge journey to beyond 82 degrees south in 1902. Now famous, Scott was chosen to lead an official expedition in 1910 in the *Terra Nova* which was again scientific in its aims, but also designed to get a party to the South Pole. Scott led four others who reached the Pole on 18 January 1912 only to find that Amundsen had preceded them there by just over a month. All five eventually perished on the horrendous walk back to their base. Scott's journal read, 'We shall stick it out to the end. . . . It seems a pity but I do not think I can write any more.' News of this epic tragedy led to national mourning, a posthumous knighthood for Scott, and the founding of the Scott Polar Research Institute. However, it is now widely believed that Scott's nobility and bravery could not compensate for the wrong decision (probably encouraged by Markham) to use man-hauled sledges for polar travel. RB

Scott, Sir Walter (1771–1832). Poet, novelist, man of letters. Scott distilled the literary and historical culture of the *Scottish Enlightenment into the first great European works of historical fiction. A patriot and publicist, he placed Scotland on the international tourist map as a land of enlightenment and romance. The son of an Edinburgh lawyer, educated for the Scottish bar, Scott remained an active lawyer for the rest of his life, becoming latterly sheriff depute of Selkirk and principal clerk of Session. His literary career began in the school playground, telling stories to his friends. He first made his mark as a poet, collecting, editing, and adapting border ballads and later writing enormously popular narrative poems of which the *Lay of the Last Minstrel* (1805) and *Marmion* (1808) are probably the best. His career as a novelist began in 1814 with the publication of *Waverley*, followed by another 24 novels which appeared at almost yearly intervals until the end of his life. In addition he edited standard editions of *Swift and *Dryden, wrote a series of lives of the novelists, a profusion of reviews, and an enormous personal correspondence. By the early 1820s he was sometimes writing more than 15,000 words per day. He built Abbotsford out of his substantial profits, turning it into an extraordinary physical embodiment of his taste for antiquities, real and phoney, and his more modern respect for creature comforts. Bankruptcy in 1825 and failing health overshadowed his later years, but yielded a *Journal*, a work of genius, posthumously published and surprisingly little read. Scott was a man universally liked, known, and admired. NTP

Scottish Enlightenment. A relatively new term, said to have been invented in 1909 when W. R. Scott described Francis *Hutcheson as the father of the Scottish Enlightenment. It became fashionable in the 1960s when social scientists began exploring the history of their disciplines, and is now used generally and imprecisely to describe the intellectual, material, and moral culture of Scotland during the long 18th cent. It is a culture associated with the middling ranks of Scottish society, with the Scottish universities, and with the clubs, societies, and salons of Edinburgh. Ideologically it was a culture concerned with the defence of the revolution settlement, the Hanoverian succession, the Act of Union, and the presbyterian establishment. It was concerned with the civilizing functions of commerce and culture and with the problems of developing the institutions and manners appropriate to the preservation of a free commercial polity. Intellectually, the Scots owed important debts to the Dutch, the French, and the English as well as to their own intellectual traditions. Philosophers like *Hutcheson, *Hume, *Smith, Ferguson, and Reid were interested in the principles of human nature, the meaning of sociability, and the truths of natural religion. Their conclusions made possible the development of a remarkable theory of progress which was instrumental in shaping the political economy of Smith, the histories of Hume and *Robertson, and the historical fiction of *Scott. Scottish medical professors developed a model for explaining the physical constitution of man which was particularly sensitive to the nervous system and to environmental determinants of health. Joseph *Black's research into the properties of heat made possible James *Hutton's revolutionary theory of the earth. Poets like Ramsay, Ferguson, *Burns, and Scott reactivated the resources of vernacular literature with the new aesthetics developed by the philosophers and historians. It is sometimes argued that the architecture and town-planning of the *Adam family and the portraiture of Allan *Ramsay and Sir Henry *Raeburn needs to be viewed in the same way. Perhaps the most lasting monument to the Scottish Enlightenment is the New Town of Edinburgh, a vast project which would testify to the civilizing power of commerce by turning Edinburgh into a modern Athens. It bankrupted the city. NTP

Scottish National Party (SNP). The SNP was formed in 1934 after a merger between the National Party of Scotland and the Scottish Party. The party is committed to securing an independent parliament for Scotland.

The SNP won their first parliamentary seat in 1945 when Dr Robert McIntyre was returned at a by-election for Motherwell. However the SNP had no great electoral success until the 1960s. In November 1967 Winnie Ewing captured Hamilton from Labour and the SNP had a high profile in the 1968 local elections. By 1974 the SNP had eleven seats in Parliament and polled over 30 per cent of the vote in Scotland. A royal commission report in 1973 recommended the creation of a separate Scottish Assembly. The SNP, despite internal disputes, supported the idea as the first step on the road to independence. A bill passed through Parliament in July 1978 providing for an elected assembly but it needed support from 40 per cent of the Scottish electorate. In a referendum on 1 March 1979 the measure failed, as only 32.85 per cent of the electorate backed it. From this point there was a waning in SNP fortunes. In the 1979 general election their share of the poll dropped to 17 per cent and they lost all but two seats. The 1980s were a period of retrenchment as the emergence of the *Social Democratic Party and their alliance with the Liberals threatened SNP support.

In the 1987 general election the SNP gained a seat, retained all three in 1992, and won the 1995 Perthshire and Kinross by-election. In 1990 Alex Salmond became party leader, confirming the SNP as a left-of-centre social democratic party. The party retains its grass-roots support in Scottish local elections and in 1995 had the second highest number of local councillors (182). A new campaign in recent years has focused on 'independence in Europe', emphasizing Scotland's potential role as a member of the European Community. RAS

Scottish Wars of Independence, 1296–1357. The name usually given to the prolonged wars between English and Scots after the sudden death of Alexander III of Scotland in 1286. The death of his heir *Margaret ('the Maid of Norway') in 1290 left a number of 'competitors' for the vacant throne, of whom the chief were John *Balliol and Robert *Bruce, grandfather of the future Robert I; in 1292 Edward I, who claimed to be 'Lord Superior of Scotland', awarded the crown to Balliol. Edward however was determined to assert what he saw as his rights to overlordship; and Balliol found it impossible to maintain the independence of his kingdom against this pressure. In 1295 the Scottish nobles took power out of Balliol's hands, made an alliance with Edward's enemy Philip IV of France, and prepared to defy Edward. A crushing campaign in 1296 forced Balliol to resign the crown. Edward took Scotland into his own hands and compelled the bulk of the Scottish landed classes to do homage to him.

This was however only the start of a struggle which was to last till 1357. There were three stages: first a 'revolt' against Edward in the name of King John, which was not finally subdued in 1304; secondly, the recovery following the rising of Robert Bruce in 1306, which ultimately secured the recognition of Scottish independence by the English government in 1328; and thirdly, the revival of attempts at English conquest under Edward III, which lasted till the treaty of *Berwick in 1357.

The first stage opened with widespread revolts in the early months of 1297, backed by many of the nobles but openly led by William *Wallace in the south, and Andrew *Murray in the north. They joined forces to win the devastating victory of *Stirling Bridge in 1297; but Wallace's defeat at *Falkirk in 1298 left the leadership in the hands of the nobles, who continued under a succession of guardians to resist Edward till 1304 when they were forced to submit. Edward then proceeded to what seems a statesmanlike reorganization of Scottish government with the support of most of the Scottish leaders.

His hopes however were shattered by the revolt of the younger Robert Bruce in 1306. The result was to reopen the rivalries between the Bruce and Balliol factions which had been obvious in the late 1280s and early 1290s. Bruce's enemies, notably the widely connected *Comyn family, were driven firmly onto the English side, and for many years the Wars of Independence took on the aspect of a civil 'War of the Scots'. Bruce was rapidly crowned as Robert I, but as rapidly defeated twice, and by the end of 1306 was in hiding. Edward however died on 7 July 1307, which gave the respite Robert needed. In the next few years he defeated his enemies and gradually eliminated the English garrisons by a masterly policy of guerrilla warfare. By 1314 few remained; and the decisive defeat of Edward II at the battle of *Bannockburn left Robert secure. It was the only occasion after 1307 when he took on the English in a set battle.

The war then became a war of raids on the north of England which caused widespread suffering, but had little effect on the stubborn Edward II. A diversion into Ireland under Robert I's brother Edward *Bruce (1315–18) alarmed the Anglo-Irish settlers but failed to get the support of the Irish themselves, and collapsed with Edward's death in 1318. Peace only became possible after Edward II's deposition. By the treaty of *Edinburgh/*Northampton of 1328, Robert I was formally recognized as king of Scots, and his son and heir, the future David II, was married to *Joan of the Tower, a sister of Edward III. In return he agreed to pay a 'contribution for peace'.

The peace did not last. Robert I died in 1329, when David was aged only 5. The temptation was too great for Edward III, who wanted to establish his prowess and authority. He encouraged the son of John Balliol, Edward *Balliol, to attempt to seize the throne; and the Scottish leaders of the time were forced to confront the invaders in battles, in which the English were twice victorious, at *Dupplin Moor (1332) under Edward Balliol, and at *Halidon Hill (1333) under Edward III himself. Balliol was established as king; much of the south was ceded into English control; and the rest was to be held as a vassal kingdom. In 1334 David II had to flee to the safety of France.

The threat was more serious than is often allowed—many, perhaps most, of the Scottish nobles contemplated at one time or another coming into Edward's peace; but a long guerrilla war, at which the Scots remained superior, gradually wore down the occupiers, and in 1341 David II was able to return. Unfortunately, he continued the policy of raids into England, in one of which he was captured in 1346 and remained a captive till 1357. This led to a renewed English occupation; and parts of southern Scotland remained in English hands for a long time. However, by 1357, after several bouts of negotiation had failed, Edward III agreed to David's release under ransom. Though the treaty of *Berwick ignored the real issues of Scottish independence, no further attempts at subjection were to be made till the 1540s, so that the Wars of Independence can be said to have ended with the treaty of 1357.

They had distorted irretrievably the relations of the two countries. In the 13th cent. Scotland and England had been developing in ever closer friendship. By 1357 they were, and long remained, enemies. This was the disastrous consequence of Edward I's political misjudgements after 1292. BW

Barrow, G. W. S., *Robert Bruce and the Community of the Realm of Scotland* (3rd edn. Edinburgh, 1988); Duncan, A. A. M., 'The War of the Scots 1306–1323', *Transactions of the Royal Historical Society*, 6th ser. (1992), 125–51; Nicholson, R., *Scotland: The Later Middle Ages* (Edinburgh, 1974); Webster, B., 'Scotland without a King, 1329–41', in Grant, A., and Stringer, K. J. (eds.), *Medieval Scotland: Crown, Lordship and Community* (Edinburgh, 1993).

Scott Memorial (Edinburgh). This tribute to the Scottish novelist Sir Walter Scott dominates Princes Street, despite being described by *Ruskin as 'a small vulgar Gothic steeple on the ground'. The design of water-colourist and self-taught architect George Meikle Kemp, it was completed in 1846, two years after Kemp was found drowned in the Union canal. The seated figure of Scott, wrapped in a shepherd's plaid, his hound Maida at his feet, was sculpted by Sir John Steell. Other sculptors carved the 84 statuettes of Scott's characters and Scottish historical figures which decorate the ornate spire. JC

Scrope, Richard (*c.*1346–1405). Archbishop of York. The third son of Henry, Lord Scrope of Masham, Scrope was chancellor of Cambridge University in 1378 and a doctor of laws. From 1381 he was an auditor at the papal court until the pope appointed him to the bishopric of Coventry and Lichfield in 1386. After some diplomatic service to Richard II, he was promoted to York in 1398. He made no opposition to Henry IV's usurpation, assisting at his coronation. In 1403, however, he may have favoured the Percy conspiracy, and in 1405 *Northumberland apparently prompted Scrope to revolt. Supported by *Norfolk, the earl marshal, he published in York a manifesto denouncing Henry's oppressive taxes and misgovernment, attracting a dangerously large following from north and west Yorkshire which assembled on Shipton Moor. Archbishop and earl were enticed to a rendezvous with Ralph Neville, earl of *Westmorland, who arrested them. After the king's arrival, they were summarily tried and executed. Scrope was buried in York minster, where his tomb attracted pilgrims. RLS

scutage or shield-money was commutation in lieu of knight service as a fixed levy on the fee. From an early period after the Norman Conquest it became difficult to raise an adequate number of knights to form the royal army, nor was their military prowess necessarily satisfactory. The person holding the fee might be old, infirm, or even a female. There were therefore advantages to both sides in allowing landowners to buy themselves out, and as early as 1100 the term scutage had come into use. But the temptation to monarchs to raise the levy and to impose scutage more often made the issue controversial. John increased both the rate of scutage and the frequency of demands and an article of *Magna Carta declared that scutage must be imposed only 'by common counsel of our kingdom'. When Edward I revived scutage in 1279 for his Welsh expedition he met with opposition, and Edward III's attempts to levy scutage for a Scottish campaign in 1327 were largely unsuccessful, the arrears of payment having to be wiped off. JAC

sea power enables a state to use the oceans for commerce and war, while denying these facilities to enemies or rivals and controlling neutral shipping. This has been true since early periods. Sea-battles such as Salamis (480 BC) and Mycale (479 BC) played a part in compelling the Persian king Xerxes to abandon his invasion of Greece. During the struggle between Carthage and Rome for control of the western Mediterranean, fleet engagements at Mylae (260 BC), Cape Ecnomus (256 BC), and the Aegates Islands (241 BC) were equally decisive. The defeat of Marcus Antonius at the naval battle of Actium (31 BC) established the Julio-Claudian imperial dynasty of Rome. Two invasions of Japan launched by the Chinese Mongol emperor Kublai Khan in 1274 and 1281 were disastrous failures because of terrible losses inflicted on their supporting fleets by storms. In 1571, the Christian victory at Lepanto crippled Ottoman naval power in the eastern Mediterranean and delivered a decisive check to Muslim western expansion. Successive Spanish armadas against the protestant English and Dutch, including major efforts in 1588 and 1639, failed because the attackers were unable to win command of the sea. Three hard-fought naval wars between Britain and the Dutch, in 1652–4, 1665–7, and 1672–4, were caused by commercial competition and rival claims to sea power. The victories of the British and Dutch fleets, now in alliance, at Barfleur and *La Hogue in 1692 safeguarded the Glorious Revolution of 1688 against a Stuart restoration backed by France. The 18th cent. saw a series of wars in which sea power was crucial, in a world in which sea-borne commerce and overseas empires had expanded markedly. The French Revolutionary and Napoleonic wars (1793–1815) saw the culmination of naval warfare in the age of the sailing warship. Nelson's victory at the *Nile in 1798 established British control of the Mediterranean, and *Trafalgar on 21 October 1805 set the seal on British naval superiority. During the 19th cent., Britain's naval predominance sustained her world-wide commercial and imperial power, despite revolutions in warship design, including steam propulsion and protective armour.

The late 19th cent. saw increased scholarly analysis of the nature of sea power. Foremost was the American naval officer A. T. Mahan. He sought to explain Britain's success in attaining maritime hegemony and claimed to draw contemporary lessons from it, stressing that command of the sea in war could only be attained by the destruction or neutralizing of the enemy fleet. His first book, *The Influence of Sea Power in History, 1660–1783* (1890), was particularly influential, appearing to provide an analysis of sea power backed by thorough historical research.

By 1914, while the heavily armed and armoured battleship was still seen as the principal naval weapon, the introduction of torpedoes and submarines had already necessitated protective screens for major warships. In the 1914–18 conflict allied sea power facilitated the dismemberment of Germany's overseas empire and enforced a blockade of Germany and Austria-Hungary. In both the First and Second World Wars, Germany's unrestricted submarine warfare at times seemed potentially decisive. Britain's dependence on overseas trade made her particularly vulnerable, though the introduction of the convoy system reduced losses and the allied navies eventually triumphed.

During the Second World War, advances in naval aviation introduced a further element into the struggle for naval supremacy. The Italian battle fleet, at anchor in its *Taranto base, was badly damaged by a tiny force of obsolescent Fleet Air Arm aircraft in a raid in November 1940. In December 1941, planes from a Japanese carrier force crippled the American Pacific battle fleet at anchor at Pearl Harbor, though fortunately the American aircraft carriers were away at sea. Japanese sea power was vital in the allied defeats in the Far East in early 1942, but the survival of the American carriers brought a major Japanese defeat in the battle of Midway in June 1942. The principal Japanese striking force suffered disastrous losses in an engagement in which the main warships involved never saw each other, strikes by carrier aircraft proving decisive. Sea power was important in the European theatre of war, in the battle of the Atlantic, and in the north African campaigns, but its most convincing demonstration was in the allied advance in the Pacific between 1942 and 1945. 'Island-hopping' campaigns, moving ever closer to the Japanese home islands, were made possible by the development of striking forces capable of keeping the sea for long periods, backed by an impressively sophisticated sea-borne supply system. Before the atomic bomb brought Japan to surrender, her defeat had been ensured by the success of American submarines and aircraft in decimating Japanese shipping, depriving the Japanese war machine of oil and other vital raw materials. Since the 1960s, the submarine armed with nuclear missiles has become the single most potent embodiment of sea power. NMcC

seaside holidays were an English invention of the mid-18th cent. Orthodox medicine adopted popular sea-bathing customs and advocated formal therapeutic bathing regimes, for patients suffering from a variety of diseases. At Scarborough, by the 1730s, visitors to the spa were combining sea-bathing with their other treatments, and a sojourn at Bath was increasingly followed in the late 18th cent. by a visit to Weymouth. Dr Russell, the great proponent of sea-bathing, based himself at Brighton, which from the mid-18th cent. became the most fashionable of the emerging genre of seaside resorts. Royal patronage from the prince of Wales, the future George IV, made Brighton fashionable and attracted pleasure-seekers as well as those seeking cures. Other resorts, especially in Kent and Sussex, followed suit. Brighton already had over 40,000 inhabitants at the 1841 census, and the railways opened out new markets. The middle-class family holiday, with bathing and sandcastles for the children and 'nigger minstrels' and German bands for their elders, became a mid-Victorian institution, as did the seaside pier. The railways also made cheap trips to the seaside for the working classes possible, and the Lancashire cotton towns pioneered the working-class seaside holiday of several days at a time from the 1870s, flocking to Blackpool in particular, as the traditional wakes holidays were transformed and fairgrounds migrated to the coast. By 1914 the British seaside resort network was well established, catering for all classes and all tastes, with huge pleasure palaces and sophisticated fairground technology at the popular resorts. The inter-war years saw a greater concentration on fresh air and a freer approach to bathing, by this time recreational rather than therapeutic. British seaside resorts reached their peak of popularity in the 1950s, after the introduction of paid holidays. But when cheap travel to new Mediterranean resorts became available, in conjunction with the popularization of sunbathing, British resorts struggled to compete. By the 1970s many smaller places were in terminal decline, and the British seaside holiday, threatened by pollution and new holiday fashions, is currently an endangered species. JKW

Sebastopol, siege of. The chief event of the *Crimean War 1853–6. From 27 September 1854 British, French, and Turkish (and later Sardinian) armies maintained the siege of Sebastopol, the main Russian naval base in the Crimea. The town was never completely surrounded, being accessible from the north throughout. Not until 1855 were the allies strong enough to assault the town's chief bastions in earnest. The French captured the White Tower on 7 June 1855 but the British assault on the Redan on 17 June was a failure. In a joint attack on 8 September the British again failed to hold the Redan but the French captured the Malakov, the key to the town. The Russians evacuated Sebastopol that night, keeping it under fire. Although the allies destroyed the docks in January 1856 they never occupied the city, which was still disputed when the war ended. SDB

Second World War. Germany made the Second World War: a necessary condition was a nationalist German government ready, even eager, to use force to secure far-reaching aims. Hitler did not create the social and economic conditions that gave him power, but he brilliantly exploited them to develop a state usable for his own purposes, which went further than most Germans would consciously have ventured. The Nazis, who preached violence to forge unity between social classes, included those whose first aim, to increase German power in the world, required the co-operation of the military, the civil service, and industrialists, and also Nazis whose first, egalitarian, aim was to destroy the influence of those privileged groups. Hitler reflected and helped to win the dominance among Nazis of those who wanted international power. His coming to power was with the help of German conservatives who combined with the Nazis to resist socialists, in preference to working with socialists to block the Nazis.

Hitler's strength lay in the support of voters; many voted Nazi through despair at the depression of 1930–2. Arguably, it was the consequence of the treaty of *Versailles after the First World War and its insistence on reparations payments by Germany which forced the maintenance of deflationary policies to keep up the exchange value of the mark, as well as recent memories of the catastrophic inflation of 1923, itself even more plausibly the result of the enforcement of reparations. Hitler, and the expansionist German nationalists he stood for, seemed a result of Versailles. Most British opinion concluded that those, especially the French, who had tried to enforce Versailles were to blame and that to soften the nationalism of Hitler's Third Reich the remaining grievances of Versailles should be remedied. Hence, British 'appeasement'. Towards Germany, even towards Hitler, conciliation seemed better than confrontation. France should be restrained and the anti-fascism proclaimed by the Soviet Union checked. Without the United Kingdom (and the British empire), restraint on the militarily reviving Germany could not be effected and though French governments attempted to work with Italy and the Soviet Union, Italy was weak in resources and the Soviet Union struggling to exploit its own. As Hitler understood, British policy determined how far he could move towards a 'purified' German nation, self-sufficient and militarily invulnerable, without engaging in war. Until 1939, with British acquiescence, Hitler won success after peaceful success: restoring compulsory military service, creating an air force, remilitarizing the Rhineland, absorbing Austria, annexing the German-inhabited areas of Czechoslovakia, and then, in March 1939, destroying Czechoslovakia altogether. Hitler's growing support in Germany, as foreign success went with full employment, steadily increased his freedom of action.

In Britain, however, appeasement became unpopular. Neville *Chamberlain, its leader, felt obliged to threaten force to compel German restraint and insisted that change to German benefit should take place only by way of negotiation. On 31 March 1939 he pledged Britain to defend Poland, and tried, at last, to build a 'peace front'. Chamberlain's policy was to persuade, or coerce, Hitler into acceptance of moderate change which would leave intact Britain's capacity to defend her independence. The British aim was to preserve the European balance of power, Hitler's to destroy it. In 1939 the British obstructed him. But the alliance attempted between Britain, France, and the USSR failed. Probably Stalin observed Chamberlain's reluctance to make a Soviet alliance because it would be too provocative to Germany and wreck chances of renewed Anglo-German concord. Stalin thought it safer to make his own bargain with Hitler, took up appeasement, and agreed to help Hitler to destroy Poland.

After an attempt to persuade Britain not to interfere, Germany attacked Poland, in theory to solve German grievances about Polish mistreatment of ethnic Germans, in fact to increase German resources, 'living space'. At dawn on 1 September 1939 began what became the Second World War. On 3 September Britain and France declared war on Germany. The unusually vicious nature of the German government already made morally desirable the defence of European balance.

As expected, Poland did not last long against German attack and was partitioned with the USSR. Anglo-French strategy was defensive, waiting to build up their armed strength. In May and June 1940 it went badly wrong. France, defeated by a German attack in May 1940, whose main weight was further south than anticipated, surrendered in June. Italy joined Germany, tempted by the prospect of participation in a prospective peace conference. Hitler could now organize Europe to support the German war effort. For the moment that effort was relaxed. Everything seemed possible: the British would surely give in. Carefully calculating, while offering inspiring calls to arms, Churchill led the cabinet to resist, assuming, correctly, that the navy and air force could prevent German troop landings in sufficient force to occupy England in 1940 and that US economic help would enable protracted defence. The victory of the *RAF in the Battle of *Britain in 1940 blocked invasion, but in 1941 German submarines nearly defeated Britain; British code-breaking came to the rescue in June.

In 1941 Hitler decided to attack the USSR before the defeat of Britain. In 1940 President Roosevelt, hesitantly, had decided to try to keep Britain fighting. In 1941, therefore, Hitler feared that the war in the west might escalate into war with the USA and decided, after tentative attempts to make a new bargain with Stalin, to defeat the USSR first. His advisers expected success in 1941. Then resources for intercontinental war, if necessary, would have been won. It went wrong. Roosevelt, concerned to maintain a world balance of power, gave help to the USSR. The 'Lend-Lease' Act permitted him to supply countries at war without payment. Like Churchill he strove to keep the Red Army fighting. The Red Army wore down the German army while the Americans made tanks, aircraft, and ships; hence Hitler's defeat.

In the 20th cent. Japan has maintained expanding population by trade, either by co-operating in the international structures or by forceful seizure of raw materials, especially fuel. In 1930–45 the Japanese authorities used force to counter trade barriers erected by foreign countries, threatening British and Dutch rubber, tin, and oil. The US government, working to maintain a world balance of power in 1940 and 1941, tried to check Japan by denying raw materials. The Japanese, with the threat from the USSR met by the Germans, decided to seize essential resources. In December 1941 Japan, encouraged by Germany, attacked the US Pacific fleet at Pearl Harbor and invaded Malaya, Burma, and the Dutch East Indies. Hitler, conscious that the USA was already an opponent, and still hopeful of victory over the USSR, clarified the conflict by declaring war on the USA. The Second World War involved Germany, Italy, and Japan against the USA, USSR, and the British empire, with France overrun by Germany, and China, divided between nationalists and communists, uncertainly united in resistance to Japanese attempts to control Chinese resources and trade.

The British empire and the USA fought a world war. Both gave priority to defeating Hitler. The main effort against Japan came from the USA. The failure of the Chinese to defend territories from which Japan could be attacked reduced the British role in Burma from the expansion of the line of communications to China to the defence of India and the eventual reassertion of British power in Malaya and Singapore.

In Europe the American army hoped to concentrate all Anglo-American resources in the United Kingdom to invade Europe at the earliest date permitted by the prior need to defeat attempts by German submarines to prevent passage between America and Britain. Churchill and the British thought Germany must first be weakened by campaigns in north Africa and Italy. Roosevelt agreed with Churchill in order to avoid delay in bringing *some* US forces into action in the European theatre; partly he wanted to maintain US public interest in the war against Hitler, partly to demonstrate US eagerness to take some burden off Soviet forces. Thus, their main operations were delayed and British and US ground forces became fully engaged against the German army only after the landings in Normandy in June 1944. By September 1944 the allies had defeated Germany; Anglo-American forces closed to the Rhine, the Red Army had taken Romania, territorial losses and bombing by overwhelming Anglo-American attack ended German ability to sustain war for much longer. However, SS coercion and fear of the allies, especially the Soviets, enabled Hitler to delay the end until May 1945.

In the Pacific, Japan, too, continued the war long after defeat brought about by attacks by US submarines on transport ships and US bombing attacks on Japanese industry. Japanese authorities, led by the emperor, accepted defeat only after the use of two atomic bombs, developed in time in the USA.

In Europe the war created a partition, which lasted for more than 40 years, between communist states, influenced or controlled by the USSR, and societies dominated by more or less tempered liberal capitalism. The partition came surprisingly peacefully, though with particular problems in Poland, accepted in the end as belonging to the communist sphere, and with increasing tension for a time in Germany, where an administrative partition agreed during the war lasted for several decades. In the East partition brought devastating and protracted conflict in China, where communists triumphed in civil war; in Korea, split in two, after a fierce war: and in Indo-China, where conflict lasted for decades. Here, as in Europe, capitalism is recovering among 'communist' states, but in Asia liberalism is less evident.

Germany, Italy, and Japan, the defeated countries, are today more agreeable to live in and far more prosperous than were the countries that precipitated the bloodshed of the Second World War. All, so far, are more tolerant societies. The Nazis demonstrated to rational human beings the dangers of the menacing idiocy of racial prejudice by carrying it through to its chilling conclusion in the mass murder of Jews, as enemies of 'Germanic and Aryan purity'.

In 1940 the United Kingdom, inspired by Churchill, continued to fight. The British preferred American domination to Hitler's. In 1945 the USA became, and has remained, the greatest power in the world. Equipped with generally benign intentions, that country, especially through political interference, has sometimes brought misery and disaster; more often it has helped to advance the good of mankind. RACP

Bell, P. M. H., *The Origins of the Second World War in Europe* (1986); Calvocoressi, P., Wint, G., and Pritchard, J., *Total War: The Causes and Courses of the Second World War* (1989); Iriye, A., *The Origins of the Second World War in Asia and the Pacific* (1987); Parker, R. A. C., *Struggle for Survival: The History of the Second World War* (Oxford, 1989); Weinberg, G., *A World at Arms* (Cambridge, 1994).

secretaries of state. Like many other great offices, the secretaryships of state grew from comparatively modest beginnings. The development from a mere clerk to a policy-maker was largely a 16th-cent. phenomenon. In medieval usage, 'secretary' retained a slightly sinister meaning as one who was privy to secrets, and was used to describe *Gaveston and *Despenser, the favourites of Edward II. As first the *great seal and then the *privy seal were regarded by monarchs as too public, the keeper of the signet rose in importance. In the reign of Edward IV, a principal secretary holding the signet was appointed, but the jump in status was not until Thomas *Cromwell became principal secretary in 1534. Two years later he added the privy seal and became the engine of government. Cecil (Lord *Burghley) held the post of secretary under Edward VI and Elizabeth (1550–3 and 1558–72) and his son Sir Robert *Cecil 1596–1600. From 1573 until 1590 the post was filled by *Walsingham. In the reign of James I the convention was established of appointing two secretaries. After the Restoration, the posts were divided into a secretary of state for the north and for the south—the former conducting diplomacy with the protestant powers of northern Europe, the latter with the catholic powers of southern Europe. This strange system, bound to cause problems, survived for more than 100 years, partly because one secretary usually took the lead: few people doubted that William *Pitt, secretary for the south 1757–61, carried more weight than his colleague the earl of Holdernesse. In 1768 a third secretary was appointed to administer the American colonies, but it was an ill-fated experiment since they declared themselves independent in 1776.

A major reorganization took place in 1782 when the southern secretaryship was converted into the *Home Office and the northern secretaryship into the *Foreign Office. After that there were periodic increases in the number of secretaryships. Henry *Dundas was made secretary for war in 1794 and also took on colonial responsibilities; a separate secretaryship for the *colonies was created in 1854; a secretaryship for India after the mutiny, in 1858; a secretaryship for air in 1918. In the 20th cent., though the foreign and home secretaries have retained their identities and importance, the others have suffered from repackaging according to the vicissitudes of time. The colonial secretary found his department shrinking when, in 1925, a separate secretaryship for dominion affairs was set up. Since his main task after the Second World War was to wind up the British empire as rapidly as possible, his reward in 1966 was abolition. The secretary for dominion affairs did not long outlast him and, having changed his name to the secretary for Commonwealth relations in 1947, was swallowed up by the Foreign Office in 1968. The secretary of state for India vanished in 1947 when India became independent, and the secretary for air disappeared when an integrated Ministry of *Defence was established in 1964. Meanwhile the proliferation of secretaryships illustrated the law that grand titles increase as power diminishes—for industry (1963), education and science (1964), employment (1968), social services (1968), environment (1970), and transport (1976).

The early evolution of the secretaryship in Scotland from the reign of David II followed a similar course to that in England, with the office emerging from the keepership of the signet. In 1558–71 it was held by William *Maitland, in 1661–80 by *Lauderdale, and after 1680 usually by two persons. At the Union of 1701 *Mar and Loudoun were reappointed as secretaries of state, but in 1709 *Queensberry became a single third secretary. This arrangement lasted until the Jacobite rising of 1745, after which no secretary of state for Scotland was appointed until 1885. A secretaryship for Wales was set up in 1964. In Ireland, the lord-lieutenant had the main responsibility, but was assisted by a powerful chief secretary who, from 1859 onwards, was usually a member of the cabinet. This post lapsed when the Irish Free State was set up in 1922, but a secretary of state for Northern Ireland was appointed in 1972 after direct rule had been imposed on the province. JAC

secret ballot was advocated as early as 1656 by James *Harrington in *Oceana*, discussed in pamphlets at the time of the Glorious Revolution, argued by *Defoe in 1708, and became a persistent radical demand in the 18th cent. It was adopted by both France and the USA for their new constitutions. Nevertheless, when the reform committee proposed it in 1831 it was struck out by *Grey and the cabinet, to the great relief of William IV. The issue was then taken up by George *Grote, became one of the *chartists' six points, and was urged in the Commons by Henry Berkeley. Opposing it in 1842, George Byng declared that 'a real Englishman would never conceal his feelings and opinions' and Sir James *Graham agreed that only 'dirty and hypocritical cowards' would wish to vote in secret. In 1856 it was introduced into the new constitutions for South Australia and Victoria. A select committee in 1869 reported in favour and in 1872 *Forster succeeded in carrying the measure against some opposition by the House of Lords. The introduction of secret ballot did not eliminate bribery and corruption but was a blow to the influence of the propertied classes, particularly when the franchise was further extended in 1884.

JAC

secret service. The British secret service traces its history back to Elizabeth I's secretary of state Sir Francis *Walsingham; but, being secret, there is no way of telling that it is not really older than that. Walsingham used it mainly to sniff out foreign-aided catholic plots. The playwright Christopher *Marlowe is supposed to have been one of his spies; or murdered by one; or both. (Espionage is a confusing field.) Most later ministers used covert intelligence to a greater or lesser extent, though never in a formal, institutional fashion. The only British secret service agency with a continuous history from the 17th cent. onwards was the *Post Office, which used to open letters, decipher them, reseal them, and send them on their way. During the Napoleonic years these activities were stepped up, as one might expect, both abroad, and also at home, in circles where French revolutionary contagion was thought likely to catch on. This continued through to 1820, when suspicions of *agent provocateur* activities by a number of government agents, including one known as *'Oliver', provoked such public outrage that the practice was discontinued.

For most of the Victorian years Britain had virtually no secret service, mainly because it was thought to be immoral, counter-productive, and foreign. (There was a 'secret service *fund*', but that was spent on other things.) It started up again around the turn of the 20th cent., with the formation first of the London *Police Special Branch in 1881–7, to look after American-Irish and continental anarchist dynamiters; and then of MI5 and MI6 in 1909, in response to the German threat. The *First World War saw their activities expand enormously. Afterwards they became a permanent though invisible feature of the British political scene.

Their achievements have been mixed. They undoubtedly contributed to the allies' victory in the *Second World War. Hitler admired them hugely, crediting their successes at lying and deception to the influence of the English public school. On the other hand they made some terrible errors; were almost immobilized by Russian 'moles' in the 1950s and 1960s; and are strongly suspected of having plotted treacherously against Labour governments in 1924 (the *Zinoviev letter) and 1976. BJP

sects. See DISSENT.

secularism was the word adopted by George Jacob *Holyoake in the early 1850s to describe a system of morals and social action shaped exclusively by this-worldly considerations, irrespective of religious beliefs. The word was derived from the secular education movement for the complete separation of religious teaching from other forms of education.

Christians in 19th-cent. Britain argued that atheists, lacking belief in divine judgement, must be immoral and incapable of exercising civil rights. Holyoake wished to avoid the negative connotations of the word *atheism by finding an alternative which stressed the positive nature of an ethical life inspired to do good for its own sake. Regarding religion as an irrelevance, he argued that secularism could extend beyond the bounds of atheism to include all enlightened reformers.

Local secular societies were formed in the 1850s, incorporating earlier groups of anticlerical and atheistic radicals who had supported Richard *Carlile and Robert *Owen. In 1866 these were brought together by Charles *Bradlaugh in the National Secular Society though, unlike Holyoake, Bradlaugh argued that atheism was a necessary precondition for secularism. Ironically, secularism as a movement declined from the mid-1880s partly because society was becoming more secularized, making the campaigns of secularism seem unnecessary, although the National Secular Society continues as a pressure group for the complete secularization of state education, repeal of the blasphemy laws, disestablishment of the Church of England, and the removal of all religious influences in politics, law, morals, and society. ER

Security, Act of [S], 1704. The Scottish Act of Security was, paradoxically, an important step towards Union. After the failure of the *Darien scheme in 1700, the Scots were bitter towards England. Proposals for a union failed and the Scottish Parliament pointedly refused to follow the English Act of *Settlement (1701), which ensured succession to the Hanoverians. Instead, their Act of Security left the Scottish succession to be resolved by Parliament later and declared that the successor in England would not be named if Scottish grievances over religion, liberty, and trade were not met. To point the threat, the Scottish militia was put in readiness. Anne refused consent but, reluctant to force the issue in the midst of a great war, gave way in 1704. The two countries were now on collision course and, after retaliation from both sides, negotiations commenced which resulted in Union in 1707. James Mackinnon called the statute 'an ultimatum rather than an Act of Parliament'. JAC

Sedgemoor, battle of, 1685. Sedgemoor was that most desperate of ventures, a surprise night attack. *Monmouth landed at Lyme Regis on 11 June 1685 and was proclaimed king at Taunton on the 20th. But he gained little support from the gentry or nobility and his scratch army failed to take Bristol or Bath. He was pursued to Bridgwater by a royal army under Lord Feversham, with John Churchill, the future duke of *Marlborough, as second in command. Monmouth's men outnumbered their opponents, but Feversham's were trained soldiers. The royal army drew up east of Bridgwater, behind the line of the Bussex rhine, a waterlogged ditch. On the night of 5 July, Monmouth led out his men in total silence, past the village of Chedzoy, hidden by darkness and night mist. But with still a mile to go, the alarm was given. Once the element of surprise had been lost, Monmouth's fate was sealed. His cavalry was soon dispersed and the infantry, firing wildly, ran short of ammunition. As dawn broke, Feversham's men advanced and the fight was over. Monmouth was found hiding in a ditch on Cranborne Chase two days later, taken to London, and beheaded on Tower Hill on 15 July. His supporters were cut down, the rest rounded up in Weston Zoyland church, transported, or hanged by Judge *Jeffreys. JAC

Seditious Meetings Act, 1795. In the autumn of 1795 high bread prices reinforced a demand for parliamentary reform and the London *Corresponding Society held a mass open-air meeting at Copenhagen House (Islington) on 26 October. Three days later, on his way to open Parliament, George III was hooted and the window of his coach shattered. *Pitt's government responded with the Seditious Meetings Act (36 Geo. III c. 8), which forbade meetings of more than 50 people without prior permission from a magistrate, and the Treasonable Practices Act (36 Geo. III c. 7), which threatened with transportation for up to seven years anyone speaking or writing against king, government, or constitution. Both bills were vigorously contested by the Foxite opposition but carried by large majorities. Though Pitt has been accused of exaggerating the threat for party advantage, there seems little doubt that he was genuinely alarmed. JAC

Seisyllwg, kingdom of. An early Welsh kingdom of obscure origin, though it may have been established by Seisyll ap Clydog, king of Ceredigion, by extending his dominion south to the Tywi valley (*c.*730). His descendant Angharad married *Rhodri Mawr, who temporarily combined it with *Gwynedd (871). Later (904), it was absorbed into the wider kingdom of *Deheubarth under *Hywel Dda; thereafter, Seisyllwg ceased to be an independent kingdom and its name fell into disuse. RAG

Selborne, Roundell Palmer, 1st earl of (1812–95). Lawyer. Palmer got off to a flying start. He was educated at both Rugby and Winchester, moved on to Christ Church, Oxford, was president of the Union, and gained a first-class degree. He studied law at Lincoln's Inn and entered Parliament in 1847 as a supporter of Sir Robert *Peel. He became solicitor-general in *Palmerston's administration in 1861 and moved up to attorney-general in 1863, holding the post until 1866. A strong churchman, he disapproved greatly of the disestablishment of the Irish church in 1869 and refused *Gladstone's offer of the lord chancellorship, with a peerage. But on the resignation of Lord Hatherley in 1872 with failing eyesight, Palmer succeeded him as lord chancellor, holding office 1872–4 and again 1880–5. He was created baron in 1872 and advanced to earl in 1882. Increasingly uneasy at the radical trend of the Liberals, he parted with them on *Irish Home Rule in 1886, writing sadly in his *Memorials*, 'my idols were broken'. Henceforth he gave independent support to the Conservatives. Palmer's brilliant intellect, vast memory, and powers of application were widely recognized, and the complete reorganization of the law courts in the *Judicature Act of 1873 was his work. His son and grandson also had distinguished political careers. JAC

Selby, battle of, 1644. In the spring of 1644, the royal army in the north, under *Newcastle, was at Durham, to prevent a junction of the Scots with the parliamentary forces under the *Fairfaxes. But on 11 April John Bellasyse, holding Selby, south of York, was badly defeated, lost 1,600 men and all his guns, and was taken prisoner. York, the king's northern capital, was in imminent danger and on 13 April, as soon as he heard the news, Newcastle struck camp and moved south to hold the city. Rupert's attempt to relieve York later in the summer led to the crushing royalist defeat at *Marston Moor. Selby was the stone that started the avalanche. JAC

Selby abbey (Yorks.) was founded *c.*1070 by King William I for Benedict, a monk of Auxerre, who had become a hermit at Selby, and who had brought with him a relic of St *Germanus of Auxerre. Its estates and its appropriated churches were concentrated in south-east Yorkshire and northern Lincolnshire and in wealth it was second only to St Mary's York amongst the *Benedictine houses of Yorkshire. Its net income in 1535 was nearly £740. This supported a community of some 30 monks in the late Middle Ages. Selby's abbot was regularly summoned to Parliament as a spiritual lord. BJG

Selden, John (1584–1654). Selden, 'the father of English legal history', was one of the most distinguished antiquarians of Stuart England. A lawyer of the Inner Temple, he served as MP for Lancaster (1623), Great Bedwyn (1626), Ludgershall (1628), and in the Long Parliament of 1640 for the University of Oxford. Selden was born in Sussex of lesser gentry stock. He practised law, but his main interests were history and politics. From 1607 he issued a stream of learned works, mainly on legal history, of which a history of tithes (1617) is best known. His legal knowledge made him useful to the opposition to Charles I, when debates often turned on precedents. He took part in attacks upon the royal favourite *Buckingham in 1626 and collaborated closely with *Coke in 1628 on *habeas corpus. The court took reprisals and from March 1629 to May 1631 he was imprisoned. In the early days of the Long Parliament he was a moderate and there were rumours that he might join the court. But he did not and in 1643 was put in charge of records in the Tower. Meanwhile, Selden continued to publish, including an important treatise on the law of the sea (1636) and another on the privileges of the baronage (1641). Many of his books and archives finished up in the Bodleian library. His *Table Talk* was published in 1689. *Clarendon paid the highest tribute to his learning and kindness. The Selden Society was established in 1886 by *Maitland and others to encourage the study of English law. JAC

self-denying ordinance, 1645. Growing dissatisfaction in Parliament with the inability of *Essex and *Manchester to finish the Civil War led to a proposal, late in 1644, for a self-denying ordinance, whereby members of both Houses of Parliament could no longer hold commissions. This was ingenious, since members of the House of Commons could, if they chose, resign their seats, but peers could not divest themselves of their titles: the House of Lords consequently rejected it. Brought forward again in 1645 after more royalist successes, it passed on 3 April. Essex, Manchester, and *Waller resigned, clearing out the old guard, and paving the way for the *New Model Army under Sir Thomas *Fairfax. *Cromwell was given special exemption from the ordinance. JAC

self-help. Social and moral doctrine that people should rely on their own efforts and not look to the state for help. In the 19th cent. self-help took two forms: collectivist, as with *friendly societies, mutual improvement societies, *co-operatives, and *trade unions; or individualistic, as with the practice of sobriety, thrift, hard work, and self-education. Self-help, as popularized by Samuel *Smiles, was middle-class advice how working people might better themselves without upsetting the status quo or seeking public relief when sick, aged, or unemployed. It also harmonized with the skilled artisan tradition of independence. JFCH

Selgovae. A British tribe in southern Scotland. This tribe, whose name is thought to mean 'hunters', is referred to by the Greek geographer Ptolemy. His information places them in the southern uplands of Scotland centred in the upper Tweed basin, sandwiched between the *Votadini to the east and the Novantes to the west. Their principal settlement was on Eildon Hill, where an initial fortified enclosure of only 3 acres was enlarged in the years before the Roman invasion to a hill-fort of some 40 acres. Inside, the remains of over 300 huts can still be traced, so that the population of the Selgovaean capital must have run into four figures. It was abandoned at the time of the Roman conquest *c.* AD 79, briefly described in *Agricola's biography written by his son-in-law *Tacitus. The native hilltop stronghold was replaced by a Roman fort, Trimontium (Newstead), at the foot of the hill. KB

Selsey, diocese of. *Wilfrid, formerly of *Ripon and *York, created this see, conterminous with Sussex, in 681. When he returned to *Hexham in 686, Selsey was united with *Winchester until Selsey's revival some years later. After the Council of London (1075), the see moved to *Chichester. WMM

Septennial Act, 1716. This Act prolonged the life of Parliament from a maximum of three years (as the 1694 Triennial Act required) to seven years. Its pretext was the Jacobite uprising in 1715. But by delaying the next election until 1722 the new Whig ministers succeeded in evading electoral judgement until they had consolidated themselves in power and weakened their Tory opponents. Following the 'rage of party' of Queen Anne's day, the longer periods between elections did much to quieten political life and entrench the

Whigs in government for the next three decades. The *Parliament Act of 1911 shortened the duration of parliaments to five years. AAH

Septimius Severus. Roman emperor 193–211. Lucius Septimius Severus was born at Lepcis Magna in north Africa. Consul in 190, he was governor of Pannonia Superior on the Danube when he was proclaimed emperor on the assassination of Commodus, gaining the support of the Senate. He was opposed by the governor of Britain, *Clodius Albinus, whom he killed at the battle of Lyons in February 197. It may have been after this that the province and army of Britain were divided in two. After a series of wars against the Parthians, Severus' attention was drawn back to Britain by trouble with the Scottish tribes. He took the field with his sons *Caracalla and Geta in 208 and reconquered the Lowlands, establishing a garrison fortress at Carpow on the Tay. Increasing ill-health led to his death early in 211 at York. ASEC

serfdom is the general term for servitude to a superior, but distinguished from slavery by being regulated by custom. The name masks a great variety of arrangements. There were large areas of England where it had never applied, particularly in Kent, the old Danelaw, and parts of the west country. Though the basic obligation of the unfree was to work for three days a week on the lord's demesne, to assist at harvest time, and to pay certain dues, the details differed from estate to estate. It was understood that serfs and their families should not be moved from their lands as chattels, but there are instances where it was done. The nearest that serfdom came to being a complete system was in the two centuries after the Norman Conquest. Before then personal vassalage was common, but a considerable proportion of peasants were slaves. By the 13th cent. the pattern was beginning to unravel as more and more villeins obtained their freedom and became copyholders. The system withered away, though it was a slow process, and as late as 1549, in *Kett's rebellion, there were demands that bond-men should be made free. In Scotland serfdom disappeared even sooner, and had gone by the 14th cent., though clan and family loyalties remained strong and *heritable jurisdictions survived until the 18th cent. By a remarkable throwback, a system akin to serfdom was introduced in Scotland in the 17th cent. to control the supply of labour in coal-mines and salt-pans, especially in Fife. In 1701 a statute declared that *habeas corpus did not apply to the miners and in 1708 it was enacted that a collier escaping could be brought back within eight years. The system was finally abolished as late as 1799 (39 Geo. III c. 56) when the colliers were declared 'free from their servitude'. JAC

serjeant at law. The order of serjeants at law, dating at least from the early 14th cent., consisted of the leaders of the legal profession and until 1846 they alone had the right to plead cases before the Court of *Common Pleas, the most important of the common law courts for medieval civil litigation. The characteristic of their office was the distinctive 'coif' and they were members of Serjeants' Inn. It was necessary to be a serjeant at law in order to become a judge in the common law courts, but by the mid-16th cent. the office had declined in importance and was often conferred merely as a preliminary to judicial appointment. The order of serjeants was dissolved in the 19th cent. MM

Settlement, Act of, 1701. This statute, 12 & 13 Wm. III c. 2, is strange and betrays the mixed motives of its authors. The immediate problem was to provide for the protestant succession after the death of Anne's son, the duke of Gloucester, in July 1700. This was done by putting aside more than 50 catholic claimants and offering the succession to *Sophia, electress of Hanover, a granddaughter of James I. But the Tory majority in Parliament took the opportunity to tack on a number of incongruous clauses designed to limit the powers of the monarch, who was not to leave the country or engage in war without parliamentary approval. Placemen were not to sit in Parliament, judges were to hold office on good behaviour, and government business was to be conducted in the *Privy Council, where counsellors were to sign their advice. Royal pardons were not to be issued against impeachments. The clauses devoted to the succession took effect in 1714, when Queen Anne was succeeded by Sophia's son George I. The other clauses were either repealed or circumvented. The clause forbidding placemen to sit in Parliament, which would have divorced legislature and executive, was nullified by the clumsy device of re-election on taking office. JAC

Settlements and Removals, Act of, 1662. The end of the Civil War period left the Elizabethan *Poor Law arrangements in confusion, since many people had left their native villages and towns, some to join armies, others to find work. Charles II's *Cavalier Parliament brought in an Act 'for the better relief of the poor of this kingdom' (13 & 14 Car. II c. 12) which governed poor relief until the reform of 1834. Though overseers and justices had often tried to move on the indigent poor there was no Elizabethan statute to justify doing so, save for 'vagrant rogues'. The Act of 1662 offered the drastic solution that any persons, not necessarily begging or asking for relief, but only 'likely to be chargeable' might be expelled to their native parishes by a removal order granted by two JPs. In addition to being a gross infringement of personal liberty, the arrangements were bound to lead to disputes between parishes which, according to Rickman in 1822, had become 'the main employment of Quarter Sessions since the Revolution'. Though there were hundreds of cases of severe hardship, the law cannot have been rigorously enforced since the cost of removal and litigation, which fell upon the parish, was considerable, and the growth of towns suggests that movement remained possible. But in *The *Wealth of Nations*, Adam *Smith wrote: 'there is scarce a poor man in England, of forty years of age, who has not, in some part of his life, felt himself most cruelly oppressed by this ill-contrived law of settlements.' The first substantial concession did not come until 1795 when it was enacted that persons should not be removed on suspicion that they might become a charge on the poor rate, but on evidence that they had become so. JAC

seven bishops, trial of the, 1688. Seven bishops, including Archbishop *Sancroft, arrested for petitioning against the public reading of James II's second *Declaration of Indulgence (1688), were tried for 'seditious libel'. The cheering which broke out among James's soldiers on Hounslow Heath when the verdict of acquittal was known was an ominous sign for the king. The trial contributed, with the birth of James II's male heir, to James's overthrow and the succession of William III and Mary II. Five of the seven subsequently refused the oath to William. WMM

Sevenoaks, battle of, 1450. In June 1450 Henry VI advanced with a sizeable force into Kent to confront Jack *Cade's rebels. But on the 18th a detachment under Sir Humphry Stafford was routed and the commander killed. Though little more than an ambush, it was enough to undermine morale in the royal army. Henry left for safer parts and Cade went on to occupy London. JAC

seventh-day adventists. Largest of a group of sects focusing on the Second Coming—the return of Christ in glory to judge the living and the dead. They originated in the USA in 1831 when William Miller, a baptist farmer, announced the Coming for 1843, recalculated to 1844. When that failed to happen Miller recanted, but Ellen (Harmon) White held that Christ had in fact come to cleanse the sanctuary of heaven, thus commencing the Final Judgement. This would take place quietly, with evildoers annihilated rather than eternally damned. Her followers observed the sabbath from Friday sunset to Saturday sunset, hence their name, adopted in 1861. They practised believer's baptism. Other distinctive beliefs included the sleep of the soul after death. Originally vegetarian and opposed to political activity and state education, they have become widely regarded for the medical and educational emphasis of their missionary work. They reached England in 1878 with a mission to Southampton. CB

Seven Years' War, 1756–63. In the years immediately after the War of the Austrian Succession, a 'diplomatic revolution' took place in Europe. France and Austria, with support from Russia, Sweden, and Saxony, aligned themselves against Frederick II of Prussia, effectively surrounding his country. In 1756 Frederick made a pre-emptive strike into Saxony, followed a year later by an advance into Bohemia. As his enemies responded by threatening Prussia from all sides, Frederick turned to Britain for aid. An 'Army of Observation' under the duke of *Cumberland was deployed to western Germany, comprising Hanoverian, Hessian, and Prussian troops, but when the French invaded, Cumberland was beaten at *Hastenbeck (26 July 1757) and forced to sign a convention to disband his army. This was countermanded by the British prime minister, William *Pitt (the Elder), who sent British units to reinforce the remains of Cumberland's army, now under the command of Ferdinand of Brunswick. As Frederick II fought for his own survival, winning victories against the French at Rossbach (November 1757) and the Austrians at Leuthen (December 1757), the British, now known as the 'Army of Execution', prepared for action in the west. Initially, the British did well, winning a victory against the French at Krefeld in spring 1758, but in the following year they were forced to pull back towards Hanover. A hard-won victory at *Minden on 1 August 1759 allowed the 'Army of Execution' to consolidate its hold over western Germany, but the war was by no means over. Further east, Frederick had managed to survive only by fighting desperate and costly battles at Zorndorf (1758) and Kunersdorf (1759); he had to fight further battles at Liegnitz and Torgau (1760) and at Schweidnitz (1762), shifting his armies from one side of Prussia to the other to defeat the French, Austrians, and Russians in turn. Only when Russia withdrew from the war on the death of the Tsarina Elizabeth in 1762 did Frederick receive any respite, aided by continued British pressure on the French. The war ended in February 1763 with the peace of *Paris.

But the fighting was not confined to Europe. Preoccupied with their war against Prussia, the French were in no position to protect their overseas possessions, and Britain took full advantage. In North America spasmodic fighting between British and French settlers had been going on for years. In 1758 Pitt dispatched an expeditionary force of 12,000 men under General *Amherst to capture the fortress of Louisbourg on Cape Breton Island and, when this proved successful, ordered a much more ambitious advance into French-held Canada. On the night of 12–13 September 1759 Major-General James *Wolfe, commanding no more than 3,000 men, mounted a surprise attack on Quebec on the upper reaches of the St Lawrence river. Carried there by a British fleet under Admiral Saunders, Wolfe's men scrambled up cliffs to the south of Quebec under cover of darkness and, as dawn broke, faced a force of about 5,000 French soldiers under the marquis de Montcalm on the Plains of Abraham. The ensuing battle was short and decisive; although both Wolfe and Montcalm were fatally wounded, the French retreated and Quebec fell. Montreal followed, leaving Britain in control of much of Canada. This was officially recognized at the peace in 1763.

By then, the British had also consolidated their power in India, where the pro-French nawab Siraj-ud-Daula was defeated by Robert *Clive at the battle of *Plassey in 1757 to give the East India Company control of Bengal. By 1761, when the French outpost at Pondicherry surrendered to General Eyre *Coote, this control had been extended into the Carnatic. JLP

Seville, treaty of, 1729. In 1727 Spain, with Habsburg support, began a siege of *Gibraltar, held by the British since 1704. It was not pressed with much vigour and an armistice was agreed in 1728. By the treaty of Seville in 1729 Spain restored Britain's commercial concessions while Britain agreed to support Spanish claims in Italy. The question of Gibraltar was tacitly abandoned. Disagreement within the British ministry obliged *Townshend, secretary of state for the north, to resign, leaving *Walpole supreme. JAC

Seychelles. These islands in the Indian Ocean were first marked on Portuguese charts in 1502 but not settled by whites until 1742 when Lazare Picault took possession of them for the French East India Company. They were named in 1756 after Louis XV's finance minister Moreau de Sechelles.

The French developed 'secret' spice plantations on them to undercut Dutch monopolies. In 1810 they were captured by the British and retained at the peace of Paris. They were administered along with *Mauritius until 1872 when they became separate under their own governor and council. The Republic of the Seychelles came into existence on 27 June 1976. DAW

Seymour, Lady Catherine (1540–68). Lady Catherine was the younger sister of Lady Jane *Grey, her grandmother being *Mary Tudor, sister of Henry VIII. She was only 13 when the disastrous abortive coup took place. Her sister and father were both executed and the earl of Pembroke, to whom she had been betrothed, broke off the contract. In 1560 she made a secret marriage to the earl of Hertford: Elizabeth sent them both to the Tower. As next in succession to the crown, Catherine was in the midst of intrigue. Philip of Spain considered the possibility of a marriage and in 1562, when the queen was believed to be dying of smallpox, it was mooted to bring Lady Catherine out of the Tower and proclaim her. But the queen recovered and Lady Catherine spent the last six years of her life under house arrest with various guardians. JAC

Seymour, Sir Edward (1633–1708). Tory politician. Opinionated, arrogant, self-seeking, and complex, Seymour was one of the most formidable parliamentarians of his age and a thorn in the side of any government. On becoming an MP in 1661, he set out as an aspiring careerist. At heart a country gentleman, he wavered between a craving for high office and an attachment to 'country principles', often giving the impression of being motivated by pure self-interest. He was a skilful if authoritarian Speaker of the Commons (1673–8, 1678–9), and opposed *'Exclusion' despite his anti-catholicism. In 1688 he joined William of Orange at Exeter, but like many Tories harboured misgivings about William's claim to be king *de jure*. After a troubled spell as a Treasury lord (1692–4), he was for the rest of William's reign a heavyweight opponent of the Whig ministers. Featuring among Anne's new 'high-church' appointments in 1702, his opposition to *Marlborough's costly land campaigns earned him dismissal in 1704. AAH

Seymour, Thomas Seymour, 1st Baron (1508–49). Seymour played for high stakes and lost. He was the brother of *Jane Seymour, Henry VIII's third wife, and the younger brother of *Somerset, protector to the young Edward VI. His spectacular rise began with his sister's marriage in May 1536. He was made a gentleman of the bedchamber and employed on important diplomatic and military missions. In 1544 he was appointed master-general of ordnance for life and lord admiral. As soon as his nephew became king in 1547 he was created a peer and given the Garter. Within months of Henry VIII's death he had married his widow *Catherine Parr, to his brother's indignation. On her death in childbirth, he seems to have aimed at marriage with Princess Elizabeth, whom he had certainly treated with familiarity. But in January 1549 he was accused of conspiring against his brother, of whom he was envious. He was said to have tried to suborn the young king with lavish presents and urged him to exert his authority. Condemned by attainder, he was executed on Tower Hill. Edward noted his uncle's death in his diary without undue grief and Elizabeth is reported to have dismissed him as 'of great wit but very little judgement'. JAC

Shackleton, Sir Ernest Henry (1874–1922). Almost the antithesis of *Scott as an explorer, Shackleton was impetuous and restless and his experience was in the merchant marine rather than the Royal Navy when he successfully applied to join Scott's Antarctic expedition of 1901–4. Sledging with Scott himself, he reached 82 degrees south in 1902. After a variety of experiences including unsuccessful parliamentary candidature, Shackleton raised enough support to take his own expedition back to the Antarctic in 1907–8 where he discovered and named the Beardmore Glacier as a route onto the 10,000-foot plateau at the centre of the continent. Shackleton himself reached 88 degrees south, only 97 miles from the Pole. Now a hero, he was later encouraged to lead an official expedition aiming to explore from the Weddell Sea and cross the continent to the Ross Sea. Ordered to go ahead despite the Great War, Shackleton lost his ship *Endurance* when it was crushed by ice in November 1915. With sledges and small boats, he led his men to Elephant Island by the following April, sailed in an open boat to South Georgia, returned to rescue his men, and then visited the Ross Sea. After some diplomatic service in South America and military service in Russia in 1919, he set out on a third Antarctic expedition in 1921 but died suddenly after reaching South Georgia. RB

Shaftesbury, Anthony Ashley Cooper, 1st earl of (1621–83). Politician. As chancellor of the Exchequer 1661–72, Shaftesbury (then Lord Ashley) was a minor but hard-working and able member of Charles II's early ministries. Promoted to the more prestigious office of lord chancellor in 1672, and made an earl, his deism and attachment to parliamentary government put him at odds with the king's increasingly obvious pro-French and pro-catholic policy and its sinister threat of royal absolutism, and he was dismissed in 1673. He then went into systematic opposition. From 1679 he led the *'Exclusion' campaign to bar the catholic duke of York from the succession, exploiting the *Popish plot to generate anti-catholic feeling. Despite poor health, he succeeded in unifying the disparate opposition groups in Parliament into an electorally successful party of 'Whigs' and employed demotic and propagandist tactics to rouse popular support. Hounded in his last months on a charge of treason, he died in Holland early in 1683. AAH

Shaftesbury, Antony Ashley Cooper, 7th earl of (1801–85). Philanthropist and social reformer. Lord Ashley (as he was styled until 1851 when he succeeded his father) was a strict evangelical who devoted his whole life to promoting, both in and out of Parliament, a succession of reform causes: the Ten Hour Bill; the 1842 Mines Act; reform of the lunacy laws; abolition of child chimney-sweeping; public health and slum housing; ragged schools; the plight of agricultural labourers; training for destitute children (the Shaftesbury homes). He was motivated by a deep religious faith which was simple, rigid, and exclusive. He believed in the literal truth of every word in the Bible. Shaftesbury was the most active champion of Victorian evangelicalism as applied to all aspects of public life. He was chairman of the Lord's Day Observance Society and the Working Men's Lord's Day Rest Association; and was influential (through his family connection with *Palmerston, the prime minister) in the appointment of evangelicals to bishoprics. Politically he was a Tory and opposed all forms of popular democracy. JFCH

Shakespeare, William (1564–1616). Dramatist and poet. Baptized in Stratford-upon-Avon on 26 April 1564, William was the son of John Shakespeare, a glovemaker and prominent Stratford citizen who became mayor and justice of the peace during William's childhood. He was educated at the Stratford grammar school, and married Anne Hathaway, daughter of a successful local farmer, eight years his senior (and already pregnant at the wedding) in 1582. Myths abound about the 'lost years', but there is negligible evidence of his activities between leaving school and beginning work as an actor and playwright in London in the late 1580s. He started as an actor, continued as a playwright, and developed as an administrator and entrepreneur: by the time of his death, on 23 April 1616, he had established his status as a major shareholder in the King's Men, the principal acting company of his time, and was a successful and wealthy man.

Shakespeare wrote approximately forty-two plays (the list has fluid boundaries, with two or three 'apocryphal' plays generally vying for inclusion), in a range of genres and styles, which occupy the principal place in the canon of English literature and which are the subject of a considerable theatrical and critical industry (as well as of substantial tourist revenue). Quotations from Shakespeare remain an often unwitting part of the everyday speech of anglophones; productions of his plays remain hugely popular, both in theatres and in the cinema; his style and verse techniques have come to define 'literariness'; and his history plays in particular are, for many people, the only source of information readily available for a considerable period of medieval history. Although it is impossible to assess Shakespeare's achievement objectively, one may none the less attempt to locate his plays and poems both historically and critically.

His earliest plays are mostly comedies and histories—*The Two Gentlemen of Verona* and *The Taming of the Shrew* are probably the very earliest—for a variety of companies and theatres. He wrote the first play (*The First Part of the Contention*, generally better known as *2 Henry VI*) in the four-play cycle known as the 'first tetralogy' in 1591, completing it with the best known of his earlier histories, *Richard III*, the following year. These plays emerged from a rapidly changing culture fascinated by historiography and particularly by the function of history in the analysis of current affairs. Shakespeare drew on contemporary histories of England, notably *Holinshed's *Chronicles*, for accounts of the events he dramatized, but he rarely left his source (already the product of careful selection, omission, and collaboration) unaltered. His portrayals of kings—most notably of Richard III—have bequeathed a fixed, but often wholly inaccurate, sense of their historical personalities and abilities.

The first tetralogy preceded Shakespeare's attachment to the Lord Chamberlain's Men in 1594; it was for that company, and for their first playhouse, the Theatre, that he wrote the 'second tetralogy', his most popular group of history plays—*Richard II, 1* and *2 Henry IV*, and *Henry V*—which turned back to the period immediately prior to that delineated in the earlier histories to plot the rise to power of Henry Bolingbroke and the accession to the throne of his son, Henry V. Both tetralogies attest to the lasting impact on English society of the Wars of the *Roses (which had occupied much of the previous century) and to the need of the Tudor dynasty, only relatively recently established, to mythologize and legitimize its claim to power. The historiographical focus of the plays shifts: where the earlier histories had adopted a wave-like, cyclical structure and a providentialist outlook—principal characters emerging and fading in succession, attention devoted to overarching issues of causation—the later histories focus on the character and the theatrical abilities of the young Henry V, edging away from providential history and depicting a world in which 'miracles are ceas'd; | And therefore we must needs admit the means | How things are perfected' (*Henry V*, I. i. 67–9). As Phyllis Rackin notes, Shakespeare's Prince Hal 'anticipates the Tudors in using the resources of theatrical role-playing to produce the perfect image of royal authority that he could not inherit from the ambiguous genealogy that left him the throne'.

The move to the new *Globe theatre in 1598–9 marked a new phase in Shakespeare's writing career and the demise of the Shakespearian history play 'proper'. The common assumption is that, as it became clearer that civil war was not likely to follow the death of the Virgin Queen Elizabeth, the plays' function as lightning rods for succession anxiety gradually diminished. For the Globe, Shakespeare turned to other genres, writing his mature comedies (*As You Like It* and *Twelfth Night*) and his major tragedies (*Hamlet*, *Othello*, *King Lear*, and *Macbeth*), as well as his later tragicomedies or romances (*Pericles*, *The Winter's Tale*, *Cymbeline*, and *The Tempest*)—these latter plays affected also by the company's acquisition of an additional playhouse, the smaller, indoor Blackfriars theatre—and putting his Holinshed aside.

But his Jacobean plays none the less exhibit a strong consciousness of their cultural and historiographical function. The Lord Chamberlain's Men had become the King's Men at James I's accession, and played regularly at court. *King Lear* and *Macbeth*, for example, by depicting dark alternatives, acknowledge the role of James I in reunifying Britain, and both *Lear* and *Cymbeline* delve far back into mythical British history in search of complex political resonances. Shakespeare's penultimate (and collaborative) play, *Henry VIII, or All is True*—echoing another underestimated Shakespearian history, the energetically ambivalent *King John*—offers a complex, and not wholly complimentary, picture of the status of history and of 'truth' in the mid-Jacobean period, representing a vacillating, casually adulterous Henry, a cruel, machiavellian *Wolsey, and a haughty yet sympathetic *Catherine of Aragon, and culminating in the birth and christening of the baby Elizabeth and a prophecy from *Cranmer that implies a certain frustration with the direction of James's policies, foreign and ecclesiastical.

Shakespeare wrote at a unique period in the history of the British theatre—for the range of his audiences, for the cultural resonance of theatrical institutions—and his plays cannot fairly be dismissed as 'mere' fiction or entertainment. It is a valuable commonplace of current literary criticism that Shakespearian drama both responded to and shaped public perspectives on history and politics at a time of considerable, and hugely productive, cultural anxiety, 'shaping fantasies' for a developing nation-state. GAM

Greenblatt, S. J., *Shakespearean Negotiations: The Circulation of Social Energy in Renaissance England* (Oxford, 1988); Rackin, P., *Stages of History: Shakespeare's English Chronicles* (Ithaca, NY, 1990); Shakespeare, William, *The Complete Works*, ed. Stanley Wells and Gary Taylor (Oxford, 1986), pp. xiii–xl; *Shakespeare Survey*, 38 (Cambridge, 1985), a review of criticism of Shakespeare's history plays.

Shannon, Richard Boyle, 2nd earl of [I] (1728–1807). Boyle's father was Speaker of the Irish House of Commons and was raised to the peerage on resigning. Boyle attended Trinity College, Dublin, and entered the Irish Parliament as soon as he was 21. He inherited the title in 1764. He acted closely with his wife's family, the Ponsonbys, and was one of the *undertakers whose power Lord *Townshend as lord-lieutenant in 1768 wished to destroy. From 1766 to 1770 he was master-general of the ordnance, vice-treasurer of Ireland 1781–9, and given a British peerage in 1786 as Baron Carleton. He wobbled on the Regency question in 1789, apparently under pressure from his wife, and was dismissed. But he served again as a lord of Treasury [I] from 1793 to 1804 and exerted himself and his great influence to carry the Act of *Union in 1801. JAC

Sharp, Granville (1735–1813). Anti-slavery campaigner. Born in Durham, son of the archdeacon of Northumberland and grandson of an archbishop of York, Sharp was employed in London as a government clerk when in 1765 he befriended Jonathan Strong, a runaway slave. The ensuing legal disputes culminated in the *Somerset case (1772) in which slavery was declared not to exist in England. In 1783 he formed the idea of an African settlement for freed slaves (*Sierra Leone, 1787), in 1787 he chaired the committee for the abolition of the slave trade, and in 1807 founded the African Institution to work for the total suppression of the trade following its abolition in the British empire. In his religious beliefs he was a millenarian churchman, founding the Society for the Conversion of the Jews in 1808 and the Protestant Union against *catholic emancipation in 1813. ER

Sharp, James (1613–79). Archbishop. Sharp was educated at Aberdeen University and appointed professor of philosophy at St Andrews. In 1649 he was admitted to the living at Crail and rapidly became a leader of the resolutioners, the more moderate presbyterian group. At the Restoration he worked closely with *Monck and was sent to Breda to negotiate with Charles II. *Burnet accused Sharp of systematic hypocrisy in praising *presbyterianism while working to restore episcopacy. He was appointed royal chaplain in Scotland, made archbishop of St Andrews in 1661, and confirmed in the primacy. He then began a determined attack upon the presbyterian clergy he had just left. In 1668 he escaped a serious attempt at assassination but in 1679 fell into the hands of a *covenanting group in Fife and was murdered. The incident led to the covenanting rising, suppressed at *Bothwell Bridge, and was used by Scott in *Old Mortality*. JAC

Shaw, George Bernard (1856–1950). Dramatist. Ambitious to write, Shaw left Dublin and his childhood's genteel poverty to join his mother and sisters in London (1876), where he spent hours voraciously in the British Museum's reading room and embraced socialism. His novels rejected, he eventually found steady work as literary, music ('Corno di Bassetto'), and theatre critic. Now orator, polemicist, and force behind the *Fabian Society, he began to write his own plays, influenced by Ibsen and trying to move the English stage away from affectations to a new *gravitas*: *Widowers' Houses* (1892), considering slum landlordism, and *Mrs Warren's Profession*, on organized prostitution, were radical, unromantic, and offensive to many. Prolific, passionate, and witty, he is now regarded as the most significant playwright in the 20th-cent. English-speaking world (Nobel prize for literature, 1925); *St Joan* (1924) is considered a masterpiece, but *Pygmalion* (1916) remains the most popular. Shaw's anti-war speeches (1914) drew much criticism, but he continued political writing into old age, outliving his time. ASH

Shawfield riots, 1725. After the *Union of 1707 taxation policy remained a delicate matter in Scotland. The imposition of the malt tax on Scotland by exasperated Tories in 1712 provoked a determined attempt at repeal of the Union and it was not levied. In 1724 a move to raise revenue by 3 pence on every bushel of malt, though half the rate in England, provoked severe riots in Glasgow. Shawfield, the home of Daniel Campbell, MP for Glasgow Burghs, was plundered. One result was that *Roxburgh, secretary of state [S], was dismissed and henceforward Walpole relied upon the earl of Islay (*Argyll). JAC

Sheffield was a comparatively late developer among the great English cities. Its situation was determined by the river Sheaf joining the Don: William de Lovetot built a castle in the angle in the 12th cent. together with a bridge. The property passed to the earls of Shrewsbury and thence to the dukes of Norfolk. As early as the 14th cent. Sheffield had a national reputation for cutlery, since *Chaucer's Miller from Trumpington had a 'Sheffield whittle', a short dagger or knife, in his hose. By *Leland's day, in the 1540s, it was 'the chief market town of Hallamshire'. Its development as a great steel town depended upon local supplies of iron, the water-power of the Loxley, Rivelin, and Porter, as well as the Sheaf and Don, and sandstone for grinding. *Camden's *Britannia* (1580s) found Sheffield 'remarkable, among many other places hereabouts, for blacksmiths, there being much iron digged up in these parts'. The Cutlers' Company was granted a charter under the master cutler in 1624. Mary, queen of Scots, was held prisoner in the castle for thirteen years in the custody of George, earl of Shrewsbury, and the castle changed hands several times during the Civil War. *Defoe in the 1720s found the town 'very populous and large, the streets narrow, and the houses dark and black, occasioned by the continued smoke of the forges, which are always at work'. Two innovations in the 1740s and improved communications brought about the vast expansion. Thomas Boulsover invented Sheffield plate, silver on copper, and Benjamin Huntsman a new process for making steel: the Don was made navigable to Tinsley in 1751 and turnpike roads were opened to Chesterfield (1756), Wakefield (1758), and Worksop (1764). By 1801, Sheffield, with a population of 31,000, was the tenth town in England. It was given parliamentary representation by the Great Reform Act of 1832, acquired a town council in 1843, and by 1861 was fifth largest, with 185,000 people. It became a city in 1893, gained a university in 1905, was given cathedral status in 1914. But perhaps it took greater pleasure from passing Leeds in population in 1911. By the 1990s communications had been further improved with the M1 motorway, the population exceeded half a million, and it was the capital of the South Yorkshire metropolitan region. JAC

Sheffield, diocese of. This see, comprising south Yorkshire, was created in 1914 out of the *York diocese. Even by the 1870s Sheffield contained one-third of the York diocese's population and the inhabitants successfully resisted inclusion in the new *Wakefield diocese of 1888. Though a suffragan see of Sheffield was established in 1901, only the rapid extension of the Doncaster coalfield and some significant political manœuvring in the Commons enabled the passage of the Three Bishoprics Bill (for Sheffield, *Chelmsford, and *Bury St Edmunds) in 1913. Despite its long, thin, unnatural shape, with three distinct areas (possibly Doncaster would have been a better centre), the see was successfully welded together by the first two bishops, Leonard Burrows (1914–39) and Leslie Hunter (1939–62), the latter being particularly noted for his devotion to social welfare. The cathedral is the former Perpendicular parish church (*c.*1430), reconstructed in 1880, with further extensions completed in 1966. WMM

Shelburne, William Petty, 2nd earl of (1737–1805). Shelburne was intelligent and able, but deemed untrustworthy by most of his social and political equals. He entered the army in 1757, became an MP in 1760, and went to the Lords in 1761, succeeding his father as earl of Shelburne and Baron Wycombe. Initially a follower of *Bute, he shifted his allegiance to the elder *Pitt (later earl of Chatham) and served under him, from 1766, as southern secretary. Chatham's illness left his ministry rudderless and prone to squabbling. Shelburne was frequently at odds with his colleagues and after a disagreement over foreign policy with the *de facto* premier, *Grafton, was marked for dismissal. Grafton only withheld sentence for fear of precipitating Chatham's resignation. From his sick-bed, Chatham misread the situation and, believing Shelburne to have been removed, resigned. This comedy of errors was straightened out, but the net result was the departure of Shelburne and Chatham. After Chatham's death in 1778, Shelburne was the leader of the Chathamites and consequently mistrusted by the *Rockinghamites, who referred to him as Malagrida, an infamous Jesuit schemer. The fall of *North in 1782 presented George III with an uncongenial recourse to opposition, which he mitigated by playing off Shelburne against the Rockinghamites. Shelburne was a willing accomplice and cultivated the king's personal favour. As home secretary (March–July 1782), he created difficulties over patronage and was at variance with the foreign secretary, Charles *Fox, over the peace negotiations, which involved both their departments. Shelburne employed his own representatives in Paris and tried to undermine the Rockinghamite policy of conceding, from the outset, American independence. Rockingham's death in July 1782 precipitated a cabinet crisis, with the king insisting on Shelburne's succession to the premiership. Fox and the firmer Rockinghamites resigned and then coalesced with the Northites to force Shelburne's resignation in February 1783. Although created marquis of Lansdowne in 1784, Shelburne never regained high office. His failings as a politician stemmed from his restless imagination, his attachment to intrigue, and his personal manner, which was alternately obsequious and stubborn. As an intellectual patron Shelburne was more successful, gathering around him such luminaries as Joseph *Priestley, Jeremy *Bentham, and Richard Price, sometimes referred to as the Bowood circle, taking their name from Shelburne's country residence. DW

Sheldon, Gilbert (1598–1677). Archbishop of Canterbury (1663–77). A graduate of Trinity College, Oxford, Sheldon was fellow, then warden (1626), of All Souls. Spiritual adviser to Charles I in the Civil War, he was ejected from All Souls (1648) and briefly imprisoned. He returned in 1659 and at the Restoration became bishop of London (1660). A keen protagonist of uniformity, he succeeded *Juxon as archbishop (1663) and arranged with *Clarendon to end separate taxation for the clergy (1664). As chancellor of Oxford (1667–9), he had the Sheldonian theatre built at his own expense with *Wren as architect. A man of deep spirituality, he was equally critical of dissent and Charles II's suspected popery. WMM

Shelley, Mary Wollstonecraft (1797–1851). Author. Only daughter of the radical philosopher William *Godwin and early feminist Mary *Wollstonecraft, pretty, bookish Mary eloped with the young Percy Bysshe *Shelley to Europe in 1814, marrying him on his wife Harriet's suicide (1816). Her most famous novel *Frankenstein* (1818), generated from *Byron's ghost-story contest one 'wet, ungenial summer' by Lake Geneva, but overseen by her husband at every stage, founded the genre of 'scientific Gothick' later exploited by horror-film makers, generally unsubtly. After the poet's death (1822), Mary returned to England and became a professional writer in order to educate her only surviving child Percy Florence Shelley. Devotion prompted editions of her husband's works to perpetuate his memory, while her letters and journal are further rich biographical sources. She also wrote articles, reviews, short stories, travel accounts, and further novels, though at the expense of health. ASH

Shelley, Percy Bysshe (1792–1822). Perhaps the least accessible of the Romantic poets, though recent attention to his radical politics has modified the Victorian picture of 'a beautiful and ineffectual angel'. Son of a Whig landowner, a precocious and unconventional career at Eton and Oxford was followed by a precipitous first marriage and, soon after, elopement to the continent with the daughter of William *Godwin and Mary *Wollstonecraft. Already he had published *Queen Mab* (1813), later revered in *chartist circles. 'Ode to the West Wind' (1819) best represents his impetuous idealism and technical accomplishment, foreshadowing *Prometheus Unbound* (1820), which imagines a bloodless revolution where 'mankind had only to will that there should be no evil and there would be none'. The sad reality was recognized in *The Masque of Anarchy* when news of the *Peterloo massacre reached him in Italy and *A Philosophical View of Reform* shows a more measured concern. Neither were published in his lifetime, abruptly ended by an accident at sea. JNRS

Sheraton, Thomas (1751–1806). English furniture designer. Sheraton was born in Stockton-on-Tees, where he learned cabinet-making, probably never returning to this trade after his move to London about 1790. He was principally occupied writing several manuals on furniture design, the most popular, *The Cabinet-Maker and Upholsterer's Drawing Book* (1791–4), including treatises on geometry, architecture, and perspective. A fervent baptist, he also published numerous religious tracts. Sheraton's many chair-back designs were simple and elegant, employing straight lines and delicate marquetry of animals, flowers, or musical instruments. Other designs were more ingenious, providing furniture with several purposes, always enhancing the beauty and qualities of the woods. Although influential, none of Sheraton's books brought him financial success and he died insane in direst poverty. Often acerbic in print, his obituary in the *Gentleman's Magazine* described him as 'a very honest, well-disposed man'. JC

Sherborne, diocese of. The see, carved out of *Winchester in 705 by King *Ine for the oversight of all west Wessex, was further split in 909 by *Edward the Elder; Sherborne retained Dorset, Devon and Cornwall went to *Crediton, Somerset to *Wells, and Wiltshire and Berkshire to *Ramsbury. In 1058 Sherborne was reunited with Ramsbury and in 1075 the combined see was moved to Old Sarum (*Salisbury). The superb fan vaulting in the Benedictine abbey church is 15th cent. WMM

Sherborne abbey (Dorset) was founded *c.*700 as a community of secular canons. It was lavishly endowed by the kings of Wessex, some of whom were buried here during the 9th cent. It was reformed *c.*998 as a house of *Benedictine monks by *Æthelred II under the guidance of Bishop Wulfsige III of Sherborne. Following the Norman Conquest the episcopal see was transferred to *Salisbury. Sherborne retained close links with Salisbury, enjoying the patronage of its bishop *Roger (1102–39). Most of its endowments were concentrated in Devon and Dorset, though it also acquired interests in and around Cydweli (Dyfed). At the *dissolution it had a net income of nearly £700. Its church, which survives, was rebuilt in the 15th cent. following a riot of townspeople in 1436 which destroyed the earlier church. BJG

Sheridan, Richard Brinsley (1751–1816). The son of an Irish actor, Sheridan achieved fame as both dramatist and politician, making his way by merit, with the additional advantage of influential friends, notably Charles *Fox and the prince of Wales. Sheridan's major works were all produced before entering Parliament in 1780: *The Rivals* (1775), *The Duenna* (1775), *The School for Scandal* (1777), and *The Critic* (1779). 'Sheridan', according to Horace *Walpole, was 'one of the most perfect comic writers . . . his plots are sufficiently deep, without clumsy entanglement' and his 'characters strictly in nature—wit without affectation'.

Sheridan was a superb political orator, achieving fame during the campaign against Warren *Hastings; one memorable speech, on 8 February 1787, lasted an astonishing 5 hours and 40 minutes. For all his ability, Sheridan never attained cabinet rank, and served only as under-secretary at the Foreign Office (1782), Treasury secretary (1783), and treasurer of the navy (1806–7). His predominant loyalty was to Fox; but Sheridan's intrigues in the *Regency crisis were not approved. Mutual antagonism between Sheridan and *Burke contributed to the disintegration of the Whig Party in the 1790s, with Sheridan flaunting his admiration for the French principles Burke despised. Sheridan never became the revolutionary some anticipated, and was a patriot with regard to Napoleonic France. His private life was eventful, even disreputable: he cheated openly on both his wives, drank to excess, and borrowed extensively from friends. He died in straitened circumstances, caused partly by losses incurred from his involvement with Drury Lane theatre. DW

Sheriffmuir, battle of, 1715. Leading the Jacobite rising, *Mar rallied his forces at Perth and commanded 9,000 men: *Argyll, with much smaller numbers, took up position at Stirling. On 13 November the armies did battle at Sheriffmuir, near Dunblane. In a confused encounter, each army's right wing carried the day, but Argyll retired to Stirling in good order. Mar was unable to follow up his advantage, abandoned Perth, retreated to Aberdeen, and, at length, took ship for France. JAC

sheriffs. Reeves were Anglo-Saxon officials, and the king's reeves had special duties to keep order and collect royal dues. By the 11th cent. English kings put each shire under a *scirgerefa* ('shire-reeve', sheriff) who administered justice and collected revenues. Their powers and duties were greatly increased by the Normans, and they became notorious for high-handedness. Henry II was driven to hold an Inquest of Sheriffs into their activities, and to remove many from office (1170), but complaints of their maladministration long continued: the sheriff of Nottingham in the *Robin Hood ballads represents the type. The crown's long-term solution was to spread the exercise of local administration and justice, especially, from the 14th cent., through *justices of the peace; since the 16th cent. sheriffs have been largely county figureheads. In Scotland, where sheriffs were introduced in the 12th cent., they have been chief judges of sheriffdoms: and in those English towns taken out of county administration, sheriffs are elected urban officials responsible to the *mayor. The sheriffs of American counties kept up, in the 19th cent., something of the role of earlier English sheriffs; and the 'posse' of the Wild West is the *posse comitatus* (force of the county) which medieval sheriffs could summon to pursue suspects and repress riots. DMP

Sherston, battle of, 1016. This was one of a series of encounters between *Edmund Ironside and *Cnut in the summer of 1016 and took place just west of Malmesbury. The Saxons were victorious but their advantage was soon cancelled by the disaster at *Ashingdon. JAC

Shetland is a group of islands in the northern North Sea, some 150 miles from the north-east tip of the Scottish mainland. Once annexed by the Vikings and subsequently part of the kingdom of Norway, Shetland (together with Orkney) became part of Scotland in 1469. It is a county of Scotland and has remained a unitary local administrative authority. More than Orkney, Shetland has asserted its cultural separateness from Scotland, most notably by the annual 'Viking' midwinter festival of Up-Helly-A. North Sea oil has had a significant effect on the economy: one of the main terminals for landing oil from pipelines is at Sullom Voe, and the local authority negotiated with the oil companies a deal which generated considerable revenue for the islands, which were able to cut local taxes and build up a development fund for the future. CML

shipbuilding was a widely scattered industry before the 18th cent., ships normally varying between 50 and 100 tons. For four centuries the Thames and Medway had been the principal shipbuilding rivers for large ships and the location of the main naval dockyards. Technical innovations threw the advantage to the Tyne, Wear and Tees, Mersey, and Clyde with relatively deep water, cheap coal and iron, and expertise in building marine engines.

The Clyde was a latecomer as a major shipbuilding river. The main hull-builders were downriver at Greenock and Port Glasgow. Deepening the river served both commerce and industry, for Glasgow's engine-builders came to dominate British shipbuilding. Labour costs in the new shipyards were lower than on the Thames, and technical innovations gave the Clyde major advantages. In 1813–14 this region produced only 4.5 per cent of the British tonnage, and this market share remained relatively constant until the 1840s. In the production of iron river steamers the Clyde falteringly led the way in the early 19th cent. but between 1840 and 1870 produced two-thirds of British steam tonnage. Early marine engines used fuel prodigally; Glasgow engineers solved this problem and also improved boilers and methods of construction and propulsion: the screw propeller replaced the paddle in the 1840s; compound engines were installed from 1853, dramatically cutting coal consumption and thereby increasing the payload; iron hulls increased the scale of shipping, reducing freight costs and encouraging the growth of international trade. Glasgow became the home base for many shipping lines, including Cunard, and their orders tended to go to Clyde yards.

Steam and iron eclipsed wood and sail in the 1850s. Steam tonnage, which in 1850 represented under 7 per cent of British output, accounted for 70 per cent by 1870. About 24,000 of 47,500 men working in shipbuilding in 1871 were resident in Scotland, all but a few employed in the Clyde yards. They produced at least one-third of British tonnage—mostly specialist vessels—every year from 1870 to 1914. The Wear initially challenged the Clyde, producing about one-third of Britain's merchant tonnage in the 1830s, but the north-east increasingly specialized in lower-cost tramp shipping, except in war. Belfast was essentially an extension of Clyde capacity, and by 1914 one firm, *Harland and *Wolff, dominated its shipbuilding just as Cammell Laird on the Mersey and Vickers-Armstrong at Barrow controlled regional output.

The integration of iron, steel, coal, and shipbuilding as major exporting industries explains why the economy which made shipbuilding regions prosperous before 1914 should be a source of economic weakness after 1920. The long decline of shipbuilding had a downward multiplier effect on these regional economies which became the depressed areas of inter-war Britain.

Demand for capital goods declined rapidly after 1920, but shipbuilding suffered most. World capacity had been grossly inflated during the First World War, but peacetime demand was reduced by the decline in world trade. In 1933 launchings from British yards fell to 7 per cent of the 1914 figure. Foreign orders for new ships were markedly reduced. Britain was slow to move into the production of motor vessels which were most in demand; foreign governments provided subsidies to retain orders within their own boundaries. In 1930 'National Shipbuilders' Security Limited' was formed to reduce the number of shipyards and excess capacity. By 1937, 28 firms had been bought and closed, with a capacity of about 3,500,000 tons. The government in 1935 sponsored an ineffective 'scrap and build' scheme whereby owners were subsidized to scrap 2 tons of shipping for every new ton they ordered.

Rearmament and the Second World War revived shipbuilding, and after 1945 the world dollar shortage drove shipowners to order in Britain. World trade expanded and kept the boom going, but increasingly foreign yards benefited from this exceptional demand. The Clyde produced a third of British tonnage in the early 1950s (although demand was greatest for tankers and cargo ships); the Wear and Tees a quarter and the Tyne about one-sixth; Belfast, the Mersey, and Barrow nearly one-quarter. In 1956 Britain was third in export sales behind Germany and Japan; by 1977 she produced 4 per cent of world output (compared with 60 per cent in 1910–14), and British owners were ordering ships from overseas. Asia, with its low labour costs and modern equipment, became the most significant continent for ship production. The government responded by further rationalization under British Shipbuilders (1977), a public corporation. Technically backward, the industry was faced with closures and redundancies until the government returned firms to private ownership and a process of private investment in the 1980s. Shipbuilding survives but subject to intense foreign competition. JB

ship money was an occasional tax on property, traditionally levied in port towns for their protection by the navy. Because Parliament, together with its power to grant taxes, had been dissolved in 1629, Charles I lacked money both for the fleet and for other expenses. In 1634 he therefore levied ship money in London, extending the tax in the following year to the whole country. In 1635, 1636, and 1637 it produced a high yield, but resistance developed and in 1638 it produced only one-third of the assessed amount. John *Hampden, a Buckinghamshire squire, and others refused to pay on principle. There followed a test case on the legality of non-parliamentary taxation, including ship money. To the perturbation of the property-owning classes, the judges found for the king, though by a majority of only 7 : 5. In 1641 Parliament declared ship money illegal. MW

Shippen, William (1673–1743). Jacobite parliamentarian. The son of a clergyman, Shippen trained as a barrister. He became a Tory MP in 1707, and, but for one short interlude (1709–10), remained in Parliament for the rest of his life. During the Tory administration (1710–14) he emerged as an outspoken member of the Jacobite wing of the party, and in 1711 took an active part in the inquiry of corruption against the duke of *Marlborough. In 1712 he married one of the wealthiest heiresses. With the ostracization of the Tory Party after George I's accession in 1714, Shippen settled into a routine of unrelenting opposition to successive Whig ministries. In the Commons he was invariably hostile to the Hanoverian dynasty, maintaining that the German connection undermined the British constitution. Such remarks earned him a spell in the Tower in 1717. Though leader of the Jacobite MPs by the later 1720s, he always shunned any form of conspiratorial activity with the pretender. AAH

shires. See COUNTIES.

shooting, as a sport, may be divided into shooting at animals or birds, or shooting at targets in competition. Pheasant- and grouse-shooting reached its peak in the vast country-house gatherings of Edwardian England: game was rigorously preserved and *poaching caused much ill-feeling in rural society. Big-game shooting, largely in Africa and India, was fashionable in the 19th and early 20th cents. A regular feature of overseas royal visits was a big-game shoot: George V on a visit to Nepal in 1912 claimed 21 tigers, 8 rhino, and 1 bear in a fortnight's shooting. Organized target-shooting in Britain dates from the mid-19th cent. The National Rifle Association was founded at Wimbledon in 1860 and transferred in 1880 to Bisley in Surrey. The Queen's Prize, first awarded in 1860, remains one of the most coveted honours. Bisley is the venue for regular summer competitions, for different classes of weapons, including small-bore rifles. Shooting was included in the first of the modern Olympics in 1896. JAC

shops. Britain has been described as a nation of shopkeepers, but shops did not really come into existence until the later Middle Ages. Before then, buying and selling occurred through fairs, market-stalls, artisans' workshops, or itinerant pedlars. Progression from open market to covered market-hall extended as the frequency of markets increased and permanent storage for merchandise was required: a shop on street level at the front of the house had workshop/service rooms behind and dwelling-rooms above, the shutter of its large unglazed window being let down to form a display counter. As trading began to separate from manufacture, London became a shop-window for the whole country, its own shops smart, seductive, and increasingly stocked with imported goods. The provinces could hold their own, though: Celia Fiennes (1698) found Newcastle's 'shops are good and are of distinct trades, not selling many things in one shop as is the custom in most country towns and cittys'.

With growth in population in the 18th cent., a burgeoning middle class, and money available for more than bare necessities, towns expanded and *retail trade gained in vigour as consumerism emerged. As shops became more numerous, hence more competitive, projecting shop-signs became larger and heavier, so increasingly dangerous, until they were banned (1762), after which they were affixed over doorways or flat against the frontage. Even though railway development enabled fresh food to reach town shops more easily, much food sold was adulterated, but it was not until 1872 that inspectors were empowered to procure samples for analysts' reports. Not only could goods be transported more quickly from producer or manufacturer to retailer, but more customers could now travel easily into towns to purchase. The number and variety of shops increased considerably, sometimes grouped in arcades, larger windows enhanced display, and large speciality stores transformed themselves into departmental stores modelled on the French pattern; by the First World War, these were widely established in cities.

As the family tradition of shopkeeping began to decline, shops were transformed from places fulfilling known needs to premises attracting new customers and creating new wants. One route to growth was the *Co-operative movement, founded in 1844 by the *Rochdale Pioneers. If a retailer opened additional shops, his chain of stores could reduce operating costs, standardize quality, and offer special price reductions yet still increase profits (W. H. *Smith, *Boots). Supermarkets, whose pattern was set in 1930s America, did not develop in Britain much before the 1960s; they operate primarily on a self-service basis, and tend to drive small independent food retailers out of business. Since the Second World War, there has been a growth in shopping precincts, then malls, often financed by real estate developers, which aim to provide for every need under a single roof in attractive, climatically controlled environments; out-of-town hypermarkets rely on car ownership, so usually provide generous, free parking. Corner shops and village stores have suffered accordingly, though mail-order retailing through catalogue houses attempts to fill the gap for non-food purchasing. ASH

Short Parliament, April–May 1640. The first *Bishops' War ended inconclusively because Charles I was not strong enough to fight the Scots. He summoned Parliament in 1640 in the expectation that it would provide the funds for him to do so. But the Commons were more concerned with grievances, in particular the growth of *arminianism and the crown's resort to prerogative taxation such as *ship money. Some members were prepared to compromise. Others, like *Pym, preferred deadlock since this would benefit the Scots, whom they regarded as allies in the struggle to preserve the true protestant faith in both kingdoms. In the end, Charles lost patience and brought proceedings to an abrupt close. RL

Shovell, Sir Clowdesley (1650–1707). Naval commander. Entering the service in 1664 as a cabin boy, Shovell achieved a reputation for unflinching courage and skill during his Mediterranean commands in the 1680s, was knighted in 1689, and promoted to rear-admiral in 1690. In the naval war against the French during the 1690s he proved an effective operational commander, with an important share in the victories at *Beachy Head (1690) and Barfleur (1692), while in 1695–6 he was second in command in a series of successful attacks on French ports. He was appointed full admiral in 1695. In the early years of Anne's reign he commanded in several Mediterranean actions including the capture of *Gibraltar and the battle off Malaga in 1704, and in 1705 assisted Lord *Peterborough to capture Barcelona. Returning from the unsuccessful Toulon mission in 1707, his flagship was wrecked off the Scilly Isles. Washed ashore, but supposedly murdered for his emerald ring, he was interred at Westminster abbey. AAH

Shrewsbury. County town of Shropshire, its old centre built on a defensive hill nearly surrounded by the river Severn. It has been a regional centre since Anglo-Saxon times, a military strong point in the Welsh marches, and a centre of cloth trading and manufacture from the Middle Ages to the 19th cent. In the 16th and early 17th cents. it was also, with *Ludlow, a centre of the *Council for Wales in the Marches. It has a fine legacy of historic buildings, especially timber-framed houses of the Tudor and Stuart period. DMP

Shrewsbury, battle of, 1403. Henry IV learned of the rebellion of Hotspur (Henry *Percy), in league with Owain *Glyndŵr, Thomas Percy, earl of *Worcester, Archibald, earl of *Douglas, and Edmund Mortimer, when he was at Burton. A forced march carried his troops westwards to Shrewsbury to join his son Henry, prince of Wales, campaigning in Wales. Possession of the bridges over the Severn would prevent a junction between Hotspur, marching south from Chester, and Glyndŵr, believed to be advancing from south Wales. Hotspur arrived to find the town in royal hands. Glyndŵr did not join him, and his father, the earl of *Northumberland, got no nearer than Pontefract. Hotspur was outnumbered and his recruits untrained, but he resolved to give battle rather than risk retreat and disintegration. He chose a small ridge 3 miles north of the town, near the village of Berwick, and dug in. The early exchanges on 31 July went in favour of the rebels but Hotspur was killed and his followers fled. Worcester was captured and executed at Shrewsbury two days later: Douglas was held in prison until 1408. The new Lancastrian dynasty had survived its first major test. JAC

Shrewsbury, Charles Talbot, 1st duke of (1660–1718). The last person to hold the office of lord treasurer. Brought up a Roman catholic, he converted to Anglicanism in 1679, and was one of the 'Immortal Seven' who, in 1688, signed the letter inviting William of Orange to invade. In 1689 he was appointed secretary of state, but became disillusioned with growing party strife, resigned in 1690, and went into opposition (being suspected of Jacobite sympathies). In 1694 he again became secretary of state and was created a duke (having succeeded as earl of Shrewsbury in 1668). Appointed lord chamberlain in 1699, he resigned on health grounds in 1700. He lived abroad (1700–7), chiefly in Rome, and upon his return became alienated from his former Whig associates. He was appointed lord chamberlain in the Tory ministry (1710–14), and lord-lieutenant of Ireland in 1713. On the dismissal of *Harley, Queen Anne appointed Shrewsbury lord treasurer (30 July–11 October 1714), thwarting *Bolingbroke's ambition, and upon the queen's death (1 August) he helped to secure the Hanoverian succession. His final office was again as lord chamberlain (1714–15). CJ

Shrewsbury, Elizabeth Talbot, countess of (1518–1608). 'Bess of Hardwick' was one of the most remarkable women in Elizabethan England. The daughter of a Derbyshire squire, she gained wealth and status through four increasingly ambitious marriages, the last (in 1567) to George Talbot, earl of Shrewsbury. Two alliances between their respective children created a dynastic structure. The Shrewsburys were given charge of Mary, queen of Scots (1569–84), but a daughter's marriage to *Darnley's younger brother (the union producing Arabella *Stuart) provoked Elizabeth I's displeasure. After the earl's death, Bess, intriguer, termagant, and by then the richest woman in the kingdom, was free to concentrate on her building and furnishing at *Chatsworth and *Hardwick Hall, and her extensive business concerns based on land and cash; her shrewdness, energy, and strength of purpose made her feared, but she could be generous and lavish. Two of her sons founded the dukedoms of Devonshire and Newcastle. ASH

Shrewsbury, John Talbot, 1st earl of (*c.*1387–1453). Talbot was the most renowned in England and most feared in France of the English captains in the last stages of the *Hundred Years War. Having fought briefly under Henry V, he returned to France in 1427, where he served until his death at *Castillon in 1453. The only battles in which he was in command (*Patay and Castillon) were defeats; his reputation rested on his persistence, dedication, and vigour, qualities which made him a master of the small-scale war of thrust and counter-thrust that characterized the defence of Normandy between 1434 and 1444. His service to the cause of Lancaster was acknowledged in 1442 by his elevation to the earldom of Shrewsbury. A tough, cruel, and quarrelsome man, he came to be regarded as the last of the old chivalric breed. AJP

shrines. These pilgrimage centres, claiming to house either relics of Jesus' life or of the saints or statues of the Virgin Mary, to be visited either for more effective prayer, to obtain indulgences, or for healing, were a central element in medieval life. England could not emulate Jerusalem, the ultimate place of *pilgrimage, Rome with its multitude of relics, or Compostella. Nevertheless, like other countries, England had shrines of great popularity, journeys to which were less arduous and expensive. Relics of Jesus' life were sparse indeed in England, though Bromholm priory (Norfolk), Waltham and Reading abbeys, and Canterbury all claimed to possess fragments of the True Cross. Canterbury's vast collection also included thorns from the Crown of Thorns and part of Jesus' seamless robe, while Reading had St James's hand and Glastonbury Joseph of Arimathea's Holy Thorn. Shrines of saints' mortal remains were almost as potent. Before 1066 the most popular included Durham (St *Cuthbert), St Albans, and Bury (St *Edmund), which all faded in the late 12th cent. before the brighter light of Westminster (St *Edward), Worcester (St *Wulfstan), and—by far the most popular—Canterbury (St Thomas *Becket). Miracles also occurred at the tombs of the less worthy—Simon de *Montfort, *Thomas of Lancaster, Archbishop Richard *Scrope of York, all opponents of kings—and of kings themselves, Edward II and Henry VI. In late medieval England as elsewhere, as devotion to the Virgin Mary intensified, her shrines at Westminster, Doncaster, Ipswich, and above all at *Walsingham grew in importance. The last was much patronized and frequently visited by Henry III, Edward I, and their successors, so that by the Reformation it attracted offerings that surpassed even those at Canterbury. Late medieval shrines, encrusted with jewels, were an easy prey for reformers and for the covetous eyes of the crown. WMM

Shropshire is a large and beautiful county. The hilly southern part includes the Wrekin, the Long Mynd, Clee Hill, and Wenlock Edge: the north, adjoining Cheshire, is flatter, with some notable meres. The Severn, running from west to south-east, bisects the county: the Teme, which forms the boundary with Herefordshire, drains the southern part, the Tern much of the north. Shrewsbury grew up as an important crossing over the Severn and as a bastion against the Welsh. Whitchurch is the chief town of the northern half, Ludlow, in Tudor times home to the *Council in the Marches of Wales, of the south.

In Roman times, the area fell between the *Cornovii and the *Ordovices; *Caratacus' last stand against *Ostorius' Roman legions may have been at Caer Caradoc, near Church Stretton. The Roman road *Watling Street ran through the county and Viriconium (*Wroxeter), where it crossed the Severn, was an important legionary base. The region was disputed between Britons and Saxons and at one stage much of it belonged to the kingdom of *Powys, whose capital, Pengwern, may have been at Shrewsbury. By the 8th cent. it formed part of the kingdom of Mercia and Offa's Dike runs through the western parts of the shire, from near Oswestry to near Clun in the south-west. Bridgnorth was mentioned in the *Anglo-Saxon Chronicle* as early as 895, when a Danish army wintered there, and Shrewsbury in 1016. For ecclesiastical purposes, the area came under *Lichfield, until the parishes south of the Severn were moved into the new diocese of *Hereford. By the 10th cent. it was in existence as a shire. The *Anglo-Saxon Chronicle* in 1006 referred to it as Scrobbesbyrigscir, after the town.

The Normans, finding Saxon pronunciation difficult, called the county Salopescira and studded it with castles, at Shrewsbury, Ludlow, Bishop's Castle, and Clun. Even so, the western parts were defended against the Welsh with difficulty. Taking advantage of English weakness during Stephen's reign, the Welsh took Oswestry in 1149 and, though it was recovered, it was once more destroyed by *Llywelyn during John's reign in 1213. The county was again at risk during *Glyndŵr's rising in the early 15th cent., when Clun was destroyed, but Glyndŵr's allies, the Percies, were defeated just north of Shrewsbury in 1403 and Henry *Percy (Hotspur) killed.

The Severn crossing and the proximity to Wales made Shropshire important during the Civil War. Charles I, having raised his standard at Nottingham in 1642, made straight for the area and delivered a recruiting speech at Wellington. Many of the men who fought in the first battle at *Edgehill came from Shropshire. The county remained royalist territory but suffered from raids and incursions. There was a vicious exchange at Stokesay castle, where adversaries fired at point-blank range between the castle and the church. The loss of Shrewsbury itself in February 1645 to a daring raid from the parliamentary garrison at Wem was a heavy blow to the royalists. Charles II took refuge at Boscobel in the east of the county after his defeat at *Worcester in 1651 and the celebrated oak tree, in which he hid, was a place of pilgrimage for years.

Until the 18th cent. Shropshire was overwhelmingly an agricultural county, famous for sheep, but the development by the *Darby family of a great mining and iron industry at *Coalbrookdale produced the strange phenomenon of blast furnaces and chimneys amid lush wooded valleys. The *Ironbridge, built in 1777, and now the centre of a splendid museum complex, was for decades regarded as one of the wonders of technological progress.

Shrewsbury retained its primacy as county town without difficulty, hosting the assizes and the parliamentary elections. When Celia Fiennes visited it in 1698 it had its own water supply and 'an abundance of people of quality', who took walks in the abbey gardens, amongst orange and lemon trees, hollies, myrtles, and aloes. Thirty years later, *Defoe found it 'beautiful, large, pleasant, populous and rich: they speak all English in the town, but on a market-day you would think you were in Wales.' A statue of Llywelyn kept guard over the Welsh bridge. In the later 18th cent. Shrewsbury became a fashionable provincial centre, with regular assemblies, horse-races, balls, and concerts. Its central position was enhanced by the coming of the railways in the mid-19th cent., which confirmed its importance as a route centre. In 1851 its population was over 20,000, with Ludlow, Whitchurch, Market Drayton, Bridgnorth, and Oswestry about the 5,000 mark. The county was not affected by the Local Government Act of 1972, but the balance of population began to change with the development of a new town in the east, absorbing Dawley, Oakengates, and Wellington. It was renamed Telford, after the great engineer who was county surveyor from 1788 to 1834. By 1991 Shrewsbury, with a population of 91,000, had been overtaken by Telford with 118,000. Yet it is also a county trapped in amber. If Dorset is Hardy country, Shropshire belongs to *Housman, buried at Ludlow, and poet of Clun, of Uricon and Wenlock Edge, 'the land of lost content'. JAC

Sickert, Walter Richard (1860–1942). British artist. Born in Munich, Sickert's Danish/Irish parents came to England in 1868. After a short career as an actor, he studied at the Slade School before joining the studio of Whistler through whom he met Degas, who became a close friend. In frequent visits to France, Sickert mixed with other artists and writers who influenced his style. His best work shows a deeply personal view of music-hall and seedy town life. He wrote extensively on diverse topics, often to *The Times*, whose obituary spoke of his 'insatiable curiosity especially in low-life'. He was intrigued by unsolved crimes, particularly the case of Jack the Ripper. In 1934 he became a Royal Academician, a position he resigned the following year over a point of principle. Sickert's work is represented in many British galleries, especially the Tate in London and the Walker in Liverpool. JC

Siddons, Sarah (1755–1831). Actress. The eldest of Roger Kemble's twelve children, her early years were spent travelling widely with the family company until marriage to the young actor William Siddons. Her first London season (1775/6) was a failure, but, having established a reputation in the provinces, she reappeared at Drury Lane and rapidly regained recognition in a theatre where neo-classicism and tragic posing were replacing the relative naturalism of *Garrick's day. Described by *Hazlitt as 'tragedy personified', painted by *Reynolds as *The Tragic Muse*, and acting with her brother John, she inspired admiration rather than affection, though as her girth increased (a Kemble characteristic) some poses threatened to become grotesque and empire-line dresses were unflattering. A strong voice and declamatory style contributed to a legend that she sustained until her farewell at Covent Garden in 1812, when she played Lady Macbeth, the role most associated with her. ASH

Sidney, Algernon (1622–83). Sidney was a famous Whig martyr and apologist. His brother, the 3rd earl of Leicester, was a strong supporter of the Commonwealth and Sidney fought for Parliament at *Marston Moor, where he was wounded. He refused to serve on the court that tried Charles I but joined the *Council of State in 1652. He disapproved of Cromwell's Protectorate but rejoined the Council of State in 1659. At the Restoration he was abroad on diplomatic missions and prudently decided to stay there. He returned to England in 1677 just as the *Popish plot was about to explode. He joined Shaftesbury's Whig opposition and, though a theoretical republican, took money from Louis XIV to embarrass Charles II, leaving *Macaulay to lament that a 'hero, philosopher and patriot' should have fallen so low. In 1683 he was tried before *Jeffreys for involvement in the *Rye House plot and convicted on shaky evidence. A manuscript discourse on government, written in reply to Filmer in 1680, and not published until after Sidney's death, was produced to show that he advocated that the people were the source of all authority and had the right to bring tyrannical monarchs to justice. In his statement at the block, Sidney wrote that he died for 'that Old Cause in which I was from my youth engaged'. Macaulay wrote that he died 'with the fortitude of a stoic' but *Burnet, while admitting Sidney's bravery and sincerity, observed that his 'rough and boisterous temper could not bear contradiction'. JAC

Sidney, Sir Henry (1529–86). Lord deputy of Ireland. Sidney, of Penshurst (Kent), was brought up with Prince Edward who was eight years younger, and on his accession was made a gentleman of the privy chamber. In 1551 he married the daughter of *Northumberland. He backed Northumberland's attempted coup on behalf of Lady Jane *Grey in 1553 but distanced himself in time to avoid disaster. Though Northumberland perished, Sidney still had *Leicester as a brother-in-law and patron. In 1556 he accompanied *Sussex to Ireland, acting as deputy in his absence. Elizabeth appointed him lord president of the marches in Wales in 1559, a post he held for the rest of his life. In 1565 he was given the Garter and sent back to Ireland as lord deputy. His first task was to deal with Shane *O'Neill who was in rebellion, but who was assassinated in 1567. By 1571 Sidney had had enough of trying to pacify Ireland and resigned. But fresh rebellions led to his recall in 1575. This time the difficulty was expense, since Elizabeth was unwilling to accept that Ireland could not be subdued on the cheap. He was replaced in 1578. Though clearly an able man, his forward policy was never adequately supported. His son was the poet Sir Philip *Sidney. JAC

Sidney, Sir Philip (1554–86). Soldier and poet. Born in the year of Mary's marriage to the king of Spain, Sidney was named Philip in his honour. Educated at Shrewsbury (his father being lord president of the Council in the Marches of Wales) and at Christ Church, Oxford, he was devoted to study. From 1572 to 1575 he was on the continent, and was in Paris on the night of the massacre of St Bartholomew. In 1583 he married the daughter of Sir Francis *Walsingham, served in Parliament, and continued to win golden opinions from all his acquaintance. But in 1585 when *Leicester, his uncle, was given command of the forces against Spain in the Low Countries, Sidney was made governor of Flushing, a key port. He volunteered to join Leicester in the attack upon Zutphen, was wounded in the thigh, and died of gangrene nearly a month later. His death was received with great grief. But the story that he gave his own bottle of water on the battlefield to a dying soldier was first reported by his friend Fulke Greville many years after his death and is suspiciously like a story of Alexander the Great. He left much unpublished work, including the sonnets, *Arcadia*, and the *Apologie for Poetrie*, but his posthumous reputation depended as much upon his character and courage as on his poetry. JAC

Sierra Leone. Former British west African colony and protectorate. British anti-slavery campaigners established a home for freed slaves in Freetown in 1797. The settlement became a British colony in 1808 and a naval base from which the British government could conduct its campaign against the slave trade. The educational opportunities provided for the freed slaves by Christian missionaries produced a reservoir of talent which, lacking an adequate outlet in Sierra Leone which was poorly endowed with natural resources, proved invaluable in extending British influence and trading interests throughout west Africa. Until the mid-20th cent. Sierra Leone continued to exert a powerful influence on the cultural development of British west Africa, especially through Fourah Bay College, founded in 1828 and attended by Africans from other British dependencies, but British economic activities were concentrated elsewhere. A British protectorate was declared over the Sierra Leonean hinterland in 1896 and the colony and protectorate together became independent in 1961. KI

Sigeberht (d. 635), king of the East Angles (*c.*630–5), became a baptized Christian when exiled in Gaul. Returning to reign, he introduced Christianity into East Anglia, aided by the Burgundian bishop *Felix, and secured the future of his church by founding a school. During his reign he received the Irish monk *Fursa, who established a monastery on the Suffolk coast. Described by *Bede as devout and learned, he ultimately resigned his earthly kingdom, entering his own monastery. Attacked by the powerful Mercian king *Penda, the East Angles tried to persuade their erstwhile distinguished royal commander to lead them. When Sigeberht refused to fight, they dragged him out of his monastery, hoping his presence would inspire the soldiers. Refusing to carry anything but a staff, he was killed by the heathen army. AM

Sigurd, jarl of Orkney (d. 1014). Sigurd succeeded his father Hlodve as jarl of Orkney, then under Norse rule, *c.*988 and extended his power over northern Scotland and the Isle of Man. In 995, under pressure from Olaf Tryggvason, king of Norway, he accepted baptism. In 1014, in alliance with Sihtric, king of Dublin, Sigurd campaigned against *Brian Boru, high king of Ireland, but was killed at *Clontarf. He was father of *Thorfinn. JAC

Sihtric (Sigtryggr) (d. 927), Norse King of York. A grandson of Ivarr the Boneless, 'king of all the Scandinavians of Ireland and Britain', Sihtric (nicknamed 'Squinty') joined forces with another grandson, Ragnall, in 917 to recover Dublin, lost in 902. Moving out from Waterford, they devastated Munster and Leinster and recaptured Dublin. Next, Sihtric won a crushing victory over Niall, king of Ulster. In 920 he left Ireland to succeed Ragnall as king of York. Sihtric refused to acknowledge *Edward the Elder as his overlord, but after his death in 924 proposed an alliance with his successor and in 926 married Eadgyth, a sister of *Athelstan of Wessex, and is said to have been converted. Roger of Wendover reported that Sihtric at once repudiated his wife and his new religion. He may have then been dispossessed, since a year later he was dead and Athelstan reigned in York. The Scandinavians succeeded in recapturing the kingdom and in 941 Sihtric's son *Olaf was in possession. SMD

Sikh wars. The wars of 1845–6 and 1848–9 originated over the Sutlej river area of north-west India between the Sikh sect in Punjab and the British. General Sir Hugh Gough defeated the numerically superior Sikh army at Mudki (18 December 1845), Ferozeshah (21 December) and Sobraon (10 February 1846). The Sikhs renounced their claims to the territory and recognized British supremacy. However in 1848 they launched a rebellion. After an initial set-back at Ramnagar on 22 November, Gough defeated the Sikhs at Jallianwalla (14 January 1849) but sustained heavy casualties. Reinforced, he finally broke Sikh resistance on 22 February 1849 at Gujrat. Thereafter the Sikhs remained loyal to the British. RAS

Silchester was a Romano-British *civitas*-capital of the *Atrebates on the present Hampshire–Berkshire border. The site was extensively if inexpertly excavated at the end of the 19th cent. and the resulting plan of Calleva remains the most comprehensive of a western Roman provincial town. In the half-century before the Claudian invasion Silchester was the site of an important *oppidum*. Development after the invasion was swift, with street-grid, large central timber structures, and possibly the baths. Eventually the developed town was surrounded by a 2nd-cent. earthwork and 3rd-cent. stone defences enclosing 100 acres. At the centre was the stone-built, Hadrianic forum. Other public buildings included the baths, an earth-and-timber amphitheatre, and temples. The Victorian excavations did not examine the buildings of the earlier Roman period, but showed that by the 4th cent. much of the interior of the town was occupied by large residences, often with mosaics, with commercial premises along the main east–west street. Also dating to the 4th cent. was a small probable church south-east of the forum. Objects indicate occupation into the 5th cent., but thereafter the site was deserted. ASEC

Silures. A British tribe and *civitas*. The Silures are mentioned by several Roman authors, among them Pliny, Ptolemy, and *Tacitus. Tacitus actually described their physical characteristics—swarthy and curly-haired—and suggested that their ancestors migrated from Spain. Their territory was south-east Wales, and for a time in the period around AD 45–57 they led the British opposition to the Roman advance westwards. Tacitus described them as a strong and warlike nation, and for ten years or more the Romans fought to contain rather than conquer them. Although defeated and occupied by the early 60s, their bitter resistance may explain the late grant of self-governing *civitas* status to them only in the early 2nd cent. A capital was established on a previously unoccupied site at *Caerwent and was given the name Venta Silurum, but it never matched in size (45 acres) or public buildings the *civitas*-capitals of southern England. KB

silver jubilees, 1935, 1977. The success of Victoria's *Golden and *Diamond Jubilees (1887, 1897) persuaded George V's advisers to celebrate his 25 years on the throne with a thanksgiving service (marred, in the king's view, only by 'too many parsons'), street parties, jubilee mugs, and the like. 'I remember so well both Queen Victoria's jubilees,' wrote the king, 'and can't yet realise that I am having one now.' The silver jubilee of his granddaughter Elizabeth II followed a similar pattern, adding a dash of colour to what had been, in many respects, a sombre reign. JAC

Simeon, Charles (1759–1836). A leading evangelical. Born in Reading, Simeon had religious experiences at Eton (1776) and again at King's College, Cambridge. A fellow of Queens' and later vice-provost of King's, after taking orders (1782) he became incumbent of Holy Trinity, Cambridge (1783–1836). Despite initial hostility his pastoral work won people over. He became well known as an evangelical. After Charles Grant, an East India Company director, had drawn his attention to missionary work in India (1788), Simeon advised on chaplaincy appointments there; he was subsequently a founder of the *Church Missionary Society (1797) and supported the British and Foreign Bible Society. He gathered a large following of young men, especially among undergraduates. Today his name is permanently commemorated in the Simeon Trust, which purchases church patronage and administers it for evangelically minded clergy. WMM

Simnel, Lambert (*c.*1475–*c.*1535). Simnel, one of the many pretenders to the throne of Henry VII, was put forward as Edward, earl of *Warwick, nephew of Richard III, escaped from the Tower. He appears to have been the son of an Oxford tradesman. He was taken up by Richard Simon, a priest, and supported by the Yorkists. In May 1487 he was crowned as Edward VI in Dublin, summoned a parliament, and the following month was brought over to England with a formidable invading force. Henry VII met it at *Stoke, 2 miles south-west of Newark, and was victorious. Simnel, a mere pawn, was pardoned and set to work as a scullion in the royal kitchens, living out the rest of his life in safe obscurity. The real earl of Warwick was executed in 1499. JAC

Simon, Sir John (1873–1954). Liberal politician and eminent barrister. Simon's collection of high offices—home secretary, foreign secretary, chancellor of the Exchequer, and lord chancellor—is unique in the 20th cent. He rose from modest beginnings through sheer brain power to achieve cabinet rank before the First World War. Thereafter his career suffered with the decline of the Liberal Party. But he returned to government in 1931 as foreign secretary at the head of his own band of Liberal National MPs. It was an inauspicious time to hold this office and Simon's reputation declined as first Japan, then Italy and Germany, challenged the authority of the League of Nations. He was more suited to the Home Office (1935–7), playing an important part in the abdication crisis, but as chancellor of the Exchequer (1937–40) his cautious financial control failed to take sufficient account of the need to rearm. In 1940 Churchill sent him to the Lords as lord chancellor, a position for which his legal talents well qualified him. Once thought of as a radical among Liberals, he was, by the end, for practical purposes a Conservative. His intellectual gifts made him reluctant to reach clear-cut decisions. But his greatest failing in public life was an inability to relate to others and a widespread—but not always deserved—reputation for insincerity. DJD

simony. Although particularly associated with the purchase of preferment or office in the church, simony is strictly the acquisition by financial means of any spiritual benefit. The name comes from that of Simon Magus, recorded in Acts 8. Consistently denounced by councils of the church throughout the centuries, it has remained a temptation not universally resisted. JRG

Simpson, Sir James (1811–70). Anaesthetic pioneer. Youngest son of a Scottish village baker, Simpson entered Edinburgh University in 1825, to graduate MD (1832) and proceed rapidly to the chair of midwifery (1839). Excited by the new use of sulphuric ether as an anaesthetic agent, but concerned to find a substance more manageable and effective, he self-experimented with other volatile fluids before settling on chloroform (1847). Despite its rapid popularity, his advocacy for its use in natural childbirth as well as surgical intervention led to intense criticism from moralists and theologians until Queen Victoria's delighted approbation after the delivery of her ninth child (1853). A baronetcy followed in 1866. Always in a hurry, but with foresight and an intensely critical mind, Simpson's contributions to obstetric science and foundation of gynaecology considerably improved their credibility, while his wider interests included hospital infection and design, acupressure, and archaeology. ASH

Simpson, Mrs Wallis (1896–1986). Wife of Edward, duke of Windsor. Born into a Baltimore family, Bessie Wallis Warfield first married an aviator, Earl Winfield Spencer, but his fondness for drink led to separation and ultimately divorce. Mrs Spencer travelled the world, but on returning to Baltimore she met an English businessman, Ernest Simpson, also in the throes of divorce. In 1928 Mrs Spencer became the second Mrs Simpson, and moved with her husband to London. Two years later an American friend, Thelma, Lady Furness, introduced her to Edward, the prince of Wales. In 1934 Mrs Simpson and Prince Edward became lovers. Mrs Simpson lacked beauty, but oozed wit and charm; Edward, infatuated, found in her the feminine sympathy and understanding he craved. In 1936 she divorced Mr Simpson, and Edward gave up his throne in order to marry her. The couple enjoyed a devoted but childless marriage of some 35 years; she is buried next to him at Frogmore. GA

Sinclair, Sir Archibald, 1st Viscount Thurso (1890–1970). Sinclair held the post of secretary of state for air from the formation of *Churchill's government in 1940 until the end of the Second World War. Son of a Scottish baronet, he entered the Life Guards in 1910 and became a close friend of Winston Churchill, his senior by sixteen years, and they served together on the western front. Sinclair was returned to Parliament in 1922 as a Lloyd George Liberal. He took office with *Samuel in the National Government of 1931 but resigned a year later on the issue of protection. When Samuel lost his seat in 1935, Sinclair took over as leader of the Liberals. He declined to serve under *Chamberlain in 1939 but accepted Churchill's invitation. Sinclair's reputation suffered from his amiability and he was regarded by some as Churchill's creature, but his place in the cabinet was political, and he was capable of standing up to Churchill over *Tedder and Sholto-Douglas. He lost his seat in 1945 but Churchill sponsored his viscountcy in 1952. JAC

Sinn Fein. The Gaelic for 'we ourselves'. Formed as a series of clubs in Ireland and led by the journalist Arthur *Griffith at the beginning of the 20th cent., until 1916 Sinn Fein was more important for ideas than organization. It stressed the need for self-sufficiency in economic and cultural affairs, advocated passive resistance and the *de facto* establishment of an Irish government as the means of achieving nationalist ends, less appropriately suggesting a dual monarchy along Austro-Hungarian lines for resolving the Ulster question. The British authorities inaccurately referred to the Sinn Fein rising 1916. From 1917 it was used as an umbrella title for the advanced nationalist party which supplanted the parliamentary party. Following its triumph in the 1918 general election, Sinn Fein formed the Dáil government, but in the Anglo-Irish War it took a back seat in the military campaign and became the political arm of the *Irish Republican Army. Splitting over the *Anglo-Irish treaty, under *de Valera it supported the republican fight in the civil war 1922–3. In 1926 Sinn Fein divided again over the issue of recognition of the Free State Dáil: the minority adhered to an abstentionist policy and retained the Sinn Fein title, the majority formed the Fianna Fail Party. In the following decades, it lost popular support, though remaining significant as the political wing of the IRA on both sides of the border. It abandoned its traditional abstentionist policy over the hunger strikes in 1981 and became increasingly popular among the catholic working class in Northern Ireland, challenging the electoral dominance of *SDLP, under the leadership of Gerry Adams in Belfast and Martin McGuinness in Derry. New Sinn Fein has been much more successful in Northern Irish politics than in the south. MAH

Singapore was an important trading port between the 11th and 16th cents. In 1819 Sir Stamford *Raffles re-established it as a counterweight to Dutch influence in the region and it became a crown colony in 1867. It developed with the exploitation of south-east Asian rubber, tin, and oil and was made a major naval base in 1921. On 15 February 1942 the Japanese received its surrender. After the war it remained separate from the Malay Union and was given its own constitution in 1955, which led to self-government in 1959. Singapore initially joined, but then withdrew from, the Malaysian Federation (1965). DAW

sinking fund. Originally devised in 1717 as one of numerous schemes to reduce the *national debt. Legislation provided that any surplus funds from government revenues were to be reserved for paying off both capital and interest accumulated before Christmas 1716. A new scheme, in 1786, administered by national debt commissioners, declared that the dividends on government stock would be used to pay off debt in the following year so that eventually the debt would be abolished. But at the end of the Napoleonic wars the national debt was £16 million greater than it would have been without the sinking fund because of the obligation to purchase stock at low interest rates during the war with funds borrowed at high rates of interest in the market. It was phased out during the 19th cent. CHL

Siward, earl of Northumbria (d. 1055). Of Danish descent and gigantic stature, Siward seems to have come to England with *Cnut and had been made earl of *Deira by 1026. He subsequently served *Harthacnut and *Edward the Confessor, becoming earl of all Northumbria. In 1054 he led an expedition to Scotland, defeated *Macbeth, and installed *Malcolm Canmore on the throne. A man of great valour, he was said by Henry of Huntingdon to have lamented in York in 1055 that he was not dying in battle but 'like a cow', and arming himself from head to foot, met death as a warrior. His earldom went to *Tostig, Harold Godwineson's brother. Siward appears in Shakespeare's *Macbeth*. JAC

Six Acts, 1819. Repressive measures to deal with the radical reform agitation which culminated in *Peterloo. The Acts (*a*) prohibited most meetings of over 50 people; (*b*) gave magistrates powers to search private houses for arms; (*c*) prohibited drilling and military training by civilians; (*d*) strengthened the laws against blasphemous and seditious libel; (*e*) limited the right of an accused to adjournment of trial to prepare his defence; (*f*) increased the stamp duty on newspapers and cheap pamphlets to 4 pence, thus hitting the radical press. However, the decline of popular radicalism after 1820 was as much due to improved economic conditions as to the Acts. JFCH

Six Articles, Act of, 1539 (31 Hen. VIII c. 14). The Act gave legal and penal authority to a set of highly reactionary statements on issues of church belief and practice. The Six Articles, decided by debate within the House of Lords and approved by convocation, upheld (*a*) the catholic doctrine of the transubstantiation of the substance of the eucharistic elements into the body and blood of Christ, in its most exclusive form; (*b*) the view that one need not receive both bread and wine in the communion; (*c*) the obligation of priests to remain celibate; (*d*) the binding character of vows of chastity; (*e*) private masses; and (*f*) auricular confession. The Act decreed that denial of the first article was to be punished by burning as a heretic; denial of the others, and priestly marriage, was ultimately punishable by hanging. In keeping with the Act's traditional nickname of the 'whip with six strings', this was not a reasoned doctrinal statement, but a legal snare designed to trap protestant believers. Bishops Shaxton of Salisbury and *Latimer of Worcester resigned their sees in protest. The passing of the Act seems to have resulted from a temporary ascendancy in the king's council of conservative opponents of Thomas *Cromwell, especially the duke of Norfolk and Bishop Stephen *Gardiner. The Act was enforced very little during the life of Cromwell, and sporadically afterwards. It was repealed in the first Parliament of Edward VI in 1547. EC

Skippon, Philip (d. 1660). Major-general of the infantry in the *New Model Army. From a Norfolk gentry family, and a man of puritan piety, Skippon distinguished himself as the leader of the London trained bands, and as commander of the infantry in *Essex's army from 1642 to 1644. At *Naseby (June 1645) he commanded the New Model foot, and was severely wounded. In the second civil war (1648) he was again put in command of the London militia, and prevented the city from falling into royalist hands, and giving assistance to the royalists in Essex and Kent. Though appointed one of the king's judges, he never attended a session of the High Court of Justice. During the Interregnum he held high office but exercised little political influence. Having acquired confiscated crown, church, and royalist land, he died rich. IJG

slave trade. The slave trade of Great Britain, and those of other European countries, transformed the indigenous African and surpassed the Muslim trades. Britain's became the largest national trade. About 75,000 Africans were carried in British ships in the 17th cent.; in 1701–1800 the numbers were about 2.5 million out of the 6.13 million slaves exported, reflecting the expanding demand from the British plantations, especially the sugar colonies, as well as exports to Spanish America. Between 1701 and 1810 British North America received about 348,000 slaves, the British Caribbean about 1.4 million.

The English trade after 1600 was first conducted by monopolistic chartered companies, of which the Guinea Company (1618) lasted until the 1650s. The Royal Adventurers into Africa (1660, 1663) was succeeded by the *Royal Africa Company (1672–1752). However, private traders were always active, even before the company's quasi-monopoly was ended in 1698, and numerous merchant partnerships were involved. The royal family's patronage of trading and colonizing companies in the 17th cent., particularly the duke of York's, and the granting of parliamentary subsidies for the maintenance of African forts and trading posts in the next, mirrored the involvement, if not the direct participation, of all classes of British society. Slaves were traded for an increasing number of English commodities, so that by the early 18th cent. groups as diverse as Devon textile producers and iron manufacturers from the Birmingham area sought to influence legislation. The trade was viewed as a pillar of the plantations and necessary to economic and commercial expansion. Lawyers, legislators, and churchmen viewed it as morally and theologically justifiable. The *quakers were unusual in their early attacks on it as contrary to Christian equality and compassion.

The slave trade has given rise to a vast historical literature. Topics examined include: the regions of west Africa from which the slaves were brought—the major regions for the European trade as a whole were roughly west central Africa (2 million), Bight of Benin (1.2 million), Bight of Biafra (814,000), Gold Coast (677,000), Sierra Leone (483,000), and Senegambia (210,000)—how these changed over time and the extent to which preferences for Africans from one or another region could affect the market; the organization of the trade on the African coast; the nature of slave voyages, the size of ships, the treatment of slaves, and their mortality rates; the sex and age ratios of the slaves taken from Africa; the volume of the trade; its impact on African societies. Econometric analyses have been complemented by studies examining the growing unease over the cruelties of the trade, part of the change in sensibilities, expressed in the literature of benevolence and sentimentalism, that found expression in the writings of, for example, William *Cowper, Samuel *Johnson, and the *Wesleys. Other studies have looked sympathetically at the black population of 18th-cent. England and have documented the lives of individual Africans.

The trade was critical to the production of major colonial commodities, especially sugar, tobacco, and rice, whose export helped shape the global market economy of the late 17th and 18th cents. as well as sectors of the British economy. Its importance for certain British ports is well known. *Liverpool's dominance is clear and Liverpudlians were in the forefront of opposition to reform. Figures for 1750–76 suggest 1,868 ships sailed from there to Africa, 588 from Bristol, and about 260 from London. However, while profits from the trade in some periods may have run at about 9 per cent, arguments that it provided important investment capital, contributing to the British industrial revolution, are now discounted. See ANTI-SLAVERY. RCS

Slim, William, 1st Viscount Slim (1891–1970). Soldier. Born in Bristol and brought up in Birmingham, Slim joined the army in 1914, emerging twice wounded from the war with the rank of major. He spent most of the inter-war years with the army in India and in 1940 was sent with a brigade to Eritrea to fight the Italians. In 1942 he was given a command in *Burma and in October 1943 took over the 14th Army. The following year he won a great victory in repelling a major Japanese offensive and was able to launch a counter-attack to recover Burma, with a brilliant diversionary movement towards Mandalay. After the war he served as chief of the imperial general staff from 1948 and was governor-general of Australia 1953–60. He was given the Garter in 1959 and a viscountcy in 1960. Slim was a fighting general, bluff and pugnacious, 'the finest general the Second World War produced' according to *Mountbatten, and known to his men as 'Uncle Bill'. JAC

Slioch, battle of, 1307. The first of two battles which confirmed Robert I, king of Scots, in his position after the death of Edward I. Probably in October, Robert captured the Comyn castle of Inverlochy, near the modern Fort William, marched up the Great Glen destroying Urquhart and Inverness castles, and attacked Elgin and Banff. He then fell seriously ill and had to retreat to a more secure position at Slioch, just east of Huntly. His enemies, the earls of *Buchan and Atholl, made an unsuccessful attack on Christmas Day. A second attempt on 31 December found Robert's position too strong, and he was able to withdraw to safety, and prepare for the decisive victory at *Inverurie. BW

Sluys, battle of, 1340. At *Halidon Hill in 1333 the Scots discovered that Edward III was rather more formidable than his father. In 1337 Edward went to war with Philip VI of France who built up a vast armada at Sluys on the Flemish coast for an invasion of England. Edward attacked it on 24 June 1340. The French lashed their ships together to form a floating platform, protected by archers and artillery. Edward's vessels crashed into them and ferocious hand-to-hand fighting lasted all day. A few French vessels made their escape but the armada was totally destroyed. JAC

Smeaton, John (1724–92). One of the founders of the civil engineering profession. Born in Leeds, where his father was a lawyer, he demonstrated a practical aptitude which won him rapid recognition as a craftsman and instrument-maker. He was commissioned to rebuild the lighthouse on Eddystone Rock, 15 miles south of Plymouth, and completed this in 1759 with a remarkably innovative design which set the pattern for all subsequent offshore lighthouses. It was after this that he set up a consultancy business, styling himself a 'civil engineer' to distinguish his profession from that of the military engineers. His commissions included canals such as the Forth–Clyde canal in Scotland, many distinguished masonry bridges such as those at Perth and Coldstream, harbours such as that at Ramsgate, and a succession of water-mills and steam-engines. In 1771 he took the lead in establishing the Society of Civil Engineers, the first professional institution for engineers. RAB

Smiles, Samuel (1812–1904). Popularizer of the dominant social values of middle-class Victorian Britain. By profession a doctor, Smiles worked for a time as a radical journalist in Leeds before settling down as secretary (i.e. chief executive officer) to a succession of railway companies. In his leisure time he wrote a series of books, of which **Self-Help* (1859) was the most successful, selling over 250,000 copies during his lifetime. Smiles's heroes were the self-made men who laid the foundations of Britain's industrial greatness. *Self-Help* was a collection of potted biographies of men who had risen from poverty and obscurity to wealth and influence, interspersed with moral reflections and proverbial wisdom. Smiles's original aim was to show how working men might better themselves. However, for large sections of the working class this was simply impracticable; and in the later 19th cent. Smiles appeared to critics of capitalism as the banal apologist for bourgeois success. JFCH

Smith, Adam (1723–90). Famous son of Kirkcaldy (Fife) and educated at Glasgow University, Smith graduated at the age of 14. After six years at Balliol College, Oxford, he became professor of logic, then moral philosophy, at Glasgow University. In 1764–6 he was tutor to the duke of Buccleuch, followed by advisory work for Charles *Townshend; in 1778 he was appointed commissioner of customs for Scotland in which role he remained until his death. Although his reputation was founded on *The Theory of Moral Sentiments* (1759), his *magnum opus* was *An Inquiry into the Nature and Causes of the *Wealth of Nations* (1776). This book was the foundation of the classical school in Britain. It analysed the operation of free market economies where the key players were motivated by self-interest and profit maximization. Out of it economists saw an 'invisible hand' at work and the division of labour, which was eventually responsible for the wealth of nations. Most interpretations have labelled Adam Smith a parent of **laissez-faire* economics, but he was much more interventionist than this. Nevertheless, he was an advocate of an economy based primarily upon *free trade, private enterprise, and 'perfect' competition wherever possible. JRP

Smith, Frederick E., 1st Lord Birkenhead (1872–1930). Lord chancellor. Educated at Birkenhead and Oxford, Smith made a name for himself as a barrister in Liverpool where (1906) he was elected as a Conservative MP. His rhetorical onslaughts against the Liberal government brought him to the attention of the Tory die-hards, and in 1911 he joined the opposition front bench. In 1915 he became solicitor-general and then attorney-general in the wartime coalition government, and in 1919 was appointed lord chancellor; from 1924 to 1928 he served as secretary of state for India. Smith has been unfairly characterized as an unmitigated reactionary. Though a supporter of Ulster's right to opt out of Home Rule, Smith did his best to bring about a compromise in the Irish question, and played a key part in the negotiations which led to the Irish treaty of 1921. He also devoted much energy to law reform; the passage of the Law of Property Act (1922) was largely due to his efforts. GA

Smith, Ian Douglas (b. 1919). Rhodesian politician, advocate of white rule. In 1961 Smith founded the Rhodesian Front, a party which rejected the proposal of the government of the Federation of Rhodesia and Nyasaland to offer more representation for blacks in Parliament. When the federation was dissolved (1963), Smith became prime minister of Southern Rhodesia in 1964. He rejected Britain's plan for black majority rule in the colony and in 1965 unilaterally declared Rhodesia's independence. He then fought a powerful rearguard action against British attempts to reverse the declaration. In response to the imposition of economic sanctions by the UN he severed Rhodesia's links with the Commonwealth and in 1970 declared the country to be a republic. The civil war subsequently waged by black nationalists against his government forced Smith to take part in negotiations in London, as a result of which black majority rule was introduced in 1979. KI

Smith, John (1938–94). Scottish QC who became leader of the Labour Party (1992–4). Smith was chosen to succeed *Kinnock both as someone who had held office (minister of state, Department of Energy 1975–6; minister of state, Privy Council Office 1976–8; secretary of state for trade 1978–9), and as a political heavyweight who possessed the gravitas that Kinnock lacked. Even so, his 'shadow budget' of 1992 had contributed to Labour's defeat. Smith, though much respected, was not perhaps as good as he was painted. He never dominated the Commons or captured the national imagination as *Wilson had done as leader of the opposition. And although he broke the trade union block vote at the 1993 party conference, his longer-term strategy for Labour was not entirely clear. Cruelly, his greatest contribution to Labour's progress was his sudden death in 1994 from a second heart attack. This brought the youthful Tony *Blair as his successor and scuppered Michael *Heseltine's chances—he had recently also suffered a heart attack—of overthrowing John *Major. AS

Smith, Sir Sidney (1764–1840). Admiral. Smith entered the navy in 1777 and saw action in the American War at Cape St

Vincent (16 January 1780) and off the Chesapeake (5 September 1781). In 1785–7 he studied French at Caen before spending a year with the Swedish navy. In 1793 he was posted to Toulon and returned with dispatches after its fall. Smith was given command of the frigate *Diamond* which he used to conduct partisan warfare along the French coast. He was captured in 1796 off Le Havre and imprisoned in the Temple, Paris. Two years later he escaped and returned to command the *Tigre* in Levant. The most famous episode in his career came in 1799 when he undertook the defence of Saint-Jean d'*Acre (3 March–8 May) and heroically repulsed Napoleon. Smith possessed a vainglorious streak to his character, but also showed great valour and judgement. He died in Paris and was buried in Père-Lachaise. RAS

Smith, Sydney (1771–1845). One of the ablest polemicists in a period of remarkable vitality. His father was severe, often in financial difficulties, and ungenerous. Sydney was educated at Winchester and New College, Oxford, where he took orders and became a fellow. After two years in Netheravon in Wiltshire as a curate, he became tutor in 1797 to Michael Hicks Beach and then to his younger brother William. The continent being closed by the war, they settled in Edinburgh. During his stay there, he launched in 1802 the **Edinburgh Review* with his friends *Brougham and *Jeffrey and contributed to it for 25 years. From 1806 Smith was rector of Foston near York, which he held until 1829, when he moved to the living of Combe Florey in Somerset. In 1807 his *Peter Plymley* letters, published anonymously and urging religious liberty, had a great success. Smith was an ardent advocate of *catholic emancipation, had a distaste for the excesses of methodists—'there is not a madhouse in England where a considerable part of the patients have not been driven to insanity by the extravagancies of these people'—and his speech at Taunton in 1831 on parliamentary reform ('Mrs Partington and the Atlantic Ocean') became an instant classic. When his Whig friends came to power in 1830, *Grey gave him a canonry at St Paul's, but he was passed over for a bishopric, which hurt him. Though Smith's facetiousness can appear mechanical, and even desperate, he was genuinely funny, and there is testimony to dinner-table companions reduced to helplessness and servants forced to leave the room in stitches. JAC

Smith, Sir Thomas (1513–77). Scholar and statesman. Smith was born in Saffron Walden of prosperous parents and educated at Queens' College, Cambridge. In the early 1540s, with his friend *Cheke, he plunged into the controversy about the pronunciation of Greek. In 1543 he was made professor of civil law. Under Protector *Somerset he prospered as a protestant. He was appointed provost of Eton, dean of Carlisle, and a secretary of state, and was given a knighthood. He survived Somerset's fall with some difficulty and took a back seat under Mary. Elizabeth restored him to favour and he was involved in negotiating the treaty of *Troyes in 1564. In 1572 he was reappointed secretary of state, using his influence on behalf of the Scottish reformers. His best-known work is his *Discourse on the Commonwealth of England*, published posthumously in 1583 and frequently reprinted. It is a description of the mechanics of government in 1565, with a famous, and disputed, account of the role of Parliament. JAC

Smith, W. H. A nation-wide chain of retail outlets of books, newspapers, stationery, computers, recordings, games, and other leisure products. William Henry Smith (1792–1865) was born in London where his widowed mother ran a small newspaper business. W. H. Smith extended it, laying the foundations for growth during the second half of the 19th cent. As the railway network expanded, the company secured concessions for kiosks to sell newspapers and periodicals at principal stations from most railway companies. Until 1960 many of the high street shops also ran lending library departments. In partnership with *Boots, the company assumed control of Do-It-All, the household goods supermarket chain. W. H. Smith's son (also W. H.), who entered politics, was satirized by *Gilbert and *Sullivan as 'ruler of the Queen's Navee' when 1st lord of the Admiralty (1877–80). IJEK

Smollett, Tobias (1721–74). Novelist. Son of a prosperous Dumbarton laird, Smollett became the best-known London-Scottish man of letters of his generation. His life was dogged by financial disaster and he took to *Grub Street out of necessity. Much of his literary career was the stuff of hack writing—translations, political and historical journalism, travel writing. But he was a cut above the rest. His 'Continuation' of *Hume's *History of England* was not only lucrative but a serious foray into contemporary history. His *Critical Review* founded in 1756 was a respected and popular literary journal. His early picaresque novels *Roderick Random* (1748) and *Peregrine Pickle* (1751) are minor classics. His last novel *Humphry Clinker* (1771), set in London, the English provinces, Wales, and Scotland, is the first genuinely British novel. It is also a major classic of comic fiction. NTP

smuggling refers to covert movement of goods into or out of the country in order to evade taxes or limitations on imports or exports, and involves practical difficulties relating to clandestine activity and risks of detection by customs and excise. It was so extensive and organized in the 18th cent. as to be considered a trade in its own right, but one able to benefit rather than suffer by the disruption of war. If hampered by high naval presence in inshore waters, smugglers could flourish when the navy's forces were stretched and revenue officers corrupt. The 1740s and 1770s were accordingly profitable, and *Wesley found his congregation at Rye in 1773 intensely reluctant to stop the habit. Although the gangs were predominantly comprised of labourers or artisans, who regarded the practice as a legitimate part of the local economy, the contraband reached all sections of society. The risks entailed encouraged ingenuity: Horace *Walpole's jacket came via a banker cousin in Paris, probably in the diplomatic bag; in 1792 Parson *Woodforde had to hide tubs of rum and brandy since he was liable to a £10 fine for each illicit purchase under 19 Geo. III c. 69 (which not only fined the supplier £50 but deliberately encouraged 'informing'); more recently, weapon parts have been disguised as engineering components, and clothes have been impregnated with powdered drugs. Flourishing wherever there are high duties (luxuries like silk, spices, wines and spirits, and tea in the 18th cent.), bans, or embargoes (narcotics in the 20th cent., arms in all periods), estimates of the value of the trade, of the loss of revenue to government, and of damage to individuals or businesses can only be conjectural. IJEK

Smuts, Jan Christian (1870–1950). South African soldier, diplomat, statesman, and scholar. Having trained as a lawyer in England, Smuts, an Afrikaner, fought against the British in the second Anglo-Boer War (1899–1902). He became one of the main architects of the unification of South Africa within the British empire, but under Afrikaner leadership (1910). During the First World War he commanded British troops in east Africa before serving with distinction in Lloyd George's war cabinet (1916–19) and in the peace negotiations in Versailles, when he was a vigorous protagonist of the *League of Nations. He was not so successful as prime minister of the Union of South Africa (1919–24 and 1939–48) because his attachment to the British empire and Commonwealth angered the Afrikaners, who also resented his intervention in the Second World War. Although critical of the apartheid policy introduced after 1948 he always believed that whites should continue to govern the country. KI

Snowden, Philip (1864–1937). Labour politician. Snowden came from humble Yorkshire weaving stock, but managed to obtain a junior post in the civil service. Through a process of self-education he converted himself to socialism, joining the *Independent Labour Party, of which he became (1903–6 and 1917–20) national chairman; he entered Parliament in 1906 as MP for Blackburn, later representing Colne Valley. During the 1920s his revolutionary ardour dimmed; he opposed the *General Strike (1926) and resigned from the ILP the following year. Snowden's grasp of fiscal matters led to his appointment as chancellor of the Exchequer in the Labour governments of 1924 and 1929–31, but far from pursuing a socialist economic policy he revealed himself as a devotee of the balanced budget and an unrepentant supporter of *free trade. Following the collapse of the minority Labour government in 1931, Snowden joined Ramsay MacDonald's National Government, thus retaining his Exchequer portfolio, but the following year (by then a viscount) he resigned on the issue of free trade. GA

Soane, Sir John (1753–1837). English architect. Following an apprenticeship and successful studies at the Royal Academy, between 1778 and 1780 Soane travelled in Italy on a scholarship awarded by George III. In 1788 he won the competition to design a new Bank of England and remained as surveyor to the Bank until 1833. Of this, his most important work, only some fine interiors remain. Two houses he designed for himself show his mature style; Pitzhanger Manor, Ealing, is now a library, while 13 Lincoln's Inn Fields is the Sir John Soane Museum, containing his collection of antiques and paintings. Dulwich College Art Gallery, another most original design, was destroyed in 1944, but faithfully rebuilt. Less successful than his great rival John *Nash, from whom he differed in every respect, Soane was probably a truer interpreter of the period's taste for the classical. He was knighted in 1831. JC

soccer. See FOOTBALL.

Social Democratic and Labour Party (SDLP). The SDLP has been the most effective institution representing the catholic minority in Northern Ireland since the province's establishment. It was formed in 1971 as a coalition between the old Nationalist Party members, republican socialists, and civil rights campaigners, and represented the enlarging catholic middle class. It was initially led by Gerry Fitt, representative of Belfast's Labour tradition. The SDLP accepted the position as opposition party within Stormont, but boycotted it over the implementation of internment in 1971. It joined the power-sharing executive of 1973–4 and suffered from its rapid collapse. In 1979 John Hume was elected leader and developed effective contact with politicians in Dublin, Brussels, and the USA. Its electoral dominance among the catholic community has been challenged by *Sinn Fein, particularly over the hunger strikes of 1981. Hume led a peace initiative in 1993–4 in talks with the Sinn Fein leader Gerry Adams; their agreement provided background to the Downing Street declaration of December 1993, and the republican cease-fire of August 1994–January 1996. Hume's international prominence tends to eclipse his party, whose future will depend on the success or failure of the peace initiative. MAH

Social Democratic Federation. Founded in June 1881, but did not add the 'Social' to its name until 1884. By then it had also become social*ist*, in a Marxist sense, under the influence of H. M. *Hyndman. Unfortunately neither Marx himself nor Engels supported it. It also suffered other early blows: by the defection of William *Morris's anarcho-socialists to form the rival Socialist League in December 1884, for example; and when it was discovered in 1885 to have accepted 'Tory gold'. It was never a mass party, but it did exert considerable influence, especially initially, and assisted in the birth of the *Labour Party in 1900. It soon denounced Labour, however, as being insufficiently dedicated to the class war; and thereafter continued as the voice of militant socialism and trade unionism, until it came to be upstaged by the Moscow-inspired *Communist Party of Great Britain after 1920. BJP

Social Democratic Party. The late 1970s saw a marked rise of the left within the *Labour Party. There were demands for the mandatory reselection of MPs, and for the choice of the party leader to be taken from MPs and lodged in an electoral college, which would include the trade unions and the constituency parties. Dissatisfaction with the *Callaghan government (1976–9) intensified such pressures. Leading ex-ministers began to contemplate breaking away from Labour to form a new party. The signal came when the party conference in January 1981 voted to vest the election of party leader in an electoral college, in which MPs would have only thirty per cent of the votes. Twelve MPs, led by Shirley Williams, Bill Rodgers, David *Owen, plus Roy *Jenkins (chancellor of the Exchequer in the 1966 Wilson government), formed a Council for Social Democracy, soon transformed into the SDP.

The first task was to create a party structure, the second to negotiate an alliance with the *Liberals. The Alliance involved a division of the constituencies between the two parties, and the nomination of a prime minister-designate, who would form a government were the Alliance to win a majority—the choice being Jenkins. In the first months, the Alliance was highly successful, winning by-elections at Croydon NE, Crosby, and Glasgow Hillhead, where Jenkins was returned. At the end of 1981, 50 per cent of a national sample said they would vote for the Alliance if a general election was held at once. By April 1982, 29 sitting Labour MPs and one Conservative had joined the SDP.

Early in 1982 polls indicated a falling-off of support, possibly instigated by quarrels between the two parties over the share-out of seats. A second factor was the *Falklands War, which rallied opinion to Mrs *Thatcher's Conservative government, and a third influence was signs of economic recovery. In the general election of 1983, the Alliance won 26 per cent of the national vote outside Northern Ireland, only 2 per cent behind Labour. But the working of the British electoral system, which penalizes evenly spread third parties, awarded the Alliance only 23 seats, against Labour's 209.

Jenkins resigned as leader of the SDP at once and was replaced by David Owen. Relations with the Liberals became more strained. The Alliance won some by-elections spectacularly and did well in local elections. But it was hampered by the retreat of the left inside the Labour Party, and in the 1987 general election the strains in the Alliance became more visible. Its vote dropped to 23 per cent and a few days after the election David Steel, leader of the Liberals, delivered an ultimatum—either a merger or the Alliance should be dissolved. Owen bitterly opposed a merger and resigned when a majority of his members supported it. The two parties then formed the new Social and *Liberal Democrat Party. Owen and two other MPs stayed aloof in an independent SDP but it had lost most of its support. Owen retired from Parliament at the 1992 election and the two other SDP MPs were narrowly defeated. The party was over.

HB

social history. G. M. Trevelyan's often quoted 'Social history might be defined negatively as the history of a people with the politics left out' is as thought-provoking as it is misleading. The result was a diffuse agenda of great breadth from family and household to furniture, dress, and photography. This was given coherence around the notion of 'Englishness'. He began in the 14th cent. because this was the period in which 'the English people first clearly appear as a racial and cultural unit'. He finished with a vision of a society experiencing increasingly rapid change and 'progress . . . particularly in education and social services'. In a book written in the shadow of an uncertain war, the last footnote ended, 'If we win this war, it will have been won in the primary and secondary schools' (1941). None the less the tradition of social history which dominated the 1950s and 1960s had come out of the side door of the *Fabian Society guided by the Hammonds and the *Webbs.

Social history inherited from the *Scottish Enlightenment a sense of a society progressing by stages to a more civilized condition. There was a keen awareness of the impact of economic structures derived from Marxism. The deep sense of national identity and purpose explicit in Trevelyan was implicit in the development of social history. The Anglocentric British state was the reference point for the bulk of research and analysis. The dominant agenda grew from the Fabian perspective. It included work and the impact of economic change, social conditions, especially health and housing, social movements, notably trade unions and organizations campaigning for social change, and social reform based upon legislation and the growth of state intervention. This writing was organized around two key assumptions. The first identified a major and disruptive change in the late 18th and early 19th cents. called the *'industrial revolution'. The second sought understanding and explanation through the concept of social *class. These assumptions were common to the work of authors as different as Asa Briggs, E. P. Thompson, and Harold Perkin. Although Edward Thompson's work initially divided its readers by political persuasion, its long-run importance was to widen the agenda of social history and to bring to the front the tension between human agency and economic determinism as a basis for explanation in social history.

The 1960s and 1970s brought an increasing engagement between social science and the understanding of the past. The initial impact was evident in the study of social class but most notable in demography and *family history. The recognition of the distinctive nature of the nuclear family-based household in Britain was one outcome. This engagement brought another tension to social history, that between the social scientist's desire to generalize and the historian's respect for the particularity of time, place, and person. This period saw a dramatic increase in the sources and methods employed by social historians: parish registers, parliamentary poll books, oral history, the early use of computers, and the interpretation of landscape were only some of the additions to the repertoire.

The 1970s and 1980s released social history from a variety of self-imposed inhibitions. There was a rapid extension of the range of 'legitimate' topics. *Urban history with its awareness of the complex interactions and variety of the town played a major part in this. Social theory, much of it from the Chicago school of urban sociology, was important here, but the urban historians also sustained a tradition of social history which sought an elegant account of the texture of the past, a sort of organized poetry of facts. The most crucial impact was probably women's history with its rapid development into gender history. Leading writers displayed a deep dissatisfaction with existing categories and agendas such as the Fabian concern with paid (mainly male) work in the cash economy.

In the past 25 years the British have written more social history than in the rest of their history-writing history. The agenda has extended to an almost unlimited range of topics. Politics, often through studies of the nature of the state, has been reintegrated. Ethnic, racial, religious, and national identities have been added to those of gender and class. The greater understanding of the 17th and 18th cents. has questioned the notion of the 'industrial revolution' as a discontinuity.

In the 1990s the British display a hunger for their own history, not just as a nation state unit in the manner of Trevelyan, but as a reflection of multiple identities, Scottish, Irish, Welsh, the regionality of the English, in terms of work, gender, religion, ethnicity, leisure interests, social and moral enthusiasms. As a result 'social history' has become part of the mainstream of British culture. The political debate of the 1980s and 1990s directly involved interpretations of social history through concepts such as 'Victorian values' and 'middle-class failure'. Leisure and cultural products as varied as tourism, television, and living space involved historical understanding through the notions of 'heritage' and 'restoration'. Social history has become not just an intellectual base for understanding the past but a crucial element in the relationship of past and present and in the multiple identities of the late 20th cent. RJM

socialism. The word first appeared in 1827 as a description of the doctrines of Robert *Owen. Socialists emphasized a social, as opposed to an individualist, approach to life, especially economic organization. Owenite socialism (also known as co-operative, utopian, or communitarian socialism) aimed to change society by the establishment of experimental communities, in which property was held in common and social and economic activity was organized on a co-operative basis. Between 1825 and 1847, seven Owenite communities were founded in Britain. None of them flourished long; but from the co-operative trading stores, established by working men to accumulate funds for starting a community, came the modern *Co-operative movement. Owenism provided a critique of capitalism and an alternative political economy based on a general labour theory of value. It did not survive as a movement beyond the later 1840s. The idea of co-operative socialism was continued by the middle-class *Christian socialists of 1848–54. Throughout the 1860s and 1870s little was heard of socialism.

In 1884 came a revival, beginning with the *Social Democratic Federation (SDF), founded in 1881 as the Democratic Federation from various radical clubs in London. It was basically Marxist and most of the leading socialists were for a short time in its ranks. The Socialist League, under the leadership of William *Morris, split off from the SDF in 1884; and in the same year the *Fabian Society was formed by a group of middle-class intellectuals who derived their socialism not from Marx but from *utilitarianism. In 1893 the *Independent Labour Party was founded at a conference in Bradford, and despite its title was committed to socialism. Local groups of socialists grew up in towns across the country.

Membership of most socialist organizations signified a commitment to certain principles (of which some version of 'the collective ownership of the means of production, distribution, and exchange' was the most important), followed by a list of 'immediate' reforms such as the eight-hour day, state pensions, and free, secular education to 16. There were also other expectations and motivations. For some, the revolt against Victorian society was paramount; some were appalled by the waste and inefficiency of capitalism and wished to replace it by a more rational system; others found in socialism a new religion; and a few believed in class struggle and revolution.

Numerically the socialists were only a small body—probably no more than 2,000 in the 1880s and perhaps 20,000–30,000 by 1900. The failure to build a mass socialist party (as in Germany or France) in the 1890s encouraged socialists to look to the *trade union movement for wider support, with the result that in 1900 a Labour Representation Committee based on an alliance of socialist societies and trade unions was formed, and in 1906 this became the *Labour Party. It did not adopt a specifically socialist programme until 1918. Thereafter the Labour Party was the main vehicle for an empirical, reformist, welfare-statist type of socialism in Britain, which reached its apogee in the Labour victory of 1945 with its ensuing programme of nationalization and welfare legislation. For many ardent socialists the Labour Party was inadequate, and their sectarian inclinations encouraged the formation of numerous minority movements, including the *Communist Party, from 1920 to the present. Their differences were mainly about the means by which socialism could be attained, especially the issue of revolutionary action (variously defined) versus constitutional, reformist measures. JFCH

socialism, Christian. The belief that Christ's teachings led to socialism and that the church should actively promote social reform. After the collapse of *Owenism and *chartism, a group of middle-class Christian socialists, disturbed by the alienation of working people from organized religion, promoted co-operative socialism among working men from 1848 to 1854, led by F. D. *Maurice, Charles *Kingsley, and J. M. Ludlow. The movement was revived in the 1880s mainly by high-church Anglicans influenced by Maurice's liberal theology. Its main institutions were Stewart Headlam's Guild of St Matthew (1877–1909), the Christian Social Union (1889–1919) founded by the Oxford scholars Charles Gore and Henry Scott Holland, and the Church Socialist League (1906–24) which drew upon the traditions of Yorkshire radicalism and the inspiration of Gore's monastic Community of the Resurrection at Mirfield, and whose best-known propagandist was Conrad Noel. Non-institutional Christian socialism was also found among nonconformists, especially *congregationalists. JFCH

Society for Constitutional Information. Founded in 1780 by Major *Cartwright and other middle-class radicals to promote parliamentary reform, the SCI flourished until 1783, but thereafter made little headway, partly because its energies were diluted by efforts in support of *anti-slavery, prison reform, and the civic emancipation of dissenters. The SCI actively promoted Paine's **Rights of Man* and other radical publications, and under the leadership of *Horne Tooke collaborated with other reform societies, metropolitan and provincial. After the government repression and treason trials of 1794, the SCI ceased to meet, without being formally dissolved. JFCH

Society for Promoting Christian Knowledge (SPCK). Founded (1698) by Thomas Bray (1656–1730) and others to provide religious literature for those without nearby libraries. As Bishop *Compton of London's Commissary for Maryland, Bray aimed to promote 'Religion and Learning in any part of His Majesty's Plantations abroad, and to provide Catechetical Libraries and free schools in the parishes at home'. Though it handed over to the *Society for the Propagation of the Gospel its American and West Indian missionary work, SPCK, albeit Anglican, supervised the German-Danish Lutheran Mission in south India, which SPG took over in 1825. As the third oldest English publisher, printing and distribution of literature remains its major task, its shop in Bath being the first (1835). SPCK was the main distributor of the Bible, though the King's Printers and Oxford and Cambridge held the publishing copyright, and has been the principal Prayer Book publisher in different languages. WMM

Society for the Propagation of the Gospel in Foreign Parts (SPG). Founded on the recommendation of Thomas Bray, founder of the *Society for Promoting Christian Knowledge (1701), with Archbishop *Tenison as its first president. Its aim was 'to settle the State of Religion as well as may be among our own people [in the plantations] . . . and then to proceed in the best Methods towards the Conversion of the Natives'. At first it aimed at the American colonies and the plantations in the West Indies. It not only requested bishops for the colonies, for which Tenison himself bequeathed £1,000, but also purchased a house for a bishop in New Jersey. Dean *Swift was rumoured to be the likely first bishop of Virginia. Queen Anne's death, however, prevented its realization. SPG was instrumental in making mission part of Anglican life. An SPG college was founded in Barbados (1716). WMM

socinians denied Christ's deity and existence before his birth as a man, holding, however, that his birth was miraculous and that he possessed divine qualities. Used, particularly in the 17th and 18th cents. as a term of abuse against any suspected of unorthodox views of the trinity, it in fact describes a stage of *unitarianism and underlines its international development, deriving from the Italians Lelio Sozzini (Socinus) and his nephew Fausto. The former (1525–62), developing protestant views *c.*1546, and received by Melanchthon and Calvin, was challenged in Geneva about the Trinity, but settled undisturbed in Zurich. His nephew (1539–1604), who published a denial of Christ's deity in 1562, lived in Poland from 1579, where the minor (reformed) church encapsulated his views in the Racovian catechism (1605). CB

Sodor and Man, diocese of. According to tradition *Patrick converted Man *c.*447. There was certainly a succession of Celtic bishops, but it was probably not until the reign of *Edward the Confessor that the present see of Sudreys (the southern isles) was founded to include the Isle of Man and the Hebrides. The title 'and Man' is probably a 17th-cent. scribe's mistake. In 1152 the see was transferred from the *York province to the Norwegian archiepiscopal province of Trondheim. Sudreys itself was returned to York in 1542 without the Scottish islands which had been detached in 1334. Between 1425 and 1553 there were both English and Scottish successions of bishops. There are Manx-language editions of the Prayer Book (1765) and the Bible (1772). The former cathedral of St German's in the island castle at Peel, now a ruin, reputedly dates from 447. WMM

Solemn League and Covenant. An agreement between the Long Parliament and the Scots brought about by the failure of Parliament's war against the king. Adopted by the Scots Estates on 17 August 1643 and sworn by members of the House of Commons on 25 September, the covenant promised to reform religion in England and Ireland on *presbyterian lines. In return, the Scots undertook to invade England with an army of 20,000. The Scots kept the bargain, which turned the tide of the Civil War against the king. But Parliament's half-heartedness in adopting presbyterianism prompted the Scots to transfer their support to the king in 1648 when he recognized the validity of the covenant as a voluntary engagement. Charles II was also required to swear the covenant when he was crowned king of Scotland in 1650. IJG

solicitor-general. The 'junior' of the two law officers of the crown. The precursor of this office was the 'king's solicitor' first mentioned in 1461 and the title 'solicitor-general' was first used in 1515. From 1525 onwards the office of solicitor-general was a 'stepping stone' to the office of attorney-general, whose deputy and subordinate he was. The solicitor-general was accepted without controversy as a member of the House of Commons and although, like the attorney-general, he was a law officer of the crown, he did not incur the same odium politically as he did not prosecute for criminal libel. The solicitor-general was more familiar with *Chancery than his colleague and for that reason, on at least one occasion, in 1733, the solicitor-general was created lord chancellor, whereas the attorney-general became lord chief justice. Despite the title, the solicitor-general is a barrister. There is a separate solicitor-general for Scotland, who acts as deputy to the *lord advocate. MM

Solomon Islands. The Solomon Islands are in the South Pacific, east of New Guinea, and export copra and coconuts. In 1886 Germany and Britain agreed to spheres of influence but the German sphere, including Bougainville, was later administered by Australia. During the Second World War there was extremely heavy fighting, particularly on Guadalcanal, where Japanese and Americans struggled for control of an important airfield. JAC

Solway Moss, battle of, 1542. When war broke out in August 1542 between Henry VIII and his nephew James V of Scotland, an English raid was defeated at Hadden Rig. James then assembled a large army for a counter-stroke towards Carlisle. But he remained at Caerlaverock, while his troops under Oliver Sinclair moved south along the Esk valley. On 24 November, at Solway Moss west of Longtown, they were surprised and routed by a much smaller English force, led by Thomas Wharton, Thomas Dacre, and John Musgrave, losing 1,200 prisoners, including many noblemen. The defeat broke the spirit of James, already in poor health, and he died in despair three weeks later. JAC

Somerled, lord of the Isles (d. 1164). Somerled claimed descent from Gofraid mac Fherghusa, son of the founder of the kingdom of *Dalriada. He established his position in Argyll and Kintyre at the expense of the Norse and fought for David I at the battle of the *Standard in 1138. About 1140 he married a daughter of Olaf, king of Man, and in the 1150s began a campaign to make himself master of Man and of the Isles. After a naval victory, he forced Gofraid of Man in 1158 to take refuge in Norway. Somerled was at peace with Malcolm IV, David's successor, in 1160, but four years later they clashed and Somerled took an expedition to Renfrew, where he was killed. The Isles were then divided between his remaining sons. JAC

Somers, John, 1st Baron Somers (1651–1716). Lawyer and Whig politician. Called to the bar in 1676, Somers made his name as an outstanding barrister. He was elected in 1689 to the Convention Parliament and was among the principal draftsmen of the *Bill of Rights. After that his advancement was rapid, becoming solicitor-general (1689), attorney-general (1692), lord keeper (1693), lord chancellor (1697), and a peer (1697). A leading *Junto Whig, he was one of the few English politicians in whom William III closely confided, but in 1700 Tory jealousy brought about his dismissal. Though out of office during Anne's early years, he helped to promote much-needed reform in the legal system, supported the war against Louis XIV, and played an important role in the passage of the Regency Act (1706) and the *Union with Scotland (1707). By 1708 the queen's coolness gave way to appreciation of his statesmanlike qualities and he became lord president, but went out with his fellow-Whigs in 1710. At George I's accession he was given a seat in the cabinet. AAH

Somerset was one of the largest counties, 70 miles from Frome in the east to Exmoor in the west. It forms the southern hinterland of the Bristol channel and has an unusual variety of topographical features—the bare Mendips north of Wells, the marshes around Glastonbury, the wooded Quantocks west of Bridgwater, and the high Cotswolds north of Bath. Since, despite a vigorous cloth industry and substantial deposits of coal, iron, and lead, it escaped the worst ravages of industrialization, it remains one of the most beautiful of shires. The largest town, *Bath, which was not lost to Avon until the reorganization of 1972, had then only 85,000 people and was twice the size of the next largest town, Taunton.

The northern parts of the shire drain into the rivers Avon and Frome, which form the border with Gloucestershire and Wiltshire, and the central parts into the Parrett and its tributaries the Cary, Yeo, and Tone. The border with Devon runs through Exmoor and the Blackdown hills, and in the east the shire merges with the chalk hills of Wiltshire west of Salisbury Plain. The northern parishes look towards Bristol and Bath, the south-western towards Taunton, and the south-eastern towards Yeovil.

In Caesar's time, the area was in the territory of the *Belgae, though it seems to have been on the fringes. It fell speedily to the Romans, who were exploiting the lead-mines of Mendip as early as AD 49. The *Fosse Way, from Lincoln to Exeter, bisected the county north-east to south-west. The hot springs at Bath were almost certainly known before Roman times and the city, Aquae Sulis, grew up quickly. Ilchester, on the Fosse, was another important development. After the Roman withdrawal, the area was shielded from Saxon advance for some time by Selwood forest to the east, and the legends of *Arthur arose from British resistance. The battle of *Mount Badon, around AD 500, has been placed at Little Solsbury Hill, near Bath, or on the Wiltshire downs to the east: a British defensive victory, it held up the Saxon advance. But in 577 a Saxon victory at *Dyrham, east of Bristol, gave them control of the northern parts, the rest falling after their victory at Peonnan in 658 when, according to the *Anglo-Saxon Chronicle*, *Cenwulf drove the Britons in flight to the Parrett. The region then became part of the kingdom of Wessex. *Ine is said to have refounded the monastery at Glastonbury and to have fortified Taunton. His nephew *Aldhelm built a church at *Wells (*c.*704), which became a see in 909 when jurisdiction was transferred from *Sherborne. By this time the region was acquiring its own identity as a shire, taking its name from Somerton, then the county town, and adding the suffix *sæte*—'the people of'.

Somerset suffered severely from the ravages of the Danes, who destroyed *Glastonbury in 873 and Somerton in 877. *Alfred's resistance was organized from the marshes around Athelney. The submission of *Guthrum, the Danish leader, was at Aller, near Somerton, and the treaty dividing up southern England was agreed in 878 at *Wedmore, near Axbridge. At the Domesday survey, Bath was a city of national importance; Ilchester, Milborne Port, Taunton, Langport, Axbridge, and Bruton of local significance.

After the Norman Conquest, Glastonbury abbey, with its traditions of Joseph of Arimathea and of Arthur, became one of the wealthiest monasteries in the kingdom. Work on the new Wells cathedral started *c.*1184. Somerton and Ilchester were in sharp decline by Tudor times, but Taunton, Frome, and Yeovil prospered as cloth towns. Glastonbury lost its estates at the *dissolution of the monasteries and its last abbot was hanged on the Tor. The most famous purchaser was 'Little Jack Horner', whose plum was the estate of Mells. The church lands seem to have been widely distributed and no overriding aristocratic interest arose, partly also because the shire was large with many market towns. Consequently it gained a reputation for independence, to which was added, in the cloth towns, a strong tradition of religious dissent. In the Civil War, the towns were largely parliamentary in sympathy. Taunton, led by Robert *Blake, withstood a protracted siege from *Goring's men in 1645 and the royalist army was later routed by *Fairfax at *Langport. At the Restoration, Taunton was punished by the forfeiture of its charter and the demolition of the town walls. It gave a warm welcome to *Monmouth in 1685 and paid for it after *Sedgemoor in corpses swinging from innumerable gallows.

The 18th and 19th cents. saw great changes in the county. Bath's greatest period of fashion came under Beau *Nash in the 1750s. Later in the century, large parts of central Somerset were reclaimed from persistent flooding by rhynes and sea-walls: one of the most ambitious, the King's Sedgemoor drain, straightening the course of the river Cary, was finished in 1791. The 19th cent. saw a diversification of the economy. In 1801 Bath was still the ninth largest town in England and retained its unique character. Street, which had been no more than a village, became a sizeable town after Clarks shoe factory was built there in 1825; Bridgwater, long a local port, added brick- and tile-making, and Shepton Mallett grew on the production of cider. The Brendon hills produced iron for south Wales until the last mine closed in 1911. The Somerset coalfield had a brief burst of prosperity. By 1868 there were 64 small pits at work around Radstock and production peaked just before the First World War. It declined sharply after 1945 and the last pit was abandoned in 1973. The most remarkable growth in the county was at Yeovil and at Weston super Mare. Yeovil had fewer than 3,000 people in 1801 but developed into a manufacturing town, specializing in aircraft. Weston's growth was even more spectacular. In 1801 it had only 138 inhabitants, but the cult of seaside holidays and the arrival of Brunel's railway in 1841 sent it into orbit. By 1914 the population had passed that of Taunton. Clevedon and Portishead, without the beaches to rival Weston, retained more of their Victorian charm.

By a strange piece of legislation in 1972 the northern parishes of the shire were hived off to form the southern part of the new county of Avon. Though Avon was itself abolished in 1996, the parishes were not returned to Somerset. Instead, the Banham commission on local government reported in 1993 in favour of the abolition of the county for all but ceremonial purposes and its replacement by three unitary authorities—West Somerset, Mid Somerset, and South Somerset. JAC

Somerset, Edmund Beaufort, 1st duke of (*c.*1406–55). Entitled count of Mortain from 1427, and earl of Dorset from 1438, Beaufort was frequently employed in the defence of Lancastrian France, with the backing of his uncle, Cardinal *Beaufort. He succeeded to the titles of his elder brother John (d. 1444), but not to his lands. To the chagrin of Richard of *York, Somerset was appointed lieutenant-general of France in 1447; by 1450 all Normandy had been lost to the French. York accused him of treason, but he became the dominant favourite of Henry VI, created duke 1448 and captain of Calais in 1451. Being a grandson of *John of Gaunt, Somerset may have been suspected of kingly ambitions while Henry was childless. He was prominent in the suppression of York's rising in 1452, but was himself imprisoned for trial during York's first protectorate. Having alienated the Nevilles by a territorial dispute with *Warwick, Somerset gained the support of the earl of *Northumberland; both were killed in the first battle of *St Albans. RLS

Somerset, Charles Seymour, 6th duke of (1662–1748). Charles Seymour succeeded to the dukedom at the age of 16 when his elder brother was shot in Italy, and married the heiress to the vast Percy estates. He was gentleman of the bedchamber to Charles II and James II and given the Garter in 1684. But in 1687 he refused to make a public introduction to the papal nuncio and was dismissed by James from his post and his lord-lieutenancies. At the Glorious Revolution, he joined William of Orange, but his support for Princess Anne in her family quarrels with her sister and brother-in-law kept him out of favour. When Anne succeeded in 1702, he was appointed master of the horse. In 1708 he gave support to *Marlborough and *Godolphin in their power struggle against *Harley and lost his post in 1712 as a consequence. In 1714 his attendance at the council on Anne's death strengthened the Hanoverian position, and he was restored to the mastership. His nickname 'the proud duke' testified to an arrogance of which many stories were circulated. Horace *Walpole thought 'his whole stupid life one series of pride and tyranny' and *Macaulay that his pride was 'almost a disease'. JAC

Somerset, Edward Seymour, 1st duke of (*c.*1500–52). The foundation of Somerset's career was that he was elder brother of *Jane Seymour, Henry VIII's third wife, and therefore uncle to Edward VI. His father had been a gentleman of good family at Wolf Hall in Wiltshire. Somerset's early career was in *Wolsey's service and he was knighted in France in 1523. His progress was by no means spectacular until his sister's marriage in May 1536. A week later he was made Viscount Beauchamp and the following year earl of Hertford. Great honours followed—the Garter in 1541, lord high admiral 1542–3, lieutenant-general in the north 1544–5, when he waged war against the Scots. On Henry VIII's death in 1547, with his nephew aged 9, he became protector of the realm and duke of Somerset. For 2½ years he was the effective power in the land. In August 1547 he consolidated his position with a third campaign against the Scots ending in victory at *Pinkie Cleugh. But his relations with his younger brother Thomas, created Baron *Seymour and made lord high admiral in 1547, were difficult. Six months after Henry's death, Thomas Seymour married his widow *Catherine Parr and when she died in September 1548 transferred his hopes to Princess Elizabeth. He was arrested in January 1549 and executed two months later.

During 1549 Somerset's position collapsed completely. The *prayer book issued under his auspices provoked a serious rising in Cornwall and Devon in June, and was followed in July by *Kett's rebellion in Norfolk. The second was put down by *Northumberland, who now emerged as Somerset's chief rival. In October Somerset was deprived of his protectorate and sent to the Tower. Though he was pardoned the following year and restored to the council, he was again sent to the Tower in October 1551 and executed in January 1552.

Somerset's character and policy have proved controversial. Kindly and amiable in the view of some Victorian commentators, one contemporary thought him 'dry, sour and opinionated', while even an ally, Sir William *Paget, warned him that 'Your Grace is grown in great choleric fashion.' The sentimental view of Somerset as 'the good duke' overthrown by the nobility because he showed too much sympathy for the people's complaints against enclosures is not easy to reconcile with his greed for estates. A better soldier than politician, Somerset lost control of the situation, made concessions to rebellion, and convinced his noble colleagues that he was a dangerous man to have in charge. More remarkable is that he was allowed a second chance by his opponents: fallen ministers did not often emerge from the Tower. JAC

Somerset, William Seymour, 1st duke of (1587–1660). William Seymour was a great-grandson of Protector *Somerset, and son of Lord Beauchamp, who died before inheriting his father's title of earl of Hertford. He had royal blood since his grandmother, Lady Catherine Grey, was a direct descendant of *Mary Tudor, Henry VIII's sister. He succeeded his grandfather as earl in 1621. In 1610 he had gone through a private marriage to Arabella *Stuart, cousin of James I. Both were placed in the Tower and Arabella died there in 1615. Seymour escaped to France and lived there until 1616, when he was allowed to return. He was created marquis of Hertford in 1641. Originally sympathetic to the moderate opposition, he joined Charles I at the outbreak of war, fought in the west, and was groom of the stole at Oxford in 1644. At the Restoration, he was given the Garter and reinstated in the dukedom a month before his death. JAC

Somerset case. In 1771 the American master of James Somerset, a negro slave, attempted to send him out of England to be sold. Abolitionists pleaded *habeas corpus on his behalf. *Blackstone, in his Oxford lectures, had already denied that English law recognized slavery. In a famous judgment on 22 June 1772, which he made with some reluctance, *Mansfield declared that slavery was odious and unknown to common law. Somerset was given his freedom. Though the implications of the judgment have been much discussed, it seems clear that slavery was not recognized in England subsequently. JAC

Somerville, Mary (1780–1872). Mathematician and scientist. Born into genteel poverty in Scotland, Mary Fairfax married secondly her cosmopolitan medical cousin William Somerville (1812), leaving Edinburgh for London in 1816. Largely self-taught but with zest and capacity for learning, she had developed an interest in mathematics, which William encouraged, and an informal apprenticeship under the foremost philosophers led to a long and distinguished career, since scientific society was then wide open to the talented and well connected. Her mastery of French mathematics and expositional skill made important contributions to the modernization of its English counterpart, while *On the Connexion of the Physical Sciences* (1834) helped define these more precisely; if not a creative scientist like *Herschel or *Faraday, her books brought knowledge and clarity to a broad public. Rational but compassionate, Mary Somerville was widely accepted as the leading scientific lady in Europe, honoured accordingly, and posthumously commemorated in the foundation of Somerville College, Oxford. ASH

Somme, battle of the, 1916. When he became commander-in-chief, *Haig wanted to advance from Ypres to liberate the Belgian coast. However, the allies had already concerted their operations for 1916, so he agreed to take part in an Anglo-French offensive further south, astride the river Somme, where the British and French armies met. This was part of a plan by which each of the allied armies would attack simultaneously and compel the Germans to sue for peace by Christmas 1916. Haig hoped that he would break through the German defences in a single day. But despite a lengthy bombardment, when his infantry advanced on 1 July, they suffered nearly 60,000 casualties and only dented the German line. The battle continued until mid-November, by which time the British had suffered approximately 400,000 casualties and advanced a maximum of only 8 miles. DF

Sophia, electress of Hanover (1630–1714). Sophia was a granddaughter of James I by his daughter *Elizabeth, who had married the elector palatine. On the death in 1700 of Anne's last surviving child, William, duke of Gloucester, Sophia was the next non-catholic heir, and was recognized in the Act of *Settlement of 1701. She died at Herrenhausen seven weeks before Anne and her son George Lewis succeeded as George I. JAC

Sophia Dorothea (1666–1726). Divorced wife of George I. Sophia Dorothea married her cousin George in 1682, but in 1694 was surprised in a rendezvous with her lover Count Königsmarck. He was never seen again, and she was divorced and honourably confined at the castle of Ahlden in Celle until her death. Her infidelity allowed the Jacobites to imply that George's children might not have been his own. JAC

South Africa, Republic of. Former British dominion. During the French Revolutionary War, British troops seized the Dutch settlement at the *Cape of Good Hope to protect Britain's trade route to the Far East. Handed back in 1802, the Cape was again captured in 1806 and became Cape Colony. The Dutch settlers (Boers/Afrikaners), spreading eastward, had come into conflict with Bantu-speaking peoples migrating southward along the coast. That conflict was inherited by the British colonial administrators and frontier skirmishes took place for a considerable part of the 19th cent. Many Afrikaners, too, were irked by British rule and migrated eastward and northward to found the self-governing republics of *Transvaal and the *Orange Free State. British policy vacillated between expansion and retrenchment, but in 1843 a British colony was declared in *Natal to the east of the Cape. Continuing clashes with the overwhelmingly numerous Bantu-speaking peoples encouraged successive British governments to press for a confederation of colonies and republics in the hope of strengthening the position of the white population, but the proposal was strongly resisted by the Afrikaners.

Diamonds were discovered at Kimberley in 1868 and Cape Colony quickly claimed ownership of the district.

When gold was found in the Transvaal in the 1880s there was no doubt about the ownership of the land but the exploitation of the vastly rich discovery depended heavily upon outside capital. This became the excuse for British intervention in the Transvaal which led to war between British and Afrikaners from 1899 to 1902. After the war the republics became British colonies and were joined with the older colonies in the Union of South Africa in 1910 under a predominantly Afrikaner government. The British government was relieved to shift responsibility for South African affairs onto other shoulders.

The majority of white South Africans supported Britain during the First World War, but with Afrikaners in the majority among the white population there was growing opposition to membership of the British empire. South Africa's participation in the Second World War was less enthusiastically received by many whites. Nevertheless, with gold as the main source of foreign exchange and with a sound agricultural and pastoral farming industry, the white population prospered. A policy of white domination had always been accepted by both British and Afrikaners, but the victory of the National Party in the 1948 elections saw the policy carried to such extremes as to arouse international condemnation, resulting in South Africa's quitting the British Commonwealth in 1961 and becoming a republic. KI

Southampton. A seaport which gave its name to Hampshire as early as 755, though it is no longer the county town. Saxon Hamwic was the chief port of the kingdom of Wessex; its successor, on a slightly different site, has been a major port since the 11th cent. Kings embarked there (including Henry V before Agincourt), and Venetian and Genoese ships traded there. It lost ground to London in Tudor and Stuart times, but recovered from the 1840s with new docks and the railway, and is now the leading British deep sea port on the Channel. DMP

Southampton, Henry Wriothesley, 3rd earl of (1573–1624). Wriothesley's father, a catholic, was imprisoned in the Tower 1571–3 under suspicion of encouraging *Norfolk's proposed marriage to Mary, queen of Scots. Wriothesley succeeded to the earldom at the age of 7 and grew up as a follower and companion of *Essex, whose cousin he married. He took a prominent part in Essex's rising in 1601, was sent to the Tower, and was considered very fortunate not to lose his head. At the accession of James I, who had worked closely with Essex, he shot into favour, being given the Garter at once and having the earldom restored. He did not however play a leading role in the reign and is of interest mainly as the patron of Shakespeare, who dedicated to him *Venus and Adonis* (1593) and *Lucrece* (1594). Southampton died of fever in 1624 while fighting as a volunteer in the Dutch service. JAC

Southcott, Joanna (1750–1814). A religious fanatic, of Devon farming stock, Joanna was in domestic service in Exeter. Originally called to *methodism (1791), she soon had religious experiences and started 'sealing' her writings. She visited Bristol (1798), published *The Strange Effects of Faith* (1801), and moved to London (1802), where she began the practice of 'sealing the faithful' who, according to the Book of Revelation, were to be 144,000. She claimed to be 'the Lamb's wife' (Rev. 12) who would give birth to 'the second Christ' in 1814; instead she died of brain disease. Her bizarre following, surviving into the 20th cent., believed she would rise again. She left a box, directed to be opened after 100 years with 24 bishops present (cf. Rev. 4: 4). When opened (1927), with one bishop present, it contained merely a night-cap, book, lottery ticket, dicebox, and some coins. WMM

South-East Asia Treaty Organization (SEATO). A US-led security pact designed to contain communism in south-east Asia to North Vietnam. Britain, France, Australia, New Zealand, the Philippines, Pakistan, and Thailand were the other signatories of the founding treaty of Manila (September 1954). SEATO never developed a NATO-style integrated command structure, and the fight against communism was carried out by the USA (culminating in the Vietnam War disaster) rather than SEATO, which was officially disbanded in 1977. CNL

Southern Rhodesia. See RHODESIA.

Southey, Robert (1774–1843). Southey had a strange career, moving from extreme radicalism in the 1790s to a gloomy conservatism and fear of revolution by the 1810s. Born in Bristol, he was educated at Westminster and Balliol College, Oxford, where he met *Coleridge and planned a liberated American settlement, Pantisocracy, on the banks of the Susquehanna. In 1794 he joined with Coleridge in a drama, *The Fall of Robespierre*. An annuity enabled him to settle at Greta Hall (Keswick), with Coleridge and *Wordsworth nearby. He was made poet laureate in 1813 and from 1835 received a pension of £300 p.a. from the government. Of greatest historical interest in his vast output was the *Life of Nelson* (1813), the *History of the Peninsular War* (1823–32), his essays for the **Quarterly Review*, and the curious *Colloquies on the Progress and Prospects of Society* (1829), which, though ridiculed by *Macaulay, contained some uncomfortable insights into the onset of unbridled industrialism. Always highly strung, his mind gave way completely after a disastrous second marriage in 1839. JAC

South Sea bubble. The 1720 financial crisis resulting from the collapse of the South Sea Company. Founded by *Harley in 1711 as a Tory alternative to the Whig financial establishment, the company in 1719 proposed (and in 1720 the ministry accepted) to take over three-fifths of the national debt (about £30 million). In return for trading privileges and accepting 5 per cent interest until 1727 and thereafter 4 per cent, the company was to pay £7 million immediately. A fever of speculation followed and its shares rose from 130 per cent to over 1,000 per cent in six months. Other companies climbed on the bandwagon, and in an effort to drive its rivals to the wall, the company spread alarm. Panic selling ensued and the market collapsed, ruining thousands of investors. *Walpole produced a plan (which helped to secure his supremacy in the ministry) to stem the disaster by transferring a proportion of the stock to the *Bank of England and the *East India Company. Subsequent parliamentary investigations, prompted by a public outcry, revealed corruption on a wide scale, which implicated some ministers and George I himself. CJ

Southwark, diocese of. The see, founded in 1905, is roughly conterminous with Greater London south of the Thames, with east and mid-Surrey; an area originally under *Winchester, but after 1877 under *Rochester. Notable bishops have been Cyril Garbett (1919–32) and Mervyn Stockwood (1959–81). Under Stockwood and his successive suffragan bishops of Woolwich, John Robinson (1959–69) and David Shepherd (1969–75), the diocese was regarded as avant-garde in many ecclesiastical fields, pastoral ministry, liturgical worship, and popularization of radical theology. Many claimed that 'South Bank religion' led the way in modernizing the Church of England. The cathedral is the former Augustinian priory church of St Mary Overie, founded in 1106 and the parish church after the dissolution. It is predominantly Early English in style with 19th-cent. renovation. WMM

Southwell, diocese of. This see, now roughly conterminous with Nottinghamshire, was created in 1884, following rapid population growth in the 19th cent. Initially it had combined Nottinghamshire, from the *Lincoln diocese, and Derbyshire, from *Lichfield, but, as the two counties proved incompatible, the new *Derby diocese was created in 1927. In 1935 Southwell moved from the Canterbury province to York. It was a return home, for Nottinghamshire had been in the York diocese before its move to Lincoln in 1837. Southwell with its medieval minster, one of three (with Ripon and Beverley) in the old York diocese, and its ancient ecclesiastical associations became the see instead of Nottingham, the industrial centre. The cathedral is the former minster church, founded in 1108, dissolved in 1540, but restored in 1558. It has a fine Norman nave and transepts with a 13th-cent. choir and chapter house, where the stonework with its distinctive Southwell foliage is unique. WMM

Southwold or Sole Bay, battle of, 1672. Naval engagement off the Suffolk coast in the third *Anglo-Dutch War on 7 June 1672 between de Ruyter with 91 ships and a slightly larger Anglo-French force, under the command of James, duke of York. Most of the fighting was between the Dutch and the English. De Ruyter lost more ships but the English fleet was badly damaged and Lord *Sandwich, admiral of the Blue, drowned. JAC

South Yorkshire. See YORKSHIRE, SOUTH.

Spa Fields riot, 1816. One of a number of popular incidents provoked by hunger and revolutionary feeling in the wake of the French wars. A great meeting in north London on 15 November addressed by Henry 'Orator' *Hunt turned into a drunken quasi-insurrection when a part of the crowd marched threateningly into the city after arming itself with weapons stolen from a gunsmith's shop. Its leaders were later tried for high treason, but acquitted when the main witness against them, the spy Castles, was revealed as a bigamist, brothel-minder, and *agent provocateur.* BJP

Spain, relations with. Recurrent quarrels with France ensured that the English were normally aligned with Spain in the early Tudor period. This changed under Elizabeth I for reasons of religion, the queen of Scots' claim to the English throne, growing English interest in the success of the Dutch revolt against Spain, and the struggle for trade in the New World. An outright confrontation from 1585 led to its first great climax, the defeat of the Spanish *Armada, in 1588. Spanish efforts to injure England continued for some time, and the English were slow to recognize the decline of Spain in relation to the rise of France and the Dutch. Good sense finally prevailed with Charles II's commercial treaty of 1667. Spain was again frequently numbered among England's enemies in the next century, partly as an ally of France, partly for reasons of empire and trade, and also because of the British possession of *Gibraltar seized during the War of the Spanish Succession. *Wellington, however, found many invaluable allies during the *Peninsular War against Napoleon (1808–14). In the 1830s, Britain and France successfully backed professedly liberal monarchists against the absolutist Carlists and the *Holy Alliance. Yet Britain and France were as much rivals as allies, with the former suffering defeat over the Spanish marriages in 1846. Neither power, however, secured lasting advantage given Spain's recurrent political instability. This reached its climax in the devastating Civil War of 1936–9 when the British government—anxious to localize the conflict—opted for non-intervention to the great dismay of those who saw this conflict primarily in terms of the struggle against fascism in Europe. CJB

Spanish blanks conspiracy, 1593. A number of Scottish noblemen were in negotiation with Philip II of Spain to restore catholicism in Scotland. In 1593 a messenger was apprehended bearing blank letters with signatures. Under torture, he implicated *Huntly, Erroll, and Angus, but the mysterious affair was eventually compromised. JAC

Spanish Succession, War of the, 1702–13. Britain's involvement in a new war with France so soon after the conclusion of the *Nine Years War in 1697 arose from William III's anxiety to prevent Louis XIV incorporating the Spanish kingdom and its possessions in the Netherlands and Italy into a French 'universal monarchy'. When the imbecile Carlos II of Spain died childless in November 1700 Louis disregarded his own agreement with William III in the *Partition treaty of 1699, whereby the Spanish possessions were to be divided between Bourbon and Austrian Habsburg claimants, preferring Carlos's will which bequeathed everything to Louis's grandson, Philip of Anjou. British politicians and public opinion were cautious about renewing war with the French, but there was little option when in 1701 Louis provocatively declared Philip king of Spain, invaded the Spanish Netherlands, and recognized James II's son as 'King James III'. At The Hague in September William III brought Britain, the United Provinces, and Austria together in a Grand Alliance which was later joined by Prussia, Hanover, and other German states.

Under *Marlborough's command Anglo-Dutch forces concentrated on driving back the French from their advanced positions in the Spanish Netherlands. The duke's superlative generalship relied upon rapid manœuvre in the field, where infantry musket-fire could be deployed with devastating effect, in contrast to the slow-paced siege warfare that had dragged out William III's campaigns in the 1690s. His close accord with Lord Treasurer *Godolphin ensured that the British war effort remained well resourced. By 1706 the British nation was shouldering an army budget of £2.75 million, half of which was spent on the war in Flanders. From 1704 the allies won a series of spectacular victories over the French. In that year, as the Franco-Bavarian forces were coming close to winning the war in Germany, Marlborough swiftly marched his 40,000-strong Flanders army up the Rhine and into Bavaria where, joining the imperial regiments under Prince Eugene, he defeated the French and their allies at *Blenheim on 14 August, thereby enfeebling French action in Germany for the rest of the war. Marlborough pressed on in Flanders and following his victory at *Ramillies in May 1706 reconquered most of the southern Netherlands. In August 1708 he repulsed a major French counter-attack at *Oudenarde.

In Spain, Britain's war to replace Louis XIV's grandson Philip V with the allied candidate, the Archduke Charles of Austria, was less successful. Portugal joined the coalition in 1703 and committed British ministers to a policy of 'no peace without Spain'. But while important strategic benefits were obtained, such as the capture of *Gibraltar (1704) and *Minorca (1708), facilitating naval control of the western Mediterranean, advances on the Spanish mainland were short-lived and provoked much dissatisfaction in Parliament. In 1709 the carnage and near-defeat for Marlborough at *Malplaquet demonstrated that the war on France's northern frontier had reached stalemate, while in Spain in December 1710 the allied army under General *Stanhope was pushed into retreat and humiliatingly beaten at *Brihuega.

In Britain the Tories, long convinced that Whig ministers were deliberately prolonging the war in the interests of wealthy city financiers, had come to power in 1710 determined to end the enormous cost and stabilize the soaring national debt. Though Marlborough continued to extend his hold over the French north-eastern border, the government denied him resources to finish the war, and in December 1711 he was removed from his command. As British troops were withdrawn from the Netherlands, the Dutch and Austrians found themselves exposed to defeat. Meanwhile, Archduke Charles's succession in April 1711 as emperor rendered the war for him in Spain unfeasible, as no one was prepared to countenance a massive Austro-Spanish monarchy. Peace negotiations commenced in January 1712, and in March 1713 the treaty of *Utrecht was signed between the allies and France. AAH

spas were places with springs or wells containing salts which were claimed to improve the physical, mental, and spiritual health of people drinking or bathing in the waters. The term became current during the 17th cent. to describe towns which emulated Spa in the Ardennes in Belgium which had just risen to fame. Several British towns owed their prosperity to the benefits of health-giving waters long before the 17th cent., for example, *Bath, whose hot springs were used in the Roman town of Aquae Sulis and which regained fame in the Middle Ages, and *Walsingham in Norfolk, a centre of *pilgrimage in the later Middle Ages.

Fashionable visitors, including royalty, gave prestige to Bath and Tunbridge Wells in the 17th cent. but these and other towns grew in prominence later. They had lodging-houses to let to wealthy patrons in the season with space for their servants to sustain comfortable living. In the early 19th cent. Cheltenham offered the first purpose-built luxury hotel. 'Taking the Waters' did not occupy all the time and energies of visitors. Elaborate provisions were made: theatres, ballrooms, libraries, specialized shops and services, excursions to places of interest, and religious devotions. Elegant buildings, residential, religious, and public, were set in well-maintained, lit, and policed streets. Success attracted imitators for the growing health and leisure business. A late entrant was Buxton in Derbyshire which remained popular throughout the 19th cent. Failed projects included Glastonbury in Somerset during the 18th cent. and Ashby de la Zouch in Leicestershire in the 19th cent. Most British spas declined in popularity during the 19th cent. because of competition from foreign resorts which catered for a much more diverse clientele. IJEK

Speaker. The office of Speaker originated as a spokesman for the House of Commons in its dealings with the crown in the course of the 14th cent. The first formal acknowledgement of the Speaker as 'prolocutor' was to Sir Peter de la Mare, knight of the shire for Herefordshire, in 1376 at the end of the reign of Edward III. He was followed in 1377 by Sir Thomas Hungerford, previously regarded as the first Speaker. The office was at first highly political. Sir Peter launched an attack on the king's advisers, clashed with *John of Gaunt, and as soon as Parliament was dissolved, was put in prison: Hungerford, chosen by the next Parliament, was John of Gaunt's steward. Clearly the royal government had decided it must command the office. The struggle for control continued for centuries and even after the crown's influence had been reduced, the election of Speaker often remained a trial of party strength. The post of Speaker was therefore one of considerable risk, physical and political, and the protestations of reluctance to serve, now a pleasant ritual, were once genuine. Though there is no evidence that de la Mare acted as a chairman of debate, such a function was a logical development from the role of spokesman, especially as legislation increased in volume. John Hooker's *Order and Usage how to Keep a Parliament* (1571) notes the Speaker's duty to 'direct and guide that House in good order', but he had probably been doing that since the 15th cent.

In the fierce disputes between the king and Parliament in the early 17th cent., the Speakers were in an extremely difficult position. Speaker Finch reminded the Commons in 1629 that 'I am not less the king's servant for being yours':

nevertheless, he was held down in the chair when he tried to carry out the king's instructions to adjourn. But in 1642, with the wind blowing the other way, Speaker Lenthall defied Charles I demanding the arrest of the *five members, and declared, 'I have neither eyes to see, nor tongue to speak in this place, but as the House is pleased to direct me.' By the end of the century, the Speaker was relatively free from royal pressure, though elections continued to be made on a party basis. In 1841, however, *Peel urged the Conservative majority not to oppose the re-election of the Liberal Speaker on the grounds that it should not be a party matter. The first Labour Speaker, Dr Horace King, was elected in 1965.

In the last 100 years or so changes in parliamentary procedure have laid new duties on the Speaker. They began with devices to overcome Irish parliamentary obstruction in the 1880s. But governments are always short of time, with more legislation than the House can consider in a session. Hence the imperative to limit debate. The two most important devices involving the Speaker are the closure, and the selection of amendments (the kangaroo). The Speaker must see that the right of the majority (normally the government) to pass legislation is balanced by respect for the rights of the opposition and the other minorities. The closure is a motion 'that the question be now put'. With a government bill, this will be moved by a whip. The Speaker must decide whether or not to accept the motion: if carried, as is likely, debate ceases forthwith. The opposition may feel that the matter has not been adequately discussed and the Speaker has to balance their view against that of the government.

A bill may attract a lot of amendments and, indeed, one way of delaying the passage of a bill is to propose many changes. The Speaker has the power of selecting amendments for debate: those not called fall by the wayside. Moreover, the chair seeks to focus debate by grouping amendments according to subject-matter. The decision whether or not to call an amendment may have important political consequences: for instance, to call an amendment tabled by a rebel faction on the government side may expose the government to defeat, at the least to unfavourable publicity.

The impact of the Speaker is even greater when the House is dealing with private members' bills. Rejection of a closure motion is inconvenient for the government but further time for debate can be found (though at a cost). With a backbench bill, failure to enforce the closure in the second reading debate may be fatal: the private member is allowed no second chance.

The modern Speaker has to be an impartial chairman. The office needs tact, sensitivity, and skills of an unusual order. The growth of the modern party system has put strains on the traditional folkways of the House. The responsibility for calling members to speak (and even more for not calling) may become contentious; the use of unparliamentary language may have to be checked; members may need protection against unfair interruptions. The Speaker has to reconcile the almost inarticulate assumptions of parliamentary government with the needs of a mass democracy.

The Speaker has a ministerial scale salary, a pension, a suite in the palace of Westminster, and a peerage on retirement. In precedence, the Speaker comes after the royal family, archbishops, lord chancellor, prime minister, and lord president of the council. In the House of Lords, the lord chancellor acts as Speaker, but may speak and vote in debate. JAC; HB

Spectator. The most famous periodical of Anne's reign appeared daily between March 1711 and December 1712, and was briefly revived in 1714. It was reprinted regularly throughout the 18th cent. Professing to be 'above party', the *Spectator*'s essays on social, moral, literary, or philosophical themes, mostly written by *Addison and *Steele, subtly promoted Whig values, *Macaulay's portrait of a Tory being clearly influenced by the character of Sir Roger de Coverley. JAD

Speenhamland poor relief system. Growth of population and acute distress during the Revolutionary and Napoleonic wars placed great strain upon the poor law system. In 1795 the price of bread, the labourer's staple diet, reached record levels. On 6 May 1795 the Speenhamland justices, meeting at the Pelican Inn (Berks.), resolved to give outdoor relief to families on a sliding scale in proportion to the cost of a loaf. The system was widely adopted but increasingly criticized as ruinously expensive, an invitation to farmers to pay low wages leaving the poor rate to make up the difference, and an encouragement to farm labourers to breed without restraint in order to get extra assistance. The *Poor Law Amendment Act of 1834 accordingly moved against the system in favour of indoor relief in workhouses. JAC

Speke, John Hanning (1827–64). British soldier and explorer. Speke became famous as the result of two exploratory journeys in eastern Africa. In the course of the first, led by another Briton, Richard *Burton, which reached Lake Tanganyika in 1858, Speke conceived the idea that Lake Victoria was the source of the White Nile. Burton and others rejected the claim and Speke led another expedition (1860–3) which confirmed his earlier opinion, but because he was unable to circumnavigate Lake Victoria or to follow the Nile along the whole of its course to the sea, his claim was again challenged. Later explorers proved him to have been right. Speke died in a shooting accident. KI

Spence, Sir Basil Urwin (1907–76). Scottish architect who leapt to prominence with his prize-winning design for Coventry cathedral (1951; completed 1962) which brought together such artists as Geoffrey Clarke, Jacob Epstein, Elisabeth Frink, John Hutton, John Piper, Patrick Reyntiens, and Graham *Sutherland. Spence trained at Edinburgh College of Art, worked for *Lutyens on the Viceroy's House, New Delhi, in 1929–30, and practised in Edinburgh during the 1930s. Spence designed the Sea and Ships Pavilion at the Festival of Britain in 1951, and with partners undertook extensive university work at Cambridge, Edinburgh, Newcastle, Southampton, Sussex, and elsewhere. His other buildings include churches, housing, schools, and the chancery at the British embassy, Rome (1971). Spence was a gifted designer and draughtsman, with a powerful belief in the creative role of the architect, and his architecture was often picturesque—as at Mortonhall crematorium, Edinburgh (1967), set in a rolling landscape and calling to mind Gunnar Asplund's Woodland Crematorium, Stockholm. Like Lutyens before him, Spence was knighted and held the Order of Merit. PW

Spence, Thomas (1750–1814). Artisan radical reformer and bookseller from Newcastle whose 'Plan' (first announced in 1775 and subsequently elaborated in later publications) argued that all land should be publicly owned. Spence believed that all injustice, inequality, and exploitation stemmed from the private ownership of land. He therefore proposed that the land and all wealth from it should be held communally by the inhabitants of each parish. Local hostility and personal misfortune in 1787 caused him to move to London, and from 1792 he was an active member of the London *Corresponding Society. His numerous radical pamphlets and token coins attracted government attention, and he was arrested and imprisoned in 1792, 1794, 1798, and 1801. Spence originally hoped to effect his plan by education, and indeed advocated language reform. But after his prison experience, he conceded the probable need for physical force, though he was not implicated in the insurrectionary activities of some of his followers. JFCH

Spencer, Herbert (1820–1903). Philosopher. Spencer was the son of a Derbyshire schoolteacher of radical and dissenting views. In the 1840s he joined Sturge's Complete Suffrage Union and in 1848 became subeditor of *The Economist*. His *Social Statics*, published in 1851, allowed the state only the minimum of defence and police functions: the struggles of individuals would, Spencer argued, strengthen the nation in an evolutionary fashion. Despite considerable nervous affliction, he published *Education* in 1861, advocating a child-centred approach and emphasizing the importance of science. He next moved into sociology and had publishing success. But his main thesis—the need to limit the intervention of the state—was at variance with the spirit of the times. The miscellany of his thought gave him influence, but he was not a trained thinker or a wide reader, and his fame faded fast. His *Autobiography* appeared in 1904 and renewed anxiety about the state led to some revival of interest in the 1980s. JAC

Spencer, John Poyntz, 9th Earl (1835–1910). A prominent Whig/Liberal politician. He was lord-lieutenant of Ireland in 1868–74 and again in 1882–5, years when the Irish question was of central importance, as social and religious protest led to political nationalism. Spencer fully supported the Liberal Irish reforms of 1868–74, though not playing a great part in promoting them. In 1882–5 he played a more direct role, combining coercion with political concession. Spencer strongly supported *Irish Home Rule in 1885–6—the most prominent Whig aristocrat to do so enthusiastically. In 1892–5 he was 1st lord of the Admiralty, in 1894 promoting naval expansion against the wishes of Gladstone (even so, Gladstone thought Spencer should succeed him as prime minister). He led the Liberals in the Lords in 1902–5, but illness spoilt his chances of the premiership in 1905. His library (sold to cover losses from the agricultural depression) forms the basis of the John Rylands library (Manchester). Spencer was known as the Red Earl from the colour of his beard (not his politics); he was the great-great-grandfather of Diana, princess of Wales. HCGM

Spenser, Edmund (1552–99). Elizabethan poet, mythographer, and colonial administrator. Educated at Merchant Taylors' School and Cambridge, Spenser briefly belonged to the household of the earl of *Leicester, and his political affiliations remained those of the Sidney/Leicester circle. His pastoral, *The Shepheardes Calender*, effectively marks the beginning of the Elizabethan 'golden age' of poetry; his masterpiece, *The Faerie Queene* (Books 1–3, 1590)—a vast, consciously archaic chivalric allegory—is the finest example both of the 'cult of Elizabeth' and of the project for a 'reformation' in English poetics. He published the sonnet sequence *Amoretti* (culminating in 'Epithalamion') and *Colin Clouts Come Home Agayne* in 1595, and a year later *Fowre Hymnes* and *Prothalamion*. His last published work, *A View of the Present State of Ireland*, advocated harsh colonial measures. His estate at Kilcolman was, perhaps fittingly, destroyed during the *Tyrone uprising, and he fled to England in 1598 where he died a year later. GAM

Spion Kop, battle of, 1900. A battle of the second *Boer War (1899–1902), famous at the time for its slaughter. The battle arose from repeated British attempts to relieve the siege of *Ladysmith. The highest point of the Tugela Heights, Spion Kop ('Lookout Mountain'), is 1,470 feet high, and was defended by a Boer force of about 7,000 under Louis Botha. Lieutenant-General Sir Charles Warren ordered a night attack by 1,700 troops under Major-General E. R. P. Woodgate to capture the heights and dig in. As the fog lifted after dawn on 24 January the British found themselves in a position completely exposed to enemy fire. Amid much confusion some reinforcements were sent, until eventually 2,500 men held the position. After dark the British retreated, having lost about 250 dead including Woodgate, and 1,000 wounded. Boer casualties were about 300. SDB

Spithead naval mutiny, 1797. While this mutiny lasted a calendar month, 16 April to 14 May, its roots had a century's growth. The Channel fleet was immobilized, with men withholding further service until grievances over pay, provisions, and leave had been redressed. Their case was firmly yet reasonably put by 33 'delegates', and the mutiny might have been terminated as early as 23 April had the royal pardon, which reached Portsmouth that day, been accompanied by evidence that Parliament had also voted the appropriate financial supply. Not until 10 May could the seamen be satisfied on this score, but Earl *Howe's prestige and conciliatoriness, buttressed by a fresh pardon, was decisive in bringing what had in effect been a strike to an end. DDA

'splendid isolation'. For most of the 19th cent. Britain was diplomatically isolated, in the sense of having what *Palmerston called 'no eternal allies' to whom she owed favours, except in circumstances where her own interests were affected. The obverse of this, of course, was that no other country owed favours to her. That served tolerably well while she and her European neighbours followed different paths in the world; but growing colonial rivalry between them at the end of the century changed all that. This was the context of Canadian premier Sir Wilfrid Laurier's description of Britain's situation in February 1896 as one of 'splendid' isolation, arising, he claimed, 'from her superiority'. Others at that time were beginning to doubt this. Joseph *Chamberlain in particular feared for the future of the *British empire if it could not find an ally in Europe, and negotiated with Germany behind his prime minister's back. That came to nothing; but early in the new century Britain did abandon isolation, at least partially, through a treaty with *Japan (1902), *'ententes' with France (1904) and *Russia (1907), and then, of course, involvement in the First World War. BJP

sport, development of. Organized competitive sport with codified rules, governing bodies, league or knock-out competitions, and restrictions on space and time is above all a product of the Victorian era. The classic case of the remaking of a traditional collective test of strength and ingenuity into a recognizable modern sport is that of *football. In the form inherited by the early Victorians, football was usually a calendar custom, often associated with Shrove Tuesday or Easter, played between neighbouring villages or parts of towns, with no restrictions on number of players, few on duration of game, and custom rather than codified rules dictating what was permissible. Rules and constraints were imposed through the playing of football of various kinds at the public schools, from which it was disseminated as part of an evangelical culture of muscular Christianity in a drive to reform the urban working class. *Rugby and association football emerged from this background as most of the traditional football games were suppressed or atrophied, though a few survived, as at Ashbourne or Workington. But as football became a popular sport in its reformed guise it developed a momentum of its own, and dominant clubs evolved, especially at first in northern industrial towns, attracting paying spectators, crystallizing local loyalties and identities, and (paradoxically) leading managements increasingly drawn from local business rather than the churches into employing professionals drawn from elsewhere. In football, by the 1880s, they came especially from Scotland, and in rugby a little later from Wales. Association football came to terms with professionalism, while it was the rock on which rugby split, with the emergence of the Northern Union in 1895, allowing payment for absence from work, opening the way to the full professionalism of what became known as rugby league. The formation of the Football League in 1888 set the seal on the new world of association football as a spectator sport, with routine five-figure attendances, and football soon became a great British cultural export. Football had been reclaimed by the industrial working class in its revised form, without the trappings of muscular Christianity, and as a focus for the communal loyalties of the manufacturing towns, although a stratified system of lesser clubs and leagues was emerging by the turn of the century, with emphasis on participation as well as spectatorship. Restrictions on dividends ensured that even when football clubs were run as businesses their main role was to maximize enjoyment and interest rather than profits.

This remaking of sport took on different guises for different games. *Cricket had been codified earlier, though rule changes continued, and a distinctive Saturday-afternoon form emerged in the late 19th cent. to suit the needs of industrial populations, although Sheffield working men were capable of taking days off in mid-week to watch Yorkshire in the distinctive local industrial setting. Prize-fighting gave way to *boxing on a similar principle to the transformation of football, though on a one-to-one level and with a wider gulf between amateur and professional. New games were invented in mid-Victorian times, with *lawn tennis (originally sphairistike) and *croquet designed to facilitate the polite mingling of the sexes in expansive suburban garden settings, the milieu for Betjeman's Miss Joan Hunter Dunn. *Rowing and *athletics saw particularly bitter conflicts between amateur and professional ethics, exacerbated by the amateurs' fear of professionals' competitive advantages arising from their work, especially as watermen on the Thames. Cricket resolved the amateur/professional problem partly through the division of labour, with bowling the duty of professionals and batting the prerogative of amateurs, though the distinction was never complete. Certain kinds of blood sports were driven underground by early Victorian legislation against cruelty to animals, although *fox-hunting never went the way of *cock-fighting or bull-baiting, and the proletarian enjoyment of coarse *fishing survived and prospered alongside the artificially exclusive world of fly-fishing. This raises the question of what constitutes a sport, and activities such as *billiards or *darts posed problems for the Victorians in this regard, as, in a more intellectual dimension, did *chess. Problems of social context, and of the physical versus the cerebral, raised their heads here. The role of women in sport was also problematic, as ideas about proper ladylike behaviour and the proper form of the female body conflicted with developing cults of health and energy at the turn of the century. The morality of sport was also difficult in relation to gambling, especially but not exclusively in the context of *horse-racing, which became a commercialized spectator sport in the later 19th cent. while continuing to be regulated, at least nominally, by the aristocratic Jockey Club. So the development of sport was raising large issues at the turn of the century in forms which were to prove enduring as the commercialization of sport proceeded in the 20th cent., and as big business interests penetrated sport to an increasing extent. The tensions between the Olympic ideal, sport for its own sake, and participation in a spirit of fairness being the dominant motive on the one hand, and professionalism, spectatorship, and the acceptance of gambling on the other, have roots which can be traced back over a century or more to the formative years of sport as we know it. JKW

Spottiswood, John (1565–1639). Archbishop. Spottiswood was born in 1565, and, though originally a strict *presbyterian, his Erastianism led him to embrace James VI and I's policy of appointing bishops to oversee the Scottish church. He was appointed archbishop of Glasgow in 1603, and, after the General Assembly in 1610 effectively abolished presbytery by agreeing that ordination and discipline should be the prerogative of the bishops, he obtained episcopal consecration in England. In 1615 he was translated to St Andrews, which at that date included Edinburgh. Under Charles I, Spottiswood did his best to temper the king's zeal and the heavy-handedness of Archbishop *Laud, and was present in St Giles in 1637 when riot ensued over attempts to impose a new liturgy. He left Scotland in 1638, and died in 1639. JRG

Spurs, battle of the, 1513. In 1513 Henry VIII began his second campaign against France, in alliance with the emperor, and laid siege to the town of Thérouanne. On 16 August a French cavalry force, attempting to relieve the town, fled in disarray, leaving many prisoners. Thérouanne surrendered the following week. Magnified as the battle of the Spurs, the skirmish testified to the military prowess of the young king. JAC

squash rackets derived from rackets and originated at Harrow. An Association was formed in 1928 and by 1939 more than 200 clubs were affiliated. The International Federation was set up in 1967. The sport was given a considerable boost by the Royal Air Force, which built courts at almost all stations, and it became fashionable in the 1980s as fierce and competitive exercise for young business executives. JAC

squire is a term which has come down in the world. Originally it applied to a young man attendant on a knight, bearing his shield, and, by the late 14th cent., entitled to his own coat of arms. *Chaucer's Squire, a dapper young man, served his father. By Tudor times, the terminology was changing. William Harrison (1577) referred to 'esquire, which we commonly call squire'. In the 17th cent. it developed into a general term for the lord of the manor, well below the level of nobility, but far above yeomen. *Addison offered an idealized version in the *Spectator* (1711/12) in the form of Sir Roger de Coverley, worshipped by his servants and tenants: in the *Freeholder* (1715–16) he drew the antithesis in Squire Foxhunter, an ignorant boor, cursing the Hanoverians and complaining that there had been no good weather since the days of Charles II. *Fielding's Squire Western in *Tom Jones* (1749) offered support for *Macaulay's much-criticized portrait of the squirearchy as drunken clowns. The term 'esquire', like that of 'gentleman', was gradually applied to any man as a suffix, and its final degradation was as a 20th-cent. term of pert familiarity. See GENTRY. JAC

Sri Lanka or Ceylon was settled during the 6th cent. BC by peoples from the Indian subcontinent, who subsequently converted to Buddhism. Hindu Tamils conquered the island in the 11th cent. AD but were eventually driven back to a northern enclave. The powerful Kandyan kingdom arose in the central region and was first encountered by the Portuguese in 1505. They established a hold over the south-west coast until moved on by the Dutch in the 17th cent. The Dutch took over virtually the entire seaboard and developed a lucrative spice trade which became the envy of the British in India. In 1795 the *East India Company invaded but mismanaged their rule. When Ceylon was finally ratified in British possession at the treaty of Amiens (1802), it was made a crown colony. The British displaced the kings of Kandy in 1818 and developed Ceylon as a plantation economy. The emergence of an important Sinhala and Tamil middle class permitted advanced constitutional experiment. A legislative council was established as early as 1912 and a universal franchise adopted in 1931. Ceylon was granted independence within the Commonwealth in February 1948 and, in 1972, adopted a republican constitution under the ancient name of Sri Lanka. DAW

Stafford, John (d. 1452). Archbishop of Canterbury. The illegitimate son of Sir Humphrey Stafford of Southwick (Wilts.), Stafford was an Oxford doctor of civil law by 1413. Like John *Kemp, he entered Henry V's service after a short career in the court of Canterbury and was his last keeper of the privy seal. While treasurer of England (1422–6), he became bishop of Bath and Wells in 1424 and was advanced to the archbishopric in 1443. As a protégé of Cardinal *Beaufort, he was appointed chancellor in 1432. He held the office for eighteen years, latterly as one of the small coterie of councillors headed by the duke of Suffolk (William de la *Pole); he resigned when Suffolk was banished. It is likely that he was rarely seen in his Kentish diocese, where the rebels in 1450 called him 'the devil's shepherd'. RLS

Stafford, William Howard, 1st Viscount (1612–80). Howard was a younger son of the earl of *Arundel and was brought up as a catholic. After marrying the sister and heiress of the 5th Baron Stafford in 1637, he was created Baron Stafford in 1640 by Charles I, and almost immediately advanced to the viscountcy. But he did little to help the royalists during the Civil War, which he spent mainly in Holland in some poverty. In 1678 he was accused by Titus *Oates of complicity in the *Popish plot, kept in the Tower until 1680, tried in Westminster Hall, and executed. James II created his son earl of Stafford in 1688. *Evelyn, who attended Stafford's trial, commented that he was 'not a man beloved, especially of his own family', but added, sensibly, 'I can hardly think a person of his age and experience should engage men, whom he never saw before,' and his guilt seems very doubtful. JAC

Staffordshire is one of the counties most affected by the industrial revolution. The county town has never dominated the shire. In pre-Conquest days, it was overshadowed by Tamworth and Lichfield, in modern times by the Black Country towns and the Potteries.

The core of the county is the river Trent, rising north of Stoke, then flowing through Stone and Rugeley to leave the shire at Burton. The Dove, joining the Trent north of Burton, forms the boundary with Derbyshire. Stafford itself is on the river Sow, which joins the Trent south-east of the town. The border with Cheshire runs along the river Dane, a tributary of the Weaver, and the north-west border with Shropshire follows the Tern. The northern parts of the shire are hilly, running up to the Peak District. Cannock Chase, south-east of Stafford, was for centuries almost impassable, and the Staffordshire rivers were not navigable until the 18th cent. Even as late as the 19th cent., Arnold *Bennett could describe his county as 'lost in the midst of England'.

In Roman times, the region was part of the territory of the *Cornovii. *Watling Street crossed the southern part of the county, intersecting with the *Icknield Way near Lichfield. It subsequently became the heartland of the kingdom of *Mercia. Tamworth, on the river Tame, was the royal city of the Mercian kings and Lichfield the ecclesiastical capital, St *Chad establishing the bishopric there in 669. Stafford, first appearing as Staefford—the ford by the landing-place—may have been where St Bertelin founded a hermitage, though its position as county town was presumably because it was more central than the others. In the later 8th and 9th cents. the power of Mercia declined, first defeated by Wessex, then overrun in the 870s by the Danes. Since, by the treaty of *Wedmore of 878, the Danes took the lands east and north of Watling Street, most of Staffordshire was in their hands, though Danish settlement was less intense than in the shires to the east. Under *Edward the Elder, the Mercians counter-attacked. *Æthelfleda, the lady of the Mercians, recovered Tamworth and Stafford in 913 and fortified them: she died in 922 at Tamworth. The outlines of the shire were now appearing and it is mentioned in the *Anglo-Saxon Chronicle* for 1016 by name.

Throughout the Middle Ages, Staffordshire remained remote and inaccessible. Poor communications and the relative insignificance of the county town meant that many market towns achieved a genuinely independent existence—Leek, Stone, Walsall, Wolverhampton, Newcastle under Lyme, Rugely, and Uttoxeter. In the assessment for *ship money in 1635, Stafford paid only £20, Walsall £25, and Lichfield £100. Industry was vigorous, but mainly local. Celia Fiennes, on her tour by horseback in the 1690s, noted near Beaudesert 'the coal pits where they were digging, they drew up the coal in baskets with a little wheel, or windlass, like a well'. *Defoe in the 1720s was greatly impressed by the horse fairs at Penkridge, but a little disappointed in Stafford—'we thought to have found something more worth going so much out of the way'. *Dickens, in the next century, was even more disparaging, describing Stafford as 'dull and dead'.

The transformation of Staffordshire's economy came in the 18th cent., with the development of potting, brewing, engineering, and mining, all greatly assisted by the new canals. The outlines of the canal network were apparent in the 1770s, when *Brindley opened the Staffordshire and Worcester to link up with the Severn; the Trent and Mersey, through Burton, Rugely, Stone, and the Potteries, brought access to the north-west; the Birmingham canal to the midlands and south; the Caldon canal, opened in 1777, linked Etruria to Froghall, with a branch to Leek. The work of the canals in bringing the county into a national orbit was completed by the railways. The Grand Junction, opened in 1837, linked Warrington and Birmingham via Stafford; the Birmingham and Derby, via Tamworth and Burton, opened 1839; the Trent valley line, via Stone, opened in 1849. The effect upon the county was dramatic. The deposits of iron and coal in south Staffordshire began to be exploited on a national scale: Matthew *Boulton started his Soho works at Handsworth in 1762 and was joined in partnership by James *Watt. In the north of the county, Josiah *Wedgwood opened his Ivy House works at Burslem in 1759, setting up as a master potter, and ten years later built the great Etruria works. Burton on Trent, favoured by such good water that brewers for miles around carried it in carts, was exporting to the Baltic by the mid-18th cent.: William Worthington set up in business in 1744, William Bass in 1777. The first census of 1801 registered the changing situation. The population of Stafford with 3,900 was already surpassed by Stone, Lichfield, Leek, Wolverhampton, Newcastle, Rowley Regis, and West Bromwich above the 5,000 mark, Burslem 6,500, Walsall 10,000, and Stoke, a comparative newcomer, at 16,000. In the course of the 19th cent. the southern parts of the shire were swallowed up in Birmingham, and the six pottery towns came together, after difficult negotiations, in 1910 to form the unique federated borough of Stoke-on-Trent. By the local government reorganization of 1972, Staffordshire lost Walsall and Wolverhampton to the new West Midlands authority. The Banham commission on local government in 1994 recommended the establishment of Stoke-on-Trent as a unitary authority but the maintenance of the two-tier system for the rest of the county. JAC

stage-coaches were road vehicles offering public scheduled stage carriage of passengers. London had its hackneys by the mid-1620s, the first stage-coach—to St Albans—was recorded in 1637, and services developed on the radial routes to the capital 1650–1715. Small (four-seat) and expensive, they offered carriage at speed and cost two to three times that by stage wagon. By the late 1750s, the London-based network was largely complete, and services differentiated between 'flying' and 'old' or 'slow' coaches, and in the last quarter of the century suburban short stages developed. Regular services between leading provincial centres developed only from the 1770s, apart from *Bath, which had coaches from Exeter, Salisbury, and Oxford 'in the season' from the 1750s. The size and appointment of coaches grew in the late 18th cent., and John Palmer's Post Coach network from 1784 set a reference point of standards for schedules as journey times were reduced. Manchester was 80 hours from London in 1750, 27 in 1808, and around 20 in 1832; the inside coach fare was £2 5*s*. in 1760, £3 3*s*. 6*d*. in 1808, and £4 4*s*. in 1832, significantly cheaper in real terms, as increased speeds eliminated many overhead costs—meals, inn accommodation, and so on—compared with the 1760s; and the market for coaches grew as the industry more than doubled its productivity. Passenger mileages grew at least tenfold 1770–1840, and in the peak year, 1836, there were around 10 million passenger journeys.

The industry originated with services run co-operatively by owner-drivers, using inns as their infrastructure. Bookings were made through them, and in central London groups of streets came to specialize in services to specific areas, like later railway stations: Aldersgate and Smithfield effectively monopolized services to Yorkshire and Lincolnshire. Debts led to innkeeper control, largely complete by 1750, and thereafter concentration grew, with large firms predominant in the London trade by the 1820s. William Chaplin (1787–1859), an innkeeper's son, was employing 68 coaches, 1,800 horses, and 2,000 men in 1838, and was the 'Napoleon of coach proprietors', then shrewdly disinvesting to become chairman of the London and South-Western railway. Stage-coaches collapsed precipitously in the 1840s and 1850s, relegated to feeder and link services, and to serving peripheral areas beyond the advancing tide of the railway. JCh

stained glass, initially a Christian art-form but subjected to changing attitudes and technical developments, is part of Britain's artistic heritage. Although the cathedral at York was glazed in the 7th cent., the use of pieces of coloured glass held together by lead strips (derived from mosaic and enamelling) did not appear in England until the 12th cent., notably at Canterbury. As Romanesque church architecture, where windows weakened structure, yielded to Gothic's soaring delicacy, partnership between mason and glazier enabled greater illumination, with supporting tracery part of the design. Medieval stained glass was essentially didactic, though the clergy were not unaware of the spiritual impact of luminescence and ever-changing light: the Scriptures were expounded, saints glorified, Jesse trees recollected Christ's ancestry, and great rose windows imagined the Apocalypse or the Last Judgement. Workshops were highly organized, while glaziers, artists in their own right and influenced by French and then Flemish models, kept stocks of cartoons (working drawings) which could be adapted for different glazing structures and then passed down from father to son. With important regional centres at Oxford, Coventry, and York, English glaziers were most prolific in the 14th cent., when glass-painting made extensive use of yellow stain and windows abounded with details of donors. The great east window at York (1405–8) typifies the high quality of the period, but purity of art-form began to decline as cathedral-building yielded to college chapels (*King's, Cambridge) and parish churches (*Fairford), and Renaissance influences encouraged naturalism and realism. The Reformation reacted iconoclastically to all religious imagery, with the loss of much stained glass, though heraldic windows for private houses and some churches were still produced. Destruction was most rampant during the Civil War, when cathedrals were sacked and men like Dowsing and Culmer gloried in their work. Simultaneous widespread warfare in Europe created a dearth of coloured glass, hence the virtual demise of the art. The Gothic Revival of the later 19th cent. led to renewed interest in both technique and history—Winston, Chance (who recreated 'antique' glass), Burne-Jones, *Morris—before art nouveau designers such as Tiffany used it decoratively for lampshades and light fitments. The bulk of significant 20th-cent. work came after the Second World War, when the use of steel frames and reinforced concrete enabled huge walls of glass, experimentation in technique and colour, and a return to its incorporation as an integral element in architectural design. ASH

Stainmore, battle of, 954. The death at Stainmore of *Erik Bloodaxe, son of Harold Fairhair of Norway, brought to an end the Scandinavian kingdom of York, which reverted to Wessex. The place of the battle, on the old route from Scotch Corner to Penrith, suggests that Erik had already been expelled from the city and was intercepted while escaping to Viking allies in Scotland or Ireland. JAC

stallers were officials in the late Anglo-Saxon household. The name derives from Danish and they were introduced during the reign of *Cnut. There were seven of them in the reign of *Edward the Confessor and they were clearly men of property and standing. Their duties included provisioning the army, a responsibility later taken by the *constable. Ralph the Staller held one of the posts before the Conquest and remained in favour, being created earl of Norfolk. His son lost the title and position after a rebellion against the Conqueror. JAC

Stamford. Small town on the Lincolnshire border, at a strategic point where the Great North Road crosses the river Welland. It originated with a Danish fortress, flourished commercially, and in the 13th cent. hosted one of the great international trading fairs of England. It declined in the late Middle Ages, and the Cecils (who lived nearby at Burghley House) stifled its development until 1872 to retain control of the properties electing MPs: Lord Exeter forced the main railway line to go through Peterborough instead. The town remains a gem, full of 17th–19th-cent. stone houses, and 'we may perhaps be grateful to the Cecils for the feudal obstinacy which kept their town from growing . . . There are too many Peterboroughs, and not enough Stamfords, in modern England' (W. G. Hoskins). DMP

Stamford Bridge, battle of, 1066. A victory for King *Harold Godwineson over *Harold Hardrada, king of Norway, and his own brother *Tostig, both of whom were killed. Harold Hardrada was seeking to enforce a purported promise of succession to the English kingdom by King *Harthacnut. Little is known about the battle, which took place on the Derwent just east of York, save that it was fiercely fought and that Harold Godwineson surprised his opponents. Harold's success indirectly assisted William the Conqueror, who was given time to establish a secure base on the south coast before the battle of *Hastings. DB

Stamp Act, 1765. The Stamp Act, introduced by George *Grenville, was the most important single piece of parliamentary legislation affecting British–American relations. It imposed duties on goods and services (legal documents, appointments to public offices, ship's papers, etc.) in the British colonies in order to raise money for military expenses in America. Protests against Parliament's right to tax the colonies, widespread discussions of political liberty, crowd violence, and trade boycotts followed. In Britain, petitions from British merchants and manufacturers led to its repeal by the *Rockingham Whigs, ostensibly for commercial reasons in

1766. This was accompanied by the *Declaratory Act's simultaneous enactment. RCS

Standard, battle of the, 1138. The border between Scotland and England was far from settled in the 12th cent. and David I of Scotland was eager to acquire Northumbria and Cumbria. The civil war in England between Stephen and *Matilda gave him an opportunity to intervene and a period of border campaigning ended in August with a Scottish foray into north Yorkshire. It was met by a local force under *Thurstan, archbishop of York, and Raoul, bishop of Durham, on the 22nd at Cowton Moor, south of Darlington. The English fought under the banners of St *Cuthbert, St Peter of York, St John of Beverley, and St *Wilfrid of Ripon, which accounted for the name 'battle of the Standard'. Though the saints were successful and the Scots defeated, the encounter was not decisive. David retained possession of the northern counties and was residing at Carlisle when he died in 1153. JAC

Stanford, Charles Villiers (1852–1924). Irish composer, teacher, conductor, and writer on music. Educated at Cambridge, where he was organist of Trinity College and conductor of the University Musical Society, Stanford studied composition at Berlin and Leipzig and met Meyerbeer, Offenbach, and Brahms, who was a profound influence. A fluent and prolific composer in almost every genre, Stanford was a leader of the late 19th-cent. 'English musical renaissance'; indeed, as professor at the *Royal College of Music from its inception in 1883 (he was also professor at Cambridge from 1887), he taught most of Britain's leading composers, including *Vaughan Williams, *Holst, Ireland, Bliss, and Howells. Stanford raised standards in British choral music and particularly in Anglican church music. The influence of Irish folk-song is reflected in his six Irish Rhapsodies, the opera *Shamus O'Brien* (1896), and the third 'Irish' Symphony (1887), although his Germanic style has earned the description 'like leaving and returning to Ireland for a holiday in Germany'. ECr

Stanhope, James Stanhope, 1st Earl (1673–1721). Soldier, diplomat, and politician. Stanhope came to prominence in the War of the Spanish Succession where he was largely responsible for the campaign of 1710, including the disaster at *Brihuega, where he was captured. He was a Whig MP 1702–13 and 1714–17, was created a viscount in 1717 and an earl in 1718. From the accession of George I, Stanhope was continuously in office as secretary of state for the southern department (1714–16), for the northern department (1716–17, 1718–21), and 1st lord of the Treasury and chancellor of the Exchequer (1717–18). Foreign policy was Stanhope's main interest, his aim being to safeguard the Hanoverian succession by ending Britain's isolation by building up a series of alliances ensuring collective security. He teamed up with the 3rd earl of *Sunderland (who was interested in domestic policy), and together they dominated the ministry until Stanhope's death (particularly during the Whig schism of 1717–20 when *Walpole and *Townshend left the government). Stanhope's diplomatic triumphs were the negotiation of the *Triple and *Quadruple Alliances in 1717 and 1718. He used the British navy in the Baltic and the Mediterranean to maintain the balance of power. At home he supported the Whig supremacy by trying to ensure the dominance of the existing ministry with the *Septennial Act (1716), the *Peerage Bill (1719), and the repeal of the *Occasional Comformity and *Schism Acts (1719). CJ

Stanley, Sir Henry Morton (1841–1904). The most effective, if ruthless, of the 19th-cent. explorers of Africa, Stanley was born in a Welsh workhouse but became a journalist in the USA. Sent to Africa by the *New York Herald*, in October 1871, he uttered the immortal words 'Dr Livingstone, I presume' on finding the explorer at Ujiji on Lake Tanganyika. In 1874–7 he led a well-financed expedition across the continent which solved nearly all the remaining puzzles of Africa's basic geography, including the course of the Zaïre (Congo) river. Engaged by King Leopold, he established the beginnings of the Congo Free State in 1879–84 and then, from 1886 to 1889, led what was a great imperialist as well as exploratory expedition through the forbidding Ituri Forest to link up Leopold's state with the Upper Nile region, thought to be held by Emin Pasha. The venture was an epic of determination on Stanley's part, but created controversy and scandal because of Stanley's methods and his high-handed attitude to his companions. RB

Stanley, Thomas, 1st earl of Derby (*c.*1435–1504). Thomas Stanley succeeded his father in 1459 as Baron Stanley and lord of the Isle of Man. He served as steward of the household to Edward IV and then to Richard III, who gave him the Garter. In December 1483 he was appointed constable of England for life. But his second wife, whom he married about 1482, was the widow of the earl of Richmond and mother of the future Henry VII. Before *Bosworth, Richard suspected Stanley's fidelity and took his son Lord Strange as hostage. Stanley took no part in the battle and his younger brother Sir William Stanley intervened against Richard at a critical stage. Stanley is said to have placed the crown of England on Henry's head. His reward was speedy. He was made steward of the duchy of Lancaster and created earl. His brother's execution for treason in 1495 does not appear to have shaken his position. JAC

stannaries (from the Latin *stannum*, tin). The region of tin-mining in Cornwall and Devon, which acquired special jurisdiction. Tin- and lead-miners, being isolated communities, had their own customs and conventions. King John's charter of 1201 empowered the lord warden of the stannaries to try all cases except land, life, or limb. The warden appointed stewards to conduct regular trials, with appeals to a vice-warden. The jurisdiction of the warden survived until 1873, that of the vice-warden until 1898. The stannaries also had parliaments for both Devon and Cornwall: each consisted of 24 representatives, nominated by the four stannary towns in each shire. The Cornish parliament met last in 1752. The jurisdiction of the stannary courts was a matter of considerable dispute, since outsiders tried to restrict it to the actions of miners against other miners, while their opponents argued for a wider interpretation. JAC

staple. A staple was a trading centre in England or occasionally abroad, where traders deposited certain important commodities, bought and sold there. Edward II is regarded as the 'father of the English Staple' since it was during his reign that the Ordinance of the Staple (1313) made the system compulsory. The aims of the system, of particular importance in the 14th and 15th cents., were to regulate commerce in important commodities, especially wool, wool cloth, leather, and tin, and, by confining trade to a few named staple towns, to facilitate the collection of tolls or customs duties, and to bring trade under the control of royal officials who could ensure the maintenance of quality. The courts of the staple decided issues within the statutes. Because of England's importance as a trading nation, the staple system was also significant politically as an instrument of diplomacy. MM

Star Chamber. The origins of the Court of Star Chamber have been disputed, but it undoubtedly arose as an offshoot of the king's *council. The origins of its name have also been debated but it probably derived from the fact that the king's council sat as a judicial tribunal in the 'camera stellata', a chamber with a starred ceiling, built in 1347 at Westminster. The court did not owe its existence to a statute of 1487 (described as the statute *pro camera stellata*) though this statute was regarded by some later commentators as its origin. The court was at first little more than an aspect of the council, but it became prominent especially under the Tudors as a court which would control 'over-mighty subjects' and prevent abuses of the courts and the justice system, as well as threats to public order. It also provided civil remedies to petitioners seeking redress which was unavailable at *common law. However its main role was the enforcement of statutes and the prevention of public disorder, including riot, libel, and sedition. It was at first popular, but under the Stuarts became hated because of its increasingly draconian rulings on libel and sedition and its savage punishments. Having become a byword for tyranny, it was abolished by the *Long Parliament in 1640. MM

statutes. See PARLIAMENT, ACTS OF.

steam-engines are machines employing steam pressure and condensation to generate motion. Thomas *Savery's device (1698) pumped water by partial vacuum, without moving parts, and while engines on his principles were still in use in the 1790s, *Newcomen's atmospheric cylinder/piston engine erected near Dudley in 1712 established the fundamental principles of steam power. James *Watt's separate condenser of 1769 (and reciprocation from 1782) became a source of much-improved technical efficiency once *Wilkinson's improved cylinder boring became available (1774), and expressed itself in economy of coal use: by the 1790s Watt engines consumed 70 per cent of the fuel of a comparable *Smeaton atmospheric device. Higher capital costs meant that coal prices determined the adoption of Watt technology, and industry located onto the cheapest available coal, still providing half its steam-power in 1800 with atmospheric engines.

Mine drainage was its primary application, where coals were cheap and many engines ran on unsaleable slack, with brewing and milling, water supply, and textiles following, the last before the 1820s often employing stationary steam-power through water-wheels for the even torque needed by early machinery. Wider applications from the 1790s owed more to *Trevithick's high-pressure non-condensing and direct acting engines, which powered the first successful marine applications with Symington's *Charlotte Dundas* (1802—though experimentally proven by Jouffroy at Lyons in 1781), and his validation of the steam carriage (1801) and locomotive (1804). Steam was proven at sea by the voyage of Dodd's *Thames* from Glasgow to London (1815) and entered general coastal service during the 1820s; and on railways by the Rainhill trials of 1829.

Steam-power in cotton more than doubled 1835–56, and was followed by woollens and linen; the Cornish boiler diffused to produce high pressures at reduced fuel costs; and *Stephenson long-boiler and Kitson outside-frame locomotives established the basic pattern of railway motive power. From the Grand Junction's establishment of Crewe (1837), generalized from the early 1850s, British railways manufactured their own locomotives, with occasional purchases from specialists such as Beyer Peacock, who were otherwise confined to export markets, producing long-term losses in standardization and technical progress. The economical compound steam-engine was little used on British railways, where coal was cheap and labour relatively under-skilled, whereas it became a standard unit for factory power, and in its ultimate triple-expansion form (after 1880) the key to British shipping and shipbuilding dominance. From the early 1900s, *Parsons's marine steam turbine provided still greater speed and economy. Plentiful coal supplies, and the extensive coal/steam engineering industrial base, hereafter represented elements of inertia slowing Britain's adoption of electricity and internal combustion. JCh

Steelboys. One of the many Irish agrarian protest movements. It was largely provoked in the early 1770s by rack-renting on the estates of the marquis of Donegal and confined mainly to presbyterian Ulstermen. JAC

Steele, Sir Richard (1672–1729). Irish writer, soldier, and politician, sometimes misleadingly called the inventor of the periodical essay. Educated at Charterhouse and Merton College, Oxford, Steele entered the army, rising to the rank of captain, before turning to writing plays. Appointed gazetteer in 1707, a post he held until 1710, Steele embarked on a hugely successful journalistic career, assisted by *Addison in the **Tatler* and then the enormously popular **Spectator.* Elected MP for Stockbridge in 1713 and recruited by the Whigs to head their propaganda campaign against the *Harley administration, Steele responded with papers like the *Guardian* and the *Englishman*, as well as *The Crisis*, the bombastic pamphlet for which he was expelled the House in March 1714. Rewarded for his services on the Hanoverian succession, Steele was knighted and appointed supervisor of Drury Lane theatre. He continued to publish pamphlets and periodicals, and had a success with his sentimental comedy *The Conscious Lovers* (1722). JAD

Steelyard. The Steelyard, on the site of Cannon Street station (London), was for more than three centuries the headquarters of the *Hanseatic traders. They were charged with the repair and defence of Bishopsgate, but were deprived of their privileges by Elizabeth in 1598 in retaliation for restrictions placed upon English merchants in the Holy Roman empire. JAC

Steenkirk, battle of, 1692. William III, defending Brussels against the French, launched a surprise attack on 3 August on Marshal Luxembourg, who was separated from Boufflers. William made use of a discovered spy to gain a temporary advantage but Boufflers's troops joined in at the end of the day. The struggle was bloody but inconclusive and the Dutch commander Solms was much blamed for not bringing his men to help the British. William confided to Heinsius, 'you can easily understand how much it grieves me that I have not been able to do better.' JAC

Stephen (*c.*1096–1154), king of England (1135–54) and duke of Normandy (1135–44), was the third son of Stephen, count of Blois, and Adela, daughter of William the Conqueror. During his reign England was plunged into a civil war in which neither side possessed the resources or the ability to achieve outright victory. Stephen was brought up at the court of his uncle Henry I, receiving extensive estates from him, and becoming one of the wealthiest of the Anglo-Norman magnates. Although he was among the first to take the oath to accept Henry's daughter *Matilda as heir to the throne, he used the opportunity created by the confusion which followed Henry's death to seize the kingdom in December 1135. Subsequently accepted in Normandy, he seemed at first to have secured his rule over the entire Anglo-Norman realm and was able to obtain papal confirmation of his right. The reasons for the subsequent decline in his fortunes have been much discussed. He seems to have lacked the capacity to command the loyalty of the magnates, and he faced very large problems which, in strategic terms, were certain to be difficult to overcome. Symptomatic of the former were the sporadic revolts which took place early in his reign, the rivalries at court which led to the defection of Earl *Robert of Gloucester in May 1138 and the attempt to arrest Bishop *Roger of Salisbury and his brothers in 1139. Manifestations of the latter were the secure bases available to his rival Matilda provided in Anjou by her husband *Geoffrey and in western England by Robert of Gloucester, disturbances in Wales, and the fact that her supporters included the king of Scots, David I. Stephen always appears to have been needed in too many places at the same time; in 1137, for example, he had to abandon his only campaign in Normandy because he believed that he ought to be in northern England to confront the Scots. Stephen's cause declined once Matilda was established in England from 1139 and—dramatically—after his capture at the battle of *Lincoln in 1141. Although he was sustained in 1141–2 by his queen *Matilda and was released from prison in 1142 after the capture by his supporters of Robert of Gloucester, his position was already seriously compromised. His enemies controlled western and parts of northern England and Count Geoffrey completed the conquest of Normandy in 1144–5; subsequent campaigns in England in the 1140s, mostly in the Thames valley, only confirmed the stalemate. The existence of two established centres of power in England and Normandy created an impossible dilemma for the Anglo-Norman magnates, especially for those with land in both territories. Most sought increasingly to withdraw from the conflict and many tried to protect their local power by treaties with their neighbours; this has wrongly been described as 'the Anarchy', when it was in fact often the only way in which some kind of order could be kept. Stephen also fell foul of the papacy because of a disagreement over the succession to the archbishopric of York, which had serious consequences when the pope (Eugenius III) refused to accept Stephen's son *Eustace as his heir in 1152, and instead transferred his support to Matilda's son, the future Henry II, as the direct descendant of Henry I. Henry's cause was further strengthened when he succeeded to the duchy of Normandy in 1150–1. In 1153, with the great magnates refusing to fight a pitched battle which would have been decisive, Stephen accepted Henry as his heir by the treaty of *Winchester. Henry's succession followed peacefully after Stephen's death on 25 October 1154, a sign that all were weary of the civil war. Stephen deserves admiration for the way he sustained a difficult cause for so long; he besieged castles successfully and he established (not always reliable) supporters in earldoms to cement local power. But he lacked the ruthlessness required to prosecute his cause successfully; in particular, the way in which he allowed Matilda and Henry respectively to escape his grasp in 1139 and 1147 did his prospects no good at all. DB

Chibnall, M., *The Empress Matilda* (Oxford, 1991); Crouch, D. B., *The Beaumont Twins* (Cambridge, 1986); Davis, R. H. C., *King Stephen* (3rd edn. 1990); Stringer, K. J., *The Reign of Stephen: Kingship, Warfare and Government in Twelfth-Century England* (1993).

Stephen, James FitzJames (1829–94). Stephen was the son and grandson of distinguished lawyers and educated at Eton, which he disliked, and at Trinity College, Cambridge. He embarked on a legal career, but augmented his income with articles in the *Saturday Review*, the *Cornhill Magazine*, and the *Pall Mall Gazette*. After 2½ years in India on the council, which he described as a second university education, he was appointed a judge in 1879. His baronetcy came in 1891 when ill-health forced him to retire early. Large and formidable, he expressed his views trenchantly, was hostile to democracy, and mistrustful of sentiment: 'the French way of loving the human race is one of their many sins which it is most difficult to forgive.' He was a great admirer of *Hobbes, the apostle of strong government. Stephen's most important works were *Liberty, Equality, Fraternity* (1873), a critique of John Stuart *Mill's *On Liberty*, and a *History of the Criminal Law* (1883). His candour is frequently refreshing, sometimes brutal. His younger brother Leslie Stephen was the founding editor of the **Dictionary of National Biography* and father of Virginia *Woolf. JAC

Stephen Harding, St (d. 1134). Third abbot of Cîteaux. A native and monk of Sherborne (Dorset), Stephen joined the abbey of Molesme near Dijon. Fervently ascetic, he helped Abbot Robert tighten Benedictine life there, but, facing opposition, they left for Cîteaux, a barren, marshy place, to follow the rule more rigorously. Stephen, the driving force, became third abbot (1109), but Cistercian austerity caused numbers to decline until Bernard's arrival (1111) with 30 followers retrieved the situation; the order revived and spread, Stephen himself founding thirteen other houses and appointing Bernard abbot of Clairvaux. He wrote *Carta caritatis* (1119), which was Cistercianism's foundation document, and with its centralized structure, its annual visitation, and general chapters became a model for all future religious foundations. Stephen's administrative ability complementing Bernard's emotional appeal made Cistercianism spread rapidly—over 100 Cistercian houses were founded in his lifetime, the first in England at Waverley, Surrey (1128). WMM

Stephens, James (1825–1901). Fenian. Stephens, a protestant railway engineer from Kilkenny, was one of the few who joined Smith *O'Brien in the abortive 1848 rising. He escaped to France and returned to Ireland in 1856. He found little nationalist enthusiasm but resolved to organize an Irish republican cause. Such a movement should have a dictator, 'perfectly unshackled' in charge, and Stephens volunteered for the role. In 1858 he founded what later became the *Irish Republican Brotherhood, drawing on his experience with revolutionary groups in France. An excellent organizer, he was said to be 'vain, despotic and overbearing beyond any man I ever saw'. On a fund-raising trip to America 1858–9 he joined in founding the *Fenian Brotherhood and in 1863 launched the *Irish People*, a weekly newspaper. But while the Fenians were still drilling, the government struck and raided the *Irish People* offices. Stephens was later arrested but escaped and fled to America. The American Fenians then organized an abortive attack upon Canada, a rather devious way of liberating Ireland. When Stephens urged a further postponement of any Irish rising, he lost all credibility, and his successors in the leadership initiated the rising of 1867. Stephens was allowed to return to Ireland in 1885. JAC

Stephenson, George (1781–1848). Son of a colliery workman, without schooling, George Stephenson became one of the most famous of all engineers, more by hard work and intuition than any grasp of engineering theory. Beginning work at the age of 8, in early manhood he earned a reputation for managing the primitive *steam-engines employed in collieries. In 1815 he invented a safety lamp for use in coalmines, after risking his life repeatedly in earlier tests. He was responsible for the adoption of locomotives by the Stockton and Darlington railway and then the Liverpool and Manchester railway. His *Rocket* was triumphantly successful in the Rainhill trials of 1829. When he recommended the use of locomotives on these early railways, he knew that the available machines could not provide the necessary power, but he was confident that these technical problems would be overcome. This moral courage, and his innate ingenuity, paved the way for later railway contracts and aided Stephenson's rise to wealth and distinction. NMcC

Stephenson, Robert (1803–59). Only son of George *Stephenson, Robert was born when his father was still an obscure north-eastern colliery workman. At first, he was dependent on his father's success, acting as his assistant in railway and other projects, and managing the Forth Bank works in Newcastle, an important centre of early railway engineering. By mid-century, he had acquired an independent reputation as one of the world's most famous engineers, with many distinctions and honours conferred upon him. His achievements at home and abroad included many railways and bridges, including the High Level bridge at Newcastle (1849), the Royal Border bridge, Berwick (1850), the Menai Straits bridge (1850) and the Victoria bridge at Montreal (1859). He was Conservative MP for Whitby from 1847 until his death. A popular figure, a generous philanthropist, and a considerate employer, he was buried in Westminster abbey amidst widespread mourning. NMcC

Sterne, Laurence (1713–68). Novelist and humorist. Son of a low-ranking infantry officer but educated through a cousin's bounty at Jesus College, Cambridge, where he embraced *Locke's philosophy and contracted tuberculosis, Sterne was ordained and collated to a Yorkshire living (1738). Voracious reader, moderately successful rural parson though a persistent philanderer, his satire on local ecclesiastical courts jeopardized preferment but encouraged him to entrust the parish to a curate and concentrate on writing. *Tristram Shandy* (1759) prompted both applause and abuse for its sentimentality and salaciousness, though, freeing the novel from straightforward narrative, it has since been seen as begetter of 'stream-of-consciousness' writing. Sterne revelled in the literary esteem and social notoriety he found in London, but was forced to forsake England briefly for France for health reasons, this providing material for his *Sentimental Journey* (1767). His corpse was exhumed by London resurrectionists but escaped dissection for secret reburial, being finally interred at Coxwold (his last Yorkshire living) in 1969. ASH

Stevenson, Robert Louis (1850–94). Writer. A spirited but sickly child, Stevenson abandoned engineering studies at Edinburgh for law but, although admitted as advocate (1875), never practised: rejecting parental calvinism for liberal bohemianism, he was determined to write. Much of his life was spent journeying in search of health after tuberculosis developed, and this provided material for future publication; it was while in France that he met his future wife, the American Fanny Osbourne. His output covered essays, short stories, poetry (*A Child's Garden of Verses*), travelogues, and collaborations with his stepson Lloyd Osbourne, while delighting readers with Scottish romances (*Kidnapped*, *Catriona*) and story-telling (*Treasure Island*, *Dr Jekyll and Mr Hyde*). Financially independent after his father's death (1887), Stevenson took the whole family to the South Seas, settling eventually at Vailima (Samoa), where his health improved partially and he gained a reputation as 'Tusitala' ('Teller of Tales'). ASH

Stewart, Alexander. See BUCHAN, 1ST EARL OF.

Stewart, Dugald (1753–1828). Philosopher. Son of a distinguished mathematician, Stewart studied under Adam Ferguson, Thomas Reid, and Adam *Smith. He was professor of moral philosophy at Edinburgh 1785–1820. A noted lecturer and teacher, Stewart's classes drew huge audiences and shaped the intellectual world of a rising generation of young Whig politicians. His philosophy was a critical distillation of the metaphysical and moral philosophy of the *Scottish Enlightenment. His metaphysics were shaped by Reid's critique of *Hume's scepticism, his moral philosophy by a critique of Smith. He gave an influential series of classes on Smith's political economy, which played an important part in disseminating that text. The **Edinburgh Review*, founded by his pupils, was an indirect but important monument to his teaching. His critical lives of Adam Smith, Thomas Reid, and William *Robertson and a long critical dissertation on the progress of metaphysics since the Renaissance are notable early essays in the history of philosophy and have played a significant part in placing the philosophy of the Scottish Enlightenment in a historical perspective. NTP

Stewart, James. See ROSS, 1ST DUKE OF.

Stigand (*c.*1000–72), archbishop of Canterbury (1052–70), was a worldly prelate, whose extensive lands placed him among the wealthiest magnates in *Edward the Confessor's England. Promoted rapidly by the king, he held the bishoprics of Winchester and Canterbury in plurality after 1052, an arrangement for which there were precedents in England, but which was illegal in canon law. His appointment to Canterbury after the Norman *Robert of Jumièges had been forced into exile was also deemed uncanonical by the papacy. He was at first apparently accepted by William the Conqueror, even though he had crowned *Harold Godwineson. This was presumably a consequence of William's early policy of trying to work with the native English. But in 1070 a case for his removal was built up from his numerous irregularities and he was deposed by a papal legate. He died a prisoner in 1072. DB

Stilicho. Late Roman general. In AD 395 Honorius became ruler of the western empire, but effective power lay with the outstanding military and political personality of his time, 'enigmatic Stilicho, half-Roman and half-German'. Stilicho's career was marked by hostility towards the eastern empire and a reluctance to deal comprehensively with the Germanic tribes threatening the western empire, whose support he might need. His career impinged on Roman Britain: in 396–8 he ordered an expedition against the barbarians troubling Britain, restoring peace in 399; but in 401–2 he withdrew troops from Britain to defend Italy. Eventually he was accused of conspiring with the German Alaric to usurp imperial power, surrendered to Honorius, and was executed in 408. ES

stipendiary magistrates are paid magistrates who are professional lawyers. The normal mode of trial of minor criminal offences is by a bench of lay magistrates, but in the 18th cent. the problem of crime in London, exacerbated by the lack of a police force, led to the establishment in 1792 of paid magistrates for the metropolis. In 1813 a stipendiary magistrate was appointed for Manchester and later legislation provided that boroughs and urban areas could request the appointment of a stipendiary. In 1839 those appointed were to be barristers; since 1949 solicitors may also be appointed. MM

Stirling Bridge, battle of, 1297. Edward I's victory at *Dunbar in 1296 did not keep Scotland subdued for long. On 11 September 1297 a large English army, under John de *Warenne, earl of Surrey, and Hugh de Cressingham, was caught by William *Wallace crossing a narrow bridge over the Forth near Stirling. Cressingham was killed and Edward's conquest had to begin again. JAC

Stirling castle, which stands on a dolorite hill over 400 feet above sea level, occupies an important strategic position controlling the main ford of the river Forth; it is thus a link between the Highlands and the Lowlands of Scotland. The castle is of unknown age, but from the time of Alexander I (d. 1124) until the union of the Scottish and English crowns in 1603 it was an important royal centre, rivalling Edinburgh as Scotland's capital. Called the 'Key to Scotland', the castle changed hands many times during the Wars of *Scottish Independence. It fell to the English in 1296, was recovered in 1297, but fell again to Edward I in 1304. It was to relieve a siege on the castle that Edward II risked a battle at *Bannockburn, 2½ miles to the south in 1314. When Robert the Bruce was victorious he had the building dismantled, so fearful was he of the consequences of losing it. Edward *Balliol surrendered the castle to Edward III in 1334 but the Scots regained it in 1339. As a result of this turbulent history, the fortifications and palace buildings within the irregular enclosure are of the 15th cent. and later. LR

Stock Exchange. The London Stock Exchange was founded in 1802, providing a mechanism for the increasing volume and complexity of financial transactions which had developed in the 18th cent. Prosperous merchants, and institutions such as insurance companies, which had massive resources, supplied the investment to the government, ever short of funds, to individuals, characteristically for improvements to landed estates, and to business. The scale of formal investment increased massively in the second half of the 19th cent., with a marked orientation towards international operations which the city of London still retains. Provincial stock exchanges also flourished rather briefly in the Victorian period, often with strong local specializations, such as Oldham in cotton and Sheffield in steel. CHL

stocks. The growth of government spending from the late 17th cent. onwards, frequently for war, stimulated the search for ways to raise funds. The issue of government stock, effectively a form of IOU, dates from this time. In 1696 the Exchequer Bill was introduced, offering 3 pence per day interest on a subscription of £100. In 1749 a plan was introduced to consolidate all the different loans taken out by the government, reducing the rate of return to a standard 3 per cent p.a., while making the loans irredeemable, meaning that there was no obligation to pay off the capital. These consolidated loans were established in 1752 as '3 per cent consols'. While this investment was free of the risk of default it was exposed to changes in prices. While the nominal rate remained fixed, the fact that consols were actively traded amongst merchants, brokers, and speculators caused the value to vary. Consols sold above par yielded a lower rate of return than 3 per cent, while those sold below par yielded a higher rate. But they proved to be a secure and flexible monetary instrument, since they could be bought conveniently through any attorney. Consols also became a useful source of government income. CHL

Stoke, battle of, 1487. Lambert *Simnel, posing as Edward, earl of *Warwick, son of the duke of *Clarence and nephew to Edward IV, raised support in Ireland and was crowned in Dublin as Edward VI. He landed near Lancaster and was supported by the earl of *Lincoln. His forces met with those of Henry VII at Stoke, near Newark, on 16 June. After heavy fighting, with perhaps 20,000 men involved, Lincoln was killed and Simnel captured. With a humour or clemency not much apparent in the Wars of the *Roses, Simnel was given menial employment at court. JAC

Stoke-on-Trent was formed in 1910 as a federation of six Staffordshire pottery towns—Tunstall, Burslem, Hanley, Stoke, Fenton, and Longton. The development of the conurbation was largely 19th cent. and owed much to the canal network, begun with the Trent and Mersey in 1775, which greatly facilitated the transport of pottery. The growing importance of the area was recognized by the Reform Act of 1832 which grouped the towns into the parliamentary borough of Stoke. By 1851 the total population was some 137,000 and by 1901 in excess of 300,000. An experiment after 1910 with the new council meeting in the six towns in turn was soon abandoned in favour of permanent headquarters at Stoke. There was considerable boundary extension and Stoke became a city in 1925. In Stoke City and Port Vale the area has two of the oldest clubs in the Football League. The population in 1992 was just over 250,000. JAC

Stonehenge (Wilts.) is the best-known archaeological site in the British Isles. It is spectacular—over 70 worked standing stones set in an incomplete circle, an inner horseshoe shape and various outliers, with capping stones used as lintels to link the standing stones at a height of up to 22 feet above ground—but what survives is but the ruin of the final phase of a structure, including earthen banks, set in a complex of other ritual and burial monuments and field systems dating from *c.*4000 to *c.*1500 BC. By what means and why Stonehenge was built has fascinated antiquarians at least from John *Aubrey (1666); in 1740 William Stukeley firmly attributed the monument to the (Iron Age) druids—an anachronistic association which has persisted with modern 'druids' and New Age travellers visiting Stonehenge to observe the midsummer sunrise. The monument was orientated to mark sunrise at the midsummer solstice (and sunset at the midwinter solstice), but whether it has further astronomical significance is debatable. The stones of which it is constructed include 'bluestones' probably from Wales—memory of the transport of which may underlie *Geoffrey of Monmouth's story that the magician Merlin moved a stone circle from Ireland to Salisbury. CML

Stopes, Marie (1880–1958). Birth control pioneer. Methodical and brilliant as a palaeobotanist, with an international reputation in her twenties, but disarrayed in her emotional life, her radical vision of an ideal marriage and clarification of sexual conduct prompted deep changes in social attitudes. Encountering fierce hostility from the catholic church and much of the medical profession, many of whom were nearly as ignorant as the public, in a background of moral panic engendered by post-First World War venereal disease figures, she faced libel and lawsuits with courage. With her second husband, she opened Britain's first birth control clinic at Holloway (1921), and published a stream of successful sociological works, but indifferent poetry and plays. Passionate but arrogant and opinionated, with a startling indifference to others' feelings, hence isolated, her crusades attacking prejudice and prudery nevertheless encouraged social reform and the economic emancipation of women. ASH

Stormont is the grandiose building in a Belfast suburb which housed the Northern Irish Parliament 1932–72. Its absurdly lengthy drive possesses an imposing statue of a defiant Sir Edward *Carson. The word became a synonym for intransigent unionism. H. M. Pollock, minister of finance in the first Northern Irish government, said: 'It was the outward and visible proof of the permanence of our institutions.' Since 1972 and direct rule from Westminster, it has been little used: the castle alongside it houses British government officials. MAH

Stow, John (1525–1605). Self-taught antiquary and historian, famous for his *Survey of London* (1598), which he revised and extended in 1603. Stow, a third-generation Londoner, began his career in 1547 as a working tailor, but by 1560 was building up an important manuscript collection. Before his *Survey,* Stow produced the *Annales of England* (revised edition, 1592) as well as other antiquarian works. His *Survey of London* takes the form of a perambulation of London by ward. Based on both manuscript and oral evidence, its most evocative passages are those where Stow includes his own personal opinions and memories. He was sympathetic to the old religion and wrote at a time when London was growing rapidly. His *Survey,* therefore, contains many observations on the decline of community spirit, regret at the destruction of monuments during the Reformation, and laments about the building of suburban slums. JPB

Stowell, William Scott, 1st Baron (1745–1836). Stowell began his life as an academic after gaining a scholarship to Corpus Christi College, Oxford, in 1761. He went on to become fellow and tutor at University College, Oxford, in 1765. After gaining his MA (1767) and BCL (1772) he became Camden reader in ancient history 1773–85. However, Stowell always desired to enter the law. In 1780 he joined Middle Temple and became a barrister working in the Admiralty and ecclesiastical courts. He served as MP for Oxford University 1801–21 and in the main opposed reform, but it was his legal career that had lasting influence. He served as a judge in the High Court of Admiralty from 1798 until 1828, and on many maritime points his judgments are still the only law. His younger brother was Lord Chancellor *Eldon. RAS

Strafford, Thomas Wentworth, 1st earl of (1593–1641). Wentworth made his name as a champion of constitutional rule by opposing the *forced loan of 1626. However, in the 1628 Parliament he suggested the compromise which culminated in Charles I's acceptance of the *petition of right. This opened the way to a career in government, and in 1633 the king sent him to rule Ireland. Strafford did so in such a despotic manner that he aroused fear and hatred in England, and when Charles, after the disastrous *Bishops' wars, called Strafford to his side and made him an earl, he promised that he would not 'suffer in his person, honour, or fortune'. Although Strafford advised Charles to summon Parliament, he planned to intimidate it by charging its leaders with treason for abetting the king's Scottish enemies. However, *Pym struck first by impeaching Strafford for the greater treason of alienating the king from his subjects. At his trial, in March 1641, Strafford defended himself so ably that acquittal seemed likely. The Commons therefore changed tack, passing a bill of attainder, which simply declared Strafford's guilt and sentenced him to death. Despite the pressure from angry mobs baying for the blood of 'black Tom the tyrant', the king delayed his response until Strafford urged him to give his assent, 'for prevention of evils which may happen by your refusal'. A few days later, Strafford was executed on Tower Hill. Charles subsequently realized that his consent had been a blunder, morally and politically. RL

Stratford, John de (d. 1348). Archbishop of Canterbury and chancellor. Born in Stratford-upon-Avon and trained in law at Merton College, Oxford, he entered royal service. While at Avignon on papal business, he was appointed bishop of Winchester (1323) by the pope, much to Edward II's annoyance. Stratford later supported Edward II's deposition (1327) in Edward III's favour. As Edward III's principal counsellor and chancellor in the 1330s and archbishop of Canterbury from 1333, he negotiated with France and Scotland and accompanied him to Flanders at the outbreak of war. On Edward's return in 1340 he furiously, but unjustly, attacked Stratford for financial incompetence. Stratford stood his ground, insisting on appealing to Parliament, thus confirming the principle of peers being tried by peers in Parliament. Reconciliation followed in 1341 but in later years Stratford only advised on ecclesiastical matters. WMM

Stratford de Redcliffe, Stratford Canning, 1st Viscount (1786–1880). Diplomat. Son of a London merchant and cousin of George *Canning, Stratford Canning was sent to Eton and King's College, Cambridge, before entering the Foreign Office. He served in Denmark, Turkey, Switzerland, and the USA. He was in Constantinople at the time of the battle of *Navarino (1827) and again as ambassador 1841–58. He urged the Turks to resist Russian demands in the exchange which led to the *Crimean War. In 1852 he was made viscount and in 1869 was given the Garter. His title, which the *Complete Peerage* understandably calls 'a strange medley', commemorates the 15th-cent. Cannynges who were associated with St Mary Redcliffe, Bristol. Canning, with a handsome presence and majestic manner, was one of the grandest of old-style diplomats. Malmesbury wrote that his talents were undisputed but that he was so 'despotic and irritable' that they were only of use in certain situations. JAC

Stratford-upon-Avon. Birthplace of *Shakespeare. For many years after the death of Shakespeare in 1616, Stratford, originally where a Roman road crossed the river, remained a small Warwickshire market town and route centre. It was known for its fair in September and for its fine late 15th-cent. bridge. It suffered considerably from fires in 1594, 1595, and 1614. The event which put it on the map was *Garrick's Shakespeare Jubilee of 1769 which, though nearly washed away by rain, attracted great attention. Present places of pilgrimage include the birthplace in Henley Street, the grammar school, Anne Hathaway's cottage at Shottery, and Holy Trinity church, where Shakespeare is buried and commemorated in an unimaginative monument. New Place, which he purchased in 1597, was subsequently pulled down, and a museum has now been erected on the site. The first Memorial theatre, completed in 1879, was destroyed by fire in 1926 and replaced by the present building in 1932. JAC

Strathclyde was the name of an ancient British kingdom, centred on the Clyde valley, with its capital at the natural fort of Dumbarton, and absorbed into Scotland *c.*1018. The name was adopted in 1963 by one of Glasgow's universities, and from 1973 to 1996 was used for an administrative region. The 1973 local government reorganization of Scotland was an attempt to rationalize the previous system of cities, burghs, and rural areas, which reflected historical rather than contemporary population patterns, into regions big enough to exploit economies of scale in services such as education, police, water, roads, and transport; smaller districts became responsible for other local authority services. Strathclyde, which incorporated Glasgow and the counties of Bute, Dunbarton, Lanark, Renfrew, Ayr, most of Argyll, and the Kilsyth area of Stirlingshire, illustrates the problems of such reorganization: it contained 2.3 million people, nearly half Scotland's population, in a little under 20 per cent of the area of Scotland. The region was unpopular with people living in its more rural parts, who felt it was dominated by Glasgow and its surrounding industrial areas (guaranteeing a large Labour majority in the regional council), and with other regions, which felt overwhelmed by its size. Government awareness of this unpopularity and concern that the two-tier administration was inefficient, reinforced perhaps by the Conservatives eventually controlling none of the regions, led to the abolition of the 1973 structure and its replacement, from 1996, by all-purpose authorities—in Strathclyde's case, nineteen new councils, corresponding roughly to the previous districts. The new authorities for Glasgow and the surrounding area will have to wrestle with the same problems as their predecessors—persistent economic difficulties, arising from an industrial structure that has been obsolescent since the 1950s, which lead (especially in some of the urban municipal housing estates) to pockets of very high unemployment and hence to social problems, aggravated in some places by a sectarian religious divide. CML

Strathclyde, kingdom of. The kingdom of Strathclyde, at its greatest extent, stretched from Loch Lomond in the north to Cumbria in the south. Its kings were Brittonic/Welsh, and were variously described by contemporaries as kings of the (northern) Britons or kings of the Cumbrians, though they are most often referred to simply as kings of Dumbarton, the fort which tops the massive rock which projects from the north bank of the Firth of Clyde, 10 miles west of Glasgow. The first king who can be identified is Coroticus (Ceredig) to whose warband St *Patrick addressed a scathing letter sometime in the 5th cent. The last Brittonic king was probably Owain the Bald who died in 1018 fighting in the army of *Malcolm II of Scotland at the battle of *Carham (12 miles south-west of Berwick).

Strathclyde was remarkable for being the only Brittonic kingdom outside Wales to survive the Anglo-Saxon onslaught of the 6th and 7th cents. *Gododdin (centred on Edinburgh), *Rheged (somewhere in northern England and southern Scotland), and *Elmet (around Leeds) vanished: others whose names are unrecorded were overrun. It survived the aggression of Picts and Gaels as well as Angles, and scored some notable victories—such as the defeat and death of Domnall Brecc, king of Dalriada (Argyll) at Strathcarron (near Falkirk) in 642, or the defeat of the Picts—who had recently conquered Argyll—in 750 at Mugdock (6 miles north of Glasgow), or the defeat and death of *Cuilén king of Scots and his brother *Eochaid in Lothian in 971. For extended periods, however, they were clients of more powerful kings. They submitted to kings of Northumbria in the 7th cent. and again after an invasion by a combined force of Picts and Angles in 756, which led to Anglian colonization of Kyle (mid-Ayrshire). The kingdom fell increasingly under the power of kings of Scots after being weakened by the destruction of Dumbarton in 870 by Vikings and ravaged by *Edmund, king of the English, in 945. It is often alleged that *Duncan I was installed as king by his grandfather *Malcolm II, following Owain the Bald's death, but the evidence for this is open to question. Kings of Scots no doubt held sway over Strathclyde for most of the 11th cent.; the last semi-independent ruler was David, brother of Alexander I of Scotland, before he became David I in 1124.

By the 11th cent. Gaelic began to eclipse Welsh, though Welsh was still spoken in some areas in the mid-12th cent. This, plus Anglian settlements in the west and Norse colonization in Cumbria, gives the place-names of the region a striking cultural mix. Cultural diversity is also apparent in the remarkable collection of 10th- and 11th-cent. sculpture at Govan (in the west end of modern Glasgow), which displays Scottish, Scandinavian, and Anglian influence. Govan was the kingdom's most important religious site at that time. Glasgow may originally have been the leading church of the kingdom with St Kentigern (or Mungo) (d. *c.*603) as its first bishop. It had its status as the chief church of the region vindicated by David in the early 12th cent. Although the kingdom disappeared as a political entity, it had an afterlife (minus Cumbria but including Teviotdale in the east) as the diocese of *Glasgow. DEB

Stratton, battle of, 1643. Much of 1643 was devoted by king and Parliament to establishing local domination. In most areas, there were divided loyalties and towns to be made secure. Even in Cornwall and Devon, royalist strongholds, there was considerable support for Parliament. *Hopton suffered an embarrassing ambush at the hands of James Chudleigh on Sourton Down, near Okehampton, on 25 April, but on 16 May caught Lord Stamford and Chudleigh at Stratton in Cornwall and defeated them heavily, taking Chudleigh prisoner. JAC

strict settlement. See ENTAIL.

Stuart, Arabella (1575–1615). The niece of *Darnley, first cousin to James VI and I, and a possible successor to Elizabeth on the throne of England. She avoided implication in the *Bye and *Main plots in 1603 but her secret marriage in 1610 to William Seymour (*Somerset), who had royal blood through his grandmother Lady Catherine Grey, alarmed the king and she spent most of her remaining years in the Tower. JAC

Stuart, Charles Edward (1720–88), the 'Young Pretender'. Elder son of James Francis Edward *Stuart, the son and heir of the exiled James II and VII, Charles was the Jacobite prince of Wales. He was born in December 1720 in Rome to James and his teenage Polish wife Clementina Sobieska. Another son, Henry *Stuart, was born in 1725 to this unstable marriage. Charles was a robust and wilful child, who was nominally blooded for war by being present at the age of 13 for a few days at the siege of Gaeta.

Early in 1744 he left Italy for France carrying his father's commission as prince regent, having been summoned to accompany a proposed French invasion of England. It was cancelled. In July 1745 Charles sailed for Scotland to raise a rebellion in the Highlands, with the hope of stimulating French aid. Total self-confidence, plus a limited grasp of reality, and the outstanding generalship of Lord George *Murray, carried him through a conquest of Scotland and march to Derby which made him a hero. His period of hiding after his defeat at *Culloden endeared him to romantics as 'Bonnie Prince Charlie'. Yet he was an embarrassment to Louis XV (who was seeking peace) on his return to France, from which he had to be expelled. The rest of his life was a protracted anti-climax, full of failed relationships and alcoholism. He died in Rome in 1788. BPL

Stuart, Cardinal Henry Benedict (1725–1807). The younger son of James *Stuart, and latterly Jacobite cardinal-king, he was born in March 1725 in Rome and was his father's favourite son. He was kept ignorant about Franco-Jacobite intrigues in 1744, but did go to France to support his brother Charles in 1745. In 1747, in political despair, he accepted a cardinal's hat. Charles, who had not been informed, was embittered. Reconciliation came late.

After the death of Charles in 1788, Henry styled himself 'Henry IX'. It was an empty title. When the French revolutionaries invaded Italy, confiscating his property, George III pensioned him. He died in Frascati in 1807, and is buried in St Peter's, Rome, with his father and brother. The monument was paid for by the prince regent, later George IV. BPL

Stuart, house of. One of Europe's most resilient royal dynasties, the Stewart or Stuart family ruled Scotland in direct descent for over three centuries from 1371 to 1688, inheriting also the thrones of England and Ireland in 1603. The family was of Breton origin, holding the office of *dapifer* or steward to the archbishops of Dol in Brittany before settling in Scotland at the invitation of David I who gave Walter FitzAlan the honorific title of high or royal steward in 1158. The title was subsequently made heritable and the family was known by the surname Stewart until the mid-16th cent. when, under French influence, it was modified to Stuart. The family's place in the royal succession came through the marriage of Walter, 6th high steward, to Marjory, daughter of Robert I Bruce. In 1371, the death without issue of Robert I's only son, David II, led to the accession of Robert Stewart (1316–90), the sole heir of Walter and Marjory, as King Robert II. The royal dynasty he founded proved remarkably durable, surviving recurrent periods of minority rule in the 15th and 16th cents. (including the succession in 1542 of a female infant), and going on to preside over the multi-kingdom empire created in 1603 when the Stuart king of Scots, James VI, inherited also the Tudor thrones of England and Ireland. Having weathered assassination (James I), rebellion (James III), deposition (Mary), and execution (Charles I), the dynasty's luck finally ran out in 1688 when the 12th Stuart monarch, James VII and II, was ousted in the *Glorious Revolution. Though his successors could legitimately claim (increasingly diluted) royal Stuart blood, the direct descent and indefeasible hereditary right of the exiled 'pretenders' provided the ideological basis of the abortive Jacobite rebellions of the 18th cent. RAM

Stuart, James Francis Edward (1688–1766), the 'Old Pretender'. Son and heir of James VII of Scotland and II of England and Ireland by his second wife, *Mary of Modena. The oddity of the catholic James II as head of the Anglican church-state was acceptable to protestant opinion only because his heir was the protestant Mary, daughter of a first marriage and wed to William of Orange. The birth of Prince James in June 1688 precipitated the Glorious Revolution. He was taken to France at his father's command in December 1688.

The propaganda querying his parentage was false, but the decision by Louis XIV to recognize him as heir to the British thrones when his father died in 1701 helped precipitate the War of the *Spanish Succession. He participated in an abortive invasion of Scotland in 1708. In 1713 he was expelled from France to Lorraine. In late 1715 he joined the Scottish rising, fleeing from Montrose in the following spring. He was in Spain during the 1719 rising in the Highlands, returning to Italy to marry the Polish princess Clementina Sobieska, by whom he had two sons, *Charles and *Henry, and little happiness. He spent the last Jacobite rising, the '45, as a papal pensioner in Rome, happy to abdicate if Prince Charles succeeded. Latterly he had little to do except attend religious services. He died in January 1766. BPL

Stubbs, George (1724–1806). English anatomist and animal painter, especially of horses, Stubbs's work captures the English gentleman's enjoyment of rural life, at its peak in the prosperity of the mid-18th cent. Stubbs's paintings of racehorses, often with owner or groom, were particularly popular both in original form and as prints. Another recurring theme, of a lion attacking a horse, recalled an event Stubbs saw on a visit to north Africa. His anatomical skills ensured that the power and beauty of animals was captured without sentimentality. In 1766 Stubbs published *Anatomy of the Horse*, the result of ten years of dissection and drawing. At his death he was working on an anatomical study (now at Yale) comparing various species. Working with Josiah *Wedgwood, he produced enamel paintings on earthenware including one of Warren *Hastings, in the Memorial Hall in Calcutta. There are examples of Stubbs's work in the Royal Collection and principal galleries throughout Britain. JC

submission of the clergy, 1532. By the submission, which convocation passed on 15 May 1532, the English church surrendered its right to make provincial ecclesiastical laws independently of the king. It followed a campaign against the legal autonomy of the church, probably managed by Thomas *Cromwell. The clergy promised to issue no new canons without royal licence, and to submit existing canons to a royally appointed committee for revision. It was passed with only seven bishops present, of whom three gave full assent. Sir Thomas *More, a supporter of church immunities, surrendered the lord chancellorship the following day. Although it was a significant humiliation for the clergy, no major revision of church law followed. The submission was enacted as statute (25 Hen. VIII c. 19), later repealed under Mary I in 1554–5. EC

subsidies are transfer payments, usually made by government to individuals, groups, or institutions, to bring about a redistribution of welfare which could not be achieved through market forces. If a particular export industry is unable to maintain production and employment because international prices are too low, a subsidy on exports from the government might increase the firms' revenues sufficiently to keep them in operation. Governments have used subsidy payments to fulfil social objectives by subsidizing the cost of public sector housing through grant payments to local authorities which, in turn, have often subsidized the rents charged to benefit tenants on low incomes. The term 'subsidy' was also used, until the 18th cent., to describe grants of taxation. CHL

Succession, Acts of, 1534, 1536, 1543. Henry VIII used statutes to make the adjustments to the succession that his complicated matrimonial history necessitated. The first Act (25 Hen. VIII c. 22) declared Mary illegitimate as a consequence of his divorce from *Catherine of Aragon. The second (28 Hen. VIII c. 7) after *Anne Boleyn's execution declared both Mary and Elizabeth illegitimate and vested the succession in any future offspring of Henry's new wife, *Jane Seymour: in the absence of legitimate issue the king was authorized to decide the matter by letters patent or will. The third Act (35 Hen. VIII c. 1), while recognizing Edward's claim, declared that should he die without heirs, Mary and Elizabeth would succeed in turn. By his will, made in December 1546, Henry repeated these arrangements but added that the succession would then go to the Suffolk line, offspring of his younger sister *Mary. The Stuart line, descendants of his elder sister *Margaret, was ignored. These repeated changes, from a man anxious to establish a clear succession, could only store trouble for the future. Lady Jane *Grey's claim in 1553 was from the Suffolk line. Ironically, the winners, 56 years after Henry's death, were the Stuarts, whom he had tried to push aside because of his dislike of the Scots. JAC

Sudan. Former Anglo-Egyptian condominium. Britain became involved in the Sudan as a result of her occupation of *Egypt in 1882. Formerly an Egyptian dependency, the Sudan was conquered by Muslim revivalist forces in 1885. Fearing that French colonial expansion in the region might threaten her control of the Red Sea route to India, Britain agreed to assist Egypt in reconquering the Sudan, which was achieved at the battle of *Omdurman in 1898. Britain and Egypt then ruled the country as a condominium and Britain tried to expand the Sudan's limited economy by encouraging cotton-growing. Independence was granted in 1956. KI

Sudbury, Simon (d. 1381). Archbishop of Canterbury. An Oxford doctor of civil law by 1349, Sudbury was an auditor in the papal court at Avignon until he was promoted to the bishopric of London in 1362. He served Edward III in embassies to Flanders and was a member of his council. Appointed archbishop in 1375 he incurred odium for supporting *John of Gaunt. In 1380 he was appointed chancellor and asked Parliament to grant the third poll tax. During the *Peasants' Revolt, his reported hostility to the rebels caused them to hunt him down; he was captured in the Tower of London and beheaded. RLS

Suetonius Paullinus. Governor of Britain 58–61. A native of Umbria, he waged a successful mountain campaign in Mauretania in 42. This experience may have influenced his posting to Britain, where he spent most of his governorship campaigning in Wales. Eventually in 60 he penned up the last resistance and the last of the druids in the island of Anglesey. Batavian auxiliaries forced the Menai Straits, the Britons were slaughtered, and the sacred groves put to the axe. At the moment of triumph, news came of the *Boudiccan revolt in East Anglia. With his cavalry Suctonius reached London, but could not save it or Verulamium, before rejoining his advancing infantry in the midlands, where he destroyed the British force in battle. The new procurator, *Classicianus, fell out with him and a commission under the imperial freedman Polyclitus removed him on a pretext, though not in disgrace. ASEC

Suez canal and crisis. The 106-mile canal links the Mediterranean, at Port Said, to the Red Sea. It was built by the international Suez Canal Company, under the guidance of Ferdinand de Lesseps, and opened in November 1869. The British gained an interest in 1875 when *Disraeli purchased 40 per cent of the shares from the khedive for the government. It operated according to the Suez canal convention, signed at Constantinople in 1888, which promised free navigation. The canal was protected by British troops from 1883 until 1956. In July 1956 the Egyptian government, under Nasser, nationalized the canal despite the fact that the Canal Company's concession ran until 1968. Anglo-French military intervention in November was unsuccessful in regaining control of the canal, which was blocked for a time but reopened in April 1957. The canal was also closed during the 'Six Day War' of June 1967 and did not reopen until 1975. RAS

Suffolk is one of the largest and most beautiful of shires and its greater distance from London has saved it from some of the ravages inflicted on its southern neighbour *Essex. The 'south folk', from whom the county took its name, formed part of the kingdom of the *East Angles, which survived from the 6th cent. until overrun by the Danes in the later 9th cent. The county boundary to the south is the Stour, to the north the Little Ouse and the Waveney. The twin pivots of the county are Bury St Edmunds, described by *Leland as 'a city more neatly seated the sun never saw', and Ipswich, in *Camden's words 'the eye of the county'. The division between east and west is of long standing and in 1888, after a parliamentary debate and vote, the two sections were given separate county councils. They were brought together in the local government reorganization of 1972.

In Roman times, Suffolk was part of the territory of the *Iceni, and the *Icknield Way cuts across the county from Thetford to Newmarket. In AD 61 *Boudicca's rebellion slaughtered thousands of Romans and their allies and burned Colchester, Verulamium, and London. Burgh castle, defending the port of Caistor-by-Yarmouth, is one of the most impressive Roman remains in the country. By the 7th cent. the kingdom of East Anglia was of importance. The *Sutton Hoo ship-burial, near Woodbridge, dating from *c.*630, is almost certainly the grave of one of their kings, probably *Raedwald, who died *c.*625 and claimed, as *bretwalda, sovereignty over the other English kingdoms. A diocese was established at *Dunwich, *c.*630, later shared with North *Elmham.

By the 8th cent. East Anglia was experiencing difficulty in fending off Mercia and Wessex and dwindled into dependency status. The area suffered severely from Danish raids from 861 onwards. In 870 King *Edmund was martyred, allegedly transfixed with arrows, and his body taken eventually to Beodricsworthe, to be known in future as Bury St Edmunds. The region fell under Danish rule from 878, when the treaty of *Wedmore allotted it to *Guthrum, but was recovered by *Edward the Elder in the 920s. Dunwich lost its episcopal status to *Thetford, and then *Norwich.

The shire of Suffolk, now taking shape, was not an administrative unit, though treated separately in Domesday. There were two large liberties in west and east, the former belonging to the abbot of Bury, the latter to the prior of Ely. The rest was 'geldable' land, paying taxes directly to the king. Even this was further divided into an Ipswich district and Beccles in the north. The geldable area contained so few hundreds that, until the reign of Elizabeth, it shared a sheriff with Norfolk.

Throughout the Middle Ages, Suffolk was dominated by the two liberties and the many other religious houses. Strife between the abbot of Bury, one of the greatest of all foundations, and the townsfolk was fierce and sustained. In 1327 the town rioted and burned much of the abbey: in 1381, during the *Peasants' Revolt, the lord chief justice and the abbot were beheaded. At the *dissolution of the monasteries, the abbey was soon ransacked, though Camden wrote in the 1580s, 'the very carcass of its ancient greatness hath something of beauty'. The estates went mainly to the gentry and nobility, and a number of their towns were given parliamentary representation—Orford in 1512, Sudbury 1559, Aldeburgh and Eye in 1571, and Bury, belatedly, in 1614. In the 18th cent. the gentry began improving their estates, and Suffolk contains splendid examples of the work of William *Kent at Euston, 'Capability' *Brown at Ickworth and Heveningham, and *Repton at Glemham Hall and Henham Hall.

Suffolk's prosperity was built on sheep, corn, and fish. The cloth trade, in the later Middle Ages, produced the profits for the fine churches at *Long Melford, Framlingham, Lavenham, Eye, and Bury. In the absence of mineral resources or heavy industry, population grew slowly. Dunwich's decline, due to erosion, was evident by the 14th cent., but Ipswich remained a busy port and Lowestoft became a major fishing harbour, particularly after the advent of the railway in 1847. But in the villages there was a steady drift from the land in the later Victorian period: of 531 parishes in the 1901 census, more than 400 had lost population since 1851. Felixstowe developed as a seaside resort in the 19th cent. and after 1945 became a substantial container-port, dealing with Europe. JAC

Suffolk, Charles Brandon, 1st duke of (1484–1545). Brandon managed a spectacular career from modest beginnings. He was a son of Sir William Brandon, standard-bearer for Henry VII at *Bosworth, where he was killed. Brandon's rise began with the accession of Henry VIII in 1509: the king was seven years his junior. They were both fond of athletic pursuits and Brandon excelled in jousting. In 1515 he was given the wardship of Elizabeth, Lady Lisle, and created Viscount Lisle. The Garter followed. He fought in the campaign in France in 1513 and in February 1514 was made duke of Suffolk a few months after the death of the last de la Pole duke. His most extraordinary advance came in 1515 when, six weeks after the death of her husband Louis XII, he married *Mary, queen of France and sister of Henry VIII. Brandon bought himself out of the king's anger with gifts. After this, despite Mary's death in 1533, he continued in favour, serving as earl marshal 1524–33, lord president 1530–45, chief justice in Eyre south of Trent 1534–45, and lord steward 1540–5. He commanded against the *Pilgrimage of Grace in 1536 and campaigned in France in 1544. His two sons died of the sweating sickness in 1551, when the dukedom became extinct. JAC

suffrage. Since suffrage (the right to vote) can be the key to political power, it has been contentious since representative institutions came into being. The original county franchise seems to have included all freemen, whether freeholders or not. But an Act of Henry VI's reign in 1429 declared that 'great, outrageous and excessive numbers of people . . . of small substance and of no value' were voting at elections, and went on to limit the franchise to freeholders with land worth 40 shillings a year, free of all charges. This remained the franchise until 1832. But the effect of inflation, particularly in the Tudor period, was to weaken the qualification and increase the total electorate. The issue became lively after the Civil War. At the *Putney army debates, *Cromwell and *Ireton opposed Rainborough and the radicals who pressed for a great extension of the franchise: where would it end, demanded Cromwell, if men 'who have no interest but the interest of breathing' were given the vote? In fact the subsequent Commonwealth regime cut the franchise dramatically to £200 p.a. property, though the old franchise was restored in 1660. *Shaftesbury was still complaining in 1679 that 'men of mean and abject fortune' were voting.

In parliamentary boroughs the franchise had always varied but there were four main groups—corporation, freeman, burgage, and inhabitant householder. They ranged from Westminster, Bristol, and Coventry with thousands of voters, to Gatton, a *rotten borough with two voters, and Malmesbury, where the thirteen members of the corporation elected the two MPs. The Scottish representation was extremely narrow, before and after the Union of 1707. The burgh electorate totalled some 1,250, the counties about 2,500. In the whole country, there were fewer voters than in Suffolk.

In the 18th cent. arguments for extending the franchise were heard with increasing frequency without quite getting onto the political agenda. *Wilkes argued in 1776 that 'the meanest mechanic, the poorest peasant and day labourer' was entitled to a vote, but nobody supported him and Lord *North retorted that he was surely 'not serious'. From 1832 onwards, however, a number of measures, several of them claiming to be final, enlarged the suffrage to full democracy. By the *Great Reform Act the urban franchise was made uniform at the £10 householder level, and in the counties the £50 copyholder was brought in to join the freeholders. The Scottish electorate rose from some 5,000 to 65,000. Radicals were far from satisfied and within a few years manhood suffrage was one of the six points of the *charter. It was strenuously opposed, *Macaulay insisting in 1842 that universal suffrage was 'utterly incompatible with the very existence of civilization'. The second Reform Act of 1867 moved one step closer, giving the vote to borough householders, including many working men, and the 1884 Act, by extending the same franchise to the counties, brought the total electorate to well over 5 million. The introduction of *secret ballot in 1872 had freed voters from landlord or employer influence, though many continued to vote deferentially.

By the later 19th cent. the campaign to give the vote to women was well under way, though they had to wait until 1918, and then were given the vote only if they were over 30. The electorate was more than doubled and, at 22 million, was fast approaching that universal suffrage Macaulay had so much feared. Women under 30 gained the vote in 1929 and in 1969 the inclusion of persons between 18 and 21 brought in another 3 million new voters. The electorate in 1992 was estimated at nearly 44 million (England and Wales just over 38 million, Scotland just under 4 million, Northern Ireland just over 1 million) out of a population of 56 million. Of these, 32,800,000 or some 75 per cent cast their votes. The vote is not available to convicted felons, certified lunatics, or peers of the realm, but is granted to resident citizens of the Republic of Eire. JAC

suffragettes were feminists who adopted militant methods to campaign for the parliamentary vote for women. Though by far the most famous members of the women's movement before 1914, their contribution to winning the vote has been much diminished by modern scholarship.

The term 'suffragette' was coined by the *Daily Mail* to distinguish them from the suffragists who had been working for the vote since 1866. The movement originated with Mrs Emmeline *Pankhurst and her daughters Christabel and Sylvia, who founded the Women's Social and Political Union in 1903. They regarded militancy as justified in view of the failure to achieve the vote after 40 years of campaigning. In particular, the Pankhursts argued that women would have to force the government to introduce its own bill instead of relying upon backbench legislation. To this end they attempted to mobilize public opinion against the post-1905 Liberal government. Initially this involved interrupting the meetings of leading politicians, attempting to enter the lobby of the House of Commons, and intervening at by-elections at which electors were urged to vote against Liberal candidates. However, the growing violence used by the police and the hostility of the public towards the suffragettes led them to change tactics so as to minimize personal injuries. This involved window-breaking, setting fire to pillar boxes and buildings, destroying the turf at golf courses, ambushing cabinet ministers, and dramatic incidents like the slashing of a painting, the *Rokeby Venus*, by Mary Richardson in 1914.

As a result the authorities began to impose prison sentences on the suffragettes, who went on hunger strikes. In order to avoid the death of a suffragette in custody attempts were made at forcible feeding. However, this proved even more dangerous to health, and thus in 1913 the government resorted to special legislation, dubbed the *'Cat and Mouse Act', to allow the authorities to release hunger-strikers but rearrest them when their health had improved. In 1913 Emily Wilding Davison foiled the government's strategy when she threw herself under the king's horse on Derby Day and died of her injuries.

Up to 1908 militancy attracted much publicity and pushed women's suffrage higher up the political agenda. This led more women to join the non-militant organizations than hitherto. The Pankhursts also proved notably successful as fund-raisers. Using Sylvia's artistic talents they marketed a wide range of products bearing suffragette slogans and colours (purple, white, and green). Mrs Pankhurst also undertook American lecture tours to raise money in 1909, 1911, and 1912.

On the other hand, their campaign clearly set back the cause, albeit temporarily, by antagonizing many non-militant women and by alienating pro-suffrage members of Parliament. But the crucial weakness lay in the Pankhursts' hostility towards the labour movement and their failure to mobilize working-class men and women. This lack of a genuine mass movement explains why the government freely employed the police against them. By 1914 the Pankhursts' autocratic style had reduced the WSPU to a beleaguered group, loyal to the family, but losing impact outside it.

The outbreak of war in August 1914 rescued them from the impasse. They quickly accepted an amnesty whereby prisoners were released and militancy suspended. Mrs Pankhurst and Christabel effectively abandoned not only militancy but the women's cause itself. During the war they attempted, with some success, to build a new role, this time in alliance with the government, by speaking on recruiting platforms and touring the industrial districts to urge workers not to go on strike. In the process they moved further to the right. In spite of, or perhaps because of, the suspension of the Pankhursts' campaign, the vote was granted to 8.4 million women in June 1918, and at the 1918 election their efforts were rewarded when the coalition leaders agreed to give Christabel their support as a parliamentary candidate in Smethwick. She was, however, defeated by Labour, and the Women's Party created to promote her candidacy promptly folded. Thereafter Mrs Pankhurst spent much of her time lecturing in North America, Christabel gave up politics for religion, and Sylvia adopted several causes including the British *Communist Party and the defence of Abyssinia against Italian occupation in the 1930s. Most ex-militants left public life, though some, such as Lady Rhondda, pioneered new women's organizations including the Six Point Group and the Open Door Council. Militant methods, however, were not resumed. MDP

suicide. Whereas in ancient Greece and Rome (for example, Socrates and Seneca) and in Japan (seppuku or harakiri) suicide was sometimes considered honourable, the Judaeo-Christian tradition and Islam have rejected the taking of one's own life as self-murder. God alone gives life and takes it away. But martyrdom, dying for a religious cause, blurs the distinction. Early Christian martyrs were almost theatrically suicidal as they went to death; mass suicide of Jews at Masada (AD 74) and at York (1190) and of cultic followers in Guyana (1978) also makes distinction difficult. Augustine (428), later church councils, and Aquinas condemned suicide as sinful and secular powers made it a crime, despite John *Donne's moderating view. The custom of burying suicides in unconsecrated ground at crossroads, with stakes driven through their hearts to prevent their ghosts causing harm, ended in 1823 and property ceased to be confiscated (1870). Though no longer criminal in Britain (1961), suicide is still widely regarded as sinful. The issue is now ethically complicated by the advance of medical science, whereby the life of the elderly or terminally ill can be greatly extended to the emotional and economic detriment of themselves, relatives, and society. Meanwhile 'living wills' to prevent unnatural lengthening of life become more commonplace. WMM

Sullivan, Sir Arthur (1842–1900). Sullivan's musical pedigree was Mendelssohnian and the influence may be traced in much of his music, particularly *Iolanthe*. He was born in Lambeth Walk (London), son of a professional musician at one time bandmaster at Sandhurst. Blessed with a fine voice, Sullivan was a chorister at the Chapel Royal and was publishing by the time he was 13. In 1856 he won the Mendelssohn scholarship and entered the Royal Academy of Music. From 1858 to 1861 he studied at Leipzig. At the age of 21 his incidental music for *The Tempest* won great acclaim. In 1866 he produced his only symphony and was offered the professorship in composition at the academy. The following year his short comic opera *Box and Cox* received its first performance. The year 1870 saw the overture *Di Ballo*—stylish and elegant—and 1873 the oratorio *The Light of the World*. The great collaboration with *Gilbert got off to a faltering start in 1871 with *Thespis* but took fire in 1875 with *Trial by Jury*. *Pinafore* (1878), *The Pirates of Penzance* (1879), and *Mikado* (1885) followed in quick succession. The Savoy theatre, specially built by D'Oyly Carte for the operas, opened in 1881. Sullivan's serious work continued with *The Golden Legend* (1886) and *Ivanhoe* (1891). The last of the collaborations, *The Grand Duke*, was put on in 1896. He was knighted in 1883 at *Gladstone's suggestion. His popular pieces included 'Onward Christian Soldiers' (1871) and 'The Lost Chord' (1877), written on the death of his brother Frederick. Sullivan possessed a wealth of melody, brilliant orchestration, considerable poetry, and much humour. The serious work is good; the comic operas incomparable. JAC

sumptuary laws appear to have reflected a view of society as a pyramid of social groups which had to be held together by preventing too great a variation in overt affluence. Such laws were enacted in many countries between the 14th and 17th cents., and sought to prevent waste by extremely ostentatious display by the wealthy, and to keep the lower orders in their place. A statute of 1337 in England restricted the wearing of furs to those with an income of £100 p.a., while a later scale confined ermine to the richest and restricted the poor to the furs of humble creatures, such as the cat, coney, or fox. By the Tudor period, English laws applied only to clothing and were repealed at the end of the 16th cent. Such laws were used for other forms of social engineering, by Peter the Great for whom western dress was a means to modernize Russia, while the English tried to impose a dress code on the Irish as a civilizing stratagem. CHL

Sunday observance. See SABBATARIANISM.

Sunday schools. The English Sunday school movement is usually associated with Robert Raikes of Gloucester (1735–1811), the founder of the Sunday School Union. From 1782 Raikes established classes, often on Saturdays as well as Sundays, for children of the poor who were in employment for the rest of the week. Adults also received instruction. The curriculum was partly secular, consisting largely of reading, writing, and religious education. The movement saw its task as the inculcation of religion and the elimination of radical ideologies which had spread since the industrial revolution. A century after the movement began, over $5\frac{3}{4}$ million children in England were attending these schools. As economic conditions improved, restrictions on the use of child labour increased and with the introduction of day schools the role of the Sunday school became restricted to religious instruction taught on Sundays. PG

Sunderland, Charles Spencer, 3rd earl of (1674–1722). Whig politician. Son of the 2nd earl, he entered Parliament in 1695 and shone as a gifted Whig spokesman. His marriage in 1700 to a daughter of the *Marlboroughs enhanced his political connections, and it was to the duchess and Lord Treasurer *Godolphin that he owed his appointment as secretary of state (southern department) in 1706, becoming the first *Junto leader to attain office under Queen Anne. Impetuous and temperamental, his determination to see *Sacheverell impeached cost him the queen's favour in 1710. Much to his mortification he was given only token office at George I's accession, and intrigued against the effective leaders *Walpole and *Townshend until in 1717 he replaced the latter as secretary of state (northern). In 1718 he became 1st lord of the Treasury and shared leadership of the administration with *Stanhope. His scheme for reducing the national debt led to the *South Sea bubble in 1720, the fall-out from which forced him to surrender the premiership to Walpole in 1721. He nevertheless retained personal influence with the king, dying suddenly in the midst of the election in 1722. AAH

Sunderland, Robert Spencer, 2nd earl of (1641–1702). Clever, urbane, and supremely self-confident, Sunderland was undoubtedly the most durable politician of the late Stuart age. After an ambassadorial career, he was appointed in 1679 secretary of state but dismissed in 1681 for supporting *'Exclusion'. Through his influence with Charles II's mistress Louise de Kéroualle he was reappointed in 1683 and for the next six years was effectively chief minister. An expert in foreign affairs, he promoted royal pro-French policies, and in addition to his control over patronage master-minded James II's catholicizing campaign, becoming a catholic himself in 1688. Upon William's 'invasion', Sunderland insisted that James reverse his policy, but was dismissed. Briefly exiled in Holland, he returned in 1690, reconverted, and by 1693 had emerged as William III's political 'manager' behind the scenes, a role which he fulfilled without taking office until 1697 when he was made lord chamberlain. Parliamentary hostility forced his resignation shortly afterwards, but the king retained him in his counsels. AAH

Super anxietatibus, 1176. William the Lion, king of Scotland, captured at Alnwick in 1174, was obliged to make sweeping concessions to Henry II at the treaty of *Falaise, including homage for his kingdom. He also promised that the Church of Scotland would be subject to the Church of England. The archbishop of York claimed authority over the bishops of Whithorn and Glasgow. But by the bull *Super anxietatibus*, Pope Alexander III forbade the archbishop to exercise that authority and, in effect, freed the Scottish church from English control. The terms were repeated by the bull **Cum universi* in 1192. JAC

Supremacy, Act of, 1534 (26 Hen. VIII c. 1). This Act, passed in the sixth session of the Reformation Parliament in November–December 1534, defined the headship of the English church, which Henry VIII had progressively asserted over the previous two to three years. The Act claimed merely to 'confirm and corroborate' the pre-existing right of the king and his successors to be supreme head on earth of the Church of England. Already in the preamble to the Act in Restraint of *Appeals of 1533, the 'Supreme Head and King' had been defined as having 'whole and entire power' over clergy and laity alike. However, whereas earlier legislation had limited itself to specific fiscal and legal aspects of church authority, the Act of Supremacy conferred personally on the king all spiritual authority to reform abuses and correct doctrine. On 15 January 1535 Henry included the supreme headship in the royal style, and around then transferred its authority to a spiritual 'vicegerent', the layman Thomas *Cromwell. Such personal control over spiritual *issues*, as well as spiritual people, was unique to the Henrician supremacy; the title of supreme head was abolished by Mary I in 1554–5 (1 & 2 P. and M. c. 8), to be replaced by the more muted title of 'Supreme Governor' under Elizabeth I. EC

Surrey, once a kingdom, became, in the course of the 19th cent., largely a suburb and dormitory of London. Its main rivers, the Mole and the Wey, drain into the Thames, which forms the northern boundary. Across the middle of the county run the chalk downlands, from Farnham to Guildford along the Hog's Back, and east to Dorking and Reigate. The southern border with Sussex is the line of the Weald, for centuries densely forested and a great obstacle to travel. Separating Surrey from Hampshire to the west were the sandy and infertile soils around Bagshot, and as late as the 19th cent. much of the county remained uncultivated. The meaning of the name—Suth-rige—as the land or region of the south people prompts the suggestion that the area may have formed part, in the early Saxon period, of a larger kingdom with *Middlesex or *Essex. So small a kingdom was bound to have difficulty in resisting more powerful neighbours, particularly *Kent, *Mercia, and *Wessex. Ecclesiastically, it came at an early period under the authority of the bishopric of *Winchester, founded in 660.

The region suffered considerably from Danish attacks from the 9th cent. onwards. In 851 a Danish force was cut to pieces at Ockley, south of Dorking, but there were further depredations in the 870s and again in the 1010s. By the latter date, Surrey had become a recognized county unit. Kingston upon Thames, close to the Wessex–Mercian border, was a royal town, and a number of Wessex coronations and burials took place there.

But as early as the *Domesday survey in 1086 the future pattern of the county could be perceived. Much of the shire was still waste and relatively inaccessible. Only two towns were separately identified—Guildford, the county town, and Southwark, itself a suburb of London: the other towns were of only local significance. Surrey remained a predominantly agricultural county, producing mainly for the London market. *Camden, visiting towards the end of Elizabeth's reign, found the shire 'exceeding pleasant: the parks are everywhere stored with deer, and the rivers with fish'. But *Defoe, surveying west Surrey 150 years later, was less impressed: 'here is a vast tract of land, some of it within seventeen or eighteen miles of the capital city, which is not only poor, but even quite sterile, given up to barrenness, horrid and frightful to look on, not only good for little, but good for nothing—much of it is a sandy desert.' Guildford was busy, though the assizes were not held there; Woking 'is very little heard of in England', Leatherhead 'a little through-fare town'. But towards London it was different. There were large numbers of gentlemen's seats, Croydon was 'a great corn-market' for the capital, and Southwark had 'a prodigious number of inhabitants'.

In the first census of 1801, we can trace the effects of the capital on the county. The inner towns were still small—Kingston 4,400, Epsom 4,400, Farnham 4,300, Godalming 3,400, Dorking 3,000, and Guildford 2,600. But Lambeth had 28,000, Newington 10,000, and Southwark 66,000. By the 1840s the railways were pushing out into the shire. In 1851 Lambeth was 139,000, Southwark more than 100,000. By 1901 the suburbs had taken over—299,000 in Lambeth, 259,000 in Camberwell, 169,000 in Battersea, 134,000 in Croydon. New towns had arisen, scarcely heard of in 1801. Putney moved from 2,000 to 24,000, Wimbledon from 1,600 to 41,000, Wandsworth from 4,000 to 68,000.

In the 1990s the pivotal point of the county may be said to be at Merstham, where the M25 crosses the Gatwick to Victoria line, reminding us that, because of its geographical position, Surrey has historically been a county of people on the move. JAC

Surrey, Henry Howard, Lord (*c.*1517–47). Grandson of Thomas, duke of *Norfolk, the victor of *Flodden. In high favour at the court of Henry VIII, he was made KB, given the Garter and, at one time, considered as a possible husband for the Princess Mary. He served against the Scots in 1542, then against the French, and 1545–6 was governor of Boulogne. But in December 1546 he was accused of treason for quartering the arms of *Edward the Confessor and beheaded on Tower Hill on 19 January 1547. His father, also attainted, escaped execution when Henry died on 28 January. Surrey, though clearly proud and indiscreet, was victim of Henry's senile suspiciousness and the machinations of his rival the earl of Hertford (*Somerset). He was a poet of some note. JAC

Surrey, kingdom of. The name 'Surrey' means the southern region, and at some time must have been linked in men's minds with Middlesex to the north of the Thames. This could have been relatively late in the story of Anglo-Saxon settlement. There is no royal dynasty associated with Surrey, and the most impressive evidence for its early history is a charter of *c.*672–4 granting land for a minster at Chertsey to Eorcenwold, bishop of London, issued by Frithuwold, a subking for the Mercian ruler *Wulfhere. Indeed the early history of Surrey must be looked for in the existence of small groups practising transhumance into the weald after the pattern of similar groups which have been identified in Sussex and Kent. These smaller units may well have developed into larger regions centred on Kingston and Wallington in central and eastern Surrey and on Woking and perhaps Godalming to the west. The political and ecclesiastical fortunes of Surrey were naturally closely bound up with the fortunes of London. The powerful Mercian kings of the 8th cent. maintained effective control, but in 825, when *Egbert of Wessex defeated the Mercians at *Ellendun, the people of Kent and Surrey and the South Saxons submitted to him because, in the words of the *Anglo-Saxon Chronicle*, 'they had been wrongfully forced away from his kinsmen'. From that time forward Surrey was an integral part of the greater Wessex which became the basis for the united kingdom of England. HL

Susa, treaty of, 1629. In 1627 Charles I, already at war with Spain, began a conflict with Louis XIII of France. Attempts to relieve the Huguenot port of La Rochelle, besieged by Richelieu's troops, having failed, peace was made at Susa in Savoy in April 1629. Louis and Charles agreed not to interfere in the religious affairs of each other's kingdoms. JAC

suspending power. Though the monarch could not arbitrarily repeal a statute, he claimed, as executive, the right to suspend its operation. This was an intelligible safeguard at a time when parliaments were summoned infrequently. Controversy began when Charles II, who disapproved of the penal laws against religious dissidents, issued a *Declaration of Indulgence in 1672 to circumvent them. He was forced by the Commons to withdraw it. James II repeated the attempt in 1687 and indicted the *seven bishops for questioning the validity of his actions. The bishops were acquitted, Sir John Powell declaring, 'if this be once allowed, there will need no Parliament.' The same day, a message was dispatched to William of Orange, begging him to rescue the liberties of the subject. By the *Bill of Rights in 1689 the suspending power of the crown was abolished. See DISPENSING POWER. JAC

Sussex was for centuries a byword for inaccessibility, cut off by the north downs and the heavily wooded weald, and proverbial for muddy lanes. It was one of the larger of the shires—80 miles from Chichester harbour in the west to Rye in the east. Almost all the rivers drain south into the Channel—the Arun, Adur, Ouse, Cuckmere, and Rother. The south downs run across the county west–south-east, falling into the sea at Beachy Head.

In Roman times the local tribe was the *Regni, ruled over in Caesar's day by *Commius. At the time of the Roman conquest, the king was *Cogidubnus, who submitted and whose title was recognized. The Roman capital was *Chichester (Regnum) and a later fort was built at Pevensey (Anderida). The Saxon settlement in the area is curiously and perhaps deceptively precise. The *Anglo-Saxon Chronicle* relates that *Ælle and his three sons came to Britain in 477 (perhaps earlier?) and that one of the sons, Cissa, took Pevensey in 491 and slew all the Britons. Some support is given by the assumption that Chichester is derived from Cissacestre. By *Bede's time, the kingdom of the South Saxons—Sussex—was well established. Though its geographical isolation did not allow for easy expansion, neither did it permit easy conquest, and the line of Sussex kings continues until the later 8th cent., when the region fell under *Mercia and then *Wessex. The first bishopric for the area was established by *Wilfrid at Selsey *c.*681, but transferred by *Stigand to Chichester soon after the Norman Conquest.

The size of the area made it a manageable unit for the shire system which developed in the 10th cent., but there were several local characteristics. First, the county was, uniquely, divided into six *rapes—strips centred on Chichester, Arundel, Bramber, Lewes, Pevensey, and Hastings. The word is of Old English origin, though it has been suggested that they were Norman military areas. Secondly, the difficulties of east–west communication meant that Sussex fell naturally into sections. The rape of Hastings was probably the territory of the Haestingas, who formed a subkingdom. Later, the county divided into a western section, based on Chichester, and an eastern section, based on Lewes. When parliamentary representation developed in the later medieval period, the convention was to choose one MP from each section. In 1832, when the county was awarded four MPs, the convention was formalized and the divisions of East and West Sussex created.

The sea coast being difficult and the only large harbours at Chichester and Rye, the Sussex ports remained local. The connection with Normandy ensured a modest prosperity but the spectacular medieval development was in iron manufacture, eked out by smuggling. *Camden, writing in the 1580s, noted that Sussex was 'full of iron mines everywhere . . . a great deal of meadow-land is turned into ponds and pools, for the driving of mills by the flashes; which beating with hammers upon the iron, fill the neighbourhood round about, night and day, with their noise.' But in the late 17th cent. cheap Swedish iron, the exhaustion of the forests, and competition from Shropshire led to a decline, and by 1788 there were only two furnaces left.

Dr John Burton, a fastidious observer, drew an unflattering portrait of Sussex farmers in the mid-18th cent., deploring 'the inelegant roughness and dull hilarity of their conversation; being illiterate, they shun the lettered, being sots the sober. Their whole attention is given to get their cattle and everything else fat.' The transformation of Sussex from a remote rural county of farms and small market towns was the result of two developments—the growing taste for seaside holidays and the coming of the railways. Brighthelmstone was described by *Defoe in the 1720s as 'a poor fishing town, old built', fast eaten away by an 'unkind' sea. In the 1750s Richard Russell, a physician, drew attention to the value of sea-bathing and built some lodging-houses. The prince regent's visit in 1782 and his plans for the Pavilion put *Brighton on the fashionable map and thereafter its growth was prodigious. By 1801 it was already nearly twice the size of Chichester and by 1851 bigger, at 65,000, than all the other Sussex towns put together. The Sussex coast, only 50 miles from London, was one of the first regions to be opened up by the railways, the London to Brighton arriving in 1841 and throwing out branches east and west in the next few years. By 1901 Brighton was well over 100,000 and had acquired county borough status in 1888. It was now pursued by other local resorts. Hove, its neighbour, had a population of 100 in 1801 but 29,000 100 years later. By 1901, Eastbourne had 42,000, Hastings 52,000, and Worthing 20,000. Bognor left its run until the 20th cent., profiting from the convalescence of George V in 1929. The concentration of population along the coastal fringe has been mitigated by the development of Crawley, one of the first post-war new towns, with a population by 1992 of 88,000.

Among the great attractions of Sussex are the Pavilion, Arundel, Goodwood, Sheffield Park, Uppark, and Battle abbey. *Kipling lived at Bateman's at Burwash in East Sussex, Hilaire Belloc at Shipley, near Horsham. Debussy wrote his tone poem *La Mer* while staying at the Grand Hotel, Eastbourne, in 1905. JAC

Sussex, East. By a long-standing tradition, the large county of Sussex had its eastern and western parts, looking to Lewes and to Chichester. The county courts, quarter sessions, and usually the assizes were held alternately, and in 1832 the Reform Act recognized the situation by giving two representatives to each division. In 1888 separate county councils were established for East and West Sussex, and this arrangement was continued by the Local Government Act of 1972. In 1994 the Banham commission on local goverment proposed that Brighton and Hove be created a unitary authority. JAC

Sussex, kingdom of. Sussex was ruled by its own kings from the time of *Ælle (*c.*477), who is said by *Bede to have been the first overlord (*bretwalda) of the southern English, to the end of the 8th cent., but for most of that period the kings (sometimes referred to not under a royal title but as *duces* or *ealdormen) were subordinate to other rulers. In spite of its relatively small size and compact geographical location from the south coast to the weald, Sussex was a complex political unit. Its earliest charters show that it was divided among a number of kings at times with a marked division between East Sussex, probably centred at Lewes, and West Sussex with a centre somewhere in the Chichester area, though apparently not Chichester itself. Hastings and its immediate surroundings always preserved individual characteristics, closer to Kent and even as late as 771 referred to specifically as the land of the *gens Hastingorum*. Socially Sussex developed in some isolation. It was the last substantial kingdom to receive Christianity, owing its conversion to St *Wilfrid during his period of exile from Northumbria in the early 680s. Wilfrid was granted an extensive estate at Selsey by Æthelwalh, who was himself a Christian, and from 709 Selsey became the centre for a bishopric, ultimately transferred to Chichester in 1075. In the 8th cent. Sussex was tributary to the Mercian kings, but after 825 the West Saxon dynasty under *Egbert and his successors took control, treating it, together with Surrey and Kent, as a suitable subkingdom for West Saxon princes. *Alfred established an important burh at Chichester, and Sussex was easily absorbed into the shire system of later Anglo-Saxon England. HL

Sussex, Thomas Radcliffe, 3rd earl of (*c.*1525–83). Radcliffe was well connected. His mother was a daughter of the 2nd duke of *Norfolk: his grandfather had married the niece of Elizabeth, Edward IV's queen. He fought with distinction in the French campaign of 1544 and at *Pinkie in 1547. Though he signed the proclamation of Lady Jane *Grey in 1553, his father was one of the first to declare for Mary and was in command of her forces at Framlingham. Radcliffe's wobble does not seem to have done him harm. He was summoned to Parliament in his father's barony of Fitzwalter, made captain of the gentlemen pensioners, and entrusted by Mary with the suppression of *Wyatt's rising. He succeeded his father as earl in 1557 and was given the Garter. In 1556 he was sent by Mary to Ireland as lord keeper with instructions to promote the catholic cause. He was active against the O'Neills in Ulster and led a punitive expedition against their allies, the Scots of the Islands. Elizabeth reappointed him, making him lord-lieutenant, but his renewed campaign against the O'Neills made little progress. He resigned in 1565 and from 1568 to 1572 was lord president of the Council of the North, helping to put down the rising of the *northern earls in 1569. From 1572 until his death he was lord chamberlain. At court he was a rival to *Leicester, of whom he spoke scathingly. JAC

Sussex, West was given a separate county council in 1888, with its county headquarters at Chichester, and the arrangement was continued in 1972. The Banham commission in 1994 recommended no change in the two-tier system for West Sussex. See SUSSEX, EAST. JAC

Sutherland, Graham (1903–80). Painter. Sutherland studied art at Goldsmiths College, London, after abandoning a railway engineering apprenticeship. His early work, influenced by Samuel *Palmer, was in etching and engraving, before he moved into ceramics and painting. During the Second World War, as an official war artist, he produced powerful studies of air-raid devastation in London and Swansea. A number of important public commissions followed, including a *Crucifixion* for St Matthew's, Northampton (1944), and, one of his most celebrated works, the design for the tapestry *Christ in Glory* in the new Coventry cathedral in 1962. A portrait of Somerset Maugham (1949), now in the Tate Gallery, was the first of several strong representations of famous people. That of Winston *Churchill was commissioned by Parliament, but destroyed by the sitter's wife. Sutherland's first love remained landscape, especially in Wales, where he established a gallery at Picton castle. JC

Sutton Hoo. A site containing up to 20 Anglo-Saxon burial barrows (*c.* AD 400–700) on the east bank of the Deben estuary in south-east Suffolk, opposite Woodbridge. Since 1982 archaeologists have shown that the barrow area, almost 10 acres, was superimposed on an extensive burial field in use since the 2nd millennium BC, and possibly associated with a stock-rearing society. The region as a whole is rich in 'find spots' over 2½ millennia: Sutton Hoo is here centrally situated, and the barrows given a context as a 'compound'.

In 1938 three barrows were excavated, one of which had been a boat-burial. In pre-AD 800 Europe the only other group of comparable burials is at Vendel-Valsgärde in central Sweden. In 1939 the largest barrow, some 120 feet in length and over 12 feet high, was opened. The depth of its extraordinarily rich deposit, almost certainly the inhumation of a king, possibly *Raedwald who died about AD 625, had protected it from robbery. The deposit lay in the centre of a 90-foot-long rowing boat, 14 foot in the beam, the largest known from this era. The objects, of supreme local craftsmanship in gold, of lesser craftsmanship in eastern Mediterranean silver, and including a whetstone sceptre and a mysterious 'iron standard', immeasurably widened a hitherto vestigial knowledge of 'Dark Age' culture. While a fragmented helmet had been unusually wrought from one piece of iron, the shield boss and sword pommel can only be paralleled by Swedish finds. Though virtually all traces of a corpse had been dissolved by the acidic sand, the evaluation of the furnishings required the expertise of 96 investigators over 30 years. This revelation of the Germanic world of the 'Age of Migrations' stands comparison with the tomb of Tutankhamun. The finds are in the *British Museum. DDA

Swan, Sir Joseph Wilson (1828–1914). Born at Sunderland and educated in local schools, Swan was apprenticed to a local pharmacist. In his spare time he carried out electrical and other experiments. He attended lectures and read scientific books and journals at the Sunderland Athenaeum, before moving to Newcastle upon Tyne, where he became a partner in a pharmacy. A photographic business and a scientific instruments department were soon added. Swan invented an improved photographic printing technique, the 'Carbon Process' (1864) and the 'Bromide Paper' (1879), which is still in use. In December 1878 and February 1879 he demonstrated his first incandescent electric bulbs. To provide his lamp filaments, Swan invented the first synthetic fibre. Legal disputes between the Swan and Edison lighting interests were solved by creating a joint venture. Swan lived in the south of England from 1883; he received many honours, including fellowship of the Royal Society in 1894 and a knighthood in 1904. NMcC

Swansea. Town of south Wales located at the mouth of the river Tawe (Abertawe). The name, Scandinavian in origin, reflects post-Roman Viking activity, but there is no evidence of settlement until the site was developed as a castle borough by Henry de Beaumont, the first Norman lord of Gower. After 1717 it became the centre of the early Welsh metallurgical industry, mainly copper, lead, and silver. Coal and coke transformed the industry and a specialization developed in coated steel plate, tinplate, and galvanized sheet. Initially production was in small mills but now only one integrated plant remains. An associated chemical industry devastated the lower Swansea valley but it has been extensively reclaimed. The port role is reflected in an oil refinery. Swansea acquired city status in 1969 and is now an industrial and administrative centre for the western coalfield. Its population in 1991 was 181,906. Ten per cent spoke Welsh. HC

Swansea and Brecon, diocese of. In 1923, three years after the disestablishment of the Church in Wales, those parts of the ancient diocese of St Davids within the counties of Breconshire, Radnorshire, and western Glamorgan were formed into a new see of Swansea and Brecon, with the cathedral at the medieval priory church of St John in Brecon itself. The name of the see reflects the two focal points. The northern part of the diocese, the old archdeaconry of Brecon, is almost entirely rural, sparsely populated, and overwhelmingly dependent upon agriculture. By contrast the southern part, centred upon the city of Swansea, is almost entirely urban and industrial. Throughout the diocese's short history there has been pressure for the see to be in Swansea, rather than in a small town 40 miles away, but it remains a diocese with two centres. In recent years the elevation of the large parish church of St Mary in Swansea, rebuilt after bombing in 1941, to collegiate status has gone some way to giving the two ends of the diocese a degree of parity. There have been seven bishops of Swansea and Brecon since the formation of the see, but none have become archbishops of Wales whilst holding it, though two did subsequently on translation to Llandaff. JRG

Swaziland. Former British high commission territory. In the 19th cent. the Bantu kingdom of Swaziland was under intermittent threat from Zulus, from would-be Boer (Afrikaner) settlers, and from British administrators in *Natal. In 1906, along with *Botswana and *Lesotho it was placed under the jurisdiction of a British high commissioner. When the Union of South Africa was created in 1910 the three territories were excluded from its authority because of British qualms about the Union's racial policy, which subsequent events were to justify. Nevertheless, Swaziland relied heavily upon its economic contacts with South Africa, which were strengthened after the country became independent in 1968. KI

Sweden, relations with. Sweden became a great power in northern Europe in the 17th cent., a matter of importance to England on account of both Baltic naval stores and Swedish championship of the 'protestant' cause. Charles XII further enhanced Sweden's importance, and the British were soon torn between concern over Russian advances in the Baltic and suspicion of Charles's own ambitions. Under George I (with his Hanoverian interests) the British briefly became the enemy of both. In the end fears of Russian preponderance meant that Britain played a leading role in seeking peace between Sweden and her western enemies, an outcome assisted by the death of Charles XII in 1718. Sweden, however, was soon in decline, and Britain enjoyed only limited success in the bewilderingly complicated rivalries in the Baltic region in the 18th cent. Between 1812 and 1814 she played a leading role in the transfer of Norway from Denmark to Sweden, as a reward for the Swedes casting their lot against Napoleon. In 1814 the British put pressure on the Norwegians to accept the change, while trying to secure for them as much autonomy as possible. CJB

Swedenborgians were followers of Emanuel Swedenborg (1688–1772), a Swedish scientist and diplomat who taught that there are correspondences between the visible forms of nature and the invisible world of the spirit. In 1787 some of his followers started the New Jerusalem church. Their teaching that the end of creation could be achieved only through man had radical implications and they were particularly strong in Manchester where they were known as *Bible Christians under the leadership of William Cowherd, a Church of England curate, Joseph Brotherton, MP for Salford, and James Scholefield, supporter of Henry *Hunt and Feargus *O'Connor. ER

Sweyn Estrithsson (d. 1074), king of Denmark (1047–74). Overshadowed by the energy and glamour of his rival *Harold Hardrada, king of Norway, Sweyn nevertheless contributed mightily to the stabilization of the Danish monarchy and at various stages posed a significant threat to the rulers of England. The son of *Cnut's sister Estrith and Jarl Ulf (Earl *Godwine's brother-in-law), Sweyn was actively interested in English affairs in the 1040s when two of his brothers, Beorn and Osbern, were prominent among the Anglo-Danish nobility at the court of *Edward the Confessor. Concentration on Danish security after 1047 precluded serious prosecution of a claim to the English throne as Cnut's heir but Sweyn's existence as a possible heir to the childless Edward and his powerful Danish fleet made him a consistent element in the tangled northern politics of the age. After the death of Harold Hardrada at *Stamford Bridge in September 1066 and the subsequent Norman conquest of England, Sweyn came to the forefront of English politics. In 1069 he sent a huge fleet which sacked York, inflicting a rare defeat on the Normans. He intervened in person in the spring of 1070 in Humberside and off the East Anglian coast in support of *Hereward's resistance at Ely. William, however, came to terms, more or less buying him off, and Sweyn's death on 28 April 1074 signals a virtual end to any revival of Cnut's Anglo-Danish kingdom. HL

Sweyn Forkbeard (d. 1014), king of Denmark (*c.*985–1014), king of England (1013–14). For some 20 years before 1013 Sweyn Forkbeard was involved in sporadic heavy raiding against England, in 994 in the company of Olaf Tryggvason of Norway, later an arch-enemy. Attacks intensified after 1004, some said in revenge for the murder of his sister Gunnhild during the massacre of *St Brice's Day, 1002. His principal effort came, however, in 1013 when, accompanied by his son *Cnut, he invaded England through the Humber and the Trent, setting up his base at Gainsborough, where he was recognized as king by most of Anglo-Danish England, east of Watling Street. He then moved south where Oxford and Winchester surrendered immediately. Only London, incongruously defended in *Æthelred's interest by the Viking chieftain Thorkell the Tall, held out against him, and when London finally submitted towards the end of the year, Æthelred was forced to flee to Normandy. For five or six weeks Sweyn was thus in control of all his newly conquered kingdom of England, but on 3 February 1014 he died at Gainsborough. Cnut was too inexperienced at that stage to do more than withdraw to Denmark, leaving behind him a reputation for cruelty and treachery, and opening the way for Æthelred's return. HL

Sweyn Godwineson (d. 1052). The eldest son of Earl *Godwine, Sweyn was awarded an earl's title in 1043 but a wild streak in his nature led to personal disaster. In 1046 he seduced the abbess of Leominster, fled to Denmark, and on his forced return to England, apparently for some unspecified crime committed in Denmark, became responsible for the murder of his own cousin, Earl Beorn, at Bosham. This further crime was regarded as especially heinous. Beorn had been interceding with King *Edward on Sweyn's behalf. By special procedures more Scandinavian than English, Sweyn was adjudged 'nithing' in an assembly of the whole army, that is to say 'a man without honour'. He was outlawed and took refuge in Flanders. The influence of his father and the support of Bishop *Ealdred enabled him to return and he was appointed to an earldom which involved extensive jurisdiction in the western shires. His new powers did not last long, and he went into exile again in the autumn of 1051, this time with the rest of the Godwine family. He died on his way back from a penitential pilgrimage to Jerusalem, and so did not live to enjoy the rewards reaped by his brothers on their successful return to England in 1052. HL

Swift, Jonathan (1667–1745). Irish writer and clergyman, Swift's disturbing satiric vision and eccentricities have given rise to countless myths and legends about his life. Educated at Kilkenny School and Trinity College, Dublin, Swift became secretary to Sir William *Temple, taking holy orders in 1695. The witty and notorious *A Tale of a Tub* (1704), an exposé of abuses in religion and learning, established Swift's reputation, and in 1710 he was recruited as a ministerial propagandist, writing the *Examiner* (1710–11) and *The Conduct of the Allies* (1711), an influential pamphlet defending the Tory government's peace overtures to France. Rewarded for his services by the deanship of St Patrick's, Dublin, Swift became embroiled in Irish politics after 1714. His later writings in prose and verse, most notoriously the scathing *Modest Proposal* (1729) for eating beggars' babies to solve the country's economic problems, largely consist of outspoken denunciations of English and Irish politicians. Despite the enduring relevance of **Gulliver's Travels* (1726), Swift's reputation has suffered from the savagery and scatology of his satire, as well as his attacks on women. Myths have accumulated in particular around his relationships with Esther Johnson and Esther Vanhomrigh (the 'Stella' and 'Vanessa' of his poems), and his mental stability, principally on account of the debilitating bouts of vertigo and deafness, the result of Menière's syndrome, from which he suffered throughout his adult life. JAD

swimming was until recently confined to those living by lakes, rivers, or near the sea. The development of public baths and pools in the 19th cent. gave, for the first time, a chance for large numbers of people to learn to swim. After some early unsuccessful attempts, the Metropolitan Swimming Association was formed in 1869 and later became the Amateur Swimming Association. Like most of the sporting associations established in the later 19th cent. the ASA emphasized amateur status, trying to ensure that swimming remained free from corruption, whether from cash prizes or gambling. The feat of Captain Matthew Webb in swimming the English Channel from Dover to Calais in 1875 captured much attention for the sport. It was included in the Olympics in 1896 and an international regulatory body established in 1908. By the late 20th cent., swimming for leisure, along with competitive swimming, diving, water polo, synchronized, and long-distance swimming, was the most popular participant sport in Britain. JAC

Swing riots, 1830. Collective action by agricultural workers began in east Kent late in August 1830 with two attacks on the hated threshing-machines, which were believed to take winter work away from agricultural labourers. The disturbances continued until December and spread to much of southern and eastern England. The protesters combined demands for higher wages and tithe reductions with destruction of the threshing-machines. Barns and hay ricks were fired, and threatening letters—often signed by the mythical 'Captain Swing'—were sent in all directions. Hobsbawm and Rudé, in their classic study of the riots, considered them to be mainly a southern and East Anglian phenomenon, but subsequent research has revealed just how widespread Swing riots really were, with virtually every county south of the Scottish border involved. More than 1,400 separate incidents have been recorded. In the wake of the disturbances 19 people were executed, 481 transported, and more than 700 imprisoned. JVB

syndicalists. Disliking capitalism and fearing that the triumph of communism would merely introduce a different form of state oppression, syndicalists argued for the transfer of power to the trade unions, if necessary through a general strike. Their theorists included Proudhon and Sorel, they formed links with anarchist groups, and had considerable influence in France, Italy, and Spain. In Britain their main contribution was to the concept of *guild socialism. British trade unionists showed little interest in the theory and their creation of the Labour Party was a direct repudiation of syndicalist tactics: Ramsay *MacDonald wrote a short book in 1912 denouncing syndicalism as class warfare. There was some syndicalist involvement in the labour unrest before 1914 and the *General Strike of 1926 was certainly condemned by some as syndicalist, though few of the strikers had such grandiose ambitions. Though the slogan 'All power to the trade unions' does not seem to have much contemporary appeal, concern at the power of the state, capitalist or communist, remains a live issue. JAC

Synge, J. M. (1871–1909). Most gifted of the dramatists in the early days of the *Abbey theatre. After studying Irish in his native Dublin and music in Germany he gravitated towards Paris, but a meeting with *Yeats in 1896 helped persuade him of the literary possibilities of his own country and language. Visits to the Aran Islands encouraged the development of a poetic prose based on the patterns of native speech. In *Riders to the Sea* (1904) he invested the life of the islands with something of the dignity of Greek tragedy and *The Playboy of the Western World* (1907) better embodied the spirit of the new literature than the more academic efforts of Yeats and Lady *Gregory. Like *In the Shadow of the Glen* (1903) it angered bigoted nationalists, reluctant to see Ireland's dirty linen washed in public; the use of the word 'shift' was found particularly offensive. JNRS

synods. A synod is a meeting of clergy, or clergy and laity, convened to discuss and decide upon matters of doctrine, church policy, and discipline. The meeting of bishops and representatives of the churches in the early centuries, the ecumenical councils, formulated through decree agreed statements of orthodoxy and belief. Throughout its history, however, all branches of the Christian church have summoned more local councils, synods, and assemblies, to debate and to rule on matters of current concern. Today in the Church of England a general synod meets once or twice a year with the traditional agenda. However, from the 19th cent. there was an increasing recognition that synods of the church should include lay as well as clerical representation, and the General Synod as now constituted contains three 'houses', the bishops, representatives of the clergy, and of the laity, the latter two made up of those successful in an electoral process. When the Church in Wales was disestablished in 1920, the synod then set up, the Governing Body, was given such a constitution. The process of democratization has spread through all levels of church life, and is common in different forms to most denominations. The fundamental purpose of the synod, however, remains the same. JRG

Tacitus. Roman historian born *c.* AD 55. He is the principal surviving historian of Roman Britain, dealing with the first forty years of the province. Unfortunately the portion of the *Annals* dealing with the Claudian invasion has not survived. Other passages of the *Annals* tell us of the governorships of *Ostorius Scapula and Didius Gallus, and there are further snippets in the *Annals* and the *Histories*. In 77 he married the daughter of *Agricola, soon to be governor of Britain, and his biography of his father-in-law survives. After a geographical introduction, he builds up to Agricola by belittling previous governors. The exceptionally long governorship of Agricola is structured by his seven seasons of campaigns, ending with the victory at Mons Graupius. In civil affairs Agricola does what a virtuous governor should. Though a very useful source, the *Agricola* should not be taken at face value. ASEC

Taff Vale judgment, 1902. Over 1,000 employees of the Taff Vale railway went on strike in 1901, and Beasley, the general manager, sought an injunction against their union, the Amalgamated Society of Railway Servants; this was first granted and then dismissed on appeal. However, the company's appeal to the House of Lords was successful, the union was sued for damages, and in December 1902 the Taff Vale Railway Company was paid £23,000. With costs, the union paid a total of £42,000. A crippling blow to trade unionism, this judgment was one reason why unions supported the infant Labour Representation Committee. JB

Táin Bó Cuailnge is the central story of the 8th-cent. Ulster cycle of heroic tales. The earliest versions are recorded in the 12th-cent. Lebor na hUidre (Book of the Dun Cow), the 12th-cent. Book of Leinster, and the 14th-cent. Yellow Book of Lecan. Set in pre-Christian Ireland, the *Táin* is the tale of a cattle-raid and invasion of Ulster by King Ailill and Queen Medb of Connacht, initiated as a result of their desire to capture the Brown Bull of Cuailnge. Cúchulainn single-handedly defends Ulster until the war-band can come to his aid. When they arrive the Connacht forces are decimated and in the end the Brown Bull is found dead. SMD

Tait, Archibald (1811–82). Archbishop of Canterbury. A Scottish presbyterian by upbringing, Tait was educated at Glasgow University and Balliol College, Oxford. He was successively headmaster of *Rugby (1842), dean of Carlisle (1849), bishop of London (1856), and archbishop (1869). Ecclesiastically he had to cope with the advance of both liberalism and ritualism. Though a low churchman, he was no evangelical—'a big man, intelligent and able and rock-like and not in the least narrow'. Having protested against Newman's *Tract 90* (1841), he viewed the Anglican church not in *tractarian terms as the catholic body in England, but as the national church, whose hallmark was comprehension. To preserve this, despite his own inclinations, he courageously and consistently vetoed prosecutions for ritualism under the Public Worship Act (1874). A conscientious bishop, he impressed Londoners by preaching in the open air in working-class areas and visiting them during a cholera epidemic. WMM

Talavera, battle of, 1809. On 28 July Wellesley's British army of 20,000 men, co-operating with Cuesta's Spanish army of 34,000 men (who saw little action), were attacked by 46,000 French commanded by King Joseph Bonaparte and Marshal Jourdan. A night attack achieved surprise but was thrown back. Then the French mounted a series of assaults against the British centre, followed by a turning movement in the north. All were unsuccessful. Although Talavera was a clear British victory, Wellesley, who had been abandoned by Cuesta, retreated to Portugal. As a reward for his victory, Wellesley was created Viscount *Wellington. GDS

Talbot, William Henry Fox (1800–77). Pioneer of photography. A prosperous country gentleman from Lacock abbey (Wilts.), Talbot went to Harrow and Trinity College, Cambridge. An amateur scientist, in 1833 he began experiments to see if permanent images could be recorded on sensitized paper. In January 1839 his progress was reported to the Royal Institution and the Royal Society, explaining how 'natural objects may be made to delineate themselves without the aid of the artist's pencil'. His work was rivalled by Daguerre in France and other inventors. Daguerre's images were clearer, but Talbot's use of the negative made for easy reproduction. In 1867 he was awarded the gold medal at the Paris Exhibition. Talbot's book *The Pencil of Nature* appeared 1844–6, including 24 photographs, one of them a famous view of the boulevards in Paris, and a magnificently evocative 'The Open Door'. JAC

Talents, Ministry of All the, 1806–7. A coalition government formed in February 1806, following *Pitt's death. Supposedly embracing 'All the Talents', it was composed of the followers of Lord *Grenville and Charles *Fox, bolstered by those of Lord Sidmouth (*Addington). Some former Pittites were, nevertheless, excluded, despite their acknowledged abilities. The resignation of the Talents in March 1807 was precipitated by George III, who rejected a limited measure of catholic relief and demanded that this question never again be raised. The king called on the excluded Pittites, under *Portland, to form a replacement ministry. This change-over did not, however, destroy the Talents' greatest achievement: the abolition of the slave trade in May 1807. DW

Taliesin (6th cent.). Bard. Taliesin and *Aneurin were two of the five great bards referred to by *Nennius in his *Historia Brittonum* (c.796). His surviving work records the deeds of Urien, king of the Britons, in *Rheged and his struggle against the Anglo-Saxons, just as Aneurin does for *Gododdin: 'And when I'm grown old, with death hard upon me, I'll not be happy save to praise Urien.' But establishing the corpus of Taliesin's work has proved difficult and only a few poems in the *Book of Taliesin* are accepted by most scholars. He may have come from Powys and settled in Rheged as a resident bard, but his very existence has been strenuously denied by some. JAC

tallage was the very valuable right of the king (and of other lords) to impose taxation on his demesne, including his boroughs. It could not be refused, though it could be negotiated, and the civic authorities were normally left to distribute the burden. Edward I's incessant warfare against Wales, Scotland, and France placed severe tax demands on his subjects. In the crisis of 1297, after he had left for France, he was urged to let tallage come under parliamentary control. But the document which was taken to be a statute, De Tallagio non concedendo, was only a preliminary demand and the Confirmatio cartarum, which the king eventually granted, was much less explicit and did not concede parliamentary control. Tallages continued to be demanded at intervals until 1340, when Edward III agreed that the consent of Parliament must be obtained. JAC

Tallis, Thomas (*c.*1505–85). English composer and organist, whose early career included short periods at Dover priory, St Mary-at-Hill in London, Waltham abbey in Essex, and Canterbury cathedral. By 1545 he was a gentleman of the Chapel Royal, where he remained, also acting as organist, until his death. Thus, unusually, Tallis served four monarchs, something apparent in his music. His early works for Henry VIII involve traditional catholic polyphony, whereas the six years of Anglican liturgy under Edward VI required new styles, reflecting Cranmer's desire for clear syllabic word-setting as in the simple four-part 'If ye love me'. The return to catholicism under Queen Mary saw some of Tallis's most elaborate music, probably including the massive six-part antiphon 'Gaude gloriosa Dei mater'. Finally, Elizabeth's catholic sympathies, despite her official protestant religion, allowed Tallis to publish his *Cantiones sacrae* jointly with Byrd (1575) and to write some of his finest Latin church music, including the two darkly emotional sets of *Lamentations* and his technical masterpiece, the 40-part motet 'Spem in alium'. A small amount of consort and keyboard music also survives. ECr

Tamworth manifesto, 1835. *Peel's manifesto to his constituents is often regarded as the foundation document of modern Conservatism. The Tory Party, badly beaten at the election of 1832, faced another general election and could hardly campaign on repealing the Great Reform Act, depriving Birmingham, Leeds, and Sheffield of their new representation, and restoring Gatton, Hindon, and Old Sarum. Peel, leading a minority government, explained that he now considered the Reform Act 'a final and irrevocable settlement, which no friend to peace would attempt to disturb' and that his general policy would be 'the firm maintenance of established rights, the correction of proved abuses and the redress of real grievances'. This left open who was to decide what was proof, what the word 'real' signified, and what would happen if the reform of abuses threatened established rights. Peel conceded that his statement was 'necessarily vague' but added detailed comments on certain contemporary issues. The manifesto has been seen as the foundation for a policy of prudent adjustment or as a recipe for continual surrender. *Disraeli in *Coningsby* (1844) took the latter view: 'the awkward question naturally arose, what will you conserve? The prerogatives of the crown, provided they are not exercised; the independence of the House of Lords, provided it is not asserted—everything, in short, that is established, as long as it is a phrase, and not a fact.' But when Disraeli took over from Peel as leader of the Conservative Party and faced a similar dilemma over the *Corn Laws, the party's pledges were conveniently forgotten. JAC

Tanzania. Formerly Tanganyika and *Zanzibar. Previously a German dependency, Tanganyika became a British mandated territory after the First World War. Having few natural resources, it proved unattractive to white settlers who were, in any case, unwelcome to British administrators because of the country's mandatory status. This, together with the absence of any dominant ethnic group with aspirations to hegemony, meant that the country developed peacefully, if unspectacularly. Its progress towards independence in 1961 was equally without serious incident. The following year Tanganyika became a republic with Julius Nyerere as president, and in 1964 joined with Zanzibar to become Tanzania. KI

Tara, hill of (Co. Meath). A sacred site for at least two millennia, going back as far as the Neolithic period, the hilltop shows evidence of many structures. The Neolithic 'Mound of the Hostages' was erected *c.*2000 BC; during the Iron Age, a hill-fort was constructed on the summit, taking advantage of the natural view of the plain. It later became a central site for the five provinces to hold assembly and conduct markets and fairs. In Irish mythology Tara is the royal seat of kings, and many rites and rituals associated with kingship were enacted there. SMD

Taranto, battle of, 1940. On 11 November 1940, 21 Swordfish aircraft from HMS *Illustrious* launched a torpedo attack at night on the Italian fleet at anchor off Taranto. Two aircraft were lost but heavy damage was done and the remaining Italian vessels sought more remote harbours. This Fleet Air Arm victory was particularly welcome at a bad time during the Second World War and was followed up in March 1941 by the naval success off Cape *Matapan.

JAC

tariff reform. See PROTECTIONISM.

Tasmania (formerly Van Dieman's Land), a 26,282-square-mile island 150 miles south of Victoria, and member state of the federal Commonwealth of Australia, has a population (1995) of 473,000. Hobart (population 194,000), established 1803, is the largest city and state capital. Its Aboriginal inhabitants, none of whose descendants now survive as full-blooded Aborigines, numbered *c.*4,000 at the coming of the British. The island's original inhabitants probably came across Bass Strait during a period of low sea level.

Discovered by Dutch navigator Abel Tasman in 1642 and named Van Dieman's Land it became infamous, following British occupation in 1803, for its ill-treatment of convicts (especially at Hell's Gate and Port Arthur) and the extermination of its Aboriginal population. Its name was changed to Tasmania in 1856 to help rid the island of its evil reputation. Until the 1860s Tasmania was Australia's major wooden shipbuilding centre and an important exporter of food to the mainland. The island lost population and was adversely affected by the discovery of gold in Victoria in 1851.

The island's agricultural settlements and typically small farms are concentrated in its northern and south-eastern lowland areas leaving the mainly rugged, mountainous, and high-rainfall forested western two-thirds largely uninhabited. The latter was for a time after 1880 important for the mining of tin, gold, lead, silver, and copper (Queenstown, Zeehan, and Mount Lyell). Today the island's mountainous centre and west's main economic resources are tourism and the production and export of hydroelectricity to lowland centres of metal-refining and paper and pulp and cement manufacture. Tasmania's natural beauty has encouraged a strong environmental movement. The island is politically notable for its adoption of the Hare-Clark system of proportional representation.

MJW

Tate Gallery. During the 19th cent. British art was poorly represented in the national collections. The 1840s and 1850s saw a number of important bequests to the nation, including that of sculptor Sir Francis *Chantrey, who left his fortune for the purchase of 'Works of Fine Art . . . [by] artists resident in Great Britain' and the enormous Turner bequest, which the National Gallery was unable to house adequately. In 1890 the sugar magnate Henry Tate gave 60 modern English paintings to the National Gallery provided that a gallery was made available. The offer was twice withdrawn as arguments delayed the provision of a suitable site and funding for a new gallery. Eventually the government offered the prison site at Millbank, London, and the Tate Gallery opened in 1897.

Wealthy benefactors have continued to aid expansion; in 1987 the Turner bequest was finally housed as the artist intended, in the extension funded by the Clore Foundation. The Tate is the showcase of British art and sculpture as well as modern foreign art. Mainly housed at Millbank, with outstations in Liverpool and St Ives, plans are made and National Lottery funds awarded for the conversion of the disused Battersea power station on the Thames to house 20th-cent. art.

JC

Tatler. A periodical edited by Richard *Steele under the pseudonym 'Isaac Bickerstaff', it appeared three times a week between April 1709 and January 1711. *Addison was an important collaborator. Mixing news, political opinion, and social comment, the *Tatler* gradually assumed the format to be made familiar by the *Spectator* of a single essay on a social, moral, literary, or philosophical theme.

JAD

Tawney, R. H. (1880–1962). Tawney made a significant impact in four interrelated roles, as Christian *socialist, social philosopher, educationalist, and economic historian. In 1908 he became the first tutorial class teacher in an agreement between the *Workers' Educational Association and Oxford University. The classes he took became renowned for their excellence. A member of the WEA executive for the next 42 years, Tawney wrote voluminously and incisively on educational matters, including contributions to several government reports such as the Hadow Report. As a socialist, he wrote *Secondary Education for All* (1922), which informed Labour policy for a generation. Other achievements included a role on the Sankey Commission (1919) and a part in writing *Labour and the Nation* in 1928. His two most influential books, *The Acquisitive Society* (1921) and *Equality* (1931), exercised a profound influence on socialists in Britain and abroad and anticipated the welfare state. Tawney was also a professor of economic history from 1931, having made his reputation with *Religion and the Rise of Capitalism* (1926). In his later years he grew unhappy at the return of affluence after wartime austerity, and at the growth of values he had devoted his life to combating.

LHM

taxation represents a transfer of resources from citizens to government. Without it government could not function. Taxation is divided into indirect taxes (levied on sales of goods and other transactions) and direct taxes (levied primarily on persons). The original objective of taxation was to raise revenue to finance public expenditure, often on wars, but taxes have subsequently been adopted (especially tariffs) to protect domestic industries and, in the 20th cent., used as an instrument for the redistribution of income. The advent of Keynesian economics in the post-Second World War period has seen taxation used as a tool of macro-economic policy with rates varied as a stabilizer against economic fluctuations. There has also been a tradition of taxes at urban and regional levels to finance local expenditures.

There is a range of criteria which governs a good tax system. Adam *Smith's four canons in the **Wealth of Nations*, that taxes should be based on a person's ability to pay, and that they should be certain, convenient, and economical, remain valid today, although the emphasis on each has changed with time. The problem is that in many instances the most certain, convenient, and economical tax to collect involves taxing those least able to pay.

While modern taxation is conducted using monetary transfers, there is a long history of taxation involving transfers in kind; most notably labour services or agricultural output. The Roman period saw the taxation of consumption and trade (customs duties) and forms of poll (*tributum*) and land taxation were employed. Inheritances were also taxed. During the Middle Ages these taxes gave way to the authority of the sovereign to levy taxes in a more or less arbitrary manner. The results were direct service obligations and *aids* (essentially gifts and tributes), although transit duties and market fees were also used. Export duties were first introduced in England on hides and wool in 1275. Gradually, a number of, often short-lived, indirect taxes were introduced (e.g. the *window tax) especially at times of national emergency. As overseas territories were acquired, new forms of taxation were developed relating to trade. These provided additional revenue but often bred resentment amongst colonists—as in North America, which felt unrepresented in the political decision-making processes.

Levies on capital or income were not considered a normal means of financing government, except in exceptional circumstances, until the 19th cent. The taxation of incomes was initiated by *Pitt the Younger in 1799 as a temporary measure to assist financing the wars with France and only became a permanent feature of the British fiscal system after its reintroduction in 1842 during a period of tariff reform. Its introduction required a more sophisticated institutional infrastructure and brought with it, as the appropriate sphere of government became more clearly defined, the development of tax law. The growth in importance of direct taxation for income redistribution policy has led to graduated rates and allowances which, combined with an explicit corporate income tax, has added to the institutional bureaucracy.

Indirect taxation has traditionally been on property, especially at the local level, either on the capital or rental value of land (rates), or levied at death (death duties). Excise duties, taxes levied on particular types of goods such as alcoholic drinks, petrol, and tobacco, have increased in importance in the 20th cent. They are often depicted as taxes on luxury goods. A general sales tax, purchase tax, was only introduced in 1940, and then seen initially as a temporary measure. It was subsequently replaced by a multi-stage value added tax, where taxes are imposed at each stage of the production process. KJB

Tay bridge. The wide estuary of the river Tay on the east coast of Scotland presented a formidable obstacle to transport. The first bridge over the estuary was designed by Thomas Bouch for the North British Railway Company. It was almost 2 miles long, consisting of 85 wrought-iron lattice-girder spans supported on cast-iron columns with masonry foundations, and was completed in 1877. Queen Victoria crossed it in the summer of 1879, and knighted its designer on the spot. But at the end of that year, on 28 December 1879, several spans collapsed in a severe storm while a train was crossing, sending 74 people to their deaths. The subsequent inquiry concluded that the bridge was 'badly designed, badly constructed and badly maintained', and found Bouch mainly responsible for these defects. The disaster alarmed the engineering profession and ensured that the replacement bridge was built within ample safety margins. A new road bridge was opened over the estuary in 1966. RAB

Taylor, Jeremy (1613–67). Bishop of Down and Connor. Born in Cambridge, and educated at Gonville and Caius College, he was successively fellow of All Souls, Oxford (1635), rector of Uppingham (1638), and chaplain to Charles I. After joining the royalist army he was captured (1645), but after release lived in Carmarthenshire as chaplain to Lord Carberry where he wrote *Liberty of Prophesying* and the devotional works *Holy Living* and *Holy Dying*. After a spell in London ministering to episcopalians (1653–8) and as lecturer at Lisburn (Ireland) (1658), he became bishop of Down and Connor (1661). The presbyterians there would 'talk with no bishop' and Taylor ejected 36 ministers. His severity ensured the establishment of presbyterians as a separate ecclesiastical community. His plea to *Sheldon for a move to England (1664) was unheeded and he died at Lisburn. WMM

Tayside. From 1973 an administrative region in east Scotland created from the city of Dundee, all Angus and Kinross, and most of Perthshire. The combination of urban and rural populations meant that none of the political parties could be confident of a majority, and Conservative, Labour, and the Scottish National Party have all provided the convenor. In 1996 it was divided into three all-purpose authorities (Angus, Dundee, Perth and Kinross) whose boundaries are almost the same as the previous districts. In addition to survival of older industries—some jute is still spun and woven—agriculture (especially soft fruit), food-processing, and manufacture of hole-in-the-wall cash machines are important to the economy; among the services in which the region specializes are wholesaling and insurance (at Perth). The most distinctive offerings to tourism are surviving Pictish monuments such as souterrains and symbol stones. ASH

technology is the study of the techniques whereby human beings make and do things. It is thus as old as humanity itself, as our species is distinguished by its intelligent use of tools and other artefacts, so that the field of enquiry in the history of technology stretches back at least 2 million years. Over most of this time, however, incremental advances in technological sophistication were slow and slight in a hunting-gathering nomadic society, although gradually improvements were made in the shaping of stone, in the control of fire, and in weapons for hunting and fighting. About 10,000 years ago, in a few well-favoured environments, advances in the techniques of growing crops and domesticating animals made possible the emergence of a more settled form of life, which encouraged the development of new techniques in cooking, baking, distilling, pottery-making, and, eventually, metalworking. This was the 'neolithic revolution', which prepared the way for the first 'civilized' communities, with their new features of social organization in towns, and the skills of literacy and numeracy.

While technology is as old as humankind, science—the systematic understanding of the environment—is only as old as civilization, because it depends for its effectiveness on the sort of cumulative knowledge which only becomes possible with literacy and numeracy. The relationship between science and technology is frequently very close, but it is important to recognize that they are different exercises: technology derives from practical techniques, and is never far from the earthiness of tools and artefacts, whereas science has a strongly conceptual and speculative element, some of which operates at a high level of abstraction. In technology, the emphasis is rightly on good design—fitness for purpose—by which an artefact can best fulfil its function.

Amongst the techniques associated with the rise of civilizations, the inventions of metalworking were most formative because they brought quantum jumps in human weaponry and thus influenced the ability of one society to dominate another. Nevertheless, modern society is characterized by an extraordinary range of techniques whereby every aspect of life has been transformed: power sources have been mastered, materials exploited, productivity increased in both agriculture and industry, and an endless stream of artefacts has been manufactured. Power to make and do things—the mainspring of technological development—has been derived from the steam-engine, the internal combustion engine, electricity, and nuclear fission. New materials have come from the *chemical industry and from the molecular engineering of new plastic substances. Old industries, like pottery, glass-making, and textiles, have employed new machinery and processes. New industries, like electronics, have sprung up to provide a myriad of everyday services. Transport has been transformed, so that rapid journeys are now feasible to all parts of the world, and previously slow methods of communication have become immediate. Information technology is currently doing much to change our perceptions, and space technology holds out a prospect of infinite exploration. Technology, always important in human societies, has become omnipresent, vastly complicated, and indispensable. RAB

Tedder, Sir Arthur (1890–1967). Tedder read history at Cambridge, then joined the RFC in the First World War. He commanded the Middle East Royal Air Force, May 1941 to February 1943. Next he was in charge of allied air forces in the Mediterranean before becoming deputy supreme commander of 'Overlord'. He was responsible for securing the co-ordination of all allied aircraft in the invasion. Tedder made compatible the independence of air forces from ground and naval forces, essential for flexibility, with quick support from the air when needed.

Tedder's contribution to allied success, especially in Normandy, 1944, involved 'interdiction': preventing enemy supplies and reinforcements from reaching the battlefield by attacking road and rail transport, direct and prompt tactical support for ground troops, using fighter-bombers as mobile artillery, and his occasional diversion of British and American heavy bombers to support big offensives. He showed tactful impartiality and lessened the damage done by the bumptious vanity of Generals *Montgomery and Patton. He became marshal of the RAF and was made viscount in 1946. RACP

Teheran conference, 28 November–1 December 1943. This was the first of the 'Big Three' wartime meetings. It was here that *Churchill became uncomfortably aware of the extent to which British power was declining in relation to his allies. He had to bow to American and Soviet insistence on limiting military operations in the Mediterranean in favour of the earliest possible second front in northern France (June 1944). Churchill did what he could to protect the future of the Polish government in exile, while broadly agreeing to the drastic post-war movement westward of Poland's frontiers. CJB

Teilo, St (6th cent.). Teilo is associated in Welsh triads with SS *David and *Cadoc as one of the Three Blessed Visitors to the Isle of Britain. Twelfth-cent. sources claim Teilo was born near Penally (Pembrokeshire), studied first under Dubricius, then with a Paulinus (St Pol). There he met St David, whom he allegedly accompanied on a pilgrimage to Jerusalem. Crossing to escape the plague, he spent some years in Brittany, staying with *Samson of Dol. His ministry was centred, however, on his monastery at Llandeilo Fawr, where he eventually died. Though his name is associated with Llandaff cathedral, the Book of Llandaff's claim that he succeeded Dubricius in the see is insubstantial. The most fantastic story relates to his death, when priests from Llandaff, Llandeilo Fawr, and Penally argued over possession of his body. During the night, it miraculously became three, resolving the dispute. AM

Tel-el-Kebir, battle of, 1882. In the third quarter of the 19th cent. Egypt's external debt became so great that Britain and France took control of the country's finances. The heavily taxed peasantry, led by an army officer, Ahmed Arabi, rebelled against their khedive (governor), whom they held responsible for their plight. British troops under Sir Garnet *Wolseley landed in Egypt to support the khedive and in a surprise attack destroyed Arabi's army at Tel-el-Kebir, 130 miles north-east of Cairo. Arabi surrendered and pleaded guilty to rebellion, but liberal opinion in England ensured that his sentence was exile rather than death. KI

television is the most powerful and influential audio-visual medium of the second half of the 20th cent. As with so many technologies, no one inventor or country can take full credit for the invention of television. But among the claims of Germany, USA, Russia, and Japan, Britain's reputation will always remain strong due to the dominating presence of John Logie *Baird. His dedication through the 1920s to developing 'seeing-by-wireless' made him a key figure in the process, though his particular mechanical model was a failure and the television we have today is the electronic model developed by his rivals, the Marconi-EMI Company team, led by Isaac Schoenberg.

From the 1870s, when the idea of the 'telephonescope' was first mooted by Edison, progress with 'seeing by electricity' was made in various countries. Key developments in Germany—Nipkow's mechanical scanning disc (1884) and

Braun's cathode ray tube (1897)—were used by Scottish scientist A. A. Campbell-Swinton in 1908 to elucidate the basic principles of modern television—the conversion of light and shade into electrical signals to be transmitted from a camera to a receiver on the same airwaves as wireless radio.

With developments interrupted by the First World War, it was not till 1923 that Baird took up the running, with his elaboration of Nipkow's mechanical system producing a primitive 30-line picture for public demonstration in 1925 and 1926, and sending images by wire across the Atlantic in 1928. His negotiations with the *British Broadcasting Corporation, who held the monopoly on broadcasting, resulted in experimental transmissions in 1930 and 1931, including an outside broadcast of the 1931 Derby, to the handful of TV sets which had begun to be manufactured.

By this time, however, the newly formed EMI had joined forces with the Marconi Co. to develop the alternative electronic scanning system that had come from the cathode ray tube. With its greater number of lines producing a clearer picture, it highlighted the clumsy limitations of Baird's mechanical system. Though Baird was able to push his definition up to 240 lines, the Marconi-EMI team reached 405 lines by the time the Selsdon Commission of 1935 had recommended that the BBC run trials of the two systems with the aim of setting up a national television service.

The world's first continuous television service started broadcasting from Alexandra Palace in November 1936, duplicating the programmes in the two rival systems. After a few months, it was clear that the electrical system had the advantage of power and consistency over Baird's, and the greater potential for future development, so it was duly adopted. Over the next few years, Baird's wayward genius was to demonstrate almost every innovation which would eventually become staples of television—colour, the giant screen, and primitive videotape recording.

Until its close-down with the war in 1939, the BBC broadcast some 20 hours per week to the 20,000 TV sets in the south-east, mixing special events such as the coronation, Remembrance Day, and Chamberlain's Munich flight with a regular diet of sport, drama, and music.

The post-war popularity of television was boosted with coverage of the 1946 Victory Parade, and, especially, the 1953 coronation. But the BBC's monopoly was soon to be broken with the 1954 Television Act introducing commercial television (or Independent Television, ITV)—a series of regional stations throughout Britain, making their own programmes and selling their own advertising, under the central regulation of the Independent Television Authority (later to become the Independent Broadcasting Authority, then the Independent Television Commission). Since then the popularity of television has mushroomed, with viewing generally shared equally by the BBC and ITV, and with new specialist stations coming from the BBC in 1962 (BBC2), and from ITV in 1982 (Channel 4).

Technological advances have included the better definition of 625 lines from 1962; colour on BBC2 from 1967 and on BBC1 and ITV from 1969; domestic video recorders from the late 1970s; and, most crucially, satellite TV, from the experimental launch of Telstar in 1962. Within 25 years, the arrival of Rupert Murdoch's Sky TV and the promise of digital broadcasting has demonstrated the power of satellite and cable, providing a massive choice of channels for the consumer, breaking down national frontiers, and presenting a major challenge to the BBC and the well-regulated traditions of British television broadcasting. DJA

Telford, Thomas (1757–1834). Civil engineer from Eskdale (Dumfries). Apprenticeship as a stonemason laid the basis for Telford's move via Edinburgh to London, where he worked on Somerset House (1782), being introduced to *Chambers and *Adam, before work at Portsmouth dockyard (1784). The patronage of William *Pulteney took him to Shrewsbury (1786), where he restored the castle, and built the gaol and the reputation that led to his appointment as 'general overlooker' of the Ellesmere canal in 1793, and his transition to civil engineer. Distinguished canal work followed with his aqueduct at Pontcysyllte (1805), the Caledonian canal (1822), contributions to Sweden's Gotha canal (1832), the Birmingham and Liverpool Junction (1835), the last main line, and his replacement tunnel at Harecastle on the Trent and Mersey (1826). As adviser to the British Fisheries Society (1796) he was invited to undertake road- and bridge-building in the Scottish Highlands, and between 1803 and 1824 was responsible for the construction or remodelling of 1,200 miles of road, all constructed on his 'Roman' principles, with adequate foundations. His creation of the Shrewsbury–Holyhead road (from 1802) was a parallel developmental project, and at Menai (1825) and Conwy (1826) led to his pioneering development of suspension bridges that was to influence *Brunel and others. Nicknamed by *Southey 'the colossus of roads', he succeeded *Rennie as Britain's leading civil engineer, and was a founding member of the Institute of Civil Engineers in 1828. JCh

temperance movement. A powerful social and political force in Victorian Britain. Though it did not succeed in eradicating drink, it helped to control it. Between 1831 and 1931, spirit consumption per head p.a. fell from 1.11 gallons to 0.22, and beer from 21.6 gallons to 13.3: in the same period, consumption of tea per head rose from 1.24 pounds p.a. to 9.67 pounds. Direct propaganda was not of course the only factor in this change: others included growing respectability, improved amenities, more comfortable homes, and a decline in occupations of heavy labour where drink was regarded as a necessity. The chief support of the temperance movement was the dissenting bodies, who carried it as an issue into the *Liberal Party, which adopted local option on the sale of drink as part of its *Newcastle Programme in 1891. As a consequence, the brewing interest gravitated increasingly to the *Conservative Party.

The movement began in the late 1820s with the formation of a number of local temperance societies. In the course of the century, there was a great proliferation of leagues and societies, but the leading organizations were the British and Temperance Society (1831), the British Association for the Promotion of Temperance (1835), the National Temperance Society (1842), and the United Kingdom Alliance (1853), a political pressure group demanding prohibition. One of the best publicized groups was the Band of

Hope, founded in Leeds in 1847 to appeal to children, organizing outings and publishing a periodical *Onward*. One reason for the multiplicity of groups was a difference of opinion which soon emerged between the advocates of moderation in drinking and those who demanded total abstinence—or teetotalism. A trusted technique was to persuade men to 'take the pledge'—an action first agreed in 1832 by seven workmen in Preston. The movement often took the form of a religious revival and was referred to as a crusade: one teetotal group was even included with the churches by the religious census of 1851, along with temperance Wesleyans and temperance Christians. Drink was 'the demon', the pledge echoed baptism, and the solemn reading of the names of backsliders was a form of excommunication. The nature and austerity of the pledge differed from group to group: many northerners preferred 'the long pledge'—refusing to offer alcohol to others as well as abstaining oneself—while the south preferred 'the short pledge'. The temperance movement was a vast and sustained effort, appealing to large numbers of ordinary people and giving them experience of recruiting, organizing, and public speaking. JAC

Templars. Established in Jerusalem in 1118 as a small group of knights pledged to protect pilgrims journeying to the Holy Places. In 1128 they gained papal support and a rule, owing much to *Cistercian custom, was compiled for them by St Bernard of Clairvaux. Until the fall of *Acre (1291) they played an important, but not uncontroversial, role (with their rivals, the *Hospitallers) in the defence of the crusading states.

Their first, and largest, house in England was established just outside the city of London and moved to a site (the 'New Temple') off Fleet Street in 1161. They attracted considerable land and cash grants, much of which was used for the order's needs in Palestine, and their estates were organized as preceptories. Their wealth (and ultimate military failure) led to accusations of heresy, particularly in France in 1307–8, where King Philip IV in association with Pope Clement V brought about the brutal demise of the order, finally suppressed in 1312. In England, as generally elsewhere, their property was ceded to the Hospitallers: many Templars were executed or imprisoned. BJG

Temple, Sir William (1628–99). Diplomat and author. Educated at Cambridge and eventually successful in his patient courtship of Dorothy Osborne, Temple moved from Ireland to England in 1663 and became *Arlington's protégé. Accredited envoy at Brussels (1665), with a baronetcy the following year, he negotiated the *Triple Alliance as ambassador at The Hague (1668), but judiciously retired to England and his orangery at Sheen as relations deteriorated; pro-Dutch, he was recalled to negotiate the 1674 treaty which ended the Dutch War, and then, with *Danby, successfully arranged the alliance between Charles's niece Mary and William of Orange (1677). Although undertaking reorganization of the Privy Council, disillusion increased, and he retired from politics (1681) to pursue gardening, fruit-growing, and writing at Moor Park, where his secretary 1689–99 was Jonathan *Swift. Temple's literary reputation rests on his essays, despite Swift's satire of his style in *The Battle of the Books*. ASH

Temple, William (1881–1944). Archbishop of Canterbury. Born in Exeter, Temple was educated at Balliol College, Oxford. He was ordained while fellow of Queen's (1904–10) only after hesitation. He was successively headmaster of Repton (1910), rector of St James's, Piccadilly (1914), bishop of Manchester (1921), archbishop of York (1929) and of Canterbury (1942). Influenced by the *Workers' Educational Association and Student Christian Movement, he was, like his friend, R. H. *Tawney, socialist in his thinking. He was essentially modern, looking for a synthesis of Christian faith and modern culture in his *Mens creatrix* (1917), *Christus veritas* (1924), and *Christianity and Social Order* (1942). Later dubbed 'intellectually the most brilliant archbishop since *Anselm', he also had great administrative ability and towered over the English ecclesiastical scene. Chairman of the Doctrine Commission (1925), he was also, with *Bell, a major architect of ecumenism. He spoke out in vain for the Jews suffering under Nazism. His early death was a blow to all. WMM

Tempsford, battle of, *c.*918. *Edward the Elder and his sister *Æthelfleda, lady of the Mercians, launched a sustained counter-attack upon Danish-held territory. In *c.*918 he stormed a large Danish camp at Tempsford, east of Bedford, killing the leader Guthrum II. Danish resistance in East Anglia crumbled. JAC

Tenant League. The Irish Tenant League was formed in 1850 to agitate for tenants' rights, in part to replace the repeal campaign. One objective was to extend the *Ulster custom, which gave some protection over rents and evictions. The league offered support to sympathetic parliamentary candidates and organized petitions, but its tenants' rights bills made little progress. The Ulster supporters, who had feared an erosion of their own rights, soon parted company from the catholic south and the revival of agricultural prosperity took the edge off discontent. *Gladstone's *Land Act of 1870 conceded some of the rights claimed. JAC

tenant right was a phrase much in use in Irish politics, especially after the famine of 1846. Since custom and practice differed from province to province and from estate to estate, the term was not precise and landlords complained that tenants devised new rights as soon as old ones were conceded. The immediate objective of the *Tenant League, formed in 1850, was to secure the *Ulster custom, whereby a tenant could sell his goodwill or interest in a farm, thus gaining some compensation for improvements. The three Fs for which the league later campaigned were free sale, fixity of tenure, and fair rent—all of which were slogans difficult to quantify and to adjudicate on. *Gladstone's *Land Act of 1870 legalized the Ulster custom where it existed. The *Irish Land League of 1879 renewed the campaign, organizing rent strikes and boycotts and resisting evictions. Gladstone's second Land Act of 1881 conceded free sale, improved security of tenure, and introduced a machinery for deciding what was a fair rent. After 1885 the Conservatives moved towards facilitating land purchases, turning tenants into independent farmers. By that time a number of landlords were only too glad to sell up and be expropriated. *Palmerston's comment—'tenant right is landlord's wrong'—was the other side of the coin. JAC

tenants-in-chief were those who, after the *Norman Conquest, held their lands directly from the king. Their names are given in *Domesday Book (1086) and are mainly those who had fought alongside William at Hastings or their descendants. The Conqueror kept about one-fifth of the land of England, the church had a quarter, and the tenants-in-chief about half. Domesday records some 1,400 of them, but land was concentrated in very few hands and some eleven magnates owned nearly half of the tenants-in-chief's share. They were under obligation to produce a quota of knights on demand, though they could sublet (subinfeudate) provided the obligation was met. The larger tenants-in-chief may be regarded as the forerunners of the later nobility. JAC

Tenerife, battle of, 1657. On 20 April 1657 *Blake won his last great victory, attacking a force of sixteen Spanish vessels at harbour in Santa Cruz, protected by shore batteries. Every enemy vessel was destroyed and all Blake's ships, some of them badly damaged, survived. The crushing blow helped to bring the long war to an end. JAC

Ten Hours Act (1847). This Act, limiting the work of women and young persons (aged 13–18) in textile mills to ten hours a day for five days in the week and eight hours on Saturday, was the result of a sustained campaign from the 1830s managed in Parliament by Lord Ashley (*Shaftesbury) and John *Fielden and in the factory districts of Yorkshire and Lancashire by Richard *Oastler and the short-time committees of working men. Although adult hours were not reduced until the system of working children in relays was suppressed in 1853, the Act was a triumph of welfare legislation over **laissez-faire* doctrine. JFCH

Tenison, Thomas (1636–1715). Archbishop of Canterbury. A graduate of Corpus Christi College, Cambridge, Tenison was ordained privately (*c.*1659). He was rector of St Martin-in-the-Fields (1680–92) and St James's, Piccadilly (1686–92), archdeacon of London (1689–92), bishop of Lincoln (1692–5), and archbishop (1695). With his friend John *Evelyn he was a zealous supporter of the 1688 revolution. As archbishop, he was close to William III and crowned Anne and George I, but, as a leading advocate of the Hanoverian succession, he was isolated by extreme Tories. He successfully steered the church through the *convocation controversy, though convocation itself was abandoned. He showed compassion for the poor, and promoted voluntary societies and charity schools, the foundation of the *Society for Promoting Christian Knowledge and the *Society for the Propagation of the Gospel, and the demand for bishops in America. 'Dull and prosaic . . . yet a great primate' is a modern assessment. *Gibson wrote of his 'great goodness and integrity' and 'natural sedateness' which preserved the church from shipwreck in stormy times. WMM

tennis. See LAWN TENNIS.

Tennyson, Alfred, 1st Baron Tennyson (1809–92). Tennyson was the first poet to be made a peer of the realm, since *Macaulay, author of *Lays of Ancient Rome*, had been an active politician. He was the son of a Lincolnshire rector and attended Louth Grammar School and Trinity College, Cambridge. His first volume of poetry in 1830 sold badly, though it contained 'Mariana': the next volume in 1832 included 'The Lady of Shalott'. His collected volume in 1842 established him as a major poet, he was given a pension in 1845, succeeded *Wordsworth as poet laureate in 1850, and was given his barony during *Gladstone's ministry in 1884, apparently at Queen Victoria's suggestion. Much of his work, though not always his best, was based upon historical or legendary themes: 'Morte d'Arthur' and 'Idylls of the King' (1842, 1859); a translation from the Anglo-Saxon of 'The Battle of Brunanburh' (1880); and several historical plays, including *Queen Mary* (Mary Tudor, 1876), *Harold* (1877), and *Becket* (1884). JAC

Territorials. With a large navy to support, it was always necessary for Britain to augment her army with a reserve force. The *militia was not always popular, nor particularly effective, and in periods of crisis was supplemented by *volunteer and fencible corps, often regarded as personal fiefdoms by their colonels. In 1907, *Haldane, Liberal secretary of state for war, determined to bring order into a confused situation by establishing a Territorial Force, which absorbed the militia. In 1921 it became the Territorial Army and remains in existence, on a reduced scale. Though intended initially for home defence, its members fought overseas in both the world wars. JAC

Terry, Ellen (1847–1928). Actress. Born into an acting family and brought up on the boards, Alice Ellen Terry left the stage for some years until concern for her children's future prompted a return in 1874 under Charles Reade. She joined *Irving as his leading lady at the Lyceum theatre (1878), where her beauty and grace of movement enhanced his productions; appearing in Britain and America, their famous partnership lasted until 1902, though she had already commenced her 'paper courtship' with *Shaw in the 1890s. Enormously popular, her vitality and stagecraft were underpinned by intelligence, yet all her successes, except in *Shakespeare, were in sentimental melodrama. An unconventional approach to life was accompanied by humour, frankness, and generosity. When Terry became too old for many roles, and eyesight and memory began to fail, she turned to lecture-recitals here and abroad. She was created dame in 1925. ASH

Test Act, 1673. Usually linked to the *Corporation Act, but a later addition to the code of laws excluding non-members of the Church of England from public office (25 Car. II c. 2). It required all office-holders under the crown, including MPs, to receive communion according to the rites of the Church of England at least once a year. They were also required to take oaths of supremacy and allegiance to the crown and to make a declaration against transubstantiation. This was aimed more particularly at recusant catholics and the repeal of the Test Act was the principal aim of the successful *catholic emancipation campaign led by Daniel *O'Connell in the late 1820s. JFC

Tettenhall, battle of, 910. With the death of *Alfred the Great in 899, his son *Edward succeeded to the Wessex crown. Together with his sister *Æthelfleda, 'the lady of the Mercians', Edward began to forge a strong English kingdom. The Danes invaded in 910 and the king marched his army to Staffordshire to intercept them. On 5 August the Saxons fought a pitched battle with the Northumbrian Danes. Edward won a convincing victory and extended his kingdom as far north as the Humber. RAS

Tewkesbury, battle of, 1471. The last and one of the bloodiest battles of the Wars of the *Roses. Queen *Margaret, still defending the claims of her husband Henry VI, landed at Weymouth the same day that Edward IV defeated *Warwick at *Barnet. She moved towards Wales and the north-west to collect support, with Edward marching from Windsor to intercept her. Yorkist supporters denied her a crossing of the Severn at Gloucester, obliging her to make for Tewkesbury. Her troops were caught before they could safely cross and forced to give battle on 4 May 1471, facing south. An attack by the duke of Somerset on the right failed and in the subsequent flight *Edward, the young Lancastrian prince of Wales, was killed, near the abbey mill. Somerset was executed, Queen Margaret captured, and Henry VI murdered the same month. The slaughter is commemorated in the name Bloody Meadow and the Lancastrian cause never recovered from the disaster. JAC

Tewkesbury abbey (Glos.) developed from a religious community founded in the 8th cent., ceded after many vicissitudes to the *Benedictine monastery of Cranborne *c.*980. Robert *Fitzhamon, lord of Gloucester, lavishly endowed Tewkesbury *c.*1090 and in 1102 Cranborne became its dependency. During the next century Tewkesbury flourished, establishing cells at Bristol and Cardiff. It continued to attract powerful patrons such as the de Clares, Despensers, and Beauchamps, many of whom were buried in the abbey. In spite of financial difficulties at the end of the 15th cent., in 1535 Tewkesbury had a net income of *c.* £1,600, making it the wealthiest monastery in the west midlands. At the *dissolution the Romanesque abbey church (which survives) became the parish church. BJG

Texel, battle of the, 1673. On 21 August was fought the last battle in the third Anglo-Dutch War. The Dutch were expecting a large convoy from the Indies and were also threatened with an invasion. De Ruyter took the initiative though at a considerable disadvantage against a joint Anglo-French fleet under *Rupert. Cornelis Tromp in the *Gouden Leeuw* fought an individual action against Sir Edward Spragge in the *Royal Prince*, much to the advantage of the former. Dutch superiority in gunnery gave them the upper hand, though no major ships were lost on either side. But the convoy came home safely and the proposed landing was abandoned. Peace followed six months later. JAC

Teyte, Dame Maggie (1888–1976). English soprano. After studying in London and Paris, Teyte made her public début while still under 18 in a Mozart festival at Paris in 1906. She was chosen and coached by Debussy in 1908 to succeed Mary Garden as Mélisande in his opera *Pelléas et Mélisande*, and he also accompanied her in recitals of his songs. Teyte sang in England with the Beecham Opera Company (later the British National Opera Company) and in the USA with the Chicago (1911–14) and Boston (1914–17) opera companies. Between the wars her British activity centred on operetta and musical comedy, but later concerts and recordings returned particularly to French song, benefiting from her interpretative insights and the clean, pure tone of her singing. ECr

Thackeray, William Makepeace (1811–63). Novelist. Born in Calcutta, the son of a collector in the East India Company, he was educated at Charterhouse and Cambridge. This Indian background and his public school were to figure prominently in *The Newcomes* (1853–5). Having studied drawing in Paris and German at Weimar (where he met Goethe) he began a career as a journalist in London. He was a notable early contributor to **Punch* (founded 1841) and to *Fraser's Magazine* (founded 1830) and in 1860 became the editor of the dynamic new *Cornhill Magazine*. His real breakthrough came with the monthly part serialization of *Vanity Fair* (1847–8), a novel set at the time of Waterloo and its aftermath. Thackeray's growing interest in the culture of the 18th cent. is reflected in his novels *Barry Lyndon* (1844), *Henry Esmond* (1852), and its sequel *The Virginians* (1857–9) and in his two lecture series published as *The English Humourists of the Eighteenth Century* (1851) and *The Four Georges* (1855–7). ASL

thanes. See THEGNS.

Thatcher, Margaret (b. 1925). Prime minister. Britain's first woman prime minister and one of the most controversial, she won three resounding election victories in a row for the Conservatives (1979, 1983, and 1987), before they unceremoniously rejected her as party leader and premier in 1990, a victim of a ruthless act of political ingratitude.

Mrs Thatcher was educated at Kesteven and Grantham Girls' School and Somerville College, Oxford, and entered Parliament in 1959. Beforehand she had been a research chemist (1947–54) and a lawyer (she was called to the bar in 1954). Between 1970 and 1974 she was secretary of state for education, a position in which she earned the sobriquet of 'Margaret Thatcher, milk snatcher' for abolishing the free supply of milk to schoolchildren. This was mild compared to the abuse she would endure later.

As leader of the opposition, between 1975 and 1979, she repudiated the legacy of her predecessor as Tory leader, Edward *Heath, and, under the influence of Sir Keith Joseph, a former colleague in Heath's cabinet, moved towards that ideal of political patriotism, low taxes, private ownership, balanced budgets, and individual initiative which later became known as Thatcherism. However, if the goal was financial stability, permanently low inflation, reduced government spending, and lower taxes, it proved illusory. Her record as prime minister began and ended with severe recessions (the worst since the 1930s) leading to a reduced industrial base and very low overall growth rates. She failed to reverse Britain's relative decline, although for a few years, until Nigel Lawson and John *Major threw it away, it looked as if she had managed to establish the right conditions for doing so. The trade unions were tamed; Arthur Scargill's miners went down to defeat after a year-long strike aimed at overthrowing the government; most state-owned companies were privatized; and income tax was significantly lowered. However, rising indirect taxes, rising interest rates, rising inflation, plus the introduction of the hugely unpopular *poll tax in an attempt to reform local government finances, meant that when a crisis erupted over Europe in 1990, Mrs Thatcher lacked the political support needed to survive.

Just as she had not been expected to win the Tory Party leadership in 1975, her rapid rise to international fame took many by surprise. There had been little in her record to suggest that she had any talent for diplomacy, yet from the start of her premiership, she made her mark in international affairs. In 1979 a peace settlement was negotiated at Lancaster House which ended the Rhodesian question and paved the way for an independent *Zimbabwe. Such a settlement had eluded international negotiators since 1965, although it must be conceded that events in Africa, plus Lord *Carrington's diplomacy, had more to do with the success than Mrs Thatcher's personal input. Her own triumph, which made her an international celebrity, came with victory over Argentina in the *Falklands War of 1982, when, having been taken by surprise by the Argentine invasion (Carrington resigned), Mrs Thatcher dispatched a battle fleet to the South Atlantic, which recaptured the colony. The bravery and efficiency displayed by the armed forces, the collapse of the reactionary Argentine dictatorship, and the leadership provided by the prime minister, with whom the war became almost personally identified, all enabled Mrs Thatcher to win a remarkable triumph in the 1983 general election. Thereafter she developed a 'very, very special relationship' with the US president, Ronald Reagan, and despite some differences (the Soviet oil pipeline, *Grenada, nuclear disarmament) worked very closely with him to end the *Cold War. She also managed to develop a close relationship with the Soviet leader Mikhail Gorbachev, of whom she remarked, after they first met: 'That is a man I can do business with.' British contacts with eastern Europe intensified and Gorbachev, like western leaders, used Mrs Thatcher as an intermediary with President Reagan. When she finally visited Moscow, she received a triumphal welcome. Other aspects of her diplomacy were more controversial. These included the *Anglo-Irish agreement of 1985, the joint agreement with Peking over the future of *Hong Kong (1984), her resistance to economic sanctions against South Africa, and the scepticism with which she greeted the prospect of German re-unification. She insisted in the latter instance that the issue was an international one and that Germany must respect its frontier with Poland.

Her policy towards the European Community was, however, most controversial of all. Her first instincts had been conventional. She had campaigned enthusiastically for a Yes vote in the 1975 referendum and always believed that her approach was a constructive one. She helped achieve closer co-operation on foreign policy, and the Single European Act which was signed in 1986 received her full backing as a means of extending Thatcherite free enterprise across a European single market, despite the concessions involved to majority voting. On the other hand, she had had to battle mightily in order to secure the annual British rebates agreed on in the Fontainebleau accord (1984) and was horrified by Jacques Delors's ideas regarding a European Social Charter, and even more so by European economic and monetary union. In her famous Bruges speech (1988), she declared her opposition to future integration, although she was persuaded by her cabinet colleagues Sir Geoffrey *Howe and Nigel Lawson to promise to enter the exchange rate mechanism, a move which came under John Major as chancellor and which proved a disaster. By 1990, however, after having rejected economic and monetary union at a summit in Rome, she was deserted by Sir Geoffrey Howe, who, bitter at having been dismissed as foreign secretary, and fearful lest his long-standing federalism be rendered futile, took his revenge by resigning from her government and challenging Michael *Heseltine to contest the party leadership. In the ensuing contest, Mrs Thatcher won the first round, but was deserted by her cabinet—over whom she had never exercised full control and who were weary of her autocratic style—and withdrew from the leadership race, rather than submit to a second ballot. She was succeeded by John Major as Tory leader.

She was accused by many of having broken with the post-war consensus in British politics and, indeed, she herself regularly denounced the concept. In fact, she had responded to a changing consensus and had influenced that change by her personality and policies. The high unemployment of her years in power had not been intended. The welfare state had grown under her as never before. Her defence and foreign policies had been totally conventional. She had made no constitutional innovations and had if anything been slow to dismiss her cabinet critics. Privatization had proved popular. So too had trade union reform. In the end she contributed to her own undoing by retaining the services of key ministers whose policies, priorities, and philosophies were fundamentally different from her own. In this sense, the Iron Lady proved an unexpectedly weak prime minister. AS

Harris, K., *Thatcher* (1988); Young, H., *One of Us* (1989).

theatre is a general term that covers plays, players, places, and spectators; although it is predominantly a pretence that entertains, with varying degrees of spectacle, themes in drama may reflect and challenge contemporary issues. There is little trace now of Roman theatre in Britain other than remnants of multi-purpose amphitheatres, a few masks, and the name of a player (Verecunda), but these suggest quite widespread, broadly based performance. Itinerant popular entertainers like dancers, mimes, minstrels, and story-tellers then preserved fundamental skills, while folk-plays developed out of seasonal celebrations and mimetic elements in dance, passed on through oral tradition; some of these became integrated into the church's liturgical calendar. The later middle ages saw a growing taste for civic pageantry and development of 'mystery cycles' (biblical histories portrayed on fixed staging or pageant-wagons hauled through the streets, often under the auspices of craft guilds). Liturgical drama began to yield to more secular morality plays, 'interludes' provided a link between *mimi* and the early professional touring companies, mummings and disguisings were indoor and court-linked (later merging into *masques), and, by the late 15th cent., nobles began to take players' troupes under their own protection. The creation of the royal household post of master of the revels (1494) not only legitimized theatre but established control over an institution that was now predominantly secular, mainly professional, and increasingly regulated.

In the 16th cent., companies of strolling players, performing in inn-yards on trestle stages or private banqueting-halls, flourished despite strong disapproval from puritan preachers and city fathers bothered about public order. The first public playhouse was built in Shoreditch, London (1576), by James Burbage, a member of the earl of *Leicester's company of players, resembling a modified inn-yard with a raised platform stage, central yard usable for other activities but unroofed, and surrounding galleries with varying admittance charges. Others soon followed south of the river Thames (Rose, Swan, *Globe) and prospered. The actors owned the theatres, ran a repertory system, and jealously guarded their unpublished scripts; absence of scenery, making act/scene divisions unnecessary, challenged playwrights' and actors' skills alike. All players had to be competent dancers and singers, but dramatists like *Marlowe, *Shakespeare, and *Jonson replaced earlier short, rhymed verse with poetic drama. As women were forbidden to perform, boy-actors took all female roles, hence their relative rarity and tendency to be breeches-parts. Private indoor theatres were mostly used by boy companies (Children of St Paul's or the Chapel Royal) presenting rather artificial dramas to a limited, wealthy audience. On James I's accession, the three leading adult companies came under royal protection, which inevitably led to adaptations tailored to royal rather than popular tastes. *Anne of Denmark, however, encouraged development of the court masque, for which extravagant, one-off entertainments Ben Jonson frequently provided the words and Inigo *Jones spectacular, Italianate scenery and costume.

Although playhouses closed briefly during episodes of plague, they were shut down altogether on the outbreak of the Civil War (1642). For the next eighteen years there was rigorous suppression, but players went 'underground' and extracts or short entertainments known as drolls were frequently performed. After the Restoration, Charles II, an avid theatre-goer, who had become familiar with European theatre during exile, issued two patents which granted a monopoly of performed drama in London until 1843. Killigrew (forming and running the King's Company) at *Drury Lane and Davenant (the Duke's Company) at Lincoln's Inn Fields initially revived old plays (though with happy endings to *King Lear* and *Romeo and Juliet*, and singing witches in *Macbeth*) until their own playwrights (Etherege, *Wycherley, then *Congreve, *Vanbrugh, and Farquhar) created bawdy comedies of manners, played to fashionable rather than popular audiences. Aphra *Behn, who produced fifteen plays (1671–89), was the first woman professional playright. Theatres were roofed, perspective scenery introduced, and actresses now permitted; initially untrained but quickly proving highly popular with the rowdy audiences, their make-up had to be exaggerated because of poor indoor illumination, and its excessiveness revolted *Pepys when he visited Nell *Gwyn.

Despite the success of marionette theatres, early 18th-cent. theatre was limited, dramatic rather than operatic but increasingly sentimental and mediocre, with audiences predominantly middle-class, more numerous but volatile. Prompted by *Fielding's attack on *Walpole and his administration, especially in *The Historical Register for 1736* (which virtually invented the satirical revue), the 1737 Licensing Act confirmed the monopoly of the two patent theatres, Drury Lane and *Covent Garden (built 1732, inheritor of Davenant's Duke's House), authorized the lord chamberlain to act as censor, and hindered expansion of smaller unlicensed theatres. Ingenuity to circumvent this was boundless: a 'concert', or sale of chocolate, punch, or toothpaste, might be accompanied by free entertainment conducted as a 'rehearsal'. Theatrical evenings became the norm, mixing full-length drama, songs, dances, and ever-popular afterpieces (farce, pantomime). Provincial theatre was provided by travelling companies on defined circuits—Tate Wilkinson ran the York circuit, Sarah Baker covered Kent, and Austin's company eventually covered *c.*1,100 miles each year in the north of England. These stock companies were training-grounds for young actors such as *Garrick, who eventually introduced a more naturalistic style of acting, improved lighting, and stage-design (though contemporary costume still prevailed) at Drury Lane, banished spectators from the stage, and resuscitated Shakespeare. The comedies of *Goldsmith (*She Stoops to Conquer*, 1773) and *Sheridan (*The School for Scandal*, 1777) typified the eventual reaction to sentimental drama, but there was a growing demand by unsophisticated audiences for popular entertainment, to be met by melodrama (to which even John Philip Kemble and Mrs *Siddons had to submit), harlequinade in pantomime (Joseph Grimaldi was a favourite clown), burlesque, and, later, *music-hall and vaudeville.

Even before the Theatres Act (1843) broke the monopoly of Drury Lane and Covent Garden, many new, small theatres had arisen, increasingly specialized to cater for differing tastes, and lit by gas which provided more controllable stage illumination; more authentic costumes and stage settings were introduced, plush seating appeared, and auditoria were darkened. Competition from music-hall and the rise of the actor-manager encouraged bravura performances and flamboyant productions under brighter electric light (eventually necessitating stage-managers), but men such as Henry *Irving helped to raise actors' status. The satirical libretti of W. S. *Gilbert and brilliant but artificial comedies of Oscar *Wilde in the late 19th cent. began to yield to the growing realism and concern with social problems that European dramatists such as Chekhov and Ibsen had begun to explore. *Shaw's 'plays unpleasant', looking at some current abuses, were considered offensive, but the importance of the dramatist was regaining ground, as also were repertory companies and the idea of a supervisory director or producer. Farce, drawing-room, and musical comedy nevertheless continued to retain popularity.

British theatre after the Second World War was fragile. Many London theatres were bomb-damaged, an entertainment tax was imposed, and competition with film, radio, and television was increasing. Actor–audience relationships were challenged, and, although a brief revival of poetic drama occurred, plays such as John Osborne's *Look Back in Anger* (1956) rejected upper-class sophistication for local accents and 'kitchen-sink' drama. Experimental work such as free improvisation and 'fringe' theatre emerged, though reaction to such 'alternative' theatre led to revivals and new musicals (*Oliver*, *Cats*). Censorship was eventually abolished in 1968. The *National Theatre finally opened on the South Bank in 1976, and its company, together with the Royal Shakespeare Company, has not only restaged classical plays but also commissioned new large-scale works (Shaffer's *Royal Hunt of the Sun*, 1964; *Nicholas Nickleby*, RSC, 1980). Most professionals now graduate from drama schools. Arts Council subsidies have proved insufficient, and industrial sponsorship of productions is heavily encouraged. ASH

thegns was a title given to those members of society in late Anglo-Saxon England who held at least five hides of land and were under the obligation of serving the king in battle. Their nearest predecessor was the gesith, their successors the knights of the post-Conquest period. The rank was hereditary but could be attained by *ceorls who came to own five hides. Though there were many gradations within the ranks of thegns, their *wergeld in Mercia and Wessex was six times that of a ceorl. The spelling has been preferred by historians to distinguish them from Scottish thanes, who were barons or clan leaders. SMD

Theobald (d. 1161). Archbishop of Canterbury. Theobald's long tenure of the archbishopric was in an exceptionally turbulent period. He became abbot of Bec in Normandy in 1137 and was appointed to Canterbury by King Stephen in 1138. In the civil war which raged Theobald managed to keep some balance between Stephen and his rival Matilda. But much of his time was devoted to beating off attacks on his authority. He suffered from the prominence of Stephen's brother *Henry of Blois, who was bishop of Winchester, a papal legate, and an ambitious cleric. In 1148 he incurred Stephen's wrath by attending a papal council at Rheims and retorted with an interdict which was little regarded. There was a further dispute in 1152 when Theobald refused to crown Stephen's son *Eustace, and another resort to interdict. He fought a long-running battle against St Augustine's monastery at Canterbury, clashed with the rival archbishop of York, and resisted the claims of the archbishop of Armagh to the primacy of Ireland. After Henry II succeeded in 1154, life was easier, with *John of Salisbury to advise and assist him. But much of his archiepiscopate looks like a dress rehearsal for the even greater convulsions under his successor Thomas *Becket. JAC

Theodore of Tarsus (*c.*602–90). Sent by Pope Vitalian as archbishop of Canterbury, with Hadrian, who became abbot of St Augustine's, Theodore arrived in 669. Two deaths had left the see vacant for five years. Plague had drastically reduced church leaders and monastic communities, and rekindled some heathenism. The church lacked organization and had not achieved the uniformity promised at *Whitby (664). Theodore toured his province, eliminating irregularities, consecrating bishops, and in 672 summoned the first synod of the whole English church at *Hertford. Deaths and depositions afforded opportunities to divide large dioceses. By his death, Theodore had built up the episcopate and created an organized, united church under Canterbury. In his primacy monasticism progressed, the use of charters confirming land grants grew, and with Hadrian, the Canterbury school flourished, attracting scholars from far afield. AM

Thirty-Nine Articles. The articles are those finally agreed by the convocations of the Church of England in 1571. They comprise a set of doctrinal statements which were intended to define the position of the reformed Church of England in respect of the disputes and questions over matters of faith and order current at the time. Printed as an appendix to the 1662 *Book of Common Prayer (where they are dated 1562, the year of their original formulation), their declared purpose is 'for the avoiding of diversities of opinions and for the establishing of consent touching true religion'. The articles encompass Trinitarian doctrine, justification, predestination and election, the authority of the church and of general councils, as well as the ordering of ministry, the disciplines expected of the faithful, and the position of the sovereign and of civil magistrates *vis-à-vis* the church. They steer a careful—and sometimes ambiguous—path between catholic and reformed doctrines. Subscription to them is still required of the clergy, but since 1865 only a general affirmation that what is expressed in them is agreeable to the Word of God and not a more particular and searching assent to each one individually is required. JRG

Thirty Years War. The war, from 1618 to 1648, was primarily a conflict between the Habsburgs and their Spanish allies against France, Sweden, and the Dutch. There were two reasons why England might be drawn into it. The *casus belli* was the decision by the Bohemians to defy the Habsburgs and offer their throne to Frederick of the Palatinate, who was married to *Elizabeth, daughter of James I. Secondly, there was a religious element to the war which, despite France's opposition to the Habsburgs, was seen by many protestants as a catholic crusade. England took little part in the conflict and for the last ten years was preoccupied with her own troubles. James resisted pressure to intervene, partly because Parliament's enthusiasm for war was not matched by enthusiasm for supply, partly because he was seeking a Spanish marriage for his son Charles. After the breakdown of the negotiations, Charles demanded war with Spain: the expedition of 1625 was a fiasco. He then compounded his difficulties by becoming involved in war with France as well, a masterpiece of incompetence, which meant that he was now fighting both sides. The expedition in 1627 to relieve La Rochelle was no more successful than that of 1625. Luckily, Charles's relations with Parliament were so bad that he was obliged to make peace with both countries and leave them to fight it out without English assistance. The conflict was concluded by the treaty of Westphalia in 1648, by which time Charles was a prisoner awaiting trial. JAC

Thistle, Order of the. The origins of this Scottish order of knighthood are unclear but it seems to have been founded by James III about 1480. It lapsed after the Reformation but was revived by James VII and II in 1687 and again by Anne in 1703. It now numbers sixteen, including the sovereign. The insignia is a star with the cross of St Andrew and a green thistle superimposed. The chapel of the order is in St Giles' cathedral, Edinburgh. JAC

Thomas, Dylan (1914–53). Poet. Born in Swansea, son of a schoolteacher, Thomas began as a journalist, publishing his first book *18 Poems* in 1934 and following it in 1936 with *25 Poems*. He married in 1937 and settled in the coastal village of Laugharne, south of Carmarthen, working for the BBC and lecturing. A collection of short stories of a strongly autobiographical nature, *Portrait of the Artist as a Young Dog*, came out in 1940. Though he knew no Welsh, Thomas's roistering life-style led some to accuse him of being a stage-Welshman. *Deaths and Entrances* (1946) and *Collected Poems 1934–52* were well received, but Thomas died on a lecture tour of the USA. His radio play *Under Milk Wood* (1954) was greatly acclaimed as a portrait of Welsh life in the fictitious village of Llareggub. JAC

Thomas of Lancaster (*c.*1278–1322) was one of the most powerful magnates during the reign of Edward II and a thorn in the side of the king. He was the son of Edmund Crouchback, a younger son of Henry III and was therefore first cousin to Edward II. Succeeding to the earldom of Lancaster in 1296, he served against the Scots during Edward I's reign. But as soon as his cousin succeeded, Thomas moved into opposition. He took an active part against the royal favourite *Gaveston, was one of the *Ordainers appointed to supervise the young king, and brought about Gaveston's execution in 1312. He refused to serve in the *Bannockburn campaign of 1314 and profited from the king's humiliation to increase his own influence. In 1316 he was appointed chief counsellor and in 1318 he and Edward were briefly reconciled at the treaty of *Leake, taking part in the unsuccessful campaign against the Scots in 1319. But by 1321 he was once more at odds with the king over the *Despensers, whom he forced into exile. In 1322 he was captured at *Boroughbridge and executed at Pontefract in the king's presence. Though the experiment with conciliar government recalls de *Montfort's career under Henry III, Thomas's activities seem to have been purely factious. Surprisingly a cult grew up at Pontefract and miracles were said to have been performed. The earldom passed to his younger brother, whose great-grandson took the throne as Henry IV. JAC

Thomas of Woodstock. See GLOUCESTER, THOMAS, DUKE OF.

Thomas, J. H. (1874–1949). Jimmy Thomas, one of the most colourful politicians of his day, was an h-dropping, hard-drinking gambler and a joy to the cartoonists. Brought up in Newport (Mon.) by a washerwoman grandmother, he became a GWR engine-cleaner and rose rapidly in the Amalgamated Society of Railway Servants. Elected as a Labour MP in 1910 for Derby, a railway town, Thomas gave strong support to the war effort. *MacDonald appointed him Colonial Secretary in 1924 when *The Times* hailed him as a man who had demonstrated Labour's fitness to govern. In 1929 he became Lord Privy Seal with a special brief to tackle unemployment, but moved in 1930 to the Dominions Office. In the crisis of 1931 he stayed with MacDonald, held his seat at Derby, and retained his cabinet post. His career ended abruptly in 1936 when he was censured for a budget leak: 'he let his tongue wag when he was in his cups', remarked *Baldwin charitably. Thomas resigned both post and seat, telling the Commons, in a moving farewell, 'my vices, if they are vices, have always been open and never disguised'. JAC

Thomson, J. J. (1856–1940). Discoverer of the electron. After study in Manchester, Thomson gained a scholarship to Trinity College, Cambridge. In 1884 he became Cavendish professor, working on electricity and gases. Michael *Faraday and then William Crookes had thought that the rays coming from the negative pole, or cathode, were charged particles, but with Wilhelm Röntgen's discovery of X-rays, most Germans supposed that cathode rays were similar, radiation akin to light. Thomson, with better vacuum pumps, devised an experiment in which the rays were deflected by a magnetic field, and then deflected back again by an electric field. This proved they were negatively charged particles, or *corpuscles* as he called them following Robert *Boyle, and he calculated their ratio of charge to mass, showing how much smaller they were than atoms. Thomson was knighted in 1908, served as president of the Royal Society 1915–20, and was master of Trinity College, Cambridge, from 1918 to his death. DK

Thorfinn, earl of Orkney (*c.*1009–*c.*1065). Though the saga sources are far from specific, it is clear that 'Thorfinn the Mighty' wielded great power. He succeeded his father *Sigurd as earl of Orkney when a small boy in 1014. He was a grandson of *Malcolm II of Scotland. He fought against *Duncan I, his cousin, and may have divided the kingdom with *Macbeth. They certainly defeated and killed Duncan, and seem to have stayed in harmony until Macbeth's own death at *Lumphanan: it is said that they visited Rome together. Thorfinn built a cathedral at Birsay in Orkney. His daughter married *Malcolm III of Scotland and his sons fought alongside *Harold Hardrada at *Stamford Bridge in 1066. JAC

Three Choirs Festival. An annual festival, originally termed 'Music Meeting', based in turn on the cathedrals of Gloucester, Hereford, and Worcester. The festival was inaugurated around 1716 in aid of charity and its early years were increasingly devoted to the music of *Handel. It has done much to foster English choral music, especially the works of *Elgar, often using choirs drawn from the three cathedrals and conducted by one of the three organists. Premières have included Elgar's *The Dream of Gerontius* and works by *Parry, *Vaughan Williams, *Holst, Bliss, Bax, Howells, and Peter Maxwell Davies. ECr

Throckmorton, Sir Nicholas (1516–71). Diplomat. Of gentry stock from Coughton Court (War.), Throckmorton was related to *Catherine Parr, Henry VIII's last wife, and joined her household. From 1545 until 1563 he was in most parliaments and was in favour during the reign of Edward VI, being a zealous supporter of the reformed religion. In Mary's reign he was accused of complicity in *Wyatt's rebellion but was acquitted: he did not serve in Mary's parliaments of 1555 or 1558. With the accession of Elizabeth, Throckmorton's career prospered and he represented her at the court of France (helping to negotiate the treaty of *Troyes). He was next employed in Scottish affairs but his sympathy for Mary, queen of Scots, caused him to fall into disfavour. His reputation as a 'machiavellist' and his equivocal conduct at the accession of Mary may have led to mistrust and he did not achieve high office. JAC

Throckmorton plot, 1583. This was one of many conspiracies to free Mary, queen of Scots, and put her on the throne in place of Elizabeth. Francis Throckmorton was son of Sir John Throckmorton, chief justice of Chester, disgraced in 1579. Francis Throckmorton, a catholic, spent the early 1580s on the continent and in 1583 was acting as go-between for Mary and Mendoza, the Spanish ambassador in London. When he was arrested a list of catholic conspirators and details of possible invasion ports were found. Throckmorton confessed under torture and was executed at Tyburn in July 1584. Mendoza was expelled, and left threatening to return with an army. JAC

Thurles, Synod of, August 1850. This was a national synod of Irish catholic bishops, whose decisions, submitted to Rome for ratification, were consequently binding. The Queen's Colleges were secular institutions, established in Ireland by Act of Parliament in 1845, to make higher education available to all denominations. They were widely criticized as 'godless'. Catholic opposition sought papal support and, by a narrow margin, the Synod of Thurles voted to forbid priests accepting posts and to urge parents against enrolling their children. AM

Thurloe, John (1616–68). The son of an Essex clergyman, Thurloe was a lawyer under the patronage of Oliver St John. He did not take up arms in the Civil War, but in 1652 was appointed secretary to the *Council of State and was soon put in charge of Commonwealth intelligence gathering. He was an MP 1654 and 1656 and a member of *Cromwell's second council. Remarkably efficient, devoted to Cromwell, Thurloe presided over an international espionage network. After Cromwell's death he transferred his allegiance to his son *Richard, and served in the Parliament of 1659 for the University of Cambridge. After the fall of Richard Cromwell, he was reappointed secretary of State and tried to dissuade *Monck from bringing back Charles II. He survived a charge of treason at the Restoration and was allowed to return to his practice at Lincoln's Inn. His vast collection of state papers found their way into the Bodleian Library, but seven bulky volumes were published by Thomas Birch in 1742. JAC

Thurlow, Edward, 1st Baron Thurlow (1731–1806). A distinguished lawyer who appeared with success in several important constitutional cases. He was solicitor-general 1770, attorney-general 1771–8, and became lord chancellor as Baron Thurlow in 1778. He was a formidable presence on the woolsack and dominated the House of Lords. *Fox remarked that 'No man could be so wise as Thurlow looked'. Except during Fox's ministry of 1783 he remained lord chancellor until 1792, but he alienated *Pitt by intriguing with the prince of Wales during the *Regency crisis of 1788–9 in the hope of retaining office if the prince became regent. Pitt tired of his independence in the cabinet, where he was regarded as the king's representative, and compelled George III in 1792 to choose between them. Thurlow then retired. EAS

Thurstan (d. 1140). Archbishop of York. Born in Bayeux, Thurstan was secretary to Henry I. As part of the unending dispute between Canterbury and York he refused consecration in 1114 by the archbishop of Canterbury and was eventually consecrated at Rheims (1119), receiving the pallium from Pope Calixtus II. With his fiery personality he vigorously championed the independence of York from Canterbury; the pope decided in York's favour (1126), though Canterbury with legatine authority could still claim obedience. He organized and inspired Yorkshire forces against David I of Scotland's invasion and defeated him at the battle of the *Standard (1138). An intimate friend of St Bernard, Thurstan strongly supported the growth of Cistercianism. *Rievaulx and *Fountains were founded with his assistance. In his last years he wanted to resign his see to become a Cistercian himself, but was refused. He became a Cluniac before dying at Pontefract abbey. WMM

Tichborne, Chidiock (*c.*1558–86). Tichborne, from Hampshire, was a devout catholic and became involved in the *Babington conspiracy to murder Queen Elizabeth and release Mary, queen of Scots, from captivity. He was arrested in August 1586, tried, and executed as a traitor with the full rigour of the law. In the Tower of London, awaiting his death, he wrote an exquisite threnody. JAC

Tien-Tsin, treaty of, 1858. The second Opium War began in October 1856 when the Chinese authorities at Canton seized the British-registered *Arrow.* In June 1856 at Tien-Tsin, the Chinese agreed to receive a British diplomat at Peking, open up more treaty ports, pay an indemnity, and legalize the opium trade. Russia, America, and France obtained similar concessions. A punitive expedition to Peking in 1860 forced the confirmation of the terms, and Kowloon, opposite Hong Kong, was ceded in perpetuity. JAC

Tierney, George (1761–1830). Whig politician, MP 1790 and 1796–1830. An early devotee of democratic principles, nicknamed 'Citizen Tierney', he joined the Association of the *Friends of the People and helped to draw up their report criticizing the state of the representative system 1792–3. He spoke frequently in Parliament after 1796, ignoring the

Whig 'secession' of 1798–1802. Disillusioned by events in France, he moderated his reformist views. After 1801 he advocated co-operation between the Whigs and *Addington, and joined Addington's government in 1803 as treasurer of the navy. An intimate of the prince of Wales, he served as president of the India Board in the *'Talents' ministry of 1806–7. Returning afterwards to opposition, Tierney acted as chief whip and parliamentary manager to the Whigs under Grey and in 1817 was elected their leader in the Commons, but he was frustrated by their disunity and lack of energy and became depressed and pessimistic. He accepted office in *Canning's cabinet as master of the mint but failed to persuade *Grey to join the government. After Canning's death he was dogged by ill-health and was less active. He was a formidable parliamentary speaker but too moody and inconsistent to be a successful leader. EAS

Tillett, Ben (1860–1943). Trade unionist. A Bristol man, Tillett spent his early years in the navy and merchant marine. Coming to the London docks he was shocked at the misery and poverty of casual labour and organized a docker's union. The great dockers' strike of 1889, for a basic wage of 6 pence an hour, was a sensation, and succeeded, partly through the mediation of Cardinal *Manning. Admitting that he hated strikes, as he had seen too much of the suffering they caused, Tillett campaigned for compulsory arbitration. He continued to build up dockers' and transport organizations, which came together in 1922 to form the Transport and General Workers' Union. Tillett threw himself into the war effort in 1914 and made recruiting speeches, to the disgust of many of his Labour colleagues. He served in Parliament for North Salford 1917–24 and 1929–31, and was chairman of the TUC 1928/9. A fine open-air speaker, Tillet was no theoretician and shocked some of his audience at the foundation meeting of the *Independent Labour Party in Bradford in 1893 with a fierce attack on doctrinaire socialists. He outlived his fame, drank too much, and reminisced. JAC

Tillotson, John (1630–94). Archbishop of Canterbury. As a graduate and fellow (1651) of Clare Hall, Cambridge, calvinistic writings impressed Tillotson. Though initially nonconforming, he was ordained (*c.*1661). As lecturer at St Lawrence Jewry (from 1664), he 'revolutionised preaching style', weaning some away from extreme puritanism. Despite some anti-catholic sermons, Charles II, who admired his preaching, appointed him royal chaplain and dean of Canterbury (1672). With *Baxter he supported comprehension of nonconformists (1674–5). Favoured by William III (1689), he became dean of St Paul's (1689) and was nominated by the Canterbury chapter to exercise archiepiscopal authority during *Sancroft's suspension, reluctantly accepting the see of Canterbury (1691) on Sancroft's deprivation. Despite his personal views, he was tolerant towards nonjurors and worked with *Nottingham, the moderate Tory secretary of state, to preserve peace in the church. WMM

Times, The. This newspaper has come to represent the 'establishment' of Britain and British journalism in popular perception. Founded in 1785 as the *Daily Universal Register*, it adopted its current title three years later, and its masthead symbol of the clock in 1804. *The Times* pioneered many of the staples of modern journalism—news gathering from foreign—especially war—correspondents; editorial independence from government; use of illustrations and advanced print technologies. After its late 19th-cent. decline, *The Times* was bought and revived by *Harmsworth in 1908, since when it has been the object of desire of most of the great newspaper magnates—Lord Astor, Lord Thomson, and currently Rupert Murdoch. DJA

Tinchebrai, battle of, 1106. Henry I and his elder brother *Robert of Normandy had been in contention over the succession to England and Normandy since 1100, when William II 'Rufus' died. In 1106 Henry sought to settle the issue. Whilst besieging Tinchebrai castle (near Vire, south-west Normandy), Henry was challenged by Robert, who had decided to risk battle. This was extremely rash since Henry enjoyed immense numerical superiority. The battle, fought on 28 September 1106, lasted barely an hour and settled the political issue once and for all. Robert's army was destroyed and he himself was taken to England where he was successively imprisoned in the castles of Wareham, Devizes, Bristol, and, finally, Cardiff. SL

Tindal, Matthew (1655–1733). One of the leading deists of the early 18th cent., Tindal came from Devon and attended Lincoln College, Oxford. In 1678 he obtained a fellowship at All Souls. After a brief flirtation with catholicism during the reign of James II, he moved into a low-church Erastian position and his book *The Rights of the Christian Church Asserted* (1706) scandalized high churchmen. Its sequel *A Defence of the Rights of the Christian Church* (1709) was burned by order of the House of Commons in 1710. His most celebrated work came out in 1730. In *Christianity as Old as Creation*, Tindal argued the case for natural religion. Though frequently accused of free thinking, he retained his fellowship at All Souls until his death. JAC

tin-mining was undertaken in Cornwall and Devon in prehistoric times and has continued into the 20th cent. Early mines exploited alluvial deposits near the surface but by the 16th cent. underground working following veins of ore had become the norm. Flood waters limited access to some tin deposits and deeper mining only became practicable during the 18th cent. when *Newcomen beam-engines made it possible to pump water from the workings. Tin combined with copper made bronze; and tin combined with lead made pewter. Both these alloys were used for many purposes for centuries. Coal replaced charcoal for smelting tin ore in the later 17th cent. as the demand for tin grew. Large quantities of coal from south Wales and Somerset were used at the tin-mines. Cornish production supplied most of the needs of Britain and Europe until the mid-19th cent. when many mines were worked out. The increased demand was met from Peru, and, later, Malaya. Demand for tin rose rapidly in the late 19th cent. to make tinplate (steel with a coating of tin) for rust-free containers for food. IJEK

Tintern (Gwent), a *Cistercian abbey, was founded in 1131 by Richard de Clare, lord of Chepstow, and was the first

Cistercian community in Wales. The majority of its endowments (most of them in south-east Wales) were acquired before 1200, by when it had established two daughter houses, at Kingswood and Tintern Minor. The patronage of the Bigod family, particularly at the end of the 13th cent., brought further property and financed the rebuilding of the abbey church. Like most Cistercian abbeys, Tintern's economy declined during the late Middle Ages, and the number of monks fell. However, some building work continued and at the time of its dissolution in 1536 Tintern was the wealthiest monastery in Wales. The surviving remains acquired fame from *Wordsworth's poem, and are amongst the finest of any Cistercian abbey in Europe. BJG

Tippermuir, battle of, 1644. Fought on 1 September 1644, this was the first in *Montrose's great run of victories. Outnumbered by more than two to one, he routed Lord Elcho's poorly trained troops just outside Perth, and went on to occupy the city. JAC

Tippett, Sir Michael (b. 1905). Composer. Of Cornish stock, hence his Celtic temperament, Tippett studied at the Royal School of Music, before further private tuition in composition. Disillusioned by the realities of the First World War, he turned to socialism, then pacifism (a conscientious objector in the Second World War, briefly imprisoned 1943). Believing, like *Britten, that music should be useful, he taught, conducted, lectured, and broadcast, and was director of music at Morley College, Southwark (1940–51), a focal point for central European musical refugees. Tippett's own music was initially conservative, but he soon developed a strongly personal idiom based on complex rhythms and long lyrical phrases; to symphonies and chamber music were added oratorio (*A Child Of Our Time*, 1941) and operas with his own librettos (*The Midsummer Marriage*, *King Priam*, *The Knot Garden*). Public recognition came late—not until the 1960s in Britain (knighthood 1966), and the 1970s in America. ASH

Tiptoft, John, 1st earl of Worcester (*c.*1427–70). Unusually for a peer's heir, Tiptoft spent three years with a tutor in University College, Oxford, immediately before his father's death in 1443. His creation as earl in 1449 coincided with his (first) marriage to the widowed duchess of Warwick. He was treasurer of England from 1452 to 1454, and probably became a sympathizer with Richard of *York. In 1458 he distanced himself by going to Jerusalem, afterwards touring Italy and studying at Padua until 1461; humanists enjoyed his patronage, and he collected books later bequeathed to Oxford University. Edward IV appointed him a councillor and constable of England. Tiptoft became notorious for his trials of traitors, allegedly by 'the law of Padua' but actually by the supranational law of arms. He was captured when *Warwick restored Henry VI, tried, and executed. RLS

Tironensians. Founded by St Bernard of Tiron (*c.*1046–1117), a former Benedictine monk of Poitiers, who became a hermit at Tiron (near Chartres), this Benedictine congregation was one of several ascetic communities established in the early 12th cent., of which the *Cistercians were the most successful. Though most of its abbeys were in France, and only a few very small houses were established in England and Wales, the Tironensians flourished in Scotland, where there were four abbeys (Kelso to which the first community founded at Selkirk *c.*1113 moved in 1128, Kilwinning, Arbroath, and Lindores), which enjoyed considerable popularity. BJG

Titanic. The largest passenger liner afloat, until the early morning of 15 April 1912, on its maiden transatlantic voyage, when it struck an iceberg and sank. Because its owners, the White Star Line, considered them an unnecessary extravagance, there were sufficient lifeboats to save no more than a minority of the passengers: 1,513 died altogether, out of a total complement of 2,224. Most of them were men, because the women were allowed into the lifeboats first (there were some compensations for not having the vote), and lower class, because they were in the most dangerous parts of the ship. The ship's band famously continued playing on the sloping deck as she sank, ending its selection with 'Nearer, my God, to thee'. The *Titanic* became a national symbol for both hubris and courage. BJP

tithe. The payment, originally in kind, of a tenth of the produce of land was at first a voluntary religious duty for the benefit of the poor, pilgrims, and churches, but by the 10th cent. it was compulsory, replacing the old church-scot for the maintenance of the church and clergy, and enforceable with heavy penalties, perhaps the loss of nine-tenths of annual income and later even excommunication. When lords built private churches on their land, tithe, at first still payable to the original church, soon went to the lord's family with only a portion to the priest. Similarly in parishes appropriated to a monastery, tithe was paid to the monastery and after the dissolution to their lay successors. With the spread of protestant nonconformity in the 17th cent., the payment of tithe became extremely contentious, leading to innumerable lawsuits. Resentment of tithe was still a factor in the *Swing riots of 1830 and the *Rebecca riots in south Wales in 1842–3. By the Tithe Commutation Act (1836) all tithe was commuted to rent-charges. Acts of 1918 and 1925 led to full, compulsory redemption of rent charges, which through the 1936 Tithe Act were replaced by redemption annuities, the crown issuing redemption stock to tithe owners with final extinction after 60 years (1996). Capital loss to the church by this Act was *c.* £17.7 million. In Scotland, tithes were known as teinds. WMM

tobacco industry. This originated in the 16th cent. and was attacked by James I in his *Counterblaste* (1604). Yet smoking spread, and snuff-taking became fashionable. There were three products, cut tobacco for pipes, roll tobacco for chewing and smoking, and snuff. The cost of entry to the industry increased and by 1840 it was beginning to concentrate in large towns. Mass production of manufactured tobacco was made possible by Robert Legg, the inventor of the automatic cutting machine (1853). Among the upper classes cigars became popular in the 1840s and late in that decade cigarettes were first introduced. Cigarettes became popular with servicemen during the *Crimean War, and their production greatly expanded after 1856. Light yellow tobacco, produced in Virginia, commonly replaced Turkish tobacco in handmade cigarettes by 1860. The introduction of the Bonsack machine (1881) led to the mass production of cigarettes and was adopted by *Wills, the leading company in the tobacco industry. Wills formed the Imperial Tobacco Company in 1901 by merging the leading British manufacturers. Since 1960 medical evidence of the effects of addiction and the correlation between smoking and lung cancer has clearly hit domestic demand, but the industry has developed extensive markets overseas. JB

Tobruk, battle of, 1941. The Libyan port of Tobruk, situated some 50 miles from the Egyptian frontier, was captured from the Italians by British forces on 22 January 1941. Axis forces under Rommel subsequently defeated the British, but it was decided to hold Tobruk, which Churchill described as a 'sally port' deep behind Axis lines. The siege of Tobruk began on 10 April 1941, and the port was relieved by the British during operation Crusader on 10 December 1941. Tobruk was subsequently captured by Rommel on 21 June 1942 and finally retaken by the British following the battle of *El Alamein in November 1942. GDS

Toc H. The movement was founded in 1915 when Revd Philip ('Tubby') Clayton acquired a house in Poperinghe, near Ypres, as a rest-home for troops. It was called Talbot House, after Gilbert Talbot, son of the bishop of Winchester, who was killed in action, and was known by its Morse-code initials. Based upon Christian and charitable principles, the movement received strong support from Edward, prince of Wales, was given a royal charter in 1922, and had more than 1,000 branches throughout Britain and the empire. Its symbol was a lamp. JAC

Toleration Act, 1689. As the Act's title, 'for exempting [dissenters] from the penalties of certain laws', indicates, it did not grant whole-hearted toleration but has been hailed as 'the grand landmark . . . in the history of dissent', for after comprehension failed, it legally sanctioned schism. Those unable to accept Anglican liturgy could worship in *unlocked* meeting-houses, licensed by the bishop, provided that the minister subscribed to the Thirty-Nine Articles except on baptism and church government. Catholics and unitarians were excluded. Non-Anglicans continued to suffer civil disabilities imposed by the *Clarendon code until 1828. By the 1720s even the Whigs, now landed gentry, despising the mainly urban dissenters, made no attempt to extend civil rights. WMM

Tolpuddle martyrs. In 1834 six agricultural labourers from the village of Tolpuddle in Dorset, who formed a trade union lodge, were sentenced to seven years' transportation under an Act of 1797 forbidding 'unlawful oaths'. Their leader, George Loveless, was a methodist and seems to have been in contact with delegates from Robert *Owen's *Grand National Consolidated Trade Union, who advised on the necessary ritual and initiation ceremony, including an oath of loyalty. Although unions were no longer illegal after the repeal of the *Combination Acts, and the Tolpuddle men sought only to resist a reduction in wages, the government feared rural unrest, including rick-burning and machine-breaking. The harsh sentence provoked a campaign of petitions and mass demonstrations organized by the GNCTU. Two years later the six were pardoned. In 1838 they returned home, but five of them later emigrated to Canada. JFCH

Tone, Wolfe (1763–98). Irish patriot. Tone was born into a middle-class protestant family in Dublin, educated at Trinity College, Dublin, and later trained as a lawyer. He was an eloquent advocate of catholic relief, gaining prominence through his *Argument on Behalf of the Catholics of Ireland* (1791) and as assistant secretary to the Catholic Committee (1792). He was intimately involved with the foundation, in 1791, of the United Irish Society, a constitutional radical organization with clubs initially in Belfast and Dublin. However, his politics grew progressively more militant, and in 1794–5 he was implicated in the indictment and trial, for treason, of a French agent, William Jackson. After a brief exile in the USA (August–December 1795), Tone served as United Irish emissary in France (1796–8), advocating French military assistance for the Irish republican cause. He was involved with two abortive French expeditions (in 1796 and 1798), being captured in October 1798. Convicted of treason by a court martial in November, he committed suicide rather than suffer a public hanging. Despite his origins as a Whig and a constitutionalist, he is widely revered as the father of militant Irish republicanism. AJ

Tonga is a group of volcanic islands, forming an independent kingdom within the Commonwealth. It lies to the east of Fiji in the South Pacific and exists on fishing and the export of copra and bananas. Cook, who visited several islands on his second and third voyage in the 1770s, called them the Friendly Islands. JAC

tonnage and poundage were customs duties which Parliament granted to Tudor monarchs for life. However, the crown's resort to *impositions led the first Parliament of Charles I to refrain from making the customary lifetime grant. The king reacted by ordering the collection of the duties on an *ad hoc* basis until such time as Parliament granted them. Parliament failed to do so, however, and the 1629 session concluded in uproar with the passing of a resolution against the collection of tonnage and poundage, framed by Sir John *Eliot. Only in 1641 did the *Long Parliament at last grant the duties, but it did so for a limited period and declared that the earlier prerogative levies were illegal. RL

Torres Vedras. The lines of Torres Vedras were a system of defensive fortifications constructed by *Wellington's engineers in 1809, and were situated 40 miles north of Lisbon to protect the city from French attack during the Peninsular War. They consisted of a series of forts and gun emplacements in three lines stretching some 30 miles from the river Tagus to the sea. Wellington fell back on the lines in October 1810 and held Masséna's French army at bay. In November Masséna was forced to retire to Spain with his army in poor condition. RAS

Torrington, battle of, 1646. By 1646, after the heavy defeats at *Naseby, *Langport, and *Philiphaugh, though Charles I still had armies in the field, the Civil War had become largely a mopping-up operation. *Hopton, one of the best royalist commanders, took over the remnants of *Goring's army in the south-west, numbering some 3,000 men. At Torrington in north Devon, while hoping to come to the relief of Exeter, he was attacked on 16 February by Sir Thomas *Fairfax's much larger force, was wounded, and forced back into Cornwall, where he was obliged to surrender the following month. JAC

torture. In his important work *De laudibus legum Angliae*, Chief Justice Fortescue (*c.*1385–1477/9) describes torture as being foreign to English law, which he praised in comparison with the civil law of the European continent. Certainly torture was a feature of the civil law system and was used to discover truth where an inquisitorial form of trial was used. However, although not used by the common law courts, it was used by the *council when investigating offences and, particularly in the reign of Henry VIII and Elizabeth I, the use of torture, notably the use of the rack, was common. Torture was also occasionally used by the Court of *Star Chamber. Although the common law itself did not use torture as a means of obtaining evidence, it did in practice torture those who refused to accept trial by jury under the *peine forte et dure. Torture was permitted under Scottish law, but was abolished immediately after the Union by 7 Anne c. 21 s. 5 (1708). MM

Tories. The Tories were one of the two main political parties which dominated public affairs between the later 17th and mid-19th cents. Their existence as a parliamentary 'party' was not continuous but evolved and changed over time in response to issues and personalities, their party pretensions sometimes weakened by division, or disappearing entirely. The term Tory (from *toraighe*, Irish for bandit or bog-trotter) was first applied by the Whigs to the court supporters of James, duke of York, during the *Exclusion crisis, 1679–81. Their notions of God-ordained kingly authority, 'divine right', to which there could be no human resistance, entailed a deep attachment to the Anglican church, and to typical Tories crown and church were the chief preservatives of the political, religious, and social order. James II's catholicism forced them into choosing between their king and their church, and though most chose the latter and guardedly accepted the revolution, many were still unwilling to regard William III as rightful king, or to accept the Whiggish notion of parliamentary authority enshrined in the *Declaration of Rights. Under King William, the country Tories (as opposed to court Tories who took office) identified with the squirearchy and pursued their prejudices against the *Junto Whigs, the toleration of dissenters, the expense of continental war, the 'monied interest', and the expansion of government influence and bureaucracy. Out of their alliance with disaffected Whigs emerged the 'new Tory Party' during the late 1690s under Robert *Harley's leadership. The Tories were more at ease under Queen Anne (1702–14), whom they regarded as a legitimate successor of James II. But despite their electoral popularity and steadfastness towards the church, they were frequently split ministerially and in Parliament over war strategy, the persecution of dissenters, and the Hanoverian succession, a situation worsened towards the close of the reign by the open rivalry between Harley (as Lord Oxford) and *Bolingbroke.

The adherence of some die-hard Tories to the *Jacobite cause after George I's accession in 1714 allowed the Whigs as champions of the new dynasty to discredit all Tories as disloyal and dangerous, and until the 1760s they were kept out of government office, with only a few admitted in the localities to the magisterial bench. But as individuals many retained their importance in local politics and administration, while as a component of opposition in the Commons, where they numbered more than 100, they displayed continued sensitivity in issues concerning the church and the royal prerogative. As a result of George III's ending of proscription during the early 1760s, the Tories went their different ways, some aligning with the government, some with the various Whig factions, and others remaining as independent country MPs. Tory values, however, with their focus on the church and the sanctity of governmental authority, continued to have an important place in political argument, featuring significantly in the debates on America and in the 'conservative reaction' towards the end of the century. Under the impact of the French Revolution, the younger *Pitt's ministry was frequently derided by the Foxite opposition as 'Tory', though this did not become a meaningful political label again until after Pitt's death in 1806. Out of the factionalism of the early 19th cent. gradually emerged the Toryism of *Liverpool and *Peel, the latter credited with the ideology of Conservatism. The term 'Tory' is still used, often pejoratively, to refer to the modern Conservative Party. AAH

Tostig, earl of Northumbria (*c.*1025–66), younger brother of *Harold, who was briefly, in 1066, king of England, and of *Eadgyth, *Edward the Confessor's queen. With Tostig's appointment to Northumbria, his family seemed set to dominate the English kingdom. But he was driven out by a local rebellion in 1065. He blamed Harold for not attempting to secure his reinstatement, and in exile raised a force which raided the English coast. Achieving little, he joined the army led by *Harold Hardrada, king of Norway, and was killed at the battle of *Stamford Bridge. Tostig's unpopularity in Northumbria may well have made the wary Harold reluctant to support him. Whatever the case, their bitter quarrel had disastrous results since, united, the two brothers would surely have been able to do much more to prevent the *Norman Conquest than was ultimately possible. DB

touching for the king's evil was an instant medieval royal tradition. On learning that their rivals the Capetian kings of France claimed divine healing powers, the kings of England, from Henry I onwards, followed suit. Curiously it was only scrofula that could be cured. The ceremony developed into a very formal one, with the monarch stroking the sufferer's throat, while a cleric intoned 'They shall lay their hands on the sick and they shall recover' (Mark 16). If they did not, they at least had a gold medallion to show for it. James I disliked the practice but Charles II is said to have stroked more than 90,000 people. William III discontinued the ceremony. Jacobites insisted that the touch had deserted a usurper but claimed that the exiled Stuarts had effected miraculous cures. Queen Anne revived it and one of the last persons to be stroked was the young Samuel *Johnson in 1712. The Hanoverians gave it up, though in France Charles X was still stroking when removed by revolution in 1830. JAC

Toulouse, battle of, 1814. On 10 April 1814 *Wellington launched an assault against the city, losing 5,000 men. However, after fierce fighting, Marshal Soult and the French were driven out with the loss of 3,000 men. The victory came hours before Napoleon's abdication in Paris on 11 April. RAS

tourism is a stage beyond trail-blazing as an explorer or adventuring in little-explored and possibly dangerous places as what might be called a traveller. It depends on an infrastructure providing guidance, accommodation, and perhaps entertainment, on however rudimentary a level, for those who seek pleasure and interest in journeys away from home territory. It follows beaten paths, and sometimes receives contemptuous responses from the more self-consciously imaginative and adventurous: even Revd Francis *Kilvert, thinking himself a little off the conventional routes of Cornwall in the early 1870s, felt able to denounce (repeatedly) the common 'tourists' he encountered. There is a case for presenting *Chaucer's Canterbury pilgrims and their medieval counterparts as early tourists, but the phenomenon of tourism has its most obvious roots in the *grand tour of Europe which British aristocrats opened out in the 17th and 18th cents., seeking cultural awakening and worldly experience in (especially) northern Italy and buying sculptures and paintings to take back to adorn their country houses. Cultural tourism was soon supplemented by landscape tourism, as the cult of the picturesque, the romantic, and the sublime led British aristocrats to alpine passes and glaciers, as well as to landscapes vivified by classical connotations; and the pursuit of the picturesque encouraged tours like those of Lord Torrington or Sir Richard Colt Hoare in search of distinctive scenery and novel sensations, which could be transmogrified into the stuff of polite cultural exchange through the sketch-book and the printed word. Architecture also became part of the fashionable passing show, as did ruins and natural history, and the country houses of the aristocracy and the birthplaces or chosen subjects of literary lions or artists also became objects of the tourist gaze.

The age of the steamship and the railway brought a widening of the tourist market in Britain, as the middling and even the lower middle classes began to aspire to travel in search of entertainment and enlightenment, and cheaper transport and more accessible arrangements made this a realistic possibility. The foremost name here is Thomas Cook, the Leicester temperance reformer, who inaugurated cut-price continental travel, with all arrangements made by his firm, after modestly inaugurating his activities with a temperance excursion from Leicester to Loughborough. Cook's tourists, as they became known, were derided by those who laid claim to effortless expertise in cultural analysis, and their passage through places such as Cologne cathedral, guidebooks in hand, eager not to miss a single point, was the subject of condescending comment in periodicals like **Punch* from the 1860s onwards. But tourism was to prove an enduring growth industry, as higher real incomes and expanded free time spread down the social scale, and the cultural rewards for being able to talk about interesting holidays became enhanced accordingly. Alongside the rise of spas and seaside resorts (from the 18th cent.), which catered for seekers after health and entertainment as well as those with more exacting aspirations, there were regions which offered mountain air and scenery, literary associations, and interesting flora and fauna as well as architecture and classical allusions; and the market for British tourism had extended throughout and beyond Europe by the turn of the century, including Cook's popular tours to the Holy Land. The growth of tourism promoted markets in souvenirs and fake works of art, and the tourist gaze transformed the societies at which it was directed. This was already a source of complaint before the First World War, though some utilitarian and progress-celebrating writers like Harriet Martineau, writing in this case about the mid-Victorian Lake District, celebrated the progress and enlightenment which tourism brought in its train, pointing out its capacity for generating employment. Not everyone was so optimistic. The problems and possibilities opened out by an ever-expanding tourist industry, and by its popularizations (especially for the affluent middle-class British market), continued to be the focus for anguished debate in the inter-war years, although it was not until the advent of cheap air travel and package tours to the Mediterranean from the 1960s that a real sense of cultural crisis could be detected on a broad front. The debates on tourism at the end of the 20th cent. differ more in degree and emphasis than in kind from those which were already being aired a century earlier. JKW

tournaments. By the later Middle Ages, the term tournament covered all kinds of armed combat, both team and individual, performed competitively in public. Originally, however, the term applied specifically to the meeting of two teams in a quasi-battlefield situation. In England and France, this form of combat was commonly described as a 'hastilude', literally a game with spears, whereas a 'joust' was generally a contest between individuals, on foot or on horseback, although the competitors often formed teams. Indeed, it has been suggested that Edward III's Order of the *Garter, founded *c.*1348, was initially intended to comprise two equal-sized tournament teams, headed by the king and his eldest son *Edward the Black Prince. Tournaments were essentially sporting and social occasions rather than a means of developing skills for war. They were often banned in England in times of overseas war (Henry V particularly disapproved of them), since they had been closely connected with baronial disquiet in the first half of the 13th cent. It was possible for young men of relatively low status to make a mark through their prowess, but in general the participants were already of noble or at least knightly birth. Moreover, it was an expensive activity, requiring increasingly sophisticated equipment, not only for show and identification, but also for protection because the combats were often exceedingly dangerous and specialized tournament armours and weapons were necessary: in these respects, a close analogy can be drawn with Formula One motor racing today. It was undoubtedly a spectator sport, involving much pageantry and ritual. Its popularity in England was boosted by the personal enthusiasm and participation of Edward I; from his reign onwards, the royal court was the focus of both leadership and patronage to a degree unparalleled elsewhere in Europe. Edward III followed in his grandfather's footsteps, developing the *Arthurian analogies to the full, but after the reign of Richard II royal patronage, and with it the tournament in England, declined until its revival under Henry VIII. AC

Tours, truce of, 1444. With the struggle in France moving against them in the 1440s, the English wished to use a marriage negotiation for Henry VI to obtain a settlement. At Tours in May 1444, Suffolk (William de la *Pole) promised to surrender Maine in exchange for a two-year truce and Henry was betrothed to *Margaret of Anjou, niece of Charles VII of France. The break in hostilities lasted only until 1449 when Charles attacked Normandy and took Rouen. JAC

Tower of London (White Tower). Built by William the Conqueror within the south-east corner of the old Roman walls of London as one of three fortresses intended to secure the city. As London became increasingly important as the centre both of government and of commerce, the castle was enlarged and updated by successive kings, especially by Edward I and Edward III, until it became a complex concentric fortification. But no royal castle in the Middle Ages was used solely for defence and the Tower became the site of a multitude of offices and departments. Its multifarious role was summed up by John *Stow in his *Survey of London* in 1598: 'This Tower is a citadel to defend or command the city [of London]; a royal palace for assemblies or treaties; a prison of state for the most dangerous offenders; the only place of coinage for all England at this time; the armoury for warlike provision; the treasury of the ornaments and jewels of the crown; and general conserver of the most records of the courts of justice at Westminster.'

Even in the later Middle Ages the kings had preferred to reside when in London at their palace at *Westminster. Traditionally, however, the new sovereign spent the night in the Tower before his coronation, going in procession to Westminster for the ceremony. The last king to make this procession was Charles II. The Tower has gradually been stripped of most of its other functions. It is still a royal castle, houses the crown jewels, and retains a small military presence but its other offices were relocated in the 19th cent.; the royal mint was moved to new premises on Tower Hill in 1811–12; and in the 1850s the documents held in the Tower were moved to the newly built Public Record Office in Chancery Lane. The historic collection of weapons in the armouries is all that remains of the arsenal, moved to Woolwich after 1841, and to Leeds in 1995.

The importance of the Tower as a prison and military strong point remained. Each political crisis caused the Tower to be placed in readiness and saw it housing a crop of political prisoners. Even the duke of Wellington, constable of the Tower 1836–52, fearing that the country was close to popular revolution and that the Tower would be a target, had its defences repaired and strengthened and new barracks built with accommodation for a garrison of nearly 1,000 men. He also argued that the Tower was 'the best if not the only good place of security' for state prisoners, although few were held there. During the two world wars some German spies were executed by firing squad in the Tower and prisoners were again housed there, the last being Rudolf Hess, after his flight to Britain in 1941. LR

towns. Since Britain was the first country in the world to urbanize, i.e. to have over half its population living in towns, but also for many centuries lagged behind other European countries in the degree of its urbanization, there is an interesting paradox at the heart of British urban history. It is also bedevilled by semantic debate: what is a town? Much older literature concentrated on legal status and discussed 'boroughs', whereas recent scholars stress more social and economic criteria. The best definition is perhaps that of Susan Reynolds, that a town is a permanent human settlement which forms a social unit distinct from the surrounding countryside, and in which a significant proportion of its population lives off non-agricultural occupations.

Though there were large settlements in Iron Age Britain which have been identified as 'proto-towns', true urbanism began with the Roman occupation of southern Britain. Leading Romano-British towns included a strikingly high proportion of those towns which topped urban league tables until the industrial revolution—*London, *Lincoln, *York, *Winchester, *Canterbury, etc. Though they are often seen as primarily administrative and social rather than economic centres, which ceased to be towns when Roman administration collapsed in the 5th cent., that may be too simple. Their strategic positions, and their reoccupation in the Middle Ages (with one or two exceptions like *Silchester and *Wroxeter) suggests that they were as well sited as they could be in relation to the economic exploitation of British pre-industrial conditions.

Some Roman towns may have continued, under native leadership and invading Anglo-Saxons, as 'central places', with royal palaces or religious centres, but true town life seems to have revived in the 7th and 8th cents. with the development of organized trade and settled states. Large trading towns (*wics* or *emporia*) developed both alongside old Roman fortified sites (London, York, and *Southampton) and in at least one case on a new, non-Roman site (*Ipswich). Meanwhile small towns developed inland around royal and ecclesiastical centres, especially after the foundation of cathedrals and major churches. Urban life may have been disrupted by the Viking raids and conquests of the 8th and 9th cents., and King *Alfred initiated or developed a system of fortified settlements (burhs) to resist them; but the Vikings themselves stimulated urban growth and trade in eastern England. Under the kings of united England (954–1066) existing towns flourished and new towns were founded, including networks of shire towns and mint towns.

The Normans after 1066 further developed towns in England and also in south Wales, many of them dominated or protected by a castle, while in Scotland towns emerged in the 11th and 12th cents. A developing commercial economy in the 12th and 13th cents. led to the expansion of many towns and the creation of many new ones, including hundreds of small market centres. Large towns acquired communal defences and chartered privileges, and London rapidly acquired a unique status as a capital city and the only British town comparable to the great continental towns. Its population may have reached 80,000–100,000 by 1300, while towns as a whole may have accounted for 15 per cent of the English population; the proportion was much lower in Wales and Scotland. The *Black Death of 1348–50 killed a high proportion of townspeople, and some historians have seen it as ushering in a period of late medieval urban decay, and even crisis. However, there is much evidence that many towns, though reduced in size, flourished, and certainly liberties were granted to many towns by both English and Scottish monarchs.

The 16th and 17th cents. saw some recovery in the size of towns, since although their mortality rates were high (bubonic plague returned periodically until the 1660s), they attracted large numbers of immigrants. The most outstanding case was that of London, which grew rapidly both in absolute and in relative terms, becoming by 1700 the largest town in western Europe and at least 20 times as large as any other English town. In the 18th cent., however, industrial and commercial development, including better communications, allowed many other towns to grow rapidly. This huge urban growth disrupted old institutions and attitudes and led to the municipal reforms imposed by Parliament from the 1830s onwards.

In the 19th and 20th cents. towns continued to grow in relative as well as absolute terms, while nearly all British people have come to share an essentially urban culture, whether or not they live in towns. The total urban population of England and Wales reached 54 per cent by 1851, 78 per cent by 1901, and 81 per cent by 1951 (for Scotland similar calculations give 52 per cent by 1851 and 65 per cent by 1891). With proportions so high, it becomes increasingly difficult to separate urban from national history, and it becomes possible to write national history from an urban perspective. DMP

Clark, P., and Slack, P., *English Towns in Transition 1500–1700* (Oxford, 1976); Corfield, P. J., *The Impact of English Towns, 1700–1800* (Oxford, 1982); Reynolds, S., *An Introduction to the History of English Medieval Towns* (Oxford, 1977); Waller, P. J., *Town, City and Nation: England 1850–1914* (Oxford, 1983).

Townshend, Charles (1725–67). Townshend dashed across the political sky in the 1760s like a comet, blazed, and was gone. A grandson of 'Turnip' *Townshend, he was returned to Parliament on the family interest at Great Yarmouth when he was 21 and held a variety of junior posts in the 1750s and early 1760s. In 1766 he became chancellor of the Exchequer in Chatham's (*Pitt) ministry. The weakness of the ostensible first minister, *Grafton, and the illness of Chatham, gave Townshend his head. In May 1767 he delighted and amazed the Commons with his 'champagne' speech, of which few reports survive. At the same time he pledged himself to raise a revenue in America by the imposition of a range of duties, a policy made all the more necessary by his failure to carry the land tax at 4 shillings, which left him short of budgetary income. Having lit the fuse for an American time-bomb, he died in September 1767 of a fever at the age of 42. Lecky called him 'the spoiled child of the House of Commons'. JAC

Townshend, Charles Townshend, 2nd Viscount (1674–1738). Townshend succeeded to his peerage and the headship of the leading Norfolk political family in 1687. Though from a Tory background, he became a Whig closely associated with the *Junto, specializing in foreign affairs. In 1713 he married Robert *Walpole's sister and the following year became secretary of state for the northern department. Shifted to the less powerful post of lord-lieutenant of Ireland in 1717, he resigned from the government along with Walpole and remained in opposition during the Whig schism until 1720 when he became lord president of the council, returning to the northern department the following year. From 1722 he and Walpole ran the administration, with Townshend concentrating on foreign affairs, and though Walpole can be considered first minister because of his control of the Treasury, the ministry should be viewed as a duumvirate until at least 1727 when Townshend began to lose ground to his brother-in-law. Disagreement over foreign policy, partly with Queen *Caroline, had led to his resignation from the ministry in 1730. In retirement he devoted himself to agriculture on his estate at Rainham, and has come down to posterity as 'Turnip Townshend'. CJ

Townshend, George (1724–1807). George Townshend, elder brother of *Charles, had a distinguished military and political career. An army officer, he was second in command to *Wolfe in Canada and took over when Wolfe was killed. He succeeded as viscount in 1764 and from 1767 to 1772 was lord-lieutenant of Ireland. During this time he tried to free the castle from the *undertaker system and made important concessions to the Irish Parliament. On his return, he was master of the ordnance throughout the rest of North's ministry and held the post again in 1783 under the coalition. He was out of office after 1784 though he became marquis in 1786 and was promoted field marshal in 1796. His brother was a brilliant mimic: George Townshend was an equally brilliant amateur caricaturist. JAC

townswomen's guilds, emerging out of the women's suffrage movement and modelled on the remarkably successful rural *women's institutes, were founded in 1928 with a programme of 'comradeship, arts and crafts and citizenship' for the urban ordinary housewife. Similarly non-party and non-sectarian, with a firm framework, their social and educational emphasis was reassuring, and guilds burgeoned throughout the UK. During the Second World War, their monthly magazine the *Townswoman*, which aided continuity, offered practical advice and encouragement, while the extent of poverty and degradation revealed by the evacuation programme encouraged subsequent public and social welfare interests. Pioneering work in adult education was accompanied by organizational strengthening and overseas links, but membership began to fall in the 1970s as structural rigidity came under challenge and younger women failed to come forward. Learning how to serve had begun to yield to women's changing aspirations and increasing economic emancipation. ASH

Towton, battle of, 1461. Towton is unique among British battles, being fought in a blinding snowstorm. It saw the largest armies ever assembled in the country, with more than 50,000 men involved, including most of the nobility. Edward IV, the 19-year-old Yorkist claimant in the Wars of the *Roses, was proclaimed king in London early in March 1461 and pursued his adversaries north. Queen *Margaret and her hapless husband Henry VI were at York. The armies clashed at Ferrybridge on 28 March and did battle the following day at Towton, 10 miles towards Tadcaster. The slaughter was great and the Lancastrians routed. Henry and his wife fled to Scotland while Edward returned to London to be crowned. JAC

tractarianism was the name applied to the first stage of the *Oxford movement, derived from a series of *Tracts for the Times* written between 1833 and 1841 by a group of Oxford high churchmen, including Hurrell Froude, *Keble, *Newman, *Pusey, and Isaac Williams. Their context, signalled by Keble's Oxford assize sermon on 'National Apostasy' (14 July 1833), was alarm at the onslaught of Roman catholicism, dissent, and 'liberalism', focused by the Whig government's abolition of ten Irish bishoprics in what appeared to be a revolution in the relations between church and state. Tractarians insisted on the church's authority to teach catholic truth to the English as the divinely commissioned agent of Christ and his apostles, and their exploration of this authority began a movement which decisively affected English Christianity's understanding of sanctity, worship, and religious practice. The furore provoked by Newman's Tract 90, on the Thirty-Nine Articles, ended the series and his reception into the Roman catholic church closed the tractarian phase, but their influence set the Anglican pace for the rest of the century. CB

trade. Economic development has, from the earliest times, been manifest in and driven by trade, which has been one of the principal mechanisms by which prosperity has increased. One of the main reasons for trade is specialization of production. Some examples are obvious. European countries are not very successful in growing bananas and other tropical foods. Similarly, the distribution of natural resources like coal, iron ore, and oil has always been unequal. Thus each country specializes in producing those commodities in which it has a comparative advantage. Even if, in a two-country world, one country was most efficient in producing everything, it would still be worth while for it to specialize and import some commodities from the other. Specialization allows economies of scale because it is more efficient to produce for a large world market than for a much smaller national market. Britain in the 19th cent. relied very heavily on export markets to sustain its textiles, engineering, and mining industries. Trade can be envisaged as an indirect form of production. The commodities imported rather than produced at home will always require less productive inputs than would be required under home production. Trade is thus an unqualified benefit to all parties, irrespective of whether trade is fair or a country is competitive.

But the fact that trade is universally advantageous does not mean that the benefits are equally distributed. Changes in the composition of output resulting from trade will produce both gains and losses. The impact of imperial free trade policies on 19th-cent. India boosted the export of raw cotton to Britain but had a devastating impact on Indian cotton manufactures. Similarly British manufacturers gained from access to overseas markets, while wheat producers suffered from competition from cheap grain from the USA. The overall gain is derived from the fact that, in principle, those who gain from trade could compensate those who lose and still be better off than they were initially. In an ideal world in which there existed unrestrained trade and free movement of labour and capital between countries, the price of inputs like labour and capital would be the same everywhere. There would be, in fact, a single integrated world market. In reality this is far from the case. Variations in natural resources, in which some countries are rich (Russia) and some are relatively very poor (Japan), and in technology, barriers to trade, and historical experience of development have maintained and augmented these differences.

There is little doubt that international trade and specialized production played a major part in the growth of the industrial economies in the 18th and especially the 19th cent. The depression of the 1930s was marked by the lowest level of international trade for centuries, while the boom in the 1950s and 1960s was as manifest in trade as in output and incomes. But many in the less developed countries have argued that trade has not been beneficial for them since they have been peripheral to those with greater comparative advantage. Indeed it has become a radical criticism of the free market system that it prospered through the exploitation of the less developed countries by the industrial nations. Attention is drawn to the experience of countries like Brazil or Egypt, which experienced growth without development through a comparative advantage in exporting raw materials, such as coffee, rubber, and cotton. Hence the support for import substitution policies and attempts to persuade the developed world to help by allowing trade on terms favourable to the less developed. Neither strategy was successful. But in the 1970s and 1980s the 'four tigers' of south-east Asia (Hong Kong, Singapore, South Korea, Taiwan) achieved unparalleled growth rates through the export of manufactures, from textiles to engineering and electrical goods, and thus provided a reminder of the benefits of trade. CHL

Trade, Board of. The origins of the department may be traced back to 1621 when, in the face of a trade recession and a difficult Parliament, a number of committees were appointed, under the guidance of *Cranfield, to consider the matter. At the Restoration, Charles II appointed separate councils for trade and for plantations, brought together by *Shaftesbury in 1672, who took the presidency. His successor, *Danby, reorganized it with William Blathwayt as secretary. In 1696 when the problem of coinage was again giving trouble, a permanent Board of Trade and Plantations was set up, with eight core members, supported by the great officers of state. The earl of Bridgwater took the presidency and John *Locke was one of the first commissioners. The business of the board was primarily colonial administration and policy. *Gibbon found, when appointed in 1779, that 'our duty is not intolerably severe' and in 1782 the board fell victim to the *economical reform of the Rockinghams. Pressure of business soon demanded a replacement. As early as March 1784 *Pitt's government appointed a new committee, upgraded in 1786 to a board, with Jenkinson as president and given a peerage as Lord *Liverpool. The post was not at first highly regarded and the president was not necessarily in the cabinet. But as extra responsibilities were acquired and economic growth became a major consideration, the prestige of the department rose and politicians of the calibre of *Gladstone, Joseph *Chamberlain, *Churchill, *Lloyd George, *Cripps, and *Wilson took it on. Since 1945 the presidency has often been held with some other post as governments reshuffled organization in desperate attempts to find the golden key to prosperity.

JAC

Trades Disputes Act, 1906. The Liberal government introduced a bill based on the recommendations of the royal commission (1903). It proposed statutory recognition of unions and the separation of their benefit funds from strike and general funds. The trade unions and Labour MPs were not satisfied with the government's bill and introduced a private member's bill. The Labour bill was accepted by the Liberals and formed the basis of the Trades Disputes Act. This indemnified unions against civil proceedings; their funds were protected against claims for damages, thus discounting the *Taff Vale judgment (1902). This very privileged position survived until 1927. JB

Trades Union Congress. At an early stage of trade union development, the idea of a co-ordinating body emerged and in 1834 the *Grand National Consolidated Trade Union was founded. It attracted many members but few funds, and the secretary absconded with what there were. It lasted less than a year. But during the next three decades there was a substantial growth of trade union membership, particularly in the skilled trades. The Amalgamated Society of Engineers was founded in 1851, the Amalgamated Society of Carpenters in 1860, together with a Glasgow trades council 1858 and a London trades council 1860. In 1868 a meeting of 34 delegates in Manchester resolved that annual meetings were desirable, though no machinery was devised. The new organization set up a parliamentary committee in 1871 to lobby on legislation. In 1900 a Labour Representation Committee was established—the forerunner of the *Labour Party in 1906. The Scottish TUC was founded in 1897. By 1893 there were more than a million trade unionists affiliated to the TUC, 6 million by 1920, and 12 million by 1979, after which membership went into marked decline. The electoral difficulties of the Labour Party after 1979 caused its relationship to the TUC to be constantly reassessed. JAC

Trade Union Act, 1871. Passed by *Gladstone's administration following the recommendations of the Royal Commission on Trade Societies (1867), the Act clarified the legality of trade unions and provided for their funds to be protected under the Friendly Society Act, 1855. Penal clauses, initially included in this Act, were incorporated in the Criminal Law Amendment Act, 1871. Intimidation, obstruction, and molestation were difficult to define at law; *Disraeli's government legalized peaceful picketing in 1875 (Conspiracy and Protection of Property Act). These measures did not solve the complex issues of behaviour during industrial disputes but they did indicate the growing electoral importance of skilled urban workers. JB

trade unions, retaining some of the benefit functions of the old craft guilds, emerged in the 18th cent. as conflicts between capital and labour increased and state protection collapsed before the rise of the *factory system. More intensive exploitation occurred in the factory, but factory workers were in a minority for most of the period 1780–1900, and skilled handicraft societies set the style of unionism. They were subject to prosecution under English common law as combinations in restraint of trade. Fear of revolution led to the *combination laws of 1799–1800; this legislation was ineffective, forcing unions underground. Eventually, unions were given legal recognition under the Act of 1825. Most unions were local, small, and based on public houses or 'houses of call', but some of them had a primitive national organization.

Owenite utopianism stimulated the rise of general unions. Older unionism existed alongside attempts to found a *Grand National Consolidated Trade Union; when this grandiose organization collapsed in 1834–5, continuity was maintained by 'the aristocracy of labour'. After the depression of the early 1840s national unions of skilled trades either revived or were founded. There is little justification for using the term 'New Model Unionism' about the formation of the Amalgamated Society of Engineers (1851); there was no radical reorganization and no new characteristics. The ASE was merely one successful example of a process proceeding from the 1820s. Skilled unions had always insisted upon efficient organization, strikes being a last resort, collective bargaining the norm, and death, sickness, or unemployment benefits provided. Trades councils were created by unions; from the London Trades Council emerged the *Trades Union Congress (1868).

Legal recognition and protection of funds became an issue after the *Hornby* v. *Close* decision revealed that unions lacked these basic rights; hence the pressure for the Acts passed in the 1870s. The revival of socialism in the 1880s coincided with depressions and the creation of new unions for the semi-skilled and the unskilled, paying lower entry fees and prepared to be militant. Membership of unions rose from about 750,000 in 1888 to over 4 million by 1913. Individual unions increased in size. Some grew organically, others as a result of amalgamation. Industrial strife was widespread in the years before 1914, provoked by falling living standards and a growing radicalism associated with *syndicalist ideas. The Triple Alliance of transport workers, miners, and railwaymen was in existence by 1914 and had a strategy of sympathy strikes in place. Thus the ground was drawn for the sharp class conflicts of the 1920s including the *General Strike of 1926. Trade union membership declined during the Great Slump, only reviving in the late 1930s.

The Second World War (1939–45) led to the direction of labour and full employment. Trade union membership increased from about 6,250,000 in 1939 to nearly 8 million in 1945. By 1979 there were about 13,500,000 members or 58 per cent of those in work. More industrial unions were created at the expense of traditional craft unions, but demarcation disputes and unofficial strikes were frequent.

After 1979 trade union membership fell to under 10,250,000 by 1988 or 37.6 per cent of the labour force, and the number of unions declined from 453 in 1979 to 330 in 1987. Hostile legislation designed to remove union power over the labour market beginning with Acts of 1980 and 1982 was a feature of the policies of *Thatcherite Conservatism. Single union agreements with 'no strike' clauses were common, as plant bargaining began to replace national negotiations. A significant change was the Labour Party's distancing itself from the union movement, with which it had been closely associated since its birth. JB

Trafalgar, battle of, 1805. Fought on 21 October 1805, 20 miles south of Cadiz and 12 miles south-west of the shoaling Cape Trafalgar, this most famous of engagements in the era of sail lasted from midday to about 5 p.m. In the course of it, 18 of the 33-strong combined fleet of France and Spain surrendered to the British under the command of Lord *Nelson, supported by Cuthbert *Collingwood heading the fleet's southerly (lee) division, and Lord Northesk, in the rear of Nelson's northerly (weather) division, which he himself headed in **Victory*. The two divisions, comprising 27 ships in all and separated north–south by a mile, advanced at right angles against the Franco-Spanish line from the west. By midday this line was on a northerly bearing for Cadiz, having a few hours before been on a southerly one, as if for the Straits. In consequence Villeneuve's and Alava's dispositions of their ships were fatally confused, though their often inexperienced crews fought with great bravery. The British engaged 'pell mell' at the closest quarters without losing a ship, Nelson's exhortation to 'every man to do his duty' being echoed by rates of fire which no other fleet of the day could approach. Nelson's victories removed all possibility of Napoleon launching an invasion of Britain.

Trafalgar was the quintessence of the implicit abandonment, in progress during the previous half-century, of opposing fleets engaging in formal parallel lines, but it was Nelson's personal genius which conferred on the battle a resonance which transcended innovation. Following his death at the battle's close, when some 500 British and at least 2,000 Spaniards and French had died (followed by many more drowned in the ensuing week-long gale), there was no active pursuit of Nelson's ideas, a retrograde conservatism being deemed the better part of audacity.

DDA

Traherne, Thomas (1637–74). Religious writer. Son of a Hereford shoemaker but enabled to study at Oxford, Traherne was ordained in 1660 and held the living of Credenhill (near Hereford) 1661–74, though he resided at London and Teddington 1669–74 as domestic chaplain to Sir Orlando Bridgman, lord keeper of the great seal. Despite his literary intensity, only *Roman Forgeries* (1673), which attempted to substantiate charges against the Roman church for tampering with early Christian church records, was published in his lifetime. *Christian Ethicks* (1675) and *Thanksgivings* (1699) were posthumous, but manuscripts for *Centuries of Meditations* (instructing a friend in the way of 'felicity') and *Poetical Works* had to await chance discovery on a London street bookstall in 1896, whilst *Poems of Felicity* was unearthed later in the British Museum. A mystic poet like *Herbert and *Vaughan, Traherne was acknowledged by contemporaries for piety and scholarship, though has since been charged with naïvety. ASH

trained bands were the county- and city-based militia regiments, which, except for London and a few counties, played little significant part in the civil wars. The London regiments were built up to a strength of 18,000, mainly infantry, by 1643. Officered by the commercial leaders of the city, their rank and file comprised mainly apprentices and hired men rather than householders. They were employed in patrolling the Thames valley, but also played a critical role at *Turnham Green, the siege of Gloucester, and the first battle of *Newbury. Increasingly unwilling to leave London, they saw their role taken over by permanent standing armies in 1643 and 1644. The attempt by the moderate peace party of Denzil *Holles to use the London trained bands in the projected presbyterian counter-revolution of 1647 was an abject failure: when summoned to defend London against the invading *New Model Army, the men refused to stir. IJG

trams. Light rail systems for passenger carriage, predominantly urban in use, named after the pre-1800 wagon-ways of the north-east, were introduced to Europe from the USA in the 1850s. With the low rolling resistance of rails, trams offered a smooth ride, with considerable economy in horsepower: a two-horse, 2-ton tram could carry 50 passengers, double the load of an omnibus with a similar team. Established in five centres in 1859–62 by George Francis Train, using unacceptably protuberant rails, Britain's tramways effectively began with the Liverpool system in 1868. The Tramways Act of 1870 facilitated growth, but its provision for municipal purchase at current value after 21 years ultimately inhibited innovation. Because of weight problems, steam traction had limited application to British tramways, but electrification was critical to advance, and was retarded by the Act. First applied on third-rail Siemens principles to the Newry tramway in the 1880s, electrification became generalized using overhead conductors, and was successfully proven in the demonstration line provided by Thomson-Houston in Leeds in 1890. Electrification spread quickly in municipalized tramways, beginning with Bristol (1895) and Glasgow from 1898, where municipal tramway enterprise reached a height.

Trams catered for the 'better-off' workers, and provided a well-lit and reliable service, producing star-profiled growth of towns and cities, as property values and development followed the tramlines outward. They proved correspondingly profitable, producing rather better dividends than railways around 1900, attracting demands for municipal regulation of monopoly. The next 25 years saw booming traffic: journeys rose from 992 million in 1899–1900 to 4,706 million at their peak in 1927–8, and route miles peaked in 1924 at 2,605. One could travel by municipal tram from Leeds to Liverpool in the 1930s, with but a short walk between end-on networks. They declined steadily thereafter, with some traffic being transferred to the trolleybuses, pioneered by Leeds and Bradford in 1911, but which, at their peak, only carried a little over 2,000 million passengers. Trams proved relatively inflexible from the 1920s, although some cities, such as Leeds, introduced new express routes in the early 1920s. They were starved of capital as their profits were milked to hold down the rates: new investment might have slowed decline, but could not prevent it, and by 1938 route mileage had fallen to half its peak level. The British urban tram largely disappeared by the mid-1950s, often amid poignant municipal ceremony. Concern over incipient urban gridlock has led in the 1990s to revivals in Manchester and Sheffield, though still with massive problems of undercapitalization, and more tramlines may yet be disinterred. JCh

transport was critical to the evolution of the nation state, and explains some of Britain's historical differences from its European neighbours, and much of its perception of distinctiveness. It helped to determine the early success of England as a political entity, its patterns of social and geographical mobility, and the close economic integration that helped to make Britain the first 'industrial nation'.

Post-Roman Britain lacked a single capital, and its transport system was diffuse, focused on the port, market, church, and seigneurial hall in a plurality of political and economic zones. In England, the gradual emergence of *London as capital city in the 13th and 14th cents. re-established the hub of a transport system, and the crown, the law, the court, the Exchequer, and associated institutions created a powerful centripetal influence, never replicated in Scotland or Wales. London's influence on Britain's transport grew thereafter, through its disproportionate demand for provisions and its dominance in international trade. Its function as central location for services, and for craft and business training, meant that by 1700 perhaps a quarter of England's population had experienced life in the capital. *Turnpikes reinforced this focus, but after 1750 *canals and *railways also reflected other urban demands, and created a transport system profiled as a St Andrew's cross, centred on the midlands, and framed by coastal shipping, and the Edinburgh–Glasgow route. The decline of traditional industries in the 20th cent., with the growth of *air travel, and the rise of services and big government, increasingly restored London as the sole hub of British transport.

Transport influenced perceptions of distance and time, and through this the sense of place. In the horse-drawn world before 1770, market and county town were objects of weekly and seasonal travel, the capital a place for temporary or life-cycle migration; a century later, London and Edinburgh were accessible to overnight visitors from most parts of England and Scotland; by the 1980s London's *rail commuting zone, bounded by the 100-minute journey, enveloped Bristol (122 miles distant), Birmingham (105), Norwich (114), and Doncaster (159), radically 'reshaping' the country. The railways also unified Britain into a single time zone in the 1850s, and the telegraph's instantaneous communication transformed the transmission of news beyond that of the fastest post or courier. With such transport change, and the induced shift in the perception of this island, the linguistic confusion of 'county' and 'country', so common before 1700, declined and disappeared.

The transport of information interacted with that of goods, and thus personal experiences of scarcity or plenty, and local and regional autonomy in the supply of food or fuel. The provisioning of medieval London, in 1400 around 4 per cent of the nation, was a complex transport problem demanding the integration of carts, river vessels, and coasters, and became the more so as that proportion rose to 11 per cent in 1700. Londoners dined on the meat of the Highland and Welsh cattle that had walked in droves south; on Dales sheep and Norfolk turkeys and geese also driven overland; on Thames-borne cheese, treated generically as 'Double Gloucester'; with Fulham or Putney vegetables, sustained by the reciprocating transport of manure; and washed them down with London porter, brewed from the dark malts shipped down the River Lea. Each shift in transport dislocated the equilibrium of supplies, and induced hostility from the threatened or the dispossessed: from the early modern grain wagon attacked by villagers as the proximate cause of their hunger, to Newcastle upon Tyne's vehement opposition to the navigation of Sunderland's river Wear, to those who mobbed James *Brindley or George *Stephenson as they came to survey their parish for canal or railway, and to the modern road 'nimby', transport has been keenly political, carrying high economic stakes. Britain's relatively small size and favourable endowment with water transport permitted its pre-railway transport systems to induce intense regional specialization, urbanization, and the economic growth of the first *'industrial revolution', where other nations attained merely developed industrial regions without complete social transformation.

Transport too provided for personal travel long before the coming of modern systems. The great *pilgrimages developing from the 14th cent., to *Canterbury, *Walsingham, or even Compostella, crowded the roads and perhaps led to the creation of commercial *inns. Medieval law implied a fifteen-mile round trip for market day, a near-universal transport experience, and marriage horizons commonly extended beyond the parish boundary, with courtship energetically pursued by foot or horse recorded in the early writings of the 18th-cent. common man.

The cheapening effect of successive transport innovations has democratized travel over the very long term, especially train, bus, and motor car, but we must not allow suburban prejudices to blind us to the extent to which their impact was creative. Neither have six centuries of transport change, mass urbanization through migration, and industrialization been sufficient wholly to dissociate surnames from the *pays* from which they stemmed. By the mid-19th cent. Britain had the transport almost perfectly to integrate its political, economic, urban, and social systems, and yet preserved specificity of place and voice long afterwards. Transport must therefore be seen as a critical contributory factor in the historical process, not a dominant determinant. JCh

transportation was a form of punishment devised in England to exile convicted criminals to the American colonies from *c.*1650 and after the War of Independence to Australia between 1788 and 1868, when it was abolished. The system arose out of England's lack of state-organized prisons and the overcrowding of what few prisons there were, including converted warships (hulks) anchored in the river Thames. Transportation, systematized by the Transportation Act of 1779, was not only a more humane alternative to hanging, but, by removing the persons out of society for at least seven years (mostly for life), achieved the same effect while, at the same time, providing the opportunity for redemption and a useful source of cheap near-slave labour in settler colonies. It is estimated that some 210,000 convicts were exiled between 1650 and 1868; 50,000 to the American colonies, the remainder to Australia. The landing of the first convicts at Sydney Cove in Port Jackson (in preference to Botany Bay which proved unsuitable) in January 1788 was the first of a series of convict settlements throughout eastern Australia, where evidence of convict labour can still be seen in roads, bridges, and public buildings. The harshest treatment was reserved for those who committed further crimes in Australia and for whom conditions at the punishment centres on Norfolk Island and Van Dieman's Land (renamed Tasmania) were almost beyond belief. A large number of those transported came from Ireland, especially after the 1798 Irish rebellion. These, by modern-day standards, were mostly political prisoners and, together with the post-famine migrants, account for the high proportion of persons of Irish descent in Australia. MJW

Transvaal. Former British colony in South Africa. Founded as an independent republic by Boers (Afrikaners) fleeing British rule in the mid-19th cent., the Transvaal was annexed by Britain in 1877 but regained its internal autonomy in 1881. The discovery of immense reserves of gold in the years which followed led to an influx of foreign, predominantly British, miners whose treatment by the Boer government was used by the British government as the pretext for demands which the Boers rejected, and which culminated in war in 1899. The Transvaal was again annexed by Britain and became part of the Union of South Africa in 1910. KI

treason. For centuries the evolution of the law of treason was to extend the number of offences and the ferocity of the punishment. Petty treason (abolished in 1848) was a breach of trust, such as the murder of a parent by a child, a husband by his wife, or a master by his servant. High treason was a crime against the state which meant, in practice, against the monarch. *Alfred's law declared that a man's life and property were forfeit if he plotted against the king. Edward I set the precedent for hideous punishments when *Dafydd ap Gruffydd at Shrewsbury in 1283 was drawn to the gallows on a sledge, hanged, cut down while alive, disembowelled, and his head and limbs exhibited in different towns. Edward III's statute of 1352, which became the basic definition, made it treason to encompass the death of the king, or to violate the queen, the king's eldest daughter (if unmarried), or the king's eldest son's wife, and added fresh offences, such as counterfeiting the *great seal or the coinage, or killing the *chancellor, *treasurer, or judges in the operation of their royal duties. New crises brought new offences. After the *Peasants' Revolt in 1381 it was made treasonable to start a riot, Henry V made it treason to clip the coinage, and Henry VI to extort money by threatening to burn down a house. The scope of treason was widened still further by 'constructive treason', which allowed judges to 'interpret' the Act of 1352. The Tudors added more than 60 treason statutes. Henry VIII made it treason to deny his royal supremacy, or to refuse to admit it, and each of his marriages, separations, or divorces was buttressed by a fresh treason law. His daughter Elizabeth made it treason to declare her a heretic or usurper. The panic over the French Revolution produced the Treasonable Practices Act of 1795 which declared that it was treason to contemplate the use of force to make the king change his counsels or to intimidate Parliament, and a high misdemeanour, punishable by transportation, to encourage hatred or contempt of the government or constitution. The Act was made permanent in 1817 and extended to cover the prince regent.

Mitigating legislation was slow in making its appearance. An Act of 1695 allowed the defendant counsel, a copy of the indictment five days before the trial, and declared that two direct witnesses were necessary. In 1814 *Romilly succeeded in carrying an Act not to cut traitors down still alive and disembowel them, though the Lords insisted that they should still be quartered. In 1870 quartering and beheading was also renounced. By the Treason Act of 1945 the procedure as in a murder trial was to apply, though by repealing the Act of 1695 the safeguard of two witnesses was removed. The first person to be tried under the new legislation and the last person to be executed as a traitor was William Joyce, 'Lord Haw-Haw'. It was at least doubtful whether he was not an American citizen, and evidence that he had broadcast from Nazi Germany was provided by only one witness, though the accused did not deny it, and presumably thousands of witnesses might have been summoned. JAC

treasurer. The official who guarded the Norman treasure at Winchester in the reign of William I seems to have been more of a custodian than a minister or counsellor. The modern office has been traced back to the reign of Henry I, *c.*1126, and quickly established itself as of major importance. When the *Exchequer split into a judicial and a financial side, the treasurer's responsibilities increased, since he was involved in the legal process, as well as presiding over the receipt of the royal revenues. The title lord treasurer, or lord high treasurer, came into use in the Tudor period. Thereafter the post was held by prominent figures such as Protector *Somerset, Lord *Burghley, and Sir Robert *Cecil. But from 1612 the practice grew up of putting the Treasury into commission and the last lord high treasurer was Lord *Rochester 1679–84. That opened the way for the 1st lord of the Treasury to become the head of government or first minister and in the 18th cent. the long tenures of *Walpole, *Pelham, *North, and *Pitt were based upon their financial expertise. As the demands on the prime minister increased and financial questions became more complex, the office of *chancellor of the Exchequer rose in importance.

In Scotland, the office of treasurer was introduced by James I, who had spent nineteen years in captivity in England as a youth. In 1617 it was formally declared to be the leading ministry, but lapsed at the Act of Union in 1707.

JAC

Treasury. The Treasury has its antecedents far back in time as all governments have faced the need to secure revenues to finance expenditure. But the recognizably modern Treasury has its principal roots in the late 17th and early 18th cents. Its emergence as a major organ of state was precipitated, like that of other financial structures, by a fairly sudden and large increase in government spending. Prior to the 20th cent. such an increase was invariably the result of military involvement, and at the beginning of the 18th cent., commitments in Ireland, Flanders, Africa, and the Caribbean accumulated a bill of £45 million. (See NATIONAL DEBT.) The increase in expenditure produced a proliferation of stratagems to pay for it. One means was, of course, new taxation, which was imposed on salt, stamps, hackney coaches, and, especially, on land. The latter was a form of embryonic income tax in that it levied a fixed quota on each county from their landed ratepayers. New customs and excise duties were introduced and there were increases in those already in operation. Such an expansion in taxation required a bureaucracy to organize the operation of the revenue system and this, in turn, needed to be managed. This became the task of the Treasury. The Exchequer and Audit Department Act of 1866 established the practice of consolidating the annual tax proposals into a single Finance Bill. This created the first effective machinery for a retrospective annual audit of government spending, and effectively established the Treasury as custodian of financial propriety. It did not exercise control at that time because hostility to centralization was widespread. But it meant that the role of the Treasury was 'cast in a narrow mould—essentially negative, harnessed to a defective concept of economy and a static concept of government. They meant adjudication, not inspiration; parsimony not efficiency; conservation, not growth.' This perception was reinforced by two major concerns of 19th-cent. policy, elimination of the national debt and the preservation of *free trade, both of which required tight fiscal control.

As government involvement in economic affairs has increased in the 20th cent. together with the massive increase in the ratio of public spending to national income, so the role and influence of the Treasury has become extremely important. Indeed, the most obvious manifestations of financial probity, including the control of public expenditure, maintenance of the exchange rate, and a tight fiscal and monetary stance to combat inflation, actual or potential, have been persistently at the heart of the economic management strategy of the Treasury, which has always strongly favoured stabilization over growth. Very often, incumbent administrations have adopted the Treasury view and followed policies consistent with its aims. Its close links with the city of London and its control over the *Bank of England have secured the primacy of financial considerations in economic policy. Thus policy was devoted to the restoration of the exchange rate after the First World War until the policy was rendered untenable by the depression at the end of the 1920s. But maintenance of the exchange rate dominated policy until the late 1960s and the eventual collapse of the Bretton Woods regime, and again in the late 1980s in the context of the Exchange Rate Mechanism. The other part of the strategy has been control of expenditure, an uphill struggle given the massive spending increases in two world wars and the demand-driven government commitments to pay pension, unemployment, and welfare benefits. The elimination of the national debt in the 1980s marked the success of a long-term Treasury aim, albeit very temporary, since the deficit reappeared at the end of the decade with a ferocious potency.

CHL

Trenchard, Hugh, 1st Viscount Trenchard (1873–1956). Soldier and airman. 'Boom' Trenchard began his service career as an infantryman. By 1912, when he learned to fly, he was a major whose career appeared to be going nowhere. But by 1915 he was a major-general in command of the *Royal Flying Corps in France. The RFC was then part of the army but when the *Royal Air Force was established as the world's first independent air force in 1918, Trenchard became its first professional head as chief of air staff, a post he held with only a brief interruption until 1929. After 1918 he fought tenaciously to preserve the RAF's independent existence by claiming that the next major war could be won by bombing alone. This theory had a powerful appeal to a nation anxious to avoid a repetition of the war on the western front, but proved to be hopelessly wrong during the *Second World War.

DF

Trent, battle on the, 679. *Æthelred, king of Mercia, defeated *Ecgfrith, king of Northumbria, and regained authority over *Lindsey. The site cannot be localized. *Bede's account has specially revealing elements. He emphasizes how Archbishop *Theodore successfully urged acceptance of a blood-price for the Northumbrian king's brother who had been killed. Long peace followed. Second, Bede relates a miracle story about Immia, a Northumbrian noble, captured by the Mercians. It shows that it was normal for captured nobles to be killed, lesser men enslaved; and that lesser captives were sold to a Frisian slave merchant, who took them, chained, to London for export. JCa

***Trent* case,** 1861. In November 1861, soon after the start of the American Civil War, a Federal warship, the *San Jacinto*, stopped the British packet *Trent* and took off two Confederate envoys, Mason and Slidell. *Palmerston suspended export of arms to the North and sent reinforcements to Canada. War seemed likely but the prince consort, a dying man, softened the cabinet's protest. The Federal government apologized, disavowed the captain, and liberated the envoys. But relations between Britain and the North were further strained by the **Alabama* incident. JAC

Trenton, battle of, 1776. *Washington's attack upon Trenton in New Jersey, though small scale, gave a welcome victory after the loss of New York in September 1776. Early in the morning of Christmas Day, the Americans attacked the Hessian garrison under the command of Colonel Rall. Nearly 1,000 Hessians were taken prisoner and their commander killed. JAC

Tresilian, Sir Robert (d. 1388). From Cornwall, Tresilian practised law in Oxford, where he advised Exeter College, served in Parliament, and was appointed a justice of King's Bench in 1377. Political feeling ran high in the early years of Richard II's reign. In 1381 Tresilian chief justice, trying, with severity, many of the participants in the *Peasants' Revolt, including John *Ball. He was associated with the royalist group in its struggle against the *appellants. In 1388, along with Suffolk (Michael de la *Pole) and *Oxford, he was indicted for treason by the *Merciless Parliament. Condemned in his absence, he was captured in February, probably in violation of sanctuary, and immediately hanged at Tyburn. JAC

Trevithick, Richard (1771–1833). Cornish engineer and inventor whose genius did not extend to business. A mine engineer from 1790 before erecting his first engine at Ding Dong (1795), he developed high-pressure, non-condensing engines from 1797 to patent both in 1802. His attainments include demonstrating the first practical steam carriage at Camborne (1801) and locomotive at Penydarran (1804), venting steam by the chimney to improve draught; a hydraulic engine and plunger pump for mines (1798); a steam barge (1805); iron storage tanks and iron ships (1808–9); a near-complete Thames tunnel (1809); a Cornish boiler and engine (1812); a portable agricultural engine (1812); a screw propeller (1815); and a tubular boiler (1816). Bankrupt in 1811, mining ventures led him to South America, 1816–27, at a loss, followed by a final flurry of patents including superheating and the jet propulsion of ships (1831). None made him a living, and he died the employee of a Kentish foundry, two of his sons succeeding where he failed in combining engineering with economy. JCh

trial by battle. Before the Norman Conquest, guilt or innocence in legal disputes were decided by *compurgation, where a party would summon a number of 'oath helpers' to swear to the reliability of his oath, or especially in cases of 'criminal' accusation by one of the ordeals, fire, cold water, hot water, or accursed morsel (see TRIAL BY ORDEAL). To these methods the Normans, with their strong militaristic tradition, added trial by battle. The parties, or champions on their behalf, would fight in formal single combat and the winner would be deemed to be the successful party in the case. Trial by battle fell into disuse, especially with the decline of the appeal of felony and the decline of writ of right in disputes over freehold land. However, it was not abolished until 1819, after the accused was challenged to combat in the case of *Ashford* v. *Thornton*. MM

trial by ordeal was used to decide the guilt or innocence of a suspected criminal by invoking divine justice. There were several forms of ordeal in Anglo-Saxon and Norman England. In one the accused held a red hot iron or put his hand in a flame. The hand was then bound up and examined after several days. If the wound was healing, the accused was deemed innocent but if it festered, this was believed to show guilt. In ordeal by cold water, used particularly for villeins, the accused was thrown, bound, into a pond or river. If he sank, he was deemed to be innocent, but if he floated he was regarded as guilty—the water was rejecting him. In ordeal by accursed morsel, the accused was required to eat a piece of meat with a feather or other foreign body in it, and was adjudged guilty if he choked. The ordeal was administered within a religious service. When in 1215 the Lateran Council of the church forbade clergy to take part in ordeals, they fell into disuse and were eventually replaced by *jury trial. MM

Triennial Acts, 1641, 1664, 1694. These were attempts to curb the prerogatives of the crown in summoning and retaining parliaments. The first, 16 Car. I c. 1, passed in February 1641 and committed Charles I to summon a Parliament at least every three years and to keep it for at least 50 days. This was repealed in 1664 and replaced by an Act, 16 Car. II c. 1, declaring that the king should summon Parliament at least every three years but providing no mechanism for enforcing it. Charles II was in breach of the Act from March 1684 and James II from November 1688. The third Act, 6 & 7 Wm. & Mar. c. 2, passed in 1694 after William had vetoed a previous measure. It laid down that Parliament must be summoned within three years of the previous one and could not be retained more than three years. The first provision was rendered nugatory by financial demands that necessitated annual sessions; the second was abrogated by the *Septennial Act of 1716. JAC

trimmer. The term acquired popularity from the publication in 1688 of *Halifax's pamphlet *The Character of a Trimmer*, which appealed for moderation in politics, condemning 'madmen in two extremes [who] agree to make common sense treason'. Why, asked Halifax, do we play the fool by throwing the names Whig and Tory at each other, as boys do snowballs? Since moderation is rarely admired, the term soon acquired a pejorative meaning of waverer or time-server. JAC

Trinidad and **Tobago** (its neighbouring island) lie off the coast of Venezuela and form an independent republic within the Commonwealth. Trinidad was discovered by Columbus and colonized by Spain. In 1797 it was captured by Sir Ralph Abercromby and ceded in 1802. Tobago, originally a Dutch colony, was taken from the French in 1793, restored by the treaty of Amiens in 1802, and recaptured in 1803. The islands were united in 1888 and became independent in 1962. The capital is Port of Spain and the population is more than $1\frac{1}{4}$ million. The main economic resources are oil, natural gas, and tourism. JAC

Trinity College, Dublin. Founded by charter of Elizabeth I dated 21 December 1591, Trinity, both a college and a university, was intended for 'the education, training and instruction of youths and students . . . that they may be better assisted in the study of the liberal arts, and in the cultivation of virtue and religion'. The Elizabethan college, situated outside the walls of the city, was largely modelled on *Cambridge. The period of growth was in the 18th cent. when the lord-lieutenant, the duke of Dorset, entered his son as a student in 1731. The college thenceforth attracted the nobility and gentry and its graduates included *Berkeley, *Burke, *Goldsmith, and *Grattan. Unlike *Oxford and Cambridge at this time, Trinity practised religious toleration, allowing both nonconformists and Roman catholics to follow a full college course, though catholics were debarred from taking a degree until the Act of 1793. PG

Trinovantes. A British tribe and *civitas*. The Trinovantes are the first British tribe to be mentioned by a Roman author, appearing in *Caesar's account of his invasion of 54 BC. Already at this early date, they seem to have been engaged in a power struggle with the neighbouring tribes to the west who were to be forged into the kingdom of the *Catuvellauni under Tasciovanus. Caesar took them under his protection, but eventually they succumbed and *c.* AD 10 were absorbed by *Cunobelinus, who moved the Catuvellaunian capital to Camulodunum (*Colchester). Thus, at the time of the Claudian conquest, the Trinovantes had no independent existence. However, the inevitable reduction of the huge Catuvellaunian kingdom provided the opportunity for the Trinovantes to be restored as a tribal entity. But the imposition of a Roman colony on their old tribal centre, and the abuses and expense which this brought, created resentments which spilled over at the time of the *Boudiccan revolt in AD 60–1. Despite their role in the rebellion, within fifteen years the Trinovantes had been given local self-governing status as a *civitas*. The seat of their government is uncertain; it may have been Camulodunum but Chelmsford (Caesaromagus) is also a possibility. KB

Triple Alliance.

1\. 1668. Alarmed at the growing power of Louis XIV's France, which was overrunning the Spanish Netherlands, the Dutch and the English formed a defensive alliance in January 1668, which was joined by the Swedes. Louis was obliged to make peace and at Aix-la-Chapelle his gains were modest. He set to work to break the alliance and succeeded in 1670, when Charles II of England signed the treaty of *Dover at the expense of the Dutch. Louis's great invasion of Holland followed in 1672.

2\. 1717. Soon after the death of Louis XIV in 1715, the Regent d'Orléans of France sought a *rapprochement* with Britain to check the ambitions of Philip V of Spain. An understanding was reached in 1716 to guarantee the succession in France and Britain and to expel the Pretender from French soil. By the accession of the Dutch in January 1717 this was converted into a Triple Alliance and when the Emperor Charles VI adhered to it in 1718 it became a *Quadruple Alliance.

3\. 1788. After the War of American Independence, Pitt's government was concerned at Britain's diplomatic isolation. Political instability in Holland in 1786 gave rise to fears of French aggrandizement and in 1787 the Prussian army intervened to suppress the pro-French party. This was followed by a series of treaties in 1788 between Prussia, Britain, and Holland to guarantee each other's territories.

4\. 1882. The adherence of Italy to the Dual Alliance of Germany and Austro-Hungary in 1882 produced the Triple Alliance, which lasted until the outbreak of war in 1914. France, Russia, and Britain responded with the Triple Entente (1894–1907), thus dividing Europe into two armed camps. JAC

Trojan legend. See BRUTUS.

Trollope, Anthony (1815–82). Trollope's reputation suffered from the frank admission in his *Autobiography* (1883) that he set out to write 1,000 words an hour, checked by his watch. Many took this as evidence that he was a mere journeyman, a word-spinner. But his stock has risen dramatically, and, like *Eliot and *Bennett, he is a historian's novelist, filling in the social background with care and detail. Though a contemporary of Dickens (1812–70), he seems to belong to a later generation, having dropped much of the moralizing, the sentimentality, and the Gothic caricaturing. His political novels are greatly admired, but there is something in the criticism that they show the political world with politics left out. Indeed Trollope was not very familiar with politics, and did not greatly enjoy what he saw of it—particularly as Liberal candidate for the corrupt borough of Beverley in 1868. Nor is it easy to retain patience with Trollope's favourite character, the duke of Omnium, a languid Whig. He is better at drawing clerics in his Barchester novels—Revd Obadiah Slope in *Barchester Towers* (1857) or Revd Septimus Harding in *The Warden* (1855); Irish plotters in his early novel *The Macdermots of Ballycloran* (1847); civil service rivalry in *The Three Clerks* (1858); or perhaps, most memorably, shady plausible swindlers like Ferdinand Lopez in *The Prime Minister* (1876), or Melmotte in *The Way We Live now* (1875), a novel that haunts after more than 100 years. Trollope's life was uneventful—that of a hard-working Post Office official, whose claim to fame was the introduction of pillar boxes in the 1850s. JAC

Trotskyites. Trotsky's condemnation of Stalinist Russia as a vicious state bureaucracy found considerable support in Britain, but his call for permanent revolution less so. After his murder in 1940, Trotskyism in Britain was disputed between the Revolutionary Socialist League and the Workers' International League, which joined forces in 1944 to form the Revolutionary Communist Party. Later parties sympathetic to his analysis were the Socialist Workers' Party and the Workers' Revolutionary Party, but more influential were supporters of Militant Tendency, whose paper *Militant* was launched in 1964 and who achieved considerable support in the *Labour Party in the early 1980s. JAC

Troyes, treaty of, 1420. By this Anglo-French treaty, ratified on 21 May, Henry V became heir and regent to the mad Charles VI of France. This was by adoption, not by virtue of his subsequent marriage to *Catherine, Charles's daughter (2 June). After the death of Charles, France and England were to be under one ruler. The dauphin (later Charles VII) was thus disinherited. Henry's triumph derived from his military success and from Burgundian support after the dauphinist murder of Duke John at Montereau (10 September 1419). The treaty preserved the laws and government of each kingdom, but gave Henry direct control of Normandy until Charles VI died. In fact Henry died first: it was his baby son Henry VI who became king of the 'double monarchy'. AC

Troyes, treaty of, 1564. At her accession in 1558, Elizabeth inherited from Mary a war against France in which *Calais, a 200-year-old possession, had been lost. By the treaty of *Cateau-Cambrésis (1559), the French promised to restore Calais after eight years or pay a large indemnity. In 1562 Elizabeth was tempted to intervene in the French wars of religion, supporting the Huguenots and taking possession of Le Havre as a pledge for Calais. But the garrison was decimated by disease and Le Havre was forced to surrender. At the treaty of Troyes in April 1564 peace was signed, both sides reserving their rights on Calais which, in effect, meant that it was lost for ever. JAC

truck, the payment of wages in food and kind, was an old form of exploitation by employers in outwork industries and spread with industrialization. In a minority of cases the practice was benign, since basic supplies were not otherwise available. Commonly, employers' shops supplied adulterated food and drink at high prices ('tommy rot'); there was unrest in communities so badly served. Codifying Acts prohibiting truck were passed in 1831 (which was generally evaded) and 1887; a royal commission in 1870 found the practice still existed in some areas. Truck died a natural death as retailing spread and workers became better organized. JB

Truro, diocese of. The see, roughly conterminous with Cornwall and the Isles of Scilly, was created in 1877. Episcopal oversight of Cornwall, previously Celtic, passed to *Canterbury after *Egbert's victory over the Cornish *c.*838, and finally to *Crediton (909). The separate see for Cornwall, *St Germans, only lasted from 931 to 1027, before reunion with Crediton and a move to *Exeter (1050). Not until 1877 did Cornwall have its own see again. Notable bishops of Truro include Edward *Benson (1877–83), later archbishop, and Walter Frere (1923–35), previously superior of the Community of the Resurrection, Mirfield (1902–13 and 1916–22), scholar, liturgist, and promoter of Christian unity. The last Anglican ritual riots occurred at St Hilary in 1932. The cathedral, consecrated in 1887 and completed in 1903, incorporated the dilapidated south aisle of St Mary's 16th-cent. parish church. The architect was J. L. Pearson and the style Early English neo-Gothic Revival. WMM

Tuam, archiepiscopal diocese of. Though this Irish see had bishops in the early 12th cent., the Council of Kells-Mellifont (1152) established it as an archbishopric, carved out of Armagh province, with six dioceses in the far west of Ireland. As late as the 16th cent. it was still part of *ecclesia inter hibernos* and all its bishops were Irish. Its cathedral, however, probably had a secular chapter after the continental pattern from the 1190s. In 1593 catholic Archbishop James O'Hely went to Spain to ask for aid against Elizabethan adventurers. Tuam is still a catholic archbishopric, but in 1839 the Anglican province of Tuam was reunited with Armagh. It thus ceased to be an archbishopric; the diocese now includes Killala and Achonry. There are cathedrals at Tuam and Killala. St Mary's Anglican cathedral at Tuam is 19th cent., but incorporates a barrel-vault chancel and a fine east window of the 12th–14th-cent. church. WMM

Tudor, house of. This is something of a misnomer. The important descent for Henry VII, who founded the dynasty when he defeated Richard III at *Bosworth, was the direct line from Edward III through *John of Gaunt and the Beaufort dukes of Somerset, and though the branch was illegitimate, it had subsequently been legitimized. The Welsh link, of which Henry and the Welsh made so much, was quite subordinate. Henry V's widow *Catherine de Valois made a private marriage with a minor courtier, Owen *Tudor, later executed at Hereford in 1461 after the battle of *Mortimer's Cross. Their son Edmund married Margaret *Beaufort, great-granddaughter of Gaunt, thus bringing a second royal link into the equation. Henry VI created his half-brother earl of Richmond in 1452. The Tudors were in essence a Lancastrian dynasty and the red rose seems to have been one of the badges of the Beauforts: it was deliberately exploited in the pageant to mark Henry VII's visit to York only eight months after Bosworth. Henry moved quickly to end the old feud with the house of York by marrying *Elizabeth, daughter of Edward IV and sister of the two princes in the Tower. The dynasty used propaganda to stress the sanctity of Henry VI and the villainy of Richard III.

Few dynasties have produced five strong-minded rulers in succession, for though Edward VI died at 15, the marks of authority were already visible. Mary, the least fortunate of the Tudors, was certainly not lacking in courage, as her behaviour during the Lady Jane *Grey *coup* and the *Wyatt rising demonstrated. Henry VII, Henry VIII, and Elizabeth were in command, even if their policies may be questioned. This must be remembered when discussing the nature of Tudor government, for it is never easy to separate political structures from purely personal and non-transferable ability. J. R. Green in the 1890s credited the Tudors with creating a 'new monarchy'. This interpretation is now in retreat, with emphasis on evolutionary developments: nevertheless, the contrast between Tudor strength and the chaos that succeeded it remains. In some respects the Tudor period was the apogee of monarchy. The Tudors were ruthless in dealing with challenges to their authority, whether from possible claimants to the throne, like the earl of *Warwick (d. 1499) or Lord *Surrey (d. 1547), or from rebels in the field (the *Pilgrimage of Grace 1536, or the Rising of the *northern earls 1569). Yet beneath authority, there were weaknesses, some of which did not fully reveal themselves until the Stuarts succeeded. Each Tudor met serious rebellion, with no standing army to quell it: within two years of Bosworth, Henry VII faced Lambert *Simnel and his supporters, and three years before the end of her reign, Elizabeth faced *Essex's rebellion. The Reformation, though greatly adding to royal power by making the monarch head of church as well as head of state, also introduced bitter schism. Having displaced the pope, the monarch had to take the blame for what was done in religious matters and found it exceptionally difficult to please all sides. The enormous wealth of the monasteries was not only dissipated by the crown but augmented the influence of the nobility. The financial position of the monarchy, built up by Henry VII, was run down by his successors, and Elizabeth handed over large debts to James I. Lastly, partly by bad luck and partly by mismanagement, the dynasty failed to provide for its own survival in the form of heirs, lasting for only three generations and 118 years. But Stuart rule soon brought back golden memories of Tudor England. JAC

Tudor, Jasper, 1st earl of Pembroke and 1st duke of Bedford (*c.*1431–95). The second son of Owen *Tudor and *Catherine of Valois, Jasper was created earl of Pembroke in 1452, at the same time as his elder brother Edmund became earl of Richmond. He was one of the few die-hard Lancastrians. Ruling Wales on behalf of Henry VI from 1457, he refused to come to terms with Edward IV after 1461. He led an expedition to Wales in 1468, and returned again in 1470 during the restoration of Henry VI. But after the defeat of the Lancastrians at *Tewkesbury in May 1471, he fled once more, taking with him his 13-year-old nephew Henry Tudor, earl of Richmond (later Henry VII). He remained in exile for fourteen years, returning in triumph in 1485. Thereafter, back in Wales, and promoted duke of Bedford, he remained until his death Henry VII's principal lieutenant in the principality and the marches. AJP

Tudor, Owen (*c.*1400–61). A humble Welsh servant of *Catherine of Valois, widow of Henry V, he secretly married her about 1428. Their first-born Edmund was the father of Henry VII. There is probably no truth in the rumour that the real father of Edmund Tudor was Edmund Beaufort, whose close friendship with Catherine was brought to a hasty end shortly before the marriage. Tudor's sons were promoted by their half-brother Henry VI. Owen Tudor was a victim of the Wars of the Roses, executed by Edward, earl of March (later Edward IV), at Hereford following the battle of *Mortimer's Cross. On the scaffold he is reputed to have declared, 'That head shall lie on the stock that was wont to lie on Queen Catherine's lap.' AJP

Tull, Jethro (1674–1741). Once considered a pioneer of the *agricultural revolution through his invention of the seed drill *c.*1700 when he was farming near Wallingford. The 'invention' was made famous by his book *The Horse-Hoing Husbandry* published in 1733, but today his role appears less influential. The seed drill (which we now know he did not originate) came into widespread use only from the 1820s. Seed drills and horse-drawn hoes were originally invented in the late 17th cent., but were adopted only slowly until improvements were made to Tull's designs in the 1780s. JVB

Tullibardine, William Murray, marquis of (1689–1746). One of the most determined Jacobite leaders. Second son to the 1st duke of *Atholl, he became heir when his elder brother was killed at *Malplaquet. He took part in the '15, fought at *Sheriffmuir, was attainted, and fled to France. In 1717 he was created duke of Rannoch by James III, the Old Pretender. He returned to Scotland in 1719 and again escaped. Despite poor health, he embarked with Prince Charles in 1745 and was given the honour of unfurling the banner at Glenfinnan. His brother James, the duke, fled from Blair Atholl, and Murray was able to entertain the prince there. After *Culloden he surrendered and was lodged in the Tower, where he died in July 1746. Lord George *Murray was his younger brother. JAC

Tunstall, Cuthbert (1474–1559). Bishop. Tunstall was a distinguished scholar and ecclesiastical statesman, whose religious balancing act, in a period of startling change, kept him in high office for almost the whole of his life. Of Lancashire gentry stock, he attended Balliol College, Oxford, before moving on to Cambridge and Padua. The patronage of *Warham, to whom he was chancellor, brought him swift promotion. By 1522 he was bishop of London, in 1527 keeper of the privy seal, and much employed by Henry VIII on diplomatic missions. Though he disapproved of Henry's adoption of the headship of the church, Tunstall continued to serve. He succeeded *Wolsey as bishop of Durham in 1530 and in 1537 became president of the Council of the North. He was out of sympathy with the reforms of Edward VI's reign and fell into disfavour on *Somerset's overthrow, being deprived of his see in 1552. Mary restored him to it but he could not accept Elizabeth's Act of *Supremacy and lost his bishopric once more in 1559, at the age of 85, a few weeks before his death. JAC

Turks and Ottomans, relations with. Serious British strategic interest in the Ottoman empire began in the late 18th cent. when it was hoped that the Turks would act as a barrier to Russia's southern and south-westward expansion. But the latter's advance continued, and British governments (especially from the 1820s) tried in various ways to ensure that the Ottoman empire itself (and such parts as broke away) should not be dominated by Russia. The future of Constantinople and the Straits caused special concern, and this increased with the development of the Suez route to India. The British also valued naval access to the Black Sea in order to threaten southern Russia (as in the *Crimean

War in 1854–6). India, it was often thought, could best be defended by command of the Black Sea. Turkey in Asia also formed part of the defences against a Russian threat to the Persian Gulf. From the 1890s, however, interest turned from the Straits to Egypt as the key to British strategy in the eastern Mediterranean. The Ottoman alliance with Germany in the *First World War was answered by British campaigns from the Persian Gulf and Egypt which brought about the collapse of Turkish rule from Mesopotamia to Syria. It was not until 1923, at the conference of *Lausanne, that the British accepted that the new Turkish republic might act as a bulwark against Bolshevik Russia in the Near East. Demands by the USSR at the end of the Second World War for more influence at the Straits caused further alarm, but by 1947 the USA had become the main executors of the latest versions of the policies of Palmerstonian Britain. CJB

Turner, Joseph Mallord William (1775–1851). British land- and seascape artist. Born in London the son of a barber, Turner was precociously talented. He entered the RA Schools in 1789, had a drawing exhibited at the academy in 1790, and was elected a full academician in 1802. He became professor of perspective in 1807. In 1792 he made the first of many sketching tours he was to undertake over the next 50 years, throughout the British Isles and Europe. A prolific artist of amazing range of subject and style, he began work in water-colours, quickly founding both a reputation and a fortune, which made him independent of changing public taste. At home in both oils and water-colours, he took the use of each almost to the limits of artistic possibility. His work was not appreciated by everyone, but his supporters included Thomas *Lawrence, John *Ruskin, and the earl of Egremont, whose large collection at *Petworth (Sussex) now belongs to the National Trust. He died in eccentric obscurity under a false name. A taciturn and miserly man, secretive of his methods, yet meticulous in documenting his artistic development, Turner's will left about 300 oils and over 19,000 water-colours and drawings to the nation. The conditions of the bequest were ignored until 1987 when a special Turner Gallery was opened at the Tate in London. *Frosty Morning* (1813), *Chichester Canal* (1828), *The Fighting Teméraire* (1839), *Rain, Steam and Speed—the Great Western Railway* (1844), hint at Turner's wide diversity of theme and style. JC

Turnham Green, battle of, 1642. Like Valmy in the French Revolution, the battle of Turnham Green had an importance out of all proportion to the actual fighting. Charles I's best hope of winning the Civil War was to bring it to a quick end before the superior resources of Parliament could be brought to bear. After the indecisive encounter at *Edgehill on 23 October, the king resumed his leisurely march on London, giving his adversaries time to regroup. By the time he reached Brentford on 12 November, the remains of *Essex's army had been reinforced by the trained bands, bringing it up to 24,000 men. After inconclusive negotiations and some skirmishing, Charles's advance came to a halt the following day at Turnham Green. Outnumbered and unable to use his cavalry, Charles retired to Oxford. He was never again as close to London until he was brought there for his trial in January 1649. JAC

turnpikes were a means of financing road maintenance by tolls charged on users, named from the gate used to restrict access. First applied to part of the Great North Road in 1663 on a temporary basis, the principle was employed from 1695 in a series of private Acts to supplant inadequate parish repair under the statute of 1555. Initially administered by justices of the peace, management by trustees was introduced in 1706, and generalized by 1714. Trusts covered on average 30 miles of road, and were a systematic response to traffic growth: most of the thirteen radial routes from London had been turnpiked by 1750, as had much of the network centred on the leading provincial towns of Bristol, Hereford, Worcester, and Leeds. 'Turnpike mania' 1750–72 saw the addition of 500 trusts, covering 15,000 miles, and the spread of the system into Wales and Scotland; further peaks occurred in the mid-1790s and 1820s, one-third in the industrial districts of Yorkshire and Lancashire. Turnpiking was limited to trunk and busy urban routes, and covered only 17 per cent of over 126,000 miles of roads by 1838.

Turnpiking represented a major transport innovation in applying use-based revenues to the increased investment that improved road quality. Mortgage finance was used from the 1750s to permit large-scale engineering work, bridge-building, and improvement of both surfaces and lines. The benefits were reflected in reduced travel times: Edinburgh, ten days from London by the fastest coach in 1754, was only four days away by 1776, and 40 hours by 1840. The cost of travel fell substantially in real terms, and road transport became up to three times more productive between the 1690s and the 1840s as a result of turnpiking. National perceptions of distance shifted fundamentally, and travel began to become a consumer good. JCh

Turpin, Dick (1706–39). Highwayman. Dick Turpin became a popular hero and the stuff of legend. He was, in fact, a leader of a gang of Essex ruffians, whose speciality was robbery with violence. He went into partnership with Tom King, whom he accidentally shot in a skirmish. Turpin escaped to York, where he traded in horses, and was hanged on 7 April 1739 for stealing a mare. The story of the celebrated ride to York to establish an alibi was told of John Nevison, or 'Swift Nick', who was hanged at York in 1685: it was given fully by Defoe in his *Tour*, published in 1724. There is no reference to the ride in contemporary accounts of Turpin's life or trial, and the story owed its Victorian popularity to W. H. Ainsworth's novel *Rookwood* (1834). Turpin and Tom King were a very popular pair of Staffordshire China figures, now collectors' items. JAC

Tuvalu became independent within the Commonwealth in 1978. It was formerly the Ellice Islands and was part of the Gilbert and Ellice colony. The nine small islands lie some 2,500 miles north-east of Australia. They were visited in 1819 by the ship *Rebecca*, which belonged to Alexander Ellice, a Montreal shipowner. JAC

Tweeddale, John Hay, 1st marquis of [S] (1625–97). Tweeddale's father Lord Hay was advanced to the earldom of Tweeddale by Charles I in December 1646, presumably as part of the negotiation for the *Engagement. The son had been sympathetic to the *covenant and fought against the king at *Marston Moor, but in 1648 supported the Engagement and joined the Scottish army which was defeated at *Preston. He attended Charles II's coronation at Scone in 1651 and succeeded to the earldom in 1653. He then came to terms with the Cromwellian regime. After the Restoration he was a member of the Privy Council [S] 1661–74, dismissed through the influence of *Lauderdale, but reinstated in 1680. He gave strong support to William and the Glorious Revolution and was raised to the marquisate in 1694. From 1692 until 1696 he was lord chancellor [S] and served as commissioner to the 1695 Parliament. In 1696 he was abruptly dismissed by William as a scapegoat for England's anger at the *Darien venture which, it was felt, would drag England into war with Spain. Burnet observed of him, not unreasonably, that 'he seemed to think that what form soever was uppermost it might be complied with'. JAC

Tweeddale, John Hay, 2nd marquis of [S] (1645–1713). Tweeddale's father played an important role in Scottish politics from the Restoration until 1696 and Tweeddale was a privy counsellor [S] 1670–4 and again in 1684. He joined his father in supporting William in 1688 and succeeded to the marquisate in 1697. In Anne's reign, he was one of the leaders of the 'Flying Squadron', a loose alliance of Scottish peers, whose political tacking earned them their name. He was plucked from opposition in 1704 and made commissioner to the Parliament. But his efforts to confirm the Hanoverian succession ran into difficulty and he was replaced by *Argyll. During 1704–5 he served as lord chancellor [S]. Tweeddale helped to carry the Union and was a representative peer 1707–8. His character was said to have been amiable and his politics moderate. JAC

Twickenham stadium (Middx.). The headquarters of the Rugby Football Union. The site was purchased by William Williams in 1907, laid out with stands and provided with a car park. It has since been added to and has a capacity of more than 60,000. JAC

Two Treatises of Government (1690). Composed by John *Locke between 1681 and 1689, the treatises were not published until 1690. Locke's purpose was twofold: in Part I to demolish the *divine right of kings theory held by Sir John Filmer; and in Part II to establish his own theory of government, resting on the consent of the governed and respect for natural rights. The book is regarded both as a justification for the Whig revolution and settlement in England in 1688–9, and as the foundation of, and inspiration for, liberal constitutionalism throughout the western world. TSG

Tyburn, the name borrowed for the Middlesex gallows from a nearby tributary of the river Thames, was the principal place of execution in London from 1388 until 1783 (near the modern Marble Arch). In the hope that witnessing an execution might prove deterrent, hanging days were public holidays, hence enormous, unruly crowds (the more affluent on grandstand seating) awaited the carts from Newgate gaol on the condemned prisoners' oft-perceived day of glory. After the spectacle, the bodies were buried nearby or removed for dissection. The bodies of *Cromwell, *Ireton and *Bradshaw were exhumed and hanged at Tyburn in January 1661. ASH

Tyler, Wat (d. 1381). The most famous leader of the *Peasant's Revolt in 1381, Tyler was a man of obscure origins. He may have worked as a tiler in Essex; he was said to have served with Richard Lyons, a wealthy London merchant in France; some sources, almost certainly wrongly, identified him with another peasant leader, Jack Straw. He first emerged as a major leader in Kent at the end of the first week in June 1381, seizing Canterbury on 10 June and heading the march to London on the next day. On 15 June he was the spokesman at Smithfield. His demands were radical. The young king Richard II ordered the mayor, John Walworth, to arrest Tyler, and in a struggle he was killed. A man of eloquence, charisma, and courage, he achieved more in two weeks than many men in a lifetime. MCP

Tyndale, William (*c.*1494–1536). Translator of the Bible. Tyndale was probably from a Gloucestershire family and entered Magdalen College, Oxford, in 1510. He became tutor to the children of Sir John Walsh of Old Sodbury, but soon removed to London and the continent, visiting Luther at Wittenberg. Meanwhile he worked on his English translation of the New Testament. Printed in Germany, copies smuggled into England were seized and burned by the authorities. In 1528 Tyndale issued *The Obedience of a Christian Man*, which argued for complete submission to temporal power, but his *Practice of Prelates* in 1530 attacked both *Wolsey and Henry VIII's proposed divorce. His subsequent controversy with *More turned on the question whether the authority of Scripture or of the church was paramount. In 1535 Tyndale was seized by servants of the Emperor Charles V and burned as a heretic at Vilvoorde near Brussels in October 1536. Tyndale's translation, based on Erasmus' Greek version, was much used by the Authorized Version issued in 1611, and his great phrases roll round the heads of Christians and non-Christians alike—'God shall wipe away all tears from their eyes'; 'And though I bestowed all my goods to feed the poor, and though I gave my body even that I burned, and yet had no love, it profiteth me nothing'; 'the last enemy that shall be destroyed is death.' JAC

Tyndall, John (1820–93). Physicist, lecturer, and foe of organized religion, Tyndall grew up in Ireland; after surveying and teaching, he went to Marburg in 1848 to study with R. W. Bunsen. In 1853 he got a professorship at the *Royal Institution, and from 1867 followed Michael *Faraday as superintendent. He worked on heat and on bacteria, translated important papers from the German, and in 1874 as president of the *British Association for the Advancement of Science delivered in Belfast an address declaring that scientists would wrest the whole of cosmology from theologians. He was an ally of T. H. *Huxley. Tyndall was an expert and enthusiastic mountaineer (and student of glaciers), calculating how high the energy in a ham sandwich would take him; his writings about the alps are suffused with pantheism. His ice-axe is preserved in the Zermatt museum. DK

Tyne and Wear was one of the six English metropolitan county councils that existed from 1974 until their abolition in 1986. The Redcliffe-Maud Report of 1969 followed the royal commissions of 1937 and 1963 in suggesting a single local authority for the industrial area of Tyneside, but the Heath government added the Wearside borough of Sunderland. The county council (always Labour controlled) had fewer conflicts with its constituent districts and a less confrontational relationship with central government than some other metropolitan counties. Tyne and Wear is still used as a geographical description for the former council's territory. CNL

Tynwald, meaning the assembly field, is an institution unique to the Isle of Man and is the successor of the Norse meeting of freemen. It meets on Tynwald Day, 5 July, on Tynwald Hill and is attended by the president of Tynwald, the lieutenant-governor, the bishop, the deemsters, the Legislative Council, and the House of *Keys. Its main task is to ratify or approve laws and to appoint boards which serve as administrative committees. The Tynwald shares with the Icelandic Althing the claim to be the oldest surviving parliamentary institution. JAC

Tyrconnel, Richard Talbot, 1st Earl (I) (1630–91). Talbot, a younger son from Co. Kildare, fought for the king in the 1640s and escaped from the destruction of Drogheda in 1649. In the 1650s he was appointed a groom of the bedchamber to the duke of York in exile and for the rest of his life his fortunes followed his patron's. He fought alongside the duke at the naval battles off *Lowestoft in 1665 and at Sole Bay (*Southwold) in 1672 and, though a catholic, was made colonel of a regiment of horse. As soon as the duke became James II, Talbot was created earl and in 1686 appointed lieutenant-general of the army in Ireland. In 1687 he succeeded *Clarendon as lord-lieutenant and began consolidating the catholic position. Tyrconnel was the 'new deputy' whom 'brother Teague' welcomed in *'Lillibullero'. After the Glorious Revolution he was made a jacobite duke, fought at the *Boyne, carried on the rearguard action, and died in Limerick just before it was forced to capitulate. A brave and well-built soldier, running to corpulence in age, Tyrconnel was regarded by most as hot-headed and lacking in judgement. Macaulay dismissed him as a drunken swaggerer. JAC

Tyrell, Sir James (d. 1502). Reputed to have been the murderer of the two princes in the Tower. His grandfather Sir John Tyrell had been Speaker of the House of Commons in Henry VI's reign. Tyrell fought on the Yorkist side at *Tewkesbury in 1471 and was knighted after the battle. Richard, duke of Gloucester, made him a knight-banneret in 1482, and after Richard's coronation Tyrell became master of the horse. He is said to have supervised the murders when the constable of the Tower, Sir Robert Brackenbury, refused. When Richard died at *Bosworth, Tyrell was at Guisnes, where he was constable. Henry VII employed him and he was granted pardons in June and July 1486. But in 1501 he surrendered Guisnes to Suffolk (Edmund de la *Pole), a claimant to the throne, was arrested, and was executed at the Tower in May 1502. He is said to have confessed to the murders before his death. The validity of this confession, if ever made, is a key element in the controversy about the fate of the two princes. JAC

Tyrone was the largest of the six counties of Northern Ireland before the local government reorganization of 1973. The border with Londonderry to the north ran across the Sperrin Mountains; to the west was Donegal in the Irish Republic, Fermanagh to the south-west, Monaghan and Armagh to the south-east. Omagh, near the centre of the county, is the chief town: it suffered a disastrous fire in 1743 and was totally rebuilt. Strabane, Dungannon, and Cookstown are local centres. The diocese of *Clogher in the south dates from the 12th cent.: the Church of Ireland cathedral was built in 1744 and is dedicated to St Macartan. Clogher is also a Roman catholic diocese, though the cathedral is in Monaghan. The main occupations are in farming, fishing, and tourism. Since the 17th cent. the county has had a mixed religious population and in 1921 the county council was dissolved after declaring allegiance to the Irish Free State. For Westminster parliamentary purposes the south is united with Fermanagh and in 1992 returned an Ulster Unionist MP: the north is the mid-Ulster constituency and returned a Democratic Unionist. JAC

Udall, Nicholas (1505–56). Dramatist. Udall was educated at Winchester and Corpus Christi College, Oxford, took up teaching, and became headmaster of Eton and, at the end of his life, at Westminster. Like most Tudor pedagogues he was reputed a heavy flogger. His sympathies were with Lutheran reform and he prospered during the reign of Edward VI but managed to survive in that of Mary. Udall translated from the classics and wrote Latin plays, but is remembered as the author of the earliest known English comedy, *Ralph Roister Doister*, an imitation of Plautus, performed about 1552. The subject-matter is the wooing of a widow by Roister, a simple-minded braggart who comes to grief, and must have owed its popularity to the opportunities it presented for knockabout humour. JAC

Uganda. Former British protectorate in eastern Africa. The search for the source of the White Nile first brought the region to Britain's attention in the 1860s. British missionaries reached Uganda in 1877 and the difficulties in which they became involved, together with Britain's interest in Egypt, to the north, led to the declaration of a British protectorate in 1894. The presence of well-organized indigenous societies was responsible for the decision, taken early in the 20th cent., to develop Uganda as an African, rather than as a white settler, dependency. This, in turn, led to the introduction of indirect administration, using modified indigenous institutions, and the policy was made economically viable by the encouragement of cotton, and later of coffee, to provide foreign exchange. The road to independence in 1962 was bedevilled only by the problem of accommodating the powerful, centrally located kingdom of Buganda in a unified state. KI

Ulster. The northern province of Ireland, comprising the counties of Antrim, Down, Armagh, Cavan, Monaghan, Fermanagh, Donegal, Tyrone, and Londonderry. It was dominated by Gaelic lords until the 17th cent.; the Normans under John de *Courcy and Hugh de Lacy establishing a foothold in eastern Ulster in the late 12th and early 13th cents.: de Lacy was created earl of Ulster by King John in 1205. The Norman intrusion was both socially and geographically confined: Ulster remained the most Gaelic, and—from the perspective of English governors in Dublin—inaccessible part of Ireland until the plantation of 1609. The flight of the Gaelic lords in 1607 after the failure of *Tyrone's rebellion opened the way to mass confiscations of land by the crown, and the redistribution of this property through a programme of colonization. The Ulster plantation embraced the six central and western counties of Ulster: an earlier plantation in Monaghan (1593) was allowed to stand, and the eastern counties, long characterized by informal British settlement, were also untouched. The destruction of Gaelic society continued during the Commonwealth, when massive confiscations occurred in eastern and southern Ulster: the Gaelic aristocracy was, by 1660, all but annihilated. The victory of the Williamite forces in Ireland by 1691 confirmed this territorial distribution, and opened the way to further British migration into Ulster. However, the weak economic condition of Ireland at the beginning of the 18th cent. stemmed this tide, and indeed produced a flow of presbyterian emigrants. The mid- and late 18th cent. was characterized by economic growth throughout most of Ireland, and at this time Ulster emerged as the centre of the Irish linen industry, and *Belfast developed as a significant industrial centre. The commercial success of especially eastern Ulster in the 19th cent., allied with the substantial British and protestant population, helped cut the region off from the rising nationalist fervour elsewhere in Ireland: by the time of the first *Home Rule Bill (1886), there was broad support for the maintenance of a constitutional link with Britain. In 1920 the island was partitioned, with the six most unionist counties—the new *Northern Ireland—obtaining a separate devolved parliament and government. This partition settlement was confirmed by the *Anglo-Irish treaty of 1921, and by the Boundary Commission of 1925: it was further underwritten by the *Ireland Act (1949), passed by the United Kingdom House of Commons after the declaration of a republic by Dublin in 1948. However, the dominant unionist social and political culture of Northern Ireland came under increasing challenge from the nationalist minority, benefiting from improved access to higher education, but still economically and culturally disadvantaged. Between 1969 and 1994, in the context of a low-grade civil war conducted between loyalist and republican paramilitaries and the Royal Ulster Constabulary and British army, an untenable position of unionist political predominance was gradually undermined. Although 'Ulster'—the old provincial label is still sometimes applied to Northern Ireland—looks set to remain with Britain, it is probable that its governing institutions will more faithfully reflect its cultural and political diversity. AJ

Ulster (Ulaid), **kingdom of.** The most powerful of the four provinces in the **Táin Bó Cuailnge*, along with Connachta (Connacht), Laigin (Leinster), and Mumu (Munster). The province of the Ulaid consisted of the whole of northern Ireland with its high seat at Emain Macha, near Armagh. In the *Táin*, the king of the Ulaid is Conchobor mac Nessa, a prince of the Érainn, and his enemy is Medb of Connachta. The *Táin*, a story of Ulster heroes, preserves a tradition which may depict an 'heroic' culture of the sub-La Tène period, dating back to the 4th cent. As a result of political upheavals and the rise of the Uí Néill in the 5th cent., Ireland was subsequently divided into fifths (coiceds). *Armagh became the most important Irish town and was subsequently the seat of an archbishopric. The kingdom of the Ulaid was gradually destroyed and partitioned by the sons of Niall Noígiallach with the aid of Connachta. This conquest established the Uí Néill in the north, whose territory included Armagh, Monaghan, Tyrone, and the greater part of Fermanagh and Derry. The result was the creation of two new kingdoms of Airgialla in the first conquest and Ailech after the conquest of Donegal *c.*428, later known as Tír Conaill (Tyrconnel) and Tír Eógain (Tyrone). The small kingdom of *Dalriada on the Antrim coast migrated to Scotland in the course of the 5th cent. The Uí Néill kingdom was greatly weakened by Viking expeditions from the 9th cent. onwards. SMD

Ulster covenant, 1912. The Parliament Act of 1911 reduced the Lords' veto to a delay and in April 1912 the third Home Rule Bill was introduced. The protestant response was to bring forward a covenant on 'Ulster Day', 28 September 1912, pledging the signatories to use 'all means which may be found necessary to defeat the present conspiracy to set up a Home Rule Parliament in Ireland'. It was signed by 237,000 Ulstermen and accompanied by a campaign to drive catholics out of employment in the dockyards. Both sides began preparing for armed conflict and the *Ulster Volunteer Force was founded in January 1913. JAC

Ulster custom was the name given to the informal rights of Ulster tenants. These included security of tenure so long as the rent was fully paid, and the freedom to sell the right of occupancy to any new tenant who met with the landlord's approval. In practice the Ulster custom was not uniformly honoured in Ulster, and was not confined to the province. The custom had initially no legal force. In 1847 the *tenant rights advocate William Sharman Crawford attempted to gain legalization for the custom, but failed. Only in 1870, through *Gladstone's Land Act, was this objective nominally attained. AJ

Ulster Special Constabulary, 1920–70. Formed as an auxiliary armed police force by the new Northern Irish government, the Ulster Specials in 1922 consisted of 'A' full-time, 'B' part-time, 'C' reserve with 5,500, 19,000, and 7,500 members respectively. Always dominated by old *Ulster Volunteer Force and *Orange order members and seen as a ruthless sectarian force by the catholic minority, it was reluctantly paid for by the British Treasury. After the early turbulent years of province, the 'A's and 'C's were disbanded. The 'B' Specials became a major target for criticism of their biased, aggressive policing of civil rights marches in the late 1960s. The Hunt Report (October 1969) recommended their replacement by a new part-time security force, soon known as the Ulster Defence Regiment. The new, avowedly non-sectarian, force again failed to recruit many catholics and was destined to be almost as controversial as the notorious 'B' Specials. MAH

Ulster Unionist Council. Created in 1904–5 as a representative body for Ulster unionism. Comprising originally 200 members (100 representing the local unionist associations, 50 representing the Orange order, and 50 co-opted members), the council was subsequently expanded and restructured: it was governed by a standing committee of 30. A new constitution was accepted in 1946. This gave belated recognition to the political institutions created by the partition settlement of 1920; it also provided for an enlarged standing committee and a new tier at the pinnacle of the representative pyramid, the executive committee. Although the representative significance of the UUC was overshadowed by the Unionist parliamentary party in the Northern Ireland House of Commons, since 1972 its strategic importance has been restored. AJ

Ulster Unionist Labour Association. Created in July 1918 as a working-class adjunct to the Ulster Unionist Party, it benefited from the social Toryism of its patron, Edward *Carson. The UULA won three of the eight Unionist seats in Belfast at the general election of December 1918; six UULA candidates were returned to the first Northern Irish Parliament in June 1921. Thereafter, the UULA parliamentary voice—a combination of deference and sectarianism—grew frailer, weakened by the retirement of Carson from politics in 1921 and by defeats in the 1925 Northern Ireland elections. AJ

Ulster Unionist Party. Formed in 1904–5 as the *Ulster Unionist Council to resist the threat of all-Ireland devolution, it consisted of representatives of local unionist institutions, the presbyterian church, the Orange order, and loyalist MPs. It brought protestant landowners, businessmen, and working class together successfully to oppose the third Home Rule Bill, 1912–14. It was led by southern unionist Sir Edward *Carson 1910–21, and then by Sir James *Craig, key organizer in the preceding period and the first Northern Ireland prime minister 1921–40. The Ulster Unionists became the single party controlling the Northern Ireland government and Parliament 1921–68, resisting constitutional reforms and concessions to the catholic minority until *O'Neill's premiership in 1963. Representing highly conservative social and economic views, it always had locally based interests at heart. Through control of local and provincial government, it was frequently accused of gerrymandering and sectarianism. The civil rights crisis from 1967 and the reluctant involvement of the British government placed enormous strains on party unity and resulted in a challenge from traditional unionist sources. It divided over the power-sharing executive 1973–4, the majority deserting Brian *Faulkner's leadership and helping its demise. It has remained the majority representative of Northern unionist opinion, despite an increasing challenge from the *Democratic Unionist Party, leaving it with primarily middle-class support. The UUP opposed the *Anglo-Irish agreement 1985, but extremely cautiously supported the Downing Street declaration of 1993. MAH

Ulster Volunteer Force (UVF). Formed in 1913, as the military backup to Ulster loyalist resistance to the third Home Rule Bill, and led by ex-British army officers and generals, the UVF achieved success in the Larne gun-running. Its membership totalled 100,000. It ceased with the First World War, but its veterans were the basis of the *Ulster Special Constabulary, formed in 1920–1. The name was resuscitated in the mid-1960s for a secret protestant paramilitary force, responsible for sectarian assassinations, preceding the outbreak of widespread violence in 1969. Outlawed in the 1970s, it remained less popular and active than the Ulster Defence Army (UDA), with which it frequently clashed. The prominence of its long-imprisoned leader, Gusty Spence, in the announcement of the loyalist cease-fire in October 1994 has inflated its significance. MAH

Ulundi, battle of, 1879. Last battle of the *Zulu–British War of 1879. A force of 10,000 men under General Chelmsford headed for Ulundi, 115 miles north-east of Durban, the seat of Zulu chief Cetewayo. On 4 July 1879 they engaged a Zulu force of 20,000 men. Chelmsford's army marched forward in a square formation with infantry forming the walls and cavalry riding within. The Zulus attacked but were cut down by rifle fire, and harried by the cavalry as they fled. They lost over 1,500 men, breaking the power of the tribe. The British lost just 15 killed and 78 wounded. RAS

unauthorized programme, 1885. Between 1883 and 1885 Joseph *Chamberlain and John *Morley organized publication in the *Fortnightly Review* of a series of articles—on land, housing, religion, education, and taxation—republished as *The Radical Programme* (1885) with a fiery preface by Chamberlain, promulgating 'a definite and practical programme for the Radical party'. The programme was 'unauthorized' as it lacked the Liberal Party leadership's approval, *Gladstone especially deploring its 'constructive' (i.e. socialistic) direction. Within a year 'Radical Joe' was allied to the Unionists, some of the items of his programme becoming even more 'unauthorized', and an embarrassment to him for the remainder of his career. HCEM

undertaker system. For many years the English administration in Dublin castle kept control of the Irish Parliament by reaching agreements with leading Irish borough patrons, who 'undertook' to construct a government majority and see through business. In exchange they received extensive patronage. Lord *Townshend, appointed lord-lieutenant in 1767, resolved to end the system, but was unable to do more than shuffle the personnel. The concessions which he made, including the *Octennial Act, paved the way for legislative independence and *Grattan's Parliament. The influence of undertakers was not fully removed until the *Union of 1801. JAC

unemployment. This apparently simple concept has been the source of great disagreement amongst economists in recent decades. Indeed the principal differences between major schools of thought are reflected in views about the nature and even the existence of unemployment. The term is an abbreviation and, fully stated, should be 'involuntary unemployment', to exclude those of working age who, for a variety of reasons, choose to be unemployed. The actual level of involuntary unemployment at any given time is a source of endless disagreement, reflected in the different mechanisms by which it can be defined and measured. In the past decade, British official statistical estimates of unemployment have changed on several occasions. But even the achievement of perfect measurement, improbable as that may be, would not resolve the disputes. Nineteenth-cent. definitions of involuntary unemployment assumed that it was the result exclusively of friction in the economic system, a term used to denote the fact that economic change entails both the creation of new jobs and the disappearance of existing ones. For this, and for many other reasons, individuals periodically choose or are obliged to change jobs. The period of adjustment between the loss of a job and the commencement of a new one represents frictional unemployment. It is generally agreed that this is a real phenomenon and that some unemployment of this type will always exist in any economy. For some authorities this constitutes both a full definition of unemployment and a complete explanation of it. Any unemployment beyond this is voluntary in that workers choose leisure rather than work at prevailing wage rates. Those who subscribe to this view of the economy agree that there is a natural rate of unemployment, which may vary, and will be the result of both frictional change and prevailing wage rates. For them the only way to reduce unemployment is for workers to choose work rather than leisure and to price themselves back into employment by accepting lower wages. There is an equally large and vociferous body of opinion which does not accept such an interpretation, holding the view that unemployment can be reduced or increased by government intervention. In the 1930s *Keynes suggested expenditure on public works as a vehicle for creating employment. More popularly, in recent decades, measures have been advocated to stimulate consumer spending, such as tax cuts, as a means of increasing opportunities for work.

Unemployment was initially recognized as a major economic and social problem between the wars, when the numbers of those unemployed increased well above the levels which could be explained as a temporary frictional readjustment, and because unemployment in industrial areas of the country including south Wales, Scotland, and much of northern England rose to very high levels. Post-war governments committed themselves to maintaining 'full employment', without actually defining what that entailed, but the problem reappeared in the 1970s and 1980s. By then inflation had replaced unemployment as the source of major anxiety for politicians and their constituents, and policies to curb inflation pushed unemployment rates upwards. The problem has thus re-emerged as a central issue dividing both economists and politicians, and the debate remains as heated and inconclusive as ever. CHL

Uniformity, Acts of, 1549, 1552, 1559, 1662. By enforcing the use of successive Prayer Books, the Acts provided liturgical conformity in Books of *Common* Prayer instead of the diverse uses of Sarum, York, Bangor, and Lincoln. Constitutionally and ecclesiastically, though not liturgically, the 1549 Act was 'a momentous moment', because Parliament set a precedent by itself authorizing doctrine and liturgy, a royal preserve since 1534. Liturgically the 1549 book, broadly an abridged Sarum rite in English, catholic in tone, made little change. The 1552 book marked a Zwinglian shift; the mass became the communion, tables replaced altars, the surplice replaced eucharistic vestments. Despite recent debate as to Elizabeth's intention, the 1559 book was decidedly comprehensive. Catholic elements were added to the 1552 book and vestments were to be as in 1548. The 1661 Prayer Book (authorized 1662) roughly followed 1559, and was uniformly used until the 20th cent., though *Anglo-catholic ritualists often illegally used Tridentine rites in English. WMM

Union, Act of (Ireland), 1801. United the parliaments of Great Britain and Ireland, abolished the Irish Parliament in Dublin, and ended Irish legislative independence granted in 1782. The Act originated from Britain's difficulties in governing Ireland especially after the *Irish rising of 1798, and was designed to strengthen British security against France. The first bill in 1799 failed because of the opposition of powerful protestant interests which dominated the Irish Parliament. They were bought off by bribery and lavish promises of honours and titles and the Act came into force on 1 January 1801. In place of her own House of Commons of 300 members, Ireland was given 100 MPs at Westminster, drawn from the counties and larger boroughs, while 28 Irish peers were elected for life by the whole Irish peerage to represent them in the Lords. Four bishops of the Church of Ireland, serving in rotation, also entered the Lords. The Act was intended to pave the way for catholic emancipation in Ireland but George III refused to consent and *Pitt, the prime minister, resigned. The Act was always unpopular in Ireland, Daniel *O'Connell and later Charles Stewart *Parnell leading the agitation for repeal, but it lasted until 1920. EAS

Union, Act of (Scotland), 1707. United England and Scotland and established the kingdom of Great Britain. In 1603 there was a union of crowns when James VI of Scotland became James I of England but, despite the king's wish the two countries remained independent states until 1707 (except for a brief legislative union during the Interregnum). After 1688 William III was anxious to promote union and in 1700 the House of Lords approved a bill authorizing the appointment of commissioners to negotiate, but the Commons did not agree. The process was restarted on the accession of Anne in 1702, but commissioners did not meet until April 1706, as there was much opposition or indifference in both countries. The English government was driven to seek a union when in 1705, to try to extract economic concessions, the Scottish Parliament passed an act allowing Scotland to choose a successor to the Scottish crown on Anne's death, putting the prospect of the Hanoverian succession in jeopardy. The articles of union negotiated by the commissioners formed the basis of the Acts passed by both the English and Scottish Parliaments.

The unitary state of Great Britain was established on 12 May 1707 with Anne as queen, and the succession guaranteed in the house of Hanover. The Scottish Parliament was abolished, and Scottish representation in the British parliament consisted of 45 MPs and 16 representative peers (the numbers based on the respective sizes of the two economies). Free trade between North Britain (Scotland) and South Britain (England) was established, and England's colonies were open to the Scots on an equal footing. The Scots retained their own legal system (though the House of Lords soon established its position as the highest court of appeal from the Scottish courts), as well as their own Privy Council (this, however, was abolished in 1708). The established churches were to remain the same: Anglican in England and presbyterian in Scotland.

The Union did not settle the problem of mistrust between the two nations, and though England secured immediately the succession and thus her northern frontier (one of her main objectives), Scotland's chief expectation of economic benefit was several decades in coming. CJ

Union, Act of (Wales). A 20th-cent. term applied to two Acts of Parliament (1536, 1542/3) in which Wales was declared 'incorporated, united and annexed' to the English realm. The 1536 Act laid down principles 'for laws and justice to be administered in Wales in like form as it is in this realm'; the Act of 1542/3 contained further details. This legislation completed social, administrative, and judicial developments in the principality and marcher lordships of Wales since Edward I's reign. It sprang from the circumstances of the 1530s: Henry VIII's divorce and the breach with Rome, royal supremacy over the church, and associated problems, and order and defence. It was also part of an attempt to bring uniformity and control to provincial government, by attacking franchises; it expressed ideas about royal sovereignty and reflected the bureaucratic genius of Thomas *Cromwell. The 1536 Act created five shires (Monmouth, Brecon, Radnor, Denbigh, and Montgomery) in addition to the six of the old principality (Carmarthen, Cardigan, Anglesey, Caernarfon, Merioneth, and Flint) and existing counties palatine, Pembroke and Glamorgan. Equality at law was granted to the Welsh, and English law, which had made great advances in Wales, became official usage. Each Welsh county had one MP (prosperous Monmouth two), and each county town had one parliamentary burgess (except poor Harlech), with 'contributory' boroughs providing support. The 1542/3 Act created the Court of Great Sessions, with twelve shires grouped in four circuits and Monmouth joining the Oxford circuit, an anomaly that created uncertainty as to whether Monmouthshire was or was not Welsh. The *Council in the Marches received statutory recognition with supervisory judicial powers. The English language, which had made considerable inroads, was the language of administration and justice, a sore point later on. The measures were welcomed by influential Welshmen and were regarded as a boon for long after; the growth of Welsh nationalism in the 20th cent. modified this view. RAG

Unionist Party of Northern Ireland. Established in September 1974 by the unionist supporters of the Sunningdale agreement (December 1973), which created the power-sharing Northern Ireland executive (January–May 1974). The Ulster Unionist leader Brian *Faulkner, who had helped to negotiate the agreement, failed to carry the majority of his party with him: his supporters at first accepted the label 'Unionist pro-Assembly', but later organized as UPNI. The party's share of the poll shrank from 7.7 per cent in the Convention elections of 1975 to 1.9 per cent in the council elections of 1981. Consistently weak performances after 1977 brought the dissolution of the party in 1981. AJ

Union Jack. National flag of the United Kingdom. The earl of Nottingham's designs after the accession of James I and VI yielded to the 1606 superimposition of the red cross of St George (England), bordered by its own white field, upon the saltire of St Andrew (Scotland) on a blue field. An Irish harp at the centre was added by Cromwell but withdrawn after the Restoration. On the union of Great Britain and Ireland (1801), the diagonal red cross of St Patrick was combined while still maintaining the individuality of each emblem. Its dramatic design has influenced many other national flags. ASH

Union of Democratic Control. Founded in September 1914 by a group of liberal intellectuals, including J. A. *Hobson, Norman Angell, and Bertrand *Russell, who believed that wars came about through secret diplomacy, and that they would cease if the people had more say. By the time it started up, the Great War had come along to prove them (as they saw it) right. During the war they agitated vigorously for a negotiated settlement, for which they—and especially their secretary, E. D. Morel—were continually harried as subversive pacifists. Afterwards they campaigned against armaments and alliances, until 1967, when the UDC was dissolved. BJP

unitarians deny the deity of Christ. They believe that only the Father should be worshipped, but their attitude to Jesus varies, reflecting their application of reasoned individual judgement to the Bible, and their reluctance to formulate creeds. Their views developed with the Reformation, notably through Michael Servetus (1511–53), the physician burned in Geneva, Bernardino Ochino (1487–1564), the friar turned Lutheran whom *Cranmer invited to England in 1547, and Lelio and Fausto Sozzini. By the 17th cent. they had communities in Poland, Hungary, and England, where John *Biddle's (1615–62) *XII Arguments* qualify him as the father of English unitarianism. They grew congregationally in the 18th cent. from *presbyterian, independent, and general *baptist churches, although avowed unitarianism only became legal in 1813. Joseph *Priestley (1733–1804) and Theophilus Lindsey (1723–1808) were that century's outstanding unitarians; the former had been an independent and the latter an Anglican clergyman. With no co-ordinating body before the British and Foreign Unitarian Association of 1825, superseded in 1928 by the General Assembly of Unitarian and Free Christian Churches, they none the less produced a distinctive social, political, and intellectual culture, represented by such families as the Martineaus, Chamberlains, Wicksteeds, and Holts, and such institutions as Manchester College, Oxford. In Scotland, where Thomas Aikenhead's mockery of the trinity led to Britain's last execution for blasphemy (1697), their corporate existence dates from 1776; in Ireland their strength lies with the non-subscribing presbyterians originating in the early 18th cent. and reinforced after 1829. CB

United Empire Loyalists was the term coined by the governor of British North America, Lord Dorchester, in 1789 to designate those citizens of the thirteen colonies who remained loyal to Britain during the American Revolution and fled to what is now Canada or returned to England. Some went to Nova Scotia, and in 1776 loyalists were transported to Halifax from Boston when the army withdrew, and again in 1783 with the fall of New York. Many settled in Nova Scotia, New Brunswick, Prince Edward Island, Quebec, and Ontario, and a small number later returned to the USA. SMD

United Irishmen. A society formed in Belfast and Dublin in 1791 by Theobald Wolfe *Tone and James Napper Tandy to agitate for parliamentary reform and equal religious rights. Revolutionary events in France made them more radical in 1793, while fears of growing catholic strength caused many protestants to secede and form the *Orange Society. In 1795 the United Irishmen were reconstituted as a secret society pledged to work for a republic. A rising with French help was thwarted when the invasion force was scattered by a storm off Bantry Bay in 1796. The government now encouraged the Orange Society to help suppress the United Irishmen, which increased its appeal to catholic peasants resentful of tithes and rents. A rising fixed for May 1798 was aborted by the arrest or flight of the leadership and the peasants were routed at *Vinegar Hill in June, shortly before Tone arrived with a small French invasion force. Irish-inspired subversion, also present in Britain in the later 1790s, was destroyed with the exposure of the Despard plot in 1802 and the failure of Robert *Emmet's rising in Ireland the following year. Though some protestants remained in the United Irishmen, the society's legacy was one of anti-protestant republican nationalism based on armed struggle. ER

United Kingdom. See GREAT BRITAIN.

United Nations. The UN replaced the failed *League of Nations after the Second World War. The term was first used in the 1942 declaration by 26 anti-axis states. Wartime negotiations between Russia, America, China, and Britain produced a blueprint for a new global security institution, rejecting *Churchill's preference for institutionalized spheres of influence. Following minor amendments at the San Francisco conference in 1945, the United Nations came into being on 24 October 1945 with 51 member states. By 1992, there were 175.

The institutions of the UN bore some similarity to those of the league, though the General Assembly was empowered to act on majority votes, rather than the principle of unanimity. But the five main powers, UK, USA, USSR, France, and China, gave themselves a power of veto in the Security Council, which Britain retains, though her right to do so has been questioned.

The effectiveness of the UN in maintaining global security has rested to a large extent on the superpowers being in agreement. UN peacekeeping activities proliferated at times of relaxation during the *Cold War, and after 1989, but were rarer when the two main powers were trading vetoes with each other in the 1950s or the 1980s. The UN was able to intervene in the *Korean War because the USSR at the time was boycotting the Security Council.

In the League of Nations, the absence of the USA and Russia allowed Britain and France to play leading roles, which have not been repeated in the UN. Britain's reliance on her understanding with the USA has limited her scope for independent initiatives. In addition, the 'clubby' traditional style of British diplomacy has fitted uneasily at times into the rhetorical style which became common in both the General Assembly and the Security Council at the height of the Cold War.

The United Nations has occasionally proved useful to Britain—for example, in relieving her of her burdensome commitments in *Palestine in 1947. Although the General Assembly condemned Britain's action over *Suez in 1956, the dispatch of peacekeepers to the canal enabled Britain to extricate herself with some dignity. British soldiers have also played a part in UN peacekeeping activities, notably in *Cyprus and in Bosnia. CNL

United Scotsmen. This small radical and revolutionary organization, closely modelled on the larger *United Irishmen, started in 1793 and was suppressed in 1799. The first group, in Glasgow, was formed shortly after the prosecutions of the leaders of the *Friends of the People made many radicals despair of peaceful agitation. The society's object was an independent republican regime. An attempted rising in Perthshire in 1797 led to an Act in July to suppress it and in January 1798 George Mealmaker was sentenced to fourteen years transportation. Other arrests followed the outbreak of the Irish rebellion of 1798 and a second Act in 1799 completed the suppression of the movement. JAC

United States of America, relations with. American success in the *American War of Independence (1776–83) was followed by a period in which trade above all helped the British and the ex-colonists to learn to coexist. This trend was interrupted by the *War of 1812, confused alike in its origins and conduct. It was inconclusive, and left *Castlereagh hoping that time would ultimately resolve such contentious issues as neutral rights. British conservatives feared the appeal of American democracy among radicals at home, while governments suspected that the USA might try to exploit British involvement in any war with a European power. Disputes over the Canadian border, however, were mostly settled by 1846, while British moves towards *free trade helped to persuade many in the USA that war was unnecessary. Although tensions during the American Civil War included a major scare with the North (the **Trent* incident in 1861–2), the British were becoming resigned to the fact that Canada could not be defended against a determined US assault. Serious imperial and naval rivalries with other powers also persuaded them after 1895 to accept such paramountcy as the USA chose to exert in the New World.

Thus the *First World War found US neutrality tempered by the fact that Britain was already viewed as the least obnoxious of the imperial powers. British interference with American trade with Germany was more than offset by huge purchases from the USA, though Anglo-American relations were paradoxically very strained during the winter of 1916–17 until the resumption and intensification of the German submarine campaign brought the USA into the war in April. Relations cooled after 1918 over such matters as trade and naval rivalries until these were eclipsed by German and Japanese aggression, and American fears of the axis—especially from 1940—led to Lend-Lease and indirect assistance at sea. The USA became a belligerent in December 1941. Even so, and despite the highly successful wartime alliance (1941–5), the Attlee government briefly showed interest in a western European/British Commonwealth Third Force.

Lack of resources and the Russian threat finally persuaded the British to opt for the 'Special Relationship' with the USA, a relationship which—though assisted by a common language and various personal and cultural ties—was based essentially on shared interests and fears. Thus the USA frequently encouraged Britain to persevere in a world role so that it could benefit from Britain's Commonwealth bases as well as its own facilities in the British Isles (America's unsinkable aircraft carrier off the coast of Europe). Even after Britain's withdrawal from east of Suez and its entry to the *EEC (1973), the two remained intimately connected in such areas as nuclear weapons, intelligence, and the pursuit of freer trade in the world. They assisted each other in the *Falklands (1982) and *Gulf (1991) conflicts. But relations were inevitably weakened by the ending of the *Cold War. CJB

universities. In the Middle Ages, the *studium generale*, a place of learning open to all, was the equivalent of the term 'university'. Instruction was by learned men and degrees were awarded as a title of honour. From the 12th cent., Paris was the intellectual centre of this activity, where luminaries such as Peter Abelard (1079–1142) were both students and teachers.

Similar institutions were established in England, at *Oxford about 1185 and at *Cambridge in 1209. For the following six centuries, the two universities, which mainly provided a liberal education for the aristocracy and gentry, retained their exclusiveness. The attempts to establish a university at Durham during the Commonwealth foundered at the Restoration in 1660. Restrictions on non-Anglicans led to the founding of University College, London, in 1828 and the University of *London eight years later, with its affiliated colleges and degree-granting powers. Scotland had a long tradition of university education which was available for dissenters. St Andrews (1410), Glasgow (1451), Aberdeen (1494), and Edinburgh (1583) attracted many English students.

Until the early 19th cent. there were no universities in the north of England. However, in 1832, the charter of Durham cathedral decided to support a university based in the Norman castle, though restricted to students who subscribed to the *Thirty-Nine Articles. The university, which received its charter in 1837, was based on the Oxford and Cambridge model. Most of its (male) graduates entered the church.

A new impetus for change and expansion in higher education came largely from the growth of science and its applications to an industrial society. One example of this was the setting up of a Royal Commission on Scientific Instruction and the Advancement of Science in 1872, chaired by the 7th duke of Devonshire. One of its main findings, published in 1875, was the need for more and better-trained science teachers, in which universities could help. Owens' College, Manchester, opened in 1851, had been a forerunner, though many of its students were part-time and did not aim at a degree.

Civic pride was also one of the prime motives for creating universities, which received benefactions from Jesse *Boot at Nottingham, Mark Firth at Sheffield, and Josiah Mason at Birmingham, which also later attracted money from the American steel millionaire Andrew *Carnegie. University colleges were set up at Southampton (1862), Newcastle (1871), Leeds (1874), Bristol (1876), Sheffield (1879), Birmingham (1880), Nottingham (1881), Liverpool (1881), Reading (1892), and Exeter (1895).

In the 1880s, one development was the northern federation of provincial colleges. Owens' College, Manchester, was joined by Liverpool in 1884 to form the federal University of Victoria, and by Leeds in 1887. Until then the students of these colleges had been prepared for external London degrees: under the new charter, the university awarded its own. The federation lasted until 1903, when individual charters were granted.

The University of Wales followed a similar pattern of an upsurge in civic awareness. Colleges were founded at Aberystwyth (1872), Cardiff (1883), and Bangor (1884). It was not until 1893 that a charter was granted to the University of Wales, giving the body degree-awarding rights in place of the London external degree. University College, Swansea, joined the federation in 1923.

The lack of opportunities for the higher education of women led to the founding of the university extension movement. Extra-mural classes had been held for women by professors at King's College, London, as early as 1847. In 1867 Josephine *Butler and Anne Clough became president and secretary respectively of the North of England Council for Promoting the Higher Education of Women. The success of the courses, which were very well attended, led Cambridge to establish university extension in 1873, sending lecturers to Nottingham, Derby, and Leicester. This was swiftly followed by the London Society for the Extension of University Teaching in 1876 and at Oxford in 1878. The newer civic universities were also soon heavily involved in the work, later developing departments of extra mural studies. Women's colleges were instituted at Cambridge—Girton (1869) and Newnham (1871), with Anne Clough as principal—and at Oxford—Lady Margaret Hall (1879) and Somerville (1879), followed by others.

Whilst the University of London had grown into a teaching institution with 24 schools by 1900, subsequent university expansion was slight; in the inter-war period, only two new colleges outside London were founded, at Hull and at Leicester. Government funding was supplied to the universities and from 1919 was administered by the University Grants Committee (UGC).

After the Second World War, there was a great demand for more university places as the birth rate rose. The University College of North Staffordshire, now Keele University, was founded in 1949, and in the years 1961–5, East Anglia, Essex, Kent, Lancaster, Sussex, Warwick, and York. Newcastle, previously linked with Durham, became a university in its own right. The Robbins Committee on Higher Education (1963) recommended that nine colleges of advanced technology (CAT) should become full universities, including Aston, Bath, Bradford, Loughborough, and Salford. At the same time Strathclyde, Dundee, and Heriot-Watt were founded in Scotland. Northern Ireland has *Queen's, Belfast, a 19th-cent. foundation, and the University of Ulster at Coleraine.

Innovations in the structure of university organizations and curricula are a recent feature of the system. The Open University (1966) provides degree and other courses for students over 21, operates an open admissions policy, and uses distance learning. The University of Buckingham (1976) is the only independent university in the United Kingdom, offering two-year honours degree courses. A more informal organization is the University of the Third Age (U3A), which provides educational opportunities for the over-50s.

Following the recommendations of the White Paper 'Higher Education: A New Framework' (1991), the 1992 Education Act abolished the distinction between polytechnics and universities. There are now almost 100 universities whose finances are determined by the Higher Education Funding Council (HEFC), which replaced the UGC. PG

Cobban, A. B., *The Medieval Universities: Their Development and Organisation* (1975); Jones, D. R., *The Origins of Civil Universities* (1988); Sanderson, M. (ed.), *The Universities in the Nineteenth Century* (1975).

'Unlearned' Parliament, 1404. This nickname was given to the Parliament summoned by Henry IV in 1404 to meet at Coventry, after the king ordered that no lawyers should be returned, since they concentrated too much on their own professional business. The instructions were resented and the rebels of 1405 demanded a free Parliament. JAC

urban history can be defined variously. Histories of individual British towns have been written for over four centuries; studies of towns and urbanization in general came later; while as an academic discipline British urban history is little over 30 years old.

An interest in the history and antiquities of towns can be traced back to Anglo-Saxon times, and by the 13th cent. London had civic annals, copied later by other leading towns. From the end of the 16th cent. true urban histories started to appear, the first published being John *Stow's *Survey of London* (1598). Between the 17th and 19th cents. many towns received substantial histories, though in general they contain undigested raw materials, 'the uncooked potatoes and not the finished meal'. A controversial literature after the 1688 revolution produced one enduring work of urban scholarship (Madox's *Firma burgi*, 1726), while another, in connection with the municipal reform of the 1830s, generated a *History of the Boroughs and Municipal Corporations of the United Kingdom* by Merewether and Stephens (1835), still a useful corpus of information.

A new direction was taken at the end of the 19th cent. under German and American influences. The most notable pioneers were Charles Gross (1857–1909) and F. W. *Maitland (1850–1906), who laid the foundations of British urban history as of so much else. They and their pupils initiated a period of meticulous scholarship (mostly on medieval municipal history) which lasted until the 1940s, though in the same period the histories of individual towns fell behind American standards. However, at the end of that period new works were appearing which heralded wider perspectives both on the periods covered (breaking out of the medieval strait-jacket) and on themes dealing with society and economy as well as institutions. Hoskins's *Industry, Trade and People in Exeter, 1688–1800* (1935) and W. H. Chaloner's *The Social and Economic Development of Crewe, 1780–1923* (1950) were notable pioneer works.

The subject was transformed in the 1960s largely through the influence and inspiration of H. J. (Jim) Dyos (1921–78). He not only wrote and edited important exemplars, but founded an Urban History Group (1962), with its own *Newsletter* (1963) and *Yearbook* (1974) on the American model. He also developed work in his own University of Leicester, formalized there since 1985 as a Centre for Urban History. Work has proliferated since the 1960s, in Wales and Scotland as well as England, and there is a separate Scottish Urban History Group. Other disciplines have been brought to bear on the subject, including archaeology, cartography, and historical geography. A large body of urban archaeological data has been produced and partly published; three volumes have so far appeared of a *British Atlas of Historic Towns*; and an Urban Morphology Research Group at the University of Birmingham has developed the pioneering approaches of M. R. G. Conzen in the historical study of town plans.

DMP

Urien was the late 6th-cent. ruler of *Rheged, the British kingdom centred on Carlisle. The 9th-cent. British writer *Nennius described his power and *Taliesin, poet at Urien's court, praised him as warrior and protector. He is said to have led a coalition against the Angles in the northern kingdom of *Bernicia and to have been killed *c.*590 besieging *Bamburgh. Through *Geoffrey of Monmouth and *Malory, Urien was brought into the Arthurian legend and his activities transferred to south Wales. AM

Ursulines. Monastic order established in 1535 by St Angela Merici, a lay Franciscan, at Brescia (Italy). Orginally intended for religious women living in their own homes as teachers, the order became communal in 1566 under the guidance of St Charles Borromeo, while from 1612 the Ursulines of Paris, and later throughout France (where the largest number of communities were concentrated) and beyond, were strictly enclosed following an *Augustinian rule. The order became famous for missionary and educational activity, particularly in North America. In 1900 most Ursuline communities (which followed differing institutes) were united in the 'Roman Union'. BJG

Uses, statute of, 1535. The use was a legal device whereby property could be held by one person for the benefit of another, e.g. when a landowner was absent on crusade. But, by extension, it might be employed to evade or avoid obligations, defraud creditors, or escape legislation against *mortmain. Henry VIII pressed strongly that uses should be restricted, arguing that his revenue was affected, but the Parliament of 1532 was unwilling to legislate and was told sharply 'not to contend with me'. In 1535 Parliament accepted 27 Hen. VIII c. 10, which complained of 'subtle inventions and practices' and restored obligations to the beneficiary. Landowners remained indignant, the rebels in the *Pilgrimage of Grace demanded redress, and Henry made concessions in the Wills Act of 1540. Chancery lawyers then began to circumvent the statute of Uses by devising new forms of trust. JAC

Ushant, battle of, 1778. After France's entry into the American war, Augustus Keppel was dispatched with a fleet of 30 ships to watch Brest. On 23 July he sighted a French fleet of similar size off the Breton coast under d'Orvilliers. Though manœuvring went on for four days and a good deal of damage was inflicted, the result was indecisive, no ships being captured or sunk. The political consequences were more spectacular. Keppel was a Whig hero and his opposition friends hinted that he had been betrayed by Sir Hugh Palliser, who had commanded the rear. Palliser demanded a court martial on Keppel, which he conducted. Keppel's political friends flocked to Portsmouth to give moral support and were jubilant when he was acquitted and the charges declared malicious and unfounded. It was then Palliser's turn to be court-martialled. Though acquitted, he was censured for not keeping Keppel fully informed. Meanwhile a French squadron had escaped from Toulon to America, where it gave substantial help to the rebels. JAC

Ussher, James (1581–1656). Archbishop of Armagh. Born in Dublin and educated at Trinity College, Dublin, Ussher was successively professor of divinity, vice-chancellor (1615), bishop of Meath (1621), and archbishop (1625). He drafted the 104 Articles approved by the Dublin convocation (1615). On returning from absence in England (1623–6), he signed the Irish bishops' protest against toleration of popery (1626). Despite his predestinarian theology, he was friendly with *Laud. During his tenure the disputed primacy of Ireland was settled in Armagh's favour and the Bible in Irish language was permitted, but Scottish settlers resented the imposition of unmodified Anglican articles. After leaving Ireland (1640), he held the see of Carlisle *in commendam*. Though suggesting modified episcopacy with synods (1641) acceptable to presbyterians like *Baxter, he remained an episcopalian royalist. Ussher was a distinguished scholar, contributing to early Irish history and biblical chronology: his argument that the world was created in 4004 BC held the field for decades. WMM

usury laws. The idea that it is wrong to profit from lending money is found in the Old Testament, and was linked to the belief that there exists a just or fair price for every commodity. In the 4th cent. the church banned clerics from making loans to each other. In the reign of Charlemagne, this instruction was extended to include all Christians. But church doctrine did not forbid interest being paid as compensation for the use of capital tied in some venture. This double standard endured throughout the medieval period. The usury laws coexisted with the widespread acceptance that payment of interest was legitimate in some circumstances, such as by merchant banks on deposits. CHL

utilitarianism is the moral philosophy which asserts that the maximization of happiness is the ultimate aim of all human conduct. Philosophers since the time of Aristotle have stressed the ethical value of happiness, but not until the 18th cent., with the work of Helvetius, Beccaria, and *Hume, was there a theory which defined moral worth exclusively in terms of happiness. According to Jeremy *Bentham, the systematizer of utilitarianism, an action is right if, and only if, it promotes the greatest happiness of the greatest number.

Bentham presented utilitarianism as a practical guide to both individual and collective decision-making, developing a 'felicific calculus' to measure the net amount of happiness producible by alternative courses of action. The practical influence of utilitarianism in shaping social policy in Britain from the mid-19th cent. has been considerable. It became the ideological driving force behind the reform movement known as *philosophical radicalism, which tested all institutions by the principle of utility. Many far-reaching changes in the social security system, the treatment of employees and tenants, and the regulation of public health owed their origin in large part to the spirit of utilitarian ideas. This influence remains strong today: the theory of welfare economics, the concepts of marginal utility and cost–benefit analysis, and the late 20th-cent. preoccupation with obtaining value for money in the public services all exemplify the utilitarian interpretation of 'is it right?' in terms of 'will it work better?'

However, utilitarianism has been much criticized. It has been objected that it is impossible to reduce complex moral issues to a simple mathematical formula, however elegant, and that no rational criterion exists for balancing the great harm done to an individual by taking away his property, against the potential happiness which could be derived by 200 other persons to whom it might be distributed. Critics argue, also, that justice demands protection of basic human rights such as life and liberty irrespective of calculations of utility. On the utilitarian principle, it is possible to justify the execution or imprisonment of an innocent person in order to defuse a revolutionary situation or even to placate an angry mob. But such an act would violate justice, according to those who, like Kant and Hegel, argue that the right is prior to the good, and that it is immoral to commit wrong for the purpose of promoting utility. John Stuart *Mill sought to answer this criticism by pointing out that the principle of justice promoted social utility in the long term, if not always in the immediate short term. Mill's position later became known as 'rule-utilitarianism' or indirect utilitarianism. Overall utility is best served by adherence to secondary rules such as justice, even though in a particular case, taken in itself, an act of injustice could have more good than evil consequences.

The critics also point out that utilitarianism is essentially an aggregative principle, and lacks a defensible distributive criterion. Whatever distribution of goods maximizes social utility is endorsed by utilitarianism irrespective of who gets what. Critics find this distributive arbitrariness unacceptable; for them justice demands that good should be distributed on the basis of some non-arbitrary criterion, such as desert, entitlement, or need. TSG

Utopia. Politico-philosophic work by Thomas *More (1516), initiating a literary genre. Steeped in literary *humanism, More sought for the best form of government through discussions with the fictitious Raphael Hythloday, addressing problems of counsel (from both monarchial and advisory viewpoints) and social concerns such as theft, before expanding into a more general analysis of Tudor England. This is followed by Hythloday's account of the 'New Island of Utopia' ('Noplace'), but its egalitarian commonwealth appears flawed since, despite religious freedom and absence of hunger and homelessness, personal freedom is restricted. If welfare democracies are anticipated, shadows of modern totalitarian regimes hover. ASH

Utrecht, treaty of, 1713. This was part of the general settlement ending the War of the *Spanish Succession. France and Spain recognized the Hanoverian succession, and France agreed to expel the old pretender from French soil. Philip V of Spain abandoned his claim to the French throne. Many territorial changes, partly designed to create strong barrier states on the borders of France, occurred. The most important were that France retained Alsace, Philip retained Spain and the Indies but lost his other possessions in the Netherlands and Italy to the Emperor Charles VI, Britain gained French territory in North America, and Gibraltar and Minorca from Spain, the Dutch were allowed to garrison *barrier towns in the former Spanish Netherlands, and Savoy gained French territory and Sicily. CJ

Uxbridge, treaty of, 1645. The so-called treaty of Uxbridge was in fact an abortive negotiation. The fluctuating fortunes of war in 1644 persuaded Parliament to propose an armistice for discussion. Commissioners met at Uxbridge on 29 January to negotiate on three main issues—the church, the militia, and Ireland. On none of these points was any progress made. Charles refused to abandon episcopacy or take the covenant; to hand over control of the militia; or to allow Ireland to be subdued by parliamentary forces. Nor would he abandon supporters like *Rupert, whom Parliament refused to include in a general pardon. The negotiation was abandoned on 22 February. The last chance of ending the war by compromise had gone. JAC

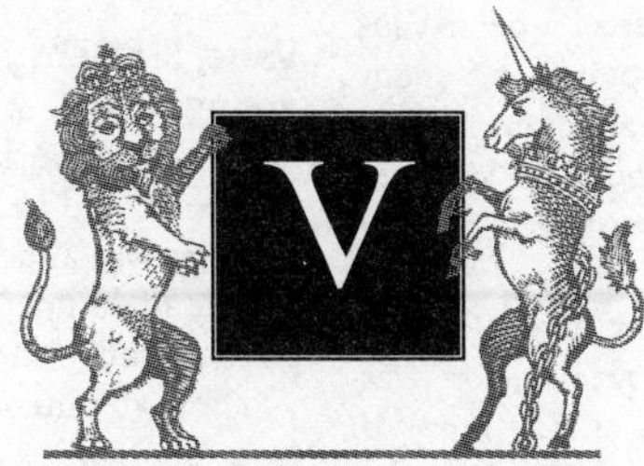

vaccination, a term first used by *Jenner (1798) for inoculating cowpox matter (*vacca* = cow) to produce immunity from the far more virulent smallpox, has since come to mean the creation of immunity from infectious diseases in general. Its benign effect on death rates from smallpox led to gradual abandonment of earlier techniques, but not without opposition. The 1840 Vaccination Act prohibited inoculation and permitted vaccination of the poor at ratepayers' expense; the 1853 extension made the practice compulsory, though it was not universally enforced. An organized movement to repeal compulsory vaccination developed after 1871, leading eventually to amendments of previous statutes (1898). Nevertheless, with compulsory notification of infectious diseases and better trained public health officers, vaccination and revaccination rapidly reduced the prevalence, morbidity, and mortality of smallpox. Subsequent vaccines (using attenuated or altered viruses) against diphtheria, polio, measles, whooping cough, and rubella have largely controlled these diseases. ASH

Vagrancy Acts. Vagrancy was a phenomenon which particularly worried late medieval and Tudor society, not merely because it often led to crime, but because 'masterless men' seemed to threaten the whole social structure. The breakdown of the authority of lords of the manor freed men and women to move, and unemployment, demobilization, enclosures, and high prices could combine to produce destitution and vagrancy. London, by far the largest town in the country, produced its own vagrants and imported others from the neighbouring counties. In 1608 Thomas Dekker, the playwright, wrote that suburbs were 'caves where monsters are bred up to devour the cities themselves'.

One of the earliest government interventions came in 1351, after the *Black Death had caused an acute shortage of labour. The statute attempted not only to control wages and enforce contracts but declared punishment for persons fleeing from one shire to another. Another flurry of legislation came after the *Peasants' Revolt of 1381. An Act of 1383 authorized JPs to apprehend vagabonds and another Act of 1388 insisted that anyone leaving his abode or service must carry letters patent from the hundred explaining the purpose of his journey. Tudor legislation on the subject was both frequent and fierce. The Parliament of Henry VII in 1495 enacted that vagabonds should be put in the stocks for three days and three nights on bread and water. Henry VIII improved upon this in 1531 declaring that an able-bodied vagrant should be 'tied to the end of a cart naked and be beaten with whips till his body be bloody', and then sent back to his place of birth or last employment. In 1535 it was announced that on a second offence any 'valiant beggar or sturdy vagabond' would lose part of his right ear, and on a third offence would be hanged. Branding was introduced in 1547 and the vagabond was to be sold into slavery. By 1572 they were to be flogged and have their ears bored and by 1604 they would be branded on their shoulder with the letter 'R' for rogue. Hanging for repeat offences was certainly no idle threat: four vagrants, including one woman, were hanged in Middlesex in 1575/6. Transportation was also introduced after 1597, mainly to the new American colonies. A different approach was *Bridewells, where work was provided: opened in London in 1553, they were soon imitated in other towns and counties. After the Restoration the problem of vagrancy diminished, partly because paupers were given help in their parishes of origin, partly because an expanding economy provided better opportunities for employment. The increasing expense of *poor relief led in the early 19th cent. to reorganization of the whole system, but vagabondage had ceased to terrify. JAC

Valence, Aymer de, earl of Pembroke (*c.*1270–1324). Valence's father William was a half-brother of Henry III, being a son of John's widow Isabella by her second marriage, and came to England in 1247. He fought on the king's side in the baronial wars and commanded against the Welsh in the 1280s. Aymer de Valence inherited in 1296 and spent his early years campaigning in Scotland, fighting at *Falkirk (1298) and defeating Robert I Bruce at *Methven in 1306. The following year he was himself defeated by Bruce at *Loudoun Hill. In 1307 he was recognized as earl of Pembroke by virtue of his mother, a granddaughter of William *Marshal, earl of Pembroke (d. 1219). In Edward II's reign he was at first an *Ordainer but switched to the king's side after the murder of *Gaveston, who was seized from his custody. He fought with the king at *Bannockburn and was subsequently employed watching the Scots and on diplomatic missions. His widow founded Pembroke College, Cambridge. JAC

Vanbrugh, Sir John (1664–1726). Dramatist and architect. A good imitation of Renaissance Man, Vanbrugh was of

Dutch descent. His grandfather settled in London as a merchant; his father moved to Chester after the Great Fire of London; his mother was the granddaughter of a peer. Vanbrugh began as a soldier, was made a captain, and spent 1688–92 in captivity in France. In 1696 he had an enormous success with his delightful comedy *The Relapse, or Virtue in Danger*, with its bravura role of Lord Foppington. He followed it in 1697 with *The Provok'd Wife*, and in 1705 *The Confederacy* was put on at the Queen's, Haymarket, which Vanbrugh had built. His last play, *The Journey to London*, was finished by Cibber and had great success as *The Provok'd Husband*. Meanwhile, Vanbrugh's career as an architect developed after he began building *Castle Howard in 1701 for the earl of *Carlisle. He was appointed comptroller of the board of works in 1702, Carlisle herald in 1703, and Clarenceux herald in 1704. His work on Blenheim palace began in 1705 and involved him in protracted and rancorous exchanges with Sarah, duchess of *Marlborough. He was knighted by George I at Greenwich on his arrival in 1714 and was appointed architect of Greenwich hospital. Among his many buildings are King's Weston, near Bristol (1710–25); Morpeth town hall (1714); the north front at Grimsthorpe (Lincs.) for the duke of Ancaster (1715–30); Eastbury (Dorset) for *Dodington (1716–18); Floors Castle for the duke of Roxburgh (1718); Seaton Delaval (Northd.) (1718–29), and much rebuilding at Lumley castle, Co. Durham (1722–4). His usual style is an extravagant and idiosyncratic baroque. Vanbrugh married late in life and his widow outlived him by 50 years: his only son was killed at *Fontenoy. JAC

Vancouver, George (*c.*1758–98). Born in King's Lynn, Vancouver was originally only a seaman on *Cook's second voyage, but rose to command in the Royal Navy. After further service with Cook, he was sent in 1791 in *Discovery* to re-establish British claims to Nootka Sound, disputed with Spain, to explore the north-east coast of the Pacific, and to seek the North-West passage. His voyage revealed the chain of islands along the coast, including the large island which bears his name. He died just before the account of his expedition was published in 1798. RB

Van Dyck, Anthony (1599–1641). Portrait painter. In the opinion of Rubens, that master's finest pupil, the Antwerp-born Van Dyck had imbibed in Italy all the influences of Titian before he encountered the connoisseurship of Charles I in England. In 1632 he became 'Principal Painter in Ordinary to their Majesties' and was knighted in 1633, undertaking large compositions to project the mystique of the king's royalist convictions. In its range and quality this *œuvre*, together with many commissions depicting the Caroline aristocracy, was without precedent in England. In the course of one decade, Van Dyck mirrored the frailest of the European monarchies with such mastery that, in British portraiture, only *Gainsborough and *Lawrence may be considered rivals. Though he never intended to settle in England, and purchased property in Flanders, Van Dyck died in London in December 1641, helplessly witnessing the extinction of a world he had himself gone far to create. As a result of the sales of the royal collection following Charles I's execution, some of Van Dyck's work of the 1630s was lost to England. DDA

Vane, Sir Henry the elder (1589–1655) and **Sir Henry the younger** (1613–62). Politicians of contrasted character. The father was a worldly minded courtier, adroit, thrusting, industrious, and bent on accumulating a great landed estate. The son was a radical puritan with mystical leanings, and in middle life a doctrinaire republican. What they shared was political skill—and some deviousness in exercising it.

Through purchase or patronage, the elder acquired a succession of posts in the royal household, won Charles I's confidence, and became a privy counsellor in 1630. Favoured also by the queen and the marquis of *Hamilton, he rose in February 1640 to secretary of state. As such, he recorded *Strafford's fatal words about using an Irish army 'to reduce this kingdom', which his son leaked to *Pym. Gradually he aligned himself with the future parliamentarians, until Charles stripped him of all his offices. With his son, he sat on the Committee of Both Kingdoms and in the *Rump.

The younger Vane sacrificed a promising career at court in 1635 for the religious liberty of Massachusetts, where within six months he was elected governor. But through supporting the unorthodox Anne Hutchinson he got deep into religious controversy, clashed seriously with the general court, resigned, and returned home in 1637. In the Long Parliament he rapidly became a leader of the war party, a close ally of *Cromwell, and after Pym's death its most influential single member. But by 1648 he and Cromwell were parting company, and he held aloof from the king's trial. He was very active, however, in the government of the *Commonwealth, and he regarded Cromwell's *Protectorate as a betrayal of its republican principles. His subversive tract *A Healing Question* (1656) cost him four months' imprisonment, but he returned to prominence with the restored Rump in 1659. He was excepted from pardon at the *Restoration, but Charles II granted the Convention's plea for his life. To the shame of the king and the Cavalier Parliament, he was nevertheless executed in 1662. AHW

Vanuatu, an independent republic in the Commonwealth, was formerly the islands of the New Hebrides, so named by Cook. They lie 1,000 miles east of Australia and have a population, largely Melanesian, of about 160,000. Their main support is agriculture (cocoa, coffee, and copra), fishing, and tourism. From 1906 they were under a condominium run by France and Britain, but became independent in 1980. JAC

vassal was the term used to describe a person who had taken a formal oath of allegiance to a superior and was derived from a Celtic word meaning 'youth'. In its simplest form it was no more than commending oneself to a lord for protection, but it became more complex when estates and benefices were granted in exchange for specified duties. It was upheld by the ceremony of *homage. In Anglo-Saxon England vassalage remained largely personal. The Normans introduced the continental practice of endowing the vassal with a *fief: this did not imply outright ownership of the land and the vassal could not alienate, though he could subcontract and create his own vassals by the process of subinfeudation. In exchange, the vassal performed carefully defined duties, such as knight service, and aids for particular occasions. The lord retained rights over marriage and wardship, since they might affect the integrity of the fief, and could demand a payment on inheritance. By the 13th cent. the arrangements were unravelling as lords increasingly paid *scutage rather than perform knight service and vassals tried to commute their own obligations. Though at the outset the greatest lords were themselves vassals of the king, as tenants-in-chief, the term eventually acquired a pejorative meaning as slave, vagabond, or miscreant. JAC

Vaughan, Henry (1622–95). Poet and mystic. After two years at Oxford, Vaughan commenced legal training in London but returned home to Breconshire at the outbreak of war in 1642. Briefly clerk to a royalist judge, and possibly on military service until 1646 when the puritans controlled south Wales, he turned his attention to medicine, apparently successfully, though no degree or licence has been traced. He began to publish poetry in 1646, but George *Herbert's influence led to rejection of 'idle books', and it is for his religious poems that he is now best known, though they were largely disregarded in his own day; *Silex Scintillans* ('The Glittering Flint', 1650, Part II 1655) and the prose *The Mount of Olives* (1652) reflect his spiritual rapture and fresh creativeness. Welsh sentiment led Vaughan to assume the title 'Silurist', since his native county had formerly been inhabited by a local tribe called the *Silures. ASH

Vaughan Williams, Ralph (1872–1958). English composer, conductor, writer, editor, and teacher, who believed passionately in the need for direct communication with his audience. Vaughan Williams studied composition with Charles Wood at Cambridge and with *Parry and *Stanford at London's *Royal College of Music, where he established a lifelong friendship with fellow-composer Gustav *Holst. He scored a great success with his first published work, the delightful song 'Linden Lea' (1902). He also took lessons with Bruch in Berlin and Ravel in Paris. Vaughan Williams drew heavily on his native heritage: he edited *The English Hymnal* (1906), and works like the *Fantasia on a Theme of Thomas Tallis* (1909) reflect his great interest in Elizabethan music. He also collected folk-songs, which influenced his modal harmony and melodic style, contributing to an influential 'Englishness'. The finest of his nine symphonies are the fiercely dissonant No. 4 (1935), the modal No. 5 (1943), whose luminous spirituality draws on the 'morality' (opera) *The Pilgrim's Progress*, and the war-torn No. 6 (1948) with its desolate hushed 'Epilogue'. His film music included *Scott of the Antarctic* (1948). ECr

Vauxhall gardens (London), just south of the Thames, opened soon after the Restoration as New Spring gardens, and were visited by *Pepys, who complained of high prices. In 1732 Jonathan Tyers arranged a grand reopening, attended by Frederick, prince of Wales. The central features were the Rotunda and a famous statue of *Handel by *Roubiliac, erected in 1738. In 1749 a rehearsal of Handel's *Music for the Royal Fireworks* in celebration of the peace of Aix-la-Chapelle, brought 12,000 people to Vauxhall. Most visitors came by water. Leopold Mozart, in London in 1764 to show off his extraordinary son, wrote: 'I thought I was in the Elysian fields, with a thousand glass lamps turning night into day.' In the 19th cent. there were increasing complaints of rowdiness and vulgarity, and the gardens closed in the summer of 1859. They were soon built over. JAC

Vereeniging, treaty of. This brought the second *Boer War to a close. At the beginning of May 1902 the Boers agreed to treat for 'limited independence'. On the 31st at Vereeniging in southern Transvaal they accepted Britain's final offer: that they stop fighting and declare themselves subjects of King Edward VII, in return for which they would get their lands back, with compensation for buildings and crops that had been destroyed; be allowed the use of their language in schools and law courts; and be given self-government as soon as possible, with a racist franchise if that was what they really desired. BJP

Verneuil, battle of, 1424. The first task of John, duke of *Bedford, regent for the infant Henry VI, was to preserve and, if possible, extend Henry V's gains in France. In the summer of 1424 he began a campaign to conquer Anjou and Maine, but was confronted at Verneuil on 17 August by a superior French force, under the command of two Scots, the earl of *Buchan, recently made constable of France, and Archibald, earl of *Douglas, veteran campaigner of Henry IV's reign. English archers repeated their success at *Agincourt, nine years earlier. Buchan and Douglas were both killed and the duc d'Alençon taken prisoner. JAC

Vernon, Edward (1684–1757). Admiral. Second son of James Vernon, secretary of state to William III, Vernon entered the navy at the age of 15, and was given his first command in 1706. In 1722 he came into Parliament as MP for Penryn but moved into opposition and lost his seat in 1734. At the outbreak of the war with Spain in 1739, Vernon offered his services and was sent to the West Indies with the rank of vice-admiral. On 21 November 1739 his forces stormed the fortress of Portobello in Panama. Vernon became a national hero. London made him a freeman, taverns were named after him, and the tiny resort outside Edinburgh commemorated his great victory. But attempts to repeat the success at Cartagena, Santiago, or Panama failed and Vernon returned home in December 1742. Returned to Parliament for Ipswich he became a noisy critic of government and though promoted admiral in 1745 was dismissed from the service in 1746 for publishing his letters to the Admiralty. 'Henceforth', wrote Namier, 'he was merely a picturesque and turbulent politician, embarrassing to his friends . . . the erstwhile firebrand had become a bore.' JAC

Versailles, treaty of, 1783. The treaty of Versailles, at the end of the *American War of Independence, was less disadvantageous to Britain than had seemed likely, partly because of *Rodney's naval victory at the *Saints in April 1782 and partly because of the failure of de Bussy's expedition to India. The independence of the thirteen American colonies had to be recognized, but that had been inevitable after the surrender at *Yorktown in 1781. The Americans retained their fishing rights off Newfoundland and Congress promised 'earnestly to recommend' the restitution of estates to the loyalists. In the West Indies, France restored her conquests, save for Tobago, and in India Britain restored France's conquered possessions. Britain gave up Florida to Spain, retained *Gibraltar, for which Spain had pressed strongly, but ceded *Minorca. In Africa, France ceded the *Gambia but gained Senegal. The Fox–North coalition succeeded in bringing down *Shelburne's government on the peace preliminaries, mainly by deploring the treatment of the American loyalists, but after taking office was unable to obtain much modification of the original terms. JAC

Versailles, treaty of, 1919. The peace treaty between Germany and the victorious allies at the end of the *First World War. It was signed on 28 June 1919 in the hall of mirrors of the palace of Versailles, where the German empire had been proclaimed in 1871. The allies tried to combine the British and, especially, the French desire for security against Germany with the USA's determination to see international relations based on new and more moral principles. Germany had to surrender Alsace and Lorraine to France and considerable territory to the reconstituted Poland. She was not to be allowed to rearm. The Germans particularly resented the fact that they had to accept liability for all war damage and pay 'reparations' to the allies. The treaty also established the new *League of Nations. MEC

Verulamium. Romano-British town, capital of the *Catuvellauni, predecessor of St Albans (Herts.). In the late Iron Age Verulamium was a major *oppidum*. The Catuvellauni seem to have been pro-Roman and after only brief military presence the new Verulamium started to develop. By the time of its destruction by *Boudicca in AD 60 it had a small street-grid and Roman-style buildings. By 79 it was able to dedicate its elaborate new forum and in due course acquired public baths, a theatre and temple complex, a *macellum* (covered market), and monumental arches, and may have been promoted a *municipium*. In the mid-2nd cent. an expansive circuit of earthwork defences with impressive stone gates was unfinished, possibly because of a disastrous fire in the town in the 150s. In the 3rd cent. the defences were completed in stone on a slightly reduced line. In the 1st and 2nd cents. private housing at Verulamium was principally artisan. From the later 2nd cent. large residences were built, dominating the town in the 4th cent. some lasting into the 5th. Verulamium was the site of the martyrdom of *Alban. Bishop *Germanus of Auxerre visited his shrine in 429, and the present cathedral may perpetuate its site. ASEC

Vespasian. Roman emperor AD 69–79. Titus Flavius Vespasianus was born in AD 9 at Reate in Sabine country. In 43 as legate of *legio II Augusta* he took part in the invasion of Britain, distinguishing himself at the *Medway battle and going on to reduce the south-west, defeating two powerful tribes and reducing twenty hill-forts. For these services he was awarded the *ornamenta triumphalia*. Late in 66 he was appointed to command the suppression of the Jewish revolt and was proclaimed emperor in 69 following Nero's suicide. Vespasian was the ultimate victor of the 'Year of the Four Emperors', founding the Flavian dynasty. His financial prudence corrected the profligacies of Nero and allowed him to build the Temple of Peace and the Colosseum in Rome. In Britain the advance north was resumed under his kinsman by marriage, *Petillius Cerialis. ASEC

Victoria (1819–1901), queen of the United Kingdom of Great Britain and Ireland (1837–1901) and empress of India (1877–1901). We know more about Queen Victoria than almost any other person in history. For more than 80 years she was the focus of attention and comment. From the age of 13 until a week before her death she kept a diary, and though much of it was later destroyed by her daughter Princess Beatrice, the early parts survived, and transcriptions and extracts were made. She maintained, particularly in her later years, a voluminous correspondence with her ever-growing and far-flung family, much of which has been printed. In 1868 she published her own *Leaves from the Journal of our Life in the Highlands* and followed it in 1884 with *More Leaves*. There are many excellent portraits of her and she is the first British monarch of whom we have photographs. We can trace her from a small girl of 7 watering the flowers at Kensington palace to a tired old lady of 81 at Osborne House, receiving news about the Boer War from Field Marshal *Roberts. When she was born the stage-coaches lumbered up the Great North Road and Nelson's **Victory* was still in service: when she died, London to Edinburgh was eight hours by train and pre-dreadnoughts were being laid down in the shipyards of Europe.

Victoria would have agreed that her life fell into three parts—before *Albert, with Albert, after Albert. The death in childbirth in November 1817 of Princess *Charlotte, only daughter and heir to the prince regent, prompted a famous 'rush to the altar', since none of the seven royal brothers had legitimate offspring, nor any of their sisters, of whom five survived. The duke of Cambridge married in May 1818. His elder brothers, the dukes of Clarence and Kent, were married in a joint ceremony a month later. Clarence's two daughters died as infants, leaving the probable succession to the duke of Kent's daughter the Princess Victoria, born 18 May 1819, christened Alexandrina, and known at first as 'Drina'. Eight months later her father was dead, taken off by pneumonia in winter at Sidmouth, leaving her to be brought up in a household almost totally female and totally German. Her mother, Princess Victoria of Leiningen, had a boy and girl by her first marriage, and was of the house of Saxe-Coburg: recently arrived in England, she found the language difficult. The other person in constant attendance was Fräulein Lehzen, brought over as governess and companion from Hanover when the princess was 6 months old. They lived at Kensington palace, Victoria sleeping in her mother's room until she came to the throne. The princess adored her half-sister Feodora, but she was twelve years older than Victoria, and went off to Germany to marry when Victoria was 8. The centre of the princess's life was her 132 dolls, given imposing names and elaborate costumes. Years later Feodora reflected on 'that dismal existence of ours'.

Victoria grew up intelligent and self-possessed. Later in life she regretted that she had not had a more systematic education, but she read widely, spoke several languages, sang well and drew competently, enjoyed music and the theatre. Her upbringing, though sheltered, endowed her with an artlessness and directness—a lack of introspection—which is rare, and never left her. Inevitably the duchess of Kent was on bad terms with George IV and even worse with his successor William IV, to whose demise she looked forward with ill-concealed relish. A clash over precedence meant that the duchess and the young princess boycotted William's coronation in 1831, the princess writing that not even her dolls could console her. 'I longed sadly for some gaiety', she wrote to her uncle Leopold at 16, 'but we have been for the last three months immured within our old palace.' Her correspondence with Leopold, king of the Belgians and avid to advise her, showed a growing interest in politics, national and international, even if she saw them, as she always did, in highly personal terms. As news of the gravity of King William's illness emerged in 1837 she wrote to Leopold: 'I look forward to the event which it seems is likely to occur soon with calm and quietness: I am not alarmed at it . . . I trust that with goodwill, honesty and courage, I shall not, at all events, fail.' Leopold redoubled his bombardment on 'the trade' of kings. She could never praise the English too much: like the French they were 'almost ridiculous in their own exaggerated praise of themselves'. At her first council, *Greville wrote that 'she appeared to be awed, but not daunted'.

Victoria's education for life started with her first prime minister *Melbourne, whom she liked from their first audience, and who stood for father-figure and first love. His kind and pleasant manner, mellow and relaxed, eased her into her new duties: after five days she wrote to Leopold, 'I do regular, hard, but to me delightful work.' Melbourne turned many things into fun. Lord Amelius Beauclerk, a naval aide-de-camp, asked permission to wear a sash: Melbourne thought not—'Your Majesty had perhaps better say that you can make no change . . . particularly considering Lord Amelius's figure.' Greville wrote, not unkindly, in 1839 when the queen's affection for Melbourne had dragged her into the *Bedchamber crisis, 'Melbourne is everything to her . . . her feelings are sexual, though she does not know it.'

She told Melbourne that she might not marry at all: 'I don't know about that,' replied Melbourne, sensibly. In October 1839 Leopold played his trump card, sending Victoria's cousin Albert over from Saxe-Coburg on approval. Victoria grew agitated, the subject of marriage was very disagreeable, and she tried to postpone the visit. In the event, one look was enough. 'It was with some emotion that I beheld Albert,' she wrote, 'who is *beautiful* . . . so excessively handsome.' Two days later, even disconcerting the urbane Melbourne, she declared that no time should be lost, and the following day she sent for Albert to propose marriage. The second phase of her life had begun.

Victoria took to matrimony *con brio*. 'We did not sleep much,' she confided to her journal after the wedding night. 'You cannot imagine how delightful it is to be married,' she told a female cousin about to embark on the same adventure. Then, to her dismay, within six weeks there were signs of pregnancy. Victoria was quite unsentimental about babies—'nasty objects'—but after the birth of the princess royal in November 1840, eight more arrived in rapid succession: the future Edward VII in November 1841, the last princess in April 1857. Victoria had no wish to look after the children herself, especially when they were tiny, but her life became a strange juxtaposition of public and private. April 1841 found her with Princess Victoria 6 months old and war with China: 'Albert is so much amused at my having got the Island of Hong Kong, and we think Victoria ought to be called Princess of Hong Kong in addition to Princess Royal.' The great chartist demonstration in April 1848 was only three weeks after the birth of Princess Louise and the royal family prudently departed to their new house at Osborne. Two months after Prince Arthur's birth in 1850, *Peel died from a fall from his horse: Victoria, who had found him 'such a cold, odd man' when he had nearly replaced Melbourne in 1839, now mourned him as a father. The Crimean War was still raging in December 1855 when the 14-year-old prince of Wales submitted a disastrous six-and-a-half-line examination paper on his ancient history course. Albert's influence grew with the years, particularly after the success of the *Great Exhibition in 1851, and in 1857 Victoria gave him the unprecedented title of prince consort. But pressure of work and his own sense of duty took its toll. 'I am sure if I had a severe illness', he once remarked, 'I should give up at once. I would not struggle against it.' In December 1861, he caught typhoid and died at the age of 42.

Victoria faced a widowhood of forty years. To some, even in her own day, her grief seemed excessive. It was not an age that took death lightly, nor is it easy to say how much other people should mourn. There was a touch of morbidness and some gestures were repeated when the estimable John Brown, her Scottish manservant, died in 1883. There was also perhaps a touch of remorse since she had always inclined to the view that Albert made a fuss about his ailments. For several years, her disappearance from public life was total. Albert's room at Osborne was left untouched, his towel laid out and his hot water brought, busts and statues commissioned, an official biography commanded from Theodore Martin, and plans laid for the erection of the Albert memorial and its afterthought, the Albert Hall. But slowly the family took over as it grew inexorably—such 'swarms of children', wrote Victoria without enthusiasm. Her nine children produced by the time of her death 40 grandchildren (31 still alive) and a further 40 great-grandchildren. Life became a welter of match-making, weddings, christenings, teething, mumps, visits, and birthdays (remembered or missed)—and, the penalty of advancing years, of deaths. In the midst of the Franco-Prussian War old Baroness Lehzen died, the last link with Victoria's childhood. In 1879 the prince imperial, Napoleon III's only son, was killed while a volunteer with the British army in South Africa—'those horrid Zulus', lamented the queen. *Disraeli, once detested for his unkindness to Sir Robert Peel, long a dear friend, died in 1881, 'the Queen bowed down with this misfortune'. In 1892 a terrible shock when 'Eddy', the prince of Wales's eldest son, succumbed to pneumonia at Sandringham. And gradually the courts and thrones of Europe filled up with Victoria's relatives and descendants. Willi, the princess royal's son, became emperor of Germany in 1888: Alix, a granddaughter, married Nicholas II, tsar of Russia, in 1894; cousin Alexander ('Sandro') was briefly king of Bulgaria and, in due course, granddaughters became queens of Sweden, Norway, Spain, Greece, and Romania. The tiny lady in the wheelchair was 'the matriarch of Europe'.

Her political influence as queen has been much debated and analysed, but the more extravagant claims should not be entertained. In the give and take of appointments over more than 60 years, the queen was bound to have victories and defeats. It has been suggested that she was personally responsible for choosing *Aberdeen and *Rosebery as prime ministers. But in 1852, when *Derby's ministry was defeated over Disraeli's budget, Derby himself advised her to send for *Lansdowne and Aberdeen, united in the new Liberal coalition. Lansdowne, at the age of 72, declined to become prime minister and the queen, agreeing that he was too old and infirm, authorized Aberdeen to form a government. She had little choice. Rosebery, in 1894, was already foreign secretary and the almost unanimous choice of the cabinet, who dreaded serving under *Harcourt. The queen did not consult *Gladstone, the outgoing prime minister, but since he would have recommended *Spencer who would have recommended Rosebery, the result would have been the same. The two politicians she most distrusted were *Palmerston ('Pilgerstein') and Gladstone ('half-crazy'), but this did not stop the former being prime minister for nearly ten years and dying in office at the age of 81, nor the latter being prime minister on four occasions. Her importance lies in her role, with Albert, in restoring the dignity and reputation of the monarchy. She rescued it from a situation in which George III had been mad for the last ten years of his reign; George IV's private life was scarcely very private since his estranged wife gatecrashed his coronation demanding to be let in; William IV had a bevy of no less than fifteen illegitimate children, the FitzClarences, to be found anywhere in the royal palaces. Though her friendship with Melbourne and her consequential Whig partisanship gave much offence at first and her seclusion after Albert's death fuelled a brief republican movement, Victoria's standing rose with the years, and she enjoyed memorable triumphs at her *Golden and *Diamond Jubilees in 1887 and 1897. Much of it, of course, was illusion, and her ministers and advisers were aware of the importance of public opinion in a way that had scarcely occurred to anyone in previous centuries. The queen mother and empress was a tiny, fat old lady, painfully short-sighted, gobbling her food and eating too much. But nobody took liberties. The ribald jokes about John Brown had bounced off her, and H. G. *Wells's mother, the housekeeper at Uppark, was not the only woman to identify with the poor widow of Windsor, 'with a passionate loyalty'. Bismarck, the arbiter of Europe, faced an audience in 1888 nervously and came out saying, 'That was a woman.' Though the queen herself did not fit the stereotype of 'Victorian England' (she never quite got over the dislike she had taken to bishops as a toddler), the phrase took hold so firmly that one wonders how other countries manage without the adjective. She remained to the end a mass of contradictions—self-centred yet considerate and dutiful; homely yet grand; excitable and passionate but with shrewd judgement. At her death Henry James the novelist, a sophisticated observer of human nature, wrote: 'we grovel before fat Edward—Edward the Caresser, as he is privately named . . . But I mourn the safe and motherly old middle-class queen, who held the nation warm under the fold of her big, hideous Scotch-plaid shawl . . . I felt her death more than I should have expected.' JAC

Longford, E., *Victoria R.I.* (1964); Strachey, L., *Queen Victoria* (1921); Weintraub, S., *Victoria* (1983).

Victoria and Albert Museum. After the success of the *Great Exhibition (1851), a museum of manufactures was quickly established in Marlborough House, but, despite maintaining strong links with the design schools established in the 1830s because of perceived lapses in design standards from the impact of mechanization upon traditional crafts, its collecting policies became increasingly antiquarian. The first director was Henry Cole, a pioneer of public relations, who oversaw the construction of new but heterogeneous buildings at South Kensington (opened 1857), a site suggested by Prince *Albert. Administrative chaos after Cole's retirement eventually led to the severance of the sciences to their own museum, and the new, renamed building designed by Webb (imposing but impractical) was completed by 1908. Arrangements on craft lines did not cede to chronological presentations until after 1948, but, likened to 'an extremely capacious handbag', the 'V. & A.' has become a leading museum for world-wide decorative art. ASH

Victoria Cross. The highest award for conspicuous gallantry, instituted in 1856 during the Crimean War. Unlike most previous honours, it was open to all ranks and unclassified. The ribbon is crimson and the inscription 'For Valour' was Queen Victoria's suggestion. But her wish that the abbreviation should be BVC (Bearer of the Victoria Cross), lest the recipient be confused with vice-chancellors, was not followed. The original crosses were made from metal of Russian guns captured at *Sebastopol. The first award went to Lieutenant Charles Lucas for gallantry in the Baltic on 21 June 1854 in seizing a live shell which had landed on the deck of HMS *Hecla* and throwing it overboard. In June 1857 the queen made awards to 62 persons in a Hyde Park ceremony. The VC is given sparingly and in 1994 there were fewer than 40 survivors. JAC

***Victory*, HMS.** The oldest warship in commission in the navy, *Victory* serves as flagship to the commander-in-chief, Naval Home Command. She was designed as a 100-gun ship by Sir Thomas Slade in 1759. Her 150-foot keel was laid that July, but she was not launched until 1765 and only first commissioned in 1778 during the American War of Independence. Though a three-decker of over 2,000 tons with a complement of 850, *Victory* sailed as well as a two-decker, and her endurance and longevity can be attributed to the six years between laying down and launching, which critically seasoned her timbers. She was the fifth ship of the name in the navy, wearing the flags of Keppel, Kempenfelt, and Lord *Howe before *Nelson hoisted his on 30 July 1803. As his flagship at *Trafalgar, *Victory* was severely damaged, but had further spells of service before being hulked at Portsmouth in 1824. In the 1920s she was dry-docked, and by the bicentenary of Trafalgar in 2005 it is expected she will have been returned to her state on the eve of the battle in every particular. DDA

Vienna, Congress of, 1814–15. Napoleon's abdication in April 1814 was followed by a preliminary settlement, the first treaty of *Paris, which restored the Bourbon monarchy, returned most of France's colonies, allowed her the boundaries of 1792, and approved the union of Belgium and Holland. But twenty years of warfare, in the course of which boundaries had been constantly changed and new states created, demanded a general European settlement. The Congress opened in September with Castlereagh representing Britain. Strong disagreement between Prussia, Russia, and Austria over the fate of Saxony threatened allied unity and allowed Talleyrand, the French representative, to play a balancing role. In March 1815 everything was thrown into the melting pot by Napoleon's escape from Elba, and not until he had been defeated in June at *Waterloo were the arrangements safe. The terms of the settlement with France were then made more severe, giving her the 1790s boundaries, and insisting on an indemnity and an army of occupation. Belgium and Holland were united in the hope that they would be a more effective barrier to French aggression than either the Spanish or Austrian Netherlands had been; Piedmont was strengthened as a barrier in Italy, where Austria, with Milan, Lombardy, and Venetia, became the dominant power; a kingdom of Poland was established under the rule of Tsar Alexander; Prussia was compensated in the west for territorial losses in the east; the neutrality of Switzerland was guaranteed; Denmark lost Norway to Sweden, which had changed sides at the last minute; Hanover's gains included East Frisia; Britain retained the Cape of Good Hope, Ceylon, Tobago, St Lucia, Malta, Mauritius, the Ionian Islands, and Heligoland. By the *Quadruple Alliance, which accompanied the second treaty of *Paris in November 1815, the system of *congresses was established to adjudicate future problems. The Congress of Vienna was a prime example of *balance of power diplomacy. The first piece of the settlement to collapse was the union of Belgium and Holland, which disintegrated in 1830. JAC

Vienna, treaty of, 1731. By the second treaty of Vienna of March 1731, Britain guaranteed Maria Theresa's succession to the Habsburg dominions under the pragmatic sanction, while the Emperor Charles VI agreed to wind up the Ostend Company, a competitor to the *East India Company. The Austro-British understanding in the War of the *Spanish Succession was thereby restored. But when Maria Theresa was attacked in 1740, British assistance was far from whole-hearted. JAC

Vigo Bay, battle of, 1702. In August 1702, at the outset of the War of the *Spanish Succession, Sir George *Rooke and the duke of *Ormond led an abortive expedition against Cadiz. On the way back they received news that a large Spanish treasure fleet and its escort was harboured in Vigo Bay, protected by a heavy boom. On 12 October they breached the boom and annihilated the enemy, sinking 11 men-of-war and taking 10 war vessels and 11 galleons. Though most of the treasure had been landed, the gains were enormous. JAC

Viking is an Old Norse term, of disputed derivation, which only came into common usage in the 19th cent. to describe peoples of Scandinavian origin who, as raiders, settlers, and traders, had major and long-lasting effects across large areas of northern Europe and the Atlantic seaboards between the late 8th and 11th cents.

Archaeological evidence suggests that trading activity between Britain and Scandinavia had existed from at least the 6th cent. In the later years of the 8th cent., however, contemporary documents record the beginnings of more aggressive contact, with Viking raids on weakly defended coastal sites in both Britain and Francia; the sacking of *Lindisfarne in 793 was but one of a series of such attacks. After a period in which Viking fleets concentrated on Ireland, raids along the English coast intensified from *c.*835, affecting trading centres like Southampton, London, and Canterbury. This pattern of attacks on England changed significantly in 850 when a Danish army overwintered on Thanet in Kent; a more permanent presence was now envisaged. In 866 the 'great raiding army' invaded East Anglia, after several years fighting in the Carolingian empire, and one branch of this group subsequently captured the commercial and political centre of *York in 867; from this base attacks were launched on *Mercia, *East Anglia, and *Wessex. In 867, under Halfdan, the army established a permanent settlement on lands around York and this was followed by a similar take-over of territories in eastern Mercia in the following year. The final years of the century saw a military and political struggle for power in southern England between the Danes and *Alfred (871–99), who ruled the only remaining Anglo-Saxon kingdom of Wessex; during this period recognition of a distinct legal and administrative system in the Scandinavian-settled areas north of the Thames–Chester line emerged with the establishment of *Danelaw *c.*886. Alfred's successors in the early years of the 10th cent. gradually re-established their power over the Anglo-Scandinavian midlands and north but it was only with the expulsion of the last Viking king of York, *Erik Bloodaxe, in 954 that England achieved a precarious political unity under a single crown. Yet, despite its subjection to southern kings, northern England remained a distinct entity for centuries, its linguistic, legal, and cultural structures long bearing the mark of its Scandinavian settlement.

The Danelaw Scandinavians in eastern England were largely of Danish origin. During the first two decades of the 10th cent., however, groups from Norway, together with second-generation settlers familiar with western Scotland, arrived in Cumbria in a colonization which is now largely detectable only in place-name evidence. There are also traces of a secondary settlement from the Norse stronghold of *Dublin in the Cheshire Wirral at about the same date.

The middle years of the 10th cent. were largely free of Scandinavian activity in England, but a second wave of widespread raids began early in the reign of King *Æthelred (978–1016); these increased in intensity until 991 when the first of a series of payments of *Danegeld was made. The ultimate aim was now political domination of England and this was eventually achieved by *Cnut who became king of England and of Denmark in 1017. Anglo-Scandinavian relationships had a complex history after his death in 1035 but the defeat of *Harold Hardrada at *Stamford Bridge immediately before the battle of *Hastings represented the last important Scandinavian attempt to conquer England. Ironically the Norman victory of 1066 ensured that the English throne then passed to a descendant of Scandinavians who had settled in northern France.

Elsewhere in Britain (outside Ireland) Scandinavian raids and colonization are less well recorded. Apart from a few coastal place-names there is little trace of any impact on Wales. By contrast archaeological and onomastic evidence in *Orkney, *Shetland, the Hebrides, and adjacent areas of the Scottish mainland, together with the *Isle of Man, points to heavy Norwegian settlement from the early 9th cent. Much of this western area remained as a recognizable political entity (the 'kingdom of the *Isles') until 1266, whilst the Scandinavian settlement of Orkney and Shetland accounts for their continued allegiance to Norway which only ended in 1469.

Why Scandinavian peoples should suddenly have emerged as such an influential element over an area reaching from North America to the Black Sea is still far from clear. Early historians sought explanations in political consolidation in Scandinavia and military weaknesses in Francia and Britain; climatic and population changes were also invoked as were patterns of inheritance which partitioned land to the point where holdings were too small to sustain a subsequent generation. More recently the emphasis has moved to explanations involving technical improvements in ships and navigation and to the manner in which growing trade in northern Europe may have attracted the increasingly aggressive involvement of entrepreneurial merchants from Denmark, Norway, and Sweden who made little distinction between legitimate and piratical trade. Equally controversial in recent years among British historians has been the problem of the number of people involved in the English raids and settlement; most historians probably now recognize that, whilst the raiding armies may have been relatively small, the linguistic evidence must argue for a large-scale settlement.

Viking activity clearly opened up new international markets for cities like York and *Lincoln. The Scandinavian presence also undoubtedly accelerated changes which were already taking place in England; thus both the decline of monasticism and the rise of Wessex at the expense of other kingdoms can be detected long before the Vikings arrived. There can however be no questioning the fact that the initial raids and subsequent land-taking were socially and politically disruptive. Monastic chroniclers may have exaggerated the extent of the devastating effect of raids—Lindisfarne, for example, continued as a monastic centre for some 75 years after its looting in 793—but the loss of church lands to settlers, with the consequent diminution of ecclesiastical resources, resulted in a major dislocation of England's diocesan organization and also accounts for the fact that the late 10th-cent. *Benedictine reform movement failed to penetrate the Anglo-Scandinavian north. RNB

Crawford, B., *Scandinavian Scotland* (Leicester, 1987); Loyn, H. R., *The Vikings in Britain* (1977); Richards, J. D., *Viking-Age England* (1991); Roesdahl, E., *The Vikings in England* (1981).

villas, Roman. 'Villa' is a Latin word for farm, which has been appropriated by antiquaries and archaeologists to denote Romano-British rural establishments which exhibit Roman-style architecture, however debased. In general this means buildings to a rectilinear plan, often involving the use of stone and recognizably different from what is known of late Iron Age structures. Modern approaches might add differences in economic basis and social make-up as distinguishing the villa. Villas develop from the late 1st cent., often overlying Iron Age buildings and are seen as the indigenous aristocracy taking on Roman ways. By the first half of the 4th cent. there were probably 1,000 villas, ranging from simple cottages to vast palatial complexes such as *Bignor and *Woodchester. The larger villas were equipped with hypocausts, mosaics, painted walls and ceilings, but they remained the centres of agricultural estates. More recent work has concentrated on two aspects. One is the excavation of the hitherto-neglected agricultural dependencies and the reconstruction of the villa economy; the other is the examination of villa plans to elucidate social structures. Villas were in decline in the later 4th cent. and passed out of use in the first half of the 5th. ASEC

Villaviciosa, battle of, 1710. Abandoning Madrid in November 1710, the allies retreated. The British and Dutch moved towards Aragon, the Austrians towards Navarre. Franco-Spanish forces pursued, catching the Anglo-Dutch at *Brihuega on 9 December. The following day Marshal Vendôme, at the head of 21,000 French soldiers, attacked General Stahremberg's 13,600 Austrians at Villaviciosa. It was a bruising engagement—the Austrian left wing was cut to pieces, while the right and centre made some headway—but neither side was strong enough to exploit its limited success. JLP

villein was the term used to describe a peasant in a state of *serfdom—i.e. subject to a lord and under obligation to perform labour services. The term 'villanus' was used in *Domesday Book without any derogatory flavour to indicate persons who lived in 'vills'—and therefore formed the largest social class. Though not free men, they were above the bordars and cottars who held less land, and well above the slaves, who had been numerous in Saxon England. But the term is not precise and status and duties varied from manor to manor, region to region, and over time. There was very little villeinage in Kent, in the old Danelaw, most of the north, and parts of the west. Villeins on crown estates were likely to have more privileges. As royal justice developed, the status of villeins sank, since they had no access to royal courts and could not serve as jurors. There were several ways in which they could escape from villeinage—by purchasing freedom from the lord (*commutation); by escaping to a town for one year and one day; by taking holy orders (with the lord's permission). By the end of the 14th cent. villeinage was clearly disintegrating, villeins changing their status to that of copyholders. JAC

Vimeiro, battle of, 1808. The first major battle of the Peninsular War. British troops under Arthur Wellesley (*Wellington) landed in Portugal at Mondego Bay on 1 August 1808 to assist the Portuguese by marching on Lisbon 30 miles to the south. The French, under Junot, numbered 14,000 and attacked on 21 August but were repulsed by Wellesley with 17,000 men. The French retreat might have become a rout but for the intervention of Wellesley's more cautious superior officer, Sir Harry Burrard, who landed during the course of the battle. The victory was later marred by the controversial terms of the convention of *Cintra. RAS

Vinegar Hill, battle of, 1798. Part of the Wexford rebels in the Irish rising made camp on Vinegar Hill, just outside Enniscorthy, where they terrorized the protestants of the neighbourhood. On 21 June 1798, having recovered from their initial surprise, government forces under General Lake stormed the hill. Pikes and numbers were no match for artillery, and the rebels dispersed and were forced back to Wexford with heavy losses. JAC

Virgin Islands. A group east of Puerto Rico, shared between Britain and the USA. The British islands form a crown colony. They were visited and named by Columbus but colonized by the English from the later 17th cent. Tourism is their chief source of income. JAC

viscounts are the fourth highest grade in the peerage, taking precedence over barons. This was the last of the five grades to be created: in 1440 Henry VI made John, Lord Beaumont, a viscount. The title was never particularly popular. In 1838, when Melbourne was educating the young Queen Victoria, she remarked that there had been very few viscounts at her coronation: 'there *are* very few viscounts,' he replied, 'they are a foreign title and not really English.' JAC

Vitoria, battle of, 1813. Decisive battle of the Peninsular War between Wellington with 75,000 men and Joseph Bonaparte with 58,000 men. Wellington launched an attack 8 miles from Vitoria with a main assault from the west and thrusts from the hills to the north and south. Despite a determined stand the French centre crumbled and both flanks were turned. Joseph lost 7,000 men, 143 guns, and much booty. The battle ended Napoleon's rule in Spain and the French retreated across the Pyrenees. Tsar Alexander ordered a Te Deum to be sung to celebrate the victory, the first time this had been done for a foreign army. RAS

Volunteer movement (Ireland). After France and Spain had entered the American War of Independence, many Irish volunteered to defend their country against invasion. By 1780, 40,000 were under arms. This also gave them political leverage which they used to wring concessions from the British government—first commercial advantages offered by *North in 1780, then the repeal of *Poynings's Law and the grant of legislative independence from the *Rockinghams in 1782. But when the Volunteers moved on to discuss parliamentary reform, they split on the rock of the catholic question. The coming of peace in 1783 also deprived them of their tactical advantage and after the Dublin convention of November 1783, the movement faded rapidly. JAC

volunteers. Since from time immemorial it had been regarded as the duty of citizens and free men to defend their country, governments could scarcely object if, in moments of crisis, volunteers came forward to offer their services. Yet they were not necessarily very efficient, often tiresome in their personal demands, and, as the case of the Irish volunteers suggests, a potential political threat. Henry *Fox in 1745 doubted whether one should trust a man to raise a regiment who could not raise half a crown and Hanbury Williams wrote of the duke of Bolton that 'he much dislikes both guns and pikes, but relishes the clothing'. Volunteer corps were raised by private donations, reinforced by public appeals, but, as weapons of war grew more sophisticated and expensive, governments had to find substantial assistance. A number of corps were raised in 1690 to deal with a threat of French invasion, again in 1715 and 1745 to cope with the Jacobite risings, and again in 1779 during the American War of Independence. But the biggest response was during the Revolutionary and Napoleonic wars, and again in 1859 when there was yet another threat of war with France. By 1901 there were 230,000 volunteers, augmented by the Royal Navy and Royal Artillery Volunteers, the *militia and the *yeomanry. *Haldane's reforms of 1907 reorganized them into the Territorial Force, later the *Territorial Army. JAC

Vortigern. A leader of the Britons in the immediate post-Roman period. The Venerable *Bede gives AD 449 as the year of the *adventus Saxonum* (the coming of the Saxons) and the story of Vortigern falls into the years following this date. Vortigern appears to have been a sub-Roman ruler in southern England, who, in order to protect his realm from Saxon incursions, is said to have invited two Saxon warriors, *Hengist and Horsa, and their troops into Britain to act as a kind of *foederatus* or mercenary force. They revolted against Vortigern and set up their own rule in Kent in the 450s. ES

Votadini. Indigenous British tribe of the Iron Age and Roman periods whose territory covered the eastern part of Lowland Scotland. The ancient geographer Ptolemy, writing in the mid-2nd cent. AD and using sources probably dating to the time of *Agricola's expeditions 70 years earlier, names four tribes inhabiting the area south of the Forth–Clyde isthmus: the Novantae, the *Damnonii, the *Selgovae, and the Votadini. Many hill-forts are known within the territory of the Votadini, notably the important tribal centre of Traprain Law; the site has yielded a number of significant Roman finds including a hoard of late Roman silver. ES

Wade, George (1673–1748). One of the best-known soldiers of early Hanoverian Britain. Wade was the grandson of a Cromwellian officer who had settled in Westmeath (Ireland). He joined the army in 1690 at the beginning of more than twenty years of almost incessant warfare and by the end of the War of the *Spanish Succession in 1714 had risen to major-general. In 1715 he was returned to Parliament for Hindon and in 1722 transferred to Bath, where he built up a powerful political base and where his fine house in the abbey courtyard still stands. From 1724 to 1740 he commanded in Scotland, where his programme of military road-building was designed to facilitate troop movements. Promoted to field marshal in 1743 he fought an unremarkable campaign in Flanders the following year. He was given charge of the army at Newcastle during the Jacobite invasion of 1745 though his conduct appears to have been sluggish. JAC

wages are the returns earned by workers for their labour. Real wages reflect the actual purchasing power of these returns adjusted by price levels, while money wages involve no adjustment for inflation. The importance of wages has grown since the *enclosure movement resulted in hired labour replacing self-employment and indenturement on the land and as industrialization produced the *factory system.

Real wages in 12th-cent. England were closely correlated to pressures of population change. Population growth in the 12th and 13th cents. reduced per capita output and famines resulted in years of bad harvests. The considerable impact of the *Black Death (1348–9) on the labour force acted as a counter-balance and following it real wages rose considerably. By the 15th cent. the wages of skilled workers attained a level not reached again until the latter half of the 19th cent. Increased population pressure in the 16th cent. brought real wages down and after 1600 the index of real wages was about half its level a century earlier. The period following the Civil War saw a gradual improvement which continued through the mid-18th cent. as the *agrarian revolution offset the effects of a rising population. Higher farm production also contained the fall in wages which accompanied the Napoleonic wars. Real wages rose slowly through the 19th cent. as industrialization expanded and have, with the marked exception of the Great Depression and the world wars, risen throughout the 20th cent.

The pattern of money wages is different, with both a remarkable consistency characterizing long periods from the 13th until the mid-20th cent. and the absence of any major falls. Real wage adjustments have generally come about through price inflation effects. Only major shocks have brought about significant upward shifts in monetary wages—the Black Death, the Tudor debasement of the currency (1532–80), and the Napoleonic wars. The recent past has seen money wages rising since the investment boom of the post-Second World War period. Initially this may have been explained by a reluctance of employers to limit wage rises when productivity was rising rapidly but subsequently expectations on the part of labour made it difficult to contain further rises.

Various theories have been developed to explain levels of real wage. The classical economists Adam *Smith and David *Ricardo in the late 18th cent., although arguing that wages are an essential material necessity of production, tended to treat them as part of a distribution process—an approach continued by Karl Marx. Alternatively, T. R. *Malthus placed considerable emphasis on the effects of population on wages—if real wages rose above subsistence population growth would push them down again. The neoclassical framework associated with Alfred *Marshall focused on the role of real wages in balancing the supply of labour and the demand for its services as reflected by its marginal product. Neo-Keynesian economists have paid more attention to imperfections in the labour market, which make structural changes difficult as aggregate levels of demand change. KJB

Waitangi, treaty of, 1840. In 1839 the British government dispatched Captain William Hobson to New Zealand where piecemeal and uncontrolled development had already undermined traditional Maori culture. At Waitangi in February 1840 a majority of the Maori chiefs present agreed to cede sovereignty to Queen Victoria in exchange for confirmation of their land and protection. Hobson declared himself lieutenant-governor and proclaimed British sovereignty in May 1840. But Maori disappointment at the persistent encroachments upon their land led to the *Maori wars from 1844 until 1872. In 1994 a New Zealand government apologized for breaches of the treaty and promised compensation. JAC

Wake, William (1657–1737). Archbishop of Canterbury. A graduate of Christ Church, Oxford, after ordination (1682) Wake was chaplain to the English ambassador in Paris. His contact with Gallican divines at the Sorbonne gave him a continuing interest in the French church. Afterwards he was successively canon of Christ Church, Oxford (1689–1702), dean of Exeter (1703–5), bishop of Lincoln (1705), and archbishop (1716). He, however, broke with the Whigs by opposing *Hoadly's appointment to Bangor (1715), the suspension of *convocation (1717), and the repeal of the *Occasional Conformity and *Schism Acts (1718). From 1723 his influence was eclipsed by *Gibson of London. Always personally tolerant, his primary objective was to preserve the traditional latitude of the Anglican church without allowing degeneration into licence. Ecumenical before his time and risking governmental antipathy, he negotiated with the French church for possible union (1717–20) and encouraged intercommunion with continental Lutheran and reformed churches. WMM

Wakefield, battle of, 1460. The Yorkist victory at *Northampton in the summer of 1460 had put Henry VI in the power of Richard, duke of *York. In October a reconciliation was effected, whereby Henry continued as monarch but recognized York as his heir. Queen *Margaret refused to accept this and raised troops in the north. York and *Warwick's father *Salisbury marched to meet her but were routed on 30 December at Wakefield, just outside York's castle of Sandal. Salisbury and York were executed after the battle, the latter's head being exhibited on the walls of the city of York, wearing a paper crown. JAC

Wakefield, diocese of. The see, comprising parts of south Yorkshire, was created in 1888 to cope with the rapidly rising population. It did not, however, include Sheffield, which remained fiercely independent. Like the other new sees of *Southwell, *St Albans, and redrawn *Rochester, created at the same time, it was not a natural unit, but this was no obstacle to the first bishop, William Walsham How (1888–97), who powerfully welded the diocese together, after a remarkable spell as suffragan bishop in east London (1879–88). The cathedral is the former All Saints' parish church, dating mostly from 14th cent. with a 15th-cent. west tower and a 20th-cent. east end by Gilbert *Scott. WMM

Wakefield, Edward Gibbon (1796–1862). Wakefield, whose father and uncle were authors, was a wild youth who demanded to be removed from Westminster School, disliked Edinburgh High School, and made a runaway marriage with a ward of Chancery. Released from that scrape by the death of his wife, he attempted a second runaway match with a schoolgirl and was sent to gaol for three years. On his release he took up the cause of colonization, urging emigration to Australia and pointing out that the policy of granting free lands produced an acute shortage of labour. In 1838 Wakefield accompanied Lord *Durham on his mission to Canada and had considerable influence on the final report. He then transferred his interest to *New Zealand, organizing a company to send out settlers and contributing to the formal annexation of that country in 1840. In 1852 he left for New Zealand but suffered a final breakdown a year after his arrival. Wakefield's achievement was to encourage a more systematic and coherent attitude towards colonial development. JAC

Walcheren landing, 1809. Britain did not find it easy to wage war against Napoleonic Europe. Despite the catastrophic failure of the landing in Holland in 1799, the British government resolved in 1809 to try again, using troops recently withdrawn from Portugal. The object was to capture Walcheren, the island on which Flushing stands, menace Antwerp, and encourage the Dutch to rise against the French. Lord Chatham commanded 40,000 men, with Sir Richard Strachan in charge of a very large fleet. There was no element of surprise, French resistance was fierce, the commanders quarrelled, and the army was decimated by dysentery and fever. Some 106 men died in action, 4,000 from disease. The enterprise was abandoned. JAC

Wales, march (or marches) **of.** Comparable to 'mark' (German) and 'marche' (French), signifying, from the 11th cent., the frontier or borderland between the English shires and unsubdued Welsh kingdoms. It was an extensive and fluctuating region covered by a large number of lordships, from the north-east coast of Wales (e.g. Denbigh lordship) to the far south-west of Wales (e.g. Pembroke lordship). It arose from the Anglo-Norman conquests from the 11th cent. onwards, and parts were a theatre of war until the late 13th. By 1300 the march enjoyed stability, politically and militarily, governmentally and socially. Its distinctive society embraced native and immigrant, Welsh, English, and French languages, and peculiar customs and laws. 'Marcher lords' enjoyed great authority to govern and exploit; the king's writ did not run and the common law did not normally operate there. Although marcher lordships had common characteristics, they formed a diverse and fragmented polity. There was no effective, supervisory authority, and the march acquired a reputation for independence and lawlessness. These matters were seriously addressed from Edward IV's reign by a *Council of the March', developing from the councils of English princes of Wales. The march played a significant role in English politics, for many marcher lords were English nobles and their lordships provided men, money, power, and a refuge in uncertain times. By the Act of *Union (1536), the marcher lordships were absorbed in new or existing English or Welsh shires; but marcher lords survived and so did some of their rights over land and tenant. RAG

Wales, principality of. The term refers to the territorial dominion of the last Welsh princes of Wales; the estate granted to English princes of Wales after 1301; and the entire land of Wales following the Act of *Union (1536). The first Welsh ruler to call himself prince of Wales (1244) was *Dafydd ap Llywelyn; he was recognized by the pope and his principality was based on *Gwynedd, of which his father *Llywelyn ab Iorwerth had been prince. Dafydd's nephew *Llywelyn ap Gruffydd (d. 1282), prince of Wales, had a more extensive principality in north, north-east, and central Wales of which he was either direct ruler or overlord; his title and principality were acknowledged by Henry III to be hereditary (1267). Llywelyn's brother *Dafydd (d. 1283) claimed to be prince of Wales, but his principality was swiftly conquered by Edward I, who annexed and united it to the English crown (1284). This modified principality, which included all royal lands in north Wales (much of Llywelyn's principality) and west Wales (formerly either royal enclaves or lordships held by Llywelyn's vassals) was bestowed in 1301 on Edward I's eldest surviving son, Edward, as the first English prince of Wales. From time to time thereafter, this principality was the territorial endowment of the heir to the throne, for whom the title of prince was reserved as a special dignity. It covered half of Wales and should 'never be separated from the crown, but should remain entirely to the kings of England for ever' (1301). The title of prince lapsed for periods (e.g. between the accession of Edward II in 1307 and the creation of the Black Prince as prince of Wales in 1343), few heirs who were created prince of Wales in the Middle Ages reached manhood, and some heirs apparent were not created princes of Wales. However, the principality of Wales had a continuous existence as part of the inseparable crown estate, to be periodically vested in the king's eldest son, to be governed and exploited by him in his interest.

Edward I outlined an elaborate scheme of government for the principality of Wales in the statute of *Wales (1284). It was based on existing arrangements and hence had two sectors, of three counties in north Wales (Anglesey, Caernarfonshire, and Merioneth) based on Caernarfon, and of two counties in west Wales (Carmarthenshire and Cardiganshire) based on Carmarthen. Each sector had a justiciar with political and judicial competence, and a chamberlain with financial competence; each county had shire officials and great sessions; more local administrative arrangements were based on the commote with Welsh and English elements. The two sectors were frequently referred to, inaccurately, as the principality of north Wales and the principality of west (or south) Wales. Ultimately responsible to the king's court, council, and officials at Westminster, or (when there was one) to the prince's council, in practice the principality of Wales was a separate and independent jurisdiction. It was a development of Llywelyn's principality, rather than a clear break with it, and it was larger than Llywelyn's in some respects, in others smaller than his: Flintshire, though a royal shire, was attached for administrative convenience to Cheshire and lay outside the principality of Wales; the English princes were overlords of several marcher lordships in the north-east which had been part of Llywelyn's principality.

The council of Edward IV's eldest son began to undertake responsibility for order not only in the principality but also (by 1476) in the marcher lordships and border English shires and so had a Wales-wide supervisory authority (as the *Council in the March) that was the germ of the arrangements made by the Act of Union (1536). These arrangements consolidated Wales administratively and constitutionally by extending the machinery of government of the principality of Wales to Wales as a whole, including Flintshire and the March. Thus, the 'country and dominion of Wales' became conterminous with the principality of Wales, and was so regarded from the 16th cent. onwards. This principality retained peculiar features of law and justice, with separate courts albeit dispensing English common law, until, first, the Council of Wales and the March was abolished as a prerogative court in 1689 and, second, the great sessions were abolished in 1830 and the judicial system assimilated to that of England. The revenues from rights of jurisdiction and lands continued to accrue to the crown and could be granted to individual princes of Wales by special Act of Parliament—though not all princes were granted them. In 1760 they were surrendered by George III along with the crown's hereditary revenues in return for a 'civil list'; thereafter, no principality lands or financial rights could be bestowed on a prince (in contrast to the duchy of *Cornwall).

Yet the concept of the principality of Wales within the United Kingdom survived, largely because of the distinctive culture, language, and sense of identity of the Welsh. Although in modern times prior to the 20th cent. princes of Wales visited their principality rarely, both prince and principality were a focus of Welsh sentiment. The investiture of Prince Edward (later Edward VIII; 1911) took place in an atmosphere of national euphoria, during a picturesque ceremony held at Caernarfon castle in deference to spurious tradition; that of Prince *Charles (1969), though more controversial, was enthusiastically welcomed by most Welsh people. RAG

Edwards, J. G., *The Principality of Wales, 1267–1967* (Caernarfon, 1969); Griffiths, R. A., *The Principality of Wales in the Later Middle Ages*, i: *South Wales, 1277–1536* (Cardiff, 1972); Jones, F., *The Princes and Principality of Wales* (Cardiff, 1969).

Wales, statute of. See RHUDDLAN.

Walker, George (1618–90). Walker, an elderly Church of Ireland clergyman, was the heart and soul of Londonderry's resistance to James II after the Glorious Revolution. He held a living at Donaghmore, near Dungannon, and began raising troops early in 1689. In April he went to Londonderry and acted as joint governor throughout the siege. After its relief he was sent to London with an address to William III, which he presented at Hampton Court, received the thanks of the House of Commons, was honoured by both universities, and was in line for promotion to the bishopric of Derry. He joined William at the start of his Irish campaign and was shot dead at the battle of the *Boyne. Walker's *True Account of the Siege of Londonderry* appeared in 1689 and is an important source. JAC

Wallace, William (d. 1305). Scottish patriot and commander at the battles of *Stirling Bridge (1297) and *Falkirk (1298). Wallace came of a middling family, retainers of the Stewarts in the neighbourhood of Paisley. Nothing reliable is known of his date of birth or early life; nor is it easy to explain his emergence as a Scottish leader in 1297.

In that year there were many prominent Scots anxious to resist Edward's 'take-over' of the previous year, including Wallace's lord, James, the hereditary steward of Scotland. But there was no co-ordinated or open rising, only miscellaneous outbreaks in the early part of the year. In May Wallace killed the English sheriff of Lanark in an affray. He was joined by Sir William Douglas in an attack on the English justiciar at Scone. Others, including Robert Bruce, earl of Carrick, the future Robert I, were also prepared to join in. This rising might easily have achieved nothing, since determined English action quickly persuaded many of the prominent leaders of the Scots to make terms; but in May another movement had started in Moray, with an attack on Inverness led by the young Andrew *Murray, son of a leading baron. These twin risings, by Wallace and Murray, attracted increasing support, including that of the earls of Fife and *Buchan, and Bruce openly took the Scottish side. By August, Murray and Wallace had joined forces and threatened Stirling. Their astute tactics at the battle of Stirling Bridge, and the ineptitude of the English commander, Earl *Warenne resulted in a dramatic victory, which put Edward I's position in Scotland in peril. Murray, however, was wounded and died a few months later.

The Scottish kingdom existed once more, and was to maintain its existence, nominally in the name of the absent King John, till 1304. By early 1298 Wallace had been knighted, and emerged as sole guardian. By June, however, Edward was leading an army of some 12,000 men to repress what he regarded as a revolt. At Falkirk, in more open ground than at Stirling, the English knights and archers were devastating. The Scots were routed and Wallace escaped into hiding, resigning his guardianship immediately.

His next task was abroad. In 1299 he led a mission to the French court trying to get more active support from Philip IV, and seems to have stayed in Paris for most of the next year. He may have gone also to Rome, though evidence is uncertain. By 1303 Wallace was back in Scotland, again fighting in the south. By 1304, Edward had triumphed. Almost all the Scottish leaders submitted on negotiated terms. On 24 July Stirling, the last castle to be held against Edward, surrendered, and only Wallace and John de Soules remained in resistance.

Wallace was now a fugitive. In August 1305 he was captured, and there followed a show trial on 23 August, and immediate execution for 'treason', of which, as he had never sworn allegiance to Edward, he could not justly be accused. From that day, Wallace has been regarded as one of the greatest heroes in Scotland's national history. BW

Waller, Edmund (1606–87). Poet. Waller mixed poetry and politics. Born in Buckinghamshire of a very wealthy family, he went to Eton and King's College, Cambridge. He was returned to Parliament for Ilchester in 1624 when he was no more than 17 and was in the *Short and *Long Parliaments in 1640. Related to both *Hampden and *Cromwell, he was outspoken in 1642 for negotiations with the king and acquired the reputation of a bold royalist. But when 'Waller's plot' to seize London for the king was unmasked in 1643, he made an abject apology and confession to Parliament, which saved his life while leaving his brother-in-law to be hanged. Waller paid a crippling fine, spent seven years in France, and then made his peace with Cromwell, on whom he wrote a famous panegyric. Nevertheless, he rescued his political career at the Restoration, served in Parliament 1661–79 and again in 1685, held office as a commissioner of trade and plantations, spoke frequently, and reminisced cheerfully. He seems to have had a genuine belief in religious toleration. Much of Waller's poetry was pleasant social verse, but occasionally he hit a deeper note with 'Go, lovely rose' and 'Of the Last Verse in the Book'. *Johnson, in his *Lives of the Poets*, devoted much space to Waller, praising his elegance and gaiety: 'he is never pathetick and very rarely sublime.' JAC

Waller, Sir William (1598–1668). MP and parliamentary general during the Civil War. Educated at Magdalen Hall, Oxford, and Gray's Inn, Waller saw military service on the continent during the Thirty Years War. He was elected to the *Long Parliament, commissioned colonel under *Essex, and later major-general for the region around Gloucester. Emboldened by early military successes, he became a critic of Essex's leadership, but his own reputation suffered with his defeats at *Roundway Down (July 1643) and *Cropredy Bridge (June 1644). His nickname 'William the Conqueror' was turned against him. Forced to resign his commission by the *self-denying ordinance in 1645, Waller turned into a supporter of the Essex–Holles faction in parliament, and an opponent of the religious toleration advocated by the *New Model Army. He was one of eleven MPs whose impeachment the army advocated. Arrested in 1648, he suffered three years' imprisonment. With the restoration of the Long Parliament in 1660 he resumed his seat, and was elected to the *Convention Parliament the same year. IJG

Wallingford, treaty of. See WINCHESTER, TREATY OF.

Wallis, John (1616–1703). Mathematician, grammarian, and founder member of the *Royal Society. A Cambridge graduate, from 1649 he was Savilian professor of geometry at Oxford. During the Civil War he worked on codes for the parliamentary side. In a famous controversy, he showed that Thomas *Hobbes had failed to square the circle; he was also involved in other disputes with contemporaries. He was an important participant in scientific groups meeting during the Interregnum, which were the nucleus for the Royal Society, founded in 1660. In 1652 Wallis published his study of English grammar. He was an important and influential mathematician, producing books on arithmetic (especially series), geometry, algebra, and mechanics. He invented our symbol for infinity, translated Greek works, including some of Archimedes, and wrote an interesting memoir of his own life. DK

Walpole, Horace, 4th earl of Orford (1717–97). The youngest son of Sir Robert *Walpole, Horace Walpole became the most gifted letter-writer in English history. When he entered Parliament in 1741 his father's long administration was tottering to its fall. Though he remained in the Commons until 1768 he made no mark and his preferred role was that of observer. The places and pensions provided by his father afforded him a comfortable bachelor existence and he lavished great attention on the Gothic villa at Strawberry Hill (Twickenham) which he purchased in 1748 and where he installed his private printing press. Much of his time was devoted to correspondence with his many friends and acquaintances. But he also wrote substantial works. *The Castle of Otranto* (1764) was an early example of the Gothick horror novel and *Historic Doubts on Richard III* (1768) fathered a minor academic industry. His *Memoirs* of the reigns of George II and George III were greatly used by 19th-cent. historians, but Walpole had much spite, lurid suspicions, and a taste for melodrama, which he worked into his narrative. Above all, he was chiefly responsible for the story that George III aimed at autocracy, a legend which poisoned the wells of scholarship for decades. Walpole succeeded to the peerage at the age of 74, but never took his seat in the Lords. JAC

Walpole, Sir Robert, 1st earl of Orford (1676–1745). Traditionally known as Britain's first prime minister. From a Norfolk gentry family, Walpole was the Whig MP for Castle Rising (1701–2) and King's Lynn (1702–12, 1713–42). His first posts were as secretary at war (1708) and treasurer of the navy (1710). His part in the administration of the War of the *Spanish Succession and his management of the trial of Dr *Sacheverell earned him the hatred of the Tory Party and he was dismissed in 1710, impeached for corruption, sent to the Tower (1711), and expelled from Parliament (1712). At the Hanoverian succession he re-joined the government, along with his brother-in-law Viscount *Townshend, as paymaster-general, being promoted to 1st lord of the Treasury and chancellor of the Exchequer in 1715. In 1717 he, Townshend, and several followers left the *Sunderland/*Stanhope ministry. During the ensuing Whig schism Walpole opposed the repeal of the *Occasional Conformity and *Schism Acts (1718), and successfully defeated the *Peerage Bill in the Commons (1719). In April 1720, with most of the schismatic Whigs, he rejoined the government in the office of paymaster-general.

Walpole was not the first 'prime minister'; several of his immediate predecessors (such as Sunderland, *Harley, and even *Godolphin) were so regarded, and the term was in common use (though often pejoratively). The starting date of Walpole's premiership is a matter of some controversy. One historian has recently suggested that it should be dated from 1720 (since he was in control of the Treasury as paymaster-general, John Aislabie, the chancellor of the Exchequer, being a figurehead), rather than from the traditional date of his promotion to the chancellorship in 1721. Despite his brilliant financial acumen, which managed to save the administration and the dynasty in 1720–1 from the disaster of the *South Sea bubble, and his control of the nation's finances and the secret service money (the major source of patronage), neither of these dates marks his true dominance of the ministry. Both Stanhope (who died prematurely in 1721), and more particularly Sunderland (who also died unexpectedly in April 1722), retained the confidence of George I until their deaths. Until 1724, when he was manœuvred into the lord-lieutenancy of Ireland, *Carteret (a protégé of Sunderland's favoured by the king) was a potential rival. Further, from the very beginning of the reconciliation of the Whigs in 1720, Townshend was a major force to be reckoned with, particularly through his control of foreign policy after 1721 (an area dear to the king) and the House of Lords after 1722 (an important aspect as the dominance of the Commons over the upper House was some way off). Townshend remained in office until his resignation in 1730, and for most of the mid- to late 1720s the ministry should be seen more as a duumvirate. Only in the late 1720s did Walpole become the unquestioned prime minister, partly through forcing the most talented of his Whig opponents, led by *Pulteney, into opposition. These self-proclaimed *'patriots' worked fitfully with the Tories in the 1730s, but were no real threat to Walpole, until he began to lose his grip in the early 1740s.

Walpole's major contribution to politics was his development of the cabinet system, of the 'party of the crown' (which he based on the work of Harley) through extensive use of patronage, and of the Commons as the centre of parliamentary power. His refusal of a peerage in 1723 (it went to his son), which astounded contemporaries, signalled the beginning of the latter development.

Following the South Sea crisis, Walpole's establishment of the Whig hegemony was largely accomplished as a result of his handling of the *Atterbury plot in 1722–3, which he used to drive home the fear of *Jacobitism, a label he had great success in attaching to his Tory opponents (though largely undeserved) and which, in the final analysis, prevented effective and sustained co-operation between them and the Whig 'patriots'. The smear of Jacobitism proved very effective for the rest of his ministry. His ruthless control of political patronage was the foundation on which he built his control of the administration. This is best illustrated by his removal in 1734 of several peers from colonelships of regiments for voting against the government, though such positions were, in effect, regarded as private property, and the dismissals caused consternation amongst the political élite.

His sure grip on politics occasionally wavered. One such occasion was the *Excise scheme in 1733, which aroused so much opposition that Walpole was forced into dropping the proposal before the second reading. Another was his loss of favour in Scotland by his too repressive measures over the *Porteous riots in 1736. Yet another was his opposition to war with Spain in 1739, to which he was forced to agree by both the patriot opposition and members of his own government. The poor handling of the war eventually led to his downfall in February 1742 as he lost control of the House of Commons, one of two essential props to his power. The other was the support of the monarch (first George I, and then George II, though the latter's was uncertain before his accession in 1727), which he retained to the end, along with that of Queen *Caroline who, until her death in 1737, provided invaluable support.

Walpole was created earl of Orford upon his resignation, and helped from the Upper House to baffle efforts to impeach him for corruption. He took part in debates in the Lords, and continued to give advice to George II when asked. He devoted much of his time to Houghton in Norfolk, the palatial house he had built and stocked with art treasures. He died in debt CJ

Cruickshanks, E., 'The Political Management of Sir Robert Walpole', in Black, J. (ed.), *Britain in the Age of Walpole* (1984); Dickinson, H. T., *Walpole and the Whig Supremacy* (1973); Holmes, G., 'Sir Robert Walpole', in Holmes, G. (ed.), *Politics, Religion and Society in England, 1679–1742* (1986); Plumb, J. H., *Sir Robert Walpole* (2 vols., 1956–60).

Walsingham. Marian shrine, Norfolk. The earliest shrine, dedicated to the Holy House of Nazareth, was built by the lady of the manor, Richeldis de Faverches, traditionally to commemorate her vision of the Blessed Virgin (1061). Both shrine and adjacent Augustinian priory gained fame and wealth from pilgrims and their bequests, until destruction 1538–9. Interest in Walsingham began to revive in 1897. The present Anglican shrine, which includes an Orthodox chapel, contains a newly carved statue of Our Lady of Walsingham, while Roman catholic devotion utilizes the reconsecrated Slipper Chapel, which marked the last stage of Walsingham Way. ASH

Walsingham, Sir Francis (*c*.1532–90). Walsingham matriculated at King's College, Cambridge, in 1548 and was taught by the prominent humanist (and *Cecil's father-in-law) Sir John *Cheke. He travelled abroad 1550–2, began common law training at Gray's Inn in 1552, and studied civil law at Padua from 1555. He became privy counsellor and principal secretary in 1571 and held the post until his death. Walsingham was a strong protestant, watchful against catholic plots and anxious for a European coalition of protestant powers. He helped to draft the 'bond of Association' in 1584 to protect Elizabeth from conspiracies, though Cecil had developed the idea in 1569. Walsingham had a reputation as an intelligence expert and in 1568 warned of a European plot to free Mary Stuart. One of his lines should stand as his epitaph: 'there is less danger in fearing too much than too little.' SA

Walter, Hubert (*c*.1140–1205). Viewed by many as one of the greatest royal ministers of all time. Introduced into Henry II's service by his uncle Ranulf *Glanvill, his career blossomed under Richard I. Created bishop of Salisbury in 1189, he accompanied Richard as his chief of staff on crusade. His performance in such challenging conditions led to his being promoted in 1193 to take charge of both secular and ecclesiastical government as *justiciar and archbishop of Canterbury. In 1195 he was made papal legate. While Richard stayed in his French dominions, Hubert administered England, supplying the king with the men and money he needed to fight Philip of France. On John's accession he was appointed chancellor; the chancery rolls, for centuries the principal records of English central government, date from his period in office. He still found time to summon and preside over reforming church councils. JE

Walter of Coutances (d. 1207). A trusted servant of the Plantagenet kings who governed England for two years while Richard I was on crusade. His diplomatic and administrative skills brought him the bishopric of Lincoln in 1183 and Rouen in 1184. He set out on crusade with Richard but news of tension in England between John and *Longchamp persuaded the king to send him back from Sicily in spring 1191 with discretion to use confidential letters appointing him *justiciar if and when he judged it necessary. When John tried to use the controversial arrest of *Geoffrey archbishop of York to topple Longchamp in October, Walter produced Richard's letters—much to John's chagrin. Walter remained in charge until December 1193, setting up the machinery for the collection of England's share of King Richard's ransom. The fall of Normandy meant that in 1204, as archbishop of Rouen, he had to invest Philip Augustus as duke of Normandy—just as earlier he had invested Richard I and John. JE

Waltham Black Act, 1722. The statute of 9 Geo. I c. 22 has long been held up as a specimen of draconian 18th-cent. legislation. It originated in response to an outbreak of organized poaching in Windsor Forest and near Waltham (Hants), and declared that to go abroad in woodland areas, commons, or on the high road in disguise or with blackened face was a felony without benefit of clergy and punishable by death. The gangs were so ruthless and intimidating that more and more offences were specified until the Act became a compendium of rural disorder—cutting down trees, maiming cattle, setting fire to ricks, breaking down fishponds, writing threatening letters, and shooting at people. In the end fifty or more offences were included in the Act. Passed for three years, it was continued until 1758 and then made permanent. It was abolished, largely at the instigation of *Mackintosh and *Peel, in 1823. JAC

Waltheof (d. 1076). Waltheof was the son of *Siward, earl of Northumberland and victor over *Macbeth, who died in 1055. Waltheof did not then inherit the earldom, presumably because he was too young, and it passed to *Tostig, brother of Harold Godwineson. But on Tostig's exile in 1065, Waltheof became earl of Huntingdon. In 1069 he joined the Danish attack on York, but submitted to William the Conqueror in 1070, and was made earl of Northumberland two years later. He was also given a niece of the king in marriage. But in 1075 he was on the fringes of another conspiracy against William, who had him executed at Winchester the following year. The cause of his downfall has been discussed, but presumably William was exasperated at a man who had rebelled once, been given a royal bride, and was disloyal again. A man of great strength and piety, Waltheof was revered by some after his death and reputed to have been a hero to the English, though his ancestry was Danish. On this showing he was technically the last Englishman to be an earl in the Norman period. JAC

Walton, Izaak (1593–1683). Biographer. Of Staffordshire yeoman stock and member of the Ironmongers' Company, this kindly Fleet Street tradesman lived through political and religious turmoil socially and spiritually at ease with the higher clergy, and sufficiently royalist to be entrusted briefly with Charles II's 'lesser George' jewel (1651). Immortalized through the quiet charm of his *Compleat Angler* (1653), where he is pastoralist rather than preceptor, he was better known to contemporaries for his lives of *Donne, Wootton, *Hooker, *Herbert, and Sanderson, and as provider of tributes for friends' works. The serenity and gentle humour of his 'mild pen' prompted sentimental rather than critical appreciation in the 18th cent., after *Johnson's admiration of the lives had led to a literary revival, but later commentators have emphasized the subjectivity and irregularities, though admitting his good intentions. Ending his days with family at Winchester, he was buried in the cathedral there. ASH

Walton, Sir William (1902–83). English composer and conductor of his own music. Walton was a chorister and undergraduate at Oxford, although he remained a largely self-taught composer. He was adopted by the Sitwell family, causing a stir with his 'entertainment' *Façade* (1921–2), in which Edith Sitwell's poems were recited through a megaphone to music whose elements of parody and jazz parallel the Parisian scene in the 1920s. The Viola Concerto, first performed by Hindemith in 1929, helped establish a less controversial reputation; the lyricism apparent here increased in later works. The dramatic paganism of *Belshazzar's Feast* (1931), although initially startling to audiences with its raw energy and powerful orchestration, lies firmly within the English choral tradition. The long gestation of the 1st Symphony (1932–5) reflects the difficulties Walton often experienced, resulting in a comparatively small output. His film music is also justly renowned, especially the score for Olivier's *Henry V* (1943–4). ECr

Wandewash, battle of, 1760. On 22 January 1760 Sir Eyre *Coote defeated the forces of the Count de Lally at Wandewash, in south India, to signal the dominance of the English *East India Company over its French equivalent. After Wandewash, Coote went on to capture the French capital of Pondicherry. The victories brought to an end hostilities which had begun in 1746. The French, especially under Governor Dupleix, enjoyed early success in the south. But Coote brought men and money from the rich province of Bengal, where the English already had power, which proved decisive. DAW

Wantage code. King *Æthelred's third law code. Issued at Wantage (Berks.) possibly in 997, it showed royal confirmation of local court customs in the five boroughs of the *Danelaw. Twelve leading *thegns in each *wapentake were to swear on relics neither to accuse an innocent man nor conceal a guilty one, the earliest reference in English law to what was effectively a sworn jury of presentment. The validity of a unanimous verdict was confirmed, but the agreement of eight thegns was allowed when opinions differed, a first assertion of this principle in England. AM

wapentakes in England were, from the 10th cent., subdivisions of shires in the *Danelaw, corresponding to *hundreds elsewhere. The terms applied in Derbyshire, part of Lancashire, Leicestershire, Lincolnshire, Nottinghamshire, Rutland, and Yorkshire, though perhaps not in the East Riding. The early 12th-cent. (unofficial) *Laws of Edward the Confessor* raise a problem. They say that when anyone accepted the headship of a wapentake, all the leading men met him at the usual meeting-place, and as he dismounted and raised his lance, they touched it with theirs. This account, whether representing truth or learning, takes the 'wapentake' back to an ancient Germanic world. JCa

Warbeck, Perkin (1474–99). Warbeck was a troublesome pretender to Henry VII's crown. He claimed to be Richard, duke of York, the younger of the two princes, sons of Edward IV. He was in fact born in Tournai. When he appeared in Cork in 1491 he was taken up by a number of people who wished to embarrass Henry, including the earls of Kildare and Desmond, Charles VIII of France, and *Margaret, dowager duchess of Burgundy. In 1494 he was recognized by Maximilian, Holy Roman emperor, as king of England and provided with an expeditionary force in 1495. James IV of Scotland welcomed him and gave him his cousin in marriage. In 1497 he landed in Cornwall, won some support, but failed to take Exeter or Taunton. He surrendered at Beaulieu and was spared his life on confession. In 1499, having attempted to escape from the Tower, he was hanged at Tyburn. His wife, daughter of the earl of Huntly, was treated kindly by Henry and made three further marriages. JAC

wardrobe. Financial institution. As its name suggests, the wardrobe was originally the place in which the king's robes were placed for safe keeping, and where cash was held from which the king's personal expenses might be paid. Under Henry III it developed its scope of action, having more moneys paid into it and thus providing an easily accessible source of funds for the king, enabling him to bypass the *Chancery and *Exchequer. The keeper of the wardrobe was also the *treasurer of the household; he received moneys for its upkeep, checked the accounts of its departments and rendered them to the Exchequer. The wars of Edward I and his successors boosted the wardrobe's significance further by making it the equivalent of a war treasury which travelled with the campaigning king, receiving war funds from the Exchequer as well as directly from other sources of royal income, and paying soldiers' wages. In the 1320s there were attempts to curb the independence of the wardrobe and to place it more firmly under Exchequer control. Subsequent rulers, however, continued to use the wardrobe for both regular household and military expenses although the Yorkist and early Tudor kings placed greater emphasis on the *chamber for their private and 'secret' expenses. The great wardrobe was abolished in 1782 and its duties concerning the royal household transfered to the *lord chamberlain. AC

Wards, Court of. This court was set up in 1540 by Henry VIII to enforce the lord's rights of wardship and marriage which had existed, since the Norman Conquest, as feudal incidents. After the statute of *Quia emptores 1290 ended the practice of subinfeudation, the crown gradually became the lord of many estates. Increasingly payments had taken the place of feudal incidents. The purpose of the Court of Wards was to enforce payment of these ancient feudal dues to the crown and thus to increase the income of the king. This court was later combined with the Court of Liveries to become the Court of Wards and Liveries. It was abolished in 1656. MM

Warenne, John de, 7th earl of Surrey (*c.*1231–1304). Warenne was a staunch supporter of Edward I. He inherited the earldom in 1240 when a boy of 9 or so. He was a little older than Edward I and in 1247 was married to Henry III's half-sister Alice de Lusignan. This gave him connections with Henry's continental relatives who were so much disliked in England. During the civil war he sided with Henry and was on the losing royal side at the battle of *Lewes in 1264. The following year he joined Prince Edward and took part in the campaign that ended with de *Montfort's death at *Evesham. He was a guardian during Edward I's absence during the early weeks of his reign, was much employed in the later 1270s and 1280s against the Welsh, and in the 1290s against the Scots. In 1296 he inflicted a sharp defeat on the Scots at *Dunbar but the following year was badly beaten by *Wallace at *Stirling Bridge, when he imprudently divided his forces. He was retained for the 1298 campaign when Edward defeated the Scots at *Falkirk. JAC

Warenne, John de, 8th earl of Surrey (1286–1347). Warenne succeeded his grandfather as earl in 1304 at the age of 18. In 1306 he married Edward I's granddaughter Joan, but the marriage was unhappy and Warenne scarcely built on his great position. He was instrumental in the capture of *Gaveston in 1312 though not in his subsequent murder. He refused to join Edward II's campaign which ended in *Bannockburn and showed little inclination for martial glory. He took an active part in 1322 against *Thomas of Lancaster, with whom he had long been at feud and remained a supporter of Edward II until his deposition. During Edward III's reign, Warenne supported the claims of Edward *Balliol, a cousin, and received the earldom of Strathearn [S] from him. Much of his energy was devoted to his complex domestic life and advancing his numerous illegitimate offspring; his political conduct seems hesitant and indecisive. JAC

Warham, William (*c.*1450–1532). Archbishop of Canterbury. Born in Hampshire and educated in law at New College, Oxford, Warham frequently served as a diplomat (1491–1502) and negotiated Prince *Arthur's marriage to *Catherine of Aragon (1496). He was successively master of the rolls (1494), bishop of London (1502), archbishop (1504), and lord chancellor (1504–15). A patron of the New Learning, he was chancellor of Oxford University (1506). From 1515 *Wolsey, as cardinal, lord chancellor, and papal legate, constantly overshadowed Warham. Though originally disapproving of Henry and Catherine's marriage, he had crowned them, but was Wolsey's assessor in the secret inquiry of 1527. Under pressure he signed the petition requesting papal consent for a divorce. Though he led convocation's offer to buy off penalties of *praemunire (1531), conscience provoked him to protest formally (1532) against the anti-papal Acts passed since 1529. Described as 'morose and inflexible', he was nevertheless competent and conscientious. WMM

War of 1812. The last conflict between Britain and the USA began when the British blockade of Napoleonic Europe and naval impressment of American sailors inflamed relations. Western American politicians campaigned for conquest of Canada to open land for settlement and eliminate Indian resistance. Congress declared war on 16 June 1812—four days after *Castlereagh had announced relaxation of the blockade. The Americans failed to overrun Canada, despite battles including *Queenston Heights (1812), Chrysler's Farm (1813), Lundy's Lane, and Chippewa (1814). The British retaliated for the destruction of York (later Toronto) in April 1813 by occupying Washington in August 1814 and burning the White House. Indians played a significant role as British allies. American pride was salved by unexpected victories at sea, and on the Lakes. The war was ended by the treaty of *Ghent, with its causes unresolved. The diversion of troops to Canada limited forces available for the *Waterloo campaign. GM

War Office. The centre of British army administration from at least 1661 until the emergence of the Ministry of Defence in 1963, the War Office was designed to impose civilian control over military affairs. Before 1855, it was run by the curiously named secretary at war, whose duties lay as much towards the monarch as Parliament, but in the light of disasters in the Crimea, all administrative duties were consolidated under the secretary of state for war, a cabinet post. This had the advantage of rationalizing what had been, hitherto, a chaotic administrative structure, but as the need for military advice to politicians grew, both in response to the development of empire and the emerging threat from Germany in the early 20th cent., clashes between the secretary of state and military men became inevitable. In 1914 these clashes were dealt with by appointing Lord *Kitchener, an experienced soldier, as secretary of state. His death two years later allowed the politicians to reassert some measure of control. Similar problems were avoided during the Second World War when Winston *Churchill, as prime minister, assumed the role of 'minister of defence' and downgraded the influence of the War Office. Moreover, the nature of the war necessitated inter-service advice, and this further undermined the importance of a strictly army organization. Although the War Office was revived after 1945, any long-term hopes of continued independence soon faded in light of a need for consolidated inter-service policies and economy. The Ministry of *Defence was the answer. JLP

Warriston, Archibald Johnston, Lord (1611–63). Johnston was born in Edinburgh, educated at Glasgow University, and became a lawyer. He helped to frame the national *covenant in 1638 and was appointed procurator of the kirk. In the temporary lull of 1641 Charles I appointed him to the Court of Session as Lord Warriston. He was much employed in negotiation with the English Parliament and strongly disapproved of the *Engagement in 1648. After the Cromwellian conquest of Scotland, he was deprived of all offices, but in 1657 was reappointed lord clerk register [S], a post he had held 1649–51. He also attended Cromwell's House of Peers and was a member of the *Council of State in 1659. After the Restoration, Warriston fled to the continent, but was seized at Rouen, taken to Scotland, and hanged at the market cross in Edinburgh. *Burnet, his nephew, wrote that *presbyterianism was 'to him more than all the world'. His son James was secretary of state [S] from 1692 to 1696. JAC

Warwick, Richard Neville, 1st earl of (1428–71), known as 'the Kingmaker'. Warwick was the mightiest of overmighty subjects, who was instrumental in putting Edward IV on the throne in 1461, deposing him in 1470, and restoring Henry VI. So powerful was he in the early years of Edward IV that one Frenchman wittily remarked of England, 'they have two rulers, Warwick and another, whose name I have forgotten'. Warwick owed his power to his vast estates, combining in his own hands no fewer than four earldoms, with lands stretching the length and breadth of England. Neville resources enabled the Yorkists successfully to overthrow Henry VI in 1461. In the next four years Warwick proved indispensable to Edward IV in securing control of the kingdom. Lavishly rewarded and allowed to take virtual control of northern England, he resented loss of influence after 1465. He first withdrew from court (1467) and eventually after two abortive rebellions (1469 and 1470) he resorted to the restoration of Henry VI. However, the restoration was short-lived and on Easter Sunday 1471 Warwick was defeated and killed by Edward IV at *Barnet. Warwick has generally had a bad press as over-ambitious. But his inherited wealth inevitably made him a power in the land. He was an astute politician, instinctively knowing how to exploit popular feelings for his own advantage. He was an inept general, and this, in the last resort, was his undoing. AJP

Warwick, Edward Plantagenet, 2nd earl of (1475–99). Warwick's father was George, duke of *Clarence (brother of Edward IV and Richard III), who was murdered when Warwick was 3. His mother was a daughter of *Warwick the Kingmaker. On the death of his only son in 1484, Richard III is said to have considered Warwick as a possible heir. After Henry VII's victory at *Bosworth, he was placed in the Tower. In 1487 Lambert *Simnel claimed to be him and was crowned in Dublin, whereupon Warwick was taken publicly to St Paul's to quell the rumours. He remained in the Tower until November 1499 when he was accused of conspiring with Perkin *Warbeck and executed. JAC

Warwick castle, sited on a cliff above the Avon, was founded by William the Conqueror in 1068 and has been the seat of the earls of Warwick from the 11th cent. It began as a motte and bailey castle, a stone castle from at least the 12th cent. The present castle owes much to the major rebuilding under the powerful Beauchamp earls, Thomas (d. 1369) and his son, also Thomas (d. 1401). The domestic range, above the river, was extensively remodelled as was the front towards the town, which was provided with an elaborate gatehouse and barbican and two wall towers, known as Guy's Tower and Caesar's Tower. The work, begun by the first Thomas, is dependent on French models, parallels work being carried out at *Windsor by Edward III, and reflects closely the power and wealth of a man who was a hero of *Crécy and *Poitiers and a founder member of the Order of the *Garter. The new towers demonstrate the integration of domestic accommodation and fortification, each being elaborately defended but having also several self-contained apartments for important members of the household. LR

Warwickshire was an archetypal Mercian shire, regular in shape and taking its name from the chief town. The southern parts are drained by the Avon and its tributaries, the northern by the river Thame, which joins the Trent. The eastern border runs along the line of Watling Street, the west along Icknield Street, and the shire is bisected north-east to south-west by the Fosse Way. *Camden placed it in the territory of the *Cornovii and divided it into the arable south, or Fielden, and the wooded north around the forest of Arden. The Fielden territory had been part of the land of the *Hwicce. The area was included in the diocese of *Lichfield in the early 7th cent. but the southern parts were hived off to the see of *Worcester. Warwickshire formed the heartland of the kingdom of Mercia: in the 8th and 9th cents. Tamworth was the chief residence of the Mercian monarchs and Warwick was refounded in 914 by *Æthelfleda, lady of the Mercians.

It remained a rural county throughout the Middle Ages. Warwick itself was a significant provincial city, *Kenilworth and *Warwick castles important until the civil wars, and *Coventry had a reputation for cloth-making. During the civil wars, the shire was held for the most part by the parliamentarians Lords Warwick and Brooke, with strong support from Coventry and Birmingham, proving too powerful for the royalist Lord Northampton. The gradual improvement in transport through inland navigation, turnpikes, and finally railways brought Warwickshire into the national orbit. In 1825, just before the railway era, the Birmingham canal was paying 70 per cent, the Coventry canal via Atherstone 44 per cent, the Oxford canal via Rugby 32 per cent, the Grand Junction linking up with the Thames 13 per cent, and the Warwick and Birmingham canal 11 per cent. The Liverpool to Birmingham railway opened in 1837, the London to Birmingham in 1838.

The modern history of the county is the development of industry in the northern parts around *Birmingham and Coventry, exploiting the proximity of woodland, coal, and iron resources. Camden described Birmingham in Elizabeth's reign as 'swarming with inhabitants and echoing with the noise of anvils'. It passed Coventry in size during the 17th cent. and by 1700 had grown to around 15,000 people. Birmingham's dissatisfaction with its lack of representation in Parliament was demonstrated in 1774 when it captured one of the two county seats, previously the preserve of Tory country gentlemen. The demand for direct representation grew. In 1812 one of the county MPs was censured for his 'inattention' to the commercial interests of the shire and in 1819, to dramatize the situation, Birmingham radicals 'elected' a legislative attorney. *Attwood's *Birmingham Political Union played an important part in the passing of the *Great Reform Act of 1832, whereby Birmingham received two MPs. In the later 19th cent. Birmingham was granted city status and under Joseph *Chamberlain led the way in progressive local government. To nail-making, small arms, cutlery, and button-making was added industry of all kinds: Cadbury's moved to Bournville in 1879 and the Austin Motor Company opened at Longbridge in 1905. By 1911 the population was well over half a million.

*Stratford-upon-Avon owed its fame as a tourist attraction largely to the Shakespeare jubilee of 1769, organized by David *Garrick. The Memorial theatre opened in 1932. The salt springs at Leamington had been known since Tudor times, but the expansion of the town was 19th cent., the Pump Room opening in 1814. Nuneaton developed as a textile centre, Courtauld's setting up a factory in 1920, and Rugby grew steadily after the opening of the London to Birmingham railway, on which it was an important junction. The county lost several parishes to *West Midlands in the local government reorganization of 1972. The Banham commission in 1994 recommended no change in the local government structure. JAC

Washington, George (1732–99). First president of the USA. Washington's ancestors came from Northamptonshire and the first of the family to settle in Virginia was John, in 1657. George Washington was his great-grandson. He inherited the Mount Vernon estate in 1752 when his half-brother died. His first military experience was gained in the Virginia militia, he was with Braddock when he was killed in 1755, appointed commander of the Virginia forces at the age of 23, and elected to the state legislature. After attending the first and second continental congresses in 1774 and 1775, he was elected commander of the congress forces. His early years in command were necessarily defensive, largely concerned with gathering, training, and retaining some sort of army. His first victory of any importance was at *Trenton in December 1776 and he held his army together through the terrible winter at Valley Forge in 1777–8. French support from 1778 onwards helped to turn the tide, though as late as 1780 Washington could write, 'I have almost ceased to hope.' At the end of hostilities, on 19 April 1783, he led the triumphal march into New York. When the Federal constitution was adopted, he was the obvious choice for the presidency, and was unanimously elected and re-elected in 1789 and 1793. He retired in 1797 to spend his last two years back in Mount Vernon. Tall, with natural authority and genuinely reluctant to serve, Washington was honest, patient, and shrewd. JAC

Washington, treaty of, 1871. The USA claimed compensation from Britain for the depredations of the **Alabama*, a Confederate warship built in England during the Civil War. Also in dispute was access to the Canadian fisheries and ownership of San Juan Island off British Columbia. The five-man British commission included Canada's prime minister, Sir John A. Macdonald, who was trapped into surrendering the fisheries to placate the Americans. Britain agreed to arbitration: San Juan was awarded to the USA, and $15.5 million was paid for the *Alabama* claims. Although a poor settlement for Britain and Canada, the treaty was a milestone in international arbitration. GM

watch and ward was an attempt at a more effective policing system, which started in 1233 with a specific incident and became firmly established. After disturbances, Henry III ordered all vills (townships) to arrange guards at night and apprehend suspicious persons. The instructions were repeated in 1242, with details on numbers of men and weapons, again in 1253, and in Edward I's reign were promulgated in the statute of *Winchester of 1285. Watch and ward was still being maintained in the 18th cent. and its modern echoes are the neighbourhood watches set up in many suburbs and villages in the 1980s. JAC

Waterford (Port Láirge), **diocese of.** Originally a Norse city and thus an object of Anglo-Norman colonization of Ireland, it was a suffragan see of *Canterbury from 1096, when Malchus, a monk of Winchester and later archbishop of *Cashel (1111–35), was consecrated by *Lanfranc. Waterford was first listed as a bishopric at the Council of Kells-Mellifont (1152), though there was no regular succession of bishops until 1175. As it was a royal town, from 1225 bishops tended to be Anglo-French. After long Irish and papal resistance, Lismore was merged with Waterford, as English influence spread. The bishopric was sometimes a reward for administrative service; Stephen Fulbourn, bishop (1274–86), was justiciar of Ireland (1281–8) and it was held by English bishops from then onwards. In the 1590s there was a Jesuit college in Waterford which sent boys to the continent for training. Waterford and Lismore is still a catholic bishopric in the province of Cashel, but the Anglican see was merged with the Cashel diocese in 1833. WMM

water industry. Water for human consumption was traditionally obtained from wells, ponds, or rivers. This remained adequate until rapid urbanization during the 17th and 18th cents., particularly the growth of London and the industrial cities elsewhere, brought about the need for better supply. The solutions, sought during the 19th cent., invariably came in response to the related problems of public hygiene and the spread of water-borne diseases, such as typhus and cholera.

Among the earliest developments were the companies established in London using water from the Thames and its tributaries, one of the first being the *New River scheme undertaken by Sir Hugh *Myddleton in 1609. During the 17th cent. other companies were established, notably the York Buildings Company, sanctioned by letters patent from Charles II in 1675 and incorporated in 1691. The water was taken from the river by canals equipped with sluices and pumped by horse-powered gins to cisterns on higher ground, from which it was conveyed to wealthy customers' dwellings by service pipes, connected to 7-inch. wooden pipes laid through the streets. Public supply in London and other towns until the early 19th cent. was by similar conduits of wooden (and later iron) pipes to carry spring or well water to lead cisterns, which fed subsidiary lead pipes supplying communal taps or water carriers.

But as population increased, water supplies became contaminated by sewage and other effluent, creating major problems of public health in the larger towns, particularly after the first *cholera epidemic in 1831–2. A series of investigations culminating in Edwin *Chadwick's *Report on the Sanitary Condition of the Labouring Population* (1842) acted as spurs to improvement. Self-cleansing sewers of improved design required a constant supply of water under pressure and this was easier to provide in some places than others.

The Metropolitan Board of Works scheme, designed by Joseph Bazalgette for the drainage of London, and the largest for the time, was not completed until 1865. As in other 19th-cent. schemes, steam power was used for pumping.

During the early stages of industrialization, canal-building and the use of water power as a prime mover led to a greater understanding of hydraulics and water engineering. Both of these developments necessitated the construction of dams, sluices, and water channels, the design of which influenced the construction of reservoirs for water supply under gravity. Two of the earliest, using earth with a core of puddled clay, were those of the Edinburgh Water Company (1822) and the Shaws waterworks for domestic and industrial supply in Greenock (1825–7). Many similar structures were built in the Pennines, south Wales, and other suitable locations. However, these dams were relatively small and their strength limited. There were disastrous collapses at Holmfirth near Huddersfield in 1852 and Dale Dike near Sheffield in 1864. Traditional methods of dam construction were abandoned and replaced by masonry dams, the first being built at Vyrnwy in Wales to supply Liverpool, begun in 1881 and completed in 1892.

As demand increased, other natural or man-made reservoirs were developed. Glasgow tapped Loch Katrine in the Trossachs, Manchester the resources of the Lake District, while Birmingham, like Liverpool, exploited the potential of Wales. There the drowning of valleys for English water supply caused considerable local resentment, particularly among Welsh nationalists. However, from the age of 'gas and water' civic pride in the 19th cent., water supply was traditionally a non-political issue, controlled by local authorities and water boards. During the 1980s, amid much political controversy, it became one of several nationalized industries to be sold to the private sector. The difficulty of maintaining a regular supply to homes and industry of such stupendous quantities of water, compounded by the occasional drought, has meant that the water industry in the 1990s has been much in the public eye. ID

Waterloo, battle of, 1815. In June 1815, Napoleon struck into Belgium, hoping to destroy *Wellington's Anglo-Dutch army and Blücher's Prussians before they could unite to crush him. After the battle of *Quatre Bras on 16 June, Wellington's inexperienced army of 67,000 men (of which less than a third were British) fell back to a ridge near Waterloo. The 89,000 strong Prussian army, although badly mauled at Ligny on the same day, also retreated. The French Marshal Grouchy pursued Blücher with 33,000 men, fighting an action at Wavre on 18 June, but failed to prevent the Prussians from marching to Wellington's aid.

The battle began on 18 June with an unsuccessful attack on Hougoumont, a fortified farmhouse on Wellington's right flank. A major attack developed in the centre, but the French infantry were driven back. Then for about 90 minutes the French made a series of fruitless attacks with unsupported cavalry on unbroken allied infantry squares. The arrival of Prussian forces compelled Napoleon to send part of his élite Imperial Guard to his right flank. By 6.30 p.m. the key farmhouse of La Haye Sainte had fallen to the French, and an all-out assault might well have broken Wellington's lines. However, Napoleon prevaricated, and only released his reserve—the Imperial Guard—at 7.00. The repulse of the Guard was the signal for the rout of Napoleon's army. With Blücher's men pouring on the field, Napoleon was finally defeated. GDS

Watling Street is the later name for the major Roman road from Dover through Canterbury to London and thence via *Verulamium and a series of smaller towns to *Wroxeter (later the basis for *Telford's Holyhead road, the A5). Whether the sections either side of London were seen as unitary in the Roman period is debatable; they are now united by their Anglo-Saxon name *Wæcelinga Stræt*, 'the street of the people of Wæcel'. ASEC

Watson, George (d. 1723). A merchant in Edinburgh, Watson became accountant to the Bank of Scotland, set up in 1695. He left a bequest for 'the maintenance and education of the offspring of decayed merchants'. Building started in 1738 and Watson's hospital opened in 1741 with twelve boys. His institution became a day school in 1870 and a girls' school opened the following year. JAC

Watson-Watt, Robert (1892–1973). Scientist. Born in Brechin of a family related to James *Watt, Watson-Watt studied engineering at University College, Dundee. During the First World War he was posted to the Royal Aircraft Factory at Farnborough, which had begun studying the use of radio to predict atmospheric storms. The work was continued after the war at Slough and then at Teddington. In the 1930s his team became involved in air defence against bombers. By 1935 Watson-Watt was able to present a paper on 'The detection of aircraft by radio method'. A successful experiment led to a new unit being set up near Felixstowe. By 1938 the basis of a radar defence system had been established and played a crucial part in the Battle of *Britain in 1940. Watson-Watt was knighted in 1942 and published an account of his work in *Three Steps to Victory* (1957). JAC

Watt, James (1736–1819). Instrument-maker to Glasgow University, where he applied principles of latent heat to the *Newcomen engine to patent the separate condenser in 1769, and found a career as leading steam engineer, conducted mainly (1775–1800) in partnership with *Boulton. Watt generated a subsequent flow of patents: principally sun-and-planet rotary motion (1781), reciprocation (1782), and parallel motion (1784), though his engines were dependent upon *Wilkinson's patent boring machinery (1774). They were high in prime cost, and their economy offset by patent premiums, and sold best where coal was expensive and higher power required, leaving others to supply more than half Britain's horsepower in 1800. Watt stopped his assistant's experiments with steam carriages, enthusiastically protected his patents, remained committed to low-pressure operation, and probably retarded steam innovations before 1800. Other research led to his patenting of a damp-paper letter copier (1780); experiments with the properties of air; the principle of the marine screw; and many measuring devices, in addition to his re-specification of *Savery's 'horsepower' as a standard unit. He retired at the expiry of the patent in 1800, and lived a gentlemanly country life at Handsworth and Rhayader. JCh

Waugh, Evelyn (1903–66). Novelist and satirist whose early books *Decline and Fall* (1928) and *Vile Bodies* (1930) chronicle the doings of the Bright Young Things at Oxford and after with an ironic detachment approaching the grotesque. He consolidated his reputation with more material drawing on his own experience, in *A Handful of Dust* (1934) of a harrowing divorce; in *Scoop* (1938) as war correspondent in Africa; but the central event in his life was conversion to Roman catholicism in 1930. Though middle-class himself, son of a successful publisher, like the narrator of *Brideshead Revisited* (1945) he cultivated the aristocracy and the old order assailed by contemporary vulgarity. If his latter-day persona as irascible country gentleman sometimes verged on self-parody, in *The Sword of Honour* trilogy (1962) he convinces us that the concept is more than another name for snobbery. JNRS

Wavell, Archibald Percival (1883–1950). British general, commander-in-chief Middle East from July 1939, he directed campaigns against Italians after June 1940. In Cyrenaica he won a series of spectacular victories in December 1940 to February 1941, taking prisoner 130,000 Italians. He was then ordered to give priority to helping Greece. There, and in Africa, German contingents inflicted defeat and in spring 1941 both Cyrenaica and Greece were lost. In July *Auchinleck took over and Wavell became C.-in-C., India. In December 1941, Wavell became C.-in-C., south-west Pacific area, and faced violent Japanese attacks: he could not stop the loss of Malaya, Singapore, the Dutch East Indies, and Burma. Promoted field marshal and viscount, he became viceroy of India in June 1943. At the end of the war he attempted the impossible search for agreement on the future of India between Hindus and Muslims, Congress and the princes. In February 1947 he was replaced by Lord *Mountbatten, who, to Wavell's dismay, accelerated the end of British rule. RACP

Wealth of Nations, The. Adam *Smith's treatise was published in 1776 when the old mercantilist system was fast breaking down. Few books have been more influential. In simple and direct language, Smith argued the case for **laissez-faire* with a minimum of government intervention, though he conceded the need for regulation to protect national security, such as fostering shipping. He did not believe that politicians had any competence in directing economic activity, nor did he like their motives—'there is no art which one government sooner learns of another than that of draining money from the pockets of the people'. In a remarkable passage, he insisted that the endeavour of each individual to better himself advanced the common good, as though 'led by an invisible hand to promote an end which was no part of his intention'. Not until *Malthus and *Ricardo were Smith's optimistic assumptions seriously challenged. JAC

Webb, Sidney (1859–1947) and **Beatrice** (1858–1943). Fabian socialists, social reformers, and historians. Married in 1882, the Webbs formed a partnership of unparalleled significance for the development and introduction of left-wing social policies in Britain. They wrote many books together on social history, and held many public offices. Sidney served on the London County Council from 1892 to 1910, became a Labour MP for Seaham in 1922, becoming president of the Board of Trade in 1924, and as Baron Passfield in 1929 serving briefly as secretary of state for the dominions and colonies.

The Webbs' approach to social reform was gradualist; they rejected Marxist theories of class struggle, and believed that socialism would be achieved by a process of 'permeation'—i.e. the inculcating of socialist ideas into the minds of the power élite in Britain. In the 1930s, however, the Webbs became disillusioned with the progress of socialism in Britain and turned their attention to the USSR, which they visited and found so impressive that in their last substantial book, *Soviet Communism: A New Civilisation?* (1935), they abandoned their piecemeal approach to political and social change. TSG

Wedderburn, Alexander, 1st earl of Rosslyn (1733–1805). Wedderburn was a member of a Scottish legal family and an associate of David *Hume and Adam *Smith's Edinburgh circle. He was called to the English bar in 1757 and entered Parliament in 1761. He supported *Bute, *Grenville, and *North, becoming solicitor-general 1771–8 and attorney-general 1778–80. He was a frequent and effective speaker in the Commons, with a reputation for intrigue and self-advancement. He was appointed lord chief justice of Common Pleas in 1780 as Baron Loughborough. He remained a follower of North and helped to negotiate the coalition with *Fox in 1783. After the French Revolution he attempted to negotiate a junction between *Pitt and the opposition to support war against France but was tempted by Pitt's offer of the lord chancellorship and crossed the House alone. He was consulted by George III as to whether the coronation oath forbade him to consent to catholic emancipation. He left office with Pitt in 1801 and received the earldom of Rosslyn. EAS

Wedgwood, Josiah (1730–95). Potter, industrialist, and social reformer. Wedgwood was born into a Staffordshire family of potters and was at work by the age of 9. Shrewd and innovative in manufacture, design, and marketing, he capitalized on 18th-cent. fashion and snobbery, setting up on his own in 1758, and opening the great Etruria factory in 1769. Aware that 'a name has a wonderful effect', he presented his newly improved creamware to Queen *Charlotte and obtained her permission to call it Queen's Ware, multiplying his sales in Britain and Europe. A notable commission came from Catherine the Great in 1774: a 952-piece service, now in the Hermitage Museum in St Petersburg, decorated with exquisite and accurate detail of 18th-cent. houses and countryside.

Wedgwood was keenly interested in the social and political problems of his day, much involved in road and canal development, and constantly reviewed the working and living conditions of his employees. His views were liberal/radical, he was sympathetic towards American independence in the 1770s, welcomed the French Revolution, and was a fervent supporter of the abolition of slavery. JC

Wedmore, treaty of, 878. The agreement made between King *Alfred and the Danish leader *Guthrum at Wedmore proved a turning-point in the Danish wars. From their fortified position at Chippenham the Danes had threatened to overrun all Wessex, but Alfred emerged from his refuge at Athelney, inflicted a severe defeat on the Danes at *Edington, and forced peace on Guthrum on condition that he would himself accept baptism and that his army would leave Wessex. There followed a series of formal ceremonies which involved Alfred standing as sponsor at baptism for the Danish leader at Aller near Athelney and the unbinding of the chrism at Wedmore. Guthrum with 30 of his chosen companions spent some twelve days with the king and was greatly honoured by him. The Danes kept the substance of the arrangement, moving the army back to Cirencester and ultimately to East Anglia. Guthrum accepted the baptismal name of Athelstan and, as far as can be judged, the Christian faith. The accord reached at Wedmore foreshadowed the partition of England into much of the south and west, which remained in English hands, and the Danelaw of the north and east. HL

weights and measures. The history of weights and measures in Britain is dominated by efforts at standardization, nationally and locally, for many variations existed for bulk, liquid, and linear measures in the different countries of the British Isles.

In England, Saxon weights and measures, based roughly on the standards prescribed by *Offa, king of Mercia, were used for centuries, being confirmed after the Norman Conquest by William I and subsequently in 1215 by *Magna Carta. The ounce was approximately 450 grains, i.e. slightly heavier than the modern one. An ordinance of Henry III in 1266 defined both coinage and commercial weights for the first time. There was some effort to relate English weights to those of the cities of the *Hanseatic league, the principal market for wool, the country's major export. This act established a 16-ounce pound for commercial weight.

A new standard of bulk weight was enacted by Edward III in 1340, when the treasury at Winchester became the repository for weights with denominations of 7, 14, 28, 56, and 91 lbs. The standard corresponded roughly with that of Florence, another major market for English wool, indicating that one stone should weigh 14 lbs. During the reign of Henry VII, weights and measures were put on a statutory basis by an Act of 1497 and later under Elizabeth I a series of ordinances, culminating with that of 1588 aimed to standardize bulk and precious metal weights. The hundredweight and the ton were standardized at 112 lb. and 20 cwt. (2,240 lb.) respectively. These Acts also set standards for liquid and linear measures, which were distributed to all the main cities and boroughs in England and Wales, though adoption was gradual and inspection difficult.

North of the border, despite similar attempts to disentangle the confusing system of Scottish weights and measures, there was no serious attack on the problem until the Restoration. In 1661 a parliamentary commission proposed the introduction of national standards with certain burghs having custody of particular weights and measures. Accordingly, Edinburgh would keep the ell for linear measure, Linlithgow the firlot for dry measure, Lanark the troy stone for weight, and Stirling the jug for liquid capacity.

The *Union of 1707 should have brought standardization throughout Great Britain but in reality it was not until the 19th cent., by an Act of 1824, that the uniformity recommended by the Carysfort parliamentary inquiry in 1758–60 was statutorily established. British standards then became known as imperial measure. More precise instruments, particularly for use in scientific experiments and in cartography, led to greater standardization of both weights and measures.

While many attempts have subsequently been made to substitute metric for imperial measure, the former, though widely used in industry, and scientific and professional spheres, has not yet replaced traditional standards. A further step towards standard metrification with Europe was taken in 1995, though, as an act of kindness, the British people were allowed to continue to drink pints of milk or pints of beer, and to travel, if they wished, in miles. ID

welfare state. The term refers to the state's assumption of responsibility for the welfare of its citizens through the delivery of incomes and services in kind. There are many theories as to why it developed, from the radical view of its serving the needs of capitalism by maintaining political stability and providing healthy, educated workers, to the democratic perspective that it arose from the demands of the working class expressed through the ballot box. It has been called 'an erratic and pragmatic response of government and people to the practical individual and community problems of an industrialised society'.

In the *laissez-faire*, capitalist, self-help ideology of the 19th cent. fears of dependency and disincentives for the poor resulted in harsh measures based on the workhouse. At the turn of the century *Booth's (London) and *Rowntree's (York) studies, revealing the facts of poverty and showing its origins in social and economic conditions, helped to raise awareness of the problem and set the stage for reform at a national level.

Measures taken by *Asquith's Liberal government, with *Lloyd George as chancellor, represent the foundations of the British welfare state. Non-contributory old-age pensions (1908), paid for by higher taxes ('the People's Budget', 1909), and the *National Insurance Act—Health and Unemployment (1911) were the most important of the reforms. In the inter-war years the problem of unemployment dominated social policy; the insurance scheme could not cope and in 1931 the dole was cut and a family means test was implemented, a return to relief based on Victorian deterrent values.

The Second World War threw people together, and in the relative social cohesion of the war years they determined that 'never again' should there be a return to the misery of the 1930s. The *Beveridge Report (*Report on Social Insurance and Allied Services,* Cmd. 6404) gave shape to these ideas.

Beveridge identified 'five giant evils of Want, Disease, Squalor, Ignorance and Idleness' and, to fight each evil, 'five giants on the road to reconstruction': social security, a national health service, housing provision, state education, and a commitment to full employment. In July 1945 a Labour government, fully committed to wholesale reform, was elected in a landslide general election victory. Led by Clement *Attlee, it lasted until 1951 and founded the modern British welfare state. Legislation took place between 1945 and 1948, most of the provisions taking effect on or before 5 July 1948, the 'appointed day'.

Poverty was to be conquered by a commitment to full employment together with social insurance. The coalition government's 1944 Employment White Paper made explicit all-party acceptance of Keynesian demand management to combat unemployment. Social insurance provisions, based on Beveridge, were a move from selectivity to comprehensive coverage. Compulsory contributions to a National Insurance scheme provided for incomes during sickness, unemployment, widowhood, and retirement; there was also a means-tested safety net, national assistance (now income support), and family allowances (now child benefit). The *National Health Service Act (1946) provided for free health care for all regardless of means, and the birth of the NHS in 1948 was a triumph for Aneurin *Bevan, minister for health. Education reform had been initiated by R. A. *Butler, Conservative education minister in the coalition government, in his 1944 Education Act. The school-leaving age was to be raised to 15 and there was free secondary education for all. Finally, council housing was to solve the problem of homelessness and squatting which followed the end of the war.

Throughout the 1950s and 1960s there was cross-party consensus on the welfare state. In the 1970s the consensus was challenged from the right by neo-liberals who wanted to 'roll back the state'. Their arguments, together with rising unemployment, reawakened concern over costs and a 'dependency culture'. The election of a Conservative government under Margaret *Thatcher in 1979 led to debate on the future of the welfare state, but few measures to reduce its scope were taken until after the third Conservative election victory in 1988. The debate continues: broadly there are two interrelated issues: the universalist One Nation approach versus a means-tested safety-net system, and the sustainability of the costs of provision. MW

Welles, Richard and Robert (d. 1470). Lionel, Lord Welles, and his son Richard, Lord Willoughby, fought against Edward IV at *Towton in 1461, when Lionel was killed and subsequently attainted. By fighting for Edward against Lancastrians in 1464, Richard earned the reversal of the attainder and thus recovered his father's title and estates. Then, in a private feud, he sacked the house of Thomas Burgh at Gainsborough. Determined to restore order, Edward summoned Richard and planned a formidable royal visitation of Lincolnshire. At this point, apparently, *Warwick and *Clarence fomented a rebellion to oppose Edward's arrival. His rapid march caught them unprepared. The locals assembled by Richard's son Robert were scattered at Empingham, in an action known as *Losecoat Field on 12 March 1470. Richard and Robert Welles were executed; Warwick and Clarence fled to France. RLS

Wellesley, Richard, 1st Marquis Wellesley (1760–1842). British administrator and the eldest brother of the duke of Wellington. In 1784 Wellesley entered parliament as MP for Beeralston where he sympathized with the free trade movement but opposed parliamentary reform. In 1793 he became a member of the India Board and from 1797 to 1805 acted as governor-general of Bengal. British rule was threatened by the French in alliance with Tipu Sahib of Mysore and the nizam of Hyderabad. Wellesley retorted by taking control of Mysore, the Carnatic, Hyderabad, and Oudh, bringing native princes under British influence. He served as foreign secretary in *Perceval's cabinet and in 1812 tried unsuccessfully to form an administration. Wellesley championed the rights of catholics in Ireland and in 1821–8 and 1833–4 acted as lord-lieutenant of Ireland. In 1835 he became lord chamberlain. RAS

Wellington, Arthur Wellesley, 1st duke of (1769–1852). Soldier and prime minister. Arthur Wellesley was the third surviving son of the earl of Mornington, an impoverished Irish peer. Educated at Eton, he was regarded by his family as a dreamy introspective youth; the army was thought to be the only possible career for him. After a year at a French military academy at Angers, he entered the army by purchasing a commission. Early experience in the campaigns in the Low Countries during the first years of the Revolutionary War showed how things should not be done. His great chance came in India, where his elder brother was governor-general. Arthur established his military reputation by winning the spectacular victories of Assaye and Argaum over the Mahrattas in 1803. His campaigns in India were invaluable in preparing him for the type of war he was to fight in Portugal and Spain. In 1808 he was sent as commander of the first detachment of British troops to Portugal. Winning the battle of *Vimeiro he was prevented from following up his victory by the caution of his superiors, and he was recalled with them to face a court of inquiry after the armistice of *Cintra, which was seen in England as craven. Wellesley had signed the agreement under orders, but was bitterly attacked by opposition politicians. Cleared by the inquiry he resumed command of the British army in Portugal after the death of *Moore. He always believed that Portugal could be denied to the French. Shrewdly exploiting natural features and the engineering skills of the British army to construct the lines of *Torres Vedras he ensured that the British army would not be pushed into the sea. Thereafter his Portuguese base was firm, and although collaboration with the Spaniards was often fraught with difficulties, he repeatedly challenged the French, proving the superiority of the British line over the French column. But he was more than a defensive general. He was bold when necessary, as the assaults on the fortresses of Badajoz and *Ciudad Rodrigo showed, and in the battles of *Salamanca, *Vitoria, and the *Pyrenees he was as resourceful in attack as he had been in defence. The end of the Peninsular War saw him as the most famous British general since the duke of Marlborough. The battle of *Waterloo in 1815 confirmed his stature and his fame. He was without vanity and had little time for romantic delusions about military glory. For Wellington the greatest misery next to a battle lost was a battle won. He cared for his men and husbanded their lives, scorned extravagant gestures, and despised popularity.

After 1815 Wellington was prominent as a diplomat and politician. He had owed much to *Castlereagh; now he became one of his trusted lieutenants in the complex diplomacy of the post-war era. He also became a member of *Liverpool's government, believing that it was his duty to serve the state in whatever capacity might be required of him. After the death of *Canning and the failure of the *Goderich ministry, Wellington became prime minister in January 1828. Many Conservatives saw him as pledged to the maintenance of the existing order in church and state, but while he did not desire catholic emancipation he was aware that it might be unavoidable. When in 1828 a crisis erupted in Ireland he chose to grant catholic emancipation rather than risk civil war. This earned him the hatred of the ultra-Tories and he fought a duel with Lord Winchilsea to demonstrate his integrity. He had already lost the support of the liberal Tories because of his dislike of Canning's foreign policy. In 1830 Wellington attempted to rally conservative opinion by affirming his resolute opposition to parliamentary reform. The tactic failed to restore confidence in his administration. In November 1830 he was defeated on the civil list in the Commons and resigned. Although Wellington opposed the Reform Bill he realized that opposition had to be attuned to the realities of politics. He therefore led 100 Tory peers from their seats in the Lords to allow the Reform Bill to pass in June 1832, preferring reform to the prospect of the Upper House being swamped by newly created peers. In 1834, during the crisis provoked by *Melbourne's resignation, Wellington became a caretaker prime minister for some three weeks and after 1835 he played an important role as an elder statesman. The service of the crown and the preservation of public tranquillity were his chief priorities. He helped to secure the repeal of the Corn Laws in 1846. His final years saw him as a popular figure and on his death in 1852 he was mourned as a great soldier and outstanding public servant.

Wellington's attitudes were those of an Anglo-Irish aristocrat. He distrusted democracy, had little time for the vagaries of popular opinion, and saw politics in terms of fending off disaster rather than inaugurating utopia. His influence upon the army was conservative, though he was more perceptive than many contemporaries in understanding the role of the army in peacetime. Gifted with a cool intellect, the capacity to penetrate to the essentials of any problem surely and quickly, and the ability to express himself with lucid incisiveness, Wellington deserves his reputation as a great commander and a man of selfless integrity. JWD

Bryant, A., *The Great Duke* (1971); James, L., *The Iron Duke* (1992); Longford, E., *Wellington: The Years of the Sword* (1969); id., *Wellington: Pillar of State* (1972).

Wells, H. G. (1866–1946). Shopkeeper's son who jumped the counter to become successful author and eventually teacher-at-large to the human race. A scholarship to what is now Imperial College, London, where he studied under T. H. *Huxley, suggested the power of science to make us free, though it was an imaginative energy which fuelled his early romances *The Time Machine* (1895) and *The War of the Worlds* (1898). Moving in literary and *Fabian circles, he saw the novel as a medium for discussing problems 'raised in such bristling multitude by our contemporary social development'. Perhaps no one did more to shape that development, and after the First World War he increasingly abandoned fiction for analysis and exhortation. The best-selling *Outline of History* (1920) offered mankind 'salvation by history', lasting world peace only to be secured by learning its lessons. Yet Wells's faith in human potential was not blind to obstacles to be overcome, and in the novels too comedy and pessimism are mingled. JNRS

Wells cathedral. See BATH AND WELLS.

Welsh language. The oldest language spoken in Britain, with an unbroken history from Brythonic origins as part of the Celtic family of Indo-European languages from which most European languages derive. Its development was powerfully affected by external linguistic influences: Latin of Rome and the Christian Middle Ages; Irish, a Goidelic form of Celtic; Norse to a minor extent; and especially English following the Germanic invasions of Britain, and French after the Norman Conquest. Germanic and English advances westward led to the separate development of Brythonic Celtic in Wales, Cumbria, and Cornwall: only Welsh survives; Cumbric died out in the 11th cent. and Cornish in the 18th. At the same time, Welsh, the language of that part of Britain which the invaders called foreign (*Wealas*), acquired its characteristics of initial mutations, a complex word order, and an accent on the penultimate syllable. Those who used this language called themselves *Cymry* (fellow-countrymen).

Welsh appeared as a recognizable language before AD 600; up to the mid-12th cent., when French and English influences became strong, Old Welsh has left few traces apart from inscriptions, manuscript glosses, and Welsh poetry in saga or prophetic vein and usually recorded in manuscripts of the 13th and 14th cents., e.g. *The Book of *Aneurin* and *The Book of *Taliesin*, and perhaps too the prose tales known as the **Mabinogi*. Middle Welsh from the mid-12th cent. to the early 15th was rich in prose and popular verse, whose writers were patronized by Welsh princes and then (after 1283) by gentry of Welsh and immigrant lineage. Several dialects also emerged: according to *Gerald of Wales (d. 1223), Welsh 'is more delicate and richer in north Wales', but 'the language of Ceredigion in south Wales . . . is the most refined'. The same influences that enriched the language set the scene for its decline, for trends in government and society, immigration and town foundation, popularized Latin, French, and especially English in the later Middle Ages. The Act of *Union (1536) sought to replace Welsh with English in official contexts; although this was not fully practicable, it discouraged its use and patronage, and the gentry gradually ceased to speak Welsh, adopting English surnames instead of Welsh patronymics.

Salvation came with printing and the Reformation, especially with the translation of the Scriptures and the Prayer Book into Welsh (1567, 1588). The dignity of William *Morgan's Bible (1588) set a standard for literary Welsh thereafter. Educational, antiquarian, publishing, and religious movements in the 17th and 18th cents. ensured its survival as a spoken and written tongue; indeed, the 18th cent. saw a renaissance in Welsh culture. Even after half a century of industrialization, in 1801 80 per cent of Wales was Welsh-speaking; the borderland and southern littoral had not been so for centuries. Industrialization was not at first an enemy to Welsh, for many migrants to the southern valleys were Welsh-speaking, and in 1851 there were more Welsh-speakers than in 1801; but as a proportion of the expanding population they were a declining number (from 80 to 67 per cent between 1801 and 1851). The popularity of English among the upper classes, the demands of British education, the cosmopolitan industrial and commercial centres, immigration, and mass media and communications undermined Wales's linguistic character and portrayed the language as old-fashioned. By 1901, 50 per cent of Wales's population spoke Welsh; thereafter the decline was relentless, the figure standing at 19 per cent in 1981 (about 500,000 people), mostly in the rural west and north-west. In North America, too, where Welsh was implanted by emigrants in the late 19th cent., social and religious changes produced decline.

Yet since the 18th cent., Welsh literary culture has shown some creativity: an interest in Welsh history and tradition (including the *eisteddfod), a vigorous Welsh press, active nonconformity, the growth of national sentiment, and the foundation of national institutions (notably a library, museum, and university) in the late 19th and early 20th cents. More recently, opinion has focused intently on the question of the language's survival. It has been buttressed by academic study and a literary renaissance, acceptance at all levels of education, as well as by pressure groups, even perhaps violent protests. Official milestones are the report on *The Legal Status of the Welsh Language* (1965), the Welsh Language Act (1967) which enshrined the principle of equal validity with English, a Welsh TV channel (1982), and the Welsh Language Board (1993) to oversee its use and fate. It remains to be seen whether this nurturing will enhance its vitality and stem its overall decline. RAG

Welsh Nationalist Party. See PLAID CYMRU.

Wembley stadium. The Great Stadium at Wembley Park, London, was built to coincide with the British Empire Exhibition of 1923. Work was completed just four days before hosting its first Football Association Cup Final on 29 April 1923. It has since been a venue for a multitude of sports, including boxing, hurling, speedway, greyhound meetings, horse shows, and show jumping events. The Rugby League Cup Final has been played at Wembley every year since 1929 (except 1932). The greatest moments in its history were the hosting of the 1948 Olympic Games and the 1966 World Cup. RAS

Wensleydale's peerage case. In 1856 Sir James Parke, judge of the Court of Exchequer, was raised to the peerage with the title of Baron Wensleydale. However, the patent which conferred the title stated his barony was to be held 'for the term of his natural life'. This was an attempt to revive a right not used since the time of Richard II. There was strong feeling in the Lord's against such a move. Lords *Lyndhurst, *Brougham, and Campbell were united in opposing the change. After great argument, the government gave way and conferred on Parke an ordinary patent of peerage. Life peerages were postponed until 1958. RAS

wergeld was the fixed amount, or blood-price, payable by a killer and his kin to his victim's kinsmen. A man's kin was obliged to seek vengeance for his untimely death, but payment of wergeld was an alternative to blood-feud, and a means of keeping order in a violent society. The amount of wergeld was also an important mark of social status. In the earliest written Anglo-Saxon law code, a nobleman's wergeld was 300 shillings, three times that of a *ceorl. AM

Wesley, Charles (1707–88). Hymn-writer. Like his brother John, Charles was educated at Oxford, ordained in the Church of England, and became a leading methodist preacher. Methodism, it has been said, was born in song; and this was facilitated by the magnificent collection of hymns written by Charles Wesley, perhaps the greatest hymn-writer England has ever known. Favourites like 'Hark! The Herald Angels Sing' and 'Jesu, Lover of my Soul' became familiar far beyond the bounds of methodism. The Wesleys understood the use of hymns for popular devotion and instruction. In Charles's eucharistic and advent hymns, or his celebration of the sacramentalism of daily life, traditional Christian teaching was restated, and indeed became part of the religious discourse for the next 200 years. Charles disapproved of John Wesley's ordinations and remained closer to the Church of England. JFCH

Wesley, John (1703–91). Founder of methodism. Educated at Christ Church, Oxford, and elected a fellow of Lincoln College, Wesley was ordained in the Church of England. At Oxford in 1729 he gathered round him a group of devout Christians who were nicknamed methodists because they sought to follow strictly the method of study and practice laid down in the statutes of the church. After a short-lived missionary journey to Georgia, during which he was much influenced by some Moravian brethren, Wesley experienced a sudden conversion (1738). He felt that after much searching he had 'found spiritual rest' and that his mission was to evangelize England. For over 50 years Wesley travelled all over Britain on horseback, averaging 5,000 miles annually, preaching thousands of sermons, often three times a day. Finding the churches closed to him, he began field-preaching and organized local religious societies and a body of lay preachers, which became virtually a church within the church. When the movement spread to America, Wesley was led to ordain a superintendent or bishop. Wesley wished methodism to remain within the Church of England, but this was not possible, given official Anglican hostility and the desire of conference (the supreme body of methodism) for independence. JFCH

Wessex, kingdom of. The origins of the kingdom of Wessex are obscure. Archaeological evidence shows that the communities of Germanic settlers established in the middle Thames region in the late 5th and early 6th cents. constituted one of the principal elements, but literary evidence emphasizes a more southerly origin in the movement of *Cerdic and his successors in the early 6th cent. from a base in the Portsmouth area into Hampshire and Wiltshire. The Isle of Wight and the Meon valley in eastern Hampshire were settled by a people of *Jutish origin. Historic shape was given to Wessex in the reign of *Ceawlin (560–91), who claimed descent from Cerdic and was described by *Bede as a *bretwalda (overlord of the Germanic settlers in Britain). At the battle of *Dyrham near Bath in 577, he won a victory over the Britons which left him in control of Bath, Cirencester, and Gloucester. His people at this stage, or possibly only the ruling group, were known as the *Gewisse*, but also as the West Saxons to distinguish them from the other Saxon folk who gave their names to Sussex, Middlesex, and Essex. They accepted Christianity in the 7th cent. and bishoprics were set up (apparently representing the duality of the predominant groups) at *Dorchester-on-Thames (634) and at *Winchester (662). Under two powerful kings, *Cædwalla (685–8) and *Ine (688–726), the West Saxons extended their political control over Devon and Somerset to the borders of still Celtic Cornwall. A significant British element of acknowledged legal status survived in the kingdom. Ine died on pilgrimage to Rome and for the rest of the 8th cent. Wessex played a subordinate part to *Mercia in English affairs. Revival came in the 9th cent. during the reign of *Egbert (802–39). After his defeat of the Mercians at *Ellendun in 825 the *Anglo-Saxon Chronicle* referred to him as *bretwalda, and indeed for a brief period he seems to have been recognized as overlord by all the English kingdoms, including Mercia (830–1). This did not prove permanent, but the south-east and East Anglia continued to acknowledge his lordship. The creation of a greater Wessex, involving effective mastery of all lands south of the Thames, can firmly be attributed to his reign. His son *Æthelwulf (839–58) and his grandsons, especially his youngest grandson, *Alfred the Great (871–99), consolidated the West Saxon hold over Sussex, Surrey, and Kent. But the whole political structure of England was changed in the second half of the 9th cent. by the Danish invasions which resulted in the conquest of more than half the country. Alfred's heroic defence resulted in the peace of *Wedmore (878) which left all England north and east of Watling Street and the river Lea in Danish hands. Alfred regained London after 886 and skilfully exploited his position as sole surviving effective representative of the ancient ruling English dynasties. He emphasized the elements of Christian kingship and legal lordship over his own people, and extended it over the Mercians and over all Christian English under Danish rule. From that point onwards the story of the kingdom of Wessex folds absolutely into the story of the kingdom of England. Danish kings and warlords were gradually conquered and their territories reabsorbed into England in the reigns of Alfred's son *Edward the Elder (899–924), and grandsons *Athelstan (924–39), *Edmund (939–46), and *Edred (946–55). After 954 and the death of *Erik Bloodaxe, the last Scandinavian ruler of York, we deal with a unitary kingdom of England. Intrinsic reasons within Wessex can be adduced to explain why Wessex emerged as the nucleus of such a kingdom: better communications, greater agrarian wealth, proximity to the continent, control of the south-east with its economic and political potential in London, Kent, and Canterbury. Geographic and strategic advantage came to Wessex from its distance from the main thrust of Danish attack across the North Sea. Full credit also must be given to the West Saxon dynasty in the critical century, 871–975, notably to Alfred and ultimately to his great-grandson *Edgar (959–75), who laid heavy emphasis on their position as Christian monarchs, extending the range of their legitimate authority beyond the West Saxon people to embrace all the Christian inhabitants of England. HL

West, Benjamin (1738–1820). History and portrait painter. West was born a British subject in Pennsylvania, remaining a loyalist all his life. He learned to paint in America, and studied for three years in Italy before settling in London in 1763. He was a founder member of the Royal Academy, becoming the second president on the death of *Reynolds. In 1769 he began a long association with George III when the king commissioned a series of pictures for Buckingham House and, later, several for the state rooms at Windsor castle. In 1772 West was appointed historical painter to the king, but he refused a knighthood. His *Death of Wolfe* (1771), described by Reynolds as revolutionary, broke with the tradition of painting heroes in classical costume and showed contemporary dress. JC

Westbury, Richard Bethell, 1st Baron (1800–73). Lawyer. Bethell was born in Bradford on Avon (Wilts.) and went to Wadham College, Oxford. After Middle Temple he began practising with great success. In 1851 he entered Parliament for Aylesbury as a Liberal, was made solicitor-general in 1852 and attorney-general in 1856. His ambition for the lord chancellorship was widely known and he obtained it, with a peerage, in 1861. He began a series of legal reforms but in 1865, peculation having been discovered in his office, a select committee found in him a 'laxity of practice and want of caution'. One of Bethell's weapons had been vituperative sarcasm, together with overweening self-confidence, which did not help him in the crisis. He was censured by the House of Commons and obliged to resign. JAC

Western European Union (WEU). This international security organization was initiated on 6 May 1955 when the Federal Republic of Germany and Italy joined the existing *Brussels Treaty Organization. This was a consequence of the refusal of the French National Assembly to ratify the European Defence Community plan (EDC). The collapse of the plan was in part due to the British government's refusal to take part in supranational (as opposed to intergovernmental) security organizations, and the emergence of the WEU can be seen as a fulfilment of British goals. The pledge made by Britain to maintain troops in Europe in peacetime was a major innovation in foreign policy.

*NATO remained the primary West European security organization, but from 1958 to 1973 the WEU structure allowed the British government to consult with the six WEU

states that had formed the *EEC without involving other NATO members. Following British accession to the EEC, ministerial meetings of the WEU ceased. The organization was reactivated from 1984 to strengthen European influence within NATO and to promote EC foreign policy co-ordination (European Political Cooperation, EPC). Britain was among the states that prevented the integration of WEU into the European Union's supranational structure, instead confirming it as an intergovernmental institution in the *Maastricht treaty. The WEU played a prominent role in the Bosnian crisis in the 1990s. CNL

Western Isles is the name given to the administrative region which since 1973 has been the local government area for the Outer Hebrides (Lewis, Harris, North and South Uist, Benbecula, Barra, Eriskay, and other small islands). Until 1973 Lewis was part of the county of Ross and Cromarty, and the other islands of Inverness-shire. Although the islands are diverse geologically, they are mostly rocky or peaty with sandy shores, supporting very limited agriculture, mainly in crofting townships, which provide some of the raw material for the woollen goods manufacture for which Harris is famed. Various attempts to diversify manufacturing (most notably Lord Leverhulme's establishment of Leverburgh, in Harris) have had very limited success). The isolation of the Western Isles has helped Scottish Gaelic to survive as a living language, with distinctive accents in the different islands, and the local authority fosters Gaelic, for example by bilingual road and street signs. CML

Western Samoa is a group of mountainous South Pacific islands with a population of about 165,000. Since 1962 they have been formed into an independent nation and joined the Commonwealth in 1970. The capital is Apia and the main crops are copra, cocoa, and bananas. In 1899 eastern Samoa was annexed by the USA, Western Samoa by Germany. In 1914 troops from New Zealand, 1,600 miles to the south, occupied Western Samoa and it became a New Zealand *mandate in 1920. JAC

West Indies is the general geographical term for the many islands of the Caribbean, the largest of which are Cuba, Hispaniola (politically Haiti and the Dominican Republic), *Jamaica, Puerto Rico, *Trinidad, Guadeloupe, and Martinique. After Columbus' landing on San Salvador in 1492, Spain claimed the whole region, concentrating first on Hispaniola, then on Cuba and Puerto Rico. Sugar plantations were established and black African slaves introduced. The first inroads into the Spanish monopoly came when Spain, in the early 17th cent., was still struggling to put down the Dutch revolt in Europe. English settlement started at *St Kitts (1623) and *Barbados (1627), followed by *Antigua and *Montserrat (1632), Anguilla (1650), and the conquest of Jamaica in 1655 by a Cromwellian expedition. The *Bahamas, claimed as early as 1629, did not receive much attention until after the Restoration. Meanwhile, France had acquired Guadeloupe and Martinique (1635), *Grenada in the 1640s, and had established a foothold on the western part of Hispaniola. Dutch settlements were on Curaçao and St Eustatius in the 1630s, and the Danes, entering the race comparatively late, acquired St Thomas in the Virgin Islands in 1666 and purchased St Croix from the French in 1733. Control by European governments was necessarily fitful and the West Indies gained its reputation for piracy and buccaneering.

The 18th cent. saw incessant warfare between the colonial powers, towns repeatedly sacked, and islands taken and retaken, often for use as bargaining counters at the peace. Tobago changed hands so often that its inhabitants were said to live in a state of betweenity: at one stage, Charles II, who did not have it, granted it to the duke of Courland. Admiral *Vernon became a national hero in Britain in 1739 when he sacked Porto Bello, Spain's base in Panama, at the start of the War of *Jenkins's Ear. At the end of the *Seven Years War in 1763, Britain retained Grenada, *Dominica, *St Vincent, and Tobago at the expense of France. When British sea power wobbled during the War of *American Independence, the French and Spanish took Grenada, Montserrat, St Kitts, St Vincent, and the Bahamas, but had to return them at the treaty of *Versailles in 1783, retaining only Tobago.

During the *Revolutionary and Napoleonic wars, Britain added Trinidad from Spain (1802) and *St Lucia from France (1814). By this time the West Indies were beginning to lose some of their economic importance to Britain, and the West Indian lobby some of its influence in Parliament. The slave trade was abolished in 1807 and slavery in the British empire in 1833. The colonial distribution did not change greatly in the course of the 19th cent. The western part of Hispaniola, ceded by Spain to France in 1697, saw a black rising in the 1790s and established its independence as Haiti in 1804: the other two-thirds of the island threw off Spanish rule in 1821, only to fall under Haitian domination, and the Dominican Republic was not established until 1844. British rule in Jamaica was shaken by a rising in 1865, and the governor Edward Eyre recalled in disgrace, but control was reasserted. As a result of the war between Spain and the USA in 1898, Puerto Rico was annexed to the USA, and Cuba was declared an independent state, though under American tutelage.

Since the Second World War, the great majority of West Indian islands of any size have become sovereign states. In 1945 only Cuba, Haiti, and the Dominican Republic were independent. In 1958 the British introduced the West Indian Federation, long an aspiration, to improve political and economic co-operation, but it rapidly fell victim to inter-island rivalries. Jamaica resented that the capital was in Port of Spain, Trinidad, 1,000 miles away, and voted in a referendum to pull out. Trinidad followed suit and the Federation was wound up in 1962. Jamaica and Trinidad then became independent, followed by Barbados (1966), Bahamas (1973), Grenada (1974), Dominica (1978), St Lucia (1979), St Vincent (1979), Antigua (1981), and St Kitts and Nevis (1983). Two of the enduring legacies of British colonialism are the use of the English language and an awesome addiction to cricket. JAC

West Midlands. The metropolitan county of West Midlands was the creation of the Local Government Act of 1972. It brought together the county boroughs of Birmingham,

Wolverhampton, Walsall, Dudley, Warley and West Bromwich, Solihull, and Coventry. In addition, Brownhills was transferred from Staffordshire; Halesowen and Stourbridge from Worcestershire; Sutton Coldfield from Warwickshire; and a number of parishes from the rural district of Meriden. The county headquarters was at Birmingham. The authority was abolished, along with the other metropolitan counties, by the Local Government Act of 1985. JAC

Westminster, palace of. From the time of Edward the Confessor to the early years of the reign of Henry VIII, Westminster was the main royal residence. The palace grew up around the abbey built by the Confessor on Thorney Island and consecrated in December 1065, a week before the king's death. The abbey was completely rebuilt by Henry III from 1245 onwards, though far from finished in his lifetime. William Rufus built the great hall and first held court in it in 1099: it was reroofed by Richard II and for centuries was the home of the law courts, the place of impeachments and state trials, and the venue for the coronation banquet. John began the building of St Stephen's chapel, which was taken over after the Reformation by the House of Commons. Henry II built domestic rooms for the household, including the great chamber, and Henry III added the painted chamber, adorned with biblical stories. In Edward III's reign the Jewel Tower was built, later to be used as the House of Lords Record Office. By the 15th cent., the palace was a rabbit warren of rooms and corridors, swarming with servants and lawyers, and liable to flooding. In 1512, soon after a grand celebration in honour of the king's young son, who died a week later, there was a disastrous fire. Henry moved to Whitehall and the palace of Westminster was totally given over to public offices. After the fire of 1834, only Rufus' great hall was left. The rest was rebuilt according to the design of Sir Charles *Barry, assisted by Augustus *Pugin. JAC

Westminster, provisions of, 1259. The provisions of Westminster formed a stage in the conflict between Henry III and his baronial opponents led by Simon de *Montfort. By the provisions of *Oxford in June 1258 Henry had agreed to a mechanism of control, including the appointment of a supervising committee of fifteen. On 13 October 1259 in Westminster Hall, a detailed and miscellaneous programme of law reform was approved in response to a number of petitions and complaints. It clarified rights of inheritance and of wardship, tried to prevent lords from forcing attendance at their courts, and forbade the transfer of property to monastic institutions without the consent of the lord. It also included populist clauses restricting the offices of state and the command of fortresses to Englishmen. The provisions were reissued in 1262 and 1264 and incorporated in the statute of Marlborough of 1267. The activities of the manorial courts were brought under closer scrutiny. JAC

Westminster, statute of, 1275. The first statute of Westminster, promulgated in Edward I's first Parliament in 1275, was a great survey of the existing law, whose 51 clauses dealt with a vast variety of problems. The intention was to redress some of the grievances which had been felt during the new king's absence and which had been revealed by the hundred roll inquiries of 1274–5. Among the items mentioned were shipwrecks, elections, rapes, coroners, bail, cattle-rustling, wardship, tolls, feudal aids, and guardianship. The statute revealed a more positive attitude towards law, accepting the need to modify and adapt it. JAC

Westminster, statute of, 1285. The lengthy statute 13 Edw. I, usually known as Westminster II, was designed to remedy miscellaneous grievances at law. The most important provisions were to tighten up the donor's rights over gifts of property; to improve the lord's command of services due to him by enabling him to sue in the royal courts; to protect the rights of the owners of advowsons; and to increase the security of property by imprisoning bailiffs suspected of dishonesty in royal gaols. The statute was part of a determined attempt by Edward I to regulate a mass of law and custom and impose fairer solutions. JAC

Westminster, statute of, 1290. The statute 18 Edw. I, known as Westminster III, was intended to prevent magnates being deprived of their feudal rights, such as *escheat, marriage, or *wardship, by the sale of estates. It was declared that, on sale, the same feudal rights must continue and that land could not 'come into *mortmain'. The statute is often known by the opening words *'Quia emptores' ('because purchasers'). It is generally accepted that the statute failed to hold the position. JAC

Westminster, statute of, 1931. The immediate cause of the statute was the complaint of Mackenzie King, prime minister of Canada, that the governor-general had acted unconstitutionally in 1926 in refusing him a dissolution. This led the imperial conference of that year to discuss constitutional relationships. *Balfour, philosopher by inclination, defined Britain and the dominions as 'autonomous communities, equal in status, in no way subordinate one to another'. The statute of Westminster, 22 Geo. V c. 4, confirmed this position, leaving the crown and membership of the Commonwealth as the only link. Governor-generals were selected on the advice of the dominion's prime minister and the Westminster Parliament specifically gave up any claim to legislate for a dominion, save at its own request. *Cosgrave, the prime minister of the Irish Free State, gave assurances that the new powers would not be used to change the 1921 settlement. His successor, *De Valera, did exactly that and a trade war ensued. The bonds of empire were tenuous indeed. JAC

Westminster, treaty of, 1462. Edward IV, hoping to recover some of the influence in Scotland lost by the Wars of the *Roses, agreed in 1462 at Westminster (sometimes called the treaty of London) with John *Macdonald, lord of the Isles and earl of Ross, and James, 9th earl of *Douglas, that they should become his vassals and help him to gain the Scottish throne. They would then share the lands north of the Forth. Nothing came of the grandiose plan and it took Edward twenty years to recapture the border fortress of Berwick. JAC

Westminster, treaty of, 1654. Though the Dutch had suffered more during the first *Anglo-Dutch War, the treaty which concluded it was mild, since *Cromwell was anxious to bring to an end this damaging quarrel between two protestant nations. The English *Navigation Act of 1651 remained on the statute book and the Estates of Holland agreed to exclude the House of Orange from public life, thus removing a potential source of assistance to the Stuarts in exile. But the issues of sovereignty, saluting the flag, fishing rights, search, and contraband, which had been so prominent at the start of the war, were compromised. JAC

Westminster, treaty of, 1674. The treaty, signed on 19 February, brought to an end the third *Anglo-Dutch War. Since the Dutch were anxious to make a separate peace in order to concentrate their resources on defeating the French, they offered concessions which did not reflect the balance of the fighting. They agreed to salute the English flag, pay a small indemnity, and return New Amsterdam, recaptured in August 1673. JAC

Westminster abbey has been the setting for the coronation of English monarchs since 1066, when William the Conqueror was crowned in the new church of *Edward the Confessor, perhaps to underline continuity; from Henry III to George II sixteen monarchs were buried there. There was a monastery on the isle of Thorney by the Thames before Edward began his great building *c.*1050 but there is no certain evidence when it had been founded. *Harold Harefoot was buried there in 1040 at the end of his short reign. Nor is there anything above ground surviving of Edward's church, dedicated on 28 December 1065, with the king absent on his death-bed. It was however on a grand scale. The present abbey was begun by Henry III in 1245 and was much influenced by contemporary French styles: it is the highest of great English medieval churches and therefore seems narrow. The body of Edward the Confessor was moved there in 1269. The chapter house where, until the Reformation, Parliament met was one of the earliest parts to be completed. Building on such a scale was inordinately expensive and progress in finishing the abbey was very slow. The nave was not completed until the reign of Henry VII, who began his own addition—the fan-vaulted chapel. Work had already started on the foundations for the two western towers.

The abbey's close connection with the monarchy saved it from the fate of most other abbeys at the Reformation, which were turned into parish churches or plundered for their stone. The abbot's house was taken over by Lord Wentworth and the bishopric established in 1540 suppressed (leaving Westminster's claim to be a city). Mary began the restoration of the monastery but at the end of her brief reign it was closed again and the buildings made over to *Westminster School. Though the abbey suffered from the iconoclasts of the 1640s, its prestige helped it during the Commonwealth: *Cromwell had the stone of *Scone taken to *Westminster hall for his inauguration as lord protector and was given an elaborate funeral in the abbey, only to be disinterred in January 1661. *Wren began the work of restoring the fabric of the abbey after years of neglect but not until 1745 were the western towers completed, to the design of Nicholas *Hawksmoor. By that time the tradition of affording the great and mighty burial in the abbey was well established, as a British pantheon. *Spenser was buried in what became known as Poets' Corner in 1599, *Newton in 1727, *Pitt in 1778, Samuel *Johnson in 1784. At length the abbey became too crowded to permit of further burials. But among the host of memorials, the most moving is that which commemorates the dead of the Great War, a brass to a 'British warrior, unknown by name or rank'. JAC

Westminster Assembly, 1643. Set up by the Long Parliament to reform the English church, it consisted of 30 members of both houses and 121 ministers of varying opinions. Though most members favoured *presbyterianism, a forceful minority of independents, to Scottish astonishment, opposed it. The Scots, despite wanting full-blown non-Erastian presbyterianism in England, agreed to the *Solemn League and Covenant (1643), which resulted in English presbyterianism being firmly under parliamentary control. The assembly produced a calvinistic *Directory of Worship* (1644) to replace the Book of Common Prayer, the presbyterian *Westminster Confession*, and two presbyterian *Westminster Catechisms*, which were its most enduring work. WMM

Westminster cathedral. Commissioned by Cardinal Herbert Vaughan, the third archbishop after the restoration of the Roman catholic hierarchy in Britain, it was designed by J. F. Bentley in neo-Byzantine rather than Gothic style and built 1895–1903; outspoken opposition from many quarters was accompanied by derision ('Vaughan's Folly'), and his attempt to establish Benedictine monks at the cathedral was unsuccessful. The neo-Renaissance exterior, which includes a lofty campanile, contrasts bands of Portland stone with terracotta brick, but the interior decoration, richly ornamented with marble and mosaic, remains unfinished. The choir has long sustained an outstanding reputation for polyphonic music. ASH

Westminster hall, built by William Rufus (1097) as an extension of Edward the Confessor's palace, is the only surviving part of the original palace of *Westminster. Used initially for feasts, then early parliaments, it developed into an administrative centre, housing the Courts of Common Pleas, King's Bench, Chancery, Exchequer, and Star Chamber. From mid-17th to mid-18th cent., legal activities proceeded alongside stalls selling books and trinkets, rendering it a fashionable haunt. The hall has suffered fires and floods, seen coronation banquets, trials (*More, Charles I), and lyings-in-state (*Gladstone, *Churchill) under its hammerbeam roof, and is now linked to the House of Commons. ASH

Westminster School was founded shortly after the building of Westminster abbey. Henry VIII made the last abbot the first dean of the school in 1540. It was refounded by Elizabeth I 20 years later, connecting the school closely with her father's foundations of Christ Church, Oxford, and Trinity College, Cambridge. The great headmaster Richard Busby during his 57 years at the school (1638–95) increased its prestige, attracting the ruling classes. In 1848 there were eight former pupils in Lord John *Russell's ministry. Following the report of the Public School Commission 1864, the school was separated from the abbey, whilst retaining a religious connection. PG

Westmorland was one of the smaller counties, about 40 miles from Stainmore in the east to Bowfell in the west. The greater part was fell country and the market towns—Appleby, Kendal, Kirkby Lonsdale, and Kirkby Stephen—were small. The southern part was drained by the rivers Lune and Kent running into Morecambe Bay, the northern by the Eden, draining into Solway Firth. Down the middle of the county ran the Tebay gorge, made by the Lune, and followed in 1846 by the railway and in 1971 by the M6 motorway. The administrative arrangements reflected the topography of the shire. It was divided into two baronies, north and south, each in turn divided into two wards. The barony of Kendal was in the diocese of York, and then of Chester: the barony of Westmorland was in the diocese of Carlisle. Not until 1856 were they both placed under Carlisle. The population was thinly spread. In 1811, the county had only 45,000 inhabitants, 7,000 in Kendal, 2,200 in Appleby, and just over 1,000 in Kirkby Lonsdale and Kirkby Stephen.

The name Westmorland seems to mean the country west of the moors—i.e. the Pennines. It formed part of *Brigantes territory, was occupied by the Romans, colonized by Anglo-Saxons pushing out the Britons, and became a rather loosely attached part of the kingdom of *Northumbria. From the early 10th cent. there was considerable Norse settlement, from Ireland and the Isle of Man, leaving evidence in words like fell, ghyll, tarn, and how. There was also much penetration south by Scottish and Pictish settlers. *Athelstan established political control in 927, negotiating with the kings of Scotland and the Picts at Eamont bridge, just south of Penrith, probably on the line of the existing frontier. But Westmorland remained very much a border area, not integrated into the kingdom of England, and too remote and too poor to receive much attention.

At the time of the Domesday survey in 1086, the Kendal barony was treated as part of Lancashire, while the northern parts of the area were not included at all. Much of the district remained under Scottish control until William Rufus in 1092 seized Carlisle and built a frontier castle there. Its establishment as a recognized county may have been as late as the 13th cent. but by 1290 it was represented in Edward I's parliaments by two knights of the shire.

The natives of Westmorland relied heavily upon sheep-farming in the south, cattle-rearing in the north, with a useful cloth industry in Kendal and some of the other towns. Appleby, the county town, suffered greatly from Scottish raids, since it was athwart an easy line of advance across Stainmore towards Durham and York. It was sacked in 1173 and again in 1388. *Camden in 1586 commented that there was 'nothing remarkable about it besides its antiquity and situation . . . it is of so little resort, and the buildings so mean, that if antiquity did not make it the chief town of the county, and the Assizes were not kept in the castle, where is the publick gaol for malefactors, it would be but very little above a village.'

*Defoe, writing in the 1720s before the Romantic movement, found Westmorland 'eminent only for being the wildest, most barren and frightful of any thing that I have passed over in England, or even in Wales'. But by the mid-18th cent. travellers were discovering the charms of the Lake District and, with Ullswater, Helvellyn, Grasmere, and Windermere, Westmorland became better known. Its status as a national treasure owed much to the Lakeland poets in the early 19th cent. By mid-century railways were probing into the region—to Windermere in 1847, Coniston 1859, Keswick 1864, and Lakeside at Newby Bridge by 1869. Purists shuddered. R. S. Ferguson wrote in 1894 that 'nowadays railways and cheap trips have opened the district to everyone. The Liverpool man and the Manchester man have claimed it as their own, and studded the banks of Windermere with villas fearfully and wonderfully made . . . steam gondolas plough the waters once dear to Wordsworth.' In the 1990s, tourism is still the salvation and despair of the region. But, with the passing of years, gondolas on Windermere, Coniston, and Ullswater and steam trains to Lakeside have come to symbolize a bygone age of tranquillity.

By the local government reorganization of 1972, the county was merged with Cumberland and north-west Lancashire to form Cumbria. JAC

Westmorland, Charles Neville, 6th earl of (1542–1601). Westmorland, a catholic, succeeded his father in the title and great estates in Durham in 1564. Five years later he joined his neighbours Lord Dacre and the 7th earl of *Northumberland in the rising of the *northern earls to release Mary, queen of Scots, from captivity and restore the old religion. After initial success, occupying Durham and Ripon and saying mass in the cathedrals, he fled before Lord *Sussex and went into exile, never to return. He survived as a pensioner of Spain, implicated in many plots against Elizabeth's life. This was the last baronial rising in England and, significantly, in the northern counties where personal loyalties remained. Raby castle and the Neville estates were taken into crown hands and sold in the 1630s to Sir Henry *Vane, father of the parliamentarian, and ancestor of the earls of Darlington, dukes of Cleveland. JAC

Westmorland, Ralph Neville, 1st earl of (*c.*1364–1425). Son of the 3rd Baron Neville, he succeeded to the title and great northern estates in 1388. He supported Richard II and was created earl in 1397. But he joined Henry Bolingbroke, his brother-in-law, in 1399 and was made marshal for life. He stayed loyal to Henry IV and was given the Garter in 1403. Neville profited considerably from the defeat of the Percies in 1403, taking many of their estates, and was primarily responsible in 1405 for crushing the rising of *Nottingham, Archbishop *Scrope, and *Northumberland, it was said by treachery. His children by two marriages numbered 23: *Warwick the Kingmaker was his grandson. JAC

Weston, Richard. See PORTLAND, 1ST EARL OF.

West Sussex. See SUSSEX, WEST.

West Yorkshire. See YORKSHIRE, WEST.

Whewell, William (1794–1866). Polymath, historian and philosopher of science, and Cambridge reformer, Whewell came from Lancashire where his father was a carpenter. At Cambridge with John *Herschel he reformed the mathematics courses; at Trinity College he served as tutor, professor of mineralogy, professor of moral philosophy, and finally master. His study of Kant made him unhappy with the prevailing understanding of science, going back to Francis *Bacon. Whewell believed that in science an intuitive leap must be associated with careful induction, and used this insight to display the history of science as a matter of finding the appropriate fundamental ideas in the various sciences. He believed that God's existence could not be proved, but that science could deepen and refine faith. Involved in numerous scientific bodies, he was greatly respected; but Sydney *Smith said that science was his forte, omniscience his foible. DK

Whigs. The Whigs were one of the two main political parties in Britain between the later 17th and mid-19th cents. The term, which derived from 'whiggamore', the name by which the Scots *covenanters had been derogatorily known, was first used by the Tories during the *Exclusion crisis to brand the opponents of James, duke of York. Whiggery thus began as a distinctly oppositional and populist ideology, which saw political authority stemming from the people, a 'contract' existing between them and their king, whom they might resist if he overrode their interests. The Whigs naturally placed emphasis on parliamentary, as opposed to monarchical, authority, while their libertarian creed made them espouse toleration for protestant dissenters. Early Whig principles played a key part in shaping the 1689 revolution settlement, though the Whigs themselves soon became divided over their attitudes to power-holding. The court Whigs ignored the party's populist attitudes and recognized the monarch's position in a 'mixed' or 'balanced' constitution. Their experience in office 1694–8 gave them a pragmatic view of government; they supported the wars against Louis XIV, sought partnership with London's extensive business interests, and made beneficial use of patronage. Under their aristocratic *Junto leaders they acquired remarkable cohesion as a parliamentary party and achieved effective electoral organization. The smaller group of country Whigs remained critical of government, and under *Harley in the later 1690s were absorbed into the 'new Tory Party'. As firm supporters of the Hanoverian succession the Whigs presided over George I's accession in 1714 and afterwards engineered the long-term proscription of their Tory rivals. The resulting 'Whig oligarchy' achieved a hitherto unseen stability in political life over the next few decades, with power concentrated in the hands of the great Whig families. Even so, Whig discontent with *Walpole's administration grew appreciably in the 1730s and helped to topple him in 1742.

By the mid-1750s the ruling 'old corps' Whigs under Pelhamite direction were losing their party motivation under the vicissitudes of factionalism, and George III's antipathy to party resulted in many being removed from office. In the 1760s all politicians regarded themselves loosely as Whigs, but the term was consciously appropriated and used by the remnants of the old corps who had regrouped as an aristocratic country party led by *Rockingham. Their consciousness as a 'party' was promoted by *Burke in the 1770s and 1780s, with economical reform and the reduction of the power of the crown essential to their evolving ideology. The political crisis at the end of the American war brought them briefly to office until Rockingham's sudden death in July 1782. In 1783 they were the driving force behind the *Fox–North coalition, but the king's long-standing hatred of Fox hastened their dismissal, enabling him to appoint the younger *Pitt to head a government of essentially nonparty Whigs. The Rockingham Whigs, now led by the duke of *Portland and Charles James Fox, split in 1794 over their reaction to the French Revolution, with 'conservative' Whigs under Portland joining Pitt's administration, and the Foxites remaining in opposition. The latter kept alive the name of Whig, associating it with political, religious, and social reform, thereby contributing to the ideological context of the *Reform Act of 1832. The mid-19th cent. saw Whiggery largely subsumed into liberalism, and the Whig label disappeared from political vocabulary. AAH

Whistler, James Abbott McNeill (1834–1903). Painter and etcher, born in Massachusetts. Dismissed from West Point, Whistler joined the US navy, where as a cartographer he learned etching and decided on a career in art. He went to Paris in 1855 before settling in London in 1859, where he enjoyed an early success, not only for his art but also for his flamboyant life-style. Often controversial, he conducted a number of campaigns against both critics and public. In 1877 he sued *Ruskin for libel and although he won his case and was awarded one farthing in damages, the expenses bankrupted him. In one year, he was able to restore his fortunes with the sale of etchings made in Venice. His later life saw both artistic and financial success, with his salon in Chelsea a fashionable gathering place. In 1890 he published *The Gentle Art of Making Enemies*, a collection of caustic letters and comment. JC

Whitby, Synod of, 664. The Northumbrian church, which began with *Paulinus and Roman Christianity, was revived by *Aidan, who introduced Celtic customs from Iona. The most controversial difference, the dating of Easter, was the main issue at Whitby. *Bede highlights the inconvenience at court when King *Oswui's Celtic Easter conflicted with his queen Eanflæd's Roman observance, claiming previous tolerance was out of respect for Aidan. As the dates rarely diverged and Aidan died in 651, it is possible the debate was prompted by political tension between Oswui and his son Alchfrith, subking of Deira. Influenced by *Wilfrid, whom he made abbot at Ripon, expelling Celtic adherents, Alchfrith had recently adopted Roman practices.

Key Northumbrians representing the Celtic cause at Whitby were Abbess *Hilda, Cedd, bishop to the East Saxons, and Bishop Colman of Lindisfarne. Wilfrid was spokesman for the visiting Frankish bishop Agilbert from Wessex, and his priest Agatho, main advocates for Rome. Oswui's decision to conform with the greater body of Roman Christianity may have been politically expedient. He probably defused a situation created by Alchfrith, and won vital papal acknowledgement of his supremacy in England. Of greater significance, Whitby prepared the way for unification of the English church by *Theodore, next archbishop of Canterbury. AM

White, Gilbert (1720–93). Naturalist. Born in his grandfather's vicarage in the village of Selborne (Hants), into a scientifically minded family, White was educated at Oriel College, Oxford (fellow, 1744), and ordained in 1747, but preferred a Hampshire curacy to a 'fat goose living' elsewhere to stay close to the family home The Wakes (inherited eventually, with tortoise). A scientific naturalist by intention and committed diarist and record-keeper, observant, accurate, and unassuming, he started a 'Garden Kalendar' in 1751 which developed into 'The Naturalist's Journal' (1768); this, with letters and papers, provided source material for *The Natural History of Selborne* (1788), subsequently an English classic, reflecting concern for the behaviour of living things rather than dead specimens, and evoking village life. Gardening was one of White's greatest pleasures, but he regularly visited London, Oxford, and relations, was essayist and poet, corresponded with other naturalists, and influenced local husbandry. ASH

Whiteboys was the name adopted by agrarian rebels in Ireland from 1761 onwards. The immediate cause of the outrages seems to have been the enclosure of common land for pasture, but grievances soon included tithes and extortionate leases. Bands of armed men rode at night with comparative impunity, levelling walls, maiming cattle, and burning houses. The centre of the movement was Munster, where the native Irish were poorest. Supported by widespread intimidation, it was difficult to deal with and continued for some decades. JAC

Whitefield, George (1714–70). Evangelist. Born at the Bell Inn, Gloucester, which his father kept, Whitefield entered Pembroke College, Oxford as a servitor in 1732. Attracted by the Oxford *methodists, he openly joined them in 1735. Ordained deacon and then priest (January 1739), he went to America for the first of seven visits in 1738. If his first sermon reputedly drove fifteen hearers mad, his breakthrough as an evangelist came in February 1739 when he preached in the open air to 200 Kingswood colliers. This daring irregularity made his name and soon he was preaching to thousands. He first used extempore prayer in 1738, giving up the surplice in America, where he also exchanged pulpits with dissenters. His championship of predestination interrupted his friendship with *Wesley in the late 1740s and the breach between calvinist and arminian methodists remained unhealed. From 1741 Whitefield's London base was Moorfields tabernacle, with other tabernacles at Norwich (1751), Bristol (1756), and elsewhere. In 1744 he met Lady *Huntingdon, proving no match for her 'tip-top gentility'. He is said to have delivered 18,000 sermons, preaching 40–60 hours a week. He visited Ireland, Scotland, and Wales as well as America, where he died, worn out, at Newbury Port, New Hampshire, in September 1770. Fair, stout, irritable, orderly, and punctual, with an inimitable voice, his weakness as an organizer has obscured his lasting influence as the *evangelical revival's greatest preacher. CB

Whitehall palace as a royal residence lasted some 150 years. It began life as the London residence of the archbishops of York and was called York Place. *Wolsey spent lavishly on it and, on his fall in 1529, it was seized by Henry VIII, who had lost the greater part of Westminster palace by fire in 1512. He added a tiltyard for tournaments, a tennis court, cockpit, and bowling alley, and bought up fields to the west which eventually became St James's Park. The palace remained ramshackle, a collection of miscellaneous buildings linked by galleries, with the main road from Charing Cross to Westminster running right through it. Elizabeth I entertained her suitor the duc d'Alençon there in 1581 in a number of makeshift canvas pavilions. Her successor James I resolved to build a fitting reception hall. His first attempt was burned down in 1619, but the second, the *Banqueting hall, designed by Inigo *Jones, was finished by 1622. Charles II used the palace a great deal after the Restoration with various suites fitted out for his assortment of mistresses, but William III disliked it and began developing *Hampton Court and *Kensington palace, in the country, as alternatives. A disastrous fire in 1698, which left only the Banqueting hall standing, provided the opportunity to abandon a palace that was too sprawling, public, and inconvenient. By the 18th cent. it was being taken over for government offices. JAC

Whitelocke, Bulstrode (1605–75). Whitelocke's father was a judge and he was called to the bar after graduating from St John's College, Oxford. Returned to the Long Parliament for Marlow in 1640, he took the parliamentary side, but was moderate in tone and prominent in peace discussions. In 1648 he was made one of four commissioners for the *great seal, a position he held several times subsequently. He took no part in the trial of the king. From 1653–4 he was ambassador to Sweden, leaving an account of his negotiations. Close to *Cromwell, he urged him to accept the crown, served in 1657 as a member of the House of Lords, and was on the *Council of State under Richard *Cromwell. At the Restoration he profited from his moderate stance, *Clarendon writing charitably that he had been 'carried away with the torrent'. He was allowed to live in retirement without harassment. Given his position, it is not surprising that Whitelocke has been regarded by many commentators as a trimmer and time-server, but he is a reminder that many men did not wish to take sides or place themselves in peril. His *Memorials of the English Affairs*, first published in 1682, is useful, but of even greater value is his diary, covering the whole of his life, first printed in 1990. JAC

White Ship. Its wreck on 25 November 1120 destroyed Henry I's plans for the succession, because his only legitimate son William died aged 17 in the disaster. An immediate second marriage to *Adela of Louvain produced no male heir, so, in 1126, Henry nominated his daughter, the Empress *Matilda, as his successor. The *White Ship* was sailing from *Normandy to England, on one of the many routine voyages made necessary by the cross-channel

Anglo-Norman realm, when it hit a rock in the Seine estuary. Two contemporary chroniclers say that the crew was drunk. DB

Whitgift, John (*c.*1530–1604). Archbishop of Canterbury (1583–1604). Born in Lincolnshire, Whitgift was educated at Pembroke Hall, Cambridge, a centre of reform, where he remained throughout Mary's reign. Ordained (1560), he was successively Lady Margaret professor of divinity (1563–7), master of Pembroke Hall (1567) and Trinity College (1567–77)—where he expelled *Cartwright—regius professor of divinity (1567–9), dean of Lincoln (1576), bishop of Worcester (1577), and archbishop in succession to *Grindal. Though strongly calvinist, he vigorously defended *episcopacy and Anglican liturgy and ritual. As archbishop, he worked hard for uniformity; his Six Articles (1583) insisted on the Thirty-Nine Articles, the Book of Common Prayer, and the royal supremacy, to be enforced by the Court of *High Commission. Despite his fierce offensive against puritans, he upheld calvinist doctrines of predestination and election in the Lambeth articles (1595). WMM

Whithorn, diocese of. Established in 731 as one of the four northern bishoprics under *York, its centre in extreme south-west Scotland was on the site of a Celtic monastery founded by *Ninian (*c.*440). It failed to survive the Danish invasions of the 9th cent. and was not revived. The site has been extensively excavated. WMM

Whittingham, William (*c.*1524–79). Translator of the Bible. Educated at Oxford, where he became a fellow of All Souls, Whittingham travelled on the continent from 1550, mixing in calvinist circles. He spent the reign of Mary in exile, succeeding John *Knox in 1559 as minister at Geneva. Much of his time was devoted to a new translation of the Bible, the 'breeches version', published in Geneva in 1560. Until the issue of the Authorized Version in 1611, this was by far the most popular translation. Returning to England in 1560, he was appointed by Elizabeth to the deanery of Durham in 1563. Objection was made to his puritan tendencies, including dislike of the surplice, and he was said not have been validly ordained. He died before these charges had been adjudicated. JAC

Whittington, Richard (d. 1423). Mercer and benefactor. Youngest son of a Gloucestershire landowner, Whittington established himself in London, dealing in valuable imported silks and velvets, and thrice becoming master of the Mercers' Company. He regularly loaned large sums of money to the crown, but his licence from Henry IV to ship wool from London without paying the normal heavy export duty and two separate terms as collector of customs and subsidy in London and Calais enabled him to recoup the debts. A city alderman in 1393, he was elected mayor three times (1397–8, 1406–7, 1419–20). Dying widowed and childless, his executors devoted his great wealth to further public works, including improvements to St Bartholomew's hospital, Guildhall, and Newgate gaol. The Whittington charity remains active. The myth introducing a cat, his early poverty, and eventual knighthood evolved in the early 17th cent., but retains its charm today in pantomime. ASH

Whittle, Sir Frank (b. 1907). Frank Whittle, the distinguished aeronautical engineer and inventor of the jet engine, began his career as an apprentice with the Royal Air Force at the RAF College, Cranwell. While still a student he developed the idea of the gas turbine or 'jet' engine, but was discouraged from pursuing it by the technical and administrative difficulties in Britain in the 1920s. However, in the lead-up to the Second World War he was assigned to a special project to develop the engine, and despite shortage of materials and much official incomprehension was brilliantly successful. His team produced a viable gas turbine and installed it in an aeroplane to create the first British jet fighter in the closing stages of the war. Other inventors, in Germany and elsewhere, had been working on similar lines but it was Whittle's expertise which was taken up in Britain and the USA to produce the radically new generation of jet aircraft for both civil and military applications after the war. RAB

Wiglaf (d. 840), king of Mercia (827–9 and 830–40). Wiglaf's family background is not known, but he came to power in 827 at a time when several cadet lines were competing for the throne and, perhaps to help consolidate his position, he married Ælfflæd, the daughter of Ceolwulf I. In 829 Wiglaf was expelled by King *Egbert of Wessex who had already greatly reduced Mercian control south of the Thames. Egbert ruled Mercia for a year, but Wiglaf returned in 830 and reasserted Mercian control in Middlesex and Berkshire. In 836 he presided over a church assembly at Croft (Leics.), which was attended by the archbishop of Canterbury and all the southern bishops. Wiglaf was the only one of his line to rule; his grandson Wigstan was murdered by the son of Wiglaf's successor Beorhtwulf and was subsequently venerated as a saint at Repton, where he and Wiglaf were buried. BAEY

Wihtred (d. 725), king of Kent (690 (as joint king), sole ruler 692, 694–725). Wihtred is chiefly remembered for laws issued in 695, the third and last of the surviving Kentish 'codes'. Much of its emphasis is ecclesiastical. The first clause grants the church immunity from taxation. Others seek to enforce the church's rules on marriage, fasting, and the observance of the sabbath. We cannot assume that such laws were necessarily much more than indicative of the aspirations of ecclesiastics who played a large part in drawing them up. But it is important that they *could* have stood for much more; for an enforced godly regime. Certainly Wihtred was a major benefactor to monasteries. A characteristic of his Kent was wealth: an abundant silver coinage of 'sceattas' was minted there, and Kent lay at a great maritime crossroads. The silver coins and the pious efforts of Wihtred's reign must relate to this and to one another in ways no less important than hard to disentangle. JCa

Wilberforce, William (1759–1833). Evangelical philanthropist and anti-slavery campaigner. Born in Hull, the son of a merchant, and educated at St John's College, Cambridge, he was MP for Hull (1780), Yorkshire (1784–1812), and Bramber (1812–25). Following his conversion (1784–85) he became a leading evangelical, helping found the Proclamation Society to prosecute blasphemy and vice (1787), the Society for Bettering the Condition of the Poor (1796), the *Church Missionary Society (1799), and the *Bible Society (1804). His *Practical View of Christianity* (1797) went through 15 English and 25 American editions by 1825. In 1787 he joined the campaign against the slave trade, which he promoted in Parliament through his friendship with Prime Minister *Pitt, though his inept tactics may have delayed success, which came only in 1807. In 1823 he joined the *Anti-Slavery Society, though ill health forced his retirement from public life in 1825. ER

Wild, Jonathan (*c.*1682–1725). Thief-taker and anti-hero. Trained as a buckle-maker, imprisonment for debt brought Wild into contact with the underworld, then into handling stolen property. He circumvented the 1707 Act which made fences accessories by deliberately planning robberies from identifiable victims, from whom he could then claim reward money on return of their property. Ostensibly an instrument of justice by apprehending criminals whose conviction would be rewarded, he simultaneously organized his own thieves into allotted gangs, supporting but controlling them by 'bringing them to justice' if he chose. His activities prompted a statute whereby receiving a reward for returning deliberately stolen goods was an offence comparable to the felony (1718), but the self-delusion that his public services outweighed his own crimes eventually ended at Tyburn. ASH

Wilde, Oscar (1854–1900). Dublin-born aesthete, dramatist, and, by his own declaration, genius. At Oxford Pater and *Ruskin entranced him more than his classical studies, though a visit to Greece confirmed his commitment to the artist's life. His early *Poems* (1881) were derivative but his personality, extravagantly displayed on an American tour the following year, was original. 'To become a work of art is the object of living,' he wrote, anticipating *The Picture of Dorian Gray* (1891), though much of his art went into his conversation. Something of its brilliance survives in essays like 'The Critic as Artist' but in the theatre he found his true *métier*: 'I took the drama, the most objective form known to art, and made it as personal . . . as the lyric or sonnet.' At the height of his powers, his ambivalent relationship to Victorian society most subtly deployed with *The Importance of Being Earnest* (1895), disaster struck. Publicly reviled, accused of sodomy, he was sentenced to two years' hard labour in Reading gaol. Five years later, neglected in Paris, he was dead. JNRS

'Wild Geese' was the name given to catholic Irish professional soldiers who served in the armies of European sovereigns, especially after the conclusion of the Williamite war (1689–91) in Ireland. In fact connections of this kind long pre-dated 1691, but the treaty of *Limerick of 1691 sent 12,000 Irish troops to join the French army, and thereafter the combination of discouragement at home and opportunity abroad kept the flow of men going. They served with distinction in the armies of France, Austria, and Spain. Their leaders inevitably began to be absorbed into the ruling class of the great catholic monarchies, especially after 1759, when the last hope of Stuart restoration vanished. The French Revolution abolished the Irish Brigade in 1791. It also destroyed their monarchical Counter-Reformation world. BPL

Wilfrid, St (*c.*634–*c.*709). Bishop of Northumbria. Noble, Northumbrian, sent by Queen Eanflæd to study at *Lindisfarne, Wilfrid then travelled to Kent, to Lyons, whose bishop offered him a marriage alliance and a secular career, and to Rome. Back home, he introduced Roman ways in the monastery of Ripon, given to him by Alchfrith of Deira, was ordained by Agilbert, Frankish bishop of Wessex, for whom he spoke at the Synod of *Whitby (664) in favour of the Roman Easter, which won the day, and was sent for consecration in Paris as bishop for the Northumbrians.

His subsequent career was very stormy, involving deprivation (664–9, 678–86, 691–706) and divisions of his see, appropriation of assets of his monasteries, disagreements with the Northumbrian kings Ecgfrith and Aldfrith and with the archbishops of Canterbury *Theodore and Berhtwald, visits to the pope to appeal (he put in some missionary work in Frisia in 678–9 *en route*), imprisonment, exile, and Northumbrian councils (Austerfield in 703 and Nidd 706). While not at home, he worked amongst the South Saxons, the West Saxons in the Isle of Wight, and in Mercia. He died as bishop of *Hexham at Oundle in 709 or 710 and was buried at Ripon. His relics were moved to Canterbury, probably in 948, by Archbishop *Oda.

The Wilfridian view, expressed in the partisan life attributed to Eddius Stephanus, was apparently that the good in the Northumbrian church was Roman, that it had been introduced by Wilfrid, and that, like a latter-day Old Testament prophet, he was persecuted by persons with ignoble motives. The historical perception of the opposition, strong at Whitby (under *Hilda), *Lindisfarne, and perhaps *Jarrow, possibly enunciated in *Bede's measured account, differed, giving Wilfrid less prominence. Various issues were at stake. Wilfrid's episcopal style and ideals resembled those in Gaul, where bishops had large sees, huge estates, and a high political profile, combining personal asceticism with public grandeur. Theodore implicitly favoured smaller sees, as more manageable and less corrupting, while Irish bishops tended to be glorified priests, inferior in most ways to abbots. There were questions of which monastery could establish precedent for supplying bishops to a particular see, Whitby having designs on York. Wilfrid may have wanted archiepiscopal status for York.

Wilfrid was in many respects—his ferocity, retinue, the loyalty of his followers, and his death-bed distribution of treasure—an ecclesiastical version of a traditional aristocratic warlord. His wealth was, however, not out of line, which suggests that other considerations irritated his kings. He refused to persuade Queen *Æthelthryth to consummate her marriage to Ecgfrith, and if, as is possible, the estates which she had given Wilfrid at Hexham would have reverted to Ecgfrith when she retired, had she not so alienated them, Ecgfrith's irritation must have been compounded. Wilfrid's promotion of Æthelthryth's cult was perhaps in part to emphasize, by association, his own sanctity. His promotion of King *Oswald's cult makes it plausible that he supported claims of Oswald's offspring to the Northumbrian kingship, against those of *Oswui's family. Ill-gained and ill-used power is ill-tolerated. Wilfrid's activities in Mercia and his friendship with Mercian kings, notably *Wulfhere and *Æthelred, might also have rendered him suspect.

The intensity of feeling Wilfrid aroused is testimony to his importance. Conversion (of Frisians and Anglo-Saxons), foundation of monasteries (including Oundle in Mercia and Selsey in Sussex), and building (his crypts at Ripon and Hexham survive) were grist to his mill. His churches were in Gallic style, proclaiming his allegiances. He also brought from Gaul esteem for the rule of St Benedict, to whose English diffusion he contributed. He was a channel for Roman influence, for instance promoting the cult of the Virgin, but he did not dramatically enhance papal authority. AER

Wilkes, John (1725–97). Described on his coffin as 'A Friend of Liberty', Wilkes was the central figure in a number of constitutional disputes which protected and extended the political rights of ordinary citizens. After a rakish and dissolute youth, he became MP for Aylesbury in 1757. A leading opponent of the government, especially of the king's favourite, Lord *Bute, Wilkes was arrested after the publication on 23 April 1763 of an article in No. 45 of his paper, the **North Briton*, and charged with seditious libel. He successfully challenged the use of *general warrants which had been issued, but could not avoid condemnation by Parliament for publishing a scandalous, obscene, and impious libel. Wilkes fled to the continent in 1764. On his return in 1768 he was treated as a popular hero and elected MP for Middlesex. However, he was imprisoned for libel and expelled from the Commons, despite repeated re-election for Middlesex. 'Wilkes and Liberty' became the slogan of the London crowds who demonstrated in his support from 1763 to 1774, when he became lord mayor of London and was able to assume his seat as MP for Middlesex. Wilkes advocated complete religious toleration and supported the American colonists. He was a champion of mass politics, henceforth one of the strands in popular radicalism. JFCH

Wilkie, Sir David (1785–1841). Scottish painter renowned for his lively representations of the commonplace in Scottish life, which influenced many Victorian artists. His first important work, now in the National Gallery of Scotland, was *Pitlessie Fair* (1804), while *The Village Politicians* (Scone palace) confirmed his reputation when it was submitted to the Royal Academy in 1806. Wilkie had many important patrons, including the duke of *Wellington and the prince regent, who commissioned *The Penny Wedding* in 1818. He was painter-in-ordinary to three monarchs and knighted in 1836. Between 1825 and 1828, Wilkie was in Europe and his later works, showing Italian and Spanish influences, were less popular. In 1840 he visited the Holy Land to paint authentic biblical scenes. On the return journey he died at sea, an event commemerated by *Turner in *Peace: Burial at Sea* (Tate Gallery). JC

Wilkins, John (1614–72). One of the most prominent of the remarkable group of amateur scientists in the mid-17th cent. He attended Oxford and took holy orders, becoming chaplain to a number of noblemen. In his first book, *Discovery of a World in the Moon* (1638), he argued that man could reach the moon and that it could be made habitable. The 'invisible college' of scientists which he organized was the forerunner of the *Royal Society, established in 1660 with Wilkins as secretary. Joining the parliamentary side in the Civil War, he was appointed warden of Wadham College, Oxford, in 1648 and in 1656 married a sister of Oliver *Cromwell, retaining his college headship. In 1659 he transferred to the mastership of Trinity College, Cambridge, and though he lost it at the Restoration, he was made dean of Ripon in 1663 and bishop of Chester in 1668. His reputation was as a conciliator and latitudinarian, anxious not to oppress the dissenters. Though some sneered at him as a time-server and trimmer, it is extraordinary that a man could live in such turbulent times and win such widespread praise. *Burnet wrote that Wilkins had 'as great a mind and as good a soul' as any man he had known, and *Evelyn, a close friend, thought him 'universally beloved by all that know him'. *Aubrey wrote that Wilkins was 'no great read man, but one of much and deep thinking, and of a working head'. JAC

Wilkinson, Ellen (1891–1947). One of Britain's best known and most successful female politicians. After completing a history degree at Manchester University, she became an organizer for the National Union of Women's Suffrage Societies and then, in 1915, for the National Women's Organization of the Amalgamated Union of Co-operative Employees. Although an early *Communist Party member, she became Labour MP for Middlesbrough (1924–31) and for Jarrow from 1935. It was in the 1930s that 'Red Ellen' made her reputation as a crusader for the unemployed with extensive involvement in the Unity campaign, the famous Jarrow march, and in the campaign against fascism in Germany and Spain. Her fiery oratory became legend. By the outbreak of war she had risen from rebel to front-bencher and was given a position in the Home Office in 1940. As minister for education 1945–7 her career has been regarded with disappointment by some. Yet she achieved much: the implementation of the 1944 Education Act, the raising of the school-leaving age to 15, despite Treasury opposition, the building of new schools, and the introduction of 'school milk'. Her achievement was more impressive given the unfavourable prevailing economic conditions. She died of bronchitis in 1947. LHM

Wilkinson, John (1728–1808). One of the most remarkable ironmasters and entrepreneurs of his day, Wilkinson was born in Cumberland. His father made money producing box-irons and then moved near to Wrexham, where he made high-quality cylinders, much used by *Boulton and *Watt. John Wilkinson established furnaces at *Coalbrookdale, using coal in place of charcoal, and diversified his output. Iron barges on the Severn carried his wares, he provided the ironwork for the great *Iron Bridge in 1779, and manufactured lead pipes. But his most profitable line was boring cannon. Said to be harsh and combative, he amassed a large fortune. His sister married Joseph *Priestley and in 1792 Wilkinson was reported to be sympathetic towards the French Revolution, paying his workmen in *assignats*. The *DNB* remarks coyly that 'his domestic arrangements were of a very peculiar character' and he left three illegitimate sons. Known popularly as 'Iron-mad Wilkinson', he was buried on his Cumberland estate near Ulverston in an iron coffin inside an iron tomb, roofed by an iron pyramid, and with an inscription, in iron letters, that he had himself composed. JAC

William I (1027/8–87), king of England (1066–87) and duke of Normandy (1035–87), known as 'the Conqueror', was born at Falaise in central *Normandy. His father was Robert the Magnificent, duke of Normandy (1027–35), and his mother was Herleva, a woman about whose origins various theories have been developed, but who was certainly an established partner of the duke. William's succession to the duchy occurred when he was 8 and had the prior agreement of the Norman magnates and of his lord, the king of France. The first years of his rule in Normandy were turbulent and his survival at times precarious. He faced rival claimants from within his own family and his illegitimate birth was sometimes mocked by contemporaries—his other nickname ('the Bastard') was used in his own lifetime—but, after defeating Norman rebels in 1047 and 1053–4, he established a formidable control within the duchy which was never thereafter seriously threatened. For reasons which are not entirely clear, his overlord the French king turned against him in the early 1050s and he had to overcome invasions led by Henry I of France and the count of Anjou, Geoffrey Martel, in 1053–4 and 1057. William began to make territorial gains to the south of Normandy in the 1050s and in 1063 acquired the large county of Maine. In 1051 he received a promise of succession to the English kingdom from *Edward the Confessor, apparently out of gratitude for the protection which Edward had been given while in exile in Normandy, and in 1066 he defeated *Harold Godwineson at the battle of *Hastings to make good his claim. William appears initially to have tried to rule conquered England with the support of an aristocracy which was a mixture of natives and Normans, but it is clear in retrospect that there was no genuine trust between the two groups and that the policy was doomed to failure. Six years of often brutal campaigning, which included the notorious 'harrying of the North' in the winter of 1069–70, were needed to complete the subjugation of William's new kingdom. He thereafter relied almost exclusively on his northern French followers, a new aristocracy whose dominance is clearly revealed by *Domesday Book. After 1072 he visited England only infrequently, usually to deal with crises such as the revolt of the earls in 1075 or the threatened invasion from Denmark in 1085. The last decade of his life was troubled by the revival of enemies in northern France, dissensions within the ruling group of Normans fomented by his eldest son *Robert Curthose, and threats of invasion of England from Scandinavia. On his death-bed, he divided his lands between Robert Curthose, who received Normandy, and his second surviving son, William Rufus, who was given England. The reasons for this division are not definitively known and have been much discussed; it is probable that years of conflict had made him distrust Robert, whose claims to Normandy were none the less undeniable, and that he was influenced by a long-standing custom whereby territorial provision was often made for the younger sons of the Norman ducal kindred.

William's achievement was based on a powerful personality, which appears to have overawed almost all who came into contact with him, and a strong physique which made him one of the most formidable warriors of his day. A capacity for often excessive cruelty and for leadership in war was combined with an unbending will and a shrewd political mind. His power base in Normandy was constructed around a small inner circle of kinsmen and associates who were ruthlessly advanced at the expense of rivals. Members of this group were also at the centre of Norman rule in England. His wife *Matilda, to whom he was faithful in a way which is remarkable among contemporary medieval kings and aristocrats, often acted as his deputy in Normandy when he was in England. He cleverly ensnared Harold Godwineson in a web of perjury, by obliging him to swear the celebrated oath at either Bonneville or Bayeux, and he skilfully used his reputation as a religious reformer to secure the papacy's sponsorship of the war of conquest of 1066 and its co-operation in the reorganization of the English church which followed, in which Archbishop *Lanfranc of Canterbury was a skilled and well-chosen collaborator. Intelligently and probably cynically, he used Edward the Confessor's promise of the succession to construct a framework of legality within which lands could be transferred from the dispossessed English to French newcomers; even if this was a disorderly process exacerbated by the rapacity of many of the conquerors (to which William himself seems at times to have turned a blind eye), the idea of legal continuity created a structure within which royal authority could sometimes operate effectively. He maintained English overlordship over Wales and Scotland. He enjoyed a measure of good fortune, most notably in the deaths in 1060 of his major rivals in France, the French king Henry I and Count Geoffrey Martel, which enabled him to intervene in England without having to be much concerned about possible threats to the duchy. He was also lucky in that Harold Godwineson's victory at the battle of *Stamford Bridge over *Harold Hardrada removed a contender whom William would otherwise have had to fight and in that *Edgar the Atheling was not a credible alternative around whom the English could unite after 1066. William's death was followed by a civil war between his sons over his inheritance, which was not finally resolved until Henry I's reunification of Normandy and England in 1106. This struggle is testimony to the solidity of William's achievements, since his sons were basically fighting to continue them. Almost every aspect of the *Norman Conquest is controversial. But there can be no doubt that it was William's formidable abilities which laid the foundations for its success. DB

Bates, D., *William the Conqueror* (1989); Douglas, D. C., *William the Conqueror* (1964); Fleming, R., *Kings and Lords in Conquest England* (1991).

William II (*c*.1060–1100), king of England (1087–1100), known as 'Rufus', the second son of William the Conqueror, was a ruler whose reputation has suffered because of the opinions of contemporary ecclesiastics, appalled by his sometimes cynical attitude to religion. William became England's king as a result of his father's death-bed bequest. Whether his succession should be interpreted as involving the disinheritance of his elder brother *Robert Curthose is a controversial matter which cannot be conclusively resolved from the existing sources. Whatever the case, the consequence was that William rapidly faced widespread revolt in England in 1088 in support of Robert, who had acquired *Normandy. A major motive for revolt, quite apart from personal loyalties towards Robert, was certainly that the great magnates holding cross-channel estates feared the implications of having the territories under two different rulers. After defeating his opponents, William set out to weaken Robert's increasingly fragile hold on the duchy, organizing expeditions there in 1091 and 1094. In 1096 Robert mortgaged the duchy to William in order to take part in the First Crusade, and from then until his death, William ruled over his father's cross-channel realm and regained some of the authority over Normandy's neighbours which his brother had lost. William also consolidated Norman rule in northern England, establishing effective royal power at Carlisle, and he supported the continuing Norman-French penetration of Wales. William's notoriety is based partly on the rapacity of his financial exactions and in particular on the way in which such established royal rights as that of administering bishoprics and abbeys during vacancies were ruthlessly exploited to divert their revenues into the royal treasury. The king also had a habit of making provocative remarks which offended the susceptibilities of more scrupulous clergy and he lacked the skill and sincerity of belief which had by and large ensured his father's good relations with the church. All of these factors contributed to his quarrel with St *Anselm, the gifted theologian and philosopher whose appointment to Canterbury had been dramatically sanctioned by the king as he lay seriously ill at Gloucester in 1093. A series of arguments culminated in the archbishop going into exile in 1097 and remaining out of England until after William's death. Historians differ as to the central causes of this conflict and where personal responsibility should be placed; it is at least certain that the king lacked tact, but it is also notable that most bishops continued to work with him and to support him. William can be seen as personifying the masculine military virtues of his age; the fact that he never married led to suggestions of homosexuality and several clerical commentators accused him of sexual depravity. In most respects, his reign was a success, but his blustering and inflammatory personality made him enemies. He was killed while hunting in the New Forest on 2 August 1100. His death was probably an accident; all arguments that he was murdered rest on highly circumstantial evidence. His death did, however, come at a very convenient time for his younger brother, the future Henry I, who was nearby and who reacted with such promptness that he was crowned king within three days of his brother's death. The nickname 'Rufus' first appeared in the early 12th cent., and refers either to red hair or to a ruddy complexion.

DB

Barlow, F., *William Rufus* (1983).

William I (*c*.1142–1214), king of Scots (1165–1214), later known as 'the Lion'. Younger brother and successor to Malcolm IV, he was granted the earldom of Northumberland by his grandfather David I in 1152, and never accepted the loss of the border counties to Henry II in 1157. When Henry faced a major rebellion in 1173–4, William invaded Northumberland and Cumberland in a disastrous bid to reassert Scottish control. Captured at *Alnwick, he had to recognize Henry as the superior lord of Scotland by the treaty of *Falaise. Scottish independence was restored by the quitclaim of *Canterbury, and in 1192 the papacy confirmed that the Scottish church was free of all external authority save the pope's. But Anglo-Scottish relations remained tense and, while Scotland retained its formal independence, King John imposed stringent terms by the treaty of *Norham. Although William's conflicts with the English crown distracted his attention from the Highlands and Isles, his long reign nevertheless saw important advances on the lines laid down by David I, and 'against his few startling failures we must set a larger though less dramatic record of unflagging achievement'. New burghs were founded outside the traditional royal heartlands; Anglo-Norman families gained new estates, especially north of the river Tay; and the bishopric of Argyll was established in about 1192. Though native lords were by no means excluded from William's favour, the intensification of royal control triggered a series of rebellions along the periphery, in Galloway, Moray, Ross, and Caithness. The crushing of these risings was striking testimony to William's resources and ability; but a contrast must still be drawn between the effectiveness of royal power in the Lowlands and its much more restricted nature in the far north and west. In addition, the Isles remained, however loosely, under the overlordship of Norway. William died at Stirling and was buried in Arbroath abbey, which he had founded in honour of St Thomas *Becket. Not until the 14th cent. was he referred to as 'the Lion', an epithet evoking his reputation as an enforcer of justice. KJS

William III (1650–1702), king of England, Scotland (as William II), and Ireland (1689–1702), prince of Orange. Appointed stadtholder of Holland and Zeeland, and captain- and admiral-general of all the Dutch provinces for life in July 1672, these posts were rendered hereditary in 1674 and 1675, when William was additionally elected stadtholder of Utrecht and Gelderland. He was the only child of William II of Orange and Mary Stuart, eldest daughter of Charles I, and was born on 4 November, eight days after his father's death, at a time of extreme crisis in Orange's relations with Amsterdam, always the seat of anti-Orangist sentiment. Twenty years of republican rule then ensued, setting the Orangist interest at a discount: it was excluded from all future participation in Holland's government, the young prince's upbringing being left to his mother and then to his redoubtable paternal grandmother, Amalia van Solms. Like his cousin and lifelong antagonist Louis XIV, William's early life was overshadowed by adversity, though this proved preparation for an astute character with a destiny of exceptional challenge. Impressively educated in sciences and languages, and severely tutored in Dutch republican doctrine, William yet had his Stuart ties, the exiled Charles II conferring the Garter on his infant nephew in 1653. Charles's restoration in 1660 in fact saw Orange's readmission to Holland's public life, the 10-year-old William being ceremonially received at Amsterdam.

During the 1660s William, puny in stature and incurably asthmatic, reached manhood. The Dutch republicans tried to bolt the door against any renewed Orange challenge. In 1667 the Holland stadtholderate was abolished, and the other six provinces following suit in 1670. William's first visit to England in November 1670, when he was received with gratifying honour, left him distrustful of Charles II, who was now planning the dismemberment of the Dutch republic in conjunction with Louis XIV. The Anglo-French attack in 1672 brought forth so strong an Orangist reaction that the Dutch savagely discarded republican government and bore the 22-year-old William upwards as the embodiment of resistance to aggression. In the formation of an anti-French front, William attained European stature and, returning to England in October 1677, was able to take momentous advantage of Charles II's embarrassed foreign policies by marrying his 15-year-old cousin Princess Mary, the elder and indubitably protestant daughter of James, duke of York, a professed catholic since 1670. William's underlying objective, frustrated by Charles II's wiles and Louis XIV's bribes, was to bring England into the anti-French front, but since Mary at this time was heir to the British crown, after her father, William manifestly enhanced his own more distant claim through his mother. The duke of York's last son by his first marriage had died in 1671, but his second duchess, the Italian *Mary of Modena, at 19 only four years the senior of Princess Mary, might well have a healthy son. From different motives the British and French monarchs resolved to acquiesce in the Orange marriage. Difficult though the marriage proved to be for two people of very different temperaments, and remaining childless, it enabled William to play the dynast and laid the foundation for his intervention in England's affairs in November 1688. His visit in July 1681 confirmed William's view that the collapse of the opposition to his father-in-law's succession would indefinitely prolong British non-alignment in Europe's struggle against France. His 'failure' to prevent *Monmouth's attempt against James II from Holland in May 1685 may have been calculated, William presuming that the expedition would end in disaster.

In November 1685 James II's assertion of the prerogative on behalf of his non-Anglican subjects alienated the most loyal Parliament a Stuart king had known. That William could prepare to intervene in England in the spring of 1688, some three months before he received the celebrated 'Invitation' of 30 June to rescue English liberties 'before it be too late', was owing to a series of reverses for France, and misjudgements by Louis XIV. The French thrust across the Rhine in September 1688, which enabled William to take 40,000 men in 400 ships across to England in autumn weather six weeks later, was occasioned by a series of diplomatic reverses which threatened the collapse of French policy towards Germany. No less consequential was Louis XIV's revocation of the Edict of Nantes in October 1685 which united behind Orange a spectrum of Dutch protestant opinion of unprecedented breadth. Further, the French government endeavoured to arrest economic decline by reimposing in 1688 its harsh tariffs of 1667, a measure devastating for Dutch textile and dairy product exports. If William's move into England brought a renewal of war between the republic and France, even Francophile Amsterdam now accepted that the French market could only be prised open by a resort to arms.

William had no illusions about English dislike of his countrymen, but his experience as a Dutch prince with more influence than real authority was providential for his exercise of Britain's 'Revolution' kingship. He never doubted, and gratefully recognized, Mary's own contribution to the device of the joint monarchy, and her death on 27 December 1694 prostrated him for months. With whatever reservations, the couple had accepted the radical drift of the traditionally based *Declaration of Rights in February 1689; and subsequent statutory changes in treason law and judicial tenure coincided with William's own preferences. But his rule in Scotland, where he delegated too much, is a blight on his record; and those terms in the Act of *Settlement of 1701 which placed limits upon the executive were unmistakably censorious. His conduct of the war against France, once Jacobite forces had been defeated in Ireland in 1691, placed him and his ministries under unrelenting parliamentary scrutiny, the more severe since coherent political parties were still in germination. How much the reforms in British public finance, for example the founding of the *Bank of England in 1694, owed to initiatives from William is uncertain, since such reforms had begun under Charles II. What is clear is that William's contribution to the disclosure of foreign policy to Parliament opened a new era in crown–Parliament relations, even if this was occasioned by strident criticism of his use of prerogative power in this area. When he died on 8 March 1702 he had won a measure of international recognition for Britain's protestant succession, and had endeavoured to resolve peaceably, in partnership with Louis XIV, the problem of the Spanish succession. No British king has stood higher than William in international renown. DDA

Baxter, S. B., *William III* (1966); Jones, J. R., 'William and the English', in Wilson, C. and Proctor, D. (eds.), *1688: The Seaborne Alliance and Diplomatic Revolution* (1989); Robb, N. A., *William of Orange: A Personal Portrait* (2 vols., 1962–6).

William IV (1765–1837) king of the United Kingdom of Great Britain and Ireland (1830–7), king of Hanover. The third son of George III, born 21 August 1765, he seemed unlikely to become king. He entered the navy at 13 as a midshipman and soon demonstrated that despite enthusiasm for the service, his talents were limited and his manners rough. He saw active service in the War of *American

Independence, and became a warm admirer and friend of *Nelson, but his naval service was accompanied by a private life which was far from respectable. George III's first serious illness led to the prince's return home in 1789. He now became duke of Clarence. In 1790 he met Mrs Jordan, an actress, with whom he was to live for many years and who bore him ten children. Although he received promotions to rear-admiral, vice-admiral, and in 1799 admiral, the navy refused his pleas for a return to active service. His long affair with Mrs Jordan ended acrimoniously in 1811, the year in which he became admiral of the fleet. In 1814 he briefly hoisted his flag at sea, commanding the naval escort for Louis XVIII's return to France from his English exile. The death of George IV's daughter Princess *Charlotte in 1818 led to William's marriage to *Adelaide of Saxe-Meiningen, a widowed Bavarian princess. The marriage was a generally happy one, with Adelaide taking care of William's illegitimate children. The duke of Kent died in 1820, leaving a single daughter, Victoria, and the duke of York, George III's second son, died without issue in 1827. George IV's health was failing. William, by now the probable successor, was already in his sixties. In 1827 he was given the resurrected dignity of lord high admiral, intended as an honorific title, but his clumsy attempts to make its nominal authority effective led to his resignation after only fifteen months. He had made serious errors of judgement, but he had also tried to improve naval gunnery, reform the promotion system, and limit flogging. He had also helped the navy to obtain its first steam vessel, the *Lightning*. George IV died on 26 June 1830, and 'Silly Billy' became king, with little in the way of helpful previous experience. He had occasionally spoken in the House of Lords, showing himself more liberal than most of his brothers, supporting catholic emancipation and opposing slavery. He marked his accession by the conferment of titles on his illegitimate children, and exhibited an obvious and sometimes undignified zest for his new role. He also showed a willingness to work hard and an antipathy to extravagance, both of them contrasting with the attitudes of his predecessor. He inherited a political crisis, as the end of a long period of Tory ascendancy approached and *Wellington's government faltered. Unlike George IV, William had no objection to Whig ministers, telling his new premier Lord *Grey that he had 'complete confidence in your integrity, judgement, decision and experience'. During the tense reform crisis of 1831–2, he was not always wise, but ultimately facilitated the enactment of that *Great Reform Act which was crucial in ensuring the peaceful evolution of Britain. William's enthusiasm for change was limited, and in November 1834, having tired of his Whig ministers and disliking the unscrupulous political manœuvres of men like *Brougham and *Russell, he dismissed the government and recalled the Tories under *Peel. This proved a premature and unsuccessful ploy. The new government made gains at the ensuing general election, but not a majority, and William was forced to take the Whig ministers back again for the remainder of his reign. William's relations with his sister-in-law, the widowed duchess of Kent, Princess Victoria's mother, were difficult, with faults on both sides. He was determined to survive to see the young princess achieve her majority and so prevent her mother's regency. He lived for a month after Victoria's 18th birthday and died on 20 June 1837. His young successor wrote of him, 'Whatever his faults may have been, . . . he was not only zealous but most conscientious in the discharge of his duties as a king. He had a truly kind heart and was most anxious to do what was right.' NMcC

Ziegler, P., *King William IV* (1971).

William the Atheling (*c*.1102–20). Heir to the thrones of England and Normandy, who died in the wreck of the **White Ship*. According to William of Malmesbury, as the son of a Norman father (Henry I) and an English mother (Queen *Matilda), he represented the hope of reconciliation between the two peoples, conquerors and conquered. But his father's careful preparations for his unchallenged succession were brought to nothing on 25 November 1120. Like nearly everyone on board the **White Ship*, he was drowned when it hit rocks—allegedly because the crew was drunk—as it left the Norman port of Barfleur. JG

William Longspee II (*c*.1212–50) was the eldest son and heir of Countess Ela of Salisbury (d. 1261) and William Longspee I (d. 1226). He is chiefly remembered for his crusading deeds and the manner of his death. He went on crusade twice, which marks him out from most of his contemporaries and suggests a genuine crusading enthusiasm. He first accompanied *Richard of Cornwall to the Holy Land in 1240–1. Then, in 1247, he took the cross again and with some 200 English knights joined Louis IX of France in Egypt in 1249. The army advanced from Damietta towards Cairo, but was halted by a waterway it was unable to cross until a ford was discovered. On 8 February 1250 the vanguard, including the English under William, crossed at dawn with instructions to secure a bridgehead and advance no further. But Count Robert of Artois rashly goaded the rest of the vanguard into an assault upon the town of Mansourah, where they were overwhelmed in the narrow streets. A legend concerning William's supposed exemplary last stand rapidly developed in England, a vehicle for adulation of the English and savage denunciation of the French. For over a century William enjoyed a considerable reputation as a national crusading hero. SL

William of Malmesbury (1095–*c*.1143) was a monk, born of Anglo-Norman parentage, who set out to write the history of the English in two books, the *Gesta Regum Anglorum* ('The Deeds of the Kings of the English') and the *Gesta Pontificum Anglorum* ('The Deeds of the Bishops of the English'). Both were completed before 1125 and are important commentaries not just on the English past, but on the Anglo-Norman present and the traumas of the *Norman Conquest. Malmesbury was exceptionally learned and widely read. He produced many other works and at the end of his life was writing a contemporary history, the *Historia Novella*, dedicated to *Robert, earl of Gloucester. He is admired as a historian because he travelled to undertake research, because he criticized and evaluated his sources, and because he wrote in a good, classically based, Latin style. DB

William of Occam (*c.*1289–1349). Occam is a village near Guildford in Surrey, from which William presumably took his name. An Oxford Franciscan, he is said to have been a pupil of *Duns Scotus and may have later studied in Paris. His thought developed when his order became involved in a protracted and acrimonious dispute with the papacy on the subject of evangelical poverty, which the Franciscans embraced. Occam's writings in defence of his order led to a summons to Avignon and a condemnation by Pope John XXII. In 1328 Occam and his superior fled to Munich, where they were given protection by the emperor, Lewis of Bavaria. The continuing controversy led Occam to examine the question of sovereignty and the relations of church and state. He argued that the papacy had no standing in temporal matters and that within the church it was subordinate to a general council: though the sovereignty of temporal rulers originally derived from the people, it could not be challenged, save for gross turpitude. In his general methodology, he emphasized both the power and limitations of logic: it could not touch revealed truth and faith, and since it dealt largely with terms of argument, the principle of economy should apply and as few assumptions as possible should be made—hence, 'Occam's razor'. JAC

William of St Carilef (d. 1096) bishop of Durham. A secular priest at Bayeux, he took monastic vows at St Carilef (Maine), became prior there, and then abbot of St Vincent. In 1080 William I chose him as bishop of Durham where, following the English pattern, he replaced the cathedral's secular canons with monks from *Monkwearmouth and *Jarrow (1083). William II made him justiciar, but after implication in the 1088 rebellion, he was arrested and tried. He surrendered his castle to the king before going into exile in Normandy. Restored in 1091, he surprisingly supported the king against *Anselm at the Council of *Rockingham (1095). After another northern rebellion, he was summoned to Windsor, where he died. A great builder, on his return from exile (1091) he brought plans for the magnificent new cathedral, started in 1093. Clever and unscrupulous, he was nevertheless loved by his monks. WMM

William of Wykeham (1324–1404). Bishop of Winchester, keeper of the privy seal, chancellor of England. Possibly the son of a Hampshire serf, he entered royal service (*c.*1348) and superintended the rebuilding of Windsor castle. As bishop of Winchester (1366), he was the greatest ecclesiastical pluralist of the century with twelve appointments, headed by the archdeaconry of Lincoln. As chancellor (1367), he was efficient rather than statesmanlike. The tide of anticlericalism forced him to resign (1371) to make way for laymen. He was briefly chancellor under Richard II (1389–91), but took no further part in politics. He is chiefly remembered for his benefactions to education by founding New College, Oxford (1379), and *Winchester College (1382), the latter a unique corporation, independent of cathedral or monastery, a model for Henry VI's *Eton and *Wolsey's Ipswich college. He also resumed the rebuilding of the cathedral at his own expense. WMM

Williams, John (1582–1650). Archbishop of York, lord keeper. A Welshman, educated at St John's College, Cambridge, Williams was successively dean of Salisbury (1619) and Westminster (1620–40), lord keeper (1621–5), bishop of Lincoln (1621–41), and archbishop (1640). Adviser to *Buckingham, he succeeded *Bacon as lord keeper. 'Pragmatic, talkative and worldly-wise', he advised Prince Charles against his journey to Madrid (1623). Though at odds with Charles I, Buckingham, and later *Laud, his difference with Laud has been exaggerated, for, like him, he preferred order to dogma. A moderate calvinist, he was nevertheless a 'supple bishop', advocating music, ornaments, and compromise over the altar's position, and criticizing Geneva as 'fit only for tradesmen and beggars'. Opposed by extreme Laudians, he was suspended (1637) and imprisoned for anonymously publishing *The Holy Table, Name and Thing* (1636). On release (1640), he worked for compromise between Anglicans and extreme puritans. Favoured by Parliament, he was translated to York, but then imprisoned for leading a bishops' protest against exclusion from Parliament. Released on bail (1642), he escaped, was enthroned at York, and, a royalist, fled to Wales where he died. WMM

Williams, Roger (*c.*1603–83). Colonist. Williams was born in London, attended Pembroke College, Cambridge, and took holy orders. In 1630 he left England for Massachusetts but his belief that magistrates should have no power over conscience gave him an uncomfortable time when he was appointed to the church at Salem. His sympathy for the local Indians also made him suspect to many of his fellow-colonists. Expelled from Massachusetts in 1636, he founded a settlement at Providence and in 1639 established a baptist church, though he subsequently became a seeker, acknowledging no creed. In 1644 he visited England and obtained a charter of self-government for Providence—the foundation of Rhode Island. The colony soon became known for its tolerant attitude and *Jews and *quakers were allowed to settle. In 1654–7 Williams served as governor. *Milton, whom he knew well, admired him as a champion of religious liberty: Cotton Mather thought he had 'a windmill in his head'. JAC

Willibrord, St (658–739). Northumbrian monk and missionary to Frisia. He was educated at *Wilfrid's Ripon, then for twelve years at Rath Melsigi (Clonmelsh, Co. Carlow) in Ireland, under Egbert, who in 690 directed him to work, as Wilfrid had, in Frisia. Consecrated archbishop (as Clement) of the Frisians by Pope Sergius I in 695, he was given Utrecht for his see by the Carolingian mayor of the palace, Pippin II. His monastery at Echternach (in modern Luxembourg), founded in 698, possibly as a base for work in Thuringia and Hesse, enjoyed Pippin's patronage. Its school and scriptorium were famous between the 8th and 10th cents. Willibrord took the cult of *Oswald to Europe and prepared the way for the missionary *Boniface, but his preaching in Denmark failed and whatever ecclesiastical administrative structure he established lapsed. He was buried at Echternach and soon venerated as a saint, his kinsman *Alcuin writing his biography. His cult flourished more in Holland and Luxembourg than in England. AER

Willoughby, Francis, 5th Lord Willoughby de Parham (*c.*1614–66). Willoughby succeeded to the barony at the age of 4. At the outbreak of the Civil War, his presbyterian sympathies led him to join the parliamentary side as cavalry commander in Lincolnshire. But he grew despondent at the turn of events and in June 1644 wrote to Lord Denbigh, 'we are all hasting to an early ruin . . . nobility and gentry are going down apace'. He remained with Parliament until in 1647 he was accused of treason, when he fled to join the royalists in Holland. Charles II appointed him governor of Barbados and he began colonizing Surinam. But in 1652 he was forced to capitulate, returned to England, and took a risky part in royalist conspiracies. At the Restoration he returned to Barbados as governor. He survived heavy fighting against the Dutch and French in 1665 but the following year was drowned in a hurricane. Bulstrode *Whitelocke, the diarist, was his brother-in-law. 'Charming, impetuous, self-opinionated and quarrelsome' is a modern verdict. JAC

Willoughby, Sir Hugh (d. 1554). A minor landowner with some military experience, Willoughby was chosen, possibly by Sebastian *Cabot, to be captain-general of the fleet sent by London merchants to find the North-East Passage in 1553. The expedition sailed around the north of Norway but Willoughby's lack of navigational skills and maritime experience may account for the disaster which overtook him. One of the other ships took *Chancellor into the White Sea, but Willoughby became lost. His journal claimed that he reached as far north as 72 degrees, presumably on Novaya Zemlya, but this is in doubt. It is certain that he and his crew wintered on the Kola Peninsula, were alive in January 1554, but perished later that winter. RB

Wills, W. H. and H. O. A tobacco firm established in Bristol and by the end of the 19th cent. the largest in Britain. In contrast with many other tobacco importers, by the mid-19th cent. the directing members of the Wills family understood the nature of retailing and in particular the significance of brand names in selling to an increasingly literate mass market. Their successes with distinctive pipe tobaccos and a diverse array of cigarettes built a strong market (Passing Clouds 1871, Three Castles 1877, Woodbine 1888). In 1883 they bought the rights to the Bonsack cigarette-making machine enabling them to dominate cigarette-manufacturing in Britain until the 20th cent. In response to international competition, Wills led mergers to form British and American Tobacco in 1902. The family members were patrons of many charities, the most significant being the University College of Bristol, granted its charter in 1909. IJEK

Wilmington, Spencer Compton, 1st earl of (*c.*1674–1743). A younger son of the earl of Northampton. He entered the Commons in his twenties and became Speaker in 1715. At the accession of George II in 1727 he was expected to become first minister, having served as treasurer to the prince, but was outmanœuvred by *Walpole without difficulty. Compensation came in the form of a barony (1728), an earldom (1730), and the lord presidency of the council from 1730 until 1742. A ponderous and formal man, he succeeded Walpole as first minister in 1742, but old, unwell, and with little taste for leadership, he merely presided for a year until his death. Lord *Hervey, one of his many critics, dismissed him as a 'plodding, heavy fellow . . . a subaltern rather than a commander'. JAC

Wilson, Harold, 1st Baron Wilson (1916–95). Prime minister. The son of an industrial chemist, Wilson won an exhibition in history to Jesus College, Oxford. In the event he read politics, philosophy, and economics, gaining a first. In 1940 he joined the war cabinet secretariat as an economist, developing a particular expertise in the area of fuel and power. Elected MP for Ormskirk in the Labour landslide of 1945, Wilson became parliamentary secretary at the Ministry of Works and in 1947 entered the cabinet as president of the Board of Trade, aged only 31. He resigned from the government in 1951 along with Aneurin *Bevan, but was careful to distance himself from Bevan by insisting that his specific quarrel was over excessive expenditure on rearmament. His action none the less established his credentials—not entirely deserved—as a left-winger when Labour began to factionalize in the 1950s.

In opposition Wilson progressed steadily up the hierarchy of the National Executive Committee and shadow cabinet and was made shadow chancellor in 1956 soon after *Gaitskell became party leader. He was out of sympathy with Gaitskell's efforts to 'modernize' the party following Labour's third successive electoral defeat in 1959 and unsuccessfully challenged him for the leadership in 1960. His action did not prevent him being made shadow foreign secretary. Wilson's opportunity came with Gaitskell's unexpected death in January 1963: in the contest for the succession he emerged victorious over George *Brown and James *Callaghan.

With hindsight it is clear that Wilson was the right man for the time. He inherited a party which had recovered its electoral credibility and proceeded to add his own distinctive contribution. His position on the centre-left enabled him to unite the Labour movement in a way Gaitskell would have found difficult. His comparative youth and his call for a technological revolution struck a chord with the optimism of the 1960s. He seemed to stand for the future just as certainly as the Conservatives' Edwardian patricians, Harold *Macmillan and Alec *Douglas-Home, represented the past. In the circumstances, Labour's victory in the election of 1964 was less surprising than the narrowness of the overall majority of four seats.

Yet hopes that Wilson's election might mark a new beginning for Britain were largely disappointed. His first cabinet was elderly and uninspiring. Wilson himself remained wedded to many traditional attitudes, especially Britain's role as a world power and the importance of sterling as an international currency. The creation of a new Department of Economic Affairs, designed to shake off the overweening control of the Treasury, proved a failure. The electorate, however, was ready to give Labour the benefit of the doubt. A parliamentary majority in single figures was scarcely a basis for innovative government and in 1966 Labour achieved a comfortable majority at the polls.

Increasingly, however, Wilson seemed to lose any sense of direction, particularly after the belated devaluation of the pound in 1967. Politics by gesture appeared to replace long-term strategical planning. Wilson's undoubted cleverness became an end in itself. The quality of pragmatism on which he prided himself seemed to degenerate into mere opportunism. Wilson maintained party unity, but at the expense of blurring over internal differences. There was no transformation of the national economy, though Roy *Jenkins, as chancellor, established a reputation for prudent administration. Britain's application to join the Common Market in 1967 came up against General de Gaulle's veto. The qualities of the government seemed to be encapsulated in Labour's attempt to reform the trade union movement. Wilson and his employment secretary, Barbara Castle, invested much of their credibility in the proposed 'In Place of Strife' legislation but were obliged to accept humiliating defeat.

Opinion polls none the less suggested another Labour victory in 1970 and Wilson's defeat at the hands of Edward *Heath came as a considerable shock. In opposition Labour's centre of gravity moved significantly leftwards, a trend which Wilson accommodated without apparent difficulty. He returned to power in 1974 still exuding self-confidence but lacking the apparent dynamism of a decade earlier. In the eyes of many, the new government allowed too much influence to the trade union leaders under the so-called Social Contract. The most threatening issue, however, as far as the internal dynamics of the party were concerned, was membership of the *EEC. Wilson had opposed Heath's action in taking Britain into the community on the somewhat spurious grounds that the terms of entry were unacceptable. In 1975, Wilson allowed the issue of continuing membership to go to a referendum with members of the cabinet openly opposing one another.

There seems little reason to doubt Wilson's assertion that he had decided to stand down early from the premiership at the time he returned to office in 1974. Wilson had perhaps lost his enthusiasm for the game of politics. He was concerned, with some justification, at the attempts of sections of the security services to destabilize his government. Yet his resignation in 1976 was met with disbelief—a commentary, no doubt, on the reluctance of other prime ministers to hand over the reins of power. He stayed on in the Commons until 1983 without playing much of a role. But his reputation rapidly declined, especially because of some curious nominations in his resignation honours list—the judgement of character had never been one of his strengths. Recent attempts at rehabilitation note his excellent record in electoral terms, his capacity to keep the Labour movement relatively united, the continuing economic problems of the last two decades and the important social legislation passed by his first administration. DJD

Pimlott, B., *Harold Wilson* (1992); Zeigler, P., *Wilson* (1993).

Wilson, Sir Henry (1854–1922). Soldier. Wilson was unusual amongst British soldiers in that he was an ardent Francophile and enjoyed the company of politicians. Between 1910 and 1914 he served as the director of military operations at the War Office, preparing plans to send the British army to France in the event of war with Germany. When that war came he served in a variety of liaison posts in France until, in February 1918, *Lloyd George dismissed Sir William Robertson and Wilson succeeded him as chief of the imperial general staff. But soon the prime minister was complaining that his new adviser was as committed to deploying the bulk of the British army on the western front as his predecessor had been. In 1922 Wilson retired from the army and became a Unionist MP for an Ulster seat, only to be murdered on his own doorstep in London by the *IRA. DF

Wilson, Richard (1714–82). Landscape painter. Born in Wales, the son of a clergyman, Wilson's formal training and early career were in portrait painting, but, while in Italy between 1750 and 1756, he decided to concentrate on painting landscape in the classical style. On his return to England, his pictures brought him fame but little employment. He was a founder member of the Royal Academy and appointed librarian in 1776, by which time he had almost ceased to paint. An abrasive character, Wilson was often critical of his contemporaries. He referred to *Gainsborough's 'fried parsley' landscapes and while serving on the hanging committee of the RA would wash over brightly coloured paintings to reduce them to his more restrained tones. He is now regarded as the first great British landscapist and an important influence on 19th-cent. landscape painting. JC

Wilton diptych. A small portable altarpiece of two hinged oak panels, painted and gilded on both sides, almost certainly intended for the private devotions of Richard II. Resplendent with exquisite tooling and expensive pigments, the artist is unknown and the date, author, and motive of commission remain uncertain, despite scholarly debate. A rich but cryptic icon of priestly views of kingship, ambiguous figures of Richard with SS Edmund, Edward the Confessor, and John the Baptist face the Virgin and Child with angels; on the exterior a white hart (Richard's personal emblem) lies couchant, adjacent to other heraldic emblems and arms. It was first recorded in the collection of Charles I, then reputedly given by James II to Lord Castlemaine, before purchase by the earls of Pembroke at Wilton House, from which it takes its name, but has been in the National Gallery since 1929. ASH

Wiltshire is one of the larger counties, more than 50 miles from north to south. It is not easy to perceive much geographical coherence and the balance of the county has constantly changed. The northern towns of Cricklade and Malmesbury had little contact with Mere or Downton in the south, save occasionally at shire meetings, held often for convenience at Devizes in the middle. For decades there was a rough understanding that the two county parliamentary seats would be shared by north and south—a convention formalized after the *Great Reform Act of 1832, which established two divisions with two seats each. Most of Wiltshire was prosperous farming country, the north famous for cheese, the south for butter, and the middle, around Salisbury plain, given over to sheep. On the western fringes, around Trowbridge, Bradford, Westbury, and Melksham, there was a domestic cloth industry, described by *Defoe in his tour of the 1720s as very flourishing.

The county took its name from Wilton, on the river Wylye, a tributary of the Salisbury Avon. As Wilton declined, prosperity shifted first to Old Sarum, then to New Sarum or Salisbury, which, by Tudor times, was one of the ten largest towns in the kingdom, with a population of 8,000. The diocese of the county, founded in 905, also moved around, beginning at *Ramsbury, moving to *Sherborne, and finishing at the two Sarums. The foundation stone of the great cathedral at Salisbury was laid in 1220. In modern times, with the development of Swindon as a railway town, the balance swung again: a hamlet of just over 1,000 people at Old Swindon in 1801 became by 1881 by far the largest town in Wiltshire, with 17,000 people, and, by the 1990s, had risen to more than 170,000.

In pre-Roman times, the area was one of the most thickly populated in the country, the settlers preferring dry chalk lands to the damp and heavily wooded valleys. Wiltshire is the richest of all counties in prehistoric remains, festooned with barrows, and in Stonehenge and Avebury claiming two of the greatest sites in Europe. Though the tribes of the *Durotriges and the *Atrebates had a reputation for bravery, the region fell easily to the Roman advance. The Romans do not seem to have found it congenial and there are comparatively few remains from that period. By the later 6th cent. it had succumbed to the Saxons, who won a decisive victory at Old Sarum in 552. In the early 9th cent. it was heavily disputed between *Mercia and *Wessex and was a centre of *Alfred's struggles against the Danes. The first evidence of its emerging identity is a reference in the *Anglo-Saxon Chronicle* for 800 to the defeat of the *Hwicce from Gloucestershire by the Wilsætes, under their ealdorman Woxtan. In 898 there was a further reference to Ædelm, 'Wiltunscire ealdorman'. The most remarkable survival from the Saxon period is the tiny church at *Bradford on Avon, used as a cottage for many years and only rediscovered in 1856.

In the 13th cent. Wiltshire acquired parliamentary representation, and eventually no fewer than sixteen of its boroughs were given seats, rivalling Cornwall in profusion. The county had a reputation for sturdy independency. Though there were several aristocratic families—the Herberts at Wilton, the Howards at Charlton, and the Bruces at Tottenham Park—the county was too large for one magnate to dominate. The nobility avoided expensive county contests, concentrated on their neighbouring boroughs, and left the shire representation largely to the country gentlemen.

During the Civil War, the region lay between royalist and parliamentary areas and saw much fighting. Wardour castle was held for the king by Lady Arundell, surrendered in 1643, but was retaken by her son and destroyed rather than let it be used by the enemy. *Hopton's victory over *Waller at *Roundway Down in 1643 delivered most of the shire into royalist hands and they held Devizes until 1645. *Penruddock's rising on behalf of Charles II in 1655 was a damp squib, captured Salisbury for one day, and fizzled out.

The 19th cent. saw considerable distress in parts of the county. The cloth industry found competition from Yorkshire hard to meet and there was agricultural depression, especially after 1815. At Great Bedwyn in 1821 *Cobbett noted 'a group of women labourers, who presented such an assemblage of rags, as I never before saw', and at Cricklade he remarked, 'the labourers seem miserably poor. Their dwellings are little better than pig-beds . . . in my whole life, I never saw such human wretchedness equal to this; no, not even among the free negroes in America.' 'This *Wiltshire*', he concluded, 'is a horrible county.' In the *Swing riots of 1830, there were more prosecutions in Wiltshire than in any other county, mainly for machine-breaking.

The diffuse character of the shire made it difficult to agree on a suitable administrative headquarters. Quarter sessions met in turn at Marlborough, Devizes, Salisbury. and Warminster, and local loyalties resisted attempts to centralize. The county council, instituted in 1888, began by meeting at Trowbridge, Salisbury, Swindon, and Trowbridge in turn. By 1930 the position was intolerable. It was carried to meet at Devizes, only for the vote to be reversed when the Trowbridge United football ground became available. County hall opened there in 1940. Wiltshire was not affected by the local government reorganization of 1972, but in 1994 the Banham commission recommended that Swindon be made a unitary authority as Thamesdown. JAC

Wimbledon. The most prestigious lawn tennis club in the world. Wimbledon is the home of 'the Lawn Tennis Championships on Grass', the oldest and most important of all the lawn tennis tournaments. The event is staged by the All England Club and the Lawn Tennis Association, the game's ruling body in England. The first championship was held on 9 July 1877 at the club's original ground in Worple Road, Wimbledon, in south-west London. In 1922 the club moved to its present ground in Church Road. In 1884 women's singles and men's doubles matches were introduced and 1968 saw the first open championship after the amateur/professional player distinction was abolished. RAS

Winceby, battle of, 1643. Sir John Henderson, royalist governor of Newark, set out in October 1643 to relieve Bolingbroke castle, near Horncastle. His force was intercepted by parliamentary cavalry under *Manchester, *Fairfax, and *Cromwell and badly cut up on the 11th. Though a small-scale action, the victory was a valuable boost to sagging roundhead morale and the ease with which the parliamentary cavalry triumphed was ominous. JAC

Winchelsey, Robert de (d. 1313). Archbishop of Canterbury. Born in Kent, educated at Paris where he was rector and at Oxford where he was chancellor (1288), Winchelsey was a distinguished scholar and administrator. Though elected archbishop in 1293, he only returned from Rome after consecration in 1295. As an unyielding upholder of ecclesiastical independence, he obeyed Boniface VIII's bull

Clericis laicos by refusing Edward I's request for clerical taxation (1296) until the pope compromised (1297). Winchelsey, with the barons, again confronted Edward at the Lincoln Parliament (1301), removing Walter Langton, the treasurer, which Edward never forgave. Suspended by Pope Clement V, Edward's former vassal (1306), Winchelsey went into exile. Restored (1307), he actively opposed *Gaveston despite sickness, and was one of the lords *Ordainers (1310). WMM

Winchester (Roman) was Venta Belgarum, capital of the probably artificial *civitas* of the *Belgae. Situated at the intersection of the north–south valley of the Itchen through the east–west chalklands, there is some evidence for late Iron Age activity and a post-conquest military site. By the late 1st cent. the town, unusually, had earthwork defences; augmented in the 2nd cent. and fronted in stone in the 3rd, they enclosed 143 acres. Limited excavation in the interior has located parts of a street-grid, the site of the forum, a temple, and a number of houses. Extensive 4th-cent. cemeteries suggest that Winchester was still a major centre of population, but they passed out of use at the beginning of the 5th cent., at the same time as the abandonment of the buildings in the interior. A few sherds of Anglo-Saxon pottery are associated with this final phase. ASEC

(post-Roman) Winchester revived as a bishop's seat (662), but urban life did not return until a planned and fortified town (burh) was laid out within the Roman walls, probably by King *Alfred. The city expanded dramatically between the 10th and 12th cents., ranking by *c.*1110, with Norwich, second in size after London, and sharing with Westminster the developing functions of a national capital. Besides the cathedral, it possessed royal and episcopal palaces, 57 parish churches, and one of the four great trading fairs of England. However, it declined from the 12th cent. as the close links with the monarchy slackened. Since the 15th cent. it has been only a modest provincial town, though Charles II commissioned a palace there in 1683, and may have toyed with creating an English Versailles. The long decline has left Winchester with a rich urban fabric, as well as 'the richest architecturally of all English bishops' sees'. Important excavations in 1961–71, the first major urban archaeological programme in Britain, have revealed the entire plan of the pre-Conquest cathedral and much else. DMP

Winchester, battle of, 1141. In February 1141 *Matilda captured her rival Stephen at Lincoln and imprisoned him at Bristol. But she quarrelled with his brother *Henry of Blois, bishop of Winchester, and began a siege of his castle. Stephen's queen then led a relief force which, on 14 September, scattered the besiegers and captured *Robert of Gloucester, Matilda's illegitimate brother and chief supporter. When Stephen and Robert were exchanged, Matilda lost the advantage she had gained at Lincoln. JAC

Winchester, diocese of. Roughly conterminous with west and central Hampshire and the Channel Islands, Winchester is the fifth senior see after *Canterbury, *York, *London, and *Durham, and with them its bishop always has a seat in the House of Lords. The first signs of a bishopric were in *c.*660, when *Cenwalh appointed Wine as bishop, but there was no regular bishopric until the West Saxon see was moved there from *Dorchester in *c.*663. In 705 the diocese was divided, Hampshire, Surrey, Sussex, the Isle of Wight staying under Winchester, the remainder west of Selwood going to the new see of *Sherborne. In *c.*909 *Edward the Elder further reduced it to Hampshire and Surrey by removing Berkshire and Wiltshire for the new diocese of *Ramsbury. Though it was marginally enlarged by the addition of the Channel Islands from *Salisbury in 1499, the bishopric was further diminished by the creation of the *Guildford and *Portsmouth dioceses in 1927. The hegemony of Wessex from *Egbert's reign onwards increased the see's importance, and in the 11th cent. Winchester became the national capital. Significant bishops include Swithin (852–62), Egbert's adviser; *Æthelwold (963–84), the monastic reformer who replaced Winchester's secular canons with monks; William Giffard (1107–29), a Benedictine, the first of nine post-Conquest Winchester bishops to be chancellors of England; *Henry of Blois (1129–71), Stephen's brother and papal legate. In *c.*1142 Henry even requested metropolitan status for Winchester. Others include Peter des *Roches (1205–38), a Poitevin, guardian in Henry III's minority; *William of Wykeham (1367–1404), founder of New College, Oxford, and *Winchester College; Cardinal *Beaufort (1404–47), Henry IV's half brother; Stephen *Gardiner (1531–51 and 1553–5), chancellor under Mary; Lancelot *Andrewes (1619–26), scholar and preacher; and Samuel Wilberforce (1869–73). The present cathedral, the longest in Europe (556 feet), begun in 1079 under Walkelin (1070–98), is still basically Norman with Early English and Perpendicular additions, though its 'new' tower (1107) displays the technological influence of the returning crusaders. The cathedral contains the remains of the Saxon kings and a shrine of St Swithin. WMM

Winchester, statute of, 1285. Edward I's reign saw a determination to enforce law and order. After complaining that local people were reluctant to do justice to strangers, the statute (13 Edw. I) declared that each district or hundred would be held responsible for unsolved crimes. Highways were to be widened and cleared of shrubbery in which robbers might lurk. Each man was to keep arms to take part in the *hue and cry when necessary. JAC

Winchester, treaty of, 1153. For many years this agreement between Stephen and his rival Matilda's son Henry was known as the treaty of Wallingford. In fact, the negotiations were at Winchester and were ratified at Westminster. The death of Stephen's son *Eustace, in his twenties, had broken the back of Stephen's cause, and on 6 November 1153 he agreed to recognize Henry as his heir. Stephen died the following year and the prince succeeded as Henry II. JAC

Winchester, William Paulet, 1st marquis of (*c.*1483–1572). 'More of a willow than an oak' was reported to have been Paulet's engaging assessment of himself and, indeed, anyone who could negotiate the vicissitudes of Tudor politics and hold high office in four reigns needed to be pliant. The son of Sir John Paulet, who held land in Somerset and Hampshire, William Paulet probably had legal training and built up a powerful local position. For many years he was associated with the profitable control of wardships—first as joint master and master of the wards 1526–40, then as master of the Court of *Wards 1540–2, then as master of wards and liveries 1542–7. In the Parliament of 1529 he sat for Hampshire. From 1537 to 1539 he was treasurer of the household for Henry VIII, created baron St John in 1539, and given the Garter in 1543. From 1543 to 1545 he was lord chamberlain, lord steward 1545–50, lord president of the council 1545–50, and lord high treasurer 1550–72. Clearly he was a more than useful work-horse. In Edward VI's reign, he backed *Northumberland against *Somerset, was created earl of Wiltshire in 1550, and marquis of Winchester 1551. The only time when his footwork faltered was in supporting Lady Jane *Grey in 1553, but he abandoned her quickly enough to retain Mary's confidence, and continued in office under Elizabeth. He remained an influential figure well into his eighties, entertaining Elizabeth grandly at Basing, which he had rebuilt. JAC

Winchester Bible. The Winchester Bible (1160–70), probably commissioned by *Henry of Blois, is the finest of several large bibles produced through 12th-cent. contact with Byzantine art in Norman Sicily. Others are at Cambridge (for Bury St Edmund's) and at Canterbury. Designed for ceremonial use rather than individual study, the volume was, like altar-missals, ornately decorated. Each book in the Bible was designed to begin with a fully decorated capital letter, usually of figures rather than foliage. It has been described as 'the giant of 12th century English Romanesque century manuscripts'—in a great period of art and culture. WMM

Winchester College. In about 1330 *William of Wykeham attended a grammar school in Winchester. He later incorporated it in a new establishment, St Mary College of Winchester, founded by charter on 20 October 1382. The school consisted of a warden, 10 fellows, 2 masters, 3 chaplains, 70 scholars, and 16 choristers. The scholars, selected on a nation-wide basis, were prepared for entry to New College, Oxford, which Wykeham had founded in 1369. Entrants to the college were trained for holy orders. Winchester became a public school and flourished under George Moberly, headmaster from 1835 to 1866. PG

Winchester palace was started by Charles II in 1682 with *Wren as architect. Substantial progress was made but it was far from finished when Charles died in 1685 and his successor, James II, beset with problems, abandoned the project. In the Seven Years War and the War of American Independence, the shell of the palace was used for thousands of prisoners of war. In the early years of the Revolutionary War it gave shelter to French refugee clergy, but in 1796 was handed over to the military for use as a gaol. What was left of it was destroyed by fire in 1894. JAC

Windham, William (1750–1810). Statesman. Educated at Eton and University College, Oxford, Windham was a close friend of Edmund *Burke and Dr *Johnson, being a pall-bearer at the latter's funeral. In 1784 he became MP for Norwich and was one of the members charged with the impeachment of Warren *Hastings. He was secretary for war in the Pitt administration of 1794 to 1801 with a seat in the cabinet. Windham opposed the peace of 1802, an unpopular view at the time which cost him his Norwich seat. He assisted *Cobbett in founding the **Political Register* and returned to government at the War and Colonial Office in *Grenville's 'Ministry of All the *Talents' (1806–7). He introduced a plan for improving the condition of the military forces by increasing pay and reducing terms of service. Windham died of a tumour in 1810. His diary was published in 1866. RAS

window tax. William III's window tax (1696) was imposed on every dwelling except cottages. The rates were 2 shillings for houses with less than 10 windows, 6 shillings for 10–20 windows, and 10 shillings for more than 20 windows. It led to the stopping up of windows, often temporarily until the assessment had passed, many houses were built with fewer windows, and in Edinburgh a row was built without bedroom windows. During the Napoleonic wars the tax was increased on several occasions and by 1815 the yield was a substantial £2 million. In 1823 the tax was halved and in 1851 abolished. Throughout its existence it was hated because of the inspections to count windows, because the wide definition of a window permitted any hole in the wall, including coal holes, to be counted, and because it was regarded as a tax on light and air. MW

Windsor, house of. The Hanoverians, who were summoned in 1714 as the nearest protestant heirs, were related to the Stuarts and previous British dynasties through *Sophia, electress of Hanover, mother of George I and granddaughter of James VI and I. The original family name was Guelph. They were often known as the Brunswick line since the correct name for Hanover was first Brunswick-Calenberg-Göttingen and then Brunswick-Lüneburg. The first six rulers, up to Edward VII, married Germans: Edward in 1863 married *Alexandra of Denmark, but his son George V married Mary of Teck, German by title, though brought up in Britain. Their cousins were the Battenburgs.

When war broke out in 1914 the German antecedents of the royal family were a source of embarrassment. Prince Louis Battenburg, 1st sea lord, was obliged to resign his post and, somewhat against his will, George V ordered the Garter banners of the kaiser and his family to be removed from the walls of St George's chapel at Windsor. In 1917, as a gesture of identification with the nation, George declared that all German titles and honours would be renounced and that the family would be known in future as Windsor. The new image was perfect and well received, save for some ribaldry from the kaiser. Various alternatives had been mooted: Tudor was rejected because of the image of Henry VIII, FitzRoy as smacking of bastardy, Plantagenet as unintelligible, and Stuart as dispiriting. The Battenburgs became Mountbattens and the Tecks were made Cambridges. In 1936 when Edward VIII abdicated he was given the title duke of Windsor. JAC

Windsor, treaty of, 1175. In 1171 Henry II took an expedition to Ireland to establish his authority. He received the submission of Normans and Irish alike, save for Rory *O'Connor, king of Connacht, who claimed the high kingship of Ireland. But in 1175 O'Connor came to terms at Windsor, becoming the king's man. In return, Henry recognized his authority as high king outside the *Pale. The arrangement did not work well and in 1185 Henry sent his youngest son John to rule Ireland. JAC

Windsor castle (Berks.) is the premier castle of England as well as its largest. It is situated beside the river Thames and on the edge of Windsor Great Park, formerly a popular hunting ground of kings. Windsor castle was founded by William the Conqueror, who adopted the typical Norman design of motte and bailey, and was first used as a royal residence by Henry I. The original wooden structure was replaced by stone from 1165 to 1179 by Henry II, who also constructed the prominent Round Tower. St George's chapel, Windsor—which has long served as the last resting place of sovereigns—was begun by Edward IV in 1475 and is notable for its fan vaulting, monuments, stalls, and stained glass. The conversion of Windsor from fortress into palace began in the 16th cent. and continued in the 17th when Charles II commissioned Hugh May (1621–84) to refurbish the royal apartments. Subsequently extensive remodelling was carried out for George III from 1796 by James Wyatt, and by his nephew Sir Jeffry Wyatville for George IV from 1820 to 1830. Prince Albert died at Windsor in 1861, and to commemorate her husband Queen Victoria converted Henry III's chapel into the present Albert memorial chapel. Set in the surrounding Home Park at Windsor is Frogmore House, whose picturesque grounds may have been designed by Sir Uvedale Price, with a lake and a Gothic temple by Wyatt, and the royal mausoleum (1862–71), domed and Romanesque, by A. Jenkins Humbert and Ludwig Grüner. In the centre of the mausoleum is a monument to the queen and prince consort, with two white marble effigies by Baron C. Marochetti of 1864–8. PW

Windward Islands. A southern continuation of the chain of islands in the Caribbean known as the Lesser Antilles, with Puerto Rico to the west and *Trinidad to the south. They include *Dominica, Martinique, *St Lucia, and *St Vincent, with *Barbados lying to the east. Martinique is a *département* of France. JAC

Wingate, Orde (1903–44). Soldier. Wingate's father was a colonel in the Indian army and Wingate was born in India. His parents were Plymouth brethren. Commissioned in the Royal Artillery in 1923, he was sent to the Sudan in 1940 to lead an invasion of Italian-held Abyssinia, and with a small force, assisted by supporters of Haile Selassie, captured Addis Ababa in May 1941. He was then put in charge of the Chindit force to operate in Burma behind the Japanese lines, using radio to keep in touch and supplied from the air. A successful sortie in 1943 led to a more ambitious campaign for 1944, but Wingate was killed in an air crash in the jungle early in the operation. In a memo of July 1943 *Churchill had called him 'a man of genius and audacity . . . quite above the ordinary level'. JAC

Winstanley, Gerrard (b. 1609). Digger leader. Born in Wigan and apprenticed in London, he failed in trade, and from 1643 worked as a cowhand in Surrey. His twenty tracts (twelve being of substantial length) were all written between 1648 and 1651, and included manifestos for the *Digger movement. Before that they were strongly *millenarian, but the Digger writings give a boldly secular twist to familiar texts and tenets. God is 'the great creator Reason'; the Fall begat property and subjection, when men's covetousness overcame the law of righteousness in their hearts; the millennium will come when they restore the land to common ownership and live as equals. But Winstanley's thought never lost its scriptural roots, and he never advocated defying the state or dispossessing landlords by force. His final work, *The Law of Freedom*, proposed a polity for those who voluntarily embrace a communistic commonwealth. It is highly authoritarian, and its penalties for breaches of its code make chilling reading. Little is known of his subsequent life. AHW

Winthrop, John (1588–1649). Governor of Massachusetts. Of a prosperous Suffolk clothier's family, Winthrop went to Trinity College, Cambridge, and then studied law at Gray's Inn. Of strong puritan principles, he became increasingly disillusioned with the state of England—'evil times are coming when the church must fly to the wilderness.' In 1630 he left for America with a group of like-minded families, having been elected governor of the tiny colony of Massachusetts, which had then no more than 700 settlers. During the first summer he founded the settlement at Boston and some thousands of new settlers came in. Winthrop was governor until 1634, and then 1637–40, 1642–4, and 1645–9. He was involved in all the religious disputes of the day, gradually adopting a more austere line towards dissent. The journal which he kept from 1630 onwards is an important source for early colonial history. JAC

Winwæd River, battle of, 655. Here *Oswui of Bernicia successfully challenged the overlordship of *Penda of Mercia and was able to take temporary control of Mercia and permanent control of Deira. Penda was killed in the battle and many of his supporters drowned when they tried to escape across the flooded river. The Winwæd has been identified as the Went, a tributary of the river Don which drains into the Humber; the battle would therefore have taken place near the Mercian/Northumbrian border. BAEY

Wiseman, Nicholas (1802–65). First cardinal-archbishop of Westminster. Born of Irish parents in Seville, Wiseman was educated in Co. Durham and at the English College, Rome, where he later became rector (1828–44) and titular bishop (1840). Pius IX sent Wiseman as pro-vicar-apostolic to the London district in 1848 and then (1850) appointed him cardinal, intending to restore the English catholic hierarchy with Wiseman as archbishop. So great was English resentment that Parliament passed the Ecclesiastical Titles Act (1851), prohibiting catholics from assuming episcopal territorial titles. Wiseman's moderation and sensitive administration assuaged suspicions; the Act was repealed (1871) without ever being invoked. Chiefly remembered for restoring the English hierarchy and placing 'Roman catholics of England on the map', Wiseman was also a linguist and scholar.

WMM

Wishart, George (*c.*1513–46). One of the first Scottish protestant martyrs. Wishart came from Pittarrow near Montrose. He seems to have taught at Montrose and, after accusations of heresy, moved to Bristol, where in 1539 a George Wishart was forced to make a public recantation. After visiting Germany and Switzerland, he became a fellow of Corpus Christi College, Cambridge, before returning to Scotland in 1543. There he commenced itinerant preaching with John *Knox as a disciple. He was arrested in 1546, taken to Cardinal *Beaton's castle at St Andrews, and tried for heresy. His defence was an appeal to Scripture against the authority of the church. Two months after Wishart was burned, Beaton himself was murdered in the castle by Wishart's friends.

JAC

witan is the plural of Old English *wita*, a wise man, a counsellor. It was used by Anglo-Saxons sometimes in composition with *gemot* (an assembly) to indicate a royal or national conciliar meeting. The significance of these meetings must, over a long period, have varied, and is debatable. Some have seen all such conciliar assemblies as essentially under royal control and disposal: to the contrary was the Victorian view that these could be 'nationally' representative. *Bede, writing *c.*731, certainly believed that decision on the conversion of a kingdom could be the subject of possibly formal, conciliar debate. The 11th-cent. evidence is just enough to indicate that some conciliar meetings had elements of formality in summons and procedure, perhaps enough to indicate some conciliar independence. The nature of councils in between these periods is even more obscure; but participation in royal elections must sometimes have been important.

JCa

witchcraft. Belief in witchcraft, the capacity to do evil or good through occult means, has been present in most human societies. Scattered references to witchcraft practices survive from all parts of the British Isles from an early date, and become more numerous when medieval sources are considered.

It was, however, the 16th cent. which saw important changes in both England and Scotland. Educated opinion in both countries was affected by a new demonological theory which reinvented the witch as a member of a demonic conspiracy against Christendom. For the populace, conversely, witchcraft meant either *maleficium*, the doing of harm by witchcraft, or seeking medical advice or other services from the 'good' witch, most often referred to in England as a cunning man or woman. The new demonological thinking allowed a harder official line against witches. An English Act of 1542 had been repealed, but 1563 saw the passing of legislation against witchcraft in both England and Scotland.

Loss of most relevant trial records makes the English situation immediately after 1563 unclear. In the south-east (notably in Essex), trials and executions for witchcraft rose steadily, peaking in the late Elizabethan period, and were declining by the 1630s. In other areas the peak came in the Interregnum. Most English prosecutions were brought against individual witches, the only large-scale panic coming in East Anglia in 1645–7. This was associated with the 'Witch-Finder General', Matthew Hopkins, and involved accusations against 250 witches, of whom perhaps 100 were executed. Trials in all areas declined after the Restoration, with the last known execution for witchcraft coming in Devon in 1685, and the last trial in 1712. It seems unlikely that more than 500 people were executed for witchcraft in England. Many others, most of them cunning folk, were tried but suffered lesser penalties.

In Scotland, a different pattern emerged. There were few trials before 1591, but in that year mass prosecutions, followed by numerous executions, occurred. Accusations revolved around an alleged satanic plot against James VI, and the experience moved him to write a tract against witches, the *Daemonologie*. Other mass persecutions came in 1597, 1629, 1649, and most ferociously in 1661–2. Although peasant concerns over *maleficium* remained important, the most consistent influence behind the mass trials was the aggressive calvinism of the Scottish kirk. Accusations were concentrated in the Lowlands, where the kirk's Christianizing campaign was most intense. Witchcraft beliefs doubtlessly flourished in the Highlands, but the encouragement to prosecute witches was lacking there. Moreover, the Scottish legal system, unlike the English, permitted the torturing of suspects in criminal investigations. Overall, perhaps 1,000 people were executed for witchcraft in Scotland.

The statutes against witches in both countries were repealed in 1736. Over the second half of the 17th cent. scepticism among the educated, never entirely absent, had become stronger. The reasons for this are not entirely clear. The notion that it was somehow related to new scientific ideas is unconvincing when subjected to close scrutiny. A more useful clue lies in the scepticism which leading judges in both Scotland and England showed when trying witches. The difficulty of proving witchcraft in particular cases provoked a more general questioning, while there was also a powerful cultural shift. Many educated people, while unable to deny the theoretical possibility of witchcraft, felt uncomfortable with what they increasingly regarded as something symptomatic not of a satanic sect, but of popular superstitions.

Belief in witchcraft was retained among the populace at large, and when folklorists began to collect materials in the 19th cent. they found witchcraft beliefs flourishing everywhere from Cornwall to the Scottish Highlands. By the 20th cent., better communications, mass schooling, and the decline of those 'face-to-face' communities where witchcraft suspicions operated eroded such beliefs. At the same time, interest in the occult was renewed among educated urban dwellers, and there are currently many people who consider themselves to be witches, and as such to be adherents to a pre-Christian religion. They have little historical basis for such opinions.

JAS

Woburn (Beds.). Woburn abbey came into the hands of the 1st earl of *Bedford, along with Covent Garden and estates in Devon, at the *dissolution of the monasteries. It was an early *Cistercian foundation of 1145. Part of the present mansion dates from the 17th cent., but the west and south ranges are 18th cent., by Flitcroft and Henry Holland: one of the best rooms is the library, built by Holland in the 1790s. The park has a bridge by *Chambers and was extensively redesigned by *Repton. The dukes of Bedford were among the earliest noblemen to perceive the commercial potential of country houses and Woburn has a zoo and amusements. JAC

Wodehouse, P. G. (1881–1975). Wodehouse was the son of a judge in Hong Kong but was born in Guildford. His parents stayed in the colony and from the age of 2 Wodehouse was brought up in England by relatives or hired governesses. Dulwich College he thought 'like heaven'. He began as a bank clerk which he hated, but made his way into journalism and in 1919 published *My Man Jeeves*. The success of these stories prompted an avalanche of Bertie Wooster novels and stories. During the Second World War Wodehouse was captured in France by the Germans, who released him and allowed him to broadcast to America. This foolish action gave great offence in Britain and after the war he lived in the USA, becoming an American citizen. He was given a knighthood a few days before his death. Wodehouse's stories acquired in time a period flavour of bright young things and made a very successful television series. Like most good writers, he created his own imaginary world, full of daft men and determined women. JAC

Wolfe, James (1727–59). Born in Westerham (Kent) into a military family, Wolfe was an intelligent and articulate professional soldier. He fought at *Culloden and with distinction in the Rochefort expeditionary force. Marked out by William *Pitt for Canadian service, he served bravely at Louisbourg in 1758, then returned to London, where he dined with Pitt and Temple, exhibiting 'gasconade and bravado'. Appointed a major-general, he led the assault on *Quebec in 1759. Suffering from poor health, he was also criticized for poor generalship by fellow-officers. However, his tactical success and youthful death in victory on 13 September 1759 ensured his entry to the pantheon of British heroes, into patriotic street literature and folk memory. His call to his soldiers to 'remember what their country expects from them', echoed in Nelson's Trafalgar signal, and his statement that he would rather have written *Gray's 'Elegy' than capture Quebec, are not forgotten. RCS

Wolff, Gustav Wilhelm (1834–1913). Co-founder of the Belfast shipyard Harland & Wolff. Wolff, of German Jewish descent, was the nephew of the Liverpool business tycoon G. C. Schwabe. He joined the Belfast shipyard Robert Hickson & Co. as personal assistant to the manager, Edward Harland, and assisted Harland in his purchase of the company in 1858. Wolff was at first in charge of the drawing office, later—in 1861—entering into a full partnership with Harland. His business acumen was of considerable value to the firm, with which he remained associated until 1906. However, his verdict on his entrepreneurial record was modest: 'Sir Edward [Harland] builds the ships, Mr Pirrie makes the speeches, and, as for me, I smoke the cigars.' Like Harland he was an active Conservative and Unionist politician, representing East Belfast in Parliament (1892–1910). Sitting together in the House of Commons, Harland and Wolff were dubbed by the parliamentary wags 'Majestic' and 'Teutonic' after two of their shipyard's finest vessels. AJ

Wollstonecraft, Mary (1759–97). Author and early feminist writer. Mary Wollstonecraft worked for a London publisher, James Johnson, until leaving England for Paris in 1792 to study the French Revolution. Returning to London, she became part of a group of radical and progressive thinkers who included William *Godwin, Thomas *Paine, William *Blake, and William *Wordsworth. In 1796 she became Godwin's lover, and they married the next year—only six months before her death, which followed the birth of their daughter Mary (future wife of Shelley and author of *Frankenstein*).

Mary Wollstonecraft wrote four books, the most influential of which was *Vindication of the Rights of Woman* (1792). This was the first major statement of feminism by an English writer, and in it Wollstonecraft argued that the French revolutionary principles of liberty and equality applied to women as much as to men. Though rambling and ill organized, it captured the public imagination by its verve and optimism for a future egalitarian society. TSG

Wolseley, Garnet, 1st Viscount Wolseley (1833–1913). Soldier. The son of an Irish major, Wolseley joined the army in 1852 and served with distinction in the Burmese War and the Crimean War, being seriously wounded on two occasions. He was in India at the time of the mutiny and took part in the second Opium War against China in 1860. From 1861 he was in Canada, where he crushed the *Red River rebellion in 1870 and then won more fame in the *Ashanti War of 1873–4. His victory at *Tel-el-Kebir in Egypt over Arabi Pasha in 1882 made him a national hero. He was promoted general and given a barony. Though his expedition in 1885 failed to rescue *Gordon, Wolseley was not held responsible and was promoted viscount. He finished in 1894 as field marshal, one of the busiest and most successful of Victorian soldiers. His appointment as commander-in-chief in 1895, in succession to the duke of *Cambridge, gave him the chance to implement some of the army reforms he had long advocated, though ill-health forced him to resign in 1899. All his victories, it has been remarked, were gained in colonial conflicts, but he did what was asked of him. Queen Victoria in 1874 found him 'thin and grey, but well, and a very smart, active, wiry-looking man, full of energy'. JAC

Wolsey, Thomas (*c*.1472–1530). Cardinal. Thomas Wolsey, cardinal-minister to Henry VIII, dominated the political and ecclesiastical life of England from 1515 to 1529. His relatively modest origins (reputedly the son of an Ipswich butcher) were not unusual for a senior cleric; it was the contrast between his origins and his life-style which drew notice. He studied at Oxford and became a fellow of Magdalen College around 1497. He soon left scholarship to serve as chaplain to Henry Deane, archbishop of Canterbury, from 1501, became a royal chaplain from 1507, and the king's almoner in 1509. For helping to organize Henry VIII's first campaign in France (1513), he was rewarded with the bishoprics of Lincoln and newly captured Tournai in 1514, and the archbishopric of York shortly afterwards. In 1515 he became both cardinal and lord chancellor of England. In 1518 the pope honoured him with the special status of legate *a latere*, outranking the legatine status held by every archbishop of Canterbury; in 1524 this title was, uniquely, given for life.

With such an accumulation of posts, and vast energy, Wolsey took responsibility under the king for nearly all areas of government policy. A primary aim was to win military and diplomatic success for Henry. After the costly first campaign in France, Wolsey tried to magnify his master through grandiose peace negotiations (the treaty of *London, 1518, and the *Field of Cloth of Gold, 1520); he also tried to steer England into a position as arbiter and broker between the much wealthier monarchies of France under Francis I and Austria-Spain-Burgundy under Charles V. However, England was drawn into invading France in 1522 and 1523, forcing heavy and much-resented taxation, for which Wolsey was blamed. Attempts to side with France after 1525 backfired: a cloth embargo on the Habsburg Netherlands in 1527–8 had to be abandoned because of the harm done to England.

In domestic affairs Wolsey used his position as lord chancellor to pursue traditional policies with unusual verve and aggression. He revived Henry VII's campaign against those gentry and nobles who 'retained' excessive numbers of supporters to overawe royal justice. In 1517 he instituted commissions to search out those who had broken the law against converting arable farms into sheep-runs. He expanded the scope of the prerogative courts' equity jurisdiction, attracting a flood of civil suits to *Star Chamber and offering redress to poor plaintiffs in what later became the Court of *Requests.

Wolsey's management of the church was less creative. He enjoyed his pro-papal status as legate, gratuitously thwarting the primate's jurisdiction at times. There is no evidence that he seriously coveted the papacy for himself, though the idea of setting him up as an anti-pope was briefly canvassed to resolve the royal marriage crisis. He had neither the moral reforming zeal of *Colet nor the taste for theological polemic of John *Fisher. However, he had a good eye for intellectual gifts in others; and his educational foundations, including the great unfinished project of Cardinal College, Oxford (later refounded as Christ Church), allow him to rank with Bishops Richard *Foxe in Oxford and John Fisher in Cambridge. Dissolving multiple monasteries to endow a college and a school, however, set a dangerous precedent.

Historians have argued unfruitfully whether Wolsey or Henry VIII was really in charge of England before 1529. Contemporaries regarded the cardinal's power as quasi-regal, and his vastly ostentatious household, larger and more ritualized than the king's, contributed to that impression. Henry notoriously did not like to read papers and absented himself from duties for long periods. However, the king could intervene decisively and stubbornly via his secretaries, and occasionally did. His penchant for war created problems Wolsey would not have chosen to set himself, and brought ill-deserved public hatred on the minister. At intervals Wolsey felt the need to protect himself against hostile courtiers close to the king: he restructured the king's privy chamber in 1519 and again in 1526, and gave his own magnificent palace of *Hampton Court to Henry in 1525.

Henry's desperate need for the annulment of his first marriage required Wolsey to ask of the papacy, which had given so much to England, the one thing it could not grant. Wolsey attempted to have the issue devolved to a commission composed of himself and the roving Cardinal Campeggio, but the queen's appeal to Rome thwarted this plan. Wolsey, who planned a diplomatic second marriage to a French bride for Henry, had no control over *Anne Boleyn, who fed the king anticlerical and anti-Wolsey propaganda in the months leading up to the sudden loss of all his offices in October 1529. Wolsey pleaded guilty to an absurd charge of *praemunire arising out of his legatine status, and temporarily retired to church affairs; but when he dabbled unofficially in diplomacy in the summer of 1530 he was denounced as a traitor, and died on his way to London to answer, at Leicester, on 29 November 1530.

Wolsey's unpopularity with the political nation has been blamed for much of the anticlerical sentiment expressed in the 1529 session of Parliament. It is, however, probably too harsh to place the subsequent misfortunes of either church or state on him. For his accumulation of offices, and many of the unpopular policies he followed, the king was personally responsible. Wolsey's moral failings and pompous style were comparable to those of other cardinal-ministers in Europe at the time. It was only in the light of the religious earnestness of the 1530s and 1540s that his ministry came to appear so incongruous. EC

women's institutes. Founded in Canada (1897) for improving women's education in domestic science, the first UK institute was formed on Anglesey (north Wales) in 1915 and the first county federation (Sussex) in 1917. Written off as a wartime experiment that would not last, their determination to better the lives of rural communities led to rapid expansion, a magazine (*Home and Country*), and self-government; non-party, non-sectarian, and well organized, they broadened interests, broke down social isolation, and began to demand a voice in public affairs (health care, adult education). Concern to protect its non-political principle led the NFWI to declare in 1938 that it could not, as an institution, take part in a war effort. It was criticized for this stance, even though individual members were quite free to join the Women's Voluntary Service, Women's Land Army, or Civil Defence. Many in fact did so, while others contributed substantially to the evacuation programme, fruit-preserving, and sock-knitting. Their love of festivals has created a popular image confined to making jam and singing Blake's 'Jerusalem', but they have demonstrated that they can be a powerful pressure group for legislative change. ASH

'Wonderful' Parliament, 1386. Parliament met on 1 October and demanded the dismissal of Richard II's chancellor and favourite, Suffolk (Michael de la *Pole). Richard refused and talked wildly of seeking aid from the king of France. But he was forced to agree to Suffolk's impeachment. JAC

Wood, Sir Henry J. (1869–1944). English conductor. Initially an organist and composer, although he also taught singing for much of his life, Wood studied at London's *Royal College of Music. He made his conducting début in 1888; he also helped *Sullivan prepare *The Yeomen of the Guard* and *Ivanhoe* and conducted the British première of Tchaikovsky's *Eugene Onegin* (1892), reflecting his lifelong promotion of new Russian music. In 1895 Wood founded the enormously influential Queen's Hall *Promenade Concerts, which he conducted until his death, introducing countless new works to the British public. He encouraged many young British performers and composers, conducting the Royal Academy of Music student orchestra for twenty years. His meticulous markings of scores and parts, his well-organized rehearsals, and his clear technique with a very long baton (described in his book *About Conducting*) allowed him to make the most of often minimal rehearsal time. His *Fantasia on British Sea-Songs*, an arrangement written in 1905 for the centenary of Trafalgar, has become an immovable part of the Last Night of the Proms. ECr

Woodchester is a major Romano-British villa in the Cotswolds near Stroud (Glos.). It originated on a small scale in the 2nd cent. By the first half of the 4th cent. it consisted of at least three courts in echelon. The outer court was probably agricultural. The middle court was flanked by a large store-building and a residence, perhaps of the agent. The principal range of the inner court contained a huge reception room, floored with the largest mosaic in Roman Britain, depicting Orpheus and the beasts. Other rooms were floored in mosaic. One was probably a sculpture gallery. ASEC

Woodforde, James (1740–1803). Woodforde was a country parson whose diary from 1758 to 1802 has survived. His life was uneventful. He was born in Somerset, son of a cleric, and educated at New College, Oxford. After ten years as a Somerset curate, he returned briefly to college before becoming rector of Weston Longueville, a college living near Norwich, where he spent the rest of his life. He had a lively interest in food, in his servants, and he played whist and went fishing. Great events largely passed him by and he devoted one hundred times the space to the king and queen's visit to Sherborne in 1789 than he did to the French Revolution. The diary is full of little vignettes—'poor Thomas Barnes, who had been a long time killing himself by liquor'; old Mr Reeve who broke Woodforde's gum—'he is too old, I think, to draw teeth, can't see very well'; Andrews the smuggler, who 'frightened us a little by whistling under the parlour window just as we were going to bed'; 'Mr Townshend's gamekeeper who goes by the name of Black Jack' and shot Woodforde's dog, Pompey. JAC

Wood's halfpence, 1722. There was a shortage of coin in Ireland in 1722 and much of it was old and worn. Since there was no mint in Ireland, a patent was granted to a Wolverhampton ironmonger, William Wood, to supply just over £100,000 in halfpennies and farthings. Though Sir Isaac *Newton, as master of the mint, testified that the coins were satisfactory, there was vociferous protest from Ireland and an almost total refusal to handle the money. Swift's anonymous *Drapier's Letters* in 1724–5 raised a flame: 'if a madman should come to my shop with a handful of dirt raked out of the kennel, I would pity or laugh at him; and if Mr Wood comes to demand any gold or silver, in exchange for his trash, can he deserve or expect better treatment?' *Walpole revoked the patent in 1725 and Wood was privately compensated. The episode suggests how tense Anglo-Irish relations were and the resentment left by the Act of 1720 which reaffirmed that Ireland was 'subordinate to the imperial crown of Great Britain'. JAC

Woodstock, Assize of, 1184. The king's hunting in royal forests was protected in the Norman period by severe laws. Henry II enforced them fiercely, partly because of his own love of the chase, partly to raise revenue. This assize, also known as the Assize of the Forest, summarized previous laws. Stubbs suggested that it was milder than previous practice, but since punishments included blinding, mutilation, and castration, that is not easy to credit. By clause 9, the clergy were brought into the sway of the forest laws and Henry encouraged foresters 'not to hesitate' to arrest them. JAC

Woodstock, treaty of, 1247. For some years the treaty of Woodstock was the high-water mark of English advance against Wales. When *Dafydd ap Llywelyn died in 1246 without sons, his nephews Owain and *Llywelyn ap Gruffydd made peace with Henry III. They gave up their lands east of the Conwy and agreed to hold north Wales by military service. But Henry III's struggle with his barons enabled Llywelyn to recover much of his power and in 1258 to declare himself prince of Wales. JAC

Woolf, Virginia (1882–1941). The daughter of Sir Leslie Stephen, editor of the *DNB*, Virginia Stephen was a sensitive child. Abused at the age of 6, the death of her mother when she was 13 caused a breakdown. She was engaged at one time to Lytton Strachey but in 1912 married Leonard Woolf. The physical side of the marriage was unappealing to her given her preference for lesbian relationships. With her husband she founded the Hogarth Press and their house became a centre for the *Bloomsbury Group of artists and writers. Despite her delicate health she sustained a large output of essays, reviews, and novels—*Mrs Dalloway* (1925), *To the Lighthouse* (1927), and *Orlando* (1928), which experimented with 'stream of consciousness' technique and was a great success. *The Common Reader*, a book of essays (1925), also sold well and a second and even better *Common Reader* came out in 1932. In 1929 she published *A Room of One's Own*, surveying the difficulties confronting women, which became a classic of feminist literature. A protracted bout of depression in 1941 led her to drown herself in the river Ouse in Sussex. SMC

woollen industry. This responded early to the possibilities presented by water power, and the fulling mill, introduced in the late 12th cent., spread widely thereafter, although hand-finishing of cloth survived in remote rural societies until the 19th cent. Distaff spinning was replaced by the wheel in the 14th cent., and the loom was improved constantly to help weaving productivity. Quality control was exercised by town guilds, but country districts were free of regulation. This aided the rise of rural clothiers who sold in cloth halls, exports to the principal European markets in the Low Countries being supplied via Blackwell Hall in London and managed by the *Merchant Venturers' Company.

Although cloth exports rose remarkably from the late 15th cent., the introduction into East Anglia from the 1560s of 'new draperies', mainly worsteds, by protestant immigrants fleeing persecution added to the product range available to both the home and foreign market. Manufacture was often controlled by merchants who put out materials, sometimes over long distances, to be made up by workers in their own homes. A few entrepreneurs tried to concentrate production, intending to raise productivity by closer supervision of the labour force and able to control quality and raw materials directly.

By 1700 the woollen industry was Britain's most important industry with a range of products from luxury to plain goods. Its links with agriculture were intimate; its parliamentary lobby was therefore strong. John *Kay's 'flying-shuttle' (1733), intended for use in the woollen industry, was only slowly adopted, compared with its use in fustian-weaving. Merchant clothiers expanded production in areas with the lowest labour costs, often building large loomshops. Improvements were made in carding and scribbling, the preparatory processes, and in the 1780s worsted-spinning was first mechanized, using *Arkwright's water frame, and wool-spinning followed (1810) with the application of *Crompton's mule. Most mills were small and in the 1830s on average employed less than 50 workers. As late as 1858 only about half those employed in the industry worked in factories. The transition to the factory system was clearly slow. However, technical change did meet resistance from the croppers or shearmen who finished off cloth and were being replaced after 1800 by the gig mill and shearing frame. The croppers and shearers were the backbone of *Luddism, especially in Yorkshire.

The industry fared well for most of the 19th cent. The home market was buoyant, and 'new' products such as tweed hosiery, mohair, and alpaca found extensive markets overseas. South Africa, Australia, and New Zealand added significantly to wool supplies from the 1850s. Wool imports increased fivefold between 1850 and 1885. Yorkshire and the west country dominated the industry, although the Scottish borders exploited the demand for tweed and hosiery until the 1970s.

From the 1870s foreign competition and tariff barriers in Europe and the USA began to hit exports. An atomized industrial structure of small family firms did not help. The combination of spinning and weaving within the single business became general and was often accompanied by the integration of finishing and dyeing. The real disaster occurred after the First World War. The contraction of world trade in the great inter-war slump hit hard. Too much equipment was obsolescent, and the lack of capital investment adversely affected productivity. However, the industry was saved by tariff protection from 1932 and the revival of the home market in the late 1930s. Man-made fibres attacked the industry from the 1950s, especially the production of carpets, and its future rested with reacting rapidly to changes in fashion and markets. Decline was rapid after 1965. JB

Worcester. Cathedral city on the river Severn, and county town of Worcestershire. A modest Roman town, it was reoccupied by a cathedral (680) and later by a fortified town (burh) *c.*890. From the 14th to the 17th cents. it flourished as a river port and cloth-making city. Its peak national ranking came in the 17th cent. (twelfth largest English town in 1662), but it suffered severely for supporting the royalists in the civil wars, especially after the battle of *Worcester. In the 18th and 19th cents. it prospered more modestly through porcelain and glove manufactures. The cathedral is a fine 13th/14th-cent. building housing the tombs of King John and Prince *Arthur; the city retains much of its historic fabric despite appalling central redevelopment in the 1960s ('the sack of Worcester'). DMP

Worcester, battle of, 1651. In July 1650 Charles II landed in Scotland and was crowned at Scone on 1 January 1651. But finding his army outflanked by *Cromwell, he moved south in August, making for the old royalist strongholds of Wales and the west midlands. Cromwell pursued him with an army almost twice the size of his own, and caught up with him at Worcester. The royalists dug in, cutting all the bridges except that between the city and the suburb of St John to the west. Cromwell's response was to bring up barges from Upton to the south and construct pontoon bridges over the Severn and the Teme. He attacked on 3 September, the anniversary of his great victory over the Scots at *Dunbar. Charles II conducted operations with considerable skill from the tower of the cathedral and a counter-attack to the east of the city made some progress. But in the end, superior numbers prevailed and his army was wiped out as a fighting force. Charles was swept out of Worcester to the north and began his extraordinary escape. In his report of the battle, Cromwell wrote, 'it is, for aught I know, a crowning mercy'. Thus the civil wars ended near Powick bridge, where they had started nine years before. JAC

Worcester, diocese of. Now roughly conterminous with Worcestershire, it was created by *Theodore in *c.*679 out of the large Mercian see for the *Hwicce people who inhabited Gloucestershire, Worcestershire, and half Warwickshire. The Worcester diocese was reduced in size by the creation of the see of *Gloucester in 1541 and *Birmingham in 1905, though it also briefly (1836–1918) included the *Coventry area until its own diocese was created. Despite the Danish invasions, there was continuity of episcopal succession. *Oswald (961–92), a monastic reformer, replaced the cathedral's secular canons with monks. He also held the archbishopric of York in plurality from 972, as did his successors until 1016 and for a short spell after 1040. An attempt to renew the practice was vetoed by Pope Nicholas II in 1061. Notable bishops were *Wulfstan (1062–95), a man of great sanctity, Hugh *Latimer (1535–55), burned at the stake, Edward Stillingfleet (1689–99), a latitudinarian scholar, and Charles *Gore (1902–5), an Anglo-catholic writer, who also successfully campaigned for the creation, out of his own see, of the Birmingham diocese of which he became first bishop (1905–11). The cathedral, though Norman in plan with Norman crypt and chapter house, was mostly refashioned in the 19th cent. with a Perpendicular cloister. It contains the shrine of Wulfstan and the tomb of King John. WMM

Worcester, pact of, 1264. After Simon de *Montfort's victory at *Lewes in May 1264, he attempted to subdue Roger *Mortimer and the marcher lords. On 12 December at Worcester, a compromise was reached whereby the lords were to go to Ireland for a year and a day, Prince Edward's possessions were to pass to de Montfort, but the prince was to be released. Everything was overturned by de Montfort's defeat and death at *Evesham in August 1265, when his head was sent as a trophy to Mortimer's wife at Wigmore. JAC

Worcester, Thomas Percy, 1st earl of (*c.*1344–1403). The younger brother of the 1st earl of *Northumberland, Percy had a distinguished career in the French war from 1369 to 1388, interrupted by service on the Scottish border, at sea, and in *John of Gaunt's expedition to Spain. From 1390 he held office in Richard II's household and was rewarded with the title of earl and a share of the spoils for his part in the destruction of the king's enemies. In 1399, however, he abandoned Richard in favour of Henry IV and served as admiral, ambassador, and lieutenant in south Wales; for a while he was apparently Henry's principal noble councillor. As the Beauforts and Nevilles gained royal favour, Percy influence was threatened, and this helped to explain why Worcester joined Henry *Percy's rebellion: as in 1399, his first loyalty was to his family. He was beheaded after the battle of *Shrewsbury. RLS

Worcester, treaty of, 1218. After John's death in 1216, he was succeeded by his son Henry III, aged 9. *Llywelyn ab Iorwerth had profited from the divisions of John's reign and controlled most of Wales. At Worcester in 1218 his power was acknowledged, he was recognized as Henry's lieutenant during the minority, and the royal castles of Carmarthen and Cardigan were placed in his hands. The accommodation soon broke down. JAC

Worcestershire is bisected by the river Severn, which enters the county at Bewdley and leaves it near Tewkesbury: it is joined from the west by the Teme and from the east by the Avon and its tributaries. It was well wooded. The Malverns formed the boundary with Herefordshire in the south-west and the other hills include Bredon Hill, beloved of poets and composers, and the Lickey, Clent, and Abberley hills. The early importance of Worcester was as a river crossing and it retained its strategic significance until the 17th cent. One form of the name was Wigornaceastre, which may derive from the people of the Wyre forest. The area formed part of the territory of the *Hwicce and then of the *Mercians. It was in the diocese of *Lichfield until Worcester was established as a separate see in the later 7th cent.

Though sheltered from Welsh attacks by Hereford to the west, the county was for centuries a border area, and fell under the jurisdiction of the *Council of the Marches in Tudor times. Four great abbeys were early established, at Pershore, Evesham, Malvern, and Worcester itself. The cathedral at Worcester was rebuilt several times before the Norman Conquest. The present building was started in 1084 by St *Wulfstan but not finished until much later.

It was a fertile and flourishing county. In the 16th cent. *Camden wrote of Worcester that it 'really deserved admiration both for its antiquity and beauty' and noted that the shire was celebrated for its perry and for the salt springs at Droitwich. The strategic position of Worcester made it of great importance during the civil wars, since its bridge dominated access to Wales and to royalist recruits. Indeed, the civil wars may be said to have begun and finished in the city. The first skirmish in September 1642 was *Rupert's cavalry action at Powick bridge and the last battle in September 1651 saw Charles II driven out of the city by Cromwell's men. The flamboyant Guildhall, built in the safer 1720s, paraded the city's loyalties with statues of Charles I and Charles II.

Worcestershire retained its prosperity in the 18th cent. but the character of the county was beginning to change. Tom Jones and Mrs Waters spent a disturbed night at the White Lion at Upton on Severn, where the landlady confessed that she sold her perry as champagne: 'to be sure it is as well tasted and as wholesome as any champagne in the kingdom.' Upton itself, in the extreme south of the county, remained a tiny market town, preserved in a lovely time warp, but in the north mining and industry was changing the face of the shire. There had always been local industries and the Severn was always a busy thoroughfare. Droitwich salt-pans went back to Domesday, Kidderminster was famous for textiles and then carpets, while there were glass manufactories at Stourbridge from Tudor times. In the 17th cent. the Foleys established nail-making at Stourbridge on a grand scale and set up a great county interest: the burned-out remains of their house at Great Witley are an impressive and sombre testimony to departed grandeur. The development of a canal and railway network brought Worcestershire more into the national context, as it did Warwickshire. Stourport was scarcely more than a solitary inn in the 1770s when it became the junction of the new Staffordshire and Worcester canal with the Severn, but subsequently developed into a busy town. Great Malvern jumped from a small local spa to a national one in the middle of the 19th cent. with the popularity of hydropathy. The southern and western towns of Evesham, Pershore, and Tenbury remained small, but the northern parts were sucked into the Black Country complex. Yardley, King's Norton, and Halesowen were swallowed up by Birmingham; Dudley developed into a great mining and industrial centre, far exceeding Worcester in population. By the local government reorganization of 1972, the county lost parishes in the north to the new *West Midlands area, but was merged with its neighbour Herefordshire. 'The Malverns are no more,' it was declared. But in 1994 the Banham commission recommended that Worcestershire and Herefordshire be separated once more. JAC

Wordsworth, William (1770–1850). Greatest of the Romantic poets for 'the union of deep feeling with profound thought' his friend *Coleridge admired in his work. From Cambridge a visit to France on the first anniversary of the Revolution fired his enthusiasm for the people's cause: 'Bliss was it in that dawn to be alive, but to be young was very heaven!' His loyalties divided by the outbreak of war and separated from the woman who bore his child, he settled in Dorset with his sister Dorothy. The conditions of the rural poor preoccupied him and a *Godwinian rationalism coloured his thinking; at this period Coleridge judged him 'at least a *semi*-atheist'. *Lyrical Ballads* (1798) was written to show that 'men who do not wear fine clothes can feel deeply' and a copy presented to Charles James *Fox. After 1800, back in his native Cumberland, a more subjective vein emerged in *The Prelude* (not published until 1850), the long poem on the growth of his own mind. A long life saw some hardening of poetical arteries and political attitudes; later commentators have generally preferred the poetry of his radical youth. JNRS

Workers' Educational Association (WEA). Founded in 1903 by Albert Mansbridge (1876–1952), a cashier at the Cooperative Permanent Building Society, whose own formal education had ended at the age of 14. Mansbridge considered that the University Extension movement, established in 1878 and originally intended for the education of the working classes, had been largely taken over by the middle classes. To remedy this, Mansbridge launched an Association to Promote the Higher Education of Working Men, changing its name to the Workers' Educational Association two years later. He sought the help of Oxford and Cambridge for the new movement, which would provide high-level education for co-operators, trade union members, and reading circles. The creation of the university tutorial class, where students pledged themselves to attend courses for three years, was probably Mansbridge's greatest achievement. By the outbreak of the First World War the movement had proved a success, with every university providing tutors. PG

workhouses. The workhouse as such was an Elizabethan invention designed to provide a disciplined and productive environment for the able-bodied poor, at a time when rising urban poverty was putting pressure on existing systems of almsgiving and emergent local taxation. Its origins lay in manufacturing towns such as Norwich. The idea was slow to spread until the 18th cent., and an Act of 1723 enabled parishes to band together to support a shared workhouse out of their income from rates (local property taxes). Many of the resulting ventures, like earlier versions, soon became places of refuge for the aged and impotent poor and for unmarried mothers rather than supervised workplaces, and it was difficult to find work (apart from the maintenance of institution and inmates themselves) which would not compete in counter-productive ways with outside workers. Some attempts were made to make relief to the able-bodied conditional on entry into the workhouse, but outdoor relief in various forms continued. The workhouse really rose to prominence with the *Poor Law Amendment Act of 1834, which required each of the new unions of parishes to provide a central workhouse which would classify the poor by age, sex, and circumstances and accommodate them under conditions which were 'less eligible' than the worst that prevailed outside. No relief was originally to be given outside these workhouses, which soon became known to potential inmates as 'bastilles' after the French Revolution symbol of repression. In practice, the system was generally less fearsome than intended. Outdoor relief continued to be provided in many places: it was cheaper and more flexible than the workhouse, in both agricultural areas of seasonal unemployment and manufacturing districts where the workhouse would have been swamped in every trade depression. In industrial areas such as south Lancashire new workhouses were not built for over thirty years in some unions, after angry demonstrations when the new system was being introduced in 1837. Many people incorporated the workhouse into personal survival strategies, using the casual ward system to sustain them in their wanderings in search of work or going inside as a refuge from inclement winter weather. But the great achievement of the 1834 Act was to attach such a stigma to poor relief, and create such a fear of the workhouse, that many proud and independent people preferred starvation or prostitution to admission into the 'bastille'. Such attitudes were fuelled by scandals such as that of the Andover workhouse where starving inmates ate the rotting bones they were grinding, and by the Anatomy Act of 1832 which provided that unclaimed pauper bodies from the workhouse could be given up for dissection. This deterred people from seeking medical relief, and although many workhouses developed hospital functions, the charitably funded infirmaries were preferred. Conditions in workhouse hospitals could still be appalling in the 1860s and 1870s, especially in the venereal and insane wards. Even when the workhouse premises passed into the National Health Service as hospitals after the Second World War, the stigma remained and many elderly people were terrified of entering them, especially as many of the staff retained Poor Law attitudes. The workhouse in English social history (it was not given such a prominent role in the different history of the Scottish Poor Law) has acted above all as symbol and reinforcement of the conversion of poor relief from a right to a source of shame, which was the main purpose and effect of the 1834 Act. JKW

working class. The 18th cent. often talked of the poor, labourers, and artisans as part of its language of ranks and orders. Somewhere in the early years of the 19th cent. such groups were identified by contemporaries and later historians as a working class, or more frequently 'the working classes'. This identity was seen as a response to their position as wage earners faced with an intensification of capitalist relationships of production, namely relationships which involved private property and production for profit, mediated by cash. The responses and experiences which accumulated to form the relationships of class included opposition to machinery, the dramatic fall in real wages experienced by hand-loom weavers, and the political inspiration of radicalism. In the 1820s and 1830s, *trade unions, especially in the textile and mining industries, became a focus of industrial conflict more extensive than anything experienced by the mainly craft associations of the earlier century. The *chartist movement of the 1830s and 1840s became a focus of many working-class ambitions and gained mass support for a political programme demanding universal manhood suffrage. Many historians see chartism as a product of the economic experiences of the working classes, and its political programme as a response to the variety of relationships within which wage-earning people found themselves. Others see chartism as a political movement which offered little analysis of economic relationships in terms of capitalist exploitation, but offered a radical attack upon political privilege and corruption as a base for explaining 'the people's' poverty. Debate also exists on the meaning of trade union conflicts. Many reflect particular trades and localities with little sense of the relationships of wage labour as a whole.

The 1860s saw the establishment of a more institutionalized trade union movement with legal status and centralized bodies like the *Trades Union Congress (1867). This period saw a move from unstable conflict to social peace often identified with the influence of a *'labour aristocracy' of skilled workers prepared to co-operate with the owners of capital. The change was more broadly based and related to improvements in working-class living standards, the acceptance of many working people into political life, especially in the Gladstonian Liberal Party, and the development of a more sophisticated employer paternalism. It was a period in which the wage relationship was still partial and imperfect. Subcontracting, payment in kind, and gender and supervisory hierarchies mediated between labour and capital.

By the 1890s, a distinctive working-class culture had emerged, based upon a sense of neighbourhood and mutual support, especially amongst women, upon old and new leisure patterns built around the public house, spectator sports like *football and the *music-hall, and upon a labour movement consisting of a variety of institutions like the retail *co-operative societies, trade unions, socialist Sunday schools, and the ILP (*Independent Labour Party). These values have been called 'populist', involving a pride in work and in mutual support in the face of poverty, a delight in having a good time, a derision of privilege, and a regional pride. Such populism could as easily move to a Union-Jack-waving nationalism as to a conflict-orientated sense of class. It represented a sense of cohesion which lasted into the 1950s and was celebrated by Richard Hoggart's *The Uses of Literacy* (1957).

Through its institutional base the working class faced major periods of conflict in the late 19th and early 20th cents. culminating in the *General Strike of 1926. This was related to the impact of new technologies, often involving de-skilling, to new management strategies, and to unstable and competitive conditions in world trade. Conflict was firmly related to wages and conditions and there is little evidence of any ambitions for revolutionary change. Socialism in the 1918 constitution of the Labour Party embodied a willingness to use any means including nationalization in the attack on poverty. Major success came with the 1945 Labour government, the *welfare state, and the nationalization of key elements of capital.

By the 1950s, the life-style of the bulk of the working class had been transformed by so-called 'Fordist' relationships, in which social stability depended upon high productivity, high wages, and the consumption of an increasing variety of goods. A mass culture of film, football, and television began to entail a more private life-style. This was threatened in the 1970s, by de-industrialization, an accelerated shift in the economic structure of Britain away from traditional industries such as coal-mining, textiles, and iron and steel, accompanied by mass unemployment and new forms of poverty.

The problems of writing and understanding working-class history in Britain lie in its political meaning. The initial writings were undertaken by those seeking the origins and inspiration for the *Labour Party in a long march of labour history from Tom *Paine's **Rights of Man*, through *chartism and the *TUC, to the achievements of the 1945 government. Others led by Edward Thompson in *The Making of the English Working Class* wanted to reposition the Marxist tradition of British history and secure a recognition for the agency and creativity of working-class people, in place of a deterministic view of the impact of economic relationships. Recent writing has reflected the uncertainties and multiple identities of the late 20th cent.

See also SOCIAL HISTORY; CLASS. RJM

working men's clubs. Clubs which brought working men together sociably took many forms, including *friendly societies for mutual insurance and gatherings in pubs or beer-houses for news and information and to enjoy shared interests and pursuits such as music and gardening. But the working men's club movement, as such, was a product of philanthropic and controlling concerns within the mid-Victorian middle classes, anxious to reclaim the working man from the pub and its temptations to alcoholic, political, and other excesses, and conscious that formal educational provisions like the *mechanics' institutes were a minority taste. Clubs in which men could gather for uncontentious reading, games without gambling, and sociability without alcohol were proliferating, especially under temperance movement auspices, by the 1850s. The prime mover in the foundation of the Workingmen's Club and Institute Union, established in 1862, was the Revd Henry Solly, a unitarian minister whose experiments in Lancaster had convinced him of the viability of this approach to social reform. After the 1867 Reform Act opened out working-class urban electorates the political parties also became involved, especially the Conservatives, whose clubs were popular because of a lack of inhibitions about beer and billiards. But the CIU itself soon threw off most of the restrictions intended by its original patrons, and beer (ostensibly in moderation, as befitted a respectable, self-controlled membership) soon appeared as part of the clubs' attractions, followed by musical and comic entertainment of a kind not envisaged by the reformers. As with other cultural initiatives promoted from above, working men took what they wanted from the CIU and rejected the rest, and by the end of the 19th cent. the movement was firmly set on the road to the current emphasis on relaxation, sociability, drink, and glamour: a far cry from the godly, righteous, sober, and improving aims of the founders. JKW

Workmen's Compensation Act, 1897. This Act, passed by Lord *Salisbury's government, was a significant step in establishing employers' liability. The foundation of the *Trades Union Congress in 1868 saw increased pressure for compensation for accidents at work, and in 1876 a select committee was set up, under the chairmanship of Robert *Lowe. It resulted in an Act of 1880 which offered up to three years' wages in damages if the employer or an authorized superintendent had been negligent. A number of employers pressed their work-force to contract out of the legislation in exchange for a company accident fund. In the 1890s Joseph *Chamberlain campaigned for compensation 'irrespective of the cause of accident' and, though colonial secretary, was largely responsible for the Act of 1897, which established that an employee was entitled to compensation for any accident not his own fault, even if there was no negligence on the part of the employer. Employers could offset the cost of the scheme by taking out insurance and the amount of compensation was carefully limited. It applied to railways, factories, mines, and quarries, but not to seamen or domestic servants. Sir William *Beveridge described workmen's compensation as 'the pioneer system of social security'. JAC

World War One. See FIRST WORLD WAR.

World War Two. See SECOND WORLD WAR.

Worms, treaty of, 1743. In an attempt to gain the balance in the War of the Austrian Succession, Lord *Carteret persuaded Maria Theresa and George II to sign the treaty of Worms with Charles Emmanuel of Sardinia, offering him subsidies and territorial concessions in exchange for support. But the move was cancelled by France bringing Spain into the war on her side and the strength of the combined Franco-Spanish fleets held out hopes of a successful Jacobite invasion of Britain. The treaty of *Aix-la-Chapelle which concluded the war in 1748 was on the basis of *status quo ante bellum*. JAC

Wren, Sir Christopher (1632–1723). Wren was an instinctive mathematician and geometrician, whence came the constructional resource evident in the span of the Sheldonian theatre, Oxford (1664–9) and the dome of St Paul's (1705–11). Perhaps these disciplines held any baroque tendencies in check, though Wren's father's high Anglicanism, family links with the court, and a visit to Paris in 1665 might otherwise have predisposed him. A more reticent individualist than Inigo *Jones, as an astronomer Wren's individualism was of the age of *Newton, in which spatial values were pre-eminent. As an architect he is only conjecturally associated with country houses. His proven work ranges from the Royal Observatory, Greenwich (1675), to *Hampton Court palace (1689–1702) and *Greenwich hospital (1696–1702). Apart from his masterpiece, St Paul's, Wren designed some 25 churches for London between 1670 and 1694. In 1669 surveyor-general of the king's works (until 1718), Wren was knighted in 1673, the year of his celebrated portrait bust by the mason-sculptor Edward Pierce. DDA

wrestling is one of the oldest sports in the world and has always had a large number of local and national variants. It was included in the Olympic Games in 704 BC. In Britain, Cumberland and Westmorland, and Cornwall and Devon, developed their own versions, and it formed an important part of the Cotswold Games which flourished at Chipping Campden in the 17th cent. Wrestling was introduced into the revived Olympic Games in two forms—the Graeco-Roman and the free-style. Sumo-wrestling and judo are Japanese variants, the latter of which has become widely popular. Professional wrestling on TV had a considerable following in the 1970s but the bouts became so ludicrous that its appeal wilted. JAC

Wright, Joseph (1734–97). Painter, known as Wright of Derby, where he was born and spent most of his life. He earned a living as a portrait painter, while he experimented with the effects of light and industrial and scientific subjects, reflecting the interests of his day and earning him the patronage of *Wedgwood and *Arkwright. Two of his best-known works come from this period, *A Philosopher Lecturing on the Orrery* (1766, Derby) and *An Experiment on a Bird in the Air Pump* (1768, Tate). During the 1770s he travelled in Italy, less inspired by the great art than by an eruption of Vesuvius, which he painted eighteen times, and a Roman firework display. Although in 1775 Wright failed to replace *Gainsborough in Bath, some of his best portraits come from the early 1780s, while in later life he concentrated more on landscape painting. His work is well represented in British galleries, especially at Derby. JC

writs. The writ was originally an administrative command issued by the king to a subject, often an official such as the sheriff. After the Norman Conquest, and especially after the reign of Henry I, the king might issue a writ to permit a subject to have his case heard before the king's person or his *curia regis. In the reign of Henry II it became necessary for any person seeking to bring an action against another in relation to title to freehold land to obtain the king's writ to institute proceedings. After this, the issue of writs by the *Chancery or writ office became the regular way of obtaining a hearing in the king's court. The common law was built up from the collection of writs issued by Chancery and the 'Register of Writs', which grew from the reign of Henry III, formed the basis of the common law. Each writ had its own procedure and special features. At times the Chancery was more ready to grant new writs, but after the development of Parliament and the provisions of *Oxford 1258, it became less easy to obtain new writs. However, the story of the common law is the story of the development of new writs or 'forms of action' and their acceptance by the courts. MM

Wrotham Heath, battle of, 1554. Widespread risings against Mary's marriage to Philip of Spain did not take place as planned, but Sir Thomas *Wyatt managed to rouse considerable numbers in Kent. Part of his force under Sir Henry Isley was caught at Wrotham Heath, between Sevenoaks and Rochester, on 28 January, and dispersed by Sir Robert Southwell, sheriff of the county. The remainder went on to threaten London, but the rebellion collapsed in early February. JAC

Wroxeter. 5 miles east of Shrewsbury was the Romano-British town of Viriconium Cornoviorum, the civitas of the *Cornovii, where Watling Street crossed the Severn. The original settlement was a fortress, manned at first by *legio XIV* and, after AD 66, by *legio XX*. When the army left in AD 90 to move to its base at *Chester, Viriconium developed as an important civilian settlement, with an aqueduct, baths, drainage, forum, and temple. The theory of a catastrophic sacking and burning by the Saxons has now been abandoned and the town seems to have suffered slow decay as people moved to *Shrewsbury instead. JAC

Wulfhere (d. 675), king of Mercia (658–75). Wulfhere was in hiding after his father *Penda's defeat and death until a successful rising in 658 expelled the Northumbrians and made him king. He was a Christian: how he became one is unknown. Events in his reign illuminate the relationship between a king's role and his faith. Wulfhere had authority over Essex; his ecclesiastical interventions there were both edifying, and less so. He sent a mission to reconvert part of Essex which had apostacized (*c.*664). He sold the see of London to Wine in the first known English act of simony (666). His relations with Sussex interweave power and piety. Its king, Æthelwalh, became converted, no doubt because Wulfhere was his overlord. When he was baptized at the Mercian court Wulfhere 'adopted him' (presumably stood as his godfather) and, as 'a sign of adoption' gave him the Isle of Wight and adjacent lands. Wulfhere's power flagged at the end of his life: he was defeated *c.*674 by the Northumbrians and lost control of Lindsey. JCa

Wulfred (d. 832). Archbishop of Canterbury. Wulfred came from a wealthy family in Middlesex and was archdeacon under his predecessor Æthelheard. As archbishop from 805 Wulfred reformed the cathedral chapter at Canterbury along lines favoured in the contemporary Frankish church and reintroduced observance of the canonical hours and a common dormitory and refectory. He also consolidated and reorganized the community's lands in Kent and the south-east, as well as building up those of his family. He opposed minster or monastic churches coming under secular ownership and became embroiled with the Mercian king *Cenwulf and his daughter Cwenthryth over control of the former proprietary churches of the Kentish royal house. As a result Cenwulf suspended Wulfred from his office between 817 and 821 and the matter was not resolved until a compromise was achieved with Cwenthryth in 826. BAEY

Wulfstan, St (*c.*1009–95). Bishop of Worcester. Born near Warwick and educated at the monasteries of Evesham and Peterborough, he took vows at Worcester where he became prior. Renowned for his sanctity and care for the poor, he reluctantly accepted the bishopric after Archbishop Aldred of York's tenure of the see in plurality had ended (1062). Politically useful, he was Harold's emissary to win loyalty in the north, but after the Norman Conquest he swore allegiance to William I. He supported William II against the Welsh (1088). Though from 1080 Wulfstan was the last surviving English member of the episcopate, he was stricter in enforcing Hildebrandine decrees on celibacy even than *Lanfranc, requiring married clergy to put away their wives. By his preaching he helped William I suppress the Irish slave trade at Bristol. He was canonized in 1203. WMM

Wyatt, Sir Thomas (*c.*1521–54). Wyatt's father was a poet, courtier, and diplomat, with extensive estates in Kent. Wyatt inherited in 1542 and was attached to Lord *Surrey, who fell into disfavour in 1547 and was executed. Wyatt was outraged in 1554 at Mary's decision to marry Philip of Spain, on national and religious grounds, and joined in what was intended as a national rising but finished up confined to Kent. He led his motley troops with some dash. The rebels suffered a set-back at *Wrotham Heath but recovered the initiative when the duke of *Norfolk led an ill-judged advance. Wyatt moved towards London but Mary refused to flee. Repulsed at London bridge and the Tower, he crossed the Thames at Kingston, but found Ludgate closed and his forces deserting. He was executed on Tower Hill on 11 April. The attempt was badly co-ordinated and unclear in its objectives and served to send Lady Jane *Grey, still confined to the Tower, to her death and place Princess Elizabeth in much peril. JAC

Wycherley, William (1641–1716). English poet and playwright, aptly said to have 'fondled his age whilst abusing it'. Educated in France, at Queen's College, Oxford, and then in the Inner Temple before establishing his reputation for witty if risqué satire on contemporary morality with his four plays, *Love in a Wood* (1672), *The Gentleman Dancing-Master* (1673), *The Country Wife* (1675), and *The Plain-Dealer* (1677), Wycherley incurred Charles II's displeasure by his secret marriage in 1679 to the widowed countess of Drogheda. By the early 18th cent., largely on account of his *Miscellany Poems* (1704), Wycherley had become mentor to aspiring poets such as Alexander *Pope. Wycherley's *Posthumous Works* were published in 1728. *The Country Wife* and *The Plain-Dealer* are still regularly performed. JAD

Wyclif, John (*c.*1329–84). Religious reformer. An Oxford-educated Yorkshireman, he was the leading philosopher of his day, briefly master of Balliol (1360) and warden of Canterbury Hall (1377). As *John of Gaunt's protégé, he was diplomat and government propagandist, persistently attacking clerical wealth and privilege, despite his own non-resident benefices, but, when condemned by the pope (1377), he was protected by Gaunt and Oxford University. The papal schism (1378) fuelled his attacks on catholic fundamentals—papal authority, confession, transubstantiation, and monasticism. His belief in the sole authority of Holy Scripture inspired Wyclif to start a translation, but his criticism of eucharistic doctrine (1379) went too far for his allies. After condemnation by Oxford (1381) and Archbishop *Courtenay, he withdrew to Lutterworth (Leics.), where he died. Highly strung, uncompromising, humourless, he was as a practical reformer 'conspicuously maladroit' and, rather than seeking martyrdom, he sought protection. Though not himself implicated, the *Peasants' Revolt (1381) discredited his ideas which became 'the touchstone of heresy', pursued by the *lollards and in Bohemia by John Hus. The Council of Constance (1415) condemned Wyclif's views, and his remains were exhumed and burned. WMM

Wyndham, Sir William (*c.*1688–1740). Politician. Wyndham owed his position as a leader of the Tories in the Walpole period to three things—his standing as a well-connected Somerset baronet, his oratorical and debating ability, and the fact that he was one of the few remaining Tories who had any experience of office. He succeeded his father at the age of 7 and entered Parliament at 21 at a by-election in Somerset in 1710, just before the great Tory victory at the general election. Pushed by *Bolingbroke, he was made master of the buckhounds 1711–12, secretary at war 1712–13, and chancellor of the Exchequer in 1713. He was dismissed at once by George I in 1714 and after Bolingbroke fled to France in 1715 planned a Jacobite rising. Arrested in bed, he spent some months in the Tower, but was released through the influence of his father-in-law, the duke of *Somerset. Thereafter Wyndham gradually loosened his Jacobite ties and protested himself a Hanoverian Tory. He worked closely with Bolingbroke and *Pulteney in the opposition to *Walpole but his early death prevented him from profiting from Walpole's fall, and left his colleagues lamenting his lost leadership. JAC

Wyvill, Christopher (1740–1822). A Yorkshire squire and clergyman, Wyvill was the main instigator of the county movement for parliamentary reform. Disillusioned by the loss of America and the policies of Lord North, the gentry of Yorkshire in 1779 formed the *Yorkshire Association to press for curbs on government expenditure and patronage (*'economical reform'), an increase in the number of independent (i.e. county) MPs, and annual parliaments. Wyvill was secretary and then chairman of the association. Through mass meetings, petitions to Parliament, and letters to the press, he organized an impressive campaign which spread to other counties. Unlike the *Wilkite and later radical reform movements, supported by merchants, tradesmen, and labouring people, the county associations drew in men of landed property. The Yorkshire Association disintegrated after the ending of the American war; and Wyvill's efforts at reform were eclipsed by more radical movements inspired by the French Revolution. JFCH

Yalta conference, 4–11 February 1945. *Churchill was increasingly fearful of the rising power of the USSR, but agreed that she was entitled to a buffer zone in eastern Europe. He agitated for some western influence in the reorganization of the Polish government and strove to promote free elections in the east. He also ensured that France was given an occupation zone in Germany, but was less successful in resisting Stalin's demands for huge reparations. Britain had little say over plans for the Far East, though a proposal to return *Hong Kong to China was dropped. Nevertheless, after Yalta Churchill briefly seemed hopeful concerning the future. CJB

Yeats, Jack B. (1871–1957). Painter. Brother of W. B. *Yeats the poet, Jack Yeats became the best-known Irish painter of his day. He was born in London, son of a good portrait painter, and attended (sometimes) the Westminster School of Art. He began as a water-colourist and illustrator before turning to oils. Most of his life was spent in Ireland, his family originating from Sligo, about which he published in 1930. He collaborated with J. M. *Synge. Yeats's work is characterized by the boldness of its drawing and the vigour of its colours. Perhaps his most immediately attractive paintings are his sketches of Irish characters, painted with gentle irony—the *Race Card Seller* (1909), the *Lesser Official* (1913), and the *Steam-boat Captain* (1925). JAC

Yeats, W. B. (1865–1939). Dublin-born poet, dramatist, and essayist. His early years were spent in England where his painter father introduced him to William *Morris and his circle. *The Wanderings of Oisin* (1889) reveals a late Romantic fired with enthusiasm for things Irish though his relationship with the nationalists remained equivocal, too much so for his more committed first love, Maud Gonne. He preferred to associate himself with the Anglo-Irish, 'bound neither to Cause nor to State . . . the people of *Burke and *Grattan'. Though in England at the time of the *Easter Rising, in poetry he recorded its 'terrible beauty'. An inveterate myth-maker, his lifelong addiction to the occult was tempered by involvement in public affairs, the resulting tensions evident in his best volume *The Tower* (1928). By now honoured with the Nobel prize and a seat in the Senate, he had little liking for *de Valera's Ireland. As the 1930s drew on, he contemplated the coming cataclysm with savage satisfaction. JNRS

Yeavering. Residence of early Northumbrian kings. *Bede records the existence of the *villa regalis* of Ad Gefrin on the river Glen where *Paulinus baptized newly converted Northumbrians in 627 in the presence of King *Edwin. Following the identification of cropmarks suggesting large halls in the vicinity of the British hilltop site of Yeavering Bell, the site was dug by Brian Hope-Taylor and the results published in 1977. His excavations uncovered not only a series of massive wooden halls, which can be paralleled on other early high-status Anglo-Saxon sites, but a number of other structures not so easily matched elsewhere. These include a palisaded enclosure, a possible pagan temple, and what appears to be part of a Roman amphitheatre. Hope-Taylor stressed the evidence the site provided for collaboration between the Northumbrian kings and their predominantly British subjects. There have been many criticisms of aspects of Hope-Taylor's report including his methods of dating, his reconstruction of the buildings, and their cultural interpretation, but these do not detract from the basic interest of the site or its importance in the debate about the nature of Anglo-Saxon conquest and the relations between Anglo-Saxons and British. BAEY

Yellow Ford, battle of the, 1598. Sometimes known as the battle of the Blackwater, this was one of the last great victories of the Irish over their English antagonists. The great Hugh O'Neill (*Tyrone) was in rebellion and even his opponents conceded that he had brought together, not a scratch army capable only of guerrilla warfare, but a trained and equipped body of troops who could engage the enemy in pitched battle. The encounter was precipitated by an English attempt to relieve an advanced fort on the Blackwater. Sir Henry Bagenal's advance was fiercely resisted on 14 August 1598 and when he was killed, his army of 5,000 fled. One result of the disaster is that Elizabeth's favourite *Essex was sent to retrieve the situation. JAC

yeomanry. A force of volunteer cavalrymen, formed on a county basis, and first embodied in 1794 to meet the challenge of the French Revolution. They were not under any obligation to serve outside the kingdom and during the *Boer War a special force of Imperial Yeomanry was raised. Despite regular training, discipline was not always good. The Irish Yeomanry, raised in 1796, was almost exclusively protestant and put down the 1798 rising with great severity. The Lancashire and Cheshire Yeomanry got into difficulties in 1819 trying to disperse the crowd at *Peterloo. The yeomanry was merged with the *Volunteers in 1907 to form the *Territorial Army. JAC

yeomen. Legally a yeoman was a freeholder who could meet the qualification for voting in parliamentary elections, but the term came to be employed more widely than this, to encompass freeholders, copyholders, and sometimes even tenant farmers. In 18th-cent. Cumbria, freeholders, customary tenants, and tenant farmers were all encompassed by the term yeoman, while in other parts of the country it was virtually unknown. In 1566 Sir Thomas *Smith defined his fellow-Englishmen as gentlemen, yeomen, and rascals, and in the early 17th cent. Thomas Wilson included in a similar list yeomen, and 'yeomen of meaner ability which are called freeholders, copyholders and cottagers'. Another contemporary distinguished in 1674 between yeomen (farmer-owners), farmers (tenant farmers), and labourers, while a law dictionary of 1720 referred to yeomen as 'chiefly freeholders, and farmers; but the word comprehends all under the rank of gentlemen, and is a good addition to a name &c'. By the early 19th cent. a slightly narrower definition seems to have been gaining ground. For the agricultural writer Arthur *Young, yeomen were only freeholders who were not gentry, and the same definition was used by witnesses before the 1833 Select Committee on Agriculture. The tables of landowners prepared by John Bateman in the 1870s on the basis of the so-called New Domesday of 1873–4 used the term of two categories: greater yeomen, those owners with between 300 and 1,000 acres, and averaging around 500 acres; and lesser yeomen with between 100 and 300 acres, averaging about 170 acres. However, he recognized that this was but a makeshift title.

The imprecision of the term yeoman has raised acute difficulties for historians concerned with the small landowner-cum-farmer. Mantoux, early in the 20th cent., used the term more or less without reserve. He was followed by Clapham—although he admitted to being aware of the 'varying uses of the word yeoman, both by contemporaries and by historians'—and others, but since the 1960s historians have increasingly eschewed the word because of its romantic and sentimental overtones, as the sturdy inhabitants of a long-departed rural idyll. Phrases such as 'small owner-occupier', 'farmer-owner', and 'owner-cultivator' are thought to be more precise as descriptors, even if they lack any contemporary justification. JVB

Yeomen of the Guard are a royal bodyguard founded in 1485 for the coronation of Henry VII. They have retained their Tudor uniforms and their duties include searching the cellars of Parliament before a state opening. The Yeomen Warders of the Tower, or Beefeaters, established in Edward VI's reign, have a similar uniform. JAC

Yevele, Henry (d. 1400). Architect. Yevele, probably from Derbyshire, began as a stonemason, moved to London, and became a freeman in 1353. In 1360 he was appointed by Edward III master mason in charge of the palace of Westminster and the Tower of London. At the palace he was responsible for the Clock and Jewel Towers. He was reappointed by Richard II in 1378 and his responsibilities widened to include general supervision of the king's works. In the 1390s he supervised the rebuilding of Westminster Hall. Yevele may have also constructed the tomb of Edward III and in 1395 was commissioned to erect a tomb for Richard II and his late wife Anne of Austria. He finished as a man of substantial property with several estates. JAC

York (Roman). A Roman legionary fortress, *colonia*, and provincial capital, Eboracum was founded in the early 70s AD as a fortress for *legio IX Hispana*. After the withdrawal of *IX Hispana*, its place was taken by *legio VI Victrix*, which remained in garrison, probably until the end of the Roman period. The fortress lay between the rivers Ouse and Foss. Originally built in timber, it was rebuilt in stone either side of 100. Excavations under the minster revealed important evidence of the headquarters building. Across the Ouse a civil settlement grew up which was promoted *colonia*, probably when York became capital of the new province of Britannia Inferior at the beginning of the 3rd cent. York remained a provincial capital in the 4th cent. and a bishop attended the Council of Arles in 314. Comparatively little is known of the *colonia*, but there were large public buildings, including baths, and private buildings with mosaics, attesting to prosperity of a provincial capital. Inscriptions and burials show a wide range of beliefs besides Christianity, and inscriptions also attest to traders with links to Rouen, Bourges, and Bordeaux. Fortress and *colonia* seem to have been abandoned early in the 5th cent. ASEC

(post-Roman) York re-emerges in historical record in 627 when the first Christian king of Northumbria was baptized there, and a bishopic established (an archbishopic from 735). By the 8th cent. it was a flourishing river port; between 866 and 954 it was in Viking hands, and was the capital of Danish and Norwegian kings, who fostered a commercial city of international importance. In 954 it was absorbed into England, and by the 12th cent. it was the fourth wealthiest English town, with one of the largest *Jewish communities (victims of a massacre in 1190). From 1212 to 1213 it acquired privileges of self-government, and intermittently between 1298 and 1337 acted as a temporary English capital during the Scottish Wars of Independence. Its golden age was the century *c.*1360–1460, when a boom in cloth-making and overseas trade made it the largest English town after London. From about 1460 it declined, despite strong support from Richard III, who had close links with the city. A modest recovery began with the residence in York of the king's *Council in the North (1561–1641), although the civil wars (especially the siege of 1644) were damaging. Late Stuart and Hanoverian York flourished greatly as a social capital, but the city fell back in relative importance in the 19th cent., though the coming of the railways allowed some industry: growth was sufficient to create the usual problems of overcrowding and poverty, made notorious by B. S. *Rowntree's classic study. Its relative lack of industrialization and war damage has left it with a rich legacy of historic buildings, including an almost intact circuit of medieval walls and gates. DMP

York, Edmund of Langley, 1st duke of (1342–1402). Edmund, the fourth surviving son of Edward III, was endowed with lands in Yorkshire in 1347 and created earl of Cambridge in 1362. Negotiations had then begun for his marriage to the count of Flanders's heiress; they foundered when the pro-French pope refused a dispensation. Edmund's marriage in 1372 to the dowerless second daughter of Peter the Cruel was arranged to protect *John of Gaunt's Castilian aspirations. He was frequently engaged in military operations from 1359 onward, always in a junior role save in an abortive expedition to Portugal in 1381–2. In English politics he was likewise overshadowed by his brothers Gaunt and *Thomas of Woodstock, although Richard II appointed him regent in his absences and he was created duke in 1385. In 1399 York was unable to raise an army against Henry (IV) and joined the Lancastrian bandwagon. RLS

York, Edward of York, 2nd duke of (*c*.1373–1415). The elder son of *Edmund of Langley (whom he succeeded as duke in 1402), in 1390 Edward was created earl of Rutland by Richard II, with whom he was a particular favourite. He was a prominent supporter of Richard's coup in 1397, when his rewards included the title of duke of Aumale, which he lost after Henry IV's usurpation. In varied quarters he was accused of murdering *Thomas of Woodstock, betraying Richard in 1399, revealing the plot to kill Henry, and in 1405 conspiring against Henry. He continued, however, to serve Henry in Wales and Gascony. Edward commanded the van of Henry V's army at *Agincourt, where he was killed. As he was childless, his nephew Richard was heir to his great estates; many were in the east midlands, where he founded Fotheringhay collegiate church, where he was buried. RLS

York, Frederick Augustus, duke of (1763–1827). The second son of George III, Frederick was made bishop of Osnabrück when he was 6 months old, but pursued a career in the army. In 1793 he commanded an expedition against the French in Flanders. After a bright cavalry victory at Beaumont in April 1794, he was badly beaten at Turcoing in May, and recalled. In 1795 he was made field marshal and in 1798 appointed commander-in-chief. A second expedition to Holland in 1799 proved even more disastrous and culminated in a humiliating capitulation at Alkmaar. In 1809 after allegations in Parliament that his mistress, Mary Anne Clarke, had used her influence to sell army commissions, he was forced to resign, but came back in 1811 and held the post until his death. His father's death in 1820 left him next in succession to his elder brother George IV, whose only daughter, Princess *Charlotte, had died in 1817. Though not a successful commander in the field, the duke was a good administrator and cared much for the army. Baron Stockmar wrote of him that he was 'very bald, and not a very intelligent face'. But he was unlucky to be remembered chiefly in a nursery rhyme. JAC

York, Richard Plantagenet, 3rd duke of (1411–60). The son of the earl of Cambridge, who had rebelled against Henry V in 1415, and the heir to the estates, titles, and claims of the earls of March. Because of his blood and claim to the throne (1447–53 he was heir presumptive) he was always kept at arm's length by the king and his court. He served twice (1436–7, 1440–5) with some distinction as the king's lieutenant in Normandy. Failure to be reappointed in 1445 led to a bitter feud with his successor Edmund Beaufort, duke of *Somerset. After the loss of Normandy he endeavoured to force his way into office, espousing the cause of financial and administrative reform. He was rescued from political oblivion by the collapse of the king's health in 1453 and his appointment as protector of the realm. The recovery of the king in 1454 led to his renewed exclusion, and thereafter he was set on a course of armed opposition which led in 1460 to his laying claim to the throne. He was killed in battle at *Wakefield two months after he had been officially recognized as Henry VI's heir and his head stuck on the walls of York with a paper crown on it. York harboured a justifiable grievance against the court, but he was not a particularly able or astute politician. It is also conceivable that Henry VI's suspicions of his motives were well founded and that he had long coveted the throne which his heir Edward IV seized three months after his death. AJP

York, house of. 15th-cent. royal dynasty. Historians from the Tudor period onward viewed the Wars of the *Roses as a dynastic contest between the houses of Lancaster and York. This interpretation appears in the papal dispensation for the marriage of Henry VII and *Elizabeth of York, daughter of Edward IV, in 1486.

The title was first created in 1385 for Edmund of Langley duke of *York, 4th surviving son of Edward III, and descended to his son Edward, duke of *York in 1402. His heir was Richard of *York, son of his brother Richard of Conisborough. A hereditary right to the throne by York was inferior to that of the Lancastrians descended from *John of Gaunt, Edward III's third son to reach maturity. From his mother, however, Duke Richard could trace descent through the Mortimer earls of March from Lionel, Edward's second surviving son. In 1460 he claimed the crown as Lionel's heir.

By this date there had been intermittent hostilities since 1455, and this was the second time victory in battle by York and his allies had won control of Henry VI's government. His friends had not fought to make him king, as was apparent by their dismayed reaction to his claim and the eventual compromise that he should be Henry's heir. After York's death, they recognized his son as King Edward IV. His claim was confirmed by battles in 1461 and again in 1471, when the main Lancastrian dynasty was extinguished; its former ministers, like John *Morton, now entered Edward's service.

The Yorkist monarchy was destroyed by Richard III's usurpation. Courtiers of Edward, believing Richard had murdered Edward's sons Edward V and Richard, agreed to accept Henry Tudor as king if he married their sister. Risings for this purpose failed in 1483; it was achieved at *Bosworth in 1485.

Continental enemies encouraged opposition to the Tudor king. Edward IV's sister *Margaret, duchess of Burgundy, assisted the pseudo-Yorkist claimants Lambert *Simnel and Perkin *Warbeck; few of Henry's subjects deserted him in their favour. *Pole and *Courtenay descendants of Richard of York, some known as 'the white rose', fell victim to Henry VIII's paranoia. Pride in his own Yorkist ancestry was shown by naming his children Edward (VI) and Elizabeth, and by his burial in Edward's chapel of St George in Windsor castle. RLS

York, kingdom of. The Viking kingdom of York has attracted great attention since the Coppergate excavations revealed so much about Jorvik and its inhabitants. Post-Roman York was in the kingdom of *Deira, taken over in 655 by its northern neighbour *Bernicia to form the kingdom of *Northumbria. In 867 York and the southern part were seized by Danish raiders from the Viking kingdom of *Dublin, led by Ivarr and his brother Halfdan. Holding the new conquest did not prove easy. Halfdan was killed in Ireland in 877 trying to assert his claim to Dublin. Halfdan II, who held the kingdom in 910, was killed at *Tettenhall in Staffordshire fighting against *Edward the Elder. York's next ruler, Ragnall, a grandson of Ivarr, submitted to Edward in 920. The later decades of the kingdom were chaotic. England's suzerainty seems to have lasted since Ragnall's successor *Sihtric was married to a sister of *Athelstan, who took over the kingdom on Sihtric's death in 927, turning out Sihtric's brother Guthfrith and ruling it until 939. Guthfrith's son *Olaf then recaptured York but died soon after. Sihtric's son *Olaf could not hold it. From 944 the kings of England took over again until 947 when *Erik Bloodaxe, the last of the York Vikings, established a shaky rule. He was killed at *Stainmore in 954, possibly fleeing to Dublin. Henceforward the kingdom formed part of England, under *Edred and *Eadwig. The connection with Dublin, which was so important, may have been via the Forth-Clyde to avoid the long journey round the Pentland Firth. The relative prosperity of Jorvik—its busy international trade, thriving workshops, and well-established mints—is perhaps a warning not to judge exclusively by chronicles, which tend to record death, destruction, and disaster, rather than peaceful progress. The archbishops of York, particularly Wulfhere and Wulfstan, seem at least to have accommodated themselves to Viking rule, perhaps to prevent the region falling to the southern English. JAC

York, metropolitan diocese of. The present province of York, founded in 735, comprises the fourteen dioceses of northern England. The York diocese itself, founded by *Paulinus in 625, is now conterminous with eastern Yorkshire. Though Roman York, capital of north Britain, had a bishop who attended the Council of Arles (314), it was not until 625 that Paulinus founded the English see, after arriving from *Canterbury; success was short-lived, for King *Edwin, whom he had converted, was defeated and killed at *Heathfield in 632 by *Penda of Mercia. Christianity returned a few years later, but under Celtic auspices from *Lindisfarne. After the Synod of *Whitby, the Roman bishopric was restored, first under *Chad (664), then under the turbulent, dynamic *Wilfrid (669–78). Pope Gregory's blueprint for a northern province of twelve sees under Paulinus as archbishop, thwarted in 632, was not fulfilled until 735 under *Egbert (*c.*732–66), the patron of *Alcuin's Northumbrian renaissance. The north was so poor that the province only contained four of the twelve planned sees. Disputes between Canterbury and York over primacy were protracted. York's claim to be a metropolitan see independent of Canterbury was enhanced by Kent's political decline and *Offa of Mercia's temporarily successful bid for a *Lichfield archbishopric. Eighth-cent. York led culturally, politically, and ecclesiastically. Under Thomas of Bayeux (1070–1100) the contest developed in earnest. With William I's support in 1072, *Lanfranc (Canterbury 1070–89) was successful in resolving the matter in his favour. The dispute, renewed in 1118 with Pope Calixtus II's support for *Thurstan of York continued for two centuries until Innocent VI (1352–1405) effected a compromise, though in Canterbury's favour. York was to have metropolitan authority over the north as 'Primate of England', while Canterbury was to have national precedence as 'Primate of all England'. Meanwhile, in 866 the Danish occupation forced the archbishop to move. So feeble was the see that from 972 to 1016 and for a short spell after 1040 it had to be held in plurality with *Worcester. *Oswald (972–92) was renowned with *Dunstan and *Æthelwold for his monastic reforms and fine episcopal administration in both sees. Among later notable archbishops who did not proceed to Canterbury were Richard *Scrope (1398–1405) executed for treason, and Thomas *Wolsey (1514–30). William *Temple (1929–42), later briefly of Canterbury, made his greatest impact while at York. The cathedral, York minster, is of mixed styles (13th to 15th cent.) with the broadest and tallest nave in England and a Norman crypt. It has the largest display in England of medieval glass from three centuries. WMM

York, statute of, 1322. Immediately after the execution of *Thomas of Lancaster, Edward II summoned a parliament at York and by this statute (16 Edw. II stat. 1) repealed the *Ordinances of 1311 which had limited his authority. It added that matters concerning the king, the realm, and the people should be debated in Parliament with the assent of magnates and the community of the realm. Stubbs argued that this was a powerful affirmation that the Commons must be present at Parliaments, that Edward was using the Commons to balance the power of the magnates, and that the statute 'embodied in a very remarkable way the spirit of the constitution'. Later historians have been more cautious, pointing out that the statute declared what had been the custom, not a novelty, that 'the community of the realm' did not necessarily mean the Commons, and warning against seeing the statute as a great leap forward in parliamentary influence. JAC

York, treaty of, 1237. The kings of Scotland had longstanding ambitions to acquire Cumberland, Westmorland, and Northumberland. In the 12th cent. David I ruled at Newcastle and died at Carlisle. But in 1237 at York, under papal auspices, Alexander II and his brother-in-law Henry III reached agreement. The Scottish king abandoned any claim to the northern counties in exchange for estates within them, notably in Tynedale and at Penrith, to be held of the king of England and subject to English jurisdiction. The arrangement had to be repeated at a meeting of the two kings at Newcastle in 1244. JAC

Yorkists. The three kings of England between 1461 and 1485 (Edward IV, Edward V, and Richard III) were so named because they were descended from Richard of *York. The term is also applied to their retainers, recognizable on effigies by their collars of suns and roses; to their supporters during the Wars of the *Roses; and to those who challenged Henry VII after 1485. Like the Lancastrians, the Yorkists were not a political party. Indeed, during the Wars of the Roses, most of the nobility and gentry bent with the wind, happy to be Lancastrian, Yorkist, or Tudor according to political circumstance and personal advantage. AJP

Yorkshire, the largest county in England, is bounded to the south by the Humber (which formed part of the ancient dividing line between northern and southern England), to the north by the Tees, and extends east–westwards from the North Sea into the Pennine hills, corresponding to lands settled by Halfdan's invading Danish army after 876. They divided it into three ridings ('thridings') for easier administration, the meeting-place for the north riding being at the Yarles tree (probably near Thirsk), that for the east riding at Craikhow (near Beverley), and possibly York for the west riding; the subdivisions called *wapentakes took their names from the meeting-places of their courts (Agbrigg from a bridge, Ewcross from a cross). The Danes were by no means the first European settlers: Eboracum (York) had been provincial capital of the Romans' Britannia Secunda, 6th-cent. Angles had formed the nucleus of the kingdom of *Deira, and some Norse immigration had occurred in the west from Lancashire and Westmorland. After the Norman Conquest, William's 'harrying of the north' left devastation, reflected in the Domesday survey. The wolds became subject to forest law, but Cistercian settlement transformed much from desolation to sheep-run—*Rievaulx abbey was founded 1131, *Fountains 1132, Byland 1147—and the monks soon became famous for their wool production. Although the see had been raised to an archbishopric in 735, enhancing the area's national importance, it was not until 1070, when Thomas of Bayeux became archbishop of York, that the struggle for precedence between Canterbury and York began, not to be settled until the 14th cent. The might of the Norman barons was symbolized by their castles (Knaresborough, Richmond, Scarborough); although their families were allowed to consolidate power to counteract repeated threats of Scottish invasion, Yorkshire medieval nobility was decimated and humbled during the Wars of the Roses. Opposition to the closure of the lesser monasteries in 1536 and resentment of an increasingly centralized government in the south found outlet in Robert *Aske's *Pilgrimage of Grace, but this failed and monastic lands passed to loyal or opportunist families (Cholmley, Fairfax, Ramsden, Ingram), creating wide estates with substantial residences, though recusancy persisted despite the failure of the rising of the *northern earls (1569). York and Beverley's decline in the Tudor wool trade was the West Riding's gain, and it became one of the three major regions of the English cloth industry; Sheffield's cutlery industry was well established, Hull became one of England's busiest outports, and Whitby a coaling port. Yorkshire's integration into national life steadily increased.

In 1642 Charles I abandoned London to set up court at York, but Hull, strategically vital, refused to admit him, and Scarborough (at this stage) was in parliamentary hands. The civil wars (when Sir Thomas *Fairfax gained military prominence) saw confused street fighting and one major battle: the clothing towns changed hands repeatedly, but York's surrender after *Marston Moor (1644) spelled the end of the royalist cause in the shire, leaving the county depressed and with a badly damaged wool trade; recovery was so slow that the Restoration was welcomed. In 1697 Celia Fiennes noted coal pits, sampled various springs in and around Harrogate, was impressed by Newby Hall but dismayed by York's mean appearance apart from the minster, *Defoe found early Georgian Yorkshire endowed with thriving market towns (Doncaster, Ripon, Richmond), though he was more impressed by its horses and stone bridges than its spas. But the pace of industry was increasing, aided by improvements in the road network, canals to implement an already extensive river system (expanded to link with Lancashire counterparts, e.g. Leeds–Liverpool canal) and accelerated enclosure; the east and north ridings remained predominantly agricultural or moorland, but the west riding was transformed, since it sat at the northern edge of a huge coalfield that additionally contained iron. Inventiveness, initiative, and mechanization changed cottage industry into the harshness of 'dark, satanic mills'; Leeds was hailed as the principal seat of woollen manufacture, Bradford the centre of the worsted trade, and Sheffield was the focal point of the iron and steel industry, all experiencing massive increases in population and associated social problems. The advent of the railway in the 19th cent. (including the heroic Settle–Carlisle line) opened up some once isolated places while York developed into an important railway centre. The First World War shifted industrial emphasis to arms manufacture and khaki cloth, and encouraged agriculture; the ensuing slump hit the county badly, but both industry and agriculture rose again to the demands of renewed warfare after 1939, this time including aircraft production (Sheffield). In the remaining decades before local government reorganization (1972), when the ridings were swept away, traditional industries (textiles, coal, iron and steel) declined, but the strong sense of community barely wavered. A separate country to many because of its intense local patriotism—cricketers born outside Yorkshire were long ineligible to play for the county—the blunt-spoken, thrifty inhabitants retain an identity that many other shires have lost. ASH

Yorkshire, North. The county of North Yorkshire was created by the Local Government Act of 1972. It was substantially different from the old North Riding, losing a slice to Cleveland, including Guisborough and Yarm, gaining Filey and Norton from the east riding, and adding a large part of the former West Riding, including Harrogate, Ripon, Knaresborough, Skipton, Selby, and Tadcaster. The county town is Northallerton. The Banham commission reported in 1994 in favour of re-constituting the area as the

North Riding, and making it a unitary authority. But it would lose Craven (Skipton), Harrogate, and Selby to a reconstituted West Riding. JAC

Yorkshire, South. Since there was no south riding to build on, the metropolitan county of South Yorkshire, set up by the Local Government Act of 1972, was a new creation. It was based on the county boroughs of Sheffield, Rotherham, Barnsley, and Doncaster, augmented by parts of the West Riding around Penistone, Cudworth, and Hemsworth, and parishes taken from Nottinghamshire, including Finningley. It was abolished under the Local Government Act of 1985. JAC

Yorkshire, West. The new metropolitan county of West Yorkshire, established by the Local Government Act of 1972, was built upon the county boroughs of Leeds, Bradford, Halifax, Dewsbury, Huddersfield, and Wakefield. There were substantial changes compared with the old West Riding, which lost large areas in the north-west to Cumbria and Lancashire; Harrogate, Ripon, and Selby to North Yorkshire; and a slice around Penistone and Cudworth to South Yorkshire. It was abolished with the other metropolitan counties in 1985. The Banham commission on local government in 1994 proposed the creation of a restored West Riding to include Skipton, Harrogate, Selby, and Goole. JAC

Yorkshire Association. Formed in December 1779 to lobby for *economical reform—a reduction of places and pensions—at a time of high taxation during the American War. Though conservatives denounced associations as potentially seditious, a number of other counties formed committees and joined with Yorkshire in petitioning Parliament. Their greatest success came in April 1780 when *Dunning's motion, deploring the influence of the crown, was carried against Lord *North, and in 1782 the short-lived *Rockingham administration undertook some useful reforms. But Christopher *Wyvill, founder of the association, had difficulty in holding his supporters in line. They soon moved on to advocate parliamentary reform and a split developed between the radicals of the Westminster Committee, pushing for manhood suffrage, and moderate reformers, content to augment the representation of the counties. The end of the war took much wind out of the association's sails, though *Pitt moved for parliamentary reform in 1783 and again in 1785. The association was a remarkable attempt to mobilize public opinion and bring it to bear on Parliament, looking back to the *Wilkites and forward to the *chartists. JAC

Yorktown, surrender at, 1781. After his costly victory at *Guilford courthouse in March 1781, *Cornwallis moved north into Virginia. Early in August he dug in on the coast at Yorktown, where communication with New York would be easier and supplies could be brought in. But the ships which arrived were French. Cornwallis, with 6,000 men, was blockaded by 9,000 Americans under Washington and 6,000 French under Rochambeau. Heavy bombardment during the first two weeks of October did great damage to Cornwallis's defences and ammunition began to run low. A rescue operation from New York took too long to get started and arrived too late. On 19 October, the British surrendered with full honours of war, marching out to the tune 'The World Turned Upside Down', when 'cats should be chased into holes by the mouse'. Back in England, *North received the news like a man taking a ball in the chest: 'oh God, it is all over', he exclaimed. JAC

Young, Arthur (1741–1820). Farmer, journalist, and agricultural writer. Often regarded as a pioneer of the *agricultural revolution, Young began his working life as a small farmer at Bradfield, his family home in Suffolk. In 1767 he took the tenancy of a 300-acre farm in Essex, from which he soon moved on—reputedly paying another man £100 to take the tenancy off him—to Hertfordshire where he held the tenancy of a farm from 1768 until 1777. After two years in Ireland (1776–8) he returned to Bradfield where he farmed and settled to work as a writer and journalist, founding in 1784 the *Annals of Agriculture* of which he edited (and often largely wrote) 46 volumes until 1809. In 1785 he inherited the small family property at Bradfield, and in 1793 he became secretary to the Board of Agriculture with a salary of £400. Despite his lack of success as a practical farmer, Young's prolific writings, his trenchantly held opinions, and his position at the Board of Agriculture all helped to build up his reputation as one of the foremost popularizers of the new ideas and practices of the agricultural revolution. JVB

Young England was a small Tory parliamentary group of the 1840s, which included Lord John Manners, George Smythe, Baillie-Cochrane, and *Disraeli. They were greatly concerned with the 'condition of the people' question and their vague solution was a restoration of the trust and respect which they believed had once existed between nobility and people and a reaffirmation of the position of the church. They drifted into hostility towards the Tory leader Sir Robert *Peel, and dissolved with his fall in 1846. Disraeli wrote of the movement in *Coningsby* (1844), *Sybil* (1845), and *Tancred* (1847). It was not difficult to ridicule. Lord John Manners believed that a reintroduction of the practice of *touching for the king's evil might raise the tone of society and produced the memorable couplet: 'Let wealth and commerce, law and learning die, But leave us still our old nobility.' *Wordsworth, provoked by the name, wrote a sonnet denouncing 'beardless boys' and the *Morning Herald* thought the movement 'tomfoolery and mental dandyism'. Yet their attitude to the poor, if condescending, was generous, and echoes of Young England survived as elements in Disraeli's later vision of Tory democracy. JAC

Younghusband, Sir Francis (1863–1942). Commissioned into the army, Younghusband transferred to the Indian Political Department in 1890. In its service, he visited Manchuria in 1886 and then made his way back to India in a pioneering journey across the Gobi Desert and the Karakoram Range. Service as a political officer in the Pamirs region included further exploration, as did his work as British commissioner to Tibet in 1902–4. His central Asian and

Himalayan explorations led to his election as president of the Royal Geographical Society after his retirement in 1910 and he enthusiastically promoted Everest expeditions. Devout Christianity allied with an interest in Eastern mysticism also led him to promote understanding between different faiths. RB

Young Ireland was a group of patriotic middle-class intellectuals associated with the repeal movement of Daniel *O'Connell: its original leaders included Thomas Davis (1814–45), John Blake Dillon (1816–66), and Charles Gavan *Duffy (1816–1903). Gavan Duffy's journalistic experience was essential to the success of the *Nation*, a newspaper founded in 1842 to promote the inclusivist nationalism of the Young Ireland movement. Growing tensions between Young Ireland and O'Connell's Repeal Association came to a head in July 1846, when a split occurred on the issue of physical force: the more militant Young Irelanders seceded from the Association, and, led by William Smith *O'Brien (1803–64), formed the Irish Confederation. The fall of the July monarchy in France, combined with pre-emptive arrests of Confederation leaders by Dublin castle, further stimulated the militants, and the organization staggered into rebellion in July 1848. This was easily suppressed, and the Confederation broken; but the intellectual legacy of Young Ireland, expressed in the secular cultural nationalism of Davis, or in the vitriolic republican polemic of John *Mitchel (1815–75), has had a lasting influence. AJ

Young Men's Christian Association (YMCA). Founded (1844) by a group of twelve young draper's assistants headed by George Williams (b. 1821) for 'the improving of the spiritual condition of young men engaged in drapery and other trades', who then lived in appalling urban conditions. Meeting for prayer and Bible study, they impressed Lord *Shaftesbury, who became the YMCA's first president (1851–85). It spread rapidly throughout Britain and, after the *Great Exhibition (1851), world-wide. The first world conference met in Paris (1855). From the first fully ecumenical, it provides social welfare for armed services in war and in 100 countries works towards 'better health, education and social welfare in the developing world' without distinction of race or creed, otherwise aiming merely at 'contagious evangelism without proselytism'. WMM

Young Women's Christian Association (YWCA). Founded independently of the *YMCA (1855, but united 1877) by Emma Robarts with her Prayer Union of 23 young women 'to offer service with their prayers', and Emily Kinnaird whose London hostel, originally for Florence *Nightingale's nurses *en route* for the Crimea, became a hostel for girls in need of safe, cheap accommodation. Lord *Shaftesbury became its first president (1878). The World YWCA was formed in 1894. Today it provides social welfare among women and girls in war and peace in 90 countries and in the UK safe, affordable housing for homeless, needy women. WMM

Zambia, previously known as Northern Rhodesia, is a republic within the Commonwealth and has a population of nearly 9 million. *Livingstone visited the Victoria Falls in 1855. The region subsequently came under the control of *Rhodes's British South Africa Company, until in 1924 it was made a British protectorate. It has zinc, lead, and coal, but the main mineral resource is copper. In 1953 it was joined with Nyasaland and Southern Rhodesia to form the Central African Federation, but this was dissolved in 1963. It became independent in 1964 with Kenneth Kaunda as first president. The capital, Lusaka, has nearly 1 million people. JAC

Zanzibar. Former British protectorate. Britain first became involved in Zanzibar in the 19th cent. because the island was one of the main depots for the export of east African slaves. A succession of able British consuls-general exerted an informal protectorate over the island, and the arrangement was regularized in 1890 when Britain became responsible for the administration of Zanzibar and the adjacent islands on the sultan's behalf. The slave trade was formally abolished in the sultan's dominions in 1897. The export of cloves succeeded the slave trade as the protectorate's main source of income. Zanzibar became independent in 1963 and joined with Tanganyika to form *Tanzania in 1964. KI

Zeppelin raids. The first air raid on Britain by German airships took place in January 1915. In theory the Zeppelin attacks were directed against naval and military targets. In reality, poor weather, limited night-time visibility, and frequent navigation errors meant that they dropped their bombs indiscriminately on civilian targets. In 51 raids the Zeppelins killed 556 people and injured 1,357. These attacks caused localized panic which interrupted industrial production but in the longer term failed to have an appreciable impact on Britain's war effort. By 1916 British defences were taking an increasing toll of the attackers. Of the 80 Zeppelins which the German navy built between 1912 and 1917, 23 were shot down or destroyed on the ground, and another 31 destroyed in accidents. By bringing home the reality of war to the civilian population, the Zeppelins only reinforced the already widespread British conviction that they were engaged in a struggle for good against evil. DF

Zimbabwe. See RHODESIA.

Zinoviev letter. Supposed to have brought down the first Labour government of 1924. It bore the signature of Grigori Zinoviev, president of the Communist International (Comintern) in Moscow, and was addressed to the *Communist Party of Great Britain, calling on it to sow subversion among the armed forces of the crown. There is a faint possibility that it was a forgery; and a stronger likelihood that it was deliberately 'leaked' by the British *secret services, who intercepted it, shortly before the October 1924 general election, in order to scare voters over to the Conservatives. Conservative central office and certain sympathetic newspapers were also in the plot. BJP

Zoffany, Johann (*c.*1733–1810). Painter of portraits, conversation pieces, and theatrical scenes, Zoffany was born in Germany and came to England about 1758 after studying in Italy. He began by painting clock faces and doing hack work, before turning to painting theatrical scenes, especially depicting David *Garrick. He was favoured by the royal family. George III nominated him for the Royal Academy in 1769 and recommended him to the duke of Tuscany. He worked in Italy from 1772 to 1779, later going to India where he made a fortune painting English colonials and Indian princes. He returned to England in 1789 but painted little after 1800. His work is of particular interest to historians for its great attention to detail. JC

zoos. The earliest zoos were miscellaneous private collections of animals for curiosity rather than scientific study. Monarchs occasionally offered strange beasts as gifts and courtesy necessitated that they should be cherished. Henry I had a menagerie at Woodstock which included lions, leopards, lynxes, camels, and a porcupine. From the 13th cent. onwards, lions were kept in the *Tower of London. They were joined by an elephant sent to Henry III in 1254 by Louis IX of France. As diplomatic contacts became more permanent, housing the gifts caused problems. The Russian ambassador presented Charles II with two pelicans, which went to the menagerie in St James's Park, the Moroccan ambassador gave two lions (sent to the Tower) and thirty ostriches (sent to the park). Private citizens made their own collections. Sir Sanders Duncombe, a physician, had a small zoo in the 17th cent., and *Pepys received from the consul at Algiers a lion cub, which he kept at Admiralty headquarters in Derby House. Animals were also exhibited for private gain. *Evelyn in 1684 gives a detailed description of the first rhinoceros to be seen in England, and a crocodile. The governor of New South Wales in 1792 sent George III the first kangaroo to be trans-shipped.

Many of these menageries were open, at least to the respectable public, for a small fee, but public zoos waited until the 19th cent. The Zoological Society of London was founded in 1826, with Sir Humphry *Davy as a supporter and Sir Stamford *Raffles as first president. Its premises in Regent's Park were opened to the public in 1828. The society's collection was augmented in 1830 by the transfer of the royal menagerie from Windsor (one of William IV's cost-cutting exercises) and in 1834 when the animals from the Tower were brought across, including more than 100 rattlesnakes. In 1843 a reptile house was opened, an aquarium in 1853, and an insect house in 1881. The first hippopotamus arrived in 1850, a sea-lion in 1856, and a gorilla in 1887 (it died), but the first giant panda not until 1938. By that time the society had opened Whipsnade on Dunstable Downs (1931), still one of the most delightful of all zoos.

Meanwhile, private and municipal zoos multiplied. George Wombwell's travelling menagerie was very popular from the 1820s, though he pepped up the entertainment with animal fights and exhibitions. The Dublin Zoo opened in 1831, Bristol in 1835, and Manchester in 1836. The Royal Zoological Society of Scotland, founded in 1909, purchased the Corstorphine estate at Edinburgh in 1913 and completed the zoo by 1927. After 1945 safari parks and country-house zoos proliferated, the 'Lions of Longleat' leading the way. Though zoos are regarded primarily as amusement and treats for the children, their work in publishing, lectures, and seminars is of critical importance, and much of their income in recent years has been devoted to preserving species. JAC

Zulu War, 1879. The war was the unforeseen result of the desire of Lord *Carnarvon, the British colonial secretary, to unite the British colonies and Boer (Afrikaner) republics in South Africa to guarantee the security of white settlers. Sir Bartle *Frere, sent out as high commissioner to implement Carnarvon's plan, concluded that Cape Colony would not co-operate as long as the Transvaal Boers were at loggerheads with their Zulu neighbours. Theophilus Shepstone, a colonial servant thought to have unparalleled knowledge of the Zulus, and who had formerly supported their claims against the Boers, had recently annexed the Transvaal for Britain and now sought to win the Boers' favour by taking up their cause. In spite of receiving the report of a boundary commission which insisted that the Transvaalers' claims against the Zulus had no justification, Frere accepted Shepstone's statement that Zulu military strength constituted a threat to stability in South Africa. Against Carnarvon's strict instructions, Frere demanded impossible concessions from the Zulu ruler and then invaded Zululand in January 1879. The British government accepted the *fait accompli* and superior British arms overcame the courage and inappropriate tactics of the Zulus who surrendered in July. It was not Britain's intention to annex Zululand so the country was first split into thirteen districts under chiefs who had little support. The renewed aggression of the Boers after the Transvaal had reasserted its internal autonomy in 1881 induced Britain to recognize their claims over a portion of Zululand and the remaining Zulu territory was incorporated into the British colony of *Natal. KI

Zutphen, battle of, 1586. During the Netherlands War of Independence, Elizabeth I sent troops under the earl of *Leicester to aid the rebels. In 1586 they laid siege to Zutphen in the eastern Netherlands, defended by a Spanish garrison under Prince Alexander of Parma. The Spanish sent a relief column and on 22 September Leicester attempted to intercept it, but without success. He was forced to retire after suffering considerable losses, including the death of his own nephew, Sir Philip *Sidney. The town was relieved and the siege abandoned. RAS

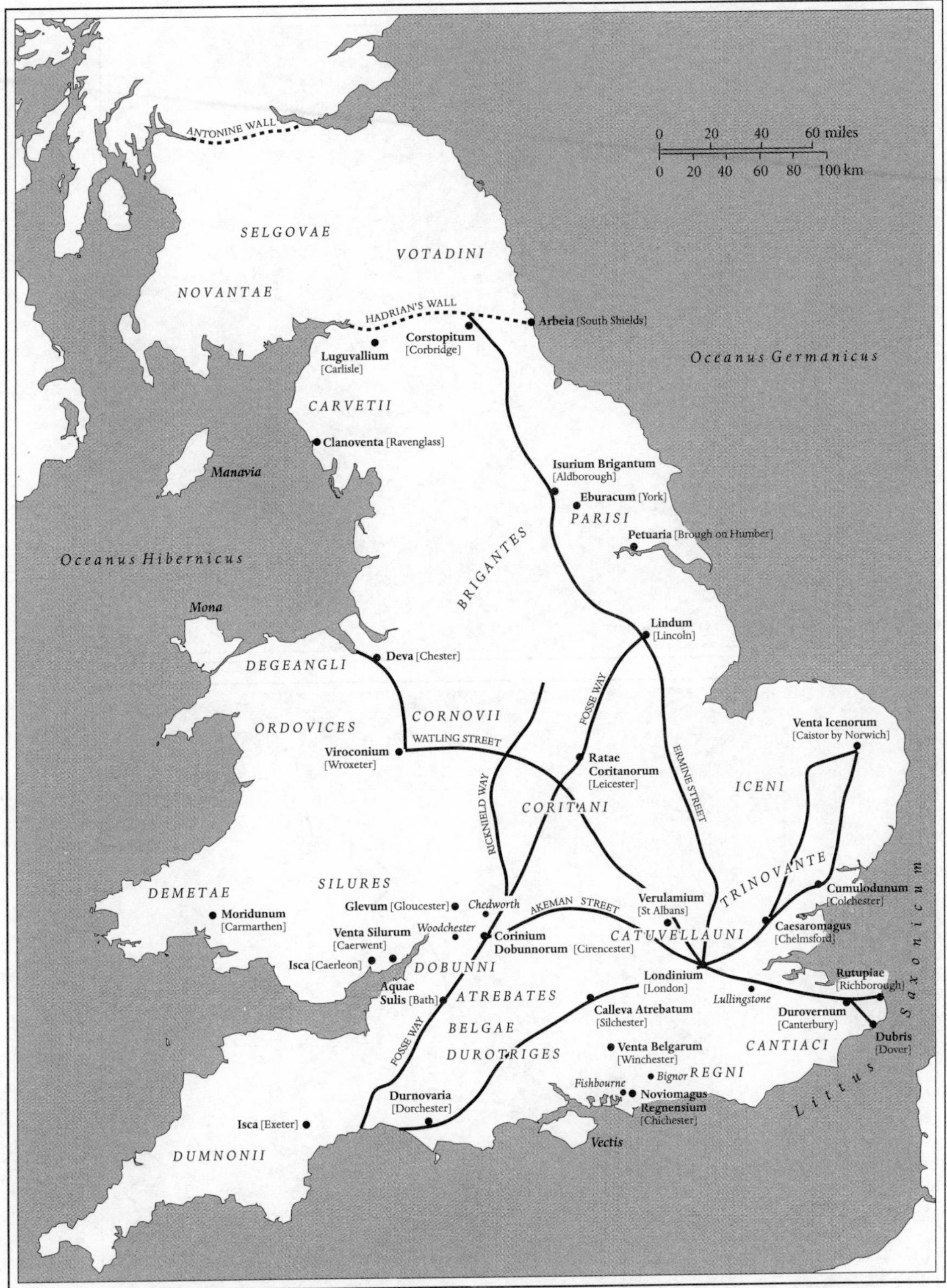

1. Roman Britain

2. Anglo-Saxon England

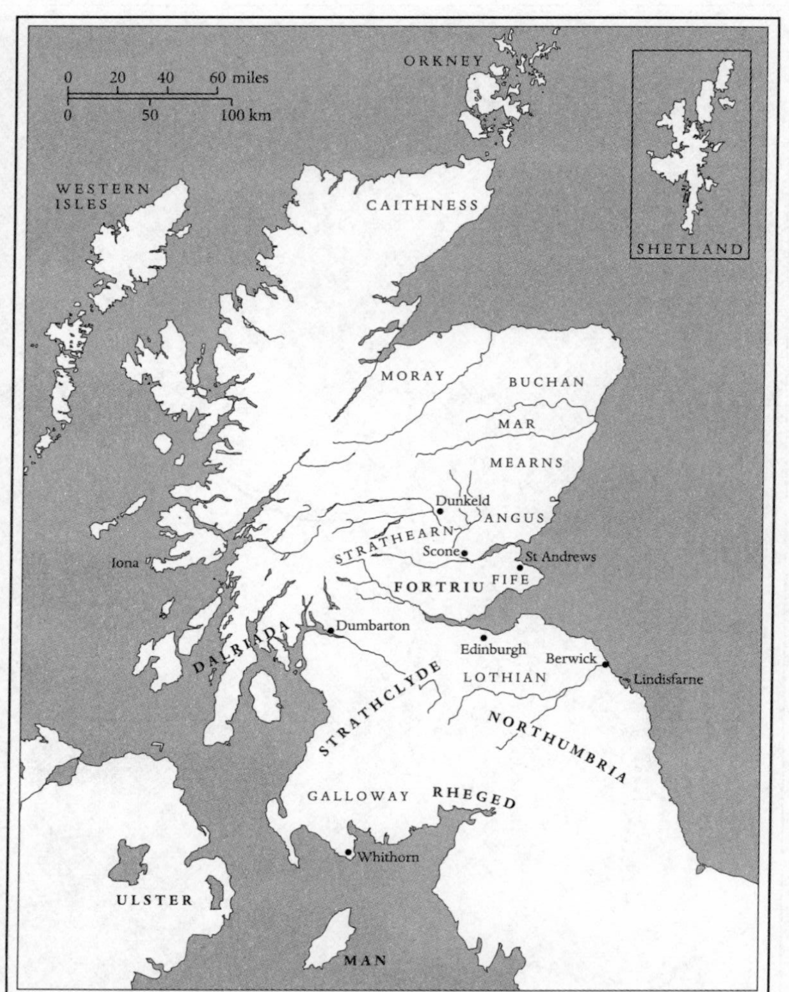

3. Early Scotland

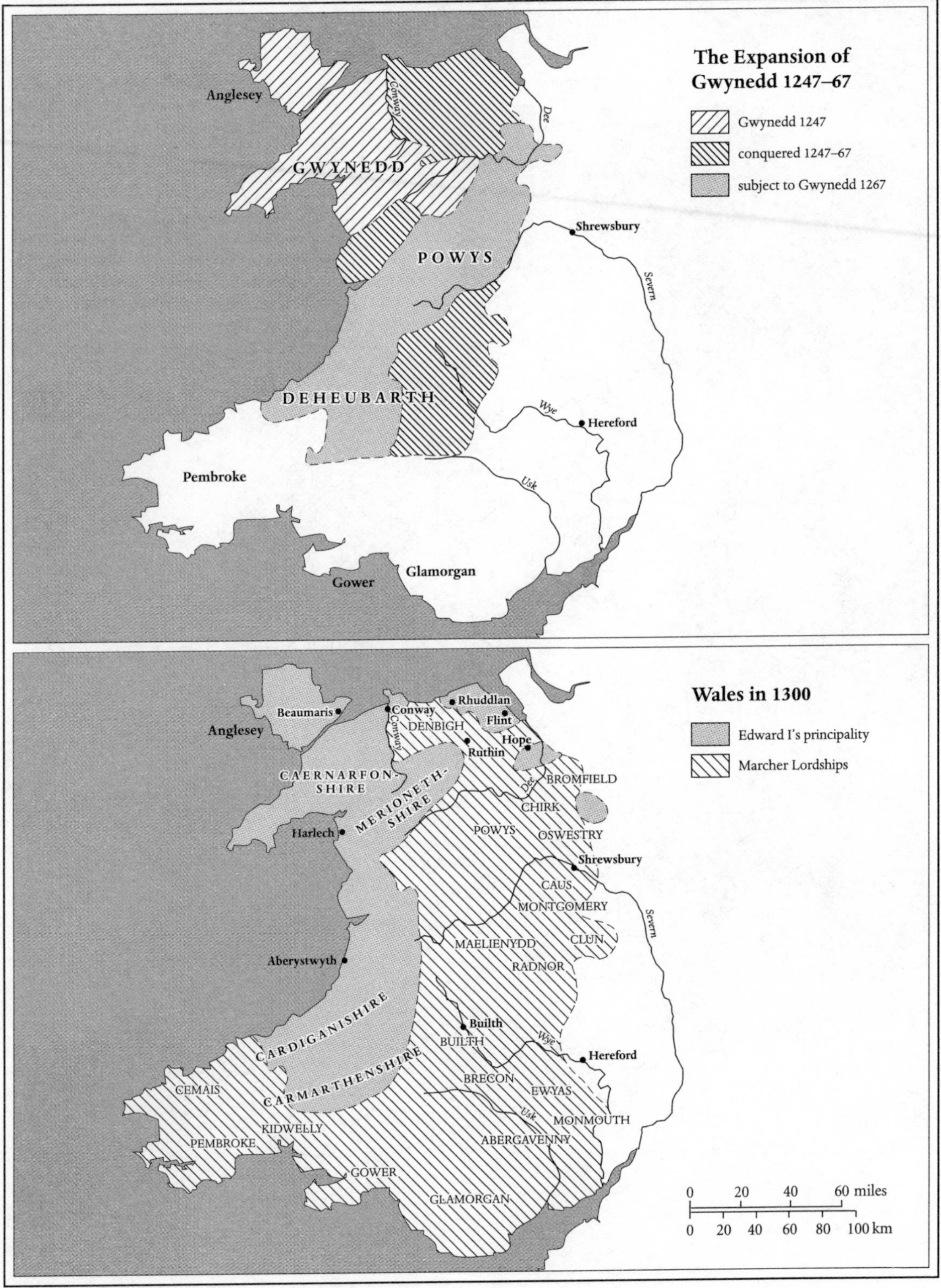
The Expansion of Gwynedd 1247–67
Gwynedd 1247
conquered 1247–67
subject to Gwynedd 1267
Anglesey
GWYNEDD
Conway
Dee
POWYS
Shrewsbury
Severn
DEHEUBARTH
Wye
Hereford
Pembroke
Usk
Gower
Glamorgan
Wales in 1300
Edward I's principality
Marcher Lordships
Beaumaris
Anglesey
Conway
Rhuddlan
Flint
DENBIGH
Ruthin
Hope
CAERNARFON-SHIRE
MERIONETH-SHIRE
BROMFIELD
CHIRK
Harlech
POWYS
OSWESTRY
Shrewsbury
CAUS
MONTGOMERY
CLUN
MAELIENYDD
RADNOR
Aberystwyth
CARDIGANSHIRE
Builth
BUILTH
Hereford
CEMAIS
CARMARTHENSHIRE
BRECON
EWYAS
KIDWELLY
MONMOUTH
PEMBROKE
ABERGAVENNY
GOWER
GLAMORGAN
0 20 40 60 miles
0 20 40 60 80 100 km

4. Wales in the 13th Century

Southampton
FLANDERS
Cherbourg
VERMANDOIS
Channel Islands
Caen
NORMANDY
CHAMPAGNE
Paris
BRITTANY
BLOIS
ROYAL DEMESNE
MAINE
ANJOU
TOURAINNE
SANS-CERRE
BERRY
NEVERS
BURGUNDY
CHATEAU-ROUX
POITOU
BOURBON
AUNIS
LA MARCHE
AUVERGNE
FOREZ
SAINTONGE
ANGOULÊME
LIMOUSIN
Bordeaux
PÉRIGORD
AGENOIS
CAHORSIN
GASCONY
ARMAGNAC
TOULOUSE
BEARN
NAVARRE
BIGORRE
ARAGON
BARCELONA
0
50
100 miles
0
50
100 km

5. The Angevin Empire

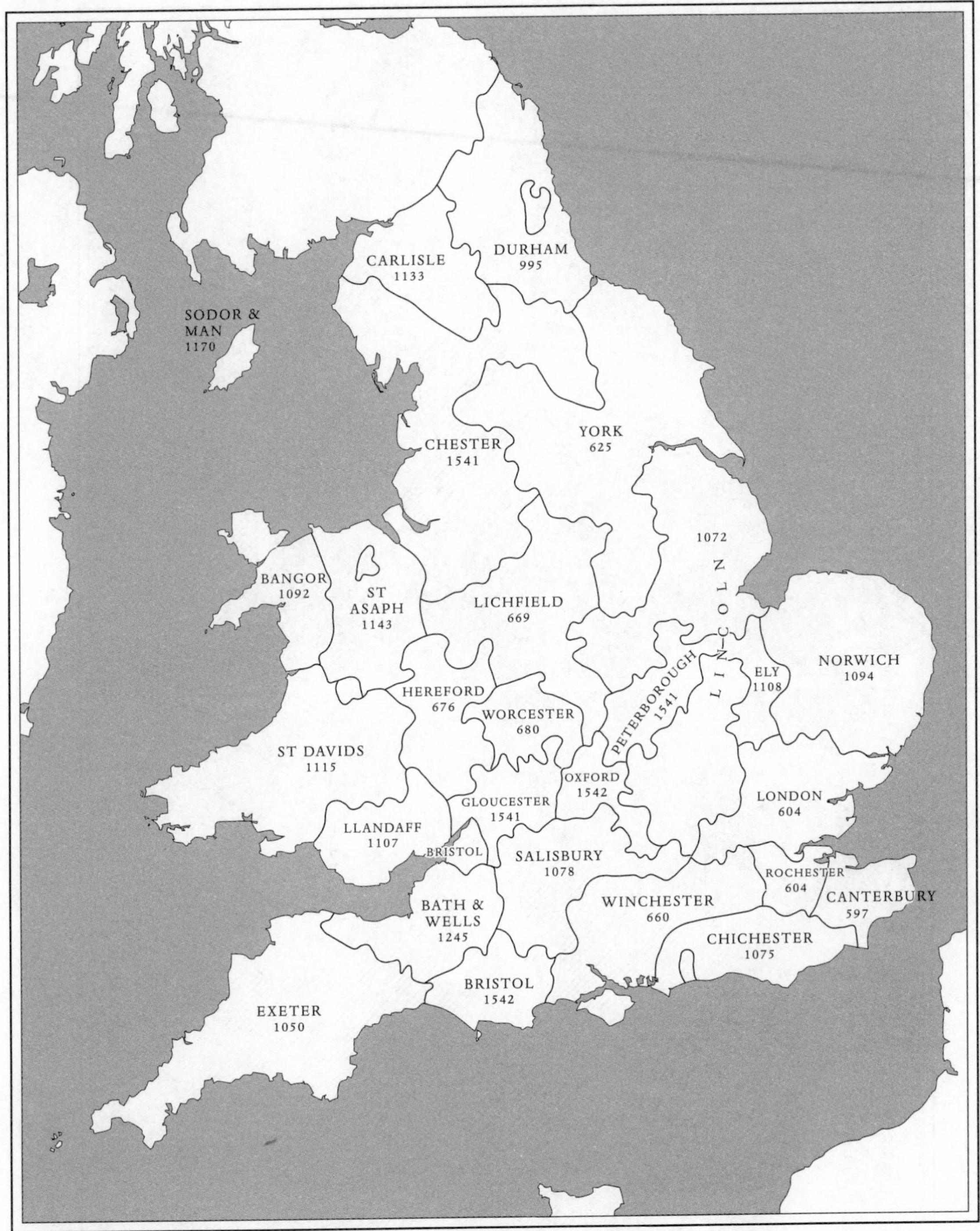
SODOR &
MAN
1170
CARLISLE
1133
DURHAM
995
YORK
625
CHESTER
1541
1072
LINCOLN
BANGOR
1092
ST
ASAPH
1143
LICHFIELD
669
NORWICH
1094
ELY
1108
PETERBOROUGH
1541
HEREFORD
676
WORCESTER
680
ST DAVIDS
1115
OXFORD
1542
GLOUCESTER
1541
LONDON
604
LLANDAFF
1107
BRISTOL
SALISBURY
1078
ROCHESTER
604
CANTERBURY
597
BATH &
WELLS
1245
WINCHESTER
660
CHICHESTER
1075
BRISTOL
1542
EXETER
1050

6. English and Welsh Dioceses, 1543

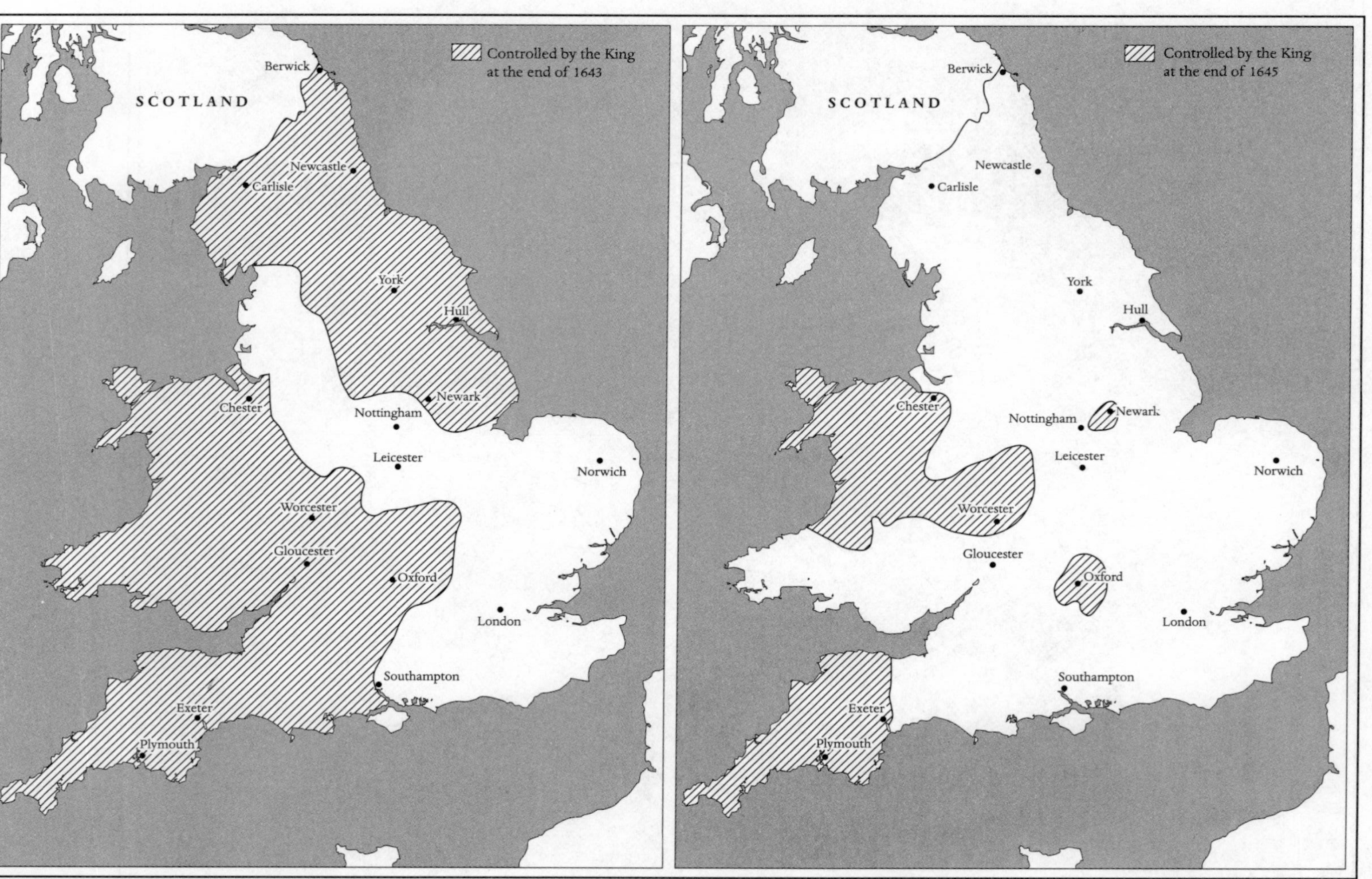

7. The English Civil War

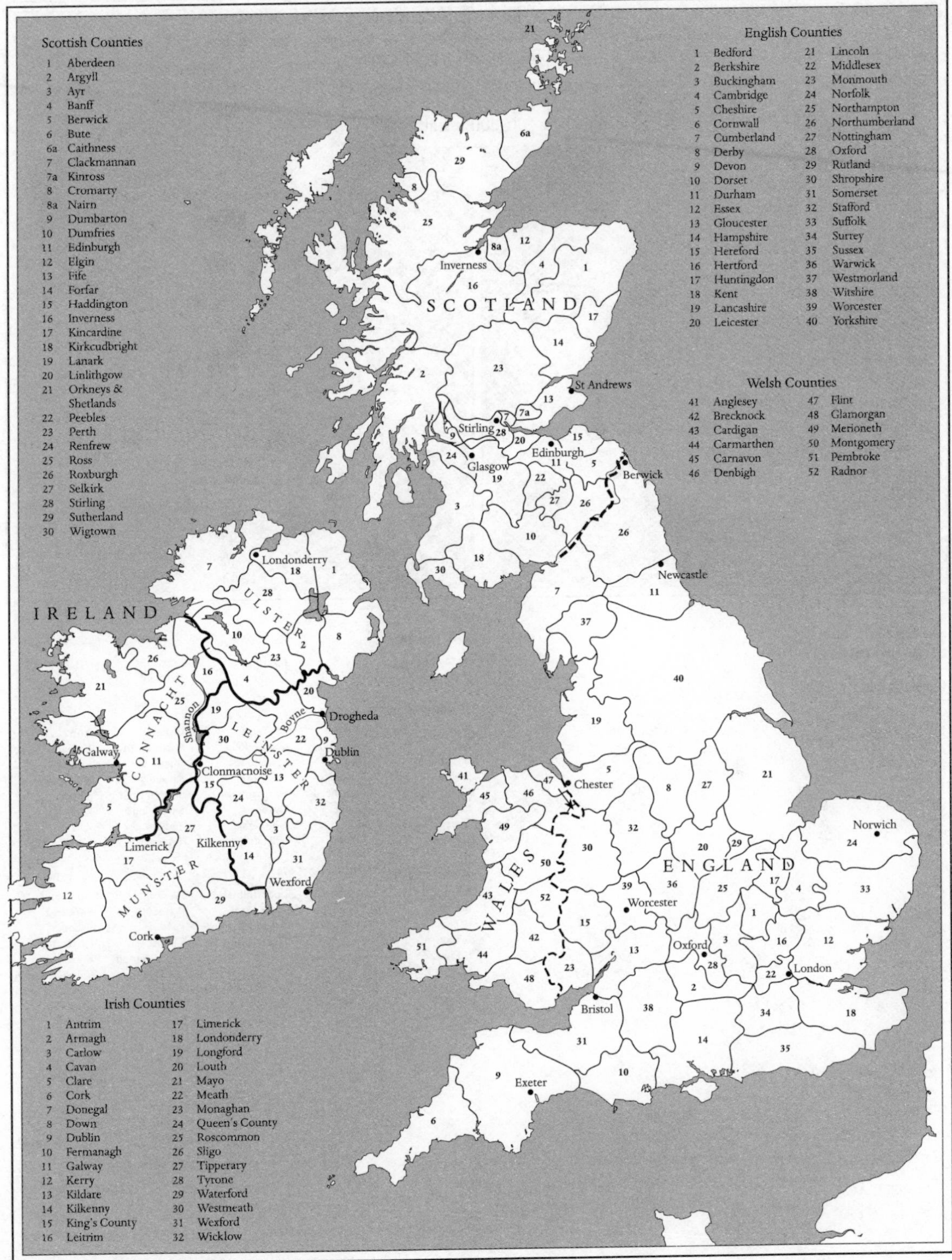

8. British and Irish Counties

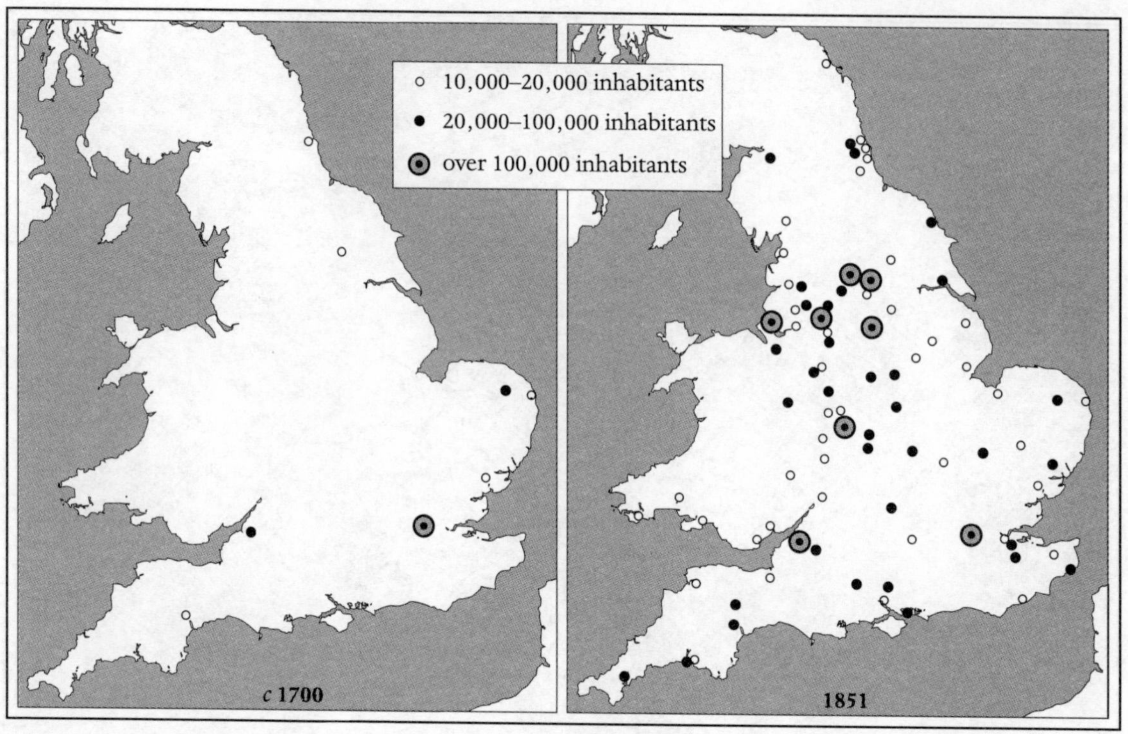

c.1700

over 100,000	London
20,000–100,000	Bristol Norwich
10,000–20,000	Colchester Exeter Gt Yarmouth Newcastle York

1851

over 100,000

Birmingham	Bristol	Liverpool	Manchester
Bradford	Leeds	London	Sheffield

20,000–100,000

Ashton-u-Lyne	Derby	Leicester	Oxford	Truro
Bath	Devonport	Macclesfield	Portsmouth	Warwick
Blackburn	Dover	Maidstone	Rochester	Wenlock
Bolton	Exeter	Newcastle	Salisbury	Winchester
Cambridge	Gateshead	Northampton	Scarborough	Wisbech
Carlisle	Halifax	Norwich	Shrewsbury	
Chester	Hull	Nottingham	Stafford	
Coventry	Ipswich	Oldham	Tiverton	

10,000–20,000

Barnstaple	Colchester	Kidderminster	Preston	Tynemouth
Bedford	Congleton	King's Lynn	Plymouth	Wakefield
Berwick	Doncaster	Lancaster	Reading	Walsall
Boston	Durham	Lincoln	Salford	Warrington
Bridgwater	Gloucester	Louth	Southampton	Wigan
Bury St Edmunds	Gravesend	Newark	South Shields	Wolverhampton
Canterbury	Hastings	Newcastle-u-Lyme	Stockport	Worcester
Cardiff	Hereford	Newport	Sunderland	Yarmouth
Carmarthen	Kendal	Pembroke	Swansea	York

9. Urban Development

10. Europe in the First World War

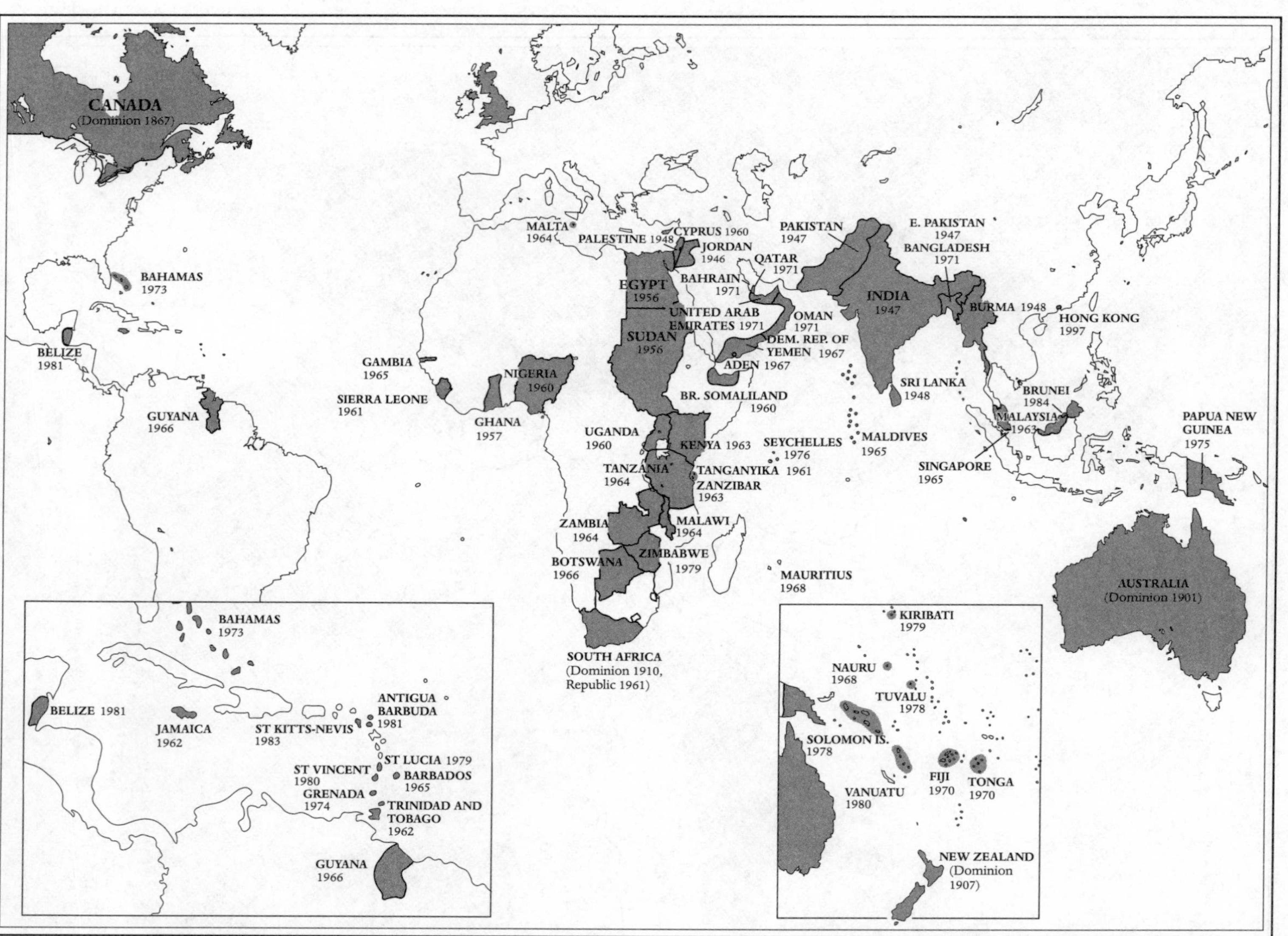
CANADA
(Dominion 1867)
BAHAMAS
1973
BELIZE
1981
GUYANA
1966
GAMBIA
1965
SIERRA LEONE
1961
GHANA
1957
NIGERIA
1960
MALTA
1964
PALESTINE 1948
CYPRUS 1960
JORDAN
1946
EGYPT
1956
SUDAN
1956
BAHRAIN
1971
QATAR
1971
UNITED ARAB
EMIRATES 1971
OMAN
1971
DEM. REP. OF
YEMEN 1967
ADEN 1967
BR. SOMALILAND
1960
UGANDA
1960
KENYA 1963
TANZANIA
1964
TANGANYIKA 1961
ZANZIBAR
1963
SEYCHELLES
1976
ZAMBIA
1964
MALAWI
1964
ZIMBABWE
1979
BOTSWANA
1966
MAURITIUS
1968
SOUTH AFRICA
(Dominion 1910,
Republic 1961)
PAKISTAN
1947
E. PAKISTAN
1947
BANGLADESH
1971
INDIA
1947
SRI LANKA
1948
MALDIVES
1965
BURMA 1948
HONG KONG
1997
BRUNEI
1984
MALAYSIA
1963
SINGAPORE
1965
PAPUA NEW
GUINEA
1975
AUSTRALIA
(Dominion 1901)
BAHAMAS
1973
BELIZE 1981
JAMAICA
1962
ST KITTS-NEVIS
1983
ANTIGUA
BARBUDA
1981
ST LUCIA 1979
ST VINCENT
1980
BARBADOS
1965
GRENADA
1974
TRINIDAD AND
TOBAGO
1962
GUYANA
1966
KIRIBATI
1979
NAURU
1968
TUVALU
1978
SOLOMON IS.
1978
VANUATU
1980
FIJI
1970
TONGA
1970
NEW ZEALAND
(Dominion
1907)

11. The Retreat from Empire

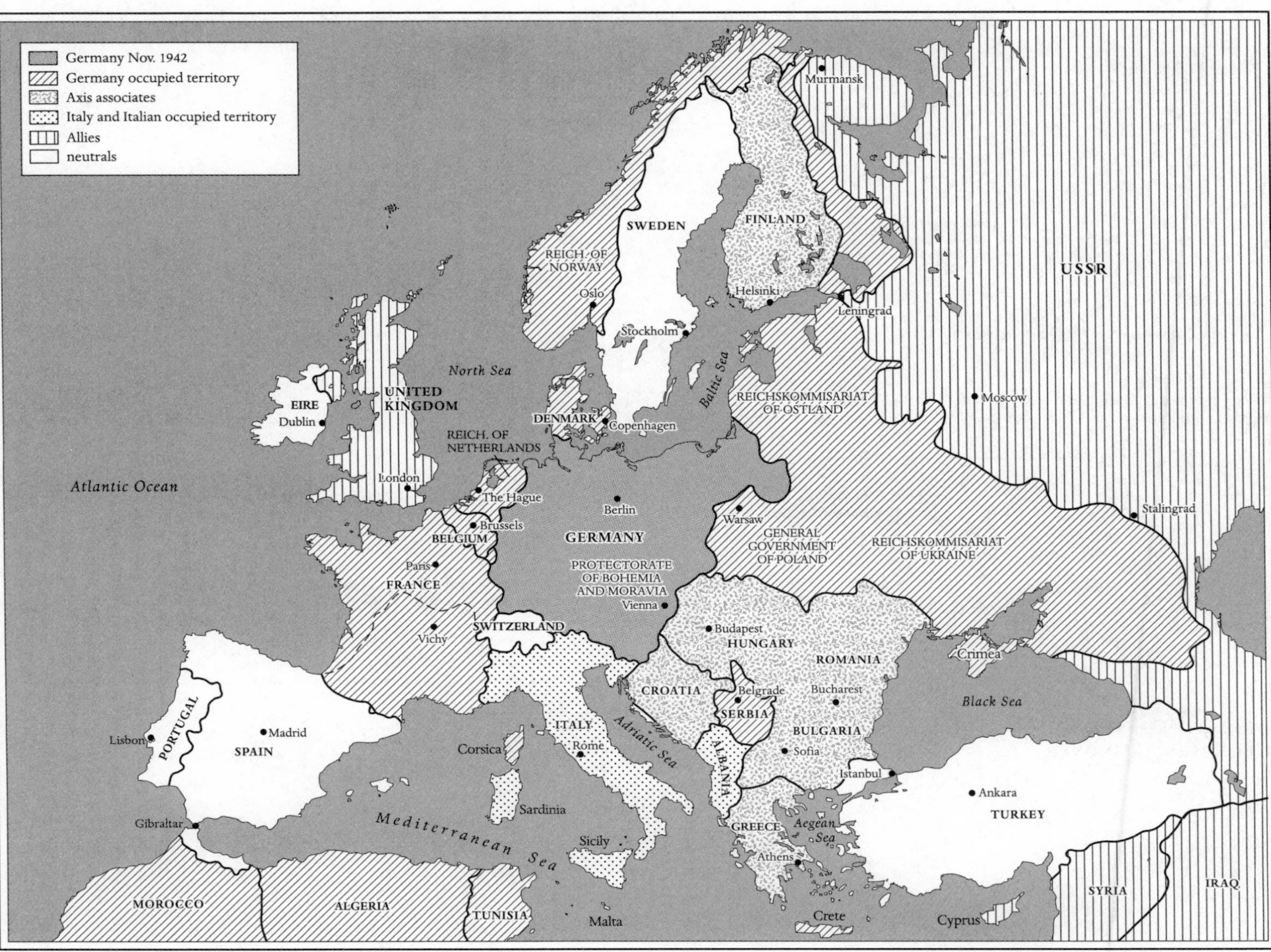

12. German Hegemony in the Second World War

SAXONS, DANES, NORMANS
[showing union of the Saxon and Norman lines]

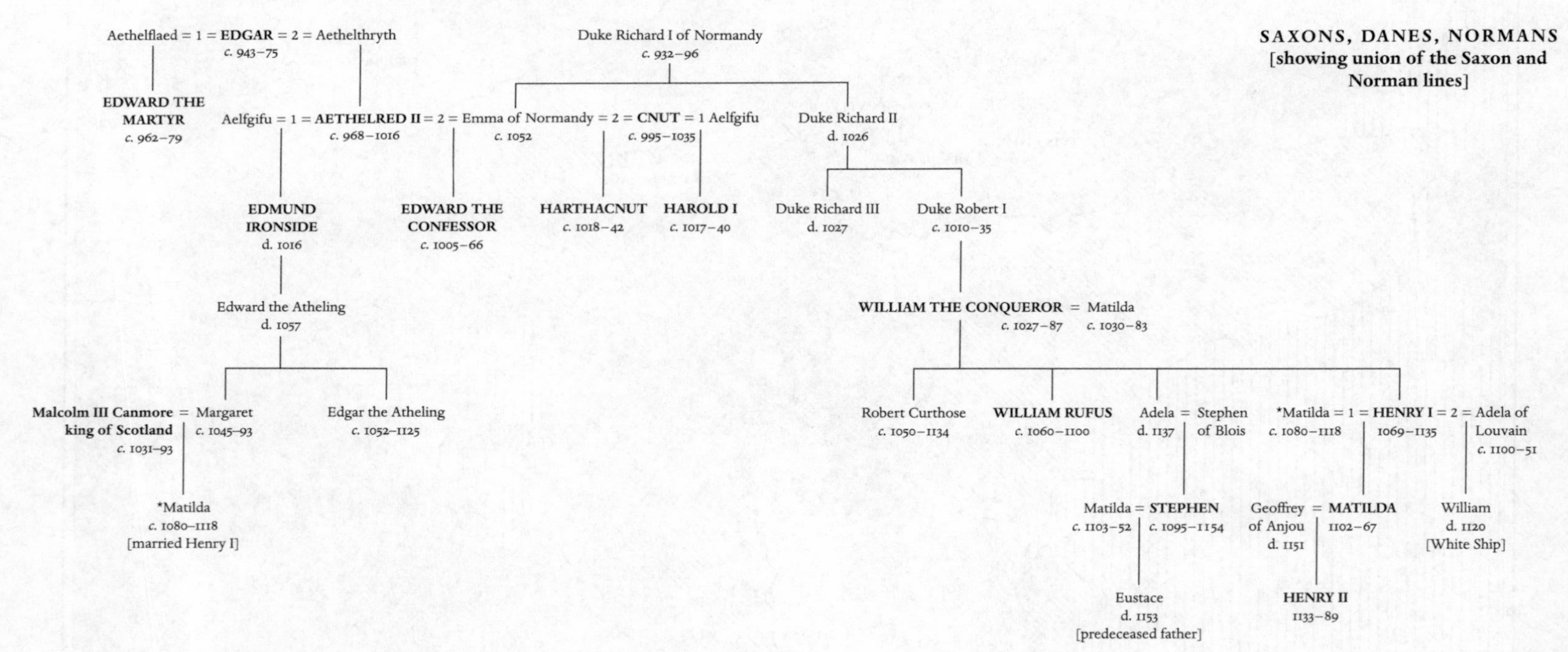

GLYNDWR'S ancestry [showing connections with princes of Deheubarth, Gwynedd, and Powys]

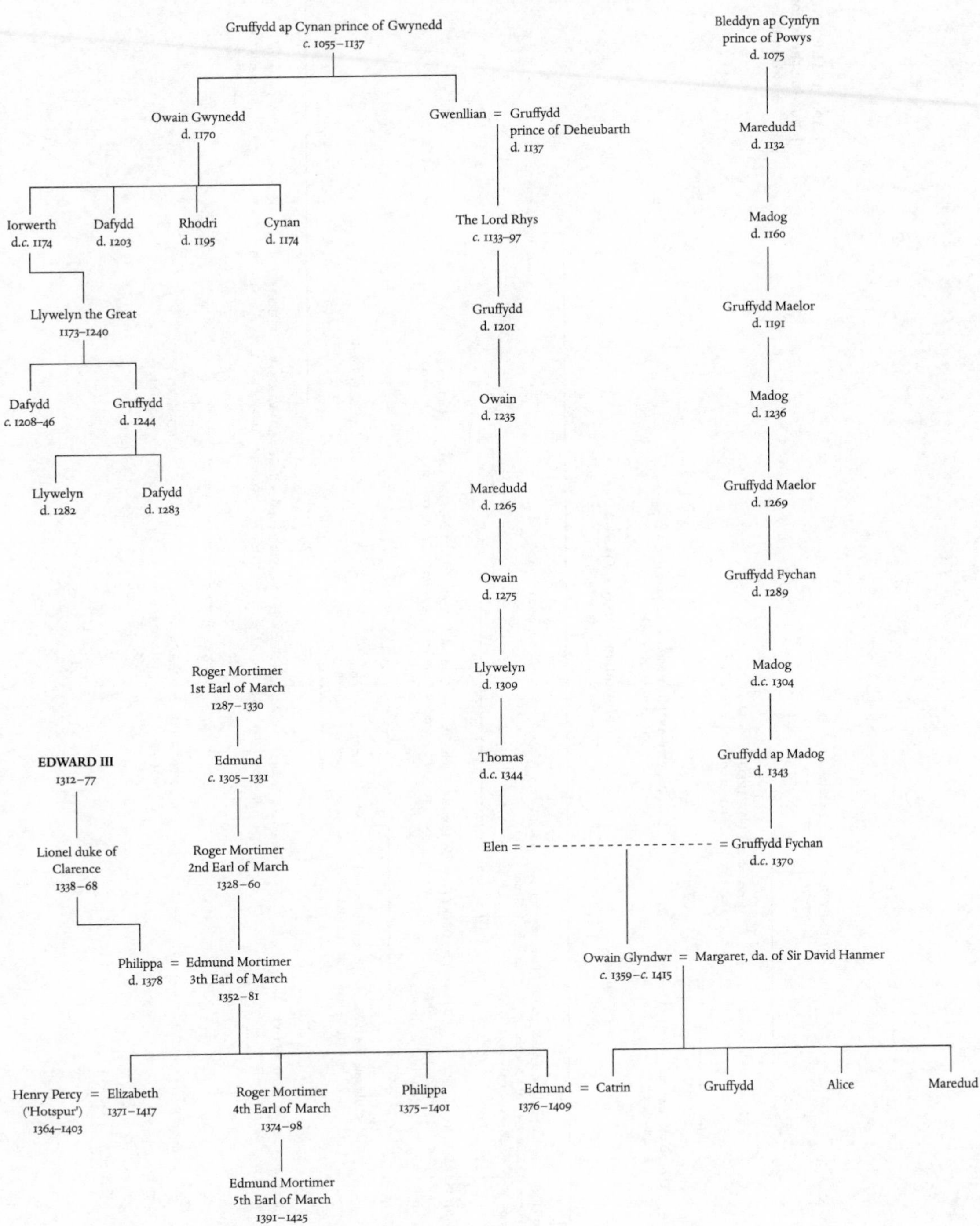

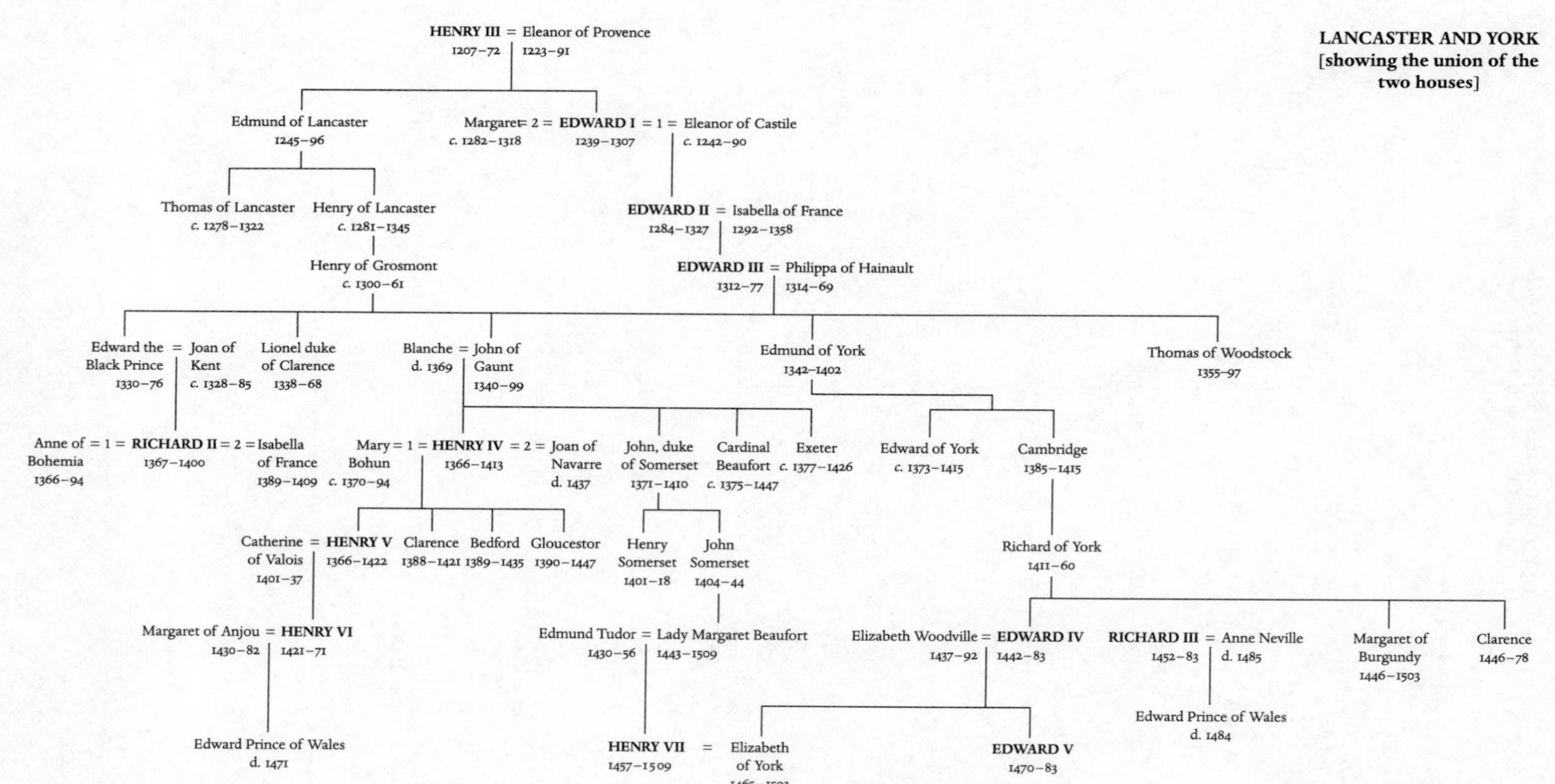
LANCASTER AND YORK
[showing the union of the two houses]
HENRY III = Eleanor of Provence
1207–72 1223–91
Edmund of Lancaster
1245–96
Margaret= 2 = EDWARD I = 1 = Eleanor of Castile
c. 1282–1318 1239–1307 c. 1242–90
Thomas of Lancaster
c. 1278–1322
Henry of Lancaster
c. 1281–1345
Henry of Grosmont
c. 1300–61
EDWARD II = Isabella of France
1284–1327 1292–1358
EDWARD III = Philippa of Hainault
1312–77 1314–69
Edward the Black Prince = Joan of Kent
1330–76 c. 1328–85
Lionel duke of Clarence
1338–68
Blanche = John of Gaunt
d. 1369 1340–99
Edmund of York
1342–1402
Thomas of Woodstock
1355–97
Anne of Bohemia = 1 = RICHARD II = 2 = Isabella of France
1366–94 1367–1400 1389–1409
Mary Bohun = 1 = HENRY IV = 2 = Joan of Navarre
c. 1370–94 1366–1413 d. 1437
John, duke of Somerset
1371–1410
Cardinal Beaufort
c. 1375–1447
Exeter
c. 1377–1426
Edward of York
c. 1373–1415
Cambridge
1385–1415
Catherine of Valois = HENRY V
1401–37 1366–1422
Clarence
1388–1421
Bedford
1389–1435
Gloucestor
1390–1447
Henry Somerset
1401–18
John Somerset
1404–44
Richard of York
1411–60
Margaret of Anjou = HENRY VI
1430–82 1421–71
Edward Prince of Wales
d. 1471
Edmund Tudor = Lady Margaret Beaufort
1430–56 1443–1509
Elizabeth Woodville = EDWARD IV
1437–92 1442–83
RICHARD III = Anne Neville
1452–83 d. 1485
Margaret of Burgundy
1446–1503
Clarence
1446–78
Edward Prince of Wales
d. 1484
HENRY VII = Elizabeth of York
1457–1509 1465–1503
EDWARD V
1470–83

TUDOR AND STUART [showing the union of the crowns under James VI & I]

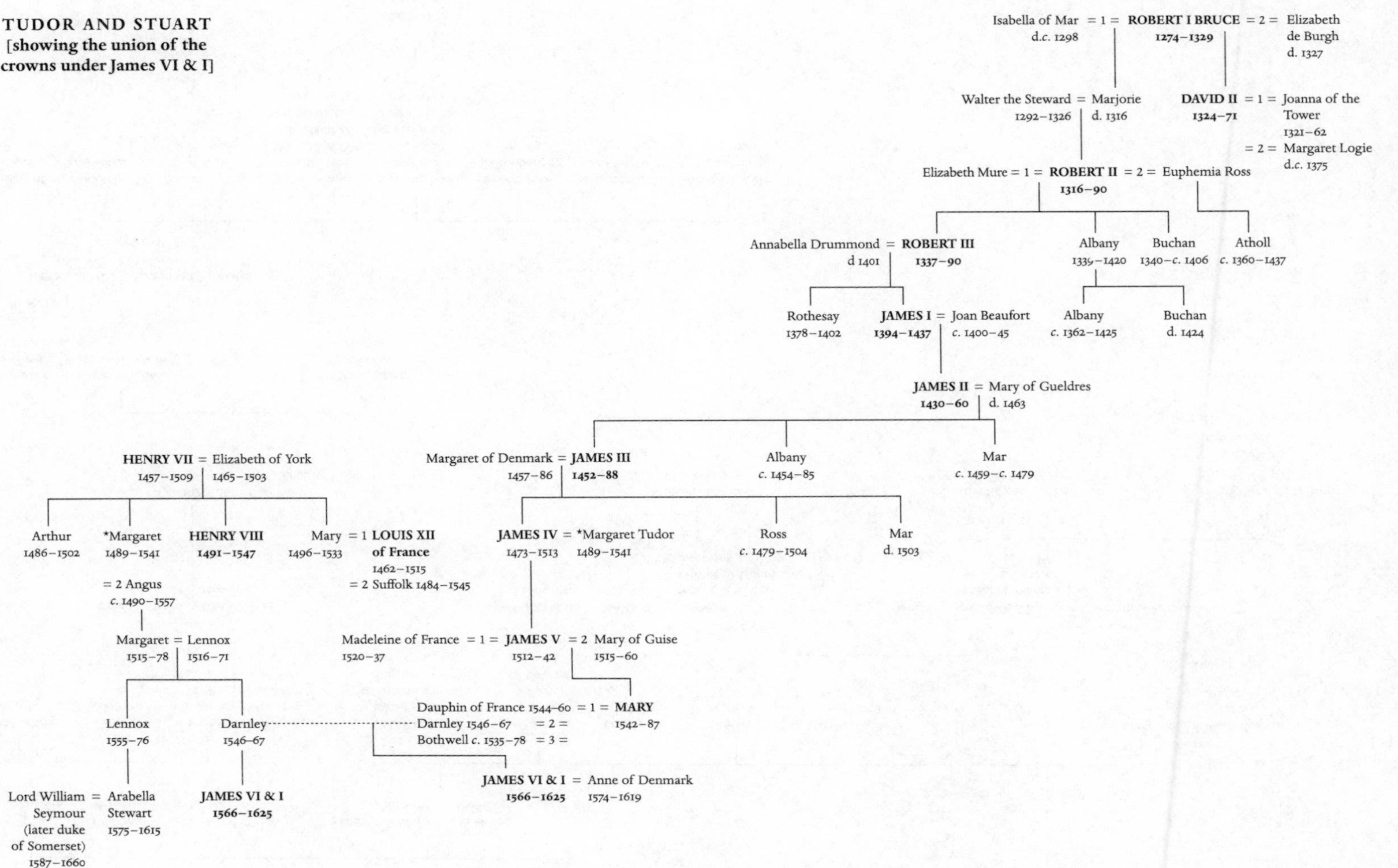

Isabella of Mar = 1 = ROBERT I BRUCE = 2 = Elizabeth de Burgh
d.c. 1298
1274–1329
d. 1327
Walter the Steward = Marjorie
1292–1326
d. 1316
DAVID II = 1 = Joanna of the Tower
1324–71
1321–62
= 2 = Margaret Logie
d.c. 1375
Elizabeth Mure = 1 = ROBERT II = 2 = Euphemia Ross
1316–90
Annabella Drummond = ROBERT III
d 1401
1337–90
Albany
1339–1420
Buchan
1340–c. 1406
Atholl
c. 1360–1437
Rothesay
1378–1402
JAMES I = Joan Beaufort
1394–1437
c. 1400–45
Albany
c. 1362–1425
Buchan
d. 1424
JAMES II = Mary of Gueldres
1430–60
d. 1463
HENRY VII = Elizabeth of York
1457–1509
1465–1503
Margaret of Denmark = JAMES III
1457–86
1452–88
Albany
c. 1454–85
Mar
c. 1459–c. 1479
Arthur
1486–1502
*Margaret
1489–1541
HENRY VIII
1491–1547
Mary = 1 LOUIS XII of France
1496–1533
1462–1515
= 2 Suffolk 1484–1545
JAMES IV = *Margaret Tudor
1473–1513
1489–1541
Ross
c. 1479–1504
Mar
d. 1503
= 2 Angus
c. 1490–1557
Margaret = Lennox
1515–78
1516–71
Madeleine of France = 1 = JAMES V = 2 Mary of Guise
1520–37
1512–42
1515–60
Lennox
1555–76
Darnley
1546–67
Dauphin of France 1544–60 = 1 = MARY
Darnley 1546–67 = 2 =
Bothwell c. 1535–78 = 3 =
1542–87
Lord William Seymour (later duke of Somerset) 1587–1660 = Arabella Stewart 1575–1615
JAMES VI & I
1566–1625
JAMES VI & I = Anne of Denmark
1566–1625
1574–1619

STUART AND HANOVERIAN [showing the disputed succession after 1688]

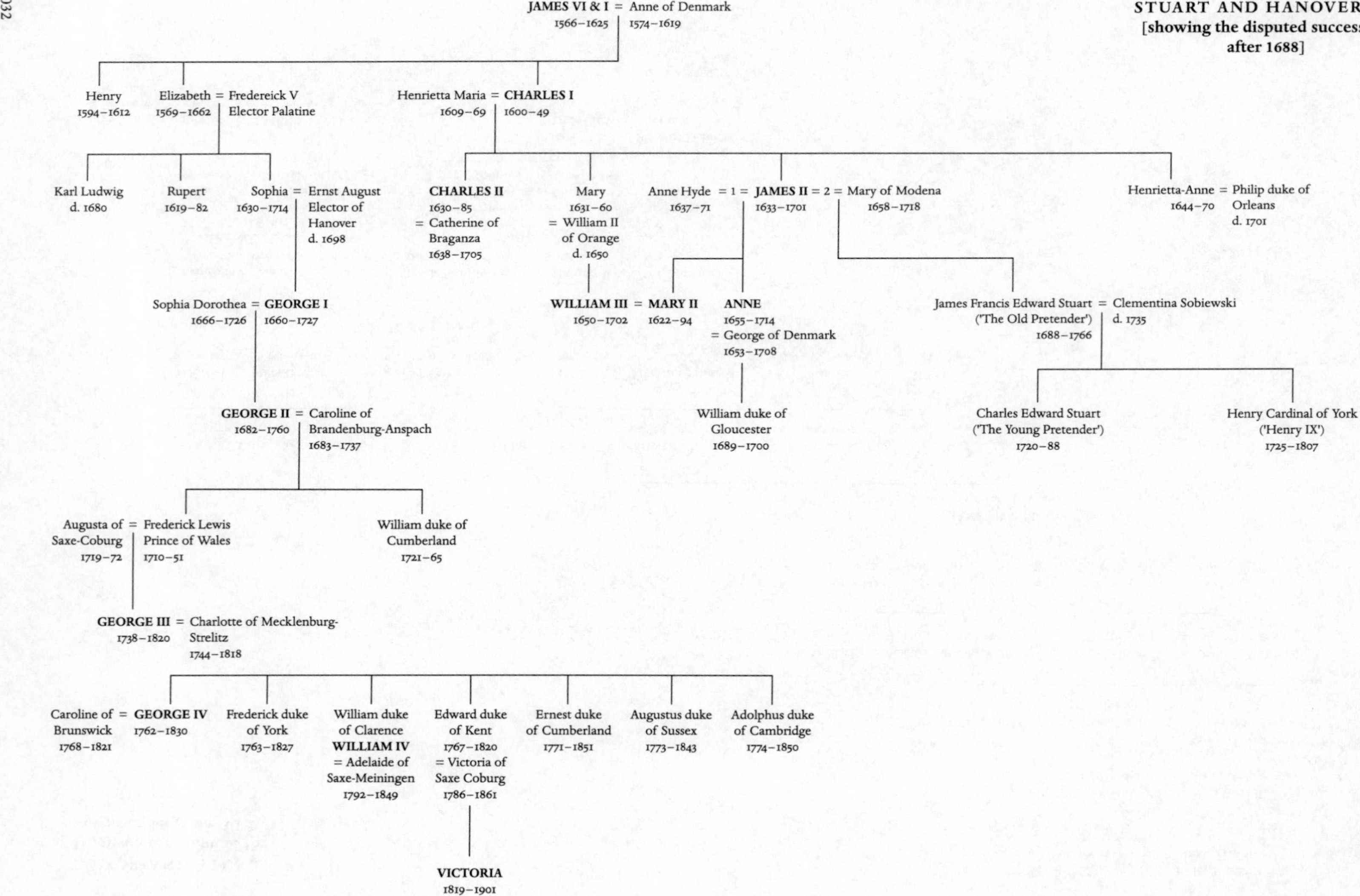

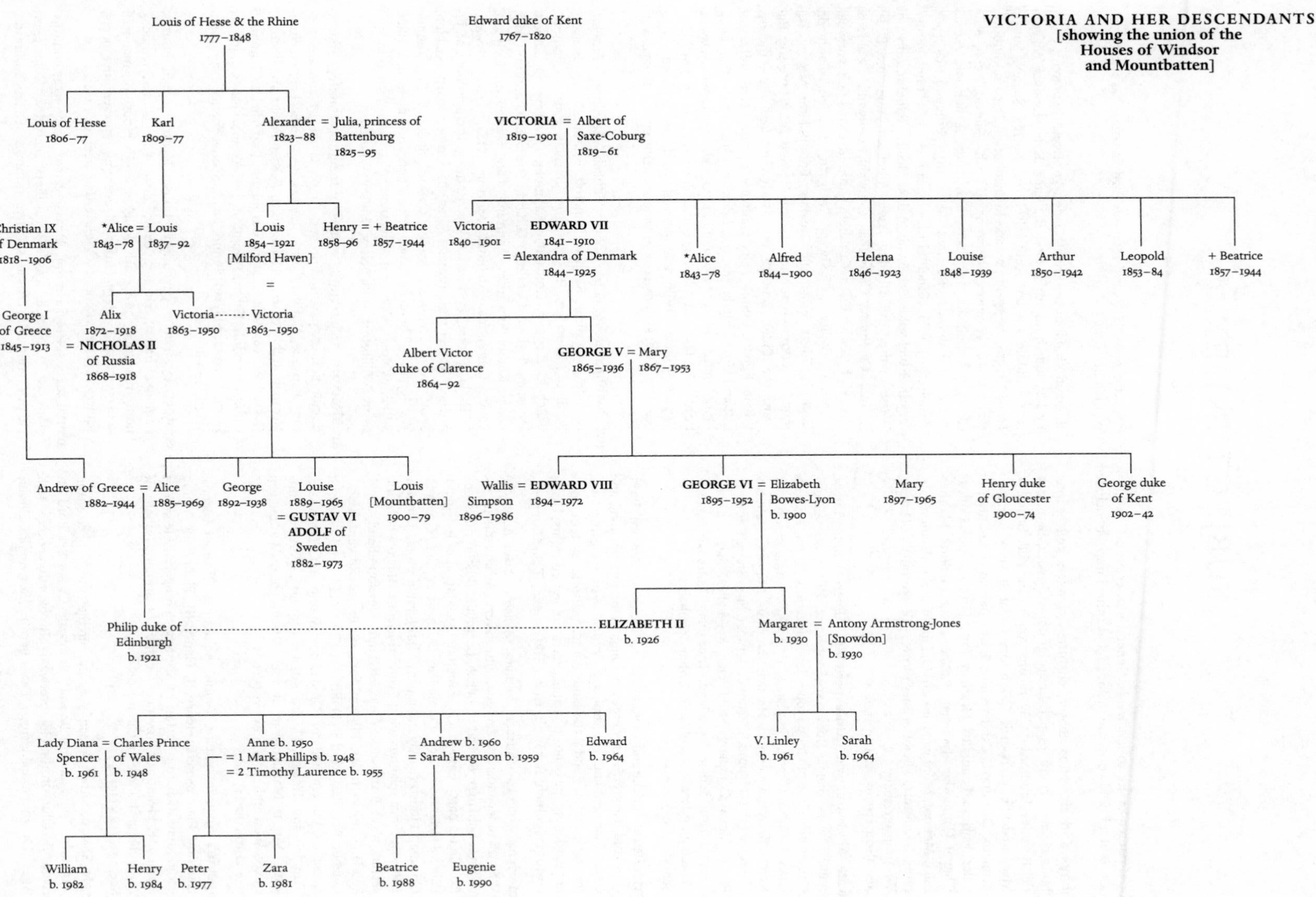
VICTORIA AND HER DESCENDANTS
[showing the union of the Houses of Windsor and Mountbatten]
Louis of Hesse & the Rhine 1777–1848
Edward duke of Kent 1767–1820
Louis of Hesse 1806–77
Karl 1809–77
Alexander = Julia, princess of Battenburg
1823–88 1825–95
VICTORIA = Albert of Saxe-Coburg
1819–1901 1819–61
Christian IX of Denmark 1818–1906
*Alice = Louis
1843–78 1837–92
Louis 1854–1921 [Milford Haven]
Henry = + Beatrice
1858–96 1857–1944
Victoria 1840–1901
EDWARD VII 1841–1910
= Alexandra of Denmark 1844–1925
*Alice 1843–78
Alfred 1844–1900
Helena 1846–1923
Louise 1848–1939
Arthur 1850–1942
Leopold 1853–84
+ Beatrice 1857–1944
=
George I of Greece 1845–1913
Alix 1872–1918
= NICHOLAS II of Russia 1868–1918
Victoria 1863–1950 ------- Victoria 1863–1950
Albert Victor duke of Clarence 1864–92
GEORGE V = Mary
1865–1936 1867–1953
Andrew of Greece = Alice
1882–1944 1885–1969
George 1892–1938
Louise 1889–1965
= GUSTAV VI ADOLF of Sweden 1882–1973
Louis [Mountbatten] 1900–79
Wallis = EDWARD VIII
Simpson 1896–1986
1894–1972
GEORGE VI = Elizabeth Bowes-Lyon
1895–1952 b. 1900
Mary 1897–1965
Henry duke of Gloucester 1900–74
George duke of Kent 1902–42
Philip duke of Edinburgh b. 1921
ELIZABETH II b. 1926
Margaret = Antony Armstrong-Jones
b. 1930 [Snowdon] b. 1930
Lady Diana = Charles Prince
Spencer b. 1961 of Wales b. 1948
Anne b. 1950
= 1 Mark Phillips b. 1948
= 2 Timothy Laurence b. 1955
Andrew b. 1960
= Sarah Ferguson b. 1959
Edward b. 1964
V. Linley b. 1961
Sarah b. 1964
William b. 1982
Henry b. 1984
Peter b. 1977
Zara b. 1981
Beatrice b. 1988
Eugenie b. 1990

SUBJECT INDEX

These references are to *headwords*. General entries are followed by more specific ones. 'See also' refers to further references *within* this index. Not all headwords are included and others may be included in two or more lists.